D0521729

Smarter *than the average quiz*

A FIRST FOR NON-MAJORS BIOLOGY

An Adaptive Student Quizzing System
Developed by the Textbook Author

Developed by Jay Phelan, the multifaceted Prep-U adaptive quizzing system offers approximately 5,000 class-tested and instructor-vetted quiz questions of outstanding quality.

✓ Prep-U for Instructors

Prep-U allows you to:

- Assign pre-populated Mastery Quizzes

- Create custom quizzes, containing questions of your choosing

- Upload your own quiz content

- Get unprecedented reporting, showing student performance

✓ Prep-U for Students

Free with all new copies of What Is Life? A Guide to Biology *and fully integrated into the BioPortal!*
Students using new copies of *What Is Life? A Guide to Biology* can access Prep-U questions correlated to the textbook at no additional cost. The Prep-U system compares individual scores to nationwide results, then generates follow-up practice quizzes geared to each student's specific improvement needs. Efficacy studies show that students who use Prep-U quizzing do 6-10% better on tests than those who do not.

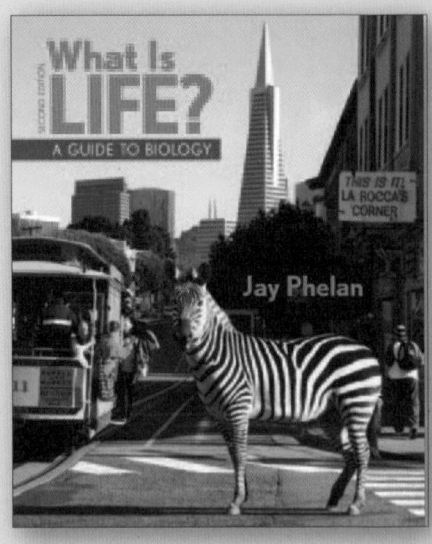

WANT ACCESS TO EVALUATE PREP-U FOR YOUR STUDENTS?

HAVE QUESTIONS ABOUT PREP-U?

Visit **www.prep-u.com**, and click on *Help Center – User Guides and Tips.*

What Is LIFE?

SECOND EDITION

A GUIDE TO BIOLOGY WITH PHYSIOLOGY

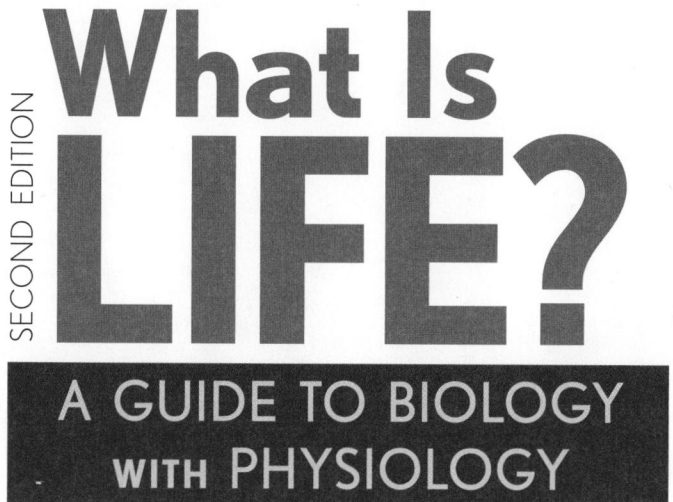

SECOND EDITION

What Is LIFE?

A GUIDE TO BIOLOGY
WITH PHYSIOLOGY

Jay Phelan

University of California, Los Angeles

W. H. FREEMAN AND COMPANY
NEW YORK

Publisher: Peter Marshall

Senior Development Editor: Elizabeth Howe

Development Editors: Jane Tufts, Alicia Moretti

Assistant Editor: Marni Rolfes

Associate Director of Marketing: Debbie Clare

Art Development Editor: Tommy Moorman

Illustrations: Tommy Moorman

Managing Editor: Philip McCaffrey

Senior Project Editor: Mary Louise Byrd

Art Director: Diana Blume

Text Design: Tom Carling, Carling Design Inc

Photo Editor: Christine Buese

Photo Researchers: Deborah Anderson, Julia Phelan

Production Manager: Susan Wein

Composition and Layout: Sheridan Sellers

Printing and Binding: Quad/Graphics

Library of Congress Control Number: 2012933462

Instructor Edition: ISBN-13: 978-1-4641-0243-1

ISBN-10: 1-4641-0243-0

Printed in the United States of America

First Printing

W. H. Freeman and Company

41 Madison Avenue, New York, NY 10010

Houndsmills, Basingstoke RG21 6XS, England

www.whfreeman.com

BRIEF CONTENTS

CONTENTS

PART 1 The Facts of Life

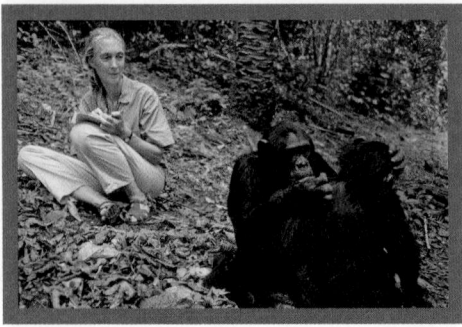

1 · Scientific Thinking

Your best pathway to understanding the world

2 • Chemistry

37

Raw materials and fuel for our bodies

3 • Cells

The smallest part of you

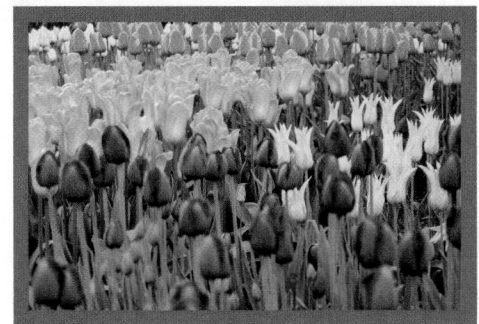

4 • Energy

129

From the sun to you in just two steps

If you feed and protect your flowers in a vase, they'll last longer.

PART 2 Genetics, Evolution, and Behavior

5 · DNA, Gene Expression, and Biotechnology 169

What is the genetic code, and how is it harnessed?

6 · Chromosomes and Cell Division

Continuity and variety

7 · Genes and Inheritance

Family resemblance: how traits are inherited

Can a gene nudge us toward novelty-seeking (and spicy foods)? Novelty-seeking and a gene that influences it.

8 · Evolution and Natural Selection

Darwin's dangerous idea

9 • Evolution and Behavior

Communication, cooperation, and conflict in the animal world

10 · The Origin and Diversification of Life on Earth

(387)

Understanding biodiversity

11 · Animal Diversification

Visibility in motion

Where are you from? "Recreational genomics" and the search for clues to your ancestry in your DNA.

12 · Plant and Fungi Diversification

Where did all the plants and fungi come from?

13 · Evolution and Diversity Among the Microbes

511

Bacteria, archaea, protists, and viruses:
the unseen world

PART 4 Ecology and the Environment

14 · Population Ecology ⓯⁴⁷
Planet at capacity: patterns of population growth

15 • Ecosystems and Communities

Organisms and their environments

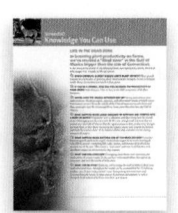
Life in the dead zone: in boosting plant productivity on farms, we've created a "dead zone" in the Gulf of Mexico bigger than the size of Connecticut.

16 · Conservation and Biodiversity

623

Human influences on the environment.

17 · Plant Structure and Nutrient Transport

663

How plants function, and why we need them

18 · Growth and Reproduction in Plants

699

Problem solving with flowers and wood

19 · Plants Respond to Their Environments

737

Defending and regulating while rooted in the ground

20 · Introduction to Animal Physiology

765

Principles of animal organization and function

21 · Circulation and Respiration

Transporting fuel, raw materials, and gases into, out of, and around the body

"Contents under pressure." Recognizing and avoiding the bends.

22 · Nutrition and Digestion

At rest and at play: optimizing human physiological functioning

"An apple a day keeps the doctor away." Silly rhyme? Sound, data-backed advice? Or something in between?

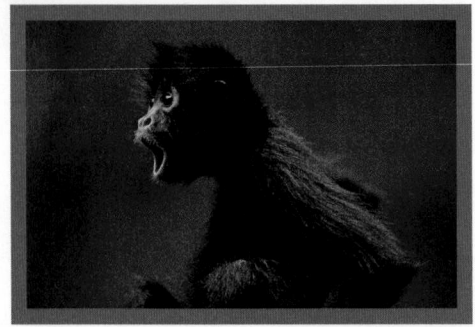

23 · Nervous and Motor Systems

Actions, reactions, sensations, and addictions: meet your nervous system

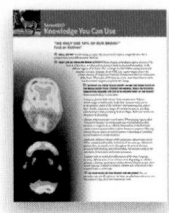

"We only use 10% of our brain!" Fact or fiction?

24 · Hormones

Mood, emotions, growth, and more:
hormones as master regulators

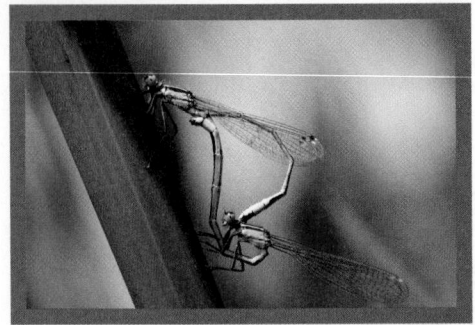

25 · Reproduction and Development

981

From two parents to one embryo to one baby

Business and science in conflict: Why is the number of multiple births—twins, triplets, and more—on the rise?

26 · Immunity and Health

How the body defends and maintains itself

Dear Reader,

My mission is to help you to help your students become scientifically literate and appreciate the beauty and the utility of biology. If students could learn anything from reading this book, I hope it would be this: *Biology is about you, and it touches your life every day, in dozens of ways. It's creative. And it's fun.*

There are two versions of this second edition of *What Is Life? A Guide to Biology*. One of them, *What Is Life? A Guide to Biology with Physiology*, includes all sixteen chapters of the other version, with an additional ten chapters on plant and animal physiology. It's not always possible to include these chapters in a one-term course, but they provide a rich introduction to the importance of biology, with particular significance for human health.

In these pages, your students will find an overview of the key themes in biology as well as detailed information and stories about meaningful topics. I hope they will find answers to questions they're curious about, and will be spurred to ask many more. You'll also find many Red **Q**s, such as:

- Do megadoses of vitamin C reduce cancer risk?

- An onion has five times as much DNA as a human. Why doesn't that make onions more complex than us?

- Why doesn't natural selection lead to the production of perfect organisms?

- Why are big, fierce animal species so rare in the world?

The Red **Q**s point toward passages where students can uncover the answers. They may not believe that the answer is found there. Ask them to look again and think some more. I want them to realize that sometimes they know things they don't realize they know. And sometimes they are learning about things beyond the specific example they're reading about. Recognizing and developing these abilities will help students reason their way through novel problems, serving them well long after they may have forgotten this or that specific fact.

At the end of each chapter, you'll find a section called **StreetBIO: Knowledge You Can Use**. These sections unpack some questions and issues that are particularly practical, such as *How clean is that food you just dropped?* (see Chapter 13).

There's much more to biology than just words. Flip through *What Is Life?* and look at the **photographs**. Images can inspire and provide an alternative hook for remembering and understanding concepts. They can also challenge students to see ideas in new ways. I have hand-picked every photo, with a goal of provoking and engaging your students while helping them make connections between complex ideas.

You'll also notice brief quotes from a variety of literary sources. There is a rich tradition of scientific imagery, references, and metaphors throughout literature. It is my hope that students will recognize that as their scientific literacy is increased, their experience and appreciation of literature will be richer.

In a world of information overload, it is more important than ever for our students to learn how to distill ideas, examples, and implications, forming hierarchies of importance. I don't want your students to lose sight of the big picture. In organizing each chapter, I have broken down the topics into **discrete, manageable sections**. And at the end of each, I highlight the **Take-Home Message** that concisely and precisely highlights and reinforces the section's most important ideas. Packaged with every new copy of the book are laminated, illustrated **To-Go** summaries of each chapter.

A detailed list of second edition changes can be found on the book's companion Web site, but here I want to mention two new pedagogical tools found in every chapter.

- An important goal in my own teaching is to help my students gain proficiency in reading and interpreting graphs. To help your students, I've included an exercise at the end of each chapter called **Graphic**

Content. This critical-thinking challenge will help students become adept at reading and analyzing visual displays of information, while identifying subtle assumptions, biases, and even manipulations.

- At the end of each chapter, the multiple-choice review questions are accompanied by a **difficulty thermometer**. This reflects the difficulty of these questions based on more than ten million responses from students nationwide, using the online adaptive learning system **Prep-U**. By noting the approximate difficulty level of the question, students can more accurately assess how proficient they are with the material.

This is just a sampling of some of the features provided in this textbook. I really hope that your students find the book engaging and valuable and that it helps you to teach your best class ever.

Sincerely,

Jay Phelan

P.S. About the cover: I wanted to convey that biology isn't something that exists far away, separate from our personal lives. Rather, it intersects with our lives and is a central part of our world.

About the Author

Jay Phelan teaches biology at UCLA, where he has taught introductory biology to more than 9,000 majors and non-majors students over the past fourteen years. He is the recipient of more than a dozen teaching awards, including UCLA's highest teaching honor, the Distinguished Teaching Award, in 2011. He received his Ph.D. in evolutionary biology from Harvard in 1995, and his master's and bachelor's degrees from Yale and UCLA. His primary area of research is evolutionary genetics, and his original research has been published in *Evolution, Experimental Gerontology*, and the *Journal of Integrative and Comparative Biology*, among other journals. His research has been featured on *Nightline*, CNN, the BBC, and National Public Radio; in *Science Times* and *Elle*; and in more than a hundred newspapers.

Jay lectures frequently on a variety of topics in education, including the nurturing of critical-thinking skills in undergraduate students, and the use and efficacy of online adaptive assessment software. His research in these areas has been published in the *International Encyclopedia of Education* and other journals.

With economist Terry Burnham, Jay is co-author of the international best-seller *Mean Genes: From Sex to Money to Food—Taming Our Primal Instincts*. Written for the general reader, *Mean Genes* explains in simple terms how knowledge of the genetic basis of human nature can empower individuals to lead more satisfying lives.

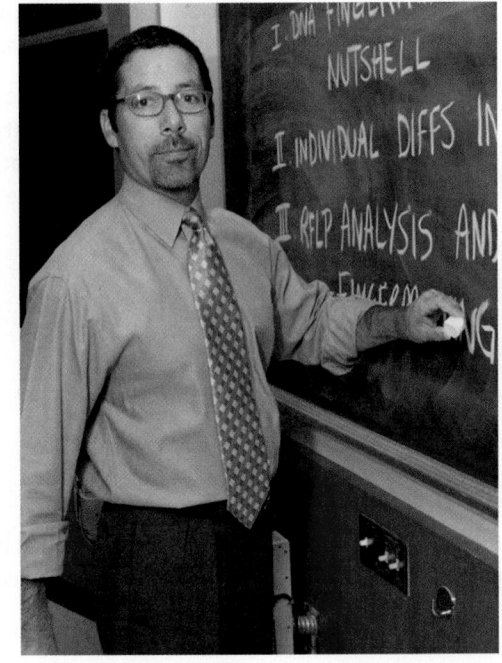

To Julia

Q HOW DOES *WHAT IS LIFE?* SO THOROUGHLY CAPTIVATE NON-MAJORS?

IT WAS CREATED WITH THEM IN MIND.

Engaging Examples

What Is Life? A Guide to Biology threads fascinating, relevant, contemporary examples throughout each chapter.

Brief Sections

Each chapter is broken down into a series of short, accessible sections.

Clear, Consistent Illustrations

Fresh and easy-to-understand figures bring the concepts to life. Collaboratively developed by the author and the scientific illustrator, the text and illustrations are seamlessly integrated, effective learning tools.

Vivid Photos

Striking images appear as unit openers and are combined with illustrations of biological processes, concepts, and experimental techniques to engage the imagination of the student.

 Once breeders recognized the existence of heredity, selective breeding—such as for reduced size in horses—became possible.

Intriguing, Often Surprising Q Questions

Q questions spark students' interest and encourage critical thinking.

Q Drinking diet soda can be deadly if you carry a single bad gene. What gene is it and why is it so deadly?

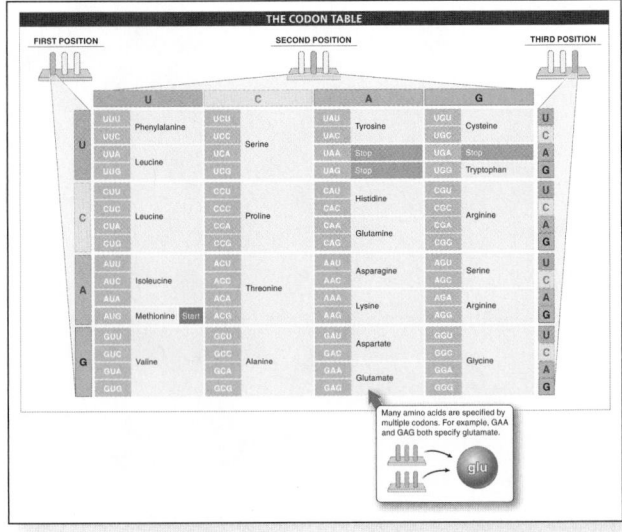

Take-Home Messages

Each section of the chapter includes a concise, memorable summary of key ideas.

TAKE-HOME MESSAGE 7·11

Many traits, including continuously varying traits such as height, eye color, and skin color, are influenced by multiple genes.

End-of-Chapter Study Tools

Each chapter includes Big Ideas—recaps of the key ideas from each section, Key Terms that are page-referenced for quick review, and Check Your Knowledge and short-answer questions.

StreetBios

STREETBIO: KNOWLEDGE YOU CAN USE features are found at the end of every chapter, and demonstrate the practicality and fun of biology. Twenty-five percent are new!

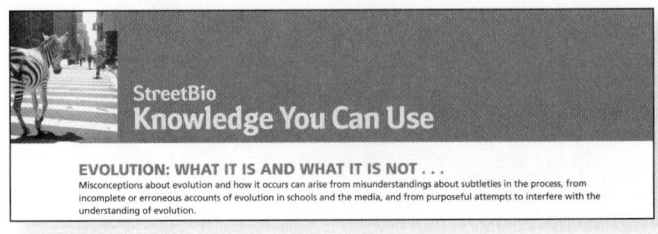

StreetBio
Knowledge You Can Use

EVOLUTION: WHAT IT IS AND WHAT IT IS NOT . . .
Misconceptions about evolution and how it occurs can arise from misunderstandings about subtleties in the process, from incomplete or erroneous accounts of evolution in schools and the media, and from purposeful attempts to interfere with the understanding of evolution.

Graphic Content Helps Students Analyze Data and Think Critically

Each chapter features a graph or chart accompanied by a series of critical-thinking questions that require students to evaluate the data presented.

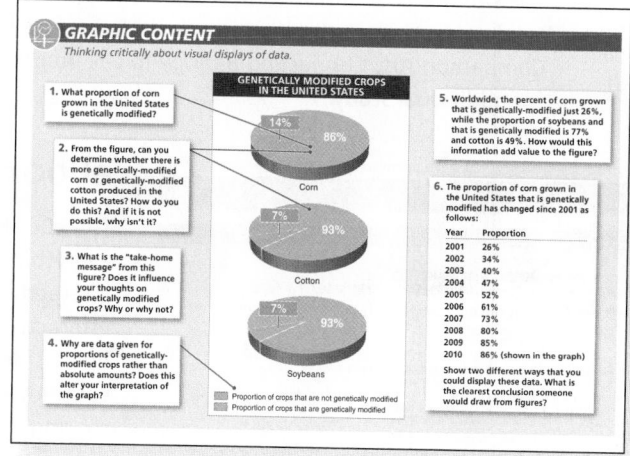

Prep-U Thermometers Rate the Question Difficulty

Thermometers appear next to each end-of-chapter Check Your Knowledge question to help students understand their current level of proficiency.

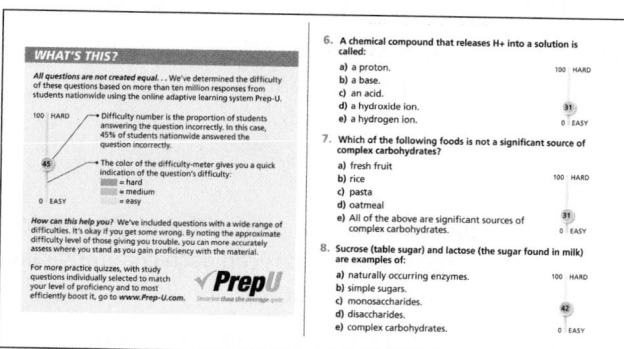

To-Go Guides Provide a Visual Summary of Each Chapter

These laminated guides offer a visual summary for each chapter and serve as a great study tool. They can be packaged with the textbook at no additional cost.

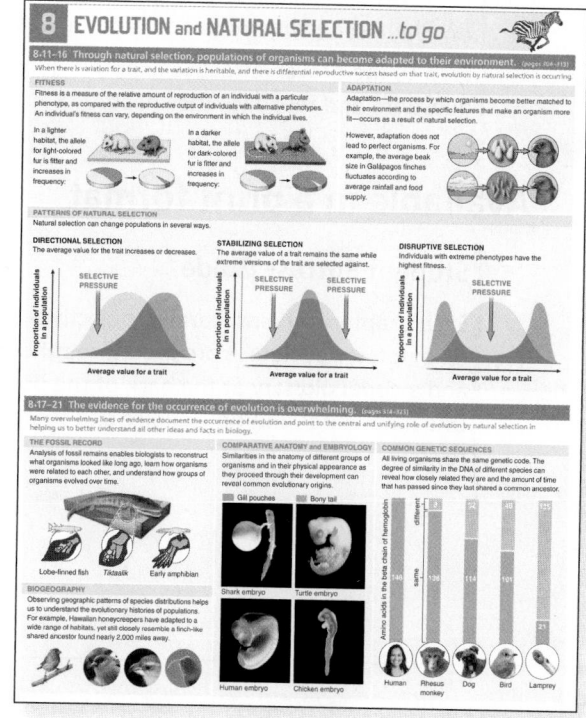

Student Study Tools

Free Book Companion Web site

The site features unrestricted student access to a variety of study tools and learning activities that build on the textbook's content and learning goals. Resources include Q Animations, Take-Home Message Podcasts, Lecture Companion Art, *Connecting Biology to Life Applications*, *Exploring Biology: Case Studies*, and Chapter Quizzes for additional study.

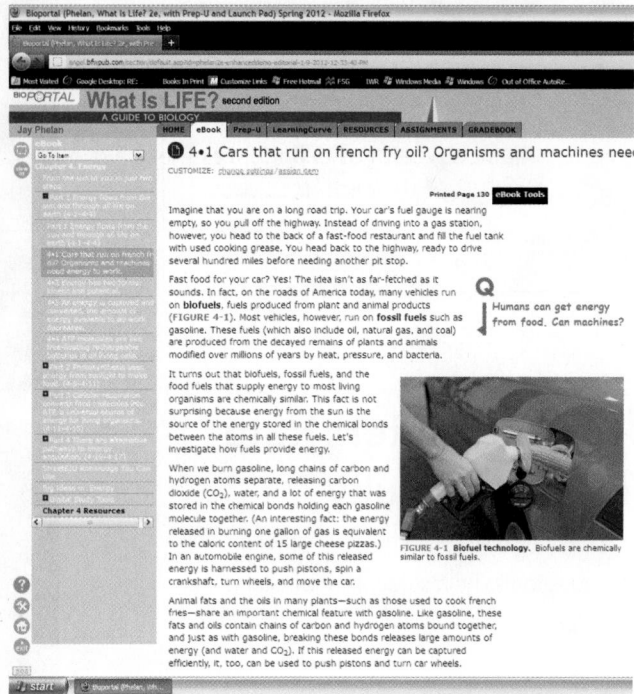

eBook

The eBook for *What Is Life? A Guide to Biology*, Second Edition, offers everything found in the printed textbook and adds the element of interactivity, giving students direct access to online study tools and interactive features like Q Animations that bring complex concepts to life. Students can personalize their eBooks by highlighting important content, adding bookmarks, and adding links, as well as creating and sharing notes. Instructors also can embed unique content to share exclusively with their own classes.

BioPortal with fully integrated Prep-U

BioPortal for *What Is Life? A Guide to Biology* offers an exceptional student experience, with online study tools and activities that help build course mastery. Here, students will find:

- A complete eBook

- All the resources in the Student Book Companion Site Mobile device-friendly Take Home Message Podcasts, which recap each chapter's Take Home Messages and related Challenge Questions

- Interactive Q Animations, which bring complex concepts to life through moving images and narration

- *Exploring Biology: Case Studies*, and *Connecting Biology to Life Applications*, which examine biology hot topics through engaging, magazine-style narratives

- Jay Phelan's Lecture Videos on high-interest biology topics relevant to students' lives

- **Prep-U,** the proven-effective adaptive quizzing program that adjusts to give each student exactly the right questions and feedback they need.

Available in a print format

Student Success Guide

Each chapter contains learning objectives and a lecture outline, in a format that encourages students to take notes. Key figures are used throughout the outline to help students associate images with concepts, and a visual glossary at the back of the book reviews key terms. Chapters conclude with Test Your Understanding—multiple-choice and short-answer practice questions to help with studying and exam review.

Acknowledgments

As a new graduate student at Harvard, I heard from experienced teaching fellows that if you were interested in learning how to be an effective teacher, it was essential to seek out extraordinary mentors. Based on word of mouth, I became involved with E. O. Wilson's course in Evolutionary Biology and Irven DeVore's course in Human Behavioral Biology. Both were known to be unusually provocative, challenging, and entertaining classes for non-science majors. I aggressively pursued teaching positions in both classes—which I held onto tightly for twelve semesters. Working under these legendary instructors, I was set on a course that inspired and prepared me to write this book.

The two courses were quite different from each other, but at their core both were built on two beliefs that are central to this book and to my thinking about education: (1) Biology is creative, interesting, and fun. (2) Biology is relevant to the daily life of every person. There was a palpable sense that, in teaching non-science majors especially, we had a responsibility to provide our students with the tools to thrive in a society increasingly permeated by scientific ideas and issues, and that one of our most effective strategies would be to convey the excitement we felt for biology and the enormous practical value it has to help us understand the world. I thank Professors Wilson and DeVore for all that they have shared with me.

My development as a scientist and, particularly, my appreciation for rigorous and methodical critical thinking have been shaped by the kind support and wise guidance of Richard Lewontin. I have also been fortunate to have as a long-time mentor and collaborator Michael Rose, who has instilled in me a healthy skepticism about any observation in life that is not fivefold replicated. And for almost daily insightful input on matters relating to scientific content, teaching, writing, and more, I thank Terry Burnham.

There are many other friends and colleagues I wish to thank for helping me with *What Is Life?*

In researching and writing the book and in developing the numerous courses I teach, I have benefited from more than a decade of perceptive and valuable contributions, too numerous to list, from Glenn Adelson, Alon Ziv, Michael Cooperson, and Alicia Moretti. I am tremendously appreciative of all they have done for me.

For a project covering so many topics and years, it is essential to have a close group of trusted, tolerant, and knowledgeable colleagues. I am grateful to Harold Owens, Greg Graffin, Brian Swartz, Greg Laden, Jeff Egger, Andy Tobias, Elisabeth Tobias, Joshua Malina, Melissa Merwin-Malina, Bill U'ren, Chris Bruno, Michelle Richmond, and Meredith Dutton, who have offered advice, guidance, and support far beyond the call of duty.

Numerous colleagues at UCLA provided assistance and support, including Steve Strand, Cliff Brunk, Fred Eiserling, Emil Reisler, Victoria Sork, Larry Loeher, Deb Pires, Lianna Johnson, Gaston Pfluegl, Bob Simons, Frank Laski, Jeff Thomas, and Tracy Newman. As a result of their commitment to excellence in the UCLA Life Science Core Curriculum, I have been able to acquire a wealth of experiences that have helped me continue improving as a teacher.

I owe a tremendous debt to Sara Tenney, without whose encouragement and support this project could never have been begun or completed.

W. H. Freeman is an extremely author-centric publisher. Throughout the process of creating this book, from the first inception of the idea through the production of all the supplementary materials, Liz Widdicombe, Brian Napack, and John Sargent have been tremendously supportive. I am grateful for their welcoming me into their publishing family. Publisher Peter Marshall has been a tenacious, versatile, and skillful manager of the entire team. I am very fortunate to have such a wise leader overseeing all aspects of this project.

The team of editors that worked with me on this book— and two people in particular—improved it immeasurably. Development editor Beth Howe oversaw every aspect of the writing and production of the book, attending to issues of content, production, and design while making insightful contributions throughout and expertly managing the thousand details necessary to put everything together. I could not have completed this book without Beth's commitment and guidance. And I cannot adequately convey my gratitude to development editor Jane Tufts, whose meticulous attention to detail, commitment to accuracy, and almost obsessive drive to create a thorough and readable book are apparent on every page.

It is impossible to teach biology without illustrations. My deepest gratitude goes to Tommy Moorman for creating such innovative and effective figures for the book. Tommy's vision for an elegant and beautiful art program completely integrated with the text is apparent on every page. Working with him to develop each illustration in this book has been (and continues to be) one of my most enjoyable and satisfying professional collaborations. Thanks also go to Alison

Kendall and to Erin Daniel for assisting with the creation of the illustrations and for work on the To Go guides. For the design of the book, I thank Tom Carling. And for excellent assistance with photo research thanks to Julia Phelan, Deborah Anderson, and Christine Buese.

I wish to thank Harvey Pough for his assistance with the first edition of *What Is Life?* for which he provided excellent drafts of Chapters 11–13 and contributions to Chapter 16.

For creating the innovative media and print materials that accompany the book, I am thankful for the contributions of Patrick Shriner, Mike Jones, and Beth McHenry, and for the extensive input of supplements editors Amanda Dunning and Marni Rolfes. I thank all the contributors and advisors who helped create the student and instructor resources— your efforts have been invaluable. I thank Jennifer Warner and Meredith Norris for their work on the Student Success Guide, and for Jennifer's willingness to share her classroom experiences with the sales force. I also appreciate the contributions of Troy Williams and the Prep-U team. Sheri Snavely provided significant input in developing pedagogical strategies throughout the book; I also appreciate her thoughtful and smart advice at nearly every step in the publishing process.

Copyeditor Linda Strange helped to ensure consistency and readability throughout the text. I thank Chris Hunt for compiling the thorough index. The rest of the life sciences editorial team at W. H. Freeman, too, have been knowledgeable and supportive, particularly Kate Parker, Marc Mazzoni, Jerry Correa, Susan Winslow, Elaine Palucki, and Lisa Samols.

For their efficiency and commitment to producing a beautiful book, I am most grateful to the W. H. Freeman production team: Sheridan Sellers, Mary Louise Byrd, Diana Blume, Susan Wein, Philip McCaffrey, and Ellen Cash.

The people on the marketing team at W. H. Freeman have contributed enormously in helping with the challenging task of introducing a new book to students and instructors across the country. Debbie Clare, Steve Rigolosi, Lindsey Veautour, and John Britch have been enthusiastic and dedicated in creating materials and strategies to assist instructors in evaluating the ways in which *What Is Life?* can aid them as they develop their own courses and strategies for success.

Finally, I thank my family—Kevin Phelan, Patrick Phelan, Erin Enderlin, and my parents—for their unwavering support and interest as I wrote this book. Reading draft after draft and following each revision, they made valuable contributions at every stage. I thank Jack, Charlie, and Sam, too. Most of all, for her generous and passionate support of this project from day one, her substantive contributions to both the content and presentation of ideas, and so much more, I thank Julia.

Contact the author with your feedback.

The content of this book has been greatly improved through the comments of reviewers and students. Your comments, suggestions, and criticism are also welcome; they are essential in guiding its ongoing evolution. Please contact the author at **jay@jayphelan.com.** I'm serious.

We thank the many reviewers who aided in the development of this text.

Second Edition Text Development

Jessica Adams, Southwestern Illinois College
Sylvester Allred, Northern Arizona University
Kim Atwood, Cumberland University
Nina Baghai-Riding, Delta State University
E. A. Bailey, Alamance Community College
Donna Becker, Northern Michigan University
Charles Biles, East Central University
Tolga Bilgen, University of Washington
Donna Bivans, Pitt Community College
TJ Bliss, Brigham Young University
Barbara Blonder, Flagler College
Judy Bluemer, Morton College
Cheryl Boice, Florida Gateway College
Lisa Boggs, Southwestern Oklahoma State University
Bruno Borsari, Winona State University
Laura Bradshaw, Illinois Central College
Judy Brooks, Blinn College
Wendy Brown, Danville Area Community College
Bruce Carroll, Lone Star College–North Harris
Michelle Cawthorn, Georgia Southern University
David Chambers, Concord University
Jianguo Chen, Claflin University
Richard Cheney, Christopher Newport University
Genevieve Chung, Broward College
Elizabeth Co, Diablo Valley College
Robert Conover, Glendale College
Erica Corbett, Southeastern Oklahoma State University
Cathy Cornett, University of Wisconsin–Platteville
Sarah Cotton, Chaffey College
James Courtright, Marquette University
Richard Cowart, University of Dubuque
Hattie Dambroski, Normandale Community College
Jim Daugherty, Glendale Community College
Buffany DeBoer, Wayne State College
Jennifer Dechaine, Central Washington University
Tracy Deem, Bridgewater College
Theresa Dehne, Chippewa Valley Technical College
Paul Delaney, Copper Mountain Community College
Danielle Dodenhoff, California State University Bakersfield
Craig Denesha, Spartanburg Community College
Hartmut Doebel, George Washington University
Brett Dooley, Patrick Henry Community College
Hawkins Dowis, Fresno City College
Dani DuCharme, Waubonsee Community College
Jacquelyn Duke, Baylor University
Michael Edgehouse, Lewis-Clark State College

Jamin Eisenbach, Eastern Michigan University
Jennifer Ellington, Belmont Abbey College
Susan Epperson, University of Colorado, Colorado Springs
Marirose Ethington, Genesee Community College
Myriam Feldman, Lake Washington Institute of Technology
Arnaldo Ferreira, Chaffey College
Ryan Fisher, Salem State University
Reza Forough, Bellevue College
Brandon Foster, Wake Technical Community College
Sarah Gall, Ashford University
Cynthia Galloway, Texas A&M University–Kingsville
Joseph Gar, West Kentucky Community and Technical College
Tom Gehring, Central Michigan University
Alexandros Georgakilas, East Carolina University
Patricia Geppert, University of Texas at San Antonio
Julie Gibbs, College of DuPage
Caitlin Gille, Pasco Hernando Community College
Brad Goodbar, College of the Sequoias
Becky Graham, Ohio Dominican University
Sherri Graves, Sacramento City College
Madoka Gray-Mitsumune, Concordia University
Jeff Green, Nashville State Community College
Cindy Gustafson-Brown, University of California, San Diego
Sue Habeck, Tacoma Community College
Mark Haefele, Community College of Denver
Kathryn Hanley, New Mexico State University
Krista Henderson, California State University, Fullerton
John Hoffman, Arcadia University
Thomas Horvath, State University of New York–Oneonta
Anne-Marie Hoskinson, Gustavus Adolphus College
Laurie Host, Harford Community College
Catherine Hurlbut, Florida State College at Jacksonville
Godwin Ifere, Clark Atlanta University
Virginia Irintcheva, Black Hawk College
Robert Iwan, Inver Hills Community College
Mark Jackson, Central Connecticut State University
Elisabeth Javazon, Morehouse College
John Jenkin, Blinn College
Mitrick Johns, Northern Illinois University
Scott Johnson, Wake Technical Community College
Richard Karp, University of Cincinnati
Cynthia Kay-Nishiyama, California State University Northridge
Elena Keeling, California Polytechnic State University
Joe Keen, Patrick Henry Community College
Amanda Kin, Jefferson State Community College
Melissa Kosinski-Collins, Brandeis University
Joe Kremer, Alvernia University
Dhirendra Kumar, East Tennessee State University

Dana Kurpius, Elgin Community College
Karen Kurvink, Moravian College
Kim Lackey, University of Alabama
Jordana LaFantasie, Fort Hays State University
Kevin Lam, Alexander College
Ellen Lamb, University of North Carolina at Greensboro
Lorraine Leiser, Southeast Community College
Laurie Len, El Camino College
Suzanne Long, Monroe Community College
Mark Manteuffel, St. Louis Community College
Brian Maricle, Fort Hays State University
John Markham, University of Manitoba
Jennifer Maupin, Santa Barbara City College
Lilly Mayer, Clackamas Community College
Tom McConnell, Ball State University
Maura McGrail, Iowa State University
Michael McLeod, Belmont Abbey College
Patricia Melloy, Fairleigh Dickinson University
Diane Melroy, University of North Carolina at Wilmington
Jon Milhon, Azusa Pacific University
Rachel Mintell, Manchester Community College
June Minter, Patrick Henry Community College
Kiran Misra, Edinboro University of Pennsylvania
Alice Monroe, St. Petersburg College
Frances Moore, Patrick Henry Community College
Ulrike Muller, California State University–Fresno
Necia Nicholas, Calhoun Community College
Zia Nisani, Antelope Valley College
Fran Norflus, Clayton State University
Chuma Okere, Clark Atlanta University
Phillip Ortiz, Empire State College
Marie Panec, Moorpark College
Wiline Pangle, The Ohio State University
Randi Papke, Southwestern Illinois College
Brian Paulson, California University of Pennsylvania
Micah Perkins, Owensboro Community and Technical College
Lori Pitkofsky, Ramapo College of New Jersey
Anita Plagge, San Diego Mesa College
Michael Plotkin, Mt. San Jacinto College
Heather Prestridge, Blinn College
Diane Purves, Crafton Hills College
Chittur Radhakrishnan, Santa Fe College
Stuart Reichler, University of Texas at Austin
Sheila Reilly, Belmont Abbey College
Carol Rhodes, Canada College
Eugenia Ribeiro-Hurley, Fordham University
Troy Rohn, Boise State University
Lori Rose, Hill College
Bill Rogers, Ball State University
John Rousseau, Whatcom Community College
Matthew Rowe, Sam Houston State University
Edward Saiff, Ramapo College of New Jersey

Eduardo Salazar, Temple College
Tom Saleska, Concordia University Wisconsin
Shamili Sandiford, College of DuPage
Jennifer Schepp, College of Charleston
Jennifer Schramm, Chemekta Community College
John Schampel, Phoenix College
Roger Seeber, West Liberty University
Brian Seymour, Edward Waters College
Dave Sheldon, St. Clair County Community College
Cara Shillington, Eastern Michigan University
Jack Shurley, Idaho State University
Gillian Schultz, Foothill College
Brian Seymour, Edward Waters College
Dale Smoak, Piedmont Technical College
Suzanne Sousa, Middlesex Community College
Agnes Southgate, College of Charleston
Richard Stiehl, Pima Community College
Lisa Strain, Northeast Lakeview College
Jackie Swanik, Wake Technical Community College
Robert Swatski, Harrisburg Area Community College–York Campus
Ignatius Tan, New York University
Kimberly Taugher, Diablo Valley Community College
John Taylor, Southern Utah University
Pamela Thinesen, Century College
Douglas Thrower, University of California, Santa Barbara
Nina Thumser, Edinboro University of Pennsylvania
Elizabeth Tomlin, University of North Carolina at Greensboro
Edward Tucker, Baruch College, City University of New York
Virginia Turner, Harper College
Kimberly Vietti, Illinois Central College
Thomas Vogel, Western Illinois University
Joannna Vondrasek, Piedmont Virginia Community College
Erikc Wada, Folsom Lake College
Judy Wallace, Middlesex Community College
Dennis Walsh, MassBay Community College
Yunqiu Wang, University of Miami
Chelsea Ward, Auburn University, Montgomery
Katherine Warpeha, University of Illinois at Chicago
David Webb, St. Clair County Community College
Michael Wenzel, California State University–Sacramento
Tina Whitney, Governors State University
Robert Whyte, California University of Pennsylvania
Rachel Wiechman, West Liberty University
Matt Wilkerson, Carson Newman College
Andrew Wold, Fond Du Lac Tribal and Community College
Donald Wood, Odessa College
Dulce Zayas-Alvarez, Southwestern Community College
David Zeigler, University of North Carolina at Pembroke
Jacquelyn Zevenbergen, Kent State University, Stark Campus
Brenda Zink, Northeastern Junior College
Gerald Zuercher, University of Dubuque

Second Edition
Focus Group Participants

(2010, Albuquerque)

Tonya Bates, University of North Carolina at Charlotte
Craig Clifford, Northeastern State University, Oklahoma
Danielle DuCharme, Waubonsee Community College
Ana Escandon, Los Angeles Harbor College
Mark Hens, University of North Carolina at Greensboro
Jessica Hopkins, University of Akron
Lorraine Leiser, Southeast Community College
Ashley Ramer, University of Akron
Sydha Salihu, West Virginia University
Jennifer Stueckle, West Virginia University
Jennifer Warner, University of North Carolina at Charlotte

(2010, New York City)

Joseph Ahlander, Northeastern State University
Tami Asplin, North Dakota State University
Caroline "Lena" Ballard, Rock Valley College
Charlotte Borgeson, University of Nevada–Reno
Susan Bower, Pasadena College
Greg Dalhem, North Kentucky University
Moon Draper, University of Texas at Austin
Gloria Hoffman, Morgan State University
Craig Jordan, University of Texas at San Antonio
Michael Koban, Morgan State University

Josephine Kurdziel, University of Michigan
Ellen Lamb, University of North Carolina at Greensboro
Jennifer Scoby, Illinois Central College

(2011, New York City)

Jennie Bever, Arizona State University
Michelle Cawthorn, Georgia Southern University
John Constable, California State University–Fresno
Elisabeth Javazon, Morehouse College
Brian Kram, Prince George's Community College
Lorraine Leiser, Southeast Community College
Cassandra Moore-Crawford, Prince George's Community College
Ulrike Müller, California State University–Fresno
Wiline Pangle, The Ohio State University
Jennifer Warner, University of North Carolina at Charlotte
Michael Wenzel, California State University–Sacramento
   and Folsom Lake Community College

(2011, Santa Monica, California)

Joseph Ahlander, Northeastern State University
Tonya Bates, University of North Carolina at Charlotte
Sara Carlson, University of Akron
Michelle Cawthorn, Georgia State University
Christina Couroux, Los Angeles Harbor College
Ana Escandon, Los Angeles Harbor College
Michael Greene, Delgado Community College
Krista Henderson, California State University–Fullerton
Gigi Saunders, Missouri State University

First Edition
Text Development

Stephanie J. Aamodt, University of Louisiana–Shreveport
M. Stephen Ailstock, Anne Arundel Community College
Sylvester Allred, Northern Arizona University
Jessica K. Baack, Montgomery Community College–Rockville
Sarah Barlow, Middle Tennessee State University
Rebecca A. Bartow, Western Kentucky University
Brian J. Baumgartner, Trinity Valley Community College
Jose Bava, El Camino Community College
Lisa L. Boggs, Southwestern Oklahoma State University
Charlotte Borgeson, University of Nevada–Reno
Peggy Brickman, University of Georgia
Jason Brown, Young Harris College
Carole L. Browne, Wake Forest University
Neil J. Buckley, State University of New York–Plattsburgh
Anne E. Bunnell, East Carolina University
Joseph Burdo, Bridgewater State University
David Byres, Florida Community College at Jacksonville
William Caire, University of Central Oklahoma
Michael S. Carr, Oakton Community College
Kelly Carrillo Burke, College of the Canyons
Thomas Chen, Santa Monica College
Thomas F. Chubb, Villanova University
Nira Clark, Southwestern College
Erica Cline, University of Washington
George Clokey, University of Wisconsin–Whitewater
Anthony D. Cornett, Valencia Community College, Osceola
Karen Curto, University of Pittsburgh
Don C. Dailey, Austin Peay State University
Douglas W. Darnowski, Indiana University–Southeast
Garry Davies, University of Alaska
Renee Dawson, University of Utah
Lewis E. Deaton, University of Louisiana–Lafayette
Tom Deaton, Auburn University
Elizabeth Anne Desy, Southwestern Minnesota State University
Doreen R. Dewell, Whatcom Community College
Mary E. Dominiecki, Slippery Rock University
Charles Dunn, Austin Community College
Frank DuRoy, Essex County College
Kari Eamma, Tarrant County Community College–Northeast
Heidi Engelhardt, Brandon University
Marirose T. Ethington, Genesee Community College
Rebecca A. Fetherson, University of Dayton
Robert C. Frankis, University of New Mexico
Monica C. Frazier, Columbus State University
Anne Galbraith, University of Wisconsin–La Crosse
Sandra Gibbons, Moraine Valley College
Philip G. Gibson, Gwinnett Technical College
Andrew Goliszek, North Carolina A &T State University
Stephen M. Gómez, Central New Mexico Community College
Becky C. Graham, University of West Alabama
Cara Gubbins, Butte College
Charles (Billy) Gunnels IV, Florida Gulf Coast University

Janelle M. Hare, Morehead State University
Carla Hass, Pennsylvania State University
Colleen Hatfield, California State University–Chico
J. L. Henriksen, Bellevue Community College
John A. Hnida, Peru State College
Thomas Horvath, State University of New York–Oneonta
Adam W. Hrincevich, Louisiana State University
Dianne Jennings, Virginia Commonwealth University
Mitrick A. Johns, Northern Illinois University
Robert D. Johnson Jr., Pierce College
Martin A. Kapper, Central Connecticut State University
Arnold J. Karpoff, University of Louisville
Todd Kelson, Brigham Young University–Idaho
Stephen T. Kenny, Yakima Valley Community College
Jennifer M. Kilbourne, Community College of Baltimore County
Joanne Kilpatrick, Auburn University–Montgomery
Brenda Knotts, Eastern Illinois University
Michael Koban, Morgan State University
Catherine Koo, Caldwell College
Jerome A. Krueger, South Dakota State University
Jim Krupa, University of Kentucky
Ellen Shepard Lamb, University of North Carolina at Greensboro
Thomas Landefeld, California State University–Dominquez Hills
Leah LaPerle Larkin, University of New Mexico
Lynn Larsen, Portland Community College
Kathleen H. Lavoie, State University of New York–Plattsburgh
Gregory P. Lewis, Furman University
Harvey Liftin, Broward Community College
Tammy J. Liles, Lexington Community College
Cynthia W. Littlejohn, University of Southern Mississippi
Jonathan Lochamy, Georgia Perimeter College
Melanie Loo, California State University–Sacramento
Juan M. Lopez-Bautista, University of Alabama
Blasé Maffia, University of Miami
Jeffrey M. Marcus, Western Kentucky University
Betsy Maxim, Austin Community College
Karen McFarland, Austin Peay State University
Mark A. McGinley, Texas Technical University
John Mersfelder, Sinclair Community College
Shahroukh Mistry, Westminster College
Jeanne Mitchell, Truman State University
Beth A. Montelone, Kansas State University
Cynthia L. Morin, Lincoln University of Missouri
Royden Nakamura, California Polytechnic–San Luis Obispo
Rocky Nation, Southern Wesleyan University
Allan D. Nelson, Tarleton State University
Tania Nezrick, Kishwaukee College
David Niebuhr, College of William and Mary
Meredith Sommerville Norris, University of North Carolina at Charlotte
Alexander E. Olvido, Virginia State University
Randi Papke, Southwestern Illinois College
Mary Paulson, Central Washington University
John M. Pleasants, Iowa State University
Gregory J. Podgorski, Utah State University
Melissa Presch, California State University–Fullerton

Eric Rabitoy, Citrus College
Karen Raines, Colorado State University
Dawn Ranish, Nova Southeastern University
Erin Rempala, San Diego Mesa College
Melody Ricci, Victor Valley
Kathleen Richardson, Portland Community College
Dave Rintoul, Kansas State University
Steven Rissing, The Ohio State University
Robert R. Robbins, Utah Valley State College
Bill Rogers, Ball State University
Troy T. Rohn, Boise State University
Susan T. Rouse, Southern Wesleyan University
Lynette Rushton, South Puget Sound Community College
Michael L. Rutledge, Middle Tennessee State University
Shamili Ajgaonkar Sandiford, College of DuPage
Fayla Schwartz, Everett Community College
Erik P. Scully, Towson University
Juanita C. Sharpe, Chicago State University
Marilyn Shopper, Johnson County Community College
Michele Shuster, New Mexico State University
Neil E. Simister, Brandeis University
Anu Singh-Cundy, Western Washington University
Jennifer Skillen, College of Southern Nevada
Kerri M. Skinner, University of Nebraska–Kearny
Marc Allen Smith, Sinclair Community College
Nancy G. Solomon, Miami University of Ohio
Roberta Lynn Soltz, Central Washington University
Bryan G. Spohn, Florida Community College at Jacksonville–Kent Campus
Amanda Starnes, Emory University
Leo Sternberg, University of Miami
Joan C. Stover, South Seattle Community College
Sukanya V. Subramanian, Collin County Community College
Franklyn Tan Te, Miami Dade Community College
William J. Thieman, Ventura College
Pamela Thinesen, Century College
Michael W. Thompson, Middle Tennessee State University
Martin A. Vaughan, Indiana University–Purdue University Indianapolis
Jack Waber, West Chester University of Pennsylvania
Jennifer M. Warner, University of North Carolina at Charlotte
John E. Whitlock, Hillsborough Community College
Elizabeth Willott, University of Arizona
Clifford Wilson, Chicago State University
Mark Woelfle, Vanderbilt University
Calvin Young, Fullerton College
Brenda Zink, Northeastern Junior College

First Edition
Art Development

Ann Aguanno, Marymount Manhattan College
Kelly Carrillo Burke, College of the Canyons
William Caire, University of Central Oklahoma
Debra Chapman, Wilkes University
Genevieve C. Chung, Broward Community College
Jeffrey Scott Coker, Elon University
Michael S. Dann, Pennsylvania State University
Renee Dawson, University of Utah

Francisco Delgado, Pima Community College
Doreen R. Dewell, Whatcom Community College
Hartmut G. Doebel, George Washington University
Diane Lynn Doidge, Grand View College
James Doyle, College of the Holy Cross
Dave Eakin, Eastern Kentucky University
Paul Farnsworth, University of New Mexico
Brandon L. Foster, Wake Technical and Community College
Patrick Galliart, North Iowa Community College
David Gordon, Pittsburg State University
Charles (Billy) Gunnels IV, Florida Gulf Coast University
Bernard Hauser, University of Florida
Jane J. Henry, Baton Rouge Community College
Mark A. Holland, Salisbury University
Virginia E. Irintcheva, Black Hawk College–Quad City Campus
Philip Jardim, City College of San Francisco
Denim M. Jochimsen, University of Idaho
Judy Kaufman, Monroe Community College
Ariel R. Krakowski, Laney College
Dan E. Krane, Wright State University
Maria Kretzman, Glendale College
Kathleen H. Lavoie, State University of New York–Plattsburgh
Mary LeFever, Columbus State Community College
Stephen Matheson, Calvin College
James McCaughern-Carucci, Quinnipiac University
Lori A. Pitkofsky, Rampano College
Michael P. Robinson, Miami University
Wendy F. Rothwell, University of California–Santa Cruz
Jason F. Schreer, State University of New York–Potsdam
Jennifer J. Scoby, Illinois Central College
Dawn Sherry, Macon State University
Cara Shillington, Eastern Michigan University
Patricia L. Smith, Valencia Community College
Jeffrey Thomas, California State University–Northridge
Bruce Tomlinson, State University of New York–Fredonia
Joy B. Trauth, Arkansas State University
Alan R. Wasmoen, Metropolitan Community College
Michael Windelspecht, Appalachian State University
David E. Wolfe, American River College
Kerry Yurewicz, Plymouth State University

First Edition
Accuracy Reviewers

Christine Bezotte, Elmira College
Michael Carr, Oakton Community College
Erica Champion
William Crampton, University of Central Florida
Michael S. Dann, Pennsylvania State University
Bernard Hauser, University of Florida
John A. Hnida, Peru State College
Kelly Hogan, University of North Carolina at Chapel Hill
Anne Houtman, California State University–Fullerton
Ariel R. Krakowski, Laney College
Michael Silva, El Paso Community College
Pamela Thinesen, Century College
Jeffrey Thomas, California State University–Northridge

Michael Wenzel, California State University–Sacramento
John E. Whitlock, Hillsborough Community College

First Edition
Focus Group Attendees
Text and Content Development

(2004, Los Angeles)
Garen Baghdasarian, Santa Monica College
Thomas Chen, Santa Monica College
Elizabeth Ciletti, Pasadena City College
Mary Colavito, Santa Monica College
Ana Ester Escandon, Los Angeles Harbor College
Phyllis Hirsh, East Los Angeles College
Melody Ricci, Victor Valley College

(2004, Memphis)
T. Wayne Barger, Tennessee Technical University
Don Baud, University of Memphis
Jay Blundon, Rhodes College
Martha P. Brown, University of Memphis
Dave Eakin, Eastern Kentucky University
Stan Eisen, Christian Brothers University
Jack Grubaugh, University of Memphis
Min-Ken Lao, Furman University

(2004, Chicago)
Sandra Bobick, Community College of Alleghany
Christopher Dobson, Grand Valley State University
Sondra Dubowsky, Allen County Community College
Eileen Gregory, Rollins College
Tracy Harris, Florida Keys Community College
Robert Krasner, Providence College
Bernard A. Marcus, Genesee Community College
Laurel B. Roberts, University of Pittsburgh
Lyndell P. Robinson, Lincoln Land Community College
Brian Schmaefsky, Kingwood College
Janet Vigna, Grand Valley State University
Daniel W. Ward, Waubonsee Community College

(2006, Florida)
Peggy Brickman, University of Georgia
Anne E. Bunnell, East Carolina University
Cara Gubbins, Butte College
Janelle M. Hare, Morehead State University
John A. Hnida, Peru State College
Mitrick A. Johns, Northern Illinois University
Kathleen H. Lavoie, State University of New York–Plattsburgh
Blasé Maffia, University of Miami
Gregory J. Podgorski, Utah State University
Susan T. Rouse, Southern Wesleyan University
Jennifer M. Warner, University of North Carolina at Charlotte

Art Development

(2007, Atlanta)
Renee Dawson, University of Utah
Charles (Billy) Gunnels IV, Florida Gulf Coast University
Bernard Hauser, University of Florida

Arnold J. Karpoff, University of Louisville
Stephen R. Kelso, University of Illinois at Chicago
Meredith Sommerville Norris, University of North Carolina at Charlotte
Therese M. Poole, Georgia State University
Mary Celeste Reese, Mississippi State University
Bill Rogers, Ball State University
Kim Cleary Sadler, Middle Tennessee State University
Amy S. Wernette, Hazard Community College

Media and Supplements

(2007, Santa Monica)
Michael Bucher, College of San Mateo
Kelly Carrillo Burke, College of the Canyons
John A. Hnida, Peru State College
Anne Houtman, California State University–Fullerton
Hinrich Kaiser, Victor Valley College
Melanie Loo, California State University–Sacramento
Gregory J. Podgorski, Utah State University
Melissa Presch, California State University–Fullerton
Calvin Young, Fullerton College

(2008, Miami)
Barbara Blonder, Flagler College
Charlotte Borgeson, University of Nevada–Reno
Kris Curran, University of Wisconsin–Whitewater
Kari Eamma, Tarrant Community College
Evelyn Frazier, Florida Atlantic University
John Janovy, University of Nebraska–Lincoln
Jennifer Schramm, Chemeketa Community College
Greg Sievert, Emporia University
Heather Vance Chalcraft, East Carolina University
Martin Vaughn, Indiana University–Purdue University Indianapolis

First Edition
Comparative Reviewers

Zulfiqar Ahmad, East Tennessee State University
Julie H. Aires, Florida Community College at Jacksonville
Mahmood Anwar, Palm Beach Community College
William Anyonge, Xavier University
Tami Asplin, North Dakota State University
Christine Barrow, Prince George's Community College
Joressia Beyer, John Taylor Community College
Randy Brewton, University of Tennessee–Knoxville
Dustin Brisson, University of Pennsylvania
Jeannie Chapman, University of South Carolina–Upstate
Thomas Chen, Santa Monica College
Cary Chevalier, Missouri Western State University
Craig Clifford, Northeastern State University
Vince Connors, University of South Carolina–Upstate
William Gareth Richard Crampton, University of Central Florida
Chris Davison, Long Beach City College
Kevin Dees, Wharton City Junior College
Doreen Dewell, Whatcom Community College
Tiffany Doan, Central Connecticut State University
Ernest F. DuBrul, University of Toledo

Contributors and Advisors

Instructor's Manual—Classroom Catalysts

Verona A. Barr, Heartland Community College
Stephen M. Gómez, Central New Mexico Community College
Paul H. Marshall, Northern Essex Community College

eBook and Non-Major's Biology Study Tools

Amy Combs
Robert Iwan, Inver Hills Community College
Eric Stavney, Pierce College

Exploring Biology: Case Studies

Michelle Cawthorn, Georgia Southern University
Jennifer L. Holzman, Emory University

Figure Conversion Engine

Ann Aguanno, Marymount Manhattan College

Hands-On Biology: Laboratories for Distance Learning

Mimi Bres, Cassandra Moore-Crawford, and Arnold Weisshaar, Prince George's Community College (all)

Image Bank Advisor

Jane J. Henry, Baton Rouge Community College

Keynote Lecture Presentation

Michael C. Bucher, College of San Mateo

PowerPoint Lecture Outlines

Kristen L. Curran, University of Wisconsin–Whitewater
Danielle DuCharme, Waubonsee Community College
Jennifer Lange, Chabot College
Mark S. Manteuffel, St. Louis Community College

Prep-U Instructor's Test Bank and Prep-U for Students

Glenn Adelson, Lake Forrest College
Jay Phelan, University of California, Los Angeles
Alon Ziv, Prep-U

Q Animations

Anne Bunnell, East Carolina University
G. Chung, Broward College
Johnny El-Rady, University of South Florida
Julie V. Gibbs, College of DuPage
Eric Stavney, North Seattle Community College

Student Worksheets

Michael C. Bucher, College of San Mateo

Reviewers

Ann Aguanno, Marymount Manhattan College
Charlotte E. Borgeson, University of Nevada–Reno
Kelly Burke, College of the Canyons
Michelle Cawthorn, Georgia Southern University
Michael S. Dann, Pennsylvania State University
Debra B. Folsom, Pasadena City College
Julie V. Gibbs, College of DuPage
Stephen M. Gómez, Central New Mexico Community College
Jane J. Henry, Baton Rouge Community College
Jane Horlings, Saddleback College
Carina Endres Howell, Lock Haven University
John Janovy, Jr., University of Nebraska–Lincoln
Hinrich Kaiser, Victor Valley College
Judy Kaufman, Monroe Community College
Charlease Kelly-Jackson, Claflin University
Patrick J. Lewis, Sam Houston State University
Cindy S. Malone, California State University–Northridge
Meredith S. Norris, University of North Carolina at Charlotte
Greg Podgorski, Utah State University
Lawrence F. Roberge, Florida Community College at Jacksonville
William D. Rogers, Ball State University
Georgianna Saunders, Missouri State University
Jason Schreer, State University of New York–Potsdam
Marilyn Shopper, Johnson County Community College
Carol St. Angelo, Hofstra University
Eric Stavney, Pierce College
Alicia Steinhardt, Hartnell College
Jamey Thompson, Hudson Valley Community College
Helen Walter, Diablo Valley College
Jennifer M. Warner, University of North Carolina at Charlotte
Michael Windelspecht, Appalachian State University

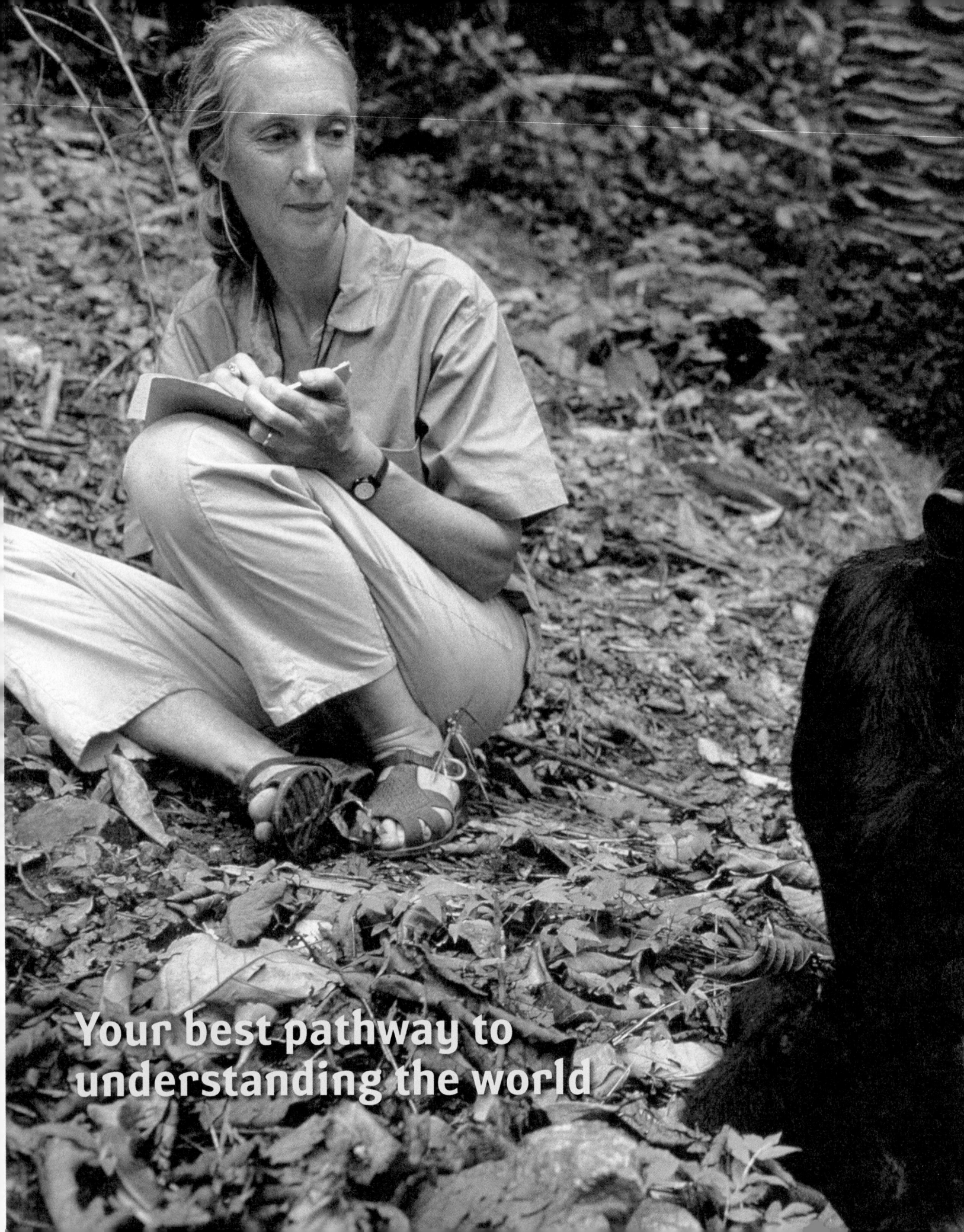

Your best pathway to
understanding the world

1

Scientific Thinking

1·1–1·3 Science is a collection of facts and a process for understanding the world.

Already a scientist? It starts with curiosity.

1·1 What is science? What is biology?

You are already a scientist. You may not have realized this yet, but it's true. Because humans are curious, you have no doubt asked yourself or others questions about how the world works and wondered how you might find the answers.

- Does the radiation released by cell phones cause brain tumors?

- Do large doses of vitamin C reduce the likelihood of getting a cold?

These are important and serious questions. But you've probably also pondered some less weighty issues, too.

- Why is morning breath so stinky? And can you do anything to prevent it?

- Why is it easier to remember gossip than physics equations?

And if you really put your mind to the task, you will start to find questions all around you whose answers you might like to know (and some whose answers you'll learn as you read this book).

- Which parent determines a baby's sex? Why?

- Why do so few women get into barroom brawls?

- What is "blood doping," and does it really improve athletic performance?

- Why is it so much easier for an infant to learn a complex language than it is for a college student to learn biology?

Still not convinced you're a scientist? Here's something important to know: science doesn't require advanced degrees or secret knowledge dispensed over years of technical training. It does, however, require an important feature of our species: a big brain, as well as curiosity and a desire to learn. But curiosity, casual observations, and desire can take you only so far. Many pressing issues require some understanding of science, what it can and can't do, and what it can and can't explain. Consider, for example, nutritional claims on foods and dietary supplements, human behavior, health and disease, the interactions of plants, animals, and their environments, global climate change, the continuity and diversity of life in all its forms. By learning more about science, you can understand your life and the world around you.

Explaining how something works or why something happens requires methodical, objective, and rational observations and analysis that are not clouded with emotions or preconceptions. **Science** is not simply a body of knowledge or a list of facts to be remembered. It is an intellectual activity, encompassing observation, description, experimentation, and explanation of natural phenomena. Put another way, science is a pathway by which we can come to discover and better understand our world.

Later in this chapter, we explore specific ways in which we can most effectively use scientific thinking in our lives. But first let's look at a single powerful question that underlies scientific thinking:

How do you know that is true?

Once you begin asking this question—of others and of yourself—you are on the road to a better understanding of the world.

The following two stories about popular and successful products show the importance of questioning the truth of many "scientific" claims you see on merchandise packages or read in a newspaper or on the internet.

Dannon yogurt. According to the Federal Trade Commission (FTC), a U.S. government agency with the mission of consumer protection, the Dannon Company claimed in nationwide advertisements that its Activia yogurt relieves irregularity and helps with "slow intestinal transit time." Dannon also claimed that its DanActive dairy drink helps prevent colds and flu (**FIGURE 1-1**). The FTC charged that the ads were deceptive because there was no substantiation for the claims and, further, that the claims had been clinically proven to be false. In an agreement finalized in 2011, Dannon agreed to pay $21 million in fines and to stop making those claims unless the company gets reliable scientific evidence demonstrating that the claims are true.

Airborne. For almost 15 years, the product Airborne has been marketed and sold to millions of customers. On the packaging and in advertisements, the makers originally asserted that Airborne tablets could ward off colds and boost your immune system (see Figure 1-1). Not surprisingly, Airborne quickly became a great success; it has generated more than $200 million in revenue. Then some consumers posed a reasonable question to the makers of Airborne: *How do you know that it wards off colds?*

Can we trust the packaging claims that companies make?

Q To prove their claims, the makers of Airborne pointed to the results of a "double-blind, placebo-controlled study" conducted by a company specializing in clinical drug trials. We'll discuss exactly what those terms mean later in the chapter; for now we just need to note that as a result of a class-action lawsuit, it became clear that no such study had been conducted and that there was *no* evidence to back up Airborne's claims. The Airborne company removed the claims from the packaging and agreed to refund the purchase price to anyone who had bought Airborne. It also removed any reference to its "clinical trials," with the company's CEO saying that people "are really not scientifically minded enough to be able to understand a clinical study."

Are you insulted by the CEO's assumption about your intelligence? You should be. Did you or your parents fall for Airborne's false claims? Possibly. But here's some more good news: you can learn to be skeptical and suspicious (in a good way) of product claims. You can learn exactly what it means to have scientific proof or evidence that something is absolutely true. And you can learn this by learning what it means to think scientifically.

Scientific thinking is important in the study of a wide variety of topics: it can help you understand economics, psychology, history, and many other subjects. Our focus in

  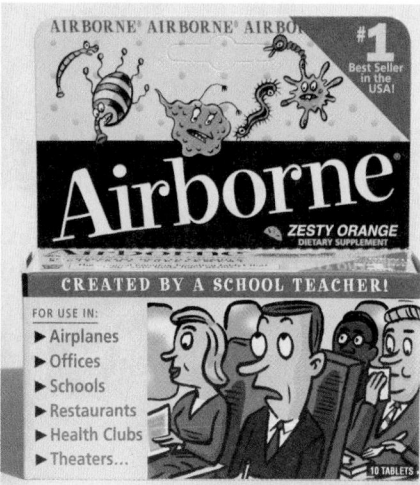

FIGURE 1-1 Some products claim to improve our health, but how do we know whether they work?

this book is **biology,** the study of living things. Taking a scientific approach, we investigate the facts and ideas in biology that are already known and study the process by which we come to learn new things. As we move through the four parts of the book, we explore the most important questions in biology.

- What is the chemical and physical basis for life and its maintenance?

- How do organisms use genetic information to build themselves and to reproduce?

- What are the diverse forms that life on earth takes, and how has that diversity arisen?

- How do organisms interact with each other and with their environment?

In this chapter, we explore how to think scientifically and how to use the knowledge we gain to make wise decisions. Although we generally restrict our focus to biology, scientific thinking can be applied to nearly every endeavor, so in this chapter we use a wide range of examples—including some from beyond biology—as we learn how to think scientifically. Although the examples vary greatly, they all convey a message that is key to scientific thinking: it's okay to be skeptical.

Fortunately, learning to think scientifically is not difficult—and it can be fun, particularly because it is so empowering. **Scientific literacy,** a general, fact-based understanding of the basics of biology and other sciences, is increasingly important in our lives, and literacy in matters of biology is especially essential.

TAKE-HOME MESSAGE 1·1

Through its emphasis on objective observation, description, and experimentation, science is a pathway by which we can discover and better understand the world around us.

1·2 Biological literacy is essential in the modern world.

A brief glance at any magazine or newspaper will reveal just how much scientific literacy has become a necessity (**FIGURE 1-2**). Many important health, social, medical, political, economic, and legal issues pivot on complex scientific data and theories. For example, why are unsaturated fats healthier for you than saturated fats? And why do allergies strike children from clean homes more than children from dirty homes? And why do new agricultural pests appear faster than new pesticides?

As you read and study this book, you will be developing **biological literacy,** the ability to (1) use the process of

FIGURE 1-2 In the news. Every day, news sources report on social, political, medical, and legal issues related to science.

scientific inquiry to think creatively about real-world issues that have a biological science component, (2) communicate these thoughts to others, and (3) integrate these ideas into your decision making. Biological literacy doesn't involve just the big issues facing society or just abstract ideas. It also matters to you personally. Should you take aspirin when you have a fever? Are you using the wrong approach if you try to lose weight and, after some initial success, you find your rate of weight loss diminishing? Is it a good idea to consume moderate amounts of alcohol? Lack of biological literacy will put you at the mercy of "experts" who may try to confuse you or convince you of things in the interest of (their) personal gain. Scientific thinking will help you make wise decisions for yourself and for society.

> ## TAKE-HOME MESSAGE 1·2
>
> **Biological issues permeate all aspects of our lives. To make wise decisions, it is essential for individuals and societies to attain biological literacy.**

1·3 The scientific method is a powerful approach to understanding the world.

It's a brand new age, and science, particularly biology, is everywhere. To illustrate the value of scientific thinking in understanding the world, let's look at what happens in its absence, by considering some unusual behaviors in the common laboratory rat.

Rats can be trained, without much difficulty, to push a lever to receive a food pellet from a feeding mechanism (**FIGURE 1-3**). When the mechanism is altered so that there is a 10-second delay between the lever being pushed and the food pellet being dispensed, however, strange things start to happen. In one cage, the rat will push the lever and then, very methodically, run and push its nose into one corner of the cage. Then it moves to another corner and again pushes its nose against the cage. It repeats this behavior at the third and fourth corners of the cage, after which the rat stands in front of the feeder and the pellet is dispensed. Each time the rat pushes the lever it repeats the nose-in-the-corner sequence before moving to the food tray.

In another cage, with the same 10-second delay before the food pellet is dispensed, a rat pushes the lever and then proceeds to do three quick back-flips in succession. It then moves to the food tray for the food pellet when the 10 seconds have elapsed. Like the nose-in-the-corner rat, the back-flip rat will repeat this exact behavior each time it pushes the lever.

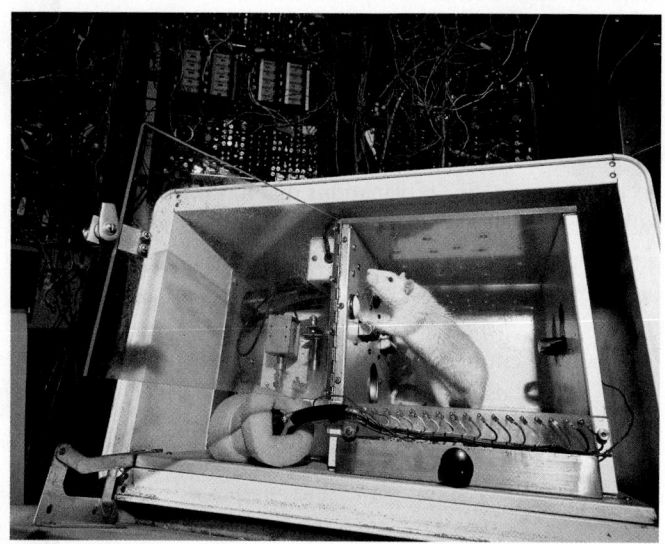

FIGURE 1-3 "In the absence of the scientific method . . ." Rats develop strange, superstition-like behaviors if there is a 10-second delay between when they push a lever and when food is delivered.

Q Why do people develop superstitions? Can animals be superstitious?

In cage after cage of rats with these 10-second-delay food levers, each rat eventually develops its own peculiar series of behaviors before moving to the food dish to receive the pellet. Why do they do this? Because it seems to work! They have discovered a method by which they can get a food pellet. To some extent, the rats' behaviors are reasonable. They associate two events—pushing the lever and engaging in some sequence of behaviors—with another: receiving food. In a sense, they have taken a step toward understanding their world, even though the events are not actually related to each other.

Humans can also mistakenly associate actions with outcomes in an attempt to understand and control their world. The irrational belief that actions that are not logically related to a course of events can influence its outcome is called **superstition.** In the absence of scientific thinking, individuals can develop incorrect ideas, such as superstitions about how the world works (**FIGURE 1-4**). For example, Nomar Garciaparra, a former major league baseball player, always engaged in a precise series of toe taps and adjustments to his batting gloves before he would bat.

Thousands of different narratives, legends, fairy tales, and epics from all around the globe exist to help people understand the world around them. These stories explain everything from birth and death to disease and healing.

As helpful and comforting as stories and superstitions may be (or seem to be), they are no substitute for really understanding how the world works. This kind of understanding begins when someone wonders about why something is the way it is and then decides to try to find out the answer. This process of examination and discovery is called the **scientific method.**

The scientific method usually begins with someone observing a phenomenon and proposing an explanation for it. Next, the proposed explanation is tested through a series of experiments. If the experiments reveal that the explanation is accurate, and if the experiments can be done by others with the same result, then the explanation is considered to be valid. If the experiments do not support the proposed explanation, then the explanation must be revised or alternative explanations that more closely reflect the experimental results must be proposed and tested. This process continues as better, more accurate explanations are found.

While the scientific method reveals much about the world around us, it doesn't explain everything. There are many other methods through which we can gain an understanding of the world. For example, much of our knowledge about plants and animals does not come from the use of the scientific method, but rather comes from systematic, orderly observation, without the testing of any explicit hypotheses. Other disciplines also involve understandings of the world based on non-scientific processes. Knowledge about history, for example, comes from the systematic examination of past events as they relate to humans, while the "truths" in other fields, such as religion, ethics, and even politics, often are based on personal faith, traditions, and mythology.

Scientific thinking can be distinguished from these alternative ways of acquiring knowledge about the world in that it is **empirical.** Empirical knowledge is based on experience and observations that are rational, testable, and repeatable. The empirical nature of the scientific approach makes it self-correcting: in the process of analyzing a topic, event, or phenomenon with the scientific method, incorrect ideas are discarded in favor of more accurate explanations. In the next sections, we look at how to put the scientific method into practice.

FIGURE 1-4 Superstitions abound. As comforting as myths and superstitions may be, they are no substitute for really understanding how the world works.

TAKE-HOME MESSAGE 1·3

There are numerous ways of gaining an understanding of the world. Because it is empirical, rational, testable, repeatable, and self-correcting, the scientific method is a particularly effective approach.

1·4–1·10 A beginner's guide: what are the steps of the scientific method?

Scientific thinking relies on rational, testable, and repeatable observations. (Shown here: A botanist in Borneo measures Rafflesia arnoldii, *which produces the largest flowers of any species.)*

1·4   Thinking like a scientist: how do you use the scientific method?

"Scientific method"—this term sounds like a rigid process to follow, much like following a recipe. In practice, however, the scientific method is an adaptable process that can be done effectively in numerous ways. This flexibility makes the scientific method a powerful process that can be used to explore a wide variety of thoughts, events, or phenomena, not only in science but in other areas as well.

The basic steps in the scientific method are:

Step 1. Make observations.

Step 2. Formulate a hypothesis.

Step 3. Devise a testable prediction.

Step 4. Conduct a critical experiment.

Step 5. Draw conclusions and make revisions.

Once begun, though, the process doesn't necessarily continue linearly through the five steps until it is concluded (**FIGURE 1-5**). Sometimes, observations made in the first step can lead to more than one hypothesis and several

testable predictions and experiments. And the conclusions drawn from experiments often suggest new observations, refinements to hypotheses, and, ultimately, increasingly precise conclusions.

THE SCIENTIFIC METHOD

STEP 1	STEP 2	STEP 3	STEP 4	STEP 5
Make observations.	Formulate a hypothesis.	Devise a testable prediction.	Conduct a critical experiment.	Draw conclusions and make revisions.

 The scientific method rarely proceeds in a straight line. Conclusions, for example, often lead to new observations and refined hypotheses.

FIGURE 1-5 The scientific method: five basic steps and one flexible process.

What should you do when something you believe in turns out to be wrong?

An especially important feature of the scientific method is that its steps are self-correcting. As we continue to make new observations, a hypothesis about how the world works might change (**FIGURE 1-6**). If our observations do not support our current hypothesis, that hypothesis must be given up in favor of one that is not contradicted by any observations. This may be the most important feature of the scientific method: *it tells us when we should change our minds.*

> *If science proves some belief of Buddhism wrong, then Buddhism will have to change.*
> —THE 14TH DALAI LAMA,
> *New York Times,* December 2005

Because the scientific method is a general strategy for learning, it needn't be used solely to learn about nature or scientific things. In fact, we can analyze an important criminal justice question using the scientific method:

- How reliable is eyewitness testimony in criminal courts?

For more than 200 years, courts in the United States have viewed eyewitness testimony as unassailable. Few things are seen as more convincing to a jury than an individual testifying that she can identify the person she saw commit a crime (**FIGURE 1-7**). But is eyewitness identification always right?

FIGURE 1-6 Hold the fries. We apply an understanding of science when we choose foods from the menu that have fewer calories and less saturated fat.

FIGURE 1-7 "With your own two eyes . . ."? How reliable is eyewitness testimony in criminal courts?

Can the scientific method tell us if whether this perception—or some other commonly held idea—is true? As we describe how to use the scientific method to answer questions about the world, it will become clear that the answer is a resounding *yes.* In the coming sections of this chapter, we also look at how the scientific method can be used to address a variety of issues. In addition to our criminal justice question, we'll answer three additional questions:

- Does echinacea reduce the intensity or duration of the common cold?

- Does chemical runoff give rise to hermaphrodite fish?

- Does shaving hair from your face, legs, or anywhere else cause it to grow back coarser or darker?

TAKE-HOME MESSAGE 1·4

The scientific method (observation, hypothesis, prediction, test, and conclusion) is a flexible, adaptable, and efficient pathway to understanding the world, because it tells us when we must change our beliefs.

1·5 Step 1: Make observations.

Scientific study always begins with observations: we simply look for interesting patterns or cause-and-effect relationships. This is where a great deal of the creativity of science comes from. In the case of eyewitness testimony, DNA technologies have made it possible to assess whether tissue such as hair or blood from a crime scene came from a particular suspect. Armed with these tools, the U.S. Justice Department recently reviewed 28 criminal convictions that had been overturned by DNA evidence. It found that in most of the cases, the strongest evidence against the defendant had been eyewitness identification. The observation here is that many defendants who are later found to be innocent were initially convicted based on eyewitness testimony.

Opportunities for other interesting observations are unlimited. Using the scientific method, we can (and will) also answer our three other questions.

Many people have claimed that consuming extracts of the herb echinacea can reduce the intensity or duration of symptoms of the common cold (**FIGURE 1-8**). We can ask: how do you know this is true?

- Does taking echinacea reduce the intensity or duration of the common cold?

Some people have noted that chemicals in sewage runoff—particularly those related to the hormone estrogen—seem to cause male fish to turn into hermaphrodites, organisms that have the reproductive organs of both sexes. Is this true?

- Does chemical runoff give rise to hermaphrodite fish?

And finally, some people have suggested that shaving hair from your face, legs, or anywhere else causes the hair to grow back coarser and darker. Is this true?

- Does hair that is shaved grow back coarser or darker?

STEP 1   STEP 2   STEP 3   STEP 4   STEP 5

STEP 1: MAKE OBSERVATIONS

OBSERVATION

To many people, consuming echinacea extract seems to reduce the intensity or duration of symptoms of the common cold.

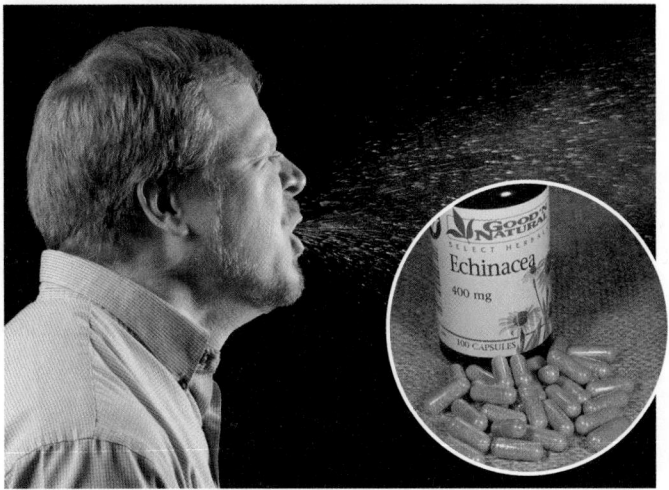

FIGURE 1-8 The first step of science: making observations about the world.

Using the scientific method, we can answer all of these questions.

TAKE-HOME MESSAGE 1·5

The scientific method begins by making observations about the world, noting apparent patterns or cause-and-effect relationships.

1·6 Step 2: Formulate a hypothesis.

Based on observations, we can develop a **hypothesis** (*pl.* **hypotheses**), a proposed explanation for observed phenomena. What hypotheses could we make about the eyewitness-testimony observations described in the previous section? We could start with the hypothesis

"Eyewitness testimony is always accurate." We may need to modify our hypothesis later, but this is a good start. At this point, we can't draw any conclusions. All we have done is summarize some interesting patterns we've seen in a possible explanation.

STEP 1   STEP 2   STEP 3   STEP 4   STEP 5

STEP 2: FORMULATE A HYPOTHESIS

HYPOTHESIS
Echinacea reduces the duration and severity of the common cold.

FIGURE 1-9 Hypothesis: the proposed explanation for a phenomenon.

To be most useful, a hypothesis must accomplish two things.

1. It must clearly establish mutually exclusive alternative explanations for a phenomenon. That is, it must be clear that if the proposed explanation is not supported by evidence or further observations, a different hypothesis is a more likely explanation.

2. It must generate testable predictions (**FIGURE 1-9**). This characteristic is important because we can evaluate the validity of a hypothesis only by putting it to the test. For example, we could disprove the "Eyewitness testimony is always accurate" hypothesis by demonstrating that, in certain circumstances, individuals who have witnessed a crime might misidentify the criminal when asked to select the suspect from a lineup.

Researchers often pose a hypothesis as a negative statement, proposing that there is no relationship between two factors, such as "Echinacea has no effect on the duration and severity of cold symptoms." Or "There is no difference in the coarseness or darkness of hair that grows after shaving." A hypothesis that states a *lack* of relationship between two

factors is called a **null hypothesis.** Both types of hypothesis are equally valid, but a null hypothesis is easier to disprove. This is because a single piece of evidence or a single new observation that contradicts a null hypothesis is sufficient for us to reject it and conclude that an alternative hypothesis must be considered. So, once you have one piece of solid evidence that your null hypothesis is not true, you gain little by collecting further data. Conversely, it is impossible to prove that a hypothesis is absolutely and permanently true: all evidence or further observations that support a hypothesis are valuable, but they do not rule out the possibility that some future evidence or observation might show that the hypothesis is not true.

> "Scientific issues permeate the law. I believe [that] in this age of science we must build legal foundations that are sound in science as well as in law. The result, in my view, will further not only the interests of truth but also those of justice. "
> — U.S. SUPREME COURT JUSTICE STEPHEN BREYER, at the annual meeting of the American Association for the Advancement of Science, February 1998

For our three additional observations, we could state each of our hypotheses in two different ways:

Hypothesis: Echinacea reduces the duration and severity of the symptoms of the common cold.

Null hypothesis: Echinacea has no effect on the duration or severity of the symptoms of the common cold.

Hypothesis: Estrogens in sewage runoff turn male fish into hermaphrodites.

Null hypothesis: Estrogens in sewage runoff have no effect in turning male fish into hermaphrodites.

Hypothesis: Hair that is shaved grows back coarser and darker.

Null hypothesis: There is no difference in the coarseness or color of hair that is shaved relative to hair that is not shaved.

TAKE-HOME MESSAGE 1·6

A hypothesis is a proposed explanation for an observed phenomenon.

1·7 Step 3: Devise a testable prediction.

Not all hypotheses are created equal. For a hypothesis to be useful, it must generate a prediction. That is, it must suggest that under certain conditions we will be able to observe certain outcomes. Put another way, a good hypothesis helps us make predictions about novel situations. This is a powerful feature of a good hypothesis: it guides us to knowledge about new situations.

All of this is rather abstract. Let's get more concrete with the four hypotheses we are considering. Keep in mind that when you do not understand some aspect of the world, any one of several possible explanations could be true. In devising a testable prediction from a hypothesis, the goal is to propose a situation that will give a particular outcome if your hypothesis is true, but will give a different outcome if your hypothesis is not true.

Hypothesis: Eyewitness testimony is always accurate.

Prediction: Individuals who have witnessed a crime will correctly identify the criminal regardless of whether multiple suspects are presented one at a time or all at the same time in a lineup.

This is a good, testable prediction because, if our hypothesis is true, then our prediction will always be true. On the other hand, if one method of presenting suspects consistently causes incorrect identification of the criminal, our hypothesis cannot be true and must be revised or discarded.

Hypothesis: Echinacea reduces the duration and severity of the symptoms of the common cold.

Prediction: If echinacea reduces the duration and severity of the symptoms of the common cold, then individuals taking echinacea should get sick less frequently than those not taking it, and when they do get sick, their illness should not last as long (**FIGURE 1-10**).

Hypothesis: Estrogens in sewage runoff turn male fish into hermaphrodites.

Prediction: If estrogens in sewage runoff turn male fish into hermaphrodites, then exposing fish to estrogens should cause more fish to turn into hermaphrodites than when fish are not exposed to estrogens.

Hypothesis: Hair that is shaved grows back coarser and darker.

Prediction: If shaving leads to coarser, darker hair growing back, then if individuals shaved one leg (or eyebrow) only, the

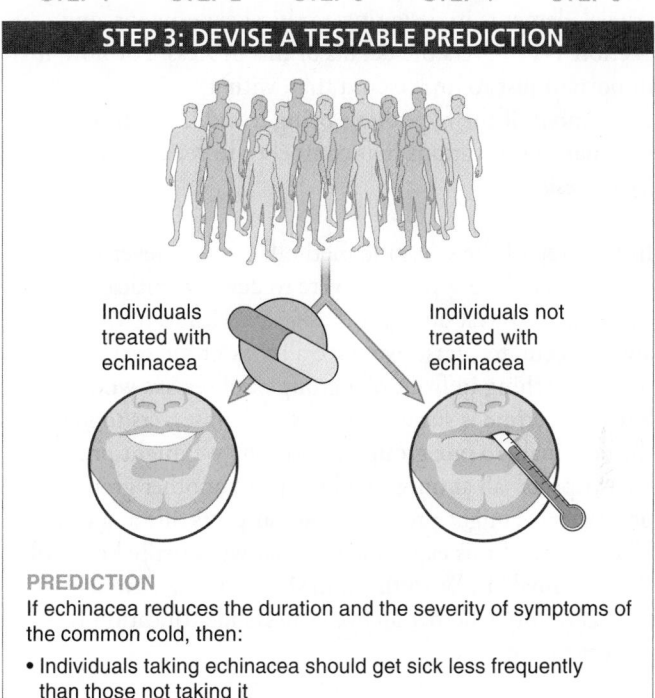

PREDICTION
If echinacea reduces the duration and the severity of symptoms of the common cold, then:
• Individuals taking echinacea should get sick less frequently than those not taking it
• Individuals who get sick should recover more quickly

FIGURE 1-10 Coming up with a testable prediction. For a hypothesis to be useful, it must generate a testable prediction.

hair that re-grows on that leg should become darker and coarser than the hair growing on the other leg.

As you begin to think scientifically, you will find yourself making a lot of "if . . . then" types of statements: "*If* that is true," referring to some hypothesis or assertion someone makes, or perhaps a claim made by the manufacturer of a new health product, "*then* I would expect . . . ," proposing your own prediction about a related situation. Once you've made a testable prediction, the next step is to go ahead and test it.

TAKE-HOME MESSAGE 1·7

For a hypothesis to be useful, it must generate a testable prediction.

1·8 Step 4: Conduct a critical experiment.

Once we have formulated a hypothesis that generates a testable prediction, we conduct a **critical experiment,** an experiment that makes it possible to decisively determine whether a particular hypothesis is correct. There are many crucial elements in designing a critical experiment, and Section 1-11 covers the details of this process. For now, it is important just to understand that, with a critical experiment, if the hypothesis being tested is not true, we will make observations that compel us to reject that hypothesis.

In this step of the scientific method, a bit of cleverness can come in handy. Suppose we were to devise a critical experiment to test our hypothesis "Eyewitness testimony is always accurate." First, we stage a mock crime such as a purse snatching in front of a group of observers who do not know the crime is staged. Next, we ask observers to identify the criminal. To one group of observers we might present six "suspects" all at once in a lineup. To another group of observers we might present the six suspects one at a time. The beauty of this experiment is that we actually know who the "criminal" is. With this knowledge, we can evaluate with certainty whether an eyewitness's identification is correct or not.

This exact experiment was done, but with an additional, devious little twist: the researcher did not include the actual "criminal" in any of the lineups or one-by-one presentations of the six "suspects." If eyewitness testimony is always accurate, however, this slight variation should not matter. We would predict that the observers in both groups (the lineup group and the one-at-a-time group) would indicate that the criminal was not present. In the next section, we'll see what happened. Right now, let's devise critical experiments for our other hypotheses.

Hypothesis: Echinacea reduces the duration and severity of the symptoms of the common cold. The critical experiment for the echinacea hypothesis has been performed, and it is about as close to a perfect experiment as possible. Researchers began with 437 people who volunteered to be exposed to viruses that cause the common cold. Exposure to the cold-causing viruses was a bit unpleasant: all of the volunteers had cold viruses (in a watery solution) dripped into their noses. The research subjects were then secluded in hotel rooms for five days, and doctors examined them for the presence of the cold virus in their nasal cavity and for any cold symptoms (**FIGURE 1-11**).

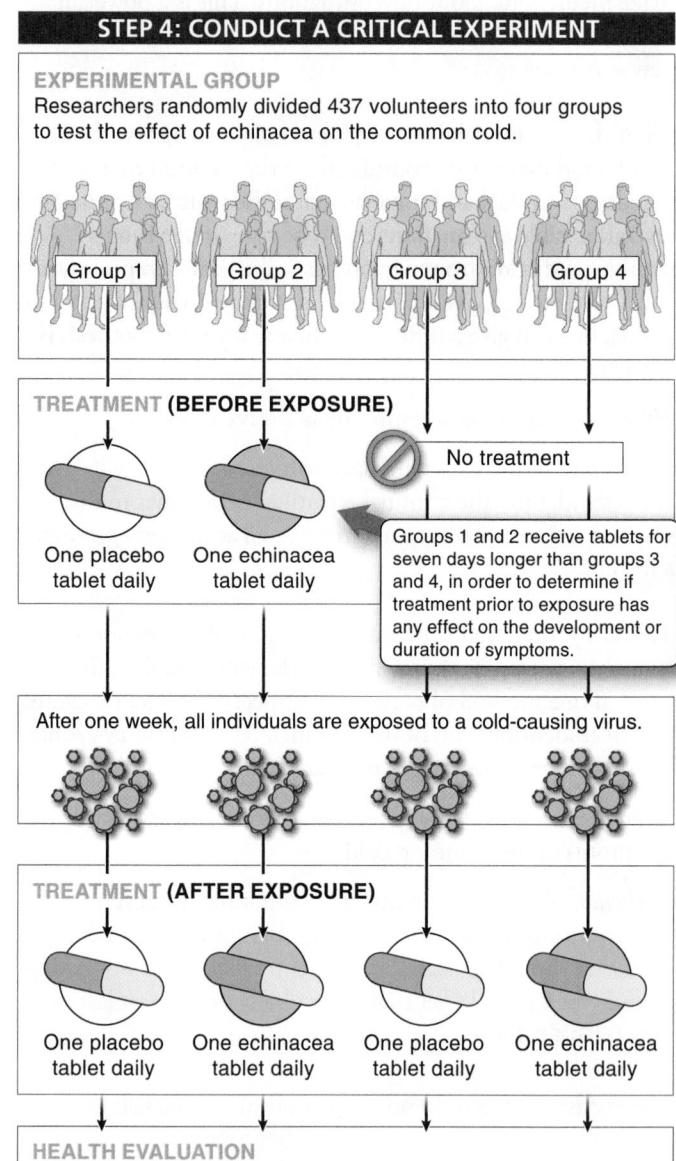

FIGURE 1-11 **"When you need to know . . ."** A critical experiment makes it possible to conclusively determine whether a hypothesis is correct.

The subjects were randomly divided into four groups. In two of the groups, each individual began taking a pill each day for a week prior to exposure to the cold virus. Those in one group received echinacea tablets, while those in the other took a **placebo,** a pill that looked identical to the echinacea tablet but contained no echinacea or other active ingredient. Neither the subject nor the doctor administering the tablets (and later checking for cold symptoms) knew what they contained. In the other two groups, the individuals did not begin taking the tablets until the day on which they were exposed to the cold virus. Again, one group got the echinacea and the other group got the placebo.

Hypothesis: Estrogens in sewage runoff turn male fish into hermaphrodites. To try to determine the validity of this hypothesis, researchers placed cages containing male trout downstream from sewage treatment plants on several rivers in England. They then examined the fish for the presence of eggs in their testes and tested their blood for the presence of an egg-production hormone that is not normally found in males.

FIGURE 1-12 **Does shaving hair cause it to grow back coarser or darker?**

Q ▶ Does shaving or cutting hair make it grow back more thickly?

Hypothesis: Hair that is shaved grows back coarser and darker. A critical experiment does not have to be complex or high-tech. All that matters is that it can decisively determine whether or not a hypothesis is correct (**FIGURE 1-12**). This point is illustrated by an experiment published in the scholarly journal *Archives of Facial Plastic Surgery.* Researchers decided to test the hypothesis that shaving hair causes it to grow back coarser or darker. A group of volunteers had one of their eyebrows, selected at random, completely shaved off. The subjects were then evaluated for eyebrow re-growth over the course of the next six months, with observers also analyzing photographs of the individuals.

In the next section we'll see how our hypotheses survive being confronted with the results of these critical experiments and how we can move toward drawing conclusions.

TAKE-HOME MESSAGE 1·8

A critical experiment is one that makes it possible to decisively determine whether a particular hypothesis is correct.

1·9 Step 5: Draw conclusions, make revisions.

Once the results of the critical experiment are in, they are pulled apart, examined, and analyzed. Researchers look for patterns and relationships in the evidence they've gathered from their experiments; they draw conclusions and see whether their findings and conclusions support their hypotheses. If an experimental result is not what you expected, that does not make it a "wrong answer." Science includes a great deal of trial and error, and if the conclusions do not support the hypothesis, then you must revise your hypothesis, which often spurs you to conduct more experiments. This step is a cornerstone of the scientific method because it demands that you must be open-minded and ready to change what you think.

Q ▶ Is eyewitness testimony in courts always right?

The results of the purse-snatching experiment were surprising. When the suspects (which, as you'll recall, did not include the actual "criminal") were viewed together in a lineup, the observers/witnesses erroneously identified someone as the purse snatcher about a third of the time. When the suspects were viewed one at a time, the observers made a mistaken identification less than 10% of the time.

In this or any other experiment, it does not matter whether we can imagine a reason for the discrepancy between our hypothesis and our results. What is important is that we have demonstrated that our initial hypothesis— "Eyewitness testimony is always accurate"—is not supported by the data. Our observations suggest that, at the very least, the accuracy of an eyewitness's testimony depends on the method used to present the suspects. Based on this result, we might adjust our hypothesis to: "Eyewitness testimony is more accurate when suspects are presented to witnesses one at a time."

We can then devise new and more specific testable predictions in an attempt to further refine our hypothesis. In the case of eyewitness testimony, further investigation suggests that when suspects or pictures of suspects are placed side by side, witnesses compare them and tend to choose the suspect that *most resembles* the person they remember committing the crime. When viewed one at a

time, suspects can't be compared in this way, and witnesses are less likely to make misidentifications.

Q Does echinacea help prevent the common cold?

Hypothesis: Echinacea reduces the duration and severity of the symptoms of the common cold. In the echinacea study, the results were definitive (**FIGURE 1-13**). Those who took the echinacea were just as likely to catch a cold as those who took placebo, and, once they caught the cold, the symptoms lasted for the same amount of time. In short, echinacea had no effect at all. Several similar studies have been conducted, all of which show that echinacea does not have any beneficial effect. As one of the researchers commented afterward, "We've got to stop attributing any efficacy to echinacea."

Although it seems clear that our initial hypothesis that echinacea stops people from catching colds and reduces the severity and duration of cold symptoms is not correct, further experimentation might involve altering the amount of echinacea given to the research subjects or the length of time they take echinacea before exposure to the cold-causing viruses.

Hypothesis: Estrogens in sewage runoff turn male fish into hermaphrodites. The results of the sewage experiment showed that, in every single river tested, male fish downstream from

STEP 1　STEP 2　STEP 3　STEP 4　STEP 5

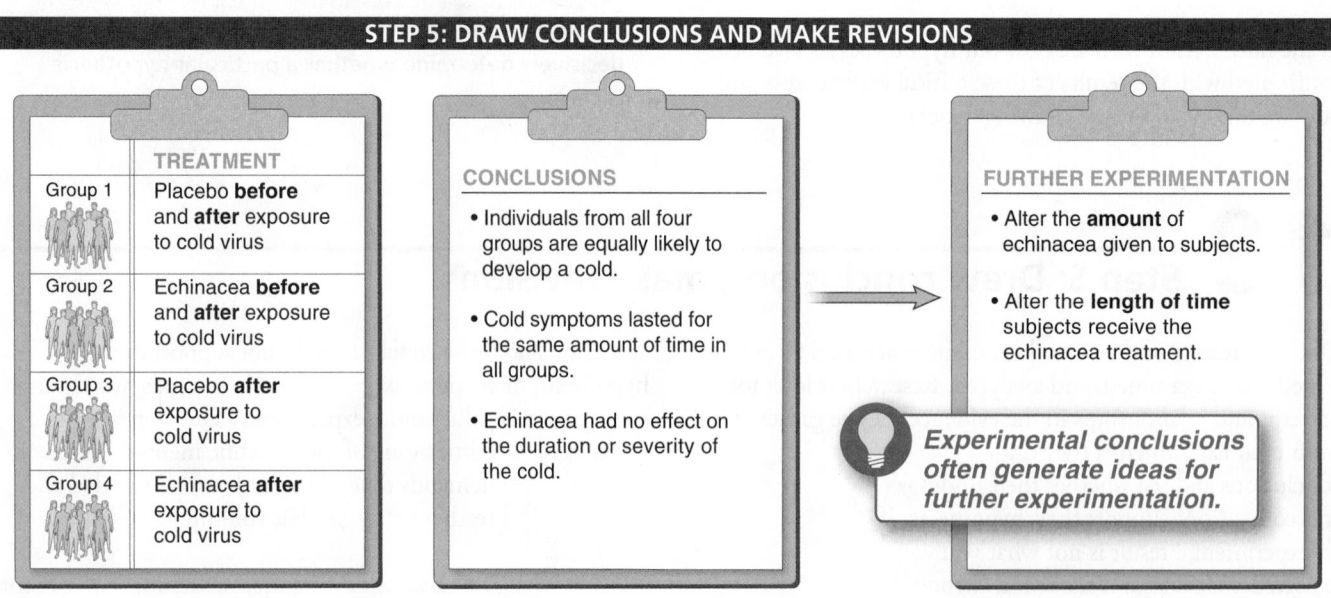

FIGURE 1-13 Using experimental conclusions to make revisions.

the runoff developed eggs in their testes and had significant levels of the egg-production hormone in their blood. Further research, stimulated by these results, has investigated a variety of common industrial chemicals to see whether they can stimulate production of the egg-development hormone in male fish under laboratory conditions, in an attempt to identify which particular chemical component in the sewage causes the male fish to change.

Hypothesis: Hair that is shaved grows back coarser and darker. In the hair-shaving experiment, the observers discovered that, after six months, it was impossible to distinguish which eyebrow had been shaved. This was not a surprise to dermatologists evaluating the study, because all of the living parts involved in hair growth are below the surface of the skin. (Plucking hairs can damage the root of the hair, potentially affecting future hair growth, but that is another story that awaits further study.)

The outcomes in all of these studies show that after the results of a critical experiment have been gathered and interpreted, it is important not just to evaluate the initial hypothesis but also to consider any necessary revisions or refinements to it. This revision is an important step; by revising a hypothesis, based on the results of experimental tests, we can explain the observable world with greater and greater accuracy.

> ### TAKE-HOME MESSAGE 1·9
>
> **Based on the results of experimental tests, we can revise a hypothesis and explain the observable world with increasing accuracy. A great strength of scientific thinking, therefore, is that it helps us understand when we should change our minds.**

1·10 When do hypotheses become theories, and what are theories?

It's an unfortunate source of confusion that, among the general public, the word "theory" is often used to refer to a hunch or a guess or speculation—that is, something we are not certain about. In fact, to scientists, the word means nearly the opposite: a hypothesis of which they are most certain. To reduce these common misunderstandings, we examine here the ways in which scientists describe our knowledge about natural phenomena.

Hypothesis As we have seen, hypotheses are at the very heart of scientific thinking. A hypothesis is a proposed explanation for a phenomenon. A good hypothesis leads to testable predictions. Commonly, when non-scientists use the word "theory"—as in, "I've got a theory about why there's less traffic on Friday mornings than on Thursday mornings"— they actually mean that they have a hypothesis.

Theory A **theory** is an explanatory hypothesis for natural phenomena that is exceptionally well supported by the empirical data. A theory can be thought of as a hypothesis that has withstood the test of time and is unlikely to be altered by any new evidence. Like a hypothesis, a theory is testable; but because it has already been repeatedly tested and no observations or experimental results have contradicted it, a

theory is viewed by the scientific community with nearly the same confidence as a fact. For this reason, it is inappropriate to describe something as "just a theory" as a way of asserting that it is not likely to be true.

Theories in science also tend to be broader in scope than hypotheses. In biology, two of the most important theories (which we explore in more detail in Chapters 3 and 8) are the *cell theory,* that all organisms are composed of cells and all cells come from preexisting cells, and the *theory of evolution by natural selection,* that species can change over time and all species are related to one another through common ancestry.

> ### TAKE-HOME MESSAGE 1·10
>
> **Scientific theories do not represent speculation or guesses about the natural world. Rather, they are hypotheses— proposed explanations for natural phenomena—that have been so strongly and persuasively supported by empirical observation that the scientific community views them as very unlikely to be altered by new evidence.**

Controlled experiments increase the power of our observations. Here, laboratory-grown wheat plants are compared.

1·11–1·13 Well-designed experiments are essential to testing hypotheses.

1·11 Controlling variables makes experiments more powerful.

From our earlier discussion of critical experiments, you have a sense of how important it is to have a well-planned, well-designed experiment. In performing experiments, our goal is to figure out whether one thing influences another thing: if an experiment enables us to draw a correct conclusion about that cause-and-effect relationship, it is a good experiment.

In our initial discussion of experiments, we just described what the experiment was without examining why the researchers chose to perform the experiment the way they did. In this section, we explore some of the ways to maximize an experiment's power, and we'll find that, with careful planning, it is possible to increase an experiment's ability to discern causes and effects.

First, let's consider some elements common to most experiments.

1. Treatment: any experimental condition applied to the research subjects. It might be the shaving of one of an individual's eyebrows, or the pattern used to show "suspects" (all at once or one at a time) to the witness of a staged crime, or a dosage of echinacea given to an individual.

2. Experimental group: a group of subjects who are exposed to a particular treatment—for example, the

individuals given echinacea rather than placebo in the experiment described above. It is sometimes referred to as the "treatment group."

3. Control group: a group of subjects who are treated identically to the experimental group, with one exception—they are not exposed to the treatment. An example would be the individuals given placebo rather than echinacea.

4. Variables: the characteristics of an experimental system that are subject to change. They might be, for example, the amount of echinacea a person is given, or a measure of the coarseness of an individual's hair. When we speak of "controlling" variables—the most important feature of a good experiment—we are describing the attempt to minimize any differences (which are also called "variables") between a control group and an experimental group other than the treatment itself. That way, any differences between the groups in the outcomes we observe are most likely due to the treatment.

Let's look at an example that illustrates the importance of considering all these elements when designing an experiment.

Stomach ulcers are erosions of the stomach lining that can be very painful. In the late 1950s, a doctor reported in the *Journal of the American Medical Association* that stomach ulcers could be effectively treated by having a patient swallow a balloon connected to some tubes that circulated a refrigerated fluid. He argued that by super-cooling the stomach, acid production was reduced and the ulcer symptoms relieved. He had convincing data to back up his claim: in all 24 of his patients who received this "gastric freezing" treatment, their condition improved (**FIGURE 1-14**). As a result, the treatment became widespread for many years.

Although there was a clear hypothesis ("Gastric cooling reduces the severity of ulcers") and some compelling observations (all 24 patients experienced relief), this experiment was not designed well. In particular, there was no clear group with whom to compare the patients who received the treatment. In other words, who is to say that just going to the doctor or having a balloon put into your stomach doesn't improve ulcers? The results of this doctor's experiment do not rule out these interpretations.

A few years later, another researcher decided to do a more carefully controlled study. He recruited 160 ulcer patients and gave 82 of them the gastric freezing treatment. The

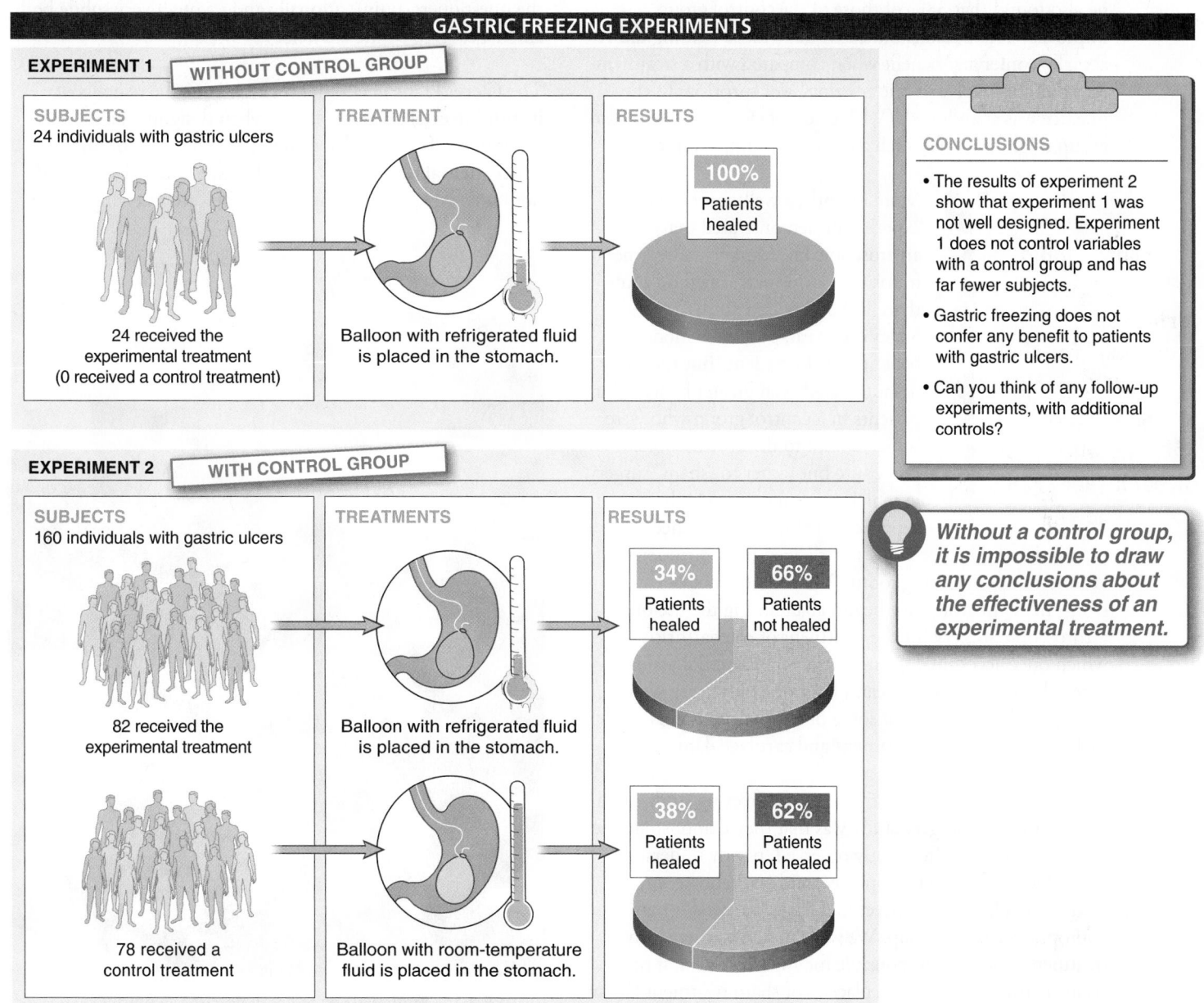

GASTRIC FREEZING EXPERIMENTS

EXPERIMENT 1 WITHOUT CONTROL GROUP

SUBJECTS
24 individuals with gastric ulcers

24 received the experimental treatment
(0 received a control treatment)

TREATMENT

Balloon with refrigerated fluid is placed in the stomach.

RESULTS

100%
Patients healed

CONCLUSIONS

- The results of experiment 2 show that experiment 1 was not well designed. Experiment 1 does not control variables with a control group and has far fewer subjects.

- Gastric freezing does not confer any benefit to patients with gastric ulcers.

- Can you think of any follow-up experiments, with additional controls?

EXPERIMENT 2 WITH CONTROL GROUP

SUBJECTS
160 individuals with gastric ulcers

82 received the experimental treatment

78 received a control treatment

TREATMENTS

Balloon with refrigerated fluid is placed in the stomach.

Balloon with room-temperature fluid is placed in the stomach.

RESULTS

34% Patients healed   66% Patients not healed

38% Patients healed   62% Patients not healed

Without a control group, it is impossible to draw any conclusions about the effectiveness of an experimental treatment.

FIGURE 1-14 No controls. Gastric freezing and stomach ulcers: a poorly designed experiment and a well-controlled "do-over."

other 78 received a similar treatment in which they swallowed the balloon but had room-temperature water pumped in. The latter was an appropriate control group because the subjects were treated exactly like the experimental group, with the exception of only a single difference between the groups—whether they experienced gastric freezing or not. The new experiment could test for an effect of the gastric freezing, while controlling for the effects of other, lurking variables that might affect the outcome.

Surprisingly, although the researcher found that for 34% of those in the gastric freezing group their condition improved, he also found that 38% of those in the control group improved. These results indicated that gastric freezing didn't actually confer any benefit when compared with a treatment that did not involve gastric freezing. Not surprisingly, the practice was abandoned. (We'll discuss below why the control group might have had such a high rate of improvement.)

Q Is arthroscopic surgery for arthritis beneficial for the 300,000 people in the United States who have it each year? How do we know?

More recently, a well-controlled experiment demonstrated that arthroscopic knee surgery, a treatment for osteoarthritis performed on more than 300,000 people in the United States each year, produced moderate benefits for the patient. But the study demonstrated even greater benefits for patients in a control group who were subjected not to the arthroscopic procedure but rather to "sham" surgery, in which the surgeon made three superficial incisions in the knee, manipulated the knee a bit, and clanged the instruments around in the operating room. As a consequence of this study, many doctors have begun abandoning the use of arthroscopic surgery for the treatment of osteoarthritis— which once accounted for more than a billion dollars in surgical procedures each year. (This type of surgery is still useful for the treatment of some other knee problems, including the repair of ligament and cartilage damage.)

A surprising result from both the gastric freezing studies and the arthroscopic surgery study was that they demonstrate the **placebo effect,** the frequently observed, poorly understood phenomenon in which people respond favorably to *any* treatment. The placebo effect highlights the need for an appropriate control group. We want to know whether the treatment is actually responsible for any effect seen; if the control group receiving the placebo or sham treatment has an outcome much like that of the experimental group, we can conclude that the treatment itself does not have an effect.

Another pitfall to be aware of in designing an experiment is to ensure that the persons conducting the experiment don't influence the experiment's outcome. An experimenter can often unwittingly influence the results of an experiment. This phenomenon is seen in the story of a horse named Clever Hans. Hans was considered clever because his owner claimed that Hans could perform remarkable intellectual feats, including multiplication and division. When given a numerical problem, the horse would tap out the answer number with his foot. Controlled experiments, however, demonstrated that Hans was only able to solve problems when he could see the person asking the question and when that person knew the answer (**FIGURE 1-15**). It turned out that the questioners, unintentionally and through very subtle body language, revealed the answers.

The Clever Hans phenomenon highlights the benefits of instituting even greater controls when designing an experiment. In particular, it highlights the value of **blind experimental design,** in which the experimental subjects do not know which treatment (if any) they are receiving, and

FIGURE 1-15 Math whiz or ordinary horse? The horse Clever Hans was said to be capable of mathematical calculations, until a controlled experiment demonstrated otherwise.

double-blind experimental design, in which neither the experimental subjects nor the experimenter know which treatment a subject is receiving.

Another hallmark of an extremely well-designed experiment is that it combines the blind/double-blind strategies we've just described in a randomized, controlled, double-blind study. In this context, "randomized" refers to the fact that, as in the echinacea study described above, the subjects are randomly assigned into experimental and control groups. In this way, researchers and subjects have no influence on the composition of the two groups.

The use of randomized, controlled, double-blind experimental design can be thought of as an attempt to imagine all the possible ways that someone might criticize an experiment and to design the experiment so that the results cannot be explained by anything other than the effect of the treatment. In this way, the experimenter's results either support the hypothesis or invalidate it—in which case, the hypothesis must be rejected. If multiple explanations can be offered for the observations and evidence from an experiment, then it has not succeeded as a critical experiment.

Suppose you want to know whether a new drug is effective in fighting the human immunodeficiency virus (HIV), the virus that leads to AIDS. Which experiment would be better, one in which the drug is added to HIV-infected cells in a test tube under carefully controlled laboratory conditions, or one in which the drug is given to a large number of HIV-infected individuals? There is no definitive answer. In laboratory studies, it is possible to control nearly every environmental variable. In their simplicity, however, lab studies may introduce difficulties in coming to broader conclusions about a drug's effectiveness under real-world conditions. For example, complex factors in human subjects, such as nutrition and stress, may interact with the experimental drug and influence its effectiveness. These interactions will not be present and taken into account in the controlled lab study.

Good experimental design is more complex than simply following a single recipe. The only way to determine the quality of an experiment is to assess how well the variables that were not of interest were controlled, and how well the experimental treatment tested the relationship of interest.

> ## TAKE-HOME MESSAGE 1·11
>
> To draw clear conclusions from experiments, it is essential to hold constant all those variables we are not interested in. Control and experimental groups should differ only with respect to the treatment of interest. Differences in outcomes between the groups can then be attributed to the treatment.

1·12 Repeatable experiments increase our confidence.

Can science be misleading? How can we know?

In 2005, a study showed that some patients being treated for HIV infection who were also taking an epilepsy drug called valproic acid had significantly reduced numbers of HIV particles in their blood. Newspaper headlines announced this finding—"AIDS Cure Possible, Study Suggests"—and raised many people's hopes. Two years later, however, a study of people who were already taking valproic acid and anti-HIV drugs concluded that those taking valproic acid had not benefited at all from the drug (FIGURE 1-16). It's not certain why the later study didn't produce the same results as the first study, but the second study did address two serious shortcomings of the first study—namely, that the first study was much smaller, involving only four patients, and that no control group was used. This pair of studies reveals the importance of repeatability in science.

A powerful way to demonstrate that observed differences between a treatment group and a control group truly reflect the effect of the treatment is for the researchers to conduct the experiment over and over again. Even better is to have other research groups repeat the experiment and get the same results. Researchers describe this desired characteristic of experiments by saying that an experiment must be "reproducible" and "repeatable."

An experiment that can be done over and over again by a variety of researchers to give the same results is an effective defense against biases (which we discuss in the next

Do megadoses of vitamin C reduce cancer risk?

NEWSCHANNEL 11
COVERAGE YOU CAN COUNT ON!
HOME   NEWS   WEATHER   HEALTHWISE   SPORT

✉ Email   🖶 Print

8/7/08
Texas Tech Researchers May Have Found AIDS Cure
Posted: Aug 7, 2008 09:59 PM

Texas Tech University in partnership with Harvard University is on the research forefront of a possible vaccine for HIV, the virus that causes AIDS.

To give you some idea of how big this story is, on Thursday it was the number one story on Newsweek's website and it will be the lead in their next magazine.

Larger, better controlled follow-up studies may reveal flaws undermining earlier, promising conclusions.

Repeatability is essential! Scientific conclusions are more reliable when experiments have been repeated (and modified, if necessary).

Valproic Acid Does Not Reduce Latent HIV Reservoir in Resting CD4 Cells

By Liz Highleyman

Some prior studies have suggested that valproic acid (Depakote), a drug used to treat epilepsy and bipolar disorder, might help eradicate HIV from the body. Two studies published in the June 19, 2008 issue of *AIDS*, however, indicate that it has little long-term effect.

Valproic Acid (Depakote)

Study 1

David Margolis and colleagues from the University of North Carolina previously reported that valproic acid plus intensified antiretroviral therapy could "flush" HIV out of long-lived latently infected CD4 T-cells and potentially reduce the resting CD4 cell reservoir. They later conducted a study to test the ability of valproic acid to deplete resting CD4 cell infection in patients receiving standard HAART.

Infection of resting CD4 cells was measured in 11 patients with stable undetectable HIV viral load using a standard HIV RNA assay twice rior to, and twice after, adding 1000 mg valproic acid to their standard antiretroviral regimen. Resting CD4 T-cell infection frequency was measured by outgrowth assay, and low-level viremia was quantified in 9 patients using a highly sensitive single-copy plasma HIV RNA assay.

FIGURE 1-16 Once is not enough. Experiments and their outcomes must be repeatable for their conclusions to be valid and widely accepted.

section) and reflects a well-designed experiment. Experiments whose results cannot be confirmed by repeated experiments or by experiments performed by other researchers are the downfall of many dramatic claims. Even though chemist Linus Pauling had not one, but two Nobel prizes, he was never able to convince the scientific community that megadoses of vitamin C are an effective treatment for cancer. Every time other individuals tried to repeat Pauling's studies, properly matching the control and treatment groups, they found no difference. Vitamin C just isn't effective against cancer—a conclusion that the vast majority of the medical community now believes. The scientific method is profoundly egalitarian: more important than a scientist's credentials are sound and reproducible results.

When a study is repeated (also referred to as "replicating" a study), sometimes a tiny variation in the experimental design can lead to a different outcome; this can help us isolate the variable that is primarily responsible for the outcome of the experiment. Alternatively, when experiments are repeated and the same results are obtained, our confidence in them is increased.

TAKE-HOME MESSAGE 1·12

Experiments and their outcomes must be repeatable for their conclusions to be considered valid and widely accepted.

1·13

We've got to watch out for our biases.

Q *Can scientists be sexist? How would we know?*

In 2001, the journal *Behavioral Ecology* changed its policy for reviewing manuscripts that were submitted for publication. Its new policy instituted a double-blind process, whereby neither the reviewers' nor the authors' identities were revealed. Previously, the policy had been a single-blind process in which reviewers' identities were kept secret but the authors' identities were known to the reviewers. In an analysis of papers published between 1997 and 2005, it turned out that after 2001, when the double-blind policy took effect, there was a significant increase in the number of published papers in which the first author was female (**FIGURE 1-17**). Analysis of papers published in a similar journal that maintained the single-blind process over that period revealed no such increase.

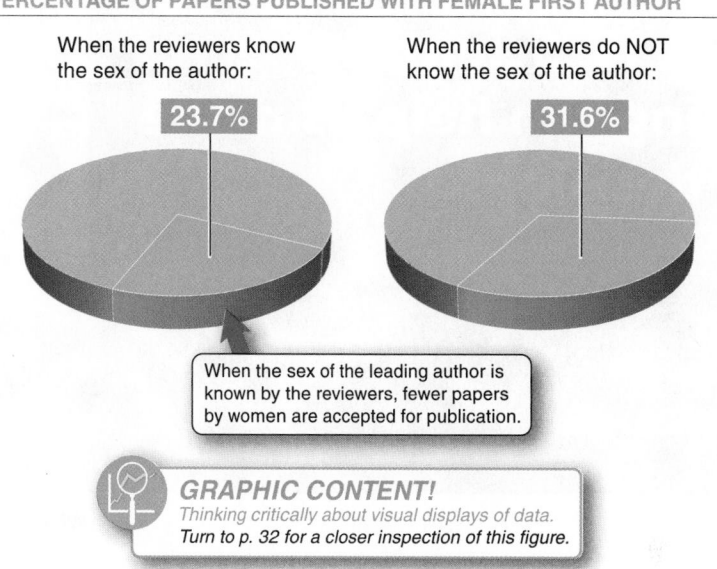

PERCENTAGE OF PAPERS PUBLISHED WITH FEMALE FIRST AUTHOR

When the reviewers know the sex of the author: **23.7%**

When the reviewers do NOT know the sex of the author: **31.6%**

When the sex of the leading author is known by the reviewers, fewer papers by women are accepted for publication.

GRAPHIC CONTENT!
Thinking critically about visual displays of data.
Turn to p. 32 for a closer inspection of this figure.

FIGURE 1-17 Bias against female scientists? The journal *Behavioral Ecology* accepted more papers from female authors when the reviewers were not aware of the author's sex.

This study reveals that people, including scientists, may have biases—sometimes subconscious—that influence their behavior. It also serves as a reminder of the importance of proper controls in experiments. If knowing the sex of the author influences a reviewer's decision on whether a paper should be published, it is also possible that researchers' biases can creep in and influence their collection of data and analysis of results. (Even the decision about what—and what not—to study can be influenced by our biases.)

It can be hard to avoid biases. Consider a study that required precise measuring of the fingers of the left and right hands—comparing the extent to which people in different groups were physically symmetrical. The researcher noted that when she measured individuals from the group she predicted would be more symmetrical, she felt a need to re-measure if the reading on her digital ruler indicated a big asymmetry. Because she was thinking that the person's left- and right-hand fingers *should* be symmetrical, she assumed she had made an error. She felt no such need to re-measure for subjects in the other group, for whom asymmetries confirmed her hypothesis. To control for this bias, the researcher connected her digital ruler to a computer and, without ever having the number displayed, transmitted the measurement directly to the computer when she pushed a button. In this way, she was able to make each measurement without introducing any regular bias.

TAKE-HOME MESSAGE 1·13

Biases can influence our behavior, including our collection and interpretation of data. With careful controls, it is possible to minimize such biases.

1·14–1·17 Scientific thinking can help us make wise decisions.

What can you believe? Reading labels is essential to evaluating products and the claims about them.

1·14

Visual displays of data can help us understand and explain phenomena.

"Let's look at the data." Using points and lines and symbols and a variety of other graphic elements to display measured quantities is a powerful tool commonly used throughout the sciences. Such visual displays of data can serve a range of purposes, which relate to both the presentation of and the exploration of the data.

Whether making a point, illustrating an idea, or facilitating the testing of a hypothesis, visual displays of data typically have one feature in common: they condense large amounts of information into a more easily digested form. In doing so, they can help readers think about and compare data, ultimately helping them to synthesize the information and see useful patterns.

There is an almost infinite variety of ways to display data, including maps, tables, charts, and graphs. Graphs are particularly prevalent in biology, and a few forms are used most frequently. These include bar graphs, line graphs, and pie charts (**FIGURE 1-18**).

Visual displays of data generally have a few common elements. Most have a title, for example, which usually appears at the top and describes the content of the display. Bar graphs and line graphs include axes, usually a horizontal axis, also called

COMMON VISUAL DISPLAYS OF DATA USED IN BIOLOGY

BAR GRAPH
Rectangular bars are used to represent data, each with a height that is proportional to the value being represented.

LINE GRAPH
A line or curve may be used to connect data points or to illustrate trends across many data points.

PIE CHART
"Slices" are used to represent data, in which each slice is a proportion of the whole.

FIGURE 1-18 Presenting what we have observed, precisely and concisely.

the *x*-axis, and a vertical axis, called the *y*- axis. Each axis has a scale, generally labeled with some gradations, indicating one dimension by which the data can be described.

The *x*-axis of a line graph, for example, might describe the number of hours a student spends studying for a class, in which case it would be labeled "Time spent studying each day (hrs)," while the *y*-axis might be labeled "Performance on midterm exams (%)." Depending on the size of the data set (the total number of observations collected in the experiment that relate an individual's performance on a midterm and the number of hours that student spent studying each day), individual data points are included on the graph, with additional information conveyed by the shape, color, or pattern of the data points (**FIGURE 1-19**). One data point might reflect that one student spent 2 hours studying per day and scored 85% on a midterm exam, while another spent 1 hour per day and scored 94% on the midterm exam. A line or curve may be used to connect data points or to illustrate a relationship between the two variables.

Rather than displaying individual data points, a bar graph has rectangular bars, each with a height proportional to the value being represented—maybe hours spent studying in a particular class. In a pie chart, each "slice" is a proportion of the whole—for instance, with each slice representing the portion of a student's total number of study hours spent on each different topic every day. A legend may be included for

the graph, identifying which information is represented by which bar or data point or pie slice.

One of the most common functions of visual displays of information is to present the relationship between two variables, such as in a graph. An **independent variable** is some measurable entity that is available (i.e., can be measured) at the start of a process and whose value can be changed as required. A **dependent variable** is one that is created by the process being observed and whose value cannot be controlled. The dependent variable is generally represented by the *y*-axis and is expected to change in response to a change in the independent variable, represented on the *x*-axis. The number of hours of sleep a student gets each night, for example, could be thought of as an independent variable, while some measure of academic performance—maybe grade point average—would be a dependent variable.

Visual displays of data can be simple and straightforward, but they can also have features that reduce their effectiveness, or even cause them to be downright misleading. These difficulties can arise from ambiguity in the axis labels or scales, or incomplete information on how each data point was collected (and how the points might have varied), or biases or hidden assumptions in the presentation or grouping of data, or unknown or unreliable sources of data, or an insufficient or inappropriate context given for the data presentation.

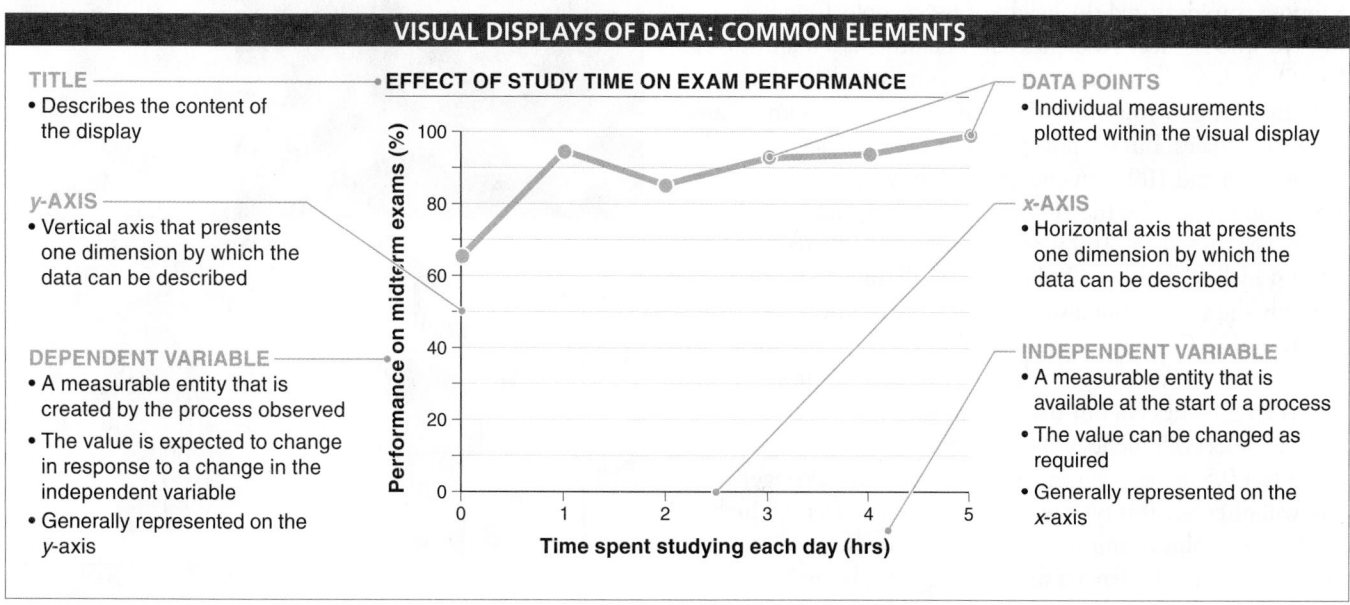

VISUAL DISPLAYS OF DATA: COMMON ELEMENTS

EFFECT OF STUDY TIME ON EXAM PERFORMANCE

TITLE
• Describes the content of the display

y-AXIS
• Vertical axis that presents one dimension by which the data can be described

DEPENDENT VARIABLE
• A measurable entity that is created by the process observed
• The value is expected to change in response to a change in the independent variable
• Generally represented on the *y*-axis

DATA POINTS
• Individual measurements plotted within the visual display

x-AXIS
• Horizontal axis that presents one dimension by which the data can be described

INDEPENDENT VARIABLE
• A measurable entity that is available at the start of a process
• The value can be changed as required
• Generally represented on the *x*-axis

FIGURE 1-19 Common elements of effective graphical presentations of data. Shown here: an example of a line graph.

In each chapter of this book, you will see that one of the visual displays of data is labeled with the "Graphic Content" icon (you'll have noticed this on Figure 1-17). For each of these figures, in the Check Your Knowledge section at the end of the chapter you'll find several questions about the figure's content. These questions will guide you in evaluating aspects of the figure (such as: "What is its main point?") and in extracting information from it. They will also help you understand when it might be warranted to approach a data display with more than the usual amount of skepticism, and when greater trust is reasonable.

TAKE-HOME MESSAGE 1·14

Visual displays of data, which condense large amounts of information, can aid in the presentation and exploration of the data. The effectiveness of such displays is influenced by the precision and clarity of the presentation, and it can be reduced by ambiguity, biases, hidden assumptions, and other issues that reduce a viewer's confidence in the underlying truth of the presented phenomenon.

1·15 Statistics can help us in making decisions.

In Section 1-12 we saw that researchers repeatedly found, through experimentation, that megadoses of vitamin C do not reduce cancer risk. If you put yourself in the researchers' shoes, you might wonder how you'd figure out that the vitamin C did not reduce cancer risk. Perhaps there were 100 individuals in the group receiving megadoses of vitamin C: some of them developed cancer and some of them did not. And among the 100 subjects in the group not receiving the megadoses, some of the individuals developed cancer and some did not. How do you decide whether the vitamin C actually had an effect? This knowledge comes from a branch of mathematics called **statistics,** a set of analytical and mathematical tools designed to help researchers gain understanding from the data they gather. To understand statistics, let's start with a simple situation.

Suppose you measured the height of two people. One is a woman who is 5 feet 10 inches tall. The other is a man who is 5 feet 6 inches tall. If these were your only two observations of human height, you might conclude that female humans are taller than males. But suppose you measured the height of 100 women and 100 men chosen randomly from a population. Then you can say, "of the 100 men, the average man is 5 feet 9.5 inches, and of the 100 women, the average woman is 5 feet 4 inches." Better still, the data can illuminate for you not only the average but also some measure of how much variation there is from one individual to another. Statistical analysis can tell you not only that the average man in this study is 5 feet 9.5 inches tall but that two-thirds of the men are between 5 feet 6.5 inches tall (3 inches less than the average) and 6 feet 0.5 inches tall (3 inches more than the average). You will often see this type of range stated as "5 feet 9.5 inches ± 3 inches" ("plus or minus 3 inches"). Similarly, the data might show that the female subjects in the study are "5 feet 6 inches ± 3 inches," indicating that two-thirds of the women are between 5 feet 3 inches and 5 feet 9 inches tall. As we discussed in Section 1-11, on experimental design, and as this example shows, larger numbers of participants are better than smaller numbers if you want to draw general conclusions

about natural phenomena such as the height of men and women (**FIGURE 1-20**).

HUMAN HEIGHT AND STATISTICS

Don't get fooled! One or two observations isn't enough to draw general conclusions about natural phenomena, such as height.

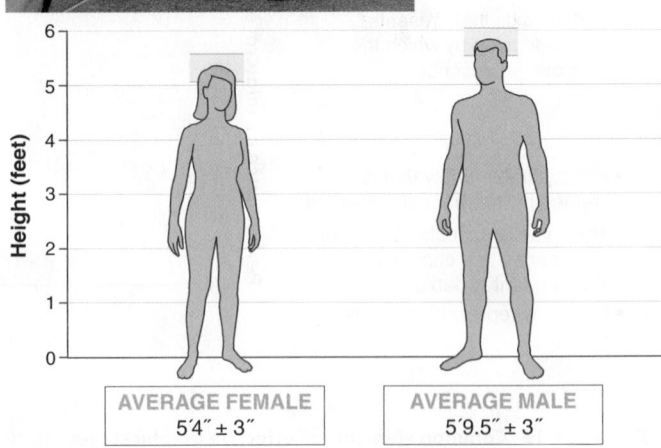

| AVERAGE FEMALE | AVERAGE MALE |
| 5′4″ ± 3″ | 5′9.5″ ± 3″ |

FIGURE 1-20 Drawing conclusions based on limited observations is risky. Measuring a greater number of people will generally help us draw more accurate conclusions about human height.

Using data to describe the characteristics of individuals participating in a study is useful, but often we want to know whether data support (or do not support) a hypothesis. If the scientific method is to be effective in helping us understand the world, it must help us make wise decisions about concrete things. For example, suppose we want to know whether having access to a textbook helps a student perform better in a biology class. Statistics can help us answer this question. After conducting a study, let's say we find that students who had access to a textbook scored an average of 81% ± 8% on their exams, while those who did not scored an average of 76% ± 7%.

In this example, it is difficult to distinguish between the two possible conclusions.

Possibility 1: Students having access to a textbook *do perform better* in biology classes. In other words, our sampling of this class reveals a true relationship between the two variables, textbook access and class performance.

Possibility 2: Students having access to a textbook *do not perform better* in biology classes. The variation in the scores for the two groups may be too large to allow us to conclude that there's any effect of having access to a textbook. Instead, the difference in average scores for the two groups may mean that more of the high-performing students just happened, through random chance, to be in the group given access to a textbook.

But what if the students with access to a textbook scored, on average, 95% ± 5%, while those without access scored only 60% ± 5%? In this case, we would be much more confident that there is a significant effect of having access to a textbook (**FIGURE 1-21**), because even with the large variation in the scores seen in each group, the two averages are still very different from each other.

Statistical methods help us to decide between these two possibilities and, equally important, to state how confident we are that one or the other is true. The greater the difference between two groups (95% vs. 60% is a greater difference than 81% vs. 76%), and the smaller the variation in each group (± 5% in the 95% and 60% groups, vs. ± 8% and ± 7% in the 81% and 76% groups), the more confident we are of the conclusion that there is a significant effect of the treatment (having access to a textbook, in this case). In other words, in the case where the groups of students scored 95% or 60%, depending on whether they did or did not have access to a textbook, it is possible that having a textbook did not actually improve performance and that this observed difference was just the result of chance. But this conclusion is very, very unlikely.

Statistics can also help us identify relationships (or lack of relationships) between variables. For example, we might note that when there are more firefighters at a fire, the fire is larger and causes more damage. This is a **positive correlation,**

INTERPRETING STATISTICS: A HYPOTHETICAL STUDY

Students without textbooks score an average of 60% ± 5%

Students with textbooks score an average of 95% ± 5%

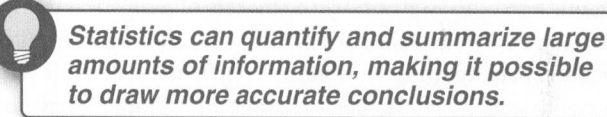

Statistics can quantify and summarize large amounts of information, making it possible to draw more accurate conclusions.

FIGURE 1-21 Drawing conclusions based on statistics. Statistical analyses can help us organize and summarize the observations that we make and the evidence we gather in an experiment.

meaning that when one variable (the number of firefighters) increases, so does the other (the severity of the fire). Should we conclude that firefighters make fires worse? No. While correlations can reveal relationships between variables, they don't tell us *how* the variables are related or whether change in one variable causes change in another. (You may have heard or read the phrase "correlation is not causation," which refers to this sort of situation.) Before drawing any conclusions about more firefighters causing larger fires, we need to know about the type of fire and its size when the firefighters arrived, because those factors will significantly influence the ultimate amount of damage. To estimate the effect of the number of firefighters on the amount of damage, we would need to compare the amount of damage from fires of similar size that are fought by different numbers of firefighters.

Ultimately, statistical analyses can help us organize and summarize the observations that we make and the evidence we gather in an experiment. These analyses can then help us decide whether any differences we measure between experimental and control groups are likely to be the result of the treatment, and how confident we can be in that conclusion.

1·16 Pseudoscience and misleading anecdotal evidence can obscure the truth.

One of the major benefits of the scientific way of thinking is that it can prevent you from being taken in or fooled by false claims. There are two types of "scientific evidence" that frequently are cited in the popular media and are responsible for people erroneously believing that links between two things exist, when in fact they do not.

1. **Pseudoscience,** in which individuals make scientific-sounding claims that are not supported by trustworthy, methodical scientific studies.

2. **Anecdotal observations,** in which, based on just one or a few observations, people conclude that there is or is not a link between two things.

Pseudoscience is all around us, particularly in the claims made on the packaging of consumer products and food (**FIGURE 1-22**). Beginning in the 1960s, for example, consumers encountered the assertion by the makers of a sugarless gum that "4 out of 5 dentists surveyed recommend sugarless gum for their patients who chew gum." Maybe the statement is factually true, but the general relationship it implies may not be. How many dentists were surveyed? If the gum makers surveyed only five dentists, then the statement may not represent the proportion of *all* dentists who would make such a recommendation. And how were the dentists sampled? Were they at a shareholders meeting for the sugarless gum company? What alternatives were given—perhaps gargling with a tooth-destroying acid? You just don't know. That's what makes it pseudoscience.

Pseudoscience capitalizes on a belief shared by most people: that scientific thinking is a powerful method for learning about the world. The problem with pseudoscience is that the scientific bases for a scientific-sounding claim are not clear. The claims generally sound reasonable, and they are persuasive in convincing people to purchase one product over another. But one of the beauties of real science is that you never have to just take someone's word about something. Rather, you are free to evaluate people's research methods and results, and then decide for yourself whether their conclusions and claims are appropriate.

FIGURE 1-22 Pseudoscientific claims are often found on food products.

We are all familiar with anecdotal evidence. Striking stories that we read or hear, or our own experiences, can shape our views of cause and effect. We may find compelling parallels between suggestions made in horoscopes and events in our lives, or we may think that we have a lucky shirt, or we may be moved by a child whose cancer went into remission following treatment involving eating apricot seeds. Yet, despite lacking a human face, data are more reliable than anecdotes, primarily because they can illustrate a broader range of observations, capturing the big picture.

Anecdotal observations can seem harmless and can be emotionally powerful. But because they do not include a sufficiently large and representative set of observations of the world, they can lead people to draw erroneous conclusions, often with disastrous consequences. One important case of anecdotal evidence being used to draw general conclusions involves autism, a developmental disorder that impairs social interaction and communication, and the vaccination for measles, mumps, and rubella (commonly called the MMR vaccine) that is given to most children.

Q | Does the measles, mumps, and rubella vaccine cause autism?

In 1998, the prestigious medical journal *The Lancet* published a report by a group of researchers that described a set of symptoms (diarrhea, abdominal pain, bloating) related to bowel inflammation in 12 children who exhibited the symptoms of autism. The parents or physicians of 8 of the children in the study said that the behavioral symptoms of autism appeared shortly after the children received MMR vaccination. For this reason, the authors of the report recommended further study of a possible link between the MMR vaccine, the bowel problems, and autism.

In a press conference, one of the paper's authors suggested a link between autism and the MMR vaccine, recommending single vaccines rather than the MMR triple vaccine until it could be proved that the MMR vaccine did not trigger autism. This statement caused a major health scare that only recently has begun to subside. Noting that there had been a significant increase in the incidence of autism in the 1990s and early 2000s, the press and many people took the claims made by the researcher at the press conference as evidence that the MMR vaccine causes autism. Over the course of the next few years, the number of children getting the MMR vaccine dropped significantly, as parents sought to reduce the risk of autism in their children (**FIGURE 1-23**).

Unfortunately, this is a notable case of poor implementation of the scientific method, with numerous flaws leading to an incorrect conclusion. Most important among these is that the study was small (only 12 children), the sample was carefully selected rather than randomized (that is, the researchers selected the study participants based on the symptoms they showed), and no control group was included for comparison (for example, children who had been vaccinated but did not exhibit autism symptoms). On top of this, the study, even flawed as it was, did not actually find or even report a link between autism and the MMR vaccine. That purported link came only from the unsupported, suggestive statements made by one of the study's authors at the press conference.

On their own, the design flaws in the study would be sufficient to invalidate the one author's claims about the link between autism and the MMR vaccine, but there are even more weaknesses in the research. It later was discovered that before the paper's publication, the study's lead author (the one who spoke at the press conference) had received large sums of money from lawyers seeking evidence to use in lawsuits against the MMR vaccine manufacturers. It also came to light that he had applied

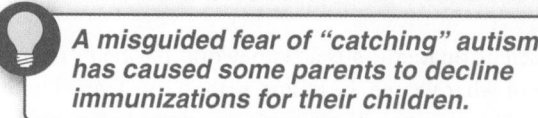

A misguided fear of "catching" autism has caused some parents to decline immunizations for their children.

FIGURE 1-23 Bad science became headline news.

for a patent for a vaccine that was a rival to the most commonly used MMR vaccine. In the light of these initially undisclosed biases, 10 of the paper's 12 authors published a retraction of their original interpretation of their results. And in 2011, the *BMJ* (*British Medical Journal*) published an article declaring that the "article linking MMR vaccine and autism was fraudulent."

In the years since the original paper was published, many well-controlled, large-scale studies have conducted critical experiments on this subject, and all have been definitive in their conclusion that there is no link between the MMR vaccine and autism. Here are a few of these studies.

1. A study of all children born in Denmark between 1991 and 1998 found no difference in the incidence of autism among the 440,655 children who were vaccinated with the MMR vaccine and the 96,648 children who were not vaccinated.

2. A 2005 study in Japan showed that after use of the MMR vaccine was stopped in 1993, the incidence of autism continued to increase.

3. A study of 1.8 million children in Finland who were followed up for 14 years after getting the MMR vaccine found no link at all between the occurrence of autism and the vaccine.

At this point, the consensus of the international scientific community is that there is no scientific evidence for a link between the MMR vaccine and autism.

> " Science is a way to call the bluff of those who only pretend to knowledge. It is a bulwark against mysticism mysticism, against superstition, against religion misapplied to where it has no business being. If we're true to its values, it can tell us when we're being lied to. "
>
> —CARL SAGAN,
> in *The Demon-Haunted World: Science as a Candle in the Dark*, 1997

So what explains the observation that there are more autism cases now than in the past? It seems that this is a function of the better identification of autism by doctors and changes in the process by which autism is diagnosed. Another reason for the perceived link between autism and the MMR vaccine was simply the coincidence that most children receive the vaccine at around 18–19 months of age, which happens to be the age at which the first symptoms of autism are usually noticed. In the end, what we learn from this is that we must be wary that we do not generalize from anecdotal observations or let poorly designed studies obscure the truth.

TAKE-HOME MESSAGE 1·16

Pseudoscience and anecdotal observations often lead people to believe that links between two phenomena exist, when in fact there are no such links.

1·17 There are limits to what science can do.

The scientific method is a framework that helps us make sense of what we see, hear, and read in our lives. There are limits, however, to what science can do.

The scientific method will never prove or disprove the existence of God. Nor is it likely to help us understand the mathematical elegance of Fermat's last theorem or the beauty of Shakespeare's sonnets. As one of several approaches to the acquisition of knowledge, the scientific method is, above all, empirical. It differs from non-scientific approaches such as mathematics and logic, history, music, and the study of artistic expression in that it relies on *measuring* phenomena in some way. The generation of value judgments and other types of non-quantifiable, subjective information—such as religious assertions of faith—falls outside the realm of science. Despite all of the intellectual analyses that the scientific method gives rise to and the objective conclusions it makes possible, it does not, for example, generate moral statements and it cannot give us insight into ethical problems. What "is" (i.e., what we observe in the natural world) is not necessarily what "ought" to be (i.e., what is morally right). It may or may not be.

Further, much of what is commonly considered to be science, such as the construction of new engineering marvels or the heroic surgical separation of conjoined twins, is not scientific at all. Rather, these are technical innovations and developments. While they frequently rely on sophisticated scientific research, they represent the application of research findings to varied fields such as manufacturing and medicine to solve problems (**FIGURE 1-24**).

FIGURE 1-24 The application of science. Applying scientific findings to solve a problem can result in sophisticated technical innovations, like this thought-controlled prosthetic arm.

As we begin approaching the world from a more scientific perspective, we can gain important insights into the facts of life, yet must remain mindful of the limits to science.

TAKE-HOME MESSAGE 1·17

Although the scientific method may be the most effective path toward understanding the observable world, it cannot give us insights into the generation of value judgments and other types of non-quantifiable, subjective information.

1·18 On the road to biological literacy: what are the major themes in biology?

Contemplating unity and diversity. An entomologist organizes and categorizes specimens.

1·18

A few important themes tie together the diverse topics in biology.

Driven forward by the power of the scientific method, modern biology is in the midst of an explosion of new and exciting developments. Now more than ever, biology is influencing and even transforming our lives. Its increasing relevance outside the world of scientists is felt in a multitude of areas, including breakthroughs in agriculture, innovative developments in criminology, and increased understanding and awareness of environmental issues and the need for widespread changes in behavior.

In this guide to biology, as we explore the many facets of biology and its relevance to life in the modern world, you will find two unifying themes recurring throughout.

Hierarchical organization. Life is organized on many levels within individual organisms, including atoms, cells, tissues, and organs. And in the larger world, organisms themselves are organized into many levels: populations, communities, and ecosystems within the biosphere.

The power of evolution. Evolution, the change in genetic characteristics of individuals within populations over time, accounts for the diversity of organisms, but also explains the unity among them.

These two major themes connect the diverse topics, as we make our way through four chief areas of focus:

1. The chemical, cellular, and energetic foundations of life

2. The genetics, evolution, and behavior of individuals

3. The staggering diversity of life and the unity underlying it

4. Ecology, the environment, and the subtle and important links between organisms and the world they inhabit

Armed with an appreciation for the scientific method and the broader themes you'll encounter in your study of biology, let's continue our exploration of life!

> ### TAKE-HOME MESSAGE 1·18
>
> Although the diversity of life on earth is tremendous, the study of life is unified by the themes of hierarchical organization and the power of evolution.

RAINY DAYS AND MONDAYS.

Q: WHAT'S THE MOST IMPORTANT OUTCOME OF SCIENTIFIC THINKING? "Scientific thinking tells us when to change our mind about the natural world." Let's consider a question that might seem silly–even trivial–and watch our minds open.

Q: IT OFTEN SEEMS TO RAIN MORE ON WEEKENDS. COULD IT BE TRUE? Before you read on, write down your one word answer (and a justification for it, if you'd like).

Q: WELL, DOES IT RAIN MORE ON WEEKENDS? At first, it seems that the answer must be "NO." How could the weather even "know" what day it is? Weather, after all, existed long before humans, calendars, and Monday mornings.

Q: RATHER THAN RELYING ON COMMON SENSE, LET'S THINK SCIENTIFICALLY.

My hypothesis: It rains more on weekends.

Restated as a null hypothesis: The amount of rainfall does not differ across the days of the week.

A testable prediction: The amount of rain rainfall should not differ depending on what day of the week it is.

And now the data . . .

In a 1998 study published in the journal *Nature,* researchers using 17 years of data analyzed rainfall along the eastern coast of North America. Here's what they found:

There was 22% more rain on Saturdays than on Mondays! (And this difference was statistically significant.)

Q: HOW CAN THIS BE? The researchers also tracked the pollutants carbon monoxide and ozone and found them both to gradually increase from Monday through Friday. This pattern, they suggested, is probably related to accumulations from driving, which is greater during the week than on weekends. They suggested that the weekly pollution cycle causes increased cloud formation and rain on weekends (while the reduced pollution on Mondays leads to reduced rainfall). In other words human activities are influencing the weather!

Q: ONE GOOD HYPOTHESIS DESERVES ANOTHER. If their suggestion is true, we should expect the "Rainy Saturday/Dry Monday" phenomenon to occur only in the vicinity of human activities. As a test of this hypothesis, the researchers measured daily rainfall patterns over the oceans in the northern hemisphere, away from large human populations. Here they found that one-seventh of the rain fell on each day, with no days rainier than others.

Q: THE TAKE HOME MESSAGE HERE? Scientific thinking rewards open minds with satisfying answers.

Big Ideas in ...
Scientific Thinking

1·1–1·3 Science is a collection of facts and a process for understanding the world.

- Through objective observation, description, and experimentation, science is a pathway by which we can understand the world around us. Biological issues permeate all aspects of our lives.
- To make wise decisions, individuals and societies must attain biological literacy.
- There are numerous ways of gaining an understanding of the world. Because it is empirical, rational, testable, repeatable, and self-correcting, the scientific method is a particularly effective approach.

1·4–1·10 A beginner's guide: what are the steps of the scientific method?

- The scientific method (observation, hypothesis, prediction, test, and conclusion) is a flexible, adaptable, and efficient pathway to understanding the world, because it tells us when we must change our beliefs.
- The scientific method begins by making observations about the world.
- A hypothesis is a proposed explanation for a phenomenon. For a hypothesis to be useful, it must generate a testable prediction.
- A critical experiment is one that makes it possible to decisively determine whether a particular hypothesis is correct. Based on the results of experimental tests, we can revise our hypothesis and explain the world with increasing accuracy.
- A great strength of scientific thinking is that it helps us understand when we should change our minds.
- Scientific theories are hypotheses—proposed explanations for natural phenomena—that have been so strongly supported by empirical observations that the scientific community views them as very unlikely to be altered by new evidence.

1·11–1·13 Well-designed experiments are essential to testing hypotheses.

- To draw clear conclusions from experiments, it is essential to hold constant all those variables we are not interested in.
- Control and experimental groups should vary only with respect to the treatment of interest. Differences in outcomes between the groups can then be attributed to the treatment.
- Experiments and their outcomes must be repeatable for their conclusions to be valid and widely accepted.
- Biases can influence our behavior, including our collection and interpretation of data. With careful controls, we can minimize such biases.

1·14–1·17 Scientific thinking can help us make wise decisions.

- Visual displays of data condense large amounts of information and can aid in the presentation and exploration of the data, but care must be taken to evaluate the presentation of the data and their underlying truth.
- Because much variation exists in the world, statistics can help us evaluate whether differences between a treatment group and control group can be attributed to the treatment rather than random chance.
- Pseudoscience and anecdotal observations often lead people to believe that links between two phenomena exist, when there are no such links.
- Although the scientific method may be the most effective path toward understanding the observable world, it cannot give us insights into non-quantifiable, subjective information.

1·18 On the road to biological literacy: what are the major themes in biology?

- Although the diversity of life on earth is tremendous, the study of life is unified by the themes of hierarchical organization and the power of evolution.

See the To-Go Guide (packaged with every new copy of this textbook) for an illustrated summary of the chapter.

Check Your Knowledge

1. What does the green portion of the pie chart represent? What does the blue portion represent? What does the "whole pie" represent?

2. Why are there two pie charts?

3. What can you conclude from this figure?

4. What might be an alternative explanation (other than bias against female scientists) for the phenomenon shown here?

5. How big was the increase in number of papers published with female first author following the institution of a double-blind review policy?

6. Why isn't the percentage of papers published with female first author 50%, even after the new review policy? Is that cause for concern? What data would help you to answer that question?

7. Do these graphs prove a general bias against female scientists?

PERCENTAGE OF PAPERS PUBLISHED WITH FEMALE FIRST AUTHOR

When the reviewers know the sex of the author: 23.7%

When the reviewers do NOT know the sex of the author: 31.6%

See Answers at the back of the book.

Key Terms in Scientific Thinking

anecdotal observation, p. 26
biological literacy, p. 4
biology, p. 4
blind experimental design, p. 18

control group, p. 16
critical experiment, p. 12
dependent variable, p. 23
double-blind experimental design, p. 19
empirical, p. 6

experimental group, p. 16
hypothesis (*pl.* hypotheses), p. 9
independent variable, p. 23
null hypothesis, p. 10
placebo, p. 13

placebo effect, p. 18
positive correlation, p. 25
pseudoscience, p. 26
randomized, p. 19
science, p. 2
scientific literacy, p. 4

scientific method, p. 6
statistics, p. 24
superstition, p. 5
theory, p. 15
treatment, p. 16
variable, p. 16

Multiple-Choice Questions

1. **Science is:**

   a) a field of study that requires certain "laws of nature" to be taken on faith.

   b) both a body of knowledge and an intellectual activity encompassing observation, description, experimentation, and explanation of natural phenomena.

   c) a process that can be applied only within the scientific disciplines, such as biology, chemistry, and physics.

   d) the only way to understand the natural world.

   e) None of the above are correct.

   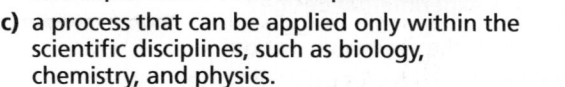

2. **All of the following are elements of biological literacy except:**

   a) the ability to use the process of scientific inquiry to think creatively about real-world issues having a biological component.

   b) reading the most important books in biology.

   c) the ability to integrate into your decision making a consideration of issues having a biological component.

   d) the ability to communicate with others about issues having a biological component.

   e) All of the above are elements of biological literacy.

3. **Superstitions are:**

   a) held by many humans, but not by any non-human species.

   b) just one of many possible forms of scientific thinking.

   c) true beliefs that have yet to be fully understood.

   d) irrational beliefs that actions not logically related to a course of events influence its outcome.

   e) proof that the scientific method is not perfect.

4. **In a recent study, patients treated with a genetically engineered heart drug were able to walk on a treadmill 26 seconds longer than those not receiving the drug, and they showed no side effects from taking the drug. Can we conclude that this drug is an effective treatment for heart disease?**

   a) No. Genetically engineered drugs cannot be tested by the scientific method; they require comparative observations.

   b) No. It is not clear how many subjects were in the study.

   c) No. It is not clear that the drug is not a placebo.

   d) Yes.

   e) No. It is not clear that the proper controls were included.

5. **Empirical results:**

   a) rely on intuition.

   b) are generated by theories.

   c) are based on observation.

   d) cannot be replicated.

   e) must support a tested hypothesis.

6. **In a well-designed experiment:**

   a) the prediction will be highly probable if the experiment shows the explanation is correct.

   b) the prediction will be highly improbable if the experiment shows the explanation is incorrect.

   c) the null hypothesis will not be tested.

   d) the prediction will most likely be correct.

   e) Both a) and b) are correct.

7. **Which of the following statements is correct?**

   a) A hypothesis that does not generate a testable prediction is not useful.

   b) Common sense is usually a good substitute for the scientific method when trying to understand the world.

   c) The scientific method can be used only to understand scientific phenomena.

   d) It is not necessary to make observations as part of the scientific method.

   e) All of the above are correct.

8. The placebo effect:

a) is the frequently observed, poorly understood phenomenon that people tend to respond favorably to any treatment.

b) reveals that sugar pills are generally as effective as actual medications in fighting illness.

c) reveals that experimental treatments cannot be proven effective.

d) demonstrates that most scientific studies cannot be replicated.

e) is an urban legend.

100 HARD

32

0 EASY

9. Before experimental drugs can be brought to market, they must undergo many rigorous trials to ensure that they deliver their medical benefits effectively and safely. One method commonly used in this process is to compare the effect of a drug with that of a placebo in double-blind tests. Which of the following correctly describes a double-blind test?

a) The researchers apply two-layered blindfolds to the study participants so that they cannot see whether they are receiving the drug or a placebo.

b) Neither the researchers nor the study participants know who is receiving the drug and who is receiving the placebo.

c) The researchers know who is receiving the drug and who is receiving the placebo, but they do not know what the supposed effects of the drug should be.

d) The researchers do not know who receives the drug or the placebo, but the participants know and tell them later.

e) None of the above is correct.

100 HARD

15

0 EASY

10. In controlled experiments:

a) one variable is manipulated while others are held constant.

b) all variables are dependent on each other.

c) all variables are held constant.

d) all variables are independent of each other.

e) all critical variables are manipulated.

100 HARD

24

0 EASY

11. If a researcher collects data by using the same experimental setup as in another study, but using different research subjects, the process is considered:

a) an uncontrolled experiment.

b) intuitive reasoning.

c) extrapolation.

d) replication.

e) exploration.

100 HARD

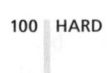

0 EASY

12. Upon hearing the males of a particular bird species calling in their natural environment, you wonder why they call. In order to answer your question, you cage one male bird and record his calling rate under several different conditions:

- in the presence of no conspecific (i.e., of the same species) birds.
- in the presence of 10 conspecific males.
- in the presence of 10 conspecific females.
- in the presence of 5 conspecific males and 5 conspecific females.

Which of the following null hypotheses could be falsified using this experimental design?

a) Males of the species do not call.

b) Males of the species call more often than do females.

c) Males of the species call at a rate that is independent of the sex composition of the audience.

d) Males of the species call less often than do females.

e) Males of the species call when called to.

100 HARD

51

0 EASY

13. An independent variable:

a) can cause a change in a dependent variable.

b) is generally less variable than a dependent variable.

c) is plotted on the y-axis in a line graph.

d) can be controlled less well than a dependent variable.

e) is typically of greater interest to the experimenter than a dependent variable.

100 HARD

10 ASY

14. Statistical methods make it possible to:

a) prove that any hypothesis is true.

b) determine how likely it is that certain results have occurred by chance.

c) unambiguously learn the truth.

d) reject any hypothesis.

e) test non-falsifiable hypotheses.

100 HARD

23

0 EASY

15. Anecdotal evidence:

a) is a more efficient method for understanding the world than the scientific method.

b) tends to be more reliable than data based on observations of large numbers of diverse individuals.

c) is a necessary part of the scientific method.

d) is often the only way to prove important causal links between two phenomena.

e) can seem to reveal links between two phenomena, but the links do not actually exist.

100 HARD

43

0 EASY

16. A relationship between phenomena that has been established based on large amounts of observational and experimental data is referred to as:

   a) a theory.

   b) a fact.

   c) an assumption.

   d) a conjecture.

   e) a hypothesis.

100 HARD

30

0 EASY

17. Which of the following issues would be least helped by application of the scientific method?

   a) developing more effective high school curricula

   b) evaluating the relationship between violence in videogames and criminal behavior in teens

   c) determining the most effective safety products for automobiles

   d) formulating public policy on euthanasia

   e) comparing the effectiveness of two potential antibiotics

100 HARD

31

0 EASY

18. What is the meaning of the statement "Correlation does not imply causation"?

   a) Just because two variables vary in a similar pattern does not mean that changing one variable causes a change in the other.

   b) It is not possible to demonstrate a correlation between two variables.

   c) When a change in one variable causes a change in another variable, the two variables are not necessarily related to each other in any way.

   d) It is not possible to prove the cause of any naturally occurring phenomenon.

   e) Just because two variables vary in a similar pattern does not mean that they have any relationship to each other.

100 HARD

49

0 EASY

Short-Answer Questions

1. A pharmaceutical company plans to test a potential anti-cancer drug on human subjects. The drug will be administered in pill form. How should this study be designed so that appropriate controls are in place?

2. Lately there have been many claims concerning the health benefits of green tea. Suppose you read a claim that alleges drinking green tea causes weight loss. You are provided with the following information about the studies that led to this claim.

People were weighed at the beginning of the study.

People were asked to drink two cups of green tea every day for 6 weeks.

People were weighed at the end of the study.

People who drank green tea for 6 weeks lost some weight by the end of the study.

It was concluded that green tea is helpful for weight loss.

This study obviously had some holes in its design. Assuming no information other than that provided above, indicate at least four things that could be done to improve the experimental design.

See Answers at the back of the book.
For additional study questions, go to www.prep-u.com.

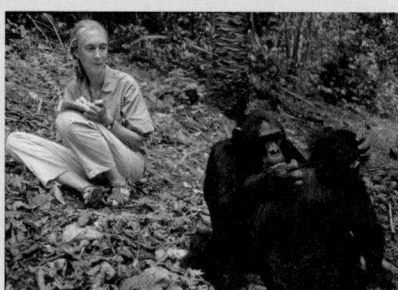

ABOUT THE CHAPTER OPENING PHOTO

Beginning in 1960 (and continuing for more than 45 years), Jane Goodall studied the social and family interactions of chimpanzees in the wild, in Gombe Stream National Park, Tanzania.

Raw materials and fuel
for our bodies

Chemistry

2·1–2·3 Atoms form molecules through bonding.

Classical atomic models: a nucleus as a packed cluster of protons and neutrons, orbited by electrons.

2·1 Everything is made of atoms.

A little bit of chemistry goes a long way in the study of biology and in understanding a great deal about your everyday life. Will eating those beans in your soup keep you up all night in gastrointestinal distress? Just knowing whether the beans are lentils or lima beans—each contains slightly different types of sugar molecules—will give you an answer. Will the butter you spread on your toast sabotage your efforts to lose weight? Understanding something about the carbon-hydrogen connections in the fat molecules can help you decide.

The chemistry that is most important in biology revolves around a few important elements, which are introduced at the end of this section. An **element** is a substance that cannot be broken down chemically into any other substances. Gold, carbon, and copper are elements you might be familiar with. Whatever the element, if you keep cutting it into ever smaller pieces, each of the pieces behaves exactly the same as any other piece. The smallest piece of pure gold will still have the softness, reflectivity, and malleability characteristic of that element (**FIGURE 2-1**).

Gold

Carbon

Copper

FIGURE 2-1 Familiar elements. Elements are substances that cannot be broken down chemically into any other substances.

If you could continue cutting, you would eventually separate the gold into tiny pieces that could no longer be divided without losing their gold-like properties. These individual component pieces of an element are called **atoms.** An atom is a bit of matter that cannot be subdivided any further without losing its essential properties. The word "atom" is from the Greek for "indivisible."

Everything around us, living or not, can be reduced to atoms. All atoms—whether of the element gold or some other element such as oxygen or aluminum or calcium—have the same basic structure. At the center of an atom is a **nucleus,** which is usually made up of two types of particles, called protons and neutrons. **Protons** are particles that have a positive electrical charge and **neutrons** are particles that have no electrical charge. The amount of matter in a particle is its **mass;** protons and neutrons have approximately the same mass (**FIGURE 2-2**).

Whirling in a cloud around the nucleus of every atom are negatively charged particles called **electrons.** An electron weighs almost nothing—less than one-twentieth of one percent of the weight of a proton. (The mass of an atom—its **atomic mass**—is made up of the combined mass of all of its protons and neutrons; for our purposes here, electrons are so light that their mass can be ignored.)

Particles that have the same charge repel each other; those with opposite charges are attracted to each other. Because all electrons have the same charge, the electrons in an atom repel each other. But because they are negatively charged, they are attracted to the positively charged protons in the nucleus. This attraction holds electrons close enough to the nucleus to keep them from flying away, while the energy of their fast movement keeps them from collapsing into the nucleus.

Atoms are tiny. Enlarge an atom by a billion times and it would only be the size of a grapefruit. Paradoxically, most of the space taken up by an atom is empty. That is, because the nucleus is very small and compact, the electrons zip about relatively far from the nucleus. If the nucleus were the size of a golf ball, the electrons would be anywhere from half a mile to six miles away.

What distinguishes one element, such as chlorine, from another, such as neon or oxygen? The number of protons in an atom's nucleus determines what element it is. As a rule, atoms of different elements have a different number of protons in the nucleus. A chlorine atom has 17 protons, a neon atom has 10 protons, and an oxygen atom has 8 protons. Each element is given a name (and an abbreviation, such as O for oxygen and C for carbon) and an **atomic number** that corresponds to how many protons it has (**FIGURE 2-3**).

THE ATOM: BASIC STRUCTURE

Nucleus

HYDROGEN ATOM
1 Proton
0 Neutrons
1 Electron

CARBON ATOM
6 Protons
6 Neutrons
6 Electrons

Nucleus:
Proton   Neutron   Electron

Forces of attraction between positive and negative charges hold the fast-moving electrons (negative) close to the nucleus (positive).

FIGURE 2-2 The atom. At the center of an atom is a nucleus containing protons and (in all elements except hydrogen) neutrons. The nucleus is surrounded by electrons whirling about in a cloud.

The mass of an atom is usually about double the element's atomic number. This is because the number of neutrons in the nucleus is usually equal to the number of protons, and

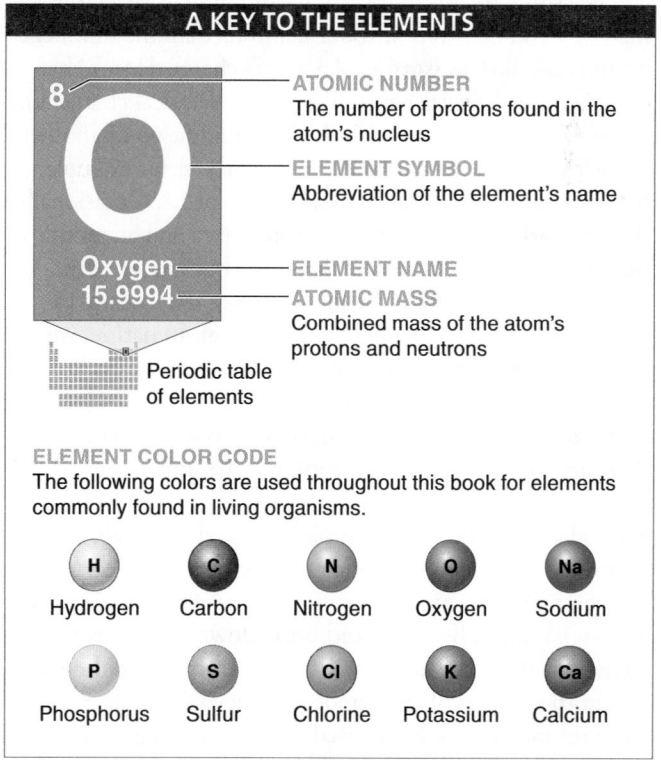

A KEY TO THE ELEMENTS

8
O
Oxygen
15.9994

ATOMIC NUMBER
The number of protons found in the atom's nucleus

ELEMENT SYMBOL
Abbreviation of the element's name

ELEMENT NAME

ATOMIC MASS
Combined mass of the atom's protons and neutrons

Periodic table of elements

ELEMENT COLOR CODE
The following colors are used throughout this book for elements commonly found in living organisms.

H — Hydrogen
C — Carbon
N — Nitrogen
O — Oxygen
Na — Sodium

P — Phosphorus
S — Sulfur
Cl — Chlorine
K — Potassium
Ca — Calcium

FIGURE 2-3 The vital statistics of atoms. This key explains how to read a periodic table of elements. A full periodic table of the elements is at the back of the book.

ISOTOPES

Atoms with the same atomic number (i.e., the same number of protons) but different atomic mass are isotopes.

	CARBON-12	CARBON-13	CARBON-14
⊕ Protons	6	6	6
◯ Neutrons	6	7	8
• Electrons	6	6	6
Atomic mass	**12**	**13**	**14**

FIGURE 2-4 Isotopes are atoms that have extra neutrons or missing neutrons.

protons and neutrons have approximately the same mass. The element oxygen, for example, has the atomic number 8 because it has 8 protons, so we expect it to have an atomic mass of 16, simply the mass of the 8 protons and 8 neutrons added together—which it generally does. (As noted above, we can ignore the mass of the electrons.)

Atoms don't always have the exact same number of protons and neutrons in their nucleus and electrons circling around it. They sometimes acquire or lose components. An atom that has extra neutrons or fewer neutrons than the number of protons is called an **isotope.** An atom's charge doesn't change in an isotope, because neutrons have no electrical charge, but the atom's mass changes with the loss or addition of another particle in the nucleus (**FIGURE 2-4**). Carbon, for example, has six protons and so usually has a mass of 12. Occasionally, though, carbon has an extra neutron or two and an atomic mass of 13 or 14. This is rare in nature, but it does occur. These isotopes are called carbon-13 (^{13}C) and carbon-14 (^{14}C) and are referred to as "heavy" carbon. In nature, we frequently see mixtures of several isotopes for a given element. So although a sample of pure carbon is predominantly ^{12}C atoms (with 6 protons and 6 neutrons), there are some ^{13}C and ^{14}C atoms in the sample, too.

Most elements and their isotopes have perfectly stable nuclei that remain unchanged virtually forever, never losing or gaining neutrons, protons, or electrons. A few atomic nuclei are not so stable, however, and break down spontaneously sometime after they are created. These atoms are **radioactive,** and in the process of decomposition they release, at a constant rate, a tiny, high-speed particle carrying a lot of energy. (The particle may be a proton, neutron, electron, or just energy.) For example, uranium-238 (which has 92 protons and 146 neutrons in its nucleus) is a radioactive

element. It spontaneously loses a particle containing 2 protons and 2 neutrons, turning it into an isotope of a different element altogether—thorium-236, in this case. The thorium is radioactive as well, one in a long chain of isotopes, each decaying into another radioactive element, until finally producing the stable element lead (with an atomic mass of 206). Radioactive atoms turn out to be useful in determining the age of fossils (see Section 8-17), in medical imaging and cancer treatment, and in the generation of vast amounts of energy.

All the known elements can be arranged in a scheme, in the order of their atomic number, called the **periodic table** (see Figure 2-3). A copy of the periodic table is provided at the back of the book. So far, about 90 elements have been discovered that are present in nature, and about 25 others can be made in the laboratory. Everything you see around you is made up of some combination of the 90 or so naturally occurring elements.

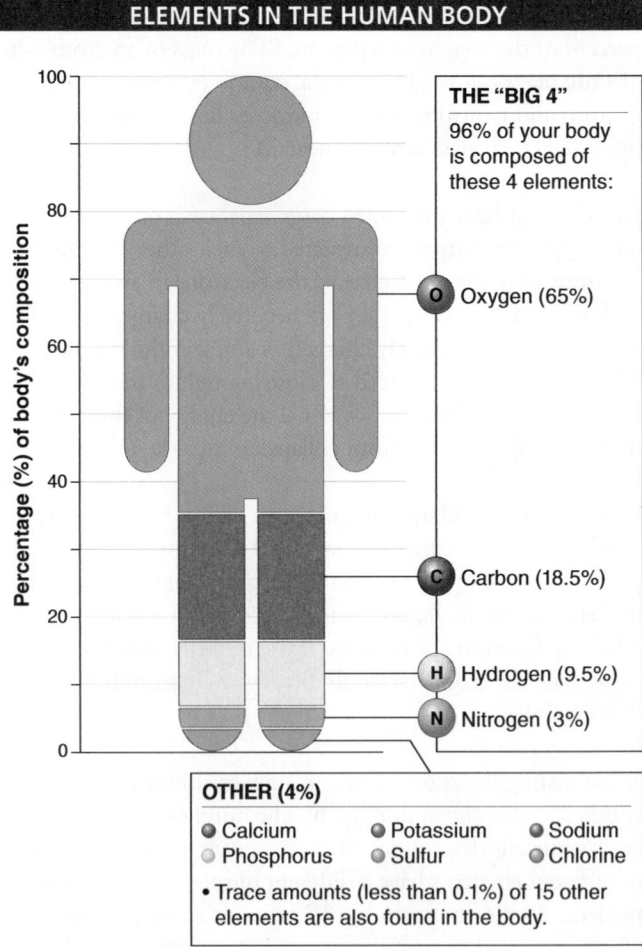

FIGURE 2-5 The body's chemistry. Just 10 elements make up 99.9% of your body. Four of these—oxygen, carbon, hydrogen, and nitrogen—are most abundant and make up about 96% of your body.

Of all the elements found on earth, only 25 are found in your body. The "Top 10" most common of these make up 99.9% of your body mass, but they are not present in equal measures (FIGURE 2-5). The "Big 4" elements, oxygen, carbon, hydrogen, and nitrogen, predominate and make up more than 96% of your body mass. With knowledge about the Big 4, you can understand a huge amount about nutrition and physiology (how your body works), so we'll focus on the properties of these four elements later in this chapter.

2·2 An atom's electrons determine how (and whether) the atom will bond with other atoms.

Although the number of protons identifies an element, it is an atom's electrons that determine how (and whether) it bonds with other atoms. Electrons move so quickly that it is impossible to determine, at any given moment, exactly where an electron is. Electrons are not just moving about haphazardly, though. Speeding around the nucleus, they tend to stay within a prescribed area. This area is called an "electron shell," and an atom may have several shells, each shell occupied by its own set of electrons. Within a shell, the electrons stay far apart because their negative charges repel one another. (Electron shells aren't actual physical tracks but, rather, are simplified placeholders for the different possible energy levels of the electrons.)

The first electron shell is closest to the nucleus and can hold two electrons (FIGURE 2-6). If an atom has more than two electrons, as most atoms do, the other electrons are arranged in other shells. The second shell is a bit farther away from the nucleus and can hold as many as eight electrons. There can be up to seven shells in total, holding varying numbers of electrons.

Atoms become stable when their outermost shell is filled to capacity. Atoms with this configuration behave like loners, neither reacting nor combining with other atoms. On the other hand, when atoms have outer shells with vacancies, they are likely to interact with other atoms, giving, taking, or sharing electrons to achieve that desirable state: a full outer shell of electrons. In fact, based on the number of electron vacancies in the outermost shell of an atom, it's possible to predict how amenable to bonding that atom will be, and even which other atoms its likely bonding partners will be.

FIGURE 2-6 **Electron interactions.** The chemical characteristics of an atom depend upon the number of electrons in its outermost shell.

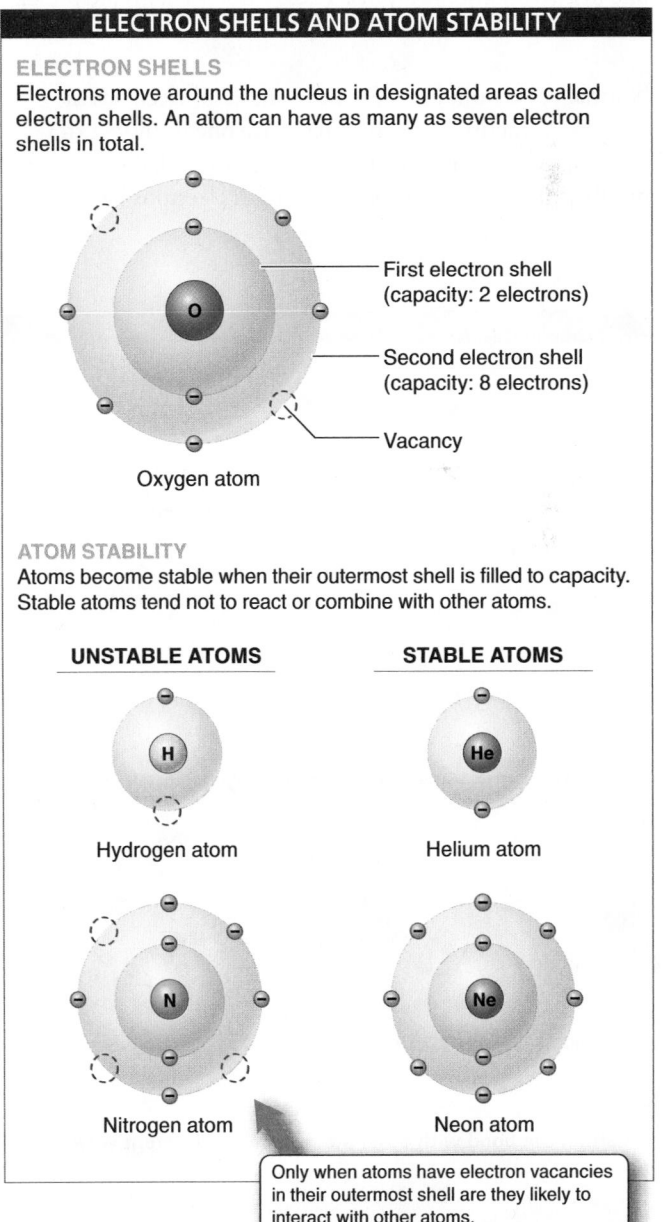

ELECTRON SHELLS AND ATOM STABILITY

ELECTRON SHELLS
Electrons move around the nucleus in designated areas called electron shells. An atom can have as many as seven electron shells in total.

First electron shell (capacity: 2 electrons)

Second electron shell (capacity: 8 electrons)

Vacancy

Oxygen atom

ATOM STABILITY
Atoms become stable when their outermost shell is filled to capacity. Stable atoms tend not to react or combine with other atoms.

UNSTABLE ATOMS | STABLE ATOMS

Hydrogen atom | Helium atom

Nitrogen atom | Neon atom

Only when atoms have electron vacancies in their outermost shell are they likely to interact with other atoms.

Let's take a brief look at one element—carbon—whose electron configuration gives it considerable versatility when it comes to bonding with other atoms and making important compounds. Carbon has 6 electrons overall: 2 in the first electron shell and 4 in the second electron shell. Because the second electron shell has a capacity of 8 electrons, carbon can share its 4 electrons in its outermost shell. This gives it an ability to bond with other atoms in a large number of different ways—including in four different directions—and makes a huge variety of complex molecules possible (**FIGURE 2-7**).

Carbon most commonly bonds with oxygen, hydrogen, and nitrogen. And because carbon atoms often bind to other carbon atoms, carbon chains are very common—and each carbon bound to two other carbon atoms can still bind with one or two additional atoms. These carbon chains are present in most organic molecules.

Normally, an atom has the same number of electrons as protons. Sometimes an atom may have one or more extra electrons or may lack one or more electrons relative to the number of protons. An atom with extra electrons becomes

IONS ARE CHARGED ATOMS

An atom that loses one or more electrons becomes positively charged, while an atom that acquires electrons becomes negatively charged. This transfer of electrons is driven by the fact that atoms with full outer electron shells are more stable.

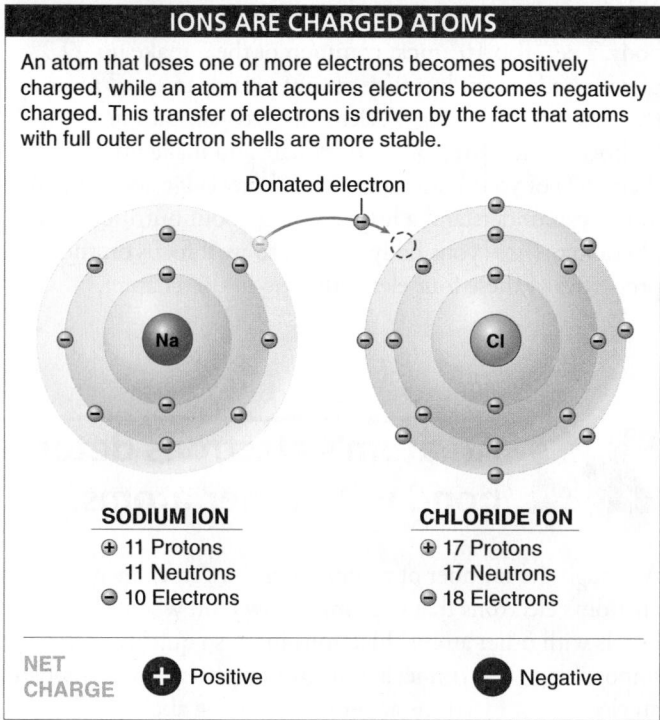

Donated electron

SODIUM ION	**CHLORIDE ION**
⊕ 11 Protons	⊕ 17 Protons
11 Neutrons	17 Neutrons
⊖ 10 Electrons	⊖ 18 Electrons

NET CHARGE   ➕ Positive   ➖ Negative

FIGURE 2-8 Ions are electrically charged atoms.

negatively charged, and an atom lacking one or more electrons is positively charged. Such a charged atom is called an **ion** (**FIGURE 2-8**). Due to their electrical charge, ions behave very differently from the atoms that give rise to them. As we see later in the chapter, ions are more likely to interact with other, oppositely charged ions.

TAKE-HOME MESSAGE 2·2

The chemical characteristics of an atom depend on the number of electrons in its outermost shell. Atoms are most stable and least likely to bond with other atoms when their outermost electron shell is filled to capacity.

THE VERSATILITY OF CARBON

First electron shell (capacity: 2 electrons)

Second electron shell (capacity: 8 electrons)

Vacancy

Carbon atom

EXAMPLES OF THE WIDE VARIETY OF CARBON COMPOUNDS

Carbon dioxide   Proteins   Sugars (glucose and fructose)

FIGURE 2-7 Carbon can bond with other atoms in many different ways.

2·3 Atoms can bond together to form molecules or compounds.

When you eat a meal, it is like filling your car's tank with gasoline; you have a source of energy that can be used to fuel activities like running, thinking, building muscle, and maintaining the machinery of life. That energy initially comes from the sun and is captured and stored by plants. When we eat plants or eat other animals that eat plants, we ingest the energy stored in the plant material. But how exactly is energy stored in plants?

Groups of atoms held together by bonds are called **molecules.** It takes a certain amount of energy to break a bond between two atoms. The amount of this energy, called the **bond energy,** depends on the atoms involved. When chemical reactions occur—such as when animals (including humans) consume molecules in their diet—some existing bonds are usually broken and some new bonds are usually formed. If the bond energy of the new bonds formed is less than the bond energy of the starting materials, the excess energy is released—and can be used to fuel the body's activities. In a sense, molecules are created as a short-term storage of energy that can be harnessed later.

Before looking at specific types of bonds that hold molecules together, let's look at how molecules are illustrated. In this book you will most often see molecular structures represented by the ball-and-stick and space-filling models.

DIFFERENT WAYS OF REPRESENTING MOLECULAR STRUCTURE

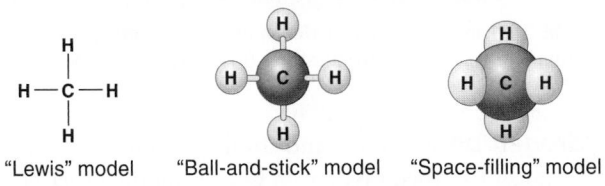

"Lewis" model   "Ball-and-stick" model   "Space-filling" model

There are three principal types of bonds that hold atoms together. The type of bonding that any atom is likely to take part in depends almost entirely on the number of electrons in its outermost shell.

Covalent bonds When two atoms share electrons, a strong **covalent bond** is formed. The simplest example of a covalent bond is the bonding of two hydrogen atoms to form a hydrogen molecule, H_2 (**FIGURE 2-9**), the simplest of all molecules. A hydrogen atom has an atomic number of 1: it has a single proton in its nucleus and a single electron circling around the nucleus in the first shell. Because the atom is most stable when the first shell has two electrons, two hydrogen atoms can each achieve a complete outermost shell by sharing electrons. The nuclei come close together (but not

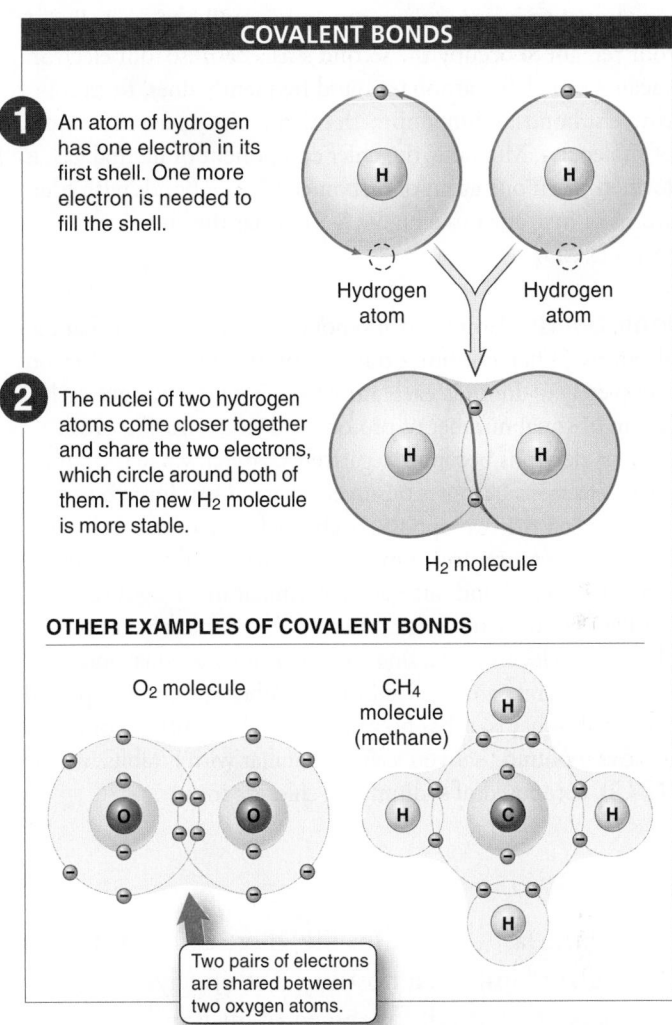

COVALENT BONDS

1 An atom of hydrogen has one electron in its first shell. One more electron is needed to fill the shell.

Hydrogen atom   Hydrogen atom

2 The nuclei of two hydrogen atoms come closer together and share the two electrons, which circle around both of them. The new H_2 molecule is more stable.

H_2 molecule

OTHER EXAMPLES OF COVALENT BONDS

O_2 molecule CH_4 molecule (methane)

Two pairs of electrons are shared between two oxygen atoms.

FIGURE 2-9 Covalent bonds: strong chemical bonds formed through electron sharing.

too close, because they are positively charged and their mutual repulsion would destabilize the molecule), and the two electrons circle around both of the nuclei, almost in a figure 8. The new H_2 molecule is very stable because, now that both atoms have two electrons in their outermost shell, they are no longer likely to bond with other atoms.

Oxygen, with an atomic number of 8, has two electrons in its innermost shell and six in its outermost shell. Consequently it needs to form two covalent bonds to fill its outermost shell. Sometimes two oxygen atoms join together to form O_2. Each oxygen atom shares a pair of electrons with the other, filling the outermost shell of both. The sharing of two electrons between two atoms is called a

double bond (see Figure 2-9). O_2 is the most common form in which we find oxygen in the world.

Carbon is a particularly "extroverted" atom. It has an atomic number of 6, meaning that two electrons fill its first shell and four remain to occupy the second shell. Because four electron vacancies are left, carbon can, and frequently does, form four covalent bonds, joining up with other atoms in a wide variety of molecules. Methane, the chief component of natural gas, is formed when one atom of carbon covalently bonds with four atoms of hydrogen (see Figure 2-9). It has the chemical formula CH_4.

Ionic bonds Atoms can also bond together without sharing electrons. When one atom transfers one or more of its electrons completely to another, each atom becomes an ion, since each has an unequal number of protons and electrons. The atom gaining electrons becomes negatively charged, while the atom losing electrons becomes positively charged. An **ionic bond** occurs when the two oppositely charged ions attract each other and form a **compound,** a molecule made up of two or more elements. Ionic bonds are generally similar in strength to covalent bonds. Unlike covalent bonds, in ionic bonds each electron circles around a single nucleus. Ions of equal and opposite charges are attracted to each other and the compound is neutral—that is, it has no charge (**FIGURE 2-10**). A common ionic compound that you may be familiar with is table salt (NaCl), composed of sodium and chloride ions.

IONIC BONDS

1 One atom transfers one or more electrons completely to another.

Donated electron

2 The result is two oppositely charged ions.

Sodium ion ⊕   ⊖ Chloride ion

OPPOSITE CHARGES ATTRACT

3 The two oppositely charged ions attract each other, forming a compound.

NaCl compound

NaCl crystals (table salt)

NaCl crystal structure

When multiple Na⁺ ions and Cl⁻ ions are attracted to each other, a NaCl crystal structure forms.

FIGURE 2-10 Ionic bonds: transfer of electrons from one atom to another. The resulting charged atoms (ions) attract each other.

> **"**In the last third of his life, there came over Laszlo Jamf . . . a hostility, a strangely personal hatred, for the covalent bond . . . That something so mutable, so soft, as a sharing of electrons by atoms of carbon should be at the core of life, *his* life, struck Jamf as a cosmic humiliation. *Sharing?* How much stronger, how everlasting was the ionic bond—where electrons are not shared, but *captured. Seized!* and held! polarized plus and minus, these atoms, no ambiguities . . . how he came to love that clarity: how stable it was, in such mineral stubbornness!**"**
>
> — **THOMAS PYNCHON,** in *Gravity's Rainbow*
> [Was Laszlo Jamf mistaken in his understanding of the relative strengths of ionic and covalent bonds?]

Hydrogen bonds Ionic and covalent bonds link two or more atoms together. **Hydrogen bonds,** on the other hand, are important in bonding molecules together. A hydrogen bond is formed between a hydrogen atom in one molecule and another atom, often an oxygen or nitrogen atom, in another molecule (or even in another part of the same molecule). This bond is based on the attraction between positive and negative charges.

The atoms taking part in hydrogen bonds are not necessarily ions, so where do the electrical charges come from? The hydrogen atom is already covalently bonded to another atom in the same molecule and shares its electron. That electron circles both the hydrogen nucleus and the nucleus of the other atom, but the electron is not shared equally. Because the other atom always has more than the one proton found in the hydrogen nucleus, it is more positively charged. As a

1 In a water molecule, oxygen's eight positively charged protons attract electrons more readily than does the single proton in the hydrogen atoms. As a result, the electrons are pulled toward the oxygen side of the molecule, making it slightly negative in charge, while the hydrogen side is slightly positive.

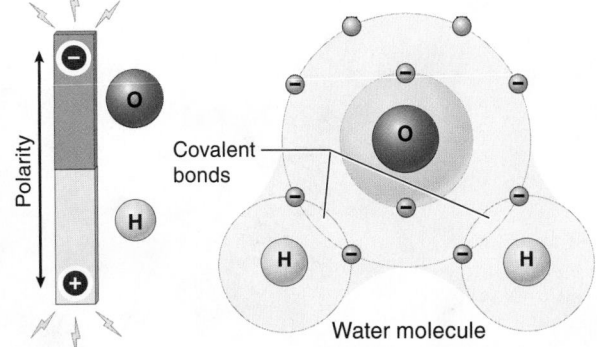

2 Hydrogen bonds are formed between the slightly positively charged hydrogen atoms of one molecule and the slightly negatively charged oxygen atom of another.

FIGURE 2-11 Hydrogen bonds: attraction between a polar atom or molecule and a hydrogen atom. As we'll see later in the chapter, the hydrogen bonding between H_2O molecules gives water some of its characteristic properties.

result, the electron contributed by hydrogen spends more of its time near the other, more positively charged nucleus than near the hydrogen nucleus. Having an extra electron nearby causes the larger atom to be slightly negatively charged, while the hydrogen atom becomes slightly positively charged (**FIGURE 2-11**).

In a sense, the covalently bonded molecules become like a magnet, with distinct positive and negative sides (see Figure 2-11), and are said to be "polar." Polar molecules are attracted to other polar molecules, lining up in particular orientations such that the positive regions of one molecule are near the negative regions of another. These attractions between polar molecules and hydrogen atoms are called hydrogen bonds. Although they are only about one-thirtieth as strong as covalent or ionic bonds, hydrogen bonds are responsible for many of the unique characteristics of water that make it one

COVALENT BOND
A strong bond formed when atoms share electrons in order to become more stable, forming a molecule.
BOND STRENGTH: STRONG

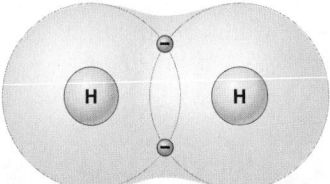

H_2 molecule

IONIC BOND
An attraction between two oppositely charged ions, forming a compound.
BOND STRENGTH: STRONG

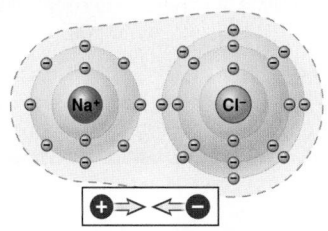

NaCl compound

HYDROGEN BOND
An attraction between the slightly positively charged hydrogen atom of one molecule and the slightly negatively charged atom of another.
BOND STRENGTH: WEAK

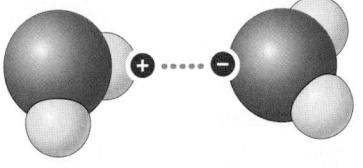

H_2O molecule H_2O molecule

FIGURE 2-12 The properties of covalent, ionic, and hydrogen bonds compared.

of the most important molecules for life on earth. See **FIGURE 2-12** for a review of the three types of bonds discussed in this section.

TAKE-HOME MESSAGE 2·3

Atoms can be bound together in three different ways. Covalent bonds occur when atoms share electrons. In ionic bonds, one atom transfers its electrons to another and the two oppositely charged ions are attracted to each other, forming a compound. Hydrogen bonds, which are weaker than covalent and ionic bonds, involve the attraction between a hydrogen atom and a polar molecule.

2·4–2·6 Water has features that enable it to support all life.

Water flowing down a Japanese waterfall.

2·4 Hydrogen bonds make water cohesive.

Every so often, a tadpole or small fish gets an unexpected—and life-ending—surprise from above as a giant spider moves quickly across the surface of the water, reaches down with its two front legs, and plucks the animal from the water. The spider, known as the fishing spider (*Dolomedes triton*), injects its prey with venom, carries it back to shore—moving across the water's surface as if across solid ground—and eats it. How can these spiders walk on water?

The fishing spider, like numerous other insects such as the water strider, makes use of the fact that water molecules have tremendous cohesion. That is, they stick together with

WATER: HIGH SURFACE TENSION

Pressure applied to water surface

Hydrogen bond

V-shaped water molecules are held together by hydrogen bonds. The bonds are just strong enough to give water a surface tension with net-like properties.

FIGURE 2-13 Walking on water! Hydrogen bonds make this possible for some animals.

unusual strength. This molecular cohesiveness is due to hydrogen bonds between the water molecules.

Each water molecule is V-shaped (**FIGURE 2-13**; see also Figure 2-11). The hydrogen atoms are at the ends of the two arms and the oxygen is at the bottom end of the V, between the two hydrogen atoms. Oxygen's strongly positively charged nucleus pulls the circling electrons toward itself and holds on to them for more than its fair share of the time. Consequently, the oxygen at the bottom of the V has a slight negative charge and the end of the water molecule containing the hydrogen atoms has a slight positive charge.

Because of their unequally shared electrons, water molecules are polar (see Figure 2-11). Consequently, large numbers of water molecules orient themselves so that the negative side of one molecule is near the positive side of another. Hydrogen bonds form between the relatively positively charged hydrogen atoms and the relatively negatively charged oxygen atoms of *adjacent* water molecules.

Hydrogen bonds are much weaker than covalent and ionic bonds and they don't last very long. Nonetheless, to the fishing spider, the cumulative effect of all the hydrogen bonds in water is to link together all the water molecules in the stream just enough to give the water a surface tension with some net-like properties.

TAKE-HOME MESSAGE 2·4

Water molecules easily form hydrogen bonds, giving water great cohesiveness.

2·5 Water has unusual properties that make it critical to life.

All life on earth depends on water; organisms are made up mostly of water and require it more than any other molecule. Hydrogen bonding among water molecules gives water several important properties that contribute to its crucial role in the biology of all organisms.

1. Cohesion. We saw in the previous section how the connection of water molecules through hydrogen bonds makes water cohesive, resulting in, for example, high surface tension. The cohesiveness of water molecules also makes it possible for tall trees to exist (**FIGURE 2-14**). Leaves need water. Molecules of water in the leaves are continually lost to the atmosphere through evaporation or are used up in the process of photosynthesis. In order to get more water, plants must pull it up from the soil. The problem for many plants, such as the giant sequoia trees, is that the soil may be 300 feet below the leaf. Hydrogen bonds, however, allow water molecules to pull up adjacent water molecules to which they have hydrogen-bonded. The chain of linked molecules extends all the way down to the soil, where another water molecule is pulled in via the roots each time a water molecule evaporates from a leaf far above.

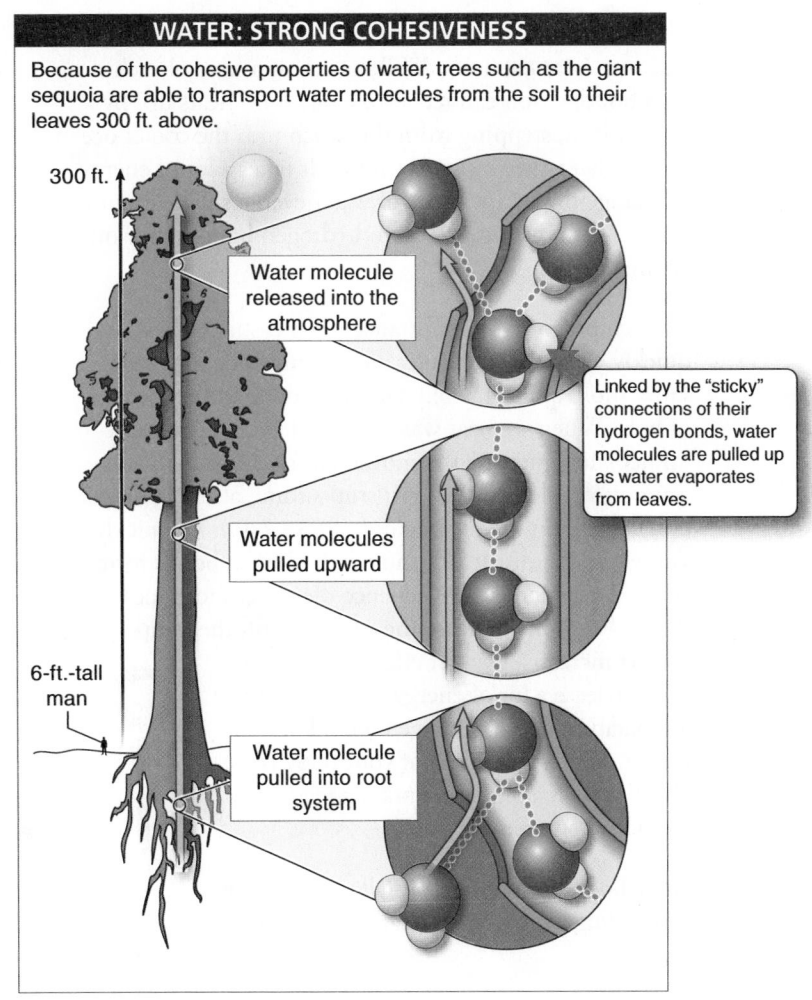

WATER: STRONG COHESIVENESS

Because of the cohesive properties of water, trees such as the giant sequoia are able to transport water molecules from the soil to their leaves 300 ft. above.

300 ft.

Water molecule released into the atmosphere

Linked by the "sticky" connections of their hydrogen bonds, water molecules are pulled up as water evaporates from leaves.

Water molecules pulled upward

6-ft.-tall man

Water molecule pulled into root system

FIGURE 2-14 **Like a giant straw.** Hydrogen bonds cause water molecules to "stick" together, so they can be pulled up through the giant sequoia.

1 Heat (energy) from the sun disrupts some of the hydrogen bonds between water molecules.

2 New hydrogen bonds are formed almost as quickly as they are disrupted.

3 While the sun's energy may make sand very hot, when the same energy hits water, much of that energy breaks hydrogen bonds (which may later re-form), rather than increasing the water's temperature.

······ Disrupted bond
······ Newly formed bond

Sun

FIGURE 2-15 Water as a moderator of temperature change. Hydrogen bonds help water resist heating.

2. Large heat capacity. Walking across a sandy beach on a hot day, you can feel how easily sand heats up. By comparison, stepping from the beach into the cooler ocean reveals that water resists warming. It takes a lot of energy to change the temperature of water even a small amount. Why? Again, we must look to hydrogen bonding for our answer.

The temperature of a substance is a measure of how quickly all of the molecules are moving. The molecules move more quickly when energy is added in the form of heat. When we heat water, the added energy doesn't immediately increase the movement of the individual water molecules. Rather, it disrupts some of the hydrogen bonds between the molecules (**FIGURE 2-15**). As quickly as they can be disrupted, though, hydrogen bonds form again somewhere else. And since the water molecules themselves don't increase their movement, the temperature doesn't increase. The net effect is that even if you release a lot of energy into water, the temperature doesn't change much. For this reason, because so much of your body is water, you are able to maintain a relatively constant body temperature.

Large bodies of water, especially oceans, can absorb huge amounts of heat from the sun

during warm times of the year, reducing temperature increases on the land. Similarly, during cold times of the year, the ocean slowly cools, giving off heat that reduces the temperature drop on shore.

3. Low density as a solid. Ice floats. This is unusual, since most substances *increase* in density when frozen; as the molecules slow down, they pack together more and more efficiently—and densely. Consequently, the solid sinks. Water, however, becomes less dense and, as you might expect by now, this is due to hydrogen bonding. As the temperature drops and water molecules slow down, rather than becoming more and more tightly packed, they become less so. Each V-shaped water molecule bonds with four partners, via hydrogen bonds, forming a crystalline lattice in which the molecules are held slightly farther apart than in the liquid, causing ice to be less dense than water (**FIGURE 2-16**).

4. Good solvent. If you put a pinch of table salt into a glass of water, it will quickly dissolve. This means that all the charged sodium (Na^+) and chloride (Cl^-) ions that were ionically bonded together become separated from one another. The sodium and chloride ions were initially attracted to each other because they are polar molecules

Q Why do coastal areas have milder, less variable climates than inland areas?

FROZEN WATER
Hydrogen bonding arranges water molecules into a crystalline lattice, keeping them slightly farther apart and, therefore, less dense.

LIQUID WATER
Water molecules move about freely, allowing them to be closer to one another.

RELATIVE AREA OCCUPIED BY THE SAME NUMBER OF H_2O MOLECULES:

Frozen water   Liquid water

FIGURE 2-16 The lattice structure of ice allows it to float.

WATER: A GOOD SOLVENT

NaCl crystal (table salt)

When placed in water, ionic compounds such as NaCl are broken down into separate Na^+ and Cl^- ions.

Dissolved Na^+ and Cl^- ions

Na^+

Cl^-

Positively charged Na^+ ions are attracted to the negatively charged side of the H_2O molecule, while negatively charged Cl^- ions are attracted to the positively charged side.

FIGURE 2-17 **Solutions.** Water pries apart ionic bonds, dissolving ionic compounds.

(ions), each carrying a slight charge. Water is able to pry them apart because, as a polar molecule, it, too, carries charges. The positively charged sodium ions are attracted to the negatively charged side of the water molecule, and the negatively charged chloride ions are attracted to the positively charged side (**FIGURE 2-17**). Many substances are, like water, polar and consequently dissolve easily in water.

Nonpolar molecules (such as oils) have neither positively charged regions nor negatively charged regions. Consequently, the polar water molecules are not attracted to them. Instead, when an oil is poured into a container of water, the water molecules distance themselves from the oil, leaving the oil molecules in clumps that never dissolve.

Q *Why don't oceans freeze as easily as freshwater lakes?*

Because so much salt is dissolved in the oceans, many of the water molecules have their positively charged sides facing Cl^- ions. Simultaneously, many molecules of water are turned the other way, with their negatively charged sides facing Na^+ ions. Consequently, the orderly lattices of hydrogen bonds found in ice cannot form in salt water, and it does not freeze well.

TAKE-HOME MESSAGE 2·5

The hydrogen bonds between water molecules give water several of its most important characteristics, including cohesiveness, reduced density as a solid, the ability to resist temperature changes, and broad effectiveness as a solvent for ionic and polar substances.

2·6

Living systems are highly sensitive to acidic and basic conditions.

There's a lot more going on in water than meets the eye. Most of the molecules are present as H_2O, but at any instant some of them break into two parts: H^+ and OH^-. In pure water, the amount of H^+ and OH^- must be exactly the same, since every time a molecule splits, one of each type of ion is produced. But in some fluids containing other dissolved materials, this balance is lost: the fluid can have more H^+ or more OH^-.

HYDROGEN IONS and HYDROXIDE IONS

| Non-ionized Water Molecule (H_2O) | Ionized Hydrogen Molecule (H^+) | Ionized Hydroxide Molecule (OH^-) |

The amount of H^+ or OH^- in a fluid gives it some important properties. In particular, the amount of H^+ in a solution is a measure of its acidity and is called **pH.** The greater the number of free hydrogen ions floating around, the more acidic the solution is.

Pure water is in the middle of the pH scale, with a pH of 7.0. Any fluid with a pH below 7.0 has more H^+ ions (and fewer OH^- ions) and is considered an **acid.** Any fluid with a pH above 7.0 has fewer H^+ ions (and more OH^- ions) and is considered a **base.** The pH scale, like the Richter scale for earthquakes, is logarithmic, although in the case of pH, the *lower* the number the *greater* the acidity: a decrease of 1 on the pH scale represents a 10-fold increase in the hydrogen ion concentration (**FIGURE 2-18**). A decrease of 2 represents a 100-fold increase. This means that a cola, with a pH of about 3.0, is 10,000 times (!) more acidic than a glass of water, with a pH of 7.0.

H^+ ions are essentially free-floating protons. Acids can donate their H^+ ions to other chemicals. In fact, H^+ is a very reactive little ion. Its presence gives acids some unique properties. For instance, the hydrogen ions in acids can bind with atoms in metals, causing them to corrode. That's why you can dissolve nails by dumping them in a bucket of acid (or cola).

Your stomach produces large amounts of hydrochloric acid (HCl dissolved in water) and has a pH between 1 and 3. (HCl is acidic because most of the hydrogen ions split off

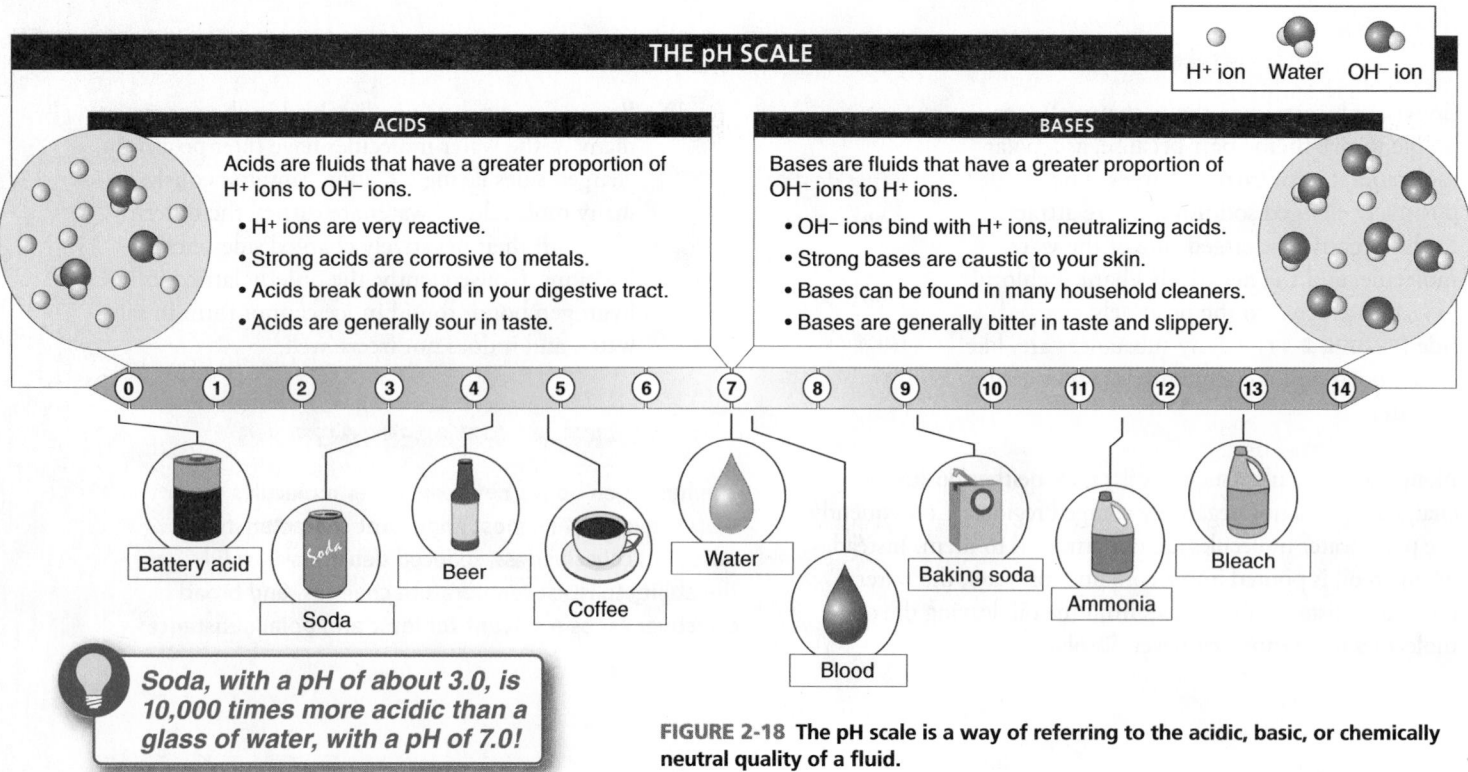

FIGURE 2-18 The pH scale is a way of referring to the acidic, basic, or chemically neutral quality of a fluid.

Is acid rain likely to have any impact on populations of microbes living in lakes, streams, and soil? Why?

from the chlorine, raising the H⁺ concentration of the fluid.) The acid in your stomach helps to kill most bacteria that you ingest. It also greatly enhances the breakdown of the chemicals in the food you eat and the efficiency of digestion and absorption. You may have learned firsthand of the high acidity of your stomach fluids if you have experienced heartburn or the sour taste of vomit.

Acids have a higher concentration of H⁺ than of OH⁻. Conversely, bases have a higher concentration of OH⁻ than of H⁺. Baking soda is a common basic substance. Some bases are called "antacids" because the OH⁻ ions in bases can bind with excess H⁺ ions in acidic solutions, neutralizing the acid. Base-containing products such as Alka-Seltzer and Milk of Magnesia reduce the unpleasant feeling of heartburn and acid indigestion that sometimes arise from the overproduction of acids by the stomach. Bases are commonly used in household cleaning products and generally have a bitter taste and a soapy, slippery feel.

The pH of blood is usually 7.4. Given that most cellular reactions produce or consume H⁺ ions, there ought to be great swings in the pH of our blood. Unfortunately, our bodies can't tolerate such swings. Most of the chemicals that aid in the chemical reactions in our blood or cells stop functioning properly if the pH swings up or down by less than half a point. Fortunately, our bodies contain some chemicals that act like bank accounts for H⁺ ions (**FIGURE 2-19**). Called **buffers,** these chemicals can quickly absorb excess H⁺ ions to keep a solution from becoming too acidic, and they can quickly release H⁺ ions to counteract any increases in OH⁻ concentration. Therefore, buffers are chemicals that act to resist changes in pH.

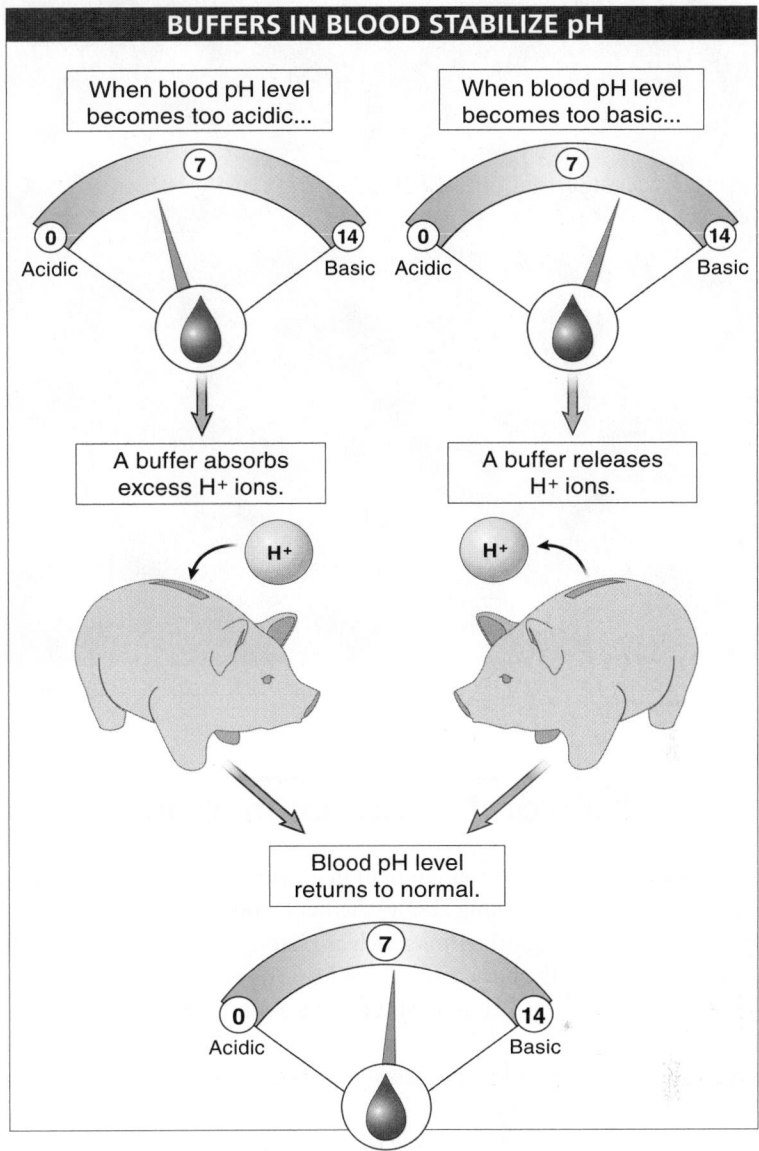

FIGURE 2-19 Maintaining a constant internal environment. Buffers in blood prevent potentially damaging pH swings.

TAKE-HOME MESSAGE 2·6

The pH of a fluid is a measure of how acidic or basic the solution is and depends on the concentration of dissolved H⁺ ions present; the lower the pH, the more acidic the solution. Acids, such as vinegar, can donate protons to other chemicals; bases, including baking soda, bind with free protons.

2·7–2·10 Carbohydrates are fuel for living machines.

Worldwide, more corn is produced (by weight) than any other grain.

2·7 Carbohydrates include macromolecules that function as fuel.

Hardly a day goes by without an item in a magazine or newspaper or on TV talking about whether carbohydrates are good or bad for us. Sports drinks such as Gatorade are filled with carbs, and in the days before a big game or race, athletes often "carbo-load" by eating bowls of pasta. Yet other dietary supplements and "power" bars tout that they are low-carb and effective in weight loss by causing the body to resort to using fat for energy. Meanwhile, nutritionists, doctors, and many diet programs exhort people to increase the amount of fiber—another type of carbohydrate—in their diet. What exactly are they all talking about?

Four types of **macromolecules**—large molecules made up from smaller building blocks or subunits—are essential to the building and functioning of living organisms: carbohydrates, lipids, proteins, and nucleic acids. **Carbohydrates** are molecules that contain mostly carbon, hydrogen, and oxygen: they are the primary fuel for running all of the cellular machinery and also form much of the structure of cells in all life forms. Sometimes they contain atoms of other elements, but they must have carbon, hydrogen, and oxygen to be considered a carbohydrate (**FIGURE 2-20**). Additionally, a carbohydrate generally has approximately the same number of carbon atoms as it does H_2O units. For instance, the best-known carbohydrate, glucose, has the composition $C_6H_{12}O_6$ (6 carbons and, as a little math will show us, 6 H_2O units; notice that $6 \times H_2 = H_{12}$ and $6 \times O = O_6$). A carbohydrate called maltose has the composition $C_{12}H_{22}O_{11}$.

Carbohydrates are classified into several categories, based on their size and their composition. The simplest carbohydrates are the **monosaccharides,** or **simple sugars.** The simple sugars contain anywhere from three to six carbon atoms and, when they are broken down, the products usually are not carbohydrates. Two common monosaccharides are glucose, found in the sap and fruit of many plants, and fructose, found primarily in fruits and vegetables, as well as in honey. Fructose is the sweetest of all naturally occurring sugars. The suffix *-ose* tells us that a substance is a carbohydrate.

SOME COMMON MONOSACCHARIDES

| Glucose | Fructose | Galactose |
| $C_6H_{12}O_6$ | $C_6H_{12}O_6$ | $C_6H_{12}O_6$ |

Carbohydrates function well as fuels because of their many carbon-hydrogen bonds; as those bonds are broken down and other, more stable bonds (primarily between carbon and oxygen) are formed, a great deal of energy is released that organisms can utilize.

In the next section we investigate glucose, the chief carbohydrate used by organisms to fuel their activities.

CARBOHYDRATES

The carbon-hydrogen bonds of carbohydrates store a great deal of potential energy and are easily broken down by organisms.

H ———ENERGY——— C

Glucose
$C_6H_{12}O_6$

Carbohydrates, such as glucose (shown above), are composed primarily of three elements:

C   H   O

Carbohydrates are the primary fuel source for cellular mechanisms.

FIGURE 2-20 All carbohydrates have a similar structure and function.

TAKE-HOME MESSAGE 2·7

Carbohydrates are the primary fuel for running all cellular machinery and also form much of the structure of cells in all life forms. Carbohydrates contain carbon, hydrogen, and oxygen, and generally have the same number of carbon atoms as they do H_2O units. The simplest carbohydrates, including glucose, are monosaccharides or simple sugars. They contain from three to six carbon atoms. As the chemical bonds of carbohydrates are broken down and other more stable bonds are formed, a great deal of energy is released that can be used by organisms.

2·8 Glucose provides energy for the body's cells.

The carbohydrate of most importance to living organisms is glucose. This simple sugar is found naturally in most fruits, but most of the carbohydrates that you eat, including table sugar (called sucrose) and the starchy carbohydrates found in bread and potatoes, are converted into glucose in your digestive system. The glucose then circulates in your blood at a concentration of about 0.1%. Circulating glucose, also called "blood sugar," has one of three fates (**FIGURE 2-21**).

1. Fuel for cellular activity. Once it arrives at and enters a cell, glucose can be used as an energy source. Through a series of chemical reactions, the glucose molecule is converted into other molecules with stronger bonds (a process explained in detail in Chapter 4). The change from weaker bonds to stronger bonds releases energy, and organisms use the released energy to fuel cellular activity, including the muscle contractions that enable you to move and the nerve activities that enable you to think.

2. Stored temporarily as glycogen. If there is more glucose circulating in your bloodstream than is necessary to meet your body's current energy needs, the excess glucose can be temporarily stored in various tissues, primarily your muscles and liver. The stored glucose molecules are linked together to form a large web of molecules called **glycogen.** When you need energy later, the glycogen can easily be broken down to release glucose molecules back into your

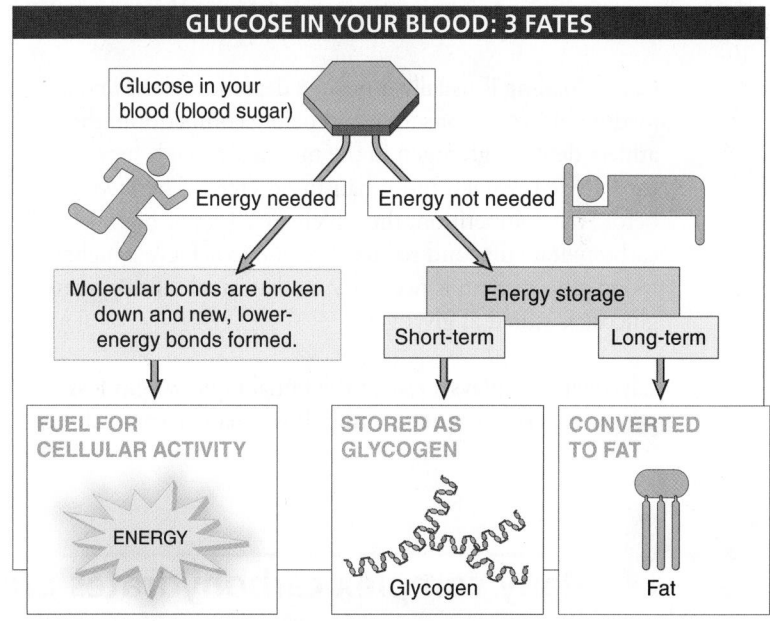

GLUCOSE IN YOUR BLOOD: 3 FATES

Glucose in your blood (blood sugar)

Energy needed | Energy not needed

Molecular bonds are broken down and new, lower-energy bonds formed. | Energy storage — Short-term | Long-term

FUEL FOR CELLULAR ACTIVITY — ENERGY

STORED AS GLYCOGEN — Glycogen

CONVERTED TO FAT — Fat

FIGURE 2-21 What happens to sugar in your blood? Depending upon whether energy is needed, glucose can be released for immediate use or stored on a short-term or long-term basis.

bloodstream. Glycogen is the primary form of short-term energy storage in animals.

3. Converted to fat. Finally, glucose circulating in your bloodstream can be converted into fat, a form of long-term energy storage.

FIGURE 2-22 **Some competitive athletes carbo-load to maintain high energy levels.**

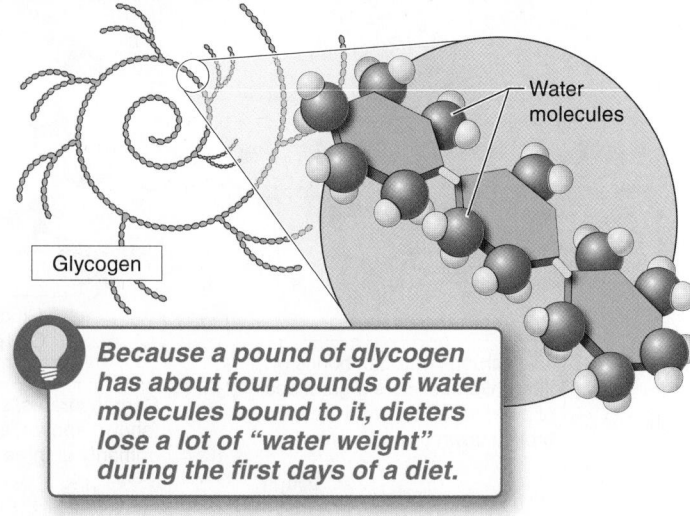

Water molecules

Glycogen

Because a pound of glycogen has about four pounds of water molecules bound to it, dieters lose a lot of "water weight" during the first days of a diet.

FIGURE 2-23 **Water weight.** Water molecules bound to glycogen account for much of the weight lost early in a diet.

"Carbo-loading" is a method by which athletes can, for a short time, double or triple the usual amount of glycogen stored in their muscles and liver, increasing the store of fuel available for extended exertion and delaying the onset of fatigue during an endurance event (**FIGURE 2-22**).

Q What is "carbo-loading"?

Carbo-loading is usually done in a depletion phase and a loading phase. Six or seven days before competition, the athlete depletes glycogen in the muscles through super-low carbohydrate intake and exhaustive exercise. Then two days before the competition, the athlete eats a super-high carbohydrate diet and reduces exercise to achieve a higher blood glucose than is necessary, so that much of the excess glucose is stored as glycogen.

Glycogen also plays a role in the initial rapid weight loss people experience when dieting. If you reduce your caloric intake such that your body is burning more calories than you are consuming, your body must use stored energy. The first, most accessible molecules that can be broken down for energy in the absence of sufficient sugar in your bloodstream are glycogen molecules in your muscles and liver. Large amounts of water are bound to glycogen. As that glycogen is removed from your tissue, so, too, is the water. This leads to the initial dramatic weight loss that occurs before your body resorts to using stored fat, and the rate of weight loss slows considerably (**FIGURE 2-23**).

TAKE-HOME MESSAGE 2·8

Glucose is the most important carbohydrate to living organisms. Glucose in the bloodstream can be used as an energy source, can be stored as glycogen in the muscles and liver for later use, or can be converted to fat.

2·9 Many complex carbohydrates are time-release packets of energy.

In contrast to the simple sugars, some carbohydrates contain more than one sugar unit or building block. When two simple sugars are bonded together they form a **disaccharide;** the joining of glucose and galactose, for example, makes the disaccharide lactose, which is the sugar found in milk. When large numbers of simple sugars are joined together— sometimes as many as 10,000 may be linked—the resulting carbohydrate is called a **polysaccharide,** or a **complex carbohydrate** (**FIGURE 2-24**). Depending on how the simple sugars are bonded together, polysaccharides may function as "time-release" stores of energy or as structural materials that may be completely indigestible by most animals. An example of such a structural material is the polysaccharide cellulose— the primary component of plant cell walls.

Like simple sugars, many disaccharides and polysaccharides are important sources of fuel for cells. Unlike simple sugars, however, disaccharides and polysaccharides must undergo some preliminary processing before the energy can be released from their bonds. Let's look at what happens when we eat sucrose, common table sugar. Sucrose is the primary carbohydrate in plant sap and is composed of two simple sugars, glucose and fructose, linked together. To use sucrose, the body must first break the bond linking the glucose and fructose. Only then can the individual monosaccharides be broken down into their component atoms and the energy that was stored in their chemical bonds be harvested and used.

Energy can also be stored in a complex carbohydrate called **starch,** which consists of a hundred or more glucose molecules joined together in a line. In plants, starch is the primary form of energy storage, found in roots and other tissues (see Figure 2-24). Grains such as barley, wheat, and rye are high in starch content, and corn and rice are more than 70% starch. Although it is composed of glucose molecules linked together, starch does not taste sweet. Because of its molecular shape, it does not stimulate the sweetness receptors on the tongue. The glycogen that stores energy in your muscles and liver is also a complex carbohydrate, so it is sometimes referred to as "animal starch" (although it has a more branched structure than starch and carries more glucose units linked together).

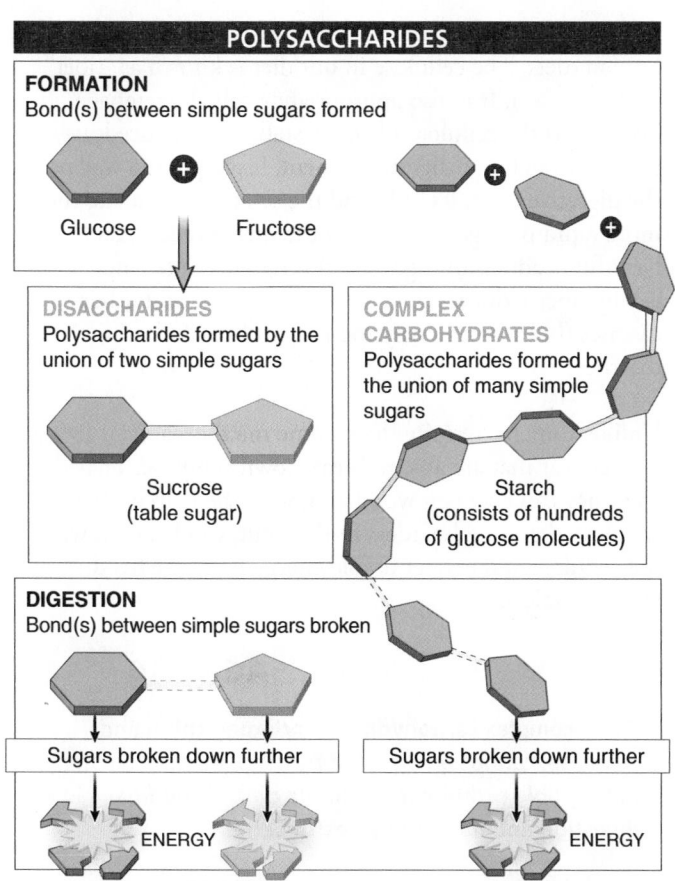

POLYSACCHARIDES

FORMATION
Bond(s) between simple sugars formed

Glucose   Fructose

DISACCHARIDES
Polysaccharides formed by the union of two simple sugars

Sucrose
(table sugar)

COMPLEX CARBOHYDRATES
Polysaccharides formed by the union of many simple sugars

Starch
(consists of hundreds of glucose molecules)

DIGESTION
Bond(s) between simple sugars broken

Sugars broken down further   Sugars broken down further

ENERGY   ENERGY

FIGURE 2-24 Chains of sugars. Polysaccharides are made from simple sugars bonded together.

Depending on their structure, dietary carbohydrates can lead to quick-but-brief or slow-but-persistent increases in blood sugar.

Blood sugar level   Fructose   Time

Blood sugar level   Complex carbohydrates   Time

FIGURE 2-25 Short-term versus long-term energy. Simple sugars and complex carbohydrates differ in the way they make energy available to you.

Many complex carbohydrates are like "time-release" fuel pellets. The glucose molecules become available slowly, as the bonds between glucose units are broken. As a demonstration, put a piece of potato or bread into your mouth and let it rest on your tongue. Initially, it does not taste sweet. After a few minutes, you will begin to taste some sweetness as the chemicals in your saliva break the starch down into glucose.

The relative amounts of complex carbohydrates and simple sugars in foods cause them to have different effects when you eat them. Oatmeal (along with rice and pasta), for example, is rich in complex carbohydrates. Fresh fruits, on the other hand, are rich in simple sugars, such as fructose. Consequently, although fruit will give a quick burst of energy as the sugars are almost immediately available, the fuel will soon be gone from the bloodstream. Simple sugars in the oatmeal will become available only gradually, as the complex carbohydrates of the oats are broken down into their simple sugar components (**FIGURE 2-25**).

Q

Before heading to the library for a long study session, students would be wise to consume oatmeal rather than fresh fruits. Why?

TAKE-HOME MESSAGE 2·9

Multiple simple carbohydrates are sometimes linked together into more complex carbohydrates. Types of complex carbohydrates include starch, which is the primary form of energy storage in plants, and glycogen, which is a primary form of energy storage in animals.

2·10 Not all carbohydrates are digestible.

Despite their general importance as a fuel source for humans, not all carbohydrates can be broken down by our digestive system. Two different complex carbohydrates—both indigestible by humans—serve as structural materials for invertebrate animals and plants: **chitin** (pronounced KITE-in) and **cellulose** (FIGURE 2-26). Chitin forms the rigid outer skeleton of most insects and crustaceans (such as lobsters and crabs). Cellulose forms a huge variety of plant structures that are visible all around us. We find cellulose in trees and the wooden structures we build from them, in cotton and the clothes we make from it, in leaves and in grasses. In fact, it is the single most prevalent compound on earth.

Surprisingly, cellulose is almost identical in composition to starch. Nonetheless, because of one small difference in the chemical bond between the simple sugar units, cellulose has a slightly different three-dimensional structure. Even tiny differences in the shape of a molecule can have a huge effect on its behavior. In this case, the difference in shape makes it impossible for humans to digest cellulose as they can starch. Consequently, the cellulose we eat passes right through our digestive system unused.

Though indigestible by humans, fiber still aids in digestion and has numerous health benefits.

FIGURE 2-27 Fiber. It's not digestible, but it's still important for our diet.

Although it is not digestible, cellulose is still important to human diets. The cellulose in our diet is known as "fiber" (FIGURE 2-27). It is also appropriately called "roughage" because, as the cellulose of celery stalks and lettuce leaves passes through our digestive system, it scrapes the wall of the digestive tract. Its bulk and the scraping stimulate the more rapid passage of food and the unwanted, possibly harmful products of digestion through our intestines. That is why fiber reduces the risk of colon cancer and other diseases (but it is also why too much fiber can lead to diarrhea).

Unlike humans, termites have some microorganisms living in their gut that are able to break down cellulose. That's why they can chew on wood and, with the help of the cellulose-digesting boarders in their gut, can break down the cellulose and extract usable energy from the freed glucose molecules.

Cellulose gives trees the rigidity to grow tall (and makes wood a desirable building material).

Chitin offers protection for the lobster.

FIGURE 2-26 Carbohydrates can serve as structural materials.

TAKE-HOME MESSAGE 2·10

Some complex carbohydrates, including chitin and cellulose, cannot be digested by most animals. Such indigestible carbohydrates in the diet, called fiber, aid in digestion and have many health benefits.

A well-insulated harp seal, in Canada.

2·11–2·13 Lipids store energy for a rainy day.

2·11 Lipids are macromolecules with several functions, including energy storage.

Lipids are a second group of macromolecules important to all living organisms. Lipids, just like carbohydrates, are made primarily from atoms of carbon, hydrogen, and oxygen, but the atoms are in different proportions. The lipids in your diet, for example, tend to have significantly more energy-rich carbon-hydrogen bonds than carbohydrates, and so contain significantly more stored energy.

What exactly is a lipid? That's not as easy to answer as you might expect. Lipids come in a wide variety of structures. They don't have any unique subunits (such as the simple sugars that make up disaccharides and polysaccharides) or particular ratios of atoms that serve as defining features. Consequently, lipids

Why does a salad dressing made with vinegar and oil separate into two layers shortly after you shake it?

are defined based on their physical characteristics. Most notably, lipids do not dissolve in water and are greasy to the touch—think of salad dressings.

Q Lipids are insoluble in water because they tend to have long chains consisting only of carbon and hydrogen atoms, which, in contrast to water, are nonpolar. Nonpolar molecules (or parts of molecules) tend to minimize their contact with water and are considered **hydrophobic** ("water-fearing"). Lipids cluster together when mixed with water, never fully dissolving. Molecules that readily form hydrogen bonds with water, on the other hand, are considered **hydrophilic** ("water-loving").

One familiar type of lipid is *fat*, the type most important in long-term energy storage and insulation

The Emperor penguin (*Aptenodytes forsteri*) benefits from the insulating effect of fat and is able to thrive in the extreme cold of Antarctica.

TYPICAL FEATURES OF LIPIDS
• Nonpolar molecules that do not dissolve in water
• Greasy to the touch
• Can be significant source of energy storage

THREE TYPES OF LIPIDS

FATS

FUNCTION
Long-term energy storage and insulation

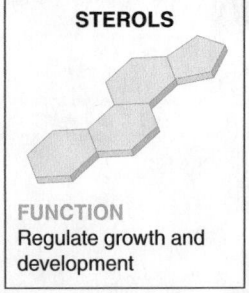

STEROLS

FUNCTION
Regulate growth and development

PHOSPHOLIPIDS

FUNCTION
Form cellular membranes

FIGURE 2-28 Lipids serve many roles in the body.

(**FIGURE 2-28**). (Penguins and walruses can maintain relatively high body temperatures, despite living in very cold habitats, due to their thick layer of insulating fat.) Lipids also include *sterols,* which include *cholesterol* and many of the sex hormones that play regulatory roles in animals, and *phospholipids,* which form the membranes that enclose cells.

TAKE-HOME MESSAGE 2·11

Lipids are insoluble in water and greasy to the touch. They are valuable to organisms for long-term energy storage and insulation, in membrane formation, and as hormones.

2·12 Fats are tasty molecules too plentiful in our diets.

All fats have two distinct components: they have a "head" region and two or three long "tails" (**FIGURE 2-29**). The head region is a small molecule called **glycerol.** It is linked to "tail" molecules known as **fatty acids.** A fatty acid is simply a long hydrocarbon—that is, a chain of carbon molecules, often a dozen or more, linked together with one or two hydrogen atoms attached to each carbon.

The fats in most foods we eat are **triglycerides,** which are fats having three fatty acids linked to the glycerol molecule. For this reason, the terms "fats" and "triglycerides" are often used interchangeably. Triglycerides that are solid at room temperature are generally called "fats," while those that are liquid at room temperature are called "oils."

Fat molecules contain much more stored energy than do carbohydrate molecules. That is, the chemical breakdown of fat molecules releases significantly more energy. A single gram of carbohydrate stores about 4 calories of energy, while the same amount of fat stores about 9 calories—not unlike the difference between a $5 bill and a $10 bill. Because fats store

STRUCTURE OF FATS (TRIGLYCERIDES)

HEAD: Glycerol

TAILS: Fatty acids

Fats are composed primarily of three elements:
C H O

Energy is stored in the many carbon-hydrogen bonds.

C H
ENERGY

Symbol for fat (triglyceride) used in this book

FIGURE 2-29 Triglycerides have glycerol heads and fatty acid tails.

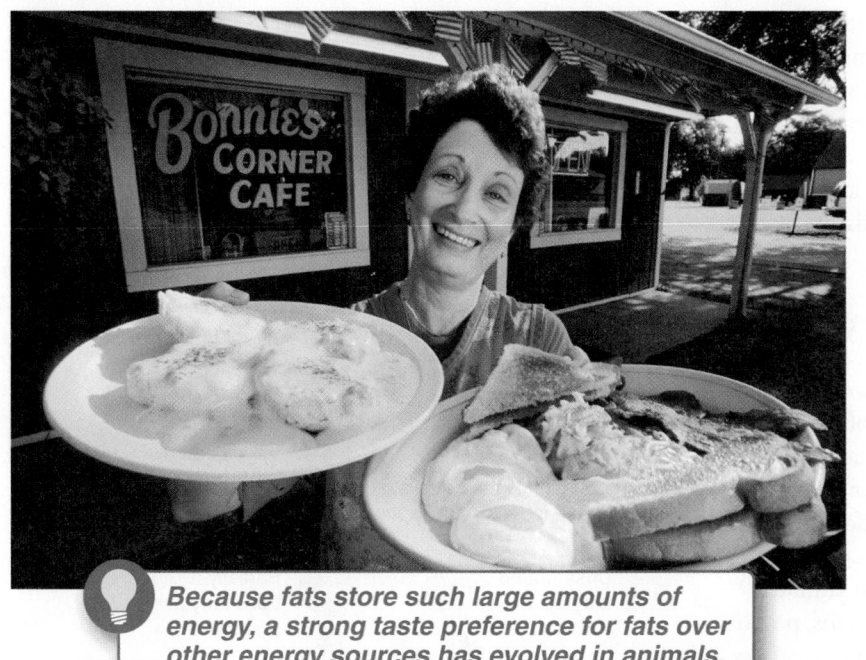

FIGURE 2-30 Animals (including humans!) prefer the taste of fats.

Because fats store such large amounts of energy, a strong taste preference for fats over other energy sources has evolved in animals.

such a large amount of energy, a strong taste preference for fats over other energy sources has evolved in animals (FIGURE 2-30). Organisms evolving in an environment of uncertain food supply will build the largest surplus by consuming molecules that hold the most amount of energy in the smallest mass. This feature helped the earliest humans to survive, millions of years ago, but today puts us in danger from the health risks of obesity now that fats are all too readily available.

An important distinction is made between "saturated" and "unsaturated" fats (FIGURE 2-31). These terms refer to the hydrocarbon chain in the fatty acids. If each carbon atom

SATURATED FATS

In saturated fats, each carbon in the hydrocarbon chain is bound to two hydrogen atoms.

Straight fatty acids can be packed together tightly. As a result, saturated fats are solid at room temperature.

UNSATURATED FATS

Double bond

In unsaturated fats, at least one carbon in the hydrocarbon chain is bound to just one hydrogen, causing the fatty acid to have a crooked shape.

Crooked fatty acids cannot be packed together tightly. As a result, unsaturated fats on their own (such as olive oil) are liquid at room temperature.

FIGURE 2-31 Degrees of saturation. Fatty acids (and thus the fats that contain them) can be unsaturated or saturated.

in the hydrocarbon chain of a fatty acid is bonded to two hydrogen atoms, the fat molecule carries the maximum number of hydrogen atoms and is said to be a **saturated fat.** Most animal fats, including those found in meat and eggs, are saturated. They are not essential to your health and, because they accumulate in your bloodstream and can narrow the vessel walls, they can cause heart disease and strokes.

An **unsaturated fat** is one in which some of the carbon atoms are bound to only a single hydrogen. Most plant fats are unsaturated. Unsaturated fats may be *mono-unsaturated* (if a fatty acid hydrocarbon chain has only one pair of neighboring carbon atoms in an unsaturated state—that is, has only one double bond) or *polyunsaturated* (if more than one pair of carbons is unsaturated—there's more than one double bond). Unsaturated fats are still high in calories, but because they can lower cholesterol, they are generally preferable to saturated fats. Foods high in unsaturated fats include avocados, peanuts, and olive oil. Relative to other animals, fish tend to have less saturated fat.

Q

How will the "chewy-ness" of a cookie differ depending on whether you make it with butter or vegetable oil as the lipid? Which is better for your health?

The shapes of unsaturated fat molecules and saturated fat molecules are different. When saturated, the hydrocarbon tails of the fatty acids all line up very straight and the fat molecules can be packed together tightly. The tight packing causes the fats, such as butter, to be solid at room temperature. When unsaturated, the fatty acids have kinks in the hydrocarbon tails and the fat molecules cannot be packed together as tightly (see Figure 2-31). Consequently, unsaturated fats, such as canola oil and vegetable oil, do not solidify as easily and are liquid at room temperature.

The ingredient list for many snack foods includes "partially hydrogenated" vegetable oils. The hydrogenation of an oil means that a liquid, unsaturated fat has had hydrogen atoms added to it so that it becomes more saturated. This can be useful in creating a food with a more desirable texture, since increasing a fat's degree of saturation changes its consistency and makes it more solid at room temperatures. By attaining just the right degree of saturation, it is possible to create foods, such as chocolate, that are near the border of solid and liquid and

Q

Many snack foods contain "partially hydrogenated" vegetable oils. Why might food producers add hydrogen atoms to a vegetable oil?

HYDROGENATION

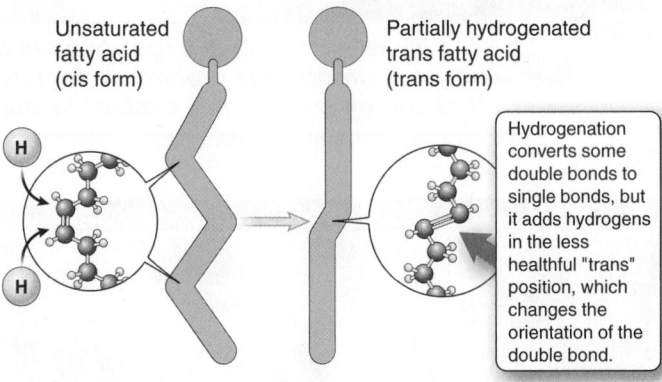

Hydrogenation is the artificial addition of hydrogen atoms to an unsaturated fat. This can improve a food's taste, texture, and shelf-life.

Unsaturated fatty acid (cis form)

Partially hydrogenated trans fatty acid (trans form)

Hydrogenation converts some double bonds to single bonds, but it adds hydrogens in the less healthful "trans" position, which changes the orientation of the double bond.

 Hydrogenation can increase the saturation of fats—for better and worse.

FIGURE 2-32 Hydrogenation improves a food's taste, texture, and shelf-life (but at a cost).

"melt in your mouth" (**FIGURE 2-32**). Unfortunately, hydrogenation also makes the food less healthful because saturated fats are less reactive—your body is less likely to break them down—and so are more likely to accumulate in your blood vessels, increasing the risk of heart disease.

Hydrogenation of unsaturated fats is doubly problematic from a health perspective because it also creates **trans fats,** the "trans" referring to the unusual orientation of some or all of the double bonds that remain following the addition of hydrogen atoms. This orientation differs from that in other unsaturated dietary fats—which have their double bonds in an orientation called "cis." Trans fats in your diet cause your body to produce more cholesterol, further raising the risk of heart disease, and they also reduce your body's production of a type of cholesterol that protects against heart disease.

Because of the well-documented links between dietary fats and heart disease, many people are trying to reduce their fat intake. "Fake fats" make this possible. They are designed to be similar to fats in taste and texture, but have one big difference: they cannot be digested by humans. One such "fake fat" is olestra. Olestra, instead of being a triglyceride fat with three fatty acid tails linked to a glycerol molecule, has eight separate hydrocarbon fatty acids attached to a molecule of sucrose. This octopus-like molecule allows the fatty acids to stimulate their usual taste buds on your tongue, telling your brain that you are eating a fat. The complex shape of the molecule, however,

prevents your body's digestive chemicals from grabbing onto it and breaking it down. As a consequence, it passes through your digestive system without being digested. It's not a perfect solution, however. Olestra reduces absorption of some vitamins, and in some people causes abdominal cramping.

Q

Olestra is a recently developed "fake fat" chemical that gives foods the taste of fat, without adding the calories of fats. What chemical structure might make this possible?

TAKE-HOME MESSAGE 2·12

Fats, including the triglycerides common in the food we eat, are one type of lipid. Characterized by long hydrocarbon tails, fats effectively store energy in the many carbon-hydrogen and carbon-carbon bonds. Their caloric density is responsible for humans' preferring fats to other macromolecules in the diet, and is also responsible for their association with obesity and illness in the modern world.

2·13 Cholesterol and phospholipids are used to build sex hormones and membranes.

Not all lipids are fats, nor do lipids necessarily function in energy storage. A second group of lipids, called the **sterols,** plays an important role in regulating growth and development (**FIGURE 2-33**). This group includes some very familiar lipids: cholesterol and the steroid hormones such as testosterone and estrogen. These molecules are all variations on one basic structure formed from four interlinked rings of carbon atoms.

Cholesterol is an important component of most cell membranes. For this reason, it is an essential molecule for living organisms. Cells in our liver produce almost 90% of the circulating cholesterol by transforming the saturated fats in our diet. Cholesterol is also present in foods and has a bad reputation in most Western cultures that is mostly well deserved. When we ingest too much cholesterol (present in animal-based foods such as egg yolks, red meat, and cream) and high levels of cholesterol circulate in our bloodstream, the cholesterol can attach to blood vessel walls and cause them to thicken. In turn, this thickening can lead to high blood pressure, a major contributor to strokes and heart attacks. For these reasons, nutritionists advise limiting the consumption of foods high in cholesterol and saturated fats.

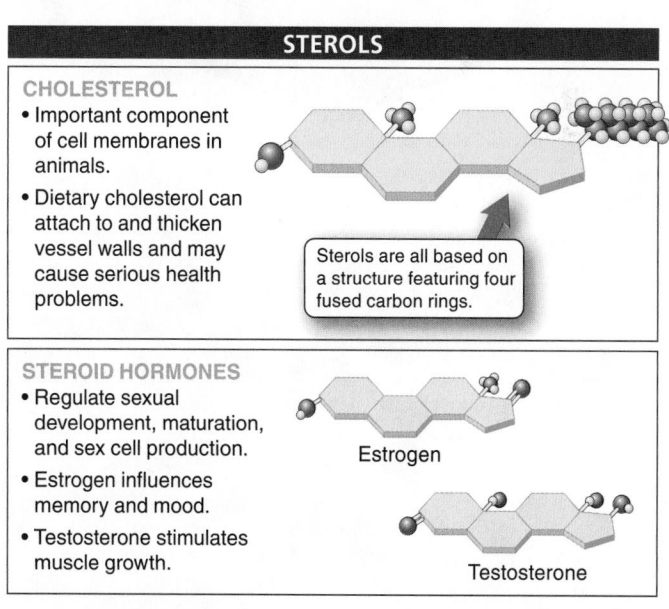

STEROLS

CHOLESTEROL
- Important component of cell membranes in animals.
- Dietary cholesterol can attach to and thicken vessel walls and may cause serious health problems.

Sterols are all based on a structure featuring four fused carbon rings.

STEROID HORMONES
- Regulate sexual development, maturation, and sex cell production.
- Estrogen influences memory and mood.
- Testosterone stimulates muscle growth.

Estrogen

Testosterone

FIGURE 2-33 Not all lipids are for energy storage. Cholesterol, estrogen, and testosterone are all lipids.

The steroid hormones estrogen and testosterone are built through slight chemical modifications to cholesterol. These hormones are among the primary molecules that direct and regulate sexual development, maturation, and sperm and egg production. In both males and females, estrogen influences memory and mood, among other traits. Testosterone has numerous effects, one of which is to stimulate muscle growth. As a consequence, athletes (particularly bodybuilders) have often been found to take synthetic variants of testosterone to increase their muscularity. But the use of these supplements is often accompanied by dangerous side effects, including extreme aggressiveness ("'roid rage"), high cholesterol, and, following long-term use, cancer. As a consequence, nearly all athletic organizations have banned their use (**FIGURE 2-34**).

Phospholipids and waxes are also lipids. **Phospholipids** are the major component of the membrane that surrounds the contents of a cell and controls the flow of chemicals into and out of the cell (**FIGURE 2-35**). They have a structure similar to

PHOSPHOLIPIDS

HYDROPHILIC HEAD (attracted to water)

Phosphate group

HYDROPHOBIC TAILS (not attracted to water)

Fatty acids

PHOSPHOLIPIDS IN WATER

Hydrophilic heads

Water

Hydrophobic tails

Phospholipids align so that their hydrophilic heads extend toward the water, while their hydrophobic tails are directed away from the water.

Symbol for phospholipid used in this book

FIGURE 2-35 Dual nature. Phospholipids have a head region that is attracted to water and a tail that is not.

fats, but with two differences: they contain a phosphorus atom (hence *phospho*lipids) and they have two fatty acid chains rather than three. We explore the significant role of phospholipids in cell membranes in the next chapter.

Waxes resemble fats but have only one long-chain fatty acid linked to the glycerol head of the molecule. Because the fatty acid chain is highly nonpolar, waxes are strongly hydrophobic; that is, these molecules do not mix with water but repel it. Their water resistance accounts for their presence as a natural coating on the surface of many plants and in the outer coverings of many insects. In both cases, the waxes prevent the plants and animals from losing the water essential to their life processes. Many birds, too, have a waxy coating on their wings, keeping them from becoming water-logged when they get wet.

FIGURE 2-34 Dangerous bulk. Steroids can increase muscularity, but with serious health consequences.

TAKE-HOME MESSAGE 2·13

Cholesterol and phospholipids are lipids that are not fats. Both are important components in cell membranes. Cholesterol also serves as a precursor to steroid hormones, important regulators of growth and development.

2·14–2·18 Proteins are versatile macromolecules that serve as building blocks.

Hair and feathers are built from proteins.

2·14 Proteins are bodybuilding macromolecules.

You can't look at a living organism and not see proteins (**FIGURE 2-36**). Inside and out, **proteins** are the chief building blocks of all life. They make up skin and feathers and horns. They make up bones and muscles. In your bloodstream, proteins fight invading microorganisms and stop you from bleeding to death from a shaving cut. Proteins control the levels of sugar and other chemicals in your bloodstream and carry oxygen from one place in your body to another. And in just about every cell in every living organism, proteins called **enzymes** initiate and assist every chemical reaction that occurs.

Although proteins perform several very different types of functions, all are built in the same way and from the same raw materials in all organisms. In the English language, every sentence is made up of words and every word is formed from one or more of the 26 letters of the alphabet. With 26 letters we can write anything, from sonnets to cookbooks to biology textbooks. Proteins, too, are constructed from a sort of alphabet. Instead of 26 letters there are 20 molecules, known as **amino acids.** Unique combinations of these 20 amino acids are strung together, like beads on a string, and the resulting protein has a unique structure and chemical behavior.

Let's look more closely at the structure of the amino acids in the protein alphabet. They all have the same basic two-part structure: one part is the same in all 20 amino acids, and the other part is unique, differing in each of the 20 amino acids.

Proteins contain the same familiar atoms as carbohydrates and lipids—carbon, hydrogen, and oxygen—but differ in an

Proteins perform a variety of different functions. They all, however, are built the same way and from the same raw materials in organisms.

STRUCTURAL
Hair, fingernails, **feathers**, horns, cartilage, tendons

PROTECTIVE
Help fight invading microorganisms, coagulate **blood**

REGULATORY
Control cell activity, constitute some **hormones**

CONTRACTILE
Allow **muscles** to contract, heart to pump, sperm to swim

TRANSPORT
Carry molecules such as **oxygen** around your body

FIGURE 2-36 Proteins everywhere! Proteins are the chief building blocks of all organisms.

important way: they also contain nitrogen. At the center of every amino acid is a carbon atom, with its four covalent bonds (**FIGURE 2-37**). One bond attaches the carbon to something called a **carboxyl group,** which is a carbon bonded to two oxygen atoms (one by a single bond and the other by a double bond). The second bond attaches the central carbon to a single hydrogen atom. The third bond attaches the central carbon to an **amino group,** which is a

The side chain is the unique part of each of the 20 amino acids, varying in size, shape, and charge.

SIDE CHAIN EXAMPLES

Alanine   Glycine

Tryptophan

FIGURE 2-37 Amino acid structure. Amino acids are made up of an amino group, a carboxyl group, and a side chain.

nitrogen atom bonded to hydrogen atoms (usually two or three). These components—the central carbon with its attached hydrogen atom, carboxyl group, and amino group—are the foundation that identifies a molecule as an amino acid and, as multiple amino acids are joined together, forms the "backbone" of the protein.

The fourth bond of the central carbon attaches to a functional group or side chain. This side chain is the unique part of each of the 20 amino acids. In the simplest amino acid, glycine, for example, the side chain is simply a hydrogen atom. In other amino acids, the side chain is a single CH_3 group or three or four such groups. Most of the side chains include both hydrogen and carbon, and a few include nitrogen or sulfur atoms. The side chain determines an amino acid's chemical properties, such as whether the amino acid molecule is polar or nonpolar.

TAKE-HOME MESSAGE 2·14

Unique combinations of 20 amino acids give rise to proteins, the chief building blocks of the physical structures that make up all organisms. Proteins perform myriad functions, from assisting chemical reactions to causing blood clotting to building bones to fighting microorganisms.

2·15 Proteins are an essential dietary component.

The atoms present in the proteins we eat—especially the nitrogen atoms—are essential to the growth, repair, and replacement that take place in our bodies. As we digest protein, breaking it down into its amino acids, our bodies use them for various building projects. Proteins also store energy in their bonds and, like carbohydrates and lipids, they can be used to fuel living processes.

The amount of protein we need depends on the extent of the building projects under way. Most individuals need 40–80 grams of protein per day. Bodybuilders, however, may need 150 grams or more a day to achieve the extensive muscle growth stimulated by their training; similarly, the protein needs of pregnant or nursing women are very high.

Contrary to the impression you might get from food labels, all proteins are not created equal. Every different protein has a different composition of amino acids. And while our bodies can manufacture certain amino acids as they are needed, many other amino acids must come from our diet. Those that we must get from our diet—about half of the 20 amino acids—are called "essential amino acids." For this reason, we shouldn't just speak of needing "*x* grams of

Q Food labels indicate how many grams of protein are contained in a food item. Why is this information only partially helpful for effectively guiding your protein intake?

protein per day." We need to consume all of the essential amino acids every day.

Many foods, containing "complete proteins," have all of the essential amino acids. Animal products such as milk, eggs, fish, chicken, and beef tend to provide complete proteins. Vegetables, fruits, and grains often contain "incomplete proteins," which do not have all the essential amino acids. If you consume only one type of incomplete protein in your diet, you may be deficient in one or more of the essential amino acids. But two incomplete proteins that are "complementary proteins," when eaten together, can provide all the essential amino acids.

Traditional dishes in many cultures often include such pairings. Examples are corn and beans in Mexico and rice and lentils in India (**FIGURE 2-38**).

TAKE-HOME MESSAGE 2·15

Twenty amino acids make up all the proteins necessary for growth, repair, and replacement of tissue in living organisms. Of these amino acids, about half are essential for humans: they cannot be synthesized by the body so must be consumed in the diet. Complete proteins contain all essential amino acids, while incomplete proteins do not.

COMPLETE vs. INCOMPLETE PROTEINS

ESSENTIAL AMINO ACID CONTENT OF COMMON FOODS

- ● Present at optimal levels
- ○ Not present at optimal levels

Optimal levels determined by the Institute of Medicine's Food and Nutrition Board

Foods: Apples, Almonds, White rice, Lentils, Milk - 2% fat, Tofu - firm (coagulated soy milk), Chicken, Beef - T-bone steak

Amino acids: Histidine, Isoleucine, Leucine, Lysine, Methionine + Cysteine, Phenylalanine + Tyrosine, Threonine, Tryptophan, Valine

GRAPHIC CONTENT!
Thinking critically about visual displays of data.
Turn to p. 76 for a closer inspection of this figure.

Traditional dishes in many cultures combine proteins, bringing together all essential amino acids.

FIGURE 2-38 All proteins are not created equal. Some foods have "complete proteins" with all the essential amino acids. Other foods have "incomplete proteins," and we must consume proteins from multiple sources to get all the essential amino acids.

2·16 A protein's function is influenced by its three-dimensional shape.

Proteins are formed by linking individual amino acids together with a **peptide bond,** in which the amino group of one amino acid is bonded to the carboxyl group of another. Two amino acids joined together form a *dipeptide,* and several amino acids joined together form a *polypeptide.* The sequence of amino acids in the polypeptide chain is called the **primary structure** of the protein and can be compared to the sequence of letters that spells a specific word (**FIGURE 2-39**).

Amino acids in a polypeptide chain don't remain in a simple straight line like beads on a string. The chain begins to fold as side chains come together and hydrogen bonds form between various atoms in the chain. The two most common patterns of hydrogen bonding between amino acids cause the chain to either twist in a corkscrew-like shape or form a zigzag folding pattern. This hydrogen bonding between amino acids gives a protein its **secondary structure.**

The protein eventually folds and bends upon itself, and additional bonds continue to form between atoms in the side chains of amino acids that are near each other. Eventually, the protein folds into a unique and complex three-dimensional shape called its **tertiary structure.** The exact form comes about as the secondary structure folds and bends, bringing together amino acids that then form bonds such as hydrogen bonds or covalent sulfur-sulfur bonds (see Figure 2-37).

Some protein molecules have a **quaternary structure** in which two or more polypeptide chains are held together by bonds between amino acids in the different chains. Hemoglobin, the protein molecule that carries oxygen from the lungs to the cells where it is needed, is made from four polypeptide chains, two "alpha" chains and two "beta" chains.

Some proteins are attached to other types of macromolecules. *Lipoproteins,* for example, circulate in the bloodstream carrying fats. They are formed when cholesterol and a triglyceride (both lipids) combine with a protein. *Glycoproteins* are combinations of carbohydrates and proteins. These are found on the surfaces of nearly all animal cells and play a role in helping the immune system distinguish between your own cells and foreign cells. (We learn more about glycoproteins in the next chapter, which discusses cells.)

The overall shape of a protein molecule determines its function—how it behaves and the other molecules it interacts with. For proteins to function properly, they must retain their three-dimensional shape. When their shapes are deformed, they usually lose their ability to function. We can see

Q Egg whites contain a lot of protein. Why does beating them change their texture, making them stiff?

STRUCTURE OF PROTEINS

PRIMARY STRUCTURE
The sequence of amino acids in a polypeptide chain, similar to the sequence of letters that spell out a specific word

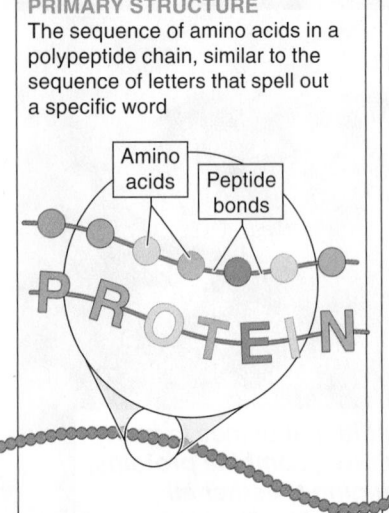

Amino acids | Peptide bonds

SECONDARY STRUCTURE
The corkscrew-like twists or pleated folds formed by hydrogen bonds between amino acids in the polypeptide chain

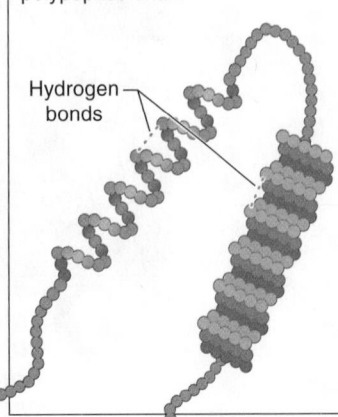

Hydrogen bonds

TERTIARY STRUCTURE
The complex three-dimensional shape formed by multiple twists and bends in the polypeptide chain, based on the side chains' interactions with each other and with the aqueous solvent.

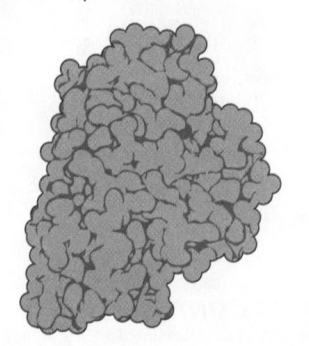

QUATERNARY STRUCTURE
Two or more polypeptide chains bonded together

FIGURE 2-39 The several levels of protein structure. The functions of proteins are influenced by their three-dimensional shape.

proteins deforming when we fry an egg. The heat breaks the hydrogen bonds that give the proteins their shape. The proteins in the clear egg white unfold, losing their secondary and tertiary structure. This disruption of protein folding is called **denaturation** (FIGURE 2-40).

Almost any extreme environment will denature a protein. Take a raw egg, for instance, and crack it into a dish containing baking soda or rubbing alcohol. Both chemicals are sufficiently extreme to turn the clear protein opaque white, as in fried egg whites.

Hair is a protein whose shape most of us have modified at one time or another. Styling hair—whether curling or straightening it—involves altering some of the hydrogen bonds between the amino acids that make up the hair protein, changing its tertiary structure. When your hair gets wet, the water is able to disrupt some of the hydrogen bonds, causing some amino acids in the protein to form hydrogen bonds with the water molecules instead. This enables you to change your hair's shape—making it straighter or, if you manipulate it around curlers, making it curlier—if you style it while it's wet. The hair can then hold this shape when it dries, as the hydrogen bonds to water are replaced by other hydrogen bonds between amino acids of the hair protein as the water evaporates. Once your hair gets wet again, however, unless it is combed, brushed, or wrapped in a different style, it will return to its natural shape.

Whether your hair is straight or curly or somewhere in between depends on your hair protein's amino acid sequence and the three-dimensional shape it confers (FIGURE 2-41).

FIGURE 2-41 **Curly or straight?** Proteins determine it!

This amino acid sequence is something you're born with (that is, it's genetically determined). The chains are more or less coiled, depending on the extent of covalent and hydrogen bonding between different parts of the coil. Many hair salons make use of the ability to alter covalent bonds to change hair texture semi-permanently. They are able to do this in three simple steps. First, the bonds are broken chemically. Second, the hair is wrapped around curlers to hold the polypeptide chains in a different position. And third, chemicals are put on the hair to create new covalent bonds between parts of the polypeptide chains. The hair thus becomes locked in a new position. (New hair will continue to grow with its genetically determined texture, of course, requiring the procedure to be repeated regularly.)

Q Why *do some people have curly hair and others have straight hair?*

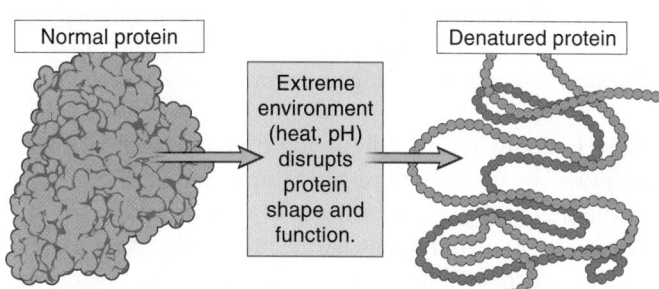

FIGURE 2-40 **Denaturation.** When proteins are unfolded, they lose their function.

TAKE-HOME MESSAGE 2·16

The particular amino acid sequence of a protein determines how it folds into a particular three-dimensional shape. This shape determines many of the protein's features, such as which molecules it will interact with. When a protein's shape is deformed, the protein usually loses its ability to function.

2·17

Enzymes are proteins that speed up chemical reactions.

Protein shape is particularly critical in **enzymes,** molecules that help initiate and accelerate the chemical reactions in our bodies. Enzymes emerge unchanged—in their original form—when the reaction is complete and thus can be used again and again. Here's how they work.

Think of an enzyme as a big piece of popcorn. Its tertiary or quaternary structure gives it a complex shape with lots of nooks and crannies. Within one of those nooks is a small area called the **active site** (FIGURE 2-42). Based on the chemical properties of the atoms lining this pocket, the active site provides a place for the participants in a chemical reaction, the reactants or **substrate** molecules, to nestle briefly.

Enzymes are very choosy: they bind only with their appropriate substrate molecules, much like a lock that can be opened with only one key (see Figure 2-42). The exposed

atoms in the active site have electrical charges that attract rather than repel the substrate molecules, and only the substrate molecules can fit into the active-site groove. Once the substrate is bound to the active site, a reaction can take place—and usually does so very quickly.

The chemical reactions that occur in organisms can either release energy or consume energy. But in either case, there is a certain minimum energy—a little "push"—needed to initiate the reaction, called **activation energy.** And although enzymes don't alter the amount of energy released by a reaction, they act as catalysts by lowering the activation energy, which causes the reaction to occur more quickly.

An enzyme can reduce the activation energy and initiate a chemical reaction in a variety of ways. These include:

1. Stressing critical chemical bonds in the substrate molecule, thus increasing the likelihood of their breaking.

2. Directly participating in the reaction, increasing the substrate's ability to make or break other bonds.

3. Creating a "micro-habitat" that favors the reaction. For instance, the active site might be a nonpolar environment, or it might have a different pH than the surrounding fluid. These slight alterations might increase the likelihood that a particular reaction occurs.

4. Simply orienting or holding substrate molecules in place so that they can be modified.

By virtue of their catalytic capacities, enzymes are at the heart of the chemistry of living organisms. Taken together, all of the chemical reactions in a living organism are its *metabolism.*

These reactions are generally arranged in sequential "metabolic pathways" by which increasingly complex molecules are synthesized or degraded. Each step of these metabolic pathways is catalyzed by an enzyme produced in the body. Proteins are the building blocks with which living organisms are built, but since nearly all enzymes are proteins, proteins can also be thought of as the *builders* of bodies, too.

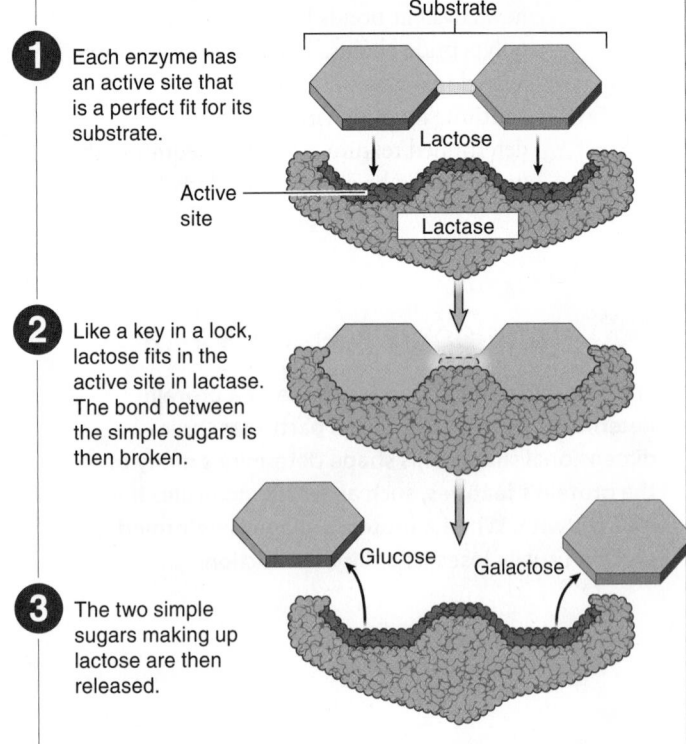

ENZYMES FACILITATE CHEMICAL REACTIONS

Enzymes can help to bring about chemical reactions in a variety of ways. The enzyme lactase, for example, breaks down the milk sugar lactose into two simple sugars that can be used for energy.

Substrate

1 Each enzyme has an active site that is a perfect fit for its substrate.

Lactose

Active site

Lactase

2 Like a key in a lock, lactose fits in the active site in lactase. The bond between the simple sugars is then broken.

Glucose   Galactose

3 The two simple sugars making up lactose are then released.

FIGURE 2-42 Lock and key. Enzymes are *very* specific about which molecules and reactions they will catalyze.

TAKE-HOME MESSAGE 2·17

Enzymes are proteins that help initiate and speed up chemical reactions. They aren't permanently altered in the process, but rather can be used again and again.

2·18 Enzymes regulate reactions in several ways (but malformed enzymes can cause problems).

If not for enzymes, it is possible that nothing would ever get done. At least not in living organisms. Enzymes don't alter the outcome of reactions, but without the chemical "nudge" they supply—often increasing reaction rates to millions of times their uncatalyzed rate—the processes necessary to sustain life could not occur.

The rate at which an enzyme catalyzes a reaction is influenced by several chemical and physical factors (**FIGURE 2-43**). These include:

1. Enzyme and substrate concentration. For a given amount of substrate, an increase in the amount of enzyme increases the rate at which the reaction occurs. Similarly, for a given amount of enzyme, an increase in the substrate concentration increases the reaction rate. In both cases, the increases occur only up to the point at which all of the enzyme molecules are bound to substrate, or vice versa, at which point additional enzyme or substrate no longer increases the reaction rate.

2. Temperature. Because increasing the temperature increases the movement of molecules, reaction rates generally increase at higher temperatures. This occurs only up to the optimum temperature for an enzyme. At temperatures above the optimum, reaction rates decrease as enzymes lose their shape or even denature. Enzymes from different species can have widely differing optimum temperatures.

3. pH. As with temperature, enzymes have an optimum pH. Above or below this pH, interactions between excess hydrogen or hydroxide ions and amino acid side chains in the active site disrupt enzyme function (and sometimes structure) and decrease reaction rates.

4. Presence of inhibitors or activators. One of the most common ways that cells regulate their metabolic pathways is through the binding of other chemicals to enzymes. This can alter enzyme shape in a way that increases or decreases the enzyme's activity. **Inhibitors** reduce enzyme activity and come in two types: **competitive inhibitors** bind to the active site, blocking substrate molecules from the site and thus from taking part in the reaction. **Noncompetitive inhibitors** do not compete for the active site but rather bind to another

FIGURE 2-43 Enzyme activity is influenced by physical factors such as temperature and pH, and by chemical factors such as enzyme and substrate concentrations.

ENZYME ACTIVITY

The rate at which an enzyme catalyzes a reaction is influenced by several chemical and physical factors.

ENZYME AND SUBSTRATE CONCENTRATION
Reaction rates increase with increased amounts of enzyme (or substrate), but only up to the point at which all of the enzyme molecules are bound to substrate. At that point, additional enzyme (or substrate) no longer increases the reaction rate.

TEMPERATURE
Reaction rates generally increase at higher temperatures, but only up to the optimum temperature for an enzyme. At temperatures above the optimum, reaction rates decrease as enzymes lose their shape or even denature.

pH
Reaction rates generally increase as pH nears the optimum level for an enzyme. Above or below this pH, enzyme function can be disrupted and reaction rates decrease.

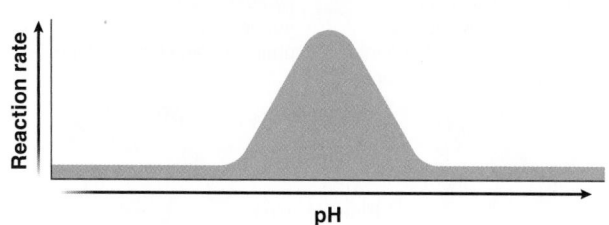

PRESENCE OF INHIBITORS OR ACTIVATORS
Reaction rates increase in the presence of activators and decrease in the presence of inhibitors.

part of the enzyme, altering its shape in a way that changes the structure of the active site, reducing or blocking its ability to bind with substrate. Often, it is the very product of a metabolic pathway that acts as an inhibitor of enzymes early in the pathway, effectively shutting off the pathway when enough of its end product has been produced.

Just as a molecule can bind to an enzyme and inhibit the enzyme's activity, some cellular chemicals act as **activators.** Instead of their binding to an enzyme "turning it off," their binding to the enzyme "turns it on," altering the enzyme's shape or structure so that it can now catalyze a reaction.

Sometimes a cell produces a protein "word" that is misspelled—that is, the sequence of amino acids is incorrect. If an enzyme is altered even slightly, the active site may change and the enzyme no longer functions (**FIGURE 2-44**). Slightly

modified, non-functioning enzymes are responsible for a large number of diseases and physiological problems (see Section 5-9). An example is the body's inability to break down the amino acid phenylalanine (in a condition known as phenylketonuria).

One health issue influenced by enzyme function is the condition called lactose intolerance. Normally, during digestion, the lactose in milk is broken down into its component parts, glucose and galactose (see Figure 2-42).

Q

Why do some adults get sick when they drink milk?

These simple sugars are then used for energy. But some people, when they become adults, are unable to break the bond linking the two simple sugars because they no longer produce the enzyme lactase that assists in this process. Consequently, any lactose in their diet passes through their stomach and small intestine undigested. Then, when it reaches the large intestine, bacteria living there consume the lactose. The problem is that, as the bacteria break down the lactose, they produce some carbon dioxide and other gases. These gases are trapped in the intestine and lead to severe discomfort. Interestingly, in regions of the world with long traditions of pastoralism (raising and consuming livestock), lactose intolerance is much rarer than in other parts of the world. Only about 10% of people from Denmark or Sweden have lactose intolerance, but among people from China, which has historically been largely non-pastoral, about 99% are lactose intolerant.

The unpleasant symptoms of lactose intolerance can be avoided by not consuming milk, cheese, yogurt, ice cream, or any other dairy products, but they can also be avoided by taking a pill containing the enzyme lactase. It doesn't matter how the enzyme gets into your digestive system; as long as it's there, the lactose in the milk can be broken down.

NON-FUNCTIONING ENZYMES

Sometimes a protein "word" is misspelled—that is, the sequence of amino acids is incorrect. If an enzyme is altered even slightly, the active site may change, which can cause the enzyme to no longer function.

FUNCTIONING ENZYME   **NON-FUNCTIONING ENZYME**

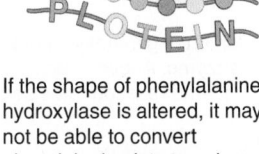

When functioning normally, the enzyme phenylalanine hydroxylase converts the amino acid phenylalanine into another amino acid, tyrosine.

If the shape of phenylalanine hydroxylase is altered, it may not be able to convert phenylalanine into tyrosine.

Non-functioning enzymes are responsible for a large number of diseases and physiological problems.

FIGURE 2-44 When a protein is "misspelled."

TAKE-HOME MESSAGE 2·18

Enzyme activity is influenced by physical factors such as temperature and pH, as well as chemical factors, including enzyme and substrate concentrations. Inhibitors and activators are chemicals that bind to enzymes and by blocking the active site or altering the shape or structure of the enzyme can change the rate at which the enzyme catalyzes reactions.

2·19–2·21 Nucleic acids store information on how to build and run a body.

Three turns of the DNA double helix (from a scanning tunneling micrograph).

2·19 Nucleic acids are macromolecules that store information.

We have examined three of life's macromolecules: carbohydrates, lipids, and proteins. We turn our attention now to the fourth: **nucleic acids,** macromolecules that store information and are made up of individual units called **nucleotides.** All nucleotides have three components: a molecule of sugar, a phosphate group (containing a phosphorus atom bound to four oxygen atoms), and a nitrogen-containing molecule (**FIGURE 2-45**). There are two types of nucleic acids: **deoxyribonucleic acid (DNA)** and **ribonucleic acid (RNA).** Both play central roles in directing the production of proteins in living organisms, and by doing so play a central role in determining all of the inherited characteristics of an individual. In both types of nucleic acids, the molecule has the same type of backbone: a sugar molecule attached to a phosphate group attached to another sugar, then another phosphate, and so on. Attached to each sugar is one of the nitrogen-containing molecules called DNA **bases** (so named because of their chemical structure). A 10-unit nucleic acid therefore would have 10 bases, one attached to each sugar within the sugar-phosphate-sugar-phosphate backbone. But the base attached to each sugar is not always the same. It can be one of several different bases. For this reason, a nucleic acid

FIGURE 2-45 The molecules that carry genetic information.
The structure of nucleic acids.

is often described by the sequence of bases attached to the sugar-phosphate-sugar-phosphate backbone.

Nucleic acids are able to store information by varying which base is attached at each position in the molecule's backbone. At each position in a molecule of DNA, for example, the base can be any one of four possible bases: adenine (A), thymine (T), guanine (G), or cytosine (C). Just as the meaning of a sentence is determined by which letters are strung together, the information in a molecule of DNA is determined by its sequence of bases. One molecule may have the sequence adenine, adenine, adenine, guanine, cytosine, thymine, guanine—abbreviated as AAAGCTG. Another molecule may have the sequence CGATTACCCGAT. Because the information differs in each case, so, too, does the protein for which the sequence codes, as we'll see.

TAKE-HOME MESSAGE 2·19

The nucleic acids DNA and RNA are macromolecules that store information in their unique sequences of bases contained in nucleotides, their building-block molecules. Both nucleic acids play central roles in directing protein production in organisms.

2·20 DNA holds the genetic information to build an organism.

A molecule of DNA has two strands, each a sugar-phosphate-sugar-phosphate backbone with a base sticking out from each sugar molecule. The two strands wrap around each other, each turning in a spiral. Although each strand has its own sugar-phosphate-sugar-phosphate backbone and sequence of bases, the two strands are connected by the bases protruding from them.

You can picture a molecule of DNA as a ladder. The two sugar-phosphate-sugar-phosphate backbones are like the long vertical sides of the ladder that give it height. A base sticking out represents a rung on the ladder. Or, more accurately, half a rung. The bases protruding from each strand meet in the center and bind to each other (via hydrogen bonds), holding the ladder together. DNA differs from a ladder slightly, in that it has a gradual twist. The two spiraling strands together are said to form a **double helix** (**FIGURE 2-46**).

The two intertwining spirals fit together because only two combinations of bases pair up together. The base A always pairs with T, and C always pairs with G. Consequently, if the base sequence of one of the spirals is CCCCTTAGGAACC, the base sequence of the other must be GGGGAATCCTTGG. That is why researchers working on the Human Genome Project describe only one sequence of nucleotides when presenting a DNA sequence—even though that DNA is double-stranded in our bodies. With that one sequence, we can infer the identity and order of the bases in the complementary sequence, and thus we know the exact structure of the nucleic acid.

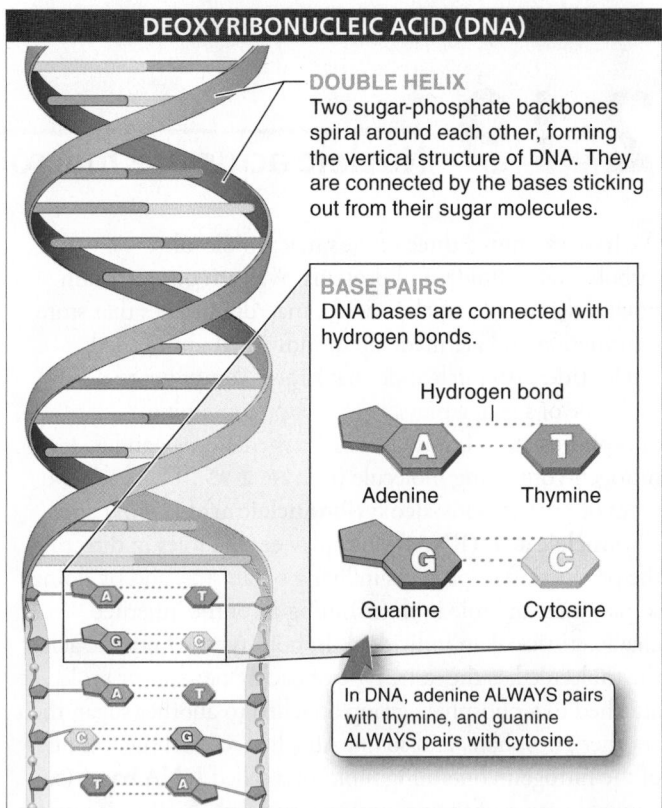

DEOXYRIBONUCLEIC ACID (DNA)

DOUBLE HELIX
Two sugar-phosphate backbones spiral around each other, forming the vertical structure of DNA. They are connected by the bases sticking out from their sugar molecules.

BASE PAIRS
DNA bases are connected with hydrogen bonds.

Hydrogen bond

A — Adenine   T — Thymine

G — Guanine   C — Cytosine

In DNA, adenine ALWAYS pairs with thymine, and guanine ALWAYS pairs with cytosine.

FIGURE 2-46 A gradually twisting ladder. The rungs of the DNA ladder are nucleotide base pairs, and the sides of the ladder are made up of two sugar-phosphate backbones.

The sequences of nucleotide bases containing the information about how to produce a particular protein have anywhere from a hundred to several thousand bases. In a human, all of the DNA in a cell, containing all of the instructions for every protein that a human must produce, contains about three billion base pairs. Almost all of this DNA is in the cell's nucleus.

2·21 RNA is a universal translator, reading DNA and directing protein production.

The process of building a protein from a DNA sequence is not a direct one. Rather, it incorporates a middleman, RNA, that is also a nucleic acid (**FIGURE 2-47**). Segments of the DNA are read off, directing the production of short strips of RNA that contain the information, taken from the DNA, about the amino acid sequence in a protein. The RNA moves to another part of the cell and then directs the piecing together of amino acids into a three-dimensional protein. We explore this in greater detail in Chapter 5.

RNA differs from DNA in three important ways. First, the sugar molecule of the sugar-phosphate-sugar-phosphate backbone differs slightly, containing an extra atom of oxygen. Second, RNA is single stranded. The sugar-phosphate-sugar-phosphate backbone is still there, as are the bases that protrude from each sugar. The bases, however, do not bind with anything else and do not form base pairs with another RNA strand. And third, while RNA has the bases A, G, and C, it replaces the thymine with a similar base called uracil (U).

Whether we're looking at the nucleotides that make up RNA and DNA or the lipids used to build sex hormones and cell membranes, we see a recurring theme in the construction of biological macromolecules: from relatively simple sets of building blocks linked together, infinitely complex molecules can be formed. Complex webs of one simple sugar, bonded together as glycogen, for instance, provide fuel for organisms. Similarly, sequences of amino acids of 20 different types, joined together, specify the structure of all the proteins found in every species on earth.

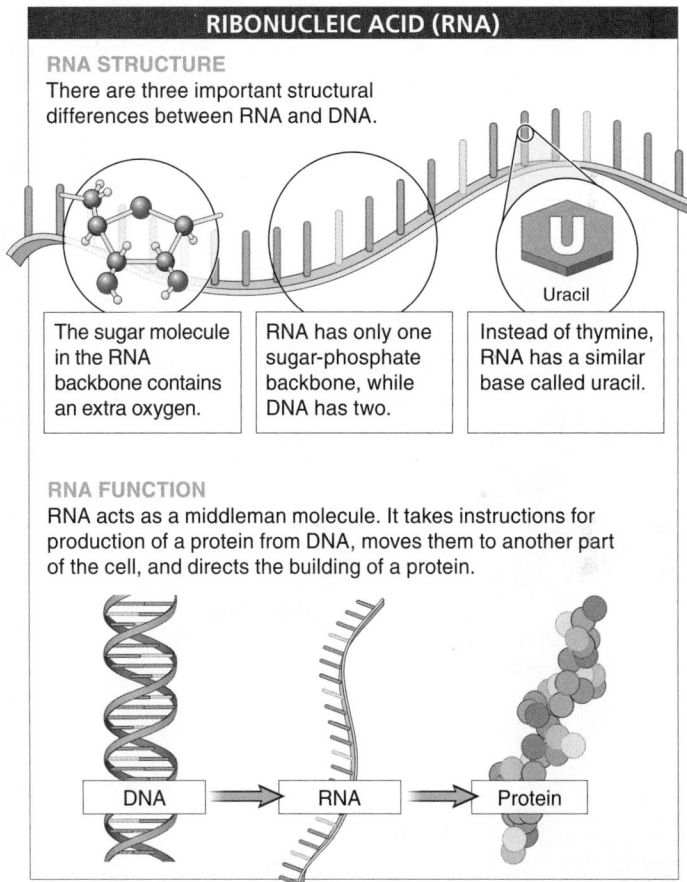

RIBONUCLEIC ACID (RNA)

RNA STRUCTURE
There are three important structural differences between RNA and DNA.

Uracil

| The sugar molecule in the RNA backbone contains an extra oxygen. | RNA has only one sugar-phosphate backbone, while DNA has two. | Instead of thymine, RNA has a similar base called uracil. |

RNA FUNCTION
RNA acts as a middleman molecule. It takes instructions for production of a protein from DNA, moves them to another part of the cell, and directs the building of a protein.

DNA → RNA → Protein

FIGURE 2-47 The middleman between DNA and protein. The structure of RNA.

MELT-IN-YOUR-MOUTH CHOCOLATE MAY NOT BE SUCH A SWEET IDEA.

Food chemists have figured out how to make chocolate that melts in your mouth. Is that a good thing?

Q: WHY ARE SOME FATS "LIQUIDY," LIKE OIL, AND OTHERS SOLID? The less saturated a fat is, the more "liquidy" it is at room temperature. Most animal fats are saturated and are solid at room temperature. Best example: butter. Most plant fats are polyunsaturated and are liquid at room temperature. Best example: vegetable oils.

Q: CAN OILS BE MADE MORE SOLID? It's possible to increase the saturation of plant fats. Just heat them up and pass hydrogen bubbles through the liquid. In creating partially hydrogenated plant oils, this process reduces the number of carbon-carbon double bonds and makes the oil more solid. (It's easy, it's cheaper than just using butter, and it increases foods' shelf-life.)

Q: DOES THAT IMPROVE THEIR TASTE? By precisely controlling the level of saturation in plant fats, it is possible to create foods that are solid but have such a low melting point that they quickly melt on contact with the warmth of your mouth. This seems great, but . . .

Q: IS THERE A DOWNSIDE? The saturation of vegetable fats creates trans fats, due to the position taken by the newly added hydrogen atoms in the molecule. Trans fats increase levels of LDL ("bad") cholesterol and decrease HDL ("good") cholesterol, narrowing blood vessel walls and increasing the risk of heart disease and strokes.

CONCLUSION: Partially hydrogenated vegetable oils can give food a perfect texture and a pleasing feel in your mouth. But the creaminess comes with a high cost when it comes to your health.

Big Ideas in ... Chemistry

2·1–2·3 Atoms form molecules through bonding.

- An atom is the smallest unit into which material can be divided without losing its essential properties.
- Atoms are made up of protons and neutrons in the nucleus and electrons that circle, far away, around that nucleus.
- Molecules are atoms linked together.

2·4–2·6 Water has features that enable it to support all life.

- Water molecules easily form hydrogen bonds, giving water great cohesiveness and the ability to resist temperature changes, and making it a versatile solvent.
- The pH of a fluid is a measure of how acidic or basic the solution is.

2·7–2·10 Carbohydrates are fuel for living machines.

- Carbohydrates, made up of carbon, oxygen, and hydrogen, are the primary fuel for all cellular machinery and also form much of the structure of cells.
- The simplest carbohydrates, including glucose, are called monosaccharides or simple sugars.
- Multiple simple sugars sometimes link together into more complex carbohydrates, including starch, which is the primary form of energy storage in plants, and glycogen, which is a primary form of energy storage in animals.
- Some carbohydrates are not digestible by humans.

2·11–2·13 Lipids store energy for a rainy day.

- Lipids are macromolecules—made up primarily of carbon, hydrogen, and oxygen—that are insoluble in water.
- Lipids are important for energy storage, hormones, and membrane structure.
- The breakdown of dietary fats releases more energy per gram than other macromolecules.

2·14–2·18 Proteins are versatile molecules that serve as building blocks.

- Cells and tissues are primarily built from proteins, sequences of amino acids that fold into complex, three-dimensional shapes.
- The atoms, especially nitrogen, present in the plant and animal proteins that an organism eats are essential to the organism's growth and repair.
- The amino acid sequence of a protein determines how it folds into a three-dimensional shape. This shape determines many of the protein's features, such as which molecules it will interact with.
- Enzymes are proteins that help initiate and speed up chemical reactions. They aren't permanently altered in the process.

2·19–2·21 Nucleic acids store information on how to build and run a body.

- The nucleic acids DNA and RNA are macromolecules that store information by having unique sequences of units called nucleotides. Both play central roles in directing protein production in organisms.
- The sequence of nucleotide bases contains the information about how to produce a particular protein.
- RNA acts like a universal translator of the genetic code into proteins. It reads DNA sequences and directs the production of a sequence of amino acids.

See the To-Go Guide (packaged with every new copy of this textbook) for an illustrated summary of the chapter.

Check Your Knowledge

GRAPHIC CONTENT

Thinking critically about visual displays of data.

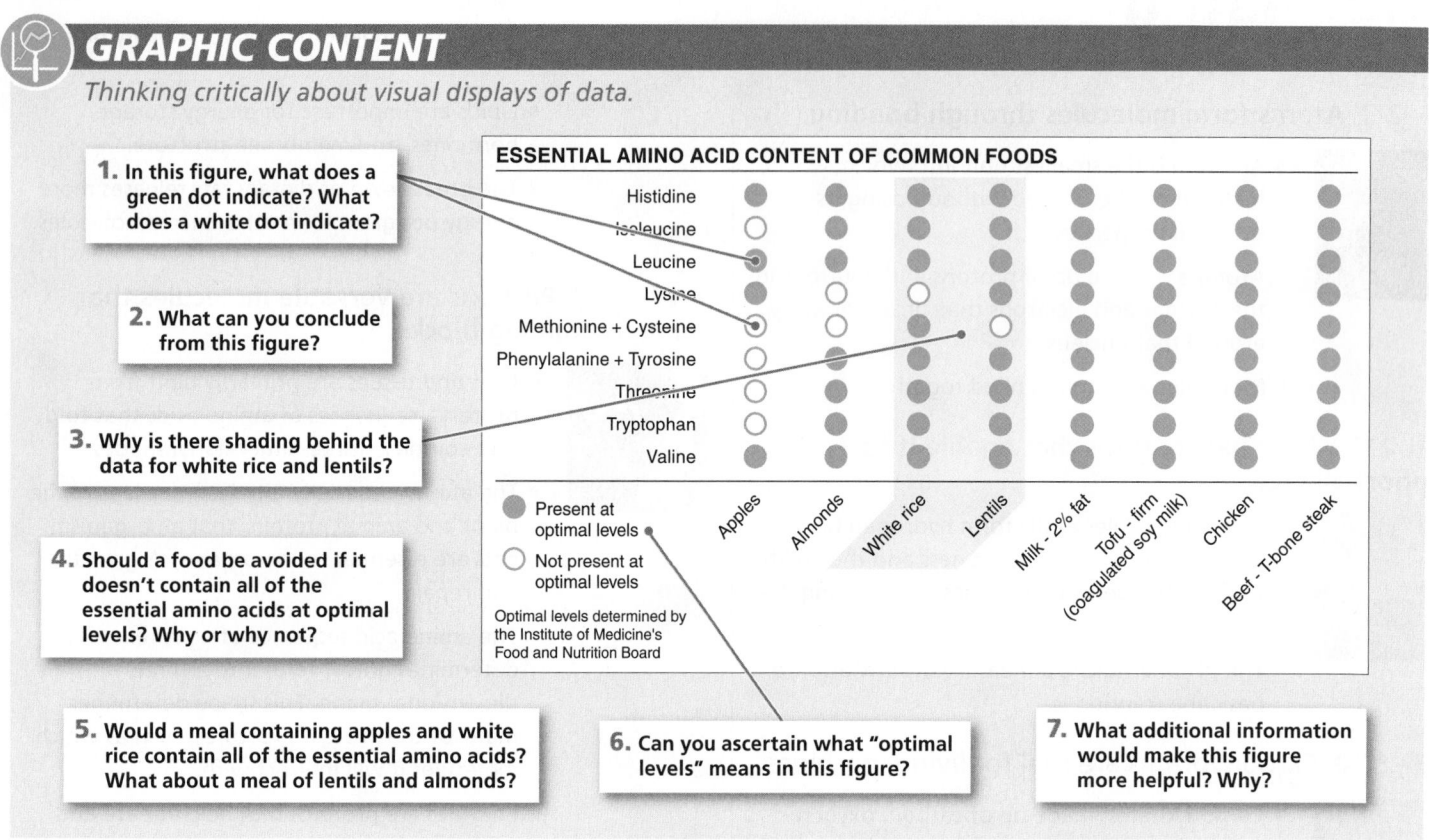

1. In this figure, what does a green dot indicate? What does a white dot indicate?

2. What can you conclude from this figure?

3. Why is there shading behind the data for white rice and lentils?

4. Should a food be avoided if it doesn't contain all of the essential amino acids at optimal levels? Why or why not?

5. Would a meal containing apples and white rice contain all of the essential amino acids? What about a meal of lentils and almonds?

6. Can you ascertain what "optimal levels" means in this figure?

7. What additional information would make this figure more helpful? Why?

See Answers at the back of the book.

Key Terms in Chemistry

acid, p. 50
activation energy, p. 68
activator, p. 70
active site, p. 68
amino acid, p. 63
amino group, p. 64
atom, p. 39
atomic mass, p. 39
atomic number, p. 39
base, p. 50
base (of DNA), p. 71
bond energy, p. 43
buffer, p. 51
carbohydrate, p. 52
carboxyl group, p. 64
cellulose, p. 56

chitin, p. 56
cholesterol, p. 61
competitive inhibitor, p. 69
complex carbohydrate, p. 54
compound, p. 44
covalent bond, p. 43
denaturation, p. 67
deoxyribonucleic acid (DNA), p. 71
disaccharide, p. 54
double bond, p. 44
double helix, p. 72
electron, p. 39
element, p. 38

enzyme, pp. 63, 68
fatty acid, p. 58
glycerol, p. 58
glycogen, p. 53
hydrogen bond, p. 44
hydrophilic, p. 57
hydrophobic, p. 57
inhibitor, p. 69
ion, p. 42
ionic bond, p. 44
isotope, p. 40
lipid, p. 57
macromolecule, p. 52
mass, p. 39
molecule, p. 43
monosaccharide, p. 52

neutron, p. 39
noncompetitive inhibitor, p. 69
nucleic acid, p. 71
nucleotide, p. 71
nucleus, p. 39
peptide bond, p. 66
periodic table, p. 40
pH, p. 50
phospholipid, p. 62
polysaccharide, p. 54
primary structure, p. 66
protein, p. 63
proton, p. 39
quaternary structure, p. 66

radioactive, p. 40
ribonucleic acid (RNA), p. 71
saturated fat, p. 60
secondary structure, p. 66
simple sugar, p. 52
starch, p. 55
sterol, p. 61
substrate, p. 68
tertiary structure, p. 66
trans fat, p. 60
triglyceride, p. 58
unsaturated fat, p. 60
wax, p. 62

Multiple-Choice Questions

1. The atomic number of carbon is 6. Its nucleus must contain:

a) 6 neutrons and 6 protons.

b) 3 protons and 3 neutrons.

c) 6 neutrons and no electrons.

d) 6 protons and no electrons.

e) 6 protons and 6 electrons.

100 HARD

41

0 EASY

2. The second orbital shell of an atom can hold _____ electrons.

a) 2

b) 3

c) 4

d) 6

e) 8

100 HARD

20
0 EASY

3. A covalent bond is formed when:

a) two nonpolar molecules associate with each other in a polar environment.

b) a positively charged particle is attracted to a negatively charged particle.

c) one atom gives up electrons to another atom.

d) two atoms share electrons.

e) two polar molecules associate with each other in a nonpolar environment.

100 HARD

16
0 EASY

4. Which of the following phenomena is most likely due to the high cohesiveness of water?

a) Lakes and rivers freeze from the top down, not the bottom up.

b) The fishing spider can walk across the surface of liquid water.

c) Adding salt to snow makes it melt.

d) The temperature of Santa Monica Bay, off the coast of Los Angeles, fluctuates less than the air temperature throughout the year.

e) All of the above are due to the cohesiveness of water.

100 HARD

51

0 EASY

5. Water can absorb and store a large amount of heat while increasing only a few degrees in temperature. Why?

a) The heat must first be used to break the hydrogen bonds rather than raise the temperature.

b) The heat must first be used to break the ionic bonds rather than raise the temperature.

c) The heat must first be used to break the covalent bonds rather than raise the temperature.

d) An increase in temperature causes an increase in adhesion of the water.

e) An increase in temperature causes an increase in cohesion of the water.

100 HARD

22
0 EASY

6. A chemical compound that releases H+ into a solution is called:

a) a proton.

b) a base.

c) an acid.

d) a hydroxide ion.

e) a hydrogen ion.

100 HARD

31

0 EASY

7. Which of the following foods is not a significant source of complex carbohydrates?

a) fresh fruit

b) rice

c) pasta

d) oatmeal

e) All of the above are significant sources of complex carbohydrates.

100 HARD

31

0 EASY

8. Sucrose (table sugar) and lactose (the sugar found in milk) are examples of:

a) naturally occurring enzymes.

b) simple sugars.

c) monosaccharides.

d) disaccharides.

e) complex carbohydrates.

100 HARD

42

0 EASY

9. Which of the following statements about starch is incorrect?

a) Starch is the primary form of energy storage in plants.

b) Starch consists of a hundred or more glucose molecules joined together in a line.

c) Starch tastes sweet because it is made from glucose.

d) Starch is a polysaccharide.

e) All of the above statements about starch are correct.

10. Which of the following statements about fiber is incorrect?

a) Dietary fiber reduces the risk of colon cancer.

b) Fiber in the diet slows the passage of food through the intestines.

c) Humans are unable to extract any caloric value from fiber.

d) The cellulose of celery stalks and lettuce leaves is fiber.

e) Fiber passing through the digestive system scrapes the wall of the digestive tract, stimulating mucus secretion and aiding in the digestion of other molecules.

11. In an unusually detailed dissection of your dinner, you isolate an unknown fatty acid. It is a liquid at room temperature (that is, has a low melting point) and contains carbon-carbon double bonds. What are you most likely to be eating?

a) a plant

b) a cow

c) a pig

d) a chicken

e) a lamb

12. An unsaturated fatty acid is one in which:

a) carbon-carbon double bonds are present in the hydrocarbon chain.

b) the hydrocarbon chain has an odd number of carbons.

c) the hydrocarbon chain has an even number of carbons.

d) no carbon-carbon double bonds are present in the hydrocarbon chain.

e) not all of the carbons in the hydrocarbon chain are bonded to hydrogen atoms.

13. Which statement about phospholipids is incorrect?

a) Because their phosphate groups repel each other, they are used as organisms' chief form of short-term energy.

b) They are hydrophobic at one end.

c) They are hydrophilic at one end.

d) They are a major constituent of cell membranes.

e) They contain glycerol linked to fatty acids.

14. Proteins are an essential component of a healthy diet for humans (and other animals). Their most common purpose is to serve as:

a) raw material for growth.

b) fuel for running the body.

c) organic precursors for enzyme construction.

d) long-term energy storage.

e) inorganic precursors for enzyme construction.

15. Dietary proteins:

a) are considered "complete" only if they contain the 8 essential amino acids required by humans.

b) consist of all 20 amino acids required in the human body.

c) are considered "complete" only if they contain the 12 non-essential amino acids required by humans.

d) are nutritionally identical, since all are broken down into their constituent amino acids in the digestive system.

e) can be obtained from animal sources but not plant sources.

16. The primary structure of proteins is often described as amino acids connected like beads on a string. In this same vein, which of the following images best describes a protein's quaternary structure?

a) threads in a cloth

b) needles in a haystack

c) rungs on a ladder

d) links on a chain

e) coils in a spring

17. Which of the following statements about enzymes is incorrect?

a) Enzymes can initiate chemical reactions.
b) Enzymes speed up chemical reactions.
c) Enzymes often induce conformational changes in the substrates that they bind.
d) Enzymes contain an active site for binding of particular substrates.
e) Enzymes undergo a permanent change during the reactions they promote.

100 HARD
 42
0 EASY

18. Which of the following nucleotide bases are present in equal amounts in DNA?

a) adenine and cytosine
b) thymine and guanine
c) adenine and guanine
d) thymine and cytosine
e) adenine and thymine

100 HARD
 22
0 EASY

19. Which type of macromolecule contains an organism's genetic information?

a) polysaccharide
b) monosaccharide
c) fatty acid
d) DNA
e) phospholipid

100 HARD
 6 ASY

20. All of the following are features of RNA except:

a) a sugar-phosphate-sugar-phosphate backbone.
b) a coiled double-stranded structure.
c) a different type of sugar than is found in DNA.
d) an ability to direct protein production.
e) a different type of base than is found in DNA.

100 HARD
46
0 EASY

Short-Answer Questions

1. An atom of sodium has an atomic number of 11 and an atom of chlorine has an atomic number of 17.

a) Indicate the number of electrons that are present in the outermost electron shell of each atom.
b) Predict what type of bond would form between these atoms, and explain why.

2. Explain how hydrogen bonding plays a part in each of the unique properties of water and, in essence, allows for life on earth.

3. There are many cleaning products on the market that advertise their ability to get rid of stubborn, oily dirt. Why is water alone not sufficient for removing oily dirt?

4. Some people who are watching what they eat may opt for a salad when they are dining out. A dinner salad may include lettuce, celery, strawberries, walnuts, chicken, and a salad dressing of oil and vinegar. Explain which category of major macromolecules each of these individual salad components falls into. Then explain the general purpose or function of each major macromolecule.

See Answers at the back of the book.
For additional study questions, go to www.prep-u.com.

ABOUT THE CHAPTER OPENING PHOTO

Hydrogen bonding between molecules gives water cohesiveness. This causes the water to bead up when on surfaces that water molecules are less attracted to, such as the waxy leaves of many plants.

The smallest part of you

3

Cells

3·1–3·3 What is a cell?

Human cell, packed with organelles.

3·1

All organisms are made of cells.

Where do we begin if we want to understand how organisms work? Given their complexity, this task can be daunting. In the case of organisms, whether we are studying a creature as small as a flea or as large as an elephant or giant sequoia, they can be broken down into smaller units that are more easily studied and understood (**FIGURE 3-1**). The most basic unit of any organism is the **cell,** the smallest unit of life that can function independently and perform all the necessary functions of life, including reproducing itself. Understanding cell structure and function is the basis for

Fungi

Elephants

Head louse

FIGURE 3-1 **What do these diverse organisms have in common?** Cells.

our understanding of how complex organisms are organized.

The term "cell" was first used in the mid-1600s by Robert Hooke, an English scientist also known for his contributions to philosophy, physics, and architecture. When he was made Curator of Experiments for the Royal Society of London, Hooke suddenly had access to many of the first microscopes available, and he began to examine everything he could get his hands on. Because Hooke thought the close-up views of a very thin piece of cork resembled a mass of small, empty rooms, he named these compartments *cellulae*, Latin for "small rooms."

Today, we know that a cell is a three-dimensional structure, like a fluid-filled balloon, in which many of the essential chemical reactions of life take place (such as the breakdown of carbohydrates for energy, the modification of cholesterol to create testosterone and estrogen, and the translation of the genetic code into protein production). Generally, these reactions involve transporting raw materials and fuel into the cell and exporting finished materials and waste products out of the cell. In addition, nearly all cells contain DNA (deoxyribonucleic acid), a molecule that contains the information that directs the chemical reactions in a cell, the formation of various cellular products within the cell, and the cell's ability to reproduce itself. (A few types of cells, including mammalian red blood cells and cells called "sieve tube elements" that form part of the plant circulatory system, lose their nuclei after they are created and are unable to divide.) We explore all of these features of cell functioning in this and the next three chapters.

To see a cell, you don't have to work in a lab or use a microscope. Just open your refrigerator. Chances are you've got a dozen or so visible cells in there: eggs. Although most cells are too small to see with the naked eye, there are a few exceptions, including hens' eggs from the supermarket. As long as they are unfertilized, which most store-bought hens' eggs are, each egg tends to contain just one cell. The ostrich egg, weighing about three pounds, contains the largest of all animal cells. (It should be noted, however, that by the time the ostrich lays a fertilized egg, the embryo inside has already gone through multiple divisions.)

In addition to being among the largest cells around, eggs are also the most valuable. Almas caviar, eggs from the beluga sturgeon, sells for nearly $700 per ounce. This value is exceeded only by that of human eggs, which currently fetch as much as $25,000 for a dozen or so eggs on the open market (**FIGURE 3-2**). (Human sperm cells command only about a penny per 20,000 cells!)

Hummingbird egg: 0.02 ounce
Elephant bird (extinct) egg: two gallons

Beluga sturgeon eggs: $700 per ounce

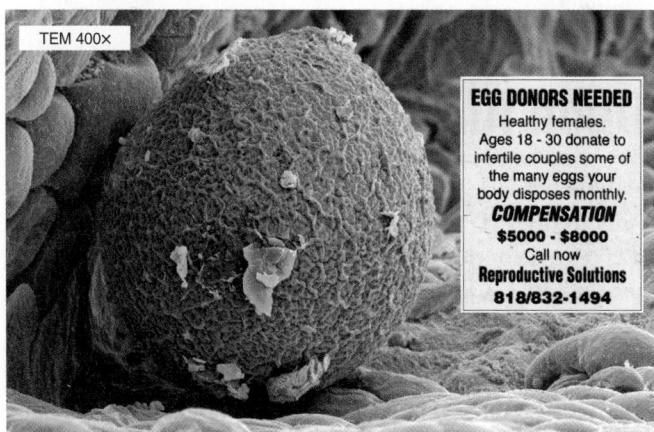

TEM 400x

Human eggs: Thousands of dollars per egg

Eggs are the largest and most expensive cells in the world!

FIGURE 3-2 Not all cells are tiny. And some cells are extremely valuable!

Most cells are much smaller than hens' eggs and ostrich eggs. Consider that, at this very moment, there are probably more than seven billion bacteria in your mouth—even if you just brushed your teeth! This is more than the number of people on earth. It is possible to squeeze so many bacteria in there because most cells (not just bacteria) are really, really tiny—so tiny that 2,000 red blood cells, lined up end to end, would just extend across a dime.

After sufficient improvements were made to early microscopes in the 19th century, the central role of the cell in biology could be understood. By the 1830s, scientists realized that all plants and animals were made entirely from cells. Subsequent studies revealed that every cell seemed to arise from the division of another cell. You, for example, are made up of at least 60 trillion cells, all of which came from just one cell: the single fertilized egg produced when an egg cell from your mother was fertilized by a sperm cell from your father.

The facts that (1) all living organisms are made up of one or more cells and (2) all cells arise from other, preexisting cells are the foundations of **cell theory,** one of the unifying theories in biology, and one that is universally accepted by all biologists. As we see in Chapter 10, the origin of life on earth was a one-time deviation from cell theory: the first cells on earth probably originated from free-floating molecules in the oceans early in the earth's history (about 3.5 billion years ago). Since that time, however, all cells and thus all life have been produced as a continuous line of cells, originating from these initial cells.

In this chapter, we investigate the two different kinds of cells that make up all of the organisms on earth, the processes by which cells control how materials move into and out of the cell, and how cells communicate with each other. We also explore some of the important structures found in many cells and the specialized roles these structures play in a variety of cellular functions. Along the way, we learn about some of the health consequences that occur when cells malfunction.

TAKE-HOME MESSAGE 3·1

The most basic unit of any organism is the cell, the smallest unit of life that can function independently and perform all of the necessary functions of life, including reproducing itself. All living organisms are made up of one or more cells, and all cells arise from other, preexisting cells.

3·2 Prokaryotic cells are structurally simple, but there are many types of them.

Although there are millions of diverse species on earth, billions of unique organisms alive at any time, and trillions of different cells in many of those organisms, every cell on earth falls into one of two basic categories.

A **eukaryotic cell** (from the Greek for "good" and "kernel") has a central control structure called a nucleus, which contains the cell's DNA. Organisms composed of eukaryotic cells are called **eukaryotes.**

A **prokaryotic cell** (from the Greek for "before" and "kernel") does not have a nucleus; its DNA simply resides in the cytoplasm. An organism consisting of a prokaryotic cell is called a **prokaryote.**

We begin our study of the cell by exploring the prokaryotes. Prokaryotes were the first cells on earth, making their appearance about 3.5 billion years ago, and, for a long time (1.5 billion years), they had the planet to themselves.

All prokaryotes are one-celled organisms and are invisible to the naked eye. Prokaryotes have four basic structural features (**FIGURE 3-3**).

1. A **plasma membrane** encompasses the cell (and sometimes is simply called the "cell membrane"). For this reason, anything inside the plasma membrane is referred to as "intracellular," and everything outside the plasma membrane is "extracellular."

2. The **cytoplasm** is the jelly-like fluid that fills the inside of the cell.

3. **Ribosomes** are little granular bodies where proteins are made; thousands of them are scattered throughout the cytoplasm.

4. Each prokaryote has one or more circular loops or linear strands of DNA.

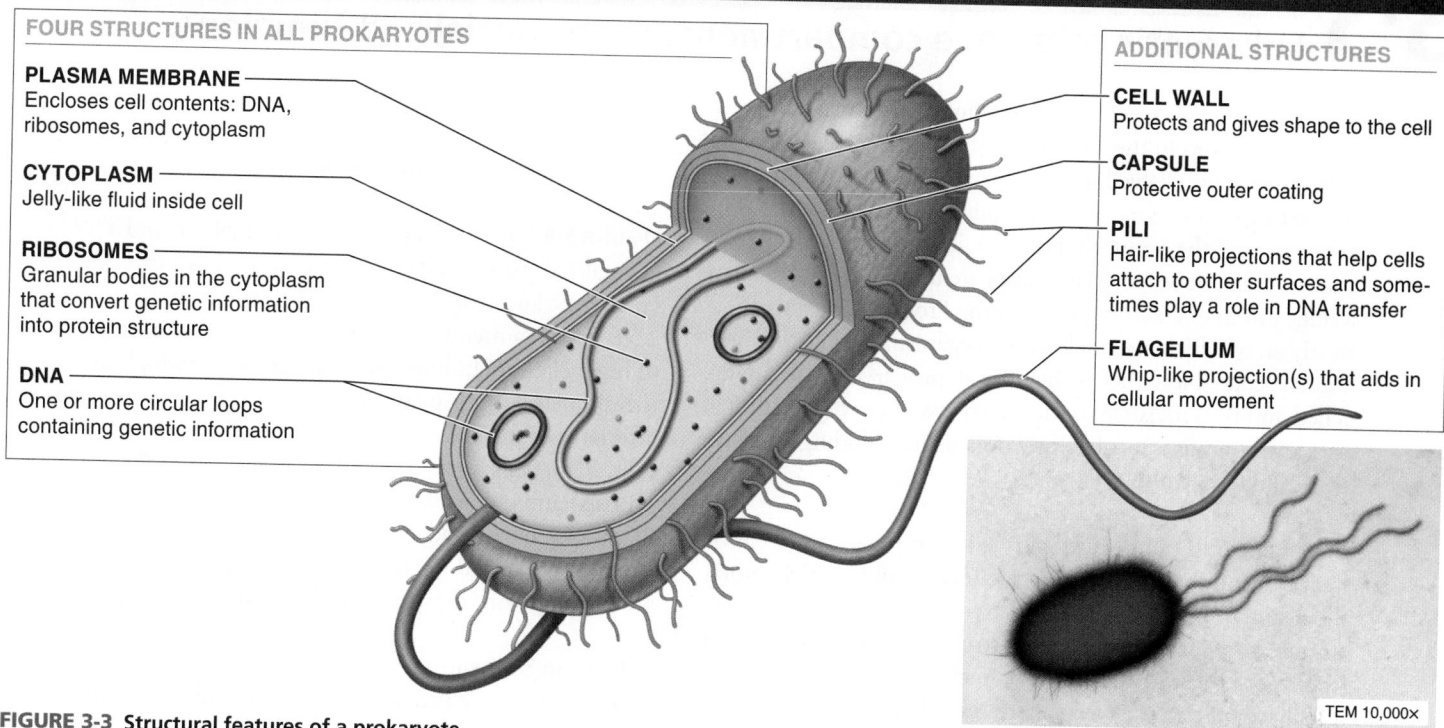

FOUR STRUCTURES IN ALL PROKARYOTES

PLASMA MEMBRANE
Encloses cell contents: DNA, ribosomes, and cytoplasm

CYTOPLASM
Jelly-like fluid inside cell

RIBOSOMES
Granular bodies in the cytoplasm that convert genetic information into protein structure

DNA
One or more circular loops containing genetic information

ADDITIONAL STRUCTURES

CELL WALL
Protects and gives shape to the cell

CAPSULE
Protective outer coating

PILI
Hair-like projections that help cells attach to other surfaces and sometimes play a role in DNA transfer

FLAGELLUM
Whip-like projection(s) that aids in cellular movement

TEM 10,000×

FIGURE 3-3 Structural features of a prokaryote.

In addition to the characteristics common to all prokaryotes, some prokaryotes have additional, unique features. Many have a rigid **cell wall,** for example, that protects and gives shape to the cell. Some have a slimy, sugary capsule as their outermost layer. This sticky outer coat provides protection and enhances the prokaryotes' ability to anchor themselves in place when necessary.

Many prokaryotes have a **flagellum** (*pl.* **flagella**), a long, thin, whip-like projection that rotates like a propeller and moves the cell through the medium in which it lives. Other appendages include **pili** (*sing.* **pilus**), much thinner, hair-like projections that help prokaryotes attach to surfaces and can serve as "tubes" through which they exchange DNA.

You may think you've never encountered a prokaryote, but you are already familiar with the largest group of prokaryotes: the bacteria. All bacteria are prokaryotes, from those such as *Escherichia coli* (*E. coli*), which live in your intestine and helps your body make some essential vitamins, to those responsible for illness, such as *Streptococcus pyogenes,* which causes strep

throat. Another recently discovered group of organisms, the archaea, are also prokaryotes.

From our human perspective, it is easy to underestimate the prokaryotes. Although prokaryotes are smaller, evolutionarily older, and structurally more simple than eukaryotes, they are fantastically diverse metabolically (i.e., in the way they break down and build up molecules). Among many other innovations, bacteria can fuel their activities in the presence or absence of oxygen, using almost any energy source on earth, depending on the type of bacteria—from the sulfur in deep-sea hydrothermal vents to hydrogen to the sun.

TAKE-HOME MESSAGE 3·2

Every cell on earth is either a eukaryotic or a prokaryotic cell. Prokaryotes, which have no nucleus, were the first cells on earth. They are all single-celled organisms. Prokaryotes include the bacteria and archaea and, as a group, are characterized by tremendous metabolic diversity.

3·3 Eukaryotic cells have compartments with specialized functions.

Eukaryotes showed up about 1.5 billion years after prokaryotes, and in the 2 billion years that they have been on earth, they have evolved into some of the most dramatic and interesting creatures, such as platypuses, dolphins, giant sequoias, and the Venus flytrap. Not all eukaryotes are multicellular, however. Many fungi are unicellular, and there is a huge group of eukaryotes, called the Protista (or protists), nearly all of which are single-celled organisms visible only with a microscope. Nonetheless, because all prokaryotes are single-celled and thus invisible to the naked eye, every organism that we see around us is a eukaryotic organism, including all plants and animals (**FIGURE 3-4**).

Eukaryotic cells can be distinguished from prokaryotic cells by their size and their numerous structural features. Chief among the distinguishing features of eukaryotic cells is the presence of a **nucleus,** a membrane-enclosed structure that contains linear strands of DNA. In addition to a nucleus, eukaryotic cells usually contain in their cytoplasm several other specialized structures. Many of these structures, called **organelles,** are enclosed separately within their own lipid membranes. Eukaryotic cells are also about 10 times larger than prokaryotes. All of these physical differences make it easy to distinguish eukaryotes from prokaryotes under a microscope (**FIGURE 3-5**).

Organelles enable eukaryotic cells to do many things that a prokaryotic cell cannot do. Most important, the physical separation of compartments means that there can be distinct areas within the same cell in which different chemical reactions can occur simultaneously. In the mostly non-compartmentalized interior of a prokaryotic cell, random molecular movements quickly blend the chemicals throughout the cell, reducing the ease with which different reactions can occur simultaneously.

FIGURE 3-6 illustrates a generalized animal cell and a generalized plant cell. Because they share a common, eukaryotic ancestor, they have much in common. Both can have a plasma membrane, nucleus, cytoskeleton, and a host of organelles, including rough and smooth endoplasmic membranes, Golgi apparatus, and mitochondria. Animal cells have centrioles, which are not present in most plant cells. Plant cells have a rigid cell wall (as do fungi and many protists) and chloroplasts (also found in some protists). Plants also have a vacuole, a large central chamber (only occasionally found in animal cells). We explore each of these animal and plant organelles in detail later in this chapter.

When you compare a complex eukaryotic cell with the structurally simple prokaryotic cell, it's hard not to wonder how eukaryotic cells came about. How did they get filled up with so many organelles? We can't go back 2 billion years to watch the initial evolution of eukaryotic cells, but there is considerable evidence for some of what occurred. In particular, a theory called **endosymbiosis** provides the best explanation for the presence of two organelles in eukaryotes: chloroplasts in plants and algae, and mitochondria in plants and animals. Chloroplasts help plants and algae convert sunlight into a more usable form of energy. Mitochondria help plants and animals harness the energy stored in food molecules. (Chapter 4, on energy, explains the details of both of these processes.)

Venus flytrap

Golden-headed lion tamarin

Yellow-fuzz cone slime mold

FIGURE 3-4 Diversity of the eukaryotes. Every organism that we can see without magnification is a eukaryotic organism.

EUKARYOTIC vs. PROKARYOTIC CELLS

Nucleus

Other organelles

TEM 6,000×

TEM 10,000×

TYPICAL EUKARYOTIC CELL FEATURES
• DNA contained in nucleus.
• Larger than prokaryotes—usually at least 10 times bigger.
• Cytoplasm contains specialized structures called organelles.

TYPICAL PROKARYOTIC CELL FEATURES
• No nucleus—DNA is in the cytoplasm.
• Internal structures mostly not organized into compartments.
• Much smaller than eukaryotes.

FIGURE 3-5 Comparison of eukaryotic and prokaryotic cells.

According to the theory of endosymbiosis, two different types of prokaryotes may have set up close partnerships with each other. For example, some small prokaryotes capable of performing photosynthesis (the process by which plant cells capture light energy from the sun and transform it into the chemical energy stored in food molecules) may have come to live inside a larger

Q

Humans, deep down, may be part bacteria. How can that be?

"host" prokaryote. The photosynthetic "boarder" may have made some of the energy from its photosynthesis available to the host.

After a long while, the two cells may have become more and more dependent on each other, until neither cell could live without the other (they became "symbiotic"), and

THE ANIMAL CELL: BASIC STRUCTURE

THE PLANT CELL: BASIC STRUCTURE

STRUCTURES FOUND IN BOTH CELLS

Nucleus
Plasma membrane
Ribosomes
Mitochondria
Rough endoplasmic reticulum
Smooth endoplasmic reticulum
Cytoplasm
Cytoskeleton
Golgi apparatus
Lysosome

STRUCTURE NOT FOUND IN PLANT CELLS

Centriole

STRUCTURES NOT FOUND IN ANIMAL CELLS

Chloroplast
Cell wall
Vacuole (occasionally found in animal cells)

FIGURE 3-6 Structures found in animal and plant cells.

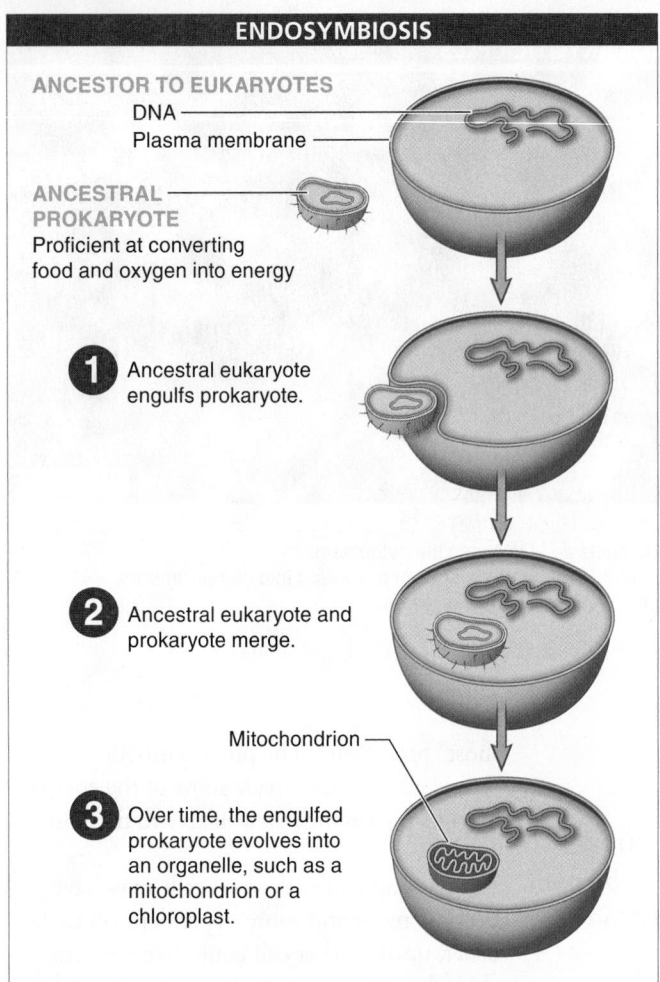

ENDOSYMBIOSIS

ANCESTOR TO EUKARYOTES
DNA
Plasma membrane

ANCESTRAL PROKARYOTE
Proficient at converting food and oxygen into energy

1 Ancestral eukaryote engulfs prokaryote.

2 Ancestral eukaryote and prokaryote merge.

Mitochondrion

3 Over time, the engulfed prokaryote evolves into an organelle, such as a mitochondrion or a chloroplast.

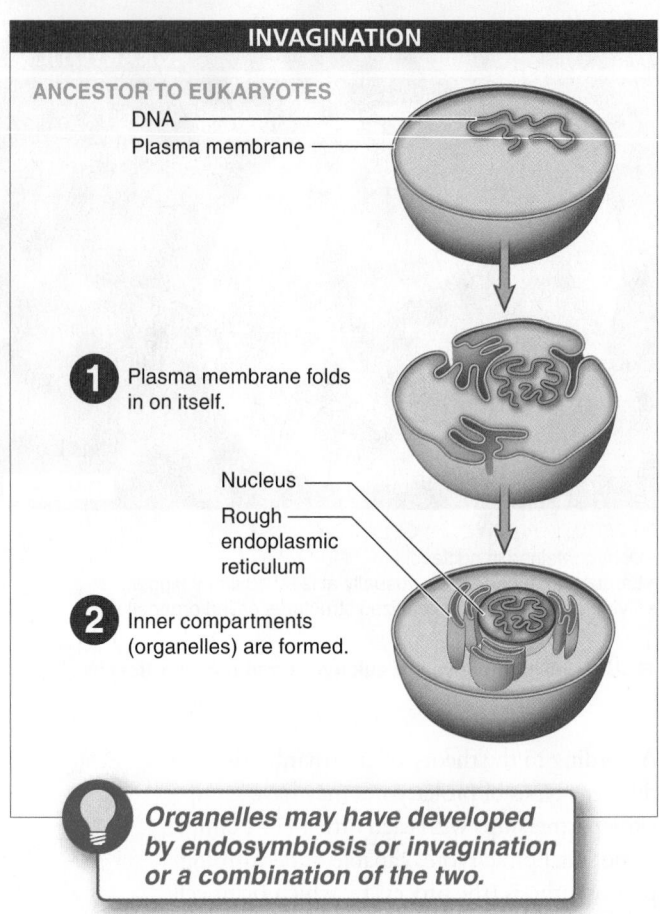

INVAGINATION

ANCESTOR TO EUKARYOTES
DNA
Plasma membrane

1 Plasma membrane folds in on itself.

Nucleus
Rough endoplasmic reticulum

2 Inner compartments (organelles) are formed.

Organelles may have developed by endosymbiosis or invagination or a combination of the two.

FIGURE 3-7 **How did eukaryotic cells become so structurally complex?** Two theories.

they became a single, more complex organism. Eventually, the photosynthetic prokaryote evolved into a **chloroplast,** the organelle in plant cells in which photosynthesis occurs. A similar scenario might explain how a prokaryote unusually efficient at converting food and oxygen into easily usable energy took up residence inside another, host prokaryote and evolved into a **mitochondrion,** the organelle in plant and animal cells that converts the energy stored in food into a form usable by the cell (**FIGURE 3-7**).

The idea of endosymbiosis is supported by several observations.

1. Chloroplasts and mitcochondria are similar in size to prokaryotic cells and divide by splitting (fission), just like prokaryotes.

2. Chloroplasts and mitochondria have internal structures called ribosomes, similar to those found in bacteria, that allow them to synthesize some of their own proteins; this ability is not found in other organelles, which rely on proteins made by cytoplasmic ribosomes.

3. Chloroplasts and mitochondria have small amounts of circular DNA, similar to the circular DNA in prokaryotes and in contrast to the linear DNA strands found in a eukaryote's nucleus.

4. Analysis of chloroplast and mitochondrial DNA has revealed that it is highly related to bacterial DNA, much more closely than it is related to eurkaryotic DNA.

The best current theory about the origin of orther organelles in eukaryotes is a process called **invagination.** The idea is that the plasma membrane around the cell may have folded in on itself to form the inner compartments, which subsequently became modified and specialized (see Figure 3-7).

TAKE-HOME MESSAGE 3·3

Eukaryotes are single-celled or multicellular organisms consisting of cells with a nucleus that contains linear strands of genetic material. The cells also commonly have organelles throughout their cytoplasm; these organelles may have originated evolutionarily through endosymbiosis or invagination, or both.

3·4–3·7 Cell membranes are gatekeepers.

Like gatekeepers, cell membranes control the movement of material into and out of the cell.

3·4 Every cell is bordered by a plasma membrane.

Just as skin covers our bodies, every cell of every living thing on earth, whether a prokaryote or a eukaryote, is enclosed by a plasma membrane, a two-layered membrane that holds the contents of a cell in place and regulates what enters and leaves the cell. Plasma membranes are thin (a stack of a thousand would be only as thick as a single hair) and flexible, and in photos or diagrams the membranes often resemble simple plastic bags, holding the cell contents in place. This image is a gross oversimplification, however. Membranes are indeed thin and flexible, but they are far from simple: a close look at a plasma membrane will reveal that its surface is filled with pores, outcroppings, channels, and complex molecules floating around within the two layers of the membrane itself (**FIGURE 3-8**).

Plasma membranes are such complex structures because they perform several critical functions beyond simply holding a cell's interior contents. Cells, after all, are perpetually interacting with their external environment. They take in food and nutrients and dispose of waste products. Cells take in water. They build and export molecules needed elsewhere in the body. They mediate communications and adhesion with the external environment and other cells. And, like the booths or checkpoints at a country's borders that control the flow of people into and out of the country, plasma membranes serve as gatekeepers that control the flow of molecules into and out of the cell.

The foundation of all plasma membranes is a layer of lipid molecules all packed together. These are a special type of lipid, called **phospholipids,** which, as you may recall from Section 2-13, have what appear to be a head and two long tails. The head consists of a molecule of **glycerol** linked to a molecule containing phosphorus (**FIGURE 3-9**). This head region is said to be **polar,** because the electrons are not shared equally among the atoms, leading to regions of partial positive and partial negative charge. As you may recall from Chapter 2, water is also a polar molecule and, for this reason, other polar molecules mix easily with water. Molecules that can mix with water are described as **hydrophilic** ("water-loving") molecules. The two tails of the phospholipid are long chains of carbon and hydrogen atoms. Because the electrons in these bonds are shared equally, the carbon-hydrogen chains are **nonpolar.** And because they are nonpolar, these tails do not mix with water and are said to be **hydrophobic** ("water-fearing"). The chemical structure of phospholipids gives them a sort of split personality: their hydrophilic head region mixes easily with water, while their hydrophobic tail region does not mix with water.

The split personality of phospholipids makes them good membrane material. Once a large number of phospholipids are packed together with all of their heads facing one way and their tails the other, we have a sheet with one side that is hydrophilic and one that is hydrophobic. In a cell's plasma membrane, two of these sheets of phospholipids are arranged

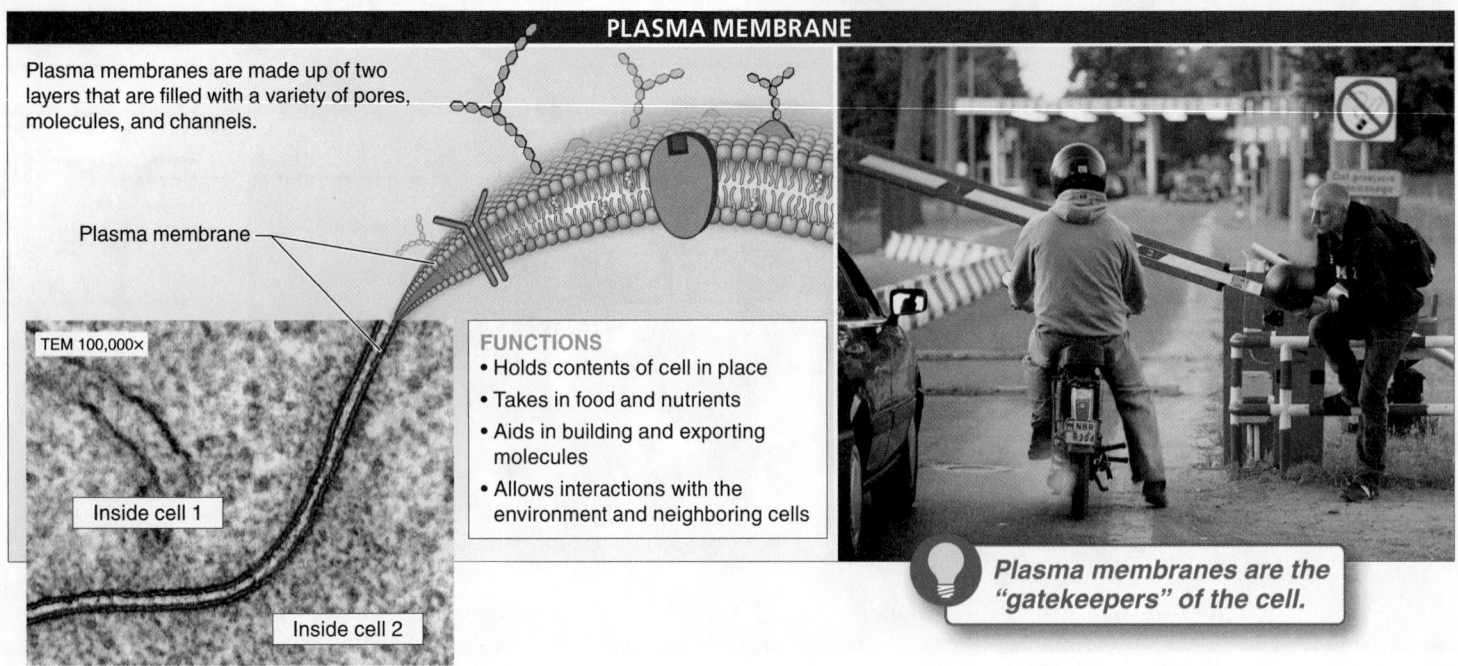

Plasma membranes are made up of two layers that are filled with a variety of pores, molecules, and channels.

Plasma membrane

TEM 100,000×

Inside cell 1

Inside cell 2

FUNCTIONS
- Holds contents of cell in place
- Takes in food and nutrients
- Aids in building and exporting molecules
- Allows interactions with the environment and neighboring cells

Plasma membranes are the "gatekeepers" of the cell.

FIGURE 3-8 More than just an outer layer. The plasma membrane performs several critical functions beyond simply enclosing a cell's interior contents.

so that the hydrophobic tails are all in contact with one another and the hydrophilic heads are in contact with the watery solution outside and inside the cell (see Figure 3-9). This arrangement gives us another way to describe the structure of the plasma membrane: as a **phospholipid bilayer.**

The phospholipids are not locked in place in the plasma membrane; they just float around their side of the bilayer. They cannot pop out of the membrane, or flop from one side to the other, because their hydrophobic tails always line up away from any watery solution. Just as similarly charged sides of two magnets push away from each other, so do the

PHOSPHOLIPID BILAYER: STRUCTURE

HYDROPHILIC HEAD (POLAR)
- Attracted to water
- Composed of a glycerol linked to a phosphorus-containing molecule

HYDROPHOBIC TAILS (NONPOLAR)
- Not attracted to water
- Composed of carbon-hydrogen chains

EXTRACELLULAR FLUID
Watery fluid outside cell

INTRACELLULAR FLUID
Watery fluid inside cell

Plasma membrane

Hydrophilic heads extend toward the intracellular and extracellular fluid, and hydrophobic tails are directed away from these watery fluids.

FIGURE 3-9 Good membrane material. The phospholipid bilayer of the plasma membrane prevents fluid from leaking out of the cell.

hydrophobic tails in the center of the membrane push away from and avoid coming into contact with water molecules. Because the center part of the bilayer membrane is made up of hydrophobic lipids, the solution on one side of the membrane cannot leak across into the solution on the other side. In this way, the plasma membrane forms a boundary around the cell's contents.

3·5 Molecules embedded in the plasma membrane help it perform its functions.

While the plasma membrane's phospholipid bilayer construction forms the cell's basic boundary with its environment, there is much more to a plasma membrane. Embedded within or attached to the phospholipid bilayer are different types of protein, carbohydrate, and lipid molecules (**FIGURE 3-10**), which serve many different roles.

The proteins found in the plasma membrane enable it to carry out most of its gatekeeping functions. For every 50–100 phospholipids in the membrane, there is one protein molecule. Some of these proteins, called **transmembrane proteins,** penetrate right through the lipid bilayer, from one side to the other. Others, called **surface proteins** or peripheral proteins, reside primarily on the inner or outer surface of the membrane.

What determines whether a protein resides on the surface or extends through the bilayer? Its tertiary structure. Remember from Chapter 2 that all the amino acids that make up each protein have side chains that differ from one another chemically. Some of these side chains are hydrophobic, others are hydrophilic, and as a protein is assembled into its final shape, these side chains can cause parts of the protein to be attracted to hydrophobic or hydrophilic regions. Because a transmembrane protein has both hydrophobic and hydrophilic regions, part of the protein can be positioned in the hydrophobic region in the center of the membrane while the other parts reside in the hydrophilic regions. Peripheral membrane proteins, on the other hand, have an entirely hydrophilic structure and reside on the membrane surface, bound only to the head regions of the phospholipids. As a consequence, they can be positioned on either the outer or the inner side of the membrane.

Once membrane proteins are in place, the hydrophobic and hydrophilic forces keep them properly oriented. Because all of the components of the plasma membrane are held in the membrane in this manner, they can float around without ever popping out.

There are four primary types of membrane proteins, each of which performs a different function (**FIGURE 3-11**).

1. Receptor proteins are surface or transmembrane proteins that bind to chemicals in the cell's external environment and, by doing so, regulate certain processes within the cell. Cells in the heart, for example, have receptor proteins that bind to adrenaline, a chemical released into the bloodstream in times of extreme stress or fright. When adrenaline binds to these heart cells, the cells increase the heart's rate of contraction to pump blood through the body more quickly. You have experienced this reaction if you've ever been startled and felt your heart start to pound.

MOLECULES WITHIN THE PLASMA MEMBRANE

Extracellular fluid

Hydrophilic region
Hydrophobic region

Carbohydrates

Plasma membrane

Transmembrane protein

Lipids

Surface proteins

Intracellular fluid

Hydrophobic and hydrophilic forces determine the orientation of proteins in the plasma membrane.

FIGURE 3-10 Protein, carbohydrate, and lipid molecules are embedded in the plasma membrane.

Extracellular fluid

CARBOHYDRATE CHAINS
Provide a "fingerprint" for the cell, so it can be recognized by other cells

CHOLESTEROL
Helps the membrane retain its flexibility

REACTIONS

Intracellular fluid

REACTIONS

RECEPTOR PROTEINS
Bind to external chemicals in order to regulate processes within the cell

RECOGNITION PROTEINS
Provide a "fingerprint" for the cell, so it can be recognized by other cells

TRANSPORT PROTEINS
Provide a passageway for molecules to travel into and out of the cell

ENZYMATIC PROTEINS
Accelerate intracellular and extracellular reactions on the plasma membrane

FIGURE 3-11 Plasma membrane molecules serve diverse roles.

2. Recognition proteins are surface or transmembrane proteins that give each cell a "fingerprint" that makes it possible for the body's immune system (which fights off infections) to distinguish the cells that belong inside your body from those that are invaders and need to be attacked. (Note that carbohydrates also play a role in recognition.) Recognition proteins also can help cells bind to or adhere to other cells or molecules.

3. Transport proteins are transmembrane proteins that help polar or charged substances pass through the plasma membrane. Transport proteins come in a variety of shapes and sizes, making it possible for a wide variety of molecules to be transported.

4. Enzymatic proteins are surface or transmembrane proteins (enzymes) that accelerate chemical reactions on the plasma membrane's surface. (A variety of enzymatic proteins exist, with some accelerating reactions on the inside of the plasma membrane and others accelerating reactions on the outside of the plasma membrane.)

In addition to the various kinds of membrane proteins, two other types of molecules—carbohydrate chains and cholesterol—can be incorporated in a cell's plasma membrane.

Short, branched carbohydrate chains that are attached to proteins or to phospholipid heads on the outside of the cell membrane serve as part of a membrane's fingerprint, along with recognition proteins. This fingerprint allows the cell to be recognized by other cells, such as those of the immune system.

The plasma membrane also can contain the lipid **cholesterol,** which helps the membrane maintain its flexibility. Cholesterol prevents the membrane from becoming too fluid or floppy at moderate temperatures and acts as a sort of antifreeze, preventing the membrane from becoming too rigid at freezing temperatures. The membranes of some cells are about 25% cholesterol; other plasma membranes, such as those of most bacteria and plants, have no cholesterol at all.

As we've seen, the plasma membrane is made up from several different types of molecules, like a mosaic, and many of those molecules float around, held in a proper orientation by hydrophobic and hydrophilic forces, but not always anchored in place. For these reasons, the plasma membrane is often described as a **fluid mosaic.**

TAKE-HOME MESSAGE 3·5

The plasma membrane is a fluid mosaic of proteins, lipids, and carbohydrates. Proteins found in the plasma membrane enable it to carry out most of its gatekeeping functions. The proteins act as receptors, help molecules gain entry into and exit from the cell, and catalyze reactions on the inner and outer cell surfaces. In conjunction with carbohydrates, some plasma membrane proteins identify the cell to other cells. And, in addition to the phospholipids that make up most of the plasma membrane, cholesterol is an important lipid in some membranes, influencing fluidity.

3·6 Faulty membranes can cause disease.

With all the complexity of plasma membranes, it's not surprising that there are many ways in which they can malfunction. One disease that results from an improperly functioning membrane is cystic fibrosis, the single most common fatal inherited disease in the United States. At any given time, about 30,000 people in the United States have cystic fibrosis.

Cystic fibrosis occurs when an individual inherits from both parents incorrect genetic instructions for producing one type of transmembrane protein that allows chloride ions to get into and out of cells. This transport protein occurs primarily in the membranes of cells in the lungs and digestive tract.

There are more than a thousand different ways in which these genetic instructions can be defective, but the result is the same: malfunction of chloride passageways in a cell's membrane that causes gradual accumulation of chloride ions within cells. In nearly all cases of cystic fibrosis, two primary effects occur: an improper salt balance in the cells and a buildup of thick, sticky mucus—particularly in the lungs. Normal mucus helps to protect the lungs by trapping dust and bacteria. This mucus is then moved out of the lungs (helped along by coughing). The mucus produced by

someone with cystic fibrosis, however, is too thick and sticky to be moved out of the lungs, so it collects there, where it impairs lung function and increases the risk of bacterial infection. Because of the improper cellular salt balance, one way to test for cystic fibrosis is to measure the concentration of salt in the sweat—abnormally high concentrations indicate that the person may have the disease.

Although many high-tech treatments have been promised for the sufferers of cystic fibrosis and a great deal of research is being done on this disease, one of the most common treatments is decidedly low-tech. Parents help their children with cystic fibrosis clear the mucus out of their lungs by holding them on a steep slant, almost upside down, and vigorously patting or thumping their chest and back. This shakes loose the mucus in their lungs and moves it to a place where they can cough it up (**FIGURE 3-12**). With careful treatment, the life expectancy of someone with cystic fibrosis can be 35–40 years or longer.

While faulty membranes can cause a disorder as serious as cystic fibrosis, pharmaceutical tinkering with cell membranes can alter cellular function in ways that have beneficial effects. For example, a group of drugs called

TREATING CYSTIC FIBROSIS

The thick and sticky mucus produced by someone with cystic fibrosis collects in the lungs, impairing lung function and increasing the risk of bacterial infection.

"Thumping" on the chest and back can loosen the mucus.

The vest, by inflating and deflating rapidly, can have a similar effect in the course of a 20-minute session.

FIGURE 3-12 Moving mucus manually, or through an inhalation vest.

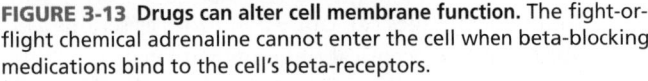

1 In stressful situations, the adrenal glands pump out adrenaline.

2 Adrenaline binds with beta-receptors on cells, causing a faster heartbeat and increased blood pressure.

3 Beta-blocker chemicals bind to receptors and prevent adrenaline from binding to the cell.

FIGURE 3-13 Drugs can alter cell membrane function. The fight-or-flight chemical adrenaline cannot enter the cell when beta-blocking medications bind to the cell's beta-receptors.

> 💡 *By binding to adrenaline receptors, beta-blockers reduce anxiety symptoms.*

"beta-blockers" is extremely effective at reducing anxiety. This effect was discovered almost accidentally—the drugs were actually developed as a treatment for high blood pressure.

Q Why do "beta-blockers" reduce anxiety?

Here's how beta-blockers work. Many cells in your body, particularly the cells of the heart, have receptor proteins on their plasma membranes that can bind to adrenaline, which helps your body cope with stressful situations. These receptor proteins are called "beta-adrenergic receptors." In stressful situations, your adrenal glands pump out adrenaline (**FIGURE 3-13**). On reaching cells in your heart (among other locations in your body) and binding to beta-receptors, the adrenaline promptly causes your heart to beat faster and more forcefully, increasing your blood pressure in the process. This reaction is fine in a short-term fight-or-flight situation, but it is not healthy over the long run because the increased pressure can damage blood vessels. Depending on its severity, this reaction can also be problematic if you are giving

a presentation or taking a test, or if you're in any other anxiety-producing situation.

When you take a beta-blocker pill, the pill dissolves and the chemicals travel throughout your body until they encounter the beta-receptors. They bind to the receptors, hold on, and block the adrenaline from doing its job. This outcome slows your heart rate, causes a reduction in blood pressure, and can bring great relief to those suffering from the sweating and trembling associated with anxiety.

TAKE-HOME MESSAGE 3·6

Normal cell functioning can be disrupted when cell membranes—particularly the proteins embedded in them—do not function properly. Such malfunctions can cause health problems, such as cystic fibrosis. But disruption of normal cell membrane function can also have beneficial, therapeutic effects, such as in the treatment of high blood pressure and anxiety.

3·7 Membrane surfaces have a "fingerprint" that identifies the cell.

As mentioned earlier, every cell in your body has a "fingerprint" made from a variety of molecules on the outside-facing surface of the cell membrane. Some of these membrane molecules vary, depending on the specific function of the cell. Others are common to all of your cells and convey to your immune system: "I belong here." Cells with an improper fingerprint are recognized as foreign and are attacked by your body's defenses.

Throughout our evolutionary history, this system has been tremendously valuable in helping our bodies fight infection. In some cases, however, this vigilance is a problem, like a car alarm that goes off even when you don't want it to. Suppose you receive a liver (or any other organ) transplant. Even if the donor is a close relative, the molecular fingerprint on the cells of the donated liver is not identical to your own. Consequently, your body sees the new organ as a foreign object and puts up a fight against it (**FIGURE 3-14**). Because your body will naturally try to reject the new organ, doctors must administer drugs that suppress your immune system. Immune suppression helps you tolerate the new liver, but, as you can imagine, it leaves you without some of the defenses to fight off other foreign invaders, such as bacteria that may cause infection. The presence or absence of certain molecular markers on plasma membranes is also responsible for a person's blood type and can lead to problems with simple blood transfusions.

Q Why is it extremely unlikely that a person will catch HIV from casual contact—such as shaking hands—with an infected individual?

The AIDS-causing virus, HIV, uses the molecular markers on plasma membranes to infect an individual's cells. These same molecular markers are also the reason that it is extremely unlikely that you can catch an HIV infection from casual contact with an infected individual, such as shaking his or her hand. The specific molecular markers involved in infection by HIV belong to a group of identifying markers called "clusters of differentiation." Abbreviated as "CD markers" and having names such as CD1, CD2, and CD3, these marker molecules are proteins embedded in the plasma membrane that enable a cell

MOLECULAR FINGERPRINTS AND ORGAN TRANSPLANTS

Liver transplant recipient

Molecular fingerprint (on membrane surfaces) of recipient

Donor liver

Molecular fingerprint (on membrane surfaces) of donor liver

POSSIBLE OUTCOMES

Liver is rejected.

Liver is accepted after drugs are administered to suppress the immune system.

FIGURE 3-14 Mismatched molecular fingerprints can cause difficulty in organ transplantation.

to bind to outside molecules and, sometimes, transport them into the cell.

One CD marker, called the CD4 marker, is found only on cells deep within the body and in the bloodstream, such as

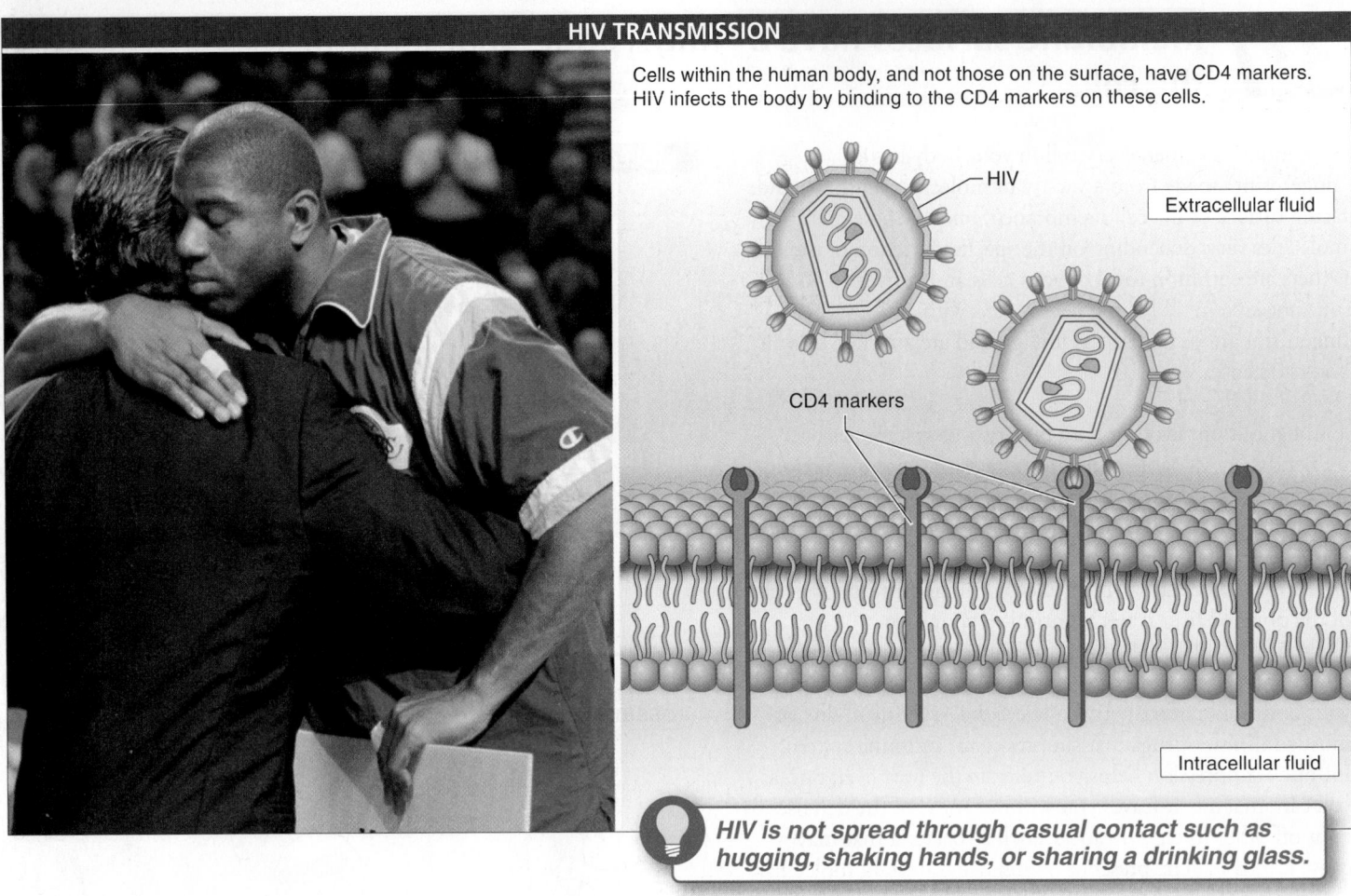

Cells within the human body, and not those on the surface, have CD4 markers. HIV infects the body by binding to the CD4 markers on these cells.

HIV

Extracellular fluid

CD4 markers

Intracellular fluid

HIV is not spread through casual contact such as hugging, shaking hands, or sharing a drinking glass.

FIGURE 3-15 HIV requires CD4 markers—not found on skin cells—to infect the body.

immune system cells and some nerve cells. It is the CD4 marker, in conjunction with another receptor, that is targeted by HIV. If the virus can find a cell with a CD4 marker, it can infect you, and because the CD4 markers *never* occur on the surface of your skin cells, casual contact such as touching is very unlikely to transmit the virus (**FIGURE 3-15**). Even if millions of HIV particles are present on a person's hands, they just can't gain access into any of the other person's surface cells.

How does HIV get transmitted? Far and away, the most common methods of transmission involve the transfer of blood, semen, vaginal fluid, or breast milk from one individual to another. Particles of the virus as well as cells infected by the virus are present in these fluids. Consequently,

the chief routes of transmission are from an infected mother to her child in breast milk, from an infected mother to her baby at birth, the use of contaminated needles, and unprotected sexual intercourse. Because an open sore or cut might expose some of the cells in your bloodstream to the outside world, however, it is not impossible for casual transmission of HIV to occur.

TAKE-HOME MESSAGE 3·7

Every cell in your body has a "fingerprint" made from a variety of molecules on the outside-facing surface of the cell membrane. This molecular fingerprint is key to the function of your immune system.

3·8–3·11 Molecules move across membranes in several ways.

Passage of proteins between cells can be tracked (junctions between these human cancer cells are stained red and green).

3·8 Passive transport is the spontaneous diffusion of molecules across a membrane.

To function properly, cells must take in food and/or other necessary materials and must move out metabolic waste and molecules produced for use elsewhere in the body. In some cases, this movement of molecules requires energy and is called active transport. (We cover active transport later in this chapter.) In other cases, the molecular movement occurs spontaneously, without the input of energy, and is called **passive transport.** There are two types of passive transport: diffusion and osmosis. (Osmosis is discussed in Section 3-9.)

Diffusion is passive transport in which a particle, called a **solute,** is dissolved in a gas or liquid (a **solvent**) and moves from an area of high solute concentration to an area of lower concentration (**FIGURE 3-16**). In the absence of other forces, molecules of a substance will always tend to move from where they are more concentrated to where they are less concentrated. This movement occurs because molecules move randomly and are equally likely to move in any direction. And when certain molecules are highly concentrated, they keep

bumping into each other and eventually end up evenly distributed. For this reason, we say that molecules tend to *move down their concentration gradient.* For a simple illustration, drop a tiny bit of food coloring into a bowl of water and wait for a few minutes. The molecules of dye are initially clustered together in a very high concentration. Gradually, they disperse down their concentration gradient until the color is equally spread throughout the bowl.

In cells, molecules such as oxygen (O_2) and carbon dioxide (CO_2) that are small and carry no charge can pass directly through the phospholipid bilayer of the membrane without the assistance of any other molecules, in a process called **simple diffusion.** Each time you take a breath, for example, there is a high concentration of O_2 molecules in the air you pull into your lungs. That oxygen diffuses across the plasma membranes of the lung cells and into your bloodstream, where red blood cells pick it up and deliver it to parts of your body where it is needed. Similarly, because CO_2 in your bloodstream is at a higher concentration than in the air in

DIFFUSION

1 A solute, such as food coloring, is dropped into a solvent, such as water.

Food coloring

2 Food-coloring molecules move about randomly, bumping into each other.

Food-coloring molecules

3 The random motion of the food-coloring molecules causes them to end up evenly distributed.

FIGURE 3-16 Diffusion: a form of passive transport that results in an even distribution of molecules.

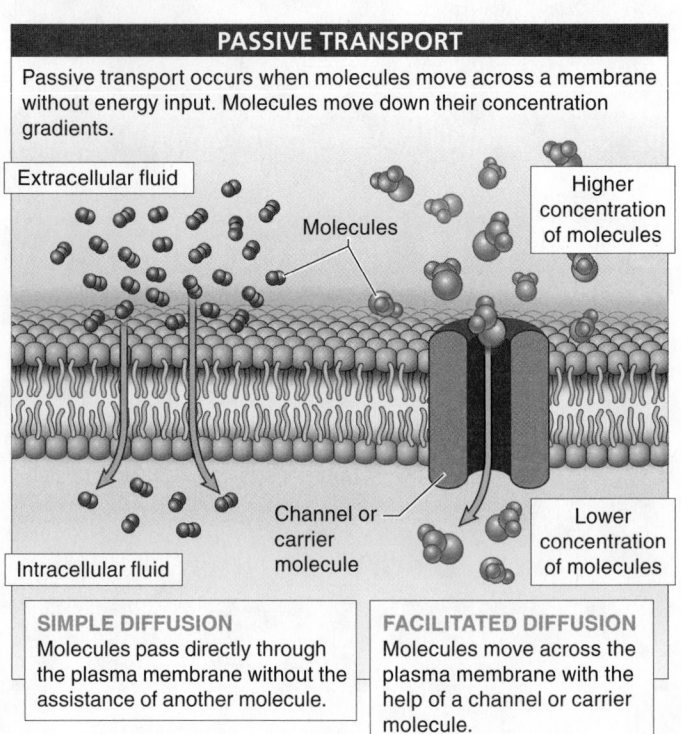

PASSIVE TRANSPORT

Passive transport occurs when molecules move across a membrane without energy input. Molecules move down their concentration gradients.

Extracellular fluid

Molecules

Higher concentration of molecules

Channel or carrier molecule

Intracellular fluid

Lower concentration of molecules

SIMPLE DIFFUSION
Molecules pass directly through the plasma membrane without the assistance of another molecule.

FACILITATED DIFFUSION
Molecules move across the plasma membrane with the help of a channel or carrier molecule.

FIGURE 3-17 Simple and facilitated diffusion: no energy required.

your lungs, it diffuses from your blood into your lungs and is released to the atmosphere when you exhale (**FIGURE 3-17**).

Most molecules, however, can't get through plasma membranes on their own. They may be electrically charged (polar) and, hence, are repelled by the hydrophobic middle region of the phospholipid bilayer. Or the molecules may be too big to squeeze through the membrane. Nonetheless, when there is a concentration gradient from one side of the membrane to the other, these molecules may still be able to diffuse across the membrane, down their concentration gradient, with the help of a channel or carrier molecule—one of the transport proteins, which we discussed in Section 3-5. Often, this transport protein spans the membrane and functions like a revolving door. When spontaneous diffusion across a plasma membrane requires a transport protein, it is called **facilitated diffusion** (see Figure 3-17).

Defects in transport proteins can reduce facilitated diffusion or even bring it to a complete stop, with serious health consequences. Many genetic diseases are the result of inheriting incorrect genetic instructions for building transport proteins. In the disease cystinuria, incorrect genetic instructions result in a malformed transport protein in the plasma membrane. When structured and functioning properly, this transport protein facilitates the diffusion of some amino acids (including cystine, from which the disease gets its name) out of the

kidneys into the urine. When the proteins are malformed, they cannot facilitate this diffusion and these amino acids build up in the kidneys, forming painful and dangerous kidney stones.

Diffusion across membranes doesn't occur just in animals—we see it in all organisms on earth. As we'll see in Chapter 4, one of the most important biological processes on earth is the diffusion of CO_2 from the atmosphere (an area of relatively high concentration) into the leaf cells of plants (areas of relatively low concentration), where it can be attached to other molecules, forming sugars through photosynthesis. At the same time, O_2 diffuses out of the leaves and into the atmosphere.

TAKE-HOME MESSAGE 3·8

For proper functioning, cells must acquire food molecules and/or other necessary materials from outside the cell. Similarly, metabolic waste molecules and molecules produced for use elsewhere in the body must move out of the cell. In passive transport—which includes simple and facilitated diffusion and osmosis—the molecular movement occurs spontaneously, without the input of energy. This generally occurs as molecules move down their concentration gradient.

3·9 Osmosis is the passive diffusion of water across a membrane.

Just as solute molecules will passively diffuse down their concentration gradients, water molecules will also move from areas of high concentration to areas of low concentration to equalize the concentration of water inside and outside the cell. The diffusion of water across a membrane is a special type of passive transport called **osmosis** (**FIGURE 3-18**). Just as solute molecules may diffuse across a plasma membrane, molecules of water also move across the membrane, equalizing the water

concentration inside and outside the cell. (Although some water can pass through the lipid bilayer, the hydrophobic region severely limits this flow. Most of the rapid movement of water in and out of cells occurs through "water channels," called *aquaporins,* that are transmembrane proteins with hydrophilic channels through which the water molecules pass in single file.)

Osmosis can have some dramatic effects on cells. It turns out that many molecules just can't move across a cell membrane. They may be too big or too charged, or there may not be any carrier molecules in the membrane that can move them. Let's imagine, for instance, that there is a high concentration of a large molecule inside a cell and that it can't pass through the cell membrane. Although the molecule can't move out of the cell and down its concentration gradient, water can move into the cell down *its* concentration gradient. As water diffuses into the cell, the cell will get larger.

When a cell is in a fluid environment (referred to as a solution), the amount of dissolved substances (solutes) in that solution may be (1) equal to, (2) less than, or (3) greater than the concentration of dissolved substances in the cell. This relationship between the concentrations of solutes inside the cell and solutes outside the cell is referred to as **tonicity** (see Figure 3-18).

Let's review how water diffuses across the cell membrane in each of these different tonicity situations.

1. If the concentration of solutes outside the cell is *equal* to the concentration inside the cell, the outside solution is **isotonic.** Although water still moves between the solution and the cell, since it moves at the same rate in both directions, there is no net change in the amount of water inside versus outside the cell.

2. If the concentration of solutes outside the cell is *lower* than the concentration inside the cell, the outside solution is **hypotonic.** In this situation, if the cell membrane is not permeable to the solutes, more water will move into the cell than out of it, and the cell will swell.

3. If the concentration of solutes outside the cell is *higher* than the concentration inside the cell, the outside solution is **hypertonic.** In this situation, if the cell membrane is not permeable to the solutes, more water will move out of the cell than into it, and the cell will shrivel.

OSMOSIS

Osmosis is a type of passive transport by which water diffuses across a membrane, in order to equalize the concentration of water inside and outside the cell. The direction of osmosis is determined by the total amount of solutes on either side of the membrane.

PLANT CELL   **ANIMAL CELL (RED BLOOD CELL)**

ISOTONIC SOLUTION
- Solute concentrations are balanced.
- Water movement is balanced.

Extracellular fluid

HYPOTONIC SOLUTION
- Solute concentrations are lower in the extracellular fluid.
- Water diffuses into cells.

Unlike plant cells, animal cells may explode in hypotonic solutions because they don't have a cell wall to limit cellular expansion.

HYPERTONIC SOLUTION
- Solute concentrations are higher in the extracellular fluid.
- Water diffuses out of cells.

 Water will always move toward a region having a greater concentration of solutes.

FIGURE 3-18 Osmosis overview.

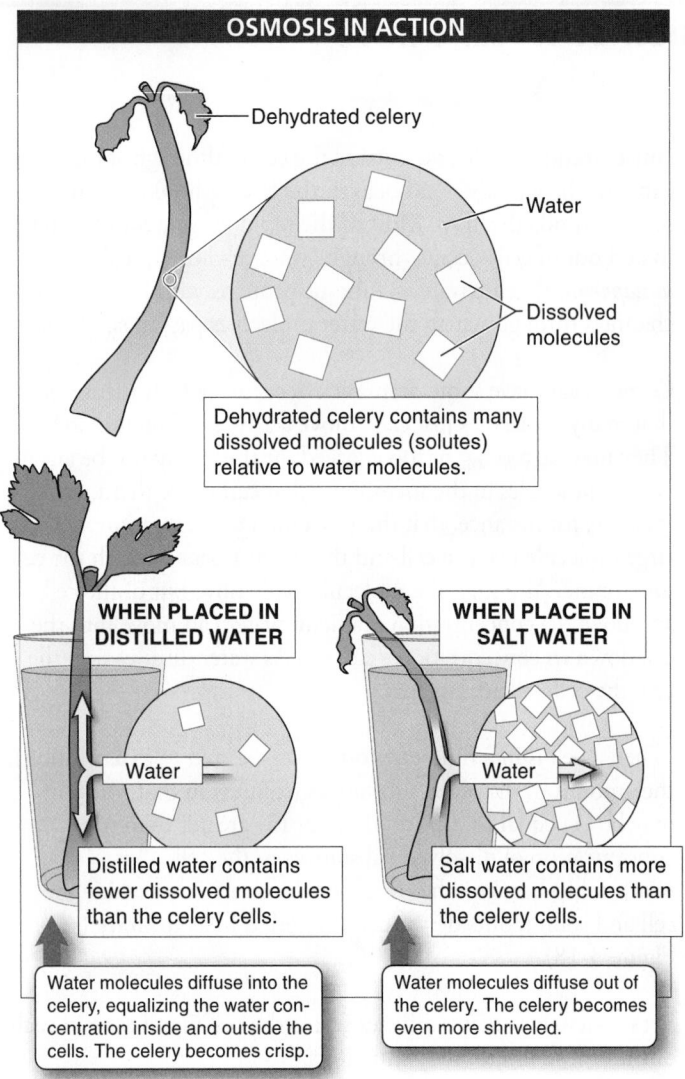

OSMOSIS IN ACTION

Dehydrated celery

Water

Dissolved molecules

Dehydrated celery contains many dissolved molecules (solutes) relative to water molecules.

WHEN PLACED IN DISTILLED WATER

Water

Distilled water contains fewer dissolved molecules than the celery cells.

Water molecules diffuse into the celery, equalizing the water concentration inside and outside the cells. The celery becomes crisp.

WHEN PLACED IN SALT WATER

Water

Salt water contains more dissolved molecules than the celery cells.

Water molecules diffuse out of the celery. The celery becomes even more shriveled.

FIGURE 3-19 Osmosis in your kitchen.

The key to understanding osmosis is to remember that water will always move toward a hypertonic solution.

You can see osmosis in action in your own kitchen (**FIGURE 3-19**). Take a stalk of celery and leave it on the counter for a couple of hours. As water evaporates from the cells of the celery stalk, it will shrink and become limp. You can make it crisp again by placing it in a solution of distilled water. Why distilled water? Because it contains very few dissolved molecules—it is a hypotonic solution. The cells in the celery stalk, on the other hand, contain many dissolved molecules, such as salt. Because those dissolved molecules can't easily pass

across the plasma membrane of the celery stalk cells, the water molecules move into the cells (moving from the pool of distilled water where they are at super-high concentration to the interior of the celery cells where water is scarcer). Would the celery regain its crispness if you placed it in concentrated salt water? No, because in the hypertonic salt solution there are more dissolved solute molecules (and fewer water molecules) outside the celery cells, so what little water remains in the celery cells actually moves, by osmosis, out of the celery, causing it to shrivel even more.

A more practical use of osmosis is seen with the laxative Milk of Magnesia. This product contains magnesium salts, which are poorly absorbed from the digestive tract. As a consequence, after a dose of the laxative, water moves by osmosis from the surrounding cells into the intestines. The water softens the feces in the intestines and increases the fecal volume, thereby relieving constipation.

Q How do laxatives relieve constipation?

It's important to note that the direction of osmosis is determined only by a difference in the *total concentration* of all the molecules dissolved in the water: it does not matter what the solutes are, only how many molecules of solutes there are. To determine which way the water molecules will move, you need to determine the total amount of "dissolved stuff" on either side of the membrane. The water will move toward the side with more stuff dissolved in it. For this reason, even small increases in the salinity of lakes can have disastrous consequences for the organisms living there, from fish to bacteria. Conversely, putting animal cells—such as red blood cells—in distilled water will cause them to explode, because water will diffuse into the cell (which contains more solutes) and the cell will swell and burst. This will not generally happen to plant cells because (as we see later in this chapter) the plant cell plasma membrane is surrounded by a rigid cell wall that limits the amount of cell expansion possible when water moves in by osmosis.

TAKE-HOME MESSAGE 3·9

The diffusion of water across a membrane is a special type of passive transport called osmosis. Water molecules move across the membrane until the concentration of water inside and outside the cell is equalized.

3·10 In active transport, cells use energy to move small molecules into and out of the cell.

Molecules can't always move spontaneously and effortlessly in and out of cells. Sometimes their transport needs energy, in which case the process is called **active transport.** Such energy expenditures may be necessary if the molecules or ions to be moved are being moved *against* their concentration gradient. In all active transport, proteins embedded in the membrane act like motorized revolving doors, pushing molecules into the cell regardless of the concentration of those molecules on either side of the membrane. There are two distinct types of active transport, primary and secondary, which differ only in the source of the fuel that keeps the revolving doors spinning.

The process of digestion provides an example of **primary active transport,** the type of active transport that occurs when energy from ATP is used to fuel the transport of molecules. To help break down the food into more digestible bits, the cells lining your stomach create an acidic environment by pumping large numbers of H^+ ions (also called protons) into the stomach contents, against their concentration gradient (**FIGURE 3-20**). (That is, there are more H^+ ions in the stomach contents than there are inside the cells lining the stomach.) All of this H^+ pumping increases your ability to digest the food but comes at a great energetic cost—in the form of usage of the high-energy molecule ATP—because the protons would not normally flow into a region against their concentration gradient. (We explore ATP in more detail in Chapter 4.)

Many transport proteins use an indirect method of fueling their activities rather than using energy released directly from ATP. In the process of **secondary active transport,** the transport protein simultaneously moves one molecule against its concentration gradient while letting another flow down its concentration gradient. Although no ATP is used directly in this process, at some other time and in some other location, energy from ATP was used to pump one of the types of molecule involved in the secondary transport process against its concentration gradient. The process is a bit like using energy to pump water up to the top of a high water tower. Later, the water can be allowed to run out of the tower over a water wheel, which can, in turn, power a process such as grinding wheat into flour. Our bodies frequently use the energy from one reaction that occurs spontaneously to fuel another reaction that requires energy.

TAKE-HOME MESSAGE 3·10

In active transport, moving molecules across a membrane requires energy. Active transport is necessary if the molecules to be moved are very large or if they are being moved against their concentration gradient. Proteins embedded in the plasma membrane act like motorized revolving doors to actively transport (pump) the molecules.

ACTIVE TRANSPORT

Active transport occurs when the movement of molecules into and out of a cell requires the input of energy. For example, in response to eating, the cells lining your stomach use ATP to pump large numbers of H^+ ions into the stomach.

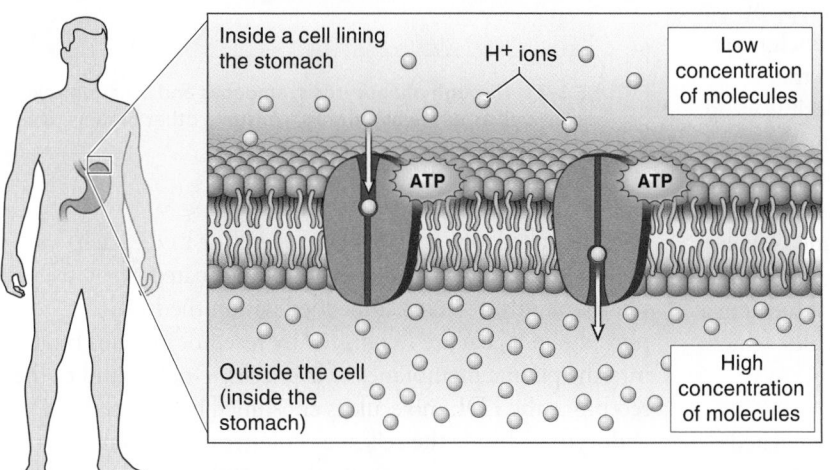

Inside a cell lining the stomach

H^+ ions

Low concentration of molecules

ATP

ATP

Outside the cell (inside the stomach)

High concentration of molecules

FIGURE 3-20 With an input of energy, molecules can be moved against concentration gradients.

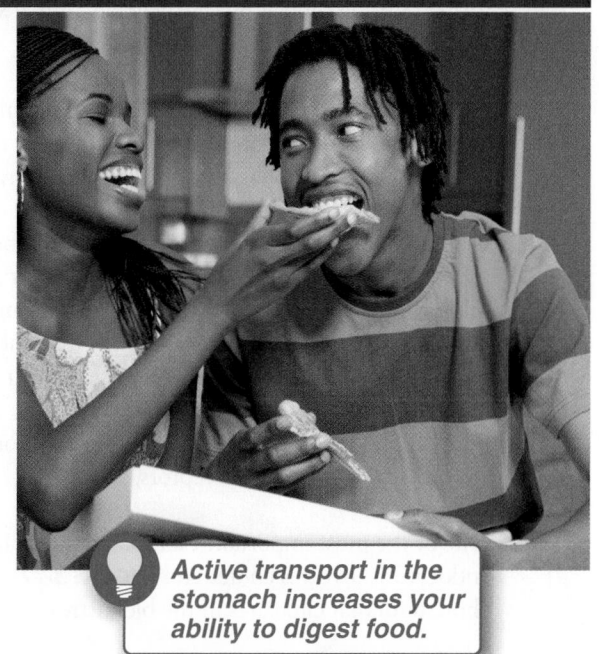

Active transport in the stomach increases your ability to digest food.

3·11

Endocytosis and exocytosis are used for bulk transport of particles.

Many substances are just too big to get into a cell by passive or active transport. To absorb large particles, such as bacterial invaders, cells engulf them with their plasma membrane in a process called **endocytosis.** Cells also have another method besides passive and active transport for moving molecules out of the cell. Cells that manufacture molecules (such as digestive enzymes) for use elsewhere in the body must get those molecules out of the cell, and they often use the process of **exocytosis** to do this.

There are three types of endocytosis: phagocytosis, pinocytosis, and receptor-mediated endocytosis. All three involve the basic process of the plasma membrane oozing around an object that is outside the cell, surrounding it, forming a little pocket called a *vesicle,* and then pinching off the vesicle so that it is inside the cell but separated from the rest of the cell contents.

Phagocytosis and pinocytosis The process by which relatively large particles are engulfed by cells is called **phagocytosis** (**FIGURE 3-21**). Amoebas and other unicellular protists, as well as white blood cells, use phagocytosis to consume entire organisms either as food or as their way of defending against pathogens (disease-causing organisms or substances). Whereas "phagocytosis" comes from the Greek for "eat" and "container," the term **pinocytosis** comes from the Greek for "drink" and "container" and describes the process of cells taking in dissolved particles and liquids. The two processes are largely the same, except that the vesicles formed during pinocytosis are generally much smaller than those formed during phagocytosis.

Receptor-mediated endocytosis The third type of endocytosis, **receptor-mediated endocytosis,** is much more specific than either phagocytosis or pinocytosis. In this process, receptor molecules on the surface of a cell sit waiting until the one type of molecule they recognize bumps into them. For one receptor it might be insulin, for another it might be cholesterol. Many receptors of the same type are often clustered together in a cell's plasma membrane. When the appropriate molecule binds to each of the receptor proteins, the membrane begins to fold inward, first forming a little pit and then completely engulfing the molecules, which are still attached to their receptors.

One of the most important examples of receptor-mediated endocytosis involves cholesterol (**FIGURE 3-22**). Most cholesterol that circulates in the bloodstream is in the form of

particles called low-density lipoproteins, or LDL. Each molecule of LDL is a cholesterol globule coated by phospholipids. Proteins embedded within the LDL's phospholipid coat are recognized by receptor proteins built into the plasma membranes of liver cells. Once bound to the receptors, the LDL molecule is consumed by the cell by endocytosis. Inside the cell, the cholesterol is broken down and used to make a variety of other useful molecules, such as the hormones estrogen and testosterone.

PHAGOCYTOSIS

Phagocytosis is a type of endocytosis by which cells engulf large particles.

TEM 4,700×

Extracellular fluid

Intracellular fluid

Large particle

Plasma membrane

1 The plasma membrane forms a pocket-like vesicle around a large particle.

2 The particle is transported into the cell in a vesicle.

Vesicle

FIGURE 3-21 Through phagocytosis, amoebas and other unicellular protists, as well as white blood cells, consume other organisms for food or for defense.

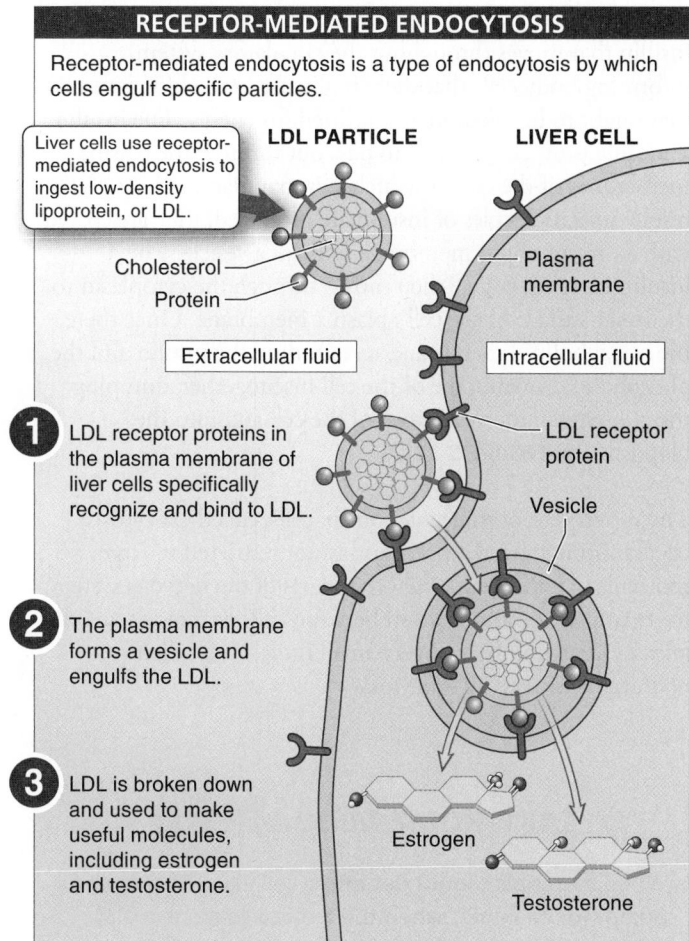

RECEPTOR-MEDIATED ENDOCYTOSIS

Receptor-mediated endocytosis is a type of endocytosis by which cells engulf specific particles.

Liver cells use receptor-mediated endocytosis to ingest low-density lipoprotein, or LDL.

LDL PARTICLE   **LIVER CELL**

Cholesterol
Protein
Plasma membrane

Extracellular fluid   Intracellular fluid

LDL receptor protein

Vesicle

1 LDL receptor proteins in the plasma membrane of liver cells specifically recognize and bind to LDL.

2 The plasma membrane forms a vesicle and engulfs the LDL.

3 LDL is broken down and used to make useful molecules, including estrogen and testosterone.

Estrogen

Testosterone

FIGURE 3-22 Receptor proteins aid in endocytosis. This process is important in the ability of your liver to remove cholesterol from your bloodstream.

Circulating cholesterol often builds up on the walls of arteries, reducing the area (that is, the diameter of the blood vessel) available for blood flow and causing the artery to harden. Because too much circulating cholesterol in LDL molecules can lead to cardiovascular disease and death (**FIGURE 3-23**), it's good to remove as much cholesterol from your bloodstream as quickly as possible. Individuals lucky enough to have large numbers of LDL receptors on the plasma membranes of their liver cells have a significantly lower risk of cardiovascular disease.

Conversely, individuals who consume food laden with too much cholesterol (such as egg yolks, cheese, and sausages), or those who have the misfortune of inheriting genes that code for faulty liver cell membranes that have only a few LDL receptors, can have a heavy load of circulating blood cholesterol. This outcome can result in the early onset of cardiovascular disease. In the extreme case where an

Q

Faulty cell membranes are a primary cause of cardiovascular disease. What modification to these membranes might be an effective treatment?

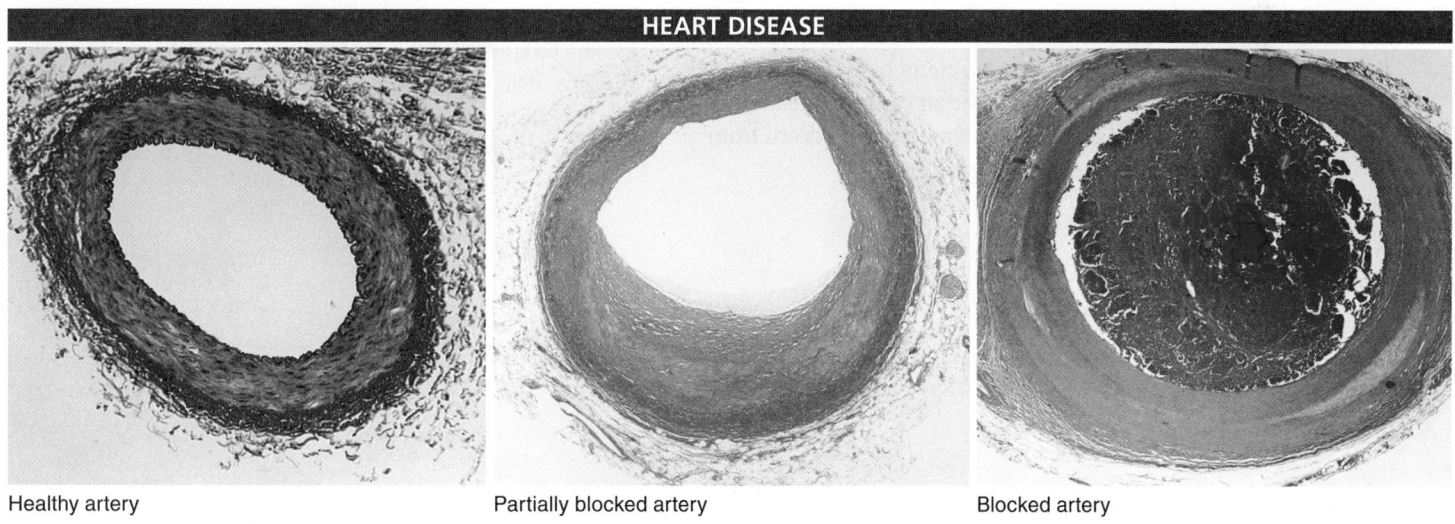

HEART DISEASE

Healthy artery   Partially blocked artery   Blocked artery

FIGURE 3-23 Comparison of a healthy artery and arteries choked by the buildup of cholesterol.

When circulating cholesterol levels exceed the LDL receptors' capacity for binding and removing the lipid, blood flow can become reduced or blocked and the risk of cardiovascular disease increases.

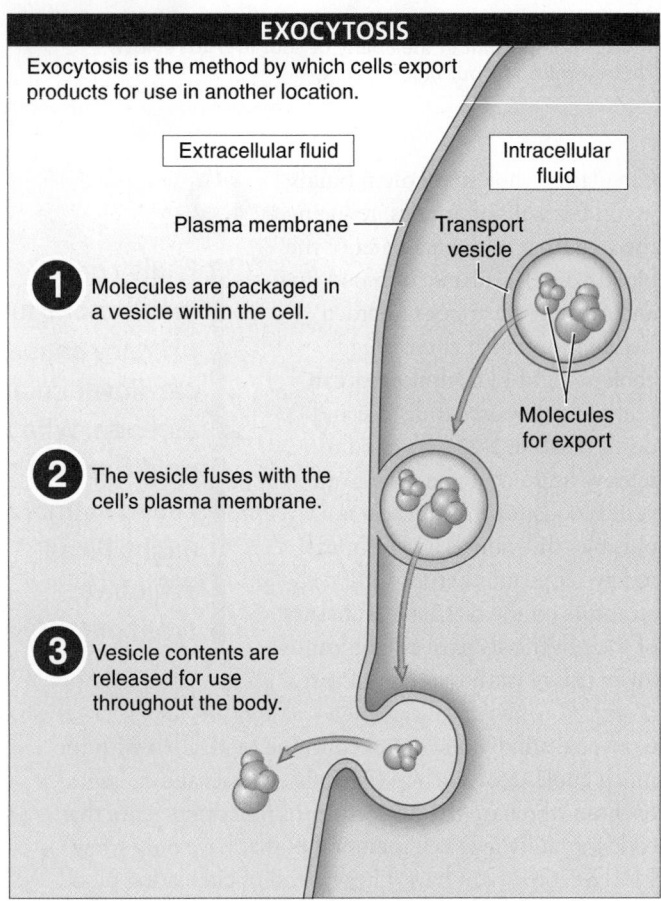

EXOCYTOSIS

Exocytosis is the method by which cells export products for use in another location.

Extracellular fluid

Intracellular fluid

Plasma membrane

Transport vesicle

1 Molecules are packaged in a vesicle within the cell.

Molecules for export

2 The vesicle fuses with the cell's plasma membrane.

3 Vesicle contents are released for use throughout the body.

FIGURE 3-24 Exocytosis moves molecules out of the cell. This is how insulin is exported from the cells where it is synthesized.

individual is born with no LDL receptors at all (a disorder called familial hypercholesterolemia), circulating cholesterol accumulates in the arteries so rapidly that cardiovascular disease begins to develop even before puberty, and death from a heart attack can occur before the age of 30.

Exocytosis Cells in the pancreas produce a chemical called insulin that moves throughout the circulatory system, informing body cells that there is glucose in the bloodstream that ought to be taken in and utilized for energy. The insulin molecule is much too large to pass out through the plasma membranes of the cells in which it is manufactured. As a result, after molecules of insulin are produced, they are coated with a phospholipid membrane to form a vesicle. The insulin-carrying vesicle then moves through the cytoplasm to the inner surface of the cell's plasma membrane. Once there, the phospholipid membrane surrounding the insulin and the phospholipid membrane of the cell fuse together, dumping the contents of the vesicle out of the cell and into the bloodstream (**FIGURE 3-24**).

The movement of molecules out of cells, called exocytosis, occurs throughout the body and is not restricted to large molecules. In the brain and other parts of the nervous system, for example, communication between cells occurs as one cell releases large numbers of very small molecules, called neurotransmitters, by exocytosis.

TAKE-HOME MESSAGE 3·11

When materials cannot get into a cell via diffusion or a pump (for example, when the molecules are too big), cells can engulf the molecules or particles with their plasma membrane in a process called endocytosis. Similarly, molecules can be moved out of a cell by exocytosis. In both processes, the plasma membrane moves to surround the molecules or particles and forms a little vesicle that is pinched off inside the cell (endocytosis) or fuses with the plasma membrane and dumps its contents outside the cell (exocytosis).

3·12 Cells are connected and communicate with each other.

Cells reach out and connect; no telephone lines required.

3·12 Connections between cells hold them in place and enable them to communicate with each other.

So far in this chapter we have examined the cell as a free-living and independent entity. The majority of cells in any multicellular organism, however, are connected to other cells. There is a variety of methods by which cells adhere to other cells, involving numerous types of protein and glycoprotein adhesion molecules. We examine three primary types of connections between animal cells: (1) tight junctions, (2) desmosomes, and (3) gap junctions (**FIGURE 3-25**).

Tight junctions form continuous, water-tight seals around cells and also anchor cells in place. Much like the caulking around a tub or sink that keeps water from leaking into the surrounding walls, tight junctions prevent fluid flow between cells. Tight junctions are particularly important in the small intestine, where digestion occurs. Cells lining the small intestine absorb nutrients from the watery fluid moving through your gut. If the fluid—and the resident bacteria—inside the intestine were to leak between the cells and into your body cavity, you would not be able to extract sufficient energy and nutrients from your food, and the

bacteria would make you sick. The tight junctions instead force fluid to pass *into* the cells that line the intestine, where the nutrients can be utilized.

Desmosomes are like spot welds or rivets that fasten cells together into strong sheets. They occur at irregular intervals and function like fastened Velcro: they hold cells together but are not water-tight, allowing fluid to pass around them. Desmosomes and other similar junctions are found in much of the tissue that lines the cavities of animal bodies. They also are found in muscle tissue, holding fibers together. Genetic disorders that reduce cells' ability to form desmosome proteins or lead to destruction of desmosomes by the immune system result in the formation of blisters, where layers of skin separate from each other.

Finally, **gap junctions** are pores surrounded by special proteins that form open channels between two cells (see Figure 3-25). Functioning like secret passageways, these junctions are large enough for salts, sugars, amino acids, and the chemicals that carry electrical signals to pass through,

TIGHT JUNCTIONS
Form a water-tight seal between cells, like caulking around a tub

DESMOSOMES
Act like Velcro and fasten cells together

GAP JUNCTIONS
Act like secret passageways and allow materials to pass between cells

FIGURE 3-25 Cell connections: tight junctions, desmosomes, and gap junctions.

but are too small for the passage of organelles or very large molecules such as proteins and nucleic acids. Gap junctions are an important mechanism for cell-to-cell communication. In the heart, for example, the electrical signal telling muscle cells to contract is passed from cell to cell through gap junctions. Gap junctions are also important in allowing a cell to recognize that it has bumped up against another cell; chemicals flowing from one cell to the next can signal the body to stop producing cells of a particular type.

masses of cells, called tumors, and their spread throughout the body. (Interestingly, treatments that cause an increase in the number of gap junctions tend to reduce tumor growth.)

Q Is a breakdown of cell-cell communication related to cancer?

Compared with normal cells, cancer cells have fewer gap junctions. And research suggests that the resulting reduction in intercellular communication among cancer cells may be important in the formation of

TAKE-HOME MESSAGE 3·12

In multicellular organisms, most cells are connected to other cells. The connections can form a water-tight seal between the cells (tight junctions), can hold sheets of cells together while allowing fluid to pass between neighboring cells (desmosomes), or can function like secret passageways, allowing the movement of cytoplasm, molecules, and other signals between cells (gap junctions).

3·13–3·21 Nine important landmarks distinguish eukaryotic cells.

Cell of the voodoo lily. How many different organelles can you spot in this plant cell?

3·13 The nucleus is the cell's genetic control center.

As we have seen, all cells are surrounded by a complex plasma membrane that actively regulates what materials get into and out of a cell. Now it's time to look at the cellular contents that are surrounded by the plasma membrane in eukaryotic cells.

The nucleus is the largest and most prominent organelle in most eukaryotic cells. In fact, the nucleus is generally larger than any prokaryotic cell. If a cell were the size of a large lecture hall or movie theater, the nucleus would be the size of a big-rig 18-wheeler truck parked in the front rows. The nucleus has two primary functions, both related to the fact that most of the cell's DNA resides in the nucleus. First, the nucleus is the genetic control center, directing most cellular activities by controlling which molecules are produced, and in what quantity. Second, the nucleus is the storehouse for hereditary information (**FIGURE 3-26**).

Three important structural components stand out in the nucleus (**FIGURE 3-27**). First is the **nuclear membrane,** sometimes called the nuclear envelope, which surrounds the nucleus and separates it from the cytoplasm. Unlike most

FIGURE 3-26 The nucleus holds the genetic information that makes it possible to build organisms. That's why identical twins, carrying the same genetic information, look so similar.

NUCLEUS

FUNCTIONS
- Acts as the genetic control center of the cell
- Stores hereditary information

NUCLEOLUS
Area of the nucleus, where ribosomal subunits are assembled

CHROMATIN/ CHROMOSOMES
Thin fibers of DNA, which carry all hereditary information

NUCLEAR MEMBRANE
Two bilayers, covered in pores, that surround the nucleus

Pore

TEM 43,000×

FIGURE 3-27 The nucleus: the cell's genetic control center.

plasma membranes, however, the nuclear membrane consists of *two* bilayers, one on top of the other, much like the double-bagging of groceries at the market. The nuclear membrane is not a sack, though. It is perforated, covered with tiny pores made from multiple proteins embedded in the phospholipid membranes and spanning both bilayers. These pores enable large molecules to pass from the nucleus to the cytoplasm and from the cytoplasm to the nucleus.

The second prominent structure in the nucleus is the **chromatin,** a mass of long, thin fibers consisting of DNA with some proteins attached to it that keep it from getting impossibly tangled. Most of the time, as the DNA directs cellular activities, the chromatin resembles a plate of spaghetti. When it's time for cell division (a process described in detail in Chapter 6), the chromatin coils up and the threads become shorter and thicker until they become visible as chromosomes, the compacted, linear DNA molecules on which all of the organism's hereditary information is carried.

A third structure in the nucleus is the **nucleolus,** an area near the center of the nucleus where subunits of the ribosomes, a critical part of the cellular machinery, are assembled. Ribosomes are like little factories in which the information stored in the DNA is used to construct proteins, including enzymes and the proteins that make up tissues such as the bark of trees or the bone of vertebrates. The ribosomes are built in the nucleolus but pass through the nuclear pores and into the cytoplasm before starting their protein-production work.

TAKE-HOME MESSAGE 3·13

The nucleus is usually the largest and most prominent organelle in the eukaryotic cell. It directs most cellular activities by controlling which molecules are produced and in what quantity. The nucleus is also the storehouse for all hereditary information.

3·14 Cytoplasm and the cytoskeleton form the cell's internal environment, provide its physical support, and can generate movement.

If you imagine yourself inside a cell the size of a big lecture hall, it might come as a surprise that you can barely see that big rig of a nucleus parked in the front rows. Visibility is almost zero, not only because the room is filled with jelly-like cytoplasm, but also because there is a dense web of thick and thin, straight and branched, ropes, strings, and scaffolding, running every which way throughout the room.

This inner scaffolding of the cell, which is made from proteins, is the **cytoskeleton** (**FIGURE 3-28**). It has three chief purposes. First, it gives animal cells shape and support—making red blood cells look like little round doughnuts (without the hole in the middle) and giving neurons their very long, thread-like appearance. Plant cells are shaped primarily by their cell wall (a structure we discuss later in the chapter), but they also have a cytoskeleton. Second, the cytoskeleton controls the intracellular traffic flow, serving as a series of

tracks on which a variety of organelles and molecules are guided across and around the inside of the cell. And third, because the elaborate scaffolding of the cytoskeleton is dynamic and can generate force, it gives all cells some ability to control their movement.

Three types of protein fibers make up the cytoskeleton. **Microtubules,** the thickest, are linear polymers of a protein and look like rigid, hollow tubes. Like intracellular conveyor belts, they are the tracks to which molecules and organelles within the cell may attach and be moved along. Microtubules also help to pull chromosomes apart during cell division. Continuously built, disassembled, and rebuilt, microtubules rarely last more than about 10 minutes in a cell. **Intermediate filaments,** a second type of cytoskeleton fiber, are durable, rope-like systems of numerous different overlapping proteins. They give cells great strength. **Microfilaments** are the

CYTOSKELETON

FUNCTIONS
- Acts as the inner scaffolding of the cell
- Provides shape and support
- Controls intracellular traffic flow
- Enables movement

Structural network of intermediate filaments

3,500×

THREE TYPES OF PROTEIN FIBERS IN THE CYTOSKELETON

MICROTUBULES
- Thick, hollow tubes
- The tracks to which molecules and organelles within the cell may attach and be moved along

INTERMEDIATE FILAMENTS
- Durable, rope-like systems of numerous overlapping proteins
- Give cells great strength

MICROFILAMENTS
- Long, solid rod-like fibers
- Help with cell contraction and cell division

FIGURE 3-28 The cytoskeleton: the cell's inner scaffolding.

FIGURE 3-29 Cilia and flagella assist the cell with movement.

With gentle beating, cilia can move fluid past cells, whereas flagella, with whip-like motions, can move the cells themselves.

thinnest elements in the cytoskeleton. Long, solid, rod-like fibers, microfilaments help generate forces, including those important in cell contraction and cell division.

A couple of microtubule-based structures are sometimes present in cells and can help to move the cell through its environment (or in stationary cells, can help move the cell's environment past the cell). **Cilia** (*sing.* **cilium**) are short projections that often occur in large numbers on a single cell (**FIGURE 3-29**). Cilia beat swiftly, often in unison and in ways that resemble blades of grass in a field, blowing in the wind. Cilia can move fluid along and past a cell. This movement can accomplish many important tasks, including sweeping the airways to our lungs to clear them of debris (such as dust) in the air we breathe.

Flagella are much longer than cilia. They occur in many prokaryotes and single-celled eukaryotes, and many algae and plants have cells with one or more flagella. But in animals, cell types with one or more flagella are very rare. One of these cell types, however, has a critical role in every animal species: sperm cells. With a flagellum for a tail, sperm are among the most mobile of all animal cells. Some spermicidal birth control methods prevent conception by disabling the flagellum and immobilizing the sperm cells.

TAKE-HOME MESSAGE 3·14

The inner scaffolding of the cell, which is made from proteins, is the cytoskeleton. Consisting of three types of protein fibers—microtubules, intermediate filaments, and microfilaments—the cytoskeleton gives animal cells their shape and support, gives cells some ability to control their movement, and serves as a series of tracks on which organelles and molecules are guided across and around the inside of the cell.

3·15 Mitochondria are the cell's energy converters.

Cars have it easy: we generally put only a single type of fuel in them, and it is exactly the same fuel every time. With human bodies it's a different story. During some meals we put in meat and potatoes. Other times, fruit or bread or vegetables, popcorn and gummy bears, pizza and ice cream. Yet no matter what we eat, we expect our body to utilize the energy in these various foods to power all the reactions that make it possible

for us to breathe, move, and think. The mitochondria are the organelles that make this possible (**FIGURE 3-30**).

Mitochondria (*sing.* **mitochondrion**) are the cell's all-purpose energy converters, and they are present in nearly all plant cells, animal cells, and every other eukaryotic cell. Although we consume a variety of foods, our mitochondria allow us to

FUNCTIONS
- Act as all-purpose energy converters
- Harvest energy to be used for cellular functions

DNA
Matrix
Outer membrane
Inner membrane
Intermembrane space

TEM 73,000×

Cells such as liver cells, which use a lot of energy, can have up to 2,500 mitochondria!

FIGURE 3-30 Mitochondria: the cell's all-purpose energy converters.

convert the energy contained in the chemical bonds of the carbohydrates, fats, and proteins in the food into carbon dioxide, water, and ATP—the molecule that is the energy source all cells use to fuel all their functions and activities. (ATP and how it works are described in detail in Chapter 4.) Because this energy conversion requires a significant amount of oxygen, organisms' mitochondria consume most of the oxygen used by each cell. In humans, for example, our mitochondria consume as much as 80% of the oxygen we breathe. They give a significant return on this investment by producing about 90% of the energy our cells need to function.

As with so many aspects of our bodies, form follows function. Cells that are not very metabolically active, such as some fat storage cells in humans, have very few mitochondria. Other cells, such as muscle, liver, and sperm cells in animals and fast-growing root cells in plants—all of which have large energy requirements—are packed densely with mitochondria (**FIGURE 3-31**). Some of these cells have as many as 2,500 mitochondria!

To visualize the structure of a mitochondrion, imagine a plastic sandwich bag. Now take another, bigger plastic bag and stuff it inside the sandwich bag. That's the structure of mitochondria: there is a smooth outer membrane and a scrunched-up inner membrane. This construction forms two separate compartments within the mitochondrion: a region

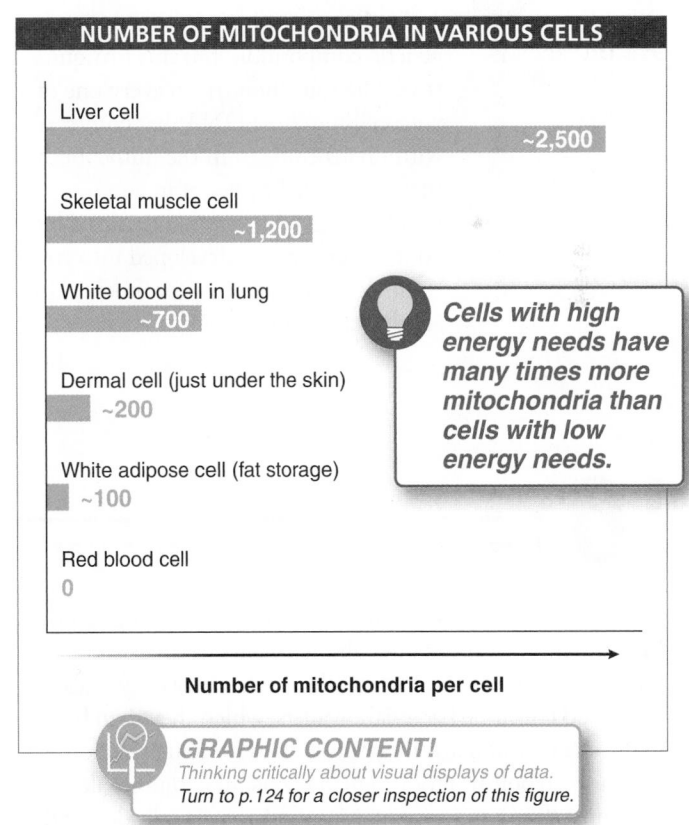

NUMBER OF MITOCHONDRIA IN VARIOUS CELLS

Liver cell
~2,500

Skeletal muscle cell
~1,200

White blood cell in lung
~700

Dermal cell (just under the skin)
~200

White adipose cell (fat storage)
~100

Red blood cell
0

Number of mitochondria per cell

Cells with high energy needs have many times more mitochondria than cells with low energy needs.

GRAPHIC CONTENT!
Thinking critically about visual displays of data.
Turn to p.124 for a closer inspection of this figure.

FIGURE 3-31 How does the number of mitochondria vary in different types of cells?

outside the inner plastic bag (called the **intermembrane space**) and another region, called the **matrix,** inside the inner plastic bag. This bag-within-a-bag structure has important implications for energy conversion. And having a heavily folded inner membrane that is much larger than the outer membrane provides a huge amount of surface area on which to conduct chemical reactions. (We discuss the details of mitochondrial energy conversions and the role of mitochondrial structure in Chapter 4.)

As we learned in our earlier discussion of endosymbiosis, mitochondria may very well have existed, billions of years ago, as separate single-celled bacteria-like organisms. They are similar to bacteria in size and shape, and may have originated when symbiotic bacteria took up permanent residence within other cells. Perhaps the strongest evidence for this is that mitochondria have their own DNA (see Figure 3-30). Mixed in among the approximately 3,000 proteins in each mitochondrion, there are anywhere from 2 to 10 copies of its own little ring-shaped DNA. This DNA carries the instructions for making 13 important mitochondrial proteins necessary for metabolism and energy production.

Q *We all have more DNA from one parent than the other. Who is the bigger contributor: mom or dad? Why?*

We're always taught that our mothers and fathers contribute equally to our genetic composition, but this isn't quite true. The mitochondria in every one of your cells (and the DNA that comes with them) come from the mitochondria that were initially present in your mother's egg, which, when fertilized by your father's sperm, developed into you. In other words: all of your mitochondria are descended from your mother's mitochondria. The tiny sperm contributes DNA, but no cytoplasm and, hence, no mitochondria. Consequently, mitochondrial DNA is something that we inherit exclusively from our mothers. This is true not only in humans but in most multicellular eukaryotes. As the fertilized egg develops into a two-celled, then four-celled, embryo, the mitochondria split themselves by a process called fission, the same process of division and DNA duplication used by bacteria—so there are always a sufficient number of mitochondria for the newly produced cells. This similarity between mitochondria and bacteria is another characteristic that supports the theory that mitochondria were originally symbiotic bacteria.

Given the central role of mitochondria in converting the energy in food molecules into a form that is usable by cells, you won't be surprised to learn that mitochondrial malfunctions can have serious consequences. Recent research has focused on possible links between defective mitochondria and diseases characterized by fatigue and muscle pain. It seems, for instance, that many cases of "exercise intolerance"—extreme fatigue or cramps after only slight exertion—may be related to defective mitochondrial DNA.

TAKE-HOME MESSAGE 3·15

In mitochondria, which are found in nearly all eukaryotic cells, the energy contained in the chemical bonds of carbohydrate, fat, and protein molecules is converted into carbon dioxide, water, and ATP, the energy source for all cellular functions and activities. Mitochondria may have their evolutionary origins as symbiotic bacteria living inside other cells.

3·16 Lysosomes are the cell's garbage disposals.

Garbage. What does a cell do with all the garbage it generates? Mitochondria wear out after about 10 days of intensive activity, for starters. And white blood cells constantly track down and consume bacterial invaders, which they then have to dispose of. Similarly, the thousands of ongoing reactions of cellular metabolism produce many waste macromolecules that cells must digest and recycle. Many eukaryotic cells deal with this garbage by maintaining hundreds of versatile floating "garbage disposals" called lysosomes (**FIGURE 3-32**).

Lysosomes are round, membrane-enclosed, acid-filled vesicles that dispose of garbage. They are filled with about 50 different digestive enzymes and a super-acidic fluid, a corrosive broth so powerful that if a lysosome were to burst, it would almost immediately kill the cell by rapidly digesting all of its component parts. The selection of enzymes in the lysosome represents a broad spectrum of chemicals designed for dismantling macromolecules that are no longer needed by the cell or are generated as by-products of cellular metabolism.

FUNCTION
• Act as floating garbage disposals for cells, digesting and recycling cellular waste products and consumed material

Membrane

Digestive enzymes and acid

Partially digested organelle

TEM 59,500×

FIGURE 3-32 Lysosomes: digestion and recycling of the cell's waste products.

Some of the enzymes break down lipids, others carbohydrates, others proteins, and still others nucleic acids. Consequently, when a cell consumes a particle of food or even an invading bacterium via phagocytosis, the cell directs the material to lysosomes for dismantling. And, ever the efficient system, the cell releases most of the component parts of molecules that are digested, such as amino acids, back into its cytoplasm, where they can be reused by the cell as raw materials.

Some immune system cells tend to have particularly large numbers of lysosomes, most likely because of their great need for disposing of the by-products of disease-causing bacteria.

Why is Tay-Sachs disease like a strike by trash collectors?

Q With 50 different enzymes necessary for lysosomes to carry out their metabolic salvaging act, malfunctions sometimes occur. A common genetic disorder called Tay-Sachs disease is the result of just such a genetic mishap. In Tay-Sachs disease, an individual inherits an inability to produce a critical lipid-digesting enzyme. Even

though the lysosomes cannot digest certain lipids, the cells continue to send lipids to the lysosomes, where they accumulate, undigested. This leads to a sort of lysosome constipation. The lysosome swells until it bursts and digests the whole cell or until it chokes the cell to death. Within the first few years of life, this process occurs in large numbers of cells and eventually leads to the child's death.

Although it has long been debated among biologists, it does seem that plant cells also contain lysosomes, compartments with similar digestive broths that carry out the same digestive processes as in animals.

TAKE-HOME MESSAGE 3·16

Lysosomes are round, membrane-enclosed, acid-filled organelles that function as a cell's garbage disposals. They are filled with about 50 different digestive enzymes and enable a cell to dismantle macromolecules, including disease-causing bacteria.

3·17 The endoplasmic reticulum is the site where cells build proteins and disarm toxins.

The information for how to construct the molecules essential to a cell's smooth functioning and survival is stored in the DNA found in the cell's nucleus. The energy used to construct these molecules and to run cellular functions comes primarily from the mitochondria. The actual production and modification of biological molecules, however, occurs in a system of organelles called the **endomembrane system** (**FIGURE 3-33**). This mass of interrelated membranes spreads out from and surrounds the nucleus, forming chambers within the cell that contain their own mixtures of chemicals. The endomembrane system takes up as much as one-fifth of the cell's volume and is responsible for many of the fundamental functions of the cell.

Lipids are produced within these membrane-enclosed compartments, products for export to other parts of the body are modified and packaged here, polypeptide chains are assembled into functional proteins here, and many of the toxic chemicals that find their way into our bodies—from recreational drugs to antibiotics—are broken down and neutralized in the endomembrane system.

Because the process of protein production follows a somewhat linear path, we explore the endomembrane system sequentially, beginning just outside the nucleus with the endoplasmic reticulum.

Rough endoplasmic reticulum Perhaps the organelle with the most cumbersome name, the **rough endoplasmic reticulum,** or **rough ER** ("endoplasmic reticulum" is derived from the Greek for "within" and "anything molded" and the Latin for "small net"), is a large series of interconnected, flattened sacs that look like a stack of pancakes. These sacs are connected directly to the nuclear envelope. In most eukaryotic cells, the rough ER almost completely surrounds the nucleus (**FIGURE 3-34**). It is called "rough" because its surface is studded with little bumps. These bumps are ribosomes, the cell's protein-making machines, and cells with high rates of protein production generally have large numbers of ribosomes. We cover the details of ribosome structure and protein production in Chapter 5.

The primary function of the rough ER is to fold and package proteins that will be shipped to other locations in the endomembrane system, the cell surface, or outside the cell. Poisonous frogs, for example, package their poison in the rough ER of the cells where it is produced before transporting it to the poison glands on their skin. Proteins that are used within the cell itself are generally produced on free-floating ribosomes in the cytoplasm.

Smooth endoplasmic reticulum As its name advertises, the **smooth endoplasmic reticulum** is part of the

OVERVIEW OF THE ENDOMEMBRANE SYSTEM

FUNCTIONS
- Produces and modifies molecules to be exported to other parts of the organism
- Breaks down toxic chemicals and cellular by-products

Rough endoplasmic reticulum

Smooth endoplasmic reticulum

Golgi apparatus

FIGURE 3-33 The endomembrane system: the rough endoplasmic reticulum, smooth endoplasmic reticulum, and Golgi apparatus.

FUNCTION
• Modifies proteins that will be shipped to other locations in the endomembrane system, the cell surface, or outside the cell

Ribosomes

Rough ER is covered in ribosomes. Ribosomes are protein-making machines.

TEM 56,500×

FIGURE 3-34 The rough endoplasmic reticulum is studded with ribosomes.

endomembrane network that is smooth, because there are no ribosomes bound to it (**FIGURE 3-35**). Although it is connected to the rough ER, it is farther from the nucleus and, besides lacking ribosomes, differs slightly in appearance. Whereas the rough ER looks like stacks of pancakes, the smooth ER sometimes looks like a collection of branched tubes.

The smooth surface gives us the first hint that smooth ER has a different job than rough ER. Because ribosomes are absolutely essential for protein production, we can guess that, with few of them, the smooth ER is not extensively involved in folding or packaging proteins. It isn't. Instead, it primarily takes part in the synthesis of lipids such as fatty acids,

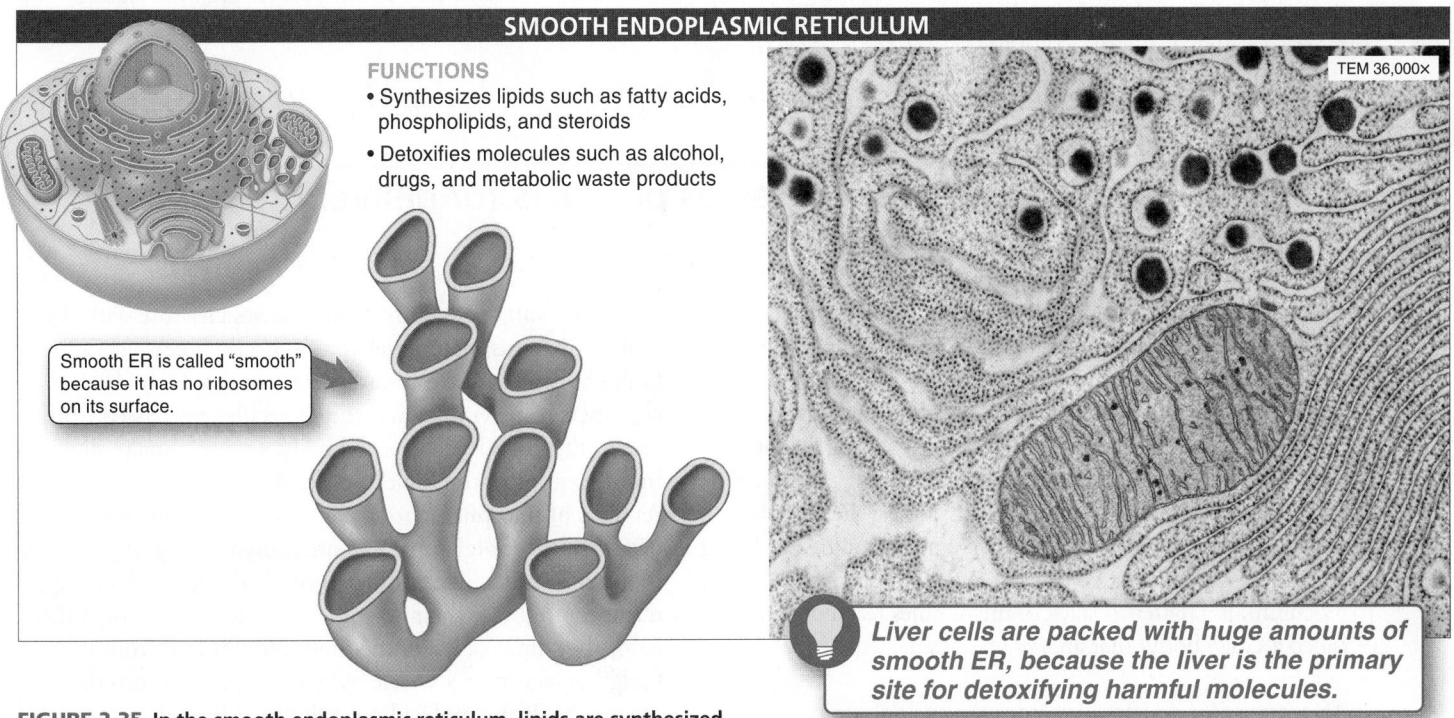

TEM 36,000×

FUNCTIONS
• Synthesizes lipids such as fatty acids, phospholipids, and steroids
• Detoxifies molecules such as alcohol, drugs, and metabolic waste products

Smooth ER is called "smooth" because it has no ribosomes on its surface.

Liver cells are packed with huge amounts of smooth ER, because the liver is the primary site for detoxifying harmful molecules.

FIGURE 3-35 In the smooth endoplasmic reticulum, lipids are synthesized and alcohol, antibiotics, and other drugs are detoxified.

phospholipids, and steroids, as well as carbohydrates. Exactly which lipids are produced varies throughout the organism and across plant and animal species. Inside the smooth ER of mammalian ovaries and testes, for example, the hormones estrogen and testosterone are produced. Inside the smooth ER of liver and fat cells, other lipids are produced. As occurs for proteins in the rough ER, following their production these lipids are packaged in transport vesicles and then sent to other parts of the cell or to the plasma membrane for export.

Another critical responsibility of the smooth ER—particularly the smooth ER in human liver cells—is to help protect us from the many dangerous molecules that get into our bodies. Alcohol, antibiotics, barbiturates, amphetamines, or other stimulants that we may consume, along with many toxic metabolic waste products formed in our bodies, are made less harmful by the detoxifying enzymes in the smooth ER. And just as a bodybuilder's muscles get bigger and bigger in response to weightlifting, our smooth ER proliferates in cells that are exposed to large amounts of particular drugs. This proliferation can be beneficial because it increases the capacity for detoxification. But as the cells become more and more efficient at detoxification, our tolerance to the very drugs the smooth ER is trying to destroy can increase.

As we see over and over in living organisms, form follows function. Not surprisingly, then, just as cells with high rates of protein production have large numbers of ribosomes, we find huge amounts of smooth ER in liver cells because they are the primary sites of molecular detoxification. Other cells that are packed with ER (both rough and smooth) include plasma cells in the blood that produce immune system proteins for export and pancreas cells that secrete large amounts of digestive enzymes.

How can long-term use of one drug increase your resistance to another, different drug that you have never encountered?

Q Chronic exposure to many drugs (from antibiotics to heroin) can induce a proliferation of smooth ER, particularly in the liver, and the smooth ER's associated detoxification enzymes. This proliferation in turn increases tolerance to the drugs, necessitating higher doses to achieve the same effect. Moreover, the increased detoxification capacity of the cells often enables them to better detoxify other compounds, even if the person has never been exposed to these chemicals. This increased detoxification capacity can lead to problems. An individual who has been exposed to large amounts of certain drugs, for example, may end up responding less well to antibiotics.

TAKE-HOME MESSAGE 3·17

The production and modification of biological molecules in eukaryotic cells occurs in a system of organelles called the endomembrane system, which includes, among other organelles, the rough and smooth endoplasmic reticulum. In rough ER, proteins that will be shipped elsewhere in the body are folded and packaged. In the smooth ER, lipids and carbohydrates are synthesized and alcohol, antibiotics, and other drugs are detoxified.

3·18 The Golgi apparatus processes products for delivery throughout the body.

Moving farther outward from the nucleus, we encounter another organelle within the endomembrane system: the Golgi (GOHL-jee) apparatus (**FIGURE 3-36**). The **Golgi apparatus** processes molecules synthesized in the cell—primarily proteins and lipids—and packages those that are destined for use elsewhere in the body. The Golgi apparatus is also a site of carbohydrate synthesis, including the complex polysaccharides found in many plasma membranes. The Golgi apparatus, which is not connected to the endoplasmic reticulum, is a flattened stack of membranes (each of which is called a Golgi body) that are *not* interconnected.

After transport vesicles bud from the endoplasmic reticulum, they move through the cytoplasm until they reach the Golgi apparatus. Here, the vesicles fuse with the Golgi apparatus membrane and dump their contents into a Golgi body. There are about four successive Golgi body chambers to be visited, and the molecules get passed from one to the next. In each Golgi body, enzymes make slight modifications to the molecules (such as the addition or removal of phosphate groups or sugars). The processing that occurs in the Golgi apparatus often involves tagging molecules (much like adding a postal address or tracking number) to direct them to some other part of the organism. After they are processed, the molecules bud off from the Golgi apparatus in a vesicle, which then moves into the cytoplasm. If the molecules are destined for delivery and use elsewhere in the body, the transport vesicle eventually fuses

GOLGI APPARATUS

FUNCTION
• Processes and packages proteins, lipids, and other molecules for export to other locations in or outside of the cell

Transport vesicles

TEM 62,500×

FIGURE 3-36 Golgi apparatus: processing of molecules synthesized in the cell and packaging of those molecules destined for use elsewhere in the body.

with the cell's plasma membrane and dumps the molecules into the bloodstream via exocytosis.

FIGURE 3-37 shows how the various parts of the endomembrane system work to produce, modify, and package molecules within a cell.

THE ENDOMEMBRANE SYSTEM AT WORK

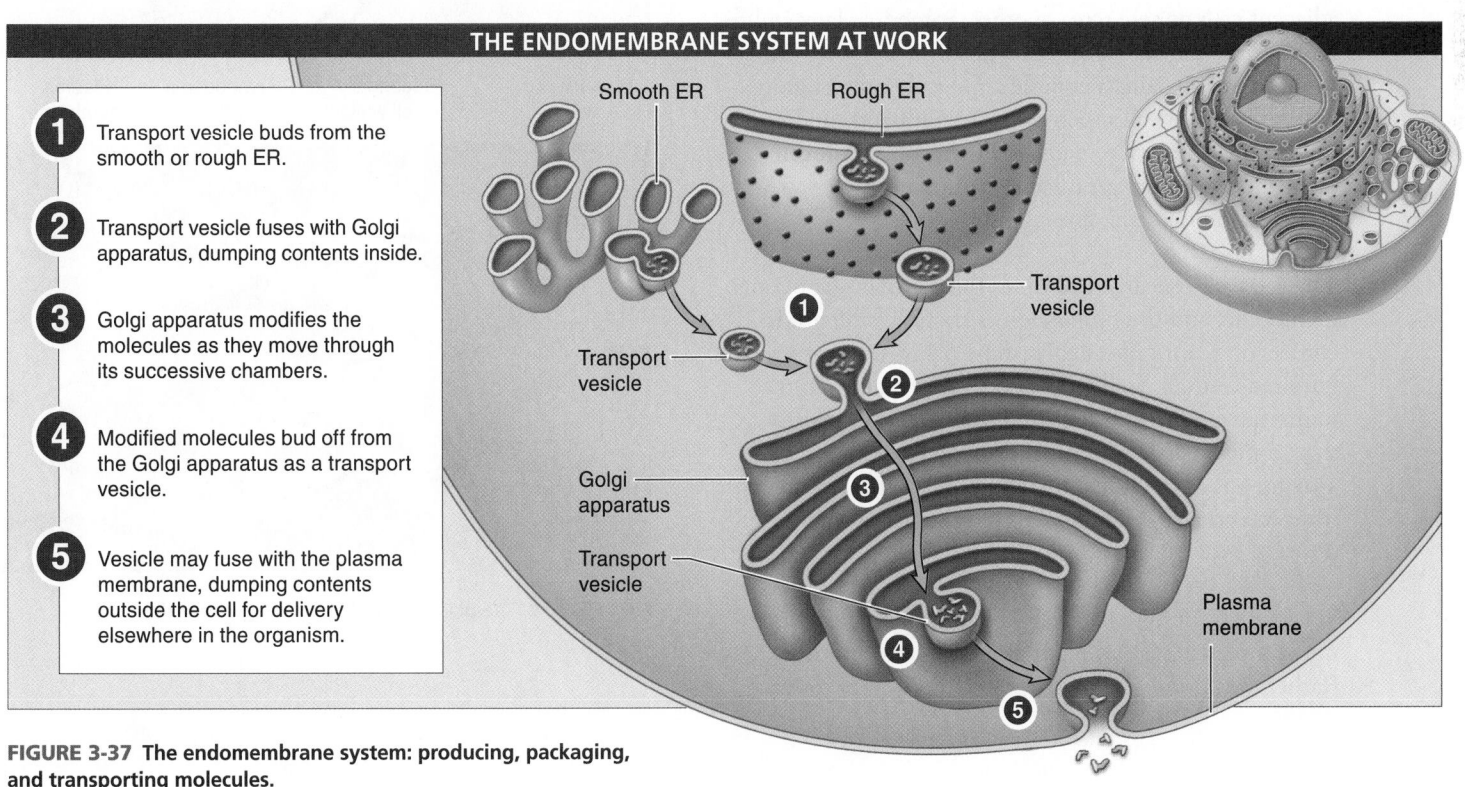

1 Transport vesicle buds from the smooth or rough ER.

2 Transport vesicle fuses with Golgi apparatus, dumping contents inside.

3 Golgi apparatus modifies the molecules as they move through its successive chambers.

4 Modified molecules bud off from the Golgi apparatus as a transport vesicle.

5 Vesicle may fuse with the plasma membrane, dumping contents outside the cell for delivery elsewhere in the organism.

Smooth ER   Rough ER

Transport vesicle

Transport vesicle

Golgi apparatus

Transport vesicle

Plasma membrane

FIGURE 3-37 The endomembrane system: producing, packaging, and transporting molecules.

3·19 The cell wall provides additional protection and support for plant cells.

Until this point, we've discussed organelles and structures that are common to both plants and animals. Now we're going to look at several structures that are not found in all eukaryotic cells. Because plants are stuck in the ground, unable to move, they have several special needs beyond those of animals. In particular, they can't outrun or outmaneuver their competitors to get more food. Nor can they outrun organisms that want to eat them. If they want more sunshine, they have few options beyond simply growing larger or taller. And if they want to resist plant-eating animals, they must simply reduce their edibility.

One structure that helps plants achieve both of these goals is the cell wall, which surrounds the plasma membrane. The cell wall is made largely from long fibers of a polysaccharide called cellulose. Note that although animal cells do not have cell walls, some non-plants such as archaea, bacteria, protists, and fungi also have cell walls; their cell walls are made of different polysaccharides rather than cellulose.

In plants, cell wall production can be a multistage process. Initially, when the cell is still growing, a primary cell wall is laid down, along with some glue that helps adjacent cells adhere to each other. Sometime later in life, a secondary cell wall is laid down. This secondary cell wall usually contains a complex molecule called lignin, which gives the wall much of its strength and rigidity. Oddly, this strength remains even after the plant cell dies—hence wood's great value to humans as a construction material, among other things.

The cell wall is nearly 100 times thicker than the plasma membrane, and the tremendous structural strength it confers on plant cells enables some plants to grow several hundred feet tall. Cell walls also help to make plants more water-tight—an important feature in organisms that cannot reduce water loss through evaporation by moving out of the hot sun—and provide some protection from insects and other animals that might eat them (**FIGURE 3-38**).

Surprisingly, despite its great strength, the cell wall does not completely seal off plant cells from one another. Rather, it is porous, allowing water and solutes to reach

PLANT CELL WALL

FUNCTIONS
- Provides the cell with structural strength
- Gives the cell increased water resistance
- Provides some protection from insects and other animals that might eat plant parts

Plasmodesmata allow water and other molecules to pass between adjacent cells.

Cell 1   Cell 2   Cell 3

Primary cell wall   Secondary cell wall   Plasmodesma   Plasma membrane

TEM 440x

FIGURE 3-38 The plant cell wall: providing strength.

the plasma membrane. Additionally, the cells in most plants have anywhere from 1,000 to 100,000 microscopic tube-like channels, called **plasmodesmata** (*sing.* **plasmodesma**) (see Figure 3-38), connecting the cells to each other and enabling communication and transport between them. In fact, because so many of the cells are connected to one another, sharing cytoplasm and other molecules, some biologists have wondered whether we should consider a plant as just one big cell. How would you respond to that idea?

TAKE-HOME MESSAGE 3·19

The cell wall is an organelle found in plants (and in some other non-animal organisms). It is made primarily from the carbohydrate cellulose, and it surrounds the plasma membrane of the cell. The cell wall confers tremendous structural strength on plant cells, gives plants increased resistance to water loss, and provides some protection from insects and other animals that might eat them. In plants, plasmodesmata connect cells and enable communication and transport between them.

3·20   Vacuoles are multipurpose storage sacs for cells.

If you look at a mature plant cell through a microscope, one organelle, the **central vacuole,** usually stands out more than all the others because it is so huge and appears empty (**FIGURE 3-39**). Although it may look like an empty sac, the central vacuole is anything but. Surrounded by a membrane, filled with fluid, and occupying from 50% to 90% of a plant cell's interior space, the central vacuole can play an important role in five different areas of plant life. (Vacuoles are also found in some other eukaryotes, including some protists, fungi, and animals, but they tend to be particularly prominent in plant cells.)

1. **Nutrient storage**—the vacuole stores hundreds of dissolved substances, including amino acids, sugars, and ions.

2. **Waste management**—the vacuole retains waste products and degrades them with digestive enzymes, much like the lysosome in animal cells.

3. **Predator deterrence**—the poisonous, nasty-tasting materials that accumulate inside the vacuoles of some plants make a powerful deterrent to animals that might try to eat parts of the plant.

4. **Sexual reproduction**—the vacuole may contain pigments that give some flowers their red, blue, purple, or other colors, enabling them to attract birds and insects that help the plant reproduce by transferring pollen.

5. **Physical support**—high concentrations of dissolved substances in the vacuole can cause water to rush into the cells through the process of osmosis. The increased

VACUOLE

FUNCTIONS
- Stores nutrients
- Retains and degrades waste products
- Accumulates poisonous materials
- Contains pigments, enabling plants to attract birds and insects that help the plant reproduce
- Provides physical support

Vacuole

TEM 5,000×

FIGURE 3-39 The vacuole: multipurpose storage.

fluid pressure inside the vacuole can cause the cell to enlarge a bit and push out the cell wall. This process is responsible for the pressure (called **turgor pressure**) that allows stems, flowers, and other plant parts to stand upright. The ability of non-woody plants to stand upright is due primarily to turgor pressure. Wilting is the result of a loss of turgor pressure.

3·21 Chloroplasts are the plant cell's solar power plant.

It would be hard to choose the "most important organelle" in a cell, but if we had to, the chloroplast would be a top contender. The chloroplast, an organelle found in all plants and eukaryotic algae, is the site of photosynthesis—the conversion of light energy into the chemical energy of food molecules, with oxygen as a by-product. Because all photosynthesis in plants and algae takes place in chloroplasts, these organelles are directly or indirectly responsible for everything we eat and for the oxygen we breathe. Life on earth would be vastly different without the chloroplast (**FIGURE 3-40**).

In a green leaf, each cell has about 40–50 chloroplasts. This means there are about 500,000 chloroplasts per square millimeter of leaf surface (that's more than 200 million chloroplasts in an area the size of a small postage stamp). Chloroplasts are oval, somewhat flattened objects. On the outside, the chloroplast is encircled by two distinct layers of membranes (similar to the structure of mitochondria). The fluid in the inside compartment, called the **stroma,** contains some DNA and much protein-making machinery.

With a simple light microscope, it is possible to see little spots of green within the chloroplasts. Up close, these spots look like stacks of pancakes. Each stack consists of numerous, interconnected little flattened sacs called **thylakoids,** and it is on the membranes of the thylakoids that the light-collecting for photosynthesis occurs. (In Chapter 4, we discuss the details of how chloroplasts convert the energy in sunlight into the chemical energy stored in sugar molecules.)

A peculiar feature of chloroplasts, mentioned in Section 3-3, is that they resemble photosynthetic bacteria, particularly with their circular DNA (which contains many of the genes essential for photosynthesis). Also, the dual

CHLOROPLAST

FUNCTION
• Site of photosynthesis—the conversion of light energy into chemical energy

Light is collected for photosynthesis on the membranes of the thylakoids within the chloroplasts.

DNA

Thylakoid

Stroma

TEM 16,000×

FIGURE 3-40 The chloroplast: location of photosynthesis.

REVIEW OF CELL STRUCTURES

STRUCTURE	ANIMALS	PLANTS	FUNCTION
Nucleus	✓	✓	Directs cellular activity and stores hereditary information
Cytoskeleton	✓	✓	Provides structural shape and support and enables cellular movement
Mitochondrion	✓	✓	Harvests energy for cellular functions
Lysosome	✓	✓	Digests and recycles cellular waste products and consumed material
Rough ER	✓	✓	Modifies proteins that will be shipped elsewhere in the organism
Smooth ER	✓	✓	Synthesizes lipids and detoxifies molecules
Golgi apparatus	✓	✓	Processes and packages proteins, lipids, and other molecules
Cell wall	🚫	✓	Provides structural strength, protection, and increased resistance to water loss
Vacuole	Sometimes	✓	Stores nutrients, degrades waste products, provides pigments and structural support
Chloroplast	🚫	✓	Performs photosynthesis

FIGURE 3-41 Review of major cellular structures and their functions.

outer membrane of the chloroplast is consistent with the idea that, long ago, a cell engulfed a photosynthetic bacterium, enveloping it with its plasma membrane in endocytosis. These features have given rise to the belief that chloroplasts might originally have been bacteria that were engulfed by a predatory cell. According to the endosymbiosis theory (see Section 3-3), the bacteria remained alive and, rather than becoming a meal, became the cell's meal ticket, providing food for the cell in exchange for protection.

FIGURE 3-41 summarizes the major parts of a cell, in animals and plants, and their functions.

TAKE-HOME MESSAGE 3·21

The chloroplast is the organelle in plants and algae that is the site of photosynthesis—the conversion of light energy into chemical energy, with oxygen as a by-product. Chloroplasts may originally have been bacteria that were engulfed by a predatory cell by endosymbiosis.

DRINKING TOO MUCH WATER CAN BE DANGEROUS!

People have long understood the risks of becoming dehydrated, particularly during activities such as marathon running in which a great deal of fluid can be lost through sweating. Only recently, however, has it been recognized that too much water—called "water intoxication"—can also be dangerous. In 2007, a 28-year-old woman competing in a water-drinking contest died just a few hours after consuming about two gallons of water without urinating. Similarly, the death of a runner during the 2002 Boston marathon was attributed to water intoxication.

Q: WHEN PEOPLE SWEAT, WHAT DO THEY LOSE? Sweat consists of water and some dissolved solids, primarily salt. As the sweat evaporates, the body is cooled.

Q: HOW DO PEOPLE RESPOND TO NAUSEA AND DIZZINESS, THE WARNING SIGNS OF DEHYDRATION? By drinking water. Because the water they drink lacks salt and other solutes, this can lead to sodium imbalances in the body, particularly in the bloodstream and the fluid around cells (extracellular fluid).

Q: WHAT IS OSMOSIS? Osmosis is the diffusion of water across a membrane toward areas where there is a greater concentration of solutes and, consequently, a lower concentration of water molecules.

Q: IF YOU DRINK LOTS OF WATER (TWO GALLONS OR MORE)—WHICH HAS FEW OR NO SOLUTES—WHERE IS IT GOING TO MOVE ONCE IT GETS INTO YOUR BLOODSTREAM AND EXTRACELLULAR FLUID? It moves by osmosis into your cells, where there is a higher concentration of solutes (primarily sodium) and a lower concentration of water molecules.

Q: WHAT HAPPENS TO YOUR CELLS IF THEY ABSORB TOO MUCH WATER? They swell, sometimes to the point of rupturing. Such swelling and rupturing in the enclosed brain cavity can cause vomiting and confusion. Disastrously, these symptoms are often mistaken for the symptoms of dehydration and so the consumption of water is recommended, making the situation worse. Further swelling can lead to seizures, coma, and even death. (The reverse situation occurs when people drink too much seawater. Their bloodstream and extracellular fluid gain in solutes, particularly salt, so water flows out of cells by osmosis. Cell dehydration and death can occur—usually from shrinkage of brain cells.)

WHAT SHOULD YOU DO? Many marathon organizers have been reducing the number of water stops they offer runners during the race and testing symptomatic runners' sodium levels in medical tents along the course. Consuming salt tablets and salty snacks helps keep blood sodium levels in a healthy range. Also, when possible, runners should weigh themselves during a race to make sure they are only replacing the fluid they have lost through sweating and are not gaining weight.

Big Ideas in ... Cells

3.1–3.3 What is a cell?

- The cell is the smallest unit of life that can perform all of the necessary activities of life, including reproducing itself.

- All living organisms are made up of one or more cells, and all cells arise from other, preexisting cells.

- Every cell on earth is either a eukaryote or a prokaryote.

- Prokaryotes, which have no nucleus and are single-celled, were the first cells on earth.

- Eukaryotes are single-celled or multicellular organisms whose cells have a nucleus that contains linear strands of genetic material.

3.4–3.7 Cell membranes are gatekeepers.

- Every cell of every living organism is enclosed by a plasma membrane, a two-layered membrane that holds the contents of a cell in place and regulates what enters and leaves the cell.

- The plasma membrane is a fluid mosaic of proteins, lipids, and carbohydrates.

- Every cell in your body has a "fingerprint," made from a variety of molecules on the outside-facing surface of the cell membrane, that is key to the functioning of your immune system.

3.8–3.11 Molecules move across membranes in several ways.

- Cells must import food molecules and other necessary materials from outside the cell and export metabolic waste and molecules produced for use elsewhere in the body.

- In passive transport, the molecular movement occurs spontaneously, without the input of energy.

- The diffusion of water across a membrane is a special type of passive transport called osmosis.

- Active transport is necessary if the molecules to be moved are very large or if they are being moved against their concentration gradient, and this transport requires energy.

- Cells can also engulf particles with their plasma membrane in a process called endocytosis. Similarly, molecules can be moved out of a cell by exocytosis.

3.12 Cells are connected and communicate with each other.

- In multicellular organisms, most cells are connected to other cells.

- The connections can form a water-tight seal between the cells (tight junctions), can hold sheets of cells together while allowing fluid to pass between the cells (desmosomes), or can function like secret passageways between cells (gap junctions).

3.13–3.21 Nine important landmarks distinguish eukaryotic cells.

- Specific structures in eukaryotic cells perform specific life-sustaining functions.

- The nucleus directs all protein production and is the storehouse for all hereditary information.

- The cytoskeleton gives animal cells shape and support.

- In mitochondria, energy from macromolecules is converted into usable energy in the form of ATP.

- Lysosomes dismantle waste and bacterial pathogens.

- The production and modification of molecules, including drug detoxification, occurs in the rough and smooth endoplasmic reticulum; and the Golgi apparatus processes molecules synthesized in the cell and packages those destined for use elsewhere in the body.

- In plants, the cell wall confers structural strength, protection from predators, and resistance to water loss. Vacuoles function as storage spaces, and chloroplasts are the site of photosynthesis.

- In plants, plasmodesmata connect cells and enable communication and transport between them.

See the To-Go Guide (packaged with every new copy of this textbook) for an illustrated summary of the chapter.

Check Your Knowledge

Thinking critically about visual displays of data.

1. What are the variables in this graph?

2. What additional information would make this figure more helpful? Why?

3. What can you conclude from this figure?

4. Is "number of mitochondria per cell" the best measure of a cell's "energy-generating capacity"? Can you think of a reason why this might not be a perfect measure? (Hint: muscle cells can be much, much larger than liver cells.)

5. Based on these data, can you make any of your own predictions?

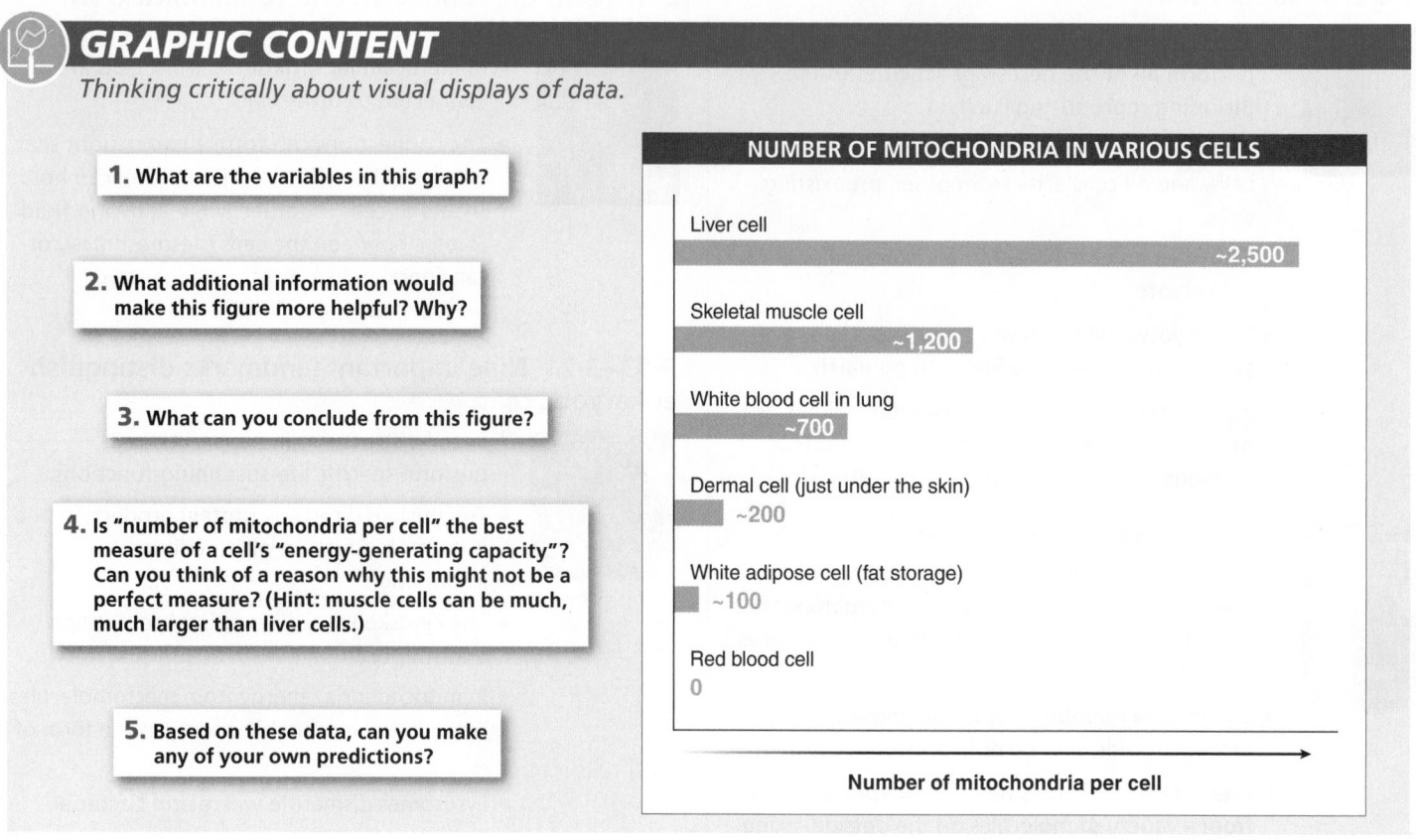

NUMBER OF MITOCHONDRIA IN VARIOUS CELLS

Liver cell ~2,500

Skeletal muscle cell ~1,200

White blood cell in lung ~700

Dermal cell (just under the skin) ~200

White adipose cell (fat storage) ~100

Red blood cell 0

Number of mitochondria per cell

See Answers at the back of the book.

Key Terms in Cells

Multiple-Choice Questions

1. **Which of the following statements about the cell theory is correct?**

   a) All living organisms are made up of one or more cells.

   b) All cells arise from other, preexisting cells.

   c) All eukaryotic cells contain symbiotic prokaryotes.

   d) All prokaryotic cells contain symbiotic eukaryotes.

   e) Both a) and b) are correct.

   100 HARD
   11
   0 EASY

2. **Which of the following statements about prokaryotes is incorrect?**

   a) Prokaryotes appeared on earth before eukaryotes.

   b) Prokaryotes have circular pieces of DNA within their nuclei.

   c) Prokaryotes contain cytoplasm.

   d) Prokaryotes contain ribosomes.

   e) Some prokaryotes can conduct photosynthesis.

   100 HARD
   51
   0 EASY

3. **Which of the following facts supports the claim that mitochondria developed from bacteria that, long ago, were incorporated into eukaryotic cells by the process of phagocytosis?**

   a) Mitochondria have flagella for motion.

   b) Mitochondria have proteins for the synthesis of ATP.

   c) Mitochondria are the "powerhouses" of the cell.

   d) Mitochondria are small and easily transported across cell membranes.

   e) Mitochondria have their own DNA.

   100 HARD
   37
   0 EASY

4. **Hydrophobic molecules can pass freely through the plasma membrane, but ions and polar molecules are impeded by the hydrophobic core. For this reason, plasma membranes can be considered:**

   a) partially permeable.

   b) impermeable.

   c) hydrophobic.

   d) hydrophilic.

   e) None of these terms properly describe plasma membranes.

   100 HARD
   15
   0 EASY

5. **Drugs called beta-blockers do all of the following except:**

   a) reduce high blood pressure.

   b) block signaling through adrenaline receptors.

   c) reduce outward symptoms of anxiety.

   d) bind to the cytoplasmic side of a receptor protein.

   e) reduce the effects of adrenaline on the heart.

   100 HARD
   44
   0 EASY

6. **Cellular "fingerprints":**

   a) are exposed on the cytoplasmic side of the membrane.

   b) are made from cholesterol.

   c) are "erased" by the HIV virus.

   d) can help the immune system distinguish "self" from "non-self."

   e) All of the above are correct.

   100 HARD
   42
   0 EASY

7. **The movement of molecules across a membrane from an area of high concentration to one of low concentration is best described as:**

   a) active transport.

   b) inactivated transport.

   c) passive transport.

   d) channel-mediated diffusion.

   e) electron transport.

   100 HARD
   31
   0 EASY

8. The transport of water across a membrane from a solution of lower solute concentration to a solution of higher solute concentration is best described as:

   a) osmosis.

   b) facilitated diffusion.

   c) receptor-mediated transport.

   d) active transport.

   e) general diffusion.

   100 HARD

   38

   0 EASY

9. In an experiment, you measure the concentration of a polar molecule inside and outside a cell. You find that the concentration is high and gradually increasing inside the cell. What is your best hypothesis for the process you are observing?

   a) facilitated diffusion

   b) passive transport

   c) simple diffusion

   d) active transport

   e) endocytosis

   100 HARD

   44

   0 EASY

10. Which of the following allow the passage of small molecules between animal cells?

    a) nucleoli

    b) tight junctions

    c) desmosomes

    d) gap junctions

    e) black holes

    100 HARD

    38

    0 EASY

11. The largest structure in a eukaryotic cell is the _____ and it is surrounded by _____ membrane(s).

    a) nucleus; one

    b) nucleus; two

    c) Golgi apparatus; one

    d) mitochondrion; two

    e) mitochondrion; one

    100 HARD

    39

    0 EASY

12. The cytoskeleton:

    a) is a viscous fluid found in all cells.

    b) fills a cell's nucleus but not the other organelles.

    c) gives an animal cell shape and support, but cannot control movement.

    d) helps to coordinate intracellular movement of organelles and molecules.

    e) All of the above are correct.

    100 HARD

    55

    0 EASY

13. Which of the following statements about mitochondria is correct?

    a) Mitochondria are found in both eukaryotes and prokaryotes.

    b) There tend to be more mitochondria in fat cells than in liver cells.

    c) Most plant cells contain mitochondria.

    d) Mitochondria may have originated evolutionarily as photosynthetic bacteria.

    e) All of the above are correct.

    100 HARD

    70

    0 EASY

14. Which of the following organelles is not present in animal cells?

    a) lysosome

    b) Golgi apparatus

    c) rough endoplasmic reticulum

    d) mitochondrion

    e) chloroplast

    100 HARD

    14

    0 EASY

15. Given that a cell's structure reflects its function, what function would you predict for a cell with a large Golgi apparatus?

    a) movement

    b) secretion of digestive enzymes

    c) transport of chemical signals

    d) rapid replication of genetic material and coordination of cell division

    e) attachment to bone tissue

    100 HARD

    59

    0 EASY

16. Cell walls:

    a) only occur in plant cells.

    b) are not completely solid, having many small pores.

    c) confer less structural support than the plasma membrane.

    d) dissolve when a plant dies.

    e) are made primarily from phospholipids.

    100 HARD

    66

    0 EASY

17. Which one of the following organelles is not found in both plant and animal cells?

    a) nucleus

    b) rough endoplasmic reticulum

    c) mitochondrion

    d) smooth endoplasmic reticulum

    e) central vacuole

    100 HARD

    41

    0 EASY

18. In plant cells, chloroplasts:

a) serve the same purpose that mitochondria serve in animal cells.

b) are the site of conversion of light energy into chemical energy.

c) play an important role in the breakdown of plant toxins.

d) have their own linear strands of DNA.

e) Both b) and d) are correct.

100 HARD

40

0 EASY

Short-Answer Question

1. Name and note the function of the organelles shown in the diagram.

See Answers at the back of the book.
For additional study questions, go to www.prep-u.com.

ORGANELLE:
FUNCTION:

ORGANELLE:
FUNCTION:

ORGANELLE:
FUNCTION:

ORGANELLE:
FUNCTION:

ORGANELLE:
FUNCTION:

ORGANELLE:
FUNCTION:

ORGANELLE:
FUNCTION:

ORGANELLE:
FUNCTION:

ORGANELLE:
FUNCTION:

ABOUT THE CHAPTER OPENING PHOTO

Color-enhanced electron micrograph of a human liver cell (hepatocyte). Hepatocytes are responsible for protein synthesis and storage; the metabolism of carbohydrate, protein, and lipid; detoxification; and the initiation of the formation and secretion of bile.

From the sun to you in
just two steps

Energy

129

4·1–4·4 Energy flows from the sun and through all life on earth

Sunlight filters through the northern California redwoods.

4·1 Cars that run on french fry oil? Organisms and machines need energy to work.

Imagine that you are on a long road trip. Your car's fuel gauge is nearing empty, so you pull off the highway. Instead of driving into a gas station, however, you head to the back of a fast-food restaurant and fill the fuel tank with used cooking grease. You head back to the highway, ready to drive several hundred miles before needing another pit stop.

Fast food for your car? Yes! The idea isn't as far-fetched as it sounds. In fact, on the roads of America today, many vehicles run on **biofuels,** fuels produced from plant and animal products (**FIGURE 4-1**). Most vehicles, however, run on **fossil fuels** such as gasoline. These fuels (which also include oil, natural gas, and coal) are produced from the decayed remains of plants and animals modified over millions of years by heat, pressure, and bacteria.

It turns out that biofuels, fossil fuels, and the food fuels that supply energy to most living organisms are chemically similar. This fact is not surprising because energy from the sun is the source of the energy stored in the chemical bonds between the atoms in all these fuels. Let's investigate how fuels provide energy.

Q *Humans can get energy from food. Can machines?*

When we burn gasoline, long chains of carbon and hydrogen atoms separate, releasing carbon dioxide (CO_2), water, and a lot of energy that was stored in the chemical bonds holding each gasoline molecule together. (An interesting fact: the energy released in burning one gallon of gas is equivalent to the caloric content of 15 large cheese pizzas.) In an automobile engine, some of this released energy is harnessed to push pistons, spin a crankshaft, turn wheels, and move the car.

Animal fats and the oils in many plants—such as those used to cook french fries—share an important chemical feature with gasoline. Like gasoline, these fats and oils contain chains of carbon and hydrogen atoms bound together, and just as with gasoline, breaking these bonds releases large amounts of energy (and water and CO_2). If this released energy can be

FIGURE 4-1 Biofuel technology. Biofuels are chemically similar to fossil fuels.

captured efficiently, it, too, can be used to push pistons and turn car wheels.

Cars that run on biofuels are more than just a technological trick. The production of biofuels requires only the plant or animal source, sunlight, air, water, and a relatively short amount of time—a few months or years, depending on the source. On the other hand, the production of fossil fuels such as coal or crude oil requires plant and animal remains and millions of years. This difference gives biofuels an important advantage over fossil fuels: they are a renewable resource. For this reason, biofuels point the way toward a future of reduced dependence on fossil fuels, the supplies of which are dwindling and the combustion of which has many harmful consequences, such as increasing global warming and releasing cancer-causing particles into the atmosphere. Are we at the point yet where all our cars can run on biofuels? Not quite: there are several significant drawbacks to the increased use of biofuels, chief among them the destruction of forests, wetlands, and other ecologically important habitats from the increased use of land to grow these fuels. This is why the search for better fuels continues.

In this chapter we explore how plant, animal, and other living "machines" run on energy stored in chemical bonds. Just as the forward motion of a car is fueled by breaking the chemical bonds in gasoline and harnessing the released energy, the activities of living organisms are fueled by breaking the chemical bonds in food molecules and harnessing the released energy.

All life depends on capturing energy from the sun and converting it into a form that living organisms can use. This energy capture and conversion occurs in two important

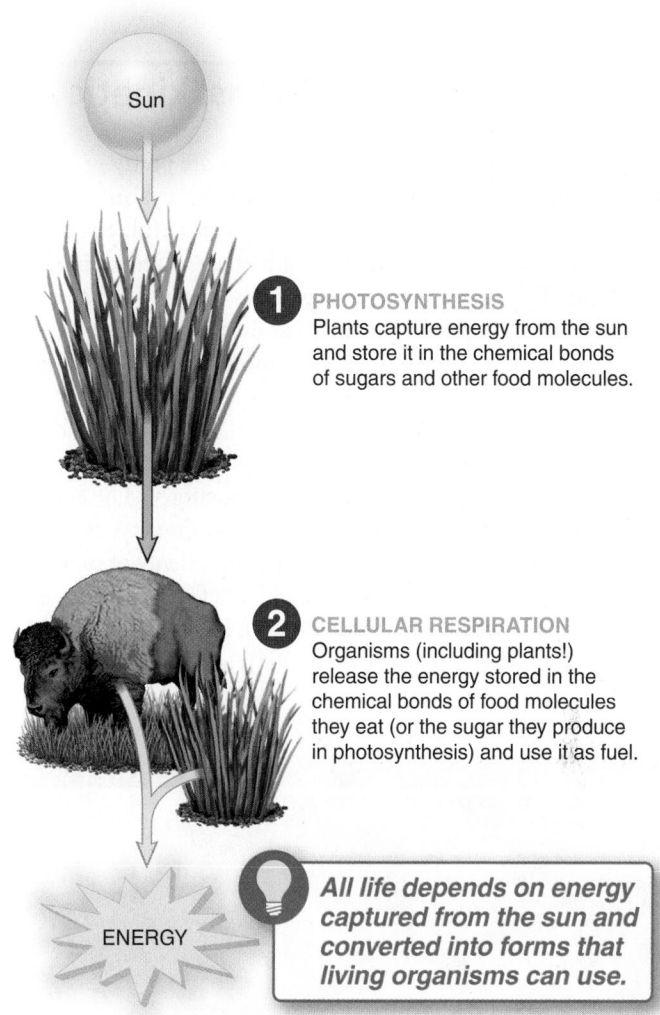

1 PHOTOSYNTHESIS
Plants capture energy from the sun and store it in the chemical bonds of sugars and other food molecules.

2 CELLULAR RESPIRATION
Organisms (including plants!) release the energy stored in the chemical bonds of food molecules they eat (or the sugar they produce in photosynthesis) and use it as fuel.

ENERGY

All life depends on energy captured from the sun and converted into forms that living organisms can use.

FIGURE 4-2 Photosynthesis and cellular respiration. The sun to you in just two steps!

processes that mirror each other: (1) **photosynthesis,** the process by which plants capture energy from the sun and store it in the chemical bonds of sugars and other food molecules they make, and (2) **cellular respiration,** the process by which all living organisms release the energy stored in the chemical bonds of food molecules and use it to fuel their lives (**FIGURE 4-2**). The sun to you in just two steps!

TAKE-HOME MESSAGE 4·1

The sun is the source of the energy that powers all living organisms and other "machines." The energy from sunlight is stored in the chemical bonds of molecules. When these bonds are broken, energy is released regardless of whether the bond is in a molecule of food, a fossil fuel, or a biofuel such as the oil in which french fries are cooked.

4·2 Energy has two forms: kinetic and potential.

"Batteries not included." For a child, those are pretty depressing words. We know that many of the toys and electronic gadgets that make our lives fun or useful (or both) need energy—usually in the form of batteries. Generating ringtones, lights, and movement requires energy. The same is true for humans, plants, and all other living organisms: they need energy for their activities, from moving to reproducing to thinking.

Energy is the capacity to do work. And work is anything that involves moving matter against an opposing force. The energy encountered in the study of living things is of two types: kinetic and potential. **Kinetic energy** is the energy of moving objects. Legs pushing bike pedals and birds flapping wings are examples of kinetic energy (**FIGURE 4-3**). Heat, which results from lots of molecules moving rapidly, is another form of

kinetic energy. Because it comes from the movement of high-energy particles, light is also a form of kinetic energy—probably the most important form of kinetic energy on earth. (When we look at photosynthesis later in this chapter, we explore how sunlight is harnessed for producing food molecules.)

An object does not have to be moving to have the capacity to do work; it may have **potential energy,** which is stored energy or the capacity to do work that results from an object's location or position. Water behind a dam, for example, has potential energy. If a hole in the dam is opened, the water can flow through, and perhaps spin a waterwheel or turbine. A concentration gradient, which we discussed in Chapter 3, also has potential energy: if the molecules in an area of high concentration move toward an area of lower concentration, the potential energy of the gradient is converted to the kinetic

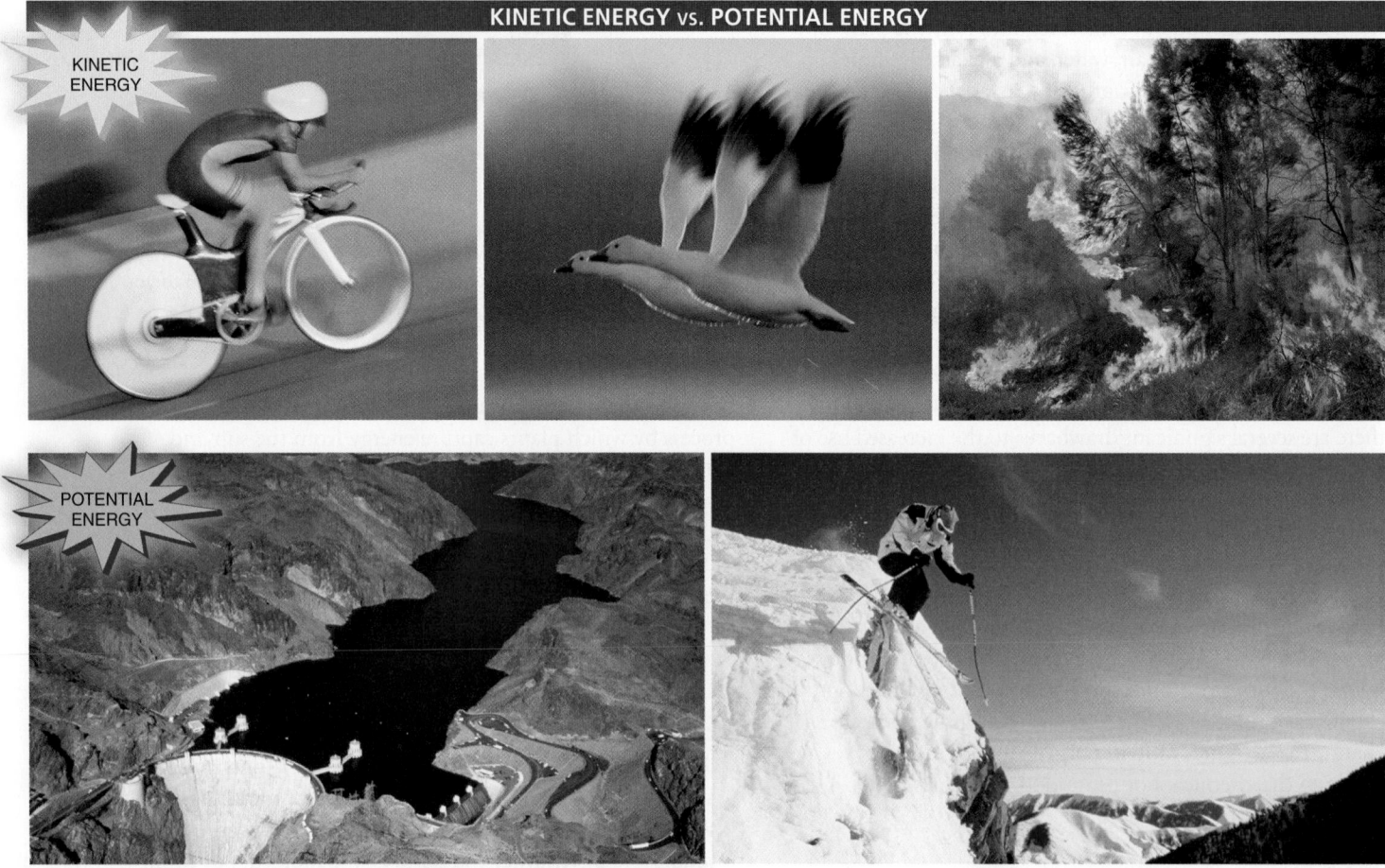

FIGURE 4-3 Two forms of energy. Kinetic energy is the energy of motion; potential energy is energy stored in an object, such as water trapped behind a dam, or a skier poised at the top of a hill.

CHEMICAL ENERGY

Glucose
$C_6H_{12}O_6$

Chemical energy is a form of potential energy stored in chemical bonds.

H — CHEMICAL ENERGY — C

Food is a form of chemical energy!

FIGURE 4-4 The energy of chemical bonds. The chemical bonds in food molecules are a form of potential energy.

energy of molecular movement, and this kinetic energy can do work. **Chemical energy,** the storage of energy in chemical bonds, is also a type of potential energy.

Because potential energy doesn't involve movement, it is a less obvious form of energy than kinetic energy. An apple has potential energy, as does any other type of food (**FIGURE 4-4**). Why? Because the chemical energy stored in the chemical bonds making up the food can be broken and the energy released during cellular respiration, enabling you to run, play, and work. We explore cellular respiration, the energy-releasing breakdown of molecules, later in this chapter. But first we need to know more about the nature of energy.

TAKE-HOME MESSAGE 4·2

Energy, the capacity to do work, comes in two forms. Kinetic energy is the energy of moving objects, while potential energy, such as chemical energy, is *stored* energy or the capacity to do work that results from the position or location of an object.

4·3 As energy is captured and converted, the amount of energy available to do work decreases.

Every minute of every day—even on cloudy ones—the sun shines brightly, releasing tremendous amounts of energy. Organisms on earth cannot capture every bit of energy released by the sun; indeed, most plants capture only a tiny fraction of the available energy. What happens to the rest? This unused energy does not simply disappear. Accountants would love to monitor the flow of energy because, as in a good accounting ledger, all of the energy numbers add up perfectly. All energy from the sun can be accounted for: some (probably less than 1%) is captured and transformed into usable chemical energy by organisms through photosynthesis (**FIGURE 4-5**). The rest of the energy from the sun is reflected back into space (probably about 30%) or absorbed by land, the oceans, and the atmosphere (about 70%) and mostly transformed into heat. Heat is not easily harnessed to do work, however, and is therefore a much less useful form of energy than the energy transformed into chemical energy in plants (and stored as carbohydrates). The same accounting also exists on a smaller level. If you eat a bowl of rice, some portion of the chemical energy stored in the bonds of the molecules that make up the rice grains is transformed into usable energy that can fuel your

cells' activities. All the rest is transformed into heat and is ultimately lost into the atmosphere.

The fact that energy can change form but never disappear is an important feature of energy in the universe, whether we are looking at the sun and the earth or a human and her rice bowl. Just as energy can never disappear or be destroyed, energy can never be created. All the energy now present in the universe has been here since the universe began, and everything that has happened since then has occurred by the transformation of one form of energy into another. In all our eating and growing, driving and sleeping, we are simply transforming energy. The study of the transformation of energy from one type to another, such as from potential energy to kinetic energy, is called **thermodynamics,** and the **first law of thermodynamics** states that energy can never be created or destroyed. It can only change from one form to another.

Because plants capture less than 1% of the sun's energy, it might seem like they are particularly inefficient. But we humans are also rather inefficient at extracting the chemical

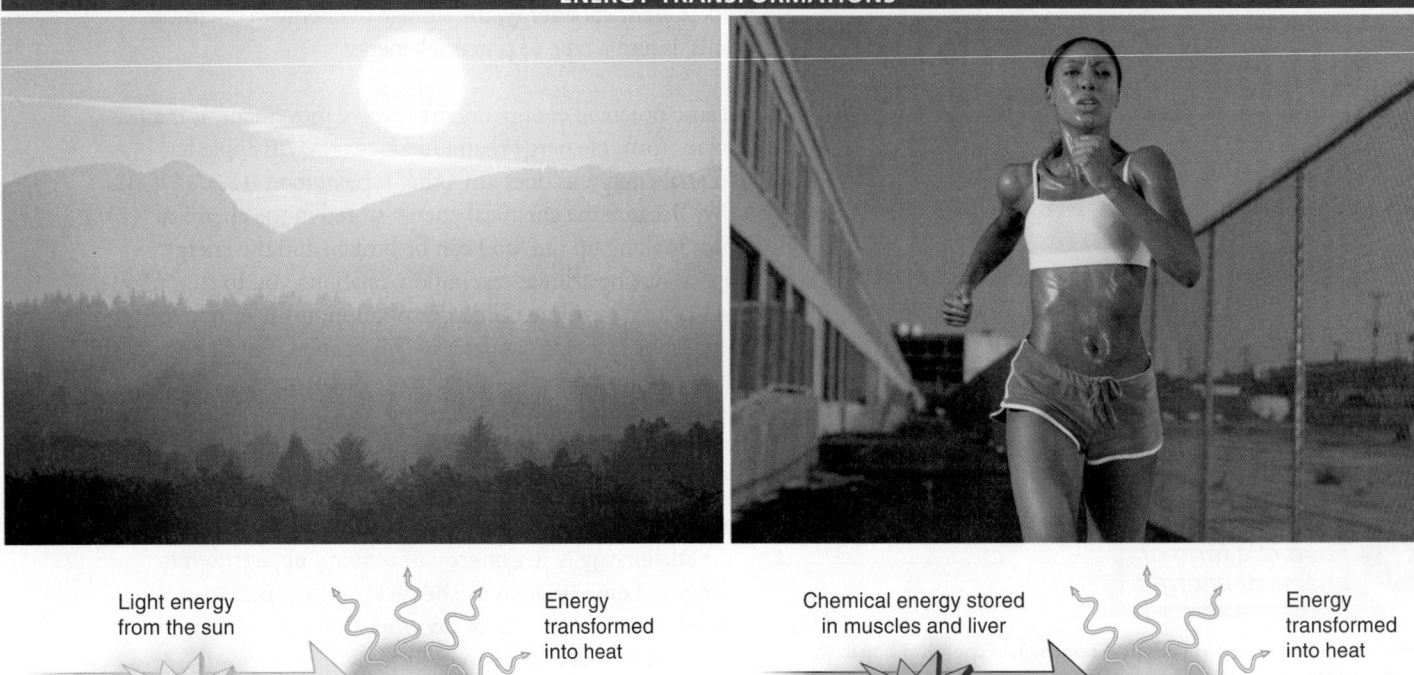

Light energy from the sun → Energy transformed into heat

Chemical energy stored in plants

Chemical energy stored in muscles and liver → Energy transformed into heat

Kinetic energy of forward motion

FIGURE 4-5 As energy is converted to do work, some energy is released as heat.

energy of plants when we eat them. These inefficiencies occur because every time energy is converted from one form to another, some of the energy is converted to heat. When a human converts the chemical energy in a plate of spaghetti into the kinetic energy of running a marathon, or when a car transforms the chemical energy of gasoline into the kinetic energy of forward motion, some energy is converted to heat, the least usable form of kinetic energy. In automobiles, for example, about three-quarters of the energy in gasoline is lost as heat (**FIGURE 4-6**). Thus, for every $10 spent on gas, only about $2.50 goes toward moving the car!

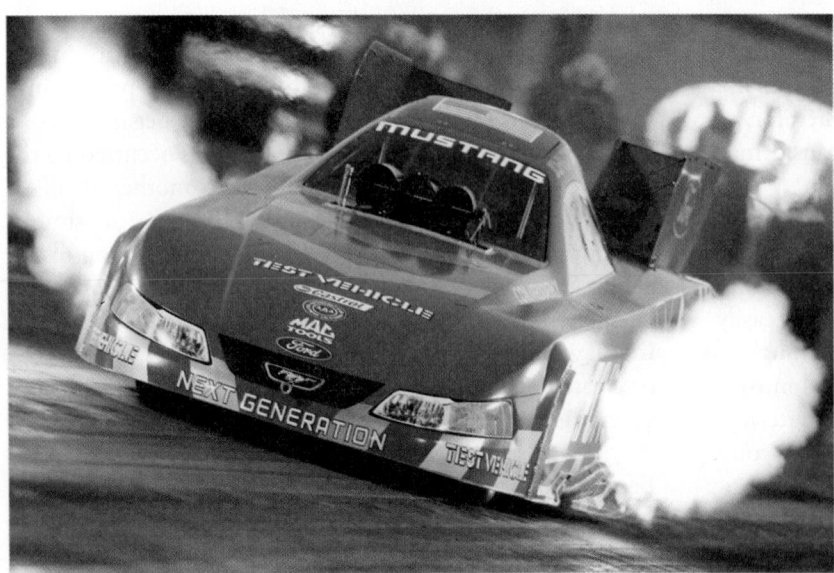

FIGURE 4-6 Inefficient conversion. Much of the energy used to fuel a combustion engine is converted to heat rather than forward motion.

The **second law of thermodynamics** states that every conversion of energy is not perfectly efficient and invariably includes the transformation of some energy into heat. Although heat is certainly a form of energy, it is almost completely useless to living organisms for fueling their cellular activity because it is not easily harnessed to do work. Put another way, the second law of thermodynamics tells us that although the quantity of energy in the universe is not changing, its quality is. Little by little, the amount of energy that is available to do work decreases. Now that we understand that organisms on earth cannot capture every single bit of energy released by the sun—and that energy conversions are inefficient—we can look at the chief energy currency of the cell: ATP.

> ### TAKE-HOME MESSAGE 4·3
>
> Energy is neither created nor destroyed but can change forms. Each conversion of energy is inefficient, and some of the usable energy is converted to less useful heat energy.

4·4 ATP molecules are like free-floating rechargeable batteries in all living cells.

Much of the work that cells do requires energy. But even though light energy from the sun carries energy, as do molecules of sugar, fat, and protein, none of this energy can be used directly to fuel chemical reactions in organisms' cells. First it must be captured in the bonds of a molecule called **adenosine triphosphate (ATP),** a free-floating molecule found in cells that acts like a rechargeable battery which temporarily stores energy that can then be used for cellular work in plants, animals, bacteria, and all the other organisms on earth. The use of ATP solves an important timing and coordination problem for living cells: a supply of ATP guarantees that the energy required for energy-consuming reactions will be available when it's needed.

ATP is a simple molecule with three components (**FIGURE 4-7**). At the center of the ATP molecule are two of these components: a small sugar molecule attached to a molecule called adenine. But it is the third component that makes ATP so effective in carrying and storing energy for a short time: attached to the sugar and adenine is a chain of

ADENOSINE TRIPHOSPHATE (ATP) AND ADENOSINE DIPHOSPHATE (ADP)

Adenine

Phosphate groups

High-energy bonds

Ribose (sugar)

P_i Separate phosphate group

ENERGY

Adenine

Phosphate groups

Ribose (sugar)

ATP — Symbol for ATP used in this book

The green halo represents ATP's potential energy.

ADP — Symbol for ADP used in this book

FIGURE 4-7 The structure of ATP and ADP. When ATP ejects one of its phosphate groups, energy is released as ATP becomes ADP.

An input of energy from the breakdown of food attaches ADP to P_i.

Energy is released as a phosphate group is ejected from ATP.

ATP can be used and recycled hundreds of thousands of times!

FIGURE 4-8 ATP is like a rechargeable battery.

three negatively charged phosphate groups (hence the "tri" in "triphosphate"). Because the bonds between these three phosphate groups must hold the groups together in the face of the three electrical charges that all repel one another, each of these bonds contains a large amount of energy and is stressed and unstable. The instability of these high-energy bonds makes the three phosphate groups like a tightly coiled spring or a twig that is bent almost to the point of breaking. With the slightest push, one of the phosphate groups will pop off, displaced by water. And in the process, a little burst of energy is released that the cell can use.

It is precisely because each molecule of ATP is always on the brink of ejecting one of its phosphate groups that ATP is such an effective energy source inside a cell. As long as plenty of ATP molecules are around, they can energize the chemical reactions that make it possible for the cell to carry out reactions that require work, such as building muscle, repairing wounds, or growing roots. Each time a cell expends one of its ATP molecules to pay for an energetically expensive reaction, a phosphate is broken off and energy is

released. What is left is a molecule with two phosphates, called ADP (adenosine *di*phosphate), and a separate phosphate group (labeled P_i).

An organism can then use ADP, a free-floating phosphate, and an input of kinetic energy to rebuild its ATP stocks (**FIGURE 4-8**). The kinetic energy is converted to potential energy when the free phosphate group attaches to the ADP molecule and makes ATP. In this manner, ATP functions like a rechargeable battery. Where does the input of energy for recharging ATP come from? When we discuss photosynthesis, we'll see that plants, algae, and some bacteria directly use light energy from the sun to make ATP from ADP and free-floating phosphate groups. Animals use the energy contained in the bonds of their food molecules. In either case, the energy is used to re-create the unstable bond in the triphosphate chain. When energy is needed, the organism can again release it by breaking the bond holding the phosphate group to the rest of the molecule. Our bodies recycle ATP molecules in this way tens of thousands of times a day.

Here's the ATP story in a nutshell. Breaking down a molecule of sugar—in a glass of orange juice, for example—leads to a miniature burst of energy in your body. The energy from the mini-explosion is put to work building the unstable high-energy bonds that attach phosphate groups to ADP molecules, creating new molecules of ATP. Later—perhaps only a fraction of a second later—when an energy-consuming reaction is needed, your cells can release the energy stored in the new ATP molecules.

TAKE-HOME MESSAGE 4·4

Cells temporarily store energy in the bonds of ATP molecules. This potential energy can be converted to kinetic energy and used to fuel life-sustaining chemical reactions. At other times, inputs of kinetic energy are converted to the potential energy of the energy-rich but unstable bonds in the ATP molecule.

4·5–4·11
Photosynthesis uses energy from sunlight to make food.

All plants are able to capture light energy and convert it to organic matter. Shown here: King protea (Protea cynaroides), the national flower of South Africa.

4·5 Where does plant matter come from? Photosynthesis: the big picture.

Watching a plant grow over the course of a few years can seem like watching a miracle, or at least a very subtle magic trick. Of course it's neither, but the process is nonetheless amazing. Consider that in five years a tree can increase its weight by 150 pounds (68 kg) (**FIGURE 4-9**). Where does that 150 pounds of new tree come from?

Q Our first guess might be the soil. Could that be it? It's easy enough to weigh the soil in a pot when first planting a tree, and weigh it again 5 years later. After 5 years, though, we find that the soil in our planter has lost less than a pound, nowhere near enough to explain the massive increase in the amount of plant material. Perhaps the new growth comes from the water? Wrong again. Although the older and much larger tree holds more water in its many cells, the water provided to the plant does not come close to accounting for the increase in the dry weight of the plant.

When humans grow, the new tissue comes from food we eat. When plants grow, where does the new tissue come from?

The amazing truth is that most of the new material comes from an invisible gas in the air. In the process of photosynthesis, plants capture carbon dioxide gas (CO_2) from the air. And using energy they get from sunlight, along with

water and small amounts of chemicals usually found in soil, they produce solid, visible (and often tasty) sugars and other organic molecules that are used to make plant structures such as leaves, roots, stems, flowers, fruits, and seeds. In the process, the plants give off oxygen (O_2), a by-product that happens to

5 LB. → 5 years → 155 LB.

FIGURE 4-9 When plants grow, where does the new tissue come from? From the dirt? From thin air?

| Euglena | Cyanobacterium | Dinoflagellates | Kelp |

LM 250× | SEM 660× | SEM 80×

FIGURE 4-10 Plants aren't the only photosynthesizers. Some bacteria and other unicellular organisms, along with kelp and other multicellular algae, are capable of photosynthesis.

FIGURE 4-11 Photosynthesis: the big picture.

be necessary for much of the life on earth—including all animal life!

Although plants are generally the most visible organisms that can capture light energy and convert it to organic matter, they are not the only organisms capable of photosynthesis. Some bacteria and many other unicellular organisms, along with kelp and other multicellular algae, are also capable of using the energy in sunlight to produce organic materials (**FIGURE 4-10**).

There are three inputs to the process of photosynthesis (**FIGURE 4-11**): light energy (from the sun), carbon dioxide (from the atmosphere), and water (from the ground). From these three inputs, the plant produces sugar and oxygen. As we'll see, photosynthesis is best understood as two separate events: a "photo" segment, during which light is captured, and a "synthesis" segment, during which sugar is built. In the "photo" reactions, light energy is captured and temporarily saved in energy-storage molecules. During this process, water molecules split and produce oxygen. In the "synthesis" reactions, the energy in the energy-storage molecules is used to assemble sugar molecules from carbon dioxide from the air.

TAKE-HOME MESSAGE 4·5

Through photosynthesis, plants use water, the energy of sunlight, and carbon dioxide gas from the air to produce sugars and other organic materials. In the process, photosynthesizing organisms also produce oxygen, which makes all animal life possible.

4·6 Photosynthesis takes place in the chloroplasts.

If a plant part is green, then you know it is photosynthetic. Leaves are green because the cells near the surface are packed full of **chloroplasts,** light-harvesting organelles, which make it possible for the plant to use the energy from sunlight to make sugars (their food) and other plant tissue (much of which animals use for food) (**FIGURE 4-12**). Other plant parts, such as stems, may also contain chloroplasts (in which case they, too, are capable of photosynthesis), but most chloroplasts are located within the cells in a plant's leaves.

Let's take a closer look at chloroplasts (**FIGURE 4-13**). The sac-shaped organelle is filled with a fluid called the **stroma.** Floating in the stroma is an elaborate system of interconnected membranous structures called **thylakoids,** which often look like stacks of pancakes. Once inside the chloroplast, you can be in one of two places: in the stroma or inside the thylakoids. The conversion of light energy to chemical energy—the "photo" part of photosynthesis—occurs inside the thylakoids. The production of sugars—which are made in the "synthesis" part of photosynthesis—occurs within the stroma.

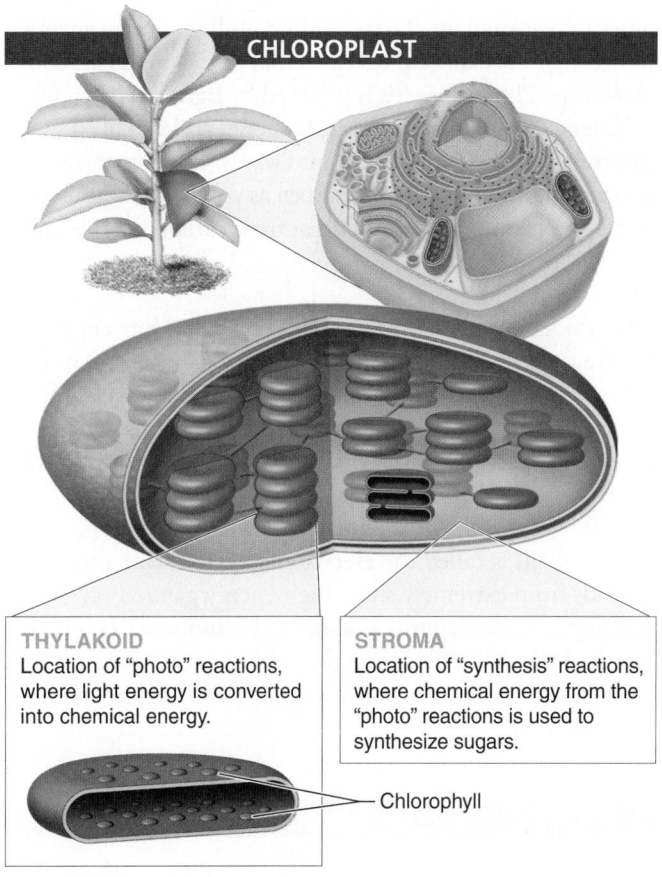

CHLOROPLAST

THYLAKOID
Location of "photo" reactions, where light energy is converted into chemical energy.

STROMA
Location of "synthesis" reactions, where chemical energy from the "photo" reactions is used to synthesize sugars.

Chlorophyll

FIGURE 4-13 Chloroplast structure. The chloroplast is where photosynthesis takes place in a plant.

Top edge of leaf

Photosynthetic cells packed with chloroplasts

Bottom edge of leaf

FIGURE 4-12 Photosynthesis factories. Cells near the leaf's surface are packed with photosynthetic chloroplasts.

We examine both the "photo" and the "synthesis" processes in greater detail later in this chapter. First, however, we examine the nature of light energy and of **chlorophyll,** the special molecule found in chloroplasts that makes the capture of light energy possible.

TAKE-HOME MESSAGE 4·6

In plants, photosynthesis occurs in chloroplasts, green organelles packed in cells near the plants' surfaces.

4·7 Light energy travels in waves: plant pigments absorb specific wavelengths.

You can't eat sunlight. That's because sunlight is *light* energy rather than the chemical energy found in the bonds of food molecules. Photosynthesis is powered by **light energy,** a type of kinetic energy made up of little energy packets called **photons,** which are organized into waves. Photons can do work as they bombard surfaces such as your face (heating it) or a leaf (enabling it to build sugar from carbon dioxide and water).

Photons have various amounts of energy, and the length of the wave in which they travel corresponds to the amount of energy carried by the photon. The shorter the wavelength, the more energy the light carries. Within a ray of light, there are super-high-energy packets of photons (those with short wavelengths), relatively low-energy packets (those with longer wavelengths), and everything in between. This range, which is called the **electromagnetic spectrum,** extends from extremely short high-energy gamma rays and X rays, with wavelengths as short as 1 nanometer (a human hair is about 50,000 nanometers in diameter), to very long low-energy radio waves, with wavelengths as long as a mile (**FIGURE 4-14**).

Just as we can't hear some super-high-pitched frequencies of sound (even though many dogs can), there are some wavelengths of light that are too short or too long for us to see. The light that we can see, visible light, spans all the colors of the rainbow. Humans (and some other animals) can see colors because our eyes contain light-absorbing molecules called **pigments.** These pigments absorb wavelengths of light within the visible range. The energy in these light waves excites electrons in the pigments, stimulating nerves in our eyes, which then transmit electrical signals to our brains. We perceive different wavelengths within the visible spectrum as different colors. The pigments in the human eye absorb many different wavelengths pretty well: that's why we can see so many colors. When plants use sunlight's energy to make sugar during photosynthesis, they also use the visible portion of the electromagnetic spectrum. Unlike the pigments in our eyes, however, plant pigments (the energy-capturing parts of a plant) absorb and use only a portion of visible light wavelengths.

Chlorophyll is the pigment molecule in plants that absorbs light energy from the sun. Chlorophyll molecules are embedded in the thylakoid membrane of chloroplasts, which are found primarily in plants' leaves. Just as light energy excites electrons in the pigments responsible for color vision in humans, electrons in a plant's chlorophyll can become excited by certain wavelengths of light and can capture a bit of this light energy.

Plants produce several different light-absorbing pigments (**FIGURE 4-15**). The primary photosynthetic pigment, called **chlorophyll *a,*** absorbs red and blue-violet wavelengths of light. Every other wavelength generally travels through or bounces off this pigment. Because chlorophyll *a* cannot efficiently absorb green light and instead reflects those wavelengths, we perceive the reflected light waves as green, and so the pigment and the leaves that contain it appear green. Another pigment, **chlorophyll *b,*** is similar in structure but

ELECTROMAGNETIC SPECTRUM

Sunlight

Radio waves | Infrared | UV light | X rays | Gamma rays

1,000 m
Longer wavelength
Lower energy

1 nm
Shorter wavelength
Higher energy

Visible light

740 nm   400 nm

FIGURE 4-14 A spectrum of energy. A ray of light emits high-energy photons, low-energy photons, and everything in between. Plants use only a fraction of the light's available energy.

PHOTOSYNTHETIC PIGMENTS

Plants produce several different light-absorbing pigments. Each photosynthetic pigment absorbs and reflects specific wavelengths.

Seasonal differences in the amount of pigment molecules present in leaves lead to the leaves changing color.

In the fall, chlorophyll *a* and *b* molecules are broken down and stored in branches.

GRAPHIC CONTENT!
Thinking critically about visual displays of data.
Turn to p.164 for a closer inspection of this figure.

FIGURE 4-15 Plant pigments. Each photosynthetic pigment absorbs and reflects specific wavelengths.

absorbs blue and red-orange wavelengths. Chlorophyll *b* reflects yellow-green wavelengths. Some related pigments called **carotenoids** absorb blue-violet and blue-green wavelengths and reflect yellow, orange, and red wavelengths.

In the late summer, cooler temperatures cause some trees to prepare for the winter by shutting down chlorophyll production and reducing photosynthesis rates, much like an animal's hibernation. Gradually, the chlorophyll *a* and *b* molecules in the leaves are broken down and their chemical components are stored in the branches. As the amounts of chlorophyll *a* and *b* in the leaves decrease relative to the remaining carotenoids, the striking colors of the fall foliage are revealed (see Figure 4-15). During the rest of the year, chlorophylls *a* and *b* are so abundant in leaves that green masks the colors of the other pigments.

Why *do the leaves of some trees turn beautiful colors each fall?*

TAKE-HOME MESSAGE 4·7

Photosynthesis is powered by light energy, a type of kinetic energy made of energy packets called photons. Photons hit chlorophyll and other light-absorbing molecules near the green surfaces of plants. These molecules capture some of the light energy and harness it to build sugar from carbon dioxide and water.

4·8 Photons cause electrons in chlorophyll to enter an excited state.

An organism can use energy from the sun only if it can convert the light energy of the sun into the chemical energy in the bonds between atoms. The most important molecule in this conversion is the pigment chlorophyll (**FIGURE 4-16**).

ENERGY MOVEMENT THROUGH CHLOROPHYLL

1 Light energy bumps an electron in the chlorophyll molecule to a higher, excited energy level.

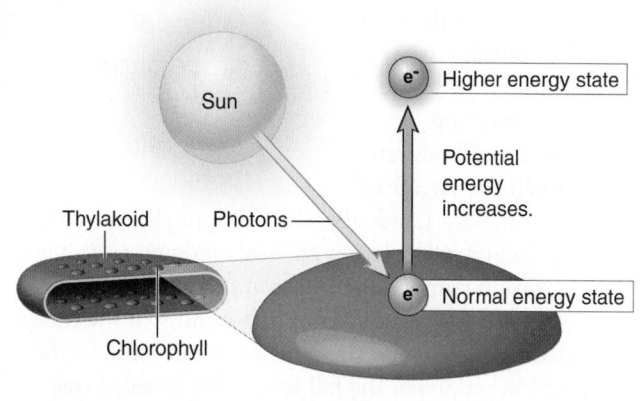

Sun

Thylakoid   Photons

Chlorophyll

e⁻   Higher energy state

Potential energy increases.

e⁻   Normal energy state

2 The excited electron generally has one of two different fates:

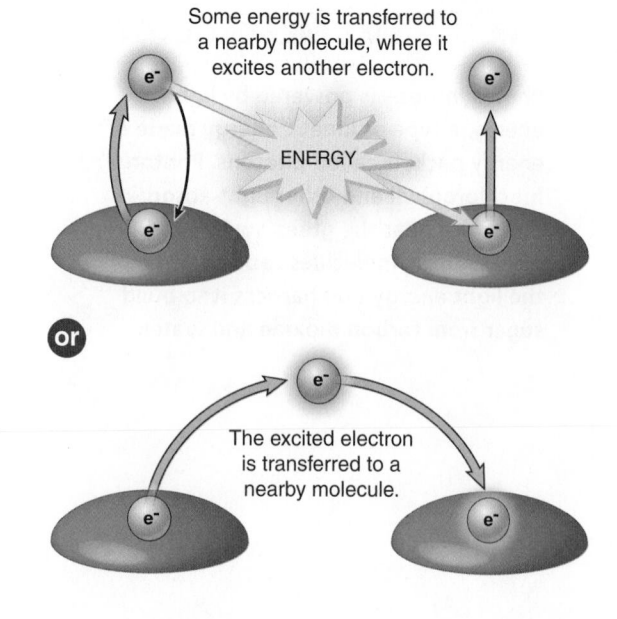

Some energy is transferred to a nearby molecule, where it excites another electron.

e⁻

e⁻

ENERGY

e⁻

e⁻

or

e⁻

The excited electron is transferred to a nearby molecule.

e⁻

e⁻

FIGURE 4-16 Capturing light energy as excited electrons. Chlorophyll electrons are excited to a higher energy state by light energy.

When chlorophyll is hit by photons of certain wavelengths, the light energy bumps an electron (e⁻) in the chlorophyll molecule to a higher energy level, an *excited* state. Upon absorbing the photon, the electron briefly gains energy, and the potential energy in the chlorophyll molecule increases.

An electron in a photosynthetic pigment that is excited to a higher energy state generally has one of two fates. (1) The electron returns to its resting, unexcited state, releasing energy in the process, some of which may bump electrons in a nearby molecule to a higher energy state (while the rest of the energy is dissipated as heat). Or (2) the excited electron itself is passed to another molecule.

The passing of electrons from molecule to molecule is one of the chief ways that energy moves through cells. Many molecules carry or accept electrons during cellular activities. All that is required is that the acceptor must have a greater attraction for electrons than does the molecule from which it receives them. This receiver molecule, in turn, hands off electrons to another acceptor with an even greater attraction for them. A molecule that gains electrons always carries greater energy than it did before receiving the electron(s). For this reason, the passing of electrons from one molecule to another can be viewed as a passing of potential energy. In this way, energy moves through cells.

This transfer of electrons is one of the first steps of photosynthesis, the process that enables a plant to harness light energy from the sun and convert it to the more readily usable chemical energy. As we see later in this chapter, the dismantling of food molecules such as glucose to generate energy is also a story of breaking and rearranging chemical bonds as electrons pass from one atom or molecule to another.

Because particles in the atmosphere can block light from the sun and reduce the excitation of electrons in chlorophyll molecules, photosynthesis depends on a relatively clean atmosphere. Any reduction in the available sunlight can have serious effects on plants. Scientists believe that if a large meteor hit the earth—as one did when the dinosaurs were

Q *Suppose a large meteor hit the earth. How could smoke and soot in the atmosphere wipe out life far beyond the area of direct impact?*

wiped out 65 million years ago—smoke, soot, and dust in the atmosphere could block sunlight to such an extent that plants in the region, or possibly all of the plants on earth, could not conduct photosynthesis at high enough levels to survive. And when plants die off, all of the animals and other species that rely on them for energy die as well. All life on earth is completely dependent on the continued excitation of electrons by sunlight.

TAKE-HOME MESSAGE 4·8

When chlorophyll is hit by photons, the light energy excites an electron in the chlorophyll molecule, increasing the chlorophyll's potential energy. The excited electrons can be passed to other molecules, moving the potential energy through the cell.

4·9 Photosynthesis in detail: the energy of sunlight is captured as chemical energy.

Photosynthesis is a complex process, but our understanding can be greatly aided by remembering one phrase: FOLLOW THE ELECTRONS. In the passages that follow, if you feel that you are losing focus or getting lost, just remember to follow the electrons. Where are they coming from? What are they passing through? Where are they going? And what will happen to them when they get there?

In the first part of photosynthesis, the "photo" part, sunlight hits a plant and, in a three-step process, some of the energy in this sunlight is captured and stored in ATP and in another molecule (NADPH) that stores energy by accepting high-energy electrons (**FIGURE 4-17**).

The energy-capturing process occurs in two **photosystems.** These photosystems are arrangements of light-catching pigments (including chlorophyll) within chloroplasts that capture energy from sunlight and transform it—first into the energy of excited electrons and ultimately into ATP and high-energy electron carriers. After these transformations, the captured energy is ready to be used to make sugar molecules in the "synthesis" part of photosynthesis. We begin following electrons as sunlight hits a leaf and the chloroplasts in it (**FIGURE 4-18**).

The chloroplasts in a leaf convert light energy from the sun into chemical energy. This conversion begins in a collection of chlorophyll molecules and other light-absorbing pigments arranged within a chloroplast's thylakoid membrane. As these pigments absorb photons from the sunlight that hits the leaves, electrons in the pigments become excited and then return to their resting state. As the electrons return to their resting state, energy (but not the electrons) is transferred to neighboring pigment molecules. This process continues until the transferred energy from many pigment molecules excites the electrons in a

"PHOTO" REACTIONS

Sunlight Water

Chlorophyll

The "photo" reactions occur in the thylakoids of the leaves' chloroplasts.

ATP NADPH

Chloroplast Energy-storing molecules Oxygen

Diffuses out of the plant

FIGURE 4-17 Overview of the "photo" reactions. Light energy is captured in the "photo" portion of photosynthesis. That energy is later used to power the building of sugar molecules.

chlorophyll *a* molecule at the center of the photosystem (see Figure 4-18). This is where the electron journey begins.

Each energy burst boosts chlorophyll's electrons to an excited state, but the chlorophyll *a* molecule at the center of the photosystem is special, differing from the other pigment molecules in one key feature. When its electrons are boosted to an excited state they do not return to their resting, unexcited state. Instead, the special chlorophyll *a* continually

1 Light energy excites electrons in a pigment molecule (such as a chlorophyll molecule). The energy from the excited electrons is transferred to nearby pigment molecules.

2 When transferred energy excites electrons in the chlorophyll *a* molecule, the primary electron acceptor grabs them and sends them to the electron transport chain.

3 To replace electrons sent to the electron transport chain, water molecules are split and oxygen and hydrogen are released as by-products.

Chloroplast   Thylakoid

AREA OF DETAIL

Sun

Primary electron acceptor

To electron transport chain

Chlorophyll *a* molecule

Pigment molecule

Oxygen released into the atmosphere

Water

The oxygen released in the photo reactions happens to be necessary for much of the life on earth— including all animal life!

FIGURE 4-18 The water-splitting photosystem. Splitting water provides electrons for photosynthesis.

loses its excited electrons to a nearby molecule, called the **primary electron acceptor,** which acts like an electron vacuum.

As electrons keep getting taken away from the special chlorophyll *a* molecule, the electrons must be replaced. The replacement electrons come from water. As long as photosynthesis is occurring, a constant supply of replacement electrons is required. Molecules of water inside the thylakoid, near the special chlorophyll *a* molecule in the thylakoid membrane, are continuously split. This split—in which four photons of light split two molecules of water into four electrons, four protons (H+), and a molecule of O_2—provides the electrons necessary to replenish chlorophyll *a*'s electron supply. A convenient and life-sustaining by-product of the splitting of water in photosynthesis is the oxygen that is released from the cell, a by-product essential for much of the life on earth, including all animal life.

Once the primary electron acceptor gets hold of the high-energy electrons from chlorophyll *a*, it passes them along like hot potatoes to another molecule, which passes them to another, which passes them to yet another, in what is called an **electron transport chain** (**FIGURE 4-19**). At each step in the electron transport chain's sequence of electron handoffs, the electrons fall to a lower energy state and a little bit of energy is released. These bits of energy are harnessed to power

Q

Why must plants get water for photosynthesis to occur?

pumps in the thylakoid membrane that move protons (which are also referred to as hydrogen ions or H+ ions) from the stroma to the inside of the thylakoid. The pumps pack the protons inside the thylakoid sac at higher and higher concentrations. Think of a pump pushing water into an elevated tank, creating a store of potential energy that can gush out of the tank with great force and kinetic energy. Similarly, the protons eventually rush out of the thylakoid sacs with great force—and the force of the protons moving down their concentration gradient is harnessed to build energy-storing ATP molecules, one of the two products of the "photo" portion of photosynthesis.

Recall that the energy-capturing and energy-transforming processes of the "photo" reactions occur in two photosystems (arrangements of chlorophyll and other light-catching molecules). The electron transport chain physically links the first photosystem to the second. As the traveling electrons continue their journey, they fill electron vacancies in the reaction center of the second photosystem, right next to the first photosystem (**FIGURE 4-20**). Like the first photosystem, the second photosystem also has numerous pigments that harness photons from the sun and pass the light energy to another special chlorophyll *a* molecule. The special chlorophyll *a* molecule at the center of this second photosystem has electron vacancies because, as in the first photosystem, when electrons in the special chlorophyll *a* molecule are boosted to an excited

1. Electrons move through the electron transport chain, releasing a little energy and falling to a lower energy state.

2. The released energy powers proton pumps that move hydrogen ions from the stroma and pack them inside the thylakoid.

3. Protons rush out of the thylakoid with great kinetic energy, which can be used to build ATP.

FIGURE 4-19 Harnessing the potential of high-energy electrons. As electrons are passed from the primary electron acceptor to a chain of molecules embedded within the thylakoid membrane, called the electron transport chain, the released energy is used to create a proton gradient.

state, they are whisked away from the chlorophyll molecule by another primary electron acceptor. This electron acceptor then passes the electrons to a second electron transport chain.

At the end of this second electron transport chain, the electrons are passed to a molecule called NADP+, creating **NADPH,** a high-energy electron carrier. NADPH is the

SUMMARY OF "PHOTO" REACTION COMPONENTS

1. **WATER-SPLITTING PHOTOSYSTEM**
Light energy is used to transfer electrons to the primary electron acceptor. Electrons are donated by water, releasing oxygen and hydrogen ions as by-products.

2. **1st ELECTRON TRANSPORT CHAIN**
High-energy electrons are used to pump hydrogen ions into the thylakoid. The kinetic energy from the release of these ions is used to build ATP.

3. **NADPH-PRODUCING PHOTOSYSTEM**
The NADPH-producing photosystem is identical to the water-splitting photosystem, except that electrons are donated by the electron transport chain.

4. **2nd ELECTRON TRANSPORT CHAIN**
High-energy electrons are passed to NADP+, creating NADPH, a high-energy electron carrier.

FIGURE 4-20 The "photo" portion of photosynthesis.

second important product of the "photo" portion of photosynthesis.

With the electrons' passage through the second photosystem and arrival in NADPH, we now have the final products of the "photo" part of photosynthesis (which are also called the light-dependent reactions): we've captured light energy from the sun and converted it to the chemical energy of ATP and the high-energy electron carrier NADPH (see Figure 4-20). But we haven't made any food yet. In the next section, we cover the "synthesis" part of photosynthesis and see how plants use the energy in ATP and NADPH to produce sugar from carbon dioxide.

4·10 Photosynthesis in detail: the captured energy of sunlight is used to make food.

The "synthesis" part of photosynthesis takes place in a series of chemical reactions called the **Calvin cycle.** All the Calvin cycle reactions occur in the stroma of the leaves' chloroplasts, outside the thylakoids. Plants carry out these reactions using the energy stored in the ATP and NADPH molecules that are built in the "photo" portion of photosynthesis. This dependency links the light-gathering ("photo") reactions with the sugar-building ("synthesis") reactions (**FIGURE 4-21**).

If there is any part of photosynthesis that appears magical, it is the Calvin cycle. Just as a magician seems to make a rabbit appear from thin air, the Calvin cycle takes invisible molecules of CO_2 from the air and uses them to assemble visible—even edible—molecules of sugar. The processes in the Calvin cycle occur in three steps (**FIGURE 4-22**).

1. Fixation. First, using an enzyme called **rubisco,** plants pluck carbon from the air, where it occurs in the form of carbon dioxide, and then attach, or "fix," it to a visible organic (carbon-containing) molecule within the chloroplast. Not surprisingly, given its role as the critical chemical that enables plants to build food molecules, rubisco is the most abundant protein on earth.

2. Sugar creation. The newly built molecule is chemically modified: a phosphate from ATP is added, and the molecule receives some high-energy electrons from NADPH. This product of the Calvin cycle is a small sugar called glyceraldehyde 3-phosphate (G3P).

Some of the G3P molecules are combined to make the six-carbon sugars glucose and fructose. These sugars can be used as fuel by the plant, enabling it to grow. They can also be used as fuel by animals that eat the plant.

3. Regeneration. Not all of the G3P molecules are used to produce sugars. In the third and final phase of the Calvin cycle, some G3P molecules are used to regenerate

"SYNTHESIS" REACTIONS

ATP NADPH

Energy-storing molecules   Carbon dioxide

CALVIN CYCLE

Sugar

The "synthesis" reactions occur in the stroma of the leaves' chloroplasts.

Chloroplast

FIGURE 4-21 Overview of the "synthesis" reactions of photosynthesis.

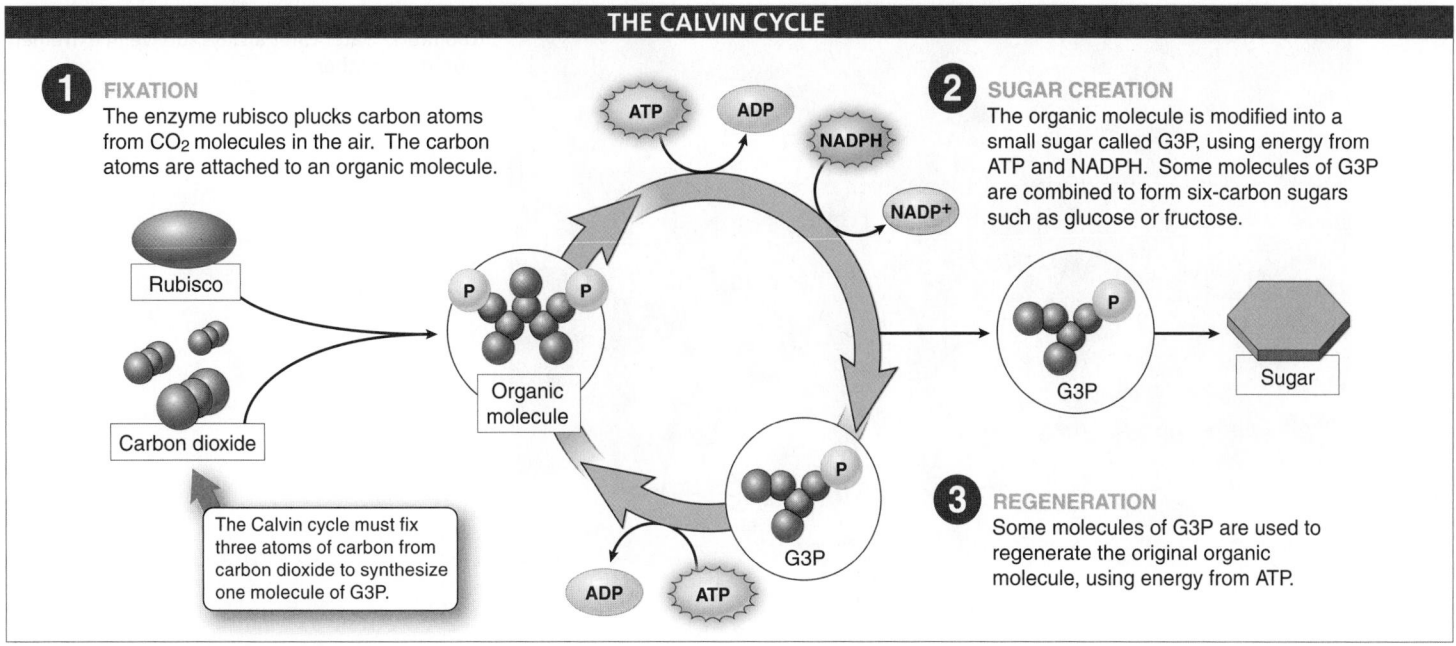

THE CALVIN CYCLE

1 FIXATION
The enzyme rubisco plucks carbon atoms from CO_2 molecules in the air. The carbon atoms are attached to an organic molecule.

Rubisco

Carbon dioxide

The Calvin cycle must fix three atoms of carbon from carbon dioxide to synthesize one molecule of G3P.

Organic molecule

ATP   ADP

NADPH

NADP+

2 SUGAR CREATION
The organic molecule is modified into a small sugar called G3P, using energy from ATP and NADPH. Some molecules of G3P are combined to form six-carbon sugars such as glucose or fructose.

G3P

Sugar

3 REGENERATION
Some molecules of G3P are used to regenerate the original organic molecule, using energy from ATP.

G3P

ADP   ATP

FIGURE 4-22 Sugar synthesis. In the Calvin cycle—the "synthesis" portion of photosynthesis—sugars are produced.

the original molecule in the chloroplast to which the carbon from CO_2 is attached. This regeneration process requires energy from ATP produced in the "photo" reactions of photosynthesis. With this regeneration, the Calvin cycle can continue to fix carbon and produce molecules of G3P.

Ultimately, to synthesize one molecule of G3P, the Calvin cycle must fix three atoms of carbon from carbon dioxide to the initial organic molecule; this process consumes nine molecules of ATP and six molecules of NADPH generated in the "photo" reactions of photosynthesis.

> ### TAKE-HOME MESSAGE 4·10
>
> The second part, or "synthesis" part, of photosynthesis is the Calvin cycle, which occurs in the stroma of chloroplasts. During this phase, carbon from CO_2 in the atmosphere is attached (fixed) to molecules in the chloroplasts, sugars are built, and molecules are regenerated to be used again in the Calvin cycle. The fixation, building, and regeneration processes consume energy from ATP and NADPH (the products of the "photo" part of photosynthesis).

4·11 The battle against world hunger can use plants adapted to water scarcity.

Sudan. Ethiopia. India. Somalia. Many of the world's regions with the highest rates of starvation also are places with the hottest, driest climates. This is not a coincidence. These climate conditions present difficult challenges for sustaining agriculture (**FIGURE 4-23**), and in the absence of stable crop yields, food production is unpredictable and the risk of starvation high. But evolutionary adaptations in some plants enable them to thrive in hot, dry conditions. Recent technological advances in agriculture use these innovative

evolutionary solutions to battle the problem of world hunger. In this section, we discuss some adaptations that allow plants to thrive when water is scarce. We also look at how humans use these adaptations to grow food in the dry, inhospitable climates where starvation rates are highest.

When it gets too hot and dry, animals can seek coolness in the shade. Plants, however, are anchored in place and do not have this option. Consequently, plants in hot, dry climates can lose

FIGURE 4-23 **Nowhere to hide.** Plants that lose too much water can't always survive in extremely hot, dry weather.

significant amounts of water through evaporation. Evaporation is a problem for plants because water is essential to photosynthesis, growth, and the transport of nutrients. Without water, plants cannot live long.

One method of combating water loss through evaporation is for plants to close their **stomata** (*sing.* **stoma**), small pores usually on the underside of leaves (**FIGURE 4-24**). These openings are the primary sites for gas exchange in plants: carbon dioxide for photosynthesis enters through these openings and oxygen generated as a by-product in photosynthesis exits through them. When open, the stomata also allow water to evaporate from the plant. Closing their

stomata solves one problem for plants (too much water evaporation) but creates another: with the stomata shut, oxygen from the "photo" reactions of photosynthesis cannot be released from the chloroplasts, and carbon dioxide cannot enter. If there are no carbon dioxide molecules for sugar production, the Calvin cycle tries to fix carbon but instead finds only oxygen. Plant growth comes to a standstill and crops fail.

In some plants, including corn and sugarcane, a process has evolved that minimizes water loss but still enables the plants to make sugar when the weather is hot and dry. In the process called **C4 photosynthesis,** these plants add an extra set of

Stoma open

Stoma closed

FIGURE 4-24 **Plant stomata.** Carbon dioxide enters a plant through stomata, but water can be lost through the same openings.

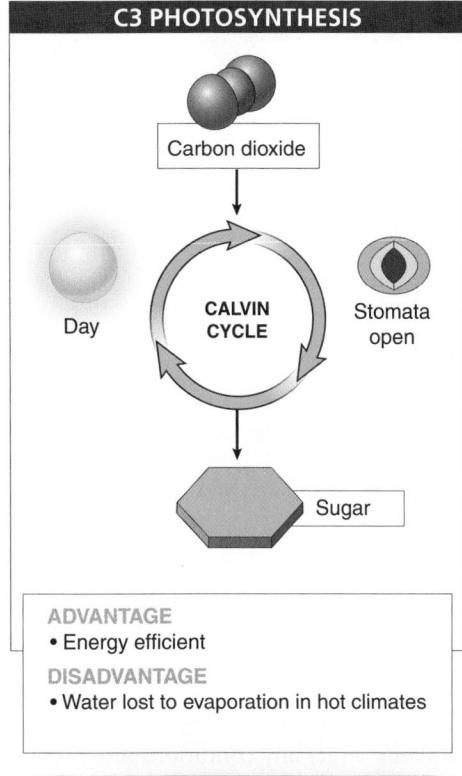

C3 PHOTOSYNTHESIS

Carbon dioxide

Day

CALVIN CYCLE

Stomata open

Sugar

ADVANTAGE
• Energy efficient

DISADVANTAGE
• Water lost to evaporation in hot climates

Common ivy

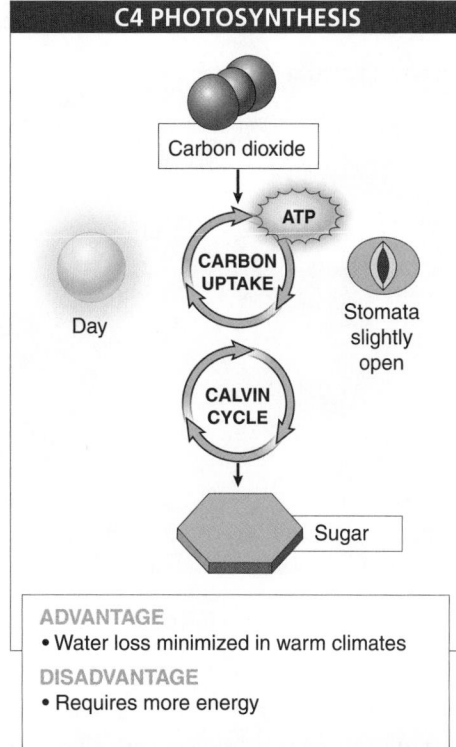

C4 PHOTOSYNTHESIS

Carbon dioxide

Day

ATP

CARBON UPTAKE

Stomata slightly open

CALVIN CYCLE

Sugar

ADVANTAGE
• Water loss minimized in warm climates

DISADVANTAGE
• Requires more energy

Corn

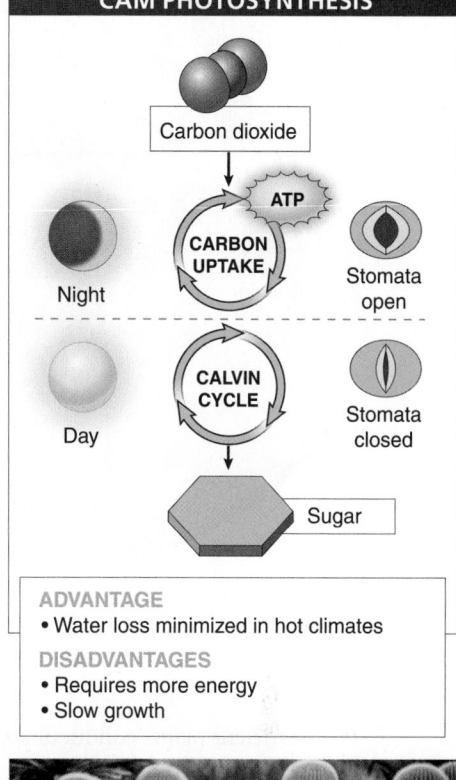

CAM PHOTOSYNTHESIS

Carbon dioxide

Night

ATP

CARBON UPTAKE

Stomata open

Day

CALVIN CYCLE

Stomata closed

Sugar

ADVANTAGE
• Water loss minimized in hot climates

DISADVANTAGES
• Requires more energy
• Slow growth

Golden Barrel Cactus

FIGURE 4-25 C3, C4, and CAM photosynthesis.

steps to the usual process of photosynthesis (**FIGURE 4-25**). In these steps, the plants produce an enzyme that functions like the ultimate "CO_2-sticky tape." This enzyme has a tremendously strong attraction for carbon dioxide; it can find and bind carbon even when CO_2 concentration is very low. (In contrast, rubisco, the usual enzyme that plants use to pluck carbon from the atmosphere, functions poorly when CO_2 is scarce.) As a consequence, stomata can be opened just a tiny bit, and let in just a little CO_2. Having the stomata closed also reduces evaporation and conserves water for the plant.

How might global warming be bad for agriculture?

Q

This seems like such a good solution that we would expect all plants to use it. There is a catch, though. The extra steps in C4 photosynthesis require the plant to expend additional energy. Specifically, every time the plant generates a molecule of the "CO_2-sticky tape" enzyme, it uses one molecule of ATP. It is acceptable to pay this energy cost only when the climate is so hot and dry that the plant would otherwise have to close its stomata and completely shut down all sugar production. If the climate is mild, however, plants conducting the more energetically expensive C4 photosynthesis would be out-competed by the

DISTRIBUTION OF PHOTOSYNTHESIS METHODS

Equator

C3 plants dominant
C4 plants dominant

FIGURE 4-26 Global distribution of C3 and C4 plants.

more efficient plants conducting standard photosynthesis (called C3 photosynthesis; see Figure 4-25). Not surprisingly, we see few C4 plants in the temperate regions of the world and little C4 photosynthesis among photosynthetic organisms living in the oceans. In hot, dry regions, however, C4 plants are dominant and displace the C3 plants wherever both occur (**FIGURE 4-26**). With global warming, many scientists expect to see a gradual expansion of the ranges over which C4 plants occur and believe that non-C4 plants will be pushed farther and farther away from the equator.

A third and similar method of carbon fixation, called **CAM** (for "crassulacean acid metabolism"), is also found in hot, dry areas. In this method, used by many cacti, pineapples, and other fleshy, juicy plants, the plants close their stomata during hot, dry days. At night, they open the stomata and let CO_2 into the leaves, where it binds temporarily to a holding molecule. During the day, when a carbon source is needed to make sugars in the Calvin cycle, the CO_2 is gradually released from the holding molecule, enabling photosynthesis to proceed while keeping the stomata closed to reduce water loss (see Figure 4-25). A disadvantage of CAM photosynthesis is that by completely closing their stomata during the day, CAM plants significantly reduce the total amount of CO_2 they can take in. As a consequence, they have much slower growth rates and cannot compete

well with non-CAM plants under any conditions other than extreme dryness.

C4 and CAM photosynthesis originally evolved because they made it possible for plants to grow better in the world's hot and dry regions. Researchers are now experimenting with these adaptations as a way to fight world hunger. They have introduced into rice several genes from corn that code for the C4 photosynthesis enzymes. Once in the rice, these genes increase the rice plant's ability to photosynthesize, leading to higher growth rates and food yields. Whether the addition of C4 photosynthesis enzymes will make it possible to grow new crops on a large scale in previously inhospitable environments is not certain. Early results suggest, however, that this is a promising approach.

TAKE-HOME MESSAGE 4·11

C4 and CAM photosynthesis are evolutionary adaptations at the biochemical level that, although more energetically expensive than regular (C3) photosynthesis, allow plants in hot, dry climates to close their stomata and conserve water without shutting down photosynthesis.

4·12–4·15 Cellular respiration converts food molecules into ATP, a universal source of energy for living organisms.

Watermelon powered! We extract energy from all the foods we eat.

4·12 How do living organisms fuel their actions? Cellular respiration: the big picture.

Food is fuel. And all the activities of life—growing, moving, reproducing—require fuel. Plants, most algae, and some bacteria obtain their fuel directly from the energy of sunlight, which they harness through photosynthesis. Less self-sufficient organisms, such as humans, alligators, and insects, must extract the energy they need from the food they eat. This energy comes from photosynthetic organisms either directly (from eating plants) or indirectly (from eating animals that eat plants) (**FIGURE 4-27**).

All living organisms extract energy from the chemical bonds of molecules (which can be considered "food") through a process

FIGURE 4-27 Living organisms require fuel (in one form or another).

Oxygen from atmosphere

Sugar and other energy-rich food molecules

CELLULAR RESPIRATION

In the cells of plants and animals, high-energy bonds of food molecules are broken down, releasing energy.

Carbon dioxide released to atmosphere

ATP

Water

INPUT		OUTPUT			
Oxygen + Sugar		→	Carbon dioxide + Water +		Energy (ATP)

FIGURE 4-28 Cellular respiration: the big picture.

called cellular respiration (**FIGURE 4-28**). This process is a bit like photosynthesis in reverse. In photosynthesis, the energy of the sun is captured and used to build molecules of sugars, such as glucose. In cellular respiration, plants and animals break down the chemical bonds of sugar and other energy-rich food molecules (such as fats and proteins) to release the energy that went into creating them. (Don't confuse cellular respiration with the act of breathing, which is also called *respiration*.) As energy is released, cells capture and store it in the bonds of ATP molecules. This plentiful, readily available stored energy can then be tapped as needed to fuel the work of the life-sustaining activities and processes of all living organisms.

In humans and other animals, cellular respiration starts after we eat food, digest it, absorb the nutrient molecules into the bloodstream, and deliver them to the cells of our bodies. At this point, our cells begin to extract some of the energy stored in the bonds of the food molecules. We focus here on the breakdown of glucose, but later in this chapter we'll see that the process is similar for the breakdown of fats or lipids. Ultimately, when a food molecule has been completely processed, the cell has used the food molecule's stored energy (along with oxygen) to create a large number of high-energy-storing ATP molecules (which supply energy to power the cell's activities), water, and carbon dioxide (which is exhaled into the atmosphere).

TAKE-HOME MESSAGE 4·12

Living organisms extract energy through a process called cellular respiration, in which the high-energy bonds of sugar and other energy-rich molecules are broken, releasing the energy that went into creating them. The cell captures the food molecules' stored energy in the bonds of ATP molecules. This process requires fuel molecules and oxygen and it yields ATP molecules, water, and carbon dioxide.

4·13 The first step of cellular respiration: glycolysis is the universal energy-releasing pathway.

To generate energy, fuels such as glucose and other carbohydrates as well as proteins and fats are broken down in three steps: (1) glycolysis, (2) the Krebs cycle, and (3) the electron transport chain. **Glycolysis** means the splitting (*lysis*) of sugar (*glyco-*) and it is the first step that all organisms on the planet take in breaking down food molecules; for many single-celled organisms, this one step is sufficient to provide all of the energy they need (**FIGURE 4-29**).

As **FIGURE 4-30** illustrates, glycolysis is a sequence of chemical reactions (there are 10 in all) through which glucose is broken down, resulting in two molecules of a substance called **pyruvate.** Glycolysis has two distinct phases: an "uphill" preparatory phase and a "downhill" payoff phase.

Just as you sometimes have to spend money to make money, before any energy can be extracted from glucose, some energy

FIGURE 4-29 Plants, animals, bacteria, and all other organisms use glycolysis to break down fuels.

Every living organism, large or small, extracts energy through glycolysis!

must be added to the molecule. This addition occurs during the "uphill" phase. The additional energy (which comes from ATP) destabilizes the glucose molecule, making it ripe for chemical breakdown. Once the glucose can be broken down chemically, the energy stored in its bonds can be harnessed as the bonds are broken.

Three of the 10 steps in glycolysis yield energy. In two of these three, as bonds from the sugar are broken, and other lower-energy bonds are formed, the energy released is quickly harnessed by the attachment of phosphate groups to molecules of ADP to create energy-rich ATP molecules. In the third energy-yielding step of glycolysis, electrons originally from the glucose are transferred to NAD^+ to become the high-energy electron carrier NADH. Later (in an electron transport chain in the mitochondria) this energy will be converted to ATP. The net result of glycolysis is that each glucose molecule is broken down into two molecules of pyruvate. During this breakdown, some of the released energy is captured in the production of energy-rich ATP molecules and molecules of the high-energy electron carrier NADH. Two molecules of water are also produced during glycolysis.

In the absence of oxygen and in many yeasts and bacteria, glycolysis is the only game in town for fueling activity. Because single-celled organisms have much lower energy needs, they can function solely on the yields of glycolysis. For many organisms (including humans), however, glycolysis is a springboard to further energy extraction. The additional energy payoffs come from the Krebs cycle and the electron transport chain.

GLYCOLYSIS

1 PREPARATORY PHASE   **2** PAYOFF PHASE

ATP (2)

Unstable molecule prepared to be broken down

Glucose

ATP (4)

NADH (2)

Water

Gycolysis takes place in the cell's cytoplasm.

Pyruvate (2)

ENERGY SPENT

−2 ATP

ENERGY ACQUIRED

+4 ATP   +2 NADH

FIGURE 4-30 Glycolysis up close.

TAKE-HOME MESSAGE 4·13

Glycolysis is the initial phase in the process by which all living organisms harness energy from food molecules. Glycolysis occurs in a cell's cytoplasm and uses the energy released from breaking chemical bonds in food molecules to produce high-energy molecules, ATP and NADH.

4·14 The second step of cellular respiration: the Krebs cycle extracts energy from sugar.

Cells could stop extracting energy when glycolysis ends, but they rarely do so because that would be like leaving most of your meal on your plate. In glycolysis, only a small fraction of the energy stored in sugar molecules is recovered and converted to ATP and NADH. Cells get much more of an "energy bang" for their "food buck" in the steps following glycolysis, which occur in the mitochondria. This is why mitochondria are considered ATP "factories." In the mitochondria, the molecules produced from the breakdown of glucose during glycolysis are broken down further, during two steps that are dramatically more efficient at capturing energy: the Krebs cycle (the subject of this section) and the electron transport chain (the subject of the next section). In breaking down the products of glycolysis, the **Krebs cycle** produces some additional molecules of ATP and, more importantly, captures a huge amount of chemical energy by producing high-energy electron carriers.

Q Aerobic training can cause our bodies to produce more mitochondria in cells. Why is this beneficial?

Before the Krebs cycle can begin, however, the end products of glycolysis—two molecules of pyruvate for every molecule of glucose used—must be modified. First, the pyruvate molecules move from the cytoplasm into the mitochondria, where they undergo three quick modifications that prepare them to be broken down in the Krebs cycle (**FIGURE 4-31**).

Modification 1. Each pyruvate molecule passes a pair of its high-energy electrons (and a proton) to the electron-carrier molecule NAD+, building two molecules of NADH.

Modification 2. Next, a carbon atom and two oxygen atoms are removed from each pyruvate molecule and released as carbon dioxide. The CO_2 molecules diffuse out of the cell and, eventually, out of the organism. In humans, for example, these CO_2 molecules pass into the bloodstream and are transported to the lungs, from which they are eventually exhaled.

Modification 3. In the final step in the preparation for the Krebs cycle, a giant compound known as coenzyme A attaches itself to the remains of each pyruvate molecule, producing two molecules called acetyl-CoA. Each acetyl-CoA molecule is now ready to enter the Krebs cycle.

ACETYL-CoA PRODUCTION

Glucose Pyruvate = Molecular model of pyruvate

1 As each pyruvate is broken down, a pair of electrons (and a proton) are passed to NAD+, producing NADH.

NAD+ NADH

2 A carbon and two oxygen atoms are released as carbon dioxide.

Carbon dioxide

3 Coenzyme A attaches itself to the remaining molecule, creating acetyl-CoA.

+ Coenzyme A

Acetyl-CoA

Modifications of pyruvate take place in the cell's mitochondria.

to Krebs cycle

FIGURE 4-31 Preparation of pyruvate. In the mitochondria, pyruvate must be modified before it can be broken down in the Krebs cycle.

There are eight separate steps in the Krebs cycle, but our emphasis is on its three general outcomes (**FIGURE 4-32**).

Outcome 1. *A new molecule is formed.* Acetyl-CoA adds its two-carbon acetyl group to a molecule of the starting material of the Krebs cycle, a four-carbon chemical called oxaloacetate, creating a six-carbon molecule.

Outcome 2. *High-energy electron carriers (NADH) are made and carbon dioxide is exhaled.* The six-carbon molecule then gives electrons to NAD+ to make the high-energy electron carrier NADH. (Don't forget that the main purpose of the Krebs cycle is the capture of energy.) The six-carbon molecule releases two carbon atoms along with four oxygen atoms to form two carbon dioxide molecules. In mammals (including humans), this CO_2 is carried by the bloodstream to the lungs, from where it is exhaled into the atmosphere.

Outcome 3. *The starting material of the Krebs cycle is re-formed, ATP is generated, and more high-energy electron carriers are formed.* After the CO_2 is released, the four-

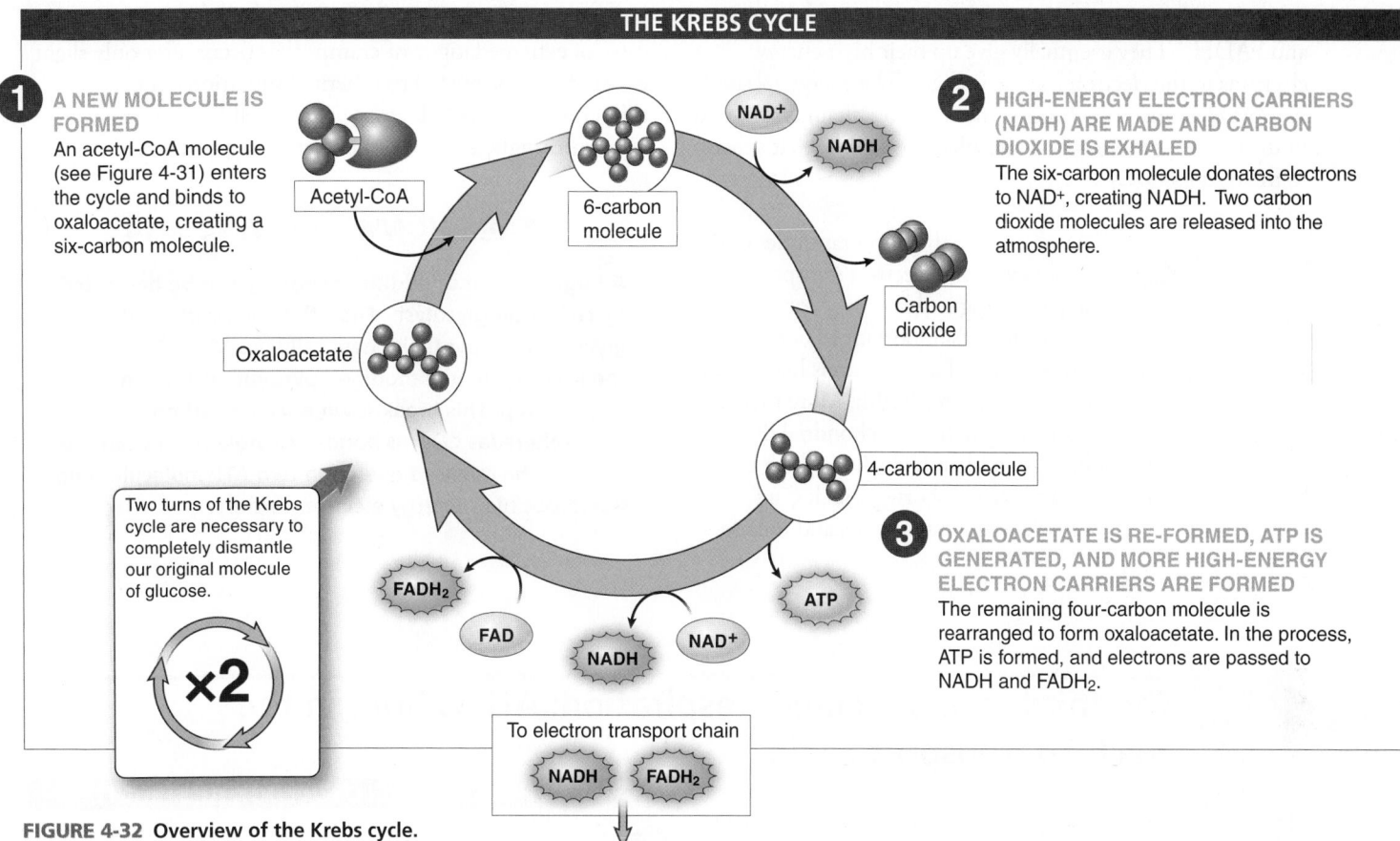

1 A NEW MOLECULE IS FORMED

An acetyl-CoA molecule (see Figure 4-31) enters the cycle and binds to oxaloacetate, creating a six-carbon molecule.

Acetyl-CoA

6-carbon molecule

NAD^+

NADH

Oxaloacetate

Carbon dioxide

2 HIGH-ENERGY ELECTRON CARRIERS (NADH) ARE MADE AND CARBON DIOXIDE IS EXHALED

The six-carbon molecule donates electrons to NAD^+, creating NADH. Two carbon dioxide molecules are released into the atmosphere.

4-carbon molecule

Two turns of the Krebs cycle are necessary to completely dismantle our original molecule of glucose.

×2

FADH$_2$

FAD

NADH

NAD^+

ATP

3 OXALOACETATE IS RE-FORMED, ATP IS GENERATED, AND MORE HIGH-ENERGY ELECTRON CARRIERS ARE FORMED

The remaining four-carbon molecule is rearranged to form oxaloacetate. In the process, ATP is formed, and electrons are passed to NADH and FADH$_2$.

To electron transport chain

NADH   FADH$_2$

FIGURE 4-32 Overview of the Krebs cycle.

carbon molecule that remains from the original pyruvate-oxaloacetate molecule formed in Outcome 1 is modified and rearranged to once again form oxaloacetate, the starting material of the Krebs cycle. In the process of this reorganization, one ATP molecule is generated and more electrons are passed to one familiar high-energy electron carrier, NADH, and a new one, FADH$_2$. The formation of these high-energy electron carriers increases the energy yield of the Krebs cycle. One oxaloacetate is re-formed, and the cycle is ready to break down the second molecule of acetyl-CoA. Two turns of the cycle are necessary to completely dismantle our original molecule of glucose.

Now that we have seen the Krebs cycle in its entirety, let's trace the path of the original six carbons in the original glucose molecule. In a sense, the carbon atoms that were first plucked from the atmosphere to make sugar during photosynthesis have been exhaled back into the atmosphere as six molecules of carbon dioxide.

1. **Glycolysis:** the six-carbon starting point. Glucose is broken down into two molecules of pyruvate. No carbons are removed.

2. **Preparation for the Krebs cycle:** two carbons are released. Two pyruvate molecules are modified to enter the Krebs cycle, and they each lose a carbon atom in the form of two molecules of carbon dioxide.

3. **Krebs cycle:** the last four carbons are released. A total of four carbon atoms enter the Krebs cycle in the form of acetyl-CoA. For each turn of the Krebs cycle, two molecules of carbon dioxide are released. So the two final carbons are released into the atmosphere during the second turn of the wheel. Poof! The six carbon atoms that were originally present in our single molecule of glucose are no longer present.

So we've come full circle. In photosynthesis, carbon atoms from the air were used to build sugar molecules, which had energy stored in the bonds between their carbon, hydrogen, and oxygen atoms. In cellular respiration, the energy previously stored in the bonds of the sugar is converted to molecules of ATP, NADH, and FADH$_2$. Carbon atoms from sugar are exhaled back into the air as CO_2, and water is produced.

What happens to the high-energy electron carriers, NADH and FADH₂? They eventually give up their high-energy electrons to the electron transport chain. The energy released as those electrons pass through the transport chain is captured in the bonds of more ATP molecules. We explore that process in the next section.

Q As we explore the important roles of the Krebs cycle and electron transport chain in generating usable energy for organisms, it's important to note that mitochondrial malfunctions have serious consequences for health. More than a hundred genetic mitochondrial disorders have been identified, all of which can lead to energy shortage, including muscle weakness, fatigue, and muscle

Why might the malfunctioning of mitochondria play a role in lethargy or fatigue?

pain. And, as noted in Section 3-15, it appears that many cases of extreme fatigue or cramps that occur after only slight exertion may be related to inherited mutations in the mitochondrial DNA. Damage to our cellular powerhouses, not surprisingly, can create a personal energy crisis.

TAKE-HOME MESSAGE 4·14

A huge amount of additional energy can be harvested by cells after glycolysis. First, the end product of glycolysis, pyruvate, is chemically modified. Then, in the Krebs cycle, the modified pyruvate is broken down step by step. This breakdown releases carbon into the atmosphere (as CO_2) as bonds are broken, and captures some of the released energy in two ATP molecules and numerous high-energy electron carriers.

4·15 The third step of cellular respiration: ATP is built in the electron transport chain.

How do we finally get a big payoff of usable energy from our glucose molecule? Glycolysis and the Krebs cycle produce a few molecules of ATP for each molecule of glucose broken down, but it is the energy held in the high-energy electron carriers NADH and FADH₂ formed in these processes that ultimately generates the largest amount of usable energy as ATP. In fact, almost 90% of the energy payoff from a molecule of glucose is harvested in the final step of cellular respiration when the electrons from NADH and FADH₂ move along an electron transport chain. This process, like the Krebs cycle, takes place in the mitochondria.

In a manner similar to that seen in the chloroplast during photosynthesis, mitochondria convert kinetic energy (from electrons) into potential energy (a concentration gradient of protons). Two structural features of mitochondria are essential to their impressive ability to harness energy from molecules.

Feature 1. Mitochondria have a "bag-within-a-bag" structure that makes it possible for a concentration gradient to form between the regions inside and outside the "inner bag" and makes it possible to harness the potential energy in the bonds of NADH and FADH₂ molecules to produce ATP (**FIGURE 4-33**).

Material inside the mitochondrion can lie in one of two spaces: (1) the intermembrane space, which is outside the inner bag, or (2) the **mitochondrial matrix,** which is inside

MITOCHONDRIA: A CLOSER LOOK AT STRUCTURE

1 **"BAG-WITHIN-A-BAG"**
Inside the mitochondrion, material can lie in one of two places:

Intermembrane space

Mitochondrial matrix

2 **INNER "BAG" STUDDED WITH MOLECULES**
These molecules create an electron transport chain that enables ATP production.

Plane of cross section

FIGURE 4-33 "A bag-within-a-bag." The structure of mitochondria makes possible their impressive ability to harness energy from food molecules.

High-energy electrons are passed from the carriers NADH and FADH$_2$ to a series of molecules embedded in the inner mitochondrial membrane called the electron transport chain.

1 At each step in the electron transport chain's sequence of handoffs, the electrons fall to a lower energy state, releasing a little bit of energy.

2 At the end of the chain, the lower-energy electrons are handed off to oxygen, which then combines with free H$^+$ ions to form water.

3 The energy is used to power proton pumps, which pack hydrogen ions from the mitochondrial matrix into the intermembrane space.

4 The protons rush back into the mitochondrial matrix with great kinetic energy, which can be used to build ATP.

FIGURE 4-34 The big energy payoff. Most of the energy harvested during cellular respiration is generated by the electron transport chain in the mitochondria.

the inner bag. With two distinct regions separated by a membrane, the mitochondrion can create higher concentrations of molecules in one area or the other. And because a concentration gradient is a form of potential energy—molecules move from the high-concentration area to the low-concentration area the way water rushes down a hill—once a gradient is created, the energy released as the gradient equalizes itself can be used to do work. In the electron transport chain, this energy is used to build the energy-rich molecule ATP.

Feature 2. The inner bag of the mitochondrion is studded with molecules, mostly electron carriers, which are sequentially arranged as a "chain." This arrangement makes it possible for the molecules to hand off electrons in an orderly sequence.

Now let's explore how these features of mitochondria make it possible to harness energy from high-energy electron carriers (**FIGURE 4-34**).

Step 1 of the electron transport chain begins with NADH and FADH$_2$ in the mitochondrial matrix (inside the inner bag) moving to the membrane. There, the high-energy electrons they carry are transferred to molecules embedded within the membrane.

Over-the-counter NADH pills provide energy to sufferers of chronic fatigue syndrome. Why might this be?

After they donate their electrons, the molecules that remain, NAD$^+$ and FAD, are recycled back to the Krebs cycle.

The membrane-embedded molecules pass the electrons to the next carrier, which passes the electrons to the next, and so on. At each handoff, a bit of energy is released. Thus, as electrons move from one carrier to another through the electron transport chain, they lose energy at each handoff.

At the end of the chain (step 2), the lower-energy electrons are handed off to oxygen, which then combines with free H$^+$ ions in the mitochondrial fluid to form water.

As shown in step 3 of Figure 4-34, most of the energy released at each handoff from one electron carrier to another in the electron transport chain is used to pump protons (H$^+$ ions) from the mitochondrial matrix across the membrane and into the intermembrane space. As more and more protons are pumped across the membrane and packed into the intermembrane space, a concentration gradient is created. This gradient represents a significant source of potential energy.

If this description seems familiar, it is. In chloroplasts, during photosynthesis, great numbers of protons are pumped from the stroma outside the thylakoid sacs to the inside

THE NATURE
OF ENERGY

PHOTOSYNTHESIS

CELLULAR
RESPIRATION

ALTERNATIVE
PATHWAYS

157

SUMMARY OF CELLULAR RESPIRATION

1 GLYCOLYSIS

Glucose

Pyruvate

ATP

CYTOPLASM

MITOCHONDRIA

2 ACETYL-CoA PRODUCTION

Pyruvate

Carbon dioxide

Acetyl-CoA

3 KREBS CYCLE

Carbon dioxide

ATP

NADH   FADH$_2$

4 ELECTRON TRANSPORT CHAIN

e⁻

e⁻

Oxygen

Water

Each step in the breakdown of food increases the amount of usable energy that is generated!

ATP

FIGURE 4-35 The steps of cellular respiration: from glucose to usable energy.

of the thylakoids. We likened this potential energy to the potential energy of water in an elevated tower, which can be released with great force. Similarly, in step 4 of the mitochondrial electron transport chain, the protons pumped into the intermembrane space rush back to the inner mitochondrial matrix through channels in the inner mitochondrial membrane. And as the protons pass through, the force of their flow fuels the attachment of free-floating phosphate groups to ADP to produce ATP.

In the end, the number of ATP molecules generated from the complete dismantling of one molecule of glucose is about 36, most of which are produced with the energy harnessed from high-energy electron carriers as they pass their electrons down the electron transport chain (**FIGURE 4-35**).

Given the central role of the electron transport chain in the generation of usable energy from the breakdown of food molecules, any interference in its functioning has dire consequences. And in fact, murder by cyanide poisoning, an old tradition in detective stories, is just such an interference. When cyanide gets into the mitochondria, it binds to a molecule in the electron transport chain, preventing it from accepting electrons. This halts the transfer of electrons and the pumping of protons across the mitochondrial membrane. As a consequence, the production of ATP that would occur when protons rush back across the membrane down their concentration gradient ceases. Halting the production of ATP removes a cell's energy source, starving it very quickly. For this reason, cyanide poisoning can cause death within minutes.

Q *Cyanide blocks the passage of electrons to oxygen in the electron transport chain. Why does this make it a toxic poison?*

TAKE-HOME MESSAGE 4·15

The largest energy payoff of cellular respiration comes as electrons from NADH and FADH$_2$ produced during glycolysis and the Krebs cycle move along the electron transport chain. The electrons are passed from one carrier to another and energy is released, pumping protons into the mitochondrial intermembrane space. As the protons rush back into the mitochondrial matrix, the force of their flow fuels the production of large amounts of ATP.

4·16–4·17 There are alternative pathways to energy acquisition.

Unlike cars, living organisms (such as this cheetah) use multiple types of fuel.

4·16 Beer, wine, and spirits are by-products of cellular metabolism in the absence of oxygen.

Every beer brewery, the entire wine industry, and all distilleries of whiskey, vodka, tequila, and other alcoholic beverages owe their existence to microscopic yeast cells scrambling to break down their food for energy under stressful conditions. To better understand how yeast metabolism produces alcohol, it helps to investigate what happens when humans and other animals try to metabolize energy from sugar molecules under some stressful conditions.

If you run or swim as fast as you can, you soon feel a burning sensation in your muscles. Why? Your muscle cells are becoming very acidic. This acid buildup occurs when we demand of our bodies bursts of energy beyond that which they can sustain (**FIGURE 4-36**). (The next-day muscle soreness is not due to acid buildup, which goes away in a matter of minutes or hours; this soreness is caused by damage to the muscle fibers. They break down a bit before growing stronger.)

With rapid, strenuous exertion, our bodies soon fall behind in delivering oxygen from the lungs to the bloodstream to the cells and finally to the mitochondria. Oxygen deficiency then limits the rate at which the mitochondria can break down fuel and produce ATP (**FIGURE 4-37**). This slowdown occurs because the electron transport chain requires oxygen as the final acceptor of all the electrons generated during glycolysis and the Krebs cycle. If oxygen is in short supply, the electrons from NADH (and $FADH_2$) have nowhere to go.

Consequently, the regeneration of NAD^+ (and FAD) in the electron transport chain is halted, leaving no recipient for the high-energy electrons harvested from the breakdown of glucose and pyruvate, and the whole process of cellular respiration can grind to a stop. Organisms don't let this interruption last long, though; most have a backup method for breaking down sugar.

FIGURE 4-36 Energy production without oxygen. Organisms have a backup method for breaking down sugar when oxygen is not present.

Among animals, there is an acceptor for the NADH electrons in the absence of oxygen: pyruvate, the end product of glycolysis. When pyruvate accepts the electrons, it forms lactic acid (see Figure 4-37). Once the NADH gives up its electrons, NAD⁺ is regenerated, and glycolysis can continue. But as lactic acid builds up, it causes a burning feeling in our muscles. It's not ideal, but to escape a predator or to exercise strenuously, the two ATP molecules generated from each glucose molecule during glycolysis—which can serve as an immediate energy source—are better than nothing.

Like humans, yeast normally use oxygen during their breakdown of food. And like humans, they have a backup method when oxygen is not available. But yeast make use of a different electron acceptor, and the resulting reaction leads to the production of all drinking alcohol.

After glycolysis in these single-celled organisms, pyruvate is usually converted to a molecule called *acetaldehyde,* generating bubbles of CO_2 (which, when yeast is used in baking, allows bread to rise). In the absence of oxygen, this molecule accepts the electrons released from NADH, allowing glycolysis to resume. Acetaldehyde's acceptance of NADH's electrons results in the production of **ethanol,** the molecule that gives beer, wine, and spirits their kick. Ethanol can also be used as a fuel source because it can be combusted in much the same way as the biofuels generated from animal fats and plant oils described earlier in this chapter.

Fermentation is the process by which cell respiration occurs in the absence of oxygen. It occurs when, following glycolysis, alternative molecules are used as electron acceptors. Interestingly, although ethanol is always the alcohol produced by fermentation, the flavor of the output of fermentation depends on the type of sugar metabolized by the yeast. Fruits, vegetables, and grains all give different results. If the sugar comes from grapes, wine is produced. If the sugar comes

Exertion without enough oxygen leads to burning cramps in animals, but to alcohol in yeast!

FIGURE 4-37 Energy production with and without oxygen.

from a germinating barley plant, beer is produced. Potatoes, on the other hand, are the sugar source usually used to produce vodka.

Because yeast prefer the more efficient process of aerobic respiration, they produce alcohol only in the absence of oxygen. Fermentation tanks used in producing wine, beer, and other spirits are built to keep oxygen out so that yeast cells are forced to use their backup respiratory pathway of fermentation (**FIGURE 4-38**).

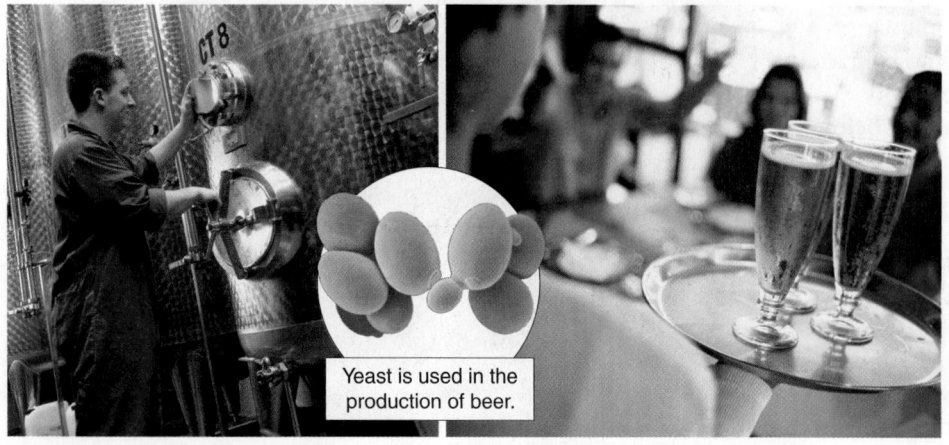

Yeast is used in the production of beer.

FIGURE 4-38 Just a by-product of metabolism under stressful conditions. Beer, wine, and spirits are by-products of cellular metabolism in the absence of oxygen.

TAKE-HOME MESSAGE 4·16

Oxygen deficiency limits the breakdown of fuel because the electron transport chain requires oxygen as the final acceptor of electrons during the chemical reactions of glycolysis and the Krebs cycle. When oxygen is unavailable, yeast resort to fermentation, in which they use a different electron acceptor, pyruvate, and in the process generate ethanol, the alcohol in beer, wine, and spirits.

4·17 Eating a complete diet: cells can run on protein and fat as well as on glucose.

Most automobiles can run on only one type of fuel, gasoline. If you run out of fuel and cannot get to a gas station, you are out of luck. In this chapter, we have examined the steps by which plants, animals, and other organisms use glucose as fuel. But living organisms are more flexible than autos when it comes to fuel sources. They also have more complex needs because their fuel must also provide raw materials for growth.

Q

How can someone on a low-carb diet fuel their body?

Evolution has built humans and other organisms with the metabolic machinery that allows them to extract energy and other valuable chemicals from proteins, fats, and a variety of carbohydrates (**FIGURE 4-39**). For that reason, we are able to consume and efficiently utilize meals comprising various combinations of molecules.

Sugars. In the case of dietary carbohydrates, many are polysaccharides—multiple simple sugars linked together—rather than solely the simple sugar glucose. Before they can be broken down by cellular respiration, the polysaccharides must first be separated by enzymes into glucose or related simple sugars.

Lipids. Dietary lipids are broken down into their two constituent parts: a glycerol molecule and fatty acids. The glycerol is chemically modified into one of the molecules produced during glycolysis. It enters the glycolysis process at that step and is broken down to yield energy. The fatty acids, meanwhile, are chemically modified into acetyl-CoA, at which point they enter the Krebs cycle.

Proteins. Proteins are chains of amino acids. Upon consumption the chains are broken down chemically, after which each amino acid is broken down into (1) an amino group that may be used in the production of tissue or excreted in the urine, and (2) a carbon compound that is converted to one of the intermediate compounds in glycolysis or the Krebs cycle, allowing the energy stored in its chemical bonds to be harnessed.

In the end, humans (indeed, all animals) are able to harvest energy from a variety of food sources beyond simple glucose. Whether a meal contains carbohydrates, lipids, proteins, or some combination thereof, the nutrients are chemically modified in some preliminary steps and then fed into one of the intermediate steps in glycolysis or the Krebs cycle to furnish usable energy for the organism (see Figure 4-39).

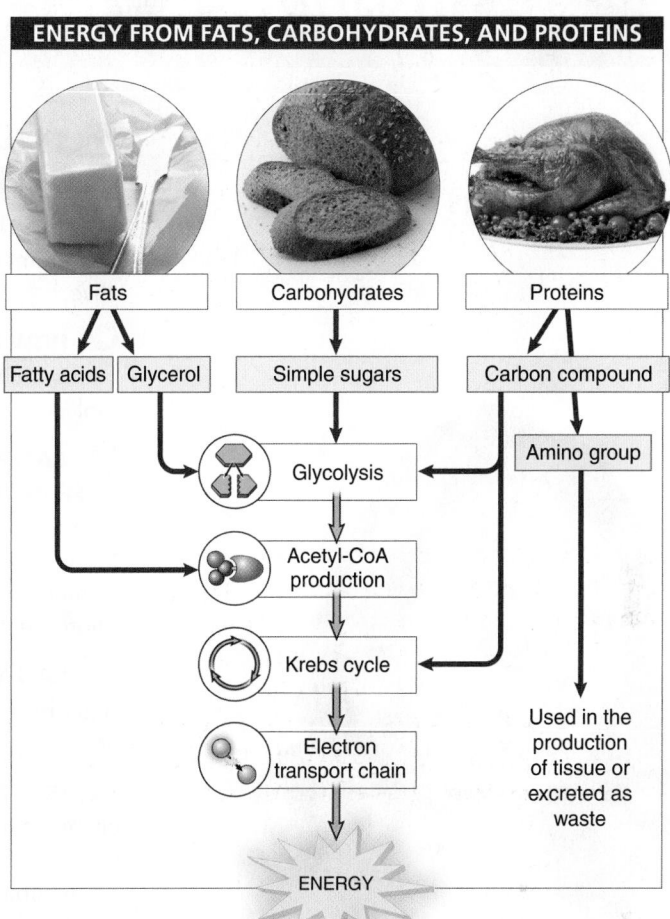

ENERGY FROM FATS, CARBOHYDRATES, AND PROTEINS

Fats → Fatty acids | Glycerol
Carbohydrates → Simple sugars
Proteins → Carbon compound

Glycolysis
Acetyl-CoA production
Krebs cycle
Electron transport chain

Amino group
Used in the production of tissue or excreted as waste

ENERGY

FIGURE 4-39 "More flexible than autos." Animals are able to harvest energy from proteins, carbohydrates, and lipids.

TAKE-HOME MESSAGE 4·17

Humans and other organisms have metabolic machinery that allows them to extract energy and other valuable chemicals from proteins, fats, and carbohydrates in addition to the simple sugar glucose.

IF YOU FEED AND PROTECT YOUR FLOWERS IN A VASE, THEY'LL LAST LONGER.

Like animals, plants require fuel for the cellular activities that keep them alive.

Q: HOW DO PLANTS GET THE ENERGY THEY NEED TO STAY ALIVE? Plants use photosynthesis to harness light energy, converting it to sugar molecules that serve as their food.

Q: CAN PLANTS STILL PHOTOSYNTHESIZE ONCE THEY'RE IN A VASE IN YOUR HOUSE? Yes, but humans don't make it easy. Once cut, plants generally cannot produce sufficient sugar through photosynthesis. Light levels in houses tend to be a bit too low, and the loss of many or most plant leaves reduces the number of chloroplasts in which photosynthesis can occur. So they're starving to death.

Q: CAN YOU SLOW THEIR DEMISE? Yes. Plants are able to take up sugar in the vase water and use it as an energy source for cell activities. So adding a bit of sugar to the vase is like putting fuel in their tank.

Q: IS IT THAT EASY? No. Putting sugar—a molecule with lots of energy stored within its chemical bonds—in the vase is like offering a free lunch. And many, many organisms are looking for a free lunch. Unfortunately, when you add sugar, bacteria on the flower stems can grow rapidly, blocking the water-conducting tubes in the stems. This slows the flow not just of sugar, but of water as well.

Q: WHAT SHOULD YOU DO? With the addition to vase water of both sugar and an antibacterial chemical such as chlorine bleach, you can feed and protect your cut flowers, significantly increasing their longevity.

CONCLUSION: Here's a useful summary from Martha Stewart (www.marthastewart.com): "Flowers last longer if their stems are cut under water. Use a sharp knife, and cut the stem on a slant so it can absorb as much water as possible. Next, place [the flowers] in a flask filled with 2 inches of warm water (no hotter than 110 degrees); this expedites the flow of water into the flower. Add either cut-flower food or a teaspoon of sugar and a couple drops of liquid bleach to a vase filled with cool water up to the point where the flower foliage will hit. After 5 minutes, transfer [the flowers] to the vase."

Big Ideas in ... Energy

4·1–4·4 Energy flows from the sun and through all life on earth.

- Energy is neither created nor destroyed but can change form.

- Energy from the sun fuels all life on earth as it is converted to different forms. Each conversion is inefficient, and some of the usable energy is converted to less useful heat energy.

- Cells temporarily store energy in the bonds of ATP molecules. This potential energy can be converted to kinetic energy and used to fuel life-sustaining chemical reactions.

4·5–4·11 Photosynthesis uses energy from sunlight to make food.

- In the "photo" part of photosynthesis, chloroplasts transform light energy into the chemical energy of ATP and NADPH, while splitting water molecules and producing oxygen.

- In the Calvin cycle, the "synthesis" part of photosynthesis, carbon from CO_2 in the atmosphere is attached to molecules in chloroplasts to build sugars. This production of sugars consumes ATP and NADPH generated in the "photo" part of photosynthesis.

- C4 and CAM photosynthesis are evolutionary adaptations at the biochemical level that, although having competitive drawbacks, allow plants in hot, dry climates to close their stomata and conserve water without shutting down photosynthesis.

4·12–4·15 Cellular respiration converts food molecules into ATP, a universal source of energy for living organisms.

- In cellular respiration, glucose and oxygen are converted to carbon dioxide, water, and energy that is stored in the high-energy bonds of ATP molecules.

- In the electron transport chain, high-energy electrons from NADH and $FADH_2$ pass from carrier to carrier, releasing energy with each step. This energy fuels the creation of a proton concentration gradient. The energy released as the protons move back down their concentration gradient is used to produce ATP.

- Overall, the cellular respiration of one glucose molecule yields about 36 molecules of ATP.

4·16–4·17 There are alternative pathways to energy acquisition.

- Organisms are built with multiple systems for acquiring energy. They can generate ATP even when oxygen is lacking or when organic molecules other than glucose, such as lipids, proteins, and polysaccharides, are consumed.

See the To-Go Guide (packaged with every new copy of this textbook) for an illustrated summary of the chapter.

Check Your Knowledge

GRAPHIC CONTENT

Thinking critically about visual displays of data.

1. What are the axes of these two graphs?

2. What variable(s) is presented? How was it measured? What do the colors represent?

3. Do you know the source of the information in the graphs? Does that matter? Why or why not?

4. Why are there two graphs? What is the difference between them?

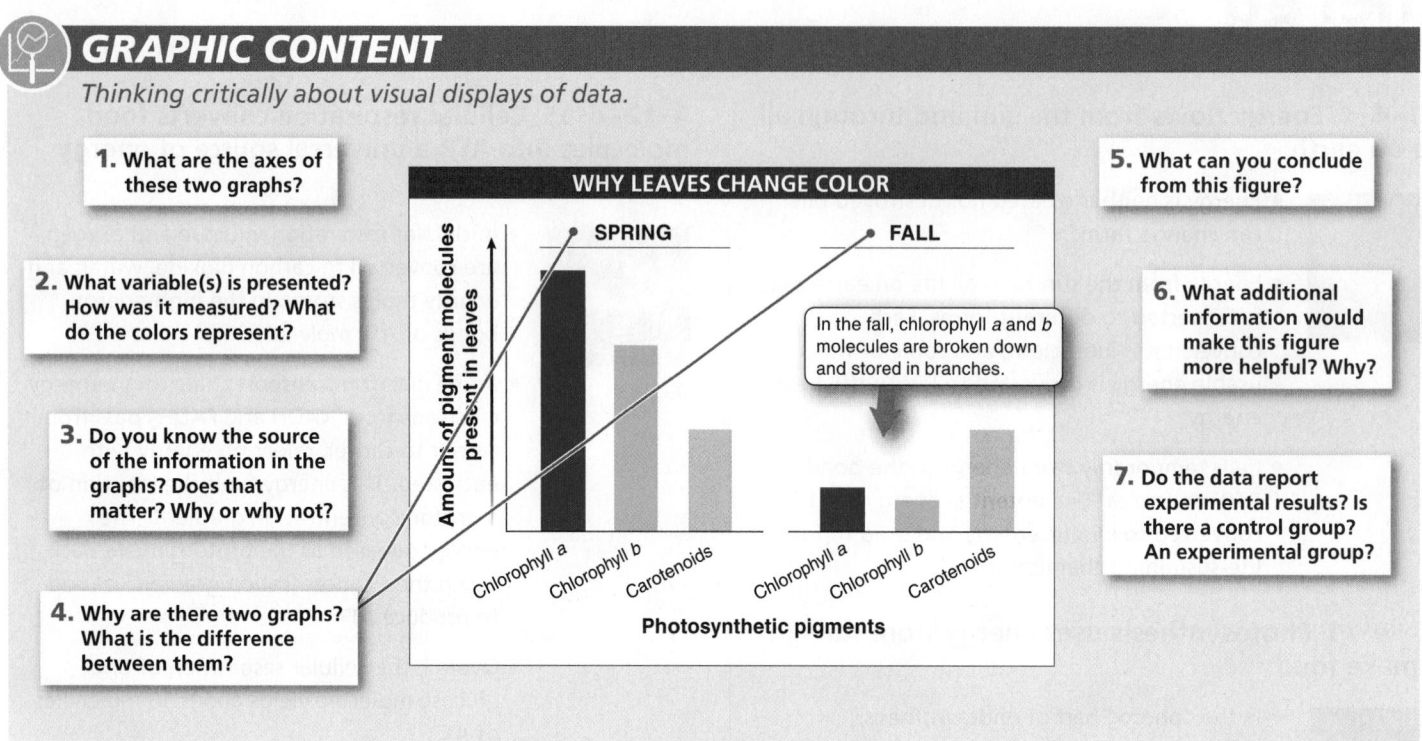

WHY LEAVES CHANGE COLOR

SPRING   FALL

Amount of pigment molecules present in leaves

In the fall, chlorophyll *a* and *b* molecules are broken down and stored in branches.

Chlorophyll *a*   Chlorophyll *b*   Carotenoids   Chlorophyll *a*   Chlorophyll *b*   Carotenoids

Photosynthetic pigments

5. What can you conclude from this figure?

6. What additional information would make this figure more helpful? Why?

7. Do the data report experimental results? Is there a control group? An experimental group?

See Answers at the back of the book.

Key Terms in Energy

adenosine triphosphate (ATP), p. 135
biofuel, p. 130
C4 photosynthesis, p. 148
Calvin cycle, p. 146
CAM (crassulacean acid metabolism), p. 150
carotenoid, p. 141
cellular respiration, p. 131

chemical energy, p. 133
chlorophyll, p. 139
chlorophyll *a*, p. 140
chlorophyll *b*, p. 139
chloroplast, p. 140
electromagnetic spectrum, p. 140
electron transport chain, p. 144
energy, p. 132

ethanol, p. 160
fermentation, p. 160
first law of thermodynamics, p. 133
fossil fuel, p. 130
glycolysis, p. 152
kinetic energy, p. 132
Krebs cycle, p. 154
light energy, p. 140

mitochondrial matrix, p. 156
NADPH, p. 145
photon, p. 140
photosynthesis, p. 131
photosystem, p. 143
pigment, p. 140
potential energy, p. 132
primary electron acceptor, p. 144

pyruvate, p. 152
rubisco, p. 146
second law of thermodynamics, p. 135
stoma (*pl.* stomata), p. 148
stroma, p. 139
thermodynamics, p. 133
thylakoid, p. 139

Multiple-Choice Questions

1. **Animal fats and plant oils are sometimes used as sources of fuel for automobile engines. How is energy harvested from these molecules?**

   a) They contain long chains of hydrogen and carbon that, when broken, release the energy stored in the bonds linking the atoms together.

   b) They contain hydrogen and carbon tails linked by disulfide bridges that, when broken, release chemical energy.

   c) They contain multiple phosphate groups that each release energy when "liberated" from the molecule chemically.

   d) They contain long hydrophobic regions that, when mixed with water, generate explosive resistances.

   e) They contain long carbon tails, and each atom has unpaired electrons that are released on exposure to extreme heat and pressure.

100 HARD

33

0 EASY

2. **A cyclist rides her bike up a very steep hill. Pick from the flowing choices the statement that properly describes this activity in energetic terms.**

   a) Potential energy in food is converted to kinetic energy as the cyclist's muscles push her up the hill.

   b) Kinetic energy is highest when the cyclist is at the crest of the hill.

   c) The cyclist produces the most potential energy as she cruises down the hill's steep slope.

   d) Potential energy is greatest when the cyclist is at the top of the hill.

   e) Both a) and d) are correct.

100 HARD

39

0 EASY

3. **Every time a source of energy is converted from one form to another:**

   a) the potential energy of the system increases.

   b) heat is required.

   c) the second law of thermodynamics is violated.

   d) the total amount of energy in the universe is reduced by a tiny amount.

   e) some of the energy is converted to heat, which is not a very usable form of kinetic energy.

100 HARD

33

0 EASY

4. **In your body, when energy is released from the breakdown of a molecule such as glucose:**

   a) adenosine monophosphate is created.

   b) adenosine diphosphate is created.

   c) some of the energy may be harnessed by building the unstable high-energy bonds that attach phosphate groups to ADP molecules.

   d) molecules of ATP are required to capture and absorb the heat generated by the reaction.

   e) all of the energy is lost as heat.

100 HARD

46

0 EASY

5. **A green plant can carry out photosynthesis if given nothing more than:**

   a) water, light, and carbon dioxide.

   b) water, light, and oxygen.

   c) carbon dioxide.

   d) oxygen.

   e) oxygen and carbon dioxide.

100 HARD

39

0 EASY

6. **The actual production of sugars during photosynthesis takes place:**
   a) within the outer membrane of the chloroplast.
   b) within the stroma, inside the thylakoids of the chloroplast.
   c) within the stroma, outside the thylakoid, but still inside the chloroplast.
   d) just outside the chloroplast, within the mitochondria.
   e) within the thylakoid membrane of the chloroplast.

7. **The leaves of plants can be thought of as "eating" sunlight. From an energetic perspective, this makes sense because:**
   a) light energy, like chemical energy released when the bonds of food molecules are broken, is a type of kinetic energy.
   b) both light energy and food energy can be converted to kinetic energy without the loss of heat.
   c) the carbon-oxygen bonds within a photon of light release energy when broken by the enzymes in chloroplasts.
   d) the carbon-hydrogen bonds within a photon of light release energy when broken by the enzymes in chloroplasts.
   e) photons are linked together by hydrogen bonds, which release energy when striking the surface of a leaf.

8. **A molecule of chlorophyll increases in potential energy:**
   a) when it binds to a photon.
   b) when a photon strikes it, boosting electrons to a higher-energy excited state.
   c) when it loses an electron.
   d) only in the presence of oxygen.
   e) None of the above. The potential energy of a molecule cannot change.

9. **Photosynthesizing plants rely on water:**
   a) to provide the protons necessary to produce chlorophyll.
   b) to concentrate the beams of light hitting a leaf, focusing them on the reaction center.
   c) to replenish oxygen molecules that are lost during photosynthesis.
   d) to replace electrons that are excited by light energy and passed from molecule to molecule down an electron transport chain.
   e) to serve as a high-energy electron carrier.

10. **During photosynthesis, which step is most responsible for a plant's acquisition of new organic material?**
    a) the "building" of NADPH during the Calvin cycle
    b) the excitation of chlorophyll molecules by photons of light
    c) the "plucking" of carbon atoms from the air and fixing of them to organic molecules within the chloroplast
    d) the loss of water through evaporation
    e) the production of ATP during the light reactions

11. **During C4 photosynthesis:**
    a) plants use less ATP when producing sugar.
    b) plants are able to continue producing sugars even when they must close their stomata to reduce water loss on hot days.
    c) plants are able to generate water molecules to cool their leaves.
    d) plants are able to reduce water loss by producing more rubisco.
    e) plants are able to produce sugars without any input of carbon dioxide.

12. **Cellular respiration is the process by which:**
    a) oxygen is used to transport chemical energy throughout the body.
    b) oxygen is produced during metabolic activity.
    c) light energy is converted to kinetic energy.
    d) ATP molecules are converted to water and sugar.
    e) energy from the chemical bonds of food molecules is captured by an organism.

13. **During cellular respiration, most of the energy contained within the bonds of food molecules is captured in:**
    a) the conversion of the kinetic energy of food to the potential energy of ATP.
    b) the Krebs cycle and electron transport chain.
    c) digestion.
    d) glycolysis.
    e) None of the above. Energy is lost, not gained, during cellular respiration.

14. Which of the following energy-generating processes is the only one that occurs in all living organisms?

    a) the Krebs cycle

    b) glycolysis

    c) combustion

    d) photosynthesis

    e) None of the above. There are no energy-generating processes that occur in all living organisms.

100 HARD

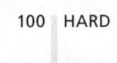 31

0 EASY

15. During the Krebs cycle:

    a) the products of glycolysis are further broken down, generating additional ATP and the high-energy electron carrier NADH.

    b) high-energy electron carriers pass their energy to molecules of sugar, which store them as potential energy.

    c) the products of glycolysis are further broken down, generating additional ATP and ethanol.

    d) cellular respiration can continue even in the absence of oxygen.

    e) the products of glycolysis are converted to acetyl-CoA.

100 HARD

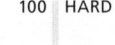 37

0 EASY

16. Mitochondria have a "bag within a bag" structure. This structure is necessary in order to:

    a) create a concentration gradient of certain molecules between the regions inside and outside the "inner bag," a form of potential energy.

    b) keep molecules of ADP in close proximity to molecules of the ATP-synthesizing enzyme.

    c) allow light-reactive accessory pigments to be embedded within the membranes.

    d) segregate the most toxic digestive enzymes from molecules of ATP and NADP$^+$.

    e) None of the above.

100 HARD

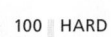 44

0 EASY

17. All alcoholic beverages are produced as the result of:

    a) cellular respiration by bacteria that occurs in the absence of oxygen.

    b) cellular respiration by bacteria that occurs in the absence of free electrons.

    c) cellular respiration by yeast that occurs in the absence of free electrons.

    d) cellular respiration that occurs in the absence of sugar.

    e) cellular respiration by yeast that occurs in the absence of oxygen.

100 HARD

18

0 EASY

18. In harvesting the chemical energy of the molecules in food:

    a) all macromolecules must first be converted to glucose.

    b) all macromolecules must first be converted to their hydrocarbon chains.

    c) all macromolecules must first be converted to glucose or another simple sugar.

    d) organisms can use sugars, lipids, and proteins.

    e) all macromolecules must first be converted to proteins or free-form amino acids.

100 HARD

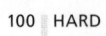 56

0 EASY

Short-Answer Questions

1. A plant and a mouse are placed in a sealed container with a watering system. For a period of time, both will survive. Explain what the two organisms can provide for each other in order to allow them, temporarily, to survive.

2. It is possible to measure the rate of the "photo" reactions in plants by measuring the levels of O_2 produced by chloroplasts. If bicarbonate solution, a source of CO_2, is provided to the plants, the rate of the "photo" reactions increases.

    a) Explain why measuring O_2 levels provides an indication of the rate of the "photo" reactions.

    b) Being as specific as possible, describe how the plants use the CO_2 provided by the bicarbonate solution.

    c) Propose an explanation of how increasing the CO_2 source for the plants affects the rate of the "photo" reactions.

3. Some plants grow much more quickly than others. For a plant that is growing at a rapid rate, propose a hypothesis on whether cellular respiration or photosynthesis is occurring at a faster rate. Justify your hypothesis.

**See Answers at the back of the book.
For additional study questions, go to www.prep-u.com.**

ABOUT THE CHAPTER OPENING PHOTO

Tulips in Skagit County, Washington, bask in the sun.

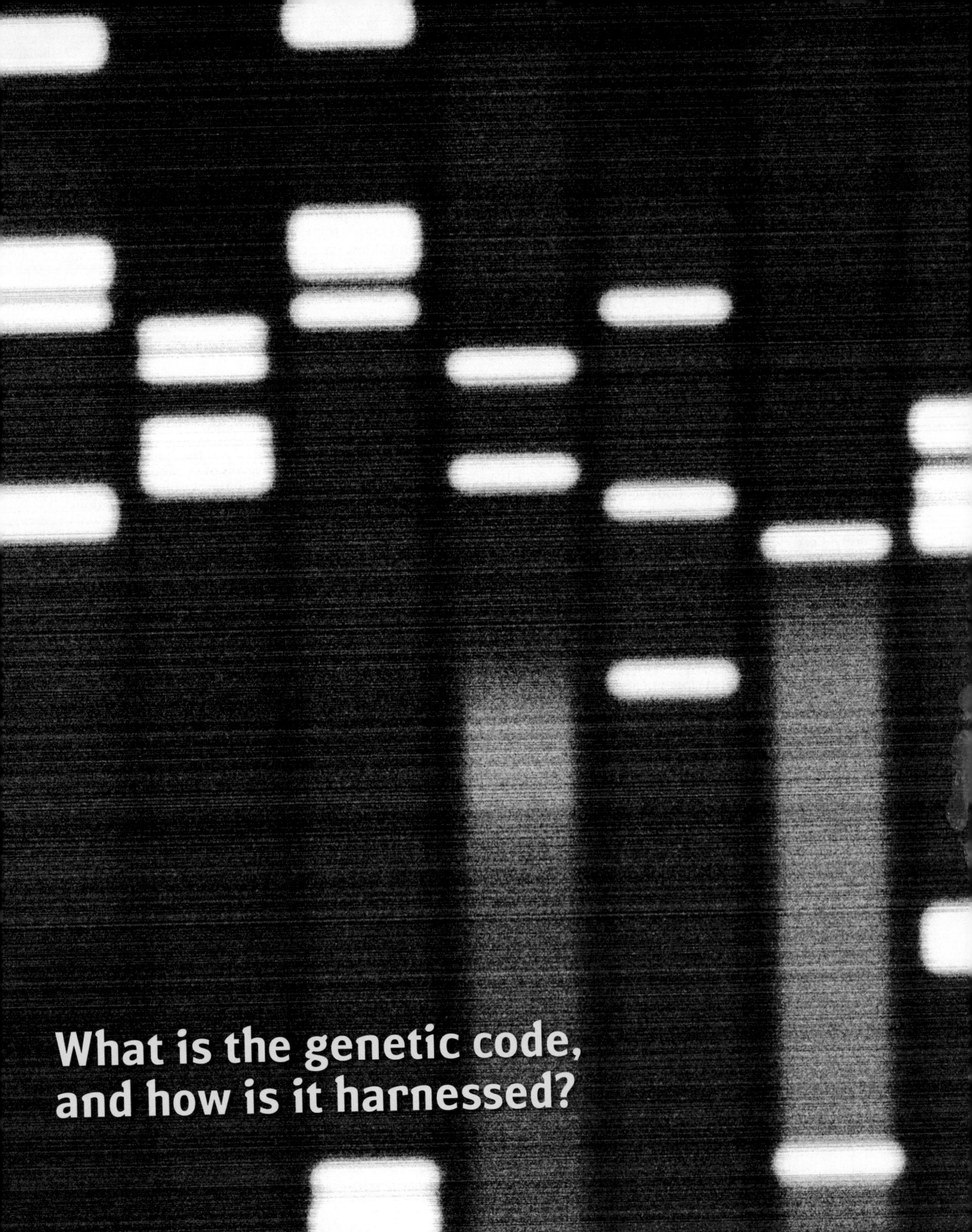

What is the genetic code,
and how is it harnessed?

5

DNA, Gene Expression, and Biotechnology

169

Visual representation of the human genome. Each color represents a different nucleotide.

5·1–5·5 DNA: what is it, and what does it do?

5·1 "The DNA 200"—knowledge about DNA is increasing justice in the world.

In 1981, Julius Ruffin, a 27-year-old maintenance worker at Eastern Virginia Medical School, got onto an elevator and lost more than 20 years of his life. Several weeks earlier, a nursing student at the school had been raped by an attacker who broke into her apartment. When Ruffin got on the elevator, the student thought she recognized him as her attacker and called the police, who immediately arrested him.

Q **What is the most common reason that DNA analyses overturn incorrect criminal convictions?**

Ruffin's girlfriend testified that he was with her at the time of the attack, but on the basis of the victim's eyewitness testimony, a jury found Ruffin guilty and sentenced him to life in prison. Ruffin maintained his innocence—to no avail, until 2003. At that time, the state's Division of Forensic Science performed a DNA analysis on a swab of evidence that remained from the investigation. The analysis revealed that Ruffin was not the attacker. Rather, the analysis showed that the DNA perfectly matched that of a man who, in 2003, was already in a Virginia prison, serving time for rape. Ruffin was freed, but only after having served more than two decades in prison (**FIGURE 5-1**).

Julius Ruffin's case is tragic, but it is not unusual. He is one of a group of 200 people in the United States who have been freed from prison as a result of DNA analyses. Called "the DNA 200," these unjustly imprisoned people spent an average of 12 years behind bars. Eighty percent had been convicted of

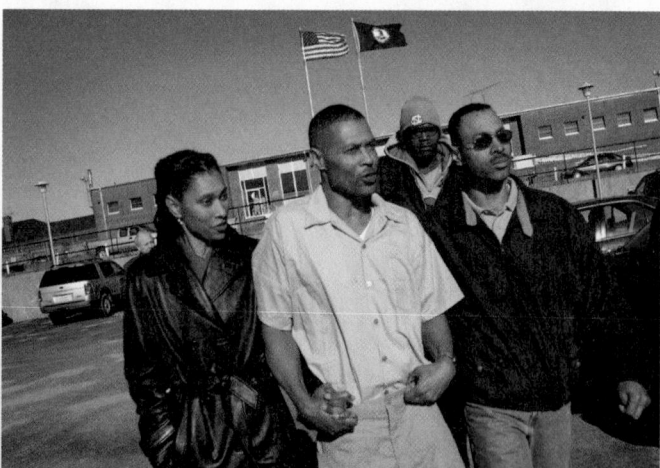

FIGURE 5-1 Vindicated by DNA evidence. Julius Ruffin was released from prison after two decades of wrongful incarceration.

sexual assault; 28% had been convicted of murder. In more than three-quarters of the cases, inaccurate eyewitness testimony played an important role in the guilty verdict. (Recall, from Chapter 1, the experiments that revealed the unreliability of eyewitness identification.)

In this chapter, we take a close look at DNA, the molecule responsible for Julius Ruffin's exoneration and the deferred justice served to the DNA 200. All living organisms—people, plants, animals, bacteria, and otherwise—carry DNA in almost every cell in their body (with just a few exceptions). Like a social security number, every person's DNA is unique (with the exception of identical twins). In addition to being contained in our living cells, our DNA exists in what we leave behind. It is in our saliva, hair, blood, and even the dead skin cells that fall from our bodies. This is why DNA can serve as an individual identifier; it is a trail we all leave that is increasingly being used to ensure greater justice in our society.

The importance of DNA goes far beyond its function as an individual identifier, however. The information carried within this molecule, which is organized into individual units called genes, is among the most important of all biological knowledge. It controls the operation of cells and carries a record of the evolutionary history of lineages of cells and organisms. And, as witnessed by the following excerpts, it is often in the news.

FIGURE 5-2 Genetics issues are in the news.

> «Selfish dictators may owe their behaviour partly to their genes, according to a study that claims to have found a genetic link to ruthlessness.»
> —*Nature,* April 2008

> «*Too Many One-Night Stands? Blame Your Genes . . .* according to a new study, it may be fair to say that while you jolly well could help cheating, your particular genes did make things more difficult.»
> —*Time* magazine, December 2010

In fact, it's nearly impossible to open a newspaper or watch a news report these days without being informed that yet another complex human characteristic or trait has been linked to a newly discovered gene (**FIGURE 5-2**). But what does that actually mean? What is this molecule that apparently exerts influence over everything from our fidelity to our ruthlessness?

We explore these issues and more in this chapter, beginning with a look at the structure of DNA itself and how it contains the information for producing organisms. In later sections of the chapter, we learn how modern manipulations of DNA are having far-reaching implications not just for human health but for agriculture as well.

TAKE-HOME MESSAGE 5·1

DNA is a molecule that all living organisms carry in almost every cell in their body. Because every person's DNA is unique and because we leave a trail of DNA behind us as we go about our lives, DNA can serve as an individual identifier. This is the basis of the DNA analysis that is increasingly being used to ensure greater justice in our society, often by establishing the innocence of individuals wrongly convicted of crimes.

5·2 The DNA molecule contains instructions for the development and functioning of all living organisms.

Beginning in the 1900s and continuing through the early 1950s, a series of experiments revealed two important features of DNA. First, molecules of DNA are passed down from parent to offspring. Second, the instructions on how to create a body and control its growth, development, and behavior are encoded in the DNA molecule.

Given that DNA must be able to hold the instructions for how to produce every possible type of structure in every living organism, scientists were in a frenzy to learn all they could about it. There was a spirited race to determine the chemical structure of DNA and to understand how the molecule was assembled and shaped so that it could hold and transmit so much information.

Many formidable scientists rose to the challenge of determining the structure of DNA. American Linus Pauling had already won a Nobel prize in chemistry for his work on elucidating the structure of molecules when he began investigating the structure of DNA. Simultaneously, Maurice Wilkins and Rosalind Franklin in England devoted their research to this task as well, and produced X-ray pictures of DNA that were critical to decoding its shape. But it was Englishman Francis Crick and American James

Watson, working in Cambridge, England, who happened to put all the pieces together and deduce the exact structure of DNA (**FIGURE 5-3**). As we'll see later in this chapter, their discovery was more than just a description of a molecule. As soon as they figured out DNA's structure, the answers to several other thorny problems in biology—such as how DNA might be able to duplicate itself—became apparent. We explore that process later, in the next chapter, but first we need to examine the structure of DNA in more detail.

DNA (deoxyribonucleic acid) is a **nucleic acid,** a macromolecule that stores information. It consists of individual units called **nucleotides,** which have three components: a molecule of sugar, a phosphate group (containing four oxygen atoms bound to a phosphorus atom), and a nitrogen-containing molecule called a **base.** The physical structure of DNA is frequently described as a "double helix." But what exactly is a double helix? Picture a long ladder twisted around like a spiral staircase and you'll have a good idea of what a DNA molecule looks like (**FIGURE 5-4**). The molecule has two distinct strands, like the vertical sides of a ladder. These are the "backbones" of the DNA molecule, and each is made from two alternating

FIGURE 5-3 Watson and Crick. James Watson (left) and Francis Crick (right) figured out the exact structure of DNA. The first sketch of the double helix, shown here, was rendered by Crick's wife, Odile.

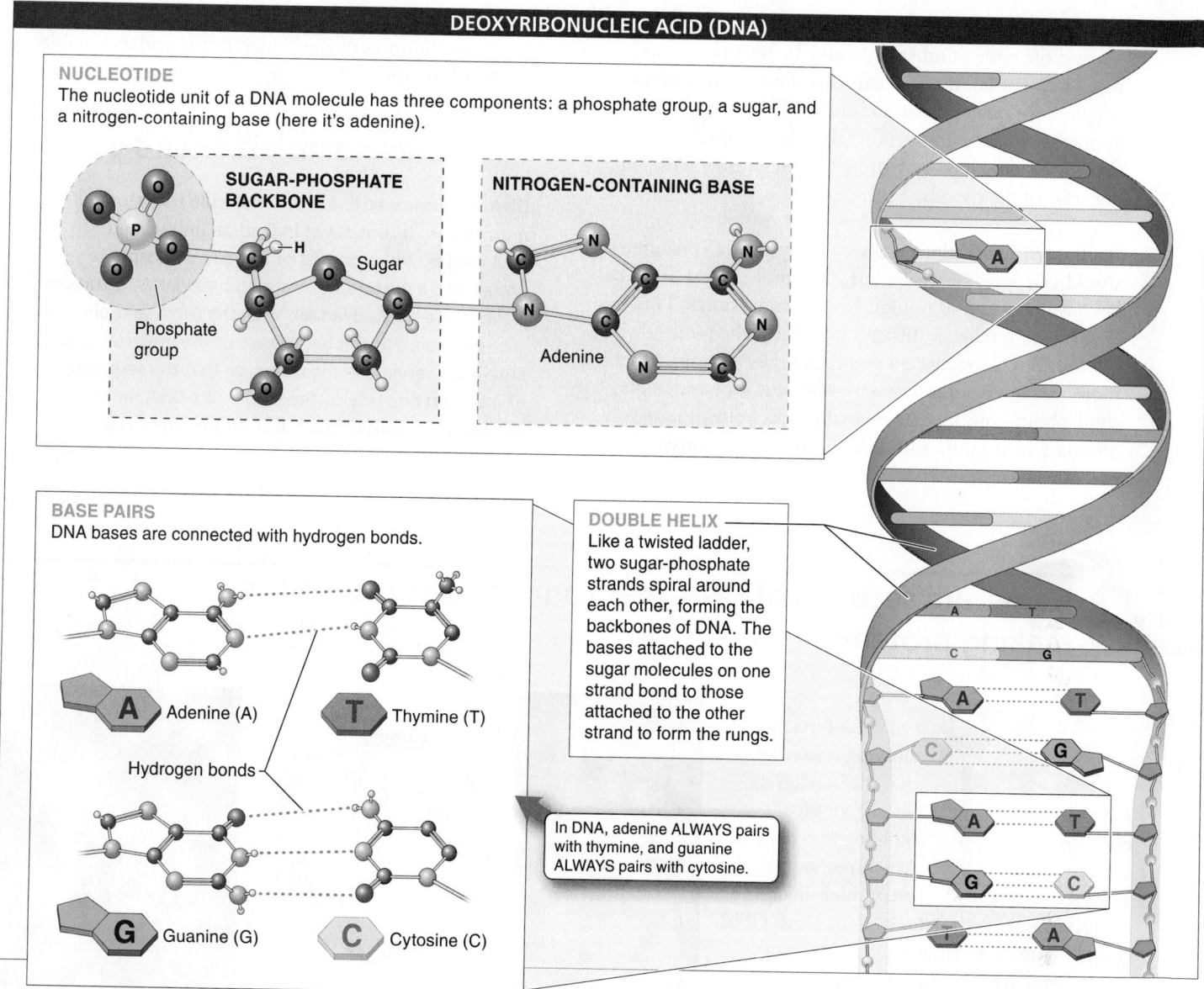

NUCLEOTIDE
The nucleotide unit of a DNA molecule has three components: a phosphate group, a sugar, and a nitrogen-containing base (here it's adenine).

SUGAR-PHOSPHATE BACKBONE

Phosphate group

Sugar

NITROGEN-CONTAINING BASE

Adenine

BASE PAIRS
DNA bases are connected with hydrogen bonds.

Adenine (A)

Thymine (T)

Hydrogen bonds

Guanine (G)

Cytosine (C)

DOUBLE HELIX
Like a twisted ladder, two sugar-phosphate strands spiral around each other, forming the backbones of DNA. The bases attached to the sugar molecules on one strand bond to those attached to the other strand to form the rungs.

In DNA, adenine ALWAYS pairs with thymine, and guanine ALWAYS pairs with cytosine.

FIGURE 5-4 Overview of the structure of DNA.

molecules: a sugar, then a phosphate group, then a sugar, then a phosphate group, and so on. The sugar is always deoxyribose and the phosphate group is always the same, too. It is the shapes of the molecules in the backbone that cause the DNA "ladder" to twist.

The alternating sugars and phosphates hold everything in place, but they play only a supporting role. The rungs of the ladder are where things get interesting. Attached to each sugar, and protruding inward like half of a rung on the ladder, is one of the four nitrogen-containing bases. Each sugar always has a base attached to it; the four bases are adenine, thymine,

cytosine, and guanine. When discussing DNA, these bases are usually referred to by their first letter: A, T, C, and G.

Both backbones of the ladder have a base protruding from each sugar. The base on one side of the ladder binds, via hydrogen bonds, to a base on the other side, and together these **base pairs** form the rungs of the ladder. They don't just pair up at random, though. Every time a C protrudes from one side, it forms hydrogen bonds with a G on the other side (and vice versa: a G always bonds to a C). Similarly, every time a T protrudes from one side, it forms hydrogen bonds with an A on the other side (and vice versa). For this reason, each DNA molecule always has the same number of Gs and Cs, and the same number of As and Ts. Because of these base-pairing rules, it also is true that if we know the base sequence for one of the strands in a DNA molecule, we know the sequence in the other. For this reason, a DNA sequence is described by writing the sequence of bases on only one of the strands.

If a human DNA molecule were really a spiraled ladder, it would be a very, very long one. One molecule of DNA can have as many as 200 million base pairs, or rungs. This length would make it difficult to squeeze the molecule into the cell. But the rungs are small, and the twisting of the molecule—twists upon twists—shortens it considerably: think about how, if you repeatedly twist your shoelace around and around, it becomes shorter and shorter. That's what happens with DNA. Let's now investigate how DNA's structure—the rungs of the ladder, in particular—enables it to carry information.

5·3 Genes are sections of DNA that contain instructions for making proteins.

Q Why is DNA considered the universal code for all life on earth?

One of DNA's most amazing features is that it embodies the instructions for building the cells and structures for almost every single living organism on earth (**FIGURE 5-5**). Thus, DNA is like a universal language, the letters of which are the bases A, T, C, and G. (Note that the sugar-phosphate backbone only serves to hold the bases in sequence, like the binding of a book. It does not convey genetic information.)

We've seen how the *structure* of DNA is like a spiral staircase. Another analogy may help you understand the *information-containing* aspect of DNA. You can think of an organism's DNA as a cookbook. Just as a cookbook contains detailed instructions on how to make a variety of foods (such as french toast, macaroni and cheese, or chocolate chip cookies), an organism's DNA carries the detailed instructions to build an organism and keep it running. And just as a book can be viewed as a

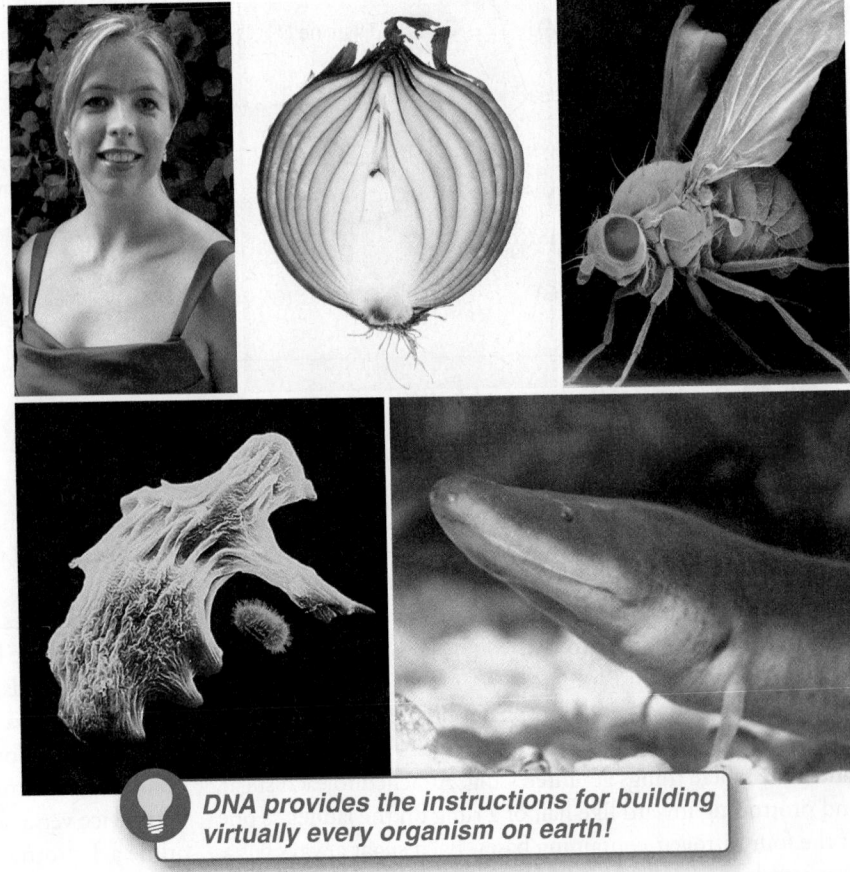

💡 *DNA provides the instructions for building virtually every organism on earth!*

FIGURE 5-5 DNA is the universal code for all life on earth.

sequence of letters, with the book's meaning determined by which letters are strung together and in what order, a molecule of DNA can be viewed as a sequence of bases. Letters don't have much meaning on their own, of course, but when they are put together into words and sentences, their order holds a great deal of information. Similarly, the sequence in which bases appear in a molecule of an organism's DNA makes up a **code** that holds the detailed instructions for the building of the organism—chiefly in the form of instructions for the amino acid sequences of polypeptides. Upon processing and folding, these polypeptides become the numerous and varied protein molecules that make up an organism—whether it is a one-celled amoeba, a giant oak tree, or a biology student.

The full set of DNA present in an individual organism is called its **genome** (FIGURE 5-6). In prokaryotes, including all bacteria, the information is contained within circular pieces of DNA. In eukaryotes, including humans, this information is laid out in long linear strands of DNA in the nucleus. Rather than being one super-long DNA strand, eukaryotic DNA exists as many smaller, more manageable pieces, called **chromosomes.** Humans, for example, have three billion base pairs, divided into 23 unique pieces of DNA (and we have two copies of each piece, one from our mother and one from our father, for a total of 46 chromosomes, and six billion base pairs in every cell).

Many mysteries about the organization of our DNA remain. The number of chromosomes, for example, varies from species to species, but is not related to how simple or complex an organism is. Corn has 10 unique chromosomes, yet fruit flies have only 4. Dogs and chickens have 39 different chromosomes, while goldfish put most other animal species to shame with 50 different chromosomes. As in humans, individuals in each of these species inherit one copy of each chromosome from each parent, so the total number of chromosomes in a cell is doubled—a dog, for example, has 78 chromosomes in each cell. Chromosomes vary in length, too. In humans, the longest chromosome has more than 200 million base pairs and the shortest has fewer than 50 million.

Within the long sequences of bases are relatively short sequences, on average about 3,000 bases long, that are the actual genes. "Gene" may seem like an impossibly nebulous concept, because the word is often used casually in the media as if it were some magical, irresistible, and mysterious force that controls our bodies and behavior. Beyond these vague descriptions, though, the word has a literal meaning. A **gene** is a sequence of bases (strictly, as we've noted, base pairs) in a DNA molecule that carries the information necessary for

FROM GENOME TO GENE

GENOME
An organism's complete set of DNA. In eukaryotes, this information can be found in the nucleus of almost every cell.

— Eukaryotic cell

— Nucleus

CHROMOSOME
One or more unique pieces of DNA—circular in prokaryotes, linear in eukaryotes—that together make up an organism's genome. Chromosomes vary in length and can consist of hundreds of millions of base pairs.

Humans have 23 unique chromosomes (and we have two copies of each: one from our mother and one from our father, for a total of 46).

GENE
A specific sequence of DNA, on average about 3,000 bases long, that contains the information necessary to produce all or part of a protein molecule.

Protein production

Protein

FIGURE 5-6 The genome unpacked.

producing a functional product, usually a polypeptide or RNA molecule. Nothing more, nothing less.

Remember that a DNA molecule is like a ladder in which half of each rung is any one of the four bases—A, T, G, or C. Strung together, a segment might be read as "AAAGGCTAGGC . . ." continuing on for another 3,000 or so bases. Returning to our cookbook analogy, just as a particular sequence of letters in a cookbook may be read and understood as the directions for baking chocolate chip cookies, the sequence of bases in DNA also carries information. Perhaps the sequence spells out part of the instructions for producing a red blood cell, for constructing the keratin that will form part of a curly strand of hair, or for assembling a chemical that alters your brain chemistry so that you exhibit a mood disorder or suicidal behavior.

ALLELES

Within a species, different individuals may have alternative versions of a gene for a given protein. These instructions can result in different versions of the same trait.

ALLELES
Different versions of a gene that code for the same trait

FIGURE 5-7 "Different versions of the same thing." Alleles are alternative versions of a gene.

Each gene is the instruction set for producing one particular molecule, usually a protein. For example, there is a gene in silk moths that codes for fibroin, the chief component of silk. And, there is a gene in humans that codes for triglyceride lipase, an enzyme that breaks down dietary fat.

Within a species, individuals sometimes have slightly different instruction sets for a given protein, and these instructions can result in a different version of the same characteristic. These alternative versions of a gene that code for the same feature are called **alleles** (**FIGURE 5-7**)—and function like alternative recipes for chocolate chip cookies. Any single characteristic or feature of an organism is referred to as a **trait.** A simple hypothetical example will clarify the meaning of these terms. The color of a daisy's petals is a trait. The instructions for producing this trait are found in a gene that controls petal color. This gene may have many different alleles; one allele may specify the trait of red petals, another may specify white petals, and yet another may specify yellow petals. Similarly, one allele for eye color in fruit flies may carry the instructions for producing a red eye, while another, slightly different allele may have instructions for brown eyes. (Ultimately, though, the trait may be influenced not just by the genes an individual carries but by the way those genes interact with the environment, too.)

TAKE-HOME MESSAGE 5·3

DNA is a universal language that provides the instructions for building all the structures in all living organisms. The full set of DNA that an organism carries is called its genome. In prokaryotes, the DNA occurs in circular pieces. In eukaryotes, the genome is divided among smaller, linear strands of DNA. An organism's DNA pieces are generally called chromosomes. A gene is a sequence of bases in a DNA molecule that carries the information necessary for producing a functional product, usually a polypeptide or RNA molecule.

5·4 Not all DNA contains instructions for making proteins.

It is debatable whether humans are the most complex species on the planet, but surely we must be more complex than an onion. "Complexity" is somewhat subjective and can be assessed in a variety of ways, such as by counting the number of different cell types in the organism. But if we measured complexity simply as the amount of DNA an organism has, we'd have to say an onion is more complex—it has more than five times as much DNA as a human (**FIGURE 5-8**)! We

Q *An onion has five times as much DNA as a human. Why doesn't that make onions more complex than humans?*

don't fare any better when compared with some other seemingly simple organisms, either. The salamander species *Amphiuma means,* for example, has about 25 times as much DNA as we do, and one species of amoeba—a single-celled organism—has almost 200 times as much!

Comparing the amount of DNA present in various species, in terms of both numbers of chromosomes and numbers of base pairs, reveals a paradox: there does not seem to be any

GENOME SIZES OF VARIOUS ORGANISMS

Fruit fly (*Drosophila melanogaster*)
180

Human (*Homo sapiens*)
3,400

Onion (*Allium cepa*)
18,000

Salamander (*Amphiuma means*)
84,000

Amoeba (*Amoeba dubia*)
670,000

Estimated genome size (millions of base pairs)

An onion has more than five times as much DNA in every cell as a human does! A salamander and an amoeba have even more.

FIGURE 5-8 Is the size of an organism's genome related to its complexity?

relationship between the size of an organism's genome and the organism's complexity.

The description earlier in this chapter about what DNA is and how genes code for proteins is logical and tidy, but it doesn't completely explain what we observe in cells. In humans, for example, genes make up only about 2% of the DNA (**FIGURE 5-9**). In many species, the proportion of the DNA that consists of genes is even smaller. In almost all eukaryotic species, the amount of DNA present far exceeds the amount necessary to code for all of the proteins in the organism. The fact is, a huge proportion of base sequences in DNA do not code for anything and have no obvious purpose. When it was first observed, some biologists even referred to this non-coding DNA as "junk DNA."

In what types of organisms do we find the most "junk DNA"? Bacteria and viruses tend to have very little non-coding DNA; genes make up 90% or more of their DNA.

It is in the eukaryotes (with the exception of yeasts) that we see an explosion in the amount of non-coding DNA (**FIGURE 5-10**). Non-coding regions of DNA often take the form of sequences that are repeated, sometimes thousands (or even hundreds of thousands) of times; often these repeats exist because some DNA sequences can make copies of themselves and move throughout the genome. Occasionally, the non-coding DNA consists of gene fragments, duplicate versions of genes, and pseudogenes (sequences that evolved from actual genes but accumulated mutations that made them lose their protein-coding ability). About 25% of the non-coding regions occur *within* genes—in which case they are called **introns.** About 75% of the non-coding regions occur *between genes* (see Figure 5-10).

In the end, the presence of this non-coding DNA is still not completely understood. Recent evidence has revealed, however, that some of the non-coding DNA actually does encode extremely short RNA molecules (~20 nucleotides

PERCENTAGES OF CODING DNA FOUND IN VARIOUS ORGANISMS

Human (*Homo sapiens*)
2%

Fruit fly (*Drosophila melanogaster*)
19%

Round worm (*Caenorhabditis elegans*)
25%

Arabidopsis (*Arabidopsis thaliana*)
28%

E. coli (*Escherichia coli*)
90%

Percentage of DNA that codes for proteins

FIGURE 5-9 "Junk DNA"? The proportion of DNA that codes for proteins or RNA varies greatly among species. Of the species listed, which has the least "junk DNA"?

CODING vs. NON-CODING DNA

Eukaryotic cell
Nucleus
Chromosome

REGIONS OF DNA THAT CODE FOR PROTEINS (color)

GENE 1   GENE 2

REGIONS OF DNA THAT DO NOT CODE FOR PROTEINS (gray)
75% of non-coding DNA occurs between genes, while 25%, called introns, occurs within genes.

💡 *Most DNA in eukaryotes does not code for any proteins!*

FIGURE 5-10 Non-coding regions of DNA. These regions are found both between and within genes.

long) that function in gene regulation; they act as a "switch" that regulates when genes are turned on or off, or as a "volume knob" that influences the rate at which gene products are produced. Non-coding DNA may also serve as a reservoir of potentially useful sequences. In any case, the label "junk DNA" is a bad description.

TAKE-HOME MESSAGE 5·4

Only a small fraction of the DNA in eukaryotic species is in genes that code for proteins; the function of the rest is still poorly understood, although at least some of it plays important roles in the cell, such as gene regulation.

5·5 How do genes work? An overview.

Just as having a recipe for chocolate chip cookies is not the same thing as having the actual cookies, having a wealth of hereditary information about how to build muscle cells or leaf cells is not sufficient to produce an organism. Think about it: an organism's every cell contains all of the information needed to manufacture every protein in its body. This means that the skin cells on your arm contain the genes for producing proteins found only in liver cells or red blood cells or muscle

tissue—but they don't produce them. Having the instructions is not the same as having the products.

The genes in strands of DNA are a storehouse of information, an instruction book, but they are only one part of the process by which an organism is built. If the genes that an organism carries for a particular trait—its **genotype**—are like a recipe in a cookbook, the physical manifestation of the instructions—

FIGURE 5-11 Overview of the steps from gene to protein.

the organism's **phenotype**—is the cookie, or any of the other foods described by the recipes. And, just as you have to assemble the ingredients, mix them, then bake the dough to get a cookie, there are several steps in the production of the molecules, tissues, and even behaviors that make up a phenotype.

How does a gene (a sequence of bases in a section of DNA) affect a flower's color or the shape of a nose or the texture of a dog's fur (the phenotype)? The process occurs in two main steps: **transcription,** in which a copy of a gene's base sequence is made, and **translation,** in which that copy is used to direct the production of a polypeptide, which then, in response to a variety of factors, including the cellular environment, folds into a protein.

FIGURE 5-11 presents an overview of the processes of transcription and translation. In transcription, which in eukaryotes occurs in the nucleus, the gene's base sequence, or

code, is copied into a middleman molecule called **messenger RNA (mRNA).** (Because prokaryotes don't have a nucleus, transcription occurs in the cytoplasm.) This is like copying the information for the chocolate chip cookie recipe out of the cookbook and onto an index card. The mRNA then moves out of the nucleus into the cytoplasm, where translation allows the messages encoded in the mRNA to be used to build proteins.

TAKE-HOME MESSAGE 5·5

The genes in strands of DNA are a storehouse of information, an instruction book. The process by which this information is used to build an organism occurs in two main steps: transcription, in which a copy of a gene's base sequence is made, and translation, in which that copy is used to direct the production of a polypeptide.

5·6–5·8 Building organisms: information in DNA directs the production of the molecules that make up an organism.

DNA microarrays measure the expression levels of many genes simultaneously.

5·6

In transcription, the information coded in DNA is copied into mRNA.

If DNA is like a cookbook filled with recipes, transcription and translation are like cooking. In cooking, you use information about how to make chocolate chip cookies to actually produce the cookies. In an organism, the information about putting together proteins is used to build the proteins the organism needs to function. In this section, we examine transcription, the first step in the two-step process by which DNA regulates a cell's activity and its synthesis of proteins (see Figure 5-11). In transcription, a copy of one specific gene within the DNA is made. Continuing our cookbook analogy, transcription is like copying a single recipe from the cookbook onto an index card. It happens in four steps (**FIGURE 5-12**).

Step 1. Recognize and bind. To start the transcription process, the enzyme RNA polymerase, recognizes a **promoter site,** a part of the DNA molecule that indicates the start of a gene and, in effect, tells the RNA polymerase, "Start here." RNA polymerase binds to the DNA molecule at the promoter site and unwinds it just a bit, so that only one strand of the DNA can be read.

Step 2. Transcribe. As the DNA strand is processed through the RNA polymerase, the RNA polymerase builds a copy—

called a "transcript"—of the gene from the DNA molecule, just as (to use another analogy) a court reporter transcribes and creates a record of everything that is said in a courtroom. This copy is called messenger RNA (mRNA) because, once this copy of the gene is created, it can move elsewhere in the cell and its message can be translated into a protein. Throughout transcription, DNA is unwound ahead of the RNA polymerase so that a single strand of the DNA can be read, and it is rewound after the polymerase passes.

The mRNA transcript is constructed from four different nucleotides, like DNA nucleotides but with a different sugar. Each pairs up with an exposed base on the now unwound and separated DNA strand, following these rules:

If the DNA strand has a thymine (T), an adenine (A) is added to the mRNA.

If the DNA strand has an adenine (A), a uracil (U) is added to the mRNA.

If the DNA strand has a guanine (G), a cytosine (C) is added to the mRNA.

If the DNA strand has a cytosine (C), a guanine (G) is added to the mRNA.

TRANSCRIPTION

DNA

1 RECOGNIZE AND BIND
Once RNA polymerase recognizes a promoter site, it binds to one strand of the DNA and begins reading the gene's message.

RNA polymerase

Promoter site

2 TRANSCRIBE
As the DNA strand is processed through the RNA polymerase, the RNA polymerase builds a single-stranded RNA copy of the gene, called the mRNA transcript.

RNA polymerase

mRNA transcript

3 TERMINATE
When the RNA polymerase encounters a code signaling the end of the gene, it stops transcription and releases the mRNA transcript.

RNA polymerase

Termination site

mRNA transcript

UNWIND AND REWIND

As the RNA polymerase moves down the strand of DNA, the helix unwinds so that the DNA can be read. At the same time, the DNA that has already been transcribed rewinds back to its original double-helix form.

Helix unwinds

Helix rewinds

4 CAP AND PROCESS
In eukaryotes, mRNAs receive extra processing before they can be translated into a protein. A cap and tail are often added for protection and to promote recognition, and non-coding sections are removed.

Cap

Tail

Non-protein-coding regions of mRNA

mRNA transcript leaves the nucleus to be translated into a protein.

Because our court reporter (RNA polymerase) transcribes a specific sequence of DNA letters (the gene), the mRNA transcript carries this specific bit of the DNA's information. And because it is separate from the DNA, the mRNA transcript can move throughout the cell, to the places where the information is needed, while leaving the original information within the DNA.

Step 3. Terminate. When the RNA polymerase encounters a sequence of bases on the DNA at the end of the gene (called a termination sequence), it stops creating the transcript and detaches from the DNA molecule. After termination, the mRNA molecule is released as a free-floating, single-strand copy of the gene.

Step 4. Capping and editing. In prokaryotic cells, once an mRNA transcript is produced and begins to separate from the DNA it is ready to be translated into a protein (it doesn't have a nuclear membrane to cross). In eukaryotes, mRNAs receive extra processing before they can be translated into a protein.

First, a cap and a tail may be added at the beginning and end of the transcript. Like the front and back covers of a book, these serve to protect the mRNA from damage and help the protein-making machinery recognize the mRNA. Second, because (as we saw earlier in the chapter) there may be some non-coding bits of the DNA that are transcribed into mRNA, those sections—the introns—are snipped out. Once the mRNA transcript has been edited, it is ready to leave the nucleus for the cytoplasm, where it will be translated into a polypeptide that will fold into a protein.

TAKE-HOME MESSAGE 5·6

Transcription is the first step in the two-step process by which DNA directs the production of proteins. In transcription (which occurs in the nucleus in eukaryotic cells), a single copy of one specific gene in the DNA is made in the form of a molecule of mRNA. When the mRNA copy of a gene is completed, it moves to the cytoplasm, where it can be translated into a polypeptide.

5·7 In translation, the mRNA copy of the information from DNA is used to build functional molecules.

Once the mRNA molecule moves out of the cell's nucleus and into the cytoplasm, the translation process begins. In translation, the information carried by the mRNA is read, and ingredients present in the cytoplasm are used to produce a protein (see Figure 5-11). The process of translation is like the combining and baking of the ingredients listed in our chocolate chip cookie recipe to produce a cookie.

Several ingredients must be present in the cytoplasm for translation to occur. First, there must be large numbers of free amino acids floating around. Recall from Chapter 2 that amino acids are the raw materials for building proteins and an essential component of our diet. Second, there must be **ribosomal subunits,** the protein-production factories where amino acids are linked together in the proper order to produce the protein. And there must also be molecules that can read the mRNA code and translate that message from a sequence of bases into a protein.

To read an encrypted message, you need to know the secret code by which to translate each of the encrypted characters into a readable character in the message. Similarly, to understand which sequence of amino acids in a polypeptide is specified by a sequence of nucleotides in a DNA molecule, you need to know a secret code of sorts.

A special type of RNA molecules holds the secret code. These molecules, called

transfer RNA (tRNA), interpret the mRNA code, translating the language of DNA—coded in the linear sequence of bases—into the language of proteins, coded in the linear sequences of amino acids.

Picture a two-sided molecule (**FIGURE 5-13**). On one side of the two-sided tRNA molecule is an attachment site consisting of a three-base sequence that matches up with a three-base sequence on the mRNA transcript. This matchup enables the

TRANSFER RNA (tRNA)

Transfer RNA (tRNA) molecules translate the mRNA code by linking specific bases on the mRNA with specific amino acids that will be used to build a protein.

Amino acid — thr

tRNA

Attachment site

Attachment sites consist of a three-base sequence that matches up with a three-base sequence on the mRNA transcript. Each three-base sequence in mRNA—called a codon—matches with a tRNA that carries one particular amino acid.

mRNA

Codon

FIGURE 5-13 Each transfer RNA attaches a particular amino acid to the mRNA.

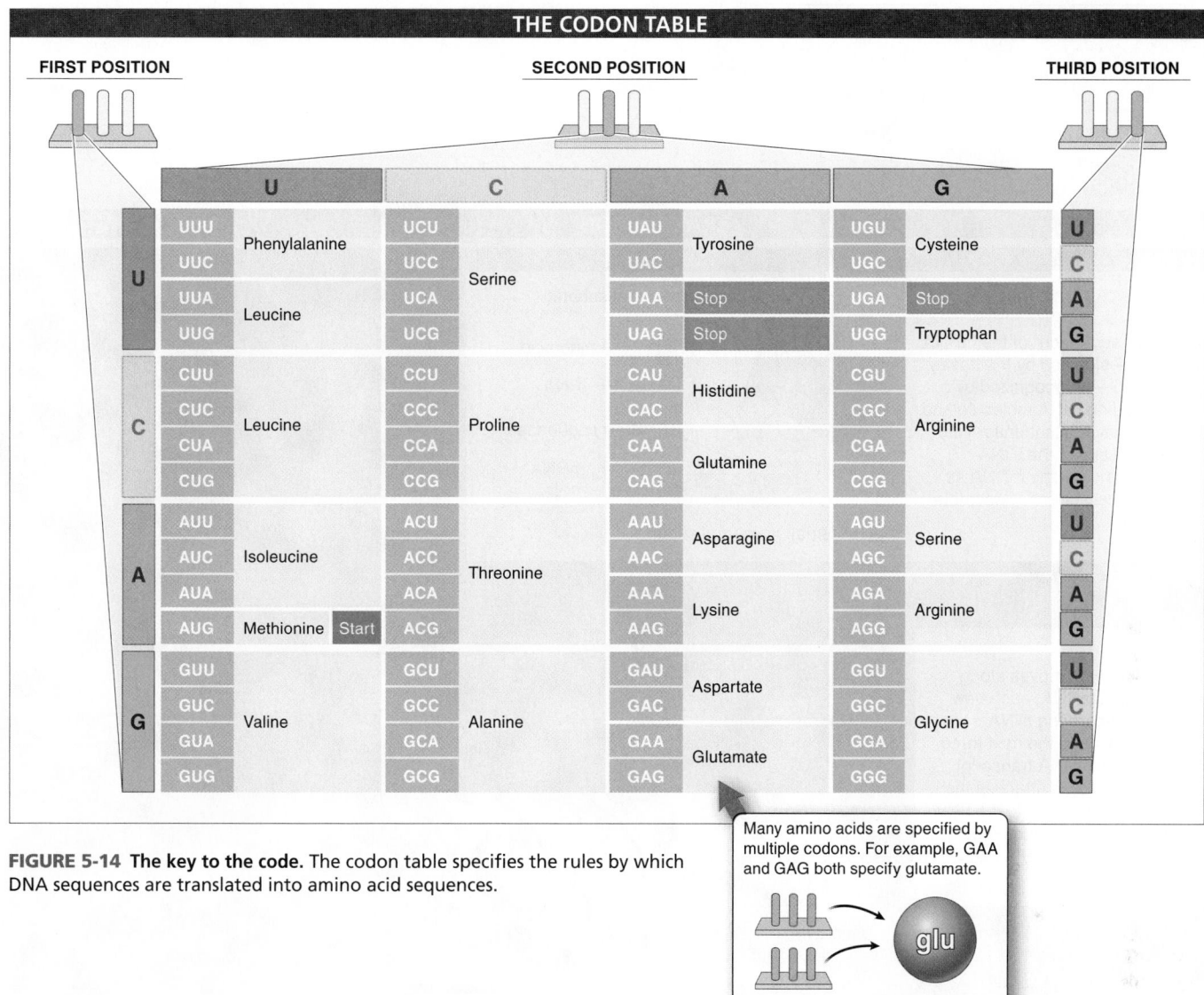

THE CODON TABLE

FIRST POSITION

SECOND POSITION

THIRD POSITION

	U	C	A	G	
U	UUU UUC Phenylalanine UUA UUG Leucine	UCU UCC UCA UCG Serine	UAU UAC Tyrosine UAA Stop UAG Stop	UGU UGC Cysteine UGA Stop UGG Tryptophan	U C A G
C	CUU CUC CUA CUG Leucine	CCU CCC CCA CCG Proline	CAU CAC Histidine CAA CAG Glutamine	CGU CGC CGA CGG Arginine	U C A G
A	AUU AUC Isoleucine AUA AUG Methionine Start	ACU ACC ACA ACG Threonine	AAU AAC Asparagine AAA AAG Lysine	AGU AGC Serine AGA AGG Arginine	U C A G
G	GUU GUC GUA GUG Valine	GCU GCC GCA GCG Alanine	GAU GAC Aspartate GAA GAG Glutamate	GGU GGC GGA GGG Glycine	U C A G

FIGURE 5-14 The key to the code. The codon table specifies the rules by which DNA sequences are translated into amino acid sequences.

Many amino acids are specified by multiple codons. For example, GAA and GAG both specify glutamate.

glu

tRNA molecule to attach to the mRNA. Attached to the other side of the tRNA molecule is an amino acid. Each three-base sequence in mRNA—called a **codon**—matches with a tRNA molecule that carries a particular amino acid. The codon ACG, for example, is recognized by the tRNA molecule that carries the amino acid threonine. And the codon CAG is recognized by the tRNA molecule that carries glutamine. For every possible codon, there is one type of tRNA molecule that will recognize and bind to the mRNA at that point, and it will always carry the same amino acid.

The codon table (**FIGURE 5-14**), also called the "genetic code," describes which amino acid is specified by each codon. With four possible bases in each of the three positions of a codon, 64 different codons are possible. Sixty-one of these codons specify amino acids and 3 are "stop" codons, indicating the

end of translation. Because there are only 20 amino acids, many amino acids are specified by multiple codons. UGU and UGC, for example, both specify cysteine. With just a few small exceptions, the genetic code is the same in every organism on earth.

The translation of an mRNA molecule into a sequence of amino acids (that will then fold into the complex three-dimensional shape of a protein) occurs in three steps (**FIGURE 5-15**).

Step 1. Recognize and initiate protein building. Translation begins in the cell's cytoplasm when the subunits of a ribosome, essentially a two-piece protein-building factory, recognize and assemble around a "start sequence" on the mRNA transcript. This start sequence is always the sequence A, U, and G (AUG). As the ribosomal subunits assemble

TRANSLATION

1 RECOGNIZE AND INITIATE PROTEIN BUILDING

The "start sequence" of the mRNA transcript—signified by the bases A, U, and G—is recognized by a corresponding tRNA molecule and the two ribosomal subunits. The attachment site of the tRNA molecule binds to the mRNA as the ribosomal subunits assemble around them.

Large ribosomal subunit

Amino acid

tRNA

Start sequence

mRNA

Small ribosomal subunit

2 ELONGATE

As the ribosome moves along the strand of mRNA, each new amino-acid-carrying tRNA molecule binds to the next three bases on the mRNA transcript. After the ribosome attaches the growing protein chain to the new amino acid, the tRNA molecule detaches from the mRNA and floats away.

Ribosome

Protein chain

tRNA

met

cys

ser

val

ile

ser

gln

mRNA

Start sequence

Stop sequence

3 TERMINATE

Once the ribosome encounters the three-base "stop sequence," protein assembly is complete. Translation ends and both the protein and the mRNA molecule are released from the ribosome.

Newly formed protein

Stop sequence

The same mRNA molecule can be translated over and over again before it is degraded, producing dozens or even hundreds of molecules of the protein.

FIGURE 5-15 Translation: reading a sequence of nucleotides and producing protein. The second step in a two-step process by which DNA regulates a cell's activity and synthesis of proteins.

themselves into a ribosome, one side of a particular tRNA molecule also recognizes the start sequence on the mRNA and binds to it. This initiator tRNA has the amino acid methionine (met) bound to its other side. Thus, methionine is always the first amino acid in any protein that is produced. (Occasionally, in eukaryotes, this initial methionine is "edited out" later in the protein-building process.)

Step 2. Elongate. After the mRNA start sequence (AUG), the next three bases on the mRNA specify which amino acid–carrying tRNA molecule should bind to the mRNA. If the next three bases on the mRNA transcript are GUU, for example, a tRNA molecule that recognizes this sequence, and carrying its particular amino acid (valine, or val), will attach to the mRNA at that point. The ribosome then facilitates the connection of this second amino acid to the first. After the amino acid carried by a tRNA molecule is attached to the preceding amino acid, the tRNA molecule detaches from the mRNA and floats away.

As this process continues, the amino acid chain grows. The next three bases on the mRNA specify the next amino acid to be added to the first two. And the three bases after that specify the fourth amino acid, and so on. This process of progressively linking together the amino acids specified by an mRNA strand is called **protein synthesis,** because all proteins are chains of amino acids, like beads on a string. Precision in this process is essential. Any skipping or backing up or misreading as the bases of the mRNA are used to specify the amino acid sequence could alter the amino acid sequence (and possibly the normal functioning) of the protein specified by the mRNA.

The mRNA continues to be "threaded" through the ribosome, with the ribosome moving down the mRNA strand reading and translating its message in little three-base chunks. Each three-base sequence specifies the next amino acid, lengthening the growing amino acid strand.

Step 3. Terminate. Eventually, the ribosome arrives at the three-base sequence on the mRNA that signals the end of translation. Once the ribosome encounters this stop sequence, the assembly of the amino acid sequence is complete. Translation ends, and the amino acid strand and mRNA molecule are released from the ribosome. As it is being produced, the amino acid sequence folds and bends, based on the chemical features in the amino acid side chains (as we saw in Chapter 2). Through the folding and bending, the protein acquires its three-dimensional structure. The completed protein—such as a membrane protein or insulin or a digestive enzyme—may be used within the cell or packaged for delivery via the bloodstream to somewhere else in the body where it is needed.

Following the completion of translation, the mRNA strand may remain in the cytoplasm to serve as the template for producing another molecule of the same protein. In bacteria, an mRNA strand may last from a few seconds to more than an hour; in mammals, an mRNA may last several days. Depending on how long it lasts, the same mRNA strand may be translated hundreds of times. Eventually, it is broken down by enzymes in the cytoplasm.

TAKE-HOME MESSAGE 5·7

Translation is the second step in the two-step process by which information carried in DNA directs the synthesis of proteins. In translation, the information from a gene that has been encoded in the nucleotide sequence of an mRNA is read, and ingredients present in the cell's cytoplasm are used to produce a protein.

5·8 Genes are regulated in several ways.

Why do some people get sick more than others? Why is one person taller or shorter than another? More generally, what makes us look and act the way we do? We say that our health, growth, and development are the result of interactions between our genes and our environment. But how do our genes and our environment actually interact?

It matters which genes a person has, but carrying a gene is not the only thing that matters when it comes to **gene expression**—the production of the protein that the gene's sequence codes for. There is also the issue of **gene regulation,** the question of whether a gene is turned on—producing its protein product—or turned off. And this, commonly, hinges on a person's environment.

A powerful tool in the study of gene regulation is the microarray, a small chip that looks like a microscope slide that can be used to monitor the expression levels of thousands of genes simultaneously. Taking cells from one part of the body, researchers examine gene expression in that tissue. Microarrays are particularly useful in exploring how gene expression differs in response to an illness, or the treatment of an illness, or in response to aging.

For example, in a five-year medical study exploring the health consequences of loneliness, microarray analyses of gene activity in immune system cells revealed that 209 genes were expressed differently in two groups of participants. One group included individuals who were experiencing chronic social isolation and loneliness, while individuals in the other group were not.

Individuals in the "lonely" group had impaired transcription (decreased activity) of some genes associated with an effective stress response. They also had increased activity in genes associated with inflammatory processes that are implicated in a variety of diseases (**FIGURE 5-16**). Related studies have shown a similarly reduced immune function among stressed-out individuals—including one study of students during a stressful exam period!

Lonely, isolated individuals have very different patterns of immune system gene expression.

FIGURE 5-16 Social isolation. Very different patterns of immune-system gene expression occur in lonely, isolated individuals.

Controlling gene expression Cells have a wide variety of mechanisms by which they can control when individual genes are expressed. One of the main ways expression is controlled is by transcription factors, proteins that bind to specific regulatory sites on the DNA. These sites are often located in front of genes. The regulation may be "positive

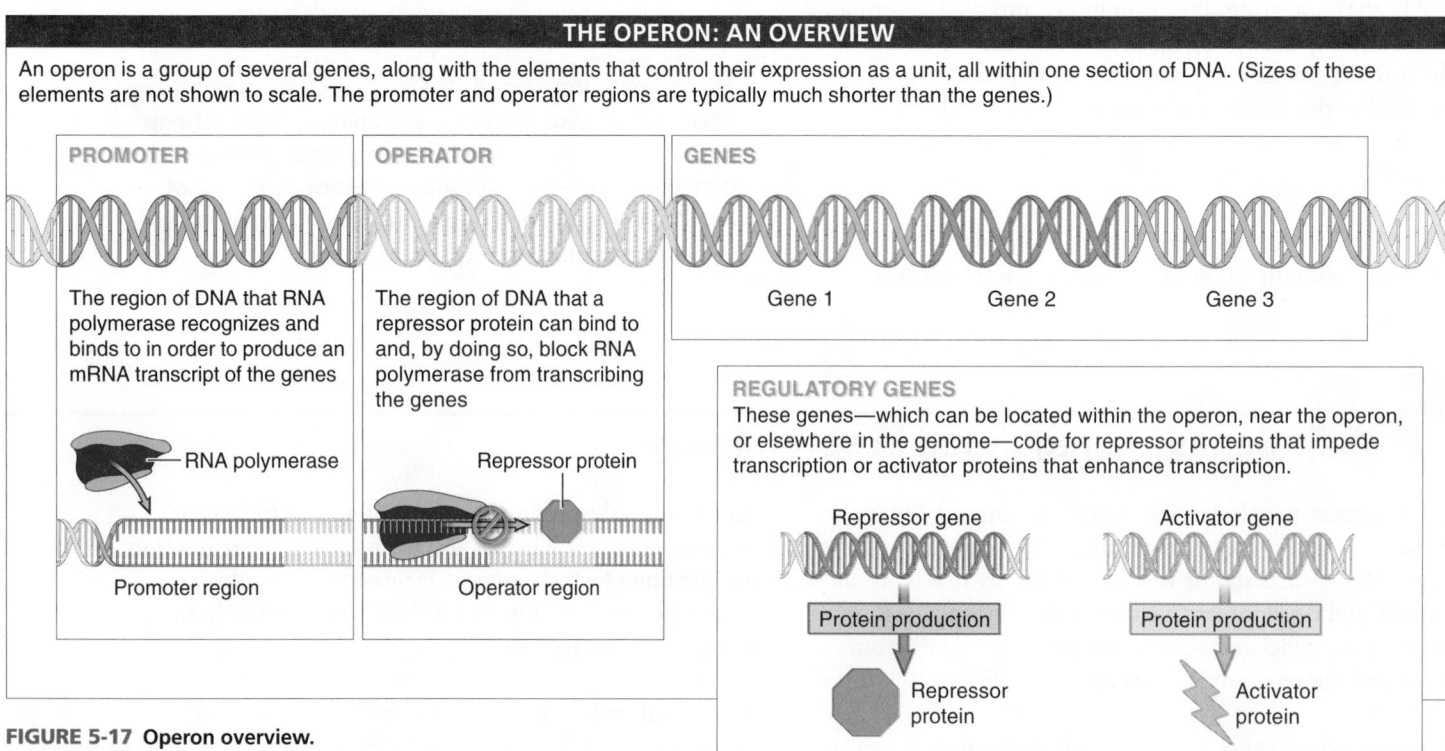

THE OPERON: AN OVERVIEW

An operon is a group of several genes, along with the elements that control their expression as a unit, all within one section of DNA. (Sizes of these elements are not shown to scale. The promoter and operator regions are typically much shorter than the genes.)

PROMOTER

The region of DNA that RNA polymerase recognizes and binds to in order to produce an mRNA transcript of the genes

RNA polymerase

Promoter region

OPERATOR

The region of DNA that a repressor protein can bind to and, by doing so, block RNA polymerase from transcribing the genes

Repressor protein

Operator region

GENES

Gene 1   Gene 2   Gene 3

REGULATORY GENES

These genes—which can be located within the operon, near the operon, or elsewhere in the genome—code for repressor proteins that impede transcription or activator proteins that enhance transcription.

Repressor gene

Protein production

Repressor protein

Activator gene

Protein production

Activator protein

FIGURE 5-17 Operon overview.

control," in which binding of the regulatory protein initiates or speeds up gene expression, or "negative control," in which the protein slows or blocks gene expression.

Regulatory proteins may come from nearby cells. During the initial development of an organism, for example, gene regulation is extremely important in directing cells to differentiate into one type of tissue—perhaps muscle, rather than bone—and proteins produced by one cell commonly influence gene expression in neighboring cells.

Prokaryotic gene control and the lac operon

Regulation may also be influenced by the nutrients an organism takes in. One well-studied example concerns the case of how the bacterium *E. coli* adjusts its diet depending on which sugars are available in its environment. More specifically, although its preference is for glucose, in the absence of glucose, it will utilize lactose as an energy source. (*E. coli* cells, many of which live in your intestine, are likely to encounter lactose, which is the chief sugar in milk.)

The absorption and digestion of lactose, however, requires transcription of three genes, and bacteria do not waste their energy transcribing these genes, translating the proteins, folding them, and sending them to the correct destinations unless lactose is actually present. That regulation is accomplished with one set of regulatory sequences called an **operon,** which is a group of several genes and the elements that control their expression as a unit, all within one section of the cell's DNA (**FIGURE 5-17**).

Promoter. For a gene to be transcribed, RNA polymerase recognizes and binds to the promoter region, the specific sequence of nucleotides in the DNA that signals the beginning of the gene.

Operator. A molecule called a repressor protein can bind to the operator, the regulatory portion of the DNA, and by doing so it blocks RNA polymerase from transcribing the genes necessary for lactose metabolism.

Regulatory gene. The regulatory gene codes for the repressor protein that, when bound to the operator region, does the blocking of RNA polymerase's binding to the promoter site.

In the absence of glucose (more on this below), here's how this operon (called the "lac operon") functions. If lactose is not present: (1) The regulatory gene produces the repressor protein. (2) The repressor protein binds to the operator region. And (3) RNA polymerase is blocked from transcribing the lactose metabolism genes (**FIGURE 5-18**).

THE LAC OPERON IN ACTION

In the bacterium *E. coli*, glucose is the preferred food source, but it can utilize lactose as a backup. The lac operon makes it possible for the bacteria to not waste energy transcribing the three genes necessary for lactose absorption and digestion unless glucose is absent and lactose is actually present. Shown here is how on/off switching of the lac operon occurs **in the absence of glucose**.

IF LACTOSE IS NOT PRESENT: OPERON OFF

A repressor protein binds to the operator, preventing RNA polymerase from binding to the promoter and transcribing the genes necessary for lactose metabolism.

IF LACTOSE IS PRESENT: OPERON ON

Lactose (slightly modified) binds to the repressor protein, preventing it from binding to the operator. RNA polymerase can then bind to the promoter and transcribe the genes necessary for lactose metabolism.

FIGURE 5-18 Operon in action. In *E. coli,* environmental conditions control the expression of the genes necessary for the metabolism of lactose.

If, on the other hand, lactose *is* present: (1) The regulatory gene produces the repressor protein. (2) Lactose binds to the repressor protein, altering its shape so that it can no longer bind to the operator. And (3) with no repressor bound to the DNA, RNA polymerase binds to the promoter and transcribes the genes necessary for lactose metabolism.

Note that the lac operon can only be switched on in the absence of glucose. Without glucose, a regulatory protein called an *activator* helps the DNA unwind in the vicinity of the lac operon, enabling RNA polymerase to bind and

TRANSCRIPTION REGULATION

POSITIVE CONTROL
- Activators can initiate or speed up gene expression
- Enhancer sequences can speed RNA polymerase binding and gene transcription

NEGATIVE CONTROL
- Repressors can block or slow down gene expression
- Chemicals can bind to DNA and block gene transcription

POST-TRANSCRIPTION REGULATION

- mRNA processing, transport, and enzymatic breakdown can be blocked or accelerated
- mRNA translation and protein processing rates can be altered

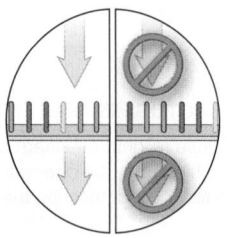

FIGURE 5-19 Regulating gene expression. Cells can increase or decrease gene expression in multiple ways.

Eukaryotic gene control   There are many other ways that genes can be regulated, besides operons. Many eukaryotes, for example, have enhancer sequences that increase transcription rates (positive control). Often far from the gene they regulate, these sequences, after binding a regulatory protein, bind "transcription factors" associated with RNA polymerase and enhance the rate at which the RNA polymerase binds to a promoter and transcribes a gene.

Additional mechanisms of gene control include the binding of chemicals to DNA that can block genes from being transcribed (negative control) and mRNA regulation. Messenger RNA can be regulated by altering mRNA processing and transport, or by altering the rate at which mRNA is broken down in the cytoplasm. Translation of mRNAs can be regulated, too, as can the processing of proteins following translation (**FIGURE 5-19**).

TAKE-HOME MESSAGE 5·8

Environmental signals influence the turning of genes on and off. By binding to DNA, regulatory proteins can block or facilitate the binding of RNA polymerase and subsequent transcription of genes. Regulation of gene expression also can occur in a variety of other ways that enhance or impede transcription, or alter mRNA's longevity and rate of degradation, or influence translation or protein processing.

transcribe genes. When glucose is present, however, activator protein cannot bind to the DNA, and this prevents RNA polymerase from binding to and transcribing the lactose metabolism genes.

5·9–5·10 Damage to the genetic code has a variety of causes and effects.

Damage to the genetic code can interfere with normal development.

5·9 What causes a mutation, and what are its effects?

Through the two-step process of transcription and translation, an organism converts the information held in its genes into the proteins necessary for life. But the process is only as good as the organism's underlying genetic information. Sometimes something occurs to alter the sequence of bases in an organism's DNA. Such an alteration is called a **mutation,** and it can lead to changes in the structure and function of the proteins produced. Mutations can have a range of effects. Sometimes they result in a serious, even deadly, problem for an organism. Sometimes they have little or no detrimental effect. And occasionally—but very rarely—they may even turn out to be beneficial to the organism.

As an example of how mutations can affect organisms, consider the case of breast cancer in humans. When two human genes, called BRCA1 and BRCA2, are functioning properly, they help to prevent breast cancer by helping to repair DNA damage, preventing cells from accumulating the changes that lead to cancer. If the DNA sequence of either of these genes is altered through mutation and the gene's normal function is lost, the person carrying the gene has a significantly increased risk of developing breast cancer. (Because a variety of other factors, including environmental variables, are involved in development of cancer, it's impossible to know for certain whether these individuals will develop breast cancer.) Currently, more than 200 different changes in the DNA sequences of these genes have been detected, each of which results in an increased risk of developing breast cancer.

Given the havoc they can cause for an organism, it's not surprising that mutations have a bad reputation. After all, because they can change the protein produced, they can disrupt normal processes and harm the individual (**FIGURE 5-20**). But there are a couple of reasons why mutations' bad reputation may not be fully deserved. First, it turns out that many—perhaps even *most*—mutations are neutral, having neither a positive nor a negative effect on an organism's phenotype. This may be the case when a mutation occurs in a non-coding region of DNA. It can also occur when a change in DNA within a gene doesn't alter the function of the protein produced. Based on a recent study, researchers estimate that the rate of germ line mutations is approximately 10^{-8} per base pair per generation.

A second reason that mutations' bad reputation may be undeserved is the paradoxical fact that mutations are essential to evolution. Those mutations that don't kill an organism, or reduce its ability to survive and reproduce, can be beneficial. Every genetic feature in every organism was, initially, the result of a mutation. (In Chapter 8, we explore the relationship between mutation and evolution.) Ultimately, most mutations you inherit from your parents will have no effect. And all of you are carrying mutations that you will never know about!

It's important to note that mutations can occur in an organism's gamete-producing cells (that is, cells that produce sperm or eggs) as well as in its non-sex cells (such as skin cells

Normal fruit fly

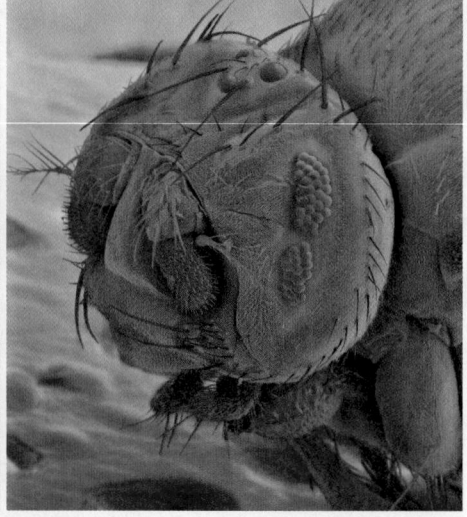
Mutant fruit fly

FIGURE 5-20 Wreaking havoc. Mutations can change the protein produced by the altered gene, with disastrous consequences.

or cells in the lungs). Mutations in non-sex cells can have bad health consequences for the person carrying them. Many forms of cancer, such as lung cancer and skin cancer, result from such mutations. On the upside, non-sex-cell mutations are not passed on to your children. Mutations in the sex cells (gametes), on the other hand, do not have any adverse health effects on the person carrying them, but these mutations can be passed on to offspring, with terrible effects such as the induction of a miscarriage or the occurrence of birth defects. Individuals inheriting certain mutations from a parent—because the mutation occurred in the parent's sex cells or because the parent inherited the mutation from his or her parent—can be at increased risk for certain diseases such as breast cancer or cardiovascular disease.

Mutations generally fall into two types: point mutations and chromosomal aberrations (**FIGURE 5-21**). In point mutations, one base pair is changed. In chromosomal aberrations, entire sections of a chromosome are altered.

Point mutations occur when one base pair in the DNA is substituted for another, or when a base pair is inserted or deleted. Insertions and deletions can be much more harmful than substitutions, because the amino acid sequence of a protein is thrown off. If a single base is added or removed, the three-base groupings in an mRNA get thrown off, and the entire sequence of amino acids stipulated "downstream" from that point will be wrong—the reading frame is shifted. It's almost like putting your hands on a computer keyboard, but offset by one key to the left or right, and then typing what should be a normal sentence. It comes out as gibberish.

Why do dentists put a heavy apron over you when they X-ray your teeth?

Chromosomal aberrations are changes to the overall organization of the genes on a chromosome. Chromosomal aberrations are like the manipulation of large chunks of text when you are editing a term paper. The aberrations can involve the complete deletion of an entire section of DNA, the relocation of a gene from one part of a chromosome to elsewhere on the same chromosome or even to a different chromosome, or the duplication of a gene, with the new copy inserted elsewhere on the chromosome or on a different chromosome. Whatever the type of aberration, a gene's expression—the production of the protein that its sequence codes for—can be altered, as well as the expression of the genes around it.

Given the potentially hazardous health consequences of mutations, it is advisable to minimize their occurrence. Can this be done? Yes and no. There are three chief causes of mutation and, although one of them is beyond our control, the risk of occurrence of the other two can be significantly reduced (**FIGURE 5-22**).

1. Spontaneous mutations. Some mutations arise by accident as long strands of DNA are duplicating themselves—at the rate of more than a thousand bases a minute in humans—when cells are dividing (you'll read more details on this process in Chapter 6). Most errors are corrected by DNA repair enzymes, but some still slip through and there's not much we can do about them.

Q

2. Radiation-induced mutations. Ionizing radiation, such as X rays, is radiation with enough energy to disrupt atomic structure—even break apart chromosomes—by removing tightly bound electrons. But even non-ionizing lower-energy radiation (which is not able to remove electrons) can damage

TYPES OF MUTATIONS

NORMAL DNA

mRNA

Normal protein: met — cys — ser — gly — arg

> Insertions and deletions can be much more harmful than substitutions because they can alter the reading frame for the rest of the gene.

POINT MUTATIONS

NUCLEOTIDE SUBSTITUTION

DNA

mRNA

Mutated protein: met — ser — ser — gly — arg

NUCLEOTIDE INSERTION

DNA

mRNA

Mutated protein: met — cys — glu — arg — lys

NUCLEOTIDE DELETION

DNA

mRNA

Mutated protein: met — cys — ala — glu — glu

NORMAL CHROMOSOME

Gene 1   Gene 2   Gene 3

CHROMOSOMAL ABERRATIONS

GENE DELETION

Gene 1   Gene 3

Gene 2 DELETED

GENE RELOCATION

Gene 2   Gene 3

Gene 1 RELOCATED to a different chromosome

GENE DUPLICATION

Gene 1   Gene 2

Gene 3 DUPLICATED

FIGURE 5-21 Point mutations and chromosomal aberrations.

 In point mutations, one nucleotide is changed, whereas in chromosomal aberrations, entire sections of a chromosome are altered.

DNA. Ultraviolet (UV) rays from the sun, for example, can be absorbed by certain bases in DNA and cause them to rearrange bonds. This can prevent them from pairing correctly with the complementary DNA strand and can transform a cell into a cancer cell. This is why long-term sun exposure can contribute to the development of skin cancer. Because ionizing rays cannot pass through lead, the lead apron a doctor or dentist puts over you when you get an X ray protects your body from the ionizing radiation.

Another source of dangerous radiation is found in the core of nuclear power plants, where radioactive atoms are used and produced in energy-generating reactions. The high energy of the radioactivity that fuels the production of usable energy can pass through your body and disrupt your DNA, causing point mutations and chromosomal aberrations. With the proper

 Q Why is it dangerous to be near the core of a nuclear power plant?

FIGURE 5-22 Gambling with mutation-inducing activities. You can increase or decrease your risk of mutations with your behavior: smoking, tanning, and radiation (but notice the protective lead apron).

safety precautions, however, nuclear power plant workers can minimize their exposure to harmful radiation.

3. Chemical-induced mutations. Many chemicals, such as those found in cigarette smoke and in the exhaust from internal combustion engines, can also react with the atoms in DNA molecules and induce mutations.

In the next section, we examine how even tiny changes in the sequence of bases in DNA can lead to errors in protein production and profound health problems.

> **TAKE-HOME MESSAGE 5·9**
>
> Mutations are alterations in a single base or changes in large segments of DNA that include several genes or more. They are rare, but when they do occur, they may disrupt normal functioning of the body (although many mutations are neutral). Extremely rarely, mutations may have a beneficial effect. Mutations play an important role in evolution.

5·10 Faulty genes, coding for faulty enzymes, can lead to sickness.

Isabella joins her friends in sipping wine during a dinner party. As the meal progresses, her companions become tipsy. Their conversations turn racy, their moods relaxed. They refill their glasses, reveling in a little buzz. Not so for Isabella. Before her first glass is empty, she experiences a "fast-flush" response: her face turns crimson, her heart begins to race, and her head starts to pound. Worse still, she soon feels the need to vomit.

How can people respond so differently to alcohol? It comes down to a difference in a single base pair in their DNA, a single difference that can influence dramatically a person's behavior, digestion, respiration, and general ability to function. The base-pair change leads to the production of a non-functional enzyme, and the lack of a functional version of this enzyme leads to physical illness. Let's look at the details.

When we consume alcohol, our bodies start a two-step process to convert the alcohol molecules from their

intoxicating form into innocuous molecules. Each of the two steps is made possible by a specific enzyme, whose assembly instructions are, for most people, coded in their DNA.

"Fast-flushers" such as Isabella complete the first step of breaking down alcohol, but cannot fully complete the breakdown because they carry defective genetic instructions for making aldehyde dehydrogenase, the enzyme that makes possible the second step of the process. A poisonous substance subsequently accumulates, and the symptoms of the fast-flush reaction are due to this substance's toxic effects in the body.

Approximately half of the people living in Asia carry a non-functional form of the gene for aldehyde dehydrogenase, a mutation that may confer a greater benefit than harm. In

Q

Why *do* many Asians have unpleasant experiences associated with alcohol consumption?

FROM MUTATION TO ILLNESS

1 A mutated gene codes for a non-functioning protein, commonly an enzyme.

DNA

mRNA

Functioning enzyme should look like this:

Non-functioning enzyme

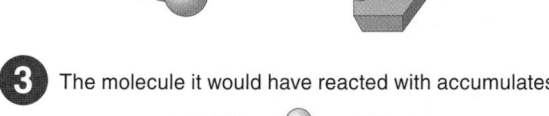

2 The non-functioning enzyme can't catalyze the reaction as it normally would.

3 The molecule it would have reacted with accumulates.

4 The accumulating chemical causes sickness (fast-flushing, for example) or death (Tay-Sachs disease, for example).

FIGURE 5-23 Faulty enzymes can interfere with metabolism.

a study of 1,300 alcoholics in Japan, not a single one was a fast-flusher, even though half of all Japanese people are fast-flushers. The minor change in the genetic code that makes alcohol consumption an unpleasant experience may be responsible for the lower incidence of alcoholism among Japanese and other Asian people.

In many other cases—perhaps in the majority of genetic diseases—the link between a particular defective DNA sequence and physical illness is equally direct. Recall from Chapter 3 the case of Tay-Sachs disease. In Tay-Sachs disease, an individual inherits genes with a mutation that causes an inability to produce a critical lipid-digesting enzyme in their lysosomes, the cellular garbage disposals. Because these organelles cannot digest certain lipids, the lipids accumulate, undigested. The lysosomes swell until they eventually choke the cell to death. This occurs in numerous cells in the first few years of life, and ultimately leads to the child's death.

Although the details differ from case to case, the overall picture is the same for many, if not most, inherited diseases. The pathway from mutation to illness includes just four short steps (**FIGURE 5-23**).

1. A mutated gene codes for a non-functioning protein, commonly an enzyme.

2. The non-functioning enzyme can't catalyze a particular reaction as it normally would, bringing the reaction to a halt.

3. The molecule with which the enzyme would have reacted (to convert it to another substance) accumulates, just as half-made products would pile up on a blocked assembly line.

4. The accumulating chemical causes sickness and/or death.

The fact that many genetic diseases involve illnesses brought about by faulty enzymes suggests some strategies for treatment. These include administering medications that contain the normal-functioning version of the enzyme. For instance, lactose-intolerant individuals can consume the enzyme lactase, which for a short while gives them the ability to digest lactose. Alternatively, lactose-intolerant individuals can reduce their consumption of lactose-containing foods to keep the chemical from accumulating, thus reducing the problems that come from lactose overabundance.

TAKE-HOME MESSAGE 5·10

Most genetic diseases result from mutations that cause a gene to produce a non-functioning enzyme, which in turn blocks the functioning of a metabolic pathway.

5·11–5·13
Biotechnology is producing improvements in agriculture.

A scientist works with transgenic plants in a greenhouse.

5·11
What is biotechnology?

Understanding a phenomenon (such as how DNA is transcribed and translated) is nice, but controlling it can take the satisfaction to an entirely new level. This may explain why there is so much excitement surrounding the field of **biotechnology,** in which organisms, cells, and their molecules are modified to achieve practical benefits. The modern emphasis in biotechnology is on **genetic engineering,** the manipulation of organisms' genetic material by adding, deleting, or transplanting genes from one organism to another.

In the remainder of this chapter, we explore the two primary areas in which biotechnology is applied: agriculture and human health. We begin by introducing the most important tools and techniques used in biotechnology.

How would you create a plant resistant to being eaten by insects? Or a colony of bacteria that can produce human insulin? Although there are many different uses of biotechnology, it employs a surprisingly small number of processes and tools that enable researchers to do the following (**FIGURE 5-24**).

1. **Chop** up the DNA from a donor organism that exhibits the trait of interest.

FIGURE 5-24 Five important tools and techniques of most biotechnology procedures.

FIVE TOOLS OF BIOTECHNOLOGY

CHOP up DNA from a donor species that exhibits a trait of interest.

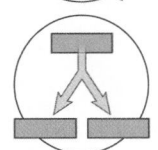

AMPLIFY small samples of DNA into more useful quantities.

INSERT pieces of DNA into bacterial cells or viruses.

GROW separate colonies of bacteria or viruses, each containing some donor DNA.

IDENTIFY colonies of bacteria or viruses that have DNA for a trait of interest.

 Not all of the tools are used in all biotechnology applications—some only utilize one or a few of these techniques.

2. **Amplify** the small amount of DNA into larger quantities.

3. **Insert** pieces of DNA into bacterial cells or viruses.

4. **Grow** separate colonies of the bacteria or viruses, each of which contains a different inserted piece of donor DNA.

5. **Identify** colonies of bacteria or viruses that have DNA for a trait of interest (and propagate them).

To be sure, it's easier said than done, but these tools capture the essence of most modern biotechnology. Not all of the techniques are used in all biotech applications; nonetheless, they all are mainstays of today's biotechnology world. Let's explore each technique in a bit more detail.

Tool 1. Chopping up DNA from a donor organism. To begin, researchers select an organism that has a desirable trait. For example, they might want to produce human growth hormone in large amounts. Their first step would be to obtain a sample of human DNA and cut it into smaller pieces. Cutting DNA into small pieces requires the use of **restriction enzymes** (**FIGURE 5-25**).

Restriction enzymes have a single function: when they encounter DNA, they cut it into small pieces. These enzymes evolved to protect bacteria from attack by viruses. Upon encountering DNA from an invading virus, a restriction enzyme recognizes and binds to a particular sequence of four to eight bases on the invader's DNA and cuts there, thus making it impossible for the virus to reproduce within the bacterial cell. Since all DNA has the same structure, these enzymes can cut DNA from any source as long as the specific four-eight base sequence is present (bacteria protect their own DNA by modifying it, or it would be cut up also). Dozens of different restriction enzymes exist, each of which cuts DNA at a different location.

Tool 2. Amplifying DNA pieces into larger quantities. In many situations, only a small amount of DNA is available for analysis or for some other biotechnology use. The **polymerase chain reaction (PCR)** is a laboratory technique that allows a tiny piece of DNA (perhaps one recovered from a crime scene) to be duplicated repeatedly (**FIGURE 5-26**).

The process involves heating up the DNA of interest, causing the two strands to separate. Then, in the presence of enzymes and plenty of free nucleotides, the DNA is cooled. As it cools, an enzyme matches free nucleotides

CHOP: RESTRICTION ENZYMES

1 The gene of interest is located on a section of DNA from the donor species.

Gene of interest

Source DNA

2 Restriction enzymes that target a particular base-pair sequence on either side of the gene are introduced.

Restriction enzymes

In this example, the restriction enzyme recognizes the sequence ATCGAT and cuts between the first A and T.

3 The restriction enzymes bind to their target base-pair sequence and cut the strand of DNA.

4 The gene of interest has now been separated from the donor's DNA.

FIGURE 5-25 Restriction enzymes are used to isolate a gene of interest.

with their complementary bases on each of the single strands, and covalently links these nucleotides together to form a new single strand across from each original. The result is two complete double-stranded copies of the DNA of interest. This process of heating and cooling can be repeated again and again until there are billions of identical copies of the target sequence.

Tool 3. Inserting foreign DNA into the target organism. In the human growth hormone example mentioned above,

AMPLIFY: POLYMERASE CHAIN REACTION (PCR)

1 A solution containing an isolated segment of DNA is heated, separating the double-stranded DNA into two single strands.

Heat

2 The enzyme DNA polymerase is added along with a large number of free nucleotides, and the solution containing the segments is cooled.

Cool

DNA polymerase

Free nucleotides

3 DNA polymerase adds complementary bases to each single strand.

4 The result is two identical copies of the original segment of DNA.

This process can be repeated again and again until there are billions of identical copies of the target sequence.

FIGURE 5-26 The polymerase chain reaction can duplicate a small strand of DNA into billions of copies.

the researchers might want to transfer the human growth hormone gene into the bacterium *E. coli,* creating **transgenic organisms.**

To create a transgenic organism (that is, an organism with DNA inserted from a different species), researchers must physically deliver the DNA from a donor species into the recipient organism. This delivery often is accomplished using **plasmids,** circular pieces of DNA that can be

incorporated into a bacterium's genome (**FIGURE 5-27**). Genes on the plasmid can then be expressed in the bacterial cell and are replicated whenever the cell divides, so both of the new cells contain the plasmid. In some cases, for the delivery process, genes are incorporated into viruses instead of plasmids. The viruses can then be used to infect organisms and transfer the genes of interest into those organisms.

Tool 4. Growing bacterial colonies that carry the DNA of interest: cloning. Once a piece of foreign DNA has been transferred to a bacterial cell, every time the bacterium divides, it creates a **clone,** a genetically identical cell that contains that inserted DNA. The term **cloning** describes

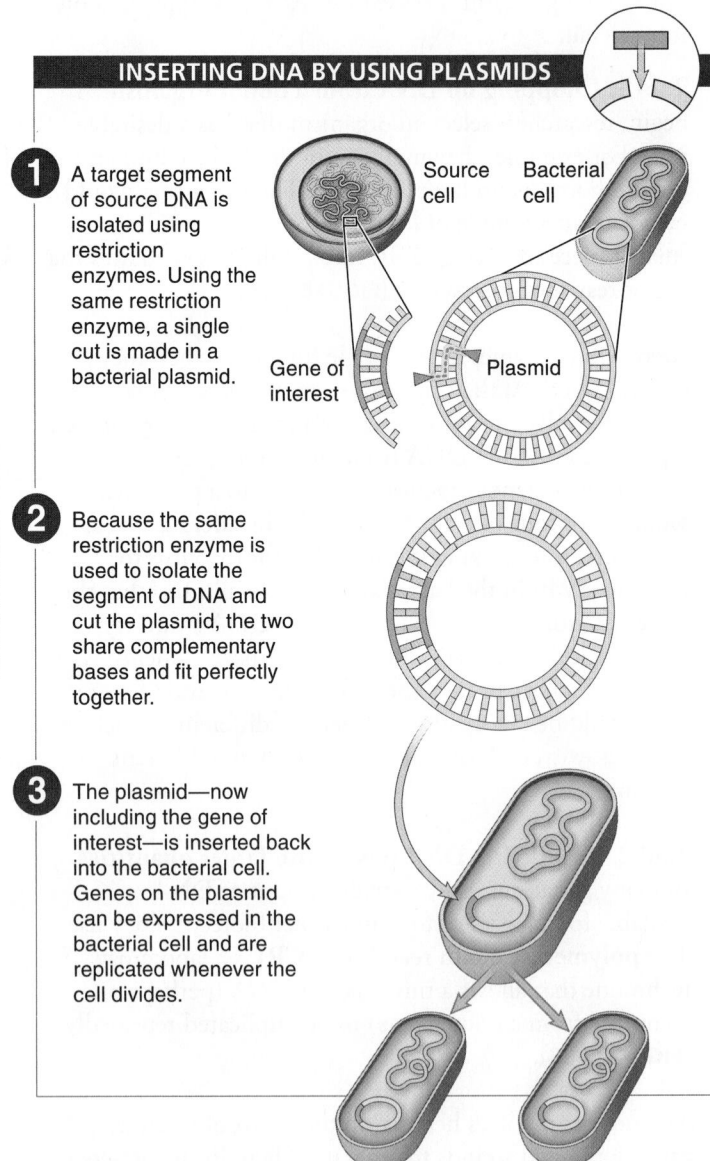

INSERTING DNA BY USING PLASMIDS

1 A target segment of source DNA is isolated using restriction enzymes. Using the same restriction enzyme, a single cut is made in a bacterial plasmid.

Source cell   Bacterial cell

Gene of interest   Plasmid

2 Because the same restriction enzyme is used to isolate the segment of DNA and cut the plasmid, the two share complementary bases and fit perfectly together.

3 The plasmid—now including the gene of interest—is inserted back into the bacterial cell. Genes on the plasmid can be expressed in the bacterial cell and are replicated whenever the cell divides.

FIGURE 5-27 A gene chauffeur. Plasmids can transfer DNA from one species to another.

the production of genetically identical cells, organisms, or DNA molecules, a process that occurs each time a bacterium divides. With numerous rounds of cell division, it is possible to produce a huge number of clones, all of which transcribe and translate the gene of interest.

In a typical experiment, a large amount of DNA may be chopped up with restriction enzymes, incorporated into plasmids, and introduced into bacterial cells. The bacteria are then allowed to divide repeatedly, with each producing a clone of the foreign DNA fragment they carry. Together, all of the different bacterial cells containing all of the

different fragments of the original DNA are called a **clone library** or a **gene library** (**FIGURE 5-28**).

Tool 5. Identifying bacterial colonies that have received the gene of interest (and propagating them). Chopping up human DNA and inserting the pieces (each of which carries different genes) into the genomes of bacteria, which divide repeatedly, leads to a large population of bacterial cells, with many carrying useful genetic information. But the information is in no particular order, much like a bookstore in which all the books are uncatalogued and in complete disarray. How can a researcher interested in working with bacterial cells that contain just the one human gene capable of producing human growth hormone identify and separate those bacteria from the other bacteria in the population?

Researchers have developed a way to make the bacteria of interest identify themselves (**FIGURE 5-29**). First, a chemical

GROW: CREATING A GENE LIBRARY

❶ To create a gene library, a large amount of DNA is chopped up using restriction enzymes. ❷ Each piece is inserted into a plasmid that is then introduced into a bacterial cell. ❸ The bacteria are allowed to divide repeatedly, each producing a clone of the foreign DNA fragment it carries. ❹ Together, all of the different bacterial cells contain all of the different fragments of the original DNA.

1

Gene A   Gene B   Gene C

2

Plasmid A   Plasmid B   Plasmid C

3

Bacterium A   Bacterium B   Bacterium C

4

GENE LIBRARY

FIGURE 5-28 DNA collection. A gene library (or clone library) is a collection of cloned DNA fragments.

IDENTIFYING A GENE BY USING A DNA PROBE

1 To locate a gene of interest among the millions of clones in a gene library, the bacteria are washed with a chemical that breaks down the DNA, making it single-stranded.

GENE LIBRARY

Gene of interest

2 A radioactive probe is then washed over the single-stranded DNA. The probe is a short length of DNA that contains a sequence of bases complementary to the gene of interest.

DNA probe

3 The DNA probe binds to the complementary base sequence found in the gene of interest and glows with radioactivity, allowing the gene to be easily identified.

G T A C T
C A T G A

T A G C T

A T C C G

FIGURE 5-29 Finding the needle in a haystack. A DNA probe is used to locate the desired clone in a gene library.

is added to the entire population of bacterial cells, separating the double-stranded DNA into single strands. Next, a short sequence of single-stranded DNA is washed over the bacteria. Called a **DNA probe,** this DNA contains part of the sequence of the gene of interest and has also been modified so that it is radioactive. Bacteria with the gene of interest bind to this probe and glow with radioactivity. These cells can then be separated out and grown in large numbers—for example, vats of *E. coli* that produce human growth hormone. (Note that because the "correct" folding of a protein depends not just on the amino acid sequence specified by a gene but also on the appropriate cellular conditions, genes transplanted from one species to another don't always produce proteins with the exact same shape. Such folding problems can lead to proteins that do not function as expected.)

We turn next to how these tools and techniques are used to develop products. Keep in mind, however, that the field is still in its infancy.

TAKE-HOME MESSAGE 5·11

Biotechnology is the use of technology to modify organisms, cells, and their molecules to achieve practical benefits. Modern molecular methods make it possible to cut and copy DNA from one organism and deliver it into another. The methods rely on naturally occurring restriction enzymes for cutting DNA, the polymerase chain reaction for amplifying small amounts of DNA, inserting the DNA into bacterial or viral vectors, and cloning and identifying the cells with the transferred DNA of interest.

5·12 Biotechnology can improve food nutrition and make farming more efficient and eco-friendly.

Your breakfast cereal is probably fortified with vitamins and minerals. And for snacking you may eat protein bars that have as much protein as a full chicken breast. It shouldn't come as a surprise, then, that farmers have begun using biotechnology to improve on the natural levels of vitamins, minerals, and other nutrients in the fruits, vegetables, and livestock they produce.

For thousands of years, humans have been practicing a relatively crude and slow form of **genetic engineering**—the manipulation of a species' genome in ways that do not normally occur in nature. In its simplest form, genetic engineering is the careful selection of the plants or animals used as the breeders for a crop or animal population. Through this process, farmers and ranchers have produced meatier turkeys, seedless watermelons, and big, juicy corn kernels (**FIGURE 5-30**). But what used to take many generations of breeding can now be accomplished in a fraction of the time, using **recombinant DNA technology,** the combination of DNA from two or more sources into a product.

In crop plants, for example, the process begins with the identification of a new characteristic, such as larger size or faster ripening time, that farmers would like in a particular crop. Traditionally, breeders would then search for an organism within the same species that had the desirable trait, breed it with their crop organisms, and hope that the offspring would express the trait in the desired way. With

recombinant DNA technology, the desired trait can come from *any* species, so the pool of organisms from which the trait can be taken becomes much larger. Organisms produced with recombinant DNA technology are referred to as genetically modified organisms, or GMOs.

Although the rewards are potentially huge, in practice the process of creating transgenic species that are more nutritious or have other desirable traits turns out to be difficult.

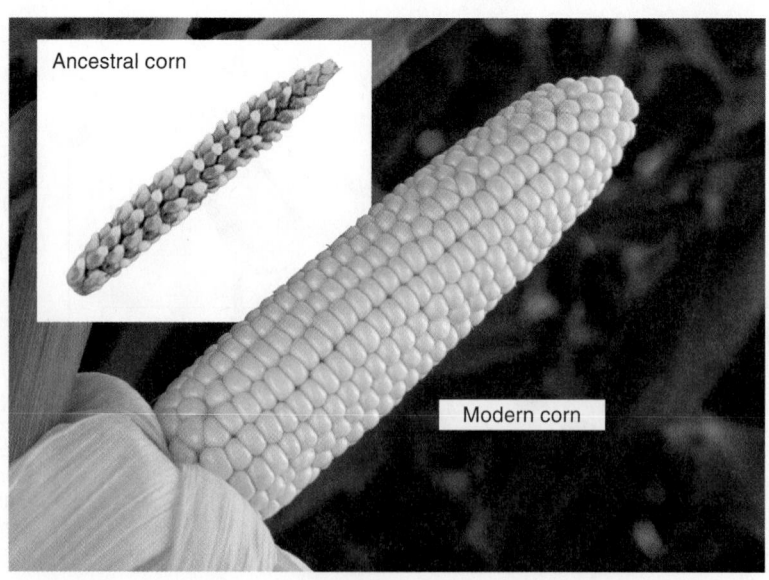

Ancestral corn

Modern corn

FIGURE 5-30 Ancestral corn and modern corn—selected for larger, juicier kernels—compared.

Q: How might a genetically modified plant help 500 million malnourished people?

Nonetheless, the results so far hint at a fruitful marriage of agriculture and technology.

Nutrient-rich "golden rice" Almost 10% of the world's population suffers from vitamin A deficiency, which causes blindness in a quarter-million children each year and a host of other illnesses in people of all ages. These nutritional problems are especially severe in southern Asia and sub-Saharan Africa, where rice is a staple of most diets. Addressing this global health issue, researchers have developed what may be the model for solving problems with biotechnology. It involves the creation of a new crop called "golden rice."

Mammals generally make vitamin A from beta-carotene, a substance found in abundance in most plants (it's what makes carrots orange), but not in the edible part of rice grains. Researchers set out to change this by inserting into the rice genome, from other species, three genes that code for the enzymes used in the production of beta-carotene: two genes from the daffodil plant and one bacterial gene (**FIGURE 5-31**). It's clear that the transplanted genes are working because the normally white rice grain takes on a golden color from the accumulated beta-carotene. And since golden rice was first developed in 1999, new lines have been produced that use only two transplanted genes, yet produce almost 25 times the vitamin A found in the original strains. Field tests of golden rice are still under way, but it is viewed as one of the most promising applications yet of biotechnology.

> **"**Italians come to ruin most generally in three ways, women, gambling, and farming. My family chose the slowest one.**"**
>
> —POPE JOHN XXIII

While the development of golden rice demonstrates that biotechnology, in the near future, may help us produce food that is more nutritious, biotechnology has already had a much more profound impact than this on agricultural practices in the United States. It is not a stretch to say that we are in the midst of a revolution—a green revolution—and that few people are aware of it. This revolution is the extent to which biotechnology has reduced the costs, both environmental and financial, of producing the plants and animals we eat.

Currently, more than 170 million acres worldwide are planted with genetically modified crops, most containing built-in insecticides and herbicide

GOLDEN RICE

Daffodil

Bacteria

Genes in the pathway for beta-carotene production are introduced into the white rice genome.

White rice

Beta-carotene

Golden rice

The addition of beta-carotene-producing genes to white rice has increased its vitamin A content almost 25-fold.

FIGURE 5-31 The potential to prevent blindness in 250,000 people each year. Engineering rice to prevent blindness by increasing its vitamin A content.

resistance, representing more than a forty-fold increase over the past 10 years. The financial benefits to farmers—at least in the short run—are so great that more and more of them are embracing the genetically modified crops.

Q: What genetically modified foods do most people in the United States consume (usually without knowing it)?

The numbers are surprising: 86% of all corn grown in the United States is genetically modified. Ninety-three percent of all cotton grown is genetically modified. And 93% of all soybeans grown are genetically modified (**FIGURE 5-32**). Two factors explain much of the extensive adoption of genetically modified plants in U.S. agriculture. (1) Many plants have had insecticides engineered into them, which can reduce the amounts of insecticides used

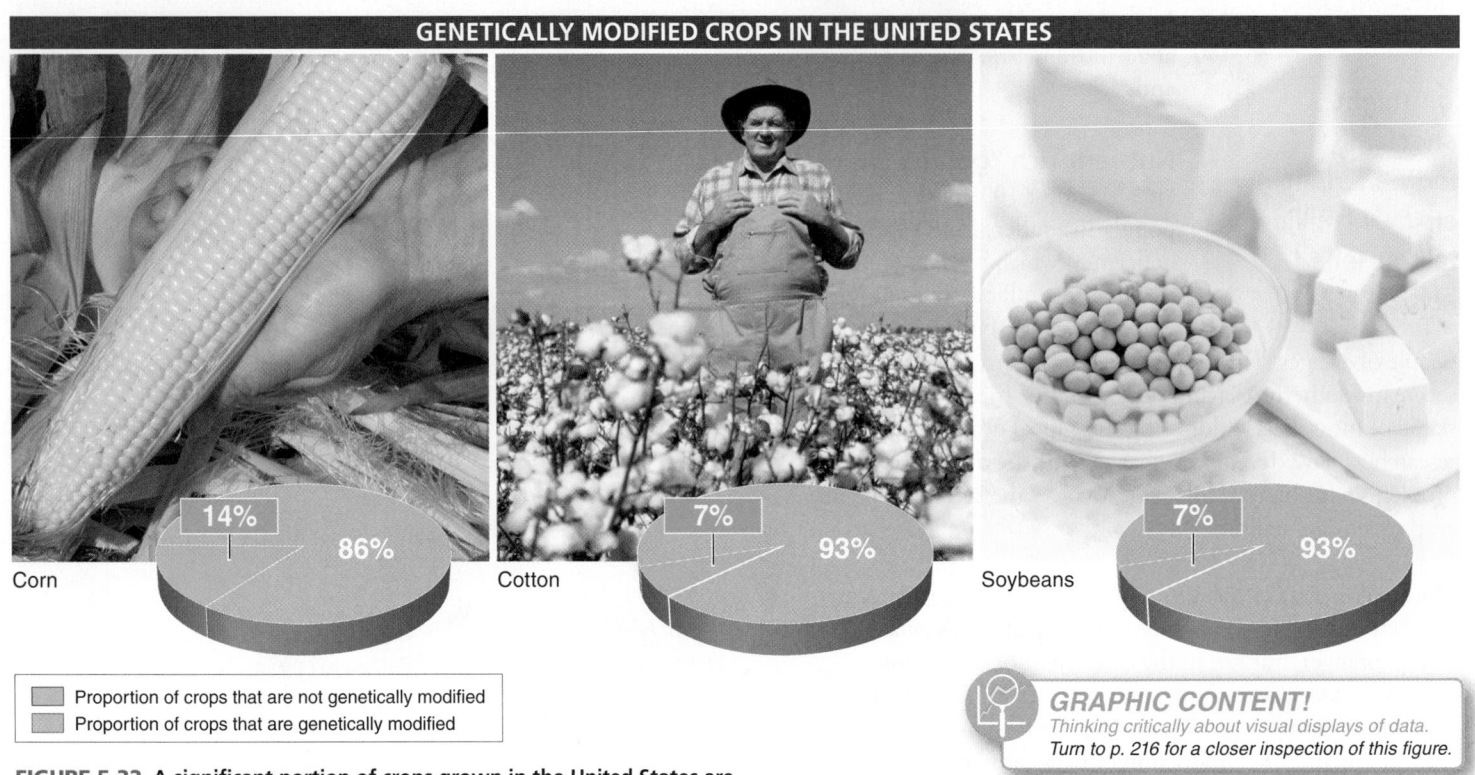

Corn 14% 86%

Cotton 7% 93%

Soybeans 7% 93%

☐ Proportion of crops that are not genetically modified
☐ Proportion of crops that are genetically modified

GRAPHIC CONTENT!
Thinking critically about visual displays of data.
Turn to p. 216 for a closer inspection of this figure.

FIGURE 5-32 A significant portion of crops grown in the United States are genetically modified.

in agriculture. (2) Many plants also have herbicide-resistance genes engineered into them. Such herbicide-resistant plants as well as insect-resistant plants can reduce the amount of plowing required around crops to remove weeds. As a consequence, then, the use of genetically modified plants can reduce both the costs of producing food and the loss of topsoil to erosion.

Here are some of the biggest successes in the application of recombinant DNA technology to agriculture.

Insect and herbicide resistance Insect pests have a field day on agricultural crops (**FIGURE 5-33**). Crops planted at high densities and nurtured with ample water and fertilizer represent a huge potential food resource for insects. Every year, about 40 million tons of corn are unmarketable as a consequence of insect damage. Increasingly, however, farmers have been enjoying greater success in their battles against insect pests.

Farmers owe much of this success to soil-dwelling bacteria of the species *Bacillus*

thuringiensis (in brief, Bt). These bacteria produce spores containing crystals that are poisonous to insects but harmless to the crop plants and to people. In insects, within an hour of

FIGURE 5-33 Competing with us for food. Insects can ravage crops.

Bt CORN

Bacterium (*Bacillus thuringiensis*)

Bt crystal gene

Plant cell

Corn genome

1 Corn plant destroyed by butterfly larvae (caterpillars).

2 Bacterial gene coding for Bt crystals, which are poisonous to the caterpillars, is inserted directly into the corn plant's DNA.

3 Bt crystals—toxic to caterpillars—are now produced by the corn plant itself and present in all cells, reducing the amount of pesticides the farmer must use.

FIGURE 5-34 Help from bacteria in growing disease-resistant corn. Corn engineered to contain spores of the bacterium *Bacillus thuringiensis* (Bt) kills insect pests but does not harm humans.

ingestion, Bt crystals cause pores to develop throughout the insects' digestive systems, paralyzing their gut and making them unable to feed. Within a few days, the insects die from a combination of tissue damage and starvation.

Q **How can genetically modified plants lead to reduced pesticide use by farmers?**

Beginning in 1961, the toxic Bt crystals were included in the pesticides sprayed on crop plants. Then in 1995, the gene coding for the production of the Bt crystals was inserted directly into the DNA of many different crop plants, including corn, cotton, and potatoes. As a consequence, farmers no longer need to apply huge amounts of Bt-containing pesticides (**FIGURE 5-34**); instead, the plants themselves produce insect-killing Bt crystals. There is no evidence that humans are harmed by the Bt crystals, even when they are exposed to very high levels.

Bacteria have come to the aid of farmers in their fight against pests in another way, too. In the 1990s, researchers discovered a bacterial gene that gives the bacteria resistance to herbicides, and they introduced the gene into crop plants. Integration of this gene into the plants' DNA gives them resistance to herbicides, allowing farmers to kill weeds with herbicides but leave the crop plants unharmed, greatly increasing yields (**FIGURE 5-35**).

Faster growth and bigger bodies Agriculture includes the cultivation not just of plants but also of animals. And for

FIGURE 5-35 Crop duster. Herbicides like the one applied by this crop duster must kill weeds while leaving the crop unharmed.

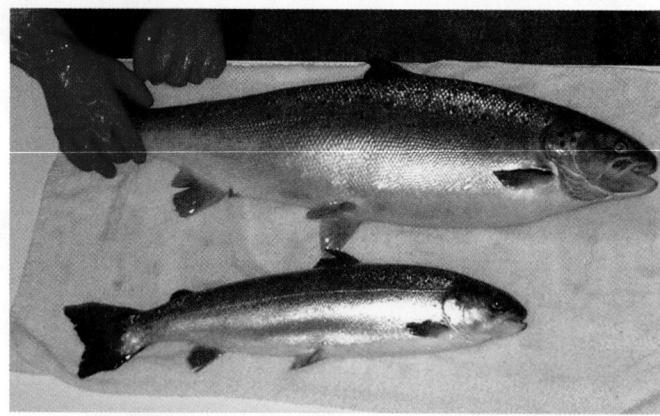

FIGURE 5-36 **Bigger salmon.** The larger salmon carries a growth hormone gene that keeps it growing year-round rather than in the summer only.

the first time, the U.S. Food and Drug Administration is close to approving for human consumption a genetically modified animal. The animal in question is a transgenic Atlantic salmon that carries a growth hormone gene from another species (Chinook salmon), along with a region of DNA from a third species (ocean pout) that acts as an "on" switch, facilitating transcription of the growth hormone gene. The transgenic fish, which is reported by its creators to taste the same as regular Atlantic salmon, grows much more quickly and reaches market size within 18 months rather than the usual three years (**FIGURE 5-36**).

The FDA has reported that the transgenic salmon "is as safe to eat as food from other Atlantic salmon." Numerous fisheries experts, food safety experts, environmental groups,

and consumer groups, however, continue to express concerns about a wide variety of safety and environmental issues and the process by which the safety and environmental impacts of the transgenic species have been evaluated. Health concerns include the possibility that consuming the salmon will cause increased rates of allergic reactions, as well as unknown effects that may stem from potentially higher levels of hormones present in the fish.

Most troubling to environmental groups is the risk that the larger, faster-growing transgenic fishes will escape from their enclosed breeding facilities and back into their natural habitat—something that many experts believe is inevitable. If this occurs, environmentalists fear that the fish might harm wild salmon populations, many of which are listed as endangered, because the transgenic salmon can consume more resources and may grow too large to be consumed by its natural predators. It is unclear what the outcome would be.

TAKE-HOME MESSAGE 5·12

Biotechnology has led to important improvements in agriculture by using transgenic plants and animals to produce more nutritious food. Even more significant is the extent to which biotechnology has reduced the environmental and financial costs of producing food, through the creation of herbicide-resistant and insect-resistant crops. The ecological and health risks of such widespread use of transgenic species are not fully understood and are potentially great.

5·13 Fears and risks: are genetically modified foods safe?

Chickens without feathers look ridiculous (**FIGURE 5-37**). But such a genetically modified breed was developed with a valuable purpose in mind: "naked" birds are easier and less expensive to prepare for market, benefiting farmers by lowering their costs and benefiting consumers by lowering prices. These chickens, however, have turned out to be unusually vulnerable to mosquito attacks, parasites, and disease, and ultra-sensitive to sunlight. They also have difficulty mating, because the males are unable to flap their wings. Researchers currently are working to address these problems.

Naked chickens teach us an important lesson about genetically modified plants and animals. Although the new breed of

featherless chickens was produced by relatively low-tech genetic engineering—the traditional animal husbandry method of crossbreeding two different types of chickens—rather than by more modern recombinant DNA technology, the new breed ended up having not just the desired trait of no feathers but also some unintended and undesirable traits. Now, as more genetically modified foods are created using modern methods of recombinant DNA technology, the same risks of also creating unintended and potentially harmful traits must be weighed. For these and other reasons—some legitimate and rational, others irrational—many people have concerns about the production and consumption of genetically modified foods (**FIGURE 5-38**). These concerns are outlined in the following discussion.

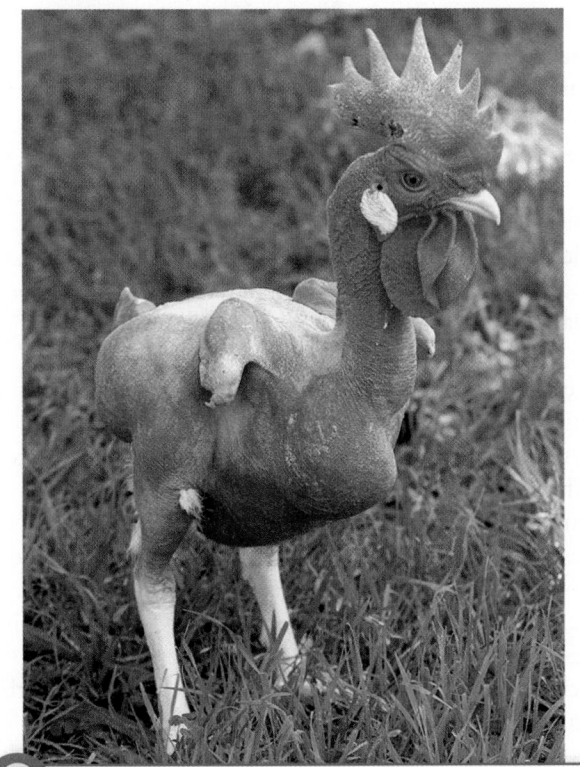

Featherless birds are cheaper for farmers and consumers. But there are unintended consequences, including vulnerability to mosquitoes and other parasites.

FIGURE 5-37 "Naked" birds. The breeding of featherless chickens has benefited farmers but led to some unanticipated consequences.

Organisms that we want to kill may become invincible. Pesticide-resistant canola plants were cultivated in Canada, making it possible for farmers to apply herbicides freely to kill the weeds but not the canola crop. But the pesticide-resistant canola plants accidentally spread to neighboring farms and grew out of control, because traditional herbicides could not kill them. Similarly, there is the possibility that insect pests will develop resistance to the Bt produced by genetically modified crops, which will also make these pests resistant to Bt pesticides applied to crops that are not genetically modified.

Organisms that we don't want to kill may be killed inadvertently. Monarch butterflies feed on milkweed plants. Recent research has demonstrated that if pollen from plants genetically modified to contain the insect-killing Bt genes accidentally lands on milkweed plants and is consumed by monarch butterflies, the butterflies can be killed, which may significantly reduce their populations. Although such an incident has not occurred outside experimental fields, it illustrates a risk that may be hard to control.

Genetically modified crops are not tested or regulated adequately. It is impossible to really know whether a new technology has been tested adequately. Still, scientists and lawmakers have been working toward an organized and responsible set of policies designed to ensure that sufficient safety testing is done. For example, laboratory procedures for working with recombinant DNA have been established, and researchers have developed techniques that make it impossible for most genetically engineered organisms to survive outside the specific conditions for which they are developed.

As an example of the degree of testing of genetically engineered foods, the Monsanto Company has had its strain of herbicide-resistant soybeans evaluated and approved by 31 different regulatory agencies in 17 different countries, including, in the United States, the Department of Agriculture, the Food and Drug Administration, and the Environmental Protection Agency. In a recent report on genetically modified animals, however, an expert committee of the U.S. National Academy of Sciences warned that GMOs still pose risks that the government is unable to evaluate. Technology is moving so fast that it is difficult to even know what the new risks might be.

> **❝**And he gave it for his opinion, 'that whoever could make two ears of corn, or two blades of grass, to grow upon a spot of ground where only one grew before, would deserve better of mankind, and do more essential service to his country, than the whole race of politicians put together.'**❞**
>
> —JONATHAN SWIFT, *Gulliver's Travels,* 1726

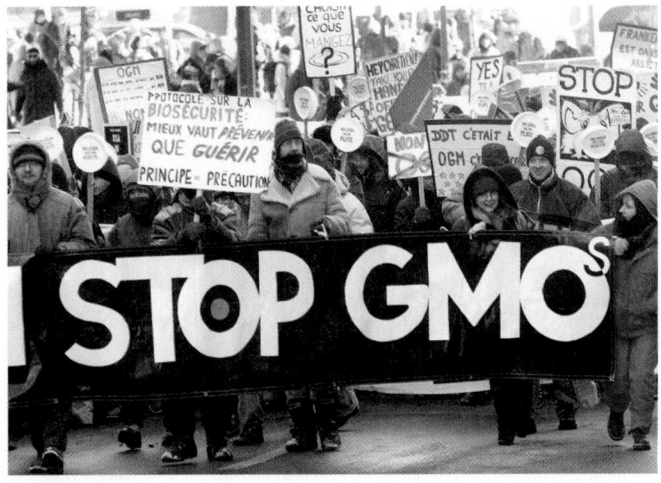

FIGURE 5-38 Consumer fears. Protesters voice opposition to the use of genetically modified organisms (GMOs).

Eating genetically modified foods is dangerous. In the 1990s, a gene from Brazil nuts was used to improve the nutritional content of soybeans. The genetically modified soybeans had better nutritional content, but they also acquired some allergy-causing chemicals previously present in the Brazil nuts but not in soybeans. This outcome illustrates the risk that some unwanted features might be passed from species to species in the creation of transgenic organisms. In this case, all of the genetically modified soybeans were destroyed and this research program was suspended. To date, no evidence has appeared to suggest that consumption of any genetically modified foods is dangerous.

Loss of genetic diversity among crop plants is risky. As increasing numbers of farmers stop using non-genetically modified crops in favor of one or a few genetically modified strains of crops, the genetic diversity of the crops declines. This can make them more vulnerable to environmental changes or pests. The Irish Potato Famine is an example of the value of genetic diversity in crops. In the mid-1800s, much of the population of Ireland depended on a diet of potatoes. Because most of the potato crops had been propagated from cuttings from the same plant, they were all genetically the same. When the crops were infected by a rot-causing mold, all of the potato plants were susceptible and most were wiped out, causing a famine responsible for the deaths of more than a million people.

Hidden costs may reduce the financial advantages of genetically modified crops. When seed companies create genetically modified seeds with crop traits desirable to farmers, the companies also engineer sterility into the seeds. As a consequence, the farmers must purchase new seeds for each generation of their crops. Such increases in long-term costs and dependency on seed companies must be factored in by the farmers.

Another argument sometimes made in opposition to genetically modified foods is that such organisms are not "natural" and, for that reason, must be harmful. This is one argument that is flawed and should not be a cause for concern. Smallpox, HIV, poison ivy, and cyanide, after all, are natural. The smallpox vaccine, on the other hand, is unnatural. Innumerable other valuable technological developments are equally unnatural. There simply is no value in knowing whether something is natural or unnatural when evaluating whether or not it is good and desirable.

In the end, we must compare the risks of producing genetically modified foods with the benefits. The cost-benefit analyses will have to include the potential to reduce food costs and the ability to reduce environmental degradation by agriculture. For example, with genetically modified, pest-resistant crops, farmworkers will greatly benefit from spending less time applying pesticides. These benefits of reduced pesticide exposure will be significantly greater for workers in the less-developed countries, where safety regulations for pesticide use are more frequently ignored. Unfortunately, the difficulties in establishing the risks of genetically modified foods—as well as the ecological magnitude of those risks— ensures that this important issue must be evaluated extremely closely and regulated carefully.

TAKE-HOME MESSAGE 5·13

More and more genetically modified foods are being created using modern methods of recombinant DNA technology. Numerous legitimate fears among the public remain, however, about the potentially catastrophic risks of these foods, given that their development relies on such new technology, and about the long-term financial advantages they offer.

5·14–5·17
Biotechnology has the potential for improving human health (and criminal justice).

With the cloning of sheep, a new era in biotechnology began.

5·14 The treatment of diseases and production of medicines are improved with biotechnology.

You can't always get what you want. In the best of all worlds, biotechnology would *prevent* humans from ever getting debilitating diseases. Next best would be to *cure* diseases once and for all. But these noble goals are not always possible, so biotechnology often is directed at the more practical goal of *treating* diseases, usually by producing medicines more efficiently and more effectively than they can be produced with traditional methods. Biotechnology has had some notable successes in achieving this goal. The treatment of diabetes is one such success story.

Diabetes is a chronic disease in which the body cannot produce insulin, a chemical that allows cells to take up and break down sugar from the blood. Complications from diabetes can include vascular disease, kidney damage, and nerve damage. As recently as 1980, if you were one of the approximately 15 million Americans with diabetes, each day you would treat the disease by injecting yourself with insulin extracted from the pancreas of cattle or pigs that had been killed for meat. For most diabetics, the insulin injections kept the disease under control. But the traditional process of collecting insulin this way was difficult and costly.

Everything changed in 1982 when a 29-year-old entrepreneur, Bob Swanson, joined scientist Herbert Boyer to transform the

Q *Why do some bacteria produce human insulin?*

potential of recombinant DNA technology. In doing so, they started the biotech revolution. Working with the scientist Stanley Cohen, Swanson and Boyer used restriction enzymes to snip out the human DNA sequence that codes for the production of insulin. They then inserted this sequence into the bacterium *E. coli,* creating a transgenic organism. After cloning the new, transgenic bacteria, the team was able to grow vats and vats of the bacterial cells, all of which churned out human insulin (**FIGURE 5-39**). The drug could be produced efficiently in huge quantities and made available for patients with diabetes. This was the first genetically engineered drug approved by the Food and Drug Administration and it continues to help millions of people every day.

Perhaps even more significant than providing a better source of insulin, Swanson, Boyer, and Cohen's application of biotechnology revealed a generalized process for genetic engineering. It instantly opened the door to a more effective method of producing many different medicines to treat diseases. Today, more than 1,500 companies work in the recombinant DNA technology industry, and their products generate more than $40 billion in revenues each year.

Several important achievements followed the development of insulin-producing bacteria. Here are just two examples.

FIGURE 5-39 Life-saving insulin. Human insulin is engineered through recombinant DNA technology.

FIGURE 5-40 Bulking up with a little (illegal) help. Sylvester Stallone—age 61 in this photo—used human growth hormone (along with strength training) to develop larger muscles for a film role.

1. Human growth hormone (HGH). Produced by the pituitary gland, human growth hormone has dramatic effects throughout the body. It stimulates protein synthesis, increases the utilization of body fat for energy to fuel metabolism, and stimulates the growth of virtually every part of the body (**FIGURE 5-40**). Insufficient growth hormone production, usually due to pituitary malfunctioning, leads to dwarfism.

When treated with supplemental HGH, individuals with dwarfism experience additional growth. Until 1994, however, HGH treatment was prohibitively expensive because the growth hormone could only be produced by extracting and purifying it from the pituitary glands of human cadavers.

Through the creation of transgenic bacteria, using a technique similar to that used in the creation of insulin-producing bacteria, HGH can now be produced in virtually unlimited supplies and made available to more people who need it.

The availability of HGH, which can increase strength and endurance, may be irresistibly tempting to some people (who don't need it for medical reasons)—even at $7,500 for a month's supply. Recent sporting scandals suggest that the illegal use of HGH occurs frequently among elite swimmers, cyclists, and other athletes.

2. Erythropoietin. Produced primarily by the kidneys, erythropoietin (also known as EPO) is a hormone that regulates the production of red blood cells. Numerous clinical conditions (nutritional deficiencies and lung disease, among others) and treatments (such as chemotherapy) can lead to anemia, a lower than normal number of red blood cells, which reduces an individual's ability to transport oxygen to tissues and cells. This lack of sufficient oxygen, in turn, can cause a variety of symptoms, including weakness, fatigue, and shortness of breath.

First cloned in 1985, recombinant human erythropoietin (rhu-EPO) is now produced in large amounts in hamster ovaries. It is used to treat many forms of anemia. Worldwide sales of EPO are in the billions of dollars.

Q *What is "blood doping"? How does it improve some athletes' performance?*

EPO has been at the center of several "blood doping" scandals in professional cycling. This hormone increases the oxygen-carrying capacity of the blood, so some otherwise healthy athletes have used EPO to improve their athletic performance. It can be very dangerous, though. By increasing the number of red blood cells, the blood can become much thicker and this can increase the risk of heart attack.

Beyond these and other medicines currently produced by transgenic organisms, plans are under way to create a variety of other useful products—including potatoes that produce antibodies enabling a more effective response to illnesses—for treating disease. In the next section we examine the strategies

for preventing genetic diseases, and the much less successful attempts to cure diseases through biotechnology.

5·15 Gene therapy: biotechnology can help diagnose and prevent diseases, but has had limited success in curing them.

Would you want to know? Once, this was just a hypothetical question: if you carried a gene that meant you were likely to develop a particular disease later in your life, would you want to know about it? Or another question: would you want to know if there's a good chance that your future children will be born with a genetic disease? Now, for better or for worse, these are becoming real-life questions that we all must address. And there is more at stake than simply peace of mind. As biotechnology develops the tools to identify some of the genetic time-bombs that many of us carry, it also carries the danger that such information may become the basis for greater discrimination than we have ever known.

Intervening to prevent diseases through biotechnology focuses on answering certain questions posed at three different points in time.

1. Is a given set of parents likely to produce a baby with a genetic disease? Many genetic diseases occur only if an individual inherits two copies of the disease-causing gene, one from each parent. This is true for Tay-Sachs disease, cystic fibrosis, and sickle-cell anemia, among others. Individuals with only a single copy of the disease-causing gene never fully show the disease, but they may pass on the disease gene to their children. Consequently, two healthy parents (that is, having no disease symptoms) may produce a child with the disease. In these cases, it can be beneficial for the parents to be screened to determine whether they carry a disease-causing copy of the gene. Such screening, combined with genetic counseling and testing of embryos following fertilization, can reduce the incidence of the disease dramatically. Since screening began in 1969, the incidence of Tay-Sachs disease, for example, has fallen by more than 75% (**FIGURE 5-41**).

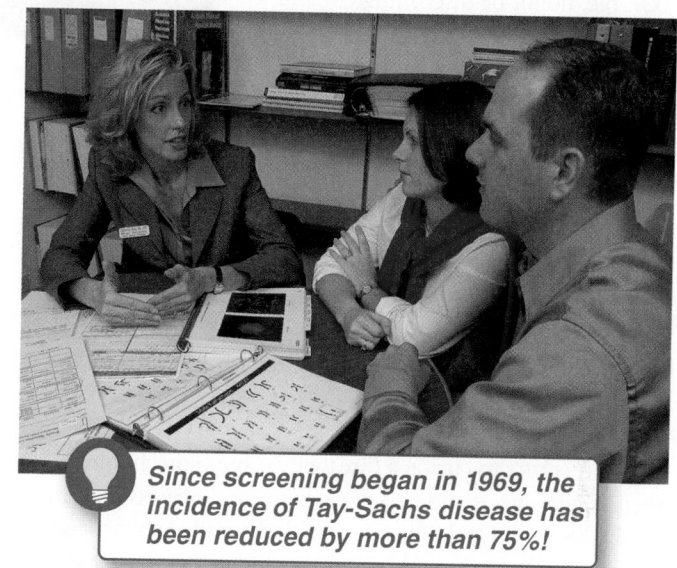

Since screening began in 1969, the incidence of Tay-Sachs disease has been reduced by more than 75%!

FIGURE 5-41 Genetic screening can determine the presence of the Tay-Sachs gene.

2. Will a baby be born with a genetic disease? Once fertilization has occurred, it is possible to test an embryo or developing fetus for numerous genetic problems. Prenatal genetic screening can detect cystic fibrosis, sickle-cell anemia, Down syndrome, and a rapidly growing list of other disorders.

To screen the fetus, doctors must examine some of the fetal cells and/or the amniotic fluid (which surrounds the fetus in the uterus and carries many chemicals produced by the developing embryo). Cells and fluid are usually collected by amniocentesis or chorionic villus sampling (CVS), techniques that we explore in detail in Chapter 6.

3. Is an individual likely to develop a genetic disease later in life? DNA technology can also be used to detect disease-causing genes in individuals who are currently healthy but are at increased risk of developing an illness later. Early detection of many diseases, such as breast cancer, prostate cancer, and skin cancer, greatly enhances the ability to treat the disease and reduce the risk of more severe illness or death.

These potential benefits of genetic technology come with significant potential costs. People who have a gene that puts them at increased risk of developing a particular disease, for example, might be discriminated against, even though they are not currently sick and may never suffer from the particular disease. Although a federal Genetic Information Nondiscrimination Act was signed into law in 2008, the law does not cover life insurance, disability insurance, and long-term care insurance. Insurance companies have already denied such coverage on discovering that an individual carries a gene that puts him or her at increased risk of disease. Additionally, parents who discover that their developing fetus will develop a painful, debilitating, or fatal disease soon after birth are confronted with the difficult question of how to proceed.

When it comes to curing a disease by using biotechnology, there is good news and bad news. The good news is that, in the 1990s, a handful of humans with a usually fatal genetic disease called severe combined immunodeficiency disease (SCID) were completely cured through the application of biotechnology. The bad news is that it has not been possible to apply these promising techniques to other diseases.

It's not for a lack of trying. There have been more than 500 other clinical trials for **gene therapies** designed to treat or cure a variety of diseases by inserting a functional gene into an individual's cells to replace a defective version of the gene. But no clear successes. Not one.

Let's examine the case of SCID, which has served as a model for gene therapy. SCID is a condition in which a baby is born with an immune system unable to properly produce a type of white blood cell. This leaves the infant vulnerable to most infections and usually leads to death within the first year of life (**FIGURE 5-42**). In gene therapy for

FIGURE 5-42 Protected by a bubble. This child with severe combined immunodeficiency lived 12 years in a protective bubble at Baylor Medical Center.

SCID, researchers removed from an affected baby's bone marrow some **stem cells,** cells that have the ability to develop into any type of cell in the body. In bone marrow, they normally produce white blood cells, but in individuals with SCID, a malfunctioning gene disrupts normal white blood cell production.

Next, in a test tube, the bone marrow stem cells were infected with a transgenic virus carrying the functioning gene. Ideally, the virus inserted the good gene into the DNA of the stem cells, which were then injected back into the baby's bone marrow. There, the cells could produce normal white blood cells, permanently curing the disease. Although this strategy worked to cure several cases of SCID, treatment has been suspended indefinitely following the recent deaths of two patients from illness related to their treatment.

Q Why has gene therapy had such a poor record of success in curing diseases?

Difficulties with gene therapy have been encountered in several different areas, usually related to the organism used to transfer the normal-functioning gene into the cells of a person with a genetic disease. They include:

1. Difficulty getting the working gene into the specific cells where it is needed.

2. Difficulty getting the working gene into enough cells and at the right rate to produce a physiological effect.

3. Difficulty arising from the transfer organism getting into unintended cells.

4. Difficulty regulating gene expression.

Beyond these technical problems, for most diseases the malfunctioning gene has not been identified or the disease is caused by more than one malfunctioning gene. And finally, it is important to keep in mind that gene therapy targets cells in the body other than sperm and eggs. Consequently, while a disease might, in theory, be cured in an individual, he or she can still pass on the disease-causing gene(s) to offspring. It's not clear what the future holds for gene therapy, but a great deal of research is still in progress.

TAKE-HOME MESSAGE 5·15

Biotechnology tools have been developed to identify whether a set of parents is likely to produce a baby with a genetic disease, whether a baby is likely to be born with a genetic disease, and whether an individual carries disease-causing genes that may have their effect later in life. These tools can help reduce suffering and the incidence of diseases, but come with significant potential costs. Gene therapy has had a poor record of success in curing human diseases, primarily because of technical difficulties in transferring normal-functioning genes into the cells of a person with a genetic disease.

5·16 Cloning—ranging from genes to organs to individuals—offers both promise and perils.

Cloning. Perhaps no scientific word more readily conjures horrifying images of the intersection of curiosity and scientific achievement. But is fear the appropriate emotion to feel about this burgeoning technology? Perhaps not.

For starters, let's clarify what the word means. "Cloning" actually refers to a variety of different techniques. To be sure, cloning can refer to the creation of new individuals that have exactly the same genome as the donor individual—a process called "whole organism cloning." That is, a clone is like an identical twin, except that it may differ in age by years or even decades. It is also possible to clone tissues (such as skin) and entire organs from an individual's cells. And, as we saw in Section 5-11, it is possible to clone genes.

Cloning took center stage in the public imagination in 1997, when Ian Wilmut, a British scientist, and his colleagues first reported that they had cloned a sheep—which they named Dolly. Their research was based on ideas that went back to 1938, when Hans Spemann first proposed the experiment of removing the nucleus from an unfertilized egg and replacing it with the nucleus from the cell of a different individual. Although the process used by Wilmut and his research group was difficult and inefficient, it was surprisingly simple in concept (**FIGURE 5-43**). They removed a cell from the mammary gland of a grown sheep, put its nucleus into another sheep's egg from which the nucleus had been removed, induced the egg to divide, and

Are there any medical justifications for cloning?

transplanted it into the uterus of a surrogate mother sheep. Out of 272 tries, they achieved just one success. But that was enough to show that the cloning of an adult animal was possible.

Shortly after news of Dolly's birth, teams set about cloning a variety of other species, including mice, cows, pigs, and cats (**FIGURE 5-44**). Not all of this work was driven by simple curiosity. For farmers, cloning could have real value. It can take a long time to produce animals with desirable traits from an agricultural perspective—such as increased milk production in cows. And with each successive generation of breeding, it can be difficult to maintain these traits in the population. But through the process of transgenic techniques and whole animal cloning, large numbers of valuable animals with such traits can be produced and maintained.

Q Medical researchers, too, see much to gain from cloning. In particular, transgenic animals containing human genes—such as the hamsters producing rhu-EPO, discussed earlier—can be very valuable. But can a human be cloned? At this point, it is almost certain that the cloning of a human will be possible. Many people wonder, though, whether such an endeavor should be pursued. There is near unanimity among scientists that human cloning to produce children should not be attempted. Some of the reasons cited relate to problems of safety for the mother and the child, legal and philosophical issues relating to the inability of

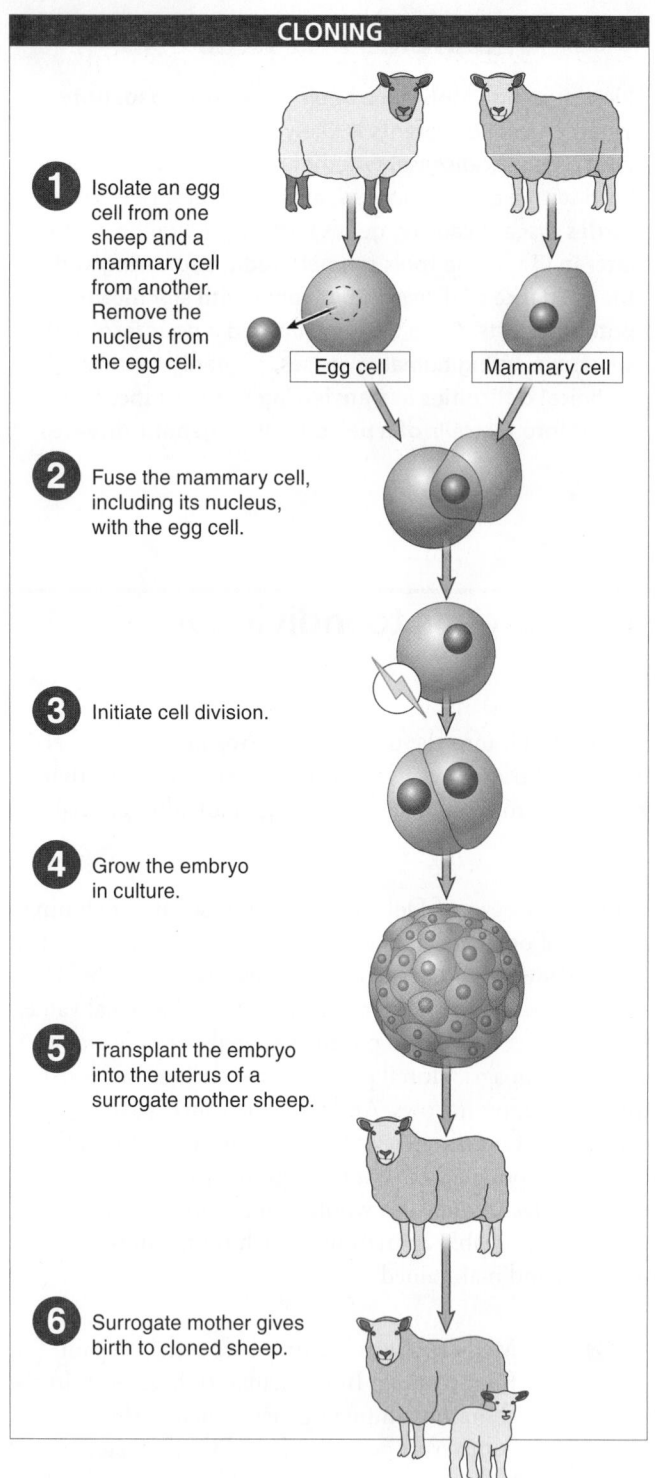

CLONING

1. Isolate an egg cell from one sheep and a mammary cell from another. Remove the nucleus from the egg cell.

   Egg cell   **Mammary cell**

2. Fuse the mammary cell, including its nucleus, with the egg cell.

3. Initiate cell division.

4. Grow the embryo in culture.

5. Transplant the embryo into the uterus of a surrogate mother sheep.

6. Surrogate mother gives birth to cloned sheep.

FIGURE 5-43 No longer science fiction. The steps used in the cloning of Dolly the sheep.

FIGURE 5-44 Genetically identical cloned animals. The cloning of animals can maintain desirable traits from generation to generation.

cloned individuals to give consent, problems of the exploitation of women, and concerns regarding identity and individuality. Governments are struggling to develop wise regulations for this new world.

TAKE-HOME MESSAGE 5·16

Cloning of individuals has potential benefits in agriculture and medicine, but ethical questions linger.

5·17 DNA is an individual identifier: the uses and abuses of DNA fingerprinting.

In another time, Colin Pitchfork, a murderer and rapist, would have walked free. But in 1987, he was captured and convicted, betrayed by his DNA, and is now serving two life sentences in prison. Pitchfork's downfall began when he raped and murdered two 15-year-old high-school girls in a small village in England in the 1980s. The police thought they had their perpetrator when a man confessed, but only to the second murder. He denied any involvement with the first murder, which perplexed the police because the details of the two crimes strongly suggested that the same person committed both.

At the time, British biologist Alec Jeffreys made the important discovery that there are small pieces of DNA in every person's chromosomes that are tremendously variable in their base sequences. In much the same way that each person has a driver's license number or social security number that differs from everyone else's, these DNA fragments are so variable that it is extremely unlikely that two people would have identical sequences at these locations. Thus, a comparison between these regions in a person's DNA sample and in DNA-containing evidence left at a crime scene would enable police to determine whether the evidence sample came from that person.

Jeffreys analyzed DNA left by the murderer-rapist on the two victims and found that it did indeed come from a single person, and that person was *not* the man who had confessed to one of the crimes. The original suspect was released and has the distinction of being the first person cleared of a crime through DNA fingerprinting. To track down the criminal, police then requested blood samples from all men in the area of the crimes who were between 18 and 35 years old—a practice that many viewed as an invasion of privacy. The police collected and analyzed more than 5,000 blood samples. This procedure led them to Colin Pitchfork, whose DNA matched perfectly the DNA left on both victims, and ultimately was the evidence responsible for his conviction (**FIGURE 5-45**). (He almost slipped through, having persuaded a friend to give a blood sample in his name. But when the friend was overheard telling the story in a pub, police tracked down Pitchfork to get a blood sample.)

DNA fingerprinting is now used extensively in forensic investigations, in much the same way that regular fingerprints have been used for the past 100 years. But traditional fingerprinting is limited in its usefulness for

FIGURE 5-45 Betrayed by his DNA. Colin Pitchfork, the first criminal brought to justice with DNA fingerprinting.

many crimes because, often, no fingerprints are left behind. DNA samples, though, more frequently are left behind, usually in the form of semen, blood, hair, skin, or other tissue. As a consequence, this technology has been directly responsible for bringing thousands of criminals to justice and, as we saw at the beginning of the chapter, for establishing the innocence of more than 200 people wrongly convicted of murder and other capital crimes. Let's examine how DNA fingerprinting is done, why it is such a powerful forensic tool, and why it is not foolproof.

The DNA from different humans is almost completely identical. More than 99.9% of the DNA sequences of two individuals are the same, because we're all of the same species and thus share a common evolutionary history. Even so, in a genome of three billion base pairs, one-tenth of a percent difference still translates to about three million base-pair differences. These differences are responsible for the fact that all individuals have their own unique genome. (The lone exception? Identical twins, whose DNA is exactly the same.) Thus, when we are trying to evaluate whether the DNA from a crime scene matches that from a suspect, the analysis focuses on the parts of our DNA that differ. There are thousands of these highly variable regions in the human genome.

Among the thousands of variable regions in the human genome, one particular type is used for the determination of a person's genetic fingerprint. These regions are called **STRs** (for **short tandem repeats**) and are characterized by having a short sequence (commonly four or five nucleotides) that repeats over and over a dozen or more times.

An individual—we'll call her Individual A—has two copies of each chromosome, one from her mother and one from her father. At one STR location (on chromosome 3, for example), the number of times the sequence repeats is likely to differ on the maternal and the paternal copies of that chromosome in Individual A. The sequence may repeat 14 times on the maternal copy of chromosome 3 and it may repeat only 3 times on the paternal copy that she carries. In such a case, Individual A is said to have two different alleles for this STR region: 14 and 3. In contrast, in Individual B, for the same STR region on chromosome 3, the sequence may repeat 5 and 11 times (**FIGURE 5-46**).

For an STR region within the human genome, there typically are about 10 different alleles that occur within a population, and each is shared by about 10% of all individuals in a population. So the likelihood that two individuals carry the same two alleles is about 1 in 100.

SHORT TANDEM REPEATS (STRs)

Short tandem repeats, or STRs, are sequences of DNA (commonly 4 or 5 nucleotides) that repeat over and over again. They occur in some of the most highly variable regions of an individual's DNA.

INDIVIDUAL A

STR locus

Chromosome from mother — Number of repeats: 14
Chromosome from father — 3

Short tandem repeat (STR)

14 / 3 — Individual A's alleles for this STR locus

INDIVIDUAL B

Number of repeats

Chromosome from mother — 5
Chromosome from father — 11

5 / 11 — Individual B's alleles for this STR locus

For a given region, it's the same sequence that repeats, but the number of times it repeats differs from individual to individual (and usually differs on the maternal and paternal copies of a chromosome that an individual carries).

FIGURE 5-46 Biotechnology in forensics. Forensic scientists can use highly variable regions of DNA to genetically link a person to DNA-containing evidence left at a crime scene.

This is unlikely, but given enough people, many are likely to carry the same alleles. If two different STR regions are analyzed, the likelihood that two individuals have the same four alleles is then $1/10 \times 1/10 \times 1/10 \times 1/10$, or 1/10,000. This is much rarer, but still would lead to multiple individuals within the same large city carrying the same four alleles. The real power of DNA fingerprinting comes from simultaneously determining the alleles an individual carries (that is, their genotype) not simply at one or two STR locations but at 13 *different* STR locations. This is the number used by the FBI in constructing DNA fingerprints in the United States, and it makes the probability that two individuals would have exactly the same genotype extremely low (see Figure 5-46).

CREATING A DNA FINGERPRINT

A DNA fingerprint is created by determining which alleles an individual carries for 13 different STR loci.

1 For each of the 13 STR loci used to construct an individual's DNA fingerprint, the DNA fragment containing each STR region is amplified using PCR, resulting in huge numbers of those fragments. The amplified DNA fragments differ in size, depending on how many times the repeating unit of that STR is repeated.

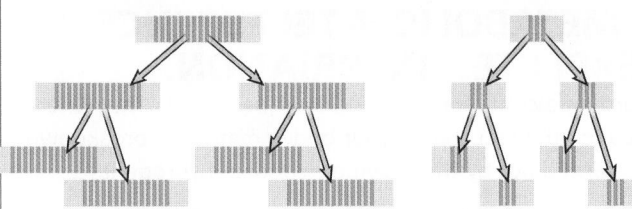

2 The amplified DNA fragments are separated by size using electrophoresis. In this process, DNA fragments are poured into a solution and an electrical charge is applied. Because DNA is a negatively charged molecule, the pieces of DNA move toward the positively charged electrode. Smaller pieces—those with fewer repeats—move more quickly than larger pieces.

Individual A's DNA sample

Direction of DNA strand movement

Electrical charge

3 Computer software is used to analyze the results. The number of repeats within an STR region (indicating an individual's genotype) is determined by comparing the length of the fragments containing that STR region to DNA fragments of known lengths.

FIGURE 5-47 Your unique identifier: a DNA fingerprint. DNA fingerprints are being used to match a suspect's DNA to DNA found at the scene of a crime. (The DNA fingerprint of the crime scene evidence matches that from Individual B.)

For each STR locus analyzed, an individual's genotype is determined by using PCR to amplify that region, then measuring the length of the STR region using electrophoresis. The length of the region can then be used to determine the number of times that the STR is repeated. For a single STR region, an individual's genotype is two numbers, reflecting the number of STR repeats in the copies inherited from the mother and from the father. And a person's full DNA fingerprint is a string of 26 numbers that includes the two numbers for each of 13 STRs.

Q What is a DNA fingerprint?

In court, a suspect's genotype might be compared with the DNA fingerprint obtained from evidence found at the crime scene. DNA samples from different people will produce different 26-number "fingerprints," whereas different samples of DNA from one person will have exactly the same genotype (**FIGURE 5-47**).

In the end, despite universally accepted methods, DNA fingerprinting still is not foolproof. Numerous incidences of human error—accidental as well as intentional—have been documented, from mislabeled test tubes to tissue from a suspect being added to evidence from a crime scene. So we should not blindly draw conclusions solely from this one type of evidence. Nonetheless, DNA fingerprinting is an increasingly valuable tool for law enforcement. The FBI, for example, has reported that nearly one-third of their suspects are cleared immediately by DNA testing, and that many more criminals, because of DNA fingerprinting, now plead guilty to the crimes they have committed.

TAKE-HOME MESSAGE 5·17

Comparisons of highly variable DNA regions can be used to identify tissue specimens and determine the individual from whom they came.

MIXING ASPIRIN AND ALCOHOL CAN LEAD TO METABOLIC INTERFERENCE AND UNEXPECTED INEBRIATION.

Ethanol is the form of alcohol found in cocktails, beer, and wine. When you consume alcohol, the first step in your body's metabolic breakdown of the ethanol is carried out by the enzyme alcohol dehydrogenase.

Q: WHAT HAPPENS TO ETHANOL MOLECULES THAT ARE *NOT* BROKEN DOWN? Any ethanol molecules in the bloodstream that are not broken down by alcohol dehydrogenase make their way to the brain. Once there, they cause you to feel a bit inebriated—or drunk, if the amount of ethanol is sufficiently large. Aspirin has the unintended side effect of disabling alcohol dehydrogenase, thus interfering with its normal functioning.

Q: WHAT HAPPENS IF SOMEONE TAKES TWO ASPIRINS AND THEN DRINKS SEVERAL ALCOHOLIC BEVERAGES? By blocking the activity of alcohol dehydrogenase, aspirin interferes with a person's ability to break down ethanol. As a consequence, the ethanol remains in the body longer and has a more pronounced effect on the brain, producing greater inebriation (26% greater, according to one study).

Q: WHAT CAN YOU CONCLUDE? Medications, even over-the-counter products, can have unexpected (and unintended) physiological consequences, particularly when mixed with alcohol consumption. Exercise great caution when taking them.

Big Ideas in ... DNA, Gene Expression, and Biotechnology

5·1–5·5 DNA: what is it and what does it do?

- DNA, the genetic material for all living organisms, is a double-helical molecule consisting of two "backbone" chains of sugar and phosphate molecules, with the chains linked by pairs of nucleotide bases.
- Genes are sequences of bases in DNA that contain the code for the construction of protein molecules. Only a small fraction of the DNA in eukaryotes consists of protein-coding genes.

5·6–5·8 Building organisms: information in DNA directs the production of the molecules that make up an organism.

- Information in the genes is transcribed into the sequences of mRNA molecules. These mRNA sequences are then translated as they direct the construction of proteins.
- Regulation of gene expression can occur in ways that enhance or impede transcription, or alter the longevity and degradation of mRNA, or influence translation or protein processing.

5·9–5·10 Damage to the genetic code has a variety of causes and effects.

- Mutations are rare alterations in a single base or changes in large segments of DNA that include several genes.
- Mutations in a gene may disrupt normal physiological functioning.
- Mutations play an important role in evolution.
- Most genetic diseases result from a mutation that causes a gene to produce a non-functioning enzyme, resulting in a blocked metabolic pathway.

5·11–5·13 Biotechnology is producing improvements in agriculture.

- Biotechnology is the use of technology to modify organisms, cells, and their molecules to achieve practical benefits.

- With modern molecular methods, researchers can cut and copy DNA and deliver it to new organisms, not necessarily of the same species.
- Biotechnology has led to important advances in agriculture by using transgenic plants and animals to produce more nutritious food. Biotechnology has also reduced the environmental and financial costs of producing food through the creation of herbicide- and insect-resistant crops.
- Some legitimate concerns among the public remain as to the safety of genetically modified foods.

5·14–5·17 Biotechnology has the potential for improving human health (and criminal justice).

- Biotechnology has had some successes in treating diseases, usually by producing medicines more efficiently and effectively than with traditional methods.
- Gene therapy has so far had a poor record of success in curing human diseases.
- With biotechnology, many tools have been developed that enable us to identify individuals carrying disease-causing genes. These tools can help reduce the symptoms and incidence of diseases, but come with significant potential costs, particularly the risk of discrimination.
- Advances in biotechnology have led to automated methods for analyzing DNA sequences. Comparisons of highly variable DNA regions have forensic value in identifying tissue specimens and determining the individual from whom they came.
- Cloning of individuals has potential benefits in agriculture and medicine, but ethical questions linger.

See the To-Go Guide (packaged with every new copy of this textbook) for an illustrated summary of the chapter.

Check Your Knowledge

GRAPHIC CONTENT

Thinking critically about visual displays of data.

1. What proportion of corn grown in the United States is genetically modified?

2. From the figures, can you determine whether there is more genetically modified corn or genetically modified cotton produced in the United States? How do you do this? And if it is not possible, why isn't it?

3. What is the "take-home message" from these figures? Does it influence your thoughts on genetically modified crops? Why or why not?

4. Why are data given for proportions of genetically modified crops rather than absolute amounts? Does this alter your interpretation of the graph?

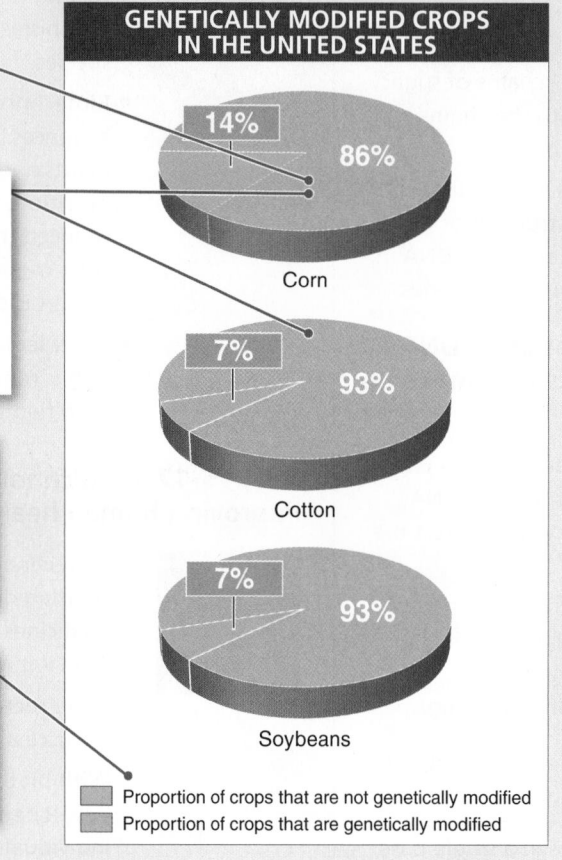

GENETICALLY MODIFIED CROPS IN THE UNITED STATES

14% — 86%
Corn

7% — 93%
Cotton

7% — 93%
Soybeans

☐ Proportion of crops that are not genetically modified
☐ Proportion of crops that are genetically modified

5. Worldwide, the percent of corn grown that is genetically modified is just 26%, while the proportion of soybeans that is genetically modified is 77% and cotton is 49%. How would this information add value to the figure?

6. The proportion of corn grown in the United States that is genetically modified has changed since 2001 as follows:

Year	Proportion
2001	26%
2002	34%
2003	40%
2004	47%
2005	52%
2006	61%
2007	73%
2008	80%
2009	85%
2010	86% (shown in the graph)

Show two different ways that you could display these data. What is the clearest conclusion someone would draw from the figures?

See Answers at the back of the book.

Key Terms in DNA, Gene Expression, and Biotechnology

Multiple-Choice Questions

1. A person's DNA is carried in: 100 HARD

a) muscle cells.

b) hair.
 28
c) saliva.
 0 EASY
d) skin cells.

e) All of the above contain a person's DNA.

2. Which of the following are always the same in every DNA molecule? 100 HARD

a) the sugar

b) the base
 37
c) the phosphate group
 0 EASY
d) Only a) and b) are always the same.

e) Only a) and c) are always the same.

3. The full set of an individual organism's DNA is called its: 100 HARD

a) complement.

b) genome.

c) nucleosome.

d) nucleotide.
 21
e) chromosome.
 0 EASY

4. In humans, genes make up _____ of the DNA. 100 HARD

a) about 75%

b) 100%

c) less than 5%

d) about 10%
 33
e) about 50%
 0 EASY

5. Genotype is to phenotype as: 100 HARD

a) cookie is to oven.

b) cookie is to recipe.

c) cookbook is to cookie.

d) recipe is to cookie.
 26
e) oven is to cookie.
 0 EASY

6. To start the transcription process, a large molecule, _____, recognizes a _____. 100 HARD

a) RNA polymerase; messenger RNA

b) DNA polymerase; termination site

c) DNA polymerase; promoter site
 39
d) RNA polymerase; promoter site
 0 EASY
e) DNA polymerase; messenger RNA.

7. During transcription, at the point at which the DNA strand being copied has an adenine, a(n) _____ is added to the _____. 100 HARD

a) thymine; tRNA

b) cytosine; DNA

c) uracil; tRNA
 46
d) adenine; mRNA
 0 EASY
e) uracil; mRNA.

8. There are different _____ molecules for each of the 20 different amino acids that are used in building proteins.

a) ribosomal subunit 100 HARD

b) tRNA

c) mRNA
 60
d) DNA

e) elongation 0 EASY

217

9. Deletions and substitutions are two types of point mutations. Which type is more likely to cause mistranslations of proteins?

a) Substitutions, because they shift the reading frame and cause downstream amino acids to be changed.

b) Substitutions, because one protein is substituted for another protein.

c) Deletions, because they shift the reading frame and cause downstream amino acids to be changed.

d) Deletions, because one protein is deleted.

e) None of the above is correct.

100 HARD
40
0 EASY

10. Which of the following statements about the metabolism of ethanol (which is present in alcoholic beverages) is incorrect?

a) Individuals who produce non-functioning aldehyde dehydrogenase exhibit "fast-flushing."

b) The process requires two enzymes: alcohol dehydrogenase and isopropyl dehydrogenase.

c) Individuals who are "fast-flushers" are less likely to become alcoholics.

d) Aspirin interferes with the action of alcohol dehydrogenase.

e) All of the above are correct.

100 HARD
69
0 EASY

11. The polymerase chain reaction (PCR):

a) makes it possible to create huge numbers of copies of tiny pieces of DNA.

b) enables researchers to determine the sequence of a complementary strand of DNA when they have only single-stranded DNA.

c) utilizes RNA polymerase to build strands of DNA.

d) can create messenger RNA molecules from small pieces of DNA.

e) All of the above are correct.

100 HARD
60
0 EASY

12. Which of the following is not a difficulty that medicine has encountered in its attempts to cure human diseases through gene therapy?

a) The transfer organism—usually a virus—may get into unintended cells and cause disease.

b) It is difficult to get the working gene into the specific cells where it is needed.

c) It is difficult to get the working gene into enough cells at the right rate to have a physiological effect.

d) For many diseases, a malfunctioning gene has not been identified.

e) All of the above are difficulties encountered in attempts to cure human diseases through gene therapy.

100 HARD
31
0 EASY

13. Golden rice:

a) grows without a husk, thereby reducing the processing required before it can be consumed.

b) can make vitamin A without beta-carotene.

c) could help prevent blindness in the 250,000 children who lose their sight each year because of vitamin A deficiency.

d) supplies more vitamin A in one serving than an individual needs in a full week.

e) is one of the most recent developments in organic farming.

100 HARD
30
0 EASY

14. Which of the following statements about Bt crystals is correct?

a) They are produced by soil-dwelling bacteria of the species Bacillus thuringiensis.

b) The gene coding for the production of Bt crystals has been genetically engineered into the genome of dairy cows, increasing their milk production sixfold.

c) They are produced by the polymerase chain reaction (PCR).

d) They are produced by most weedy species of plants.

e) All of the above are correct.

100 HARD
58
0 EASY

15. Highly repetitive sequences of DNA:

a) are characteristic of genes that code for biochemical traits rather than structural traits.

b) are used in biotechnology when creating a clone.

c) are produced when a mutation occurs in a non-sex cell.

d) can be used to produce a DNA fingerprint.

e) are produced when a mutation occurs in a sperm-producing or egg-producing cell.

100 HARD
60
0 EASY

Short-Answer Questions

1. After sequencing a molecule of DNA, you discover that 20% of the bases are cytosine. What percentage of the bases would you expect to be thymine? Explain why.

2. A cell is in the process of transcription. The single strand of DNA that is being copied has the sequence ATC GAC GGA TCC. Indicate the mRNA strand that will be synthesized from this strand, listing the correct sequence of bases. Explain why transcription is important in the process of producing protein.

3. What is being "translated" in translation? What is the role of transfer RNA molecules in this step?

4. The genetic disorder known as sickle-cell disease results in an altered form of the protein hemoglobin, which ultimately can affect the structure of red blood cells. A portion of the sequence of the normal hemoglobin allele is:

CTG ACT CCT GAG GAG AAG TCT

Individuals with the sickle-cell disorder have the following sequence:

CTG ACT CCT GTG GAG AAG TCT

Identify the type of mutation and explain how it would result in an altered (in this case non-functional) protein.

5. Describe three major applications of biotechnology and their impact on human health.

See Answers at the back of the book.
For additional study questions, go to www.prep-u.com.

Continuity and variety

6

Chromosomes and Cell Division

6·1–6·5 There are different types of cell division.

Cell division by fission in Staphylococcus aureus, *a disease-causing bacterium having resistance to multiple antibiotics.*

6·1

Immortal cells can spell trouble: cell division in sickness and in health.

Once you are fully grown, do you have just one set of cells that live as long as you do? The answer is *no:* your cells are continually dying off, and the ones that remain divide and replace the cells you've lost, in an ongoing process. But how long can this last? Can it go on forever? And does a cell even know how old it is?

Actually, a cell does have a measure of how old it is. Just as a car comes with an odometer, which keeps track of how far the car has been driven, animal cells have a sort of counter that keeps track of how many times a cell has divided. This "counter" is a section of non-coding, repetitive DNA, called a **telomere,** that serves as a protective cap and is located at each tip of every chromosome, right next to the genes that direct the processes that keep the organism alive (**FIGURE 6-1**). Every time a cell divides, making an exact copy of itself, its

DNA divides as well. However, each time the DNA divides, the telomere at each end of every chromosome gets a bit shorter. Eventually, after some critical number of cell divisions, the telomeres can become so short that additional cell divisions cause the loss of functional, essential DNA, and that means almost certain death for the cell.

At birth, the telomeres in most human cells are long enough to support about 50 cell divisions. Occasionally, however, individuals are born with telomeres that are much shorter than normal. In these people, the normal functioning of many genes is disrupted, and their cells and tissues begin to appear aged very soon after birth (**FIGURE 6-2**). As a consequence, children born with this disorder rarely live beyond the age of 13.

Just as someone might think it's a good idea to disconnect the car's odometer, you might think that disconnecting the cellular odometer by continually rebuilding the telomere would be an effective strategy for allowing a cell and its descendants to function for a longer time than normal. Such a line of cells

> "Cancer cells are those which have forgotten how to die."
> — HAROLD PINTER, playwright, from the poem "Cancer Cells," 2002

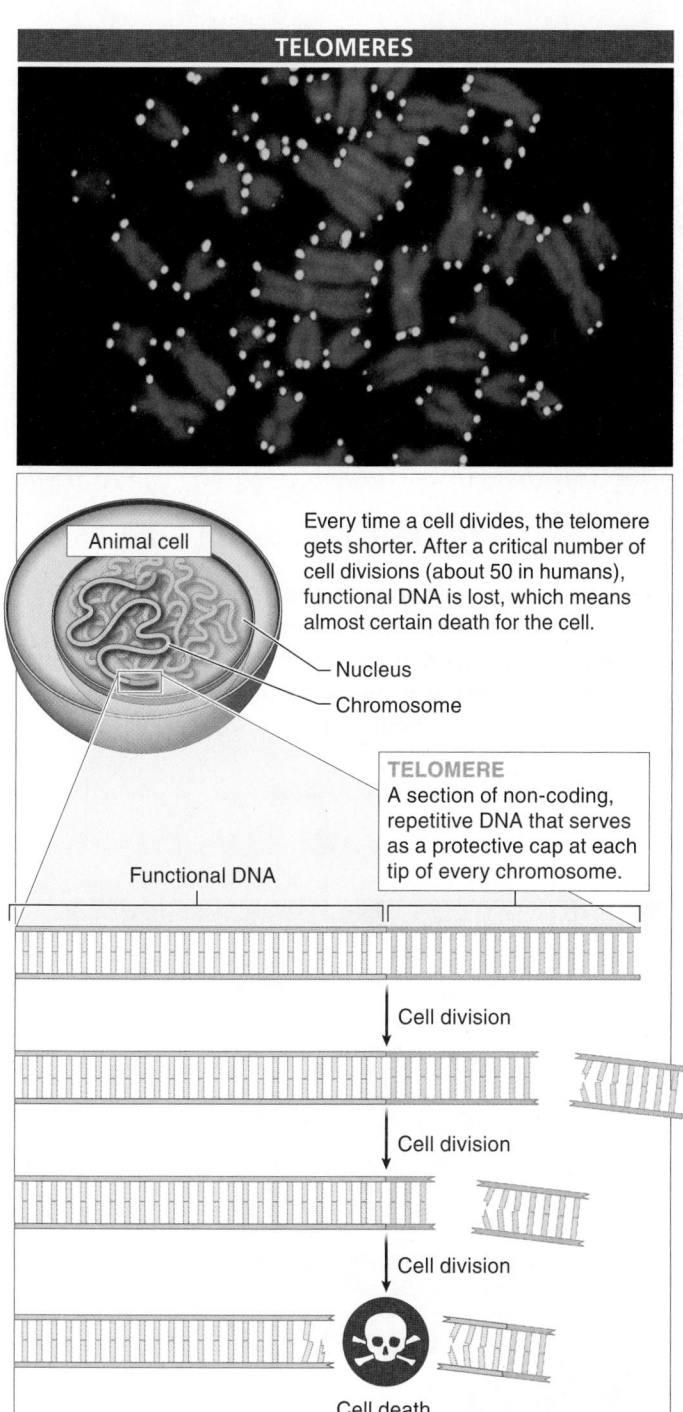

Every time a cell divides, the telomere gets shorter. After a critical number of cell divisions (about 50 in humans), functional DNA is lost, which means almost certain death for the cell.

Animal cell

Nucleus

Chromosome

TELOMERE
A section of non-coding, repetitive DNA that serves as a protective cap at each tip of every chromosome.

Functional DNA

Cell division

Cell division

Cell division

Cell death

FIGURE 6-1 A cellular "odometer." Telomeres limit cells to a fixed number of divisions. The photo shows chromosomes (in blue) with the telomeres highlighted in yellow.

would never die—so you'd think that a constantly rebuilding telomere would be like a fountain of youth. It's not. We know this because there are some cells with a sort of perpetually resetting odometer. These cells rebuild their telomeres after each cell division, restoring the chromosomes' protective caps. Unfortunately, most cells that rebuild their telomeres with

FIGURE 6-2 Just a child. Individuals with the genetic condition known as Hutchinson-Gilford progeria syndrome are born with shorter-than-normal telomeres and appear to age at a rapid rate.

each cell division present a big problem: they don't know when to stop dividing. There is a word for such cells: cancer. Because cancer is runaway cell division, discovering a cure for cancer will necessarily involve a deep understanding of cell division.

In this chapter, we investigate the processes that enable cells to divide and create new cells. Prokaryotes exhibit one method of cell division (called binary fission), and it serves all of their cell division needs. Eukaryotes exhibit two methods of cell division, mitosis and meiosis, each of which has a specific purpose in a eukaryote's life cycle. We'll explore normal cell division and discuss what happens when cell division does not proceed in the normal way.

TAKE-HOME MESSAGE 6·1

Cell division is an ongoing process in most organisms and their tissues; disruptions to normal cell division can have serious consequences. In eukaryotic cells, a protective section of DNA called the telomere, at each end of every chromosome, plays a role in keeping track of cell division, getting shorter every time the cell divides. If telomeres become too short, additional cell divisions cause the loss of essential DNA and cell death. Cells that rebuild their telomeres with each division can become cancerous.

6·2

Some chromosomes are circular, others are linear.

As a method for storing genetic information, DNA has complete market saturation. All life on earth uses it. This is pretty remarkable considering the tremendous diversity of life that exists on our planet—from single-celled bacteria to multicellular plants and animals. One way in which different organisms' DNA varies is in how it is organized into chromosomes.

In most bacteria and archaea, the genetic information is carried in a single, circular chromosome, a strand of DNA that is attached at one site to the cell membrane (**FIGURE 6-3**). Eukaryotes, which have much more DNA than do bacteria, organize it into free-floating linear chromosomes within the nucleus. As we saw in Chapter 5, a eukaryotic organism may have as few as 2 chromosomes or as many as 1,000. For plants and animals, the number is usually between 10 and 50.

The most important part of a eukaryotic chromosome may be the DNA molecule, which carries information on how to carry out the processes needed to support the life of the organism. But eukaryotic chromosomes (and some prokaryotic chromosomes) are made of more than just DNA. The long, linear strand is wrapped around proteins called **histones,** which keep the DNA from getting tangled and enable it to be tightly and efficiently packed in an orderly manner inside the cell (see Figure 6-3). In the next sections we examine how prokaryotic and eukaryotic chromosomes behave during cell division.

TAKE-HOME MESSAGE 6·2

In most bacteria and archaea, the genetic information is carried in a single, circular chromosome, a strand of DNA that is attached at one site to the cell membrane. Eukaryotes have much more DNA than do bacteria and organize it into free-floating linear chromosomes within the nucleus.

PROKARYOTIC AND EUKARYOTIC CHROMOSOMES

PROKARYOTIC CELLS
Prokaryotic cells have a single circular chromosome attached to the cell membrane.

EUKARYOTIC CELLS
Eukaryotic cells contain free-floating linear chromosomes within a nucleus.

FIGURE 6-3 **Chromosomes compared.** Prokaryotic cells have a single circular chromosome attached to the cell membrane. Eukaryotic cells contain free-floating linear chromosomes within a nucleus.

Prokaryotes divide by binary fission.

When it is time for bacteria and archaea to reproduce, they use a method called **binary fission,** which means "division in two" (**FIGURE 6-4**). This process begins with **replication,** the method by which a cell creates an exact duplicate of each chromosome. Replication begins as the double-stranded DNA molecule unwinds from its coiled-up configuration. Once the strands are uncoiled, they split apart like a zipper. As the double-stranded molecule unzips, free-floating nucleotide bases attach to the growing DNA backbone, with bases exposed on each of the two separated, single-stranded circular molecules of DNA, matching A to T and G to C, thus creating two identical double-stranded DNA molecules. The newly created circular chromosomes of DNA attach to the inside of the plasma membrane at different spots from each other. The original cell, called the **parent cell,** then pinches in until it divides into two new cells, called **daughter cells.** Each of the daughter cells has an exact and precise two-stranded copy of the original two-stranded circular chromosome.

In some prokaryotes, such as the bacteria called *E. coli* that live in our digestive system, the complete process of binary fission can occur very quickly—often in as little as 20 minutes. Binary fission is considered **asexual reproduction** because the daughter cells inherit their DNA from a single parent cell and thus are genetically identical to the parent cell. In **sexual reproduction,** a combination of DNA from two separate individuals is passed on to offspring, resulting in offspring that are genetically different both from one another and from their parents. We discuss sexual reproduction in more detail later in this chapter.

TAKE-HOME MESSAGE 6·3

Bacteria divide by a type of asexual reproduction called binary fission: first, the circular chromosome duplicates itself, then the parent cell splits into two new, genetically identical daughter cells.

PROKARYOTIC CELL DIVISION: BINARY FISSION

Prokaryotic parent cell

Double-stranded DNA

Attachment site

REPLICATION
An exact copy of the cell's DNA is created.

Cell elongates and begins to pinch in two.

Daughter cells are formed.

Binary fission results in two genetically identical daughter cells.

FIGURE 6-4 **Dividing in two.** Asexually reproducing prokaryotes reproduce rapidly through binary fission.

6·4 There is a time for everything in the eukaryotic cell cycle.

In life, we often go through phases that are defined by the primary focus of our interests and activities. For many years we go to school. For a while we may tend to our career. Then, for a spell, our personal life may take center stage. Most eukaryotic cells go through phases, too. They spend long periods of time occupied with activities relating solely to their growth and then may suspend those activities as they segue into a period devoted exclusively to reproducing themselves. This alternation of activities between processes related to growth and processes related to cell division is called the **cell cycle** (FIGURE 6-5).

Before we go any farther in discussing the cell cycle, we need to note an important distinction among the cells of the body. All the cells of a multicellular eukaryotic organism can be divided into two types: **somatic cells** are the cells forming the body of the organism; **reproductive cells** are the sex cells, or **gametes.** The processes of cell division by which somatic cells and reproductive cells are produced differ from each other. In this section, we focus on cell division as it occurs in somatic cells. Later in the chapter, we examine cell division that leads to the production of sex cells.

The cell cycle describes the series of phases in somatic cell division. There are two main phases in the cell cycle: **interphase,** during which the cell grows and prepares to divide, and the **mitotic phase** (or **M phase**), during which first the nucleus and genetic material within the cell divide, then the rest of the cellular contents divide. Interphase is further divided into three distinct subphases, described below. A eukaryotic somatic cell moves through the phases in precise order and, at any given moment, the cell is at some point in this cycle.

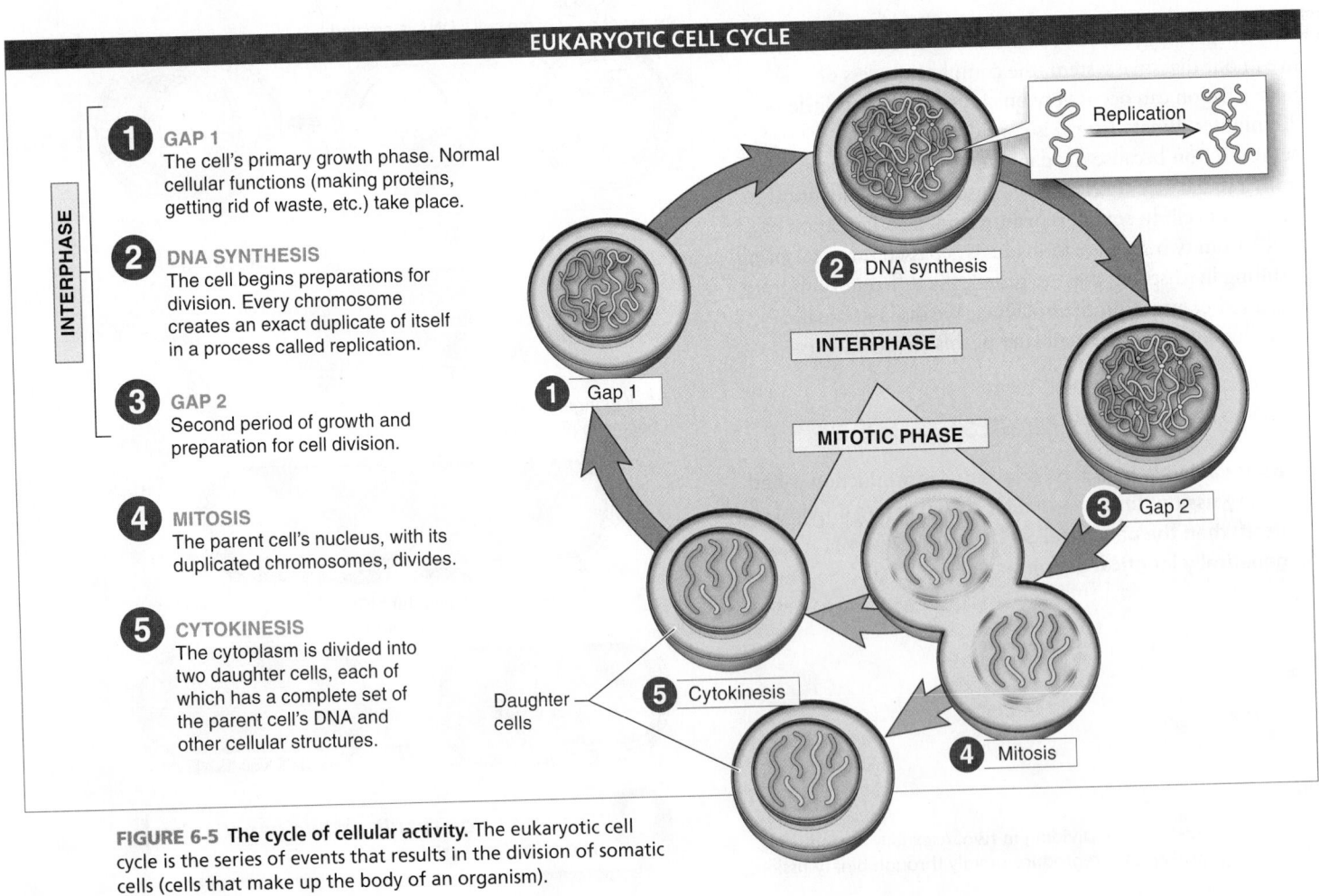

EUKARYOTIC CELL CYCLE

INTERPHASE

1 GAP 1
The cell's primary growth phase. Normal cellular functions (making proteins, getting rid of waste, etc.) take place.

2 DNA SYNTHESIS
The cell begins preparations for division. Every chromosome creates an exact duplicate of itself in a process called replication.

3 GAP 2
Second period of growth and preparation for cell division.

4 MITOSIS
The parent cell's nucleus, with its duplicated chromosomes, divides.

5 CYTOKINESIS
The cytoplasm is divided into two daughter cells, each of which has a complete set of the parent cell's DNA and other cellular structures.

Replication

2 DNA synthesis

INTERPHASE

1 Gap 1

MITOTIC PHASE

3 Gap 2

5 Cytokinesis

Daughter cells

4 Mitosis

FIGURE 6-5 The cycle of cellular activity. The eukaryotic cell cycle is the series of events that results in the division of somatic cells (cells that make up the body of an organism).

Interphase The three subphases of interphase can be summarized as follows.

Gap 1. During this period, a cell grows and performs all cellular functions (making proteins, getting rid of waste, and so on). Cells that divide infrequently, such as most neurons and heart muscle cells, spend most of their time in the Gap 1 phase.

DNA synthesis During this phase, the cell begins to prepare for cell division, first by creating an exact duplicate of each chromosome by replication. Before replication, each chromosome is a long, linear piece of genetic material. After replication, each chromosome has become a pair of identical long, linear pieces, held together near the center; the region where the two pieces are in contact is called the **centromere.** (The centromere also serves as the point to which spindle fibers can attach.)

Gap 2. In this phase, the cell continues to grow and prepare for division. This phase differs from Gap 1, though, because the genetic material has now been duplicated. Gap 2 is usually much shorter than Gap 1.

Mitotic phase This period begins with **mitosis,** a process in which the parent cell's nucleus, including its chromosomes, duplicates. Mitosis is generally followed by **cytokinesis,** during which the cytoplasm is divided into two daughter cells, each of which has a complete set of the parent cell's DNA and other cellular structures. (Note that each daughter cell becomes a parent cell in the next cell cycle.) The mitotic phase is usually the shortest period in the eukaryotic cell cycle.

The transition from one phase of the cell cycle to the next is triggered by specific events. For instance, a cell moves from the Gap 1 phase (denoted G_1) to DNA synthesis only if environmental conditions outside the cell are favorable for cell division. Until conditions are favorable, the cell remains in G_1. Likewise, a cell begins mitosis only when the genetic material has been successfully duplicated. Later in this chapter we'll see that errors in this orderly, step-by-step process can lead to out-of-control cell division and cancer.

TAKE-HOME MESSAGE 6·4

Eukaryotic somatic cells alternate in a cycle between cell division and other cell activities. The cell division portion of the cycle is called the mitotic phase. The remainder of the cell cycle, called interphase, consists of two gap phases (during which cell growth and other metabolic activities occur) separated by a DNA synthesis phase during which the genetic material is replicated.

6·5 Cell division is preceded by replication.

In one of the great understatements in the scientific literature, James Watson and Francis Crick wrote the following sentence in their paper describing the structure of DNA: "It has not escaped our notice that the specific pairing we have postulated immediately suggests a possible copying mechanism for the genetic material." The researchers' ability to explain how DNA copied itself was a critical feature of their description of DNA's structure. After all, every single time any cell in any organism's body divides, that cell's DNA must first duplicate itself so that each of the two new daughter cells has all of the genetic material of the original parent cell. The process of DNA duplication, as we've seen, is called replication.

What is it about DNA's structure that makes duplication so straightforward? Watson and Crick were referring to the feature of DNA called **complementarity,** the characteristic that in the double-stranded DNA molecule, the base on one strand always has the same pairing partner (called the **complementary base**) on the other strand: A pairs with T (and vice versa), and G pairs with C (and vice versa).

With this consistent pattern of pairing, when the DNA molecule separates into two strands, it is possible to perfectly reconstruct all the information on the missing half because one strand carries all the information needed to construct its complementary strand. Just before cells divide, the DNA molecule unwinds and "unzips," and each half of the unzipped molecule serves as a template on which the missing half is reconstructed. At the end of the process of reconstructing the missing halves, there are two DNA molecules—each identical to the original DNA molecule— one for each of the two new cells.

So, the process of DNA replication occurs in two steps: unwinding and rebuilding (**FIGURE 6-6**).

1. **Unwinding.** Replication begins when the coiled, double-stranded DNA molecule unwinds and separates into two strands, like a zipper unzipping.

2. **Rebuilding.** In the rebuilding process, each of the single strands becomes a double strand as the

appropriate complementary base pairs with the exposed base, and an enzyme links the nucleotides of the new strand together. If an A is exposed, a T binds to it; if a C is exposed, a G binds to it.

The end result of replication is two double-stranded DNA molecules, each identical to the cell's original double-stranded DNA molecule. DNA replication occurs in all types of cells, somatic and reproductive, prior to cell division.

A variety of mutations (such as mismatched bases and added or deleted segments) can occur during replication, but many of these errors are caught and repaired during or after replication. If an error remains, however, the sequences in a replicated DNA molecule (including the genes) can be different from those in the parent molecule. A changed sequence may then produce a different mRNA sequence, which may in turn produce a different amino acid sequence. As a result, the changed sequence may lead to the production of a different protein. In this way, new genes can enter a population and be acted on by evolution. We explore the relationship between mutation and evolution in more detail in Chapter 8.

Q Errors sometimes occur when DNA duplicates itself. Why might that be a good thing?

DNA REPLICATION

1 UNWINDING
The coiled, double-stranded DNA molecule unwinds and separates into two strands.

2 REBUILDING
Enzymes connect a nucleotide with the appropriate base to the growing new strand, as the base bonds with the exposed, complementary base.

Complementary nucleotide bases attached

3 Each of the single strands becomes a double strand, each identical to the cell's original double-stranded DNA molecule.

Adenine
Cytosine
Guanine
Thymine

FIGURE 6-6 How DNA replicates: unwinding and rebuilding.

6·6–6·9 Mitosis replaces worn-out old cells with fresh new duplicates.

For most of the cell cycle, chromosomes resemble a plate of spaghetti more than the familiar condensed, replicated "X" seen in photos.

6·6 Most cells are not immortal: mitosis generates replacements.

Look around your dorm room. Dust is everywhere. What is it? It is primarily dead skin cells. In fact, you (and your roommates) slough off millions of dead skin cells each day—yet your skin doesn't disappear. Why not? Because your body replaces the sloughed-off cells. When the cells wear out, your body

Q What is dust? Why is it your fault?

creates replacements through the process of mitosis.

Mitosis has just one purpose: to enable existing cells to generate new, genetically identical cells. There are two different reasons for this need (**FIGURE 6-7**).

THE NEED FOR NEW CELLS: GROWTH AND REPLACEMENT

The tip of the root is a site of particularly rapid cell division in most plants.

The act of shaving damages thousands of cells, which must be replaced.

FIGURE 6-7 Reasons for mitosis. Mitosis is important in organism growth and the replacement of cells.

1. Growth. During development, organisms get bigger. Growth happens in part through the creation of new cells. In fact, if you want to see cell division in action, one surefire place to find it is at the tip of a plant root: at a growth rate of about half an inch per day, the root is one of the fastest-growing parts of a plant.

2. Replacement. Cells must be replaced when they die. The wear and tear that come from living can physically damage cells. The daily act of shaving, for example, damages thousands of cells on a man's face. It's nothing to worry about, though. Microscopic views of human skin reveal several distinct layers, with the outermost layers—the layers under assault during shaving—made up primarily of dead cells. These cells help protect us from infection and also reduce the rate at which the underlying living cells dry out. The living cells that exist just below the layers of dead cells are produced at a high rate by mitosis.

FIGURE 6-8 The red blood cells in your body carry oxygen to your organs and tissues and are replaced about every 120 days.

Some other cells that must be replaced actually die on purpose, in a planned process of cell suicide called **apoptosis** (A-pop-TOE-siss). This seemingly counterproductive strategy is employed in parts of the body where the cells are likely to accumulate significant genetic damage over time and are therefore at high risk of becoming cancer cells (a process described later in this chapter). Cells targeted for apoptosis include many of the cells lining the digestive tract as well as those in the liver, two locations where cells are almost constantly in contact with harmful substances.

Every day, a huge number of cells in an individual must be replaced by mitosis. In humans this number is in the billions. Nearly all the somatic cells of the body—that is, all cells except sperm- and egg-producing cells—undergo mitosis. There are a few notable exceptions. Brain cells and heart muscle cells, in particular, do not seem to divide, or, if they do divide, they do so at very, very slow rates. (We don't know why this is so.)

The rate at which mitosis occurs in animals varies dramatically for different types of cells. The most rapid cell division takes place in the blood and in the cells lining various tissues and organs. The average red blood cell, for example, is in circulation only for about two to four months and then must be replaced (**FIGURE 6-8**). The cells lining the intestines are replaced about every three weeks. Hair follicles, too, are among the most rapidly dividing cells.

TAKE-HOME MESSAGE 6·6

Mitosis enables existing cells to generate new, genetically identical cells. This makes it possible for organisms to grow and to replace cells that die.

6·7

Overview: mitosis leads to duplicate cells.

For mitosis to begin, the parent cell replicates its DNA, creating a duplicate copy of each chromosome. Once this task is completed, the remainder of mitosis can take place, in which the chromosomes are separated into identical sets in two separate nuclei, and then the cell can divide into two duplicate cells, the daughter cells (**FIGURE 6-9**).

FIGURE 6-9 These two human embryonic stem cells have just completed mitosis.

Mitosis occurs in just four steps. It begins with the condensing (or compacting) of the chromosomes, all of which are uncondensed and tangled during interphase, a bit like a big plate of spaghetti. Next, all the duplicated, condensed chromosomes move to the center of the cell. Each chromosome is then pulled apart from its duplicate. In the final step, new membranes form around each complete set of chromosomes to create the new nuclei, after which the cytoplasm and the rest of the cell are divided into two cells that pinch apart. Where once there was one parent cell, now there are two daughter cells (**FIGURE 6-10**).

TAKE-HOME MESSAGE 6·7

Mitosis is the process by which cells duplicate themselves. Mitosis follows chromosome replication and leads to the production of two daughter cells from one parent cell.

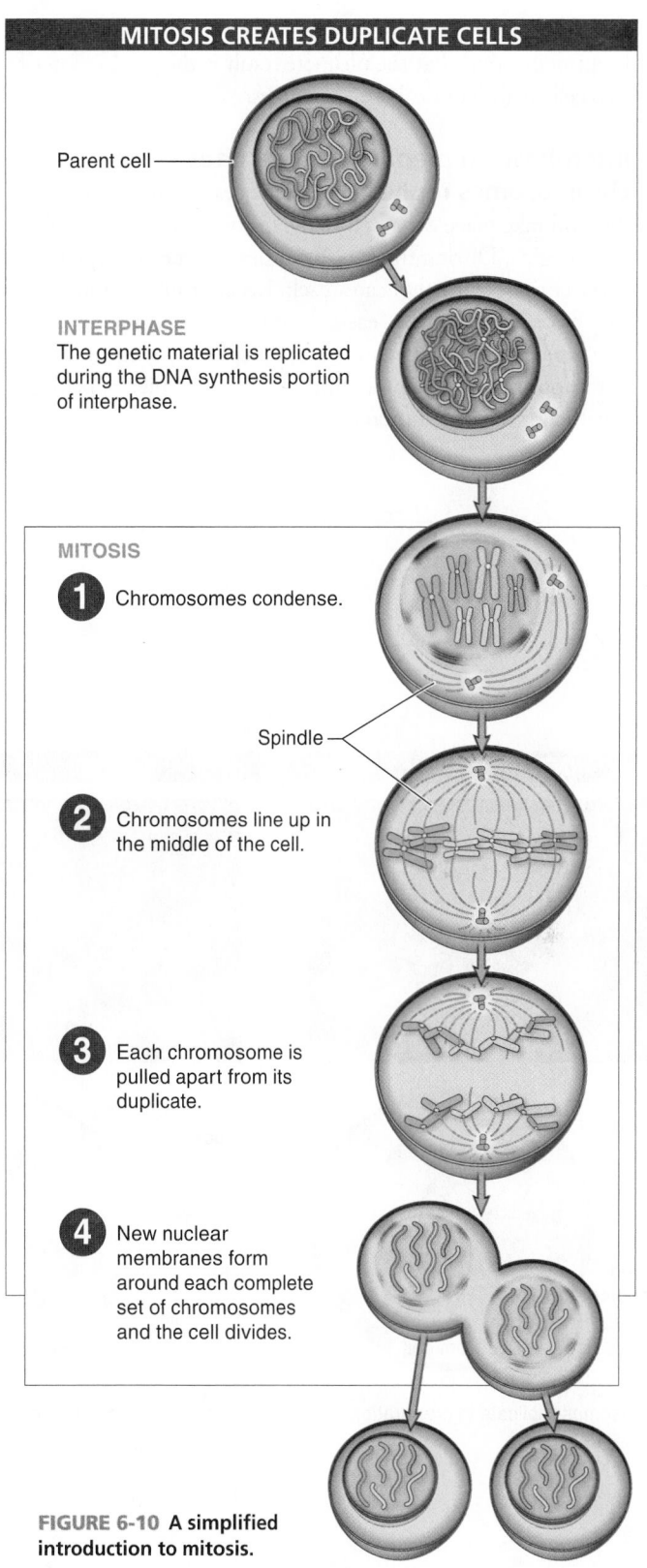

MITOSIS CREATES DUPLICATE CELLS

Parent cell

INTERPHASE
The genetic material is replicated during the DNA synthesis portion of interphase.

MITOSIS

1 Chromosomes condense.

Spindle

2 Chromosomes line up in the middle of the cell.

3 Each chromosome is pulled apart from its duplicate.

4 New nuclear membranes form around each complete set of chromosomes and the cell divides.

FIGURE 6-10 A simplified introduction to mitosis.

6·8

The details: mitosis is a four-step process.

Let's look at the process of mitosis in a bit more detail, keeping in mind that the ultimate result is the production of two cells with identical chromosomes.

Interphase: in preparation for mitosis, the chromosomes replicate
Processes essential to cell division take place even before the mitotic phase of the cell cycle begins. During the DNA synthesis part of interphase, every chromosome replicates itself. Recall from Section 6-4 that prior to replication, each chromosome is just a long, linear piece of genetic material; after replication, each chromosome is a *pair* of identical long, linear pieces, held together at the centromere.

Single chromosome — Replication → Centromere

Mitosis The actual process of cell division occurs in four steps (**FIGURE 6-11**).

1. Prophase: the long, linear chromosomes that have replicated condense. When you look at a cell through a microscope, you generally won't see any chromosomes because the cells you're looking at are in some part of their interphase. During all of the cell cycle except mitosis, chromosomes are uncoiled and spread out in a diffuse way, like a mass of spaghetti. Because they are so stretched out, they are not dense enough to be visible. Mitosis begins with prophase, when the chromosomes in the cell's nucleus become more and more tightly coiled. As they condense, they become thick enough to be seen through a light microscope.

At this point, in prophase, each chromosome looks like the letter X. This appearance is misleading; chromosomes are not actually X-shaped. They are *linear*. Each X consists of two identical linear DNA molecules—a chromosome and its

---

INTERPHASE	MITOSIS

Nucleus

Spindle fibers

Nuclear membrane
Centromere
Replicated chromosome
Parent cell

Nuclear membrane
Sister chromatids
Centriole
Spindle fibers

INTERPHASE
• Chromosomes replicate in preparation for mitosis.

1 PROPHASE
• Nuclear membrane breaks down.
• Sister chromatids (replicated chromosomes) condense.
• Spindle forms.

2 METAPHASE
• Sister chromatids line up at the center of the cell.

FIGURE 6-11 Mitosis: cell duplication, step by step.

Animal chromosomes are linear. Why do they look like the letter X in pictures?

identical, replicated copy—joined at the centromere. (Each of the identical DNA molecules is called a **chromatid;** together, the two are called **sister chromatids.**) The reason for the X shape in most photos of chromosomes is that the only time the chromosome is coiled tightly and thus thick enough to be seen (and photographed) is during cell division.

Centromere

Sister chromatids

Because a lot of room is required for the duplicated chromosomes to separate, the membrane around the nucleus is dismantled and disappears near the end of this first stage of mitosis. At the same time, a structure called the **spindle** is assembled. The spindle, which is part of the cell's cytoskeleton, can be thought of as a group of parallel threads stretching across the cell between its two ends, or poles—where the threads connect at each pole to a structure called the **centriole.** These threads (known as **spindle fibers**) pull the sister chromatids to the middle of the cell and will eventually be used to pull the chromatids apart as cell division proceeds.

2. Metaphase: the chromosomes congregate at the cell center. After condensing, the pairs of chromatids seem to move aimlessly around the cell, but eventually they line up at the cell's center, pulled by spindle fibers attached to the centromere of each pair. Metaphase can be considered the half-time of mitosis. At the end of metaphase, all the chromatid pairs are lined up in an orderly fashion, straddling the center in a "single-file" congregation that is called the metaphase plate. All the chromatids are at their most condensed during this part of mitosis.

3. Anaphase: the chromatids separate and move in opposite directions. In anaphase, the fibers attached to the centromeres begin pulling each chromatid in the sister chromatid pairs toward opposite poles of the cell. From each pair of sister chromatids, one strand of DNA is pulled in one direction and the other, identical strand is pulled in the opposite direction. At the end of anaphase, one full

---

CYTOKINESIS

Chromosomes

Spindle fiber

Nuclear membrane

Daughter cells

3 ANAPHASE
• The sister chromatid pairs are pulled apart by the spindle fibers. One full set of chromosomes goes to one side of the cell and another identical set goes to the other.

4 TELOPHASE
• The chromosomes begin to uncoil as the nuclear membrane reassembles around them.
• The cell begins to pinch in two.

CYTOKINESIS
• Cytoplasm is divided into the two daughter cells.

set of chromosomes is at one end of the cell and another, identical full set is at the other end. These chromosome sets will eventually reside in the nucleus of each of the two new daughter cells that result from the cell division.

4. Telophase: new nuclear membranes form around the two complete chromosome sets. With two full, identical sets of chromosomes collected at either end of the cell, the cell is prepared to divide into two genetically identical cells. In this last step, called telophase, the chromosomes begin to uncoil and fade from view, nuclear membranes reassemble, and the cell begins to pinch into two.

The process of mitosis, the division of a cell's nucleus into two nuclei, each of which includes an identical set of chromosomes, is generally followed by cytokinesis, during which the cell's cytoplasm is also divided into approximately equal parts, with some of the organelles going to each of the two new cells. When cytokinesis is complete, the two new daughter cells, each with an identical nucleus containing identical genetic material, enter interphase and begin the business of being cells.

Usually, mitosis occurs without errors and only when needed. In rare cases, however, something goes wrong that can cause cell division to proceed unchecked. In such cases, cancer can arise.

> **TAKE-HOME MESSAGE 6·8**
>
> The ultimate result of mitosis and cytokinesis is the production of two genetically identical cells.

6·9 Cell division out of control means cancer.

Too much of a good thing can be bad. This is especially true when cell division runs amok, a situation that can lead to cancer. **Cancer** is defined as unrestrained cell growth and division that can damage adjacent tissues. Some cancers can metastasize, or spread to other locations in the body. Cancer can cause serious health problems and is the second leading cause of death in the United States, responsible for more than 20% of all deaths. Only heart disease causes more deaths.

Cancer occurs when some disruption of the DNA in a normal cell interferes with the cell's ability to regulate cell division. DNA disruption can be caused by chemicals that mutate DNA or by sources of high energy such as X rays, the sun, or nuclear radiation. Cancer can even be caused by some viruses. However it begins, once a cell loses control over its cell cycle, cell division can proceed unrestrained (**FIGURE 6-12**).

Cancer cells have several features that distinguish them from normal cells; the three most significant differences are:

1. Cancer cells lose their "contact inhibition." Most normal cells divide until they bump up against other cells or collections of cells (tissues). At that point, they stop dividing. Cancer cells, however, ignore the signal that they are at high density and continue to divide.

2. Cancer cells can divide indefinitely. As we saw in Section 6-1, a normal cell can divide approximately 50 times. After that point, the cell may continue living but it loses the ability to divide. Cancer cells, on the other hand, never lose their ability to divide and continue to do so indefinitely, even in the presence of conditions that would normally halt the cell cycle before cell division. (Cancer cells can divide indefinitely because they are able to rebuild their telomeres following each cell division.)

3. Cancer cells have reduced "stickiness." Cells are normally held together by adhesion molecules, proteins within cell membranes. And cancer cells, too, usually group together, forming a tumor. But the membranes of cancer cells tend to have reduced adhesiveness, causing them to stick to each other less than do non-cancerous cells.

Tumors caused by excessive cell growth and division are of two very different types: benign and malignant. Benign tumors, such as many moles, are just masses of normal cells that do not spread. They can usually be removed safely without any lasting consequences. Malignant tumors, on the other hand, are the result of unrestrained growth of cancerous cells. They grow continuously and shed cells (**FIGURE 6-13**). The shedding of cancer cells from malignant tumors is how cancer spreads, a process called metastasis (meh-TASS-tuh-siss) In this process, cancer cells separate from a tumor and invade the circulatory system, which spreads them to different parts of the body where they can cause the growth of additional tumors.

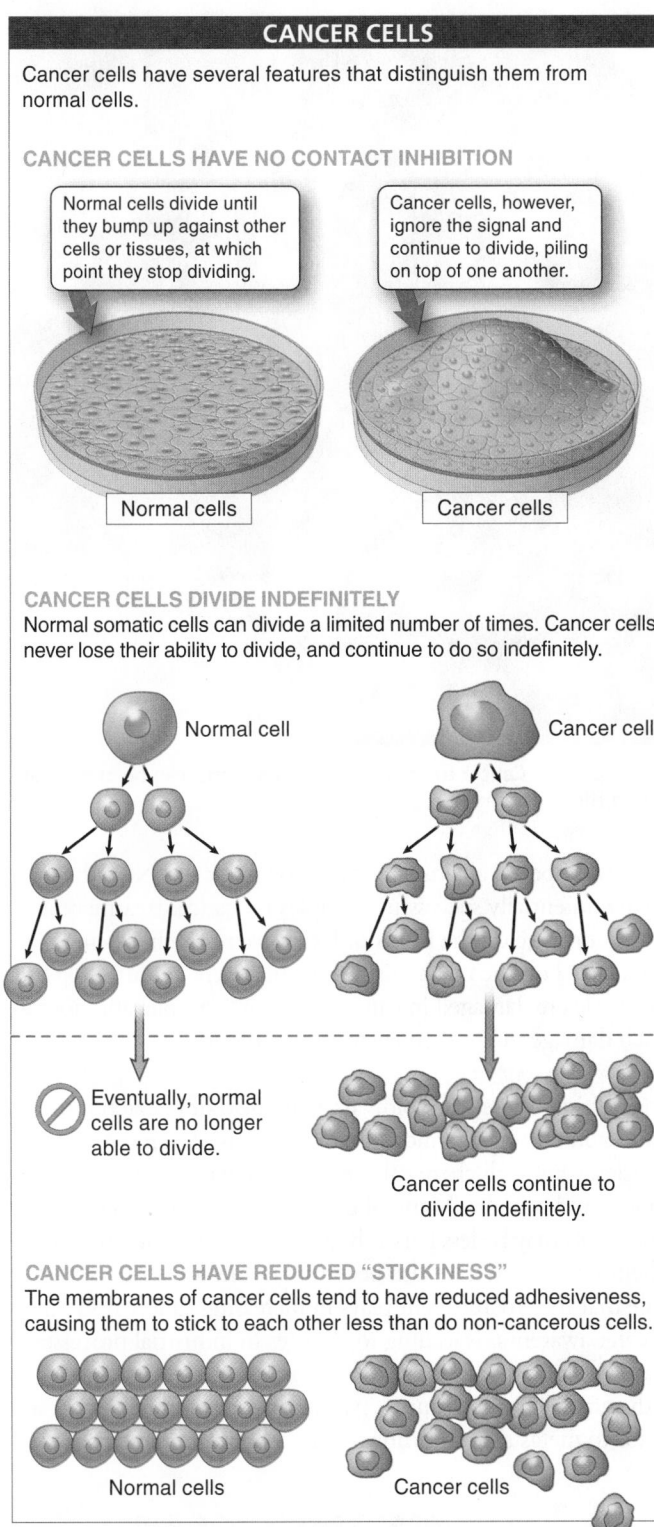

CANCER CELLS

Cancer cells have several features that distinguish them from normal cells.

CANCER CELLS HAVE NO CONTACT INHIBITION

Normal cells divide until they bump up against other cells or tissues, at which point they stop dividing.

Cancer cells, however, ignore the signal and continue to divide, piling on top of one another.

Normal cells

Cancer cells

CANCER CELLS DIVIDE INDEFINITELY

Normal somatic cells can divide a limited number of times. Cancer cells never lose their ability to divide, and continue to do so indefinitely.

Normal cell

Cancer cell

Eventually, normal cells are no longer able to divide.

Cancer cells continue to divide indefinitely.

CANCER CELLS HAVE REDUCED "STICKINESS"

The membranes of cancer cells tend to have reduced adhesiveness, causing them to stick to each other less than do non-cancerous cells.

Normal cells

Cancer cells

FIGURE 6-12 Problem cells. Cancer occurs when there is a disruption in cells' ability to regulate cell division and a reduced adhesion among those cells.

METASTASIS Cancer cells, shown here in white, can separate from a tumor and spread throughout the body via the circulatory system.

When a tumor metastasizes, cancer spreads, treatment becomes difficult, and the prognosis worsens.

FIGURE 6-13 Multiple tumors. Metastasis spreads cancer cells throughout the body.

How does cancer actually cause death? Somewhat surprisingly, it's not because of some chemical or genetic property of the cancer cells themselves. It's simpler than that. As a tumor gets larger, it takes up more and more space, and presses against neighboring cells and tissues (**FIGURE 6-14**). Eventually, the tumor may block other cells and tissues from carrying out their normal functions and even kill them. This cell dysfunction or cell death can have disastrous consequences when the affected normal tissue controls processes critical to life, such as breathing, heart function, or the detoxification processes in the liver.

Q What is cancer? How does it usually cause death?

To treat cancer, the rapidly dividing cells must be removed surgically or killed, or their division at least slowed down. Currently, the killing and slowing down are done in two ways: by chemotherapy and by radiation. In chemotherapy, drugs that interfere with cell division are administered,

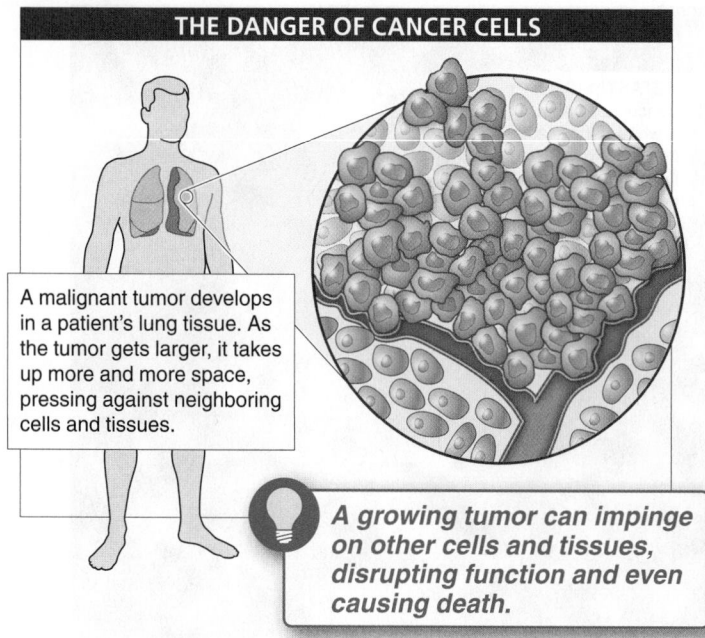

THE DANGER OF CANCER CELLS

A malignant tumor develops in a patient's lung tissue. As the tumor gets larger, it takes up more and more space, pressing against neighboring cells and tissues.

A growing tumor can impinge on other cells and tissues, disrupting function and even causing death.

FIGURE 6-14 Cancer's effects. Cancer cells harm the body by crowding and disrupting normal cells.

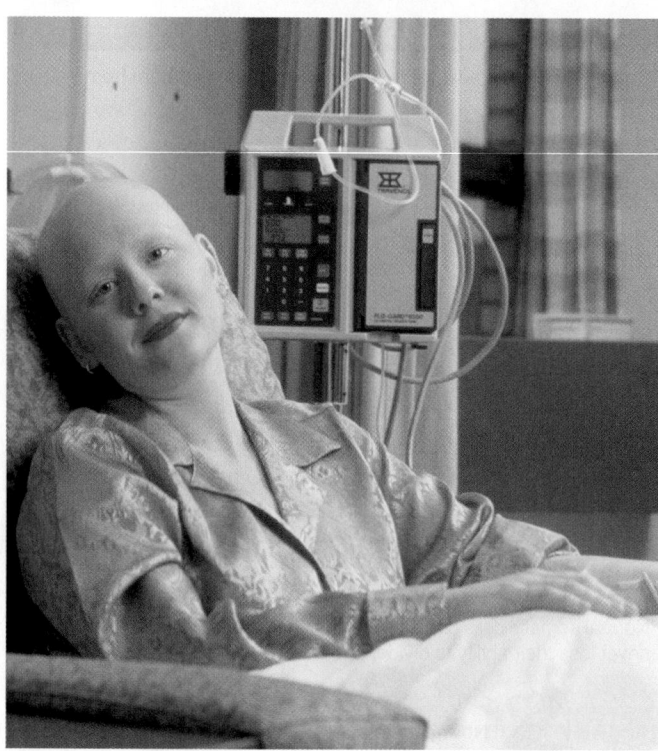

FIGURE 6-15 Cancer treatments. The treatments can be as painful and difficult as the disease.

slowing down the growth of tumors. Because these drugs interfere with rapidly dividing cells throughout the body (not just the rapidly dividing cancer cells), they can have very unpleasant side effects. In particular, chemotherapy drugs disrupt normal systems that rely on the rapid and constant production of new cells. For instance, chemotherapy often causes extreme fatigue and shortness of breath because it reduces the rate at which red blood cells are produced, thus limiting the amount of oxygen that can be transported throughout the body. By interfering with the division of bone marrow stem cells, chemotherapy also reduces the production of platelets and white blood cells and thus increases bruising and bleeding, and increases susceptibility to infection. Another location of rapidly dividing cells commonly affected by chemotherapy and radiation is the hair follicle. Many people lose their hair when undergoing chemotherapy (it usually grows back when treatments stop).

Like chemotherapy, radiation works by disrupting cell division. Unlike the drugs used in chemotherapy, however, which circulate throughout the entire body, radiation therapy directs high-energy radiation only at the part of the body where a tumor is located. Like chemotherapy, the radiation process is not perfect and nearby tissue is often harmed as well. The significant negative effects of chemotherapy and radiation treatment on normal tissue and the suffering this leads to have caused some patients to comment that the treatment for cancer can initially feel as bad as the disease itself—especially because patients may be asymptomatic at the time of treatment (**FIGURE 6-15**).

Is there hope for a complete cure soon? Not yet. Nonetheless, many potentially successful therapies for cancer treatment and prevention are on the horizon. Extensive research is being conducted on the mechanisms by which genes controlling the cell cycle are damaged in cancer cells, for example, and how such damage might be prevented or reversed.

In addition, there is a rapidly growing field of research into cancer-inhibiting chemicals that have evolved in many plant species. One such chemical is resveratrol, which is found in grapes and peanuts. Many of these naturally occurring chemicals may be less harsh than the drugs currently used in chemotherapy. We are also becoming more conscious of the role that the environment plays in increasing cancer risk; our greater awareness is leading to changes in industrial processes and, on the individual level, to dietary or lifestyle changes. Advances in early screening, particularly in identifying cancer prior to metastasis, continue to have significant benefits as well.

TAKE-HOME MESSAGE 6·9

Cancer is unrestrained cell growth and cell division, which lead to large masses of cells that may cause serious health problems. Treatment focuses on killing or slowing down the fast-growing and dividing cells, usually using chemotherapy and/or radiation.

6·10–6·14 Meiosis generates sperm and eggs and a great deal of variation.

Human gametes: sperm attempting to fertilize an egg.

6·10 Overview: sexual reproduction requires special cells made by meiosis.

There are two ways in which an organism can reproduce. Many organisms, including bacteria, fungi, and even some plants and animals, undergo asexual reproduction, in which a single parent produces identical offspring. Other organisms, including most animals and plants, undergo sexual reproduction, in which offspring are produced by the fusion of two reproductive cells in the process of **fertilization.** And some species, particularly among plants, can use both methods.

Sexually reproducing organisms, humans included, have a problem to solve when it comes to cell division. When offspring are created, they carry the genetic material from two individuals. But think about the difficulties this presents. If reproductive cells were produced through mitosis, both parents would contribute a full set of genes—that is, 23 pairs of chromosomes in humans—to create a new individual, and the new offspring would inherit 46 pairs of chromosomes in all. And when that individual reproduced, if he or she contributed 46 pairs of chromosomes and his or her mate also contributed 46 pairs, their offspring would have 92 pairs of chromosomes. Where would it end? The genome would double in size every generation. That wouldn't work at all. At

the very least, within a few generations the cells would be so overloaded with chromosomes that they would explode.

In sexually reproducing organisms, a way has evolved to avoid such chromosome overload. The solution is **meiosis,** a process that enables organisms to make special reproductive cells, the gametes, which have only half as many chromosomes as the rest of the cells in the organism's body (the somatic cells). In other words, in anticipation of combining one individual's genome with another's during fertilization, meiosis reduces each individual's genome by half in the gametes. In humans, for example, each gamete cell has only one set of 23 chromosomes, rather than two sets. In genetics, the term **diploid** refers to cells that have two copies of each chromosome (in humans that is two sets of 23 chromosomes, for 46 chromosomes in total), and the term **haploid** refers to cells that have one copy of each chromosome. Thus, somatic cells are diploid, and gametes, the cells produced in meiosis, are haploid. At fertilization, two haploid cells, each with one set of 23 chromosomes, merge and create a new individual with the proper diploid human genome of 46 chromosomes. And when the time comes to reproduce, this new individual, through meiosis, also will produce haploid gametes that have only a single set of 23 chromosomes. With sexual reproduction, then, diploid organisms produce haploid gametes that fuse at fertilization to restore the diploid state (**FIGURE 6-16**). In this way, meiosis maintains a stable genome size in a species.

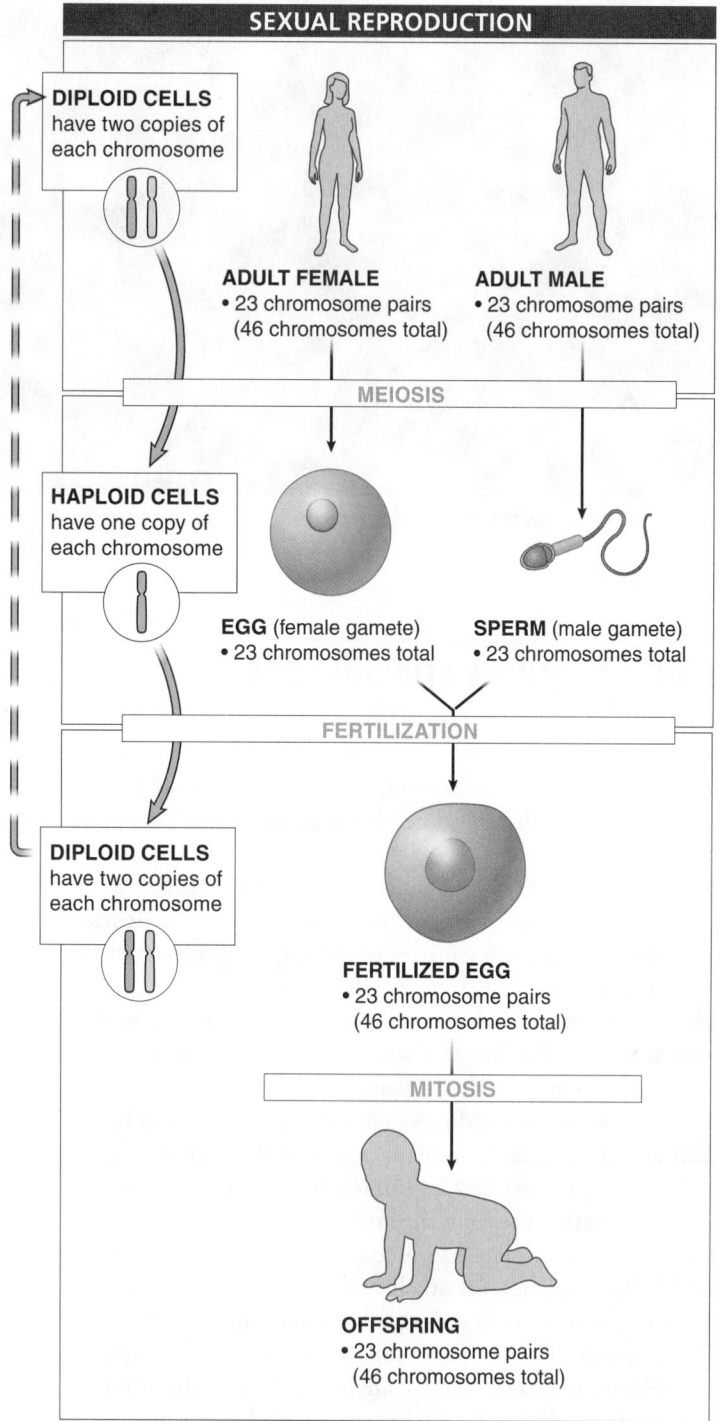

FIGURE 6-16 Sexual reproduction. Diploid organisms produce haploid gametes that fuse at fertilization and return to the diploid state.

Although there are some variations on this pattern of alternation between the haploid and diploid states, in most cases, multicellular animals produce simple haploid cells for reproduction. And after two of those gametes come together to form a diploid fertilized egg, multiple cell divisions via mitosis again produce a diploid, multicellular animal.

Meiosis achieves more than just a reduction in the amount of genetic material in gametes. As a diploid individual, you have two copies (i.e., two alleles) of every gene in every somatic cell: one from your mother and one from your father. When making haploid cells from cells that are diploid, an individual creates cells that have one allele for each trait rather than two. Which of these two alleles is included in each gamete cannot be predicted.

Each egg or sperm is produced with a varied combination of maternal and paternal alleles so that all of the gametes an individual makes carry a unique set of alleles. As a consequence, each offspring inherits a slightly different assemblage of each parent's alleles. All offspring resemble their parents, yet none resembles them in exactly the same way. This variation among offspring can be seen among the five Jackson brothers in the photo that opens this chapter (and among the Kennedy brothers in **FIGURE 6-17**).

FIGURE 6-17 One mother, one father: varied offspring. Variation generated in the production of sperm and eggs causes each sibling to carry a unique set of alleles.

In all, then, meiosis has two important outcomes:

1. It reduces the amount of genetic material in gametes.
2. It produces gametes that differ from one another with respect to the combinations of alleles they carry.

In the next sections, we examine the exact steps by which these outcomes occur and investigate the consequences of all the variation that meiosis and sexual reproduction can generate.

TAKE-HOME MESSAGE 6·10

Meiosis is the process by which reproductive cells are produced in sexually reproducing organisms. It results in gametes that have only half as much genetic material as the parent cell and that differ from one another in the combinations of alleles they carry.

6·11 Sperm and egg are produced by meiosis: the details, step by step.

Mitosis is an all-purpose process for cell division. It occurs all over the body, all the time. Meiosis, on the other hand, is a special-purpose process. It takes place in just a single place: the **gonads** (the ovaries and testes in sexually reproducing animals). And it takes place for just a single reason: the production of gametes (reproductive cells). To better understand meiosis, let's examine in detail the steps by which a diploid cell creates haploid cells, each of which is different from the other.

Meiosis starts with a diploid cell—not just any diploid cell, but one of the specialized diploid cells, found in the gonads, that is capable of undergoing meiosis. Thus, for humans, meiosis starts with a cell that has 46 chromosomes: a maternal copy and a paternal copy of each of the 23 human chromosomes. Together, the maternal and paternal copies of a chromosome are called a **homologous pair,** or **homologues.** This means that there are 23 homologous pairs in a diploid human cell (**FIGURE 6-18**).

Before meiosis can occur (and just as we saw with mitosis), each of these 46 chromosomes is duplicated during the cell's interphase. So now, instead of having just a maternal and paternal copy of, say, chromosome 1, we have two copies of the maternal copy of chromosome 1, bound together as sister chromatids, and two copies of the paternal copy of chromosome 1, bound together as sister chromatids. This means that when meiosis begins, we have 92 (2 × 46) strands of DNA, after replication.

Unlike mitosis, which has only one cell division, cells undergoing meiosis divide twice. In the first division, the homologues separate. In other words, for each of the 23 chromosome pairs, the maternal sister chromatid pairs and the paternal sister chromatid pairs separate into two new cells. In the second division, each of the two new cells

HOMOLOGUES AND SISTER CHROMATIDS

Homologues are the maternal and paternal copies of a chromosome. A sister chromatid is one of the two identical copies of a chromosome created during replication. The two sister chromatids are held together at a centromere.

FIGURE 6-18 Chromosome vocabulary: homologues and sister chromatids.

divides again, and this time the sister chromatids separate from each other into two newer cells. At the end of meiosis, there are four new cells, each of which has 23 strands of DNA—that is, 23 chromosomes (**FIGURE 6-19**). Note that none of these four cells will undergo any further cell division—they do not become parent cells for a next cycle of cell division. And remember, only specialized types of diploid cells located in the gonads can undergo meiosis.

Interphase: in preparation for meiosis, the chromosomes replicate Before meiosis begins, preparations for cell division occur that are similar to those taking place in the interphase of mitosis in the somatic cell cycle. In particular, every chromosome creates an exact duplicate of itself by replication. The chromosomes that were each a single, long, linear piece of genetic material become a pair of identical long, linear pieces, held together at the centromere.

MEIOSIS: REDUCING THE GENOME BY HALF

INTERPHASE
Each chromosome in a homologous pair replicates to form a sister chromatid.

(Chromosomes shown condensed here for diagrammatic purposes.)

Diploid parent cell
— Homologues
— Maternal chromosome
— Paternal chromosome

— Sister chromatids

MEIOSIS I
In the first division of meiosis, the homologous pairs separate.

Haploid daughter cells (gametes)

MEIOSIS II
In the second division of meiosis, the sister chromatids separate. This results in four haploid cells, each containing just one copy of each chromosome, rather than a homologous pair.

FIGURE 6-19 Meiosis reduces the genome by half in anticipation of combining it with another genome.

Meiosis begins following this replication step during interphase; it proceeds through eight steps (**FIGURE 6-20**).

Meiosis division I: the homologues separate
The first meiotic division takes place in four stages.

1. Prophase I: chromosomes condense and crossing over occurs. This is by far the most complex of all the phases of meiosis. It begins with all of the replicated genetic material condensing.

As the sister chromatids become shorter and thicker, the homologous chromosomes come together. That is, the maternal and paternal sets of sister chromatids for chromosome 1 come together so that there are *four* versions of this chromosome lined up together. The maternal and paternal sets of chromosome 2, 3, 4, and so on, also line up. Under a microscope, the two homologous pairs of sister chromatids appear as pairs of X's lying on top of each other.

At this point, the sister chromatids that are next to each other do something that makes every sperm or egg cell genetically

---

INTERPHASE

MEIOSIS DIVISION I: HOMOLOGUES SEPARATE

Centromere
Replicated chromosome

Nuclear membrane

Homologues

Spindle

Piece of maternal chromatid now on paternal chromatid following crossing over

Spindle fiber

INTERPHASE
• Chromosomes (uncondensed in this phase) replicate in preparation for meiosis.

1 PROPHASE I
• Replicated chromosomes condense.
• Spindle is formed.
• Homologous pairs of sister chromatids come together and cross over.
• Nuclear membrane disintegrates.

2 METAPHASE I
• Homologues move toward the center of the cell (at this point, referred to as the metaphase plate) and line up.

3 ANAPHASE I
• Homologues separate and are pulled to opposite poles. Sister chromatids going to each side are a mix of maternal and paternal genetic material.

FIGURE 6-20 Meiosis: generating reproductive cells, step by step.

unique: they swap little segments of DNA. In other words, when this is happening inside of you, some of the genes that you inherited from your mother get swapped onto the strand of DNA you inherited from your father, and the corresponding bit from your father is inserted into the DNA strand from your mother. This event is called **recombination** or **crossing over,** and it can take place at several spots (up to dozens) on each chromatid. As a result of crossing over, every sister chromatid ends up having a unique mixture of the genetic material that you received from your two parents. Note that crossing over occurs only during the production of gametes, in meiosis. It does not occur during mitosis. Following crossing over, the nuclear membrane disintegrates.

We explore crossing over in more detail in Section 6-13. The remaining steps of meiosis are relatively straightforward.

2. Metaphase l: all chromosomes line up along the center of the cell.

After crossing over, each pair of homologous chromosomes (that is, the pairs of X's lying on top of each other) moves to the center of the cell, pulled by the spindle fibers to form the arrangement called the metaphase plate. Remember that each pair of homologous chromosomes includes the maternal and paternal versions of the chromosome (with crossed-over segments) *and* the replicated copy of each—four strands in all.

3. Anaphase l: homologues are pulled to either side of the cell.

This phase is the beginning of the first cell division that occurs during meiosis. In anaphase, the homologues are pulled apart toward opposite poles of the cell. One of the homologues (consisting of two sister chromatids) goes to one pole, the other to the opposite pole. At this point, something else occurs that, along with crossing over, contributes to making all the products of meiosis genetically unique. The maternal and paternal sister chromatid pairs are pulled to the ends of the cell in a random fashion. As a result, the pairs of sister chromatids gathered at each pole are a mix of maternal and paternal sister chromatids.

Imagine all the different combinations that can occur in a species with 23 pairs of chromosomes. For chromosome pair 1, perhaps the maternal homologue goes to the "top" pole and the paternal to the "bottom" pole. And for pair 2, perhaps the maternal homologue also goes to the top and the paternal to the bottom. But maybe for pair 3 it is the paternal homologue that goes to the top and the maternal homologue to the bottom. For each of the 23 pairs, you cannot predict which will go to the top and which will go to the bottom. There is a *huge* number of possible combinations. (Can you figure out how many? Here's a hint: if there were 2 chromosome pairs, the answer would be 4; if there were 3 chromosome pairs, the answer would be 8.)

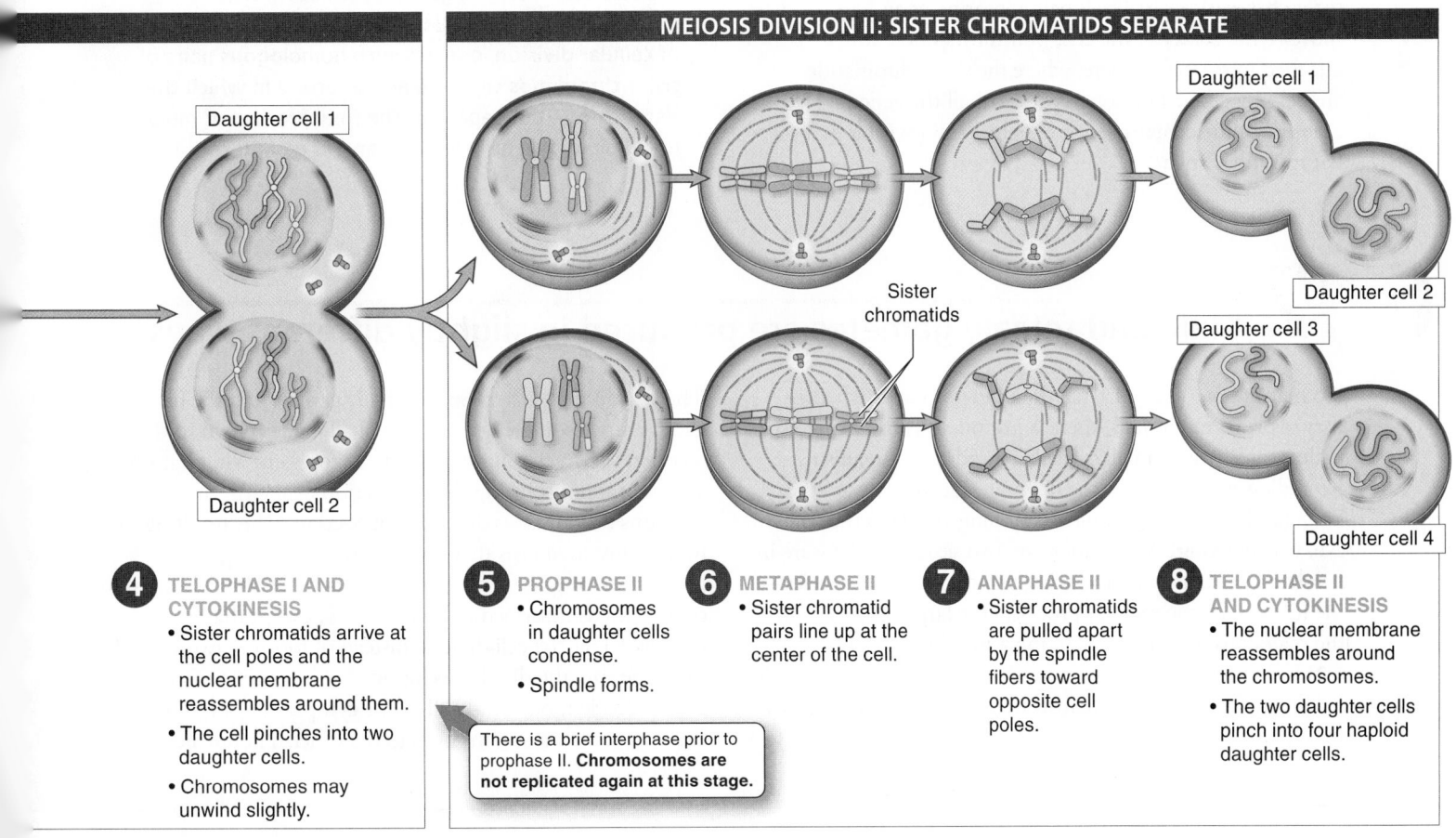

MEIOSIS DIVISION II: SISTER CHROMATIDS SEPARATE

Daughter cell 1

Daughter cell 2

Daughter cell 1

Daughter cell 2

Daughter cell 3

Daughter cell 4

Sister chromatids

4 TELOPHASE I AND CYTOKINESIS
- Sister chromatids arrive at the cell poles and the nuclear membrane reassembles around them.
- The cell pinches into two daughter cells.
- Chromosomes may unwind slightly.

There is a brief interphase prior to prophase II. **Chromosomes are not replicated again at this stage.**

5 PROPHASE II
- Chromosomes in daughter cells condense.
- Spindle forms.

6 METAPHASE II
- Sister chromatid pairs line up at the center of the cell.

7 ANAPHASE II
- Sister chromatids are pulled apart by the spindle fibers toward opposite cell poles.

8 TELOPHASE II AND CYTOKINESIS
- The nuclear membrane reassembles around the chromosomes.
- The two daughter cells pinch into four haploid daughter cells.

4. Telophase I and cytokinesis: nuclear membranes reassemble around sets of sister chromatid pairs, and two daughter cells form. After the pairs of chromatids arrive at the two poles of the cell, nuclear membranes re-form, then cytokinesis occurs: the cytoplasm divides, and the cell membrane pinches the cell into two daughter cells. Each daughter cell has its own nucleus that contains the genetic material—two sister chromatids for each of the 23 chromosomes in humans.

Meiosis division II: separating the sister chromatids

There is a brief interphase after the first division of meiosis. In some organisms, the DNA molecules (now in the form of chromatid pairs) briefly uncoil and fade from view. In others, the second part of meiosis begins immediately. *It is important to note that in the brief interphase before prophase II, there is no replication of any of the chromosomes.* The second part of meiosis, like the first division of meiosis, is a four-phase process.

5. Prophase II: chromosomes re-condense. The second division of meiosis begins with prophase II. In this phase, the genetic material in each of the two daughter cells once again coils tightly, making the pairs of chromatids visible under the microscope. (Unlike prophase I, no crossing over occurs during prophase II.)

6. Metaphase II: sister chromatid pairs line up at the center of the cell. In each of the two daughter cells, the sister chromatid pairs (each pair appearing as an X) move to the center of the cell, pulled by spindle fibers attached to the centromere, where the sister chromatids are held together. The congregation of all the genetic material in the center of each daughter cell is visible as a flat metaphase plate.

7. Anaphase II: sister chromatids are pulled to opposite sides of the cell. This phase starts with 46 pieces of DNA in each cell created by meiosis I: that is, 23 sister chromatid pairs. During this anaphase, the fibers attached to the centromere begin pulling each chromatid in the 23 sister chromatid pairs toward opposite poles of the daughter cell. When anaphase II is finished, each of what will become the four daughter cells (you could think of them as granddaughter cells!) has one single copy of each of the 23 chromosomes.

8. Telophase II and cytokinesis: nuclear membranes reassemble and the two daughter cells pinch into four haploid gametes. After the sister chromatids for all 23 chromosomes have been pulled to opposite poles, the cytoplasm then divides. The cell membrane pinches each cell into two new daughter cells, nuclear membranes begin to re-form, and the process comes to a close.

In humans, the outcome of one diploid cell undergoing meiosis is the creation of four haploid daughter cells, each with just one set of 23 individual chromosomes. These chromosomes contain a combination of traits from the individual's diploid set of chromosomes.

> ### TAKE-HOME MESSAGE 6·11
>
> Meiosis occurs only in gamete-producing cells. It is preceded by DNA replication and consists of two rounds of cellular division, one in which homologous pairs of sister chromatids separate and a second in which the sister chromatids separate. The final product of meiosis in a diploid organism is four haploid gametes.

6·12 Male and female gametes are produced in slightly different ways.

No matter how small or large they are, no matter whether they're plants or animals, there is just one way to distinguish males from females in all sexually reproducing organisms. Regardless of the species, the defining feature is always the same (and if you're thinking of anything visible to the naked eye, you're wrong). When there are two sexes—as there are in nearly every sexually reproducing plant and animal species—the females are the sex that produces the larger gamete, and the males produce the smaller, more motile, gamete (**FIGURE 6-21**). Because all gametes are produced through meiosis, it is a slight variation in how meiosis works in males and females that leads to this difference.

The size difference between the male gamete and the female gamete (sperm and eggs in animals) all comes down to the fact that sperm cells have very little cytoplasm, while eggs have a huge amount. During the production of sperm, the two divisions occur just as described in Section 6-11, resulting in four evenly sized cells that become sperm. During the production of eggs, things are a bit different. The first division occurs just as described in Section 6-11, except that in telophase I, as the cell divides, instead of forming two cells of the same size, the division is lopsided. The genetic material is evenly divided, but nearly all of the cytoplasm goes to one of the cells and almost none goes to the other. The smaller cell is

> The definition of male vs. female is always the same: females produce the larger gamete, males produce the smaller, more motile gamete.

FIGURE 6-21 **Egg and sperm.** In sexually reproducing organisms, the female produces the larger gamete.

called a **polar body** and degrades almost immediately in most animal cells (although it sometimes goes through with a second division, after which, in most animal cells, both of those polar bodies degrade; we see in Chapter 18 that polar bodies have some function in producing nutritive tissue for the developing embryo in flowering plants). Then, in the second meiotic division of the larger cell, there is again an unequal division of cytoplasm.

As in the first division, one of the new cells gets nearly all of the cytoplasm and the other gets almost none, forming another polar body. The net result of meiosis in the production of eggs is one large egg with lots of cytoplasm and two or three small polar bodies with very little cytoplasm that degrade and never function as gametes (**FIGURE 6-22**).

Ultimately, whether eggs or sperm are produced, each gamete ends up with just one copy of each chromosome. That way, the fertilized egg that results from the fusion of sperm and egg carries two complete sets of chromosomes, so the developing individual will be diploid. The extra cytoplasm carried by the egg contains a large supply of nutrients and other chemical resources to help with the initial development of the organism following fertilization.

TAKE-HOME MESSAGE 6·12

In species with two sexes—including nearly every sexually reproducing plant and animal species—females are the sex that produces the larger gamete, and males produce the smaller gamete. Whether it is male or female gametes that are being produced, each gamete ends up with just one copy of each chromosome.

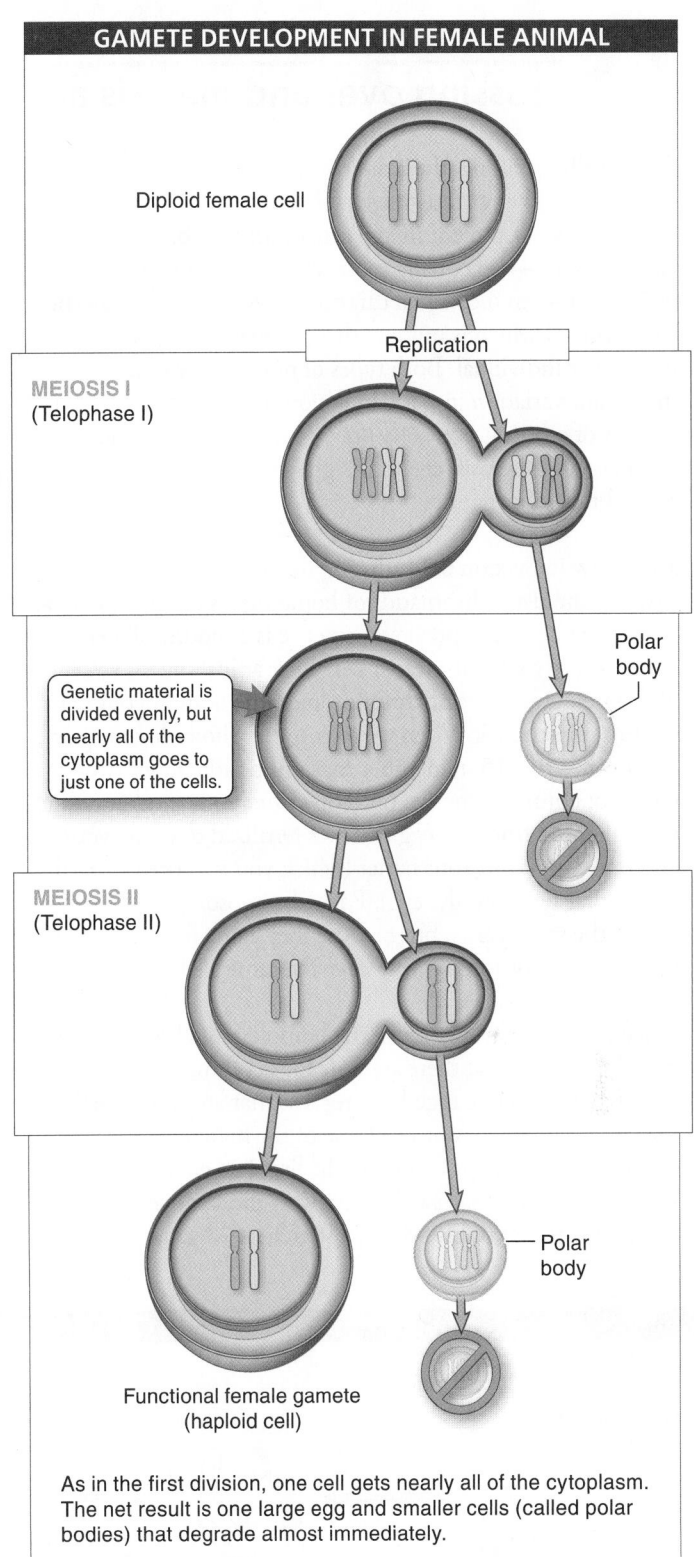

GAMETE DEVELOPMENT IN FEMALE ANIMAL

Diploid female cell

Replication

MEIOSIS I
(Telophase I)

Polar body

Genetic material is divided evenly, but nearly all of the cytoplasm goes to just one of the cells.

MEIOSIS II
(Telophase II)

Polar body

Functional female gamete
(haploid cell)

As in the first division, one cell gets nearly all of the cytoplasm. The net result is one large egg and smaller cells (called polar bodies) that degrade almost immediately.

FIGURE 6-22 **Unequal distribution of cytoplasm results in one large egg.**

6·13

Crossing over and meiosis are important sources of variation.

Genetically speaking, there are two ways to create unique individuals. The obvious way is for an organism to carry an allele that is not present in any other individuals. Alternatively—and equally successful in creating uniqueness—an individual can carry a *collection* of alleles, no single one of which is unique, that has never before occurred in another individual. Both types of novelty introduce important variation into a population of organisms. The process of crossing over (FIGURE 6-23), which occurs during prophase I in meiosis, creates a significant amount of the second type of variation.

As we saw in Section 6-11, during the first prophase of meiosis, the sister chromatids of homologous chromosomes all come together. That previous sentence is a mouthful! Let's review exactly what it means. Let's look at just one of your 23 homologous pairs of chromosomes, the homologous pair of chromosome 15. When we refer to the "homologous pair" of chromosome 15, remember that this pair includes two copies of chromosome 15: one copy from your mother (which you inherited from the egg that was fertilized to create you) and one copy from your father (which you inherited from the sperm that fertilized the egg). Each chromosome in the pair carries the same genes, but because they came from different people, they don't necessarily have the same alleles.

Once the sister chromatids of the homologous chromosome pairs line up (so that there are now four chromatids in two pairs lying very close together), regions that are close together can swap segments. A piece of one of the maternal chromatids—perhaps including the first 100 genes on the strand of DNA—may swap places with the same segment in a paternal chromatid. Elsewhere, a stretch of 20 genes in the middle may be swapped from the other maternal chromatid with one of the paternal chromatids. Every time a swap of DNA segments occurs, an identical amount of genetic material is exchanged, so all four chromatids still contain the complete set of genes that make up the chromosome. The *combination* of alleles on each chromatid, though, is now different.

Suppose there are genes relating to eye color, hair color, and height on a particular chromosome. After crossing over, the linear strands still have instructions for all of those traits. But whereas one chromatid previously may have had instructions for brown eyes, brown hair, and short height, it may now have some differences—perhaps brown eyes, blond hair, and tall height. All of the alleles from your parents are still carried on one DNA molecule or another. But the *combination of traits* that are linked together on a single chromatid is new. And when a gamete, let's say it's an egg, carrying a new combination of alleles is fertilized by a sperm, the developing individual will carry a completely novel set of alleles. And so without creating new versions of any traits (such as yellow eyes or purple hair), crossing over still creates gametes with collections of alleles that may never have existed together. In Chapter 8, we'll see that this variation is tremendously important for evolution.

> ### TAKE-HOME MESSAGE 6·13
>
> Although it doesn't create new versions of any traits, crossing over during the first prophase of meiosis creates gametes with combinations of traits that may never have existed before; this variation is important for evolution.

CROSSING OVER

HOMOLOGOUS CHROMOSOMES

Sister chromatids

Maternal copy   Paternal copy

Crossing over between the sister chromatids of the homologous chromosomes

Homologous chromosomes after the exchange of genetic information

Each of these 4 chromatids gets packaged into a haploid gamete (sperm or egg cell).

Chromatids with recombined DNA

Crossing over doesn't create new alleles but it does create new combinations of alleles on a chromatid.

FIGURE 6-23 **Swapping DNA.** Crossing over creates new combinations of alleles on each chromatid.

6·14

What are the costs and benefits of sexual reproduction?

As we've seen, there are two fundamentally different ways by which cells and organisms can reproduce. On the one hand there is mitosis and asexual reproduction via binary fission; on the other hand, meiosis and sexual reproduction. Is one method better than the other? It depends. In fact, the more appropriate question is, what are the advantages and disadvantages of each method and under what conditions do the benefits outweigh the costs?

What are the advantages of sexual reproduction?

Sexual reproduction leads to offspring that are genetically different from one another and from either parent, through three different routes (**FIGURE 6-24**).

1. **Combining alleles from two parents at fertilization.** First and foremost, with sexual reproduction, a new individual comes from the fusion of gametes from two different individuals. Each of these parents comes with his or her own unique set of genetic material.

2. **Crossing over during the production of gametes.** As we saw, crossing over during prophase I of meiosis causes every chromosome in a gamete to carry a mixture of an individual's maternal and paternal genetic material.

3. **Shuffling and reassortment of homologues during meiosis.** Recall that as the homologues for each chromosome are pulled to opposite poles of the cell during the first division of meiosis, maternal and paternal homologues are randomly pulled to each pole. This means that there is an extremely large number of different combinations of maternal and paternal homologues that could end up in each gamete.

Q *Bacteria reproduce asexually, whereas most plants and animals reproduce sexually. Which is the better method?*

The variability among the offspring produced by sexual reproduction enables populations of organisms to cope better with changes in their environment. After all, if the environment is gradually changing from one generation to the next, individuals producing many genetically different offspring increase the likelihood that one of their offspring will carry a set of genes particularly suited to the new environment. Over time, populations of sexually reproducing organisms can quickly adapt to changing environments. It's like buying different lottery tickets—the more tickets you buy, the more likely it is that one of them will be a winner.

SOURCES OF GENETIC VARIATION

There are multiple reasons why offspring are genetically different from their parents and one another.

ALLELES COME FROM TWO PARENTS
Each parent donates his or her own set of genetic material.

CROSSING OVER
Crossing over during meiosis produces a mixture of maternal and paternal genetic material on each chromatid.

REASSORTMENT OF HOMOLOGUES
The homologues and sister chromatids distributed to each daughter cell during meiosis are a random mix of maternal and paternal genetic material.

FIGURE 6-24 Crossing over and meiosis: creating many different combinations of alleles. As a result of crossing over and meiosis, each individual developing from a separate fertilized egg is genetically unique.

What are the disadvantages of sexual reproduction?
In the yellow dung fly (*Scathophaga stercoraria*), males sometimes wrestle each other for mating access to a female. The female awaits the outcome of the battle in a pile of dung. Occasionally, females drown in the dung pile as they wait. Males, too, can be at risk during

reproduction. This is seen most dramatically in species such as praying mantises and black widow spiders in which the female will attempt to eat the male (and often succeed in doing so) during or after mating, gaining not just gametes but a nutritious meal as well (**FIGURE 6-25**)!

Dangers associated with mating are just one of the downsides to sexual reproduction. There are several others. First, when an individual reproduces, only half of its offsprings' alleles will come from that organism. The other half will come from the other parent. With asexual reproduction, an individual produces nearly identical offspring, so there is a very efficient transfer of genetic information from one generation to the next. Also, with sexual reproduction it takes time and energy to find a partner. This is energy that asexual organisms can devote to additional reproduction. Moreover, as we see with the dung flies, sex can be a risky proposition because organisms make themselves vulnerable to predation, disease, and other calamities during mating and reproduction. And finally, as we'll see later in this chapter, the complex cellular division required for sexual reproduction offers opportunities for mistakes, sometimes leading to chromosomal disorders.

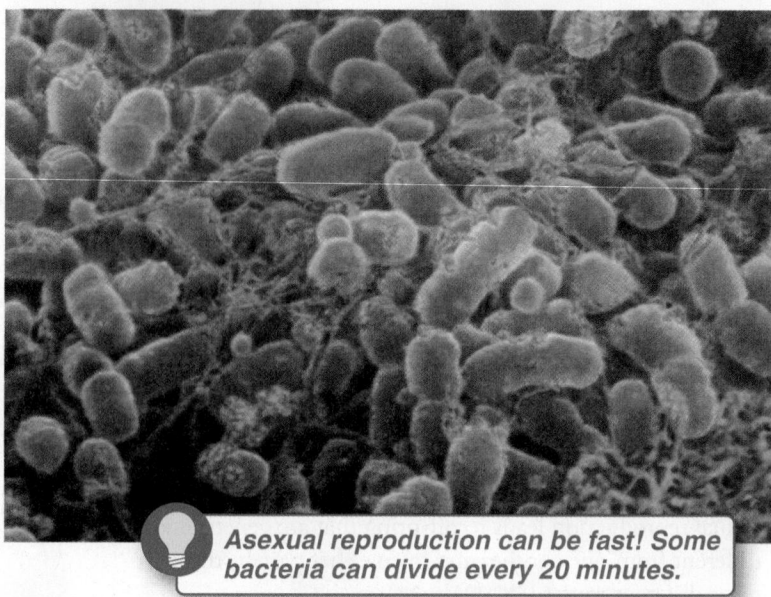

Asexual reproduction can be fast! Some bacteria can divide every 20 minutes.

FIGURE 6-26 Pluses and minuses. This asexually reproducing bacterial colony can reproduce quickly and efficiently, but because each new cell's genome is an exact duplicate of the parent genome, there is no genetic variety to enable adaptation should the environment change.

beneficial for organisms to produce offspring as similar to themselves as possible.

What are the disadvantages of asexual reproduction?
The downside to asexual reproduction is that the more closely an offspring's genome resembles its parent's, the less likely it is that the offspring will be suited to the environment when it changes.

In the end, we still see large numbers of species using asexual reproduction and large numbers, including the vast majority of animals and plants, that reproduce sexually. It seems that conditions favoring each occur in the great diversity of habitats in the world. That we see both sexual and asexual reproduction also highlights the recurring theme in biology that there often is more than one way to solve a problem.

FIGURE 6-25 Sexual reproduction has its risks. Female black widow spiders attempt to eat the male during or after mating.

What are the advantages of asexual reproduction?
With asexual reproduction, the advantages and disadvantages are more or less reversed. Because asexual reproduction involves only a single individual, it can be fast and easy. Some bacteria can divide, forming a new generation, every 20 minutes (**FIGURE 6-26**). And for organisms in isolated habitats or when establishing new populations, asexual reproduction can be advantageous as well. Asexual reproduction is efficient, too. Offspring carry all of the genes that their parent carried—they are genetically identical. If the environment is stable, it is

TAKE-HOME MESSAGE 6·14

There are two fundamentally different ways that cells and organisms can reproduce: (1) mitosis and asexual reproduction via binary fission, and (2) meiosis and sexual reproduction. Asexual reproduction can be fast and efficient, but leads to genetically identical offspring that carry all of the genes that their parent carried, which could be disadvantageous in a changing environment. Sexual reproduction leads to offspring that are genetically different from one another and from either parent, but takes more time and energy and can be risky.

6·15–6·16 There are sex differences in the chromosomes.

XX and XY: only one of the 23 chromosome pairs determines sex in humans.

6·15

How is sex determined in humans?

Q

Which parent determines a baby's sex? Why?

In humans, the sex of a baby is determined by its father. The sequence of events involved in sex determination is instigated by one special pair of chromosomes, the sex chromosomes, which carry information that directs a growing fetus to develop as a male or as a female.

Let's take a closer look at the human sex chromosomes. We noted that there are 23 pairs of chromosomes in every somatic cell. These can be divided into two different types: 1 pair of sex chromosomes and 22 pairs of non-sex chromosomes. The human sex chromosomes are called the **X and Y chromosomes** (**FIGURE 6-27**).

How do the X and Y chromosomes differ from the other chromosomes? As we described earlier, all of the genetic information is stored on the chromosomes in all the cells of an organism's body. But most of this information is not sex specific—that is, if you are building an eye or a neuron or a skin cell or a digestive enzyme, it doesn't matter whether it is for a male or for a female; the instructions are the same for both sexes. Some genetic information, however, instructs the body to develop into one sex or the other. That information is found on the sex chromosomes.

FIGURE 6-27 X and Y: the human sex chromosomes. (The X chromosome is on the left.)

An individual has two copies of all the non-sex chromosomes. One copy is inherited from the mother, one from the father. Individuals also have two copies of the sex chromosomes, but not always two copies of the same kind. Males have one copy of the X chromosome and one copy of the Y chromosome. Females, on the other hand, don't have a Y chromosome but instead have two copies of the X chromosome.

So how does the father determine the sex of the baby? During meiosis in females, the gametes that are produced carry only one copy of each chromosome. This is true for the sex chromosomes, too. So from the two copies of the X chromosome carried by females, half of the gametes end up with a copy of one of those X chromosomes while the rest of the gametes inherit the other X chromosome. Thus, every egg has an X for its one sex chromosome. During meiosis in males, the sperm that are produced also carry one copy of each chromosome, including the sex chromosomes, but in this case, half of the sperm produced inherit the X chromosome and the other half inherit the Y chromosome. At fertilization, an egg bearing a single X chromosome (and one copy of all the non-sex chromosomes) is fertilized by a sperm bearing one copy of all the non-sex chromosomes and *either* an X chromosome or a Y chromosome. When the sperm carries an X, the baby will have two X chromosomes and will develop as a female. When the sperm carries a Y, the baby will have an X and a Y and so will develop as a male (**FIGURE 6-28**).

Q **We know that no genetic information on the Y chromosome is essential for producing a normally functioning human. Why?**

Given the distribution of X and Y chromosomes into males and females, it must be true that no essential genetic information is carried on the Y chromosome. Why? Because females don't have a Y chromosome in any of their cells, yet they are able to develop and live normal, healthy lives. For this reason, we know that nothing on the Y chromosome is absolutely necessary for the development of a normally functioning human.

Physically, the X and Y chromosomes look very different from each other. The X chromosome is relatively large and carries a great deal of genetic information relating to a large number of non-sex-related traits. The Y chromosome is tiny and carries genetic information about only a very small number of traits. The genetic instructions on the Y chromosome instruct the fetal gonads to develop as testes rather than ovaries. Once this is done, very little additional genetic input from the Y chromosome is necessary. Instead, the hormones produced by the testes or ovaries generally direct the rest of the body to develop as a male or female.

HOW SEX IS DETERMINED IN HUMANS

Individuals have two copies of the sex chromosomes in every cell.

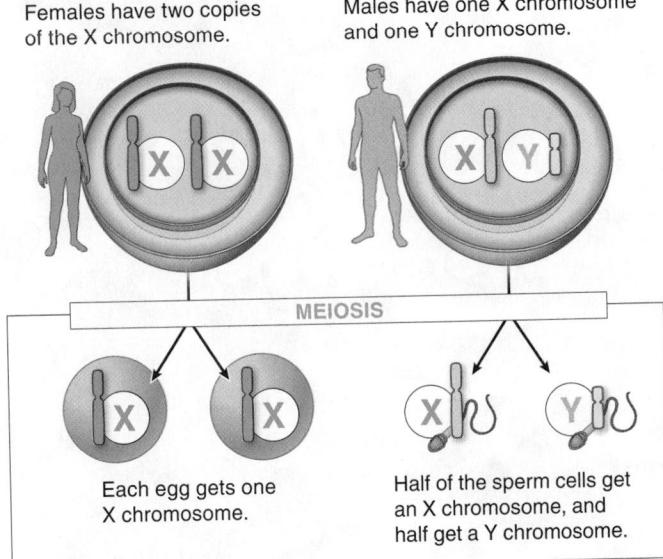

Females have two copies of the X chromosome.

Males have one X chromosome and one Y chromosome.

MEIOSIS

Each egg gets one X chromosome.

Half of the sperm cells get an X chromosome, and half get a Y chromosome.

FERTILIZATION

When the sperm carries an X, the baby will have two X chromosomes and develop as female.

When the sperm carries a Y, the baby will have an X and a Y and develop as male.

FIGURE 6-28 Sex determination in humans. The sex of offspring is determined by the father.

In the next sections we investigate some of the ramifications of males having two different sex chromosomes and look at some of the systems for sex determination that have evolved in other groups of organisms.

TAKE-HOME MESSAGE 6·15

In humans, the sex chromosomes carry information that directs a growing fetus to develop as either a male (if a Y chromosome is present) or a female (if no Y chromosome is present). Sex determination depends on the sex chromosome inherited from the father.

6·16 The sex of offspring is determined in a variety of ways in non-human species.

For something as fundamental to a species as sex determination, you might imagine that one method evolved and all species use it. The world is more diverse than that. In most plants there aren't even distinct males and females. In corn, for example, every individual produces both male and female gametes. All earthworms and garden snails are also capable of producing both male and female gametes. Such organisms are called **hermaphrodites,** because male and female gametes are produced by a single individual. But even among the species with separate males and females there are several different methods of sex determination. The human method, in which having both an X and a Y chromosome makes you male and having two X chromosomes makes you female, is common among eukaryotes and is seen in all mammals. But at least three other methods are used by organisms for determining sex (FIGURE 6-29).

Birds In birds (as well as in some fish and butterfly species), the mother determines the sex in much the same way that fathers determine sex in humans. Females have one copy of two different sex chromosomes, called the Z and the W chromosomes, while males have only one type, carrying two copies of the Z chromosome. Consequently, the sex of bird offspring is determined by the mother rather than the father.

Ants, bees, and wasps In these insects, sex is determined by the number of chromosome sets an individual possesses. Males are haploid, having a *single* set of chromosomes, and females are diploid, carrying two sets of chromosomes. In this method, females produce haploid eggs by meiosis. They mate with males and store the sperm in a sac. As each egg is produced, the female can fertilize it with sperm she has stored, in which case the offspring will be diploid and female. Alternatively, she can lay the unfertilized egg, which develops into a haploid, male individual. Just think, in these species, males don't have a father, yet they do have a grandfather!

Turtles In some species, sex determination is controlled by the environment rather than by the number or types of chromosomes an organism has. In most turtles, for example, offspring's sex is determined by the temperature at which the eggs are kept. Eggs kept relatively hot during incubation become females, while eggs incubated at cooler temperatures become males. The sex of some lizards and crocodiles is also determined this way.

TAKE-HOME MESSAGE 6·16

A variety of methods are used for sex determination across the world of plant and animal species. These include the presence or absence of sex chromosomes, the number of chromosome sets, and environmental factors such as incubation temperature.

SEX DETERMINATION IN VARIOUS OTHER SPECIES

BIRDS
In birds, the mother determines the sex in a way that is similar to how fathers determine sex in humans.

FEMALE   MALE

ANTS, BEES, AND WASPS
In ants, bees, and wasps, sex is determined by the number of chromosome sets an individual possesses.

FEMALE   MALE

TURTLES
In most turtles, sex is determined by the temperature at which the eggs are incubated.

FEMALE   MALE

FIGURE 6-29 **Other methods of sex determination.** In some species, sex is determined by the type of chromosomes, the number of chromosomes, or incubation temperature of the eggs.

6·17–6·18 Deviations from the normal chromosome number lead to problems.

Karyotype displaying the chromosome pairs of a normal human female.

6·17 Down syndrome can be detected before birth: karyotypes reveal an individual's entire chromosome set.

Reproduction becomes riskier for women as they become older. Increasingly, their gametes contain incorrect numbers of chromosomes or chromosomes that have been damaged (**FIGURE 6-30**). These problems can lead to effects on the offspring that range from minor to fatal.

To find out whether their offspring may have a disorder associated with incorrect numbers of chromosomes, parents can request a quick test for some common genetic problems even before their baby is born. This information is available from an analysis of an individual's **karyotype,** a visual display of a complete set of chromosomes. A karyotype can be made for adults or children, but it is most commonly done for a fetus. A karyotype is a useful diagnostic tool because it can be prepared very early in the fetus's development to assess whether there is an abnormality in the number of chromosomes or in their structure. And because it shows all of the chromosomes, even the sex chromosomes, it also reveals the sex of the fetus.

Preparing a karyotype takes five steps. (1) First it is necessary to obtain some cells from the individual. (2) The cells are then encouraged to divide by culturing them in a test tube with nutrients. (3) After a few days to two weeks of cell

DOWN SYNDROME AND MOTHER'S AGE

Incidence of Down syndrome per 1,000 live births (y-axis: 0, 5, 10, 15, 20, 25)
Age of mother (x-axis: 20, 25, 30, 35, 40, 45)

GRAPHIC CONTENT!
Thinking critically about visual displays of data.
Turn to p. 256 for a closer inspection of this figure.

FIGURE 6-30 Reproduction risks and maternal age. Down syndrome incidence increases as the age of the mother increases.

division, the cells are treated with a chemical that stops them exactly midway through cell division—a time when the chromosomes are coiled thickly and more visible than usual. (4) The cells are then placed on a microscope slide and a

FIGURE 6-31 A human karyotype. A visual display of a complete set of chromosomes.

stain is added that binds to the chromosomes, making them more easily visible. (5) And finally, the chromosomes are arranged by size and shape and displayed on a monitor or in a photograph (**FIGURE 6-31**).

The first step—obtaining cells to prepare the karyotype—is relatively easy in an adult or child. Usually cells are collected from a small blood sample. Collecting cells from a fetus, on the other hand, poses a special problem. Two different methods for collecting cells have been developed.

1. Amniocentesis. This procedure can be done approximately three to four months into a pregnancy (**FIGURE 6-32**). In one quick motion (and without the use

FIGURE 6-32 Amniocentesis. Fluid surrounding a fetus (containing some of its cells) is extracted and analyzed to determine the genetic composition of the developing fetus.

FIGURE 6-33 Trisomy 21. An extra copy of chromosome 21 causes Down syndrome.

of anesthetic), a 3- to 4-inch needle is pushed through the abdomen, through the amniotic sac, and into the amniotic fluid that surrounds and protects the fetus. Using ultrasound for guidance, the doctor aims for a small pocket of fluid as far as possible from the fetus and withdraws about 2 tablespoons of fluid. This fluid contains many cells from the fetus, which can then be used for karyotype analysis. Any chromosomal abnormalities in the fetus will be present in these cells.

2. Chorionic villus sampling (CVS). In this procedure, rather than sampling cells from the amniotic fluid, a small bit of tissue is removed from the **placenta,** the temporary organ that allows the transfer of gases, nutrients, and waste products between a mother and fetus. A needle is inserted either through the abdomen or through the vagina and cervix, again using ultrasound for guidance. Then a small piece of the finger-like projections from the placenta is removed via the syringe. Because the fetus and placenta both develop from the same fertilized egg, their cells have the same genetic composition. The chief advantage of CVS over amniocentesis is that it can be done several weeks earlier in the pregnancy, usually between the 10th and 12th weeks.

The resulting karyotype, whether from amniocentesis or CVS, will reveal whether the fetus carries an extra copy of any of the chromosomes or lacks a copy of one or more chromosomes. Of all the chromosomal disorders detected by karyotyping, Down syndrome is the most commonly observed. Named after John Langdon Down, the doctor who first described it, in 1866, the syndrome is revealed by the presence of an extra

copy of chromosome 21 (**FIGURE 6-33**). (For this reason, the condition that causes Down syndrome is also called "trisomy 21.") Striking about 1 of every 1,000 children born, Down syndrome is characterized by a suite of physical and mental characteristics that includes learning disabilities, a flat facial profile, heart defects, and increased susceptibility to respiratory difficulties.

Down syndrome and other disorders caused by a missing chromosome or an extra copy of a chromosome are a consequence of **nondisjunction,** the unequal distribution of chromosomes during meiosis. Nondisjunction can occur at two different points in meiosis: homologues can fail to separate during meiosis I, or sister chromatids can fail to separate during meiosis II (**FIGURE 6-34**). In both cases, nondisjunction results in an egg or sperm with zero or two copies of a chromosome rather than a single copy. Any of the chromosomes can fail to separate during cell division, but the ramifications of trisomy (having an extra copy of one chromosome in every cell) are greater for chromosomes with larger numbers of genes. When trisomy occurs for chromosomes with greater numbers of genes, the likelihood that the developing embryo will survive to birth is reduced. Consequently, we tend to see cases of trisomy that involve only the chromosomes with the fewest genes, such as chromosomes 13, 15, 18, 21, and 22. In fact, observations show that trisomy 1 is never seen (all such fertilized eggs die before implantation in the uterus), trisomy 13 occurs in 1 in 20,000 newborns (and most die soon after birth), while trisomy 21, as we've seen, occurs in 1 in 1,000 newborns (many of whom live long lives).

Nondisjunction is the unequal distribution of chromosomes during meiosis. The resulting gametes have zero or two copies of a chromosome, rather than a single copy.

METAPHASE I — Homologues

ANAPHASE I — Homologues do not separate.

METAPHASE II

RESULTING GAMETES

Both gametes are missing a chromosome.

Both gametes have an extra chromosome.

FIGURE 6-34 An error during meiosis produces gametes with too many or too few chromosomes.

As we mentioned at the beginning of this section, as women become older there are increased problems associated with reproduction. Older women, for example, have more babies with Down syndrome. Why does the risk of having a baby with Down syndrome or some other disorder that results from trisomy increase with increasing age for women but significantly less so for men? As women age, their gametes tend to have more errors. The problem is that those eggs began meiosis near the time the woman was born, and they may not complete it until she is 40 or more years old. During those decades, the cells may accumulate defects that interfere with normal cell division. In men, the cells that undergo meiosis are relatively young because new sperm-producing cells are produced every couple of weeks after puberty.

Whereas lacking a non-sex chromosome or having an extra chromosome usually has serious consequences for health, we'll see in the next section that lacking or having an extra X or Y chromosome has consequences that are much less severe.

Q Why do older women have more babies with Down syndrome?

TAKE-HOME MESSAGE 6·17

A karyotype is a visual display of a complete set of chromosomes. It is a useful diagnostic tool because it can be prepared early in a fetus's development to assess whether there is an abnormality in the number of chromosomes or in their structure, such as in Down syndrome. Down syndrome is caused by having an extra copy of chromosome 21.

6·18

Life is possible with too many or too few sex chromosomes.

It is usually fatal to have one too many or one too few of the non-sex chromosomes. When it comes to the sex chromosomes, however, the situation is less extreme. Many individuals are born lacking one of the sex chromosomes or with an additional X or Y chromosome, and they usually survive. We can get a glimpse into the role of the sex chromosomes by looking at the physical and mental consequences of having an abnormal number of sex chromosomes. In each of the cases below, the condition is caused by nondisjunction of the sex chromosomes during the production of sperm or eggs (**FIGURE 6-35**).

Turner syndrome: X Approximately 1 in 5,000 females carry only one X chromosome (and no Y chromosome), exhibiting a condition called Turner syndrome, denoted as X_ (or sometimes XO). This is the only condition in humans in which a person can survive without one of a pair of chromosomes. Instead of having 46 chromosomes in every cell, these individuals have only 45. As common as Turner syndrome is, in 98% of the fertilized eggs in which this condition occurs, the egg is spontaneously aborted long before a fetus can come to term.

There are both physical and mental consequences of the absence of a second sex chromosome.

- Women with Turner syndrome are usually relatively short, averaging 4 feet 8 inches in height.
- They develop a web of skin between the neck and shoulders.
- The ovaries never fully mature, so the women are almost always sterile.
- The breasts and other secondary sex characteristics develop incompletely.
- Intelligence is usually normal, but some learning difficulties are common.

Klinefelter syndrome: XXY An individual who has two X chromosomes is female; an individual with an X and a Y is male. But what happens when both of those conditions are true? An individual who carries two X chromosomes and a Y chromosome, a condition known as Klinefelter syndrome, develops as male. This is because, as we saw earlier, the Y chromosome carries genetic

Q *If a person has two X chromosomes but also has a Y chromosome, is the individual male or female?*

instructions that cause fetal gonads to develop as testes; if these instructions are absent, the fetal gonads develop as ovaries. The extra X chromosome, however, does cause Klinefelter males to be somewhat feminized, although this effect can be reduced through treatments such as testosterone supplementation. Approximately 1 in 1,000 males have the genotype XXY, making this one of the most common genetic abnormalities in humans.

TOO MANY OR TOO FEW SEX CHROMOSOMES

FIGURE 6-35 Characteristics of individuals with too many or too few sex chromosomes.

Klinefelter syndrome has some physical and mental consequences:

- Men with this syndrome have testes, but they are smaller than average. Because the testes are small, levels of testosterone are low and the men are almost always infertile.

- They develop some female features, including reduced facial and chest hair and some breast development.

- They have long limbs and are slightly taller than average (about 6 feet on average).

- They learn to speak at a later age than average and tend to have language impairments.

- Some individuals have further additional X chromosomes, exhibiting the karyotypes XXXY or even XXXXY. These males also exhibit Klinefelter syndrome but more frequently have mental retardation.

Q Do human hermaphrodites exist?

A hermaphrodite is an individual with functioning male and female reproductive organs capable of producing both male and female gametes. Often it is mistakenly assumed that a person with Klinefelter syndrome must be a hermaphrodite because he has both two X chromosomes (which would usually make an individual a female) and an X and a Y chromosome (usually making the individual a male). Although hermaphroditism is common among invertebrates and occurs in some fish and other vertebrates, contrary to urban legends, human hermaphrodites do not exist. Some men with Klinefelter syndrome may have some features of the opposite sex; however, they do not produce female gametes and so are not hermaphrodites.

XYY males There is no official name for the condition in which an individual has one X chromosome and two Y chromosomes, although such individuals are sometimes referred to as "super males." This chromosomal abnormality occurs in approximately 1 in 1,000 males (and in about 1 in 325 males who are 6 feet or taller). There are no distinguishing features at birth to indicate that an individual carries an extra Y chromosome, and the vast majority live their lives normally without knowing they have an extra chromosome in every cell.

Several consequences of the XYY condition have been well documented:

- XYY males are relatively tall (about 6 feet 2 inches on average).

- They tend to have moderate to severe acne.

- Their intelligence usually falls within the same range as that of XY males, although the average may be slightly lower.

Because, in the United States, about 3 to 5 times as many XYY males are found in prisons as in the population as a whole, there has been tremendous controversy over whether the extra Y chromosome predisposes individuals to criminal behavior. These observations were not part of randomized, controlled, double-blind experiments, however, so they are open to numerous alternative interpretations.

In one study, for example, researchers identified all male Danish citizens born in Copenhagen between 1944 and 1947, and obtained sex chromosome determinations for the 4,139 of these men who were taller than 6' 0.4" (184 cm). From this sample, they found that the level of intellectual functioning (as indicated by scores on an army selection test taken by the men) was significantly lower among the XYY males as compared to XY males. Based on this finding, they suggested that the increased representation of XYY males in prison may be more likely due to the fact that males of lower intelligence are more likely to be apprehended, regardless of which chromosomes they carry. The controversy remains unresolved, and the vast majority of XYY males are not in prison.

Although an error during meiosis in either the father or the mother can cause Klinefelter or Turner syndrome, it is only an error in meiosis in a male that can give rise to an XYY child. Why? Because only males carry Y chromosomes. Consequently, an XYY child must receive both of his Y chromosomes from his father. This means that the father's sperm cell must have contained two copies of the Y, a result of nondisjunction during meiosis in the father.

XXX females Sometimes called "metafemales," individuals with three X chromosomes occur at a frequency of about 1 in 1,000 women. Very few studies of this condition have been completed, although initial observations suggest that some XXX females are sterile but otherwise have no obvious physical or mental problems.

TAKE-HOME MESSAGE 6·18

Although it is usually fatal to have one too many or one too few of the non-sex chromosomes, individuals born with only a single sex chromosome that is an X, or with an additional X or Y chromosome, usually survive—though often with physical and/or mental problems.

CAN YOU SELECT THE SEX OF YOUR BABY?
(Would you want to?)

Some fertility clinics now promise that for as little as $200 they can help a couple choose the sex of their baby.

Q: GIVEN OUR KNOWLEDGE OF THE BEHAVIOR OF THE X AND Y CHROMOSOMES, IS IT MORE LIKELY THAT THESE SEX-SELECTION TECHNIQUES INVOLVE MANIPULATIONS OF SPERM OR OF EGGS? WHY? Because all eggs have X chromosomes, the X chromosome doesn't play a role in determining the sex of a baby. Instead, the fertility clinics must somehow sort and separate sperm cells based on whether they carry an X or a Y chromosome (men produce approximately equal numbers of each).

Q: WHAT FEATURE OF SPERM MUST BE USED IN SEPARATING THEM? This process must be based on a way of distinguishing between sperm carrying an X chromosome and sperm carrying a Y chromosome. After the two types of sperm are distinguished, they must then be separated. Sperm with the desired sex chromosome are then used to fertilize the woman's egg (which may be done within her body, using artificial insemination, or in a Petri dish, after which a fertilized embryo is transferred into the woman's reproductive tract).

Q: WHAT TECHNIQUES MIGHT MAKE IT POSSIBLE TO SEPARATE SPERM WITH AN X CHROMOSOME FROM THOSE WITH A Y CHROMOSOME? One method involves determining, by weighing sperm, which cells have more DNA. The heavier sperm must be carrying the X rather than the Y chromosome because the X is so much larger. Another method is to add a fluorescent dye to sperm that temporarily attaches to DNA. Because sperm with an X chromosome have more DNA, more of the dye attaches to them and they are more fluorescent. A machine then sorts the sperm one by one, and at ovulation, insemination is performed using the sperm with the desired sex chromosome.

Q: DOES IT WORK? The technique is still fairly new, but initial results suggest that the procedures have a success rate of 70% to 90%.

CONCERNS FOR YOU TO PONDER. What are the ethical concerns raised by selecting the sex of one's baby? Are there some circumstances in which such a selection would be more acceptable than in others? Would it be acceptable to select for a baby with one eye color versus another? Why would that process be more difficult than selecting for sex?

Big Ideas in ...
Chromosomes and Cell Division

6·1–6·5 There are different types of cell division.

- In eukaryotic cells, a protective section of DNA called the telomere, at each end of every chromosome, plays a role in keeping track of cell division, getting shorter every time the cell divides. If telomeres become too short, additional cell divisions cause the loss of essential DNA and cell death. Cells that rebuild their telomeres with each division can become cancerous.

- In most prokaryotes, genetic information is carried in a single, circular DNA strand (chromosome). Eukaryotes have much more DNA, organized into linear chromosomes in the nucleus.

- Bacteria divide by a type of asexual reproduction called binary fission.

- In the cell cycle, eukaryotic somatic cells alternate between division, called the mitotic phase, and other cell activities, called interphase, which consists of two gap phases separated by a DNA synthesis phase.

- Every time a cell divides, its DNA must first replicate so that each of the two new cells has all the genetic material of the parent cell.

6·6–6·9 Mitosis replaces worn-out old cells with fresh new duplicates.

- In mitosis, cells generate new, genetically identical cells, enabling organisms to grow and replace cells.

- Mitosis occurs in four steps, following replication of the chromosomes, to produce two genetically identical daughter cells from one parent cell.

- Cancer is unrestrained cell growth and division, leading to large masses of cells (tumors). Treatment focuses on killing or slowing down cell growth and division.

6·10–6·14 Meiosis generates sperm and eggs and a great deal of variation.

- Meiosis occurs only in gamete-producing cells of sexually reproducing organisms.

- Gametes have only half as much genetic material as the parent cell, and differ from one another in the allele combinations they carry.

- Meiosis is preceded by DNA replication and consists of two rounds of cell division: separation of homologous pairs of sister chromatids, then separation of the sister chromatids. The final product in a diploid organism are haploid gametes.

- In species with two sexes, the female is the sex producing the larger gamete, while males produce the smaller gamete.

- Crossing over during the first prophase of meiosis creates gametes with new collections of alleles which may never have existed together; this variation is important for evolution.

- Cells and organisms can reproduce by mitosis and asexual reproduction via binary fission or by meiosis and sexual reproduction.

6·15–6·16 There are sex differences in the chromosomes.

- In humans, the sex chromosomes carry information that directs a fetus to develop as male (if a Y chromosome is present) or female (no Y present). The sex is determined by the sex chromosome inherited from the father.

- Several methods for sex determination occur in plant and animal species.

6·17–6·18 Deviations from the normal chromosome number lead to problems.

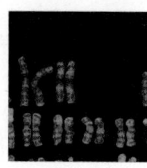

- A karyotype is a display of a complete set of chromosomes. It can be prepared very early in fetal development to detect abnormalities in the chromosome number or structure.

- Having one too many or one too few non-sex chromosomes is usually fatal, but individuals born with a single sex chromosome that is an X, or with an additional X or Y, usually survive, but often with physical and/or mental problems.

See the To-Go Guide (packaged with every new copy of this textbook) for an illustrated summary of the chapter.

Check Your Knowledge

Thinking critically about visual displays of data.

1. According to this figure, what is the probability (i.e., 1 out of 800, or 1 out of 256, etc.) that a baby born to a 35-year-old woman will have Down syndrome?

2. Is a woman of age 45 who gives birth more likely than not to have a baby with Down syndrome? What is the exact probability that her baby will not have Down syndrome?

3. From this figure, can you conclude that most babies with Down syndrome are born to women older than 35?

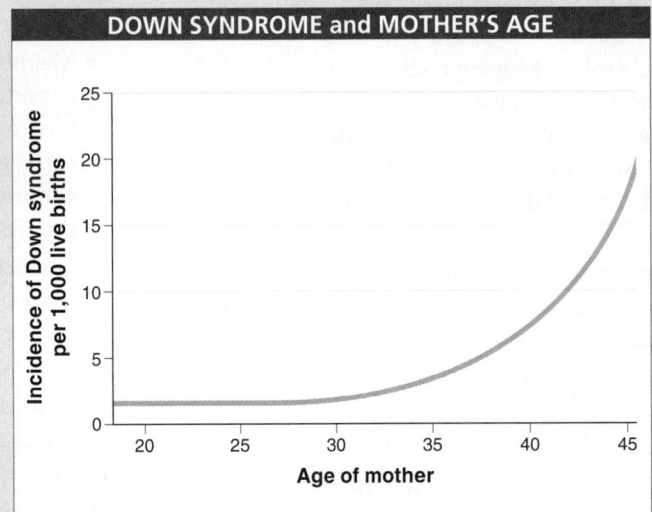

DOWN SYNDROME and MOTHER'S AGE

4. Why does the graph not show data for women older than 45?

5. Among women aged 35 and higher (but not among women younger than 35), the incidence of fetuses produced that have an extra copy of chromosome 21 may be higher than the graph indicates. Why?

See Answers at the back of the book.

Key Terms in Chromosomes and Cell Division

anaphase, p. 233
apoptosis, p. 230
asexual reproduction, p. 225
binary fission, p. 225
cancer, p. 234
cell cycle, p. 226
centriole, p. 233
centromere, p. 227
chromatid, p. 233

complementarity, p. 227
complementary base, p. 227
crossing over, p. 241
cytokinesis, p. 227
daughter cell, p. 225
diploid, p. 237
fertilization, p. 237
gamete, p. 226
gonad, p. 239

haploid, p. 237
hermaphrodite, p. 249
histone, p. 224
homologous pair (homologues), p. 239
interphase, p. 226
karyotype, p. 250
meiosis, p. 237
metaphase, p. 233

mitosis, p. 227
mitotic phase (M phase), p. 226
nondisjunction, p. 252
parent cell, p. 225
placenta, p. 252
polar body, p. 243
prophase, p. 232
recombination, p. 241
replication, p. 225

reproductive cell, p. 226
sexual reproduction, p. 225
sister chromatids, p. 233
somatic cell, p. 226
spindle, p. 233
spindle fiber, p. 233
telomere, p. 222
telophase, p. 234
X and Y chromosomes, p. 247

Multiple-Choice Questions

1. **Which of the following statements about telomeres is incorrect?**

   a) They function like a counter, keeping track of how many times a cell has divided.

   b) At birth, they are long enough to permit approximately 50 cell divisions in most cells.

   c) They are slightly shorter in prokaryotic cells than in eukaryotic cells.

   d) They function like a protective cap on chromosomes.

   e) They contain no critical genes.

   100 HARD
   62
   0 EASY

2. **Prokaryotic cells can divide via:**

   a) mitosis.

   b) binary fission.

   c) meiosis.

   d) both mitosis and binary fission.

   e) None of the above.

   100 HARD
   31
   0 EASY

3. **In multicellular organisms, cells that undergo mitotic division but not meiotic division are called _____ cells.**

   a) somosis

   b) skin

   c) interphase

   d) somatic

   e) germ

   100 HARD
   22
   0 EASY

4. **The _____ marks the break in the cell cycle between the end of mitosis and beginning of the DNA synthesis stage.**

   a) mitotic phase

   b) synthesis phase

   c) Gap 2 phase

   d) Gap 1 phase

   e) None of the above.

   100 HARD
   64
   0 EASY

5. **Mitosis results in:**

   a) daughter cells with twice as much genetic material as the parent cell and a unique collection of alleles.

   b) eight daughter cells.

   c) daughter cells with the same number and composition of chromosomes.

   d) gametes.

   e) daughter cells with the same number of chromosomes but different combinations of alleles.

   100 HARD
   45
   0 EASY

6. **Using a light microscope, it is easiest to see chromosomes:**

   a) during mitosis and meiosis, because the condensed chromosomes are thicker and therefore more prominent.

   b) during interphase, when they are concentrated in the nucleus.

   c) in the mitochondria, because the chromosomes are circular.

   d) during asexual reproduction.

   e) during interphase, because they are uncoiled and have a more linear structure.

   100 HARD
   35
   0 EASY

7. **The division of the cytoplasm during cell division is referred to as:**

   a) cytoplasm splicing.

   b) cytokinesis.

   c) vegetative growth.

   d) cytodivision.

   e) hybridization.

   100 HARD
   0 **10** EASY

8. Which of the following statements about tumors is incorrect?

   a) Benign tumors pose less of a health risk than do malignant tumors.

   b) Malignant tumors shed cancer cells that can spread to other parts of the body.

   c) Tumors are caused by excessive cell growth and division.

   d) Cancer cells from malignant tumors can travel to other parts of the body in a process called metastasis.

   e) They contain cells with abnormally high contact inhibition.

100 | HARD

 48

0 | EASY

9. During meiosis but not during mitosis:

   a) haploid gametes are produced that are all identical in their allelic composition.

   b) division of the cytoplasm occurs.

   c) chromosomes line up in the center of the cell during metaphase.

   d) genetic variation among the daughter cells is increased.

   e) two identical daughter cells are produced.

100 | HARD

52

0 | EASY

10. Sister chromatids are:

   a) the result of crossing over.

   b) identical molecules of DNA resulting from replication.

   c) homologous chromosomes.

   d) produced in meiosis but not in mitosis.

   e) single-stranded.

100 | HARD

39

0 | EASY

11. Which of the following events does not occur during prophase I of meiosis?

   a) Spindle fibers form.

   b) Homologous pairs of chromosomes align at the metaphase plate.

   c) Homologues come very close together.

   d) Crossing over occurs between sister chromatids.

   e) Chromosomes condense.

100 | HARD

43

0 | EASY

12. Which of the following is the best way to distinguish male from female?

   a) Males are larger.

   b) Males are more brightly colored.

   c) Males produce motile gametes.

   d) Males are more aggressive.

   e) All of the above statements are correct.

100 | HARD

32

0 | EASY

13. A potential disadvantage of asexual reproduction is that:

   a) it increases the time required to find a mate.

   b) it allows perpetuation of a population even when the members are isolated.

   c) it allows population size to increase rapidly.

   d) it produces genetically uniform populations.

   e) it requires additional rounds of meiosis, which is energetically much more costly than mitosis.

100 | HARD

 35

0 | EASY

14. Which of the following is not a method of chromosomal sex determination that occurs in nature?

   a) In birds, the mother's sex chromosomes determine the sex of the offspring.

   b) In sea turtles, eggs laid in hot sand become females and eggs laid in cooler sand become males.

   c) In humans, the presence of a Y chromosome makes an individual male, even if he also possesses two X chromosomes.

   d) In bees, the eggs that the queen allows to be fertilized become females and the eggs she doesn't fertilize become males.

   e) All of the above are naturally occurring examples of sex determination.

100 | HARD

 38

0 | EASY

15. A karyotype reveals:

   a) the shape of the spindle.

   b) 23 pairs of chromosomes.

   c) the number, shapes, and sizes of chromosomes in an individual cell.

   d) the sex chromosomes but not the non-sex chromosomes.

   e) the non-sex chromosomes but not the sex chromosomes.

100 | HARD

 20

0 | EASY

16. What type of chromosomal abnormality leads to the phenotype known as Down syndrome?

   a) trisomy 21

   b) monosomy 21

   c) monosomy 22

   d) trisomy 22

   e) disomy 21

100 | HARD

20

0 | EASY

17. Nondisjunction:

   a) is the unequal division of the genetic material during cell division.

   b) occurs during meiosis but not mitosis.

   c) occurs in males but not females among mammals, and in females but not males among birds.

   d) leads to a missing chromosome or extra chromosome.

   e) Both a) and d) are correct.

100 | HARD

 36

0 | EASY

18. Of all the varying types of sex chromosome abnormalities, one possibility—that of an individual having one Y but no X—has never been reported. Which of the following statements is the most likely reason that medical researchers have yet to report a person having a karyotype with one Y and no X?

a) There is no meiotic event that could produce an egg that does not have an X chromosome.

b) Individuals are probably born with this karyotype; however, because the phenotypic abnormalities caused are so slight, they live out their lives normally and are unaware of this genetic anomaly.

c) The Y chromosome needs the X chromosome to be present in the cell in order for its genes to be expressed.

d) The X chromosome contains genes that are unrelated to sex determination and are essential for life.

e) Our current technology for karyotyping would not reveal such an abnormality.

100 | HARD

65

0 | EASY

Short-Answer Questions

1. Seventy to ninety percent of the genetic material in a sperm or egg cell made in your body could be inherited from your mother. Why isn't there always a 50/50 split (half from your mother and half from your father)? Is the reverse situation (more genetic material from your father than from your mother) possible?

2. Healthy individuals may have just one sex chromosome, as long as it is an X chromosome. Why can't a person survive with a Y chromosome and no X chromosome?

3. Some organisms can switch between sexual and asexual reproduction. Under what conditions would you expect them to reproduce sexually? What conditions would be more conducive to asexual reproduction? How would you test your hypotheses under laboratory conditions?

See Answers at the back of the book.
For additional study questions, go to www.prep-u.com.

ABOUT THE CHAPTER OPENING PHOTO

Sibling similarities—such as those seen among the Jackson brothers (shown here performing in 1973)—illustrate the phenotypic consequences of genetic similarity; but the subtle differences also reveal variability among the offspring in sexually reproducing species. The phenotypic variation stems from a variety of sources, including crossing over, the shuffling and reassortment of homologues during meiosis, and the contributions from two parents.

Family resemblance:
how traits are inherited

7

Genes and Inheritance

Mirror image? Not quite, but a canine parent and happy puppy reveal parent-offspring similarity.

7·1–7·5 Why do offspring resemble their parents?

7·1 Family resemblance: your father and mother each contribute to your genetic makeup.

Q *How can a single bad gene make you smell like a rotten fish?*

Can a gene be cruel? Of course not. But if one could, consider this candidate: in humans, there is a gene for an enzyme called FMO3 (flavin-containing mono-oxygenase-3), which breaks down a chemical in our bodies that smells like rotting fish. Some unfortunate individuals inherit a defective FMO3 gene and can't break down the noxious chemical. Instead, their urine, sweat, and breath excrete it, causing them to smell like rotting fish. Worst of all, because the odor comes from within their bodies, they cannot wash it away no matter how hard they try. Called "fish odor syndrome," this disorder often causes those afflicted by it to suffer ridicule, social isolation, and depression. (Currently, there is no cure for fish odor syndrome, although there are a few ways of reducing the odor such as reducing consumption of eggs, fish, and some meats that contain certain chemicals, including sulfur.)

For individuals born with this malady, beyond their own suffering there looms a scary question: "Will I pass this condition on to my children?" They might also wonder how

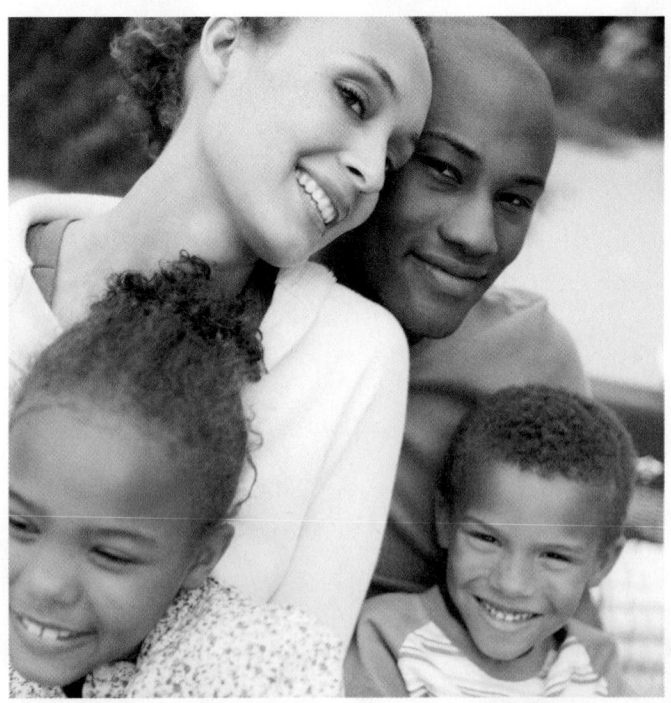

FIGURE 7-1 Where do we begin and our parents end? Family resemblances reveal that many traits are inherited.

INHERITANCE OF GENES

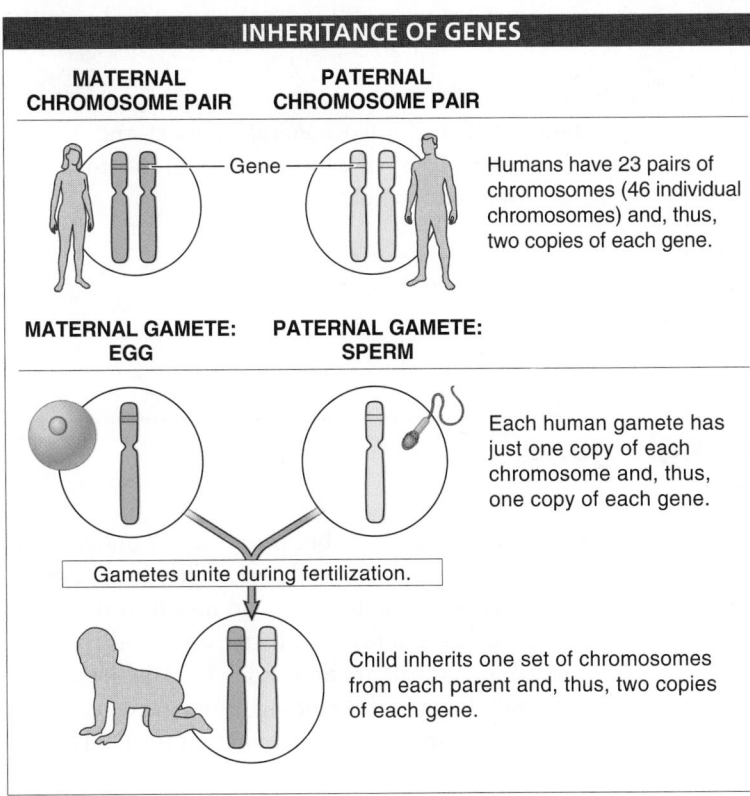

MATERNAL CHROMOSOME PAIR **PATERNAL CHROMOSOME PAIR**

Gene

Humans have 23 pairs of chromosomes (46 individual chromosomes) and, thus, two copies of each gene.

MATERNAL GAMETE: EGG **PATERNAL GAMETE: SPERM**

Each human gamete has just one copy of each chromosome and, thus, one copy of each gene.

Gametes unite during fertilization.

Child inherits one set of chromosomes from each parent and, thus, two copies of each gene.

FIGURE 7-2 How we inherit our genes. Each human offspring inherits one maternal set of 23 chromosomes and one paternal set.

they came to have the disorder, particularly if neither of their parents suffered from it.

Fortunately, most of us do not have to worry about fish odor syndrome, but we do wonder about many other inherited traits that we may or may not pass down to our children. Whom do I blame for my straight hair (or curly hair or big feet)? Hearing a new baby described as having "his father's nose" and "his grandmother's lips" could make someone think that we're all cobbled together from a bunch of used parts. Where do we begin and our parents end (**FIGURE 7-1**)?

In many cases, the answers to questions about heredity are simple. Fish odor syndrome, for example, is just such a case. Recall from Chapter 6 that sexually reproducing organisms generally carry two copies of every chromosome in every cell (except their sex cells), because they inherit one copy of each chromosome from each parent. Humans, for example, have 23 pairs of chromosomes (46 individual chromosomes). At each location on the two chromosomes of a pair is the same gene: one copy from the mother and one from the father (**FIGURE 7-2**). As we noted in Chapter 5, each of the two copies of the gene is called an **allele**. The gene for FMO3 is on chromosome 1. There is a normal version—or allele—of the gene for FMO3, which most people carry, and there is a

rare, defective version that is responsible for fish odor syndrome. As long as a person has at least one normal version of the FMO3 gene, he or she will produce enough of the enzyme to break down the fishy chemical. But if a person inherits two copies of the defective version of the fish odor gene, one from each parent, that person will inherit the disorder (**FIGURE 7-3**).

When it comes to having children, there is a bright side, at least. Although individuals with fish odor syndrome carry two defective copies of the allele and will pass on one set of the bad instructions in every sperm or egg cell that they make, their children won't necessarily inherit the disease. As long as the other parent supplies a normal version of the FMO3 gene, the child will not have fish odor syndrome. The unaffected children, though, will carry a silent copy of the fish odor allele, and if, when they have children, it comes together with a defective FMO3 allele from another person, the fish odor trait will be expressed. In this way, some alleles can exist in a population without always revealing themselves.

FISH ODOR SYNDROME

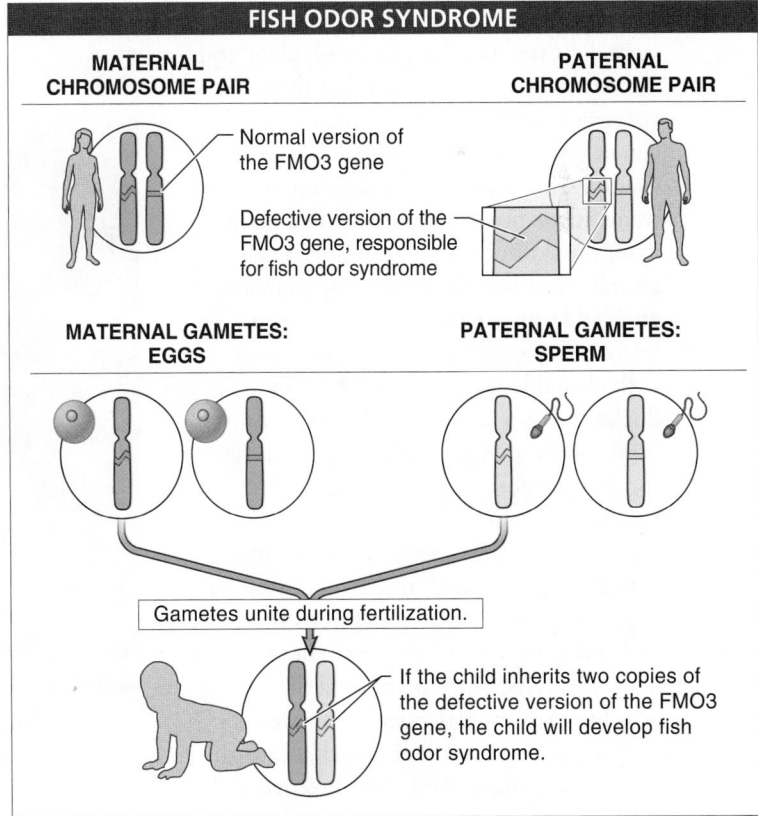

MATERNAL CHROMOSOME PAIR **PATERNAL CHROMOSOME PAIR**

Normal version of the FMO3 gene

Defective version of the FMO3 gene, responsible for fish odor syndrome

MATERNAL GAMETES: EGGS **PATERNAL GAMETES: SPERM**

Gametes unite during fertilization.

If the child inherits two copies of the defective version of the FMO3 gene, the child will develop fish odor syndrome.

FIGURE 7-3 Unlucky catch. A baby inheriting two copies of the defective FMO3 gene will develop fish odor syndrome.

In this chapter, we explore how heredity works. Inheritance follows some simple rules that allow us to make sense of the patterns of family resemblance we see, and even to predict accurately how many offspring are likely to inherit particular traits—or, put another way, predict the likelihood that an offspring will inherit a trait. We'll also examine why the behavior of some traits is easy to predict while many other traits have less straightforward patterns of inheritance, yet still can be studied experimentally and yield predictable patterns.

7·2 Some traits are controlled by a single gene.

Like father, like son. No one will ever seek a paternity test to prove that Michael Douglas is the son of Kirk Douglas. All it takes is a quick look at the legendary dimpled chins shared by the two actors and we are sure that the men are related. We see all around us that offspring resemble their parents more than they resemble other random individuals in the population—a consequence of the passing of characteristics from parents to offspring through their genes. This is **heredity.**

Observing heredity is easy. Elucidating how it works is not. For thousands of years before the mechanisms of heredity were discovered and understood, plant and animal breeders recognized that there is a connection from parents to offspring across generations. In ancient Greece, for example, the poet Homer extolled the tremendous benefits to society that came from the skillful breeding of horses. The awareness of beneficial breeding practices enabled farmers to systematically create strains of crops, livestock, and even pets with desirable traits (**FIGURE 7-4**). From flocks of sheep and herds of reindeer to litters of puppies and fields of wheat, the similarity among relatives is clear. Once breeders recognized the existence of heredity, they began selecting individual plants or animals with the desired traits to breed with each other, in the hope that their offspring would also have those desirable traits. Since then, it has been possible to create a rich world of sweeter corn, loyal dogs, docile livestock, beautiful flowers, and more. And these breeders did it all without ever really understanding how heredity works.

Practical successes were many, but people didn't understand exactly how the outcomes were achieved. They knew the result of selective breeding, but why and how it worked, or didn't always work, was a mystery. Patterns of similarity among related individuals are impossible to make sense of without an underlying understanding of *how* heredity works. This understanding is the province of the field of genetics.

Mechanisms of heredity are like a puzzle, and they become a bit easier to grasp when we focus on aspects of family resemblances that are commonplace. Virtually everyone

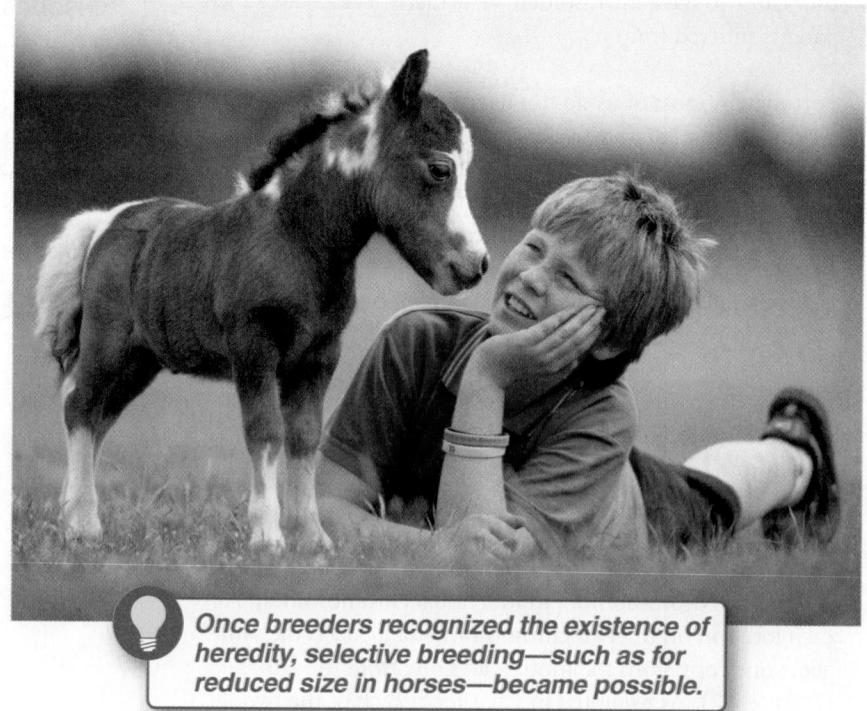

Once breeders recognized the existence of heredity, selective breeding—such as for reduced size in horses—became possible.

FIGURE 7-4 Honey, I shrunk the horse! Selective breeding was used to produce this tiny horse.

EXAMPLES OF SINGLE-GENE TRAITS

Cleft chin

Non-cleft chin

Unattached earlobes

Attached earlobes

Widow's peak

Straight hairline

Tongue-roller

Non-tongue-roller

FIGURE 7-5 Chins, ears, hairlines, and tongue-rolling: single-gene traits. Some traits are determined by the instructions a person carries on one gene.

with a cleft chin, for instance, has a similarly dimpled parent. Everyone who has earlobes that hang from their ears rather than being attached directly to their head has at least one parent with the same feature. Everyone who has a widow's peak has a parent with the same hairline. Everyone who is farsighted has a similarly farsighted parent. The list goes on and on. In fact, there are more than 9,000 human traits that exhibit these straightforward patterns of inheritance. Traits that are determined by the instructions a person carries on one gene are called **single-gene traits** (FIGURE 7-5).

> **HEREDITY**
>
> I AM the family face;
> Flesh perishes, I live on,
> Projecting trait and trace
> Through time to times anon,
> And leaping from place to place
> Over oblivion.
>
> The years-heired feature that can
> In curve and voice and eye
> Despise the human span
> Of durance—that is I;
> The eternal thing in man,
> That heeds no call to die.
>
> —THOMAS HARDY, in *Moments of Vision and Miscellaneous Verses*, 1917

It is important to note here that most human characteristics are influenced by multiple genes as well as by the environment. However, because the mechanism by which single-gene traits pass from parent to child is the easiest pattern of inheritance to decipher, we first explore this process. Then we'll expand our model of heritability to account for the passing on of more complex traits.

TAKE-HOME MESSAGE 7·2

Many human traits are determined by instructions a person carries on a single gene, and these traits exhibit straightforward patterns of inheritance.

7·3 Mendel learned about heredity by conducting experiments.

What do parents "give" their offspring that confers similarity? In other words, how is a physical entity, such as a cleft chin, inherited? How is such a trait passed from parent to offspring? It wasn't until the mid-1800s that any real headway was made on answering these questions. At that time, Gregor Mendel, a monk living in what is now the Czech Republic, began some studies that not only shed light on these questions but practically answered them completely. Mendel understood the essence of the genetics puzzle and set out to piece it all together.

When Mendel turned to these questions about heredity, there were no obvious answers. One idea put forth suggested that perhaps an entire, pre-made human—albeit a very, very tiny one—was contained in every sperm cell (**FIGURE 7-6**). That idea had been popular since the late 1600s. It doesn't take much imagination to see why it ran into difficulty, though, because children resemble both their mothers and their fathers, not just their fathers. Another popular idea was that offspring reflect a simple blending of their two parents' traits via the blood. But this couldn't explain how brown-eyed parents could give birth to blue-eyed children. Or why one tall and one short parent sometimes produced a tall

Q Individuals who share common ancestry are called "blood relatives," yet they don't actually share any blood. How might the phrase "blood relatives" be a reflection of early conceptions of inheritance?

child, rather than always producing children of intermediate height.

Sometimes scientific breakthroughs are made because an innovative new technique is invented or a lucky observation is made by chance. Neither played a role in Mendel's success. He didn't do anything radically new, but simply applied the tried and true methodical experimentation and scientific thinking (as described in Chapter 1) that had been a boon to chemists and physicists. In particular, three features of Mendel's research were critical to its success (**FIGURE 7-7**).

1. He chose a good organism to study: the garden pea. It's not that Mendel had a particular fondness for vegetables. In fact, his goals were to understand inheritance in all organisms, not just plants. Pea plants were simply the right tool. Cats and dogs or even mice wouldn't have served his purposes very well, because they would have been too hard to take care of in the large numbers—thousands and thousands of individuals—that Mendel required. Humans, too, would have made a terrible study organism. We take too long to breed (and won't produce offspring on command). Pea plants, on the other hand, have a lot going for them as experimental organisms. They are relatively easy to fertilize manually by "pollen dusting." It is easy to collect dozens or even hundreds of offspring from a single **cross**, the process in which male pollen (carrying the sperm) is used to fertilize female eggs. And, on top of all this, pea plants are fast enough breeders that Mendel could conduct experiments that lasted for multiple generations.

2. Mendel chose to focus on easily categorized traits. For instance, shape: all peas of the variety that Mendel studied are either round or wrinkled in shape, with nothing in between. In addition, all peas are either yellow or green in color, never any intermediate shade. In all, Mendel looked at seven different traits of the pea plants but, for each trait, only two variants ever appeared, so he and his research assistants could easily observe and unambiguously identify them.

3. Mendel began his studies by first repeatedly breeding together similar plants until he had many distinct populations, each of which was unvarying for a particular trait. He described these plants as **true-breeding** for that trait because they always produced offspring with the same

💡 The mistaken idea that a tiny, pre-made human existed in every sperm cell was introduced in the 1600s. This theory remained popular through the 1800s.

FIGURE 7-6 The "pre-made human." Tiny humans in every sperm cell? Why would children have any resemblance to their mothers?

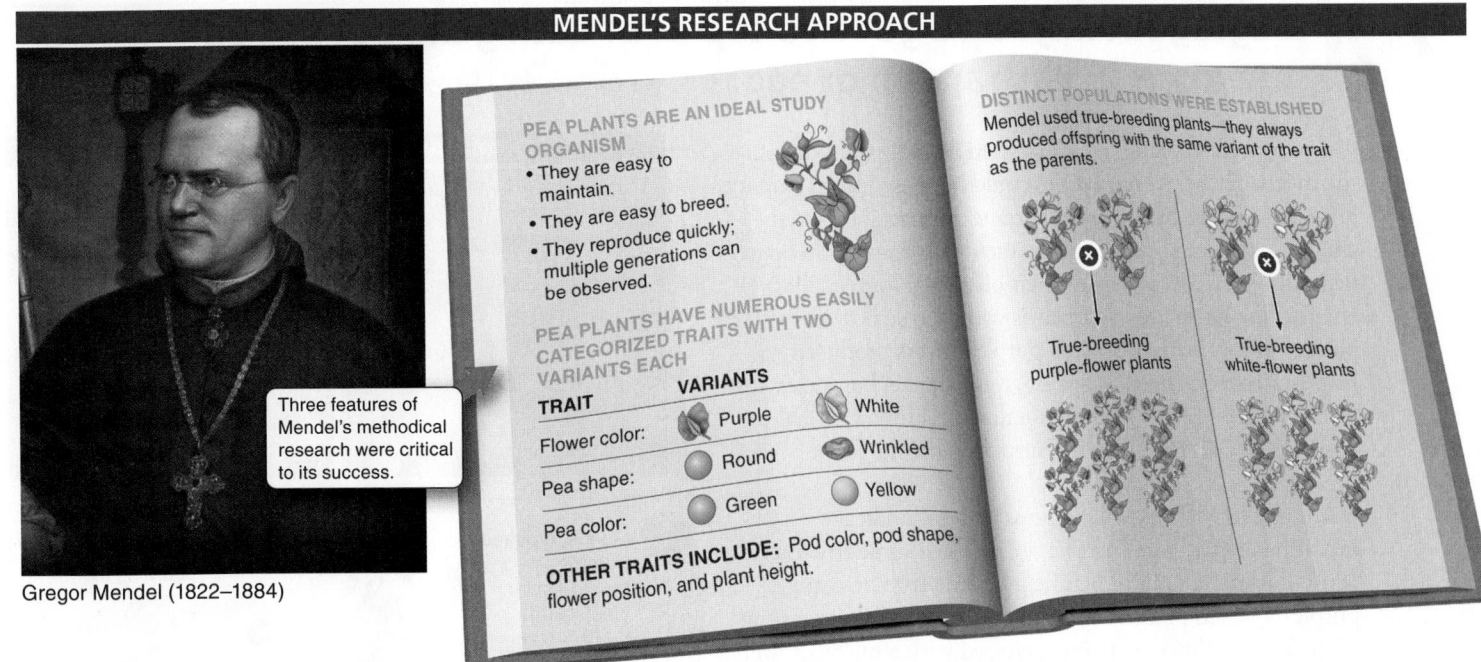

Gregor Mendel (1822–1884)

Three features of Mendel's methodical research were critical to its success.

PEA PLANTS ARE AN IDEAL STUDY ORGANISM
- They are easy to maintain.
- They are easy to breed.
- They reproduce quickly; multiple generations can be observed.

PEA PLANTS HAVE NUMEROUS EASILY CATEGORIZED TRAITS WITH TWO VARIANTS EACH

TRAIT	VARIANTS	
Flower color:	Purple	White
Pea shape:	Round	Wrinkled
Pea color:	Green	Yellow

OTHER TRAITS INCLUDE: Pod color, pod shape, flower position, and plant height.

DISTINCT POPULATIONS WERE ESTABLISHED
Mendel used true-breeding plants—they always produced offspring with the same variant of the trait as the parents.

True-breeding purple-flower plants

True-breeding white-flower plants

FIGURE 7-7 Mendel's notebook. Careful planning and a well-selected study organism contributed to the success of Mendel's experiments.

variant of the trait as the parents. True-breeding round-pea plants always produced plants with round peas when they were crossed together. True-breeding purple-flowered pea plants always produced purple-flowered offspring, while true-breeding white-flowered pea plants always produced white-flowered offspring. It took a lot of prep work to establish these populations, but once Mendel had them, he was in a position to set up all of the different crosses that enabled him to piece together the genetics puzzle.

Once he had obtained his groups of true-breeding plants, Mendel began a straightforward process of experimentation. He crossed plants with different traits—for example, he crossed plants with green peas and plants with yellow peas—and observed large numbers of their offspring, counting the number of plants that produced green peas and the number of plants that produced yellow peas. (This cross, written as "green × yellow cross," always resulted in plants that produced only yellow peas.) Mendel devised a hypothesis that would explain his observations and generate predictions about the outcomes of further crosses. Then he conducted those crosses to see whether the predictions generated by his hypothesis were borne out.

There was a simple elegance to Mendel's work: his predictions were always in the form of simple questions that could be answered by his experiments, such as, "If I cross a plant that produces wrinkled peas with a plant that produces smooth peas, will the offspring plants produce wrinkled or smooth peas?" His crosses would come out either one way or the other. Everything was black and white. This process of performing well thought-out, rigorous experiments was a radical innovation for biology. In the end, Mendel's patience, perseverance, and cleverness paid off. We explore his results in the next section and see that they allowed Mendel to clearly and definitively describe how the traits he studied were inherited.

TAKE-HOME MESSAGE 7·3

In the mid-1800s, Gregor Mendel conducted studies that help us understand heredity. He focused on easily observed and categorized traits in garden peas and applied methodical experimentation and rigorous hypothesis testing to determine how traits are inherited.

7·4 Segregation: you've got two copies of each gene but put only one copy in each sperm or egg.

One odd and recurring result spurred Mendel to figure out the mechanism by which traits could be passed from parent to offspring. Just as brown-eyed parents can have blue-eyed children, sometimes traits that weren't present in either parent pea plant would show up in their offspring. Crosses that entailed the fertilization of plants with purple flowers by pollen from other plants with purple flowers produced *mostly* purple-flowered offspring, for instance, but *sometimes* they produced plants with white flowers. How was that possible? Where did the whiteness come from?

Here's where Mendel's meticulous and methodical experiments paid off. First, he started with some true-breeding white-flowered plants. Then he got some true-breeding purple-flowered plants. He wondered: which color wins out when a white-flowered plant is crossed with a purple-flowered plant? The answer was definitive: purple wins (**FIGURE 7-8**). All of the offspring from these crosses were purple, every time. For this reason, Mendel called the purple-flower trait **dominant,** and he considered the white-flower trait to be the **recessive** trait. In general, a dominant trait masks the effect of a recessive trait when an individual carries both the dominant and the recessive versions of the instructions for the trait.

Things got a bit more interesting when Mendel took the purple-flowered plants that came from the cross between true-breeding purple- and white-flowered plants and bred these purple offspring with each other. He found that these mixed-parentage plants were no longer true-breeding. Occasionally, they would produce white-flowered offspring. (To be exact, of the 929 offspring plants Mendel examined, 705 had purple flowers, and 224 had white flowers.) Apparently, the directions for building white flowers—last seen in one of their grandparents—were still lurking inside their purple-flowered parent plants. The existence of traits that could disappear for a generation and then show up again was quite perplexing. Mendel devised a simple hypothesis to explain these observations (**FIGURE 7-9**).

Mendel's hypothesis for explaining this pattern of inheritance incorporated three ideas that then helped him (and now help us) make predictions about crosses he hadn't yet done.

1. Rather than passing on the trait itself, **each parent puts into every sperm or egg it makes a single set of instructions for building the trait.** Today, we call that instruction set a *gene*.

2. Offspring receive two copies of the instructions for any trait. Often, both sets of instructions are identical

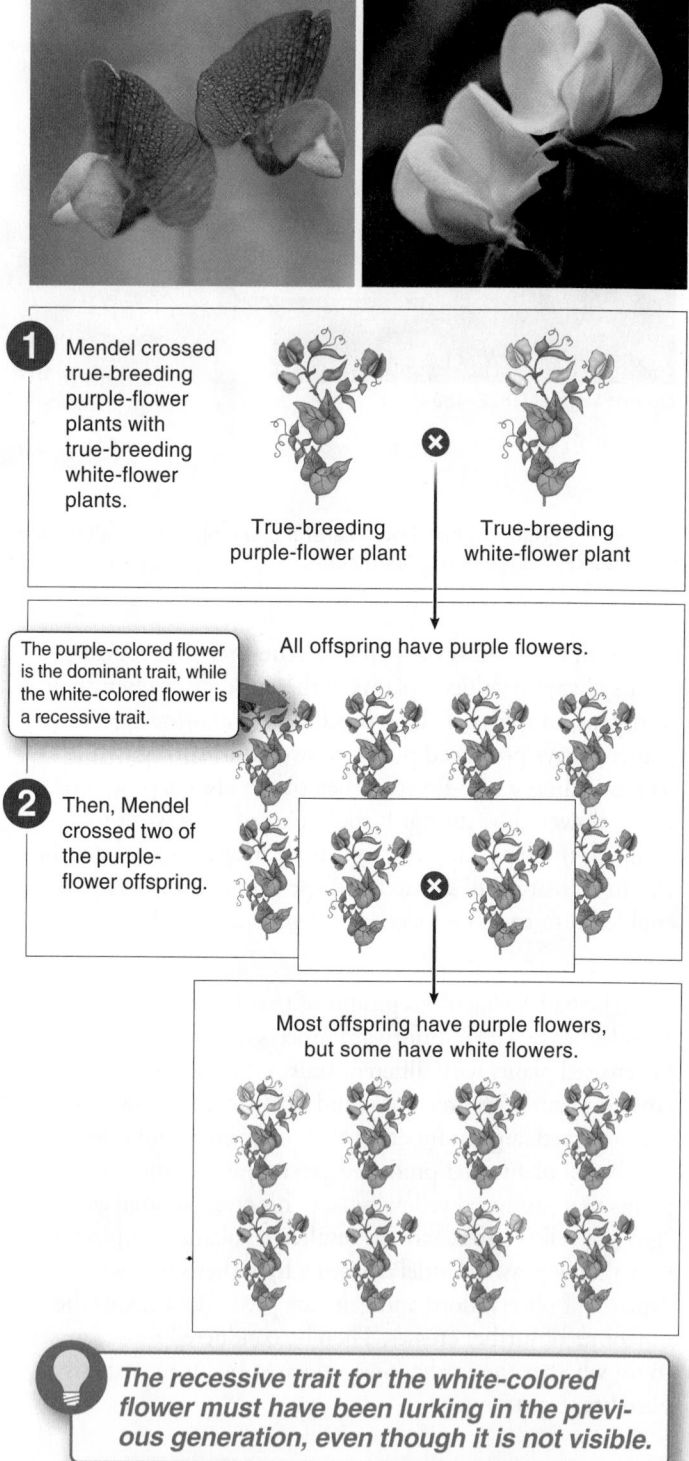

DOMINANT AND RECESSIVE TRAITS

1 Mendel crossed true-breeding purple-flower plants with true-breeding white-flower plants.

True-breeding purple-flower plant

True-breeding white-flower plant

The purple-colored flower is the dominant trait, while the white-colored flower is a recessive trait.

All offspring have purple flowers.

2 Then, Mendel crossed two of the purple-flower offspring.

Most offspring have purple flowers, but some have white flowers.

The recessive trait for the white-colored flower must have been lurking in the previous generation, even though it is not visible.

FIGURE 7-8 White or purple? By careful and repeated crosses among pea plants, Mendel determined that there were "dominant" and "recessive" traits.

According to Mendel's law of segregation, only one of the two alleles for a gene is put into a gamete. At fertilization, offspring receive from each parent one allele for each gene.

Heterozygous pea plant   Heterozygous pea plant

Two different alleles (white, purple) for the same gene (flower color)

MEIOSIS Each gamete gets one copy of each gene.

FERTILIZATION Each fertilized egg gets two copies of each gene.

Homozygous recessive   Heterozygous   Heterozygous   Homozygous dominant

FIGURE 7-9 Segregation of alleles in meiosis. Organisms have two copies of each gene but place only one copy into each gamete during the process of meiosis (as described in Chapter 6).

and the offspring produce the traits according to those instructions. Other times, though, each parent contributes a slightly different set of instructions—that is, a different allele—for the trait. So, for example, in pea plants there are two alleles for flower color: a purple-flower allele and a white-flower allele. Each is a different allele, but because both specify instructions for producing color in flowers,

they are both genes for flower color. Same gene (flower-color gene), different alleles (purple and white).

3. The trait observed in an individual depends on the *two* copies of the gene it inherits from its parents. When an individual inherits the same two alleles for this gene, the individual's genotype for that gene is said to be **homozygous** and the individual shows the trait specified by the instructions embodied in those alleles. When an individual inherits a different allele from each parent, the individual's genotype for that gene is said to be **heterozygous.** Dominant and recessive alleles are defined by their action when they are in the heterozygous state: if one of the alleles is fully apparent in the individual while the other is not, the first is called the dominant allele and is said to "mask" the effect of the other allele, which is called the recessive allele.

> **"There were no questions."**
> —Entry in meeting notes following Mendel's first public presentation of his ideas on how heredity works. (*Tragically, no one in the audience of scientists had any idea what he was talking about. Not until about 40 years later did the world understand his discoveries.*)

Later, when an offspring grows up and gets ready to reproduce, it only gets to contribute one of its two copies of the gene to its own offspring. The other parent will contribute the other allele. So, when sperm and eggs are made, each sex cell gets only one copy of the gene—as opposed to the two copies present in every other cell in the body. For a male who is heterozygous, for example, it means that half of the sperm he produces will have one of the alleles and half will have the other. The idea that, of the two copies of each gene everyone carries, only one of the two alleles gets put into each gamete is significant and important enough that it is called **Mendel's law of segregation.**

TAKE-HOME MESSAGE 7·4

Each parent puts a single set of instructions for building a particular trait into every sperm or egg it makes. This instruction set is called a gene. The trait observed in an individual depends on the two copies (alleles) of the gene it inherits from its parents.

7·5 Observing an individual's phenotype is not sufficient for determining its genotype.

Things are not always as they appear. Take skin coloration, for example. Humans and many other mammals have a gene that contains the information for producing melanin, one of the chemicals responsible for giving our skin its coloring (**FIGURE 7-10**). This gene is one of many that influence skin color. Unfortunately, there is also a defective, non-functioning version of the melanin gene that is passed along through some families. An individual who inherits two copies of the defective version of the gene cannot produce pigment and has a condition known as albinism, a disorder characterized by little or no pigment in the eyes, hair, and skin. But it is impossible to tell whether a normally pigmented individual carries one of these defective alleles just by looking at his or her appearance—we would need to get a genetic analysis done to discover this information.

The inability to deduce an individual's genetic makeup through simple observation is a general problem in genetics: physical appearances don't always exactly reflect the underlying genes. A normally pigmented individual may have two copies of the pigment-producing allele or may have only one copy. In either case, the individual will look the same. The outward appearance of an individual is called its **phenotype.** A phenotype includes features visible to the naked eye such as flashy coloration, height, or the presence of antlers.

A phenotype also includes less easily visible characteristics such as the chemicals an individual produces to clot blood or digest lactose. An individual's phenotype even includes the behaviors it exhibits.

Underlying the phenotype is the **genotype.** This is an organism's genetic composition. We usually speak of an individual's genotype in reference to a particular trait. For example, an individual's genotype might be described as "homozygous for the recessive allele for albinism" (e.g., two recessive alleles of the gene or two dominant alleles of the gene.) Another individual's genotype for the melanin gene might be described as "heterozygous" (e.g., a recessive allele and a dominant allele.) Occasionally, the word "genotype" is also used as a way of referring to *all* of the genes an individual carries.

When an organism exhibits a recessive trait, such as albinism, we know with certainty what its genotype is for the melanin gene. When it shows the dominant trait, on the other hand, it's impossible to distinguish whether the organism carries two copies of the dominant allele (homozygous dominant) or carries one copy of the dominant allele and one of the recessive (heterozygous). Because it's not possible to discern the genotypes of two individuals with the same phenotype just by looking at them, much of genetic analysis must make use of clever experiments and careful record-keeping to determine organisms' genotypes. Let's explore a useful method of analyzing the relationships between genotypes and phenotypes.

How do we analyze and predict the outcome of crosses? First, we must assign symbols to represent the different variants of a gene. Generally we use an upper-case letter for the dominant allele and lower-case letter for the recessive allele. In the case of the albino giraffe, we represent the albino individual as *aa*, because it must carry two copies of the recessive allele, *a*. A giraffe that is pigmented must have the genotype *AA* or *Aa*. If we don't know which of the two possible genotypes the pigmented individual has, we can write *A_*, where _ is a placeholder for the unknown second allele, whose identity we aren't certain of.

PHENOTYPE: Little or no pigment in the eyes, hair, and skin
GENOTYPE: Homozygous for the recessive allele for albinism

FIGURE 7-10 An albino giraffe stands out from its peers. Carrying two non-functioning versions of the gene that produces the pigment melanin causes albinism.

We can trace the possible outcomes of a cross between two individuals using a handy tool called the **Punnett square.** In **FIGURE 7-11** we illustrate the

A Punnett square is a useful tool for determining the possible outcomes of a cross between two individuals.

FIGURE 7-11 Predicting the outcome of crosses. A Punnett square helps in determining the likelihood of inheriting albinism.

cross between a true-breeding pigmented individual, *AA,* and an albino, *aa.* Along the top of the square we list, individually, the two alleles that one of the parents produces, and along the left side of the square we list the two alleles that the other parent produces. We split up an individual's two alleles in this way because, although the individual carries two alleles, only one of the alleles is contained in each sperm or egg cell that it produces.

In the four cells of the Punnett square, we enter the genotypes of all the possible offspring resulting from our cross—a cell contains the allele given at the head of the column, which is one parent's contribution, and the allele at the left of the row, which is the other parent's contribution. The two gametes that come together at fertilization produce the genotype of the offspring. In Cross 1 illustrated in Figure 7-11, every possible offspring would be heterozygous and would be normally pigmented, because it receives a dominant allele from the pigmented parent and a recessive allele from the albino parent.

In the bottom half of Figure 7-11 (Cross 2), we trace the cross between two heterozygous individuals. Note that each parent produces two kinds of gametes, one with the dominant allele and one with the recessive allele. This cross has three possible outcomes: one-quarter of the time the offspring will be homozygous dominant (*AA*), one-quarter of the time the offspring will be homozygous recessive (*aa*), and the remaining half of the time the offspring will be heterozygous (*Aa*). Phenotypically, three-quarters of the offspring will be normally pigmented (*AA* or *Aa*) and one-quarter will be albino (*aa*).

TAKE-HOME MESSAGE 7·5

It is not always possible to determine an individual's genetic makeup, known as its genotype, by observation of the organism's outward appearance, known as its phenotype. For a particular trait, an individual may carry a recessive allele whose phenotypic effect is masked by the presence of a dominant allele. Much genetic analysis therefore makes use of clever experiments and careful record-keeping, often using Punnett squares, to determine organisms' genotypes.

FAMILY
RESEMBLANCE

GENETICS
AND CHANCE

TRANSLATION
OF GENOTYPES

GENE
LINKAGE

273

7·6–7·8 Probability and chance play central roles in genetics.

Because of the role of chance in genetics, we cannot always predict the exact outcome of a genetic cross.

7·6 Chance is important in genetics.

Sometimes genetics is a bit like gambling. Even with perfect information, it can still be impossible to know the genetic outcome with certainty. It's like flipping a coin: you can know every last detail about the coin, but you still can't know whether the coin will land on heads or tails. The best you can do is define the probability of each possible outcome.

The rules of probability (the same ones that govern coin tosses and the rolling of dice) have a central role in genetics, for two reasons. The first is a consequence of segregation, the process Mendel described, in which each gamete an individual produces receives only one of the two copies of each gene that the individual carries in most of its other cells. As a result, it is equally likely that the haploid gamete—the sperm or egg—will include one allele or the other allele of the two that the individual carries. It is impossible to know which allele it will be. The second reason probability plays a central role in genetics is that fertilization, too, is a chance event. All of the sperm or eggs produced by an individual are different from one another, and any one of those gametes may be the gamete involved in fertilization. Thus, knowing everything about the alleles a parent carries is not enough to be able to determine with certainty which alleles his or her offspring will carry.

Let's explore how we can make predictions in games of chance, as well as in matings, based on probabilities. As with the probability of getting heads in a coin flip, any gamete produced by an individual heterozygous for a trait has a 50% probability of carrying the dominant allele and a 50% probability of carrying the recessive allele. If an individual is homozygous for a trait, 100% of his or her gametes will carry that allele. Let's use these probabilities in an example.

If a male is heterozygous for albinism (*Aa*) and a female is albino (*aa*), what is the probability that their child will be homozygous for albinism (*aa*)? To get the *aa* outcome, two events must occur. First, the father's gamete must carry the recessive allele (*a*), and second, the mother's gamete must carry the recessive allele (*a*). In this case, the probability of a homozygous recessive offspring is 0.5 (the probability that the father's gamete carries *a*) times 1.0 (the probability that the mother's gamete carries *a*), for a probability of 0.5. This is a general rule when determining the likelihood of a complex event occurring: if you know the probability of each component that must occur, you multiply all the probabilities together to get the overall probability of that complex event occurring (**FIGURE 7-12**).

Consider another example, involving Tay-Sachs disease. As described in Chapter 3, Tay-Sachs is caused by malfunctioning lysosomes that do not digest cellular waste properly. It leads to death in early childhood. Tay-Sachs occurs if a child inherits two recessive alleles for the

IF...
The mother is albino, and the father is heterozygous.

aa — 100%
a   a

Aa — 50%
A   a

THEN...
There is a 100% chance that the mother's egg will carry the recessive *a* allele and a 50% chance that a sperm will carry the recessive *a* allele.

1.0 × 0.5 = 0.5 or 50% chance the offspring will be albino.

Multiply the two components together to determine the overall probability.

AND...

aa

FIGURE 7-12 Using probability to determine the chance of inheriting albinism.

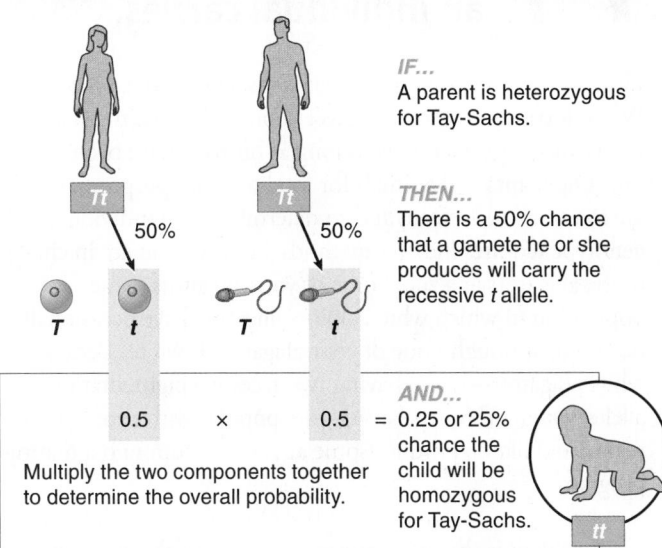

IF...
A parent is heterozygous for Tay-Sachs.

Tt — 50%
T   t

Tt — 50%
T   t

THEN...
There is a 50% chance that a gamete he or she produces will carry the recessive *t* allele.

0.5 × 0.5 = 0.25 or 25% chance the child will be homozygous for Tay-Sachs.

Multiply the two components together to determine the overall probability.

AND...

tt

FIGURE 7-13 The chance of inheriting Tay-Sachs disease. The probability that a child will inherit Tay-Sachs disease from two heterozygous parents is 25%.

Tay-Sachs gene. If each parent is heterozygous for the Tay-Sachs gene, what is the probability that their child will have Tay-Sachs disease?

To solve this, break down the event of the child having Tay-Sachs into two separate events: first, it must inherit a recessive allele, *t,* from its heterozygous father. Because half the father's sperm will have the dominant *T* allele and half will have the *t* allele, the probability of the child inheriting the *t* allele is 0.5. Second, the child must also inherit a recessive allele from its heterozygous mother. Because half of the mother's eggs will have the *T* allele, while the other half have the *t* allele, the probability of the child inheriting the *t* allele from its mother is also 0.5. So the overall probability of the child having Tay-Sachs disease is 0.5 × 0.5 = 0.25, or 1 in 4 (**FIGURE 7-13**). Of course, if the couple has only one child, we can't predict *with certainty* whether the child will have Tay-Sachs. The mathematical probability is, however,

that if the couple had an infinite number of children, we could be certain that one-fourth of them would have Tay-Sachs disease. This fact may not be much help for heterozygous couples trying to decide whether to have a child or not.

TAKE-HOME MESSAGE 7·6

Probability plays a central role in genetics. In segregation, each gamete that an individual produces receives only one of the two copies of each gene the individual carries in its other cells, but it is impossible to know which allele goes into the gamete. Chance plays a role in fertilization, too: all of the sperm or eggs produced by an individual are different from one another, and any one of those gametes may be the gamete involved in fertilization.

7·7 A test-cross enables us to figure out which alleles an individual carries.

How can you see something that is invisible to the naked eye? When it comes to genetics, this is a practical issue that has been causing problems for as long as humans have been breeding plants and animals for food or other purposes. Genes are too small to be seen, and so determining an individual's genotype requires indirect methods. Suppose you are in charge of the alligators at a zoo. Some of your alligators come from a population in which white, albino alligators have occasionally occurred, although none of your alligators is white. Because white alligators—those having two recessive pigmentation alleles, *mm* ("m" for melanin)—are popular with zoo visitors, you would like to produce some at your zoo through a mating program.

The problem is that you cannot be certain of the genotype of your alligators. They might be homozygous dominant, *MM,* or they might be heterozygous, *Mm.* In either case, their phenotype is normal coloration. How can you figure out which of these two possibilities is the genotype of a particular alligator? This is a challenge to animal breeders, but not an insurmountable one. Genes may be invisible, but their identity can be revealed by a simple tool called the **test-cross.**

In the test-cross, you take an individual exhibiting a dominant trait but whose genotype is unknown. You cross (i.e., mate) that individual with an individual that is homozygous recessive and look at the phenotypes of their offspring. In the case of your breeding program for albino alligators, you could borrow an albino alligator from another zoo and breed your unknown-genotype alligator (genotype: *M_*) with that albino alligator (genotype: *mm*). There are two possible outcomes, and they will reveal the genotype of your unknown-genotype alligator (**FIGURE 7-14**). If your alligator is homozygous dominant (*MM*), it will contribute a dominant allele, *M,* to every offspring. Even though the albino alligator will contribute the recessive allele, *m,* to all its offspring, all the offspring of this cross will be heterozygous, *Mm,* and none of them will be albino.

If, on the other hand, your unknown-genotype alligator is heterozygous, *Mm,* half of the time it will contribute a recessive allele, *m,* to the offspring. In every one of those cases, the offspring will be homozygous recessive and thus albino.

FIGURE 7-14 A test-cross can reveal an unknown genotype. In this test-cross, a homozygous white female alligator is bred with a normally colored male of unknown genotype. The color of their offspring will help identify whether the male is homozygous dominant or heterozygous.

TEST-CROSS: WHITE ALLIGATORS

Test-cross

MOTHER
white
homozygous
mm

FATHER
pigmented
unknown genotype
*M_*
(*MM* or *Mm*)

GAMETES — m | m

GAMETES — M | M or m

Unknown allele could be *M* or *m.*

Mm | Mm
Mm *or* | Mm *or*
mm | mm

OFFSPRING (if unknown genotype is *MM*)

	GENOTYPE	PHENOTYPE
	All heterozygous *Mm*	All pigmented

OFFSPRING (if unknown genotype is *Mm*)

	GENOTYPE	PHENOTYPE
	2/4 heterozygous *Mm*	2/4 pigmented
	2/4 homozygous recessive *mm*	2/4 white

So the cleverness of the test-cross is that when you cross your unknown-genotype organism with an individual showing the recessive trait (and so having the known genotype of *mm*), the offspring will reveal the previously unknown makeup of the parent. For example, if your alligator sometimes produces offspring with the recessive trait (and if it does, it will do so half the time, on average), its genotype must be heterozygous. If it never produces offspring with the recessive trait, it must be homozygous for the dominant allele. To be confident in concluding that the unknown-genotype alligator has the *MM* genotype, though, you'd have to observe many, many offspring. After all, even if its genotype is *Mm*, quite a few offspring in a row might be normally pigmented, with the genotype *Mm*. Eventually, however, a heterozygous individual is likely to produce an offspring with the homozygous recessive genotype, *mm*, and the albino phenotype.

7·8 We use pedigrees to decipher and predict the inheritance patterns of genes.

People want to know things about the future, such as: what is the likelihood that I will have a child with a particular genetic disease, say hemophilia? Or what is my own risk of developing a genetic disease, such as Huntington's disease, later in my life? Geneticists who study these and other diseases want to know other things: how is a particular disease or trait inherited? Is it recessive or dominant? Is it carried on the sex chromosomes or on one of the other chromosomes? A **pedigree** is a type of family tree that can help answer these questions.

In a pedigree, information is gathered from as many related individuals as possible across multiple generations (**FIGURE 7-15**). Starting from the bottom, each row in the chart represents a generation, listing all of the children in their order of birth, their sex, and whether or not they have a particular trait. Working up the pedigree, the children's parents are indicated and, above them, their parents' parents, for as far back as data are available. Squares represent males and circles represent females, and these shapes are shaded to indicate that an individual exhibits the trait of interest. Sometimes the genotype (as much of it as is known) is also listed for each individual.

By analyzing which individuals manifest the trait and which do not, it may be possible to deduce a pattern of inheritance for the trait—or, at least, rule out certain patterns. For example, for dominant traits, all affected individuals must have at least one parent who exhibits the trait. In contrast, an individual can exhibit a recessive trait even if both parents are unaffected (i.e., do not exhibit the

trait). In this case, the individual's parents must be heterozygous for that trait, each carrying one dominant and one recessive allele. Similarly, it is sometimes possible to determine whether a trait is carried on the sex chromosomes (X or Y, which we discuss in Section 7-13) or on one of the non-sex chromosomes (also called "autosomes"). Traits that are controlled by genes on the sex chromosomes are called **sex-linked traits.** Recessive sex-linked traits, for example, appear more frequently in males than in females, whereas dominant sex-linked traits appear more frequently in

PEDIGREE

A pedigree is a useful tool to document a trait of interest across multiple generations of family members.

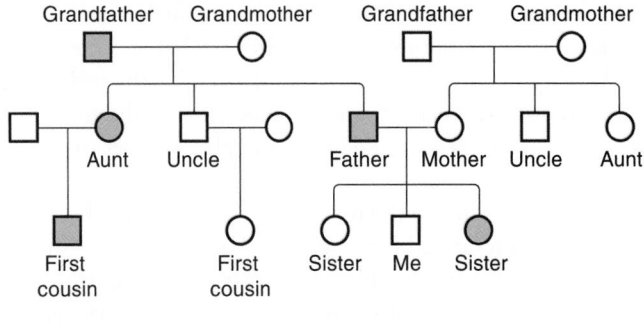

○ Female exhibiting trait of interest   ■ Male exhibiting trait of interest
○ Female not exhibiting trait   □ Male not exhibiting trait

FIGURE 7-15 Family tree. A pedigree maps the occurrence of a trait in a family.

Anury is a condition in dogs and other animals in which they are born without a tail. The condition is inherited as a recessive trait.

IF...
A dog has no tail, but both parents do (such as individual "3").

THEN...
We know with certainty each parent's genotype. (Can you figure out the genotypes of 1 and 2?)

PEDIGREE

Female with anury
Female not exhibiting anury
Male with anury
Male not exhibiting anury

This puppy definitely inherits a recessive allele from its father. It will have anury if (1) its mother has a recessive allele **and** (2) she passes that allele to the puppy. What is that probability?

FIGURE 7-16 Pedigree puzzle: tracing the occurrence of anury in a family of dogs.

females. These patterns may become obvious only on inspection of a large pedigree.

An example of how pedigrees can help determine how traits are inherited is given in **FIGURE 7-16**. Anury is a condition seen in dogs and some other animals in which the animal has no tail. The pedigree reveals that anury is inherited as a recessive trait, because unaffected parents can have offspring with the disorder.

Can you determine the genotype of the individual labeled "1" in Figure 7-16? Why must that female be heterozygous (*Aa*) for anury? (By the way, an individual that carries one allele for a recessive trait, and so does not exhibit the trait but can have offspring that do, is referred to as a **carrier** of the trait.) Must her mate have the same genotype?

On the same pedigree, note that two individuals in the second generation have a puppy (indicated by "?"). What is the probability that this puppy has anury? Examine the pedigree carefully and see whether you can come up with the answer; the next paragraph will guide you through if you get stuck.

In the cross producing the mystery puppy, the father has anury and so must be homozygous recessive; he will definitely pass on one *a* to the son. The mother's genotype can be *AA*, *Aa*, or *aA*, given that both of her parents are heterozygous. Consequently, she has a ⅔ (2 in 3) probability of being a carrier of the *a* allele. If she is, then there is a ½ (50%) chance that she will pass it on to her offspring, and he will have anury. The probability, therefore, is ⅔ × ½ = ⅓, or a 1 in 3 chance that the puppy will have anury.

As we'll discuss in later sections of this chapter, some traits may not show complete dominance and many traits are also influenced by the environment, so it is not always completely obvious what a trait's mode of inheritance is. In such cases, the more individuals we can include in the pedigree, the more accurate the analysis. Some human pedigrees contain thousands of individuals and stretch back six or more generations. With some other species it is possible to analyze tens of thousands of individuals per generation for a dozen or more generations. This is why plants and small insects (among other organisms) are excellent for studying inheritance patterns.

Q *Why do breeders value "pedigreed" horses and dogs so much?*

Dog and horse breeders often speak of "pedigreed" animals, a feature that adds tremendous value to the animals. This is because, with knowledge of an animal's family tree, or complete lineage, it is much less likely that any genetic surprises will occur as the animal develops and reproduces.

Once we have an idea about how a trait is inherited, it is possible to make informed predictions about a couple's risk of having a child with a particular disorder. This can be useful in conjunction with prenatal testing and treatment. It also enables the identification of individuals who are carriers of a recessive trait.

TAKE-HOME MESSAGE 7·8

Pedigrees help scientists, doctors, animal and plant breeders, and prospective parents determine the genes that individuals carry and the likelihood that the offspring of two individuals will exhibit a given trait.

Phenotype diversity has multiple sources and is all around us.

7·9 Incomplete dominance and codominance: the effects of both alleles in a genotype can show up in the phenotype.

As Mendel saw it, the world of genetics was straightforward and simple. We should be so lucky. Unfortunately, the world in which each trait is coded for by a single gene with two alleles—one completely dominant and one recessive—and with no environmental effects at all doesn't quite capture the complexity of the world beyond Mendel's pea plants. So, here and in the next sections, we build up a more complex model of how genes influence the building of bodies. We begin with the observation that, sometimes, the phenotype of heterozygous individuals differs from that of either of the homozygotes, and instead reflects the influence of both alleles rather than a clearly dominant allele.

One situation in which complete dominance is not observed is called **incomplete dominance,** in which the phenotype of a heterozygote is intermediate between the phenotypes of the two homozygotes. In humans, there is a plasma membrane receptor that allows cells (chiefly those in the liver) to remove cholesterol from the bloodstream (see Section 3-11), and the gene that codes for this receptor exhibits incomplete dominance. Individuals that carry two recessive alleles for this gene produce few (or even no) LDL receptors, and cardiovascular disease develops early, at a very young age. Individuals carrying one recessive allele and one dominant allele (that codes for normal-functioning LDL receptors) have significantly reduced levels of circulating cholesterol and a corresponding lower risk of cardiovascular disease. Individuals carrying two copies of the dominant allele produce twice as many LDL receptors as heterozygotes and experience significantly lower levels of circulating cholesterol and a much lower risk of cardiovascular disease.

An example of incomplete dominance that can be easily observed is the flower color of snapdragons (**FIGURE 7-17**). We can obtain true-breeding (homozygous) lines of snapdragons with red flowers, and true-breeding (homozygous) lines that produce only white flowers. When plants from these two populations are crossed, we would expect—if one allele were dominant over the other—either all red or all white flowers. Instead, such crosses always produce plants with pink flowers. Interestingly, when we cross two plants with pink flowers, we get ¼ red-flowered plants, ½ pink-flowered plants, and ¼ white-flowered plants.

How can we interpret this cross? It seems that the plants with white flowers have the genotype $C^W C^W$ and produce no pigment. At the other extreme, the plants with red flowers have the genotype $C^R C^R$ and produce a great deal of pigment. The letter "C" refers to the fact that the gene codes for **c**olor, and the superscript "W" or "R" refers to an allele producing no pigment (**w**hite) or **r**ed pigment. We use these designations for the genotypes because it isn't clear that either white or red is dominant over the other, and so neither should be upper-case or lower-case. The pink flowers receive one of the pigment-producing C^R alleles and one of the no-pigment-producing C^W alleles, and so produce an intermediate amount of pigment. Ultimately, the intensity of pigmentation just

Incomplete dominance occurs when a heterozygote exhibits an intermediate phenotype between the two homozygotes.

Cross 1

MOTHER
white-flowered
homozygous
$C^W C^W$

Because neither allele is dominant, we can't use upper case and lower case for the alleles. Instead, the superscript **W** represents the allele that produces the white flower, and **R** represents the red flower allele.

GAMETES C^W C^W

FATHER
red-flowered
homozygous
$C^R C^R$

GAMETES C^R C^R

	$C^W C^R$	$C^W C^R$
	$C^W C^R$	$C^W C^R$

OFFSPRING	GENOTYPE	PHENOTYPE
	All heterozygous $C^W C^R$	All pink flowers

Cross 2

MOTHER
pink-flowered
heterozygous
$C^W C^R$

GAMETES C^W C^R

FATHER
pink-flowered
heterozygous
$C^W C^R$

GAMETES C^W C^R

	$C^W C^W$	$C^W C^R$
	$C^W C^R$	$C^R C^R$

OFFSPRING	GENOTYPE	PHENOTYPE
	1/4 homozygous $C^R C^R$	1/4 red flowers
	2/4 heterozygous $C^W C^R$	2/4 pink flowers
	1/4 homozygous $C^W C^W$	1/4 white flowers

FIGURE 7-17 Pink snapdragons demonstrate incomplete dominance. When true-breeding white and red snapdragons are crossed, offspring have pink flowers.

CODOMINANCE

FIGURE 7-18 With codominance, a heterozygous individual shows features of both alleles.

depends on the amount of pigment chemical that is made by the flower-color gene.

A second situation in which complete dominance is not observed is called **codominance,** in which the heterozygote displays characteristics of both homozygotes, playfully represented in **FIGURE 7-18** (although "shirt phenotype," of course, has no genetic basis). In codominance, neither allele masks the effect of the other. An actual example of codominance occurs with feather color in chickens. When white chickens are crossed with black chickens, the offspring all have both white and black feathers.

TAKE-HOME MESSAGE 7·9

Sometimes the effects of both alleles in a heterozygous genotype are evident in the phenotype. With incomplete dominance, the phenotype of a heterozygote appears to be an intermediate blend of the phenotypes of the two homozygotes. With codominance, a heterozygote has a phenotype that exhibits characteristics of both homozygotes.

7·10 What's your blood type? Some genes have more than two alleles.

What is your blood type? It can be O, A, B, or AB. Each of these different blood types indicates something about the physical characteristics of your red blood cells and has implications for blood transfusions—both giving and receiving blood. The blood groups are also interesting from a genetic perspective, because they illustrate a case of **multiple allelism,** in which a single gene has more than two alleles. Each individual still carries only two alleles—one from the mother and one from the father. But if you survey all of the alleles present in the *population,* you will find more than just two alleles.

Inheritance of the ABO blood groups provides the simplest example of multiple allelism, because there are only three alleles. We can call these alleles *A, B,* and *O.* The *A* and *B* alleles are both completely dominant to *O,* so individuals are considered to have blood type A whether they have the genotype *AA* or *AO* (**FIGURE 7-19**). Similarly, an individual with the genotype *BB* or *BO* is considered to have blood type B. If you carry two copies of the *O* allele, you have blood type O. The *A* and *B* alleles are codominant with each other, so the genotype *AB* gives rise to blood type AB. Consequently, with these three alleles in the population, individuals can be one of four different blood types: A, B, AB, or O.

What are the phenotypes of these alleles? An individual's blood-type alleles carry instructions that direct construction of a specific set of chemicals, called *antigens,* that protrude from every red blood cell. Antigens are proteins that jut from the surface of a cell and can "turn on" its defenses against foreign invaders. The *A* allele directs the production of A antigens all over the surface of red blood cells. Similarly, the *B* allele directs the production of B antigens on all red blood cells.

MULTIPLE ALLELISM: BLOOD TYPE

Multiple allelism occurs when there are three or more alleles for a gene within a population. An individual still inherits only two alleles—one from each parent.

Gene that determines blood type

Three alleles possible:
- **A** (dominant to **O** and codominant with **B**)
- **B** (dominant to **O** and codominant with **A**)
- **O** (recessive to **A** and **B**)

Type A — A A or A O
Type B — B B or B O
Type AB — A B
Type O — O O

Red blood cells have 6 different genotypes (**AA**, **AO**, **BB**, **BO**, **AB**, and **OO**). These genotypes result in 4 different phenotypes (type A, type B, type AB, and type O).

FIGURE 7-19 Multiple allelism. There are three different alleles—*A, B,* and *O*—for blood type in humans.

The *O* allele does not code for either type of antigen. This means that individuals with blood type AB have red blood cells with both A and B antigens, while individuals with blood type O have red blood cells with a "smoother" surface because they produce no A or B antigens (**FIGURE 7-20**).

BLOOD TYPE, ANTIGENS, AND ANTIBODIES

BLOOD TYPE

	TYPE A	TYPE B	TYPE AB	TYPE O
ANTIGENS Chemicals on the surface of some cells. They act as signposts that tell the immune system whether the cell belongs in the body.	A antigens	B antigens	A and B antigens	Neither A nor B antigens
ANTIBODIES Immune system molecules that attack cells with foreign antigens.	B antibodies	A antibodies	Neither A nor B antibodies	A and B antibodies

Individuals produce antibodies to the antigens they don't have on their cells.

FIGURE 7-20 Friend or foe? Antigens are signposts that tell the immune system whether or not a cell belongs in the body.

Antigens on red blood cells play a role in the body's disease-fighting immune system. Antigens are like signposts, telling the immune system whether a cell belongs in the body or not. If a red blood cell with the wrong antigens enters your bloodstream, your immune system recognizes it as a foreign invader and destroys it. Such an attack is initiated by molecules in the bloodstream called *antibodies,* which attack only foreign antigens. Individuals with only A antigens on their red blood cells produce antibodies that attack B antigens. If they encounter a red blood cell with B antigens, they attack it. Such an immune response can lead to destruction of red blood cells, low blood pressure, and even death. Under normal circumstances, antibodies do not encounter a red blood cell with foreign antigens. Such an event may occur, however, if red blood cells with foreign antigens are accidentally injected into the person's bloodstream in a transfusion.

Individuals with only B antigens on their red blood cells produce antibodies that attack A antigens. Individuals with blood type O, who have neither A nor B antigens on their red

> **Q** Why are people with type O blood considered "universal donors"? Why are those with type AB considered "universal acceptors"?

blood cells, produce antibodies that attack both A and B antigens. Individuals with blood type AB don't produce either type of antibody (or else they would have antibodies that attacked their own blood cells). From this information, we can deduce which blood types can be used in transfusions. Individuals with blood type O are universal donors because their red blood cells have no antigens and so do not trigger a reaction from either type of antibody. And individuals with blood type AB are universal recipients because they do not produce antibodies to either the A or B antigen. This is shown in **FIGURE 7-21**.

Another marker on the surface of red blood cells is the Rh blood group marker. This marker results from the effects of a single gene with just two alleles. Individuals' red blood cells carry the Rh cell surface marker if they have one or two copies of the dominant Rh marker allele, and they are said to be "Rh-positive." This "positive" (or "+") is then noted in their blood type, in addition to their ABO blood type, as in "O-positive" or "B-negative." Individuals who have two copies of the recessive allele for this gene do not have any

THE SCIENCE BEHIND BLOOD DONATION

BLOOD TYPE	CAN DONATE TO	CAN RECEIVE FROM
TYPE A • Red blood cells have A antigens. • Individual produces antibodies that attack B antigens.	Type A Type AB	Type A Type O
TYPE B • Red blood cells have B antigens. • Individual produces antibodies that attack A antigens.	Type B Type AB	Type B Type O
TYPE AB • Red blood cells have A and B antigens. • Individual produces neither A nor B antibodies. • Individual is universal recipient.	Type AB	ANYONE! Type A Type B Type AB Type O
TYPE O • Red blood cells have neither A nor B antigens • Individual produces antibodies that attack A and B antigens • Individual is universal donor.	ANYONE! Type A Type B Type AB Type O	Type O

💡 *Individuals with type O blood are universal donors. Individuals with type AB are universal recipients.*

FIGURE 7-21 Mapping blood compatibility. Individuals mount an immune response to blood cells if they produce an antibody that attacks an antigen present on the donated red blood cells.

Rh markers, and they are described as "negative," as in "O-negative" or "A-negative." If individuals who are Rh-negative are exposed to Rh-positive blood, their immune system attacks the Rh antigens as foreign invaders—an immune response that can vary from mild, and passing unnoticed, to severe, which can lead to death. Thus, the Rh marker further restricts whose blood a person can receive in a transfusion.

Beyond the ABO and the Rh marker groups, there are many, many genes with multiple alleles—a dozen or even more alleles in some cases. In fact, one gene for eye color in fruit flies has more than 1,000 different alleles!

TAKE-HOME MESSAGE 7·10

In multiple allelism, a single gene has more than two alleles. Each individual still carries only two alleles, but in the population, more than just two alleles exist. This is the case for the ABO blood groups in humans.

7·11 Multigene traits: how are continuously varying traits such as height influenced by genes?

When babies are born, the parents are often curious about how tall their child will grow to be. Old wives' tales suggest a couple of ways for predicting height. If the baby is a boy, they say to add 5 inches to the mother's height and average that with the father's height. If it is a girl, subtract 5 inches from the father's height and average that with the mother's height. Alternatively, the lore says, just take the child's height at two years of age and double it.

While these methods can be surprisingly accurate at making predictions, they don't really help us understand the underlying reason *why* height can be predicted so well. The reason these methods work is that genes play a strong role in influencing height, and so offspring do resemble their parents in measurable ways. But unlike the simple case of Mendel's pea plants, where a single gene with two alleles determines the height of the plant, for humans and most animals, adult height is influenced by many different genes. Such a trait is said to be **polygenic.**

Recent research has identified two genes that help determine height in humans. Individuals with the "tall" allele for both genes are taller than those with the tall allele for only one. Individuals with one tall allele, in turn, are taller than people who do not have a tall allele for either gene. The term **additive effects** describes what happens when the effects of alleles from multiple genes all contribute to the ultimate phenotype. One of these height genes is on chromosome 15 and codes for an enzyme that converts testosterone to estrogen. This enzyme influences height because estrogen helps bones fuse at their ends and thus stop growing. In all, the two height genes identified in humans account for only about 2 inches of a person's height, but they exemplify how multiple genes can influence a single characteristic. The variety of heights from very short to very tall, with every height in between, reflects the fact that height is a trait influenced by contributions from multiple genes as well as the environment (**FIGURE 7-22**).

Many other physical traits are influenced by multiple genes, including eye color in humans. Long believed to be controlled by a single gene with a dominant brown-eye allele and a recessive blue-eye allele, it now seems that eye color is the result of the interactions between at least two genes and

POLYGENIC TRAITS

FIGURE 7-22 From many genes, one trait. Height and skin color are multigene traits.

possibly more—a situation that makes more sense, given the significant continuous variation in eye color seen among adults.

Many behavioral traits are influenced by multiple genes. The developmental disorder known as autism, for example, seems to be the result of alterations in numerous—perhaps as many as 10 or even 20—different genes. Individuals with autism have difficulty interacting with others, particularly in making emotional connections. Autistic individuals also tend to have narrowly focused and repetitive interests. Autism is notoriously difficult to study, though, because its symptoms are varied, as is their intensity. It turns out that these variations in the disorder may result from the different combinations of the many genes involved in autism, much as different alleles for several height genes may work together to produce a variety of heights.

Interestingly, the genes responsible for autism may also influence some desirable characteristics. Behaviors that cause problems when manifest in the extreme may turn out to be beneficial when less extreme, such as unusual abilities of

perception, analytical skills, and focus. This idea—called the "geek theory of autism"—was first suspected when an upsurge in cases of autism in children was noticed in areas with large numbers of high-tech workers, including Silicon Valley in California and near Cambridge, England, in the heart of the United Kingdom's high-technology industry. Subsequently, researchers have published findings showing an over-representation of autistic children among parents working in the fields of engineering, physics, computer science, and math (although the researchers point out that autistic children are born to parents across all professions and socio-economic backgrounds). Perhaps alleles for genes that contribute to making individuals good at computer programming and solving complex technology problems can produce autism when an individual carries too many of them.

> **TAKE-HOME MESSAGE 7·11**
>
> Many traits, including continuously varying traits such as height, eye color, and skin color, are influenced by multiple genes.

7·12 Sometimes one gene influences multiple traits.

Just as multiple genes can influence one trait, some individual genes can influence multiple, unrelated traits, a phenomenon called **pleiotropy.** In fact, this may be true of nearly all genes. Consider sickle-cell anemia (also called sickle-cell disease), a potentially fatal condition in which individuals produce defective red blood cells that change their shape, becoming sickle-shaped, when they lose the oxygen they carry. The defective blood cells cannot effectively transport oxygen to tissues, and they accumulate in blood vessels, causing extreme pain. Individuals with sickle-cell disease suffer shortness of breath and numerous other problems that lead to a significantly reduced lifespan. The gene responsible for sickle-cell disease encodes the molecule hemoglobin, the oxygen-carrying molecule in red blood cells: Hb^A is the allele for normal hemoglobin, and Hb^S is the abnormal, "sickle-cell" allele. Anemia occurs in individuals homozygous for the sickle-cell allele, Hb^SHb^S, but not in individuals carrying at least one copy of the normal allele, Hb^A (although heterozygous individuals produce both

Q What is the benefit of "almost" having sickle-cell disease?

normal and sickling red blood cells, just not enough to cause sickle-cell anemia).

This hemoglobin gene is pleiotropic because individuals homozygous or heterozygous for the sickle-cell allele, Hb^SHb^S or Hb^AHb^S, are resistant to the parasite that causes malaria. The resistance is due to the fact that the malarial parasite—which lives in red blood cells—cannot survive well in cells that carry the defective version of the hemoglobin gene. And because even individuals who are heterozygous for the sickle-cell allele have a significant number of sickling red blood cells, their bloodstream is just not a hospitable environment for the malarial parasite (**FIGURE 7-23**). Consequently, this one gene influences two traits: both the building of hemoglobin and the susceptibility to malaria.

Another example of pleiotropy is the SRY gene. Named for "**s**ex-determining **r**egion on the **Y** chromosome," this gene causes fetal gonads to develop as testes shortly after fertilization. Following the gonads' secretion of testosterone, a

Pleiotropy occurs when one gene influences multiple, different traits.

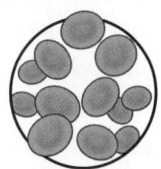

Hb^A Hb^A HOMOZYGOTE
• Does not have sickle-cell disease
• Is susceptible to malaria

Hb^S Hb^A HETEROZYGOTE
• Does not have sickle-cell disease
• Is immune to malaria

Hb^S Hb^S HOMOZYGOTE
• Has sickle-cell disease
• Is immune to malaria

Malarial parasite infecting a red blood cell

Someone with no sickled cells does not have sickle-cell anemia but is susceptible to malaria.

FIGURE 7-23 From one gene, multiple traits. The allele for sickle-cell disease is pleiotropic: it causes red blood cells to form an unusual, sickled shape, and it also provides resistance to malaria.

cascade of other developmental changes then occurs, such as development of the internal and external male reproductive structures. Ultimately, the SRY gene is responsible for numerous behavioral characteristics as well. These characteristics are described further in Chapter 9.

TAKE-HOME MESSAGE 7·12

In pleiotropy, one gene influences multiple, unrelated traits. Most, if not all, genes may be pleiotropic.

7·13 Why are more men than women color-blind? Sex-linked traits differ in their patterns of expression in males and females.

The patterns of inheritance of most traits do not differ between males and females. When a gene is on an autosome (one of the non-sex chromosomes), both males and females inherit two copies of the gene, one from their mother and one from their father. The likelihood that an individual inherits one particular genotype versus another does not differ between males and females.

Traits coded for by the sex chromosomes, on the other hand, have different patterns of expression in males and females. One of the most easily observed examples of this phenomenon is red-green color-blindness. On the X chromosome in humans, there is a gene that carries the instructions for producing light-sensitive proteins in the eye that, when produced normally, respond differently to red wavelengths and green wavelengths of light. These proteins make it possible to distinguish between the colors red and

green. As long as an individual has at least one functioning copy of the gene carrying the instructions for production of these light-sensitive proteins, he or she produces sufficient amounts of the protein to have normal color vision.

There is a rare allele for this gene, however, that produces a non-functioning version of the protein. Having some of this non-functioning protein is not a problem as long as the person also carries another, normal version of the gene and produces some of the functioning protein. But this poses a problem for males, because they have only one X chromosome. In contrast, females inherit two X chromosomes.

Here's the problem: men get only one chance to inherit the normal version of the gene that codes for red-green color vision. It must be on the X chromosome they inherit from

SEX-LINKED TRAITS: COLOR-BLINDNESS

A sex-linked trait is carried on the X chromosome. Women carry two copies of the X chromosome, while men carry an X chromosome and a Y chromosome.

Gene with instructions for light-sensitive proteins within the eye

Two alleles possible:
- **R** (produces functioning light-sensitive proteins)
- **r** (produces defective light-sensitive proteins)

TO BE COLOR-BLIND...

Male must inherit color-blindness allele (**r**) from his mother.

Female must inherit color-blindness allele (**r**) from both parents.

TO HAVE NORMAL VISION...

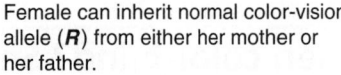

Male must inherit normal color-vision allele (**R**) from his mother.

Female can inherit normal color-vision allele (**R**) from either her mother or her father.

FIGURE 7-24 Sex-linked traits such as color-blindness are not expressed equally among males and females.

their mother. Women get two chances. Although a woman may inherit the defective allele from one parent, she can still inherit the normal allele from the other parent. As long as she inherits the normal gene from one parent, she will have normal color vision. (If she inherits the defective allele from both parents, she will be red-green color-blind.) As we would predict, then, the frequency of red-green color-blindness is significantly greater in males than in females (**FIGURE 7-24**). Approximately 7% to 10% of men exhibit red-green color-blindness, while fewer than 1% of women are red-green color-blind.

Although males exhibit sex-linked recessive traits more frequently than do women, the situation is reversed for sex-linked dominant traits. In these cases, because females have two chances to inherit the allele that causes the trait, they are more likely to have the allele and thus exhibit the trait than are males, who have only one chance to inherit the allele.

Q If a man is color-blind, did he inherit this condition from his mother, his father, or both parents?

TAKE-HOME MESSAGE 7·13

The patterns of inheritance of most traits do not differ between males and females. However, when a trait is coded for by a gene on a sex chromosome, such as color vision on the X chromosome, the pattern of expression differs for males and females.

7·14 Environmental effects: identical twins are not identical.

It is a very serious warning, in boldfaced capital letters: "PHENYLKETONURICS: CONTAINS PHENYLALANINE." But it's not next to a skull and crossbones on a glass bottle in a chemistry lab, it's on cans of diet soda intended for human consumption (**FIGURE 7-25**). Most of us either don't notice the warning or ignore it. Still, it's always there, and to some people it's a matter of life and death. What does it mean?

Q Drinking diet soda can be deadly if you carry a single bad gene. What gene is it and why is it so deadly?

At the most fundamental level, this warning is on products that contain phenylalanine because an organism's phenotype is a product of its genes in combination with its environment. In this case, specifically, the warning is for people who have a particular genotype that, in the presence of phenylalanine, can be deadly.

Phenylalanine is one of the amino acids. Sometimes our bodies use phenylalanine directly to

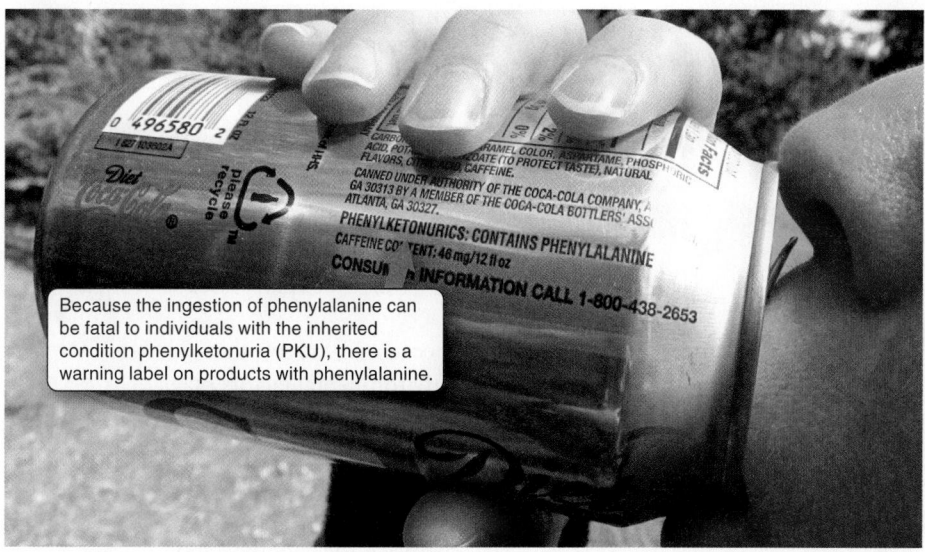

FIGURE 7-25 Change the environment, "cure" the disease. The ingestion of phenylalanine in diet soda can be fatal to individuals with the inherited condition phenylketonuria (PKU).

> Because the ingestion of phenylalanine can be fatal to individuals with the inherited condition phenylketonuria (PKU), there is a warning label on products with phenylalanine.

build proteins, adding it to a growing amino acid chain. At other times, phenylalanine is chemically converted into another amino acid, called tyrosine. The body then uses tyrosine to build proteins and in a variety of other ways.

The problem is this: at birth, some people carry two copies of a mutant version of the gene that is supposed to produce the enzyme that converts phenylalanine into tyrosine. The mutant gene produces a malfunctioning enzyme, and none of the body's phenylalanine is converted into tyrosine. Perhaps this doesn't seem as though it should be a big problem, but it is. Little by little, as these individuals consume phenylalanine, it builds up in their bodies because none of it is converted into tyrosine. Eventually, so much accumulates that it reaches toxic levels and poisons the brain, leading to mental retardation and death. The disease is called phenylketonuria, or PKU.

Here's where the warning label comes in. By limiting the amount of phenylalanine in their diet (from diet soda and other sources), individuals with the two mutant alleles for processing phenylalanine can avoid the toxic buildup of the amino acid in their brain. In essence, they modify their environment (their diet) so that it contains little or no phenylalanine. And in that environment, the PKU mutant alleles are harmless. This example highlights the fact that genes by themselves do not "code" for physical characteristics. Rather, genes interact with the environment to produce physical characteristics. Unless you have information about

Q *Could you create a temporarily spotted Siamese cat with an ice pack? Why?*

both the genes *and* the environment, it is not usually possible to know what the phenotype will be.

A non-life-threatening illustration of the interaction of genes with the environment can be seen at a pet shop. Siamese cats (as well as Himalayan rabbits) carry genes that produce dark pigmentation. These genes interact strongly with the environment and are heat-sensitive. Dark pigment is produced only in relatively cold areas of the animal's body, while warm areas remain very light in color. This is why the fur on the coldest parts of the body—the ears, paws, tail, and tip of the face—becomes the darkest, while the fur on the rest of the body remains cream-colored or white (**FIGURE 7-26**). For Siamese cats living in cold climates and that spend a lot of time outside, it's interesting to notice that they become significantly darker in color during the winter months. Those that lounge indoors all winter remain lighter in color.

There are thousands of other cases in which genes' interactions with the environment influence their ultimate effects in the body. The very fact that identical twins—who inherit exactly the same set of alleles at the time of fertilization—don't die on the same day at the same moment and from the same cause, for example, reveals that environmental variation influences the expression of genes. The scope of environmental influences ranges from traits with large and obvious environmental effects, such as body weight and its relationship with caloric intake, to traits such as eye color that are barely influenced by environmental effects, to traits with complex and subtle interactions with the environment, such as intelligence or personality.

Because of the role that environmental factors play in influencing phenotypes, DNA is not like a blueprint for a house. There is nearly always significant interaction between the genotype and the environment that influences the exact phenotype produced. The use of this metaphor is problematic to the extent that it suggests the phenotype is determined *solely* by the genotype. If that were the case, there would be no reason to invest in better schools, physical fitness regimens, nutritional monitoring, self-help efforts, or any other process by which individuals or societies try to improve people's lives (i.e., alter phenotypes) by enriching their environment.

Q

James Watson, the co-discoverer of DNA, once wrote that when we completed the Human Genome Project, we would have "the complete genetic blueprint of man." Why might that be a poor metaphor?

Some pigment genes produce dark pigment only under cold conditions—such as on the tail, nose, ears, and feet of these animals.

TAKE-HOME MESSAGE 7·14

Genotypes are not like blueprints that specify phenotypes. Phenotypes are generally a product of the genotype in combination with the environment.

Different genes influence red hair and freckles, so why are they often inherited together?

7·15–7·16 Some genes are linked together.

7·15

Most traits are passed on as independent features: Mendel's law of independent assortment.

Sometimes you can be right about something for the wrong reason. This happened to Gregor Mendel. He didn't know that genes were carried on chromosomes. He believed that the units of heredity were just free-floating entities within cells. Given this perspective, it made sense to him that the inheritance pattern of one trait wouldn't influence the inheritance of any other trait. He believed that all genes behaved independently.

It helps to consider an example. Earlier in this chapter we saw that the characteristic of having a dimpled chin is caused by a single dominant gene. Imagine that you had a true-breeding population of people with dimpled chins (remember, "true-breeding" for a trait means that all offspring always manifest the trait; in the case of dimples, all have the genotype *DD*). Now suppose that an individual in this population had children with someone from a population of true-breeding, non-dimple-chinned people (everyone has the genotype *dd*). In this case, all of their children would have dimpled chins, but they would be heterozygous (*Dd*), getting a dominant allele from their dimple-chinned parent and a recessive allele from the other parent. If two heterozygotes had children together, though, they would produce three-quarters dimpled and one-

quarter non-dimpled children, with genotypes in the ratio of ¼ *DD*, ½ *Dd*, and ¼ *dd*. That is just what Mendel observed for traits in pea plants.

But what if we concurrently observed another characteristic of these people? Suppose the original true-breeding population of dimpled-chin people (*DD*) was also true-breeding for albinism (all *aa*), a disorder caused by carrying two recessive alleles for a single gene. And suppose that individuals in the normal-chinned population (*dd*) were also true-breeding for normal pigmentation (all *AA*). The question is, do the alleles an individual inherits for the dimpled-chin trait influence which alleles that individual inherits for pigmentation? And the answer is that, in most cases, they do not (**FIGURE 7-27**). Rather, the first cross of a dimple-chinned albino with a normal-chinned, normally pigmented individual would result in a child heterozygous for both traits, expressing each of the dominant traits. Phenotypically, this and all other offspring of this cross would be dimple-chinned and normally pigmented. In a mating between two doubly heterozygous individuals, three-quarters of their children would have the dominant trait and one-quarter would have the recessive trait, regardless of which trait you are tallying. In other words,

Mendel's law of independent assortment states that one trait does not influence the inheritance of another trait.

IF...
Parents are both homozygous for both traits. (But each parent is homozygous for a different allele than the other parent.)

MOTHER
albino
homozygous **aa**
dimpled chin
homozygous **DD**

GAMETES
All are *aD*

FATHER
pigmented
homozygous **AA**
non-dimpled chin
homozygous **dd**

GAMETES
All are *Ad*

All are *Aa Dd*

THEN...
All offspring are heterozygous for both traits (i.e., "doubly heterozygous"): **Aa Dd** (and exhibit the dominant trait in their phenotype).

OFFSPRING	GENOTYPE	PHENOTYPE
	All heterozygous **Aa**	All pigmented
	All heterozygous **Dd**	All dimpled chin

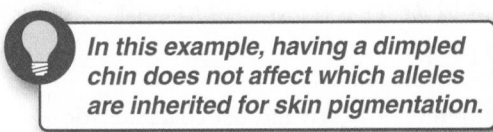
In this example, having a dimpled chin does not affect which alleles are inherited for skin pigmentation.

FIGURE 7-27 Independent assortment of genes.

IF...
Parents are both heterozygous for both traits (i.e., "doubly heterozygous"). Four different types of gametes are produced by each: **AD**, **Ad**, **aD**, and **ad**.

MOTHER
pigmented
heterozygous **Aa**
dimpled chin
heterozygous **Dd**

FATHER
pigmented
heterozygous **Aa**
dimpled chin
heterozygous **Dd**

GAMETES	AD	Ad	aD	ad
AD	AA DD	AA Dd	Aa DD	Aa Dd
Ad	AA Dd	AA dd	Aa Dd	Aa dd
aD	Aa DD	Aa Dd	aa DD	aa Dd
ad	Aa Dd	Aa dd	aa Dd	aa dd

THEN...
The genotype proportions for **A/a** are still ¼ **AA**, ½ **Aa**, and ¼ **aa**. And the genotype proportions for **D/d** are still ¼ **DD**, ½ **Dd**, and ¼ **dd**.

OFFSPRING	GENOTYPE	PHENOTYPE
	1/4 homozygous dominant **AA**	3/4 pigmented
	2/4 heterozygous **Aa**	
	1/4 homozygous recessive **aa**	1/4 albino
	1/4 homozygous dominant **DD**	3/4 dimpled chin
	2/4 heterozygous **Dd**	
	1/4 homozygous recessive **dd**	1/4 non-dimpled chin

neither trait influences the inheritance pattern for the other trait; all traits are inherited independently of each other. This is known as **Mendel's law of independent assortment.**

In the next section we'll see that, despite Mendel's correct understanding that separate traits are inherited independently, his belief that this happened because all genes just float freely around in the cell was not correct. The genes, as we now know, are carried on chromosomes. And this fact leads

occasionally to some situations in which independent assortment does *not* occur.

TAKE-HOME MESSAGE 7·15

Genes tend to behave independently, such that the inheritance pattern of one trait doesn't usually influence the inheritance of any other trait.

7·16 Red hair and freckles: genes on the same chromosome are sometimes inherited together.

Most redheads have pale skin and freckles. This simple observation is problematic for the law of independent assortment as Mendel imagined it. After all, in his law, he asserted that the inheritance of one trait does not influence the inheritance of another. But clearly that doesn't happen in this case. Having one of the traits, such as red hair, seems to influence the presence of another trait, pale skin (**FIGURE 7-28**). Strictly speaking, Mendel's second law is not true for *every* pair of traits. Sometimes the alleles for two genes are inherited together and expressed almost as a package.

Q Why do most redheads have pale skin?

In the case of humans, for example, there are about 23,000 genes in our genome. Yet we have only 23 unique chromosomes (two copies of each). Thus, genes influencing different traits must be on the same chromosome, maybe even right next to each other. When they are close together, we say that they are **linked genes.** One 2008 study, for example, demonstrated a link between human genes that influence hair color and skin pigmentation (including freckles).

Why are linked genes inherited together? To answer this, we must revisit the behavior of chromosomes during the production of gametes, discussed in Chapter 6. When you made that sperm or egg by meiosis, only one of the two copies of each of your chromosomes ended up in the gamete. It may have been the one from your mother or it may have been the one from your father. In either case, all of the alleles that were on the chromosome from that one parent were passed on as a group to the child that resulted from the fertilization involving that gamete. This process continues generation after generation. The linked alleles never get split up unless, during meiosis, recombination occurs between them, moving one or more to

FIGURE 7-28 Violating the law of independent assortment. Red hair and freckles are often inherited as a package deal.

the other chromosome in the pair so that they now become linked with the alleles on that chromosome (**FIGURE 7-29**).

When alleles are linked closely on the same chromosome, Mendel's second law doesn't hold true. It is very surprising—and was fortunate for Mendel—that of the seven pea plant traits he chose for his studies, none of them were close together on the same chromosome. For this reason, they all behaved as if they weren't linked.

TAKE-HOME MESSAGE 7·16

Sometimes, having one trait influences the presence of another trait. This is because the alleles for two genes are inherited and expressed almost as a package deal when the genes are located close together on the same chromosome.

LINKED GENES

HOMOLOGOUS CHROMOSOMES

Linked genes

Maternal copy   Paternal copy

When crossing over occurs, linked genes usually stay together.

Homologous chromosomes after the exchange of genetic information

If this gamete is fertilized, the linked genes will be passed on to the offspring together as a group.

Each of the four chromatids gets packaged into a gamete.

FIGURE 7-29 Gene linkage. Alleles that are closely linked on the same chromosome will be passed on to offspring in one bundle.

If genes are far apart on a chromosome or are on different chromosomes, the inheritance of one gene does not influence the inheritance of another.

CAN A GENE NUDGE US TOWARD NOVELTY-SEEKING (AND SPICY FOODS)?
Novelty-seeking and a gene that influences it.

On human chromosome 11 there is a gene called DRD4. This gene carries the instructions for building a protein embedded in the membranes of many of your brain cells. The protein is a receptor for the brain chemical dopamine, which is active in several areas of the brain called "pleasure centers" and influences initiative and motivation.

Although all humans have some form of the DRD4 gene, there are several different alleles that a person might carry (though only two per person, of course). One aspect of the gene that varies is a short sequence near the beginning of the gene, called "promoter polymorphism –521C/T," that alters the activity of the brain's pleasure centers. There are two different alleles, C and T, and it appears that having one or two copies of the T allele leads to reduced transcription of the dopamine receptor gene, while having the CC genotype is associated with greater gene activity.

Q: CAN A SINGLE GENE INFLUENCE YOUR PERSONALITY? In 2000, researchers reported that individuals carrying two copies of the C allele for the DRD4 gene, as opposed to zero or one copy of the C allele, were more likely to exhibit certain personality traits, particularly novelty-seeking. The subjects in the study responded to a commonly used questionnaire, called the temperament and character inventory. On the questionnaire, subjects ranked how well certain statements described them, such as "I have sometimes done things just for kicks or thrills" or "I think things through before coming to a decision." The subjects were then evaluated for seven dimensions of personality traits. When it came to their score for "novelty-seeking," there was a small but statistically significant difference in how the subjects scored, depending on their genotype for this DRD4 gene:

GRAPHIC CONTENT!
Thinking critically about visual displays of data.
Turn to p. 294 for a closer inspection of this figure.

By 2008, 11 studies had been published on the relationship between the CC genotype and novelty-seeking. In a "meta-study" of all the published findings, researchers concluded that, taken together, these studies demonstrated a significant association between novelty-seeking and the –521C/T genotype. They summarized the results graphically:

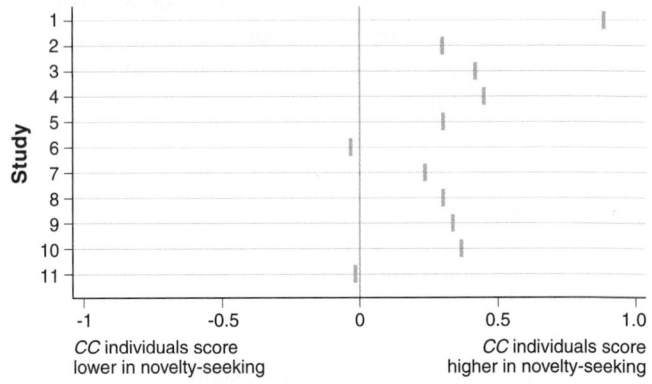

Novelty-seeking score of CC individuals compared with CT and TT individuals

Researchers have subsequently reported a variety of behavioral differences among people with higher novelty-seeking scores, including increased propensities for engaging in high-risk sports, alcohol and drug consumption, and attraction to vocations with a higher degree of risk. These people have even been reported to show a preference for spicy foods!

Q: DO YOU WANT YOUR EMPLOYERS OR INSURANCE COMPANIES TO KNOW WHICH ALLELES YOU CARRY FOR THE DRD4 GENE? Information about your genetic predisposition for diseases such as breast cancer or colon cancer can put you at risk for genetic discrimination. Might a person be at risk for discrimination based on whether his or her genotype is CC or CT or TT for this one variant of the DRD4 gene? Should it be taken into account that the personality differences influenced by DRD4 are small, that they seem to be affected by numerous other genes, and that there is tremendous variation in personality traits that is unrelated to the DRD4 gene? Would you want to know what your genotype is? Why?

Big Ideas in ...
Genes and Inheritance

7·1–7·5 Why do offspring resemble their parents?

- Offspring resemble their parents because they inherit genes—instruction sets for biochemical, physical, and behavioral traits, some of which are responsible for diseases—from their parents.

- Gregor Mendel conducted studies on garden peas that help us understand how traits are inherited, by applying methodical experimentation and rigorous hypothesis testing and by focusing on easily observed and categorized traits in the pea plants.

- Each parent puts into every sperm or egg it makes a single set of instructions for building a particular trait. The trait observed in an individual depends on the two copies of the gene that it inherits from its parents.

- It is not always possible to determine an individual's genotype through observation of its phenotype. Much genetic analysis therefore makes use of clever experiments and careful record-keeping to determine organisms' genotypes.

7·6–7·8 Probability and chance play central roles in genetics.

- Probability plays a central role in genetics. In segregation, each gamete that an individual produces receives only one of the two copies of each gene the individual carries in its other cells; it is impossible to know which allele this will be.

- Chance plays a role in fertilization, too: all of the sperm or eggs produced by an individual are different from one another, and any one of those gametes may be the gamete involved in fertilization.

- Test-crosses and pedigrees help scientists, doctors, plant and animal breeders, and prospective parents determine which genes individuals carry and the likelihood that the offspring of two individuals will exhibit a given trait.

7·9–7·14 The translation of genotypes into phenotypes is not a black box.

- Sometimes the effects of both alleles in a heterozygous genotype are seen in the phenotype.

- Many traits are influenced by multiple genes, and many genes may influence multiple unrelated traits.

- When a trait is coded for by a gene on the sex chromosomes, the pattern of expression differs for males and females.

- Genotypes are not like blueprints that specify phenotypes. Rather, phenotypes are a product of the genotype in combination with the environment.

7·15–7·16 Some genes are linked together.

- Many genes tend to behave independently, such that the inheritance pattern of one trait doesn't usually influence the inheritance of any other trait.

- When genes are located close together on the same chromosome, the alleles for the genes are inherited and expressed almost as a package deal.

See the To-Go Guide (packaged with every new copy of this textbook) for an illustrated summary of the chapter.

Check Your Knowledge

Thinking critically about visual displays of data.

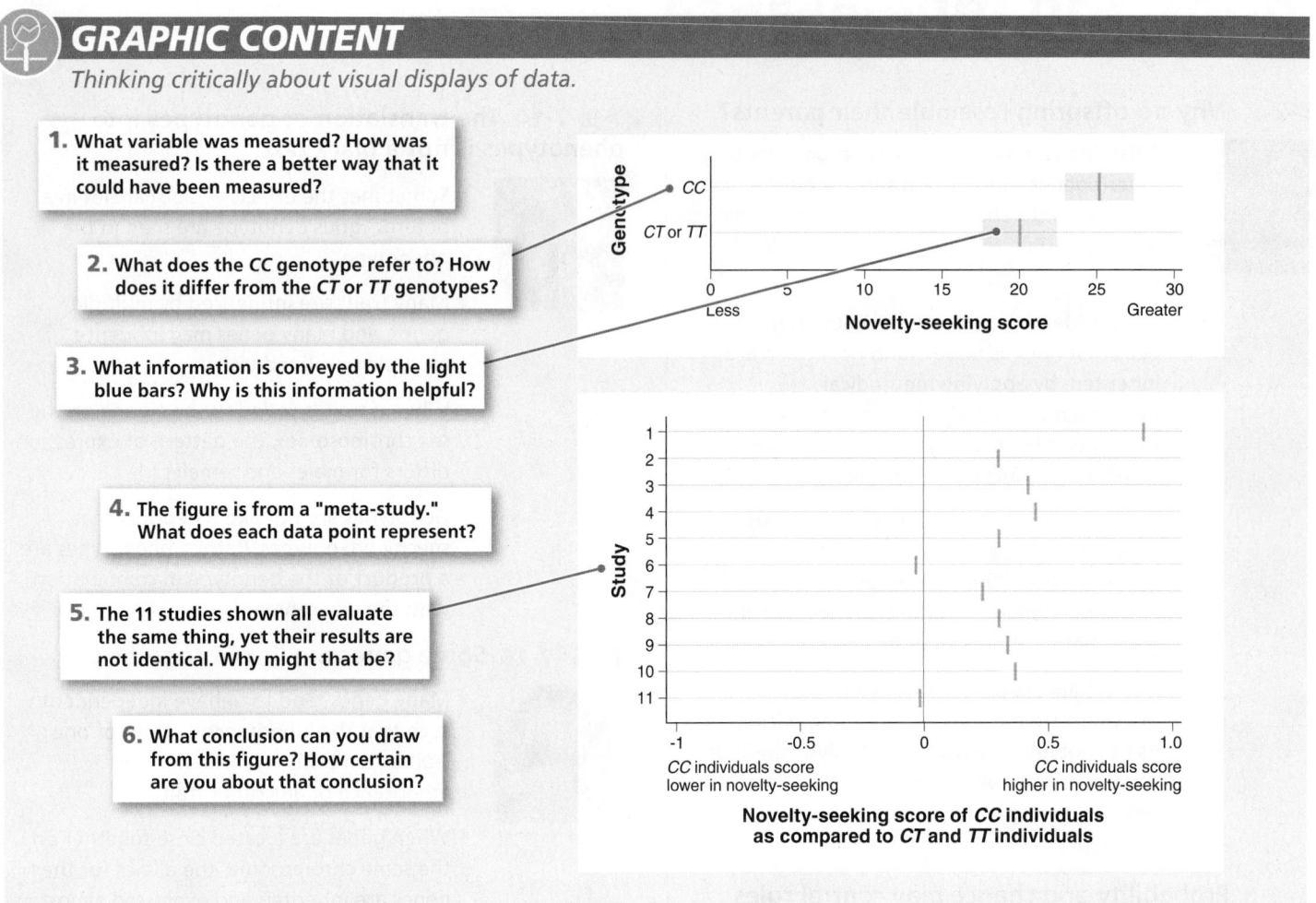

1. What variable was measured? How was it measured? Is there a better way that it could have been measured?

2. What does the *CC* genotype refer to? How does it differ from the *CT* or *TT* genotypes?

3. What information is conveyed by the light blue bars? Why is this information helpful?

4. The figure is from a "meta-study." What does each data point represent?

5. The 11 studies shown all evaluate the same thing, yet their results are not identical. Why might that be?

6. What conclusion can you draw from this figure? How certain are you about that conclusion?

See Answers at the back of the book.

Key Terms in Genes and Inheritance

Multiple-Choice Questions

1. Most genes come in alternative forms called:

   a) alleles.

   b) heterozygotes.

   c) gametes.

   d) chromosomes.

   e) homozygotes.

100 | HARD
23
0 | EASY

2. Traits that are determined by a single gene:

   a) occur in single-celled organisms, but not in humans.

   b) are common in humans.

   c) must occur on the X chromosome, because males have only a single X and so the gene must be able to function in the absence of its homologous allele.

   d) include eye color and skin color.

   e) can have only two alleles.

100 | HARD
69
0 | EASY

3. Pea plants were well suited for Mendel's breeding experiments for all of the following reasons except:

   a) Peas exhibit variations in a number of observable characteristics, such as flower color and seed shape.

   b) Mendel and his staff could control the pollination between different pea plants.

   c) It is easy to obtain large numbers of offspring from any given cross.

   d) Many of the characteristics that vary in pea plants are not linked closely on the same chromosome.

   e) Peas have a particularly long generation time.

100 | HARD
31
0 | EASY

4. The law of segregation states that:

   a) the transmission of genetic diseases within families is always recessive.

   b) an allele on one chromosome will always segregate from an allele on a different chromosome.

   c) gametes cannot be separate and equal.

   d) the number of chromosomes in a cell is always divisible by 2.

   e) each of two alleles for a given trait segregate into different gametes.

100 | HARD
30
0 | EASY

5. In pea plants, purple flower color is dominant to white flower color. If two pea plants that are true-breeding for purple flowers are crossed, in the offspring:

   a) all of the flowers will be purple.

   b) three-quarters of the flowers will be purple and one-quarter will be white.

   c) half of the flowers will be purple and one-quarter will be white.

   d) one-quarter of the flowers will be purple and three-quarters will be white.

   e) all of the flowers will be white.

100 | HARD
23
0 | EASY

6. Pea flowers may be purple (*P*) or white (*p*). Pea seeds may be round (*R*) or wrinkled (*r*). What proportion of the offspring from a cross between purple-flowered, round-seeded individuals (heterozygous for both traits) will have both white flowers and round seeds?

   a) $^1/_{16}$

   b) $^1/_2$

   c) $^3/_{16}$

   d) $^3/_4$

   e) $^9/_{16}$

100 | HARD
57
0 | EASY

7. The test-cross:

   a) makes it possible to determine the genotype of an individual of unknown genotype that exhibits the dominant version of a trait.

   b) is a cross between an individual whose genotype for a trait is not known and an individual homozygous recessive for the trait.

   c) sometimes requires the production of multiple offspring to reveal the genotype of an individual whose genotype is unknown (but who exhibits the dominant phenotype).

   d) Only a) and b) are correct.

   e) Choices a), b), and c) are correct.

100 HARD · 43 · 0 EASY

8. Which of the following statements is correct regarding pedigree analysis?

   a) Darkened squares or circles always represent individuals with the trait being traced.

   b) White squares or circles always represent heterozygous individuals.

   c) Horizontal lines connect siblings.

   d) The length of the vertical lines is dependent on the relatedness between two individuals.

   e) Squares represent females, and circles represent males.

100 HARD · 33 · 0 EASY

9. All of the offspring of a black hen and a white rooster are gray. The simplest explanation for this pattern of inheritance is:

   a) multiple alleles.

   b) codominance.

   c) incomplete dominance.

   d) incomplete heterozygosity.

   e) sex linkage.

100 HARD · 44 · 0 EASY

10. A woman with type B blood and a man with type A blood could have children with which of the following phenotypes?

   a) AB only

   b) AB or O only

   c) A, B, or O only

   d) A or B only

   e) A, B, AB, or O

100 HARD · 27 · 0 EASY

11. Which of the following traits shows a polygenic method of inheritance?

   a) flower color in snapdragons

   b) blood type in humans

   c) seed color in peas

   d) sickle-cell disease in humans

   e) skin color in humans

100 HARD · 44 · 0 EASY

12. The impact of a single gene on more than one characteristic is called:

   a) incomplete dominance.

   b) environmentalism.

   c) balanced polymorphism.

   d) pleiotropy.

   e) codominance.

100 HARD · 31 · 0 EASY

13. A rare, X-linked dominant condition in humans, congenital generalized hypertrichosis, is marked by excessive hair growth all over a person's body. Which of the following statements about this condition is incorrect?

   a) The son of a woman with this disease has just slightly more than a 50% chance of having this condition.

   b) The daughter of a man with this condition has a 100% chance of having this condition.

   c) The daughter of a woman with this disease has just slightly more than a 50% chance of having this condition.

   d) The son of a woman with this disorder has a 100% chance of having this condition.

   e) Males with this condition almost always have a more severe phenotype, because women usually have at least one normal allele that dilutes the effect of the mutated allele.

100 HARD · 69 · 0 EASY

14. Individuals carrying two non-functioning alleles for the gene producing the enzyme that converts phenylalanine into tyrosine:

   a) will develop phenylketonuria (PKU).

   b) may or may not develop phenylketonuria, because the environment (diet, in this case) also plays a role in determining their phenotype.

   c) will develop both PKU and Tay-Sachs disease, because the genes causing the two traits are on the same chromosome.

   d) will develop both PKU and Tay-Sachs disease, because one pleiotropic gene influences both traits.

   e) do not need to worry about their phenylalanine consumption, because PKU depends on both genes and the environment.

100 HARD · 58 · 0 EASY

15. Because of Mendel's law of independent assortment:

   a) individuals with red hair are more likely to have freckles.

   b) skin color and hair texture tend to be inherited together.

   c) we can deduce that genes cannot exist as free-floating entities within a cell but must be carried on chromosomes.

   d) the alleles coding for one trait do not usually influence the inheritance pattern for another trait.

   e) Both a) and b) are correct.

100 HARD · 51 · 0 EASY

16. Thousands (or even tens of thousands) of different traits make up an individual. For this reason:

   a) in a species with 23 different chromosomes, some traits must be coded for by genes on the same chromosome.

   b) the environment must influence more than half of our traits.

   c) all (or nearly all) genes must be pleiotropic.

   d) knowing an individual's phenotype is not sufficient for determining the person's genotype.

   e) All of the above are correct.

100 | HARD
76
0 | EASY

Short-Answer Questions

1. Two healthy parents have two children, both of whom have a degenerative muscular disorder called SMA (spinal muscular atrophy).

   a) Explain how SMA must be inherited and what the genotypes of the parents must be.

   b) The parents wish to have a third child and are contemplating adopting versus having a biological child. They seek the guidance of a genetic counselor and ask what the probability of having another child with SMA would be. What does the genetic counselor tell them? Explain.

2. Mackenzie's favorite flower is the hydrangea. She plants a large hydrangea bush in her yard and enjoys the big purple blossoms. Her sister, Anna, would like some hydrangeas for her yard as well, so they transplant a small portion of the large bush to Anna's yard. Anna is surprised when, the first time the plant in her yard blooms, the blossoms are pink instead of purple. If the genotype of this plant has not changed, what might have influenced a change in the phenotype?

3. Your friend explains to you that her father has hemophilia, a genetic disorder that affects the process of blood clotting, but her mother does not.

   a) Knowing that the inheritance pattern for this disorder is sex-linked, explain to your friend why it is more common for males to inherit a sex-linked trait.

   b) Using a Punnett square, indicate the probability that a brother of your friend would have hemophilia, assuming that her mother carries two functional copies of the gene involved in this sex-linked recessive disorder. Explain your answer.

See Answers at the back of the book.
For additional study questions, go to www.prep-u.com.

Darwin's dangerous idea

8

Evolution and Natural Selection

8·1 Evolution is an ongoing process.

What big eyes you have! The glasswing butterfly, Cithaerias aurorina, *from Peru.*

8·1 We can see evolution occurring right before our eyes.

What's the longest that you've ever gone without food? Twenty-four hours? Thirty-six hours? If you've ever gone hungry that long, you probably felt as if you were going to die of starvation, but humans can survive days, even weeks, without food. In 1981, for example, 27-year-old Bobby Sands, a political prisoner in Northern Ireland, went on a hunger strike. Forsaking all food and consuming only water, he gradually deteriorated and ultimately died—after 66 days without food.

Each hour without food is even more dangerous when you're tiny. How long do you think a fruit fly can last without food? The answer is just under a day—20 hours, give or take a few (**FIGURE 8-1**). Fruit flies can't live long without food because their tiny bodies don't hold very large caloric reserves. But could you breed fruit flies that could live longer than 20 hours, on average? Yes.

First, start with a population of 5,000 ordinary fruit flies. In biology, the term **population** specifically means a group of organisms of the same species living in a particular geographic

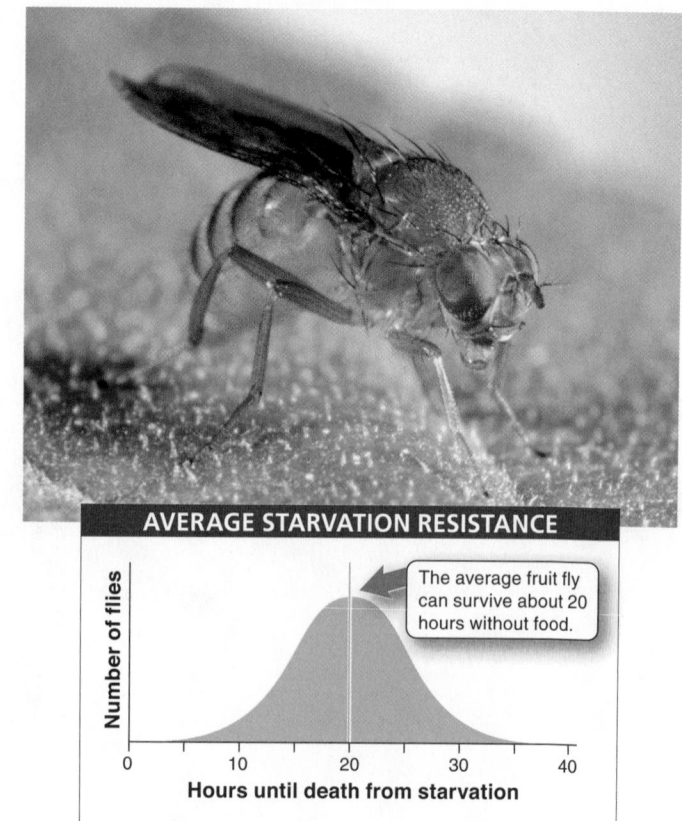

AVERAGE STARVATION RESISTANCE

The average fruit fly can survive about 20 hours without food.

Number of flies

0   10   20   30   40
Hours until death from starvation

FIGURE 8-1 **How long can a fruit fly survive without food?**

region. The region can be a small area such as a test tube or a large area such as a lake. In your experiment, your population occupies a cage in your laboratory.

From these 5,000 fruit flies, you choose only the 20% of flies that can survive the longest without food:

1. Remove the food from the cage with the population of 5,000 flies.

2. Wait until 80% of the flies starve to death, then put a container of food into the cage.

3. After the surviving flies eat, they'll have the energy to reproduce. When they do, collect and transfer the eggs to a new cage.

You can now start a new generation populated only by the offspring of those fruit flies able to survive without food for the longest amount of time. When these eggs hatch, do you think the flies in this new generation will live longer than 20 hours without food? Indeed, these flies do show increased resistance to starvation. The average fly in the new generation can live for about 23 hours without food. And again, some of the new flies survive for more than 23 hours, some for less. The longest-surviving flies tend to be those that pack on the fat when the food is available. The new starvation-resistance curve for this second generation is similar to that of the original flies, but shifted to the right a bit so that the highest part of the curve occurs at 23 hours, indicating that most flies of the new generation survive for an average of 23 hours without food (**FIGURE 8-2**).

What if you kept repeating these three steps? Start each new generation using eggs only from the fruit flies in the top 20% of starvation resistance. After five generations, would the average starvation-resistance time for a fly in your latest

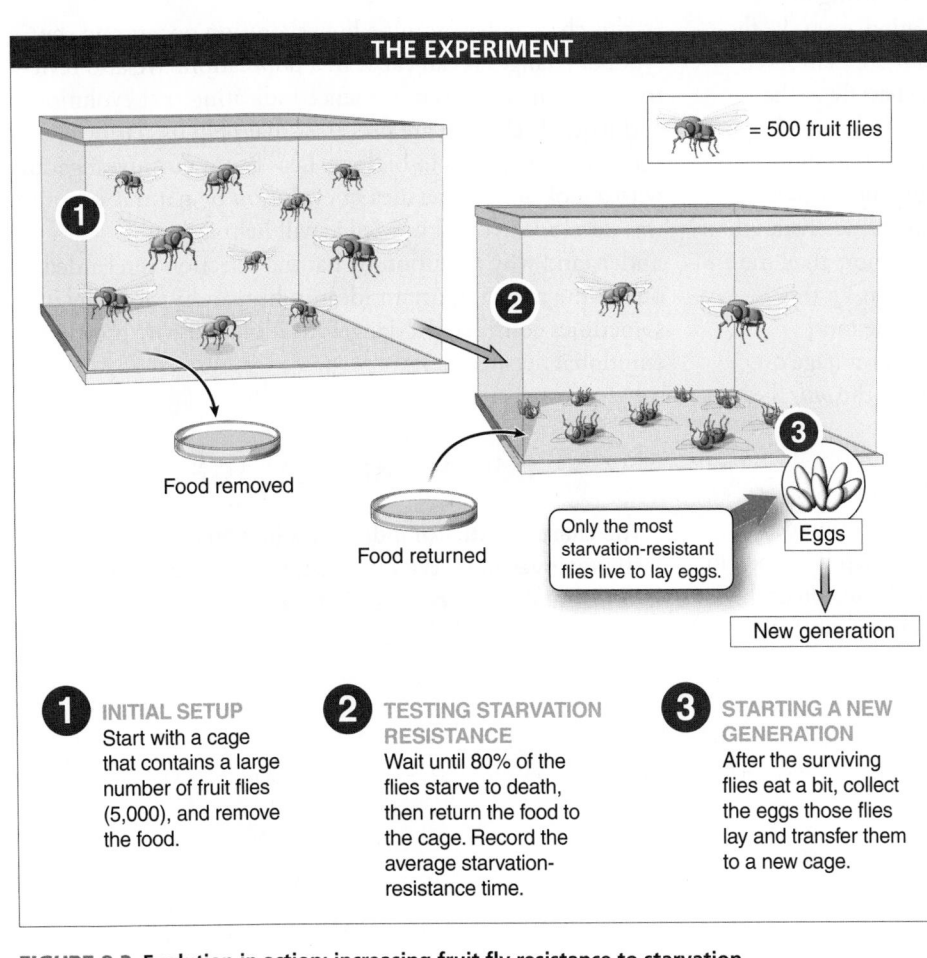

THE EXPERIMENT

Food removed

Food returned

Only the most starvation-resistant flies live to lay eggs.

= 500 fruit flies

Eggs

New generation

1 INITIAL SETUP
Start with a cage that contains a large number of fruit flies (5,000), and remove the food.

2 TESTING STARVATION RESISTANCE
Wait until 80% of the flies starve to death, then return the food to the cage. Record the average starvation-resistance time.

3 STARTING A NEW GENERATION
After the surviving flies eat a bit, collect the eggs those flies lay and transfer them to a new cage.

FIGURE 8-2 Evolution in action: increasing fruit fly resistance to starvation.

THE RESULTS

Number of flies
GENERATION 1
Average starvation resistance:
20 HR.
0 40 80 120 160 200
Hours until death from starvation

Number of flies
GENERATION 2
Average starvation resistance:
23 HR.
0 40 80 120 160 200
Hours until death from starvation

Experiment continues through 60 generations.

Number of flies
GENERATION 60
Average starvation resistance:
160 HR.
0 40 80 120 160 200
Hours until death from starvation

Over many generations of natural selection, the population changes. Originally, the flies couldn't survive a day without food. Now they survive almost an entire week!

population be even higher? In fact, it would. With each new generation, you would see a slight increase, and with the fifth generation, the population's average survival would be about 32 hours.

One benefit to conducting research on fruit flies is that they have very short lives—they reach maturity at about two weeks and live for one month, on average. Such an experiment can be continued for many generations. After 60 generations of allowing the flies that are best at surviving without food to reproduce, how has the population changed? Amazingly, the *average* fly in the resulting population can survive for more than 160 hours without food (see Figure 8-2). In 60 generations, the flies have gone from a starvation resistance of less than a day to one of nearly a week! At the point where the food is removed, the flies in generation 60 are noticeably fatter than the flies in generation 0.

What happened? In a word: **evolution.** That is, there was a genetic change in the population of fruit flies living in the cage. Every fly in the generation 60 population, even the fly with the worst starvation resistance, is still more than seven times better at resisting starvation than the best fly in the original population. Later in this chapter we'll discuss the mechanisms by which evolution can occur, but, in short, in this situation it is the consequence of certain individual organisms in a population being born with characteristics that enable them to survive better and reproduce more than the offspring of other individuals in the population. In this experiment, the 20% of fruit flies that were the most starvation resistant had a huge reproductive advantage over less starvation-resistant flies because they were the *only* flies in the population that survived to reproduce.

This experiment answers a question that is sometimes perceived as complex or controversial: does evolution occur? The answer is an unambiguous *yes.* We can watch it happen in the lab whenever we want. Recall from our discussion of the scientific method (see Chapter 1) that for an experiment's

results to be valid, they must be reproducible. To be certain of these results, researchers carried out the starvation-resistance experiment described above five separate times. The results were the same every time.

In this experiment we changed starvation resistance in fruit flies, but what if we used dogs instead of flies and, instead of allowing the most starvation-resistant individuals to reproduce, we allowed only the smallest dogs to reproduce? Would the average body size of individual dogs decrease over time? Yes. What if the experiment were done in a natural habitat, in the absence of human intervention, on rabbits, and only the fastest rabbits escaped death from predation by foxes? Would the average running speed in rabbits increase over time? Yes. We know these answers because each of these experiments has already been done. An unfortunate example of evolution in action is the evolution of resistance to antibiotics in numerous illness-causing bacteria, including some bacteria responsible for pneumonia and tuberculosis.

In this chapter, we examine how evolution occurs and the types of changes it can cause in a population. We also review the five primary lines of evidence indicating that evolution and natural selection are processes that help us clarify all other ideas and facts in biology. Let's begin our investigation with a look at how the idea of evolution by natural selection was developed. This knowledge will help us better understand why evolution by natural selection is regarded as one of the most important ideas in human history, why it is sometimes considered a dangerous idea, and why it generates emotional debate.

TAKE-HOME MESSAGE 8·1

The characteristics of individuals in a population can change over time. We can observe such change in nature and can even cause it to occur.

8·2–8·5 Darwin journeyed to a new idea.

The *Galápagos tortoise*, Geochelone elephantopus.

8·2 Before Darwin, many people believed that all species had been created separately and were unchanging.

Charles Darwin grew up in an orderly world. In the Victorian British society he inhabited, many beliefs about humans and our place in the world had changed little over the previous two centuries. Biblical explanations were sufficient for most natural phenomena: the earth was thought by most people to be about 6,000 years old. With the occasional exception of a flood or earthquake or volcanic eruption, the earth was believed to be mostly unchanging. People recognized that organisms existed in groups called species. (In Chapter 10, we discuss in more detail what a species is; for now, we'll just say that individual organisms in a given species can interbreed with each other but not with members of another species.) People in Darwin's society also generally believed that all species, including humans, had been created at the same time and that, once created, they never changed and never died out.

Before he left this world, Darwin had thrown into question long- and dearly held beliefs about the natural world, and he forever changed our perspective on the origins of humans and our relationship to all other species. He didn't smash his society's worldview to pieces all at once, though, and he didn't do it by himself (**FIGURE 8-3**).

In the 1700s and 1800s, scientific thought was advancing at a rapid pace. In 1778, the respected French naturalist

Georges Buffon shook things up by suggesting that the earth must be about 75,000 years old. He arrived at this age by estimating that 75,000 years was the minimum time required for the planet to cool from a molten state. In the 1790s, Georges Cuvier began to explore the bottoms of coal and slate mines and found fossil remains that had no obvious similarity to any living species. Many interpreted the Bible in such a way that made Cuvier's discoveries unthinkable, believing that biblical accounts did not allow for species to be wiped out. Cuvier's publications documented giant fossils (including the Irish elk, the mastodon, and the giant ground sloth) that bore no resemblance to any currently living animals (**FIGURE 8-4**). And although Cuvier was not a proponent of the idea of evolution, the fossils he discovered allowed only one explanation: extinction was a fact. Troubling as this observation was for the prevailing Western worldview, it was only the beginning.

Not only was it starting to seem that species could disappear from the face of the earth, but several scientists, including Darwin's own grandfather, Erasmus Darwin, began to suggest that living species might change over time. And in the early 1800s, the biologist Jean-Baptiste Lamarck put forth a popular idea about the mechanisms by which this change might occur. Lamarck's idea was wrong—he thought that

GEORGES BUFFON
(1707–1788)
Suggested that the earth was much older than previously believed.

GEORGES CUVIER
(1769–1832)
By documenting fossil discoveries, showed that extinction had occurred.

JEAN-BAPTISTE LAMARCK
(1744–1829)
Suggested that living species might change over time.

CHARLES LYELL
(1797–1875)
Argued that geological forces had gradually shaped the earth and continue to do so.

The young Charles Darwin

FIGURE 8-3 Scientists who shaped Darwin's thinking.

change came about chiefly through the use or disuse of features—but the increased willingness among scientists to question previously sacred "truths" contributed to an atmosphere of unfettered scientific thought in which it was possible to challenge convention.

Perhaps the revolutionary ideas that most inspired Darwin were those of the geologist Charles Lyell. In his 1830 book *Principles of Geology,* Lyell argued that geological forces had shaped the earth and were continuing to do so, producing mountains and valleys, cliffs and canyons, through gradual but relentless change. This idea that the physical features of the earth were constantly changing would most closely parallel

Darwin's idea that the living species of the earth, too, were gradually—but constantly—changing.

TAKE-HOME MESSAGE 8·2

In the 18th and 19th centuries, scientists began to overturn many commonly held beliefs in the Western world, including that the earth was only about 6,000 years old and that all species had been created separately and were unchanging. These gradual changes in scientists' beliefs helped shape Charles Darwin's thinking.

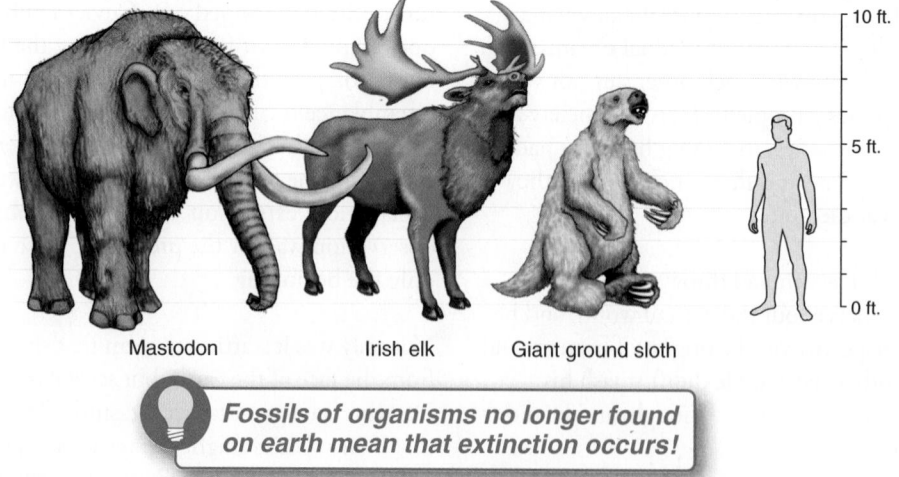

Mastodon   Irish elk   Giant ground sloth

Fossils of organisms no longer found on earth mean that extinction occurs!

FIGURE 8-4 Extinction occurs. Deep in coal mines, Cuvier discovered the fossilized remains of very large animals no longer found on earth.

8·3 A job on a 'round-the-world survey ship allowed Darwin to indulge and advance his love of nature.

Charles Darwin was born into a wealthy family in England in 1809, and his early life was unremarkable. Charles was never at the top of his class and professed to hate schoolwork. Nonetheless, at 16, he went to the University of Edinburgh to study medicine, following his father's footsteps. He was bored, though, and left at the end of his second year, when the prospect of watching gruesome surgeries (in the days before anesthesia) was more than he could bear.

Upon the abrupt ending of Charles's medical career, his father urged him to pursue the ministry and sent him to study theology at Cambridge University. Although he never felt great inspiration in his theology studies, Darwin was in heaven at Cambridge, where he could pursue his real love, the study of nature.

Shortly after graduation in 1831, Darwin—with significant help from his botany professor—landed his dream job, a position as a "gentleman companion" for the captain of the HMS *Beagle,* on a five-year, 'round-the-world surveying expedition (**FIGURE 8-5**). This job came as a huge relief to the young Darwin, who was not really interested in becoming a minister.

Once on the *Beagle,* Darwin found that he didn't actually like sea travel. He was seasick for much of his time on board, writing to his cousin: "I hate every wave of the ocean with a fervor which you . . . can never understand." To avoid nausea, Charles spent as much time as possible on shore. It was there that he found that fieldwork was his true calling. At each stop, he would eagerly investigate the new worlds he found. In Brazil, he was enthralled by tropical forests. In Patagonia, near the southernmost part of South America, he explored beaches and cliffs, finding spectacular fossils from huge extinct mammals. Elsewhere, he explored coral reefs and barnacles, always packing up specimens to bring back to museums in England and recording his observations for later use. He was like a schoolboy on permanent summer vacation.

DARWIN'S 'ROUND-THE-WORLD VOYAGE

Galápagos Islands

FIGURE 8-5 Like a schoolboy on permanent summer vacation. In 1831, Darwin set out on the HMS *Beagle* on a five-year surveying expedition that took him around the globe.

TAKE-HOME MESSAGE 8·3

After initially training in medicine and theology, Charles Darwin was able to focus on studying the natural world when, in 1831, he got a job on a ship conducting a five-year, 'round-the-world survey.

8·4 Observing geographic similarities and differences among fossils and living plants and animals, Darwin developed a theory of evolution.

The only book Darwin brought with him on the *Beagle* was Lyell's *Principles of Geology,* which he read again and again. Intrigued by the book's premise that the earth has been, and continues to be, constantly changing, Darwin's mind was ripe for fresh ideas—particularly as he began observing seemingly inexplicable things. How could he explain marine fossils high in the Andes, hundreds of miles from the nearest ocean? The idea that the earth was an ever-changing planet was seeping into Darwin's mind. That idea would serve him well when, a few years into its journey, the *Beagle* stopped at the Galápagos Islands, off the northwest coast of South America.

This group of volcanic islands was home to many unusual species, from giant tortoises to extremely docile lizards, which made so little effort to run away that Darwin had to avoid stepping on them. Darwin was particularly intrigued by the wide variety of birds, especially the finches, which seemed dramatically more variable than those he had seen in other locations.

Darwin noticed two important and unexpected patterns on his voyage that would be central to his discovery of a mechanism for evolution. The first involved the finches he collected and donated to the Zoological Society of London. Darwin had assumed that they were the equivalent of tall and short, curly-haired and straight-haired people. That is, he thought that all the finches were of the same species but with different physical characteristics or **traits,** such as body size, beak shape, or feather color. The staff of the Zoological Society, however, could see from the birds' physical differences that the birds were not reproductively compatible and that there were 13 unique species—a different species for every one of the Galápagos Islands that Darwin had visited. Moreover, although the birds were different species, they all resembled very closely the single species of finch living on the closest mainland, in Ecuador (**FIGURE 8-6**).

This resemblance seemed a suspicious coincidence to Darwin. Perhaps the island finches resembled the mainland species because they used to be part of the same mainland population.

DARWIN'S OBSERVATIONS

FPO

RESEMBLANCE OF ISLAND FINCH SPECIES TO MAINLAND FINCH SPECIES
Although the finches found on the Galápagos Islands had slightly different physical characteristics, they still resembled the single mainland finch.

600 mi

Galápagos Islands

Ecuador (mainland)

Mainland finch

GALÁPAGOS FINCHES

Ground finch

Tree finch

Warbler finch

RESEMBLANCE OF EXTINCT SPECIES TO LIVING SPECIES IN SAME AREA
Around the world, there is a striking similarity between the fossils of extinct species and the living species in that same area.

10 ft

Glyptodont (extinct)

Hairy armadillo (alive today)

FIGURE 8-6 Darwin observed unexpected patterns.

Over time they may have separated and diverged from the original population and gradually formed new—but similar—species. Darwin's logic was reasonable, but his idea flew in the face of all the scientific thinking of the day.

The second important but unexpected pattern Darwin noted was that, throughout his voyage, at every location there was a striking similarity between the fossils of extinct species and the living species in that same area. In Argentina, for instance, he found some giant fossils from a group of organisms called "glyptodonts." The extinct glyptodonts looked just like armadillos, a species that still flourished in the same area. Or rather, they looked like armadillos on steroids: the average armadillo today is about the size of a house cat and weighs 10 pounds, while the glyptodonts were giants at 10 feet long and more than 4,000 pounds (see Figure 8-6).

If glyptodonts had lived in South America in the past, and armadillos were currently living there, why was only one of the species still alive? And why were the glyptodont fossils found only in the same places that modern armadillos lived? Darwin deduced that glyptodonts resembled armadillos because they were their ancestors. Again, it was a logical deduction, but it contradicted the scientific dogma of the day that species were unchanging and extinction did not occur.

The wheels were turning in Darwin's head, but he didn't have a great "Eureka!" moment until several years after his voyage, when he was back in England. He was reading "for amusement" *Essay on the Principle of Population,* by the economist Thomas Malthus. Malthus prophesied doom and gloom for populations, including humans, based on his belief that populations had the potential to grow much faster than food supplies could. Darwin speculated that, rather than the future holding certain catastrophe for all, maybe the best

individuals would "win" in the ensuing struggle for existence, and the worst would "lose." If so, he suddenly saw that "favourable variations would tend to be preserved, and unfavourable ones to be destroyed."

In 1842, Darwin finally prepared a draft of his ideas in a 35-page paper, written in pencil, and fleshed it out over the next couple of years. He knew that his idea was important—so important that he wrote a letter to his wife instructing her, in the case of his sudden death (an odd request, given that he was only 35 years old), to give his "sketch" to a competent person, along with about $1,000 and all of his books, so that this person could complete it for him.

He also had an inkling that his ideas would rock the world. In a letter to a close friend, he wrote: "At last gleams of light have come, and I am almost convinced (quite contrary to the opinion I started with) that species are not (it is like confessing to murder) immutable." But "confessing to murder" was apparently more than Darwin was ready for. Inexplicably, he put his sketch into a drawer, where it remained for 14 years.

TAKE-HOME MESSAGE 8·4

Darwin noted unexpected patterns among fossils he discovered and living organisms he observed while on the voyage of the *Beagle.* Fossils resembled but were not identical to the living organisms in the same area where they were found. And finch species on each of the Galápagos Islands differed from each other in small but significant ways. These observations helped Darwin develop his theory of how species might change over time.

8·5 In 1859, after decades of mulling and procrastinating, Darwin published his thoughts on natural selection.

In a letter to Darwin, Alfred Russel Wallace (FIGURE 8-7), a young British biologist in the throes of malaria-induced mania in Malaysia, laid out a clear description of the process of evolution by natural selection, after having read Malthus's book. He asked Darwin to "publish it if you think it is worthy." Although he may have been inspired by his fever to put his thoughts in writing, they were careful, precise, and resulted from many years of thought and exposure to the writings of many of the same scientists who influenced Darwin. Crushed at having been scooped, Darwin wrote that "all my originality will be smashed." He had numerous friends

among the most prominent scientists of the day, however, and they arranged for a joint presentation of Wallace's and Darwin's work to the Linnaean Society of London. As a result, both Darwin and Wallace are credited for the first description of evolution by natural selection.

Darwin then sprang into action, rapidly putting together his thoughts and observations and completing, 16 months later, a full book. In 1859, he published *The Origin of Species* (its full title is *On the Origin of Species by Means of Natural Selection, or the Preservation of Favoured Races in the Struggle for Life*).

FIGURE 8-7 **Alfred Russel Wallace.** Darwin and Wallace independently identified the process of evolution by natural selection.

EVOLVING BELIEFS IN DARWIN'S WORLD

BEFORE:
- Organisms were all put on earth by a creator at the same time.
- Organisms are fixed: no additions, no subtractions.
- Earth is about 6,000 years old.
- Earth is mostly unchanging.

First published in 1859

AFTER:
- Organisms change over time.
- Some organisms have gone extinct.
- Earth is more than 6,000 years old.
- The geology of earth is not constant, but always changing.

FIGURE 8-8 **Reconsidering the world.** Commonly held ideas before and after Darwin.

The book was an instant hit, selling out on its first day, provoking public discussion and debate and ultimately causing a wholesale change in the scientific understanding of evolution. Where once the worldview was of a young earth, populated by unchanging species all created at one time, with no additions or extinctions, now there was a new dynamic view of life on earth: species could and did change over time, and as some species split into new species, others became extinct (**FIGURE 8-8**).

Darwin's theory has proved to be among the most important and enduring contributions in all of science. It has stimulated an unprecedented diversity of theoretical and applied research, and it has withstood repeated experimental and observational testing. With the background of Darwin's elegant idea in hand, we can now examine its details.

TAKE-HOME MESSAGE 8·5

After putting off publishing his thoughts on natural selection for more than 15 years, Darwin did so only after Alfred Russel Wallace independently came up with the same idea. The two men published a joint presentation on their ideas in 1858, and Darwin published a much more detailed treatment in *The Origin of Species* in 1859, sparking wide debate and discussion of natural selection.

8·6–8·11 Four mechanisms can give rise to evolution.

Barn owl swoops to seize a mouse.

8·6
Evolution occurs when the allele frequencies in a population change.

Suppose you were put in charge of a large population of tigers in a zoo. Almost all of them are orange and brown with black stripes. Occasionally, though, unusual all-white tigers are born. This white phenotype is the result of a rare pair of alleles that suppresses the tiger's production of most fur pigment (**FIGURE 8-9**). (Recall from Section 7-1 that alleles are variants of a gene, and that most mammals inherit one allele from

their mother and one from their father for each gene.) Because visitors flock to zoos to see the white tigers, you want to increase the proportion of your tiger population that is white. How would you do so?

One possibility is that you could alter the population by trying to produce more animals with the white phenotype.

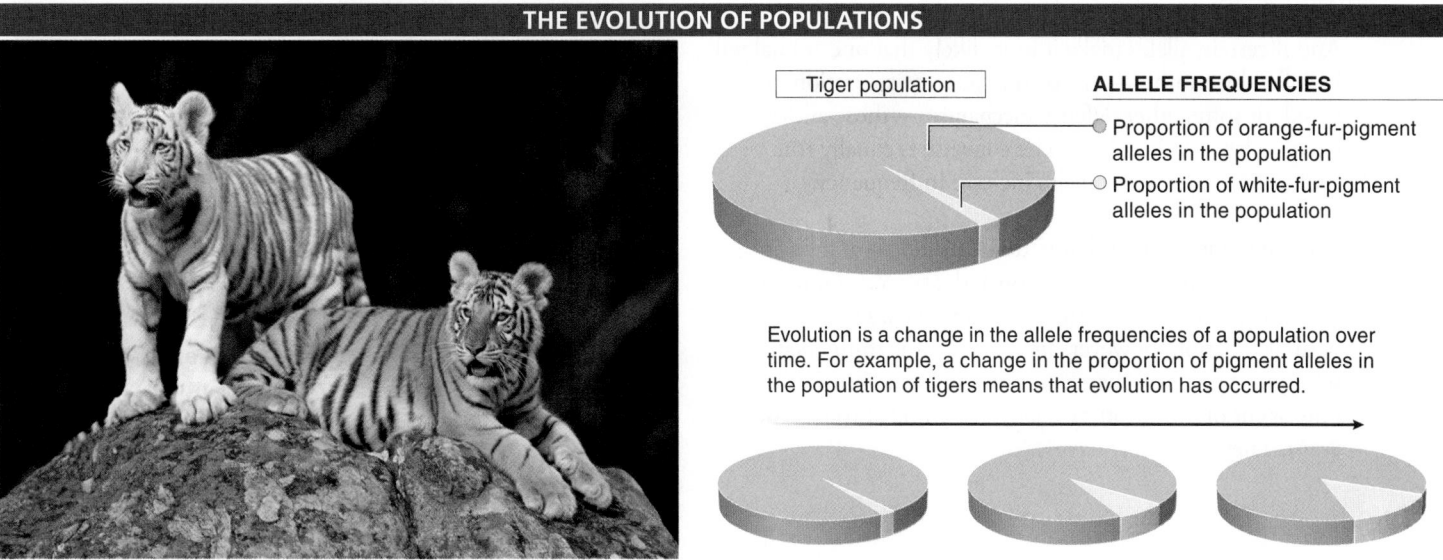

THE EVOLUTION OF POPULATIONS

Tiger population

ALLELE FREQUENCIES
- Proportion of orange-fur-pigment alleles in the population
- Proportion of white-fur-pigment alleles in the population

Evolution is a change in the allele frequencies of a population over time. For example, a change in the proportion of pigment alleles in the population of tigers means that evolution has occurred.

FIGURE 8-9 Evolution defined. Evolution is a change in allele frequencies in a population.

In this case, your best strategy would be to try to breed the white tigers with each other. Over time, this would lead to more and more white tigers. And as the generations go by (this will take a while, though, since the generation time for tigers is about eight years), your population will include a higher proportion of white tigers. When this happens, you will have witnessed evolution, a change in the allele frequencies of the population.

Another way you might increase the proportion of white tigers in your population would be to acquire some white tigers from another zoo. By directly adding white tigers to your population, the population would include a higher proportion of white tigers (you might even trade some of your orange tigers, which would further increase the proportion of your population that is white). By adding white tigers or removing orange tigers, you will again have witnessed evolution in your population.

As this example illustrates, evolution doesn't involve changing the genetics or physical features of *individuals*. Individuals do not evolve. Rather, you change the proportions of the alleles in the *population*. Within a population, for a particular allele type, the proportion of all the alleles that are of this type is that allele's frequency, like its "market share." In the tiger example, the white-fur alleles initially had little market share, perhaps as small as 1%. Over time, though, they came to make up a larger and larger proportion of the total fur-pigment alleles in the population. And as this happened, evolution occurred.

Any time an allele's market share changes, evolution is occurring. Perhaps the most dramatic way we see this is in acts of predation. When one organism kills another, the dead animal's alleles will no longer be passed on in the population. And if certain alleles make it more likely that one animal will be killed by another—maybe they alter its coloration, or speed, or some other defense mechanism—those alleles are likely to lose market share. The converse is equally true: evolution occurs when alleles increase in frequency.

Darwin demonstrated that natural selection could be an efficient mechanism of evolution and a powerful force in adapting populations to their environments. Evolution and natural selection, however, are not the same thing. Natural selection is one way that evolution can occur, but it is not the only agent of evolutionary change. It is one of four (**FIGURE 8-10**). They are:

THE MECHANISMS OF EVOLUTION

MUTATION
An alteration of the base-pair sequence in the DNA of an individual's gamete-producing cells that changes an allele's frequency.

GENETIC DRIFT
A random change in allele frequencies, unrelated to any allele's influence on reproductive success.

MIGRATION
A change in allele frequencies caused by individuals moving into or out of a population.

NATURAL SELECTION
A change in allele frequencies that occurs when individuals with one version of a heritable trait have greater reproductive success than individuals with a different version of the trait.

FIGURE 8-10 The four ways in which evolution can occur.

1. Mutation

2. Genetic drift

3. Migration

4. Natural selection

Keeping in mind that evolution is genetic change in a population, we'll now explore each of these four agents that are capable of causing such genetic changes.

TAKE-HOME MESSAGE 8·6

Evolution is a change in allele frequencies within a population. It can occur by four different mechanisms: mutation, genetic drift, migration, and natural selection.

8·7 Mutation—a direct change in the DNA of an individual—is the ultimate source of all genetic variation.

In describing the first of the four mechanisms of evolution, it is helpful to keep in mind our precise definition of evolution: a change in the allele frequencies found in a population. **Mutation** is an alteration of the base-pair sequence of an individual's DNA, and when this alteration occurs in the DNA that codes for a particular gene, the change in the DNA sequence may change that allele. (See Section 5-9 for a detailed discussion of the mutation process.) Say, for example, that a mutation changes one of a person's two blue-eye alleles into a brown-eye allele. If this mutation occurs in the sperm- or egg-producing cells, it can be passed on to the next generation; the offspring may carry the brown-eye allele. When this happens, the proportion of blue-eye alleles in the population is slightly reduced, and the proportion of brown-eye alleles is slightly increased. Evolution has occurred.

When considering mutation as an agent of evolution, it is important to remember that the cells of a multicellular eukaryotic organism can be divided into two types: somatic cells and reproductive cells. Somatic cells—the cells forming the body of an organism—are not passed from parent to offspring. Only reproductive cells are. For that reason, only mutations that affect reproductive cells can be inherited, and so we consider only those mutations as altering the allele frequencies within a population. The causes of mutations, however, are the same for somatic and reproductive cells.

Mutations can occur spontaneously during the complex process of cell division and, as we saw in Chapter 5, can be induced by a variety of environmental factors—including radiation, such as X rays, and some chemicals. But although these factors can induce mutations and influence the rate at which mutations occur, they do not generally influence exactly *which* mutations occur. Thus, mutations are random, and whether a mutation happens or not is unrelated to how useful or harmful it might be. Treatment of an agricultural pest with harmful chemicals, for example, might increase the number of mutations occurring in that pest population, but it does not increase the likelihood that a particular mutation is beneficial or detrimental.

There are many potential DNA-damaging threats in our world today. These include tanning beds, for example, which cause individuals to become tan by bombarding the skin with ultraviolet rays similar to those

produced by the sun. These rays induce tanning just as exposure to the sun does: by stimulating pigment-producing cells to produce more melanin, a pigment that darkens skin color. But because ultraviolet rays are a form of energy, they can damage DNA, just as the sun's rays can. Not surprisingly, researchers have found that the greater an individual's exposure to ultraviolet rays, the greater the likelihood of DNA damage and, as a consequence, of skin cancer.

Another potential source of DNA-damaging energy is of concern to many more people: mobile phones. The scientific community is still divided on this question, however. Although mobile phones do emit electromagnetic radiation, that radiation is sufficiently low level that it is generally unable to break chemical bonds and therefore cause mutations. The majority of studies have not found any consistent causal relationship between mobile phone usage and any short- or medium-term health hazards.

Since 2004, however, several studies have suggested that further investigation is warranted. A study from 12 laboratories found evidence of DNA damage in cell cultures exposed to levels of radiation similar to those produced by mobile phones. Another study found that individuals who had used mobile phones for 10 years or more had an increased risk of brain tumors. A third study discovered an increased risk of brain tumors only for the side of the head on which the phone was used. Stay tuned for more information on this important question. (And, as with tanning beds, it is important to note that any cell phone–induced mutations are almost certainly *somatic* cell mutations, and so unlikely to influence evolution.)

In addition to being an agent of evolutionary change, mutation has another important role relevant to all agents of evolution, including natural selection: mutation is the ultimate source of genetic variation in a population. We saw that a mutation may lead to the conversion of one allele to another that is already found within the population, as in our blue eye and brown eye example. More importantly, though, a mutation may create a completely novel allele that codes for the production of a new protein (**FIGURE 8-11**). That is, a change in the base-pair sequence of a person's DNA may cause the production of a gene product that has never existed before in the human

Q

Tanning beds and mobile phones expose people to radiation. Can they damage DNA?

EVOLUTIONARY CHANGE: MUTATION

Mutation causes evolution when an alteration of the base-pair sequence in the DNA of an individual's gamete-producing cells changes an allele's frequency.

DNA

Mutagen

Normal base-pair sequence

Mutated base-pair sequence

Normal protein

Mutated protein

Normal phenotype

Mutated phenotype

💡 *Despite mutation's vital role in the generation of variation, mutations almost always cause early death or lower the reproductive success of an organism.*

FIGURE 8-11 Agents of evolutionary change: mutation.

population: instead of blue or brown eyes, the mutated gene might code for yellow or red eyes. If such a new allele occurs in the sperm- and egg-producing cells, and if it does not significantly reduce an individual's "fitness" (which we'll consider below), the new allele can be passed on to offspring and remain in the population. At some future time, the mutation might even confer higher fitness, in which case natural selection could cause it to increase in frequency. For this reason, mutation is critical to natural selection: all variation—the raw material for natural selection—must initially come from mutation.

Despite this vital role in the generation of variation, however, nearly all mutations reduce an organism's fitness by causing early death or reducing its reproductive success. Suppose you wrote a 10-page paper. If you were to randomly select one letter in the paper and change it to another letter, is the change likely to make your paper better or worse? The answer is obvious: except in *very* rare situations (can you imagine one?) the change will hurt your paper. Similarly, mutations usually change a normally functioning allele that codes for a normally functioning protein into an allele that codes for a non-functioning protein. Almost inevitably, that reduces an organism's fitness. For this reason, our bodies protect our sperm- or egg-producing DNA with a variety of built-in error-correction mechanisms. As a result, mutations are rare (on the order of 1 mutation in every 30 million base pairs each generation in humans).

TAKE-HOME MESSAGE 8·7

Mutation is an alteration of the base-pair sequence in an individual's DNA. If such an alteration changes an allele in an individual's gamete-producing cells, this constitutes evolution within the population. Mutations can be caused by high-energy radiation or chemicals in the environment, and also can appear spontaneously. Mutation is the only way that new alleles can be created within a population, and thus it generates the variation on which natural selection can act.

8·8 Genetic drift is a random change in allele frequencies in a population.

Along with mutation, another evolutionary agent is **genetic drift,** a random change in allele frequencies in a population. For example, imagine that there are two alleles for a particular trait, let's say a cleft chin. This is a dominant trait, so individuals with either one or two copies of the dominant allele (*CC* or *Cc*) exhibit the cleft chin (**FIGURE 8-12**). Now suppose that two heterozygous (*Cc*) people have one child. Which combination of alleles will that child receive? This is impossible to predict, because it depends completely on which sperm fertilizes which egg—the luck of the draw. If the couple's sole child inherits a recessive allele from each parent, will the *population's* allele frequencies change? Yes. The new individual's two recessive alleles (*cc*) increase the proportion of recessive alleles in the population. It is equally likely that this couple's only child will receive two dominant alleles (*CC*). In either case, because a change in allele frequencies has occurred, evolution has happened.

This impact of genetic drift is much greater in small populations than in large populations. In a large population, any one couple having a child with two recessive alleles is likely to be offset by another couple having one child with two dominant alleles. When that happens, the overall allele frequencies in the population do not change, and evolution has not occurred.

One of the most important consequences of genetic drift is that it can lead to **fixation** for one allele of a gene in a population (see Figure 8-12). Fixation occurs when an allele's frequency in a population reaches 100% (and the frequency of all other alleles of that gene becomes 0%). If this happens, there is no more variability in the population for this gene; all individuals will always produce offspring carrying only that allele (until new alleles arise through mutation). For this reason, genetic drift reduces the genetic variation in a population.

The important factor that distinguishes genetic drift from natural selection is that the change in allele frequencies is not related to the alleles' influence on reproductive success. A cleft chin does not affect an individual's ability to reproduce.

FIGURE 8-12 Agents of evolutionary change: genetic drift. Genetic drift has the greatest impact in small populations.

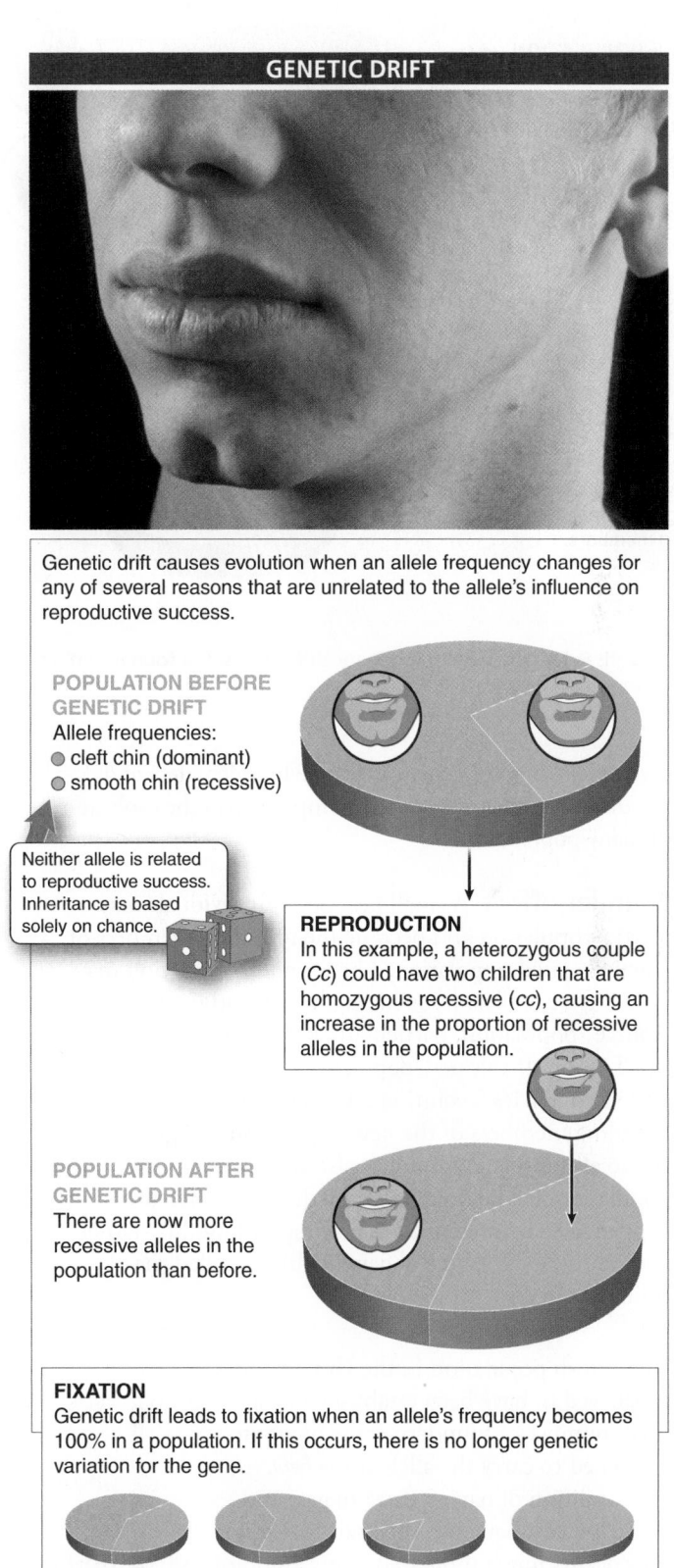

GENETIC DRIFT

Genetic drift causes evolution when an allele frequency changes for any of several reasons that are unrelated to the allele's influence on reproductive success.

POPULATION BEFORE GENETIC DRIFT
Allele frequencies:
- cleft chin (dominant)
- smooth chin (recessive)

Neither allele is related to reproductive success. Inheritance is based solely on chance.

REPRODUCTION
In this example, a heterozygous couple (*Cc*) could have two children that are homozygous recessive (*cc*), causing an increase in the proportion of recessive alleles in the population.

POPULATION AFTER GENETIC DRIFT
There are now more recessive alleles in the population than before.

FIXATION
Genetic drift leads to fixation when an allele's frequency becomes 100% in a population. If this occurs, there is no longer genetic variation for the gene.

Genetic drift occurs via the founder effect when the founding members of a new population have different allele frequencies than the original source population.

SOURCE POPULATION
Allele frequencies:
- 5 digits per hand (recessive)
- >5 digits per hand (dominant)

A group of individuals may leave a population and become the founding members of a new, isolated population.

NEWLY FOUNDED POPULATION
The new population will be dominated by the genetic features present in the founding members.

FIGURE 8-13 One way that genetic drift occurs: the founder effect.

Two special cases of genetic drift, the founder effect and population bottleneck effect, are important in the evolution of many populations.

Founder effect A small number of individuals may leave a population and become the founding members of a new, isolated population. The founder population may have different allele frequencies than the original, "source" population, particularly if the founders are a small group. If this new population does have different allele frequencies, evolution has occurred. Because the founding members of the new population will give rise to all subsequent individuals, the new population will be dominated by the genetic features that happened to be present in that group of founding fathers and mothers. This type of genetic drift is called the **founder effect.**

The Amish population in the United States is believed to have been established by a small number of founders, some of whom happened to carry the allele for *polydactyly*—the condition of having extra fingers and toes. As a consequence, this trait, while rare, now occurs much more frequently among

the Amish than among the rest of the U.S. population (**FIGURE 8-13**).

Population bottleneck effect Occasionally, a famine, disease, or rapid environmental change causes the deaths of a large proportion of individuals in a population. Because the population is quickly reduced to a small fraction of its original size, this reduction is called a **bottleneck.** If the catastrophe is equally likely to strike any member of the population, the remaining members are essentially a random, small sample of the original population. For this reason, the remaining population may not possess the same allele frequencies as the original population. Thus, the consequence of such a population bottleneck would be evolution through genetic drift (**FIGURE 8-14**).

Just such a population bottleneck occurred with cheetahs near the end of the last ice age, about 10,000 years ago. Although the cause is unknown— possibly environmental cataclysm or human hunting pressures—it appears that nearly all cheetahs died. And although the population rebounded, all

Q Why are Amish people more likely than other people to have extra fingers and toes?

Genetic drift occurs via the bottleneck effect when famine, disease, or rapid environmental change causes the deaths of a large, random proportion of the population, and the surviving individuals have different allele frequencies than the original population.

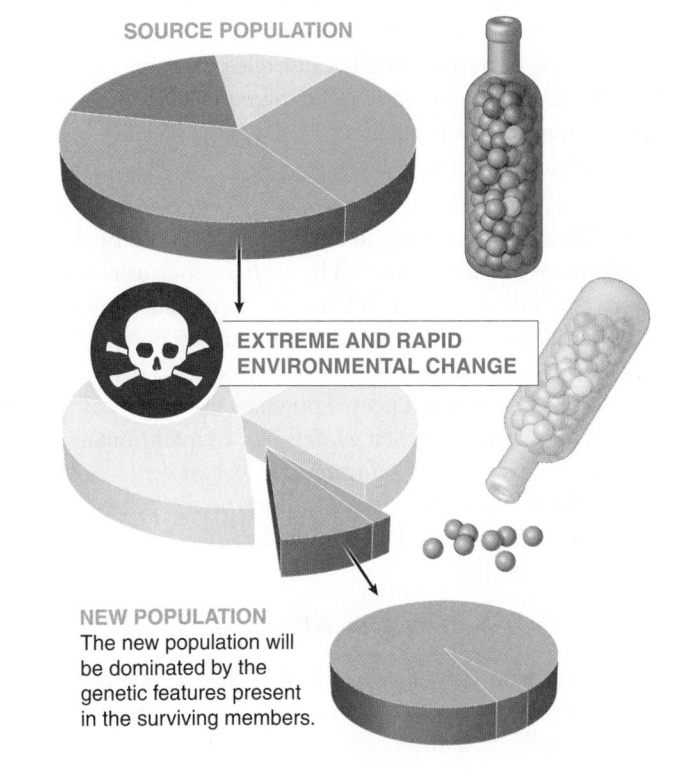

SOURCE POPULATION

EXTREME AND RAPID ENVIRONMENTAL CHANGE

NEW POPULATION
The new population will be dominated by the genetic features present in the surviving members.

FIGURE 8-14 Another way that genetic drift occurs: the bottleneck effect.

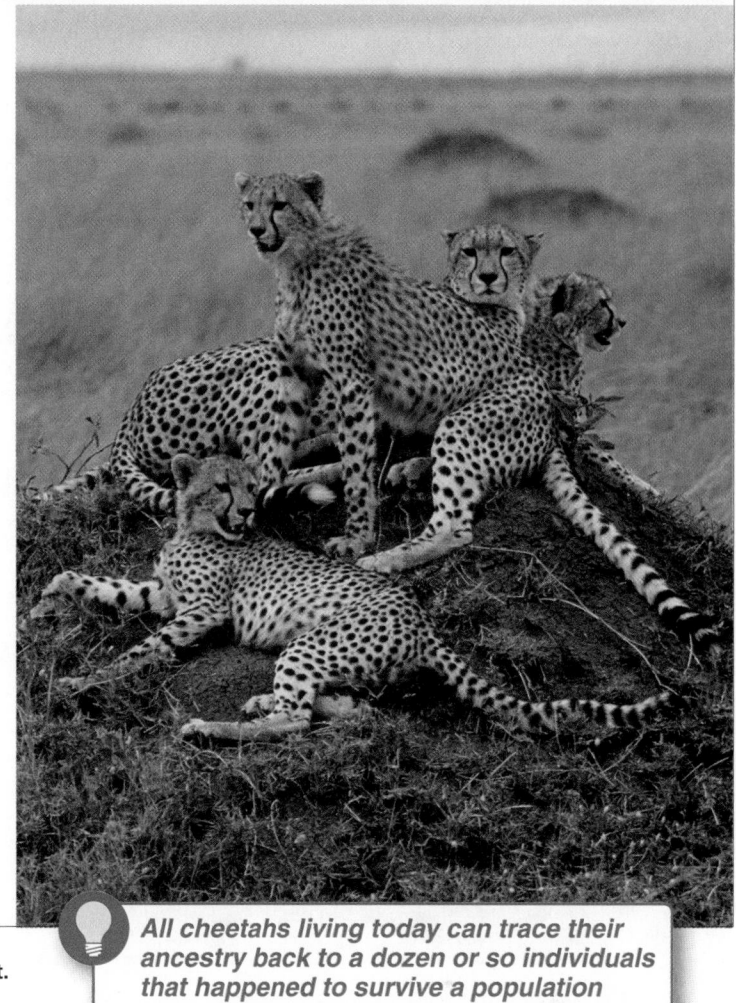

All cheetahs living today can trace their ancestry back to a dozen or so individuals that happened to survive a population bottleneck about 10,000 years ago!

cheetahs living today can trace their ancestry back to a dozen or so lucky individuals that survived the bottleneck. As a result of this past instance of evolution by genetic drift, there is almost no genetic variation left in the current population of cheetahs. (And, in fact, a cheetah is able to accept a skin graft from any other cheetah, much as identical twins can from each other.)

TAKE-HOME MESSAGE 8·8

Genetic drift is a random change in allele frequencies within a population, unrelated to the alleles' influence on reproductive success. Genetic drift is a significant agent of evolutionary change, primarily in small populations.

8·9 Migration into or out of a population may change allele frequencies.

The third agent of evolutionary change is **migration.** Migration, also called **gene flow,** is the movement of some individuals of a species from one population to another (**FIGURE 8-15**). This movement from population to

population within a species distinguishes migration from the founder effect, in which individuals migrate to a new habitat, previously unpopulated by that species. If migrating individuals survive and reproduce in the new population, and

MIGRATION (GENE FLOW)

Gene flow causes evolution if individuals move from one population to another, causing a change in allele frequencies in either population.

1 BEFORE MIGRATION
Two populations of the same species exist in separate locations. In this example, they are separated by a mountain range.

Population 1   Population 2

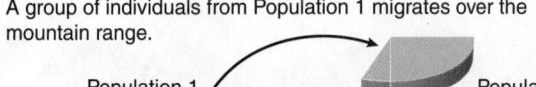

2 MIGRATION
A group of individuals from Population 1 migrates over the mountain range.

Population 1   Population 2

3 AFTER MIGRATION
The migrating individuals are able to survive and reproduce in the new population.

Population 1   Population 2

FIGURE 8-15 Agents of evolutionary change: migration (gene flow).

if they carry a different proportion of alleles than the individuals in their new home, then the recipient population experiences a change in allele frequencies and, consequently, experiences evolution. And because alleles are simultaneously lost from the population that the migrants left behind, that population, too, will experience a change in its allele frequencies and, thus, will evolve.

Gene flow between two populations is influenced by the mobility of the organisms and by barriers, such as mountains or rivers. And as we'll see in Chapter 16, human activities, too, can dramatically influence the migratory potential of organisms, as we sometimes transport species. This can occur intentionally—as when people purchase exotic pets or non-native species for their garden—or unintentionally—such as when marine species get trapped in ballast water tanks of cargo ships, later to be released in ports on the other side of the world when the tanks are flushed.

TAKE-HOME MESSAGE 8·9

Migration, or gene flow, leads to a change in allele frequencies in a population as individuals move into or out of the population.

8·10 When three simple conditions are satisfied, evolution by natural selection is occurring.

The fourth agent of evolutionary change is **natural selection.** This is the mechanism that Darwin identified in *The Origin of Species,* in which he noted that three conditions are necessary for natural selection to occur:

1. There must be variation for the trait within a population.

2. That variation must be heritable (that is, capable of being passed from parents to offspring).

3. Individuals with one version of the trait must produce more offspring than those with a different version of the trait.

Let's examine these conditions more closely.

Condition 1: Variation for a trait Close your eyes and imagine a dog. What does the dog look like? If 50 people were asked this question, we would probably get 50 different dog descriptions (**FIGURE 8-16**). Some are big, some are small. Some have short hair, some long. They vary in just about every way you can imagine. Likewise, if 50 people were to imagine a human face, a similarly broad range of images would pop into their heads. Variation is all around us. Beyond making the world an interesting place to live in, variation serves another purpose: it is the raw material on which evolution feeds.

Variation is not limited to physical features such as fur color or face shape. Organisms vary in physiological and

FIGURE 8-16 The first condition for natural selection is variation for a trait.

biochemical ways, too. Some people can quickly and efficiently metabolize alcohol, for example. Others find themselves violently ill soon after sipping a glass of wine. The same goes for digesting milk. Similarly, we vary in our susceptibility to poison ivy or diseases such as malaria. Behavioral variation—from temperament to learning abilities to interpersonal skills—is dramatic and widespread, too. So impressed was Darwin with the variation he observed throughout the world, he devoted the first two chapters of *The Origin of Species* to a discussion of variation in nature and among domesticated animals. Darwin knew that variation was an essential component of evolution by natural selection and considered it the first of three necessary conditions for natural selection.

Condition 2: Heritability The second condition that Darwin identified as necessary for natural selection was a no more complex discovery than the first: for natural selection to act on a trait within a population, offspring must inherit the trait from their parents. Although inheritance was poorly

understood in Darwin's time, it was not hard to see that, for many traits, offspring look more like their parents than like some other, random individual in the population (**FIGURE 8-17**). Animal breeders had long known that the

FIGURE 8-17 The second condition for natural selection is heritability. Goldie Hawn and daughter Kate Hudson resemble each other.

fastest horses generally give birth to the fastest horses. Farmers, too, understood that the plants with the highest productivity generally produce seeds from which highly productive plants grow. And everyone knew that children resemble their parents, from their appearance to their behavior to their temperament. It was enough to know that this similarity between offspring and parents exists—it was not necessary to understand how it occurs or to be able to quantify it. We call the transmission of traits from parents to their children through genetic information **inheritance** or **heritability.**

Condition 3: Differential reproductive success

It would be nice to say that Darwin made a stunning and insightful discovery for the third of the three conditions necessary for natural selection to occur, but he didn't. Rather, he derived the third condition for natural selection from three fairly simple observations. First, more organisms are born than can survive. Second, organisms are continually struggling for existence. Lastly, some organisms are more likely than others to survive and reproduce. In a world of scarce, limited resources, finding food or shelter is a zero-sum game: if one organism is feasting, another is more likely to be starving.

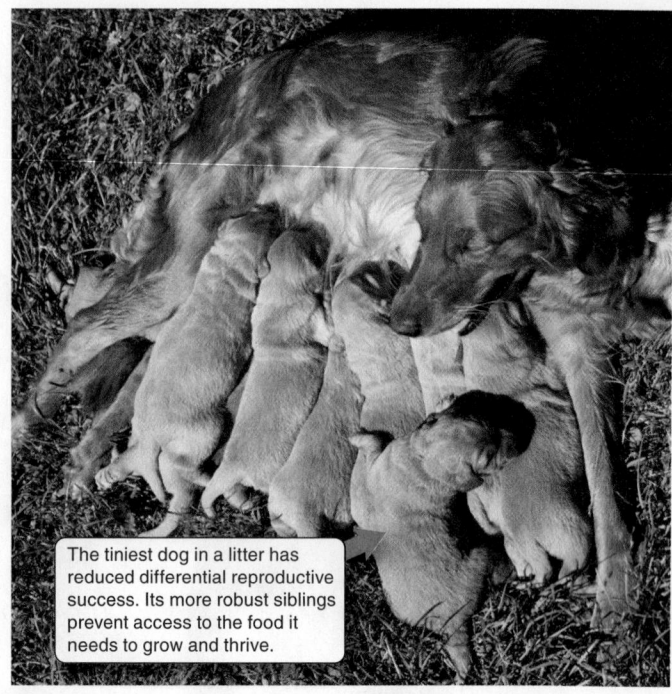

The tiniest dog in a litter has reduced differential reproductive success. Its more robust siblings prevent access to the food it needs to grow and thrive.

FIGURE 8-18 The third condition for natural selection is differential reproductive success.

EVOLUTION BY NATURAL SELECTION: A SUMMARY

Natural selection causes evolution as individuals with one version of a heritable trait have greater reproductive success than individuals with a different version of the trait.

1 VARIATION FOR A TRAIT
Different versions of a trait are present within a population.

+

2 HERITABILITY
The different versions of a trait may be passed from parents to offspring.

+

3 DIFFERENTIAL REPRODUCTIVE SUCCESS
Individuals with the version of a trait most suited to reproduction in their environment generally leave more offspring than individuals with other versions of the trait.

NATURAL SELECTION
When these three conditions are satisfied, the population's allele frequencies change and, consequently, evolution by natural selection occurs.

FIGURE 8-19 Agents of evolutionary change: natural selection.

This three-part observation led Darwin to his third condition for natural selection, which goes by the name **differential reproductive success:** from all the variation existing in a population, individuals with traits most suited to reproduction in their environment generally leave more offspring than do individuals with other traits (**FIGURE 8-18**). For example, in the fruit fly food experiments, we saw that the flies that inherit the ability to pack on fat when food is available end up leaving more offspring than those inheriting a poor ability to pad their little fruit fly frames with fat deposits. The portly fruit flies have greater reproductive success than other individuals in the population.

That's it. Natural selection—certainly one of the most influential and far-reaching ideas in the history of science— occurs when three basic conditions are met (**FIGURE 8-19**):

1. Variation for a trait

2. Heritability of that trait

3. Differential reproductive success based on that trait

When these three conditions are satisfied, evolution by natural selection is occurring. It's nothing more and nothing less. Over time, the traits that lead some organisms to have greater reproductive success than others will increase in frequency in a population, while traits that reduce reproductive success will fade away.

When it comes to some traits, the reason they confer greater reproductive success is that they make the individual more attractive to the opposite sex. Such traits—including the brightly colored tail feathers of male peacocks, the large antlers of male red deer, and a variety of other "ornaments" that increase an individual's status or appeal—increase in frequency because they satisfy the three conditions for natural selection. This natural selection for mating success is called **sexual selection.**

Q Most agricultural pests evolve resistance to pesticides. How does this happen?

Another way of looking at natural selection is to focus not on the winners (the individuals who are producing more offspring), but on the losers. Natural selection can be viewed as the elimination of some heritable traits from a population. If you carry a trait that makes you a slower-running rabbit, for example, you are more likely to be eaten by a fox (**FIGURE 8-20**). If running speed is a heritable trait (and it is), the next generation in a population contains fewer slow rabbits. Over time, the population is changed by natural selection. It evolves.

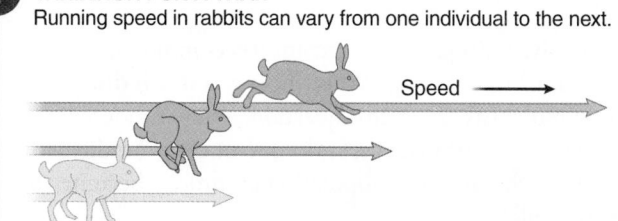

NATURAL SELECTION IN NATURE

1 VARIATION FOR A TRAIT
Running speed in rabbits can vary from one individual to the next.

Speed →

2 HERITABILITY
The trait of running speed is passed on from parents to their offspring.

3 DIFFERENTIAL REPRODUCTIVE SUCCESS
In a population, rabbits with slower running speeds are eaten by the fox, and their traits are not passed on to the next generation.

FIGURE 8-20 Removing the losers. Natural selection can be thought of as the elimination from a population of traits that confer poor reproductive success.

One of Darwin's contemporaries, Thomas Huxley, supposedly cursed himself when he first read *The Origin of Species,* saying that he couldn't believe he didn't figure it out on his own. Each of the three basic conditions is indeed simple and obvious. The brilliant deduction, though, was to put the three together and appreciate the consequences.

TAKE-HOME MESSAGE 8·10

Natural selection is a mechanism of evolution that occurs when there is heritable variation for a trait, and individuals with one version of the trait have greater reproductive success than do individuals with a different version of the trait. Natural selection can also be thought of as the elimination of alleles that reduce the reproductive rate of individuals carrying those alleles, relative to the reproductive rate of individuals who do not.

8·11 A trait does not decrease in frequency simply because it is recessive.

Do recessive traits gradually become less common in a population? In the early 1900s, there was much discussion among biologists about this question. They wondered: "If the allele for brown eyes is dominant over the allele for blue eyes, why doesn't a population eventually become all brown-eyed?"

R. C. Punnett (originator of the Punnett square, described in Chapter 7) posed this question to G. H. Hardy, a mathematician with whom Punnett played cricket. Hardy replied the next day, and published his answer in *Science* in 1908. It turns out that Wilhelm Weinberg answered the question independently six months earlier. But because he published his findings in an obscure journal, scientists didn't appreciate his results for another 35 years.

Their result underlies all evolutionary genetics and is referred to as the Hardy-Weinberg Law. It reveals several things, including that the answer to the question of whether recessive traits become rarer in a population is *no*. A trait does not decrease in frequency simply because it is recessive. Here's how Hardy and Weinberg demonstrated it.

First, we refer to the frequency of the dominant allele in the population, *A*, as "*p*" and the frequency of the recessive allele, *a*, as "*q*." Since every allele in the population has to be either *A* or *a*, we can say that $p + q = 1$. The percentage of the two alleles must total 100%. If we know the frequency of either allele in the population, we can subtract it from 1 to calculate the frequency of the other allele.

Next, we can predict how common each genotype in the population will be (**FIGURE 8-21**). The frequency of *AA* is just the probability that an individual gets two copies of allele *A*, which is $p \times p$, or p^2. Applying the same math, the frequency of *aa* individuals in the population is simply $q \times q$, or q^2. Predicting the frequency of heterozygous individuals, *Aa*, is slightly more complicated. Because the dominant allele may come from either the mother or the father, the frequency of the *Aa* genotype is $2 \times p \times q$, or $2pq$.

Consider an example. Suppose a population of 1,000 kangaroo rats has the following phenotype and genotype frequencies: 16 are dark brown (*BB*), 222 are spotted (*Bb*), and 762 are light brown (*bb*). The trait shows incomplete dominance, with the allele for dark brown color, *B*, dominant over the allele for light brown color, *b*, and the

heterozygote having a spotted phenotype. Because every individual in the population has two alleles for the coat-color gene (one from each parent), there are twice as many alleles as members of the population. So a population of 1,000 kangaroo rats has 2,000 alleles of the gene for coat color.

Now let's look at the allele frequencies. Each *BB* individual has two copies of *B*, and each *Bb* individual has one copy:

Frequency of $B = (2 \times 16 + 222)/2,000 = 0.127 = p$

Frequency of $b = (2 \times 762 + 222)/2,000 = 0.873 = q$

Since we know the allele frequencies, *p* (0.127) and *q* (0.873), we can determine the genotype frequencies of the offspring produced in this population. According to the equations above, they should be:

Frequency of $BB = p^2 = (0.127)^2 = 0.016$

Frequency of $Bb = 2pq = 2(0.127)(0.873) = 0.222$

Frequency of $bb = q^2 = (0.873)^2 = 0.762.$

If 1,000 kangaroo rats are produced, we expect to see genotype frequencies that are the same as in the parent generation:

16 *BB*, 222 *Bb*, and 762 *bb*. And from these genotype frequencies, we expect the following allele frequencies among the offspring they produce:

Frequency of $B = (2 \times 16 + 222)/2,000 = 0.127 = p$

Frequency of $b = (2 \times 762 + 222)/2,000 = 0.873 = q$

Notice that the frequencies are unchanged. The allele frequencies 0.127 and 0.873 will always produce the same genotype frequencies—0.16, 0.222, and 0.762—which, in turn, will always have the same allele frequencies. Put another way: the recessive allele *doesn't* decrease over time! It doesn't change at all.

This is true as long as individuals are not dying off specifically because they carry the recessive allele (or because they carry the dominant), in which case the allele frequencies would be changing due to natural selection. It also holds true only if mutations aren't changing the allele frequencies, and if migration or genetic drift isn't altering the allele frequencies. In each of these exceptions, the allele

HARDY-WEINBERG EQUILIBRIUM

If a population is in Hardy-Weinberg equilibrium, and the allele frequencies of the population are known, predictions can be made about the genotypes of the offspring that the population produces.

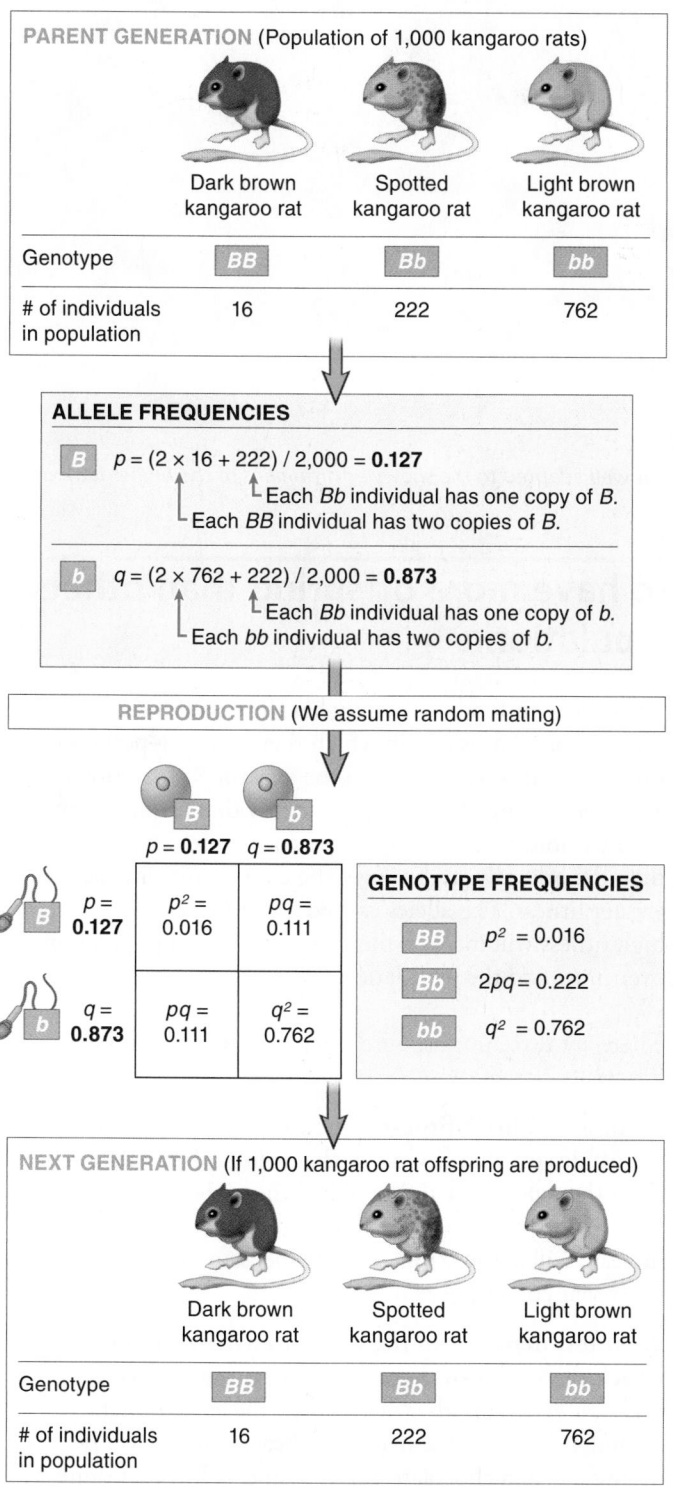

PARENT GENERATION (Population of 1,000 kangaroo rats)

	Dark brown kangaroo rat	Spotted kangaroo rat	Light brown kangaroo rat
Genotype	BB	Bb	bb
# of individuals in population	16	222	762

ALLELE FREQUENCIES

B $\quad p = (2 \times 16 + 222) / 2{,}000 = \mathbf{0.127}$
Each Bb individual has one copy of B.
Each BB individual has two copies of B.

b $\quad q = (2 \times 762 + 222) / 2{,}000 = \mathbf{0.873}$
Each Bb individual has one copy of b.
Each bb individual has two copies of b.

REPRODUCTION (We assume random mating)

$p = 0.127 \quad q = 0.873$

	$p = 0.127$	$q = 0.873$
B $\quad p = 0.127$	$p^2 = 0.016$	$pq = 0.111$
b $\quad q = 0.873$	$pq = 0.111$	$q^2 = 0.762$

GENOTYPE FREQUENCIES

BB $\quad p^2 = 0.016$
Bb $\quad 2pq = 0.222$
bb $\quad q^2 = 0.762$

NEXT GENERATION (If 1,000 kangaroo rat offspring are produced)

	Dark brown kangaroo rat	Spotted kangaroo rat	Light brown kangaroo rat
Genotype	BB	Bb	bb
# of individuals in population	16	222	762

💡 *As long as there is random mating and no evolution, the frequencies of recessive alleles and dominant alleles do not change over time.*

FIGURE 8-21 Recessive alleles don't necessarily disappear from populations.

frequencies would be changing through evolution. The Hardy-Weinberg conclusion also assumes random mating, in which the alleles are randomly coming together in all possible genotypes.

As long as these assumptions hold true—that is, random mating and no evolution—allele frequencies will not change over time, and the Hardy-Weinberg equations allow us to predict the genotype frequencies we should see.

What if we examine a population and find that the genotype frequencies we observe are *not* those predicted by the Hardy-Weinberg equations? There may be, for example, fewer heterozygotes than predicted. If this occurs, we say that the population is not in *Hardy-Weinberg equilibrium,* and we know that either evolution is occurring, or non-random mating, or both. If there are fewer heterozygotes than we expected, for example, it may be that more heterozygotes are dying than homozygotes, for some reason—perhaps predation. Or maybe individuals are preferentially mating with individuals having a similar phenotype. In either case, our calculations help us better understand the forces influencing the population and suggest further lines of investigation.

TAKE-HOME MESSAGE 8·11

If we know the frequency of each allele in a population, we can predict the genotypes and phenotypes we should see in that population. If the phenotypic frequencies in a population are not those predicted from the allele frequencies, the population is not in Hardy-Weinberg equilibrium, because an assumption has been violated. Either non-random mating or evolution is occurring. But as long as the Hardy-Weinberg assumptions are not violated, recessive alleles and dominant alleles do not change their frequencies over time.

The polar bear is well adapted to the snowy environment of the higher latitudes.

8·12 Traits causing some individuals to have more offspring than others become more prevalent in the population.

"Survival of the fittest." This is perhaps one of the most famous but misunderstood phrases. Taken literally, it seems to be circular: those organisms that survive *must* be the fittest. If being fit is defined as the ability to survive. But we'll see that in evolution, the word *fitness* is not defined by an organism's ability to survive or its physical strength or its health. Rather, fitness has everything to do with an organism's reproductive success.

Here's an interesting side note: the phrase "survival of the fittest" was coined not by Darwin but by Herbert Spencer, an influential sociologist and philosopher. Moreover, the phrase did not appear in *The Origin of Species* when Darwin first published it. It wasn't until the fifth edition, 10 years later, that he used the phrase in describing natural selection.

Before we see how fitness affects natural selection and a population's adaptation to its environment, let's define fitness. **Fitness** is a measure of the relative amount of reproduction of an individual with a particular phenotype, compared with the reproductive output of individuals of the same species with alternative phenotypes.

Suppose there are two fruit flies. One fly carries the genes for a version of a trait that allows it to survive a long time without food. The other has the genes for a different version of the trait that allows it to survive only a short

while without food. Which fly has the greater fitness? If the environment is one in which there are long periods of time without food, such as in the experiment described at the beginning of the chapter, the fly that can live a long time without food is likely to produce more offspring than the other fly, and so over the course of its life has greater fitness. The alleles carried by an individual with high fitness will increase their proportion in a population over time, and the population will evolve.

There are three important elements to an organism's fitness.

1. An individual's fitness is measured relative to other genotypes or phenotypes in the population. Those traits that confer on an individual the highest fitness will generally increase in frequency in a population, and their increase will always come at the expense of alternative traits that confer lower fitness.

2. Fitness depends on the specific environment in which the organism lives. The fitness value of having one trait versus another depends on the environment. A sand-colored mouse living in a beach habitat will be more fit than a chocolate-colored mouse. But that same sand-colored mouse will practically call out to potential predators if it lives in the darker brush away from the beach. An organism's fitness, although genetically based,

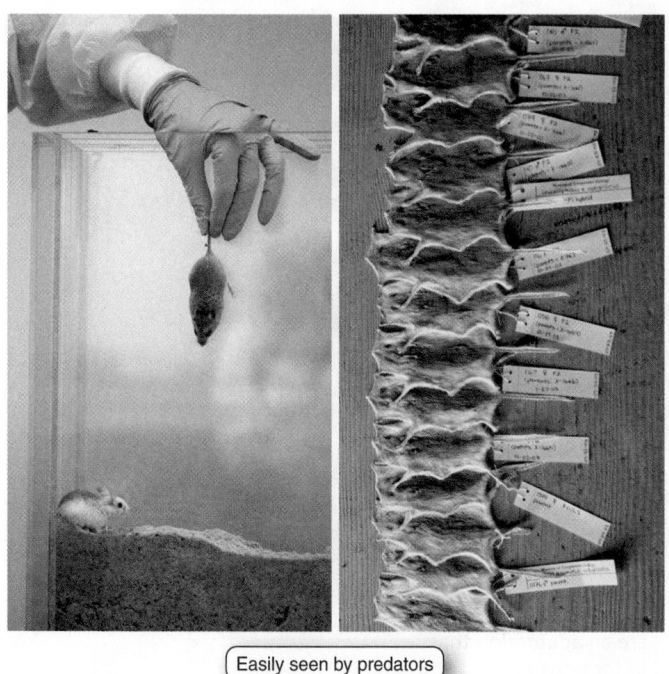

Easily seen by predators

In a lighter habitat, the allele for light-colored fur is fitter and increases in frequency:

In a darker habitat, the allele for dark-colored fur is fitter and increases in frequency:

FIGURE 8-22 An organism's fitness depends on the environment in which it lives.

is not fixed in stone and unchanging—it can change over time and across habitats (**FIGURE 8-22**).

3. Fitness depends on an organism's reproductive success compared with other organisms in the population. If you carry an allele that gives you the trait of surviving for 200 years, but that also causes you to be sterile, your fitness is zero; that allele will never be passed down to future generations, and its frequency in the population will soon be zero. On the other hand, if you inherit an allele that gives you a trait that causes you to die at half the age of everyone else, but also causes you to have twice as many offspring as the average individual, your fitness is increased. It is reproductive success that is all-important in determining whether particular traits increase in frequency in a population.

Q *"Survival of the fittest" is a misnomer. Why?*

"Survival of the fittest" is a misleading phrase because it is the individuals with the greatest *reproductive output* that are the most fit in any population. It becomes a more meaningful phrase if we consider it as a description of the fact that those alleles that increase an individual's fitness will "survive" in a population more than those that decrease an individual's fitness.

> **TAKE-HOME MESSAGE 8·12**
>
> Fitness is a measure of the relative amount of reproduction by an individual with a particular phenotype, compared with the reproductive output of individuals with alternative phenotypes. An individual's fitness can vary, depending on the environment in which it lives.

8·13 Organisms in a population can become better matched to their environment through natural selection.

If you put a group of humans on the moon, will they flourish? If you take a shark from the ocean and put it in your swimming pool, will it survive? In both cases, the answer is *no*. Organisms are rarely successful when put into novel environments. And the stranger the new environment, the less likely it is that the transplanted organism will survive. Why is that?

As Darwin noted over and over during his travels, the organisms that possess traits that allow them to better exploit the environment in which they live will tend to produce more offspring than the organisms with alternative traits. With passing generations, a population will be made up of more and more of these fitter organisms. And, as a consequence, organisms will tend to be increasingly well matched or adapted to their environment.

Adaptation refers both to the process by which organisms become better matched to their environment *and* to the specific features that make an organism more fit. Examples of adaptations abound. Bats have an extremely accurate type of hearing (called echolocation) for navigating and finding

FIGURE 8-23 **Adaptations increase fitness.** Quills are an adaptation that reduces (but doesn't eliminate) the risk of predation for porcupines.

food, even in complete darkness. Porcupine quills make porcupines almost impervious to predation (**FIGURE 8-23**). Mosquitoes produce strong chemicals that prevent blood from clotting, so that they can extract blood from other animals.

> **TAKE-HOME MESSAGE 8·13**
>
> Adaptation, which refers to the process by which organisms become better matched to their environment and to the specific traits that make an organism more fit, occurs as a result of natural selection.

8·14 Natural selection does not lead to perfect organisms.

In Lewis Carroll's *Through the Looking-Glass,* the Red Queen tells Alice that "in this place it takes all the running you can do, to keep in the same place." She might have been speaking about the process of evolution by natural selection. After all, if the least fit individuals are continuously weeded out of the population, we might logically conclude that, eventually, fitness will reach a maximum, and all organisms in all populations will be perfectly adapted to their environment. But this never happens. That is where the Red Queen's wisdom comes in.

Consider one of the many clearly documented cases of evolution in nature: beak size of Galápagos finches. Over the course of a multidecade study, biologists Rosemary and Peter Grant closely monitored the average size of the finches' beaks. They found that the average beak size within a population fluctuated according to the food supply. During dry years— when the finches had to eat large, hard seeds—bigger, stronger

beaks became the norm. During wet years, smaller-beaked birds were more successful, since there was a surplus of small, soft seeds.

> ❝I was taught that the human brain was the crowning glory of evolution so far, but I think it's a very poor scheme for survival.❞
>
> —KURT VONNEGUT, American writer

The ever-changing "average" finch beak illustrates that adaptation does not simply march toward some optimal endpoint (**FIGURE 8-24**). Evolution in general, and natural selection specifically, does not guide organisms toward "betterness" or perfection. Natural selection is simply a process by which, in each generation, the alleles that cause organisms to have the traits that make them most fit in that environment

GALÁPAGOS FINCHES: FOOD SUPPLY AND BEAK SIZE

In dry years, finches had to eat large, hard seeds, and bigger beaks were selected for.

In wet years, finches could eat small, soft seeds, and smaller beaks were selected for.

GRAPHIC CONTENT!
Thinking critically about visual displays of data.
Turn to p. 342 for a closer inspection of this figure.

FIGURE 8-24 What's fit in one time and place may not be fit in another. Beak size in Galápagos finches changes along with the average rainfall.

Adaptation does not march toward an optimal endpoint. Average beak size within a population continues to fluctuate according to food supply.

tend to increase in frequency. If the environment changes, the alleles that are most favored may change, too.

Why doesn't natural selection lead to perfect organisms?

In the next to last paragraph of *The Origin of Species,* Darwin wrote: "as natural selection works solely by and for the good of each being, all corporeal [physical] and mental endowments will tend to progress towards perfection." In this passage, he overlooks several different factors that prevent populations from progressing inevitably toward perfection:

1. Environments change quickly. Natural selection may be too slow to adapt the organisms in a population to such a constantly moving target.

2. Variation is needed as the raw material of selection— remember, it is the first necessary condition for

natural selection to occur. If a mutation creating a new, "perfect" version of a gene never occurs, the individuals within a population will never be perfectly adapted.

3. There may be different alleles for a trait, each causing individuals to have the same fitness. In this case, each allele represents an equally fit "solution" to the environmental challenges.

TAKE-HOME MESSAGE 8·14

Natural selection does not lead to organisms perfectly adapted to their environment, because (1) environments can change more quickly than natural selection can adapt organisms; (2) mutation does not produce all possible alleles; (3) there is not always a single, optimum adaptation for a given environment.

8·15 Artificial selection is a special case of natural selection.

In practice, plant and animal breeders understood natural selection before Darwin did; they just didn't know that they understood it. Farmers bred crops for maximum yield, and dog, horse, and pigeon fanciers selectively bred the animals with their favorite traits to produce more and more of

the offspring with more and more exaggerated versions of those traits.

The process used by animal breeders and farmers is called **artificial selection,** but the underlying genetic process does not differ from natural selection because the three conditions are satisfied. Artificial selection is considered a special case of natural selection, however, because the differential reproductive success is being determined by humans rather than by nature. Apple growers, for example, use artificial selection to produce the wide variety available. What is important is that it is still differential reproductive success, and the results are no different. It was a stroke of genius for Darwin to recognize that the same process farmers were using to develop new and better crop varieties is occurring naturally in every population on earth, and always has been.

8·16 Natural selection can change the traits in a population in several ways.

Certain traits are easily categorized—blue eyes and brown eyes, white tiger fur and orange tiger fur, cleft chin and smooth chin. Other traits, such as height, are influenced by many genes and environmental factors, so that a continuous range of phenotypes occurs (**FIGURE 8-25**). Whether a given trait is influenced by one gene or by a complex interaction of many genes and the environment, it can be subject to natural selection and be changed in any of several ways.

TRAIT CATEGORIZATION

SPECIFIC CATEGORY
Some traits, such as chin shape, can be easily placed into one category or the other.

or

Cleft chin | Smooth chin

CONTINUOUS RANGE
Other traits, such as height, may fall into a wide range of values.

Traits influenced by a single gene or by multiple genes interacting with the environment can be changed in various ways by natural selection.

FIGURE 8-25 Some traits fall into clear categories, others range continuously.

FIGURE 8-26 More milk? Cows have been selected for their ability to produce more and more milk.

Directional selection In **directional selection**, individuals with one extreme of the range of variation in the population have higher fitness. Milk production in cows is an example. There is a lot of variation in milk production from cow to cow. As you might expect, farmers select for breeding those cows with the highest milk production and have done so for many decades. The result of such selection is not surprising: between 1920 and 1945, average milk production increased by about 50% in the United States (**FIGURE 8-26**).

Those at the other end of the range, the cows that produce the smallest amounts of milk, have reduced fitness, since the farmers do not allow them to reproduce, limiting the number of "less milk" alleles in the next

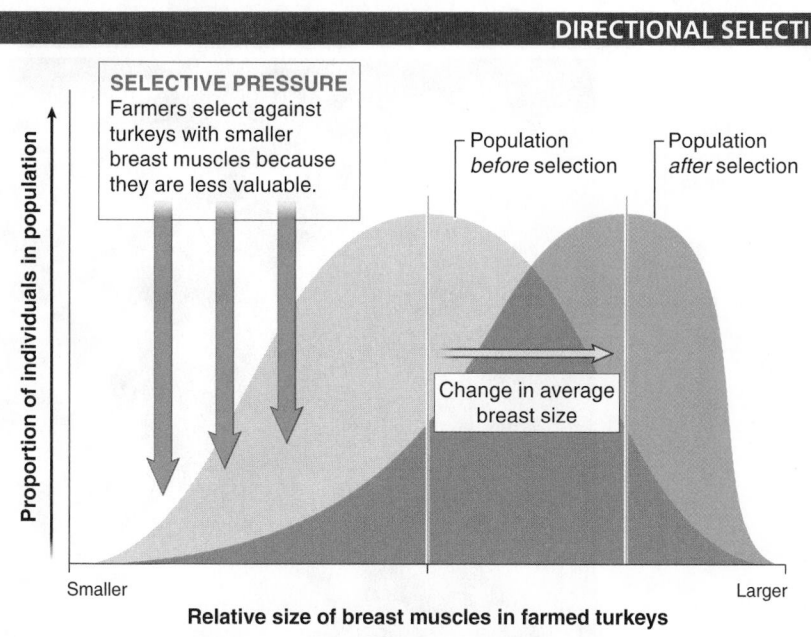

SELECTIVE PRESSURE Farmers select against turkeys with smaller breast muscles because they are less valuable.

Population *before* selection

Population *after* selection

Change in average breast size

Proportion of individuals in population

Smaller

Larger

Relative size of breast muscles in farmed turkeys

FIGURE 8-27 Patterns of natural selection: directional selection.

Turkeys on poultry farms can no longer mate naturally! Their breast muscles have become so large that artificial insemination is required.

generation. In subsequent generations, the average value for the milk-production trait increases. Note, however, that the variation for the trait in the cow population decreases a bit, too, because the alleles contributing to one of the phenotypic extremes are eventually removed from the population.

Hundreds of experiments in nature and laboratories and on farms demonstrate the power of directional selection. In fact, it is one of the marvels of laboratory selection and animal breeding that nearly any trait chosen to be exaggerated via directional selection responds dramatically—sometimes with absurd results (**FIGURE 8-27**). Turkeys, for instance, have been selected for increased size of their breast muscles, which makes them more profitable for farmers. Directional selection has been so successful that the birds' breast muscles are now so large that it has become impossible for them to mate. All turkeys on large-scale, industrial poultry farms must now reproduce through artificial insemination!

Q

Turkeys on poultry farms have such large breast muscles that they can't get close enough to each other to mate. How can such a trait evolve?

Stabilizing selection How much did you weigh at birth? Was it more than 10 pounds? More than 11? Was it close to the 22½ pounds that Christina Samane's child weighed

when born in South Africa in 1982? Or was it 5 pounds or less? Unlike directional selection, for which there is increased fitness at one extreme and reduced fitness at the other, **stabilizing selection** is said to occur when individuals with intermediate phenotypes are the most fit. The death rate among babies, for example, is lowest between 7 and 8 pounds, increasing for both lighter and heavier babies (**FIGURE 8-28**). This outcome has kept the average weight of a baby constant over many generations; but at the same time, the variation in birth weight has decreased as stabilizing selection has reduced the frequencies of genes associated with high and low birth weights.

Modern technologies, including Caesarean deliveries and premature-birth wards, allow many babies to live who would not have survived without such technology. This has the unintended consequence of reducing the selection against any alleles causing those "extreme" traits, reducing the rate of their removal from the population.

Disruptive selection There is a third kind of natural selection, in which individuals with extreme phenotypes experience the highest fitness, and those with intermediate phenotypes have the lowest. Although examples of this type of

STABILIZING SELECTION

SELECTIVE PRESSURE
Babies with low birth weights are more vulnerable to complications.

Population *before* selection

Population *after* selection

SELECTIVE PRESSURE
Babies with high birth weights are more vulnerable to complications.

Proportion of individuals in population

3 4 5 6 7 8 9 10 11 12

Birth weight of human baby (lbs.)

FIGURE 8-28 Patterns of natural selection: stabilizing selection.

selection, called **disruptive selection,** are rare in nature, the results are not surprising. Among some species of fish—the coho salmon, for instance—only the largest males acquire good territories. They generally enjoy relatively high reproductive success. While the intermediate-size fish regularly get run out of the good territories, some tiny males are able to sneak in and fertilize eggs before the territory owner detects their presence. Consequently, we see an increase in the frequency of small and large fish with a reduction in the frequency of medium-size fish (**FIGURE 8-29**).

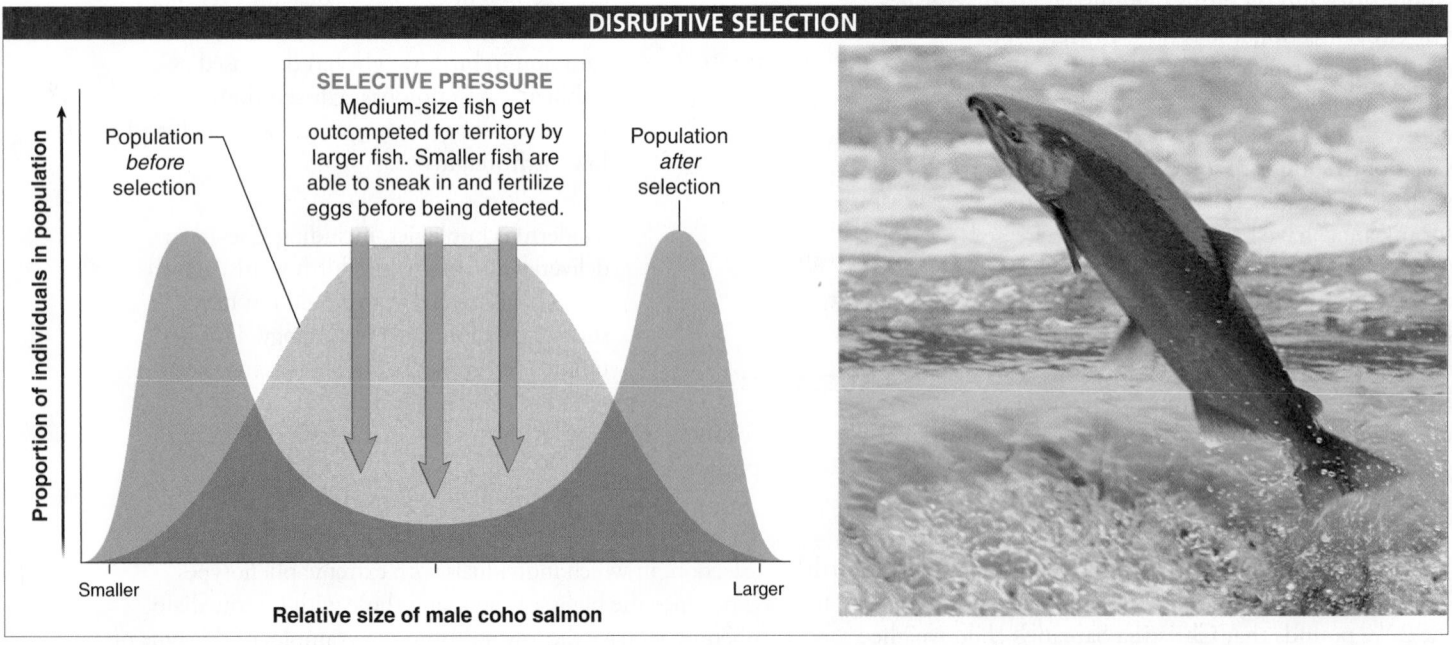

DISRUPTIVE SELECTION

Population *before* selection

SELECTIVE PRESSURE
Medium-size fish get outcompeted for territory by larger fish. Smaller fish are able to sneak in and fertilize eggs before being detected.

Population *after* selection

Proportion of individuals in population

Smaller   Larger

Relative size of male coho salmon

FIGURE 8-29 Patterns of natural selection: disruptive selection.

8·17 Natural selection can cause the evolution of complex traits and behaviors.

We have seen that natural selection can change allele frequencies and modify the frequency with which simple traits, such as fur color or turkey-breast size, appear in a population. But what about complex traits, such as behaviors, that involve numerous physiological and neurological systems? For instance, can natural selection improve maze-running ability in rats?

The short answer is *yes*. Remember, evolution by natural selection is occurring, changing the allele frequencies for traits, whenever (1) there is variation for the trait, (2) that variation is heritable, and (3) there is differential reproductive success based on that trait. These conditions can easily be satisfied for complex traits, including behaviors.

In 1954, to address this question, William Thompson trained a group of rats to run through a maze for a food reward (**FIGURE 8-30**). There was a huge amount of variation in the rats' abilities: some rats learned much more quickly than others how to run the maze. Thompson then selectively bred the fast learners with each other and the slow learners with each other. Over several generations, he developed two separate populations: rats descended from a line of fast maze-learners and rats descended from a line of slow maze-learners. After only six generations, the slow learners made twice as many errors as the fast learners before mastering the maze, while the fast learners were adept at solving complex mazes that would give many humans some difficulty. Fifty-five years later, it still is unclear which particular genes are responsible for maze-running behavior, yet the selection experiment still demonstrates a strong genetic component to the behavior.

> **❝** All things must change
> To something new, to something strange. **❞**
> —HENRY WADSWORTH LONGFELLOW

Natural selection can also produce complex traits in unexpected, roundabout ways. One vexing case involves the question of how natural selection could produce an organ as complex as a fly wing, when 1% or 2% of a wing—that is, an incomplete structure—doesn't help an insect to fly. In other words, while it is clear how natural selection can preserve and increase the frequencies of fitness-increasing traits in populations, how do these soon-to-be-useful traits increase

---

NATURAL SELECTION FOR COMPLEX TRAITS

SLOW LEARNERS
Rats making most errors in maze are selected and bred with each other.

After 6 generations of selection, the rats selected for fast learning made only half as many errors as the slow learners.

FAST LEARNERS
Rats making fewest errors in maze are selected and bred with each other.

Average number of errors committed (y-axis: 100, 140, 180, 220, 260, 300)
Generation (x-axis: 1, 2, 3, 4, 5, 6)

💡 *Natural selection can produce and alter complex traits, including behaviors.*

FIGURE 8-30 "Not too complex . . ." Natural selection can produce and alter complex traits, including behaviors.

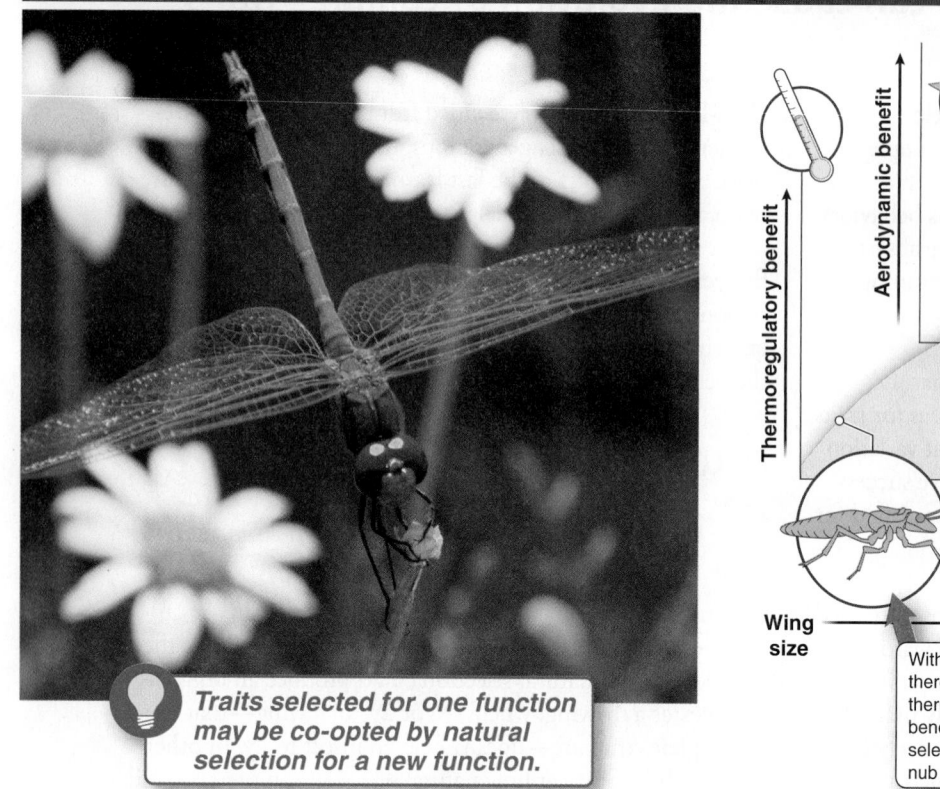

Traits selected for one function may be co-opted by natural selection for a new function.

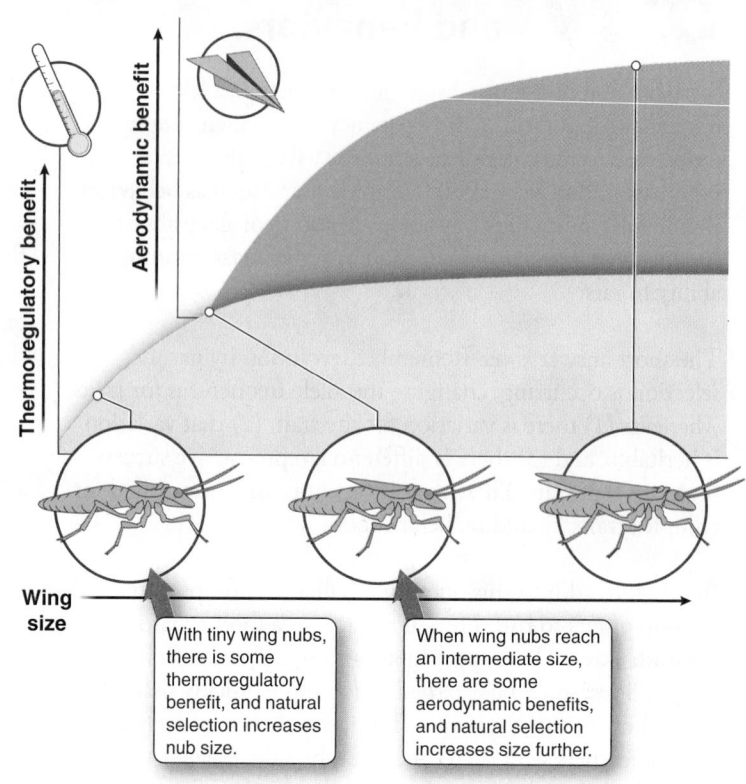

With tiny wing nubs, there is some thermoregulatory benefit, and natural selection increases nub size.

When wing nubs reach an intermediate size, there are some aerodynamic benefits, and natural selection increases size further.

FIGURE 8-31 How could natural selection produce an insect wing, when the primitive wing nub had no aerodynamic benefits?

during the early stages if they don't increase the organism's fitness (**FIGURE 8-31**)?

How can a wing evolve if 1% of a wing doesn't help an organism fly or glide at all?

The key to answering this question is that 1% of a wing doesn't actually need to function as a wing to increase an individual's fitness. Often, structures are enhanced or elaborated on by natural selection because they enhance fitness by serving some other purpose. In the case of little nubs or "almost-wings" on an insect, experiments using models of insects demonstrated that, as expected, the nubs confer no benefit at all when it comes to flying. (They don't even help flies keep their orientation during a "controlled fall.") The incipient wings *do* help the insects address a completely different problem, though. They allow much more efficient temperature control, so that an insect can gain heat from the environment when the insect is cold and dissipate heat when the insect is hot. Experiments on heat-control efficiency, in fact, show that as small nubs become more and more pronounced, they are more and more effective, probably conferring increased fitness

on the individual in which they occur—but only up to a point.

Eventually, the thermoregulatory benefit stops increasing, even if the nub length continues to increase. But it is right around this point that the proto-wing starts to confer some aerodynamic benefits (see Figure 8-31). Consequently, natural selection may continue to increase the length of this "almost-wing," but now the fitness increase is due to a wholly different effect. Such functional shifts explain the evolution of numerous complex structures that we see today, and these shifts may be common in the evolutionary process.

TAKE-HOME MESSAGE 8·17

Natural selection can change allele frequencies for genes involved in complex physiological processes and behaviors. Sometimes a trait that has been selected for one function is later modified to serve a completely different function.

The pygmy seahorse (Hippocampus bargibanti) is so well camouflaged by the coral it lives near that the first specimens were discovered only after coral had been collected and put in an aquarium.

8·18 The fossil record documents the process of natural selection.

> **❝** It is indeed remarkable that this theory [evolution] has been progressively accepted by researchers, following a series of discoveries in various fields of knowledge. The convergence, neither sought nor fabricated, of the results of work that was conducted independently is in itself a significant argument in favor of this theory. **❞**
> —POPE JOHN PAUL II, 1996

In the some 150 years since Darwin first published *The Origin of Species,* thousands of studies involving his theory of evolution by natural selection have been conducted, both in the laboratory and in natural habitats. A wide range of modern methodologies has also been developed, all contributing to a much deeper understanding of the process of evolution. This ongoing accumulation of evidence overwhelmingly supports the basic premise that Darwin put forward, while filling in many of the gaps that frustrated him.

In the remainder of the chapter we review the five primary lines of evidence demonstrating the occurrence of evolution:

1. **The fossil record**—physical evidence of organisms that lived in the past

2. **Biogeography**—patterns in the geographic distribution of living organisms

3. **Comparative anatomy and embryology**—growth, development, and body structures of major groups of organisms

4. **Molecular biology**—examination of life at the level of individual molecules

5. **Laboratory and field studies**—implementation of the scientific method to observe and study evolutionary mechanisms

The first of the five lines of evidence is the fossil record. Although it has been central to much documentation of the occurrence of evolution, it is a very incomplete record. After all, the soft parts of an organism tend to decay rapidly and completely after death. And there are only a few environments (such as tree resin, tar pits, and the bottom of deep lakes) in which the forces of decomposition are so reduced that an organism's hard parts, including bones, teeth, and shells, can be preserved for thousands or even millions of years. These remains, called **fossils,** can be used to reconstruct what organisms must have looked like long ago. Such reconstructions

FIGURE 8-32 Evidence for evolution: the fossil record. Fossils can be used to reconstruct the appearance of organisms that lived long ago.

often provide a clear record of evolutionary change (**FIGURE 8-32**).

The use of **radiometric dating** helps in painting a clearer picture of organisms' evolutionary history by telling us the age of the rock in which a fossil is found (**FIGURE 8-33**). In Darwin's time, it was assumed that the deeper in the earth a fossil was found, the older it was. Radiometric dating goes a step further, making it possible to determine not just the *relative* age of fossils, but also their *absolute* age. This is accomplished by evaluating the amounts of certain radioactive isotopes present in the fossil-containing rocks. Radioactive isotopes in a rock begin breaking down into more stable compounds as soon as the rock is formed, and they do so at a constant rate. Nothing can alter this. By measuring the relative amounts of the radioactive isotope and its leftover decay product in the rock where a fossil is found, the age of the rock, and thus of the fossil, can be calculated.

Radiometric dating confirms that the earth is very old. Rocks more than 3.8 billion years old have been found on all of the earth's continents, with the oldest so far found in northwestern Canada. By using the radioactive isotope uranium-238, with a half-life of 4.5 billion years, researchers have determined that the earth is about 4.6 billion years old and that the earliest organisms appeared at least 3.5 billion years ago. Radiometric dating also makes it possible to put the fossil record in order. By dating all the fossils discovered in one locale, paleontologists can learn whether and how the organisms were related to each other and how groups of organisms changed over time.

Paleontologists must deal with the fact, however, that fossil formation is an exceedingly unlikely event, and when it does

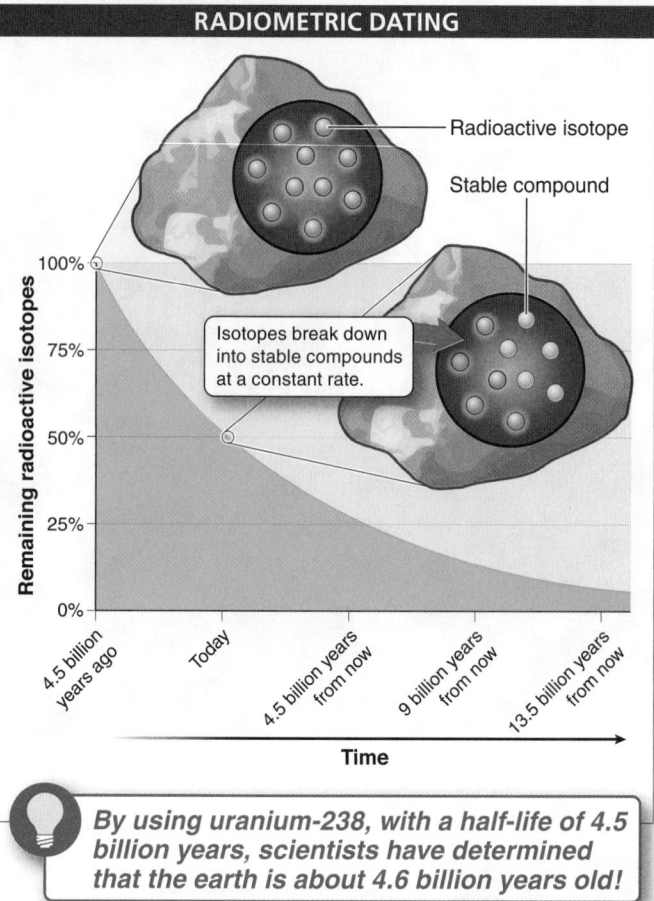

RADIOMETRIC DATING

Radioactive isotope

Stable compound

Isotopes break down into stable compounds at a constant rate.

By using uranium-238, with a half-life of 4.5 billion years, scientists have determined that the earth is about 4.6 billion years old!

FIGURE 8-33 How old is that fossil? Radiometric dating using uranium-238 helps to determine the age of rocks and the fossils in them.

occur it represents only those organisms that happened to live in that particular area and also had physical structures that could leave fossils. For this reason, the fossil record is annoyingly incomplete. Entire groups of organisms have left no fossil record at all, and some others have numerous gaps. Still, fossils have been found that link all of the major groups of vertebrates.

The evolutionary history of horses is among the most well preserved in the fossil record. First appearing in North America about 55 million years ago, horses radiated around the world, with more recent fossils appearing in Eurasia and Africa. These fossils exhibit distinct adaptations to those differing environments. Later, about 1.5 million years ago, much of the horse diversity—including all North American horse species—disappeared, leaving only a single remaining genus, or group of species, called *Equus*. Because there is now only one horse genus on earth, it is tempting to imagine a simple linear path from modern horses straight back through their 55-million-year evolutionary history. But that's just not how evolution works. In reality, there have been numerous branches of horses that have split off over evolutionary time,

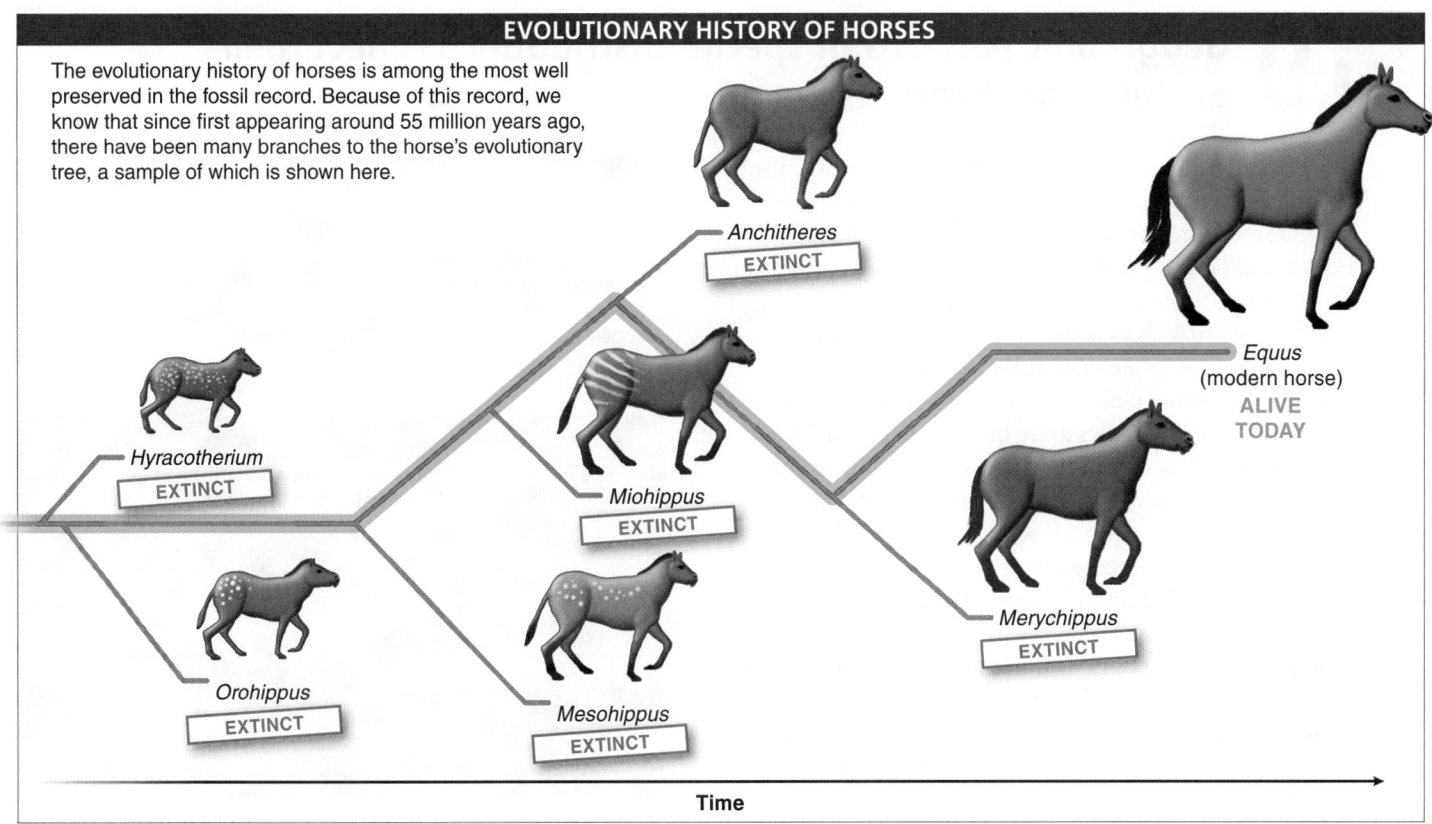

EVOLUTIONARY HISTORY OF HORSES

The evolutionary history of horses is among the most well preserved in the fossil record. Because of this record, we know that since first appearing around 55 million years ago, there have been many branches to the horse's evolutionary tree, a sample of which is shown here.

Anchitheres
EXTINCT

Hyracotherium
EXTINCT

Miohippus
EXTINCT

Orohippus
EXTINCT

Mesohippus
EXTINCT

Merychippus
EXTINCT

Equus
(modern horse)
ALIVE
TODAY

Time

FIGURE 8-34 An evolutionary family tree. The branching evolutionary tree of the horse.

flourished for millions of years, and only recently gone extinct. What we see living today is only a single branch of a greatly branched evolutionary tree (**FIGURE 8-34**).

The fossil record provides another valuable piece of evidence for the process of natural selection, in the form of "missing links." These are fossils that demonstrate a link between groups of species believed to have shared a common ancestor. One such "missing link" is *Tiktaalik* (**FIGURE 8-35**). First found in northern Canada and estimated to be 375 million years old, *Tiktaalik* fossils seem to represent a transitional phase between fishes and land animals. These creatures, like fishes, had gills, scales, and fins, but they also had arm-like joints in their fins and could drag their bodies across land in much the same way as a marine mammal such as a seal.

TAKE-HOME MESSAGE 8·18

Radiometric dating confirms that the earth is very old and allows scientists to determine the age of fossils. By analyzing fossil remains, biologists can reconstruct what organisms looked like long ago, learn how organisms were related to each other, and understand how groups of organisms evolved over time.

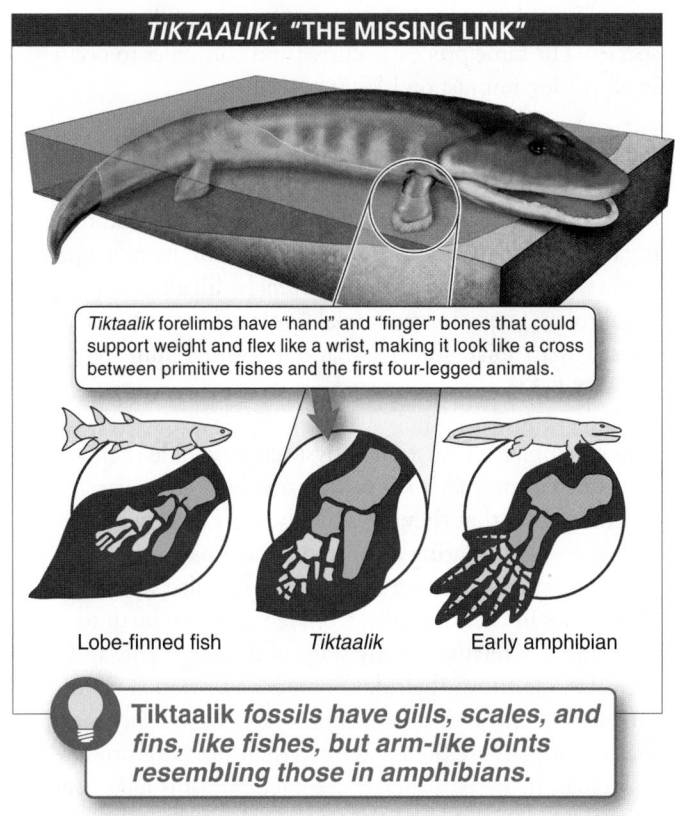

TIKTAALIK: "THE MISSING LINK"

Tiktaalik forelimbs have "hand" and "finger" bones that could support weight and flex like a wrist, making it look like a cross between primitive fishes and the first four-legged animals.

Lobe-finned fish   *Tiktaalik*   Early amphibian

💡 Tiktaalik *fossils have gills, scales, and fins, like fishes, but arm-like joints resembling those in amphibians.*

FIGURE 8-35 A missing link? *Tiktaalik* seems to be a transitional phase between fishes and land animals.

333

EVOLUTION
IS ONGOING

DARWIN'S
JOURNEY

FOUR MECHANISMS

NATURAL SELECTION

EVIDENCE
FOR EVOLUTION

8·19 Geographic patterns of species distributions reflect their evolutionary histories.

The study of the distribution patterns of living organisms around the world is called **biogeography.** This is the second line of evidence that helps us see that evolution occurs and better understand the process. The patterns of biogeography noticed by Darwin and by many subsequent researchers provide strong evidence that evolutionary forces are responsible for these patterns. Species often more closely resemble other species that live less than a hundred miles away but in radically different habitats than they resemble species living thousands of miles away in nearly identical habitats. On Hawaii, for example, nearly every bird is some sort of modified honeycreeper, from seed-eating honeycreepers to curved-bill nectar-feeding honeycreepers (**FIGURE 8-36**).

When it comes to species distributions, history matters. Species were not designed from scratch to fill a particular niche. Rather, whatever arrived in a geographic region first—usually a nearby species—took up numerous different lifestyles in numerous different habitats, and the populations ultimately adapted to and evolved in each environment. In Hawaii, it seems that a finch-like descendant of the honeycreepers arrived 4–5 million years ago and rapidly evolved into a large number of diverse species. The same process occurred and continues to occur in all locales, not just on islands.

Large isolated habitats also have interesting biogeographic patterns. Australia and Madagascar are filled with unique organisms that are clearly not closely related to organisms elsewhere. In Australia, for example, marsupial species, rather than placental mammals, fill all of the usual roles. There are marsupial "wolves," marsupial "mice," marsupial "squirrels," and marsupial "anteaters" (**FIGURE 8-37**).

The marsupials of Australia physically resemble their placental counterparts for most traits, but molecular analysis shows that they are actually more closely related to one another, sharing a common marsupial ancestor. Their relatedness to each other is also revealed by similarities in their reproduction: females give birth to offspring at a relatively early stage of development, and the offspring finish their development in a pouch. The presence of marsupials in Australia does not simply mean that marsupials are better adapted than placentals to Australian habitats. When placental organisms have been transplanted to Australia they do just fine, often thriving

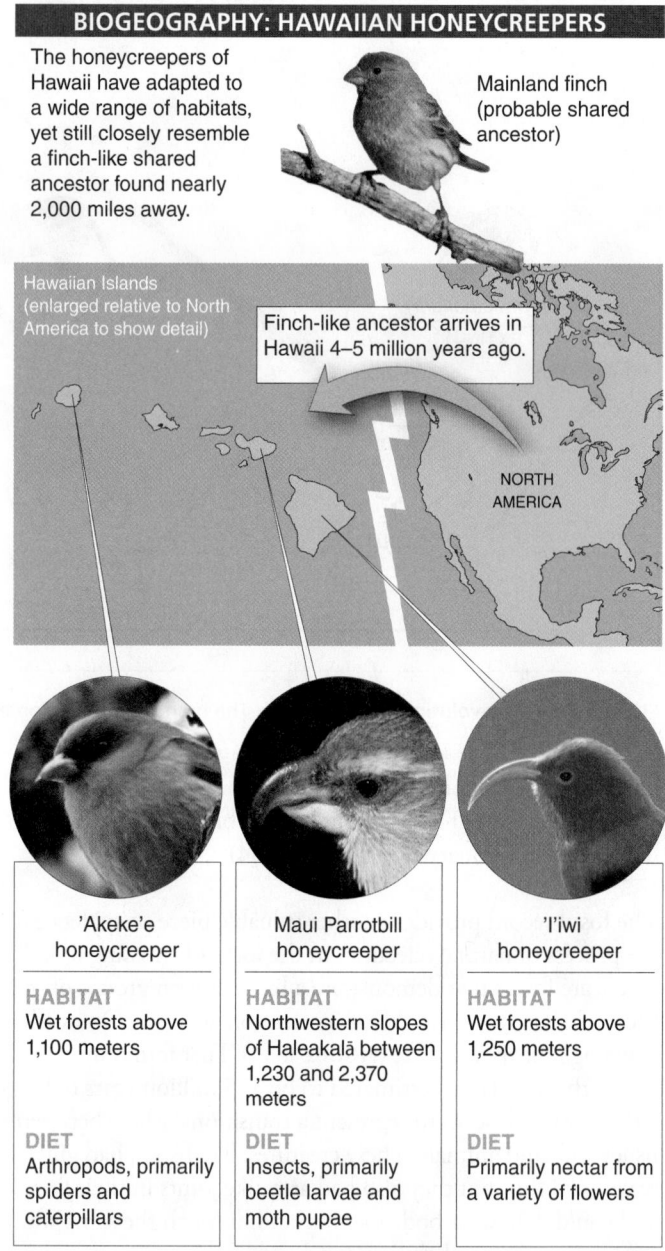

FIGURE 8-36 Evidence for evolution: biogeography. The Hawaiian honeycreepers resemble a common ancestor from mainland North America, but all have unique features.

to the point of endangering the native species. Instead, it appears that the terrestrial placental mammals in Australia disappeared about 55 million years ago—although the reasons are not clear—giving the marsupials the chance to flourish and diversify.

AUSTRALIAN MARSUPIALS

Sugar glider

Numbat

Tasmanian wolf

PLACENTAL COUNTERPARTS

Flying squirrel

Giant anteater

Gray wolf

FIGURE 8-37 Evidence for evolution: biogeography. Many Australian marsupials resemble placental counterparts, though they are not closely related.

 Though less related to each other than you are to a shrew, these marsupials and their placental counterparts have come to resemble each other as natural selection has adapted them to similar habitats.

Biogeographic patterns such as those seen in honeycreepers and in the marsupials of Australia illustrate that evolution doesn't necessarily lead to the same "solutions" each time a particular set of environmental conditions occurs. Rather, the traits in populations that happen to be in a particular location gradually change, and those species become better adapted to the habitats they occupy.

TAKE-HOME MESSAGE 8·19

Observing geographic patterns of species distributions—noting similarities and differences among species living close together but in very different habitats and among species living in similar habitats but located far from one another—helps us understand the evolutionary histories of populations.

8·20 Comparative anatomy and embryology reveal common evolutionary origins.

If you observe any vertebrate embryo, you will see that it passes through a stage in which it has little gill pouches on the sides of the neck. It will also pass through a stage in which it has a long bony tail. This is true whether it is a human embryo or that of a turtle or a chicken or a shark. The gill pouches disappear before birth in all but the fishes. Similarly, we don't find humans with tails. Why do these features exist during an embryo's development? Such common embryological stages indicate that the organisms share a common ancestor, from which all have been modified (**FIGURE 8-38**). Study of these developmental stages and the adult body forms of organisms provides our third line of evidence for the occurrence of evolution.

Among adult animals, several features of anatomy reveal the ghost of evolution in action. We find, for example, that many related organisms show unusual similarities that can be explained only through evolutionary relatedness. The

HOMOLOGOUS STRUCTURES: EMBRYO STAGE

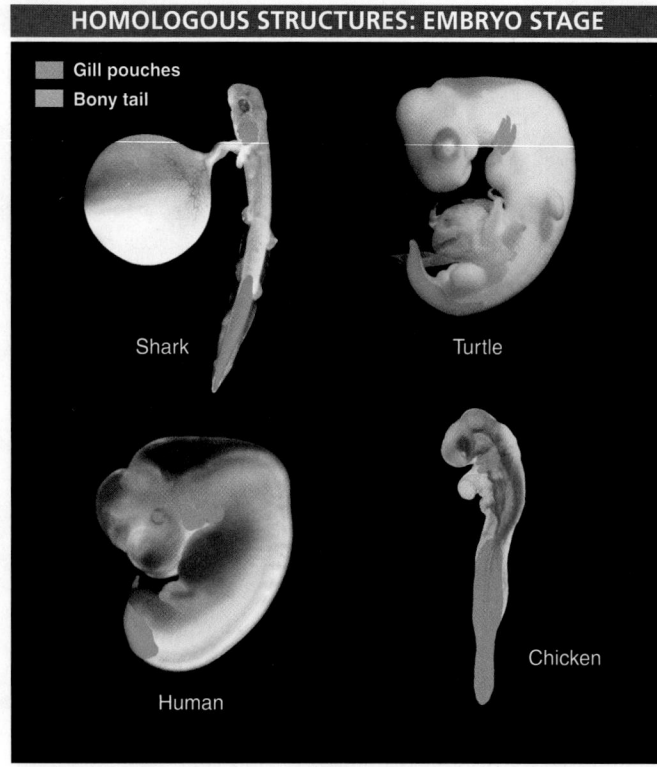

Gill pouches
Bony tail

Shark

Turtle

Human

Chicken

FIGURE 8-38 Evidence for evolution: embryology. Structures derived from common ancestry can be seen in embryos.

that betray the fact that they share a common ancestor. These features are called **homologous structures.**

At the extreme, homologous structures sometimes come to have little or no function at all. Such evolutionary leftovers, called **vestigial structures,** exist because they had value ancestrally. Some vestigial structures in mammals include the molars that continue to grow in vampire bats, even though these bats consume a completely liquid diet (**FIGURE 8-40**); eye sockets (with no eyes) in some populations of cave-dwelling fishes; and in whales, pelvic bones that are attached to nothing (but in nearly all other mammals serve as an important attachment point for leg bones). Even humans may have a vestigial organ—the appendix. It is greatly enlarged in our relatives the great apes, acting as host to cellulose-digesting bacteria that aid in breaking down the plants in the ape diet, but in humans it seems to serve no purpose (although recent studies suggest it provides some immune system support).

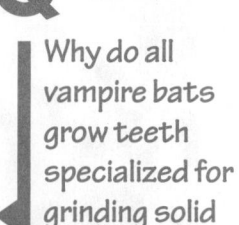

Why do all vampire bats grow teeth specialized for grinding solid food, when the bats have a completely liquid diet?

Not all organisms with adaptations that appear similar actually share recent ancestors. We see flying mammals (bats) and flying insects (locusts) (**FIGURE 8-41**). Likewise, dolphins and penguins live in similar habitats and have flippers that help them swim. In both examples, however, the analogous structures developed from different original structures. Natural selection, in a process called **convergent evolution,** may act on different starting

forelimbs of mammals are used for a variety of very different functions in bats, porpoises, horses, and humans (**FIGURE 8-39**). If each had been designed specifically for the uses necessary to that species, we would expect dramatically different designs. And yet, in each of these species, we see the same bones—modified extensively—

HOMOLOGOUS BONE STRUCTURES

Humerus

Radius
Ulna

Phalanges
Metacarpals
Carpals

Human

Horse

Bat

Porpoise

FIGURE 8-39 Evidence for evolution: comparative anatomy. Homologous bone structures among some mammals.

The similarities in the bone structure of the forelimbs of mammals demonstrate common ancestry.

Vampire bat skull

Molars

Like their ancestors, vampire bats have molars (adapted for grinding food), even though they consume a completely liquid diet and so have no use for the molars.

FIGURE 8-40 Evidence for evolution: vestigial structures.

materials (such as a flipper or a forelimb) and modify them until they serve similar purposes—much as we saw in the marsupial and placental mammals in Figure 8-37.

TAKE-HOME MESSAGE 8·20

Similarities in the anatomy and development of different groups of organisms and in their physical appearance can reveal common evolutionary origins.

CONVERGENT EVOLUTION

Different starting materials come to perform the same function through convergent evolution.

FIGURE 8-41 Evidence for evolution: convergent evolution and analogous structures.

8·21 Molecular biology reveals that common genetic sequences link all life forms.

New technologies for deciphering and comparing the genetic code provide our fourth line of evidence that evolution occurs. From microscopic bacteria to flowering plants to insects and primates, the molecular instructions for building organisms and transmitting hereditary information are the same: four simple bases, arranged in an almost unlimited variety of sequences. All living organisms share the same genetic code.

When we examine the similarity of DNA among related individuals within a species, we find that they share a

greater proportion of their DNA than do unrelated individuals. This is not unexpected; you and your siblings got all of your DNA from the same two parents, while you and your cousins got half of your DNA from the same two grandparents. The more distantly you and another individual are related, the more your DNA differs.

We can measure the DNA similarity between two species by comparing their DNA sequences for individual genes. For example, let's look at the gene that codes for a polypeptide used to build hemoglobin. In vertebrate animals, hemoglobin is found inside red blood cells, where its function is to carry oxygen throughout the body. It is made up of two types of chains of amino acids, the alpha chain and the beta chain. In humans, the beta chain has 146 amino acids. In rhesus monkeys, this beta chain is nearly identical: of the 146 amino acids, 138 are the same as those found in human hemoglobin, and only 8 are different. In dogs, the sequence is still somewhat similar, with 114 of the same amino acids. When we look at non-mammals such as birds, we find about 101 amino acid similarities with humans. And between humans and lamprey eels (still vertebrates, but with more than 500 million years since our last common ancestor), there are 21 amino acid similarities.

The differences in the amino acid sequence of the beta hemoglobin chain (and thus the alleles that govern this structure) seem to indicate that humans have more recently shared a common ancestor with rhesus monkeys than with dogs. And that we have more recently shared an ancestor with dogs than with birds or lampreys. These findings are just as we would expect, based on estimates of evolutionary relatedness made from comparative anatomy and embryology, as well as from the fossil record. It is as if a molecular clock is ticking. The longer two species have been evolving separately, the greater the number of changes in amino acid sequences—or "ticks of the clock" (**FIGURE 8-42**).

TAKE-HOME MESSAGE 8·21

All living organisms share the same genetic code. The degree of similarity in the DNA of different species can reveal how closely related they are and the amount of time that has passed since they last shared a common ancestor.

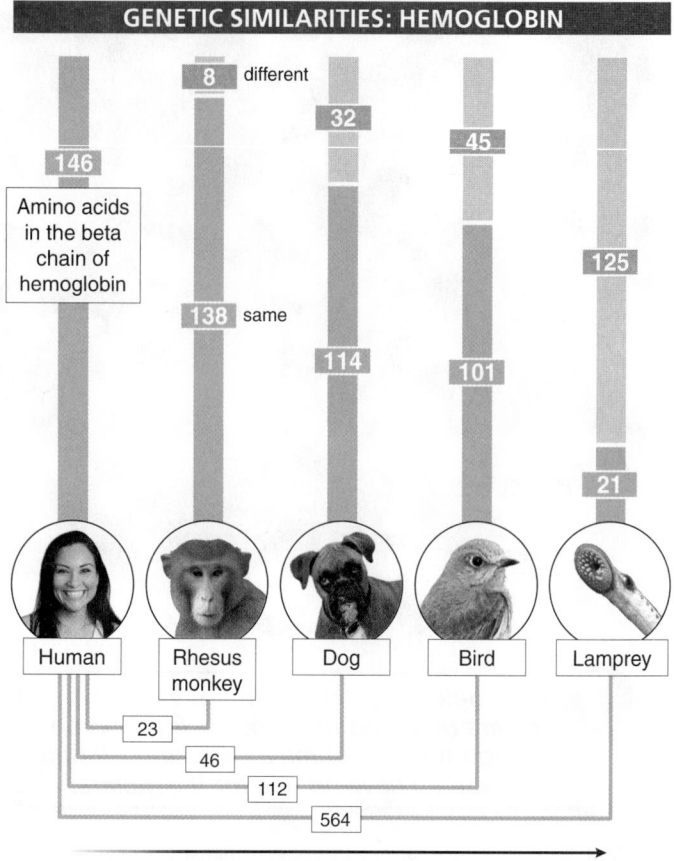

GENETIC SIMILARITIES: HEMOGLOBIN

Amino acids in the beta chain of hemoglobin

Time elapsed since common ancestor was last shared (millions of years)

 The longer two species have been evolving on their own, the greater the number of genetic differences that accumulate.

FIGURE 8-42 An evolutionary clock? Genetic similarities (and differences) demonstrate species relatedness.

8·22 Laboratory and field experiments enable us to watch evolution in progress.

A fifth line of evidence for the occurrence of evolution comes from multigeneration experiments and observations. People once thought that evolution was too slow a process to be observed in action. However, by choosing the right species—preferably organisms with very short life spans—and designing careful experiments, we can observe and measure evolution as it is happening.

In one clever study, researchers looked at populations of grass on golf courses—a habitat where lawn-mower blades represent a significant source of mortality. Although all the grass on golf courses was of the same species, on the putting greens it was cut very frequently, whereas on the fairways it was cut only

occasionally, and in the rough it was almost never cut at all (**FIGURE 8-43**). Over just a few years, significant changes occurred in these different grass populations. The grass plants on the greens came to be short lived, with rapid development to reproductive age and a very high seed output. For the plants in these populations, life was short and reproduction came quickly. (For those in which it did not come quickly, it did not come at all; hence their lack of representation in the population.) Plants on the fairways had slightly slower development and a reduced seed output, while those in the rough had the slowest development and the lowest seed output of all. When plants from each of the habitats were collected and grown in greenhouses under identical conditions, the dramatic differences

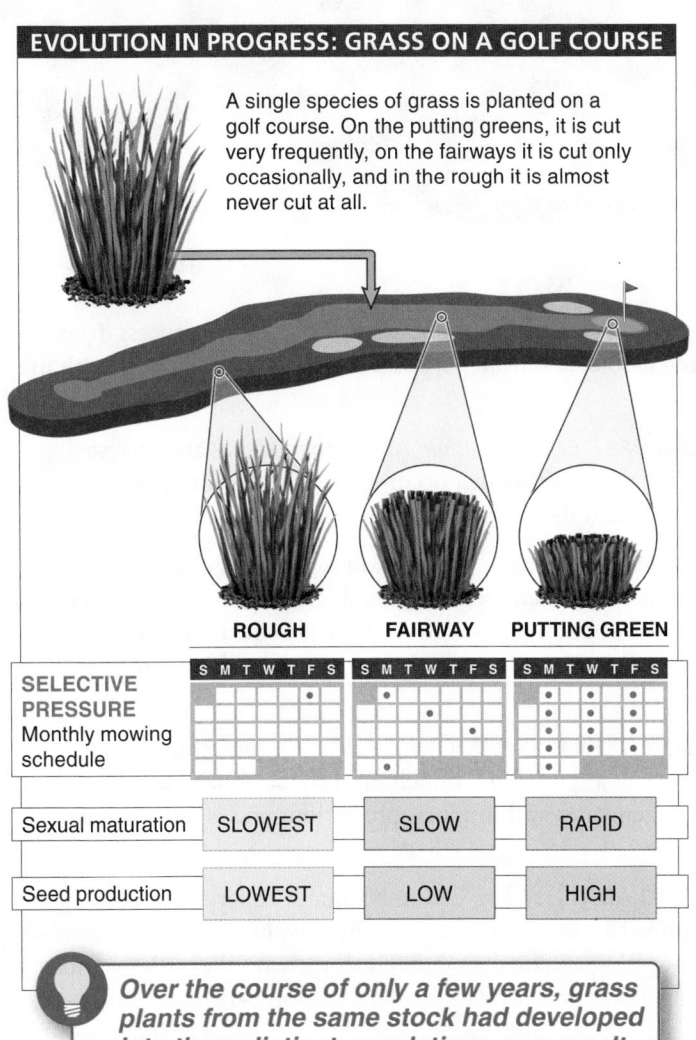

A single species of grass is planted on a golf course. On the putting greens, it is cut very frequently, on the fairways it is cut only occasionally, and in the rough it is almost never cut at all.

ROUGH   FAIRWAY   PUTTING GREEN

SELECTIVE PRESSURE Monthly mowing schedule																					

Sexual maturation	SLOWEST	SLOW	RAPID
Seed production	LOWEST	LOW	HIGH

💡 *Over the course of only a few years, grass plants from the same stock had developed into three distinct populations as a result of the frequency at which they were cut.*

FIGURE 8-43 Evolution in progress: grasses. Different mowing patterns can cause evolution in the grass on a golf course.

When first used as medicine in the 1940s, penicillin was uniformly effective in killing the bacterium *Staphylococcus aureus*. Today, natural selection has led to an increase in antibiotic-resistance alleles, and humans are increasingly at risk from untreatable *Staphylococcus* infections.

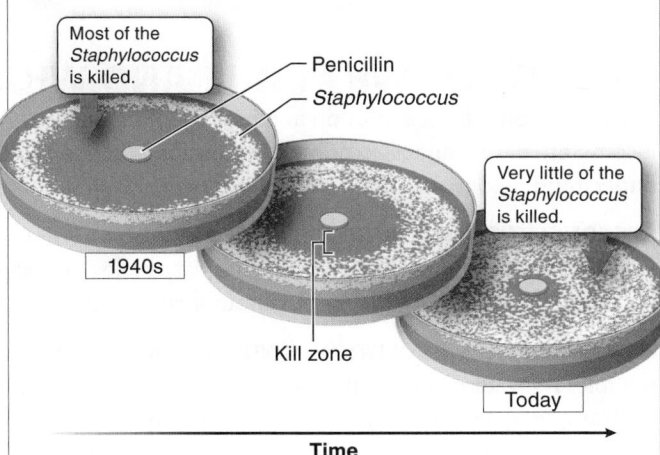

Most of the *Staphylococcus* is killed.
Penicillin
Staphylococcus
Very little of the *Staphylococcus* is killed.
1940s
Kill zone
Today
Time

FIGURE 8-44 Evolution in progress: disease-causing bacteria. Antibiotic resistance has evolved in *Staphylococcus*.

pneumonia and meningitis. In the 1960s, the antibiotics methicillin and oxacillin had nearly complete effectiveness against *Staphylococcus*. Today, though, nearly a third of staph infections are resistant to these antibiotics as well. The meaning of such unintentional natural selection "experiments" is clear and consistent: evolution is occurring all around us.

Finally, let's return to the starvation-resistant fruit flies introduced at the beginning of this chapter. They are an unambiguous demonstration that natural selection can produce dramatic changes in a population, and that it can bring about these changes very quickly. And, perhaps most important, we saw that replicating the same evolutionary process over and over again produced the same predictable results. In the laboratory, on the farm, in the doctor's office, and in deserts, streams, and forests, evolution is occurring.

Reflecting on both the process and products of evolution and natural selection, in the final paragraph of *The Origin of Species* Darwin eloquently wrote: "There is grandeur in this view of life . . . and that . . . from so simple a beginning endless forms most beautiful and most wonderful have been, and are being, evolved."

---

in growth, development, and life span remained, confirming that the frequencies of the various alleles controlling the traits of life span and reproductive output in the three populations had changed. In other words, evolution had occurred.

One particularly disturbing line of evidence for the occurrence of evolution in nature comes from the evolution of antibiotic-resistant strains of bacteria that cause illness in humans. In the 1940s, when penicillin was first used as a treatment for bacterial infections, it was uniformly effective in killing *Staphylococcus aureus*. Today, more than 90% of isolated *S. aureus* strains are resistant to penicillin (**FIGURE 8-44**). Because penicillin has become such a pervasive toxin in the environment of *Staphylococcus*, natural selection has led to an increase in the frequency of alleles that make these strains resistant to the drug. As a consequence, humans are increasingly at risk for becoming infected with *Staphylococcus* and getting diseases such as

TAKE-HOME MESSAGE 8·22

Replicated, controlled laboratory selection experiments and long-term field studies of natural populations allow us to watch and measure evolution as it occurs.

EVOLUTION: WHAT IT IS AND WHAT IT IS NOT . . .

Misconceptions about evolution and how it occurs can arise from misunderstandings about subtleties in the process, from incomplete or erroneous accounts of evolution in schools and the media, and from purposeful attempts to interfere with the understanding of evolution.

MISCONCEPTION: EVOLUTION IS A THEORY ABOUT THE ORIGIN OF LIFE. *Clarification:* Although scientists are interested in (and investigating) how life began, evolutionary biology is focused on the processes that occurred (and still occur) *after* life began, including those responsible for diversification and branching of species and those adapting populations to their environments.

MISCONCEPTION: EVOLUTION IS NOT OBSERVABLE OR TESTABLE. *Clarification:* Evolution is both observable and testable. Long-term, controlled and replicated, laboratory experiments on many species have demonstrated evolution (see an example in Section 8-1), including speciation. Numerous studies of natural populations have also documented evolution occurring (see Section 8-14). And, as in astronomy and geology, sophisticated hypothesis testing can be done using observations in the natural world.

MISCONCEPTION: EVOLUTION IS ONLY A THEORY AND HASN'T BEEN PROVED. *Clarification:* This misconception stems from confusion between the colloquial definition of a theory as a "guess" or "hunch" and the scientific definition of a theory as an explanation, based on many lines of evidence, that generates and supports predictions and is tested in many ways (see Section 1-10).

MISCONCEPTION: INDIVIDUALS EVOLVE (AND ARE "TRYING" TO ADAPT). *Clarification:* Natural selection can lead to populations of organisms adapted to their environment (see Section 8-13). But the process does not involve "trying" to adapt—it is simply a consequence of some individuals passing on their genes at a higher rate than individuals carrying alternative versions of those genes, and it is the population rather than any one individual that changes over time (see Section 8-12).

MISCONCEPTION: EVOLUTION IS GOAL-ORIENTED AND LEADS TO PROGRESS AND "OPTIMAL" SOLUTIONS. *Clarification:* Alleles that make it impossible for the individuals carrying them to live in a particular environment are weeded out of the population. But this is not the same as creating perfect or optimal organisms. Rather, the traits and features of organisms that increase in frequency within a population are simply those that cause the organisms carrying them to leave more descendants than are left by individuals with alternative traits (see Section 8-10). As the environment changes, so do the traits that are most fit. Several factors can prevent populations from becoming better adapted to a particular environment (see Section 8-14).

MISCONCEPTION: THERE ARE NO TRANSITIONAL FOSSILS; THE GAPS IN THE FOSSIL RECORD DISPROVE EVOLUTION. *Clarification:* Because fossils are formed only under a narrow range of environmental conditions, biologists do not expect to find all transitional forms, so the gaps do not disprove evolution. Numerous transitional fossils *have* been found, including those between dinosaurs and modern birds, and those between whales and their terrestrial mammalian ancestors (see Section 8-18).

MISCONCEPTION: THE THEORY OF EVOLUTION SAYS THAT LIFE ORIGINATED, AND EVOLUTION PROCEEDS, RANDOMLY, BY CHANCE. *Clarification:* Although chance is one element of evolution—there is a random element to the generation of mutations, for example—many non-random factors are central to how evolution proceeds. For example, the differential reproductive success of some variants—such as bacteria with antibiotic-resistance genes—that leads to natural selection is not random (see Section 8-13).

MISCONCEPTION: MOST BIOLOGISTS HAVE REJECTED EVOLUTION. *Clarification:* All modern theories of science are continually tested, verified, and modified as new and deeper understandings of the natural world emerge. That is how science works. The presidents of the National Academy of Sciences, the American Association for the Advancement of Science, and the National Science Teachers Association recently wrote a joint statement, saying that "evolutionary theory has stood the test of time in serving as the most comprehensive scientific explanation for the diversity of life on Earth and it is accepted by the overwhelming majority of scientists." There have been no credible challenges to the basic principles of evolution and how it proceeds.

Big Ideas in ... Evolution and Natural Selection

8·1 Evolution is an ongoing process.

- The characteristics of individuals in a population can change over time. We can observe such change in nature and can even cause such change to occur.

8·2–8·5 Darwin journeyed to a new idea.

- Following years of observations on worldwide patterns of the living organisms and fossils of plant and animal species, Charles Darwin developed a theory of evolution by natural selection that explained how populations of species can change over time.

8·6–8·11 Four mechanisms can give rise to evolution.

- Evolution—a change in the allele frequencies in a population—can occur by genetic drift, migration, mutation, or natural selection.

8·12–8·17 Through natural selection, populations of organisms can become adapted to their environments.

- When there is variation for a trait and the variation is heritable, and there is differential reproductive success based on that trait, evolution by natural selection is occurring.

- Fitness is an individual's relative reproductive output. The alleles that yield traits conferring the highest fitness on the individuals that carry them will increase their frequency in a population over time, but this process does not necessarily lead to "perfect" organisms.

- Artificial selection, in which humans determine which individuals will have the highest reproductive success, is a type of natural selection.

- Directional, stabilizing, and disruptive selection can alter the average value of a trait and/or the variation for a trait in a population.

- Natural selection can produce and modify complex traits, including behaviors. This modification may occur as traits selected for one purpose later confer increased fitness for a different purpose.

8·18–8·22 The evidence for evolution is overwhelming.

- Many lines of evidence document the occurrence of evolution and point to the central and unifying role of evolution by natural selection in helping us better understand all other ideas and facts in biology.

See the To-Go Guide (packaged with every new copy of this textbook) for an illustrated summary of the chapter.

Check Your Knowledge

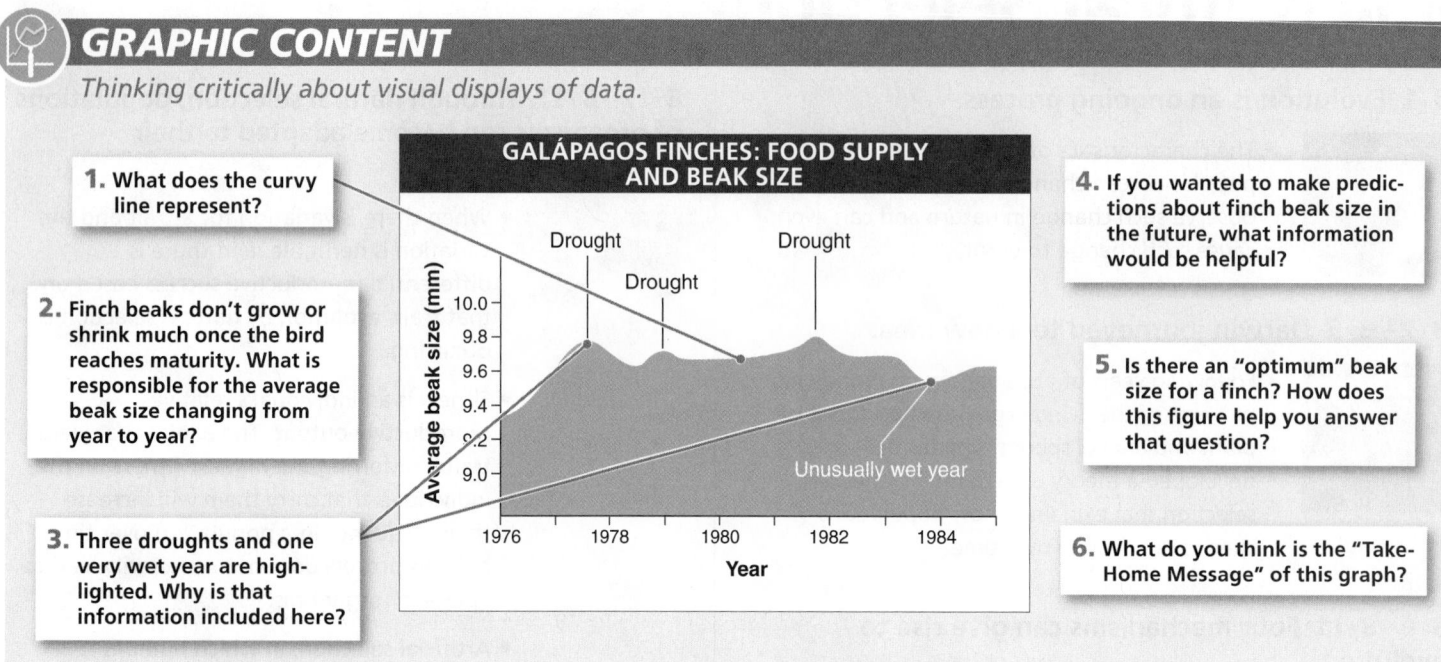

1. What does the curvy line represent?

2. Finch beaks don't grow or shrink much once the bird reaches maturity. What is responsible for the average beak size changing from year to year?

3. Three droughts and one very wet year are highlighted. Why is that information included here?

4. If you wanted to make predictions about finch beak size in the future, what information would be helpful?

5. Is there an "optimum" beak size for a finch? How does this figure help you answer that question?

6. What do you think is the "Take-Home Message" of this graph?

GALÁPAGOS FINCHES: FOOD SUPPLY AND BEAK SIZE

See Answers at the back of the book.

Key Terms in Evolution and Natural Selection

Multiple-Choice Questions

1. **The average time to death from starvation in a fruit fly is about 20 hours. Selecting for increased starvation resistance in fruit flies:**

   a) has no effect, because starvation resistance is not a trait that influences fruit fly fitness.

   b) has little effect, because ongoing mutation continuously reduces starvation resistance, counteracting any benefits from selection.

   c) cannot increase their survival time, because there is no genetic variation for this trait.

   d) has no effect, because starvation resistance is too complex a trait, dependent on the effects of too many genes.

   e) can produce populations in which the average time to death from starvation is 160 hours.

   100 HARD
   36
   0 EASY

2. **Georges Cuvier's discovery of fossils of Irish elk and giant ground sloths:**

   a) supports scientific evidence for extinction.

   b) was possible because of Buffon's determination that the earth was more than 6,000 years old.

   c) was possible only following Darwin's publication of *The Origin of Species.*

   d) was made in deep ocean trenches.

   e) suggested that species are immutable.

   100 HARD
   31
   0 EASY

3. **While on the voyage of the HMS *Beagle*, Darwin:**

   a) wrote *The Origin of Species.*

   b) nurtured his love of studying nature, exploring plant and animal diversity, and collecting fossils.

   c) discovered a love for sea travel.

   d) studied Malthus's book *Essay on the Principle of Population.*

   e) corresponded extensively with Alfred Russel Wallace about their ideas on evolution.

   100 HARD
   22
   0 EASY

4. **Which one of the following statements best describes the difference between artificial and natural selection?**

   a) Natural selection is limited to physical traits and artificial selection is not.

   b) Artificial selection has produced many of the most delicious food items for humans; natural selection has not.

   c) Natural selection acts without the input of humans; artificial selection requires human input.

   d) Charles Darwin understood natural selection but, at that time, was unaware of artificial selection.

   e) Natural selection works on all species; artificial selection works only on laboratory-raised species.

   100 HARD
   30
   0 EASY

5. **Which of the following statements about Charles Darwin is incorrect?**

   a) He spent five years traveling the world, observing living organisms and collecting fossils.

   b) He was under constant pressure from his father to make something of himself.

   c) He dropped out of medical school.

   d) He was enthusiastic about unleashing his theory of natural selection on the world as soon as he thought of it.

   e) He and Alfred Russel Wallace independently came up with the theory of evolution by natural selection.

   100 HARD
   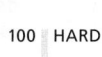
   19
   0 EASY

6. **Evolution occurs:**

   a) only when the environment is changing.

   b) only through natural selection.

   c) almost entirely because of directional selection.

   d) only via natural selection, genetic drift, migration, or mutation.

   e) by altering physical traits but not behavioral traits.

   100 HARD

   19
   0 EASY

7. **Which of the following statements about mutations is incorrect?**
   a) Mutations are almost always random with respect to the needs of the organism.
   b) A mutation is any change in an organism's DNA.
   c) Most mutations are harmful or neutral to the organism in which they occur.
   d) The origin of genetic variation is mutation.
   e) All of these statements are correct.

8. **Genetic drift has the strongest effects in populations that are:**
   a) small.
   b) large.
   c) characterized by extensive gene flow.
   d) in Hardy-Weinberg equilibrium.
   e) undergoing natural selection.

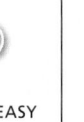

9. **When a group of individuals colonizes a new habitat, the event is likely to be an evolutionary event, because:**
   a) members of a small population have reduced rates of mating.
   b) gene flow increases.
   c) mutations are more common in novel environments.
   d) new environments tend to be inhospitable, reducing survival there.
   e) small founding populations are rarely genetically representative of the initial population.

10. **To establish that evolution by natural selection is operating in a population, one must demonstrate variability for a trait, heritability of that trait, differential reproductive success based on that trait, and:**
    a) increased complexity of the organism.
    b) random mating.
    c) progress.
    d) continuous change in the environment.
    e) nothing else.

11. **"Survival of the fittest" may be a misleading phrase to describe the process of evolution by natural selection, because:**
    a) it is impossible to determine the fittest individuals in nature.
    b) survival matters less to natural selection than does reproductive success.
    c) natural variation in a population is generally too great to be influenced by differential survival.
    d) during population bottlenecks, it is the least fit individuals that have the greatest survival.
    e) reproductive success on its own does not necessarily guarantee evolution.

12. **Evolutionary adaptation:**
    a) refers both to the process by which populations become better matched to their environment and to the features of an organism that make it more fit than other individuals.
    b) cannot occur in environments influenced by humans.
    c) is possible only when there is no mutation.
    d) is responsible for the fact that porcupines are at an unusually high risk of predation.
    e) occurs for physical traits but not behaviors.

13. **Adaptations shaped by natural selection:**
    a) are magnified and enhanced through genetic drift.
    b) are unlikely to be present in humans living in industrial societies.
    c) may be out of date, having been shaped in the past under conditions that differed from those in the present.
    d) represent perfect solutions to the problems posed by nature.
    e) are continuously modified so that they are always matched to the environment in which a population lives.

14. **Artificial selection was used on corn to produce a single strain of corn with increased growth rates and greater resistance to a fungus. Although farmers have continued to select for these traits, the productivity of this strain is no longer increasing. This suggests that:**
    a) the population size has been decreasing.
    b) all or most of the natural variation for these traits has been eliminated.
    c) gene migration is a major evolutionary agent in corn.
    d) long-term disruptive selection may lead to speciation.
    e) artificial selection is not as strong as natural selection.

15. **In a population in which a trait is exposed to stabilizing selection over time:**
    a) neither the average value nor the variation for the trait changes.
    b) both the average value and the variation for the trait increase.
    c) the average value increases or decreases, and the variation for the trait decreases.
    d) the average value for the trait stays approximately the same, and the variation for the trait decreases.
    e) the average value for the trait stays approximately the same, and the variation for the trait increases.

16. Maze-running behavior in rats:

a) is too complex a trait to be influenced by natural selection.

b) is a heritable trait.

c) is not influenced by natural selection, because it does not occur in rats' natural environment.

d) shows no variation.

e) is influenced primarily by mutation in the laboratory.

100 HARD

52

0 EASY

17. A fossil is defined most broadly as:

a) the preserved pieces of hard parts (e.g., shell or bone) of extinct animals.

b) any preserved remnant or trace of an organism from the past.

c) the preserved bones of vertebrates.

d) a piece of an organism that has turned into rock.

e) the process of preservation of intact animal bodies.

100 HARD

41

0 EASY

18. Which of the following statements about marsupial mammals is correct?

a) They fill many niches in Australia that are occupied by placental mammals in other parts of the world.

b) They are less fit than placental mammals.

c) They have become extinct as a result of the greater fitness of placental mammals.

d) They are more closely related to each other than they are to placental mammals.

e) Both a) and d) are correct.

100 HARD

46

0 EASY

19. Convergent evolution can occur only when two species:

a) have a recent common ancestor.

b) live in the same geographic area.

c) are separated by a barrier such as a new river.

d) evolve under similar selective forces.

e) are both unpalatable to predators.

100 HARD

54

0 EASY

20. What can be concluded about comparing differences in molecular biology between different species?

a) Extremely different species are fundamentally unrelated in any way.

b) Only DNA sequences can be used to compare relatedness between species.

c) Birds are more closely related to humans than dogs are.

d) Genetic similarities and differences demonstrate species relatedness.

e) The longer two species have been evolving on their own, the fewer the genetic differences between them.

100 HARD

47

0 EASY

21. Evolution:

a) occurs too slowly to be observed in nature.

b) can occur in the wild but not in the laboratory.

c) is responsible for the increased occurrence of antibiotic-resistant bacteria.

d) does not occur in human-occupied habitats.

e) None of these statements is correct.

100 HARD

48

0 EASY

Short-Answer Questions

1. Distinguish between evolution and natural selection. (Restrict your answer to 30 words or fewer.)

2. What is genetic drift? Why is it a more potent agent of evolution in small populations than in large populations?

3. In *The Origin of Species,* Charles Darwin wrote: "We may look with some confidence to a secure future of great length. And as natural selection works solely by and for the good of each being, all corporeal and mental endowments will tend to progress towards perfection." Describe three reasons why he is wrong.

4. How does the increasing frequency of antibiotic-resistant strains of bacteria represent an example of the occurrence of evolution?

See Answers at the back of the book.
For additional study questions, go to www.prep-u.com.

ABOUT THE CHAPTER OPENING PHOTO

Camels in the Sahara are adapted to life in the hot, dry desert. They have a "flexible thermostat," which allows their body temperature to drop during cool nights, storing coolness, and to increase over the course of a hot day. They have two rows of eyelashes, which protect them from blowing sand. And they have webbed feet, which help them to avoid sinking in the sand.

Communication, cooperation,
and conflict in the animal world

9

Evolution and Behavior

9·1–9·4 Behaviors are traits that can evolve.

From taste preferences to mate preferences, behaviors can evolve just as physical features can. (Shown here, a chimpanzee forages for termites.)

9·1 Behavior has adaptive value, just like other traits.

What are your favorite things to eat? Perhaps donuts or hot fudge sundaes top your list. Or maybe pizza, or cheeseburgers and french fries. One thing is almost certain about the food preferences of any human: the list is filled with calorie-rich substances. Put another way, when it comes to eating, humans show an almost complete aversion to dirt or pebbles or other substances from which no energy can be extracted (**FIGURE 9-1**).

In controlled studies, humans demonstrate a clear and consistent preference for sweet and fatty foods. Specifically, when people are presented with different mixtures, their preferences increase as the sugar concentration in the food increases—up to a point, after which adding more sugar makes the food less preferable. But the preference becomes stronger and stronger as the food's fat content increases. In short, we prefer sweet (but not too sweet) foods that are packed with as much fat as possible (**FIGURE 9-2**).

Watch birds in a field and you'll see that they, too, have preferences. A starling, for example, does not eat everything in its path. Rather, it walks through the grass, probing the ground and only occasionally picking up something to eat, such as a beetle larva. Shore crabs, too, have definite preferences. When presented with mussels of different sizes, shore crabs prefer the mussels that provide the greatest amount of energy relative to the amount of energy a crab

FIGURE 9-1 Mud pie for dinner? Humans show an aversion to eating dirt (and other substances from which we cannot extract nutrition).

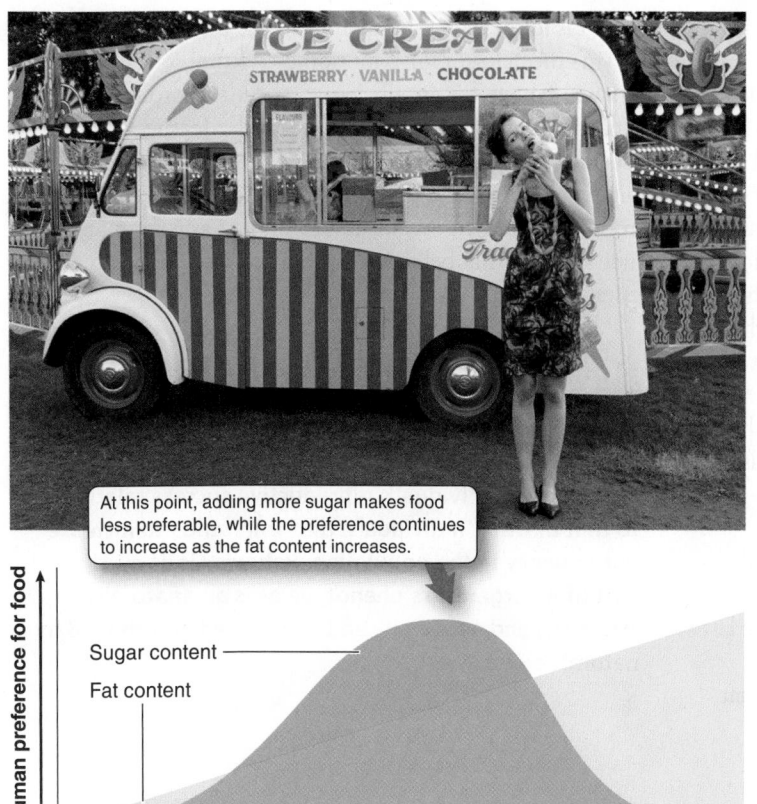

At this point, adding more sugar makes food less preferable, while the preference continues to increase as the fat content increases.

Human preference for food

Sugar content ———
Fat content

Sugar and fat content in food

 In controlled experiments, humans exhibit preferences for sugary foods, high in fat. And the more fat, the stronger the preference is.

FIGURE 9-2 Fatty and sweet. Across cultures, humans prefer sweet, but not too sweet, foods that are packed with fat.

offspring they can produce. As a consequence, natural selection can shape feeding behaviors just as it can bring about changes in physical structures.

Before we continue, let's define exactly what we mean by "behavior." **Behavior** encompasses any and all of the actions performed by an organism, often in response to its environment or to the actions of another organism. Feeding behavior is only one of many behaviors influenced by natural selection.

The scope of animal behavior is vast and varied. Even a brief listing of well-studied topics in animal behavior is impressively long:

- Conflict, aggression, and territoriality
- Cooperation, alliance building, and sociality
- Competing for food and predator avoidance
- Migration and navigation
- Behavioral control of body temperature
- Courtship and mate choice
- Pair bonding and fidelity
- Breeding and parental behavior
- Communication
- Learning and tool use

must expend to open the mussel. The largest mussels take too long to open and so are less preferred; the smallest mussels are easily opened but don't provide enough caloric content to make the effort worthwhile (**FIGURE 9-3**). Thus, the research shows, shore crabs prefer medium-size mussels.

Humans, starlings, shore crabs, and all other animals have taste preferences for the same reason: animals (including humans), unlike plants, cannot create their own food, so they must consume materials from which they can extract the most energy and acquire essential nutrients. If they don't, they die. We may believe that some things simply taste good while others do not, but these preferences are a direct result of the actions of molecules within our taste buds. And those molecules are produced by a large number of genes that have been shaped by natural selection.

Taste preferences directly influence the evolutionary fitness of organisms; the feeding choices of animals affect the number of

ENERGY-EFFICIENT FEEDING BEHAVIOR HAS EVOLVED

The feeding behavior of shore crabs has evolved; they preferentially choose mussels that provide the most energy relative to the effort it takes to open the shell.

FIGURE 9-3 Efficient eater. A shore crab feeds on a mussel.

In Chapter 8, we learned about the evolutionary origins of many *physical traits*. We did not investigate every physical trait that occurs in organisms, however. It was sufficient to look at a few examples, such as birth weight in babies, milk production in cows, and fur color in tigers, to understand the general process by which natural selection acts and how it can lead to the evolution of organisms adapted to their environments. Similarly, in this chapter, although we explore the evolution of *behavioral traits,* we won't investigate each and every behavioral trait in organisms. Rather, we'll explore three broad areas of animal behavior—cooperation and conflict, communication, and mating and parenting—focusing on why those behaviors evolved. That is, we'll be answering this question: How do these behaviors contribute to an organism's fitness, survival, and reproduction?

Our approach to the study of evolution and behavior parallels our approach to the study of the evolution of non-behavioral traits. Recall from the discussion of natural selection in the last chapter that when a heritable trait increases an individual's reproductive success relative to that of other individuals, that

trait tends to increase in frequency in the population. This is Darwin's mechanism for evolution by natural selection and, as we saw in Chapter 8, its effects are evident all around us, from the fancy ornamentation of male peacocks' feathers produced by sexual selection to the cryptic coloration that camouflages so many organisms. In this chapter, we see that *behavior* is just as much a part of an organism's phenotype as is its anatomical structures, and that behavior is produced and shaped by natural selection.

TAKE-HOME MESSAGE 9·1

Behavior encompasses any and all of the actions performed by an organism. When a heritable trait increases an individual's reproductive success relative to that of other individuals, that trait tends to increase in frequency in the population. Behavior is as much a part of an organism's phenotype as is an anatomical structure, and as such it can be produced and shaped by natural selection.

9·2 Some behaviors are innate.

In his study of pea plants, Gregor Mendel described a single gene for plant height that caused a plant to be either tall or short. The production of a trait such as plant height, however, is not completely genetically determined. Certain environmental conditions, such as the type of soil and the availability of water, nutrients, and sunlight, also have a role

SOME BEHAVIORS ARE INNATE

In geese, the sight of an egg outside the nest triggers a fixed action pattern: the goose uses a side-to-side egg-retrieval movement all the way back to the nest, even if the egg is taken away during the process.

Male stickleback during non-breeding season

Male stickleback during breeding season

During breeding season, a red belly on any other male stickleback fish triggers an aggressive response.

FIGURE 9-4 No learning required. Egg-retrieval behavior in geese and the aggressive behavior of male sticklebacks are fixed action patterns.

to play. Nearly all physical traits of all organisms are the products not only of genes but also of environmental conditions. When it comes to the production of behaviors, the environment also plays an important role.

The degree to which a behavior depends on the environment for expression, however, varies a great deal. At one extreme are behaviors—called **instincts** or **innate behaviors**—that don't require any environmental input to develop. Innate behaviors are present in all individuals in a population and do not vary much from one individual to another or over an individual's life span. An example of innate behavior is a **fixed action pattern.** Triggered in response to a specific signal called a **sign stimulus,** a fixed action pattern is a sequence of behaviors that requires no learning, does not vary, and, once started, runs to completion. Here are just two examples of fixed action patterns.

Egg retrieval in geese. When a goose spots an egg outside its nest (a sign stimulus), a fixed action pattern is triggered. The goose gets out of the nest and rolls the egg back, using a side-to-side motion, keeping the egg tucked underneath its bill. Once started, a goose continues the behavior, even if the egg is taken away on the way to the nest (**FIGURE 9-4**).

Aggressive displays and attacks by stickleback fish. The bellies of male stickleback fish turn bright red when the breeding season arrives. During this time, a male stickleback reacts aggressively to the sight of a red belly (a sign stimulus) on any other male stickleback. In fact, the males become antagonistic at the sight of anything remotely resembling a red belly. One researcher even noticed that his sticklebacks performed aggressive displays every day when a red mail truck drove by his window.

> ### TAKE-HOME MESSAGE 9·2
>
> The degree to which a behavior depends on the environment for expression varies a great deal. At one extreme are instincts, innate behaviors present in all individuals in a population that do not vary much from one individual to another or over an individual's life span. Innate behaviors develop without any environmental input.

9·3 Some behaviors must be learned (and some are learned more easily than others).

In contrast to innate behaviors are those behaviors that are influenced to a much greater degree by the individual's environment. Requiring some degree of **learning,** these behaviors are altered and modified over time in response to past experiences. There can be tremendous variation among behaviors that require learning: some come relatively easily and are learned by most individuals in a population, while other behaviors are less easily learned.

Consider a trait common to most primates, including humans: fear of snakes. In the wild, rhesus monkeys are afraid of snakes. The sight of a snake causes the monkeys to engage in fear-related responses, including making alarm calls and rapidly moving away from the snake.

Observations of monkeys in captivity, however, reveal that they aren't born with a fear of snakes. Captive Rhesus monkeys will reach over a plastic model of a snake to get a peanut. Experiments also show that monkeys learn to fear snakes if they see another monkey

Why is it so much easier for an infant to learn a complex language than for a college student to learn biology?

terrified at the sight of a snake (**FIGURE 9-5**). Even if they see only a videotape of another monkey expressing fear at the sight of a snake, monkeys immediately and permanently become afraid of snakes. They will no longer reach over a snake model to get a peanut, even when they are very hungry. Instead, they scream and move as far away from the artificial snake as possible. Studies on humans show an equally easily learned fear of snakes. Rather than shrieking and cowering in the corner of a cage, however, we respond with sweaty palms and an increased heart rate.

Q When behaviors are learned easily and by all (or nearly all) individuals, it is called **prepared learning.** In addition to the snake-fearing behavior of monkeys, examples of prepared learning abound. The acquisition of language in humans is a dramatic example. Most children don't talk until they are a year old, but by the age of three they understand most rules of sentence construction, and the average six-year-old who is a native English-speaker already has a vocabulary of about 13,000 words. These skills are impressive, particularly given that, at this age, children are

PREPARED LEARNING

1 BEFORE EXPOSURE TO FEAR OF SNAKES
A captive monkey will reach over a plastic snake for food.

Monkey has no fear of snakes.

2 EXPOSURE TO FEAR OF SNAKES
A captive monkey views another monkey expressing fear at the sight of a snake.

In real life   or   On video

3 AFTER EXPOSURE TO FEAR OF SNAKES

Monkey expresses fear of the plastic snake.

A monkey quickly learns to fear snakes if it sees another monkey express such fear.

FIGURE 9-5 Learning to be afraid. The monkey can easily learn to fear snakes by observing fear in other monkeys. This is a type of prepared learning.

generally not competent in reading, writing, and fine motor coordination.

Examples of prepared learning also underscore the fact that organisms don't learn everything with equal ease. For example, researchers demonstrated how easily monkeys learned to fear snakes, but in a related experiment, they demonstrated that the monkeys were not prepared to learn everything with equal ease. The researchers altered the videotape that previously showed a monkey expressing fear on encountering a snake. On the modified tape, a monkey was shown having the same

fear reaction in response to a flower or a toy rabbit. The captive monkeys—which had never seen flowers or rabbits or snakes—did not learn to fear flowers or rabbits the way they learned to fear snakes.

These observations point to an evolutionary basis for the acquisition of certain behaviors. It seems that organisms are well-prepared to learn behaviors that have been important to their ancestors' survival and reproductive success over the course of their evolutionary history, and are less prepared to learn behaviors irrelevant to their evolutionary success. Consider, for example, that although human babies quickly and easily develop a fear of snakes, they don't easily develop a fear of guns. Given that more than 30,000 people are killed by guns in the United States each year, while fewer than three dozen people are killed by snakes, it would seem that we ought to be very afraid of guns and relatively unconcerned about snakes. But we are built in just the opposite way (**FIGURE 9-6**). The likely explanation is that evolution can be slow in producing populations that are

Q Human babies quickly and easily develop a fear of snakes. Yet they don't easily develop a fear of guns. Why?

FIGURE 9-6 Instincts out of date. A human infant is born with a fear of snakes.

adapted to their environments—that is, evolutionary change cannot always keep up with a rapidly (in evolutionary terms) changing environment.

Like all genes, any genes involved in behaviors have been handed down to us from our ancestors. Snakes caused many human deaths over the course of our evolutionary history. In contrast, guns didn't kill a single person until very recently on the evolutionary time scale. Accordingly, we still fear our ancient enemy, the snake, and have no instinctual response to novel threats, regardless of how deadly.

TAKE-HOME MESSAGE 9·3

In contrast to innate behaviors are those behaviors that are influenced more by the individual's environment, requiring some learning, and are often altered and modified over time in response to past experiences. Organisms are well-prepared to learn behaviors that have been important to the reproductive success of their ancestors, and less prepared to learn behaviors irrelevant to their evolutionary success.

9·4 Complex-appearing behaviors don't require complex thought in order to evolve.

Why do humans and other animals have sex? Is it because they are thinking, robot-like: "Must maximize reproductive success. Must maximize reproductive success"? Of course not. Yet they go about their lives behaving as if they were.

In actuality, natural selection produces organisms that exhibit relatively simple behaviors in response to certain situations or environmental conditions—behaviors that to us may seem complex and sophisticated. Let's look at an example. An animal that experiences pleasure when it has sex has the incentive to seek out additional opportunities to experience that pleasure. As long as reproductive success is enhanced in the process, it is not necessary (from the reproductive-success standpoint) for the animal to deliberately seek that outcome. In other words, natural selection doesn't have to produce animals consciously trying to maximize reproductive success. It only needs to produce animals that behave in a way that actually results in reproductive success, and this outcome will occur if organisms experience a pleasurable sensation by having sex. It's like an evolutionary shortcut. Behaviors that lead to a specific outcome that increases the animal's relative reproductive success will be favored by natural selection.

We can investigate experimentally whether natural selection works in this way by tricking animals. Consider the example of egg retrieval in geese. When an egg falls out of the nest, a goose retrieves it in exactly the same way every time. Is a goose able to do this because it vigilantly keeps tabs on all of

Q Animals don't consciously try to maximize their reproductive success, yet they behave as if they do. How does this happen?

its eggs? This seemed to be the case, until researchers decided to trick some geese. The researchers learned that putting *any* object that remotely resembles an egg near a goose's nest triggers the retrieval process. Geese will retrieve beer cans, door knobs, and a variety of other objects that will not increase the animal's reproductive success. Moreover, if multiple egg-like items are just outside the nest, the goose will retrieve the largest item first.

To test the limits of the retrieval behavior, researchers began putting larger and larger models of eggs outside the nests. When given a choice between an actual goose egg and an artificial egg the size of a basketball, the goose always tried to retrieve the giant egg. Rather than keeping tabs on their eggs, geese seem to be following a rule of thumb to retrieve any nearby egg-like objects, preferentially retrieving the larger objects first (**FIGURE 9-7**). Thus, natural selection can produce organisms that exhibit silly and clearly maladaptive (i.e., fitness-decreasing) behaviors in experiments—the goose trying to retrieve a basketball-sized egg—if, in nature, individuals' performance of these simple actions nearly always leads to fitness-increasing behaviors.

Taking an evolutionary approach to the study of the behavior of animals, including humans, is not new. Charles Darwin wrote in *On the Origin of Species:* "In the distant future I see open fields for far more important researches. Psychology will be based on a new foundation." And in the past several decades, Darwin's prediction has

RETRIEVING BEHAVIOR IN GEESE

FIGURE 9-7 Programmed to retrieve. The goose will retrieve any egg-like object outside its nest.

NATURALLY OCCURRING FIXED ACTION PATTERN

By following simple rules that have evolved, an animal can exhibit complex-appearing behaviors.

When an egg rolls out of a nest, a goose retrieves it in exactly the same way every time.

EXPERIMENTAL FIXED ACTION PATTERN

A goose retrieves any object near its nest that remotely resembles its eggs.

A goose retrieves the largest egg-like object first instead of the actual goose eggs.

Setting up a situation that would never occur in nature, we can reveal that an animal is following simple behavioral rules.

increasingly proved true. In a synthesis of evolutionary biology and psychology, researchers taking an approach called "evolutionary psychology" have begun to view the human brain and human behaviors, including emotions, as traits produced by natural selection, selected as a result of their positive effects on survival and reproduction. So, too, has the evolutionary approach to studying behavior begun to influence the field of economics. The 2002 Nobel prize for economics was awarded to researchers who used insights from evolutionary biology and psychology in their analyses of human decision making.

In the rest of this chapter, working from the understanding that organisms' traits, including their behaviors, have evolved by natural selection, we examine the question of why organisms behave as they do. We begin with an exploration of selfishness and cooperation in animals, investigating in particular how natural selection has produced organisms that engage in apparent acts of altruism.

TAKE-HOME MESSAGE 9·4

If an animal's behavior in natural situations usually increases its relative reproductive success, the behavior will be favored by natural selection. The natural selection of such behaviors does not require the organism to consciously try to maximize its reproductive success.

9·5–9·9 Cooperation, selfishness, and altruism can be better understood with an evolutionary approach.

Placing herself at risk, a female arctic ground squirrel alerts the colony to approaching danger.

9·5 "Kindness" can be explained.

If we look closely, we see many behaviors in the animal world that *appear* to be **altruistic behaviors**—that is, they seem to come at a cost to the individual performing them while benefiting a recipient. When discussing altruism, we define costs and benefits in terms of their contribution to an individual's fitness.

Take the case of the Australian social spider (*Diaea ergandros*). After giving birth to about 50 hungry spiderlings, the mother's body slowly liquefies into a nutritious fluid that the newborn spiders consume. Over the course of about 40 days, her offspring literally eat her alive; they ultimately kill their mother, but start their lives well-nourished. The cost to the mother is huge—she is unable to produce any more offspring—but there is a clear benefit to her many gene-bearing recipients (**FIGURE 9-8**).

Such altruistic-appearing behavior is common enough in the natural world that it puzzled Darwin. Natural selection, he believed, generally works to produce selfish behavior. The alleles that cause the individual carrying them to have the greatest reproductive success should increase their market share—that is, should increase as a proportion of all the alleles for that gene within the population—in any given generation. At the same time, alleles that cause the individual carrying

This mother spider is actually being selfish—not altruistic—when she lets her offspring eat her alive.

FIGURE 9-8 Parental care to the extreme. The female *Diaea ergandros* spider feeds her offspring with her own body.

them to help increase other individuals' reproductive success should decrease their relative frequency in a population. Put another way, natural selection should never produce altruistic behavior. Darwin worried that if the apparent instances of altruism were indeed truly altruistic, they would prove fatal to his theory.

As it turns out, Darwin's theory is safe. Virtually all of the apparent acts of altruism in the animal kingdom prove, on closer inspection, to be not truly altruistic; instead, they have evolved as a consequence of either **kin selection** or **reciprocal altruism.**

Kindness toward close relatives: kin selection. Kin selection can lead to the evolution of apparently altruistic behavior toward close relatives. Suppose that, for one gene, you carry allele *K,* which causes you to behave in a way that increases the fitness of a close relative of yours, while decreasing your own fitness. Allele *K* might actually increase its frequency in the population, because you and your relatives tend to share many of the same alleles—including allele *K.* Thus the increased fitness of the relatives you help might compensate for your own reduced fitness, because allele *K* will, overall, increase its frequency in the population when you help your relatives increase their reproductive output.

Kindness toward unrelated individuals: reciprocal altruism. Reciprocal altruism can lead to the evolution of apparently altruistic behavior toward unrelated individuals. Suppose that, for another gene, you carry allele *R,* which causes you to help individuals to whom you are not related. This helps to increase their fitness and decreases yours in the process. Allele *R* might still increase its market share in the population, if the individuals whom you help become more likely to return the favor and help you in the future, increasing your fitness.

Seen in this light, both kin selection and reciprocal altruism can lead to the evolution of behaviors that are *apparently* altruistic but, in actuality, are beneficial—from an

evolutionary perspective—to the individuals engaging in the behaviors.

In the next two sections, we explore kin selection and reciprocal altruism in more detail. We also investigate some of the many testable predictions about when acts of apparent kindness should occur, whom they should occur between, and how we could increase or decrease the frequency of their occurrence through a variety of modifications to the environment.

> "It is not from the benevolence of the butcher, the brewer, or the baker that we expect our dinner, but from their regard to their own interest. We address ourselves, not to their humanity, but to their self-love, and never talk to them of our own necessities, but of their advantages."
>
> —ADAM SMITH, *An Inquiry into the Nature and Causes of the Wealth of Nations,* 1776

Occasionally, we see individuals engaging in behavior that *is* genuinely altruistic. We'll examine how and why certain environmental situations cause individuals to behave in a way that decreases their fitness and, as such, is evolutionarily maladaptive. It is also important to note that even as genes play a central role in cooperation and conflict, humans' ability to override impulses toward selfishness is responsible for some of the rich diversity in behavior that we see around us.

TAKE-HOME MESSAGE 9·5

Many behaviors in the animal world appear altruistic. In almost all cases, the apparent acts of altruism are not truly altruistic and have evolved as a consequence of either kin selection or reciprocal altruism and, from an evolutionary perspective, are beneficial to the individual engaging in the behavior.

9·6 Apparent altruism toward relatives can evolve through kin selection.

The grasslands of the western United States are home to large colonies of Belding's ground squirrels, living in underground burrows. Because the colonies are as large as hundreds or thousands of individuals, they attract many birds of prey, which succeed in killing a squirrel in about 10% of attempts. Squirrels have a system for reducing predation risk that

resembles a neighborhood watch program. When an aerial predator approaches, it is common for a squirrel standing on top of a burrow to produce a loud whistle-like alarm call, warning the colony of the impending danger. On hearing an alarm call, squirrels quickly take cover in their burrows, reducing their risk of death. Making an alarm call is a very

An individual Belding's ground squirrel will warn members in its colony that a predator is nearby. Eighty percent of squirrels making the alarm calls are older females, who have more relatives to protect in the colony.

Predator

Making an alarm call seems like a bad idea—a calling squirrel frequently is killed in the process—but because she protects her relatives, the alarm-calling behavior is favored by natural selection.

FIGURE 9-9 Protecting relatives by making an alarm call. At great risk to herself, a female Belding's ground squirrel will make an alarm call likely to save her family members from a predator.

dangerous activity: about half the time that an alarm call is made, the caller is killed by the predator (**FIGURE 9-9**).

Some squirrels see predators and make alarm calls, while other squirrels see predators and keep their mouths shut. Why would any squirrel make an alarm call? And which squirrels are most likely to engage in this altruistic-appearing behavior? It certainly isn't random: about 80% of the squirrels making alarm calls are female. Moreover, older females are five times more likely than young females to make alarm calls.

These differences reveal that alarm calling is about protecting relatives. The more kin an individual is likely to have, the more likely that individual is to sound the alarm. Because males travel long distances to live in new colonies shortly after reaching maturity, most adult males don't live near their parents, siblings, or any other relatives except their own offspring. Females, on the other hand, remain near the area where they were born and are likely to have many close relatives nearby. Older females, then, are likely to have the largest number of relatives.

The biologist W. D. Hamilton expressed the idea of "kin selection," that one individual assisting another could compensate for its own decrease in fitness if it helped a close relative in a way that increased the relative's fitness. After all,

he realized, the recipient of the aid is likely to have at least some genes in common with the altruistic individual. And the more genes they share (i.e., the more closely the individuals are related), the more likely it is that the alleles being propagated by the recipient of the altruistic-like behavior are the same alleles found in the altruistic individual.

Thus, altruistic-appearing behavior will most likely occur when the benefits to close relatives are greater than the cost to the individual performing the behavior. That is, the more closely related two individuals are, the more likely they are to act altruistically toward each other. It seems that individuals are acting selflessly/altruistically, but they are really acting in their genes' best interests.

Belding's ground squirrels probably don't know exactly how closely they are related to the squirrels around them, so it is likely that natural selection has led to an evolutionary shortcut that allows them to behave as if they did know. In a clever experiment that tested this idea, researchers trapped adult female squirrels and relocated them to distant ground squirrel colonies in which they had no close relatives. If the transplanted females were able to determine exactly how closely they were related to the squirrels around them, they would not make alarm calls. To do so would put the caller at risk without benefiting her genes. What the researchers

INAPPROPRIATE ALARM CALLING IN UNNATURAL SITUATIONS

Researchers transplanted an older female Belding's ground squirrel from her original colony to a new colony, where she had no relatives. Even though this older female is not related to any individuals in the colony, she behaves as if she were and is likely to make an alarm call.

Predator

Transplanted ground squirrel (not related to any individuals in the colony)

 As with the egg-retrieval experiments in geese, by tricking an animal, setting up a situation that would never occur in nature, we can reveal that the animal is following simple behavioral rules.

FIGURE 9-10 Following simple behavioral rules. A transplanted female Belding's ground squirrel that is not related to the squirrel colony behaves as though she is.

found, though, was that transplanted females were just as likely to sound the alarm in the colony of strangers as they were in their home territories, surrounded by close relatives (**FIGURE 9-10**). It seems that female ground squirrels have evolved to follow a simple rule that says, "If I am an older female, I behave as if I have many close relatives around me."

Q *Who are people most likely to bequeath money to in their wills?*

Another example of apparent altruistic behavior toward kin is seen in how people give their money and property away when they die. Kin selection theory gives rise to the prediction that people will bequeath their assets based on their degree of relatedness to others. In an analysis of 1,000 randomly chosen wills, researchers tested and supported two hypotheses: (1) that individuals would leave more of their estates to genetic kin, including their parents, children, and siblings (or spouses, who, the researchers assumed, would eventually distribute the assets to the dead person's

genetic kin), and (2) that closer relatives would be left greater amounts than more distant relatives (**FIGURE 9-11**).

Based on the idea of kin selection, it is necessary to redefine an individual's fitness. An individual's fitness is not just measured by his or her total reproductive output (this is called **direct fitness**). Fitness also includes the reproductive output that individuals bring about through their seemingly altruistic behaviors toward their close kin. This is called an individual's **indirect fitness.** The sum of an individual's indirect and direct fitness is called **inclusive fitness.**

No two individuals—with the exception of identical twins—are genetically identical. And because different individuals do not share all of the same alleles, we expect that they should experience some conflict. One disturbing example of such conflict takes place between a pregnant woman and her developing fetus.

A mother's and a fetus' interests differ when it comes to the question of how much food—doled out as nutrients in the blood flow across the placenta—the fetus ought to get. There is a point at which it is in the mother's best interests

Q *James Joyce wrote: "Whatever else is unsure in this stinking dunghill of a world, a mother's love is not." According to the concept of kin selection, he may not be completely right. Why?*

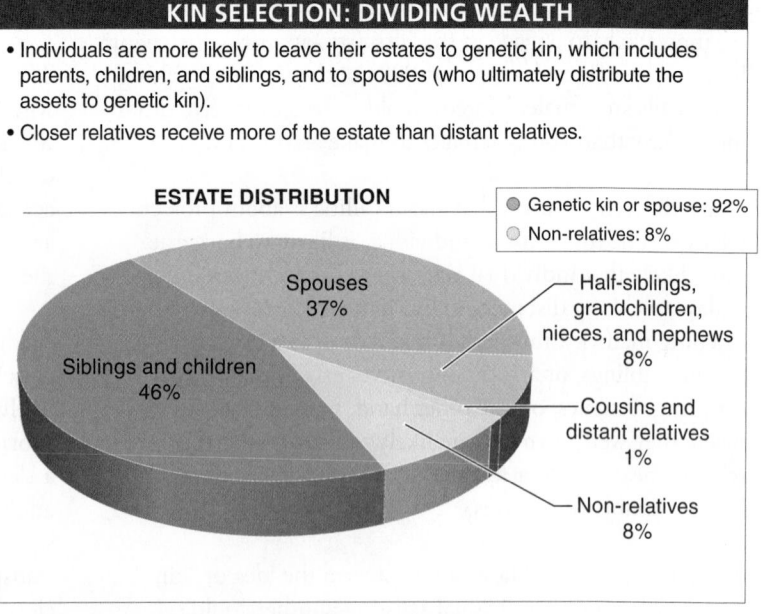

KIN SELECTION: DIVIDING WEALTH

• Individuals are more likely to leave their estates to genetic kin, which includes parents, children, and siblings, and to spouses (who ultimately distribute the assets to genetic kin).

• Closer relatives receive more of the estate than distant relatives.

ESTATE DISTRIBUTION

● Genetic kin or spouse: 92%
○ Non-relatives: 8%

Spouses 37%

Half-siblings, grandchildren, nieces, and nephews 8%

Siblings and children 46%

Cousins and distant relatives 1%

Non-relatives 8%

FIGURE 9-11 Reading the will. How likely are you to inherit money from a family member?

to reduce the amount of glucose and other nutrients given to the fetus. Her genes gain if she saves some of her resources for future fetuses, to whom she will be related as closely as to the present fetus.

Now consider the fetus' "point of view." Future siblings will carry some but not all of the same genes as the fetus. Consequently, the fetus does not necessarily benefit from sacrificing nutritional intake for the sake of future siblings. In a sense, it is a sibling rivalry that starts before the sibling is even conceived! The conflict results in a physiological battle throughout pregnancy. The fetus produces chemicals that increase the diameter of the mother's blood vessels, thus increasing the amount of sugar delivered to the fetus. In response, the mother produces more insulin, a chemical that has exactly the opposite effect, causing a reduction in the amount of sugar in the bloodstream available to the fetus. In some mothers this conflict causes gestational diabetes, an inability to properly regulate her blood sugar levels—a condition that disappears as soon as the baby is born. In all pregnancies, though, the conflict escalates until the mother is producing a thousand times the normal amount of insulin.

Gestational diabetes might also be the result of conflict between the fetus's alleles that come from its father and those that come from its mother. The parents may have different interests concerning how much to invest in the current offspring versus how much to save for future offspring. (Paternally inherited genes may benefit from greater resource uptake by the fetus, while maternally inherited genes may benefit from reduced resource uptake.)

Just as close relatives are more likely to help each other than are strangers, the converse is also true: the less closely related two individuals are, the more likely they are to experience conflict. Male lions, for example, upon taking over a pride usually kill unrelated cubs (although females defend their young aggressively), causing the females to become reproductively ready sooner than they would if they continued nursing their cubs.

The idea of kin selection gives rise to another prediction about conflict among relatives and non-relatives. Specifically, it generates the prediction that children in step-families will be injured or killed more frequently than those living with their biological families. And in fact, evidence from numerous studies across many different cultures, including evaluation of 20,000 reports from the American Humane Association in the United States, supports what has been called the "Cinderella syndrome." These findings included, for example, an estimate that the risk of abuse for a preschooler is about 1 in 3,000 for a child living with two biological parents (with whom he or she shares considerable genetic relatedness) and 40 in 3,000 for a child living with a step-parent (with whom he or she has no genetic relatedness). This difference in risk for children living in a home with a step-parent versus those living with their biological parents remains even when socioeconomic factors are taken into account. Although the effect has been noted in multiple other cultures, it is important to note that in the overwhelming majority of step-families no abuse occurs.

Q

Is a child living with one or more step-parents at greater risk of abuse than a child of the same age living with his or her biological parents?

TAKE-HOME MESSAGE 9·6

Kin selection describes apparently altruistic behavior in which an individual that assists a genetic relative compensates for its own decrease in direct fitness by helping increase the relative's fitness and, consequently, its own inclusive fitness.

9·7 Apparent altruism toward unrelated individuals can evolve through reciprocal altruism.

It is ironic that studies of altruism among animals reveal that natural selection has primarily produced selfish behavior. And, as we saw in the previous section, when behavior appears altruistic, it is frequently because individuals are helping kin and, by doing so, are promoting the reproduction of the copies of the genes (i.e., the alleles) that they share with close relatives. Does any apparently altruistic behavior toward non-relatives occur in the animal world? Yes, but there's not much of it. Here we'll explore the conditions that give rise to reciprocal altruism, how it may have arisen, and why it is so common among humans but so rare among most other animal species.

We start by examining one species with well-documented altruistic-appearing behavior: the vampire bat. Vampire bats live in social groups of 8–12 mostly unrelated adults, roosting primarily in caves and hollow trees. They feed by landing on large mammals such as cattle, horses, and pigs, piercing the skin with their razor-sharp teeth, and drinking the blood that flows from the wound. A chemical in their saliva keeps the blood from clotting, and thus allows the bats to feed for a longer period of time.

Because of their small body size (about the size of your thumb) and their very high metabolic rate, vampire bats must consume almost their entire body weight in blood each night. If they go for more than about 60 hours without finding a meal, they are likely to die from starvation. Here's where the apparent altruism comes in: a bat that has not found food and is close to death will beg food from a bat that has recently eaten. In many cases, the bat that has just eaten will regurgitate some of the blood it has consumed into the mouth of the hungry bat, saving it from starvation. This act obviously has very high benefit for the recipient of the blood, but it comes at a cost to the sharing bat, which loses some of the caloric content of a meal it has just obtained (**FIGURE 9-12**).

RECIPROCAL ALTRUISM IN VAMPIRE BATS

A vampire bat may vomit up a blood meal for an unrelated individual—saving that individual's life. Bats do this only for individuals that will return the favor, so their own survival is improved in the long run and the behavior is favored by natural selection.

FIGURE 9-12 The gift of life.

Kin selection is responsible for some of the blood sharing (females often regurgitate blood for their own offspring), but, in many cases, individuals give blood to unrelated individuals. How might this behavior have arisen? To answer the question, it is important to note three other features of vampire bats. First, they are able to recognize more than a hundred distinct individuals. Second, bats that receive blood donations from non-relatives reciprocate significantly more than average with the bats that have shared blood with them. And third, bats that are not familiar with each other (and do not have a history of helping each other) generally do not regurgitate for each other.

One method proposed to explain the evolution of this apparent altruism is that the bats giving blood to other bats in need are repaid the favor when they are in need of blood. In other words, the act only seems to be selfless, when in actuality it is selfish. With such reciprocal altruism, both individuals (at different encounters) give up something of *relatively* low value in exchange for getting something of great value at a later time when they need it most. In other words, they are storing goodwill in another individual, in much the same way that a person might put money in a bank for a rainy day. In both cases, individuals are protected from some of the world's uncertainties.

Reciprocal altruism has also been documented in vervet monkeys. Monkeys that would otherwise be searching for food or, perhaps, for a mate spend time grooming other monkeys instead (mostly by picking parasites from their fur). In return for their grooming behavior, the monkeys are more likely to receive assistance in response to their solicitations for aid (**FIGURE 9-13**).

Taken together, studies of primates, bats, and other mammals show that reciprocal altruism can evolve if certain conditions are met:

1. Repeated interactions among individuals, with opportunities to be both the donor and the recipient of altruistic-appearing acts

2. Benefits to the recipient that are significantly greater than the costs to the donor

3. The ability to recognize and punish cheaters, individuals that are recipients of altruistic-appearing acts but do not return the favor

In the absence of these conditions, selfishness is expected to be the norm among unrelated individuals. But in the presence of all three conditions, reciprocity masquerading as altruism is likely to occur, as it does with blood sharing among the vampire bats.

RECIPROCAL ALTRUISM IN GROOMING BEHAVIOR

Time that could be spent finding food? Individuals that groom others are more likely to receive assistance if they ever are in danger.

FIGURE 9-13 You scratch my back, I'll scratch yours.

The three conditions required for the evolution of reciprocal altruism are not satisfied in many animal species, which may be why altruistic-appearing behavior among unrelated individuals is rare. But there are some exceptions. The cleaner fish, for example, is a small fish that is allowed to swim right into the mouth of a grouper, a much larger fish, where it eats the grouper's parasites. Stomach analyses reveal that groupers almost never eat the cleaner fish, opting to pass up this opportunity for a meal. And so, while the grouper is cleaned of parasites, the cleaner fish gets to eat a meal of parasites. In this case, it is easy to rule out kin selection as the reason for the altruistic-appearing behavior; the fishes are from different species and can't possibly be close relatives. Many such mutually beneficial relationships seem to develop when the environment is stressful. In other words, behaviors can evolve that help organisms live more harmoniously with one another—when doing so improves their reproductive success.

As rare as it is in other species, reciprocal altruism is very common among humans. Friendship, among other human relationships, is built on reciprocity and is almost universal.

The opportunity for friendship may be enhanced by our long life span and our ability to recognize thousands of faces and keep track of cheaters. These features are essential in individuals engaging in reciprocal altruism, because an individual becomes very vulnerable when he or she acts in an altruistic manner toward an unrelated individual. The risk is that the altruism will not be repaid, in which case the cheater enjoys greater fitness than the altruist.

Q *Why are humans among the few species to have friendships?*

While cooperators, those who repay altruistic-appearing behavior, have evolutionary advantages over loners, this advantage disappears if the cooperators are the givers all or most of the time, never, or rarely, getting anything in return. The importance of keeping track of cheaters and of identifying good potential reciprocity partners (i.e., other cooperators) may be why humans are so interested in social information and seemingly trivial gossip. As with many of the complex behaviors we have explored, humans probably use some rules of thumb when making decisions about reciprocal altruism. This might include keeping track of *all* available social information to best determine any promising individuals with whom to engage in reciprocal altruism. This includes information about health, generosity, social status, and reproduction. Researchers have even hypothesized that the evolution of maintaining an interest in social information, while valuable in most contexts, may now have maladaptive manifestations. We may find ourselves interested in and distracted by the social lives of Angelina Jolie, Brad Pitt, or other individuals whom we will most likely never meet.

Q *Why is it easier to remember gossip than physics equations?*

TAKE-HOME MESSAGE 9·7

In reciprocal altruism, an individual engages in an altruistic-appearing act toward another individual. Although giving up something of value, the actor does so only when likely to get something of value at a later time. Reciprocal altruism occurs only if individuals have repeated interactions and can recognize and punish cheaters, conditions satisfied in humans but in few other species.

9·8 In an "alien" environment, behaviors produced by natural selection may no longer be adaptive.

A transplanted female squirrel makes an alarm call, putting herself in grave danger to help out dozens of squirrels that share none of her genes. A person in the United States donates money to refugees in Africa. Or someone craves high-fat food even as she knows it may increase her risk of heart disease and shorten her life.

These situations have something in common. In each, genetically influenced traits, behaviors favored by natural selection over evolutionary time, cause individuals to behave in a way that *reduces* their fitness. But how can that be? How can natural selection lead to fitness-reducing behaviors?

To better understand these situations, it is helpful to return to our discussion of fitness in Chapter 8. Recall that fitness not only is an individual's reproductive success, relative to that of other individuals in the population, but also depends on the specific environment in which the organism lives. An adult female Belding's ground squirrel that makes alarm calls generally increases her inclusive fitness by doing so, because all around her are individuals who share her genes. For this reason, such behavior has been favored by natural selection and has increased in frequency in the population.

The world in which alarm calling evolved did not include biologists with pickup trucks who trapped female squirrels, drove them long distances, and released them into colonies of unrelated individuals. So, when a female squirrel suddenly finds herself in that world, her evolved behaviors can no longer be expected to be adaptive—no more than a human could be expected to survive on the moon. And an individual's genes and all the behaviors they influence cannot change overnight. Adaptation to a new environment takes time, and the more quickly an environment changes, the more likely it is that the evolved behaviors of a population will no longer be appropriate.

Let's return to the donations to refugees on another continent. To understand how natural selection could lead to this behavior, we need to understand a bit about human evolutionary history. We know from archaeological deposits that for more than two million years, our ancestors lived as hunter-gatherers in small groups of a few hundred people, at most. Their success depended on joint efforts against predators and in killing prey; being "nice" paid off when the prospect of hunting alone or sleeping

outside the camp meant almost certain death. The loners died, so we are descended from those who could work well with others.

It is only recently, the blink of an eye in evolutionary time, that humans invented agriculture, industrialization, and the means of food production and distribution. As a result of these changes, group size has increased dramatically; on a given day, you may see 10 or even 100 *times* as many people as a hunter-gatherer ancestor might have seen. Additionally, if you were a hunter-gatherer, all of the people in your group would be a regular part of your life. You would have many opportunities to help them and, in turn, to be helped by them. Reciprocity paid. And we evolved so that "altruistic" acts gave us pleasure, stimulating parts of our brain in ways that made us want to repeat such actions.

It is with this brain that you approach the issue of refugees halfway across the world, or a homeless person somewhere in the United States. It is almost certain that you will not have repeated interactions with any of those people. And you will probably never be in a position to be helped by them. From an evolutionary perspective, your action almost certainly will not increase your fitness. But in the world that humans evolved in, such altruistic-appearing behavior would most likely have been reciprocated at some future time—and thus your instincts guide you to, and reward you for, your kindness (**FIGURE 9-14**).

In addition to having small population sizes, our ancestors' hunter-gatherer world was characterized by unpredictable food sources that could not be stored for long periods of time. In response to this environment, humans evolved to have great appetites and taste preferences for calorie-laden foods. Fitness increased with food consumption and the storage of fat, helping to protect individuals during regular times of starvation. From an evolutionary perspective, today's world is truly an alien environment: most of us have easy access to unlimited amounts of food, including fat-laden fast foods. Because humans have not yet adapted to this environment of plentiful food, our instincts to consume large amounts are strong, making it difficult for most people to control their body weight.

From battles against obesity to charitable contributions to alarm calling in transplanted squirrels, when organisms of any

MALADAPTIVE BEHAVIOR

In the small hunter-gatherer groups common for much of human evolutionary history, altruistic behaviors would probably have been reciprocated. Today, the pleasure we feel in response to such behaviors remains—even though in our world we may behave altruistically to people unable to ever return the favor, making our act of kindness maladaptive.

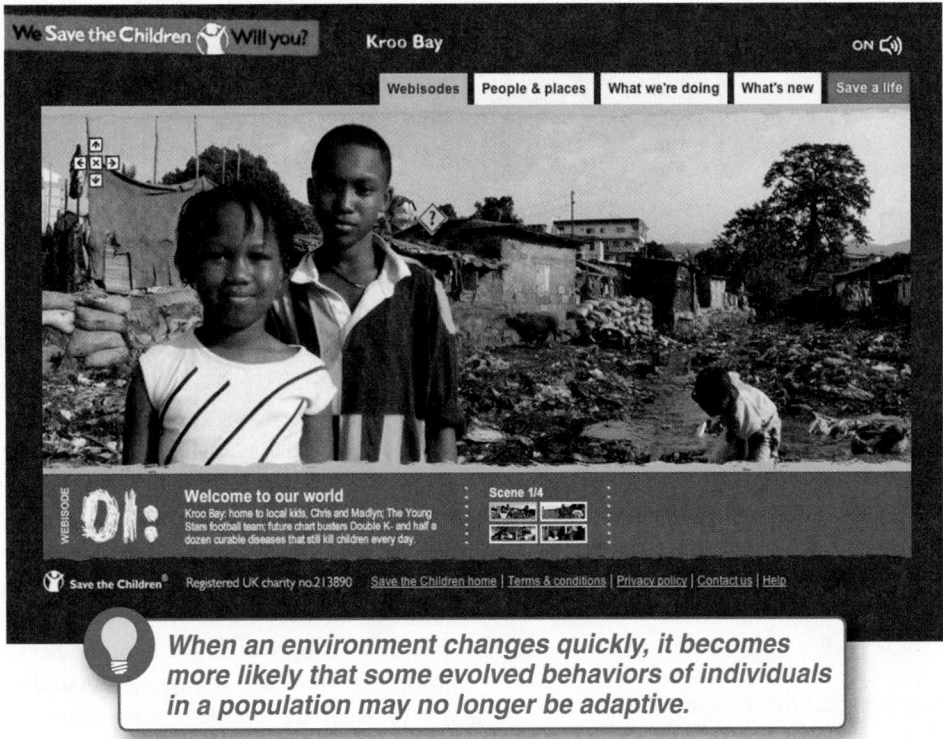

When an environment changes quickly, it becomes more likely that some evolved behaviors of individuals in a population may no longer be adaptive.

FIGURE 9-14 Charitable acts can give us pleasure (but in today's world can be evolutionarily maladaptive).

species find themselves in an environment that differs from the environment to which they are evolutionarily adapted, we expect (and see) behaviors that appear to be (and are) not evolutionarily adaptive. Still, understanding the process of natural selection can help us make sense of these behaviors (which in some cases can even seem nonsensical).

Can you think of other ways in which the modern industrial environment differs from the environment to which humans are adapted? How do these differences lead to situations in

which our behavior, like the behavior of the transplanted Belding's ground squirrel, may not be adaptive from an evolutionary perspective?

TAKE-HOME MESSAGE 9·8

When organisms are in environments that differ from the environment to which they are adapted, the behaviors they exhibit are not necessarily evolutionarily adaptive.

9·9 Selfish genes win out over group selection.

Kin selection and reciprocal altruism can evolve in a population of animals, as we have seen; and examples of kin selection abound in nature. As a consequence, casual observers of nature frequently see individuals acting in ways

that appear altruistic, even though these individuals are truly acting—from the perspective of evolutionary fitness— in their own selfish interests. This nearly universal selfishness raises the question of whether evolution ever

DOES GROUP SELECTION OCCUR?

Group selection describes the evolution of a trait that is beneficial for the species or population while decreasing the fitness of the individual exhibiting the trait.

ALLELE FREQUENCIES

- proportion of **selfless behavior** allele in the population ("do what's best for the group, even though it reduces your own reproductive output")

- proportion of **selfish behavior** allele in the population ("do what's best for you, even if it hurts the group")

> Regardless of the initial frequencies, over time, selfish behavior alleles increase their market share relative to alleles for selfless behaviors.

Time

> *Because group selection decreases the reproductive success of individuals, it very rarely occurs.*

FIGURE 9-15 Can a "selfless" gene increase in frequency in a population?

leads to behaviors that are good for the species or population but detrimental to the individual exhibiting the behavior, a process called **group selection.**

It might seem that evolution would favor individuals that behave in a manner that benefits the group, even if it comes at a cost to the individual's reproductive success. But this does not happen. Behaviors that reduce an individual's reproductive output (relative to that of other individuals in the population) are not likely to evolve. Natural selection favors individuals producing more offspring relative to those producing fewer offspring.

Let's look at an example. Imagine that a new allele appears in a population (perhaps through mutation) that causes the individual carrying the allele to double its reproductive output, even though this might spell doom for the species as individuals over-use their resources. An individual carrying this "selfish" allele will pass it to more offspring than an individual carrying the alternative allele, coding for the production of fewer offspring, will pass its allele—and this will lead to excessive, "selfish" consumption of the species' resources. And the selfish offspring also will pass on the selfish allele at a higher rate than the alternative allele is passed on. This scenario may lead to extinction of the species, yet it still occurs. With its market share perpetually increasing, the selfish allele eventually is favored by evolution and will predominate (**FIGURE 9-15**).

Just because a behavior (determined by an "unselfish" allele) leads to a better outcome for the group doesn't mean that natural selection will favor that behavior. In the end, natural selection generally causes increases in the alleles that benefit the *individual* carrying them, even when this comes at the expense of the group. In some special situations, it is possible for natural selection to lead to group selection. But the stringent conditions necessary for this to occur are so rarely found in nature that we almost never see it.

TAKE-HOME MESSAGE 9·9

Behaviors that are good for the species or population but detrimental to the individual exhibiting such behaviors are not generally produced in a population under natural conditions.

9·10–9·15 Sexual conflict can result from disparities in reproductive investment by males and females.

"Look at me!" The red-crowned crane (Grus japonensis) extends its wings during a courtship display as potential mates look on.

9·10 There are big differences in how much males and females must invest in reproduction.

As we've seen, many behaviors have evolved that influence the ways in which animals interact with each other, reducing conflict and sometimes leading to cooperation. One aspect of life that necessarily involves interaction—for sexually reproducing species—is reproduction, from courtship and mating to parental investment and the forming and breaking of ties. In this and the next few sections, we'll explore these behaviors and the factors that influence them.

How many babies can a woman produce over her lifetime? The number is probably higher than you would guess: a Russian woman had 69 children (in 27 pregnancies). But even this high number is greatly exceeded by the 888 offspring produced by one man (the Emperor of Morocco from 1672 to 1727). The large difference between the number of offspring that can be produced by females and males is less surprising. Among other species of mammals, the pattern is consistent: a male elephant seal can produce 100 offspring, while the maximum produced by a female over her lifetime is 8; a male red deer can produce 24 offspring, while the maximum produced by a female is 14. Here we examine the physical differences between males and females and how they lead to differences in sexual behavior.

The very definition of "male" and "female" hinges on a physical difference between the sexes. Recall from Chapter 6

that in species with two distinct sexes, a **female** is defined as the sex that produces the larger gamete, while a **male** produces the smaller gamete (**FIGURE 9-16**). At conception, the mother's material and energetic contribution to the offspring, the

At conception, the mother's energetic contribution to the offspring, her reproductive investment, exceeds the father's.

FIGURE 9-16 Small sperm, big egg.

energy she will expend in the growth, feeding, and care of offspring—her **reproductive investment**—exceeds the father's. This is true for all animals, whether mammals, birds, insects, or sharks. (It is also true for plants.) Not only are female gametes larger, they tend to be relatively immobile and produced in smaller numbers. Male gametes, on the other hand, while smaller, are more plentiful and very motile.

This discrepancy in size and quantity between the sperm produced by a male and the eggs produced by a female sets the stage for evolutionary developments that magnify this initial difference in reproductive investment. For starters, the difference in the number of gametes that males and females can produce means that males have the potential to produce many, many more offspring than females. Put another way, a male's **total reproductive output,** the lifetime number of offspring he can produce, tends to increase as the number of females he is able to fertilize increases. A female, on the other hand, does not generally increase her reproductive success by mating with additional males beyond the first (**FIGURE 9-17**).

Q

Why do males usually compete for females rather than the opposite?

Because additional matings usually lead to greater increases in reproduction (and fitness) for males, selective pressure has resulted in the evolution of some differences in male and female reproductive behavior. For males, the most effective way to maximize reproductive success often is to find and gain access to mating opportunities with additional females. For females, an effective way to maximize reproductive success often is to put more effort into parenting and less effort into mating.

Two physical differences that can exist between males and females are particularly important when it comes to reproduction. First, in species with internal fertilization, which includes most mammals, fertilization takes place in the female. The offspring also grow and develop within the female's body. The amount of energy females invest in reproduction is therefore much greater than males' investment. Females' reproductive investment also limits their reproductive output; they can be pregnant only once at a time. A second important physical difference between females and males occurs in the mammals: lactation takes place in females and not in males (with a very small number of exceptions). In these species, then, nurturing during both pregnancy and lactation can be accomplished only by the female. This difference in reproductive investment has led to the evolution of some very different reproductive behaviors between males and females.

Although the gamete size difference is consistent across all animals (i.e., the egg is always bigger and energetically more

GRAPHIC CONTENT!
Thinking critically about visual displays of data.
Turn to p. 382 for a closer inspection of this figure.

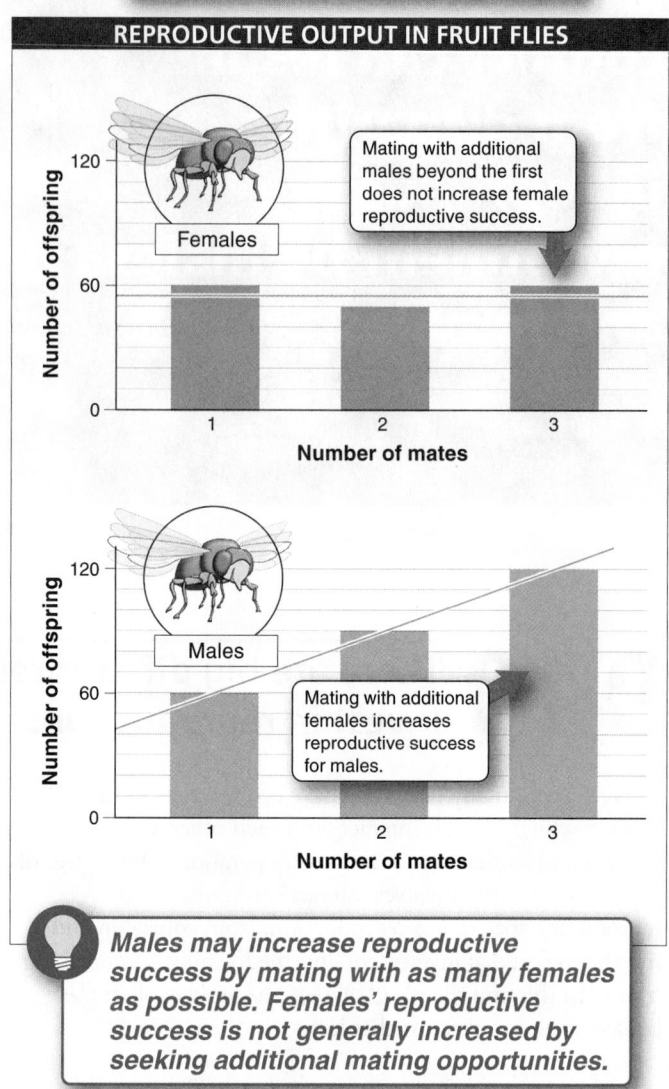

FIGURE 9-17 Maximizing reproductive success in fruit flies.

costly to make than the sperm), the physical differences between the sexes in the early nurturing (i.e., gestation and feeding) of offspring can vary considerably across animal species. In some cases, male and female investments become more nearly equal after fertilization. In birds, for example, before emergence of the chicks, much of the development of the fertilized egg is external: the female lays an egg, but either the male or the female can protect and incubate the developing embryo. Further, birds do not lactate. Once hatched, the chicks must be fed—a task that can be done by both parents.

Accordingly, in many bird species, the maximum lifetime reproductive output of males and females is similar. In the

The female mammal invests much energy in the production and care of offspring.

Amphibian eggs are left to develop on their own; there is very little maternal or paternal reproductive investment after fertilization.

Among most bird species, males and females have an equal reproductive investment.

FIGURE 9-18 Male and female reproductive investment differs across species. Female investment is greatest when offspring develop internally and are fed by lactation after birth. In animals whose offspring develop externally, males or females (or neither parent) can provide the care.

kittiwake gull, for example, the largest number of offspring produced by a male is 26, while for a female the number is 28. External fertilization in fish and amphibian species further reduces the reproductive investment of the female—she does not spend any energy as the fertilized eggs begin developing into embryos (**FIGURE 9-18**).

We have seen, then, that in species in which fertilization occurs inside the female body, there is an unequal energetic investment in reproduction, and as a result the female expends more energy in the growth and care of offspring (much more so for mammals than for birds). Another profound consequence of internal fertilization is that a male cannot be 100% certain that any offspring a female produces are his progeny. Because it is possible for a female to mate with multiple males, any of whom could be the father, male mammals and birds will always have some degree of **paternity uncertainty.**

In the next few sections, we'll continue to explore how the physical differences between males and females in reproductive investment, along with paternity uncertainty, have led to the evolution of differences in male and female reproductive behavior.

TAKE-HOME MESSAGE 9·10

In mammals and many other animals, there are important physical differences between males and females relating to reproduction. Fertilization usually takes place in the female. Lactation takes place only in the female. And in species in which fertilization occurs inside the female, males cannot be certain that offspring are their progeny. These physical differences have led to the evolution of differences in male and female reproductive behavior.

9·11 Males and females are vulnerable at different stages of the reproductive exchange.

Suppose you are on your college campus and a person of the opposite sex comes up to you and says, "Hi. I have been noticing you around campus. I find you very attractive. Would you go out with me tonight?" What percentage of men would answer *yes?* And women? In a study conducted at Florida State University in 1978 and 1982, the percentage answering *yes* was 50% for both males and females.

Now imagine the question was "Would you have sex with me tonight?" Among the men, 75% said *yes;* among the women, not a single one said *yes*. It is tempting to interpret such results as a consequence solely of the culture of Western society, characterized by significant differences in the expectations and tolerances of male and female sexual conduct. However, cultural expectations don't adequately explain the consistency of the pattern found across Western and non-Western societies: men and women differ in their approach to sexuality.

Studies of male-female differences in selectiveness about sexual partners, drawing on a wide range of human cultures—including many as far removed from Western influence as possible, such as the Trobriand Islanders of Melanesia in the South Pacific—reveal a consistent difference in men's and women's willingness to have sex. Why might this difference exist?

Humans, like nearly all mammals, are characterized by a greater initial reproductive investment by females. Women are more hesitant to take a mating opportunity, while men are much more willing. For females, the cost of a poor mating choice can have significant consequences—pregnancy and lactation, with offspring from a low-quality male or a male who does not provide any parental investment or access to valuable resources (**FIGURE 9-19**). For a male, the consequences of a poor choice are less dire—little beyond the time and energy involved in mating.

Two differences in the sexual behavior of males and females have evolved:

1. The sex with the greater energetic investment in reproduction is more discriminating about mating.

2. Members of the sex with the lower energetic investment in reproduction compete among themselves for access to the higher-investing sex.

A dramatic illustration of how a high reproductive investment leads to the evolution of choosiness in mating behavior comes from the insect world. When bush crickets mate, the male loses about a quarter of its body weight contributing a massive ejaculate (the equivalent of nearly 50 pounds of semen in a human), which the female then uses for energy (**FIGURE 9-20**). (It can represent up to one-tenth of her lifetime caloric intake.)

Not surprisingly, male crickets are very choosy when selecting a mate. They reject small females that would produce relatively few offspring. (Females, you won't be surprised to learn, spend a great deal of effort courting males.)

The sex with the greater reproductive investment must be choosy: a poor choice of mate could be disastrous. The sex with the lower initial reproductive investment (usually males), on the other hand, is not made vulnerable through its mating choices, because the matings are of little energetic consequence. However, there is a point at which males *are* vulnerable in the reproductive exchange.

The point of greatest vulnerability for males comes when they provide parental care to offspring. Due to paternity uncertainty, there is some chance that the male may be investing in offspring that are not his own. This has significant evolutionary costs: rather than increasing his own fitness, he is increasing the fitness of another male. Females, conversely, are less vulnerable at the point of providing parental care to offspring, because a female can be completely certain that the offspring she gives birth to are her own.

In the next two sections, we explore the evolution of reproductive behaviors that help males and females reduce their vulnerability and maximize their reproductive success. First we explore competition and courtship tactics used in

FIGURE 9-19 The choosier sex. Males and females differ in their attitude toward mating opportunities. For the female more than the male, the choice of the wrong mate could have expensive consequences.

When bush crickets mate, the male loses about a quarter of his body weight contributing a massive ejaculate that the female uses for energy. This makes males very choosy.

FIGURE 9-20 A costly decision. Because of the investment the male bush cricket is required to make when fertilizing a female, he chooses a mate very carefully.

selecting and securing a mate, then we investigate the various strategies of "mate guarding" employed by males to increase their paternity certainty.

As we explore some general patterns of reproductive behavior among males and females, it is important to keep two critical points in mind.

1. There is tremendous variability across species in male and female behaviors. For example, the use of DNA fingerprinting to identify the parents of bird offspring has led to some surprising revelations. In significantly more cases than researchers originally predicted, offspring have different fathers than observers assumed. It seems that things are not always as they appear to observing biologists. As a consequence, much of the new research calls into question some long-held assumptions about the behavioral consequences of physical differences in reproductive investment among birds versus mammals. There are general behavioral patterns among animals, but as is becoming increasingly clear, these patterns are not universal features of their biology, and a reasonable skepticism is important when identifying and interpreting broad trends across large groups of species.

2. Throughout history, there have been many cases of people using observations and scientific findings to justify a wide variety of discriminatory thoughts and behaviors—for example, that if male mammals "naturally" tend to be less faithful to their mates, this reduces individual responsibility for behaviors among humans. Such thinking ignores both the tremendous variation in behavior among species and the power of cultural norms and socialization to influence and shape human behavior, while encouraging the inappropriate assumption that biology can supply meaningful insights into morality or ethical decision making.

TAKE-HOME MESSAGE 9·11

Differing patterns of investment in reproduction make males and females vulnerable at different stages of the reproductive process. This has contributed to the evolution of differences in their sexual behavior. The sex with greater energetic investment in reproduction is more discriminating about mates, and members of the sex with a lower energetic investment in reproduction compete among themselves for access to the higher-investing sex.

9·12 Tactics for getting a mate: competition and courtship can help males and females secure reproductive success.

Female choosiness (and the male-male competition it leads to) tends to increase the likelihood that a female will select only those males that have plentiful resources or relatively high-quality genes, either of which is beneficial to the female, causing her to produce more or better offspring—where "better" may mean increased disease resistance or physical traits that will be found attractive by future mates. Female choosiness is manifested by four general rules.

1. Mate only after subjecting a male to courtship rituals. In many bird species, including the western grebe, the female requires the male to perform an elaborate and time-consuming courtship dance before she will mate with him. For the grebe, this courtship dance involves fancy dives into water, graceful hovering, various head movements, and flamboyant twists and turns. The courtship process can go on for several days. But if the male passes the time-

COURTSHIP RITUALS
A female grebe requires the male to perform a courtship dance before she will mate with him.

GIFTS UP FRONT
A female hanging fly will not mate with a male unless he brings her a large offering of food.

CONTROL OF VALUABLE RESOURCES
Female yellow-bellied marmots prefer rock outcroppings that provide retreats for predator escape and for hibernation (and are controlled by dominant males).

GOOD LOOKS
A female peacock is attracted to a male with the most beautiful tail feathers.

FIGURE 9-21 Four factors that influence a female's choice of mate.

consuming audition, he can generally be counted on to stick around to see a brood through hatching and early care (**FIGURE 9-21**).

Among bower birds, a courting male builds a small thatched structure, at which he makes displays that can involve complex dance steps and dramatic poses. The female walks around the structure and inspects it. Only if she deems it satisfactory will she mate. A male that is rejected by multiple females usually tears down his bower and rebuilds it from scratch to try again to attract a female.

2. Mate only with a male who controls valuable resources. Territorial defense is a common means by which males compete for access to females. Among arctic ground squirrels, for example, a female chooses a mate based, in part, on the territory he defends, which is where she will reside after mating. With greater quality and quantity of resources in his territory, a male is better able to attract females, whose reproductive success can be increased if the territory is rich in resources.

> *It is a truth universally acknowledged, that a single man in possession of a good fortune must be in want of a wife.*
> —JANE AUSTEN, *Pride and Prejudice*, 1813

3. Mate only with a male who contributes a large parental investment up front. Better than a believable pledge to commit resources to future offspring is an actual, on-the-spot exchange in which a female requires a male to give her his parental investment up front, in the form of resources that will help her maximize her reproductive success. In the hanging fly, for example, a female will not mate with a male unless he brings her a big piece of food—usually a dead insect. If a male offers an acceptable food item or other token, called a **nuptial gift,** as part of his courtship behavior, she will mate with him (see Figure 9-21). The larger the food item, the longer she will mate; and the more she eats, the larger the number of eggs she will lay. After about 20 minutes of mating, though, when a male has transferred all of the sperm that he can, he is likely to break off the mating and take back whatever remains of the "gift," which he may use to try to attract another mate. Nuptial feeding is common among birds and insects.

4. Mate only with a male that has a valuable physical attribute. Male-male competition for the chance to mate with females can also take a more literal form: actual physical contests. Across the animal kingdom, from dung beetles to hippopotamuses, male-male contests determine the dominance rankings of males. Females then mate primarily with the highest-ranking males.

In a similar process, rather than choosing the best-fighting or largest males, females sometimes base their choice on some physical attribute, such as antler size in red deer, the bright red chest feathers of frigate birds, or the elaborate tail feathers of the male peacock (see Figure 9-21). In each case, for the female, the physical feature serves as an indicator of the relative quality of the male, possibly because the feature is correlated with the male's health.

Why do so few women get into barroom brawls?

Q With so many examples of male-male fighting as part of the courtship rituals that have evolved for attracting a mate, it is reasonable to ask: Why is it so rare for females to fight?

And why do females generally not have to advertise their health with flashy feathers or other ornamentation? The answer is that as long as females are making the greater investment in reproduction, nearly any male will mate with them. Consequently, there is nothing more to be gained by trying to outcompete other females or otherwise attract the attention of males.

Moreover, among humans, social and cultural values have powerful influences over mating behavior, complicating interpretation. We are not lumbering robots, destined to follow some genetic program. Researchers have noted some subtle manifestations of female health and fertility, including waist-to-hip ratios and patterns of facial and body symmetry. There is a rich and complex world of mating tactics, many of which we do not fully understand.

TAKE-HOME MESSAGE 9·12

As a consequence of male-female differences in initial reproductive investment, males tend to increase reproductive success by mating with many females and have evolved to compete among themselves to get the opportunity to mate. Females increase their reproductive success not through extra matings but rather by being choosy about selecting a mate and by caring for their offspring.

9·13 Tactics for keeping a mate: mate guarding can protect a male's reproductive investment.

If a male simply abandons a female after mating and searches for other mating opportunities, rather than making any investment in the potential offspring, he has no risk of investing further energy in offspring that are not his. This is one way to minimize the potential costs associated with paternity uncertainty. If you don't play, you can't lose.

This strategy, however, is not necessarily the most effective way for a male to maximize his reproductive success. If a male has a hundred or even a thousand matings, but no offspring survive, that behavior is not evolutionarily successful. Consequently, in species for which offspring's survival can be enhanced with greater parental investment—including those species not well-developed at birth, such as humans—there is an incentive for a male to provide some additional investment

in offspring, even though such behavior makes him vulnerable to paternity uncertainty.

In situations in which males provide parental care, it is common for the male to reduce his vulnerability through some form of **mate guarding.** In addition to simply reducing opportunities for a female to mate with other males (which can benefit all males), mate guarding can improve a male's reproductive success by increasing his paternity certainty and thus reducing his vulnerability when he makes investment in offspring. As long as the offspring emerge from the female's body, she can be certain that they contain her genes. In contrast, a male inhabits a "danger zone" that lasts as long as the female is fertile. If she mates with any other males during this time, the offspring she produces may not be his. If he is going to make any investments of time or energy that will benefit the offspring, he benefits by minimizing his risk in the danger zone. It is during this period that mate guarding is particularly common.

Q **Why do so few females guard their mates as aggressively as males do?**

Mate-guarding methods range from the simple to the macabre. If a male wants to ensure that a female does not mate with another male, why bother to stop mating at all? In many species, males take this approach to reduce their risk in the danger zone. Among house flies, even though the male has completed the transfer of sperm to the female in 10 minutes of copulation, he does not separate from her for a full hour. Moths go even farther and continue to mate for a full 24 hours. And in the extreme case of this strategy, certain frog species continue individual bouts of mating for several months (**FIGURE 9-22**). In humans, this would be equivalent to almost 10 years for a single round of intercourse.

In a slightly subtler form of mate guarding that occurs in reptiles, insects, and many mammalian species, after copulation, males block the passage of additional sperm into

Some frog species carry on individual bouts of mating for several months continuously. If humans mated for a similar percentage of our lives, a single round of intercourse would last almost ten years!

FIGURE 9-22 Preventing paternity uncertainty. A prolonged period of mating prevents the female from accessing other males, assuring the male of reproductive success.

The male black widow spider ensures his paternity certainty by breaking off his sexual organ inside the female after mating—precluding her mating again. (He also is eaten by her in many cases, giving her a resource to help produce more and healthier offspring.)

FIGURE 9-23 A reasonable trade-off? The male black widow spider ensures his paternity by an extreme form of mate guarding.

the female by producing a copulatory plug. Formed in the female reproductive tract from coagulated sperm and mucus, copulatory plugs can be very effective. Male garter snakes that encounter a female snake with a copulatory plug, for example, do not attempt to court or mate with her, treating her instead as if she were not available.

A much more extreme form of mate guarding occurs in the black widow spider: the male breaks off his sexual organ inside the female, preventing her from ever mating again. Interestingly, when the act is completed, the female usually kills and eats the male (**FIGURE 9-23**). In sealing his mate's reproductive tract, the male assures himself of fathering the offspring, and in consuming her mate's nutrient-filled body, the female gets resources that help her produce the offspring.

TAKE-HOME MESSAGE 9·13

Mate guarding can, in general, increase reproductive success by reducing additional mating opportunities for a partner, and can improve a male's reproductive success by increasing his paternity certainty and thus reducing his vulnerability when he makes investment in offspring.

9·14 Monogamy versus polygamy: mating behaviors can vary across human and animal cultures.

As we continue our tour of animal mating behavior, we turn again to the elephant seal. In December of each year, the males appear on islands off the coast of northern California, where they compete with each other for possession of the beach. Through bloody fights they establish dominance hierarchies, with the biggest males—which are 13 feet long and weigh more than 2 tons—generally winning.

In mid-January, the females arrive and are ready to mate. They congregate in large groups on just a few prime beaches. Because the females stick close together, the biggest males, who control the prime beaches, can dominate the other males in the competition for sexual access to females (**FIGURE 9-24**). In one study that observed 115 males, the 5 highest-ranking males fathered 85% of the offspring. While nearly every female will mate and produce offspring, the majority of males never get the chance to mate during the 10–20 years of their lives.

The elephant seals' mating pattern exemplifies **polygamy,** a system in which some individuals attract multiple mates while other individuals attract none. Polygamous mating systems can be subdivided into **polygyny,** in which individual males

mate with multiple females, and **polyandry,** in which individual females mate with multiple males. Polygamy can be contrasted with **monogamy,** in which most individuals mate and remain with just one other individual. Polygamy and monogamy are two types of **mating systems,** which describe the patterns of mating behavior in a species. In this section, we explore the features of environments and species that influence mating systems and survey the range of mating systems observed in nature.

As we have seen, throughout the animal world, males tend to make less parental investment than females. As a consequence, females are choosy about which males they mate with, and males compete for access to mating opportunities. Not surprisingly, multiple females often end up selecting the same male—usually a male on a territory rich in resources or a male with unusually pronounced physical features, such as antler size. Such female selection is the reason for the fancy ornamentation we see in male peacocks. Although the male peacock's tail is like a giant bull's-eye to predators, the number of eyespots on the tail is directly related to how well he can attract a mate: below 140 eyespots, he gets no mates; at 150, he gets two to three mates on average; and with 160 eyespots

POLYGAMY IN ELEPHANT SEALS

In a polygamous mating system, some individuals have multiple mates, while others have few or none.

FIGURE 9-24 King of the beach. The biggest, best-fighting male elephant seals control the beach and mate with as many females as possible.

💡 *In an extremely polygynous mating system, such as in elephant seals, the vast majority of males have no reproductive success at all.*

he gets six or more mates (see Figure 9-21). Given their greater parental investment, virtually *all* females are able to attract a mate, regardless of fitness or status.

Mating systems are not as easy to define as the elephant seal example might lead us to believe. Three issues, in particular, complicate the task. First, there are often differences between animals' mating behavior and their bonding behavior. That is, it may seem that a male and female have formed a **pair bond**—in which they spend a high proportion of their time together, often over many years, sharing a nest or other "home" and contributing equally to parental care of offspring in what appears to be a monogamous relationship. Closer inspection (often including DNA analysis of the offspring) sometimes reveals, however, that the male and/or the female may be mating with other individuals in the population, and perhaps the mating system is better described as a variation on polygamy. A second difficulty in defining a species' mating system arises because the mating system may vary within the species. That is, some individuals may be monogamous, while others are polygamous. And the mating system may even change over the course of an individual's life. A third difficulty is that males and females often differ in their mating behavior. In the elephant seals described above, it could be said that the females are all mating monogamously, while the males are polygamous.

Within almost any large group of related animal species, there will be a variety of species with each type of mating system, so it is not usually possible to make generalizations. In a recent surprising discovery, researchers were able to alter the behavior of males of a polygynous species of meadow voles by inserting into their brains a single gene from a related but monogamous prairie vole species. With the new gene, the formerly polygynous males showed a preference for their current partner over other females, and the males' ability to form a long-term bond with their partner increased.

Examination of birds and mammals in general, however, reveals one sharp split. As we discussed in Section 9-10, the vast majority of female mammals have a greater parental investment than male mammals. In birds, females and males have a more equal parental investment.

Does the difference in parental investment patterns in birds and mammals lead to different mating systems? Yes. In mammals, polygyny is the most common mating system

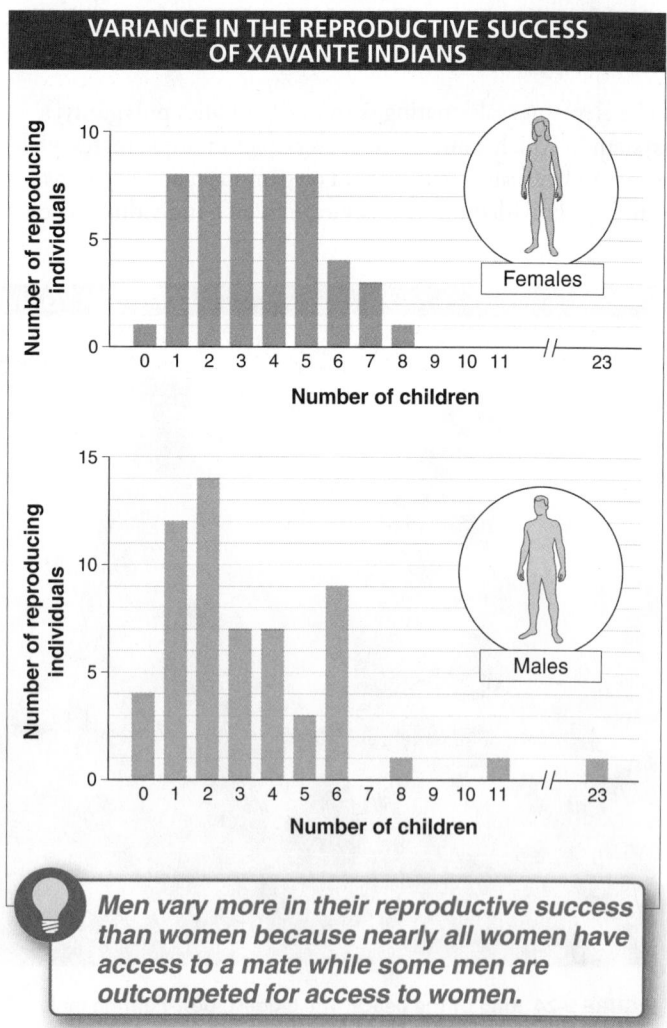

MONOGAMOUS BIRDS

💡 *Of the approximately 10,000 species of birds, more than 90% appear to be monogamous.*

FIGURE 9-25 Let's stay together. Parental investment that is roughly equal often leads to monogamous mating behavior in birds.

VARIANCE IN THE REPRODUCTIVE SUCCESS OF XAVANTE INDIANS

💡 *Men vary more in their reproductive success than women because nearly all women have access to a mate while some men are outcompeted for access to women.*

FIGURE 9-26 Larger male variance in reproductive success. Studies of the Xavante Indians of Brazil show that the range in number of offspring over their lifetime is much greater for men than for women.

across all large groups, from rodents to primates. Polygyny is a consequence of the significant female investment and lesser male investment. Males can generally benefit more by seeking additional mating opportunities, leading to male-male competition. In birds, the relatively equal parental investment by males and females has led to much less polygyny. More than 90% of the approximately 10,000 bird species we know about appear to be monogamous (although in most cases, it is serial monogamy) (**FIGURE 9-25**).

Q **Are humans monogamous or polygamous?**

And what of humans? Across a variety of cultures, males consistently have greater variance in reproductive success than females—that is, some males have very high reproductive success and many others have little or none. **FIGURE 9-26**, for example, presents data from one of the first investigations of this phenomenon. It is from a study of the Xavante Indians of Brazil. The Xavante were selected because they were a pre-industrial population subsisting primarily as hunter-gatherers, with no access to reliable birth control and with almost no contact with Western cultures. The average number of children (3.6) does not differ from men and women, but some men have very large numbers (as many as 23!), and many have none. There is significantly less variability in reproductive success

from one woman to another. Interestingly, a 2010 study using data from 7,710 women and men living in the contemporary United States similarly found significantly greater variance in reproductive success among men as compared to women.

Such differences in the variance in reproductive success among males and females, which can be significantly influenced by socialization and other cultural forces, are generally associated with polygynous mating systems. However, the difference between the sexes found in the Brazilian study is quite small when compared with many other mammalian species, such as elephant seals, and is close to that seen in populations with a monogamous mating system. Humans, consequently, seem to have a mating system close to, but not completely, monogamous.

TAKE-HOME MESSAGE 9·14

Mating systems—monogamy, polygyny, and polyandry—describe the variation in number of mates and the reproductive success of males and females. They are influenced by the relative amounts of males' and females' parental investment.

9·15 Sexual dimorphism is an indicator of a population's mating behavior.

Male elephant seals are three to four times the size of female elephant seals. In contrast, the males and females of most bird species are the same size. In these species, even expert bird-watchers often cannot distinguish between the sexes, except when the female bird is carrying eggs (**FIGURE 9-27**). When the sexes of a species do differ in size or appearance, this is called **sexual dimorphism.** Why do species have such dramatic differences in the degree to which males and females resemble each other?

Body size is an important clue to behavior. We have seen how male elephant seals have a winner-take-all tournament for control of the beach, and as the winner, a male has access to mating opportunities. Because the largest individual will have the most offspring, there is selection for larger and larger body size. The smaller males have relatively low reproductive success. There is no selection for larger body size among female elephant seals,

Q **It's almost impossible to distinguish males from females in most bird species. Why does this tell us they are monogamous?**

because females of any size can mate. Hence the dramatic size difference between the sexes.

In addition to body size, coloration is also a clue to behavior. Because females of some polygynous species choose the males with the brightest or flashiest coloration, rather than the largest males, male-male competition sometimes results in differences in physical appearance between the sexes rather than (or in addition to) differences in size.

What happens when there is little male-male competition for mates? Among bird species, males can provide significant investment in offspring. Eggs have to be incubated, and because many chicks emerge in a very poorly developed condition, it takes two parents to raise them. So a pair tends to stay together for a season or longer. If each female can pair up with only one male, there really isn't much

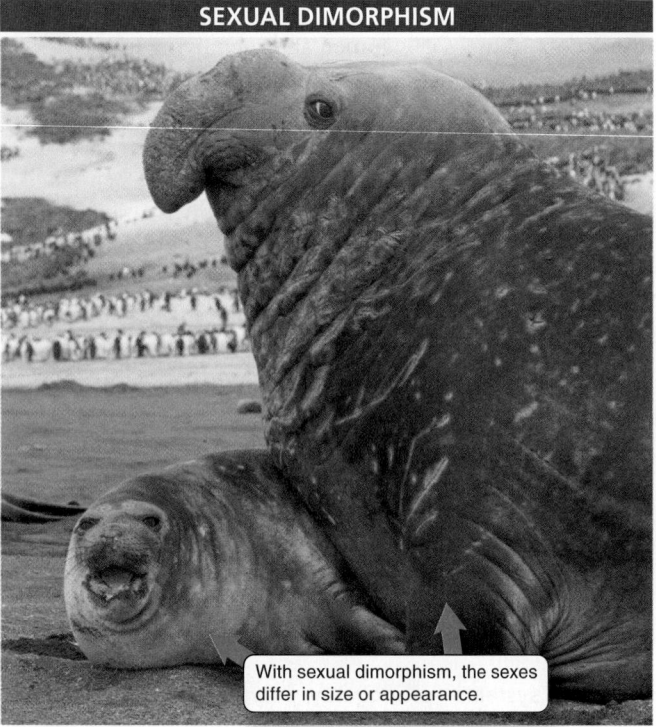

SEXUAL DIMORPHISM

With sexual dimorphism, the sexes differ in size or appearance.

BEHAVIORS ASSOCIATED WITH SEXUAL DIMORPHISM
• One parent invests more in caring for the offspring.
• Mating system tends toward polygamy.
• One sex (usually females) is choosier when selecting a mate.
• One sex (usually males) competes for access to mating opportunities with the other sex.

SEXUAL MONOMORPHISM

With sexual monomorphism, the sexes are indistinguishable.

BEHAVIORS ASSOCIATED WITH SEXUAL MONOMORPHISM
• Both parents invest (approximately) equally in caring for the offspring.
• Mating system tends toward monogamy.
• Both sexes are equally choosy when selecting a mate.

FIGURE 9-27 Size says a lot. Species with large males and small females are very likely to be polygamous. Species with similarly sized males and females are likely to be monogamous.

Q Men are bigger than women. What does that tell us about our evolutionary history of monogamy versus polygamy?

competition for mates. And without male-male competition, there is little selection for increased size. As a consequence, little sexual dimorphism occurs in most bird species.

In turn, we can predict a great deal about the parental practices of a species just by looking at a picture of a male and a female and examining the ratio of body sizes. If the two are dramatically different, as in elephant seals, you can be confident that the smaller sex is doing most of the care of the offspring and that the species is more likely to be polygamous than monogamous.

TAKE-HOME MESSAGE 9·15

Differences in the level of competition among individuals of each sex for access to mating opportunities can lead to the evolution of male-female differences in body size and other aspects of appearance. In polygynous species, this results in larger males that are easily distinguished visually from females. In monogamous species, there are few such differences between males and females.

Howling strengthens the social bonds among wolves in a pack.

9·16

Animal communication and language abilities evolve.

The challenge of communication is central to the evolution of animal behaviors, whether they relate to cooperation, conflict, or the many interactions inherent to selecting a mate. An animal must be able to convey information about its status and intentions to other individuals. And equally important, animals must be able to interpret and assess the information they get from other individuals so as to reduce the likelihood of being tricked or taken advantage of. In this section and the next, we explore the evolution of a variety of methods of animal communication and the ways in which communication can influence fitness and the evolution of other behaviors.

Not all animals need to open their mouths when they have something important to communicate. When the female silkworm moth is ready to mate, for example, she releases a potent chemical called bombykol into the air. As molecules of the chemical come in contact with the bushy antennae of a male silkworm moth—who might be as far as three miles away—he recognizes the mate attractant and responds by flying upwind, looking for the source of the chemical, until he zeroes in on the female and they mate (**FIGURE 9-28**).

This is just one example—a chemical one—of **communication,** an action or signal on the part of one individual that informs or alters the behavior of another individual. But a huge range of animal behaviors requires communication, including defending territory, alerting individuals to threats, announcing one's readiness for mating, establishing one's position in a dominance hierarchy, and caring for offspring.

Animals communicate with many different types of signals. Three types are most common.

1. **Chemical.** Molecules released by an individual into the environment that trigger behavioral responses in other individuals are called **pheromones.** They include the airborne mate attractant of the silkworm moth, territory markers such as those found in dog urine, and trail markers used by ants. They are even used by humans: there are chemicals that influence the length of the menstrual cycle in women and are responsible for the synchronization of menstrual cycles that occurs in women living in group housing situations, such as in dormitories and prisons.

2. **Acoustical.** Sounds that trigger behavioral responses are abundant in the natural world. These include the alarm calls of Belding's ground squirrels described earlier, the complex songs of birds, whales, frogs, and crickets vying for mates, and the territorial howling of wolves.

3. **Visual.** Individuals often display visual signals of threat, dominance, or health and vigor. Examples include the male baboon's baring of his teeth and the vivid tail feathers of the male peacock.

With increasingly complex forms of communication, increasingly complex information can be conveyed. One extreme case is the honeybee **waggle dance.** When a honeybee scout returns to the hive after successfully locating a source of food, she performs a set of maneuvers on a honeycomb that resemble

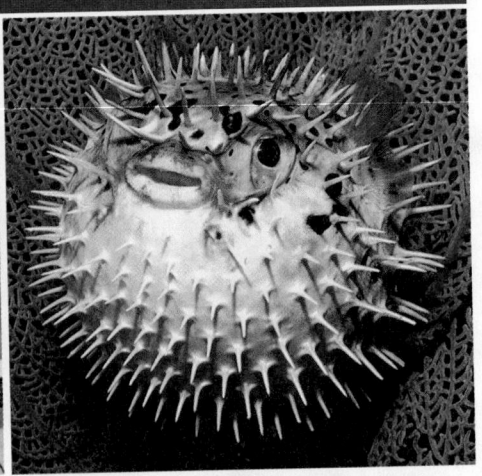

CHEMICAL COMMUNICATION
Pheromones released by one individual and detected by another using its antennae can trigger behavioral responses.

AUDITORY COMMUNICATION
Sounds, such as the howl of a coyote, are a common method of triggering behavior responses.

VISUAL COMMUNICATION
Organisms can convey information, such as threat or receptivity, with visual displays. Here, a balloon-fish puffs up its body in response to a predator.

FIGURE 9-28 Chemical, auditory, and visual communication. Many animal behaviors require communication: the ability to convey and receive information from other animals.

a figure 8, while wiggling her abdomen. Based on the specific angle at which the scout dances (relative to the sun's position in the sky) and the duration of her dance, the bees that observe the dance are able to leave the hive and quickly locate the food source.

The complexity and power of the waggle dance raises an important question: at what point does communication become **language?** Language is a very specific type of communication in which arbitrary symbols represent concepts, and a system of rules, called grammar, dictates the way the symbols can be manipulated to communicate and express ideas (**FIGURE 9-29**).

It's not always easy to identify language. Consider one type of communication in vervet monkeys. Vervet monkeys live in groups, and when an individual sees a predator coming, it makes an alarm call to warn the others. Unlike in most other alarm-calling species, the vervet monkey's alarm call differs depending on whether the predator is a hawk, a snake, or a leopard. And the response of other vervet monkeys to the call is appropriate to the type of predator approaching. The snake alarm causes individuals to stand on their toes and look down. The leopard alarm causes individuals to quickly climb the nearest tree. And the hawk alarm causes vervet monkeys to look to the sky.

Does alarm calling in vervet monkeys or the honeybee waggle dance constitute language? This is debatable. Is the form of American Sign Language taught to chimpanzees and gorillas a language (see Figure 9-29)? There are opinions on both sides.

FIGURE 9-29 Dancing, signing, and speaking. A variety of ways have evolved in animals to convey complex information to others.

Interestingly, the great apes have shown a capacity for creating new signs, expressing abstract ideas, and referring to things that are distant in time or space—important features of human language. One thing that is certain, however, is that human language is near the most complex end of the communication continuum.

Language influences many of the other behaviors discussed throughout this chapter. The evolution of reciprocal altruism, for example, may be influenced by language, as this makes it easier for individuals to convey their needs and resources to other individuals. Similarly, in courtship and the maintenance of reproductive relationships, language gives individuals a tool for conveying complex information relating to the resources and value they may bring to the interaction.

9·17 Honest signals reduce deception.

Among Natterjack toads, found in northern Europe, males produce booming calls to attract females. Because females desire large males and size determines the volume of the calls, females will push their way through murky swamps until they reach the loudest croaker. They are drawn by calls that can be heard a mile away and are often louder than the legal noise limit for a car engine (**FIGURE 9-30**).

The Natterjack's call is an **honest signal,** a signal that cannot be faked and is given when both the individual making the signal and the individual responding to it have the same interests. An honest signal is one that carries the most accurate information about an individual or situation, and animals that respond to signals of any sort have evolved to value most highly those signals that cannot be faked. A loud Natterjack's call, for example, cannot be faked by a small Natterjack toad. And so there is evolutionary pressure for animals to both produce and respond to honest signals, because these behaviors enable them to maximize their fitness by selecting the best possible mate.

HONEST SIGNAL

The volume of a male Natterjack toad's call impacts females' mating decisions. Loud calls can only be made by large males—smaller males can't fake it—so it is an honest signal, carrying accurate information.

FIGURE 9-30 Loud and true.

When one animal can increase its fitness by deceiving another, deception can also be expected to evolve. An example might be baby birds begging for food from their parent. If an allele that causes a chick to exaggerate its need for food leads to faster growth and better health for that individual, the allele is likely to increase in frequency in the population.

Communication and signaling, therefore, are features of populations that are continually evolving. We would expect this evolutionary "arms race" between honest signals and deception to lead, over time, to both increasingly unambiguous signals and ever more sophisticated patterns of deception.

In this chapter, we've seen how our understanding of the behavior of animals, including humans, has been greatly expanded by applying scientific thinking, an experimental approach, and careful consideration of the process by which the evolutionary mechanism of natural selection shapes populations. We return to an important point highlighted at the beginning of this chapter: an organism's phenotype is not limited to its physical traits but includes its behaviors as well. Consequently, behaviors respond to selective pressures and evolve.

HOW TO WIN FRIENDS AND INFLUENCE PEOPLE

As we have seen, in the animal world, it is very, very rare to find individuals engaging in costly behaviors that benefit unrelated individuals; with few exceptions, we see little that resembles animal "friendship."

Humans are a rare exception—every day, in myriad ways, we see friendly behaviors. Just as we put money in the bank for a rainy day, we buffer ourselves from the world's uncertainties by storing goodwill in our neighbors. Cooperators have evolutionary advantages over loners.

Q: WHY IS "KINDNESS" A RISKY BEHAVIOR EVOLUTIONARILY? From an evolutionary perspective, we remain vulnerable. With each costly act we perform for unrelated individuals, strangers and friends alike, there is the risk that our efforts will be in vain, our energies lost. For that reason, in our evolution as reciprocal altruists, we acquired a cautiousness, a hesitancy to stick our necks out.

Q: HOW CAN WE HELP OTHERS FEEL LESS VULNERABLE AND MORE WILLING TO COOPERATE? Our ability to override the impulses that often push us toward selfishness is one of the hallmarks of being human. Still, there is no reason to put people in situations where they may be better off rejecting friendship. In each interaction, there is an individual on the other side who is also feeling vulnerable. By taking steps, often absurdly simple, to address the unconscious vulnerabilities that others feel, we can increase the likelihood that they choose cooperation, reciprocity, and friendship.

- Learn and use other people's names. It tells them you recognize them specifically and, consequently, that you understand exactly who it is that you "owe." Smile and make eye contact—even when attempting to change lanes in traffic. These gestures feel like the beginning of a relationship, thus stimulating favor-granting instincts.

- Embrace etiquette. Acknowledge your debts to others. Be effusive and public in your thanks for kindnesses done to you. Send thank-you cards.

- Take the first step in reciprocity. Human cooperation is so tied to reciprocal exchange that even tiny gestures of good faith can play an important role in building relationships. Whenever possible, give gifts. Even small ones. Even when they are not required. Especially when they are not required.

- Develop a good reputation. Become known for generosity, for loyalty, for remembering and acknowledging kindnesses done to you.

CAN YOU THINK OF OTHER STEPS?

Big Ideas in ...
Evolution and Behavior

9·1–9·4 Behaviors are traits that can evolve.

- Behavior encompasses all of an organism's actions.
- Behavior is as much a part of an organism's phenotype as are its anatomical structures and, as such, can be produced and shaped by natural selection.
- Innate behaviors are present in all individuals in a population and do not vary much from one individual to another or over an individual's life span.
- Organisms are well-prepared to learn behaviors that have been important to their reproductive success over the course of their evolutionary history and less prepared to learn behaviors irrelevant to their evolutionary success.
- It is not necessary for an organism to consciously try to maximize its reproductive success in order for a behavior to evolve.

9·5–9·9 Cooperation, selfishness, and altruism can be better understood with an evolutionary approach.

- Many behaviors in the animal world appear altruistic. In almost all cases, such acts are not truly altruistic and have evolved as a consequence of kin selection or reciprocal altruism, and from an evolutionary perspective are beneficial to the individual engaging in the behavior.
- Kin selection describes apparently altruistic behavior in which an individual's assistance to a genetic relative helps increase the relative's fitness and, consequently, its own inclusive fitness.
- Reciprocal altruism describes altruistic-appearing acts in which the individual performing the act is likely to get something of value at a later time.
- Behaviors that are good for the species or population but detrimental to the individual exhibiting the behavior are not generally produced under natural conditions.

9·10–9·15 Sexual conflict can result from disparities in reproductive investment by males and females.

- In mammals and many other animals, there are important physical differences between males and females relating to reproduction. These differences have led to the evolution of differences in male and female reproductive behaviors.
- Males tend to increase their reproductive success by mating with many females and have evolved to compete among themselves to get the opportunity to mate. Females do not increase their reproductive success through extra matings, but rather by caring for their offspring and being choosy when selecting a mate.
- Mate guarding reduces additional mating opportunities for a partner and can improve a male's reproductive success by increasing his paternity certainty, reducing his vulnerability when investing in offspring.
- Mating systems describe the variation in mate number and reproductive success of males and females.
- Differences in the level of competition among the individuals of each sex for access to mating opportunities can lead to the evolution of male-female differences in body size and other aspects of appearance.

9·16–9·17 Communication and the design of signals evolve.

- Methods of communication—chemical, acoustical, and visual—have evolved in animal species, enabling individuals to convey information about their condition and situation. These abilities influence fitness and the evolution of almost all other behaviors.
- Animals have evolved to rely primarily on signals that cannot easily be faked, in order to gain the maximum amount of information from them.

See the To-Go Guide (packaged with every new copy of this textbook) for an illustrated summary of the chapter.

Check Your Knowledge

GRAPHIC CONTENT

Thinking critically about visual displays of data.

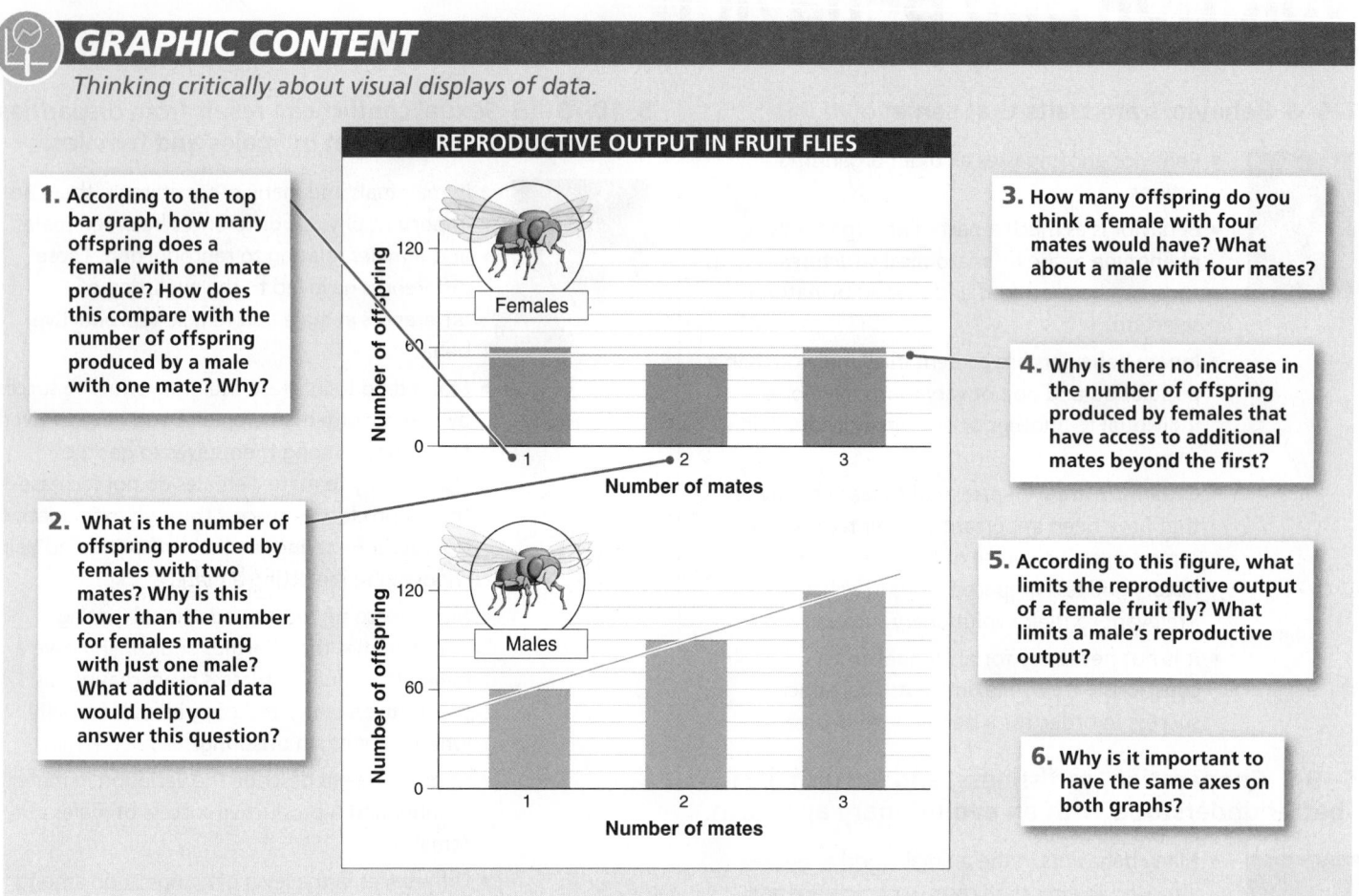

REPRODUCTIVE OUTPUT IN FRUIT FLIES

1. According to the top bar graph, how many offspring does a female with one mate produce? How does this compare with the number of offspring produced by a male with one mate? Why?

2. What is the number of offspring produced by females with two mates? Why is this lower than the number for females mating with just one male? What additional data would help you answer this question?

3. How many offspring do you think a female with four mates would have? What about a male with four mates?

4. Why is there no increase in the number of offspring produced by females that have access to additional mates beyond the first?

5. According to this figure, what limits the reproductive output of a female fruit fly? What limits a male's reproductive output?

6. Why is it important to have the same axes on both graphs?

See Answers at the back of the book.

Key Terms in Evolution and Behavior

altruistic behavior, p. 355
behavior, p. 349
communication, p. 377
direct fitness, p. 358
female, p. 365
fixed action pattern, p. 351
group selection, p. 364

honest signal, p. 379
inclusive fitness, p. 358
indirect fitness, p. 358
innate behavior, p. 351
instinct, p. 351
kin selection, p. 356
language, p. 378

learning, p. 351
male, p. 365
mate guarding, p. 371
mating system, p. 373
monogamy, p. 373
nuptial gift, p. 370
pair bond, p. 374

paternity uncertainty, p. 367
pheromone, p. 377
polyandry, p. 373
polygamy, p. 373
polygyny, p. 373
prepared learning, p. 351
reciprocal altruism, p. 356

reproductive investment, p. 366
sexual dimorphism, p. 375
sign stimulus, p. 351
total reproductive output, p. 366
waggle dance, p. 377

Multiple-Choice Questions

1. Why do human taste preferences exist?

a) They are culturally generated; consumers are influenced by suggestive advertising.

b) Human feeding choices influence energy intake and, consequently, fitness.

c) Humans can extract energy from a variety of non-food sources, so taste preferences cause us to focus on foods that are more plentiful in our environment.

d) Fats actually do taste better than sugars.

e) Vitamins and minerals give foods unusual tastes, which causes us to seek them out.

2. From an evolutionary perspective, behavior can best be viewed as:

a) a trait that arises by learning, not by natural selection.

b) non-heritable.

c) a trait subject to drift and mutation, but not natural selection.

d) part of the phenotype.

e) All of the above are correct.

3. Why is it so much easier for an infant to learn a complex language than for a college student to learn biology?

a) Language involves memorization only, without the need for understanding rules, while biology involves both.

b) Language is a feature with great evolutionary relevance for humans.

c) Learning biology was not a behavior with evolutionary relevance for humans.

d) Biology involves much more vocabulary than learning a complex language.

e) Both b) and c) are correct.

4. Babies in the United States quickly and easily develop a fear of snakes. Yet they don't easily develop a fear of guns. Why?

a) Humans cannot develop fears of inanimate objects.

b) Evolution can be slow in producing populations that are adapted to their environments.

c) Babies are more likely to encounter snakes than guns as they develop in the United States.

d) Fewer individuals are killed by guns than by snakes in the United States each year.

e) All of the above are correct.

5. In Belding's ground squirrels, why are females much more likely than males to engage in altruistic behavior by sounding alarm calls?

a) Belding's ground squirrels have a sex ratio that is biased toward females.

b) Females invest more in foraging and food storage, so they are more likely to lose their lives or their food if a predator attacks.

c) Belding's ground squirrels have a sex ratio that is biased toward males.

d) Females tend to remain in the area where they were born, so the females that call are warning their own kin.

e) Males forage alone, so their alarm calls are useless.

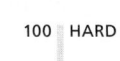

6. Gestational diabetes is thought to be the consequence of:

a) pregnant women decreasing their average daily amount of activity.

b) a mother withholding investment in future offspring in order to invest more in the current pregnancy.

c) a mother consuming too much sugar during gestation.

d) conflict between the mother and fetus with respect to how much food the fetus should be given; the mother is equally related to the fetus and to any future offspring, while the fetus is not equally related to itself and any subsequent siblings.

e) physiological constraints on the amount of insulin a mother can provide for the fetus.

7. Vampire bats:

a) sometimes regurgitate blood into the mouth of another bat that is close to starving, but the likelihood is a function of whether the individuals are genetically related.

b) are unusual in that they are one of the few animal species that exhibit kin selection.

c) sometimes regurgitate blood into the mouth of an unrelated bat that is close to starving.

d) exhibit reciprocal altruism but not kin selection.

e) There are no such things as vampire bats; they're found only in a Dracula novel.

100 HARD
37
0 EASY

8. Altruistic behavior in animals may be a result of kin selection, a theory maintaining that:

a) genes promote the survival of copies of themselves when behaviors by animals possessing those genes assist other animals that share those genes.

b) aggression within sexes increases the survival and reproduction of the fittest individuals.

c) companionship is advantageous to animals because, in the future, they can recognize those that have helped them and provide help to those individuals.

d) aggression between the sexes increases the survival and reproduction of the fittest individuals.

e) companionship is advantageous to animals because, in the future, they can recognize those that have helped them and request help once again.

100 HARD
25
0 EASY

9. All of the following conditions are necessary for reciprocal altruism to evolve in a species except:

a) the ability to recognize different individuals.

b) the ability to punish cheaters who do not reciprocate.

c) repeated interactions with the same individuals.

d) at least one of the sexes must not disperse so that some individuals always live near their kin.

e) None of the above is necessary for the evolution of reciprocal altruism.

100 HARD
31
0 EASY

10. In a situation in which males guard eggs and care for the young without help from the female, which of the following statements would most likely be correct?

a) Males are large and more brightly colored in order to attract the very best females.

b) Males and females are equally brightly colored, but males court females aggressively.

c) The population is monogamous with no sexual dimorphism.

d) A single male controls a harem of females to which he has exclusive reproductive access.

e) Females are more brightly colored than males and court males aggressively.

100 HARD
44
0 EASY

11. In mammals, as well as many other species, males generally compete for females. The best explanation for this phenomenon is:

a) males are more aggressive.

b) males, on average, have higher fitness.

c) females have a higher parental investment.

d) males are choosy.

e) females are better looking.

100 HARD
26
0 EASY

12. Mate guarding is a reproductive tactic that functions to:

a) reduce paternity uncertainty.

b) increase the female's investment in offspring.

c) reduce the male's reproductive investment.

d) reduce the female's fitness.

e) increase the number of mates to which a male has access.

100 HARD
32
0 EASY

13. Relative to birds, more mammalian species are:

a) polygynous.

b) monogamous.

c) polyandrous.

d) hermaphroditic.

e) sexually monomorphic.

100 HARD
59
0 EASY

14. In a species such as pigeons, in which males are almost indistinguishable in appearance from females, the most likely mating system is:

a) monomorphism.

b) monogamy.

c) polygyny.

d) polyandry.

e) It is impossible to predict the mating system with only this information.

100 HARD
37
0 EASY

15. If you find a species of fish in which males are much more brightly colored and larger than females, what might you infer about their mating system?

a) The degree of sexual dimorphism does not give any information about the mating system.

b) They are simultaneous hermaphrodites.

c) They exhibit parallel monogamy.

d) They are serially monogamous.

e) They are polygynous.

100 HARD
39
0 EASY

16. Polygynous species:

a) usually employ external fertilization.

b) are usually sexually dimorphic, with males larger and more highly ornamented.

c) are usually sexually dimorphic, with females larger and more highly ornamented.

d) usually have males and females that are physically indistinguishable.

e) are more commonly found among birds than among mammals.

100 HARD
29
0 EASY

Short-Answer Question

1. Female moorhens are larger and more aggressive than males. They also compete among themselves for access to the smaller, fatter males. Which sex do you think provides more parental care? Explain your answer.

See Answers at the back of the book.
For additional study questions, go to www.prep-u.com.

Understanding biodiversity

10

The Origin and Diversification of Life on Earth

387

10·1–10·2 Life on earth most likely originated from non-living materials.

Life on earth arose in a very different environment than we experience today. (Shown here: the formation of volcanic rock in Hawaii.)

10·1 Complex organic molecules arise in non-living environments.

In the beginning, there was nothing. Now there is something. That, in a nutshell, describes one of the most important, yet difficult to resolve, questions in science: How did life on earth begin? We open our investigation by describing a few things that we do know and exploring how they help us speculate about the things we do not yet know. First, let's give a basic definition of what we mean by "life." **Life** is defined by the ability to replicate and by the presence of some sort of metabolic activity (the chemical processes by which molecules are acquired and used and energy is transformed in controlled reactions). In the next section we expand on this definition and explore the transition from non-living to living.

Earth formed about 4.5 billion years ago from clouds of dust and gases, and as it very gradually cooled, a crust formed at the surface and condensing water formed the oceans. This probably took several hundred million years. The oldest rocks, found in Canada, are about 3.8 billion years old. And the earliest life forms appeared not long after these first rocks formed: fossilized bacteria-like cells have been found in rocks that are 3.4 billion years old.

From that initial point in earth's formation, there is now tremendous **biodiversity**—variety and variability among all genes, species, and ecosystems. In this chapter we explore how

this biodiversity might have come to be, how we name groups of organisms, and how we determine the relatedness of these groups to one another. We begin by returning to the question of the origin of life on earth.

How did these first organisms arise? Some have suggested that life may have originated elsewhere in the universe and traveled to earth, possibly on a meteor. It is hotly debated, however, whether microbes could even survive the multi-million-year trip to earth in the cold vacuum of space with no protection from ultraviolet and other forms of radiation. Experimental data have been unable to answer this question definitively. Most scientists believe, instead, that life originated on earth probably in several distinct phases.

Phase 1: The formation of small molecules containing carbon and hydrogen The conditions on earth around the time of the origin of life were very different from those of today. In particular, chemical analyses of old rocks reveal that no oxygen gas was present. The atmosphere included large amounts of carbon dioxide, nitrogen, methane, ammonia, hydrogen, and hydrogen sulfide. Most of these molecules were produced by volcanic eruptions. It was this environment that probably served as the cradle of life, or what Darwin called the "warm little pond" (**FIGURE 10-1**).

Earth's early atmosphere had almost no oxygen and was filled with many compounds released during volcanic eruptions.

Small organic molecules eventually formed, providing the building blocks of life.

FIGURE 10-1 Darwin's "warm little pond." The first life on earth tolerated an atmosphere without oxygen.

Critical to the origin of life was the formation of small molecules containing carbon and hydrogen. Because of their chemical structures, these molecules bond very easily and so have a huge variety of forms and functions, making them indispensable for the chemical processes of life. There are several plausible scenarios for how the creation of these small organic molecules may have occurred. The most likely comes from some simple but revealing four-step experiments done in 1953 by a 23-year-old student named Stanley Miller and his advisor, Harold Urey (**FIGURE 10-2**).

1. They created a model of the "warm little pond" and their best estimate of earth's early atmosphere: a flask of water with H_2, CH_4 (methane), and NH_3 (ammonia).

2. They subjected this mini-world to sparks, to simulate lightning.

3. They cooled the atmosphere so that any compounds formed in it would rain back down into the water.

4. They waited and then examined the contents of the water to see what happened.

They didn't have to wait long to get exciting results. Within a matter of days—not millions of years or even a few months—they discovered many organic molecules, including five different amino acids, in their primordial sea. (Using more sensitive equipment, recent re-analyses revealed that all 20 amino acids present in living organisms were produced during the course of these experiments.) This was the first demonstration that complex organic molecules

In 1953, Stanley Miller (shown) and Harold Urey developed a simple four-step experiment that demonstrated how complex organic molecules could have arisen in earth's early environment.

1. They created a model of the "warm little pond" and atmosphere early in the earth's history.

2. The atmosphere was subjected to sparks, to simulate lightning.

3. The atmosphere was cooled so that any compounds in it would rain back down into the water.

4. They examined the water, looking for organic molecules.

Electrical discharge

Cool

Heat

Within a matter of days, they discovered many organic molecules (including five different amino acids) in their primordial sea.

FIGURE 10-2 A promising first step. The Urey-Miller experiment generated organic molecules from hydrogen, methane, and ammonia.

could have arisen in earth's early environment. However, questions remain, such as whether the environment that Urey and Miller assumed to exist on the early earth was reasonable. Still, the experiments are a promising first step, suggesting that complex organic compounds—including amino acids, the primary constituents of proteins and an essential component of living systems—could have been produced from inorganic chemicals and lightning energy in the primitive environment of earth.

In the next section, we consider the final two phases by which these small organic molecules may have given rise to living organisms.

10·2 Cells and self-replicating systems evolved together to create the first life.

After the generation of numerous organic molecules such as amino acids, the second phase in the generation of life from non-life was probably the assembly of these building block molecules into self-replicating, information-containing molecules. This is where things get a bit more speculative. It's complicated enough to generate a complex organic molecule, but it's a whole lot more complicated to generate an organic molecule that can replicate itself. Researchers believe that to get to the replication phase, enzymes were required.

Phase 2: The formation of self-replicating, information-containing molecules

Recently, researchers discovered that the nucleic acid RNA can do what proteins do—catalyze reactions necessary for replication—meaning that this single, relatively simple molecule could have been a self-replicating system and a precursor to cellular life. These findings have given rise to the so-called **RNA world hypothesis,** which proposes that the world may have been filled with RNA-based life before it became filled with the DNA-based life we see today.

These self-replicating molecules raise an important question: When exactly was the threshold between living and non-living crossed? In the RNA world, self-replicating nucleic acid molecules carried the information of how to replicate *and* served as the machinery to actually carry out the replication. Is that enough? At this point, it is reasonable to ask, again: What exactly is "life"?

Fossils of 3.4-billion-year-old cells have been found in rocks in South Africa and Australia. These cells appear to be prokaryotic cells, similar to living bacterial cells, with no nucleus, no organelles, and a circular strand of genetic information (**FIGURE 10-3**). Some even look as if they are in the process of dividing. Although, superficially, the fossilized cells look like just a couple of circles, several lines of evidence

THE EARLIEST LIFE ON EARTH?

Fossils of 3.4-billion-year-old cells that may have been among the first living organisms on earth.

FIGURE 10-3 Ancient prokaryotic cells.

support the idea that they are indeed remnants of cells. These include: (1) the age of the rocks themselves has been reliably determined, (2) the size of the circles is similar to that of modern-day prokaryotes, and (3) the ratio of two carbon isotopes ($^{12}C/^{13}C$) is more characteristic of fossilized organisms than of typical rocks that do not contain fossils. But many questions remain. Were these cells the first living organisms on earth? And were they descendants of earlier, self-replicating molecules of RNA? Because no earlier fossils have been found, it is difficult to answer these questions.

Among humans, it's obvious whether someone is living or non-living. But this distinction becomes difficult to make when discussing simpler collections of molecules. Although no perfect, precise definition exists, most scientists agree that life is defined by two characteristics: the ability to replicate and the ability to carry out some sort of metabolism. So the self-replicating RNA molecules were right on the border, satisfying the first condition for life (replicating) but not the second (carrying out metabolism). We now explore the critical third phase in the generation of life from non-life: the development of a membrane that separated these self-replicating small molecules from their surroundings, thus making cells and facilitating metabolic activity.

Phase 3: The development of a membrane, enabling metabolism and creating the first cells

One way that self-replicating molecules could have acquired chemicals and used them in the controlled reactions of metabolism was by packaging the molecules within membranes. As we saw in Chapter 3, cell membranes are semi-permeable barriers that separate the inside of cells from their external environment. Membranes make numerous aspects of metabolism possible. In particular, they make it possible for chemicals inside the cell to be at higher concentrations than they are outside the cell. Differences in chemical concentrations inside and outside a cell are essential to most life-supporting reactions.

So, if we could combine a self-replicating molecule and some metabolic chemicals into a unit, surrounded by a membrane, life would be possible. But how could this have happened initially? Some evidence suggests that the first cells may simply have come together spontaneously. Specifically, researchers have found that mixtures of phospholipids placed in water or salt solutions tend to spontaneously form small spherical units that resemble living cells. These units may even "sprout" new buds at their surface, appearing to divide. Because these cell-like units don't pass on any genetic material, however, they cannot be considered to be alive. But if, at some point, units like these incorporated some self-replicating molecules inside, maybe by forming around them, such **microspheres** might have been important in the third phase in the generation of life from non-life: the compartmentalization of self-replicating, information-containing molecules into cells. If this did occur, the final step in the creation of something from nothing would be complete (**FIGURE 10-4**).

The exact process by which life on earth originated is still uncertain, and research continues. What is clear, however, is

FIGURE 10-4 How did life arise?

that life now abounds in great diversity. In the next sections, we explore that diversity and how it is generated. We start with an investigation of what a species is and how individual species split and create additional species.

TAKE-HOME MESSAGE 10·2

The earliest life on earth, which resembled bacteria, appeared about 3.5 billion years ago, not long after the earth was formed. Evidence supports the idea that self-replicating molecules—possibly RNAs—may have formed in earth's early environment and later acquired or developed membranes, enabling them to replicate and making metabolism possible, the two conditions that define life.

10·3–10·6 Species are the basic units of biodiversity.

A world of beauty. There are more than 230,000 species of flowering plants.

10·3 What is a species?

A cat and a mouse are different things. Oprah Winfrey and Bill Gates, on the other hand, are different *versions* of the same thing. That is, although they are different individuals, both are humans. We generally distinguish between different kinds of living organisms: a rose versus a daisy, a wasp versus a fly, a snake versus a frog. Similarly, we lump some organisms into the same group and recognize them as different versions of the same thing: red roses and yellow roses, Chihuahuas and Dalmatians. How do we know when to classify two individuals as members of different groups and when to classify them as members of the same group (**FIGURE 10-5**)?

Biologists use the word **species** to label different kinds of organisms. According to the **biological species concept,** species are populations of organisms that interbreed, or could possibly interbreed, with each other under natural conditions, and that cannot interbreed with organisms from other such groups (**FIGURE 10-6**).

Notice that the biological species concept completely ignores physical appearance when defining a species and instead emphasizes **reproductive isolation,** the inability of individuals from two populations to produce fertile offspring with each other, thereby making it impossible for gene exchange between the populations to occur.

Let's clarify two important features of the biological species concept. First, it says that members of a species are actually interbreeding or *could possibly* interbreed. This emphasis means that just because two individuals are physically separated, they aren't necessarily of different species. A person living in the United States and a person living in Iceland, for example, may not be able to mate because of the distance, but if they were brought to the same location, they could. So, although the people are not in the same population, we do not consider them to be reproductively isolated. Second, our definition refers to

     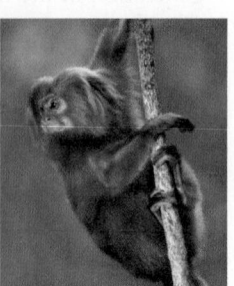

FIGURE 10-5 The same but not the same. We recognize Bill Gates and Oprah Winfrey as members of the same species, but can you tell whether the Persian buttercup and the pink rose or the Bornean orangutan and the golden lion tamarin are from the same species? (They're not.)

WHAT MAKES A SPECIES?

SPECIES ARE...

- Populations of organisms that interbreed with each other
- Or could possibly breed, under natural conditions

FIGURE 10-6 An interbreeding population. This herd of Dall sheep lives in the remote regions of Denali National Park, Alaska.

Even if they can be produced in captivity, organisms that do not naturally occur in the wild—such as the "zorse"—are not considered species.

FIGURE 10-7 Interbreeding is not enough. This "zorse" is the offspring of a zebra and a horse, two species that will interbreed, but only in captivity.

"natural" conditions. This distinction is important because occasionally, in captivity, individuals may interbreed that would not interbreed in the wild, such as zebras and horses (**FIGURE 10-7**).

There are two types of barriers that prevent individuals of different species from reproducing: prezygotic and postzygotic barriers (**FIGURE 10-8**). (Remember, an egg that has been fertilized by a sperm cell is a *zygote*.)

REPRODUCTIVE ISOLATION: KEEPING SPECIES SEPARATE

PREZYGOTIC BARRIERS

- Individuals are physically unable to mate with each other.
  OR
- If individuals are able to mate, the male's reproductive cell is unable to fertilize the female's reproductive cell.

POSTZYGOTIC BARRIERS

- Matings produce hybrid individuals that do not survive long after fertilization.
  OR
- If hybrid offspring survive, they are infertile or have reduced fertility.

FIGURE 10-8 Barriers to reproduction. With postzygotic barriers to reproduction, even if fertilization does occur, the resulting animal (such as the mule, on the right) is usually sterile.

Prezygotic barriers make it impossible for individuals to mate with each other or, if they can mate, make it impossible for the male's reproductive cell to fertilize the female's reproductive cell. These barriers include situations in which the members of the two species have different courtship rituals or have physical differences that prevent mating or fertilization.

Postzygotic barriers occur after fertilization and generally prevent the production of fertile offspring from individuals of two different species. These barriers are responsible for the production of **hybrid** individuals that either do not survive long after fertilization or, if they do, are infertile or have reduced fertility. Mules, for example, are the hybrid offspring of horses and donkeys, and although they can survive, they cannot produce their own offspring.

At first glance, the biological species concept seems to make it possible to determine unambiguously whether individuals belong to the same or different species. For plants and animals this is usually true. For many other organisms, however, it is impossible to apply the biological species concept. We examine those species in Section 10-5 and explore some alternative methods of identifying species. Even though it is not perfect, however, the biological species concept gives us an important tool for conceptualizing and categorizing the tremendous diversity of organisms found on earth.

TAKE-HOME MESSAGE 10·3

Species are generally defined as populations of individuals that interbreed with each other, or could possibly interbreed, and that cannot interbreed with organisms from other such groups. This concept can be applied easily to most plants and animals, but is not applicable for many other types of organisms.

10·4 How do we name species?

Keeping track of a large group of anything requires an organizational system. Many libraries, for example, catalog their books by using the Dewey Decimal System, which organizes books into 10 different classes, further subdivides each class into 10 divisions, and each division into 10 sections.

With the huge number of species on earth, a classification system is particularly important. Biologists use the system developed by the Swedish biologist Carolus Linnaeus in the mid-1700s. Here's how it works (**FIGURE 10-9**). Every species is given a scientific name that consists of two parts, a **genus** (*pl.* genera) and a **specific epithet.** Linnaeus named humans *Homo sapiens,* meaning "wise man." *Homo* is the genus and *sapiens* is the specific epithet. (The genus is capitalized, and both genus and specific epithet are italicized.) The redwood tree has the name *Sequoia sempervirens.* The strength of Linnaeus's system is that it is hierarchical—that is, each element of the system falls under a single element in the level just above it.

In the Linnaean system, the species is the narrowest classification for an organism. The name for every species within a genus is unique, but many different species may be in the same genus. Similarly, many genera are grouped within a **family.** And many families are grouped within an **order.** Orders are grouped within a **class.** Classes are grouped within a **phylum.** And, as Linnaeus originally set it up, all phyla were classified under one of three **kingdoms:** the animal kingdom, the plant kingdom, or the "mineral kingdom."

Today, many of the species classifications that Linnaeus described have been revised, and some of his designations, such as the "mineral kingdom," have been left out, while two other kingdoms (fungi and protists) have been added. Also, all of the kingdoms are now classified under an even higher order of classification, the **domain.** But Linnaeus's basic hierarchical structure remains, and all life on earth is still named using this system, with all organisms belonging to one of the three domains: the bacteria, the archaea, and the eukarya.

When new species are discovered, they are given names based on the Linnaean system. The higher-level groups into which a new species should be classified are generally clear—that is, it's usually obvious whether something is in the animal or plant kingdom, or whether it is in the mammalian or amphibian class. But when scientists are assigning a specific epithet, they frequently have a little fun. In recent years, for example, an amphibian fossil was named *Eucritta melanolimnetes,* which translates roughly into "creature from the black lagoon." And in honor of Elvis Presley, a wasp species was named *Preseucoila imallshookupis.* A variety of other celebrities also have had species named after them, including the Beatles, Mick Jagger, Kate Winslet, and Steven Spielberg.

THE ORGANIZATION OF LIFE

DOMAIN
Bacteria   Archaea   Eukarya

KINGDOM
Protista   Plantae   Fungi   Animalia

PHYLUM
Chordata

CLASS
Mammalia

ORDER
Perissodactyla

FAMILY
Equidae

GENUS
Equus

SPECIES
Equus quagga

FIGURE 10-9 Name that zebra. Each species on earth, like *Equus quagga,* is given a scientific name and is categorized according to hierarchical groups.

Plants and animals often are referred to by common names, which are different from their "official" names in the Linnaean system and are based on similarities in appearance. These common names, however, can cause confusion. "Fish" for example is used as part of the names of jellyfish, crayfish, and silverfish, none of which are closely related to the vertebrate group of fishes that includes salmon and tuna. Later in this chapter we'll see how an important goal of modern classification and the naming of organisms is to link an organism's classification more closely with its evolutionary history than with its physical characteristics.

> **TAKE-HOME MESSAGE 10·4**
>
> Each species on earth is given a unique name, using a hierarchical system of classification. Every species falls into one of three domains.

10·5 Species are not always easily defined.

Biologists, like all humans, can be biased. When investigating the natural world, for example, they often focus on plants and animals, to the exclusion of the rest of the earth's rich biodiversity. This gets them into trouble when it comes to an idea such as the biological species concept. While the biological species concept is remarkably useful when

describing most plants and animals, it falls short of representing a universal and definitive way of distinguishing many life forms (**FIGURE 10-10**).

Difficulties in classifying asexual species The biological species concept defines species as populations of

THE BIOLOGICAL SPECIES CONCEPT DOESN'T ALWAYS WORK

The biological species concept is remarkably useful when describing most plants and animals, but it doesn't work for distinguishing all life forms.

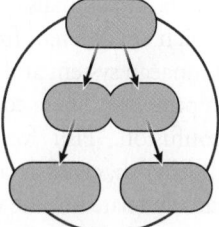

CLASSIFYING ASEXUAL SPECIES
Asexual reproduction does not involve interbreeding, so the concept of reproductive isolation is no longer meaningful.

CLASSIFYING FOSSIL SPECIES
Differences in size and shape of fossil bones cannot reveal whether there was reproductive isolation between the individuals from which the bones came.

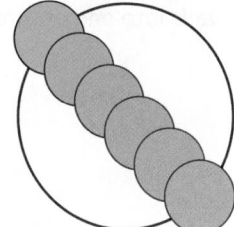

DETERMINING WHEN ONE SPECIES HAS CHANGED INTO ANOTHER
There is rarely a definitive moment marking the transition from one species to another.

CLASSIFYING RING SPECIES
Two non-interbreeding populations may be connected to each other by gene flow through another population, so there is no exact point where one species stops and the other begins.

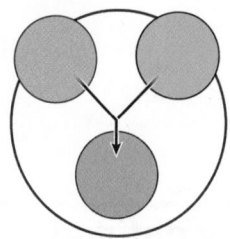

CLASSIFYING HYBRIDIZING SPECIES
Hybridization—the interbreeding of closely related species—sometimes occurs and produces fertile offspring, suggesting that the borders between the species are not clear-cut.

FIGURE 10-10 A useful concept that can't always be easily applied.

interbreeding individuals. But this is a useless distinction for the asexual species of the world. Recall from Chapter 6 that asexual reproduction, common among single-celled organisms

(including all bacteria), many plants, and some animals, is a form of reproduction that doesn't involve fertilization or even two individuals. Rather, the cell (or cells) of an individual simply divides, creating new individuals. Because asexual reproduction does not involve partners or interbreeding, the concept of reproductive isolation is not meaningful and it might seem that every individual should be considered a separate species. Clearly, that's not a helpful rule to follow.

Difficulties in classifying fossil species When classifying fossil species, differences in the size and shape of fossil bones from different individuals can never definitively reveal whether there was reproductive isolation between those individuals. This makes it impossible to apply the biological species concept.

Difficulties in determining when one species has changed into another Based on fossils, it seems that modern-day humans, *Homo sapiens,* probably evolved from a related species called *H. heidelbergensis* about 250,000–400,000 years ago. This seems reasonable, until you consider that your parents—who are in the species *H. sapiens*—were born to your *H. sapiens* grandparents, who were born to your *H. sapiens* great-grandparents, and so on. If humans evolved from *H. heidelbergensiss,* at what *exact* point did *H. heidelbergensis* turn into *H. sapiens?* It may not be possible to identify the exact point at which this change occurred.

Difficulties in classifying ring species Living in central Asia are some small, insect-eating songbirds called greenish warblers. Unable to live at higher elevations of the Tibetan mountain range, the warblers live in a ring around it. At the southern end of the

Q Chihuahuas and Great Danes generally can't mate. Does that mean they are different species?

mountain range, in northwest India, the warblers interbreed with each other. Along either side of the range, the warbler population is split, and warblers on one side do not interbreed with those on the other, because the mountain range separates them. Where the two "side" populations meet up again at the northernmost end of the mountain range, in the forests of Siberia, they can no longer interbreed.

What happened? Gradual changes in the warblers on each side of the mountain range accumulated so that the two populations that meet up in Siberia are sufficiently different, physically and behaviorally, that they have become reproductively incompatible. But because the two non-interbreeding populations in the north are connected by gene flow through other populations farther south, there is no exact point at which one species stops and the other begins. So where do you draw the line? The greenish warblers are just one example of more than 20 such **ring species** that have been described.

Difficulties in classifying hybridizing species

Increasingly, **hybridization**—the interbreeding of closely related species—has been observed among plant and animal species. This phenomenon fits with the biological species concept as long as postzygotic barriers have evolved, so that the hybrids are unable to reproduce. But in some cases, such as among butterflies in the genus *Heliconius,* the hybrids have high survival rates *and* are fertile, whether interbreeding with one another or with individuals of either of the two parental species. This suggests that the borders between the species are not clear-cut.

All of these shortcomings have prompted the development of several alternative approaches to defining what a species is. These alternatives tend to focus on aspects of organisms other than reproductive isolation as defining features. The most commonly used alternative is the **morphological species concept,** which characterizes species based on physical features such as body size and shape. Although the choice of which features to use is subjective, an important aspect of the morphological species concept is that it can be used effectively to classify asexual species. And because it doesn't require knowledge of whether individuals can actually interbreed, the

morphological species concept is a bit easier to use when observing organisms in the wild.

When it comes to species definitions, although the biological species concept is the most widely used and can be applied without difficulty to most plants and animals, we should not expect one size to fit all, and there will probably never be a universally applicable definition of what a species is. From asexual species to ring species to hybridizing species, the diversity of the natural world is simply too great to fit into neat, completely defined and distinct little boxes. Nonetheless, scientists can generally use a species definition that is satisfactory for a particular situation.

TAKE-HOME MESSAGE 10·5

The biological species concept is useful when describing most plants and animals, but it falls short of representing a universal and definitive way of distinguishing many life forms. Difficulties arise when trying to classify asexual species, fossil species, species arising over long periods of time, ring species, and hybridizing species. In these cases, alternative approaches to defining species can be used.

10·6 How do new species arise?

Biologists don't really have a clue about exactly how many species there are on earth. Estimates vary tremendously, from 5 million to 100 million. Biologists do know, however, the process by which all species arose.

The process of **speciation,** in which one species splits into two distinct species, occurs in two phases and requires more than just evolutionary change in a population. The first phase of speciation is *reproductive isolation,* through which two populations come to have independent evolutionary fates. The second phase is *genetic divergence,* in which two populations evolving as separate entities adapt differently to features of their separate environments, including to different predators and different types of food, thereby accumulating physical and behavioral differences over time.

The initial reproductive isolation necessary for speciation often comes about, as we've seen, when two populations are geographically separated. Although this is an effective and common way for speciation to occur, speciation can also occur without it.

Speciation with geographic isolation: allopatric speciation Suppose one population of squirrels is split into two separate populations because the local climate grows wetter and a river forms and splits the habitat in two. Because the squirrels cannot cross the river, the population on one side is reproductively isolated from that on the other. Over time, the two populations have different evolutionary paths as they adapt to particular features of their separate habitats, which may differ. Eventually, the two populations might genetically diverge so much that even if the river separating them disappeared and the populations came back into contact, squirrels from the two groups could no longer interbreed. In fact, two species of antelope ground squirrels formed on the north and south rims of the Grand Canyon as a result of this type of speciation, known as **allopatric speciation** (FIGURE 10-11).

Another example of allopatric speciation is seen in the various finch species of the Galápagos Islands. Individual finches from the nearest mainland, now Ecuador, originally colonized one or more of the islands. (And later, additional islands may have

ALLOPATRIC SPECIATION

Allopatric speciation occurs when a geographic barrier causes one group of individuals in a population to be reproductively isolated from another group.

1 INITIAL POPULATION

2 REPRODUCTIVE ISOLATION

Suppose a river forms through the squirrels' habitat, separating the population. Because the squirrels cannot cross the river, the two groups are now reproductively isolated.

3 GENETIC DIVERGENCE

Over time, the populations on either side diverge enough genetically that they are no longer able to interbreed.

Harris's antelope ground squirrel

White-tailed antelope ground squirrel

been colonized by birds from the mainland or from previously colonized islands.) But because the islands are far apart, the finches tended not to travel between them, and because colonization events are rare, the populations remained reproductively isolated from one another. Consequently,

FIGURE 10-11 Geographic isolation can result in genetic divergence. Two species of antelope ground squirrel that have evolved on the north and south rims of the Grand Canyon.

14 different finch species have evolved in the Galápagos Islands, each of which specializes in eating certain of the wide range of insects, buds, and seeds found on the islands (**FIGURE 10-12**). Only one species of finch is found in mainland Ecuador.

The barrier doesn't have to be an expanse of water. A forming glacier could split a population into two or more isolated populations. Or a drop in the water level of a lake might expose strips of land that divide the lake into detached, smaller bodies of water, separating one large population of fish into two distinct populations. In each case, the result is the same: geographic isolation that enforces reproductive isolation.

Researchers can easily create new species in the lab, using an analogous strategy. In one experiment, a single population of fruit flies (*Drosophila pseudoobscura*) was divided into two. The two populations were then maintained on different diets—one on the sugar maltose and the other on a starch-based food. After only eight generations of enforced reproductive isolation and adaptation to their differing nutritional environments, the populations had diverged sufficiently to form separate species; when the populations were mixed, the fruit flies from one population would no longer interbreed with flies from the other population.

Q Could you create a new species in the laboratory? How?

Speciation without geographic isolation: sympatric speciation

Speciation can also occur among populations that overlap geographically. This is called **sympatric speciation.** Among vertebrates, it is rare for populations of the same animal to become reproductively isolated when they coexist in the same area, so this method of speciation is relatively uncommon. But it *is* common among plants, and it occurs in one of two ways (**FIGURE 10-13**, page 400).

During cell division in plants (both in reproductive cells and in other cells of the plant body), an error sometimes occurs in which the chromosomes are duplicated but a cell does not divide. This creates a new cell that can then grow into an individual with twice as many sets of chromosomes as the parent from which it came. The new individual may have four sets of chromosomes, for example, while the original individual had two. This doubling of the number of sets of chromosomes is called **polyploidy.** The individual with four

Large cactus finch   Vampire finch   Large ground finch

Woodpecker finch   Small tree finch   Mainland finch

Due to allopatric speciation, fourteen different species of finches have evolved in the Galápagos Islands. Only one species of finch is found on the nearest mainland.

FIGURE 10-12 Five of the 13 Galápagos Island finch species. Each species of finch specializes in eating the insects, buds, and/or seeds found in its island habitat.

sets of chromosomes can no longer interbreed with individuals having only two sets, because their offspring would have three sets (two sets from the parent that had four, and one set from the parent that had two), which could not divide evenly during cell division. The individual with four sets can, however, propagate through self-fertilization or by mating with other individuals that have four sets. As a consequence, the individuals with four sets of chromosomes have achieved instant reproductive isolation from the original population and are therefore considered a new species. Although rare in animals, speciation by polyploidy has occurred several times among some species of tree frogs.

A much more common method of sympatric speciation occurs when plants of different (but closely related) species interbreed, forming a hybrid. The hybrid may not be able to interbreed with either of the parental species, but it may be able to propagate asexually—as many plants can. And meiosis often is disrupted in hybrids, causing a chromosome doubling (polyploidy). When this occurs, the hybrids with a doubled number of chromosome sets can interbreed with each other (see Figure 10-13). This method of speciation has led to the production of a large number of important crop plants, including wheat, bananas, potatoes, and coffee.

When reproductive separation occurs, for whatever reason, the new populations are isolated from each other. But because the biological species concept considers individuals from populations that could *potentially* interbreed as still belonging to the same species, speciation is not complete until sufficient differences have evolved in the two populations that they could no longer interbreed even if

Sympatric speciation results in the reproductive isolation of populations that coexist in the same area. Two scenarios, common in plants, lead to this method of speciation.

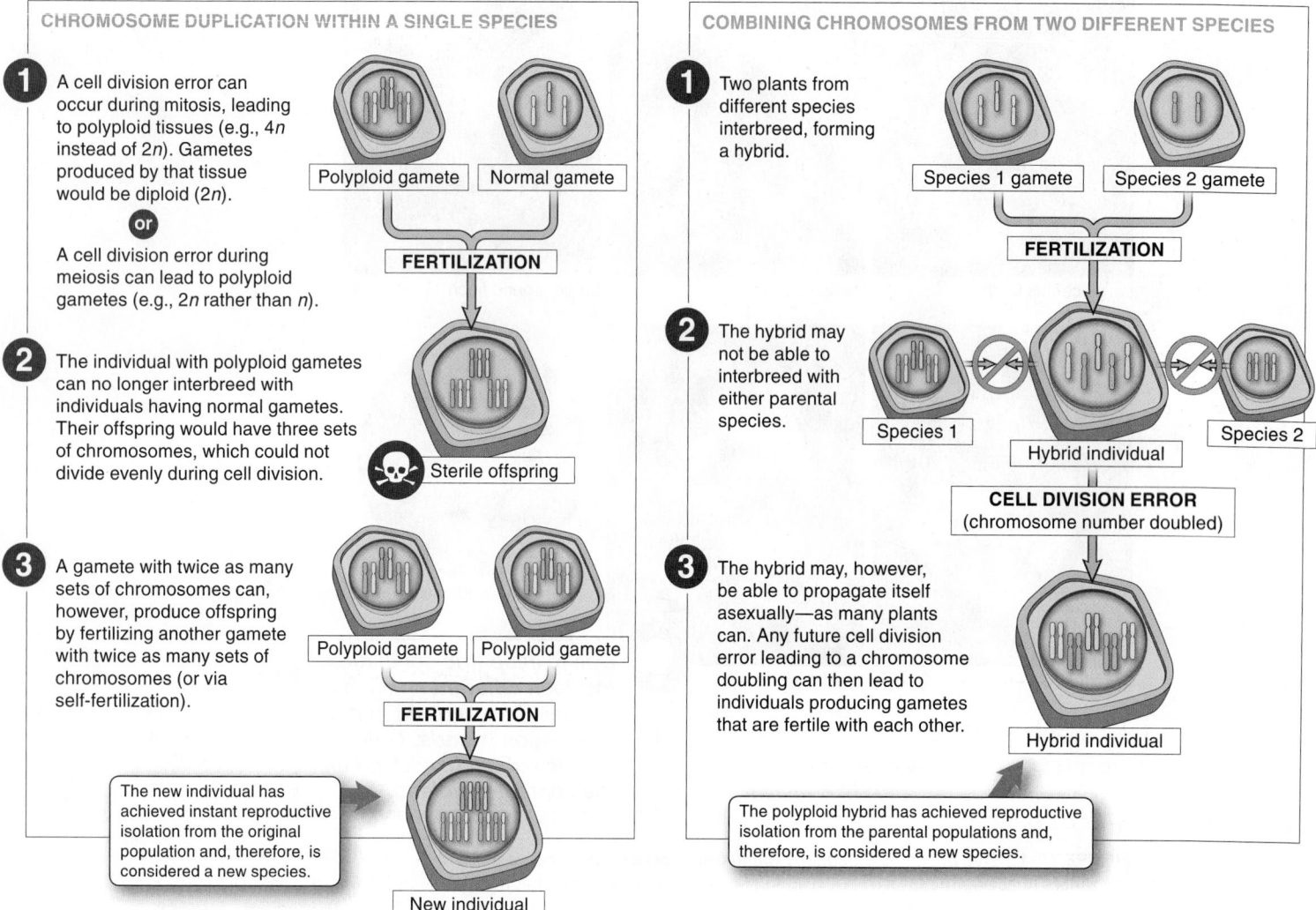

CHROMOSOME DUPLICATION WITHIN A SINGLE SPECIES

1 A cell division error can occur during mitosis, leading to polyploid tissues (e.g., 4*n* instead of 2*n*). Gametes produced by that tissue would be diploid (2*n*).

or

A cell division error during meiosis can lead to polyploid gametes (e.g., 2*n* rather than *n*).

Polyploid gamete | Normal gamete

FERTILIZATION

2 The individual with polyploid gametes can no longer interbreed with individuals having normal gametes. Their offspring would have three sets of chromosomes, which could not divide evenly during cell division.

Sterile offspring

3 A gamete with twice as many sets of chromosomes can, however, produce offspring by fertilizing another gamete with twice as many sets of chromosomes (or via self-fertilization).

Polyploid gamete | Polyploid gamete

FERTILIZATION

The new individual has achieved instant reproductive isolation from the original population and, therefore, is considered a new species.

New individual

COMBINING CHROMOSOMES FROM TWO DIFFERENT SPECIES

1 Two plants from different species interbreed, forming a hybrid.

Species 1 gamete | Species 2 gamete

FERTILIZATION

2 The hybrid may not be able to interbreed with either parental species.

Species 1 | Hybrid individual | Species 2

CELL DIVISION ERROR
(chromosome number doubled)

3 The hybrid may, however, be able to propagate itself asexually—as many plants can. Any future cell division error leading to a chromosome doubling can then lead to individuals producing gametes that are fertile with each other.

Hybrid individual

The polyploid hybrid has achieved reproductive isolation from the parental populations and, therefore, is considered a new species.

FIGURE 10-13 Speciation without geographic isolation. Plants may genetically diverge through sympatric speciation.

they did come in contact. It is in isolation from each other, however, that two populations generally diverge into separate species—that is, the prezygotic and/or postzygotic mechanisms evolve that form the biological barriers to genetic exchange between the two new species.

Reproductive separation can occur relatively quickly—as long as it takes for a new river (or freeway) to divide one large population into two. But the genetic divergence that causes true reproductive isolation—no successful interbreeding even when individuals come into contact with each other—can

take a very long time, sometimes thousands of years. For this reason, speciation can be difficult to study and observe.

TAKE-HOME MESSAGE 10·6

Speciation is the process by which one species splits into two distinct species that are reproductively isolated. It can occur by polyploidy or by a combination of reproductive isolation and genetic divergence.

10·7–10·9
Evolutionary trees help us conceptualize and categorize biodiversity.

The diversity of life on earth can be thought of as branching like a tree.

10·7 The history of life can be imagined as a tree.

Although Carolus Linnaeus's method for naming species was an important step in categorizing and cataloguing earth's biodiversity, his underlying assumption about where species came from was wrong. He believed, as did all biologists of his day, that all species had been created at the same time and were unchanging. For this reason, his classification of organisms into hierarchical groups was based on nothing more than his own evaluation of how physically similar various organisms appeared.

A hundred years later, however, Charles Darwin proposed and documented that species could, in fact, change and give rise to new species. With Darwin, the classification of species acquired a new goal and a more important function. In *The Origin of Species* Darwin wrote: "Our classifications will come to be, as far as they can be so made, genealogies." That is, Darwin proposed that the classifications of organisms would resemble family trees that link generations of parents and offspring over long periods of time. With these words, Darwin was the first to link classification with evolution.

Linnaean classification involved placing organisms within groups as a function of their apparent similarity with each other. The modern incarnation of Darwin's vision of classification is called **systematics** and has the broader goal of reconstructing the **phylogeny,** or evolutionary history, of

organisms. That is, through systematics, all species—even extinct species—are named and arranged in a manner that indicates the common ancestors they share and the points at which the species diverged. A complete phylogeny of all organisms is like a family tree for all species, past and present.

A phylogenetic tree not only shows the relationships among organisms but also presents a hypothesis about evolutionary history (**FIGURE 10-14**). At the beginning of life on earth there was the first living organism, one that could replicate itself. Then a **speciation event** occurred, after which the population of the first living organism split into independent evolutionary lineages. The phylogenetic tree had its first branch, and there was biodiversity. Over hundreds of millions of years, speciation events continued to occur, and today the tree has branches with millions (or possibly tens of millions) of tips that represent all the species on earth. Moving up a branch of any evolutionary tree from its trunk toward its tips, we can see when groups split, with each branching point representing a speciation event. And it doesn't stop here—speciation continues to add new branches all the time.

It is important to remember that phylogenies are hypotheses and, like any hypotheses, they are subject to revision and modification. In the next section, we explore how phylogenetic trees are constructed and look at the rich

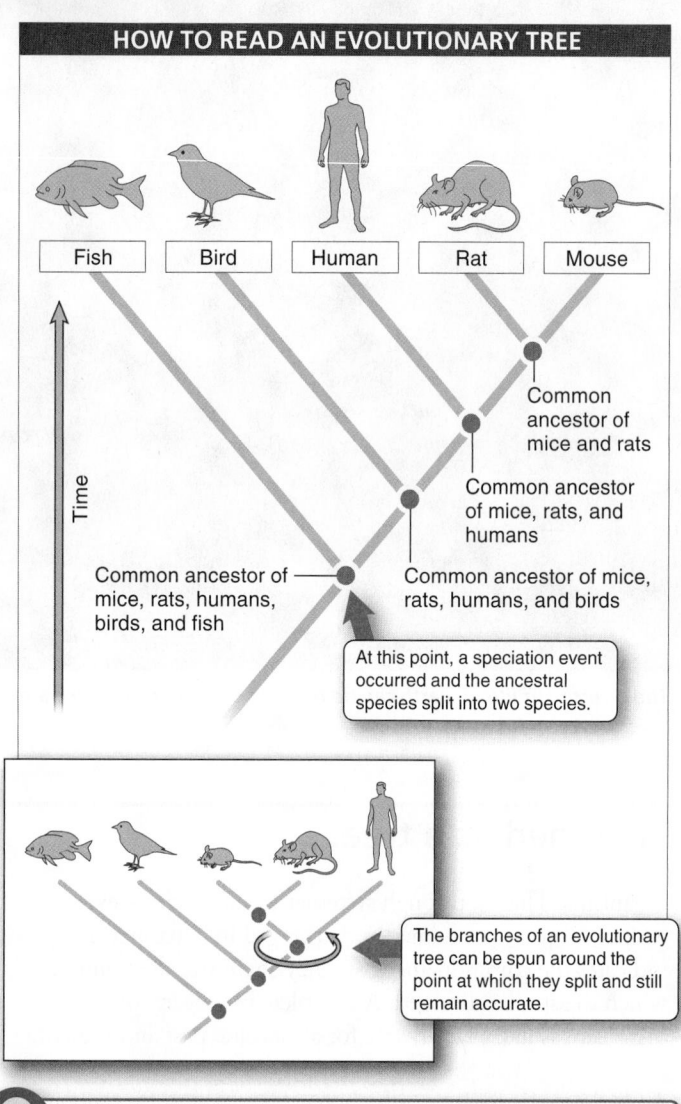

HOW TO READ AN EVOLUTIONARY TREE

Fish | Bird | Human | Rat | Mouse

Time

Common ancestor of mice and rats

Common ancestor of mice, rats, and humans

Common ancestor of mice, rats, humans, and birds

Common ancestor of mice, rats, humans, birds, and fish

At this point, a speciation event occurred and the ancestral species split into two species.

The branches of an evolutionary tree can be spun around the point at which they split and still remain accurate.

Evolutionary trees do not show which groups are more primitive or advanced, just which groups are more closely related to which other groups.

FIGURE 10-14 Mapping common ancestors. Evolutionary trees reveal the evolutionary history of species and the sequence of speciation events that gave rise to them.

information they convey about the history of life on earth. We also investigate the modern methods of molecular systematics and see how, with new molecular and DNA evidence, biologists are revising many earlier phylogenies that were based on organisms' physical features.

TAKE-HOME MESSAGE 10·7

The history of life can be visualized as a tree; by tracing from the branches back toward the trunk, we can follow the pathway back from descendants to their ancestors. The tree reveals the evolutionary history of all species and the sequence of speciation events that gave rise to them.

10·8 Evolutionary trees show ancestor-descendant relationships.

Many human traditions have a sacred "Tree of Life." The bodhi tree that the Buddha sat beneath to achieve the ultimate truth is the Tree of Enlightenment; the apple tree in the Garden of Eden is the Tree of Knowledge. The history of the relationship between all organisms that constitute life on earth is another tree of life.

The trunk and branches of an evolutionary tree represent ancestor-descendant relationships that link living organisms with all life that has ever existed on earth. The evolutionary tree of life can be thought of as one giant tree, but as a

practical matter, biologists often study only particular branches. These branches can be illustrated as big trees or little trees and can be expanded to include whatever organisms the biologist is studying: the tree might, for example, include all animals or just the rodents.

In evolutionary trees, it does not matter on which side of the tree you put a particular group of organisms. Any branches can be spun around the **nodes** at which they split (see Figure 10-14). This pinwheel effect means that you cannot assume that rats are more evolutionarily advanced than mice, or vice versa. They are equally advanced in the sense that both groups derived from the same speciation event.

> **Are humans more advanced, evolutionarily, than cockroaches? Can bacteria be considered "lower" organisms?**

Q Evolutionary trees tell us many things, but one thing they do not tell us is which groups are most "primitive" and which are most "advanced." This property of phylogenetic trees can serve to undermine some of our most sacred beliefs, such as the one that humans are the pinnacle of evolution. Many trees can be drawn to support this idea, including Figure 10-14. But notice that if you rotate this tree around any one of its nodes, you can get a number of different trees.

What trees do tell us is which groups are most closely related to which other groups. One of the most interesting revelations of "tree thinking" is that—despite appearances—fungi, such as mushrooms, yeasts, and molds, are more closely related to animals than to plants (**FIGURE 10-15**). We investigate this surprising fact in Chapter 11.

> *"We all should know that diversity makes for a rich tapestry, and we must understand that all the threads of the tapestry are equal in value no matter what their color."*
>
> — MAYA ANGELOU,
> in *Wouldn't Take Nothing for My Journey Now,* 1993

Biologists use the term **monophyletic** to describe any group in which all of the individuals are more closely related to each other than to any individuals outside that group. Monophyletic groups are determined by looking at the nodes of the trees. For example, birds and crocodiles, taken together, compose a monophyletic group because they share a more recent common ancestor (designated by node A in **FIGURE 10-16**) than either group shares with lizards or mammals. Lizards and crocodiles, taken together, do not compose a monophyletic group, because their common ancestor (at node B) is also shared by birds. But birds, crocodiles, and lizards, all taken together, *do* compose a monophyletic group, by virtue of all three sharing the common ancestor at node B. Similarly, birds, crocodiles, lizards, and mammals also compose a monophyletic group.

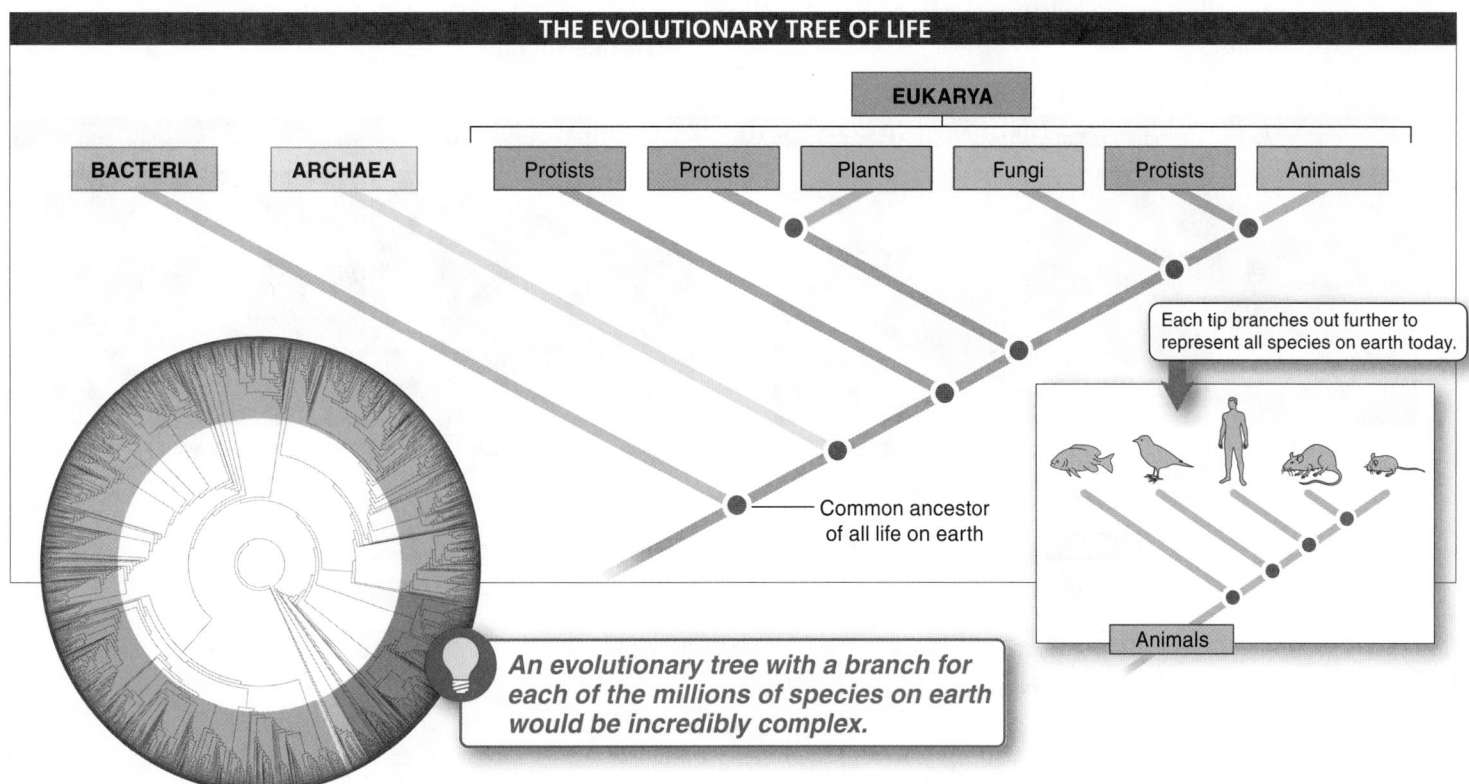

FIGURE 10-15 A growing tree. The evolutionary tree of life has branches with millions of tips representing all species on earth. As speciation events occur, new branches are added to the tree.

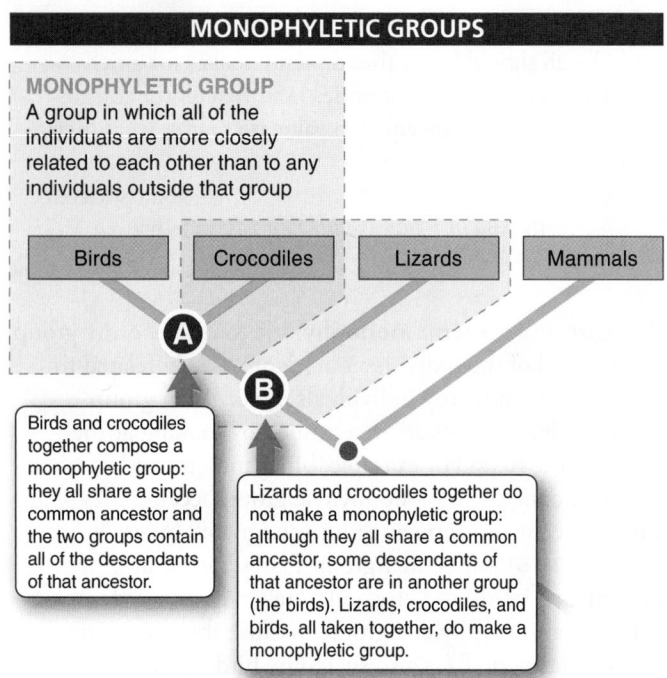

MONOPHYLETIC GROUPS

MONOPHYLETIC GROUP
A group in which all of the individuals are more closely related to each other than to any individuals outside that group

Birds | Crocodiles | Lizards | Mammals

A

B

Birds and crocodiles together compose a monophyletic group: they all share a single common ancestor and the two groups contain all of the descendants of that ancestor.

Lizards and crocodiles together do not make a monophyletic group: although they all share a common ancestor, some descendants of that ancestor are in another group (the birds). Lizards, crocodiles, and birds, all taken together, do make a monophyletic group.

FIGURE 10-16 Members of a monophyletic group share a common ancestor, and the group contains all of the descendants of that ancestor.

Notice also that in Figure 10-15, the **protists** (or "Protista"), a kingdom of mostly single-celled eukaryotes, are not actually a monophyletic group, contrary to original expectations.

Constructing evolutionary trees by comparing similarities and differences among organisms

Reading an evolutionary tree reveals which groups are most closely related and approximately how long ago they shared a common ancestor. But how are evolutionary trees—which might hypothesize historical events, such as the cat-dog split, that happened 60 million years ago—constructed in the first place?

Until recently, these trees were assembled by looking carefully at numerous physical features of species and generating tables that compared these features across the species. **FIGURE 10-17** is a simple example of such a table, showing a clear split between the characteristics of the lion and the hyena, on the one hand, and those of the wolf and the bear, on the other. For most of the 20th century, biologists classifying organisms would often use 50 or more traits to generate a tree.

Then, beginning in the 1980s, biologists began using molecular sequences rather than physical traits to generate evolutionary trees. The rationale for this approach is that organisms inherit DNA from their ancestors and so, as species diverge, their DNA sequences also diverge, becoming increasingly different. As more time passes following the splitting of one species into two, the differences in their DNA sequences become greater. By comparing how similar the DNA sequences are between two groups, it is possible to estimate how long ago they shared a common ancestor (**FIGURE 10-18**).

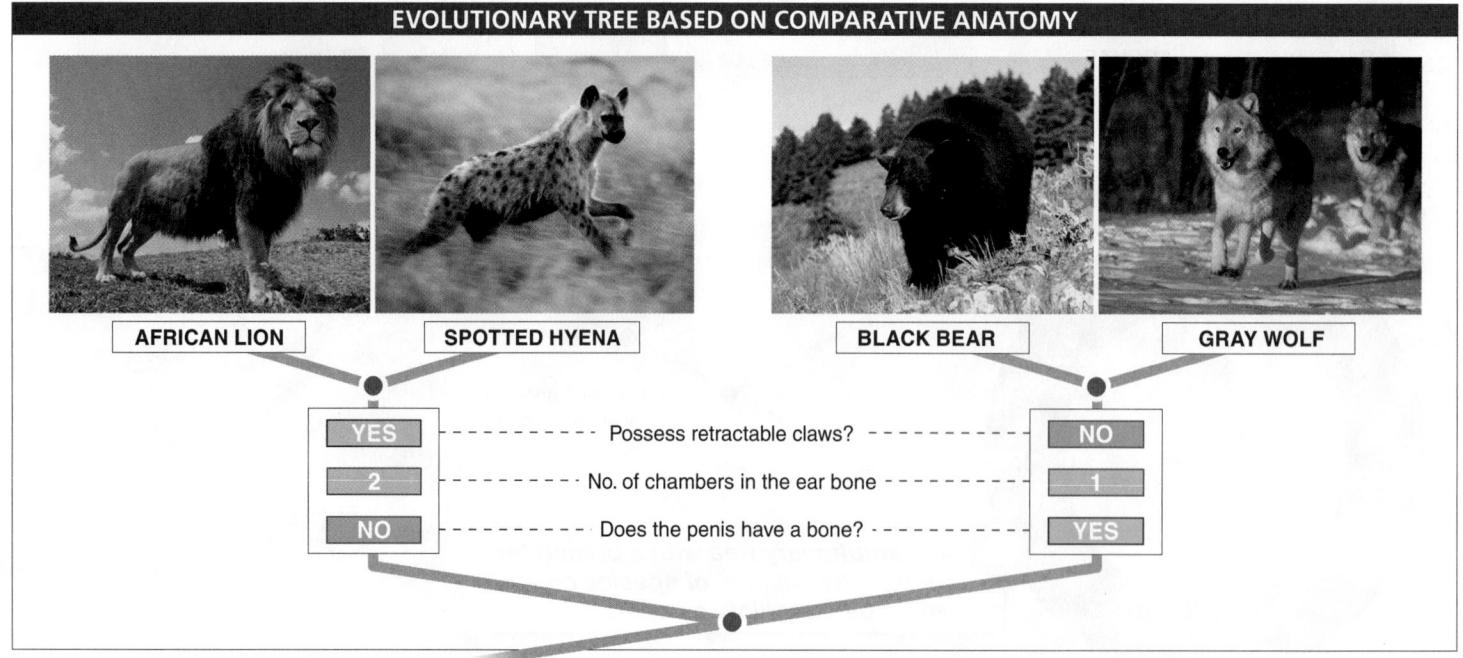

EVOLUTIONARY TREE BASED ON COMPARATIVE ANATOMY

AFRICAN LION | **SPOTTED HYENA** | **BLACK BEAR** | **GRAY WOLF**

YES	Possess retractable claws?	NO
2	No. of chambers in the ear bone	1
NO	Does the penis have a bone?	YES

FIGURE 10-17 Looking for clues in body structures. Before DNA sequencing became available, physical features of species were used to determine evolutionary relatedness.

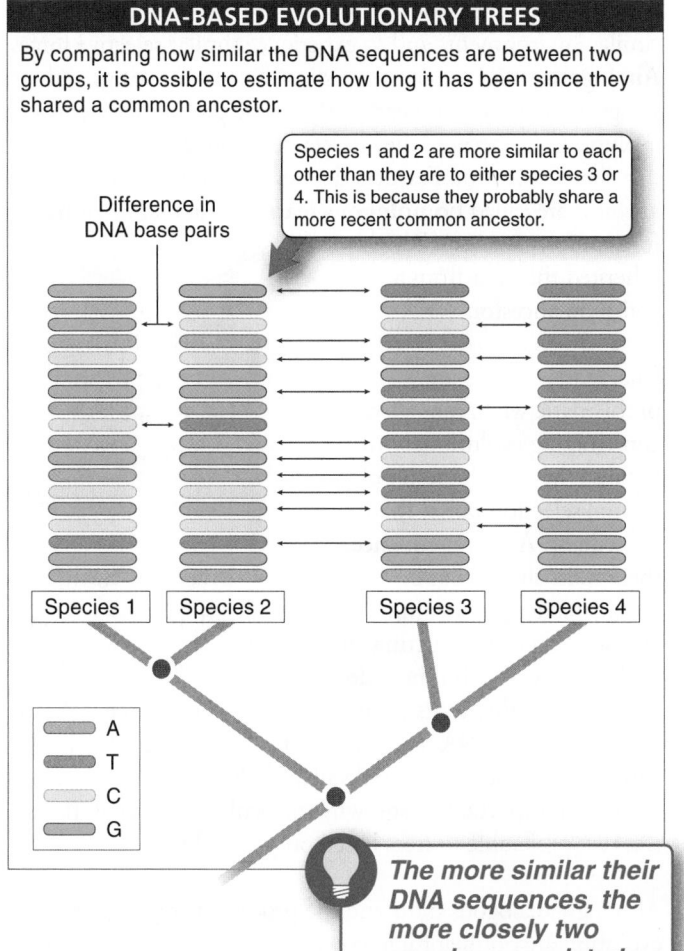

DNA-BASED EVOLUTIONARY TREES

By comparing how similar the DNA sequences are between two groups, it is possible to estimate how long it has been since they shared a common ancestor.

Difference in DNA base pairs

Species 1 and 2 are more similar to each other than they are to either species 3 or 4. This is because they probably share a more recent common ancestor.

Species 1   Species 2   Species 3   Species 4

- A
- T
- C
- G

The more similar their DNA sequences, the more closely two species are related.

FIGURE 10-18 DNA sequences reveal evolutionary relatedness.

In theory, the construction of evolutionary trees using DNA sequences is not really different from using physical traits. Each DNA base pair can be thought of as a "trait," and many, many more such "traits" can be compared.

Although most evolutionary trees are now produced by using molecular sequence comparisons, when it comes to actually naming species we still use Linnaeus's system, assigning a species name and fitting the new species within the other categories such as kingdom, class, and family. This can be difficult, because there is no objective way to assign groups above the level of species—for example, deciding whether multiple genera should be grouped in the same or different families, or whether multiple families should be grouped in the same or different orders.

TAKE-HOME MESSAGE 10·8

Evolutionary trees constructed by biologists are hypotheses about the ancestor-descendant relationships among species. The trees represent an attempt to describe which groups are most closely related to which other groups.

10·9 Similar structures don't always reveal common ancestry.

Whales and sharks have fins; bats and many insects have wings. Do bats have wings because they are most closely related to insects and inherited their wings from a common, winged ancestor, or did insects' and bats' wings evolve independently? As the evolutionary tree in **FIGURE 10-19** makes clear, insects' wings and bats' wings evolved independently—an adaptation that arose separately on more than one occasion.

The mapping of species' characteristics onto phylogenetic trees provides us with the story of evolution. Before the 1980s, biologists had tried to decode the process of evolution by comparing physical features of organisms. Then, with the advent of methods for comparing DNA sequences, tracing the history of life on earth became a more rigorous science. Let's look at a case that illuminates why the original methods were weaker (**FIGURE 10-20**).

Initially, biologists thought that African golden moles belonged in the order known as insectivores, which includes shrews, hedgehogs, and other moles. This belief seemed reasonable because the moles have many characteristics in common with these other animals: they are small, they have long, narrow snouts, their eyes are tiny, and they live in underground burrows. Biologists thought that this group of characteristics evolved just once, and that all species in the insectivore order possessed these characteristics because they inherited them from a common ancestor.

Recent evidence from DNA sequencing, however, surprised everyone who studies these animals. The DNA evidence reveals that African golden moles are more closely related to elephants than to the insectivores, including all of the other mole species! Why do they look so similar to the insectivores? Because of a phenomenon called **convergent evolution,**

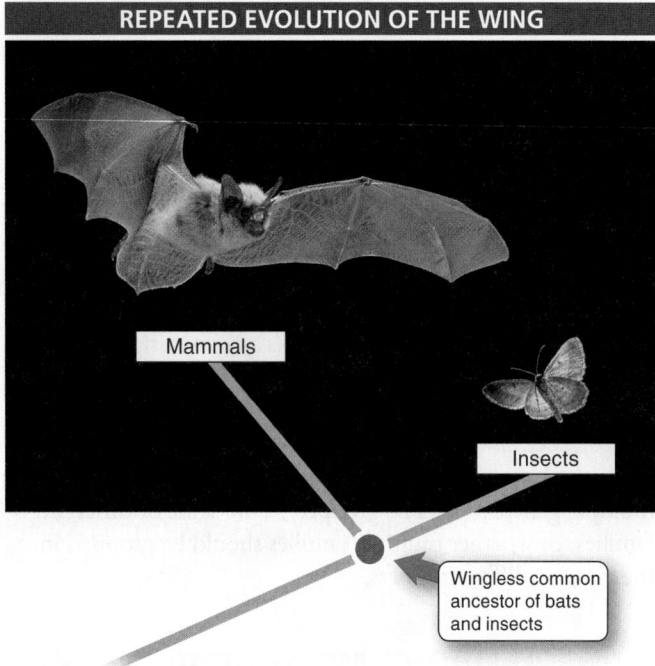

REPEATED EVOLUTION OF THE WING

Mammals

Insects

Wingless common ancestor of bats and insects

Bats and insects share a wingless common ancestor, proving that bat and insect wings evolved wings independently.

FIGURE 10-19 Because wings are an adaptation that has evolved independently many times in populations living in similar environments under similar selective pressures, the presence of wings does not necessarily indicate evolutionary relatedness.

Common shrew

African golden mole

African elephant

The African golden mole resembles a shrew, but DNA sequence comparisons reveal that it is more closely related to an elephant.

FIGURE 10-20 Looks can be deceiving. Which two of these three animals are more closely related? Can you tell just by looking?

which occurs when populations of different organisms live in similar environments and so experience similar selective forces. **Analogous traits** are characteristics (such as bat wings and insect wings) that are similar because they were produced by convergent evolution, not because they descended from a common structure in a shared ancestor. Features that are inherited from a common ancestor are called **homologous features.** All mammals have hair, for example, because they inherited this trait from a common ancestor.

Analogous features are problematic when biologists are constructing evolutionary trees, because they are the result of natural selection rather than relatedness. As a consequence, these traits should not be considered a sign of common ancestry when constructing an evolutionary tree. But how do we know whether traits are homologous or analogous? Through DNA analysis. DNA sequences do not become similar during convergent evolution, so molecular phylogenies cannot be fooled. This is an important reason why molecular-based evolutionary trees are preferable to trees based on physical features.

Q Humans have several fused vertebrae at the bottom of their spinal cord that look like a tiny, internal "tail." Are we evolving a tail or losing a tail?

Although analogous traits and the process of convergent evolution are not helpful in constructing evolutionary trees, that doesn't mean they are useless to biologists. Far from it. Convergence provides some of the best evidence for the power of natural selection. For example, from the 19th to the 20th centuries in industrialized parts of Europe, a large number of distinct butterfly and moth species became darker and darker. This change was not the result of their sharing a common ancestor, but instead came about because industrialization had caused an accumulation of dark soot on the bark of many trees. This soot accumulation caused light-colored moths and butterflies to stand out against the background when they landed on trees, making them an easier target for predators than dark-colored individuals. As a consequence, natural selection led to a rapid evolution of body color, with many species converging on a darker coloration at the same time.

TAKE-HOME MESSAGE 10·9

Evolutionary trees are best constructed by comparing DNA sequences among organisms rather than comparing physical similarities, because convergent evolution can cause distantly related organisms to appear closely related, but it doesn't increase their DNA sequence similarity.

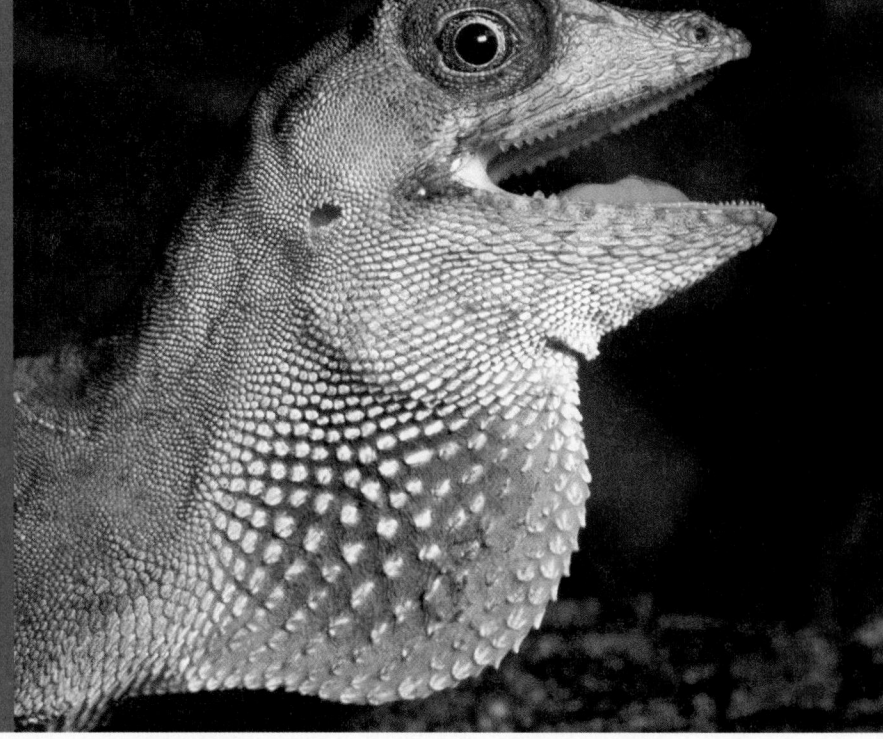

10·10–10·13
Macroevolution gives rise to great diversity.

More than 400 Anolis lizard species exist. (Shown here: A blue-throated anole, Anolis chrysolepsis, from Ecuador.)

10·10 — Macroevolution is evolution above the species level.

When water runs over rocks, it wears them away. The process is simple and slow, yet powerful enough to have created the Grand Canyon. To be sure, water running over rocks does not always make a Grand Canyon. Nonetheless, no additional physical processes are necessary. The process of evolution has a lot in common with a stream of water running over rocks: in the short term, it produces small changes in a population, yet the accumulation of these changes over the long term can be "canyonesque" (**FIGURE 10-21**). Let's consider some examples.

The production of 200-ton dinosaurs from rabbit-size reptile ancestors. The diversification from a single species of flowering plants into more than 230,000 species. These large-scale examples, which are the products of evolutionary change involving the origins of entirely new groups of organisms, are referred to as **macroevolution.** These examples can be contrasted with phenomena involving changes in allele frequencies in a population—referred to as **microevolution**—such as the increase in milk production in cows during the first half of the 20th century, or the gradual change in the average beak size of birds with changing patterns of rainfall (**FIGURE 10-22**).

These micro and macro events might seem like two very different processes, but they are not. Evolution, whether at the micro or macro level, is one thing only: a change in allele frequencies over time. In the short term, over one or a few generations, evolution can appear as a slight and gradual change within a species. But

No additional processes necessary! Just as a stream of water running over rocks can create the Grand Canyon, accumulated microevolutionary changes can lead to dramatic macro-evolutionary changes.

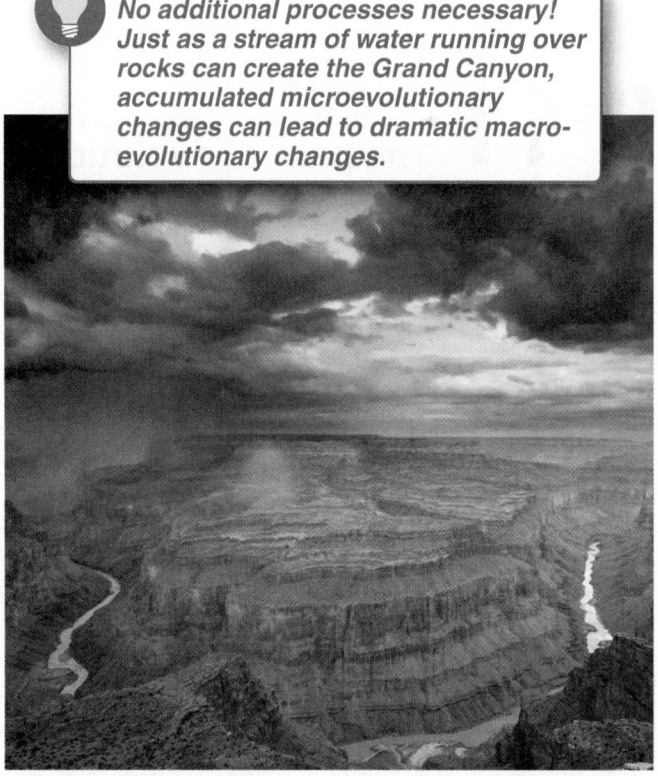

FIGURE 10-21 From a trickle of water to the Grand Canyon. The Grand Canyon is a product of small changes to the landscape occurring over millions of years.

EVOLUTION: MICRO vs. MACRO

Evolution is one thing only: a change in allele frequencies within a population. But over time, these changes can lead to new species and groups of species that vary tremendously.

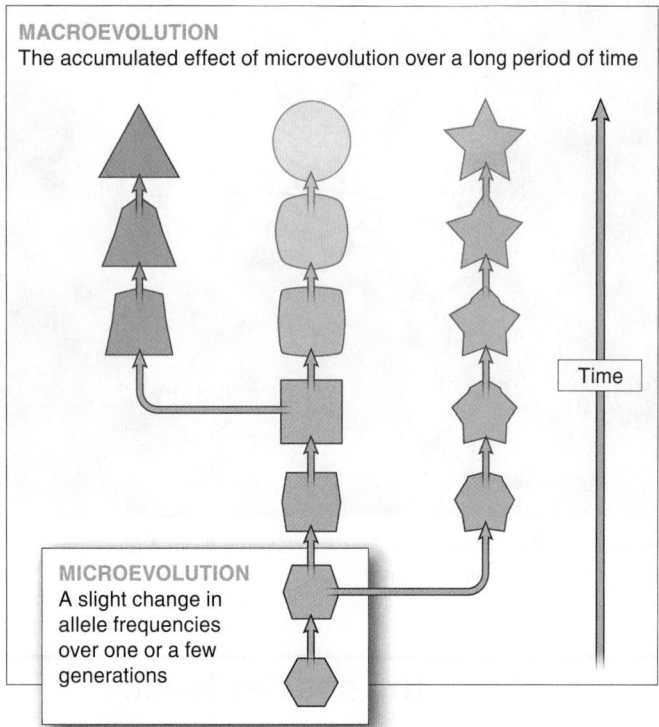

MACROEVOLUTION
The accumulated effect of microevolution over a long period of time

Time

MICROEVOLUTION
A slight change in allele frequencies over one or a few generations

FIGURE 10-22 The scale of evolution. Microevolutionary changes in allele frequencies in a population over time can lead to macroevolution, changes on a grand scale, including vast diversification of species.

over a longer period of time, the accumulated effects, acting continuously and combined with reproductive isolation of populations, can lead to the dramatic phenomena described as macroevolution. Just as a trickle of water, given enough time, produced the Grand Canyon, so evolution has created the endless forms of diversity on earth. In a sense, microevolution is the process and macroevolution is the result.

TAKE-HOME MESSAGE 10·10

The process of evolution—changes in allele frequencies within a population—in conjunction with reproductive isolation is sufficient to produce speciation and the rich diversity of life on earth.

10·11 The pace of evolution is not constant.

If you listened in on some scientists debating their research, you might hear one side describing "evolution by jerks" and the other side making light of "evolution by creeps." They're not gearing up for a fight out in the schoolyard. They're just debating the pace of evolution.

The traditional model of how evolutionary change occurred was that populations changed slowly but surely, gradually accumulating sufficient genetic differences for speciation—hence the phrase "evolution by creeps." Spurred on by findings from the fossil record that do not always support this view, however, researchers have come to believe that evolution may often occur in a different way: brief periods of rapid evolutionary change immediately after speciation, followed by long periods with relatively little change—hence "evolution by jerks." This newer view of the pace of evolution, in which long periods of relatively little evolutionary change are punctuated by bursts of rapid change, is called **punctuated equilibrium** (**FIGURE 10-23**).

In nature, we can find examples of both gradual change and the irregular pattern of punctuated equilibrium. For many groups of organisms, such as many mollusks and mammals, there are a lot of fossils for a particular species and they reveal that it seems to have persisted with little change for very long periods of time. Then, a large number of newer mollusk or mammal fossils appear in the fossil record that are similar enough to the older fossils that they seem to be in the same evolutionary lineage, yet there are no fossils representing the gradual transition between the newer and older fossils. For other groups, such transitional fossils do exist. For example, very complete sets of fossils reveal the transitional sequence from fox-like ancient terrestrial mammals to modern whales.

Punctuated equilibrium has erroneously been portrayed as a "problem" for evolutionary biology, for two primary reasons. First, it is mistakenly believed that the rapid evolutionary changes of punctuated equilibrium are the result of some new mechanism of evolution—thus seeming to undermine

The pace of evolution varies for different species. Some species have evolved gradually over time, while others spend vast amounts of time with little change.

GRADUAL CHANGE
Evolution by creeps: The pace of evolution occurs gradually in incremental steps.

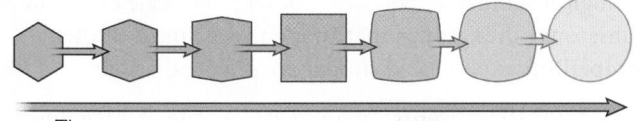

Time

PUNCTUATED EQUILIBRIUM
Evolution by jerks: Long periods of relatively little evolutionary change are punctuated by bursts of rapid change.

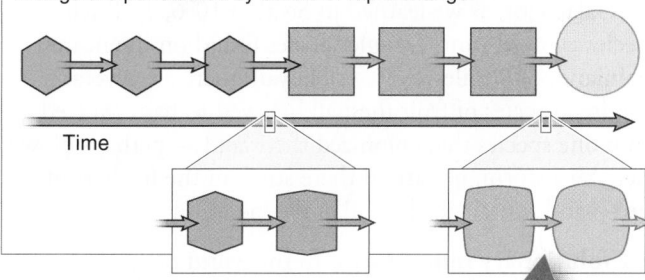

Time

Even though this period of rapid evolutionary change may cover only 1% of the species' evolutionary history, it still may cover hundreds or thousands of generations. This could take tens of thousands of years in a primate or a matter of months in bacteria.

FIGURE 10-23 The pace of evolution can be rapid or slow.

evolutionary theory. In actuality, although the punctuated change appears lightning-fast on a geological time scale, the per-generation rates of change necessary to produce it are relatively slow and not at all beyond the rates of change that have been measured in evolving populations.

Second, the existence of "gaps" in the fossil record seems to imply that the transitional species did not exist—again seeming to contradict evolutionary theory. To the contrary,

though, punctuated equilibrium should generate exactly the patterns found. Consider an example. In a large population, speciation is most likely to occur at the edges of the species' range. At the edges, small populations are more likely to be separated and geographically isolated from the rest of the population. The population is also likely to experience the most extreme selective pressures at the edges of its range, where the habitat differs most from the rest of its range and may represent the edge of the species' ecological tolerance. This border region is where speciation and rapid evolutionary change are most likely to occur. But because the individuals there represent only a tiny fraction of all the individuals in the population, they will make up only a tiny fraction of the fossil record.

In the end, there is no single rate at which evolution occurs across all species. Some species have spent vast periods of time with little change at all. The coelacanth species of fish, for example, seems to have undergone almost no physical changes over more than 300 million years. Other species have clearly changed gradually, over time, for their entire evolutionary history. For any organisms, the rate of evolutionary change depends on the selective forces acting on the population. Strong and directional forces may act over long periods of time and lead to rapid change, while stabilizing selection may lead to very little change.

Darwin foreshadowed the discussion about the pace of evolution in *The Origin of Species,* writing, "the periods during which species have undergone modification, though long as measured in years, have probably been short in comparison with the periods during which they retain the same form."

TAKE-HOME MESSAGE 10·11

The pace at which evolution occurs can be rapid or very slow. In some cases, the fossil record reveals long periods with little evolutionary change punctuated by rapid periods of change. In other cases, species may change at a more gradual but consistent pace.

10·12 Adaptive radiations are times of extreme diversification.

Even the greatest of success stories often owe something to a bit of luck. As mammals, it might seem that we owe a little of our success to luck. Flash back to 65 million years ago. Our mammalian ancestors had their place among the organisms on

earth, but these rodent-size, insect-eating, nocturnal creatures didn't remotely possess the dominant position we hold today. It was the dinosaurs' time, and the giant reptiles dominated the earth.

All that changed in an instant when the earth was struck by an asteroid, about 6 miles (10 km) in diameter, near what is now the eastern part of Mexico. This caused the environmental conditions on earth to change quickly and drastically. We'll explore the details of this catastrophic event in the next section, but one outcome was extreme: almost all of the dinosaur species were wiped out. Our mammalian ancestors, though, survived and found themselves living on a planet where most of their competitors had suddenly disappeared. We were in the right place at the right time.

What followed was an explosive expansion of mammalian species. In a brief period of time, a small number of species diversified into a much larger number of species, able to live in a wide diversity of habitats. Called an **adaptive radiation,** such a large and rapid diversification has occurred many times throughout history (**FIGURE 10-24**).

Three different phenomena tend to trigger adaptive radiations. After one of these events, surviving species find themselves in locations where they suddenly have access to plentiful new resources.

1. Mass extinction events. With the near-total disappearance of the dinosaurs, a world of "opportunities" opened up for the mammals. Where previously the dinosaurs had prevented mammals from utilizing resources, mammals suddenly had few competitors. Not surprisingly, the number of mammalian species increased from a very small number—perhaps a few hundred—to more than 4,000 species in about 130 genera. This happened over about 10 million years, barely the blink of an eye by geological standards. Following other large-scale extinctions, numerous other groups that suddenly lost most of their competitors experienced similar adaptive radiations.

2. Colonization events. In a rare event, one or a few birds or small insects will fly off from a mainland and end up on a distant island group, such as Hawaii or the Galápagos Islands. Once there, they tend to find a large number of opportunities for adaptation and diversification. In the Galápagos, as we learned in Section 10-6, 14 finch species evolved from a single species found on the nearest mainland, 600 miles away. In Hawaii, there are several hundred species of fruit flies, all believed to have evolved from one species that colonized the islands—perhaps blown there by a storm, or carried there stuck in the feathers of a bird—and experienced an adaptive radiation.

3. Evolutionary innovations. In the world of computers, software developers are always looking for the "killer app"— the new application so useful that it immediately leads to huge success, opening up a large new niche in the software market or greatly expanding an already-existing niche. The first spreadsheet, email program, and web browser were all killer apps. In nature, evolution sometimes produces killer apps, too. These are innovations such as the wings and rigid outer skeleton that appeared in insects and helped them diversify into the most successful group of animals, with more than 800,000 species today (more than a hundred times the number of mammalian species). The flower is another innovation that propelled an explosion of diversity and evolutionary success of flowering plants relative to the non-flowering plants, such as ferns and pine trees. Today, about 9 out of 10 plant species are flowering plants.

ADAPTIVE RADIATION

Adaptive radiation occurs when a small number of species diversify into a larger number of species. Three phenomena tend to trigger adaptive radiation.

MASS EXTINCTION EVENTS
With their competition suddenly eliminated, remaining species can rapidly diversify.

COLONIZATION EVENTS
Moving to a new location with new resources (and possibly fewer competitors), colonizers can rapidly diversify.

EVOLUTIONARY INNOVATIONS
With the evolution of an innovative feature that increases fitness, a species can rapidly diversify.

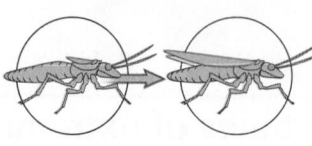

FIGURE 10-24 A rapid diversification of species.

TAKE-HOME MESSAGE 10·12

Adaptive radiations—brief periods of time during which a small number of species diversify into a much larger number of species—tend to be triggered by mass extinctions of potentially competing species, colonizations of new habitats, or the appearance of evolutionary innovations.

There have been several mass extinctions on earth.

> « Forests keep disappearing, rivers dry up, wild life's
> become extinct, the climate's ruined and the land
> grows poorer and uglier every day. »
> — ANTON CHEKHOV, *Uncle Vanya,* 1899

If the past is a guide to the future, we know this: no species lasts forever. Speciation is always producing new species, but **extinction,** the complete loss of all individuals in a species population, takes them away. Extinction, which is always occurring, is faced by all species.

For any given time in earth's history, it is possible to estimate the rate of extinctions, and the evidence reveals that these rates are far from constant (**FIGURE 10-25**). Although the details differ in most cases, extinctions generally fall into one of two categories: "background" extinctions or mass extinctions.

TWO CATEGORIES OF EXTINCTIONS

Extinctions generally fall into two categories:

● **MASS EXTINCTIONS**
A large number of species become extinct over a short period of time due to extraordinary and sudden environmental change.

● **BACKGROUND EXTINCTIONS**
These extinctions occur at lower rates during times other than mass extinctions.

FIGURE 10-25 Extinction never sleeps.

Background extinctions are the extinctions that occur at lower rates during periods other than those of mass extinctions. Background extinctions occur mostly as the result of natural selection. Competition with other species, for example, may reduce a species' size or the range over which it can roam or grow. Or a species might be too slow to adapt to gradually changing environmental conditions and becomes extinct as its individuals die off.

Mass extinctions are periods during which a large number of species on earth become extinct over a relatively short period. There have been at least five mass extinctions on earth and, during each of these extinctions, 50% or more of the animal species living at the time became extinct.

There is a fundamental difference between background and mass extinctions that goes beyond differences in rates. They have different causes. Mass extinctions are due to extraordinary and sudden changes to the environment (such as an asteroid impact). As a consequence, nothing more than bad luck is responsible for the extinction of species during mass extinctions; fit and unfit individuals alike perish.

Of the five mass extinctions during the past 500 million years, the most recent is also the best understood. Sixty-five million years ago, an almost unimaginable catastrophe occurred. A massive asteroid smashed into the Caribbean near the Yucatán Peninsula of Mexico (**FIGURE 10-26**). The impact left a crater more than 100 miles wide, and probably created an enormous fireball that caused fires worldwide, followed by a cloud of dust and debris that blocked all sunlight from the earth and disturbed the global climate for months. In the aftermath of this catastrophe, about 75% of all species on earth were wiped out, including almost all dinosaurs, a tremendously successful group that had been thriving for 150 million years. (Among the rare surviving dinosaurs were those that would become the birds.)

As bad as the dinosaur-devastating asteroid event was, from a biodiversity perspective it is not the worst catastrophe in earth's history. That distinction falls to a mass extinction that took place 250 million years ago, called the Great Dying (see Figure 10-25). Although the cause is not clear—hypotheses include an asteroid impact, continental drift, a supernova (a star explosion), or extreme volcanic eruptions—more than 95% of all marine life became extinct, along with almost 75% of all terrestrial vertebrates. The causes of the three other mass

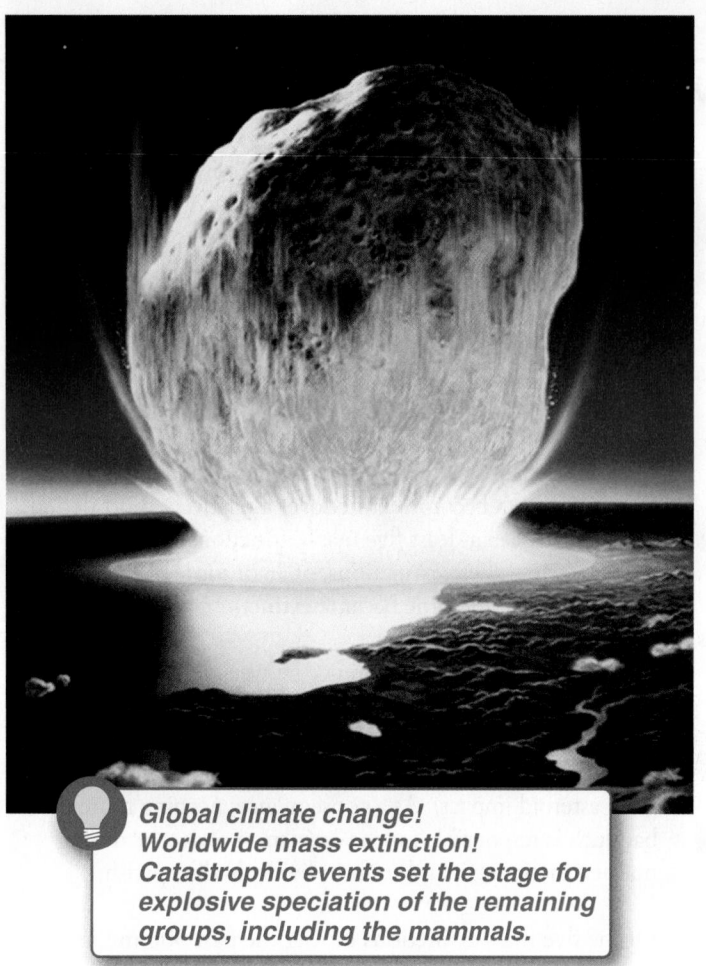

FIGURE 10-26 Catastrophic collision. Sixty-five million years ago, an asteroid 6 miles in diameter smashed into earth near the Yucatán Peninsula of Mexico and wiped out three-fourths of all species on earth, including almost all the dinosaurs.

Global climate change! Worldwide mass extinction! Catastrophic events set the stage for explosive speciation of the remaining groups, including the mammals.

extinctions also are poorly understood, but the evidence in the fossil record of the tremendous upheavals is clear.

It is interesting to note that although, from time to time, sudden and extreme events lead to mass extinctions that wipe out a large proportion of the species on earth, in every case these mass extinctions are followed by a time of explosive speciation in the groups that survive. An important question now being debated is whether we are currently in the midst of a human-caused mass extinction event. We'll explore whether this is true—and why—in Chapter 16.

TAKE-HOME MESSAGE 10·13

As new species are being created, others are lost through extinction, which may be a consequence of natural selection or large, sudden changes in the environment. Mass extinctions are periods during which a large number of species on earth become extinct over a short period of time. These events are usually followed by periods of unusually rapid adaptive radiation and diversification of the remaining species.

The flower hat jellyfish (Olindias formosa), a rare species that lives in the oceans off Brazil, Argentina, and southern Japan.

10·14 All living organisms are classified into one of three groups.

Biological diversity can be humbling. At the very least, it makes it harder to believe that humans are particularly special. We are not at the center of earth's "family tree." Nor are we at its peak. We are simply one branch.

When Linnaeus first put together his system of classification, he saw a clear and obvious split: all living organisms were either plant or animal. Plants could not move and could make their own food. Animals could move but could not make their own food. So in Linnaeus's original classification, all organisms were put in either the animal kingdom or the plant kingdom (his third, "mineral" kingdom, now abandoned, included only non-living matter).

With the refinement of microscopes and subsequent discovery of the rich world of **microbes**—microscopic organisms—the two-kingdom system was inadequate. Where did the microbes belong? Some could move, but many of those could also make their own food, seeming to put them somewhere between plants and animals. And the problems didn't stop with the microbes: mushrooms and molds, among other organisms originally categorized as plants, didn't move but they didn't make their own food either—they digested the decaying plant and animal material around them.

The two-kingdom system gave way in the 1960s to a five-kingdom system. At its core, the new system was a division based on the distinction between *prokaryotic* cells (those without nuclei) and *eukaryotic* cells (those with nuclei). The prokaryotes were put in one kingdom, where the only residents were the bacteria: single-celled organisms with no nucleus, no organelles, and genetic material in the form of a circular strand of DNA. The eukaryotes—having a nucleus, compartmentalized organelles, and individual, linear pieces of DNA—were divided into four separate kingdoms: plants, animals, fungi, and protists.

The classification of organisms took a huge leap forward in the 1970s and 1980s, and the five-kingdom system had to be discarded. Until that point, organisms had been classified primarily based on their appearance. But because the ultimate goal of classification had changed to reconstructing phylogenetic trees that reflected the evolutionary history of earth's diversity, Carl Woese, an American biologist, and his colleagues began classifying organisms by their nucleotide sequences.

Woese assumed that the more similar the genetic sequences were between two species, the more closely related they were,

THE THREE DOMAINS OF LIFE

EUKARYA

BACTERIA ARCHAEA Protists Protists Plants Fungi Protists Animals

Common ancestor of all life on earth

FIGURE 10-27 All living organisms are classified into one of three groups.

How can one molecule support the claim that all living organisms probably evolved from a single common ancestor?

and he built phylogenetic trees accordingly. The only way Woese could compare the evolutionary relatedness of all the organisms present on earth today was by examining one molecule that was found in *all* living organisms and looking at the degree to which it differed from species to species. He discovered a perfect candidate for this role: a molecule called ribosomal RNA, which helps translate genes into proteins (see Chapter 5). Ribosomal RNA has the same function in all organisms on earth, almost certainly because it comes from a common ancestor. Over time, however, its genetic sequence (i.e., the DNA that codes for it) has changed a bit. Tracking these changes makes it possible to reconstruct the process of diversification and change that has taken place.

The trees that Woese's genetic sequence data generated had some big surprises. First and foremost, the sequences revealed that the biggest division in the diversity of life on earth was not between plants and animals. It wasn't even between prokaryotes and eukaryotes. The new trees revealed instead that the diversity among microbes was much, much greater than ever imagined— particularly because of the discovery of a completely new group of prokaryotes called **archaea** (*sing.* archaeon), which thrive in some of the most extreme environments on earth and differ greatly

from bacteria. The tree of life was revised to show three primary branches, called domains: the bacteria, the archaea, and the eukarya (**FIGURE 10-27**). The domain names are often capitalized: Bacteria, Archaea, and Eukarya.

Woese put the domains above the kingdom level in the Linnaean system. In Woese's new system, which is the most widely accepted classification scheme today, the bacteria and archaea domains each have one kingdom and the eukarya domain has four. Because both bacteria and archaea are microscopic, it can be hard to believe that the two domains are as different from each other as either domain is from the eukarya. However, each of the three domains is monophyletic, meaning that each contains species that share a common ancestor and includes all descendants of that ancestor. Close inspection even reveals that the archaea are more closely related to the eukarya than they are to the bacteria.

The three-domain, six-kingdom approach is not perfect and is still subject to revision. As we saw earlier, for example, within the eukarya, the single-celled protists have turned out to be much more diverse than initially thought and, problematically, are not a monophyletic group. Increasingly, it is recognized that they should be split into multiple kingdoms. Also problematic is that bacteria sometimes engage in **horizontal gene transfer,** which means that, rather than passing genes simply from "parent" to "offspring," they transfer genetic material directly into another species. This process complicates the attempt to determine phylogenies based on sequence data, because it creates situations in which two organisms might have a similar genetic sequence, not because they share a common ancestor, but as a result of a direct transfer of the sequence from one species to another.

Are viruses alive?

Additionally, a fourth group of incredibly diverse and important biological entities, the **viruses,** is not even included in the tree of life, because they are not considered to be living organisms. Viruses can replicate, but can have metabolic activity only by taking over the metabolic processes of another organism.

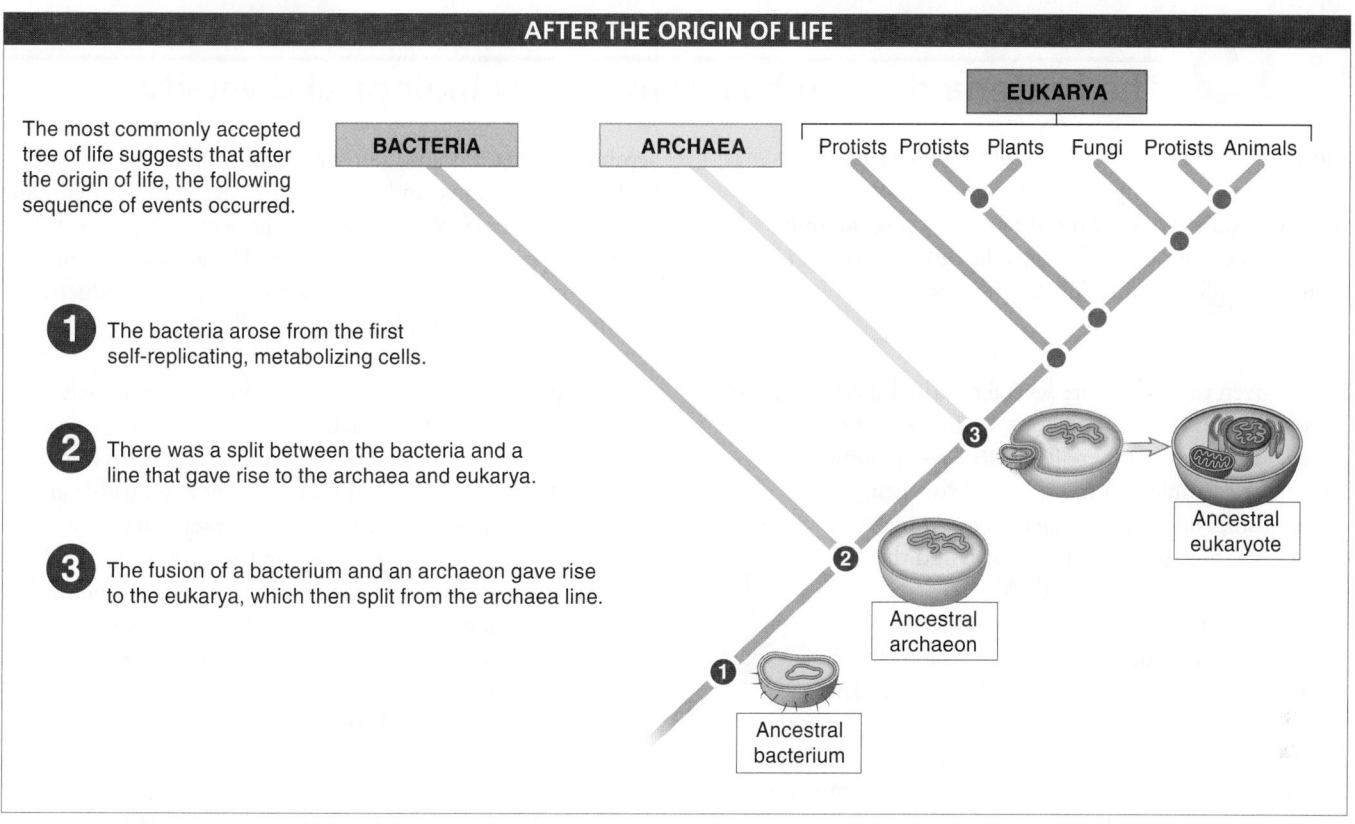

The most commonly accepted tree of life suggests that after the origin of life, the following sequence of events occurred.

1 The bacteria arose from the first self-replicating, metabolizing cells.

2 There was a split between the bacteria and a line that gave rise to the archaea and eukarya.

3 The fusion of a bacterium and an archaeon gave rise to the eukarya, which then split from the archaea line.

Ancestral bacterium

Ancestral archaeon

Ancestral eukaryote

FIGURE 10-28 From self-replicating, metabolizing cells to complex organisms. The biggest branches on the tree of life separate the three domains.

Their lack of metabolic activity puts viruses just outside the definition of life that we use in this book, but some scientists do view viruses as living.

The most commonly accepted tree of life suggests that, after the origin of life, the following sequence of events occurred (**FIGURE 10-28**).

1. The bacteria arose from the first self-replicating, metabolizing cells.

2. There was a split between the bacteria and a line that gave rise to the archaea and eukarya.

3. The fusion of a bacterium and an archaeon gave rise to the eukarya, which then split from the archaea line.

The next three sections introduce each of the three domains, surveying the broad diversity that has evolved within each domain and the common features that link all the members of each. Chapters 11, 12, and 13 cover the domains in greater detail.

TAKE-HOME MESSAGE 10·14

All life on earth can be divided into three domains— bacteria, archaea, and eukarya—which reflect species' evolutionary relatedness to each other. Plants and animals are just two of the four kingdoms in the eukarya domain, encompassing only a small fraction of the domain's diversity.

10·15

The bacteria domain has tremendous biological diversity.

Morning breath is stinky. And learning the cause of the offensive smell may make the situation even worse. You see, when you wake up, your mouth contains huge amounts of bacterial waste products. Perhaps the only consolation is that it gives us a glimpse into just how diverse and resourceful bacteria are.

At any given time, there are several hundred species of bacteria in your mouth—mostly on your tongue—all competing for the resources you put there (**FIGURE 10-29**). Some of the bacteria are aerobic, requiring oxygen for their metabolism, and others are anaerobic. At night, because the flow of saliva slows down and the oxygen content of your mouth decreases, the anaerobic bacteria get the upper hand in terms of growth and reproduction. These bacteria metabolize food bits in your mouth, plaque on your teeth and gums, and dead cells from the lining of your mouth, breaking down proteins in these materials to use as their energy source. Because proteins are made from amino acids, some of which contain the smelly chemical sulfur, their breakdown leads to the odor in the accumulating waste products.

Once you wake up, you breathe more and produce more saliva, both of which increase the oxygen level in your mouth. This tips the battle for space and food back in favor of the

Q Why is morning breath so stinky?

aerobic bacteria. Because aerobic bacteria prefer carbohydrates as their energy source and because carbohydrates don't contain sulfur, the sulfur smell goes away as the aerobic bacteria start to outcompete the anaerobic bacteria. The aerobic bacteria are, of course, also filling your mouth with waste products, it's just that their waste products don't smell as bad.

On a small scale, your mouth reveals some of the tremendous biological versatility of the bacteria: hundreds of species can live in a tiny area—a teaspoon of soil, for example, is home to more than a billion bacteria—they can thrive in a variety of unexpected habitats, they can utilize a variety of food sources, and they can survive and thrive with or without oxygen. Looking around the world, we find the clear dominance of bacteria. By any measure, it is their planet: the biomass of bacteria (if they were all collected, dried out, and weighed) exceeds that of all the plants and animals on earth. Bacteria live in soil, air, water, arctic ice, and volcanic vents (**FIGURE 10-30**). Many can even make their own food, utilizing light from the sun or harnessing energy from chemicals such as ammonia.

While the various species differ in many ways, the bacteria are a monophyletic group, sharing a common ancestor. For this reason, they all have a few features in common. All bacteria are single-celled organisms with no nucleus or organelles, with one or more circular molecules of DNA as their genetic material, and using several methods of exchanging genetic information. Because they are asexual—they reproduce without a partner, just by dividing—the biological species concept cannot be applied to bacteria when classifying them into narrower categories. Thus, bacteria are classified on the basis of physical appearance or, preferably, genetic sequences.

Many people think of bacteria as illness-causing organisms. However, although bacteria are responsible for many diseases, including strep throat, cholera, syphilis, pneumonia, botulism, anthrax, leprosy, and tuberculosis, disease-causing bacteria are only a small fraction of the domain, and bacteria seem to get less credit for their many positive effects on our lives. Consider that bacteria (*E. coli*) living in your gut help your body digest the food you eat and, in the process, make certain vitamins your body needs. Other bacteria

FIGURE 10-29 Bacteria thrive on your tongue and in your mouth.

Bacteria have a biomass greater than that of all the plants and animals on earth. They thrive in a variety of habitats including arctic ice, volcanic vents, and the human intestine.

FIGURE 10-30 **We're outnumbered.** Shown here: bacteria thriving on the bristle of a toothbrush.

(actinomycetes) produce antibiotics such as streptomycin. Still others live symbiotically with plants as small fertilizer factories, converting nitrogen into a form that is usable by the plant. Bacteria also give taste to many foods, from sour cream to cheese, yogurt, and sourdough bread. Increasingly, bacteria are used in biotechnology—from those that can metabolize crude oil and help in the cleanup of spills to transgenic bacteria used in the production of insulin and other medical products, as described in Chapter 5.

We explore the great diversity of the bacteria in more detail in Chapter 13.

10·16 The archaea domain includes many species living in extreme environments.

In a bubbling hot spring in Yellowstone National Park, the temperature ranges from the 212° F (100° C) of boiling water down to a relatively cool 165° F (74° C) at the surface. It would seem a most inhospitable place for life. Yet researchers have found 38 different species of archaea thriving there. Perhaps even more surprising, the genetic differences among these species are more than double the genetic differences between plants and animals.

In the freezing waters of Antarctica, too, archaea abound. More than a third of the organisms in the Antarctic surface waters are archaea. In swamps, completely devoid of oxygen, and in the extremely salty water of the Dead Sea, the story is the same: where once it was assumed that no life could survive, the archaea not only exist but thrive and diversify (FIGURE 10-31).

If biologists ever find themselves thinking that we have a handle on the breadth of life that is possible on earth, they

FIGURE 10-31 **Archaea can thrive in the most inhospitable-seeming places.** Archaea live in a diversity of environments; they resemble bacteria but are actually more closely related to eukarya.

Q

Will life be found elsewhere in the universe? How does the discovery of archaea alter that likelihood?

would be wise to remember the archaea. Until relatively recently, our perception of life on earth was that there were bacteria and there were eukaryotes, such as the plants and animals. But in the past several decades, as researchers have explored some of the most unlikely of habitats, they have found archaea thriving. There are entire worlds of life on earth that we never even imagined.

Analyses of genetic sequences indicate that the archaea and the bacteria diverged about 3 billion years ago and that the eukarya split off from the archaea approximately 2.5 billion years ago. The archaea are grouped in one kingdom within the domain archaea, but we have no idea how many species exist. Given that they are the dominant microbes in the deep seas, it may very well be that archaea—which we were completely ignorant of until recent decades—are the most common organisms on earth. It is still too early to tell.

We do know that, like bacteria, all archaea are single-celled prokaryotes. For that reason, under a microscope they look very similar to bacteria. Several physical features distinguish them from the bacteria, however. Specifically, the archaeal cell walls contain polysaccharides not found in either bacteria or eukaryotes. The archaea also have cell membranes, ribosomes, and some enzymes similar to those found in the eukarya.

The archaea exhibit tremendous diversity and are often divided into five groups based on their physiological features:

1. Thermophiles ("heat lovers"), which live in very hot places

2. Halophiles ("salt lovers"), which live in very salty places

3. High- and low-pH-tolerant archaea

4. High-pressure-tolerant archaea, found as deep as 4,000 meters (about 2.5 miles) below the ocean surface, where the pressure is almost 6,000 pounds per square inch (compared with an air pressure of less than 15 pounds per square inch at sea level)

5. Methanogens, which are anaerobic and produce methane

There also seem to be large numbers of archaea living in relatively moderate environments that are also commonly home to bacteria. We explore the great diversity of the domain archaea in more detail in Chapter 13.

TAKE-HOME MESSAGE 10·16

Archaea, many of which are adapted to life in extreme environments, physically resemble bacteria but are more closely related to eukarya. Because they thrive in many habitats that humans have not yet studied well, including the deepest seas and oceans, they may turn out to be much more common than currently believed.

10·17 The eukarya domain consists of four kingdoms: plants, animals, fungi, and protists.

After exploring the archaea and bacteria domains, turning to the eukarya feels like coming home. We are most familiar with this domain: all of the living organisms that we can see are eukarya. Plants, mushrooms, slime molds, insects, fish, birds, and, of course, mammals, including humans. There are three kingdoms of eukarya that can be seen with the naked eye: plants, animals, and fungi (**FIGURE 10-32**). All are made up from eukaryotic cells—they have a membrane-enclosed nucleus—and each kingdom is almost entirely multicellular.

A fourth kingdom contains the protists, which are most often invisible to the naked eye, and is a sort of grab bag

that includes a wide range of mostly single-celled eukaryotic organisms, including amoebas, paramecia, and algae. Discovery of new species of protists, as with the other microscopic organisms on earth (the bacteria and archaea), continues at a very high rate. As we noted earlier, biologists now know that the protists are not a monophyletic group and are increasingly splitting them into multiple kingdoms within the eukarya.

The eukarya split from the archaea about 2.5 billion years ago. At the time, the eukarya were single-celled and probably resembled modern protists more than they did any other modern eukarya. The split may have occurred when symbiotic

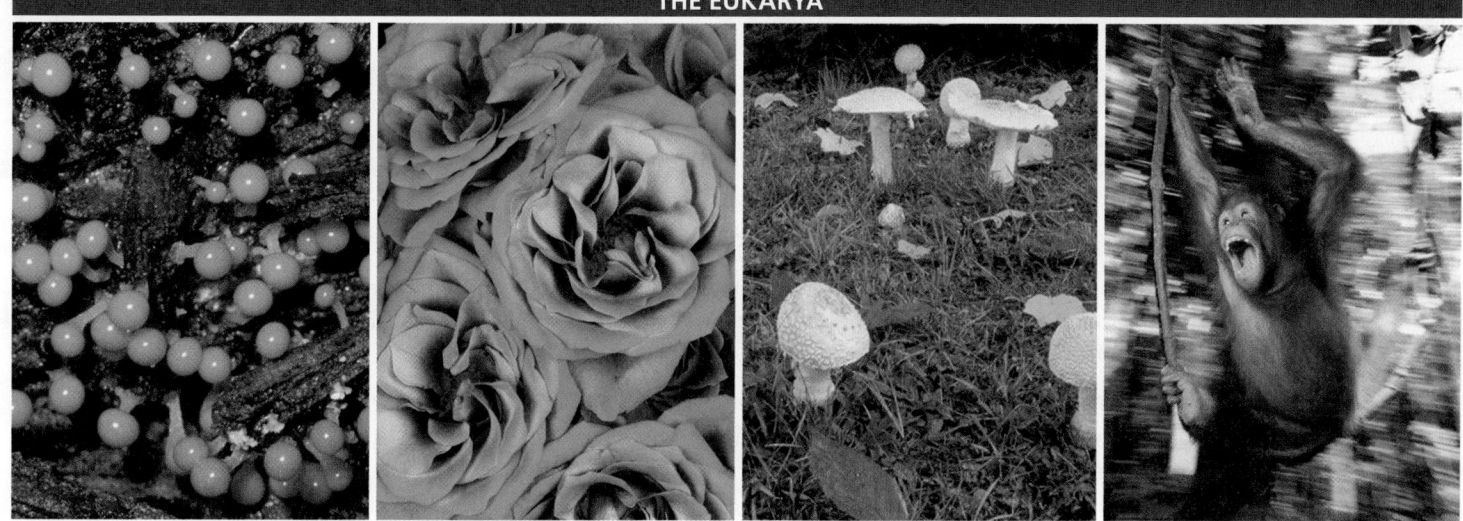

FIGURE 10-32 All shapes and sizes. The slime mold, passion flower, mushrooms, and an orangutan reflect the diversity of eukaryotic organisms.

bacteria became incorporated within an ancestor of the eukaryotes, resulting in what would become mitochondria. Later, approximately 1.5 billion years ago, a second important symbiosis between bacteria and eukarya resulted in what would become chloroplasts (see Chapter 3).

Because they are so much easier to see than bacteria and archaea, a disproportionate number of the named species on earth are in the domain eukarya. In fact, of the 1.5 million named species, the majority are eukarya, with about half being insects. This is more a result of the interests and biases of biologists than a reflection of the relative numbers of

actual species in the world. We explore the great diversity of the eukarya in Chapters 11 (on animals) and 12 (on plants and fungi).

TAKE-HOME MESSAGE 10·17

All living organisms that we can see with the naked eye (and many that are too small to be seen) are eukarya, including all plants, animals, and fungi. The eukarya are unique among the three domains in having cells with organelles.

DO RACIAL DIFFERENCES EXIST ON A GENETIC LEVEL?

In a fraction of a second, we are aware of someone's size, gender, approximate age—and race. But what is race? Does race have biological meaning? And can humans be categorized into groups that can scientifically be called races?

Q: WHAT IS RACE, BIOLOGICALLY SPEAKING? The biological species concept hinges on a straightforward question: can two individuals interbreed under natural conditions? The concept of race, conversely, is not straightforward. Some biologists have proposed that races are groups of interbreeding populations that are phylogenetically distinguishable but reproductively compatible. But it is important to note that, in humans, beyond phylogenetic distinctions, religion, culture, ethnicity, and geography are common aspects of many legal, social, and political conceptions of race. So do such social constructions of "race" reflect meaningful divisions?

Q: WHAT DO HUMAN RACIAL GROUPINGS REFLECT? Are blacks and whites genetically different? The answer is obviously yes; black-skin alleles differ from white-skin alleles. Moreover, the prevalence of some genetic diseases varies by race and ethnicity. Sickle-cell anemia, for example, is relatively common among Africans and Southeast Asians because the genes that cause it also improve a person's resistance to malaria, a disease prevalent in Africa and Southeast Asia.

Yet Africans from the southernmost part of the continent have no greater risk of sickle-cell anemia than do the Japanese, because malaria is similarly rare in both of their homelands. Should we use this trait rather than skin color when determining a person's race? If we did, southern Africans would be grouped with the Japanese and northern Africans with southern Europeans (who share their genetic resistance to malaria and the higher risk of sickle-cell anemia).

This observation reveals an important problem with racial groupings, which DNA sequence comparisons also show: *similarity in skin color between two people doesn't tell you anything about overall genetic similarity.* There is, for example, a huge variation in blood type among Africans: some are type O, some AB, others A or B. But the same goes for Asians and Turks, Russians and Spaniards. Yet we do not group people according to blood type or any other physiological and biochemical variations.

Q: WHAT IS THE FUTURE OF RACE? Racial groupings such as "Hispanic" or "black" or "Asian" do not reflect consistent genetic differences. Still, race remains an important part of individual, social, cultural, and ethnic identity for many, and its use is mandated by federal agencies. For these reasons, it will remain a powerful social construct, even as scientific consensus emerges that racial groupings do not reflect meaningful genetic distinctions.

Big Ideas in ... The Origin and Diversification of Life on Earth

10·1–10·2 Life on earth most likely originated from non-living materials.

- Under conditions similar to those on early earth, small organic molecules form that have some chemical properties of life.

- Self-replicating molecules—possibly RNA—may have acquired or developed membranes, enabling them to replicate and making metabolism possible, the two conditions that define life.

- However it came about, the earliest life, which resembled bacteria, appeared about 3.5 billion years ago, not long after the earth formed.

10·3–10·6 Species are the basic units of biodiversity.

- Species are distinct biological entities, named using a hierarchical system of classification.

- Reproductive isolation and genetic divergence together lead to speciation.

- The distinction between two species is not easily defined for all types of organisms.

10·7–10·9 Evolutionary trees help us conceptualize and categorize biodiversity.

- The history of life can be visualized as a tree; by tracing from the branches back toward the trunk, we can follow the pathway back from descendants to ancestors.

- A phylogenetic tree of life reveals the evolutionary history of every species and the sequence of speciation events that gave rise to them.

- Evolutionary trees are best constructed by comparing genetic similarities among organisms, because convergent evolution can cause distantly related organisms to appear much more closely related.

10·10–10·13 Macroevolution gives rise to great diversity.

- The process of evolution—changes in allele frequencies within a population—in conjunction with reproductive isolation is sufficient to produce speciation, diversification, and the rich diversity of life on earth.

- The pace at which evolutionary change occurs can be rapid or very slow.

- As new species are being created, others are lost through extinction, which may be a consequence of natural selection or large, sudden changes in the environment.

- Mass extinctions are usually followed by periods of unusually rapid adaptive radiation and diversification of the remaining groups or organisms.

10·14–10·17 An overview of the diversity of life on earth: organisms are divided into three domains.

- All life on earth can be divided into three domains, which reflect species' phylogeny, their evolutionary relatedness to each other.

- Bacteria have a much broader diversity of metabolic and reproductive abilities than eukarya.

- Archaea, many of which are adapted to life in extreme environments, physically resemble bacteria but are more closely related to eukarya.

- The eukarya are unique in having cells with organelles.

See the To-Go Guide (packaged with every new copy of this textbook) for an illustrated summary of the chapter.

Check Your Knowledge

GRAPHIC CONTENT

Thinking critically about visual displays of data.

1. What is the approximate rate of background extinctions over the time period shown here?

2. What distinguishes the mass extinctions from the background extinctions in this figure?

3. Why do you think the graph records the percentage of families becoming extinct rather than the percentage of species becoming extinct?

4. Why isn't the green line indicating the rate of background extinctions a straight line?

5. Rates of extinction are generally estimated based on the fossil record. Why might this not be an accurate measure of the magnitude of a mass extinction?

6. Conservation biologists believe it is important that we keep a close watch on the current rate of extinctions. Why might that be?

TWO CATEGORIES OF EXTINCTIONS

MASS EXTINCTIONS
A large number of species become extinct over a short period of time due to extraordinary and sudden environmental change.

BACKGROUND EXTINCTIONS
These extinctions occur at lower rates during times other than mass extinctions.

The Great Dying

Extinction of almost all dinosaur species (and ¾ of all species on earth)

Extinction rate (percentage of families that became extinct)

Time (millions of years ago)

See Answers at the back of the book.

Key Terms in The Origin and Diversification of Life on Earth

adaptive radiation, p. 410
allopatric speciation, p. 397
analogous trait, p. 406
archaea, p. 414
background extinction, p. 411
biodiversity, p. 388
biological species concept, p. 392
class, p. 394
convergent evolution, p. 405

domain, p. 394
extinction, p. 411
family, p. 394
genus, p. 394
homologous feature, p. 406
horizontal gene transfer, p. 414
hybrid, p. 394
hybridization, p. 397
kingdom, p. 394
life, p. 388

macroevolution, p. 407
mass extinction, p. 411
microbe, p. 413
microevolution, p. 407
microsphere, p. 391
monophyletic, p. 403
morphological species concept, p. 397
node, p. 402
order, p. 394

phylogeny, p. 401
phylum, p. 394
polyploidy, p. 398
postzygotic barrier, p. 394
prezygotic barrier, p. 394
protist, p. 404
punctuated equilibrium, p. 408
reproductive isolation, p. 392
ring species, p. 397

RNA world hypothesis, p. 390
speciation, p. 397
speciation event, p. 401
species, p. 392
specific epithet, p. 394
sympatric speciation, p. 398
systematics, p. 401
virus, p. 414

Multiple-Choice Questions

1. In a set of classic experiments performed in the early 1950s, Urey and Miller subjected an experimental system composed of H_2, CH_4 (methane), and NH_3 (ammonia) to electrical sparks. A few days later, they found _____ in their system.

   100 | HARD

   a) amino acids
   b) DNA
   c) microspheres
   d) cells
   e) RNA

   13 | EASY

2. What kind of molecule is thought to have been the first genetic material?

   100 | HARD

   a) protein
   b) DNA
   c) carbohydrate
   d) RNA
   e) microsphere

   25 | EASY

3. According to the biological species concept, species are natural populations of organisms that have the potential to interbreed and are _____ isolated from other such populations.

   100 | HARD

   a) behaviorally
   b) prezygotically
   c) postzygotically
   d) geographically
   e) reproductively

   31 | EASY

4. The classification rank that includes genera but not orders is:

   100 | HARD

   a) species.
   b) domain.
   c) class.
   d) kingdom.
   e) family.

   50 | EASY

5. Populations of *Larus* gulls around the North Pole show an unusual pattern of reproductive isolation: each population is able to interbreed with its neighboring populations, but populations separated by larger geographic distances are not able to interbreed. *Larus* gulls are an example of a(n) _____ species.

   100 | HARD

   a) ring
   b) polyploid
   c) circular
   d) Escher
   e) linked

   62

   0 | EASY

6. In animals, it is believed that the most common mode of speciation is:

   100 | HARD

   a) autopolyploidy.
   b) chromosomal.
   c) directional.
   d) allopatric.
   e) sympatric.

   54

   0 | EASY

7. Polyploidy:

   a) arises only when there is an error in meiosis resulting in diploid gametes instead of haploid gametes.
   b) is a common method of sympatric speciation for animals.

   100 | HARD

   c) arises when allopatric speciation causes plants to have fewer sets of chromosomes than their parent plants.

   46

   d) is an increased number of sets of chromosomes.

   0 | EASY

   e) always results in allopatric speciation.

8. In the plant kingdom, all of the species are descended from a single common ancestor. In terms of phylogeny, what type of tree of life is this?

   a) monophyletic

   100 | HARD

   b) uniphyletic
   c) punctuated
   d) sympatric
   e) allopatric

   27

   0 | EASY

9. Phylogenetic trees should be viewed as:

a) true genealogical relationships of species.

b) the result of vertical, but never horizontal, gene transfer.

c) intellectual exercises, not to be interpreted literally.

d) representations of allopatric speciation events.

e) hypotheses regarding evolutionary relationships of groups of organisms.

100 HARD / 34 / 0 EASY

10. The difference between microevolution and macroevolution is that:

a) they take place on different time scales.

b) macroevolution occurs with physical structures, whereas microevolution occurs with physiological traits.

c) microevolution occurs with physical structures, whereas macroevolution occurs with physiological traits.

d) microevolution has been proven, whereas macroevolution is very speculative.

e) microevolution occurs in prokaryotes, whereas macroevolution takes place among eukaryotes.

100 HARD / 47 / 0 EASY

11. The idea of punctuated equilibrium challenges which component of Darwin's theory of evolution?

a) steady change

b) gradualism

c) species stasis

d) Both a) and b) are correct.

e) None of the above is correct.

100 HARD / 45 / 0 EASY

12. Which of the following scenarios would best facilitate adaptive radiation?

a) A population of birds native to an island archipelago is forced to relocate to the mainland by a storm.

b) A population of cheetahs goes through an event in which all genetic diversity in the population is wiped out.

c) Darker-colored moths have a selective advantage over lighter-colored moths due to industrial soot on trees.

d) A population of birds becomes stranded on an island archipelago.

e) All of the above would facilitate adaptive radiation equally.

100 HARD / 78 / 0 EASY

13. The mass extinction that occurred on earth 65 million years ago was immediately followed by:

a) the rise of archaea.

b) the emergence of the first non-photosynthetic organisms.

c) the rise of the reptiles, including the dinosaurs.

d) an increase in atmospheric oxygen levels.

e) the rapid divergence and radiation of modern mammals.

100 HARD / 46 / 0 EASY

14. Prokaryotes are classified into _____ domain(s).

a) 1

b) 2

c) 3

d) 4

e) 5

100 HARD / 42 / 0 EASY

15. All protists are alike in that all are:

a) bacterial.

b) photosynthetic.

c) eukaryotic.

d) prokaryotic.

e) archaeal.

100 HARD / 42 / 0 EASY

16. Which of the following domains share the most recent common ancestor?

a) archaea and eukarya

b) bacteria and eukarya

c) archaea and bacteria

d) None of the above; all three domains evolved from different ancestors.

e) None of the above; all three domains are equally related to each other.

100 HARD / 57 / 0 EASY

17. Which of the following groups would be placed nearest the fungi in an evolutionary tree based on DNA sequences?

a) plants

b) bacteria

c) animals

d) archaea

e) protists

100 HARD / 41 / 0 EASY

Short-Answer Questions

1. Explain the difference between defining a species according to the biological species concept and according to the morphological species concept. Include an example of why one method might be more appropriate than the other for certain situations.

2. Evolutionary trees are important in helping to explain the history of life. Outline the difference between how evolutionary trees were constructed in the 20th century and how they are constructed today. Explain what types of information these trees can and cannot convey.

3. In mammals, the shape of the skull, as well as the shape and size of teeth, often reflects the method of feeding. A skull with a more rounded jaw and shorter, narrower teeth indicates a mammal that is well adapted to pulling bunches of leaves off trees and grinding them up. A skull with a more square jaw indicates a mammal adapted to grazing and cropping vegetation at the ground level. Explain how the adaptations of long, flat teeth and a more square jaw or muzzle could have triggered adaptive radiation in horses.

See Answers at the back of the book.
For additional study questions, go to www.prep-u.com.

Visibility in motion

11

Animal Diversification

11·1–11·3 Animals are just one branch of the Eukarya domain.

A scarlet macaw in flight (Ara macao), Tambopata National Reserve, Peru.

11·1

What is an animal?

Looking at a kangaroo, it's obvious that it is an animal. The same goes for a mosquito, earthworm, or jellyfish. It gets a bit more difficult, though, when you look at a sponge. Is it an animal? Or is it a plant? Or is it something else? This is when it is helpful to have some guidelines for identifying and organizing the biodiversity we can see on earth.

For the sponge, the answer is that it is classified as an animal. Here's why. When defining what is or is not an animal, we look for certain features that are common to all animals. Surprisingly, considering the enormous differences among even the few animals mentioned above, just three characteristics are generally sufficient to define **animals** (**FIGURE 11-1**).

WHAT IS AN ANIMAL?

ANIMALS EAT OTHER ORGANISMS
All animals acquire energy by consuming other organisms.

ANIMALS MOVE
All animals have the ability to move—at least at some stage of their life cycle.

ANIMALS ARE MULTICELLULAR
Animals consist of multiple cells and have body parts that are specialized for different activities.

FIGURE 11-1 Characteristics of an animal. Left to right: A garter snake eating a grasshopper, dolphins, and a nudibranch.

1. All animals eat other organisms. That is, rather than manufacturing their own food, as plants and some bacteria do through photosynthesis, animals consume plants, bacteria, other animals, fungi, or some combination of these. And because the best way to catch other organisms is to move toward them or chase after them, that brings us to the second characteristic that sets animals apart from plants.

2. All animals move—*at least at some stage of their life cycle.* That qualifying phrase is important because some animals move only during a period called the "larval stage" that comes early in their lives, and when they become adults they fasten themselves to a surface and stay there. If you visit a rocky seashore, you can find two of these animals— mussels and barnacles—living on rocks in the tidal zone. Organisms that are fastened in place, such as adult mussels and barnacles, are said to be **sessile,** but even animals that are sessile as adults moved when they were larvae.

3. All animals are multicellular, and they generally have body parts that are specialized for different activities. For example, most animals possess sensory organs (eyes, ears, nose, tongue, antennae, whiskers, and so on) that enable them to acquire information about their environment and, among other things, detect potential prey and predators.

There are a few other general features of animals—most reproduce sexually, for example—but these three are the easiest criteria to use in determining whether or not you're looking at an animal.

> **TAKE-HOME MESSAGE 11·1**
>
> Animals are organisms that share three characteristics: all of them eat other organisms, all can move during at least one stage of their development, and all are multicellular.

11·2 Four key distinctions divide the animals.

More than two-thirds of the almost two million species on earth that have been identified are animals. All of these animals share a common ancestor, an ancestral protist. (This last common ancestor to all of the animals is thought to have been a free-living unicellular organism resembling a sperm in size and shape.) With such a large number of animals to organize and identify, it is useful to divide them into a few large categories, based on their evolutionary relatedness.

Analyses of DNA and RNA sequences have helped biologists identify four major groupings into which we can classify all animals. Each of these groupings hinges on a particular adaptation and on the question of whether or not an animal has descended from an ancestor with that adaptation (**FIGURE 11-2**). At any level of classification, of course, there are additional characteristics that can be used to further subdivide and classify the animals. We'll explore many of those characteristics throughout this chapter, but first let's look at four of the key distinctions.

1. Does the animal have specialized cells that form defined tissues? If an animal has no tissues—groups of cells with a common structure and function—then it belongs to the phylum Porifera, better known as the sponges. Sponges are aggregations of similar cells, with little coordination of activities among the cells. All other animals have clearly defined tissues. Humans, for example, have

highly specialized cells such as skin cells, muscle cells, and sensory cells.

2. Does the animal develop with radial symmetry or bilateral symmetry? All animals with defined tissues develop in a shape that has some sort of symmetry: radial or bilateral. **Radial symmetry** describes animals with a body structured like a pie, such as jellyfishes, corals, and sea anemones. Slow-moving or free-floating, radially symmetrical animals have no front or back ends, and it is possible to make multiple slices, all going through the center, that divide the organism into identical pieces. In contrast, organisms with **bilateral symmetry** (such as humans, cows, and scorpions) have left and right sides that are mirror images. These animals can move adeptly, searching for food and avoiding predators.

Radial symmetry   Bilateral symmetry

Classification of animals as bilaterally or radially symmetrical is based on the pattern of symmetry seen in

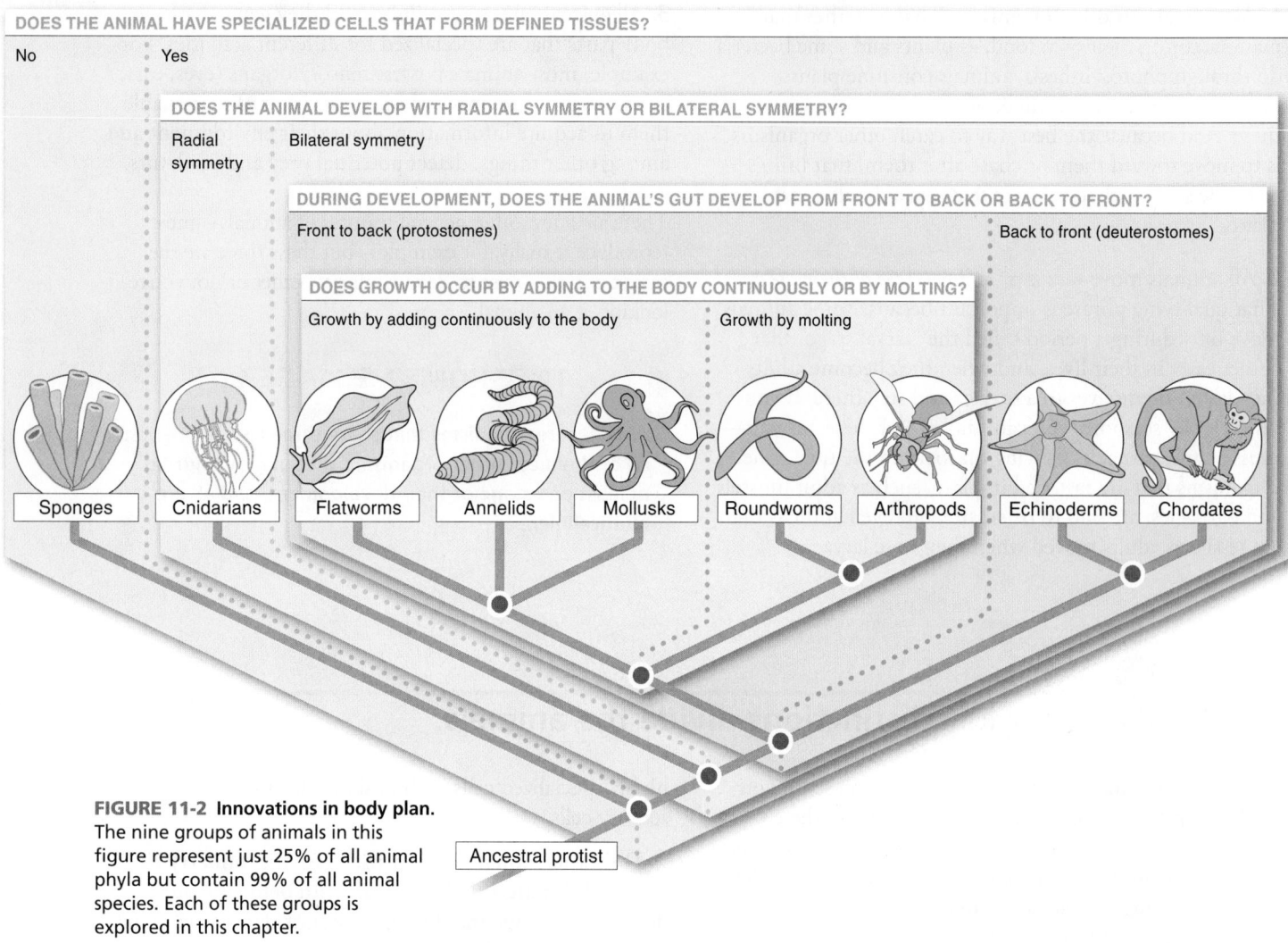

DOES THE ANIMAL HAVE SPECIALIZED CELLS THAT FORM DEFINED TISSUES?

No | Yes

DOES THE ANIMAL DEVELOP WITH RADIAL SYMMETRY OR BILATERAL SYMMETRY?

Radial symmetry | Bilateral symmetry

DURING DEVELOPMENT, DOES THE ANIMAL'S GUT DEVELOP FROM FRONT TO BACK OR BACK TO FRONT?

Front to back (protostomes) | Back to front (deuterostomes)

DOES GROWTH OCCUR BY ADDING TO THE BODY CONTINUOUSLY OR BY MOLTING?

Growth by adding continuously to the body | Growth by molting

Sponges | Cnidarians | Flatworms | Annelids | Mollusks | Roundworms | Arthropods | Echinoderms | Chordates

FIGURE 11-2 Innovations in body plan. The nine groups of animals in this figure represent just 25% of all animal phyla but contain 99% of all animal species. Each of these groups is explored in this chapter.

Ancestral protist

the embryo. As we'll see, in some animals, such as starfish, embryonic development is bilaterally symmetrical, but then the animal becomes radially symmetrical as an adult.

3. During development, does the animal's gut develop from front to back or from back to front? Early in the evolution of animals—about 630 million years ago—a major split occurred that allows us to separate the bilaterally symmetrical animals with defined tissues into two distinct lineages: the **protostomes** (which can be translated as "mouth first") and the **deuterostomes** ("mouth second"). These names refer to the way the gut develops—from front to back or from back to front. In protostomes, the gut develops from front to back, so the first opening that forms becomes the mouth of the adult animal, and the last opening becomes the anus. In deuterostomes, the gut develops from back to front. The anus is the first opening to form, and the second is the mouth. Although it's something you can see only when closely observing animals' embryonic development, the

protostome-deuterostome split is the most basic division of animals, in terms of revealing their evolutionary relatedness to one other.

4. Does growth occur by molting or by adding continuously to the skeletal elements? Among the bilaterally symmetrical animals that are protostomes, there is an important distinction between animals that molt and those that do not. Animals that molt (such as lobsters and insects) shed their exoskeleton (a hard outer layer) and replace it with a larger one at regular intervals during development. Other animals (such as clams, octopuses, cats, and humans) grow by adding to the size of their body in a continuous matter.

Although all animals share a common ancestor, the ancestral protist, these four distinctions help us identify and organize all of the approximately 36 phyla of living animals. And these four distinctions divide the animals into monophyletic groups. Recall from Chapter 10 that biologists use the term "monophyletic" to describe any group in which all of the individuals are more closely related to one another than to any individuals outside that group. Additional evolutionary transitions have occurred within the groups created by these four distinctions, allowing further categorization of animals into monophyletic groups. These categories help us understand the sequence of evolutionary events that have resulted in the tremendous animal diversity we see in the world today.

TAKE-HOME MESSAGE 11·2

The animals probably originated from an ancestral protist. Four key distinctions divide the extant animals into monophyletic groups: (1) tissues or not, (2) radial or bilateral symmetry, (3) protostome or deuterostome development, and (4) growth through molting or through continuous addition to the body.

11·3

Everything that is not extinct is evolutionarily successful.

"Never use the word higher or lower." This is a note that Charles Darwin wrote to himself in the margin as he was reading a book that proposed a theory of cosmic and biological evolution. It was an important insight, but one that can be difficult to adhere to—particularly as we turn our attention to the animals.

What is "success," evolutionarily speaking? There are two possible states for a species. It can be *extant*, meaning that it currently exists. Or it can be *extinct*. From an evolutionary perspective, every living species is successful. The fact that a species exists means it can do the things all organisms must do: find food, escape predators, and reproduce. Earthworms and tigers live very different lives, and the characteristics that work well for one species would not work at all for the other. But the earthworm is as successful at being a worm as the tiger is at being a very large cat (**FIGURE 11-3**).

Throughout his writings, Darwin emphasized adaptation among the species he described and their relationship to their environment. One species was never better or worse than another. Rather, each species was differentiated from the others, showing specializations that adapted individuals of that species to the particular niche in which they lived. Different environments posed different challenges. All extant species, as evidenced by their existence and persistence, are able to overcome those challenges.

Our tour through the animal kingdom begins with animals having a simple body plan, such as sponges, jellyfishes, and worms, continues through the more complex invertebrates, the mollusks and arthropods, and culminates in the complexity of the vertebrates—mammals (including humans), amphibians, reptiles (including birds), and fishes. Taking this path allows us to explore the major evolutionary transitions in the chronological order in which they occurred. This order does not provide any information about the relative success of any species. Nor does it imply that humans are the "crown of creation."

Although each extant species represents an evolutionary success, certain adaptations have led to the rapid and extensive diversification of particular *groups* of species. We investigate nine of the phyla with the most species (shown in Figure 11-2) and the evolutionary innovations that contributed to their success. These groups represent only a quarter of all animal phyla, but they account for about 99% of the animal species on earth today.

From an evolutionary perspective, every living species is successful.

FIGURE 11-3 Two equally successful organisms: the earthworm and the tiger.

TAKE-HOME MESSAGE 11·3

From an evolutionary perspective, all extant species are successful. Among the higher levels of taxonomic grouping, however, some groups are represented by more species than others. Of the 36 animal phyla, 9 phyla account for more than 99% of all described animal species.

11·4 Invertebrates are animals without a backbone.

Sea nettles (Chrysaora quinquecirrha) are voracious invertebrate predators of zooplankton in Atlantic estuaries (where rivers meet the ocean), such as Chesapeake Bay.

11·4

Invertebrates are the largest and most diverse group of animals.

All animals are divided into the four large categories, described in Section 11.2, which are based on patterns of evolutionary relatedness. A distinction that is perhaps more commonly used, however, is whether the animal has a backbone or not. **Invertebrates** are animals that do not have a backbone; **vertebrates** are animals that do have a backbone.

We begin our tour of the animal kingdom with the invertebrates. This group takes the prize for diversity and abundance, accounting for more than 95% of species in the animal kingdom (**FIGURE 11-4**). An example of this diversity is seen in body structure: some invertebrates (such as worms) have soft bodies, others (including snails) have soft bodies inside a shell, and still others (including insects and crustaceans such as lobsters) have a rigid external covering called an **exoskeleton.**

No invertebrate can be considered to represent the group as a whole, but the phylum Arthropoda (the **arthropods**) has the largest number of species: more than 75% of the animals on earth are arthropods. This phylum includes the most familiar invertebrates: insects, spiders, scorpions, lobsters, crabs, shrimp, and their relatives.

As "animals without backbones," the invertebrate grouping has a convenient and easy-to-apply definition, but the invertebrates are not a monophyletic group. All invertebrates are protostomes—except for one large group, whose members are all deuterostomes. Called echinoderms, and including sea stars, sea urchins, and sand dollars, this animal phylum shows the same from-back-to-front gut development as the vertebrates, and these animals are, in fact, the vertebrates' closest relatives.

The invertebrates include eight separate evolutionary lineages with an enormous diversity of body forms, body sizes, habitats, and behaviors. Sections 11-5 through 11-12 examine these lineages in detail.

TAKE-HOME MESSAGE 11·4

Invertebrates, defined as animals without a backbone, are the largest and most diverse group of animals, comprising more than 95% of all living animal species. The invertebrates are not a monophyletic group, however, and include protostomes and deuterostomes.

Orange lumpy encrusting sponge

Moon jellyfishes (cnidarians)

Liver flukes (flatworms)

Giant earthworm (annelid)

Nudibranch (mollusk)

Hookworm (roundworm)

Florida predatory stink bug (arthropod)

Peppermint sea star (echinoderm)

INVERTEBRATES

VERTEBRATES

Sponges | Cnidarians | Flatworms | Annelids | Mollusks | Roundworms | Arthropods | Echinoderms | Chordates

FIGURE 11-4 Phylogeny of invertebrates.

11·5–11·12 Across several evolutionary transitions, the invertebrate animals diversified.

The most diverse animals on earth? More than 25% of all described species are beetles. Shown here: a wood-boring beetle (Lampropepia rothschildi) from Madagascar.

11·5

Sponges are animals that lack tissues and organs.

In the natural world, we see many things that are hard to believe. Consider this: sponges (phylum Porifera) are animals. They are multicellular, they eat other organisms, and (for part of their life) they are mobile (**FIGURE 11-5**). Let's investigate this group that may be the least "animal-like," and simplest, of all the animals.

Sponges have no specialized tissues or organs, and most lack any symmetry. Despite their simplicity, however, sponges are remarkably efficient at obtaining food. Living as sessile suspension-feeders, sponges strain suspended matter and food particles from water. You can think of the anatomy of an adult sponge as a cylinder with pores in its walls. Although they have no tissues, sponges do have several different cell types. Epidermal cells—flattened, skin-like cells, connected to each other—cover the outside of the sponge. Collar cells, each of which has a long, whip-like flagellum, cover the inside. The middle layer is a gel, with embedded fibers that stiffen the sponge's body (**FIGURE 11-6**).

The beating of each collar cell's flagellum creates a current that carries water upward and out through the opening at the top of the sponge. That water is replaced by an inward flow of water through the pores on the sides of the sponge. The incoming water carries bacteria and algae, other microscopic organisms, and small particles of organic material into the sponge's body. The volume of water moving through its body daily can be as much as 20,000 times the volume of the sponge.

In the "collars" of the collar cells, sticky mucus covering the cells' thin cilia traps food particles. The cilia move these food particles inward, and some particles are taken up into the cells by endocytosis (see Section 3-11). Sponges have no circulatory systems to move nutrients from one place to another. Instead, a special kind of sponge cell, called an amoebocyte cell, picks up some of the food particles from the collar cells and moves around through the sponge's body, transferring the food particles to epidermal cells. Amoebocytes can move freely because sponges lack tight junctions (see Section 3-12) between their cells.

Sponges are hermaphrodites. That is, each individual contains both male and female reproductive organs, but it produces only one kind of gamete (eggs or sperm) at a time. Sponges that are acting as males release a cloud of sperm that swim to other sponges, which are acting as females, and fertilize their eggs. The eggs develop into larvae, which are released into the water and then drift for a few days before settling on a rock or coral outcrop and developing into a sessile adult sponge.

Sponges also reproduce asexually: small buds form on the outside of the sponge and eventually break off, settle to the bottom, and grow into new sponges. Even a piece

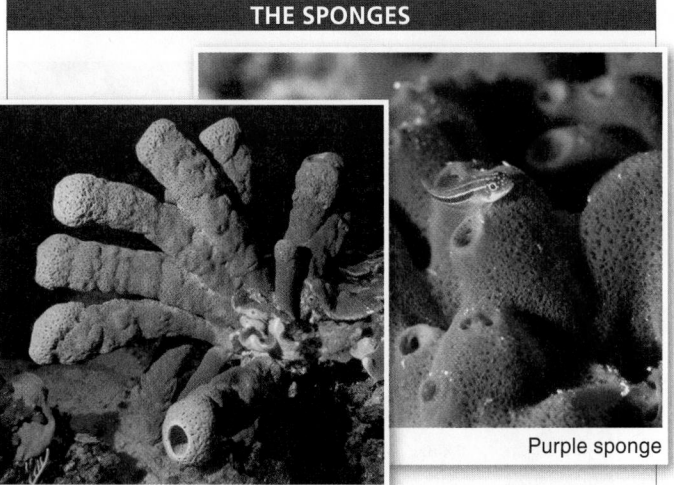

Purple sponge

Brown tube sponge

COMMON CHARACTERISTICS
- No tissues or organs
- Body consists of a hollow tube with pores in its wall
- Feed by pumping in water, along with bacteria, algae, and small particles of organic material, through their pores
- Free-swimming larvae
- Sessile as adults

MEMBERS INCLUDE
- About 5,000 species

FIGURE 11-5 An overview of the sponges.

accidentally broken off by wave action or a collision with a passing fish will grow into a new sponge. Most remarkable is the ability of sponge cells to reassemble. Picture this experiment. You put a living sponge into a food blender and puree it, then strain the liquid through a fine sieve to remove all the chunks, leaving a suspension of individual cells, which you then dump into an aquarium. Within a day you'll see small clumps of sponge forming as the individual cells move around and attach to each other when they meet, and within a week a new sponge will form. For an even more dramatic demonstration, you can repeat the experiment with two sponge species of different colors. Not only do the sponges reassemble, but the cells from each species assemble only with other cells of the same species, so you'll have two sponges, each with only the cells of its own species.

THE ANATOMY OF A SPONGE

Water — Epidermal cells
— Collar cell
— Flagellum
Pore — Amoebocyte
— Gel layer

A fist-size sponge can filter more than 1,000 gallons (5,000 liters) of water every day!

FIGURE 11-6 Sponge structure.

Because the dried skeletons of some sponges are soft and absorbent, humans have long made use of them. Sponges have been used as padding in helmets and as a tool for painting, for example. And in ancient Rome, a sponge on a stick was commonly used as toilet paper. Some true sponges are still marketed for use in personal hygiene, but these are far from living. They are just a matrix of soft, elastic fibers of a protein called spongin, isolated from dried sponges. Because over-fishing has dramatically reduced the populations of these sponges, they are not widely available. Rather, the "sponges" used in most kitchens and bathrooms today are nearly always produced from synthetic materials. Loofah sponges, contrary to their name, are made from plant material.

Q Is your kitchen sponge an animal? Is it alive?

TAKE-HOME MESSAGE 11·5

Sponges are among the simplest of the animal lineages. A sponge consists of a hollow tube with pores in its wall; it has no tissues or organs. Sponges reproduce sexually (by producing eggs and sperm) and asexually (by budding). The fertilized eggs grow into free-swimming larvae that settle and develop into sessile, filter-feeding adult sponges.

11·6 Jellyfishes and other cnidarians are among the most poisonous animals in the world.

If you feel a sting when you are swimming in the ocean, you have met a jellyfish. If you are lucky, it will be one of the thousands of species that feed on tiny floating organisms called plankton, because these species have only mild stings. If it is a species that feeds on larger prey such as fish or shrimp, however, you are definitely unlucky. These jellyfishes have powerful stings that can cause extreme pain or even death.

The jellyfishes, along with sea anemones and corals, belong to the phylum Cnidaria (pronounced nigh-DARE-ee-ah). As with all animals except the sponges, the 11,000 species in this phylum have defined tissues. The cnidarians also all have a simple body plan, with radial symmetry (**FIGURE 11-7**).

There are two types of cnidarian bodies: a sessile polyp and a free-floating medusa, which is the form most people picture when they think of a jellyfish. In some species, individuals spend part of their life cycle as a polyp and part as a medusa. Other species exist only as medusas or, as in corals and sea anemones, only as polyps.

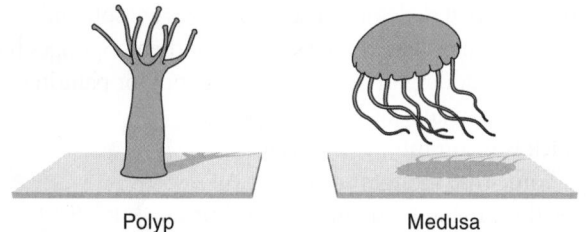

Polyp   Medusa

Cnidarians are carnivores and use their tentacles to capture and feed on a wide variety of marine organisms, from protists to fish and shellfish. Their method of capturing prey relies on a sort of weapon that is unique to the cnidarians—a stinging cell called a cnidocyst. All cnidarians have tentacles, located near their mouth, that are armed with rows of stinging cnidocysts. Each cnidocyst has a coiled thread with barbs inside and a "trigger" on the outside. When something comes in contact with the trigger, perhaps a prey item (or perhaps your leg as you swim in the ocean), the coiled thread is ejected and, like a harpoon, can penetrate the prey, often injecting a toxin (**FIGURE 11-8**). The Portuguese man-o'-war is one of the dangerously poisonous species of cnidarians. Being stung by a Portuguese man-o'-war is painful (extremely painful if the unlucky swimmer becomes entangled in the tentacles and receives hundreds of stings), but these encounters are rarely fatal.

We explore here some of the great diversity among the three major groups of cnidarians.

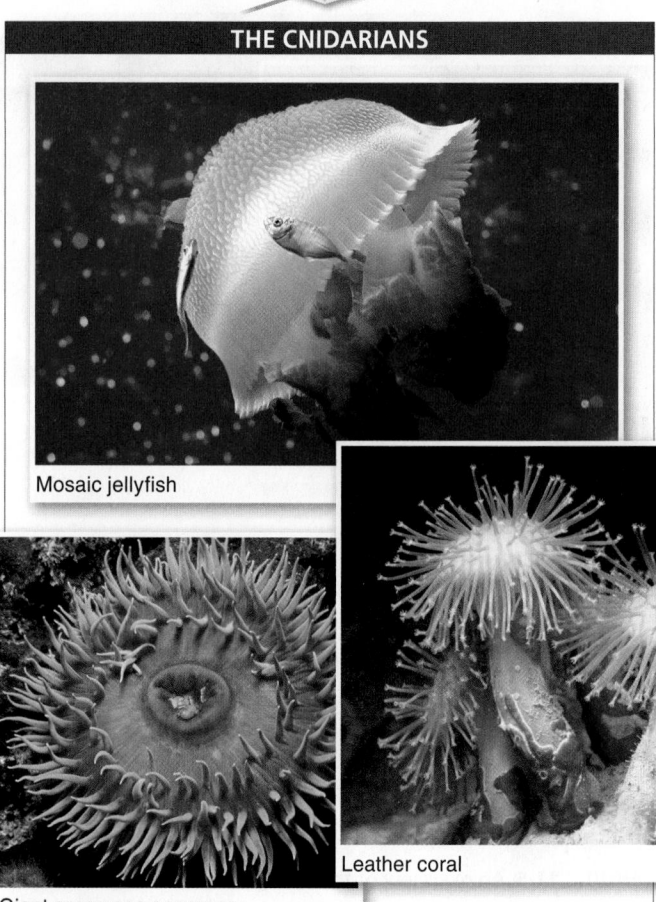

THE CNIDARIANS

Mosaic jellyfish

Leather coral

Giant green sea anemone

COMMON CHARACTERISTICS
• Radially symmetrical
• Tentacles armed with rows of stinging cells, used to paralyze prey

MEMBERS INCLUDE
• Jellyfishes
• Sea anemones
• Corals

FIGURE 11-7 Understanding cnidarians.

Corals The corals live as small (just a few millimeters) polyps in large colonial groups. Corals secrete the chemical calcium carbonate, which gives them a hard outer structure. But if you look inside this hard external structure you'll find

CNIDOCYST IN ACTION

Cnidarians capture prey using stinging cells called cnidocysts.

1 Each cnidocyst has a coiled thread with barbs inside and a "trigger" on the outside.

Coiled thread
Trigger

2 When something comes in contact with the trigger, such as a prey item, the coiled thread is ejected and can penetrate the prey, often injecting a toxin.

FIGURE 11-8 Stinging cells are used to capture prey.

animals that are soft-bodied, with stinging tentacles surrounding a mouth. Corals use the tentacles to catch small fish and plankton, which are directed into the mouth by the tentacles, then digested in the stomach. Corals most commonly reproduce sexually, with both external fertilization (releasing sperm and eggs into the water, where they can fuse and form larvae) and internal fertilization (in which only sperm are released and can fertilize eggs within female corals). Corals can also reproduce asexually.

Corals grow in a wide variety of shapes—from free-standing spherical or branched forms to crusts growing on rocks or other corals. A coral reef is a complex three-dimensional structure formed as polyps produce and secrete calcium carbonate. Coral reefs provide an environment that is home to a greater diversity of species than any other marine habitat. The Great Barrier Reef, located in the Coral Sea, off the coast of Queensland, Australia, extends more than 1,500 miles (about 2,600 km) from north to south. A truly awesome display of biological productivity, this reef is the largest biological structure in the world and is easily visible from the International Space Station.

Q

How is global warming affecting the coral reefs of the world?

Among the first casualties of global warming are coral reefs. Although coral polyps can catch prey using their cnidocysts, they obtain most of their nutrition from algae, called zooxanthellae, that live symbiotically within the polyps. Each partner contributes and receives something of value in the relationship. The algae use the carbon dioxide produced by the polyps to conduct photosynthesis, and the polyps gain oxygen and nutrients produced by the algae. Strangely, when coral polyps get too hot they expel their zooxanthellae. Because the zooxanthellae are responsible for the colors of many corals, as well as much of their nutrition, when coral polyps expel their zooxanthellae, the coral turns white—a phenomenon called coral bleaching. The zooxanthellae may return to the polyps when the water cools, but repeated bleaching events often lead to the death of the coral polyps. The world's oceans are already warming, and coral bleaching events are becoming more and more frequent (**FIGURE 11-9**).

Sea anemones The sea anemones resemble flowers, and some of the colorful species are popular additions to saltwater aquaria. The polyp form of a sea anemone looks a bit like an upside-down medusa form of a jellyfish—the tentacles with

Healthy coral

Bleached coral

With warming water, corals eject their photosynthetic symbionts, causing coral "bleaching." The polyps turn white and may die, endangering the coral reef and the diversity it supports.

FIGURE 11-9 Coral bleaching.

their stinging cells are at the top of the anemone's body, surrounding its mouth. Sea anemones have a larval stage that swims freely, then settles on a rock and metamorphoses into the adult form. Even as adults, many sea anemones can crawl a few inches a day, and wandering sea anemones are often found in seaweed.

Jellyfishes The jellyfishes (which are not fish!) range tremendously in size. The Asian giant jellyfish is more than 6 feet (about 2 m) across and weighs nearly 500 pounds (more than 200 kg). When swarms of this giant jellyfish appear, they clog the nets of fishing boats with a sticky mass of toxic stingers. At the opposite end of the size scale is the Irukandji jellyfish, about the size of a hen's egg. This species is so deadly that, in 2007, the sighting of just five Irukandji in Hervey Bay, Queensland, completely halted the filming of a major Hollywood movie (*Fool's Gold*), which had to be completed in the safety of a studio.

TAKE-HOME MESSAGE 11·6

Corals, sea anemones, and jellyfishes are radially symmetrical animals with defined tissues, in the phylum Cnidaria. All cnidarians are carnivores and use specialized stinging cells located in their tentacles to capture prey.

11·7 Flatworms, roundworms, and segmented worms come in all shapes and sizes.

It's a good thing that biologists don't run bait shops—if they did, a simple trip to buy worms for fishing would be way too complicated. The name "worm" is commonly applied to a long, skinny, slimy animal without a backbone, but you can find animals fitting that description in eight different phyla. You will never encounter most of them, and that's a good thing, because many are parasites that cause really unpleasant diseases. In this section, we consider just three phyla—**flatworms** (phylum Platyhelminthes), **roundworms** (phylum Nematoda), and **segmented worms,** or **annelids** (phylum Annelida)—that illustrate most of the diversity of the animals we call worms.

All of the worms described here have defined tissues and are protostomes—the gut develops from front to back. Unlike the cnidarians, however, the worms (along with all of the remaining animals we discuss in this chapter) develop with a body plan, characterized by bilateral symmetry, which adapts them for forward movement.

It is important to note, however, that worms do not make a monophyletic group. Their general body plan has evolved several times independently, and their evolutionary relationships are not always obvious. The segmented worms (annelids), for example, are believed to be more closely related to mollusks (including snails, clams, and octopuses) than to the roundworms. And the roundworms are believed to be more closely related to the arthropods (insects) than to either the flatworms or the segmented worms (see Figure 11-3).

Flatworms Unlike the roundworms and segmented worms, flatworms have no body cavity. That is, the space between the body wall and the digestive tract is not a fluid-filled cavity. As a consequence, the flatworms have a reduced capacity for diffusion of gases and nutrients. Like the segmented worms, but unlike the roundworms, the flatworms grow by adding body mass, rather than by molting (**FIGURE 11-10**). Flatworms have well-defined head and tail regions, with clusters of light-sensitive cells called eyespots that help them orient themselves within their environment. Most flatworms are hermaphroditic, each individual producing both male and female gametes, and they engage in both sexual and asexual reproduction. Flatworms include more than 20,000 species and can be parasites (the flukes and the tapeworms) or brilliantly colored, free-living aquatic creatures.

Although many flatworms have a digestive system, one feature of the free-living flatworms (but not the annelids or roundworms) that many humans find distasteful is that their gut has only one opening, requiring them to both consume food and eliminate undigested waste through the same opening. Tapeworms, by contrast, completely lack a digestive system; these parasitic worms live in their host's gut and absorb nutrients from the host directly through their body wall.

All 5,000 species of tapeworms are parasites, and most have a two-stage life cycle that is split between two different host species. For example, the common tapeworm that infects dogs spends the other half of its life cycle in fleas, while the human pork tapeworm splits its life cycle between pigs and humans. Tapeworms have long, flat bodies made up of repeated segments, each of which is a reproductive unit. Mature tapeworms spread by breaking off segments, which are then shed in the feces of an infected individual.

THE FLATWORMS

Tapeworm of the mammalian intestine

Liver fluke

COMMON CHARACTERISTICS
- Well-defined head and tail regions
- Hermaphroditic and can engage in both sexual and asexual reproduction
- Some have a single opening in the body, which serves as a mouth and an anus

MEMBERS INCLUDE
- Tapeworms
- Flukes

FIGURE 11-10 Overview of the flatworms.

Roundworms The roundworms, also called nematodes, are probably the most abundant animals on earth—a spoonful of garden soil contains several thousand individuals, and some species produce more than 200,000 eggs every day. Unlike segmented worms and flatworms, they grow by molting. More than 90,000 roundworm species have been named, and there may be five times as many species that have not yet been identified (**FIGURE 11-11**).

Many soil-dwelling roundworms live in the roots of plants, damaging or even killing the plant. About 15,000 species of roundworms are parasites of other animals, and roundworms are responsible for a large number of human diseases. Most roundworms are transmitted by fecal contamination of soil or food.

THE ROUNDWORMS

Root-knot nematode

Whipworm

COMMON CHARACTERISTICS
- Long, narrow unsegmented body
- Bilaterally symmetrical
- Surrounded by a strong, flexible cuticle
- Must molt in order to grow larger

MEMBERS INCLUDE
- More than 90,000 species (scientists estimate there may be five times as many species that have not yet been identified)

FIGURE 11-11 Roundworm diversity.

Tiny parasitic roundworms called *filariae* are responsible for several tropical diseases, including some that have an enormous social and economic impact in certain parts of the world. Elephantiasis, for example, is a disease in which filariae transmitted by the bite of a mosquito block the lymph ducts so that fluid accumulates in the limbs or scrotum, causing grotesque swelling. These filariae occur in

India, Africa, South Asia, Pacifica, and tropical regions of the Americas.

Segmented worms (annelids) The segmented worms, or annelids, number about 13,000 species and are easy to recognize by the grooves running around the body that mark the divisions between segments—if you've seen an earthworm, you are familiar with those grooves. The segmented worms are protostomes with defined tissues, and they do not molt. They are organized into three different groups: marine polychaetes (pronounced POL-lee-keets), terrestrial oligochaetes, and leeches (**FIGURE 11-12**).

Polychaetes are marine worms, living on the seafloor. *Polychaete* means "many bristles," and the combination of segments and bristles makes polychaetes easy to recognize. Some species burrow through the mud and extract organic material from it. Tube worms use sand grains or limestone to make a tube in which they live, with just their waving tentacles exposed. Small particles of food are trapped in mucus on the tentacles and transported to the worm's mouth.

Earthworms, which belong to the group called *oligochaetes* ("few bristles"), are the annelid worms you are most likely to have seen. The night crawler is a typical earthworm. It gets its name from its habit of emerging from its burrow on rainy nights to crawl across the surface of the ground. More than 4,000 earthworm species have been named, ranging in size from less than half an inch (about a centimeter) to the enormous length of the giant Gippsland earthworm, 7–10 feet (2–3 m)!

Earthworms are bulk-feeders—that is, as an earthworm burrows, it consumes particles of soil and organic material. The organic material is digested as it passes through the worm's gut, and the fecal material plus the inorganic part of the soil is excreted as feces, called castings. Earthworm castings are valued by gardeners as soil supplements, and an earthworm can produce its own weight in castings every day. Earthworms' activities mix the soil components, create a more even mixture of nutrients, and expedite the breakdown of organic materials in soil, thus making the nutrients available for plants. Because they perform all of these tasks, earthworms have enormous economic value to agriculture. A government study published in 2008 estimated the economic value of earthworms in Ireland alone to be more than $1 billion per year.

Have you ever waded in a pond or swamp and emerged to find a long, dark brown worm clinging to your leg? If so, you have met the third major group of annelids, the *leeches.* Probably you pulled the leech off (not an easy thing to do, because leeches are both slippery and stretchy) and threw it as

THE ANNELIDS

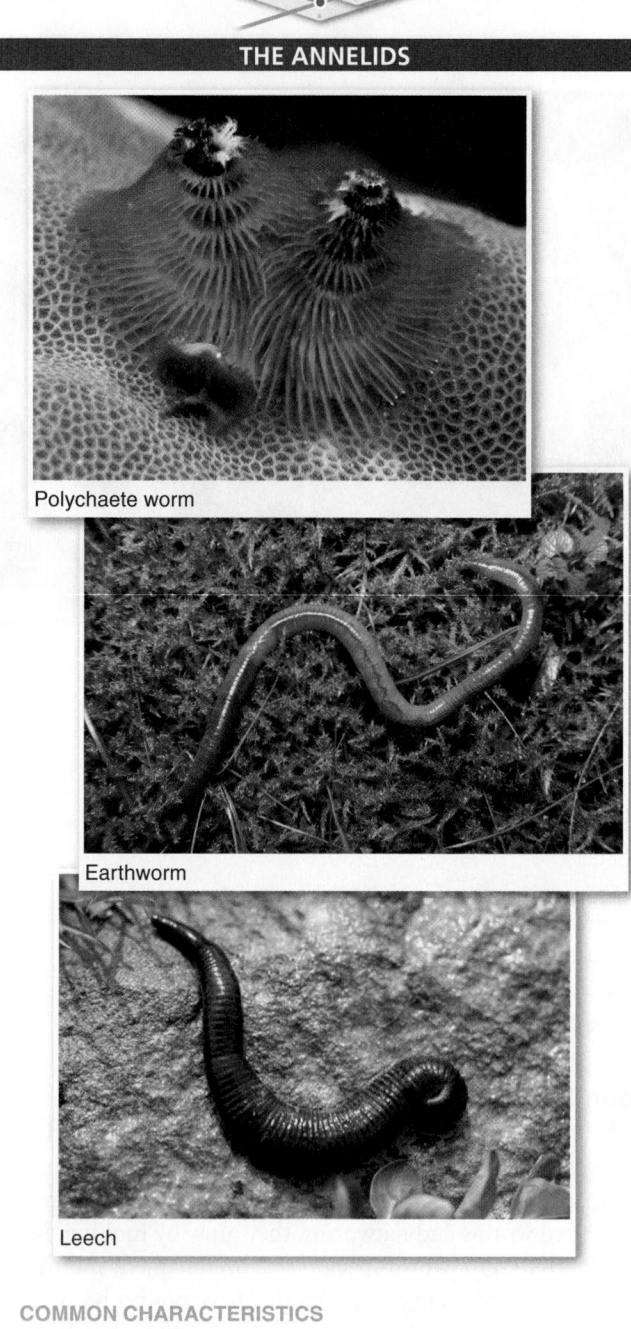

Polychaete worm

Earthworm

Leech

COMMON CHARACTERISTICS
• Segmented body

MEMBERS INCLUDE
• Marine polychaetes (about 9,000 species)
• Earthworms (more than 4,000 species)
• Leeches (about 500 species)

FIGURE 11-12 Annelid diversity.

far as you could. If you had looked at it carefully, though, you'd have noticed that, like earthworms, leeches have segmented bodies.

If you have had a close encounter with a leech, you'll also have noticed that the wound it made on your leg continued to ooze blood for several hours. That's because the saliva of blood-sucking leeches contains an anticoagulant substance that prevents blood from clotting. If the leech is undisturbed while it is feeding, blood keeps flowing and the leech inflates like a small balloon.

Not all leeches are blood-suckers—in fact, more than half the leech species are predators. The horse leech, for example, which reaches a length of 8 inches (about 20 cm), feeds on smaller annelid worms, snails, and aquatic insect larvae.

TAKE-HOME MESSAGE 11·7

Worms are found in several different phyla and are not a monophyletic group. All are bilaterally symmetrical protostomes with defined tissues. The flatworms and segmented worms (annelids) do not molt; the roundworms do. Flatworms include parasitic flukes and tapeworms, many of which infect humans. Many roundworms are parasites of plants or animals and are responsible for several widespread human diseases. Earthworms are annelids that play an important role in recycling dead plant material.

11·8 Most mollusks live in shells.

Just because they are related, organisms don't always share much physical resemblance. Consider these animals: A colossal predatory squid, more than 40 feet long, with eyes the size of beach balls and a razor-sharp beak. A small snail—*escargot* in French—from among the more than 700 million consumed in France each year. An oyster, with its nearly 2,000-year-old reputation as an aphrodisiac (unsupported by any scientific proof, it turns out). All of these are mollusks, among the most diverse groups of animals and occupying an impressive and impressively varied position within the human imagination.

More than 100,000 mollusk species have been named (and many more have not yet been named). The members of this large phylum (Mollusca) of animals live in the ocean, in fresh water, and on land and include many familiar creatures in addition to those mentioned above, including clams, scallops, mussels, and octopuses. They are so diverse that it is difficult to describe any single defining characteristic. The position of mollusks within the animal phylogeny, however, reflects several important characteristics that they all share: they have defined tissues, are bilaterally symmetrical, and are protostomes. Further, all mollusks grow by adding tissue, rather than by molting.

Several additional features are also common to many mollusks. These include a shell that protects the soft body, a mantle (the tissue that secretes calcium carbonate to form the shell), and a sandpaper-like tongue structure, called the radula, that is used during feeding.

There are three major groups of mollusks. The animals in these groups share most of the features common to mollusks, but with very different body plans: **gastropods, bivalve mollusks,** and **cephalopods** (FIGURE 11-13).

Gastropods Snails and slugs are gastropod mollusks. *Gastropod* means "belly foot," and these mollusks get their name because they have an expanded foot on the bottom of their body, which allows them to climb a vertical surface as easily as they glide across a horizontal one. Snails have a one-piece, curled shell, and slugs are snails that have reduced the shell to a tiny remnant that is not even visible because it is covered by the mantle. Found in both aquatic and terrestrial environments, snails and slugs account for three-quarters of all mollusks.

The snail's shell is its primary protection against predators, but for terrestrial slugs and sea slugs, with very little shell material, other defense mechanisms are necessary. A terrestrial slug relies on slime for defense: when a slug is attacked, it secretes slime that sticks to the predator. Worse still, anything that touches the slime coating the predator sticks to it, so a bird that attacks a slug quickly finds that its beak and face are covered by pieces of dead leaves, clods of soil, and twigs. Sea slugs have other methods of defense. Some species synthesize toxic chemicals, and others, which feed on sponges, recycle sponge toxins into their own slime. One of the most remarkable uses of another animal's defense equipment is found among sea slugs that eat sea anemones. Anemones are protected by

THE MOLLUSKS

COMMON CHARACTERISTICS
- Most have a shell that protects the soft body
- Mantle (tissue that forms the shell)
- Radula (sandpaper-like tongue structure used during feeding) Found in all mollusks except bivalves

MEMBERS INCLUDE
- Gastropods (about 35,000 species)
- Bivalves (about 8,000 species)
- Cephalopods (about 600 species)

Caribbean reef octopus (cephalopod)

Banana slug (gastropod)

Giant clam (bivalve)

Nudibranch (gastropod)

FIGURE 11-13 Mollusks: an overview.

stinging cells, and the sea slugs that eat anemones transfer some of those cells to their own skin, enabling them to sting other creatures.

Bivalve mollusks The bivalve mollusks are soft-bodied animals protected by a pair of shells hinged together by a ligament. Clams, scallops, oysters, and mussels are examples of bivalves. There are about 8,000 bivalve species and most of them live in the ocean, although there are some freshwater species. Clams spend their lives buried in mud or sand, scallops live on the seafloor, and oysters and mussels fasten themselves to underwater objects, such as rocks, the pilings that support piers, and the hulls of boats. All bivalves are filter-feeders that draw a current of water in through a tube called the "incurrent siphon," across their gills, where tiny food particles are captured, and out through the "excurrent siphon."

When a grain of sand is trapped in the shell of a bivalve, the mantle may secrete layer after layer of a shell-like protein

material that covers the sand grain and forms the iridescent gem called a pearl. Oysters are the best known source of pearls, but clams and other bivalve mollusks also form pearls.

Cephalopods The third major group of mollusks is the cephalopods (**FIGURE 11-14**). It includes 6 nautilus species and more than 600 species of squids and octopuses. The nautilus has an external shell that resembles a snail shell, except that it is not twisted. Squids have very small shells that are covered by the mantle, and octopuses have lost the shell entirely. In all these species, the tentacles appear to grow directly from the head, which explains the name: *cephalopod* translates as "head-footed."

The most obvious feature of cephalopods may be their tentacles, which they use to walk and swim and to capture prey. Squids—many of which are ferocious predators—have eight short tentacles called arms and two long, sucker-bearing tentacles that are used to capture prey. Squids are often more than 3 feet (about 1 m) long, and members of some species

SQUIDS
- 8 short tentacles and 2 long sucker-bearing tentacles
- Free-swimming
- About 300 species

OCTOPUSES
- 8 short tentacles called arms
- Bottom-dwellers, living in coral reefs and rocky coasts
- About 300 species

NAUTILUSES
- Chambered shell used for protection
- Free-swimming
- 6 species

FIGURE 11-14 Cephalopod diversity.

may exceed 40 feet (about 13 m). When a squid is in a hurry, it swims tail-end first, using jet propulsion. Water is expelled through the siphon at the tentacle end of the body, shooting the animal backward.

After a slow approach to its unsuspecting prey, a squid propels its tentacles forward with astonishing speed—accelerations of more than 800 feet (about 250 m) per second per second have been measured, the equivalent of your car accelerating from 0 to 6,000 mph in 10 seconds! The suckers on the tentacles adhere to the prey and draw it back toward the squid, where the arms take over, turning and manipulating the prey as it is bitten by the squid's sharp beak and pulled into the mouth by the tongue-like radula.

Octopuses, which can have tentacles that spread 12 feet (about 4 m), are bottom-dwellers that live in coral reefs and on rocky coasts. Because they have completely lost the shell, octopuses can squeeze through astonishingly small openings,

and their ability to escape from even carefully covered tanks is a perpetual challenge for the keepers of zoos and aquaria. Keepers are accustomed to arriving in the morning and finding an octopus wandering around the room.

In the next section we further explore the cephalopods and consider the question of whether their skills of manual dexterity make them the smartest of the invertebrates.

TAKE-HOME MESSAGE 11·8

Mollusks are protostome invertebrates that do not molt. They are the second most diverse phylum of animals and include snails and slugs, clams and oysters, and squids and octopuses. Most mollusks have a shell for protection, a mantle of tissue that wraps around their body, and a specialized tongue called a radula.

11·9 Are some animals smarter than others?

Squids and octopuses are wide-ranging predators that must locate, capture, and subdue other animals so they can eat them. This is a far more active lifestyle than that of bivalves or snails, and it requires quick movements and rapid responses to stimuli. All of these features are conspicuous

elements of the behavior of an octopus as it moves through a coral reef, inserting a tentacle into every opening. In fact, as an expert multi-tasker, an octopus can capture a prey item with one of its tentacles, use a second tentacle to hold something else, and still keep the remaining six tentacles in

FIGURE 11-15 An octopus attempts to open a jar.

motion, searching for more prey. In addition, octopuses are very good at manipulating things with their tentacles. It doesn't take a captive octopus long to learn how to unscrew the top on a glass jar to reach a fish that's swimming inside—after all, that's just a minor variation on twisting a clam to open it (**FIGURE 11-15**).

Q **Are octopuses smart?**

Because of their manipulative skills and easily observed exploratory behavior, octopuses are sometimes featured on TV shows and in magazine articles, where they are often described as the smartest invertebrates and their intelligence compared to that of mammals. But this is the sort of claim that must be viewed skeptically.

What is intelligence, after all? The concept of intelligence loses its meaning when animals that live in completely different worlds and respond to entirely different stimuli are compared. We can say that octopuses are very good at doing the things that octopuses need to do—searching for prey, capturing it,

and manipulating it, all within their marine environment, for example. But is following a complex sequence of actions the same thing as intelligence? Spiders, for example, construct elaborate webs that are strategically placed in the flight paths of insects; they detect the impact of an insect on the web and rush out to wrap the insect in silk before it can escape. Does that require more or less intelligence than opening a glass jar to eat a fish? And what about the red squirrels of northern Europe? Every fall they hide more than 3,000 acorns, cones, and nuts, then recover more than 80% of their hidden nuggets of food over the course of the winter. A human probably couldn't manage that.

If intelligence is defined, in part, as the ability to do some problem-solving task valued by humans, the concept of "intelligence" may actually be relevant only to humans. Applying the question of intelligence to non-human species may just be an assessment of how well they can accomplish tasks that are essential to their survival. For this reason, questions of comparative animal intelligence are not generally useful. Rather, animals' abilities should be considered as evolutionary responses to particular selective pressures imposed by their environment, and the fact that a species currently survives should be taken as an indication of some mastery of its particular niche. As stated earlier in this chapter, from an evolutionary perspective, any species alive today must be considered a success.

TAKE-HOME MESSAGE 11·9

The predatory behavior of octopuses involves exploration and manipulation, behaviors often considered as intelligent by humans. But the concept of intelligence cannot be applied objectively to other species, which have evolved in response to the selective forces at work in their own particular niches.

11·10 An external skeleton and metamorphosis produced the greatest adaptive radiation ever.

When it comes to species diversity, the insects take the cake, outnumbering all other forms of life. Flies, alone, comprise 90,000 species; bees, wasps, and ants number 150,000 species; and butterflies and moths, 120,000 species. But even those numbers are dwarfed by beetles, with 320,000 species! To put it in perspective, there are more species of beetles than there are species of plants, and nearly six times as many species of

beetles as there are species of all birds, mammals, fishes, amphibians, and reptiles combined.

All of these insects belong to the phylum of arthropods (Arthropoda), which contains protostome invertebrates that have a segmented body (i.e., with a distinct head, midsection, called the thorax, and abdomen), an external skeleton (called an exoskeleton) made of a stiff carbohydrate known as chitin, and legs with joints (think of all the joints in a lobster's claw). The four major lineages of arthropods are:

- Arachnids (including spiders, mites, ticks, and scorpions)

- Crustaceans (including lobsters, crabs, shrimp, and barnacles)

- Millipedes and centipedes

- Insects

In all, the phylum contains almost one million recognized species, or approximately 75% of all animal species and 60% of *all species* on earth (**FIGURE 11-16**). Taken together, there are more than a billion billion (1 followed by 18 zeroes) arthropods alive at any given time! And about 80% of these are insects. (Put another way, on earth, right now, there are more than 150 million insects for every single human.)

Insects and other arthropods have diversified so much that arthropod species of one kind or another thrive in nearly every habitat on earth. Insects, in particular, abound in terrestrial habitats (every species of plant, for example, is eaten by at least one insect species) and in fresh water, and crustaceans thrive across marine habitats. If diversification is a measure of evolutionary success, the arthropods are unmatched.

Two characteristics of insects that have been central to their success are flight and the way they cope with the change in body size as they grow. With flight, insects are able to avoid many predators and can efficiently search for food and for mates. Flight also enables organisms to more quickly leave one location and disperse to another that is potentially more hospitable.

Most arthropods have a modular body plan and a rugged exoskeleton, to which their muscles are attached. Like a suit of armor, the exoskeleton provides excellent protection from injury and predators. It also helps individuals conserve water and resist drying out. One challenge associated with having an exoskeleton, however, is that it prohibits

Mammals get bigger and bigger the more they eat. Why don't insects?

THE ARTHROPODS

COMMON CHARACTERISTICS
- Segmented body with a distinct head, thorax, and abdomen
- Exoskeleton made of chitin
- Jointed appendages

MEMBERS INCLUDE
- Insects (more than 800,000 species)
- Arachnids (about 60,000 species)
- Crustaceans (about 52,000 species)
- Millipedes and centipedes (about 10,000 species)

Elephant hawk moth (insect)

Blue millipede

Spiny orb-weaver spider (arachnid)

Hermit crab (crustacean)

FIGURE 11-16 Arthropod diversity: insects, millipedes and centipedes, arachnids, and crustaceans.

Arthropods make up about 75% of the animal species on earth.

---

growth. Many arthropods, including most insects, overcome this constraint with a process of growth (shared by the roundworms, of phylum Nematoda) that is very different from the pattern seen in other animals, such as mammals. Their life is divided into three completely different stages (FIGURE 11-17).

1. Larva. An egg hatches into a **larva** (*pl.* larvae), which looks completely different from the adult form. A caterpillar is the larval stage of a butterfly or moth, and a grub is the larval stage of a beetle. A larva's job is to eat and grow large enough to enter the next life stage, the pupa. Larvae are able to grow by passing through numerous stages (usually 4–8) in which they shed their exoskeleton, increase in size, and develop a new, slightly larger exoskeleton, in the process of molting.

2. Pupa. Eventually, a larva completely covers itself with a casing. Covered by the case—which has different names (such as cocoon or chrysalis) in different insect groups—the insect is now called a **pupa.** In the pupa, genes are activated that code for the adult body form, and the proteins that made up the larva are broken down to amino acids, which are recycled to synthesize adult proteins and reassembled into the adult form. This rebuilding process is called **metamorphosis,** from two Greek words meaning "change

of form." The entire process requires several days, and by the end of the pupal stage, the adult insect is curled tightly inside the pupal case. The pupal case then splits and the adult squirms out. While inside the pupal case, the wings of butterflies and moths are tightly folded; once freed, they require time to expand and stiffen before the adult is ready to fly.

3. Adult. When the **adult** form hatches, it is at its full size. Insects do not grow after they emerge from their pupae—for this reason, some adults do not even eat. Rather than eating and growing, the job of an adult insect is reproduction.

The developmental process called **complete metamorphosis,** which includes these three stages, allows the larva and adult to act as if they were animals from different species, each optimized to perform very specialized tasks. Caterpillars eat leaves, for example, and spend their entire larval period on a single plant. In contrast, butterflies feed on nectar that they collect by flying from flower to flower. As a larva, the animal feeds and grows. As an adult, it reproduces. The genes that control the larval body form are different from the genes that determine the adult form, so natural selection can act on the larval and adult stages independently.

METAMORPHOSIS

COMPLETE METAMORPHOSIS

Complete metamorphosis is the division of an organism's life history into three completely different stages (occurs in 83% of insect species).

LARVA
An egg hatches into a larva, which eats (and eats), growing as it molts several times until large enough to enter the pupal stage.

PUPA
The larva encloses itself in a case, body structures are broken down, and new structures are assembled into the adult form.

ADULT
The adult emerges from the pupa and no longer grows. Its primary function is to reproduce.

INCOMPLETE METAMORPHOSIS

Incomplete metamorphosis is the pattern of growth and development in which an organism does not pass through separate, dramatically different life stages (occurs in 17% of insect species).

 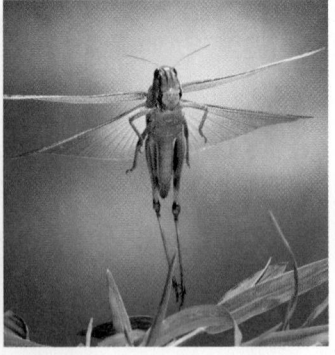

NYMPH
An egg hatches into a nymph, resembling a small version of the adult (but without wings or reproductive organs), growing as it molts several times.

ADULT
Upon reaching adult size, the nymph stops molting and the adult forms.

 The separation of life stages has contributed to the enormous ecological diversity of insects.

FIGURE 11-17 From larva to adult monarch butterfly. Some insects have a life history divided into unique stages, each with a distinct purpose.

About 83% of insect species have complete metamorphosis, and this separation of the life stages has been an important factor in helping insects diversify into nearly 20 times as many named species as vertebrates. Among those insect species that do not undergo the dramatic changes of complete metamorphosis, typically the eggs hatch as nymphs (the juvenile form), and resemble a smaller version of the adult. These juveniles do not have wings or reproductive organs, but they live in the same habitats as adults and eat the same foods. They then undergo several molts as they grow, and stop molting when they reach adult size. This pattern of growth and development is called **incomplete metamorphosis,** and it occurs in grasshoppers and cockroaches, among many other species.

TAKE-HOME MESSAGE 11·10

The arthropods are protostome invertebrates, and with nearly one million species (and probably at least as many more yet to be identified), they outnumber all other forms of life in species diversity. The ability to fly and the development of a body with a rugged exoskeleton have contributed to the enormous ecological diversity of insects. The life cycle of most insects includes a larval stage that is devoted to feeding and growth, a pupal stage during which metamorphosis occurs, and an adult stage in which the insect reproduces.

11·11 Other arthropods include arachnids, crustaceans, millipedes, and centipedes.

The arthropod phylum is so large that, even if we excluded all the insects, it would still contain more species than any other phylum. In this section we survey the other major groups of arthropods: the millipedes and centipedes, the crustaceans, and the arachnids (**FIGURE 11-18**).

Millipedes and centipedes The names *millipede* and *centipede* translate to "a thousand feet" and "a hundred feet" and refer to the enormous numbers of legs on these long, skinny animals. They don't really have a thousand—or even a hundred—feet, but millipedes do have more legs than

centipedes, and that is the easiest way to tell them apart. Millipedes and centipedes have long, segmented bodies that seem almost worm-like, but their jointed legs and hard exoskeletons are characteristics of arthropods. Both live among fallen leaves, especially in forests where the leaf litter layer is usually cool and moist. Millipedes feed on decaying plant material, while centipedes are predators that use fangs equipped with venom to kill insects and even snakes and small mammals. Unlike spiders and scorpions (which liquefy their prey for easy digestion), centipedes use their jaws to tear prey into pieces that are small enough to swallow.

GROUPS OF ARTHROPODS

Japanese slave-making ant

Giant desert centipede

A jumping spider

Sally Lightfoot crab

INSECTS
- Three pairs of walking legs
- Legs are located on the thorax
- Life cycle consists of separate life stages

MILLIPEDES AND CENTIPEDES
- Many pairs of legs (two pairs per segment in millipedes; one pair per segment in centipedes)
- Long, segmented body

ARACHNIDS
- Usually four pairs of walking legs
- Legs are located on the thorax
- Specialized mouthparts
- Predators

CRUSTACEANS
- Many pairs of legs
- Usually five pairs of appendages that extend from the head
- Mostly aquatic

FIGURE 11-18 Exploring the arthropods.

Arachnids There are 60,000 species of arachnids, land-dwelling arthropods that include spiders, scorpions, mites, and ticks. Most have four pairs of walking legs and a specialized feeding apparatus. Arachnids are distinguished from other arthropods by the positioning of their legs: they have legs only on the middle section of their body (the thorax), whereas other arthropods have legs on the posterior section of their body (the abdomen) as well as on the thorax.

Arachnids are predators. Many spiders construct webs by spinning silk fibers (which consist of interconnected protein molecules). Orb-weaving spiders construct intricate spiral-shaped webs that trap (and sometimes even lure) flying insects. Spiders generally place their webs across the routes followed by flying insects, such as between plants, and when an insect gets trapped in the web, run out to wrap the prey in silk threads. Other spiders produce tangled webs, commonly called cobwebs, or funnel-shaped webs.

When a spider captures prey, it uses its fangs to inject venom that contains two types of enzymes. The first set of enzymes disrupts the prey's nervous system and paralyzes it, then other enzymes dissolve its internal organs. When the prey's innards have liquefied, the spider sucks out the contents.

The venom of most spiders is usually harmless to animals as large as humans, but two North American spiders are dangerous. The black widow spider is easily identified by a red hourglass marking on the bottom surface of the female. The brown recluse spider lacks distinctive markings, so it is harder to identify—but it is more dangerous. Both species are likely to move indoors, constructing webs in little-used spaces such as closets and cabinets and behind furniture. Brown recluse bites can create open wounds that can last for months or years and sometimes require repeated skin grafts to close.

Scorpions look dangerous to humans, but their sting is no worse than a bee's. Scorpions are lethal to insects, hunting them at night They seize prey with their claws and use their stinger only if the prey struggles. Some of the scorpion's mouth structures are covered with spines that grind the prey, while glands secrete enzymes that liquefy it and the scorpion sucks up the soup.

Crustaceans If arachnids are the most feared arthropods, the aquatic crustaceans—lobsters, crayfish, crabs, and shrimp—may be the most desirable arthropods, at least at meal time. In the United States, the top three fishery crops, by annual market value, are shrimp, crabs, and lobsters. There are about 52,000 species of crustaceans, and although crustaceans can look very different—from sessile barnacles to mobile, tiny krill—they have one feature in common: five pairs of appendages extending from the head. Three of these appendages are used for feeding, and two are antennae that sense the environment.

Crustaceans have many pairs of legs, and their legs are modified for many purposes. Shrimp and barnacles (which are essentially shrimp that spend their adult lives within a shell, fastened to a rock) have legs with comb-like projections that they use to capture plankton. Free-living crustaceans (shrimp, crabs, lobsters) have modified limbs in the abdominal region that are used to hold eggs or newly hatched young.

Although most crustaceans are aquatic, the inconspicuous wood lice (also known as pill bugs, sow bugs, or roly-polies) are terrestrial forms that you can find when you turn over a rock in your garden. Wood lice are herbivores and play an important role in recycling dead plant material.

> ### TAKE-HOME MESSAGE 11·11
>
> Centipedes are predators with fangs that inject venom, and millipedes are herbivores that feed on dead plant material. Spiders and scorpions are predatory arthropods that eat insects and, occasionally, small vertebrates. Lobsters, crabs, shrimp, and barnacles are predatory marine crustaceans.

11·12 Echinoderms are vertebrates' closest invertebrate relatives and include sea stars, sea urchins, and sand dollars.

Appearances can be deceiving. Sea stars and other members of the phylum Echinodermata live in the oceans, are radially symmetrical (as adults), and are covered by spiny plates. And yet, because they are deuterostomes (their gut forms from back to front), it turns out that they are more closely related to humans than to any other invertebrate group. Echinoderms stand as an example of how classifying organisms based on evolutionary relatedness rather than physical similarity can reveal a great deal about the force of natural selection and its dramatic effects on body form in adapting populations of organisms to their environment.

The echinoderms include about 6,000 species of marine animals, most of them enclosed by a hard skeleton beneath an

THE ECHINODERMS

Leather sea star

Sand dollar

Club sea urchin

Sea cucumber

COMMON CHARACTERISTICS
- Enclosed by a hard skeleton under spiny skin
- Larvae are bilaterally symmetrical and share some anatomical features with chordates
- Adults are radially symmetrical
- Undersides are covered with tube feet that aid in locomotion and grasping

MEMBERS INCLUDE
- Sea stars (about 1,600 species)
- Sea urchins and sand dollars (about 940 species)
- Sea cucumbers (about 1,100 species)

FIGURE 11-19 What is an echinoderm?

outer covering of spiny plates (**FIGURE 11-19**). Adult sea stars (starfishes and brittle stars), probably the most recognizable echinoderms, have five or more appendages evenly distributed around their body circumference. They are radially symmetrical and have no front or back ends. They move with equal ease in any direction, and their sensory organs are distributed around their circumference. Adult sea urchins and sand dollars don't have projecting arms, but they are also radially symmetrical.

Although radial symmetry is characteristic of adult echinoderms, their larvae are bilaterally symmetrical, having a left and right side of the body, and this distinguishes them from other radially symmetrical animals such as jellyfishes and the other cnidarians. Bilaterally symmetrical larvae are evidence that echinoderms evolved from bilaterally symmetrical ancestors, and their radial symmetry as adults is an evolutionary characteristic associated with their mode of locomotion and feeding specializations.

Echinoderms do not have a brain. They have a nervous system that consists of a central ring of nerves, with branches that extend into each of their appendages and help them gain information about and respond to their environment. Echinoderms creep on little tube feet that are extensions of an internal system of water-filled tubes radiating throughout the body. The undersides of a sea star's arms and of the bodies of sea urchins and sand dollars are carpeted with tube feet that extend and contract in waves, grasping and releasing the surface on which they move (the substrate) as the animal glides along.

Although each tube foot is tiny, there are thousands of them, and their combined force allows a sea star to pull the two shells of a clam or mussel apart. Once it has the shells apart, an extraordinary and unexpected thing happens. The sea star pushes its stomach out through its mouth and inserts it into the opened shells. The stomach then secretes digestive enzymes that break down the clam or mussel tissue, and the sea star absorbs the soup that results. Sea urchins feed on algae, scraping them loose from rocks with sharp tooth-like surfaces made of calcium. Sand dollars capture floating particles of algae and other organic matter by trapping them in streams of mucus, which are moved toward their mouth by beating cilia.

TAKE-HOME MESSAGE 11·12

Because they are deuterostomes (as are vertebrates), echinoderms are the invertebrates that are the closest evolutionary relatives to the vertebrates (and other chordates). Their aquatic larvae are bilaterally symmetrical and share some anatomical features with chordates, but adult echinoderms are radially symmetrical.

Animals in motion: these x-ray images show a tuatara (a New Zealand reptile) walking.

11·13

All vertebrates are members of the phylum Chordata.

Vertebrates are deuterostome animals, having defined tissues and bilateral symmetry. Vertebrates are all part of a phylum called Chordata (the chordates) that includes three subphyla in total; the two other subphyla are the tunicates and the lancelets (**FIGURE 11-20**). For at least a portion of their life cycle, members of all three subphyla possess four distinct chordate body structures that are found in no other animal groups (**FIGURE 11-21**).

1. The **notochord,** a rod of tissue extending from head to tail, is the structure that gives chordates their name (from the Latin for "cord"). The notochord stiffens the body when muscles contract during movement. The simplest chordates—those most distantly related to the vertebrates—retain the notochord throughout life. In the more complex chordates such as vertebrates, however, the notochord is present only in the early embryo and is replaced by the backbone (vertebral column) as the embryo develops.

2. A **dorsal hollow nerve cord** extends along the animal's back (its dorsal side) from its head to its tail. In vertebrates, this nerve cord eventually forms the central nervous system, which consists of the spinal cord and the brain. Other kinds of animals (worms, insects, and so on) also have a nerve cord, but it lies in the lower portion of the front (ventral) part of the body and is solid instead of hollow.

3. Pharyngeal slits are present in the embryos of all chordates, but in many chordates (including humans) the slits disappear as the animal develops. The earliest chordates were aquatic, and to breathe and feed they passed water through slits in the pharyngeal region (the area between the back of the mouth and the top of the throat). In humans, pharyngeal slits are present only in the embryo; our gills were lost far back in evolutionary time.

4. A **post-anal tail** is another chordate characteristic. The posterior (back) end of the digestive system is the anus. The region of the body extending beyond the opening of the anus is referred to as "post-anal." All vertebrates have a tail in this location, but some, including humans, have a tail only for a brief period, during embryonic development.

Although all chordates share these four characteristic structures, the chordates exhibit tremendous physical and ecological diversity (**FIGURE 11-22**).

Tunicates (subphylum Urochordata; about 2,000 species) are invertebrate marine animals that have defined tissues, bilateral symmetry, and, as deuterostomes, from-back-to-front gut development. The adults are about the size of your thumb and look like balls of brownish green jelly. You can find them attached to docks and the mooring lines of boats. It is the free-swimming larvae of tunicates that reveal their chordate characteristics. Tunicates are filter-feeders: cilia draw a current of water through the mouth into the pharynx and out through the pharyngeal slits, and microscopic food items are trapped by the bars between the slits. Microscopic food items are trapped by the bars between the slits.

Lancelets (subphylum Cephalochordata; about 20 species), also bilaterally symmetrical deuterostomes, are slender, eel-like invertebrate animals, about the length of your little finger, that live in coastal waters. Unlike tunicates, adult

FIGURE 11-20 **Understanding the chordates.**

THE CHORDATES

COMMON CHARACTERISTICS

All chordates possess four common body structures, although in many chordates, these structures are only present during specific life stages.

- Notochord
- Dorsal hollow nerve cord
- Pharyngeal slits
- Post-anal tail

MEMBERS INCLUDE

- Tunicates (about 2,000 species)
- Lancelets (about 20 species)
- Vertebrates (about 56,000 species)

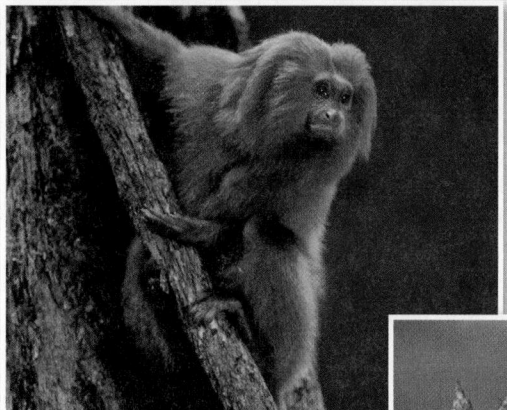

Golden lion tamarin (vertebrate)

Compound ascidians (tunicate)

Thorny devil lizard (vertebrate)

Pacific double saddle butterfly fish (vertebrate)

THE DISTINCT BODY STRUCTURES OF CHORDATES

The members of Chordata are defined by four distinct body structures present in all chordates but in no other animal groups.

NOTOCHORD

A rod of tissue extending from the head to the tail

- Simpler chordates retain the notochord throughout life
- In more complex chordates, the notochord in early embryos is replaced by a backbone

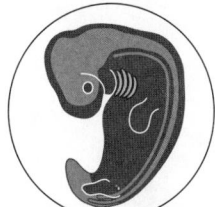

PHARYNGEAL SLITS

Slits through which water is passed in order to breathe and feed

- In many chordates (including humans), the slits disappear as the animal develops

DORSAL HOLLOW NERVE CORD

Nerve cord that extends along the animal's back (its dorsal side)

- In vertebrates, the nerve cord eventually forms the spinal cord and brain

POST-ANAL TAIL

Tail that extends beyond the posterior (back) end of the digestive system

- Some vertebrates (including humans) have a tail only briefly, during embryonic development

FIGURE 11-21 **Characteristic chordate body structures.**

TUNICATES
- Filter-feeding marine animals
- Can often be found attached to docks
- Larvae are free-swimming

LANCELETS
- Filter-feeding marine animals
- Live in coastal waters

VERTEBRATES
- The most diverse subphylum of chordates
- Range in size from the tiny hummingbird to the enormous blue whale
- Can be found in most of the habitats on earth

FIGURE 11-22 Representing the subphyla of chordates. Shown here (*left to right*) are a sea squirt, a lancelet, and a flap-necked chameleon.

lancelets have all the chordate characteristics. Lancelets are also filter-feeders.

Vertebrates (subphylum Vertebrata; about 56,000 species) are the most diverse group of chordates (**FIGURE 11-23**). Because they are deuterostomes, they are bilaterally symmetrical, with defined tissue and from-back-to-front gut development. Vertebrates differ from the other chordates in two important ways:

1. They have a backbone, formed when a column made from hollow bones (or cartilage in some organisms), called vertebrae, forms around the notochord. This backbone surrounds and protects the dorsal hollow nerve cord.

2. They have a head, at the front (anterior) end of the organism, containing a skull, a brain, and sensory organs.

The size range of vertebrates extends from tiny hummingbirds and shrews that weigh only a tenth of an ounce (about

THE VERTEBRATES

FIGURE 11-23 Vertebrate phylogeny.

3 grams) to blue whales, which weigh in at more than 130 tons (120,000 kg). Vertebrates move by swimming, burrowing, crawling, walking, running, and flying, and they are present in all habitats on earth. But despite all these differences, all vertebrates have the four chordate characteristics at some stage of their lives. In the remaining sections we focus on the vertebrates, which are by far the most diverse and widely dispersed group of chordates.

TAKE-HOME MESSAGE 11·13

All chordates have four characteristic structures: a notochord, a dorsal hollow nerve cord, pharyngeal slits, and a post-anal tail. The three subphyla of chordates are superficially very different, but are united by possessing these four structures at some stage of their life cycle.

11·14 The evolution of jaws and fins gave rise to the vast diversity of vertebrate species.

The earliest vertebrates were fish-like animals that lived more than 500 million years ago and did not have jaws. Two kinds of jawless vertebrates still exist: the lampreys (with 41 species) and the hagfishes (with 43 species). Lampreys are parasitic; they attach to other fishes by creating suction with a circular oral disk that is studded with sharp spines. First, the spines scrape an opening through the scales and skin. Then, a protein produced by the lamprey keeps the wound from closing, and the lamprey feeds on the blood and body fluids that seep out. Hagfishes feed on dead animals, using two spiny dental plates that they embed in their prey.

Lampreys and hagfishes are about as basic as an animal can be. And because they do not have jaws, they cannot seize prey or chew food before swallowing it. The evolution of fins and jaws is

Q

Why are jaws needed?

what set the stage for the evolutionary explosion of diversity in the vertebrates.

Fishes swim the same way that lampreys and hagfishes swim—that is, by bending the body from side to side to create an S-shaped wave that moves from head to tail. A typical fish has seven fins serving different purposes: to drive the fish forward, to minimize rolling from side to side, and for steering and stopping. The combined effects of the seven fins allow the fish to swim rapidly in a straight line when it is in open water or to weave its way through a dense stand of plants or corals, with great maneuverability.

The evolution of fins was paralleled by the evolution of jaws, because the two structures work together. Fins get you to the organism you are going to eat, and jaws capture and kill it (**FIGURE 11-24**).

THE EVOLUTION OF JAWS AND FINS

FISHES WITHOUT JAWS OR FINS
• Tail propels organism through water
• Feed by attaching oral disk to prey

Oral disk

FISHES WITH JAWS AND FINS
• Fins provide controlled movement through water
• Jaws lined with sharp teeth allow for seizing and chewing prey

FIGURE 11-24 The lamprey and the shark. The lamprey (*left*) has an oral disk that it uses for sucking in a meal. The shark has a powerful jaw lined with sharp teeth, and pairs of fins that allow it to move rapidly through the water and attack prey.

The development of fins and jaws set the stage for the evolutionary explosion of vertebrate diversity.

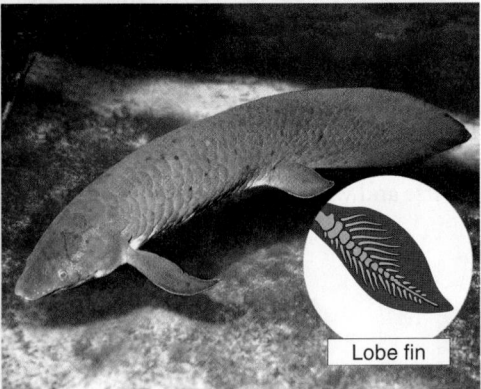

CARTILAGINOUS FISHES
- Characterized by a skeleton made completely from cartilage
- About 880 species, including sharks and rays

RAY-FINNED FISHES
- Characterized by rigid bones and fins lined with hardened rays
- Possess a swim bladder, which aids in flotation
- About 27,000 species, including almost everything you think of as "fish"

LOBE-FINNED FISHES
- Characterized by two pairs of sturdy fins on the underside of their body
- 6 species of lungfish and 2 species of coelacanths

FIGURE 11-25 Fishes with jaws: cartilaginous, ray-finned, and lobe-finned fishes. Shown here (*left to right*) are a stingray, rainbow trout, and Australian lungfish.

The development of jaws and fins allowed great diversification in vertebrate body shapes and composition. There are two major categories of jawed fish. **Cartilaginous fishes,** with about 880 species, include the sharks and rays (**FIGURE 11-25**). Cartilaginous fishes are characterized by a skeleton made entirely of cartilage, a solid but slightly flexible connective tissue—the same tissue that gives your nose and ears their shape. **Ray-finned fishes** have a rigid skeleton made from bone, which, like cartilage, is a solid connective tissue consisting of specialized cells and an extracellular material (matrix) that the cells secrete. Bone, however, is much less flexible than cartilage because its extracellular matrix is mineralized by crystals of calcium phosphate. Ray-finned fishes have a mouth at the narrow tip, or apex, of the body, and their fins, made from webs of skin, are supported with hardened rays made of bone.

More than 97% of fishes reproduce by laying eggs, which develop and hatch outside the mother. Fertilization most commonly takes place externally, with males and females releasing their gametes into the water. However, numerous species of sharks have internal fertilization, after which the female lays the fertilized eggs. There also are some fish species, including guppies, that have internal fertilization followed by development of the eggs within the mother and live birth.

Ray-finned fishes are the largest group of jawed fishes and the most diverse group of vertebrates, with about 27,000 species. This group includes almost everything you think of as "fish," from salmon to goldfish.

An important evolutionary development in the ray-finned fishes was the swim bladder, a gas-filled organ that keeps the fish from sinking. This bladder is the evolutionary precursor of the lungs of land-dwelling (terrestrial) vertebrates. Cartilaginous fishes, which have no swim bladder, must constantly move through the water or they will sink.

A third group of jawed fishes, the **lobe-finned fishes,** are represented by just eight species. These fishes have sturdy pelvic and pectoral fins on the underside of their body (see Figure 11-25), which, unlike other fins, have a central appendage containing numerous bones and muscles that connect the fins to the body. As we see in the next section, lobe-fins were useful in initiating the move onto land.

TAKE-HOME MESSAGE 11·14

The development of two structures in fishes—fins and jaws—set the stage for the enormous diversity of modern vertebrates.

11·15 The movement onto land required lungs, a rigid backbone, four legs, and eggs that resist drying.

Movement from water onto land required four major evolutionary innovations: lungs, a backbone, four legs, and eggs that won't dry out. All four of these characteristics are necessary for a land animal, and all four evolved in predatory fishes that lived in shallow water, the immediate ancestors of terrestrial vertebrates.

Q Where did legs and lungs come from?

As we've noted, lungs developed from the swim bladder found in ray-finned fishes. All of the terrestrial vertebrates—amphibians, reptiles (including birds), and mammals—are descendants of the lobe-finned fishes that lived during the Devonian period, some 400 million years ago. At this time, the lobe-finned fishes had lungs and the rudiments of limbs, but they were still fully aquatic and living near the shore. The four sturdy fins on the underside of their body helped them move through shallow water, and lungs allowed them to breathe air when the oxygen concentration in the warm, stagnant water was low. Thus, these fishes already had some of the basic characteristics of terrestrial animals—they could walk using their fins, and they could exchange gases (getting oxygen into and carbon dioxide out of the bloodstream), using oxygen from air passing through their lungs instead of from water passing through their gills. The jointed bones in the fins of lobe-finned fishes don't look much like your arms and legs, but they are evolutionarily homologous structures.

To move onto land, a vertebrate needs more than just legs and lungs, however. It needs structural support to resist the pull of gravity. Each vertebra of a terrestrial vertebrate has projections that interlock with projections from the vertebra ahead of it and the vertebra behind it. These interlocking projections prevent the backbone from sagging under the pull of gravity, and the body weight is transmitted through the limbs to the ground.

The last innovation necessary to move onto land is an egg that resists drying out (**FIGURE 11-26**). When eggs are deposited on land, they are exposed to air and lose water by evaporation. The eggs of terrestrial animals need a waterproof covering—a membrane and a shell—to prevent them from drying out before they hatch. The appearance of eggs with a shell (about 380 million years ago) marks the final step in the evolution of entirely terrestrial vertebrates, the groups that evolved into mammals and reptiles (including birds). The eggs of terrestrial vertebrates have a water-tight membrane that keeps the embryo surrounded by a bath of fluid called amniotic fluid.

FROM WATER TO LAND

The transition of vertebrates from life in water to life on land required overcoming three main obstacles. Four major evolutionary innovations allowed for this transition.

PROBLEM: RESPIRATION

Aquatic animals use gills to acquire dissolved oxygen from water. The transition onto land required the ability to breathe air.

SOLUTION: LUNGS
Gas exchange was transferred from gills to lungs, which evolved from the swim bladder found in ray-finned fishes.

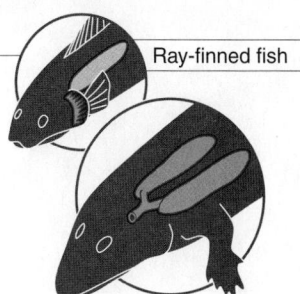
Ray-finned fish

Early terrestrial vertebrate

PROBLEM: GRAVITY

The transition onto land required structural support to resist the pull of gravity.

SOLUTIONS: LIMBS and MODIFIED VERTEBRAE
Limbs evolved from the jointed fins found on the underside of lobe-finned fishes.

Vertebrae were modified to transmit the body weight through the limbs to the ground.

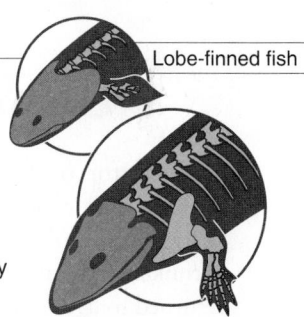
Lobe-finned fish

Early terrestrial vertebrate

PROBLEM: EGG DESICCATION

The transition onto land required an egg that resisted drying out when exposed to air.

SOLUTION: AMNIOTIC EGG
Terrestrial animals developed a waterproof eggshell, which prevents eggs from drying out before they hatch.

FIGURE 11-26 How did vertebrates make the transition from life in water to life on land?

TAKE-HOME MESSAGE 11·15

In the transition of vertebrates from life in water to life on land, fins were modified into limbs, vertebrae were modified to transmit body weight through the limbs to the ground, and the site of gas exchange was transferred from gills and swim bladders to lungs. The only entirely new feature to appear in the early development of terrestrial vertebrates was an egg that resisted drying out.

11·16–11·20 All terrestrial vertebrates are tetrapods.

Although they reach 140 pounds as adults (with one recorded at more than 230 pounds!), capybara (Hydrochoerus hydrochaeris) are rodents. Shown here: parents with baby, in Brazil.

11·16 Amphibians live a double life.

The ancestors of all vertebrates that live on land had lungs and four legs. Some modern vertebrates, such as whales and snakes, have evolved so that their limbs are reduced to a few shrunken and unused bones. Whales and some snakes have returned to living in water, and some salamanders have lost lungs and breathe through their skin, but these are recent changes, occurring in species whose ancestors had lungs and four legs. Taxonomically, all terrestrial vertebrates are **tetrapods** (*tetra* = four; *poda* = feet).

Terrestrial vertebrates are divided into two main groups: (1) animals (called **non-amniotes**) such as amphibians that reproduce in water and do not have desiccation-proof amniotic eggs; and (2) animals (called **amniotes**) such as reptiles and mammals that have amniotic eggs. We discuss amphibians here, then reptiles and mammals in the next two sections.

The first terrestrial vertebrates were **amphibians,** from the Greek word *amphibios,* meaning "living a double life." There

THE AMPHIBIAN LIFE CYCLE

Amphibians, such as frogs, toads, and salamanders, are terrestrial vertebrates (tetrapods) with non-amniotic eggs. Most species live on land as adults, but develop in water.

EGGS
Amphibians have non-amniotic eggs, which must be laid in water to prevent desiccation.

JUVENILES
Amphibians spend their juvenile stage underwater and undergo metamorphosis to develop legs and lungs.

ADULTS
Only the adults are true land animals; however, most of the species in this group stay close to water to lay their eggs.

FIGURE 11-27 From egg to larva to adult: the amphibian life cycle.

are two stages in most amphibians' lives: a water-breathing juvenile form and an air-breathing adult form. The adults of many amphibian species lay their eggs in water (**FIGURE 11-27**). Most of the 6,000 species in this group are still significantly tied to life in the water, because they must always be near water to lay their eggs, which are simple structures, not unlike fish eggs. Frogs and toads make up the vast majority of amphibians (about 5,400 species). Other amphibians include salamanders (550 species) and caecilians, a group of legless, burrowing animals (170 species).

The juvenile stage of the frog, called a tadpole, lives in water, lacks legs, and eats algae. A few weeks (or up to many months in some species) after hatching, metamorphosis occurs and the tadpole develops legs, lungs, and a digestive system fit for its

adult life as a carnivore. Adult frogs have thin, moist skin through which much of their gas (oxygen and carbon dioxide) exchange with the air takes place.

The past two decades have seen a stunning decline in amphibian populations throughout the world, attributable to a combination of causes: climate change, habitat degradation, fungal diseases, and increased pollution.

TAKE-HOME MESSAGE 11·16

Amphibians are terrestrial vertebrates, but the adults of most species still lay eggs in water. The eggs hatch into aquatic juveniles.

11·17 Birds are reptiles in which feathers evolved.

Soon after amniotic vertebrates appeared, two different evolutionary lineages began to diverge (**FIGURE 11-28**). One of these lineages is the mammals, the group to which humans belong. The other lineage is the one referred to in this chapter as "reptiles (including birds)." That is an awkward term, but the evolutionary tree shows why it is necessary. Surprisingly, birds (about 9,700 species) are one branch of the reptile lineage that also includes snakes and lizards (about 8,000 species), turtles (about 300 species), crocodiles and alligators (23 species), the New Zealand tuatara (2 species)—and the dinosaurs.

Q Birds are reptiles?

The characteristics that hold the bird-crocodile-dinosaur group together are mostly similarities in bones (especially the bones of the skull and legs) and DNA sequences. Reptiles are amniotes and thus have amniotic eggs. You are familiar with the hard-shelled eggs of birds, and some lizard, snake, and turtle eggs also have hard shells. Other species in these groups have eggs with a paper-like shell.

Most people find it confusing that birds are grouped with turtles, lizards and snakes, and alligators and crocodiles, and that confusion is

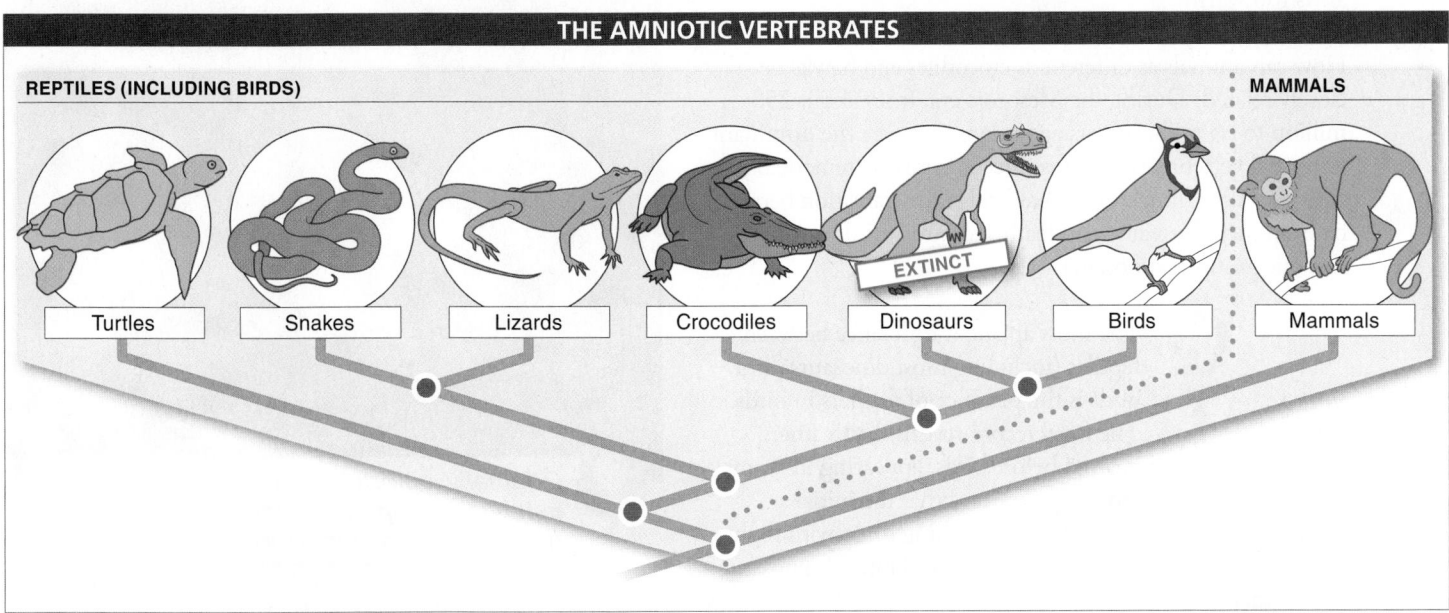

THE AMNIOTIC VERTEBRATES

REPTILES (INCLUDING BIRDS)

MAMMALS

| Turtles | Snakes | Lizards | Crocodiles | Dinosaurs (EXTINCT) | Birds | Mammals |

FIGURE 11-28 **Amniotic vertebrate phylogeny.**

REPTILES
- Skin is covered in scales
- Body temperature is controlled by external conditions, such as air temperature (exothermic)
- Include snakes and lizards (about 8,000 species), turtles (about 300 species), crocodiles and alligators (23 species), and tuatara (2 species)

BIRDS
- Skin is covered in feathers, enabling flight and providing insulation
- Body temperature is maintained by heat generated from cellular respiration (endothermic)
- Include about 9,700 species

FIGURE 11-29 Comparison of reptiles and birds.

easy to understand (**FIGURE 11-29**). After all, birds are covered by feathers and can fly, whereas the other reptiles have bare skin and do not fly. And there is an important physiological difference as well: birds are **endotherms,** meaning they use the heat produced by cellular respiration to raise their body temperature above air temperature, whereas other reptiles are **ectotherms**—they bask in the sun to raise their body temperature and seek the shade when the air is too warm.

How can animals as different as crocodiles and hawks be closely related? During the Mesozoic era, from about 250 million to 65 million years ago, dinosaurs were the dominant terrestrial vertebrates. The fossil record shows a remarkably clear series of animal forms that bridge the transition between bare-skinned dinosaurs and feathered birds. Birds are, in fact, just one group of dinosaurs.

Q

What were the first feathers used for?

The most apparent difference between reptiles (including most dinosaurs) and birds is the presence of feathers in birds. The fossil record reveals that feathers evolved before birds, appearing in many reptile species, and that the initial evolution of feathers probably had nothing to do with flight. In fact, feathers evolved in many different kinds of dinosaur, and feathered dinosaurs continued to live for millions of years after birds appeared.

Among reptiles, many different species had feathers. A small, agile dinosaur called *Sinosauropteryx,* for example, living about 120 million years ago, had feathers that were simple spiky

Originally, colorful feathers were used for behavioral displays. In modern birds, feathers provide insulation and aid in flight.

FIGURE 11-30 *Sinosauropteryx:* **an early feathered, flightless dinosaur.**

filaments on the neck, back, and tail, along with shorter filaments covering the body. These filaments were probably brightly colored and used by male *Sinosauropteryx* for courtship displays to females, as well as for aggressive displays to other males. *Sinosauropteryx* and many of the other feathered dinosaurs were latecomers, however. The pigeon-sized *Archaeopteryx,* which was among the first bird species, was already, by 147 million years ago, using its feathers to fly; by 140 million years ago, the skies were filled with birds.

If *Archaeopteryx* and a host of other early birds already had the specialized feathers needed for flight, why did later, non-flying dinosaurs still have primitive feathers? The answer is that feathers have many functions, of which flight is only one. *Sinosauropteryx,* as we saw above, probably used its feathers for courtship or territorial displays, and it may also have used them as insulation (**FIGURE 11-30**).

Another big difference between birds and reptiles is that, as noted earlier, birds use internally generated heat to maintain a high body temperature, whereas reptiles rely on the sun to heat their bodies. This evolutionary change may have been related to feathers. As feathers evolved for display and flight, they may also have provided some insulation. This insulation may then have enabled the evolution of high rates of cellular respiration and the maintenance of a high and constant body temperature.

TAKE-HOME MESSAGE 11·17

Birds are a branch of the reptile lineage but, unlike other reptiles, possess feathers and can generate body heat. The complex anatomical and physiological systems that we see in extant animals, such as feathers and endothermy in birds, are the products of hundreds of millions of years of step-by-step changes that began with simple structures. Feathers were originally colorful structures used for behavioral displays; additional functions such as insulation and flight evolved later.

11·18 Mammals are animals that have hair and produce milk.

Long before the first birds appeared, the mammals evolved from the reptiles, originally as small, nocturnal insect-eaters. These early mammals remained small and, judging from the scarce fossil record, they were never in great abundance while the dinosaurs were around. Early mammals had several features in common that are still present in all mammals today. Two important features are **hair**—dead cells filled with the protein keratin—which serves as an insulator, and **mammary glands** in female mammals, which enable them to produce nutritious, calorie-rich milk and nurse their young.

As the earliest mammals evolved, there was a gradual transition from bodies with short legs that projected out horizontally from the trunk, like the legs of an alligator, to bodies with long legs held vertically beneath the trunk, like those of a dog (**FIGURE 11-31**). These anatomical changes would have allowed the earliest mammals to run faster and farther to capture prey. But an increase in muscle activity for running had to be accompanied by an increase in the rate of cellular respiration to provide the energy to keep the leg muscles working. With this increase in metabolism, along with the evolution of hair, the early mammals could trap the heat produced and use it for temperature regulation, setting

FIGURE 11-31 How did endothermy evolve in early mammals?

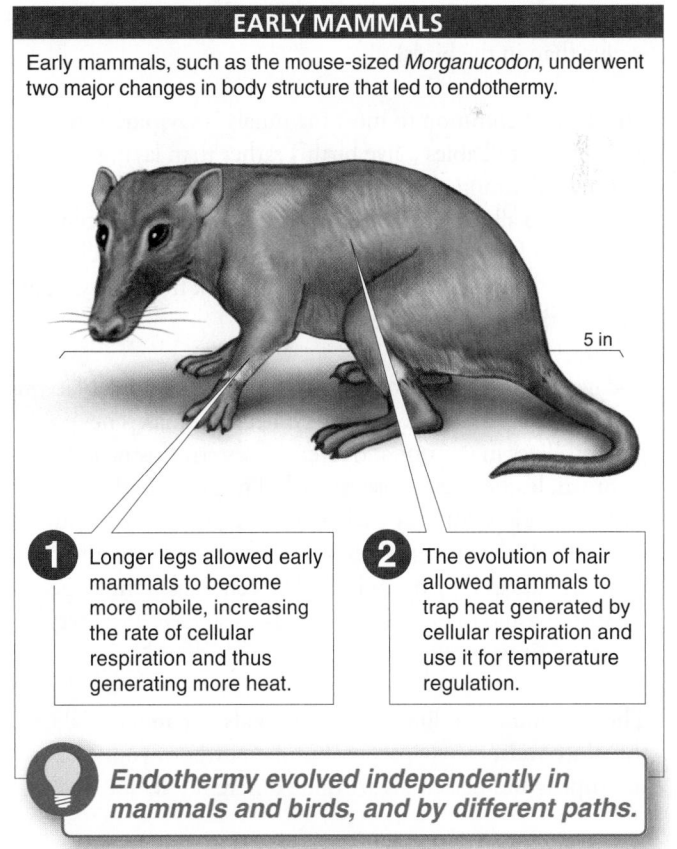

EARLY MAMMALS

Early mammals, such as the mouse-sized *Morganucodon*, underwent two major changes in body structure that led to endothermy.

5 in

1 Longer legs allowed early mammals to become more mobile, increasing the rate of cellular respiration and thus generating more heat.

2 The evolution of hair allowed mammals to trap heat generated by cellular respiration and use it for temperature regulation.

Endothermy evolved independently in mammals and birds, and by different paths.

Mammals are endothermic vertebrates that have hair and produce milk for their young.

MONOTREMES
- Females lay eggs
- Females produce milk, but do not have nipples—babies suck milk from the hairs on their mother's chest
- Only 5 species survive—the platypus and 4 species of spiny animals called echidnas

MARSUPIALS
- Females give birth after a short period of development
- Females of most species have a pouch where the young complete their development
- About 300 species, including kangaroos, koalas, wallabies, and possums

PLACENTAL MAMMALS
- Females have a placenta that provides oxygen and nutrients to embryos in the uterus
- About 4,500 species

FIGURE 11-32 Three groups of mammals: monotremes, marsupials, and placentals. Shown here (*left to right*) are a platypus, a kangaroo, and a giraffe.

the stage for endothermy (but through a different sequence of events than in the birds).

One feature common to most mammals is **viviparity,** or giving birth to babies ("live birth") rather than laying eggs, but it is not a defining mammalian characteristic—it isn't common to all mammals. **Monotremes** retain the ancestral condition of laying eggs. Monotremes do produce milk, but they do not have nipples—babies suck milk from the skin and hairs on their mother's chest.

Today, only five species of monotremes survive—the platypus and four species of spiny animals called echidnas. The platypus lives in streams and rivers in eastern Australia. It uses its broad, leathery, electrosensitive bill to probe under rocks and sunken logs for prey such as aquatic insect larvae and crayfish, which it finds by sensing the electrical activity of their muscles as they try to hide. The echidnas—three species in Australia and one in New Guinea—also have a leathery electrosensitive snout.

The remaining two lineages of mammals, the **marsupials** and the **placentals,** are viviparous, but the newborn young of marsupials and placentals are quite different (**FIGURE 11-32**).

Marsupials are called the "pouched mammals" because the female of most marsupial species has a pouch on her abdomen in which the young complete their development, following a short period of embryonic life in the uterus.

Placental mammals (including humans) take their name from the *placenta,* which is the structure responsible for the transfer of nutrients, respiratory gases, and metabolic waste products between the mother and the developing fetus. Dense capillary beds in the placenta send finger-like projections into the wall of the uterus, where they are surrounded by blood from the mother's circulation.

TAKE-HOME MESSAGE 11·18

Hair and mammary glands are defining characteristics of mammals. Monotremes are egg-laying mammals. Marsupial mammals give birth after a short period of development in the uterus, and the newborn completes its development in the mother's pouch. Placental mammals have a placenta that provides oxygen and nutrients to the fetus as it undergoes a longer development in the uterus.

11·19

Humans tried out different lifestyles.

The primates, the evolutionary lineage to which humans belong, originated about 55 million years ago. We can get an idea of what the ancestral primate looked like from the modern species of tree-living (arboreal) mammals commonly called prosimians—a group that includes the lemurs. Many of the anatomical characteristics of humans and the other primates can be traced to our arboreal origin. Our forward-directed eyes and binocular vision that allow us to judge distances accurately, our shoulder and elbow joints that allow our arms to rotate, and our 10 fingers and 10 toes that allow us to grasp objects—all these are traits we inherited from our arboreal ancestors (**FIGURE 11-33**).

Humans are part of the primate lineage that includes the groups commonly referred to as the New World and Old World monkeys (both of which have tails) and the apes (which lack tails). Among the apes, gibbons and orangutans live in pairs or alone, while gorillas and chimpanzees live in social groups that consist of one or more adult males and several females—the ancestral social structure for human societies. Within the apes, genetic and anatomical characteristics show that chimpanzees are our closest living relatives (**FIGURE 11-34**). Human and

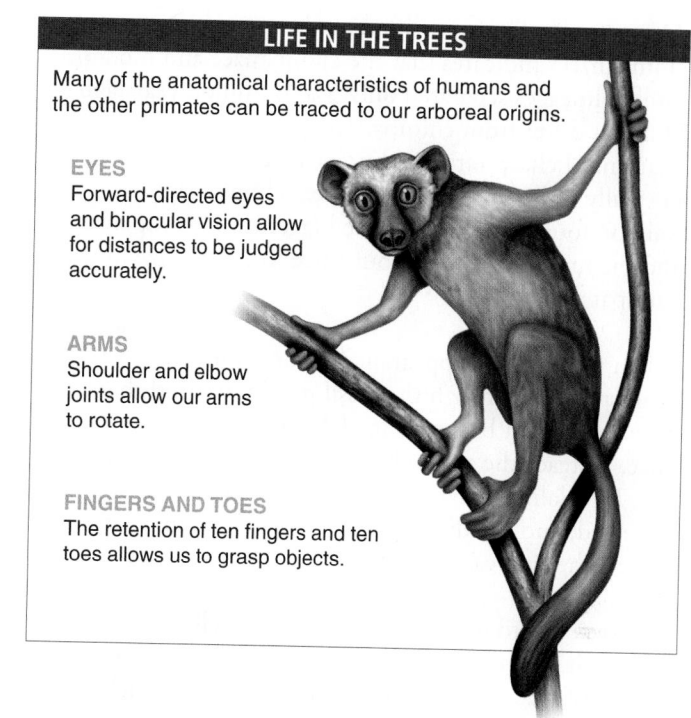

LIFE IN THE TREES

Many of the anatomical characteristics of humans and the other primates can be traced to our arboreal origins.

EYES
Forward-directed eyes and binocular vision allow for distances to be judged accurately.

ARMS
Shoulder and elbow joints allow our arms to rotate.

FINGERS AND TOES
The retention of ten fingers and ten toes allows us to grasp objects.

FIGURE 11-33 The ancestors of modern primates lived in trees.

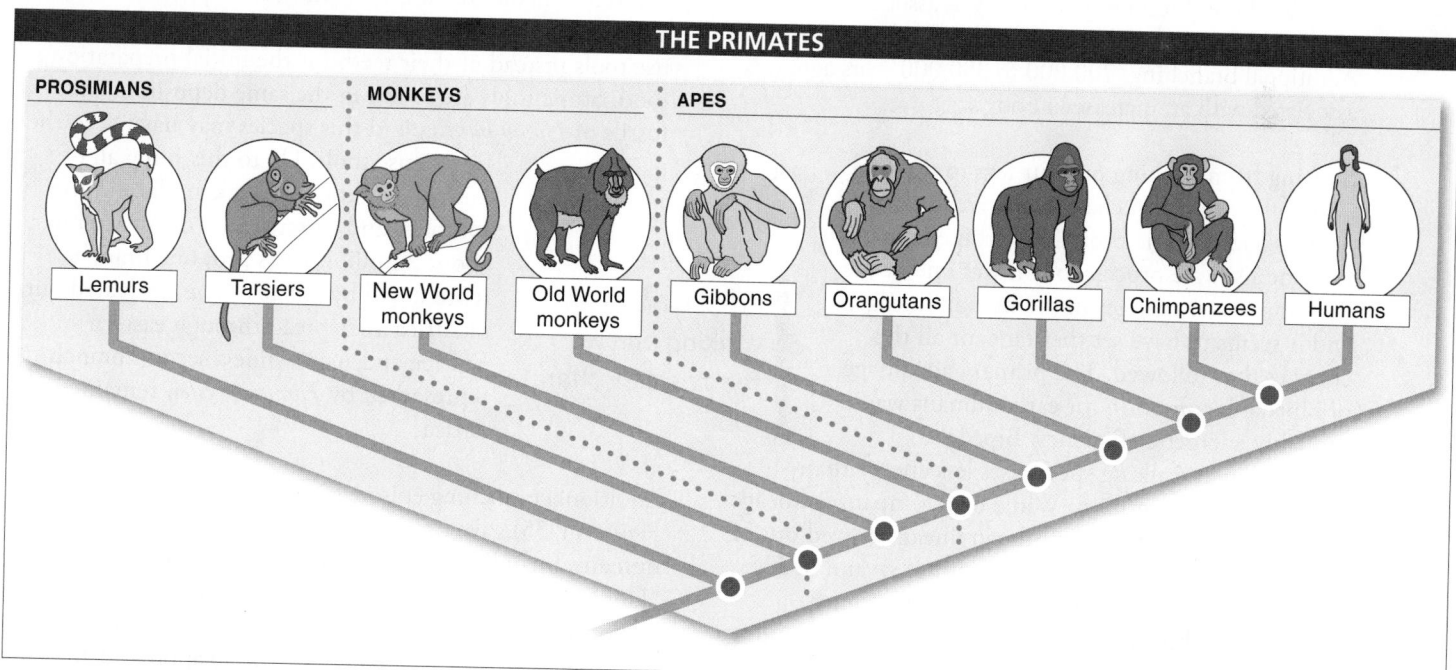

FIGURE 11-34 Phylogeny of primates.

chimpanzee genes are very similar: their base sequences differ by about 1%, and one-third of human and chimpanzee genes are identical.

The amount of genetic difference between humans and chimpanzees indicates that the chimpanzee and modern human lineages separated only 5 or 6 million years ago. Humans differ from chimpanzees in three major anatomical characteristics: humans are bipedal (we normally walk on two legs, whereas chimpanzees usually walk on four legs), humans are bigger than chimpanzees, and the human brain is about three times the size of the chimpanzee brain.

When we trace the appearance of these human characteristics through the fossil record, we find that humans did not become bipedal, big, and brainy all at once. Instead, the three characteristics evolved one by one. Bipedality evolved first, then brain volume increased, and finally body size increased, accompanied by a further increase in brain size.

The fossil record of human evolution looks like a bush with several episodes of branching that produced clusters of species. The first branching episode, which occurred about 4 million years ago, resulted from changes in the jaws and teeth associated with a changing diet (a shift to increased dietary flexibility, allowing consumption of a wider variety of food types). A second branching episode, about 2 million years ago, was associated with increased brain size and probably with the first use of tools. Additional branching, 200,000 to 350,000 years ago, was associated with an increase in body size.

Shifting from walking on four legs to walking on two legs required changes in several parts of the skeleton. The evolution of bipedality was not a simple process, but it was one of the first important changes in the human lineage, and it seems to have set the stage for all the changes that followed. The primary advantage of bipedal locomotion for early humans was probably energetic efficiency. Bipedal locomotion at walking speed uses less energy than quadrupedal locomotion. While the chimpanzee lineage remained in the forest, the human lineage moved out of the forest and onto the grasslands of the savannas. There are numerous hypotheses about the evolutionary advantages of bipedalism for human ancestors, including increasing the energetic efficiency of traveling and freeing the hands for carrying and for tool use. The issue is still being debated as research continues.

Q What are the advantages of walking on two feet rather than four?

About 3.5 or 4 million years ago, several bipedal groups, the australopithecines, appeared (**FIGURE 11-35**). They were no larger than chimpanzees and had the same brain volume, just a bit larger than a pint jar (350–400 cc). The fossil known as Lucy was the first of many australopithecines to be discovered. An adult female, Lucy was only 3 feet (about 1 m) tall and probably weighed no more than 60 pounds (a bit less than 30 kg). The group of australopithecines to which Lucy belonged lived in grassy habitats with scattered trees; their hands and feet retained the curved finger and toe bones that are characteristic of arboreal animals.

Lucy and the other closely related species of australopithecines probably foraged on the ground for food and climbed into trees to escape predators and perhaps, at night, to sleep. With jaws and teeth much like the jaws and teeth of chimpanzees, their diet was probably also like that of chimpanzees, a mixture of leaves, soft fruits, and nuts.

Following the appearance of bipedal primates—which may have occurred in conjunction with a shift to roots rather than leaves as the secondary, or "fallback," food when fruit was in short supply—a second branching episode in human evolution originated among the australopithecines and produced the earliest species in our own genus, *Homo* (from the Latin word for "human"). These earliest humans had brain volumes about twice those of chimpanzees, but little increase in body size. The species in this radiation had markedly smaller teeth than their australopithecine ancestors, a change that might indicate they had started to use tools instead of their teeth for the initial preparation of food. Stone tools are found in the same deposits as the fossils of *Homo habilis,* and this species may have been the first to use tools. Up to this time, all of human evolution had taken place in the southern and eastern parts of Africa, but about 2 million years ago, one branch, represented by *Homo erectus,* migrated out of Africa and spread through eastern Europe and Asia, while a second branch, represented by *Homo ergaster,* remained in Africa.

Additional branching episodes in human evolution (see Figure 11-35) gave rise to several species of advanced humans, including Neandertals (*Homo neanderthalensis*), "Flores man" (*Homo floresiensis,* described in the next section), and our own species (*Homo sapiens*). This radiation coincided with an increase in body size to approximately the height and weight of modern humans and an increase in brain volume to nearly twice that of earlier ancestors. In

GRAPHIC CONTENT!
Thinking critically about visual displays of data.
Turn to p. 468 for a closer inspection of this figure.

THE EVOLUTIONARY HISTORY OF HUMANS

The evolutionary history of humans did not follow a straight line. Since first appearing around 4 million years ago, there have been many branches to the human evolutionary tree, a sample of which is shown here.

Homo habilis

Ardipithecus

Australopithecus (gracile)

Homo ergaster

Homo heidelbergensis

Homo neanderthalensis

Homo sapiens

Homo floresiensis

Homo erectus

—— Probable relationship
- - - Possible relationship

Australopithecus (robust)

Time

| 4 million years ago | 3 million years ago | 2 million years ago | 1 million years ago | 500,000 years ago | 250,000 years ago | Today |

FIGURE 11-35 Branching episodes in human evolution.

Humans' success can be traced to an increase in brain size combined with an omnivorous diet.

addition, the body form of the species that evolved during this branching episode looked like that of modern humans, with shorter arms and longer legs.

The evolutionary lineage to which *H. sapiens* belongs became bipedal, started using tools, and developed larger brains and larger bodies. These features, along with an omnivorous diet and an increase in caloric intake associated with the development in cooking, turned out to be a winning strategy. Other lineages closely related to that of *H. sapiens* became extinct while our lineage survived.

TAKE-HOME MESSAGE 11·19

Humans' forward-looking eyes, hands and feet with 10 fingers and 10 toes, and shoulder and elbow joints that allow the arms to rotate are characteristics retained from our arboreal ancestors. The early ancestors of humans left the trees and took up life on the ground, where they walked on two legs. Our success can be traced to an increase in brain size, possibly in conjunction with an omnivorous diet and increased caloric intake.

11·20 How did we get here? The past 100,000 years of human evolution.

A bit more than 100,000 years ago, a new human species evolved in Africa—the first modern *Homo sapiens*. One hundred thousand years is a ballpark figure based on a combination of molecular and fossil evidence. At that time, a small group—probably no more than 100—of these modern humans left Africa and ultimately spread across the earth.

Mitochondrial DNA shows that the initial human migration out of Africa followed three major pathways (**FIGURE 11-36**). One group turned west after leaving Africa and spread into Europe. A second group turned southeast and spread into southern Asia and through the Indo-Australian Archipelago to Australia. The third group moved northeast, populating northern Asia. This is the group that crossed the Bering Straits bridge about 15,000 years ago and spread southward through the Americas. Even as some groups migrated from Africa, many individuals remained.

There was something about the world that those *H. sapiens* groups moved into as they left Africa that we would find bizarre—*they were not alone*. Populations of at least three other species of humans (i.e., species in the genus *Homo*) were already present in some of the

areas that modern humans were moving into. That situation is totally different from the world we know today, in which we are the only human species. What would it be like to live with species that were as similar to us as dogs are to wolves, coyotes, and jackals? How would you interact with an individual who was clearly human, but not human in exactly the same way that you are?

This is the situation that the first modern *H. sapiens* encountered when they left Africa. Neandertals (*H. neanderthalensis*) had already spread across Europe and the Middle East. Neandertals were about the same size as modern humans, but they were more robust and muscular. Fossils of Neandertals often include bones that had been broken and healed. These injuries provide two types of information about Neandertals.

1. Neandertals must have lived in organized groups that included a social support system, because these fossils reveal serious injuries. The injured individuals would have been incapacitated for days or even weeks until they healed, and family or clan members must have cared for them during this

> **Q** Were two species of humans ever alive at the same time? If so, what happened?

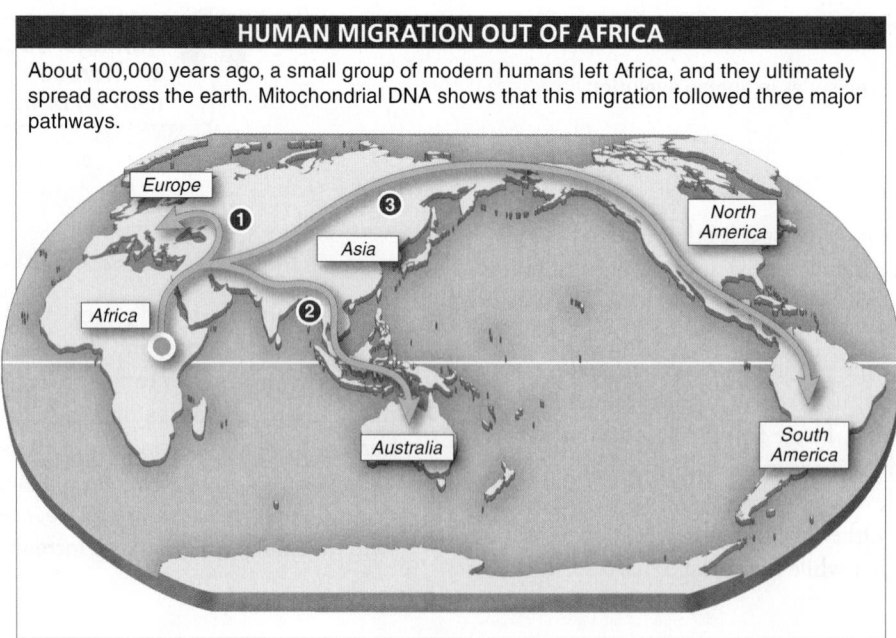

FIGURE 11-36 *Homo sapiens* on the move: three migratory paths out of Africa.

period. Ritual burials of Neandertals have also been found, and these provide additional support for the hypothesis that they lived in organized social groups.

2. The pattern of injuries found in Neandertal skeletons is distinctive—the only modern counterpart is found in professional rodeo bull and bronco riders, people who come in very close contact with large, angry animals. Neandertals probably hunted large mammals (bison, mammoths, wooly rhinoceroses) with short spears that were used for close-up jabbing instead of being thrown from a safe distance.

The *H. sapiens* who migrated through the Indo-Australian Archipelago encountered two species of humans: *H. erectus* and *H. floresiensis*. *Homo erectus* had migrated to Asia at least a million years earlier and was still present on the island of Java when modern humans arrived, about 50,000 years ago. Although *H. erectus* was the same size as modern humans, it had a smaller brain—an average brain volume of just over a quart (about 1,000 cc) for *H. erectus* compared with a quart and a half (about 1,400 cc) for *H. sapiens*. Nonetheless, *H. erectus* had technological skills. These may have been the first humans to use fire (the evidence on this is not definitive), and they almost certainly built boats that allowed them to move along coasts and from island to island.

In 2003, stone tools and fossils of a species of human only 3 feet (about 1 m) tall and with a brain volume of just over a pint (about 350 cc) were discovered on Flores Island, which lies east of Java. The paleontologists who discovered this species gave it the scientific name *Homo floresiensis* ("Flores man"), but the world press promptly called it the Hobbit because of its tiny size. When the dwarf human *H. floresiensis* lived, Flores Island was also home to a dwarf elephant, which

H. floresiensis probably ate, and a giant monitor lizard that probably ate *H. floresiensis*.

After modern *H. sapiens* groups spread into the areas occupied by the three other human species, these three other species disappeared. Neandertals became extinct about 30,000 years ago, *H. erectus* about 27,000 years ago, and *H. floresiensis* about 12,000 years ago. Why did these three species vanish? Broadly speaking, there are two possible explanations. They might have interbred with *H. sapiens,* in which case modern humans would carry genes from the three recently extinct species. No evidence supports that possibility, however, and it is more likely that *H. sapiens* exterminated the other species, either by monopolizing access to food and living space or by killing them in battles for food and space.

Now we are the only extant human species, a situation that is unique in the evolutionary history of humans. Ever since the first branching event, about 4 million years ago, multiple, closely related species of humans have coexisted. We are the first human species to be alone.

TAKE-HOME MESSAGE 11·20

Modern humans (Homo sapiens) evolved in Africa between 200,000 and 100,000 years ago, and all living humans are descended from that evolutionary radiation. About 100,000 years ago, a small group of modern humans moved out of Africa, and the descendants of this group ultimately populated Europe, Asia, and the Americas. Three other species of humans were living at this time, all of which became extinct between 30,000 and 12,000 years ago, after modern humans had spread into the areas where they were living.

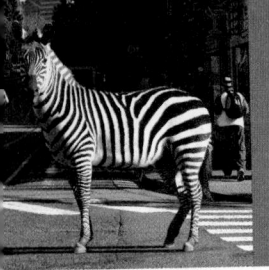

StreetBIO
Knowledge You Can Use

WHERE ARE YOU FROM? "Recreational Genomics" and the Search for Clues to Your Ancestry in Your DNA

How much do you know about your ancestral heritage? Is it enough to know that you are Italian and Asian? More than two dozen companies now offer a promise to help you discover your genetic ancestry—usually for $100 to $1,000. Can they deliver what they promise?

Q: ARE CLUES TO YOUR ANCESTRY HIDDEN WITHIN YOUR DNA? The short answer is *yes*. Researchers use comparisons of DNA sequences to explore personal ancestries *within* our species, even preparing pie charts that purport to identify a person's ancestral proportions (for example, 10% West African, 70% Middle Eastern / North African, and 20% European).

Q: HOW IS DNA USED TO BUILD A FAMILY TREE? Most tests are based on one of three types of analysis. (1) Mitochondrial DNA tests evaluate highly variable sequences in maternally inherited mitochondrial DNA. (2) Y-chromosome tests look at variation in the paternally inherited Y chromosome. (3) Autosomal DNA tests examine highly variable sections of DNA scattered throughout the chromosomes. In each case, a sample of cells is collected (usually by swabbing the inside of the cheeks), base sequences at a number of locations (a few dozen to several hundred) are determined, and those sequences are compared with sequences from thousands of individuals in populations around the world. The matching of your sequences with those of other samples is then interpreted as potential evidence of shared ancestry.

Q: GENETIC ANCESTRY TESTING MAY BE GOOD FUN, BUT IS IT GOOD SCIENCE? Unfortunately, the limitations of commercially available tests of genetic ancestry are significant. These are among the most important limitations:

- High genetic variation among individuals of most populations makes it difficult to identify specific sequences that can reliably indicate membership in a population. As an analogy: if Native Americans are highly variable for a trait (e.g., height), we can't use that trait to prove someone's Native American ancestry.

- High rates of gene flow between populations reduce the reliability with which any sequence can demonstrate membership in one particular population. As an analogy: dark hair is extremely common in Asia, but having dark hair doesn't necessarily indicate Asian ancestry.

- Evaluating too few genetic loci, of which just a small number happen to be similar, can lead to the conclusion that individuals are much more genetically similar than they actually are.

- A DNA match between two individuals living today is *not* a match with an ancestor. Rather, it suggests that the two people may have inherited the DNA sequence from a common ancestor.

Q: WHAT CAN YOU CONCLUDE? Until we have a much more comprehensive catalog of genetic variation—including precise estimates of how much variation exists within populations and how much exists between populations—the results of genetic ancestry testing remain overly speculative and insufficiently reliable. Conclusions may be incorrect and misleading. But, because the conceptual underpinnings are solid, the future of genetic ancestry testing is promising.

Big Ideas in ...
Animal Diversification

11·1–11·3 Animals are just one branch of the Eukarya domain.

- Animals are multicellular organisms that feed on other organisms and can move during at least one stage of their life.
- Animals probably originated from an ancestral protist.
- Four key distinctions divide the extant animals: defined tissues or not, radial or bilateral symmetry, protostome or deuterostome development, and growth with or without molting.

11·4 Invertebrates are animals without a backbone.

- Invertebrates, defined as animals without a backbone, are the largest and most diverse group of animals, comprising 96% of all living animal species. The invertebrates are not a monophyletic group, however, and include protostomes and deuterostomes.

11·5–11·12 Across several evolutionary transitions, the invertebrate animals diversified.

- Sponges are among the simplest of the animal lineages. A sponge consists of a hollow tube with pores in its wall; it has no tissues or organs.
- Corals, sea anemones, and jellyfishes are cnidarians, radially symmetrical carnivorous animals with defined tissues and stinging cells called cnidocysts.
- Worms are found in several different phyla and are not a monophyletic group. All are bilaterally symmetrical protostomes with defined tissues. The segmented worms (annelids) and flatworms do not molt; the roundworms (nematodes) do.
- Mollusks, the second most diverse phylum of animals, are protostome invertebrates that do not molt.
- Arthropods are protostome invertebrates. With nearly one million species, they outnumber all other forms of life in species diversity. The ability to fly and the development of a body with a rugged exoskeleton have contributed to the enormous ecological diversity of the insects.
- Echinoderms are deuterostome invertebrates and are the closest evolutionary relatives to the vertebrates (also deuterostomes).

11·13–11·15 The phylum Chordata includes vertebrates, animals with a backbone.

- There are three groups of chordates, including the vertebrates, and all share four characteristic structures: a notochord, a dorsal hollow nerve cord, pharyngeal slits, and a post-anal tail.
- The development of two structures in fishes—fins and jaws—set the stage for the enormous diversity of modern vertebrates.
- In the transition of vertebrates from life in water to life on land, fins were modified into limbs, vertebrae were modified to transmit body weight through the limbs to the ground, and the site of gas exchange was transferred from gills and swim bladders to lungs. A new feature in the early evolutionary development of terrestrial vertebrates was an egg that resisted drying out.

11·16–11·20 All terrestrial vertebrates are tetrapods.

- Amphibians are terrestrial vertebrates (tetrapods), but most species still lay eggs in water and the eggs hatch into aquatic larvae.
- Feathers were originally colorful structures used for behavioral displays in reptiles. Their current uses in insulation and flight developed later.
- Hair and lactation are defining characteristics of mammals.
- Modern humans evolved in Africa between 200,000 and 100,000 years ago, and all living humans are descended from that evolutionary radiation.
- The evolutionary success of humans can be traced to an increase in brain size combined with an omnivorous diet.

See the To-Go Guide (packaged with every new copy of this textbook) for an illustrated summary of the chapter.

Check Your Knowledge

Thinking critically about visual displays of data.

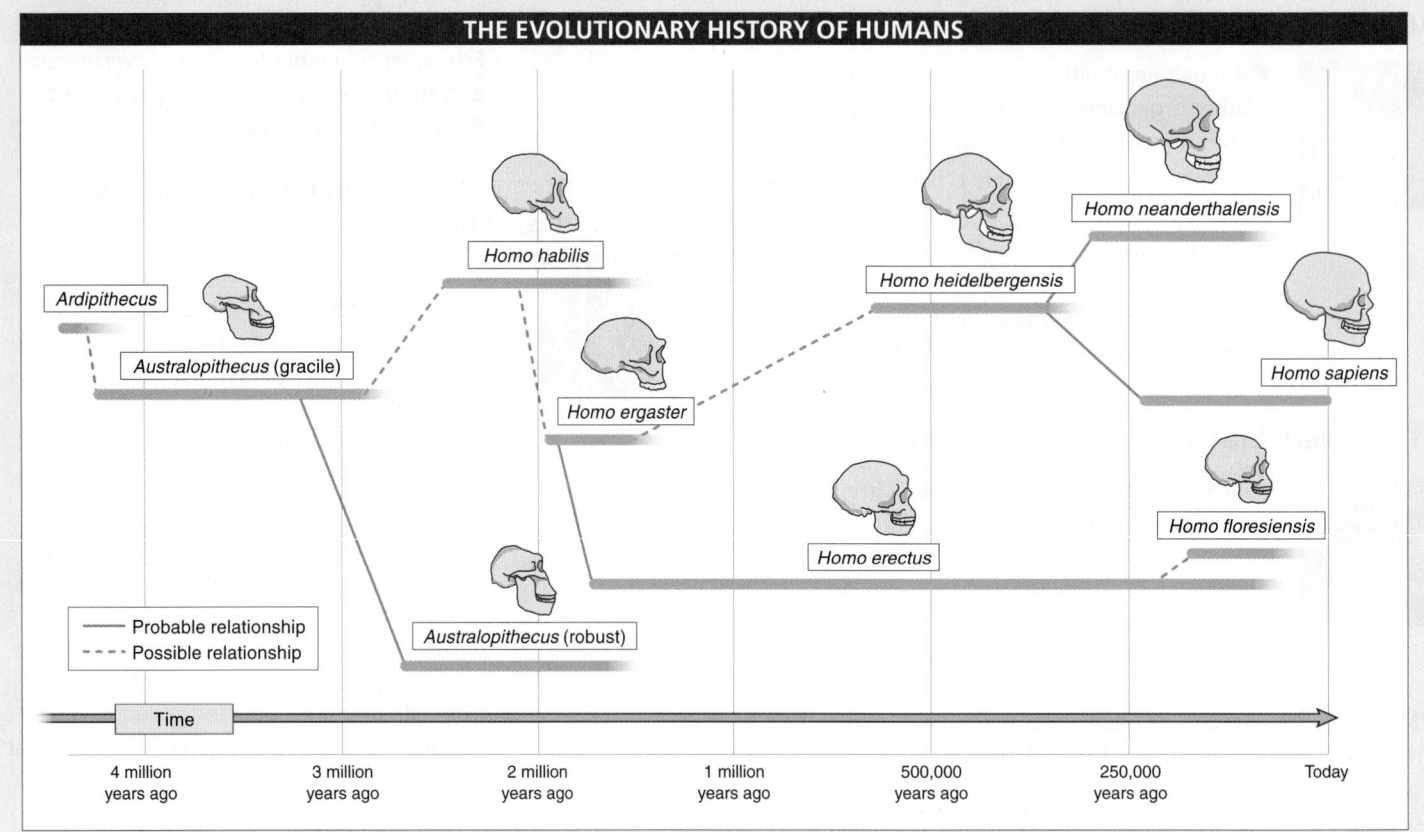

THE EVOLUTIONARY HISTORY OF HUMANS

Homo neanderthalensis

Homo habilis

Ardipithecus

Homo heidelbergensis

Australopithecus (gracile)

Homo sapiens

Homo ergaster

Homo floresiensis

Homo erectus

—— Probable relationship
- - - Possible relationship

Australopithecus (robust)

Time

| 4 million years ago | 3 million years ago | 2 million years ago | 1 million years ago | 500,000 years ago | 250,000 years ago | Today |

1. Moving back in time from today, which species are the most likely to be the direct ancestors of modern humans? Which are not? Why?

2. When did the genus *Homo* first appear? How did it differ from earlier species in this evolutionary tree?

3. What is the difference between the dotted purple lines and the solid purple lines? Why might that information change over time?

4. What is the largest number of different species on the human "family tree" that were alive at the same time? When was that?

5. How long ago did *Homo sapiens* become the only living representative of the genus *Homo*?

See Answers at the back of the book.

Key Terms in Animal Diversification

Multiple-Choice Questions

1. **Which of the following is not a characteristic of all animals?**

   a) They are able to move at some point in their life.

   b) They get their energy by eating other organisms.

   c) They are multicellular.

   d) They are reproducing sexually at some point in their life cycle.

   e) All of the above are characteristics of all animals.

   100 HARD
   77
   0 EASY

2. **The lineage that first separated from the common ancestor of all animals, and retains many of those primitive features to this day, includes which of the following modern organisms?**

   a) the grasshopper

   b) the jellyfish

   c) the sponge

   d) the earthworm

   e) the sea turtle

   100 HARD
   39
   0 EASY

3. **Which of the following extant species is the most evolutionarily successful?**

   a) the house mouse (*Mus domesticus*)

   b) the housefly (*Musca domestica*)

   c) the Western gorilla (*Gorilla gorilla*)

   d) Irukandji, the toxic jellyfish (*Carukia barnesi*)

   e) All of the above species are equally successful because they are not extinct.

   100 HARD
   14
   0 EASY

4. **Sponges are sessile, meaning that they:**

   a) reproduce asexually.

   b) are parasitic and depend on their host for a constant supply of nutrients.

   c) have exoskeletons that they must shed as they grow.

   d) live within shells they find on the ocean floor.

   e) live attached to a solid structure and do not move around.

   100 HARD
   17
   0 EASY

5. **In cnidarians, cnidocysts are primarily used for:**

   a) creation of water flow across the body wall.

   b) formation of free-living medusas.

   c) secretion of digestive enzymes.

   d) prey capture and defense.

   e) muscular contraction during movement.

   100 HARD
   24
   0 EASY

6. **The mollusk's mantle is used primarily for:**

   a) feeding.

   b) gas exchange.

   c) producing the shell.

   d) excretion.

   e) reproduction.

   100 HARD
   35
   0 EASY

7. **Which of the following insect groups has the most species currently named by scientists?**

   a) bees, wasps, and ants

   b) beetles

   c) grasshoppers and crickets

   d) flies

   e) butterflies and moths

   100 HARD
   36
   0 EASY

8. **Which is the only animal phylum to have more than a million described species?**

   a) chordates

   b) arthropods

   c) flatworms

   d) nematodes

   e) mollusks

   100 HARD
   42
   0 EASY

9. The phylum Arthropoda includes all of the following kinds of animals except:

   a) snails.
   b) crabs.
   c) crayfish.
   d) butterflies.
   e) scorpions.

   100 HARD
   53
   0 EASY

10. Which of the following traits is unique to arthropods?

    a) a ventral nerve cord
    b) an exoskeleton
    c) segmentation
    d) a large ratio of brain size to body size
    e) wheeled appendages

    100 HARD
    46
    0 EASY

11. Which of the following are chordates?

    a) fishes
    b) humans
    c) frogs
    d) All of the above are chordates.
    e) Only a) and c) are chordates.

    100 HARD
    38
    0 EASY

12. The two most important evolutionary innovations in vertebrates, which resulted in their eventual domination among the large animals, were:

    a) air-breathing lungs and a more efficient heart.
    b) opposable thumbs.
    c) jaws and amniotic eggs.
    d) the ability to walk or fly.
    e) air-breathing lungs and endothermy.

    100 HARD
    54
    0 EASY

13. Which of these animals is a tetrapod that does not produce amniotic eggs?

    a) salamander
    b) human
    c) monkey
    d) elephant
    e) python

    100 HARD
    51
    0 EASY

14. Why is the amniotic egg considered a key evolutionary innovation?

    a) It prohibits external fertilization, thereby facilitating the evolutionary innovation of internal fertilization.
    b) It has an unbreakable shell.
    c) It greatly increases the likelihood of survival of the eggs in a terrestrial environment.
    d) It enables eggs to float in an aquatic medium.
    e) It extends the time of embryonic development.

    100 HARD
    37
    0 EASY

15. Which came first, the chicken or the egg?

    a) The chicken, because the amniotic egg did not evolve until the first chicken appeared.
    b) The egg, because the amniotic egg evolved well before the first birds.
    c) The chicken, because, during speciation, the adult stage always precedes the juvenile stage.
    d) The egg, because the chicken is not a real species.
    e) It is impossible to determine, because eggs leave no fossils.

    100 HARD
    40
    0 EASY

16. Which of the following is not a reptile?

    a) sparrow
    b) snake
    c) frog
    d) turtle
    e) dinosaur

    100 HARD
    49
    0 EASY

17. Marsupials and which of the following groups combine to make a monophyletic group?

    a) birds
    b) carnivores
    c) primates
    d) monotremes
    e) placental mammals

    100 HARD
    43
    0 EASY

18. According to the fossil record, the first humans appeared approximately _____ years ago.

    a) 6 million
    b) 6,000
    c) 190 million
    d) 100,000
    e) 1 million

    100 HARD
    54
    0 EASY

Short-Answer Questions

1. The cheetah is an amazingly fast cat that hunts its prey on the African savannas, sprinting for short distances at speeds approaching 70 miles per hour. The sloth in the Amazon rain forests of South America is a very slow creature that hangs from a tree by all four limbs and eats vegetation. How can this difference—that the cheetah can sprint at high speeds, while the sloth moves almost in slow motion—be explained in evolutionary terms? What modifications might occur to the cheetah's ability to run if it were to occupy the same niche as the sloth, assuming the cheetah had no natural enemies there?

2. Explain why an ectotherm, such as a snake, requires only an occasional meal, while an endotherm, such as a mouse, requires more frequent meals to survive?

3. A caring pet owner brings her boa constrictor to the veterinarian because it has been more sluggish than normal and seems to be ill. The veterinarian is concerned when she sees that the owner has placed a thick sweater, specially knitted, on the snake. Why might the sweater worry the veterinarian?

4. You have a friend who confuses a terrestrial slug with a segmented worm (annelid). Describe some of the characteristics of the slug that you could point out to him that are not found in any annelids.

See Answers at the back of the book.
For additional study questions, go to www.prep-u.com.

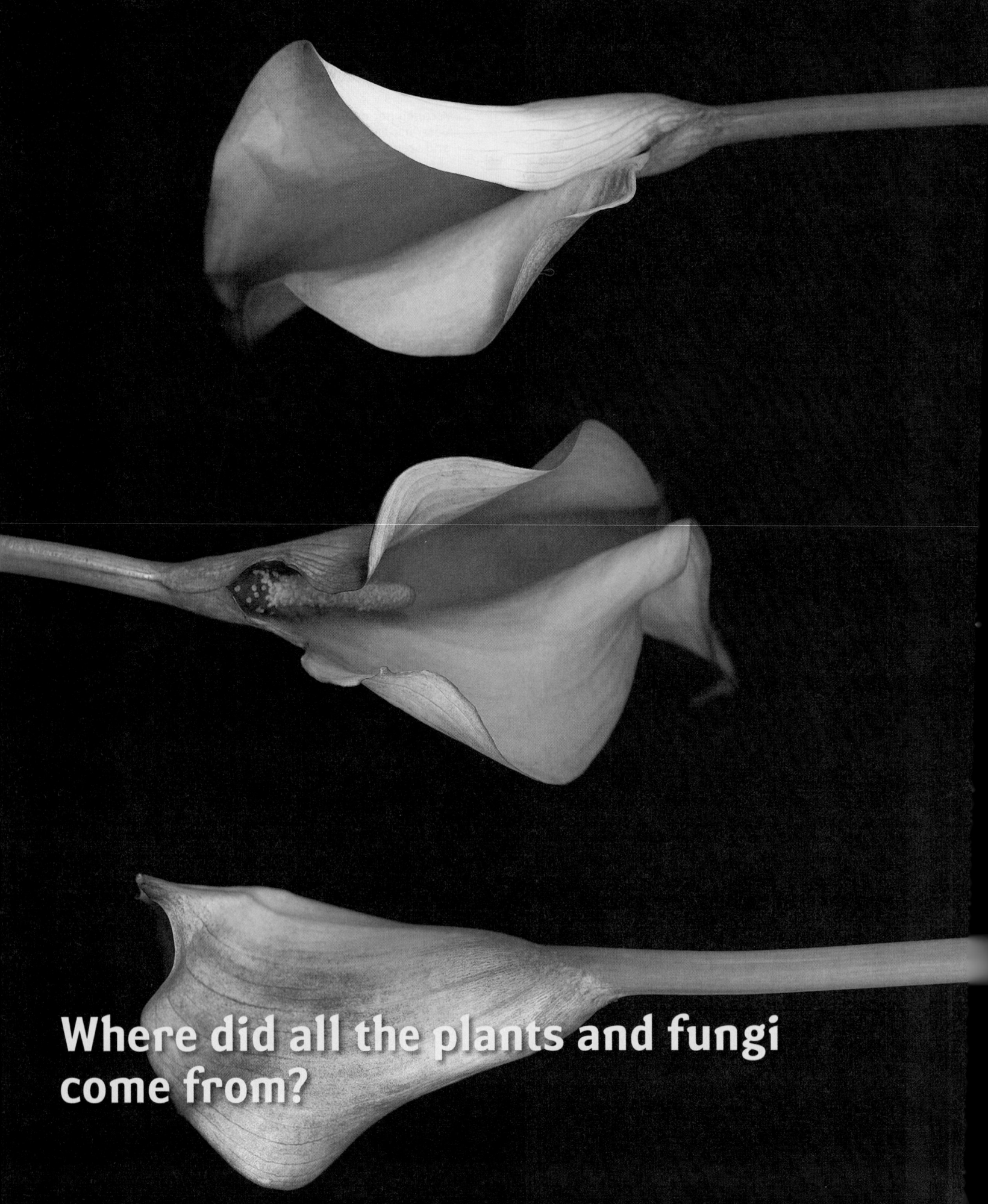

Where did all the plants and fungi come from?

12

Plant and Fungi Diversification

12·1 Plants are just one branch of the eukarya.

The land plant Psilotum nudum, *growing in Hawaii Volcanoes National Park.*

12·1 What makes you a plant?

An animal can move from place to place to get food or water, to avoid being eaten, or to find a mate. It's harder for a plant. It must do all the things an animal does—obtain food and water, protect itself from predators, and reproduce—*but* it can't move a centimeter in the process. Wherever a seed puts down roots, that's where the plant stays anchored for its entire life.

So, plants are organisms that are fixed in place, but that's only one aspect of being a plant. A **plant** is a multicellular eukaryote that produces its own food by photosynthesis—that is, it carries out photosynthesis, using energy from

sunlight to convert carbon dioxide and water to sugar—and has an embryo that develops within the protected environment of the female parent (**FIGURE 12-1**). Plants occur almost exclusively on land, and vary in size from less than 0.04 inch (1 millimeter) to 380 feet (117 meters) tall. (Note that although there are a small number of exceptions to our definition of a plant, it applies to the vast majority of the more than 280,000 species of plants on earth today.)

There are other multicellular and photosynthetic eukaryotes on earth, including many species of algae, such as seaweed, as well as species that are the closest relatives of land plants.

WHAT IS A PLANT?

PLANTS CREATE THEIR OWN FOOD
Almost all plants carry out photosynthesis, using energy from sunlight to convert carbon dioxide and water into sugar.

PLANTS ARE SESSILE AND (MOSTLY) TERRESTRIAL
Plants are anchored in place at their bases and occur almost exclusively on land.

PLANTS ARE MULTICELLULAR
Plants consist of multiple cells and have structures that are specialized for different functions.

FIGURE 12-1 Defining characteristics of a plant.

They differ from plants, however, in that they live only in water or on very moist land surfaces. This is in sharp contrast to most plants, which can live even in deserts.

As we have said, most plants make their own food by the process of photosynthesis. However, a plant can't live on carbohydrate alone, the product of photosynthesis. A plant needs nitrogen to build proteins, phosphorus to make ATP, and salts to create concentration gradients between the inside and outside of cells. Plants use **roots,** the part of a plant below ground, to obtain these needed substances from the soil. Above ground, plants have a **shoot** that consists of a stem and leaves. The stem is a structure that supports the main photosynthetic organ of a plant: its leaves.

When we think of plants, we often think of them as "chlorophyll-containing," but some plants have no chlorophyll—their ancestors had chlorophyll (which is why they are classified as plants), but they have lost almost all of it over evolutionary time—and they can't carry out photosynthesis. Instead, they live as parasites that steal nutrients from other plants. Dodder is an example of a parasitic plant that almost completely lacks chlorophyll and gets its sugar from the host plant it grows on (**FIGURE 12-2**). You can probably find dodder growing on plants in a nearby vacant lot or at the roadside.

Plants that carry out photosynthesis need sunlight, and that creates a challenge for some plants. Think about plants growing on the floor of a forest. It's mostly shady under the tree canopy, with just a few sunny spots where light penetrates the tree branches overhead. If a seed sprouts (germinates) in the shade, the young plant needs to

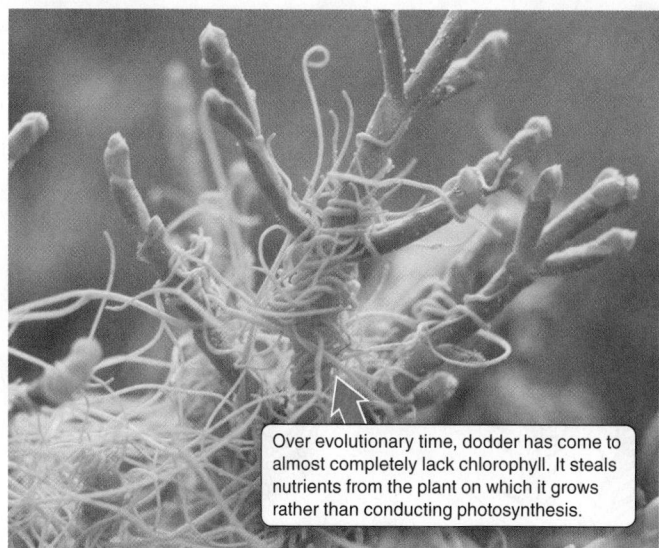

Over evolutionary time, dodder has come to almost completely lack chlorophyll. It steals nutrients from the plant on which it grows rather than conducting photosynthesis.

FIGURE 12-2 Dodder: a parasitic, non-photosynthetic plant.

somehow get to the nearest sunny spot. Plants can do that, of course, but not by moving. Instead, they grow toward the light (**FIGURE 12-3**). You may have seen a plant called "lucky bamboo" (it's not really a bamboo), which can grow in spirals or loops. The growers have produced these shapes by moving the light source every few days, forcing the plant to bend to follow the light. If you buy a lucky bamboo, you must continue rotating the light source or it will start to grow straight, like any other plant.

Q If a plant growing in the shade can't move to a new, sunnier location, how can it reach the available sunlight?

STATIONARY LIVING CREATES CHALLENGES

Diploid ferns

Haploid fern

OBTAINING FOOD
Because plants can't move to reach sunlight, they bend in place and grow toward light.

FINDING A MATE
Male and female plants can't meet to reproduce, so they have developed ways of getting the male gamete to the female gamete, including alternating haploid and diploid life stages, and using other organisms to transport the male gametes.

RESISTING PREDATION
Plants can't run from predators, so they have developed adaptations such as thorns to defend themselves.

FIGURE 12-3 Plants must overcome the constraints of being immobile.

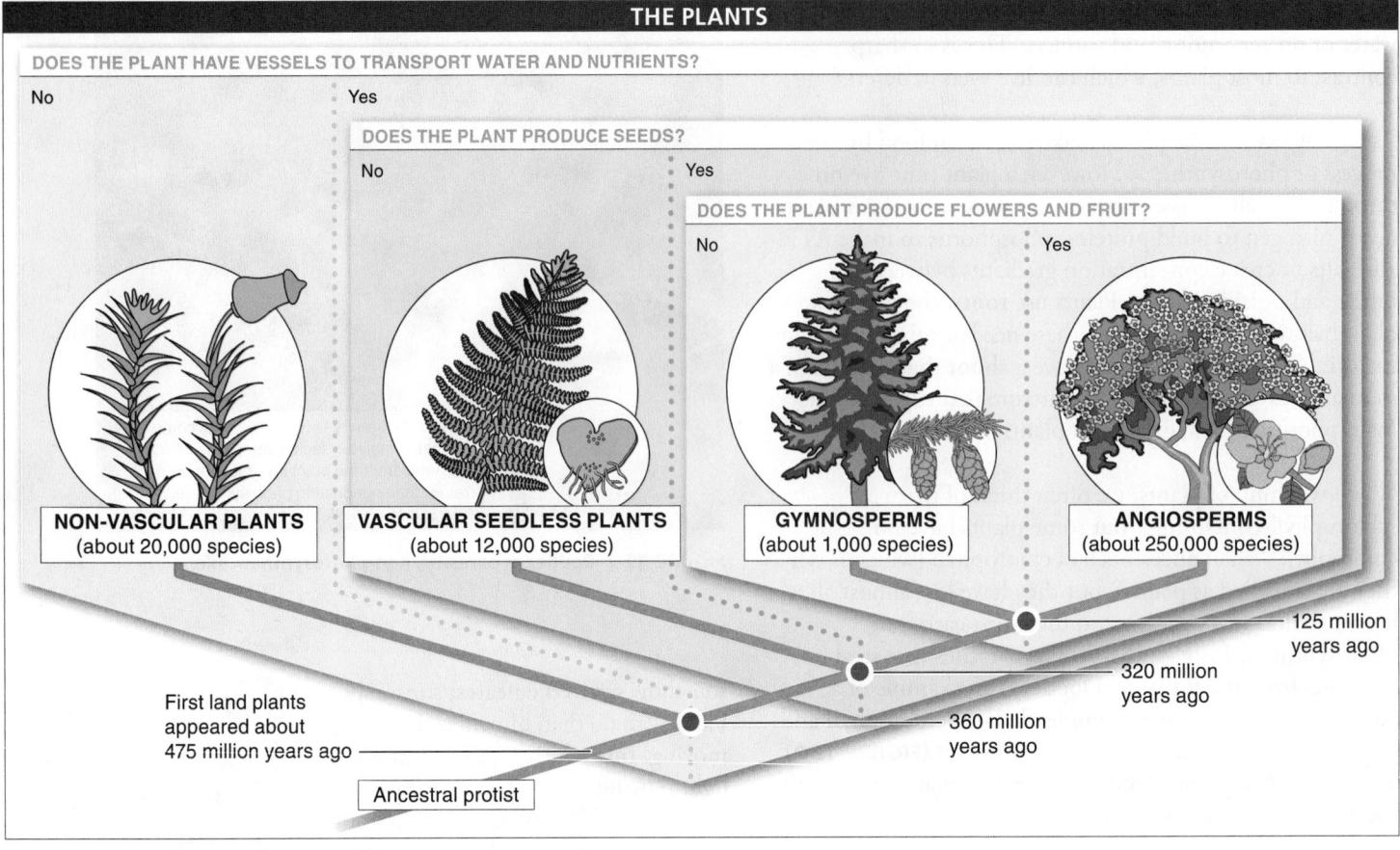

DOES THE PLANT HAVE VESSELS TO TRANSPORT WATER AND NUTRIENTS?

No

Yes

DOES THE PLANT PRODUCE SEEDS?

No

Yes

DOES THE PLANT PRODUCE FLOWERS AND FRUIT?

No

Yes

NON-VASCULAR PLANTS
(about 20,000 species)

VASCULAR SEEDLESS PLANTS
(about 12,000 species)

GYMNOSPERMS
(about 1,000 species)

ANGIOSPERMS
(about 250,000 species)

125 million years ago

320 million years ago

First land plants appeared about 475 million years ago

360 million years ago

Ancestral protist

FIGURE 12-4 Phylogeny of the plants.

Sex can also be a challenge for an organism that is anchored in place by its roots. Not surprisingly, plants have a sex life very different from that of animals. Consider humans as a typical animal. From the moment an egg is fertilized by a sperm, a human has the diploid number of chromosomes—that is, two sets of chromosomes, one set from each parent. Only the egg and sperm are haploid—an egg or a sperm has only one set of chromosomes. In plants, the haploid stage allows the male and female to reproduce, even though they will never meet because they can't move. Some plants enlist the help of animals to carry the male gamete to the female gamete.

Resisting predators is another challenge for organisms that cannot move. Running away is how most animals react to a predator, but plants have found other ways to defend themselves. Thorns, for example, are an anatomical defense that plants use to avoid predation (see Figure 12-3). Plants also use chemicals to deter predators, as many people learn when they develop an itchy rash from poison ivy.

The earliest land plants were the first multicellular organisms to live on land. They were **non-vascular,** meaning that they had no vessels to transport water and nutrients (**FIGURE 12-4**). The subsequent evolution of land plants was a series of radiations of forms with characteristics that made them increasingly independent of water. The evolutionary tree of plants shows these stages clearly: first the development of vessels to conduct water from the soil through the plant (the vascular plants), then seeds that provide nutrients to get the next generation off to a good start (the gymnosperms), and finally flowers that allow plants to entice or trick insects and birds into spreading the plant's male gametes (the angiosperms). We'll look at each of these plant adaptations in this chapter. We also explore the ecologically important kingdom of fungi. Although fungi are not plants, they are very closely associated with plants.

TAKE-HOME MESSAGE 12·1

Plants are multicellular organisms that spend most of their lives anchored in one place by their roots. The inability of plants to move shapes the way they obtain food, reproduce, and protect themselves from predation. Characteristics evolved that made it possible for plants to succeed on land despite their inability to move.

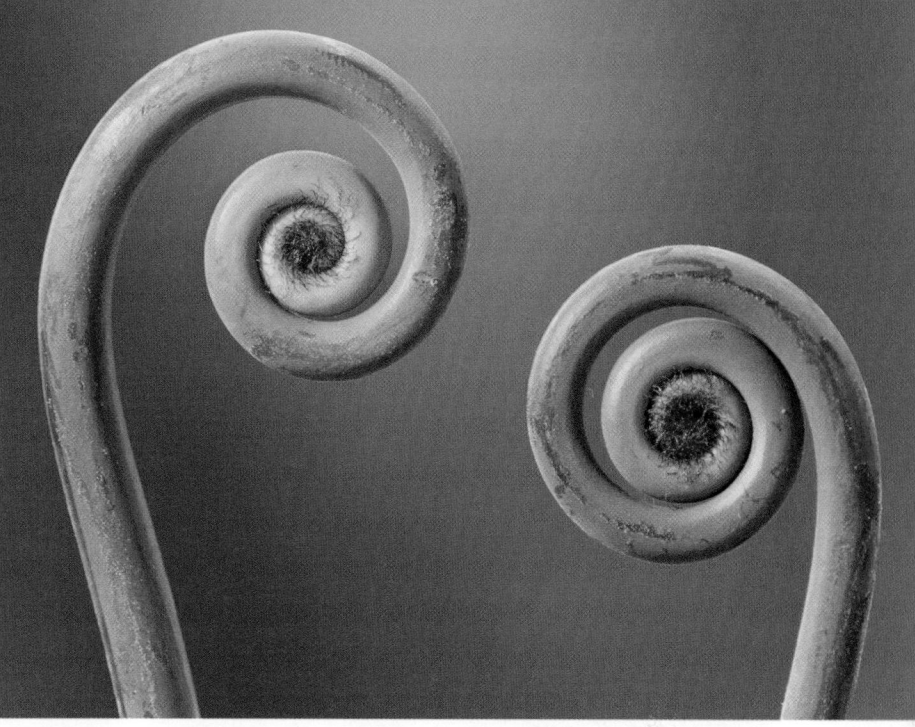

12·2–12·4 The first plants had neither roots nor seeds.

Uluhe ferns, Dicranopteris linearis, *growing in Hawaii Volcanoes National Park.*

12·2 Colonizing land brings new opportunities and new challenges for plants.

The aquatic ancestors of land plants were green algae, which are classified by many taxonomists as part of the plant kingdom. Like the land plants, green algae are multicellular, photosynthetic eukaryotes, but green algae live only in water or on very moist land surfaces. As water dwellers, green algae do not require specialized structures to obtain water and nutrients; water simply enters their cells by osmosis, and the nutrients they require are in solution in the water that surrounds them. Some green algae, such as sea lettuce and stoneworts, even look like land plants. But there is enough uncertainty among taxonomists about the best classification of green algae that some classify green algae within the protist kingdom, and they consider some green algae that look like slime on rocks—organisms called coleochaetes (pronounced кон-lee-oh-keets)—to be the closest relatives of plants (**FIGURE 12-5**). An individual coleochaete is about the size of a pinhead and is only one cell-layer thick. Coleochaetes can withstand exposure to air, so they survive when the water level in a lake falls and leaves them high and dry. This resistance to drying out was the first evolutionary step that plants took as they moved from water to land.

The first land plants appeared about 475 million years ago. They weren't impressive-looking, just some patches of low-growing green stems at the water's edge. They did not

Coleochaetes, a type of green alga, are the closest relative to plants. They can withstand exposure to air when water levels fall.

💡 *Ancestors of plants began the transition from water to land with the evolution of resistance to drying.*

FIGURE 12-5 Plants' closest relative: a green alga called a coleochaete.

When plants emerged onto land, they faced the same two challenges that terrestrial animals faced 25 million years later.

PROBLEM: GRAVITY

SOLUTION: The earliest plants grew very close to the ground, as mosses do today, in order to resist the pull of gravity.

PROBLEM: DESICCATION

SOLUTION: Plants developed an outer waxy layer called a cuticle that covers their entire surface.

FIGURE 12-6 Leaving the water.

have any of the structures we associate with plants today—no roots, leaves, or flowers. But from an evolutionary perspective, those early plants were enormously important because, until terrestrial plants evolved, there was nothing on land for other land organisms to eat. Thus, the first land plants not only set the stage for the tremendous diversity of plant life that we know today but also paved the way for the evolution and diversification of land animals.

As land plants emerged, they faced the same two challenges that were to confront the first terrestrial animals, some 25 million years later: supporting themselves against the pull of gravity and reducing evaporation so they didn't dry out. The second of these problems was the more urgent. The

earliest plants did not have to grow upward—they could creep along the ground—but they *did* have to avoid drying out (**FIGURE 12-6**). The material that protects all land plants from drying is a shiny, waxy layer on the stem and leaves called the **cuticle.**

> **TAKE-HOME MESSAGE 12·2**
>
> The first land plants were small, had no leaves, roots, or flowers, and could grow only at the water's edge. Nonetheless, these inconspicuous little plants set the stage for the enormous diversity of terrestrial plants and animals on earth today.

12·3 Mosses and other non-vascular plants lack vessels for transporting nutrients and water.

The earliest land plants were low-growing for a reason: they had no structures that could transport water and nutrients from the soil upward into the plant. The only way that these substances could move was by diffusing from one cell into an adjacent cell, and so on. Diffusion is a slow process, and plants that rely on diffusion can grow only a few centimeters tall.

Despite the limitations of diffusion, three groups of plants, all known as **bryophytes,** still use diffusion to move substances through their bodies, rather than having any sort of "circulatory system." They are the liverworts, hornworts, and mosses. More than 12,000 species of mosses grow in habitats extending from arctic and alpine regions to the tropics. Liverworts and hornworts are small (less than an

THE NON-VASCULAR PLANTS

Moss

Liverwort

Hornwort

COMMON CHARACTERISTICS
• Distribute water and nutrients throughout plant by diffusion
• Release haploid spores, which grow and produce gametes
• Life cycle with multicellular haploid and diploid phases

MEMBERS INCLUDE
• Mosses (about 12,000 species)
• Liverworts (about 8,000 species)
• Hornworts (about 100 species)

FIGURE 12-7 Overview of the non-vascular plants.

inch in height), simple plants that grow in moist and shady places and resemble flattened moss. These three types of bryophyte plants are referred to as "non-vascular" because they do not have vessels to transport water and food. Water and nutrients are absorbed into the outermost layer of cells

by projections that penetrate a few micrometers into the soil. Because these projections are so short, non-vascular plants must either live in places where the soil is always moist or become dormant when the soil surface dries out (**FIGURE 12-7**).

To adapt to land, the non-vascular plants had to develop a method of reproduction that protected the plant embryo from drying out and provided it with a source of nutrients. The innovation that made this possible was a life cycle of alternating haploid and diploid generations, which is radically different from the life cycle of humans and most other animals. In animals, the haploid gametes, at fertilization, produce a new, diploid cell that becomes a multicellular organism, which, in the adult stage, starts the process all over again. In plants, however, there is an "alternation of generations."

The life cycle of a moss provides a useful example of how the alternation of generations works. When you look at a spongy mass of moss (or any other non-vascular plant), what you see is the *haploid* (or **gametophyte**) part of the life cycle, rather than the *diploid* (or **sporophyte**) part of the life cycle (**FIGURE 12-8**). For this reason, mosses are described as having a dominant gametophyte. The adult moss plants are haploid plants—that is, all the cells have only one set of chromosomes. There are male and female moss plants that have male and female reproductive structures located among the feathery leaves at the tips of the stems. Water collects here during rainstorms, allowing the sperm to "swim" (or be splashed) from the male structures to fertilize eggs in the female structures. Once the egg is fertilized in the female structure, a diploid zygote is formed, and it divides to become an embryo.

The embryo is sheltered within the female reproductive structure, which provides water and nutrients for the growing embryo. Eventually, the female structure elongates to such a degree that it breaks in two and forms a capsule extending over the top of the plant like a raised fist. Inside the capsule are haploid **spores**—single cells, containing DNA, RNA, and a few proteins. When a capsule ruptures, it releases hundreds of spores. The spores that land in moist, sheltered spots grow into new (haploid) male or female moss plants.

Some non-vascular plants are economically or ecologically important. "Peat moss" (*Sphagnum* moss), found in many parts of the world, is sold as a soil enhancer for gardening. In areas where trees are scarce, peat is dried and burned as fuel. In places with monsoon seasons, such as Malaysia and

MOSS LIFE CYCLE

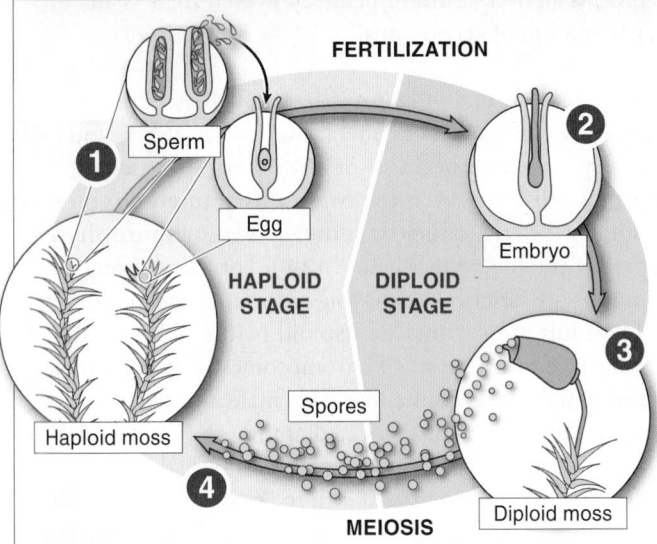

FERTILIZATION

Sperm

Egg

1

2

Embryo

HAPLOID STAGE

DIPLOID STAGE

3

Spores

Haploid moss

4

Diploid moss

MEIOSIS

1 When there is sufficient water on the leaves—such as after rainfall—sperm swim from male reproductive structures to female reproductive structures, where they fertilize the egg.

2 A diploid embryo forms and develops into an adult diploid moss.

3 The diploid moss develops a capsule, which bursts and releases haploid spores.

4 A spore lands on moist soil and grows into an adult haploid moss.

FIGURE 12-8 Alternation of generations in mosses. The spongy part of the moss, at ground level in the photograph, is the haploid form. Hovering above, on stalks, are the spore capsules, the diploid form.

Indonesia, peat bogs—consisting of partially decayed moss—are important in flood control, because they can absorb enormous amounts of water and release it over a period of months. Another commercial application: mounds

Non-vascular plants such as peat moss have many important economic and ecological uses, from flood control to gardening to the production of Scotch whisky (shown here).

FIGURE 12-9 Uses of peat. Peat can be dried and then burned as fuel to heat homes. In traditional Scotch whisky production, the burning of peat during the distillation process provides the smoky flavor.

of burning peat are used to dry the barley used in producing Scotch whisky. This gives Scotch its distinctive smoky taste (**FIGURE 12-9**).

Unlikely as it seems, non-vascular plants can grow in deserts, and mosses (along with lichens and cyanobacteria) are important components of the biological crust that holds desert soils in place. The crust cements the soil particles together and allows the soil to resist wind erosion, but it is extremely fragile and very slow to regenerate. When people or cattle walk over the crust, they break it into small pieces that cannot resist wind, and erosion can then strip a meter or more of soil in a few decades, leaving tree trunks supported in mid-air by their roots (**FIGURE 12-10**).

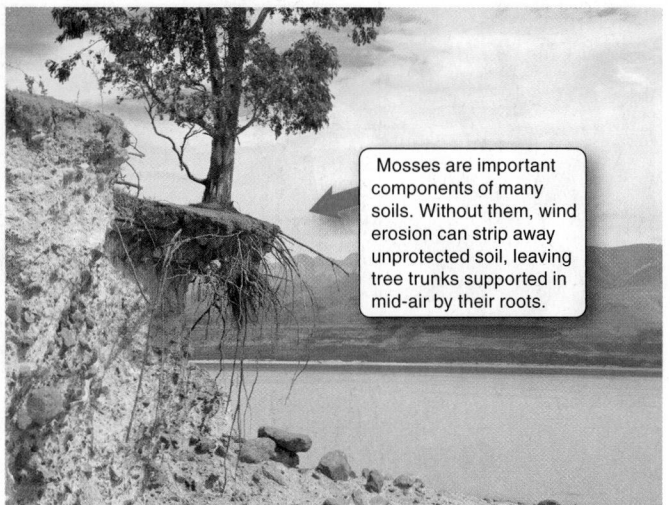

Mosses are important components of many soils. Without them, wind erosion can strip away unprotected soil, leaving tree trunks supported in mid-air by their roots.

FIGURE 12-10 Non-vascular plants reduce erosion. Without mosses, soils are more fragile. Shown here: a eucalyptus tree with eroded roots in New Zealand.

12·4

The evolution of vascular tissue made large plants possible.

What a difference some tubes make. That's all vascular tissue is—a sort of infrastructure of tubes that begins in a plant's roots and extends up its stem and out to the tips of its leaves. The evolution of vascular tissue allowed early land plants to transport water and nutrients faster and more effectively than the cell-to-cell diffusion that non-vascular plants must rely on. Vascular plants' roots penetrate far enough into the soil to reach moisture even when the soil surface is dry. Roots that reach deep into the soil also provide the support that a plant needs to grow upward without falling over. As a consequence, **vascular plants** can grow taller than non-vascular plants and are more successful in areas where the surface of the ground dries out between rains (**FIGURE 12-11**).

Ferns are the most familiar of the primitive vascular plants. During the Carboniferous period, which extended from 360 to 300 million years ago, ferns were a major component of the huge swamp forests that eventually formed the coal deposits we now mine. A related group of plants, the horsetails, like their Carboniferous ancestors, grow in wet habitats where the oxygen concentration around the roots is low because the spaces between soil particles are filled with water (rather than air). To adapt to this wet environment, horsetails developed hollow stems that allow oxygen from the air to diffuse down to the roots. The thin leaves of horsetails have a single nutrient- and water-carrying vessel extending from the base to the tip.

Simply having vessels, as horsetails do, is an important evolutionary innovation, but ferns took a further step. In addition to the central vessel in each leaflet, the leaves of ferns have vessels branching from the central vessel to the edges of the leaflet. This arrangement places a channel for the movement of water and nutrients close to each cell in the leaf.

Like non-vascular plants, horsetails and most ferns reproduce with spores. In horsetails, the central hollow stem is topped by a conical structure where the haploid spores are produced and released. Many ferns have **sporangia** (*sing.* **sporangium**) on the undersides of the leaves where spores are produced (**FIGURE 12-12**). Because the haploid gametophyte is much smaller and simpler than the diploid sporophyte, ferns are described as having a dominant sporophyte.

Horsetails and ferns are taller than non-vascular plants, so their spores can be blown by the wind when they are released, and they may settle some distance from the parent plant. This increased dispersal ability was an important adaptation—the non-vascular plants are so low-growing that wind can't play much of a role in moving their spores.

A spore that lands on moist soil grows into a tiny heart-shaped structure called a **prothallus,** which is the

FERN LIFE CYCLE

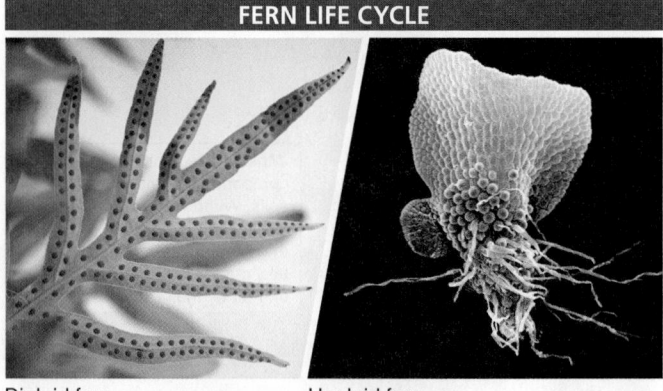

Diploid fern   Haploid fern

THE VASCULAR SEEDLESS PLANTS

Katote tree ferns

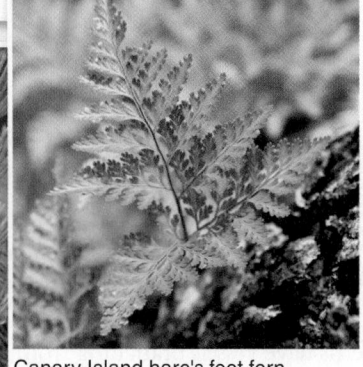

Canary Island hare's foot fern

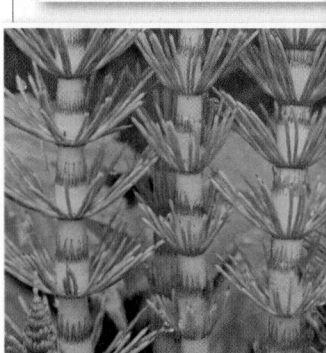

Common horsetail

COMMON CHARACTERISTICS
- Distribute water and nutrients throughout the plant with a "circulatory system" of vascular tissue
- Release haploid spores, dispersed by the wind, which grow and produce gametes
- Life cycle (unlike in animals) with multicellular haploid and diploid phases

MEMBERS INCLUDE
- Ferns (about 12,000 species)
- Horsetails (about 15 species)

FIGURE 12-11 Snapshot of the vascular seedless plants: ferns and horsetails.

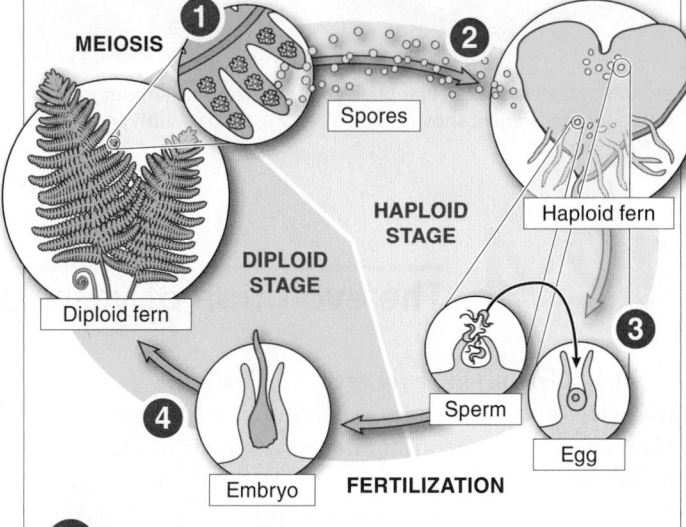

1 Adult ferns release haploid spores, which are carried by the wind to a new location.

2 A spore lands on moist soil and grows into a haploid fern called a prothallus.

3 When there is sufficient water on the leaves—such as after rainfall—sperm swim from male reproductive structures to female reproductive structures, where they fertilize the egg.

4 A diploid embryo forms and continues to grow into an adult diploid fern.

FIGURE 12-12 Haploid and diploid life stages in ferns. The photograph shows the sporangia, the spore-producing bodies, located on the underside of most fern leaves—on the diploid plant. The diploid and haploid plants in the fern life cycle are very different in appearance.

free-living haploid life stage of a fern (see Figure 12-12). The prothallus produces the haploid gametes: some cells produce eggs and others produce sperm. Sperm "swim" through drops of rainwater to fertilize an egg, and the fertilized egg (a diploid zygote with two sets of chromosomes) grows into an adult fern.

TAKE-HOME MESSAGE 12·4

Vessels are an effective "circulatory system" to carry water and nutrients up from the soil to a plant's leaves. The first vascular plants—including the earliest ferns and horsetails—were able to grow much taller than their non-vascular predecessors.

12·5–12·7 The advent of the seed opened new worlds to plants.

Forests surrounding Mistaya Lake in Banff National Park, Alberta, Canada.

12·5

What is a seed?

As we've seen, the evolutionary development of vascular tissue allowed plants to grow larger. Vascular plants could colonize areas where the soil at the surface of the ground was not always wet, because their roots could penetrate the soil to reach water and nutrients. The next big innovation in plant evolution was the **seed,** an embryonic plant with its own supply of water and nutrients encased within a protective coating (**FIGURE 12-13**).

Seeds are goodbye gifts that adult plants give to their offspring—they contain the materials needed to begin a new life. Unlike spores, which are single cells that contain only

SEEDS: STRUCTURE AND GROWTH

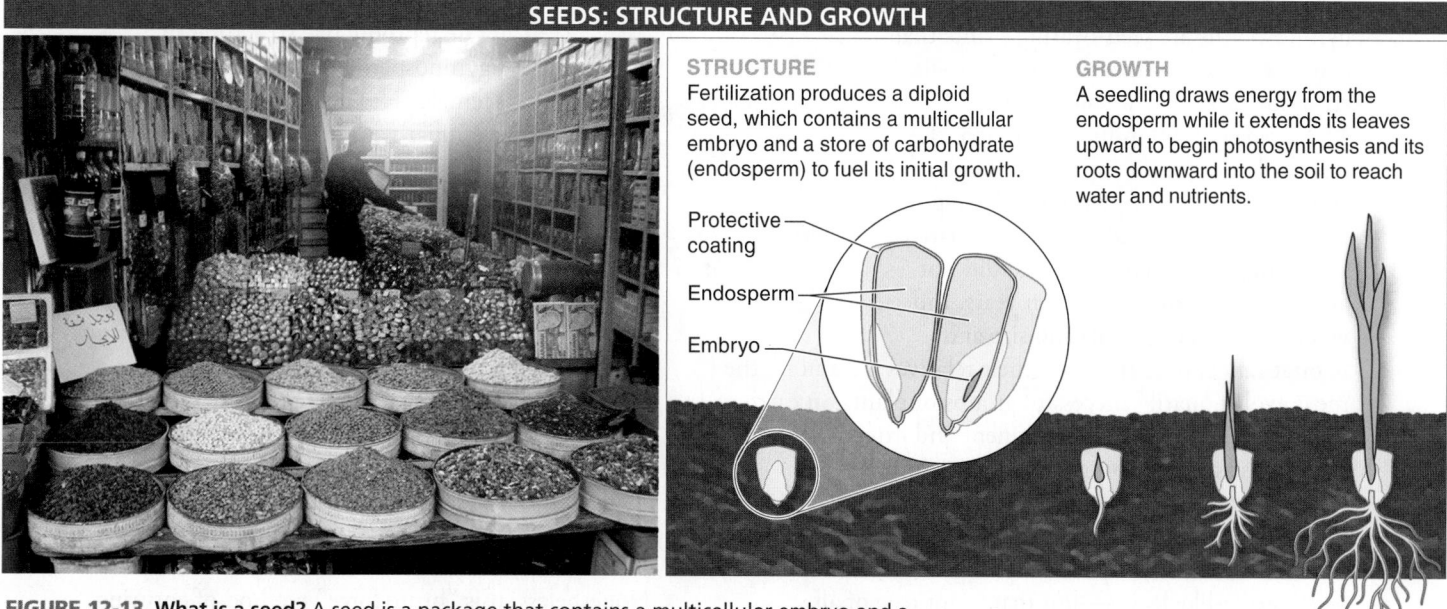

STRUCTURE
Fertilization produces a diploid seed, which contains a multicellular embryo and a store of carbohydrate (endosperm) to fuel its initial growth.

Protective coating

Endosperm

Embryo

GROWTH
A seedling draws energy from the endosperm while it extends its leaves upward to begin photosynthesis and its roots downward into the soil to reach water and nutrients.

FIGURE 12-13 What is a seed? A seed is a package that contains a multicellular embryo and a store of carbohydrate, the endosperm, to fuel its initial growth. This makes many seeds desirable as food sources. Shown here are seeds for sale at a market in Jordan.

DNA, RNA, and a few proteins, seeds contain both a multicellular embryo and a store of nutrients, mostly starch. This nutritive tissue—called **endosperm** in flowering plants and trees—can fuel the seed's initial growth. A seedling draws energy from the endosperm while it extends its leaves upward to begin photosynthesis and its roots downward to reach water and nutrients in the soil. There are two modern groups of seed-producing plants: **gymnosperms** (including pines, firs, and redwoods) and **angiosperms** (all of the flowering plants and trees).

Q Do plants have sex? How are seeds formed?

Like plants that do not produce seeds, seed plants have a life stage, called the gametophyte, that produces haploid gametes (sperm and egg). This is analogous to an individual human, which produces haploid gametes. Because the gametophyte is much smaller than the sporophyte in seed plants, these plants are considered sporophyte dominant. **Pollen grains** and **ovules** are the male and female gametophytes, respectively, of seed plants. In brief (we expand on this later in the chapter), a haploid female gamete (egg) forms inside the ovule. When a pollen grain lands near the ovule, it produces a tube that grows into the ovule. Sperm from the pollen grain move through the pollen tube into the ovule and fertilize the egg. The external layer of the ovule then forms the seed coat.

Another of the challenges that plants face is dispersing their seeds. The seed stage is the only opportunity most plants have to send their offspring away from home, and seeds and seed pods have many ways to do this. These range from the forceful send-off of exploding seed pods, to seeds that hitch a ride in or on passing animals, to those that are so small and light that they can float in water or air (such as dandelion seeds)—not to mention the use of fruits in seed dispersal. As we'll see later in the chapter, many methods for dispersing seeds have evolved.

TAKE-HOME MESSAGE 12·5

Seeds are the way that plants give their offspring a good start in life. A seed contains a multicellular embryo plus a store of carbohydrate and other nutrients. Seeds are distributed by wind, animals, or water.

12·6 With the evolution of the seed, gymnosperms became the dominant plants on earth.

Gymnosperms include four major groups: the conifers, cycads, gnetophytes, and ginkgo (just one species) (**FIGURE 12-14**). All of the 900 or more species of gymnosperms are seed-bearing plants that produce ovules on the edge of a cone-like structure. During the middle of the Mesozoic era, 160 million years ago, the forests that dinosaurs walked through consisted entirely of gymnosperms—pine trees, redwoods, cycads, and their relatives. Flowering plants (angiosperms) did not appear for another 35 million years. Indeed, when it comes to population size and habitat range, pine trees and their relatives are among the most evolutionarily successful groups of plants on earth, growing on every ice-free continent and extending from sea level to the tree line on mountains (**FIGURE 12-15**).

Pines, spruces, firs, redwoods, and their relatives are familiar to residents of the temperate regions: many of these conifers have needle-like leaves—but that is not true of all gymnosperms. The ginkgo has distinctive fan-shaped leaves, and cycads have palm-like fronds with many small leaflets

(see Figure 12-15). Both are nearly identical to fossils from the Mesozoic.

Q Why does tree pollen coat the windshield of cars parked outside in the spring?

The reproductive structures of gymnosperms—the cones—are male or female. The pine cones you are probably familiar with are the female cones, which produce the ovules and, eventually, the seeds (**FIGURE 12-16**). The male cones are smaller and release pollen that is blown by the wind, and some of it reaches the ovules, which lie beneath the protruding scales of the female cones. The quantity of pollen released by conifers is beyond imagination—pollen-heavy air in a pine forest becomes hazy, and every surface is coated with yellow. Wind dispersal is clearly an inefficient method of **pollination** (getting the pollen to the vicinity of the ovule): billions of pollen grains are wasted for each grain that lands on a female cone and produces sperm to fertilize an egg in an ovule. Nonetheless, this "brute force" method of ensuring fertilization works: for more than 200 million years, pines have been successfully pollinated by wind.

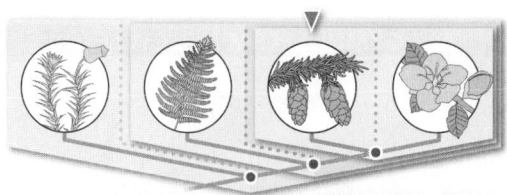

THE GYMNOSPERMS

COMMON CHARACTERISTICS
- Distribute water and nutrients throughout the plant with a "circulatory system" of vascular tissue
- Reproductive structures called cones produce the gametes
- Fertilization produces seeds

MEMBERS INCLUDE
- Conifers (about 600 species)
- Cycads (about 300 species)
- Gnetophytes (about 65 species)
- Ginkgo (1 species)

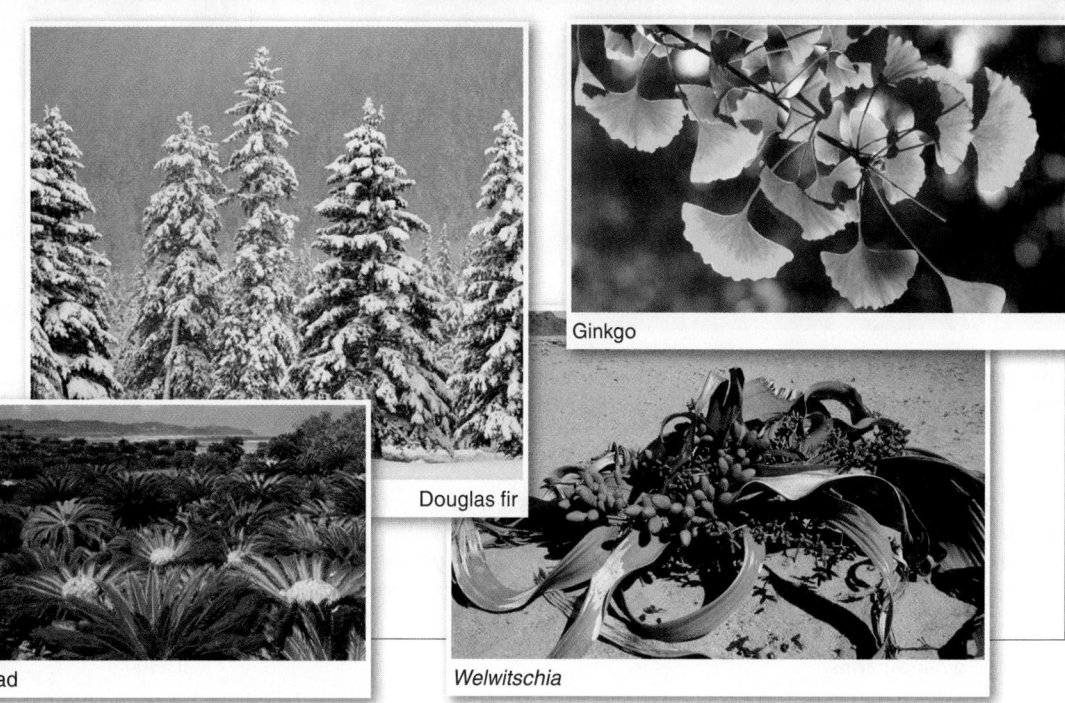

Ginkgo

Douglas fir

Cycad

Welwitschia

FIGURE 12-14 Overview of the gymnosperms: non-flowering plants with seeds.

GROUPS OF GYMNOSPERMS

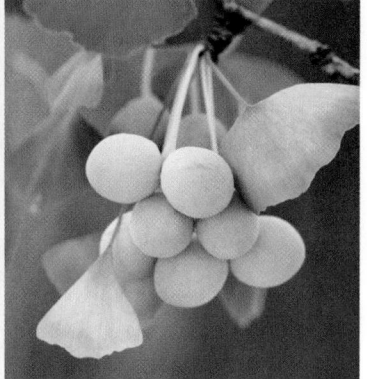

CONIFERS
- Most commonly found in colder temperate and sometimes drier regions of the world
- Commonly have needle-shaped leaves
- Important source of timber
- Include pines, spruces, firs, cedars, hemlocks, yews, larches, cypresses

CYCADS
- Slow-growing gymnosperms of tropical and subtropical regions
- Most resemble palm trees
- Several species are facing extinction in the wild

GNETOPHYTES
- Composed of 3 groups: *Gnetum, Ephedra,* and *Welwitschia*
- Most gnetophyte species are *Ephedra,* a shrub-like plant sometimes used as a herbal remedy for respiratory ailments

GINKGO
- *Ginkgo biloba* is the only remaining species
- Distinctive fan-shaped leaves
- The outer covering of the seeds emits a foul odor

FIGURE 12-15 Major groups of gymnosperms: conifers, cycads, gnetophytes, and ginkgo.

MALE CONE
The male cone releases pollen grains that require wind to reach a female cone.

FEMALE CONE
The female cone has ovules on the protruding scales. They produce seeds when fertilized by pollen.

 Although billions of pollen grains are wasted for each one that fertilizes an egg, gymnosperms have successfully used wind pollination for more than 200 million years.

FIGURE 12-16 Cones are the reproductive structures of gymnosperms.

When the pollen arrives at the female cone, a pollen tube forms and transports the haploid sperm to the ovule, where fertilization occurs and a diploid embryo begins to grow. The embryo develops slowly within the female cone over the course of many months, until the scales of the cone open and release the seed, ready to sprout into a new plant (**FIGURE 12-17**). With the evolution of seeds, gymnosperms developed a life history with no free-living haploid stage such as we see in non-vascular plants.

This evolutionary change in life history probably reflects the different degrees of evolutionary fitness of haploid versus diploid organisms. A haploid organism has just one copy of each chromosome, which means it has just one copy of each allele. If the haploid organism carries a defective allele for a critically important gene, the organism is doomed, because it has only that one defective version of the gene. In contrast, diploid organisms have two sets of chromosomes and thus two copies of each allele. If one copy is defective, the second copy can function as a backup, enabling the plant to produce the gene product. As a result, mutations are much less likely to be lethal for diploid organisms than for haploid organisms.

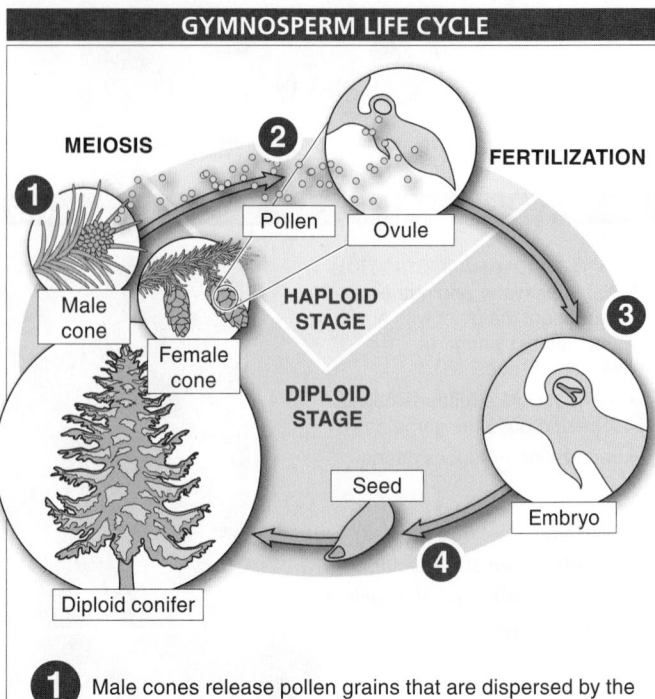

1. Male cones release pollen grains that are dispersed by the wind to ovules found beneath the scales of female cones.

2. Pollen grains release sperm that fertilize an egg within the ovule.

3. Fertilization creates a diploid embryo that matures into a seed.

4. Eventually, the seed is released from the female cone and grows into an adult tree.

 The evolution of seeds in gymnosperms eliminated the free-living haploid life stage seen in mosses and ferns.

FIGURE 12-17 Assisted by the wind: the life cycle of gymnosperms.

TAKE-HOME MESSAGE 12·6

Gymnosperms (pine trees and their relatives) were the earliest plants to produce seeds. This mode of reproduction offered advantages over the spores of earlier plants and gave gymnosperms the boost they needed to become the dominant plants of the early and middle Mesozoic era. Gymnosperms depend on wind to carry their pollen—not an efficient method of dispersal. Conifers protect the developing seeds in the female cone.

12·7 Conifers include the tallest and longest-living trees.

In addition to having the widest geographic range and the greatest number of species among the gymnosperms, the cone-bearing trees—that is, the conifers—include both the tallest and the oldest living organisms on earth (**FIGURE 12-18**). The four tallest trees in the world are conifers: a coast redwood that is 380 feet (113 m) tall, a Douglas fir and a Sitka spruce, each 318 feet (97 m), and a Sierra redwood at 311 feet (95 m). But not all conifers are big: there are also miniature species of conifers, such as the shore pine, which can be just 20 centimeters tall. The oldest tree trunk belongs to a Great Basin bristlecone pine, the Methuselah tree, which has lived for more than 4,800 years. (A slightly older tree was cut down in 1964.) There's more to a tree than its trunk, though, and trunks can be replaced. That is what a Norway spruce in Sweden has been doing: the current trunk is about 600 years old, but the roots are 9,550 years old. This tree has persisted by sending up a new trunk each time the old one dies.

Trees can grow large and live to great ages because woody plants can be exceptionally strong and resistant to attack by herbivores. A cross section of a tree trunk shows the structural characteristics that allow a tree to stand erect and transport water to leaves more than 100 meters above the ground. Rigidity is provided primarily by the heartwood, which is a core of dead tissue that contains complexly cross-linked molecules.

Bark covers the outside of the tree trunk and branches. The outer layers of bark are dead tissue that can be shed without damage to the tree, protecting the living tissue from attack by plant-eating insects. Part of the success of conifers can also be traced to their ability to defend themselves by exuding a sticky pine pitch that can engulf and smother insects.

TALLEST AND OLDEST

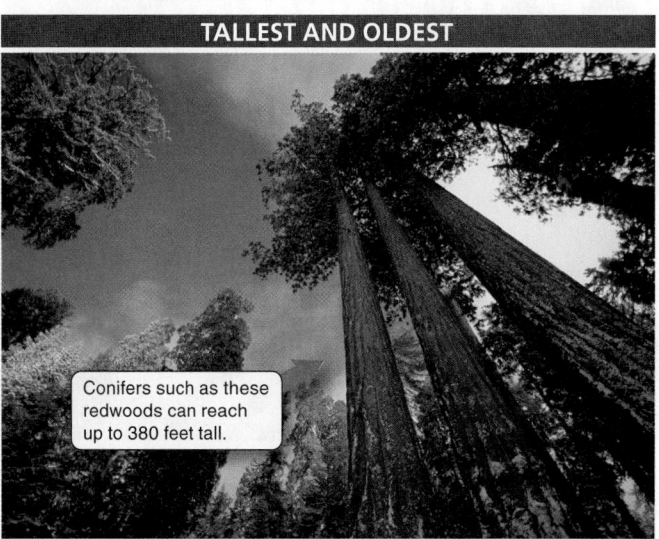

Conifers such as these redwoods can reach up to 380 feet tall.

Conifers such as these bristlecone pines can live for more than 4,800 years.

Conifers have grown taller and reached older ages than any other plants.

FIGURE 12-18 Towering and ancient gymnosperms.

TAKE-HOME MESSAGE 12·7

Conifers are the success stories among gymnosperms, with more species and a larger geographic range than all of their relatives combined. Rigidity, an exterior layer of bark, and the ability to exude sticky pitch protect conifers, allowing them to grow taller and reach older ages than any other plants.

12·8–12·10 Flowering plants are the most diverse and successful plants.

Bleeding heart flowers, surrounded by neat, heart-shaped leaves.

12·8

Angiosperms are the dominant plants today.

The appearance of flowering plants (angiosperms) about 135 million years ago set the stage for the botanical world we know today, with flowering trees, flowering bushes, and all the grasses and herbaceous (non-woody) plants we see around us. The vast majority of plants on earth are flowering plants in the angiosperm group (**FIGURE 12-19**). Many of the early flowering plants would look familiar to us, and angiosperms dominate the plant world now, with some 250,000 species, compared with approximately 1,000 species of gymnosperms.

Flowers come in a bewildering variety of sizes, shapes, and colors, but they all have similar structures: a supporting stem with modified leaves—the flashy petals and the sepals, which are a (usually) green wrapping that encloses the flower while it is in bud. Most angiosperms combine the male and female reproductive structures in the same flower. The male structure is the **stamen** and includes the **anther,** which produces the pollen, and its supporting stalk, the **filament.** The female reproductive structure is the **carpel.** It has an enclosed **ovary** at its base, which contains one or more ovules in which eggs develop; a stalk (the style), extending from the ovary; and a sticky tip (the stigma) (**FIGURE 12-20**).

Pollination, in angiosperms, is the transfer of pollen from the male reproductive structures to the female reproductive structures of a flower—sometimes the same flower, and sometimes a different flower (either on the same individual or a different individual). Pollination is a multi-step process

in which a pollen grain sticks to the stigma, forms a tube that grows until it reaches the ovule, and thus provides a route for sperm to travel down the tube to fertilize the egg. In the next section, we explore the tremendously rich and varied methods by which angiosperms get the male gametes to the female gametes.

Although most flowers contain both male and female structures, several thousand species of plants produce flowers that are only male or only female. Sometimes, male and female flowers are borne on different individual plants, but in quite a few angiosperm species, the same plant has some male flowers and some female flowers, often side by side. Maize (corn) is a familiar plant with male and female flowers in different places on the same plant, although you might not recognize the reproductive structures as flowers. The tassel at the top of the plant is the male flower, and the ear is formed by female flowers.

TAKE-HOME MESSAGE 12·8

Flowering plants appeared in the Cretaceous period, more than 100 million years ago, and diversified rapidly to become the dominant plants in the modern world. A flower houses a plant's reproductive structures. Most flowers have both male and female reproductive structures, but some species have flowers with only male or only female structures.

THE ANGIOSPERMS

COMMON CHARACTERISTICS
- Distribute water and nutrients throughout the plant with a "circulatory system" of vascular tissue
- Produce flowers, which produce gametes
- Seeds are enclosed within an ovule

MEMBERS INCLUDE
- Flowering trees, bushes, herbs, and grasses (about 250,000 species)

Apple tree

Water lily

Victoria plums

French lavender

FIGURE 12-19 Snapshot of the angiosperms.

FLOWER STRUCTURE

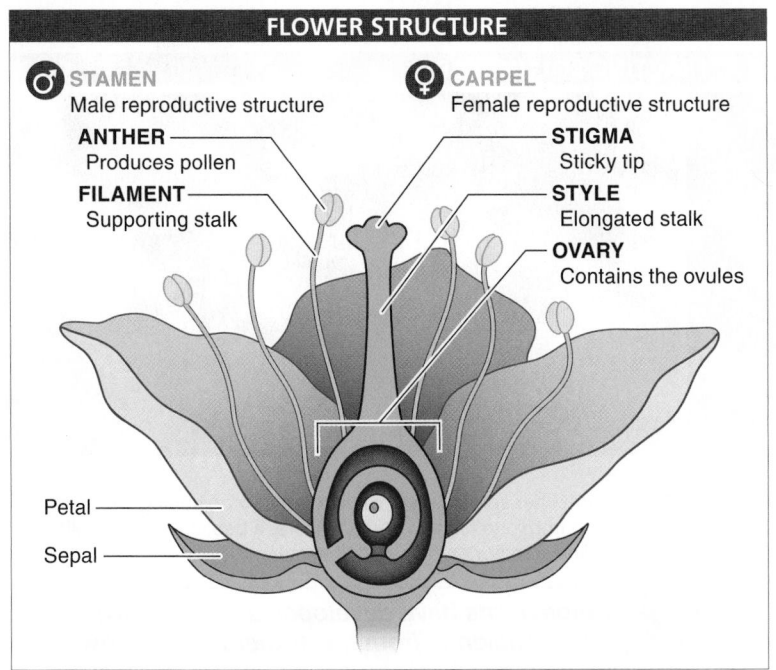

♂ STAMEN
Male reproductive structure

ANTHER —
Produces pollen

FILAMENT —
Supporting stalk

♀ CARPEL
Female reproductive structure

STIGMA
Sticky tip

STYLE
Elongated stalk

OVARY
Contains the ovules

Petal

Sepal

FIGURE 12-20 A flower houses a plant's reproductive structures.

PLANTS ARE A BRANCH OF EUKARYA

PLANTS WITHOUT ROOTS OR SEEDS

THE ADVENT OF THE SEED

FLOWERING PLANTS

PLANTS AND ANIMAL RELATIONSHIPS

FUNGI

489

A flower is nothing without a pollinator.

Flowers may play only a tiny role in the sex lives of humans—did you give or receive any last Valentine's Day?—but they play the lead part in the sex lives of most plants. Here we examine how it is possible for individual plants, rooted in the ground in different locations, to bring their gametes together in sexual reproduction.

Picture a flower. What does it look like? Flowers differ hugely from one to another, and we all have our favorites. There are giant sunflowers and colorful roses and some rotten-smelling orchids and lilies, to name just a few. The label "flower" would seem to indicate little beyond the fact that flowers are usually brightly colored, frequently have a prominent odor, and generally sit at the end of a plant's branches. Closer inspection, however, reveals that, with very few exceptions, all flowers have the same four fundamental structures: sepals, petals, stamens, and carpels.

Fertilization occurs when the male gamete merges with the female gamete. But that's a lot easier said than done: the male gamete has to get to where the female gamete is. The first step toward this is pollination—when a pollen grain makes the journey to the stigma.

A small number of angiosperms achieve pollination by releasing tremendous amounts of pollen into the wind, as do the gymnosperms, or into water—on the slim chance that some will land on the female reproductive organs of another plant of the same species. Most angiosperms,

though, have a different way of moving pollen from the anthers of one flower to the stigma of another: they use animals to carry it (**FIGURE 12-21**).

To ensure that animals will visit a flower, picking up and delivering their pollen cargo, two strategies for achieving pollination have evolved among the flowering plants.

Q Why are some flowers so flashy?

1. Trickery. The plant deceives some animals into carrying its pollen from one plant to another. Some orchid species, for example, produce flowers that resemble female wasps. The mimicry is so good that male wasps mount the flower and attempt to mate with it. The male wasp twirls wildly on the flower, like a cowboy on a bucking bronco, repeatedly whacking his head against the strategically located anthers and getting pollen stuck all over his head and body. That is not enough for the plant to achieve pollination—but it's a start. If that male wasp gets fooled again by another orchid flower and mounts it in an attempt to mate, he will inadvertently deposit some of the pollen from his body onto the also strategically placed stigma of that flower. In the end, the wasp does not gain from his actions, but the orchids have used an effective system of pollination.

2. Bribery. The plant bribes some animals to carry its pollen from one plant to another. Rather than just using trickery, the plant offers something of value to the animal. For this

STRATEGIES FOR ATTRACTING POLLINATORS

TRICKERY
Some plants deceive animals into carrying pollen from one plant to another. Shown here: This isn't a bee! It's actually an orchid flower. Pollen is picked up and delivered by male bees that attempt to mate with the flower.

FIGURE 12-21 Delivering precious cargo (inadvertently).

BRIBERY
Some plants offer something of value to an animal, bribing the animal to carry pollen from one plant to another. Here, a bee, covered in pollen, flies from flower to flower in search of nectar.

 Angiosperms have developed a way to transfer pollen efficiently from the anthers of one flower to the stigma of another: get an animal to carry it!

COLORS AND PATTERNS
WHITE: Nocturnal pollinators, such as moths and bats
BRIGHT COLORS: Visually oriented diurnal pollinators, such as birds, butterflies, and bees

FLOWER STRUCTURE
TUBE: Pollinators with long tongues, such as moths
INTRICATE/CLOSED: Pollinators such as bees

ODORS
SWEET: Pollinators with a good sense of smell, such as moths, butterflies, and bees
STINKY: Pollinators looking for rotten meat on which to lay eggs, such as flies
NO ODOR: Pollinators with a poor sense of smell, such as birds

NECTAR
ABUNDANT: Pollinators with high energy needs, such as bees, birds, and butterflies
ABSENT: Pollinators, such as flies, looking for a place to lay eggs, or such as beetles, looking for petals, pollen, and other parts to eat

FIGURE 12-22 Evolving together: plants and pollinators. You can often determine the type of animal that pollinates a flower just by examining the features of the flower.

method to work, the plant must produce (a) a sticky pollen, (b) a flower that catches the attention of the pollinator, and, most important, (c) something of value to the pollinator. The payoff for the pollinator can be food, such as nutritious nectar rich in sugars and amino acids, or perhaps a safe, hospitable location for an insect to lay its eggs.

The variety of flower structures is tremendous. They differ in shape, color, smell, time of day they are open, whether or not they produce nectar, and whether or not their pollen is edible. So, too, is the variety of pollinators: birds (mostly hummingbirds), bees, flies, beetles, butterflies, moths, and even some mammals (mostly bats) (**FIGURE 12-22**). In each case, there has been strong coevolution between the plants and their pollinators: the plants get more and more effective at attracting the pollinators and deterring other species from visiting the flower, while the pollinators get more and more effective at exploiting the resources offered by the plants. Because of this strong coevolution between the plant and

animal species, for most flowers we can determine, just by examining the features of the flower, the type of animal that will pollinate it.

Pollination is just one step toward fertilization. Fertilization itself doesn't happen until the male and female sex cells meet and fuse. We explore this process in the next section.

TAKE-HOME MESSAGE 12·9

Angiosperms have found a way to transfer pollen from the anthers of one flower to the stigma of another: let an animal carry it. Flowers are conspicuous structures that advertise their presence with colors, shapes, patterns, and odors. Using flowers, plants are able to trick or bribe animals into transporting male gametes to female gametes, where fertilization can occur.

12·10

Angiosperms improve seeds with double fertilization.

The process of fertilization—the fusion of two gametes to form a zygote—*begins* when a pollen grain lands on a stigma of a flower, but that is far from the end. In angiosperms, the process is called **double fertilization,** because there are two separate fusions of male nuclei (each carrying a complete set of the organism's genetic material) from the pollen grain with female nuclei in an ovule. As we'll see, double fertilization is a more efficient system than the type of fertilization in gymnosperms, because whenever an embryo is produced at fertilization (and only then), so, too, is a more substantial, ready-made food source.

When we left off in the previous section, a pollen grain—which will deliver the haploid male gamete—had just arrived on the female's stigma. The pollen grain forms a tube that extends downward through the stigma and style to the ovary, ultimately entering an ovule. As the pollen tube grows, two haploid sperm are formed within it by mitosis, and both move down the pollen tube (**FIGURE 12-23**).

While the pollen tube is growing, a cell within the ovule undergoes meiosis, forming four haploid cells, called spores. Three of these usually degenerate. The surviving haploid spore enlarges and undergoes mitosis, forming an embryo sac. A large, central cell in the embryo sac has two haploid nuclei. One of the other cells in the embryo sac is the haploid female gamete (the egg), which remains near the place where the pollen tube will be guided into the ovule by two other haploid cells within the embryo sac.

When the pollen tube reaches the ovule, one of the two sperm fuses with the egg to form a zygote. The other sperm fuses with the two nuclei in the middle of the embryo sac to form the endosperm, which has *three sets* of chromosomes (i.e., is triploid). The process is called double fertilization because two sperm enter the ovule and combine with female cells in two separate events, forming (1) a zygote (with two sets of chromosomes) and (2) an endosperm (with three sets of chromosomes).

The final steps in producing a seed occur as the diploid zygote cell undergoes multiple mitotic divisions to form an embryo, while the triploid cells multiply mitotically to produce the endosperm that will provide nutritional support for the seedling through its initial growth stages. The outer layers of the ovule form the seed coat that will protect

FIGURE 12-23 Double fertilization fortifies the seeds of angiosperms.

ANGIOSPERM LIFE CYCLE

Pollen

Pollen tube

MEIOSIS

Ovary

HAPLOID STAGE

DIPLOID STAGE

Diploid flower

Seed

FERTILIZATION

1 Pollen grains are released from the male anthers of a flower, delivering the male haploid gamete to the stigma—the sticky tip of the female reproductive structure.

2 The pollen grain produces a tube that extends through the stigma to the ovary. Meanwhile, a cell within the ovule undergoes meiosis, forming four haploid cells, called spores. Three of these usually degenerate.

3 The surviving haploid spore undergoes mitosis, forming an embryo sac that contains seven haploid cells. One cell becomes the egg, another cell—with two nuclei—will form the endosperm following fertilization by a sperm cell.

4 When the pollen tube reaches the ovule, two sperm are released. In a process called double fertilization, one of the two sperm fuses with the egg to form a zygote. The other sperm fuses with the two nuclei in the middle of the embryo sac to form the endosperm, which nourishes the embryo.

5 The zygote and the endosperm continue to develop within the ovule, forming a seed that will eventually be released and grow into a mature plant.

the seed until it sprouts. The enclosure of the seed within the ovary is a distinction between angiosperms and gymnosperms. The seeds of a gymnosperm are unenclosed and are sometimes referred to as "naked."

Q What advantage does double fertilization give to angiosperms?

In gymnosperms, single sperm fuses with an egg to form a zygote in an ovule that contains hundreds of other female cells that are used as a source of nutrients for the resulting embryo. By contrast, there are two important advantages that double fertilization offers angiosperms.

1. Double fertilization initiates formation of endosperm only when an egg is fertilized. Waiting to be sure that an egg is fertilized is a good strategy, because making endosperm is a large energy investment for a plant. Gymnosperms invest that energy up front, and nutrients in ovules that are not fertilized are wasted because those "seeds" do not contain an embryo. In contrast, angiosperms do not waste energy forming endosperm in ovules that will not contain embryos.

2. Angiosperms can produce smaller gametes than gymnosperms, because the large energetic reserves will be produced only *after* fertilization occurs. The small size of the male and female gametes of angiosperms ensures that seeds are produced quickly. **FIGURE 12-24** shows that as different reproductive strategies have evolved in plants, their gametes have become progressively smaller. Rapid production of seeds allows angiosperms to grow as annual plants (that is, plants that complete their life cycle from sprouting to seed production in one growing season), which is something gymnosperms cannot do.

Q Do flowers with both male and female structures fertilize themselves?

Outbreeding, the combination of haploid cells from two different individuals, produces offspring with greater genetic diversity (that is, carrying a greater diversity of alleles) than offspring that result from inbreeding, the combination of a male and female gamete from the same individual. Angiosperms have a variety of ways to increase the chance that only sperm from another individual will fertilize the female gamete. Plants that have male and female reproductive structures in different flowers or even on different individuals, for example, increase the chance that a pollen grain landing on a stigma comes from a different plant. But many flowers with both male and female parts also have mechanisms to prevent self-fertilization. For example, the anthers may mature before the

HAPLOID AND DIPLOID LIFE STAGES

HAPLOID STAGE	DIPLOID STAGE

NON-VASCULAR PLANTS
The majority of the life cycle is spent in the haploid stage.

VASCULAR SEEDLESS PLANTS
The haploid and diploid stages are both multicellular and physically independent from one another.

GYMNOSPERMS
The evolution of seeds almost completely eliminates the prominent haploid stage seen in mosses and ferns.

ANGIOSPERMS
Haploid gametes are further reduced in size, enabling more rapid seed production.

 As plants have developed different reproductive strategies, they have progressed from having a prominent haploid stage of life to simply having haploid gametes.

FIGURE 12-24 Overview of the haploid and diploid stages of plant life cycles.

stigma, so the stigma is not ready to receive pollen when the anthers are active. And when the stigma becomes functional, the anthers are no longer producing pollen. Other plants use a molecular recognition system to prevent inbreeding: proteins on the surface of the stigma will not allow pollen from the same individual to form a pollen tube.

TAKE-HOME MESSAGE 12·10

Angiosperms undergo a process of double fertilization, which ensures that a plant does not invest energy in forming endosperm for an ovule that has not been fertilized. Angiosperms have also developed methods to reduce the occurrence of self-fertilization and increase genetic variation among offspring.

12·11–12·12 Plants and animals have a love-hate relationship.

Fruits such as these peaches are structures that contained fertilized seeds.

12·11 Fleshy fruits are bribes that flowering plants pay animals to disperse their seeds.

Leaving home is an inevitable part of growing up. But as difficult as it may be, imagine you had to move away but didn't have a car or moving van—or even legs. How would you do it? This is yet another issue facing plants. Ingenious methods have evolved for transporting the male gametes to the female sex organs for fertilization, but that still results in all the fertilized eggs, and all the new offspring they develop into, living right on the female plant—or in nearly the same location, if they manage to fall off the parent plant. This is a problem because parent and offspring would end up competing for the same light, space, soil nutrients, and other resources.

The solution is the fruit, a structure that aids in dispersing seeds—the reproductive packets made up of the embryo, some food reserves, and a hard coat. The fruit usually develops from the ovary (and sometimes from nearby tissue), right around the seeds, which develop from the ovules. This should cause you to look at a field of flowers differently. Given that the ovary is part of a flower, after pollination and fertilization, that flower will turn into a fruit. Another way of looking at it is that every fruit you eat was once a flower.

Pea pods, sunflower seeds, corn kernels, and hazelnuts are fruits. These are "dry fruits," and the seeds they contain are transported by wind, water, or animals (**FIGURE 12-25**). Many angiosperms, though, make **fleshy fruits** that consist of the ovary plus some additional parts of the flower. For

example, the core of an apple is the ovary and the flesh of the apple is derived from adjacent parts of the flower. Blueberries, watermelons, oranges, tomatoes, and peaches are other examples of fleshy fruits.

The fleshy part of a fruit is often larger than the ovary, and an angiosperm invests a lot of energy in producing fleshy fruits. The payoff comes when an animal eats the fruit and then defecates the seeds at a location far from the parent plant. In other words, fleshy fruit is the bait that some flowering plants use to get animals to disperse their seeds.

When you look at fruits, you can see several characteristics that help this system work.

- Fruits are colorful—red is the most common color for fruits, followed by yellow and orange. All of these colors contrast with green foliage and make fruits conspicuous.

- Fruits typically taste good—plants pour sugars into fruits, and their sweetness appeals to many animals.

- Fruit is good for animals, serving as a significant source of sugar, enabling animals to produce ATP for their needs. Additionally, fruit has other nutritional value; many birds incorporate the red and yellow colors of fruits into their own color patterns, and colorful male birds are appealing to female birds. Thus, male birds that eat fruit are likely to produce a lot of offspring who also eat fruit—a good deal for the plant.

HITCHING A RIDE
Some seed pods have spines or projections that attach them to passing animals.

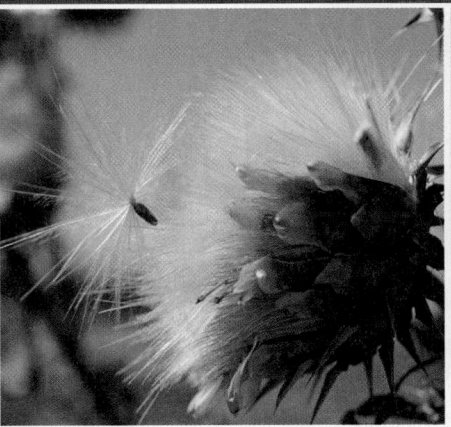

FLYING AND FLOATING
The structure of the seed allows it to be carried away from the parent plant by wind or water.

PROVIDING A FOOD SOURCE
Fleshy fruit is a form of bait that lures an animal to eat the seed and carry it far from the parent plant before eliminating it.

FIGURE 12-25 Methods of dispersing seeds.

Q

Can seeds still sprout after being eaten by an animal?

Of course, there's one more requirement to make fruit a successful way for a plant to disperse its seeds: the seeds must survive passage through the animal's digestive tract and be able to germinate when they come out. That's not a problem—seeds are fully viable when they emerge. It's easy enough to test this yourself. The next time you eat fresh tomatoes, check the toilet about 24 hours later. The seeds that have passed through your digestive system are still intact. If you want to test their viability, that's easy—recover a few, rinse them off, and put them on a wet paper towel in a sealed plastic bag. If you want to do a controlled experiment, you can take some seeds directly from a tomato and put them in another bag. Put both bags in a warm, dark place, and check them in a couple of days. You'll find that both sets of seeds have sprouted. (Or, you can just take our word for it.)

Seeds not only survive being eaten by animals—some seeds will not germinate *unless* they are eaten. For some plants, the pulp that surrounds the seeds in the fruit inhibits germination, and it must be digested away before the seed will sprout. The seeds of other plants have chemicals in the seed coats that must be removed by the acidity of an animal's stomach before the seeds will germinate. And there's another plus to this system: the seeds are deposited with a bit of manure that provides nutrients for the seedlings.

TAKE-HOME MESSAGE 12·11

Following pollination and fertilization, plants often enlist animals to disperse their fruits, which contain the fertilized seeds, depositing them at a new location where the seedlings can grow. Fruits are made from the ovary and, occasionally, some surrounding tissue.

12·12 Unable to escape, plants must resist predation in other ways.

The interactions of plants and animals are not simple. On the one hand, plants depend on animals to pollinate their flowers and disperse their seeds. On the other hand, many kinds of animals eat plants, and plants are vulnerable because they can't run away.

Just because plants can't run away from plant-eating animals, however, they are not defenseless. A host of defensive devices

that have evolved in plants give them some protection against being eaten. These defenses fall into two categories: anatomical structures, such as thorns, and chemical compounds, including hallucinogens (**FIGURE 12-26**).

Spines, prickles, and thorns are a common way to discourage herbivores, and some of these structures are impressively large. The acacias, a group of plants that grow as large

PLANT DEFENSES

ANATOMICAL STRUCTURES
Some plants have spines, spikes, and thorns that deter predators. Some trees have thick layers of bark that are shed in order to get rid of attacking insects.

STICKY TRAPS
Conifers exude pitch, a sticky substance that can engulf and smother attacking insects.

Locoweed contains substances that, when eaten, can cause cattle and horses to become lethargic and stop feeding.

Stinging nettles have needle-like hairs that inject a chemical that causes a stinging sensation when contacted by an animal.

CHEMICAL COMPOUNDS
Some plants synthesize chemicals that induce physiological and behavioral changes in the animals eating them.

FIGURE 12-26 Spines, sticky traps, and toxic compounds. Plants have developed a range of defenses against predation.

bushes or small trees, are notoriously spiny. In these plants, the deterrent effects of spines are sometimes enhanced by the presence of ants that live in the swollen bases of the spines

and fight off other animals—from insects to mammals, including humans—that would feed on their host acacia. Spines on palm fronds carry bacteria that infect the wounds that the spines create, providing a long-lasting reminder that it's not a good idea to try to eat a palm frond. In most plants, the surfaces of leaves and stems have microscopic hairs that protect the plant against insect herbivores by exuding a sticky fluid trap, but stinging plants such as nettles use larger hairs to inject a potent fluid into any animal that brushes against a leaf.

Many chemical defenses make plants bitter or otherwise unpalatable, but some plants play hardball by producing chemicals that affect the nervous or reproductive systems of their predators. Locoweeds, which occur all over western North America, contain alkaloids that can cause permanent damage to the nervous system. When cattle and horses eat locoweed, they tire quickly and stop eating. Other defensive chemicals are hallucinogens. Tetrahydrocannabinol, or THC, in the leaves and buds of marijuana plants disorients mammals and causes them to stop eating.

Many of the chemicals that plants produce to protect themselves have physiological effects in humans, and for thousands of years humans have used plants for medicinal purposes. The aboriginal peoples of North America and Eurasia, for example, knew that extracts of the bark from willows and aspens could relieve pain. Salicin is the compound in the bark that relieves pain, and we still use acetylsalicylic acid (aspirin) for pain relief. Opium poppies produce a more powerful pain reliever; foxglove flowers contain a compound that slows the heart rate; and a compound from the ipecacuanha plant can induce vomiting.

Plants with medicinal uses are sought after (called "bioprospecting"), and representatives of pharmaceutical companies trudge through rain forests and deserts to find them. The rewards from such a discovery can be great. For example, artemisin from Chinese sweet wormwood is effective in treating malarial infections that are resistant to conventional pharmaceutical compounds.

There's another role that chemicals can play in a plant's defense systems. Although plants can't move, they do send messages. They release volatile chemicals when they are attacked by insects, and these airborne chemicals can warn nearby plants of the impending threat or can call protective insects to their aid.

When plants are nibbled by insects, they release the chemical methyl jasmonate (MJ), which is carried with the breeze to

Some plants living in nitrogen-deficient soil have turned the tables, becoming predators on insects.

FIGURE 12-27 Carnivorous plants feed on insects. A true bug nymph trapped in the insectivorous northern pitcher plant, *Sarracenia purpurea*, growing in an acidic bog in Michigan.

them. Insects can also detect MJ, and insects that prey on other insects are attracted to plants emitting the chemical, because it signals the presence of prey. When corn and cotton plants are attacked by caterpillars, release of MJ summons parasitic wasps that deposit their eggs inside the caterpillars. When the eggs hatch, the wasp larvae eat the caterpillars from the inside out.

About 900 species of plants turn the tables—and eat insects. They use the protein in their insect meals to supplement the nitrogen compounds they get from the soil. Insectivorous plants are most common in boggy areas, because boggy soil often has low nitrogen concentrations (**FIGURE 12-27**). Pitcher plants are an example—their name comes from conspicuous pitcher-shaped structures that capture insects. It's easy for an insect to enter the open top of a pitcher, but hard to get out, because the inner walls are lined with hair-like structures that point downward, forcing the insect into a pool of liquid. Some pitcher plants merely absorb the nitrogen that is released when the trapped insects decay, but other species secrete digestive enzymes into the pool. These enzymes, which are basically the same as the enzymes in your stomach, digest the insects and make the nitrogen available more rapidly.

nearby plants. When these plants detect the presence of MJ, they ramp up production of their own defensive chemicals so that they are prepared if the insects move on to feast on

TAKE-HOME MESSAGE 12·12

Plants have a wide range of defenses against herbivorous animals: from physical defenses such as thorns to chemicals that have complex effects on animals' physiology. Plants respond to insect attack by synthesizing chemicals that make the plant less palatable. Some plants living in soil that is deficient in nitrogen have switched roles, preying on insects.

12·13–12·15 Fungi and plants are partners but not close relatives.

Cup fungi, Cookeina tricholoma, *from Borneo.*

12·13

Fungi are closer to animals than they are to plants.

Think about your toes for a minute. Have you ever had an itchy burning sensation between them? Almost everyone has athlete's foot at some time during his or her life. One study found that 15% of all people in the United Kingdom had this fungal infection.

Fungi make up their own monophyletic kingdom within the eukarya domain. Most fungi are multicellular, sessile decomposers (**FIGURE 12-28**). Although they were originally thought to be plants lacking chlorophyll, it turns out that they have little in common with plants. In fact, DNA sequence comparisons reveal that fungi are more closely related to animals than they are to plants (**FIGURE**

12-29). As eukaryotes, fungi have all the basic cellular components you would expect to find: nuclei, mitochondria, an endomembrane system, and a cytoskeleton. They also have cell walls, but the cell walls, instead of including cellulose, as in plants, are made of the carbohydrate chitin, a chemical also important in producing the exoskeleton of insects.

Fungi most likely arose from a unicellular, flagellated, aquatic protist more than 500 million years ago (and possibly as long as 1.3 billion years ago). Close to 100,000 species have been described, but the total number of species is estimated to be about 1.5 million. These species are

WHAT IS A FUNGUS?

FUNGI ARE DECOMPOSERS OR SYMBIONTS
Fungi acquire energy by breaking down the tissues of dead organisms or by absorbing nutrients from living organisms.

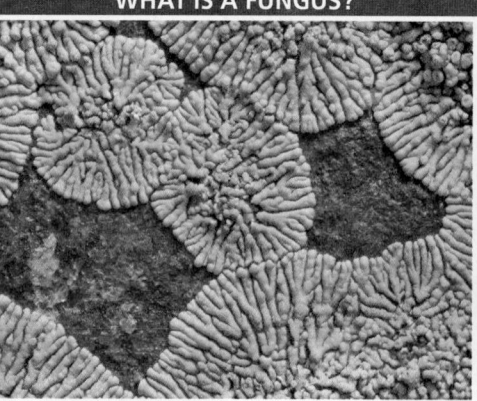

FUNGI ARE SESSILE
Fungi are anchored to the organic material on which they feed.

FUNGI HAVE CELL WALLS MADE OF CHITIN
Fungi have cell walls made of chitin, a chemical that is also important in producing the exoskeleton of insects.

FIGURE 12-28 The defining characteristics of fungi.

THE FUNGI

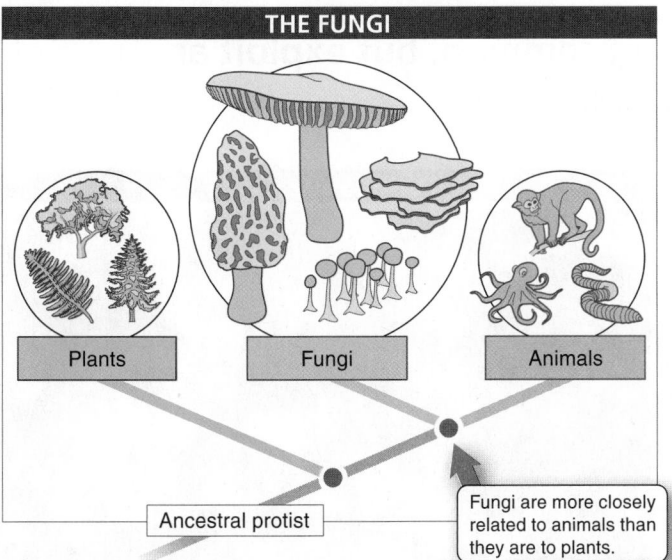

Plants

Fungi

Animals

Ancestral protist

Fungi are more closely related to animals than they are to plants.

FIGURE 12-29 Where the fungi fit in.

divided into about seven phyla, but the overall phylogenetic classification is still very much in flux, with many of the relationships unresolved. Molecular evidence increasingly is guiding the process. About 98% of the described species belong to two monophyletic phyla, Ascomycota (about 64,000 species) and Basidiomycota (about 31,000 species). Besides these phyla, the two phyla with the largest number of described species are Microsporidia, with about 1,300 species, and Chytridiomycota, with about 700 species. These two groups, however, are not monophyletic.

The most commonly encountered types of fungi are (1) yeasts (the only single-celled fungi), truffles, and morels of the phylum Ascomycota; (2) mushrooms, of the phylum Basidiomycota; and (3) molds (which are not a phylogenetic grouping), such as *Penicillium*—the source of the antibiotic penicillin—of the phylum Ascomycota, and black bread mold, of the monophyletic phylum Glomeromycota (**FIGURE 12-30**).

The fungus that causes athlete's foot is multicellular and consists of thread-like structures made up of long strings of cells called **hyphae** (pronounced HIGH-fee). Because of their thinness and length, hyphae have an enormous surface area. This means they are very good at taking up nutrients from your skin, but it also makes them very vulnerable to drying out. The fungus responsible for athlete's foot grows best in moist places—like on the skin between your toes.

Unless you actually have an active athlete's foot infection right now, your most recent encounter with a fungus (or, at least, with evidence that a fungus was once present) was most likely when you last ate bread. Bread rises because yeast cells are mixed into the dough, which is then kept in a warm place while the yeast consumes sugar and produces carbon dioxide through fermentation. The carbon dioxide released by the yeast makes the dough swell into a loaf.

TAKE-HOME MESSAGE 12·13

Fungi are eukaryotes with the same internal cellular elements as other eukaryotes—and one distinctive feature: a cell wall formed from the carbohydrate chitin. Some fungi, the yeasts, live as individual cells; most other fungi are multicellular.

FAMILIAR FUNGI

Portobello mushrooms

Penicillium chrysogenum, a mold (above). Black bread mold (inset).

Candida albicans, a yeast (above). Baker's yeast (inset).

FIGURE 12-30 **The fungi that humans know best.** There are more than 1.5 million fungal species, usually divided among seven phyla. Those most recognizable to humans are mushrooms of the Basidiomycota (basidiomycetes), yeasts of the Ascomycota (ascomycetes), and molds (a term that does not refer to a monophyletic group), which occur in multiple phyla.

12·14 Fungi have some structures in common, but exploit an enormous diversity of habitats.

As we've seen, most fungi are multicellular and are composed of long strings of barely visible, thread-like hyphal cells. The hyphae interconnect to form a mass of tissue called a **mycelium,** the form in which a fungus spends most of its time, usually underground or in a decaying tree or log. Unless you dug down to reach the mycelium, you would not know a fungus was there.

The structure that most people associate with fungi is the mushroom. But a mushroom is just a temporary reproductive structure (or "fruiting body"), part of a complex reproductive cycle that includes both sexual and asexual reproduction in some fungi (**FIGURE 12-31**).

1. Underground, genetically distinct haploid hyphal cells join together. But their nuclei *don't* fuse, so instead of being diploid, they are "dikaryotic," meaning that each cell in the hypha has two nuclei.

2. The dikaryotic mycelium can grow and spread for years.

3. At some point, tightly packed dikaryotic hyphae may form a mushroom.

4. The haploid nuclei in the dikaryotic hyphae fuse in some cells, putting the mushroom into a diploid state.

5. In meiosis, the diploid cells produce huge numbers of haploid spores (up to a billion in a single mushroom!), which are dispersed by wind or water or on the bodies of animals.

6. After landing in a hospitable place, the spores grow as haploid hyphae, and the cycle begins anew.

Q What is the largest living organism in the world?

Fungi have an unusual and effective method of getting nutrition. Unlike humans, they digest their food outside their "body." While growing underground, hyphae secrete strong enzymes that break down the organic molecules around them, and the hyphae then absorb the nutrient-rich fluid. How effective are fungi at absorbing nutrients and growing? Quite good. In fact, in eastern Oregon, a yellow honey mushroom fungus covers an area of about 4 square miles (nearly 10 square kilometers) (**FIGURE 12-32**). This fungus is estimated to be at least 2,400 years old, and it may be more than 8,000 years old, which would place it in the category of the oldest living organism. Moreover, by area, it is the largest. Huge as it is, the fungus is nonetheless hard to detect, because the

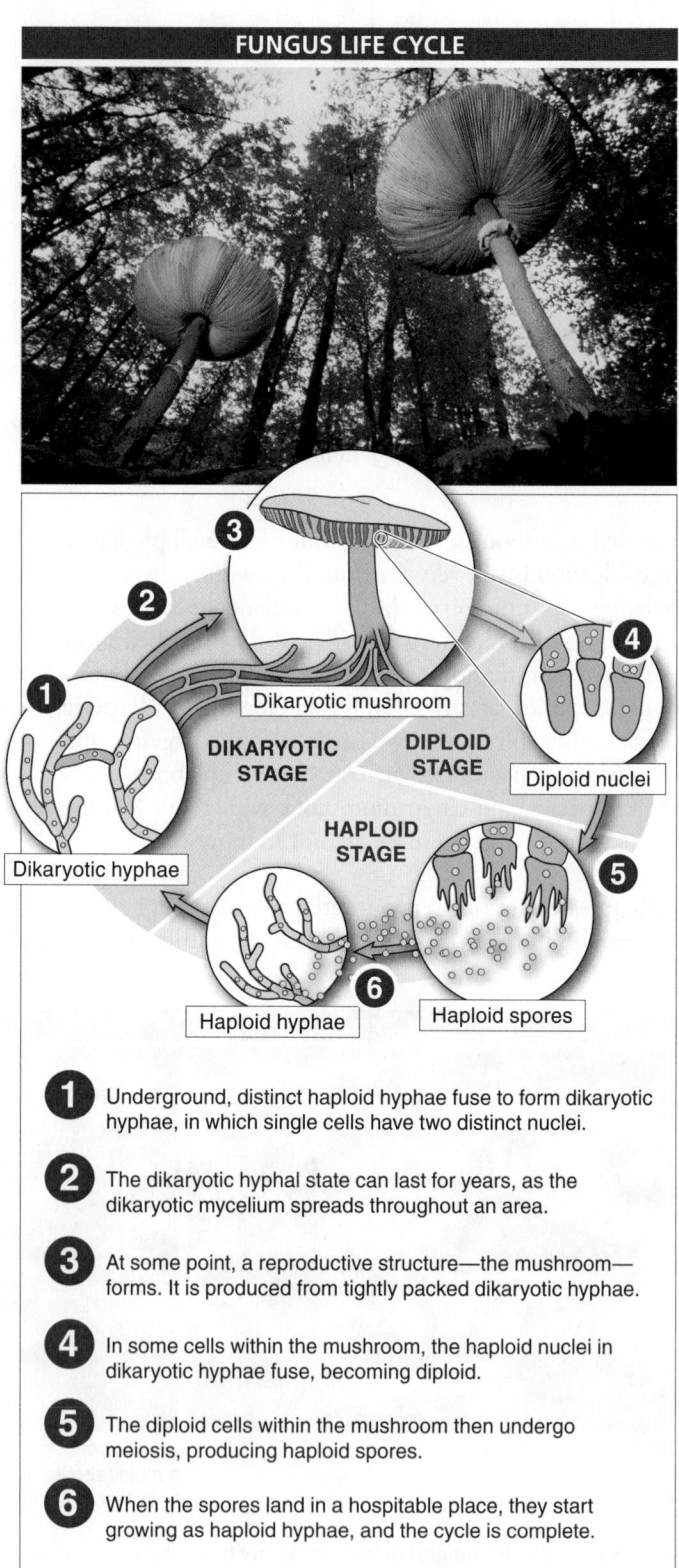

FUNGUS LIFE CYCLE

Dikaryotic mushroom

DIKARYOTIC STAGE

DIPLOID STAGE

Diploid nuclei

Dikaryotic hyphae

HAPLOID STAGE

Haploid hyphae

Haploid spores

1 Underground, distinct haploid hyphae fuse to form dikaryotic hyphae, in which single cells have two distinct nuclei.

2 The dikaryotic hyphal state can last for years, as the dikaryotic mycelium spreads throughout an area.

3 At some point, a reproductive structure—the mushroom—forms. It is produced from tightly packed dikaryotic hyphae.

4 In some cells within the mushroom, the haploid nuclei in dikaryotic hyphae fuse, becoming diploid.

5 The diploid cells within the mushroom then undergo meiosis, producing haploid spores.

6 When the spores land in a hospitable place, they start growing as haploid hyphae, and the cycle is complete.

FIGURE 12-31 The three-stage reproductive cycle of a fungus.

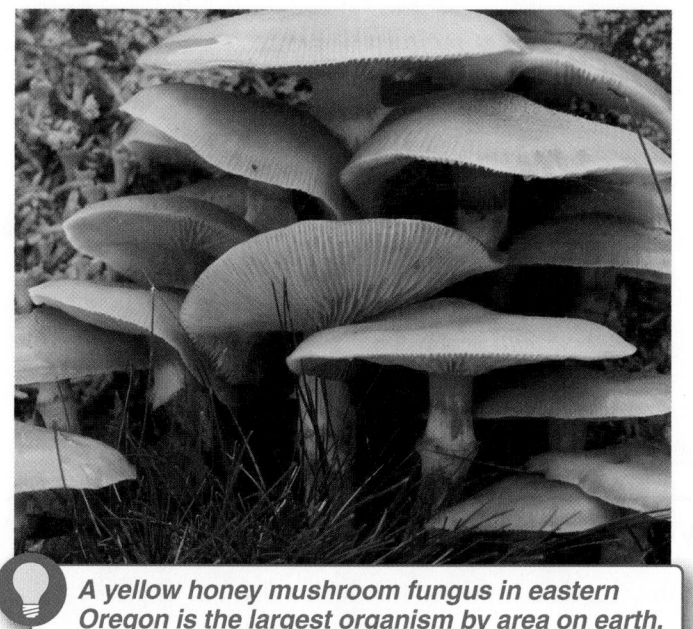

A yellow honey mushroom fungus in eastern Oregon is the largest organism by area on earth, covering four square miles, mostly underground.

FIGURE 12-32 **The largest organism in the world: a yellow honey mushroom fungus.** Shown here is just a small cluster of the fungus's temporary reproductive structures—what we call "mushrooms."

mycelium is underground. The fungus appears on the surface only as mushrooms (edible, but not particularly tasty) and as hyphae in dying and dead trees. Indeed, no one even knew that this enormous fungus existed until 2000, when Oregon foresters sought an explanation for an epidemic of dead and dying trees in the Malheur National Forest. (They discovered that the fungus was killing trees by causing their roots to rot.)

Many mushrooms are gastronomic delicacies, and commercially grown portobello and shiitake mushrooms, for example, command high prices. Truffles—the underground reproductive structures of a fungus called *Tuber*—can sell for as much as $3,500 per pound. Because truffles grow underground, there is nothing on the surface to indicate their presence, and truffle hunters use trained pigs or dogs to locate them by scent.

Fungi can grow in many different habitats because, as **decomposers,** all they need for their nutrient supply is some sort of organic material that they can break down. Fungi play an enormously important ecological role in speeding the decay of organic material in forests. They don't need light, so they can grow underground or inside dead trees and logs.

Fungi can also thrive in poorly ventilated spaces in buildings (**FIGURE 12-33**). Molds are multicellular fungi that are

responsible for many unpleasant effects. People living or working in a "sick building" can experience burning or watering eyes, a runny nose, and itchy skin—allergic reactions to the proteins in fungal spores. More severe effects, such as cancers and miscarriages, are probably produced by toxins released when the fruiting bodies of the fungi disintegrate. Curing a sick building can be so expensive that in some cases the entire building is destroyed and rebuilt.

If you break down the tissues of dead organisms, you are a decomposer, and if you break down the tissues of living organisms, you are a parasite. Just as fungi can live off dying trees, they can also grow in and on people. "Mycosis" is a general term for a disease that is caused by a fungus, such as athlete's foot, or related fungi that cause jock itch, beard itch, scalp itch, ringworm, and toenail fungus. These fungi get their nutrition by digesting some of the organic molecules of your body! And all of these fungal diseases are quite contagious, because they are spread by spores that can linger on moist surfaces and in clothing, so they tend to be a problem in places like dormitories, gymnasiums, and fitness centers.

It wouldn't be fair to mention so many undesirable effects of fungi on humans without describing some of the many beneficial fungi, particularly one that has benefited millions of humans: the fungus that produces penicillin. Alexander Fleming was a researcher studying bacteria. In 1928, just prior to taking a month-long vacation, he stacked some of his used Petri dishes containing bacterial colonies in a corner of his lab. When he returned from his vacation, he found

Molds can contaminate poorly ventilated buildings, causing a variety of irritating and potentially dangerous health problems.

FIGURE 12-33 **Cleaning out toxic mold.** A building overrun with mold spores may cause its occupants to become ill.

that some of the dishes had been contaminated by a fungus. Before discarding them, he noticed that near the fungal infection, the bacterial colonies were dead, while farther away from it, they continued to grow. Suspecting that the fungus might be producing something toxic to the bacteria, he cultured it and discovered that it did produce a substance that killed many different types of bacteria. He identified the fungus as *Penicillium*. Following the development by others of a method to purify the antibacterial compound produced by the fungus, penicillin became a "wonder drug," responsible for saving millions of lives by helping to treat bacterial infections.

12·15   Most plants have fungal symbionts.

If you examine the roots of a plant with a microscope, you will find round structures and fibers closely associated with the fine rootlets and root hairs. These are root fungi, or **mycorrhizae** (pronounced my-koh-RYE-zay). Some mycorrhizae have hyphae that press closely against the walls of root hair cells. Others send hyphae through the root cell walls and into the space between the cell wall and the plasma membrane (**FIGURE 12-34**).

Beneficial associations between roots and fungi are ancient—they have been found in 400-million-year-old fossils of early land plants—and nearly all species of modern plants have them. Lumber companies have found that they have greater success when replanting areas they have clear-cut if the conifer seedlings are first grown in soil that has been inoculated with mycorrhizal fungi. Home gardeners can buy potting soil with mycorrhizal spores or

buy spores compressed into tablets that can be placed in the soil when seedlings are transplanted. The association between mycorrhizal fungi and plants is beneficial to both partners. The mycorrhizal fungus benefits by drawing sugar from the plant, which it uses to support its own cellular respiration. The fungus extracts phosphorus and nitrogen from the soil and releases them inside the roots of the plant, allowing it to grow faster and larger. Research on the impact of root fungi on their plant hosts even demonstrated that the *offspring* of parental plants with mycorrhizae had significantly better survival than the offspring of parental plants without mycorrhizae (**FIGURE 12-35**). (In this case, unfortunately, the fungi are enhancing the growth and survival of an invasive plant called velvetleaf, which causes hundreds of millions of dollars of damage each year to corn crops in the United States.)

MYCORRHIZAE

Mycorrhizal fungi grow in association with the roots of plants, receiving sugar from the plant while transferring nitrogen and phosphorus from the soil to the plant.

Hyphae

Cell wall

Root hair

Plasma membrane

Some mycorrhizae have hyphae that press closely against the walls of root hair cells, while others send hyphae through the root cell walls and into the space between the cell wall and the plasma membrane.

FIGURE 12-34 The association between mycorrhizal fungi and plants is beneficial to both.

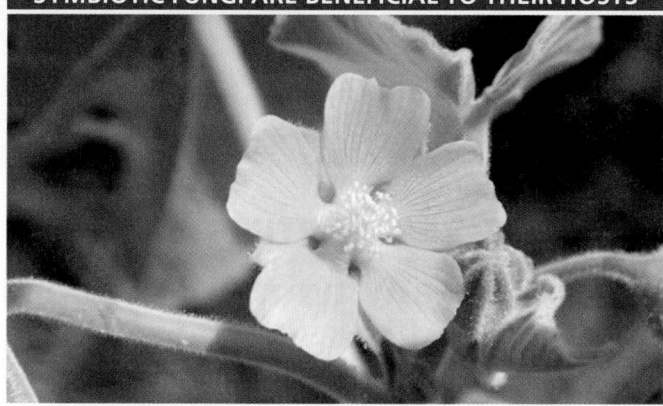

SYMBIOTIC FUNGI ARE BENEFICIAL TO THEIR HOSTS

Researchers investigating the invasive velvetleaf plant evaluated how well offspring survived. They compared the survival of offspring from parents grown with and without symbiotic root fungi and reported the data below.

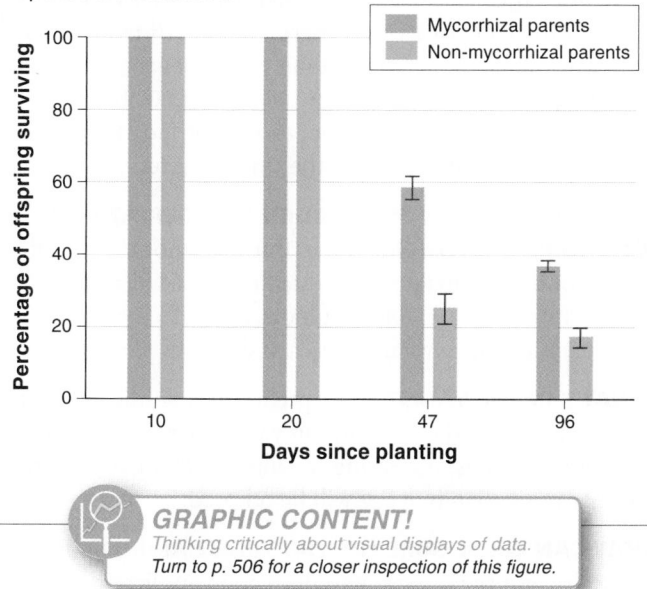

GRAPHIC CONTENT!
Thinking critically about visual displays of data.
Turn to p. 506 for a closer inspection of this figure.

FIGURE 12-35 Plant partners. Root fungi (mycorrhizae) can improve plant functioning.

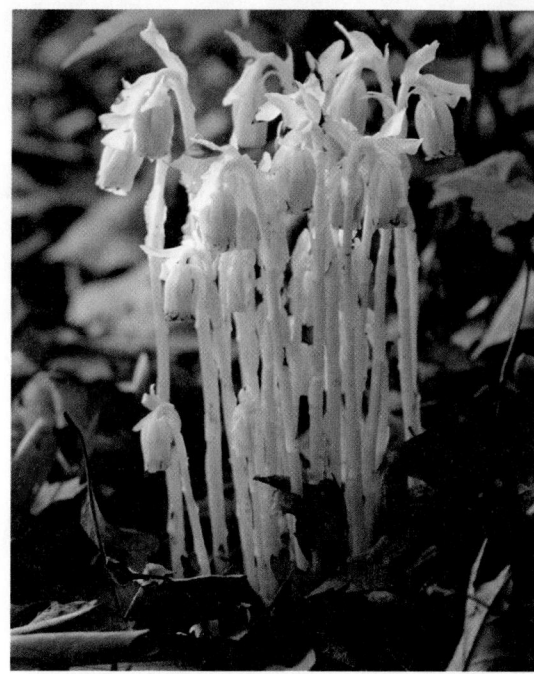

FIGURE 12-36 Not all plants play fair. Ghost pipe is a plant that parasitizes mycorrhizae for nutrients.

Not all plants play fair, however. Some take nutrients from the fungus and give nothing in return. One of the best known of these mycorrhizal parasites is the ghost pipe, which grows in forests in the northern hemisphere (**FIGURE 12-36**). The ghost pipe is an angiosperm related to heaths and heathers. The plant's name comes from its ghostly white appearance. The roots of the ghost pipe are associated with mycorrhizal fungi that are also connected to the roots of trees. The ghost pipe obtains all its nutrients from or through the mycorrhizae: nitrogen and phosphorus are provided by the mycorrhizal fungus, and sugar travels through the fungus from tree roots to the ghost pipe.

Some plants manipulate mycorrhizae to gain a competitive advantage over other plants. Garlic mustard, for example, was brought to North America by European colonists to add a tangy flavor to salads. Initially it was planted in kitchen gardens, but it escaped into the wild, where it has proved itself to be an extremely successful invasive species. Garlic mustard excretes compounds from its roots that interfere with the partnership between mycorrhizal fungi and local native plants. Because the native plants *do* need mycorrhizal fungi to prosper, the destruction of these fungi by garlic mustard weakens the plants. This chemical warfare is so successful that garlic mustard has wiped out entire populations of native woodland plants and is threatening many forests in the central United States.

Fungi also form mutually beneficial relationships with chlorophyll-containing bacteria and/or algae. These two-way or three-way partnerships are called **lichens,** and they grow on surfaces such as tree trunks and rocks. The fungus is fed by its photosynthetic partner and helps it absorb water and nutrients. In addition, the fungus provides nutrients for its partners by excreting enzymes that dissolve organic material and acid that dissolves rock.

TAKE-HOME MESSAGE 12·15

Plants and fungi have a close and mutually beneficial association in mycorrhizae. Mycorrhizal fungi grow in intimate association with the roots of most plants, receiving sugar from the plant and transferring nitrogen and phosphorus to the plant.

YAMS: NATURE'S FERTILITY FOOD?

Do you know any twins? Have you ever wondered how common twins are?

In the United States and Europe, about 12 in every 1,000 births are twin births. In Asia, the number is slightly lower, at 8 sets of twins per 1,000 births. Elsewhere, the rates are similar—except for southwest Africa, particularly in Nigeria, a place that has been called "The Land of Twins." There, the rate of twin births among the Yoruba people is more than four times that in the United States, with about 50 pairs of twins per 1,000 births. (Triplet births are unusually common, too, occurring 16 times more frequently in Nigeria than in the United States.)

Q: WHY ARE SO MANY TWINS BORN IN NIGERIA? IS IT SOMETHING IN THE WATER? Nope. But that's not too far off. It's the diet of the Yoruba people. A staple in their diet is the white yam, a starchy vegetable that looks a bit like a potato; many people eat yams several times each day.

Q: WHAT'S IN THE YAMS? Some preliminary studies suggest that an estrogen-related compound in yams is responsible for stimulating the ovaries, increasing the likelihood, in any given month, that more than one egg will be released.

Q: HOW CAN WE BE SURE IT'S THE YAMS? At this point, no one is certain, and the question awaits a good application of the scientific method. In one intriguing laboratory study, rats fed a diet rich in yams *doubled* their litter size. As yet, however, a definitive link between yams and increased rates of twin births in humans has not been demonstrated.

Q: SO, WILL IT WORK FOR YOU? It's unclear. Anecdotes abound about women having twins after purposely increasing their yam consumption. But a randomized, controlled, double-blind study has yet to be conducted. How would you set up and analyze a study like that? (It is important to note that the yams consumed in Nigeria are not the same as American yams, which are sweet potatoes and do not contain the steroid levels of yams grown in Nigeria.)

Big Ideas in ...
Plant and Fungi Diversification

12·1 Plants are just one branch of the eukarya.

- Plants are multicellular eukaryotic organisms that produce their own food by photosynthesis and have an embryo that develops within the protected environment of the female parent.
- Plants' inability to move shapes the way they obtain food, reproduce, and protect themselves from predation.
- The evolutionary history of plants reveals the progressive appearance of characteristics that allow plants to succeed on land.

12·2–12·4 The first plants had neither roots nor seeds.

- The first land plants were small, had no leaves, roots, or flowers, and could grow only near water.
- Non-vascular plants—mosses, liverworts, and hornworts—resemble the earliest land plants. They lack roots and vessels to move water and nutrients from the soil into the plant.
- Vessels are an effective way to carry water and nutrients from the soil to the leaves, and the first vascular plants were able to grow much taller than their non-vascular predecessors.

12·5–12·7 The advent of the seed opened new worlds to plants.

- A seed, which contains a multicellular embryo and a store of nutrients, is a way for plants to give their offspring a good start in life.
- Seeds are distributed by air, water, or animals.
- Gymnosperms were the earliest plants to produce seeds, which offer advantages over the spores of earlier plants, but they depend on wind to carry their pollen.
- Conifers are the most successful gymnosperms, with more species and a larger geographic range than all of their relatives combined.

12·8–12·10 Flowering plants are the most diverse and successful plants.

- Flowering plants (angiosperms) appeared in the Cretaceous period, over 100 million years ago, and diversified rapidly to become the dominant plants in the modern world.
- A flower advertises a plant's reproductive structures with colors, patterns, and odors which are used to trick or bribe animals into transporting male gametes to female gametes, where fertilization can occur.
- Double fertilization in angiosperms ensures that a plant does not invest energy in endosperm for an ovule that has not been fertilized.

12·11–12·12 Plants and animals have a love-hate relationship.

- Overcoming a challenge of immobility, plants often use the assistance of animals to disperse their fruits, which contain fertilized seeds, depositing them at a new location where the seedlings can grow.
- Fruits are made up from the ovary and, occasionally, some surrounding tissue.
- Overcoming another challenge of immobility, plants have a wide range of defenses against herbivorous animals, from physical defenses such as thorns to chemicals with complex effects.
- Some plants living in nitrogen-deficient soil have switched roles, preying on insects.

12·13–12·15 Fungi and plants are partners but not close relatives.

- Fungi are eukaryotes with a cell wall made of chitin. They can attain enormous sizes.
- Some fungi (yeasts) live as individual cells, but most are multicellular.
- Fungi are decomposers.
- Fungi have complex life cycles, with sexual and asexual phases, and the parts of fungi that are most often visible are their temporary spore-producing bodies.
- Mycorrhizal fungi grow in intimate association with the roots of most plants, receiving sugar from the plant and transferring nitrogen and phosphorus to the plant.

See the To-Go Guide (packaged with every new copy of this textbook) for an illustrated summary of the chapter.

Check Your Knowledge

Thinking critically about visual displays of data.

1. What can you conclude from this graph?

2. There are error bars for the percentage of offspring surviving at 47 days and at 96 days after planting. Why are there no error bars at 10 days and 20 days after planting?

3. What does it mean to say that the differences in offspring survival between mycorrhizal and non-mycorrhizal parents are "statistically significant"?

4. What percentage of the offspring from parents with mycorrhizal fungi were surviving after 47 days? What was the percentage surviving from parents without mycorrhizal fungi?

5. If you could have offspring survival data for one additional point in time, when would it be (i.e., how many days after planting)? Why?

SYMBIOTIC FUNGI ARE BENEFICIAL TO THEIR HOSTS

See Answers at the back of the book.

Key Terms in Plant and Fungi Diversification

angiosperm, p. 484
anther, p. 488
bryophyte, p. 478
carpel, p. 488
cuticle, p. 478
decomposer, p. 501
double fertilization, p. 492

endosperm, p. 484
filament, p. 488
fleshy fruit, p. 494
flower, p. 488
gametophyte, p. 479
gymnosperm, p. 484
hyphae, p. 499

lichen, p. 503
mycelium, p. 500
mycorrhizae, p. 502
non-vascular plant, p. 476
ovary, p. 488
ovule, p. 484
plant, p. 474

pollen grain, p. 484
pollination, p. 484
prothallus, p. 481
root, p. 475
seed, p. 483
shoot, p. 475
sporangium, p. 481

spore, p. 479
sporophyte, p. 479
stamen, p. 488
vascular plant, p. 481

Multiple-Choice Questions

1. In the plant kingdom, all the different species are descended from a single common ancestor. In terms of phylogeny, what type of tree is this?

   a) monophyletic
   b) unbranched
   c) biphyletic
   d) uniphyletic
   e) branched

   100 HARD
   20
   0 EASY

2. Which of the following is a significant new challenge that plants faced when they moved from their aquatic environment onto the land?

   a) light availability
   b) desiccation
   c) nutrient availability
   d) predation
   e) the need for osmotic regulation

   100 HARD
   51
   0 EASY

3. Which is the best brief description of the vascular system of the very first terrestrial plants?

   a) The first plants developed specialized vessel cells that conducted water.
   b) The first plants did not possess a vascular system.
   c) The first plants had a very basic vascular system with a simple method of internal transport.
   d) The first plants had only long, needle-like leaves, from which water could evaporate easily.
   e) None of the above answers is correct.

   100 HARD
   56
   0 EASY

4. Which of the following statements about ferns is incorrect?

   a) Their sporophyte is dominant.
   b) They require liquid water for fertilization.
   c) Their seeds are dispersed by the wind.
   d) They have vascular tissue for distributing water and nutrients throughout the plant.
   e) Their spores are contained in sporangia.

   100 HARD
   64
   0 EASY

5. Mosses and ferns differ from gymnosperms and angiosperms in their reproductive strategies in which of the following ways?

   a) Mosses and ferns rely on liquid water for fertilization, whereas angiosperms and gymnosperms do not need liquid water for fertilization.
   b) Mosses and ferns have much larger seeds than do angiosperms and gymnosperms.
   c) Mosses and ferns use wind pollination, whereas angiosperms and gymnosperms use insects for pollination.
   d) Mosses and ferns are primarily diploid in their adult (reproductive) form, whereas gymnosperms and angiosperms are primarily haploid.
   e) Mosses and ferns are primarily haploid in their adult form, whereas gymnosperms and angiosperms are primarily diploid.

   100 HARD
   53
   0 EASY

6. **Which of the following is characteristic of gymnosperms?**
   a) They are more diverse than the angiosperms.
   b) They are wind-pollinated.
   c) The gametophyte generation is dominant.
   d) They are water-pollinated.
   e) All of the above are correct.

100 HARD
43
0 EASY

7. **In terms of their adaptation to living on land, how are reptiles similar to the seed plants?**
   a) Both reptiles and seed plants became completely independent of water.
   b) Reptiles eat plants.
   c) Seed plants and reptiles have developed structures such as cuticles and impermeable skin to minimize desiccation.
   d) Reptiles and seed plants have developed structures that house their gametes and protect them from the surrounding environment.
   e) Both c) and d) are correct.

100 HARD
35
0 EASY

8. **Angiosperms and gymnosperms differ from each other in that:**
   a) angiosperms have vascular systems, but gymnosperms do not.
   b) angiosperms produce seeds, but gymnosperms do not.
   c) angiosperms tend to rely on animal pollinators, whereas gymnosperms tend to rely on wind pollination.
   d) angiosperms use pollen, whereas gymnosperms use cones.
   e) angiosperms have a single fertilization process, whereas gymnosperms use double fertilization.

100 HARD
45
0 EASY

9. **Anthers and stigmas are found on:**
   a) bryophytes.
   b) fungi.
   c) angiosperms.
   d) gymnosperms.
   e) all of the above.

100 HARD
40
0 EASY

10. **Which of the following is not an example of a group of angiosperms?**
    a) cacti
    b) cherry trees
    c) pine trees
    d) grasses
    e) orchids

100 HARD
51
0 EASY

11. **Over the evolutionary history of plants:**
    a) the sporophyte has become smaller, though more independent.
    b) the gametophyte and sporophyte have grown increasingly independent of each other.
    c) there has been a trend toward gametophyte dominance.
    d) there has been a trend toward gametophyte dependence on the sporophyte.
    e) the gametophyte has become larger, though more dependent.

100 HARD
75
0 EASY

12. **Which of the following comparisons and contrasts between fungi and plants is incorrect?**
    a) Fungi cannot photosynthesize, but plants can.
    b) Both fungi and plants use chitin as a structural stabilizer.
    c) Fungi are heterotrophs (i.e., cannot fix carbon and so must use organic carbon for growth), but plants are not.
    d) Both fungi and plants have cell walls.
    e) Both fungi and plants have a sexual stage in their reproductive cycle.

100 HARD
25
0 EASY

13. **Dispersal of fungal spores is typically done by:**
    a) movement of cilia.
    b) insects.
    c) hummingbirds.
    d) wind.
    e) movement of flagella.

100 HARD
25
0 EASY

14. **You are taking a hike down a forest trail and see the familiar sight of a mushroom on the ground. This visible portion of a fungal body is the structure also referred to as a:**
    a) hypha.
    b) fruiting body.
    c) thallus.
    d) spore sac.
    e) mycelium.

100 HARD
26
0 EASY

15. **In most cases, the relationship between roots and fungi in mycorrhizae can best be described as:**
    a) mycelium.
    b) competition.
    c) trickery.
    d) symbiosis.
    a) parasitism.

100 HARD
36
0 EASY

Short-Answer Questions

1. What distinguishes a vascular plant from a non-vascular plant? How do these differences affect their geographic distribution?

2. How do fungi benefit plants? What benefit do the fungi derive from this relationship?

3. How does development of a fleshy fruit benefit plants?

4. If all animals became extinct, what changes would occur in plant communities? Why?

See Answers at the back of the book.
For additional study questions, go to www.prep-u.com.

ABOUT THE CHAPTER OPENING PHOTO

Three hanging calla lilies.

Bacteria, archaea, protists, and viruses: the unseen world

13

Evolution and Diversity Among the Microbes

13·1–13·2 There are microbes in all three domains.

Dental plaque, a film that forms on teeth, is caused by the growth of bacterial colonies (shown here). It can generally be removed by brushing, but, if left, can lead to tooth decay.

13·1

Microbes are the simplest but most successful organisms on earth.

Humans are large organisms, and being large comes with a lot of baggage. We need a skeletal system to support our weight, and a respiratory system to take in oxygen and get rid of carbon dioxide. We need a circulatory system to move oxygen and carbon dioxide and other molecules around our bodies, and a digestive system to take in food and break it down. We even need a nervous system so that our brain knows what distant parts of our body are doing.

Microbes—the most abundant organisms on earth—don't have skeletal, respiratory, circulatory, digestive, or nervous systems, because they are too small to need them. In fact, "microbe" is a combination of Greek words that means "small life," and the "small" part of the name fits these organisms well. Take an amoeba, for example—it has a volume about a million billion (10^{15}) times smaller than a human. When you are that tiny, the force of gravity becomes trivial, so the amoeba needs no skeleton to support it. Plenty of oxygen diffuses inward across its cell membrane,

Q How can a microbe function when its body is just a single cell?

and carbon dioxide diffuses outward, so an amoeba does not need a respiratory system; and because every part of its interior is close to the body surface, it doesn't need a circulatory system to transport gases. An amoeba eats by enclosing food items in a piece of its cell membrane and digests the food with the same enzymes it uses to recycle its own proteins, lipids, and carbohydrates, so it does not need a digestive system. And no part of an amoeba is far enough from another part to require a specialized nervous system for communication.

Most microbes are even smaller than an amoeba: a typical bacterium or archaeon is about one thousand million billion (10^{18}) times smaller than a human, and an influenza virus is about one thousand billion trillion (10^{24}) times smaller than you are (**FIGURE 13-1**).

They may be invisible, but microbes could never be considered unsuccessful just because of their (lack of) size. To the contrary, they are more successful than humans in almost every imaginable way.

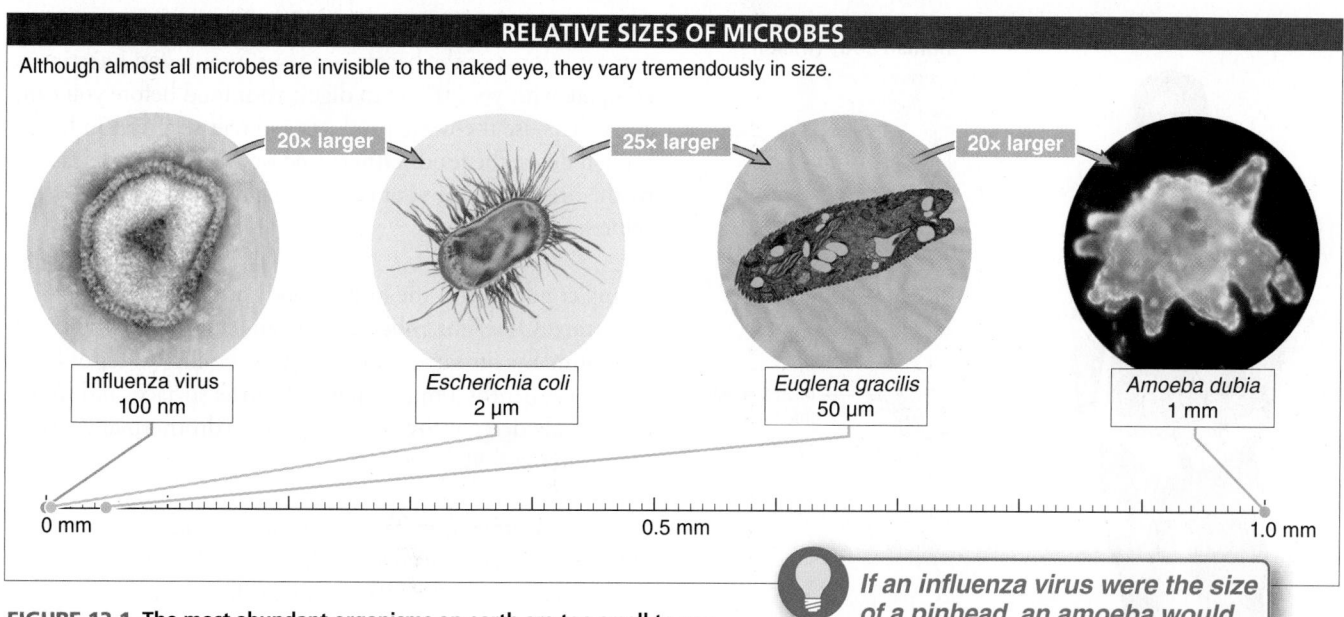

RELATIVE SIZES OF MICROBES

Although almost all microbes are invisible to the naked eye, they vary tremendously in size.

20× larger   25× larger   20× larger

Influenza virus
100 nm

Escherichia coli
2 µm

Euglena gracilis
50 µm

Amoeba dubia
1 mm

0 mm   0.5 mm   1.0 mm

FIGURE 13-1 The most abundant organisms on earth are too small to see.

If an influenza virus were the size of a pinhead, an amoeba would be the size of an oak tree.

Microbes are genetically diverse. More than 500,000 kinds of microbes have been identified by their unique nucleotide sequences, and further studies will almost certainly distinguish millions of additional microbial species.

Q How would you decide whether a group of organisms can be considered successful?

Microbial species live in almost every habitat on earth; among them, they can eat almost anything. As you read these lines, more than 400 species of microbes are thriving in your intestinal tract, 500 more species thrive in your mouth, and nearly 200 species call your skin home (**FIGURE 13-2**).

MICROBES CAN LIVE ALMOST ANYWHERE

Escherichia coli (inset), a bacterium, lives in the human intestine.

Thermus aquaticus (inset), a bacterium, lives in geothermal pools that can reach temperatures greater than 160° F.

Halobacteria (inset) are archaeons that live in extremely salty environments, such as the Great Salt Lake.

FIGURE 13-2 Microbes are everywhere on earth.

Microbes live in nearly every kind of environment, including water at temperatures of up to 750° F and as low as 5° F!

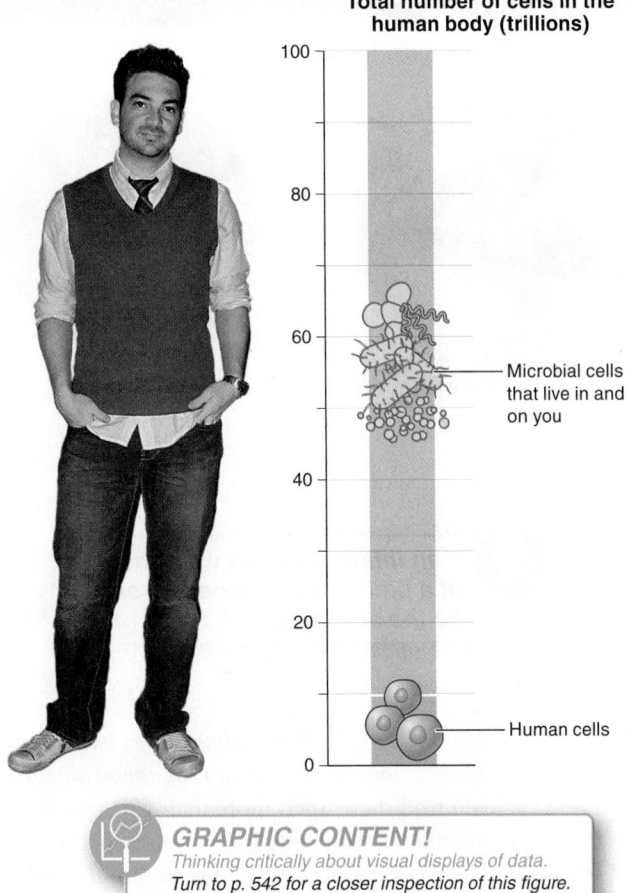

Total number of cells in the human body (trillions)

Microbial cells that live in and on you

Human cells

GRAPHIC CONTENT!
Thinking critically about visual displays of data.
Turn to p. 542 for a closer inspection of this figure.

FIGURE 13-3 Microbe majority. Your body has more microbial cells than human cells.

The microbes that live in you and on you eat mostly what you eat—some of the bacteria in your mouth and intestine compete with you, trying to digest your food before you can, and others use the waste products you release after you have broken down the food. Others feed on the leftovers released by the breakdown of your cells during the normal process of cell renewal.

Living conditions in the human body are relatively moderate. Other microbes inhabit some of the toughest environments on earth—in the almost boiling water of hot springs, at depths a mile below the earth's surface, and more than a mile deep in the oceans, where hydrothermal vents emit water at 400° C (750° F).

Microbes are abundant. Surface seawater contains more than 100,000 bacterial cells per milliliter, and diatoms (protists in the eukarya domain) are as abundant there as are the bacteria. These densities translate to about 8,000 million billion trillion (8×10^{30}) individuals of just these two kinds of microbes in the world's oceans. Your own body is a testament to the abundance of microbes: it contains about 100 trillion cells, but only one-tenth of those cells are actually human cells—the remaining 90 trillion cells are the microbes that live in and on you (**FIGURE 13-3**). You're a minority in your own body.

TAKE-HOME MESSAGE 13·1

Microbes are very small, simple organisms, but they do everything that larger, multicellular organisms do. They can live anywhere, from moderate to extreme environments. There are millions of different kinds of microbes on earth, in enormous numbers.

13·2   Not all microbes are closely related evolutionarily.

"Microbes" is an appropriately descriptive name, but it's sloppy. We could use it to point to any one of many different types of organisms too small to see without magnification. In Chapters 3 and 10 we introduced two very different kinds of microbes: bacteria and viruses. In this chapter we explore bacteria and viruses in more detail, and also include two other kinds of microbes—the protists and the archaea. The amoeba, a kind of protist, may be familiar to you, but the archaea are probably very unfamiliar to you. That's not surprising, because archaea were only recently recognized as a distinct group of microbes. The group

doesn't even have a common name (unless you like "the group formerly known as archaebacteria"). We'll just call them archaea.

It is hard to make generalizations about microbes, because they are grouped together simply because they are small, not because they all share a recent common ancestor. In fact, microbes occur in all three domains of life—bacteria, archaea, and eukarya—and so the various types of microbes could not be more widely separated (**FIGURE 13-4**). In this chapter we focus on the tiny organisms from each of these

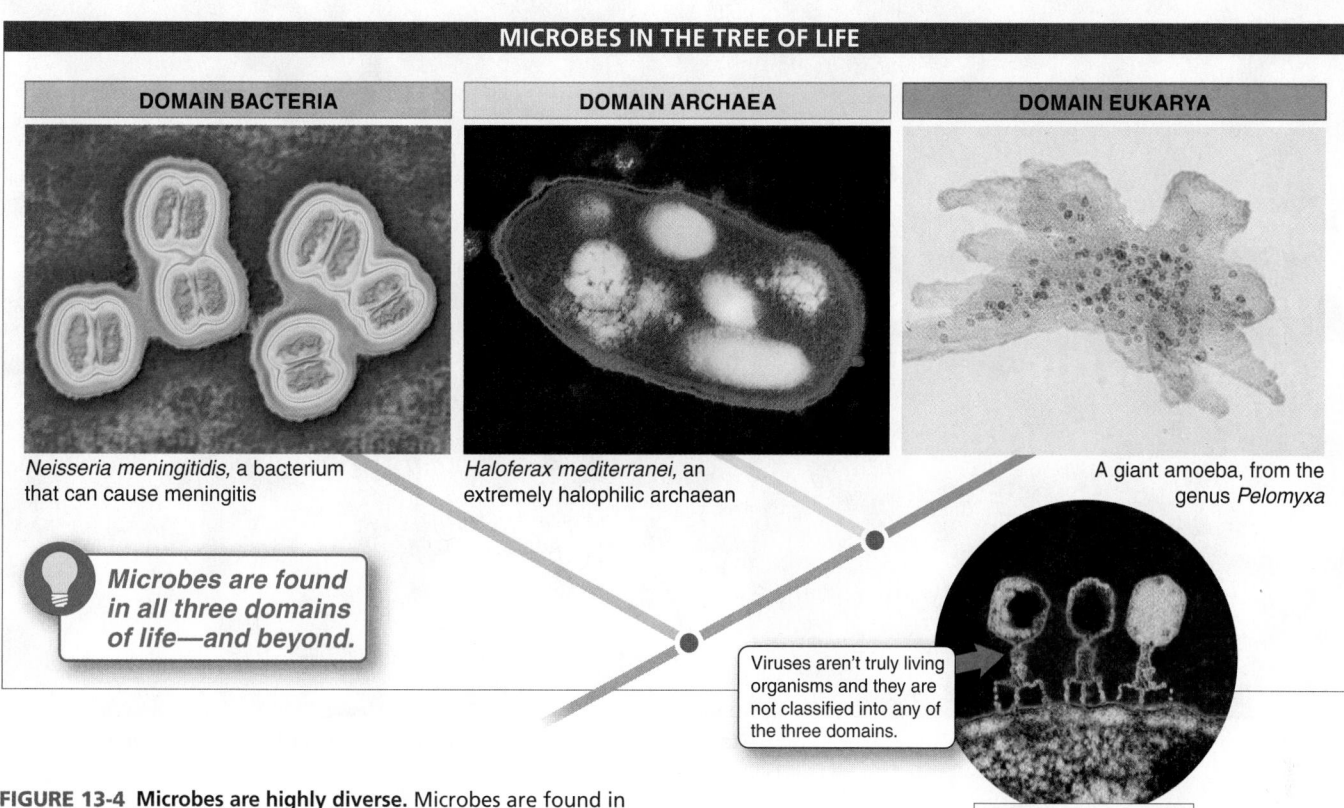

MICROBES IN THE TREE OF LIFE

DOMAIN BACTERIA

Neisseria meningitidis, a bacterium that can cause meningitis

DOMAIN ARCHAEA

Haloferax mediterranei, an extremely halophilic archaean

DOMAIN EUKARYA

A giant amoeba, from the genus *Pelomyxa*

Microbes are found in all three domains of life—and beyond.

Viruses aren't truly living organisms and they are not classified into any of the three domains.

Bacteriophage virus

FIGURE 13-4 Microbes are highly diverse. Microbes are found in every domain of life.

domains. The microbes in the domains bacteria and archaea are prokaryotic, although archaea have some characteristics like those of prokaryotes and others like those of eukaryotes. Protists are the mostly microbial members of domain eukarya. And viruses, another type of microbe, are not classified into any domain at all, because they are only at the borderline of life.

TAKE-HOME MESSAGE 13·2

Microbes are grouped together only because they are small, not because of evolutionary relatedness. They occur in all three domains of life, and also include the viruses, which are not included in any of the domains.

13·3–13·5 Bacteria may be the most diverse of all organisms.

Staphylococcus aureus *(green) on the surface of the small intestine.*

13·3 What are bacteria?

A bacterium is the simplest organism you can imagine—and in many ways, it is the most efficient. A bacterium has a cell envelope consisting of a plasma membrane and, in most cases, a cell wall—that's what it needs to maintain conditions inside that are different from conditions outside. Inside the cell envelope it has cytoplasm—the substance that fills all kinds of cells (including your own). Proteins in the cytoplasm carry out essential functions, such as digesting molecules of food and transferring the energy gained to ATP. DNA in the cytoplasm carries the instructions for making those proteins, and messenger RNAs carry this information to ribosomes, where the proteins are synthesized. That's it—everything an organism needs, with no extra baggage.

Bacteria may be classified by their shape: some are spherical cells (known as the cocci), some are rod-shaped (the bacilli), and others are spiral-shaped (the spirilli) (**FIGURE 13-5**). Bacteria usually reproduce by binary fission, and in a few hours, a single cell can form a culture containing thousands of cells.

As a bacterial cell divides, the number of cells doubles every generation, producing a colony of cells, each of which is a clone of the original cell. Colonies of different species of bacteria look different. The familiar human intestinal bacterium *Escherichia coli*, for example, forms beige or gray colonies that have smooth margins and a shiny, mucus-like covering. Species of *Proteus*, which are often responsible for spoiling food because they can grow at refrigerator temperatures, form colonies with a surface that looks like a contour map.

Microbiologists can often identify bacteria simply by looking at the colors and shapes of their colonies. They can get additional information by examining a single cell under a microscope, but living bacterial cells are transparent, so you can't see them with an ordinary microscope unless they have been dyed. In 1884, Hans Christian Gram, a Danish microbiologist, described a method of dyeing the cell walls of bacteria to make them visible under a microscope, and a **Gram stain** is still the first test microbiologists use when they are identifying an unknown bacterium (**FIGURE 13-6**).

Gram-positive bacteria are colored purple by the stain, because they have a thick layer of a glycoprotein called **peptidoglycan** on the outside of the cell wall. In *Gram-negative bacteria,* the layer of peptidoglycan is thinner and lies beneath an additional membrane, and it is not stained by the dye. Penicillin is effective in treating infections by Gram-positive bacteria because it interferes with the formation of

BACTERIA: CLASSIFICATION AND STRUCTURE

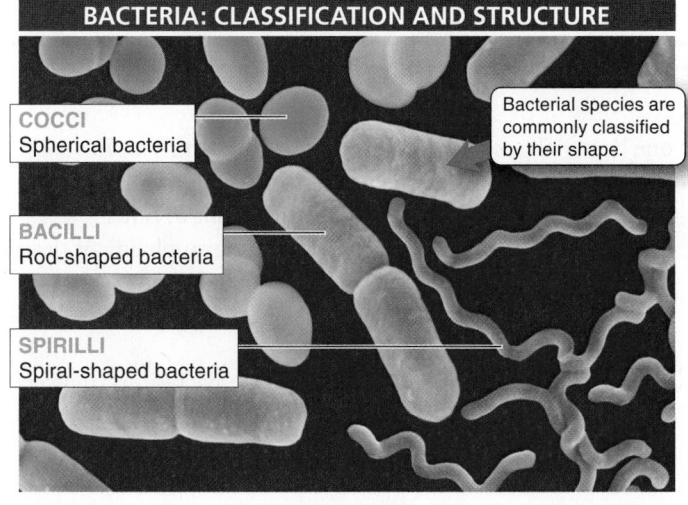

COCCI
Spherical bacteria

Bacterial species are commonly classified by their shape.

BACILLI
Rod-shaped bacteria

SPIRILLI
Spiral-shaped bacteria

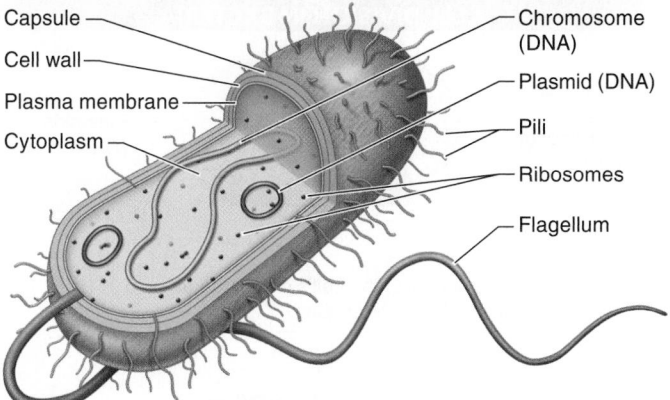

Capsule
Cell wall
Plasma membrane
Cytoplasm

Chromosome (DNA)
Plasmid (DNA)
Pili
Ribosomes
Flagellum

FIGURE 13-5 Bacteria basics. Bacteria are single-celled organisms that lack a nucleus.

peptidoglycan cross-links. Penicillin is less effective on Gram-negative bacteria because it does not pass through the outer membrane that covers the peptidoglycan layer.

Being able to distinguish these two groups of bacteria is a big help to microbiologists trying to identify a bacterium, but the peptidoglycan is there because it is important for the bacterial cells—not to make life easier for microbiologists. The extensive interlocking bonds of the long peptidoglycan molecules provide strength to the cell wall. Many bacteria also have a **capsule** that lies outside the cell wall. This capsule may restrict the movement of water out of the cell and allow bacteria to live in dry places, such as on the surface of your skin. In other cases, the capsule may be important in allowing the bacteria to bind to solid surfaces such as rocks or to attach to human cells.

TAKE-HOME MESSAGE 13·3

Bacteria are efficient single-celled organisms, with an envelope surrounding the cytoplasm, which contains the DNA (they have no nuclei and no intracellular organelles). Bacterial cells undergo binary fission, and a single cell can grow into a colony of cells.

METHODS OF IDENTIFYING BACTERIA

Some bacteria can be identified by looking at the colors and shapes of their colonies.

GRAM-POSITIVE BACTERIA
The glycoprotein layer is on the outside of the cell wall and can be stained with purple dye.

GRAM-NEGATIVE BACTERIA
The glycoprotein layer lies beneath an additional membrane and cannot be stained with the dye.

Gram-negative bacteria—due to their cell membrane composition—are resistant to penicillin.

FIGURE 13-6 Bacterial IDs. Bacteria are often identified by the appearance of an entire colony or of the cells' response to Gram staining.

13·4 Bacterial growth and reproduction is fast and efficient.

The time it takes for a bacterium to reproduce can be very short; most bacteria have generation times between 1 and 3 hours, and some are even shorter. *Escherichia coli,* for example, has a generation time of 20 minutes in optimal conditions, so a single *E. coli* could give rise to a population of 20 billion cells in less than 12 hours.

Bacteria carry genetic information in two structures: the chromosome and plasmids. The genes that provide instructions for all of the cell's basic life processes are usually located in a circular DNA molecule, the bacterial chromosome. Most bacteria have just one chromosome, but some have more than one. A bacterial chromosome is organized more efficiently than a eukaryotic chromosome, in two ways. First, in bacteria, the genes that code for proteins with related functions—enzymes that play a role in a pathway that breaks down food for energy, for example—are often arranged right next to one another on the chromosome. This makes it possible to efficiently control the transcription of all the genes together. Second, almost all the DNA in a bacterial chromosome codes for proteins, so bacteria do not use time and energy transcribing mRNA that will not be translated. As we saw in Chapter 5, as much as 90% of the DNA in the chromosomes of eukaryotes does not code for genes and is edited from mRNA after it has been transcribed and before it is translated into protein.

A second type of structure that carries genetic information is a circular DNA molecule called a **plasmid.** Plasmids carry genes for specific functions. For example, *metabolic plasmids* carry genes enabling bacteria to break down specific substances, such as toxic chemicals; *resistance plasmids* carry genes enabling bacteria to resist the effects of antibiotics; and *virulence plasmids* carry genes that control how sick an infectious bacterium makes its victim. Many bacteria have one or more (sometimes more than a hundred) plasmids. The strain of *E. coli* that occasionally sickens patrons of fast-food restaurants carries a virulence plasmid that magnifies the effects of a gene for a sometimes-lethal toxin. (*E. coli* strains without that virulence plasmid are normal components of the bacterial community of the human intestine.)

Q Would it be useful to be able to transfer genetic information from one adult human to another?

When a bacterium divides, it creates two new daughter cells, each carrying the genetic information that was present in the chromosome of the mother cell. Thus, binary fission transmits genetic information from

one bacterial generation to the next (**FIGURE 13-7**). However, bacteria can also transfer genetic information laterally—in other words, not just to their "offspring," but to other individuals *within* the same generation—through any of three different processes: conjugation, transduction, and transformation (**FIGURE 13-8**).

Conjugation is the process by which one bacterium transfers a copy of some of its genetic information to another

CELL DIVISION IN BACTERIA

Bacterium cell

Chromosome (DNA)

Plasmids (DNA)

REPLICATION
Exact copies of the cell's chromosomal and plasmid DNA are created.

Cell elongates and begins to pinch in two.

Daughter cells are formed.

Fission can be extremely fast—in less than 12 hours, a single E. coli *could give rise to a population of 20 billion cells (three times the number of humans on earth)!*

FIGURE 13-7 Binary fission. This asexual cell division method is used by prokaryotes.

METHODS OF GENETIC EXCHANGE IN BACTERIA WITHIN THE SAME GENERATION

CONJUGATION
A bacterium transfers a copy of some or all of its DNA to another bacterium, giving the second bacterium genetic information it did not have before.

Donor bacterium

Recipient bacterium

TRANSDUCTION
A virus containing pieces of bacterial DNA inadvertently picked up from its previous host infects a new bacterium, and passes new bacterial genes to the bacterium.

Virus

Recipient bacterium

TRANSFORMATION
A bacterium can take up DNA—potentially including alleles it did not carry—from its surroundings (usually from bacteria that have died).

DNA fragments

Recipient bacterium

FIGURE 13-8 Lateral transfer of genetic information: conjugation, transduction, and transformation.

bacterium—even when the two bacteria are different species. It's very much like plugging your iPod into a computer to transfer songs from the computer to the iPod. This is not reproduction, because you start with one iPod and one computer, and that's what you have when you finish. But the iPod now contains songs that it did not have before. Plasmid transfer does exactly that for a bacterium—you still have just two bacterial cells, but the newly acquired plasmid has given the recipient bacterium genetic information that it did not have before. These genes could enable the bacterium to make an enzyme that allows it to metabolize a new chemical or to defend itself against a new antibiotic.

Transduction occurs when a kind of virus called a bacteriophage (one type is shown in Figure 13-4) infects a bacterial cell. The virus reproduces inside the bacterial cell, and sometimes, inadvertently, the new virus particles are filled with pieces of bacterial DNA in addition to or instead of the viral DNA. When these viruses are released and infect new bacterial cells, the bacterial DNA can be inserted into the host bacterium's chromosome, passing new bacterial genes to that bacterium.

Transformation is the process by which bacterial cells scavenge DNA from their environment. This DNA comes from other bacterial cells that have burst open, releasing their cellular contents. The circular chromosomes break into short lengths of DNA, which can then be taken up by living bacterial cells and inserted into their own chromosomes, potentially adding genes they did not originally have.

TAKE-HOME MESSAGE 13·4

Bacteria grow rapidly. They have efficiently organized chromosomes—genes are organized in groups with related functions and virtually all the DNA codes for proteins. Bacteria sometimes carry genes for specialized traits on small DNA molecules called plasmids, which can be transferred from one bacterial cell to another by conjugation. DNA can also be transferred laterally between bacterial cells by transduction or transformation.

13·5 Metabolic diversity among the bacteria is extreme.

One important feature making bacterial diversity possible is that bacteria can metabolize almost anything. (Not all bacteria can metabolize everything. Rather, there is a huge variety of bacteria, each type with its own particular set of metabolic specializations.) Some can even use energy from light to make their own food. Microbiologists place bacteria into different "trophic" (feeding) categories that reflect their metabolic specialization.

Chemical organic feeders (**chemoorganotrophs**) are bacteria that consume organic molecules, such as carbohydrates. You probably see the products of organic

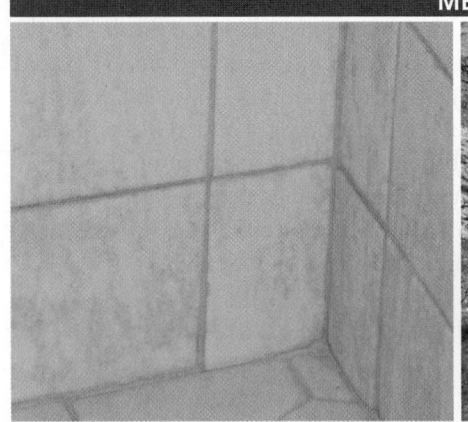

CHEMOORGANOTROPHS
Feed on organic molecules

CHEMOLITHOTROPHS
Feed on inorganic molecules (Shown here: a stream in Spain orange with oxidized iron minerals.)

PHOTOAUTOTROPHS
Use energy from sunlight to produce glucose via photosynthesis

Bacteria are resourceful and can extract food from a huge range of sources: the sun, inorganic molecules in your drainage pipes, and even your shower curtain/door!

FIGURE 13-9 A bigger palate than yours. Bacteria can metabolize almost anything.

feeders every time you take a shower—they are responsible for the pink deposits on the shower curtain and other discolorations on the floor of the shower (**FIGURE 13-9**). Most of the bacteria that live in and on your body are also organic feeders. Some compete with you to metabolize the food you eat. Others digest things you can't digest or can't eat.

Chemical inorganic feeders (**chemolithotrophs,** meaning "rock feeders") are able to use a completely different type of food as their source of energy: inorganic molecules such as ammonia, hydrogen sulfide, hydrogen, and iron. The most common inorganic feeders are the iron bacteria responsible for the brown stains that form on plumbing fixtures in regions where tap water contains high levels of iron. Sulfur bacteria are associated with iron bacteria, and are responsible for the slimy black deposits that you will probably find if you lift the stopper out of the drain in your bathroom sink.

On a larger scale, inorganic feeders are responsible for the acidic drainage that is a by-product of mining. The desirable ore makes up only a small part of the total amount of rock that is removed from a mine. The portion that does not contain ore is discarded on the ground surface in piles called "tailings." This material is often rich in minerals such as pyrites (iron sulfides). Inorganic feeders can gain energy by oxidizing these minerals and, in the process, they release compounds that combine with rainwater to produce strong acids, such as sulfuric acid. When this acidic water drains into streams, it can kill fish and aquatic plants and insects.

"Light self-feeders" (**photoautotrophs**)—bacteria that use the energy from sunlight—contain chlorophyll and use light

energy to convert carbon dioxide to glucose by photosynthesis. The floating mats of gooey green material that you see in roadside ditches are a type of photoautotroph called cyanobacteria.

The cyanobacteria living today closely resemble the first photosynthetic organisms that appeared on earth about 2.6 billion years ago. Cyanobacteria could use solar energy to build organic compounds from carbon dioxide, and in the process they broke down water molecules to release free oxygen. Before cyanobacteria, the earth's atmosphere contained no free oxygen—instead, air consisted almost entirely of nitrogen and carbon dioxide. The accumulation of oxygen released by cyanobacteria is called the **Oxygen Revolution.** Oxygen—which humans depend on—now makes up about 21% of the volume of air, and cyanobacteria still release important quantities of oxygen into the atmosphere. One of the common ways that bacteria are classified is as aerobic or anaerobic, depending on whether they require or do not require oxygen for growth—although some bacteria, called facultative anaerobes, utilize oxygen if it is present but can also switch to anaerobic respiration when oxygen is absent.

TAKE-HOME MESSAGE 13·5

Some bacteria eat organic molecules, some eat minerals, and still others carry out photosynthesis. About 2.6 billion years ago, the photosynthesizing bacteria were responsible for the first appearance of free oxygen in the earth's atmosphere.

13·6–13·9 In humans, bacteria can have harmful or beneficial health effects.

Colored scanning electron micrograph of Escherichia coli *bacteria (blue and purple) taken from the small intestine of a child.* E. coli *are part of the normal community of organisms in the human gut.*

13·6

Many bacteria are beneficial.

Do you like the taste of yogurt? You can thank bacteria for that—*Lactobacillus acidophilus* and several other species of bacteria are added to milk to create yogurt. As the bacterial cells use the milk sugar for energy, the by-product is lactic acid, which reacts with the milk proteins to produce the characteristic taste and texture of yogurt. If you buy a brand of yogurt that is labeled as containing "live cultures," you are consuming living bacterial cells as you eat the yogurt (**FIGURE 13-10**). Bacteria are also used to produce many other foods, such as cheeses, and bacteria (along with yeasts) are used in the production of beer, wine, and vinegar. Industrial microbiology is a multi-billion-dollar industry.

But you can thank bacteria for more than just tasty snacks—you owe your life to bacteria. Hundreds of species of bacteria grow in and on your body; these microbes are called your "normal flora." The normal flora take up every spot on your body that a disease-causing bacterium could adhere to, and they consume every potential source of nutrition, making it difficult for a disease-causing bacterium to gain a foothold. Thus, maintaining a robust population of these benign bacteria is your first line of defense against infection by harmful bacteria.

Probiotic therapy is a method of treating infections by deliberately introducing benign bacteria in numbers large

Many bacteria are beneficial. Those living in yogurt, for example, can take up residence in your digestive tract and improve your extraction of nutrients from food.

FIGURE 13-10 Yogurt contains beneficial bacteria.

enough to swamp the harmful forms. *Lactobacillus acidophilus,* which is a normal inhabitant of the human body, is used to treat gastrointestinal upsets, such as traveler's diarrhea, and urinary tract infections. In addition to growing so vigorously that it crowds out harmful bacteria, *L. acidophilus* releases lactic acid, which interferes with the growth of other bacteria and prevents them from adhering to the walls of the urinary tract and bladder.

13·7 Bacteria cause many human diseases.

The number of **pathogenic** (disease-causing) bacteria is very small compared with the total number of bacterial species, but some pathogens kill millions of people annually, despite advances in medicine and sanitation. Some bacteria are always pathogenic (such as those that produce cholera, plague, and tuberculosis), but others (the ones responsible for acne, strep throat, scarlet fever, and "flesh-eating" necrotizing fasciitis) are normal parts of the communities of bacteria that live in or on humans. These bacteria in our "normal flora" become pathogenic only under special circumstances.

The great cholera epidemic that devastated London in 1854 became a milestone in epidemiology (the study of the occurrence of disease outbreaks), when Dr. John Snow identified the Broad Street pump as the source of infection by mapping the pattern of deaths from cholera (**FIGURE 13-11**. When Dr. Snow persuaded the authorities to shut down the pump by removing the handle, new cases of cholera in the area dropped sharply.

Cholera epidemics are a continuing threat, especially in areas without effective sanitation. Epidemics of cholera are occurring now in parts of Iraq where the sewage systems have been destroyed and in Haiti, following the earthquake of 2010. The strains of cholera found in these areas are especially potent; as the bacteria multiply inside their hosts, they cause severe diarrhea with a massive loss of water. Victims of these severe strains of cholera are incapacitated and soon die, but before they die they release billions of cholera bacteria in diarrhea—an effective strategy for the cholera bacteria, because they contaminate the water used for drinking or bathing and rapidly infect new victims.

Streptococcus pyogenes is a normal part of the bacterial community of your nose and mouth. Normally it is harmless, and many people never experience any of the diseases it can cause. But when the population of *S. pyogenes*

By mapping the pattern of deaths from cholera, Dr. John Snow was able to identify the Broad Street water pump as the source of the infection.

● Deaths from cholera (size of circle proportionate to number of deaths)
⬦ Street pump

FIGURE 13-11 Contaminated! Water from the Broad Street pump in London was the source of a cholera outbreak that killed more than 500 people.

is not held in check by competition with other members of the bacterial community, it can become a pathogen. Strep throat (more formally known as "streptococcal pharyngitis") is the most common disease caused by *S. pyogenes;* it produces a severe sore throat and a distinctive rash of red abscesses with white pus at the top of the throat (**FIGURE 13-12**). Some strains of *S. pyogenes* produce a toxin that is released into the bloodstream and produces a red rash that spreads across the skin—the disease called scarlet fever. Most threatening of all is an infection caused by strains of

Streptococcus pyogenes *is usually harmless, but some strains are responsible for strep throat, scarlet fever, and necrotizing fasciitis (flesh-eating bacteria).*

S. pyogenes that have a toxin that allows them to enter body tissues, where they produce necrotizing fasciitis. These strains of *S. pyogenes* are known by their well-earned name, "the flesh-eating bacteria."

TAKE-HOME MESSAGE 13·7

Some bacteria always cause disease, and others do no harm except under certain conditions. For example, *Streptococcus pyogenes* can be harmless, but under some conditions it releases toxins that are responsible for strep throat, scarlet fever, and necrotizing fasciitis (caused by the flesh-eating strains).

13·8 Bacteria's resistance to drugs can evolve quickly.

Penicillin was the first antibiotic to be manufactured and used widely in the battle against illness-inducing bacteria. It came into use during the Second World War and caused a revolution in the care of the wounded. But antibiotic-resistant infections soon appeared, and the number of resistant bacteria has increased rapidly ever since (**FIGURE 13-13**). Now, 70 years after the first use of antibiotics, many bacteria are resistant to many, or even to most, antibiotics. In the United States, more people now die of *Staphylococcus aureus* infections that are resistant to many different antibiotics (MRSA infections) than die of HIV/AIDS. A few years ago, antibiotic-resistant staph infections were acquired only in hospitals, but now these infections have spread from hospitals to the community at large. Instead of contracting antibiotic-resistant staph infections in hospitals, patients (or their visitors) are now bringing the resistant bacteria into the hospital with them!

Microbes live everywhere they can, and compete for the best places to attach themselves and for the richest sources of food to eat. This competition takes many forms: rapid growth to crowd competitors out of a living space, superior ability to take in nutrients to starve competitors, and—this is the key to both the benefits of antibiotics and the problem of antibiotic resistance for humans—production of chemicals that kill other microbes, or at least stop them from growing. Antibiotics are produced by microbes to help them compete with other microbes, and most of the antibiotics we use today are derived from microbes.

Bacteria and other microbes have developed a variety of ways to resist antibiotics. For example, some bacteria pump an antibiotic out of their cells as fast as it enters, so it never reaches a lethal concentration inside the bacterial cell. Other bacteria have proteins that bind to the antibiotic molecule and block its lethal effect. Still others carry that approach a step further—they have enzymes that break down the antibiotic molecules, which are then used as fuel to help the bacteria grow faster! Antibiotic resistance within a population of bacteria can spread quickly, because many of the genes that code for resistance are on plasmids. This means that a bacterium carrying a resistance gene can transmit the gene to other bacteria by conjugation; there's no need to wait for multiple generations of natural selection

Q Where do antibiotics come from, and why do they so quickly lose their effectiveness?

Q Why is it essential to take every dose of an antibiotic prescribed by a doctor?

When an antibiotic is taken as prescribed—that is, at the times specified on the label and until all the pills have been consumed—the population of target bacteria is greatly reduced. All of the target bacteria that remain are resistant to the antibiotic, but there are not very many of them. The growth of these resistant bacteria will be held in check by competition with other types of bacteria. But,

ANTIBIOTIC RESISTANCE IN BACTERIA

1 INFECTION

Patient A and Patient B both have an infection caused by a harmful strain of bacteria.

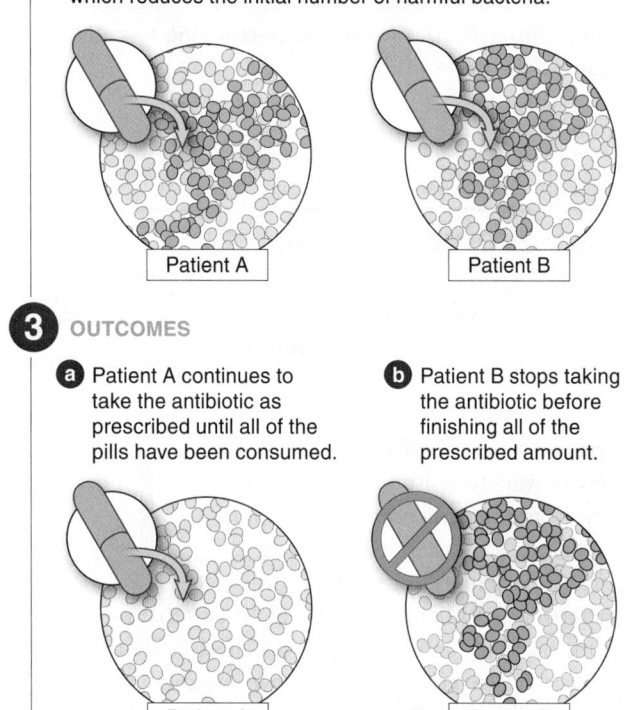

● Harmful bacteria
○ Harmless bacteria

Patient A   Patient B

2 ANTIBIOTICS

Both patients are prescribed an antibiotic to treat the infection, which reduces the initial number of harmful bacteria.

Patient A   Patient B

3 OUTCOMES

a Patient A continues to take the antibiotic as prescribed until all of the pills have been consumed.

b Patient B stops taking the antibiotic before finishing all of the prescribed amount.

Patient A   Patient B

Harmful bacterial population is significantly reduced (and can be held in check by competition with other, harmless bacteria).

The harmful bacterial cells still alive are the most resistant to the antibiotic and can proliferate, leading to future health problems.

FIGURE 13-13 Evolution of resistance. Sixty years after the appearance of antibiotics, many bacteria are resistant to many, or even most, antibiotics.

if you stop taking the antibiotic before you have finished all of the prescription, many of the target bacterial cells will remain alive, including the ones that are most resistant to the antibiotic. These resistant cells will be the founders of a new population of bacteria in your body, so the next time you take that drug it will be ineffective. Even worse, taking antibiotics when they are not needed—to treat a viral

Livestock are given antibiotics to prevent diseases easily spread in crowded living conditions.

Agriculture in the United States uses about 25 million pounds of antibiotics each year—about eight times more than is used for all human medicine!

FIGURE 13-14 Antibiotics are used in agriculture. Livestock are given antibiotics to prevent diseases easily spread in crowded living conditions.

infection, for example—selects for resistant bacteria without providing any benefit. Antibiotics have no effect on viruses.

The use of antibiotics in agriculture is another reason for the spread of antibiotic resistance. Low concentrations of antibiotics are routinely added to the feed for cattle, hogs, chickens, and turkeys. This can be beneficial in the short term, promoting growth and minimizing disease in the crowded conditions of commercial meat and milk production (**FIGURE 13-14**). But in the long run it can have disastrous consequences, as the practice can lead to selection for bacteria resistant to the antibiotics. The antibiotics can also pass through the food chain to humans. Data gathered by the Union of Concerned Scientists indicate that agriculture in the United States uses about 25 million pounds of antibiotics each year—about eight times more than is used for all human medicine!

TAKE-HOME MESSAGE 13·8

Antibiotic resistance routinely evolves in microbes. The genes that allow bacteria to combat antibiotics are located on plasmids, and plasmid transfer allows an antibiotic-resistant bacterium to pass that resistance to other bacteria. Excessive use of antibiotics in medicine and agriculture has made several of the most important pathogenic bacteria resistant to every known antibiotic, and infections caused by these bacteria are nearly impossible to treat.

13·9 Sexually transmitted diseases reveal battles between microbes and humans.

To many microbes, the human genitals and reproductive tract are desirable places to find shelter, nourishment, and opportunities for reproducing and dispersing. Unfortunately, these microbes can cause problems for humans in the form of **sexually transmitted diseases (STDs).** STDs produce symptoms of varying severity, from mild to extreme discomfort, to sterility, or even death. It is estimated that more than 300 million new cases of STDs occur each year worldwide.

STDs are caused by all types of microbes—bacteria, viruses, fungi, protists—and even by some arthropods. The organisms are passed from the mucous membranes (of the genitals, anus, and mouth) of one individual to those of another during sexual contact; sometimes they are transmitted by needles used for drug injections.

Although most STDs are curable with drugs, two characteristics of STDs make them nearly impossible to completely eradicate from a population: (1) their symptoms may be mild or absent, causing many people to unwittingly pass an infection to their partners, and (2) to prevent reinfection, both partners must be treated simultaneously. Furthermore, because most microbes have such high reproductive rates, populations of a microbe can evolve quickly and become resistant to existing drugs. The treatment of STDs is one of the most pressing public health issues in the world today (**FIGURE 13-15**).

TAKE-HOME MESSAGE 13·9

Sexually transmitted diseases (STDs) are caused by a variety of organisms, including bacteria, viruses, protists, fungi, and arthropods. Worldwide, more than 300 million people are newly infected each year.

SEXUALLY TRANSMITTED DISEASES

CAUSE	EXAMPLES	SYMPTOMS	TREATMENT
BACTERIUM	• Gonorrhea	Often none; sometimes painful urination, genital discharge, or irregular menstruation	Several antibiotics can successfully cure gonorrhea; however, drug-resistant strains are increasing.
	• Syphilis	Often no symptoms for years; eventual sores, skin rash, and if untreated, organ damage	Penicillin, an antibiotic, can cure a person in the early stages of syphilis.
	• Chlamydia	Often none; sometimes painful urination, genital discharge	Chlamydia can be easily treated and cured with antibiotics.
VIRUS	• HIV/AIDS	Initial symptoms range from none to flu-like; late stages involve severe infections and death	Currently no cure. Antiretroviral treatment can slow progression. Drug-resistant strains occur.
	• Genital herpes	Often none; outbreaks include sores on genitals, flu-like symptoms	Currently no cure. Antiviral medications can shorten and prevent outbreaks.
	• Human papilloma virus (HPV)	Often none; some types can lead to genital warts, others can cause cervical cancer	A vaccine prevents HPV, and is recommended for girls age 11–12. Warts and cancerous lesions can be removed.
PROTIST	• Trichomoniasis	Painful urination and/or vaginal discharge in women; often no symptoms in men	Trichomoniasis can usually be cured with prescription drugs.
FUNGUS	• Yeast infections	Genital itching or burning, and/or vaginal discharge in women; genital itching in men	Yeast infections can usually be cured with antifungal suppositories or creams.
ARTHROPOD	• Crab lice	Visible lice eggs or lice crawling or attached to pubic hair; itching in the pubic and groin area	Crab lice can be treated with over-the-counter lotions.

FIGURE 13-15 The most common STDs.

13·10–13·12 Archaea exploit some of the most extreme habitats.

Grand Prismatic Spring hydrothermal vent in Yellowstone National Park, Wyoming. Hot springs are home to many microbes, including thermophilic archaea.

13·10 Archaea are profoundly different from bacteria.

When you look at the photograph of archaea in **FIGURE 13-16**, you may find it hard to believe that they are even a little bit different from bacteria, let alone *profoundly* different. Both live as single cells or colonies of cells, both are surrounded by a plasma membrane, and both have species with flagella that twirl like propellers. In fact, until the 1970s, biologists considered the archaea to be bacteria. Only then did comparisons of DNA reveal that archaea are as different from bacteria as humans are.

Those studies of archaeal nucleotide sequences stimulated other comparisons, which identified additional differences among bacteria, archaea, and eukarya. For example, the chemical compositions of the plasma membranes, cell walls, and flagella of archaea are qualitatively different from those of bacteria. And beyond the large DNA sequence differences and the differences in plasma membranes, cell walls, and flagella, a third difference reflects the position of archaea between bacteria and eukarya on the tree of life (see Figure 13-4): eukaryotes have a distinct cell nucleus that is separated from the cytoplasm by a nuclear membrane, whereas bacteria and archaea have neither a nucleus nor a nuclear membrane. The presence of a nucleus protects the chromosomes of a eukaryotic cell and allows the cell to control what molecules interact with its DNA.

Archaea look very much like bacteria. But closer inspection—of their physiology, biochemistry, and DNA—reveals them to be profoundly different from all bacteria.

FIGURE 13-16 Appearances are deceiving.

TAKE-HOME MESSAGE 13·10

Archaea show a set of characteristics that places them between bacteria and eukaryotes on the tree of life. Archaea and bacteria may look similar, but they have large and significant differences in their DNA sequences, as well as differences in their plasma membranes, cell walls, and flagella. Furthermore, neither archaea nor bacteria resemble eukarya in one key way: only eukarya have a distinct cell nucleus and nuclear membrane.

Archaea thrive in habitats too extreme for most other organisms.

Archaea are famous for their ability to live in places where life would seem to be impossible, such as in water around hydrothermal vents that emerge from the seafloor, which would be boiling if it were at sea level. At 2,000 meters below the surface, the water pressure reaches 200 atmospheres, or almost 3,000 pounds per square inch, and the 400° C water coming from the vent cannot boil. Archaea thrive there. Most organisms die at temperatures between 40° and 50° C, because their protein molecules are denatured, so the ability of archaea to survive at temperatures above 100° C is truly remarkable.

Equally impressive is the ability of archaea to live in water as acidic as pH 0 or as salty as a saturated NaCl solution, and to metabolize an extraordinary range of compounds—including sulfur, iron, and hydrogen gas—to obtain energy (**FIGURE 13-17**). Some bacteria also can tolerate extreme physical and chemical conditions, and the organisms that can live in these conditions, both bacteria and archaea, are called **extremophiles** ("lovers of extreme conditions").

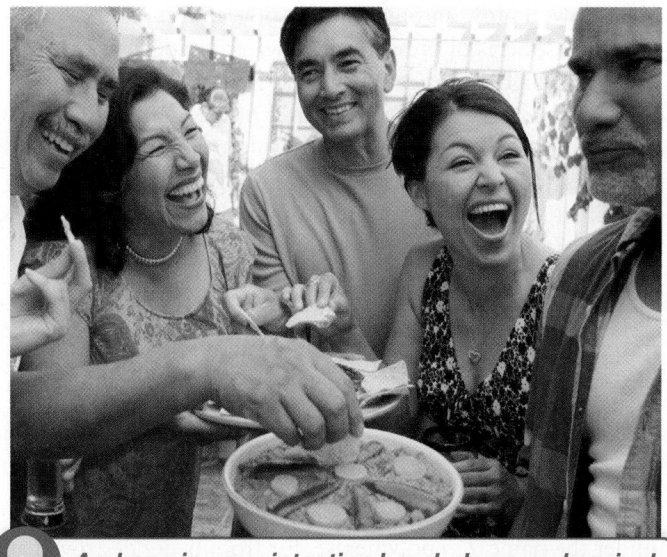

Archaea in your intestine break down a chemical bond found in beans (a bond humans cannot break) … but the process generates gas, which can cause discomfort as it tries to escape.

FIGURE 13-18 Helping you digest tough bonds. Intestinal archaea help you digest some chemical bonds in beans.

But not all archaea are extremophiles. Archaea live everywhere that bacteria do, and many of them live in places you would find comfortable. In fact, you are home to many archaea and, on occasion, some of them make their presence all too obvious. Beans are notorious for their tendency to produce gas in the intestine, but archaea are actually the culprits. Beans contain a couple of carbohydrates with chemical bonds that are not broken down very well by any human enzymes (**FIGURE 13-18**). Methane-producing archaea, on the other hand, have no such difficulties, producing an enzyme that targets those bonds. As a result, it is the archaea in your intestine that digest most of these carbohydrates. But in the process of breaking these bonds, they produce gases that, as they escape the digestive system, can cause considerable distress.

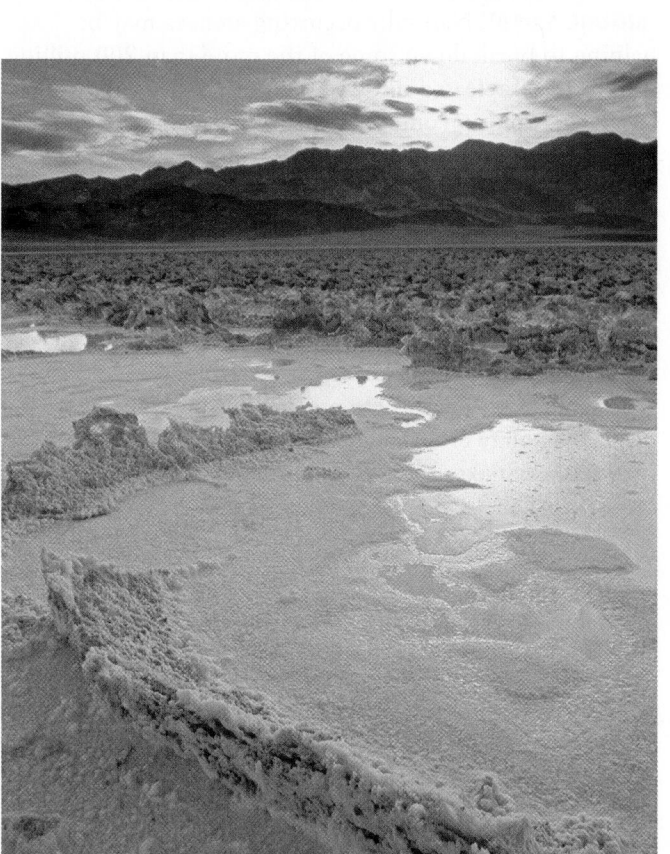

FIGURE 13-17 Living in the harshest environments. Archaea thrive in many extreme environments, such as this salt pond.

TAKE-HOME MESSAGE 13·11

Archaea can tolerate extreme physical and chemical conditions that are impossible for most other living organisms, but some live in moderate conditions and even in the human intestine.

13·12 Much archaeal diversity has yet to be discovered.

How do you grow an organism in your lab if it requires 200 atmospheres of pressure and a water temperature of 100° C or higher, and eats a gas that is toxic to humans? It's not easy, and only about one-quarter of the identified archaeal species have been cultured in the lab. We know that the other species exist, because their transfer RNA has been identified in samples taken from the environment, and biologists are confident that thousands, perhaps millions, of species of archaea await discovery.

Extremophile archaea may have important applications in bioengineering and environmental remediation. For example, *Thermus aquaticus,* an extremophile archaeon that lives in hot springs where the water is nearly boiling, produces an enzyme important in making PCR possible (see Chapter 5), and this enzyme is now sold for laboratory use under the name *Taq* polymerase. Far from being destroyed at high temperatures, *Taq* polymerase works best at 75° C, a temperature at which most human enzymes would simply fall apart.

FIGURE 13-19 Practical applications for archaea. The metabolic activity of archaea has potential for use in the cleanup of oil spills.

> " He was a killer, a thing that preyed, living on the things that lived, unaided, alone, by virtue of his own strength and prowess, surviving triumphantly in a hostile environment where only the strong survive. "
>
> —JACK LONDON, *The Call of the Wild,* 1903

Bioengineers and biotechnologists believe that extremophile archaea and bacteria that thrive at high temperatures and pressures and metabolize toxic substances have enormous potential for industries that have to carry out activities under such conditions. Recent experiments have demonstrated the ability of some archaea to efficiently degrade hydrocarbons, making it possible for them to be used in the removal of sludge that accumulates in oil refinery tanks and, potentially, in the cleanup of contaminated environments such as oil slicks (**FIGURE 13-19**). Naturally occurring archaea may be helping to break down some of the more than 200 million gallons of oil released into the Gulf of Mexico following an oil rig explosion and subsequent massive leak in 2010. Other archaea show promise in clearing mineral deposits from pipes in the cooling systems of power plants.

TAKE-HOME MESSAGE 13·12

Archaea are hard to study because many require extreme heat or pressure to grow, and these conditions are not easy to provide in a laboratory. But the ability of archaea to grow in such extreme conditions makes them potentially valuable for industrial and environmental purposes.

13·13–13·15 Most protists are single-celled eukaryotes.

Diatoms, single-celled photosynthetic algae that form an important part of the plankton, have mineralized cell walls that provide protection and support.

13·13 The first eukaryotes were protists.

For the first 2 billion years of life on earth, organisms were really, really small—bacteria and archaea less than 10 micrometers across, one-eighth the diameter of a human hair. But in rocks about 1.9 billion years old, we find fossils of new kinds of organisms that are 10 times larger (**FIGURE 13-20**). These are a group of organisms called acritarchs (a name that can be translated as "confusing old things"). They were the first eukaryotes.

> In these ancient fossilized eukaryotes, organelles are visible.

FIGURE 13-20 Ancient protists. These acritarch fossils represent the first eukaryotes on earth. The oldest fossils of this type were found in rock 1.9 billion years old.

The larger size is the first thing you notice about these fossil cells, but the internal changes in the cells are even more significant, because they are the basis for the success of the entire eukaryote lineage, including humans. For the first time in the history of life, cells had internal structures that carried out specific functions. These structures, the cellular organelles, perform the specialized activities that make eukaryotic cells more complex than prokaryotes.

The nucleus is an evolutionary innovation that appeared for the first time in protists. The nucleus is a region inside the cell that is enclosed by its own double-layered membrane. The nuclear membrane was probably formed by the fusion of folds of the plasma membrane that surrounded the cell. We know that many modern prokaryotes have complex infoldings of their plasma membranes—these increase the total surface area of the cell and allow better exchange of material between the cell and the external environment —and infoldings of this type may have played a role in endosymbiosis and the formation of the first organelles (see Figure 3-7). Infoldings probably fused around the DNA, for example, creating a membrane-enclosed compartment containing DNA. Thus, the cell nucleus was formed, separated by a double membrane from the cytoplasm of the cell.

Subsequently, these first nuclear membranes developed two specializations: they incorporated proteins that controlled the movement of molecules into and out of the nucleus, and they extended outward from the nucleus to form a folded membrane called the endoplasmic reticulum. The endoplasmic reticulum is the part of a eukaryotic cell where some proteins are assembled. Further development of internal membranes produced the Golgi apparatus, where newly synthesized proteins are given some final processing steps, and sac-like structures called lysosomes, which contain enzymes that break down damaged molecules. Finally, a lineage of protists took in a guest—a bacterial cell that subsequently became specialized as the mitochondrion, the organelle that produces most of the ATP synthesized by a eukaryotic cell.

13·14 There are animal-like protists, fungus-like protists, and plant-like protists.

Six major lineages of protists have been named, but even that classification does not capture the huge diversity of the group, and some of the best-known protists do not fit into any of the six lineages. Protists include forms that are very much like animals, others that seem a lot like fungi, and still others that look like plants (**FIGURE 13-21**).

Animal-like protists Some protists propel themselves quickly around their environment and appear to hunt for prey. These animal-like protists, which include *Paramecium,* are the ciliates, and get their name from the cilia (hair-like projections) that cover their body surfaces and propel the cells through water. *Paramecium* feeds by the process of **phagocytosis:** cilia in a funnel-shaped structure called the gullet create an inward flow of water that carries bacteria and other small particles of food with it. These particles accumulate at the inner end of the gullet, where a portion of the plasma membrane bulges inward and eventually breaks free, forming a food vacuole that drifts into the interior of the cell. Enzymes and hydrochloric acid enter the food vacuole from the cytoplasm, and in this acidic environment the engulfed food items are broken down into molecules that diffuse from the vacuole into the cytoplasm. When all of the digestible material has been consumed, the undigested contents of the vacuole are expelled.

Fungus-like protists Some protists resemble fungi: living as heterotrophs (organisms that are unable to fix carbon through photosynthesis, but require carbon for growth), establishing sheet-like colonies of cells on surfaces (such as the grout in shower stalls), using spores to reproduce, and sometimes producing fruiting bodies. These

DIVERSITY OF PROTISTS

ANIMAL-LIKE PROTISTS
Some protists, such as *Trichomonas vaginalis* shown here, move around and hunt for prey like an animal.

FUNGI-LIKE PROTISTS
Some protists, such as the plasmodial slime mold shown here, live as heterotrophs and form sheet-like colonies of cells like a fungus.

PLANT-LIKE PROTISTS
Some protists, such as the kelp forest shown here, are multicellular and photosynthetic like a plant.

FIGURE 13-21 Protists come in all shapes and sizes.

are the slime molds. They generally spread without any individual cells moving, but rather by adding new cells at the edges of the colony. Some slime molds, however, called plasmodial slime molds, are oozing masses of gooey material that flow along a surface, engulfing bacteria, fungi, and small bits of organic material as they go. The streaming of a slime mold in its feeding phase is easy to observe with a microscope, and such a slime mold can flow around, over, or through almost anything—it can even flow through a window screen and reassemble itself on the other side! You may have seen an irregularly shaped blob of yellow material in a moist, shaded garden—this was a plasmodial slime mold.

Remarkably, a plasmodial slime mold is a very large, single cell (but has multiple nuclei). Slime molds divide by binary fission, just like other cells, but in this case a single cell may cover an area of several square centimeters! All of the nuclei in the cell undergo mitosis simultaneously.

Plant-like protists Other members of the protist kingdom grow in water and resemble plants. These include the protists referred to colloquially as seaweeds. The term "seaweed" generally refers to the macroscopic, multicellular marine algae, many of which are used as a source of food for humans. And although they are all protists, seaweeds encompass several groups that do not share a common multicellular ancestor. These include some red algae and some green algae (from which the land plants most likely evolved), as well as some of the brown algae—such as the giant kelp that grows in water 30 meters deep. (The seaweeds, of course, represent parts of the protist kingdom that obviously are not "microbial.")

Brown algae cover large portions of the rocks in the intertidal zone. Giant kelp, growing in temperate regions of the North and South Pacific and off the Atlantic coast of South Africa, are among the fastest growing organisms on earth, with some growing as much as 60 meters in a single year. Kelp forests are an enormously diverse habitat; more than 1,000 species of fishes, crustaceans, snails, and mammals make their homes in these marine "forests." Sea otters wrap a kelp frond around their waist when they sleep, and gray whales hide in kelp forests to escape from killer whales.

Although many protists are unicellular, there are many exceptions. As we've seen, many green and brown algae are multicellular, composed of many different cells and cell types, performing different functions. Additionally, some other protists, such as spirogyra, are colonial, living as collections of cells, each of which can carry out all of its life processes independent of the other cells.

Also among the plant-like protists are the diatoms. These organisms live in ponds, lakes, and rivers as well as in the

FIGURE 13-22 **Diatoms are aquatic photosynthetic protists.** Shown above: krill (shrimp-like crustaceans) feeding on phytoplankton (including diatoms), on the underside of ice in Antarctica.

oceans. They are so small that, for some species, 30 individuals could be lined up across the width of a human hair. A characteristic of the diatoms is that they are enclosed in a shell made of silica (**FIGURE 13-22**). Many species of diatoms float in the water, forming part of the phytoplankton—the collection of microscopic organisms that fix carbon dioxide and release oxygen. Phytoplankton can reach densities of hundreds of thousands of cells per liter, and it accounts for about one-quarter of the photosynthetic production of oxygen on earth, occupying a critical position in marine food chains. Small fishes and shrimp-like organisms called copepods feed on phytoplankton, and these small predators are eaten by larger predators, which are eaten by still larger predators. Thus the diversity of life in the marine habitat relies on diatoms and the other microbes that make up the phytoplankton.

TAKE-HOME MESSAGE 13·14

Protists are a diverse group of mostly unicellular eukaryotic organisms. The ciliates, such as *Paramecium*, are animal-like protists. Plasmodial slime molds are fungus-like protists. Colonial protists and multicellular protists such as the giant kelp can be enormous and are plant-like in appearance.

13·15 Some protists can make you very sick.

A **parasite** is an organism that lives in or on another organism, called a **host,** and damages it. A parasitic protist called *Plasmodium* that is transmitted by a mosquito is responsible for a worldwide epidemic disease—malaria. Malaria occurs in tropical parts of Africa, Asia, and Latin America, and it is common in the eastern Mediterranean as well. Between 350 million and 500 million people have clinical cases of malaria, and about 1 million people die of malaria each year. Malaria is the leading cause of death for children younger than 5 years old in sub-Saharan Africa; somewhere on the African continent, about every 30 seconds, a child dies of malaria.

These are sobering statistics, and neither the incidence of malaria nor the rate of mortality has changed very much since *Plasmodium* was identified as the cause of malaria nearly a century ago. The reason for the lack of progress in combating malaria is the nature of *Plasmodium*—it has a complex development that makes it nearly invisible to the host's immune system (**FIGURE 13-23**).

The human immune system has a difficult time fighting a malarial infection because, to survive from one generation to the next, *Plasmodium* parasites go through a series of distinct developmental stages. And as the *Plasmodium* cells change from one stage to another, the parasite produces different cell surface proteins. Thus *Plasmodium* stays ahead of the human immune system by constantly changing the way it appears.

Although the immune system doesn't usually have much success fighting malarial infection, some individuals produce red blood cells that are inhospitable to the *Plasmodium* parasite, conferring a resistance to the malaria-causing protist. These individuals carry an allele, called Hb^S, which (as we learned in Chapter 7) codes for a variant of the normal adult hemoglobin that causes hemoglobin molecules to stick together in long chains that distort the red blood cell (see Figure 13-23), giving the cell a sickled shape. The sickled red blood cells are inhospitable to *Plasmodium* because they are leaky, and the substances that leak out happen to be essential to *Plasmodium*. Although carrying a copy of the Hb^S allele confers resistance to malaria, individuals who carry two copies of the Hb^S allele suffer from sickle-cell anemia—a severe genetic disease that is more debilitating than malaria. Individuals with the single Hb^S allele are said to have "sickle-cell trait."

MALARIA: A PROTIST-CAUSED ILLNESS

1 Following the bite of a *Plasmodium*-infected mosquito, malaria-causing protists take up residence in healthy red blood cells.

Plasmodium parasite infecting a red blood cell

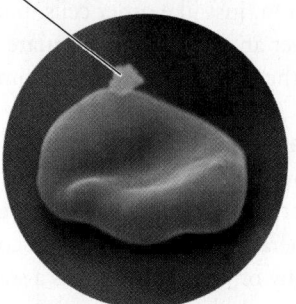

2 Once inside a red blood cell, *Plasmodium* cells modify the cell's surface proteins, making it difficult for the immune system to fight the malarial infection.

RESISTANCE TO MALARIA

In individuals with sickle-cell trait, the sickle shape of some red blood cells makes the cells inhospitable to the protist. This makes these individuals resistant to malaria.

FIGURE 13-23 Malaria-infected blood cells and sickled blood cells. The malaria parasite grows inside red blood cells and destroys them. Because sickle-cell trait changes the shape of some red blood cells, these cells resist infection by malaria parasites.

TAKE-HOME MESSAGE 13·15

Some protists cause debilitating diseases. *Plasmodium,* the protist responsible for malaria, is one of these. *Plasmodium* has characteristics that protect it from the human immune system, but some humans do have a defense against malaria: people with sickle-cell trait make red blood cells that are inhospitable to the parasite.

13·16–13·19 Viruses are at the border between living and non-living.

Colored transmission electron micrograph of T2 bacteriophage viruses (red) attacking an E. coli *bacterium.*

13·16 Viruses are not exactly living organisms.

A virus is not a cell, and that is why viruses do not fit into any of the three domains of life. A virus particle (called a virion) consists of genetic material inside a container made of protein. Some viruses also contain a few enzymes. That's all there is to a virus. The protein container is called the **capsid,** and the genetic material can be either DNA or RNA. Some viruses wrap themselves in a bit of the plasma membrane of the host cell as they are released. A virus of this type is called an enveloped virus—the flu virus is an example. Non-enveloped viruses are enclosed only by the protein container; the virus that causes the common cold is an example of a non-enveloped virus (**FIGURE 13-24**).

There is almost nothing inside the capsid of a virus except DNA or RNA. A virus particle does not carry out any metabolic processes, and it does not control the inward or

BASIC STRUCTURE OF A VIRUS

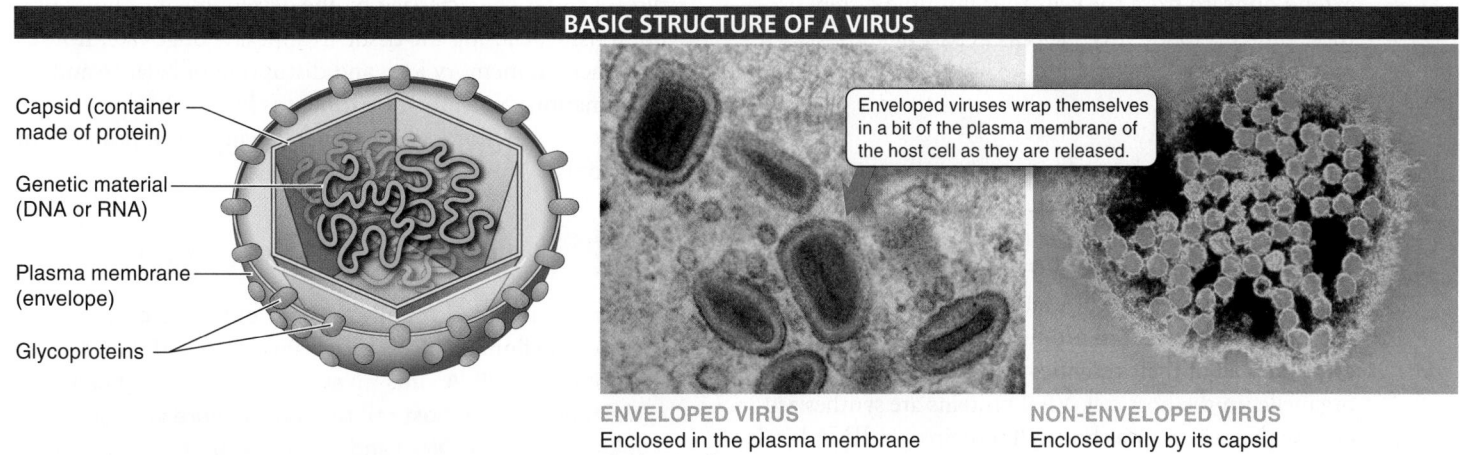

Capsid (container made of protein)

Genetic material (DNA or RNA)

Plasma membrane (envelope)

Glycoproteins

Enveloped viruses wrap themselves in a bit of the plasma membrane of the host cell as they are released.

ENVELOPED VIRUS
Enclosed in the plasma membrane of a host cell

NON-ENVELOPED VIRUS
Enclosed only by its capsid

FIGURE 13-24 The simple structure of viruses. All viruses have a container (the capsid) that holds their genetic material, and sometimes the capsid is wrapped in a membrane (an envelope).

1. After the virus binds to the host cell's membrane, the viral DNA is taken into the cell.

2. Viral DNA is replicated into dozens of new copies, using the host's metabolic machinery and energy.

3. Viral mRNA is transcribed from the viral DNA.

4. New viral proteins are synthesized, again using the host's protein-production molecules.

5. The new viral DNA and proteins assemble, forming many new virus particles.

FIGURE 13-25 Making more viruses. A virus duplicates its own genetic material (DNA in the example shown here) by taking over the resources and metabolic machinery of a host cell.

 Because they are dependent on their hosts' metabolic machinery for replication, viruses are not considered "living."

outward movement of molecules to make conditions inside the virus particle different from conditions outside. Viruses just wait for a chance to insert their genetic material into a living cell.

We speak of "catching" a cold, but what actually happens is that a virus catches us. Viruses identify the cells that they can infect by recognizing the structure of glycoprotein molecules on the surfaces of cells. Every cell in your body has these molecules. They are embedded in the plasma membrane and extend outward from the cell. Your immune system uses these proteins to identify the cells as part of you—as self rather than non-self—and it does not react to proteins that it recognizes as self.

Viruses have cracked the glycoprotein code, and when they find a cell with the appropriate glycoprotein on its surface, they bind to that cell's plasma membrane and insert their genetic material into the cell (**FIGURE 13-25**). Inside the host cell, the viral DNA or RNA takes over the cellular machinery and uses it to produce more viruses. Viruses carry out nearly all of their activities by hijacking materials and organelles in the host cell. Viral proteins are synthesized in exactly the same way as host cell proteins—mRNA binds to ribosomes, and tRNA matches the correct amino acid to each mRNA codon. The mRNA is produced from the virus's DNA or RNA, but all of the protein-building machinery

comes from the host cell, as does the ATP required to synthesize the new viral protein.

There are also some other types of non-living infectious agents. Prions, for example, are misfolded proteins that form plaques and interfere with normal tissue. Usually acquired through ingestion of an infected animal (or its bodily fluids), prions can cause a variety of degenerative neurological diseases in humans. One of these, Creutzfeldt-Jakob disease, is sometimes referred to as a human form of mad cow disease and is characterized by the development of holes in brain tissue, causing the tissue to appear sponge-like. It leads to dementia, memory loss, and disruption of balance and coordination. No cure or treatment is known, and few victims survive more than a year following the appearance of symptoms.

TAKE-HOME MESSAGE 13·16

A virus is not alive, but it can carry out some of the same functions as living organisms, provided that it can get inside a cell. A virus takes over the protein-making machinery of the host cell to produce more viral genetic material (RNA or DNA) and more viral protein. The viral proteins and genetic material are assembled into new virus particles and released from the cell.

13·17

Viruses are responsible for many health problems.

Many diseases are caused by viruses. Some viral diseases, such as the common cold, are not usually serious, but others have been responsible for worldwide epidemics, called pandemics. The influenza pandemic of 1918–1919 killed at least 20 million people, and possibly as many as 50 million. In the current HIV/AIDS pandemic, nearly 40 million people have been infected, with an annual mortality of about 3 million.

Herpes is a common viral infection in humans, caused by two related viruses. Oral herpes is an infection near the mouth and can cause cold sores, which last two to three weeks. More than three-quarters of all adults in the United States are infected with the virus, with more than 50 million people experiencing outbreaks each year. Genital herpes, a sexually transmitted disease, affects about one in six people between the ages of 14 and 49 in the United States. The viruses causing herpes are present in and released from sores and spread from one person to another by skin-to-skin contact, but infection can also occur when no symptoms are present. Although a variety of treatments are available for both types of herpes, including antiviral drugs that can reduce the severity and duration of symptoms, there is currently no cure.

DNA viruses have base-pair sequences that are stable over time, because the enzymes that replicate the DNA check for errors and correct them during replication. From a health perspective, the fact that DNA viruses do not change rapidly makes it much easier to fight and treat diseases caused by these viruses, using vaccines. Vaccination against a DNA virus such as smallpox, for example, provides years of protection.

RNA viruses, by contrast, change quickly, because the enzymes that carry out RNA replication do not have error-checking mechanisms. As a consequence, because the RNA-replicating enzymes make errors as they assemble new RNA molecules, RNA viruses are continuously mutating into new forms. The common influenza virus that causes outbreaks of flu every year, for example, is an RNA virus. And because flu viruses mutate so fast, the virus that causes health problems changes from one flu season to the next, necessitating a different flu vaccine every year.

Q Why do flu viruses change so quickly?

About every 50 years, a new variety of influenza causes a pandemic. The 20th century had three major influenza pandemics, and all of them originated in the same peculiar way. In each of these pandemics, a bird flu virus gained the ability to infect human cells by passing through pigs, and then the virus spread rapidly through the human population worldwide. The most famous of these pandemics was that of 1918–1919, mentioned above (**FIGURE 13-26**). It was called the Spanish influenza,

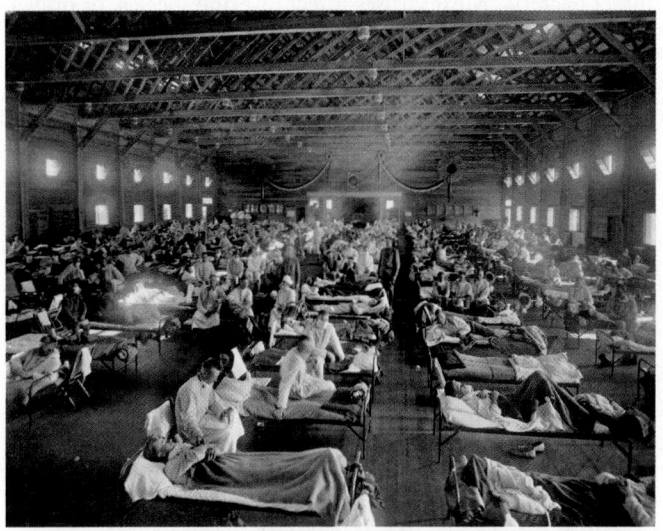

The influenza pandemic of 1918–1919 killed millions.

In 2002–2003, the virus that causes severe acute respiratory syndrome (SARS) infected several thousand people around the world.

FIGURE 13-26 Viral outbreaks can threaten large populations.

because it seemed to enter Europe through Spain, but it originated in Asia. The Asian flu and Hong Kong flu pandemics also originated in Asia, as did smaller viral outbreaks, such as Korean flu (1947), swine fever (1976), and SARS (severe acute respiratory syndrome, 2002–2003), which did not become pandemics.

TAKE-HOME MESSAGE 13·17

Many diseases are caused by viruses. DNA viruses are relatively stable, because DNA-replicating enzymes check for errors and correct them during replication. RNA viruses change quickly, however, because RNA-replicating enzymes do not have error-checking mechanisms.

13·18 Viruses infect a wide range of organisms.

Viruses are practically everywhere. There are viruses that infect animals, viruses that infect plants, even viruses that infect bacteria. Most viruses infect just one species, or only a few closely related species, and enter only one kind of cell in that species. But some viruses can infect a wide range of hosts—the rabies virus, for example, can infect any mammal. Pet dogs and cats are routinely immunized against rabies, but wild mammals, such as bats, skunks, and raccoons, can get rabies. That is why, if you are bitten by one of those wild animals, your treatment includes rabies shots as a precaution.

Q *What role does a pig play in the transmission of virus from a bird to a human?*

The glycoproteins on the surface of a virus determine which host species the virus can infect and which tissues of the host it can enter. Influenza A viruses (the ones that cause outbreaks of flu every year), for example, have two types of glycoprotein that have different functions. One glycoprotein matches that of a host cell, and allows the virus to enter the cell. The other glycoprotein allows the virus to get back out of the cell, releasing new virus particles that can infect other cells (**FIGURE 13-27**).

Influenza A is an example of a virus that can move from one species to another, and as we noted above, all of the influenza pandemics in the past century began with the transmission of a bird flu virus to humans. Here's how "species jumping" can occur.

Viruses that infect birds don't bind well to glycoproteins in human cells, making it difficult for bird flu viruses to infect humans. However, the cells of pigs have glycoproteins that allow both human and bird flu viruses to bind to them. Thus, a pig cell can be infected by a

INFLUENZA A STRUCTURE

SURFACE GLYCOPROTEINS

- Bind to receptors on the surface of the host cell and allow the virus to enter

- Allow the virus to break free from the host cell

Surface glycoproteins are the "keys" that allow a virus into and out of a host cell.

FIGURE 13-27 A virus's surface proteins. The influenza virus has surface glycoproteins that allow it to bind to and exit a host cell.

human flu virus and a bird flu virus at the same time. Influenza viruses are not very careful when they incorporate newly synthesized RNA into new particles, though. If RNA strands from a human flu virus and a bird flu virus happen to be in a pig cell at the same time, some virus particles released from the cell might include some RNA from the bird virus and some from the human virus. These influenza viruses are a new strain, and they may be able to infect humans (**FIGURE 13-28**).

Since 1997, one strain of bird flu has spread from Hong Kong through most of Asia and into Turkey, France, Germany, and England. This bird flu is the most recent avian influenza virus to also infect humans (not needing pigs as intermediary). The virus readily infects birds, and tens of millions of chickens, turkeys, and ducks have been killed in attempts to eradicate the infection. And because the virus's

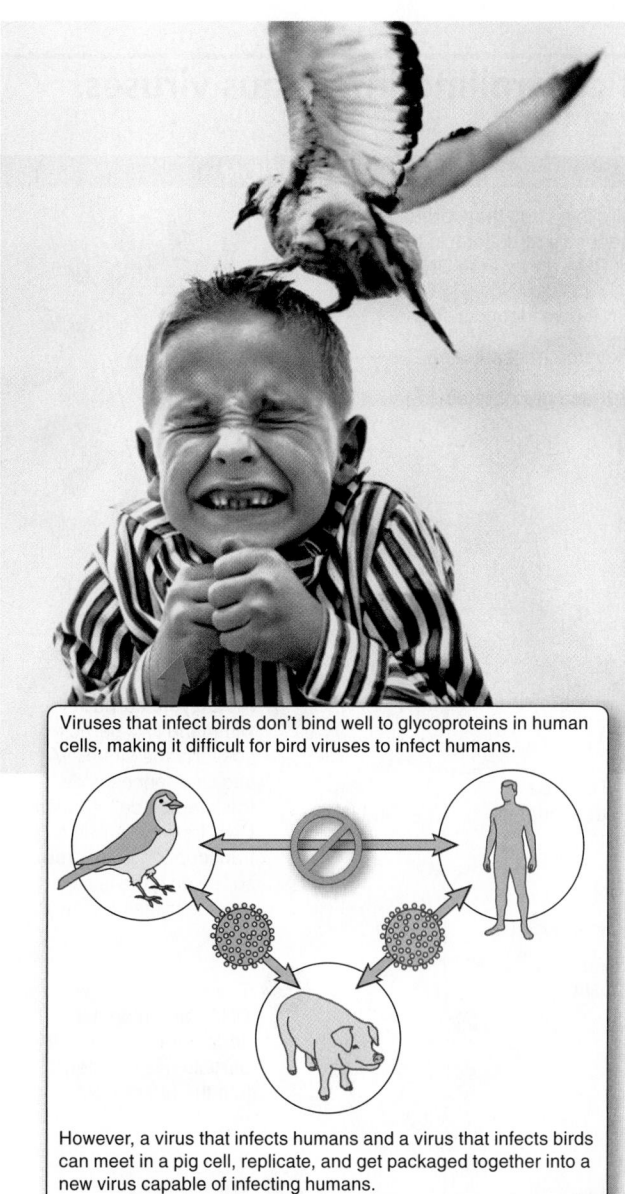

Viruses that infect birds don't bind well to glycoproteins in human cells, making it difficult for bird viruses to infect humans.

However, a virus that infects humans and a virus that infects birds can meet in a pig cell, replicate, and get packaged together into a new virus capable of infecting humans.

FIGURE 13-28 The pig connects human viruses with bird viruses. A virus that infects humans and a virus that infects birds can meet in a pig cell (as described in the text), replicate, and, because viral RNA replication is error-prone, get packaged together into a new virus particle capable of infecting humans.

host-entry glycoproteins do not bind well to human cells, the virus does not easily infect people and does not readily spread from human to human. So far, nearly all the people who have been infected by the avian influenza virus have contracted it through close contact with infected flocks of birds or by eating birds that had died of the viral infection. Only a half-dozen cases are known in which the virus seems to have been transmitted from one person to another. However, avian flu can be deadly when it does infect humans—more than half of the human cases reported have ended in death.

The World Health Organization and national health agencies are preparing for a worldwide pandemic of this bird flu virus that can also infect humans. Their alarm is based on a possibility involving pigs. If a pig infected with the bird flu virus is also infected with a human flu virus, and if the viruses are not careful when packing new RNA into new capsids, then a pig cell could contain RNA from both humans and birds, and some of the new viruses released from this cell could contain a mixture of RNA from the human and the bird flu viruses. A mixture of this type might produce a new form of the virus that carries both the genes that make the bird flu lethal to humans *and* the gene that codes for the host-entry glycoprotein. This virus would infect human cells and spread easily from person to person. The World Health Organization has estimated that a pandemic that started in this way could kill as many as 100 million people worldwide.

TAKE-HOME MESSAGE 13·18

Glycoproteins on the surfaces of viruses determine the types of cells a virus can invade. Most viruses infect just one species, or only a few closely related species, and enter only one kind of cell in that species.

13·19

HIV illustrates the difficulty of controlling infectious viruses.

New infectious diseases—some caused by bacteria and others by viruses—emerge quite frequently. Many of these new diseases originate in other species of animals and subsequently acquire the ability to infect humans. There are enough of these new diseases to fill the monthly issues of the journal *Emerging Infectious Diseases,* which is published by the Centers for Disease Control and Prevention. But even in that crowd, **acquired immunodeficiency syndrome (AIDS)** stands out. AIDS is caused by the **human immunodeficiency virus (HIV),** which is derived from a strain of the simian immunodeficiency virus (SIV) that jumped from chimpanzees to humans in the early 1900s. HIV has all of the characteristics that make viral diseases hard to control— plus an additional characteristic of its own.

HIV mutates easily. HIV is a **retrovirus,** that is, an RNA-containing virus that also contains a viral enzyme called reverse transcriptase that uses a strand of viral RNA as a template to synthesize a single strand of DNA. That DNA strand, in turn, is used as a template to make a complementary strand of DNA, and the resulting double-stranded DNA is integrated into the host cell's DNA. From here, the DNA is used by the host cell's machinery to make more viral RNA (**FIGURE 13-29**). Reverse transcriptase is so error-prone, however, that virtually every copy of HIV in an infected individual's body has a different mutation.

This enormous genetic variation in the HIV particles circulating in an infected person's body makes the infection hard to treat. Virus particles with different mutations can have different proteins on their surfaces, and these surface proteins change each time the virus replicates inside a host cell. Each new generation of HIV in the infected individual contains viruses with surface proteins that his or her immune system has never seen. Furthermore, some of the HIV mutations will confer resistance to the drugs that are being used to treat the patient, and new drugs must be used.

HIV attacks white blood cells. All of those problems would apply to any disease caused by a retrovirus, but HIV offers an additional challenge: it targets cells in the host's immune system, especially white blood cells, and particularly those

FIGURE 13-29 HIV infection. This RNA virus takes over the replicating machinery of a white blood cell to produce a new generation of HIV particles. HIV mutates rapidly during this process, because the reverse transcriptase enzyme is highly error-prone.

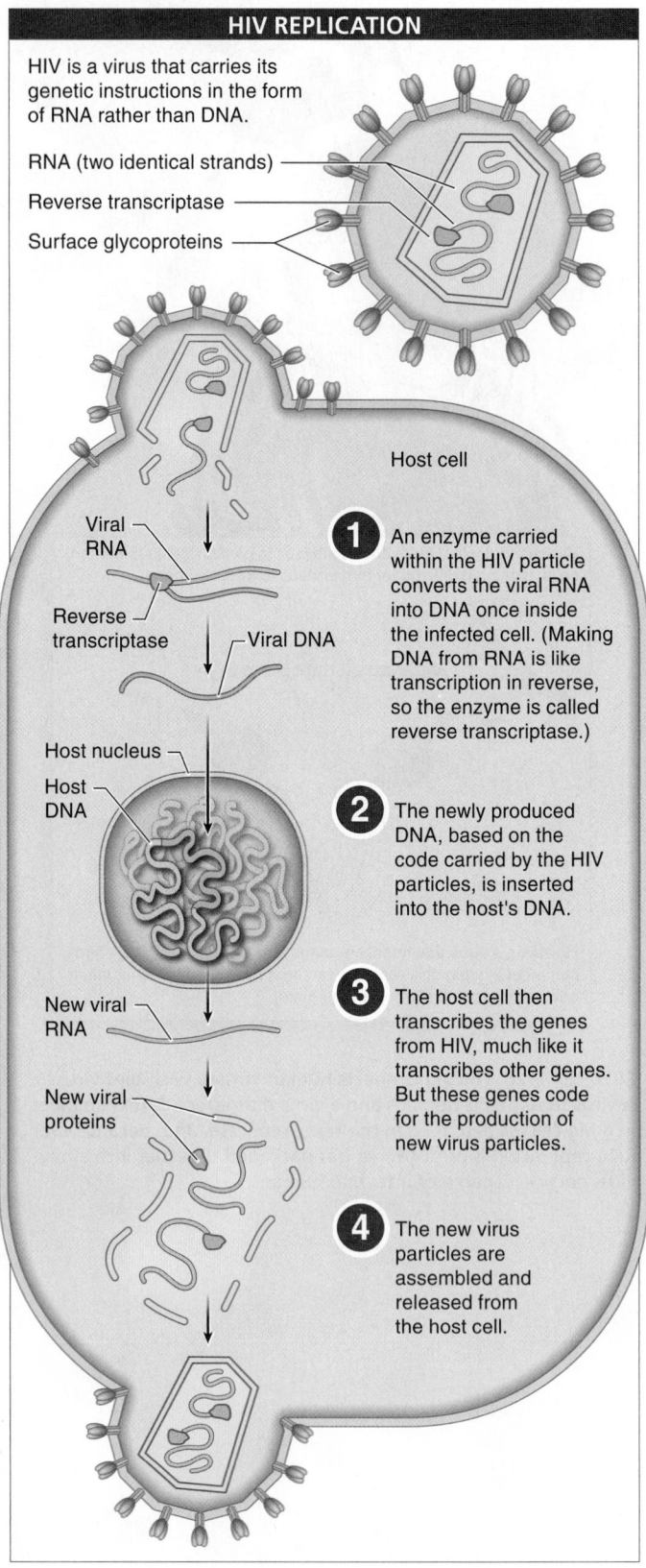

HIV REPLICATION

HIV is a virus that carries its genetic instructions in the form of RNA rather than DNA.

RNA (two identical strands)

Reverse transcriptase

Surface glycoproteins

Host cell

Viral RNA

Reverse transcriptase

Viral DNA

Host nucleus

Host DNA

New viral RNA

New viral proteins

1 An enzyme carried within the HIV particle converts the viral RNA into DNA once inside the infected cell. (Making DNA from RNA is like transcription in reverse, so the enzyme is called reverse transcriptase.)

2 The newly produced DNA, based on the code carried by the HIV particles, is inserted into the host's DNA.

3 The host cell then transcribes the genes from HIV, much like it transcribes other genes. But these genes code for the production of new virus particles.

4 The new virus particles are assembled and released from the host cell.

FIGURE 13-30 HIV attacks white blood cells essential for identifying foreign invaders.

that search for and attack invading bacteria or viruses. During the incubation period, which can last for many years, HIV infects white blood cells. New white cells are produced to replace the ones killed by the virus, however, and the infected person has virtually no symptoms. Nonetheless, HIV is present in the individual's body fluids during the incubation period and can be transmitted to other individuals. HIV testing is used to detect infections during this stage.

Each time HIV infects another white blood cell, the reverse transcriptase makes errors in transcribing the RNA to DNA, and eventually one of the mutations allows the virus to bind to the glycoprotein on the surface of a specialized type of white blood cell—a bacteria- and virus-hunting white blood cell that is critically important in identifying disease-causing threats. A suitable mutation may occur in a couple of years, but more often it takes about 10 years or longer. But when it does happen, it signals a new stage in the HIV infection: the development of AIDS (**FIGURE 13-30**).

The immune system collapses. Normally, white blood cells all work together to identify and destroy cells that have been infected by a virus. When HIV begins to kill the cells that hunt for viruses and bacteria, the immune system begins to fail—it can no longer respond to HIV, or to any other infectious agent. Patients with AIDS develop multiple infections, bacterial and viral, as well as cancers, because they have lost the immune system cells that would normally have marked infected and cancerous cells for destruction.

TAKE-HOME MESSAGE 13·19

HIV infection is especially difficult to control. Mutations change the properties of the retrovirus so that it is hard for the immune system to recognize it, and they produce variants that are resistant to the drugs used to treat the HIV infection.

THE FIVE-SECOND RULE
How clean is that food you just dropped?

In 2007, two students at Connecticut College decided to test the "five-second rule": the idea that it's safe to eat food you've dropped on the ground as long as you pick it up within 5 seconds. They dropped apple slices and Skittles candies on the floor of the cafeteria and a snack bar, let the foods lie there for 5, 10, 30, or 60 seconds, and then tested them for bacteria.

Q: IS THE FIVE-SECOND RULE VALID? The students found no bacteria on the food picked up within 30 seconds. After a minute, the apple slices had picked up some bacteria, but the Skittles had none (they found bacteria on Skittles only after 5 minutes). The students concluded that the five-second rule should get an extension, proposing that you have 30 seconds to pick up moist foods and more than a minute to pick up dry foods without risk of bacterial contamination.

Q: SHOULD WE RELAX ABOUT EATING FOODS DROPPED ON THE FLOOR? This question is a serious one and warrants more study. Each year in the United States there are more than 76 million cases of illness caused by contaminated food, including more than 5,000 that are fatal.

Q: SCIENTIFIC METHOD AND DRAWING CONCLUSIONS: CAN YOU GENERALIZE FROM A SMALL NUMBER OF OBSERVATIONS TO ALL POSSIBLE SITUATIONS? In the Connecticut College study, the students examined two food types, dropped in just two locations, and onto surfaces with unknown concentrations of bacteria. In another study, published in the *Journal of Applied Microbiology,* researchers focused on *Salmonella* bacteria. Because it has been documented that bacteria can survive on clothes, hands, sponges, cutting boards, and utensils for several days, the researchers decided to drop food on surfaces known to be covered in bacteria.

Q: WHICH FACTOR IS MORE IMPORTANT FOR DROPPED FOOD: LOCATION OR DURATION? Armed with slices of bologna and pieces of bread, the researchers found that when dropped on surfaces covered with *Salmonella* and left for a full minute, both types of food took up 1,500–80,000 bacteria. And although picking up the food quickly—within just 5 seconds—reduced by 90% the number of bacteria present, 150–8,000 bacteria still had time to hitch a ride on the food in that first 5 seconds.

A GRUBBY CONCLUSION. It's probably safe to say that if you're in the Connecticut College cafeteria, you can eat your dropped food as long as you pick it up quickly. But for all other situations, a bit more caution is advised—particularly, taking notice of the "drop zone." Unsanitary surfaces likely to have microbes will contaminate your food almost immediately. So hold on tight.

Big Ideas in ... Evolution and Diversity Among the Microbes

13·1–13·2 There are microbes in all three domains.

- Grouped together because they are small, not because they are evolutionarily related, microbes are found in all three domains of life.
- Viruses, which are on the border between living and non-living, are not classified in any domain.
- Because they are so small, microbes can also be structurally simple.

13·3–13·5 Bacteria may be the most diverse of all organisms.

- Bacteria are single-celled organisms with no nucleus and no intracellular organelles.
- Different species of bacteria are found virtually everywhere and can eat virtually anything.
- The entire bacterial chromosome (unlike eukaryotic chromosomes) consists of functional genes, and bacteria reproduce rapidly and efficiently by binary fission.
- Genes for specialized functions, such as antibiotic resistance, are carried on small DNA molecules called plasmids that can be transferred from one bacterium to another.
- The combination of short generation times and plasmid transfer allows antibiotic resistance to spread rapidly.
- Some bacteria eat organic molecules, some eat minerals, and still others carry out photosynthesis. Some require oxygen to live, others do not.
- Photosynthesizing bacteria produced the first free oxygen in the earth's atmosphere.

13·6–13·9 In humans, bacteria can have harmful or beneficial health effects.

- Some bacteria always cause disease, and others do no harm except under certain conditions.
- Microbes routinely develop resistance to antibiotics.
- Excessive use of antibiotics in medicine and agriculture has made several of the most important pathogenic bacteria resistant to every known antibiotic.

- Sexually transmitted diseases (STDs) are caused by a variety of organisms, including bacteria, viruses, and protists (as well as some fungi and arthropods).

13·10–13·12 Archaea exploit some of the most extreme habitats.

- Although archaea resemble bacteria, they are more closely related to the eukarya.
- Archaea thrive in extreme conditions, and they can eat a variety of substances toxic to other organisms.

13·13–13·15 Most protists are single-celled eukaryotes.

- Most (but not all) protists are single-celled eukaryotes.
- Amoebas and *Paramecium* are animal-like protists that eat bacterial cells.
- Some protists, such as the seaweeds (a name referring to a non-monophyletic group of species), are macroscopic and multicellular. Other protist species are colonial.
- It is likely that the green algae gave rise to the land plants.
- Plasmodial slime molds are fungus-like protists, having large single cells with multiple nuclei.

13·16–13·19 Viruses are at the border between living and non-living.

- Viruses consist of genetic material (RNA or DNA) packed inside a protein coat.
- The virus hijacks the machinery of a cell and uses it to make more viral particles.
- RNA viruses (such as those that cause influenza) mutate rapidly.
- Human immunodeficiency virus (HIV) is an RNA retrovirus that causes AIDS, a condition in which the immune system fails, allowing infections and cancers to have much more serious impact on health and mortality.

See the To-Go Guide (packaged with every new copy of this textbook) for an illustrated summary of the chapter.

Check Your Knowledge

GRAPHIC CONTENT

Thinking critically about visual displays of data.

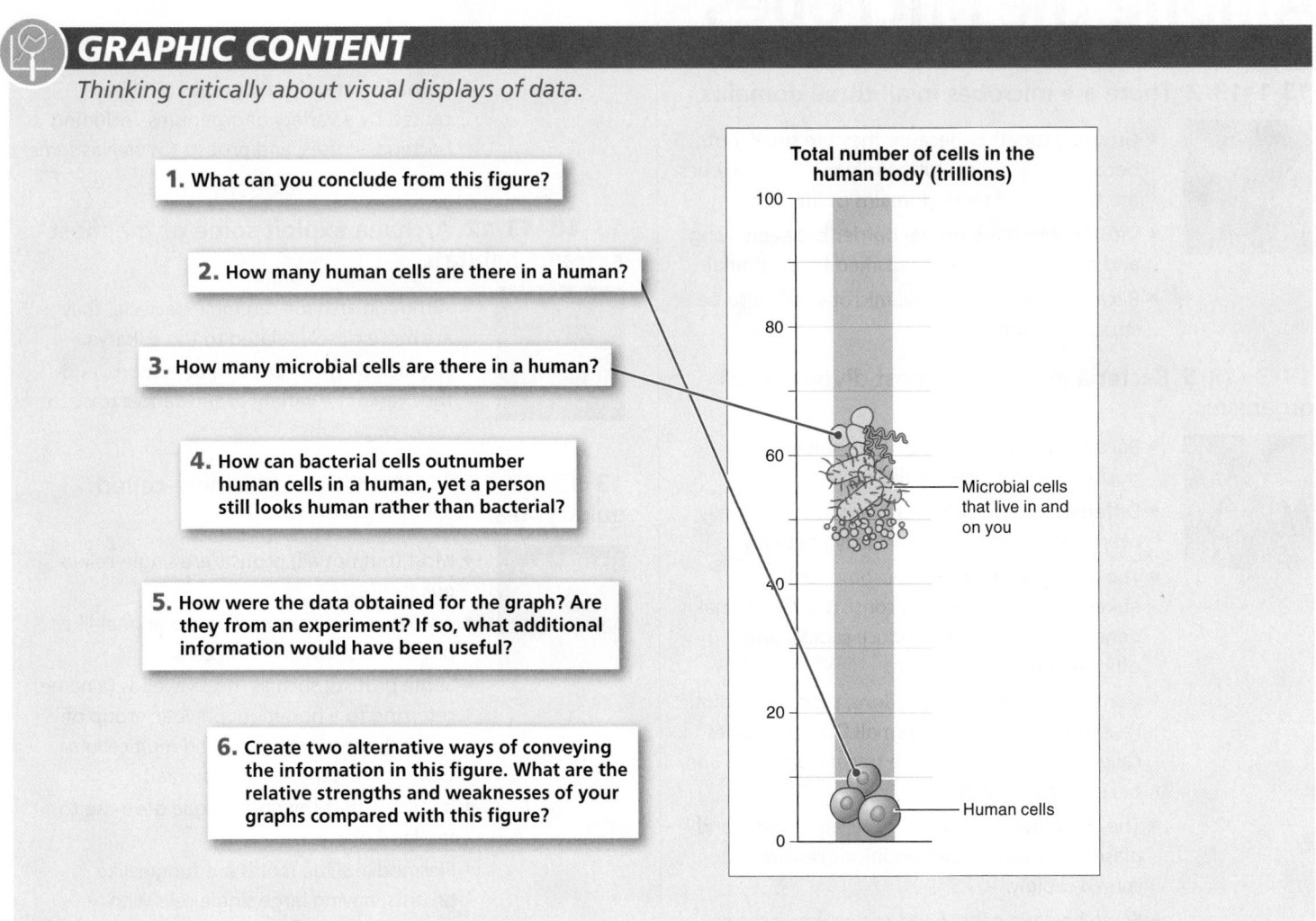

1. What can you conclude from this figure?

2. How many human cells are there in a human?

3. How many microbial cells are there in a human?

4. How can bacterial cells outnumber human cells in a human, yet a person still looks human rather than bacterial?

5. How were the data obtained for the graph? Are they from an experiment? If so, what additional information would have been useful?

6. Create two alternative ways of conveying the information in this figure. What are the relative strengths and weaknesses of your graphs compared with this figure?

Total number of cells in the human body (trillions)

Microbial cells that live in and on you

Human cells

See Answers at the back of the book.

Key Terms in Evolution and Diversity Among the Microbes

acquired immunodeficiency syndrome (AIDS), p. 538
capsid, p. 533
capsule, p. 517
chemolithotroph, p. 520
chemoorganotroph, p. 519

conjugation, p. 518
extremophile, p. 527
Gram stain, p. 516
host, p. 532
human immunodeficiency virus (HIV), p. 538

microbe, p. 512
Oxygen Revolution, p. 520
parasite, p. 532
pathogenic, p. 522
peptidoglycan, p. 516

phagocytosis, p. 530
photoautotroph, p. 520
plasmid, p. 518
probiotic therapy, p. 521
retrovirus, p. 538

sexually transmitted disease (STD), p. 525
transduction, p. 519
transformation, p. 519

Multiple-Choice Questions

1. **In the human body:**
   a) there are more microbial cells than human cells.
   b) archaea can survive, but bacteria are killed by the immune system.
   c) bacterial cells can survive only inside the eukaryotic cells.
   d) the diversity of bacterial cells living in the mouth is exceeded by the diversity living on the skin.
   e) the bacterial cells are larger than the eukaryotic cells.

2. **From an evolutionary perspective, the most basic division among all organisms on earth is among:**
   a) plants, animals, and bacteria.
   b) bacteria, archaea, and eukarya.
   c) plants, animals, and eukarya.
   d) bacteria, animals, and eukarya.
   e) bacteria, archaea, and protists.

3. **Which of the following statements about prokaryotes is incorrect?**
   a) Prokaryotes contain ribosomes.
   b) Some prokaryotes can conduct photosynthesis.
   c) Prokaryotes have circular pieces of DNA within their nuclei.
   d) Prokaryotes appeared on earth prior to eukaryotes.
   e) Prokaryotes contain cytoplasm.

4. **"Establishing a phylogeny for bacteria is more difficult than establishing a phylogeny for plants or animals." This statement is:**
   a) correct, because of the quick generation time of bacteria.
   b) incorrect, because lateral gene transfer makes creating a phylogeny simpler.
   c) incorrect, because the metabolic diversity of bacteria makes classification impossible.
   d) correct, because it is difficult to obtain enough morphological data from bacteria.
   e) correct, because bacteria can engage in lateral gene transfer.

5. **A population of *Escherichia coli* can double every _____ in an ideal laboratory culture.**
   a) 20 seconds
   b) 2 minutes
   c) 2 days
   d) 20 minutes
   e) 2 hours

6. **Plasmids containing genes for antibiotic resistance can be exchanged between bacterial cells in a culture by:**
   a) conjugation.
   b) artificial exchange.
   c) cloning.
   d) transduction.
   e) conduction.

7. **Which group of organisms utilizes the largest variety of energy sources?**
   a) prokaryotes
   b) fungi
   c) protists
   d) invertebrate animals
   e) vertebrate animals

8. Which of the following statements about antibiotics is incorrect?

a) Penicillin was the first antibiotic isolated from bacteria and was widely used to fight bacterial infections.

b) Antibiotics help microbes compete with other microbes.

c) Antibiotic-resistant microbes are selected for in humans who are taking antibiotics.

d) Antibiotics, though effective against viruses, are not effective against bacteria.

e) Antibiotics are used not just in human health care but also in agriculture.

9. Which of the following domains are the most closely related, in that they share a unique common ancestor?

a) archaea and bacteria

b) archaea and eukarya

c) bacteria and eukarya

d) None of the above; all three domains evolved from different ancestors.

e) None of the above; all three domains are equally related to one another.

10. Unlike other microbes, archaea are able to thrive:

a) in very extreme (with respect to temperature, salinity, pressure, etc.) environments.

b) in all the same places that bacteria are found.

c) in the human body.

d) in lakes and rivers (i.e., in fresh water).

e) in well-aerated soils.

11. *Taq* polymerase:

a) is produced in viruses and bacteria.

b) is denatured at temperatures above the normal human body temperature.

c) is useful in catalyzing the polymerase chain reaction.

d) can break down the sludge in oil refinery tanks.

e) can reduce the mineral deposits from rusting pipes.

12. All protists are alike in that they all are:

a) photosynthetic.

b) eukaryotic.

c) parasitic.

d) colonial.

e) multicellular.

13. Which of the following is not a protist?

a) *Paramecium*

b) slime mold

c) brown alga

d) diatom

e) All of the above are protists.

14. Which of the following statements about *Plasmodium* is correct?

a) It causes sickle-cell anemia.

b) Because it changes its surface proteins frequently, it is largely invisible to the immune system.

c) It is transmitted by *Paramecium*.

d) It confers resistance to malaria.

e) It is most common in North America.

15. Many biologists do not consider viruses to be alive. Which of the following characteristics of viruses leads to this conclusion?

a) Viruses lack a metabolic system.

b) Viruses do not respond to external stimuli.

c) Viruses are unable to reproduce on their own.

d) All of the above are correct.

e) Only a) and c) are correct.

16. The genetic information in all viruses is:

a) DNA.

b) RNA.

c) protein.

d) polymerase enzymes.

e) DNA or RNA.

17. Viruses are able to infect:

a) humans.

b) plants.

c) bacteria.

d) birds.

e) All of the above.

18. Which of the following statements about HIV is incorrect?

a) It is a virus.

b) It attacks red blood cells.

c) It mutates frequently.

d) It is derived from a simian immunodeficiency virus.

e) It contains RNA but not DNA.

Short-Answer Question

1. Complete the chart on the characteristics of microbes.

See Answers at the back of the book.
For additional study questions, go to www.prep-u.com.

	Prokaryotes		Eukaryotes	Viruses
	Bacteria	Archaea	Protists	
Unicellular, colonial, or multicellular?				
Plasma membrane?				
Peptidoglycan in cell wall?				
Flagella? What type?				
Presence of nucleus?				
Intracellular organelles?				
Type of genetic material (DNA, RNA, or both possible)?				
Chromosome structure (linear or circular)?				

ABOUT THE CHAPTER OPENING PHOTO

A T4 bacteriophage virus (orange) attacking an *E. coli* bacterium. The phage consists of a large DNA-containing head and a tail composed of a central sheath with several fibers that can attach to the host cell surface. DNA from the virus is injected into the cell through the sheath. It instructs the host to build copies of the virus, which are released when the host bursts. (Colored transmission electron micrograph.)

Planet at capacity: patterns
of population growth

14

Population Ecology

14·1–14·6 Population ecology is the study of how populations interact with their environments.

African elephants (Loxodonta africana) at the Chobe River in Botswana.

14·1

What is ecology?

Lobster tastes delicious. Many people consider it one of the finest delicacies. It's not surprising, then, that catching and selling lobsters is big business. Generating almost $200 million a year for the State of Maine alone, it is among the most economically important businesses in New England. Now imagine for a minute that you were in charge of the lobster industry. The 6,000 lobstermen in Maine depend on your managing the industry so that not only can they catch and sell enough lobsters to survive, but that sufficient numbers of lobsters are left to ensure there will be lobsters to catch in all the years to come. How would you do it? You would be faced with some tough questions:

- How many lobsters should you allow each lobsterman to take each day? Each year?

- Should you require that certain lobsters be thrown back? If so, should they be the biggest or the smallest? Males or females?

- Is it better to increase the lobster population size or maintain it at current levels?

- But wait a minute. Forget about these obviously complex questions and start with a seemingly simpler question: how many lobsters currently live in the waters off the coast of Maine? Is it even possible to know what this number is (**FIGURE 14-1**)?

Welcome to ecology.

These difficult questions, and many others like them, are all part of **ecology,** a subdiscipline of biology defined as the study of the interactions between organisms and their

💡 *Ecologists have a challenging task managing natural populations when it's difficult to count the number of individuals present or determine how many the environment can support.*

FIGURE 14-1 Managing valuable resources. Population growth models can help.

environments. But don't be fooled by the simple definition. Ecology encompasses a very large range of interactions and units of observation and is studied at different levels (**FIGURE 14-2**). These include:

- *Individuals:* How do individual organisms respond biochemically, physiologically, and behaviorally to their environments?

- *Populations:* How do groups of interbreeding individuals change over time, in terms of growth rates, distributions, and genetic compositions?

- *Communities:* How do populations of different species in a locale interact?

- *Ecosystems:* At the highest level of organization in ecology, how do the living and non-living elements interact in a particular area, such as a forest, desert, or wetland?

> ❝ I wandered lonely as a cloud
> That floats on high o'er vales and hills,
> When all at once I saw a crowd,
> A host, of golden daffodils. ❞
> —WILLIAM WORDSWORTH, *Daffodils*, 1804

We explore ecology at all of these levels throughout this and the next two chapters. We focus in this chapter on **population ecology,** a subfield of ecology that focuses on populations of organisms of a species and how they interact with the environment. We also examine the special case of human population growth and its impact on the environment, as well as the ways in which ecological knowledge can contribute to effective conservation policies. In the next chapter, we move to communities and ecosystems, where our focus will be on how species interact with each other and with their environments, and how this influences their own evolution and the environment itself.

TAKE-HOME MESSAGE 14·1

Population ecology is the study of the interactions between populations of organisms and their environments, particularly their patterns of growth and how they are influenced by other species and by environmental factors.

WHAT IS ECOLOGY?

Ecology is the study of interactions between organisms and their environments. It can be studied at many levels, including:

INDIVIDUALS
Individual organisms

POPULATIONS
Groups of individual organisms that interbreed with each other

COMMUNITIES
Populations of different species that interact with each other within a locale

ECOSYSTEMS
All living organisms, as well as non-living elements, that interact in a particular area

FIGURE 14-2 From individuals to ecosystems. Ecologists study living organisms and their relationship to the environment.

14·2 A population perspective is necessary in ecology.

As we begin our study of population ecology, a subtle but critical shift in perspective is required. It is a shift from viewing the individual as the primary focus to viewing the population—a group of organisms of the same species living in a particular geographic region. Most ecological processes cannot be observed or studied within an individual. Rather, they emerge when considering the entire group of individuals that regularly exchange genes in a particular locale.

As an example of how a population perspective is needed, consider the case of adaptations produced by natural selection. Genetic changes don't occur within an individual. That is, a longer neck did not evolve in one individual giraffe. Instead, the genetic changes occurred within a population of giraffes over time. As a consequence of differential reproductive success among the individuals of a population with different neck lengths, there came to be more individuals with longer necks over time. Birth rates, death rates, and immigration and emigration rates, too, are features not of individuals but of populations (**FIGURE 14-3**).

In the next sections, we explore how populations grow, a question important both to the management of consumable natural resources—as in the lobster fisheries described above—and to the conservation of rare and endangered species.

Population ecology examines features that cannot be studied on an individual organism, such as population size.

FIGURE 14-3 A change in perspective. Ecology requires a focus on populations rather than on isolated individuals.

TAKE-HOME MESSAGE 14·2

Most ecological processes cannot be observed or studied within an individual. Rather, we need to consider the entire group of individuals that regularly exchange genes in a particular locale.

14·3 Populations can grow quickly for a while, but not forever.

In a stable population, how many of the five million eggs laid by a female cod over the course of her life survive and grow to adulthood? How many babies that an elephant gives birth to survive to adulthood and reproduce? These may seem like difficult questions to answer, requiring complex mathematical models of population growth and special knowledge about cod or elephants. But actually, the most fundamental fact about population growth is ridiculously simple. How many of the female cod's eggs and female elephant's babies will, on average, make it to adulthood?

Just two. If a population is not growing, each individual is ultimately replacing itself with a new individual. This is true

Q *Who leaves more surviving offspring, a pair of elephants or a pair of rabbits?*

for all species. Two of those cod eggs will make it. And two of those baby elephants will make it. (For a stable population, two survive, on average, rather than one, because both a male and a female contributed to each offspring. If each pair produced only one surviving offspring, the population would get smaller and smaller.) What happens to the rest of the eggs and offspring? Along the way from gamete to adult, they may not survive. For example, an egg may not get fertilized. Or a fertilized egg may not survive to give rise to an offspring. Predation and other factors may prevent a young offspring's surviving to adulthood. Or an adult may not find a mate. There are too many risks to name them all.

What would happen if more than two cod or two elephants survived? If there were more than one offspring per individual, the population would grow and grow and grow until the earth was covered with cod, elephants, and every other species. But that hasn't happened, and it can't. Let's investigate why.

> There is no exception to the rule that every organic being naturally increases at so high a rate that, if not destroyed, the Earth would soon be covered by the progeny of a single pair.
> —CHARLES DARWIN, *The Origin of Species*, 1859

We start by figuring out how a population grows if each individual does more than just "replace" itself. To calculate the **growth rate** of a population—that is, the change in the number of individuals in the population in some unit of time, such as a year—we need two pieces of information: the number of individuals in the population now, N, and the per capita growth rate, r, which is simply the birth rate minus the death rate. The growth of the population in a year is the growth rate times the number of individuals present to start with, written as: $r \times N$.

If the birth rate is greater than the death rate, the population gets bigger. If the death rate is bigger than the birth rate, the population gets smaller. For example, if there are 500 individuals in a population ($N = 500$) and, over the course of a year, 125 offspring are born, the birth rate is 125/500, or 0.25 births per individual. And if 25 of the 500 individuals die during the same year, the death rate is 25/500, or 0.05 deaths per individual. In this population, then, the growth rate, r, is 0.25 – 0.05, or 0.20 individuals per individual per year. But how many individuals is that?

Since there were 500 individuals to start with, the population would increase by 0.20 × 500, or 100 individuals, during a year (the time period observed). After a second year, if it grew at the same rate, the population growth would be 0.20 × 600, or 120 new individuals. This would mean the population now has 720 individuals.

With the same calculations, we could predict the population size for the next 10, 50, or even 100 years (**FIGURE 14-4**). When a population's size increases at a rate proportional to its current size—in other words, the bigger the population, the faster it grows—the growth is called **exponential growth.** As the J-shaped graph reveals, the size of a population growing exponentially becomes astronomical

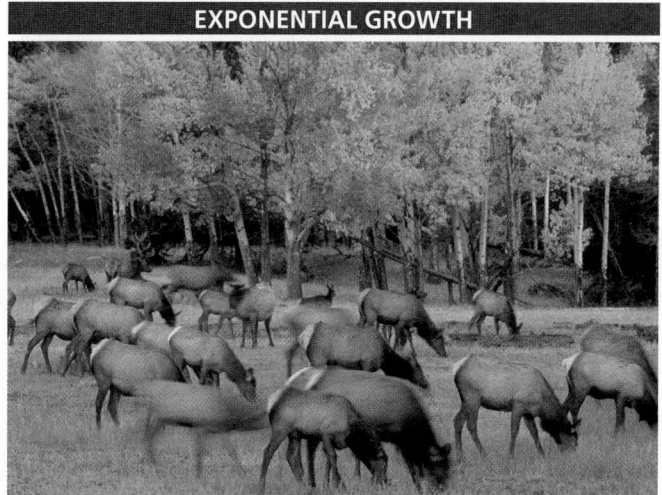

EXPONENTIAL GROWTH

Exponential growth occurs when each individual produces more than the single offspring necessary to replace itself. According to realistic (and moderate) estimates of birth and death rates, a population of just 500 elk would grow to more than a billion individuals within 80 years and eventually would cover the earth.

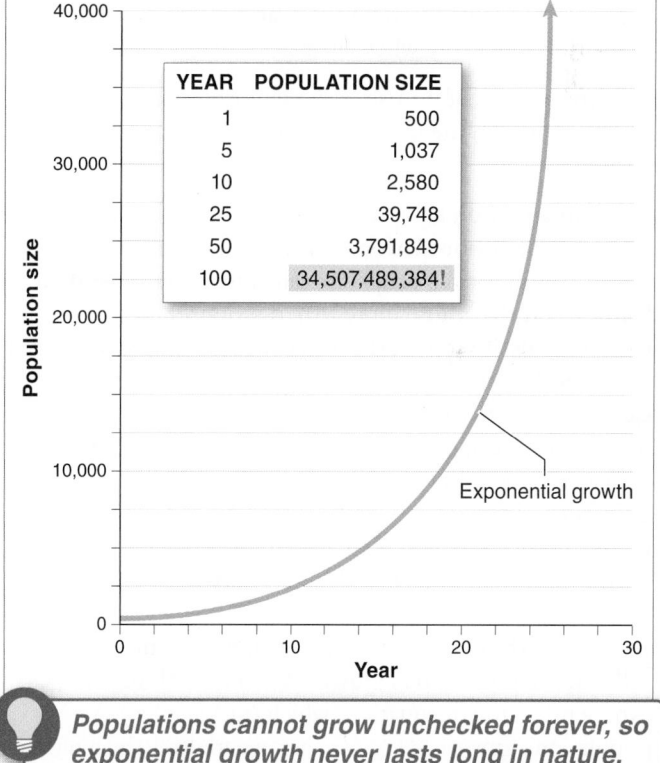

YEAR	POPULATION SIZE
1	500
5	1,037
10	2,580
25	39,748
50	3,791,849
100	34,507,489,384!

Populations cannot grow unchecked forever, so exponential growth never lasts long in nature.

FIGURE 14-4 Unchecked growth. Any animal or plant species that grew exponentially would eventually cover the planet.

very quickly. In 10 years, the population of 500 individuals would grow to 2,580. In 50 years, it would reach almost four million. And after 80 years, the population would surpass a billion individuals. It's clear that exponential population growth ends badly.

But the world isn't overrun with people or cod or elephants, so, clearly, exponential growth doesn't occur for long. In the next section, we explore why populations cannot keep growing unchecked forever, and we add some realism to the exponential growth description.

14·4

A population's growth is limited by its environment.

Life gets harder for individuals when it gets crowded. Whether you are an insect, a plant, a small mammal, or a human, difficulties arise in conjunction with increasing competition for limited resources. In particular, as population size increases, organisms experience:

- Reduced food supplies, due to competition

- Diminished access to places to live and breed, also due to competition

- Increased incidence of parasites and disease, which spread more easily when their hosts live at higher density

- Increased predation risk, as predator populations grow in response to the increased availability and visibility of prey

The limitations on a population's growth that are a consequence of **population density**—the number of individuals in a given area—are called **density-dependent factors,** and they cause more than discomfort. With increased density, a population's growth is reduced as limited resources slow it down. This ceiling on growth is the **carrying capacity, K,** of the environment. And as a population size approaches the carrying capacity, death rate increases, emigration rate increases (as individuals seek more hospitable places to live), and a reduction in birth rate usually occurs, too, as low food supplies result in poor nutrition, which, in turn, reduces fertility (**FIGURE 14-5**).

Here's how the carrying capacity of an environment influences a population's growth. We start with our exponential growth equation, which calculated a population's growth as $r \times N$. Then we multiply by a term, $[(K - N)/K]$, that can slow down exponential growth.

When N, the population size, is small relative to the carrying capacity, K, it means there are plenty of resources to go around. In this situation, the term $[(K - N)/K]$ is close to 1. To prove this to yourself, choose a large number for K, say, 100,000, and a small number for N, say, 1,000. In this case, the term $[(K - N)/K]$ equals $[(100,000 - 1,000)/100,000]$. This reduces to 99,000/100,000, which is the same as 99/100, or 0.99.

DENSITY-DEPENDENT FACTORS
LIMIT POPULATION SIZE

DENSITY-DEPENDENT FACTORS
- Food supply
- Habitat for living and breeding
- Parasite and disease risk
- Predation risk

FIGURE 14-5 Fighting over scarce resources.

And so, in this situation, we are multiplying normal exponential growth by 0.99. This is almost the same as multiplying it by 1, which doesn't change it. As a consequence, the population is growing exponentially (or very, very close to exponentially).

On the other hand, if the population size, N, is close to the value of K, it means that the environment is nearly full to capacity, and the term $[(K - N)/K]$ is close to 0. Let's plug in some numbers again. We can use 100,000 again for K. But let's use 99,000 for N. In this case, $[(K - N)/K]$ equals $[(100,000 - 99,000)/100,000]$. This reduces to 1,000/100,000, which is the same as 1/100, or 0.01. In this situation, we multiply normal exponential growth by 0.01, which reduces it to almost zero. In other words, population growth slows more and more as the population size nears the environment's carrying capacity.

LOGISTIC GROWTH

Logistic growth describes population growth that is gradually reduced as the population nears the environment's carrying capacity.

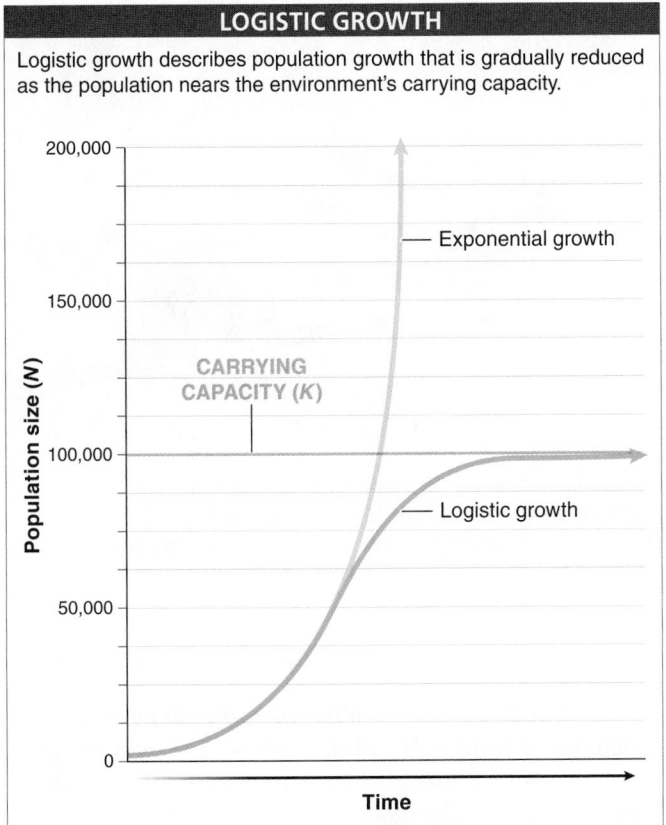

FIGURE 14-6 **Lack of resources limits growth.** Logistic growth is population growth that has stabilized because of limited resources.

When a population grows exponentially at first, but then slows as the population size approaches the carrying capacity, the growth is called **logistic growth** and makes an S-shaped curve (**FIGURE 14-6**). Logistic growth is a much better approximation than exponential growth of how populations grow in the real world.

Density-independent factors can also knock a population down, like "bad luck" limits to population growth. These forces strike populations without regard for population size, by increasing the death rate or decreasing the number and rate of offspring produced. They are mostly weather- or geology-based, including calamities such as floods, earthquakes, and fires. They also include habitat destruction by other species, such as humans. The population hit by the disaster may be at its carrying capacity, or it may be in the initial stages of exponential growth, before its growth is slowed by the carrying capacity of the environment. In either case, the density-independent force simply knocks down the size. The population then resumes logistic growth.

In an environment where these "bad luck" events repeatedly occur, a population might never have time to reach the carrying capacity. Instead, as the series of jagged curves in **FIGURE 14-7** show, the population might perpetually be in the exponential growth portion of the logistic growth curve, with periodic massive mortality events.

The growth of populations doesn't always appear as a smooth S-shaped logistic growth curve. For some populations, particularly humans, the carrying capacity

How many people can the earth support? Why does the number keep increasing?

DENSITY-INDEPENDENT FACTORS LIMIT POPULATION SIZE

Density-independent forces include natural disasters such as floods, earthquakes, and fires.

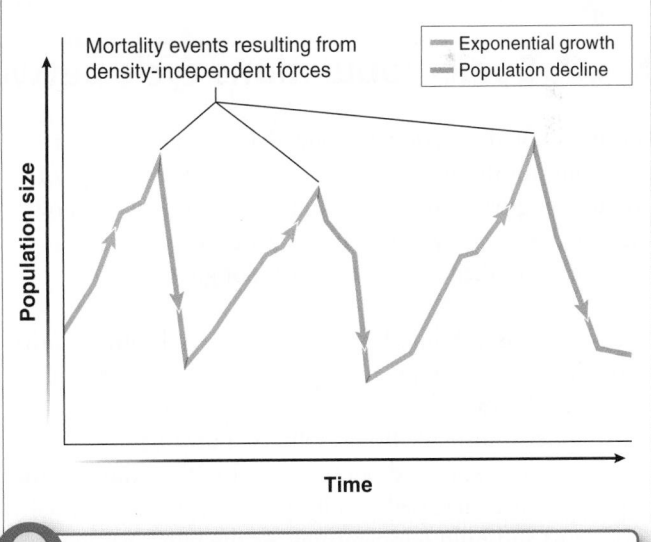

In an environment in which a "bad luck" event repeatedly occurs, a population can be in a perpetual state of exponential growth with periodic massive mortality events.

FIGURE 14-7 **Events can limit population growth.** Fires, floods, and earthquakes are density-independent forces that can dramatically reduce population size.

FIGURE 14-8 Efficient crop production. Advances in agriculture make it possible to feed the world's growing population.

Development of agricultural technologies is one example of how carrying capacity can be increased.

of an environment is not set in stone. Consider that, in 1883, an acre of farmland in the United States produced an average of 11.5 bushels of corn. By 1933, this was up to 19.5 bushels per acre. By 1992, it had increased to 95 bushels per acre. And by 2008, it had increased to 154 bushels per acre! How did this happen? The development of several agricultural technologies—including the use of vigorous hybrid varieties of corn, rich fertilizers, crop rotation, and effective pest management—has allowed farmers to produce more and more food from the same amount of land. This is just one example of how carrying capacity can be increased (**FIGURE 14-8**). Of course, over this same time, the carrying capacity has most likely been *decreased* for many other species trying to live in the same environment as humans and their crops.

TAKE-HOME MESSAGE 14·4

A population's growth can be reduced both by density-dependent factors related to crowding and by density-independent factors such as natural or human-caused environmental calamities.

14·5 Some populations cycle between large and small.

Nature is not always tidy. Exponential and logistic growth equations, for instance, help us understand the concept of population growth, but real populations don't always show such "textbook" growth patterns. Instead, they sometimes vary greatly in their rates and patterns of growth.

Locust swarms of biblical proportions certainly attest to the unpredictability of population growth (**FIGURE 14-9**). In northwest Africa, the desert locusts (migrating grasshoppers) normally live as solitary individuals in relatively small, scattered populations. In 2004, though, the population size increased rapidly, probably due to unusually good rains and mild temperatures. As the rainy season ended and green areas gradually shrank, the locusts became progressively concentrated in smaller and smaller areas. At this point, for reasons related to overcrowding but not completely understood, the locusts behaved like a mob, rather than solitary individuals. Giant swarms—some including tens of millions of insects—began flying across huge expanses of land in search of food. They completely

FIGURE 14-9 Population explosion! Sometimes, populations don't grow logistically, as occasionally happens for desert locusts.

1. A growing hare population provides more food for the lynx, which then reproduce at higher rates.

2. Lynx eat too many hares, thereby reducing their food source and causing their own population to crash, which enables the hare population to grow.

FIGURE 14-10 Predator and prey. The snowshoe hare and lynx populations rise and crash on a 10-year cycle. The population numbers are based on the number of pelts sold to the Hudson's Bay Company by trappers.

consumed giant swaths of farmland, causing more than $100 million in damage.

There is more than one way for population growth to deviate from the standard pattern. The explosive locust population growth, for example, occurs at unpredictable intervals. Another unusual pattern is the oscillations of the lynx and snowshoe hare populations of Canada. As seen in **FIGURE 14-10**, rather than undergoing smooth logistic growth, the populations of both the snowshoe hare and their predators, the lynx, cycle regularly between increases to very large numbers and crashes to much smaller numbers. Thanks to the Hudson's Bay Company, which kept detailed records for decades on the number of pelts it purchased from fur trappers, this population cycling is well documented.

Although its cause is not fully certain, to some extent, the predator and the prey cause their own cycling:

1. The hare population size grows,

2. providing more food for the lynx,

3. which then reproduce at a higher rate,

4. causing them to eat too many of the hares,

5. thereby reducing their food source,

6. causing the lynx population to crash,

7. enabling the hare population to grow, and the cycle to begin anew.

In discussing these examples of unusual population growth, we must not lose sight of the fact that, for the most part, regularly cycling populations and populations with periodic outbreaks of huge numbers are more the exception than the rule. In general, the logistic growth pattern describes populations better than any other model.

One population-growth myth that demands debunking is the story of lemmings and their supposed suicides. Do lemmings jump off cliffs when their population becomes too large? In a word: *no.* This is an urban legend. Lemming populations do occasionally experience large increases in size. Then, just as locust behavior changes when population density gets too great, lemming behavior changes, and many individuals migrate in search of less crowded habitats and more food. As they enter unfamiliar territory, some lemmings may suffer increased rates of death. But these deaths are not suicides, and they do not occur in large groups (**FIGURE 14-11**).

Do lemmings commit suicide by jumping off cliffs when their populations get too big?

FIGURE 14-11 An urban myth debunked. Lemmings do not jump off cliffs.

How did the myth of lemming mass suicides become so prevalent? In the filming of a 1958 Disney documentary, *White Wilderness,* many lemmings were placed on a giant snow-covered turntable so that it would appear they were migrating. In a later scene, many lemmings were filmed on a cliff overlooking a river and then chased into the water as if in a mad rush. None of these scenes were of actual lemming migrations, and in nature, lemmings never behave like this.

There are practical reasons for predicting population sizes and growth rates, as we'll see. But it can be difficult to translate simple growth models into feasible management practices.

14·6 "Maximum sustainable yield" is a useful but nearly impossible-to-implement concept.

Suppose you work for a logging company and are responsible for selecting which trees in an eastern hardwood forest to cut down. Or suppose you are in charge of the lobster fisheries discussed at the beginning of this chapter, responsible for deciding harvest limits. In either case, your responsibilities would be similar. In the case of the hardwood forest, how many trees would you cut down for maximum wood yield?

This is a trick question. The maximum yield on any given day would be obtained by cutting *everything* down (also known as clear-cutting). No other strategy could yield more right now. But such a harvest can be done only once, so it isn't really a management strategy. A more sensible strategy would include harvesting some individuals and leaving others for the future. With that type of strategy, which trees (or lobsters) would you harvest so as to minimally affect the

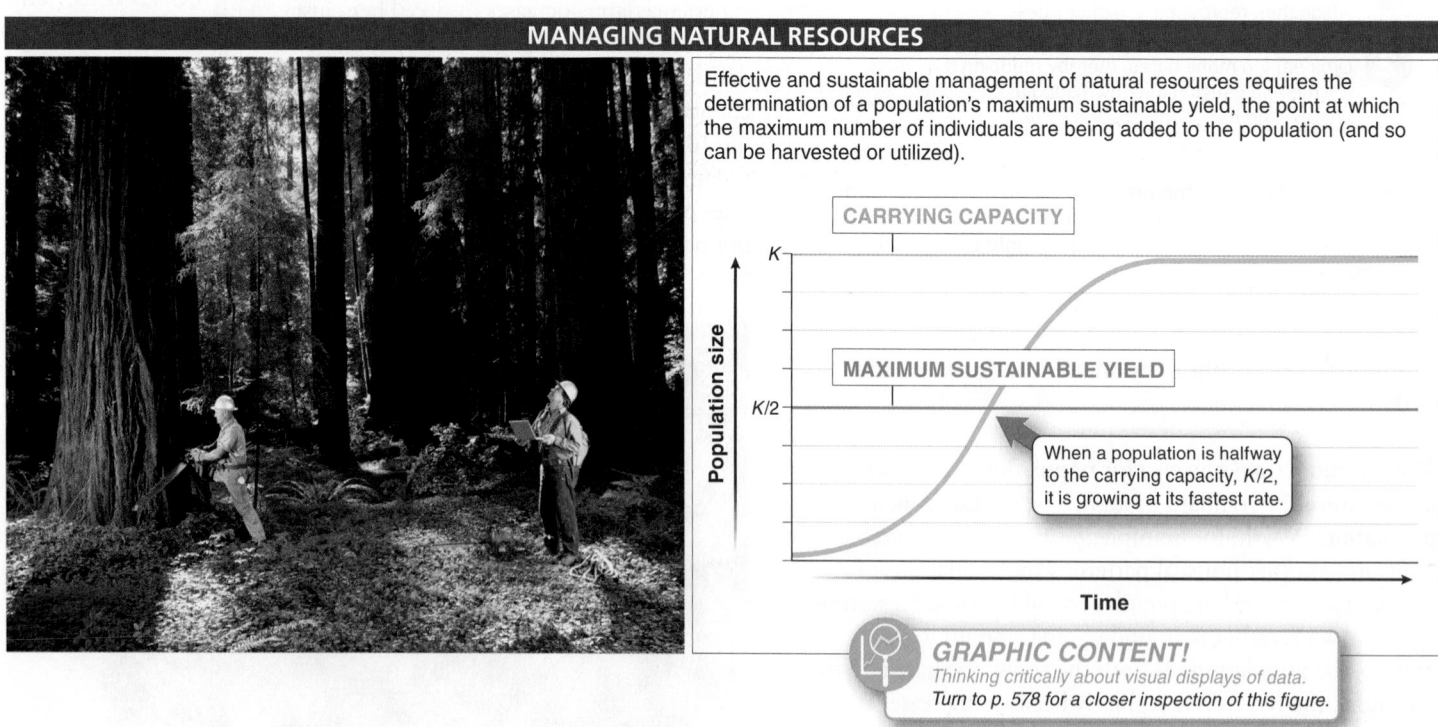

MANAGING NATURAL RESOURCES

Effective and sustainable management of natural resources requires the determination of a population's maximum sustainable yield, the point at which the maximum number of individuals are being added to the population (and so can be harvested or utilized).

CARRYING CAPACITY

Population size

K

$K/2$

MAXIMUM SUSTAINABLE YIELD

When a population is halfway to the carrying capacity, $K/2$, it is growing at its fastest rate.

Time

GRAPHIC CONTENT!
Thinking critically about visual displays of data.
Turn to p. 578 for a closer inspection of this figure.

FIGURE 14-12 Tree harvest. Wood is a renewable resource, but how many trees can we cut down (and which ones?) without irreversibly depleting the supply?

population's growth? Ideally, you would harvest those individuals that are no longer contributing to the population growth. But there may not be many post-reproductive individuals in the population, or it may be too hard to identify them.

What's the better solution? For long-term management, it is better to harvest some but leave others still growing and reproducing for harvest at a later time, so the population can persist indefinitely. The special case in which as many individuals as possible are removed from the population without impairing its growth is called the **maximum sustainable yield** (**FIGURE 14-12**). The value in such a harvest is that it can be carried out repeatedly, clearly yielding more in the long run than the shortsighted strategy of a complete, one-time harvest.

Your first step as manager is to determine the maximum sustainable yield for the resource, calculated as the point at which the population is growing at its fastest rate. In Figure 14-6, we can see that the population is getting larger at the fastest rate when its size is equal to half the carrying capacity. At this midpoint, scarcity of mates is not a problem, as it can be at low population levels, nor is competition a problem, as it can be near the carrying capacity—one of the reasons that the population doesn't grow at all when it reaches the environment's carrying capacity.

Q Almost all natural resource managers working for the U.S. government fail to do their job exactly as mandated. Why?

Maximum sustainable yield is a useful concept, applicable not just to tree or lobster harvesting but also to livestock, agriculture, and nearly every other natural resource. In fact, there are 31 official U.S. government agencies mandated to utilize the maximum sustainable yield concept in determining harvest levels. But here's the rub: this is nearly always an impossible task. Why is that so?

There are numerous reasons, most of which become apparent only when you leave the simplicity of the theoretician's desk and head into the messy real world. For starters, if maximum sustainable yield occurs when a population is at half its carrying capacity, do we first wait until the population stabilizes at its carrying capacity to determine what half of that carrying capacity would be? But isn't it inefficient to sit around waiting for the population to reach its carrying capacity, when we want to maintain it at half that size? Or can we just estimate carrying capacity and then calculate half of it? But, for lobsters, won't that be difficult, given that they live underwater (**FIGURE 14-13**)? Put simply, we rarely know the value of K.

And the problem gets worse. For one thing, with many species, not only do we not know the carrying capacity, we don't even know the number of individuals currently living. It is difficult to accurately count humans, so imagine how hard it is to count individuals of species that live underwater or fly or are microscopic.

And if we were to solve the mysteries of counting individuals and knowing the carrying capacity, we would still have to figure out whether carrying capacity is stable from year to year. If it depends on levels of resources, it may be cyclic, for instance. And even if we can figure out the carrying capacity and the population size, we would not be certain which individuals to harvest. Often, all individuals in a population are not contributing equally to population growth. The post-reproductive individuals, as mentioned above, do not contribute to this growth.

Maximum sustainable yield is a useful concept, but it is difficult to put into practice because it is hard to accurately determine population size and carrying capacity in nature.

FIGURE 14-13 How many lobsters can be harvested sustainably?

The concept of maximum sustainable yield generates insights into fighting biological pests such as cockroaches.

FIGURE 14-14 Population explosion. Population growth models don't just guide us to maximum production of valuable resources. They can help us efficiently reduce pest populations, too.

As a natural resource manager, you do your best, knowing that the theory behind maximum sustainable yield can almost never be put into practice perfectly.

As it turns out, harvesting natural resources for maximum efficiency generates insights into how to fight biological pests, such as cockroaches or termites (**FIGURE 14-14**). The problem is just turned on its head: which individuals in the pest population would you concentrate on killing so as to most effectively slow population growth? Those at the age of maturity, with the highest reproductive value, contribute most to the growth of the population. Similarly, because a population can still grow very rapidly with only a few males—given that any one male can fertilize a large number of females—it is effective to focus pest control on females.

Patterns of population growth and the environmental features that influence them can lead to evolutionary changes in populations, shaping features such as life span, age of reproduction, number of offspring produced, and amount of offspring care—the topics we turn to next.

TAKE-HOME MESSAGE 14·6

Based on models of population growth, it might seem easy to efficiently and sustainably utilize natural resources. In practice, however, difficulties such as estimating population size and carrying capacity complicate the implementation of such strategies.

14·7–14·9 A life history is like a species summary.

A female grizzly bear and cubs in Katmai National Park, Alaska.

14·7 Life histories are shaped by natural selection.

Q

Do any animals mate themselves to death? If so, why?

Some animals reproduce with a "big bang." *Antechinus* is an Australian mouse-sized marsupial, and the males are classic big-bang reproducers

(**FIGURE 14-15**). At one year of age, they enter a two- to three-week period of intense mating activity, copulating for as long as 12 hours at a time. Shortly after this, the males undergo rapid physical deterioration—they lose weight, much of their fur falls out, their resistance to parasites falls—

VARIATION IN LIFE HISTORIES

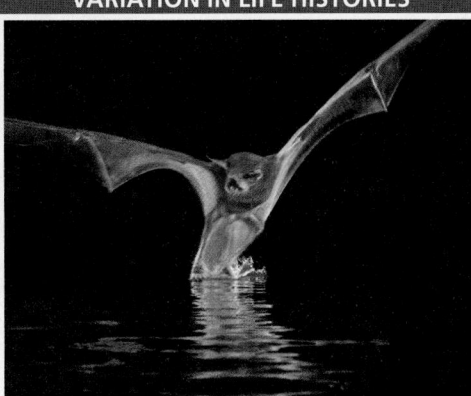

Antechinus

BIG-BANG REPRODUCTION
- Reaches sexual maturity at one year
- Mates intensely over a three-week period
- Males die shortly after mating period
- Females usually die after weaning their first litter

Greater bulldog bat

SLOW, GRADUAL REPRODUCTIVE INVESTMENT
- Reaches sexual maturity at one year
- Produces about one offspring per year

House mouse

FAST, INTENSIVE REPRODUCTIVE INVESTMENT
- Reaches sexual maturity at one month
- Produces litters of six to ten offspring every month

FIGURE 14-15 Reproductive strategies. There are many strategies for reproducing, from the big bang of *Antechinus,* to the slow but sure methods of the little brown bat, to the early, fast, abundant reproduction of the house mouse.

and then they die. (Although occasionally a female will live for two or three years, most die following the weaning of their first litter.)

Other animals are a bit—but only a bit—more restrained in their reproduction. The house mouse reaches maturity in about one month and produces litters of 6–10 offspring nearly every month, sometimes generating more than a hundred offspring in its first year of life.

And some animals could not be farther from big-bang reproducers. The little brown bat is also mouse-sized, yet does not reach maturity until one year of age and typically produces only a single offspring each year. It can, however, live more than 33 years in its natural habitat.

Why all the variation? And is one strategy better than the others, evolutionarily? One of the most important recurring themes in biology is that evolution nearly always finds more than one way to solve a problem. As the marsupial mouse, house mouse, and little brown bat illustrate, there are many possible responses to the challenge of when to reproduce, how often to reproduce, and how much to reproduce in any given episode. The answers to these questions make up an organism's **life history**—the species' vital statistics, including age at first reproduction, probabilities of survival and reproduction at each age, litter size and frequency, and longevity. Life histories are a little short on warm fuzzy stories about how plants and animals live, but they tell us as much about a species as possible in a small amount of information.

Life histories vary from the big-bang reproductive strategy in *Antechinus,* in which the male's **reproductive investment**—all of the material and energetic contribution that an individual will make to its offspring—is made in a single episode, to strategies, such as that of humans, in which organisms have repeated episodes of reproduction. Plants, too, have life histories, and, like animals, they have a range of strategies. Annuals, such as corn, wheat, rice, peas, marigolds, and cauliflower, usually reproduce once and die. Perennials, such as apples, raspberries, grapes, ginger, and garlic, on the other hand, reproduce repeatedly, often living for many years.

Returning to the question posed above—which life history strategy is best?—we need to consider two questions.

1. What is the cost of reproductive investment during any reproductive episode? Producing offspring is risky in several ways. Gametes can be costly to produce. The act of reproducing can be risky (by increasing the likelihood of an individual's being eaten by a predator, for example). And the wear and tear of reproduction on an individual's body takes its toll. Thus, the number of offspring an organism produces can only go so high before it becomes detrimental.

An organism might produce four offspring in an episode, for example, without significantly increasing its risk of dying from the effort. But if, by chance, it produces five or six, this may take such a toll that the individual is unlikely to live to have another litter. Thus, for many organisms, a smaller litter is favored by natural selection because it enables the individual to have additional litters in the future, maximizing its *lifetime* reproductive success.

2. What is an individual's likelihood of surviving to have future reproductive episodes? If predation rates or other sources of mortality are very high, an individual might not be alive in one month. If so, it makes less sense to defer reproduction. Why save for a future unlikely to come?

Taken together, the answers to these questions help us understand the variety of life history strategies we see in nature.

Toward the fast extreme of reproductive strategy are rodents. They experience very high mortality rates in the wild, and natural selection has consequently favored early and heavy reproductive investment. Rodents provide

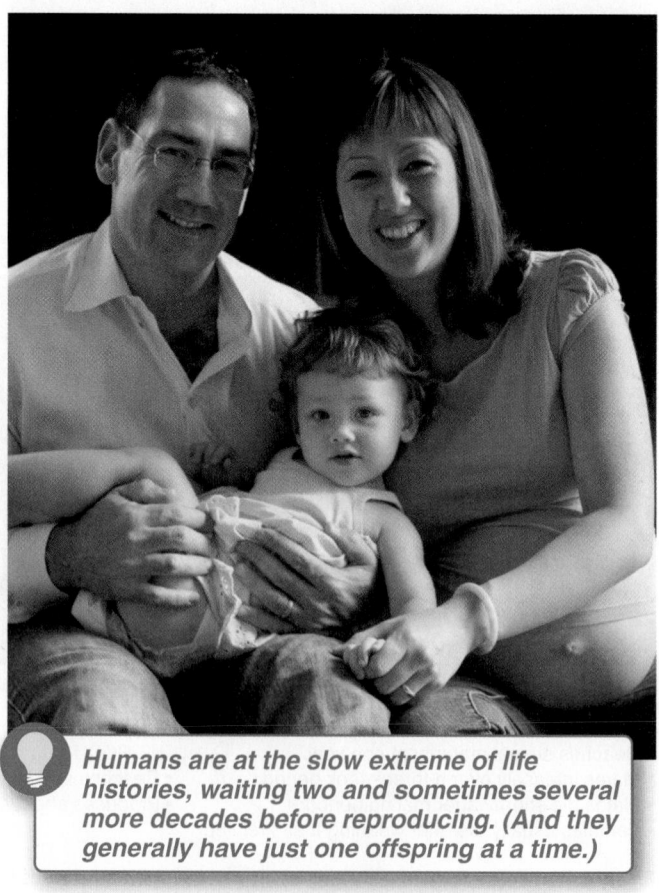

Humans are at the slow extreme of life histories, waiting two and sometimes several more decades before reproducing. (And they generally have just one offspring at a time.)

FIGURE 14-16 With such a low probability of dying in any given year, humans can defer reproduction.

relatively little parental care but produce many litters, each with many offspring. Organisms with this type of life history tend to have relatively poor competitive ability but a high rate of population growth; each individual's likelihood of surviving is low, but so many are produced that the odds of one offspring surviving are high.

enabling them to have just one offspring at a time but to invest significant parental effort in maximizing its likelihood of surviving. Organisms with this type of life history generally have evolved in such a way that their competitive ability—that is, the likelihood of an individual surviving—is high, although their rate of population growth is low. That is, not many offspring are produced, but those that are have a high likelihood of surviving (**FIGURE 14-16**).

Q

Why do humans put off mating so much longer than do cats or mice?

At the slow extreme, humans have such a low probability of dying in any given year that they can defer reproduction, or at least reproduce in small amounts—once every few years—without much risk,

---

TAKE-HOME MESSAGE 14·7

An organism's investment pattern in growth, reproduction, and survival is described by its life history.

14·8 Populations can be described quantitatively in life tables and survivorship curves.

Biologists have learned some important lessons from insurance agents. Because insurance companies need to estimate how long an individual is likely to live, they invented something called the **life table** (**FIGURE 14-17**). It ought to be called a death table, though, because the table tallies the number of people in a population within a certain age group, say 10 to 20 years old, and the number of individuals within that age range who die. From these numbers, they can predict an individual's likelihood of dying or surviving within a particular age interval. For the insurance companies, making money hinges on making accurate life span predictions. For biologists, a life table is like a quick window into the lives of the individuals of a population, showing how long they're likely to live, when they'll reproduce, and how many offspring they'll produce.

From life tables, biologists create **survivorship curves,** graphs showing the proportion of individuals of a particular age that are now alive in a population. Survivorship curves

indicate an individual's likelihood of surviving through a particular age interval. And they reveal a huge amount of information about a population, such as whether most offspring die shortly after birth—think back to the five million eggs produced by some fish—or whether most survive to adulthood and are likely to live long lives, such as humans in the United States.

Three distinct types of survivorship curves are shown in **FIGURE 14-18**. The curves plot the proportion of individuals surviving at each age, across the entire range of ages seen for that species.

Type I. At the top of Figure 14-18, in blue, is the survivorship curve seen in most human populations, and shared by the giant tortoise. We and the tortoise have a very high probability of surviving every age interval until old age, then the risk of dying increases dramatically. Species with a type I survivorship curve, which includes most large

---

LIFE TABLE				
AGE (beginning of interval)	**NUMBER ALIVE** (beginning of interval)	**PROPORTION ALIVE** (beginning of interval)	**DEATHS DURING INTERVAL**	**PROBABILITY OF DYING DURING INTERVAL**
0	210	1.00	140	0.67
3	70	0.33	28	0.40
6	42	0.20	28	0.67
9	14	0.07	10	0.71
12	4	0.02	4	1.00
15	0	0.00	n/a	n/a

In species with type II survivorship curves, individuals experience approximately the same risk of death at any age.

FIGURE 14-17 Summarizing life and earth in a table. Shown here: a life table for the cactus ground finch on one of the Galápagos Islands.

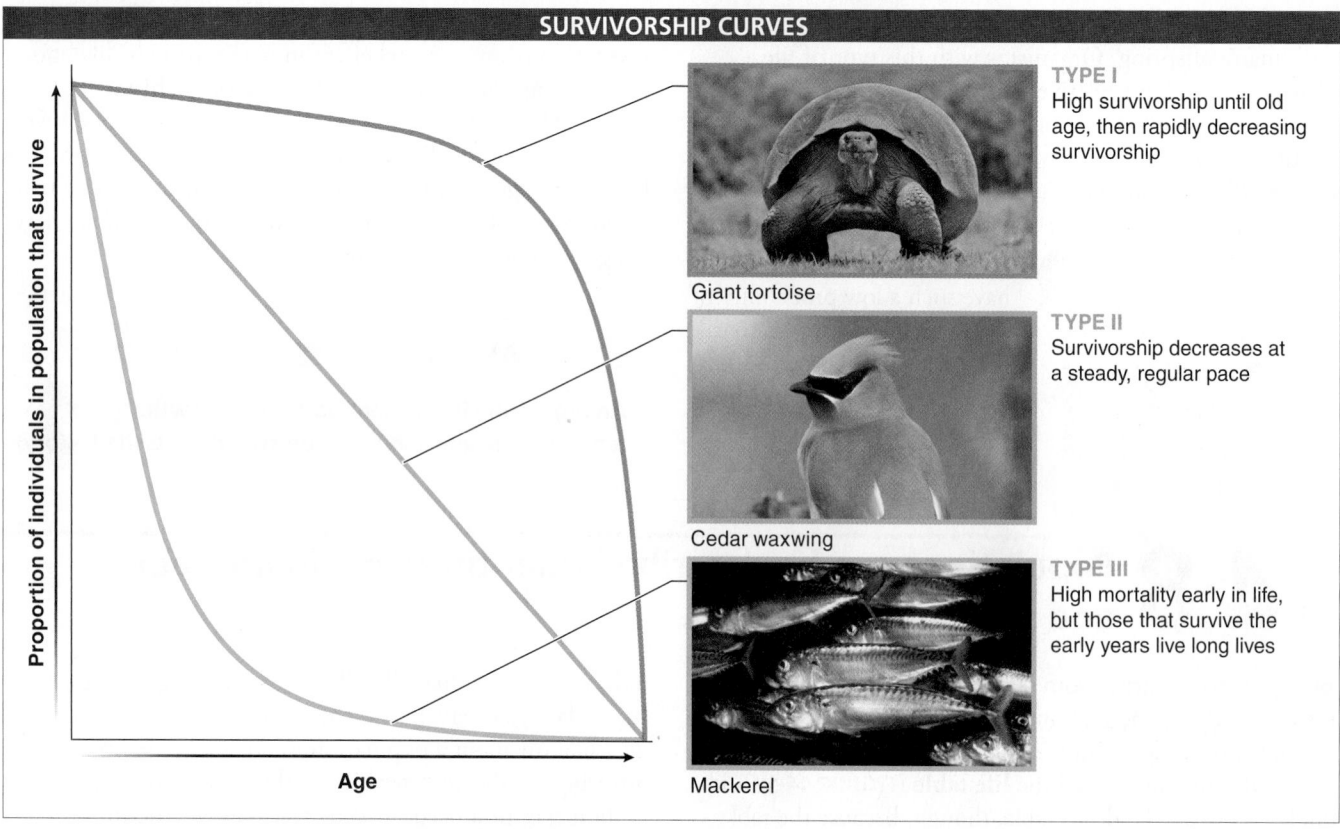

SURVIVORSHIP CURVES

Proportion of individuals in population that survive (y-axis)

Age (x-axis)

TYPE I
High survivorship until old age, then rapidly decreasing survivorship

Giant tortoise

TYPE II
Survivorship decreases at a steady, regular pace

Cedar waxwing

TYPE III
High mortality early in life, but those that survive the early years live long lives

Mackerel

FIGURE 14-18 Three types of survivorship. Survivorship curves show the proportion of individuals of a particular age that are alive in a population.

mammals, usually have a few features in common. They have few natural predators, so they are likely to live long lives. They tend to produce only a few offspring—after all, most will survive—and they invest significant time and effort in each offspring.

Type II. In the middle of the figure, in green, is a survivorship curve seen in many bird species, such as the cedar waxwing, and in small mammals such as squirrels. The straight line indicates that the proportion alive in each age interval drops at a steady, regular pace. In other words, with a type II survivorship curve, the likelihood of dying in any age interval is the same, whether the bird is between 1 and 2 years old, or between 10 and 11.

Type III. At the bottom, in purple, is a survivorship curve in which most of the deaths occur in the youngest age groups. Common in most plant and insect species, as well as in many marine species such as oysters and fishes, the type III curve describes populations in which the few individuals lucky enough to survive the first few age intervals are likely to live a much longer time. Species with this type of survivorship curve tend to produce very large numbers of offspring, because most will not survive. They also tend not to provide much parental care, if any. A classic example is the mackerel.

One female might produce a million eggs! Obviously, most of these (on average, 999,998) do not survive to adulthood, or the planet would be overrun with mackerel.

In reality, most species don't have survivorship curves that are definitively type I, II, or III. They may be anywhere in between. These three types, though, represent the extremes and help us make predictions about reproductive rates and parental investment without extensive observations of individual behavior. Survivorship curves can also change over time or location. Humans in developing countries, for example, tend to have higher mortality rates in all age intervals—particularly in the earliest intervals—relative to individuals in industrialized countries.

TAKE-HOME MESSAGE 14·8

Life tables and survivorship curves summarize the survival and reproduction patterns of the individuals in a population. Species vary greatly in these patterns: the highest risk of mortality may occur among the oldest individuals or among juveniles, or mortality may strike evenly at all ages.

14·9 There are trade-offs between growth, reproduction, and longevity.

If you were designing an organism, how would you structure its life history for maximum fitness? (Recall from Chapter 8 that fitness is an organism's reproductive output relative to that of other individuals in the population.) Ideally, you would create an organism that (1) produces many offspring (beginning just after birth and continuing every year), (2) while growing tremendously large, to reduce predation, and (3) living forever.

Unfortunately, evolution operates with some constraints. Some of these traits are just not possible, because selection that changes one feature tends to adversely affect others. When evolution increases one life history characteristic, another characteristic is likely to decrease. Life history trade-offs can be better understood in the context of the three areas to which an organism allocates its resources: growth, reproduction, and survival. When resources are limited, increased allocation to one of these areas tends to reduce allocation to one or both of the others. Some examples of the best studied trade-offs follow.

1. Reproduction and survival. Among big-bang reproducers such as the marsupial mouse, *Antechinus,* and salmon, investment in reproduction is exceedingly high, followed shortly by death (**FIGURE 14-19**). If individuals are physically prevented from reproducing, however, they can live many more years.

Q With one simple surgical procedure, most men could add more than 10 years to their life span. Why doesn't anyone opt for it?

2. Reproduction and growth. Beech trees grow more slowly during years when they produce many seeds than in years when they produce no seeds. Similarly, female red deer kept from reproducing in their first year of life grow significantly larger during that year.

3. Number and size of offspring. The females of one lizard species, *Uta stansburiana,* can lay more eggs if the eggs are smaller, but a higher proportion of the offspring survive if the female lays larger eggs. Evolution has led to a medium-size egg that tends to maximize the number of surviving offspring.

There are many other trade-offs, such as the number of offspring produced and amount of parental care given. Additionally, among mammals, litter size increases with latitude (distance from the equator). This trend may be due to the trade-off between litter size and frequency. Closer to the equator, animals can breed for a longer portion of the year (year-round near the equator). Farther from the equator, the breeding season is shorter. To compensate for having fewer litters at higher latitudes, mammals produce more offspring per litter. Can you think of other trade-offs?

TAKE-HOME MESSAGE 14·9

Because constraints limit evolution, life histories are characterized by trade-offs between investments in growth, reproduction, and survival.

LIFE HISTORY TRADE-OFFS

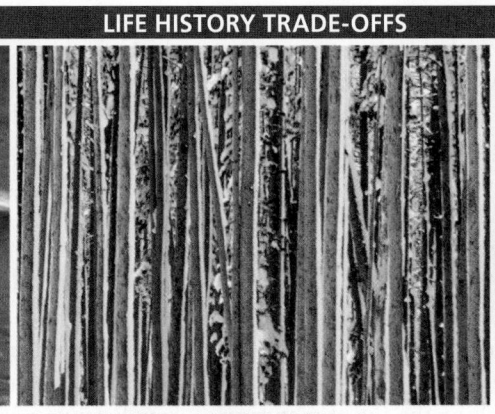

REPRODUCTION AND SURVIVAL
Big-bang reproducers such as salmon make a single, exceptionally high investment in reproduction, then die shortly afterward.

FIGURE 14-19 Life history trade-offs.

REPRODUCTION AND GROWTH
Beech trees grow much more slowly in the years when they produce many seeds than they do in years when they produce few seeds.

NUMBER AND SIZE OF OFFSPRING
Female lizards (*Uta stansburiana*) produce medium-size eggs as a compromise between many small eggs (with poor survival of offspring) and few large eggs (with better survival of offspring).

Bison pair in a blizzard in Minnesota.

14·10 — Things fall apart: what is aging and why does it occur?

Attempting to define what was obscene, an exasperated justice of the United States Supreme Court once concluded that he might never be able to define obscenity, "but I know it when I see it." Aging is like that. Picture your grandparents or people in their seventies or eighties. Clearly they have aged. But what exactly does that mean? And does it differ from the way that people in their thirties or forties have aged? Sometimes it involves sagging skin. Sometimes it involves weakened muscles and bones. Sometimes it involves senility.

The difficulty comes when we realize that no two people age in exactly the same way, yet without fail everyone ages (**FIGURE 14-20**). So we must retreat to a somewhat vague definition. For an individual, aging is the gradual breakdown of the body's machinery. With this definition, we see how each individual can experience aging differently. But aging can be seen much more clearly by examining a population as a whole.

From a population perspective, **aging** emerges as a definitive and measurable feature: it is simply an increased risk of dying with increasing age, after reaching the age of maturity. For example, among humans, people are more likely to die between the ages of 70 and 71 than between 60 and 61. Similarly, they are more likely to die between the ages of

44 and 45 than between 34 and 35. The causes of death at these ages often differ, but the shuffle toward death becomes more and more dire, with no respite. This is the most useful definition of aging for ecologists, and it doesn't apply only to humans. Aging can be measured and assessed for any species in the same way.

Jeanne Louise Calment lived for more than 122 years, the longest life span ever documented for a human. While this is spectacularly long relative to most organisms on earth (and is significantly longer than the average human life span in the United States, 78 years), it pales in comparison with some of the longest-lived organisms. Bristlecone pine trees are the longest-lived, surviving for thousands of years. The growth rings of one bristlecone pine showed that it was more than 7,000 years old!

Among the animals, lobsters and quahogs (a type of clam) are the longest-lived invertebrates (up to 100 and 200 years, respectively). Long-lived vertebrates include striped bass, which can exceed 120 years, and tortoises, which can reach 150 years. Toward the other end of the spectrum, rodents may live just a couple of years, and fruit flies and many other insects generally live and die within the span of a few weeks. Interestingly, bird and bat species live 5–10 times longer than similarly sized rodents. These data prompt the

FIGURE 14-20 **What does "aging" mean?** Aging differs from one individual to another, but we recognize individuals of different ages without any difficulty. Shown here: group portraits of the same 16 women, taken 26 years apart. (The inscription in the upper left reads "For the future.")

questions: Why is there so much variation? And what controls how long the individuals of a species live? We explore those questions in the next section, but first we consider the more general question of why organisms age at all.

> Things fall apart; the centre cannot hold;
> Mere anarchy is loosed upon the world,
> The blood-dimmed tide is loosed, and everywhere
> The ceremony of innocence is drowned;
> The best lack all conviction, while the worst
> Are full of passionate intensity.
> —WILLIAM BUTLER YEATS, *The Second Coming*, 1919

Aging, in fact, is not a mystery. The question of why we age is one of the great solved problems in biology. Oddly, though, it may also be one of the best-kept secrets in science. Let's investigate.

It is easier to *state* the evolutionary explanation for why we age than to *understand* it. But that's where we start. The explanation is based on this one fundamental fact: the force of natural selection lessens with advancing age. What does this mean?

1. Imagine a mutation that causes a person carrying it to die at age 10. Will that person pass the mutation on to many offspring? Of course not. The carrier of that mutant allele will die before she gets a chance to pass it on. Alternative versions of the gene that don't cause death will be the only ones that persist.

Q Many genetic diseases kill old people, but almost none kill children. Why not?

2. Now imagine a mutation that causes a person carrying it to die at the age of 150. Will that person pass it on? Yes! The carrier of this fatal allele will already have had children—passing on the mutation to them—long before she even knows she carries it. In fact, she will no doubt die long before this mutation has the opportunity to exert its disastrous effect. The same thing happens if the mutation has its negative effect at age 100 . . . or 70 . . . or even 50.

In the first example, we see that natural selection "weeds out" alleles that cause sickness and death early in life. Those alleles never get passed on (**FIGURE 14-21**). No one inherits them, and they disappear from the population without fail. Individuals with the alternative versions of the gene pass on the good versions at a higher rate. Consequently, those good alleles end up as the only versions of the gene in the population. These are the genes that we inherited from our ancestors, and this is why very few people have genetic diseases that kill them in their teens. We sometimes think of natural selection as only acting positively to increase or improve a trait—the length of a giraffe's neck, for example. But natural selection can also select *against* a trait—in this case, disease.

Natural selection isn't so effective with some other genes. The second example describes mutations that arise and only later in life make their carriers more likely to die. Examples include mutations that increase the risk of cancers or heart disease or other ailments. Unfortunately, the carriers of these mutant alleles will already have reproduced

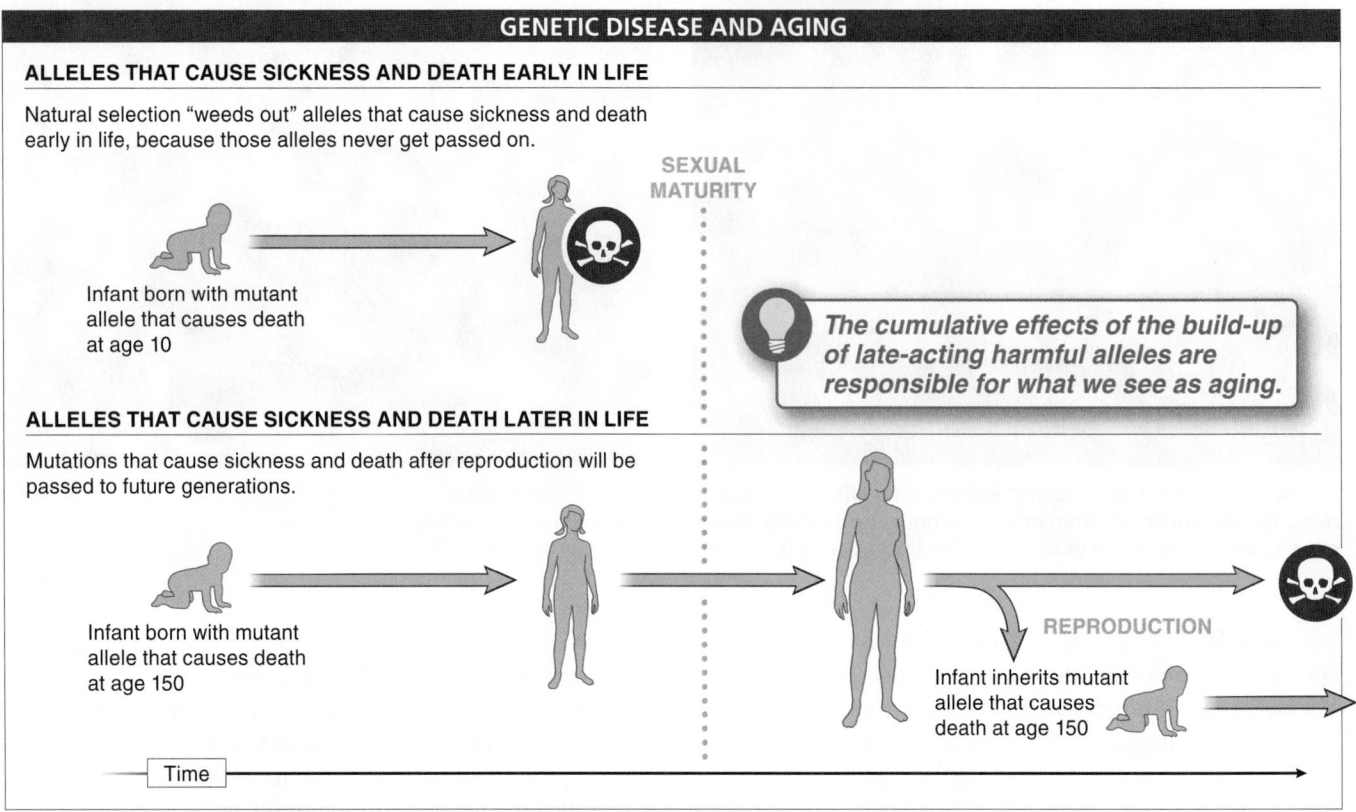

ALLELES THAT CAUSE SICKNESS AND DEATH EARLY IN LIFE

Natural selection "weeds out" alleles that cause sickness and death early in life, because those alleles never get passed on.

SEXUAL MATURITY

Infant born with mutant allele that causes death at age 10

The cumulative effects of the build-up of late-acting harmful alleles are responsible for what we see as aging.

ALLELES THAT CAUSE SICKNESS AND DEATH LATER IN LIFE

Mutations that cause sickness and death after reproduction will be passed to future generations.

Infant born with mutant allele that causes death at age 150

REPRODUCTION

Infant inherits mutant allele that causes death at age 150

Time

FIGURE 14-21 Carrying a time bomb. Natural selection can't weed out genetic defects that wait until we've already reproduced to harm our health. Those mutations that act early in life will be passed on to subsequent generations at a greatly reduced frequency. The cumulative effects of the buildup of late-acting harmful alleles are responsible for what we see as aging.

and passed on the alleles before they have had their negative effect. In other words, it doesn't matter whether you carry one of these mutants or an alternative allele that does not harm you, the number of offspring you produce—your **reproductive output**—is the same. Consequently, these mutants are never "cleaned" out of a population. The practical result is that we all have inherited many of these mutant alleles that have arisen over the past hundreds and thousands of generations.

Q *A cure for cancer may be discovered, but not for aging. Why the difference?*

These mutant alleles that have their adverse health effects later in life—after we are likely to have reproduced—are responsible for aging. The later in life they have

their effect—and therefore the more likely it is that they are passed on to offspring—the more common they will be in the population. This is why there are *many* causes of death, and why it seems as if all of our bodily systems fall apart as we get older.

TAKE-HOME MESSAGE 14·10

Natural selection cannot weed out harmful alleles that do not diminish an individual's reproductive output. Consequently, they accumulate in the genomes of individuals of nearly all species. This leads to the multiple physiological breakdowns that we see as aging.

What determines the average longevity in different species?

Can individuals live forever? No. Just because they are not at risk from internal, genetic sources of mortality doesn't mean there aren't things in the world around them that might kill them. Predators. Lightning. Drought. Disease. The list is long. And for different species, these risks are more or less serious. Rodents, for example, are at *very* high risk of predation nearly every minute of every day, so they are likely to be dead within a few years (**FIGURE 14-22**).

Because death from some external source is likely to come so early, organisms living in high-risk worlds must reproduce early. Natural selection favors this strongly. (If they didn't reproduce early, they wouldn't leave any descendants.) Now, when a harmful mutation arises that causes its damage at an early age—say, 1 or 2 years of age—the rodent has probably already reproduced and passed the mutation on. And so that harmful allele increases in frequency in the population, causing individuals to age earlier.

Tortoises, by contrast, live in relatively low-risk worlds. Because they have armor-like shells that protect them from danger, death from external sources is low. Early, intensive investment in reproduction is not necessary and so has not been favored by natural selection. In such species, when a harmful mutation arises that has its effect at 5 or 10 years of age, the individual carrying it is likely to die before it has reproduced. Consequently, the mutation isn't passed on; natural selection weeds it out of the population.

The age at time of reproduction, then, is a key factor determining longevity. Factors that favor early reproduction also favor early aging; factors that don't favor early reproduction—or actively favor later reproduction—favor later aging. But then, what determines when an organism reproduces?

We can think of each population as evolving in a world with a specific **hazard factor** (see Figure 14-22). This factor includes

ENVIRONMENTAL RISKS AND AGING

Rodent

Tortoise

HIGH HAZARD FACTOR
- Relatively high risk of death at each age
- Individuals tend to reproduce earlier
- Earlier aging
- Shorter life spans

2 years

Longevity

LOW HAZARD FACTOR
- Relatively low risk of death at each age
- Individuals tend to reproduce later
- Later aging
- Longer life spans

150 years

Longevity

In environments characterized by low mortality risk, populations of slowly aging individuals with long life spans evolve. In environments characterized by high mortality risk, the opposite occurs.

FIGURE 14-22 Hazard factor. The mouse and the tortoise face different risks of dying.

the risks of death from all types of external forces. When the hazard factor is low, as it is for tortoises and humans, individuals of a species tend to reproduce later, and so natural selection can weed out all harmful mutations except those that have their effects late in life. Individuals in these species will live a long time before they succumb to aging. A high hazard factor, on the other hand, will lead to earlier reproduction and therefore early aging and shorter life span.

Which species should age more slowly in captivity, a porcupine or a guinea pig? The difference is large, revealing unambiguously that it's good to be a porcupine. Few predators want to eat you. Or rather, few predators *can* eat you. Because of their sharp quills, porcupines have evolved in a world with little risk of predation and with a lower hazard factor.

Meanwhile, guinea pigs, who have no protective quills, live with a high risk of predation. Because they've been evolving in a world characterized by a high hazard factor, they reproduce much sooner, age more quickly, and die younger. A guinea pig in captivity lives less than 10 years, whereas a captive porcupine can live 21 years. In the wild the difference is even greater: 15 years for the porcupine and only 3 or 4 years for the guinea pig.

What difference in longevity would you expect between poisonous and non-poisonous snakes, or between bats (which can fly) and mice?

TAKE-HOME MESSAGE 14·11

The rate of aging and pattern of mortality are determined by the hazard factor of the organism's environment. In environments characterized by low mortality risk, populations of slowly aging individuals with long life spans evolve. In environments characterized by high mortality risk, populations of early-aging, short-lived individuals evolve.

14·12 Can we slow down the process of aging?

Life extension is possible. Real, honest-to-goodness doubling of the normal life span. Not only is it possible, researchers have demonstrated it repeatedly . . . in fruit flies.

Although the results of these life-extension studies are astonishing, the methods by which they were achieved are simple. Researchers kept several large populations of fruit flies in the laboratory, in small Plexiglas cages. The flies would feed and lay eggs on a small plate of food. Every few days, a fresh plate would be put in the cage and the old one discarded. At 2 weeks, eggs were collected and used to start the next generation of flies. Propagated in this way, the fly populations were maintained for hundreds of generations. When the longevity of flies in these populations was measured, the researchers found that the flies started to experience the physiological breakdowns associated with aging after a few weeks, and after about a month the flies died.

One researcher thought that changing the force of natural selection on the flies might produce an evolution in their aging pattern. So, instead of collecting eggs at 2 weeks to start the

Q Is it possible, with our current knowledge, to double longevity in humans?

new generation, he cleverly waited longer and longer (**FIGURE 14-23**). The first new generation had parents that must have lived for 3 weeks. If any fly carried a mutation that caused it to die between 2 and 3 weeks, that fly did not contribute to the next generation and that mutation was not passed on.

After several generations, eggs were collected at 4 weeks instead of 3 weeks. At this point, all the flies making up the new generation had parents that had survived for 4 weeks. Any flies that died before 4 weeks of age didn't contribute to the new generation. Natural selection was now able to reduce the prevalence of mutant genes responsible for early aging.

The experiment continued, progressively increasing the generation time to 5 weeks, then 6, 7, and ultimately 10 weeks — equivalent to decreasing the hazard factor of the fly population. At this point, only those flies with a genome free of mutations that might cause death in the first 10 weeks of life could contribute to the new generation. The net result was the creation of a

FIGURE 14-23 Creating longer-lived organisms through evolution in the laboratory.

population of flies with much "cleaner" genomes. When put under ideal conditions outside the cages, these "super" flies did not experience aging until long after the original flies would have died. In fact, the average life span of the flies hatching from eggs harvested from parents of 10 weeks of age was more than 60 days—double that of the original flies!

TAKE-HOME MESSAGE 14·12

By increasing the strength of natural selection later in life, it is possible to increase the mean and maximum longevity of individuals in a population. This occurs in nature (as in porcupines, bats, and so on) and has also been achieved under controlled laboratory conditions.

Earth's population is increasing by 80 million people each year. Is that sustainable?

14·13 Age pyramids reveal much about a population.

The "baby boom." It happened half a century ago, yet young people in the United States today may end up paying a price for it. What was it? And why does it still matter? Imagine that you run a grade school. How many teachers will you need for the first grade? That all depends on how many students will be entering. If it was 50 students last year, will it be 50 students again this year? Probably. The number of students is likely to be similar from year to year. But it can change. If we set aside changes due to migration, it depends on how many babies were born six years ago. If that number was higher than in the previous year, you may need more teachers at your school. Or you may need fewer teachers if fewer babies were born.

Increasing birth rates caused the baby boom. Beginning just after World War II, and continuing through the early 1960s, families in the United States had about 30% more babies per month than they would have had if they had followed their parents' pattern. Then the birth rates began to return to their earlier

Q What is the baby boom? Why is it bad news for young people today?

levels, where they have remained ever since. As the babies from the boom years grew to school age, schools had to increase in size to accommodate all the children. Then the schools had to downsize once the baby boomers had graduated. Now, as these individuals approach retirement age, the question of how their retirement and health care needs will be met is one of the biggest issues facing American society.

Populations often vary across space—dense in the cities and more sparse in rural areas. The baby boom illustrates that populations have an "age distribution" as well. Just as there may be more individuals in some areas and fewer in others, there may be more individuals in certain age groups and fewer in others.

Describing populations in terms of the proportion of individuals in each age group reveals interesting population features. A population can be divided into the percentages of individuals that are in specific age groupings, called *cohorts,* such as 0–4 years, 5–9 years, 10–14 years, and so on, in an "age pyramid." People have radically different likelihoods of dying or reproducing, for instance, depending on their age. A 10-year-old isn't going to produce any offspring, but a 30-year-old has a relatively high likelihood of reproducing. And a 10-year-old is less likely to die than an 80-year-old.

It can be useful, therefore, for a society to know the relative numbers of 10-, 30-, and 80-year-olds in its population. The age data can be used to determine whether a society would be better off investing in new schools or fertility wards or convalescent homes, among other social issues. Companies, too, rely on such demographic data to best plan their strategies for producing the goods that people will want and need.

Around the world, countries vary tremendously in the age pyramids describing their populations. If two populations are the same size but have different age distributions, they will have some very different features. Most industrialized countries are growing slowly or not at all; most of the population is middle-aged or old. In these countries, such as Norway, the age pyramid is more rectangular than pyramid-shaped (**FIGURE 14-24**). Because birth rates are

low, the bottom of the pyramid is not very wide. And because death rates are low, too, the higher age classes in the pyramid don't get significantly narrower. Instead, the cohorts remain about the same size all the way into the late sixties and seventies, at which point high mortality rates finally cause them to narrow. This gives the pyramid a more or less rectangular shape.

A more triangular shape is seen in the age pyramids of developing countries. Kenya, for example, has very high birth rates, reflected as a large base in its age pyramid (see Figure 14-24). But high mortality rates, usually due to poor health care, cause a large and continuous reduction in the proportion of individuals in older age groups. In these countries, most of the population is in the younger age groups.

Notice the "bulge" in the U.S. age pyramid (**FIGURE 14-25**). The shape of the age pyramid in the United States has economists worried that the social security system (including Social Security and Medicare) will not be able to offer older citizens sufficient benefits in the next 10–30 years. Because of the unusually large number of babies born about 50–65 years ago, an unusually large number of people are now reaching retirement age. Since the baby

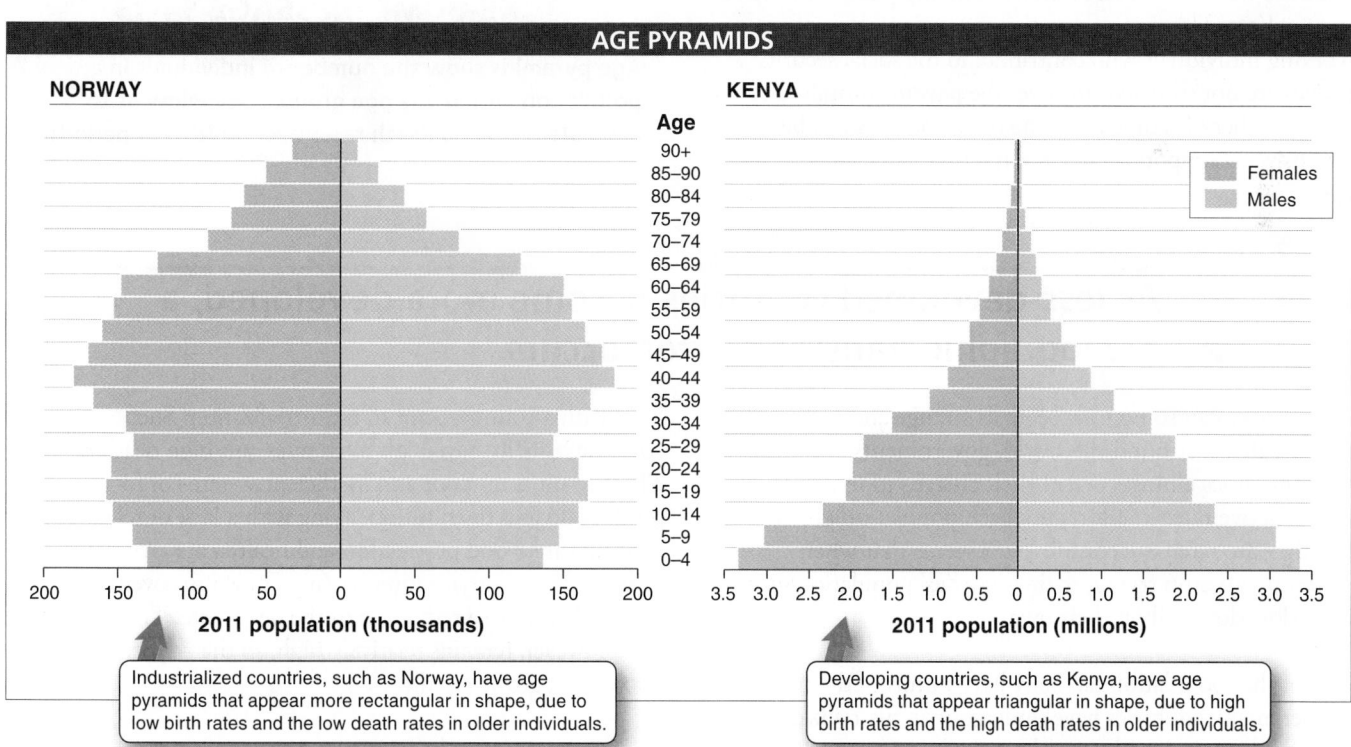

FIGURE 14-24 A visual representation of population growth. Age pyramids go from triangular to rectangular when population growth stabilizes.

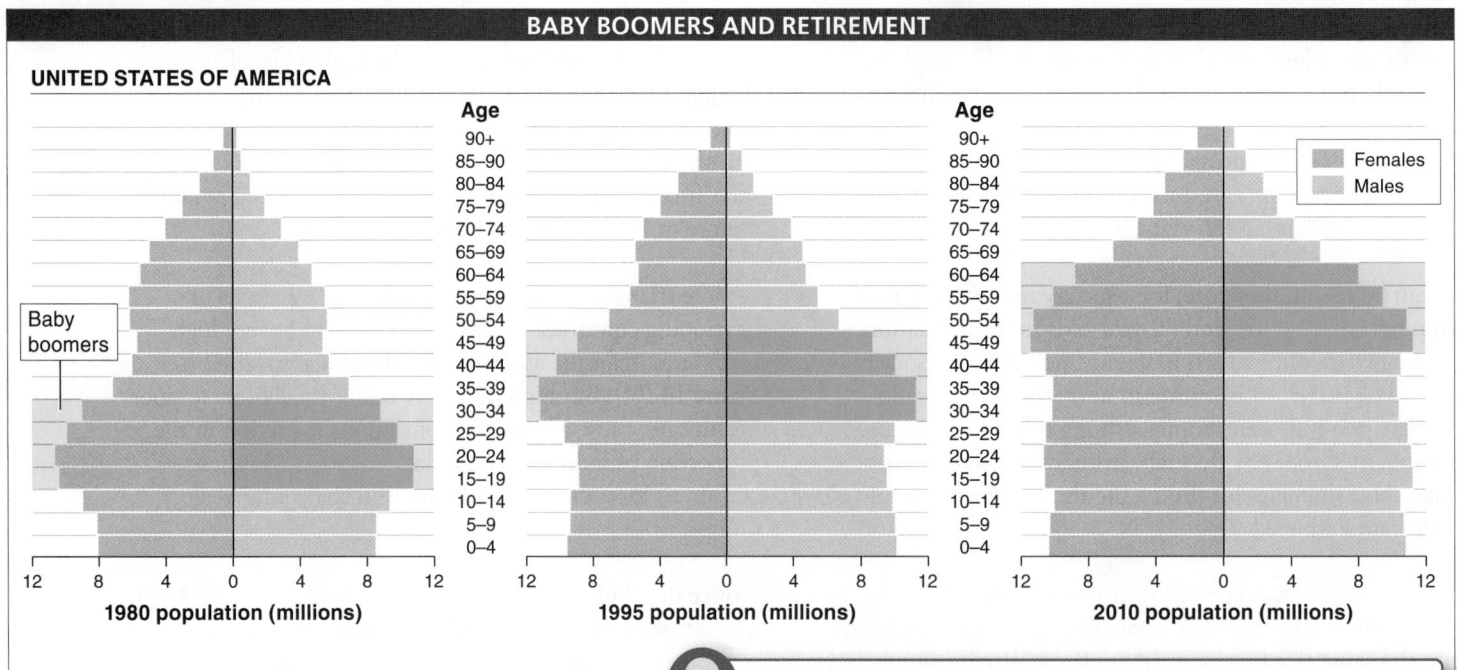

FIGURE 14-25 **The retirement boom.** As baby boomers reach retirement, the population bulge may strain the social security system in the United States.

Because birth rates were unusually large for a brief time about 50–65 years ago, those age classes appear as a bulge moving up the age pyramid. And the younger age classes may not be large enough to support them.

boomers were born, there haven't been any years with such a large cohort. This means that the current numbers of working individuals who contribute to the social security system are not sufficient to cover the payouts promised to the large number of retirees, and the baby boomers will be expensive to support as they reach retirement.

TAKE-HOME MESSAGE 14·13

Age pyramids show the number of individuals in a population within any age group. They allow us to estimate birth and death rates over multi-year periods.

14·14 As less-developed countries become more developed, a demographic transition often occurs.

Populations can sometimes seem as strange and stubborn as individuals. Around the world, governments encourage (or sometimes almost coerce) their citizens to reduce their reproductive rates in efforts to check population growth, but they are rarely successful. Yet it seems that when governments stop trying, their countries' population growth rates slow down all on their own.

It's not that populations actually have minds of their own. Rather, many countries have undergone industrialization, with increases in health, wealth, and education. And in the process, their patterns of population growth follow common paths, marked first by periods of faster growth and later by slower growth. The sequence of changes is remarkably consistent.

Start with a country prior to industrialization. Such countries usually have high birth rates and high death rates. These result from poor and inefficient systems of food production and distribution, along with a lack of reliable medical care. Food production and health care typically improve as industrialization begins. These improvements inevitably lead to a reduction in the death rate. The birth rate, however, remains relatively high, so the country's population grows rapidly.

As industrialization continues, further changes occur. Most importantly, the standard of living increases. This results from higher levels of education and employment, and, in conjunction with improved health care, this finally causes a reduction in the birth rate. The new, lower birth rate then slows the population's growth. The progression from:

1. high birth rates and high death rates (slow population growth) *to*

2. high birth rates and low death rates (fast population growth) *to*

3. low birth rates and low death rates (slow population growth)

is called the **demographic transition** (**FIGURE 14-26**).

Q Population growth is alarmingly slow in Sweden and alarmingly fast in Mexico. Why this difference?

The demographic transition can take decades to complete, so it is not always easy to identify it as it occurs. A survey of countries around the world reveals that many are at different points along the transition. Sweden, for example, has a low fertility rate (1.7 children born per woman) and a low death rate (10.4 deaths per 1,000 people). At the other extreme, Nigeria has a very high fertility rate (5.5 children born per woman) and death rate (17.2 deaths per 1,000). Mexico, in the midst of a clear demographic transition, has a moderately high fertility rate (2.45 children born per woman) yet a very low death rate (4.7 deaths per 1,000).

In the past few decades, the demographic transition has been completed in Japan, Australia, the United States, Canada, and most of Europe, leading to a slowing of population growth. In Mexico, Brazil, Southeast Asia, and most of Africa, on the other hand, the transition is not complete and population growth is still dangerously fast.

The demographic transition illustrates how health, wealth, and education can lead to a reduction in the birth rate without direct government interventions. But because more than three-quarters of the world's population lives in developing countries and less than a quarter in the developed countries, the slowed population growth that generally accompanies the demographic transition is unlikely to be sufficient to keep the world population at a manageable level. Instead, population growth will continue to rise quickly. What are the potential consequences of such explosive growth? We explore this next.

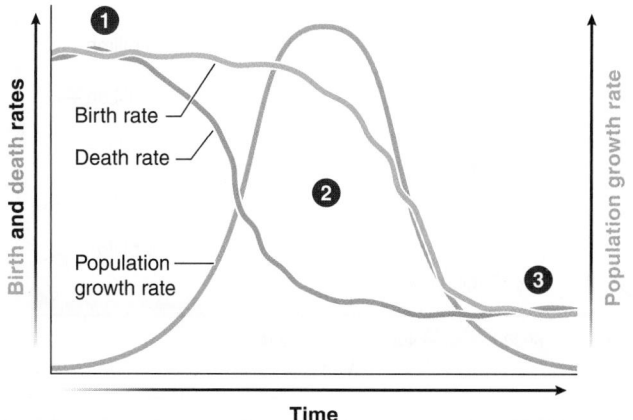

DEMOGRAPHIC TRANSITION

The demographic transition is a pattern of population growth that is experienced as a country industrializes. It is characterized by slow growth, then fast growth, and then slow growth again.

1 SLOW GROWTH
- High birth rates and high death rates
- Populations with inefficient systems of food production and distribution, along with a lack of reliable medical care, usually have high birth rates and death rates, leading to slow population growth.

2 FAST GROWTH
- High birth rates and low death rates
- As industrialization begins, both food production and health care improve, leading to a reduction in the death rate. The birth rate remains relatively high, and so the country's population grows rapidly.

3 SLOW GROWTH
- Low birth rates and low death rates
- As industrialization continues, the birth rate decreases as a result of higher levels of education and employment, along with improved health care. The new, lower birth rate then slows the population's growth.

FIGURE 14-26 With industrialization, death rates drop and, later, birth rates drop, too.

TAKE-HOME MESSAGE 14·14

The demographic transition tends to occur with the industrialization of countries. It is characterized by an initial reduction in the death rate, followed later by a reduction in the birth rate.

14·15 Human population growth: how high can it go?

Humans are a phenomenally successful species. The numbers don't lie: there are more than 7 billion people alive today (**FIGURE 14-27**). And we add 80 million people to the total each year, because birth rates greatly exceed death rates. But for all of our success, the laws of physics and chemistry still apply. We all need food for energy and space to live. We

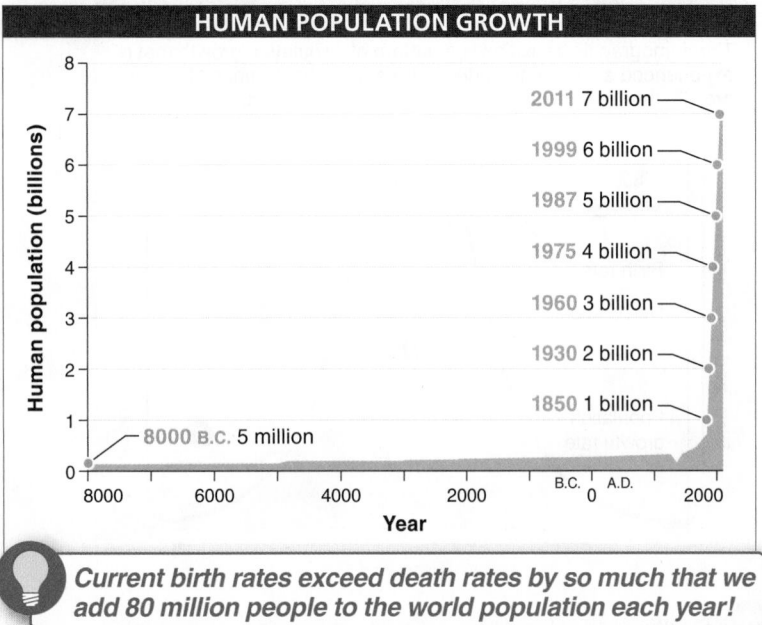

HUMAN POPULATION GROWTH

8000 B.C. 5 million

2011 7 billion
1999 6 billion
1987 5 billion
1975 4 billion
1960 3 billion
1930 2 billion
1850 1 billion

Current birth rates exceed death rates by so much that we add 80 million people to the world population each year!

FIGURE 14-27 The world's human population: a slow start, but rapidly picking up steam.

need other resources, too, and we need the capability of processing and storing all of the waste our societies generate. Because of these limits to perpetual population growth, we may become victims of our own success.

This we know for certain: human population growth cannot continue forever at the current rate. As is the case for every other species, our environment has a carrying capacity beyond which the population cannot be maintained indefinitely. The question is, how high can it

go? What is the earth's carrying capacity for humans? This, unfortunately, is a difficult question to answer.

For more than 300 years, biologists have been making estimates, starting when Anton van Leeuwenhoek (the inventor of the microscope) made an estimate of just over 13 billion people. The median of all the estimates is just over 10 billion, and the United Nation suggests that the carrying capacity is somewhere between 7 and 11 billion.

There is huge variation from one biologist's estimate to the next. Why is it so hard to figure this out? After all, it's important that we know so that we can work to avoid a global catastrophe. The problem, it seems, goes back to the reasons behind the tremendous human success in the first place. We are so clever that we seem to keep increasing the carrying capacity before we ever bump into it. We do this in a variety of ways, all made possible by various technologies that we invent. In particular, we make advances on three fronts (**FIGURE 14-28**):

1. **Expand into new habitats.** With fire, tools, shelter, and efficient food distribution, we can survive almost anywhere on earth.

2. **Increase the agricultural productivity of the land.** With fertilizers, mechanized agricultural methods, and selection for higher yields, fewer people can now produce much more food than was previously thought possible.

3. **Circumvent the problems that usually accompany life at higher densities.** Public health and civil engineering advances make it possible for higher and higher densities of people to live together with minimal problems from waste and infectious diseases.

LIMITLESS CARRYING CAPACITY?

One reason that the carrying capacity for the human population is difficult to estimate is that we can increase it in a variety of ways.

Dubai, United Arab Emirates

EXPANDING INTO NEW HABITATS
With fire, tools, shelter, and efficient food distribution, we can survive almost anywhere on earth.

Juehnsdorf, Germany

INCREASING THE AGRICULTURAL PRODUCTIVITY OF THE LAND
With fertilizers, mechanized agricultural methods, and selection for higher yields, fewer people can now produce much more food than was previously thought possible.

New York City, United States

FINDING WAYS TO LIVE AT HIGHER DENSITIES
Public health and civil engineering advances make it possible for higher and higher densities of people to live together with minimal problems from waste and infectious diseases.

FIGURE 14-28 Three ways of increasing the carrying capacity for the human population.

FIGURE 14-29 How high can the population go? As population growth continues, so, too, does our consumption of resources. Shown here: a poultry plant in China that processes and packages 375,000 chickens every day.

But the question remains: how high can the population go? The most difficult problem in determining the earth's carrying capacity for humans may be assessing just how many resources each person needs. It is possible to estimate the **ecological footprint** of an individual or an entire country by evaluating how much land, food, water, and fuel, among other things, are used. This method reveals that although some countries (e.g., New Zealand, Canada, and Sweden) have more resources available than are required to support the needs of their population, resource use in the world as a whole is significantly greater than the resources available, implying that we are already at our planet's carrying capacity. The populations of many countries—including the United States, Japan, Germany, and England—currently consume an unsustainable level of resources (**FIGURE 14-29**).

> ❝There is in every American, I think, something of the old Daniel Boone—who, when he could see the smoke from another chimney, felt himself too crowded and moved further out into the wilderness.❞
> —HUBERT HUMPHREY, 38th U.S. Vice President, 1966

Another difficulty in estimating the earth's carrying capacity is that populations can and do occasionally alter their fundamental growth properties. Relatively small changes in the worldwide birth rate can have dramatic effects on the ultimate population size of the planet.

The difficulties in estimating the earth's carrying capacity illuminate an important issue. We must be more specific when we ask: how high can it go? We must add: and at what level of comfort, security, and stability, and with what impact on the other species on earth? There are trade-offs.

The ecological footprint of the 1 billion people currently living in India, for example, is much smaller than that of Japan or Norway or Australia. It is possible, we know, to live with much less impact on the environment per person. But how much do we want to sacrifice to enable a larger number to live stably on the planet? Is our goal to maximize the number? Or to reduce the number and increase the resources available to each person? Or should our goal be something else entirely? The answers to these questions will influence whether the ultimate carrying capacity is even higher than 11 billion, or perhaps lower than the current 7.1 billion people now alive.

The problem is indeed a difficult one. And it gets even more difficult because the world population currently has significant momentum. That is, even if today we immediately and permanently reduced our fertility rate to the replacement rate of just two children per couple, the world population would continue to grow for more than 40 years, putting us up to at least 8 billion. This is because there are so many young people alive that, each year, more and more of them will enter the reproductive population. As we get closer to (or exceed) the earth's carrying capacity for humans, we should be better able to recognize it, but by then it may be too late to take preemptive measures—to avoid the resource depletion that may doom us to the much more unpleasant experience of natural population controls.

TAKE-HOME MESSAGE 14·15

The world's human population is currently growing at a very high rate, but limited resources will eventually limit this growth, most likely at a population size between 7 and 11 billion.

LIFE HISTORY TRADE-OFFS AND A MINI-FOUNTAIN OF YOUTH

What is the relationship between reproduction and longevity?

It's well documented that there is a trade-off between reproduction and longevity. In a wide variety of animals, decreasing reproductive effort has been shown to increase longevity.

Q: DOES THIS HAVE ANY PRACTICAL APPLICATIONS? Yes: spay or neuter your pet to increase its life span!

Q: DOES THIS WORK? Yes! Data from more than 1,000 cat autopsies showed that non-sterilized females lived a mean of

3.0 years, whereas sterilized females lived significantly longer, with a mean life span of 8.2 years. The results for males were similar. (Perhaps the most dramatic example of the reproduction-longevity trade-off is that of the marsupial mouse, *Antechinus stuartii,* in which castration led to a doubling or even tripling of the usual life span. Similarly, following castration, Pacific salmon lived up to 8 years, double their usual life span.)

NOT THAT YOU ASKED . . . In a study in the early 1900s of men institutionalized for mental retardation, those who were castrated lived 13 years longer (69.3 years vs. 55.7 years) than non-castrated men at the same institution, matched for age and intelligence.

Q: WHAT IS RESPONSIBLE FOR THE TRADE-OFF BETWEEN REPRODUCTION AND LONGEVITY? If it were a question of sterilized individuals living longer simply because they don't have to expend energy on reproduction, perhaps similar life span increases could be achieved by simply giving animals access to more energy. In practice, however, this doesn't work (and usually *decreases* life span). Rather, it seems that a significant part of the "cost" of reproduction, at least in mammals, is an increased incidence of cancer, caused by the higher levels of circulating hormones in "reproductively ready" (that is, fertile and receptive) animals.

POSSIBILITIES TO THINK ABOUT. The link between maintaining reproductive readiness and reduced longevity has led some researchers to contemplate the design of birth control pills that might have the additional effect of increasing longevity. Stay tuned.

Big Ideas in ...
Population Ecology

14·1–14·6 Population ecology is the study of how populations interact with their environments.

- Population ecologists study the interaction between populations of organisms and their environments, particularly patterns of growth and how they are influenced by other species and by environmental factors.

- Populations tend to grow exponentially until limited resources cause the growth to slow to logistic rates.

- A population's growth can be reduced both by density-dependent factors related to crowding and by density-independent factors, such as floods, fires, and earthquakes.

- Difficulties such as estimating population size and carrying capacity complicate the management of populations for maximum sustainable yield.

14·7–14·9 A life history is like a species summary.

- An organism's pattern of investment in growth, reproduction, and survival is described by its life history.

- Life tables and survivorship curves summarize the survival and reproduction patterns of the individuals of a population, varying greatly across species.

- Because constraints limit evolution, life histories are characterized by trade-offs between investments in growth, reproduction, and survival.

14·10–14·12 Ecology influences the evolution of aging in a population.

- Natural selection cannot weed out harmful alleles that do not diminish an individual's relative reproductive success. Consequently, these alleles accumulate in the genomes of organisms of nearly all species. This leads to the multiple physiological breakdowns that we see as aging.

- The rate of aging and pattern of mortality for a species are determined by the hazard factor of its environment.

- By increasing the strength of natural selection later in life, it is possible to increase the mean and maximum longevity of the individuals in a population.

14·13–14·15 The human population is growing rapidly.

- Age pyramids show the number of individuals within any age group in a population. They allow us to estimate birth and death rates over multi-year periods.

- The demographic transition tends to occur as countries industrialize. It is characterized by an initial reduction in the death rate, followed later by a reduction in the birth rate.

- The world population is currently growing at a very high rate, but limited resources will eventually limit this growth, most likely at a population size between 7 and 11 billion.

See the To-Go Guide (packaged with every new copy of this textbook) for an illustrated summary of the chapter.

Check Your Knowledge

GRAPHIC CONTENT

Thinking critically about visual displays of data.

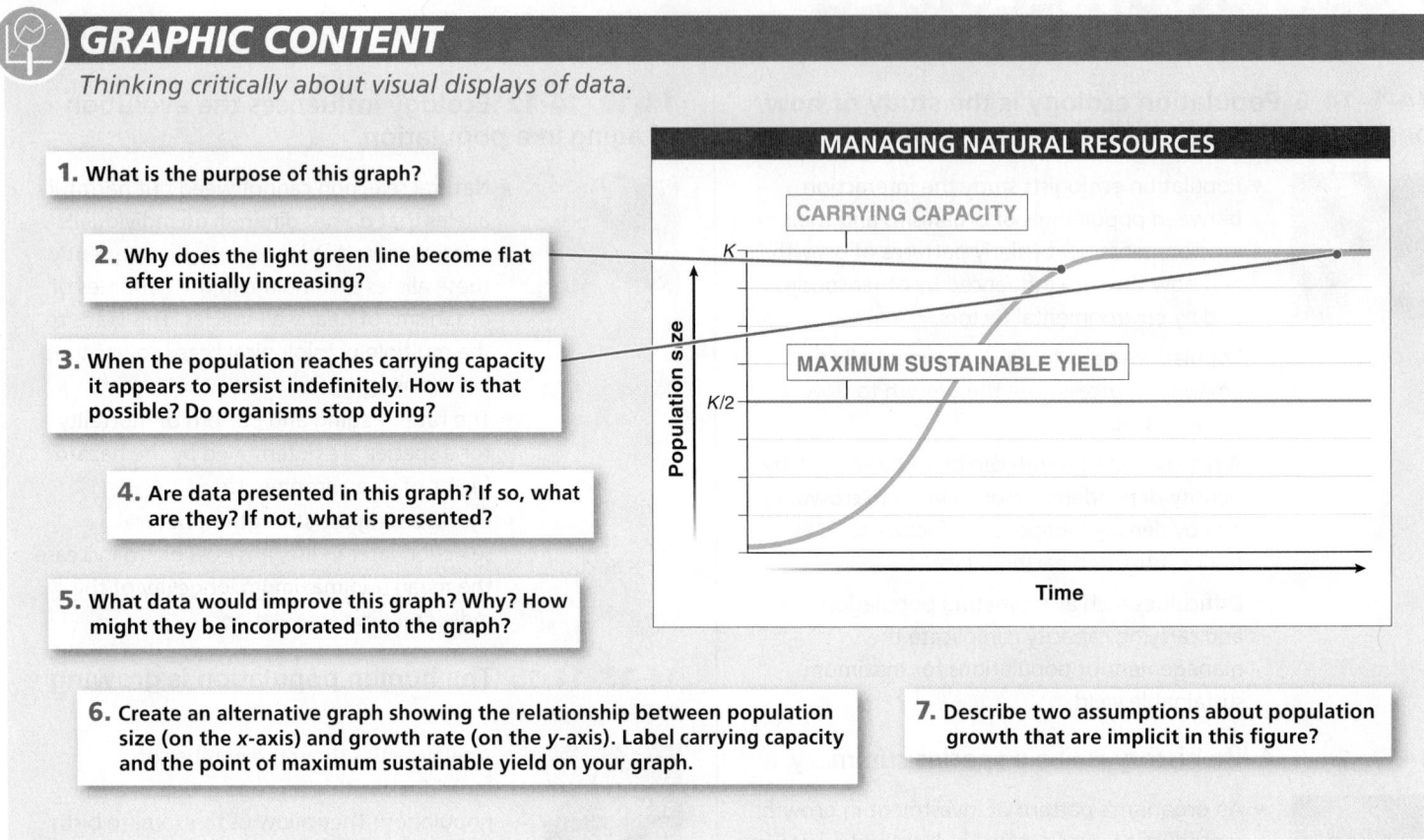

1. What is the purpose of this graph?

2. Why does the light green line become flat after initially increasing?

3. When the population reaches carrying capacity it appears to persist indefinitely. How is that possible? Do organisms stop dying?

4. Are data presented in this graph? If so, what are they? If not, what is presented?

5. What data would improve this graph? Why? How might they be incorporated into the graph?

6. Create an alternative graph showing the relationship between population size (on the *x*-axis) and growth rate (on the *y*-axis). Label carrying capacity and the point of maximum sustainable yield on your graph.

7. Describe two assumptions about population growth that are implicit in this figure?

MANAGING NATURAL RESOURCES

CARRYING CAPACITY

MAXIMUM SUSTAINABLE YIELD

Population size

K

K/2

Time

See Answers at the back of the book.

Key Terms in Population Ecology

Multiple-Choice Questions

1. **Ecology is best defined as the study of:**

   a) the relationships between all living organisms and their environments.

   b) the relationships between parasites and their hosts.

   c) aquatic organisms.

   d) interactions between predator and prey populations.

   e) the preservation of habitats.

2. **On average, which leaves more offspring that survive to become adults and reproduce: a pair of elephants or a pair of rabbits?**

   a) The pair of elephants, because elephants live much longer and have more breeding seasons.

   b) The pair of rabbits, because they have so many more offspring per breeding season than do elephants.

   c) The pair of rabbits, because they reach sexual maturity more rapidly.

   d) The pair of elephants, because any individual elephant born is more likely to survive to become an adult and reproduce.

   e) If both populations are stable, the pair of elephants and the pair of rabbits will leave the same number of offspring that survive to become adults and reproduce.

3. **In a population exhibiting logistic growth, the rate of population growth is greatest when N is:**

   a) 0.5 K.

   b) 0.

   c) above the carrying capacity.

   d) K.

   e) All of the above are correct; the rate of population growth is constant in logistic growth.

4. **In a population, as N approaches K, the logistic growth equation predicts that:**

   a) the carrying capacity of the environment will increase.

   b) the growth rate will approach zero.

   c) the population will become monophyletic.

   d) the population size will increase exponentially.

   e) the growth rate will not change.

5. **The number of individuals that can be supported in a given habitat is:**

   a) the innate capacity for increase.

   b) one-half of the maximum sustainable yield.

   c) a density-independent effect.

   d) generally increasing over time.

   e) the carrying capacity.

6. **Which of the following statements about maximum sustainable yield is incorrect?**

   a) The maximum sustainable yield for a population is the population growth rate at K/2.

   b) The maximum sustainable yield for a population can be difficult to determine, because it is not always possible to accurately measure N.

   c) The maximum sustainable yield for a population can be difficult to determine, because it is not always possible to accurately measure K.

   d) The maximum sustainable yield for a population is a useful management guideline for harvesting plant products such as timber, but is not helpful for managing animal populations.

   e) The concept of maximum sustainable yield can generate useful information for fighting the growth of pest species.

7. Dr. David Reznick has studied life history evolution in guppies that live in streams in Trinidad. Guppies are found in two different types of habitat: sites where predation is high, and sites where predation is low. Which of the following life history characteristics would you expect to evolve in a guppy population living in a high-predation site?

a) bright colors and courtship displays
b) increased egg number
c) a female-biased sex ratio
d) increased egg size
e) delayed sexual maturation

8. The death rate of organisms in a population exhibiting a type III survivorship curve is:

a) unrelated to age.
b) usually correlated with density-independent causes.
c) higher in the post-reproductive than in the pre-reproductive years.
d) lower after the organisms survive beyond the earliest age groups.
e) more or less constant throughout their lives.

9. Which of the following is a major trade-off in life histories?

a) size of offspring for amount of parental investment
b) size of offspring for number of reproductive events
c) growth for reproduction
d) size for life span
e) number of reproductive events for number of offspring per reproductive event

10. Natural selection:

a) does not influence aging, because aging is determined by an individual's environment.
b) cannot reduce the frequency of alleles that cause mortality among individuals who have not yet reached maturity.
c) cannot weed out from a population any alleles that do not reduce an individual's relative reproductive success, even if these alleles increase an individual's risk of dying.
d) can influence aging but not longevity.
e) leads to an increase in the frequency of any illness-inducing alleles that have their effect when an organism can reproduce.

11. Which of the following statements about the hazard factor of a population is incorrect?

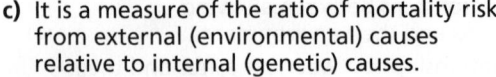

a) It is a measure of organisms' risk of death from external sources.
b) It is lower for a population of porcupines than for a population of guinea pigs.
c) It is a measure of the ratio of mortality risk from external (environmental) causes relative to internal (genetic) causes.
d) It is responsible for the rate of aging among individuals in the population.
e) It is a measure of how quickly the individuals in a population age.

12. Life extension:

a) is not possible, because natural selection cannot weed out disease-causing alleles that have an effect only after the age when reproduction is no longer possible.
b) can be achieved in species by selectively breeding individuals with the earliest age of maturity.
c) works in insects but could not work in humans.
d) has been achieved using laboratory selection for delayed reproduction.
e) None of the above are true.

 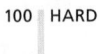

13. A population pyramid:

a) represents the number of individuals in various age groups in a population.
b) can be constructed from the data in a life table.
c) directly predicts future age distributions of the population.
d) shows the current birth and death rates of a population.
e) predicts survival and mortality rates for an individual at a given age.

  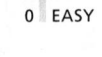

14. A primary difference between the age pyramids of industrialized and developing countries is that:

a) mean longevity is significantly greater in developing countries.
b) in developing countries, much larger proportions of the population are in the youngest age groups.
c) developing countries show a characteristic "bulge" that indicates a baby boom.
d) in developing countries, females live significantly longer than males, whereas in industrialized countries the reverse is true.
e) developing countries have significantly more individuals than industrialized countries.

15. Which statement best describes expectations for the world's human population by the year 2015?

 a) It will exceed 10 billion if the current rate of increase continues.

 b) Negative growth in the United States and Europe will counterbalance positive growth in the developing countries.

 c) It will exceed 7.5 billion if the current rate of increase continues.

 d) It will drop below 6 billion if the current rate of decrease continues.

 e) The problem is too complex to make any predictions.

100 HARD

33

0 EASY

Short-Answer Questions

1. Explain the differences between density-dependent and density-independent factors that can limit a population's growth. Give an example of each.

2. Describe the characteristics of an organism with a type I survivorship curve. How would the life history change if this organism had a type III survivorship curve?

3. Explain why some species of organisms live very long lives and others do not. How could the life span be extended?

See Answers at the back of the book.
For additional study questions, go to www.prep-u.com.

ABOUT THE CHAPTER OPENING PHOTO

Lesser flamingoes on Lake Nakuru, Kenya. (Aerial surveys have documented a flock of more than 25,000 flamingoes at this lake.)

Organisms and their environments

15

Ecosystems and Communities

15·1–15·2 Ecosystems have living and non-living components.

Lesser flamingoes (Phoenicopterus minor) feeding in Lake Nakura National Park, Kenya.

15·1 What are ecosystems?

Picture a lush garden: some greenery, a bit of rotting wood, and abundant wildlife. Grazing animals abound, while predators feed on other animals and their eggs. Parasites are poised, looking for hosts, and, just below the surface, scavengers find meals among the organic detritus. It would seem to be the quintessential **ecosystem,** a community of biological organisms plus the non-living components with which the organisms interact. But now imagine that the entire scene gets up and walks away! The "camera" in your mind pulls back to reveal that the scene is playing out on the back of a beetle no more than two inches long (**FIGURE 15-1**).

The host of this mini-ecosystem is a beetle from New Guinea called the large weevil. The weevil is camouflaged from its predators by lichens—which consist of fungi and photosynthetic algae living together—while the lichens are given a safe surface on which to live. And the garden of lichens supports a wide range of other organisms, from tiny mites to a variety of other microscopic invertebrates, some free-living and others parasitic.

Not all ecosystems are the obvious assemblages of plants and animals that we usually picture—ponds, deserts, or tropical forests. A similar scene can just as easily be found in your large intestine, where several hundred bacterial species flourish. These ecosystems are contained within ecosystems that are contained within ecosystems. The

💡 *Ecosystems are found not just in obvious places like ponds and tropical rain forests, but also in some unexpected places, like on the back of a beetle!*

FIGURE 15-1 "Be it ever so humble . . ." A small-scale ecosystem can exist on the large weevil of New Guinea.

scale can vary tremendously. The closer you look, the more you find.

What is important is that the two essential elements of an ecosystem are present: the biotic environment and the physical (abiotic) environment (**FIGURE 15-2**).

ECOSYSTEMS

All ecosystems share two essential features:

BIOTIC ENVIRONMENT
- The living organisms within an area
- Often referred to as a community

PHYSICAL (ABIOTIC) ENVIRONMENT
- The chemical resources and physical conditions within an area
- Often referred to as the organisms' habitat

FIGURE 15-2 What makes up an ecosystem?

1. The **biotic** environment consists of all the living organisms within an area and is often referred to as a **community.**

2. The physical, or **abiotic,** environment, often referred to as the organisms' **habitat,** consists of:

   • the *chemical resources* of the soil, water, and air, such as carbon, nitrogen, and phosphorus, and

   • the *physical conditions,* such as the temperature, salinity (salt level), moisture, humidity, and energy sources.

Biologists view communities of organisms and their habitats as "systems" in much the same way engineers might, hence the term eco*system.* Biologists monitor the inputs and outputs of the system, tracing the flow of energy and various molecules as they are captured, transformed, and utilized by organisms and later exit the system or are recycled. They also study how the activities of one species affect the other species in the community—whether the species have a conflicting relationship, such as predator and prey, or a complementary relationship, such as flowering plants and their pollinators. On a small scale, such as the back of a beetle, making these measurements is easy. But there are also some well-studied giant ecosystems, such as the Hubbard Brook Experimental Forest in New Hampshire, which covers 7,600 acres. Regardless of size, the same principles of ecosystem study apply: observe and analyze organisms and their environments, while monitoring everything that goes into and comes out of the system.

Why should researchers bother with such a methodical—and tedious—analysis of ecosystems? This straightforward approach has led to numerous valuable discoveries, from understanding how clear-cutting of forests dramatically reduces soil quality, to understanding the link between the use of fossil fuels and the creation of destructive acid rain. As we see in this chapter and the next, humans, perhaps more than any other species in history, are significantly affecting most of the ecosystems on earth. And, in addition to improving our understanding of environmental issues, ecosystem studies can also tell us about the microbial ecosystems living inside humans and thus lead to advances in public health.

TAKE-HOME MESSAGE 15·1

An ecosystem is a community of biological organisms plus the non-living components in the environment with which the organisms interact. Ecosystems are found not just in obvious places such as ponds, deserts, and tropical rain forests but also in some unexpected places, such as the digestive tracts of organisms or the shell of a beetle.

15·2 A variety of biomes occur around the world, each determined by temperature and rainfall.

Dense vegetation surrounds you. Above you is a canopy of evergreen trees, 30–40 meters tall. Climbing vines hang from virtually all the trees. And dozens or even hundreds of species of insects are flourishing around you. Even if you've never been there, the description of a tropical rain forest is easy to recognize. But where exactly would you be if you were in this scenario? It could be South America or Africa or Southeast Asia. The species are different, but the general pattern of life forms is the same. The same holds for arctic tundra: whether you were in northern Asia or North America, the view would be similar. These are examples of the largest of the earth's ecosystems, the **biomes.**

Biomes cover huge geographic areas of land or water—the deserts that stretch almost all the way across the northern part of Africa, for example. Terrestrial (land) biomes are defined and usually described by the predominant types of plant life in the area. But looking at a map of the world's terrestrial biomes, it is clear that they are mostly determined by the weather. Specifically, when defining terrestrial biomes, we ask four questions about the weather:

TERRESTRIAL BIOMES

Biomes are large ecosystems that cover huge geographic areas. The nine chief terrestrial biomes are determined by the temperature and amounts of precipitation in conjunction with the magnitude of seasonal variation in these factors.

FIGURE 15-3 Terrestrial ecosystem diversity.

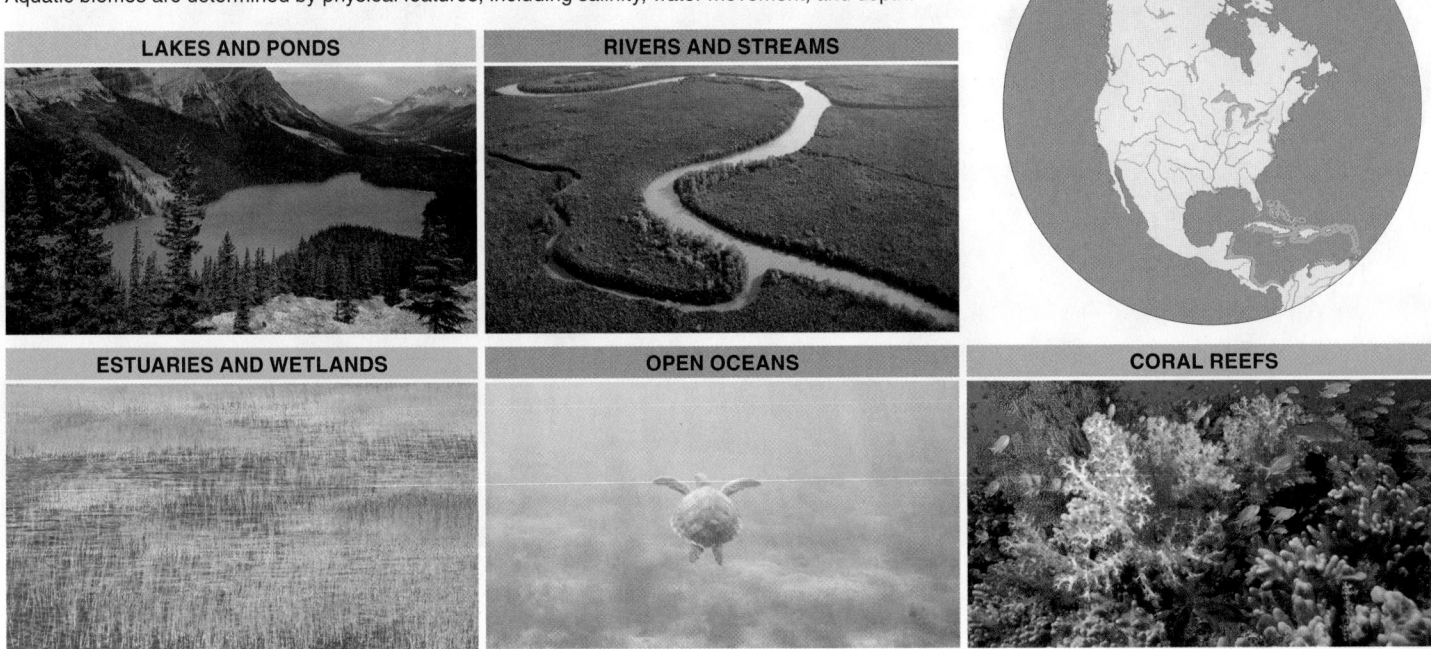

AQUATIC BIOMES

Aquatic biomes are determined by physical features, including salinity, water movement, and depth.

LAKES AND PONDS

RIVERS AND STREAMS

ESTUARIES AND WETLANDS

OPEN OCEANS

CORAL REEFS

FIGURE 15-4 Aquatic ecosystem diversity.

1. What is the average temperature?

2. What is the average rainfall (or other precipitation)?

3. Is the temperature relatively constant or does it vary seasonally?

4. Is the rainfall relatively constant or does it vary seasonally?

By knowing the answers to these questions, we can predict, with great accuracy, the type of biome. This is because temperature and precipitation dictate the **primary productivity** levels, or the amount of organic matter produced, mainly through photosynthesis. And the numbers and types of **primary producers**—the organisms responsible for the primary productivity, such as grasses, trees, and agricultural crops—are, in turn, the chief determinants of the amount and diversity of other life in the region.

For example, where it is always moist and the temperature does not vary across the seasons, **tropical rain forests** develop. And where it is hot but with strong seasonality that brings a "wet" season and a "dry" season, **savannas** or **tropical seasonal forests** tend to develop. At the other end of the spectrum, in dry areas with a hot season and a cold season, **temperate grasslands** or **deserts** develop. **FIGURE 15-3** shows examples of the nine chief terrestrial biomes; all are determined, in large part, by the precipitation and temperature levels.

Aquatic biomes are defined a bit differently, usually based on physical features such as salinity, water movement, and depth. Chief among these environments are (1) lakes and ponds, with non-flowing fresh water; (2) rivers and streams, with flowing fresh water; (3) **estuaries** and wetlands, where salt water and fresh water mix in a shallow region characterized by exceptionally high productivity; (4) open oceans, with deep salt water; and (5) coral reefs, highly diverse and productive regions in shallow oceans (**FIGURE 15-4**).

If the terrestrial biomes of the world are determined by the temperature and rainfall amounts and seasonality, what determines those features? In other words, what makes the weather? We investigate next how the geography and landscape of the planet—the shape of the earth and its orientation to the sun, and patterns of ocean circulation—cause the specific patterns of weather that create the different climate zones and the biomes characteristic of each. Then we'll see how energy and chemicals are made available for life to flourish in these biomes.

TAKE-HOME MESSAGE 15·2

Biomes are the major ecological communities of earth, characterized mostly by the vegetation present. Different biomes result from differences in temperature and precipitation, and the extent to which both vary from season to season.

15·3–15·5 Interacting physical forces create weather.

A "weather sampler": rainbows, blue skies, and storm clouds over Utah.

15·3 Global air circulation patterns create deserts and rain forests.

> There was a hot desert wind blowing that night. It was one of those hot dry Santa Anas that come down through the mountain passes and curl your hair and make your nerves jump and your skin itch. On a night like that every booze party ends in a fight. Meek little wives feel the edge of a carving knife and study their husbands' necks. Anything can happen.
>
> —RAYMOND CHANDLER, "Red Wind," 1938

Temperature and rainfall, that's all. The type of terrestrial biome depends on little else besides these two aspects of the weather. But what determines the temperature and rainfall in a particular part of the world? Differences in both ultimately result from one simple fact: the earth is round. As we'll see, the earth's curvature influences temperature, and rainfall patterns are an inevitable consequence of the variation in temperature across the globe.

Wherever you are, begin walking toward the equator. As you get closer, does it get hotter or colder? Hotter, of course. Nearly everyone is aware of this universal trend (and the reverse as well: it gets colder as you move away from the equator and approach the North or South Pole). What is responsible for the increased warmth at the equator? This is most easily explained with a drawing (FIGURE 15-5).

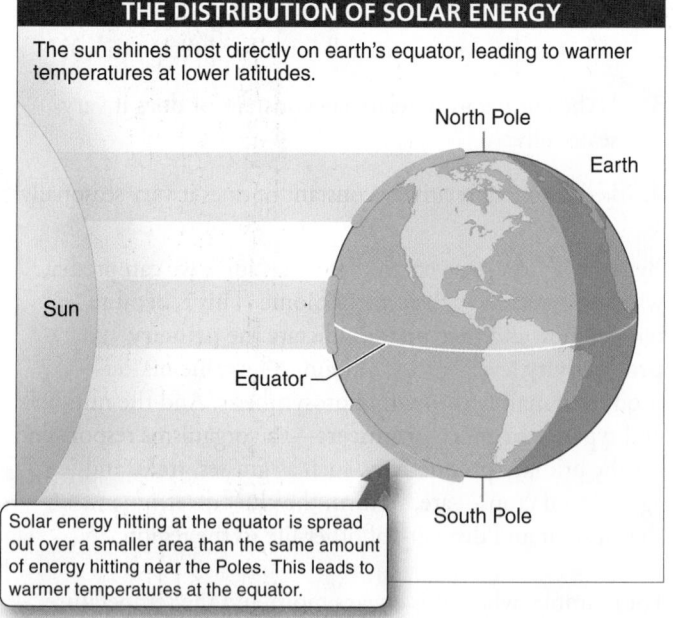

THE DISTRIBUTION OF SOLAR ENERGY

The sun shines most directly on earth's equator, leading to warmer temperatures at lower latitudes.

Solar energy hitting at the equator is spread out over a smaller area than the same amount of energy hitting near the Poles. This leads to warmer temperatures at the equator.

FIGURE 15-5 The curvature of the earth. The sun shines most directly on the equator. Closer to the Poles, the curvature of the earth causes sunlight to be spread out over a larger area, reducing its heating effect in any one spot.

The sun shines most directly on the equator. At the equator, solar energy hits the earth and spreads out over a relatively small area. Away from the equator, the earth curves toward the North and South poles. Because of this curvature, the

FORMATION OF RAIN

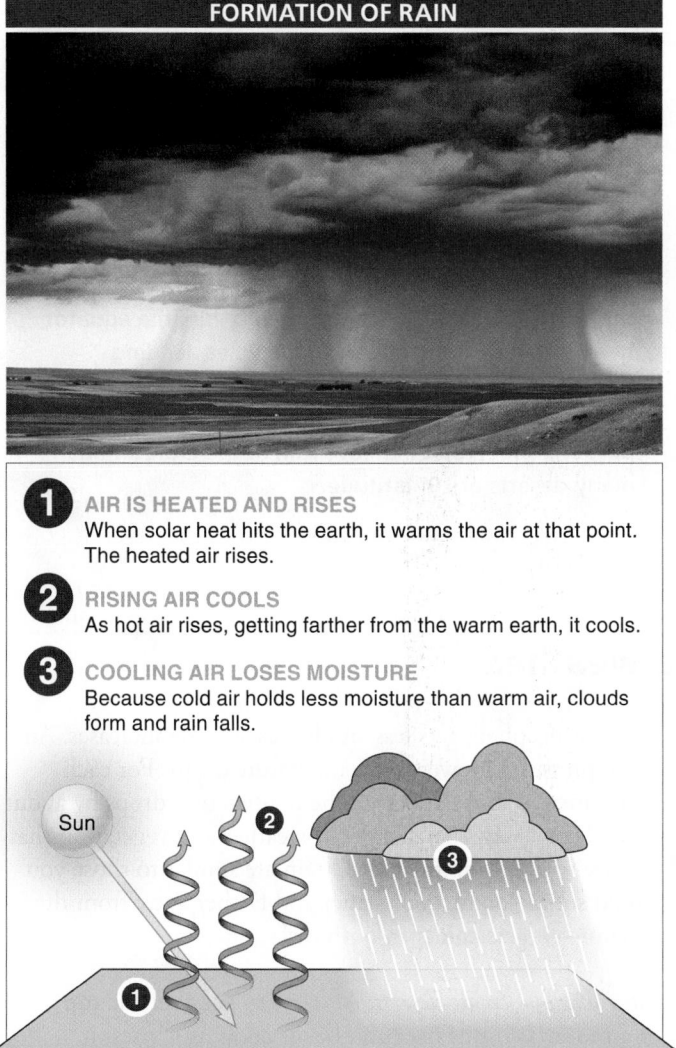

1 **AIR IS HEATED AND RISES**
When solar heat hits the earth, it warms the air at that point. The heated air rises.

2 **RISING AIR COOLS**
As hot air rises, getting farther from the warm earth, it cools.

3 **COOLING AIR LOSES MOISTURE**
Because cold air holds less moisture than warm air, clouds form and rain falls.

Sun

FIGURE 15-6 **Rainmaking.**

same amount of solar energy hitting the earth at the Poles is spread out over a much larger area and also travels a greater distance through the atmosphere, which absorbs or reflects much of the heat. With the energy dispersed over a large area, there is less warmth at any one point on the earth's surface. It's similar to the fact that at noon, the sun's rays hit the earth at a more direct angle than they do later in the day. That is why the sun provides less warmth late or early in the day. It is also why the risk of sunburn and skin cancer is greatest around noon and the nearer you are to the equator.

Global patterns of rainfall can be predicted just as easily, by taking into account that warm air holds more moisture than cold air. We'll start at the equator again. This is where the greatest warming power of the sun hits the earth, and some of that energy radiates back, warming the air. This starts a three-step process that ends with rain. (1) Hot air rises. (2) As it rises high into the atmosphere, it cools. And (3) because cool air holds less moisture, as the air rises,

clouds form, and the moisture that can no longer be held in the air falls as rain (**FIGURE 15-6**). The equator is hot, but it is also very wet.

The high, cold air in the atmosphere over the equator expands outward, to about 30° north and south. Here, the cold air, which is heavier than warm air, begins to fall downward toward the earth. As it falls, the air is warmed by heat radiated off the earth's surface. And as the air gets warmer, it can hold more and more moisture, rather than releasing it as rain. That is, moisture can be held in the air instead of being released as rain. In fact, the falling and rapidly heating air can hold so much moisture that it sometimes sucks up moisture from the land itself. For this reason, at around 30° north and south, around the world, there is very little rainfall, the ground is very dry, and deserts form (**FIGURE 15-7**). The Atacama Desert of South America,

Q Nearly all of the world's deserts occur a third of the way from the equator toward the Poles, at 30° latitude. Is this just a coincidence?

THE FORMATION OF DESERTS

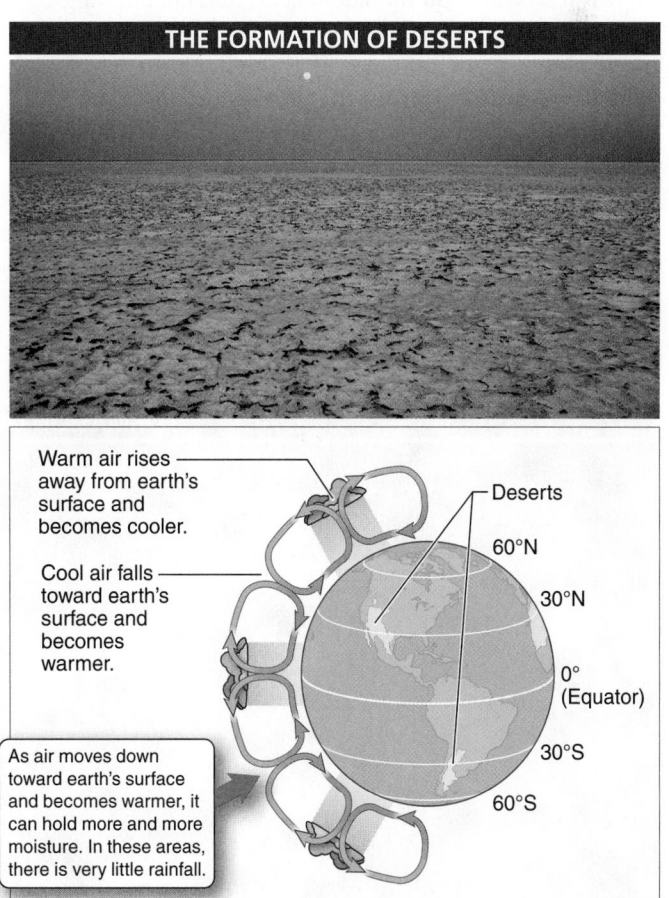

Warm air rises away from earth's surface and becomes cooler.

Cool air falls toward earth's surface and becomes warmer.

As air moves down toward earth's surface and becomes warmer, it can hold more and more moisture. In these areas, there is very little rainfall.

Deserts

60°N
30°N
0° (Equator)
30°S
60°S

FIGURE 15-7 **Desert formation.** Circulating masses of air, caused by solar energy hitting different parts of the earth at different angles, determine rainfall patterns throughout the world. The photo shows a desert in Botswana.

which lies at approximately 30° south of the equator, is an extreme example. In some parts of this large desert, *no rainfall* has ever been recorded. Other great deserts of the world are also at 30° latitude, including the Sahara, Kalahari, Mojave, and Australian deserts (although some deserts do occur at other latitudes). These areas stand in stark contrast to the equator, where it is not uncommon for an area to receive more than three meters (!) of rain in a year.

As the air falls near 30° north and south and hits the earth, it spreads equally toward the equator and toward the Poles, gradually getting warmer, until, at around 60° latitude, it begins to rise because of its accumulated heat. Again, the rising air loses its moisture as rainfall. And so at 60° latitude, two-thirds of the way toward the Poles from the equator, it's not particularly warm but there is a great deal of rain. Not surprisingly, at these latitudes lie huge temperate forests with extensive plant growth. And finally, around the Poles, air masses again descend. And as they do, because they can hold more moisture, very little rain falls. The Poles are cold, but with little precipitation—they resemble frozen desert.

> **TAKE-HOME MESSAGE 15·3**
>
> Global patterns of weather are largely determined by the earth's round shape. Solar energy hits the equator at a more direct angle than at the Poles, leading to warmer temperatures at lower latitudes. This temperature gradient generates atmospheric circulation patterns that result in heavy rain at the equator and many deserts at 30° latitude.

15·4 Local topography influences the weather.

Why is it so windy on the sidewalk around tall buildings? And why does it rain all the time on one side of some mountain ranges, while deserts form right on the other side? And is it actually warmer in the city than in the country? The answers reflect how the physical features of land, its **topography**—including features created by humans—can have dramatic but predictable effects on temperature, precipitation, and wind.

High altitudes have lower temperatures. With increasing elevation, the air pressure drops—this is because the weight of the atmosphere gets less and less as altitude increases. And when pressure is lower, the temperature drops. For each 1,000 meters above sea level, the temperature drops by about 6° C. This is why the changes in weather and vegetation that you see while climbing a mountain are similar to those you would see as you moved farther and farther away from the equator—it gets colder in both cases.

Rain shadows create deserts. Air rises to get over the top of a mountain. But because the air cools as it rises, it can't hold much moisture. So clouds form and rain falls.

FORMATION OF RAIN SHADOWS

Mountain range

Rain shadow desert

1 Wind blows from oceans toward land, rising when it hits mountains.

2 Rising air cools and holds less moisture, leading to cloud formation and rain.

3 Air passes over mountain top and falls, becoming warmer and increasing the moisture it can hold. This reduces rainfall and results in dry areas.

FIGURE 15-8 The rain shadow effect.

122

Temperature (°F)

32

Asphalt, cement, and building tops absorb heat, raising the temperature.

Tall buildings force wind downward.

FIGURE 15-9 Human engineering. When humans alter the land, this can have unintended consequences, such as alterations in temperature and in wind speed and direction.

As the air eventually passes over the top of the mountain, it falls and warms. And because warm air holds onto moisture, there is rarely any rain on the back side of the mountain. In fact, often the air will pull moisture from the ground, intensifying the already dry conditions, creating **rain shadow** deserts (**FIGURE 15-8**). Along the west coast of the United States, the Sierra Nevada and the Cascade mountain range are responsible for the Mojave Desert in California and the Great Sandy Desert in Oregon.

Q Is it warmer or cooler in urban areas relative to nearby rural areas?

Asphalt, cement, and tops of buildings absorb heat, raising the temperature. Modern landscapes also influence the weather, creating "urban heat islands." When energy from the sun hits concrete or pavement or the dark roof of a building, some of it is reflected, heating the air around it, and most of the rest is absorbed by these man-made surfaces and held until night. In the darkness, the surfaces lose heat to the sky, which is colder by comparison, through radiation. In contrast, when sunlight hits trees or other plant life, the solar energy evaporates water in the leaves. The ground surface doesn't get much hotter, and neither does the air. It's not surprising, then, that cities tend to be 1° to 6° C warmer than surrounding rural areas. And not only is it hotter in cities, but the rising warm air also alters rainfall patterns both in and around cities.

A variety of steps are being taken to create "greener" cities that absorb and release less heat from the sun, and use less energy for air conditioning. These methods include the creation of buildings with lighter-colored rooftops, the planting of trees around buildings and along roads, and the development of rooftop gardens rich with vegetation.

Tall buildings channel wind downward. Tall buildings are responsible for the perpetual winds you feel when walking on a city sidewalk. Here's why. Winds blow more strongly when they are higher above the earth, freed from the earth's frictional drag (from plants, dirt, rocks, and water) that slows wind as it gets near the surface. When these strong, elevated winds suddenly encounter tall buildings, they are deflected. Some of the wind goes up and over the building, but much of it is pushed downward, reaching double or even triple its initial speed by the time it reaches street level (**FIGURE 15-9**).

Q Why is it so windy on streets with tall buildings?

TAKE-HOME MESSAGE 15·4

Local features of topography influence the weather. With higher altitude, the temperature drops. On the windward side of mountains, rainfall is high; on the back side, descending air reduces rainfall, causing rain shadow deserts. Urban development increases the absorption of solar energy, leading to higher temperatures, and creates wind near the bottom of tall buildings.

15·5   Ocean currents affect the weather.

Weather is not just affected by circulating air masses. It is also affected by the oceans. The ocean is vast and deep, warmed almost exclusively by the sun. And water is continuously moving and mixing, due to a combination of forces, including wind, the earth's rotation, the gravitational pull of the moon, temperature, and salt concentration. These forces create several large, circular patterns of flow in the world's oceans, as illustrated in **FIGURE 15-10**.

Much of water's effect on weather stems from its great capacity to absorb and hold heat—a 10,000 times greater capacity than air. This means that temperatures fluctuate much more in air than in water. At the beach, the air temperature can go from mild to very hot and back to mild over the course of a day, while the heat of the sun will have a tiny, almost negligible effect on the water temperature. Thus, during summers, much of the heat of the sun is absorbed and held by the ocean water in coastal towns, rather than causing hot air temperatures. Conversely, during cold winter months, heat from the water can reduce the coldness of the air.

One of the strongest ocean currents is the Gulf Stream. It travels north through the Caribbean, carrying warm water up

Q

Why do beach communities have milder weather than inland communities (not as hot in summer, not as cold in winter)?

the east coast of the United States and then across the Atlantic Ocean toward Europe. Because the current begins in a warm part of the globe, close to the equator, it is still warm when it reaches the east coast of the United States and then Europe. The warm water also warms the climate in these areas. In fact, if it weren't for the Gulf Stream, much of Europe—given its high latitudes—would have a climate more like Canada's. Because all ocean currents in the northern hemisphere rotate in a clockwise direction, water reaching the beaches of California, unlike water reaching east coast beaches, has just come from the north, near Alaska, where it gets very cold.

Every two to seven years, a dramatic climate change driven by ocean currents, called **El Niño,** causes a sustained surface temperature change in the central Pacific Ocean (**FIGURE 15-11**). It is blamed for flooding, droughts, famine, and a variety of other extreme climate disruptions. We can more easily understand El Niño if we contrast it with the more common climate pattern.

In a typical year:

1. Steady winds blow across the Pacific Ocean from South America toward Southeast Asia and Australia.

2. These winds push the warm surface water away from the coast of South America and raise the sea level in Southeast Asia and Australia by about half a meter. The warmth of the water heats the air above it, causing the air to rise and produce great tropical rainstorms. (To experience this effect, fill your bathtub with hot water and feel the room get warmer and moister.)

3. Off the coast of South America, an upwelling of colder water from deep in the ocean replaces the water that is pushed west. The cold upwelling cools the air above it, causing extremely dry weather.

4. The upwelling of deep water brings up rich nutrients from below, enabling plankton to flourish and nourishing huge populations of fish.

In an El Niño year:

1. The usual South America–to–Southeast Asia winds ease just a bit. No one knows why this happens.

2. Without wind pushing it, the warm water piling up in the west flows back toward South America. This water warms the air, which rises and produces huge amounts

OCEAN CIRCULATION PATTERNS

There are several large, circular patterns of flowing water in the oceans due to a combination of forces including wind, the earth's rotation, the gravitational pull of the moon, temperature, and salt concentration.

Beaches on the east coast of the United States have warmer water than west coast beaches at the same latitudes.

← Warm ocean currents
← Cold ocean currents

North Pacific Ocean

North Atlantic Ocean

Pacific Ocean

South Pacific Ocean

South Atlantic Ocean

Indian Ocean

FIGURE 15-10 Ocean currents influence weather.

El Niño occurs every two to seven years and is blamed for flooding, droughts, famine, and a variety of other extreme climate disruptions.

USUAL CONDITIONS

1 Steady winds blow westward across the Pacific Ocean from South America toward Southeast Asia.

2 These winds push warm surface water away from the coast of South America, heating the air above it, which causes air to rise and produce tropical rainstorms.

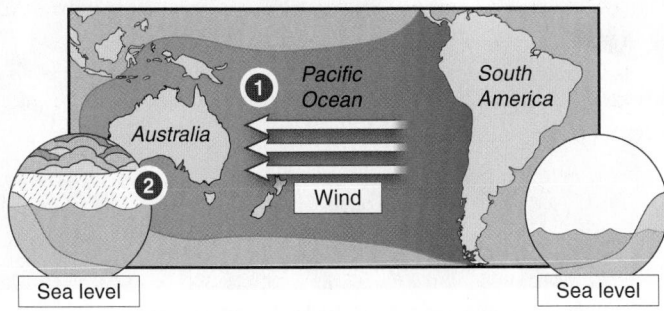

3 Off the coast of South America, colder water upwells from the ocean depths. The cold water cools the air above, causing extremely dry weather.

4 Water from the depths of the ocean brings up rich nutrients, enabling plankton to flourish and feed the huge populations of fish.

EL NIÑO CONDITIONS

1 The usual South America–to–Southeast Asia winds ease just a bit.

2 Without the push of the wind, warm water flows back toward South America. The cooled water around Australia and the Philippines cools the air and causes dry weather that can lead to droughts.

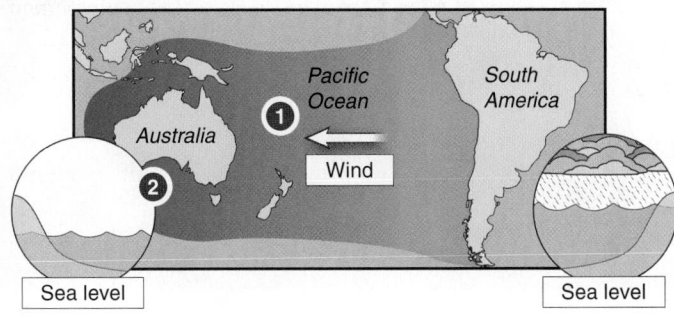

3 Without the warm surface water being blown west, colder water from the ocean depths cannot upwell. The warm surface water warms the air, resulting in rainfall.

4 With no upwelling of cold water and nutrients, plankton levels drop dramatically and fish stocks are wiped out.

> *Changes during an El Niño event start a chain reaction of unusual weather around the globe: increased rainfall in the U.S. Midwest, storms in coastal California, and warmer weather in South Africa and Japan.*

FIGURE 15-11 Domino effect. A reduction in the usual east-to-west ocean breeze can cause a cascade of disastrous weather.

of rainfall on the coast of South America where it is normally dry, often causing flooding.

3. Without the warm surface water being blown west, the normal upwelling of cool, deep water with high nutrient content cannot occur. The plankton levels drop to a fraction of their normal levels, and the typically rich fish stocks are wiped out.

4. Meanwhile, in the absence of warm water from the east, Indonesia, the Philippines, and Australia experience drastic climate changes. The cooler water cools the air above and causes unusually dry weather, which can lead to droughts and, in extreme years, famines.

These predictable changes during an El Niño event can start a global pattern of unusual weather. Although the mechanisms aren't clear, in El Niño years, more rain falls in the midwestern United States and storms form off the coast of California, while South Africa, Japan, and Canada enjoy warmer weather than usual. The counterpart of the El Niño phenomenon is called **La Niña** and is characterized by the reverse effects of El Niño. During La Niña periods, ocean surface temperatures are lower than usual and the climate effects are approximately opposite to El Niño effects.

TAKE-HOME MESSAGE 15·5

Oceans have global circulation patterns. Disruptions in these patterns occur every few years and can cause extreme climate disruptions around the world.

15·6–15·8 Energy and chemicals flow within ecosystems.

The veiled chameleon (Chamaeleo calyptratus) catching a cricket.

15·6

Energy flows from producers to consumers.

All life on earth is made possible because energy flows perpetually from the sun to the earth. Looking at an ecosystem such as a desert savanna, for example—trying to understand how all of the species, from grasses and trees to birds and mammals and worms, interact with one another, and what role each plays within the system—can seem overwhelming. But if we focus on just one aspect of the ecosystem—the pathways energy takes as it flows through the system—a simple and logical order becomes clear.

The sun is where our pathway of energy flow begins. Most of the energy is absorbed or reflected by the earth's atmosphere or surface, but about 1% of it is intercepted and converted to chemical energy through photosynthesis. That intercepted energy is then transformed again and again by living organisms, making about four stops as it passes through an ecosystem. Let's examine what happens at each of the stops, known as **trophic levels** (FIGURE 15-12).

First stop: primary producers. When it comes to energy flow, all the species in an ecosystem can be placed in one of two groups: producers and consumers. Plants (along with some algae and bacteria) are, as we noted earlier, the *primary producers*. They convert the sun's light energy into chemical energy through photosynthesis, as discussed in Chapter 4. We use another word to describe that chemical energy: food.

Second stop: primary consumers—the herbivores. Cattle grazing in a field, gazelle browsing on herbs, insects

devouring the leaves of a crop plant—these are the **primary consumers** in an ecosystem, the animals that eat plants. Plant material such as cellulose can be difficult to digest. Consequently, most **herbivores,** the animals that eat plants, need a little help in digesting their food. Primary consumers, from termites to cattle, often have bacteria living in their digestive system. These microorganisms benefit the organism in which they live by breaking down the cellulose, enabling the herbivore to harness the energy held in the chemical bonds of the plants' cells.

Third stop: secondary consumers—the carnivores. Energy originating from the sun is converted into chemical energy within a plant's tissues. The herbivore that eats the plant breaks down the chemical bonds, releasing the energy. This energy fuels the herbivore's growth, reproduction, and movement, but the energy doesn't remain in the herbivore forever. **Carnivores,** such as cats, spiders, and frogs, are animals that feed on herbivores. They are also known as **secondary consumers.** As they eat their prey, some of the energy stored in the chemical bonds of the carbohydrate, protein, and lipid molecules is again captured and harnessed for their own movement, reproduction, and growth.

Fourth stop: tertiary consumers—the "top" carnivores. In some ecosystems, energy makes yet another stop: the **tertiary consumers,** or "top carnivores." These are the "animals that eat the animals that eat the animals that eat the plants." They are several steps removed from the initial capture of solar energy by a plant, but the general process is the same. A top carnivore, such as a tiger, eagle, or great white shark, consumes other carnivores, breaking down their tissues and releasing energy stored in the chemical bonds of the cells. As in each of the previous steps, the top carnivores harness this energy for their own physiological needs.

This path from primary producers to tertiary consumers is called a **food chain.** We see later in this chapter why a food chain almost never extends to a fifth stop.

The food chain pathway from photosynthetic producers through the various levels of animals is a slight oversimplification. In actuality, food chains are better thought of as **food webs,** because many organisms are **omnivores** and can occupy more than one position in the chain (see Figure 15-12). When you eat a simple meal of rice and chicken, after all, you're simultaneously a carnivore and a herbivore. On average, about 30% to 35% of the human diet comes from animal products and the remaining 70% to 65% from plant products. Many other animals, from bears to cockroaches, also have diets that involve harvesting energy from multiple stops in the food chain.

In every ecosystem, as energy is transformed through the steps of a food chain, organic material accumulates in the form of animal waste and dead plant and animal matter. **Decomposers,** usually bacteria or fungi, and **detritivores,** including scavengers such as vultures, worms, and a variety of arthropods, break down the organic material, harvesting energy still stored in the chemical bonds (**FIGURE 15-13**). Decomposers are distinguished from detritivores because the decomposers are able to break down a much larger range of

ENERGY FLOW WITHIN AN ECOSYSTEM

Energy from the sun is intercepted and converted into chemical energy, which passes through an ecosystem in about four stops.

Sun

1 PRIMARY PRODUCERS
Plants convert light energy from the sun into food through photosynthesis.

2 PRIMARY CONSUMERS
Herbivores are animals that eat plants.

3 SECONDARY CONSUMERS
Carnivores are animals that eat herbivores.

4 TERTIARY CONSUMERS
Top carnivores are animals that eat other carnivores.

The food chain is a simplified pathway. In actuality, **food webs** are often a better representation, because many organisms can occupy more than one position in the chain.

FIGURE 15-12 Follow the fuel.

EARTH'S RECYCLERS

Mold decomposes an orange.

Compost beetles (detritivores) feed on decomposing matter.

> 💡 *Decomposers and detritivores break down organic wastes, releasing chemical components that can then be reused by plants and other primary producers.*

FIGURE 15-13 Dust to dust. Upon dying, organisms from every level in the food chain provide sustenance for decomposers and detritivores, and important chemical components are recycled through the food chain.

organic molecules. Both groups, nonetheless, release many important chemical components from the organic material, which can eventually be recycled and used by plants and other primary producers.

Energy flows from one stop to the next in a food chain, but not in the way that a baton is passed by runners in a relay race. The difference is that at every step in the food chain, much of the usable energy is lost as heat. An animal that eats five pounds of plant material doesn't convert that into five new pounds of body weight. Not by a long shot. In the next section, we'll see how this inefficiency of energy transfers ensures that most food chains are very short.

15·7 Energy pyramids reveal the inefficiency of food chains.

Look out of the nearest window. What organisms can you see? Almost without fail, you will see green plant life. Maybe some trees, possibly bushes and grasses as well. You'll have to look longer and harder to see any animals, but you'll probably see a few, most likely small animals and various insects that eat plants. On the other hand, you might stare out of the window all day and not see any animals (other than some fellow humans) that eat other animals. Why is that? And why are big, fierce animals so rare? And why are there so many more plants than animals?

The answers to these questions are closely related to our earlier observation that an animal consuming five pounds of plant material does not gain five pounds in body weight from its meal. The actual amount of growth such a meal can support is far, far less. The fraction turns out to be about 10%, and this is fairly consistent across all levels of the food chain. So the herbivore consuming five pounds of plant material is likely to gain only about half a pound in new growth, while the remaining 90% of the meal is either expended in cellular respiration or lost as feces. Similarly, a carnivore eating the herbivore converts only about 10% of the mass it consumes into its own body mass. Again, 90% is lost to metabolism and feces. Additionally, non-predatory deaths reduce the transfer of energy from one trophic level to the next. And the same inefficiency holds for a top carnivore as well. Let's explore how this 10% rule limits the length of food chains and is responsible for the rarity of big, fierce animals outside your window and across the world

Biomass is the total weight of living or non-living organic material in a given volume, such as a single organism, or, on a

Q Why are big, fierce animal species so rare in the world?

larger scale, the weight of all plant and animal matter in, say, an ecosystem. Given the 10% efficiency with which herbivores convert plant biomass into their own biomass, how much plant biomass is necessary to produce a single 1,200-pound (500 kg) cow? On average, that cow would need to eat about 12,000 pounds (5,000 kg) of grain in order to grow to weigh 1,200 pounds. But that 1,200-pound cow, when eaten by a carnivore, could only add about 120 pounds of biomass to the carnivore, and only 12 pounds to a top carnivore. That's a huge amount of plant biomass required to generate a tiny amount of our top carnivore, which explains why big, fierce animals are so rare (and why vegetarianism is more energetically efficient than meat-eating). After all, multiply that 5,000 kg of grain by several hundred (or thousands, more appropriately) to get an idea of how much plant matter would be necessary to support even a small population of top carnivores: millions of kilograms of grain can support only a few top carnivores.

How much would be required to support an even higher link on the food chain? Ten times as much, so much that there might not be enough land in the ecosystem to produce enough plant material. And even if there were, the area required would be so large that the "top, top carnivores" might be so spread out and so busy trying to eat enough that they'd be unlikely to encounter each other in order to mate. Hence, the 10% rule limits the length of food chains.

We can illustrate the path of energy through the organisms of an ecosystem with an **energy pyramid,** in which each layer of the pyramid represents the biomass of a trophic level. In FIGURE 15-14, we can see that for terrestrial ecosystems, the biomass (in kilograms per

ENERGY PYRAMID: INEFFICIENT ENERGY FLOW

Only about 10% of the biomass from each trophic level is converted into biomass in the next trophic level. The rest of the available energy is lost to the environment, a consequence of several factors, including non-predatory deaths, incomplete digestion of prey/food, and respiration.

TERTIARY CONSUMERS

SECONDARY CONSUMERS

10% converted to biomass

PRIMARY CONSUMERS

10% converted to biomass

10% converted to biomass

PRIMARY PRODUCERS

GRAPHIC CONTENT!
Thinking critically about visual displays of data.
Turn to p. 618 for a closer inspection of this figure.

FIGURE 15-14 The 10% Rule. Inefficiencies in the transfer of energy from one trophic level to the next account for the fact that there are so many more plants than animals.

VARIATIONS IN PRIMARY PRODUCTIVITY

■ Biomass of top consumers
□ Biomass of primary producers

LARGE-BASED PYRAMID
• Supports a relatively large biomass of consumers
• Common in rain forests, marshes, and algal beds

SMALL-BASED PYRAMID
• Reduced ability to support consumers
• Common in deserts, tundras, and open oceans

INVERTED PYRAMID
• Small biomass of producers supports a relatively large biomass of consumers
• Occurs in some aquatic ecosystems where plankton are primary producers

FIGURE 15-15 Relative biomass of producers and consumers. Across ecosystems, there is huge variation in primary productivity.

where the primary producers are plankton. Because plankton have such short life spans and rapid reproduction rates, a relatively small biomass can support a large biomass of consumers, giving rise to an inverted pyramid (see the bottom pyramid in Figure 15-15). If you quantified the amount of energy available to consumers (rather than biomass), however, the pyramid would resemble those seen in terrestrial ecosystems.

square meter) found in photosynthetic organisms, at the base of the pyramid, is reduced significantly at each step, given the incomplete utilization by organisms higher up the food chain. **FIGURE 15-15** illustrates the huge variation in primary productivity across a variety of ecosystems. It is highest in tropical rain forests, marshes, and algal beds, and lowest in deserts, tundra, and the open ocean. In each case, the shapes of the energy and biomass pyramids are similar. With a smaller base, though, the ability of an ecosystem to support higher levels in the food chain is reduced. One dramatic exception is seen in some aquatic ecosystems

TAKE-HOME MESSAGE 15·7

Energy pyramids reveal that the biomass of primary producers in an ecosystem tends to be far greater than the biomass of herbivores. Similarly, the biomass transferred at each successive step along the food chain tends to be only about 10% of the biomass of the organisms consumed. As a consequence of this inefficiency, food chains rarely exceed four levels.

15·8 Essential chemicals cycle through ecosystems.

What is necessary for life? Energy and some essential chemicals top the list. New energy continually comes to earth from the sun, fulfilling the first need. And everything else is already here. The chemicals just cycle around and around, using the same pathway taken by energy—the food chain. Plants and other producers generally take up the molecules from the atmosphere or the soil. Then as animals consume the plants or other animals, the chemicals move up the food chain. And as the plants and animals die, detritivores and decomposers return the chemicals to the abiotic environment. From a chemical perspective, life is just a continuous recycling of molecules.

Chemicals cycle through the living and non-living components of an ecosystem. Each chemical is stored in a non-living part of the environment called a "reservoir." Organisms acquire the chemical from the reservoir, the chemical cycles through the food chain, and eventually is returned to the reservoir.

This is a useful overview, but we can get a deeper appreciation of the functioning of ecosystems and the ecological problems that can occur when they are disturbed—particularly by humans—by investigating a few of these cycles in more detail. Here we'll explore three of the most important chemical cycles: carbon, nitrogen, and phosphorus.

Carbon Carbon is found largely in four compartments on earth: the oceans, the atmosphere, terrestrial organisms, and fossil deposits. Plants and other photosynthetic organisms obtain most of their carbon from the atmosphere, where carbon is in the form of carbon dioxide (CO_2). As we saw in Chapter 4, photosynthetic organisms use carbon dioxide in photosynthesis, separating the carbon molecules from CO_2 and using them to build sugars and other macromolecules. Carbon then moves through the food chain as organisms eat plants and are themselves eaten (**FIGURE 15-16**). The oceans contain most of the earth's carbon. Here, many organisms use dissolved carbon to build shells (which later dissolve back into the water after the organism dies).

Most carbon returns to its reservoir as a consequence of organisms' metabolic processes. Organisms extract energy from food by breaking carbon-carbon bonds, releasing the energy stored in the bonds, and combining the released carbon atoms with oxygen. They then exhale the end product as CO_2.

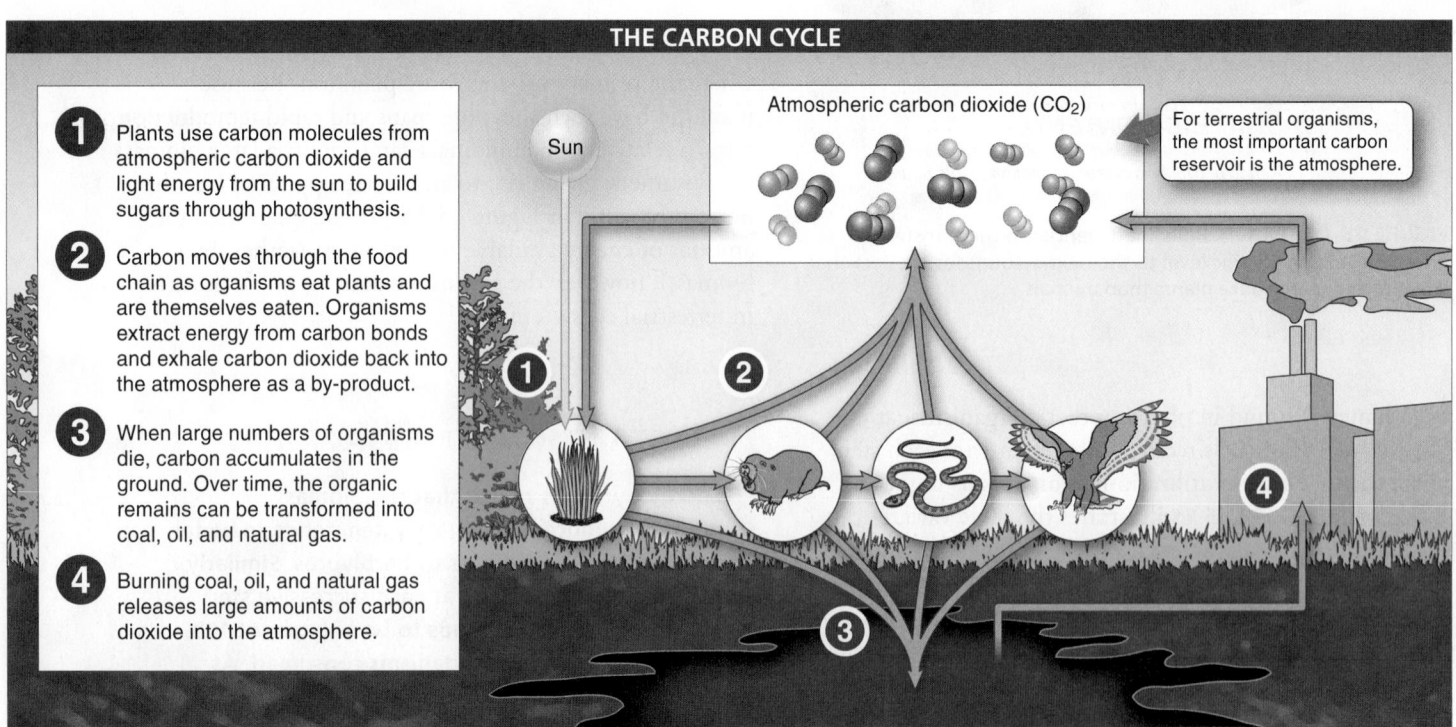

THE CARBON CYCLE

1 Plants use carbon molecules from atmospheric carbon dioxide and light energy from the sun to build sugars through photosynthesis.

2 Carbon moves through the food chain as organisms eat plants and are themselves eaten. Organisms extract energy from carbon bonds and exhale carbon dioxide back into the atmosphere as a by-product.

3 When large numbers of organisms die, carbon accumulates in the ground. Over time, the organic remains can be transformed into coal, oil, and natural gas.

4 Burning coal, oil, and natural gas releases large amounts of carbon dioxide into the atmosphere.

Atmospheric carbon dioxide (CO_2)

For terrestrial organisms, the most important carbon reservoir is the atmosphere.

Sun

FIGURE 15-16 Element cycling: carbon.

The burning of fossil fuels is adding significantly to the atmospheric carbon reservoir. Fossil fuels are created when large numbers of organisms die and are buried in sediment lacking oxygen. In the absence of oxygen, at high pressures, and after very long periods of time, the organic remains are transformed into coal, oil, and natural gas. Trapped underground or in rock, these sources of carbon played little role in the global carbon cycle until humans in industrialized countries began using fossil fuels to power various technologies. Burning coal, oil, and natural gas releases large amounts of carbon dioxide, thus increasing the average CO_2 concentration in the atmosphere—the current level of CO_2 in the atmosphere is the highest it has been in almost half a million years. This has potentially disastrous implications, as we'll see in Chapter 16.

Although, on average, the level of CO_2 in the environment is increasing, there is a yearly cycle of ups and downs in the CO_2 levels in the northern hemisphere. This cycling is due to fluctuations in the ability of plants to absorb CO_2. Many trees lose their leaves each fall and, during the winter months, relatively low rates of photosynthesis lead to low rates of CO_2 consumption, causing an annual peak in atmospheric CO_2 levels. During the summer,

Q Why are global CO_2 levels rising?

Q Global CO_2 levels are rising in general, but they also exhibit a sharp rise and fall within each year. Why?

trees have their leaves, sunlight is strong, and photosynthesis (consuming CO_2) occurs at much higher levels, causing a drop in the atmospheric CO_2 level.

Nitrogen Nitrogen is necessary to build a variety of molecules critical to life, including all amino acids, the components of every protein molecule. Just as for carbon, the chief reservoir of nitrogen is the atmosphere. But even though more than 78% of the atmosphere is nitrogen gas (N_2), for most organisms this nitrogen is completely unusable. The problem is that atmospheric nitrogen consists of two nitrogen atoms bonded tightly together, and these bonds need to be broken to make the nitrogen usable for living organisms. Only through the metabolic magic (chemistry, actually) of some soil-dwelling bacteria, the nitrogen-fixers, can most nitrogen enter the food chain (**FIGURE 15-17**).

These bacteria chemically convert, or "fix," nitrogen by attaching it to other atoms, including hydrogen, to produce ammonia and related compounds. These compounds are then further modified by other bacteria into a form that can be taken up by plants and used to build proteins. And once nitrogen is in plant tissues, animals acquire it in the same way they

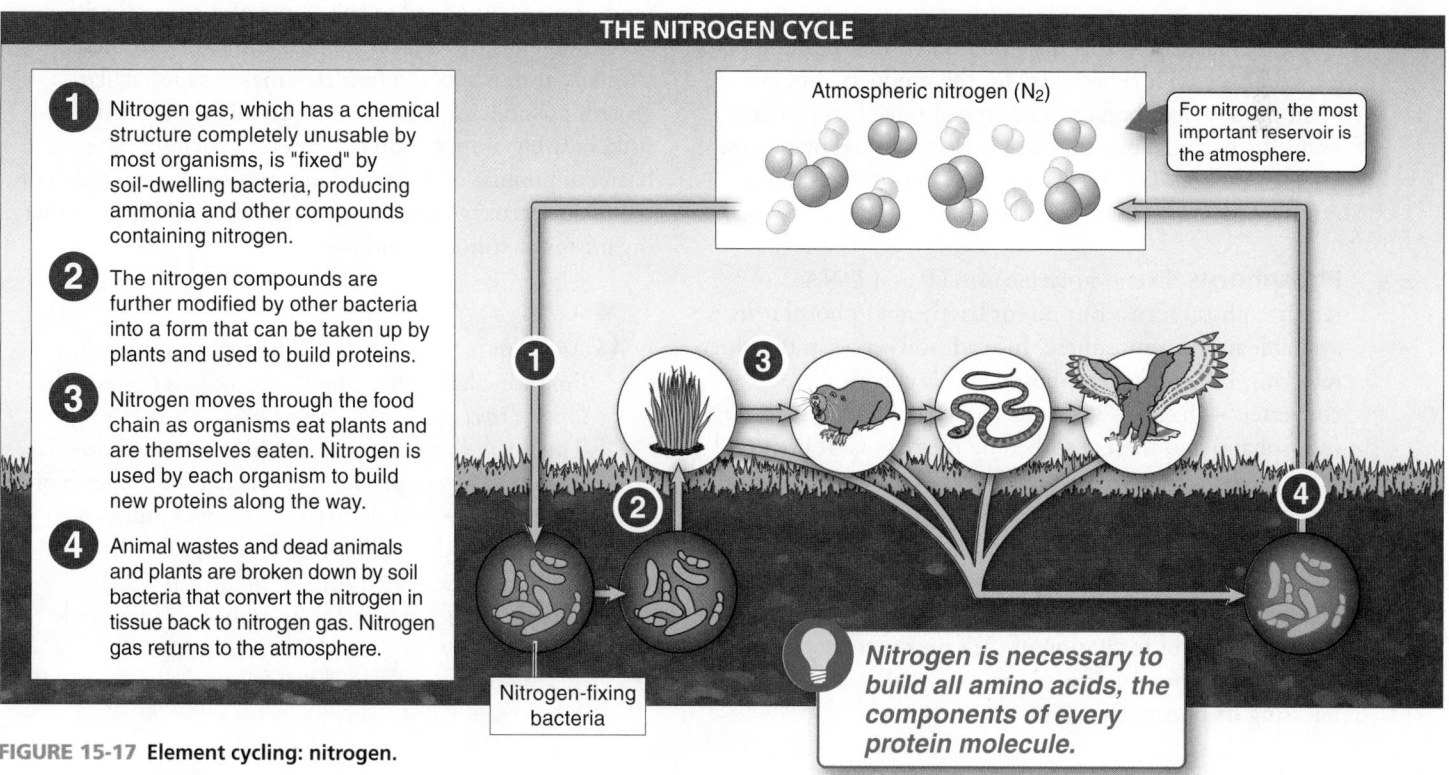

THE NITROGEN CYCLE

1 Nitrogen gas, which has a chemical structure completely unusable by most organisms, is "fixed" by soil-dwelling bacteria, producing ammonia and other compounds containing nitrogen.

2 The nitrogen compounds are further modified by other bacteria into a form that can be taken up by plants and used to build proteins.

3 Nitrogen moves through the food chain as organisms eat plants and are themselves eaten. Nitrogen is used by each organism to build new proteins along the way.

4 Animal wastes and dead animals and plants are broken down by soil bacteria that convert the nitrogen in tissue back to nitrogen gas. Nitrogen gas returns to the atmosphere.

Atmospheric nitrogen (N_2)

For nitrogen, the most important reservoir is the atmosphere.

Nitrogen-fixing bacteria

Nitrogen is necessary to build all amino acids, the components of every protein molecule.

FIGURE 15-17 Element cycling: nitrogen.

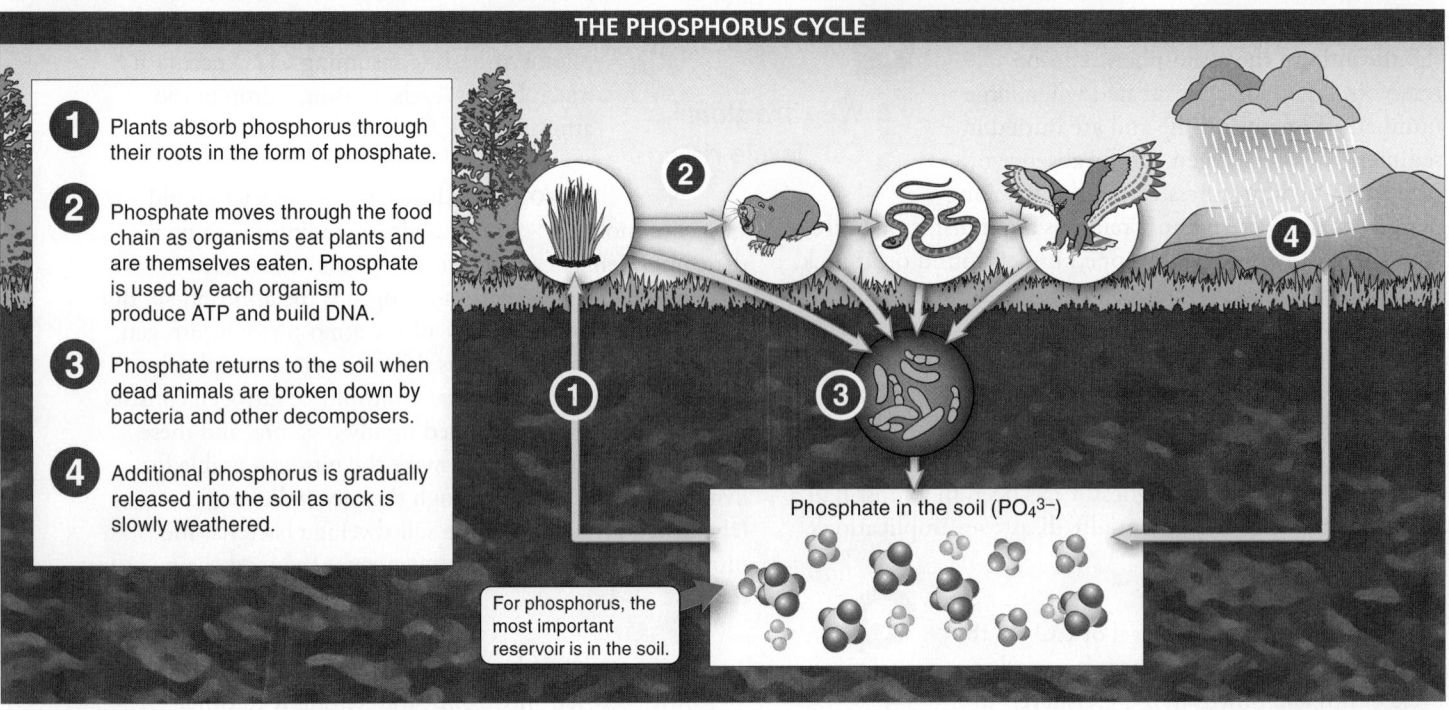

THE PHOSPHORUS CYCLE

1 Plants absorb phosphorus through their roots in the form of phosphate.

2 Phosphate moves through the food chain as organisms eat plants and are themselves eaten. Phosphate is used by each organism to produce ATP and build DNA.

3 Phosphate returns to the soil when dead animals are broken down by bacteria and other decomposers.

4 Additional phosphorus is gradually released into the soil as rock is slowly weathered.

Phosphate in the soil (PO_4^{3-})

For phosphorus, the most important reservoir is in the soil.

FIGURE 15-18 Element cycling: phosphorus.

acquire carbon: by eating the plants. Nitrogen returns to the atmosphere when animal wastes and dead animals are broken down by soil bacteria (decomposers) that convert the nitrogen compounds in tissues back to nitrogen gas.

The availability of nitrogen is like a bottleneck limiting plant growth. Because it is necessary for the production of every plant protein, and because all nitrogen must first be made usable by bacteria, plant growth is often limited by nitrogen levels in the soil. For this reason, most fertilizers contain nitrogen in a form usable by plants.

Phosphorus Every molecule of ATP and DNA requires phosphorus. But no (or barely any) phosphorus is available in the atmosphere. Instead, soil serves as the chief reservoir. Like nitrogen, phosphorus is chemically converted—"fixed"—into a form usable by plants (phosphate) and then absorbed by their roots. It cycles through the food chain as herbivores consume plants and carnivores consume herbivores. As organisms die, their remains are broken down by bacteria and other organisms, returning the phosphorus to the soil. The pool of phosphorus in the soil is also influenced by the much slower process of formation of rock on the seafloor, its uplifting into mountains, and its eventual weathering, releasing its phosphorus (**FIGURE 15-18**).

Like nitrogen, phosphorus is often a limiting resource in soils, constraining plant growth. Consequently, fertilizers usually contain large amounts of phosphorus. This is beneficial in the short run, but it can have some disastrous unintended consequences. As more and more phosphorus (and nitrogen) is added to soil, some of it runs off with water and ends up in lakes, ponds, and rivers. In these habitats, also, it acts as a fertilizer, making spectacular growth possible for algae. But eventually the algae die and sink, creating a huge source of food for bacteria. The bacterial population increases and may use up too much of the dissolved oxygen, causing fish, insects, and many other organisms to suffocate and die.

❝ An atom of phosphorus 'X' had marked time in the limestone ledge since the Paleozoic seas covered the land. *Time, to an atom locked in a rock, does not pass.* The break came when a bur-oak root nosed down a crack and began prying and sucking. In the flash of a century the rock decayed, and X was pulled out and up into the world of living things. He helped build a flower, which became an acorn, which fattened a deer, which fed an Indian all in a single year. ❞

—ALDO LEOPOLD, *A Sand County Almanac*, 1949

EUTROPHICATION

Eutrophication—the increase in nutrients in an ecosystem, particularly nitrogen and phosphorus—often leads to the rapid growth of algae and bacteria in aquatic ecosystems. These organisms then consume much of the oxygen, leading to large die-offs of animals.

Due to extensive runoff of fertilizers from agriculture, eutrophication now affects more than half of the lakes in Asia, Europe, and North America.

FIGURE 15-19 Too much of a good thing?

The increase in nutrients, particularly nitrogen and phosphorus, in an ecosystem, is called **eutrophication.** The consequent rapid growth of algae and bacteria, followed by large-scale die-offs of other organisms, is increasingly a problem in both small and large bodies of water, including more than half of the lakes of Asia, Europe, and North America (**FIGURE 15-19**). Lake Erie, on the U.S.-Canadian border, for example, has experienced eutrophication as a result of all the phosphorus- and nitrogen-containing wastewater that drains into the lake from the extensive surrounding farmlands. Given the lower use of fertilizers in South America and Africa, eutrophication is less common there.

TAKE-HOME MESSAGE 15·8

Chemicals essential to life—including carbon, nitrogen, and phosphorus—cycle through ecosystems. They are usually captured from the atmosphere, soil, or water by growing organisms, passed from one trophic level to the next as organisms eat other organisms, and returned to the environment through respiration, decomposition, and erosion. These cycles can be disrupted as human activities significantly increase the amounts of chemicals added to soils for use by plants or released to the environment.

A pair of anemone fish (Amphiprion sp.) in an anemone, Solomon Islands.

15·9 Interacting species evolve together.

There is a moth in Madagascar with a tongue that is 11 inches long! This might seem absurdly long—until the moth approaches a similarly odd-looking orchid. The orchid's flower has a very long tube, also about 11 inches long, that has a bit of nectar at the very bottom. The moth's tongue, although usually rolled up, straightens out as fluid is pumped into it and can be inserted into the long nectar tube. As its tongue reaches the bottom, the moth slurps up the nectar, gaining nourishment and energy. The moth also gets a bit of pollen stuck to it in the process, pollen that gets brushed onto the reproductive parts of the next orchid flower it visits (FIGURE 15-20).

Q **Which came first, the long-tongued moths or the long-tubed flowers?** It's clear that having an 11-inch tongue is useful, even necessary, to extract nectar from an 11-inch nectar tube. And it's clear that putting nectar at the bottom of an 11-inch tube is a strategy to restrict access to only those pollinators that will reliably pass pollen from plant to plant of the same species. But how did such a system ever originate? Which came first, the long-tongued moths or the long-tubed flowers? Each trait only seems to make sense in a world where the other already exists. The answer is that neither came first. They both evolved—**coevolved**—together.

As a consequence of natural selection, populations of organisms commonly become better adapted to their environment. As long as there is variation for a trait, and the trait is heritable, differential reproductive success will lead to a change in the population. It is easy to imagine populations becoming more and more efficient at making use of non-living resources. But natural selection does not distinguish between biotic and abiotic resources as selective forces. Either can cause individuals with certain traits to reproduce

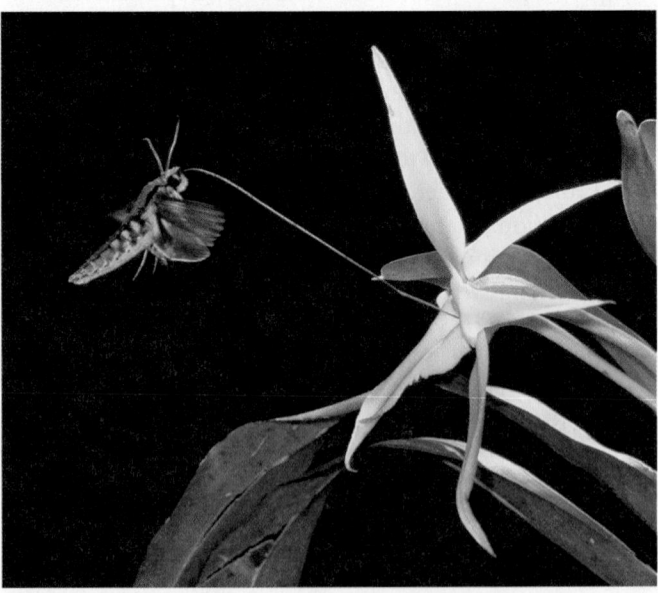

FIGURE 15-20 **A perfect match?** Long-tubed orchids and long-tongued moths in Madagascar each influence the evolution of the other.

at a higher rate than others, and so either can cause evolution. So small changes in the moth lead to small changes in the orchid, which select for further small changes in the moth . . . and the process continues on. In the end, species become adapted not just to their physical environment but also to the other species around them.

15·10 Each species' role in a community is defined as its niche.

Within a society, most humans seem to find their niche. Each person plays a particular role, defined by the nature of his or her work, activities, and interactions with others. Other species do the same thing. Within their *communities*—geographic areas defined as loose assemblages of species, sometimes interdependent, with overlapping ranges—each species has its own niche.

We can think of an organism's **niche** as its place in the community. More than just a *place* for living, however, a niche is a complete *way* of living. In other words, an organism's niche encompasses (1) the space it requires, (2) the type and amount of food it consumes, (3) the organisms for which it is a food source, (4) its influence on competitors, (5) the timing of its reproduction (its life history), (6) its temperature and moisture requirements, and almost every other aspect that describes the way the organism uses its environment and influences the other organisms in that environment (**FIGURE 15-21**).

Although a niche describes the role a species *can* play within a community, the species doesn't always get to have that exact role. Consider the rats of Boston. Until the 1990s, they lived in relative peace in the sewers beneath the city's streets. But when the city embarked on the largest underground highway construction project in U.S. history, engineers displaced and forcibly drove out thousands of rats from much of their habitat. In essence, there was suddenly an overlap between the rat niche and the human niche, and the rats were now restricted to just some portions of the sewers. As a result, the rats' **realized niche,** the narrower role that they may occupy in a community, is now just a subset of their **fundamental niche,** the full range of environmental conditions under which they can live.

It is common for species to find themselves competing with other species for parts of a niche. When this occurs, generally one of the species is restricted from its full niche. We'll examine next the various possible outcomes when such niche overlap occurs.

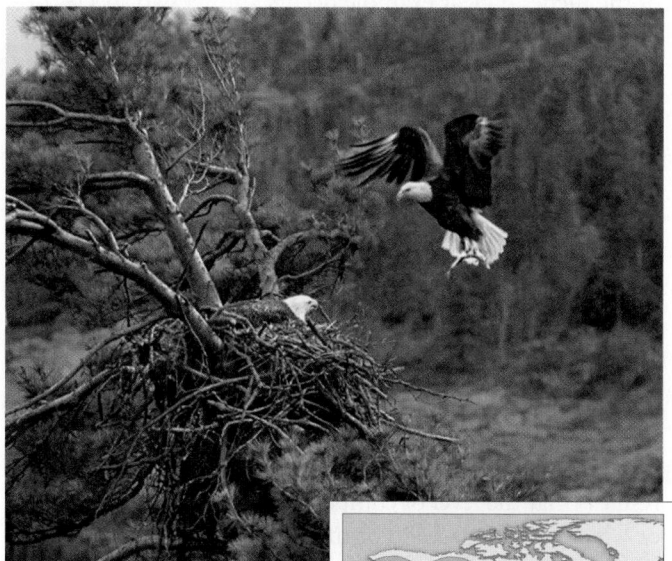

NICHE FEATURES
- The space an organism requires
- The type and amount of food an organism utilizes
- The timing of an organism's reproduction
- An organism's temperature and moisture requirements and other necessary living conditions
- The organisms for which it is a food source
- Its influence on competitors

Bald eagle range

Constrained by competitors (or other factors), a species' realized niche may be smaller than its fundamental niche.

FIGURE 15-21 A way of living. "Niche" describes all of the ways in which an organism utilizes the resources of the environment.

15·11 Competition can be hard to see, yet it influences community structure.

Some species, particularly closely related species, have similar niches. This can lead to conflict as they try to exploit the same resources. Almost invariably, when the fundamental niches of two species overlap, competition occurs. This competition doesn't last forever, though. Inevitably, one of two outcomes occurs: competitive exclusion or resource partitioning (FIGURE 15-22).

1. In **competitive exclusion,** two species battle for resources in the same niche until the more efficient of the two wins and the other species is driven to extinction in that location ("local extinction"). In the 1930s, this was demonstrated in simple laboratory experiments using *Paramecium,* a single-celled organism. Populations of two similar *Paramecium* species were grown either separately or together in test tubes containing water and their bacterial food source. When grown separately, each species thrived. When grown together, though, one species always drove the other to extinction.

WHEN NICHES OVERLAP

1 When grown alone under a particular set of environmental conditions, each of two similar *Paramecium* species thrives.

2 When both species are grown together, because their niches overlap, the species compete and two outcomes are possible:

or

COMPETITIVE EXCLUSION
One species within the niche utilizes resources more efficiently, driving the other species to local extinction.

RESOURCE PARTITIONING
The species each alter their use of the niche, dividing the resources.

When the fundamental niches of two species overlap, competition occurs.

FIGURE 15-22 **Overlapping niches: competitive exclusion and resource partitioning.**

2. Resource partitioning is an alternative outcome of niche overlap. Individual organisms and species can adapt to changing environmental conditions, and resource partitioning can result from an organism's behavioral change or a change in its structure. When this occurs, one or both species become restricted in some aspect of their niche, dividing the resource. In other experiments with *Paramecium,* for example, one of the two species was replaced with a third species. As in the initial experiment, each species thrived when grown alone. But when the two species were grown together in the same test tube, they ended up dividing the test tube "habitat." One species fed exclusively at the bottom of the test tube, and the other fed only at the top. Simple behavioral change made coexistence possible.

In many situations, resource partitioning is accompanied by **character displacement,** an evolutionary divergence in one or both of the species that leads to a partitioning of the niche. A clear example occurs among two species of seed-eating finches on the Galápagos Islands. On islands where both species live, their beak sizes differ significantly. One species has a deeper beak, better for large seeds, while the other has a shallower beak, better for smaller seeds, and they do not compete. On islands where either species occurs alone, beak size is intermediate between the two sizes (FIGURE 15-23).

Competition between species has one very odd feature: it is hard to actually see it occurring because it causes itself to disappear. That is, after only a short period of competition, one of the species becomes locally extinct or leaves the area where the niches overlap, or character displacement occurs, largely reducing the competition. In either case, the net result is that the level of competition is significantly reduced or wiped out altogether. For this reason, biologists often have to look for character displacement—the "ghost of competition past"—to identify areas where competition once occurred. Moreover, even while it is occurring, competition tends to be indirect, rather than head-to-head battles. Like a game of musical chairs, it's more a question of both species trying to use a particular resource, with one being a bit better at it.

Biologists do have the opportunity to see competition in the occasional natural experiments in which a new species is introduced to a community. This happened, for example, when the American mink, a weasel-like mammal, was introduced into Europe, where previously only the European

COMPETITION AND CHARACTER DISPLACEMENT

Character displacement occurs when natural selection reduces the competition between two species by producing an evolutionary divergence in one or both species.

1 Two finch species have medium-size beaks when the species live on separate islands.

2 When the birds inhabit the same island, they compete for the same resources. An evolutionary shift in the beak size in each species occurs, a change called character displacement.

Character displacement is an evolutionary adaptation that makes resource partitioning possible.

FIGURE 15-23 Allowing organisms to divide resources. Character displacement is an evolutionary adaptation that makes resource partitioning possible.

mink had lived. Within 10 years, in the area where their ranges overlapped, the European mink increased in size while the American mink decreased in size, as biologists documented the evolution. In the next chapter, we'll investigate in greater depth why newly introduced species frequently win the competition with native species.

TAKE-HOME MESSAGE 15·11

Populations with completely overlapping niches cannot coexist forever. Competition for resources occurs until one or both species evolve in ways that reduce the competition, through character displacement, or until one becomes extinct in that location.

15·12 Predation produces adaptation in both predators and their prey.

Some words of advice in case you ever think about quickly approaching a horned lizard: be afraid. Be very afraid. Here's why: as you get close to the lizard, it may zap you with streams of blood squirted from its eyes. In all likelihood, you will flinch. And as you flinch, the horned lizard will scurry away. The display is shocking, but the fact that evolution has produced extreme and effective anti-predator adaptations is not.

Predation—an interaction between two species in which one species eats the other—is one of the most important forces shaping the composition and abundance of species in a community. Predation, though, isn't restricted to the obvious interactions involving one animal chasing down and killing another. Herbivores' eating of leaves, fruits, or seeds is a form of predation, even though it doesn't

Why do exotic species often flourish when released into novel habitats, even though natural selection has not adapted them to this new environment?

necessarily kill the plant. And predators are not necessarily physically imposing. Each year more than a million humans die as a result of disease from mosquito bites, compared with fewer than a dozen from shark attacks.

Q Predators are a potent selective force: organisms eaten by predators tend to have reduced reproductive success. Consequently, in prey species, a variety of features have evolved (and continue to evolve)—including the blood-squirting-eyeball effect—that reduce their predation risk. But as prey evolve, so do predators. This coevolution is a sort of arms race with ever-changing and escalating predation-effectiveness adaptations causing more effective predator-avoidance adaptations, and vice versa. (In this light, it may seem unexpected that exotic species often flourish when released into novel habitats, even though natural selection has not adapted them to their new environment. As it turns out, just as these species are not fully adapted to their new environment, they also have few predators there. And with low predation risk, they often can flourish.) We'll examine some common adaptations of both predators and prey.

Prey adaptations for reducing predation There are two broad categories of defenses against predators: physical and behavioral.

Physical defenses include mechanical, chemical, warning coloration, and camouflage mechanisms.

1. Mechanical defenses. Predation plays a large role in producing adaptations such as the sharp quills of a porcupine, the prickly spines of a cactus, or the tough armor protecting an armadillo or sow bug. These, as well as claws, fangs, stingers, and other physical structures, can reduce predation risk (**FIGURE 15-24**).

2. Chemical defenses. Further prey defenses can include chemical toxins that make the prey poisonous or unpalatable. Plants can't run from their predators, so chemical defenses are especially important to them. Almost all plants produce some chemicals to deter organisms that might eat them. The toxins can be severe, such as strychnine from plants in the genus *Strychnos,* which kills most vertebrates, including humans, by stimulating nonstop convulsions and other extreme and painful symptoms leading to death. At the other end of the spectrum are chemicals toxic to some insects but relatively mild to humans, such as those found in cinnamon, peppermint, and jalapeno peppers. Ironically, many plants

PHYSICAL DEFENSES FOR REDUCING PREDATION

MECHANICAL DEFENSES

CHEMICAL DEFENSES

WARNING COLORATION

CAMOUFLAGE

FIGURE 15-24 Prey defenses: some physical means for avoiding predation. Shown (*from top left, clockwise*) are Cape porcupine, azure poison dart frog, praying mantis, and monarch butterfly.

that evolved to produce such chemicals to deter predators are now cultivated and eaten specifically *for* these chemicals. One organism's toxic poison is another's spicy flavor.

Some animals can also synthesize toxic compounds (or perhaps more commonly can safely acquire them from the organisms they eat). The poison dart frog has poison glands all over its body, making it toxic to the touch. The fire salamander, too, is toxic, with the capacity to squirt a strong nerve toxin from poison glands on its back. Some animals, including milkweed bugs and monarch butterflies, can safely consume toxic chemicals from plants and sequester them in their tissues, becoming toxic to predators who try to eat them.

3. Warning coloration. Species protected from predation by toxic chemicals frequently have bright color patterns to warn potential predators. They are essentially carrying a sign that says: "Warning, I'm poisonous, so keep away." To make it as easy as possible for predators to learn, different poisonous species often have the same color patterns. It's as if devising a single common sign saying "Danger: poison" is more effective than multiple species coming up with their own specific signs.

In a clever twist on this, some species that are perfectly edible to their predators also have evolved the same bright colors, in a phenomenon known as **mimicry.** Their coloration mimics the same warning sign but without the toxins. As long as they are relatively rare compared with the toxic individuals they mimic—reducing the chance that predators might catch on to their trickery— the evolutionary ruse is quite successful.

4. Camouflage. An alternative to warning coloration, and one of the most effective ways to avoid being eaten, is simply to avoid being seen. An adaptation in many organisms is patterns of coloration that enable them to blend into their surroundings. Examples include insects that look like leaves or twigs and hares that are brown for most of the year but turn white when there is snow on the ground.

Behavioral defenses include both seemingly passive and active behaviors: hiding or escaping, and alarm calling or fighting back.

1. Hiding or escaping. Anti-predator adaptations need not involve toxic chemicals, physical structures, or special coloration. Many species excel at hiding or running, or both. With vigilance, it is

BEHAVIORAL DEFENSES THAT REDUCE PREDATION

HIDING OR ESCAPING

FIGHTING BACK

FIGURE 15-25 Prey defenses: behavioral means for avoiding predation. Fish may travel in huge schools, finding safety in numbers. And fish may mob a predator, here, a shark, to make it harder for the predator to attack any one member of the school. The bird can project vomit at a predator, frightening it away.

possible to get advance warning of impending predator attacks, and then quickly and effectively avoid the predator. A variation of this strategy comes from safety in numbers: many species, including schooling fish and emperor penguins, travel in large groups to reduce their predation risk (**FIGURE 15-25**).

On many islands, animals show no fear of humans. Rather than encountering skittish lizards, for example, a human visitor to the Galápagos Islands must be careful not to step on them. The animals are not afraid because, given the small size of most islands, the number of predators is restricted. As a consequence, there has

Q *On islands, animals frequently have no fear of humans (in contrast to animals' more skittish behavior on the mainland). Why?*

been no selection for skittishness and hypervigilance, traits that normally evolve in response to predation risk.

2. Alarm calling and fighting back. In many species, especially birds and mammals, individuals warn others with an alarm call. Although risky for the caller, such alarm calling can give other individuals—often close kin that are nearby—enough advance warning to escape (recall, from Chapter 9, the warning calls of Belding's ground squirrels). Some prey species also turn the tables, mobbing predators to keep them from successfully completing their task. This category might also include the blood-squirting lizard described above, or the fulmar, a seabird that defends its nest from attacks with projectile vomiting aimed at the intruder.

Predator adaptations for enhancing predation

Just as prey use physical and behavioral features to reduce their risk of predation, predators evolve in parallel ways to increase their efficiency. As milkweed plants have evolved to produce toxic chemicals, sequestered within the structures of the plant, that kill their predators, milkweed bugs have evolved to produce toxic-avoidance methods that allow them to eat the toxic plants without suffering harm. And as prey have become better at hiding and escaping, predators have developed better sensory perception to help them detect hiding prey, and faster running ability to catch them. Predators, too, make use of mimicry. The angler fish, the tasseled frogfish, and the snapping turtle all have physical structures that mimic something—usually a food item—that is of interest to potential prey. As the prey come closer to inspect, the predator snaps them up (**FIGURE 15-26**).

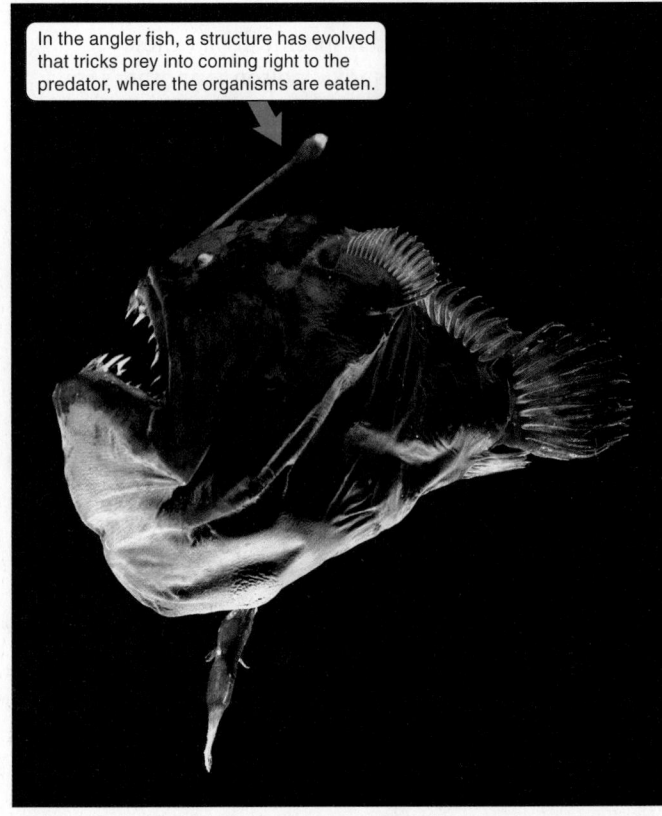

In the angler fish, a structure has evolved that tricks prey into coming right to the predator, where the organisms are eaten.

FIGURE 15-26 A better predator. Some adaptations enhance predation.

Q Why don't predators become so efficient at capturing prey that they drive the prey to extinction?

Although natural selection leads to predators with effective adaptations for capturing prey, the adaptations are rarely so efficient that the prey species are driven to extinction. The explanation for this is referred to as the "life-dinner hypothesis." Selection for "escape ability" in the prey is stronger than selection for "capture ability" in the predator. When, for example, a rabbit can't escape from a fox, the cost to the rabbit is its life—and it will never reproduce again. On the other hand, when a fox can't keep up with a rabbit, all it loses is a meal; it can still go on to capture prey and reproduce in the future. In other words, the cost of losing in the interaction is much higher for the rabbit.

TAKE-HOME MESSAGE 15·12

Predators and their prey are in an evolutionary arms race; as physical and behavioral features evolve in prey species to reduce their predation risk, predators develop more effective and efficient methods of predation. The coevolutionary process can result in brightly colored organisms, alarm calling, and many types of mimicry.

Parasitism is a form of predation.

For most people, the word "predation" conjures images of a large animal such as a cheetah, chasing and killing another large animal such as a gazelle. But there is another world of predation, largely unseen but equally deadly: **parasitism,** defined as a symbiotic relationship in which one organism (the **parasite**) benefits while the other (the **host**) is harmed. In fact, this hidden world of parasites is thriving with activity: parasites are probably the most numerous species on earth, with three or four times as many species as non-parasites!

Two general types of parasites make life difficult for most organisms. *Ectoparasites* (*ecto* = outside) include organisms such as lice, leeches, and ticks. One species of Mexican parrot is all too aware of ectoparasites: it has 30 different species of mites living on its feathers alone. And many of the parasites even have parasites themselves! *Endoparasites* are parasites that live inside their hosts (*endo* = inside). They are equally pervasive. Endoparasites infecting vertebrates include many different phyla of both animals and protists, the single-celled eukaryotes (**FIGURE 15-27**). In all of these parasite-host interactions, as with all predator-prey interactions, the predator or parasite benefits and the prey or host is harmed.

Even though they are considered predators, parasites have some unique features and face some unusual challenges relative to other predators. The most obvious of these features is that in parasitism, the parasite generally is much smaller than its host and stays in contact with the host for extended periods of time, normally not killing the host but weakening it as the parasite uses some of the host's resources. Being located right on your food source all the time can be advantageous. But this also leads to what is perhaps the greatest challenge that parasites face: how to get from one individual host to another. A parasite can't survive long once its host dies, after all. The methods by which parasites accomplish such dispersal are unexpected and surprising. Many of their complicated life cycles involve passing through two (or more) different species (and could have come about only through coevolution with each of the host species). These life cycles are likely to give us a new appreciation for the ingenuity of these microorganisms—or rather, for the evolutionary process that has produced them. Let's look at a few representative examples.

Case 1: Parasites can induce foolish, fearless behavior in their hosts. Rats fear cats. During their evolution, rats have developed a protective wariness of their feline predators and

---

PARASITES

Parasites are predators that benefit from a symbiotic relationship with their hosts.

ECTOPARASITES
Parasites that live on their host

ENDOPARASITES
Parasites that live inside their host

 There may be three to four times as many parasitic species as non-parasitic species on earth!

FIGURE 15-27 Parasites: predators dwarfed by their prey.
A bedbug (*Cimex lectularius*), an ectoparasite of humans, is shown in extreme close-up. *Trypanosoma brucei* is an endoparasite that invades a human host and is the cause of African sleeping sickness.

The rabies parasite (a virus) is more effectively passed from one animal to another by causing its host to foam at the mouth and aggressively bite.

Parasites have surprising ways of solving a challenging problem: how to get from one individual host to another.

FIGURE 15-28 Spreading disease. Rabies symptoms aid the disease-causing virus in spreading to new hosts.

areas in which cats have been roaming. *Toxoplasma* is an organism that changes this. This single-celled parasite of rats must also spend part of its life cycle in cats. It does this by altering the brain of its rat host so that the rat no longer fears cats. In fact, *Toxoplasma*-infected rats not only lose their fear of cats, they become attracted to them. Is this an accident? No. This behavioral change, while quite dangerous for the rat, is exactly the change that increases the likelihood that the rat will be attacked by a cat, spreading the parasite in the process.

Case 2: Parasites can induce inappropriate aggression in their hosts. Rabid animals don't behave normally. They froth at the mouth and become unusually aggressive (**FIGURE 15-28**). Is this an accident? No. Rabies is caused by a virus that infects warm-blooded animals, mostly raccoons,

skunks, foxes, and coyotes. It is passed from one host to another via saliva. Inducing these "rabid" behaviors, of course, is exactly the change in behavior that will most help the virus to spread.

Case 3: Parasites can induce bizarre and risky behavior in their hosts. The lancet fluke is a parasitic flatworm. It has also been described as a "zombie-maker." This fluke spends most of its life in sheep and goats, but the fluke's eggs pass into snails that graze on vegetation contaminated by sheep and goat feces. Once inside the snail, the fluke eggs grow and develop, eventually forming cysts that the snail surrounds with mucus and then excretes. Continuing on their complex life cycle, the fluke cysts find their way into ants that eat the snail mucus. The flukes' journey back to a sheep or goat is now expedited by the so-called zombie-making. In an infected ant, the flukes grow into the ant's brain, altering its behavior. Whereas ants normally remain low to the ground, when infected by the lancet fluke, an ant climbs to the top of a grass blade or plant stem and clenches its mandibles on a leaf. Is this an accident? No. This behavioral change puts the ant much more at risk of being eaten by a grazing mammal—a bad outcome for the ant, but just what the parasite needs to complete its life cycle.

These parasite-induced behavior modifications are among the most dramatic, but there are many others that are more subtle yet equally effective at allowing a parasite to thrive attached to or within its host's body. This subset of predation is an active and exciting area of ecological and physiological investigation.

TAKE-HOME MESSAGE 15·13

Parasitism is a symbiotic relationship in which one organism benefits while the other is harmed. Parasites face some unusual challenges relative to other predators, particularly in how to get from one individual host to another, and some complex parasite life cycles have evolved.

15·14 Not all species interactions are negative: mutualism and commensalism.

It's easy to get the idea that all species interactions in nature are harsh and confrontational, marked by a clear winner and a clear loser. That is largely the case when it comes to competition and predation. Nonetheless, not all species

interactions are combative. Every flower you see should be a reminder that evolution produces beneficial species interactions as well. These types of interactions fall into two categories: mutualism and commensalism.

MUTUALISM
Interaction in which both species benefit

COMMENSALISM
Interaction in which one species benefits and the other neither benefits nor is harmed

FIGURE 15-29 **Not always "red in tooth and claw."** Mutualisms and commensalisms abound in nature.

Mutualism: everybody wins Corals that gain energy from photosynthetic algae living inside their tissues. Termites capable of subsisting on wood, but only with the assistance of cellulose-digesting microbes living in their digestive system. Flowers pollinated by animals that are nourished by nectar. Each of these relationships is an

example of **mutualism,** an interaction in which both species gain and neither is harmed (FIGURE 15-29). Mutualism is common in almost all communities. Plants, particularly, have numerous such interactions: with nutrient-absorbing fungi, with nitrogen-fixing bacteria, and with animals that pollinate them and disperse their fruits.

Mutualistic interactions are so widespread and ecologically important that they are described in significant detail throughout the book. The relationship between plants and mycorrhizae bacteria, for example, is discussed in Section 12-15. Plants and the rich variety of mutualistic relationships they have with animal pollinators and fruit dispersers are covered throughout Sections 12-9 and 12-11. Lichens, the symbiotic association of fungi and photosynthetic algae or bacteria, are discussed in Section 12-15.

You need not look further than your own gut for an important mutualistic relationship. Living within your large intestine are huge populations of *E. coli* bacteria that synthesize a significant portion of the vitamin K—essential for several metabolic processes and blood clotting—you need each day.

Commensalism: an interaction with a winner but no loser Some species interactions are one-sided. The cases in which one species benefits and the other neither benefits nor is harmed are called commensal relationships, or **commensalism.** Cattle egrets have just such a relationship with grazing mammals such as buffalo and elephants (see Figure 15-29). As the large mammals graze through grasses, they stir up insects. The birds, which feed near the mammals—particularly near the forager's head—are able to catch more insects with less effort this way. The grazers are neither helped nor harmed by the presence of the birds.

TAKE-HOME MESSAGE 15·14

Not all species interactions are combative. Beneficial species interactions evolve as well. In commensalism, one species benefits and the other is neither harmed nor helped. Mutualism, in which both species benefit from the interaction, is widespread and critically important to all ecosystems.

15·15–15·16
Communities can
change or remain
stable over time.

A pair of colorful ochre starfish, keystone predators within intertidal zones in the Pacific Ocean.

15·15   Many communities change over time.

Human "progress" and development can completely transform an environment—turning a patch of desert into Las Vegas, for example. Urban landscapes, too, can obliterate any signs of the nature that was once there. This is why it can be surprising (and heartening) to observe what happens when humans abandon an area. Little by little, nature reclaims it. The area doesn't necessarily recover completely, and change is slow. Still, this process is almost universal and virtually unstoppable. Nature responds similarly to other disturbances, too, from a single tree falling in a forest, to a massive flood or fire, to massive volcanic eruptions.

The process of nature reclaiming an area and of communities gradually changing over time is called **succession.** It is defined as a change in the species composition over time, following a disturbance. There are two types of succession. *Primary succession* is when the process starts with no life and no soil. *Secondary succession* is when an already established habitat is disturbed, but some life and some soil remain.

Primary succession   Primary succession can take thousands or even tens of thousands of years, but it generally occurs in a consistent sequence. It always begins with a disturbance that leaves an area barren of soil and with no life. Frequently the disturbance is catastrophic. The huge volcanic eruption on Krakatau, Indonesia, in 1883, for

example, completely destroyed several islands and wiped out all life and soil on others. Primary succession has also begun, in a less dramatic fashion, in regions where glaciers have retreated, such as Glacier Bay, Alaska. Although succession does not occur in a single, definitive order, several steps are relatively common (**FIGURE 15-30**).

- The first arrivals, or **colonizers,** in a lifeless, soil-less area are usually bacteria or fungi or other photosynthetic microorganisms, floating in on the air.

- Lichens, symbiotic associations between a fungus and a photosynthetic alga or bacterium, are also common first colonizers. They can grow on rocks and are able to generate energy through photosynthesis. As they grow, lichens change their environment, too, secreting acids that break down the rocks and release useful minerals, making the terrain more hospitable for other organisms.

- Mosses also tend to arrive in the early stages, making use of many of the nutrients freed up by lichens. They trap moisture and can provide a hospitable site for germination of the seeds of other plants.

- Following mosses, small herbs often arrive. Later, some shrubs may begin to thrive, shading out the mosses and herbs.

- Shrubs, in turn, are eventually outcompeted and shaded out by small trees.

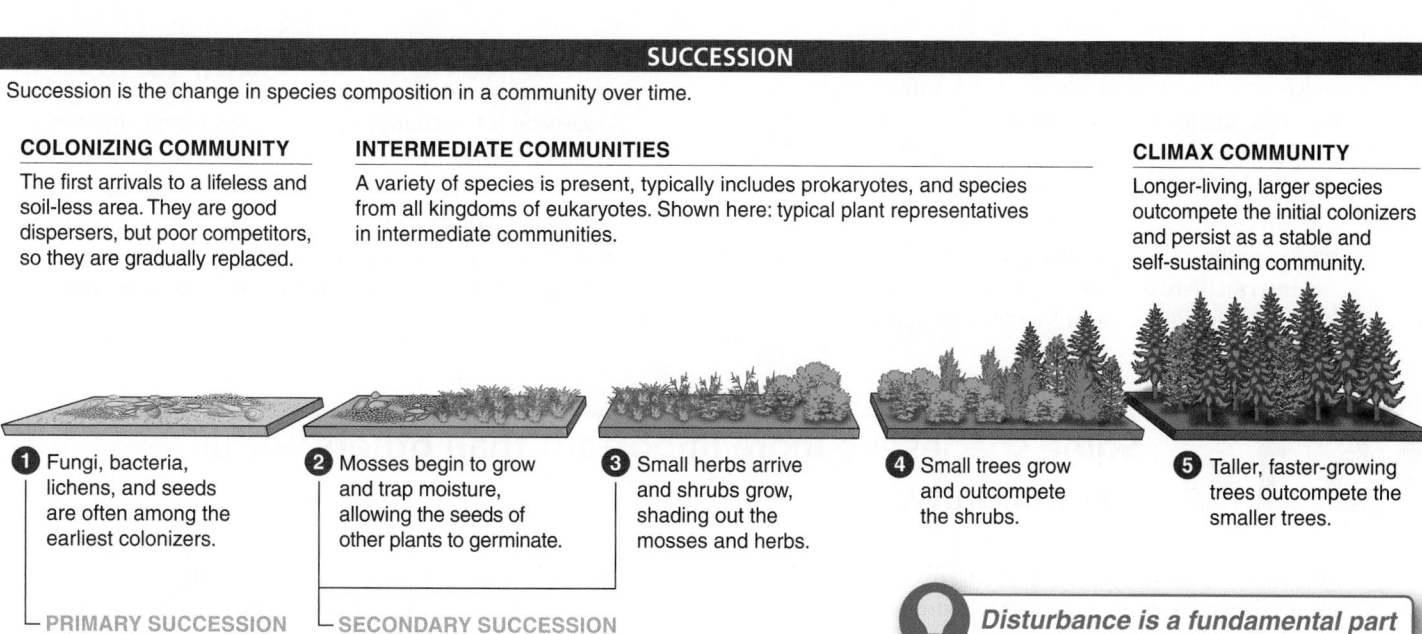

SUCCESSION

Succession is the change in species composition in a community over time.

COLONIZING COMMUNITY

The first arrivals to a lifeless and soil-less area. They are good dispersers, but poor competitors, so they are gradually replaced.

INTERMEDIATE COMMUNITIES

A variety of species is present, typically includes prokaryotes, and species from all kingdoms of eukaryotes. Shown here: typical plant representatives in intermediate communities.

CLIMAX COMMUNITY

Longer-living, larger species outcompete the initial colonizers and persist as a stable and self-sustaining community.

1 Fungi, bacteria, lichens, and seeds are often among the earliest colonizers.

2 Mosses begin to grow and trap moisture, allowing the seeds of other plants to germinate.

3 Small herbs arrive and shrubs grow, shading out the mosses and herbs.

4 Small trees grow and outcompete the shrubs.

5 Taller, faster-growing trees outcompete the smaller trees.

PRIMARY SUCCESSION
Primary succession begins after a disturbance leaves an area barren of soil and with no life.

SECONDARY SUCCESSION
Secondary succession is like primary succession with a head start. It begins when a disturbance opens up part of a community to the development and growth of species previously outcompeted by other species in the area.

Disturbance is a fundamental part of most ecosystems and can repeatedly set a community back to an earlier stage of succession.

FIGURE 15-30 The species composition of a community changes over time.

- And the first trees generally are outcompeted by taller, faster-growing trees.

An important feature of the colonizers seen in the earliest stages of primary succession—whether plants, animals, or other species—is that while they are good **dispersers,** able to move away from their original home (hence their early arrival in a newly available locale), they are not particularly good *competitors.* That's why they are gradually replaced.

Ultimately, it is the longer-living, larger species that tend to outcompete the initial colonizers and persist within a stable and self-sustaining community, called a **climax community.** The particular species present in the climax community depend on physical factors such as temperature and rainfall.

Secondary succession Secondary succession is much faster than primary succession, because life and soil are already present. Rather than the thousands or even tens of thousands of years that primary succession may take, secondary succession can happen in a matter of centuries, decades, or even years. It frequently begins with organisms colonizing the decaying remains of dead organisms. This may involve fungi

Why doesn't succession occur on front lawns?

establishing themselves in the decaying trunk of a fallen tree, and these being replaced over time by different species of fungi.

Or secondary succession may begin with weeds springing up in formerly cultivated land. If the weeds are allowed to grow, they are eventually outcompeted and replaced by perennial species, and then shrubs, and eventually larger trees. The process is similar to primary succession, but with a head start. Ultimately, if undisturbed, secondary succession also leads to establishment of a stable, self-sustaining climax community.

Given that primary and secondary succession both progress toward climax communities, it might seem surprising that, at any given time, so many communities are in states far from climax. This paradox reflects the fact that succession leads to climax communities in the *absence of disturbance.* But disturbance is a fundamental part of most ecosystems. Massive disturbances, such as the fires that destroyed a third of Yellowstone Park in 1988 or the volcanic eruptions of Mount St. Helens, can send a community back to square one. Minor disturbances, on the other hand, may undo just a small degree of the succession that has already occurred. Interestingly, it is at intermediate levels of disturbance that communities tend to support the greatest number of species. With very high or very low disturbance levels, the community is restricted to the top colonizers—those with the best dispersal or fastest reproductive rates—or the top competitors, respectively. At the intermediate level, a larger variety of species with intermediate combinations of features can persist.

TAKE-HOME MESSAGE 15·15

Succession is the change in the species composition of a community over time, following a disturbance. In primary succession, the process begins in an area with no life and no soil; in secondary succession, the process occurs in an area where life is already present. In both types, the process usually takes place in a predictable sequence.

15·16 Some species are more important than others within a community.

Not all species are created equal. In this chapter, we have examined the ways in which species interact with one other and with their habitats, noting the dependence of species on each other. But not all species have equal dependence on or

influence over others. Within a community, the presence of some species, called **keystone species,** greatly influences which other species are present and which are not (**FIGURE 15-31**). That is, if a keystone species is removed, the species

KEYSTONE SPECIES

A keystone species, such as the sea star, has an unusually large influence on the presence or absence of numerous other species in the community.

COMMUNITY WITH KEYSTONE SPECIES

COMMUNITY WITH KEYSTONE SPECIES REMOVED

When sea stars were removed from an intertidal zone, species diversity decreased drastically—only mussels remained.

Preserving just one keystone species has the effect of preserving many additional species at the same time.

FIGURE 15-31 Preserving biodiversity. Keystone species can keep aggressive species in check, allowing more species to coexist.

mix in the community changes dramatically. The removal of other species, conversely, causes relatively little change.

Bison are a keystone species. Experiments were set up in which a herd of bison was allowed to graze in certain parts of a prairie in Kansas, while being excluded from other areas. The areas without the bison were soon dominated by a single species of tall grass. The grass was like a bully to other plant species. The areas where the bison grazed, on the other hand, had significantly greater species diversity. When kept in check by the grazing bison, the bully grass was unable to outcompete the other plant species, which were able to thrive.

Sea stars, too, are a keystone species (see Figure 15-31). On the rocky seashores of the Pacific Northwest, they consume mussels, which tend to crowd out other species. In a five-year study, sea stars were removed and kept out of certain areas of the intertidal zone but allowed in other areas. As with the bison study, species diversity dropped dramatically where sea stars were excluded. In fact, ultimately, just the mussels remained. In the areas with sea stars, mussels also remained but in reduced numbers. More important, 28 other species of animals and algae were also able to live there.

Suppose you are in charge of conserving biodiversity in a large region of a country. With limited funds, you cannot simply purchase and restrict access to the entire region. It

Q When it comes to conservation, are some species more valuable than others? Why?

is not possible to preserve everything. Instead, you must make difficult decisions and prioritize species for preservation. Knowing that keystone species exist can make your job considerably easier. There is real practical value in identifying keystone species and focusing conservation efforts on these. After all, in the sea star experiment, preservation of the sea stars alone would have the "side effect" of preserving 28 other species.

Keystone species make it possible to get more "bang for your buck" when your aim is to conserve biodiversity. Consequently, identifying keystone species is an important part of conservation biology. Besides bison and sea stars, some other keystone species are dam-building beavers, elephants of the African savanna, and lichens in the desert. We'll explore these questions of conservation in greater detail in the next chapter.

TAKE-HOME MESSAGE 15·16

Keystone species have a relatively large influence on which other species are present in a community and which are not. Unlike other species, when a keystone species is removed from the community, the species mix changes dramatically. For this reason, preserving keystone species is an important strategy in preserving biodiversity.

LIFE IN THE DEAD ZONE

In boosting plant productivity on farms, we've created a "dead zone" in the Gulf of Mexico bigger than the size of Connecticut.

In the water at the mouth of the Mississippi River, each spring and summer, there is so little oxygen that virtually no life can survive.

Q: WHICH CHEMICAL ALMOST ALWAYS LIMITS PLANT GROWTH? Plant growth requires the production of proteins, all of which contain nitrogen. Access to nitrogen nearly always determines how much a plant grows.

Q: IF YOU'RE A FARMER, HOW CAN YOU INCREASE THE PRODUCTIVITY OF YOUR CROPS? Add nitrogen. This, in fact, is the chief component of all plant fertilizers.

Q: WHERE DOES THE UNUSED NITROGEN END UP? Spring and summer rains wash nutrients, dissolved organic materials, and other runoff (much of which comes from human sources) from the middle of the United States into nearby rivers and thus, eventually, into the Mississippi River. From there they flow into the Gulf of Mexico.

Q: WHAT HAPPENS WHEN LARGE AMOUNTS OF NITROGEN ARE DUMPED INTO A BODY OF WATER? Organisms such as plankton and algae living near the mouth of the Mississippi grow like crazy with all the extra nitrogen and nutrients that are washed into the Gulf of Mexico. But the rapid increase in their productivity disrupts the food chain as they decay, increasing the organic matter that sinks to the bottom and feeds the bacteria there. As the bacteria thrive, they consume ever-increasing amounts of oxygen.

Q: WHAT HAPPENS WHEN BACTERIA USE UP TOO MUCH OXYGEN? Excessive bacterial growth depletes the supply of dissolved oxygen in the water, starving all other life of oxygen—including fish, crabs, oysters, and shrimp, all of which die or move out of the area. This creates a "dead zone" and ruins local fisheries, with significant impact on the economies they support.

Q: WHAT CAN YOU CONCLUDE? Disrupting food chains, even increasing the productivity of certain trophic levels, can have unintended effects throughout an ecosystem, and even thousands of miles away.

Q: WHAT CAN BE DONE? Reducing and reversing the Gulf of Mexico's dead zone (and other dead zones throughout the world) can be accomplished by (1) reducing fertilizer use, (2) preventing animal wastes from getting into waterways, and (3) controlling the release of other sources of nutrients (phosphorus as well as nitrogen) from industrial facilities into rivers and streams.

Big Ideas in ...
Ecosystems and Communities

15·1–15·2 Ecosystems have living and non-living components.

- Ecosystems are the living organisms and the physical environment within specific areas.
- The largest ecosystems in the world are called biomes.
- The characteristic organisms and physical features present in each terrestrial biome depend largely on the temperature and rainfall patterns.

15·3–15·5 Interacting physical forces create weather.

- The greater amount of solar energy hitting earth at the equator causes global air circulation patterns that are responsible for heavy rainfall near the equator and deserts at 30° latitude, north and south.
- Global patterns of ocean circulation also influence patterns of temperature and rainfall.
- Local topography, from mountain ranges to human-made structures, can also influence rainfall, temperature, and wind patterns.

15·6–15·8 Energy and chemicals flow within ecosystems.

- Energy pyramids describe the energy flow through ecosystems, from primary producers to herbivores to carnivores.
- At each step of the food chain, energy capture and conversion are inefficient, with only 10% of energy transferred from one trophic level to the next.
- While all energy comes from the sun and flows in a pathway through food chains, chemicals repeatedly cycle from the physical environment through living organisms and back into the environment.

15·9–15·14 Species interactions influence the structure of communities.

- Interacting species in a community coevolve in a variety of ways, some antagonistic and others mutually beneficial.
- The organisms of a population fill a unique niche, defined by how they utilize the resources in their environment.
- Organisms with overlapping niches compete until character displacement or local extinction occurs.

15·15–15·16 Communities can change or remain stable over time.

- Most communities change over time. The patterns of succession, in which species composition changes within an ecosystem, depend on the rate and magnitude of disturbances.
- In a community, species vary in the degree to which they influence diversity. Keystone species are the most influential.

See the To-Go Guide (packaged with every new copy of this textbook) for an illustrated summary of the chapter.

Check Your Knowledge

GRAPHIC CONTENT
Thinking critically about visual displays of data.

1. Why is the drawing of the hawk so much smaller than those of the other organisms?

2. What does the size of each "pie" represent? Why aren't they all the same size?

3. What does the slice of the pie represent in each drawing?

4. Why isn't there a slice taken from the top pie?

5. Would this figure be different if it included data from consumers that ate both plants and other animals? How?

6. What can you conclude from this figure about the relative numbers of predators vs. herbivores in any environment?

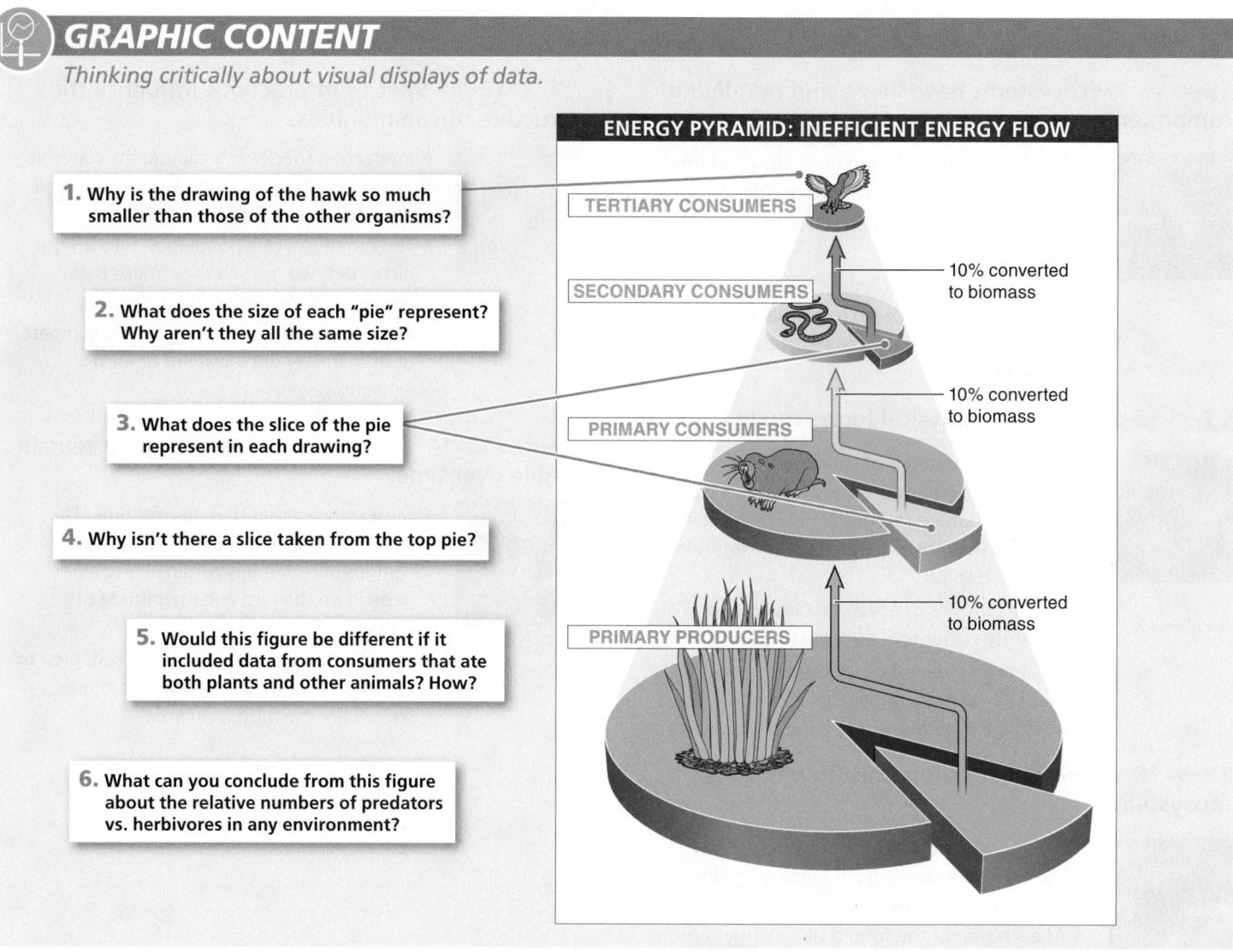

ENERGY PYRAMID: INEFFICIENT ENERGY FLOW

TERTIARY CONSUMERS

SECONDARY CONSUMERS — 10% converted to biomass

PRIMARY CONSUMERS — 10% converted to biomass

PRIMARY PRODUCERS — 10% converted to biomass

See Answers at the back of the book.

Key Terms in Ecosystems and Communities

abiotic, p. 585
behavioral defense, p. 607
biomass, p. 596
biome, p. 586
biotic, p. 585
carnivore, p. 594
character displacement, p. 604
climax community, p. 613
coevolution, p. 602
colonizer, p. 613
commensalism, p. 611

community, p. 585
competitive exclusion, p. 604
decomposer, p. 595
desert, p. 587
detritivore, p. 595
disperser, p. 613
ecosystem, p. 584
El Niño, p. 592
energy pyramid, p. 596
estuary, p. 587
eutrophication, p. 601
food chain, p. 595

food web, p. 595
fundamental niche, p. 603
habitat, p. 585
herbivore, p. 594
host, p. 609
keystone species, p. 614
La Niña, p. 593
mimicry, p. 607
mutualism, p. 611
niche, p. 603
omnivore, p. 595
parasite, p. 609

parasitism, p. 609
physical defense, p. 606
predation, p. 605
primary consumer, p. 594
primary producer, p. 587
primary productivity, p. 587
rain shadow, p. 591
realized niche, p. 603
resource partitioning, p. 604
savanna, p. 587
secondary consumer, p. 594

succession, p. 613
temperate grassland, p. 587
tertiary consumer, p. 594
topography, p. 590
trophic level, p. 594
tropical rain forest, p. 587
tropical seasonal forest, p. 587

Multiple-Choice Questions

1. **An ecosystem consists of _____ in a given area.**
   a) all the photosynthetic organisms
   b) all the living organisms
   c) all the abiotic factors that influence living organisms
   d) all the living organisms and non-living materials
   e) the plant life and climate

   100 HARD
   17
   0 EASY

2. **Earth's largest terrestrial ecosystems, the biomes, are defined primarily by:**
   a) the average rainfall.
   b) the average temperature.
   c) the seasonal variability in temperature.
   d) the seasonal variability in rainfall.
   e) All of the above.

   100 HARD
   0 **11** EASY

3. **Why is it hotter at the equator than at the Poles?**
   a) The angle at which sunlight hits the earth leads to a given amount of solar energy being spread over a smaller area at the equator than at the Poles.
   b) The increased rotational speed of the earth at the Poles creates strong winds that increase radiant cooling.
   c) Greater cloud cover at the equator leads to a greater "greenhouse" effect than at the Poles.
   d) The water in the oceans has a high heat capacity, and there is significantly more water near the equator than at the Poles.
   e) All of the above are responsible for the higher average temperature at the equator than at the Poles.

   100 HARD
   23
   0 EASY

4. **Why do beaches on the west coast of the United States have colder water than beaches on the east coast?**
   a) The ocean currents in the northern hemisphere rotate in a clockwise direction, so water off the coast of California has just come from the cold north, while water off the coast of New York has just come from the warm south.
   b) West coast beaches are not colder than east coast beaches. Ocean temperatures depend only on latitude.
   c) The Pacific Ocean is deeper than the Atlantic Ocean, so more of the sun's heat is absorbed by the colder, deep water, reducing the water temperature at the west coast beaches.
   d) Trade winds blowing north from the Tropic of Cancer in the Pacific Ocean sweep the warm air away from the west coast, taking with it much of the warmth of the water.
   e) Deep water upwellings bring cool water to the west coast beaches, while the surface currents on the east coast cause downwellings, sending warm surface water to depths where it is less likely to be lost through evaporation.

   100 HARD
   27
   0 EASY

5. **When moist wind from an ocean blows onshore toward a mountain range:**
   a) as the air rises, it pulls moisture from the ground, causing the higher elevations to be drier.
   b) as the air goes over the top of the mountain and falls back down toward lower elevations, it holds less moisture, creating a "rain shadow" zone of unusually high precipitation.
   c) as the air rises, it holds less moisture, causing the dissipation of all clouds.
   d) as the moist air goes over the top of the mountain and falls back down toward lower elevations, it holds even more moisture, creating a "rain shadow" desert with very little precipitation.
   e) None of the above are correct.

   100 HARD
   42
   0 EASY

6. **"Top" carnivores:**
   a) are more common than secondary consumers.
   b) rely directly on primary producers for energy.
   c) consume primarily herbivores.
   d) consume primarily carnivores.
   e) rely on symbiotic bacteria living in their digestive systems to help digest cellulose.

   100 HARD
   26
   0 EASY

7. The 10% rule of energy-conversion efficiency:

a) explains why big, fierce animals are so rare.

b) explains why the biomass of herbivores must exceed that of carnivores.

c) limits the length of food chains.

d) suggests that 90% of what an organisms eats is used in cellular respiration or is lost as feces.

e) All of the above are correct.

8. Nitrogen enters the food chain:

a) primarily through soil-dwelling bacteria that "fix" nitrogen by attaching it to other atoms.

b) from the atmosphere when "fixed" by the photosynthetic machinery of plants.

c) when rocks dissolved by rainwater become soil, which is then utilized for plant growth.

d) through soil erosion followed by runoff into streams and ponds.

e) through methane, produced by herbivores as a by-product of the breakdown of plant material.

9. Which of the following statements about an organism's niche is incorrect?

a) It encompasses the space the organism requires.

b) It includes the type and amount of food the organism consumes.

c) It is not always fully exploited.

d) It may be occupied by two species, as long as they are not competitors.

e) It reflects the ways in which the organism utilizes the resources of its environment.

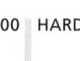

10. The "ghost of competition past" refers to the fact that:

a) competition often leads to character displacement, which remains even after direct competition is reduced.

b) competition cannot be seen in nature.

c) competition inevitably leads to the extinction of one of the competitors.

d) competition inevitably leads to the extinction of both competitors.

e) the fossil record is a record of competitive interactions.

11. Chemical defenses are more common among plants than animals because:

a) plants cannot move to escape predators and so must develop other deterrents.

b) the cell wall can contain the chemicals more effectively than a simple plasma membrane.

c) mechanical defenses against predators can evolve only in animals.

d) parasite loads are significantly higher in plants than in animals.

e) All of the above are correct.

12. Rabid animals:

a) froth at the mouth so as to increase the likelihood that the rabies-causing virus is passed on to another host.

b) have been infected by parasitic bacteria.

c) must die before their host can be passed on.

d) are infected by a viral ectoparasite.

e) often show reduced aggression, which increases their ability to get closer to other animals, thereby spreading the infection.

13. In a commensal relationship:

a) one species pollinates the other.

b) neither species benefits or is harmed, but the community itself benefits.

c) one species provides nutrients, usually cellulose, for the other.

d) one species benefits while the other neither benefits nor is harmed.

e) the "loser" has reduced reproductive output.

14. Coevolution:

a) is responsible for all the beautiful flowers in the world.

b) is responsible for nectar production by plants.

c) reveals that both biotic and abiotic resources can serve as selective forces.

d) can produce an insect with a tongue as long as its body.

e) All of the above are correct.

15. The chief difference between primary and secondary succession is that:

a) primary succession occurs among the plants in a habitat, whereas secondary succession occurs among the animals.

b) primary succession begins with no life or soil, whereas secondary succession begins with both.

c) secondary succession alters the biotic environment, and primary succession alters the abiotic environment.

d) primary succession occurs more quickly than secondary succession.

e) primary succession can occur in terrestrial and aquatic habitats, but secondary succession can occur only in terrestrial habitats.

16. **Keystone species:**

a) occur only in intertidal zones.

b) play an unusually important role in determining the species composition in a habitat.

c) can be removed from a habitat without any impact on the remaining species in the community.

d) are primary producers and therefore usually are plants.

e) are more expendable than commensal species, from a conservation perspective.

100 | HARD

0 | **11** | EASY

Short-Answer Questions

1. What changes in climate occur on moving from the equator toward the Poles? Which two aspects of weather determine the type of biome found at any location?

2. Describe the energy flow that occurs through an ecosystem. How does this energy flow influence the number of top carnivores?

3. What is a niche? What is the potential fate of two species that occupy the same niche?

See Answers at the back of the book.
For additional study questions, go to www.prep-u.com.

ABOUT THE CHAPTER OPENING PHOTO

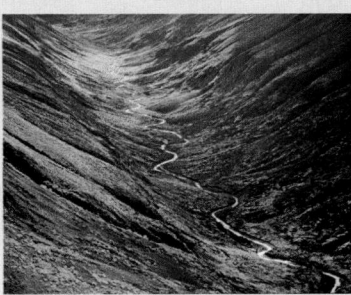

The fall colors in Wrangell-St. Elias National Park, Alaska. At more than 20,000 square miles, Wrangell-St. Elias is the largest national park in the United States and includes 9 of the 16 highest peaks in the United States, as well as an active volcano, glaciers, and the largest subpolar ice field in North America.

Human influences
on the environment

16

Conservation and Biodiversity

Baobab trees along a dirt road in Madagascar.

16·1–16·4
Measuring and defining biodiversity is complex.

16·1

Biodiversity benefits humans in many ways.

In the Pacific Northwest of the United States, a medium-size tree grows. This conifer, the Pacific yew tree (*Taxus brevifolia*), isn't the biggest tree in the forest, nor is it the most common. It's not the sort of tree that usually warrants attention in a textbook. But within the bark of the Pacific yew there is a chemical, called taxol, that has some important properties—it acts as an anti-cancer agent, interfering with the division of cells that come into contact with it (**FIGURE 16-1**). The role taxol plays for the Pacific yew is not clear; it may reduce the rate at which other organisms feed on the plant. But in humans, taxol is effective in the treatment of ovarian cancer, breast cancer, and lung cancer (generating more than $1 billion a year in pharmaceutical sales).

Consider also the following:

- The chemicals vinblastine and vincristine, isolated from the Madagascar periwinkle (*Catharanthus roseus*), are so effective in treating leukemia and Hodgkin's lymphoma that both diseases, formerly incurable, now are curable in the vast majority of people.

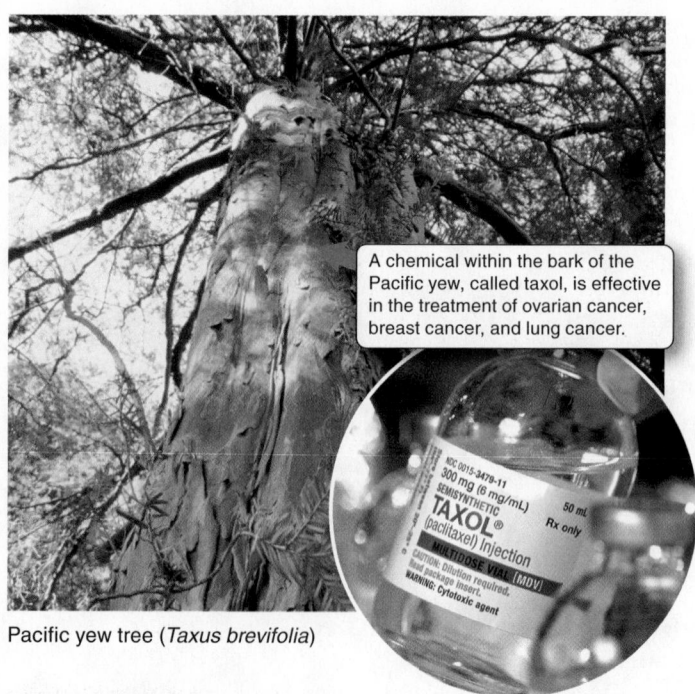

A chemical within the bark of the Pacific yew, called taxol, is effective in the treatment of ovarian cancer, breast cancer, and lung cancer.

Pacific yew tree (*Taxus brevifolia*)

FIGURE 16-1 Taxol is cancer medicine derived from a tree.

- The chemical ancrod, found only in the Malayan pit viper (*Agkistrodon rhodostoma*), dissolves blood clots and is effective in treating some heart attack and stroke patients.

- Epibatidine, a poisonous compound in the saliva of a small frog (*Epipedobates tricolor*) that lives in Ecuador, is 200 times more effective than morphine in relieving pain and is non-addictive.

These are just a few examples—there are many, many more—illustrating that medically important compounds often come from some unlikely organisms living in locations around the world. Usually, toxin production evolved in these organisms as a method of protecting them from other organisms. Co-opting the chemicals for human use reveals that one important value of biodiversity is as a sort of universal medicine cabinet.

But the beneficial effects of the world's biodiversity aren't limited to disease-fighting chemicals from plants and animals. This has been particularly apparent in the Gulf of Mexico during 2010 and 2011. In April of 2010, an explosion on a floating oil rig that was drilling a well about a mile under the surface of the water caused a massive leak of crude oil (**FIGURE 16-2**). Initially gushing oil at a rate of more than 2.5 million gallons per day, the well released more than 200 million gallons of oil into the Gulf over the almost three months it took to cap the well.

The oil spill caused extensive damage to the coastal and marine environments and was responsible for killing

Researchers believe that bacteria are responsible for the faster-than-expected "mopping up" of large amounts of oil and methane released in the 2010 Gulf of Mexico oil spill.

FIGURE 16-2 Can bacteria help clean up an oil spill?

thousands of animals, including birds, dolphins, sea turtles, mollusks, and crustaceans. The longer-term consequences of the oil spill for the region—including the eight U.S. national parks threatened—are not yet clear. One bit of good news, however, came to light as scientists began asking the question: where will the oil go? Reporting in the journal *Science,* researchers using sensors at 207 locations in the Gulf were surprised to find huge regions in which the large amounts of methane released in the spill were basically gone. Oxygen levels in these regions were also very low, suggesting that bacteria in those areas—which use oxygen when consuming methane—were responsible for the rapid "mopping up" of the methane. Fragments of methane-consuming bacteria found by the researchers supported their hypothesis.

Additionally, other researchers taking samples from deepwater sites throughout the area of the spill found high concentrations of microbes (including some never before described), related to several previously observed oil-eating bacterial species. The significant drop in oxygen saturation of the water (down from 67% to 59%) suggested that the bacteria were consuming the oil more rapidly than anyone had initially expected. The researchers believe that, because the bacteria were already present in the Gulf, feeding on the slow, natural seepage of oil from the ocean bottom, they were able to respond quickly to the spill. Nonetheless, not all scientists agree with the analyses suggesting rapid bacterial consumption of the oil, and the research is continuing.

On other fronts, *Brocadia anammoxidans* is another bacterial species that may turn out to have great value to humans. This species is able to break down an important component of human waste and, more important, it can do so without oxygen. For this reason, when treating human waste with *B. anammoxidans,* it is unnecessary to aerate the sewage sludge. Normal waste treatment utilizes bacteria that need oxygen and, consequently, it requires costly, power-hungry equipment. Still other bacteria, with sulfur-metabolizing properties, are now being used to remove the stench of sewage. In these cases, as with the medicines and oil cleanups described above, the value of biodiversity to humans is utilitarian: from other species we can obtain products or make use of processes that make our lives better.

These are just a few examples of how humans use the chemicals produced naturally by plants and animals, and sometimes whole organisms themselves, in various human enterprises.

Biodiversity is the variety of genes, species, and ecosystems on earth. And, as we've seen from these examples, there is

UTILITARIAN VALUE
Biodiversity can provide materials or processes that make our lives better.

AESTHETIC VALUE
Biodiversity can be beautiful to look at and pleasant to experience.

SYMBOLIC VALUE
Biodiversity can provide imagery that conveys meaningful abstract ideas.

NATURALISTIC VALUE
Biodiversity can provide the satisfaction that comes from direct contact with nature.

FIGURE 16-3 Biodiversity has value to humans in many different ways.

tremendous value that can come from earth's biodiversity, and it often comes from unexpected places. For these reasons, the loss of biodiversity—including genes, species, and ecosystems—can be hugely detrimental to humans.

But viewing the value of biodiversity only in the context of our abilities to extract medicines or to better process the messes we make—the utilitarian view—is to take much too narrow a view. Biodiversity provides significant, perhaps less tangible, benefits by helping regulate the climate, in the form of trees that both create shade and take up carbon dioxide from the atmosphere. Biodiversity also benefits humans in numerous other ways that are difficult to quantify, but are no less valuable than medicinal plants and oil- and sludge-eating bacteria (**FIGURE 16-3**):

- *Aesthetic value.* We think of a field of flowers or a deer in the woods as beautiful to look at and pleasant to experience.

- *Symbolic value.* Humans are so connected to the natural world that images of animals and plants can convey meaningful abstract ideas: the dove as a symbol of peace; the oak as a symbol of strength; the butterfly as a symbol of transformation; the owl as a symbol of wisdom; the rose as a symbol of love.

- *Naturalistic value.* People can get great strength, solace, and satisfaction from direct contact with nature,

including the sense of awe and fascination that can come from gaining an understanding of nature's complexity and diversity.

When we recognize that people can view the same object (or organism) and value it in different ways, we are on our way to making wiser conservation decisions. This knowledge, for example, can help us anticipate potential conflict when it comes time to invest limited conservation resources in the conservation of biodiversity, and can help us seek out methods for balancing conflicting desires. We explore some strategies for making these difficult decisions later in this chapter. First, we investigate the question of where the greatest amounts of biodiversity are to be found.

TAKE-HOME MESSAGE 16·1

Biodiversity—the variety of genes, species, and ecosystems on earth—provides significant benefits to humans in numerous utilitarian ways, such as the production of medicines and other products and processes. Biodiversity also provides important value to humans in less tangible ways, including aesthetic, symbolic, and naturalistic values.

16·2 Biodiversity is not easily defined.

Which habitat has greater biodiversity, one with 3 or 4 species each of birds, reptiles, mammals, plants, and insects, or one with 38 unique species of fruit flies, or one with 100 radically different species of prokaryotes? This question illustrates that it's not always clear exactly what a person means when using the term "biodiversity." In the media, discussions make it appear that there is a consensus on what biodiversity means, but there isn't.

All definitions of biodiversity refer, in a general sense, to the variety of living organisms on earth, and most reflect that biodiversity can be considered at multiple levels, from entire ecosystems to species to genes and alleles (**FIGURE 16-4**). Defining biodiversity as the variety of genes, species, and ecosystems on earth, however, is not sufficiently practical. Cataloguing all the genes in all species is not practical. And counting (or even identifying) all species is also impractical (and likely impossible). Similarly, it is difficult to determine where one ecosystem ends and another begins.

And so, returning to our original question: If you were given the task of overseeing the conservation of biodiversity in a region where these three habitats occur, which habitat would you protect first? In making your decision, you might first define biodiversity—maybe as the number of different classes or families of organisms in a habitat, or maybe as the number of distinct species in the habitat, which is, in fact, the most commonly used definition of biodiversity—to support your decision. In doing so, however, you are acknowledging that biodiversity can be defined in many ways and that the definition is not completely objective. Rather, it is a function of your values, biases, and interests. But this recognition helps us to discuss, manage, use, and conserve biodiversity in a practical and more productive manner.

Conservation biology is the interdisciplinary field that addresses how to understand and preserve the natural biological resources of earth, including its biodiversity at all levels (**FIGURE 16-5**). For this reason, the complexities of defining biodiversity directly affect the decisions that conservation biologists make. In this chapter, we explore how the actions of humans can have significant, even disastrous, consequences for biodiversity and natural resources, and we also explore the strategies that have been developed for effective conservation.

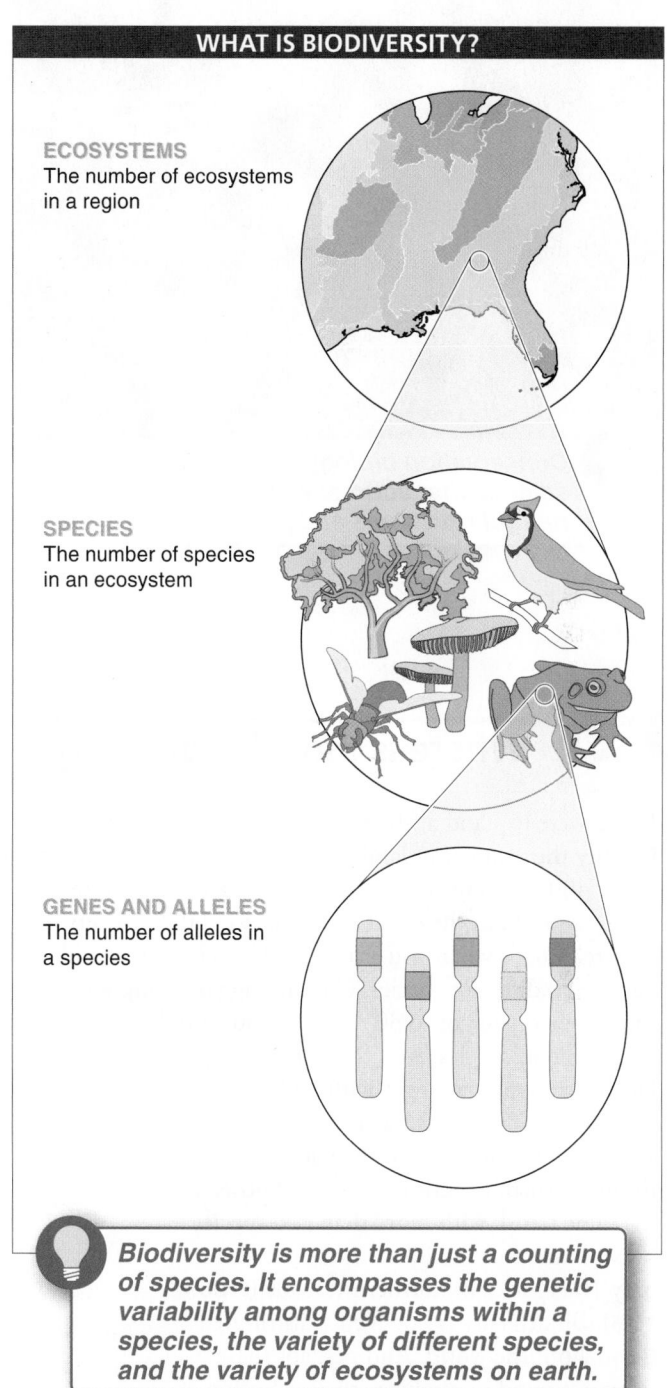

WHAT IS BIODIVERSITY?

ECOSYSTEMS
The number of ecosystems in a region

SPECIES
The number of species in an ecosystem

GENES AND ALLELES
The number of alleles in a species

Biodiversity is more than just a counting of species. It encompasses the genetic variability among organisms within a species, the variety of different species, and the variety of ecosystems on earth.

FIGURE 16-4 Biodiversity is found on many different scales.

FIGURE 16-5 Preserving the earth's natural resources.

Conservation biology is a multidisciplinary science that addresses how to preserve natural resources and protect biodiversity.

Underpinning many of the difficulties in conservation biology is that biodiversity, as we've noted, can have value for humans in so many different ways. Throughout the chapter, we'll see how that complexity makes it difficult to balance competing interests when they are in conflict.

TAKE-HOME MESSAGE 16·2

Defining biodiversity is difficult because it can be considered at multiple levels, from entire ecosystems to species to genes and alleles. In practice, it is most often defined as the number of distinct species in a habitat, which has important implications for conservation biology—the field that addresses questions of how to preserve the natural resources of earth.

16·3

Where is most biodiversity?

If you were to stand at the equator in South America and identify the number of land mammals, you would count about 400 different species. If you then started walking south, away from the equator, and assessed the diversity of land mammals when you got to 20° latitude, you would find about 350 different species. Continuing your long walk south, when you got to 30° latitude you would find only 200 different species. And the trend would continue for as far south as you could go, with 100 species at 40° latitude and fewer than 50 species at 50° latitude. On a similar walk north from the equator, through North America, you would observe the same trend, with more than 300 species of land mammals at 20° latitude, reduced to only 100 species in northern Canada (**FIGURE 16-6**). Biodiversity is not evenly distributed throughout the world. And perhaps the strongest trend in biodiversity distribution is just what we've described: as you move away from the equator in either direction, diversity is reduced with increasing latitude.

The strong biodiversity gradient from the tropics to the Poles occurs not just in land mammals but in

Q Why are there more species in an acre of tropical rain forest than in an acre farther from the equator, such as in a temperate forest or prairie?

nearly any group of plants or animals observed—recent surveys have documented the trend in woody plants, herbaceous plants, and mangrove trees. Interestingly, even the diversity of organisms in the oceans follows this trend. One survey of marine copepods—tiny crustacean animals, including plankton—found the same trend moving north from the tropical region of the Pacific Ocean (80 species present) to the Arctic Ocean (fewer than 10 species). Similar patterns have been documented in fishes, mollusks, marine and terrestrial arthropods, corals, and marine protists.

Numerous factors that influence species richness—that is, the number of species in an area—are responsible for producing the tropical-to-temperate-to-polar gradient in biodiversity. Three, in particular, play strong roles (**FIGURE 16-7**).

1. Solar energy available. Perhaps the simplest predictor of species diversity is the amount of solar energy available in an area. Solar energy is, after all, the fuel for all life. As we saw in Figure 15-5, the sun shines most directly

GRAPHIC CONTENT!
Thinking critically about visual displays of data.
Turn to p. 658 for a closer inspection of this figure.

WHERE IS MOST BIODIVERSITY?

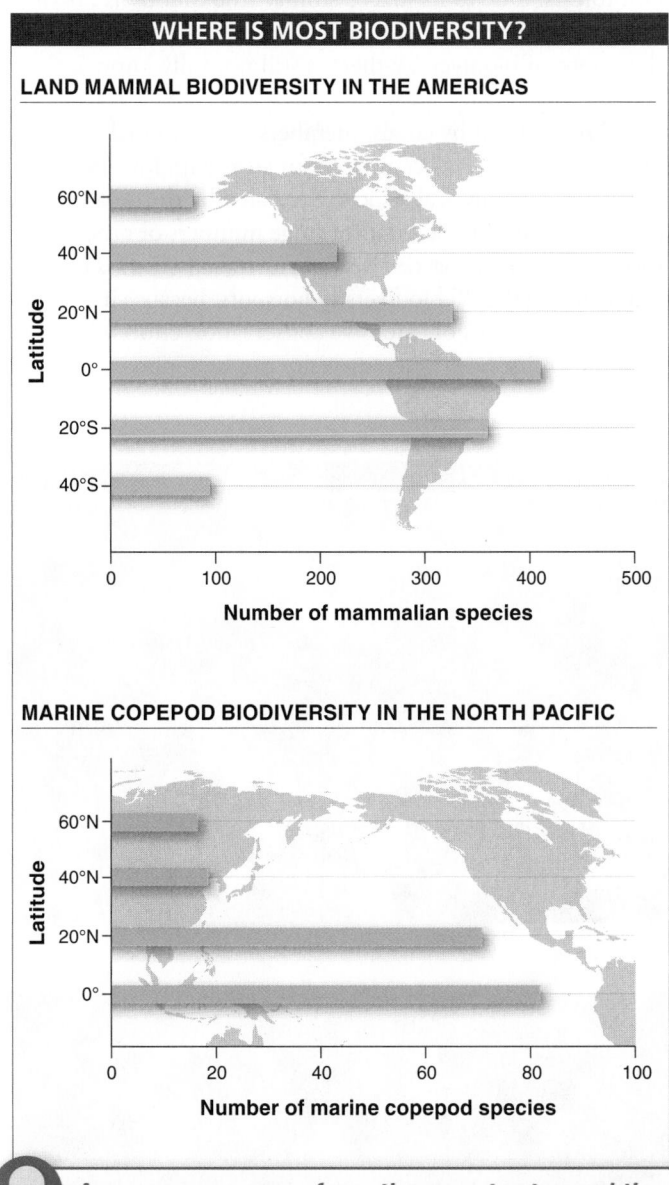

LAND MAMMAL BIODIVERSITY IN THE AMERICAS

MARINE COPEPOD BIODIVERSITY IN THE NORTH PACIFIC

> As you move away from the equator toward the Pole in either direction, biodiversity is reduced.

FIGURE 16-6 Biodiversity is unevenly distributed.

on the equator, and, as we move away from the equator, the earth's curvature causes the solar energy hitting the earth to be spread out over increasingly large areas. This leads to less solar energy at any one point as latitude increases. In a variety of species of plants and animals, researchers have documented strong relationships between energy availability and species richness.

FACTORS THAT INFLUENCE BIODIVERSITY

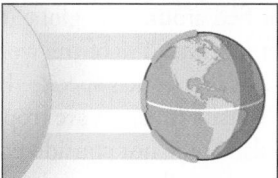

SOLAR ENERGY AVAILABLE
Greater access to solar energy, the fuel for all life, provides increased species richness.

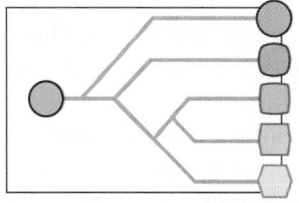

EVOLUTIONARY HISTORY OF AN AREA
Communities diversify over time. The more time that passes without a climatic event, such as an ice age, the greater the diversity in an area.

RATE OF DISTURBANCE
A habitat with an intermediate amount of disturbance tends to have the greatest species richness.

FIGURE 16-7 What determines species richness in an area?

2. Evolutionary history of an area. Communities diversify over time. Consequently, the more time that passes, generally speaking, the greater is the diversity in an area. A high level of biodiversity in an area, however, can be knocked back down by climatic disasters such as glaciations. Thus, for example, biodiversity declines due to glaciations may have disproportionately occurred in temperate and polar regions (and on the tops of some mountains), which have been affected more frequently than tropical regions as glaciers have advanced and retreated over hundreds of millions of years.

3. Rate of environmental disturbance. Over time, the best competitor for a resource is expected to outcompete other species, excluding them from the community and reducing species richness. However, communities may be kept from reaching this species-depleted state. Factors such as predation, or environmental disturbances such as floods, fires, and volcanic eruptions, which may wipe out most species in an area, can prevent any one species from excluding others. For this reason, a habitat with an *intermediate* amount of environmental disturbance is expected to have the greatest species richness.

Conservation biologists are increasingly interested in **biodiversity hotspots,** those regions of the world having significant reservoirs of biodiversity that are under threat of destruction. Twenty-five biodiversity hotspots have been identified around the globe (**FIGURE 16-8**). These hotspots cover less than 1% of the world's area, but have 20% or more of the world's species. Habitats included among the biodiversity hotspots are tropical rain forests, coral reefs, and islands. While not considered a hotspot, the deepest regions of the oceans have recently proved to hold great biodiversity.

Tropical rain forests. These habitats are common near the equator in Asia, Australia, Africa, South America, and Central America, as well as on many Pacific islands. An important, but still poorly studied, region of tropical rain forests is the canopy, the uppermost region of a forest, where nearly all of the sunlight is intercepted. The canopy (which can be up to 30 feet thick) is the most diverse part of the tropical rain forests; estimates suggest that as many as half of all species on earth reside in the canopy of tropical rain forests. Due to its inaccessibility (the canopy is 20–40 m above the ground), the canopy is not easily studied and the extent of biodiversity there is still not fully known.

Coral reefs. Built by corals, members of the animal kingdom, coral reefs occur in ocean areas with low levels of nutrients. The physical structures created by the corals provide a home and habitat for huge numbers of other species. The Great Barrier Reef of Australia (which is not listed among the 25 biodiversity hotspots, because it currently is a focus of extensive conservation efforts) is an example of just how much diversity can be supported by

BIODIVERSITY HOTSPOTS

CORAL REEFS: Philippines

TROPICAL RAIN FORESTS: Costa Rica

ISLANDS: Madagascar

FIGURE 16-8 Biodiversity hotspots are significant reservoirs of biological diversity.

 There are 25 biodiversity hotspots around the world; they cover less than 1% of the world's area, but have 20% or more of the world's species.

coral reefs. It is the largest coral reef system in the world and covers such a large area (almost the size of California) off the northeast coast of Australia that it can be seen from space. It is home to numerous species of whales, dolphins, sea turtles, sharks, and stingrays, as well as 1,500 species of fishes and 5,000 species of mollusks. Five hundred species of algae are found there, too. Above the Great Barrier Reef, more than 200 species of birds are supported by the rich diversity of life below. Other coral reefs are not as well protected by laws and conservation efforts, and the world's second largest coral reef, in New Caledonia in the southwestern Pacific, is one of the 25 biodiversity hotspots.

Islands. Because of their generally smaller size, which limits the population size of organisms living on them, islands can be regions where biodiversity is at risk. Madagascar, located in the Indian Ocean off the southeastern coast of Africa, is the fourth largest island in the world (just a bit smaller than Texas). It is home to 5% of the world's species, 80% of which are **endemic** (exclusively native to a place)—a higher percentage of endemic plants and animals than in any comparably sized area on earth. One of the 25 biodiversity hotspots, Madagascar is an area unusually rich in species diversity.

Deep oceans. The oceans that cover two-thirds of the earth's surface can be much more difficult to explore than terrestrial habitats. Deep ocean regions, in particular, are much less studied than the terrestrial parts of the world. Once thought to be completely devoid of life, the deepest regions of the oceans have recently been found to be teeming with biodiversity. One survey of the deepest parts of the Antarctic Ocean, sampling at a depth of more than 18,000 feet (6,000 m), discovered 585 new species of crustaceans alone.

TAKE-HOME MESSAGE 16·3

Biodiversity is not evenly distributed over the earth. For nearly all groups of plants and animals, both marine and terrestrial, biodiversity is greatest near the equator and progressively falls toward the North and South Poles. Factors that influence the species richness in an area include the amount of solar energy available, the area's evolutionary history, and the rate of environmental disturbance. Biodiversity hotspots are regions of significant biodiversity under threat of destruction.

16·4 Island biogeography helps us understand the maintenance and loss of biodiversity.

"Can you help me exterminate all the insects on a few islands?" In 1966, when E. O. Wilson started calling exterminators in Florida, asking them to help him put tents over several islands and then pump ethyl bromide into them to kill all of the insects, he had trouble being taken seriously. Most of the exterminators opted to pass on the job, but eventually he found one (**FIGURE 16-9**).

Why would a biologist (of all people) want to wipe out all insect life on six islands? Six years earlier, Robert MacArthur and Wilson had developed a theory, and now Wilson and one of his students, Daniel Simberloff, had an idea for a controlled experiment with which they could test the theory.

MacArthur and Wilson's theory, called the "theory of island biogeography," is an attempt to explain and predict the patterns of species diversity on islands. The theory has two fundamental components (**FIGURE 16-10**).

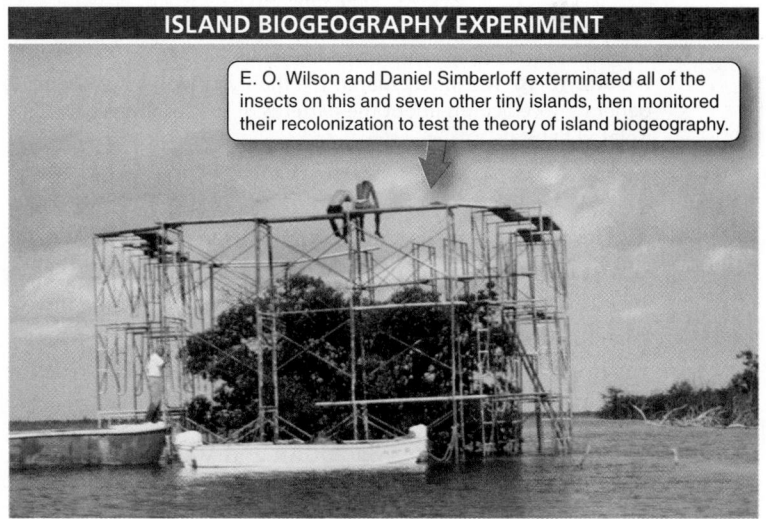

ISLAND BIOGEOGRAPHY EXPERIMENT

E. O. Wilson and Daniel Simberloff exterminated all of the insects on this and seven other tiny islands, then monitored their recolonization to test the theory of island biogeography.

FIGURE 16-9 Experiment in insect eradication and recolonization: explaining patterns of species diversity on islands.

The theory of island biogeography is designed to explain and predict patterns of species diversity on islands. It has two fundamental components:

THE AREA EFFECT
There is a close relationship between the number of species inhabiting an island and the island's area—the larger an island is, the more species it holds.

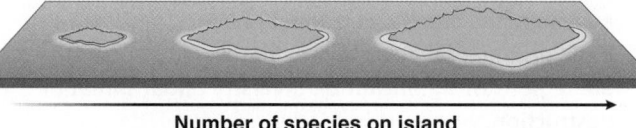

Number of species on island

THE DISTANCE EFFECT
There is a close relationship between the number of species inhabiting an island and how isolated an island is—the farther an island is from the mainland, the fewer species it holds.

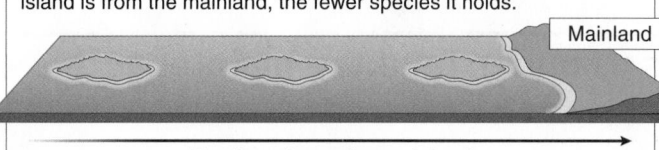

Mainland

Number of species on island

FIGURE 16-10 The lonely island. The theory of island biogeography generates predictions about the patterns of species diversity in isolated habitats.

1. The area effect. MacArthur and Wilson noted that observations of islands in the West Indies had revealed a close relationship between the number of species inhabiting an island and the island's area: the larger the island, the greater the number of species present. This relationship held true for bird species as well as plants, beetles, and snails.

2. The distance effect. MacArthur and Wilson's observations of islands in the Pacific Ocean revealed a close relationship between how isolated an island was, measured as its distance from the nearest mainland, and the number of species that inhabited the island: the farther from the mainland the island was, the fewer species it held.

1 RATE OF IMMIGRATION
Islands closer to the mainland have higher rates of immigration; the mainland serves as a pool of new species. The rate of immigration of new species to the island decreases as the number of species on the island increases.

2 RATE OF EXTINCTION
Smaller islands have higher rates of extinction than large islands (due to smaller population sizes). The rate of extinction of species on the island increases as the number of species on the island increases.

Rate of immigration

Rate of extinction

Island close to mainland

Small island

Equilibrium number

Island far from mainland

Large island

Number of species on island

3 The number of species on an island reflects a balance between immigration to the island by new species and extinction of species on the island.

Time

The composition of species on an island is not fixed; rather, it might change over time. An island might have five species of birds, but exactly which five species occur on the island may change over time.

FIGURE 16-11 Same number, but possibly different species. On islands, species composition changes over time.

From these observations, MacArthur and Wilson concluded that the number of species on an island represents a balance between the rate of immigration of new species to the island and the rate of extinction of species on the island. They proposed that the rate of immigration to an island would primarily be determined by how close the island was to the mainland, with the mainland serving as a pool of new species. And they proposed that the rate of extinction on an island would primarily be determined by the island's size: smaller islands generally support a smaller population size, making the population more vulnerable to extinction. Beyond enabling them to predict the number of species on an island, MacArthur and Wilson's theory also suggested to them that the composition of species on the island would not be fixed; rather, it might change over time. In other words, once it was "full," an island might have 10 species of birds, but exactly *which* 10 species occurred on the island could change over time (**FIGURE 16-11**).

So, in 1966, Wilson's reason for exterminating all of the insects on multiple islands was so that he could monitor the islands as they were recolonized following the exterminations. He chose the mangrove islands in the Florida Keys because they include thousands of small islands, some only yards across. He and Simberloff selected eight islands, 33–54 feet (11–18 m) in diameter. The islands varied in how far they were from the nearest mainland, with the closest just 6 feet (2 m) away and the farthest more than half a mile (1,188 m) away.

After selecting two islands as control islands, the biologists and their assistants fumigated the others, verifying that all of the insects were killed. They then surveyed the islands regularly over the next year. Here's what they found—as predicted.

1. The closer islands were recolonized more quickly than the distant islands.

2. On all of the islands, the number of insect species after fumigation returned to about the same number as before fumigation.

3. The composition of insects on each island changed over the course of the study, even on the two control islands.

The theory of island biogeography is not just about real islands—lakes and mountain tops and other geographic sites can be thought of as islands, too. The theory makes testable predictions about the biodiversity levels that occur in such areas. Perhaps most important, conservation biologists can gain insights from island biogeography into the design of nature preserves. The importance of developing nature preserves as close as possible to sources of new species, for example, is one such insight. We explore others later in this chapter, when discussing the strategies for preservation of biodiversity.

TAKE-HOME MESSAGE 16·4

The theory of island biogeography generates predictions about the patterns of species diversity in isolated habitats (including not only islands but lakes and mountain tops, too). Both the size of the habitat and its distance from a pool of new species influence the number of species present. Ideas gained from island biogeography have important implications for the development of nature preserves.

The Bengal tiger has been hunted, captured, and poisoned to near extinction.

16·5
There are multiple causes of extinction.

Imagine that you are on a deserted island. Alone. It would be hard and it would be lonely. The hope of rescue someday, however, would probably make things bearable. "Martha," a passenger pigeon living in the Cincinnati zoo in the early 1900s, found herself in a situation of this sort—minus the hope. Passenger pigeons in the wild had been completely wiped out by a combination of factors, including hunting of the birds for meat, loss of their habitat due to deforestation in North America, and possibly disease. And so, except for the small flock that Martha was part of, the species was gone. One by one, those birds died as well, and when the second-to-last passenger pigeon died in 1912, Martha was all alone. She lived for two more years, with no possibility for ever reproducing; she died on September 1, 1914 (**FIGURE 16-12**).

On average, species persist for about 10 million years, although some may last for hundreds of millions of years. An extinction occurs when all individuals in a species have died. And whether you look at biodiversity from a utilitarian, aesthetic, or symbolic perspective, extinction is a tragic loss.

As we discussed in Chapter 10, extinctions can be divided into two general categories: mass extinctions and background extinctions (**FIGURE 16-13**), which are distinguished by the numbers of species affected. A mass extinction occurs when a large proportion of species on earth are lost in a short period of time (typically less than two

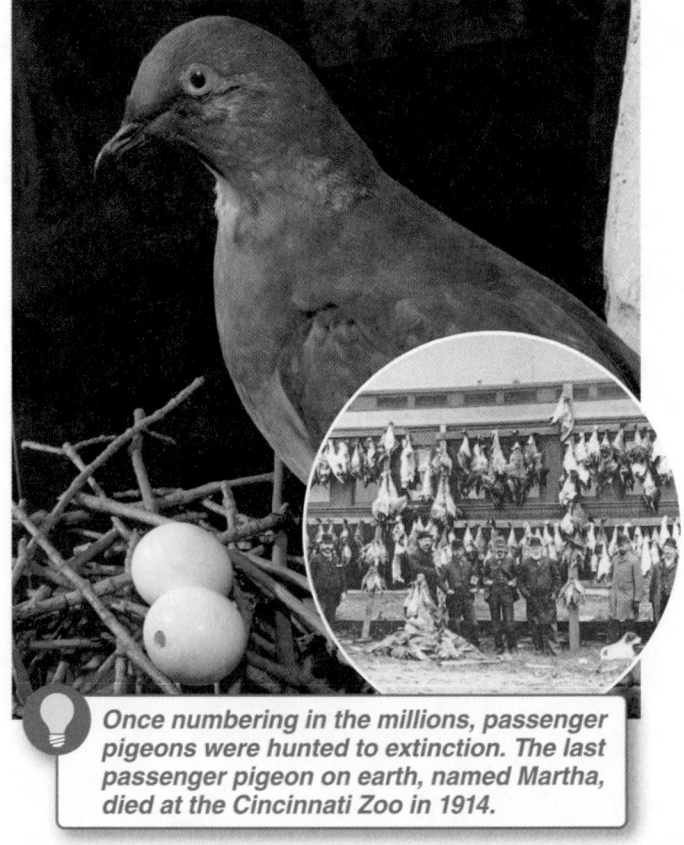

Once numbering in the millions, passenger pigeons were hunted to extinction. The last passenger pigeon on earth, named Martha, died at the Cincinnati Zoo in 1914.

FIGURE 16-12 The only way to see one today. The passenger pigeon is a species completely lost to the earth. Shown here: a stuffed passenger pigeon from the Cincinnati Zoo. *Inset:* the aftermath of a pigeon-hunting expedition; in a single day as many as 50,000 birds could be killed.

TWO CATEGORIES OF EXTINCTIONS

Extinctions generally fall into two categories:

- **MASS EXTINCTIONS**
  A large number of species (even entire families) become extinct over a short period of time due to extraordinary and sudden environmental change.

- **BACKGROUND EXTINCTIONS**
  These extinctions occur at lower rates during times other than mass extinctions.

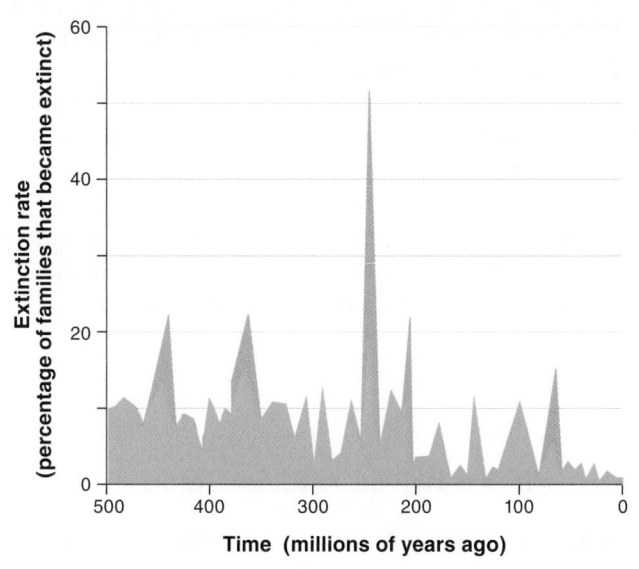

FIGURE 16-13 Background and mass extinctions.

million years, and in some cases much less)—such as when an asteroid struck earth 65 million years ago and about 75% of all species were wiped out. These extinctions are above and beyond the normal rate of extinctions that occur in any given period of time, referred to as the background extinction rate.

Q Does extinction only happen to weak, unfit species?

Both background and mass extinctions result in the same outcome for the species involved, but the causes tend to differ. In mass extinctions, the particular features of a species' biology—its biochemistry, physiology, behavior—don't play a role; rather, it's more like really bad luck. Background extinctions, by contrast, tend to be a consequence of one or more aspects of a species' biology.

For any species, there is always a risk of extinction. This risk can be larger or smaller, depending on certain features. Here we look at three important aspects of a species' biology that can influence its extinction risk (**FIGURE 16-14**).

FACTORS THAT INFLUENCE THE RISK OF BACKGROUND EXTINCTION

GEOGRAPHIC RANGE:
EXTENSIVE **vs.** RESTRICTED
Species restricted in their range are more vulnerable than those with extensive ranges.

LOCAL POPULATION SIZE:
LARGE **vs.** SMALL
Species with small population sizes are at increased risk of extinction.

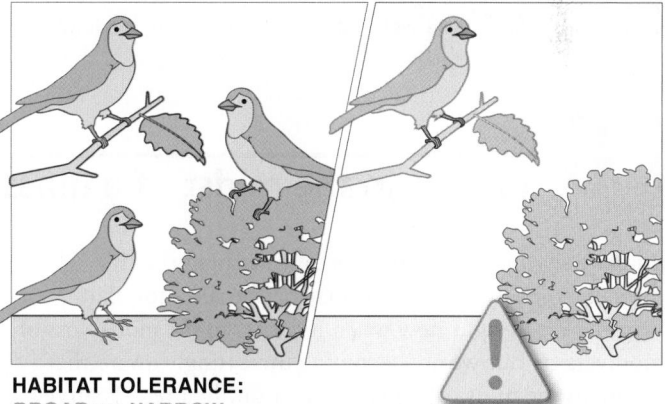

HABITAT TOLERANCE:
BROAD **vs.** NARROW
Species with narrow habitat tolerances are at greater risk of extinction than species with broader habitat tolerances.

FIGURE 16-14 Range, population size, and tolerance influence risk of extinction.

1. Geographic range: extensive versus restricted. Species restricted in their range—including those limited to small bodies of water and those confined to islands—are more vulnerable than species with extensive ranges. The Tasmanian devil is a marsupial carnivore about the size of a dog. Although these animals once thrived in Australia, they now are confined to the island of Tasmania, smaller than the state of Maine. Unable to expand their range, Tasmanian devils are more vulnerable to extinction than if their range was not limited. The house mouse, on the other hand, is found nearly everywhere in the world and so has a much lower risk of extinction.

2. Local population size: large versus small. Tigers and California condors, along with *Welwitschia,* a slow-growing, long-lived plant in southwest Africa, are examples of species that—as a consequence of their small population sizes—are at increased risk of extinction. With a small population size, a species is more susceptible to extinction due to a variety of factors that can kill individuals, including fire, diseases, habitat destruction, and predation. Put simply, the more individuals that are alive, the more likely it is that some of them will survive such events. In addition, having more individuals to breed with typically leads to greater genetic variation. When a population is small, inbreeding is increased, which generally reduces the fertility and longevity of individuals.

3. Habitat tolerance: broad versus narrow. "Habitat tolerance" describes the breadth of habitats in which a species can survive. Some plant species, for example, can tolerate large swings in water availability or soil pH or temperature. Others are limited to very narrow habitat ranges. The now-extinct passenger pigeons could only build nests in a specific type of forest and needed large numbers of individuals, breeding communally, in order to breed successfully. As forests were cut down and as the birds were hunted, the size of their flocks diminished. Their narrow habitat tolerance made them extremely vulnerable to extinction. In general, because species with narrow habitat tolerance cannot adapt in the face of habitat degradation and loss, they are at greater risk than species with broader habitat tolerance.

One species that is enormously successful, thanks to its extensive geographic range, large local population sizes, and broad habitat tolerance, is our own. Humans are growing and expanding their range at a staggering rate, consuming resources in an unprecedentedly voracious fashion. By any measure, humans are one of the most successful species in earth's history. This success, unfortunately, is having an increasingly negative effect on the species with which we share the planet, causing extinctions at a significantly higher rate than ever before. We next explore in more detail the conflict between humans' success as a species and the survival of other species.

TAKE-HOME MESSAGE 16·5

Extinctions occur for fundamentally different reasons. Mass extinctions are the result more of bad luck than of the particulars of a species' biology, including its biochemistry, physiology, and behavior. Background extinctions tend to be a consequence of one or more features of the species' biology. Small population size, limited habitat range, and narrow habitat tolerance contribute to background extinctions.

16·6 We are in the midst of a mass extinction.

Sometimes you can be so close to something that it's difficult to really see it. That may be the situation that humans are in right now when it comes to the global loss of biodiversity. But we are becoming increasingly aware that we are in the midst of a mass extinction. In a recent survey by the American Museum of Natural History, 70% of biologists indicated that they believed this is true and that steps must be taken by governments and individuals to stop this massive loss of species.

Data on current rates of extinction in every well-studied group of plants and animals support the hypothesis that a mass extinction is under way. Among the mammals, 11% of all species are currently *endangered,* under imminent threat of extinction, and 14% are *threatened,* characterized as vulnerable to extinction. Among birds, 4% of all species are endangered and 50% are in decline. Almost a third of all amphibian species are threatened. Among fishes, mollusks, insects, fungi, and plants, the story is the same.

Historically, background extinction rates are about one extinction per million species per year. Currently, as the numbers above suggest, extinction rates are 1,000 times (or more) greater than usual. It is difficult to know the exact magnitude of the problem because, as we saw in Chapter 10, biologists don't have much of an idea about

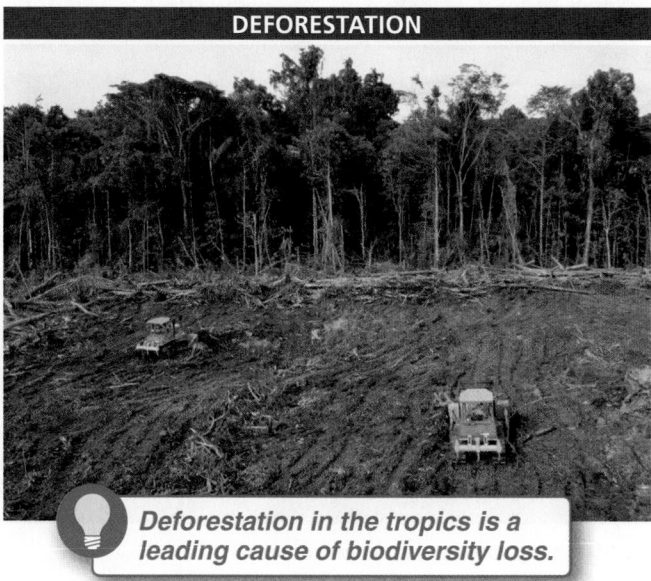

DEFORESTATION

Deforestation in the tropics is a leading cause of biodiversity loss.

FIGURE 16-15 Removing habitat through deforestation.

Bonobos, the closest living relative of humans, have been driven close to extinction, in part due to hunting.

FIGURE 16-16 Exploitation of species: the bonobo.

how many species there are on earth—the estimates range from 5 million to 100 million.

Unlike the last mass extinction event, in which the dinosaurs and most other species were wiped out in the wake of an asteroid's collision with earth, this current mass extinction seems to be the result of the activity of one species—humans. Ironically, it is the unprecedented success of humans that is responsible for this situation. The resource needs of so many people have inevitably interfered with the ability of other species to coexist with us.

The chief reason for the loss and impending loss of so many species is habitat loss and habitat degradation. Particularly harmful is habitat loss in earth's tropical rain forests, where biodiversity is greatest. In the past 25 years, half of the world's tropical rain forests have been destroyed, usually by burning to make way for agricultural use of the land or by logging (**FIGURE 16-15**). Urban development, too, is responsible for destruction of rain forests, as the growing human populations continue to expand. Intensive agriculture, livestock grazing, and the development of urban centers have led to the destruction and fragmentation of habitats worldwide.

The loss of biodiversity-supporting habitat is not restricted to the tropics. In the Pacific Northwest, as well, logging of forests has occurred at an unsustainable rate, leading to significant reductions in a diverse range of populations.

Beyond habitat loss, another factor that reduces biodiversity is overexploitation of species. Such overexploitation includes the killing of animals for food, pelts, tusks or other body parts, and medicinal products. Bonobos (*Pan paniscus*), for example, a type of chimpanzee and our closest living relatives, are almost never seen in the wild. As a consequence of habitat loss and their exploitation as a source of food in parts of central Africa, they have been driven to near extinction (**FIGURE 16-16**). And, as we'll see later in this chapter, the introduction of exotic species into habitats where they would not naturally occur is also having a significantly adverse effect on biodiversity. Consequences of the loss of biodiversity, beyond the values of biodiversity discussed earlier, are largely unknown, but most likely include a serious reduction in the capacity of the environment to provide clean air and water and to recover from environmental and human-induced disasters.

Later in this chapter, we discuss some strategies by which the current high rate of biodiversity loss can be reduced.

TAKE-HOME MESSAGE 16·6

Most biologists believe that we are currently in the midst of a mass extinction, that it is the result of human activities, and that it poses a serious threat to the future survival of humans.

Rain forest next to city sprawl, Rio de Janeiro, Brazil.

16·7

Some ecosystem disturbances are reversible, others are not.

When you fly over southern New England today, you look down on an undulating carpet of forest that covers hills and valleys. Roads traverse the forest, and here and there you see towns and cities or cultivated land and pastures, but most of what you see is the tops of trees.

If you could have flown over the same route 200 years ago, things would have looked very different. In the early 1800s, most of the forest in southern New England had been cleared and the land was in cultivation. Homesteads consisting of farmhouses, barns, stables, and other outbuildings were scattered across the countryside. Stone walls extended across hills and valleys, separating cropland from pastures.

Going back farther, the same flight 400 years ago would have taken you over mostly forested land. Here and there, Indian villages would have stood among cleared fields, but most of what you saw then would have looked much like what you see today.

The change from forest 400 years ago to cleared land 200 years ago was a major ecosystem disturbance, but now the area has returned to forest. Today, the stone fences found deep in the New England woods are the only obvious trace of the agricultural history of the area. The fences still snake their way up and down hills, but now they run through solid forest instead of between fields and pastures.

By the middle 1800s, New England settlers were abandoning farms on marginal land and moving west. The fields they had cultivated began a process of ecological succession that returned them to forests (see Section 15-15).

In the first year after a field is abandoned, its bare soil provides a harsh environment for plants. Sunlight blazes down, heating the ground surface and baking moisture from the soil. It takes a tough plant to sprout and grow under those conditions, but there are plants that can do it. We call those pioneering species of plants "weeds," and we see them growing in disturbed habitats—along roadsides, in vacant lots, and even in cracks in pavement.

As weeds grow and die, year after year, their organic matter enriches the soil and helps it retain moisture. And every year, the plants grow more densely so that they shade the ground surface, which no longer gets quite so hot and dry. Additional species of plants can grow in these milder conditions. These plants are taller, so they provide still more shade and the ground becomes still cooler and more moist. At this stage, the seeds of bushes and small trees can sprout. As these woody plants grow, they make the ground cool and shady enough to allow the seeds of forest trees (oak, maple, or beech) to sprout. More saplings of forest trees sprout and grow every year, and eventually they are so closely packed that little sunshine penetrates their leafy canopies to reach ground level. At this point, the forest stops changing, because the mature trees have created conditions in which only their own seeds can sprout and grow.

An ecosystem disturbance is reversible when the disturbance alters the biotic (living organisms) and abiotic (decaying

Q Once land is cultivated or developed, can it ever return to its natural state?

May 1980   September 1980   July 2011

FIGURE 16-17 The forest returning. Just two decades after an explosive eruption of Mount St. Helens, in Washington State, shrubs and small trees have returned to the plain at the foot of this active volcano.

organisms, soil, rocks) nature of the habitat, but does not result in the complete extinction of any species, so species can re-establish their populations. The example of New England forests is based on a disturbance that was caused by humans—clearing land for agriculture in the 1700s—but wind storms, forest fires, floods, and volcanic eruptions have been clearing forests throughout the history of life (**FIGURE 16-17**).

> **"**Any fool kid can step on a beetle. But all the professors in the world can't make one.**"**
> — ARTHUR SCHOPENHAUER, German philosopher
> (1788–1860)

If an ecosystem disturbance involves the complete loss of a species to extinction, however, the disturbance is irreversible. Each species is the result of a long and uninterrupted

evolutionary history, involving an interplay of random and selective forces, and producing a unique genome. Once lost, a species can never be created again (**FIGURE 16-18**). For this reason, ecosystem disturbances that involve the loss of species can have more devastating consequences than those that do not lead to extinctions, no matter how great the changes to the abiotic environment might be.

TAKE-HOME MESSAGE 16·7

An ecosystem disturbance is reversible when the disturbance does not include the complete extinction of any species, so they can re-establish their populations. An ecosystem disturbance that involves the complete loss of a species to extinction is irreversible because a species, once lost, can never be created again.

EXTINCT   EXTINCT   ENDANGERED

Tasmanian wolves   Chinese river dolphin   Blue whale

FIGURE 16-18 The end of a species.

Once lost, a species will never exist again. The blue whale—the largest animal ever to have lived on earth—is at risk of being lost forever.

16·8 Disruptions of ecosystems can be disastrous: 1. Introductions of exotic species.

In the rain and sleet of a Chicago winter, the idea of colorful birds flying about is very appealing to some people, and you might see exactly that, in the form of the monk parakeet. These small green members of the parrot family are about a foot (30 cm) from head to tail tip. And if they look out of place in Chicago, it's because they are. Monk parakeets are just one example of an **exotic species** (also called **introduced species**), which refers to species introduced by human activities, intentionally or accidentally, to areas other than the species' native range.

Native to southern South America, monk parakeets were imported to the United States as pets in the 1960s and 1970s. Some of those pet birds escaped, and free-living populations of monk parakeets now occur in 11 states across the country, including Oregon, Florida, and New York, in addition to those mentioned above, in Illinois (**FIGURE 16-19**).

The phrase "exotic species" suggests colorful birds and butterflies winging through a forest, but the ecological reality of such species can be much darker. Because although some introduced species do not cause harm to their new habitat, in many cases they can cause harm—including economic or environmental harm, or harm to human health.

Monk parakeets were imported from South America as pets. Some escaped and now make a nuisance of themselves in cities such as Chicago, where they build huge nests on utility poles, transformers, and floodlights.

FIGURE 16-19 A parakeet in the Midwest.

When species are introduced and cause harm, they are referred to as **invasive species.**

The appearance of these free-living monk parakeets in the United States was greeted with alarm because they are regarded as agricultural pests in South America. Records from the Inca civilization that flourished before Pizarro's invasion of Peru in 1532 attest to crop damage by monk parakeets. And when Charles Darwin visited Uruguay in 1833, he was told that monk parakeets attack fruit orchards and grain fields. Fortunately, the dire predictions that these parakeets would devastate crops in the United States have not been fulfilled as yet, but monk parakeets do make a nuisance of themselves in cities such as Chicago, where they build nests on utility poles, transformers, and floodlights. There is nothing delicate about a monk parakeet nest—it is a large mass of sticks and twigs, and a nest that has been soaked with rain is heavy enough to bring down wires, interrupting electrical service to entire neighborhoods.

While monk parakeets were initially introduced to the United States intentionally, in many cases exotic species introductions have been unintentional, as was the case with the brown tree snake, which reached Guam sometime before 1952 by stowing away in shipments of military equipment just after the Second World War. In either case, two characteristics, in particular, can lead to introduced species becoming harmful, invasive species (**FIGURE 16-20**).

1. Exotic species have no predators in their new habitat, so their populations may grow unchecked.

2. Native plants and animals have no mechanisms to compete with or defend themselves against invading exotic species.

Q Why should we worry about exotic species?

Guam, which lies in the middle of the South Pacific Ocean, had no native snakes and no predators specialized to eat snakes. But Guam did have a magnificent fauna of native birds that had evolved in isolation on the island for thousands of years. Because the species of birds on Guam had never experienced predation by snakes, they had no defense mechanisms against them—and brown tree snakes have eradicated most of the native species of birds. Extraordinary efforts are being made to prevent brown tree snakes from spreading to other Pacific islands, such as Hawaii. Like Guam, these islands are home to species of birds that occur

PROBLEM
Exotic species can threaten native populations.

CAUSE
Exotic species are often introduced, both accidentally and intentionally, by humans. Once introduced, these species can multiply, unchecked by predation, overwhelming competitors and irreversibly altering ecosystems.

STRATEGIES FOR SOLUTION
Better regulation and restriction of intentional introductions; better vigilance against accidental introductions

FIGURE 16-20 **Understanding exotic species.**

nowhere else in the world, and the islands have no native species of snakes and no native predators of snakes.

One current promising strategy used by the U.S. Department of Agriculture is to airdrop dead mice that have tablets of acetaminophen—the active ingredient in Tylenol—packed into them. In addition to killing live animals, brown tree snakes scavenge dead animals such as mice. And it turns out that acetaminophen interferes with the oxygen-carrying capability of the snake's hemoglobin, and a child's dose of Tylenol will kill a brown tree snake. While initial results are promising, it is too early to predict the long-term success of this program.

We don't have to look beyond the borders of the continental United States, though, to find examples of exotic species that are responsible for massive ecological shifts and economic costs. Purple loosestrife is an attractive flowering plant that is native to Eurasia. It was imported to

the United States in the 1800s as a garden plant. Once here, it rapidly escaped from cultivation and invaded wetlands in every state except Florida. It produces thousands of seeds a year, and also spreads by sending out underground stems. This aggressive growth overwhelms native grasses, sedges, and flowering plants, replacing diverse wetland communities with monocultures of loosestrife that provide poor-quality habitats for bog-dwelling insects, birds, reptiles, amphibians, and mammals (**FIGURE 16-21**).

The title of Most Destructive Invaders in North America may belong to the zebra mussels and quagga mussels. These thumbnail-size freshwater mussels are native to eastern Europe and western Asia. In the early 1800s, the mussels spread to western Europe, and they came to North America in the 1980s, after completion of the Saint Lawrence Seaway allowed oceangoing ships (which carried mussels in their ballast water) to travel from the Atlantic Ocean to the Great Lakes. Female mussels produce more than a million eggs per year, and the larvae settle on any solid surface. Sometimes they settle so thickly that they clog the intake pipes of water-treatment plants and factories and the cooling systems of power plants.

The ecological threat that zebra mussels represent is far more serious than the damage they cause to industrial facilities. The Great Lakes fisheries are based on game species (lake trout, salmon, walleye) and commercial species (whitefish, perch, herring), and they produce revenues of more than $1.5 billion annually. Most of the commercially valuable fish feed on small fish species, such as smelt, and the small fish feed on microscopic plants and animals (phytoplankton and zooplankton). Zebra and quagga mussels are exceptionally efficient at filtering phytoplankton and zooplankton from the

EXOTIC SPECIES: ACCIDENTAL INTRODUCTIONS

BROWN TREE SNAKE
Brown tree snakes, introduced to the island of Guam, have eradicated most of the native species of birds, which had never experienced predation by snakes and had not developed defense mechanisms.

PURPLE LOOSESTRIFE
Purple loosestrife, introduced to the United States as a garden plant, escaped from cultivation and has invaded wetlands in every state except Florida. The aggressive plant outgrows native grasses, sedges, and flowering plants.

ZEBRA MUSSELS
Zebra mussels, introduced to the Great Lakes, can cause damage to industrial facilities by clogging water-intake pipes. They also deplete resources available to small fish, eliminating the food supply for larger game fish.

FIGURE 16-21 **Unwanted guests.** Exotic species sometimes get into natural habitats accidentally. The results can be devastating.

Introduced to Australia to control agricultural pests, cane toad populations exploded and have become an ecological nightmare, killing indigenous snakes, lizards, birds, and even crocodiles.

FIGURE 16-22 Cane toad infestation.

water—so good that they are depleting the resources available to the small fish. Without enough food, the populations of small fish are crashing and that, in turn, is eliminating the food supply for the large game and commercial fish. The Great Lakes contain nearly one-fifth of the fresh water in the world, but this enormous ecosystem is being irreversibly degraded by just two exotic species.

One legendary pest is the cane toad. Ironically, it was initially imported into Australia to control a native sugarcane pest, the cane beetle. Unfortunately, not only were the cane toads unsuccessful at controlling the pest populations, but the cane toad populations exploded—preying on numerous species of amphibians, reptiles, mammals, and even birds— and spread throughout much of the continent. They now number more than 200 million and have become a nuisance in much of the country, as conservation workers struggle to determine how to control their numbers (FIGURE 16-22). The cane toad illustrates a common problem encountered when species are intentionally introduced, say, as a method of biologically, "naturally" controlling pests: the effects of a species on an ecosystem in which it does not naturally occur are unpredictable and often terrible.

TAKE-HOME MESSAGE 16·8

Exotic or introduced species are species intentionally or accidentally introduced into a new habitat. They are considered invasive species if they cause harm in their new habitat. Exotic species often come to be considered invasive because in a new habitat there often are no natural predators to reduce their population size and they often encounter prey that have few or no defenses. Invasive species can dominate and irreversibly alter communities and entire ecosystems.

16·9 Disruptions of ecosystems can be disastrous: 2. Acid rain and the burning of fossil fuels.

"What goes up must come down." That's a saying that applies to molecules just as much as it does to larger objects. The difference is that when molecules come down, they may not be in the same form as when they went up. In particular, some chemicals rise into the atmosphere as gases and return to earth as solutions of acid. Fog, sleet, snow, or rain—all forms of precipitation can be acidic.

We use the term "fossil fuels" to describe oil, natural gas, and coal. These substances are composed largely of carbon and hydrogen, and they form carbon dioxide (CO_2) and water (H_2O) when they burn. Although they are referred to as hydrocarbons, fossil fuels are not *pure* hydrocarbons. In addition to carbon and hydrogen, they also contain substantial quantities of other elements. In

How can normal rain be made ten times more acidic?

particular, it is the sulfur and nitrogen in fossil fuels that cause acid precipitation (FIGURE 16-23).

Q When sulfur burns, it produces the gas sulfur dioxide (SO_2), and nitrogen produces nitrogen dioxide (NO_2). These gases react with water vapor in the atmosphere to produce sulfuric acid (H_2SO_4) and nitric acid (HNO_3), and these acids fall to earth as acid precipitation (FIGURE 16-24).

In North America, precipitation has an average pH as low as 4.3 in some parts of the Northeast, more than 10 times as acidic as clean rain, which has a pH of about 5.6. (Clean rain is more acidic than pure water because carbon dioxide in the air dissolves in the water to form carbonic acid, making the rain slightly acidic as it breaks down.) High

1. Burning fossil fuels releases the gases sulfur dioxide and nitrogen dioxide.

2. When combined with water vapor in the atmosphere, these compounds form sulfuric acid and nitric acid.

3. The acids fall to earth as acid precipitation.

SO_2 (+) H_2O → H_2SO_4
NO_2 (+) H_2O → HNO_3

FIGURE 16-23 Formation of acid rain.

FIGURE 16-24 Acid precipitation: the problem and its cause.

Pacific Ocean. Precipitation in Europe and Asia is also acidified by local and distant sources of pollution.

Both terrestrial and aquatic organisms are harmed by acid precipitation, and the effects of acid precipitation can be direct or indirect. Direct effects result from contact of living tissues with acidic water, whereas indirect effects are produced by interactions between non-living and living systems.

Dramatic evidence of the direct effects of acid precipitation on vegetation can be found in mountain forests that are often blanketed by fog. When trees are exposed to acid fog, year after year, their leaves are damaged, their rates of photosynthesis decrease, and eventually, many of the trees die (**FIGURE 16-26**).

concentrations of sulfuric and nitric acids in the atmosphere are to blame, and several factors play a role. The Northeast has more people per square mile than the rest of the United States, and that means there are more houses, factories, and automobiles burning the oil, coal, and gasoline that create acid precipitation (**FIGURE 16-25**).

But not all of the pollution that causes acid precipitation is local. In the United States, the Midwest and Southeast have a large number of electric power plants that burn coal, and wind currents carry the sulfur dioxide and nitrogen dioxide from these power plants across the Northeast. The precipitation in the western states is not as acidic as that in the Northeast (but it's still nearly 100 times more acidic than pure water). Much of this region's acid precipitation comes from sulfur dioxide and nitrogen dioxide from Asia, which are converted to acids as they blow eastward across the

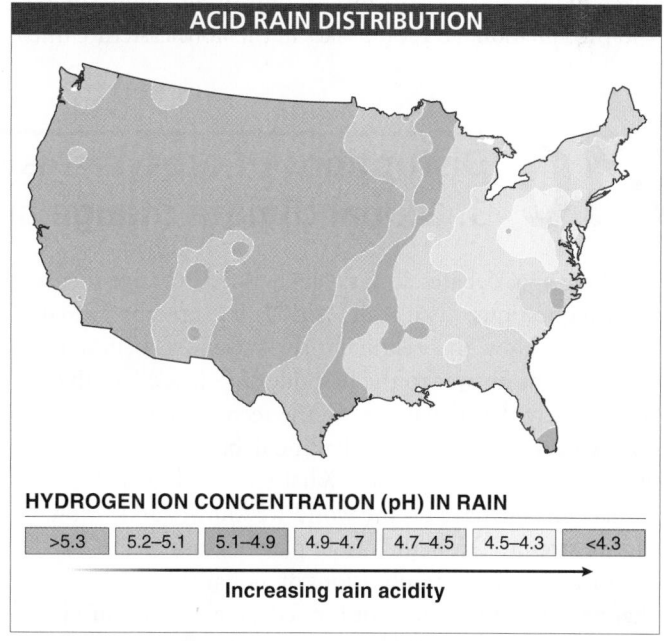

ACID RAIN DISTRIBUTION

HYDROGEN ION CONCENTRATION (pH) IN RAIN

| >5.3 | 5.2–5.1 | 5.1–4.9 | 4.9–4.7 | 4.7–4.5 | 4.5–4.3 | <4.3 |

→ **Increasing rain acidity**

FIGURE 16-25 Acid precipitation across the United States. Pure water has a neutral pH of 7.

Trees exposed to acid rain and acid fog have damaged leaves and decreased rates of photosynthesis. Eventually, many of the trees die.

FIGURE 16-26 Acid precipitation can kill trees.

The indirect effects of acid precipitation on forests are not as conspicuous as the direct effects, but they are more far-reaching. As acid falls on the soil, it carries away calcium, potassium, magnesium, and sodium ions. These ions are essential nutrients for plants, and when they are leached out of the soil, the rate of plant growth is reduced. Some forest animals also feel the impact of this change in soil chemistry—when calcium is depleted, for example, the shells of snails are thinner than usual. As a result of the thinning of snail shells, birds that eat snails receive less calcium than normal, and these birds lay eggs with shells so fragile that they can crack while the parents are incubating them.

Lakes and streams are also affected directly and indirectly by acid precipitation, and some lakes in the northeastern United States and in northern Europe have pH values as low as 4.0–4.3, which is 1,000 times more acidic than pure water. Very few species of insects, mollusks, crustaceans, fishes, or amphibians can live in water that acidic. Still worse, acid precipitation dissolves aluminum in soil and carries the dissolved metal (aluminum ions)—which is toxic to animals—into lakes and streams, where it can kill most forms of aquatic animal life.

Acid rain is a solvable problem, because the deposition of acids from acid rain can be both prevented and cleaned up. The best approach is to prevent or reduce the emissions of sulfur dioxide and nitrogen dioxide. Preventive measures include improving energy efficiency, reducing the use of coal, switching to use of natural gas, and increasing the use of renewable energy resources, such as wind energy and solar energy. In the United States, many coal-burning plants have now installed special "scrubbers" on their smokestacks. The scrubbers extract hot gases from the power plant and function like sponges, removing sulfur dioxide before it is released into the atmosphere and converting it to a less hazardous form that can be physically removed from the tower and disposed of.

TAKE-HOME MESSAGE 16·9

Burning fossil fuels releases the gases sulfur dioxide and nitrogen dioxide, and these compounds form sulfuric and nitric acids when they combine with water vapor in the atmosphere. Rain, fog, sleet, and snow that contain these acids can be more than 10 times more acidic than clean rain. Acid precipitation kills plants and aquatic animals directly, by contact with living tissues, and indirectly, through changes in soil and water chemistry.

16·10 Disruptions of ecosystems can be disastrous: 3. Global climate change and the greenhouse effect.

Not long ago, debates about global climate change focused on two questions: "Is it real?" and "Is it caused by human activities?" Now, the vast majority of scientists believe it is clear that the answer to the first question is *yes*, and that it is very likely that the answer to the second question is also *yes*. As a consequence, the scientific debate has increasingly moved to questions such as "What effect will global climate change have on the world we know?" and "How can we stop it?" Nonetheless, in part because of the significant political implications of global climate change—including, but not limited to, global warming—and because of the complex nature of the data establishing its occurrence, global climate change and the role of human activities remains a controversial topic.

Some of the evidence that the earth's atmosphere is warming comes from weather records that extend back into the 1700s. Those records show that the average temperature has increased rapidly during the past 50 years and that the 10 hottest years on record have occurred since 1990. Three centuries is a substantial time from the perspective of an individual human, but it's less than the blink of an eye in the history of the earth. We can extend the temperature records back to more than 400,000 years ago by examining ice cores from Antarctica. Although these cores do reveal short-term and long-term variations in temperature, nothing in the past 400,000 years approaches the speed of temperature change we have seen in the past 50 years.

1 Energy from the sun passes easily through the atmosphere to warm earth's surface.

2 Some energy is reflected back toward space and escapes the atmosphere.

3 Some energy is absorbed by greenhouse gases and remains trapped in the atmosphere, heating the air.

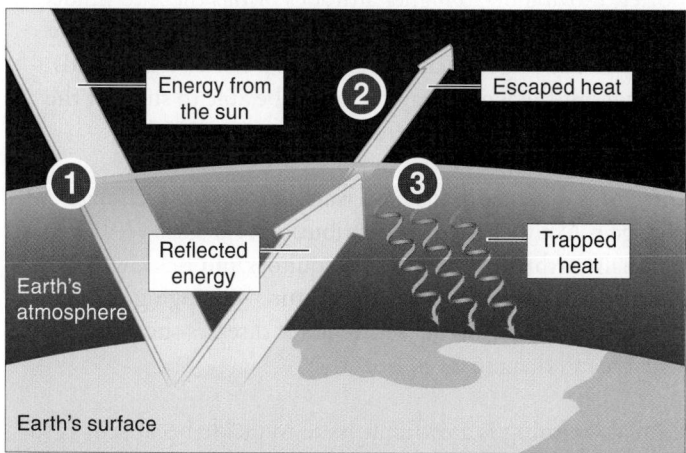

Energy from the sun
Escaped heat
Reflected energy
Earth's atmosphere
Trapped heat
Earth's surface

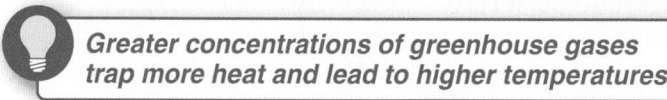

Greater concentrations of greenhouse gases trap more heat and lead to higher temperatures.

FIGURE 16-27 The earth is warmed by the greenhouse effect.

The term "greenhouse effect" describes the process by which energy from the sun warms the earth's atmosphere. The light we see lies in the visible portion of the light spectrum, and visible wavelengths of light pass easily through the atmosphere to warm the earth's surface. Some energy in the infrared part of the spectrum flows from earth back toward space, and several gases in the atmosphere absorb this energy, heating the air (**FIGURE 16-27**). These gases act like the glass panels that make up the roof of a greenhouse: they allow light energy to pass through, but they keep heat from escaping—hence the name "greenhouse gases." Carbon dioxide and methane are among the most important of the greenhouse gases. Without them, heat would escape into space and the earth's average temperature would be lower.

Q Why do we blame global warming on humans?

Humans have increased the amount of greenhouse gases in the atmosphere. And we've done it for primarily one reason: we rely on the burning of fossil fuels—coal, oil, gasoline, and natural gas—for much of the energy we use. The burning of fossil fuels, which have been stored deep in the earth for millions of years, releases carbon dioxide, and clearing land and plowing soil to cultivate crops releases both carbon dioxide and methane. The same Antarctic ice cores that reveal the unprecedented rate of global warming over the past 50 years also show that the current levels of carbon dioxide and methane in the atmosphere are far higher than any that have occurred during the 400,000-year span of the cores (**FIGURE 16-28**).

The Intergovernmental Panel on Climate Change, a scientific body set up in 1988 by the World Meteorological Organization and the United Nations, has predicted an increase in the average annual temperature of 2° to 12° F (1° to 6.4° C) during the 21st century. Sea levels will rise by 7–24 inches (18–59 cm) as warmer temperatures accelerate the melting of glaciers and ice sheets near the North and South Poles. Rainfall is predicted to decrease overall, and droughts will become more frequent and more severe. The impact of droughts will be most severe in areas that are currently on the borderline of aridity, such as Australia, the American Midwest, and sub-Saharan Africa.

Both environmental and biological evidence already reveal the effects of global warming. The Arctic Ocean ice cap is melting, and the glaciers that cover Antarctica and Greenland have also been melting at unprecedented rates—and those rates are increasing (**FIGURE 16-29**). During 1996, 21.6 cubic miles (90 cubic kilometers) of the Greenland ice sheet melted, and by 2010, the annual rate of melting was more than 57 cubic miles per year—faster than in any of the 53 years over which measurements have been made. This melting will cause an increase in ocean levels, creating flooding problems for many of the world's population centers in coastal areas, including New York City, Tokyo, and Amsterdam, and in the world's small island nations.

Biological systems are also showing the effects of climate change. Trees and flowers in northern latitudes are blooming

DISASTROUS DISRUPTIONS | **INCREASED GREENHOUSE GAS EMISSIONS**

PROBLEM
The average temperature has increased rapidly during the past 50 years, affecting both the physical environment and the biological world.

CAUSE
Burning fossil fuels and clearing land to cultivate crops have significantly increased levels of greenhouse gases in the atmosphere.

STRATEGIES FOR SOLUTION
Reduced emissions of greenhouse gases (particularly from the burning of fossil fuels)

FIGURE 16-28 Increasing greenhouse gases: the problem and its cause.

1979

2007

FIGURE 16-29 Disappearing ice pack. The satellite image at the top shows the minimum concentration of Arctic sea ice in 1979. The lower image shows the concentration of sea ice recorded on September 14, 2007.

earlier in the spring than they used to; migratory birds are arriving at their summer ranges earlier than they did even a decade ago; and birds and butterflies are extending their geographic ranges northward.

The changes to the physical environment caused by global warming, such as the thinning and shrinking of the Arctic Ocean ice or the flooding of coastal estuaries, can have profound effects on biodiversity at the species and ecosystem levels. For example, in 2004, a research ship in the Arctic Ocean found nine walrus calves swimming alone in deep water. Normally, adult female walruses leave their babies on ice floes in shallow water while they dive to the seafloor to feed on clams and crabs, and then return to the ice to nurse their babies. But the Arctic ice cap over shallow water has melted, driving the female walruses to the remaining ice, which is in deep water. The mother walruses cannot dive deep enough to reach the sea bottom, and they seem to be abandoning their calves.

Other consequences of global warming reveal the tremendous interconnectedness of so many ecosystem elements. Many bird and butterfly species' migratory patterns have been altered as they search for lower temperatures. Many populations of small mammals living near high-altitude peaks increasingly are constrained as they attempt to move toward milder temperatures during the summer months—if they move to lower altitudes it gets hotter; moving up to higher altitudes brings them to milder temperatures, but if they are already at the peak, they've got nowhere else to go when it gets too hot. Massive croplands throughout the world may no longer be able to support the crops previously grown there.

Infectious disease experts have warned that global climate change is likely to alter the distribution of disease vectors—especially arthropods such as mosquitoes and ticks, which are particularly sensitive to temperature—changing and potentially increasing the incidence of diseases such as malaria and dengue fever.

Global warming is a difficult issue to tackle because it is so large in scope; it encompasses every biome, every ecosystem, every species, every body of water, and its solutions require individual efforts in all nations as well as international cooperation among governments. Fundamentally, however, the science is straightforward: carbon emissions must be reduced significantly. This can be done by individuals who choose to cut down on their own fossil fuel use, improve the energy efficiency of their homes and cars, and support the development of carbon-free renewable energy sources. Internationally, it can be done through efforts to reduce deforestation while increasing the replanting of forests, and by developing and implementing transportation and industrial innovations that reduce dependence on the fuels that produce greenhouse gases. Innovative technologies, such as the underground sequestration of carbon, may also contribute to the reversal of global warming.

TAKE-HOME MESSAGE 16·10

Carbon dioxide and methane are called "greenhouse gases," because they trap heat in the atmosphere. As humans burn fossil fuels and clear forests, the concentrations of greenhouse gases have been increasing and global temperatures have been rising. Ecological changes in plant and animal communities have already been observed and are likely to become more serious unless there is a global reduction in emissions of greenhouse gases.

16·11

Disruptions of ecosystems can be disastrous:
4. Depletion of the ozone layer.

You are familiar with the oxygen you breathe—it comes in molecules formed by two oxygen atoms and is represented by the chemical formula O_2. Ozone is a different molecular arrangement of oxygen that packs three oxygen atoms into a molecule; its chemical formula is O_3. Ozone irritates the respiratory pathways and lungs, causing coughing and wheezing, and exposure to ozone can induce asthma attacks. If you live in a city, you are likely to hear radio and television warnings of high ozone levels during the summer. These warnings announce that ozone is expected to exceed safe levels that day. Children and adults with lung disease are advised to remain indoors during an ozone alert.

If ozone makes people sick, why would anyone worry about *depletion* of ozone in the atmosphere? Isn't that a *good* thing? The answer is, in the words of the old saying about what determines the value of real estate: "Location, location, location." At ground level, ozone is bad for you, but ozone in the upper part of the stratosphere, which is 30 miles (50 km) above the earth's surface, protects you from ultraviolet radiation, the rays that cause sunburn and skin cancer. Ozone is a Jekyll-and-Hyde molecule, and one set of environmental regulations tries to reduce the formation of ozone at ground level while a different set of regulations tries to protect ozone in the stratosphere.

There are two types of "ozone depletion": the general reduction in the amount of ozone in the stratosphere and the formation of areas with very low ozone concentration (called "ozone holes") over the North and South Poles every winter. Synthetic chemicals known as chlorofluorocarbons (CFCs) are the villains in both forms of ozone depletion. CFCs, which were developed in the 1930s, have a wide range of applications, including use as coolants in refrigeration systems. When CFC molecules leak into the atmosphere, they rise to the stratosphere, where sunlight knocks a chlorine atom off the CFC molecule. These free chlorine atoms then catalyze the breakdown of ozone to oxygen (**FIGURE 16-30**).

In the 1970s, it was noted that the amount of ozone in the stratosphere was decreasing by about 4% per decade. The cold temperatures and circular flows of air that develop over the Poles during the winter concentrate CFCs, forming ozone holes in those locations. The Antarctic ozone hole, which lasts for several months, covers the

Should we be concerned about an ozone hole in our atmosphere?

DISASTROUS DISRUPTIONS | **OZONE LAYER DEPLETION**

PROBLEM
Increased levels of ultraviolet light reach the earth's surface, leading to a greater incidence of health problems in animals and decreased rates of photosynthesis in plants.

CAUSE
Synthetic chemicals known as chlorofluorocarbons (CFCs) leak into the atmosphere, where they cause the breakdown of ozone.

STRATEGIES FOR SOLUTION
Reduced production and emission of CFCs

FIGURE 16-30 Depletion of the ozone layer: the problem and its cause.

entire continent of Antarctica and extends northward to include the southern tips of South America and Australia (**FIGURE 16-31**). The Arctic ozone hole is smaller than the Antarctic hole and does not last as long, but it is large enough to extend southward into northern Europe, Asia, and North America.

Ozone depletion allows short-wavelength ultraviolet light (UVB light, with wavelengths of 270–315 nanometers) to reach the earth's surface. The 4%-per-decade reduction in global stratospheric ozone levels has increased the intensity of UVB radiation everywhere on earth, particularly under the ozone holes.

Not surprisingly, humans tend to think first about the effects of elevated UVB on human health. A 1% increase in UVB intensity increases the incidence of skin cancer by 2% to 3%. Exposure to UVB radiation also promotes the formation of cataracts and reduces the effectiveness of our immune system. Domestic animals suffer the same kinds of damage that humans do, and a few studies indicate that wild animals are also affected.

Q But we may be looking at the wrong problem. The damage to ecosystems could be a more serious consequence of ozone depletion than damage to human health. UVB radiation reduces the rate of photosynthesis by plants, and reduced photosynthesis in agricultural ecosystems means that crop yields will decline just when the worldwide cost of food is increasing.

September 1979   September 1988   September 2000   October 2010

FIGURE 16-31 Monitoring the ozone hole. The satellite images show changes in the ozone hole over the Antarctic during the past 30 years. The darkest blue color indicates the lowest ozone concentration.

Depletion of the ozone layer and the formation of an ozone "hole" over earth's polar regions have occurred as a result of human activities.

The creation of the ozone holes is an example of how some scientifically developed industrial processes and products can have unintended and severe consequences. When CFCs were first invented, they were considered harmless, and so their use as coolants, as aerosol propellants, and in the production of materials such as Styrofoam became widespread. But the recognition that CFCs eventually reach the highest levels of the atmosphere and catalyze the destruction of the protective ozone layer prompted relatively quick reaction: an example of the power of science to help identify environmental problems and to help find solutions (**FIGURE 16-32**). With the adoption by most countries in the 1980s of an agreement to discontinue the use of CFCs, ozone depletion was slowed, and in 2010 it was shown that the atmospheric levels of ozone had stabilized. A full recovery could occur by 2050.

It's important to note that depletion of the ozone layer is not the mechanism of global warming. Ultraviolet radiation represents less than 1% of the sun's energy. And the greenhouse gases discussed in the previous section do not reduce the atmosphere's ozone layer. Global warming and ozone depletion are largely unrelated environmental issues, linked only by their common cause: human activities. The response to ozone depletion, however, represents an encouraging example of how nations can work together to address and correct human-caused environmental problems.

REDUCING CFCs

Products made from ozone-depleting CFCs, such as Styrofoam hamburger boxes and hair sprays with damaging propellants, have been phased out in the hope of spurring a recovery of the ozone layer.

FIGURE 16-32 Taking simple steps to reduce ozone depletion.

TAKE-HOME MESSAGE 16·11

Ozone in the stratosphere prevents short-wavelength ultraviolet light (UVB) from reaching the earth's surface, but for many decades the amount of ozone was decreasing, largely due to synthetic chemicals called chlorofluorocarbons (CFCs). An increase in UVB light reaching the earth's surface can seriously damage ecosystems and has adverse effects on health, including increasing the incidence of skin cancer in humans and other animals. A decline in the production and use of CFCs is reducing atmospheric ozone depletion.

16·12

Disruptions of ecosystems can be disastrous:
5. Deforestation of tropical rain forests.

Towering trees, colorful birds and butterflies, maybe a glimpse of Tarzan swinging past on a hanging vine—that is the popular image of a tropical rain forest. And it is a reasonably accurate picture (minus the Tarzan part). But it is also a picture that is rapidly fading, as agriculture, logging, gold mines, and oil wells destroy tropical forests (**FIGURE 16-33**).

DISASTROUS DISRUPTIONS DEFORESTATION

PROBLEM
Tropical rain forests are being cleared at unprecedentedly high rates, endangering countless species and increasing the concentration of greenhouse gases in the atmosphere.

CAUSE
The land is cleared for agriculture, logging, gold mines, and oil wells.

STRATEGIES FOR SOLUTION
Reduced destruction of high-biodiversity habitats, particularly tropical rain forests

FIGURE 16-33 Deforestation: the problem and its cause.

Tropical rain forests grow in a region extending just a bit north and south of the equator, in South America, Africa, Asia, and Australia. As recently as a few centuries ago, that belt of rain forest covered about 6 million square miles (15.5 million square kilometers). More than half of that forest has already been destroyed, most of it in just the past 200 years (**FIGURE 16-34**).

The destruction of a tropical rain forest means an enormous loss of species, because these forests are the most diverse terrestrial habitats on earth. More than 170,000 species of plants grow in tropical rain forests, more than 60% of the total number of living plant species in the world. A survey of a Brazilian rain forest found 487 different species of trees in just 2.5 acres (1 hectare), an area less than half the size of one city block in Manhattan. To put that number in perspective, consider that only 700 species of trees are found in the 5 *billion* acres of the United States and Canada combined!

Agriculture is responsible for the greatest loss of tropical forests, and it takes a variety of forms. Sometimes, a relatively small area is affected—"slash-and-burn agriculture" refers to cutting trees, burning them, and planting crops in the newly opened area. Usually, just a few acres of forest are cleared, but the land is fertile for only two or three years after it has been cleared. Then that plot is abandoned and more forest is cleared, so the cumulative effect of slash-and-burn agriculture is substantial. At the other end of the size scale, multinational corporations clear hundreds of acres of forest to plant bananas, coffee, or oil palms, and thousands of acres of forest to create pastures for cattle.

Pollution from oil wells and mining in tropical rain forests has an impact that can extend far beyond the areas that are actually cleared. Leaking oil contaminates streams and groundwater, and acidic water drains from mines. Even worse, gold miners use mercury to extract gold, and some of

DEFORESTATION: TROPICAL RAIN FORESTS

TROPICAL RAIN FOREST COVER BEFORE HUMAN INFLUENCE

CURRENT TROPICAL RAIN FOREST COVER

FIGURE 16-34 Worldwide loss of tropical rain forests.

the mercury enters streams, where it is converted to methyl mercury—a toxic compound that accumulates in plant and animal tissue as it moves up the food chain.

Agriculture and mining both require roads to bring equipment to the sites and take crops or minerals to market. Roads have an impact on forests that greatly exceeds the relatively small area they occupy, because they make access to the forest easy. Traveling through a virgin tropical rain forest is difficult—bogs and natural tree falls often prevent travel in a straight line; slopes are often steep and the wet soil is slippery; and the ground-level vegetation can be both dense and thorny. No wheeled vehicle larger than a motorcycle can penetrate most rain forests, and traveling by motorcycle is slower than walking. These difficulties protect rain forests, but as soon as a road is bulldozed through a forest, people flock to it. They and their activities then spread into the forest on both sides of the road, creating new clearings that spread like cancers, farther and farther into the forest.

Destruction of tropical rain forests has two serious environmental impacts: reducing the earth's biodiversity and increasing the concentration of greenhouse gases in the atmosphere, which in turn affects global climate change.

1. Reducing biodiversity. Tropical rain forests of Africa, Asia, the Pacific, and Central and South America contain an unusually large number of species of plants and animals and probably other groups of organisms. Half of the world's biodiversity hotspots are in tropical rain forests.

2. Increasing greenhouse gases. Photosynthesis in tropical rain forests removes an estimated 610 billion tons (550 trillion kg) of carbon dioxide from the atmosphere each year. As we learned earlier, accumulation of carbon dioxide in the atmosphere is the major cause of global warming. Thus, the continued photosynthetic activity of tropical rain forests is important in slowing the rate of warming. The huge quantity of carbon stored in rain forests has a downside, however, because that carbon is released into the atmosphere when forests are cleared and burned. And tropical forests are being cleared at a frightening rate—more than 50,000 square miles (an area larger than the state of New York!) each year between 2000 and 2010.

Because deforestation alters characteristics of land cover, changing the proportion of solar radiation reflected and absorbed, rain forest destruction can have additional significant effects on climate—including rainfall amounts and seasonality. These changes can further accelerate climate change, with potentially significant impacts on ecosystems.

Planting new trees can undo some deforestation damage.

FIGURE 16-35 Growing seedlings for reforestation.

The problem of tropical deforestation is among the most difficult of any environmental problems to solve, and solving it will involve multiple strategies and rely on international cooperation. The most diverse areas must be identified and protected. The poverty that necessitates the destruction of tropical rain forests for human activities must be addressed. Alternative sources of food and income must be developed. Population growth must be reduced. And education about the value of preserving biodiversity is central to these issues. At present, we have not progressed much beyond identifying the problem, but that, at least, is a necessary first step (**FIGURE 16-35**).

TAKE-HOME MESSAGE 16·12

Tropical rain forests are being destroyed at an alarming rate. This deforestation is devastating for two main reasons. First, tropical rain forests contain more species of plants and animals than all other terrestrial habitats combined, and half of the earth's biodiversity hotspots are in these forests. Second, tropical rain forests remove more carbon dioxide from the atmosphere than any other terrestrial habitat and, as a result, these forests are enormously important in limiting global warming. Deforestation further influences climate change by altering land cover characteristics.

16·13–16·14
We can develop strategies for effective conservation.

A worker carries a tree to plant at the edge of Maowusu Desert, China. Trees are planted to prevent the desert from expanding.

16·13 With limited conservation resources, we must prioritize which species should be preserved.

Is it preferable to save one beautiful, well-studied bird species or 1,000 species of bacteria, none of which have even been described or named? And what about the 1,200 species of beetles in Panama that live in the evergreen tree *Luehea seemannii*, almost 200 of which live *only* in this one species of tree—how should we prioritize these species for conservation relative to, say, a single primate species? From locale to locale the particulars of these questions may change, but the underlying issue remains: in a world where species are being driven to extinction faster than we can save them, which should be singled out for preservation and which should we leave to almost certain extinction (**FIGURE 16-36**)? This is a question that biologists, policymakers, and, ultimately, citizens must address.

When setting conservation priorities, it is essential to articulate a goal. In an ideal world, the goal might be to protect "all biodiversity." Barring that, options include protecting "most biodiversity," the most diverse subset of biodiversity (in terms of genes, species, and ecosystems), or the most valuable biodiversity. There are numerous

WHAT SHOULD WE PROTECT?

FIGURE 16-36 Prioritizing conservation efforts. How do we decide among the many options? Shown here: giant pandas and soil bacteria.

Conservation efforts can focus on preserving individual species (such as orangutans) or important habitats (such as rain forests).

FIGURE 16-37 Which to preserve? Limited resources and great demand make preservation choices difficult.

arguments in favor of each goal, and each has significant flaws as well. Once a goal is decided on, a related step in the decision-making process is needed—a plan that outlines priorities for achieving the goal. Frequently, such a plan involves an assessment of the degree to which various components of biodiversity are threatened. We can rank species, for example, as relatively intact, relatively stable, vulnerable, endangered, or critical. These rankings can then be used, in conjunction with measures of the biological value of the biodiversity to humans, in formulating a plan.

As we saw earlier in the chapter, biodiversity can be valued in many different ways, and its worth cannot be easily quantified or weighed. Sooner or later, many difficult and subjective decisions must be made in the goal-setting and prioritizing process. The undiscovered bacterial species may harbor the metabolic secrets to curing a devastating medical condition in humans, but the beautiful bird species may be much loved by bird-watchers or may serve as a powerful icon of strength or freedom, inspiring generations of people. The decisions are difficult, but not facing them is, in most cases, the same as making a decision.

In the United States, much conservation policy involves response to the **Endangered Species Act (ESA),** a law that defines **endangered species** as those in danger of extinction throughout all or a significant portion of their range. The law is designed to protect those species from extinction. As we noted earlier in the chapter, species that are dwindling are listed as endangered or threatened, according to an assessment of their risk of extinction. Once a species is listed, legal tools are available to help rebuild the population and

protect the habitat critical to its survival. Seemingly straightforward, the ESA has had the effect of focusing most conservation efforts on the preservation of individual species (and populations), sometimes at the expense of other elements of biodiversity and sometimes at the expense of efforts to reduce the loss of ecologically important habitats (**FIGURE 16-37**). Other difficulties are also associated with the ESA. Consider the task of determining the critical population size below which a population is endangered—is it 500 individuals or 5,000 or 50,000? With its emphasis on preservation of single species, the ESA does not effectively address ecosystem decline, which is an equally urgent and serious problem.

In spite of these difficulties, the species-focused approach to conservation has had some success in the United States. Since it became law in 1973, approximately 40 species that were listed as endangered—including the bald eagle, the peregrine falcon, the gray whale, and the grizzly bear—have been taken off the list as their numbers have recovered. In the final section, we examine other strategies that have been used in efforts to preserve biodiversity.

TAKE-HOME MESSAGE 16·13

Effective conservation requires the setting of goals on the elements of biodiversity (genes, species, or ecosystems) to be conserved and priorities among those elements. The U.S. Endangered Species Act has focused much conservation effort on the preservation of species.

16·14 There are multiple effective strategies for preserving biodiversity.

In a survey asking which animal they would like to be, men and women gave very different answers. Among men, the top answer was eagle, followed by tiger, lion, and dolphin. As their first choice, women chose cat, followed by butterfly, swan, and swallow. It's just a silly survey, but the differences in male and female selections parallel the fact that people have very different preferences when it comes to preserving biodiversity. One person may view as unthinkable the loss of a particular species or habitat, while another may view other species or habitats as much more valuable.

Most approaches to conservation biology, as we've seen, have focused on the preservation of individual species. Increasingly, however, conservation biology is shifting toward the preservation of important habitats, focusing on conserving communities and ecosystems. This habitat-conserving approach also leads to the preservation of individual species, but it has the added benefit of preserving, at the same time, many different species within a habitat, including many that have not yet been identified, particularly microbes and fungi.

One example of an effort aimed at the preservation of important habitat is the World Wildlife Fund's "Global 200," an identification of all of the most biologically distinct habitats on earth. The identification of these habitats, which include terrestrial, freshwater, and marine habitats, is part of an innovative strategy, often called **landscape conservation,** that is geared toward conserving not just species but habitats and ecological processes (e.g., large-scale migrations and predator-prey interactions). In an age of scarce conservation resources and limited time, this approach prioritizes the conservation of biologically unique habitats on earth.

The habitat conservation approach is not new. The very first attempts at conservation in the United States were the creation of Yellowstone Park in 1872 and Yosemite in 1890, both large-scale efforts geared not simply toward the preservation of one or a few species but rather toward the preservation of the "wilderness." In the time since then, significant efforts have been made to establish national parks, wilderness areas, and recreation areas (**FIGURE 16-38**).

As conservation biologists have started to better understand population dynamics and biogeography, the design of natural preserves has evolved. Using insights gained from

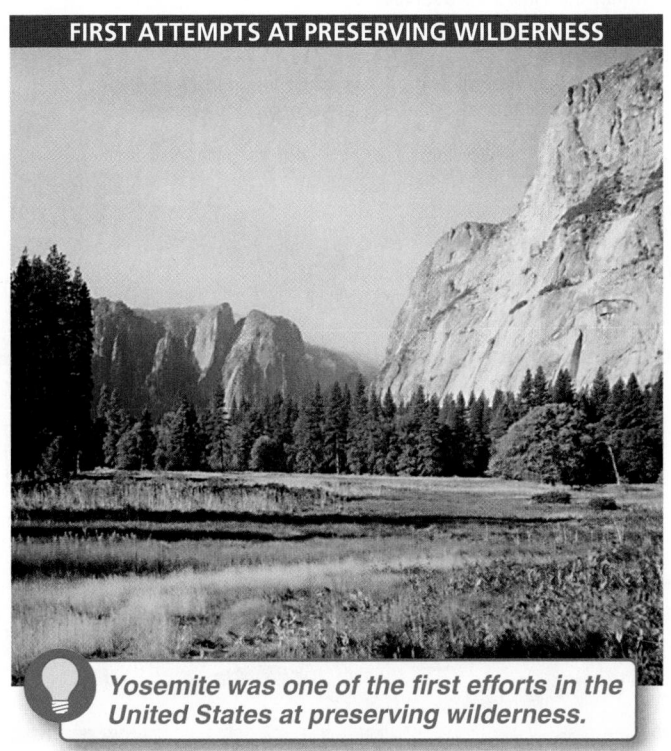

FIRST ATTEMPTS AT PRESERVING WILDERNESS

Yosemite was one of the first efforts in the United States at preserving wilderness.

FIGURE 16-38 The natural beauty of Yosemite.

the theory of island biogeography, modern preserve design focuses not simply on maximizing the variety of habitats and biodiversity preserved but on using several design features that maximize the efficiency of the preserves (**FIGURE 16-39**).

- Larger, rather than smaller, preserves (including a preference for a single, undivided preserve over several smaller preserves)

- Circular, rather than linear, preserves

- Corridors—even just relatively narrow strips of land—that connect larger natural preserves, allow gene flow, and reduce inbreeding among distinct populations in the different preserves

- Buffer zones (which permit limited amounts of human activity) around core areas (which contain the habitat to be conserved)

As conservation plans aimed at preserving habitats increase, efforts focusing on individual species still continue to be effective. Several strategies targeting individual species for

FIGURE 16-39 Carefully planned nature preserves focus on features that maximize biodiversity.

conservation have been particularly successful at preserving large amounts of biodiversity beyond that single species.

1. Flagship species. Some species, because they are particularly charismatic, distinctive, vulnerable, or otherwise appealing, can engender significant public support. Examples include the giant panda of China, the golden lion tamarin of Brazil's coastal forest, the mountain gorilla of Central Africa, the orangutan of Southeast Asia, the leatherback sea turtle, the Indian tiger, and the African elephant. Preservation of these species, given their habitat needs, can serve to preserve many other species as well.

2. Keystone species. As we saw in Chapter 15, keystone species have a disproportionate effect on the biodiversity of a community. Their removal can lead to massive changes in the composition of species in an ecosystem, often causing huge loss of biodiversity. Examples include kelp, California mussels, grizzly bears, beavers, and sea stars.

3. Indicator species. These are species whose presence within an ecosystem indicates the presence of a large range of other species. For example, the presence or absence of lichens is an indicator of air quality, because they are sensitive to sulfur dioxide, a component of industrial fumes. When lichens disappear from trees, it is usually an indicator of increased pollution, which endangers the entire ecosystem. Conversely, when lichens are present and healthy, they indicate that the ecosystem is healthy.

4. Umbrella species. These include wide-ranging species with such large needs for habitat and other resources that their preservation ends up protecting the numerous other species within that same habitat, without having to identify these other species as conservation targets. Umbrella species tend to be large, wide-ranging vertebrates.

For more critically endangered species and degraded habitats, all hope is not necessarily lost. Captive breeding programs and habitat restoration have had some success in bringing back biodiversity from the brink of extinction. Zoos and botanical gardens have taken the lead in many of these efforts. In the 1980s, for example, when the population size of the California condor had dropped to 22 individuals, due to poaching, lead poisoning, and habitat loss, all of the birds were caught and taken to zoos, where a captive breeding program began. With the success of these breeding programs, by 2011 the population had reached 400, including close to 200 birds in the wild and the remainder in zoos. Breeding programs are not a complete conservation solution on their own, however. It is essential that the species' habitats are not destroyed or altered if the species are to flourish again under natural conditions.

Restoration ecology, which uses the principles of ecology to restore degraded habitats to their natural state, has also been an important tool of conservation biologists. Wetlands that have been degraded by dredging and development, in particular, have benefited. Reintroduction of the native plant species and restoration of water and stream flow patterns can be instrumental in restoring these habitats.

Taken together, the strategies used by conservation biologists represent an important step toward reducing the adverse effects of one hugely successful (from a population growth perspective) species—humans—on other species. Although we are far from living with minimal disturbance of the environment in which we live, continued conservation efforts offer our best hope for a sustainable future.

THE PERILS OF (EXOTIC) PETS!

Some significant threats to biodiversity may come from your own neighborhood. And they're often aided by well-meaning small businesses: pet stores!

Q: HOW MIGHT OTHERWISE-RESPONSIBLE CITIZENS WREAK HAVOC ON THEIR ENVIRONMENT? The purchase of exotic, non-native animals as pets can have unintended and harmful consequences.

Q: WHAT'S WRONG WITH KEEPING AN EXOTIC FISH IN YOUR AQUARIUM OR A TROPICAL BIRD IN A CAGE? In an aquarium or in a cage, non-native species are unlikely to harm any natural environment. But the problem is that they escape, they get flushed down toilets, they're "set free" by owners who no longer want them, or, in some other way, they get into the environment. And it's not their native habitat.

Q: WHAT HAPPENS WHEN NON-NATIVE SPECIES ARE INTRODUCED TO A NOVEL ENVIRONMENT? In some cases, non-native species do no harm. But in many others, non-native or exotic species can alter habitat and crowd out, outcompete, or directly prey on beneficial native species. They can spread exotic diseases, for which native species have no resistance. And they can disrupt and harm fisheries, crops, and other valuable industries, costing millions of dollars. Consider just a few common examples.

FISH. Catfish can alter river vegetation and shorelines, making them uninhabitable for native species. Lionfish from home aquariums have been released into the ocean off the coast of Florida. Expert predators, they kill a wide variety of smaller fishes, mollusks, and other invertebrates. In 2008, their population densities in some new habitats were found to have increased by 700% in just five years. China's giant snakehead fish is a voracious eater and preys on numerous species of smaller fishes and amphibians. Traced to the aquarium industry, non-native populations off the east coast of the United States have wiped out numerous populations of native species. The snakehead fish can even crawl from one pond to another, surviving as long as four days out of water! Numerous other types of popular aquarium fish, including emperor angelfish, the yellow tang, and the orbicular batfish, have been found thriving in non-native habitats in the United States.

BIRDS. More than 150 non-native bird species have been documented in Florida, including 30 different parrot species, all of which were former pets, and many of which now cause significant crop damage, consuming fruits, berries, flowers, and seeds. Monk parakeets often build nests on electrical transformers and lampposts and have been responsible for power outages and other damage.

AMPHIBIANS AND REPTILES. Terrapins (a type of turtle) and bullfrogs often outgrow their aquariums. If released into ponds, they can wipe out native fish, amphibian, and even small mammal populations.

PLANTS. Numerous popular aquarium plant species, such as the fast-growing seaweed *Caulerpa,* have become invasive in the Mediterranean Sea and in Southern California. Freed from their natural predators, they thrive and have caused millions of dollars in damage.

Q: WHAT CAN YOU DO? The best advice here is to avoid purchasing exotic pets (or using non-native plant species when landscaping or planting a garden). You can also let your representatives in government know of the dangers of non-native species and the importance of restricting the import of such species into the country—an issue that is not always high on their list of priorities.

Big Ideas in ...
Conservation and Biodiversity

16·1–16·4 Measuring and defining biodiversity is complex.

- Biodiversity can be defined as the variety of genes, species, and ecosystems on earth.
- Biodiversity provides significant benefits to humans in utilitarian ways, such as the production of medicines, and provides important value in less tangible ways, including aesthetic, symbolic, and naturalistic.
- There is a strong latitudinal gradient in biodiversity, decreasing from the tropics to the Poles for nearly all groups of plants and animals.
- Biodiversity hotspots are regions of significant biodiversity under threat of destruction.
- The theory of island biogeography generates predictions about patterns of species diversity and has implications for the development of nature preserves.

16·5–16·6 Extinction reduces biodiversity.

- Mass extinctions tend to result from bad luck rather than from features of a species' biology, whereas background extinctions tend to be a consequence of a species' biological characteristics.
- Small population size, limited habitat range, and narrow zones of habitat tolerance contribute to background extinctions.
- Most biologists believe that we are in the midst of a mass extinction, that it is the result of human activities, and that it poses a serious threat to human survival.

16·7–16·12 Human interference generally reduces biodiversity.

- Because they have no natural predators in their new habitat and their prey have no defenses against them, exotic species can multiply unchecked, overwhelming competitors and dominating and irreversibly altering communities and entire ecosystems.

- Burning fossil fuels releases sulfur dioxide and nitrogen dioxide, and these gases combine with water vapor to form acid precipitation, harming plants, animals, and the abiotic environment.
- Carbon dioxide and methane are greenhouse gases, trapping heat in the atmosphere. Produced by the burning of fossil fuels and clearing of forests, greenhouse gases are increasing and global temperatures rising. Avoiding increasingly serious consequences requires a global reduction in emissions of greenhouse gases.
- Ozone in the stratosphere has been depleted through the effects of CFCs, with health consequences for humans and animals. A reduction in CFC production appears to be restoring the ozone to safer levels.
- Tropical rain forests contain more species than all other terrestrial habitats combined, and half of the earth's biodiversity hotspots are in tropical rain forests. Destruction of these forests is likely to have serious environmental consequences.

16·13–16·14 We can develop strategies for effective conservation.

- Effective conservation requires setting goals on which elements of biodiversity (genes, species, or ecosystems) to conserve and setting priorities among those elements.
- Although the U.S. Endangered Species Act has focused most conservation efforts on individual species, there is now a shift toward conserving communities and ecosystems. Several methods focusing on single species remain useful, however, particularly when they require preservation of an amount and type of habitat that simultaneously preserves many other species.

See the To-Go Guide (packaged with every new copy of this textbook) for an illustrated summary of the chapter.

Check Your Knowledge

GRAPHIC CONTENT

Thinking critically about visual displays of data.

1. What are the axes for these graphs? What are the variables being observed?

2. Which variable is independent? Which is dependent? Do these graphs conform to typical norms for the placement of the independent and dependent variables? Why or why not?

3. At what latitude do the largest numbers of species occur?

4. Why are data presented both for mammalian species *and* for marine copepod species (rather than just one or the other)? Why aren't data for *all* species presented?

5. At 20° north latitude, are there more mammalian or marine copepod species? What aspect of the graphs may be responsible for someone answering this question incorrectly?

6. Bar graphs often have error bars, indicating some measure of variance in the data. Why do the data bars in these graphs have no such error bars?

WHERE IS MOST BIODIVERSITY?

LAND MAMMAL BIODIVERSITY IN THE AMERICAS

MARINE COPEPOD BIODIVERSITY IN THE NORTH PACIFIC

See Answers at the back of the book.

Key Terms in Conservation and Biodiversity

Multiple-Choice Questions

1. Biodiversity is considered important because of:

a) the direct economic benefits to humans, such as medicines and food.

b) the symbolic value that elements of the natural world can provide.

c) the aesthetic value it holds.

d) its potential for helping humans understand the processes that gave rise to the diversity we see.

e) All of the above are correct.

2. Biodiversity hotspots are defined by which two criteria?

a) species richness and ecosystem integrity

b) size and distance from nearest alternative hotspot

c) species endemism and degree of threat

d) species richness and size

e) ecological diversity and species diversity

3. Madagascar is unusually important to conservation because it:

a) has more species per unit area than any other place on earth.

b) is the fourth largest island in the world.

c) is home to more endangered species than any other country.

d) has a higher percentage of endemic plants and animals than any comparably sized area on earth.

e) is the native habitat of the rosy periwinkle, a rain forest plant that helps cure childhood lymphocytic leukemia.

4. By fumigating several islands in the Florida Keys with methyl bromide, E. O. Wilson and Daniel Simberloff demonstrated that:

a) the equilibrium number of insect species was a function of island size and distance from the mainland.

b) colonization of an island by new species can no longer occur once the island is "full."

c) for plant but not insect species, the relation of area to species number holds true for all islands.

d) the effects of global warming will be greater on islands than on the mainland.

e) species turnover rates are highest on small, more distant islands.

5. When an island has the equilibrium number of species:

a) extinction no longer occurs.

b) immigration rates to the island are reduced to zero.

c) both the number and composition of species on the island remain the same.

d) both the number and composition of species on the island are changing.

e) the composition of species on the island may change, but the number of species present remains the same.

6. Which of the following attributes of a species might render it especially susceptible to extinction?

a) It lives in a marine habitat.

b) It exists as two distinct subpopulations.

c) It is an invasive species.

d) It is short-lived.

e) It has a narrow dispersal range.

7. What bird, once the most abundant in North America, was hunted to extinction by shooting and trapping during the 1800s?

a) California condor
b) blue-footed booby
c) dodo
d) passenger pigeon
e) great auk

100 HARD
53
0 EASY

8. How many species do biologists estimate to be currently existing on earth?

a) fewer than 1 million
b) between 3 million and 5 million
c) more than 1 billion
d) between 5 million and 100 million
e) between 1 million and 2 million

100 HARD
45
0 EASY

9. Which of the following is currently the leading cause of extinction?

a) pollution
b) habitat loss
c) disease
d) exotic species
e) overexploitation

100 HARD
29
0 EASY

10. Exotic species can disrupt ecosystems because:

a) they frequently have no predators in their new habitat and grow unchecked.
b) they are favored by ecotourists.
c) they have no natural prey items and so must rely on humans for their survival.
d) they have better dispersal capability than endemic species.
e) All of the above are correct.

100 HARD
42
0 EASY

11. Even though there is a carbon cycle, carbon dioxide levels around the world seem to be rising. Which of the following best explains why this is so?

a) Animals give off carbon dioxide during their normal metabolism.
b) As the atmosphere heats up, it can contain more carbon dioxide.
c) The destruction of coral reefs leads to increased levels of carbon dioxide.
d) More carbon dioxide is being given off by ocean waters as they heat up.
e) The burning of fossil fuels releases more carbon dioxide into the atmosphere.

100 HARD
19
0 EASY

12. Ozone depletion is cause for concern because:

a) without atmospheric ozone, greenhouse gases can escape earth's atmosphere, leading to global warming.
b) without ozone, fossil fuels are more likely to react with water vapor in the atmosphere, increasing levels of precipitation throughout the world.
c) without the protection against solar radiation provided by ozone, rates of skin cancer are likely to increase.
d) without ozone, solar radiation can irradiate the Antarctic ice shelf, causing unsafe levels of radioactive isotopes.
e) reduced levels of ozone can increase the rate of respiratory problems in humans, particularly children.

100 HARD
0 11 EASY

13. Which of the following statements about habitat loss is correct?

a) Small animals are not vulnerable to habitat destruction.
b) Fragmented habitats can support only small populations of the species living in them.
c) Corridors between habitat areas are of use only to active organisms such as vertebrates.
d) Corridors can replace habitat areas for migratory species.
e) Large animals are not vulnerable to habitat destruction.

100 HARD
41
0 EASY

14. An umbrella species:

a) is a species whose removal will severely damage or cause the collapse of its ecosystem.
b) is a non-native species, usually introduced to an area by accident.
c) is any species that has a larger than expected effect on its ecosystem.
d) is a popular species that the public tends to rally behind and support.
e) is a species whose preservation results in the preservation of many other species as well.

100 HARD
50
0 EASY

Short-Answer Questions

1. Where, geographically, is the greatest biodiversity? What are the primary threats to this biodiversity?

2. Why were the ecosystem disturbances created by humans in New England reversible? What changes would have made the ecosystem disturbances in New England irreversible?

3. What is the primary cause of tropical rain forest deforestation? How does this affect the biodiversity of plants and animals?

See Answers at the back of the book.
For additional study questions, go to www.prep-u.com.

How plants function,
and why we need them

17

Plant Structure and Nutrient Transport

17·1–17·3 Three basic tissue types give rise to diverse plant characteristics.

Thriving in the desert: an agave plant and flowers from Parry's Penstemon, a wildflower native to southern Arizona and northern New Mexico.

17·1 Older, taller, bigger: plants are extremely diverse (but share a basic structural organization).

Plants are better than animals. Actually, that's an absurd thing to say. But only because biology isn't a contest, and from the perspective of evolution, any species that is not extinct can be considered a success. By many measures, though, plants do surpass animals, having developed a stunning diversity of structures and features during their evolution.

Consider some vital statistics on plants and animals (**FIGURE 17-1**).

1. Longevity. The longest-living plants live 10 times longer than the longest-living animals. Bristlecone pines, found in the western United States, can live for more than 4,800 years. Among animals, the ocean quahog (a clam-like mollusk, found off the east coast of North America) can live about 200 years, and giant tortoises, found on some tropical islands, can live almost 200 years.

2. Height. The tallest plants are 20 times taller than the tallest animals. Coast redwoods, found along the west coast of North America, have grown to more than 379 feet (115 m). The tallest giraffe grew to just under 20 feet (6 m).

3. Weight. The heaviest plants weigh almost 20 times as much as the heaviest animals. The largest giant sequoias

> **Q** Plants versus animals: Which can live longer? Grow larger?

are estimated to weigh more than 3,300 tons (almost 3 million kg). The largest blue whales—believed to be the largest animals ever to inhabit the earth—weigh in at approximately 170 tons (154,000 kg).

4. Energy acquisition. Most important is that plants can make their own food by capturing energy from the sun and converting it into a usable chemical form, but animals cannot. Consequently, animals rely on primary producers such as plants for energy. This is why the total amount of plant matter on earth is more than 10 times the biomass of all the animals. But, as we said, it is not a contest. That plants have a host of strategies vastly different from those that have evolved in animals, for growth, competition, defense, and reproduction, illustrates dramatically one of the fundamental truths of biology: there are multiple pathways to evolutionary success.

In this and the next two chapters, we explore the structural and physiological features of plants and how they represent adaptive solutions—often very different from those employed by animals—to the constraints of living on earth. We discuss the three main vegetative

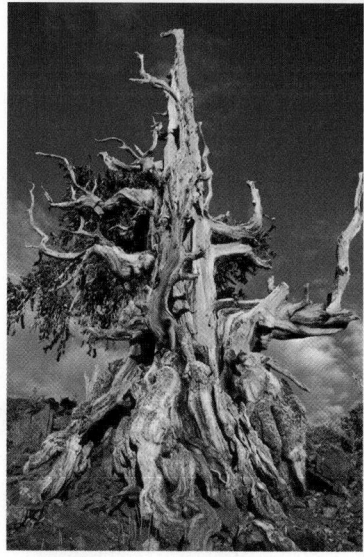

LONGEVITY
The longest-lived plants live ten times longer than the longest-living animals. Bristlecone pines have been documented to live for more than 4,800 years.

HEIGHT
The tallest plants are twenty times taller than the tallest animals. Coast redwoods have grown to be more than 379 feet.

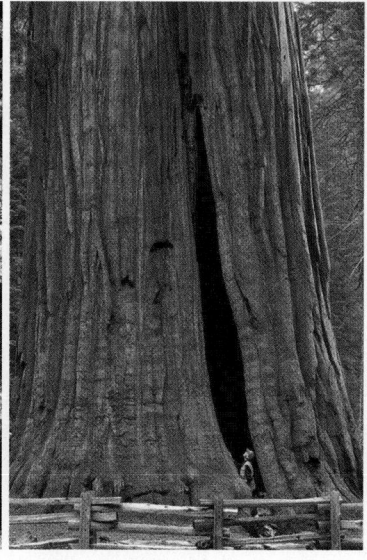

WEIGHT
The heaviest plants weigh almost twenty times as much as the heaviest animals. The largest giant sequoias are estimated to weigh more than 3,300 tons.

ENERGY
Plants can make their own food by capturing energy from the sun and converting it into a usable chemical form, but animals cannot.

FIGURE 17-1 The diversity of plant structures and features.

VASCULAR PLANT STRUCTURE

LEAVES
• The primary site of photo-synthesis, the conversion of energy from the sun into food for the plant

STEMS
• Provide structural support for the plant
• Position leaves so that they can be exposed to sunlight for photosynthesis
• Conduct food, water, and nutrients throughout the plant

ROOTS
• Absorb water and minerals from the soil
• Anchor the plant in place

Shoot system

Root system

FIGURE 17-2 Three distinct plant structures: roots, stems, and leaves.

structures in vascular plants: the roots, stems, and leaves (**FIGURE 17-2**), and how their vascular (or "circulatory") system works. We discuss plant reproductive structures in Chapter 18.

In later sections we explore plant nutrition and the methods by which water, sugars, and other nutrients move from their site of uptake or production to the parts of the plant where they are needed. And we look at some of the cellular specializations in plants that make their unique tissue types possible. First, we look at one important distinction, based on structural differences, that separates most angiosperms— the flowering plants—into two groups.

TAKE-HOME MESSAGE 17·1

Plants are an extremely diverse and successful group of organisms, generally composed of three distinct parts: roots, stems, and leaves.

The flowering plants are classified into two major groups, based on some prominent structural features of their seeds, leaves, stems, flowers, and roots. The names of the groups derive from a structure in the plant embryo within the seed, called a **cotyledon** (pronounced COT-uh-LEE-din), which usually becomes the first embryonic leaf or leaves of the plant. Plants in which one cotyledon forms are called **monocots,** and plants in which two cotyledons form are called dicots. The dicots, however, are not a monophyletic group, and include many different lineages. A large subset of the dicots, however, called the **eudicots** (pronounced you DIE cots), is a monophyletic group.

In addition to their differences with respect to cotyledons, the monocots (about 70,000 species) also differ from the eudicots (just under 200,000 species) with respect to four other common structural features (**FIGURE 17-3**).

1. *Leaves.* Monocots generally have parallel veins in their leaves, while eudicots have branching veins.

2. *Stems.* Within the stems of monocots, the vascular tissue—the tissue responsible for nutrient transport—is arranged as numerous, randomly scattered bundles.

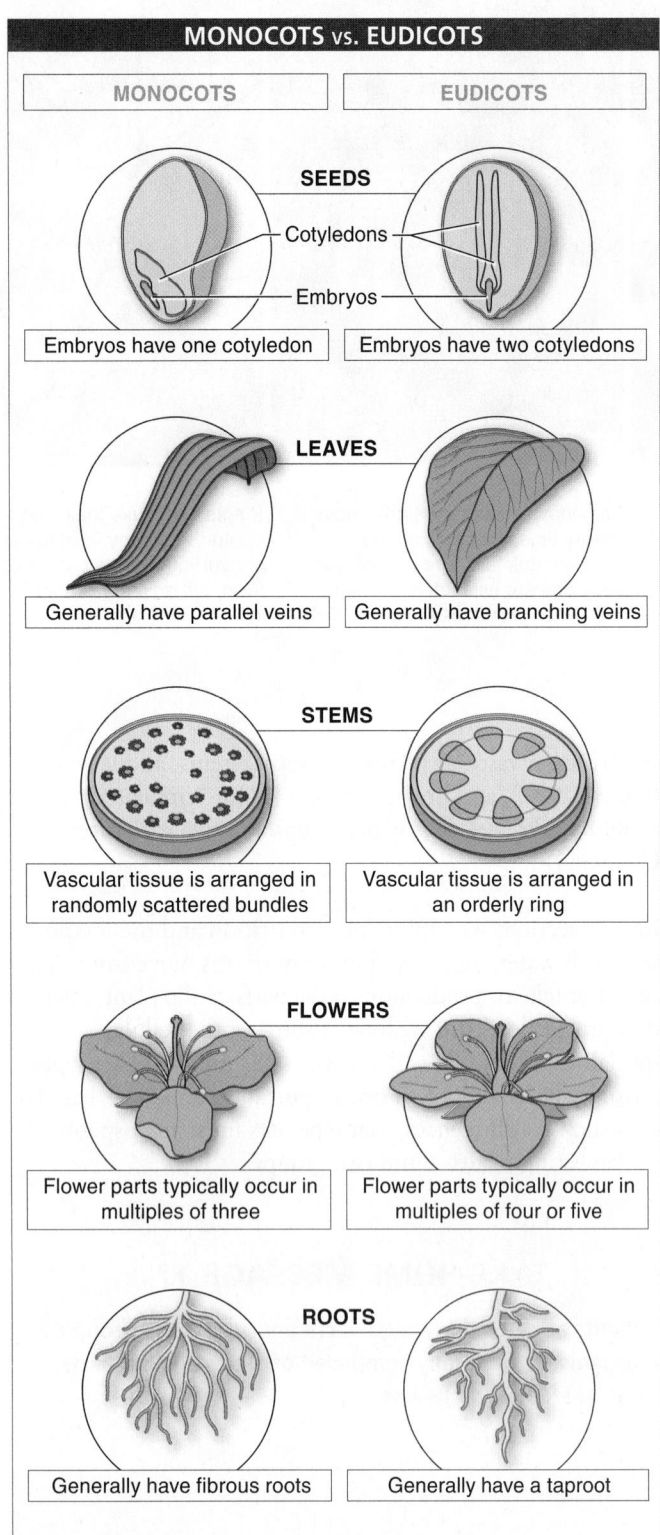

MONOCOTS vs. EUDICOTS

MONOCOTS	EUDICOTS
SEEDS	
—Cotyledons—	
—Embryos—	
Embryos have one cotyledon	Embryos have two cotyledons
LEAVES	
Generally have parallel veins	Generally have branching veins
STEMS	
Vascular tissue is arranged in randomly scattered bundles	Vascular tissue is arranged in an orderly ring
FLOWERS	
Flower parts typically occur in multiples of three	Flower parts typically occur in multiples of four or five
ROOTS	
Generally have fibrous roots	Generally have a taproot

FIGURE 17-3 Monocots and eudicots are two major groups of flowering plants that differ in several structural features.

Asparagus stem cross section (monocot)

Sunflower stem cross section (eudicot)

FIGURE 17-4 Cut through an asparagus spear and you can see the vascular tissue (shown here in purple), which is arranged in bundles and scattered throughout its stem.

You can see this if you cut through an asparagus spear (**FIGURE 17-4**). In eudicots, the vascular tissue is arranged in an orderly ring.

3. *Flowers.* The flower parts (such as petals) of monocots typically occur in multiples of three, while in eudicots they occur in fours or fives.

4. *Roots.* Monocots typically have many fibrous roots branching from the stem. Eudicots usually have a taproot, a single primary root with smaller roots branching from it.

Some common monocots are palm trees, orchids, lilies, and all of the grasses, including most of the grains used in food products. Common eudicots include roses, daisies, coffee, potatoes, apples, pears, peaches, strawberries, and most large trees, including maples and oaks.

TAKE-HOME MESSAGE 17·2

The flowering plants are divided into two major groups, the monocots and the eudicots, based on structural features of their seeds, leaves, stems, flowers, and roots.

17·3 Plants are organized into tissues, each with specific functions.

Take a look at some common plants—perhaps a rosebush, a cactus, and a redwood tree. They have some things in common: they are rooted in the ground and they have green parts. Beyond these basic characteristics, rosebushes, cacti, and redwoods don't look much like one another. If we cut them open and examine their internal structure, however, we find great similarity across all the vascular plants. (Recall from Chapter 12 that the vast majority of all plant species are vascular. In contrast to mosses, which are non-vascular, all vascular plants have a sort of circulatory system of vessels for moving water and nutrients into and throughout the organism.)

Vascular plants, which we focus on in this chapter, are all organized around the same basic body plan and built up from the same three types of tissues. Leaves, stems, roots, and flowers—all consist of these tissue types (**FIGURE 17-5**).

1. **Dermal tissue,** which covers and protects the surface of the plant, much like skin covers the human body.

2. **Vascular tissue,** which transports water and nutrients throughout the plant body, much like the circulatory system in vertebrates. (It's important to note, however, that circulation in plants differs in one huge way from circulation in animals: plants have no heart. In fact they have no pump at all.)

3. **Ground tissue,** which makes up the bulk of the plant and is where most of the plant's metabolic activities are carried out.

Each of the three tissue types, discussed in detail in the following text, is composed of one or more different types of plant cells. Recall from Chapter 3 that plant cells commonly differ from other eukaryotic cells in several ways: they may

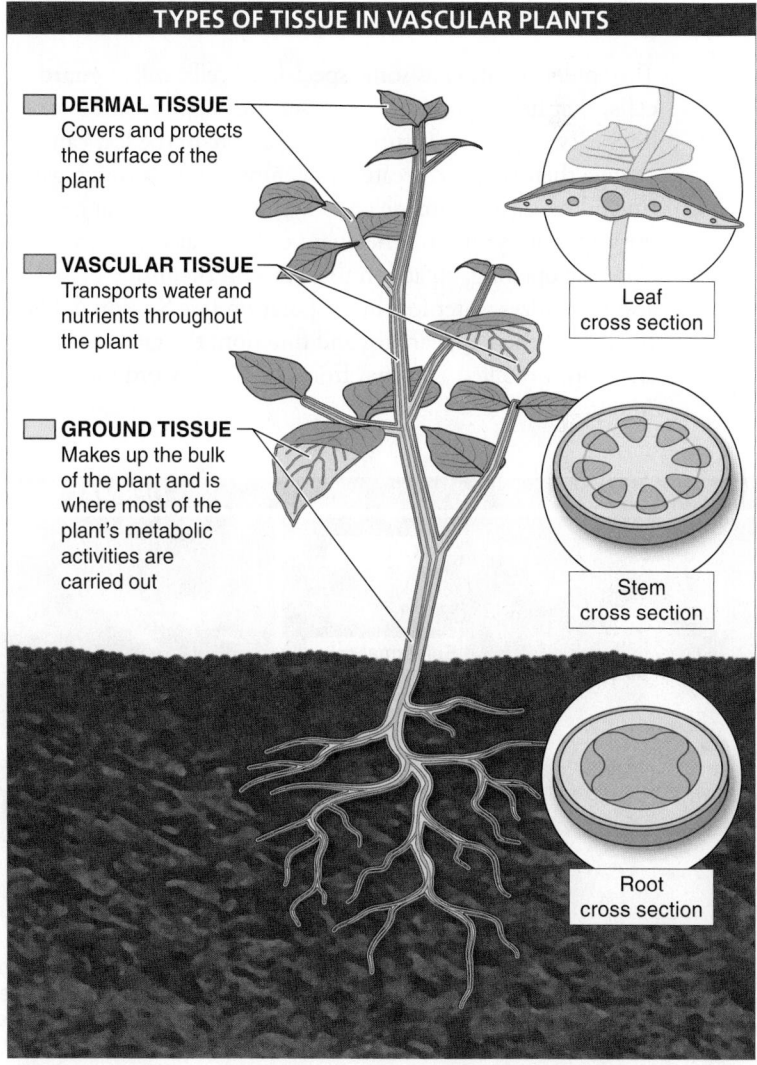

TYPES OF TISSUE IN VASCULAR PLANTS

DERMAL TISSUE
Covers and protects the surface of the plant

VASCULAR TISSUE
Transports water and nutrients throughout the plant

GROUND TISSUE
Makes up the bulk of the plant and is where most of the plant's metabolic activities are carried out

Leaf cross section

Stem cross section

Root cross section

FIGURE 17-5 Basic tissue types found in all vascular plants. Plants take a huge variety of shapes and sizes, but inside they are all composed of the same three types of tissue.

contain chloroplasts (the sites of photosynthesis), they may contain a large central vacuole (serving several functions, including storage of nutrients, waste products, or both; see Section 3-20), and they have a cellulose-containing cell wall surrounding the cell membrane.

Dermal tissue Like the skin of an animal, a plant's dermal tissue covers and protects the entire plant (**FIGURE 17-6**). Dermal tissue usually consists of a single layer of tightly packed, very thin cells, called **epidermis.** Because it may be exposed to dry air and a plant can't get out of the sun on a hot day, the epidermis produces a waxy covering, called the **cuticle,** that helps reduce some of the water loss due to evaporation. The cuticle also offers a small level of protection from pathogens and microorganisms that might want to eat the plant. The epidermal cells of roots, however, do not secrete a cuticle, because one of the root cell's primary functions is to absorb water and a cuticle would reduce the cell's ability to do this.

The epidermis also has some specialized cells, called **guard cells,** that help to regulate the gases coming into and out of leaves. Two guard cells surrounding a pore in the leaf can change their shape to create an opening through which gases (including carbon dioxide and oxygen) can be exchanged during photosynthesis. The guard cells can also expand to close the opening, an action that seals off the inside tissues and minimizes water loss by evaporation (see Section 4-11). Because of their appearance and function, the guard cells and pore are called a **stoma,** from the Greek word for "mouth."

In many vascular plants, as the plant continues to grow and increases in girth, the epidermis covering the stems and roots is replaced by a thicker, more protective dermal covering. This protective covering consists mostly of dead **cork cells.** Cork cells contain a waxy, fatty substance that makes the tissue impermeable to water and resistant to fire and decay, while small pores interspersed among the cork cells allow gas exchange. On trees, this protective covering forms the outer layer of bark. The thick covering balances two conflicting needs: the need to protect the living tissue inside the tree from risks such as fire and predation and the need to absorb CO_2 from and release O_2 into the surrounding air.

Vascular tissue As we saw earlier, plants can grow to be very large, and when they are large, they must have a system for getting nutrients to and removing waste products from all parts of the plant, from the bottommost roots to the topmost leaves. The delivery and movement of these molecules is the function of vascular tissue, which plays a role analogous to that of the circulatory system in animals (**FIGURE 17-7**). Most sugar, for example, is produced in the leaves (high up on the plant), while most water is absorbed through the roots (located underground). Because all plant cells require both water and sugar to survive, the physical separation of the leaves and roots is overcome by the vascular tissue that links them.

There are two parallel transport systems in vascular plants, each made from a different type of vascular tissue and each transporting a fluid called **sap.** (Keep in mind that, unlike animal circulatory systems, plant systems simply transport

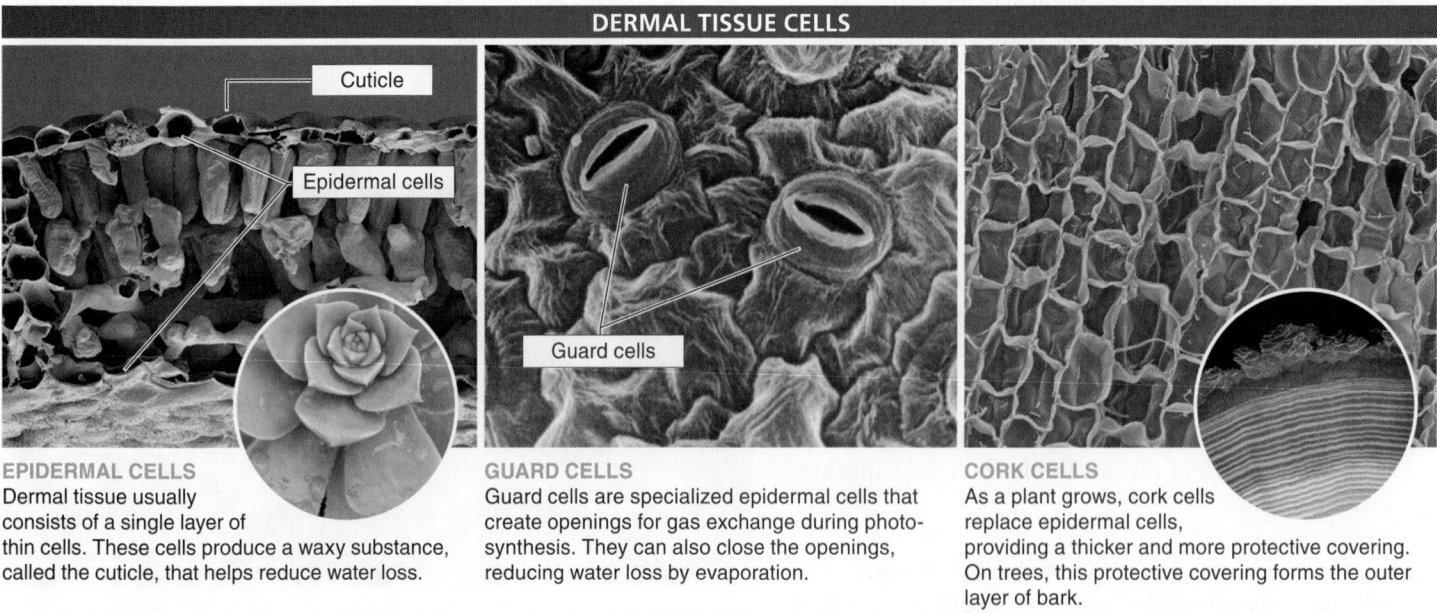

DERMAL TISSUE CELLS

Cuticle

Epidermal cells

Guard cells

EPIDERMAL CELLS
Dermal tissue usually consists of a single layer of thin cells. These cells produce a waxy substance, called the cuticle, that helps reduce water loss.

GUARD CELLS
Guard cells are specialized epidermal cells that create openings for gas exchange during photosynthesis. They can also close the openings, reducing water loss by evaporation.

CORK CELLS
As a plant grows, cork cells replace epidermal cells, providing a thicker and more protective covering. On trees, this protective covering forms the outer layer of bark.

FIGURE 17-6 Dermal tissue protects the entire plant.

Plants have two parallel transport systems, each made from a different type of vascular tissue, that transport water, sugar, and other nutrients to where they are needed.

Xylem

Phloem

Xylem, made of dead cells with rigid cell walls, provides the plant with structural support. Phloem, made of live cells with thinner cell walls, does not provide support.

XYLEM
Conducts water and dissolved minerals absorbed by the roots to tissues throughout the plant

PHLOEM
Conducts sugar produced by photosynthesis in the leaves to tissues throughout the plant

Sugar

Water

Sieve tube

FIGURE 17-7 Vascular tissue transports water, sugars, and minerals throughout the plant body.

fluids from one place to another in the plant rather than *circulating* them.) One type of vascular tissue is called **xylem** (pronounced ZY-luhm). It conducts xylem sap, containing water and dissolved minerals, from the roots to the rest of the plant body. The other vascular tissue type, called **phloem** (pronounced FLOW-uhm), conducts phloem sap, consisting mostly of water but also containing sugar—the plant's fuel source—and some minerals, to all the tissues that need sugar to fuel their activities.

Plants build some structures in ways completely unheard of in animals. For example, the tubes of the xylem are made from cells that are *dead*. The cells grow close together and, after their death, become connected to one another to form the outer surface of a pipeline. Water then flows through the pipeline and reaches all the living cells in the plant through tiny holes in the cell walls, in much the same way that a gardener's soaker hose, with hundreds of small holes, waters a large area of grass or garden. The rigid cell walls that make up the pipeline also give the plant structural support, like the girders of a building.

The other transport system, the phloem, is built from cells that remain alive while functioning as another sort of pipe. Unlike pipes, however, these cells, arranged end to end to form **sieve tubes,** have openings in their side walls through which sugar can be delivered to cells outside the phloem.

Q Cells that have already died are among the most important parts of a plant. Why?

Because phloem cells have much thinner cell walls than xylem, they don't offer much structural support to the plant.

Ground tissue The third type of tissue found in plants is called ground tissue. Because ground tissue includes everything that is neither the outer covering (dermal tissue) nor the inner vascular tissue (xylem and phloem), it makes up most of the plant body. There are three different types of ground tissue (**FIGURE 17-8**).

1. **Parenchyma cells** make up the majority of plant tissue, including most of the soft, flexible tissue found in leaves, flowers, stems, roots, and fruits. Parenchyma cells are the workhorses of the plant body, and they carry out most of the plant's metabolic activities. Depending on their location, parenchyma cells have the capacity to photosynthesize, store food molecules, produce ATP through cell respiration, or produce and release hormones. When you eat a carrot or a potato, the carbohydrate-packed cells you consume are primarily parenchyma cells that were storing energy for the plant to use at a later time. When a plant is damaged, it is parenchyma cells that divide to repair the injured tissue.

2. **Collenchyma cells** are elongated, stringy cells with thickened cell walls. This might at first seem like sloppy cell construction, but it is this construction that gives a plant great flexibility, enabling it to twist and bend.

PARENCHYMA CELLS
- Make up the majority of plant tissue, including most of the soft, flexible tissue found in leaves, flowers, stems, roots, and fruits
- Responsible for photosynthesis, food storage, and the production and release of hormones

COLLENCHYMA CELLS
- Elongated, stringy cells with thickened cell walls
- Give the plant flexibility, enabling it to twist and bend

SCLERENCHYMA CELLS
- Not living when mature
- Have very thick cell walls, containing lignin, an important component of wood
- Function like the steel girders of a building, enabling plants to resist the force of gravity and grow tall

FIGURE 17-8 Ground tissue makes up most of the plant body. Shown in the inset circles, from left to right: parenchyma cells of an apple, collenchyma cells of a sunflower, and sclerenchyma cells of a balsa tree.

An example of collenchyma tissue is the strings on the outside of a celery stalk.

3. Unlike the other types of ground tissue, **sclerenchyma cells** are not living when they are mature. They have very thick cell walls containing **lignin,** a substance that is one of the chief chemical components of wood and that makes the cell walls in woody plants indigestible to nearly all organisms. Sclerenchyma cells are very strong and can function like the steel girders of a building, enabling plants to resist the force of gravity and grow very tall. Fibrous sclerenchyma cells are used to make cloth, rope, and paper.

TAKE-HOME MESSAGE 17·3

All vascular plants are organized around the same basic body plan and built from the same three types of tissue. Dermal tissue covers and protects the surface of the plant. Vascular tissue transports water, sugars, and minerals throughout the plant body. And ground tissue, which makes up the bulk of the plant, is where most of the plant's metabolic activities are carried out.

17·4–17·7 Most plants have common structural features.

Take a deep breath: a stoma—where carbon dioxide is taken in and water is lost—from the underside of an American beech tree leaf.

17·4
Roots anchor the plant and take up water and minerals.

Roots don't garner the attention enjoyed by flowers, fruits, or the trunks and branches of tall trees. But they are essential to plant growth and survival, and they perform three primary functions (**FIGURE 17-9**).

1. *Absorption.* Roots take up water and dissolved minerals from the soil. In deserts, water absorption can be a difficult task: mesquite plants send roots straight down as deep as 175 feet to reach water, while some cacti send roots outward 50 feet in all directions to collect moisture. Roots also obtain oxygen from soil.

2. *Anchorage.* Roots secure the plant in place.

3. *Storage.* Sugar produced in the leaves can be sent to fleshy roots, where it is converted to starch and packed away for later use, much like humans store energy as lipids in fat cells around their waists. Sweet potatoes, carrots, radishes, and turnips are examples of starch-filled roots. Water, too, is sometimes stored in roots.

> **❝**If the roots are not severed, all is well—and all will be well—in the garden.**❞**
>
> — JERZY KOSINSKI, *Being There* (1971)

THE PRIMARY FUNCTIONS OF ROOTS

ABSORPTION
Roots take up water, minerals, and oxygen from the soil for use by the plant.

ANCHORAGE
Roots secure the plant in place.

STORAGE
Sugar produced by photosynthesis and converted to starch, as well as water absorbed by roots, can be packed away in the roots for later use.

FIGURE 17-9 Mostly unseen, but essential. Roots serve functions that are necessary for growth and survival.

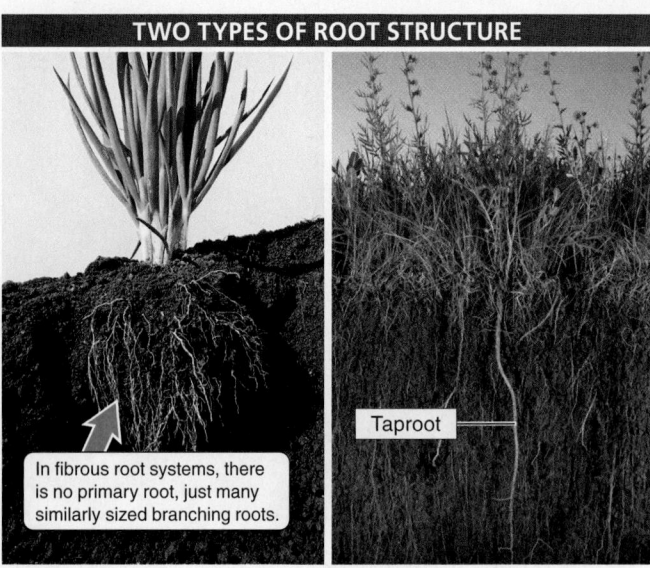

TWO TYPES OF ROOT STRUCTURE

In fibrous root systems, there is no primary root, just many similarly sized branching roots.

Taproot

FIBROUS ROOTS
- Characterized by similarly sized roots all branching out from the stem
- Tend to occupy the upper, shallow parts of the soil and spread outward
- Found primarily in monocots

TAPROOTS
- Characterized by thicker primary roots with many smaller roots branching out from them
- Often grow deep down into the soil (commonly clogging sewer pipes and damaging housing foundations)
- Found primarily in eudicots

FIGURE 17-10 Taproots and fibrous roots.

There are two types of root systems: taproots and fibrous roots (**FIGURE 17-10**). **Taproots** often grow deep down into the soil. They are characterized by a thick primary root with many smaller roots branching out from it. Found primarily in dicots, taproots commonly clog sewer pipes or burrow into and through house foundations, creating problems. Taproot systems can be thought of as more expensive to produce (energetically), but providing greater storage and depth of penetration. **Fibrous roots** are more commonly associated with monocots (but also found in some eudicots). They have numerous similarly sized roots all arising from the stem and branching out. They tend to occupy the upper, shallow parts of the soil and spread outward. Fibrous root systems are energetically less expensive to produce, characteristic of situations in which plants have greater spread and faster growth.

The organization of all root tissue is simple (**FIGURE 17-11**). A cross section of a root reveals the usual three tissue types. In most eudicots, the vascular tissue (xylem and phloem) is a central column, surrounded by ground tissue, and at the outer edge is dermal tissue. The xylem—a tube-like system in which water moves up into the plant—is in the center of the root, with arms radiating outward. Around the xylem arms are phloem strands, which conduct high-energy sugars to the roots from the leaves. Most monocot roots have a different

organization, with a central core of soft, spongy parenchyma tissue, called **pith,** surrounded by a ring of vascular tissue.

When the ground tissue in a root is used to store energy in the form of starch, the root becomes enlarged and fleshy. Plants store excess energy for the times when rapid growth or flower production is demanding a lot of energy.

Q How are sweet potatoes like the "love handles" on a person's waist?

Having so much food all in one place, though, can be risky. Animals are often tempted to find such storehouses and eat them. Many humans, for instance, like to dig up and eat large roots such as beets, turnips, carrots, and sweet potatoes.

The outer surface of the root is epidermis. Perhaps the most important components of a root's epidermis are the epidermal cells that elongate and become tiny hairs. These hairs greatly

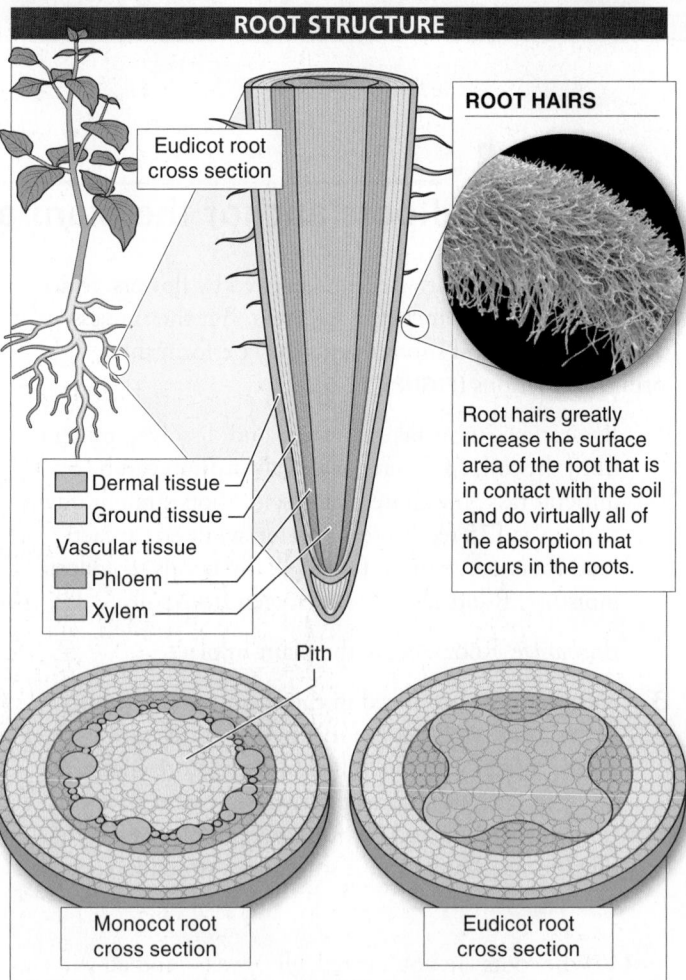

ROOT STRUCTURE

Eudicot root cross section

ROOT HAIRS

Root hairs greatly increase the surface area of the root that is in contact with the soil and do virtually all of the absorption that occurs in the roots.

Dermal tissue
Ground tissue
Vascular tissue
Phloem
Xylem

Pith

Monocot root cross section

Eudicot root cross section

FIGURE 17-11 Organization of tissues within the root. In monocots, vascular tissue is dispersed throughout the ground tissue in the stem. In eudicots, the vascular tissue of the stem is arranged in a ring.

increase the surface area of the root that is in contact with the soil. Root hairs do virtually all of the absorption that occurs in the roots. The epidermal cells are extremely permeable to water and absorb it easily. The water then moves through and between the cells of the root's ground tissue until it reaches the xylem, from where it is distributed throughout the plant.

The many spaces between root cells allow oxygen to diffuse in so that the root's cells can respire (make ATP and exchange gases with the environment). Mangroves grow in water-logged soil, a habitat in which very little air can get into their roots. As a consequence, they produce odd-looking long roots—with numerous little pores in them—that remain above the water (**FIGURE 17-12**). The pores open up to the loosely packed cells, creating a column of air that extends down to the underwater roots.

TAKE-HOME MESSAGE 17·4

Roots have three primary functions in plants: (1) absorption, the uptake of water and dissolved minerals from soil; (2) anchorage, securing the plant in place; and (3) storage of water and excess starch for future use.

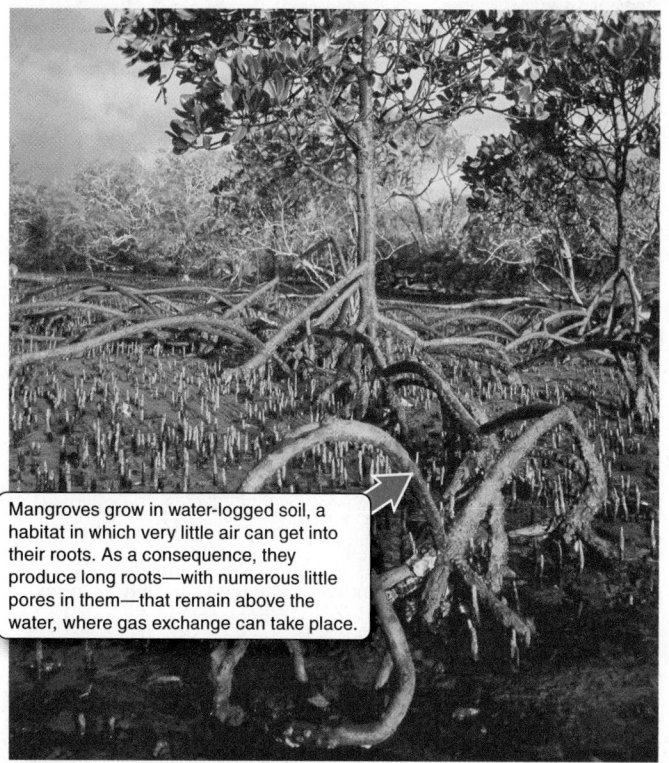

Mangroves grow in water-logged soil, a habitat in which very little air can get into their roots. As a consequence, they produce long roots—with numerous little pores in them—that remain above the water, where gas exchange can take place.

FIGURE 17-12 "Snorkel roots." Mangroves lift some of their roots out of the water for better "breathing."

17·5
Stems are the backbone of the plant.

When an organism must reach toward the sun for the energy to make its own food, gravity can be the enemy. The body of a plant is one continuous structure, with the root system below and the shoot system above the ground. The above-ground portion, the **shoot,** is divided into two parts: stems and leaves. In some species, the shoot system also includes flowers and fruits, the reproductive structures, which we discuss in Chapter 18.

Serving as the backbone of the plant, the **stem** allows the plant to grow and orient itself toward the sun. But providing structural support and positioning leaves toward the light are just two of the three main functions served by stems. The third function is housing the plant's transport infrastructure—the xylem and the phloem—through which the distribution of water, sugars, and other nutrients occurs (**FIGURE 17-13**).

In plants, growth occurs in regions called **meristems,** made up of undifferentiated cells. These cells divide, often at very

FIGURE 17-13 Stems provide support and the transport infrastructure needed for the distribution of water, sugars, and other nutrients.

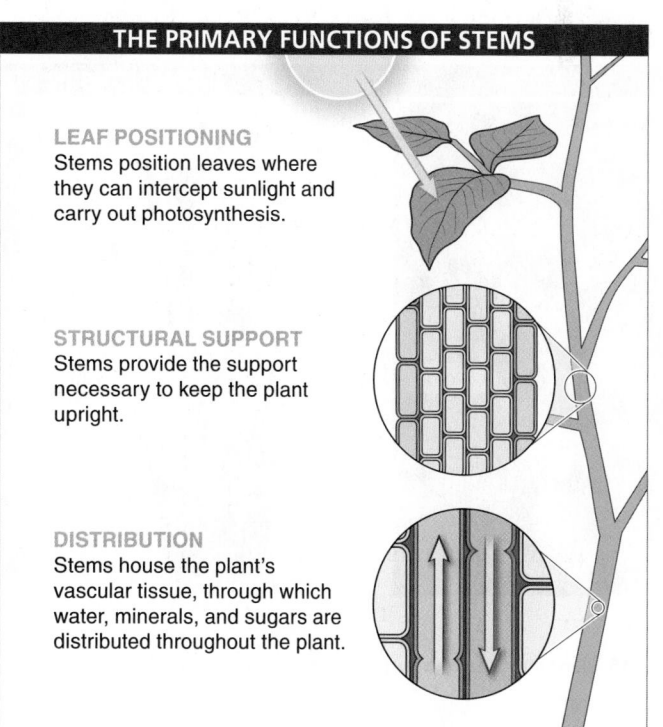

THE PRIMARY FUNCTIONS OF STEMS

LEAF POSITIONING
Stems position leaves where they can intercept sunlight and carry out photosynthesis.

STRUCTURAL SUPPORT
Stems provide the support necessary to keep the plant upright.

DISTRIBUTION
Stems house the plant's vascular tissue, through which water, minerals, and sugars are distributed throughout the plant.

STEM STRUCTURE

Eudicot stem cross section

Apical meristem

Nodes

Dermal tissue
Ground tissue
Vascular tissue
Phloem
Xylem

Vascular bundles

Lateral meristems (cambium)

Pith

Cortex

Monocot stem cross section

Eudicot stem cross section

FIGURE 17-14 Organization of tissues within the stem.

high rates, generating additional meristem cells along with cells that differentiate into epidermis, vascular tissue, or ground tissue. At the tip of a root or stem, the meristem is called an **apical meristem,** and division of cells there causes the root or stem to increase in length. **Lateral meristems,** on the other hand, consist of a layer of cells, called cambium, that cause a stem or root to become thicker, as opposed to longer, when they divide. We discuss plant growth in more detail in Chapter 18.

Stem growth is similar to the growth of roots, with the added complexity that it is segmented (**FIGURE 17-14**). That is, the stem grows a bit and then produces **nodes,** little lumps of tissue from which leaves, flowers, cones, or additional stems (or even a branch) may grow.

The stems of flowering plants contain vascular bundles. (Recall that there are two types of pipelines through which sap, containing essential fluids and chemicals, is transported: water and minerals move through the xylem, and sugars move through the phloem.) As we saw in Section 17-2, these bundles are arranged in one of two distinct patterns. In eudicots, a ring of vascular bundles is arranged near the outside of the stem. At any point that you slice a cross section of the stem, you will see a ring of bundles, like a clock face. Where each of the numbers might be, there is a double pipeline. The outer pipe is the phloem and the inner pipe is the xylem. This ring of vascular bundles divides the stem's

VARIATIONS IN STEM STRUCTURE

Potato — Stems

Daffodil — Stem

Asparagus — Stem

Strawberry — Stems

FIGURE 17-15 Plant stems take a surprising number of forms.

 Stems can become modified—sometimes into structures almost unrecognizable as stems.

ground tissue into two distinct areas: one inside and one outside the ring. The inner tissue is the pith and the outer tissue is the **cortex.** In monocots, such as corn, the vascular bundles seem less organized: they are dispersed throughout the stem. In all vascular plants, because each node of the stem may be the site of a leaf or a branch, some of the vascular bundles turn outward at this point and enter the leaf or branch.

If we started slicing up the stems of all the plants around us, it would quickly become clear that there isn't one single design for all stems. While the stems of all flowering plants are variations on the two themes described here, they vary tremendously (**FIGURE 17-15**). Most of the bulbs that gardeners plant each year, such as those for daffodils and lilies, are stems. They have many modified leaves attached to them and, after planting, the roots emerge from the bottom.

Some of our favorite foods come from modified stem tissue. Asparagus spears are fleshy stems. If you look closely, you can see what appear to be scales along the spear, and at the tip are very tiny leaves that haven't branched off very far from the stem. Broccoli and cauliflower also include modified stem. Also, the horizontal runners of a strawberry plant are stems, from which roots emerge at regular intervals to anchor the plant and stems to the ground. And growing underground, potatoes, too, are highly modified branching stems—not roots. When potatoes sprout, the "eyes" contain lateral buds that branch out. Similar-appearing foods that are true roots, such as sweet potatoes, never form such "eyes."

As stems grow and branch, they increase in girth and length, becoming stronger and better able to position leaves where they can have adequate exposure to the sun for making food through photosynthesis. In the next chapter, we investigate the process by which stems develop into tree trunks and, in doing so, produce wood—perhaps the most important non-food plant product on earth.

TAKE-HOME MESSAGE 17·5

Stems serve three chief functions in plants: (1) they put leaves in positions where they can intercept sunlight and carry out photosynthesis; (2) they provide structural support for the plant; and (3) they contain the xylem and phloem, through which water, minerals, and sugars are distributed throughout the plant body.

17·6 Leaves feed the plant.

One of the recurring themes in comparing plants and animals is that acquiring energy and nutrients can be difficult when you can't move. **Leaves** solve this problem handily. They have one primary purpose—producing food for the plant—and a dazzling array of forms has evolved that allow them to accomplish this purpose efficiently and effectively. Like the solar collectors that can heat houses (but much more efficient), leaves intercept sunlight and, by putting chloroplast-containing photosynthetic cells in the path of that light, convert the potential energy of the sun into the usable chemical energy of sugars. Plants don't need to move to get energy—they utilize the energy that comes to them.

The arrangement of cells inside the leaf clearly serves the purpose of capturing the energy of sunlight to make sugar and then efficiently transporting that food out of the leaf to the rest of the plant. Starting at the upper surface and moving inward, let's examine the leaf's layered structure (**FIGURE 17-16**).

1. The epidermis forms the upper surface. The non-photosynthetic, protective epidermal cells secrete a waxy cuticle that protects the leaf from damage and reduces the rate at which water evaporates from the leaf in the hot sun.

2. Below the epidermis are a few layers of photosynthetic cells. The cells in the first layer, called the palisade mesophyll, are closely packed parenchyma cells, rich in chloroplasts. This is the part of the leaf where the highest rates of photosynthesis occur. In the next layer or two, parenchyma cells are irregularly shaped and more loosely arranged, causing numerous air pockets that make the layers somewhat spongy—hence this portion of the leaf is called spongy mesophyll. The shape and loose arrangement of the cells in the spongy layer cause most of cells to be in contact with the air surrounding the leaf, enhancing the diffusion of gases, including CO_2—essential to photosynthesis—from the air and into the plant's photosynthetic cells.

3. Running throughout the middle, the veins of the leaf are photosynthetic layers composed of vascular tissue, xylem and phloem. Much like the veins, arteries, and capillaries in humans, they reach out to all the cells to deliver water and essential minerals and haul away the

LEEF STRUCTURE

Legend:
- Dermal tissue
- Ground tissue
- Vascular tissue
  - Phloem
  - Xylem

1 WAXY CUTICLE

2 NON-PHOTOSYNTHETIC EPIDERMAL CELLS

3 PHOTOSYNTHETIC CELLS
- Palisade mesophyll cell
- Spongy mesophyll cell

4 VASCULAR TISSUE
- Xylem
- Phloem

5 NON-PHOTOSYNTHETIC EPIDERMAL CELLS AND STOMATA
- Epidermal cell
- Guard cells
- Stomata

FIGURE 17-16 A five-part "photosynthetic-cell sandwich." In a leaf cross section we see (1) a waxy cuticle on top; (2) a layer of non-photosynthetic epidermal cells; (3) a few layers of photosynthetic cells, with (4) xylem and phloem "piping" moving essential molecules in and out; and (5) a bottom layer of non-photosynthetic epidermal cells interspersed with stomata, the breathing holes.

sugar products of photosynthesis for use elsewhere in the plant.

4. Like the top of the leaf, the bottom layer is composed of non-photosynthetic epidermal cells. Interspersed among these cells are **stomata** (see Section 17-3), the pore-like openings through which the plant takes in CO_2 and releases O_2, one of the by-products of photosynthesis.

Nearly all leaves are thin blades attached to a stem by a small stalk, but they vary tremendously in appearance (**FIGURE 17-17**). A plant can have a small number of huge leaves. Water lily leaves, for example, can reach almost 7 feet across and inspired Monet's mural-sized paintings, which are more than 6 feet high and 42 feet wide (**FIGURE 17-18**). At the other end of the spectrum, plants can have a large number of small leaves. Duckweed is such a plant: twenty-five duckweed leaves laid end to end cover less than an inch. Both strategies can be effective ways of creating large surface

areas for intercepting sunlight. But plants can't change the laws of physics, and those laws dictate that the energy in sunlight can't pass through very many layers of cells without being absorbed or reflected. For this reason, even though leaves come in all shapes and sizes, they are all thin. If leaves were more than a few layers thick, the cells near the bottom would not get enough energy to run the sugar-making machinery.

Q Leaves come in a huge number of shapes, but nearly all leaves are very, very thin. Why?

VARIATIONS IN LEAF STRUCTURE

CONIFER LEAVES

MONOCOT LEAVES

EUDICOT LEAVES

FIGURE 17-17 Some physiological "problems" have many solutions. Leaves come in all shapes and sizes, but they all have in common an ability to make food from sunlight and carbon dioxide. Plants are listed from top to bottom, left to right: spruce, Scots pine, Chile pine, corn lilies, bamboo, banana leaf, mixed deciduous leaves, branching veins of a eudicot leaf, cactus.

FIGURE 17-18 Monet was inspired by the large leaves of water lilies and painted them on a huge canvas. Water lilies produce some of the largest leaves of any plants.

shapes and styles is shown in Figure 17-17.

Perhaps the most extremely modified plant leaves are the hard, dry spines of most cacti. The spines don't contribute to photosynthesis—that occurs in the stems, which we see as the prominent green parts of the plant—but they do help adapt cacti for desert living. They slow the speed of the warm winds as they pass over the plant, for instance, reducing the water lost to evaporation. The spines also help moisture from the cooler night air condense, enabling the plant to capture a bit of the most limited desert resource. Spines go a long way toward discouraging birds and mammals from eating the plant, as well. In Chapter 19, we explore some of the chemicals that plants sequester in their leaves that also help protect them from being eaten.

Among the flowering plants, many monocots can generally be identified by their long, flat leaves that are oriented vertically, as in the grasses, in a pattern that keeps them from shading each other. Eudicot leaves come in two types: simple leaves, each with just a single blade, and compound leaves, with multiple leaflets that radiate outward from a single point. Each of these two types can vary greatly, from sharp-edged to smooth-edged. Gymnosperms—seed plants, such as the conifers, that don't produce flowers—have a variety of leaf structures, including needle-like leaves, such as those of pine trees. A sampling of the wide range of leaf

> ## TAKE-HOME MESSAGE 17·6
>
> Leaves are thin and have a three-layered structure that enables them to effectively capture energy and transport water and nutrients. In leaves, plants convert the potential energy of sunlight into the usable chemical energy of sugar. Leaves also have vascular tissue through which food is transported out to the rest of the plant, and water and minerals are transported in.

17·7 Several structures help plants resist water loss.

If you're lying on a beach, working in a field, or walking in the mountains, the sun's heat can feel relentless. But humans can seek shade when the heat becomes too intense and drink water whenever we're thirsty. Plants don't have these options. Consequently, they are perpetually at risk of losing too much water as it evaporates from their tissues. Because water is essential to nearly every chemical reaction in every living organism, water loss is not a small issue. Not surprisingly, plants have multiple adaptations that solve the "sun problem" and keep them from becoming dangerously dehydrated. We see three of these important adaptations right on the surfaces of most leaves (**FIGURE 17-19**).

1. **The cuticle.** Dermatologists have instructed people for decades that good skin care and protection starts with maintaining the skin's moisture. Many plant structures have evolved that are consistent with this advice. As we've seen, the top layer of most leaves, secreted by their epidermal cells, is the cuticle. This waxy, water-repelling substance keeps water inside a leaf from diffusing through the leaf and evaporating into the atmosphere. It seals in water almost completely. Carnauba wax, from the cuticle of Brazilian palm trees, is an ingredient in many sunscreen products for humans, as well as in a popular car polish.

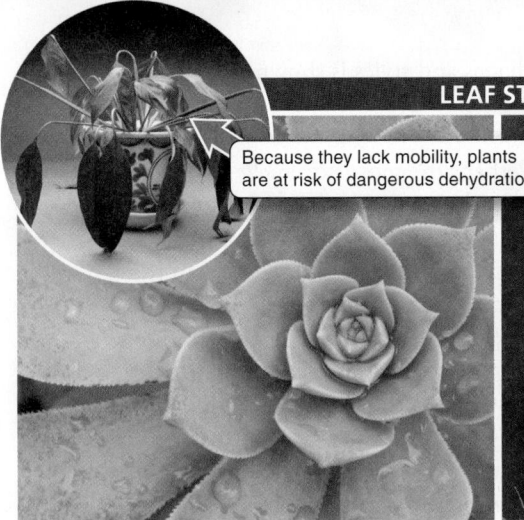

Because they lack mobility, plants are at risk of dangerous dehydration.

CUTICLE
This waxy, water-repelling substance keeps water inside the leaves from diffusing through the leaf and evaporating away into the atmosphere.

LEAF HAIRS
These tiny hairs can reflect sunlight and reduce the speed at which breezes move over the leaf's surface, decreasing water loss through evaporation.

GUARD CELLS
Guard cells can increase in size to seal off stomata or decrease in size to create a small opening through which carbon dioxide can pass and through which water can be lost.

FIGURE 17-19 Plants have multiple adaptations that keep them from becoming dangerously dehydrated.

2. **Leaf hairs.** Some of the surface cells on leaves become modified as tiny hairs. These hairs can reduce water loss by reflecting some of the sunlight (thus reducing the temperature inside the leaf) and reducing the speed at which breezes move over the leaf's surface, taking water with them—through evaporation. Standing in the sun, who would experience more evaporative cooling, a person with shaved legs or someone with hairy legs?

3. **Guard cells.** The cuticle would solve the problem of water loss in plants almost completely if it covered the entire leaf. Unfortunately, the cuticle is also impervious to CO_2, which is an essential ingredient for photosynthesis. So, just as a castle needs a front door—which then becomes a major point of vulnerability to attack—leaves must have openings to the environment. These openings, the stomata—as many as 10,000 per square centimeter—are on the underside of the leaves (and, to a lesser extent, on stems). Their structure reflects an important water-conservation adaptation. A pair of guard cells (seen in Figure 17-6) surrounds each pore, one cell on either side. The guard cells can increase in size to seal off the opening or decrease in size to create a small opening through which CO_2 can enter and water can be lost. The opening and closing of the stomata is controlled by osmotic pressure in the guard cells and appears to occur in response to changes in temperature, humidity, light intensity, or CO_2 concentration.

Stomata are the chief sites where plants "breathe." If you were to do a cruel experiment and coat the underside of the leaves of some plants with Vaseline, what do you think would happen? With no way for air to enter, the plants would become starved for CO_2 and eventually the leaves would die.

Q How could smearing Vaseline on leaves cause a plant to "suffocate"?

TAKE-HOME MESSAGE 17·7

Plants have multiple adaptations that enable them to resist becoming dangerously dehydrated. These adaptations include the cuticle, leaf hairs, and guard cells.

17·8–17·10 Plant nutrition: plants obtain sunlight and usable chemical elements from the environment.

A corn seedling emerges from soil.

17·8 Four factors are necessary for plant growth.

Gardening is harder than it looks. Plants need sunlight, water, and air to thrive. But that's not enough. Just as humans will not grow and remain healthy without a nutritious diet, plants will get sick, wither, and even die if they don't have adequate nutrition (**FIGURE 17-20**). Let's examine just what that means.

Plants generally require four things for proper nutrition. The first three are (1) sunlight for the energy to build molecules of sugar; (2) water, for numerous reasons, including as a source of electrons for photosynthesis (see Section 4-9); and (3) air as a source of carbon dioxide and oxygen. The carbon dioxide is a source of carbon atoms used in the construction of sugar during photosynthesis, and the oxygen serves as an electron acceptor in cellular respiration as a plant breaks down sugar for energy (just as animals and other organisms do; see Chapter 4). And (4) plants usually need soil. But how does soil contribute to plant nutrition?

For a plant to grow, it must build new cells, which are then assembled into new tissues. These new cells must have cell walls, DNA, mitochondria, and all the other cell components. Aside from the carbon and oxygen obtained from CO_2 in the air and hydrogen from water, plants must get all of these raw materials elsewhere, usually from the soil. In all, there are 13 different minerals (each of which is an element) that plants require for proper survival and growth.

FIGURE 17-20 The components necessary for maintaining plant health.

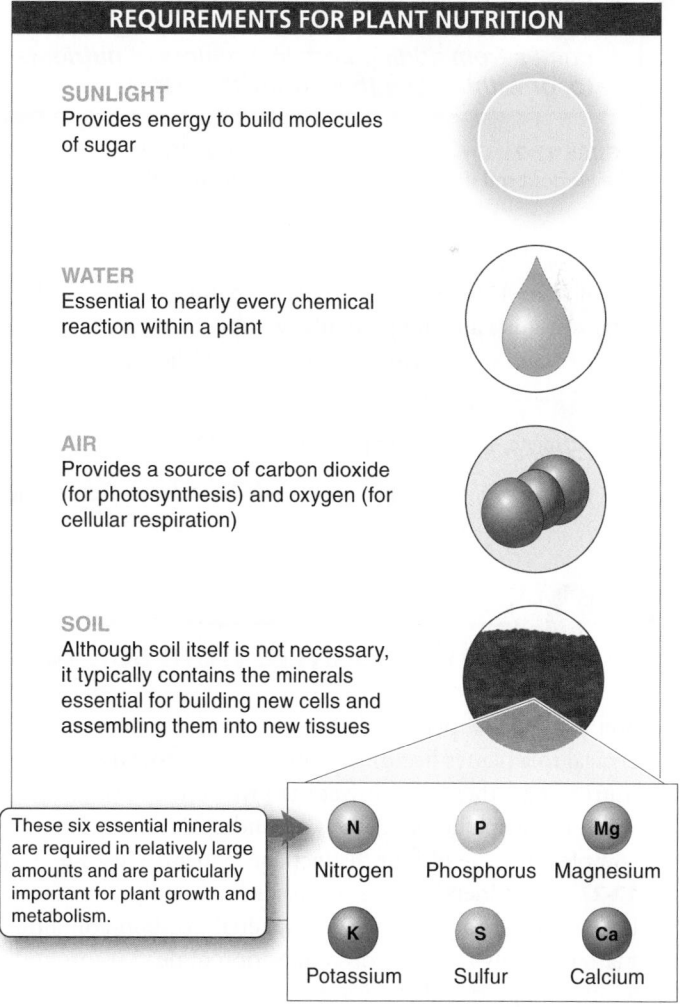

REQUIREMENTS FOR PLANT NUTRITION

SUNLIGHT
Provides energy to build molecules of sugar

WATER
Essential to nearly every chemical reaction within a plant

AIR
Provides a source of carbon dioxide (for photosynthesis) and oxygen (for cellular respiration)

SOIL
Although soil itself is not necessary, it typically contains the minerals essential for building new cells and assembling them into new tissues

These six essential minerals are required in relatively large amounts and are particularly important for plant growth and metabolism.

N	P	Mg
Nitrogen	Phosphorus	Magnesium
K	S	Ca
Potassium	Sulfur	Calcium

Hydroponically grown plants are grown without soil. Much of what we know about plant nutrition comes from adding certain amounts of nutrients to, or withholding them from, the water.

FIGURE 17-21 Growing plants hydroponically. Plants can grow just fine without soil if the essential nutrients are added to their water.

magnesium, for making chlorophyll

potassium, for making enzymes and controlling water balance

sulfur, for making proteins and vitamins

calcium, for a large number of different cell functions

Plants need seven additional elements in much smaller amounts: chlorine, iron, boron, manganese, zinc, copper, and molybdenum. How small are the amounts needed? A plant could get all the chlorine it needs just from being touched by a human with sweaty fingertips. Similarly, a tiny amount of one of these minerals may be present in the seed that the plant grows from, and this amount may be enough to supply the plant for its entire life. In other cases, the plant must "reach out" to obtain these elements from the soil by growing roots that reach to where the elements are.

Much of what we know about plant nutrition comes from **hydroponically grown plants** (**FIGURE 17-21**). These plants are grown without soil. Instead, they are grown in water that has chemicals added. By adding or withholding exact amounts of certain chemicals, it is possible to determine which are essential and in what amounts. These findings are important in helping farmers determine what types of fertilizers they need for crops, as the farmers try to coax more growth out of each acre of land than would occur naturally.

Q Can a plant grow without soil? How?

Six of these 13 essential elements are required in relatively large amounts and are particularly important for producing proteins and the enzymes that catalyze all the reactions taking place in plants:

nitrogen, for making proteins and DNA

phosphorus, for making ATP, DNA, and cell membranes

TAKE-HOME MESSAGE 17·7

Plant growth depends on four important factors: (1) sunlight for energy, (2) water, (3) air as a source of carbon dioxide and oxygen, and (4) minerals, usually obtained from soil.

17·9 Nutrients cycle from soil to organisms and back again.

Soil is an almost perpetual source of nutrients that are critical to a plant's health and survival. But how do the nutrients get there? To answer that, we need to realize that soil is not just a homogeneous mound of dirt. Soil is a complex mixture of four distinct components (**FIGURE 17-22**): (1) minerals: inorganic particles, usually from the breakdown of rock; (2) organic materials: carbon-containing matter, usually from the decomposition of dead plants and animals; (3) air; and (4) water.

Minerals About half of the total volume of soil is inorganic materials. These materials come primarily from the weathering of rocks, which decay physically and chemically over time, releasing minerals. The inorganic particles are grouped into three sizes: sand, silt, and clay. As you may know from feeling sand at the beach, there's plenty of air between the particles, so sand doesn't hold water very well. That's why it is so easy to grab handfuls of it and let the grains fall through your fingers. Silt particles are smaller, as you would feel if you grabbed a handful of soil from the bottom of a riverbed. Clay particles, the smallest of all, pack together very densely. Because minerals passing through the soil cling to clay, it is a valuable component of soil; clay holds the essential minerals in place for plants to absorb as

GRAPHIC CONTENT!
Thinking critically about visual displays of data.
Turn to p. 694 for a closer inspection of this figure.

COMPOSITION OF SOIL

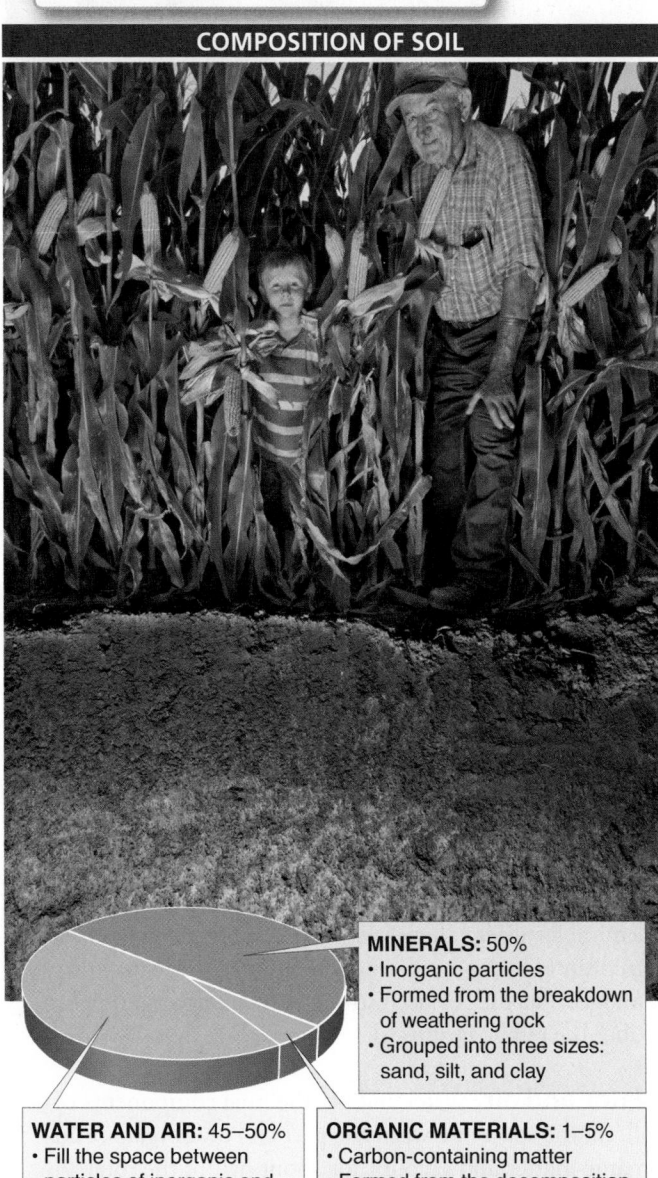

MINERALS: 50%
- Inorganic particles
- Formed from the breakdown of weathering rock
- Grouped into three sizes: sand, silt, and clay

WATER AND AIR: 45–50%
- Fill the space between particles of inorganic and organic matter

ORGANIC MATERIALS: 1–5%
- Carbon-containing matter
- Formed from the decomposition of dead plants and animals

Soil, a mixture of minerals, organic matter, air, and water, is a source of nutrients that are critical to a plant's health and survival.

FIGURE 17-22 The components of soil.

SOIL pH AND FLOWER COLOR

Although all hydrangeas are colored by the same pigment, when the soil is acidic (pH = 5–5.5) more aluminum is available to the plant, causing the flowers to bloom in blue, and when the soil is less acidic (pH= 6-6.5) they bloom in pink.

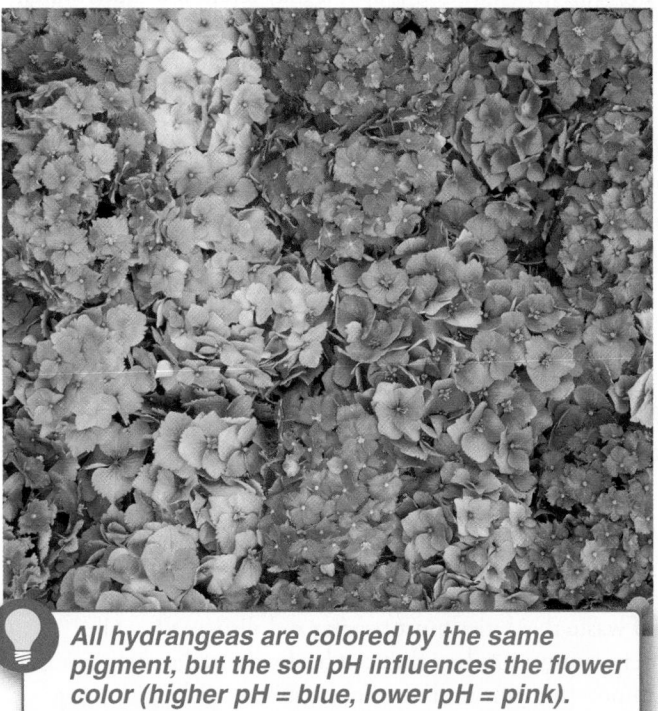

All hydrangeas are colored by the same pigment, but the soil pH influences the flower color (higher pH = blue, lower pH = pink).

FIGURE 17-23 Multicolored hydrangeas.

needed. However, too much densely packed clay in soil can limit the supply of air available for plant roots to absorb, leading to poor plant growth.

The best soils have about equal amounts of each type of particle. The minerals present in soil determine the pH of the soil and can affect how well plants grow; they can even influence the color of flowers (**FIGURE 17-23**).

Organic materials Leaves fall and animals die, but **decomposition** returns their chemicals to the soil, making reuptake by plant roots possible. Animal droppings are very important to plants, too, serving as highly concentrated bits of nitrogen, perhaps the most important of the essential plant nutrients. Called **humus** (pronounced HYOO-muhss),

> "I bequeath myself to the dirt
>   to grow from the grass I love,
> If you want me again
>   look for me under your boot-soles."
>
> — WALT WHITMAN, *Leaves of Grass*

TYPES OF PLANT TISSUES   STRUCTURAL FEATURES OF PLANTS   **PLANT NUTRITION**   NUTRIENT TRANSPORT IN PLANTS   **681** all these organic decay products make up about 1% to 5% of the soil (**FIGURE 17-24**). The humus also absorbs and releases water easily and, in the process, releases many nutrients. With too little humus, the soil may be deficient in nutrients. With too much, it may retain too much water.

Most of the decomposition of organic matter is carried out by huge populations of bacteria, fungi, insects, and earthworms that live in soil. Aristotle called earthworms "the intestines of the earth." Passing soil through their guts as they feed on organic matter, earthworms increase tremendously the amount of nitrogen available for plants.

Q What is composting? Why is it useful? Is it dangerous? A very practical application of the decomposition of organic matter can be seen in the process of **composting,** in which bacteria are utilized to process organic wastes—such as kitchen garbage, manure, yard clippings, and even sewage—metabolizing the material and in the process converting it into fertilizer (**FIGURE 17-25**). Compost heaps can speed the process of organic breakdown and greatly reduce the volume of waste that cities must process and dispose of, while generating a product that can be distributed to help return important plant nutrients to the soil.

The growing populations of bacteria in compost generate large amounts of heat—a compost heap can reach temperatures above 60° C (140° F), which is why so much steam is coming out of the overturned earth pictured in Figure 17-25—and the heat can kill many of the original organisms, which are replaced by more heat-tolerant species that are not harmful to

Composting can greatly reduce the volume of waste that cities must process and dispose of, while generating a product that can return important nutrients to the soil.

FIGURE 17-25 The practice of composting converts organic waste into useful fertilizer.

humans. For many centuries, and up until the middle of the 20th century, the use of human feces, called "night soil," as fertilizer was a common practice. In much of rural Japan and China, the purchase, collection, and distribution of night soil was a large industry. The night soil from wealthier villages even sold for higher prices; because they had better diets, there were more nutrients (particularly nitrogen from protein) in their waste products. For sanitary reasons (and as a consequence of increased availability of chemical fertilizers), however, the use of night soil has become significantly less common. Because human waste may carry pathogens, its use has been strongly discouraged in order to reduce the public health risk.

Q Does human waste have value as fertilizer?

Water and air Water and air, the final components of soil, fill the spaces between the particles of inorganic and organic matter and account for about half of the total volume of soil.

DECOMPOSITION OF ORGANIC MATTER

The decomposition of organic matter is facilitated by huge populations of bacteria, fungi, insects, and earthworms that live in the soil.

BEFORE
Decaying organic matter

AFTER
Humus

FIGURE 17-24 Decomposition (such as in the compost bin shown here) returns the chemicals inside animal and plant remains to the soil.

TAKE-HOME MESSAGE 17·9

Soil is a mixture of minerals, organic materials, air, and water that serves as an almost perpetual source of nutrients critical to a plant's health and survival.

Plants acquire essential nitrogen with the help of bacteria.

There is a sad irony to floating in a lifeboat in the ocean. Despite being surrounded by water, a person is likely to die from lack of water, because salt water just isn't drinkable for a human. Plants encounter a similarly ironic situation when it comes to one of the most important components in their diet: nitrogen.

Q **Burying dead fish in their fields can help farmers produce more food. Why?**

Nitrogen is the most common element in our atmosphere. Almost 80% of the air around us is nitrogen. But despite its abundance, lack of nitrogen is the factor, after lack of water, that limits most plant growth. Nearly every terrestrial plant outside the tropics would grow more with more nitrogen. Early farmers recognized this fact and would bury dead fish along with their corn crops. As the fish decomposed, the rotting organic material increased the nitrogen in the soil that was available for the plants' use, significantly improving the size and health of the corn plants. Today, people regularly treat their crops, flowers, and lawns with nitrogen-rich fertilizers.

Adding nitrogen to the soil in which a plant lives commonly increases the plant's growth, because every protein the plant builds contains nitrogen, every bit of DNA the plant synthesizes contains nitrogen, and every molecule of chlorophyll it creates contains nitrogen. In order to grow and survive, plants need nitrogen. If nitrogen is so plentiful in the air, why can't plants make use of it directly?

The problem is that nitrogen in the atmosphere exists as a molecule of two nitrogen atoms (N_2) bound very tightly and stably together (**FIGURE 17-26**). The nitrogen becomes usable for plants and animals only when it is converted to a molecule with a single nitrogen atom, such as ammonium (NH_4+) or nitrate (NO_3-). Breaking apart the strong, stable bond between the two nitrogen atoms in the nitrogen molecule is no easy task,

Q **Are all bacterial infections bad for plants?**

however, and plant evolution did not produce the metabolic know-how to do it. Bacteria, on the other hand, are metabolic wizards, and several species can break nitrogen molecules apart, using an enzyme they produce called nitrogenase, and get the nitrogen into a plant-usable form—a process called **nitrogen fixation.** A mutually

NITROGEN FIXATION

Atmospheric nitrogen (N_2)

Nitrate (NO_3^-) Ammonium (NH_4^+)

1 Atmospheric nitrogen does not exist in an easily usable form in nature and must first be chemically modified by bacteria.

2 Bacteria break apart the strong and stable bonds of atmospheric nitrogen.

3 Nitrogen is converted into molecules with a single nitrogen atom, and is then usable by plants.

Nitrogen is the most common element in our atmosphere, but it is in a form not easily used by plants without the help of bacteria in the soil.

FIGURE 17-26 **The conversion of atmospheric nitrogen into a form that plants can use.**

beneficial relationship has evolved that enables plants to gain access to the nitrogen fixed by these bacteria.

The alliance between plants and nitrogen-fixing bacteria can occur in several ways. In legumes—alfalfa, peas, beans, and soy, for example—the symbiosis develops in these simple steps (**FIGURE 17-27**).

1. A plant's roots secrete a bacteria-attracting compound.

2. Bacteria enter the inner cells, multiplying to form, in some cases, a big, round lump called a **nodule.**

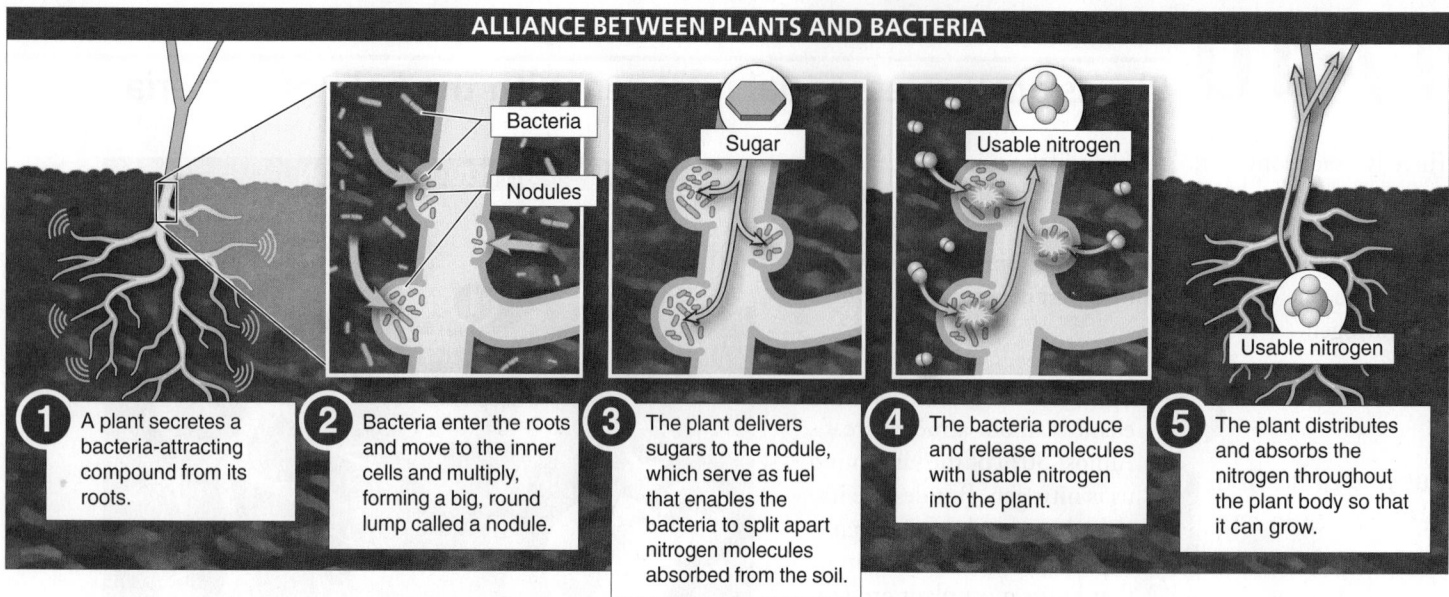

ALLIANCE BETWEEN PLANTS AND BACTERIA

Bacteria
Nodules
Sugar
Usable nitrogen
Usable nitrogen

1 A plant secretes a bacteria-attracting compound from its roots.

2 Bacteria enter the roots and move to the inner cells and multiply, forming a big, round lump called a nodule.

3 The plant delivers sugars to the nodule, which serve as fuel that enables the bacteria to split apart nitrogen molecules absorbed from the soil.

4 The bacteria produce and release molecules with usable nitrogen into the plant.

5 The plant distributes and absorbs the nitrogen throughout the plant body so that it can grow.

FIGURE 17-27 Nitrogen fixation: a product of the symbiotic relationship between plants and bacteria.

3. The bacteria split apart nitrogen molecules absorbed from the soil—an energetically expensive process, fueled by the plant's sugars.

4. The bacteria convert and release the nitrogen into the plant. Any excess of the amount required by the plant is released into the soil.

5. The nitrogen is absorbed throughout the plant body for growth. (And, we should add here, animals eat plants, from which all of their nitrogen ultimately comes.)

Not all soil conditions are conducive to the growth of nitrogen-fixing bacteria, and some plants have alternative ways to acquire nitrogen. Insect-eating (insectivorous) plants, for example, generally grow in very acidic soils in which nitrogen-fixing bacteria do not thrive. The Venus flytrap (**FIGURE 17-28**) captures insects rich in nitrogen-containing molecules, digests them, and recovers the nitrogen for its own uses.

Some plant species are not able to form the mutually beneficial alliance with nitrogen-fixing bacteria and instead must scavenge for usable nitrogen in the soil. For this reason, it can be productive for farmers to rotate their crops every few seasons, alternating between plants that have nodules of nitrogen-fixing bacteria (such as peas, soybeans, and alfalfa) and those that don't. As excess nitrogen fixed by the bacteria is released, usable nitrogen in the soil is replenished like a natural fertilizer. Also, because these plants are plowed under prior to rotation of the crops, they decay and add nitrogenous compounds to the soil—a process called "green manure"—which can reduce the need for additional fertilizer (and the costs to the farmers). The soil is now ready for a non-nitrogen-fixing crop.

The Venus flytrap—a plant that generally grows in acidic soils in which nitrogen-fixing bacteria do not thrive—acquires nitrogen by dissolving the insects that it captures.

FIGURE 17-28 Another way to acquire nitrogen: the Venus flytrap. Some plants have ways of harvesting nitrogen from insects.

TAKE-HOME MESSAGE 17·10

Among the minerals, nitrogen is the one that most commonly limits plant growth, because it is required in nearly all the cells and tissues produced by plants but does not exist in an easily usable form in nature. A mutually beneficial relationship has evolved that enables plants to gain access to nitrogen that is "fixed"—that is, chemically modified into a usable form—by bacteria.

17·11–17·13 Plants transport water, sugar, and minerals through vascular tissue.

A beech tree growing in Gloucestershire, England.

17·11 Plants take up water and minerals through their roots.

Plants absorb water and minerals from the soil through their roots. Water absorption relies on osmosis and is straightforward: the cell membranes of the root hair cells are permeable to water, and as long as the root reaches water in the soil that has a lower concentration of dissolved minerals than the fluid inside the cells, water will move into the root (**FIGURE 17-29**).

The absorption of minerals requires an intervening step (**FIGURE 17-30**). Because most minerals are chemically charged, they cannot pass through the cell membranes unaided. For this reason, plants take them up from the soil only with the help of transport proteins embedded in their root cell membranes. If the minerals are at higher concentrations outside the root cell than inside, the minerals can move across the membranes by simple facilitated diffusion (a process that does not require the plant cells to expend any energy). If the mineral is at higher concentration inside the cell, it can still be taken up by the plant, but only through active transport (see Section 3.10), in which the plant expends energy to move the mineral into the root cell against its concentration gradient.

When it comes to acquiring water and minerals, plants again benefit from collaboration with other organisms, in this case fungi (**FIGURE 17-31**). Most plants have fungi

FIGURE 17-29 The root hair cells are permeable to water. The absorption of minerals requires an intervening step.

ABSORBING MINERALS

Because most minerals are chemically charged, they must pass through transport proteins embedded within the membranes of root cells.

WHEN MINERAL CONCENTRATIONS ARE GREATER OUTSIDE THE CELL
Minerals move down their concentration gradient into the cell by *facilitated diffusion*.

Outside root cell
Root cell wall
Root cell membrane
Inside root cell

WHEN MINERAL CONCENTRATIONS ARE GREATER INSIDE THE CELL
Minerals move against their concentration gradient into the cell by *active transport*.

ATP

ATP

During active transport, the plant must expend energy in order to move the minerals into the cell.

FIGURE 17-30 Taking up minerals into the plant. The absorption of minerals through the cell membranes of plant roots requires the aid of transport proteins and sometimes energy.

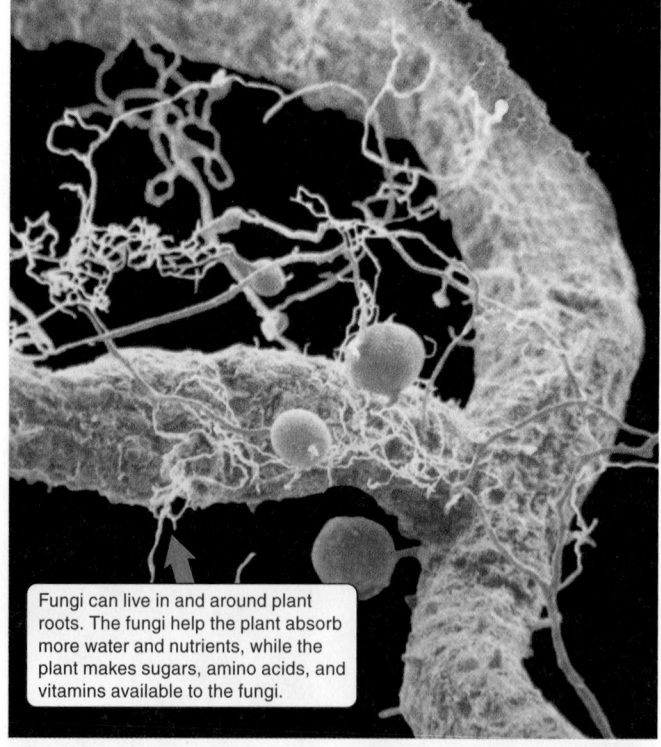

Fungi can live in and around plant roots. The fungi help the plant absorb more water and nutrients, while the plant makes sugars, amino acids, and vitamins available to the fungi.

FIGURE 17-31 Mutualistic relationship between plants and fungi.

growing all around and even within their roots, forming mutualistic associations known as **mycorrhizae.** Tiny, thread-like fungi trap water like a sponge and hold it around the roots. The fungi's huge surface area dramatically increases the amount of water and minerals that can be absorbed. The fungi don't do all that work for free, of course. In exchange, they receive sugars, amino acids, and vitamins. The association between plants and fungi is so important to plants that many trees can't grow at all if they don't have fungi around their roots.

TAKE-HOME MESSAGE 17·10

Plants absorb water from the soil through osmosis in their root hairs. Mineral absorption also occurs in the roots, but it requires the help of transport proteins in root cell membranes. In a mutualistic association called mycorrhizae, fungi growing into and around plant roots increase the plant's water and mineral absorption, while gaining access to energy and nutrients from the plant.

Evaporation is relentless. Leave a glass of water on your desk for a day or two and you can watch the water level gradually drop. Because there is less water in the dry air than in the glass, the liquid water continuously turns to vapor. Eventually, all the water will evaporate away. If you pour the water onto a plate so that it spreads out, it will evaporate even faster because more of the water is in direct contact with the air.

Q | How does water get to leaves at the top of a giant tree?

Evaporation steals the moisture from leaves, too. And although transpiration can cool leaves and help move water and ions up a plant, perpetual water loss to the atmosphere is a real problem for plants, especially trees. In one day, a big tree in a North American forest can lose 100 gallons of water or more! That is 100 gallons of water that the tree's roots absorbed but the plant does not get to use for its physiological needs. Water loss through evaporation also presents a physical challenge for the plant. Most water is lost from the leaves, high in the tree, but all of the water comes from the ground. Somehow, water must be constantly delivered to the leaves—dozens of gallons or more every hour. Not only is this a large amount of water that must be absorbed by the roots, it is also a very heavy load to lift hundreds of feet into the air (**FIGURE 17-32**). How do trees manage to get the water up there?

Water transport is the job of the xylem. As we saw earlier, the xylem is one of the two transport systems in plants. It is responsible for directing the flow of water and dissolved minerals from the roots to all of the plant's cells.

In the absence of a pump like the pump animal circulatory systems have, there are two possible explanations for how

> **"** To believe that columns of water should hang in [the xylem] . . . and should . . . transmit downwards the pull exerted on them . . . by the transpiring leaves, is to some of us equivalent to believing in ropes of sand. **"**
>
> — FRANCIS DARWIN, botanist (Charles Darwin's son), ca. 1900. (His disbelief in Henry Dixon's 1896 cohesion tension theory of water transport in plants is understandable but wrong.)

Evaporation is relentless. Large trees can lose a hundred gallons of water or more in a single day.

FIGURE 17-32 Trees can lose significant amounts of water to the atmosphere through evaporation.

water can be transported from the roots to the leaves—which might be 200 or 300 feet off the ground. The first possibility is that the column of water is pushed up by pressure from below. This would require the water in the soil and roots to be under very high pressure, which it isn't. The alternative explanation is that water is *pulled* up to the highest leaves. Although this possibility seems improbable, it turns out to be true.

There are three important components to the process by which water is moved throughout a plant (**FIGURE 17-33**).

1. *Evaporation.* Because of low water concentration in the air relative to that in the leaf, molecules of water, one by one, are vaporized and lost from the leaf.

WATER TRANSPORT

Plants use a cohesion-tension mechanism to transport water and dissolved minerals from the roots and transport them throughout the plant.

Direction of water flow

Water molecules

Xylem

Stomata

Xylem

Hydrogen bonds

1 EVAPORATION
Due to low water concentration in the air relative to the water concentration in the leaf, molecules of water are vaporized, one by one.

2 TENSION
Water molecules form hydrogen bonds with one another and these bonds cause the molecules to stick together. So as one molecule evaporates, it creates a tension, pulling on all the other water molecules that are stuck to it.

3 COHESION
The cohesion, or stickiness, of the water molecules links them together all the way down to the roots of the tree. As one molecule evaporates and pulls up the molecule next to it, that molecule pulls up the molecule next to it, and so on, all the way down to the roots.

Moving heavy fluid—water and nutrients—around a plant could be energetically expensive. However, the cohesion of water molecules causes them to be "pulled" through the plant, from the roots to the leaves, as evaporation occurs.

FIGURE 17-33 The cohesion-tension mechanism of fluid movement in the xylem.

2. *Tension.* Recall from Chapter 2 that hydrogen bonds cause water molecules to stick together. As one molecule evaporates, it creates a tension, pulling the chain of water molecules stuck to it.

3. *Cohesion.* Through this cohesion, or stickiness, water molecules all the way down to a tree's roots are pulled up as molecules evaporate one by one from the leaf.

The beauty of this system—called the **cohesion-tension mechanism**—is that the plant does not need to expend any energy to pump water and minerals up from the roots to all the cells in every branch and leaf. Just as a mechanism evolved to take advantage of nitrogen-fixing bacteria to produce a usable source of nitrogen for plants, so, too, an efficient way evolved to avoid the energetic expense of moving heavy fluid around in the plant body. And so, even though losing water to evaporation is generally bad for plants, the fact that they use the process to move water through the body turns it into a positive effect.

Although this system works well, it does have its downside: it places a limit on how tall a tree can grow. Leaves at the top of very tall trees have trouble getting enough water. They must

Q *Is there a limit to how tall a tree can grow? Why?*

"pull" it up against the ever-increasing force of gravity pulling downward on the long column of water in the xylem. And although the collective strength of the hydrogen bonds causing all the water molecules to stick to each other is impressive, it is limited. As a consequence, the leaves at the top of the tallest trees resemble desert leaves: they are small, grow slowly, photosynthesize at a slow rate, and otherwise behave like a parched leaf. Researchers estimate that the physical constraint of lifting water against the force of gravity will restrict any tree to a maximum height of about 400 feet.

Q *Maple syrup comes from trees. What is it?*

The sap in the xylem doesn't always contain just water and dissolved minerals. Sometimes the fluid contains sugars, too. (Recall that phloem is generally the sugar-transporting pipeline.) Throughout the late summer and early fall, just before maple trees (*Acer saccharum*) lose their leaves, they begin storing the sugar from photosynthesis as starch in their roots, much like a bear storing body fat prior to hibernation. In late winter, the

SAP: STORAGE AND TRANSPORT

Phloem

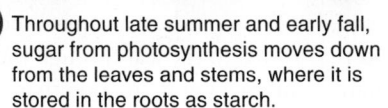

Starch

1 Throughout late summer and early fall, sugar from photosynthesis moves down from the leaves and stems, where it is stored in the roots as starch.

Xylem

2 As the temperature rises in late winter, starch in the roots begins to break down and is released into the xylem.

Xylem

Leaf bud

3 Increased pressure caused by the added sugar moves sap upward toward newly forming leaf buds.

FIGURE 17-34 In late winter and early spring, sugar-carrying sap moves upward from the plant roots to nourish the forming leaf buds.

Sugar from photosynthesis can be stored in the roots as starch. Later, the sugar can provide energy for new leaf buds.

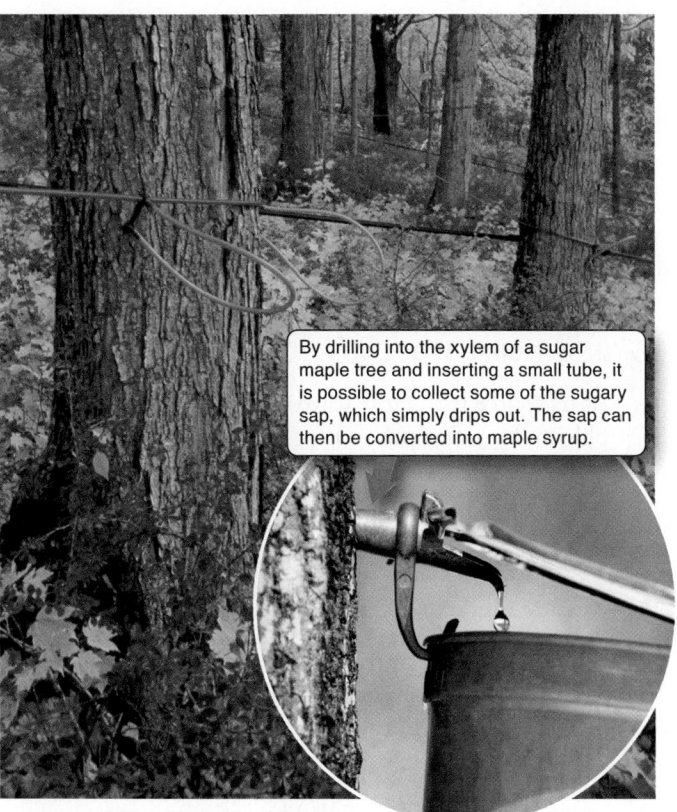

By drilling into the xylem of a sugar maple tree and inserting a small tube, it is possible to collect some of the sugary sap, which simply drips out. The sap can then be converted into maple syrup.

FIGURE 17-35 Tapping a maple tree.

temperature rises and the starch in the roots begins to break down into sugar and is released into the xylem (**FIGURE 17-34**). The sap moves upward toward the newly forming leaf buds, which need energy to develop. Humans have long recognized that by drilling into the xylem and inserting a small tube, it is possible to collect some of the sugary sap—it simply drips out. At about 1% to 5% sugar, the sap is not sweet enough to be poured on your pancakes, so it is boiled to evaporate much of the water, concentrating the sugar. When the sap reaches about 85% sugar, it makes a tasty maple syrup. About 1 gallon of sap can be collected from a tree over the several weeks during which it flows, not enough to harm the tree. But it takes about 50 gallons of sap to make 1 gallon of syrup (**FIGURE 17-35**).

TAKE-HOME MESSAGE 17·12

Xylem directs the flow of water and dissolved minerals from the roots to all the tissues of the plant. The force driving this flow of fluid (the xylem sap) comes from evaporation of water from the leaves, which pulls water up from the roots.

TYPES OF PLANT
TISSUES

STRUCTURAL FEATURES
OF PLANTS

PLANT
NUTRITION

NUTRIENT TRANSPORT
IN PLANTS

689

17·13 Sugar and other nutrients are distributed through the phloem.

SUGAR TRANSPORT

The phloem controls sugar movement throughout the plant in five steps.

① Sugar molecules

③

Phloem

Xylem

②

Water molecules

④

⑤

① Sugar is loaded by active transport into the phloem from sites of production (primarily leaves).

② The increased sugar concentration in the phloem immediately causes water to move from the xylem into the phloem by osmosis.

③ As the water moves into the phloem, it increases the fluid pressure inside the phloem.

④ The increased phloem pressure causes the fluid in the phloem to move elsewhere in the plant, such as to the roots, much like a tube of toothpaste being squeezed.

⑤ As the sugar is pushed through the plant body, it is moved out of the phloem by active transport at various locations where it is needed—such as into root cells for storage and/or growth.

FIGURE 17-36 The pressure-flow mechanism of fluid movement in the phloem.

Phloem is the food-delivery service of plants. Through a branching network of highways, sugars produced in the leaves (the "source") are transported throughout the plant to places (called "sinks") where they are needed, such as regions of rapid growth (roots, leaf buds) or fruit production, or to roots and stems where they can be stored.

When a leaf is young, it cannot produce adequate food for itself; instead, food is provided to the leaf through the phloem. Once the leaf is mature and making more food than it can use, the transport direction is switched to move sugars out of the leaf to other places in the plant where they are needed. So, unlike mammalian circulatory systems, the phloem isn't necessarily a system of one-way highways. Rather, the direction of flow depends on the plant's needs at the time.

Phloem vessels are visible to the naked eye. Along with the xylem vessels, they make up the veins in a leaf. The phloem vessels are living cells lined up end to end so that they form a pipeline, called a sieve tube. The cells of the sieve tubes have many small openings in their walls (primarily in the ends of the cells) and so can quickly move the sugar produced in the leaves throughout the plant to roots, stems, buds, flowers, and fruits. The process is called the **pressure-flow mechanism.**

Phloem controls sugar movement throughout the plant in five steps (**FIGURE 17-36**).

1. At its source (primarily leaves), sugar is loaded into the phloem by active transport.

2. Water moves from the xylem into the phloem by osmosis because of the increased sugar concentration in the phloem.

3. Pressure inside the phloem increases as water moves in.

4. The increased pressure (particularly higher up in the plant, where photosynthesis is occurring) causes the fluid in the phloem to move to other parts of the plant.

5. Sugar is moved out of the phloem at various locations where it is needed (the sinks) by active transport.

Sometimes, important science questions can be answered by unexpected methods. Consider this question: what exactly is the fluid circulating in the phloem? To answer the question, researchers used aphids—insects that use their mouthparts to pierce the outer part of a plant stem to gain access to the sugar-rich sap in the phloem (**FIGURE 17-37**). The fluid

FIGURE 17-37 Drinking from a fire hose on a small scale. The sugary fluid in the phloem is under such high pressure that aphids drinking it can't always consume it all, and some is forced through their digestive system and out of their anus (at which point, ants may consume the fluid).

simply flows into their gut. Just as mosquitoes feed on human blood, aphids are able to live on the energetically valuable fluid circulating in the phloem.

The researchers found plants on which aphids were feeding, then ripped the bodies off the aphids, leaving their mouthparts sticking into the phloem like tiny syringes. As the sap dripped out, the researchers collected and analyzed

it. As it turns out, phloem sap is a sugar solution with about 10% to 25% dissolved solids that include some lipids and amino acids. In most plants, about 90% of the phloem sugar is sucrose, the same molecule we use as table sugar.

Aphids helped answer an important question about plants, but they also create problems. If you have ever wondered why your car gets covered in a sticky substance under some trees, you can blame aphids. When aphids are attacking a tree, puncturing holes in the plant tissues to feed on the phloem sap, the pressure in the phloem fluid can cause more of the fluid to come out than the aphids can utilize. The excess sugary (and sticky) fluid secreted by the aphids, called honeydew, drops onto the ground (or your car) below.

In the next chapter, we see that as a tree grows, phloem also takes on a secondary, protective function.

TAKE-HOME MESSAGE 17·13

The phloem consists of a branching network of vessels made from living cells lined end to end to form sieve tubes, with small openings in their side walls. Sugar, usually sucrose, is moved in the phloem from sites of production (sources) to sites of use or storage (sinks). The direction of flow is not always the same: a plant part may be a source at one time and a sink at another.

ORGANIC FOODS: ARE THEY WORTH THE PRICE?

Q: WHAT ARE "ORGANIC" FOODS? Organic foods account for about 1% of all foods sold worldwide, generating more than $40 billion per year. In order to be labeled and sold as "organic," a food must be grown without the use of chemical fertilizers or non-organic pesticides. They also cannot have been genetically modified or irradiated, or had hormones added during processing.

Q: DON'T BE FOOLED BY SNEAKY LABELING. Products labeled "100% organic" must contain only organic ingredients with the exception of water and salt, according to the U.S. Department of Agriculture. But be careful, because products can be labeled "organic" if they contain at least 95 percent organic ingredients. And a product can be labeled "made with organic ingredients" as long as it is made with at least 70 percent organic ingredients.

Q: ARE THERE DOWNSIDES TO ORGANIC FOODS? The biggest downside comes at the cash register. Organic fruits and vegetables cost more than other produce, typically 13 to 36 cents more per pound. And hormone- and antibiotic-free milk sells for $6 per gallon on average versus $3.50 per gallon for non-organic certified milk.

Q: ARE ORGANIC FOODS NUTRITIONALLY SUPERIOR TO CONVENTIONALLY PRODUCED FOODS? In a 2009 review of 55 published articles on the nutritional content of organic foods, researchers funded by the U.K. Food Standards Agency examined 13 nutrient categories and found no evidence that organic foods were superior in nutritional content when compared with conventionally produced foods.

Q: MIGHT ORGANIC FOODS HAVE SOME OTHER BENEFITS? Although the results of the review seem to suggest that it might not be worth paying a premium for organic foods, there is reason to withhold final judgment. The study examined only *nutritional* content. There may be other benefits relating to safety, heart health, environmental degradation, and farmworker risks.

- *Safety:* There may be a reduced risk of *E. coli* contamination from grass-fed cattle, which are maintained with less crowding. When it comes to pesticide exposure, however, it is less clear whether there are benefits. In its published *Guidelines on Nutrition for Cancer Prevention*, the American Cancer Society has stated: "At present there is no evidence that residues of pesticides and herbicides at the low doses found in foods increase the risk of cancer."

- *Heart health:* Beef from grass-fed cattle has been shown to have less fat and higher levels of omega-3 acids, which may reduce the risks of cancer and heart disease.

- *Environmental degradation:* Organic farming reduces the addition of synthetic pesticides to the environment, potentially improving water supplies and long-term soil quality.

- *Farmworker risks:* Reduced exposure to synthetic pesticides and chemical fertilizers benefits farmworkers, decreasing their contact with potential carcinogens and other harmful chemicals.

So extensive research continues on the question of whether organic foods are worth the price, and it is difficult at this time to give a definitive answer.

Big Ideas in ...
Plant Structure and Nutrient Transport

17·1–17·3 Three basic tissue types give rise to diverse plant characteristics.

- Plants are an extremely diverse and successful group of organisms. The flowering plants are divided into two major groups, the monocots and the eudicots, based on structural features of their seeds, leaves, stems, flowers, and roots.

- All vascular plants are organized around the same basic body plan and built up from the same three types of tissues. Dermal tissue covers and protects the surface of the plant. Vascular tissue transports water and nutrients throughout the body. And ground tissue is where most of the plant's metabolic activities are carried out.

17·4–17·7 Most plants have common structural features.

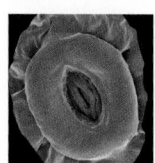

- The body plans of plants are organized around three structures. Roots absorb water and minerals from the soil and anchor the plant. Stems provide structural support and position leaves where they can intercept sunlight. Leaves are the chief sites of photosynthesis.

17·8–17·10 Plant nutrition: plants obtain sunlight and usable chemical elements from the environment.

- There are four factors essential for plant growth: (1) sunlight, (2) water, (3) air as a source of carbon dioxide, and (4) minerals, usually obtained from soil.

- Among the minerals, nitrogen is the chemical that most limits plant growth, because it is required in nearly all plant cells and tissues but does not exist in an easily usable form in nature.

17·11–17·13 Plants transport water, sugar, and minerals through vascular tissue.

- Nutrient transport in plants occurs in two separate systems: the xylem and phloem.

- Xylem directs the flow of water and dissolved minerals from the roots to all other plant tissues. The force driving the flow comes from evaporation of water from leaves, which pulls water up the xylem from the roots.

- Phloem is the food-delivery service of plants. Sugars produced in the leaves are transported through a branching network of vessels to sites of growth, reproduction, or storage throughout the plant.

See the To-Go Guide (packaged with every new copy of this textbook) for an illustrated summary of the chapter.

Check Your Knowledge

 GRAPHIC CONTENT

Thinking critically about visual displays of data.

1. What is the purpose of this pie chart?

2. What is the source of the data in the chart? What is an assumption underlying this presentation of data?

3. Are the data presented in the chart valid for all types of soil? How might such comprehensive data be presented?

4. Bar graphs can present not just an average value for data, but also an estimate of variation. Can that be done with a pie chart? How?

5. What is the benefit to presenting these data as a pie chart rather than a bar graph with three bars? If they were presented as a bar graph, what would the axis labels be?

6. Because the pie chart is shown in three dimensions and the "water and air" portion is rotated toward the front, more blue coloring than purple coloring is visible in the pie chart. Does that mean the blue "slice" represents a larger number than the purple "slice"? Could this method of data presentation be used to mislead viewers?

COMPOSITION OF SOIL

MINERALS: 50%
- Inorganic particles
- Formed from the breakdown of weathering rock
- Grouped into three sizes: sand, silt, and clay

WATER AND AIR: 45–50%
- Fill the space between particles of inorganic and organic matter

ORGANIC MATERIALS: 1–5%
- Carbon-containing matter
- Formed from the decomposition of dead plants and animals

See Answers at the back of the book.

Key Terms in Plant Structure and Nutrient Transport

Multiple-Choice Questions

1. **What are the embryonic precursors to leaves in a seedling called?**

   a) seedling leaves
   b) cotyledons
   c) angiosperms
   d) needles
   e) monocots

100 | HARD
36
0 | EASY

2. **All of the following are ground tissue cell types except:**

   a) parenchyma.
   b) meristem.
   c) collenchyma.
   d) sclerenchyma.
   e) All of the above are components of ground tissue.

100 | HARD
36
0 | EASY

3. **What role does soil play in the life of a terrestrial plant?**

   a) The plant is anchored in the soil.
   b) The plant obtains water and nutrients from the soil.
   c) The roots of the plant obtain oxygen from the soil.
   d) All of the above are correct.
   e) Only a) and b) are correct.

100 | HARD
32
0 | EASY

4. **Which of the following is most important in providing structural support in vascular plants?**

   a) xylem
   b) apical meristem
   c) phloem
   d) epidermis
   e) cortex

100 | HARD
55
0 | EASY

5. **Leaves are generally thin, with a three-layered structure that includes all of the following except:**

   a) veins of vascular tissue.
   b) non-photosynthetic epidermal cells.
   c) a few layers of photosynthetic cells.
   d) apical meristem cells.
   e) stomata.

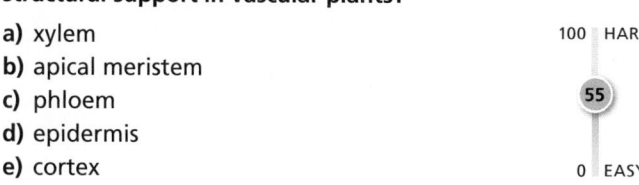

100 | HARD
0 **12** EASY

6. **The cuticle of a leaf is:**

   a) responsible for delivering water to the leaves.
   b) responsible for much of the photosynthesis in plants.
   c) the site where most of the photosynthetic products of plants are used.
   d) a waxy non-living layer that minimizes water loss.
   e) All of the above are correct.

100 | HARD
 28
0 | EASY

7. **When mineral concentrations are higher inside root cells than in the soil:**

   a) ATP is used to import more minerals into root cells.
   b) minerals move by diffusion from the soil into root cells.
   c) energy is used to export minerals into the soil.
   d) absorption of water is blocked.
   e) plants will lose minerals passively to the environment.

100 | HARD
 47
0 | EASY

8. For a typical green plant to thrive, it needs:

a) sunlight, water, carbon dioxide, oxygen, and minerals.

b) only water.

c) only minerals.

d) only sunlight.

e) sunlight, water, oxygen, and minerals.

100 | HARD

0 | 10 | EASY

9. Plants do not grow well in pure clay soils because:

a) the soil packs so tightly that the roots cannot penetrate it.

b) the soil packs so tightly that the amount of oxygen reaching the roots is limited.

c) water drains too rapidly.

d) the mineral content is very low.

e) clay holds water and will not release it to the roots.

100 | HARD

33

0 | EASY

10. The enzyme known as _____ catalyzes the fixation of nitrogen in nitrogen-fixing bacteria.

a) nitrogen reductase

b) nitrogenase

c) rhizobiase

d) ammoniase

e) nitrogen fixase

100 | HARD

29

0 | EASY

11. The process of water absorption by plant roots generally relies on _____ across the membranes of cells in _____.

a) osmosis; root hairs

b) active transport; root hairs

c) osmosis; the apical meristem

d) active transport; the apical meristem

e) facilitated diffusion; stomata

100 | HARD

35

0 | EASY

12. Evaporation from the leaves of a tree pulls water up from the roots as an unbroken column throughout the entire height of the tree. This feat is possible because of which characteristic(s) of water?

a) high heat capacity

b) cohesion and kinetic energy

c) cohesion

d) low heat capacity

e) absorption

100 | HARD

20

0 | EASY

13. Sugars produced in the leaves of a plant are transported elsewhere in the plant through:

a) the movement of symbiotic bacteria that carry the sugars.

b) the stoma apparatus.

c) sap vesicles.

d) sieve tubes that make up the xylem.

e) sieve tubes that make up the phloem.

100 | HARD

26

0 | EASY

Short-Answer Questions

1. Compare and contrast the major characteristics of the monocots and eudicot flowering plants.

2. How does the cohesion-tension mechanism allow vascular plants to transport water without the utilization of energy? How does this affect the maximum height that can be attained by trees?

3. Why would a monocot be more likely to survive having a tight wire wrapped around it causing a shallow cut than a eudicot plant suffering from the same injury?

See Answers at the back of the book.
For additional study questions, go to www.prep-u.com.

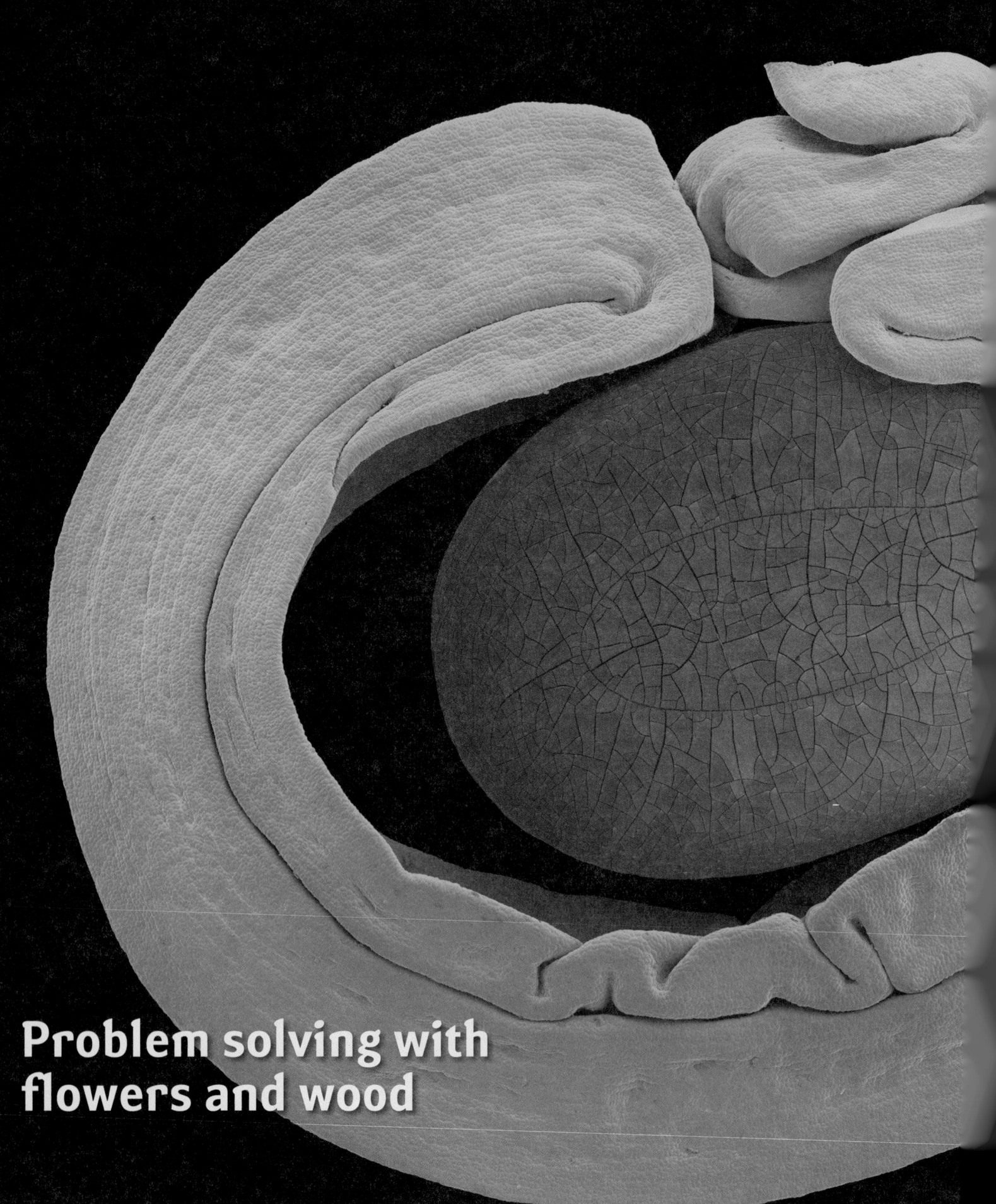

Problem solving with
flowers and wood

18

Growth and Reproduction in Plants

699

18·1–18·3 Plants can reproduce sexually and asexually.

Winged sumac (Rhus copallina), with red leaves, growing alongside tulip poplar trees.

18·1

Plant evolution has given rise to two methods of reproduction.

Why do flowers have such a hold on people? Brides clutch roses during wedding ceremonies. Suitors and partners give flowers during courtships and relationships. We send flowers to those in mourning and to those celebrating. And many people spend countless hours and dollars tending to flowering plants in their gardens.

We are innocent bystanders, as it turns out, unintentionally ensnared by plants' chief calling card: the sweet smells and captivating colors, textures, and shapes of flowers. Floral displays, though, are intended for a wide range of other animals and are the means by which plants enlist the assistance of animals in transporting male gametes to female gametes, thus using sexual reproduction to produce seeds and increase the genetic variability among their offspring.

Take carrion flowers, for example (**FIGURE 18-1**). Some insects feed on feces, rotting flesh, and other decaying organic matter, and they also lay their eggs in damp, stinky places. Carrion flowers lure these insects into their foul-smelling blossoms and, in doing so, ensure the transport of male gametes to female gametes. *Rafflesia arnoldii*, of the rain forests of Sumatra and Borneo, is a carrion flower that occasionally produces giant blooms of up to 3 feet in

diameter, each flower weighing as much as 25 pounds. These gigantic flowers emit an odor like that of a stinking corpse, attracting carrion beetles and flies—which, when they move from male flowers to female flowers, transport pollen (containing the male gamete), enabling sexual reproduction even as the plants remain immobile.

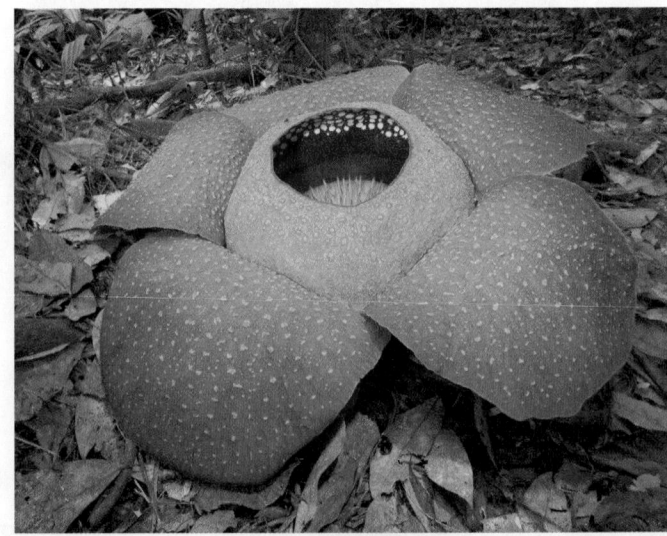

FIGURE 18-1 The carrion flower *Rafflesia arnoldii*.

FIGURE 18-2 **Aspen trees.** Aspen root suckers, by which a plant can give rise to new individuals asexually, are shown in the inset photo.

But sexual reproduction isn't the only method of reproduction for flowering plants. Most are able to make use of an alternative method, producing offspring asexually under certain conditions. Aspens, for example (**FIGURE 18-2**), are a species of tree that thrives in the cool regions of Europe, Asia, and North America. Occasionally, however, they take root in inhospitable places. But, unlike a human who finds herself on an impossibly cold or barren plot of land and quickly packs up and retreats, aspens don't have that option. They're plants, after all. They can't escape.

Evolution seems to have compensated plants for their lack of mobility with a life-saving bit of adaptability. Consider the aspen populations on the Orkney Islands, at the northernmost tip of Scotland. Unlike the aspen populations farther south, the harsh climate on the Orkney Islands does not seem to allow aspen seeds to germinate and generate new trees. This inability to reproduce, possibly a consequence of inadequate soil moisture and limited light availability, would seem to be a fatal limitation to aspens' survival on these islands. Yet there the trees are, and records indicate that they have persisted there for centuries. How do they do it?

In the Orkneys, the aspens reproduce asexually. They forgo any sexual reproduction and, instead, develop suckers, which are shoots that sprout from the roots and can give rise to new, genetically identical trees. One tree can give rise to dozens or even hundreds of new trees, all genetically identical.

Such asexual reproduction turns out to be prevalent among plants, wherever they occur in marginal habitats. Such habitats may limit the survival of seeds or, because of small population sizes, may reduce the likelihood that an individual finds a sexual partner.

In this chapter, we examine why evolution may have led to most plants having two very different options for reproduction, and we also investigate how plants grow. We begin by exploring the process of asexual reproduction and its advantages and disadvantages.

TAKE-HOME MESSAGE 18·1

Most plants have two very different options for reproduction: asexual and sexual reproduction.

18·2 Many plants can reproduce asexually when necessary.

Cloning isn't new. Gardeners have been doing it for centuries. And before that, plants were doing it for millennia—without any help from humans. Cloning is just a more modern term to describe a reproductive process by which one organism gives rise to another genetically identical individual. The process, also called asexual reproduction, is very rare among animals but is quite common among plants. As we will see in this chapter, for the vast majority of plant species, sexual reproduction is the predominant mode of reproduction, but nearly all plant species have also retained the ability to reproduce without any participation from another individual.

Most of the trees or shrubs we see in gardens are, in fact, the result of asexual reproduction. So, too, are nearly all houseplants purchased from nurseries. How does asexual

Parent plant — Genetically identical new individual

Parent plant — Genetically identical new individuals

Parent plant — Genetically identical new individuals

FIGURE 18-3 Reproduction without a partner. Most plants—including raspberries, potatoes, and *bryophyllum*—have the option of asexual reproduction. No partner is required, so it is quick and efficient, but no genetic variability is present among the cloned offspring.

The process of asexual reproduction in plants is simple. It always involves the growth of new individual plants directly from the tissue of an established plant via normal mitosis.

reproduction in plants occur? The process is simple. New individual plants are grown directly from the tissue of established plants through normal mitosis. There is no meiosis to generate gametes, and there is no fertilization of one gamete by another. Asexual reproduction is also called vegetative reproduction, because it starts with a vegetative structure of the plant (such as a stem or root or leaf) not involved in sexual reproduction, which becomes separated from the parent plant and continues to grow to form a new individual.

Raspberry plants, for example, can be propagated by cutting sprouts from their roots (**FIGURE 18-3**). And potato plants can be generated from their underground storage stems (that is, the potato itself). Thus, a new potato plant can be generated just by planting a potato and waiting for it to sprout into a genetically identical individual. We consider the new plant and "parent" plant distinct individuals because they have become separated and can grow and function independent of one another. In a group of plant species called *bryophyllum*, small "plantlets" grow right along the edges of the leaves, eventually dropping to the soil, taking root, and growing as independent plants. The critical feature in every case of asexual reproduction is that the bit of the plant that is used to start a new individual must have some undifferentiated cells, cells—like stem cells in humans—that have the developmental potential to become any type of cell and tissue. Later in the chapter, in our discussion of plant growth, we talk more about what undifferentiated cells are and where they are located.

The ability to reproduce asexually is an evolutionary adaptation that helps plants overcome the fact that they are rooted in the ground and cannot easily seek out sexual partners. By removing the need to locate a suitable partner, asexual reproduction confers important benefits. It is not a perfect solution, however. In most situations, there is a critical disadvantage to asexual reproduction. The advantages and disadvantage can be summarized quite simply.

Advantages of asexual reproduction There are three main advantages to reproducing asexually (**FIGURE 18-4**).

1. *Energetically efficient.* No energy is wasted by producing flowers, pollen, and fruits—plant tissues used exclusively for reproduction. Instead, the plant's energy can be invested in producing roots, support and nutrient-transport tissues, leaves, and other vegetative matter for growth and increased photosynthetic capacity.

2. *Faster.* Participation of another individual is not required, nor is a means of bringing together the male and female gametes. As a result, new individuals can be produced at a much faster rate, which enhances an individual's reproductive success and fitness.

3. *Preserving winning allele combinations.* If a plant is well adapted to a particular environment, all the individuals it produces by asexual reproduction will carry the same well-adapted set of alleles and are likely to flourish just as the parent plant did.

FIGURE 18-4 Asexual reproduction. It is fast and efficient but reduces genetic variation.

Disadvantage of asexual reproduction Although it has some advantages, asexual reproduction has one huge disadvantage relative to sexual reproduction: it leads to no new genetic variation among the offspring. Asexually reproduced individuals are identical to their parents (with the rare exception of any mutations that might occur). If the environment is changing—perhaps the climate is changing or a new variety of pest species is on the increase—the new individuals are less likely to be adapted to the changed environment. Moreover, as more and more of the individuals in an area are produced by asexual reproduction, if those individuals then reproduce together sexually, there will be less genetic variation among their offspring than if the parents were not genetically identical. Each parent plant will simply draw from the same set of alleles when producing gametes. This reduced variety in genetic material can leave plant populations in a vulnerable state, with a reduced capacity to evolve.

We turn next to how plants produce genetically varied offspring through sexual reproduction.

TAKE-HOME MESSAGE 18·2

Many plants can reproduce asexually. This process involves the growth of new, individual plants directly from the tissue of an established plant through mitosis. The new individual is genetically identical to the individual from which it was produced. Asexual reproduction can be energetically efficient and fast and can preserve successful genetic combinations, but it also has the important disadvantage that it does not lead to genetic variability among an individual's offspring.

18·3 Plants can reproduce sexually, even without moving.

For all its efficiency and advantages, asexual reproduction just doesn't measure up to sexual reproduction in plants. In fact, despite the difficulties associated with being anchored in one place, the ability of plants to reproduce sexually is at the heart of their evolutionary success. Because sexually reproducing populations generate large amounts of genetic diversity, they can keep up with changing conditions better than asexually reproducing plants by adapting to new environments.

Sexual reproduction, whether in plants or in animals, enhances the genetic diversity among an individual's offspring in several important ways (**FIGURE 18-5**). First, because the genetic material comes from two distinct individuals, the offspring isn't a duplicate of either parent but, instead, carries a mixture of traits from each. This outcome is analogous to having two people try to solve a group of problems together versus one person going it alone. The pair will likely arrive at better solutions. Second, as we saw in Chapter 6, during the process of producing sperm or eggs in an individual, recombination occurs during crossing over, causing each gamete to carry a mixture of alleles from that individual's mother and father, combinations of alleles

● ● ●   ● ● ●   ● ● ●   ● ● ●
ASEXUAL AND SEXUAL   REPRODUCTION IN   POLLINATION   PLANT GROWTH
REPRODUCTION   FLOWERING PLANTS   AND FERTILIZATION

703

Sexual reproduction enhances the genetic diversity among an individual's offspring in several important ways.

GENETIC MATERIAL COMES FROM TWO INDIVIDUALS
Offspring carry a mixture of traits from each parent plant.

RECOMBINATION DURING GAMETE PRODUCTION
Each gamete carries a mixture of alleles that have most likely never occurred before.

REASSORTMENT OF HOMOLOGUES
The homologues and sister chromatids distributed to each daughter cell during meiosis are a random mix of maternal and paternal genetic material.

FIGURE 18-5 Sexual reproduction.

that have most likely never occurred before. Every gamete is different from every other gamete, so each of an individual's offspring ends up with a different set of genes. And the third mechanism by which genetic variation is enhanced during sexual reproduction occurs during reassortment of the

homologues during meiosis—randomly assorted with respect to whether they are maternal or paternal in origin (see Section 6-14).

Sexual reproduction (and the resulting genetic variation in a population) is especially important in agriculture, because plant breeders can selectively breed plants for the most sought-after features—maybe the size of the corncob, the speed at which the oranges ripen, or the scent or color of a rose. There must be genetic variation in a population of plants if the population is to be changed through natural selection (or artificial selection by plant breeders). Tremendous gains in agricultural productivity have come from selective breeding programs, particularly with major crops such as wheat, rice, corn, and soybeans (**FIGURE 18-6**).

In plants and animals, the process of sexual reproduction has some common steps. Meiosis is an essential part of the process by which individuals produce gametes. The gametes then come together to produce a fertilized egg, which develops and grows by mitosis. Finally, the fertilized egg is transported to a place where it can survive and grow. These steps occur in all organisms that reproduce sexually. Sexual reproduction in animals and in plants always involves meiosis and fertilization, and because these

Sexual reproduction—and the genetic variation it introduces into a population—is particularly important in agriculture, enabling plant breeders to selectively breed plants with the most desirable features.

FIGURE 18-6 Breeding a better crop.

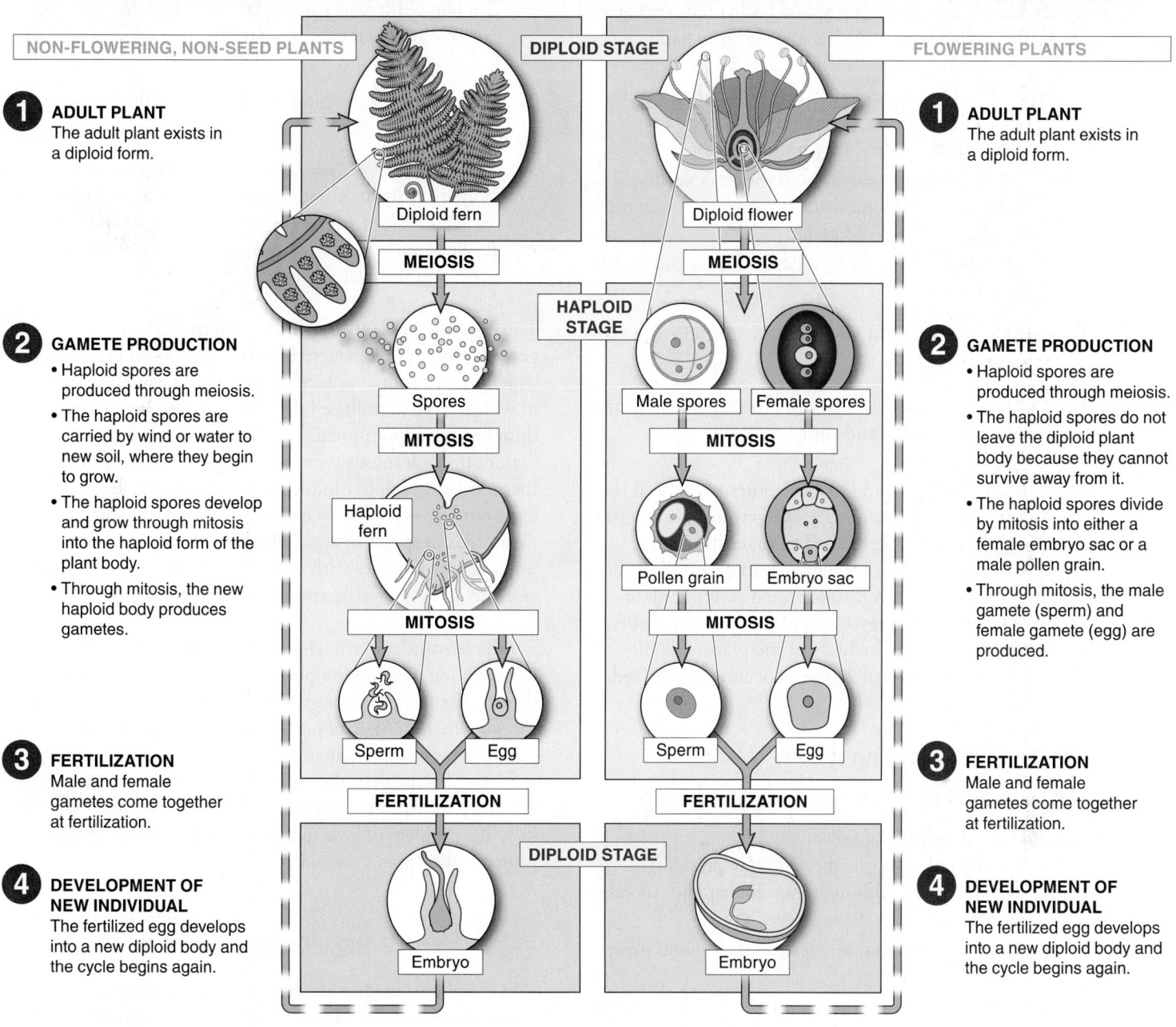

FIGURE 18-7 Life cycles of non-flowering, non-seed plants and flowering plants.

processes are repeated in every generation, they are called a **life cycle.**

Because plants cannot move, however, their life cycle includes steps that increase their ability to safely deliver the male gamete to the female gamete—delivery that must occur without the parent plant uprooting itself to find an individual with which to mate. We trace the life cycles of non-flowering, non-seed plants and flowering plants—the angiosperms (which all have seeds)—in **FIGURE 18-7**. (For more details, see Sections 12-6 and 12-10.)

Life Cycle of Non-Flowering, Non-Seed Plants (Such as Ferns)

1. One form of the plant "body" that we see is diploid (but there also are multicellular haploid forms).

2. Production of gametes:

    a. Through meiosis, the diploid body produces haploid cells called **spores.** Although spores are haploid, they *are not* gametes.

    b. The haploid spores are carried by wind or water to new soil, where they **germinate**—that is, after a period of dormancy, they begin to grow.

    c. Through mitosis, the haploid spores develop and grow into the second form of the plant "body" that we see: a new haploid plant.

    d. Through mitosis, the new haploid body produces gametes.

3. Fertilization: Male and female gametes come together at fertilization.

4. The fertilized egg develops and grows, by mitosis, into a new diploid body, and the cycle begins again.

Note that in non-flowering plants, spores are carried by wind or water to soil where they can germinate and grow into a gamete-producing form. The male and female gametes also are assisted, usually by rain or wind, in coming together for fertilization. The flowering plants have a slightly different strategy for dealing with immobility. The spores never leave the body of the plant, but the plants find a way for fertilization to occur, as described in Section 18-7.

Life Cycle of Flowering Plants

1. The plant "body" that we see is diploid.

2. Production of gametes:

    a. Through meiosis, the diploid body produces haploid spores. Although they are haploid, spores *are not* gametes.

    b. The haploid spores do not leave the diploid plant body.

    c. Within a flower on the plant body, the spores divide by mitosis to form either a haploid female embryo sac or a haploid male pollen grain.

    d. Through mitosis, the haploid embryo sac produces a haploid female gamete (an egg), and the haploid pollen grain produces a haploid male gamete (a sperm).

3. Fertilization: Male and female gametes come together at fertilization.

4. The fertilized egg (which typically has been moved away from the plant on which fertilization occurred— see Section 18-11 for a discussion of dispersal methods) develops and grows, by mitosis, into a new diploid body, and the cycle repeats.

The life cycle in plants is called an **alternation of generations** and is characterized by an extended period in which a plant is in a multicellular haploid form and a period in which it is in a multicellular diploid form. If the same thing happened in humans, it would be the stuff of science fiction: the cells in our testes or ovaries, instead of producing sperm or eggs, would produce a special creature that would leave our bodies, live elsewhere on its own for a while, and then produce sperm or eggs, which would then find some way to come together with eggs or sperm from another such creature, undergo fertilization, and produce babies.

For the remainder of this chapter, we focus on the sexual reproduction of flowering plants (the angiosperms), because they are the predominant group of plants on earth, accounting for more than 90% of all plant species. All angiosperms produce flowers, the structures in which the gametes develop and in which much of the reproductive activity takes place. We begin by exploring the role of flowers in helping plants solve the problem of how to bring male gametes to female gametes when plants are rooted in the ground.

TAKE-HOME MESSAGE 18·3

Many plants can benefit from producing genetically varied offspring via sexual reproduction, with the flower as the chief structure for sexual reproduction.

18·4–18·6 Flowers have several roles in plant reproduction.

Red petals surround the reproductive structures of this tulip.

18·4 The flower is the chief structure for sexual reproduction.

Take a look at **FIGURE 18-8**, which showcases the diversity of flower shapes and colors. If we investigate more closely, though, and dissect some flowers, we see that with only a few exceptions, all flowers have the same fundamental structures. The consistency we see there brings order to the seemingly infinite array of flower forms.

FLOWER SHAPE DIVERSITY

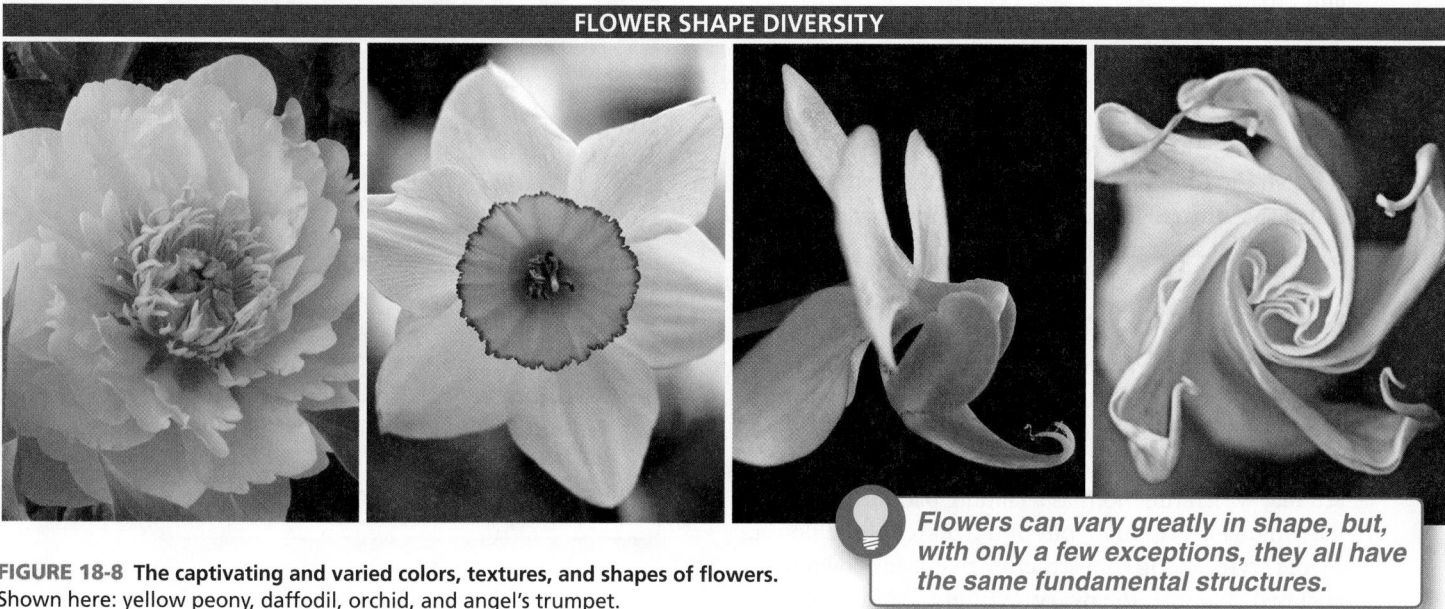

FIGURE 18-8 **The captivating and varied colors, textures, and shapes of flowers.** Shown here: yellow peony, daffodil, orchid, and angel's trumpet.

Flowers can vary greatly in shape, but, with only a few exceptions, they all have the same fundamental structures.

FLOWER STRUCTURE

♀ CARPEL
Female reproductive structure

- **STIGMA**
  Sticky landing site for pollen
- **STYLE**
  Supportive stalk
- **OVARY**
  Enclosed chamber containing the ovule(s)

PETALS
Leaf-like structures—often brightly colored—that help attract pollinators to the flower

♂ STAMEN
Male reproductive structure

- **ANTHER**
  Site of pollen grain production
- **FILAMENT**
  Supportive stalk

SEPALS
Leaf-like structures—found at the point where the flower is connected to the plant— that surround and protect the flower bud during its development and sometimes are brightly colored like flowers

FIGURE 18-9 Most flowers are organized on the same general body plan.

Specifically, flowers have four distinct parts (**FIGURE 18-9**).

1. *Sepals.* **Sepals** are leaf-like structures located at the point where the flower is connected to a main support structure of the plant, such as a branch, stem, or stalk. Sepals grow in a ring surrounding the outside of the flower, and they protect the flower bud during its development. Although sepals are usually green, in some flowers they are brightly colored and closely resemble the petals.

2. *Petals.* Just inside the ring of sepals is another ring of leaf-like structures, the **petals.** They are usually brightly colored—helping the flower to attract pollinators—and frequently have unusual shapes, from long and thin to short and broad.

3. *Stamens.* Moving inward toward the center of the flower, the next structures are the **stamens,** the male reproductive parts. There are usually several stamens, each of which appears like a head on top of a long, thin stalk. The stalk is called the **filament** and the head-like top structure is called the **anther.** The anthers are the sites where the **pollen grains**—the structures that contain the male gametes, or sperm—are produced. The typical anther on a cornflower produces about 3,000 pollen grains.

4. *Carpel.* In the very center of the flower is the **carpel,** the female reproductive structure. There is usually only one carpel, and it is usually shaped like a long-necked vase. At the very top of the carpel is a flat, sticky surface called the **stigma,** which functions as a landing pad for pollen. The stigma is held high, out of the center of the flower, by the **style,** a long thin structure that leads down to an enclosed chamber, the **ovary.** Within the ovary are one or

Saffron

Valued for its taste and vivid color, saffron—from the stigma and style of Crocus sativus—*is the world's most expensive spice.*

FIGURE 18-10 Saffron: the world's most expensive spice.

more **ovules,** which produce the female gametes (eggs). After an egg is fertilized, the ovule develops into a seed.

The prize for the most valuable stigma probably goes to *Crocus sativus,* a flowering plant native to Southwest Asia that is more commonly known as the saffron crocus (**FIGURE 18-10**). Collected and dried, the stigma and style produce a deep yellow powder, valued by food lovers for its taste, sometimes described as slightly bitter and earthy. Common in Persian and Indian dishes, saffron is the world's most valuable spice, with a pound (requiring the stigma and style from about 75,000 flowers) selling for more than $2,000.

Not all flowers have all four structures described. We'll see later in this chapter that some plants produce flowers that have only male or only female reproductive parts. Still others may lack sepals or petals.

> **TAKE-HOME MESSAGE 18·4**
>
> Flowers are plant structures specialized for sexual reproduction. Most flowers have the same fundamental structures: sepals, petals, stamens, and a carpel.

18·5 The male reproductive structure produces pollen grains.

Humans have a great love of flowers, but it's not unconditional. Tens of millions of people suffer sneezing, coughing, and watery eyes from allergies to certain types of pollen.

What exactly causes so many people so much misery? In plants, the haploid cells produced by meiosis are called spores. Spores produced in the anthers of flowers are called microspores, and spores produced in the ovules are called megaspores. As the anther grows, four chambers— sometimes called "spore sacs"— form, and each is filled with diploid cells called microspore mother cells. (To see the four spore sacs, slice the anther of a flower in half.) The microspore mother cells divide by meiosis, producing four haploid microspores each. The microspores then quickly

divide by mitosis, forming two-cell grains of pollen with very complex, water-tight, sticky surfaces. This two-celled structure is the pollen grain, a reproductive packet containing two haploid cells (**FIGURE 18-11**). One of the cells will eventually grow to form a **pollen tube** (**FIGURE 18-12**), aiding in fertilization. The other will divide once to produce two **sperm** cells. But those steps don't usually occur until the pollen grain has made its way from the anther into the environment and come to rest on a stigma somewhere.

Why does pollen cause allergy attacks in so many people? The trouble begins each spring and summer, as plants release billions and billions of tiny pollen grains into the air. Proteins project from the cell wall of every one of these

MALE GAMETE DEVELOPMENT

Anther

POLLEN PRODUCTION
Pollen grains—structures that contain the male gametes—develop from the microspore mother cells located within the spore sacs of the anther.

Pollen grains contain two haploid cells. One of the cells will eventually grow to form a pollen tube that aids in fertilization. The other will divide once to produce two sperm cells.

Spore sacs

Microspore mother cells

Microspore mother cell (diploid) → **MEIOSIS** → Microspores (haploid) → **MITOSIS** → Pollen grains (haploid)

FIGURE 18-11 The anther of a flower produces pollen grains containing the male gametes.

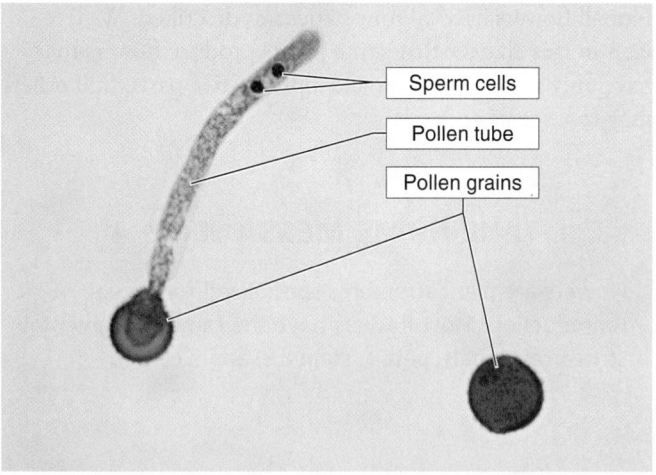

FIGURE 18-12 **A pollen grain contains two haploid cells.** One forms a tube used as a conduit for fertilization. The other cell divides once and forms two sperm cells.

Sperm cells
Pollen tube
Pollen grains

Pollen grain
Mucus
Nose hair

FIGURE 18-14 **The pollen on this nose hair may be flushed from the body by mucus (or a sneeze)!**

Because the immune system identifies pollen grains such as these as foreign invaders, our bodies mount responses against the pollen that may include a runny nose, sneezing, coughing, and congestion.

FIGURE 18-13 **Pollen grains can cause misery for those who suffer with allergies.**

pollen grains, increasing the pollen's stickiness. Inevitably, we breathe in some pollen grains, and our bodies immediately detect the pollen's surface proteins and identify them as foreign invaders (**FIGURE 18-13**). In response to this invasion, our immune system attacks and tries to flush the pollen from our bodies, as shown in **FIGURE 18-14**. Mucus on the nose hair helps move the pollen outside the nose. However, sometimes the response is extreme. The runny nose, sneezing, coughing, and congestion common to pollen allergies are all manifestations of the body's over-reaction.

Q Is pollen the equivalent of plant sperm?

TAKE-HOME MESSAGE 18·5

The male reproductive structure produces pollen grains, each grain a two-cell structure that is water-tight and sticky. One of the cells in the pollen grain will form a pollen tube, and the other will divide to produce two sperm cells.

18·6 Female gametes develop in embryo sacs.

Production of the female gametes (eggs) doesn't cause the suffering in humans that pollen grains do, primarily because the production is confined to the closed structure of the ovary. Within the ovary, one or more diploid cells differentiate into ovules. Each ovule is made of outer protective cells that surround a diploid egg-producing cell, called a megaspore mother cell. The megaspore mother cell undergoes meiosis to produce haploid megaspores. Within a flower, one of the haploid megaspores undergoes mitosis several times to produce the **embryo sac,** the structure in which fertilization will occur (**FIGURE 18-15**). The embryo sac is an unusual collection of seven cells. Six of these cells—including one that is the egg—have haploid nuclei, and the seventh cell, the central cell, has two distinct haploid nuclei. The embryo sac waits for a male gamete to arrive.

TAKE-HOME MESSAGE 18·6

Within the ovary, diploid cells differentiate into ovules. Each ovule is a group of protective cells surrounding a diploid egg-producing cell, which produces diploid megaspores. One of these megaspores produces the embryo sac, the structure that contains the egg and the place where fertilization occurs.

FEMALE GAMETE DEVELOPMENT

Carpel — Stigma — Style

Ovary — Ovule — Megaspore mother cell

EMBRYO SAC PRODUCTION
The embryo sac—a structure that contains the female gametes—develops from the megaspore mother cell located within an ovule.

Several megaspores are produced and one of these undergoes several rounds of mitosis, producing the seven-celled embryo sac.

Megaspore mother cell (diploid) → MEIOSIS → Megaspores (haploid) → MITOSIS → Embryo sac (haploid) — Egg cell

FIGURE 18-15 Female gametes are produced within the ovary of a flower.

18·7–18·11 Pollination, fertilization, and seed dispersal often depend on help from other organisms.

A honeybee coated with pollen can transport male gametes.

18·7 Plants need help getting the male gamete to the female gamete for fertilization.

The ancestors of plants, the green algae, could simply release their gametes into the water, so some were bound to find their way to the gametes of another individual of their species. For mosses and ferns, reproduction is still tied to water; they must rely on the presence of water for transporting male gametes to the female gametes, or else the gametes dry out. For this reason, mosses and ferns must live in moist habitats or reproduce when moisture is available. With the transition to land during evolution, seed plants had to reduce their reproductive dependence on water, and a number of ways evolved that bring together male and female gametes (**FIGURE 18-16**). Often, this process involves enlisting animals to carry the male gametes.

How does a flowering plant get an animal to transport its gametes? It attracts the animal with its flowers' visual cues (color, shape), olfactory cues (smell), or even tactile cues (soft, bristly, hard, rough, smooth). Regardless of the

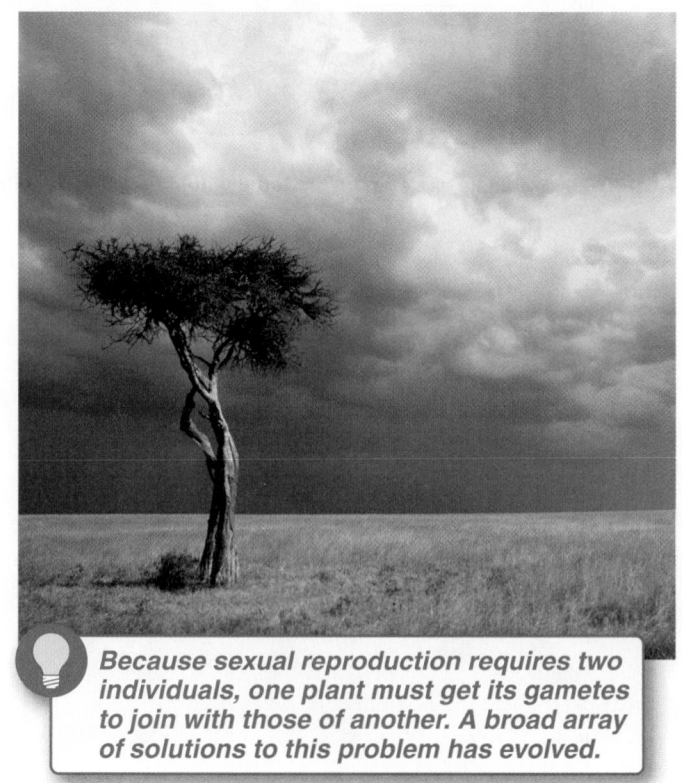

Because sexual reproduction requires two individuals, one plant must get its gametes to join with those of another. A broad array of solutions to this problem has evolved.

FIGURE 18-16 Even seemingly isolated plants can reproduce sexually.

method of attraction, the goal is always the same: to physically attach some male gametes to an animal so that they rub off on the female reproductive parts of another plant, where fertilization can then occur. That is, a pollen grain from a plant must journey to the stigma of another plant of the same species. This process is called **pollination.**

About 10% of plant species achieve pollination by simply releasing their pollen into the wind (as do grasses and pine trees) or into water (as does eelgrass, for example), on the slim chance that—through luck—some of the pollen will land on the female reproductive organs of another plant of the same species. Given the astronomically low probability of any one pollen grain actually doing so, wind- and water-pollinated plants respond in the only reasonable way: they produce tremendous amounts of pollen, tens of millions of pollen grains per plant. It's not particularly efficient, but it works.

In the other 90% of plants, animals act as "go-betweens," moving pollen from one plant to another. Among these plants, most are pollinated by insects, with numerous other species pollinated by birds or mammals (mostly bats) and even in a few cases by lizards (**FIGURE 18-17**). It is important to note that the data in Figure 18-17 are very imprecise estimates. There are several difficulties in establishing the exact proportion of plants pollinated by any group of animals. These include the observation that the vast majority (~90%) of flowering plant species are visited by more than one animal pollinator species, and the fact that it is difficult to demonstrate that an animal is actually a pollinator of a plant (rather than a predator or even just a harmless visitor).

Two different and clever strategies for achieving pollination occur (**FIGURE 18-18**): (1) bribery—plants bribe some animals to carry their pollen from one individual plant to another; and (2) trickery—they deceive animals into doing the job.

1. *Bribery.* The most common strategy for achieving pollination involves a plant offering something of value to an animal in exchange for transport of its pollen from one flower to another. For bribery to work, the plant must produce sticky pollen and a flower that catches the attention of the pollinator. Most important, the plant must produce something of value to the pollinator. The payoff can be food, such as nutritious **nectar,** a solution rich in sugars (and also containing amino acids), or it may be a safe, hospitable location for an insect to lay its eggs.

Q

Why do some flowers smell nice while others don't smell at all?

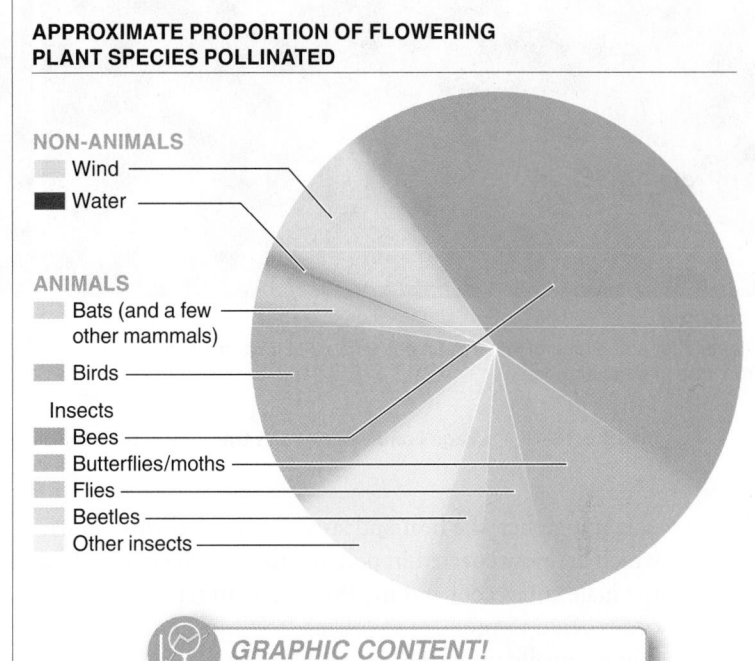

METHODS OF POLLINATION

Several factors make it impossible to give more than loose approximations of the proportion of flowering plant species pollinated by each different type of pollinator. Demonstrating that an animal is actually a pollinator (rather than an herbivore or nectar thief) is difficult, for example. Moreover, approximately 90% of flowering plant species are visited by more than one animal pollinator species.

APPROXIMATE PROPORTION OF FLOWERING PLANT SPECIES POLLINATED

NON-ANIMALS
- Wind
- Water

ANIMALS
- Bats (and a few other mammals)
- Birds

Insects
- Bees
- Butterflies/moths
- Flies
- Beetles
- Other insects

GRAPHIC CONTENT!
Thinking critically about visual displays of data.
Turn to p. 732 for a closer inspection of this figure.

FIGURE 18-17 Options for getting the male gamete to the female gamete. Flowering plants employ a variety of methods for transporting their male gametes.

2. *Trickery.* The second strategy for achieving pollination is more selfish. Rather than bribing an animal to carry its pollen, the plant just tricks the animal into thinking it is going to get something of value, while not actually giving it anything. Among the tricksters are a species of plants called cycads. Cycads are gymnosperms (they look a bit like palm trees) that produce cones once every year or so. Within the male cones, pollen is produced in large amounts. It might seem as though cycads use the strategy of bribery for pollination, because their pollen attracts huge numbers of small insects called thrips, and the thrips consume the pollen. But providing a source of food isn't enough to achieve pollination in cycads. That's where the trickery comes in.

For a few hours each day during the period that they have cones, the cycads are able to increase the temperature inside the male cones by up to 25° F. They do this by metabolizing sugars and fats within the cone. As they do so, they also produce a powerful stench.

By coordinated changes in their smell and temperature, cycad plants are able to "trick" small insects called thrips into pollinating their flowers.

BRIBERY
Plants offer something of value to an animal so that it carries pollen from one plant to another.

TRICKERY
Plants use methods of deception to trick animals into carrying pollen from one plant to another.

FIGURE 18-18 Package handlers. Animals transport pollen for plants.

Taken together, the heat and stink cause the thrips—most of which are now covered in pollen—to leave the cones. And as the male cones cool and the thrips start to return, the female cones begin to produce a pleasing (to thrips) odor, similar to that originally produced by the male cones. The attractive odor lures in some thrips, thinking that they will find pollen. But there is no pollen. And by the time the thrips realize this, they have usually brushed some of the pollen that covered their bodies onto the reproductive parts of the female cone.

The variety of flower structures is tremendous. They differ in shape, color, smell, time of day when they are open, whether or not they produce nectar, and whether their pollen is edible. Just as the variety of flower types is wide, so, too, is the variety of pollinators: birds (mostly

hummingbirds), bees, flies, beetles, butterflies, moths, and even some mammals (mostly bats). In each case, there has been strong coevolution between the plants and their pollinators: the plants have become more and more effective at attracting the pollinators and deterring other species from visiting the flower, while the pollinators have become more and more effective at exploiting the resources offered by the plants (see Figure 12-21).

TAKE-HOME MESSAGE 18·7

Plants usually utilize trickery or bribery to get the assistance of animals in carrying the male gametes to the female gametes. There has been strong coevolution between plants and their animal pollinators.

18·8 Fertilization occurs after pollination.

Pollination is a bit like sexual intercourse in mammals: it brings the male and female gametes close to each other, but it isn't quite fertilization. Fertilization requires that the male and female gametes fuse so that their genetic material can be combined. We examine here the male gamete's last steps on its journey to the female gamete.

Recall that the pollen grain is made from two cells encased in a sticky, spiky wall. When the pollen grain lands on a stigma of a flower of its own species, it sticks to the stigma

through interactions between the pollen grain's outer coating and the cells of the stigma. Pollen grains from other species have the wrong identifiers on the surface and slide off the stigma easily, keeping it open to the "right" pollen grains (**FIGURE 18-19**).

Within 12 to 36 hours of the pollen landing on a stigma, one cell in the pollen grain starts to grow into a pollen tube. This growth does not occur through cell division but by an elongation of the tube cell, which stretches itself and pushes

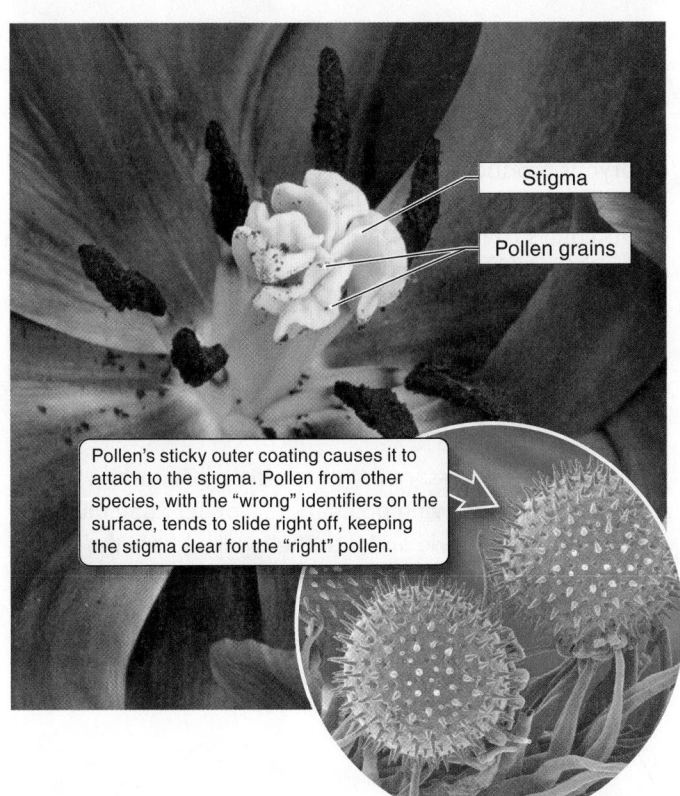

FIGURE 18-19 **Built to stick.** Pollen grains adhere to the stigma of a flower.

Stigma

Pollen grains

Pollen's sticky outer coating causes it to attach to the stigma. Pollen from other species, with the "wrong" identifiers on the surface, tends to slide right off, keeping the stigma clear for the "right" pollen.

the sperm-producing cell through the stigma, down the style of the female reproductive structure's carpel, closer and closer to the ovary. This growth isn't an easy stroll down the style, however. It's more like running a gauntlet. The cells within the style test the tube cell to check whether it is too closely related to the plant on which the pollen has landed (as it would be if the plant self-pollinated). If the tube cell is too closely related, it is killed—often by a chemical reaction, breaking down the cytoskeleton of the pollen tube. If it is not too closely related, the pollen tube is allowed to continue growing toward the ovary.

If the pollen tube survives its journey down the style and into the ovule, it grows right into the embryo sac (**FIGURE 18-20**). Meanwhile, the sperm-producing cell within the

---

DOUBLE FERTILIZATION

Pollen grain — Stigma
— Sperm-producing cell
— Pollen tube
— Style
Ovary — Ovule

Pollen tube

Embryo sac — Sperm cells

Pollen tube — Embryo sac
— Central cell
— Sperm cells
— Egg cell

Endosperm (3n)
Zygote (2n)

1 POLLEN TUBE FORMS
Once a pollen grain lands on a flower's stigma, one cell in the pollen grain starts to grow into a pollen tube and begins its journey toward the ovary, taking the sperm-producing cell with it.

2 SPERM CELLS ARE PRODUCED
The pollen tube continues to grow directly into the embryo sac. Meanwhile, the sperm-producing cell within the pollen tube divides once, producing two sperm cells.

3 TWO FUSIONS OF MALE AND FEMALE NUCLEI
As the pollen tube pushes its way into the embryo sac, it releases the two sperm cells. One of them fertilizes the egg cell, while the other fuses with the central cell of the embryo sac.

4 ENDOSPERM AND ZYGOTE FORM
The fertilization of the egg cell results in a in a diploid zygote (that will divide and become a multicellular embryo). The fusion of the other sperm cell with the central cell produces a triploid cell called the endosperm.

With double fertilization, only when a zygote is produced does a plant expend energy to produce a food source, the endosperm.

FIGURE 18-20 **Fertilization in the flowering plants.** In the process of double fertilization, there are two fusions of male and female nuclei: one produces the plant embryo and the other produces the endosperm.

pollen tube divides once, producing two sperm cells. As the pollen tube pushes its way into the embryo sac, it releases the two sperm cells, and one of them fertilizes the egg cell inside the embryo sac. When the sperm and egg fuse in fertilization, a diploid cell called the **zygote** results, which will develop by mitosis into the new diploid plant.

The other sperm cell fuses with the central cell of the embryo sac, which, as we learned earlier, has two haploid nuclei. This second fusion produces a triploid cell with three sets of genes. The triploid cell is called the **endosperm.** As the embryo starts to grow and divide, so, too, does the endosperm. It continues to do so at a high rate, turning into nutritional tissue that nourishes the developing embryo.

Q *What part of the plant supplies the majority of calories to humans?*

Because, in this fertilization, there are two separate fusions of male nuclei with female nuclei—one producing the embryo and the other producing the endosperm—the whole process is called **double fertilization.** This process, which is unique to flowering plants, is an efficient system because whenever an embryo is produced, so, too, is a ready-made food source. A large proportion of the calories we ingest when we eat plants comes from endosperm, including the sweet material in corn on the cob, rice, and the flour we eat as pasta and bread.

TAKE-HOME MESSAGE 18·8

Pollination is necessary but not sufficient for achieving fertilization. Following pollination, a pollen tube must grow down the style and into the ovule, where the sperm-producing cell divides to both fertilize the egg cell and to fuse with the diploid central cell of the embryo sac to form the endosperm, the tissue that will nourish the developing embryo.

18·9 Most plants can avoid self-fertilization.

The efficiency of flower structure is remarkable. Flowers commonly contain the male reproductive parts and gametes as well as the female reproductive parts and gametes, so a pollinator can easily assist in sexual reproduction. A visiting bee, for example, can pollinate a flower such as an apple blossom with pollen from another blossom it previously visited, while simultaneously picking up pollen for later fertilization of other individuals. But this *hermaphroditism*—having both male and female reproductive parts—can lead to some unintended and detrimental consequences. What happens, after all, if a plant's male gamete fertilizes one of its own eggs? Such self-fertilization leads not only to less genetically varied offspring, but also to offspring that are more likely to express one or more lethal or negative genes because of the extreme inbreeding. How can plants avoid self-fertilization?

Numerous mechanisms for avoiding self-fertilization occur in plants, including (as we saw in Section 18-8), chemical reactions within the cells of the style that destroy a growing pollen tube if it is too closely related. Three of the

Q *What are the risks and benefits of a plant producing "bisexual" flowers?*

most effective general mechanisms for reducing self-fertilization are described here (**FIGURE 18-21**).

1. *Separate male and female flowers.* In some plants, an individual produces some flowers with only male reproductive parts and others with only female reproductive parts. Overall, the plant is still a hermaphrodite, but such unisexual flowers minimize the likelihood of self-pollination and self-fertilization. Examples of plants with separate male and female flowers include corn and most fig species.

2. *Staggered maturation of male and female reproductive parts.* To prevent self-fertilization in hermaphrodite flowers, the flowers of some plants have male parts that develop before the female parts, or vice versa. An example of this pattern occurs in geraniums.

3. *Separate male and female plants.* The most extreme method of avoiding self-fertilization is for some plants within a population to produce only flowers with male reproductive parts, while others produce only flowers with

METHODS OF REDUCING SELF-FERTILIZATION

SEPARATE MALE AND FEMALE FLOWERS
Some plants produce some flowers with only male reproductive parts and other flowers with only female reproductive parts.

STAGGERED MATURATION
The flowers of some plants have male parts that develop before the female parts, or vice versa.

SEPARATE MALE AND FEMALE PLANTS
Some plants within a population produce only flowers with male reproductive parts, and other plants produce only flowers with female reproductive parts.

 Plants have several effective mechanisms for reducing the potentially detrimental incidence of self-fertilization.

FIGURE 18-21 Avoiding inbreeding. Several mechanisms can reduce the incidence of self-fertilization, enhancing genetic diversity among the offspring in flowering plants.

female reproductive parts. As in humans, then, there are two separate sexes. This makes self-fertilization impossible, but it also reduces the likelihood that any given visit by a pollinator will result in pollination and fertilization. Examples of plants with separate male and female plants include poplars, American holly, and willows.

TAKE-HOME MESSAGE 18·9

Plants can reduce the likelihood of self-fertilization in any of several ways: producing separate male and female flowers, staggering the time of maturation of male and female reproductive parts, or producing separate male and female plants.

18·10 Following fertilization, the ovule develops into a seed.

After fertilization within the ovule, numerous cell divisions occur rapidly. The developing embryo forms a **root meristem** and a **shoot meristem,** each of which is a cluster of active, dividing embryonic cells that will generate new tissue. (We discuss the unique qualities of meristems in more detail in Section 18-13.) Also, one or two **cotyledons** form, structures in the embryo that usually become the embryonic leaves (see Section 17-2). As the embryo matures, the outer cells of the ovule develop into a hard casing forming a **seed**—a sort of "plant in waiting" that is made of embryo (meristems and cotyledons) and any remaining endosperm (**FIGURE 18-22**).

At the same time the seed is forming, the ovary wall—surrounding one or more seeds—develops into a **fruit,** which in many species is fleshy, juicy, and edible, but in other species may be dry or inedible. The seed is protected within the fruit, which, we'll see, aids in its dispersal. Metabolism and oxygen consumption grind to a halt, and the seed dries out, reducing its water content to about 15% of its total weight. And then the waiting begins.

Q *What is popcorn?*

Humans have learned a trick that turns one type of seed into an unusual snack. Each kernel of popcorn comes from a single kernel of corn on a cob and is

1 RAPID INITIAL CELL DIVISION
Following fertilization within the ovule, numerous rapid cell divisions occur.

2 MERISTEMS AND COTYLEDONS FORM
The developing embryo forms a root meristem and a shoot meristem, as well as one or two cotyledons.

3 SEED COAT FORMS
The ovule tissue surrounding the developing embryo hardens to become a protective seed coat.

4 OVARY DEVELOPS INTO A FRUIT
At the same time that seed formation is occurring, the ovary wall develops into a fruit, protecting the seed.

FIGURE 18-22 Protected for later dispersal. Seeds are protected by a casing and nestled within a fruit.

the equivalent of a fruit: it includes a fertilized egg surrounded by a nutritious, edible outer layer, formed from the ovary wall. (If you plant some popcorn kernels, they will grow!) There is also moisture within the kernel—some oil and some water—and the kernel is surrounded by a moisture-proof coat. Heating the kernel turns the moisture inside to steam and chemically alters the starch and protein in the seed, making it soft and a bit gelatinous. With continued heating, the pressure from the steam rises and ultimately blasts through the seed coat with a pop. The fluffy white material is the starch and protein that surrounded the seed.

Before a seed can grow into a new plant, it must leave the parent plant. In the next section we look at how ever-immobile plants ensure that their seeds are moved and prepared for growth.

TAKE-HOME MESSAGE 18·10

Following fertilization, the ovule develops into a seed, containing a root meristem, a shoot meristem, and one or two cotyledons, surrounded by a hard casing. The seed is protected within a fruit, which aids in its dispersal.

18·11 Fruits exist to help plants disperse their seeds.

Every fruit you eat used to be a flower: tangerines, peaches, raspberries, cherries, pumpkin, and squash, among others. Fruits are produced by plants to aid in dispersing the seeds that will grow into their new offspring. By encasing seeds in a juicy, nutritious structure—the fruit—plants create a package that entices hungry animals. Animals eat the fruit, gaining valuable nutrients and energy. Then, at a later point—and in a location far away from the parent plant—the animals eliminate the seeds, which pass unharmed through their digestive system. At the new location, often

surrounded by a bit of the animal's feces that serves as fertilizer, the seed can grow.

There is a huge variety of fruits beyond those adapted for consumption. And although they all serve the function of dispersing the seeds, not all require the assistance of animals. Just as with dispersal of pollen, plants can also use wind or water to transport their seeds. **FIGURE 18-23** presents a small sampling of the rich variety of fruits and seeds produced by plants. As is apparent, the term "fruit" applies to a much

METHODS OF FRUIT AND SEED DISPERSAL

WIND-DISPERSED

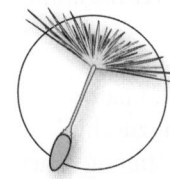

HAIRY
Seeds within fruits that have bushy hairs can float in the air.

WINGED
Seeds within fruits that have wing-like structures can float away from a tree as they slowly descend.

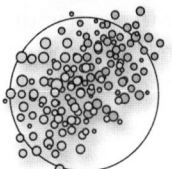

TINY, DUST-LIKE
Seeds that are tiny and light as dust are able to float in the air.

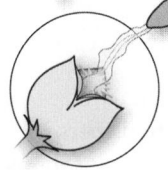

EXPLOSIVE
Seeds are propelled from the plant as the ripened fruits explode.

WATER-DISPERSED

Seeds within floating fruits can be dispersed by rivers or oceans.

ANIMAL-DISPERSED

CARRIED
Seeds within fruits that have sharp or clingy burrs can catch on the fur of animals and be carried away.

CONSUMED
Seeds within fruits that are consumed by animals can be dispersed as they pass through the animal's digestive tract and are eliminated at some distant location.

FIGURE 18-23 Wind, water, and animals can disperse seeds.

broader range of structures than is typically associated with it. And the makeup of each fruit clearly reflects the method by which it is dispersed—wind, water, or animals.

Wind-dispersed fruits and seeds Wind dispersal can be achieved by means of several characteristics of fruits and seeds.

1. *Hairy.* Bushy hairs allow the fruits of dandelions and milkweed to float in the air.

2. *Winged.* Usually released from tall trees such as elms and maples, winged fruits and seeds float away from the tree as they slowly descend.

3. *Tiny, dust-like.* Many orchids have seeds that are as tiny and light as dust and so float in the air.

4. *Explosive.* Many fruits, such as those of mistletoe, explode when ripe, propelling the seeds as far as 50 feet (about 15 meters) away at speeds of 60 miles (about 100 kilometers) per hour.

Water-dispersed fruits and seeds Some plants produce floating fruits, such as the coconut, that can be dispersed by rivers or oceans.

Animal-dispersed fruits and seeds Animals act as dispersers simply by carrying or eating fruits.

1. *Carried.* Some plants produce fruits that have sharp or clingy burrs on the outside. These burrs catch on the legs or fur of animals (including humans) and are carried away until the animal grooms itself and removes the fruit, leaving the seeds to germinate and grow in the new location. Burrs were the inspiration for Velcro.

2. *Consumed.* Many fruits are sugar- and nutrient-laden fleshy structures eaten by animals, usually vertebrates. In some cases (such as the peach), the fruit develops from a single ovary; in others (such as blackberries or pineapple), it forms from multiple ovaries from numerous flowers. It does not benefit a plant to have its seeds dispersed before they are ready to go. Consequently, fruits generally do not ripen and become sweet and edible until the seeds are fully developed. In fact, most fruits remain green until the seeds are ready for dispersal, at which point the fruit sweetens and turns a bright color to attract the attention of dispersers.

Q Why do fruits taste so bad before they are ripe?

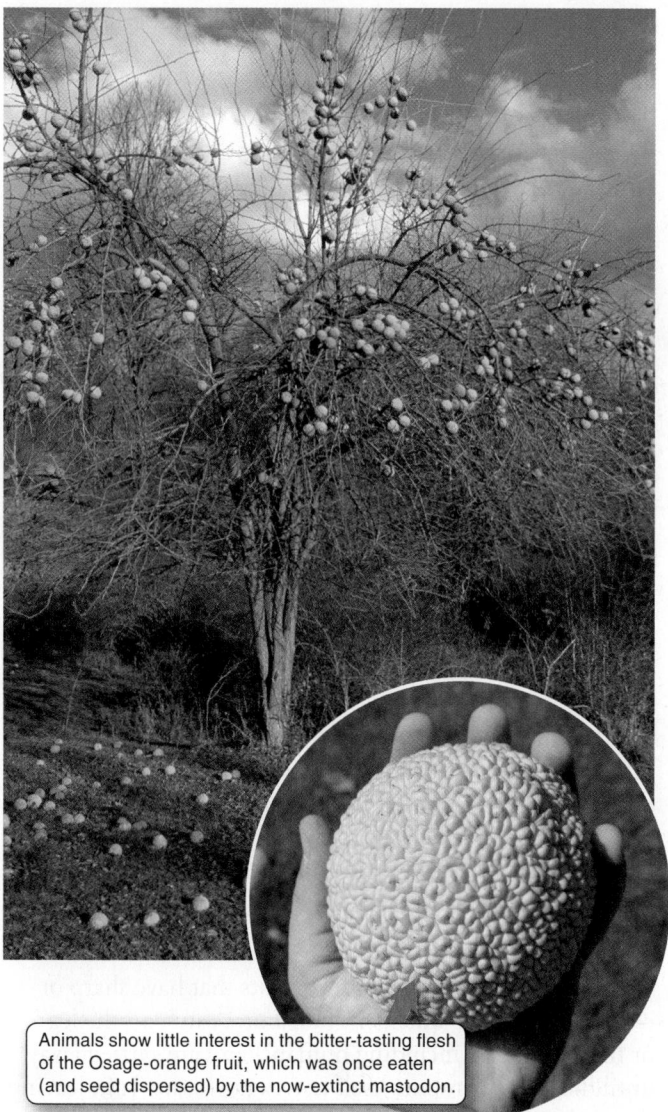

Animals show little interest in the bitter-tasting flesh of the Osage-orange fruit, which was once eaten (and seed dispersed) by the now-extinct mastodon.

FIGURE 18-24 **The fruit of the Osage orange *Maclura pomifera* (sometimes called the hedge apple) lie rotting beneath the tree.** Contemporary animals show little interest in its bitter-tasting flesh, although super-sized (now extinct) North American mammals such as mastodons once fed on it.

The seed's coating is tough enough to pass through an animal's digestive tract without being destroyed, and the seed can germinate and begin growing wherever the animal defecates (or, in the case of birds, regurgitates).

The various animal-dispersed fruits include tomatoes, grapes, cherries, olives, apples, pears, squash, zucchini, all beans and peas, corn kernels, and avocados, among others. Because there appears to be no species of animal alive today that disperses avocado seeds, researchers have speculated that the avocado plant evolved in concert with some large species of animal that has since become extinct. Today, avocado plants rely on humans to disperse their seeds. A similar situation appears to also be the case with the seed of the Osage-orange tree, whose fruit was once eaten (and seeds dispersed) by the now-extinct mastodon (**FIGURE 18-24**).

TAKE-HOME MESSAGE 18·11

Following pollination and fertilization, plants utilize the assistance of animals, water, or wind to disperse their fruits and seeds, depositing them at new locations where the seeds can germinate and new plants can grow.

Trees grow along a canal in the Netherlands.

18·12—18·15 Plants have two types of growth, usually enabling lifelong increases in length and thickness.

18·12

How do seeds germinate and grow?

With the seed, plants have created an impressive little time capsule. In suspended animation, the embryo patiently waits until the conditions for its new life are just right, at which point it bursts forth with growth. Let's examine what makes up a seed and how it emerges from its dormancy and begins life.

The seed does not start to grow until the water, temperature, and oxygen conditions are good for germination and growth (FIGURE 18-25). Sometimes this means waiting a matter of days or weeks before germination. For some species, though, the seeds remain dormant even in the face of ideal environmental conditions. Their seeds require something more before they will germinate. They may require passage through the gut of a bird or mammal to roughen up and weaken the seed coat. Or they may require exposure to

Q The seeds of plants used in agriculture have thinner coats and more stored energy than the seeds of wild, naturally occurring plants. Why?

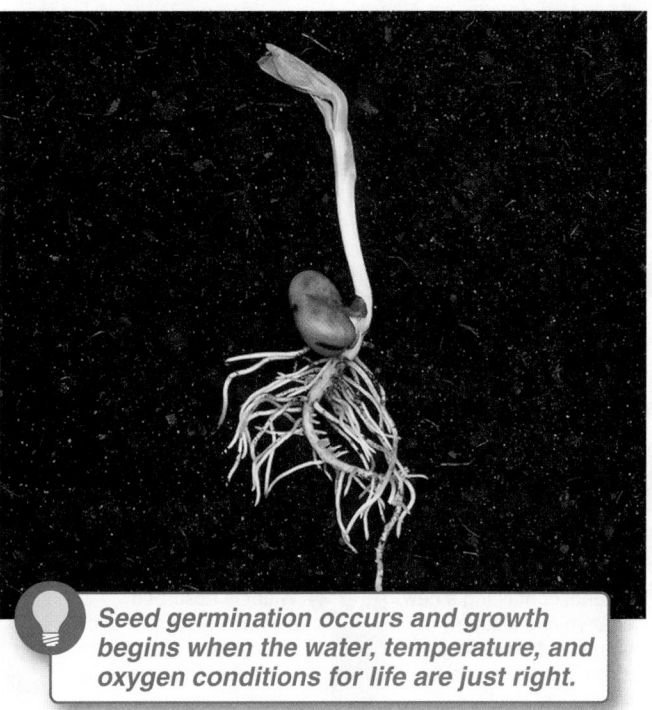

Seed germination occurs and growth begins when the water, temperature, and oxygen conditions for life are just right.

FIGURE 18-25 The emerging plant.

fire. Such seeds can remain dormant for dozens or even hundreds of years before finally germinating. Conversely, over the course of many generations of plant domestication, plant breeders are likely to have selected the seeds that germinate most quickly and have the fastest initial growth. These features may be optimal under agricultural conditions, where fields are cleared, pests are removed, and competition is limited.

There can be benefits to producing seeds with coats that require extra "processing" before they can germinate. (1) This can prevent the germination of seeds that have not been dispersed widely enough. (2) It can ensure that seeds are always left in a dollop of natural fertilizer. Or (3) it may ensure that there are clearings where competing trees have been burned down and light is available before the seeds germinate.

> **"**Though I do not believe that a plant will spring up where no seed has been, I have great faith in a seed. Convince me that you have a seed there, and I am prepared to expect wonders.**"**
>
> — HENRY DAVID THOREAU, *Faith in a Seed*

Such features, though, can also dangerously link the evolutionary success of the plant to the behavior of another species or specific ecological conditions. For example, some of the plants producing seeds that require the extreme heat or smoke from a fire to induce germination are in trouble. As humans have reduced the incidence of wildfires, so, too, have we reduced the ability of many plants to germinate.

The whole purpose of a seed is to package an embryo with a ready-made supply of nutrients and energy so that it has the fuel to start growing before it can photosynthesize for itself. That high-energy package, of course, is exactly what animals are looking for in a food source, too. Consequently, seeds can be a valuable snack, rich in calories. They are also flavorful when ground up, producing spices.

Q Animals (including humans) love to eat seeds. Why?

On a somewhat minor note, a confusing issue—though not very important biologically—is the question "Is a seed a nut?" In short, botanists have given the word "nut" a very specific and technical definition. (It is one particular type of fruit having a hard shell with no suture lines, or "seams," and with a single seed inside. An acorn is an example of a nut.) There is a much less restrictive, culinary definition of a nut, however, that encompasses most seeds. By this broader definition, virtually every seed that we eat is considered a "nut," including peanuts, almonds, cashews, and macadamia nuts—even though none of them would be classified as a nut by the botanist. The whole fruitless debate is a consequence of the common problem of words (such as "theory" or "evolution" or "altruism") having narrow, specific meanings in scientific disciplines but broader—perhaps sloppier, but usually more widely known—definitions in the everyday world outside science.

But back to the seed, ready to begin its growth. With the proper processing and sufficient warmth, oxygen, and water, germination can finally begin. As germination

SEED GERMINATION

Seed coat
Embryo
Endosperm

Water

Shoot
Root

Sunlight

1 A seed, containing a new embryo and a supply of nutrients, begins to grow when the conditions for life are just right.

2 Water is absorbed, increasing the size of the embryo and causing the seed coat to burst.

3 The plant first sends a root downward and then sends the shoot upward, each with an apical meristem near its tip.

4 The leaflets then begin photosynthesis, providing even more energy for the plant to grow.

FIGURE 18-26 From seed to seedling: the initial growth of a plant.

begins, water is absorbed, causing the embryo to enlarge and the seed coat to burst. Utilizing the fat and starch reserves of the endosperm and embryo, metabolic activity increases dramatically and the plant begins growing (FIGURE 18-26). It first sends down a root and then sends up the shoot. In many plants, the cotyledons (after their energy reserves are used) can photosynthesize, providing even more energy for the plant. This early seedling growth involves the apical meristems, which we explore in Section 18-14.

18·13 Plants grow differently from animals.

So far we have explored the reproductive processes of plants. First they make pollen and eggs. Then they manage to get the pollen to an egg and achieve fertilization. The embryo then remains dormant as a seed, carried within a fruit until it is dispersed and arrives at a place to live. Once there and ready, the seed germinates and begins to grow. In this and the following sections we examine how growth occurs.

Plants and animals grow very differently. Three particular features stand out. First, in most animals, growth is determinate. In other words, after a period of maturation

and "growing up," the growth more or less comes to an end. Most plants, though, keep on growing taller and thicker their whole lives. Second, perhaps more oddly, despite their continuous growth, most trees are largely made up of dead cells. Within the branches and roots, all the water-conducting cells are actually dead (see Section 17-3), and the majority of a large tree trunk—the wood—is dead, too. And finally, a distinctive aspect of growth in plants opposed to growth in most animals is that plants lose relatively large structures, such as branches and leaves, all the time, without adverse effects (FIGURE 18-27). Unlike limbs in mammals—

FEATURES OF PLANT GROWTH

INDETERMINATE GROWTH
Most plants continue to grow—both taller and thicker—for their entire life.

CONSIST OF BOTH LIVING AND DEAD CELLS
Many plant cells, including water-conducting cells and those that make up wood, are dead.

LOSS OF STRUCTURES
Plants are able to lose relatively large structures, such as limbs and leaves, without adverse effects.

FIGURE 18-27 Defining characteristics of plant growth.

 Several features of plant growth are very different from growth in animals.

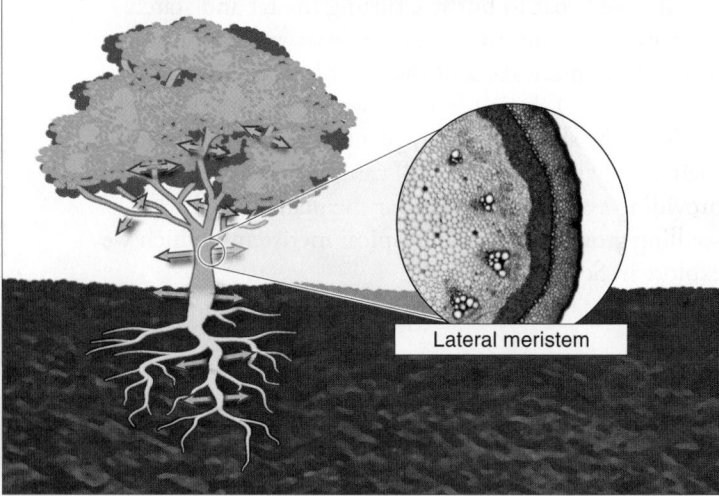

PRIMARY GROWTH
• Makes a plant taller and roots and branches longer
• Due to cell division within apical meristems present at the tips of shoots and roots

SECONDARY GROWTH
• Makes a plant stronger and roots and branches thicker
• Due to cell division within lateral meristems

FIGURE 18-28 Apical and lateral meristems are the source of plant growth.

critical appendages intended to last a lifetime—many plant structures function more like our skin cells that are regularly sloughed off and replaced by new ones.

Plants have two different methods of growing, each for a different direction of growth, which we explore in more detail in the next two sections. **Primary growth** causes plants to get taller, and **secondary growth** makes them thicker (and stronger). For both types, the cellular processes are similar and involve regions called **meristems.** These are clusters of active, dividing cells. Acting like human stem cells, the meristems contain perpetually youthful cells that can (1) repeatedly divide and (2) develop into any type of plant tissue. Nowhere else in an adult plant body are there cells with these unlimited developmental options. So, even in a 4,000-year-old bristlecone pine tree, every time a bud breaks open and produces a shoot, the meristem cells have all of the growth and development potential of a cell in a brand new plant.

The two different types of plant growth depend on the activities of two different types of meristem (**FIGURE 18-28**).

1. *Apical meristems* are clusters of meristem cells at the ends of roots and shoots or branches that repeatedly divide to produce primary growth,

making the plant taller and plant parts (roots and branches) longer. This process is in dramatic contrast to human growth. It would be as if we grew by continuously adding more material on top of our heads and at the ends of our hands and feet.

By cutting the top meristem of a shoot, axillary buds that are lower on the plant (and inhibited from growth as long as the apical meristem is present) increase their growth.

FIGURE 18-29 Taken to extremes. It is possible to "train" plants to grow into dramatic shapes with pruning.

This causes the plant to grow "out" more than "up." Taking this approach to the extreme, gardeners have found that it is possible to cause plants to grow into dramatic shapes through continued pruning (FIGURE 18-29).

2. *Lateral meristems*—not present in all plant species—give rise to secondary plant growth, the thickening of trunks and branches and the formation of wood and bark.

18·14 Primary plant growth occurs at the apical meristems.

So, as we've seen, primary growth makes shoots taller and roots and branches longer, and it forms new tissues such as buds and leaves.

All primary growth occurs as a result of cell division in apical meristems (FIGURE 18-30). The cells in meristems are *totipotent,* meaning they have the potential to develop into any type of cell the plant produces. Growth occurs as a meristem cell divides and creates two new cells. One differentiates into a specific type of tissue, such as xylem, phloem, or perhaps a storage cell. The other cell remains a meristem cell. Thus, the process of growth and differentiation can occur while the meristem remains a perpetual source of new cells. Recall that apical meristem cells are present at all root tips and shoot tips. They reside just behind a small cap of cells, at the very end of the tip that protects the meristem.

Apical meristem cells are also responsible for the production of branches as a plant grows. In the shoot, as the meristem cells divide, pushing the top of the plant higher and higher, some meristem cells are left behind at regular intervals. The meristem cells left behind are able to begin dividing at any time—usually after stimulation by hormones, which we discuss in Chapter 19. They push outward to form a branch. As the branch grows, the meristem again leaves behind some cells near each bud, allowing further branching. Some of the new cells become xylem and phloem, and the vessels join up with the central circulatory vessels within the stem.

Q **What are the knots in wood?**

Most timber used in construction comes from pieces of wood cut from the tree along the length of its trunk. Knots are places where branches were connected to the trunk and where their vascular tissue merged with that of the trunk. Knots become more and more deeply embedded within the trunk as secondary growth makes the trunk thicker.

PRIMARY GROWTH

Primary growth occurs as a result of cell division in meristem cells, present at all shoot and root tips.

Shoot apical meristem

■ Dermal tissue
■ Vascular tissue
■ Ground tissue

Growth occurs as a meristem cell divides, creating two new cells. One cell differentiates into a specific type of plant tissue, while the other cell remains a meristem cell, a perpetual source of new cells.

PRIMARY GROWTH AND BRANCHING

As a plant shoot grows, some meristem cells are left behind at regular intervals. The meristem cells left behind are dormant but can begin dividing at any time, pushing outward and forming the plant's branches.

Apical meristem   Dormant meristem cell

FIGURE 18-30 Growing taller: primary growth.

Secondary growth produces wood.

Wood is amazing. And not just from an aesthetic or utilitarian perspective—although it is quite remarkable in that way, too (**FIGURE 18-31**). Wood is mostly amazing as an almost impossibly elegant evolutionary solution that allows plants to grow to dizzying heights. A shoot cannot simply grow taller and taller by continued cell division at the apical meristem for the same reason that a small house cannot have floor upon floor added until it is a hundred stories tall. The plant and the house would tip over. Increased height demands increased structural rigidity. In addition, the top floors of the tall building must receive plumbing and electrical service, just as the top of a tree must have vascular tissue. The beauty of wood is that it serves both purposes: it confers strength, keeping the tree from toppling over, while simultaneously serving as the plumbing conduit for water and minerals. And it does this while being tremendously lightweight.

Once the apical meristems have moved past a location in a stem or trunk during primary growth, that part of the plant can no longer elongate or become taller. It can, however, grow outward and become thicker. Here we investigate the process of secondary growth by which eudicots and some other angiosperms produce wood, increasing capacity for water conduction and becoming thicker and sturdier in the process.

How does secondary growth occur? Imagine a cross section of a woody plant. It is packed with concentric cylinders, one within another, progressing outward from the center (**FIGURE 18-32**). First, from the center to about halfway to the outer circumference, extends the **pith**, soft spongy parenchyma cells. Just beyond this is a thin cylinder of vascular tissue: the xylem. A bit farther out is another cylinder of vascular tissue: the phloem. And beyond that is the epidermis and outer covering of the trunk. Sandwiched between the xylem and phloem lies the **vascular cambium**—a layer of lateral meristem cells. Recall that meristems contain perpetually youthful cells that can repeatedly divide and develop into any type of plant tissue.

As the cells of the vascular cambium divide, they produce two rings of cells—one toward the outer circumference of the trunk and one toward the center. The cells produced toward the outside are called **secondary phloem** and conduct sugars throughout the plant body. The cells closer to the center are **secondary xylem** cells and conduct water and minerals, while also providing structural support to the plant. We call these secondary xylem cells, collectively, "wood." Because the vascular cambium is producing cells toward the inside of the stem or trunk, it is gradually pushed farther and farther out, away from the center. As it is pushed farther out, it leaves ring after ring of wood to the inside, thickening the tree trunk.

Although most xylem initially acts like a long straw through which water can pass, older xylem is like a clogged artery

FIGURE 18-31 Wood is of great value to humans.

Humans utilize the strength, durability, and beauty of wood in a variety of applications.

SECONDARY GROWTH

Secondary growth occurs as cells in the lateral meristem divide, resulting in increased water conduction capacity and becoming thicker and sturdier in the process.

1 Sandwiched between the xylem and phloem is a layer of lateral meristem cells called vascular cambium.

Xylem
Phloem
Vascular cambium
Pith

2 The cells of the vascular cambium divide, producing a ring of cells closer to the center of the trunk called the secondary xylem.

Secondary xylem

3 The cells of the vascular cambium also produce a ring of cells to the outside called the secondary phloem.

Secondary phloem

As the vascular cambium is gradually pushed farther and farther out, it leaves ring after ring of wood to the inside and the tree trunk becomes thicker.

FIGURE 18-32 **Becoming thicker and sturdier: secondary growth.**

Looking at a cross section of a tree, we find that the color of the wood reveals the relative amounts of heartwood and sapwood. It can also reveal the age of the tree, in the growth rings. In temperate climates, more growth—that is, greater rates of cell division in the vascular cambium—occurs during

Q | Why can you tell a tree's age by counting its rings?

WOOD STRUCTURE

Heartwood | Sapwood

The color of the wood reveals the relative amounts of heartwood and sapwood in a tree, and the number of growth rings can reveal the tree's age.

Most of the cells are secondary xylem, also known as wood, and are dead. Secondary growth occurs in a ring called the vascular cambium, a lateral meristem, which produces new xylem on the inside and new phloem to the outside.

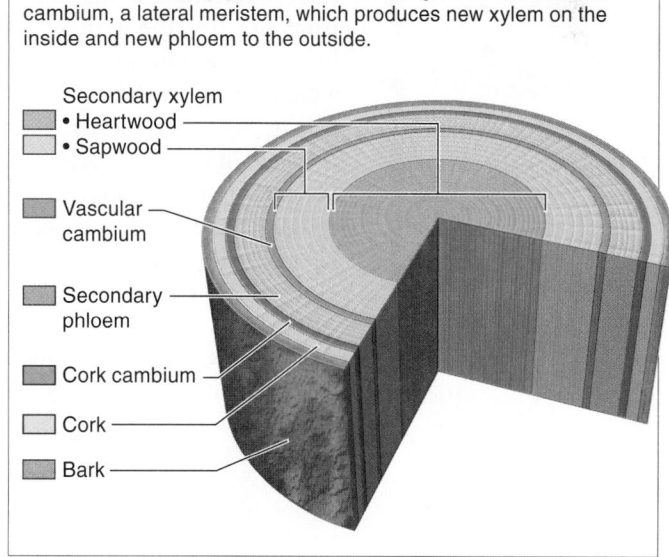

Secondary xylem
• Heartwood
• Sapwood
Vascular cambium
Secondary phloem
Cork cambium
Cork
Bark

FIGURE 18-33 **Cross section of a tree trunk.**

through which less and less blood can flow. Because the clogging of xylem is a progressive condition, the older the xylem, the more likely it is to be clogged. And the closer it is toward the center of the trunk, the older the xylem is. The clogged xylem is called "heartwood" and is darker, due to the accumulated resins and other non-soluble metabolic waste molecules. Although heartwood cannot conduct water, it still is valuable to the plant for the structural support it provides. Farther toward the outside, closer to the vascular cambium, is the xylem that was more recently created and, consequently, is better at conducting water. This xylem is called "sapwood" (**FIGURE 18-33**).

the spring and summer, causing a wider, lighter band. During winter and fall, growth is slower and produces a darker band. Wider bands also indicate wetter years, and narrower bands drier years. By counting the number of rings we can accurately determine the age of the tree. In the tropics, there is less variation in growth from one season to another, so trees don't always lay down rings, and it isn't always possible to accurately establish their ages.

As the vascular cambium increases the girth of a tree and is pushed farther and farther out, the epidermal cells that make up the bark continuously split and fall from the tree. This tissue is replaced by the cork cambium—a cylinder of lateral meristem cells close to the outer edge of the trunk. The cork cambium plays an important role in the perpetual task of maintaining the protective covering of bark. As its cells divide, they produce a cylinder of waxy cork cells on the outside, a layer of cells that protects the outer surface of the trunk from water loss, fire, and microbe infection. Secondary phloem, too, is pushed toward the outer surface of the trunk and eventually is sloughed off. For this reason, at any given time, although there may be a huge amount of functioning xylem, there is only a very thin layer of functioning phloem, and it is very close to the outer surface of the trunk. Often only the phloem that has been produced within the past year functions in the conduction of sugars throughout the plant.

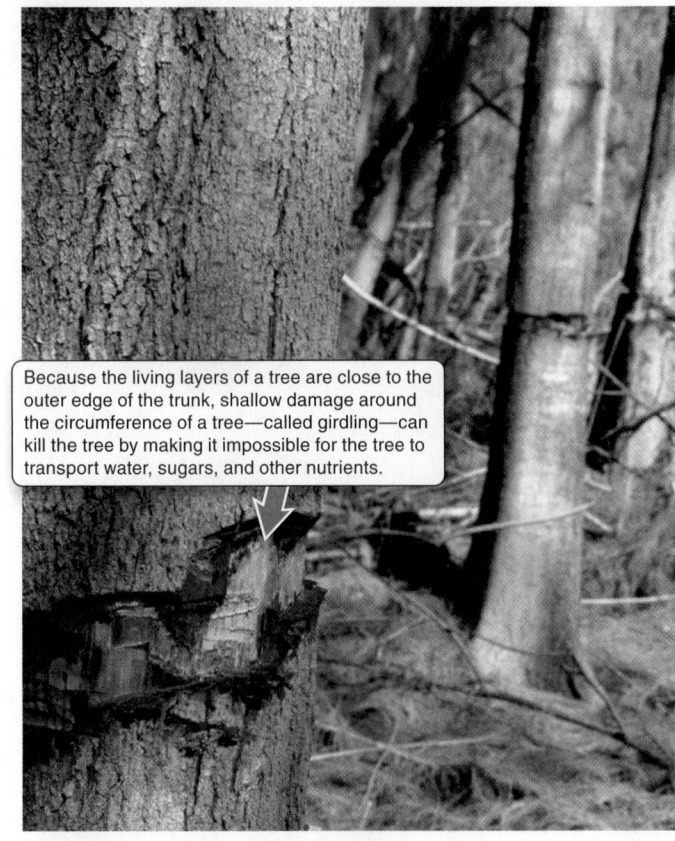

Because the living layers of a tree are close to the outer edge of the trunk, shallow damage around the circumference of a tree—called girdling—can kill the tree by making it impossible for the tree to transport water, sugars, and other nutrients.

FIGURE 18-34 Girdling a tree can kill it.

Q If you thoughtlessly carved your initials in the trunk of a tree 4 feet above the ground and came back in 10 years, would your initials be at the same height or higher? Why? What if you came back in 20 years?

Secondary growth increases the girth of a tree but doesn't elongate it. So if you were to carve your initials in the trunk of a tree, the section below where your initials are would never increase in height. Moreover, because increases in girth can cause the outer layers of bark and epidermis to fall off, replaced by new cells pushing outward, your initials would eventually completely disappear from the tree trunk.

An action that damages the bark of a tree all the way around its circumference is called "girdling." It is possible to girdle a tree with a "weed whacker" or a lawn mower. Girdling can actually kill a tree, even if the tree is very thick and the damage is not particularly deep. Because the phloem and vascular cambium layers are so close to the outer edge of the trunk, relatively shallow injuries to the trunk can destroy the secondary phloem and, if the damage goes just a bit deeper, the cells that give rise to new phloem.

Q Bumping into a tree repeatedly with a lawn mower or "weed whacker" can kill the tree. Why?

When such damage occurs, the tree is still able to transport water from the roots to all of the tissues because the xylem is much closer to the center of the trunk and isn't damaged. But damage to the phloem makes it impossible for the tree to transport sugars and other nutrients from the sites of photosynthesis down to the roots where it is needed and stored. Shortly after the damage occurs, the tree may die (FIGURE 18-34).

Roots can be girdled, too. This kind of girdling can happen when trees are planted with wire or mesh netting around their roots. As the roots grow in girth, the metal or nylon can gradually destroy the vascular cambium as it grows outward, killing the tree about 5 to 10 years after it is planted.

It is an odd fact about plants, especially trees, that most of the cells are dead. Remember (from Section 17-3) that all xylem cells, including the secondary xylem cells that make up wood, are dead at maturity. In a huge oak tree, for example, most of the tree's mass is in the wood, and more than 98% of the cells may be dead. Nonetheless, the tree has buds that keep forming and growing, and it has vascular cambium cells that continue to divide and produce new xylem and phloem. And as long as there are living cells in a tree, it can grow and is considered alive.

TAKE-HOME MESSAGE 18·15

Secondary growth results from cell divisions in a thin cylinder of tissue between the primary xylem and the primary phloem—the vascular cambium, a lateral meristem. As this tissue divides, it produces a ring of non-living xylem cells, close to the center of the trunk, that conduct water and minerals, while also providing structural support to the plant. We call these cells, collectively, wood.

When is a fruit not a fruit?
Or, You can't always trust your government when it comes to botany.

Q: WHAT IS A FRUIT? A fruit is defined as a structure that aids in dispersing seeds—it is the reproductive packet that is made up of the embryo, some food reserves, and a hard coat, and usually develops from the ovary, right around the seeds, which develop from the ovules. This should cause you to look at a field of flowers differently: the ovary is part of every flower, so all the flowers you see, after they are pollinated and fertilized, turn into fruits. Or conversely: every fruit you eat used to be a flower.

Q: HOW DO FRUITS DIFFER FROM VEGETABLES? Vegetables, unlike fruits, are simply edible parts of a plant that develop from structures other than the reproductive structures—and hence do not have seeds.

GET YOUR LAWS OUT OF MY SALAD! In 1893, in a bizarre legal case at the intersection of law and biology, the U.S. Supreme Court made a foray into botany. It started when the U.S. government instituted a 10% tax on all vegetables imported into the country. Fruits, on the other hand, were not subject to any tariffs. The tax collector then tried to collect from a company that imported tomatoes. The company refused to pay, however, arguing that tomatoes are fruits. But sometimes, a fruit is not a fruit. Here is what the Supreme Court ruled: "Botanically speaking, tomatoes are the fruit of a vine, just as are cucumbers, squashes, beans, and peas. But in the common language of the people . . . all these are vegetables which are grown in kitchen gardens, and . . . usually served at dinner . . . or after the soup, fish, or meats which constitute the principal part of the repast, and not, like fruits generally, as dessert." And so it was decided: tomatoes would be taxed and, in the eyes of the law, they are vegetables.

Big Ideas in ...
Growth and Reproduction in Plants

18·1–18·3 Plants can reproduce sexually and asexually.

- Most plants have two very different options for reproduction: asexual and sexual reproduction.

- Asexual reproduction—the growth of new plants directly from the tissue of an established plant through mitosis—can be energetically efficient and fast and can preserve successful genetic combinations. But it also has the disadvantage of producing offspring with reduced genetic variability.

- Sexually reproducing angiosperms produce flowers as the chief structure for sexual reproduction.

18·4–18·6 Flowers have several roles in plant reproduction.

- Flowers are plant structures specialized for sexual reproduction, and all flowers generally have the same fundamental parts: sepals, petals, stamens, and a carpel.

- The male reproductive structure produces pollen grains, two-cell structures that are water-tight and have a sticky surface. One of the cells forms a pollen tube, and the other produces two sperm cells.

- Within the ovary, diploid cells differentiate into ovules, each of which is a group of outer protective cells around a diploid egg-producing cell. The egg-producing cell undergoes meiosis to form haploid megaspores, one of which undergoes mitosis several times to produce the embryo sac, the structure that contains the egg and is the site of fertilization.

18·7–18·11 Pollination, fertilization, and seed dispersal often depend on help from other organisms.

- Sexual reproduction requires that two plants must get their gametes together. Plants trick or bribe animals into bringing this union about.

- Following pollination, a pollen tube must grow into the ovule, where one sperm cell fertilizes the egg cell in the embryo sac, and another fuses with the diploid central cell of the embryo sac to form endosperm, which nourishes the developing embryo.

- Plants can reduce the occurrence of self-fertilization in several ways.

- Following fertilization, the ovule develops into a seed, surrounded and protected by a fruit. Plants use the assistance of animals or water or wind to disperse their seeds and fruits.

18·12–18·15 Plants have two types of growth, usually enabling lifelong increases in length and thickness.

- Unlike most animals, plants generally grow for their entire lives.

- Plants have two types of growth. Primary growth makes shoots taller and roots and branches longer and forms new tissues. Secondary growth makes plants thicker and sturdier and is responsible for the production of wood.

See the To-Go Guide (packaged with every new copy of this textbook) for an illustrated summary of the chapter.

Check Your Knowledge

Thinking critically about visual displays of data.

1. What idea is conveyed by the "fuzzy" borders of each slice of the pie? How else could these data (and the uncertainty associated with them) be conveyed?

2. What is the reason for the color scheme used in this graph (two different shades of blue, multiple shades of green, yellow, and red)?

3. Would it be helpful to have actual percentages included with each slice of the pie? Why might those numbers have been excluded?

4. Which pollinator is used by the largest number of flowering plant species? Approximately what proportion of plant species is pollinated by this group of pollinators? Which pollinators come in second?

5. Why might it be useful to know the specific habitats surveyed in collecting the data reported here?

6. What are two important conclusions you can draw from this pie chart?

7. The total pie represents "all flowering plant species." Why would the pie chart differ if it instead reported the proportion of all plants (individuals, rather than species) that are pollinated by each type of pollinator?

8. What are the risks of reporting and interpreting data described as "loose approximations"? Are there benefits that outweigh the risks?

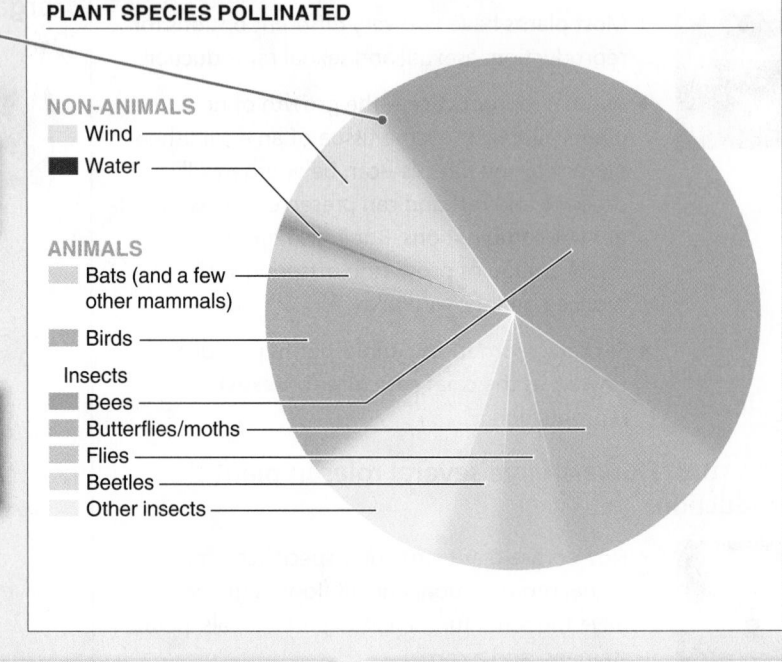

APPROXIMATE PROPORTION OF FLOWERING PLANT SPECIES POLLINATED

NON-ANIMALS
- Wind
- Water

ANIMALS
- Bats (and a few other mammals)
- Birds

Insects
- Bees
- Butterflies/moths
- Flies
- Beetles
- Other insects

See Answers at the back of the book.

Key Terms in Growth and Reproduction of Plants

Multiple-Choice Questions

1. **Asexual reproduction in plants:**
   a) tends to be particularly common in a population growing in a marginal habitat.
   b) still requires meiosis.
   c) requires reproductive cells that are produced in flowers.
   d) is energetically more expensive than sexual reproduction.
   e) Both b) and c) are correct.

   100 HARD
    56
   0 EASY

2. **Most of the trees or shrubs in backyard gardens:**
   a) are haploid.
   b) are the products of asexual reproduction.
   c) require both male plants and female plants in close proximity.
   d) utilize cell respiration rather than photosynthesis.
   e) must exhibit an alternation of generations when propagated asexually.

   100 HARD
    64
   0 EASY

3. **In angiosperms, the _____ are the specialized reproductive organs whose main function is to bring together the sperm and egg.**
   a) seeds
   b) pollen grains
   c) cones
   d) leaves
   e) flowers

   100 HARD
   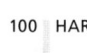 24
   0 EASY

4. **Each angiosperm pollen grain contains how many sperm cells?**
   a) two
   b) one
   c) millions
   d) thousands
   e) hundreds

   100 HARD
    53
   0 EASY

5. **Mosses and ferns differ in their reproductive strategies from gymnosperms and angiosperms in which of the following ways?**
   a) Mosses and ferns have much larger seeds than do angiosperms and gymnosperms.
   b) Mosses and ferns use wind pollination, whereas angiosperms and gymnosperms use insects for pollination.
   c) Mosses and ferns are primarily diploid in their adult (reproductive) form, whereas gymnosperms and angiosperms are primarily haploid.
   d) Mosses and ferns are primarily haploid in their adult form, whereas gymnosperms and angiosperms are primarily diploid.
   e) Mosses and ferns rely on liquid water for fertilization, whereas angiosperms and gymnosperms do not need liquid water for fertilization.

   100 HARD
    53
   0 EASY

6. **The common term for the action of transferring pollen grains from an anther onto a stigma is:**
   a) pollination.
   b) reproduction.
   c) fertilization.
   d) intercourse.
   e) None of the above is correct.

   100 HARD
   28
   0 EASY

7. **Flowering plants attract animals to assist in pollination. Which of the following animal groups is not a common pollinator of flowering plants?**
   a) bats
   b) bumblebees
   c) moths
   d) beetles
   e) All of the above are common pollinators of flowering plants.

   100 HARD
   57
   0 EASY

8. "Double fertilization" in angiosperm plants refers to the:

   a) release of two sperm from a single pollen grain.
   b) production of two or more eggs in the ovary.
   c) fusion of the ovary with the anther.
   d) fusion of a sperm cell with two nuclei of the endosperm-forming cell.
   e) fusion of one sperm cell with the egg and another with two nuclei of the endosperm-forming cell.

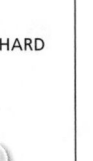

100 HARD

18

0 EASY

9. Which of the following is a likely way in which plants increase dispersal of their fruit?

   a) Fruits are conspicuously colored.
   b) Fruits taste good.
   c) Fruit stems are highly elastic.
   d) Both a) and b) are true.
   e) Both a) and c) are true.

100 HARD

53

0 EASY

10. Which of the following is the proper sequence of events when a flowering plant reproduces?

   a) meiosis; pollination; fertilization; embryo formation
   b) fertilization; meiosis; nuclear fusion; endosperm formation
   c) growth of the pollen tube; pollination; germination; fertilization
   d) meiosis; fertilization; growth of the pollen tube; germination
   e) mitosis; embryo formation; pollination; seed development

100 HARD

55

0 EASY

11. For angiosperms, which of the following statements about growth is the most correct?

   a) Vascular cambium increases girth; cork cambium increases length.
   b) Apical meristems increase length; vascular cambium increases girth.
   c) Cork cambium increases length; apical meristems increase girth.
   d) Apical meristems increase length; apical meristems increase girth.
   e) Apical meristems increase girth; vascular cambium increases length.

100 HARD

32

0 EASY

12. When, after seed germination, does photosynthesis begin?

   a) when the seed coat breaks open
   b) when the first stem is formed
   c) when the shoot emerges from the soil
   d) the second the seed begins to germinate
   e) when the root is formed

100 HARD

37

0 EASY

13. The scientific term for wood is:

   a) primary phloem.
   b) cork.
   c) secondary xylem.
   d) epidermis.
   e) pith.

100 HARD

37

0 EASY

14. When you are seven years old, you scratch your name 4 feet above the ground into a 12-foot-tall bamboo plant. You spend the next ten years in a special home for vandals. When you get out, the bamboo is 24 feet tall. At that time, how far above the ground will your name be?

a) 16 feet

b) 4 feet

c) 8 feet

d) 12 feet

e) 2 feet

100 | HARD

65

0 | EASY

Short-Answer Questions

1. A strawberry plant sends out about a dozen above-ground runners that have small crowns at the ends. When these crowns touch the soil, they send out roots, and each crown can develop into a new plant. Why is this good news for someone trying to create a strawberry patch?

2. Potato plants can reproduce sexually, producing flowers, fruits, and seeds. A potato farmer can collect the seeds and plant them. Alternatively, she can plant some of the potatoes instead. Why might it be preferable to plant potatoes instead of seeds? And which potatoes should be chosen for planting?

See Answers at the back of the book.
For additional study questions, go to www.prep-u.com.

ABOUT THE CHAPTER OPENING PHOTO

A seed (in red) from the coastal wattle *(Acacia cyclops)*, a small shrub/tree native to southwestern Australia. Surrounding the seed (in orange) is a covering modified from the stalk by which the ovule was attached to the ovary wall. (Actual size is 9 mm.)

Defending and regulating
while rooted in the ground

19

Plants Respond to Their Environments

19·1–19·2 Plants defend themselves from herbivores and survive extreme environments.

One plant defense: the thorn of a rose.

19·1

Plants actively resist being eaten.

Plants are under almost constant attack. From microbes to fungi, animals, and even other plants, organisms make varied and persistent efforts to access the valuable resources in plants. In some cases, the attackers can kill the plant outright. In most cases, though, they simply siphon off resources—such as stored chemical energy—reducing the amount available to the plant for its own growth, maintenance, and reproduction.

Plants have evolved to fight back, however. They have numerous defenses that can help them reduce the competitive and predatory "tax" they constantly face. These defenses fall into four general categories: mechanical defenses, chemical defenses, mimicry or camouflage, and enlisting help from elsewhere.

Mechanical defenses Several types of plant defenses involve physical structures or movements (**FIGURE 19-1**).

Thorns, spines, and hairs. If you've ever tried to pick blackberries or raspberries, you probably encountered sharp prickles on the stems. And while these may have been only a nuisance to you, they can be enough of a deterrent to many herbivores—in some cases, harming or even killing them—to significantly reduce herbivory. Some plants, such as the acacias common on Central American savannas, produce spines, primarily on the outside of the plant. And in many plants, fine leaf hairs can reduce herbivores' ability to eat them.

Waxes and saps. Producing leaves covered with waxy compounds can also reduce herbivory. Researchers have documented, for example, that beetles spend more time slipping and falling off waxy leaves—such as holly leaves—than they do off non-waxy leaves. Some plants produce and exude sticky saps or resins that can deter or even drown potential insect pests.

Defensive (and offensive) movements. The Venus flytrap is the most dramatic example of a plant making use of rapid movement. As we will see in Section 22-2, however, this can be considered more offensive than defensive, because it is a

MECHANICAL DEFENSES IN PLANTS

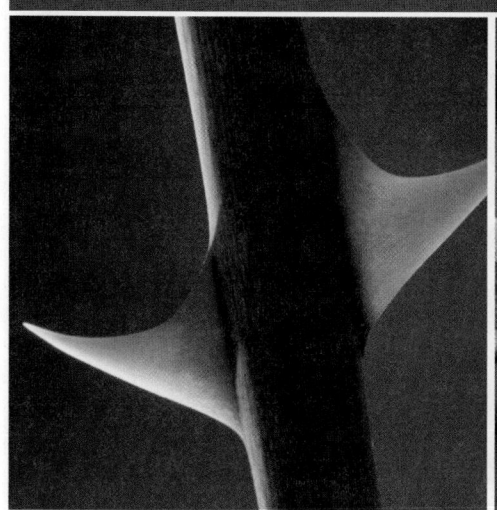

THORNS, SPINES, AND HAIRS
Structures such as sharp spines or fine hairs can significantly reduce herbivory.

WAXES AND SAPS
Leaf secretions such as slippery waxy compounds or sticky saps significantly reduce herbivory.

DEFENSIVE MOVEMENTS
Rapid movements, such as flattening leaves in response to touch, can decrease the available surface area and significantly reduce herbivory.

FIGURE 19-1 Plants have physical defenses to ward off predation by insects and other animals.

method of acquiring nitrogen (released as the prey is dissolved and digested by the plant). Many plants—particularly those in the mimosa family—use a similar movement mechanism to rapidly flatten their leaves in response to touch. This quickly decreases the surface area available to potential pests, reducing herbivory.

Chemical defenses One of the most common methods that plants use to fight herbivory is the production of chemical defenses. These are chemical compounds (sometimes called "secondary compounds") produced to deter herbivores by making the plant toxic or reducing its digestibility so as to lessen its value to the herbivore.

One common strategy, used by more than 3,000 species of plants, is to produce cyanide-containing molecules called cyanogenic glycosides. When consumed by herbivores, these molecules break down into cyanide, which blocks electron transport in cellular respiration—killing or seriously harming the animal.

In a sort of evolutionary arms race, evolution has led to individuals of some species having the ability to eat toxic secondary compounds without suffering ill effects. Monarch butterfly caterpillars, for example, can eat milkweed plants, consuming the toxic cardiac glycosides that kill most insects and induce heart attacks in vertebrates (**FIGURE 19-2**). Moreover, the monarchs store the toxic chemicals within their cell vacuoles and then become poisonous to their predators.

CO-OPTING A TOXIN

Monarch butterfly caterpillars feed on milkweed and are able to tolerate the plant's cyanide-containing molecules. The caterpillars store the toxic chemical, which makes them poisonous to potential predators.

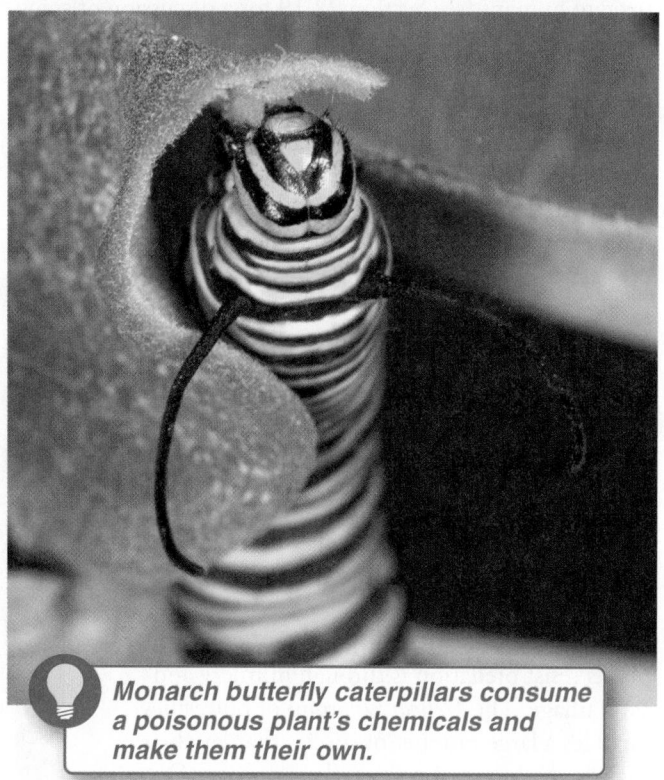

Monarch butterfly caterpillars consume a poisonous plant's chemicals and make them their own.

FIGURE 19-2 Some plants contain chemical toxins that poison (most) predators.

Other common toxins produced by plants to reduce herbivory include the neurotoxic chemicals in hemlock—which was used in carrying out the death sentence of the Greek philosopher Socrates. And ricin, a chemical found in castor beans, is among the most toxic of plant compounds and has been investigated as an agent of chemical and biological warfare. It was reportedly used in a KGB assassination—delivered by stabbing the target in the leg with an umbrella.

Many plants also secrete toxic chemicals from their roots that block the germination of seeds and reduce the growth of nearby plants, conferring a competitive advantage. Because of the toxic chemicals secreted by the roots of black walnut trees, for example, few plants grow underneath these trees.

The chemical compounds produced by plants to reduce herbivory can also have medicinal effects in humans.

FIGURE 19-3 "Bio-prospectors" search for plant chemicals that have medicinal properties.

Q Can humans benefit from plants' attempts to avoid being eaten?

Beneficial effects of secondary compounds Humans have long made use of some of the "defensive" compounds produced by plants.

Spices. Spicy foods, such as mustard, usually get their flavor from secondary plant compounds that may make the plant toxic or unpalatable to an insect but are not toxic to humans (see Section 22-19 for a discussion of spicy foods as natural antibiotics).

Medicines. Many of our medicines come from secondary compounds developed by plants. After all, a chemical that disrupts a microbe's metabolism can have its effect whether the microbe is on a plant or inside a human. These medicines include taxol, a compound with anti-mitotic properties isolated from the Pacific yew *(Taxus brevifolia),* which is now used to treat a wide variety of cancers (see Section 16-1). And quinine, an anti-herbivore compound isolated from the bark of *Cinchona* trees in South America, is an effective treatment for malaria. There has been a large increase in the number of researchers—sometimes called "bio-prospectors"—looking for plant compounds with potential medicinal uses (**FIGURE 19-3**).

Mimicry and camouflage Another way that plants resist predation is through mimicry and camouflage. The *Heliconius* group of butterflies includes a large number of species that lay their eggs on the leaves of passion flower plants. On hatching, the insects begin eating the plant, often causing significant damage. By producing leaves that appear to be already covered with butterfly eggs, one species of passion flower reduces the likelihood that butterflies will lay eggs on its leaves (**FIGURE 19-4**). Females will not lay their eggs on a leaf that already has *Heliconius* eggs, because the first eggs would hatch sooner and the larvae would eat the leaves, destroying the eggs of the second butterfly.

Enlisting other organisms for "security"
Researchers have even discovered mutualistic situations in

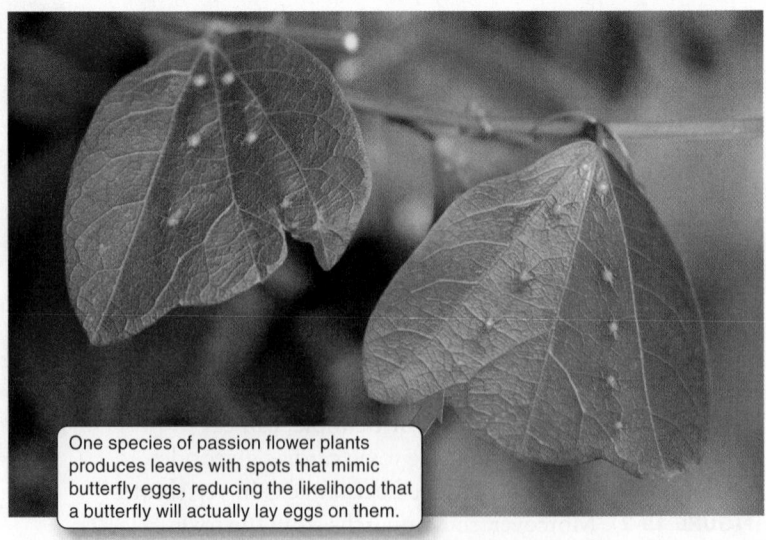

One species of passion flower plants produces leaves with spots that mimic butterfly eggs, reducing the likelihood that a butterfly will actually lay eggs on them.

FIGURE 19-4 No room for additional eggs.

which plants seem to outsource some of their defenses to another species. Acacia plants produce a sweet nectar that attracts ants. The ants hollow out thorns in the plants and live inside them. In exchange for their "room and board," the ants quickly and aggressively attack leaf-eating insects, effectively reducing the predators' ability to feed on the plant. The ants also typically trim back competing plants from their acacias, dramatically reducing competition for both water and light for the host plant.

Plants, rooted in the ground, are unable to employ many of the strategies used by animals and other organisms for resisting predation and responding to inhospitable environments. In this chapter, we explore the variety of physical and biochemical methods by which they reduce the impact of such challenges.

> ## TAKE-HOME MESSAGE 19·1
>
> Rooted in the ground, plants are targets for predators and pathogens. They actively resist infection and herbivory by several methods, including the production of toxic chemicals that make them distasteful, poisonous, or difficult to consume.

19·2 Special adaptations help some plants thrive in extreme habitats.

Just as evolution has produced plant adaptations to deter herbivory, so, too, have a variety of plant adaptations evolved as responses to the non-living components of the environment. We see particularly dramatic adaptations in plants that manage to thrive in some of the world's most extreme habitats.

Super-dry habitats In deserts, groundwater is scarce, and moisture loss due to evaporation in the hot temperatures can further constrain a plant's ability to retain water. Plants have responded to these difficult conditions with several different types of adaptations (**FIGURE 19-5**).

Succulent leaves and stems. The evolution of thick, fleshy, water-storing tissue in the leaves and stems of cacti and other succulents reduces the surface-area-to-volume ratio of their photosynthetic parts, which helps minimize water loss due to evaporation. Although this adaptation reduces plants' capacity for gas exchange and thus their overall rate of sugar production relative to plants with thinner leaves, it enables

METHODS OF SURVIVING DRY HABITATS

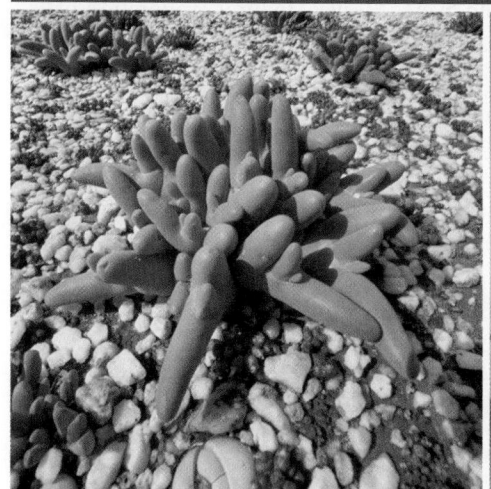

SUCCULENT LEAVES AND STEMS
Cacti and other succulent plants have thick, fleshy, water-storing tissue within their leaves and stems that helps minimize evaporation.

DEEP TAPROOTS
Plants such as mesquite send down unusually hardy and deep taproots that can utilize water far beneath the surface.

LONG-DORMANT SEEDS
Many plants have seeds that can remain dormant for long periods of time, then quickly germinate and grow in response to brief periods of moisture.

FIGURE 19-5 Survival strategies for dry climates.

them to survive in the hot, dry desert habitats where thin-leaved plants are likely to dry out and die.

Deep taproots. If water conservation is one strategy of dry-habitat plants, "water mining" is the flip side. Plants such as mesquite establish strong and deep taproots, often boring into the soil a dozen meters or more to find sources of water far beneath the surface.

Long-dormant seeds. Because rain is highly unpredictable and rare in super-dry habitats—several years may pass between rains in the deserts of Chile, for example—many dry-adapted plants have seeds that can remain dormant for long periods of time. They wait out the dry times and quickly germinate and grow in response to brief periods of moisture.

Salty environments Marshes and intertidal zones may have pleasant temperatures and plenty of moisture, but extreme levels of salt from the ocean and large fluctuations in salt concentrations can make it difficult for cells to maintain a constant water balance and carry out normal metabolic processes (**FIGURE 19-6**). Plants adapted to saltwater environments are generally unable to reduce the large amounts of salt they absorb with the water through their roots. So how do they survive? They transport much of the absorbed salt to vacuoles within their cells, thus isolating

> Plants living in cold and windy habitats tend to grow close to the ground and have smaller-than-average leaves and shallow root systems.

FIGURE 19-7 Survival in cold, windy habitats.

and containing it where it has little impact on cellular metabolism. Some plants—such as mangroves—are also able to move much of the salt to the leaves for excretion. The salt dries out on the leaf surfaces and blows away.

Cold and windy habitats At both extreme latitudes and extreme elevations, life can be hard: the air is cold, sunlight is limited, the growing season is short, and the winds can be brutal and relentless. As a consequence, plants living in these habitats tend to grow close to the ground and have smaller-than-average leaves (to limit evaporation of water). Grasses, in particular, do well under such conditions (**FIGURE 19-7**).

Arctic habitats present an additional challenge. Because the first few meters of soil below the ground surface stay perpetually frozen (called **permafrost** if it remains below freezing for two or more years), root growth is limited, and any water that is present from precipitation or melting cannot drain well. In high-altitude habitats, drainage is good, but the soil is still thin and poor in nutrients. In each case, plant life is usually limited to smaller plants with diffuse, shallow root systems.

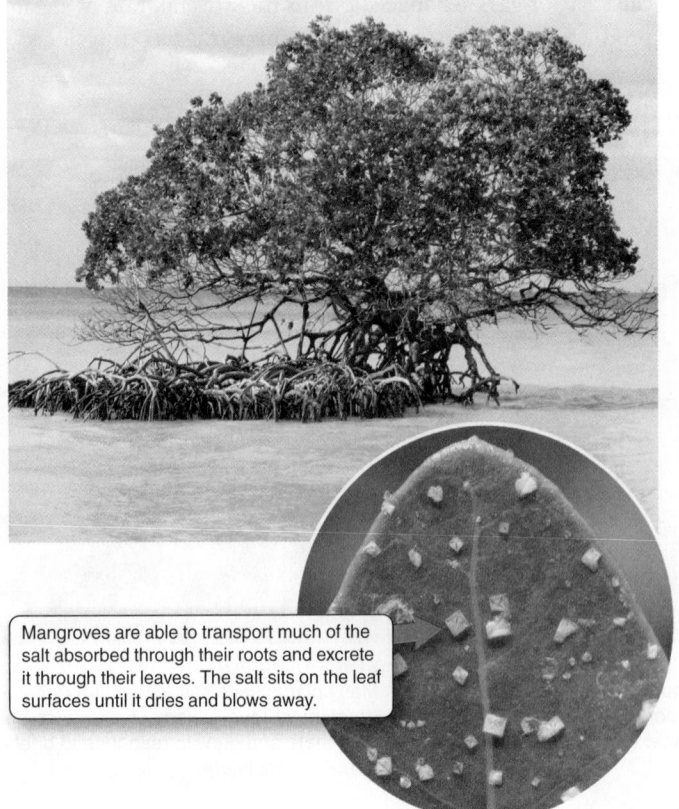

> Mangroves are able to transport much of the salt absorbed through their roots and excrete it through their leaves. The salt sits on the leaf surfaces until it dries and blows away.

FIGURE 19-6 Survival in salt water.

TAKE-HOME MESSAGE 19·2

Evolution has produced plants with adaptations to some of the most extreme of the world's habitats, including super-dry regions, salty environments, and cold, windy habitats.

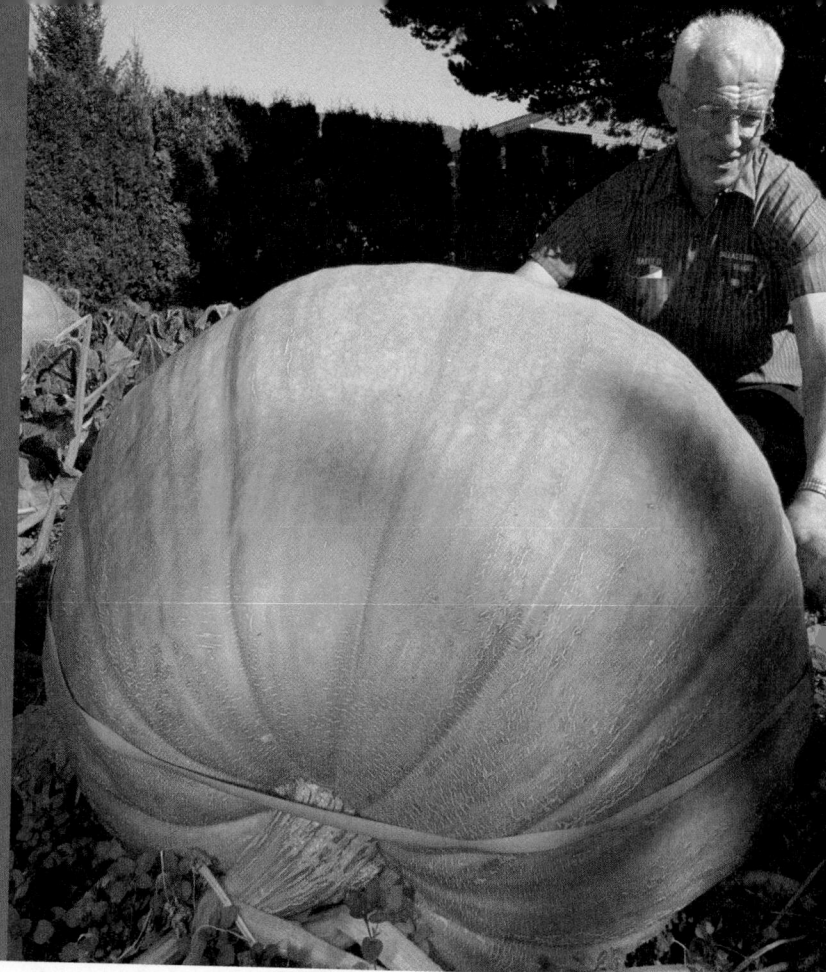

Plant hormones regulate the growth of this enormous pumpkin.

19·3–19·6 Hormones regulate growth and development.

19·3

Hormones help plants respond to their environments.

Plant **hormones** are chemical signals that enable plants to respond quickly and appropriately to changing environmental variables (such as amount of moisture, amount and direction of sunlight, and temperature). Five major types of plant hormones influence the growth and development of plants amid changes in their environmental conditions.

Consider a simple experiment with the arrowleaf plant (*Sagittaria sagittifolia*) as an example. First, from a single plant, take three cuttings—sections of the plant containing part of the stem that includes a meristem and can be used to produce a new plant, genetically identical to the original. Plant each cutting in a different habitat: one in deep water, the second in shallow water, and the third on land. Each new plant has the exact same set of genes; they are like identical triplets. But in the deep water, the plant will grow long, ribbon-like leaves. In the shallow water, the plant will develop large, round leaves resembling lily pads.

And on land, the plant will form the arrow-shaped leaves from which it gets its name (**FIGURE 19-8**).

The arrowleaf plant is not "hard-wired" to produce any one type of leaf shape. Rather, the physical form of the plant depends on the environment in which it grows. How does the plant change its growth patterns to respond to different environments? Hormones. These chemicals convey information about the physiological state of the plant's tissues or the environment in which the plant finds itself and then regulate some aspect of the metabolism of the plant's cells. Sometimes, a hormone may stimulate a certain response—such as growth—in the target cell. Other times, the hormone may suppress an action in the target cell.

Unlike the hormones in humans and other animals, which are generally produced in specific glands or tissues and then transported (commonly in the bloodstream) to different locations to exert their influence, many plant hormones are

PLANTS RESPOND TO THEIR ENVIRONMENT

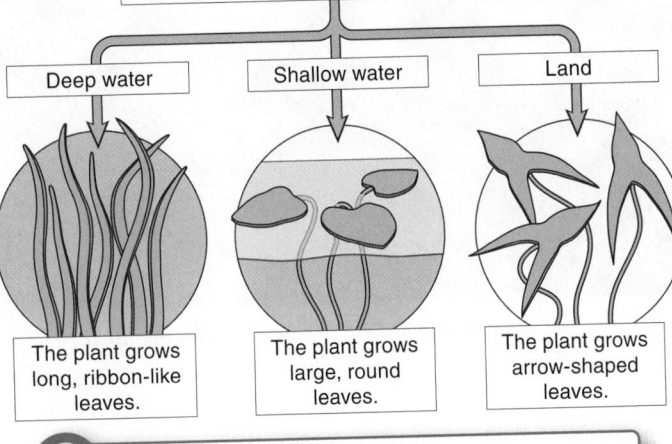

Three cuttings are taken from the same plant and grown in different environments.

Deep water	Shallow water	Land

The plant grows long, ribbon-like leaves.

The plant grows large, round leaves.

The plant grows arrow-shaped leaves.

💡 *The leaves of the arrowleaf plant take on dramatically different forms depending on the environment in which the plant grows.*

FIGURE 19-8 Environment affects the growth patterns of the arrowleaf plant. The differences in growth forms are mediated by hormones.

PLANT HORMONES

HORMONE	FUNCTION	LOCATION
Gibberellins	Increase the speed of seed germination; promote stem elongation; induce early blooming of flowers; increase fruit size	Shoot and root apical meristems; seeds
Auxins	Stimulate stem elongation; control seedling orientation; stimulate root branching; promote fruit development	Apical meristems; immature plant tissue
Ethylene	Increases the speed at which fruit ripens; stimulates leaf dropping and the death of flowers	All parts of the plant including the fruits
Abscisic acid	Inhibits growth and reproduction; inhibits seed germination; stimulates closure of stomata	Leaves; fruits; root tips; seeds
Cytokinins	Cause rapid cell division, in conjunction with auxin; induce seed germination; initiate new branches from lateral buds	Roots and fruits, primarily

FIGURE 19-9 The location and function of five types of plant hormones.

produced in numerous places and may have their effects in those same places or may be transported to another part of the plant before taking effect. As we will see, the effects of plant hormones are usually predictable and easily observed.

There are five major types of plant hormones: gibberellins, auxins, ethylene, abscisic acid, and cytokinins. **FIGURE 19-9** provides a brief summary of the functions of these hormones. We explore them in greater detail in the next three sections.

TAKE-HOME MESSAGE 19·3

Plant hormones are chemical signals produced by plant cells that enable the plant to respond to environmental variables (such as amount of moisture, amount and direction of sunlight, and temperature) and that influence its growth and development.

19·4 Seed germination and stem elongation are stimulated by gibberellins.

Gibberellins are a group of about 125 related hormones that regulate a plant's growth processes, primarily by stimulating cell division and cell elongation. Gibberellins are produced in growing areas of a plant and are found throughout all plant structures. They occur in the largest amounts in seeds but are also found in high concentrations in the shoot and root apical meristems. The areas that have the greatest concentrations of gibberellins experience the most dramatic growth.

Gibberellins have four main types of effects (**FIGURE 19-10**):

1. Initiating seed germination. Gibberellins within the seed stimulate the production of enzymes that make possible the breakdown and metabolism of nutrients stored in the seed's endosperm. When additional gibberellins are applied to seeds, whether by the plant biologist, farmer, or horticulturist, the seeds can more quickly and efficiently use their energy reserves to germinate.

2. Elongating stems. Some gibberellins increase stem elongation by spacing the nodes farther apart, thus increasing the distance between branch points.

3. Inducing blooming of flowers. Some plants do not produce flowers until the nights are sufficiently short or long to trigger flowering (as we discuss in Section 19-9), or until the plant is exposed to a certain degree of coldness. The application of gibberellins to such plants can cause flower production in the absence of the triggering event.

4. Enlarging fruits. One of the most important economic uses of gibberellins in the United States is the production of table grapes. When seedless grapes are sprayed with large amounts of gibberellins, the grapes grow larger, and due to the stem-elongation effect also induced by gibberellins, there is more space between the grapes on the bunch. Both of these effects increase the attractiveness of a bunch of grapes to shoppers. (Normally, plants don't ripen their ovary walls, producing fruits, unless they have set seeds and those seeds need to mature. After all, that would be a waste of energy.)

Q

How can farmers grow radishes the size of beach balls?

Gibberellins are about as close to "miracle grow" chemicals as exist. If one type of gibberellin is sprayed on radish plants as they are growing, the radishes exhibit explosive growth. Normally smaller than a golf ball, gibberellin-treated radishes can reach the size of beach balls.

THE EFFECTS OF GIBBERELLINS

SPEED SEED GERMINATION
Gibberellins initiate the production of enzymes that help break down nutrients stored within the seed's endosperm, allowing quicker and more efficient use of the seed's energy reserves.

PROMOTE STEM ELONGATION
Gibberellins affect stem elongation by increasing the distance between nodes, thus spacing the branch points farther apart.

INDUCE EARLY BLOOMING OF FLOWERS
Gibberellins can cause flower production in the absence of a triggering event from the external environment.

PROMOTE FRUIT ENLARGEMENT
Seedless grapes sprayed with large amounts of gibberellins grow larger and, due to the stem-elongation effects, have more space between the grapes on the bunch.

FIGURE 19-10 Physiological effects of gibberellins.

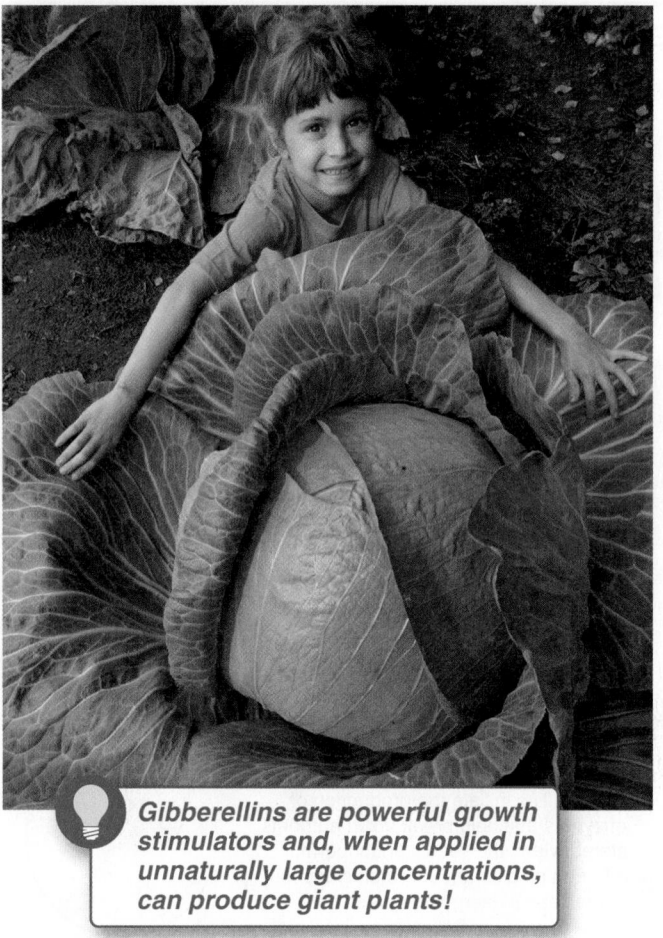

Gibberellins are powerful growth stimulators and, when applied in unnaturally large concentrations, can produce giant plants!

FIGURE 19-11 A giant, gibberellin-treated cabbage.

Equally dramatic is the effect of another type of gibberellin on cabbage plants (FIGURE 19-11). Normal cabbage plants are 1 to 2 feet high. When sprayed with a gibberellin, though, the plants can grow to more than 10 feet tall! In these extreme cases, plants are exposed to far greater hormone concentrations than they ever would encounter under natural conditions. Nonetheless, these examples reveal the powerful growth-stimulating effects of gibberellins.

If plants grow more when they have greater amounts of gibberellins, why don't all plants simply produce more gibberellins so that they can outgrow other plants competing for sunlight? The answer is that, as in most aspects of life, there are trade-offs. The fast-growing cabbages, for instance, can grow to great heights only if humans secure them to a stake for support. Under natural conditions, they wouldn't have our help, nor would their stems naturally have the strength to stand at a height of 10 feet. Instead, the cabbage plants would fall over, wilt, and die. It seems that under natural conditions, plants produce just about the right amount of gibberellins to maximize their successful growth and reproduction.

> **TAKE-HOME MESSAGE 19·4**
>
> Gibberellins are a group of about 125 related hormones, produced primarily in meristems and seeds, that regulate a plant's growth processes, mainly by stimulating cell division and cell elongation.

19·5 Seedlings grow and properly orient themselves under the direction of auxins.

Auxins are a small group of naturally occurring hormones (and a larger group of synthetic variants that chemists can produce) that play several important roles in stimulating and regulating a plant's growth and development. They are found primarily in shoot tips and immature plant tissue, such as young leaves. The primary role of auxins in plant growth is to stimulate the expression of genes that promote cell division, stem elongation, the formation of roots, and the formation of vascular cambium. Auxins also influence a plant's orientation—its growth in response to directional light and gravity.

The chief effects of auxins are of four types (FIGURE 19-12):

1. Stimulating shoot elongation. Auxins enhance the effect of gibberellins in shoot elongation. As we saw in Section 18-13, primary growth in plants causes them to get taller as apical meristems—clusters of active, dividing cells—at the ends of roots and shoots or branches repeatedly divide. This causes plants to grow "up." There are numerous other buds, called lateral buds, lower on the stem that also are capable of rapid cell division and growth, but typically these lateral buds remain dormant.

By cutting the top meristem of a shoot, however, lateral buds that are lower on the plant increase their growth. The inhibition of the lateral buds by the apical meristem is called *apical dominance,* and is caused by the large amount of auxin produced by the apical bud. Cutting the top meristem removes the inhibiting source of auxin, which is why the lateral buds then grow. This is the basis for "pruning," and makes it possible to control the branching pattern and shape of plants.

THE EFFECTS OF AUXINS

STIMULATE SHOOT ELONGATION
Auxins enhance the effect of gibberellins in shoot elongation.

CONTROL SEEDLING ORIENTATION
Auxins direct the growth of shoots and roots, making sure the correct ends are up and down.

STIMULATE ROOT BRANCHING
Auxins induce the formation of roots.

PROMOTE FRUIT DEVELOPMENT
Auxins produced within an embryo promote the maturation of the ovary wall and development of the fruit.

FIGURE 19-12 Physiological effects of auxins. Shown at top: buttercups reaching toward the sunlight.

2. Controlling seedling orientation. Charles Darwin and his son Francis were the first to document that seedlings exposed to light bend in whichever direction the light is coming from, whether up, down, or sideways. Immediately

after emerging from the seed, the shoot grows as if it knows which way is up. Whether a shoot grows down into the earth or up toward the light, though, actually depends on (1) where the auxins are located and (2) how the auxins influence the cells in those specific locations. Like gibberellins, auxins are produced near the growing tips of shoots and branches, but unlike gibberellins, they don't remain there. The auxin molecules move in two directions within a cell: they are pulled downward by gravity, and they move laterally away from light. These two movements distribute the auxin molecules unevenly within the plant. In regions of higher auxin concentration, cells in the stem elongate more rapidly than those in regions of lower auxin concentration (**FIGURE 19-13**). This difference in growth occurs because auxins increase the flexibility of the usually rigid cell wall (so that it can grow) and increase its permeability (so that it can take on more water and expand). The overall effect on growth is best seen when a

AUXINS' INFLUENCE ON PLANT ORIENTATION

Sunlight

Auxin molecules

1 Auxins are produced near the growing tips of shoots, roots, and branches.

2 The auxin molecules are directed downward by gravity and move away from light.

3 In regions of higher auxin concentration, cells elongate more rapidly than in regions of lower auxin concentration, causing the shoot to bend toward the light.

FIGURE 19-13 Auxins cause a plant to grow toward light.

plant is tipped onto its side. First, the auxins flow downward to the bottom side of the now-horizontal shoot. The bottom side then elongates more rapidly than the top side, causing the shoot to bend upward, against gravity.

3. Stimulating root branching. Auxins induce the formation of roots. In fact, you can buy auxin powders that can be dusted onto the bottom of plant stem cuttings. The powder causes the stems to send out numerous roots (transforming some stem cells into root cells), so that the cuttings can be planted and will form new plants.

Q How can we trick plants into producing seedless fruits for our convenience?

4. Promoting fruit development. Auxins produced within an embryo have several roles in the development of fruit. First, they promote maturation of the ovary wall, and then they promote several steps in the full development of the fruit. It is even possible to trick plants into producing fruits when their flowers have not been fertilized. Applying auxins to unfertilized flowers can cause them to develop into fruits. Because there has been no fertilization, such fruits are always seedless (for example, seedless tomatoes). Auxins applied to fruiting plants can also prevent the fruits from prematurely dropping from the tree or vine. This makes it easier and more inexpensive to harvest fruits, because they can all be picked at one time.

Too much of a good thing can be terrible, and this is particularly true when it comes to plant hormones. Auxins, for example, are among the chief growth-stimulating hormones in plants, but in extreme concentrations they are deadly. While this is bad news if you are a plant, it can be good news if you are a human trying to kill weeds (**FIGURE 19-14**). When synthetic auxins are sprayed on plants in higher concentrations than any plant would normally experience, they cause the plants to begin growing uncontrollably. This doesn't last long, though. Like a mismanaged start-up company, the plants devote so much of their energy budget to growth that they quickly find themselves without sufficient energy for essential metabolic maintenance functions. And then they die. One type of synthetic auxin, called 2,4-D, is a particularly useful weed killer because it kills only eudicots—such as dandelions—while not harming monocots, including

Synthetic auxins are used to control weeds, causing such a high rate of growth that death results.

FIGURE 19-14 Too much of a good thing. Excess auxins can induce lethal growth.

grasses and cereals such as corn, rice, wheat, and barley, which have significant agricultural value. (The reason for this difference is not fully understood.)

Synthetic auxins aren't just used by gardeners and farmers to get rid of weeds. During the 1960s, the United States sprayed the synthetic, auxin-based herbicide called Agent Orange on more than 3,000 villages in Vietnam, in an attempt to reduce the brush under which opposing military forces could hide. But the manufacture of Agent Orange creates a highly toxic by-product called dioxin. Agent Orange contaminated with dioxin was unexpectedly responsible for causing birth defects, leukemia, liver diseases, and other disorders and is considered a serious environmental hazard. Its use has been stopped.

TAKE-HOME MESSAGE 19·5

Auxins are a small group of naturally occurring hormones found primarily in shoot tips and immature plant tissue (and a larger group of synthetic auxin variants) that play several important roles in stimulating and regulating a plant's growth and development, often by increasing the usually rigid cell wall's flexibility and permeability.

19·6 Other plant hormones regulate flowering, fruit ripening, and responses to stress.

Auxins and gibberellins are the primary plant regulators when it comes to growth and orientation. But there is a lot more to regulating a plant's responses to the environment so that the plant germinates, sprouts, and fruits at just the right times. The other three types of hormones—ethylene, abscisic acid, and cytokinins—also play critical roles in directing germination, sprouting, fruiting, and other activities when the environmental conditions are favorable.

Q

How can farmers ensure that every banana they ship to market ripens at exactly the right time?

Ethylene Suppose you wanted to pick 10,000 bananas in Central America and deliver them to market in the United States so that they all turned yellow at just the right time. This could be a logistical nightmare, but with the help of plant hormones it doesn't have to be. The hormone **ethylene** is a gas produced in every part of a plant, and it has several important effects, including speeding up the rate at which many fruits ripen. Thus, ethylene can help with the banana problem: you can pick the fruits in Central America before they are ripe (when they are green), and just prior to their arrival in the United States, you can inject ethylene into the cargo hold of the ship and initiate the ripening of all the bananas simultaneously (**FIGURE 19-15**).

Not all fruits ripen in response to ethylene—strawberries, for example, do not, and so they must be picked from the vine only when ripe. Still, the use of ethylene for ripening fruits is probably the single most important agricultural use of any plant hormone. You can see this effect on a smaller scale by putting one ripe or rotting fruit (which produces very large amounts of ethylene) in a bag or container with fruits that haven't yet ripened. The ripe or rotten fruit will cause all of the other fruits to ripen very quickly. Alternatively, you can delay the ripening of fruits by separating them from those that are already ripe.

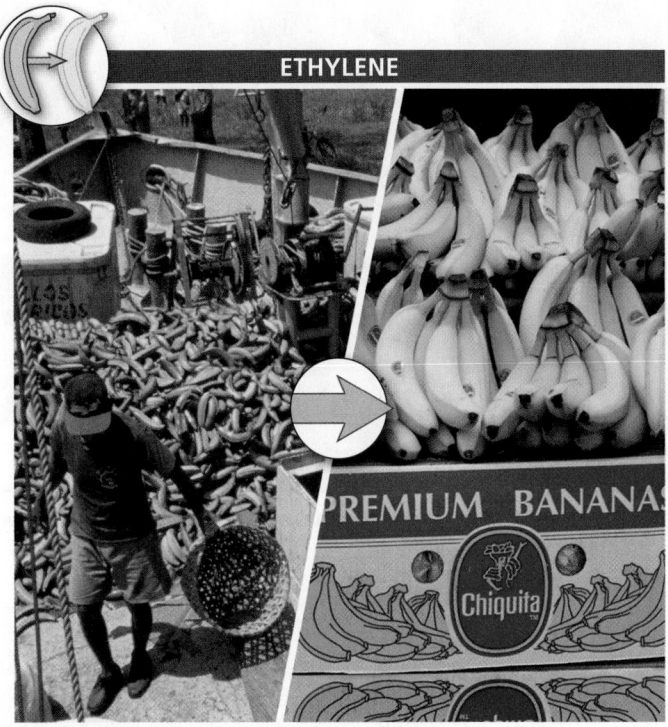

ETHYLENE

THE PRIMARY EFFECTS OF ETHYLENE
• Speeds up the rate at which many fruits ripen
• Hastens the dropping of leaves from trees and the death of flowers at specific times

 Bananas are picked prior to ripening and exposed to ethylene gas just before delivery to market, so that all ripen simultaneously.

FIGURE 19-15 Ethylene speeds fruit ripening.

Ethylene also hastens the aging and dropping of leaves from trees and the death of flowers at specific times. A plant has to maintain a flower's ovary until the seeds and fruit are mature, but it does not maintain the petals or stamens after fertilization. Most plants produce many more flowers than they can mature into fruits, so they use ethylene to abort some flowers to reduce the number of fruits the plant must mature. But, though beneficial to the plant, these effects can be seen as undesirable by humans, such as those who want to sell

Some flower merchants briefly soak cut-flower stems in a chemical solution of silver salts, which inhibits the deteriorating effects of ethylene on a flower's petals.

FIGURE 19-16 Florists fight the withering effects of ethylene on flowers.

Abscisic acid Under stressful conditions, such as water shortage, the plant hormone **abscisic acid** is produced in relatively large amounts. Synthesized primarily in leaves, fruits, and root tips (but also in other plant parts), this hormone has the general effect of inhibiting growth and reproductive activities under adverse environmental conditions (**FIGURE 19-17**). In seeds, for example, abscisic acid can inhibit germination. In a sense, it serves to tell a plant that times are tough and environmental conditions are not good enough for growth and reproduction. When roots encounter unusually dry or cold or salty conditions, the production of abscisic acid increases and, in addition to inhibiting growth, it signals the stomata on the plant's leaves to close, thereby increasing water conservation. In effect, abscisic acid causes a

cut flowers. Some flower merchants fight the effects of ethylene by briefly soaking cut-flower stems in a chemical solution of silver salts, which inhibits the effect of ethylene on the petals (**FIGURE 19-16**).

Recently, researchers were able to genetically engineer a type of tomato that does not produce ethylene. Tomatoes with blocked ethylene production can be left on the vine longer, without the risk of ripening before they can be picked and shipped to market. This allows the tomatoes to grow larger and also results in their tasting more like the tomatoes someone might grow in a home garden, where they can be left on the vine until they reach perfect ripeness. Otherwise, tomatoes must be picked long before they are ripe so that they are tough enough to transport without damaging them. Ethylene is then applied so that the tomatoes are ripe when they are sold. Although tomatoes with inhibited ethylene production were briefly tested in the market, patent disputes have led to their being discontinued.

ABSCISIC ACID

THE PRIMARY EFFECTS OF ABSCISIC ACID
• Inhibits growth and reproductive activities when environmental conditions are stressful
• Signals the stomata on a plant's leaves to close, increasing water conservation

FIGURE 19-17 Not a good time to invest in growth. Abscisic acid inhibits plant growth in times of stress, such as during a spring ice storm.

THE PRIMARY EFFECTS OF CYTOKININS
- Cause rapid cell division, in conjunction with auxins
- Initiate new branches from lateral buds
- Induce seed germination
- Retard leaf aging and death

FIGURE 19-18 Cytokinins stimulate cell division. New leaf shoots are growing from a pruned buddleia ("black night") stem.

plant to hunker down and ride out the difficult conditions before embarking on new growth.

Cytokinins The **cytokinins** are primarily stimulators of cell division throughout the body and throughout the lifetime of the plant. Although they are produced primarily in the roots and fruits, cytokinins exert their influence in all parts of the plant. They usually work in conjunction with auxins to produce four main types of effects (**FIGURE 19-18**):

1. Causing rapid cell division and promoting primary growth.

2. Initiating new branches from lateral buds.

3. Inducing seed germination. Application of cytokinins to seeds will even cause germination in the dark of seeds that normally germinate only in the light.

4. Retarding leaf aging and death. Even when applied to a leaf that has already fallen off a tree, cytokinins will cause the leaf to remain green longer than it otherwise would.

TAKE-HOME MESSAGE 19·6

In addition to auxins and gibberellins, three other types of hormones play critical roles in plant regulation. Among their multiple functions, ethylene induces and speeds fruit ripening, abscisic acid inhibits growth and reproduction under stressful environmental conditions, and cytokinins stimulate cell division throughout the plant body.

19·7–19·9 External cues trigger internal responses.

Soybean seedlings grow toward the light.

19·7 Tropisms influence plants' direction of growth.

A plant's immobility affects virtually every aspect of its structural design and function and has influenced the nature of the evolutionary solutions that enable plants to grow, develop, and reproduce successfully. Like animals, for example, plants must respond to their environment as it changes. But whereas animals can move from a problematic, changing environment to one with more suitable conditions, plants use a variety of growth patterns, known as **tropisms**— such as bending, curving, and twisting—to grow toward or away from various environmental stimuli such as light, gravity, and physical obstacles. Three of the most common tropisms are phototropism, gravitropism, and thigmotropism.

Phototropism If you have indoor plants, you've probably noticed that they always seem to grow toward a window. Even if you turn a plant around, within a few days it will grow to face the light again. This is **phototropism**—growth in response to a directional light source. It occurs when the cells in a plant's stem grow unevenly, adjusting their directional rate of growth so that the stem bends toward the light (**FIGURE 19-19**). The reason that evolution has generated such a pattern of growth is not surprising: if a plant can orient itself so that its photosynthesizing cells (in leaves and stems) can intercept more light, the plant can photosynthesize more efficiently and generate more energy for growth and reproduction.

It was the study of phototropism that led to the discovery of the plant hormone auxin (which turned out to be a group of similar hormones). When light hits a plant from a particular direction, auxins produced in the plant cells move away from the light source and end up on the opposite, shaded side of the stem. There, the auxins stimulate a slightly greater rate of growth than on the lighter side, where there is less auxin. As a consequence, the uneven growth causes the stem to bend toward the light.

Phototropism appears to be a response simply to "light," but that's not exactly right. Recall from Chapter 4 that "light" is made up from many different wavelengths. The pigments in plants responsible for phototropism are actually receptors that respond only to part of the full spectrum of light—the wavelengths that correspond to blue light.

One special type of phototropism, first described by Leonardo da Vinci, is called **heliotropism**—growth in response to the position of the sun. It describes the movement by some leaves and flowers—"heliotropic" flowers, such as the alpine buttercup—as they track the sun's movement across the sky each day. Cells in regions of the plant away from the light elongate as potassium ions are pumped into them and the subsequent movement of water into the cells increases turgor pressure (see Section 3-20), which changes the orientation of the flowers or leaves.

Gravitropism Plants' growth is also affected by gravity, and their response, known as **gravitropism** (also first described by Leonardo da Vinci), is the reason that stems grow upward and roots grow downward. You can see that plants actively control

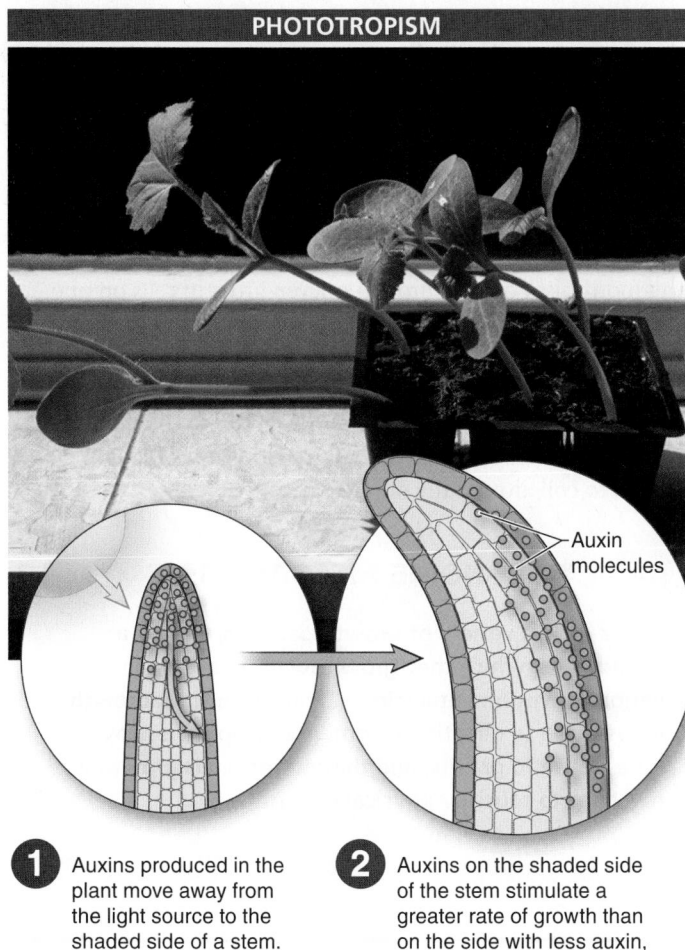

1 Auxins produced in the plant move away from the light source to the shaded side of a stem.

2 Auxins on the shaded side of the stem stimulate a greater rate of growth than on the side with less auxin, causing the plant to bend toward the light.

FIGURE 19-19 Phototropism is plant growth that is influenced by the presence of light.

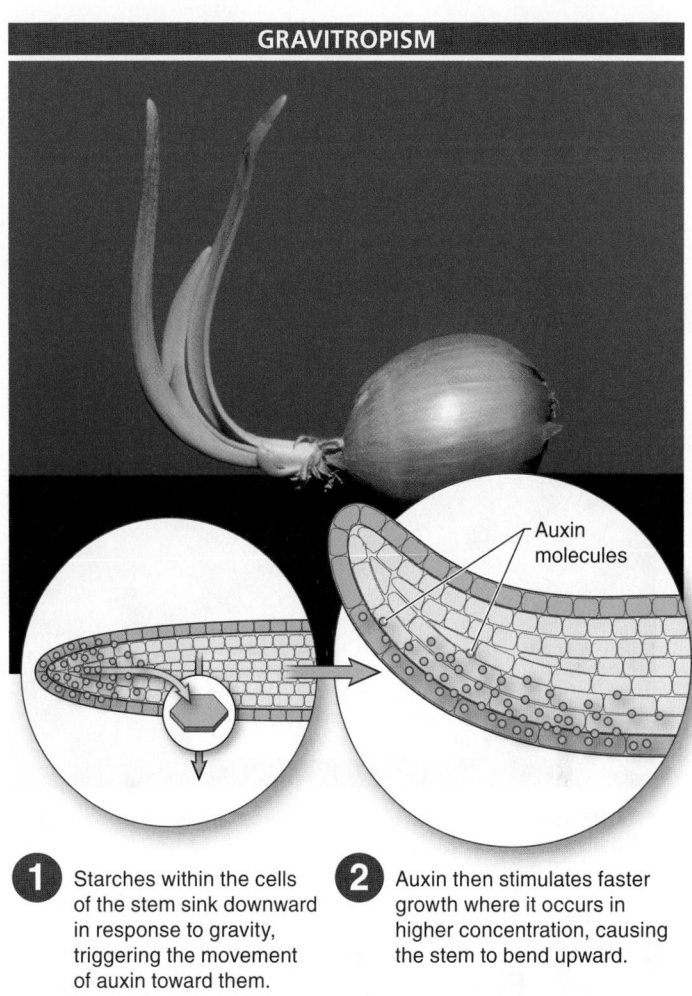

1 Starches within the cells of the stem sink downward in response to gravity, triggering the movement of auxin toward them.

2 Auxin then stimulates faster growth where it occurs in higher concentration, causing the stem to bend upward.

FIGURE 19-20 Plant stems grow away from the force of gravity.

this growth pattern if you take a potted houseplant and tip it on its side. Within a matter of days, the plant will grow upward. It doesn't matter what direction the pot faces (it can even be suspended upside down); roots will grow downward, in response to the force of gravity—and in the direction in which they are most likely to find water—and stems will grow upward, in the opposite direction, which will reliably put them in position to intercept maximal amounts of light (**FIGURE 19-20**).

Gravitropism occurs as a result of the uneven distribution of auxins, much as in the case of phototropism. How do the auxins detect the force of gravity? It seems that there are small bodies within plant cells that contain starches. Like marbles in a bottle of fluid, these starch-containing bodies, pulled by gravity, sink toward the bottom of the cell, regardless of the plant's orientation. Once there, the starch bodies trigger the migration of auxin molecules toward them, and the auxin again causes uneven cell growth so that the stems and roots grow in the right direction.

In a plant turned on its side, the starch-containing bodies in the cells of the stem sink to the bottom of the cells in response to gravity and trigger the movement of auxin toward them. The auxin, in turn, causes the stem to grow in an uneven pattern (faster on the side with the auxin), and the stem bends upward. If an apparatus is set up so that the sideways plant is slowly rotated, however, the starch bodies never get a chance to settle on the bottom of the cells (because "the bottom" is constantly changing). Consequently, the auxin never concentrates at the bottom and uneven growth is never stimulated. The plant doesn't know which way is up, because "up" keeps changing.

Q A plant turned on its side will grow upward. How would a slowly rotating plant grow?

Thigmotropism In **thigmotropism,** plant growth occurs in response to touch or physical contact with an object (*thigmo-* derives from the Greek word for "touch"). For example, many climbing plants, such as cucumbers and morning glories, will wrap around structures—other plants,

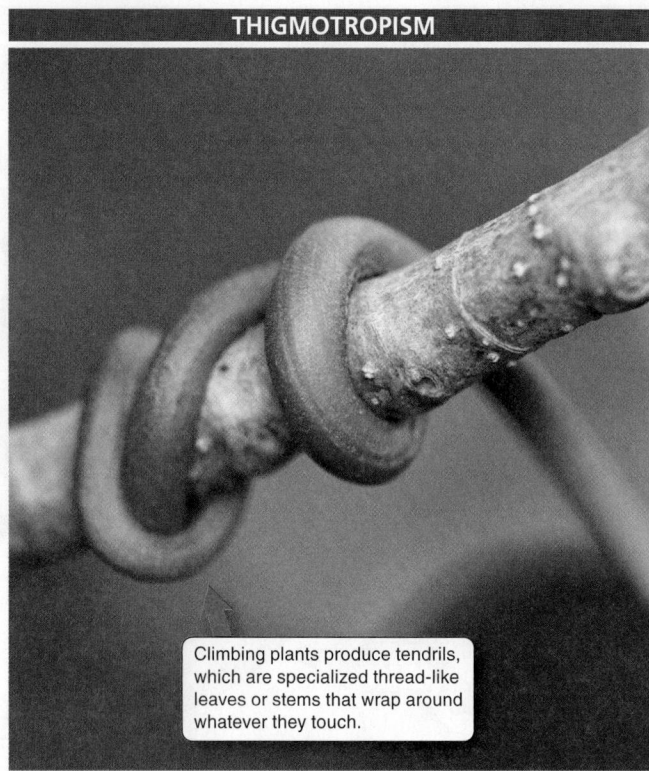

Climbing plants produce tendrils, which are specialized thread-like leaves or stems that wrap around whatever they touch.

FIGURE 19-21 Plant growth can be affected by touch or contact with physical objects.

wires, posts, trellises, or anything that might support them as they grow upward. Climbing plants produce **tendrils,** which are specialized thread-like leaves or stems or branches that wrap around whatever they touch (**FIGURE 19-21**). In some species, a tendril can grow so fast that it wraps completely around something in less than an hour.

As in the case of gravitropism and phototropism, thigmotropism occurs through uneven growth: cells on one side of a shoot (the side in physical contact with the object) elongate less quickly than cells on the opposite side. This, again, involves auxins. The cells in contact with the object produce auxins and transport them to cells not touching the object, where they induce the cells to elongate, causing the tendril to coil around the object.

TAKE-HOME MESSAGE 19·7

Plants have a variety of growth patterns, known as tropisms, by which they grow toward or away from various environmental stimuli. Phototropism is growth in response to directional light, gravitropism is growth in response to gravity, and thigmotropism is growth in response to touch or physical contact.

19·8 Plants have internal biological clocks.

Plants are not as immobile as they appear. If you were to photograph or film a plant over a 24-hour period, as some botanists have done, you would observe many slow but sure movements. The common bean plant, for example, opens its leaves and orients them so that they face the sun during the day. Then each night, the plant pulls its leaves close to the stem (**FIGURE 19-22**). Similarly, in many moth-pollinated tobacco plants, the white trumpet-shaped flowers open each evening for their night-time pollination and close again in the morning. Do the plants respond to environmental cues to schedule their daily activities at the proper times? Or do they have some sort of built-in alarm clock?

The answers are yes and yes. Plants do have a "biological clock," an internal method of keeping time that tells the plant when to turn on or off the expression of certain genes, which results in the plant's perpetually precise behavior—such as properly orienting leaves for efficient photosynthesis or making flowers accessible when pollinators are available. We know this because, even if the bean plants or tobacco plants described above are taken indoors and maintained in a room with constant, dim light, they still open their leaves or flowers on a daily schedule.

But this biological clock is not like a regular watch. As in so many aspects of biology, the events inside the organism are influenced by the world outside the organism. In other words, the internal clock of plants is continuously adjusted by environmental cues. When maintained under constant light conditions in the absence of external cues, the plants have anywhere from a 21-hour to a 27-hour cycle. Consequently, after a while, they tend to get out of synch with the natural pattern of daylight and darkness. However, left outside with access to natural environmental cues, the plants constantly adjust their clocks to those cues and maintain a cycle that always corresponds to the daily light-dark cycle. It's as if plants know that the environment is always the "correct" time and, if their clock is out of synch, they change it accordingly.

The most important environmental cues that set and reset a plant's biological clock are light-dark cycles and temperature cycles. The precise mechanism by which plants keep track of time is not known for all species. In many plants, however, it seems to be regulated by pigments in the leaves that are sensitive to particular wavelengths of light. Because the specific wavelengths of light present in sunlight vary throughout the day, plants reliably have more of the

6 a.m.

Noon

6 p.m.

Midnight

FIGURE 19-22 Great timing. Plants adjust their biological clocks in response to environmental cues such as light and dark cycles and temperature cycles.

 Plants have internal methods of timekeeping—influenced by the external environment—and so can initiate actions at the right time (such as orienting leaves horizontally during the day and vertically at night).

pigments activated during the day, and different pigments are activated as the sun sets and night begins.

Q Could we tell time accurately just by looking at some flowers?

In the mid-1700s, Swedish botanist Carolus Linnaeus used his understanding of plants' biological clocks to design what he called a "floral clock," based on flowers that opened and closed at specific times of day. By planting a garden with 41 species that differed in their flowers' opening and closing times,

Linnaeus was able to tell the time of day just by noting which flowers were open and which were closed.

TAKE-HOME MESSAGE 19·8

Plants have internal methods of keeping time that enable them to initiate various biochemical and physiological actions at the appropriate times. They constantly adjust their biological clocks to environmental cues, such as light-dark cycles and temperature cycles.

9·9 With photoperiodism and dormancy, plants detect and prepare for winter.

Flower production is an energetically expensive task, and because it is so costly, plants benefit by flowering only when it will most effectively enhance their reproductive success. The optimal flowering time differs from species to species, depending on the activity of pollinators, the time it takes for

fruits to develop and be dispersed, and a variety of other factors.

Plants must respond not just to environmental changes over the course of a 24-hour cycle but also to seasonal changes

When it comes to producing flowers—an energetically expensive task—a plant's life can depend on choosing the right moment.

FIGURE 19-23 Plants flower and become dormant in accordance with the seasons.

over the course of a year. For some plants, the best time to flower is in the spring or summer. For others, it is best to wait until early autumn. In other words, plants need more than just a biological clock—they need a "biological calendar." When it comes to producing flowers or scaling back metabolic activity and becoming dormant for winter, for example, a plant's life can depend on choosing the right moment (**FIGURE 19-23**). Timing is everything.

How do plants know when it is spring or summer? What environmental change should they use as a cue to the beginning or end of a season? Temperature? Precipitation levels? Both do tend to change with the seasons—particularly as you get farther and farther from the equator—but they are too variable for a plant to rely on. A plant doesn't want to be fooled by a cloudy spell in summer or an unseasonably dry winter. There is, however, one consistent and unvarying cue to the time of year: the number of hours of daylight or

darkness. Plants use one of these cues—the length of the dark period in a day—in a process known as **photoperiodism,** to regulate their flowering time and numerous other responses to seasonal changes.

All flowering plants fall into one of three categories when it comes to regulating flower production. There are (1) long-day plants, (2) short-day plants, and (3) day-neutral plants (**FIGURE 19-24**). The groups are so named because the amount of daylight seems to determine when they produce flowers. Long-day plants begin producing flowers only when the length of daylight exceeds a critical amount. Short-day plants are the opposite: they flower only when the length of daylight becomes less than some threshold amount. The critical amounts of daylight occur at different times of the year, when conditions are best suited for reproduction for a particular species, generally in spring for long-day plants and in late summer or fall for short-day plants. Day length has no effect on day-neutral plants, which flower when they reach a sufficient state of growth and maturity.

Although short-day and long-day plants are named for the amount of daylight that, apparently, determines when they flower, experiments have shown that short-day and long-day plants are actually sensitive to the length of the night rather than the day. That is, flowering in short-day plants is triggered when the nights become longer than some threshold period, and flowering in long-day plants is triggered by the onset of short nights. This seemingly unimportant distinction had disappointing implications for the California Department of Transportation. The department wanted to line a highway with bright-red flowering poinsettias. Unfortunately, these short-day plants never flowered as expected, because the car headlights on the

GRAPHIC CONTENT!
Thinking critically about visual displays of data.
Turn to p. 760 for a closer inspection of this figure.

PHOTOPERIODISM

All flowering plants fall into one of three categories when it comes to regulating their flower production.

LONG-DAY PLANTS
- Flower production is triggered by decreasing periods of darkness (generally in spring)
- Species include: carnations and clovers

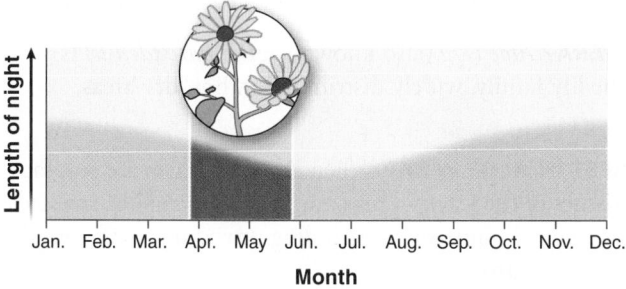

SHORT-DAY PLANTS
- Flower production is triggered by increasing periods of darkness (generally in late summer or fall)
- Species include: poinsettias and strawberries

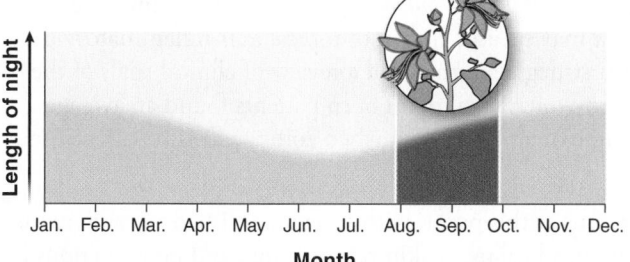

DAY-NEUTRAL PLANTS
- Flower production is triggered by a sufficient state of maturity and not by periods of darkness
- Species include: roses and tomatoes

Some plants are triggered to produce flowers when the nights are long (and the amount of daylight is relatively small). Others are triggered when nights are shorter and the daylight lasts longer.

FIGURE 19-24 Day length and flowering. In long- and short-day plants, flowering is regulated by hours of darkness. In day-neutral plants, light and darkness do not affect flowering.

highway kept interrupting the plants' measurement of the night length. As a consequence, the poinsettia plants—which require at least 14 uninterrupted hours of darkness if they are to flower—never detected an appropriately long night (and thus short day), and they remained green.

How do plants regulate photoperiodism? It seems to be related to the varying ratio of different light-sensitive pigments in their leaves at different points during the day and night. Earlier in this chapter we saw that phototropism occurs as photoreceptors in plants respond to blue light. Photoperiodism, on the other hand, is regulated in large part by plant pigments that are sensitive to red and far-red wavelengths of light. These pigments also play important roles in regulating seed germination and elongation, as well as in several aspects of leaf growth and shape.

Issues relating to photoperiodism can cause difficulties in cultivating flowers indoors. It can be particularly difficult to trigger flowering in short-day plants, as people who keep poinsettias as houseplants discover. With the artificial lights in houses, plants don't usually experience the long, uninterrupted period of darkness required for blooming. Long-day flowers, on the other hand, are easier to cultivate indoors, because flashes of light or continuous light during the night can trick the plants into behaving as if the night is short, leading to flowering. Day-neutral plants are not influenced by artificial lights.

TAKE-HOME MESSAGE 19·9

Plants exhibit photoperiodism, responding to seasonal changes over the course of a year and timing their production of flowers or initiation of winter dormancy, for example, according to environmental factors such as the length of darkness each night.

PRACTICAL BOTANY AND *ALOE VERA*

Can *Aloe vera* lessen the pain or duration of burns?

Q: **WHAT IS *ALOE VERA*?** *Aloe vera* (also known as *Aloe barbadensis*) is a succulent plant in the lily family, widely distributed in hot, dry areas, particularly in Africa.

Q: **WHY THE INTEREST IN *ALOE VERA*?** When *Aloe vera* leaves are cut, sap oozes from the inner tissues of the leaves. This clear fluid has long been touted as having a variety of medicinal properties—including providing relief from the pain of burns (including sunburn).

Q: **DOES IT WORK?** Despite a long history of the use of *Aloe vera* to treat burns, the scientific evidence has often been conflicting. Numerous published research studies on *Aloe vera* have reported (1) antibacterial properties, (2) anti-inflammatory activity, and (3) direct stimulation of the immune system. In a 2008 report in the *New England Journal of Medicine,* for example, doctors suggested that *Aloe vera* may be used in lieu of topical anti-inflammatory drugs to reduce the pain of first-degree burns. And a review of clinical trials of the use of *Aloe vera* for burn-wound healing in burn patients found an average reduction in healing time of almost 9 days when compared with patients not treated with *Aloe vera.*

Still, there is no consensus at this point, with several published research reports finding no increase in burn healing or skin regeneration, and no reductions in bacterial counts. One study even found that *Aloe vera* "hindered the healing process" when compared with an antibacterial cream.

Q: **WHY WOULD A PLANT'S COMPOUND SOOTHE HUMAN SUNBURN?** *Aloe vera* contains a large number of compounds that are toxic to many herbivores, making it resistant to most insect pests. Researchers believe that these molecules, particularly some organic compounds called anthraquinones, salicylic acid (an aspirin-like compound), and some sterols with anti-inflammatory effects, are responsible for the soothing, healing effects of *Aloe vera* when applied to the skin. So far, though, researchers have been unable to figure out exactly how the process works.

Big Ideas in ...
Plants Respond to Their Environments

19·1–19·2 Plants defend themselves from herbivores and survive extreme environments.

- Rooted in the ground, plants are targets for predators and pathogens. They actively resist infection and herbivory by producing toxic chemicals that make the plants distasteful, poisonous, or difficult to consume.

- In the course of evolution, plants have become adapted to some of the world's most extreme habitats, including super-dry regions, salty environments, and cold, windy habitats.

19·3–19·6 Hormones regulate growth and development.

- Plant hormones are chemical signals produced by plant cells that enable the plant to respond to environmental variables (such as amount of moisture, amount and direction of sunlight, and temperature) and that influence its growth and development.

- Gibberellins are a group of related hormones, produced primarily in meristems and seeds, that regulate a plant's growth processes, mainly by stimulating cell division and cell elongation.

- Auxins are a group of hormones found primarily in meristems and immature plant tissues that play several important roles in stimulating and regulating a plant's growth and development, often by increasing the usually rigid cell wall's flexibility and permeability.

- Three other types of hormones play critical roles in plant regulation. Among their multiple functions: ethylene induces and speeds fruit ripening, abscisic acid inhibits growth and reproduction under stressful environmental conditions, and cytokinins stimulate cell division throughout the plant body.

19·7–19·9 External cues trigger internal responses.

- Plants have a variety of growth patterns known as tropisms—including phototropism, gravitropism, and thigmotropism—by which they grow toward or away from various environmental stimuli.

- Plants have internal methods of timekeeping that enable them to initiate various biochemical and physiological actions at the appropriate time of day and time of year, based on environmental cues.

See the To-Go Guide (packaged with every new copy of this textbook) for an illustrated summary of the chapter.

Check Your Knowledge

Thinking critically about visual displays of data.

1. **What does this shaded region represent?**

2. **What does the purple area on the graph represent? What does the yellow area represent?**

3. **What are the actual data presented in each graph?**

4. **What can you conclude from these graphs about the environmental factor that causes flowering? Assuming that the information in the graphs is correct (that is, the periods during which flowers are produced and are not produced), what additional information could undermine your conclusion?**

5. **In the southern hemisphere, the amount of daylight is greatest in late December and is least during late June. What are the implications of this for long-day and short-day plants?**

6. **How is the information in these graphs useful for landscape architects and gardeners?**

PHOTOPERIODISM

All flowering plants fall into one of three categories when it comes to regulating their flower production.

LONG-DAY PLANTS
- Flower production is triggered by decreasing periods of darkness (generally in spring)
- Species include: carnations and clovers

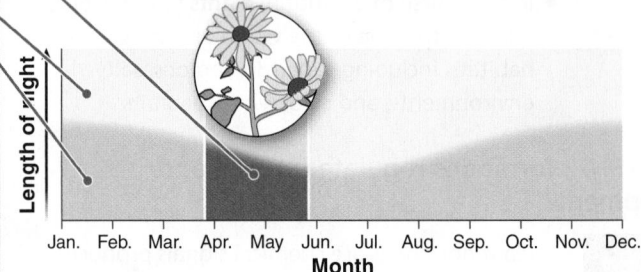

SHORT-DAY PLANTS
- Flower production is triggered by increasing periods of darkness (generally in late summer or fall)
- Species include: poinsettias and strawberries

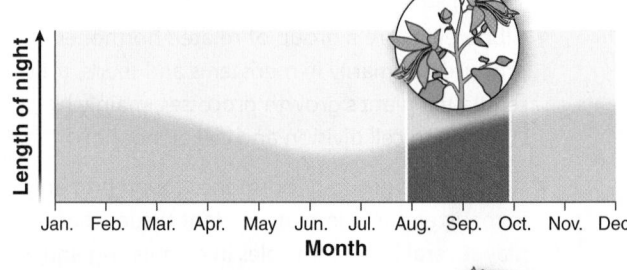

DAY-NEUTRAL PLANTS
- Flower production is triggered by a sufficient state of maturity and not by periods of darkness
- Species include: roses and tomatoes

See Answers at the back of the book.

Key Terms in Plants Respond to Their Environments

abscisic acid, p. 750
auxins, p. 746
cytokinins, p. 751

ethylene, p. 749
gibberellins, p. 745
gravitropism, p. 752

heliotropism, p. 752
hormone, p. 743
permafrost, p. 742

photoperiodism, p. 756
phototropism, p. 752
tendril, p. 754

thigmotropism, p. 753
tropism, p. 752

Multiple-Choice Questions

1. **What adaptations have occurred in desert plants that reduce the impact of the hot, dry environment?**
   a) thick, fleshy, water-storing leaves and stems
   b) strong and deep taproot
   c) seeds that can remain dormant for long periods of time
   d) All of the above are correct.
   e) Only a) and c) are correct.

   100 HARD
   9
   0 EASY

2. **Unlike animals, which produce each hormone _____, plants produce hormones _____.**
   a) in a specific part of the body; in many cell types
   b) only in certain seasons; continuously
   c) in many cell types; in a specific part of the organism
   d) continuously; only in certain seasons
   e) in high concentrations; in low concentrations

   100 HARD
   31
   0 EASY

3. **Which plant hormone or group of hormones do grape-growers spray on their crop in order to get seedless grape plants to grow fruits as large as grapes with seeds?**
   a) gibberellins
   b) ethylene
   c) cytokinins
   d) auxins
   e) abscisic acid

   100 HARD
   20
   0 EASY

4. **High concentrations of _____ stimulate root production.**
   a) gibberellins
   b) cytokinins
   c) auxins
   d) ethylene
   e) abscisic acid

   100 HARD
   42
   0 EASY

5. **Cytokinins promote the growth of:**
   a) shoots.
   b) axillary buds.
   c) pollen tubes.
   d) roots.
   e) vascular cambium.

   100 HARD
   58
   0 EASY

6. **Which hormone or group of hormones stimulates the ripening of fruit?**
   a) auxins
   b) ethylene
   c) cytokinins
   d) gibberellins
   e) abscisic acid

   100 HARD
   11
   0 EASY

7. **Which plant hormone or group of hormones is responsible for bud and seed dormancy?**
   a) auxins
   b) ethylene
   c) cytokinins
   d) gibberellins
   e) abscisic acid

   100 HARD
   47
   0 EASY

8. **Which of these hormones or group of hormones are primarily synthesized in the roots and travel to other regions of the plant?**
   a) cytokinins
   b) gibberellins
   c) 2,4-D
   d) auxins
   e) cytochromes

   100 HARD
   53
   0 EASY

9. **Phototropism in plants is:**

   a) a process that produces glucose.

   b) caused by ethylene.

   c) mediated by cytokinins.

   d) the bending of roots away from the light.

   e) the bending of the shoot tip toward a light source.

10. **Which hormone or group of hormones is involved in phototropism?**

   a) ethylene

   b) gibberellins

   c) cytokinins

   d) auxins

   e) abscisic acid

11. **What is the effect of a short burst of light during a short-day plant's dark period?**

   a) The plant will not flower if the burst of light makes the longest period of continuous darkness shorter than the critical dark period.

   b) The plant will flower, because the length of day remains unchanged.

   c) The plant's flowering does not depend on light, so the burst of light will have no effect.

   d) The plant will not flower, because the burst of light restarts its biological clock.

   e) The plant will flower perpetually, because the burst of light makes the longest period of continuous darkness shorter than the critical dark period.

Short-Answer Questions

1. A houseplant near a window often grows so that most of its leaves face the window. If you rotate the plant, within a few days the leaves will again be facing the window. How does this occur?

2. Why is ethylene so valuable to those who sell fruit?

3. Using an example, explain why so many plants contain spicy chemicals.

4. Fill out the table at the right; list the location and function of each plant hormone.

See Answers at the back of the book.
For additional study questions, go to www.prep-u.com.

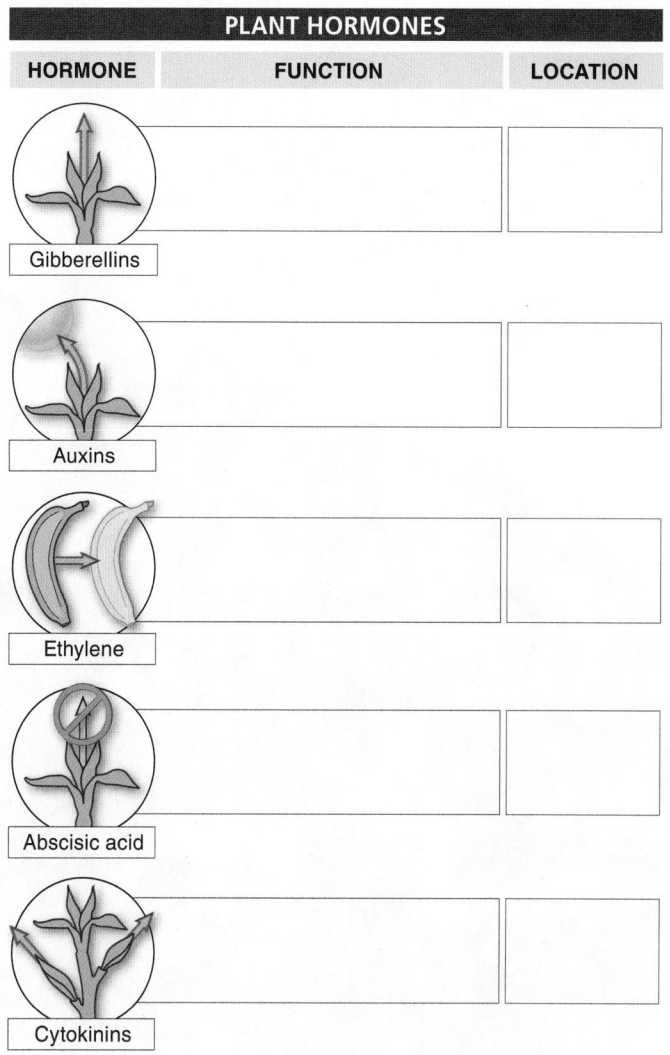

PLANT HORMONES		
HORMONE	FUNCTION	LOCATION
Gibberellins		
Auxins		
Ethylene		
Abscisic acid		
Cytokinins		

ABOUT THE CHAPTER OPENING PHOTO

Phototropism in action: flowering shamrock (genus *Oxalis*) bending toward light source.

Principles of animal
organization and function

20

Introduction to Animal Physiology

A lemon shark (Negaprion brevirostris) reveals its long, thin teeth that help it to catch slippery fish, which make up much of its diet.

20·1–20·6 Animal body structures reflect their functions.

20·1 Most animal bodies are organized in a hierarchy from cells to tissues, organs, and organ systems.

Form follows function. This simple statement captures one of the most universal relationships in the living world. For example, fast-swimming organisms, from penguins to tuna to sharks, share a common streamlined body shape (**FIGURE 20-1**). If a structure is adaptive—the product of natural selection—then its physical features closely reflect its function. And just as form follows function for large animal structures, the relationship also holds true for molecules, organelles, and cells. Form fits function in each.

Animals are multicellular organisms. And multicellularity makes it possible for animals to attain much larger sizes and much greater physiological complexity than single-celled organisms. Increased size and complexity bring many benefits, including fewer potential predators, more potential prey, and, more generally, some protection from the influence of the external environment. For these reasons, among others, the transition from a single-celled to a multicellular body is one of the most important evolutionary transitions.

FIGURE 20-1 Adapted for the life aquatic: the streamlined body of the dolphin.

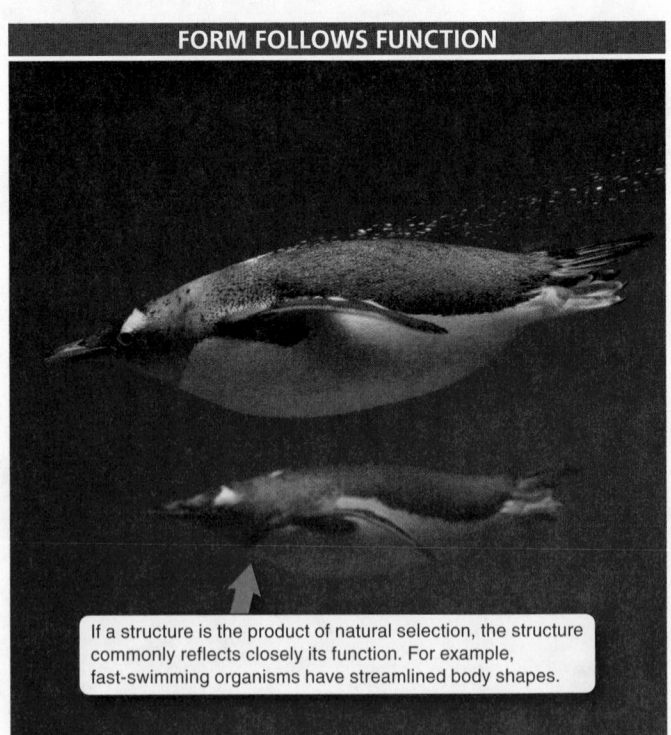

FORM FOLLOWS FUNCTION

If a structure is the product of natural selection, the structure commonly reflects closely its function. For example, fast-swimming organisms have streamlined body shapes.

ORGANIZATION OF ANIMAL BODIES

One of the fundamental features of the organization of the animal body is that it is hierarchical, containing four levels of organization.

CELL
The smallest unit of organization in all organisms

Muscle cell

TISSUE
Group of cells that share similar structure and function

Smooth muscle tissue

ORGAN
Group of tissues that perform specialized functions (most organs, including the stomach, contain all four tissue types)

Stomach

ORGAN SYSTEM
Group of organs that work together to accomplish one or a few, usually related, physiological functions

Digestive system

Multicellularity allows for larger body size and greater physiological complexity through the specialization of cell and tissue functions.

FIGURE 20-2 From cells to organ systems.

Possibly the chief benefit of multicellularity is that it makes possible a division of labor and specialization at the cellular level. It is unnecessary for each cell to carry out every single process (such as generating movement, detoxifying harmful chemicals, digesting macromolecules, and sensing and responding to environmental changes). Instead, cells can be organized into groups, and groups organized into larger groups, to carry out specific life-sustaining functions such as exchanging gases between the organism and its

environment, thinking and feeling, and fighting pathogens (**FIGURE 20-2**).

One of the fundamental features of the animal body is its hierarchical organization. Cells, as you'll recall from Chapter 3, are the smallest units of organization in all organisms. Even sponges, the structurally simplest of all animals, have cells specialized to perform a few distinct tasks. Some cells form the covering of the sponge's body, and others obtain food to provide nutrition and energy to sustain the sponge's activities. At the other end of the spectrum are humans— with 210 different cell types.

In most animals, groups of cells with similar structure, along with some products of those cells, form **tissues,** in which the cells act together to perform specific functions in the body. Adult animals generally have four main types of tissue (**FIGURE 20-3**). We'll discuss them in more detail in Sections 20-2 through 20-5, but we introduce them here.

Connective tissue consists of cells embedded in a large amount of extracellular material, called **matrix,** which together contribute to body structure and support. Found throughout the human body, connective tissue can also serve to anchor cells, regulate communication between cells, and influence growth and wound healing. Some of the most important structures formed from connective tissue include tendons, cartilage, blood, adipose (fat), and bone.

Epithelial tissue covers and lines most exterior and interior surfaces of the body. Skin is an epithelial tissue, as are the tissues that line the nose, throat, lungs, blood vessels, and digestive tract.

Muscle tissue is made up of cells that can contract. This characteristic gives muscle tissue the ability to generate movement or pump fluids through the body.

Nervous tissue, found throughout the human body, is specialized to send and receive electrical and chemical signals and, in doing so, can store and transmit information. The brain and spinal cord are made up of large amounts of nervous tissue.

Just as cells with similar functions are grouped into tissues, so tissues are often grouped into organs or organ systems. **Organs** are structures that serve specialized functions, and they can contain several (or even all four) types of tissue. The heart, liver, kidneys, and brain are examples of organs in the

CONNECTIVE TISSUE
- Composed of cells interspersed throughout a matrix
- Provides structure and support, anchors cells, and regulates communication between cells

EPITHELIAL TISSUE
- Composed of cells that cover and line most surfaces of animal bodies
- Forms the skin and the lining of the lungs, digestive tract, and blood vessels

MUSCLE TISSUE
- Composed of cells that can contract
- Generates movement, pumps fluid, and moves substances

NERVOUS TISSUE
- Composed of specialized cells that send and receive electrical signals
- Stores and transmits information

FIGURE 20-3 Tissues perform specific functions in the body.

human body. **Organ systems** are groups of organs that work together to accomplish one or a few, usually related, functions. The circulatory system, for example, includes the heart, blood vessels, and blood.

In the remaining chapters of the book, we explore animal physiology—the complex functions carried out by each of the organ systems in animals. We describe the structures that are part of each system, how they function, and how they have evolved. As we do this, we see that an organism is greater than the sum of its parts. The working together of cells to form tissues, and of tissues to form organs and organ systems, enables multicellular organisms to reproduce, defend themselves, and communicate (among many other abilities), in ways that are not possible for a single cell or a single type of tissue.

TAKE-HOME MESSAGE 20·1

Animal bodies are highly organized, and at all levels of organization, the physical features are closely related to function. In most animals, cells with similar structure and function are organized into tissues. There are four types of tissue: connective tissue, epithelial tissue, muscle tissue, and nervous tissue. Tissues are often organized into organs, which serve specialized functions and can contain several types of tissue. In turn, organs can be organized into organ systems that accomplish highly complex tasks.

Connective tissue provides support.

Connective tissue is usually the most abundant type of tissue in an animal. Most activities rely heavily on connective tissue, often in conjunction with muscle tissue. Playing tennis, for example, relies on blood to deliver oxygen to muscle, tendons that connect muscles to bones, and cartilage that cushions the joints (**FIGURE 20-4**). (Collagen from the intestines of cows is even used as a material for producing the strings in some tennis rackets.) Connective tissue is sometimes called "cellular glue," because it holds cells together and, as bone and cartilage, for example, gives shape, structure, and support to other tissues, structures, and organs throughout the body.

Regardless of the function it performs or the form it takes, all connective tissue consists of cells that are embedded in matrix—a mass of non-living extracellular material (**FIGURE 20-5**). Matrix, in vertebrates, consists chiefly of polysaccharides and protein (and some minerals, in the case of bone), which are produced and secreted by various cells within the matrix. The matrix can be liquid, jelly-like, or solid. With the exception of blood, all connective tissue contains cells called *fibroblasts*, which produce and secrete the matrix proteins **collagen** and (in most cases) **elastin.** So common is connective tissue that collagen, which often forms a sort of net surrounding organs, is the most abundant protein in humans and other mammals.

FIGURE 20-4 Most activities, such as tennis, rely heavily on connective tissue, often in conjunction with muscle tissue.

CONNECTIVE TISSUE STRUCTURE

Connective tissue is a collection of cells arranged within an extracellular matrix that gives shape, structure, and support to other body tissues.

FIBROBLASTS
Cells that produce and secrete the proteins collagen and elastin (present in every type of connective tissue except blood)

MATRIX
A non-living, extracellular mass of protein fibers and surrounding liquid, jelly-like, or solid material
• Collagen protein
• Elastin protein
• Surrounding material

FIGURE 20-5 Connective tissues consist of cells embedded in an extracellular matrix.

A type of tissue called **connective tissue proper** functions much like the body's packing material. It can be loosely or densely packed. In loose connective tissue, the cells are in a semi-fluid, flexible matrix that generally has many fibers, usually collagen, embedded in it (**FIGURE 20-6**). Loose connective tissue includes the soft padding under your skin, the tissue surrounding most organs, and adipose (fat) tissue, which aids in cushioning, lubricating, and insulating other tissues.

Dense connective tissue is stronger than loose connective tissue. It also has collagen as its chief matrix element, but it

TYPES OF CONNECTIVE TISSUE

CONNECTIVE TISSUE PROPER
Connective tissue with a soft and flexible extracellular matrix

LOOSE CONNECTIVE TISSUE
- Semi-fluid, flexible matrix
- Cushions, lubricates, and insulates other tissues
- Examples: soft padding under the skin, tissue surrounding most organs, and adipose tissue

DENSE CONNECTIVE TISSUE
- Matrix is tightly packed with many collagen fibers
- Connects bones to muscles and other bones
- Examples: tendons and ligaments

SPECIAL CONNECTIVE TISSUE
Connective tissue that has a liquid or rigid extracellular matrix

BONE
- Matrix is hardened with calcium into a solid material
- Provides protection and structural support

CARTILAGE
- Strong but flexible matrix rich in protein fibers
- Provides structural support and cushioning in joints

BLOOD
- Liquid matrix (called plasma) consists primarily of water
- Transports gases and other substances throughout the body

FIGURE 20-6 Connective tissues: the most abundant tissues in most animals.

What is a sprained ankle?

has many more tightly packed collagen fibers than loose connective tissue. Examples of dense connective tissue include **tendons,** which connect muscle to bone, and **ligaments,** which bind bone to bone. A sprained ankle is a common injury in which a twisting of the ankle overstretches and tears part of a ligament in the foot.

The second type of connective tissue, called **special connective tissue,** differs from connective tissue proper in that it is rigid or liquid. Bone, cartilage, and blood (see Figure 20-6) are examples.

In **bone,** the mineral calcium is incorporated into the extracellular matrix, which then hardens into a solid material. Bones can give significant protection to organisms (the skull protects the brain, the ribs protect the lungs and heart) or can provide structural support, as the backbone does.

Cartilage, a dense connective tissue with an extracellular matrix rich in collagen, elastin, and proteins bound to long carbohydrate chains, has a hardness between that of bone and that of tendons. Strong, but also flexible, cartilage is found in the ears and tip of the nose in humans, and it cushions the bones in joints throughout the body. In some organisms, including sharks, the entire skeleton is made of cartilage.

Blood is unique among the connective tissues because it has a liquid extracellular matrix. This liquid matrix, called plasma, is made up mostly of water, but also contains dissolved proteins, sugars, and other molecules. Blood cells, including red blood cells and white blood cells, and the cellular fragments called platelets (see Chapter 21), are suspended within plasma as they transport gases and other substances throughout the body.

All connective tissues in the body, as we've seen, have essentially the same structure: cells embedded within an extracellular matrix that may

The most common form of arthritis is called "wear and tear" arthritis. Why?

be solid, soft and flexible, or fluid. An inflammation or malfunction in connective tissue is the cause of many diseases with widespread effects, including scleroderma and Marfan syndrome. The most common type of arthritis, osteoarthritis, results from the breakdown of connective tissue, usually the cartilage, around joints. The reduced cushioning often leads to inflammation of tissue around the joint, with stiffness and pain, and is commonly treated with anti-inflammatory drugs, including aspirin and ibuprofen.

20·3 Epithelial tissue covers most interior and exterior surfaces of the body.

From the tough soles of the feet that allow you to walk barefoot on a rough, hot sidewalk, to the lining of your mouth that burns when you eat a hot pepper, epithelial tissue (also called **epithelium**) is a sheet-like tissue that covers the surfaces of your, and every other vertebrate's, body. It is made up of a single layer or a few layers of cells,

called epithelial cells, that are tightly bound together so that fluids and gases must pass through the cells, rather than around or between the cells, to get into or out of the body (**FIGURE 20-7**). When you look at a vertebrate, most of what you see is epithelium, because skin is an epithelial tissue.

FUNCTIONS OF EPITHELIAL TISSUE

Epithelium, a sheet-like tissue that separates different parts of the body, plays important roles in protection, transport, and secretion.

PROTECTION
- Acts as a barrier between the inside and outside of an organism
- Keeps fluids from leaking into or out of tissue

TRANSPORT
- Regulates the movement of nutrients and other molecules into and out of body tissues

SECRETION
- Can form exocrine glands, which secrete products such as saliva, sweat, and mucus
- Can form endocrine glands, which secrete hormones

FIGURE 20-7 The multiple roles of epithelial tissue.

FORM REFLECTS FUNCTION   THE INTERNAL ENVIRONMENT   HOW DOES HOMEOSTASIS WORK?

771

Epithelial tissue is not just found on the outer surfaces of organisms, however. It also forms **glands**—collections of cells producing secretions for use elsewhere in the body—and lines the internal tubes and cavities of the body, such as the stomach and intestines, lungs, and blood vessels. In each location, epithelium always has two distinctive sides. The "outside" can be in contact with the outside of the body or with an internal cavity such as the stomach, where it plays a protective role. The "inside" (or underside) faces away from the surface and is generally secured to underlying tissues. Epithelium plays multiple roles in organisms. Three of its most important functions are protection, transport, and secretion (see Figure 20-7).

Q

Damage to the lining of the stomach can have painful consequences. Why?

1. Protection. Acting as a barrier, epithelial cells are linked closely by tight junctions and desmosomes (see Section 3-12), which keep fluids from leaking into or out of tissue. If the strong acids in the stomach, for example, were to leak into surrounding tissue, they would seriously damage the tissue. This is what occurs in individuals with stomach ulcers, open sores in the lining of the stomach. The tight fit between epithelial cells is also why the skin of terrestrial vertebrates is usually waterproof.

2. Transport. Epithelium forms small finger-like projections in the lining of the small intestine, where nutrients are absorbed from digested food into the bloodstream. In blood vessels, epithelium controls which molecules can enter other tissues of the body. And in the kidneys, epithelium helps to regulate which molecules from the bloodstream are eliminated in the urine.

3. Secretion. Epithelium can also form glands. **Exocrine glands** generally secrete products—including earwax, sweat, saliva, milk, mucus, and, in the case of some frogs, toxic poisons—into ducts that lead to the external environment. **Endocrine glands,** on the other hand, are ductless glands that produce hormones, which are released into the fluid surrounding the glands and usually enter the bloodstream for distribution to other parts of the body, where they act as chemical messengers (see Chapter 24).

Because epithelial cells are often in contact with a large variety of materials, they tend to experience more damage than other tissues. For this reason, they tend not to last long and are replaced frequently. Human skin cells, for example, are replaced approximately every two weeks. (Dandruff is mostly dead skin cells.) Cells lining the digestive tract last about five days, and because liver epithelium experiences slightly less wear and tear, it lasts a year or two before replacement.

TAKE-HOME MESSAGE 20·3

Epithelium is a very thin, sheet-like tissue that covers most of the exterior and interior surfaces of an animal's body. Made up of a single layer or a few layers of cells that are tightly bound together, epithelium acts as a barrier between the inside and outside of an organism. It also can be specialized to aid in the secretion and transport of molecules.

20·4 Muscle tissue enables movement.

Most animals move. And muscle tissue, made up of elongated cells capable of generating force by contracting, is responsible for much of that movement. Most muscle tissue cells are packed with protein filaments that slide past one another as they break down ATP, causing the entire cell to shorten and thus the muscle to contract. The action of muscle cells enables organisms to generate force and motion. There are three types of muscle tissue: skeletal, cardiac, and smooth muscle (**FIGURE 20-8**).

Skeletal muscle (sometimes called voluntary muscle) is usually attached to bones and is responsible for generating most movement we see in animals, including facial expressions and breathing. Skeletal muscles can be under conscious control, such as when you choose to flex your biceps, or unconscious control, such as the muscles that control breathing or moving your eyes around. Muscles account for about 40% of human body weight. The individual skeletal muscle cells are called **muscle fibers.** The muscle fibers are

SKELETAL MUSCLE
- Generates most of the movement seen in animals
- Under both conscious and unconscious control

CARDIAC MUSCLE
- Muscle in the heart that pumps blood through the body
- Under unconscious control

SMOOTH MUSCLE
- Generates slow, rhythmic contractions that can gradually move food or other substances through the body, or alter blood pressure
- Under unconscious control and can generate contractions without nervous stimulation

FIGURE 20-8 Muscle tissue is made up of elongated cells capable of generating force when they contract.

very long and contain multiple nuclei, and the repeating units of protein filaments in the cells give the fibers a striped, or striated, appearance. Skeletal muscles are controlled by the nervous system, and the individual nerve cells (neurons) connected to each muscle fiber stimulate its contraction.

Cardiac muscle, as the name indicates, is located only in the heart. It is not under conscious control and causes the heart to pump blood through the body. Because of the tremendous amount of energy used by cardiac muscles, constantly contracting throughout our life, the cells contain many more mitochondria than do other types of muscle cells. The cells of heart muscle are fused together and connected by gap junctions (see Section 3-12). The electrical signals that initiate each contraction of the cardiac muscle pass through these gap junctions.

Smooth muscle is found in the walls surrounding blood vessels, the stomach and intestines, the bladder, and many other organs and internal tubes within the body. Smooth muscle generates slow, rhythmic contractions that can

gradually move food or other substances through the tube or alter blood pressure by increasing or decreasing the diameter of blood vessels. Not under conscious control (so sometimes called involuntary muscle), smooth muscle is regulated by other physiological systems and can generate contractions in several ways without nervous stimulation (including by the opening and closing of ionic channels, such as those controlling movement of calcium ions).

TAKE-HOME MESSAGE 20·4

Muscle tissue consists of elongated cells capable of generating force when they contract. Skeletal muscle is responsible for generating most of the movement we see in animals. Cardiac muscle causes the heart to pump blood through the body. Smooth muscle, surrounding blood vessels and many internal organs, generates slower contractions that can gradually move food or other substances and alter blood pressure.

20·5

Nervous tissue transmits information.

STRUCTURE OF NERVOUS TISSUE

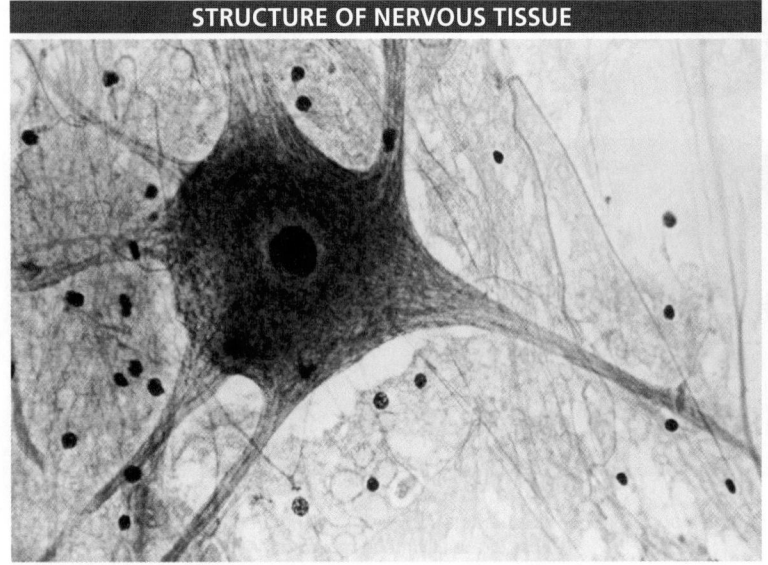

The fourth type of animal tissue is nervous tissue, specialized to store and transmit information. It is responsible for much of the communication that occurs within an animal's body. Nervous tissue enables animals to sense and respond to stimuli such as the smell of food, the sight, smell, or sounds of a predator or a potential mate, or the heat of a fire.

There are two types of nervous tissue cells: neurons and glial cells (**FIGURE 20-9**). **Neurons** are the "excitable" cells that receive and transmit a signal. Neurons have three distinctive elements: dendrites, a cell body, and an axon. **Dendrites** are a bit like an antenna system, specialized for receiving signals from the external environment or from other neurons. The **cell body** contains the nucleus and other cellular machinery found in eukaryotic cells. And the **axon** is a single projection that

There are two types of nervous tissue cells: neurons and glial cells.

NEURONS
Cells that can receive and transmit signals

External signal

DENDRITES
Receive signals from the external environment or from other neurons

CELL BODY
Contains the nucleus and other cellular machinery

AXON
A single projection from the cell body that transmits impulses away from the cell body

GLIAL CELLS (NEUROGLIA)
Assist neurons by insulating, protecting, and regulating their chemical environment, holding them in place, destroying pathogens, and providing nutrients and oxygen

FIGURE 20-9 Neurons and glial cells. Photo shows large neuron cell body and surrounding glial cells.

ORGANIZATION OF THE VERTEBRATE NERVOUS SYSTEM

In vertebrates, the nervous system is divided into the central nervous system and the peripheral nervous system.

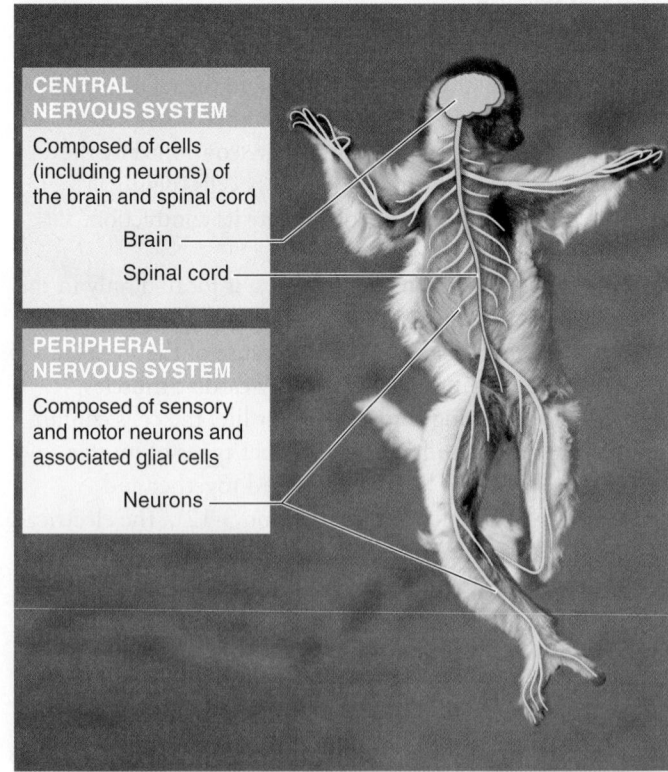

CENTRAL NERVOUS SYSTEM
Composed of cells (including neurons) of the brain and spinal cord

Brain

Spinal cord

PERIPHERAL NERVOUS SYSTEM
Composed of sensory and motor neurons and associated glial cells

Neurons

FIGURE 20-10 The vertebrate nervous system: brain, spinal cord, and neurons.

transmits impulses away from the cell body and can extend over very long distances—sometimes 3 feet (1 m) or more!

Glial cells, also called **neuroglia,** are like the support staff to neurons. They do not carry signals but assist and nourish neurons. There are numerous types of glial cells, and they vastly outnumber neurons. Together, the various types of glial cells produce insulation for neurons, protect and regulate the chemical environment around neurons, hold the neurons in place, destroy pathogens, and provide nutrients and oxygen.

All of the nervous tissue of an organism makes up its nervous system (**FIGURE 20-10**). In vertebrates, the nervous system is divided into the **central nervous system,** which includes the brain and spinal cord, and the **peripheral nervous system,** which includes the neurons that detect a stimulus (sensory neurons) and the neurons that transmit signals to the muscles (motor neurons) and glands in response to that stimulus (**FIGURE 20-11**). (The nervous system is discussed in detail in Chapter 23.)

TAKE-HOME MESSAGE 20·5

Nervous tissue is specialized to store and transmit information. There are two types of nervous tissue cells: neurons, which can receive and transmit a signal, and glial cells, which assist and provide nutrients for neurons.

20·6 Each organ system performs special tasks.

With the exception of sponges and some cnidarians, all animals have some tissues that are organized into organs—structures such as the heart, brain, lungs, and liver—that serve specialized functions and consist of multiple tissue types. And just as cells make up tissues and tissues make up organs, organs, too, are part of larger functional units, the organ systems, which carry out the various physiological processes necessary for the growth, development, maintenance, and reproduction of organisms.

We briefly describe 11 animal organ systems in **FIGURE 20-12**, and we'll discuss them in greater detail

DIGESTIVE SYSTEM
Disassembles and absorbs food so the body can acquire the nutrients it needs to function

CIRCULATORY SYSTEM
Transports gases, nutrients, waste products, hormones, and immune system cells throughout the body

RESPIRATORY SYSTEM
Provides a site for gas exchange between the external environment and an organism's circulatory system

REPRODUCTIVE SYSTEM (MALE)
Produces sperm and delivers them to the female reproductive system, where fertilization may occur

REPRODUCTIVE SYSTEM (FEMALE)
Produces eggs and provides an environment that can nurture a developing embryo and fetus, if fertilization occurs

NERVOUS SYSTEM
Acts as the control center of the body and interprets, stores, and transmits information, using electrical impulses and chemical signals

FIGURE 20-12 The major organ systems of vertebrates.

in Chapters 21–26. It's important to keep in mind that these systems do not operate in isolation: in carrying out its tasks, each system depends on the proper functioning of one or more of the other systems and, in turn, often influences the functioning of other systems. The act of running, for example, might be initiated when the *nervous system* detects a threat and sends impulses to the *musculoskeletal system* (which causes the body to move), to the *respiratory system* (which increases the rate of oxygen consumption), and to the *circulatory system* (which increases the rate at which the heart pumps blood and thus increases the oxygen available to muscle tissue).

IMMUNE AND LYMPHATIC SYSTEM
Attacks pathogens that threaten the body and plays a supporting role in circulation by recycling fluid that leaks from the circulatory system

URINARY/EXCRETORY SYSTEM
Purifies the blood by filtering out wastes and transports wastes out of the body

ENDOCRINE SYSTEM
Regulates body activities by releasing hormones that travel through vessels in the circulatory system to reach target cells

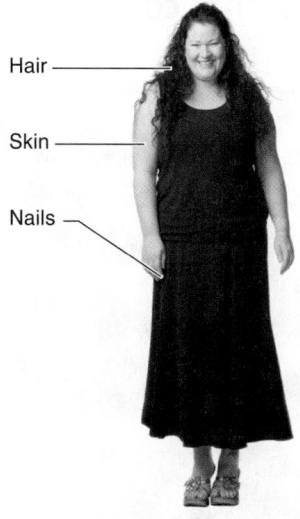

Hair
Skin
Nails

INTEGUMENTARY SYSTEM
Provides protection by forming a barrier between the inside and outside of an organism and can aid in the secretion and transport of molecules

SKELETAL SYSTEM
Supports and protects the body and internal organs, manufactures blood cells, and provides a surface for muscle attachment, creating a foundation for movement

MUSCULAR SYSTEM
Generates force through contraction, which enables movement of the body and of blood, food, and other substances throughout the body

As we explore organ systems in more detail in the following chapters, we'll pay particular attention to the ways in which the form and function of the systems' components are intimately related and what this relationship reveals about how these systems (and the organisms of which they are a part) evolved.

TAKE-HOME MESSAGE 20·6

In nearly all animals, some tissues are organized into organs that serve specialized functions and consist of multiple tissue types, and the organs into organ systems that carry out the various physiological processes necessary for the organism's growth, development, maintenance, and reproduction.

FORM REFLECTS FUNCTION   THE INTERNAL ENVIRONMENT   HOW DOES HOMEOSTASIS WORK?

20·7–20·8 Animals have an internal environment.

Although Arctic temperatures can drop far below freezing, polar bears (Ursus maritimus) maintain an internal body temperature of 98.6° F (37° C).

20·7 Our bodies function best within a narrow range of internal conditions.

Following an extremely rigorous practice in the summer of 2001, 27-year-old Minnesota Vikings football player Korey Stringer walked into an air-conditioned tent to recover. Almost immediately, however, the 6 foot 4 inch, 335-pound all-pro player began to feel weak and dizzy; his breathing became rapid and his blood pressure dropped. He was rushed to the hospital, but as a consequence of his body temperature allegedly reaching 108.8° F (42.7° C), many of his organs failed, and he died that night.

Normal body temperature is approximately 98.6° F (37° C). **Hyperthermia** occurs when too much heat is produced or when high environmental temperature and humidity overwhelm the body's ability to dissipate heat. (It is unlike a fever, in which the body sets its core temperature slightly higher in response to an infection by pathogens.) Korey Stringer's death is an example of the disastrous consequences that can result from extreme hyperthermia, called **heat stroke,** and illustrates the danger when organisms fail to maintain an internal environment within a safe range.

Q What is heat stroke? Why is it dangerous?

Although the environmental temperature range you experience every day may involve a 20°, 30°, or even 40° F

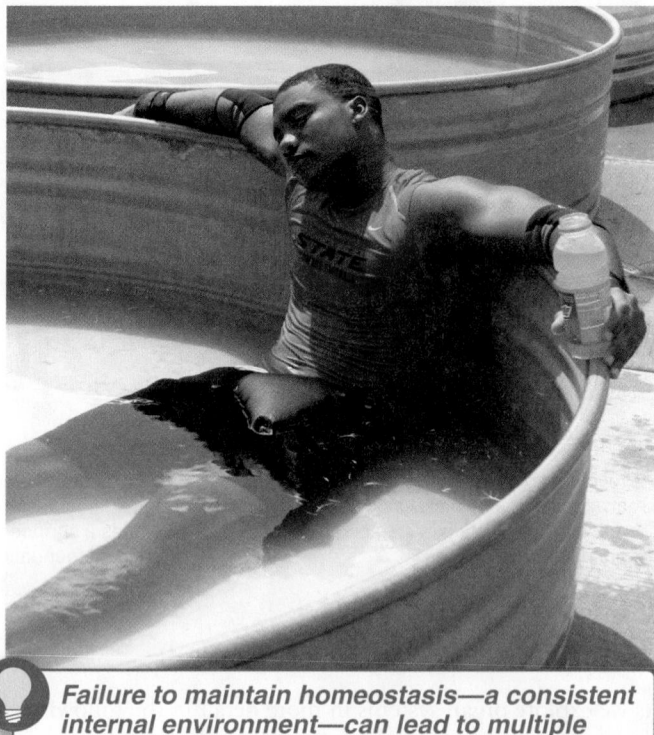

💡 *Failure to maintain homeostasis—a consistent internal environment—can lead to multiple problems in the normal functioning of cells, tissues, and organs, and can result in death.*

FIGURE 20-13 A cooling soak after a tough workout can prevent hyperthermia.

difference between high and low, humans cannot tolerate such large internal temperature swings. Even deviations of less than 10° F can lead to a cascade of biochemical problems with serious health implications. For mammals, the risks of getting too hot include reduced enzyme activity and, at extreme temperatures, the complete breakdown of enzymes. Excessive water loss, too, can occur, leading to numerous problems—including organ failure. For these reasons, heat stroke can be life-threatening (**FIGURE 20-13**).

At the other extreme, **hypothermia,** or extremely low body temperature, can cause difficulties in coordination and movement, along with disorientation and confusion, irregular heartbeat, and, ultimately, death. Similarly disastrous consequences can result from the failure to maintain a consistent internal environment in other ways, including blood sugar levels, blood pH, and tissue concentrations of oxygen and carbon dioxide.

In the remainder of this chapter, we explore a fundamental characteristic of organism function, **homeostasis,** the body's use of physical and chemical processes to maintain a consistent internal environment, even in the face of changing external and internal environmental forces.

TAKE-HOME MESSAGE 20·7

Failure to maintain a consistent internal physical and chemical environment can lead to multiple problems in the normal functioning of cells, tissues, and organs, and can result in death.

20·8 Animals regulate their internal environment through homeostasis.

When it comes to **physiology**—all of the functions and activities of an organism—taking care of business is straightforward in single-celled organisms. Food and other necessary materials for life do not have far to go to get into the cell—all they have to do is cross a plasma membrane. Moving waste products out of the cell is similarly simple. Such are the advantages to living close to the external environment. But direct contact with the external environment has its costs, too. Perhaps most important among these costs is that the single-celled organism is, to a large extent, at the mercy of its external environment. Changes in the environment—such as in temperature or pH—can have a great impact on the cell itself.

Like single-celled organisms, multicellular animals also must acquire food and other materials, as well as get rid of waste. These tasks become increasingly complex when cells are not in direct contact with the external environment. On the other hand, a cell can be protected from harsh or changing environmental conditions if it's not in direct contact with the environment.

With multicellularity and increasing size, then, an animal's internal environment takes on greater importance than the external environment in influencing cell functioning. In vertebrates, this internal environment consists of the **extracellular fluid** (also called the **interstitial fluid**) that fills the space between cells, bathing the cells. This fluid is primarily water, but also contains nutrients and raw materials for growth and development, as well as waste products that have diffused out of or been removed from cells. The volume of interstitial fluid is not insignificant. In fact, one-third of the water in the human body is in interstitial fluid, with more than two and a half gallons (10 liters—picture five 2-liter soda bottles!) surrounding and bathing the cells.

One of the hallmarks of animal physiology, however, is that organisms generally maintain homeostasis, or the ability to return to a narrow range of physical and chemical conditions, even in the face of changing external environmental forces. In this relatively constant, steady, internal environment, variables such as temperature, water-solute balances, pH, blood sugar levels, and O_2 and CO_2 concentrations in blood and other tissues are maintained within narrow ranges by the activities of cells within the organism's tissues, organs, and organ systems (**FIGURE 20-14**).

Homeostasis is of huge value to the organism. Cellular functioning (from DNA replication to protein production to intercellular communication) depends, in large part, on the activities of enzymes. In turn, an enzyme's activity depends critically on the temperature and other characteristics of its immediate environment. Even slight

Although external environmental conditions may vary widely for humans, a variety of internal physiological variables, such as body temperature, blood pH, and blood sugar level, are kept within a relatively narrow range.

EXTERNAL TEMPERATURE
110°F

INTERNAL TEMPERATURE
98.6°F

EXTERNAL TEMPERATURE
19°F

FIGURE 20-14 Homeostasis: maintaining a stable internal environment.

changes in these variables can disrupt, reduce, or even stop enzyme functioning. And this can have catastrophic consequences, such as in the case of heat stroke described in Section 20-7.

Enzyme activity is just one of many facets of cell function influenced by temperature and other physical features of the cell's internal environment; membrane permeability and the rates at which materials diffuse across membranes also respond to changes in the environment. Through homeostasis, organisms maintain optimum metabolic functioning—the processes by which organisms take up nutrients from their environment and use them for growth, movement, reproduction, and all the other actions necessary

for life. In the next section, we explore how homeostasis is maintained.

TAKE-HOME MESSAGE 20·8

Although the internal environment of multicellular animals is continuously influenced by their external environment, many animals maintain homeostasis: they keep a variety of internal physiological variables—including temperature, water-solute balances, pH, blood sugar levels, and blood gas concentrations—within a relatively constant range.

20·9–20·12 How does homeostasis work?

By adjusting its postures, a red-veined dropwing dragonfly (Trithemis arteriosa) is able to cool down on a hot day.

20·9
Negative and positive feedback systems influence homeostasis.

For animals to maintain homeostasis with regard to a particular physiological variable, that variable must have a **set point,** a target value or range to which the organism can return. Most vertebrates have set points for a variety of physiological variables, including body temperature, water-solute balances, blood sugar levels, blood pH, and tissue O_2 and CO_2 concentrations.

In the face of changes in its external environment, how does an organism maintain its homeostasis, its constant internal environment? The most common method involves the regulatory mechanism of **negative feedback,** in which sensors detect a change in the internal environment and trigger structures called **effectors** to oppose or reduce the change. This cycle of detection, response, and change is called a negative feedback loop (**FIGURE 20-15**).

An example of a negative feedback loop that we encounter in everyday life is the regulation of room temperature in a house, which involves a sensor (the thermostat) and two effectors (a furnace and an air conditioner). The thermostat

FIGURE 20-15 A negative feedback loop restores the internal environment to a set point.

NEGATIVE FEEDBACK LOOP

In a negative feedback loop, sensors detect change in the internal environment and trigger effectors to oppose or reduce the change.

TOO COLD   TOO HOT

SENSOR:
THERMOSTAT
Detects temperature

EFFECTOR:
FURNACE
Increases temperature

EFFECTOR:
AIR CONDITIONER
Decreases temperature

DESIRED TEMPERATURE

In animals, negative feedback systems are the most common method used to maintain the internal environment within a narrow range.

FORM REFLECTS FUNCTION · THE INTERNAL ENVIRONMENT · HOW DOES HOMEOSTASIS WORK?

781

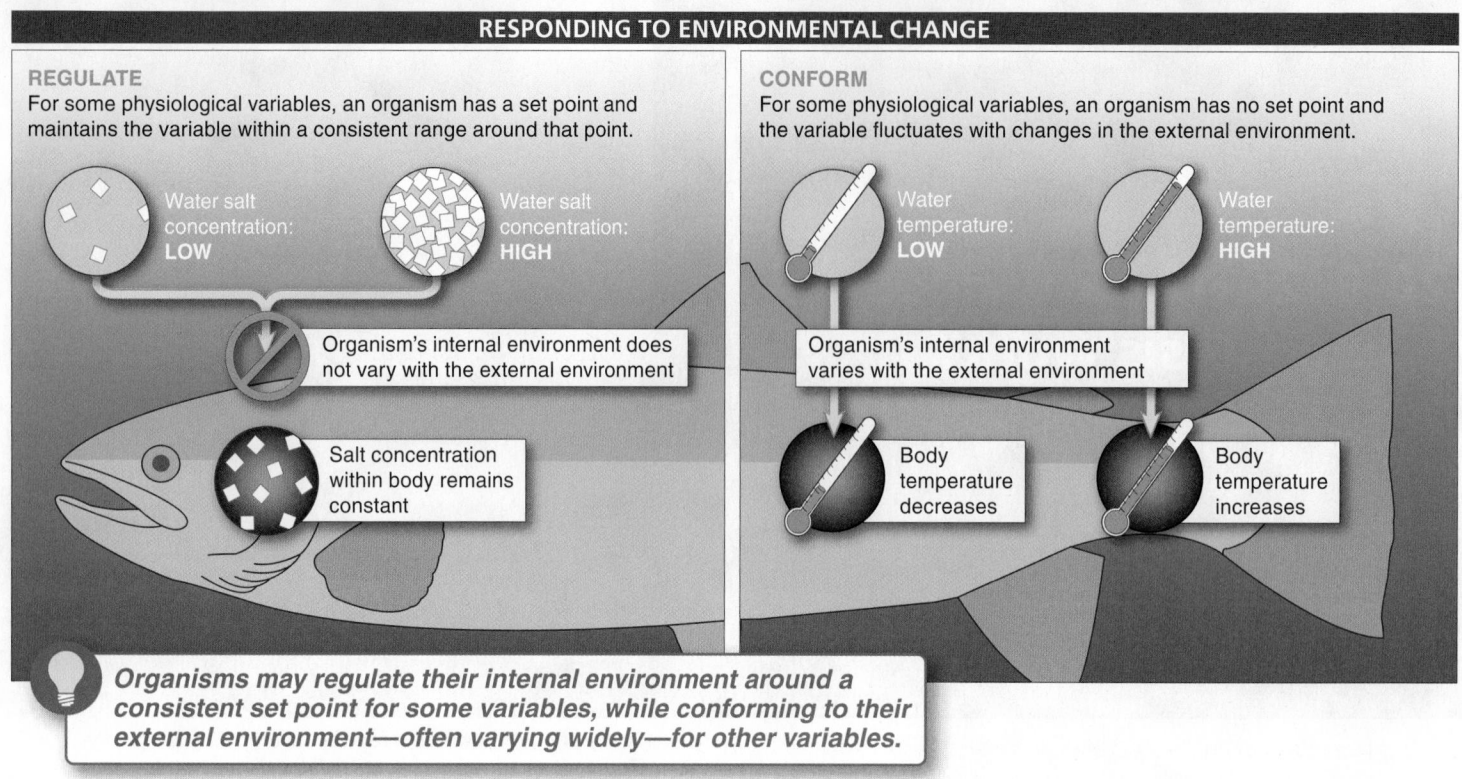

REGULATE
For some physiological variables, an organism has a set point and maintains the variable within a consistent range around that point.

Water salt concentration: **LOW**

Water salt concentration: **HIGH**

Organism's internal environment does not vary with the external environment

Salt concentration within body remains constant

CONFORM
For some physiological variables, an organism has no set point and the variable fluctuates with changes in the external environment.

Water temperature: **LOW**

Water temperature: **HIGH**

Organism's internal environment varies with the external environment

Body temperature decreases

Body temperature increases

Organisms may regulate their internal environment around a consistent set point for some variables, while conforming to their external environment—often varying widely—for other variables.

FIGURE 20-16 Regulate or conform? Two strategies to cope with a changing environment.

contains a sensor that detects the temperature in the house. If the temperature drops too low, the thermostat triggers an effector—the furnace—to turn on, bringing the room temperature back up to the desired level. Once the temperature reaches a specified level, the thermostat tells the furnace to shut off. Similarly, if the temperature gets too high, the thermostat can trigger the air conditioner to turn on, which brings the temperature back down to the desired level, after which the air conditioner shuts off. In both cases, a negative feedback system senses a change in the temperature, triggers events that reverse the change, and restores the house's internal environment to its desired level.

In the human body, negative feedback systems are the most common method used to maintain the internal environment within a narrow range. These systems include those that maintain body temperature, regulate levels of sugar in the bloodstream, and control the levels of salt and other solutes in body fluids. We explore these systems in detail later in this chapter.

It is important to note that while some groups of organisms, called **regulators,** maintain homeostasis for a certain variable (as we've just described for temperature), other organisms, called **conformers,** may have no set point for that variable, and the variable may fluctuate with external changes. Animals differ

Why don't we bleed to death when we get a cut?

in the traits for which they are regulators and those for which they are conformers. Most fishes, for example, are conformers with regard to the temperature of the surrounding water, but are regulators when it comes to the concentration of salt in their blood and tissues (**FIGURE 20-16**).

In addition to negative feedback systems, organisms also have a small number of **positive feedback** systems, in which deviations from conditions normally found in the internal environment cause an increase or acceleration of the change, in the same direction. Such systems push the body away from homeostasis and often initiate cascading processes that increase the rate at which the system deviates from the normal range. For this reason, positive feedback systems, if unchecked, can become highly unstable.

An example of a positive feedback system is the blood-clotting process (**FIGURE 20-17**). Injury to a blood vessel causes platelets—cellular fragments involved in clotting—to release their Super Glue–like contents, which begin to seal any rip or tear in the blood vessel (see Section 21-7). Within the bloodstream, the contents released from a platelet have another effect as well: they cause other platelets to release their contents. This is a positive feedback system, because the release of some blood-clotting molecules into the bloodstream causes the

In positive feedback systems, a change away from conditions normally found in the body causes an increase or acceleration of the change.

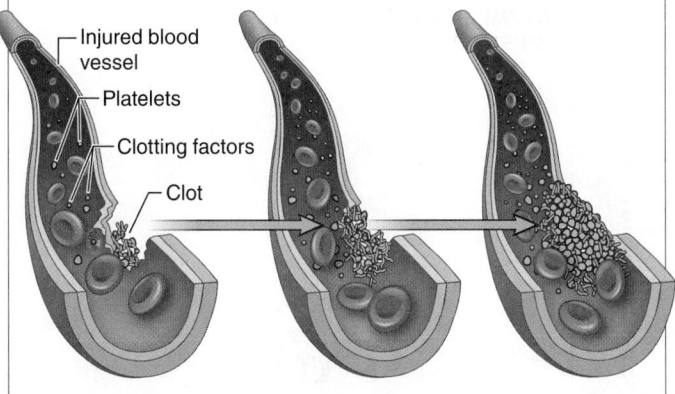

An injured blood vessel triggers platelets to form a clot.

The release of blood-clotting molecules into the bloodstream causes the release of more such molecules, which causes the release of still more, to aid in forming the clot.

Positive feedback is generally part of a larger, negative feedback system; after a period of positive feedback, the variable is brought back within its typical range.

FIGURE 20-17 Patching a tear. The blood clot that forms after an injury is a result of a positive feedback system.

release of more such molecules, which causes the release of still more. The result is that a dangerous situation, injury to a blood vessel, is quickly remedied.

Generally, positive feedback systems are part of larger, negative feedback systems, which, after a short period of positive feedback, bring the variable (and the organism) back to within its original, normal range of internal environmental conditions. After blood clotting has stopped the loss of blood from a damaged vessel, other chemical signals interrupt the positive feedback loop, stop the further release of blood-clotting molecules, and even begin to break down blood clots that no longer serve a function.

TAKE-HOME MESSAGE 20·9

For animals to maintain homeostasis with regard to a particular physiological variable, that variable must have a set point to which the organism can return. Through negative feedback, sensors detect a change in the internal environment and trigger effectors to oppose or reduce the change. Positive feedback systems, much less common, oppose homeostasis in response to a change, pushing the body away from normal conditions and increasing change in the same direction.

20·10 Temperature control is a component of homeostasis.

As we saw in the case of Korey Stringer, one of the most important environmental factors that affect animals is temperature. And for many animal species, the control of temperature, called **thermoregulation,** is an important component of homeostasis. Some of the important benefits to controlling body temperature include enhancing enzyme stability and efficiency (just a small change in temperature often significantly reduces the rate at which an enzyme catalyzes a reaction), giving organisms more independence in the timing of their daily activities, and resisting freezing.

In thermoregulation, the biggest distinction among animal species is in how they generate their body heat. **Endotherms** (sometimes described as "warm-blooded") generate their heat internally, within their own bodies. Most mammals and birds are endotherms.

Q *Why do some cold-blooded animals have "hot" blood and some warm-blooded animals have "cold" blood?*

Ectotherms (sometimes described as "cold-blooded") get their heat primarily from the environment, usually the sun. Invertebrates, fishes, amphibians, and reptiles are all ectotherms (**FIGURE 20-18**).

There are costs and benefits associated with being an endotherm versus an ectotherm. Between 27° and 36° C, for example, endotherms are able to maintain a constant internal body temperature without any energy expenditures. Within this range, called the **thermoneutral zone,** their resting metabolic rate can remain constant, as they maintain their constant body temperature by using passive methods of regulation such as heat loss through the skin. In ectotherms, on the other hand, metabolic rate increases continuously across this range of temperatures. Below the endotherms'

ENDOTHERMS
- Animals that generate body heat internally
- Sometimes described as "warm-blooded"
- Include most mammals and birds

ECTOTHERMS
- Animals that get their heat primarily from the environment
- Sometimes described as "cold-blooded"
- Include invertebrates, fishes, amphibians, and reptiles

FIGURE 20-18 Strategies to heat the body.

thermoneutral zone, the situation is reversed: metabolic rate increases significantly as they must use active heating to maintain their body temperature. At these same colder temperatures, metabolic rate in ectotherms decreases as they let their body temperature drop along with the ambient temperature (**FIGURE 20-19**).

Endotherms and ectotherms are often distinguished as "warm-blooded" and "cold-blooded," but on closer investigation, such terms do not always accurately describe the two groups. Some animals, including numerous mammalian species, **hibernate,** going into a state of reduced metabolic activity for days or weeks, during which their body temperature can drop considerably. The body

Endotherms generate their heat within their own bodies. Ectotherms get their heat primarily from the environment, usually the sun.

AMBIENT TEMPERATURE'S EFFECT ON BODY TEMPERATURE

There are energetic costs and benefits to being an endotherm versus an ectotherm, including:

- Between 27° and 36° C, endotherms can maintain constant body temperature without energy expenditure; ectotherms' metabolic rate increases continuously
- Below 27° C, endotherms' metabolic rate increases steeply as they generate heat to maintain body temperature; ectotherms' metabolic rates decrease

AMBIENT TEMPERATURE'S EFFECT ON METABOLIC RATE

GRAPHIC CONTENT!
Thinking critically about visual displays of data.
Turn to p. 794 for a closer inspection of this figure.

FIGURE 20-19 Energy expenditure and thermoregulation.

temperature of some hibernating ground squirrels, for example, can drop below freezing for more than three weeks. While some hibernating mammals can become quite cold, some lizards basking in the sun can get very warm.

These observations highlight another important aspect of thermoregulation. Some organisms (such as humans) are **homeotherms,** meaning that they maintain a relatively constant body temperature. Other organisms (such as lizards and the hibernating mammals) are **heterotherms,** and their body temperatures, at times, fluctuate as the environmental temperature changes (**FIGURE 20-20**). As a consequence, animals are most accurately categorized by describing their source of heat (internal or external) *and* the degree to which they maintain a constant temperature or have a temperature that fluctuates.

Whether or not an animal generates its own heat and maintains a constant body temperature, all animals exchange heat with the environment. Ultimately, an organism's temperature is a function of the heat produced by its body in conjunction with the heat transferred from the environment to its body or from its body to the environment. This heat exchange can occur in four ways.

1. *Conduction* is the transfer of heat that occurs when two objects at different temperatures come in contact. Holding an ice cube or sitting on a hot car seat dramatically reveals conduction in action.

2. *Convection* is the transfer of heat from an object to a medium such as water or air as it passes next to the object. This is particularly noticeable to us when a cold breeze blows.

3. *Radiation* is the transfer of heat, without direct contact, from a warmer object to a colder object. You are experiencing radiant heat when you feel the warmth of the sun on your face or the heat from a fireplace on your feet.

4. *Evaporation* is the loss of heat that occurs as a liquid substance, such as liquid water, turns to a gas. When you sweat and the sweat evaporates, it cools you off.

We'll find further examples of each of these mechanisms as we look at four of the methods—physical, behavioral, physiological, and cellular—by which animals regulate body temperature (**FIGURE 20-21**).

Numerous physical features have evolved in organisms that influence their body temperature. These include body size,

MAINTAINING BODY TEMPERATURE

HOMEOTHERMS
Body temperature remains relatively constant.

Reptiles can often be found on the edges of roads in the afternoon and early evening, using the warmth of the road to elevate their body temperature.

HETEROTHERMS
Body temperature fluctuates as environmental temperatures change.

FIGURE 20-20 Stable body temperature versus variable body temperature.

surface area, and levels of insulation. The thick, lipid-rich coat of blubber in walruses, whales, and many other marine mammals, for example, can account for up to 50% of their body weight and provides effective insulation, helping to maintain a constant body temperature.

An organism can also use behavioral strategies to regulate its body temperature. Most lizards, for example, bask in the morning sun, increasing their body temperature. Later, when the day is at its hottest, they may retreat to a burrow to reduce their body temperature. Many large mammals that cannot get to shade orient their bodies to minimize the angle at which the sunlight strikes them. The African ground squirrel even shades itself with its tail as it forages.

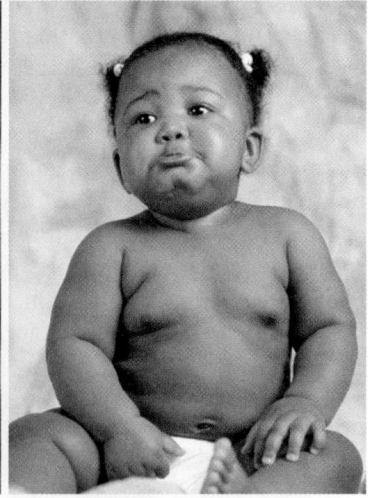

PHYSICAL METHODS
The walrus has a thick coat of blubber that provides insulation from the external environment.

BEHAVIORAL METHODS
The African ground squirrel shades itself with its tail while foraging, to minimize heat from the sun.

PHYSIOLOGICAL METHODS
By panting, dingos make use of the efficient loss of heat due to evaporation.

CELLULAR METHODS
Human infants have a special type of fat that produces heat, rather than ATP, when broken down.

FIGURE 20-21 Adaptations that aid in temperature regulation.

Animals also employ many physiological methods of thermoregulation. One specific example of this occurs as cells maintain concentration gradients of various ions, such as potassium (K^+) and sodium (Na^+). Many cell membranes are somewhat permeable to K^+ and Na^+ ions. The ions "leak" across the membrane, requiring active transport to restore and maintain the concentration gradients necessary for some cellular processes. Because the reactions involved in active transport are not perfectly efficient in their use of energy, some energy is released as heat with each reaction. This heat can help maintain an organism's body temperature. Interestingly, cell membranes in endotherms, such as humans, are leakier than cell membranes in ectotherms, such as fishes, suggesting that such "leakiness" is an adaptation that helps endotherms generate heat internally. It is also likely that the reason endotherms have, on average, three to four times as many mitochondria per cell as ectotherms is that mitochondria are the sites of greatest heat generation.

Another physiological method by which animals—both ectotherms and endotherms—can regulate their body heat is by controlling the flow of blood to the skin. To lose heat, such as during periods of extreme exertion or at extremely high external temperatures, animals increase blood flow to the skin, allowing greater heat loss by convection. Through panting and sweating, too, many animals make use of the efficient loss of heat due to evaporation (**FIGURE 20-22**). Alternatively, in cold environments, the loss of heat can be

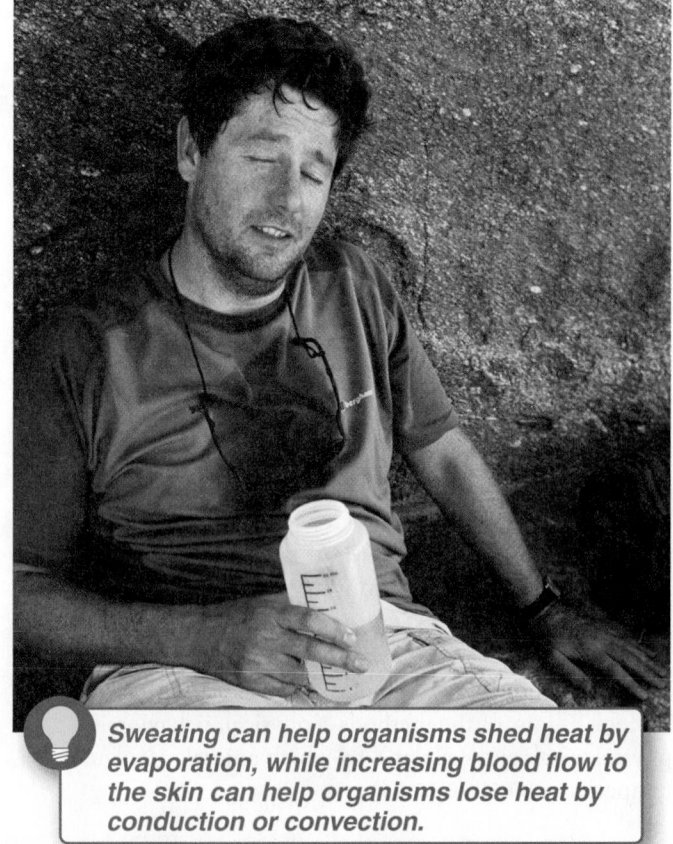

Sweating can help organisms shed heat by evaporation, while increasing blood flow to the skin can help organisms lose heat by conduction or convection.

FIGURE 20-22 Heat exchange. Sweating can help cool us off through evaporation. By leaning up against a cool rock wall, we can also lose some heat through conduction.

reduced by reducing the flow of blood to the skin and by shivering, through which animals can increase their heat production.

Q Why does "baby fat," unlike regular fat, act like a built-in heating pad?

One cellular method of temperature regulation is particularly important to human babies. It takes place in a special type of connective tissue called "brown fat." Unlike the cells of "white fat," or adipose tissue (most of the fat in adult's bodies), which have few mitochondria, the cells of brown fat have a high density of mitochondria along with the stored fat. When brown fat cells oxidize their fat, however, they don't generate ATP. Instead, a special protein causes protons to leak directly across the mitochondrial membrane, rather than passing through the enzyme that synthesizes ATP (see Section 4-15), causing the production of heat rather than ATP from the fat breakdown. Human infants have significantly more brown fat than adults. This difference probably evolved because infants' small body size gives them a large surface-area-to-volume ratio, which results in a relatively large surface area over which they can lose heat and a relatively small body mass in which they can generate heat.

TAKE-HOME MESSAGE 20·10

The control of body temperature, called thermoregulation, is an important component of homeostasis. Body temperature is a function of internal heat production and heat transfer between an organism and its environment. Heat transfer to and from the environment is regulated physically, behaviorally, physiologically, and at the cellular level.

20·11 Animals must balance their water content within a narrow range.

Organisms, whether they live in the water or on land, require water. But they can't take in too much or they will burst. And they can't lose too much or they will shrivel up and die. **Osmoregulation,** an important component of homeostasis in animals, is the regulation of water content and of the concentrations of dissolved solutes that influence osmosis. The most abundant solutes in animal fluids are sodium, chloride, potassium, magnesium, and calcium ions.

Although a variety of mechanisms of water regulation have evolved in animals, there are just four ways that animals get water: by drinking it, by eating foods that contain it, by absorbing it through osmosis, and as a by-product of cellular respiration. Similarly, there are four ways that animals lose water: urination, defecation, evaporation (including panting, breathing, and sweating), and osmosis.

Osmoregulation revolves around controlling and regulating these mechanisms of water loss and gain. Through osmosis (see Section 3-9), water flows from areas of low solute concentration to areas of high solute concentration. Thus organisms often control their water content indirectly by regulating their solute content. They generally balance the total amount of solutes—which influences the direction and magnitude of osmosis—and the concentration of each solute individually. Imbalances in the concentrations of certain solutes (minerals and electrolytes) can cause serious health problems, from muscle spasms to confusion to paralysis, and even death.

Because animals live in such a wide range of habitats, they encounter a similarly wide range of osmoregulatory challenges. The challenges are very different for aquatic organisms than for terrestrial organisms, for example. And among the aquatic organisms, the challenges faced by organisms living in saltwater habitats are very different from—almost the opposite of—those faced by organisms living in fresh water.

Different strategies have evolved for coping with such diverse osmoregulatory challenges. Most invertebrates that live in salt water are **osmoconformers,** meaning that they let the solute concentration of their body fluids reflect that of their environment. Most vertebrates, on the other hand, are **osmoregulators,** maintaining their fluids and solute concentrations within narrow ranges that differ from those of their environment (**FIGURE 20-23**; see also Figure 20-16).

A variety of structures have evolved that enable animals to regulate their water balance. In insects, for example, very small tubes branch off the digestive tract, near its end at the rectum. These extensions from the gut, called Malpighian tubules, function as insects' chief excretory organs. Using active transport (see Section 3-10), the insect moves

OSMOREGULATORY STRATEGIES

OSMOCONFORMERS

Osmoconformers are organisms that let the composition of their body fluids reflect that of their environment.

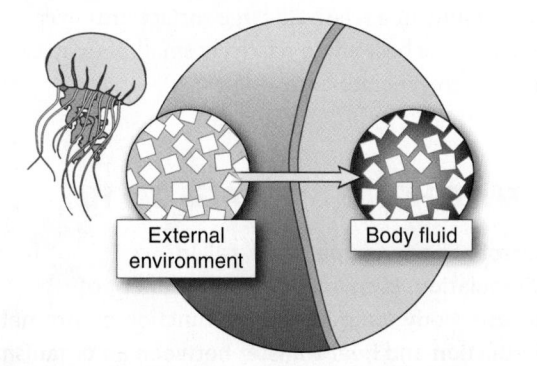

External environment → Body fluid

OSMOREGULATORS

Osmoregulators are organisms that maintain their fluids and solute concentrations within narrow ranges that differ from those of their environment.

Circulatory system

High solute concentration in circulatory system

Digestive tract

Regulated solute concentration

Excess solutes (waste)

MALPIGHIAN TUBULES (IN INSECTS)
These small tubes regulate osmotic balance in insects by removing excess solutes from the circulatory system.

High solute concentration in circulatory system

Regulated solute concentration

Excess solutes (waste)

KIDNEY (IN VERTEBRATES)
This complex organ regulates osmotic balance in vertebrates by removing either excess solutes or excess water from the circulatory system, depending on the organism's external environment.

FIGURE 20-23 Two strategies for regulating the amount of salt and water in the body.

potassium ions (K^+) and cellular waste products from its body cavity—where its blood is—into the Malpighian tubules. As a consequence of the increase in solutes in the tubules, water moves into them by osmosis. The K^+ ions, water, and waste products move down the digestive tract until, near its end, the K^+ ions and water are mostly reabsorbed into the circulatory system. This is a very effective system for conserving water, leaving mostly waste products to be excreted as feces.

Another osmoregulatory structure is the vertebrate kidney. The kidney, as we shall see, is a complex organ that filters blood, removing metabolic waste products—particularly excess nitrogen from the breakdown of proteins and nucleic acids—and other solutes while regulating the organism's water balance. The specific details of kidney function vary across the different groups of vertebrates. Let's consider, for example, the challenges faced by two groups of aquatic vertebrates: freshwater and saltwater fishes. A freshwater fish faces the problems of high concentrations of water entering its body and of solutes leaving its body. A saltwater fish, on the other hand, tends to lose water to its environment while taking in high concentrations of solutes from the environmental water. As a consequence, vertebrate kidneys—depending on the type of animal—may function either to conserve water or to remove it. (This explains why a freshwater fish does not drink water, but a saltwater fish drinks large amounts.)

Do fish drink water?

In the next section, we examine the details of kidney functioning, focusing specifically on the human kidney and how it can produce urine that has a solute concentration more than four times that of blood, and how it can eliminate the many potentially harmful molecules contained in the food and drink consumed in the diet.

TAKE-HOME MESSAGE 20·11

Many organisms maintain their water content within a narrow range. To maintain osmotic balance, organisms must be able to take up water and get rid of water, and they must be able to regulate concentrations of ions in their body fluids. Various mechanisms and strategies have evolved for coping with these challenges.

20·12 In humans, the kidneys regulate water balance.

The kidney is an organ in vertebrates that helps maintain homeostasis by regulating water balance and solute concentration in body fluids. It accomplishes this by filtering blood—as much as 2,000 liters (or 275 times the total volume of blood in your body!) pass through the human kidneys each day—and reabsorbing water and other substances needed by the body. The kidneys accomplish three primary functions:

1. **Filtration.** As blood passes through the kidneys, it is filtered. During this process, water, ions, and other dissolved substances are removed from the blood as a filtrate, leaving behind just cells and large proteins.

2. **Reabsorption.** The filtrate is then processed and modified, as water, nutrients (including glucose and amino acids), and some ions are reabsorbed into the blood, concentrating the filtrate.

3. **Secretion.** Following concentration of the filtrate, the substances not needed by the body are excreted in the urine.

The amount of urine excreted each day depends on an individual's fluid intake and water loss (such as due to perspiration) and typically ranges from 0.7 to 2.0 liters. In controlling the amount of water excreted in urine or reabsorbed, the kidneys play an important role in preventing dehydration, even as fluid consumption and fluid loss may vary tremendously from day to day.

The filtering of blood by the kidneys begins as blood flows into blood vessels within each kidney via a renal artery. The filtered blood leaves the kidney via a renal vein, while waste products isolated during filtration and any excess water removed from the bloodstream pass to the bladder, and from there are excreted as urine (**FIGURE 20-24**).

A human has two kidneys, each about the size of a fist, located on either side of the spine, just above the waist. Each kidney is made up of approximately a million nephrons, the structural units that accomplish the work of the kidneys. A **nephron** consists of two basic components: a nephron tubule and a mass of blood vessels that work together to accomplish the tasks of filtration, reabsorption, and secretion (**FIGURE 20-25**). The blood-filtering unit of the nephron is a mass of capillaries called a **glomerulus,** and the ball-like structure that surrounds it is called **Bowman's capsule.** Each Bowman's capsule is connected

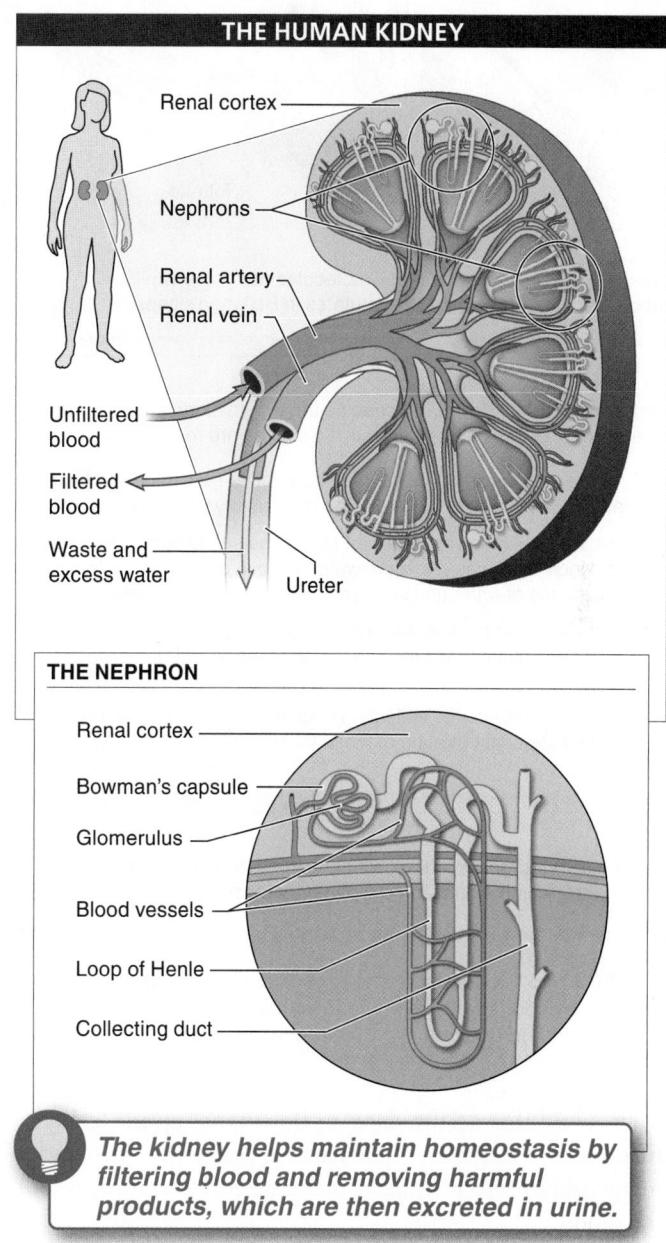

The kidney helps maintain homeostasis by filtering blood and removing harmful products, which are then excreted in urine.

FIGURE 20-24 Structure of the kidney. Human kidneys filter blood, reabsorb water and solutes, and excrete waste.

to a single, long, urine-producing tube that excretes its filtered fluid into a collecting duct.

The capillaries in the glomerulus are porous, and blood pressure forces out water and small molecules and ions (but not blood cells or most proteins) through the capillary

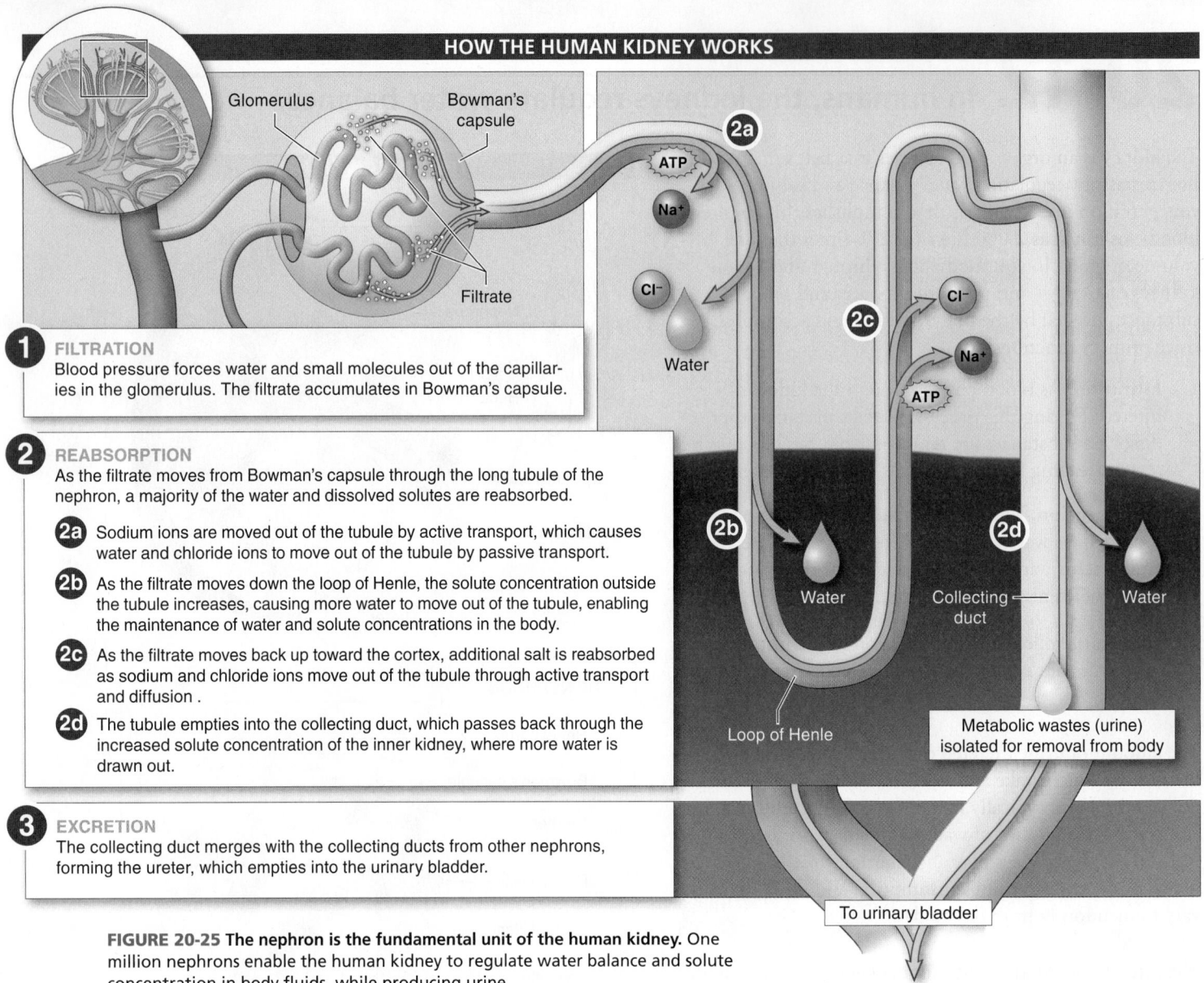

1 FILTRATION
Blood pressure forces water and small molecules out of the capillaries in the glomerulus. The filtrate accumulates in Bowman's capsule.

2 REABSORPTION
As the filtrate moves from Bowman's capsule through the long tubule of the nephron, a majority of the water and dissolved solutes are reabsorbed.

2a Sodium ions are moved out of the tubule by active transport, which causes water and chloride ions to move out of the tubule by passive transport.

2b As the filtrate moves down the loop of Henle, the solute concentration outside the tubule increases, causing more water to move out of the tubule, enabling the maintenance of water and solute concentrations in the body.

2c As the filtrate moves back up toward the cortex, additional salt is reabsorbed as sodium and chloride ions move out of the tubule through active transport and diffusion .

2d The tubule empties into the collecting duct, which passes back through the increased solute concentration of the inner kidney, where more water is drawn out.

3 EXCRETION
The collecting duct merges with the collecting ducts from other nephrons, forming the ureter, which empties into the urinary bladder.

FIGURE 20-25 The nephron is the fundamental unit of the human kidney. One million nephrons enable the human kidney to regulate water balance and solute concentration in body fluids, while producing urine.

walls. Fluid that accumulates in Bowman's capsule, called **filtrate,** contains salts, sugars, amino acids, vitamins, and many other molecules, all at the same concentration as in the blood.

As the filtrate moves from Bowman's capsule through the urine-collecting tubule of the nephron, the vast majority of its water and dissolved solutes must be reabsorbed. In fact, of the 2,000 liters of blood that pass through the kidneys each day, only about 1.5 liters of urine are produced and excreted.

Reabsorption in the long tubule of the nephron is a complex process. It begins with the active transport of sodium ions out of the tubule, which causes water and chloride ions to follow, moving out by passive transport.

The tubule (and the filtrate it contains) then loops from the outer part of the kidney, called the cortex (see Figure 20-24), down into the innermost part of the kidney and back again, in a path called the loop of Henle. As the tubule passes to the innermost part of the kidney, it encounters a higher solute concentration in the interstitial fluid, outside the tube. This creates an osmotic gradient, which causes more and more water to be drawn out of the tubule, moving from the filtrate into the interstitial fluid.

Then, as the filtrate moves up toward the kidney cortex again, more salt is lost, through diffusion and active transport. From the cortex, the tubule passes into the collecting duct, which passes through the innermost part of the kidney again, returning additional water to the interstitial fluid and further concentrating the urine for excretion. The collecting duct eventually merges with collecting ducts from other nephrons, forming the ureter, which empties into the urinary bladder. From the bladder, urine passes through the urethra and is excreted from the body.

Q

Why do some desert mammals never need to drink water?

Filtering the blood and producing urine not only follows a complicated path but is very energetically expensive. Considerable amounts of energy are expended in the active transport of solutes that leads to the recovery of water. Nonetheless, some animals, such as kangaroo rats, are so efficient at reabsorbing water that they can recover nearly all of the water filtered by their kidneys. They never have to drink water at all; the water contained in their food and the water generated as a by-product during cellular respiration are sufficient.

Among the most important of the metabolic waste products that must be filtered and removed from the blood by the kidneys are those containing nitrogen. Produced from the breakdown of proteins and nucleic acids, this nitrogen tends to be in the form of ammonia, which is generally very toxic to organisms. Some organisms—mostly aquatic organisms— are able to rid their bodies of excess nitrogen by simply excreting the ammonia. Terrestrial animals (and many marine animals), however, cannot consume sufficient water to keep ammonia diluted enough so that it is not toxic. Instead, these organisms combine ammonia with carbon dioxide to produce urea, which can be stored for longer periods of time and at higher concentrations (thereby requiring much less water). There is a cost to this system, however; the production of urea from ammonia and carbon dioxide is energetically expensive. Besides ammonia and urea, there is a third form in which nitrogenous wastes can be excreted, as a paste called uric acid. This method requires even less water than urea excretion, but is even more energetically expensive. It is used by insects, terrestrial snails, birds, and many reptiles.

The human kidneys are so effective at filtering blood and concentrating the many waste products of metabolism in urine that it is possible to detect the use of many drugs through urinalysis. Most drug-screening urinalysis does not actually involve testing for the presence of the drugs themselves, which may remain in the body for only a short

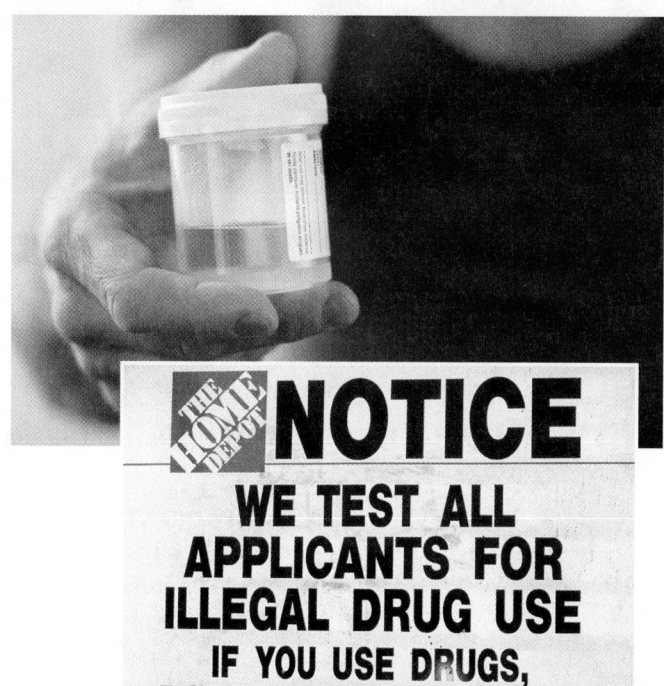

FIGURE 20-26 Detectable remainders. Drugs break down into metabolites, chemicals that sometimes linger in the body and can be detected in the urine.

time. Instead, the tests look for the presence of chemicals, called metabolites, that result from breakdown of the drugs (**FIGURE 20-26**). Metabolites have been identified for many drugs, including Ecstasy, cocaine, methamphetamines, and marijuana. In the case of marijuana, the metabolites are fat-soluble. This means that they are stored in fat cells indefinitely and released only when fat from those cells is metabolized for energy. As a consequence, marijuana can be detected a month or longer after the last use.

Q

How can some drugs be detected by urinalysis even months after the last intake?

TAKE-HOME MESSAGE 20·12

The kidney is the organ in vertebrates that helps maintain homeostasis by regulating water balance and solute concentrations in body fluids, filtering blood, and removing potentially harmful ions and metabolic waste products, excreting them in the urine.

YOUR BODY SOMETIMES DELIBERATELY UPSETS HOMEOSTASIS. (And you might not want to fight it.)

Q: WHAT DO YOU USUALLY DO WHEN YOU HAVE A FEVER? At the first sign of fever, many people take aspirin, Tylenol, Advil, or Motrin.

Q: WHAT IS THE RESULT? Aspirin, acetaminophen (Tylenol), and ibuprofen (Advil and Motrin) quickly reduce a fever.

Q: WHY DID YOU HAVE A FEVER? Generally, fever is not itself an illness. Rather, it is your body's response to cues that there is a bacterial or viral infection. In response to infection, your temperature set point is raised, because pathogens are more easily brought under control by the body's defenses at higher temperatures. (Ectotherms use a similar strategy, moving to warmer areas when they have an infection!)

Q: HOW DOES REDUCING A FEVER INTERFERE WITH YOUR BODY'S DEFENSES? Blocking a fever by taking aspirin or other medication may reduce your body's ability to fight infection. A recent well-controlled study demonstrated, for example, that chicken pox lasts longer, on average, when aspirin is used to treat it, compared with placebo.

Q: IS THE LESSON HERE ABOUT MORE THAN FEVER? Yes. There are other "symptoms" of infection that, as defenses rather than part of the illness itself, maybe shouldn't be fought. For example: (1) *Coughing:* the use of codeine to block coughing after surgery increases the risk of pneumonia; the coughing is *helpful.* (2) *Diarrhea:* anti-diarrhea medications delay recovery and slow the eradication of bacteria from the digestive tract; the diarrhea is *helpful.* (3) *Vomiting* and *inflammation,* too, appear to be important parts of our evolved defenses and, as such, blocking them can have serious health consequences.

WHAT CAN YOU CONCLUDE? *Is this the dawn of Darwinian medicine?* This new perspective on when to treat and when not to treat symptoms is called "Darwinian medicine." It represents a newfound appreciation for the fact that many protective responses have evolved that may be useful to the organism. Of course, suffering is not always the solution. There can be real costs to vomiting, diarrhea, coughing, fever, and other body defenses. Opting not to treat them isn't necessarily the best solution if, for example, antibiotics can bring an infection under control easily. Either way, bringing an evolutionary perspective to medical decision making can be valuable.

Big Ideas in ... Introduction to Animal Physiology

20·1–20·6 Animal body structures reflect their functions.

- At all levels of animal organization, from molecules to whole organisms, the physical features of a structure are closely related to its function.

- Cells with similar structure and function are organized into groups, called tissues, that work together. There are four types of tissue: connective tissue, epithelial tissue, muscle tissue, and nervous tissue.

- In nearly all animals, some tissues are organized into organs that serve specialized functions and consist of multiple tissue types, and organs into organ systems that carry out the various physiological processes necessary for growth, development, maintenance, and reproduction.

20·7–20·8 Animals have an internal environment.

- Failure to maintain a consistent internal environment can lead to multiple problems in the normal functioning of cells, tissues, and organs, and can result in death.

- Organisms maintain a variety of internal physiological variables—including temperature, water-solute balances, pH, blood sugar levels, and blood gas concentrations—within relatively constant ranges. The process of maintaining an organism's internal environment is called homeostasis.

20·9–20·12 How does homeostasis work?

- Organisms generally maintain homeostasis through negative feedback, in which sensors detect a change in the internal environment and trigger structures, called effectors, to oppose or reduce the change.

- For animals to maintain homeostasis, the variable must have a set point, a target value or range to which the organism can return.

- Methods for controlling temperature, blood sugar levels, and water and solute concentrations, among many other variables, are important components of homeostasis.

- To maintain osmotic balance, organisms must be able to take up water and get rid of water, and must also be able to regulate concentrations of ions in their fluids. The kidney is the organ in vertebrates that helps maintain homeostasis by regulating water balance and solute concentration in body fluids, filtering blood, and removing potentially harmful ions and metabolic waste products and excreting them in urine.

See the To-Go Guide (packaged with every new copy of this textbook) for an illustrated summary of the chapter.

Check Your Knowledge

1. Is the body temperature of cats influenced by the ambient temperature? Provide data to support your answer.

2. What would you expect the lizard body temperature to be when the ambient temperature is 10° C? Why?

3. What is the unit of measure for metabolic rate? Is the rate higher in cats or lizards?

4. Body weight in cats is typically much greater than in lizards. How is this difference accounted for in the lower graph?

5. In lizards, what is the percentage increase in metabolic rate between 27° and 36° C? What is the percentage increase for cats across that range?

6. Suggest a way to re-plot these data that would better highlight the greater rate of increase in the metabolic rate of lizards relative to cats between 27° and 36° C. What is a drawback of your alternative version of the graph?

7. Based on this graph, what is meant by the phrase "thermoneutral zone"? Is there a thermoneutral zone for lizards? Why or why not?

8. From the perspective of relative metabolic costs, under what conditions is it more efficient to be an endotherm? Under what conditions is it more efficient to be an ectotherm?

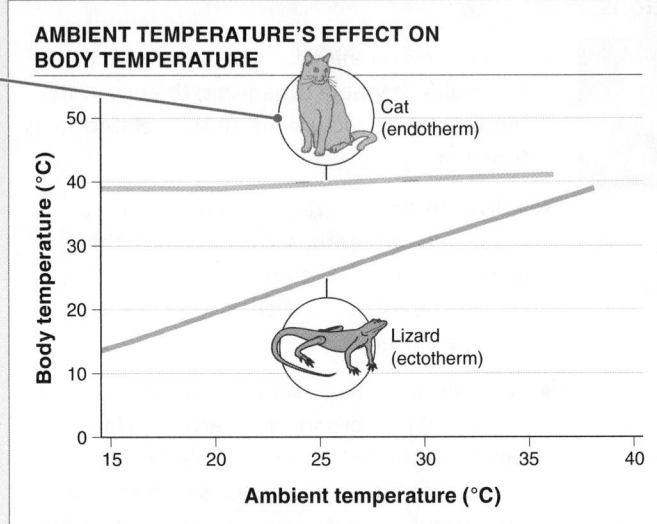

AMBIENT TEMPERATURE'S EFFECT ON BODY TEMPERATURE

AMBIENT TEMPERATURE'S EFFECT ON METABOLIC RATE

See Answers at the back of the book.

Key Terms in Introduction to Animal Physiology

axon, p. 774
blood, p. 770
bone, p. 770
Bowman's capsule, p. 789
cardiac muscle, p. 773
cartilage, p. 770
cell body, p. 774
central nervous system, p. 775
collagen, p. 769
conformer, p. 782
connective tissue, p. 767
connective tissue proper, p. 769
dendrite, p. 774
ectotherms, p. 783
effector, p. 781

elastin, p. 769
endocrine gland, p. 772
endotherms, p. 783
epithelial tissue, p. 767
epithelium, p. 771
exocrine gland, p. 772
extracellular fluid, p. 779
filtrate, p. 790
gland, p. 772
glial cells, p. 775
glomerulus, p. 789
heat stroke, p. 778
heterotherm, p. 785
hibernate, p. 784
homeostasis, p. 779

homeotherm, p. 785
hyperthermia, p. 778
hypothermia, p. 779
interstitial fluid, p. 779
ligament, p. 770
matrix, p. 767
muscle fiber, p. 772
muscle tissue, p. 767
negative feedback, p. 781
nephron, p. 789
nervous tissue, p. 767
neuroglia, p. 775
neuron, p. 774
organ, p. 767
organ system, p. 768

osmoconformer, p. 787
osmoregulation, p. 787
osmoregulator, p. 787
peripheral nervous system, p. 775
physiology, p. 779
positive feedback, p. 782
regulator, p. 782
set point, p. 781
skeletal muscle, p. 772
smooth muscle, p. 773
special connective tissue, p. 770
tendon, p. 770
thermoneutral zone, p. 783
thermoregulation, p. 783
tissue, p. 767

Multiple-Choice Questions

1. **"Form follows function" refers to the fact that:**

   a) organisms' physical structures often are adaptations, shaped by natural selection, and so reflect their physiological functions.

   b) organisms' physical structures generally come to reflect their physiological function only *after* that function has been fine-tuned by evolution.

   c) natural selection can produce adaptations in physical structures but not in physiological processes.

   d) natural selection can produce adaptations in physiological processes but not in physical structures.

   e) all structures that have the same function also have the same structure.

   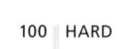
   100 HARD
   54
   0 EASY

2. **Which of the following is not a type of connective tissue?**

   a) bone
   b) cartilage
   c) blood
   d) collagen
   e) ligament

   100 HARD
   50
   0 EASY

3. **Epithelium plays all of the following roles in organisms except:**

   a) secretion.
   b) transport.
   c) protection.
   d) preventing leakage of fluids from an organ system into surrounding tissue.
   e) cushioning, lubricating, and insulating other tissue.

   100 HARD
   36
   0 EASY

4. **Smooth muscle:**

   a) is usually attached to bones.
   b) generates slow, rhythmic contractions.
   c) is usually under conscious control.
   d) generally contains more mitochondria than cardiac or skeletal muscle.
   e) All of the above are correct.

   100 HARD
   25
   0 EASY

5. Neurons generally have all of the following components except:

a) dendrites.

b) a cell body.

c) an axon.

d) glial processes.

e) a nucleus.

100 HARD

29

0 EASY

6. With the exception of _____, all animals have some tissues organized into organs.

a) sponges and some cnidarians

b) insects

c) roundworms and flatworms

d) sponges and insects

e) amphibians

100 HARD

41

0 EASY

7. The term "homeostasis" describes:

a) the body's use of physical and chemical processes to maintain a consistent internal environment.

b) the biochemical processes associated with the maintenance of body temperature.

c) the metabolic patterns of active (versus stationary) animals.

d) the metabolic patterns of stationary (versus active) animals.

e) the health benefits of a sedentary lifestyle.

100 HARD

21

0 EASY

8. Interstitial fluid:

a) is found exclusively within the spinal cord, surrounding the nerve bundles.

b) is found exclusively within the skull, surrounding the brain.

c) is mostly water.

d) is found exclusively within the skull and spinal cord, surrounding nervous tissue.

e) occurs within the organelles of all eukaryotic cells.

100 HARD

23

0 EASY

9. Negative feedback loops:

a) generally lead to highly unstable internal physiological conditions.

b) cause internal conditions to deviate from the normal range.

c) are part of larger, positive feedback systems.

d) rely on sensors to trigger effectors to alter an organism's internal environment.

e) None of the above.

100 HARD

38

0 EASY

10. A set point:

a) is the target value or range for a physiological variable, to which it generally returns following perturbation.

b) is a physiological state that occurs in animals called "conformers," but not in "regulators."

c) can occur in fishes but not in terrestrial animals.

d) is the target value or range for a physiological variable regulated through positive feedback, but not negative feedback.

e) Both a) and c) are correct.

100 HARD

44

0 EASY

11. It is not necessarily accurate to refer to endotherms as "warm-blooded," because:

a) some endotherms allow their body temperature to drop significantly during hibernation.

b) on average, their body temperature is colder than that of "cold-blooded" animals.

c) they generate their heat primarily within their own bodies.

d) most do not actually have blood in their bodies.

e) some are homeotherms rather than heterotherms.

100 HARD

50

0 EASY

Short-Answer Questions

1. What is the hierarchical organization of cells in a multicellular organism? Name the four types of tissue they form, and note their general functions.

2. What are the two kinds of connective tissue? What are their general characteristics?

3. What are the three types of muscle tissue? What are their general characteristics?

4. What is homeostasis? How does hyperthermia illustrate the failure of the body to maintain homeostasis? What are the potential consequences of this failure?

See Answers at the back of the book.
For additional study questions, go to www.prep-u.com.

Transporting fuel, raw
materials, and gases into,
out of, and around the body

Circulation and Respiration

21·1–21·3
The circulatory system is the chief route of distribution in animals.

The rhino needs a strong muscular heart to pump blood through its massive body.

21·1

What is a circulatory system, and why is one needed?

Size matters. When life first arose on earth, the tiny, single-celled organisms were small enough to acquire fuel and raw materials in a straightforward way: those materials could simply diffuse across the cell membrane and be used as needed. Similarly, metabolic waste products could diffuse out of the cell. Today, single-celled organisms and small multicellular organisms in which all cells are in contact with (or just a few cells away from) the external environment acquire raw materials and dispose of metabolic waste in this same way.

The evolution of large body sizes opened up a world of new niches in which organisms could live. Physiologically, however, large body sizes created a host of new challenges. With increasing size, most of an animal's cells were no longer in direct contact with the outside world, the environment from which the animal obtained the oxygen, nutrients, water, and other substances it needed to survive. Consequently, essential substances could no longer just

diffuse in, and waste products could no longer diffuse out adequately. As body size increased, dedicated delivery and removal systems became a necessity.

In animals, the primary distribution system is the circulatory system, which consists of tens of thousands of miles of hollow, tube-like vessels that reach all tissues of the body. In vertebrates, circulatory systems have three principal functions: transport, body temperature regulation, and protection (**FIGURE 21-1**).

1. Transport. Like a system of highways for delivering important goods and removing garbage, the circulatory system transports oxygen, nutrients, waste products, hormones, and immune system cells in the blood throughout the body.

- In vertebrates, blood vessels take oxygen from the lungs or gills and deliver it to the tissues for energy-releasing cellular respiration. Blood arriving from the

TRANSPORT
The circulatory system transports oxygen, nutrients, waste products, immune system cells, and hormones in the blood throughout the body.

TEMPERATURE REGULATION
The circulatory system helps to maintain body temperature within the optimum range for metabolic functioning.

PROTECTION
The circulatory system contains a variety of cells and chemicals that contribute to the individual's defenses against infection by pathogens.

FIGURE 21-1 Like a set of highways for the body. Circulatory system functions: transport, temperature regulation, and protection. Shown here: penis blood vessels; black-tailed jackrabbit; white blood cell phagocytosing *E. coli* on the outer surface of a lung blood vessel.

lungs or gills is loaded with oxygen and is said to be oxygenated or oxygen-rich.

- Simultaneously, blood vessels whisk away carbon dioxide and other metabolic wastes that are produced by cellular respiration and other cell processes and must be removed from the body. Blood that carries a lot of carbon dioxide is said to be deoxygenated or oxygen-poor.

- Once food particles are digested, the nutrients must be absorbed and delivered to all the tissues of the body, for activity, growth, and reproduction.

- The circulatory system delivers hormones (chemicals produced throughout the body by glands and other tissues) to target tissues to regulate growth, development, and reproduction.

2. Body temperature regulation. By expanding or contracting the blood vessels closest to the exterior of the body, animals can release or absorb (or at least minimize

the loss of) heat, a process that helps maintain body temperature within the optimum range for metabolism.

3. Protection. A variety of cells and chemicals contribute to the individual's defenses against infection by pathogens. White blood cells, or leukocytes, have the ability to engulf and destroy many disease-causing microorganisms. Platelets and certain chemicals in the blood provide protection by limiting blood loss and infection when the skin or other tissues are damaged.

TAKE-HOME MESSAGE 21·1

In animals, the circulatory system is the chief distribution system. It transports gases, nutrients, waste products, hormones, and immune system cells to and from tissues throughout the body. The circulatory system also helps animals regulate their body temperature and protect against infection.

21·2 Circulatory systems can be open or closed.

There's more than one way to build a circulatory system. And, in fact, not all multicellular organisms even need a circulatory system. In spite of their relatively large size and multicellularity, for example, flatworms, as well as jellyfish

and other cnidarians, have a body plan that gives every cell easy access to oxygen and nutrients through simple diffusion (**FIGURE 21-2**). This access is possible because every cell is close to the external surface of the cnidarian's body or to its

CIRCULATORY SYSTEMS AREN'T ALWAYS NECESSARY

Some animals, such as jellyfish and other cnidarians, do not have circulatory systems. Instead, they obtain oxygen and nutrients, and eliminate waste, through diffusion.

External surface
Gastrovascular cavity

Oxygen and nutrients diffusing into cells

Waste products diffusing out of cells

Mouth

Nutrient- and oxygen-rich fluid
Nutrient- and oxygen-poor fluid

Cells have easy access to oxygen and nutrients via diffusion because each cell is located close to the external surface of the body or the gastrovascular cavity.

FIGURE 21-2 No circulatory system required.

CIRCULATORY SYSTEMS

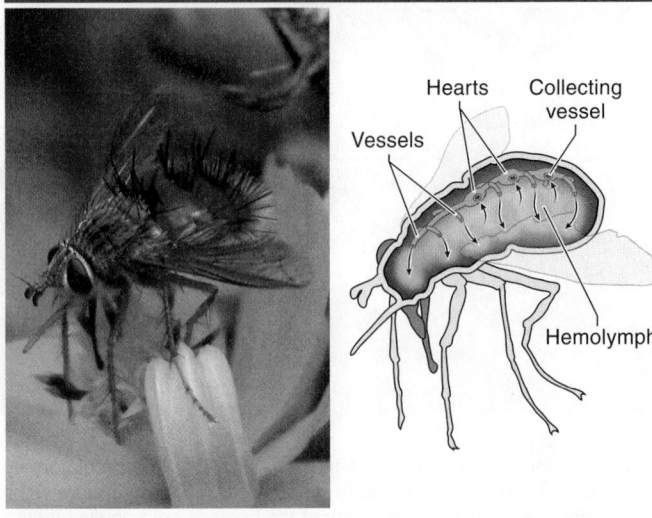

Hearts   Collecting vessel

Vessels

Hemolymph

OPEN CIRCULATORY SYSTEM
- No clear distinction between the circulating fluid and interstitial fluid
- Heart(s) pump the fluid mixture—called hemolymph—throughout the extracellular spaces inside the body
- Occurs in insects and most mollusks

Vessels

Heart

CLOSED CIRCULATORY SYSTEM
- Blood is contained within vessels that separate it from interstitial fluid
- Muscular heart propels blood through vessels to tissues throughout the body
- Occurs in all vertebrates

FIGURE 21-3 There are open and closed circulatory systems.

internal gastrovascular cavity. Although the gastrovascular cavity is not a true circulatory system, it serves many digestive ("gastro") and circulatory ("vascular") functions by directing water into the central mouth and through an elaborate system of channels. Cells lining the mouth and the channels can absorb nutrients and exchange gases by diffusion. The nutrients then diffuse to other cells, none of which are very

far away. Once nutrients have been extracted (and waste products picked up), fluid in the gastrovascular cavity is flushed back out of the mouth, and the process is repeated.

Among other multicellular animals, there are two distinct types of circulatory systems: open and closed (**FIGURE 21-3**). Open circulatory systems are found in insects and most mollusks, and closed circulatory systems are found in all vertebrates. The defining feature of an **open circulatory system** is that it has one fluid, called **hemolymph,** that not only circulates to transport nutrients, gases, and waste products but also surrounds each cell in the body. In other words, there is no clear distinction between the circulating fluid and the **interstitial fluid,** the fluid outside the cells that bathes all the body tissues. There is a heart (or sometimes many hearts!) that pumps the hemolymph, but it essentially squirts the fluid throughout the extracellular spaces. Large collecting vessels then channel the hemolymph back to the heart, where it can be pumped throughout the body again. These collecting vessels have little valves that close when the heart pumps, preventing the hemolymph from being pumped back through the same vessel from which it was collected. This one-way collection system gives some order to the circulation of hemolymph throughout the organism's body.

In **closed circulatory systems,** the circulating fluid—called **blood**—is always contained in a vessel as it is pumped throughout the animal's body, and it is physically and chemically separated from the interstitial fluid that bathes each cell. A muscular **heart** serves as a pump, and with each contraction it propels blood at high pressure through vessels called **arteries.** Like a highway system with numerous exits and connecting roads, the arteries branch extensively so that blood can be delivered to all the tissues of the body.

At the organs and tissues, arteries branch into thousands upon thousands of ever-smaller vessels, eventually becoming the narrowest and thinnest-walled, the **capillaries.** The thin walls of the capillaries allow gases, nutrients, and other molecules to diffuse easily into and out of the tissue, down their concentration gradients (**FIGURE 21-4**). After passing through the capillaries, blood returns to the heart in vessels called **veins,** which increase in diameter as they near the

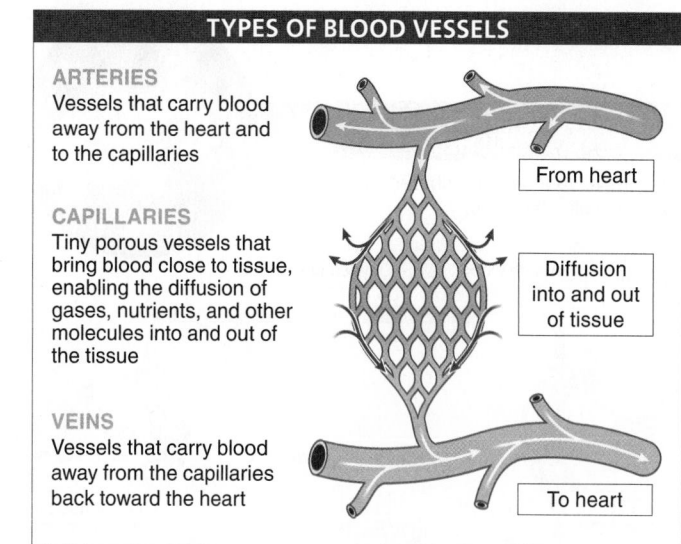

TYPES OF BLOOD VESSELS

ARTERIES
Vessels that carry blood away from the heart and to the capillaries

From heart

CAPILLARIES
Tiny porous vessels that bring blood close to tissue, enabling the diffusion of gases, nutrients, and other molecules into and out of the tissue

Diffusion into and out of tissue

VEINS
Vessels that carry blood away from the capillaries back toward the heart

To heart

FIGURE 21-4 Blood flows from arteries to capillaries to veins.

heart. We discuss the structure and function of blood vessels in more detail in Section 21-6.

TAKE-HOME MESSAGE 21·2

Animals (such as flatworms and cnidarians) that can acquire all the nutrients and oxygen they need by diffusion do not have circulatory systems. Among animals that do have circulatory systems, the system can be open, with no clear distinction between the circulating fluid and the interstitial fluid that bathes tissues, or closed, with a clear distinction. In closed circulatory systems, the circulating fluid (blood) and interstitial fluid surrounding cells and tissues are kept completely separate.

21·3 Vertebrates have several different types of closed circulatory systems.

Among the vertebrates, there are several variations of the closed circulatory system. These variations evolved in concert with numerous dramatic adaptations that accompanied and made possible the transition from life in the seas to life on land. As some vertebrates developed lungs and the ability to extract oxygen from the air rather than water, their circulatory systems increased in complexity. Here we give a broad overview of the structures and functions of the various types of closed circulatory systems. In the

sections that follow, we discuss the components of these systems (heart, blood vessels, blood) in more detail.

In fishes, the flow of blood follows a circular path (**FIGURE 21-5**). In tracing its flow, we can begin with the two-chambered heart. Blood first passes into the **atrium,** the collecting chamber, and from there is pumped into the **ventricle,** the chamber from which blood is pumped to the gills. Blood flows through the gills, where it picks up

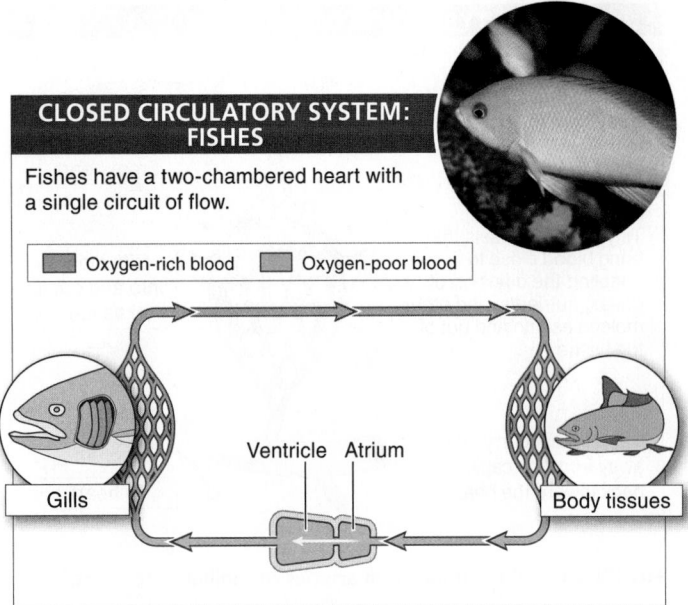

FIGURE 21-5 Blood flow in fishes.

oxygen. The friction the blood encounters as it flows through the millions of blood vessels in the gills causes the blood to lose most of the pressure it had as it was pumped from the heart. From the gills, the blood flows to the tissues of the body, delivering the oxygen. After passing through the body tissues, the oxygen-poor blood flows back to the heart, and the cycle begins again as that blood is pumped to the gills.

In contrast to the two-chambered heart of fishes, birds and mammals have a four-chambered heart with two atria and two ventricles (**FIGURE 21-6**). Twice as many chambers are required because, rather than having a single circuit of flow, birds and mammals have two circuits of flow. The two circuits can be visualized as a figure 8: oxygen-poor blood flows through the body into the right atrium and through to the right ventricle (see Figure 21-6). From there it is pumped out to the lungs, where it picks up oxygen, and then it returns to the heart. This first circuit of blood flow, between the heart and the lungs, is called the **pulmonary circuit.**

The oxygen-rich blood that returns from the lungs to the heart collects in the left atrium. The blood immediately passes into the muscular left ventricle and from there is pumped at great pressure to the rest of the body. After passing through the body and delivering its nutrients and oxygen to body tissues, the now oxygen-poor blood travels back to the right atrium, and the cycle begins again. This second circuit of blood flow, between the heart and the rest of the body, is called the **systemic circuit.**

Mammalian and bird hearts vary widely in size—from hummingbird hearts no bigger than a pencil eraser to blue whale hearts, which are bigger than a small car and pump 25 gallons with every beat. Regardless of size, all of these hearts share the same basic layout. And almost always, because the left ventricle has to pump blood to the entire body rather than just to the lungs, the left ventricle becomes much larger and more muscular than the right ventricle.

Q The left side of mammalian and bird hearts is always bigger than the right. Why?

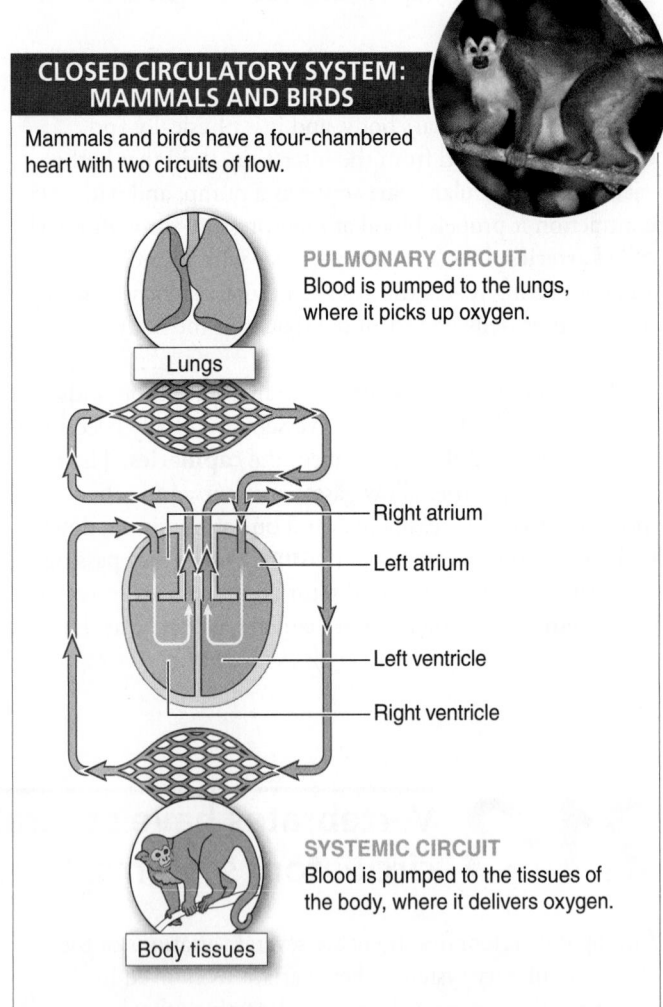

FIGURE 21-6 Blood flow in mammals and birds. Note that the right side of the animal's heart is on the left side in this diagram, and the left side is on the right. This is because drawings of the heart are made as if the animal were facing you.

PULMONARY CIRCUIT
Blood is pumped to the lungs, where it picks up oxygen.

Lungs

Right atrium

Left atrium

Ventricle

SYSTEMIC CIRCUIT
Blood is pumped to the tissues of the body, where it delivers oxygen.

Body tissues

FIGURE 21-7 Blood flow in amphibians.

greater amounts of oxygen delivered to the muscles and organs. Nonetheless, the large number and diversity of fishes on earth suggests that they have been able to thrive with their single-circuit system.

Amphibians have circulatory systems that are similar, but not identical, to the mammalian and bird systems (**FIGURE 21-7**). They have two circuits of flow, but have hearts with only three chambers rather than four. Blood from the lungs and from the rest of the body collects in the left and right atria, respectively, but it then flows into a single ventricle. Surprisingly, though, little mixing of the oxygenated blood from the lungs and the deoxygenated blood from the rest of the body occurs in the ventricle. Rather, the two types of blood flow side by side and are pumped into arteries, vessels that direct the oxygenated blood to the body and the deoxygenated blood to the lungs.

With the exception of birds, most reptiles also have three-chambered hearts, although the ventricle is partially divided into two. In one group of reptiles (the crocodilians), however, the division is complete; they also have an extra little artery through which blood can be pumped from the right ventricle to the rest of the body rather than to the lungs. This extra artery is an adaptation that allows the crocodile to bypass sending blood to the lungs when the animal is underwater. There is no sense in pumping blood to the lungs if there is no oxygen to be picked up there. Instead, the blood is sent back to the body, where the remaining oxygen in the blood can be utilized.

With two circuits of flow, mammalian and bird hearts are better than fish hearts at delivering oxygen to body tissues. In fishes, as we learned earlier, all the oxygenated blood flowing to the body has low pressure and velocity, because it passes first through the blood vessels in the gills. With the two circuits of flow in birds and mammals, all the oxygenated blood flowing to body tissues is at higher pressure, because it is pumped directly from the left ventricle and does not first pass through the pressure-robbing blood vessels of the lungs. This makes it possible for bird and mammalian hearts to sustain greater levels of activity, with

TAKE-HOME MESSAGE 21·3

Vertebrates' circulatory systems vary in structure. Fishes have two-chambered hearts, with one circuit of flow: from the heart through the gills through the body and back to the heart. Birds and mammals have four-chambered hearts and two circuits of flow: from the heart to the lungs and back to the heart, then from the heart to the body and back to the heart. This enables blood to be pumped to the body at higher pressure. Amphibians and most reptiles have a three-chambered heart and two circuits of blood flow.

21·4–21·10
The human circulatory system consists of a heart, blood vessels, and blood.

Red blood cells are packed in a capillary.

21·4
Blood flows through the four chambers of the human heart.

Clench your fist. That is the size of your heart. Now clench it and relax it a hundred thousand times. That is what you require your heart to do, every day, as it beats for 70 or more years. The human heart is at the center of our circulatory system, and it's one of the most durable and reliable pumps ever produced (**FIGURE 21-8**).

In our earlier overview of the circulatory system, we saw that the four-chambered heart sends blood on a figure 8, two-circuit path through the body, sending all blood first to the lungs for loading up with oxygen and then, on its second circuit, to the tissues and organs. Let's explore the workings of this heart, tracing the flow of blood as it cycles through the heart, lungs, and tissues of the body (**FIGURE 21-9**). We start with the arrival of oxygen-depleted blood from the organs and tissues. (The various types of blood vessels involved in the system are described in more detail in Section 21-6.)

1. Deoxygenated blood from the organs and tissues enters the right atrium. The blood arriving from the lower half of the body enters through a large vein called the

FIGURE 21-8 Heart and blood vessels. An overview of the human circulatory system.

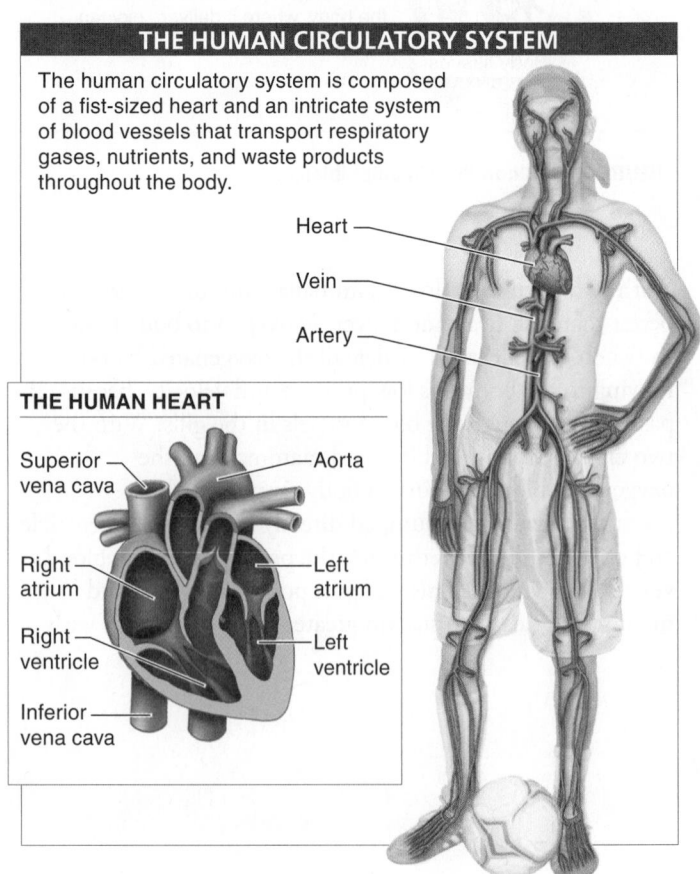

THE HUMAN CIRCULATORY SYSTEM

The human circulatory system is composed of a fist-sized heart and an intricate system of blood vessels that transport respiratory gases, nutrients, and waste products throughout the body.

Heart

Vein

Artery

THE HUMAN HEART

Superior vena cava

Aorta

Right atrium

Left atrium

Right ventricle

Left ventricle

Inferior vena cava

1 Deoxygenated blood from the organs and tissues enters the right atrium.

2 Blood is pumped through the right atrium into the right ventricle.

3 Blood is pumped out of the right ventricle, through the pulmonary arteries, to the lungs.

4 As blood passes through the lungs, it picks up oxygen and loses carbon dioxide.

5 Oxygenated blood returns to the heart, arriving in the left atrium.

6 Blood is pumped through the left atrium into the left ventricle.

7 Blood is pumped out of the left ventricle, through the aorta, sending some blood to the arms and head and the remainder to the trunk and legs.

8 Depleted of oxygen after passing through the capillary beds of the head, trunk, and legs, the blood trickles in veins back to the heart.

FIGURE 21-9 The path of blood flow in the human body.

inferior vena cava. Blood arriving from the head and arms enters through the superior vena cava.

2. Most of the blood passes directly through the right atrium into the right ventricle. A contraction pushes the remainder of the blood in the right atrium into the right ventricle.

3. The contraction continues, pumping the blood out of the right ventricle and into the pulmonary artery. This large artery immediately forks, sending half of the blood to the left lung and half to the right lung.

4. As the blood passes through the pulmonary capillaries in the lungs, it picks up oxygen and loses carbon dioxide.

5. The oxygenated blood then enters the left and right pulmonary veins and returns to the left atrium of the heart.

6. Most of the blood passes directly through the left atrium and into the left ventricle. A contraction pushes the remaining blood from the left atrium into the left ventricle.

7. As the contraction continues, the oxygenated blood is pumped up and out of the ventricle at tremendous pressure into the aorta, the largest artery in the body. After making a sharp turn (called the aortic arch), the aorta forks and sends some blood to the arms and head and the remainder to the trunk and legs.

8. After passing through the capillary beds in the tissues of the head, arms, trunk, and legs, the blood moves at low pressure through the veins. This deoxygenated blood returns to the heart by way of the superior and inferior venae cavae and collects in the right atrium, and the cycle repeats.

If you place your ear on the center of someone's chest in a quiet room, you can hear the heart working. "Lub dup, lub dup, lub dup." Over and over, the same two sounds. These are the sounds that a doctor hears when using a stethoscope. What is the source? It's not the contraction of the heart. Surprisingly, the muscular contractions don't make much noise. Rather, the sounds come from two sets

of valves that help keep blood flowing in the proper direction (**FIGURE 21-10**).

The first set of valves is the atrioventricular (or AV) valves. Located between the atrium and ventricle on each side of the heart, these two valves allow blood to flow from the atrium to the ventricle. (The AV valve on the left side is also called the *mitral valve,* while the AV valve on the right side is also called the *tricuspid valve.*) But when the ventricle contracts, these flaps of tissue slam shut, preventing blood from being pushed back into the atria: "lub." With no other escape, the blood flows out through the pulmonary arteries on the right side and the aorta on the left. At these two primary exits from the heart are two more valves. These semilunar valves, so called because of their half-moon shape, close and prevent blood from flowing back into the ventricles: "dup."

When the atrioventricular or semilunar valves do not completely close, some blood can squirt back through them, flowing in the wrong direction. The blood moving backward through the valve can be heard, with a stethoscope, making a buzzing or swishing noise; these noises are called **heart murmurs.** Most heart murmurs are not life-threatening, and the individual suffers no ill effects.

Sometimes a doctor will hear additional sounds besides the "lub" and "dup" of normal heart valve functioning. What is the source of such heart murmurs?

THE SOUND OF A HEARTBEAT

The sounds of a heartbeat ("lub dup, lub dup, lub dup") come from two sets of valves that help keep blood flowing in the proper direction and, surprisingly, not from the heart's muscular contractions.

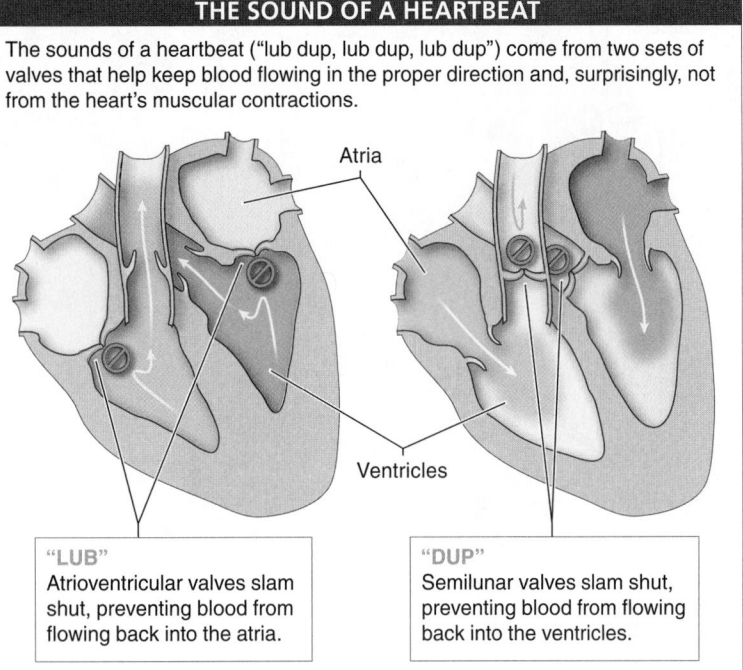

Atria

Ventricles

"LUB"
Atrioventricular valves slam shut, preventing blood from flowing back into the atria.

"DUP"
Semilunar valves slam shut, preventing blood from flowing back into the ventricles.

FIGURE 21-10 Audible heartbeats. Like doors slamming shut, the heart valves make noises that you can hear with your ear pressed to someone's chest.

TAKE-HOME MESSAGE 21·4

The human heart, at the center of our circulatory system, is an extremely durable pump. It sends blood on a figure 8, two-circuit path through the body, first to the lungs for loading up with oxygen and then, on its second circuit, to the tissues and organs of the body. Valves in the heart keep blood flowing in one direction.

21·5

Electrical activity in the heart generates the heartbeat.

Vertebrate hearts have a small piece of modified muscle tissue, the sinoatrial (SA) node, that initiates the regular, rhythmic contractions of the heart. Unlike most muscular tissue, which must be stimulated by a nerve before it contracts, the sinoatrial node spontaneously fires an

electrical impulse that initiates contractions in the heart muscle. It begins this spontaneous firing early in fetal development and continues to give rise to every heartbeat for your entire life. As the pacemaker of the heart, the SA node initiates a carefully choreographed muscle contraction

HEART CONTRACTION

In the heart, regular and rhythmic contractions initiated by the sinoatrial node can be measured using an electrocardiogram, or EKG.

1 Sinoatrial (SA) node fires and the contraction spreads to both atria.

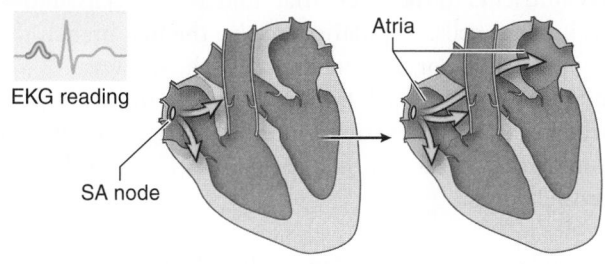

EKG reading

Atria

SA node

2 Wave of contraction passes down the center of the heart and bounces back up, causing the ventricles to contract.

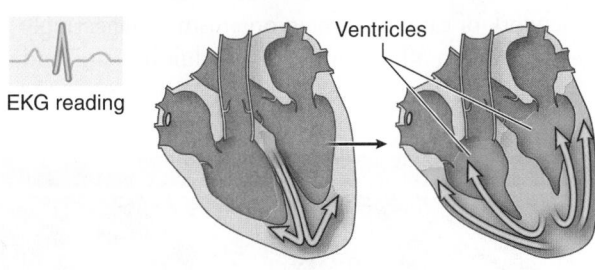

EKG reading

Ventricles

3 Ventricles relax and the process begins again.

EKG reading

As the pacemaker of the heart, the SA node is responsible for initiating the contractions that pump blood through the body.

FIGURE 21-11 Rhythmic contractions of the heart.

that results in the efficient pumping of blood to the lungs and to the rest of the body.

Beginning just above the right atrium, the electrical impulse in the SA node quickly spreads to the left atrium as well. As the atria contract, blood is pushed into the ventricles. The atria then enter a "relaxation" phase, and the wave of contraction continues, passing down the center of the heart and pausing briefly as it passes between the two ventricles. On reaching the bottom of the heart, the contraction appears to almost "bounce" back upward, causing a deep contraction that pushes the blood up from the bottom of both ventricles and into the pulmonary arteries (from the right ventricle) and the aorta (from the left ventricle), much like squeezing a tube of toothpaste from the bottom up. The ventricles then enter a relaxation phase, and the SA node starts the contraction anew (**FIGURE 21-11**).

Because the contraction of muscle tissue is a powerful electrical event, it can be recorded by electrodes placed on the skin that detect the changing electrical charges as the heart beats. The electrical signals are then traced into an electrocardiogram, or EKG (from the German *Elektrokardiogramm*). These readings allow quick and easy display and analysis of the cardiac cycle.

In some individuals, the sinoatrial node does not function properly or may have been damaged by infection. This malfunctioning can lead to a heartbeat that is too slow or erratic and can cause reduced blood flow, leading to problems such as fainting. An artificial pacemaker is a battery-operated electronic device that generates stimulation to the heart, causing a more regular heartbeat.

Q What is an artificial pacemaker?

TAKE-HOME MESSAGE 21·5

The sinoatrial node, modified muscle tissue in the vertebrate heart, initiates regular, rhythmic contractions. A heart contraction begins with an electrical impulse in the SA node in the right atrium. The contraction quickly spreads to the left atrium, passes down the center to the bottom of the heart, then moves upward, pushing blood from both ventricles out through the pulmonary arteries and aorta.

21·6

Blood flows out of and back to the heart in blood vessels.

Blood flows from the heart to the tissues of the body and back to the heart again through a series of blood vessels. There are three distinct types of blood vessels: arteries, capillaries, and veins (**FIGURE 21-12**).

1. Arteries. Leaving the heart, blood flows through arteries. The pulmonary arteries, arising from the right ventricle, carry deoxygenated blood to the lungs. The arteries arising from the left ventricle carry oxygenated blood, first to the aorta, then to the brain and the other tissues and organs of the body.

Arteries are lined with a sheet of endothelium (a type of epithelial tissue) and surrounded by smooth muscle and a layer of connective tissue. These layers of tissue, along with collagen and other, elastic connective tissue fibers, enable arteries to stretch, accommodating the high pressure generated by each beat of the heart, and then recoil, pushing the blood forward. The thickness of the artery walls is sufficient to minimize the exchange of materials between the blood and the tissues. Arteries branch repeatedly, becoming arterioles, which become smaller and smaller in diameter as they reach into all the tissues and organs. Blood then flows from the arterioles into capillaries.

2. Capillaries. The tiniest of blood vessels are the capillaries, which bring blood so close to all the cells of the body that diffusion can move the necessary molecules from the blood into the cells and from the cells into the blood. Each capillary has an inner diameter so narrow that blood cells must pass through in single file. In contrast to arteries, the walls of capillaries are thin—just a single layer of endothelial cells—and somewhat porous, permeable to water, ions, and some small molecules.

Capillaries are the last branch of the circulatory system to carry nutrients to the interstitial fluid around cells, and thus into the cells. Capillaries are also the first branch to carry nutrient-poor, carbon-dioxide-rich, and waste-product-rich blood back from cells toward the heart. Carbon dioxide and waste products diffuse from cells into the interstitial fluid and then through capillary walls and into the blood.

The capillaries are arranged in capillary beds, a network of vessels that supplies blood to tissues and organs. Although the diameter of capillaries is very tiny, cumulatively they have a much greater volume than the arterioles and arteries. The network of capillaries in an organism is staggeringly large—more than 50,000 miles in an adult human! And this

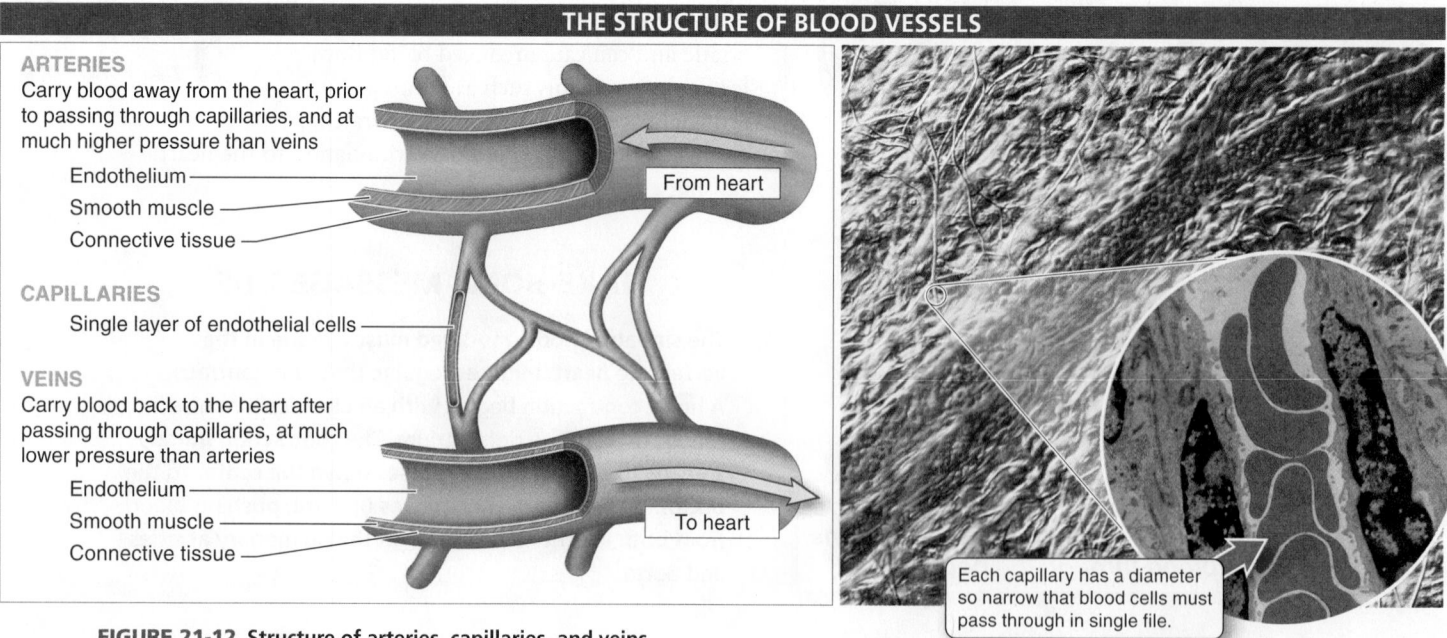

THE STRUCTURE OF BLOOD VESSELS

ARTERIES
Carry blood away from the heart, prior to passing through capillaries, and at much higher pressure than veins

Endothelium
Smooth muscle
Connective tissue

From heart

CAPILLARIES
Single layer of endothelial cells

VEINS
Carry blood back to the heart after passing through capillaries, at much lower pressure than arteries

Endothelium
Smooth muscle
Connective tissue

To heart

Each capillary has a diameter so narrow that blood cells must pass through in single file.

FIGURE 21-12 Structure of arteries, capillaries, and veins.

number is constantly in flux: the gain of a single pound of fat, for example, is accompanied by the addition of more than a mile of new capillaries. Surprisingly, the vast majority of the capillaries have little or no blood flowing through them at any given time, and the body is constantly directing blood flow to the tissues where it is most needed.

In this directing of blood flow through the circulatory system, capillaries play a key role. Consider this: when you go out in very cold weather, your face or hands may get very cold and may even turn bluish in color. Why does this

happen? Flow of blood in the capillaries is controlled by smooth muscle around the arterioles, the smaller vessels that branch off arteries and lead to capillaries. When these muscles, called precapillary sphincters, contract, blood flow can be cut off to capillaries and shunted elsewhere in the body (**FIGURE 21-13**). As a consequence of the activity of these muscles, bodies can reduce blood flow (and the heat it brings) to parts such as the face or hands when such blood flow could lead to excessive and energetically wasteful heat loss. (Simultaneously, these muscles enable the body to always direct blood to critical parts of the body, including the

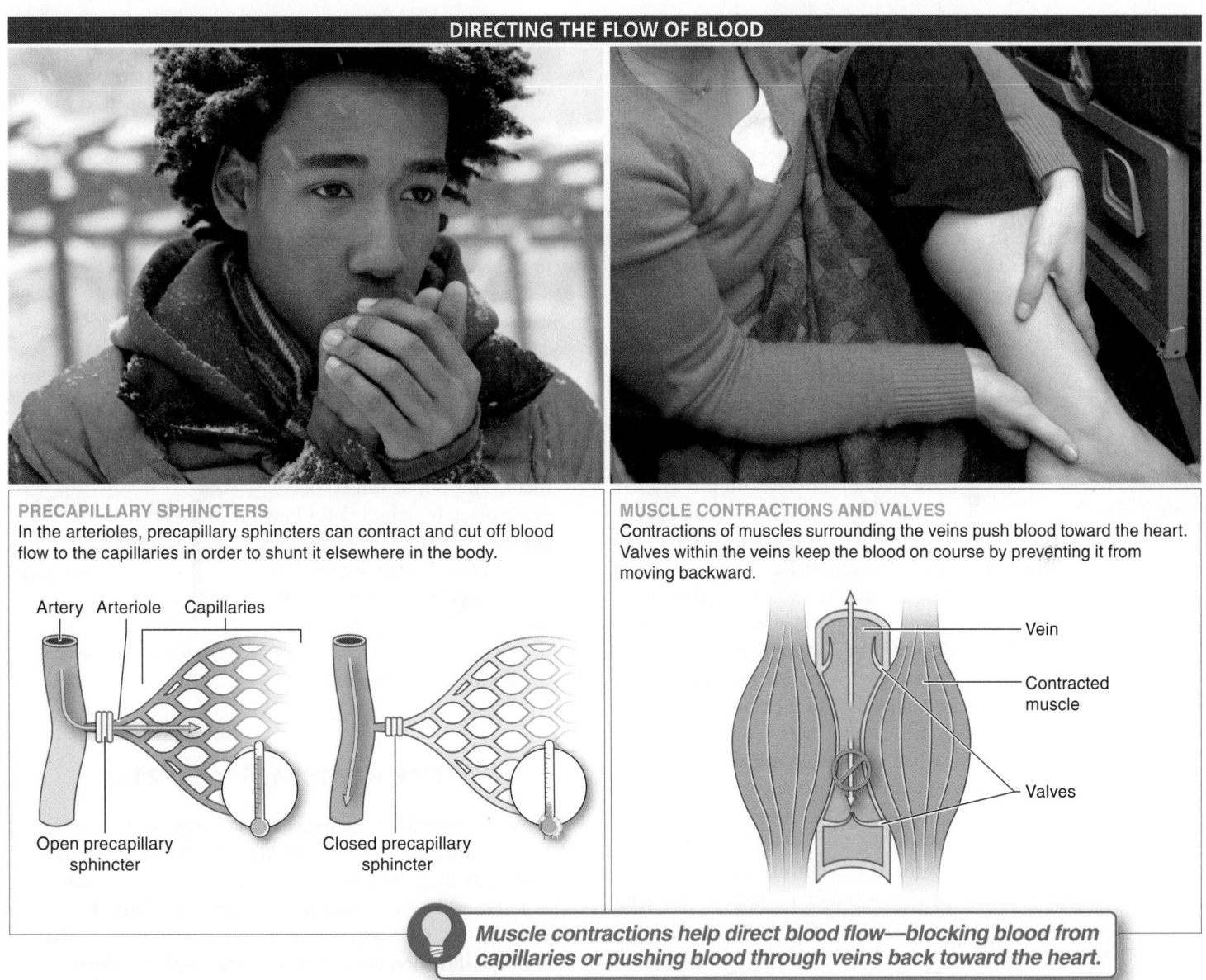

DIRECTING THE FLOW OF BLOOD

PRECAPILLARY SPHINCTERS
In the arterioles, precapillary sphincters can contract and cut off blood flow to the capillaries in order to shunt it elsewhere in the body.

Artery Arteriole Capillaries

Open precapillary sphincter

Closed precapillary sphincter

MUSCLE CONTRACTIONS AND VALVES
Contractions of muscles surrounding the veins push blood toward the heart. Valves within the veins keep the blood on course by preventing it from moving backward.

Vein

Contracted muscle

Valves

Muscle contractions help direct blood flow—blocking blood from capillaries or pushing blood through veins back toward the heart.

FIGURE 21-13 Controlling blood flow. Precapillary sphincters can reduce blood flow to hands or feet in cold weather, saving the blood's warmth for vital organs. When traveling on a long flight, move your feet and legs to help push blood back toward your heart.

brain, heart, liver, and kidneys.) Blushing is the opposite situation: precapillary sphincters relax and blood flow to the face and neck increases.

"Food coma," that feeling of lethargy following a large meal, results from a similar shunting of blood. In this case, more blood is allowed to flow through the capillaries surrounding the digestive tract, while less flows to other parts of the body. Alternatively, during strenuous exercise, more blood is directed toward the skeletal muscles in use. This accounts for the feeling of being "pumped up" during and shortly after a weightlifting session.

Q *What is "food coma"?*

3. Veins. Once blood has passed through the capillaries, it flows back to the heart through veins. Veins have a structure similar to that of arteries: they are lined with a sheet of endothelium and surrounded by smooth muscle and a layer of connective tissue. The layer of smooth muscle surrounding veins, however, is much thinner than that surrounding arteries, making the walls of veins much more expandable. In a person at rest, as much as 60% of the total blood volume can be in his or her veins.

Q *Is it more dangerous to cut the carotid artery or the jugular vein? Why?*

The pressure of blood in the veins is only about one-tenth of the pressure in the arteries. This reduced pressure occurs because, in the capillaries, an increasing proportion of the blood is in direct contact with the inside surface of the vessel (in this case, capillary) wall. This contact increases the friction and slows the blood flow. As the blood moves from the capillaries through the veins, the pressure of the blood is further reduced. In fact, in most animals, blood will spurt and gush when an artery is cut, but will only trickle out of a cut vein. Because blood flows through arteries at higher pressure, it is not surprising that most arteries are not as close to the skin as are veins. It would be too risky if they were there. This is why people who cut their wrists when attempting suicide rarely die. They generally cut only the veins, which are closer to the surface, and rarely bleed enough to cause death.

Like the capillaries, veins, too, aid in the control of blood flow. After sitting for a very long time, such as on a long plane or car ride, you may notice that your feet become swollen and it is difficult to put your shoes back on. What is the cause of this? The answer has to do with the way blood flows back to the heart after passing through capillary beds. Remember that capillaries, with their small diameter and thin, leaky walls, reduce the pressure and

speed of flowing blood. By the time it begins collecting in veins, blood has very little pressure. It is able to "limp" back to the heart only with the assistance of two important features. First, as muscles surrounding veins contract and relax during normal movement, they squeeze the veins, pushing the blood through. And second, within veins, at regular intervals, are one-way valves. Similar in function to the atrioventricular and semilunar valves of the heart, these venous valves allow blood to flow in one direction— toward the heart—but not in the reverse direction (see Figure 21-13).

Regulating blood flow by means of valves in the veins and the contractions of muscles surrounding the veins usually works fine. As we've noted, though, you can encounter a problem if you sit on a plane for several hours. Blood pumped to your feet must somehow climb up your legs, yet in the absence of contractions of your calf and thigh muscles, this doesn't occur so well. Instead, the blood pools in your feet, causing them to get more swollen and increasing the risk of blood clots. This is why it is good to get up and move around occasionally, or to exercise your leg muscles as you sit.

One serious circulatory problem is called varicose veins, a painful condition that occurs when the valves preventing backflow of blood malfunction and blood pools in the veins, stretching them. This can be caused or exacerbated by standing for long periods of time. Several methods are effective for treating varicose veins, including laser surgery or injections that cause the veins to slowly fade and disappear, with deeper veins taking over the circulation in that region.

Q *Some individuals develop enlarged, twisted, and visible veins, a painful condition called varicose veins. Why might this occur?*

TAKE-HOME MESSAGE 21·6

Blood flows from the heart to the tissues of the body and back to the heart again through a series of endothelium-lined blood vessels. Arteries are elastic and carry blood at high pressure from the heart to capillaries. Capillaries are tiny, thin-walled vessels, the site of diffusion of nutrients, gases, waste products, and other materials between tissues and blood. Blood returns to the heart in veins, at low pressure, and this movement is aided by contractions of skeletal muscles.

If circulatory systems are like highways throughout our bodies, routes for the transport of goods and garbage, then blood is the traffic. Blood is a salty, protein-rich mixture of cells and fluid, with a consistency like that of motor oil. The average human body has 4–5 quarts of blood, and the blood makes up just under 10% of our total body weight. Blood's functions revolve primarily around its transport and delivery capabilities, including the transport of (1) respiratory gases such as oxygen and carbon dioxide, (2) vitamins and minerals, (3) nutrients, (4) hormones, (5) cells of the immune system, and (6) metabolic wastes. Blood also helps to maintain body temperature and homeostasis (see Chapter 20).

Blood has several distinct components, which we can identify by putting a sample of blood in a test tube and spinning it rapidly in a centrifuge (**FIGURE 21-14**). The lighter-weight part of the blood, the creamy yellow layer in the test tube, is the **plasma,** the liquid part of the blood. Plasma is 90% salty water. Dissolved within this water is a huge variety of molecules: metabolites and wastes, salts and ions, and hundreds of plasma proteins that serve to transport lipids, vitamins, and a host of other chemicals that need molecular escorts to get to the tissues where they are required. Most of the carbon dioxide produced in tissues as a by-product of cellular respiration is carried to the lungs dissolved in the plasma.

The heaviest components of blood get forced to the bottom of the test tube when spun in a centrifuge. This layer consists of tightly packed blood cells of various types and is usually dark red in color. The proportion of the blood that consists of cells is called the **hematocrit.** In humans, a hematocrit of about 45% is normal. Individuals living at high elevations for a few weeks or longer, however, have hematocrits of around 48% or 49%. Why? The increased hematocrit is a response to the reduced oxygen concentrations in the air at high elevations. To continue to deliver enough oxygen to the body's tissues, there must be more blood cells to carry it.

Blood cells are made in the bone marrow (the material that fills the interior of our bones) by specialized cells, called **stem cells,** that are able to develop into a diverse range of cell types. Stem cells throughout the bones in our body produce blood cells at a rate of about two million cells per second. There are two types of blood cells suspended in the plasma, red blood cells and white blood

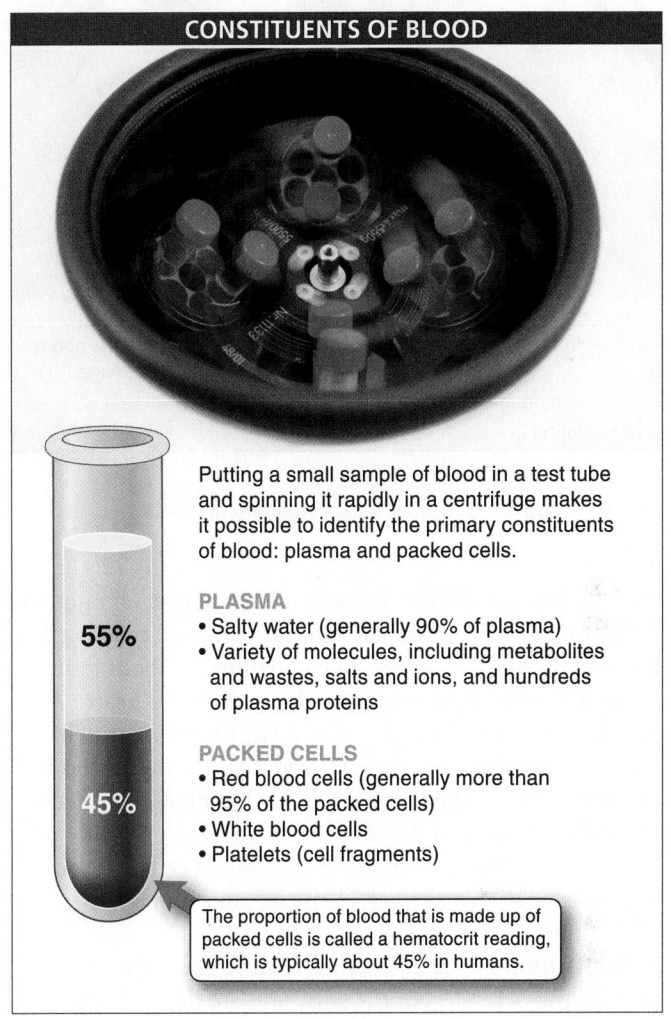

CONSTITUENTS OF BLOOD

Putting a small sample of blood in a test tube and spinning it rapidly in a centrifuge makes it possible to identify the primary constituents of blood: plasma and packed cells.

PLASMA
- Salty water (generally 90% of plasma)
- Variety of molecules, including metabolites and wastes, salts and ions, and hundreds of plasma proteins

PACKED CELLS
- Red blood cells (generally more than 95% of the packed cells)
- White blood cells
- Platelets (cell fragments)

55%

45%

The proportion of blood that is made up of packed cells is called a hematocrit reading, which is typically about 45% in humans.

FIGURE 21-14 What makes up blood?

cells, as well as platelets, which are cellular fragments (**FIGURE 21-15**).

1. Red blood cells (also called **erythrocytes**). These workhorses of the circulatory system are the most common blood cells. In a human being, about 95% of the blood cells circulating at any given time are red blood cells. They are oxygen-transporting specialists, and their structure maximizes their effectiveness. Externally, they are shaped like flexible disks, so they can squeeze through capillaries in single file. Internally, they have hardly any organelles; they have no nucleus, mitochondria, or protein-making machinery. What are they filled with? Each red blood cell contains about 250 million molecules of **hemoglobin,** an oxygen-carrying protein molecule (which we discuss in

RED BLOOD CELLS (ERYTHROCYTES)
- Transport oxygen from the lungs to the rest of the body
- Flexible disks containing few organelles
- Packed full of hemoglobin

WHITE BLOOD CELLS (LEUKOCYTES)
- Destroy pathogens and foreign organisms in the bloodstream and interstitial fluid
- There are several types of white blood cells that differ in their methods of fighting disease and responding to foreign materials

PLATELETS
- Slow blood loss by initiating the constriction of blood vessels and the formation of a clot
- Composed of small pieces of cytoplasm
- Contain no organelles

FIGURE 21-15 Erythrocytes, leukocytes, and platelets.

detail in Section 21-12). Because it lacks almost all internal cellular machinery for repair and upkeep, a red blood cell doesn't last long, remaining in circulation for about four months. (For comparison, many brain cells and heart muscle cells are never replaced and last for your entire life. Fat cells often last for a decade or more.) During its short life, a red blood cell will travel about 900 miles, repeatedly picking up oxygen in the lungs and releasing it to body cells that need it. (We cover more on how blood cells transport oxygen later in this chapter, in the sections on respiration.)

2. White blood cells (also called **leukocytes**). These cells are the defenders of the body and are the primary components of the body's immune response system. Five different types of white blood cells can be found circulating in the blood: neutrophils, lymphocytes, monocytes, eosinophils, and basophils (see Chapter 26 for more on these white blood cells and the immune system). Like red blood cells, white blood cells arise from stem cells in bone marrow. Once in the bloodstream, they patrol for **pathogens,** disease-causing foreign organisms circulating in the blood. White blood cells also spend much of their time outside the circulatory system, diffusing out of the capillaries and moving about in the interstitial fluid, where many pathogens such as viruses and bacteria may be and where the white blood cells may encounter and destroy cancerous body cells or cells infected by pathogens. The number of leukocytes circulating in an individual can vary greatly, depending on his or her health status. Under normal conditions, there is approximately one leukocyte

for every thousand red blood cells, but the number of leukocytes increases as much as twofold to threefold during an infection.

3. Platelets. With more than 50,000 miles of blood vessels in our bodies, it is inevitable that there will be occasional cuts or punctures (**FIGURE 21-16**). Fortunately, the platelets are ready to swing into action when this happens. **Platelets** are cellular fragments rather than full-fledged cells. In the bone marrow, large cells called megakaryocytes repeatedly pinch off little bits of cytoplasm that have no nuclei or other organelles. These cell fragments, the platelets, are filled with enzymes and chemicals that are essential for patching damaged blood vessels. Hundreds of thousands of platelets circulate at any given time, with each platelet generally lasting about a week. You can envision platelets as fragile glass jars full of Super Glue. When they bump into the edge of a cut in a blood vessel, they shatter and release their contents, initiating constriction of the blood vessel and production of fibrin threads that form a blood clot to reduce blood loss.

Some individuals lack platelets with properly functioning clotting factors, and they experience uncontrolled bleeding from even minor cuts or scrapes. These problems can be due to an inherited malfunctioning gene (as in hemophilia), or they can be acquired, or environmental. If the liver, where many of the clotting enzymes are produced, is damaged by disease (such as cirrhosis, which can result from alcoholism), uncontrolled bleeding can occur. Conversely,

If platelets lack properly functioning clotting factors, cuts and scrapes can lead to uncontrolled bleeding.

such clots block circulation in vessels that supply blood to the muscle tissue of the heart itself, a heart attack occurs.

Iron deficiency is the most common cause of anemia. Anemia occurs when an individual has too few red blood cells. Because red blood cells deliver oxygen to the body's cells, one consequence of anemia is a reduction in the oxygen available to cells, essentially suffocating them. This causes people with anemia to feel tired and run-down. A reduction in the number of red blood cells is also associated with an increased susceptibility to infection, apparently by weakening the immune system's ability to mount a response to pathogens. Iron is a critical element that enables oxygen to be carried by red blood cells. If iron is in short supply, red blood cells can't deliver sufficient oxygen to the tissues where it's needed. Both men and women can be anemic, but anemia affects women much more commonly, because of the blood loss during menstruation. The relationship between iron deficiency and anemia has been known for a long time. An old folk remedy for anemia—which actually worked(!)—was sipping liquid daily from a jug containing rusty iron nails and water. Even food cooked in an iron skillet has a significantly increased iron content (**FIGURE 21-17**).

Q What is anemia? Why are women more susceptible than men?

problems of blood clotting *too* readily can also lead to health problems. Thrombosis, for example, is the formation of clots of coagulated blood within a blood vessel. When

FIGURE 21-17 Cooking in a cast-iron skillet can significantly increase the iron content of foods!

TAKE-HOME MESSAGE 21·7

Blood is a salty, protein-rich mixture of cells and fluid that transports (1) respiratory gases, (2) vitamins and minerals, (3) nutrients, (4) hormones, (5) components of the immune system, and (6) metabolic wastes. Blood also helps maintain a constant internal environment, including body temperature. Blood cells are produced throughout life by stem cells in bone marrow. There are two types of cells suspended in the plasma, red blood cells (oxygen transport) and white blood cells (defense from infections), as well as cellular fragments called platelets (repair).

21·8 Blood pressure is a key measure of heart health.

Feel your pulse. With no fancy equipment at all, it is possible to get very useful information about the functioning of your heart. For some arteries, such as those on the underside of your wrist or on the side of your neck, you can feel with your fingers the pressure increase as a blood surge stretches the arteries with each contraction of the heart. Taking a person's pulse provides a quick and easy determination of the rate and rhythm of the heartbeats.

Additional information about heart health can be gained with measurement of **blood pressure,** which measures the force with which blood flows through a person's arteries. This force tells us the magnitude of each heart contraction and gives important clues about an individual's cardiovascular health. There are two different parts to a blood pressure reading (**FIGURE 21-18**). The first, called **systolic pressure,** is the pressure when the heart contracts. The powerful contraction pumps blood into the arteries, momentarily causing them to stretch as they accommodate the large pulse of blood. The second blood pressure reading is called **diastolic pressure.** This is a measure of the force that blood exerts on the artery walls while the heart is between beats. Because blood isn't being actively pumped at that moment, the diastolic pressure is always lower than the systolic pressure.

Blood pressure can be measured in four easy steps, using a blood pressure cuff.

1. The cuff is fastened around the upper arm and pumped up, clamping off the arteries in the arm so that no blood gets through.

2. Gradually, pressure on the cuff is released.

3. When the pulsing of blood getting pushed through the arteries under the cuff can first be heard—as a little squirt—with a stethoscope held to the arteries just below the cuff, the pressure reading is noted. This is the systolic pressure. Each contraction of the heart is just strong enough to push blood through the barrier of that much pressure.

4. Additional pressure in the cuff is released until the squirting sound disappears. The pressure at that point is the diastolic pressure. Blood is flowing through the arteries with this amount of pressure between heart contractions.

If your blood pressure is "120 over 80," it means that the systolic pressure is 120 and the diastolic pressure is 80. This

BLOOD PRESSURE

Blood pressure readings consist of two measurements:

SYSTOLIC PRESSURE
- The force that blood exerts on the artery walls when the heart contracts and pumps blood into the arteries
- Normal range is between 90 and 140 mm Hg

DIASTOLIC PRESSURE
- The force that blood exerts on the artery walls while the heart is between beats
- Normal range is between 60 and 90 mm Hg

BLOOD PRESSURE GUIDELINES
According to the United States National Heart, Lung, and Blood Institute

	Systolic pressure (mm Hg)	Diastolic pressure (mm Hg)
Normal	<120	<80
Prehypertension	120–139	80–89
Stage 1 Hypertension	140–159	90–99
Stage 2 Hypertension	≥160	≥100

 With a blood pressure above 120/80, your heart must work harder at all times and your arteries can lose some of their elasticity. This increases your health risks.

FIGURE 21-18 Blood pressure readings can reveal heart health.

is written as 120/80, and the units of measure are millimeters of mercury (mm Hg), representing how high a column of mercury could be lifted by such pressure.

Blood pressure above 120/80 is a potential health hazard. In its guidelines concerning high blood pressure (also called **hypertension**), the U.S. National Heart, Lung, and Blood Institute released the following definitions:

Normal: less than 120 / less than 80 mm Hg

Prehypertension: 120–139 / 80–89 mm Hg

Stage 1 Hypertension: 140–159 / 90–99 mm Hg

Stage 2 Hypertension: 160 or greater / 100 or greater mm Hg

Why is high blood pressure cause for concern? Imagine a pair of shorts with an elastic waistband. If you were to stretch the waistband as far as possible and hold it in that position for a long time, what would happen? The waistband would lose its elasticity. This is similar to what happens to your arteries if they are stretched by high pressures for long periods of time. With high blood pressure, not only must your heart work harder at all times, potentially weakening it, but your arteries have a reduced ability to expand and accommodate the increasing pulses of blood during times of exertion. Moreover, more cholesterol sticks to artery walls when they are rigid than when they are elastic, and as the cholesterol buildup narrows the diameter of the blood vessel, it further reduces the efficiency of the circulatory system and taxes the heart. These problems all increase the risk of catastrophic heart attacks and strokes, which we discuss in Section 21-9. Although both systolic pressure and diastolic pressure are important, the systolic blood pressure is more important in identifying and controlling hypertension.

Low blood pressure, or **hypotension,** at the other extreme, is defined as a pressure of 90/60 or lower and can cause symptoms such as dizziness, particularly just after a person stands up, due to inadequate blood flow to the brain. Sometimes caused by medications, low blood pressure can also be associated with weakness or depression. Most often it is not a problem, and it rarely carries long-term risks.

Relative heart size and blood pressure are consistent among the mammals, with one notable exception: giraffes. With their necks stretching 8 feet (2.5 meters) or more, giraffes must pump blood up a pretty steep slope (**FIGURE 21-19**). Not surprisingly, their hearts are much bigger—about four times bigger (relative to body size)—than a human heart, and their blood pressure is more than twice as great. Scientists have begun studying giraffe circulation in the hope of learning physiological secrets to help humans cope with high blood pressure. Why, for example, with twice the blood pressure of a human, doesn't a giraffe's head explode when it is lowered to drink from a pond?

To pump blood up the steep slope to their head, giraffes have a heart four times the size of a human's, relative to body size, and blood pressure more than twice as high.

FIGURE 21-19 Contents under pressure. The large heart of a giraffe pumps blood through its long neck all the way to its head.

TAKE-HOME MESSAGE 21·8

Blood pressure measurement gives important clues about an individual's cardiovascular health. A blood pressure reading consists of two measures. The first, systolic pressure, is the force that blood exerts on the artery wall when the heart contracts and pumps blood into the arteries. The second, diastolic pressure, is the force that blood exerts on the artery wall while the heart is between beats. With high blood pressure, the heart must work harder at all times, the arteries can lose some of their elasticity, and health risks are increased.

21·9 Cardiovascular disease is a leading cause of death in the United States.

The heart is among the most neglected organs. Most people take it for granted. But diseases of the heart, including heart attacks, result in more deaths in the United States every year than any other single cause. They also are among the most avoidable of all causes of death. In 2009, just over 24% of the deaths in the United States were caused by diseases of the heart. Heart attacks are brought on by an interruption in the flow of blood through one of the **coronary arteries**—the blood vessels that deliver

oxygen and nutrients to the heart muscle itself. When cells in the heart muscle are deprived of oxygen, the heart may beat irregularly or cease to beat, and the heart muscle cells deprived of oxygen die. This has serious and long-term implications, because heart cells are among the rare cells of the body that do not reproduce themselves. Once they are gone, they are really gone. Heart attacks rarely strike out of the blue. Although the heart attack itself is a sudden event, it usually occurs after decades of progressive

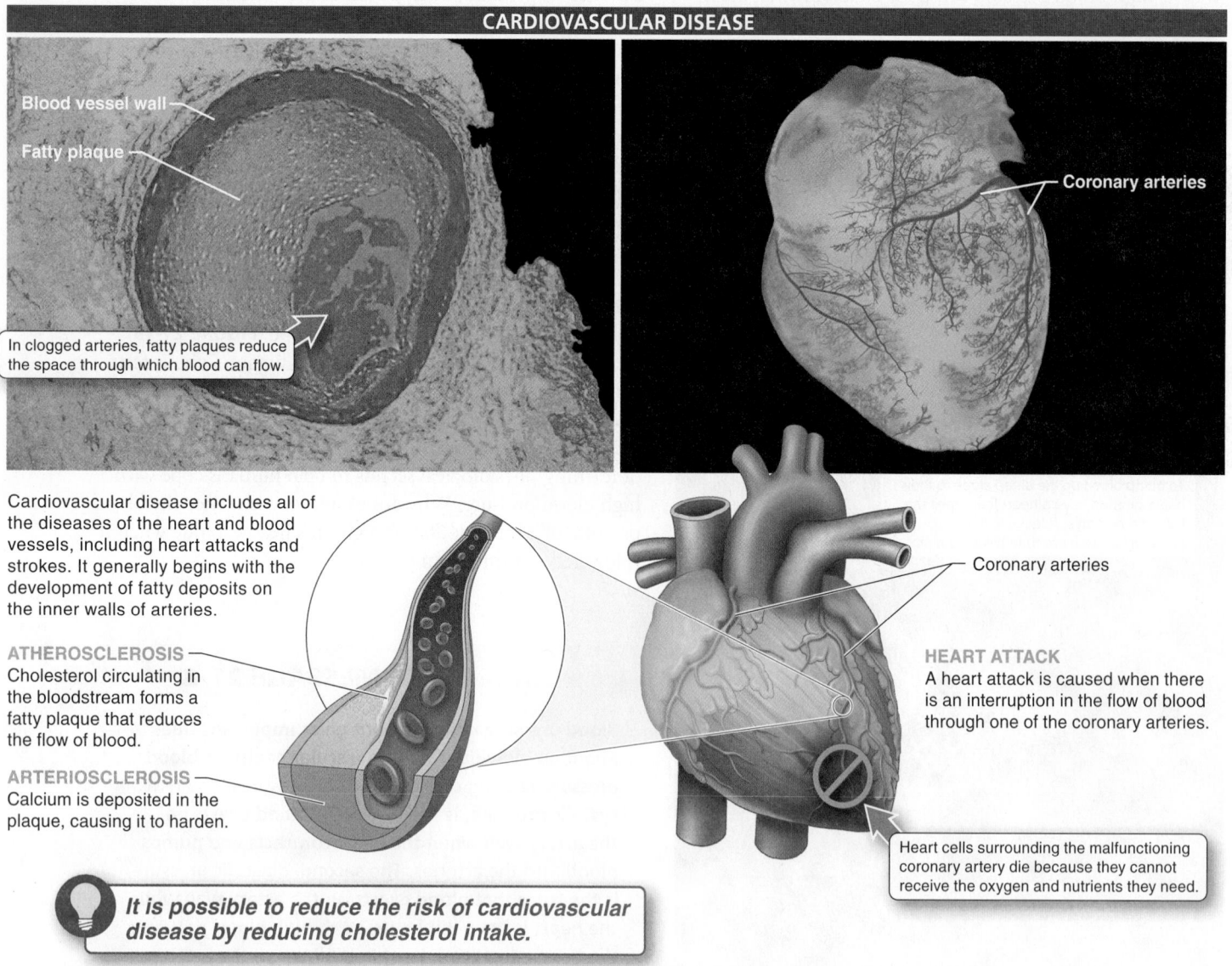

CARDIOVASCULAR DISEASE

Blood vessel wall

Fatty plaque

In clogged arteries, fatty plaques reduce the space through which blood can flow.

Coronary arteries

Cardiovascular disease includes all of the diseases of the heart and blood vessels, including heart attacks and strokes. It generally begins with the development of fatty deposits on the inner walls of arteries.

ATHEROSCLEROSIS
Cholesterol circulating in the bloodstream forms a fatty plaque that reduces the flow of blood.

ARTERIOSCLEROSIS
Calcium is deposited in the plaque, causing it to harden.

Coronary arteries

HEART ATTACK
A heart attack is caused when there is an interruption in the flow of blood through one of the coronary arteries.

Heart cells surrounding the malfunctioning coronary artery die because they cannot receive the oxygen and nutrients they need.

It is possible to reduce the risk of cardiovascular disease by reducing cholesterol intake.

FIGURE 21-20 Diseases of the heart and blood vessels. Fatty deposits and damage to arteries can disrupt blood flow and interfere with proper circulation.

deterioration of the arteries and other degradations of the circulatory system, collectively called **cardiovascular disease** (FIGURE 21-20).

> *Broken heart. A pump after all, pumping thousands of gallons of blood every day. One fine day it gets bunged up and there you are.*
>
> — JAMES JOYCE, *Ulysses*

Cardiovascular disease includes all diseases of the heart and blood vessels and is ultimately responsible for close to half of all deaths in the United States. In addition to heart attacks, strokes are a common outcome of advanced cardiovascular disease. Caused by blocked arteries or blood clots in the brain, strokes also lead to cell death in the brain tissues starved of oxygen. There is, however, some cause for optimism: the death rate from heart disease has been declining steadily for the past 50 years, including a 25% drop in the past 20 years. These reductions have come, not from advances in heart transplants and other surgical interventions, but rather from improvements in diet and exercise as well as advances in diagnosis and preventive medicine.

Cardiovascular disease generally begins with the development of fatty deposits called plaques on the inner walls of arteries. Plaques increase the risk of formation of blood clots and, by narrowing the artery, reduce the flow of blood. This narrowing of arteries, called **atherosclerosis,** is often followed by the depositing of calcium at the plaques, causing them to harden in a process known as **arteriosclerosis.** The initial formation of plaques is usually a consequence of circulating cholesterol in the bloodstream. Because most of this circulating cholesterol comes from cholesterol in our diet, we can reduce our risk of atherosclerosis by reducing our cholesterol intake.

All cholesterol is the same chemically, but you may hear references to "good" cholesterol and "bad" cholesterol. Why is this? As we discussed in Chapter 3, most cholesterol circulating in the bloodstream is packaged as LDL, or low-density lipoproteins. These molecules consist of thousands of molecules of cholesterol surrounded by a phospholipid coat. Because the LDL particles are sticky, they adhere to artery walls and can initiate the buildup of dangerous plaques. Other circulating particles, high-density lipoproteins (HDL), are considered "good" cholesterol. Less well understood than LDL, these particles seem to remove cholesterol from arteries and deliver it to

liver cells, where it can be broken down. This process can actually reduce the progression of cardiovascular disease. By including in your diet fish and other foods that contain a specific type of fatty acids, called omega-3 fatty acids, you can increase your HDL levels.

Both nature and nurture play a role in cardiovascular disease. As we saw in Chapter 3, the tendency to develop cardiovascular disease is inherited. Individuals differ in the number of LDL receptors they produce on their liver cells, and the more receptors an individual has, the better that individual is able to remove atherosclerosis-causing cholesterol from circulation. You cannot alter the genes you inherit for LDL receptor production. But you *can* alter the amount of cholesterol or type of cholesterol (that is, LDL vs. HDL) that is circulating in the first place. Several different behavioral changes, such as increasing aerobic exercise, not smoking, and eating a low-cholesterol, low-fat diet, can reduce the level of circulating cholesterol and the risk of cardiovascular disease (FIGURE 21-21).

With aerobic training, such as running, the muscle fibers of the heart get bigger (in much the same way that skeletal muscle gets bigger when you lift weights), and cardiovascular health is improved. When people are sedentary, though, their hearts may have to work harder for reasons such as hypertension or poor diet. The increased load on the heart causes the heart to get bigger, but in a pathological manner that increases the risk of heart failure, rather than in a manner that increases strength and efficiency.

Cardiovascular disease continues to be the most prevalent disease and leading cause of death in the United States. But, as mentioned above, the situation has been improving over the past several decades. The onset and progression of cardiovascular disease are strongly influenced by factors within an individual's control, and with the proper dietary strategies and lifestyle changes, most people can reduce their risk.

In summarizing its research-based recommendations for reducing risk factors for heart disease, heart attack, and stroke, the American Heart Association suggests a focus on "A, B, and C":

Avoid tobacco

- Stop using all types of tobacco products and minimize your exposure to tobacco smoke. Because cigarette smokers are two to three times more likely to die from heart disease, this behavioral change can lead to significant improvements in health and longevity.

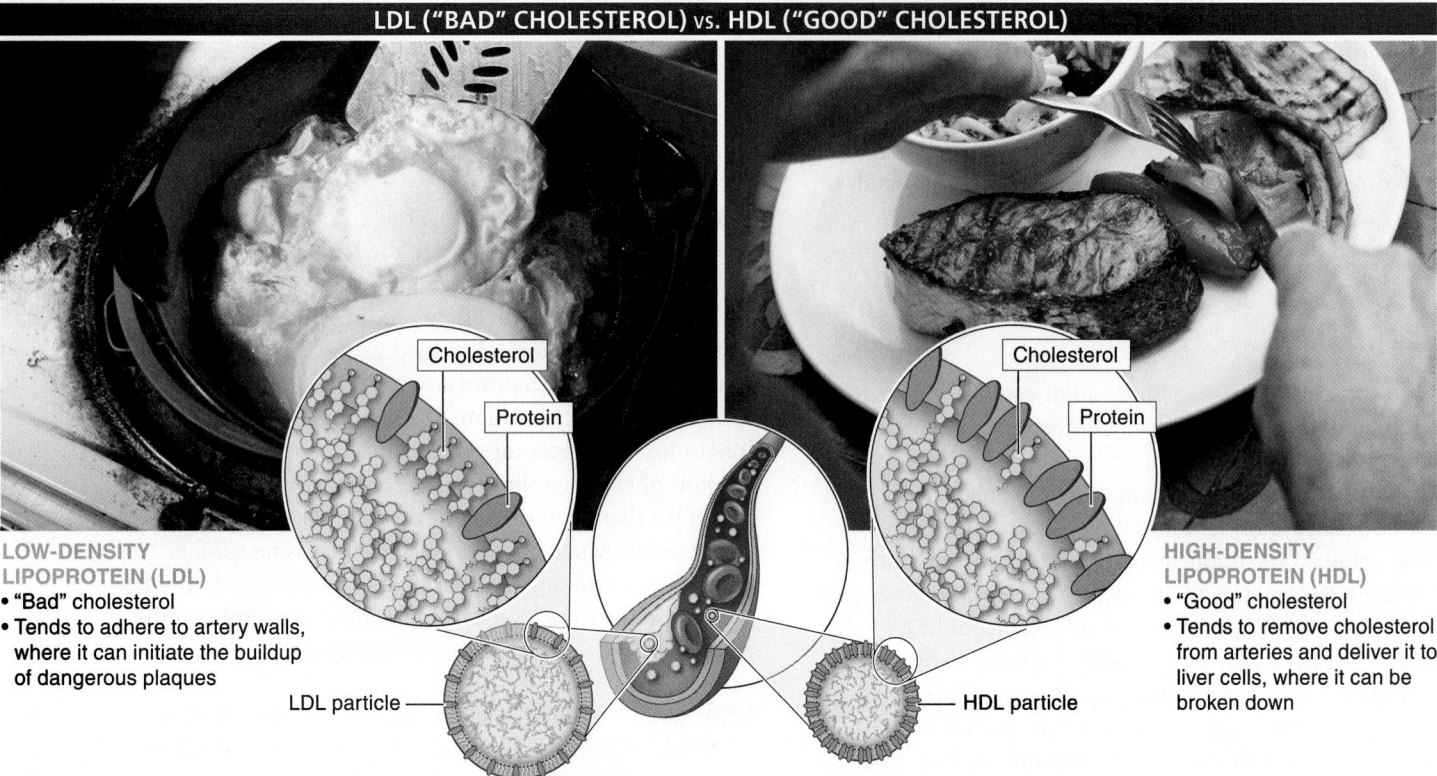

LOW-DENSITY LIPOPROTEIN (LDL)
- "Bad" cholesterol
- Tends to adhere to artery walls, where it can initiate the buildup of dangerous plaques

Cholesterol

Protein

LDL particle

HIGH-DENSITY LIPOPROTEIN (HDL)
- "Good" cholesterol
- Tends to remove cholesterol from arteries and deliver it to liver cells, where it can be broken down

Cholesterol

Protein

HDL particle

FIGURE 21-21 Cholesterol can be helpful or harmful.

Be more active

- Participate in at least 30 minutes of moderate-intensity physical activity (such as brisk walking) on five or more days each week (or vigorous-intensity activity, such as jogging, on three or more days). Additionally, every adult should perform activities that increase or maintain muscle strength, including progressive weight training and/or stair climbing, on a minimum of two days each week.

Choose good nutrition

- Eat a diet that balances energy intake with exercise to prevent weight gain. If you are overweight, take steps to increase physical activity and decrease energy intake to establish a healthy body weight (see also Section 22-16).

- Choose a diet rich in vegetables, fruits, and whole grains, particularly those that are high in fiber.

- Limit your intake of saturated fat, trans fat, and cholesterol by choosing lean meats, vegetables, and low-fat dairy products. Read food labels to check for hydrogenated fats (see Section 2-12 for a refresher on hydrogenated and trans fats).

- Limit alcohol to one drink daily for women and two drinks daily for men.

These behavioral changes are much easier said than done, but because they include the most effective strategies for reducing the risk of cardiovascular disease, the payoffs are significant.

TAKE-HOME MESSAGE 21·9

Cardiovascular disease includes all diseases of the heart and blood vessels, including heart attacks and strokes, and is the leading cause of death in the United States. It generally begins with the development of fatty deposits on the inner walls of arteries that increase the risk of blood clots and reduce the flow of blood in coronary arteries that supply oxygen to the heart (atherosclerosis). Because the hardening of arteries (arteriosclerosis) is usually initiated by circulating cholesterol, it is possible to reduce the risk of cardiovascular disease by reducing cholesterol intake.

The lymphatic system plays a supporting role in circulation.

Our bodies have another circulatory system (**FIGURE 21-22**). In addition to the cardiovascular system, and running close to it throughout the body, is the lymphatic system. Why the seeming redundancy? The lymphatic system has a supporting role in the process of circulation. It has three important functions (**FIGURE 21-23**).

1. Recycling. As diffusion occurs between the capillaries and the interstitial fluid surrounding cells, much fluid is lost from the blood. Here's where the lymphatic system comes in. Intertwined around blood vessels, the lymphatic capillaries take in, by diffusion, fluid, proteins, and other substances that have leaked into the interstitial fluid from the blood. Once recovered, this fluid, now called **lymph,** travels through progressively larger lymphatic vessels that eventually join up with veins in the shoulders. At this point, the recovered

Q It's not necessarily a good idea to have your tonsils taken out, even if they are painfully swollen. Why?

proteins and fluid (which amounts to several liters each day) are returned to the blood as it makes its way back to the heart.

2. Fighting illness. As it moves through the lymphatic system, lymph passes through patches of connective tissue called **lymph nodes.** These compartmentalized sacs are filled with pathogen-fighting white blood cells that remove dangerous materials (including bacteria, cancer cells, and viruses) from the body. This is why your lymph nodes—including your tonsils, the largest lymph nodes of all—become swollen when your body is fighting an infection.

3. Retrieving nutrients. The lymphatic system has numerous little projections that extend into the small intestine and absorb lipids from the food you have eaten and shuttle them from the digestive tract to the bloodstream.

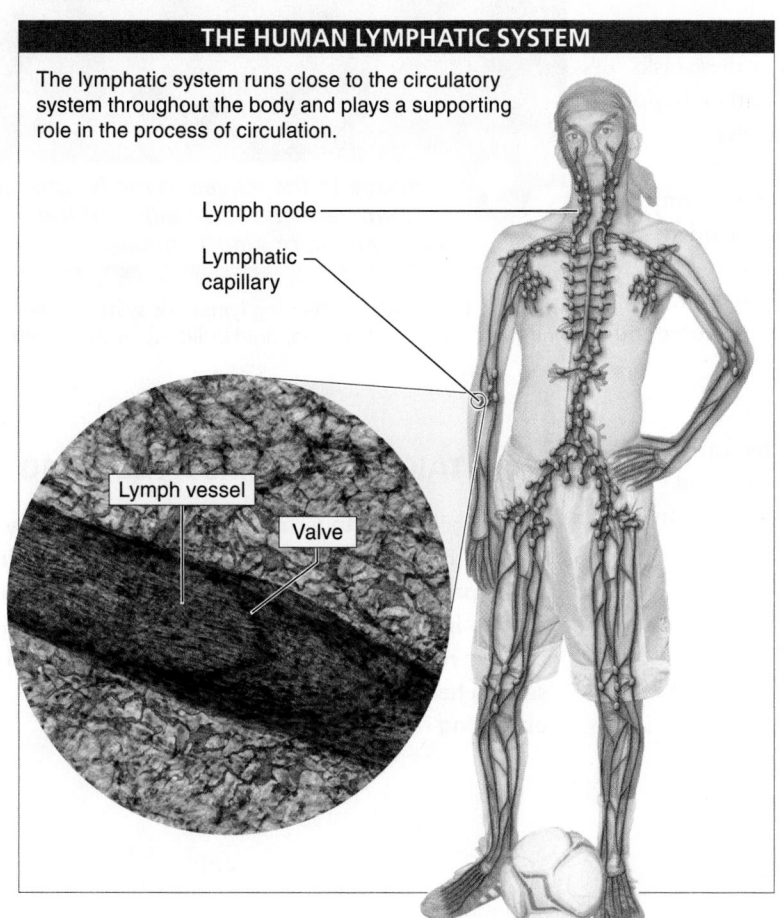

THE HUMAN LYMPHATIC SYSTEM

The lymphatic system runs close to the circulatory system throughout the body and plays a supporting role in the process of circulation.

Lymph node

Lymphatic capillary

Lymph vessel

Valve

FIGURE 21-22 The "other" circulatory system. An overview of the human lymphatic system.

RECYCLING
The lymphatic system recycles fluid and proteins that diffuse from the blood capillaries during circulation back into the bloodstream.

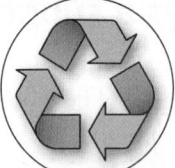

FIGHTING ILLNESS
As lymph circulates through the body, white-blood-cell-packed lymph nodes remove dangerous materials, including bacteria, cancer cells, and viruses.

RETRIEVING NUTRIENTS
Little projections that extend into the small intestine absorb lipids from the digestive tract and shuttle them to the bloodstream.

FIGURE 21-23 The lymphatic system supports the circulatory system while fighting illness.

In humans, the lymphatic system accomplishes these tasks without a pump. There is no "lymph heart." Rather, lymph is pushed through the system when muscles adjacent to lymph vessels contract and squeeze the fluid onward. Lymph vessels (like veins) have valves that keep the lymph flowing in one direction. When you sit for an extended period of time, lymph can accumulate in vessels. You can help move it along by contracting the muscles in your extremities and progressively contracting muscles closer and closer to your shoulders.

Infection by some parasitic worms can cause the scarring of lymph vessels. When lymph vessels are scarred, fluid recovered by the lymphatic system cannot be returned to the circulatory system, and the extremities swell, often tremendously (**FIGURE 21-24**). This disease is called elephantiasis. Because the parasitic worms causing elephantiasis are transmitted by mosquitoes, the condition is most common in tropical regions. The condition can be treated with antibiotics that kill the symbiotic bacteria necessary for the parasitic worm to live.

Damage to the valves in the lymphatic system can lead to swelling of the extremities, or elephantiasis.

FIGURE 21-24 A malfunctioning lymphatic system. When the lymphatic system is damaged, fluid builds up in the extremities.

TAKE-HOME MESSAGE 21·10

The lymphatic system runs close to the circulatory system throughout the body and plays a supporting role in the process of circulation, by performing three main functions: recycling fluid that leaks out of the capillaries of the circulatory system, marshaling white blood cells to help fight dangerous cells and pathogens, and absorbing nutrients from the digestive system.

Humpback whales spouting (exhaling) while feeding, in Alaska.

21·11 Oxygen and carbon dioxide must get into and out of the circulatory system.

As we've seen, circulatory systems are like trucking systems and the highways on which they move. Of the substances they transport, among the most important are the respiratory gases. After all, aerobic respiration requires cells to take up oxygen and release carbon dioxide. But how do these gases get into and out of the circulatory system? Where and how does gas exchange take place? In the remainder of this chapter, we investigate the structures where gas exchange occurs and the transport molecules that make it possible.

In single-celled and very small multicellular organisms, gas exchange can occur by direct diffusion. In larger multicellular organisms, however, gas exchange becomes a two-stage process (**FIGURE 21-25**). First comes the exchange between the external environment and the organism's circulatory system. Later comes the exchange between the circulatory system and the cells involved in cellular respiration.

The first of these two stages can occur in several different types of organs specialized for respiration, such as lungs or gills. In all cases, however, it requires a respiratory

GAS EXCHANGE IN ANIMALS

In large, multicellular organisms, gas exchange is a two-stage process.

1 Respiratory gases are exchanged between the external environment and the organism's circulatory system.

2 Respiratory gases are exchanged between the circulatory system and the cells involved in cellular respiration.

FIGURE 21-25 Overview of respiratory gas exchange in animals.

medium—air or water—that serves as a reservoir for the gases, and a moist respiratory surface across which the gas exchange can occur. The many different systems that

DIVERSITY IN GAS-EXCHANGE SYSTEMS

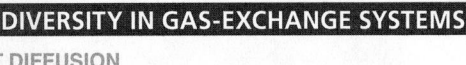

DIRECT DIFFUSION
- Gas exchange occurs directly between cells and the environment
- Occurs in single-celled organisms and small organisms with low metabolic demands

PROTRUDING RESPIRATORY SACS
- Balloon-like sacs that increase surface area for gas exchange
- Occur in sea stars and other echinoderms with low metabolic demands

GILLS
- Elaborate extensions of the body that exchange significant amounts of gases dissolved in water
- Occur in fishes and many marine invertebrates such as lobsters and clams

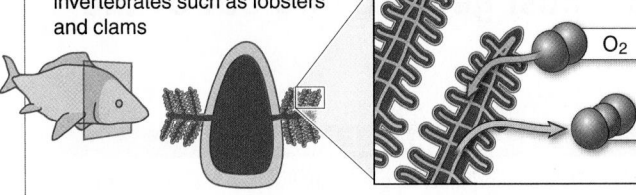

TRACHEAE
- Network of branching tubes connected to tiny openings on the body called spiracles
- Occur in most terrestrial insects

LUNGS
- Internal organs with highly branched, moist surfaces
- Occur in most land vertebrates

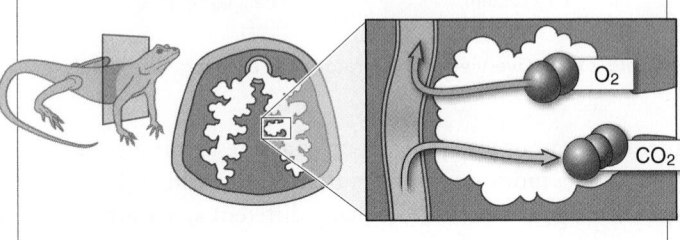

have evolved for gas exchange fall into five categories (**FIGURE 21-26**).

1. Direct diffusion. Single-celled organisms and many small multicellular organisms with low metabolic demands, such as marine flatworms, can accomplish respiration by direct diffusion between the cells and the environment.

2. Protruding respiratory sacs. Many slightly larger organisms also have low metabolic needs. Sea stars and other echinoderms have little balloon-like sacs that protrude from their skin—greatly increasing the surface area—and exchange gases between the body cavity and the environment.

3. Gills. Fishes and many aquatic invertebrates, such as lobsters and clams, have **gills.** These extensions of the body are tremendously elaborate structures in which the large surface area allows extensive exchange of gases between the water and the blood vessels of the circulatory system.

4. Tracheae. Although insect bodies look rather solid, they have a huge number of tiny openings—the spiracles—leading to tubes that branch extensively throughout the body. These inner tubes make it possible for gases in the air to come in direct contact with most of the organism's cells.

5. Lungs. Most land vertebrates have **lungs.** These are internal organs, characterized by highly branched, moist respiratory surfaces, across which gases in the air breathed in are exchanged with gases dissolved in the blood circulating through the lung tissue. Birds, reptiles, and mammals do virtually all of their respiration through their lungs, but amphibians (such as frogs) also exchange gases through their skin, which serves as a supplemental respiratory system. Their skin stays moist because of their largely aquatic lifestyle.

TAKE-HOME MESSAGE 21·11

In single-celled and very small multicellular organisms, gas exchange can occur by direct diffusion. In larger multicellular organisms, gas exchange is a two-stage process: (1) exchange between the external environment and the organism's circulatory system, which usually takes place in lungs, tracheae, or gills, and (2) exchange between the circulatory system and the cells involved in cellular respiration.

Oxygen is transported while bound to hemoglobin.

Red blood cells are filled with a molecule called hemoglobin. Hemoglobin is like an oxygen "shuttle bus," transporting oxygen around the body. In the lungs, it picks up O_2 and hangs on to it as the blood cell returns to the heart and is pumped to the body. Only when it reaches tissues such as organs or muscles that are in need of oxygen but are far from sources of the vital gas does the hemoglobin release its O_2 "passengers." Having released some (or all) of its oxygen, the hemoglobin then returns to the lungs, where it can load up on oxygen again. It is the oxygen-carrying hemoglobin that gives our blood its red color. When it gives up its O_2, hemoglobin turns more of a purplish-maroonish color. That's why books often show oxygenated blood in arteries as red and deoxygenated blood in veins as blue or purple.

Hemoglobin is a tiny molecule—so tiny that there are about 250 million copies of it in every single red blood cell. Built right inside the blood cell, the hemoglobin remains there for the cell's entire life. Each molecule of hemoglobin is a tangled mass of four polypeptide chains. Nestled within the molecule are four cozy compartments, each of which can carry one molecule of oxygen gas on a seat of iron. This iron attaches to the O_2 that diffuses into the red blood cell, temporarily making it part of the hemoglobin molecule (**FIGURE 21-27**). As we saw earlier, a shortage of iron in your diet can lead to anemia. This is because when iron is in short supply, less oxygen can be bound by hemoglobin and transported by each red blood cell, causing muscles and organs to be starved of oxygen and leading to feelings of fatigue and weakness.

Although it is banned by the Olympics and most sports organizations, "blood doping" has been used by some athletes to improve their performance. One method involves withdrawing red blood cells during the weeks and months leading up to a big competition, storing them, and re-injecting them in the few days just before the competition. Because red blood cells are filled with hemoglobin, the oxygen-carrying pigment, blood doping can increase the athlete's capacity for delivering O_2 to his or her tissues. In addition to being against the rules in most competitions, however, blood doping also carries some health risks, because it increases the viscosity of the blood. In the 1990s, dozens of apparently healthy, elite cyclists died inexplicably from heart failure. It was suspected that their blood had become so thick with red blood cells from blood doping that the burden on the heart to pump their sludge-like blood became too great.

HEMOGLOBIN

Each molecule of hemoglobin is a tangled mass of four polypeptide chains with four molecules of iron that create four "seats" to which oxygen can attach.

Red blood cell

Hemoglobin

Iron   Oxygen

Polypeptide chains

The hemoglobin molecule is like an oxygen "shuttle bus" that picks up oxygen in the lungs and transports it to tissues.

FIGURE 21-27 Hemoglobin: the oxygen transporter.

Oxygen binds to hemoglobin, but hemoglobin doesn't hold on to the oxygen so tightly that it never lets go. Like Post-it notes, which are useful because they are sticky enough to attach to surfaces but not so sticky as to become permanently affixed, hemoglobin functions as if it "knows" when to bind to O_2 and when to release it. This hinges on something called the partial pressure of the oxygen (denoted as Po_2), the force of oxygen particles in the air pressing against the body (**FIGURE 21-28**). The partial pressure of oxygen can be thought of as a measure of the amount of oxygen present.

Where in a body might hemoglobin encounter relatively high or low partial pressures of oxygen? When you breathe air that has a large amount of oxygen, all four O_2 compartments in hemoglobin promptly bind oxygen molecules. Deep in the tissues of your body, though, oxygen is not in great supply—especially if you are exerting yourself and your muscles have been consuming oxygen as they contract. When these tissues become depleted of oxygen, any hemoglobin in the vicinity encounters a reduced amount (a low partial pressure) of oxygen (Po_2). And what does hemoglobin do when it encounters a small amount of oxygen? Because the oxygen it carries is not held

Air pressure is the force of all of the particles in the air pressing against you. This force decreases as elevation increases, since there are fewer particles pressing against you.

PARTIAL PRESSURE OF OXYGEN

The partial pressure of oxygen is the force of oxygen in the air pressing against you.

The partial pressure of oxygen is usually about 21% of the total air pressure.

FIGURE 21-28 The force of particles on you. Air pressure and the partial pressure of oxygen are reduced at higher altitudes.

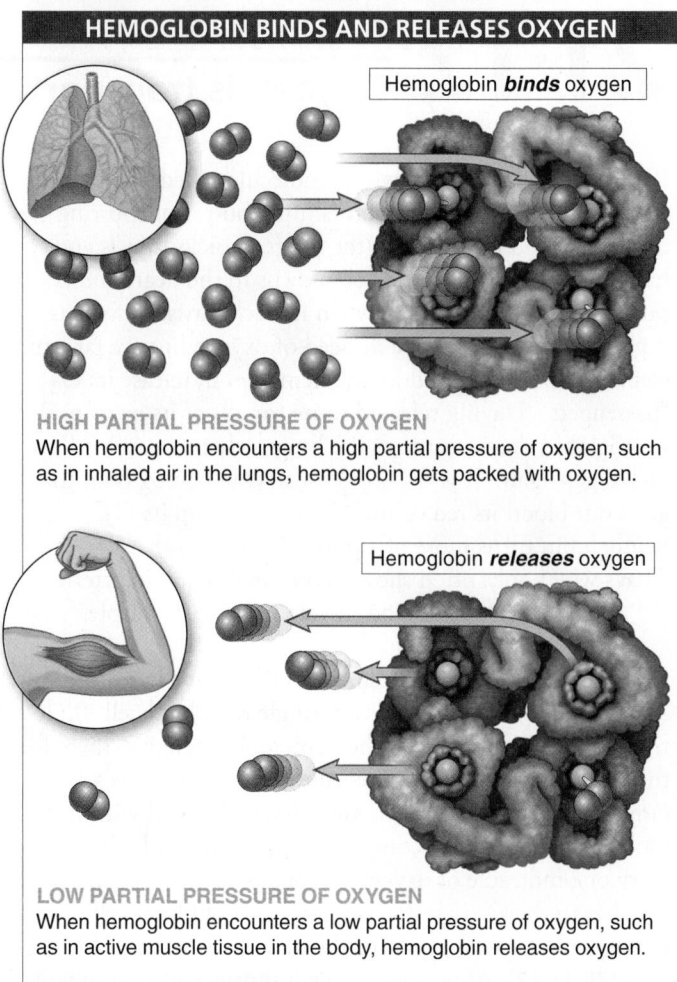

Hemoglobin *binds* oxygen

HIGH PARTIAL PRESSURE OF OXYGEN
When hemoglobin encounters a high partial pressure of oxygen, such as in inhaled air in the lungs, hemoglobin gets packed with oxygen.

Hemoglobin *releases* oxygen

LOW PARTIAL PRESSURE OF OXYGEN
When hemoglobin encounters a low partial pressure of oxygen, such as in active muscle tissue in the body, hemoglobin releases oxygen.

FIGURE 21-29 Hemoglobin binds and releases oxygen, depending on the partial pressure of oxygen in the vicinity.

too tightly, some of it is released (**FIGURE 21-29**). This oxygen is quickly soaked up by the tissue, which can then continue to generate ATP.

When you are sitting at your desk, the amount of oxygen in your tissues isn't very low. Not many of your muscles are contracting, and your breathing rate isn't especially high. Much like a car coasting downhill, you aren't using much fuel. In these circumstances, hemoglobin typically gives up only one of its four molecules of bound oxygen gas before returning to the lungs to load up again. Back and forth it

cycles between getting packed with four oxygens in your lungs and being reduced to three oxygens in your tissues.

This seems wasteful. If your hemoglobin usually oscillates between picking up a single molecule of oxygen in the lungs and dropping off that O_2 in the organs or muscles, what is the point of its carrying around the other three oxygen molecules? These are its emergency reserves for when you need a lot more oxygen to fuel some energetic activity. If you are exercising vigorously, for instance, the amount of oxygen in your tissues can drop so low that hemoglobin gives up another of its oxygen molecules. In extreme cases of exertion, it might give up three or even all four of the oxygens it carries. **FIGURE 21-30** shows an oxygen binding curve for hemoglobin, illustrating the relationship between the amount of oxygen (measured as its P_{O_2}) and the proportion of oxygen molecules that hemoglobin holds onto.

OXYGEN BINDING CURVE FOR HEMOGLOBIN

OXYGEN DELIVERED DURING NORMAL METABOLISM
Hemoglobin only gives up one oxygen molecule in the body tissues before returning to the lungs.

OXYGEN DELIVERED DURING HIGH PHYSICAL EXERTION
Hemoglobin dips into its reserves, releasing two, three, or even all four of its oxygen molecules before returning to the lungs.

GRAPHIC CONTENT!
Thinking critically about visual displays of data.
Turn to p. 840 for a closer inspection of this figure.

FIGURE 21-30 "Sticky, but not too sticky." A graph showing hemoglobin's affinity for oxygen.

When a woman is pregnant, the growing fetus does not breathe air. This does not mean that the fetus doesn't need oxygen, however. During development, oxygen needs are actually very high. How does a fetus get the O_2 it needs? It has to scavenge oxygen molecules released by the mother's hemoglobin. Fetuses do this by producing their own special type of hemoglobin that is a bit stickier than normal adult hemoglobin. At a Po_2 that is low enough for the mother's hemoglobin to release oxygen, the fetal hemoglobin—with its greater stickiness (or oxygen affinity)—binds to the oxygen. It can then deliver that oxygen to its own, fetal tissues (**FIGURE 21-31**).

If hemoglobin isn't put together exactly right, the health consequences can be serious and painful, as is seen in sickle-cell disease. A single change in the genetic instructions for building hemoglobin causes a malfunction in the hemoglobin molecules (see Chapter 7). When they lose their oxygen molecules—such as when an individual is exercising—the hemoglobin molecules suddenly become misshapen and stick together, causing the entire red blood cell to collapse into a sharply pointed sickle. Once sickled, red blood cells cause a whole host of problems. Many break

FIGURE 21-31 How a fetus gets oxygen. The fetus produces hemoglobin that binds oxygen released by the mother's hemoglobin.

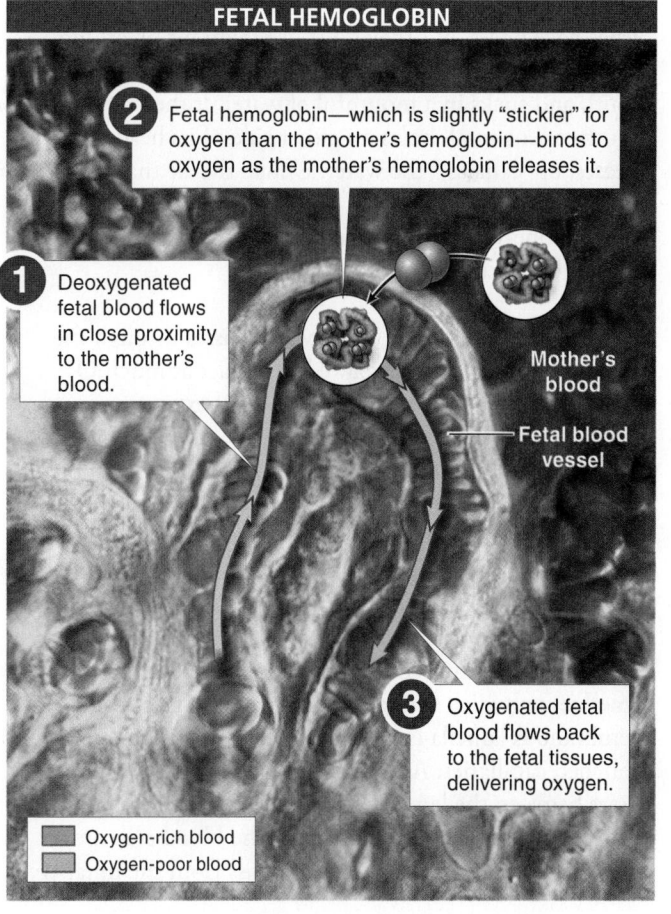

FETAL HEMOGLOBIN

2 Fetal hemoglobin—which is slightly "stickier" for oxygen than the mother's hemoglobin—binds to oxygen as the mother's hemoglobin releases it.

1 Deoxygenated fetal blood flows in close proximity to the mother's blood.

Mother's blood

Fetal blood vessel

3 Oxygenated fetal blood flows back to the fetal tissues, delivering oxygen.

☐ Oxygen-rich blood
☐ Oxygen-poor blood

open, which can cause anemia if the cells aren't replaced promptly. Others clump together, often blocking capillaries where, normally, they pass through one at a time. This leads to intense pain, especially in the joints and muscles, and can cause strokes if it occurs in the brain. About 70,000 people in the United States live with sickle-cell disease. They can minimize the effects by avoiding strenuous activity or other situations in which the amount of oxygen in their muscles and other tissues drops too low.

Q What is carbon monoxide poisoning?

In an unfortunate coincidence, carbon monoxide (CO) also binds to hemoglobin, but with a higher affinity than oxygen. In areas with high carbon monoxide concentrations—such as around a faulty furnace or a kerosene heater or lamp without adequate ventilation—the carbon monoxide will outcompete oxygen for hemoglobin's binding sites. And, to make this situation even worse, not only is carbon monoxide odorless and colorless, but hemoglobin also doesn't bind it loosely, like a Post-it note—instead, it binds CO very tightly. Thus, when the hemoglobin travels to the body tissues, it has no oxygen to release. In the absence of O_2, cellular respiration cannot generate the ATP the tissue needs (see Chapter 4). Consequently, the tissue is suffocated even as the person takes deeper and deeper breaths.

TAKE-HOME MESSAGE 21·12

Red blood cells are filled with hemoglobin, a molecule that picks up oxygen in the lungs and transports it around the body. Hemoglobin releases its oxygen in organs and tissues, such as muscles, where it is needed for cellular respiration.

21·13 Gas exchange takes place in the gills of aquatic vertebrates.

Fishes have noses, but they don't use them for breathing. Respiration begins, instead, with a gulp. The fish opens its mouth and sucks in a mouthful of water. It then closes its mouth, opens small holes on either side of its head, and releases, or "exhales," the water. Unlike the air that humans and other mammals breathe in and out, water follows a one-way path into and out of the fish, never changing direction.

Gas exchange takes place as the water passes through the gills, complex structures adapted to extract as much O_2 as possible from water (**FIGURE 21-32**). This extraction is a difficult task, because water has only 5% of the oxygen concentration found in air. The gills generally consist of four bony or cartilaginous gill arches on either side of the head. Similar in appearance to the teeth of a comb, these arches support the gill. Long filaments of tissue extend like an accordion from each gill arch, spreading out and creating as much surface area as possible. The filaments are stacks of hundreds of disk-like structures, called **lamellae,** on which the gas exchange takes place. Each membranous lamella is a semicircular disk of elaborately branched capillaries. As water rushes across the gills, it passes between the lamellae, coming in almost direct contact with the capillaries. Because the blood cells are so close to the water, dissolved O_2 can pass from the inhaled water to the blood by direct diffusion, and dissolved CO_2 can pass by direct diffusion from the blood to the exhaled water.

Blood circulation in gills is set up in a simple pattern that is highly efficient at extracting oxygen from the water. In each filament, the blood vessels are arranged so that the blood is moving in the opposite direction from the water flowing past the gills. Called a "countercurrent exchange system," this layout is much more efficient than if the blood flowed in the same direction as the water. If the blood and water flowed in the same direction, the gills would extract a maximum of about 50% of the oxygen in the water; with the countercurrent system, the gills extract as much as 85% of the oxygen in the water.

Fishes are not the only aquatic animals with gills. Many other groups of vertebrates and invertebrates have gills, including mollusks, such as clams, and arthropods, such as lobsters. Gills range from simple to complex,

> ❝Relationships are like sharks; they have to keep moving or they die.❞
>
> — WOODY ALLEN, *Annie Hall*

Gas exchange in fishes takes place in the gills—complex structures adapted to extract oxygen from water, generally consisting of four gill arches on either side of the head.

GILL ARCH
Cartilaginous structure that provides support for the filaments

LAMELLAE
Disk-like structures stacked along the filaments that contain the capillaries where gas exchange takes place

- Oxygen-rich blood
- Oxygen-poor blood

Gills

FILAMENTS
Thread-like structures—composed of hundreds of lamellae—that spread out and create as much surface area as possible

- Oxygen-rich water
- Oxygen-poor water

By orienting vessels so that the blood is flowing in the opposite direction to the water, gills make it possible to extract significantly more oxygen from the water than if blood and water flowed in the same direction.

FIGURE 21-32 Gills. The remarkable structure of gills makes gas exchange possible in fishes.

and there is a great deal of variation in the associated structures. Most sharks, for example, move water past their gills, not by gulping in water as do most fishes, but just by swimming forward all the time. If the shark stops moving forward, the oxygen in the water surrounding its gills is quickly depleted and the shark will suffocate. Consequently, most sharks spend their whole lives moving forward.

TAKE-HOME MESSAGE 21·13

In aquatic vertebrates, respiration begins when an organism opens its mouth, takes in water, and moves the water out through its gills. Gas exchange takes place in the gills, which extract as much as 85% of the oxygen from the water.

21·14 Respiratory systems of terrestrial vertebrates move oxygen-rich air into the lungs and carbon-dioxide-rich air out of the lungs.

Life on land is very different from life underwater, but the fundamental energetic needs remain. ATP is still the chemical that provides the energy for all the reactions necessary for life, and cells still need oxygen to produce ATP. Consequently, an organism must put air in contact with the cells that need it. Ultimately, oxygen must get into the cells and carbon dioxide must get out. These are universal challenges facing all terrestrial animals.

Terrestrial vertebrates have a general solution to these challenges. First, they suck in air through their mouth or

nose. The air moves down a trachea, or windpipe, into lungs. In the lungs, O_2 diffuses from air to blood, while CO_2 diffuses from blood to air. Finally, the oxygen-depleted air is exhaled and the process begins again. The specific design of the lungs and respiratory system differs a bit from one taxon to another—we review the most notable distinctions below—but the general process is the same.

Mammalian respiration begins with a deep breath. Let's trace the air through the respiratory process (**FIGURE 21-33**). Air enters through the nose, filling the nasal cavity, where it

THE HUMAN RESPIRATORY SYSTEM

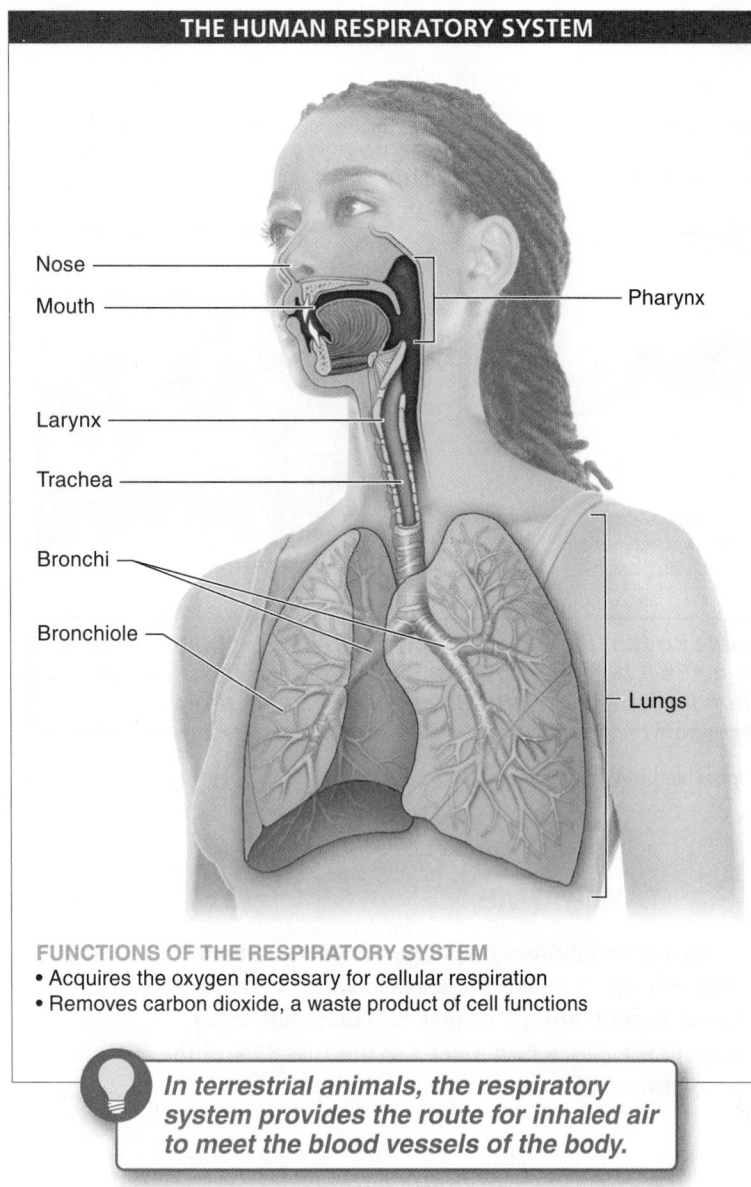

Nose
Mouth
Pharynx
Larynx
Trachea
Bronchi
Bronchiole
Lungs

FUNCTIONS OF THE RESPIRATORY SYSTEM
• Acquires the oxygen necessary for cellular respiration
• Removes carbon dioxide, a waste product of cell functions

In terrestrial animals, the respiratory system provides the route for inhaled air to meet the blood vessels of the body.

FIGURE 21-33 A terrestrial mammal. Overview of the human respiratory system.

becomes warm and moist. Additional air can be taken in through the mouth. In either case, these two entry points for air join together at the throat (also called the pharynx), at the back of the mouth. The air passes through the throat and moves through the voice box, or vocal cords—also called the larynx. The voice box can be seen as the bump on the front of your neck, called the "Adam's apple." From the larynx, the air moves into the trachea (also called the windpipe), a long tube that takes the air into the chest cavity. Once there, the trachea branches into two smaller tubes called bronchi. One bronchus goes to the left lung and the other goes to the right lung.

When the bronchi enter the lungs, which are like stretchy, elastic bags, they branch again. And again. And again. With each successive branching, the bronchi get smaller. Under a certain size they are called bronchioles. And they all just keep branching and spreading out. Eventually, the bronchioles reach a dead end. These dead ends are tiny elastic sacs, the alveoli, and it is here that the air meets the blood vessels (**FIGURE 21-34**).

GAS EXCHANGE THROUGH ALVEOLI

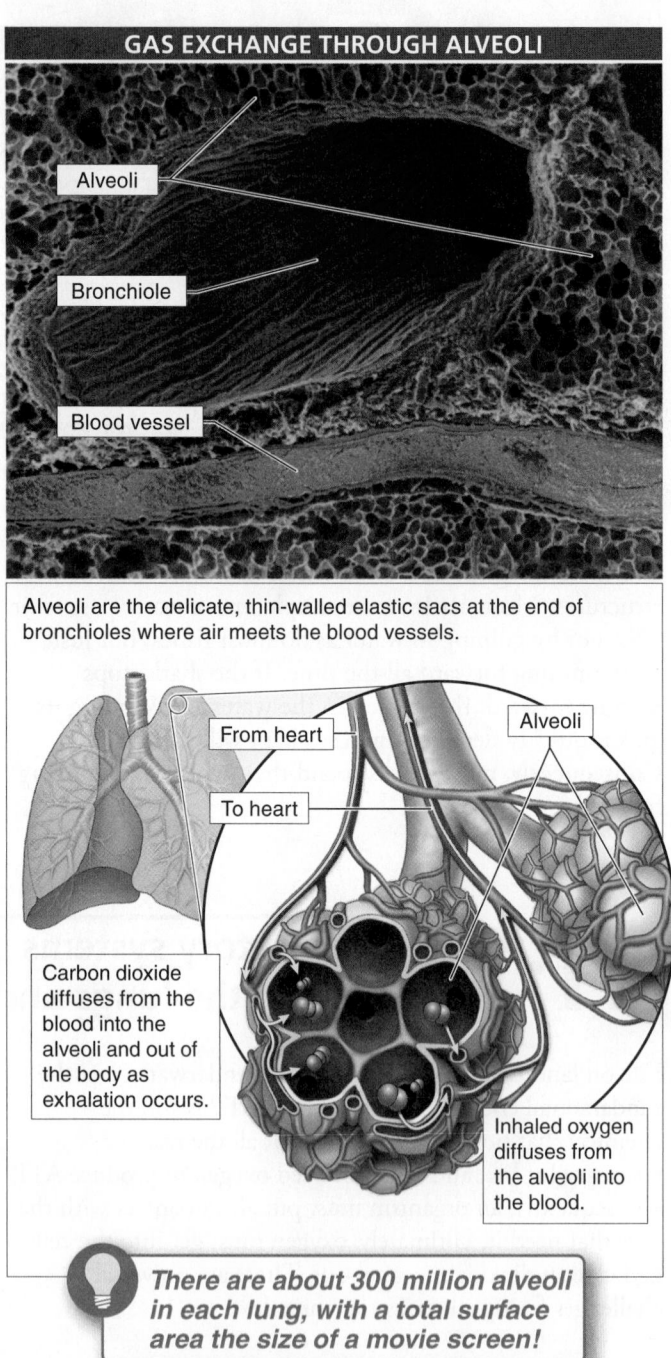

Alveoli
Bronchiole
Blood vessel

Alveoli are the delicate, thin-walled elastic sacs at the end of bronchioles where air meets the blood vessels.

From heart
To heart
Alveoli

Carbon dioxide diffuses from the blood into the alveoli and out of the body as exhalation occurs.

Inhaled oxygen diffuses from the alveoli into the blood.

There are about 300 million alveoli in each lung, with a total surface area the size of a movie screen!

FIGURE 21-34 Alveoli in the lungs: where air meets blood.

TWINS: SMOKER AND NON-SMOKER

DAMAGE CAUSED BY SMOKING
- Toxic particles damage the cilia lining the trachea
- Chemicals can kill immune cells that help fight off infections
- Chemicals trigger mucous secretions that can block the airways
- Walls of alveoli become brittle, reducing respiratory capacity
- Carcinogenic chemicals can trigger cancer

 Although smoking is destructive in numerous ways, stopping smoking at any point can begin the process of reversing some of the damage.

FIGURE 21-35 Effects of smoking. One of these identical twins is a smoker. Can you figure out which one? (She's on the left.)

There are about 300 million alveoli in each human lung, with a total surface area roughly the size of a movie screen. Alveoli are made up of the most delicate cells in our bodies and have ultra-thin walls. Completely surrounding the alveoli, the way your fingers might completely surround a small ball you are grasping, are tiny capillaries; like the alveoli, the capillaries have extremely thin walls. Oxygen in the air in the alveoli dissolves in moisture on the cells lining them. It can then pass right through the two sets of thin membranes—alveolar and capillary—and get picked up by the bloodstream. Simultaneously, carbon dioxide can diffuse from the blood into the alveoli. In the short time you hold it in your lungs, the breath you inhaled is changed. When exhaled, it is depleted of O_2 and laden with CO_2.

Amphibians and reptiles are almost identical to mammals when it comes to the respiratory system. The lungs of amphibians are a bit smaller in relation to body size, but amphibians make up for some of this reduced lung capacity by conducting a bit of gas exchange through their skin. This is why they must keep their skin moist at all times. Reptiles are generally too thick-skinned and scaly to achieve any respiration through their skin, but they have slightly larger lungs than amphibians to pick up the slack. Among the terrestrial vertebrates, birds are the champions of respiratory efficiency. We explore some of their unique adaptations in Section 21-15.

Smoking introduces thousands of different chemicals into the respiratory system, many of which—such as formaldehyde, ammonia, and benzene—have powerfully destructive effects on its cells (**FIGURE 21-35**). Toxic particles in tobacco smoke can damage the tiny, hair-like cilia on the cells lining the trachea, thus reducing their ability to filter out dirt and microorganisms from the air we breathe. The dangerous chemicals can also kill immune system cells that help fight off infections, further reducing our immune response to pathogens. The chemicals in smoke also trigger mucous secretions that can block airways and lead to other respiratory difficulties. After chronic exposure to smoke, the walls of the alveoli become brittle, reducing respiratory capacity. Finally, and perhaps most significantly, carcinogenic chemicals in tobacco smoke can trigger unrestrained cell multiplication in lung tissues, causing cancer.

Q How does smoking damage the lungs? Can the damage be reversed?

Although smoking is destructive in numerous ways—it causes almost half a million deaths in the United States every year—stopping smoking at any point can begin the process of reversing some of the damage. By the end of the first year of non-smoking, the risk of death from lung cancer and heart disease begins to decrease, and after 15 years of non-smoking, the risk of death from these causes returns to the same levels as for individuals who have never smoked.

TAKE-HOME MESSAGE 21·14

In terrestrial vertebrates, respiration begins as air is sucked in through the mouth or nose. The air moves down a trachea into lungs, where O_2 diffuses from the air into capillaries and thus into the bloodstream, while CO_2 diffuses from blood to air. Finally, the oxygen-depleted air is exhaled and the process begins again.

21·15 Birds have unusually efficient respiratory systems.

Birds take breathing to new heights. Because they often spend time in high-altitude, low-oxygen habitats, and fly for long periods of time, they need *a lot* of oxygen for ATP production (**FIGURE 21-36**). These extreme needs can be met by several key evolutionary adaptations that make it possible for birds to exchange gases much more efficiently than other terrestrial vertebrates.

For starters, birds' respiratory adaptations enable them to keep oxygen-rich air flowing through the lungs twice as long as in mammals. In mammals, air is inhaled and reaches a dead end at the alveoli. On the exhale, it changes direction and is breathed out. During the exhale, no new oxygen reaches the lungs, a problematic situation during times of exertion. In birds, a more efficient system ensures that oxygen-containing

air never runs into a dead end and the lungs never experience "stale" air. Here's how they do it (**FIGURE 21-37**).

When the bird inhales, some of the air passes through the lungs, where oxygen can diffuse into the blood. The rest of the air fills temporary holding structures called the posterior air sacs. Then, when the bird exhales, the posterior air sacs contract and push more oxygen-rich air through the lungs. With this system, even during exhales, when no "new" air is being breathed in, oxygen-rich air is passing through the lungs.

When a bird is inhaling, air moving through the lungs passes into other temporary holding structures, called anterior air sacs. Then, as the bird exhales, oxygen-poor air passing from the lungs *and* oxygen-poor air from the anterior air sacs

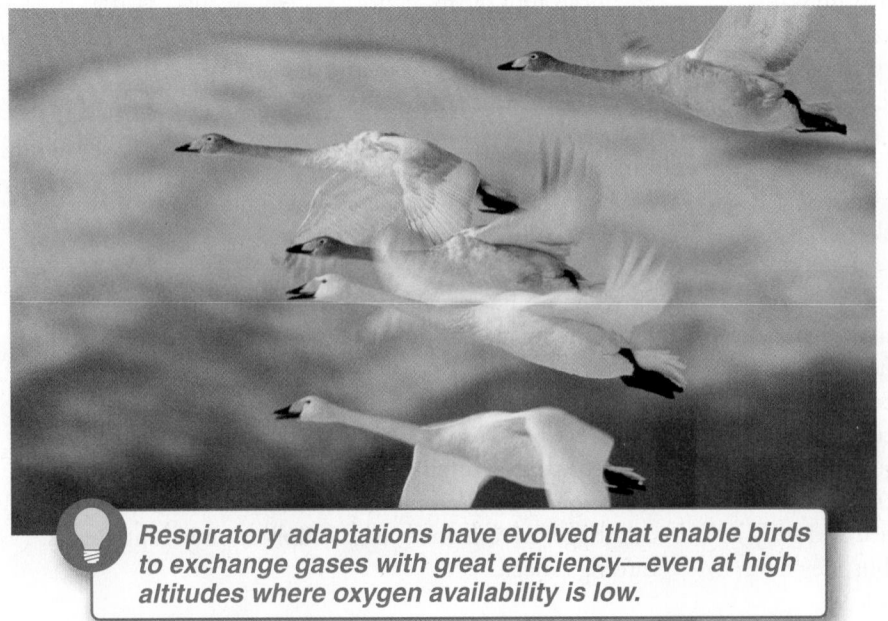

Respiratory adaptations have evolved that enable birds to exchange gases with great efficiency—even at high altitudes where oxygen availability is low.

FIGURE 21-36 High-altitude respiration. Adaptations enable birds to function even when oxygen is in short supply. Shown here: whooper swans, which have been recorded migrating at altitudes up to 8,200 m, where the ambient temperature is −40° C.

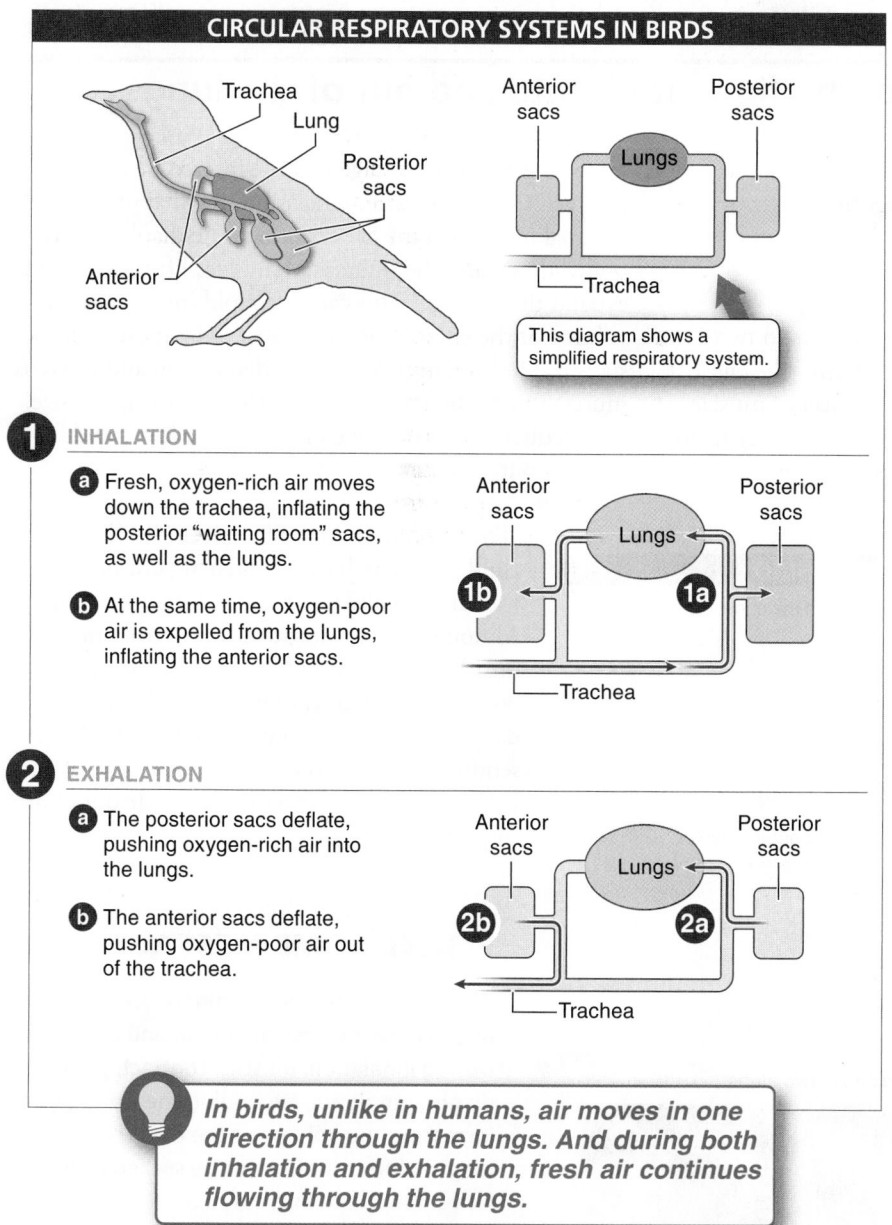

CIRCULAR RESPIRATORY SYSTEMS IN BIRDS

Trachea
Lung
Posterior sacs
Anterior sacs

Anterior sacs
Posterior sacs
Lungs
Trachea

This diagram shows a simplified respiratory system.

1 INHALATION

a Fresh, oxygen-rich air moves down the trachea, inflating the posterior "waiting room" sacs, as well as the lungs.

b At the same time, oxygen-poor air is expelled from the lungs, inflating the anterior sacs.

Anterior sacs
Posterior sacs
Lungs
1b
1a
Trachea

2 EXHALATION

a The posterior sacs deflate, pushing oxygen-rich air into the lungs.

b The anterior sacs deflate, pushing oxygen-poor air out of the trachea.

Anterior sacs
Posterior sacs
Lungs
2b
2a
Trachea

In birds, unlike in humans, air moves in one direction through the lungs. And during both inhalation and exhalation, fresh air continues flowing through the lungs.

FIGURE 21-37 Meeting extreme needs. The highly efficient gas-exchange system of birds supports the oxygen demands of flight.

together move into the trachea, and this mix is expelled from the bird's body.

How is bird breathing less like mammalian breathing and more like fish "breathing"?

Q With their circular system made possible by the air sacs and by the lungs' unique pass-through channels, birds maintain a continuous and unidirectional flow of oxygen-rich air through the lungs. These adaptations make it possible for geese to fly over Mount Everest, nearly six miles above sea level. A mammal deposited at that height would pass out almost instantly from insufficient oxygen.

TAKE-HOME MESSAGE 21·15

Birds often spend time in high-altitude, low-oxygen habitats and may fly for long periods of time, both of which require a great deal of oxygen. These extreme needs are met by a circular system of air flow, which makes it possible for birds to exchange gases more efficiently than other terrestrial vertebrates.

21·16 Muscles control the flow of air into and out of the lungs.

Breathe in. Breathe out. It all seems simple enough. You don't even have to think about it. But over the course of your life, this simple process will happen 500 million times without fail. How does it work?

In reptiles, birds, and mammals, breathing occurs in two steps: inhalation and exhalation (**FIGURE 21-38**). The chest cavity is bordered on the bottom by a large sheet of muscle called the **diaphragm,** which separates the chest cavity from the abdominal cavity. The rest of the chest cavity is surrounded by the rib cage and the intercostal muscles between the ribs. During inhalation, the diaphragm and external intercostal muscles contract; the diaphragm is pulled down and the intercostal muscles lift the ribs and expand the rib cage. This causes a rapid increase in the volume of the chest cavity and lungs, which causes air to be sucked into the lungs. When the diaphragm and intercostal muscles relax, the chest cavity returns to its original size. This reduction in volume compresses the lungs and forces air back out.

"I'm going to hold my breath until I die." As a child, you may have threatened your parents this way. It's actually not possible to do this, however. Although we can consciously control our breathing to some extent, chemical sensors in the body detect when carbon dioxide levels rise dangerously high, and our brain responds by sending signals to the muscles that control our breathing, spurring them to override our efforts to stop breathing.

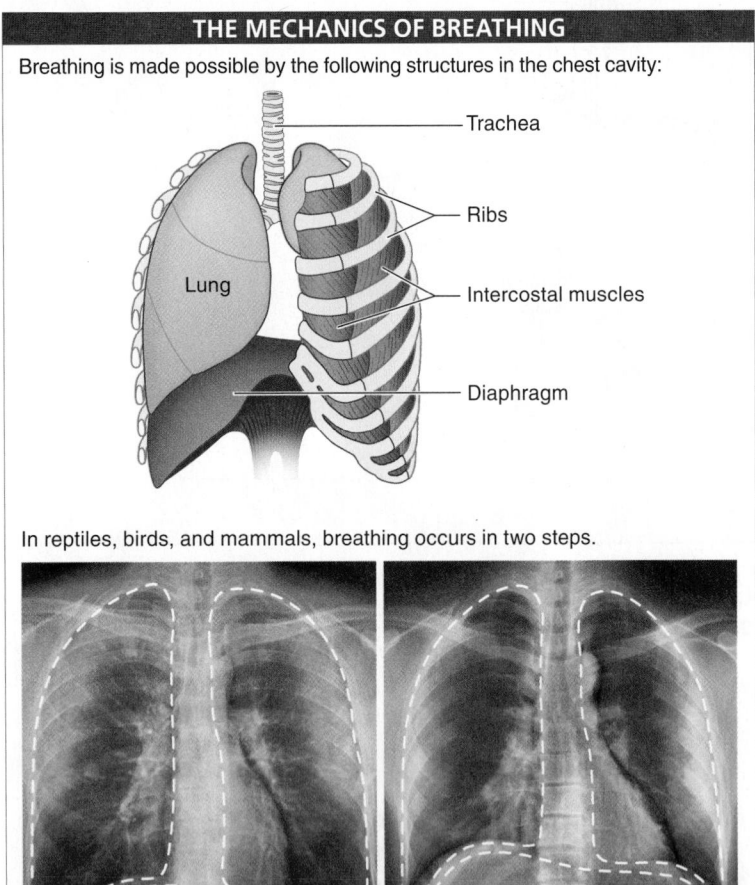

THE MECHANICS OF BREATHING

Breathing is made possible by the following structures in the chest cavity:

- Trachea
- Ribs
- Lung
- Intercostal muscles
- Diaphragm

In reptiles, birds, and mammals, breathing occurs in two steps.

1 INHALATION
- Diaphragm and intercostal muscles contract
- Diaphragm is pulled lower and rib cage expands
- Air is sucked into the lungs

2 EXHALATION
- Diaphragm and intercostal muscles relax
- Chest cavity returns to its original size
- Air is forced back out to the trachea

TAKE-HOME MESSAGE 21·16

In reptiles, birds, and mammals, breathing occurs in two steps: inhalation and exhalation. During inhalation, muscles contract, pulling the diaphragm down, expanding the rib cage, and increasing the volume of the chest cavity and lungs, which causes air to be sucked into the lungs. When the muscles relax, the chest cavity returns to its original size and air is forced out of the lungs.

FIGURE 21-38 Body structures that make breathing possible.

A rare white yak near Goyko Lake, in the Himalayas, almost 5,000 m above sea level.

21·17 Animals living at high elevations have special adaptations to the low-oxygen conditions.

Breathing is more difficult in some places than others. Because the diffusion of gases between the outside and inside of an animal depends on several physical factors, animals differ widely in their respiratory efficiency. One of the most important constraints on the rate at which oxygen diffuses into the blood is air pressure.

At high altitudes, much less oxygen is available. You don't even need to go climbing in the Himalayas to experience this. A relatively short walk up a much smaller mountain will convince you. At 15,000 feet above sea level, for example, the air pressure is half of what it is at sea level. This is because there is less atmosphere above the air, pushing down on it. With lower pressure from above, less oxygen is squeezed into a given volume. The lower air pressure makes it hard to push air into lungs and to drive the oxygen across the alveolar and capillary membranes and into the blood. We struggle at high elevations, because our hemoglobin isn't designed to pick up oxygen at such a low pressure; the hemoglobin isn't sticky enough.

Mountain climbers often carry canisters of pressurized oxygen with them. In the lungs, the high-pressure oxygen can more easily diffuse into the bloodstream. But llamas and other animals living at high elevations don't have cans of oxygen. How do they survive with less available oxygen (**FIGURE 21-39**)? Their hemoglobin has a difficult task: it

BREATHING AT HIGH ALTITUDES

Llamas can thrive in high-altitude, low-oxygen environments because they produce a "stickier" form of hemoglobin that has a higher affinity for oxygen.

FIGURE 21-39 Gas exchange is more difficult in some environments than others.

must pick up oxygen at very low pressure (a condition under which hemoglobin typically has a low affinity for oxygen) so that it can release it to muscles.

Living at elevations of about 3.1 miles (5,000 meters) above sea level, llamas solve this problem by producing a slightly different form of hemoglobin. Under the low-oxygen conditions of high elevations, llama hemoglobin has a higher affinity for oxygen than human hemoglobin. It's stickier. This stickiness enables the hemoglobin to become saturated with four molecules of oxygen even when the llama breathes in relatively "oxygen-poor" air. Because oxygen is being consumed by cellular respiration, the oxygen bound to the hemoglobin is still released to muscles to allow normal activity.

21·18 Humans become acclimated to low-oxygen conditions.

Is it just a coincidence that an unusually large percentage of the world's most accomplished mountain climbers are Sherpas, who live year-round in high-elevation Nepal? No. Although llamas are adapted for high elevations from the day they are born, humans are not—but they acclimate well, and Sherpas are among the most impressively acclimated high-elevation dwellers (**FIGURE 21-40**).

You don't need to live on Mount Everest, however, to become physiologically acclimated to the low-oxygen conditions found at high elevations. Athletes around the world have long known that they can increase their strength, speed, and stamina by training at high elevations. And, as with llamas, human acclimation to low-oxygen conditions comes from modifications (though they are acquired rather than inherited) to hemoglobin.

Training for three to five weeks at high elevations, usually 6,000–7,000 feet above sea level, triggers several physiological changes—the process of acclimation. These changes include

FIGURE 21-40 Humans acclimate to high-elevation living with improved respiratory efficiency. Shown here: A Sherpa carrying a load along a mountain ridge in Nepal.

FIGURE 21-41 High-elevation training.

BENEFITS OF HIGH-ELEVATION TRAINING
• Additional red blood cell production
• Increased blood and capillary volume
• Increased number of mitochondria
• Increased diphosphoglyceric acid (DPG) in red blood cells, which reduces hemoglobin's stickiness and releases more of the oxygen it carries

At high elevations, hemoglobin releases more oxygen to the tissues at any P_{O_2}.

DPG-modified hemoglobin

stimulating the production of additional red blood cells, increasing blood and capillary volume, and increasing the number of mitochondria. High-elevation training also causes an increase in a chemical called diphosphoglyceric acid (DPG) in red blood cells. This acid combines with hemoglobin in the red blood cells and alters the protein's shape ever so slightly. In doing so, it reduces hemoglobin's stickiness, giving it a lower affinity for oxygen. With this reduced oxygen affinity, the DPG-modified hemoglobin releases—at any elevation—more of the O_2 that it carries (**FIGURE 21-41**). Athletes who train at high elevations find that with the additional oxygen released to their tissues, they can improve their performance by about 3%. This difference was manifested dramatically during the 1968 Olympics in Mexico City (elevation 7,500 feet) when the top five finishers in the 10,000-meter race were all year-round high-elevation

Q How can high-elevation training help athletes?

residents. The benefits of high-elevation training remain after an athlete returns to sea level—increasing performance significantly. But just as humans become acclimated to high elevations, we also become acclimated to low elevations, and the DPG (and the performance enhancement it can bring) has returned to low-elevation levels by about three to five weeks after returning to sea level.

TAKE-HOME MESSAGE 21·18

Humans living at high elevations become acclimated to low-oxygen conditions over the course of three to five weeks. This acclimation includes increasing the production of diphosphoglyceric acid (DPG) in red blood cells and thereby reducing hemoglobin's affinity for oxygen, leading to release of higher levels of oxygen to muscles during exertion.

"CONTENTS UNDER PRESSURE."
Recognizing and avoiding the bends.

Q: WHAT DO SCUBA DIVERS AND BOTTLES OF CHAMPAGNE HAVE IN COMMON? Under high pressure, large amounts of a gas can be dissolved in fluid. This is why huge amounts of carbon dioxide can be present in a bottle of champagne. It is also what happens to divers who, with tremendous water pressure on their bodies, must breathe highly pressurized air in order for oxygen to dissolve in their bloodstream.

Q: WHY ARE BUBBLES BAD NEWS FOR DIVERS? When a champagne bottle is uncorked, the pressure is suddenly released. Under low pressure, not nearly as much carbon dioxide can be held in the fluid, so it quickly bubbles out. Similarly, when a scuba diver returns too quickly to the surface, the pressure on the body is rapidly reduced, as is the capacity of the blood to hold gases. And, like champagne after the cork is popped, many gases in the diver's blood—particularly nitrogen, which is the biggest component of air—quickly bubble out and can almost cause the diver to explode from within, in a condition known as "the bends." Something similar to the bends can occur if someone flies in an unpressurized plane and suddenly climbs very high, where the air pressure is lower. This was sometimes reported by pilots in World War II.

Q: WHAT CAN YOU CONCLUDE ABOUT AVOIDING THE BENDS? Just as the solution to opening a bottle of champagne without its bubbling over is to release the pressure very slowly by removing the cork slowly, a diver must reduce the pressure on his or her blood very slowly by rising gradually from the depths of the water. Alternatively, a diver can be placed in a chamber (called a hyperbaric chamber) to be gradually depressurized.

Big Ideas in ...
Circulation and Respiration

21·1–21·3 The circulatory system is the chief route of distribution in animals.

- In animals, the circulatory system is the chief distribution system, with important functions in transport of gases, nutrients, waste products, immune system cells, and hormones, as well as maintenance of homeostasis.
- Circulatory systems can be open, with no clear distinction between circulating fluid and interstitial fluid, or closed, with a clear distinction.
- Fishes have two-chambered hearts and one circuit of blood flow; birds and mammals have four-chambered hearts and two circuits of flow, which enables them to pump blood to the body at higher pressure.

21·4–21·10 The human circulatory system consists of a heart, blood vessels, and blood.

- The human heart is a muscular pump at the center of the circulatory system. It sends blood on a figure 8, two-circuit path through the body, first to the lungs and then, on its second circuit, to the tissues and organs.
- Blood is a salty, protein-rich mixture of cells and fluid, important in homeostasis and in the transport of respiratory gases, vitamins and minerals, nutrients, hormones, components of the immune system, and metabolic wastes.
- Blood flows from the heart to the tissues of the body and back to the heart through a series of endothelium-lined blood vessels.
- Arteries are elastic and carry blood at high pressure from the heart to capillaries. Capillaries are tiny, thin-walled vessels that are the site of diffusion of nutrients, gases, waste products, and other materials between tissues and blood. Blood returns to the heart through veins, at low pressure, and aided by contractions of skeletal muscles.
- High blood pressure and cardiovascular disease impair circulatory system functioning.

- The lymphatic system has a supporting role in circulation: it recycles fluid back into the circulatory system, moves white blood cells around the body to help fight pathogens, and absorbs nutrients from the digestive system.

21·11–21·16 The respiratory system enables gas exchange in animals.

- In very small organisms, gas exchange can occur by direct diffusion. In larger organisms, gas exchange is a two-stage process: exchange between the external environment and the organism's circulatory system, and exchange between the circulatory system and the cells involved in cellular respiration.
- Red blood cells are filled with hemoglobin, which picks up oxygen in the lungs and transports it around the body, releasing it in organs and tissues for cellular respiration.
- In aquatic vertebrates, gas exchange takes place as oxygen-carrying water passes through the gills. In terrestrial vertebrates, breathing occurs in two steps: inhalation and exhalation; in the lungs, O_2 diffuses across capillaries from the air to the blood, while CO_2 diffuses from blood to air.

21·17–21·18 Evolutionary adaptations maximize oxygen delivery.

- Some animals living at high elevations cope with the reduced oxygen by producing hemoglobin that has a higher affinity for oxygen.
- Humans living at high elevations become acclimated to the low-oxygen conditions by increasing production of diphosphoglyceric acid (DPG), thus reducing hemoglobin's affinity for oxygen in the tissues.

See the To-Go Guide (packaged with every new copy of this textbook) for an illustrated summary of the chapter.

Check Your Knowledge

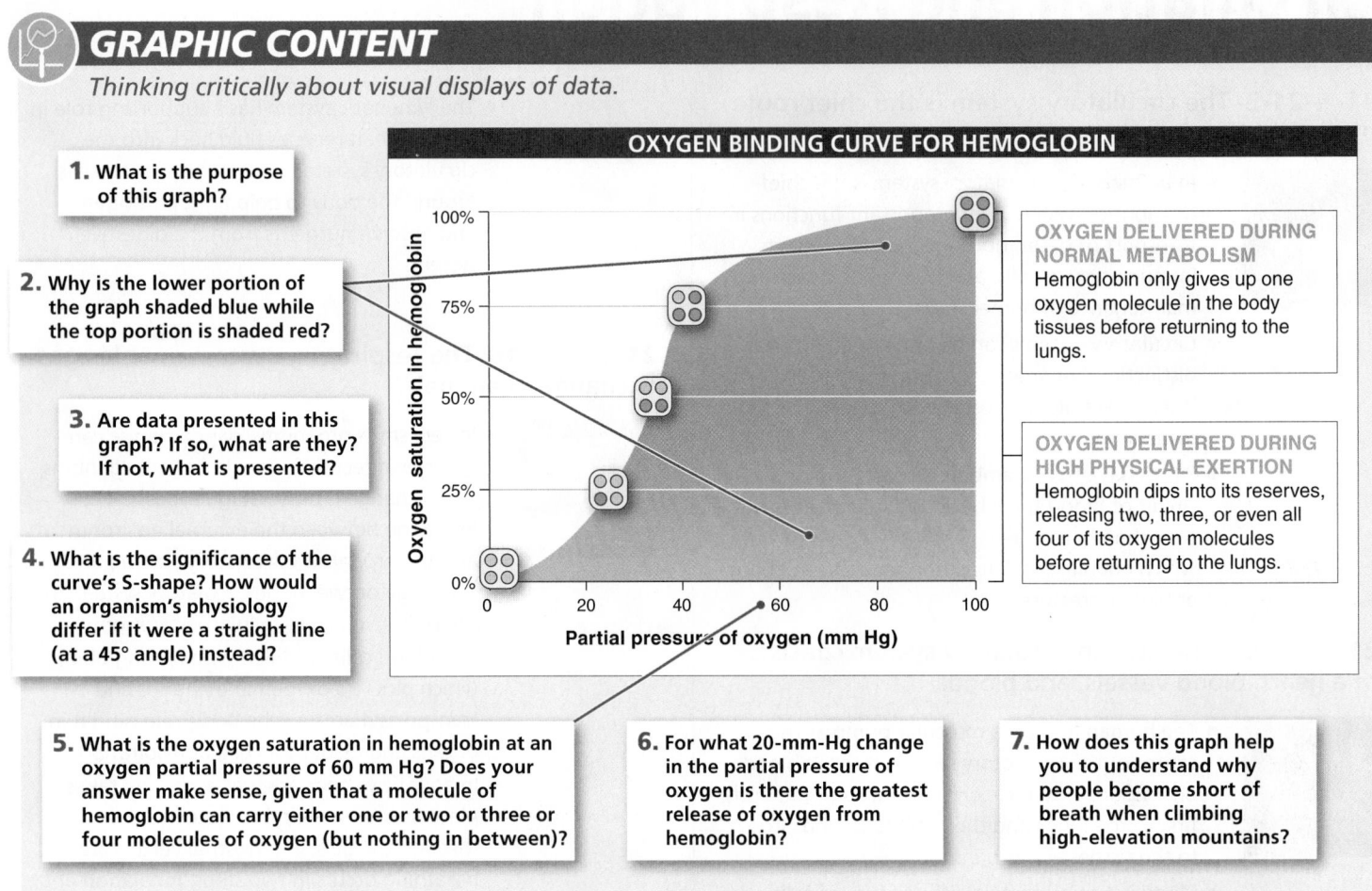

OXYGEN BINDING CURVE FOR HEMOGLOBIN

1. What is the purpose of this graph?

2. Why is the lower portion of the graph shaded blue while the top portion is shaded red?

3. Are data presented in this graph? If so, what are they? If not, what is presented?

4. What is the significance of the curve's S-shape? How would an organism's physiology differ if it were a straight line (at a 45° angle) instead?

OXYGEN DELIVERED DURING NORMAL METABOLISM
Hemoglobin only gives up one oxygen molecule in the body tissues before returning to the lungs.

OXYGEN DELIVERED DURING HIGH PHYSICAL EXERTION
Hemoglobin dips into its reserves, releasing two, three, or even all four of its oxygen molecules before returning to the lungs.

Oxygen saturation in hemoglobin — 100%, 75%, 50%, 25%, 0%
Partial pressure of oxygen (mm Hg) — 0, 20, 40, 60, 80, 100

5. What is the oxygen saturation in hemoglobin at an oxygen partial pressure of 60 mm Hg? Does your answer make sense, given that a molecule of hemoglobin can carry either one or two or three or four molecules of oxygen (but nothing in between)?

6. For what 20-mm-Hg change in the partial pressure of oxygen is there the greatest release of oxygen from hemoglobin?

7. How does this graph help you to understand why people become short of breath when climbing high-elevation mountains?

See Answers at the back of the book.

Key Terms in Circulation and Respiration

Multiple-Choice Questions

1. Which of the following is the name of the fluid in an insect's open circulatory system?

a) blood

b) hemoglobin

c) lymph

d) hemolymph

e) tracheal lymph

100 HARD

29

0 EASY

2. How can flatworms, simple animals with a flat body shape, survive without a circulatory system?

a) Flatworms do not have internal body fluids that need to be sectioned off and transported by vessels.

b) Because all cells in flat-bodied animals are in direct contact with the external environment, direct diffusion is sufficient for all their respiratory needs.

c) In flatworms, all cells are located near central body branches or near the body surface, so diffusion alone can transport important nutrients.

d) Flatworms use the water currents in their aquatic environment to circulate the necessary nutrients throughout their body.

e) Flatworms have multiple hearts and so can pump blood directly into tissues without needing a circulatory system.

100 HARD

25

0 EASY

3. Fishes have:

a) a two-chambered heart.

b) multiple hearts.

c) an open circulatory system.

d) a four-chambered heart.

e) Both a) and c) are correct.

100 HARD

29

0 EASY

4. Blood pressure tends to fall with increasing distance from the heart. On the basis of this information, which of the following lists the types of blood vessel, in order, from highest blood pressure to lowest?

a) veins, arteries, capillaries

b) arteries, capillaries, veins

c) veins, capillaries, arteries

d) capillaries, veins, arteries

e) arteries, veins, capillaries

100 HARD

60

0 EASY

5. The heartbeat in a vertebrate:

a) is initiated by modified muscle tissue, the sinoatrial (SA) node, that contracts without nerve stimulation.

b) is triggered by rhythmic stimulation from the cardiac nerve.

c) begins at the bottom of the ventricles and moves upward through the heart.

d) cannot be recorded by an EKG, but the neurons that control it can be.

e) is initiated by the atrioventricular node.

100 HARD

18

0 EASY

6. Both red blood cells and white blood cells are derived from cells in the:

a) heart.

b) liver.

c) spleen.

d) lungs.

e) bone marrow.

100 HARD

10

0 EASY

7. In a person at rest, most of his or her blood is likely to be in the:

a) heart.
b) capillaries.
c) veins.
d) arteries.
e) interstitial fluid.

100 HARD
25
0 EASY

8. Which of the following components of human blood is a cell fragment?

a) spiracle
b) red blood cell
c) white blood cell
d) plasma
e) platelet

100 HARD
0 **15** EASY

9. How are the blood-circulation system and the lymphatic system related to each other?

a) Blood carries nutrients to cells. The lymphatic system removes waste from cells.
b) Blood carries nutrients and oxygen to cells and removes their waste. The lymphatic system removes bacteria and debris from the blood.
c) Blood carries nutrients and oxygen to cells and removes their waste. The lymphatic system takes the cellular waste to the kidneys.
d) Blood carries oxygen to all the cells. The lymphatic system removes carbon dioxide from the blood and carries it to the lungs.
e) Blood carries carbon dioxide from tissues to the lungs. The lymphatic system carries oxygen from the lungs to the body tissues.

100 HARD
40
0 EASY

10. Why do most fishes swim with their mouths open?

a) They do this to take in any food particles suspended in the water.
b) This is a cooling mechanism to help regulate body temperature.
c) This allows a fish to swim faster.
d) This helps prevent infection by mouth parasites.
e) They do this to ventilate their gills.

100 HARD
0 **7** EASY

11. Carbon dioxide transport differs from oxygen transport in the circulatory systems of mammals, because:

a) CO_2 is transported mostly in the plasma, while O_2 is transported mostly in the red blood cells.
b) CO_2 is transported mostly in the platelets, while O_2 is transported mostly in the red blood cells.
c) CO_2 is transported mostly via the lymphatic system, while O_2 is transported mostly in the red blood cells.
d) CO_2 is bound primarily to receptors within the red blood cell membrane, while O_2 is bound primarily to hemoglobin inside the red blood cells.
e) CO_2 is transported mostly in the plasma, while O_2 is transported mostly in hemoglobin within the plasma.

100 HARD
61
0 EASY

12. Breathing in birds is more like "breathing" in fishes than in mammals, because:

a) water and high-altitude air have similar viscosity.
b) oxygen never runs into a dead end.
c) both birds and fishes have gill arches.
d) the blood vessels in bird lungs, like those in fish gills, are insulated with a fatty coating, reducing heat loss.
e) in birds and fishes, but not mammals, the heart pumps in a two-circuit system of blood flow.

100 HARD
70
0 EASY

13. Which of the following are the main muscles used in breathing?

a) back muscles and thoracic muscles
b) intercostal muscles and pectoral muscles
c) diaphragm and thoracic muscles
d) diaphragm and back muscles
e) intercostal muscles and diaphragm

100 HARD
44
0 EASY

14. Under regular metabolic conditions, what percentage of oxygen is released from the blood to the tissues?

a) 1%
b) 75%
c) 25%
d) 100%
e) 50%

100 HARD
32
0 EASY

15. Why is carbon monoxide (CO) so dangerous?

a) CO prevents hemoglobin from binding to and transporting O_2 to the body tissues, resulting in oxygen starvation and death.
b) CO prevents CO_2 from dissolving in the blood, and CO_2 builds up to toxic levels.
c) CO modifies the structure of hemoglobin, making it more difficult for O_2 to be transported and released in the body.
d) CO coats the inside of the alveoli, preventing diffusion of O_2 from the lungs into the blood.
e) CO binds to hemolymph, so tissues cannot remove O_2 from the red blood cells and the tissue dies.

100 HARD
26
0 EASY

16. Which of the following has the highest binding affinity for oxygen?

a) hemolymph
b) human hemoglobin
c) llama hemoglobin
d) plasma
e) All have equal binding affinity for oxygen.

100 HARD
41
0 EASY

17. Why does llama hemoglobin have a higher oxygen-binding affinity than human hemoglobin?

a) Like humans, llama fetuses use a form of hemoglobin with a higher binding affinity than the mother's hemoglobin, but unlike humans, llamas continue to use this form of hemoglobin after birth.

b) Because llamas are more active than humans, they require hemoglobin with a greater maximum oxygen saturation.

c) Llama blood has a higher CO_2 concentration than human blood, resulting in a need for hemoglobin with a higher binding affinity.

d) Llamas live at higher elevations than most humans and require a means to bind O_2 when oxygen is at a lower concentration in the air.

e) Llamas produce hemoglobin molecules that carry six oxygen molecules rather than the four carried by human hemoglobin.

100 HARD
20
0 EASY

18. Diphosphoglyceric acid (DPG):

a) causes the release of more O_2 to body tissues.

b) makes it possible for blood to carry more CO_2.

c) is the main reason that breathing is difficult at high elevations.

d) increases the binding affinity of adult hemoglobin for O_2.

e) encourages the production of more hemoglobin.

100 HARD
41
0 EASY

Short-Answer Questions

1. Why has the evolution of multicellular organisms led to the development of circulatory systems? What characteristic distinguishes closed and open circulatory systems?

2. What is the difference between single- and double-circuit cardiovascular systems? Which would be better suited for a higher energy demand? Why?

3. Name the three main types of cells (or cell fragments) that are found in blood and describe their primary functions.

4. How is gas exchange accomplished in organisms with gills and in those with lungs?

See Answers at the back of the book.
For additional study questions, go to www.prep-u.com.

ABOUT THE CHAPTER OPENING PHOTO

Blood vessels. This photo was made by injecting resin into blood vessels within connective tissue, followed by chemical digestion of the tissue surrounding the vessels. Magnification: ×125.

At rest and at play: optimizing human physiological functioning

22

Nutrition and Digestion

22·1–22·3 Food provides the raw materials for growth and the fuel to make it happen.

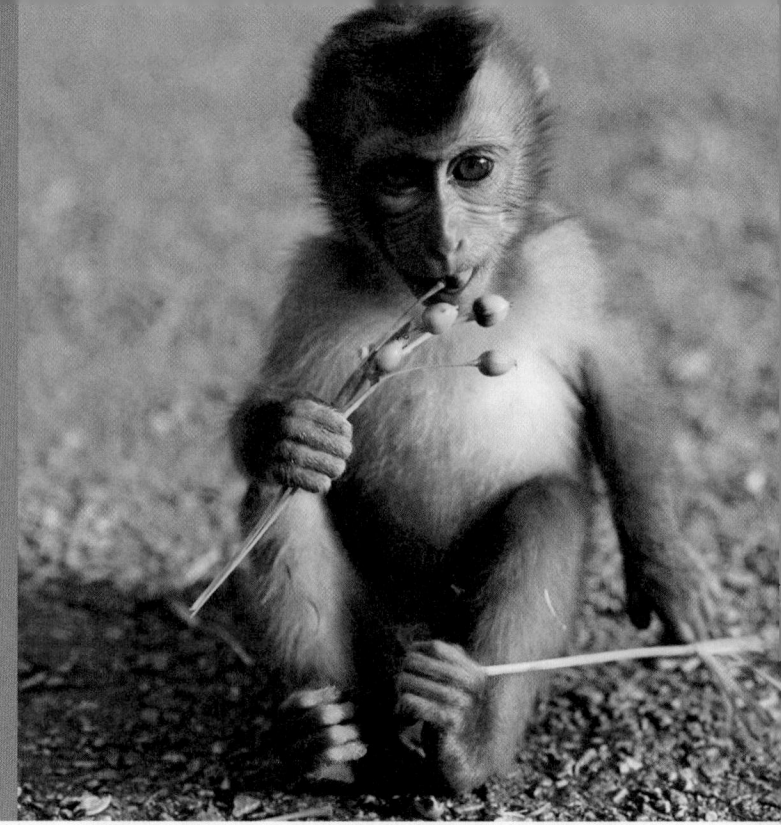

Living organisms need raw materials and fuel to function.

22·1

Why do organisms need food?

Lamb roulade with leek basil stuffing and a red wine sauce. Chili fries. Lime-marinated tofu kabobs. A big vanilla milkshake. We dress food up in an almost infinite variety of combinations. We garnish it, we heap on condiments, we daydream about it, and we even write books about it. But despite all the fuss, it really boils down to two simple biological needs: raw materials and fuel. Just as a carpenter needs wood and a car needs fuel, living organisms need raw materials and fuel to function.

Here's why: every second of every day, chemical reactions are occurring inside us. We build complex molecules. We reproduce. We respond to stimuli. Our need for fuel is one of the two reasons why we must eat: building a body, moving around, reproducing, and just staying alive all require energy. Food provides that energy. And the other reason is that to grow and build the myriad complex molecules required for life, we need raw materials: molecules of carbon and nitrogen and phosphorus, to name just a few. Food provides these raw materials.

FIGURE 22-1 Made possible by food. Living organisms need raw materials and fuel to function.

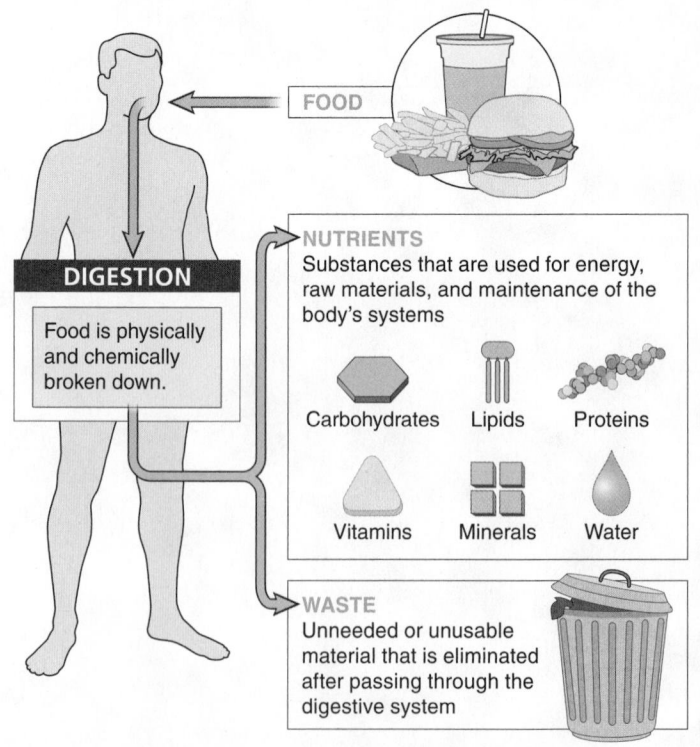

FOOD

DIGESTION

Food is physically and chemically broken down.

NUTRIENTS
Substances that are used for energy, raw materials, and maintenance of the body's systems

Carbohydrates   Lipids   Proteins

Vitamins   Minerals   Water

WASTE
Unneeded or unusable material that is eliminated after passing through the digestive system

What exactly happens to the food we eat? We'll examine this question in detail throughout the chapter. In **FIGURE 22-1**, though, we can see that the food we eat is physically and chemically broken down into its fundamental macromolecular components in the process of **digestion.** Our body quickly breaks down food and separates it into the usable and unusable. The usable materials are carbohydrates, lipids, proteins, vitamins, minerals, and water. These six groups of **nutrients** are the substances that are used for energy, raw materials, and maintenance of the body's systems. Anything we consume that doesn't fall into one of these categories is unusable. You can't get nutrients from dirt or rocks. They just pass through the digestive system and are eliminated.

Ultimately, an organism's body weight represents the balance between the energy carried within the molecular bonds of the food it consumes and the energy burned in the process of living. Any surplus calories are stored, usually as fat or as glycogen (see Section 2-8), a form of carbohydrate stored primarily in muscle and liver tissue.

TAKE-HOME MESSAGE 22·1

Animals must eat for two reasons: to acquire the energy needed for all growth and activity, and to acquire the raw materials required for life.

22·2 What's on the menu? Animals have a variety of diets.

All organisms need food—but there are some very different ways to get it. Plants and other photosynthetic organisms (including many bacteria and protists) make their own food, through photosynthesis. But animals do not have the cellular machinery to do this and so they must eat other organisms. Most animals eat plants (that make their own chemical energy), while some animals eat other animals (that eat plants). Some animals even eat animals that eat animals that eat animals (that eat plants)—but that's pretty rare (see Section 15-7). In every case, though, while some organisms are able to capture solar energy to make food, all animals must acquire that energy indirectly by consuming other organisms.

In the animal world, species fall into three groups based on their diets (**FIGURE 22-2**).

Carnivores The **carnivores** are predatory animals that consume only other animals. They include spiders and snakes; mammalian species such as wolves, seals, bats, and cats; and hawks, owls, and other birds of prey. Some carnivores don't actually kill their prey but instead just suck nutrient-rich fluids from them. Mosquitoes and ticks are carnivorous fluid-feeders.

Herbivores Food: easy to get, but hard to digest. That sums up life as a

herbivore, an organism that consumes only plants. Because plants are plentiful in most habitats and can't run away, they are easy targets for predation. To protect themselves, however, plants tend to carry many toxic compounds that are difficult or impossible for animals to break down chemically. Nonetheless, many herbivores have developed digestive adaptations to overcome these difficulties. We'll explore a couple of them in detail in Section 22-13. Examples of herbivores include sea turtles and caterpillars, as well as many species of seed-eating birds and nut-eating squirrels and a variety of large grazing mammals such as cows, horses, and deer. And just as there are fluid-feeding carnivores, there are fluid-feeding herbivores. Aphids, for example, pierce the surface of plants and suck their sugary sap.

Omnivores Most humans, as **omnivores,** eat plants and animals and can digest both efficiently. We share this diet with numerous other species, including cockroaches. Omnivores come in all sizes, from bears to raccoons, from chickens to flies and wasps.

Q *Humans grow and tend plants and animals with the sole purpose of eating them. Are there any other species with agriculture?*

Watching farmers cultivate plants and animals for food, it might seem reasonable to assume that humans are unique in this endeavor. Agriculture is not limited to humans, however. Leaf cutter ants chop up leaves, but rather than eating them, they spit out the mulch, mold it into a

TYPES OF ANIMAL DIETS

CARNIVORES
Animals that consume only other animals. (Shown here: A leopard seal feeding on a penguin)

HERBIVORES
Animals that consume only plants. (Shown here: A white-tailed deer feeding on an apple)

OMNIVORES
Animals that consume both plants and animals. (Shown here: A western scrub-jay feeding on an acorn (left) and an insect larva (right))

FIGURE 22-2 Animal diets: carnivores, herbivores, and omnivores.

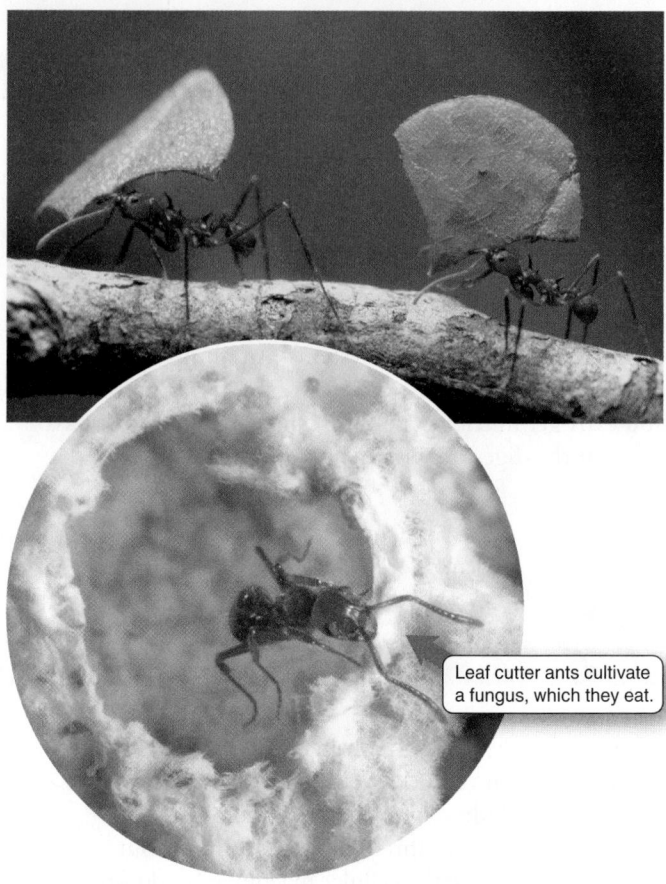

Leaf cutter ants cultivate a fungus, which they eat.

FIGURE 22-3 Fungus-farming ants. Leaf cutter ants harvest leaves in order to grow fungus, which they then consume.

honeycomb shape, and then grow fungus on the mulch (**FIGURE 22-3**). They then eat the fungus at their leisure. These ants are the only species that scientists know of, other than humans, with a system of agriculture (and they've been doing it for significantly longer than we have).

TAKE-HOME MESSAGE 22·2

All animals require food. Plants and other photosynthetic organisms produce food through photosynthesis, and animals have one of three types of diet. Carnivores consume only other animals. Herbivores consume only plants. And omnivores, including most humans, consume both plants and animals.

Have you ever gone a whole day without eating? Or have you ever spent a few weeks trying to reduce your caloric intake? Living in a state of hunger can be torturous. In the early 1990s, eight human "guinea pigs" learned this the hard way. Living in the Biosphere 2 dome—a self-contained, 3.2-acre world filled with plants and animals that was designed to explore sustainable living with minimal environmental impact—they took part in an experiment on the effects of a low-calorie diet, among other things. The findings were not surprising: all the participants lost weight, but they also became very unhappy. They argued constantly and frequently squabbled over meal portions in what they dubbed "the hunger dome" (**FIGURE 22-4**). In an earlier study, people were kept hungry for six months. Over time, study participants filled increasing hours with food fantasies. Recipes even displaced sex as the favorite topic of discussion. Put simply, humans (and all other living organisms) need a steady and sufficient flow of energy to function well.

The energetic value of food is measured in very small amounts of energy called **calories,** with a single calorie defined as the energy required to raise the temperature of 1 gram of water by 1° C. However, the term can be a bit confusing: in discussing human consumption, the term "calorie" actually refers to a **kilocalorie (kcal)**, which is 1,000 calories. So when the label on a package of cookies says that a cookie provides "100 calories," the cookie actually provides 100 *kilocalories* or 100,000 *calories.*

So what do we actually need to survive? We examine first the body's energy needs and then, in the following sections, the various nutrients necessary for growth and maintenance.

We first determine the minimal energetic needs of an individual who is doing nothing more than the equivalent of sitting on a couch all day. This is called the **basal metabolic rate,** or **BMR,** and refers to the amount of energy expended at rest, with no food in the digestive tract, in a neutral-temperature environment. For humans, the BMR can be roughly approximated as 1 calorie per hour per gram of body weight, or about 1,400 kcal/day for a woman (weighing 120 pounds) and about 1,700 kcal/day for a man (weighing 160 pounds). The difference between the sexes is mostly a function of the difference in body size: the male has more cells to power.

The BMR allows easy comparisons across species because it is so clearly defined, but to accurately evaluate organisms' energy

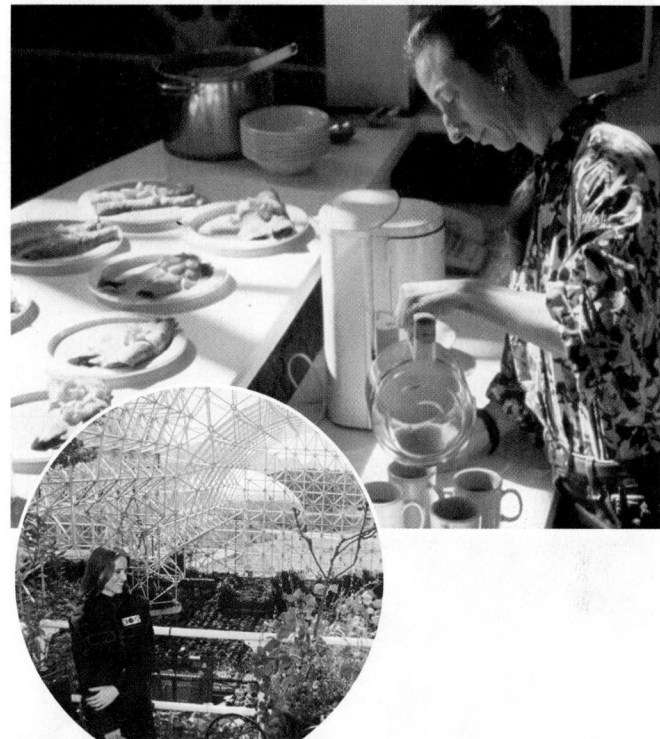

❝ If we ever all start talking to each other, that would be a major accomplishment. **❞**

— ONE OF THE PARTICIPANTS OF BIOSPHERE 2

FIGURE 22-4 Hungry Biosphere 2 crew. Living on a low-calorie diet led to weight loss and a cranky disposition for Biosphere 2 participants.

needs, we must have a sense of how active they are. Someone moving around and involved in physical exertion will require more energy than someone sitting at a desk all day, and a very large person will require more than a small person (**FIGURE 22-5**). In actuality, individuals need about 50% to 100% more kilocalories per day than their BMR. A 120-pound woman requires 1,800–2,400 kcal/day, and a 160-pound man requires about 2,400–3,200 kcal/day.

From one animal species to another basal metabolic rates differ tremendously. For the tiny shrew, for instance, BMR is about 35 times higher than that of a human (**FIGURE 22-6**). The shrew's heart beats more than 500 times per minute *at rest!*

COMPONENTS OF ENERGY EXPENDITURE

BASAL METABOLIC RATE (BMR)
The minimal energy expenditure of an organism at rest

Average kcal/day to cover the minimal energetic needs of an organism at rest

ACTUAL DAILY ENERGY EXPENDITURE
The basal metabolic rate *plus* the energy required for all activity

Individuals generally need about 50% to 100% more kilocalories per day than their BMR.

Average kcal/day to cover all of the energetic needs of an organism (including all activity)

FIGURE 22-5 How many calories do you need? Energy expenditure varies depending on body size and activity level.

Let's estimate what a shrew needs to eat each day. If it weighs 5 grams and has a BMR of 35 calories per hour per gram, we can calculate as follows:

Body weight		Energy needed each hour		Hours per day		Animal's caloric needs
	×		×		=	
5 grams	×	35 cal/ gram/hr	×	24 hr/ day	=	4,200 cal/day

BMR varies tremendously among different animal species. The tiny shrew has a BMR about 35 times higher than that of a human, relative to weight.

FIGURE 22-6 Live fast. This tiny shrew must meet the high calorie demands of its fast-beating heart.

Thus, the shrew would need 4.2 kcal/day if it were at rest. But if it needed another 4 kcal/day for its normal activities, it would have to eat about 8 kcal/day. As we'll see below, a pure source of carbohydrate or protein carries about 4 kcal/gram. Thus, every day, the shrew must find and consume at least 2 grams of food. This is no small challenge when you only weigh 5 grams. The task is equivalent to a 200-pound man finding and eating 80 pounds of food every day.

The shrew is not the only species with extreme caloric needs. Animals that fast or hibernate for long periods of time must prepare by consuming many kilocalories. Male elephant seals, for example, eat little or nothing during their 100-day breeding season, instead spending their time battling with other males for dominance and mating with females. During these 100 days, a large male that begins the season at 6,600 pounds (3,000 kg) may lose one-third of his body weight. Consequently, the male seal's caloric requirements increase in the months leading up to the breeding season.

TAKE-HOME MESSAGE 22·3

To function well, living organisms need sufficient energy, measured in kilocalories. The minimal energy needed by an individual not engaged in any activity is called its basal metabolic rate, or BMR.

22·4–22·7 Nutrients are grouped into six categories.

A jaguar takes a drink at a watering hole in Belize.

22·4 Water is an essential nutrient.

All animals need water to survive. In the early 1900s, an Italian man sentenced to death reportedly volunteered to determine how long he could live without food or water. The fatal "experiment" lasted only 17 days before he died. Water, which is considered an essential nutrient, constitutes about 60% to 65% of the body weight in most mammals. This water plays important roles in both the intracellular fluid and the extracellular fluids, including blood, in humans and other animals (**FIGURE 22-7**). Water in body fluids serves a variety of critical purposes, all of which can be impaired when the animal becomes dehydrated.

- Water transports nutrients and waste materials throughout the body.

- It takes part in chemical reactions.

- It serves as a solvent for many vitamins and minerals, amino acids, and sugars.

- It lubricates many joints, the spinal cord, and the eyes.

- It helps regulate body temperature.

A person expending about 2,000 kcal/day needs about 2–3 liters of water each day. This can come directly from drinking water, but there are many other sources of water in

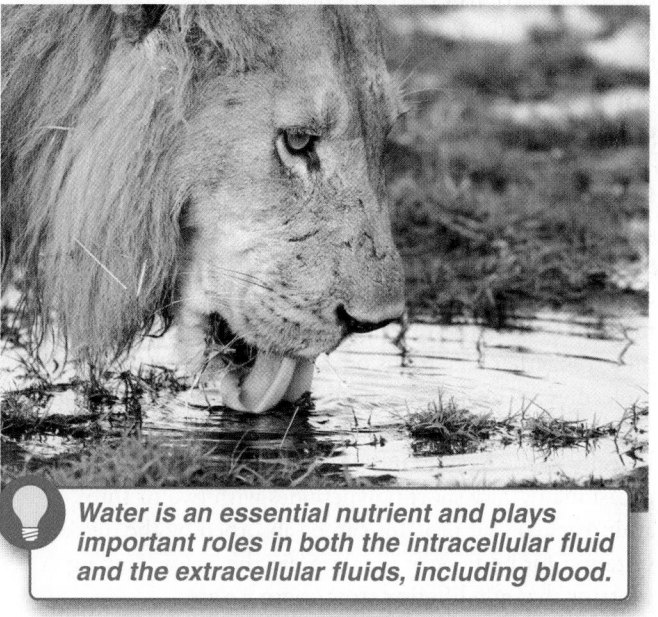

Water is an essential nutrient and plays important roles in both the intracellular fluid and the extracellular fluids, including blood.

FIGURE 22-7 Water is an essential component of the diet.

our diet, including milk, which is about 90% water, juices, and food, and the water released as a by-product of many chemical reactions. Water intake must offset the water lost in urine, feces, respiration, and sweating. It is important to remember, too, as we saw in the Chapter 3 StreetBio, that drinking too much water too quickly can also be dangerous. The consumption of too much water can lead to water intoxication—which sometimes happens to marathon runners during a race. When coupled with the loss of salt through sweating, over-consumption of water can lead to severe sodium imbalance. This imbalance causes dizziness, nausea, confusion, and swelling of the extremities. And in serious cases, it can lead to swelling of the brain, which can cause death.

Q If water is so important, why are there some desert animals that never need to drink?

Water usage varies among animal species. Tremendous water efficiency has evolved in some desert mammals—the kangaroo rat, for example—and some of

these animals do not need to drink any water at all. Rather, they get all the water they need from their food and metabolic processes. Among the marine birds and reptiles, most are able to drink salt water. They can do this with the aid of salt glands that remove and excrete the excess salt they consume.

TAKE-HOME MESSAGE 22·4

Water is probably the single most important component of an animal's diet. It constitutes 60% to 65% of the body weight of most mammals. It transports nutrients and waste materials throughout the body, takes part in metabolic reactions, serves as a solvent, lubricates many body parts, and helps regulate body temperature.

22·5

Proteins in food are broken down to build proteins in the body.

When you are on the verge of starvation, any type of food can save you. So from that perspective, it's true that calories are all that matter. But for optimum health, organisms must consume many types of nutrients. In this section and the next, we investigate the chief nutritional features of the three types of calorie sources: proteins, carbohydrates, and fats. We begin by investigating protein, a vital component of the diet and essential structural material in the body.

Proteins: Raw Material for Growth

What are proteins, and what is their role in the diet? Protein in our diet is principally a building material. As described in detail in Sections 2-14 through 2-18, protein molecules are made of long chains of smaller molecules—amino acids—linked together, like beads on a string. Once eaten, protein molecules are broken down into the individual amino acids, much like removing the beads from the string one at a time. It's only in the form of individual amino acids (and, occasionally, very short polypeptides with two or three amino acids) that proteins can be absorbed by the digestive system. Our bodies can then reorder the beads, making proteins that are different from those we ate.

The process of protein digestion and protein rebuilding does seem a bit inefficient: we consume entire, intact proteins such as muscle cells or hemoglobin molecules, from chicken or fish or some other animal, which we then break down and may ultimately use to construct similar versions of the same

protein molecules. Nonetheless, animal digestive systems are able to absorb only the simpler building blocks of proteins, not entire proteins themselves, so we must first break down all the proteins we eat and later reassemble new ones.

Besides serving as building materials, the proteins we build from amino acids function as enzymes, catalyzing reactions throughout the body (see Sections 2-17 and 2-18). Proteins, whether from our diet or from tissue in our bodies, can also be broken down to release energy or to be stored as fat. Protein breakdown happens, for example, when we are consuming too few (or too many) calories to sustain necessary growth and activities. It also happens during a long exercise session. Our bodies can use protein as fuel because we have a variety of methods of converting one type of chemical to another to release or store energy (see Section 4-17). The breakdown of proteins for energy generates 4 kilocalories per gram. But the reverse reaction—building proteins from fat or carbohydrates—cannot be done. Only the proteins in our diet contain nitrogen, which is necessary for protein building. Thus, all of the proteins we build contain parts of proteins we have consumed. When a protein is broken down for energy, the nitrogen it carries is excreted in our urine.

There are a great many sources of dietary protein, from both plants and animals (**FIGURE 22-8**). Animal sources include egg whites, shrimp, tuna, lobster, chicken, turkey, and all

FUNCTION
Once proteins are broken down, the amino acids are used as the raw materials to build new complex proteins, such as hemoglobin and muscle.

SOURCE
- Animals: egg whites, shrimp, tuna, poultry, and meat
- Plants: grains, vegetables, nuts, seeds, and legumes

STORAGE
- Amino acids are usually stored for less than half a day before being reassembled into proteins throughout the body
- Can be converted to fat and stored in fat cells

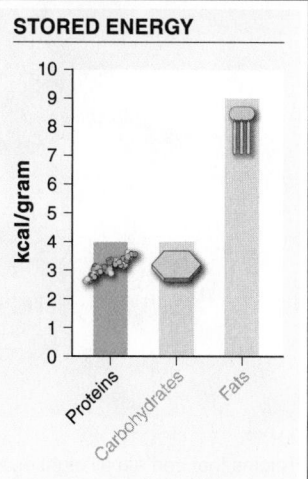

FIGURE 22-8 **Versatile proteins.** Besides serving as building materials, proteins can be broken down to release energy or can be stored as fat.

meat products. Plant sources of protein include grains, vegetables, nuts, seeds, and legumes, such as beans.

Try this. Put one can of Coke and one can of Diet Coke somewhere that they will get hot, and leave them for a few days. Then taste them. The Diet Coke will lose its flavor and taste bitter, even if you cool it down, while the Coke will taste fine. What's going on? Diet Coke, but not regular Coke, is sweetened with aspartame (NutraSweet is the brand name). Aspartame is made by linking together two amino acids, aspartic acid and phenylalanine—each of which tastes bitter by itself. When the two are joined as aspartame, however, the taste is very sweet. The reaction by which aspartic acid and phenylalanine are linked together can be reversed by heat. So if you leave a can of Diet Coke in a hot area, the aspartame decomposes to the bitter amino acids. They're not harmful, but they aren't very tasty either.

Q *Why does Diet Coke (but not regular Coke) taste bitter if you leave it in the sun for a few days?*

Are all proteins the same, or do they vary in important ways? Animals, including humans, require 20 different amino acids to make proteins. Most animals, however, can produce only about half of these amino acids themselves—for example, we can make only 12 of the 20 amino acids. The 8 amino acids we cannot produce we must get from the food we eat. For that reason, the 8 amino acids we must consume in food are called the **essential amino acids,** and the remaining 12 are called **non-essential amino acids.**

All proteins are not created equal. Protein-containing animal products vary in their amino acid composition. All eight of

the essential amino acids are found in milk, eggs, meat, poultry, cheese, and fish; these animal products have "complete" proteins (**FIGURE 22-9**). On the other hand, most proteins that we get from eating plants are not complete. Corn proteins, for example, have only six of the essential amino acids, as do beans (although they don't have the same six). In fact, with the exception of soybeans, no single plant food has all eight. A healthy diet is one containing not just a sufficient *amount of protein* but a sufficient amount of each of the eight essential amino acids that we need to make proteins. Consequently, we must know about the amino acid content of the proteins we eat in addition to how much protein the food contains.

How and where do we store proteins? Proteins and the amino acid pool they generate on digestion cannot be stored very long in our bodies, usually less than a day. By that point, they are broken down and the nitrogen we don't need is excreted. Because our bodies are making proteins constantly, it is important to take in all of the essential amino acids over the course of each day.

Q *Why is it beneficial for vegetarians to eat beans and corn over the course of the same day?*

The recommended daily intake of protein is approximately 0.8 grams per kilogram of body weight. This translates to about 45 grams of protein for a 120-pound woman (and about 25 additional grams per day for pregnant or lactating women) and 60 grams for a 160-pound man. Exercising

COMPLETE PROTEINS
Proteins that contain all eight essential amino acids

INCOMPLETE PROTEINS
Proteins that do not contain all eight essential amino acids

 Almost all plant proteins are incomplete, while virtually all animal proteins are complete.

FIGURE 22-9 Animal versus plant proteins. Animal proteins contain all eight of the essential amino acids. Plant foods contain varying amounts and types of essential amino acids.

athletes can require double or even triple this amount, but it is important to remember that it is the exercise that generates the additional need. Protein on its own does nothing to stimulate muscle growth; it simply serves as the source for the raw materials.

Animals aren't the only organisms that need protein. Every organism—even plants—must build enzymes and so needs protein. This is dramatically apparent in the Venus flytrap, a plant that captures and consumes insects in order to acquire protein. It does this with highly elastic, curved leaves. Water pressure inside the V-shaped leaf causes it to expand into an unstable, stretched-open position that is on the verge of snapping closed. When an insect or spider lands on the leaf, it triggers an electrical signal that causes a brief, rapid change in the water pressure inside the leaf. The change in water pressure is enough to cause the leaf to snap shut, capturing the insect. The plant then releases digestive juices that break down the insect into its usable nutrients. Venus flytraps grow in places where the soil is poor and, especially, where the soil is low in nitrogen; they can extract nitrogen from the animal prey they capture. The green leaves and stems of Venus flytraps, however, should serve as a reminder that these plants are also photosynthetic. And, in fact, they gain nearly all of their energy by harnessing the energy in sunlight to build sugars. The nitrogen they need (and resort to carnivory to obtain) helps them build the enzymes necessary to conduct photosynthesis.

> **TAKE-HOME MESSAGE 22·5**
>
> Animals consume three different types of macro-molecules for calories: proteins, carbohydrates, and fats. Proteins provide raw materials for growth and for the production of enzymes. Food sources of protein vary in amino acid composition. Humans require 20 amino acids for building proteins, and 8 of these, called essential amino acids, can only be supplied by the diet.

22·6 Carbohydrates and lipids provide bodies with energy and more.

Reading these words requires carbohydrates in your body, obtained from your diet, to fuel your brain—and your muscles as well, as they help you sit up and hold your book. Food fat, too, a subset of the group of macromolecular nutrients called lipids (see Sections 2-11–2-13), provides energy for your body's functioning and gives food delicious flavor (while contributing to weight gain and heart disease if consumed in too large a quantity). In this section, we

evaluate the macromolecules carbohydrates and lipids. These two crucial nutrients supply nearly all the energy that fuels your daily activities.

Carbohydrates: Fuel for Living Machines

What are carbohydrates, and what is their role in the diet? Carbohydrates are the primary fuel on which animal bodies run. In humans, nearly all of the energy used by our brain

FUNCTION
Carbohydrates provide energy to fuel movement, growth, and all cellular activities in the body.

SOURCE
Fruits, vegetables, and grains

STORAGE
- Carbohydrates are stored in the liver and muscle cells as glycogen for about a day before being broken down to provide energy
- Can be converted to fat and stored in fat cells

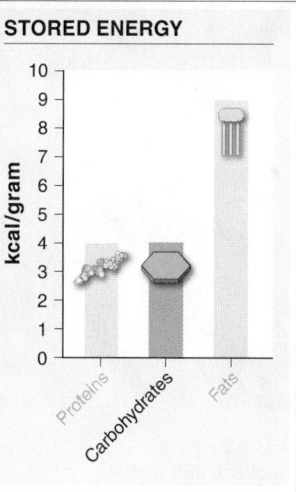

STORED ENERGY

FIGURE 22-10 **Carbohydrate is the primary fuel on which animal bodies run.**

every day comes from the simple carbohydrate glucose. As we saw in Chapter 2, all carbohydrates are made primarily from carbon, hydrogen, and oxygen. When the bonds between these atoms are broken, energy is released that can be captured by the body and used to fuel movement, growth, and all the other cellular activities that require energy.

We get the majority of our dietary carbohydrates from fruits, vegetables, and grains (**FIGURE 22-10**). And, as with proteins, the breakdown of carbohydrates for energy generates 4 kilocalories per gram.

Are all carbohydrates the same, or do they vary in important ways? Although, structurally, all carbohydrates are variations on a simple theme—molecules formed from carbon, hydrogen, and oxygen in the approximate proportions of CH_2O (see Figure 2-20)—they vary dramatically in their complexity and break down in the body at different rates (**FIGURE 22-11**). Animals consume carbohydrates in the form of simple sugars (monosaccharides), disaccharides and digestible complex sugars, and fiber (indigestible complex sugars).

Simple sugars. These include glucose and fructose. They are linear or ring structures with three to seven carbon atoms. Animals can break them down directly through the steps of glycolysis (see Section 4-13), rapidly releasing the stored energy from the bonds of the sugar.

Disaccharides and digestible complex sugars. Multiple simple sugars can bond together to form complex but digestible molecules. Disaccharides, such as sucrose (table sugar), are just two simple sugars joined together. Complex sugars, such

as starch and glycogen, are large molecules that may consist of hundreds or thousands of glucose molecules connected in dense, branching patterns. For an animal to have access to the energy stored in the bonds of the individual simple sugars, it must first break the bonds that link those sugars together. As these bonds are broken, simple sugars become available for the energy-releasing reactions of glycolysis.

Fiber. This is a complex carbohydrate, such as cellulose, that forms the structural parts of plants. Fiber differs from starch and other digestible complex sugars by having a different bond connecting the simple sugars together. In humans, this bond cannot be broken by any digestive enzyme, making fiber indigestible. As we'll see later in this chapter, although fiber isn't broken down for energy or other molecules used by the body, it still plays an important role in digestion and is necessary in the diet to maintain health.

How and where do humans store carbohydrates? Carbohydrates in our body are stored mostly as glycogen (see Section 2-8) in liver and muscle cells. At any given time, we can store only about one day's worth of energy. After we start exercising, or when our bodies need energy for an activity, a signal is sent causing the release of enzymes that break the bonds holding together the highly branched glycogen. This glycogen breakdown produces a flood of glucose into the bloodstream and in the muscles where the energy is needed.

Large amounts of water are bound to stored glycogen: 4 pounds of water for every pound of glycogen. Consequently, as glycogen in your liver and muscles is used, the water bound to it is released from the tissue and lost as urine. This is why, as stores of glycogen are depleted in the initial stages of a diet,

TYPES OF CARBOHYDRATES

SIMPLE SUGARS
- Glucose, fructose, and others
- Breakdown by glycolysis releases energy rapidly

DIGESTIBLE COMPLEX SUGARS
- Simple sugars bonded together, such as sucrose (table sugar) or starch
- Bonds between simple sugars must be broken before the energy-releasing reactions of glycolysis occur

FIBER
- Complex carbohydrate that forms structural parts of plants
- Indigestible in humans, but has a significant role in digestion

FIGURE 22-11 Carbohydrate complexity. Some carbohydrates are readily broken down for fuel, but fiber passes through the human body undigested.

there is a dramatic initial weight loss from the loss of water that was bound to the glycogen. As your body starts utilizing stored fat, the rate of weight loss slows considerably.

Fats: Long-Term Energy Storage Experts

What are fats, and what is their role in the diet? Fats in the animal diet, described in detail in Chapter 2, function primarily as a dense source of energy that can be efficiently stored in the body (**FIGURE 22-12**). The average person has about four or five weeks' worth of stored energy in the form of fat. Compared with carbohydrates or proteins, a given amount of fat contains more than twice as much stored energy: 1 gram of fat produces 9 kilocalories. Another feature that makes fats particularly efficient as energy-storage molecules is that, because they are hydrophobic, fats are stored without binding to water.

FATS: LONG-TERM ENERGY STORAGE

FUNCTION
Fats provide a dense source of energy that can be efficiently stored in the body, and they aid in keeping the body warm.

SOURCE
Butter, cheese, oils, eggs, and meat

STORAGE
Fats are stored in fat cells throughout the body.

STORED ENERGY

FIGURE 22-12 Energy-rich fats. At 9 kilocalories per gram, fats are rich in stored energy.

Because fats are poor conductors of heat, fats stored in a layer just beneath the skin can help to keep the body warm. Penguins and walruses, for example, can maintain relatively high body temperatures despite living in very cold habitats, because of their thick layer of insulating fat.

Q *If fats contain more than double the amount of energy found in the same amount of carbohydrates or proteins, why aren't fats a better fuel to consume before exercising?*

Here's a perplexing fact: although the total amount of energy in a gram of fat is greater than that found in carbohydrates or proteins, fat isn't the optimum nutrient for most situations. When it comes to exercise, for example, muscle cells need quick access to energy. The problem is that, in muscles, fat burns very slowly for energy. Remember from Chapter 4 that the universal source of chemical energy in the body is ATP. This means that the energy in fat or carbohydrate or protein must be captured as ATP before it is of use to muscle cells. It turns out to be much easier for the body to break down muscle glycogen and blood glucose to make ATP than to break down fat. In fact, the rate of ATP synthesis from carbohydrates is about double the rate from fats.

Are all fats the same nutritionally, or do they vary in important ways? With proteins, we saw that there are essential and non-essential amino acids. Similarly, with dietary fats, there are essential and non-essential fatty acids. Humans are able to produce nearly all necessary lipids. But the essential fatty acids—including linoleic acid, from the omega-6 family of fatty acids—must be consumed. Linoleic acid is essential as a building block for signaling molecules, such as some hormones; a deficiency can lead to infertility and difficulty lactating. Another essential fatty acid, important in a variety of metabolic processes, is linolenic acid, from the omega-3 family of fatty acids. Linolenic acid is used by the body to make fatty acids that are essential for normal growth and development, especially in the eyes and brain.

Another important distinction among dietary fats is between saturated and unsaturated fats (**FIGURE 22-13**). In our diet, fats usually come in the form of fatty acids, long chains of carbon atoms with hydrogens attached. If each carbon within the chain is bonded to two hydrogen atoms, the molecule carries the maximum number of hydrogen atoms and is said to be saturated. (For a refresher, see Figure 2-31.) Conversely, if some of the carbons are bound to only a single hydrogen, the fatty acid is unsaturated.

SATURATED vs. UNSATURATED FATS

SATURATED FATS
- Fatty acids have straight tails and can be packed together tightly
- Tend to be solid at room temperature
- More likely to be stored as fat in the body

UNSATURATED FATS
- Fatty acids have kinked tails and cannot be packed together tightly
- Tend to be liquid at room temperature
- Less likely to be stored as fat in the body

FIGURE 22-13 Saturated and unsaturated fats compared.

When saturated, fatty acids are very straight and the fat molecules can be packed together tightly. This causes saturated fats to be solid at room temperature, like butter. When unsaturated, the fatty acids have kinks in the hydrocarbon tail and cannot be packed together as tightly. Consequently, unsaturated fats do not solidify so easily and tend to be liquid at room temperature, like vegetable oil. Because unsaturated fatty acids can accept one or more hydrogen atoms, they are a bit less stable and more reactive—that is, they will take part in a greater variety of chemical reactions—than saturated fatty acids, making them less likely to be stored as body fat.

Trans fats have been in the news because of their tendency when consumed to raise levels of low-density lipoprotein cholesterol, increasing the risk of coronary heart disease. Trans fat is made when hydrogen is added to vegetable oil—a process called hydrogenation (see Section 2-12 for a review of trans fat chemistry). Trans fat often can be found in some of the same foods as saturated fat, such as vegetable shortenings,

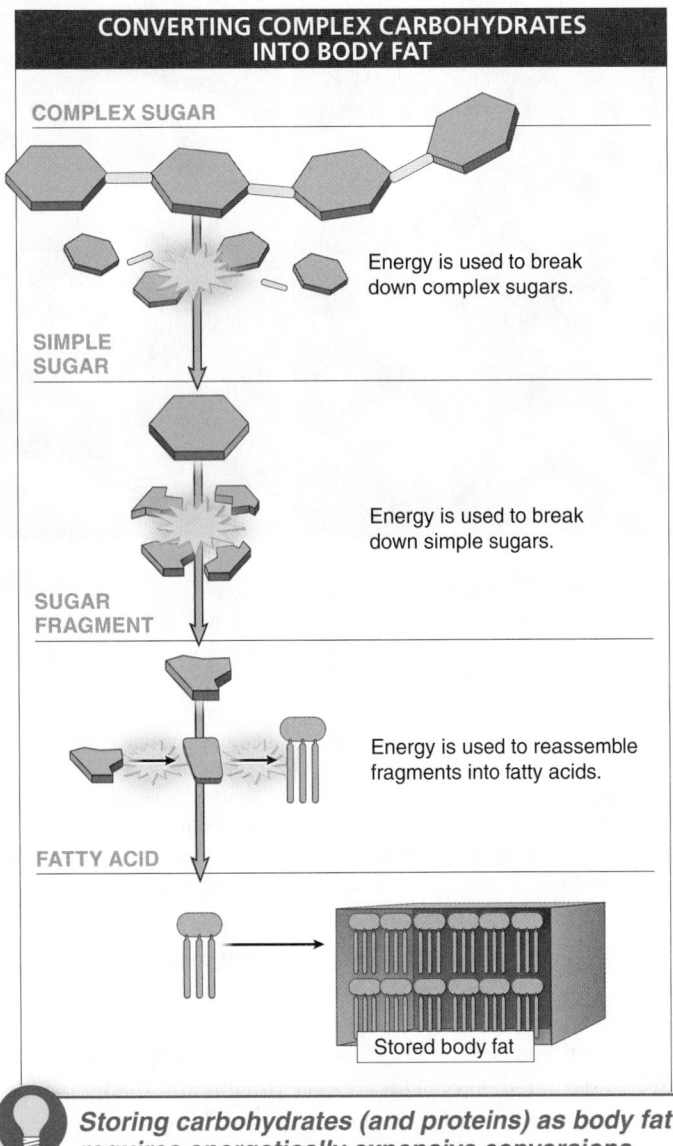

CONVERTING COMPLEX CARBOHYDRATES INTO BODY FAT

COMPLEX SUGAR

Energy is used to break down complex sugars.

SIMPLE SUGAR

Energy is used to break down simple sugars.

SUGAR FRAGMENT

Energy is used to reassemble fragments into fatty acids.

FATTY ACID

Stored body fat

Storing carbohydrates (and proteins) as body fat requires energetically expensive conversions, reducing the amount of fat stored.

FIGURE 22-14 **Inefficient conversion to body fat.** By the time carbohydrates can be stored as body fat, much of the original energy has been lost in fueling the conversion.

crackers, candies, cookies, snack foods, fried foods, baked goods, and other foods made with partially hydrogenated vegetable oils. The American Heart Association recommends that these fats be minimized in the diet.

How and where do we store fats? If a human consumes more calories than he or she burns, most of the excess (regardless of whether these calories were consumed as carbohydrate, fat, or protein) gets converted to fat and stored in fat cells distributed throughout the body. A pound of body fat holds 3,600 kilocalories worth of energy. It is like a savings account for an uncertain future.

Given that our bodies can convert excess calories into body fat, regardless of whether the calories were initially ingested as carbohydrates or proteins, why is it still an effective weight-management strategy to minimize dietary fat intake? The answer rests in the number of chemical conversions carbohydrates and proteins must undergo to become body fat. In the case of carbohydrates, complex sugars must first be broken down into simple sugars—a process that requires energy. Then the simple sugars must be broken down and the fragments reassembled as fatty acids—another process that requires energy. By the time those fatty acids can be stored as body fat, much of the original energy stored in the carbohydrates has been lost in fueling all the chemical conversions (**FIGURE 22-14**). And for someone trying to minimize body fat, that's good news. Storing protein as body fat also requires several energetically expensive conversions that reduce the ultimate quantity of fat stored.

TAKE-HOME MESSAGE 22·6

Carbohydrates are the primary fuel on which animal bodies run. Dietary fats function primarily as a dense source of energy that can be efficiently stored in the body.

22·7

Vitamins and minerals are necessary for good health.

« Vitamins can double your health! »
—DR. ATKINS, on *The Larry King Show* (making perhaps the most nonsensical nutritional claim ever)

It would be nice if we could take a pill that would make us more healthy or fit. Vitamins are not such a miracle pill. They're a bit like security guards at a museum: above a certain number, they don't make the museum any better, but in their absence, the museum is likely to become a whole lot worse. And while vitamin supplements are not a health panacea, vitamins and minerals do have an important role in nutrition.

Vitamins are organic compounds that are essential nutrients required by the body in small amounts for normal growth and health. **Minerals** are the chemical elements, other than those commonly found in organic molecules—carbon, hydrogen, oxygen, and nitrogen—some of which are required in the diet in small amounts. There are three features common to all vitamins and minerals.

1. They don't yield any usable energy. Rather, they serve as collaborators with enzymes to enable the processing of the proteins, carbohydrates, and fats we eat, and they catalyze a wide range of other chemical reactions around the body.

2. They need to be consumed in much smaller amounts than proteins, carbohydrates, and fats in our diet. This is because they tend to serve as reaction catalysts and so can be recycled and reused again and again.

3. If we have a healthy diet, we tend to consume sufficient quantities of vitamins and minerals in our food.

Although their biological roles are frequently similar, vitamins and minerals have a fundamental chemical difference. Vitamins are organic molecules, meaning they contain carbon, whereas minerals are inorganic nutrients. Because vitamins are organic, they are more fragile, easily destroyed by heat and other chemical or physical extremes. Minerals, on the other hand, are elements, so they can't be broken down further or lose their chemical identity. They stay in your body until they are excreted. In fact, the only way they can be lost is if they are leached away—such as from food into the water as the food is cooked and the water is then thrown away. Seventeen minerals have been identified that are essential to the human diet. They are described in **FIGURE 22-15**.

Thirteen vitamins essential to humans, also described in Figure 22-15, have been discovered. They fall into two groups, based on whether they are soluble in fat or water. The water-soluble vitamins include eight vitamins that are part of the vitamin B complex, plus vitamin C. There is some variation among species in the ability to manufacture (rather than needing to ingest) vitamins. Cats and dogs, for instance, can make vitamin C and do not need to consume it.

There are four fat-soluble vitamins: A, D, E, and K. Because they are stored in fatty tissue and the liver until they are needed, they don't need to be consumed as regularly as water-soluble vitamins. Also, because excess water-soluble vitamins can be removed by the kidney and excreted in urine, they are less likely to reach toxic levels than fat-soluble vitamins.

Currently, more than half of the U.S. population takes regular vitamin supplements (**FIGURE 22-16**). Should so many people be taking these supplements? It is difficult to give a yes-or-no answer to this question. Nonetheless, it is well established that in the United States, few adults suffer from any vitamin and mineral deficiency diseases. This is because nearly all adults get all of the nutrients they need from the food they eat. For this reason, nutritionists believe that high doses of vitamins and minerals are not therapeutic, and they suggest that most people do not need to take regular supplements.

Usually, taking vitamin supplements is a costly but harmless behavior. The consumption of increasing amounts of vitamins often just leads to a plateau of maximum benefit, after which greater consumption has no additional benefits. Occasionally, however, taking vitamin and mineral supplements is both costly and harmful: in many cases, above a certain point, additional consumption of fat-soluble vitamins can lead to toxicity and cause serious health problems. Excessive consumption of vitamin A, for example, can lead to hair loss in men, while over-consumption of vitamin D can lead to growth retardation. Liver damage, too, is a common result of excessive vitamin and mineral consumption. Moreover, research has definitively discredited claims that vitamin E supplementation slows or prevents aging or improves physical performance, and no supplement has been demonstrated to "relieve stress"—despite the extravagant claims of marketers.

So, we can conclude that most people in the United States have no need to take vitamin and mineral supplements. Under special circumstances, however, supplementation is necessary.

- Women who lose unusually large amounts of blood during menstruation may need iron.

- Post-menopausal women and those allergic to milk may not get enough calcium in their diet to prevent bone degeneration.

- Pregnant and breast-feeding women may need additional vitamins and minerals to support a developing fetus or rapidly growing infant.

- Pregnant women, or women who may become pregnant, may need additional folate, which helps prevent neural tube defects.

ESSENTIAL VITAMINS AND MINERALS IN THE HUMAN DIET

VITAMIN	MAJOR FUNCTION	SOURCES
WATER-SOLUBLE		
B₁ (thiamin)	Coenzyme in cellular respiration	Liver, legumes, whole grains
B₂ (riboflavin)	Coenzyme in FAD	Dairy foods, meat, eggs, green leafy vegetables
B₆ (pyridoxine)	Coenzyme in amino acid metabolism	Liver, whole grains, dairy foods
B₁₂ (cobalamin)	Formation of nucleic acids, proteins, and red blood cells	Liver, meat, dairy foods, eggs
Biotin	Found in coenzymes	Liver, yeast, bacteria in gut
C (ascorbic acid)	Formation of connective tissues; antioxidant	Citrus fruits, tomatoes, potatoes
Folic acid	Coenzyme in formation of heme and nucleotides	Vegetables, eggs, liver, whole grains
Niacin	Coenzyme in NAD and NADP	Meat, fowl, liver, yeast
Pantothenic acid	Found in acetyl-CoA	Liver, eggs, yeast
FAT-SOLUBLE		
A (retinol)	Found in visual pigments	Fruits, vegetables, liver, dairy foods
D (cholecalciferol)	Absorption of calcium and phosphate	Fortified milk, fish oils, sunshine
E (tocopherol)	Muscle maintenance; antioxidant	Meat, dairy foods, whole grains
K (menadione)	Blood clotting	Intestinal bacteria, liver

MINERAL	MAJOR FUNCTION	SOURCES
MAJOR MINERALS (essential minerals found in the human body in amounts larger than 5 g)		
Calcium (Ca)	Found in bones and teeth; blood clotting; muscle action	Dairy foods, eggs, green leafy vegetables, whole grains
Chlorine (Cl)	Water balance; principal negative ion in extracellular fluid	Table salt (NaCl), meat, eggs, vegetables, dairy foods
Magnesium (Mg)	Required by many enzymes; found in bones and teeth	Green vegetables, meat, whole grains, nuts, milk, legumes
Phosphorus (P)	Found in nucleic acids, ATP, and phospholipids	Dairy foods, eggs, meat, whole grains, legumes, nuts
Potassium (K)	Nerve and muscle action; principal positive ion in cells	Meat, whole grains, fruits, vegetables
Sodium (Na)	Nerve and muscle action; water balance	Table salt, dairy foods, meat, eggs
Sulfur (S)	Found in proteins and coenzymes; detoxification	Meat, eggs, dairy foods, nuts, legumes
TRACE MINERALS (essential minerals found in the human body in amounts smaller than 5 g)		
Chromium (Cr)	Glucose metabolism	Meat, dairy foods, whole grains, legumes, yeast
Cobalt (Co)	Found in vitamin B₁₂; formation of red blood cells	Meat, tap water
Copper (Cu)	Found in enzymes and electron carriers; hemoglobin production	Liver, meat, fish, shellfish, legumes, whole grains, nuts
Fluorine (F)	Found in teeth; helps prevent tooth decay	Most water supplies
Iodine (I)	Found in thyroid hormones	Fish, shellfish, iodized salt
Iron (Fe)	Found in many enzymes, hemoglobin, and myoglobin	Liver, meat, green vegetables, eggs, whole grains, legumes
Manganese (Mn)	Activates many enzymes	Organ meats, whole grains, legumes, nuts, tea, coffee
Molybdenum (Mo)	Found in some enzymes	Organ meats, dairy foods, whole grains, green vegetables
Selenium (Se)	Fat metabolism	Meat, seafood, whole grains, eggs, milk, garlic
Zinc (Zn)	Found in some enzymes and some transcription factors	Liver, fish, shellfish, and many other foods

FIGURE 22-15 Overview of essential vitamins and minerals.

- People on extremely low-calorie diets may need vitamin and mineral supplements.

- People with limited consumption of milk or sun exposure may need additional vitamin D. Because of insufficient levels of ultraviolet energy from the sun at latitudes above 42° (covering a line approximately from the northern border of California across to Boston), individuals in these regions are unable to produce sufficient vitamin D from sun exposure alone.

- People with absorption problems (such as when taking antibiotics, or having an infection, or following surgery) may need vitamin and mineral supplementation.

Individuals who do not fall into these groups, however, generally get all of the essential vitamins and minerals simply by eating a varied diet, rich in nutritious foods.

More than half of the U.S. population takes regular vitamin supplements. However, nearly all adults get all of the nutrients they need from the food they eat.

TAKE-HOME MESSAGE 22·7

Vitamins and minerals are organic and inorganic molecules in the diet. They are used in the production and action of enzymes and other molecules involved in the processing of food and other biochemical reactions. While vitamins and minerals are essential in small amounts, most people in the United States do not benefit from taking them as supplements.

22·8–22·13 We extract energy and nutrients from food.

A kingfisher dives to catch a fish.

22·8
We convert food into nutrients in four steps.

The human digestive system is like an assembly line running backward. Imagine starting with an assembled car and dismantling it into its many parts: the tires, doors, windshield, steering wheel. The food entering the digestive system is like the intact car. It enters the assembly line and then passes through four distinct phases, during which the food is progressively chewed up and broken down, the nutrients absorbed by the body, and the non-usable portion of the raw materials discarded as waste products (**FIGURE 22-17**).

In the next several sections, we examine in detail the four stages in the processing of food: ingestion, digestion, absorption, and elimination. Throughout these sections, it will be useful to picture the digestive system as a long tube with an opening at each end, the mouth and the anus, and some glands along the way that produce the necessary chemicals to help the process along.

TAKE-HOME MESSAGE 22·8

The digestive process in humans includes four distinct phases during which food is progressively chewed up, broken down, and absorbed by the body, after which the non-usable portion of the raw materials is discarded as waste.

DIGESTIVE PROCESS FROM START TO FINISH

The digestive process in humans includes four distinct phases.

1 INGESTION
Food is taken into the body.

2 DIGESTION
Large pieces of food are dismantled by physically and chemically breaking them into absorbable molecules.

3 ABSORPTION
Energy-rich food molecules are taken into the cells of the body, where they can be used for energy and building materials.

4 ELIMINATION
The remaining parts of the consumed foods—mostly indigestible materials—are discarded as waste products, and much water reabsorption occurs.

FIGURE 22-17 There are four steps in the body's processing of food.

Ingestion is the first step in the breakdown of food.

It will take you longer to read about **ingestion,** the intake of food into your body, than it would to just do it (**FIGURE 22-18**). Typically lasting less than a minute, ingestion primarily involves four parts of your anatomy: your mouth, teeth, tongue, and esophagus. We'll look at each in some detail. To start, imagine that you take a big bite of a hamburger, containing bread, lettuce, and the meat.

Putting food in your mouth stimulates your salivary glands. (In fact, just thinking about food can stimulate saliva secretion!) Via tiny ducts throughout your mouth, the salivary glands secrete mucus that lubricates the food to help it pass into your stomach. They also secrete an enzyme called alpha-amylase that initiates the process of digestion. Alpha-amylase breaks the bonds holding together the starch molecule (a highly branched carbohydrate pieced together from hundreds of linked glucose molecules) and releases a bit of glucose that can be used for energy. About 20% of the ingested starch is broken down in the mouth. Protein and fat molecules, on the other hand, are not broken down at all.

You start chewing food in your mouth in order to tear and grind it into little bits. This is a first important step toward completely breaking down and harvesting the energy stored in the chemical bonds of the food. Several different types of teeth have evolved in mammals and other animal species that allow different types of food items to be processed. Incisor and canine teeth, in the front, are used for biting and tearing food. Behind them are premolars and molars, used for grinding and crushing food. Just by looking at the type of teeth an animal has, we can learn a lot about its diet. Herbivores have molars primarily for grinding and crushing the tough cell walls of the plants they eat. Carnivores have sharp and lethal canines and incisors for killing and tearing apart the flesh of other animals.

Birds have no teeth. This explains why they can sometimes be seen eating gravel. Although the gravel has no nutritional value, it collects in the gizzard, one of the two chambers of their stomach, where it helps to grind up food. This is an important digestive step for birds because, lacking teeth, they must swallow their food whole. Consequently, when it first arrives in the stomach, the food hasn't been ground up at all, which can reduce the efficiency of digestive enzymes.

Q *Why do many birds eat gravel?*

While you are chewing your food, your tongue assists in the process by forming the food into a ball shape that can be swallowed. The ball of partly crushed, saliva-coated food is pushed to the back of your mouth by your tongue. There, your throat opens to two passageways into your torso, the **trachea** and the **esophagus** (**FIGURE 22-19**). The trachea, also called the windpipe, connects to your lungs, while the esophagus connects to your stomach. Food destined for your stomach is kept from entering your trachea by a fast but critical maneuver in which your voice box moves up (due to muscle contractions), causing a flap of tissue (called the epiglottis) to be pushed over the entrance to the trachea

INGESTION: THE MOUTH

Ingestion begins in the mouth as the teeth tear and grind food while mucus from the salivary glands helps lubricate the food for swallowing.

Molars

Incisors

Canine

Premolars

Salivary glands

Salivary glands also aid in the digestive process by releasing alpha-amylase, an enzyme that breaks down starch.

FIGURE 22-18 Ingestion, the intake of food into the body, begins in the mouth.

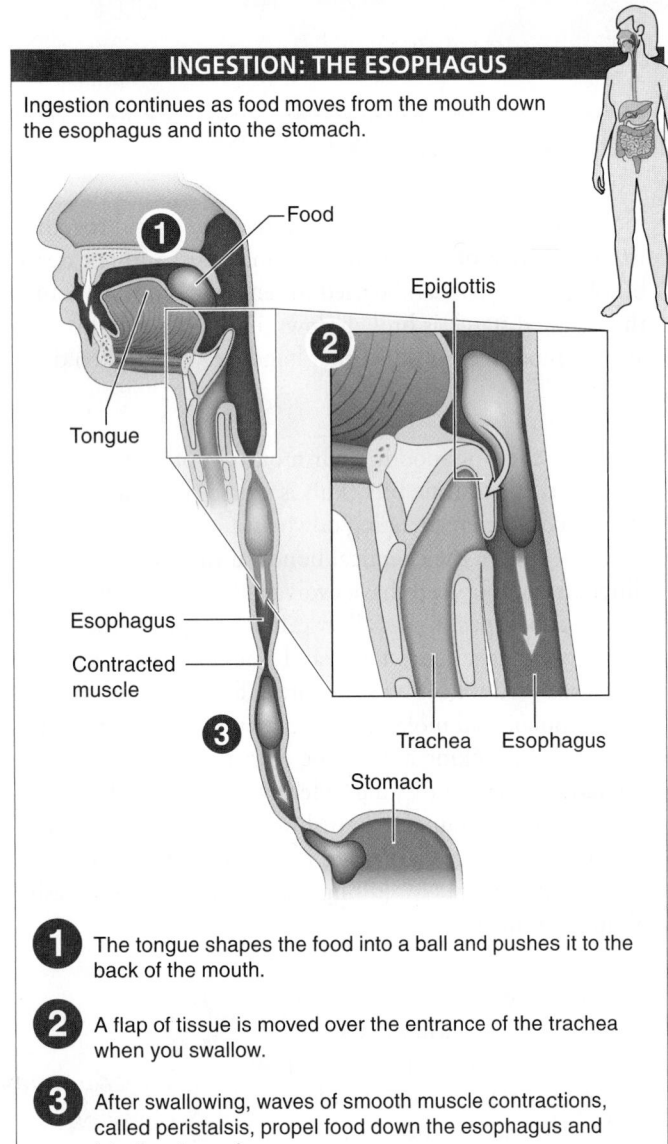

INGESTION: THE ESOPHAGUS

Ingestion continues as food moves from the mouth down the esophagus and into the stomach.

Food

Epiglottis

Tongue

Esophagus

Contracted muscle

Trachea   Esophagus

Stomach

1 The tongue shapes the food into a ball and pushes it to the back of the mouth.

2 A flap of tissue is moved over the entrance of the trachea when you swallow.

3 After swallowing, waves of smooth muscle contractions, called peristalsis, propel food down the esophagus and into the stomach.

FIGURE 22-19 Ingestion is complete when food passes from the mouth through the esophagus to the stomach.

just as you begin to swallow. If the ball of food you swallow is too big, it can get stuck at the beginning of the esophagus, wedging against the flap of tissue in front of the trachea—and this can cause you to choke by blocking all air from getting into your lungs.

Once the ball of chewed food makes its way into the esophagus, waves of smooth muscle contractions, called **peristalsis,** propel the food down the esophagus and into the stomach, where digestion continues. Because of peristalsis, it's not necessary for you to be sitting upright or standing when you eat. Even if you are standing on your head, the food is pushed down the esophagus to the stomach.

> ### TAKE-HOME MESSAGE 22·9
>
> **Ingestion is the first phase of the digestive process. Usually lasting less than a minute, ingestion involves tearing and grinding food in preparation for passing it to the stomach. Digestion also begins during this phase, with some starch being broken down by enzymes in saliva.**

22·10   Digestion dismantles food into usable parts.

Food is fuel. But it is useless to an animal until it has been completely broken down into its fundamental chemical constituents. Only then can it be absorbed into the bloodstream and used constructively. The process of dismantling the large pieces of food, physically and chemically breaking them down into absorbable molecules, is digestion. It occurs primarily in the stomach and small intestine.

The stomach The bite of hamburger moving through the digestive system empties from the esophagus directly into the **stomach,** a muscular J-shaped organ with thick, elastic

walls that can expand greatly in size to accommodate a large meal—as much as 4 liters of material! At the point where the esophagus connects to the stomach, there is a ring of muscle, called a **sphincter.** It seals off the stomach once the food has entered, preventing regurgitation of the stomach's acidic contents into the esophagus—even if you are eating while standing on your head.

The stomach has three functions.

1. It physically breaks down and mixes food, through churning of the muscles surrounding the stomach.

2. It secretes acid to further break down food chemically and to kill bacteria.

3. It begins some chemical digestion of proteins.

The presence of food in the stomach causes cells in crevices within the stomach lining, called gastric pits, to rapidly produce hydrochloric acid and pepsinogen, a precursor molecule quickly converted to the protein-dismantling enzyme **pepsin** (FIGURE 22-20). The acid corrodes proteins in the food, breaking them into smaller pieces, which can then be broken into their constituent amino acids by the pepsin.

Q What is indigestion? How do antacids cure it?

The burning sensation of indigestion occurs when the sphincter between the esophagus and the stomach doesn't completely prevent the acidic contents of the stomach from moving back up the esophagus. It usually occurs when a person eats too much or too quickly. Antacids can neutralize acid from the stomach. Remember, though, that the high acidity in the stomach is important for digestion, so while reducing it may alleviate heartburn, antacids can reduce the digestive efficiency of the stomach.

The end result of all the churning and digesting is that the food you have eaten is no longer recognizable. It becomes a creamy, very acidic liquid called **chyme.** At the other end of the stomach is another ring of muscle. About every 20 seconds, it opens just a tiny bit and squirts a few tablespoonfuls of chyme into the small intestine. While some of the hamburger's carbohydrates and proteins have been partly or completely digested in the stomach, the lettuce is undigested, as are the lipids from the meat, which are suspended as greasy droplets within the chyme.

Besides helping to chemically break down food in your stomach, the strong acid also kills most of the bacteria that you might consume. Most bacteria just can't survive when the pH gets so acidic (although some microbes occasionally manage to sneak through by hiding in pockets of food with higher pH as the food passes through the stomach).

Q Humans use heat for cooking and often marinate foods in vinegar or lemon juice. How do these processes help with digestion?

Interestingly, across dozens and dozens of cultures, humans have developed common ways of preparing their food, including using heat and marinating food in acidic solutions, such as vinegar or lemon juice. Because harsh

DIGESTION: THE STOMACH

Digestion is the process of dismantling large pieces of food, physically and chemically breaking them down into absorbable molecules.

Esophagus

Sphincter

Food

Churning muscle

A sphincter seals the stomach after food enters, preventing back-flow of stomach acids into the esophagus. Another sphincter seals the stomach from the small intestine.

Small intestine

Chyme

1 Muscles in the stomach churn and physically break down and mix food.

2 Gastric pits produce hydrochloric acid to activate pepsin, which disassembles protein.

Gastric pits

3 The food mixture, called chyme, then passes into the small intestine.

FIGURE 22-20 The role of the stomach in digestion.

conditions such as heat and acid help to disrupt the tissue of food items, they increase the efficiency with which digestive enzymes can make contact with the food and break it down.

The small intestine Digestion only begins in the mouth and stomach. Most chemical digestion actually occurs in the **small intestine,** a long thin tube connected to the stomach. It is about 20 feet long and winds all around your abdominal cavity (how else could 20 feet of tubing be packed into such a small area?). The small intestine begins its job of chemical digestion once the sphincter at the end of the stomach relaxes, creating an opening through which small amounts of chyme are squirted. The creamy substance slowly moves through the small intestine, pushed by the rhythmic contractions of peristalsis. As the chyme

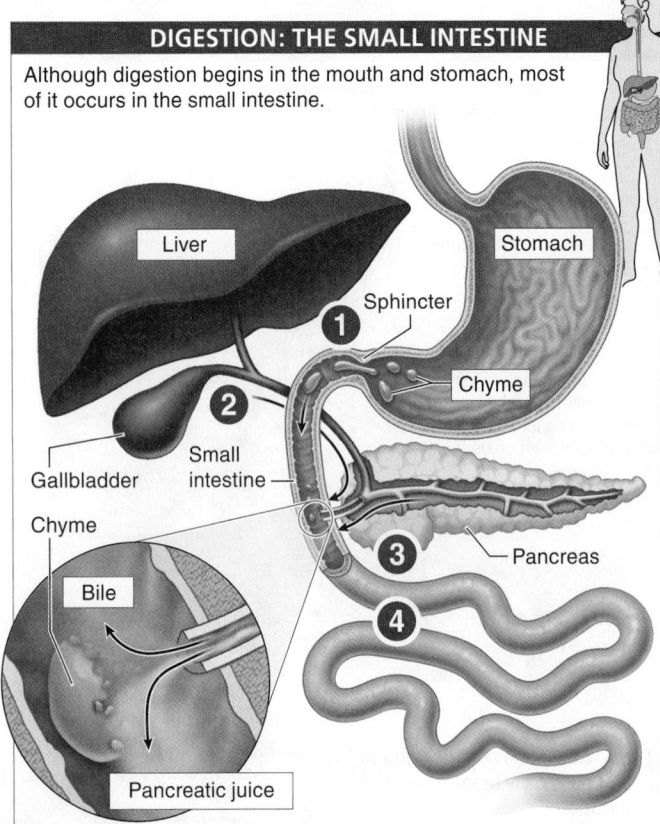

DIGESTION: THE SMALL INTESTINE

Although digestion begins in the mouth and stomach, most of it occurs in the small intestine.

Liver

Stomach

1 Sphincter

2

Chyme

Gallbladder

Small intestine

Chyme

3 Pancreas

Bile

4

Pancreatic juice

1 As a sphincter at the end of the stomach relaxes, small amounts of chyme are squirted into the small intestine.

2 The liver produces bile, which travels from the gallbladder, where it is stored, to the small intestine, where it separates globules of fat into tiny, more easily digested and absorbed droplets.

3 The pancreas secretes pancreatic juice, which neutralizes the chyme and aids in the digestion of carbohydrates, proteins, and fats.

4 Cells within the walls of the small intestine produce enzymes that further digest fats, carbohydrates, and proteins.

 Digestion is completed in the small intestine, at which point carbohydrates, proteins, and fats have been broken down into simple sugars, amino acids, and fatty acids.

FIGURE 22-21 The role of the small intestine in digestion.

makes its way through the small intestine, the macromolecules are gradually digested, with help from the pancreas and the liver (**FIGURE 22-21**)

The **pancreas,** nestled at the point where the stomach connects to the small intestine, plays a central role in digestion by secreting pancreatic juice through a duct into the very beginning portion of the small intestine. This juice is a mixture of (1) chemicals that neutralize the acidic

chyme, and (2) enzymes that digest carbohydrates, proteins, and fats. Another organ that assists the small intestine with digestion is the **liver,** which produces **bile,** a juice that aids in the breakdown of fats. The liver sends the bile to the gallbladder, and from there it passes through a small duct into the small intestine, where the bile initiates the first step in fat digestion.

Because lipids are not water-soluble, the fat from the hamburger is still suspended in the chyme, never dissolving into the watery substance of the digestive tract. In the small intestine, bile initiates the first step in fat digestion, separating globules of ingested fat into tiny, more easily digested and absorbed droplets that pancreatic enzymes can successfully break down. Besides the digestive enzymes produced by the pancreas and the liver, other enzymes are generated by cells within the walls of the small intestine. These enzymes further digest fats, carbohydrates, and proteins.

Q *Occasionally people must have part of their small intestine surgically removed. How would this affect digestion?*

Digestion is completed in the small intestine when the consumed carbohydrates, proteins, and fats have been broken down into their component parts: simple sugars, amino acids, and fatty acids. These simple molecules can then be absorbed into the bloodstream, a process that we explore in the next section.

But first, have you noticed that certain types of food commonly give people gas? Some types of beans can cause such digestive distress. Enzyme deficiencies and metabolically versatile bacteria are the culprits. The beans contain the sugars raffinose and stachyose, which are indigestible by many people. When the sugars pass undigested through the small intestine and reach the large intestine, they are digested by bacteria. And the by-product of the bacterial feeding frenzy is gas, cramps, and flatulence. The product Beano contains enzymes that help digest the trouble-making sugars before our resident bacteria can get to them.

TAKE-HOME MESSAGE 22·10

Digestion—the process of dismantling large pieces of food, physically and chemically breaking them down into absorbable molecules—is the second phase of the breakdown of food in animals. It occurs primarily in the stomach and small intestine.

22·11

Absorption moves nutrients from your gut to your cells.

Chewing, tearing, churning, acidifying, dismantling. You put a lot of energy into reducing food to its simplest component molecules. Eventually, though, there is a payoff. That payoff is **absorption,** the process by which the energy-rich food particles are taken from the digestive tract into the bloodstream and then into cells throughout the body, where they can be used for energy and building materials. Absorption occurs mainly in the small intestine; however, a few molecules are absorbed in the stomach, including aspirin and alcohol, which explains why drinking alcohol on an empty stomach can lead to unexpectedly rapid inebriation.

The secret to effective absorption is simple: surface area. For a molecule such as a sugar or an amino acid to be absorbed by the body, the molecule must be in direct contact with the cell membrane of the cell that is going to absorb it. The greater the number of cells that can come in contact with the chyme passing through the small intestine, the greater the amount of nutrients that can be absorbed. For this reason, the tremendous surface area of the small intestine, as well as other structural characteristics, allow for very efficient absorption of nutrients (**FIGURE 22-22**).

1. As we noted in Section 22-10, the small intestine is long—about 20 feet.

2. Rather than being a straight, smooth tube, it has many folds.

3. The interior lining of the small intestine is made up of thousands of small finger-like projections, called villi. These create lots of nooks and crannies where chyme can come in contact with absorptive cells.

STRUCTURE OF THE SMALL INTESTINE

Villi

Microvilli

Small intestine

SMALL INTESTINE
20 feet long with many folds

VILLI
Finger-like projections that line the small intestine

MICROVILLI
Thread-like projections that line cells in the villi

FIGURE 22-22 The small intestine has a very large area for absorbing nutrients.

 The tremendous surface area of the small intestine allows for very efficient absorption of nutrients.

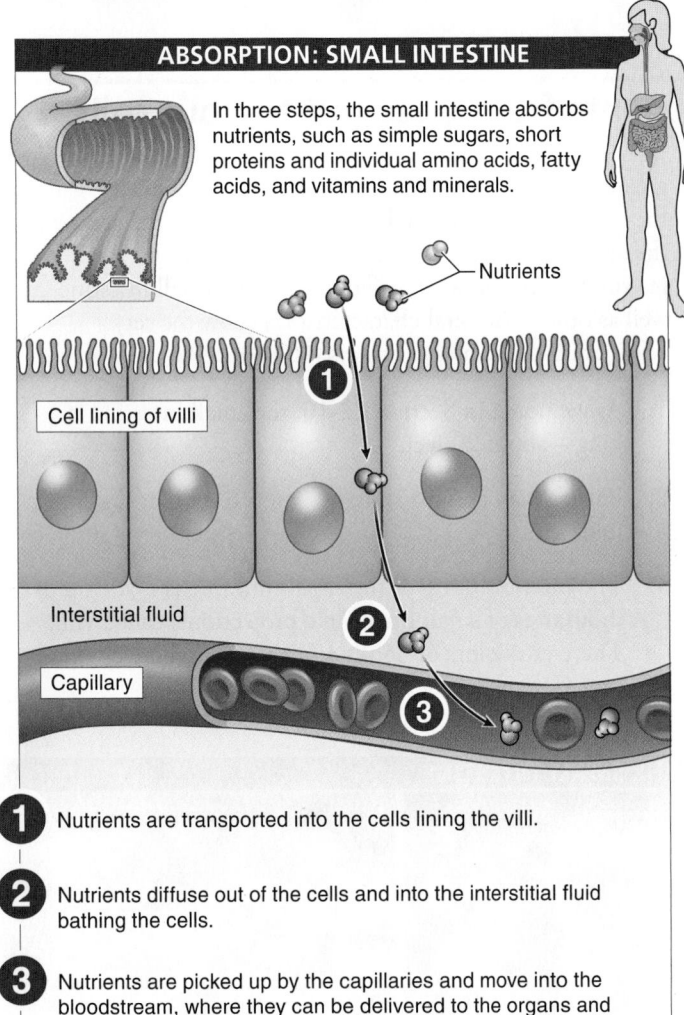

ABSORPTION: SMALL INTESTINE

In three steps, the small intestine absorbs nutrients, such as simple sugars, short proteins and individual amino acids, fatty acids, and vitamins and minerals.

Nutrients

Cell lining of villi

Interstitial fluid

Capillary

1 Nutrients are transported into the cells lining the villi.

2 Nutrients diffuse out of the cells and into the interstitial fluid bathing the cells.

3 Nutrients are picked up by the capillaries and move into the bloodstream, where they can be delivered to the organs and tissues that need them.

FIGURE 22-23 Absorption moves nutrients into the bloodstream.

4. Each of the cells along the villi has hundreds of its own tiny thread-like projections, called microvilli. These create micro-nooks and micro-crannies that allow more of the molecules in chyme to directly touch the membranes of absorptive cells.

The molecules that can be absorbed in the small intestine include simple sugars, individual amino acids (and, occasionally, short chains of two or three amino acids), fatty acids, vitamins, and minerals. When a nutrient molecule is small enough to be absorbed, it gravitates toward the villi lining the interior of the small intestine. The tiny particles become trapped in the microvilli and are drawn across the cell membranes into the cells (**FIGURE 22-23**). The nutrients then diffuse out of the cells and into the interstitial fluid bathing the cells. Finally, from here, the nutrients are picked up by capillaries and thus move into the bloodstream, where they can be delivered to the organs and tissues that need them.

There is a food myth that if certain foods are combined, digestion is impaired. This is not true. The myth ignores a couple of facts: the body is able to produce its digestive enzymes for fats, proteins, and carbohydrates simultaneously, and it can absorb nutrients regardless of which other nutrients are also in the digestive tract. In fact, the contrary is often true. Many foods enhance the absorption of nutrient molecules in other foods. Vitamin C in citrus fruits, for example, increases the efficiency of iron absorption from a meal of beef or beans.

Q Is it true that certain food combinations should not be eaten together?

TAKE-HOME MESSAGE 22·11

Absorption is the process by which energy-rich food particles are taken up from the digestive tract into the cells of the body, where they can be used for energy and building materials. Absorption takes place primarily in the small intestine.

22·12 Elimination removes unusable materials from your body.

You are much better at conservation and recycling than you imagine. Especially when it comes to the fluids and solids you consume. The last phase in the breakdown of food, **elimination,** takes place as what's left of the chyme—mostly indigestible materials—leaves the small intestine and enters the **large intestine,** also called the **colon.** Much larger in

diameter than the small intestine (about 3 inches vs. 1 inch for the small intestine) but only about 3–6 feet long, the large intestine serves to absorb water, salts, and some vitamins (**FIGURE 22-24**). The last part of the large intestine is the rectum and serves as a storage compartment for the remaining parts of consumed food, the feces, which can then be defecated.

ELIMINATION: COLON

Colon

Small intestine

Rectum

Feces

Water, salts, and some vitamins are absorbed

1 The remaining chyme—mostly indigestible materials—leaves the small intestine and enters the large intestine, or colon.

2 Water, salts, and some vitamins are absorbed.

3 The rectum serves as a storage compartment for the feces, which consists of dead bacterial cells and the remaining, indigestible parts of consumed food.

FIGURE 22-24 Elimination is the final step in the digestive process.

Q **Fiber is an indigestible carbohydrate. If we can't digest it, how can it be essential in our diet?**

Fiber—including gums and cellulose—cannot be digested or absorbed. For this reason, when fiber is consumed, it increases fecal mass and speeds the movement of chyme through the colon. With additional mass, more water is attracted, softening the feces and making it easier to eliminate (that's why too much fiber can lead to diarrhea). Fiber also binds to bile, causing some of it to be eliminated, thereby reducing the body's ability to absorb cholesterol from food. It is important to achieve just the right balance of water absorption in the large intestine. If too much is absorbed, the remaining indigestible material becomes too solid and can't move easily through the last part of the digestive system, causing constipation. Alternatively, if too little water absorption occurs, the body loses more water through diarrhea.

Huge colonies of bacteria live in the colon. Before we are born, our guts are sterile and free of bacteria. During birth,

we acquire some of our mother's vaginal and fecal bacteria. By the age of two, all of the numerous bacterial species present in adults have been acquired from food and the environment. We generally have more bacterial cells than our own body cells at any given time (see Figure 13-3). The bacteria are usually harmless and live off the undigested materials that end up in the colon. Bacteria also release important metabolic by-products, such as vitamin K and one of the B vitamins, biotin. About half of the feces that we excrete each day is made up of dead bacterial cells, and the rest is mostly indigestible materials such as cellulose from the cell walls of plant matter and other types of fiber.

Antibiotics frequently (and unintentionally) kill a large proportion of the colon bacteria, in addition to whatever illness-causing microbe they were prescribed to kill. This can have multiple negative side effects. First, the transit of undigested materials through the colon may not be slowed down as much as usual, in which case less water is removed and

Q **Why can taking antibiotics lead to vitamin deficiencies?**

diarrhea results. Also, a reduction in production of vitamin K and biotin can lead to deficiencies.

Q Laxatives contain salts. How can this help them reduce constipation?

In the colon, water is removed from feces through osmosis. First, salts are pumped out of the colon into surrounding cells, and then water moves out by simple diffusion (to an area where there are more ions). This process can be manipulated as a treatment for constipation. Laxatives contain magnesium salts, which are so slowly absorbed that they are still largely intact when they reach the colon.

Laxatives work by increasing the salt concentration in the colon, so that more water remains. This additional water makes it easier to excrete feces (but can cause diarrhea in some cases).

TAKE-HOME MESSAGE 22·12

The last phase of food breakdown takes place as the mostly indigestible materials leave the small intestine and enter the large intestine. There, water and ions are absorbed before the remaining materials are defecated.

22·13 Animals have some alternative means for processing their food.

Cellulose could feed the world. It is everywhere—it's the major carbohydrate making up the cell wall around plant cells—and there is a tremendous amount of energy stored in its chemical bonds. But most animals don't produce (or acquire in any other way) the enzymes that break down cellulose. Those with the appropriate enzymes, though—and some species do have them—gain access to one of the most plentiful sources of chemical energy on the planet. Let's investigate how some animals do it.

Ruminant animals, such as cows, bison, deer, goats, and sheep, have complex four-part stomachs in which they can digest plant matter that humans cannot (**FIGURE 22-25**). First, the grazing animals chew on the plant material for a while, grinding the tough cell walls. Then they swallow it, and it passes into the first part of their stomach, which contains a huge pool of enzymes and cellulose-digesting bacteria. There, the plant material gets broken down, and much of the cellulose is digested. To increase their energy-extraction efficiency, the animals then regurgitate the food back into the mouth, chew it some more, and swallow it again.

Called "chewing the cud," the additional chewing further breaks up the plant cell walls so that the bacteria can have

Q Silverfish are insect pests in libraries rather than in kitchens. Why might this be? (Hint: they are one of only a few species of animals to produce enzymes that digest cellulose.)

easier access to the cellulose, digesting more of it. From the first part of the stomach, the food then passes through the remaining chambers, where some additional digestion takes place, before moving into the small intestine and continuing the usual path of digestion. Cellulose-digesting bacteria have some of the most dangerous working conditions on earth: although cellulose is the primary component of the ruminant diet, ruminants also get a significant amount of protein every day by digesting many of the bacteria working in their gut.

Some insects, including silverfish, produce cellulose-digesting enzymes. These enzymes make it possible for them to eat books and paper, which are made of plant products containing cell walls made from cellulose.

There's more than one way to skin a plant. Some other animals, lacking the large bacteria-filled stomach of ruminants, also employ cellulose-digesting bacteria to enable them to extract energy from cellulose. In these animals, including horses, rodents, rabbits, and koalas, the bacteria live within an outcropping of the small intestine called the cecum. This is a separate chamber where the food goes for a while and the cellulose gets digested, before the food continues down the intestine. In animals that don't break down cellulose, the cecum is much smaller. The cecum is almost nonexistent in the meat-eating coyote, for example, while the similarly sized koala has a cecum that is 2 meters long. Within this lengthy chamber, bacteria convert shredded eucalyptus leaves into usable food (**FIGURE 22-26**). In humans, no cellulose-digesting bacteria live in the cecum (called the appendix in humans). Recent research suggests,

FOUR-PART STOMACH

In ruminant animals, a complex four-part stomach has evolved that can digest the plant matter that humans cannot digest.

Cellulose-digesting bacteria

Esophagus

Four-part stomach

Cellulose

Small intestine

1 Plant material is swallowed and passed to the first part of the stomach, where it is broken down and digested by enzymes and cellulose-digesting bacteria.

2 Food is regurgitated, chewed more, then swallowed and passed to the first chamber again.

3 Food passes through the remaining chambers, where additional digestion takes place before it moves into the small intestine.

FIGURE 22-25 Ruminants can digest plant material that humans cannot.

THE CECUM

KOALA BEAR CECUM
Two-meter long outcropping of the small intestine that contains cellulose-digesting bacteria

HUMAN CECUM
Small outcropping of the small intestine that has no digestive function at all

Stomach

Stomach

Appendix

☐ Small intestine   ☐ Cecum   ☐ Large intestine

FIGURE 22-26 Koalas can eat foods that are indigestible for humans. The cecum is the site of cellulose digestion in some animals.

FIGURE 22-27 Coprophagy can have nutritional benefits.

however, that the appendix may play a role in immune function.

Rabbits and rodents can't increase their cellulose-digesting efficiency by regurgitating their food and chewing the cud, because the cellulose-digesting bacteria reside in the small intestine, not in the stomach. But they've mastered another way to increase their ability to extract energy from their food: they pass it through their entire digestive system twice. Called **coprophagy,** eating some of their feces allows them to significantly increase their nutritional intake from their cellulose-laden diet. Numerous other species—including pigs, elephants, cats, gorillas, and chimps—also resort to coprophagy from time to time, although the reasons are not always clear and may be related to vitamin and mineral absorption, or the acquisition of bacteria to aid in digestion (**FIGURE 22-27**).

TAKE-HOME MESSAGE 22·13

Most animals don't produce enzymes that break down cellulose. In ruminant animals, complex four-part stomachs have evolved with which the animals can digest plant matter that humans cannot, in part due to the presence of symbiotic cellulose-digesting bacteria. Other animals have alternative methods of utilizing cellulose-digesting bacteria.

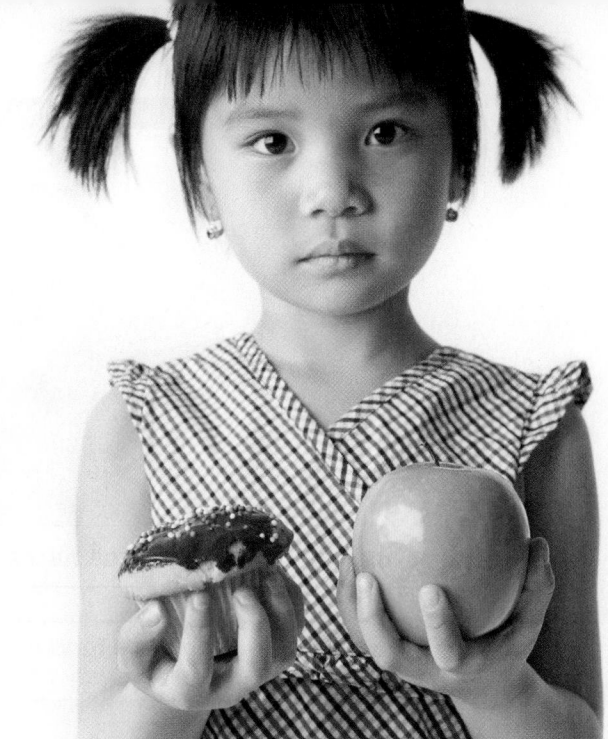

22·14–22·18 What we eat profoundly affects our health.

Two sweet foods can have very different nutritional compositions.

22·14

What constitutes a healthy diet?

Choosing a healthy diet can be very difficult. There are more than 50,000 different foods we can choose from, and we must also consider how much of each to consume each day. Fortunately, there is not a single "best" diet, so it's possible to work within any person's particular likes and dislikes.

At the most basic level, just two requirements—quality and quantity—must be satisfied in the design of a healthy diet (**FIGURE 22-28**). First, a diet must contain sufficient amounts of each of the six categories of nutrients: water, proteins, carbohydrates, lipids, vitamins, and minerals (described in Sections 22-4–22-7). And second, a healthy diet must contain sufficient energy to support an individual's metabolic needs without containing a surplus of calories. But it is not easy to find the best strategy to satisfy these requirements.

Balance in a diet is important, because no one food is completely adequate. Milk, for example, is a very good source of protein and calcium but does not contain sufficient iron for most adults. Meats, on the other hand, are rich in iron (as well as protein) but generally are poor sources of calcium. Every type of food, in fact, while providing some nutritional value, also falls short in some other essential nutrient,

FIGURE 22-28 Food quality and quantity are the main factors to consider in choosing a healthy, balanced diet.

A healthy diet should contain sufficient amounts of each of the six categories of nutrients and just enough energy to support an individual's metabolic needs.

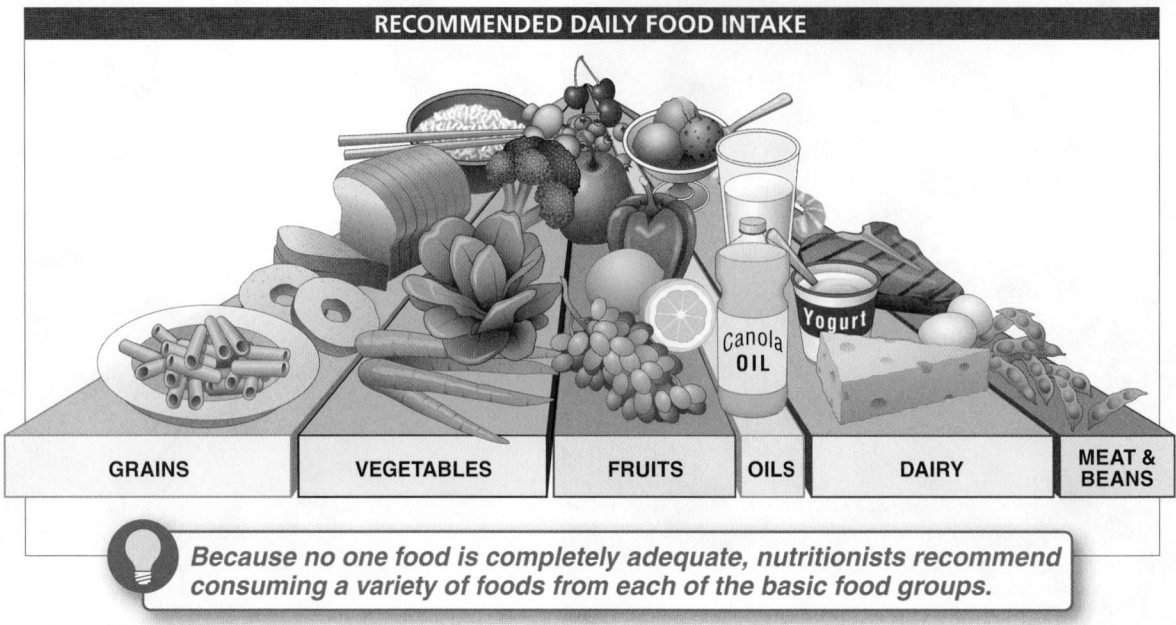

RECOMMENDED DAILY FOOD INTAKE

GRAINS VEGETABLES FRUITS OILS DAIRY MEAT & BEANS

Because no one food is completely adequate, nutritionists recommend consuming a variety of foods from each of the basic food groups.

FIGURE 22-29 **What nutritionists recommend.**

whether a protein or a specific vitamin or mineral. For this reason, nutritionists recommend consuming a variety of foods from each of the basic food groups—(1) grains, (2) vegetables, (3) fruits, (4) milk and other dairy products, and (5) meats, poultry, and beans—and small quantities of unsaturated fats, such as olive and canola oil, and exercising daily to manage body weight (**FIGURE 22-29**).

The U.S. Department of Agriculture (USDA) has established dietary guidelines to help people plan a healthy diet. The USDA updates the guidelines every five years in order to incorporate advances in nutritional science. In addition to urging people to take steps to ensure that their food is safe to eat, the USDA also recommends the following:

1. Keep your weight within the recommended range.

2. Be physically active.

3. Choose a variety of fruits, vegetables, grains—particularly whole grains—and nonfat or low-fat milk and milk products.

4. Keep your diet low in saturated fat, cholesterol, and total fat.

5. Keep your diet low in sugars relative to complex carbohydrates and fiber.

6. Keep your diet low in salt.

7. If you consume alcoholic beverages, do so in moderation.

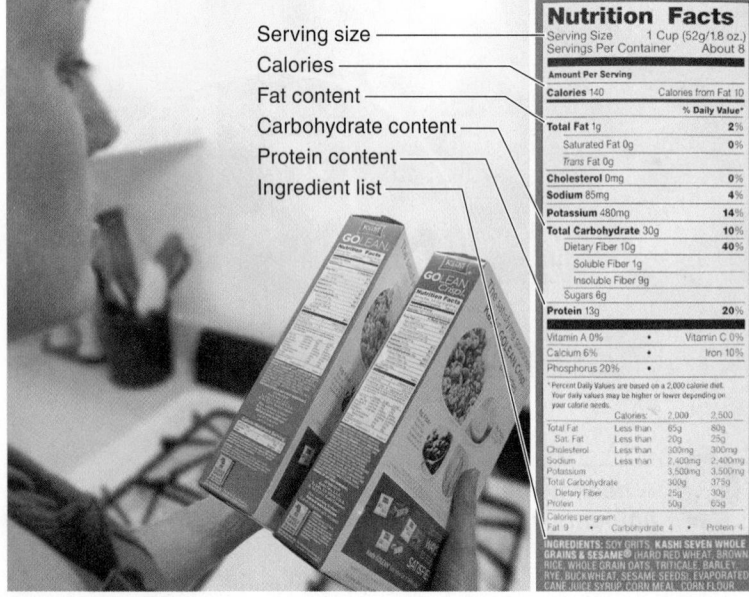

Serving size
Calories
Fat content
Carbohydrate content
Protein content
Ingredient list

FIGURE 22-30 **Food labels provide a wealth of nutritional information.**

Food labels are an often overlooked tool that can help in adhering to these guidelines and selecting a balanced diet (**FIGURE 22-30**). Ingredient lists, too, are very valuable, listing every ingredient in order of amount (by weight). Ultimately, following these guidelines can help reduce the incidence and severity of chronic diseases such as stroke and other manifestations of cardiovascular disease, diabetes, and cancer.

Q *Why is it increasingly difficult to maintain a healthy weight as we get older?*

Complicating the USDA's dietary guidelines is the fact that we need to reduce our caloric intake as we get older. Metabolic rate falls slowly but surely, beginning around age 30. Consequently, without an increase in activity, eating the same amount of food—even if it is a healthy diet—leads to a surplus of calories, a surplus that becomes larger and larger with each passing year. On average, most adults gain about half a pound every year throughout their thirties, forties, and fifties.

It is important to note that people who do not consume meat, poultry, fish, and/or milk products can still have a balanced diet. Legumes, seeds, and nuts can provide many of the same nutrients found in meat, including protein. Dark leafy vegetables can provide iron, another nutrient plentiful in meat. And in fact, because such diets tend to be lower in fat content, they can be valuable in helping to maintain a healthy body weight.

TAKE-HOME MESSAGE 22·14

A balanced diet contains adequate amounts of essential nutrients and energy, but not surplus amounts, and is low in substances—including saturated fats, cholesterol, sugar, salt, and alcohol—that can have adverse health effects when consumed in greater quantities.

22·15 Obesity can result from too much of a good thing.

Jerry and Louis Kahn are two brothers who really love to eat. The pair tip the scales at about 500 pounds each—and their hunger never subsides. What is unusual about the Kahns' difficulty controlling their weight is that doctors have pinpointed the exact physiological source of their problem. They both possess an altered gene that renders their bodies unable to recognize the internal measure of food intake and register "enough," much like a broken thermostat that never shuts off a heater. Jerry and Louis are eternally hungry because their brains never get the "we're full" message from their stomachs.

Like the Kahns, we all have inherited genes from our parents that significantly influence our body weights. All humans inherit dozens (possibly hundreds) of genes that influence body weight, and even in their "normal" condition, these genes are likely to lead to weight problems (**FIGURE 22-31**). But this raises a couple of questions. Why would it be in our genetic interests to

Genes for large appetites may have had benefits in our ancestral world. In our modern world, they may lead to weight-management problems.

FIGURE 22-31 Are your genes making it difficult for you to maintain a healthy weight?

have huge appetites? Why would natural selection favor such genes? To answer these questions, we must consider the harsher, less predictable environment in which *Homo sapiens* evolved.

Our ancestors lived off the land by hunting animals and gathering plants. Under such conditions, it was unclear where the next meal was coming from. Powerful, instinctual hunger kept our ancestors going in that tough, energetically demanding world. Those individuals who were enthusiastic rather than restrained eaters were most likely to survive periods of food shortage and live to reproduce. Recent studies using PET scans (positron emission tomography, a type of imaging) have supported this, demonstrating that just the sight of food sets off activity in the brain's pleasure centers—a mechanism that generally leads to the consumption of food when it is available.

The consequence of our perpetual hunger is not news: one of every four Americans is obese. In terms of size, plumpness gets labeled "obesity" when our body mass index hits 30. **Body mass index,** or **BMI,** equals body weight in kilograms divided by height in meters squared (kg/m^2). A BMI of 30 translates to about 209 pounds if you are 5 feet 10 inches tall, and 180 pounds if you are 5 feet 5 inches. With a BMI of 25 or higher but under 30, you are only considered "overweight." BMI isn't the only way to evaluate obesity, and it has its problems. Because the measure does not consider body composition, professional athletes and bodybuilders with unusually large muscle mass may have BMIs that fall

BODY MASS INDEX (BMI)

1 Find your height on the *y*-axis.　　**2** Move right across the row until you get to the column with your weight.　　**3** Move up to the top of the row to find out what your BMI is.

Height	UNDER-WEIGHT (<18.5)	HEALTHY WEIGHT (18.5–24.9)						OVERWEIGHT (25–29.9)					OBESE (>30)					
BMI	18	19	20	21	22	23	24	25	26	27	28	29	30	31	32	33	34	35
6´4˝	148	156	164	172	180	189	197	205	213	221	230	238	246	254	263	271	279	287
6´3˝	144	152	160	168	176	184	192	200	208	216	224	232	240	248	256	264	272	279
6´2˝	141	148	155	163	171	179	186	194	202	210	218	225	233	241	249	256	264	272
6´1˝	136	144	151	159	166	174	182	189	197	204	212	219	227	235	242	250	257	265
6´0˝	132	140	147	154	162	169	177	184	191	199	206	213	221	228	235	242	250	258
5´11˝	129	136	143	150	157	165	172	179	186	193	200	208	215	222	229	236	243	250
5´10˝	126	132	139	146	153	160	167	174	181	188	195	202	209	216	222	229	236	243
5´9˝	122	128	135	142	149	155	162	169	176	182	189	196	203	209	216	223	230	236
5´8˝	118	125	131	138	144	151	158	164	171	177	184	190	197	203	210	216	223	230
5´7˝	115	121	127	134	140	146	153	159	166	172	178	185	191	198	204	211	217	223
5´6˝	112	118	124	130	136	142	148	155	161	167	173	179	186	192	198	204	210	216
5´5˝	108	114	120	126	132	138	144	150	156	162	168	174	180	186	192	198	204	210
5´4˝	105	110	116	122	128	134	140	145	151	157	163	169	174	180	186	192	197	204
5´3˝	102	107	113	118	124	130	135	141	146	152	158	163	169	175	180	186	191	197
5´2˝	98	104	109	115	120	126	131	136	142	147	153	158	164	169	175	180	186	191
5´1˝	95	100	106	111	116	122	127	132	137	143	148	153	158	164	169	174	180	185
5´0˝	92	97	102	107	112	118	123	128	133	138	143	148	153	158	163	168	174	179

Body Weight (Pounds)

FIGURE 22-32 One indicator of healthy body weight: body mass index. The BMI indicates the ratio between height and body weight; the chart shows healthy body-weight ranges.

Fat cells increase in number during the years of childhood and early teens, making it especially important to avoid obesity then.

FIGURE 22-33 It's important to maintain a healthy body weight during childhood.

10 pounds. But because of the "famine-fearing" genes we carry, this is easier said than done.

From the cellular perspective, the specific causes of obesity are an increase in the size and number of the fat cells an individual carries. Excess calories can be converted to fat regardless of whether they come from fats, carbohydrates, or proteins. Whatever the source, the fat molecules are added right to the fat cells in the body's adipose tissue. Fat cells increase in number primarily during the late years of childhood and in the early teens (**FIGURE 22-33**). After that, the cells tend to grow in size rather than number with excess caloric intake, although when a fat cell becomes too large it will divide. The reverse, unfortunately, is not true. When people lose weight, their fat cells become smaller but are never lost completely. Consequently, it is especially important to avoid obesity early in life.

The problems of obesity are not restricted to humans. Most primates in zoos are also overweight, as are many pets and most laboratory research animals. In each case, the reason is the same as for humans. In their natural world, food is limited and unpredictable. Animals overeat when they do not need to expend much energy to acquire food and food is plentiful. In the next section, we explore some weight-loss diets and why they are almost universally unsuccessful.

> ### TAKE-HOME MESSAGE 22·15
>
> Food supplies were unpredictable for our early ancestors, leading to the evolution of strong appetites. In the modern industrial world, such instincts have problematic consequences, leading most people to overeat and to weigh more than they would prefer and more than is healthy. Zoo animals, laboratory animals, and domesticated animals have a similar problem.

within the obese range. Still, it is a useful and easily obtained measure (**FIGURE 22-32**). Repeatedly, around the world, as societies get richer and as individuals age, they tend to become fatter. Most of us would reduce our risk of heart disease, stroke, and diabetes if we lost even as little as

22·16 Weight-loss diets are a losing proposition.

> ❝I can reason down or deny everything, except this perpetual Belly: feed he must and will, and I cannot make him respectable.❞
> —RALPH WALDO EMERSON, *Representative Men,* 1850

Weight loss is both a simple and a complicated problem. It is simple because there is one complete and perfect plan that guarantees success; it requires only five words of description: "Eat less. Move around more." Regardless of the genes it carries, any animal of any species will lose weight when it expends more calories than it consumes.

"Eat less. Move around more." A successful diet plan must incorporate one or both of these changes.

FIGURE 22-34 Weight-loss diets make for popular reading.

The equation holds whether the calories are consumed in hamburgers or in fresh, organic vegetables. Similarly, it doesn't matter whether energy is expended in the weight room or on the couch.

But weight loss is also complex: we know that eating less and moving around more are all that is necessary, but while almost all short-term "diets" work in the short term, in the long run, with very few exceptions, they fail (FIGURE 22-34). More than half of the advice books currently on the *New York Times* bestseller list promise new plans for losing weight. Five years ago that was also true—although the bestsellers were different books. It may seem as if there are plenty of new ideas about how to lose weight, yet the problem has not gone away. Rather, it has gotten worse.

Current interventions designed to facilitate weight loss range from mild to extreme. They fall into three categories: drugs, surgery, and behavior modification. Each has both promising and problematic elements (FIGURE 22-35).

Drugs and Other Chemical Interventions

Xenical. The most promising of recently developed weight-control drugs is Xenical, a product that interferes with fat digestion by binding to lipases (fat-digesting enzymes) and blocking them from doing their job. As a consequence, some of the fat in the digestive system passes through the body without absorption. In randomized, double-blind, placebo-controlled clinical studies—the gold standard for experimental design—Xenical has succeeded in helping people lose about 10 pounds over the course of one year. In the second year, these people regained some of their weight, but still ended up a bit lighter and with reduced circulating cholesterol and lower blood pressure. These findings are promising, but no long-term studies have been conducted to assess the permanence of the weight loss or potential side effects. Additionally, at a cost of more than $1,000 per year, Xenical is too expensive for most people to use.

Meridia. Approved for the treatment of obesity, this appetite suppressant has shown promise as a weight-loss product. It reduces the rate at which the chemical serotonin, associated with satiation, is removed from the space between nerve cells in the brain. Concerns over possible adverse effects on the cardiovascular system, however, have prompted some opposition to continued availability of this prescription drug.

Olestra and NutraSweet. Some artificially created molecules, such as Olestra and NutraSweet, can cause the same perception as if a molecule of fat or sugar, respectively, were present. Olestra, for example, contains fatty acids and is designed to have a taste and texture similar to digestible fats, but in an indigestible molecule (see Section 2-12). Because it is a complex molecule containing eight fatty acids rather than the three fatty acids that are part of triglycerides in our diet, it ultimately is excreted rather than being digested and absorbed. For this reason, Olestra does not yield any energy. (Of concern to nutritionists are the findings that Olestra's complex structure causes it to attach to and remove important nutrients, including fat-soluble vitamins and carotenoids.) Still, in several published research studies, subjects who unknowingly ingested fewer calories as a consequence of consuming products containing either NutraSweet or Olestra responded by increasing their caloric consumption in the following days. We're not tricked quite so easily. For this reason, low-calorie versions of food are unlikely to be successful on their own in generating permanent weight loss.

Caffeine and other stimulants. A variety of products claim to increase the expenditure of energy without an offsetting increase in appetite. This approach is theoretically sound, but there are no published data on either the safety or the efficiency of these unregulated products. While clinical trials demonstrate that stimulants such as caffeine can produce short-term weight loss in the range of 5–10 pounds, long-term studies reveal that most of the short-term losses do not last.

DRUGS AND OTHER CHEMICAL
INTERVENTIONS

SURGERY

BEHAVIOR MODIFICATIONS:
WEIGHT-LOSS DIETS

FIGURE 22-35 There is a wide variety of strategies employed in the quest for weight loss.

Placebo. During clinical studies for diet pills, one observation was quite unexpected. As we learned in Chapter 1, researchers testing new compounds always have a "placebo" group. Subjects in this group go through all the same motions but get pills with none of the test drug. Because the placebo pills and the test drug pills are identical in appearance, no one knows which patients are getting the drug candidate and which are getting blanks. The goal is to separate the effects of the test drug from the effects of the monitoring process. As expected, some new drugs work and others fail, but here's the strangest finding: people in placebo groups always lose weight. In a study on the effectiveness of Xenical, for instance, more than 25% of the people in the placebo group lost at least 10 pounds. How can this be? While those in the placebo group aren't using drugs, they are keeping track of their weight and are more aware of their food intake than usual. This mindfulness may be the only "secret" behind the success of some crazy and non-scientific diets that advocate, for example, eating only food of a certain color (but "as much as you want") on a certain day. Careful monitoring proves to be a crucial component of weight control.

Surgery

Liposuction. Liposuction is fast becoming one of the most popular surgical procedures in the United States, with close to half a million performed each year. In this procedure, doctors directly remove fat cells from various parts of the body, using a hollow tube and a suction device. Over time, however, individuals who have undergone liposuction tend to regain all the lost weight. In fact, the only follow-up study on liposuction found that within a few months, nearly half of the patients weighed more than they did before the surgery. This is because body weight is a function of caloric intake and energy expenditure; fat cells can be removed, but without a change in the inputs and outputs, eventually the body will achieve the same composition.

Bariatric surgery and stomach banding. More invasive surgical procedures are also possible. The most effective is also the most extreme. In a type of procedure known as bariatric surgery, surgeons bypass a significant portion of the small intestine and seal off, by stomach banding, most of a person's stomach. This has two effects. First, it reduces the amount of food people can eat before becoming full—they actually become violently ill if they consume more than a few tablespoons at one time. And second, it reduces the ability of their small intestine to digest and absorb nutrients. Before all of the nutrients that they consume can be absorbed, the food material passes through the shortened digestive system and is excreted. The surgery carries significant risks, though, and leads to major nutritional deficiencies in almost a third of all cases. Still, something can be said for bariatric surgery that cannot be said unequivocally for any drug or diet: it works. One study of more than 600 patients found that after 14 years, the average

FOOD FOR ENERGY
AND GROWTH

NUTRIENTS

DIGESTION AND ABSORPTION

DIET AND HEALTH

879

weight loss was 100 pounds! Additionally, many health problems such as diabetes, high cholesterol, and high blood pressure went away.

Behavior Modification: Weight-Loss Diets

Portion control and general caloric restriction. Can we change our eating habits permanently? To answer this question, researchers put a group of monkeys on a very low calorie diet. The monkeys shed pounds initially, then stabilized at much lower weights for two years. After two years they were given unlimited access to food. Did they maintain their new weights? Absolutely not. After spending close to 10% of their lives at a constant, low weight, these monkeys quickly returned to their original, pre-diet weights.

This monkey example suggests that there might be a "set point" for body weight. A variety of human and non-human studies do, in fact, reveal that just like a thermostat for a room, when weight is below the set point, the body induces calorie-seeking behavior, and when weight is above the set point, the mind and body are free to pursue other goals. In a human study equivalent to the hungry monkey study, researchers observed a group of successful dieters over time. The newly skinny people had lost an average of 70 pounds per person through a comprehensive program. Three years after completing the program, the participants had, on average, regained all of their lost weight.

Low-carbohydrate diets. These are the latest in a long series of fad diets that enjoy popularity before being discarded for failing to deliver on the claims of their proponents and the promise of their short-term success. They are based on the incorrect assumption that carbohydrates universally cause rapid increases in blood sugar, followed by large releases of insulin from the pancreas, leading to immediate and efficient conversion of the blood sugar into fats, which are then stored throughout the body. While this scenario is correct for some carbohydrates, other carbohydrates, such as whole wheat pasta, produce less of an insulin response than a similar amount of high-protein beef. Similarly, many high-fiber fruits and vegetables are also rich in carbohydrates yet increase blood sugar levels only very gradually and elicit very small insulin responses. As a consequence, blanket avoidance of carbohydrates can lead to insufficient fiber intake, as well as vitamin and mineral deficiencies. Unlimited consumption of fat, too, can lead to a caloric surplus and weight gain. Low-carbohydrate diets do lead reliably to impressive *initial* weight loss. This is because, in the absence of dietary carbohydrates, glycogen (and the large amount of water bound to it) in the liver and muscles is quickly used up.

General Problems with Weight-Loss Diets

The main problems with most popular weight-loss diets are that (1) they focus on reducing weight (even weight due to water) rather than reducing body fat; (2) they reduce muscle mass, the body tissue best able to burn fat; (3) because they reduce body weight too rapidly, they trigger several defense mechanisms designed to preserve the body's energy reserves; and (4) they don't focus enough on the other side of the energy equation: exercise (**FIGURE 22-36**). This generally leads to four problems.

1. Nutritional deficiencies. Consider how a family facing a financial crunch may be forced to defer important work, such as fixing the car's brakes. Similarly, when the body

GENERAL PROBLEMS WITH WEIGHT-LOSS DIETS
- They focus on reducing weight (even weight due to water) rather than body fat
- They reduce muscle mass, the body tissue best able to burn fat
- Because they reduce body weight too rapidly, they trigger several defense mechanisms designed to preserve the body's energy reserves, generally leading to even more problems
- They don't focus enough on the other side of the energy equation: exercise

FIGURE 22-36 Weight-loss diets often fail.

goes into efficiency mode to combat a shortage of calories, a variety of systems get modulated down or turned off. Hungry lab animals, for example, almost completely lose their sex drive and may be less adept at fighting infection. Nearly all popular diets are seriously deficient in vitamins, minerals, and fiber.

2. Metabolic rate reduction. Sudden caloric restriction leads to a rapid reduction in basal metabolic rate, and this lower rate remains for several weeks after resuming normal caloric intake. With a reduced BMR, your body burns fat at a slower rate.

3. Loss of muscle mass and body fluids rather than body fat. Low-calorie diets lead to weight loss, but as much as 45% of the weight loss comes from the loss of muscle mass. Muscle tissue is significantly more metabolically active than the relatively inert fat cells. As a consequence, the body's fat-burning capacity is significantly reduced along with its muscle mass. Weight loss, as we've noted, is also commonly due to loss of the water bound to glycogen in muscles and the liver.

4. Increased lipoprotein lipase activity. With a reduction in caloric intake, your body increases the activity of an enzyme called lipoprotein lipase. This enzyme is responsible for converting nutrients in the bloodstream to fats for storage. As with the metabolic rate reduction, the increased activity of lipoprotein lipase continues for weeks following resumption of a normal diet.

An evaluation by the National Institutes of Health of *all* the major diet programs concluded that there was no good evidence that any of the programs reliably led to long-term weight loss. A large study published in the *New England Journal of Medicine* came to a similar conclusion in 2009. The claims made by weight-loss programs rely on anecdotal accounts of individuals that are not at all representative of the average outcome. Unfortunately, this means that there are no easy solutions to the problem of weight control. Living in our modern, zoo-like environment of plenty, we're going to struggle with natural systems that relentlessly seek out and efficiently store calories. Nonetheless, the National Institutes of Health notes that even modest weight loss (5% to 10% of total body weight) is likely to produce significant health benefits, and that it can be achieved through consumption of a moderate and balanced diet, in conjunction with moderate exercise.

> **TAKE-HOME MESSAGE 22·16**
>
> Weight loss is both a simple and a complicated problem. There is only one complete and perfect plan that guarantees success: reduced caloric intake and increased caloric expenditure. Interventions designed to facilitate weight loss involve drugs, surgery, or behavior modification, none of which is reliably successful and safe.

22·17 Diabetes is caused by the body's inability to regulate blood sugar effectively.

When it functions properly, the human body can resemble a finely tuned, responsive machine. Nowhere is this more evident than in the processing of food. After you digest and absorb food, there's an increase in the amount of glucose circulating in your bloodstream. This triggers the release of insulin by your pancreas. Insulin is a storage-stimulating hormone that causes your body's cells, especially muscle cells and fat cells, to pull the glucose in. They can then either use it for energy or convert it to glycogen or fat for storage until the energy is needed some other time. This leads to a reduction in glucose in the bloodstream and brings your blood sugar level back down to normal.

Foods differ in the extent to which they cause a surge in blood sugar and subsequent release of insulin. Foods that

cause a rapid and large surge—such as orange juice, honey, and white potatoes—are classified as having a high **glycemic index** and are less desirable in the diet. More desirable are foods that cause only a slow, moderate increase, having a low glycemic index. These include whole grains and beans. With a reduced insulin response comes a more efficient utilization of the sugar and lipids in the bloodstream and a reduction in fat storage. Insulin surges can also be reduced by eating smaller meals or, if you consume foods that have a high glycemic index, eating them with other foods as part of a meal.

Even finely tuned machines can malfunction. More than 10 million Americans (and 100 million people worldwide) have problems with their insulin-response systems, referred

Insulin—a hormone produced by the pancreas in response to increased blood sugar—causes your body's cells to pull glucose in from blood vessels.

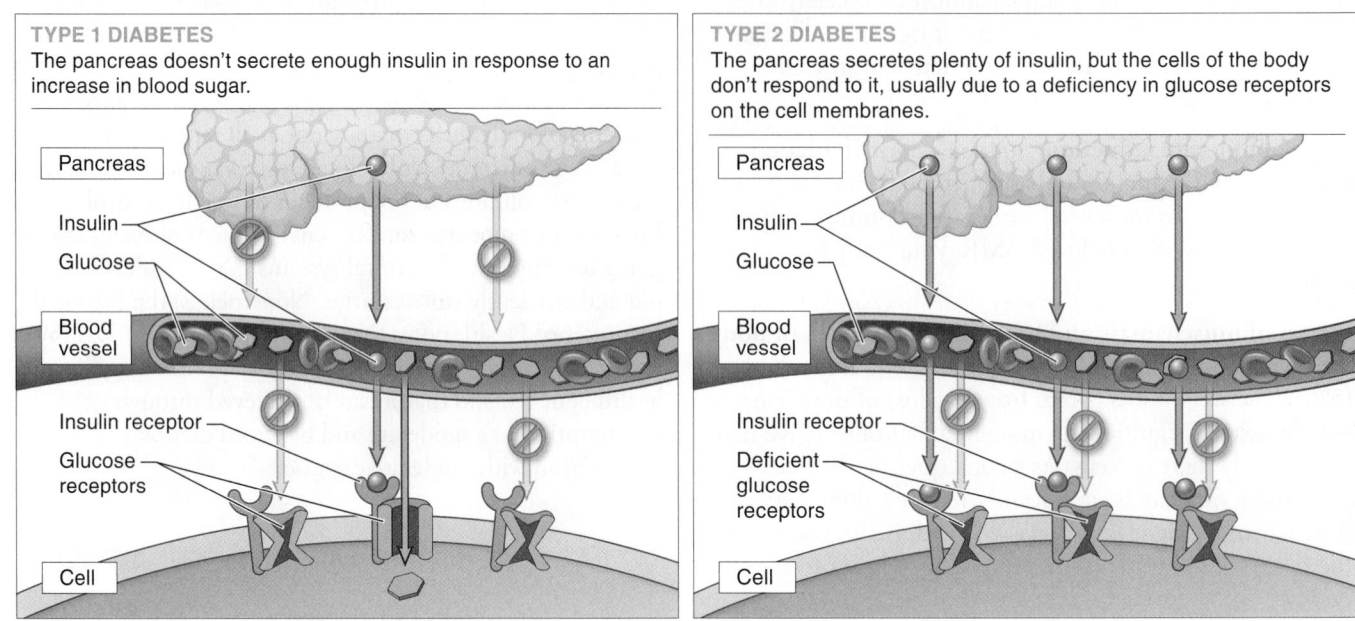

TYPE 1 DIABETES
The pancreas doesn't secrete enough insulin in response to an increase in blood sugar.

Pancreas
Insulin
Glucose
Blood vessel
Insulin receptor
Glucose receptors
Cell

TYPE 2 DIABETES
The pancreas secretes plenty of insulin, but the cells of the body don't respond to it, usually due to a deficiency in glucose receptors on the cell membranes.

Pancreas
Insulin
Glucose
Blood vessel
Insulin receptor
Deficient glucose receptors
Cell

FIGURE 22-37 Diabetes is a disruption in the body's regulation of blood sugar.

to as **diabetes.** These problems are chiefly of two types (**FIGURE 22-37**): either (1) the pancreas doesn't secrete enough insulin in response to an increase in blood sugar, or (2) the pancreas secretes plenty of insulin, but the cells of the body don't respond to it, usually due to a deficiency in glucose receptors on their cell membranes. In both cases, blood sugar remains high, and a host of problems can result from such persistence of glucose in the bloodstream.

Q

Why must diabetics inject insulin rather than taking it in pill form?

The first type of diabetes (called type 1) is believed to be an autoimmune disease and is most often diagnosed in children or young adults. Generally, people with type 1 diabetes have a pancreas that doesn't secrete enough insulin, thus they can be treated by insulin injections (**FIGURE 22-38**). (Unfortunately, because insulin is a protein, it is digested by stomach acids and the enzymes of the small intestine, so diabetics must inject the insulin in order to get it into their bloodstream intact.) The second type of diabetes (type 2) is about 10 times more common. It generally develops after the age of 40, and in about 90% of cases is a consequence of obesity. It appears that chronic

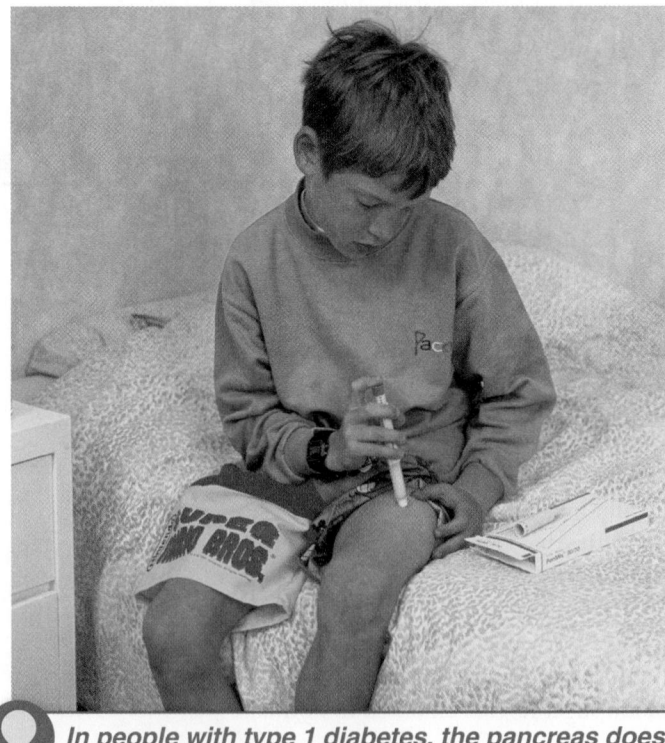

💡 *In people with type 1 diabetes, the pancreas does not secrete sufficient insulin. They can, however, modulate their blood sugar by injecting insulin.*

FIGURE 22-38 Type 1 diabetes is treated with insulin injections.

and excessive amounts of sugar in the diet (and, later, in the bloodstream) reduce the sensitivity and/or number of cellular insulin receptors that help control blood sugar. This causes even greater releases of insulin, which can, ultimately, wear out the insulin-producing cells of the pancreas. Type 2 diabetes is treated by minimizing the glucose fluctuations in the bloodstream. Weight loss is also encouraged, as it reduces insulin resistance.

Because chronically high levels of blood sugar affect nearly all the cells of the body, the health effects can be far-reaching and severe. Cells in the eye lens can become deformed, causing blurry vision; blood vessels can be damaged, causing circulatory system and kidney malfunction; and nerves can also be damaged. Taken together, the varied problems

resulting from diabetes make it the sixth leading cause of death in the United States.

TAKE-HOME MESSAGE 22·17

Digesting and absorbing food leads to an increase in the amount of glucose circulating in the bloodstream, which triggers the release of insulin by the pancreas, causing the body's cells, especially muscle cells and fat cells, to pull the glucose in for energy or storage. Problems with regulation of blood sugar, called diabetes, affect millions of people and are caused by heredity and poor diet.

22·18   Food and infection: spicy foods may act as natural antibiotics.

Have you ever tasted salsa so spicy that it brought tears to your eyes? After you gulped down a beverage to extinguish the fire in your mouth, did you ignore the distress signals from your taste buds and head right back for more? Why would anyone seek out such culinary torture? The answer may be surprisingly simple, although not immediately apparent. We'll start by asking the question: what *are* spicy foods?

Spices come from plants. Plants are rooted in the ground, and their immobility makes them easy targets for their natural enemies. But although they can't run away, they don't just give in to those organisms that want to eat them. They fight back chemically. Plants have evolved to produce a large number of toxic compounds to help in this fight. The presence of these noxious chemicals makes the plant toxic to would-be predators, either killing them outright or being so unpleasant-tasting that predators search elsewhere for a meal.

Humans, somewhat unexpectedly, actually seek out these toxins. We don't think of them as toxins, though. We call them spices, and as long as they're not too toxic, they make our food taste better. There also may be a deeper, more evolutionarily relevant reason we find our food to be more appealing with spices added. In some cases, they seem to help us in our own battles with natural enemies. "Food poisoning"—which affects about 1 in 10 people in the United States each year—is a misleading term. It isn't the

food that poisons us. Instead, it is microorganisms, particularly bacteria, that poison us. Humans and plants must perpetually fight against infection from microorganisms. This task is difficult, because bacteria find easy entry into our bodies via the food we eat. After sitting out at room temperature for just a few hours, food can acquire huge amounts of bacteria. But by adding spices to our food, we may be taking advantage of plant defenses to strike back at the microbes, killing some of them before they make it to our digestive systems.

The "spices kill bugs" hypothesis emerged from extensive observations and analyses. It has generated several predictions that have been tested.

Prediction 1: The magnitude of spice use in any part of the world should be related to the amount of microbial growth in that part of the world.

Observations: Put another way, this is a prediction that in warm, wet countries (where microbial growth occurs more readily), spice use should be greater, while in cooler climates, spice use should be less. In an analysis of more than 4,500 meat-based recipes and 2,100 vegetable-based recipes from 36 countries, this prediction was overwhelmingly supported. There is a strong correlation between regions with high average temperatures and their use of spices with antimicrobial effects (FIGURE 22-39). Spices were included in every single recipe, for example, from Ethiopia,

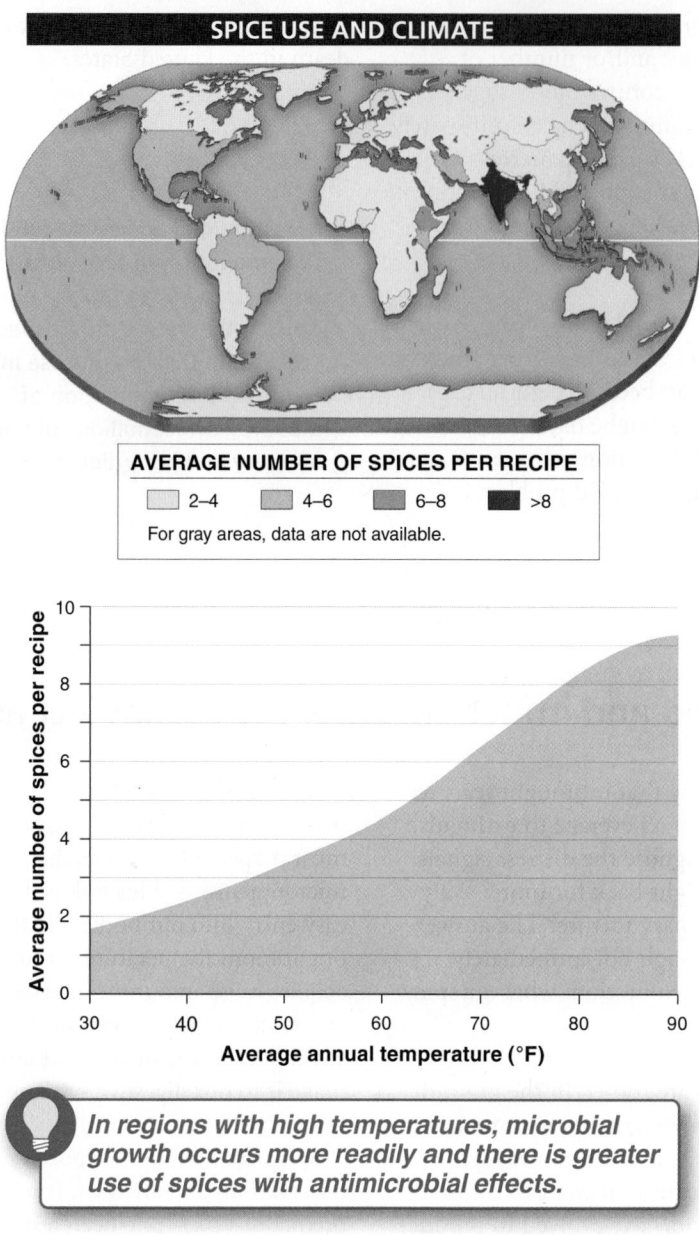

AVERAGE NUMBER OF SPICES PER RECIPE

2–4   4–6   6–8   >8

For gray areas, data are not available.

In regions with high temperatures, microbial growth occurs more readily and there is greater use of spices with antimicrobial effects.

FIGURE 22-39 Fighting natural enemies. Antimicrobial spices are used much more in regions where temperatures are high.

Greece, India, Indonesia, Iran, Kenya, Malaysia, Morocco, Nigeria, and Thailand. Conversely, two-thirds of all recipes from Finland and Norway called for no spices at all.

Two observations suggest that this relationship between spice use and climate cannot be attributed to the fact that more spices grow in the countries with hotter, wetter climates. First, onion and garlic, two of the most potent antimicrobial spices, grow in all of the countries studied but are used more frequently in the warmer countries. And second, although the warmer countries do have larger numbers of local spices to choose from, they use a greater proportion of the available spices than do the cooler countries.

Prediction 2: Spices with the strongest antimicrobial effects should be used most frequently, and the weaker antimicrobial agents used less frequently.

Observations: In a test of 42 spices, in which each was added to individual plates of bacteria, nearly all exhibited antimicrobial properties—sometimes quite dramatically, other times much less so—when used in the amounts called for in recipes. For example, the toxic compound in cilantro

GRAPHIC CONTENT!
Thinking critically about visual displays of data.
Turn to p. 888 for a closer inspection of this figure.

SPICE USE AND ANTIMICROBIAL PROPERTIES

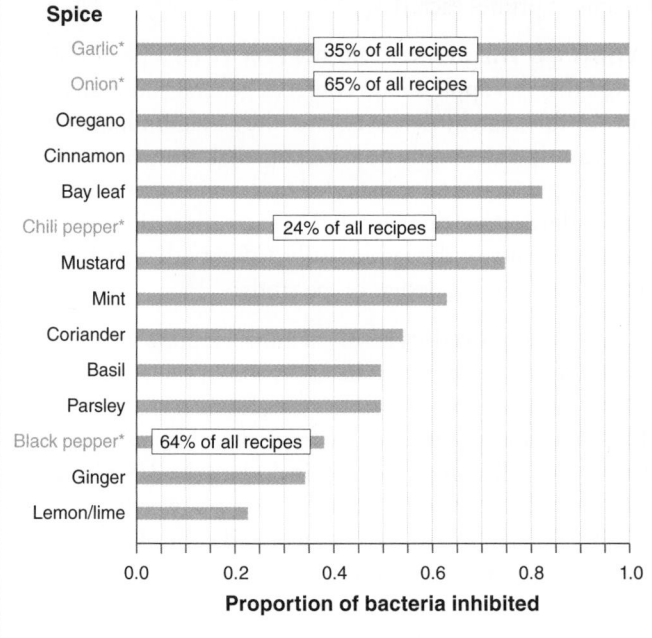

* The four most commonly used spices are shown in red.

Spices with the strongest antimicrobial effects are used more frequently in food preparation.

FIGURE 22-40 Recipe ingredients with antimicrobial properties. (Photo shows woman with drying chili peppers.)

was twice as effective at killing *Salmonella* bacteria as was the commonly used antibiotic drug gentamicin. Most of the spices tested were broad in their effects, too, killing most of the 30 different types of common food-borne bacteria tested. Overall, onions, which had the best antimicrobial effects (they killed all species of bacteria they came into contact with), were used most frequently, appearing in 65% of all recipes. They were followed by black pepper (in 64% of all recipes), garlic (in 35%), chili peppers (in 24%), and lemon and lime juice (in 23%). Other commonly used spices include parsley, ginger, bay leaf, coriander, and cinnamon (**FIGURE 22-40**).

Prediction 3: Because bacterial growth is faster and more common on meat than on vegetables, meat recipes should call for more spices than vegetable recipes.

Observations: The vegetable recipes called for, on average, 2.4 spices, while the meat recipes called for almost twice as many, with an average of 3.9.

Research on the connection between the use of spices and their antimicrobial properties continues. Current research focuses on evaluating the minimum concentrations of spices that are necessary for inhibitory activity. After all, it's not helpful if the amount of a spice required to have an antibiotic effect is much greater than the amount typically used. Additionally, it is important to evaluate the specific bacterial species inhibited by each spice, in order to determine the real-world value of a spice as an antimicrobial agent.

Nonetheless, the observations above are consistent with the suggestion that humans may have initially incorporated spices into food preparation because of their antimicrobial properties. And this example shows how seemingly arbitrary behaviors may reflect evolutionary adaptations.

TAKE-HOME MESSAGE 22·18

Plants produce toxic compounds that make the plant distasteful to would-be predators, either killing them outright or being so unpleasant-tasting that predators search elsewhere for a meal. Humans may seek out these toxins, using them as spices that help us fight off illness-inducing microorganisms.

"AN APPLE A DAY KEEPS THE DOCTOR AWAY."

Silly rhyme? Sound, data-backed advice? Or something in between?

Q: WHAT IS THE CLAIM? A 2011 research study—described in media around the world, including *Time, MSNBC,* and *CBS*—touted the first experimental support for the adage "an apple a day keeps the doctor away."

Q: WHAT IS THE PURPORTED "APPLE ADVANTAGE"? The media articles reported that participants in the study experienced:

1. A 23% decrease in LDL (low-density lipoprotein, which is associated with a higher risk of cardiovascular disease).

2. A 4% increase in HDL (high-density lipoprotein, which is associated with a reduced risk of cardiovascular disease).

3. A 32% decrease in C-reactive protein (a protein that is associated with inflammation and is a marker for cardiovascular disease).

4. A 33% decrease in lipid hydroperoxide (a chemical associated with plaque formation in arteries).

5. A loss of 3.3 pounds of body weight by each subject, on average.

Q: HOW DID THE RESEARCHERS EVALUATE THE BENEFITS OF APPLES? The study lasted for one year and included 160 post-menopausal women, aged 45–65, who were randomly assigned to one of two groups. In the "treatment" group, subjects were assigned to eat 75 grams (2.7 ounces) of dried apples each day. In the "control" group, subjects were assigned to eat 100 grams of prunes each day.

Q: WHAT DO THE RESULTS MEAN FOR YOU? The headlines suggested that "an apple a day" confers a general and dramatic benefit. Unfortunately, that overstates the actual findings. After all, the study included only post-menopausal women, it observed them for only a year, and it included health measures relating only to cardiovascular disease risk. Do these limitations reduce the generalizability of the results? Why? What other problems can you identify in the design of the study?

More importantly, overlooked in the media reports was the fact that, of the five important results listed above, the researchers found statistically significant differences for only two findings—the LDL decrease and the lipid hydroperoxide decrease. In other words, the other findings reported, including the 3.3-pound weight loss and the 4% increase in HDL levels, were not sufficiently different between treatment and control groups to confidently reject a null hypothesis of no difference between the two groups.

Q: WHAT CAN YOU CONCLUDE? BEWARE OF HYPERBOLE. When a study is presented in the form of a media-friendly sound bite, much can be lost in translation. There is a limit to what researchers can reasonably conclude from any study. In this case, there are two very promising results. In post-menopausal women, daily apple consumption might improve two measures of heart health: (1) LDL level, an important measure of the risk of cardiovascular disease, is reduced, and (2) lipid hydroperoxide, an indicator of plaque formation in arteries, is reduced. Though encouraging, these results fall far short of the claims made by news reports that apples are a "miracle fruit" and that "everyone can benefit from consuming apples." At this point, perhaps the most reasonable conclusion to draw is that it is essential to read the news with a critical eye.

Big Ideas in ...
Nutrition and Digestion

22·1–22·3 Food provides the raw materials for growth and the fuel to make it happen.

- Animals must eat for two reasons: to acquire the energy needed for all growth and activity, and to acquire the raw materials required for life.
- Carnivores consume only other animals. Herbivores consume only plants. Omnivores consume both plants and animals.
- The minimal energetic needs of an individual not engaged in any activity are called the basal metabolic rate, or BMR.

22·4–22·7 Nutrients are grouped into six categories.

- Water is probably the single most important component of a balanced diet, while proteins, carbohydrates, and fats provide calories and raw materials.
- Vitamins and minerals are, respectively, organic and inorganic molecules in the diet that are used in the production and action of enzymes and other molecules.
- Humans and other animals show an evolved preference for fatty foods over carbohydrate- or protein-laden foods.

22·8–22·13 We extract energy and nutrients from food.

- The digestive process in humans includes four distinct phases: ingestion, digestion, absorption, and elimination.
- Ingestion involves tearing and grinding food in preparation for passing it to the stomach.
- Digestion, the process of dismantling large pieces of food, physically and chemically breaking them down into absorbable molecules, occurs primarily in the stomach and small intestine.
- Absorption, in the small intestine, is the process by which energy-rich food particles are taken into the cells of the body.
- Water and ions are absorbed before the indigestible portions of consumed food are defecated.

22·14–22·18 What we eat profoundly affects our health.

- Ancestral humans experienced unpredictable food supplies, leading to the evolution of strong appetites. In the modern industrialized world, such instincts have problematic consequences for weight control.
- Although there is, in theory, one complete and perfect plan that guarantees successful weight control—reduced caloric intake and increased caloric expenditure—the many interventions designed to help people lose weight are rarely successful.
- Problems with regulation of blood sugar, called diabetes, affect millions of people and are often caused by poor diet.
- Somewhat ironically, humans may seek out toxic compounds that are produced by plants to ward off predators. Such compounds, used as spices, may help us fight off illness-inducing microorganisms.

See the To-Go Guide (packaged with every new copy of this textbook) for an illustrated summary of the chapter.

Check Your Knowledge

1. What feature of the spice is shown on the *x*-axis? Why does the *x*-axis only go up to 1.0?

2. Which spice is the second most frequently used in recipes? How do you know this?

3. Why are garlic and onion both at the top of the graph, when garlic is used in only about half as many recipes as onion?

4. What can you conclude about the frequency of recipes that contain oregano? Why?

5. What can you infer about the relative frequency of use of coriander versus ginger in recipes? Why?

6. In a city close to the equator, would you expect fewer food poisoning cases to come from a Swedish restaurant or an Indian restaurant? Why? How certain of your "prediction" are you? Why?

7. What additional data would be helpful in this figure?

8. Propose two alternative ways that you could plot the data included here. What would be an advantage to each of your alternative versions? What would be a disadvantage of each?

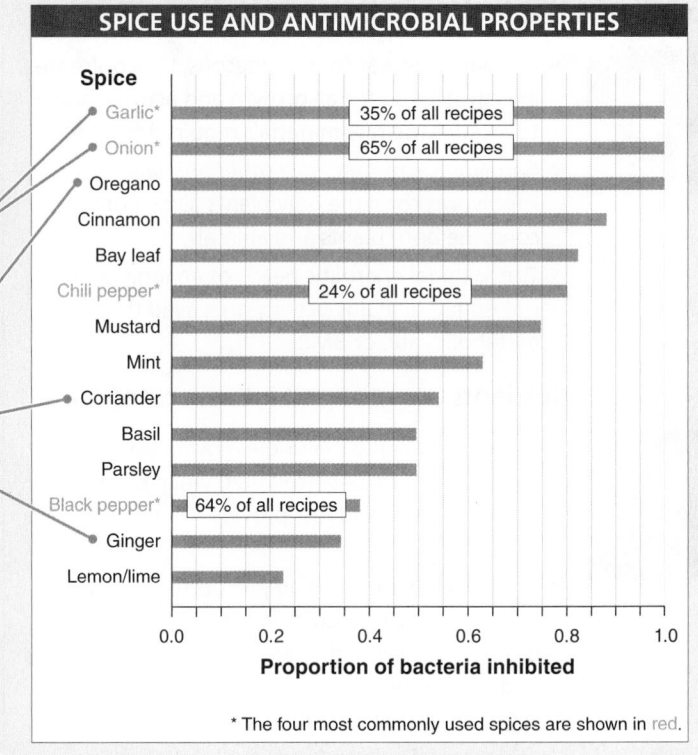

SPICE USE AND ANTIMICROBIAL PROPERTIES

Spice
- Garlic* — 35% of all recipes
- Onion* — 65% of all recipes
- Oregano
- Cinnamon
- Bay leaf
- Chili pepper* — 24% of all recipes
- Mustard
- Mint
- Coriander
- Basil
- Parsley
- Black pepper* — 64% of all recipes
- Ginger
- Lemon/lime

Proportion of bacteria inhibited (0.0, 0.2, 0.4, 0.6, 0.8, 1.0)

* The four most commonly used spices are shown in red.

See Answers at the back of the book.

Key Terms in Nutrition and Digestion

Multiple-Choice Questions

1. **Based on the types of food they consume, spiders and owls are considered:**
   a) carnivores.
   b) omnivores.
   c) herbivores.
   d) primary producers.
   e) fluid-feeders.

   100 HARD — 24 — 0 EASY

2. **Basal metabolic rate:**
   a) depends to a large degree on how active an individual is.
   b) does not vary across mammalian species.
   c) is a measure of the minimal energetic needs of an individual not engaged in any activity.
   d) is the same for males and females of any given species.
   e) All of the above are correct.

   100 HARD — 18 — 0 EASY

3. **Water has many functions in animal bodies. These include all of the following except:**
   a) lubricating many joints, the spinal cord, and the eyes.
   b) serving as a solvent for many vitamins and minerals.
   c) transporting nutrients and waste materials throughout the body.
   d) regulating growth and development.
   e) All of the above are functions of water in animal bodies.

   100 HARD — 44 — 0 EASY

4. **Why do dieters lose large amounts of "water weight" during the first few days of a diet?**
   a) The first, most accessible, molecules that can be broken down for energy are glycogen molecules in muscles and liver. Because large amounts of water are bound to glycogen, as the glycogen is removed from tissues, so too is the water.
   b) Dieters tend to reduce their consumption of all food and beverages—including their consumption of water—during the first days of a diet.
   c) Dieting causes a slight increase in body temperature, which leads to increased evaporative cooling and the loss of water.
   d) The fat cells of the body are primarily filled with water. As these cells are utilized for energy, the water is also lost.
   e) This a is a myth. Dieters do not lose "water weight" during the first few days of a diet.

   100 HARD — 24 — 0 EASY

5. **On food packages, "fiber" refers to plant material that we can't fully digest but is important for maintaining a healthy digestive tract. "Fiber" refers to a type of:**
   a) carbohydrate.
   b) nucleic acid.
   c) lipid.
   d) amino acid.
   e) protein.

   100 HARD — 32 — 0 EASY

6. **Proteins are an essential component of a healthy diet for humans (and other animals). Their most common purpose is to serve as:**
   a) fuel for running the body.
   b) raw material for growth.
   c) inorganic precursors for enzyme construction.
   d) organic precursors for membrane construction.
   e) long-term energy storage.

   100 HARD — 59 — 0 EASY

7. Various types of vitamin and mineral supplements are generally necessary for individuals in all of the following categories except:

a) post-menopausal women.

b) healthy people with good diets.

c) people on extremely low-calorie diets.

d) pregnant women.

e) people with limited milk consumption or sun exposure.

100 HARD

37

0 EASY

8. Why do birds eat gravel?

a) Gravel contains most of the essential minerals for a bird's diet.

b) Birds have poor vision and have difficulty distinguishing gravel from small seeds.

c) By chewing on gravel, birds are able to sharpen their teeth, increasing their ability to crack open hard nuts or catch their prey.

d) The gravel collects in the gizzard (one of the two chambers of the bird stomach), where it helps to grind up the food they eat.

e) Because they have such a small brain relative to body size, birds tend to be the least intelligent of the vertebrates.

100 HARD

16

0 EASY

9. Across dozens of cultures, humans have developed common ways of preparing their food, including using heat and marinating food in acidic solutions, such as vinegar or lemon juice. How might these be adaptations that help with digestion?

a) Harsh conditions such as heat and acid help to disrupt the tissue of food items. This increases the efficiency with which digestive enzymes can make contact with the food molecules and break them down.

b) These methods of food preparation reduce the necessity for producing chyme and so increase the caloric efficiency of food intake.

c) Because even the weakest acids are toxic to all bacteria, these methods of food preparation reduce the incidence of dietary-induced bacterial infection.

d) These methods increase the body's ability to extract energy from normally indigestible cellulose.

e) These methods of food preparation reduce the need for water consumption.

100 HARD

53

0 EASY

10. Which of the following statements about the small intestine is incorrect?

a) It is the primary site of digestion and absorption of nutrients into the bloodstream.

b) It is the chief site of absorption of water by the digestive system.

c) It is the longest part of the digestive tract.

d) It receives secretions from the gallbladder.

e) It is the part of the digestive tract where all food macromolecules can be broken down into absorbable monomers.

100 HARD

38

0 EASY

11. To leave the digestive tract and enter the cells of the body, a substance must cross a cell membrane. During which stage of digestion does this take place?

a) peristalsis

b) absorption

c) elimination

d) chemotaxis

e) ingestion

100 HARD

33

0 EASY

12. Digestion and absorption:

a) involve the breakdown of food into small nutrient molecules (absorption) and the passage of those molecules into the bloodstream (digestion).

b) both occur primarily in the large intestine, or colon.

c) are terms that describe the same process.

d) both occur primarily in the stomach.

e) involve the breakdown of food into small nutrient molecules (digestion) and the passage of those molecules into the bloodstream (absorption).

100 HARD

10

0 EASY

13. In the mammalian digestive system, vitamin-synthesizing symbiotic bacteria live primarily in the:

a) small intestine.

b) esophagus.

c) mouth.

d) large intestine.

e) stomach.

100 HARD

45

0 EASY

14. **Though essentially the same organ, the human appendix is much smaller than the koala's cecum. This is because:**

   a) humans take supplements to obtain enough vitamins and do not need the extra vitamins produced by the bacteria housed in the appendix.

   b) humans aid the digestive process by marinating and cooking foods, so they do not require a large appendix to aid food digestion.

   c) humans maintain bacteria in their intestine rather than in their appendix, so the organ does not need to be as large as a koala's cecum.

   d) in humans, no cellulose-digesting bacteria live in the appendix and, unlike the koala's cecum, it has no digestive function at all.

   e) humans get a greater proportion of their nutrients from meat than do koalas, so they do not need as large an organ to digest the plant matter they eat.

   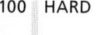
   100 | HARD
   31
   0 | EASY

15. **Cows have large populations of bacteria in their digestive systems. Which of the following best explains why?**

   a) The mutualistic microbes combat the harmful microbes that may enter a cow's body with its food.

   b) Cows are able to use cellulose-producing bacteria to help them digest their food.

   c) Most cows do not actually have large populations of bacteria in their digestive systems. Only infected cows have these microbes.

   d) Scientists put the microbes there, so that they can study how the microbes affect cows' digestion.

   e) The microbes metabolize the cellulose in the plants that cows eat.

   100 | HARD
   41
   0 | EASY

16. **The spices that many humans use to season their food:**

   a) are generally compounds produced by plants to reduce their risk of being eaten.

   b) are actually dead microorganisms.

   c) consist primarily of amino acids.

   d) are the chief cause of ulcers.

   e) can only be grown in tropical regions of the world.

   100 | HARD
   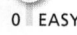
   28
   0 | EASY

Short-Answer Questions

1. What are the six groups of nutrients? What is their primary role in human health?

2. What are the four distinct phases used by humans to extract nutrients from food? For each phase, what significant activity takes place that contributes to nutrient harvesting and absorption?

3. Describe how some mammals, which do not have enzymes to break down cellulose, are able to extract nutrients from cellulose-containing food.

4. Describe the two forms of diabetes. What are the risk factors and treatments?

See Answers at the back of the book.
For additional study questions, go to www.prep-u.com.

ABOUT THE CHAPTER OPENING PHOTO

Although kingfishers feed on a variety of prey, many species hunt and eat fish. Typically, they perch 3-6 feet above the water and dive for small fish, such as minnows, swimming 1-2 feet below the surface.

Actions, reactions, sensations, and addictions: meet your nervous system

23

Nervous and Motor Systems

23·1–23·3 What is the nervous system?

The snowy owl relies on its excellent vision and hearing as it hunts for rodents and other small mammals, as well as birds and fish.

23·1 Why do we need a nervous system?

Imagine a world without pain. Think of all that you could achieve. You could work harder, run farther, and just plain feel better. Maybe that's why so many products are marketed as "painkillers."

But would it really be a better world? Think again.

The case of Gabby Gingras tells us that we wouldn't really be happier in a pain-free world. Gabby feels no pain. She was born that way. At first it seemed like a blessing: just after birth, when nurses drew blood from her, she did not cry but instead slept peacefully through the procedure. When, as a toddler, she fell down, she didn't cry. But rather than being a gift that makes her life easier, Gabby's inability to feel pain is a crippling curse. As she has grown older, some unexpected consequences of her condition make this clear. First, she inadvertently damaged her eyes—permanently scratching one of her corneas—by poking her fingers into them. Later, chewing on plastic toys, she cracked most of her teeth. Another girl, also born without the ability to feel pain, encountered even more severe problems. Holding her hand over a hot stove, she was severely burned—moving her hand only when she smelled the burning flesh. This condition is called "heritable sensory autonomic neuropathy," and it reveals that, no matter how unpleasant pain is to experience,

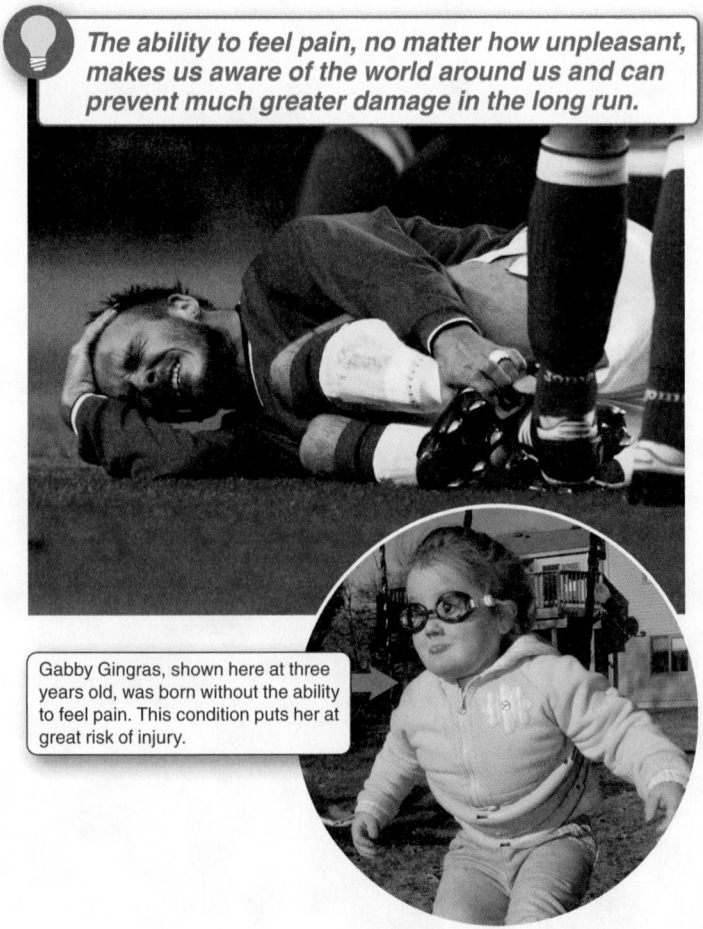

The ability to feel pain, no matter how unpleasant, makes us aware of the world around us and can prevent much greater damage in the long run.

Gabby Gingras, shown here at three years old, was born without the ability to feel pain. This condition puts her at great risk of injury.

FIGURE 23-1 Avoiding danger. The sensation of pain gives us important information about the world.

it does have a very large benefit. The pains we feel alert us to the need to extricate ourselves from a dangerous situation and can prevent much greater suffering in the long run (**FIGURE 23-1**).

The survival and well being of organisms depends on their awareness of the world around them and their ability to limit exposure to physically harmful situations. Our **nervous system** accomplishes these tasks by letting us see, hear, feel, taste, smell, remember (and forget!), think about, act on, and react to various events and stimuli around us. Present in all multicellular animals other than sponges (and not found in plants), the nervous system is a network of cells that collects information about an organism's internal and external environments, processes that information, and sends signals to effectors, which are muscles and glands that are capable of responding to the information.

Nervous systems have three critical features (**FIGURE 23-2**):

1. They receive input (stimuli) from the surrounding world.

2. They process that information.

3. They initiate responses to the internal and external environments, when necessary.

In this chapter, we examine the organization and structures found in nervous systems and the diversity of nervous system specializations that have evolved in the animal world, including specializations that allow humans to discern light from dark, to identify subtle differences in touch, temperature, and color, and to use language and abstract reasoning to perform and coordinate complex social behaviors. We also explore how the nervous system, interacting with the muscular and skeletal systems, can generate movement. And we examine how various drugs (legal and illegal) affect, often adversely, the functioning of the nervous system.

FUNCTIONS OF THE NERVOUS SYSTEM

The nervous system—present in almost all multicellular animals—has three primary functions.

RECEIVE STIMULI
The nervous system collects information about the internal and external environments.

Stimulus

PROCESS INFORMATION
The nervous system interprets the incoming stimuli and determines a response.

INITIATE RESPONSE
The nervous system sends signals to muscles and glands in response to the internal and external environments.

Cellular response

FIGURE 23-2 Overview of nervous system functions.

TAKE-HOME MESSAGE 23·1

Present in all multicellular animals other than sponges, the nervous system is a network of cells that collects information about the organism's internal and external environments, processes that information, and sends signals to muscles and glands in response to the information.

23·2

Neurons are the building blocks of all nervous systems.

The **neuron** is a type of cell that is specialized for generating and conducting electrical impulses and is found in all animals, with the exception of sponges. It is the building block of all nervous systems (**FIGURE 23-3**). No matter how complex or simple that system is, it consists of neurons. Each neuron is very small and has but a single option at any point in time: "fire" or "don't fire" (meaning that the neuron

either generates an electrical signal that can convey information to nearby cells, or does not). But, put together a few hundred billion neurons, and things start to get interesting. Taken together, groups of neurons bundled together with connective tissue—into structures called **nerves**—connect us to our world by enabling us to sense light, sound, touch, tastes, and smells and to respond to all

NEURON STRUCTURE

Neurons—individual cells that specialize in carrying electrical signals—are the building blocks of the nervous system. They are composed of three distinct elements.

Stimulus

DENDRITES
Sense and respond to stimulation from outside the cell and send that information toward the cell body

CELL BODY
Contains the nucleus and other cellular machinery

AXON
Long tube-like projection that extends from the cell body and transmits signals to other cells

Signal

GLIAL CELLS
Support cells that protect, insulate, and nourish the neurons

FIGURE 23-3 The neuron is the building block of the nervous system.

of that sensory information. The accumulated information carried by all of our neurons—whether they are firing or not firing—is also responsible for information storage and retrieval and all thought in our brain.

Neurons are powerful cells, but they are also fragile. In the time it takes you to read this sentence, one of your neurons will die. If you read it again, another one will die. And neither will be replaced; unlike most cells in your body, very few neurons are able to replace themselves. This need not be cause for alarm, though. Even with about 9,000 neurons dying on a good day—significantly more if you consume any alcohol or happen to inhale any gasoline fumes—the 100 billion to one trillion you were born with are more than enough for you to keep your wits about you.

Even though they perform such varied and significant functions, neurons are relatively standard eukaryotic cells. Each has a **cell body** that contains a nucleus, mitochondria, endoplasmic reticulum, and so on. But neurons also have two specialized structures that make them unusually adept at interacting with the external environment and with other cells.

The first of these two important specializations is the **dendrite.** A dendrite is the part of a neuron that is like an antenna: it senses and responds to stimulation from outside the cell and sends that information toward the cell body of the neuron. Numerous dendrites branch out from the neuron cell body.

The neuron's second important specialization is the **axon.** An axon can transmit a signal, much as an electrical wire does, over great distances. The axon is a long—sometimes *very* long—tube-like extension of the main cell body that transmits the signals picked up by the dendrites to the rest of the organism's body. The end of the axon is specially modified in a way that allows it to transmit the signals to another cell. The longest cells in the world are neurons. Some neurons are several feet long. The sciatic (sigh-AT-ick) nerve, for example, runs from your spinal cord all the way to the tips of your toes. Most of this distance is covered by a single axon.

Although neurons do all the actual work of the nervous system, they do it with a lot of help from other cells. Throughout the nervous system, in addition to the neurons there are large numbers of non-neuronal cells, called **glial cells,** which function like a support staff to protect, insulate, and nourish the neurons. In the human brain, there are approximately nine times as many glial cells as there are neurons. And unlike most neurons, glial cells regularly divide. Not surprisingly, then, virtually all brain tumors in adults are formed from glial cells, the supporting cells of the brain.

Q If neurons rarely (if ever) divide, how can people get brain tumors, which are the result of unstoppable cell division?

Just as corporations keep their big computers locked up in super-clean, secure rooms to keep them functioning at an optimal level, the brain is protected from potentially harmful molecules in the blood. Support cells line the blood vessels that supply the brain, forming a semi-permeable barrier. Called the "blood-brain barrier," it allows essential nutrients and gases to pass through, while barring harmful molecules such as metabolic wastes produced throughout the body. The blood-brain barrier is not perfect, though. Many small molecules, including anesthetics and alcohol, can make it through to influence the brain. The barrier also can be broken down by hypertension, radiation, and a variety of infectious organisms.

SENSORY NEURONS
- Collect information from an animal's environment
- Dendrites modified to respond to external stimulation, such as temperature, touch, taste, smell, light, or sound

MOTOR NEURONS
- Initiate an animal's response to stimuli
- Stimulate action by conveying signals to muscles or glands

INTERNEURONS
- Interpret signals coming in from sensory neurons and relay them to motor neurons
- Located only in the brain and the spinal cord

FIGURE 23-4 Three types of neurons work together in the vertebrate nervous system.

To carry out the activities of the nervous system, neurons come in three types, with names that reveal their functions (**FIGURE 23-4**).

1. **Sensory neurons** collect information from an animal's environment and have dendrites modified to respond directly to internal and external stimulation. This stimulation can include temperature, touch, taste, smell, light, or sound.

2. **Motor neurons** stimulate action by conveying signals to muscles or glands and initiating a body's response to stimuli.

3. **Interneurons** integrate the signals coming in from the sensory neurons and relay them to the motor neurons.

These "middlemen" are located only in the brain and the spinal cord.

In the next section, we'll look at how these three types of neurons interact and the general organization of the vertebrate nervous system.

TAKE-HOME MESSAGE 23·2

The neuron is a type of cell specialized for carrying electrical signals and is the building block of all nervous systems. Each neuron is very small, but groups of neurons bundled together enable us to sense light, sound, touch, tastes, and smells and to respond to them.

23·3 The vertebrate nervous system consists of the peripheral and central nervous systems.

In most animals, including all vertebrates, the nervous system is divided into two components: the peripheral nervous system and the central nervous system (**FIGURE 23-5**). The **peripheral nervous system (PNS)** is the network of (1) sensory cells modified to receive information from the environment and (2) motor pathways that transmit signals to effectors, the muscles and glands that are capable of

responding to that stimulus. But the information received by the body's sensory cells does not generally go straight to the cells that control the muscles and glands. First it passes through the **central nervous system (CNS),** which is made up of the spinal cord and brain. Not directly connected to sensory organs or to muscles, the central nervous system processes information that it receives from sensory cells

FIGURE 23-5 **Organization of the vertebrate nervous system.**

THE VERTEBRATE NERVOUS SYSTEM

In vertebrates, the nervous system is divided into the central nervous system and the peripheral nervous system.

CENTRAL NERVOUS SYSTEM

Composed of interneurons and other supporting cells that process information from sensory cells and send out instructions to other nervous tissue to act in response to that sensory information.

- Brain
- Spinal cord

PERIPHERAL NERVOUS SYSTEM

Detects stimuli and transmits signals

SENSORY PATHWAYS

- Sensory neurons that receive information from the environment

MOTOR PATHWAYS

- Motor neurons that transmit signals to the muscles and glands

SOMATIC NERVOUS SYSTEM
(Voluntary motor pathways)

- Relays signals to skeletal muscles
- Under conscious control

AUTONOMIC NERVOUS SYSTEM
(Involuntary motor pathways)

- Relays signals to glands and to smooth muscle tissue and cardiac muscle
- Not under conscious control

Sympathetic nervous system

- Responsible for coordinating the body's fight-or-flight response to stress

Parasympathetic nervous system

- Responsible for controlling activities relating to digesting food and eliminating waste

a fork. The **autonomic nervous system** relays signals to your glands and your smooth muscle tissue and cardiac muscle. These signals, which are not under conscious control, cause the muscles surrounding your stomach and intestine, for example, to contract and to move food through the digestive tract. The central nervous system controls both the somatic and the autonomic nervous systems.

Because it enables you to initiate movements consciously, the somatic nervous system is commonly referred to as the voluntary nervous system. When a sensory neuron in the peripheral nervous system—say, in your hand—senses an irritation (such as a mosquito landing on your skin), it sends a signal to convey this information to the spinal cord, where the sensory neuron connects with an interneuron that extends to the brain (**FIGURE 23-6**). The signal is interpreted and a response is determined (probably that you want to make the mosquito go away), and this information is sent through another interneuron back down your spinal cord to a motor neuron that is attached to a muscle. The signal from the brain to the muscle causes you to swat at the mosquito—removing the source of irritation. This whole process takes only a tiny fraction of a second.

Within the somatic nervous system, some signals can generate a response without any processing by the brain, traveling directly from a sensory neuron to an interneuron in the spinal cord that connects directly to a motor neuron. This kind of direct sensory-motor response is called a **reflex,** and it causes reaction to a sensation that does not need to be processed through the brain. Reflexes enable an organism to respond faster to an imminent danger (**FIGURE 23-7**). Your brain learns about it just a bit later.

In contrast to the somatic nervous system, the autonomic nervous system—which can be thought of as the "automatic" or involuntary nervous system—carries the signals by which the central nervous system regulates the heartbeat, breathing, glandular secretions, the muscles surrounding blood vessels that regulate circulation, and the

about the organism's surroundings and sends out instructions to other nervous tissue to act in response to that sensory information. Later in this chapter, we discuss the elaborate specializations—from memory to language and abstract reasoning—that have evolved in the most complex vertebrate brains.

The motor pathways of the peripheral nervous system have two major divisions: the somatic and the autonomic nervous systems. The **somatic nervous system** relays signals to your skeletal muscles and enables you to contract those muscles and move your limbs consciously, such as when you pick up

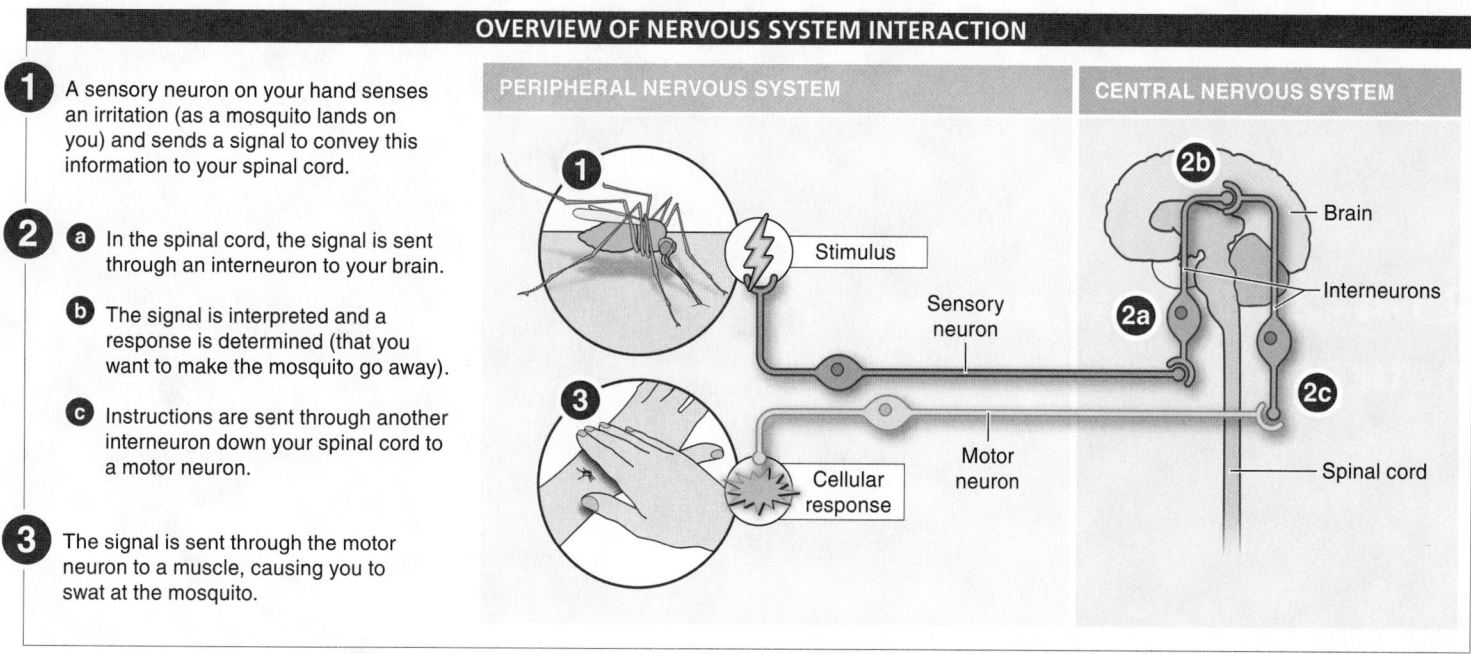

OVERVIEW OF NERVOUS SYSTEM INTERACTION

PERIPHERAL NERVOUS SYSTEM

CENTRAL NERVOUS SYSTEM

1 A sensory neuron on your hand senses an irritation (as a mosquito lands on you) and sends a signal to convey this information to your spinal cord.

2 a In the spinal cord, the signal is sent through an interneuron to your brain.

b The signal is interpreted and a response is determined (that you want to make the mosquito go away).

c Instructions are sent through another interneuron down your spinal cord to a motor neuron.

3 The signal is sent through the motor neuron to a muscle, causing you to swat at the mosquito.

Stimulus

Sensory neuron

Cellular response

Motor neuron

Brain

Interneurons

Spinal cord

FIGURE 23-6 The peripheral nervous system interacts with the central nervous system.

movement of food through the digestive tract. It is through the autonomic nervous system, in large part, that the central nervous system regulates homeostasis.

There are two components to the autonomic nervous system: the sympathetic nervous system and the parasympathetic nervous system. The **sympathetic nervous system** is responsible for coordinating the body's fight-or-flight response to stress, including increasing the heart and breathing rates and providing muscles with additional blood flow. The **parasympathetic nervous system,** in contrast, is responsible for controlling activities related to digesting food and eliminating waste, tending to slow the heart and breathing rates as these processes occur. Although the two systems tend to coordinate opposing effects, most muscles, organs, and glands receive input from both the sympathetic and the parasympathetic nervous systems.

Reflexes enable an organism to respond faster to an imminent danger.

FIGURE 23-7 Quick reaction. Reflexes can generate a response to a stimulus without need for processing of the signal by the brain.

TAKE-HOME MESSAGE 23·3

In all vertebrates, the nervous system is divided into the peripheral nervous system and the central nervous system. The central nervous system is made up of the spinal cord and brain. The peripheral nervous system carries signals to and from the sensory and motor pathways. The motor pathways carry signals from both the somatic and autonomic nervous systems, which relay signals that can be controlled consciously, and other signals that cannot be controlled consciously.

WHAT IS THE NERVOUS SYSTEM?

HOW DO NEURONS WORK?

THE SENSES

MUSCULAR AND SKELETAL SYSTEMS

THE BRAIN

DRUGS HIJACK PLEASURE PATHWAYS

899

23·4–23·7 How do neurons work?

The branching neurons (colorized green), found in the cerebellum, are some of the largest and most complex cells in the mammalian brain.

23·4

Dendrites receive external stimuli.

"Fire!" "Don't fire!" "Fire!" "Don't fire!" Dendrites are on the receiving end of an almost constant barrage of (sometimes conflicting) signals. A neuron may have hundreds or even thousands of dendrites, which give it a huge amount of surface area over which to make connections with other neurons and receive signals.

Dendrites receive stimuli in one of two ways. Those on motor neurons and interneurons generally connect with and receive signals from other neurons. Sensory neuron dendrites, on the other hand, are modified to respond to a specific external stimulus such as a touch or sound, light, or a chemical (**FIGURE 23-8**).

When a neuron is not transmitting a signal, it is still metabolically active. Using active transport, proteins within the plasma membrane of the neuron pump sodium ions (Na^+) out of the cell and potassium ions (K^+) into the cell, through ion channels. With the accumulation of sodium ions outside the neuron, there is a greater positive charge outside the cell than inside the cell. This difference in charge, referred to as a membrane potential, is called the

resting potential. The cell is described as "polarized" and can be thought of as "ready to fire."

On stimulation, receptors in the cell membrane of the dendrite respond by briefly opening up ion channels (usually the sodium channels). These channels allow the passage of charged ions (usually sodium ions), down their concentration gradient. This ion flow momentarily alters the negative electrical charge carried within the cell prior to stimulation, when the cell is at rest. Opening the channels may make the neuron more negatively charged (that is, the electrical charge inside the cell relative to that in the fluid surrounding the cell becomes even more negative), which says, "Don't fire!" Or it may make the neuron more

> ❝The trees grew heavy with blackbirds, branches like dendrites of the nervous system fattening, deep in twittering nerve dusk, waiting for some important message. ❞
>
> — THOMAS PYNCHON, *Gravity's Rainbow*

DENDRITES RECEIVE EXTERNAL STIMULI

1 Stimulus

Positively charged ions

Receptor proteins

Cell membrane

2

Ion channels

RESTING POTENTIAL

Prior to stimulation, there is a greater positive charge outside the cell than inside the cell. This difference in charge—called the resting potential—is produced by active transport of ions and results in a polarized cell that is "ready to fire."

Dendrites

Axon

3

Positively charged ions tell the neuron "Fire!" while negatively charged ions tell the neuron "Don't fire!"

Action potential

1 Receptor proteins within the cell membrane of the dendrite respond to stimuli by briefly opening up little channels.

2 Open channels allow charged ions to enter the dendrite, momentarily altering the electrical charge within the cell from the negative charge that it carried prior to stimulation.

3 Signals from all of the dendrites of a neuron converge. If the sum total of signals coming in is significantly positive, then the cell initiates an action potential that travels down the axon.

FIGURE 23-8 "Fire!" (or "Don't fire!"). Dendrites receive signals and forward them to the cell body of the neuron.

positively charged, such as when sodium channels open and sodium ions rush into the cell, which says, "Fire!"

As stimuli cause channels to open in the dendrites of a neuron—some making the neuron more negatively charged, others making the neuron more positively charged—the changes in the cell's electrical charge, occurring in all these dendrites, converge at the cell body. The cell body then integrates them, much like tallying the votes in an election. If the sum total of signals coming in is sufficiently positive—exceeding a threshold favoring "Fire!"—then the neuron initiates an **action potential,** an electrical signal that travels down its axon. If the sum total is negative, no action potential is generated.

TAKE-HOME MESSAGE 23·4

Dendrites receive external stimuli in one of two ways. Dendrites on motor neurons and interneurons generally connect with and receive signals from other neurons, whereas sensory neuron dendrites are modified to respond to a specific external stimulus such as a touch or sound, light, or a chemical.

23·5 The action potential propagates a signal down the axon.

We owe a great deal to giant squids. Much of what we know about human nervous systems has come from studying squid neurons. Neurons function almost exactly the same in all animals, and giant squids just happen to also have giant neurons. While a human neuron might be 0.02 millimeters in diameter, a squid's may be more than 100 times wider, up

WHAT IS THE NERVOUS SYSTEM?   HOW DO NEURONS WORK?   THE SENSES   MUSCULAR AND SKELETAL SYSTEMS   THE BRAIN   DRUGS HIJACK PLEASURE PATHWAYS

901

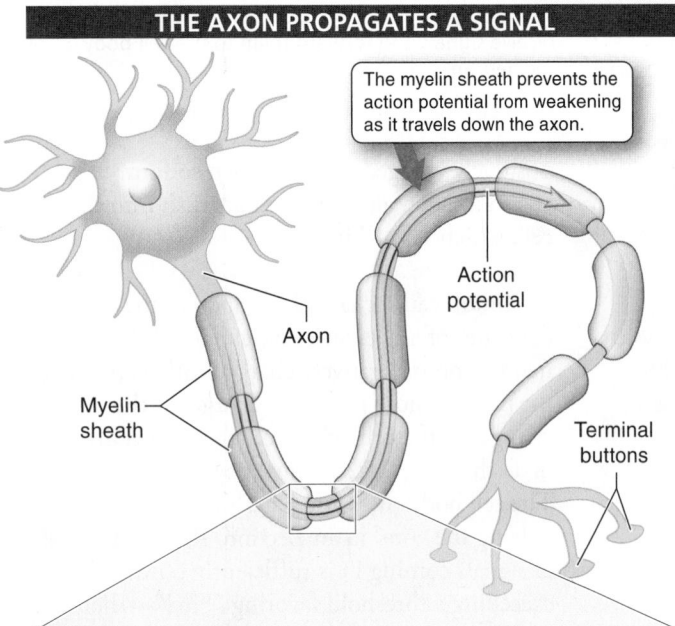

The myelin sheath prevents the action potential from weakening as it travels down the axon.

Action potential

Axon

Myelin sheath

Terminal buttons

As the action potential moves down an axon, ion channels allow positively charged sodium ions to rush in, changing the cell's charge to positive in that region and thus propagating the action potential.

Action potential   Sodium ions

FIGURE 23-9 An action potential moves down an axon.

to double the thickness of a human hair. This makes squid neurons much easier to manipulate and observe.

Regardless of the species under observation, each neuron has one axon. This projection leaves the cell body and can extend several feet or more. At its end, the axon branches into several (or hundreds of) axon terminals, also called **terminal buttons,** which are knob-like ends of the axon, positioned very close to a muscle cell or gland or to the dendrites of another neuron. And in response to an action potential, these axon terminals release the contents of vesicles, small sacs of chemicals inside the axon terminal, into the space between the cells, potentially influencing adjacent cells (**FIGURE 23-9**). We discuss this process in more detail in the next two sections.

We've said that axons are like the electrical wires of the nervous system. In your home, electrical wires are usually covered with rubber. Besides reducing the likelihood of

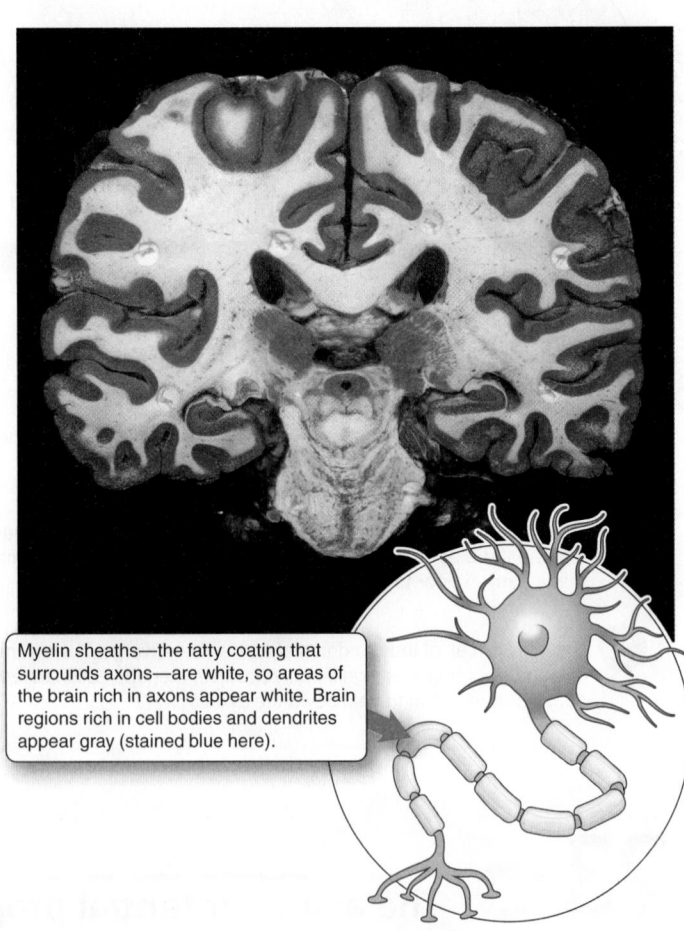

Myelin sheaths—the fatty coating that surrounds axons—are white, so areas of the brain rich in axons appear white. Brain regions rich in cell bodies and dendrites appear gray (stained blue here).

FIGURE 23-10 White matter and gray matter. The appearance of white and gray (stained blue here) matter in the brain reflects whether mostly axons or mostly cell bodies and dendrites are present.

someone receiving an electric shock from the current running through the wire, this insulation also has another function: it causes the electrical charge to move through the wire more quickly and reduces dissipation of the signal. Axons are similarly insulated, by a fatty coating called the **myelin sheath,** preventing the action potential from weakening as it travels down the axon. But, unlike in a wire's insulation, there are gaps in the fatty insulation provided by the myelin sheath. And as the action potential moves down an axon, it is at the gaps in the myelin sheath that ion channels in the axon membrane allow charged sodium ions to rush in. In doing so, the ions make the cell's charge sufficiently positive in that region to cause the opening of ion channels at the next gap in the myelin sheath, thereby propagating the action potential along the axon.

Because the fatty myelin is white, in cross sections of the brain, those areas where axons are densely packed together appear white (**FIGURE 23-10**). Other parts, where there are more cell bodies and dendrites, appear gray. These different regions are often referred to as white matter and gray matter.

What do you think would happen to signals traveling down an axon in your leg if the myelin sheath insulator were not there? You can observe this effect by watching babies when they first start trying to walk, at around 10 or 11 months of age. At that time, myelin hasn't completely formed around all of their axons and, consequently, their gross motor control isn't very good (**FIGURE 23-11**). So, although the baby's brain may be saying "Walk!" the signal never makes it to the leg muscles. Walking is especially difficult to master because the areas of the brain that control the feet and legs don't develop until after the areas controlling the rest of the body.

FIGURE 23-11 Unsteady on his feet. Incomplete development of the myelin sheath makes walking difficult for infants.

for the brain to send signals to muscles—the same difficulty babies have when first learning to walk—and can lead to a gradual loss in motor control, balance and coordination, and bladder and bowel control.

Q Some symptoms of multiple sclerosis resemble difficulties that babies have when learning to walk. Why?

Multiple sclerosis (MS) is a disease that affects the central nervous system. In MS, myelin is gradually lost, leaving scar tissue called sclerosis. As myelin is lost, the neuron gradually loses its ability to conduct electrical impulses. This makes it progressively more difficult

TAKE-HOME MESSAGE 23·5

Each neuron has one axon, a projection that extends from the cell body, sometimes several feet or more. At its end, the axon branches into numerous axon terminals (terminal buttons), positioned close to a muscle cell or a gland or to the dendrites of another neuron. In response to an action potential, the axon terminals release chemicals into the extracellular space, potentially influencing adjacent cells.

At the synapse, neurons interact with other cells.

An action potential moving rapidly down an axon quickly runs out of axon. This is the end of one neuron, but not necessarily the end of the signal. As we've seen, the end of an axon—the axon terminal or terminal button—is always right next to a receiving cell, which can be another neuron, a muscle cell, or a gland. The point where these cells meet is called a **synapse,** and several possible things can happen there. The signal arriving at the end of the axon may stimulate an action potential in the adjacent cell, or it may cause a muscle to contract or relax, or it may initiate a secretion by a gland. Or the signal may end altogether. In each case, though, the events at the synapse are remarkably similar across all animal species. Let's explore them in sequence (**FIGURE 23-12**).

1. *Sacs called vesicles release neurotransmitters into the synaptic cleft.* When the action potential reaches the axon terminal, it causes little sacs called **vesicles** to merge with the axon's cell membrane, called the **presynaptic membrane.** The sacs

open up and release their contents, chemical messengers called **neurotransmitters,** into the **synaptic cleft,** the space between the axon and the cell receiving the signal (muscle, gland, or neuron).

2. *Neurotransmitter diffuses and binds to nearby receptor sites.* As the neurotransmitter molecules float around in the fluid in the synaptic cleft, they diffuse away from the axon until they bump into the adjacent neuron, muscle, or gland. Some of the neurotransmitter molecules attach to receptor sites on the **postsynaptic membrane** of the adjacent cell (called the *postsynaptic cell*).

3. *Gates open in the postsynaptic cell membrane, and the signal enters the postsynaptic cell.* When neurotransmitter binds to a receptor in the postsynaptic cell membrane, this causes a gate to open, which allows ions (often sodium ions) to flow into the cell. The resulting chemical change in the postsynaptic cell can cause an electrical

THE SYNAPSE

Action potential

Presynaptic membrane

Vesicles

Neurotransmitter molecules

Synaptic cleft

Postsynaptic membrane

Receptor proteins

Positively charged ions

Ion channels

Enzymes

1 When the action potential reaches the axon terminal, neurotransmitter-filled vesicles fuse with the presynaptic membrane, releasing neurotransmitter molecules into the synaptic cleft.

2 The neurotransmitter molecules diffuse away from the axon and bind to receptor sites on the postsynaptic membrane of the adjacent cell.

3 When a neurotransmitter binds to the receptor, it causes a channel to open, allowing ions to flow into the adjacent cell, stimulating or inhibiting it.

4 The neurotransmitter molecules are then released from postsynaptic receptors, and either are taken back in and recycled by the initial axon terminal from which they were released, or are broken down by enzymes and cleared from the synapse so that the synapse can be used again.

FIGURE 23-12 The sequence of events when an action potential reaches the synapse.

change and, consequently, initiate an action potential (if the postsynaptic cell is a neuron), a contraction (if it's a muscle), or a secretion (if it's a gland).

4. *Neurotransmitter is released from the postsynaptic cell receptors and recycled or broken down.* The receptors then release the bound neurotransmitter molecules back into the fluid in the synaptic cleft. Eventually, the neurotransmitter molecules are either taken back up through the presynaptic membrane and recycled by the axon terminal from which they were released, or they are broken down within the synaptic cleft by enzymes, clearing out the area so that the synapse can be used again.

A contraction may occur if the postsynaptic cell is a muscle, and a secretion may occur if the postsynaptic cell is a gland, but how do neurotransmitters affect a neuron? In some cases, the released neurotransmitters are excitatory and excite the next neuron, increasing the likelihood that it will fire its own action potential. In other cases, the neurotransmitters are inhibitory and reduce the likelihood that the next cell will produce an action potential. And for some neurotransmitters, whether it is excitatory or inhibitory depends on the receptor. With the giant web of connections between neurons—each neuron synapses with hundreds or thousands of other neurons—the ultimate outcome of whether or not an action potential is initiated depends on a neuron democratically weighing all of its inputs and assessing whether most of its synapses are urging it to fire (pass on the signal) or not to fire (stop the signal from getting through).

At first it might seem odd that the total of all the signals received by a cell might tell it not to do anything, not to fire a signal, but this capacity enables the nervous system to control which signals get through. By having neurons connected by synapses (rather than one long, continuous "wire" constantly conducting electrical signals), it is possible to modulate and filter some of the overwhelming amount of sensory information coming into the brain. It's like call-screening for your brain.

This "filtering" characteristic of the nervous system is one of the main reasons that organisms don't have single, long

At synapses, not all signals are propagated. Some sensory "noise" may be filtered out—reducing the barrage of stimuli to the brain.

FIGURE 23-13 Like call-screening for your brain. Not every signal is propagated.

neurons running from their sensory receptors right to their brain or muscles. It's not always best to have every signal propagated (**FIGURE 23-13**). With continuous stimulation, too, most neurons gradually reduce the amount of neurotransmitter they release, and thus reduce the strength of the signal. It's as if the neurons are saying, "Enough already. We get the message."

TAKE-HOME MESSAGE 23·6

At the synapse, a neuron interacts with other cells. In response to an action potential, neurotransmitters are released into the synaptic cleft, diffuse, and may bind to receptors on an adjacent neuron, muscle cell, or gland, potentially stimulating an action potential, muscle contraction, or secretion. Neurotransmitters may then be taken back in by the axon terminal or enzymatically broken down in the synaptic cleft.

23·7 There are many types of neurotransmitters.

The neurotransmitters released by neurons can be thought of as the chemicals that initiate or modify a wide variety of actions, moods, feelings, or other sensations. Some make us feel happy or sad, restless or sedate. Some stimulate muscles to contract. Others influence learning or memory. In all,

about 25 neurotransmitters have been identified, each of which has a sort of personality based on its specific actions. A detailed discussion of all 25 neurotransmitters is beyond the scope of this book. Here we discuss four that are particularly important.

Acetylcholine Acetylcholine is the neurotransmitter released by motor neurons at the point where they synapse with muscle cells. When enough acetylcholine binds to a muscle cell, the muscle contracts. Botulinum toxin—a protein produced by several species of bacteria—is the most toxic substance known: less than a microgram is lethal if injected into a person or inhaled. Also known as Botox, this toxin is an increasingly popular drug used in cosmetic procedures, with more than a billion dollars spent on it worldwide each year (**FIGURE 23-14**). What does this have to do with neurotransmitters? When injected into muscles, Botox blocks the fusion of acetylcholine-filled vesicles with the presynaptic neuron's membrane, preventing release of acetylcholine into the synapse and thus paralyzing the muscle. A tiny amount of Botox can prevent a muscle from contracting for three or four months!

Q Why would someone pay to get injections of the most toxic substance known? (Hint: it's also known as "Botox.")

Why would a healthy person want to get near the most toxic substance known? Tiny injections of Botox can smooth lines in the forehead and can also reduce "crow's-feet" wrinkles around the eyes. Because Botox essentially paralyzes muscles, however, it can lead to problems. At the extreme, if Botox spreads to muscles other than those intended, it can interfere with the muscles needed for swallowing and breathing. Most of the 180 reported cases of life-threatening problems resulting from Botox injections between 1997 and 2006 stemmed from problems of this nature. Less life-threatening, but disturbing to many, is the severe reduction in individuals' ability to move parts of their face that can result from Botox injections, often causing droopy eyelids or a mask-like face and an inability to express emotions.

Glutamate Another neurotransmitter is glutamate. Although its mechanism of action isn't well understood, it appears to be involved with learning and memory. Mice that were genetically engineered to have more sensitive glutamate receptors, for instance, learned tasks better and became much better at running mazes than normal mice.

Dopamine Dopamine is important in initiating and coordinating movement. Loss of dopamine neurons may be responsible for Parkinson's disease, for which the symptoms include tremors of a hand or foot, stiffness or inflexibility of muscles, and impaired balance and coordination. Dopamine is also one of the body's chief "happiness" neurotransmitters. Its release in certain parts of the brain is associated with feelings of intense pleasure. In studies of brain functioning, for example, when subjects are shown their favorite food items, the levels of dopamine released in the brain skyrocket. We explore dopamine in greater detail later in this chapter.

Serotonin Serotonin generally functions as an inhibitory neurotransmitter. It affects appetite, sleep, anxiety, and mood, and produces feelings of contentment and satiation when released. Women make serotonin only about two-thirds as quickly as men, an observation that may be related to why depression is twice as common among women as men. As we see later in the chapter, antidepressant medications such as Prozac increase the amount of serotonin in the synapse and are effective at elevating the mood of someone who is depressed.

FIGURE 23-14 **Controlled paralysis.** By preventing acetylcholine release, botulinum toxin (Botox) paralyzes muscles. In tiny amounts, this can reduce wrinkles. Shown here: fashion stylist Rachel Zoe, in 2006 (left) and 2009.

TAKE-HOME MESSAGE 23·7

About 25 neurotransmitters have been identified, each of which has several actions, depending on the synapse where it occurs. Acetylcholine is the neurotransmitter released by motor neurons at the point where they synapse with muscle cells. Glutamate is an excitatory neurotransmitter involved with learning and memory. Dopamine is important in initiating and coordinating movement and in producing feelings of intense pleasure. Serotonin, an inhibitory neurotransmitter, affects appetite, sleep, anxiety, and mood, and produces feelings of contentment and satiation.

23·8–23·14 Our senses detect and transmit stimuli.

The greater kudu (Tragelaphus strepsiceros), *a type of antelope in South Africa. Kudu have very sensitive hearing, effective in alerting them to predators.*

23·8

Sensory receptors are our windows to the world around us.

Q Why *do animals have only one head? Why is it in the front?*

Did you ever wonder why animals tend to have only one head and why it's always in the front of the body? When organisms became bilaterally symmetrical—that is, having mirror-image left and right sides—suddenly they had a "front" and a "back." As such animals move through their environment, their "front" part encounters new things in the environment first; with the sensory equipment up front, the organism is able to decide what to do—eat or run—as quickly as possible (**FIGURE 23-15**), which may have conferred evolutionary benefits. And as the decisions to be made get more and more complex, the circuitry required for the animal to "make up its mind" becomes more complex. In fact, only then does it really become necessary to have a mind. And so the brain and head (which always go hand in hand) have tended to become more and more pronounced.

Our senses—sight, hearing, smell, taste, and touch—make us physically aware of the environment around us. They are our windows to the world. Each of our senses puts us in touch with and brings us information about a different and unique slice of the world, but the senses also have much in common (**FIGURE 23-16**).

💡 *Sensory equipment is concentrated at the "front" of bilaterally symmetrical animals, because this part of the animal encounters new things in the environment first.*

FIGURE 23-15 Eyes up front. Most of an animal's sensory organs are located in its head. Shown: a lemur.

WHAT IS THE NERVOUS SYSTEM? — HOW DO NEURONS WORK? — **THE SENSES** — MUSCULAR AND SKELETAL SYSTEMS — THE BRAIN — DRUGS HIJACK PLEASURE PATHWAYS

907

THE FIVE SENSES

HEARING

TOUCH

TASTE

SMELL

SIGHT

 Our senses—hearing, touch, taste, smell, and sight—are our windows to the world. Each brings us information about a different slice of the world, but the senses have much in common.

FIGURE 23-16 Making us aware of our environment: the senses. (Note that most of the body parts—such as our hands or tongue—may have more than one function.)

The process by which all of our senses work is basically the same. A receptor—commonly a modified dendrite on a sensory neuron (in the eye, nose, tongue, ear, or skin)—is stimulated by some aspect of the outside world (light, odor, taste, sound, or touch). This outside stimulus causes a change in the neuron, causing the sensory neuron to either (1) fire an action potential itself, which shoots down the axon and ultimately reaches a part of the brain where the signal is perceived as a particular smell or sound, for

VARIATIONS IN SENSATION INTENSITY

WEAK STIMULUS (lightweight rubber ball)

STRONG STIMULUS (bowling ball)

Sensory neurons

Less intense sensation

More intense sensation

We experience gradations of sensation depending on the number of neurons that fire.

FIGURE 23-17 Heavy or light? We experience gradations of sensation depending on the number of neurons that fire.

example, or (2) alter its rate of neurotransmitter secretion so that it increases or reduces the rate of firing of action potentials in a neighboring neuron.

How is it possible to experience variations in the intensity of sensation, when an action potential is an all-or-nothing event? As we've seen, it either occurs or doesn't occur as the result of dendrite stimulation. After all, our experience of sensations is not "all or nothing." We are able to feel gradations of intensity. A 10-pound bowling ball resting in your left hand will feel very heavy (and perhaps cooler and smoother) compared with a lightweight rubber ball in your right hand (**FIGURE 23-17**). How can the "fire" versus "don't fire" event still produce such a range of sensations? The intensity of the sensation an individual feels is modulated by the number of action potentials per unit of time and the number of neurons stimulated. The rubber ball causes a small number to fire, and the bowling ball causes many more to fire.

In the following sections, we present information about each of the five primary senses, exploring how the specific senses are variations on a theme, fine-tuned by natural selection to give an animal specific information about its environment to help it respond appropriately.

23·9 Taste: an action potential serves up a taste sensation to the brain.

Look at your tongue in the mirror. It is covered with bumps. Embedded within these bumps are taste buds—more than 10,000 in all. Within each taste bud are 60–80 sensory receptor cells, called **chemoreceptors** (which are modified epithelial cells that synapse with sensory neurons), that are stimulated when particular chemicals in food dissolve in saliva and bind to proteins on the receptor cell surface. Much as a lock will open only when the proper key is inserted,

particular taste receptors allow only specific food molecules, with exactly the right shape, to bind (**FIGURE 23-18**).

Taste chemoreceptors fall into five groups, depending on which type of molecule chemically stimulates them: sweet, salty, sour, bitter, or a recently discovered, but difficult to describe, savory taste called umami. These different types of chemoreceptors occur all across the tongue (although the

FIGURE 23-18 From taste buds to delicious flavor. How the sensation of taste is generated in the brain.

different groups tend to be concentrated in different regions of the tongue). A rich variety of tastes is possible because most foods stimulate unique combinations of the different taste receptors. Foods also release molecules into the air in the mouth, which stimulate smell receptors within the nasal cavity.

Not all animals use their mouth to taste things. Some insects have chemoreceptors on their legs, and they "taste" things just by touching them. Other animals have taste receptors on their antennae or tentacles. Regardless of where the food meets the taste receptors, the process is the same: chemical binding triggers an action potential that delivers a taste sensation to the brain.

Q How can artificial sweeteners taste like sugar while not actually being sugar?

Because of the way that humans sense taste, it's possible to fool your brain. Your brain never actually "knows" the true identity of the food on your tongue. Rather, it senses a particular taste based solely on the combination of receptor cells that is stimulated. If a molecule that is not sugar has a chemical structure closely resembling sugar, it can stimulate the same taste-bud receptors and be perceived by the brain as sugar (**FIGURE 23-19**). Many non-nutritive sugar-substitute molecules, such as saccharin and sucralose, do exactly this. They have three-dimensional arrangements of atoms that are similar to sugar molecules such as sucrose, glucose, or fructose, but have structures that cannot be broken down by any enzymes in the human body. Consequently, when we consume them, we sense the sweet taste of sugar but don't actually derive any energy from the molecules. Instead, they pass through our digestive tract unaltered.

Aspartame also resembles sugar closely enough to stimulate sugar receptors in taste buds. Molecularly, however, it is quite different: it is made from two amino acids. Unlike the other artificial sweeteners, it can be broken down and releases energy

FIGURE 23-19 Fooling the brain. Sugar substitutes stimulate receptor cells that produce a sweet taste.

(and hence contains calories), but it is so efficient at stimulating sweet-taste receptors that it can generate a strong sugary taste even when used in tiny amounts.

TAKE-HOME MESSAGE 23·9

Your tongue has about 10,000 taste buds, each of which contains 60–80 chemoreceptors, which are stimulated when particular chemicals in food bind to receptor proteins on the cell surface. Some animals have chemoreceptors on their antennae or tentacles, and the binding of chemicals to these receptors similarly triggers an action potential that delivers a taste sensation to the brain.

23·10 Smell: receptors in the nose detect airborne chemicals.

Our sense of smell works in almost exactly the same way as our sense of taste. Neurons that can detect smells have dendrites modified with tiny, hair-like projections. These dendrites—densely packed within the nasal cavity—are covered with chemoreceptors. Airborne chemicals move through mucus in the nasal cavity and bind to the smell receptors, triggering action potentials that shoot down the axon, all the way into the smell center of the brain, where the signal is perceived as a particular odor. There are more than a thousand different types of receptors—modified neurons—in

a human nose, each capable of detecting a different scent (**FIGURE 23-20**). (These are the only neurons in the body that are in direct contact with the outside world.)

In humans, the senses of smell and taste are closely connected, because the air in the mouth, throat, and nasal passages circulates around all these areas. You may have noticed that when you have a cold and your nose is stuffed up, you taste little beyond the basic salt, sweet, bitter, and sour tastes on your tongue, and you can't smell anything at

Smell receptor proteins

Ion channels

Action potential sent to brain

Nasal cavity

Airborne molecules

Positively charged ions

Chemoreceptor cells

A smell is sensed when the chemoreceptor proteins that trigger perception of that particular smell are stimulated by the appropriate airborne molecules in the nasal cavity.

FIGURE 23-20 How the sensation of smell is generated.

Q Why are your senses of smell and taste dulled when you have a cold?

all. Your senses of taste and smell are dulled because increased mucus in your nasal passages reduces the rate at which airborne chemicals can reach the smell receptors and taste receptors on dendrites in your nose and on your tongue.

Animals vary greatly in their sensitivity to smells, and humans don't fare too well in the competition. Recent evidence even suggests that fewer and fewer of the genes coding for the different smell receptors in humans function properly any more. Interestingly, human females are significantly better than males at detecting, distinguishing, and identifying odors, a sensitivity that is even greater during the days surrounding ovulation.

Dogs are among the most smell-sensitive vertebrates, having as many as 40 times more smell receptors than a human— hence their tremendous proficiency at detecting drugs or explosives (**FIGURE 23-21**). Some moths, such as gypsy moths and silkworm moths, put even dogs to shame and may be the champions of chemoreception. The tiny hairs on the males' antennae can detect just a few molecules of the sex attractant released by females. By moving in the direction of increasing concentration of the airborne molecules, a male can track down a female two miles away. Snakes, with chemoreceptors on their tongue, are actually "smelling" their environment as they stick their tongue out.

Q People are much worse than dogs at sniffing out drugs. Why?

Dogs have as many as 40 times more smell receptors than a human—hence their keen sense of smell, which gives them tremendous proficiency at detecting drugs or explosives.

FIGURE 23-21 Smelling champ: the bomb-sniffing dog.

TAKE-HOME MESSAGE 23·10

Neurons that can detect smells have dendrites modified with tiny, hair-like projections covered with chemoreceptors, densely packed within the nasal cavity.

Vision: seeing is the perception of light by the brain.

What we lack in smell proficiency, we more than make up for in visual acuity, a consequence of our image-forming, **single-lens eyes.** (This type of eye has evolved independently twice: in vertebrates and in a group of mollusks that includes the squid.) Light hits the eye and enters the eye's interior through an **iris.** The pupil, an opening in the iris, opens and closes to control the amount of light that gets into the eye. Once the light is through the pupil, a lens focuses it onto the **retina,** nervous tissue containing light-sensitive cells called **photoreceptor cells** (**FIGURE 23-22**).

The retina lines the inner surface of the eye and transmits impulses to the vision center of the brain via the **optic nerve.** The two types of photosensitive cells in the retina are **rods,** which are highly sensitive to even tiny amounts of light and make it possible to see at night and in low-light situations, and **cones,** which are less sensitive to light and so are more effective during daylight. Humans have three kinds of cone cells: red-, green-, and blue-sensitive. Our ability to detect color is based on the combination of cones being stimulated. Some individuals (usually men) produce non-functioning red or green cones—the result of mutant genes. In either of these cases, it is impossible for the individual to distinguish red from green, so the person is said to be **color-blind.**

Vision is one of the senses in which our capabilities exceed those of most other animals. Still, as with nearly every trait, there are plenty of species—including many birds and some spiders—whose abilities exceed ours. In any case, despite the great diversity of light-sensing capabilities, the basic functioning of light-absorbing cells is quite consistent among all animals, although in some ways the process works in a fashion opposite to what we see for other types of sensory reception. Here's how these cells work (**FIGURE 23-23**).

Within the eye or other light-detecting structure, there are photon-sensitive neurons, the photoreceptor cells, with light-sensitive molecules embedded in their cell membranes. In the dark, these photoreceptor cells continuously release an inhibitory neurotransmitter. Like the depressing of a brake pedal, this inhibitory message reduces the ability of adjacent cells to excite the neurons that send information to the brain. In a sense, darkness blocks the ability of optic nerves to send visual signals to the brain.

When light hits one of the light-sensitive molecules in the membrane of a photoreceptor cell, the light energy causes some of the chemical bonds in the molecule to become stretched. (A similar capture of light energy occurs in plants during photosynthesis.) This closes sodium channels in the photoreceptor cell membranes and reduces the amount of inhibitory neurotransmitter that is released. Without the inhibitory neurotransmitter at the synapse, the adjacent neurons are able to excite the neurons that send visual signals to the brain. The particular wavelength perceived by the brain depends on the particular light-sensitive molecules stimulated.

In addition to the single-lens eye, two other types of eyes have evolved (**FIGURE 23-24**)—the eye cup and the

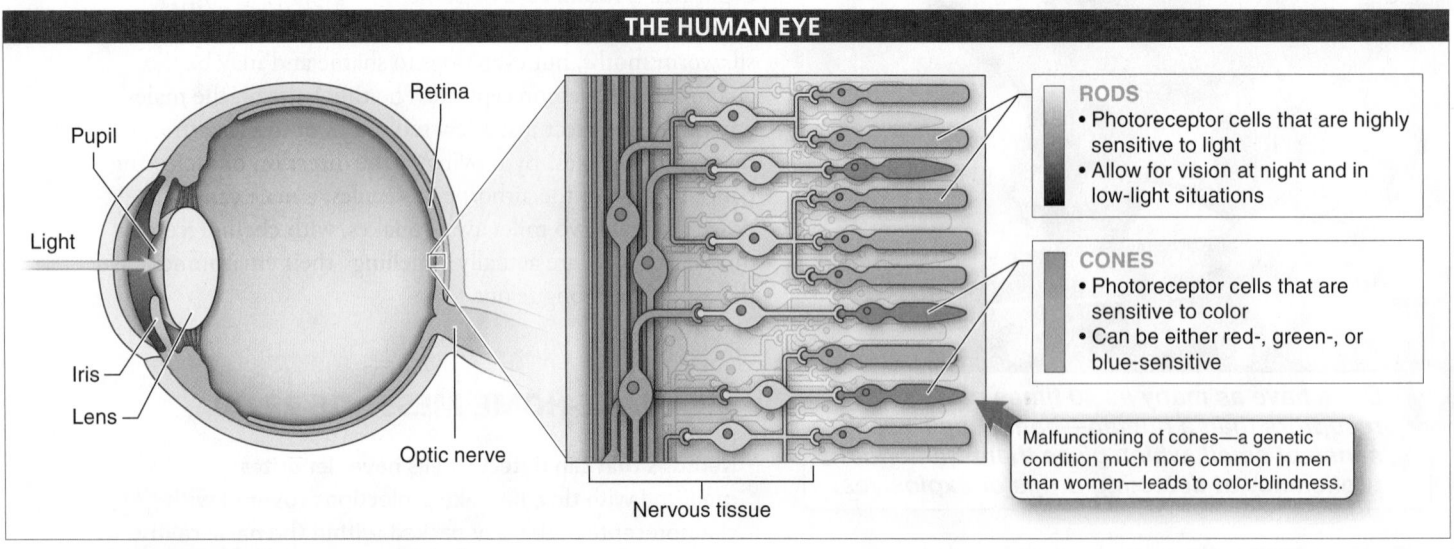

THE HUMAN EYE

Retina
Pupil
Light
Iris
Lens
Optic nerve
Nervous tissue

RODS
• Photoreceptor cells that are highly sensitive to light
• Allow for vision at night and in low-light situations

CONES
• Photoreceptor cells that are sensitive to color
• Can be either red-, green-, or blue-sensitive

Malfunctioning of cones—a genetic condition much more common in men than women—leads to color-blindness.

FIGURE 23-22 The structures of the human eye.

HOW PHOTORECEPTOR CELLS WORK

Photoreceptor cell

No light

① Sodium channel

Na⁺

Light-sensitive molecule

Inhibitory neurotransmitters

②

③ Optic nerve

Photoreceptor cell

Light

① Sodium channel

Na⁺

Light-sensitive molecule

② Inhibitory neurotransmitters

③

④ Optic nerve

IN THE DARK

① Sodium channels, located within photoreceptor cell membranes, are open, allowing the photoreceptor cells to continuously release inhibitory neurotransmitters.

② The inhibitory transmitters reduce the ability of adjacent neurons to excite the neurons that signal the brain.

③ An action potential is not sent through the optic nerve and light is not perceived by the brain.

IN LIGHT

① Light energy causes light-sensitive molecules to change shape, closing sodium channels in the photoreceptor cell membranes.

② The closing of sodium channels reduces the amount of inhibitory neurotransmitter released by the photoreceptor cells.

③ No longer inhibited, adjacent neurons excite the neurons that signal the brain.

④ An action potential is sent through the optic nerve and light is perceived by the brain.

FIGURE 23-23 Photoreceptors responding to light enable vision.

TYPES OF EYES

Photoreceptor cells

EYE CUPS
Contain photoreceptor cells that are able to detect the presence and intensity of light, but cannot form images

Photoreceptor cells

Lenses

COMPOUND EYES
Contain many separate light-sensing units—each with its own lens—that direct light onto about a dozen photoreceptor cells

Photoreceptor cells

Lens

SINGLE-LENS EYES
Contain a single lens that focuses light onto highly sensitive photoreceptor cells

FIGURE 23-24 Eye structure suits the needs of the organism. Shown (left to right): flatworm, fruit fly, and eye flash squid.

Some flowers build ultraviolet-light-reflecting petals that guide insects—which see this part of the light spectrum—to the nectar, ensuring pollination of the flowers.

Some spiders lure insects by mimicking the UV reflectance patterns of flowers.

The cross-like patterns in the webs of the Saint Andrew's Cross spider reflect certain wavelengths of light and, like the ultraviolet-reflecting petals of some flowers, lure insects. But in this case, the UV-reflecting patterns lure the insects to their deaths.

FIGURE 23-25 Insects see things differently than we do.

compound eye. The simplest form is **eye cups,** found in the flatworms, such as planaria, which live in ponds and streams. Eye cups are made up of photoreceptors, and although they cannot form images, they are able to detect the presence and intensity of light. Unless light is directly in front of the worm, it shines more intensely on one eye than the other. This allows the animal to sense which direction the light is coming

from. Usually, this information tells the animal which way to move: toward or away from the light. Planaria, for example, move away from the light.

Insects have much more refined visual capabilities (**FIGURE 23-25**). They possess **compound eyes** made of dozens to thousands of separate light-sensing units, each with its own image-forming lens that directs light onto about a dozen photoreceptors. The photoreceptors then send signals along neurons. When the signals reach the brain, the brain interprets these signals as an image. Because some insect photoreceptor cells—such as those in honeybees—contain a broader range of light-sensitive pigments than is found in humans, these insects can see wavelengths of light in the ultraviolet spectrum that are invisible to us.

Plants sometimes capitalize on this ability of insects to detect the ultraviolet spectrum by constructing flowers with UV-reflecting petals that look like the landing lights at an airport, guiding insects to their nectar reward (while ensuring pollination of the flowers). Devious spiders capitalize on this ability, too. Some build webs with UV-reflecting threads that trick insects into thinking the web is a flower. Once it flies into the web, the insect finds no nectar and ends up as a meal for the spider.

Q Insects don't just fly into spiders' webs accidentally. Sometimes they do it on purpose. Why?

TAKE-HOME MESSAGE 23·11

Vision results from the stimulation of light-sensitive sensory neurons, called photoreceptor cells. The photoreceptor cells have a variety of molecules, embedded within their membranes, that are chemically altered by light. Signals are conveyed to the brain and interpreted as an image. The particular wavelength perceived depends on which version of the light-sensitive molecules in the photoreceptor cell membranes is stimulated.

23·12 Hearing: sound waves are collected by the ears and stimulate auditory neurons.

Hearing is yet another variation on a theme. As with the previous senses described, something in the external world stimulates modified neurons, and the stimulation initiates an action potential that passes along a series of neurons until it reaches the brain. In this case, the stimuli from the outside world are sound waves, tiny fluctuations in air pressure, collected and amplified by the ears, which then pass information to the brain. While tastes and smells are detected by chemoreceptors and sight is made possible by photoreceptors, hearing is a result of the stimulation of **mechanoreceptors,** specialized neurons with receptors that respond to mechanical pressure.

Although there is some variation in the details of how hearing works in different species, this general, six-step hearing model is consistent (**FIGURE 23-26**).

1. The outer part of the ear collects sound waves and, because of its shape, funnels them down the **ear canal,** a channel that conducts sound waves.

2. At the end of the ear canal, the sound waves bang into the **eardrum**—a thin membrane that divides the outer ear from the middle portion of the ear—causing it to vibrate.

3. Small bones on the other (inner) side of the eardrum pass the vibrations on to the inner ear membrane.

4. The vibrations are conducted by fluid inside the inner ear, which consists of fluid-filled canals in the bones of the skull. The semicircular canals function in balance, and the coiled cochlea is involved in hearing. This fluid movement bends hair-shaped

HEARING

1. Sound waves are funneled down the ear canal.

2. Sound waves cause the eardrum to vibrate.

3. Vibrations pass to the inner ear membrane.

4. Fluid in the inner ear conducts the vibrations, bending hair-shaped receptor cells and releasing neurotransmitters.

5. The neurotransmitters cause auditory neurons to fire an action potential.

6. The signal is passed to the brain, where it is interpreted as sound.

Inner ear

Sound waves

Semicircular canals

Cochlea

Ear

Eardrum

Ear bones

Fluid-filled chambers

Receptor cells

Auditory neurons

Action potential sent to brain

FIGURE 23-26 The process of hearing.

receptor cells, which release neurotransmitters. (The more vigorous their bending—in response to stronger sound waves—the greater the amount of neurotransmitter released.)

5. Auditory neurons respond to the neurotransmitters released by the hair cells by firing an action potential.

6. The signal continues along a path of neurons to the brain, where it is interpreted as sound.

Q How can you get motion sickness without moving at all?

The fluid in the semicircular canals of the inner ear also acts like an inner motion detector, telling your body about its orientation, whether it is moving, and in which direction. It's not a foolproof system, though. Sitting in an IMAX theater watching a movie filmed from the seat of a roller coaster, shown on a huge screen, it is possible to feel motion sickness without actually moving. Your eyes tell your brain that you are moving, while your inner ear senses no motion at all. The conflicting signals can confuse your brain and lead to feelings of nausea. Some people experience similar effects when playing certain videogames.

Q How can loud music lead to hearing loss?

Long-term exposure to loud noises, including music, can be damaging to hearing, because such stimulation can wear out the cochlea of the inner ear. The hair cells in the inner ear are very fragile and are irreplaceable, so chronic over-stimulation due to loud noises can damage them. This reduces their ability to release neurotransmitters and stimulate auditory neurons, causing hearing loss (**FIGURE 23-27**).

Are ears necessary for hearing? Not really. Most insects, for example, don't have ears but still can hear a wide range of sounds, often with even greater sensitivity than humans. They do it with delicate hairs on their antennae, or on other parts of the body, that bend slightly in response to sound waves, much like the inner-ear hair cells described above. These insects tend to produce noises (that is, communicate by sound) by rubbing parts of their body together, rather than using their mouth. Male mosquitoes identify females by the vibrations of their wings as they fly. Cricket chirping, on the other hand, requires a bit more work; like miniature violinists, crickets rub their wings together to create their special mating calls.

Chronic over-stimulation due to loud noises can damage the hair cells in the inner ear, reducing their ability to stimulate auditory neurons and leading to hearing loss.

FIGURE 23-27 Loud noises can cause hearing loss.

ECHOLOCATION

Bats are able to sense where things are in their environment—even in the dark—by emitting high-pitched squeaks and then waiting to hear the sounds as they bounce off surfaces around them.

High-pitched call

Echoed response (after bouncing off prey)

FIGURE 23-28 Hearing through echolocation.

Among the mammals, bats have a unique system for hearing, called **echolocation.** Most bats spend nearly all of their time in the dark, and such a sensitive call-and-response system of hearing has evolved that they can sense where everything is in their environment, even with terrible sight. They do this by emitting high-pitched squeaks (that are generally inaudible to humans) and then waiting to hear the sounds as they bounce off surfaces around them. This system is so sensitive that bats can detect even a small moth as it flies in their vicinity (**FIGURE 23-28**).

23·13 Touch: the brain perceives pressure, temperature, and pain.

The last of the traditional five senses in humans is touch. Touch is actually a class of sensations generated by numerous different types of sensory neurons that are sensitive to pressure (mechanoreceptors), temperature (thermoreceptors), or pain (pain receptors). These sensory receptors are located throughout the body, and in particularly dense concentrations in places such as the fingertips in primates and the side of the body (called the lateral line) in most types of fish.

Whether they are mechanoreceptors or pain receptors or thermoreceptors—and any given part of the body usually has many of each of these sensory neuron types—they function similarly. External stimulation, such as the prick of a pin, the tickle from a feather, or the heat of a pan, can cause a change in the shape of the neuron's membrane, momentarily altering

its permeability. This change in permeability then increases or decreases the rate at which ions enter the cell, converting the stimulus into action potentials and, ultimately, sensations perceived by the brain (**FIGURE 23-29**).

Pain-killing drugs such as morphine reduce the ability of various pain receptors to send their signals to the brain. They do this by blocking the receptors' ability to respond to stimuli, thereby blocking neurons in the brain from sensing stimuli that would normally be identified as pain. It's as if the phone line between that part of the body and the brain is cut.

Conversely, and eerily, most amputees report that they sometimes experience tingling, prickly sensations or even

FIGURE 23-29 How the sensation of touch is produced.

PHANTOM PAIN

Many amputees experience "phantom pain" that seems to come from their missing limb, as neurons in the brain that had synapses with touch receptors in the lost limb are stimulated, usually by nearby neurons.

Mirror therapy—the practice of trying to move a phantom limb while looking at a reflection of its present counterpart in a mirror—can reduce the effect of phantom pain.

FIGURE 23-30 Sensory neurons may be gone, but real pain can remain.

shooting pains that come from where their amputated limb once was. Called "phantom pain," these sensations are very real and occur when neurons in the brain that used to receive information from touch receptors in the lost limb are firing, usually due to stimulation from other, nearby neurons (**FIGURE 23-30**).

Q Amputees sometimes feel real pain where their limb once was. How can this be?

TAKE-HOME MESSAGE 23·13

Touch is a class of sensations generated by mechanoreceptors, thermoreceptors, and pain receptors located throughout the body. Stimulation of these receptors causes a change in the shape of the sensory neuron's membrane, altering its permeability, generating action potentials, and causing the perception of touch by the brain.

23·14 Other senses help animals negotiate the world.

Often, we think of the senses as being limited to taste, smell, vision, hearing, and touch. But in actuality, there are several more senses that some animals use. As with the five senses described above, these additional senses are made possible by neurons that are specially modified to respond to external stimuli by generating action potentials that convey information to the brain about the outside world.

Balance and motion Many invertebrates (including jellyfish, lobsters, and crayfish) and all vertebrates have sensory cells that enable them to orient themselves with respect to gravity and to detect changes in velocity or orientation. These sensory cells are always some sort of hair cells that can be pushed in one direction or another, much as grass is blown by the wind. The force exerted on the hair cells (which, as we've seen, are located in the

FIGURE 23-31 Traveling south. Beluga whales during migration.

Animals from a wide range of migrating species, including beluga whales, are able to detect the earth's magnetic field and use it to help them navigate.

inner ear in vertebrates) gives information about the movement of the organism. In a variation on the sense of touch, in many mammals the sensations detected by whiskers can also convey information about balance and motion.

Electricity Marine animals of many types are sensitive to tiny electrical changes in the water around them. Sharks have sensory cells, embedded within sacs in their skin, that are open to the external surroundings. These cells are so sensitive to electrical changes around them that they can sense the muscle contractions of a fish swimming nearby. This ability to sense changes in electrical charge helps sharks to track down prey.

Magnetism Compass needles point north because of the faint magnetic field produced by the earth. A wide range of species, from birds to eels and sharks to migrating beluga whales, and even some bacteria, are able to detect this magnetic field and use it to help them navigate (**FIGURE 23-31**). In some clever but devious experiments, researchers placed strong magnets around some bird cages, deflecting the earth's magnetic field. This caused the birds to shift their orientation within the cages by exactly the amount that the magnetic field had been moved. Very little is known about how sensory cells have evolved to detect and respond to magnetism.

Heat Unlike the way you sense heat by touching a hot plate or feeling warm when the air around you is hot, pythons, vipers, and some other snakes can "see" heat differences in their environment without having to touch it. Using "pit organs" located on either side of the head, they can sense—even in complete darkness—a mouse or other prey animal nearby, solely from the body heat that it produces (**FIGURE 23-32**).

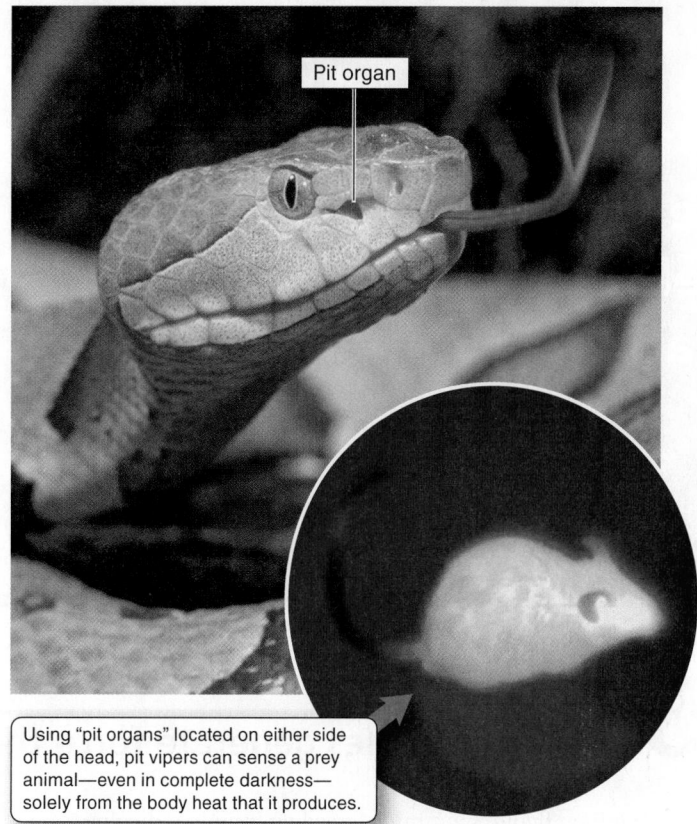

Pit organ

Using "pit organs" located on either side of the head, pit vipers can sense a prey animal—even in complete darkness— solely from the body heat that it produces.

FIGURE 23-32 Some snakes can "see" heat.

TAKE-HOME MESSAGE 23·14

Among animals, there are several senses in addition to taste, smell, vision, hearing, and touch, including those that perceive and respond to balance and motion, electricity, magnetism, and heat production in the animal's environment.

WHAT IS THE NERVOUS SYSTEM? · HOW DO NEURONS WORK? · THE SENSES · MUSCULAR AND SKELETAL SYSTEMS · THE BRAIN · DRUGS HIJACK PLEASURE PATHWAYS

919

23·15–23·16
The muscular and skeletal systems enable movement.

Eastern grey kangaroos (Macropus giganteus) *in Victoria, Australia.*

23·15 Muscles generate force through contraction.

Running, flying, swimming, crawling, walking, digging, dancing. Animals, with very few exceptions, move. And in vertebrates, this movement is generally initiated by cells of the nervous system that stimulate contractions in muscle tissue that pull on a rigid skeletal system. In this section, we examine the three types of muscle tissue, how contractions are generated within that tissue, and how input from the nervous system can initiate and control muscle contractions. We also investigate how the size and strength of muscles reflects their use and how physical training can increase muscle strength.

As we saw in Section 20-4, muscle tissue is made up of elongated cells capable of generating force when they contract, and there are three types of muscle tissue.

1. *Skeletal muscle* is responsible for generating most of the movement we see in vertebrates. Skeletal muscle attaches to bones and is controlled by individual neurons attached to each muscle fiber. It makes up about 40% of human body weight. The muscular system of humans contains about 700 skeletal muscles in all.

2. *Cardiac muscle* causes the heart to pump blood through the body. Not initiated by the nervous system or under conscious control, cardiac muscle contractions and relaxations occur continuously throughout life, with the muscle cells containing more energy-releasing mitochondria than other types of muscle cells.

FIGURE 23-33 Movement: the work done by skeletal muscles.

SKELETAL MUSCLE GENERATES MOVEMENT

- Origin point
- Biceps
- Triceps
- Upper arm bone
- Insertion point
- Lower arm bones
- Tendons

Two muscles generally work in opposition so that contracting one muscle (shown here: the biceps) moves a bone in one direction, while contracting the other muscle (the triceps) moves the bone in the opposite direction.

3. *Smooth muscle,* which is not under conscious control, surrounds blood vessels and many internal organs. In some cases, smooth muscle contractions are stimulated by the autonomic nervous systems, and in other cases, smooth muscle is able to contract without any stimulation from the nervous system. Compared with the other muscle types, smooth muscle generates slower contractions, which can gradually move blood, food, or other substances through vessels and organs.

Our focus here is on skeletal muscle. To facilitate movement, skeletal muscles are attached to bones by connective tissue. Often, a muscle tapers at each end into tendons, which attach the muscle at the two ends—the "insertion" and the "origin" of the muscle—to bones. The contraction of the muscle then pulls the attachment points closer together and causes a movement of the bone. The biceps muscle of the upper arm, for example, has its origin in the shoulder and its insertion in one of the bones of the forearm. Contraction can rotate the forearm or bring the lower part of the arm closer to the shoulder. Two muscles generally work in opposition, so that one contracts to move a bone in one direction, and the other—the triceps in the upper arm—has its insertion and origin located so that its contraction moves the bone in the opposite direction (**FIGURE 23-33**).

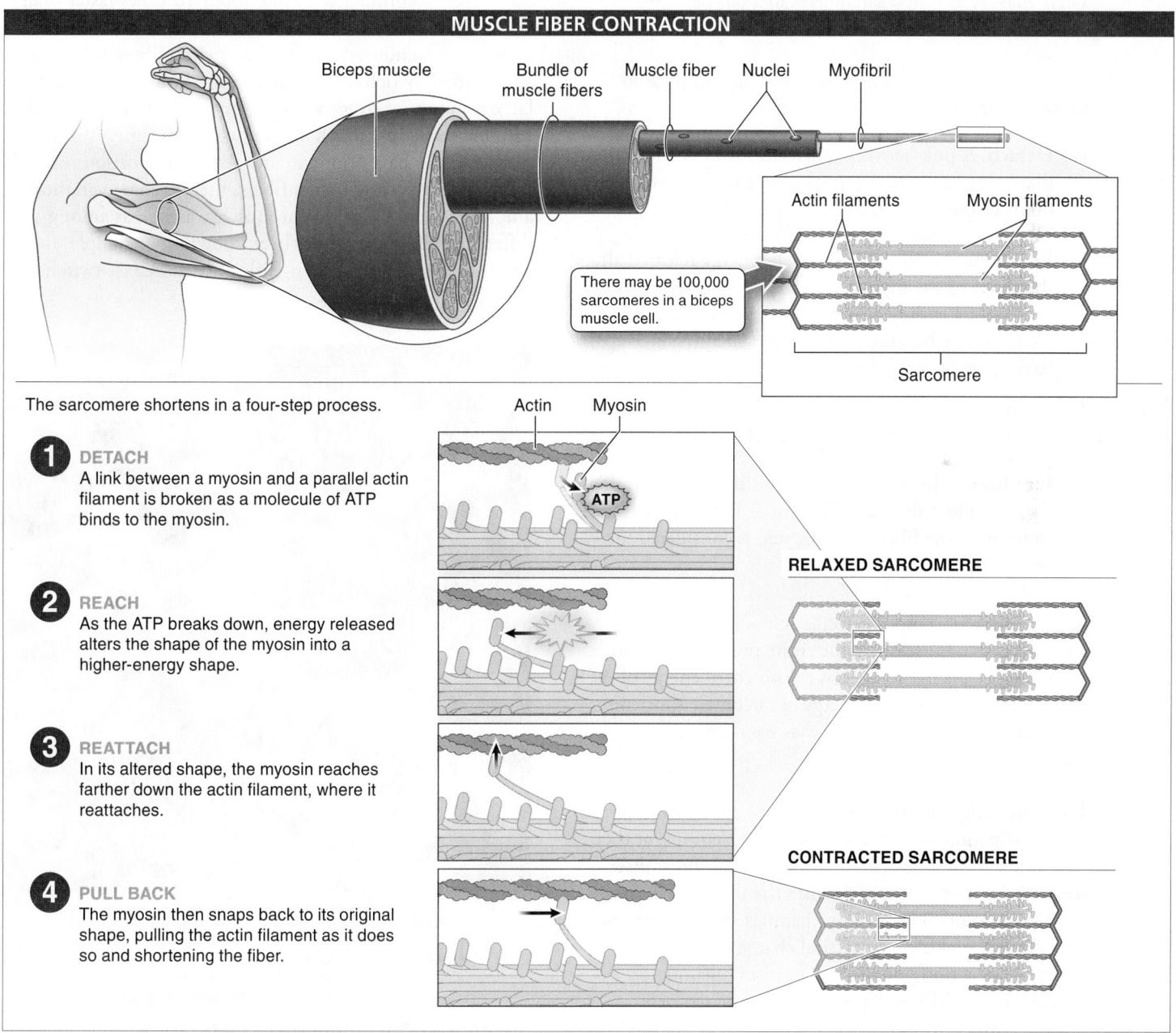

FIGURE 23-34 Muscle fibers contract to generate force.

WHAT IS THE NERVOUS SYSTEM? HOW DO NEURONS WORK? THE SENSES MUSCULAR AND SKELETAL SYSTEMS THE BRAIN DRUGS HIJACK PLEASURE PATHWAYS

921

The skeletal muscle is made up of a bundle of fibers. Each fiber is a single cell, but has multiple nuclei and numerous **myofibrils,** cylindrical organelles that shorten when they contract. A myofibril contains repeating units called **sarcomeres,** which are where the contraction takes place.

The sarcomeres are composed of large numbers of long filaments, overlapping and parallel to each other. The filaments come in two types: thin filaments made mostly from the protein **actin,** and thick filaments made mostly from the protein **myosin.** There may be 100,000 sarcomeres in a biceps muscle cell.

> Marathon runners tend to have smaller leg muscles than sprinters. Why?

The sarcomere shortens in a four-step process (**FIGURE 23-34**; see previous page).

1. **Detach.** A link between a myosin filament and an actin filament parallel to it is broken as a molecule of ATP binds to the myosin.

2. **Reach.** As the ATP breaks down, energy released alters the shape of the myosin into a higher-energy shape, much like bending a twig—the bent twig is in a higher-energy shape because it can release energy as it snaps back to its original shape.

3. **Reattach.** In its altered shape, the myosin reaches farther down the actin filament, where it reattaches.

4. **Pull back.** The myosin then snaps back to its original shape, pulling the actin filament as it does so and shortening the fiber. This last step is considered the "power stroke."

As the contraction process occurs across numerous sarcomeres in a muscle cell, the entire muscle can shorten. From the perspective of energy, the potential energy of ATP is converted to the kinetic energy of sarcomere shortening, which can do work (for instance, as your arm curls a dumbbell).

The contraction of sarcomeres cannot happen without the participation of the nervous system. Neurons, at their synapses with muscle cells, release the neurotransmitter acetylcholine. Acetylcholine causes the muscle cell membrane to open its sodium channels. Sodium ions flow into the cell, making its electrical charge positive, and initiating an action potential that causes calcium channels in the cell's endoplasmic reticulum to open. Calcium rushes from the endoplasmic reticulum into the cytoplasm, diffuses toward the myofibrils, and binds to a protein molecule surrounding the actin. When calcium binds to the protein molecule, that molecule acts as a switch and moves another molecule that normally covers binding sites on the actin filament. After the binding sites are exposed, myosin can attach to actin, and contraction can occur.

Q When a muscle contracts, the duration between a contraction and a relaxation is called a **twitch.** Muscle fibers within a muscle vary in how quickly they can twitch, with two general types. Fast-twitch fibers, which tend to function anaerobically, can contract and relax about 10 times faster than slow-twitch fibers, but have relatively weak endurance. The slow-twitch fibers, which are surrounded by rich oxygen-delivering capillary beds and large numbers of oxygen-storing myoglobin molecules, can sustain activity for much longer periods of time. Although most muscles have approximately equal proportions of fast-twitch and slow-twitch fibers, there is some variation among the fibers of different muscles, as well as among different individuals. It has been shown, for example, that world-class sprinters have significantly more fast-twitch

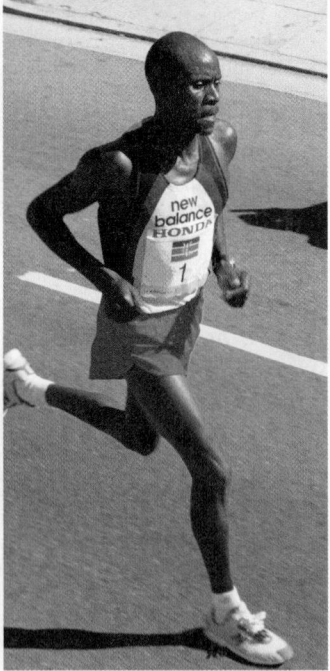

World-class sprinters have more fast-twitch fibers (which enlarge in response to heavy use) in their leg muscles, while world-class long distance runners tend to have more slow-twitch fibers in their leg muscles.

FIGURE 23-35 Fast-twitch and slow-twitch muscles.

fibers in their leg muscles, while world-class long distance runners tend to have more slow-twitch fibers in their leg muscles (**FIGURE 23-35**).

When muscles are used for high-intensity work against increasing resistance, as in many weight-training programs, muscle fibers increase in size as the fast-twitch fibers become thicker. Endurance training, on the other hand, does not cause an increase in the size of muscle cells.

23·16 Skeletal systems enable movement, among several other important functions.

By serving as a structural frame, the skeletal system interacts with the muscular system to enable movement. But this is just one of many important functions of a skeleton (**FIGURE 23-36**). A skeletal system can also provide support for the organism, providing shape and structure and a means of securing the organs and other structures within the animal's body. And in addition to enabling movement and providing support, a skeletal system offers protection—the brain, for example, is protected from harm within the skull, and the heart is protected within the rib cage. In some organisms, including humans, the skeletal system also provides a site for the production of important blood and immune cells, a process that occurs in bone marrow (see Section 26-3). Bones also serve as a reservoir of some minerals, such as calcium, absorbing excess quantities from the bloodstream or releasing minerals when their concentration in the blood is low (see Section 24-5).

There are three distinct types of skeletal systems (**FIGURE 23-37**). In a *hydrostatic skeleton*—such as is found in earthworms, jellyfish, and squid—pressure created within a fluid-filled cavity creates sufficient rigidity that the muscles surrounding it can generate movement, including, in earthworms, the ability to dig. An *exoskeleton* is a rigid outer covering that supports and protects an animal's body. An exoskeleton may be the shell of a turtle, the rigid calcium-based covering of some mollusks, or the polysaccharide-based, chitinous exoskeleton of insects, crabs and lobsters, and spiders. Exoskeletons can also be valuable in reducing some animals' vulnerability to drying out. The third type of skeleton—an *endoskeleton*—is a support structure of hard mineralized tissue, as is found in echinoderms (such as sea

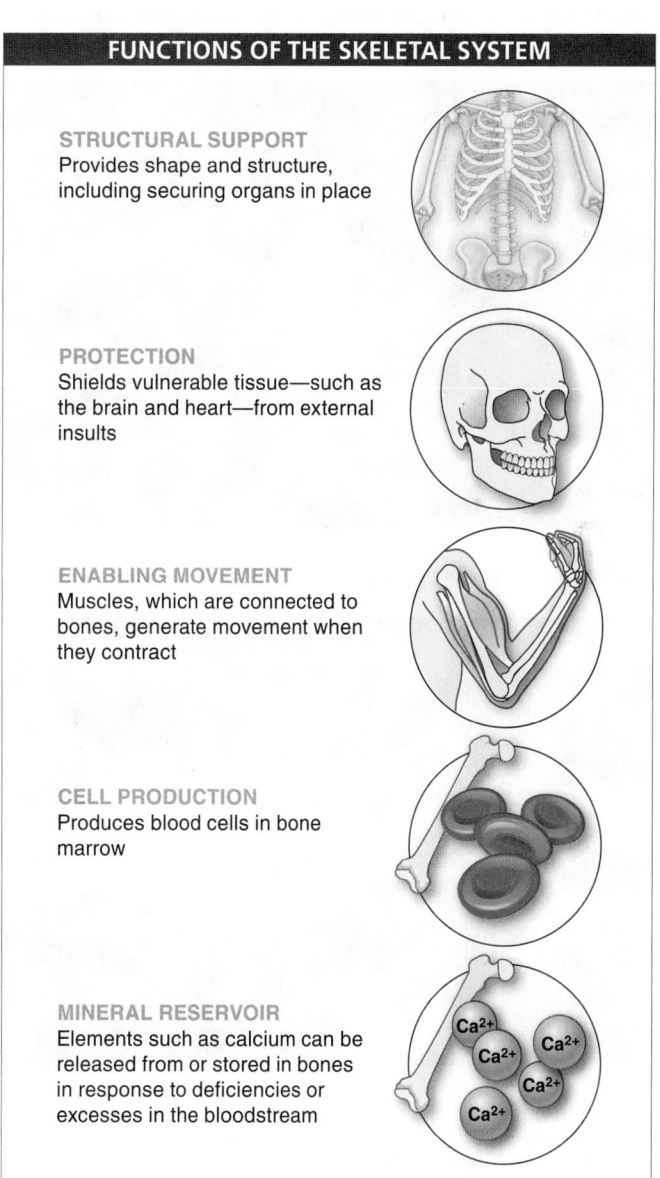

FUNCTIONS OF THE SKELETAL SYSTEM

STRUCTURAL SUPPORT
Provides shape and structure, including securing organs in place

PROTECTION
Shields vulnerable tissue—such as the brain and heart—from external insults

ENABLING MOVEMENT
Muscles, which are connected to bones, generate movement when they contract

CELL PRODUCTION
Produces blood cells in bone marrow

MINERAL RESERVOIR
Elements such as calcium can be released from or stored in bones in response to deficiencies or excesses in the bloodstream

FIGURE 23-36 The skeletal system serves multiple purposes.

TYPES OF SKELETAL SYSTEMS

HYDROSTATIC SKELETON
A fluid-filled cavity with sufficient rigidity so that muscles surrounding it can generate movement

EXOSKELETON
A rigid outer covering that supports and protects an animal's body

ENDOSKELETON
An internal support structure composed of hard mineralized tissue

FIGURE 23-37 There are three distinct types of skeletal systems in animals. Shown (top to bottom): bell jellyfish, lobster, and toad.

stars and sand dollars) and in all vertebrates, including humans.

The composition of the endoskeleton differs between echinoderms and vertebrates, and among the vertebrates. Echinoderm endoskeletons consist of a rigid, calcium-based structure, similar to bone. Among the vertebrates, the jawless fishes and sharks have a flexible but strong skeleton made from cartilage. The other vertebrates have a skeletal system made primarily from bone, a harder, but still resilient connective tissue material (described in Section 20-2).

Most vertebrate skeletons are divided into an axial skeleton, which includes the skull, sternum, ribs, and vertebrae, and an appendicular skeleton, which includes the limbs (or fins, in the case of fishes), the pelvic girdle, and the pectoral girdles (of the shoulder region) (**FIGURE 23-38**).

At the locations in the skeleton where bones meet, several types of joints occur. These may allow movement while maintaining support, such as in the shoulder, hip, knee, and elbow joints. Or they may enable little movement

What is osteoarthritis? Why is it so painful?

VERTEBRATE SKELETON STRUCTURE

AXIAL SKELETON
Includes the skull, sternum, ribs, and vertebrae

APPENDICULAR SKELETON
Includes the limbs, the pelvic girdle, and the pectoral girdles (of the shoulder region)

FIGURE 23-38 Vertebrate skeletons are divided into axial and appendicular regions.

Healthy bone

Osteoporotic bone

FIGURE 23-39 Osteoporosis weakens bone.

Osteoporosis results in reduced bone density and a change in the chemical composition of bone, leading to an increased risk of bone fracture.

(such as the joints between vertebrae) or no movement at all (such as the "joints" that are the sutured connections between the bones of the skull). Arthritis is a condition in which joints have become damaged. There are different forms of arthritis. In the most common type, osteoarthritis, a breakdown of connective tissue, usually cartilage, reduces the cushioning of the bones and can lead to inflammation of tissue around the joint, and accompanying pain.

Another type of breakdown in the skeletal system is osteoporosis, a disease that occurs as the density of bone is reduced and the chemical composition of the bones changes (**FIGURE 23-39**). Occurring most commonly in women, particularly following menopause, osteoporosis increases the risk of bone fractures and falls. Dietary modifications, including increased intake of calcium and vitamin D that can strengthen bones, along with lifestyle changes such as increased exercise that can build bone mass and strengthen muscles, can reduce osteoporosis and the risks associated with it.

TAKE-HOME MESSAGE 23·16

Among animals, three distinct types of skeletal systems occur: hydrostatic skeletons, exoskeletons, and endoskeletons. The vertebrate skeletal system, an endoskeleton, can enable movement, provide support, offer protection, provide a site for production of important blood and immune cells, and serve as a reservoir of minerals, including calcium.

An fMRI image of the brain and spinal cord of an adult male.

23·17

The brain is organized into several distinct regions.

An adult brain weighs only a bit over 3 pounds, or 1.4 kilograms. It's fairly uniform in color, a drab whitish-gray, the surface is soft and gently wrinkled, and it's just a bit stiffer than Jell-O. You'd hardly know that you were looking at something far more complex and powerful than the most advanced supercomputers ever built.

From a cellular perspective, all animal brains function in the same general way. A neuron is a neuron is a neuron. But this isn't the whole picture. Each region of the brain is characterized by neurons that are shaped slightly differently, have different axon and dendrite branching patterns and complexities, and use different neurotransmitters at their synapses. Each of these regions is the control center for various activities in the body.

Among different species, evolutionary changes have resulted in differences in the relative amount of the brain dedicated to various structures. These differences have, in turn, led to corresponding differences in abilities and behaviors. In the cerebral cortex, for example, humans have significantly more neurons than do other species. The extra brain matter in this particular part of the brain (which we examine in more detail later in the chapter) is associated with many abilities that are particularly well developed in humans, including abstract thought, perception, and language. Similarly, the unusually large number of neurons (relative to overall brain size) devoted to the smell-sensing section of a rat's brain give it a particularly powerful sense of smell. This powerful sense, which is much more sensitive to scent stimuli than is a human's sense of smell, contributes to the rat's abilities to find food.

In this section and the next, we explore the three principal regions of the vertebrate brain—the hindbrain, the midbrain, and the forebrain—and the functions they control (**FIGURE 23-40**).

Hindbrain The central nervous system is made up of the brain and the spinal cord. The spinal cord extends from the brain down through the backbone (though not down the entire length of the backbone), protected by the vertebral column. Branching off from the spinal cord at regular intervals are bundles of axons, some carrying motor information to muscles and glands, others carrying in sensory information from the senses to the brain. The top of the spinal cord is the beginning of the brain. Here, the spinal cord expands into the **hindbrain.** Three important structures are located in the hindbrain: the **medulla,** the **pons,** and the **cerebellum.** Because these structures are not

---

The title in the sidebar:

23·17–23·18 The brain is organized into distinct structures dedicated to specific functions.

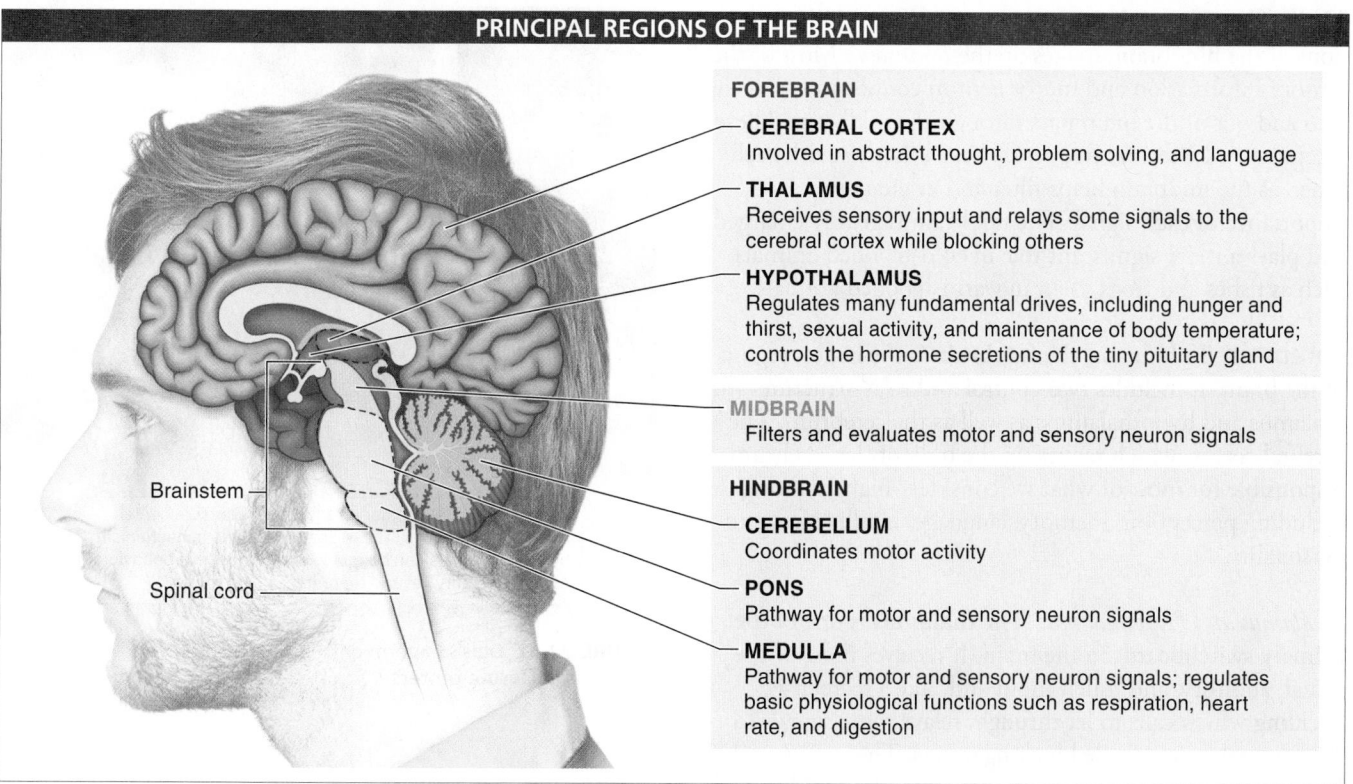

PRINCIPAL REGIONS OF THE BRAIN

FOREBRAIN

CEREBRAL CORTEX
Involved in abstract thought, problem solving, and language

THALAMUS
Receives sensory input and relays some signals to the cerebral cortex while blocking others

HYPOTHALAMUS
Regulates many fundamental drives, including hunger and thirst, sexual activity, and maintenance of body temperature; controls the hormone secretions of the tiny pituitary gland

MIDBRAIN
Filters and evaluates motor and sensory neuron signals

HINDBRAIN

CEREBELLUM
Coordinates motor activity

PONS
Pathway for motor and sensory neuron signals

MEDULLA
Pathway for motor and sensory neuron signals; regulates basic physiological functions such as respiration, heart rate, and digestion

Brainstem

Spinal cord

FIGURE 23-40 The brain is divided into three main regions: forebrain, midbrain, and hindbrain.

involved in higher thought, hindbrain damage can lead to paralysis without harming consciousness.

Medulla and Pons. Running through these structures are the many motor neurons traveling from the brain to the spinal cord and the many sensory neurons traveling from the body into the brain. Additionally, within the medulla are lots of collections of neurons that regulate basic physiological functions such as respiration, heart rate, and digestion. Consequently, injury to these structures—such as occurred when President John F. Kennedy was shot in 1963—nearly always leads to death.

Cerebellum. This structure coordinates numerous types of motor activity. When it works properly, graceful motion is possible. The coordination of many complex movements is overseen by the cerebellum. Knitting or typing, for example, involves a wide range of complex muscle movements that must be executed in precise sequences. Once learned, these movements run on "auto-pilot": we don't have to think consciously about these activities, because the cerebellum directs them (**FIGURE 23-41**). If you are typing rapidly and suddenly think consciously about the motions your fingers are engaged in, you start to make all kinds of errors. Why? Because your conscious thought draws on a part of the brain other than the cerebellum.

After complex muscle movements are learned, such as the precise sequences of knitting, they can then be done without much conscious direction, on a sort of "auto-pilot" as the cerebellum directs them.

FIGURE 23-41 Coordinated by the cerebellum. Once learned, knitting does not require conscious thought.

WHAT IS THE NERVOUS SYSTEM? · HOW DO NEURONS WORK? · THE SENSES · MUSCULAR AND SKELETAL SYSTEMS · THE BRAIN · DRUGS HIJACK PLEASURE PATHWAYS

927

Midbrain The **midbrain,** along with the medulla and pons of the hindbrain, makes up the *brainstem.* Most of the sensory information and motor neuron connections coming into and out of the brain pass through the midbrain. These receptors and effectors frequently have synapses with each other, as the midbrain helps filter and evaluate the importance of each signal. The midbrain is greatly enlarged and plays a more significant role in cold-blooded animals, such as fishes and frogs, than in warm-blooded animals.

Forebrain In humans, the **forebrain** is the largest region of the brain. It includes two control and relay structures, the thalamus and hypothalamus, as well as the cerebrum. The cerebral cortex, which makes up the bulk of the cerebrum, is responsible for most of what we consider "higher" thought, including perception, memory, language, intelligence, and personality.

Thalamus and Hypothalamus. The **thalamus** is one of the primary switchboards in the brain. It receives most of the visual, auditory, and touch input and, like a secretary deciding which calls to let through, relays some signals to the cerebral cortex while blocking others. The **hypothalamus** (part of the limbic system, discussed later in this section) is one of the chief regulatory centers of the brain. It regulates many fundamental drives, including hunger and thirst, sexual activity, and maintenance of body temperature. It also controls the hormone secretions of the tiny pituitary gland, located right next to it, which play important roles in reproduction and development.

> "The mind is its own place, and in itself Can make a heaven of hell, a hell of heaven."
> —JOHN MILTON, *Paradise Lost,* 1667

In the 1950s, James Olds discovered something very peculiar about the hypothalamus. When he inserted a tiny electrode into the hypothalamus of a rat's brain, the animal seemed to experience great pleasure. Of course, Olds couldn't be certain that it was pleasure the rats were experiencing, but he hypothesized that this was so by noting how the rats would work very hard (for instance, by learning to run very complex mazes) to get the stimulation. When he set up the apparatus so that an animal could administer the stimulation to its own brain simply by pushing a lever, the rats became lever addicts, pushing the lever more than a hundred times a minute for many hours (**FIGURE 23-42**). They would even choose to push the lever over eating food or drinking water, with some rats starving to death while pushing the lever rather than taking even a short break to eat.

James Olds's 1950s' studies identified "pleasure centers" in the hypothalamus. These centers provide a mechanism by which animals can be motivated to engage in behaviors essential to survival and reproduction.

FIGURE 23-42 Olds's experiments led to the discovery that the brain has "pleasure centers."

This discovery that the brain has "pleasure centers" or "do-it-again centers" was important because it revealed a mechanism by which animals could be motivated to engage in evolutionarily important behaviors by which they might increase their own reproductive success relative to other individuals in the population. Drinking when thirsty or eating when hungry produces stimulation in this brain area, thereby reinforcing behaviors essential to survival and reproduction.

Cerebral Cortex. For humans, the **cerebral cortex** is the most sophisticated part of the brain. Involved in abstract thought, problem solving, language, and more, this is the part of the brain most responsible for the traits that set us apart from other animal species.

One of the most dramatic demonstrations of the complexity of the cerebral cortex resulted from a tragic accident and apparently miraculous recovery. In 1848, a railroad worker named Phineas Gage was packing explosives into a hole when they exploded unexpectedly, blasting a three-and-a-half-foot iron bar right through his face, just below his left eye, through the front part of his head, and out through the top of his skull (**FIGURE 23-43**). Amazingly, he recovered from the accident. Soon after his recovery, though, it became clear that something in Gage's personality had changed. Before the accident he was serious and industrious, but after the accident he became vulgar, unpleasant, uninhibited, and irresponsible.

Damage to Phineas Gage's frontal cortex radically altered his personality.

FIGURE 23-43 Phineas Gage's accident. Gage suffered damage to his frontal cortex, which caused dramatic changes in his behavior.

Gage died about 13 years after the accident, and his skull was preserved. Recent analyses of the skull indicate that Gage suffered from severe damage to part of his frontal cortex. In other case studies of patients with damage to the same part of their frontal cortex, such as that caused by certain tumors, similar personality changes have been noted, with patients frequently exhibiting radically changed emotional responses.

The highly folded cerebral cortex is by far the largest brain structure, covering all of the brain except for the cerebellum (**FIGURE 23-44**). The cerebral cortex makes up 80% to 85% of the brain mass in humans, with about 10 billion neurons and hundreds of billions of synapses. Although the brain (including the cerebral cortex) looks fairly symmetrical, functions are not divided in a symmetrical way. The brain is divided into a left and a right hemisphere, connected by a broad, thick band of neurons, called the **corpus callosum.** The **left hemisphere** in most, but not all, individuals is the site of areas specializing in language, logic, and mathematical skills, while the **right hemisphere** is more commonly home to larger areas dedicated to emotions, intuitive thinking, and artistic expression.

Each hemisphere of the cerebral cortex has four different lobes: frontal, temporal, parietal, and occipital. Each lobe is associated with specific functions (but each also has many other subareas that control a variety of additional functions; see Figure 23-44).

1. **Frontal lobe:** important in speech production, motor control, smell detection, problem solving, and many aspects of personality.

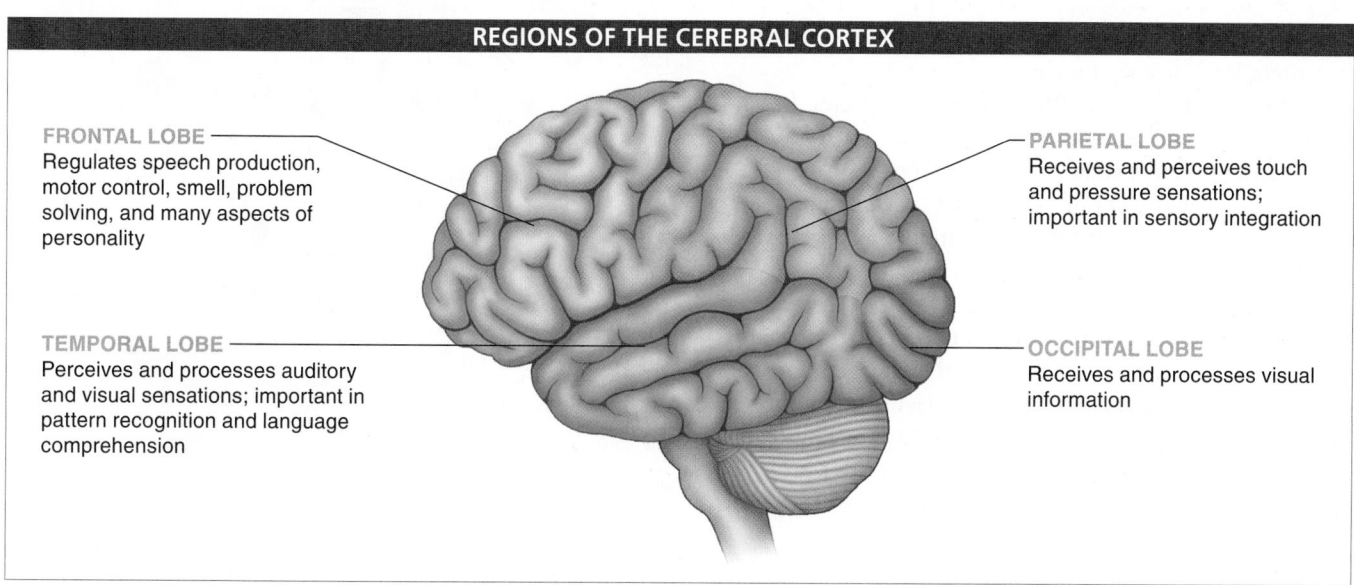

REGIONS OF THE CEREBRAL CORTEX

FRONTAL LOBE
Regulates speech production, motor control, smell, problem solving, and many aspects of personality

TEMPORAL LOBE
Perceives and processes auditory and visual sensations; important in pattern recognition and language comprehension

PARIETAL LOBE
Receives and perceives touch and pressure sensations; important in sensory integration

OCCIPITAL LOBE
Receives and processes visual information

FIGURE 23-44 The lobes of the cerebral cortex.

2. **Temporal lobe:** perceives and processes auditory and visual sensations; also important in pattern recognition and language comprehension. Damage to part of the right temporal lobe—usually due to a stroke or tumor—has been implicated in a condition known as prosopagnosia or face blindness. Individuals with this condition find it difficult or impossible to recognize faces.

3. **Parietal lobe:** receives and perceives touch and pressure sensations; also important in **sensory integration,** the process of incorporating information from all of the senses to form a single perception of something.

4. **Occipital lobe:** receives and processes visual information.

Limbic System. Within the forebrain, near the center of the brain, is a set of structures that together make up the **limbic system.** It includes parts of the cerebral cortex and two structures deeper within the center of the brain, the **hippocampus** and the **amygdala,** and is responsible for many of our physiological drives and instincts. Together, these structures also play an important role in emotions, learning, and memory, which we discuss below.

TAKE-HOME MESSAGE 23·17

There are several distinct regions in the brain, each of which is the control center for various activities in the body. The hindbrain regulates basic physiological functions such as respiration, heart rate, and digestion, and coordinates numerous types of motor activity. The midbrain, part of the brainstem, helps filter and evaluate the importance of sensory and motor information. In humans, the forebrain is the largest region of the brain, responsible for most of what we consider higher thought, including perception, memory, language, intelligence, and personality.

23·18 Specific brain areas are involved in the processes of learning, language, and memory.

Brains are capable of myriad amazing feats. Learning and memory, along with the use of complex language, are among the most sophisticated and enigmatic of these functions. But while these abilities rank among the greatest mysteries of the brain, we're unlocking more and more of the secrets every day.

Language What is language exactly? In its most broad interpretation, **language** is simply the means of communication between individuals of any species. In humans, language has evolved to its most complex level. Words and sentences allow us to convey not just simple information but also complex thoughts such as things and events distant in space or time, something rarely if ever seen in other species.

Several distinct brain structures, and two in particular, are necessary for the acquisition and use of language. One is required for the understanding of speech, including the linking of words with meaning (**FIGURE 23-45**). This region is called **Wernicke's area,** and it is located in the left temporal lobe. People with damage to Wernicke's area (from a stroke or head injury) are able to produce sounds properly, such as when repeating things they hear, but they cannot understand speech and can speak only gibberish. It's as if

SPEECH CENTERS IN THE BRAIN

BROCA'S AREA
Coordinates the muscles necessary for speech production

WERNICKE'S AREA
Responsible for language comprehension

FIGURE 23-45 Areas of the brain controlling the ability to produce speech and understand language.

they've lost the ability to link words with their meanings. The second structure, **Broca's area,** controls the muscles involved in the actual process of speaking. It is located in the front part of the left frontal lobe.

Q Do men or women have a better chance of language recovery following a stroke? Why?

Brain science is still in its infancy, and we're still discovering some perplexing and unexpected things about this most complex of all organs. Consider this: in 2008, an American woman named Cindy Lou Romberg had a chiropractic adjustment that apparently aggravated a severe brain injury that she had suffered 17 years earlier. Much to her surprise, she found that she suddenly had a foreign accent! In her whole life she had never spoken with such an accent—which sounds like a sort of mixture of German, French, and Russian—nor had she ever studied any foreign languages or even been to Europe (**FIGURE 23-46**). It seems that parts of her language production areas had been damaged, and this altered the way she spoke. Although the exact mechanism for this change is not understood, this strange phenomenon has been reported several other times, the first being in 1941, when a Norwegian woman had a stroke and afterward spoke with what sounded like a German accent.

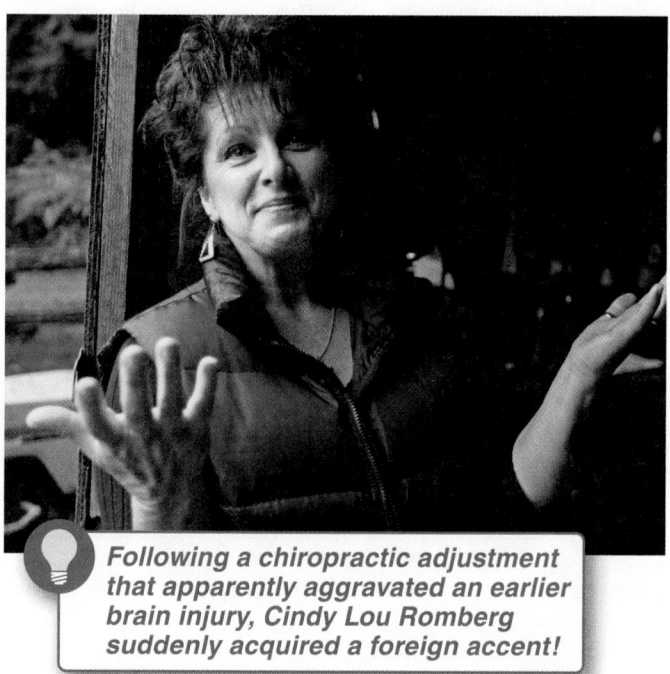

Following a chiropractic adjustment that apparently aggravated an earlier brain injury, Cindy Lou Romberg suddenly acquired a foreign accent!

FIGURE 23-46 Changing accent.

MEMORY CENTERS IN THE BRAIN

AMYGDALA
The area of the brain that appears to associate emotional feelings and sensory input with memories

HIPPOCAMPUS
The area of the brain that is important in the storage and retrieval of memories and the transfer of short-term memories

FIGURE 23-47 Areas of the brain associated with memories.

Interestingly, women are much more likely to regain the ability to speak after a stroke. This may be related to the fact that, on average, women have a thicker corpus callosum, the band of fibers connecting the left and right hemispheres of the brain. The additional thickness may facilitate another part of the brain's ability to take over language functions after the stroke-induced death of brain tissue.

Another recent discovery suggests that children have a propensity to learn language, regardless of what language they are exposed to. In a study of children raised by parents who spoke using sign language only, observations of their children revealed that the infants "babbled" with their hands. Much as babies with parents who speak begin to put together nonsense words made up from fragments of words and sounds, from age six months to one year, the babies of signing parents used their hands to produce fragments of hand signs. The babies of speaking parents did not exhibit such hand babbling.

Learning and memory are understood even less well than language. Still, certain cellular changes seem to occur in neurons when we learn and remember things. Two parts of the limbic system are critical in storing memories, the amygdala and the hippocampus. The amygdala seems to associate emotional feelings and sensory input with memories (**FIGURE 23-47**). This is why it is not uncommon for certain smells or tastes, for example, to elicit memories.

The hippocampus is also important in the storage and retrieval of memories, as well as in the transfer of short-term memories—things that are stored in our brain only briefly, such as a phone number or the name of a person we have just met—into long-term memories that can be recalled days, years, or even decades later. Memories and associations of sensations are stored throughout much of the cerebral cortex, too.

Humans don't have a monopoly on powerful memory. Each fall, for example, red squirrels each hide more than 3,000 acorns and other nuts. Come winter, each squirrel is able to remember the locations of more than 80% of those nuts and recover them for food. Similarly, birds such as the black-capped chickadee store large numbers of nuts for the winter. Researchers looking for neurological changes in these birds found that the hippocampus is significantly larger in the fall, when the birds must remember all of their nut-stash locations, than in the spring, when they no longer need to rely on stored nuts for food.

For many years, it was believed that no new neurons are added to the human brain once development is completed in early childhood. While this is largely true, recent observations suggest that some parts of the hippocampus are an exception, adding cells even into adulthood, possibly as a function of use. On the flip side, amnesia usually comes from damage to the amygdala or hippocampus from a stroke or head injury.

What happens to the neurons at a cellular level during the processes of learning and forming memories? When repeated action potentials are generated by a neuron, changes occur at the synapse. There are two types of change that generally occur. One is called **long-term depression** and the other is called **long-term potentiation.** In each, as neurotransmitters are repeatedly released by the presynaptic membrane, the adjacent neuron responds by initiating an action potential, but also by becoming less likely (long-term depression) or more likely (long-term potentiation) to respond to future stimulation with an action potential. That's the learning: future responses are modified by past experience. This makes sense when we consider that perhaps the simplest form of learning comes from repeated attempts at doing something, during which the individual becomes better and better at it.

FIGURE 23-48 "Use it or lose it!" With extensive navigational experience come changes in taxi drivers' brains.

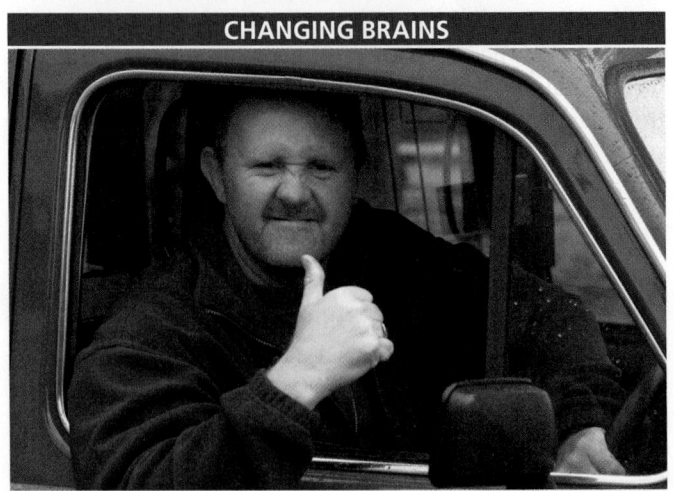

CHANGING BRAINS

The posterior hippocampus—a structure important in spatial navigation in rodents and monkeys—was found to be larger in taxi drivers than in a control group of non-taxi drivers. (The total volume of the hippocampus did not differ between the groups; the anterior hippocampus was larger in the control subjects.)

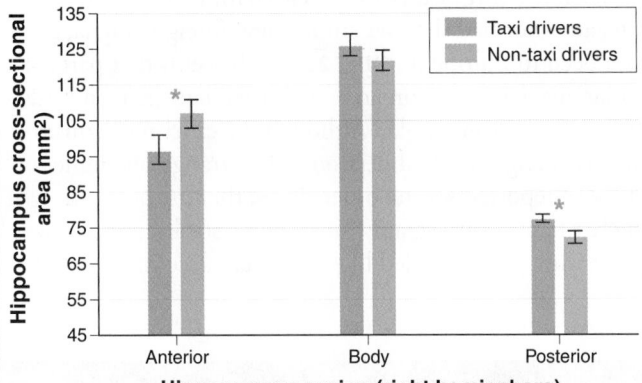

* Difference in size is statistically significant

The volume of the posterior hippocampus correlated with the amount of time spent as a taxi driver.

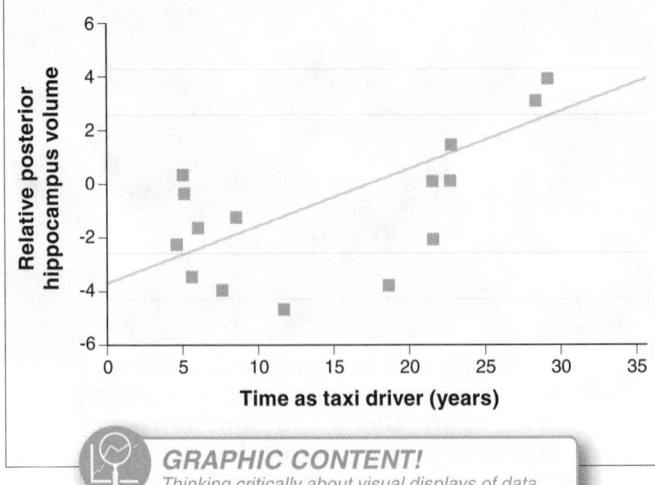

GRAPHIC CONTENT!
Thinking critically about visual displays of data.
Turn to p. 942 for a closer inspection of this figure.

Can we generate
new brain cells?
How?

Q

"Use it or lose it." That is a frequent assertion by weightlifters in reference to their muscles. The same expression might be used about the spatial-memory-forming components of our limbic system. Using a type of brain scan called **functional MRI,** or **fMRI,** which can visualize the size and activity of different brain structures, researchers in England recently discovered that in London cab drivers, the posterior portion of their hippocampus was significantly larger than the same region in the brains of non-cabbies. The researchers suggest that this may be a result of the formation of new neurons, due to the greater demands placed on the posterior hippocampus as the cab drivers navigate the streets of London. Their hypothesis was supported by the observation that the longer an individual had been a cab driver, the larger his posterior hippocampus was (**FIGURE 23-48**).

The synapse isn't just the site of "normal" signal propagation. We explore next how, by tinkering with the synapse and modifying the amount or duration of stimulation occurring, it is possible to use drugs and medications to artificially create feelings of happiness, satiation, euphoria, and more. It's also possible to create medically valuable anesthetics and deadly toxins.

TAKE-HOME MESSAGE 23·18

Learning and memory, along with the use of complex language, are among the most sophisticated functions of the brain. Although brain science is still in its infancy, we are gaining a clearer picture of the brain structures—primarily, for language, in the left frontal and left temporal lobes and, for learning and memory, in the amygdala and hippocampus—that are chiefly responsible for these functions.

WHAT IS THE
NERVOUS SYSTEM?   HOW DO
NEURONS WORK?   THE SENSES   MUSCULAR
AND SKELETAL
SYSTEMS   THE BRAIN   DRUGS HIJACK
PLEASURE
PATHWAYS   933

23·19–23·21 Drugs can hijack pleasure pathways.

The French poet Jacques Prevert tinkers with synaptic activity in his brain, in Paris, 1955.

23·19 Our nervous system can be tricked by chemicals.

Stimulation of the reward centers in the brain spurs animals to behave in certain ways. We're built this way on purpose: when we behave in ways important to our evolutionary fitness, our brain releases neurotransmitters such as dopamine. Exposed to such neurotransmitters, our pleasure centers produce the sensation of bliss. And that bliss spurs us to seek out that feeling again once it fades. Usually this system works well.

Our brain's signaling system can be tricked, however, and with potentially disastrous consequences. Drugs—whether recreational or therapeutic, whether found in nature or made in the laboratory—can work by mimicking neurotransmitters. When we take a pleasure-causing drug, our brain experiences the same sensations as if appropriately released neurotransmitters were flooding the system. The brain cannot distinguish this artificial high from a natural high. There are several different methods by which drugs can influence our nervous system. We explore some of them here.

Cocaine When someone snorts a bit of cocaine, it crosses the blood-brain barrier and quickly reaches the brain's pleasure centers. Once there, the cocaine binds to the sites on the presynaptic membrane where dopamine is normally reabsorbed from the synaptic cleft by the cells that originally released it. As long as these reuptake sites are blocked by the drug, dopamine released by that neuron remains in the synaptic cleft, repeatedly stimulating the postsynaptic cell and causing nonstop activity in the pleasure center (**FIGURE 23-49**).

Prozac and Zoloft Antidepressants work by a mechanism almost identical to that of cocaine. In addition to dopamine, another neurotransmitter important in our brain's pleasure centers is serotonin. The antidepressants Prozac and Zoloft block serotonin from being reabsorbed and recycled by the presynaptic cells that released it, prolonging its effect (see Figure 23-49). This is why these drugs are called **selective serotonin reuptake inhibitors (SSRIs).** The net result is that people taking these drugs generally experience an elevated mood because of serotonin's prolonged stay in the synaptic cleft.

Morphine and heroin Some chemical messengers we ought to be especially thankful for are the endorphins, our body's natural painkillers. Produced by our brain, endorphins block pain messages arriving from throughout the body. Under a variety of situations of extreme stress—

Blood vessel

Drug molecules

Neurons in the brain

Blood-brain barrier

1 After the drug is taken, it crosses the blood-brain barrier and quickly reaches the brain's pleasure centers.

2 Drug molecules bind to sites on the presynaptic membrane where neurotransmitters are normally reabsorbed by the cells that originally released them.

3 As long as reuptake sites are blocked by drug molecules, the neurotransmitters previously released by that neuron remain in the synaptic cleft.

4 The neurotransmitters repeatedly stimulate the postsynaptic cell and cause nonstop activity in the pleasure centers of the brain.

Presynaptic membrane

Reuptake sites

Drug molecules

Neurotransmitters

Postsynaptic cell

FIGURE 23-49 Prolonging pleasure sensations. Reuptake inhibitors cause prolonged action of a neurotransmitter in the synapse.

such as if an individual has just been seriously injured in a fight or is in mile 12 of a half-marathon—the body responds by releasing endorphins.

The popular opiates morphine and heroin mimic endorphins and bind to their receptor sites. With a large enough dose, opiate users can give themselves an "endorphin rush" and feelings of euphoria far more intense than anything possible with their own natural supply of these pleasure compounds. The respiratory slowdown that comes with heroin use can occur quickly and, with large doses of heroin, can be fatal.

Nicotine One of the most commonly used drugs is nicotine. Shortly after entering the bloodstream, nicotine begins mimicking one of the body's most common and important neurotransmitters, acetylcholine. Fooled by the nicotine binding to acetylcholine receptors, cells release adrenaline and other stimulating chemicals, including pleasure-causing dopamine. Nicotine causes rapid surges, then rapid depletions, of these chemicals, leaving smokers happy for a short while but soon yearning for another cigarette.

When we consume drugs such as those described above, our bodies soon respond to the perception that there are larger amounts than usual of certain neurotransmitters. Usually the response is a reduction in sensitivity to the drug. Although tolerance is inevitable, its magnitude and consequences vary with the type of drug. In one study, volunteers were injected with a uniform daily dose of heroin and monitored for their level of euphoria. Initially they were ecstatic, but their bodies reacted by reducing the number of receptors that bind heroin. With fewer and fewer receptors, the euphoric heroin effects dropped almost to zero in just three weeks. Similar changes occur in response to using caffeine, nicotine, or alcohol.

Do human drug addictions and dependencies reflect differences in our genes? Recent data suggest that they might at least be influenced by the alleles a person carries. In one study of 283 individuals, a third of the people who

Q *Can a gene nudge you toward risk-taking?*

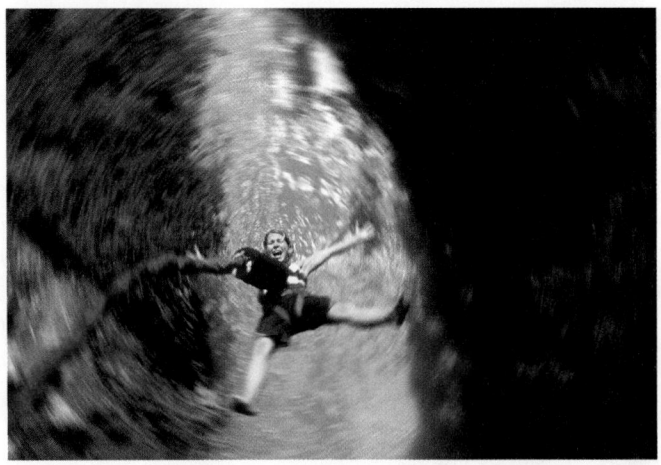

FIGURE 23-50 Can a gene nudge you toward risk-taking?

The allele of the DRD4 gene implicated in this study of drug dependency was the same one we discussed in the StreetBio at the end of Chapter 7, a gene that appears to influence a variety of personality traits associated with risk-taking and novelty-seeking behavior (**FIGURE 23-50**).

In the next section we look at a popular and effective drug that acts, not by blocking neurotransmitter reuptake, but rather by blocking the postsynaptic receptors.

smoked had a version (i.e., an allele) of an important gene that almost none of the non-smokers carried. This gene, labeled DRD4, codes for the receptor that enables the pleasure centers of our brain to respond to dopamine.

TAKE-HOME MESSAGE 23·19

Our brain's signaling system can be tricked by drugs, whether recreational or therapeutic, that mimic neurotransmitters. Such drugs—including cocaine, Prozac, heroin, and nicotine—can produce euphoric sensations, can reduce depression, and can block pain, but the effects often come with significant health risks.

23·20 A brain slows down when it needs sleep. Caffeine wakes it up.

Many drugs can interfere with normal neuron functioning, and caffeine is perhaps the most frequently used drug of all that have this effect. Worldwide, more caffeine-containing tea is consumed every day than any beverage other than water. A close second is coffee (**FIGURE 23-51**). And in the United States, 90% of the soda consumed contains caffeine. The average American drinks about a hundred gallons a year of these three beverages. From philosophers and writers to scientists and musicians, caffeine has been revered as a necessity for stimulating the creative juices. In his "Coffee Cantata" of 1732, J. S. Bach wrote, "Ah! How sweet coffee tastes! Lovelier than a thousand kisses, sweeter far than muscatel wine!"

> ❝If it weren't for coffee, I'd have no discernible personality at all.❞
>
> —DAVID LETTERMAN

The centuries of strong praise are well founded. Caffeine has powerful effects on nearly every animal species. For instance, all rats can eventually be trained to race through mazes, but some learn quickly while others languish in remedial maze-running classes. What they all have in common, however, is that when they are given a caffeine pick-me-up before their maze lessons, they learn the solutions faster and remember them better.

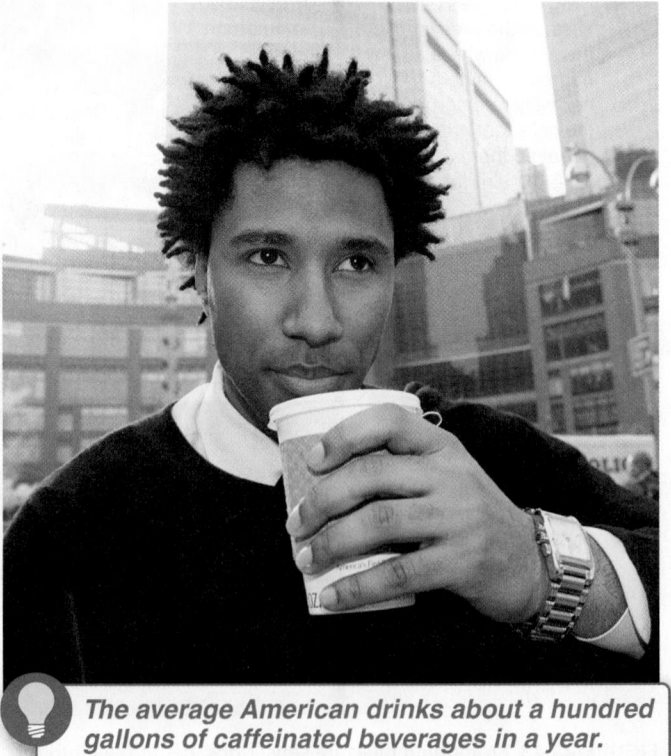

The average American drinks about a hundred gallons of caffeinated beverages in a year.

FIGURE 23-51 Many people take pleasure in drinking tea and coffee.

How does caffeine work its magic? As long as we are awake, our brain is working hard and consuming about 20% of the energy we take in. Much as a running motor generates exhaust fumes, however, all of this neural activity leads to a buildup of cellular waste products. Neuron "exhaust" takes the form of a variety of molecules, including one called adenosine. As a cell releases adenosine, it fills adenosine receptors on nearby cells, particularly those in the brainstem. When a molecule of adenosine binds to an adenosine receptor, this reduces a neuron's likelihood of initiating an action potential. Adenosine has been described as putting a brake on neuron activity. Consequently, as the production of adenosine continues throughout our day, more and more receptors on more and more neurons are filled, and the neurons in our brain become less likely to fire, regardless of how strongly they are stimulated. We perceive this as tiredness. Then, as we sleep, the cellular waste products such as adenosine are reabsorbed and recycled. Upon awaking, we feel better because we are, literally, more clear-headed.

Caffeine has its effect by blocking the message to reduce activity and to sleep. Here's how it accomplishes this effect. The caffeine we ingest quickly circulates to our brain, and once there, it diffuses around the cells. Because the shape of the caffeine molecule is similar to that of the adenosine molecule, the caffeine slips into some of the receptors intended for adenosine (**FIGURE 23-52**). It doesn't have the same effect as adenosine, however. Adenosine receptors with bound caffeine molecules do not reduce a neuron's propensity to respond to other stimuli with an action potential. Thus, when many of the adenosine receptors are blocked by caffeine, the adenosine is unable to pass on the message that we need to sleep. Instead, we feel surprisingly alert, as caffeine interrupts one of the normal sleep-signaling systems.

Surprisingly, caffeine seems to be safe for most people. Despite considerable searching for ill effects, there is no clear evidence that moderate consumption of caffeine increases our risk of anything beyond the occasional jitters. For healthy people, there appears to be no increased risk of heart, lung, or kidney disease or even cancer.

TAKE-HOME MESSAGE 23·20

Normal neural activity leads to a buildup of cellular waste products. One of these, adenosine, fills adenosine receptors on nearby neurons, reducing the likelihood that a neuron will initiate an action potential and causing fatigue. Caffeine binds to adenosine receptors, but without reducing their likelihood of firing, thus blocking the fatigue-inducing message of adenosine.

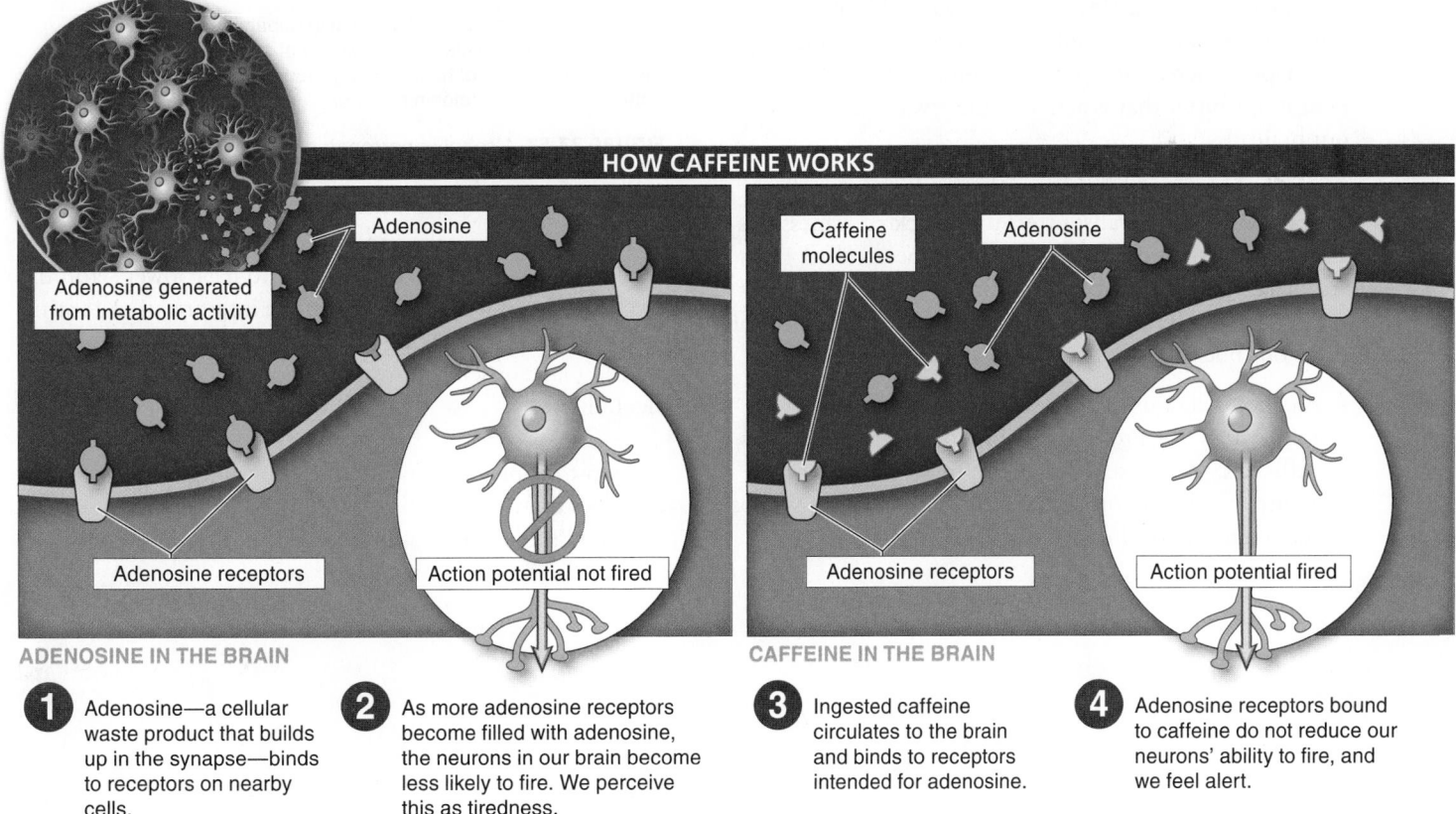

HOW CAFFEINE WORKS

Adenosine

Adenosine generated from metabolic activity

Adenosine receptors

Action potential not fired

ADENOSINE IN THE BRAIN

Caffeine molecules

Adenosine

Adenosine receptors

Action potential fired

CAFFEINE IN THE BRAIN

1 Adenosine—a cellular waste product that builds up in the synapse—binds to receptors on nearby cells.

2 As more adenosine receptors become filled with adenosine, the neurons in our brain become less likely to fire. We perceive this as tiredness.

3 Ingested caffeine circulates to the brain and binds to receptors intended for adenosine.

4 Adenosine receptors bound to caffeine do not reduce our neurons' ability to fire, and we feel alert.

FIGURE 23-52 How caffeine reduces the feeling of fatigue.

Alcohol interferes with many different neurotransmitters.

So far, we've seen that drugs frequently can alter our brain functioning by mimicking the neurotransmitters used by our neurons during normal functioning. Their specific effects are quite predictable, as long as we know the neurotransmitter that a particular drug mimics. Their work is like a surgical strike, altering our neurochemistry in one specific way.

But what happens if the drug is more of an everyman, looking enough like many different neurotransmitters to impersonate them all? This is the case with alcohol. More specifically, it is the case with ethanol, the "alcohol" molecule in alcoholic beverages. Alcohol is a great neurotransmitter impersonator, fooling at least four different receptor molecules. Let's look at some of its effects (**FIGURE 23-53**).

1. Alcohol slows us down, "relaxing" our neurons. By blocking receptors for glutamate (see Section 23-7), one of the brain's chief excitatory neurotransmitters, alcohol slows our reaction times and slurs our speech. It may also have more serious effects: many animals can't learn as well when their glutamate receptors are blocked.

2. Alcohol gives us a pleasant buzz. Acting like cocaine—but much weaker—alcohol blocks dopamine reuptake at synapses, increasing the concentration of this neurotransmitter that is active in the reward centers of our brain.

3. Alcohol blocks pain. By stimulating the release of endorphins—neurotransmitters that block pain messages—alcohol causes the same feeling that has been called "runner's high." Resembling morphine and heroin in this respect, but again at a greatly reduced magnitude, alcohol spurs our body to produce a little opiate-like high.

4. Alcohol makes us happier, at least while it's in our system. Much like Prozac, alcohol modifies and increases the efficiency of our serotonin receptors, increasing the contentment that accompanies serotonin release at synapses in the brain. Interestingly, rats that have been bred for a

EFFECTS OF ALCOHOL
- Slows reaction time and slurs speech by blocking receptors for glutamate
- Provides a pleasant buzz by blocking dopamine reuptake
- Blocks pain by stimulating the release of endorphins
- Increases feelings of happiness by modifying and increasing the efficiency of our serotonin receptors

FIGURE 23-53 Alcohol impersonates several neurotransmitters, with several consequences.

high preference for alcohol turn out to have lower serotonin levels than normal rats. One possible interpretation for this is that the alcohol-seeking animals are trying to compensate for their lack of serotonin stimulation by looking for the alcohol effects.

For most people, moderate alcohol consumption is pleasant and does not have significant health risks. For some, however, alcohol abuse and alcoholism can lead to serious

FIGURE 23-54 Alcohol intake lowers inhibitions and, in excess, can increase the likelihood of risky behavior.

problems. Nearly 14 million Americans abuse alcohol, and the consequences can be serious. Beyond the effects it creates by mimicking neurotransmitters, alcohol has a variety of other physiological effects in our bodies that can become harmful when alcohol is consumed in large amounts or for long periods of time. These include increasing the risk for some types of cancer, increasing the risk of liver disease (because the liver must metabolize and detoxify all the ethanol molecules that are consumed), increasing the likelihood of harm to the fetus during pregnancy, increasing the likelihood of taking part in risky sexual and other behaviors, and increasing the risk of automobile crashes (**FIGURE 23-54**).

TAKE-HOME MESSAGE 23·21

Alcohol affects the functioning of multiple neurotransmitters—including glutamate, endorphins, dopamine, and serotonin—slowing reaction times, slurring speech, blocking pain, and increasing contentment.

"WE ONLY USE 10% OF OUR BRAIN!"
Fact or fiction?

Q: **WELL, DO WE?** Besides being just plain silly, this pervasive myth is completely false. But it prompts some reasonable questions. Read on.

Q: **HOW CAN WE MEASURE BRAIN ACTIVITY?** Brain imaging technologies capture pictures of the brain as it functions, revealing activity patterns, based on increased metabolism, in the different regions of the brain. One technique is called fMRI scanning (functional magnetic resonance imaging). In an fMRI scan, a giant magnet detects the relative amounts of oxygenated blood and deoxygenated blood in various parts of the brain. When parts of the brain are active, more blood flows to them and the sensitive magnet can pick up the change.

Q: **SO WHAT DO THESE SCANS SHOW? DO WE USE SOME PARTS OF THE BRAIN MORE THAN OTHERS? DO MENTAL TASKS OR PHYSICAL SENSATIONS REQUIRE THE USE OF A SPECIFIC PART OF THE BRAIN?** Some recent findings include these:

Seeing your favorite foods activates brain reward centers. Subjects shown images of their favorite foods show increased brain activity in the pleasure centers of the forebrain. And recovering drug addicts have a similar response to images of a syringe (or even an anti-drug advertisement), often prompting them to relapse. Both cases underscore the power of advertising.

Altruistic behavior activates reward centers. When playing a game called "Prisoner's Dilemma," in which people gain rewards based on their decisions to cooperate or act selfishly, brain activity in the forebrain's reward center is increased when a player chooses to cooperate. This may indicate that our brains are built to produce a physiological "prodding" toward kindness in certain situations.

People with Alzheimer's disease exhibit significantly reduced brain activity. When compared with healthy individuals of the same age, Alzheimer's patients show decreased activity throughout the parts of the brain associated with thinking and understanding, but normal activity in the areas active in movement and sensory perception.

Language tasks are localized in different parts of the brain. Language uses very different parts of the cerebral cortex, depending on whether someone is hearing, speaking, or reading. Among bilingual people, their second language is stored in a slightly different part of the brain if they acquired it past a certain age.

Q: **SO HOW MUCH OF OUR BRAINS *ARE* WE USING?** For any particular task, not all regions of the brain are called into action, but over the course of a day, all of your neurons are used.

Big Ideas in ...
Nervous and Motor Systems

23·1–23·3 What is the nervous system?

- Nervous systems are found in nearly all animal species. Primarily utilizing cells called neurons, these systems (1) receive input from the surrounding world, (2) process that information, and (3) initiate responses when necessary.

- In vertebrates, the nervous system is divided into the peripheral and the central nervous systems.

- The peripheral nervous system carries signals to and from the sensory and motor pathways. The motor pathways carry signals from both the somatic and the autonomic nervous systems, which relay signals that can be controlled consciously, as well as other signals that cannot be controlled consciously.

23·4–23·7 How do neurons work?

- Neurons are cells specialized for receiving information via their dendrites and transmitting this information through action potentials down their axons.

- An action potential is a self-propagating, all-or-none change in membrane potential that travels down an axon, causing the release of neurotransmitters, which diffuse across the synapse, bind to receptors, and excite or inhibit the postsynaptic cell—which may be a muscle, a gland, or another neuron.

23·8–23·14 Our senses detect and transmit stimuli.

- All of our senses are variations on a theme: sensory cells respond to physical or chemical stimuli by opening or closing ion channels in the membranes of receptor cells and stimulating or blocking action potentials, which, when received by the brain, are perceived as taste, smell, light, sound, or touch.

23·15–23·16 The muscular and skeletal systems enable movement.

- Muscle tissue—including skeletal, cardiac, and smooth muscle—is made up of elongated cells capable of generating force when they contract.

- A muscle fiber is a single cell containing myofibrils that shorten with the making and breaking of bonds connecting parallel actin and myosin filaments.

- Muscles are attached to parts of the skeletal system. In vertebrates, the skeletal system can enable movement, provide support, offer protection, provide a site for production of important blood and immune cells, and serve as a reservoir of minerals, including calcium.

23·17–23·18 The brain is organized into distinct structures dedicated to specific functions.

- There are several distinct regions in the brain— the hindbrain, midbrain, and forebrain—each of which is the control center for various activities in the body.

- The forebrain, the largest region of the brain, is responsible for most of what we consider higher thought, including perception, memory, language, intelligence, and personality.

23·19–23·21 Drugs can hijack pleasure pathways.

- Drugs that interfere with the functioning of neurotransmitters can have various effects, some of which are used in the treatment of diseases and some of which are used to create sought-after euphoric or excited states.

- The mechanisms by which drugs interfere with synaptic events include blocking or over-facilitating the release of a neurotransmitter, increasing or decreasing the rate at which neurotransmitter is removed from the synaptic cleft, or blocking or over-facilitating the binding of neurotransmitter to its receptors.

See the To-Go Guide (packaged with every new copy of this textbook) for an illustrated summary of the chapter.

Check Your Knowledge

Thinking critically about visual displays of data.

1. What is the take-home message of these graphs?

2. The taxi-driver bar is higher than the control group bar for both the middle and right measures. Why isn't there an asterisk above the middle measures?

3. Propose two different possible explanations for taxi drivers having a larger posterior hippocampus.

4. How does the lower graph help you to decide between the two possible explanations you proposed?

5. What does each blue square represent? What does the angle of the line reflect? What was the average "length of time as taxi driver" for the subjects in this study?

6. Each taxi driver was measured at only one point in time. What could you learn from later measurements of the same drivers that you cannot determine from these graphs?

7. Propose an explanation for the difference between the groups in the anterior hippocampus size.

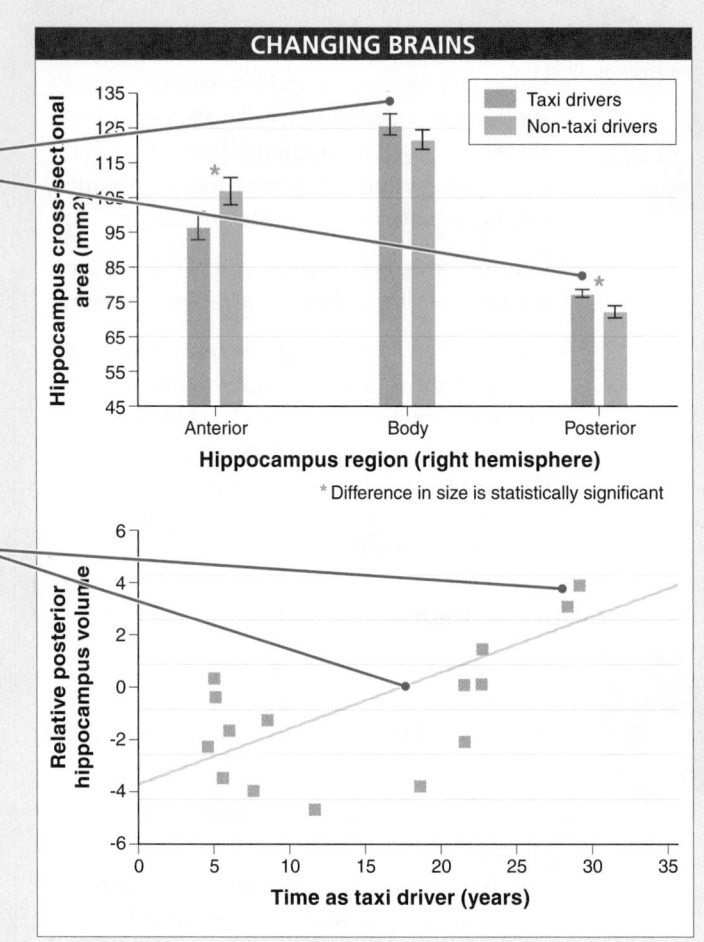

See Answers at the back of the book.

Key Terms in Nervous and Motor Systems

Multiple-Choice Questions

1. Animal nervous systems have several principal features. These include all of the following except:

   a) they coordinate long-term growth and development in an organism.

   b) they receive input from the world around the organism.

   c) they initiate responses to the information they receive from the world, when necessary.

   d) they process the information from the world that an organism receives.

   e) All of the above are principal features of animal nervous systems.

100 HARD
46
0 EASY

2. Which of the following statements about plants and nervous systems is correct?

   a) Plants can feel pain in their trunks and stems, where they have neurons, but not in their leaves.

   b) Plants can feel pain in their leaves, where they have neurons, but not in their trunks or stems.

   c) Plants can feel pain because they have a nervous system that extends throughout all of their tissues.

   d) Plants can feel pain in their trunks, where they have neurons, but not in their stems or leaves.

   e) Plants cannot feel pain, because they do not have nervous systems.

100 HARD
0 **11** EASY

3. What is the difference between a nerve and a neuron?

   a) A nerve is a bundle of neurons, whereas a neuron is a single cell.

   b) Nerves have synapses with muscle cells, whereas neurons have synapses with other neurons.

   c) Nerves have dendrites that can be modified into sensory cells, whereas neurons do not have dendrites.

   d) "Nerve" is the name given to nervous system cells specialized for receiving and transmitting information, whereas "neuron" describes a nerve cell in humans.

   e) There is no difference. They are different words for the same structure.

100 HARD
0 **18** EASY

4. In a neuron, the cell body:

   a) contains the nucleus, mitochondria, and other cell organelles.

   b) does not contain a nucleus.

   c) has a membrane that is impermeable to water and intracellular solutes.

   d) is highly modified and coated in a fatty myelin sheath.

   e) is considered the primary structure of the "central" nervous system.

100 HARD
20
0 EASY

5. Dendrites:

   a) conduct action potentials away from the cell body.

   b) are present in mammalian nervous systems but not in the nervous systems of other vertebrates.

   c) receive information from other neurons or from the external environment.

   d) are coated in a fatty substance called the myelin sheath, which speeds up the rate at which signals are conducted.

   e) are bundles of axons.

100 HARD
0 **12** EASY

6. In individuals with multiple sclerosis, myelin is gradually lost. What symptoms would you expect these individuals to exhibit?

a) Their membranes have reduced numbers of sodium channels.

b) Their sensory neurons lose the ability to initiate action potentials.

c) Their brain becomes smaller.

d) They are able to continue athletic activity long after pain would cause most individuals to stop.

e) Their neurons gradually lose their ability to conduct electrical impulses.

100 HARD

25

0 EASY

7. Which of the choices below properly describes the difference between the gray and white matter of the nervous system?

a) The white matter is composed of non-myelinated fibers, and the gray matter is composed of myelinated fibers.

b) The white matter is composed of neuron bodies, and the gray matter is composed of axons and dendrites.

c) The white matter is composed of sensory neurons, and the gray matter is composed of motor neurons.

d) The white matter is composed of myelinated fibers, and the gray matter is composed of non-myelinated fibers.

e) None of the above is correct.

100 HARD

48

0 EASY

8. The synapse consists of:

a) the release of neurotransmitter into a synaptic cleft.

b) a presynaptic neuron and its neurotransmitters.

c) the membrane depolarization that occurs at gaps in the myelin sheath.

d) the interface between a neuron and another neuron or a muscle cell or gland.

e) None of the above.

100 HARD

48

0 EASY

9. Neurotransmitters in a synaptic cleft have all of the following possible fates except:

a) reuptake by the presynaptic neuron.

b) enzymatic breakdown in the synaptic cleft.

c) inactivation by acetylcholine in the synaptic cleft.

d) binding to a receptor in the postsynaptic cell membrane.

e) All of the above are possible fates of neurotransmitters in a synaptic cleft.

100 HARD

49

0 EASY

10. An action potential in the optic nerve triggered by light striking the eye is the same as:

a) an action potential triggered by air vibrating in the ear.

b) an action potential triggered by salt on the tongue.

c) an action potential triggered by an odorous substance entering the nose.

d) Answers a), b), and c) are correct.

e) None of the above is correct.

100 HARD

24

0 EASY

11. When you put a piece of chocolate on your tongue, your brain registers a sensation of sweetness. What aspect of a molecule is responsible for its having a particular taste?

a) the molecule's shape

b) the total number of protons in the molecule

c) the number of hydrogen bonds in the molecule (more hydrogen bonds = sweeter taste)

d) the ratio of covalent bonds to ionic bonds joining the atoms of the molecule

e) the speed of melting in your mouth

100 HARD

22

0 EASY

12. Because cone cells are less sensitive to light than are rod cells:

a) cones are better suited for daylight vision.

b) cones are better suited for night vision.

c) cones are better suited for peripheral vision.

d) Both a) and c) are correct.

e) Both b) and c) are correct.

100 HARD

46

0 EASY

13. Sensory receptors in your skin include:

a) mechanoreceptors, thermoreceptors, and pain receptors.

b) mechanoreceptors, thermoreceptors, and electromagnetic receptors.

c) chemoreceptors, thermoreceptors, and electromagnetic receptors.

d) mechanoreceptors, thermoreceptors, chemoreceptors, and pain receptors.

e) mechanoreceptors, thermoreceptors, chemoreceptors, electromagnetic receptors, and pain receptors.

100 HARD

44

0 EASY

14. The connective tissue that connects a muscle to a bone is also known as:

a) collagen.

b) a ligament.

c) cartilage.

d) a tendon.

e) None of the above.

100 HARD

27

0 EASY

15. Which of the following is not one of the many functions of an endoskeleton?

    a) storage of important vital minerals

    b) production of blood and immune cells

    c) protection of the body's internal structures

    d) supporting the animal against gravity

    e) All of the above are important functions of an exoskeleton.

 100 HARD   45   0 EASY

16. The brain is divided into which three main regions?

    a) hindbrain, cerebellum, and hypothalamus

    b) midbrain, cerebrum, and brainstem

    c) hypothalamus, medulla oblongata, and cerebrum

    d) brainstem, cerebellum, and cerebrum

    e) hindbrain, midbrain, and forebrain

 100 HARD   35   0 EASY

17. The blood-brain barrier:

    a) is formed from muscle tissue.

    b) is a semi-permeable barricade that allows essential nutrients and gases to pass through.

    c) prevents harmful molecules such as metabolic wastes from passing into the brain.

    d) restricts the passage of molecules to neurons but not to glial cells.

    e) Both b) and c) are correct.

100 HARD   17   0 EASY

18. A boy is born with a specific brain defect in which the two hemispheres of his cerebrum are unable to "talk" to each other (they are not connected). This boy is born without a:

    a) hippocampus.

    b) brainstem.

    c) medulla oblongata.

    d) corpus callosum.

    e) hypothalamus.

100 HARD   35   0 EASY

19. Caffeine blocks what type of receptors in the human nervous system?

    a) dopamine

    b) adenosine

    c) acetylcholine

    d) serotonin

    e) glutamate

100 HARD   51   0 EASY

20. Which of the following is not an effect of alcohol on the nervous system?

    a) Alcohol increases the activity of some serotonin receptors, boosting the effective serotonin level in the synapse.

    b) Alcohol stimulates endorphin release.

    c) Alcohol blocks glutamate receptors, leading to slurred speech and reduced reaction times.

    d) Alcohol leads to modestly increased dopamine levels.

    e) Alcohol blocks reuptake of acetylcholine, creating an energized feeling.

 100 HARD   49   0 EASY

Short-Answer Questions

1. Compare and contrast the structure and role of neurons and glial cells of the nervous system.

2. Describe the structure of the myofibril of skeletal muscle that makes contraction possible. What changes occur that allow contraction?

3. List the primary types of sensory receptor cells, their functions, and which of the five traditional senses they are associated with.

See Answers at the back of the book.
For additional study questions, go to www.prep-u.com.

ABOUT THE CHAPTER OPENING PHOTO

The black faced spider monkey of the Amazon rain forest. Spider monkeys get their name from their very long skinny limbs and tail relative to their torso. They are fruit-eaters and spend most of their time in the upper canopy of rain forests.

Mood, emotions, growth, and more: hormones as master regulators

Hormones

24·1–24·3
Hormones are chemical messengers regulating cell functioning.

A lowland gorilla and baby. Mother-offspring bonding is influenced by hormones such as oxytocin.

24·1 The "cuddle" chemical: oxytocin increases trust and enhances pair bonding.

"Trust me." It's easy enough to say, but can be very difficult to do. Recently, however, some researchers discovered a way to actually make people more trusting. Here's how they did it.

Study participants, called investors, were given an amount of money. Each investor could keep the money or transfer some or all of it to another person, called a trustee. Any amount the investor chose to transfer to the trustee was tripled, and the trustee could then return to the investor some portion of the significantly increased pot of cash. Or, the trustee could simply keep it all. For the investors, this created a dilemma. They could lose money. But trusting behavior could also reward them with a big payoff.

Using a double-blind experimental design, the researchers created two different groups of investors. Before making the decision whether to entrust some of their money to the trustee, one group of investors used a nasal spray to inhale a dose of **oxytocin**—a chemical normally found in humans and other vertebrates, but in smaller amounts than used in the study. Investors in the other group inhaled a placebo, rather than oxytocin.

The results were dramatic and unambiguous. The oxytocin group was significantly more trusting than the placebo

group: more than twice as many of those receiving oxytocin entrusted the maximum amount of their money to the trustee, compared with investors who did not inhale oxytocin. And more than twice as many of those in the placebo group transferred the smallest amounts of cash to the trustee, apparently exhibiting a greater fear of betrayal.

This result is consistent with some findings of research on other animals. In those studies, exposure to oxytocin reliably caused animals to let down their guard, initiate interaction, and form social attachments with other individuals at a much higher rate than they typically would. It appears that this chemical had a similar effect on humans in the investor-trustee study.

One particularly clever and valuable feature of this study's experimental design is that in a follow-up study, the same methods were used but with one exception: the investors were told that the "trustee" in the game was a computer rather than another person. In these cases, the investors receiving oxytocin did not transfer greater amounts of money to the trustee; they behaved exactly like those in the placebo group. This finding suggests that oxytocin specifically increased the investors' trust of another human, rather than just increasing their willingness to take a financial risk.

Oxytocin, a chemical signal produced in the body, can influence complex emotions and behaviors, such as increasing trust, making milk available to nursing babies, and forming social attachments.

FIGURE 24-1 Oxytocin: the cuddle chemical.

Researchers believe that these findings give some insight into the biological basis for trust that might even lead to effective treatments for people with extreme shyness. And the results provide a pretty clear demonstration that complex emotions and behaviors can be influenced by chemical signals produced in the body.

It is important to note that oxytocin influences much, much more in humans than a propensity for trust (**FIGURE 24-1**). Research has demonstrated that oxytocin plays significant roles in making milk available to nursing babies and in facilitating birth. In fact, the name "oxytocin" is from the Greek word meaning "quick birth," based on the recognition of its role in stimulating uterine contractions. Oxytocin has also been shown, as noted above, to increase the propensity to form social attachments—an effect that has caused some researchers to refer to oxytocin as "the cuddle drug."

In this chapter, we see that oxytocin is just one of several dozen influential chemical signals in vertebrates and many other eukaryotes. We explore just what these chemicals are, where they are produced, and how they have their effects. We also explore their pervasive influence in nearly every aspect of vertebrate life, from emotions to physical structures, behavior, and health and physiology.

> ## TAKE-HOME MESSAGE 24·1
>
> Complex emotions and behaviors can be influenced by chemical signals produced in the body. Exposure to oxytocin, for example, causes humans to be more trusting of others, as well as facilitating birth, making milk available to nursing babies, and increasing the propensity to form social attachments.

24·2 Hormones travel through the circulatory system to influence cells elsewhere in the body.

You wouldn't use the postal service to notify the fire department that your house is burning down. Even with overnight delivery, the information wouldn't arrive in time to be of use. Similarly, you probably wouldn't use the phone to convey the complex details of a contractual agreement or architectural plans—the mail service might be preferable, to ensure that the details are conveyed precisely. For almost all

types of communication, some modes of delivery are more effective than others.

Animals need ways to respond to the outside world: ways of sending signals about certain conditions and giving instructions to tissues to respond to those conditions. There are two systems in animals for carrying out this internal

Animals have two systems for carrying out internal communication in response to external conditions.

THE NERVOUS SYSTEM

- Messages sent via chemical and electrical signals down the axons of neurons and across synapses to target cells
- Generally responsible for controlling rapid movement and sensations in response to environmental changes

THE ENDOCRINE SYSTEM

- Messages sent via chemical signals (hormones) secreted by endocrine cells into the circulatory system that influence target cells at a distance
- Generally responsible for slower, longer-term regulation, such as growth and development as well as a variety of secretions

FIGURE 24-2 The nervous and endocrine systems work together in animals.

communication and regulation (**FIGURE 24-2**). As we saw in Chapter 23, the nervous system generally is responsible for controlling rapid movement and sensations in response to environmental changes. In multicellular animals, including humans, there is another system, as well, with a special type of messenger. **Hormones** (from the Greek word meaning "that which sets in motion or urges forward") are a type of chemical messenger, secreted by cells into the circulatory system (the bloodstream or, in insects, the hemolymph), that influences the actions of cells elsewhere in the body, as part of an internal communication and regulation system. Oxytocin, described in Section 24-1, is an example of an animal hormone.

Cells that secrete hormones are called **endocrine cells,** and the cells that receive their signals are called **target cells.** The hormone-secreting cells may be individual cells such as the endocrine cells in the lining of the stomach and small intestine, which aid in digestion. Larger collections of hormone-secreting cells—including the pituitary gland, the pancreas, and the ovaries and testes—are called **endocrine glands.** Together, all of the hormone-secreting cells in an animal make up its **endocrine system** (**FIGURE 24-3**).

While the nervous system controls rapid movements and sensations, the endocrine system controls chemical signals that influence cells close to and far from the secreting cells. In contrast to the nervous system, the endocrine system is generally responsible for longer-term, slower regulation, such

FIGURE 24-3 Organization of the endocrine system.

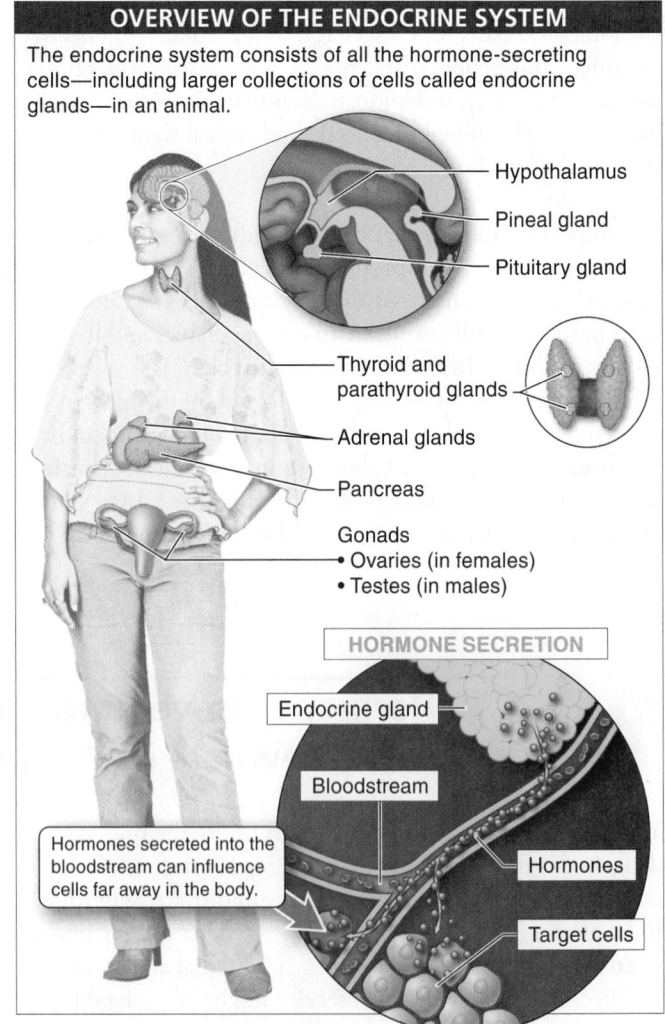

OVERVIEW OF THE ENDOCRINE SYSTEM

The endocrine system consists of all the hormone-secreting cells—including larger collections of cells called endocrine glands—in an animal.

- Hypothalamus
- Pineal gland
- Pituitary gland
- Thyroid and parathyroid glands
- Adrenal glands
- Pancreas
- Gonads
  - Ovaries (in females)
  - Testes (in males)

HORMONE SECRETION

Endocrine gland

Bloodstream

Hormones secreted into the bloodstream can influence cells far away in the body.

Hormones

Target cells

as growth and development, as well as a variety of secretions (see Figure 24-2). It's important to note, however, that there are some nervous system cells that secrete hormones, so the systems are not completely distinct but rather can overlap somewhat in function. Interestingly, although they don't have nervous systems, most plants do have hormones (see Chapter 19), suggesting that hormone systems predate nervous systems evolutionarily.

When a hormone gets to a target cell, it elicits a response. Commonly, the hormone's effect on a target cell is to alter the animal's physiology to help the organism maintain homeostasis. In doing so, the hormone may alter the target cell's metabolism or growth, or it may spur cell division, or it may initiate some developmental pathway.

Another type of chemical messenger, called a **pheromone,** is considered an "ecto-hormone," because it is transported to the outside of an animal and can cause a behavioral or physiological change in another individual. Pheromones serve many different purposes. They include territorial pheromones, such as those found in dogs' urine, that mark the boundaries of a territory (**FIGURE 24-4**); alarm pheromones, such as those that signal the presence of a predator and can trigger aggression or flight in a group of individuals; and trail-marking pheromones, such as those produced by ants that serve as a guide to the nest. The first pheromones discovered were those signaling sexual receptivity. In some butterfly species, for example, males can

FIGURE 24-4 **High hopes.** The dog marks its territory and also exaggerates its size by lifting its leg during urination.

detect a female's sex pheromones from more than six miles away and fly in the direction of increasing pheromone concentration to locate the female.

TAKE-HOME MESSAGE 24·2

Hormones are chemical messengers, secreted into the circulatory system by endocrine cells and endocrine glands, that influence the actions of target cells elsewhere in the body, as part of an internal communication and regulation system.

24·3 Hormones can regulate target tissues in different ways.

If you turn on a radio, you can hear music. This is because, somewhere, a radio station is broadcasting a signal and your radio picks up that signal. If you turn the radio off, the music stops. The signal from the radio station, however, is still there. But without the proper receiver, the signal goes unnoticed. Hormones function much like radio signals. Glands produce and release hormones, which then make their way through the body, often distributed by the bloodstream, and bump into cells throughout the body. But, like a person without a radio, a cell doesn't respond to a hormone unless it has a specific receptor for that hormone. The hormone may even diffuse right through a cell that has no intracellular receptors, without any effect.

There are dozens of hormones and even more ways that they regulate target tissues, but the general process by which hormones affect a particular cell doesn't vary much.

1. **Signal is sent.** A hormone is released by a gland.

2. **Signal is received.** Although the hormone has no effect on most tissues it comes in contact with, cells with the proper receptor in their cytoplasm or on their plasma membrane receive the signal.

3. **Cell responds.** When the hormone binds to an appropriate receptor, it causes a response in the target cell. The response can be a change in gene expression in the target cell's nucleus, which may cause the cell to start (or stop) producing a protein, or may alter the rate at which it produces the protein. A single hormone may cause different responses in different target cells.

Most hormones are one of two types: (1) the peptide and protein hormones (such as insulin), which are chains of amino acids, or (2) the steroid hormones (such as estrogen and testosterone), which are lipids, most of which are synthesized from cholesterol. Differences in the chemical structure of these two hormone types determine whether a hormone can pass through the cell membrane (**FIGURE 24-5**). Peptide and protein hormones, the most common type of hormones, are water-soluble, as opposed to lipid-soluble. This means they cannot pass through membranes, which are high in lipids and hydrophobic. Because steroid hormones are built from cholesterol, which is a lipid, they are lipid-soluble. They diffuse right through cell membranes and into the cytoplasm.

The chemical structure of the hormone also determines how it regulates activity in a target tissue. For example, the receptors for peptide and protein hormones are embedded within, and extend through, cell membranes. Once a peptide or protein hormone binds to a receptor on the outside of the cell, it alters the receptor (perhaps changing its shape) and causes any one of a number of changes within the cell (into which the receptor extends). The hormone may activate an enzyme, initiating or speeding a reaction in the cell. Or it may alter the cell membrane's permeability, facilitating absorption or secretion of certain molecules. Or it may alter proteins within the cell, causing them to move into the nucleus and bind directly to the DNA, influencing

the rate of transcription of one or more genes (turning on or turning off, for example, the cell's production of some protein products).

Steroid hormones, on the other hand, pass through the cell membrane and bind to receptors in the cytoplasm or nucleus of target cells. If binding occurs in the cytoplasm, the hormone-receptor complex generally passes into the nucleus. Once in the nucleus, it may bind to the DNA, influencing the rate of transcription of one or more genes.

By traveling through the bloodstream, steroid hormones and peptide and protein hormones secreted by glands in one part of the body are able to regulate cell function in another part of the body. However, some glands produce regulators that act more locally. Called **paracrine regulators,** these molecules generally diffuse from the tissue in which they are produced into nearby tissue, binding to receptors on or in neighboring cells and influencing their activity. *Prostaglandins* are one of the most important and common groups of paracrine regulators, produced by almost every cell and nearly every organ in an animal's body. Prostaglandins have numerous effects, such as causing dilation or constriction of blood vessels and affecting tissue inflammation.

FIGURE 24-5 Most hormones belong to one of two main groups, differing in chemical properties. Hormones influence gene expression in different ways, depending on their chemical structure.

One of the chief reasons that aspirin is such an effective pain reliever is that it inhibits an enzyme necessary for the production of prostaglandins (**FIGURE 24-6**). As a consequence, aspirin reduces inflammation (and the pain that often accompanies it). But, because aspirin also inhibits another, similar enzyme that is involved in maintaining the lining of the stomach, taking too much aspirin can cause stomach bleeding and other problems. The development of the drug celecoxib, sold as Celebrex, has been hugely beneficial to people suffering from arthritis, who need regular, long-term anti-inflammation medication. Celecoxib inhibits the prostaglandin-producing enzyme without inhibiting the stomach-lining-maintaining enzyme, making long-term use of this painkiller possible.

Q Why might long-term, heavy use of aspirin cause stomach bleeding?

Unlike hormones, paracrine regulators—such as prostaglandins—influence cells nearby or adjacent to the cells in which they are produced. Prostaglandins, which influence nearby tissue in many ways, have been implicated in causing painful inflammation that is associated with arthritis.

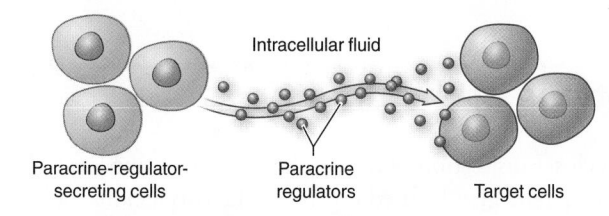

Intracellular fluid

Paracrine-regulator-secreting cells

Paracrine regulators

Target cells

FIGURE 24-6 Arthritis hurts. Prostaglandins can cause sometimes painful inflammation in the body.

TAKE-HOME MESSAGE 24·3

Hormones can regulate the activities of a target tissue only if the cells have a receptor for the hormone. Most hormones are one of two types: (1) peptide and protein hormones, which cannot pass through cell membranes and so interact with receptors embedded in the membrane, or (2) steroid hormones, which can diffuse through cell membranes, then interact with their receptors in the cytoplasm or nucleus of the target cell. Both types of hormones, once bound to a receptor, cause changes in the target cell, such as influencing the rate of transcription of genes.

24·4–24·5 Hormones are produced in glands throughout the body.

A pituitary gland cell producing growth hormone. The hormone is in the numerous granules (brown) within the cell cytoplasm (yellow).

24·4 The hypothalamus controls secretions of the pituitary.

As we have seen, animals have both the nervous and endocrine systems to send signals and regulate body functions in response to their external environment. And although one system or the other tends to be more effective for particular tasks, there is considerable interaction between the two. The **hypothalamus,** part of the underside of the brain, functions as a liaison between the nervous and endocrine systems (**FIGURE 24-7**). It receives input from neurons throughout the brain and the rest of the body, and using this information about the external environment and the physiological state of the body, it sends out the appropriate hormones (and nervous signals) to regulate nearly every aspect of the organism's physiology, including body temperature, hunger, thirst, and water balance.

Attached to the hypothalamus by a thin stalk is a gland about the size of a pea, called the **pituitary gland.** Signals from the hypothalamus directly influence the pituitary gland. The hypothalamus may release hormones that cause the pituitary to increase its production and release of hormones. Or the hypothalamus may direct the pituitary to reduce or stop the release of hormones.

On closer inspection of the pituitary gland, it appears to be two separate glands fused together. The two regions look different, originate from different embryonic tissues, produce different hormones, and are regulated differently. We consider the two regions separately.

The **posterior pituitary** has a fibrous appearance, because it contains a large amount of nervous tissue, particularly axons coming straight from the hypothalamus—from which the posterior pituitary develops. The posterior pituitary produces no hormones of its own. Instead, two important peptide hormones are produced in neurons within the hypothalamus and travel down the axon tracts into the posterior pituitary, from which they are released.

1. **Oxytocin,** the "cuddle hormone," discussed in Section 24-1, influences people's trust in others and increases the propensity to form social attachments, as well as directing the ejection (or "let-down") of milk for nursing babies and stimulating muscular contractions in the uterus during childbirth.

2. **Antidiuretic hormone (ADH)** influences water retention by the kidneys. With increased levels of

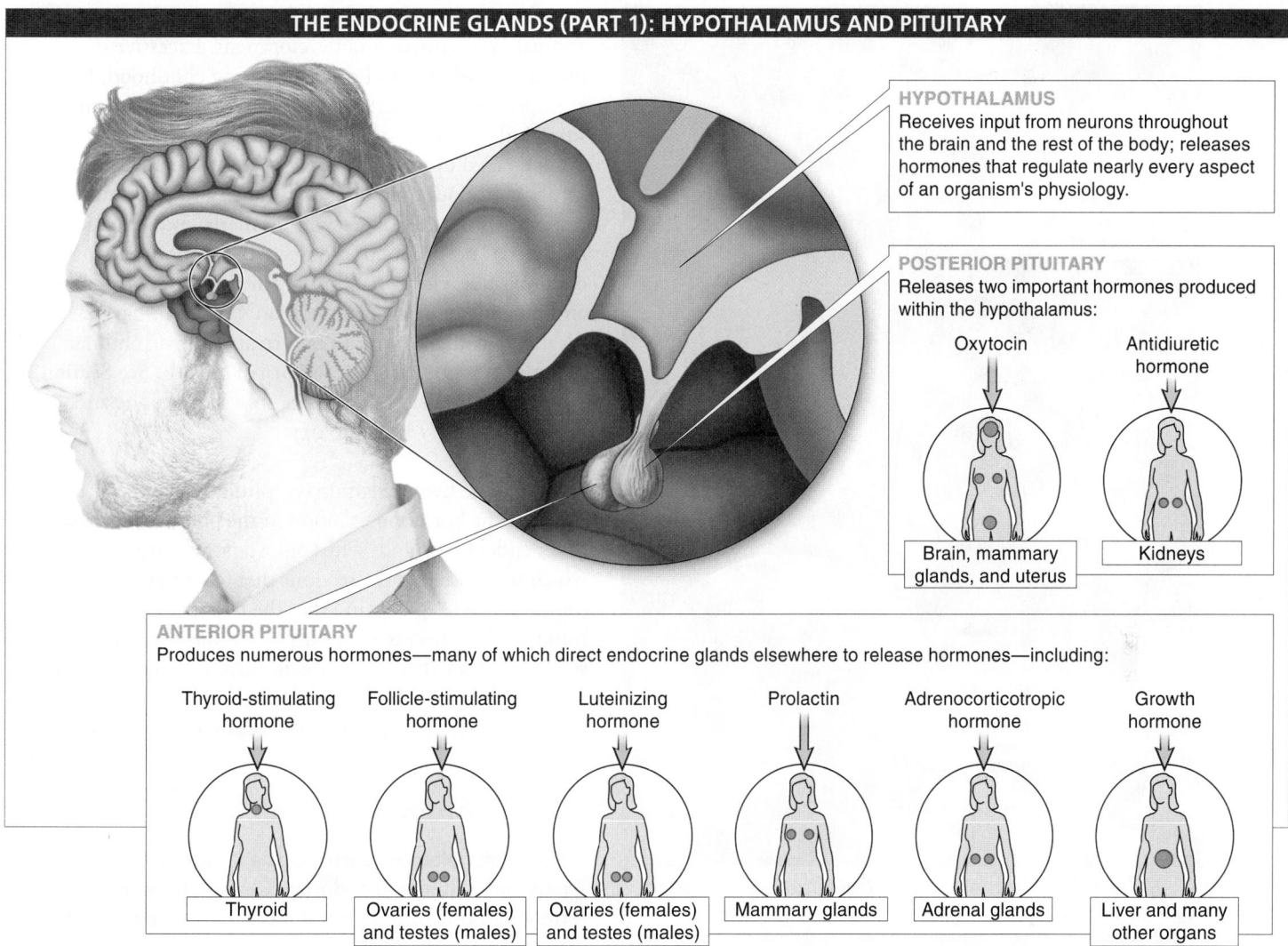

FIGURE 24-7 Functions of the glands of the endocrine system: hypothalamus and pituitary.

ADH, more water is saved, reducing the amount of urine produced while increasing its concentration.

The **anterior pituitary** has a more glandular appearance than the posterior pituitary, developing not from nervous tissue but rather from epithelial cells near the roof of the mouth during embryonic development. The anterior pituitary produces numerous hormones in response to commands by the hypothalamus. Many of the anterior pituitary hormones direct endocrine glands elsewhere to release hormones. Some of the most important hormones produced by the anterior pituitary in mammals include the following:

1. **Thyroid-stimulating hormone (TSH)** causes the thyroid to produce thyroxine, important in cellular respiration, which we discuss further in Section 24-5.

2. **Follicle-stimulating hormone (FSH)** stimulates follicles in the ovaries to begin development, and **luteinizing hormone (LH)** triggers ovulation. In males, FSH stimulates sperm maturation and LH stimulates testosterone production.

3. **Prolactin** stimulates the mammary glands to produce milk.

4. **Adrenocorticotropic hormone (ACTH),** also known as **corticotropin,** stimulates the adrenal glands to produce cortisol and other stress-related hormones.

5. **Growth hormone** has several effects, including stimulating the liver to release chemicals that spur the growth of bones, cartilage, and many other tissues.

Excessive production of growth hormone during childhood can cause extreme growth, with some individuals reaching 8 feet in height.

Reduced production or an absence of growth hormone during childhood can lead to pituitary dwarfism.

Improper functioning of the pituitary can lead to anomalies in growth and development.

FIGURE 24-8 Pituitary malfunction can affect stature in humans.

Improper functioning of the pituitary can lead to some anomalies in growth and development. Excessive production of growth hormone during childhood, for example, can cause extreme growth, called gigantism, with some individuals reaching 8 feet in height (**FIGURE 24-8**). If the increased exposure to growth hormone doesn't occur until adulthood, only the hands, face, and feet tend to respond with unusual growth. Similarly, individuals with reduced or no production of growth hormone during childhood develop a condition called pituitary dwarfism, and they may not grow more than 4 feet tall. Early diagnosis of this condition and treatment with human growth hormone can restore normal growth. See Section 5-11 for a discussion of human growth hormone and recombinant DNA technology.

Although the hypothalamus and pituitary gland control much of the hormone secretion in the body, there are several other endocrine glands with important regulatory roles, which we explore in the sections that follow. And it is important to keep in mind that the hypothalamus and pituitary don't necessarily *control* all of the hormone secretions; they themselves are, in turn, regulated in large part by the glands that they regulate, through numerous feedback loops. (See Section 20-9 for a discussion of feedback loops.)

TAKE-HOME MESSAGE 24·4

The hypothalamus functions as a liaison between the nervous system and endocrine system. It receives input from neurons throughout the brain and the rest of the body, and using this information about the internal and external environments, it sends out the appropriate hormones (and nervous signals), often directing the pituitary gland to release hormones with important regulatory control over body tissues.

24·5 Other endocrine glands also produce and secrete hormones.

As we've seen, the hypothalamus and pituitary gland play large roles in the regulation of body functions in animals, but they are joined by many other glands in using hormones to signal and regulate physiology. From the anxiety some people feel about public speaking, to the changes in sleep patterns after flying to a new time zone, to the changes in metabolism that accompany aging, endocrine glands throughout the body are responsible for detecting and

responding to signals reflecting an organism's internal and external environments. Here we explore the signals of some of the most important of these other endocrine glands (**FIGURE 24-9**).

Adrenal glands Regulating an organism's response to stress is largely a function of the secretions of the two **adrenal glands,** which sit just above the kidneys and secrete

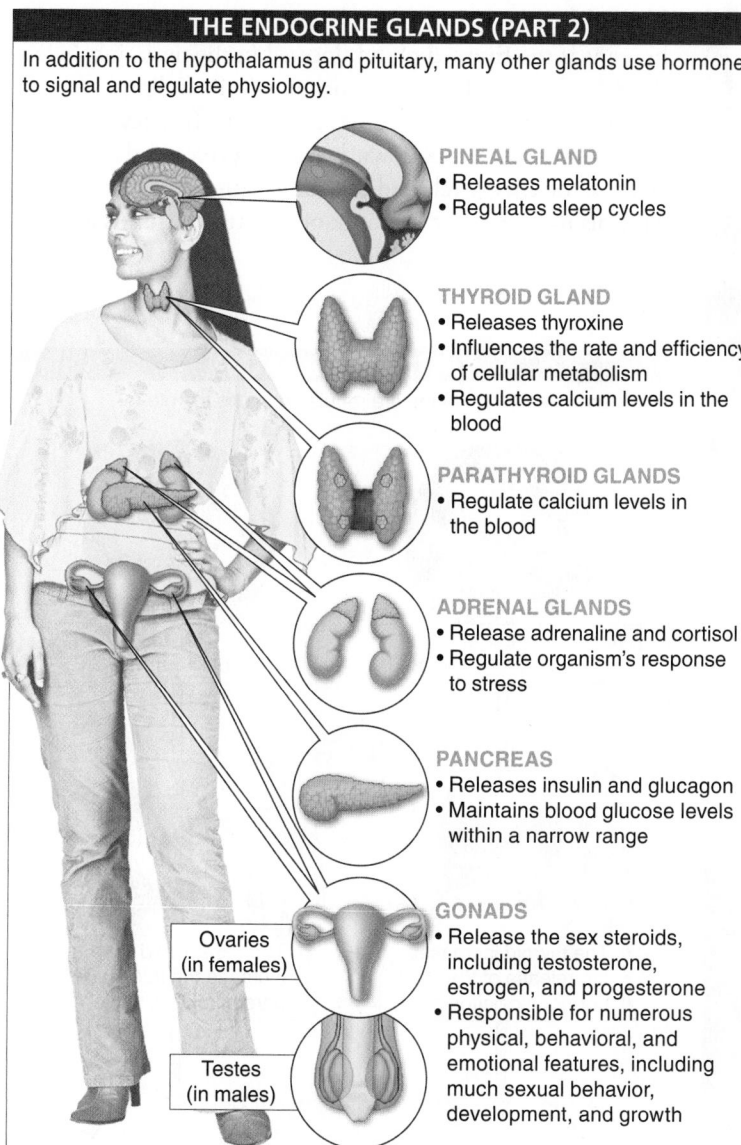

In addition to the hypothalamus and pituitary, many other glands use hormones to signal and regulate physiology.

PINEAL GLAND
• Releases melatonin
• Regulates sleep cycles

THYROID GLAND
• Releases thyroxine
• Influences the rate and efficiency of cellular metabolism
• Regulates calcium levels in the blood

PARATHYROID GLANDS
• Regulate calcium levels in the blood

ADRENAL GLANDS
• Release adrenaline and cortisol
• Regulate organism's response to stress

PANCREAS
• Releases insulin and glucagon
• Maintains blood glucose levels within a narrow range

GONADS
Ovaries (in females)
Testes (in males)
• Release the sex steroids, including testosterone, estrogen, and progesterone
• Responsible for numerous physical, behavioral, and emotional features, including much sexual behavior, development, and growth

FIGURE 24-9 Functions of the glands of the endocrine system: pineal, thyroid, parathyroids, adrenals, pancreas, and gonads.

breakdown in the liver and skeletal muscles, the release of stored fatty acids, and a dilation of bronchioles in the lungs that enables greater absorption of oxygen, for delivery to needy tissues.

The stress pathways are modulated by negative feedback loops. As an animal takes action in response to a stressful situation and the source of the stress is then removed, the secretions of cortisol and adrenaline are reduced. This is how the stress response usually works in nature. But when there is no outlet by which an organism can deal with the stress, long-term consequences of a chronic stress response include ulcers, cardiovascular problems, decreased immune function, and illness. With an increased understanding of the stress response and its function as a short-term physiological state that helps organisms quickly and effectively respond to stressful situations, researchers are gaining insights into how to better treat anxiety.

Pineal gland The 17th century philosopher René Descartes believed that the **pineal gland** was where the soul connected with the body— which he believed largely because the pea-sized gland is located near the center of the brain, is singular (that is, there's just one, not one on the left side of the brain and another on the right), and, so he thought, is unique to humans (it isn't). This view has been abandoned by scientists (and we now know that the pineal gland is present in all vertebrates), but there's still considerable scientific interest in this gland. The pineal gland has neuron connections with the retina of the eye, and it controls secretion of the hormone melatonin, which is derived from the amino acid tryptophan and affects diurnal-nocturnal wake and sleep patterns, called *circadian cycles*.

Q Why is adrenaline given to people experiencing an asthma attack?

the hormones cortisol and adrenaline (also called epinephrine), among others. Simply the sight of a predator is enough to initiate the "fight-or-flight" response— the secretions of adrenaline and cortisol that prepare the body for action (**FIGURE 24-10**). Within seconds, these secretions—in a case of positive feedback—can cause goose bumps, an increased heart rate, an increased rate of glycogen

> *My whole aim in life is to get near to God, that is, to get nearer to myself. That's why it doesn't matter to me what road I take. But music is very important. Music is a tonic for the pineal gland. Music isn't Bach or Beethoven; music is the can opener of the soul. It makes you terribly quiet inside, makes you aware that there's a roof to your being.*
> —HENRY MILLER, *Tropic of Cancer*, 1934

Simply the sight of a predator is enough to initiate the "fight-or-flight" response in an animal, and within seconds, secretions of adrenaline and cortisol generate a number of physiological changes that prepare the body for action.

FIGURE 24-10 Who will win in this conflict? Adrenal glands influence the fight-or-flight response in animals.

Although the exact mechanism by which melatonin influences circadian cycles is not understood, it has been shown to have slight benefits in synchronizing individuals' sleep and wake cycles to the environment and in treating some types of insomnia, and melatonin is now sold throughout the United States.

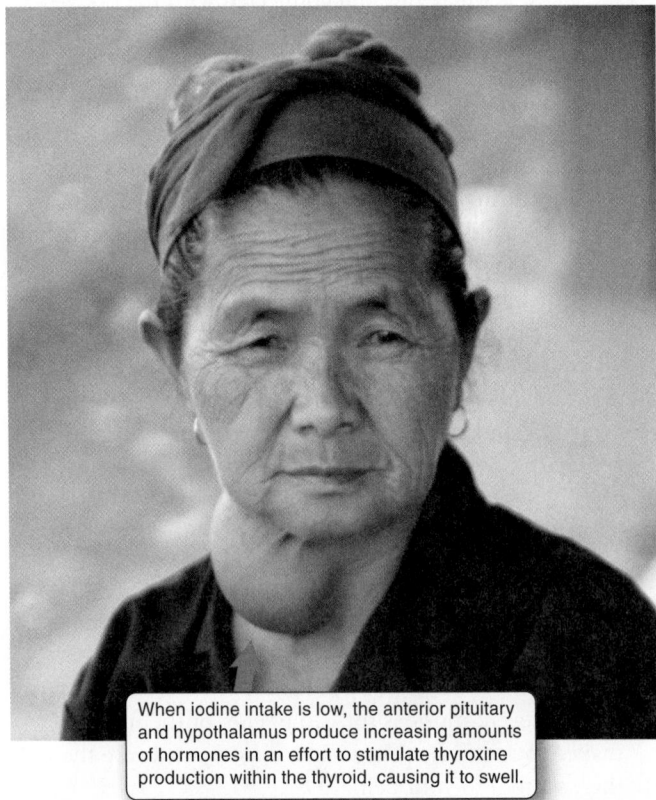

When iodine intake is low, the anterior pituitary and hypothalamus produce increasing amounts of hormones in an effort to stimulate thyroxine production within the thyroid, causing it to swell.

FIGURE 24-11 An enlargement of the thyroid gland in the neck is called a goiter.

Thyroid gland One of the largest endocrine glands in humans is the **thyroid gland,** located in the neck, just below the Adam's apple. It secretes hormones—including **thyroxine**—that influence the speed and efficiency with which body cells break down macromolecules in the diet and use the energy released to produce proteins. In short, it controls most of what we think of as metabolism. As a

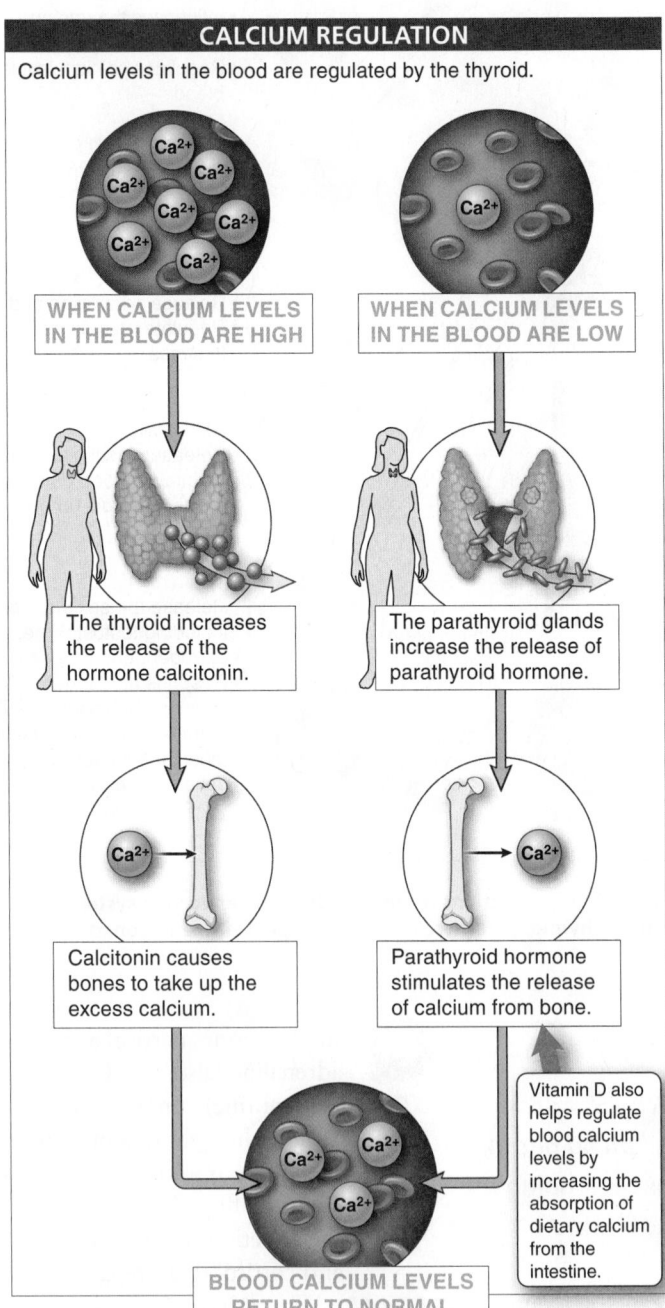

CALCIUM REGULATION

Calcium levels in the blood are regulated by the thyroid.

WHEN CALCIUM LEVELS IN THE BLOOD ARE HIGH

WHEN CALCIUM LEVELS IN THE BLOOD ARE LOW

The thyroid increases the release of the hormone calcitonin.

The parathyroid glands increase the release of parathyroid hormone.

Calcitonin causes bones to take up the excess calcium.

Parathyroid hormone stimulates the release of calcium from bone.

Vitamin D also helps regulate blood calcium levels by increasing the absorption of dietary calcium from the intestine.

BLOOD CALCIUM LEVELS RETURN TO NORMAL

FIGURE 24-12 The body's use of calcium is regulated by the thyroid and parathyroid glands.

consequence, poor thyroid function is believed to be at the root of many metabolic disorders, with underactive thyroid responsible for fatigue and weight gain, and overactive thyroid responsible for jitteriness, rapid heartbeat, weight loss, and irritability.

Goiter is a common health problem caused by an enlargement of the thyroid gland (**FIGURE 24-11**). There are several causes of goiters, and they are particularly common in areas with low iodine consumption. When iodine intake is low, the thyroid is unable to produce thyroxine (which contains iodine). This causes thyroxine levels in the body to drop. In the absence of the normal negative feedback telling the body to slow its production of thyroxine, the hypothalamus and anterior pituitary produce increasing amounts, respectively, of thyroxine-releasing hormone and thyroxine-stimulating hormone. These cause the thyroid to swell into a visible lump—a goiter—as it tries unsuccessfully to make thyroxine. In the United States, the widespread use of table salt fortified with iodine prevents most iodine deficiencies, but they are common in Asia, Central Africa, and parts of South America.

The thyroid also regulates levels of calcium in the blood. Calcium is necessary for building and maintaining bones and teeth, and it influences the functioning of nerves and muscles. When there is too much calcium in the blood, the thyroid increases its release of **calcitonin,** a hormone particularly important in babies and children, which causes bones to take up the excess calcium. Additionally, embedded in the surface of the thyroid are the four small **parathyroid glands.** They produce parathyroid hormone, which plays a central role in regulating calcium levels in adults (**FIGURE 24-12**). Throughout life, bone is continually broken down and remade as minerals are lost and added. Parathyroid hormone is important in stimulating much of this continued turnover of bone, including reabsorption of old bone and production of new bone. Parathyroid hormone further reduces calcium loss in the urine, regulates the release of calcium from bone, and in conjunction with vitamin D (from the diet and produced in response to sun exposure), helps increase the body's ability to utilize the calcium supplied in the diet.

Pancreas Located next to the stomach and connected to the small intestine via a short duct, the **pancreas** is an endocrine gland that is most important in controlling the levels of blood glucose. As we saw in Section 22-17, the pancreas maintains blood glucose within a narrow range—a typical blood glucose concentration in humans is 90 mg/ 100 mL—through the coordinated secretions of insulin and glucagon (**FIGURE 24-13**).

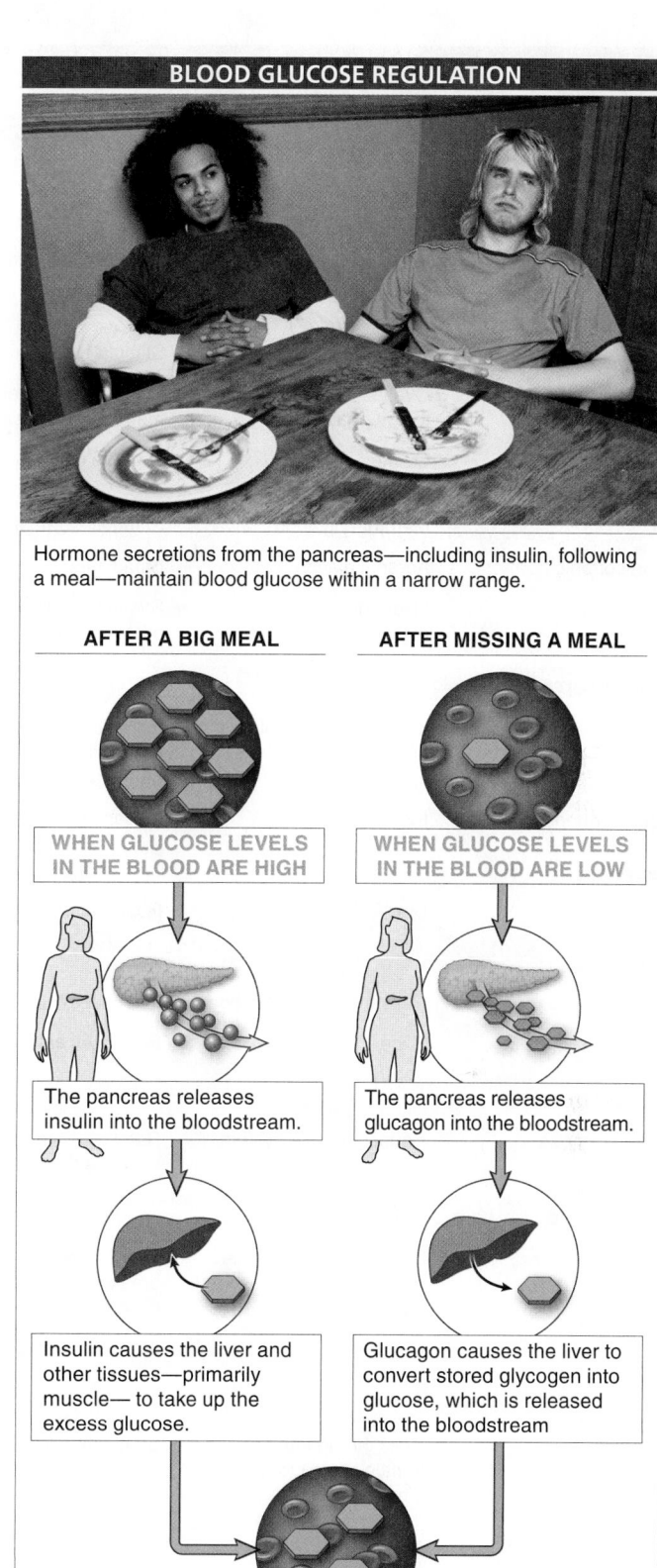

BLOOD GLUCOSE REGULATION

Hormone secretions from the pancreas—including insulin, following a meal—maintain blood glucose within a narrow range.

AFTER A BIG MEAL

WHEN GLUCOSE LEVELS IN THE BLOOD ARE HIGH

The pancreas releases insulin into the bloodstream.

Insulin causes the liver and other tissues—primarily muscle— to take up the excess glucose.

AFTER MISSING A MEAL

WHEN GLUCOSE LEVELS IN THE BLOOD ARE LOW

The pancreas releases glucagon into the bloodstream.

Glucagon causes the liver to convert stored glycogen into glucose, which is released into the bloodstream

BLOOD GLUCOSE LEVELS RETURN TO NORMAL

FIGURE 24-13 Even after a heavy meal, a healthy person can maintain blood glucose levels within a narrow range.

OVERVIEW OF THE ENDOCRINE GLANDS AND THEIR HORMONES

ENDOCRINE GLAND AND HORMONE	TARGET AREA	PRIMARY FUNCTION
HYPOTHALAMUS		
Regulatory hormones	Anterior pituitary	Increase the production and release of hormones, or reduce or stop the release of hormones
Posterior pituitary hormones	Posterior pituitary	(See posterior pituitary hormones below)
ANTERIOR PITUITARY		
Thyroid-stimulating hormone	Thyroid	Stimulates the production of thyroxine, important in cellular respiration
Follicle-stimulating hormone	Ovaries (females), testes (males)	Stimulates follicles in the ovaries to begin development (females); stimulates sperm maturation (males)
Luteinizing hormone	Ovaries (females), testes (males)	Triggers ovulation (females); stimulates testosterone production (males)
Prolactin	Mammary glands	Stimulates the production of milk
Adrenocorticotropic hormone	Adrenal glands	Stimulates the production of cortisol and other stress-related hormones
Growth hormone	Liver and many other organs	Stimulates the release of chemicals that spur the growth of bones, cartilage, and many other tissues
POSTERIOR PITUITARY		
Oxytocin	Brain, mammary glands, uterus	Influences people's trust in others and increases the propensity to form social attachments; directs the ejection of milk for nursing babies and stimulates muscular contractions in the uterus during childbirth
Antidiuretic hormone	Kidneys	Influences water retention by the kidneys
PINEAL GLAND		
Melatonin	Brain	Regulates sleep cycles
THYROID GLAND		
Thyroxine	Cells throughout the body	Influences the rate and efficiency of cellular metabolism
Calcitonin	Bone	Regulates calcium levels in the blood
PARATHYROID GLANDS		
Parathyroid hormone	Bone, digestive system	Regulates the release of calcium from bone, and in conjunction with vitamin D, helps increase the body's ability to utilize calcium in the diet
ADRENAL GLANDS		
Adrenaline	Smooth muscle, cardiac muscle, skeletal muscle, blood vessels	Initiates the body's response to stress: increases heart rate, increases rate of glycogen breakdown, initiates dilation of the bronchioles in the lungs enabling greater absorption of oxygen
Cortisol	Cells throughout the body	Initiates and modulates the body's response to long-term stress; raises blood glucose level
GONADS		
Estrogen	Cells throughout the body, female reproductive structures	Stimulates development of female secondary sex characteristics and growth of sex organs at puberty; stimulates monthly preparation of uterus for pregnancy
Progesterone	Uterus, breasts	Stimulates development of breasts; completes preparation of uterus for pregnancy
Testosterone	Cells throughout the body, male reproductive structures	Stimulates development of male secondary sex characteristics and growth spurt at puberty; stimulates development of sex organs; stimulates sperm production

FIGURE 24-14 Summary of endocrine glands, hormones, and their primary functions.

Following a meal (particularly one rich in carbohydrates), the concentration of blood glucose rises. This stimulates release of **insulin** by the pancreas. Insulin in the bloodstream causes the liver and other tissues—primarily muscle—to take up glucose, which reduces the blood glucose level. As blood glucose levels fall, there is a reduction in insulin secretion.

Conversely, after a few hours of fasting, the blood glucose level gradually drops. The reduced blood glucose triggers release of **glucagon** by the pancreas. Glucagon has the reverse effect of insulin, causing the liver to convert stored glycogen into glucose, which is released into the bloodstream. Rising blood glucose concentration then causes the pancreas to reduce its glucagon secretion, maintaining homeostasis through negative feedback.

Gonads The sex steroids, including **testosterone, estrogen,** and **progesterone,** are produced largely by the gonads—the testes in males and the ovaries in females. These hormones are responsible for numerous physical, behavioral, and emotional features, including much sexual behavior and growth, sexual development (embryonically, in puberty, and continuing into adulthood), and maintenance of gamete production throughout an organism's reproductive life. In Chapter 25 we discuss the sex hormones in detail.

A summary of the major animal hormones and their actions is in **FIGURE 24-14**.

In the next few sections, we investigate some of the gonadal hormones and see how closely linked they are to athletic performance and the attributes necessary to excel physically. We'll also see a dark side to hormones, in the dramatic physical changes and improvements in athletic performance resulting from illegal use of hormone supplements. We also note the extreme health consequences that accompany such hormone abuse.

TAKE-HOME MESSAGE 24·5

Endocrine glands throughout the body are responsible for detecting and responding to internal and external signals. The adrenal glands regulate responses to stress. The pineal gland regulates sleep cycles. The thyroid gland influences cellular metabolism. The pancreas maintains blood glucose. And hormones from the gonads are responsible for many physical, behavioral, and emotional features, such as sexual behavior, development, and growth.

24·6–24·10 Hormones influence nearly every facet of an organism.

Growth hormones influence stature.

24·6
Hormones can affect physique and physical performance.

The Tour de France is one of the world's most grueling tests of strength and endurance. The annual bike race occurs over three weeks, as riders cover more than 2,200 miles (3,500 km), in 21 separate stages. In 2006, an American rider named Floyd Landis, in 11th place overall, turned in a performance in stage 17 that was so improbably fast that some commentators called it "the greatest performance ever." His win brought him within 30 seconds of the overall lead and propelled him, over the final four stages, to the Tour de France victory (**FIGURE 24-15**).

But Landis's glory was not to last. Less than a week after his victory, it was announced that he had tested positive for unusually high levels of testosterone, which a second test confirmed. The typical ratio of testosterone relative to the hormone epitestosterone in men is 1:1 or 2:1. While the Tour de France allows ratios of up to 4:1, Landis's level was 11:1. Moreover, the lab tests detected a synthetic form of testosterone in his bloodstream, in addition to the naturally produced hormone. Landis was stripped of his title and banned from the sport for two years.

While the revelation that a competitor had resorted to illegal supplementation in an effort to boost physical performance

FIGURE 24-15 Unsporting conduct. Many athletes have tested positive for illegal testosterone supplementation.

After winning the Tour de France in 2006, Floyd Landis was found to have unusually high levels of testosterone (and to have synthetic testosterone) in his blood and was stripped of his title and temporarily banned from the sport.

For years, competitors have resorted to illegal steroid supplementation in an effort to boost physical performance.

was disappointing, it was certainly not a new or isolated occurrence. The recent history of sports is littered with drug scandals, usually involving testosterone or its variants. Olympic gold medalist Ben Johnson, for example, was stripped of his medal and the world record in 1988 when he tested positive for a synthetic steroid hormone similar to testosterone. In 2003, 104 Major League Baseball players (of 750 in the league) tested positive for illegal performance-enhancing drugs, and in 2005, 111 professional football players did. And the scandals are not limited to men. Marion Jones won five Olympic gold medals in 2000, only to have all of them taken away when she admitted that she had illegally taken performance-enhancing drugs, including a muscle-building "designer steroid" called tetrahydrogestrinone, or "the clear."

Q *Do steroids affect a person's physique and performance? If so, how?*

Testosterone and many structurally similar steroid hormones definitely affect the composition of the body. Experimental studies of testosterone supplementation in men reported weight gains of 5–12.5 pounds within 10 weeks. The gains were due primarily to increases in lean muscle mass in the shoulders, upper chest, and upper arms, areas with the highest concentrations of testosterone receptors. In randomized, controlled studies, researchers also documented strength increases of 5% to 20% in both experienced and novice athletes.

Testosterone has also been shown to influence locomotor performance—speed and endurance, in particular—in animals. In an experimental study on lizards (the northern fence lizard, *Sceloporus undulatus*), two to three weeks of supplemental testosterone caused a 24% increase in sprinting speed and a 17% increase in stamina.

Such testosterone "doping" causes changes in physique and physical performance by activating processes that lead to increased muscle mass. Produced primarily by the testes in males (but also by the adrenal glands of both males and females), testosterone binds to receptors in target cells, then moves to the nucleus and influences gene expression (see Figure 24-5). The cells increase their protein synthesis and grow, resulting—in the case of muscle cells—in increased muscle mass (and simultaneously reducing the rate of production of fat-storage cells). Supplemental testosterone also increases cell division among satellite cells, small cells found in muscle tissue that aid in muscle repair. Additional responses to testosterone supplementation include the development of secondary sex characteristics, including chest and facial hair and a deepened voice—effects seen in both males and females (**FIGURE 24-16**).

THE EFFECTS OF TESTOSTERONE

INCREASE IN LEAN MUSCLE MASS

IMPROVED SPEED AND STAMINA

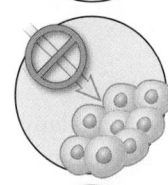
REDUCED PRODUCTION OF FAT-STORAGE CELLS

DEVELOPMENT OF SECONDARY SEX CHARACTERISTICS

THE ADVERSE EFFECTS OF SUPPLEMENTAL TESTOSTERONE

- Increased blood pressure and risk of heart disease
- Kidney and liver damage
- Development of breast tissue in males
- Atrophy (shrinkage) of the testes
- Increased risk of many types of cancer

FIGURE 24-16 The normal effects of testosterone in the body, and the harmful effects of testosterone supplementation.

There are numerous adverse effects to supplemental steroid hormones, including increased blood pressure and risk of heart disease, as well as damage to the kidneys and the liver (where the steroids are metabolized), development of breast tissue in males, and atrophy (shrinkage) of the testes as negative feedback leads to reduced production of testosterone in response to the increased levels of circulating testosterone. Also, because testosterone increases cell division—increasing muscle mass, for example—it increases the risk of unrestrained cell division in many tissues and, consequently, increases the risk of many types of cancer.

TAKE-HOME MESSAGE 24·6

Hormones affect a person's physique and physical performance by influencing gene expression and protein synthesis in cells with testosterone receptors. For example, testosterone increases muscle mass while reducing fat storage and can increase speed and stamina.

HORMONES ARE CHEMICAL MESSENGERS • HORMONES ARE PRODUCED IN GLANDS • WIDE-RANGING EFFECTS OF HORMONES • CHEMICALS CAN DISRUPT HORMONE FUNCTION

963

24·7

Hormones can affect mood.

In a randomized, controlled, double-blind study, researchers injected 47 men each week for six weeks with large amounts of testosterone and made numerous measurements of each subject's physical state. The testosterone caused more than just physical changes, though; after six weeks, one subject said, "I feel great! I'm confident, positive, happy, and productive. I want to be on this stuff forever!" The researchers said that this was a common response among the subjects.

Not only do hormones affect our physical traits and performance, they can also influence how we *feel*. Many hormones have pronounced effects on **moods,** defined as relatively long-lasting emotional states (shorter-lasting than a person's temperament, but longer-lasting and less specific than a single emotion). Here we describe just a few of the documented effects of hormones on mood in humans.

Estrogen In women, the levels of estrogen in the bloodstream change throughout life. And the incidence of depression follows a similar pattern. The large increases in estrogen levels at puberty, the sharp drop-off in estrogen levels after a woman gives birth, and the reduced estrogen levels at the onset of menopause are all associated with increased occurrence of depression (**FIGURE 24-17**). Estrogen as part of hormone replacement therapy is effective at reducing depression in women going through menopause.

Interestingly, researchers investigating the effect of hormones on mood discovered that women exposed to a male partner's semen during sex rated their mood as happier than those using condoms. The effect is believed to be a consequence of the mood-altering effects of the testosterone and estrogen that are present in semen and are absorbed through the vagina. (With unprotected sex, however, the potential for sexually transmitted diseases or unwanted pregnancy must also be factored into any long-term assessment of mood, complicating the research findings.)

Testosterone Many studies have demonstrated a link between testosterone and mood in human males, including increased self-esteem and a sense of overflowing with new ideas. In the study discussed above, the men were described by their significant others as energetic, euphoric, confident, and charismatic. In a small number of cases, however, subjects became uncharacteristically aggressive and exhibited verbal hostility. The researchers even had to withdraw one subject

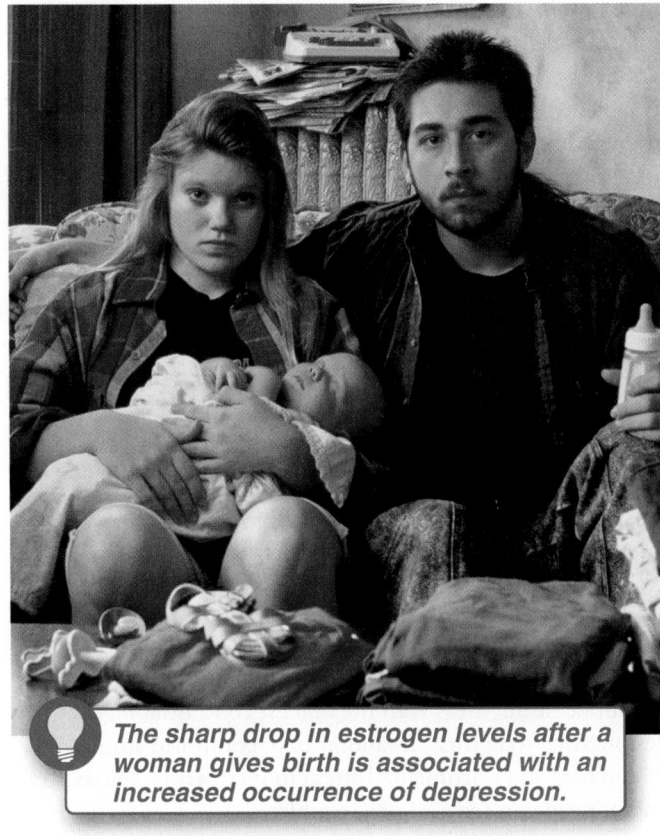

The sharp drop in estrogen levels after a woman gives birth is associated with an increased occurrence of depression.

FIGURE 24-17 Drastic changes in estrogen levels affect mood. For example, the changes can cause "the baby blues" in some women shortly after giving birth.

from the study when he became "alarmingly" aggressive—consistent with anecdotal claims of so-called 'roid rage resulting from supplemental testosterone.

Several studies on competitive male athletes have documented that testosterone levels—and the mood changes they influence—rise prior to a competition. After the contest, testosterone levels in the losers of the competition drop quickly and dramatically, while testosterone levels in the winners remain high and sometimes even increase (**FIGURE 24-18**).

Q How can the exhilaration of watching your favorite team win a game resemble the feeling you get from winning a sports contest yourself?

Recent studies reveal that sports fans share in this biological "victory dance." Measurements of testosterone levels in male fans of Brazilian and Italian soccer teams during World Cup finals (and replicated in fans of a college basketball team) revealed

Exposure to cortisol for two weeks or more caused rodents to exhibit anxiety-like behavior, including reluctance to enter a brightly lit area.

FIGURE 24-19 Hiding in the dark. Rodents exposed to cortisol show anxious behavior.

conditions, oral melatonin can induce hypnotic, sedative-like effects and improve sleep efficiency. Other studies showed that, in comparison with placebo treatment, melatonin supplementation significantly reduced subjects' self-reported vigor, while increasing their fatigue and confusion.

Cortisol The majority of individuals suffering from Cushing's disease, a condition in which the adrenal glands release unusually large amounts of cortisol, experience depression and anxiety. Also, an atypically high number of individuals treated with cortisone (a chemical variant of cortisol) to reduce tissue inflammation suffer from anxiety and depression. As a consequence of these observations, researchers conducted a controlled study exposing rodents to cortisol in their drinking water. Two weeks or more of cortisol exposure caused the animals to take significantly longer to emerge from small, dark compartments into a brightly lit area—a measure of anxiety-like behavior in rodents—as compared with animals not exposed to the cortisol (**FIGURE 24-19**).

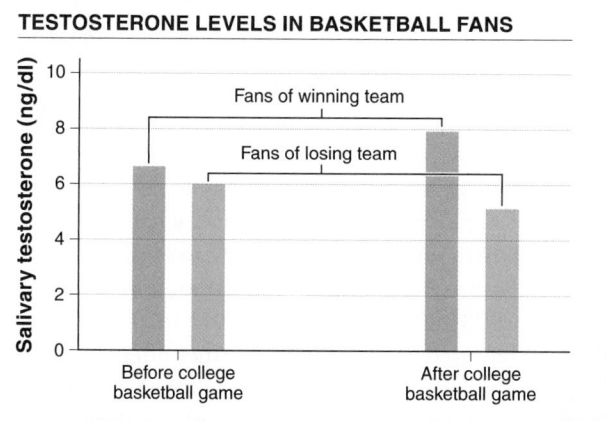

Prior to a competition, testosterone levels rise in the competitors. After the contest, levels in the losers drop quickly, while remaining high in the winners. Similar results—such as those shown below—have been reported for the testosterone levels among fans of sports teams, as well!

TESTOSTERONE LEVELS IN BASKETBALL FANS

Salivary testosterone (ng/dl)

- Fans of winning team
- Fans of losing team

Before college basketball game / After college basketball game

FIGURE 24-18 Biological victory dance. Testosterone levels surge in victorious competitors and in fans, too.

that the testosterone levels of the fans of the winning team rose, but not those of the losing team.

Melatonin In randomized, controlled, double-blind studies, researchers have demonstrated that under certain

---

TAKE-HOME MESSAGE 24·7

Many hormones, including estrogen, testosterone, melatonin, and cortisol, have pronounced effects on moods.

24·8 Hormones can affect behavior.

It can be hard to imagine how a little more or a little less of a chemical could influence an animal's behavior, but experimental research on hormones and behavior has documented literally *thousands* of such effects. The scholarly journal *Hormones and Behavior,* for example, in its 61st volume as of 2012, publishes five issues a year, each containing 25 or more articles describing laboratory and field studies on hormones and their influences on the development and expression of behaviors (**FIGURE 24-20**). In these studies, researchers take a variety of experimental approaches. Just two of these are described here.

Genetic manipulation of hormone levels. Researchers bred some lab mice that were unable to make the enzyme aromatase, which is essential to the production of estrogen. With this deficiency, the lower-estrogen animals had two striking behavioral differences: they ran excessively on their exercise wheels and, when sprayed lightly with water, spent significantly longer grooming themselves than do typical mice. Both of these behaviors are indicators of obsessive-compulsive disorder in mice.

Physiological supplementation of hormone levels. Researchers implanted testosterone capsules in male juncos, a type of songbird. These males produced a song that was more attractive to females, and they produced more offspring than control-group males that received a capsule containing no testosterone. (In similar studies, male birds with supplemented testosterone tended to have increased muscle mass and were able to establish and maintain larger territories than non-supplemented males.) The increased reproductive success did not come without a cost, however. Male birds with testosterone implants spent less time with their offspring and gave the offspring less food. The testosterone-supplemented birds were also more susceptible to disease and had shorter life spans.

The dramatic and close link between hormones and behavior has caused people to debate whether sex offenders should be castrated to modify their behavior (**FIGURE 24-21**). Whether or not castration—removal of the testes, with a resultant near-complete drop in testosterone levels—can reliably rehabilitate violent sex offenders is intensely debated. In the Czech Republic, one of the very few countries where sex offenders may be castrated, 94 prisoners underwent castration between 1998 and 2008. None of these men have been reported to commit any further offenses. Similarly, in a Danish study of 900 castrated sex offenders, the rate of repeat offense dropped to approximately 2%, from close to 80% among non-castrated sex offenders.

Q Is castration an effective and humane treatment for sex offenders?

Opponents of the castration of sex offenders argue that the evidence cannot be trusted, because it relies partly on self-reporting by the castrated men. Moreover, the opponents of castration argue that having such an option is coercive, because many convicted sex offenders will feel obligated to opt for the surgery, leading to a violation of the prisoners' rights. Some

💡 *Thousands of research articles have described the wide variety of hormone effects on behavior.*

FIGURE 24-20 The influence of hormones on behavior is an area of active scientific research.

Castrated sex offenders experience a dramatic drop in testosterone levels, but whether the procedure prevents future crimes is uncertain.

FIGURE 24-21 Is castration of convicted sex offenders an ethical procedure?

argue for the reversible form of castration by injection of chemicals that block the effects of testosterone, but this is opposed by many on the grounds that it relies on the released offenders voluntarily undergoing treatment, which they may stop at any point.

TAKE-HOME MESSAGE 24·8

Many laboratory and field studies have demonstrated the influence of hormones on the development and expression of behaviors.

24·9 Hormones can affect cognitive performance.

Repeat this phrase five times, as quickly as you can: "A box of mixed biscuits in a biscuit mixer." Researchers found that, at the midpoint in their ovulatory cycle, women in the study group could do this in about 14 seconds. During this time, women's estrogen levels are at their highest and about 50 times higher than they are in men. During the period just after menstruation, estrogen levels in women are at their lowest, but are still about 3 times higher than in men. Post-menstruation, the women took 17 seconds to repeat the tongue twister. At both times, women were able, on average, to recite the tongue twister significantly faster than men.

The methods used in this widely reported study have been criticized for several reasons, including (1) the study was not blind, because the researchers knew what phase of their reproductive cycle the subjects were in, and the subjects knew why they were being tested, and (2) actual measures of estrogen were not taken—the subjects simply self-reported where they were in their cycle. Nonetheless, this type of research has led to numerous, better-controlled research efforts to evaluate whether cognitive abilities—mental processes involving perception, memory, judgment, and reasoning—are influenced by hormones, particularly the reproductive hormones estrogen and testosterone.

Studies on the effects of hormones on cognitive performance have primarily focused on two types of measures, designed to reflect different aspects of cognition: (1) motor and verbal tasks, and (2) spatial tasks (**FIGURE 24-22**).

1. Motor and verbal tasks include tests of articulation speed, such as the tongue twister, or complex wrist and hand movements and fine-muscle movements, such as those required in surgery and machine repair.

Most tests of hormone effects on motor and non-verbal tasks involve comparisons of the performances of men and women or of girls and boys at these tasks. There is consistent and significant evidence that females perform better than males and that the disparity between male and female performances is greatest at points of high estrogen levels in the female reproductive cycle and smallest at the points of lowest estrogen levels.

2. Spatial tasks include tests such as predicting the shapes of boxes when they are unfolded and flat, and mental rotations, in which a pair of two- or three-dimensional objects are compared to see whether they represent the same object, either rotated or as a mirror image.

Repeat this sentence five times, as quickly as you can:

"A box of mixed biscuits in a biscuit mixer."

Identify which of the four shapes on the right represent the target shape on the left in alternative positions.

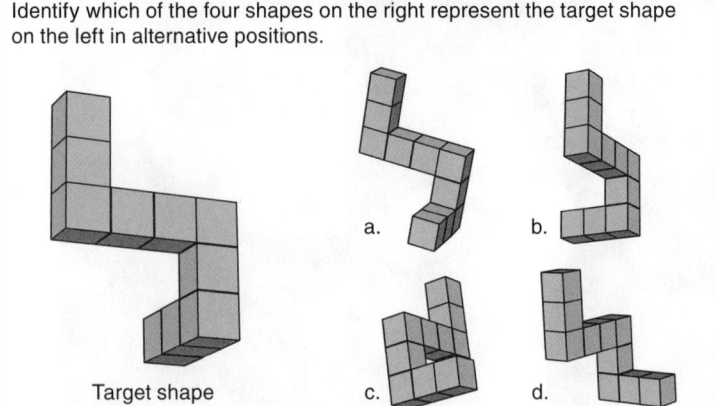

Target shape   a.   b.   c.   d.

MOTOR AND VERBAL TASKS
- Females tend to perform better than males on tests of articulation speed and fine-muscle movement.
- The disparity between male and female performance is greatest at points of high estrogen levels in the female reproductive cycle and least at the points of lowest estrogen levels.

SPATIAL TASKS
- Males tend to perform better than females on tests of spatial ability, such as mental rotations of two- or three-dimensional objects.
- Evidence suggests that this performance difference reflects effects of testosterone—although the mechanisms are unclear.

FIGURE 24-22 Different talents. Men and women have slightly different abilities in certain areas, based on the abundance or lack of the hormones testosterone and estrogen.

In humans and other animal species, performance on tests of spatial ability is, on average, higher in males than females. A large body of evidence suggests that this performance difference reflects effects of testosterone—although the mechanisms are poorly understood. Some of the suggestive findings include:

- As men get older and their testosterone levels decrease, so does their performance on tests of spatial ability.

- In older men, testosterone supplementation improves performance on spatial tasks, while administration of chemicals that reduce the production of testosterone (for treatment of prostate cancer) causes a decrease in spatial abilities.

- Women with one form of congenital adrenal hyperplasia have higher than typical levels of circulating testosterone and increased performance on tests of spatial ability.

As with tests of motor and verbal tasks, it is not clear exactly how—or whether—performance on tests of spatial ability affects individuals in contexts more relevant to everyday life. Each year since 1989, the National Geographic Society has held a "National Geography Bee" contest. In the 23 years of the contest (through 2011), 221 of the 230 finalists (and 21 of the 23 winners) have been boys (**FIGURE 24-23**). While interest in such competitions is unquestionably influenced by cultural and societal forces, researchers conducting this study suggested that the results stem from male-female differences in spatial

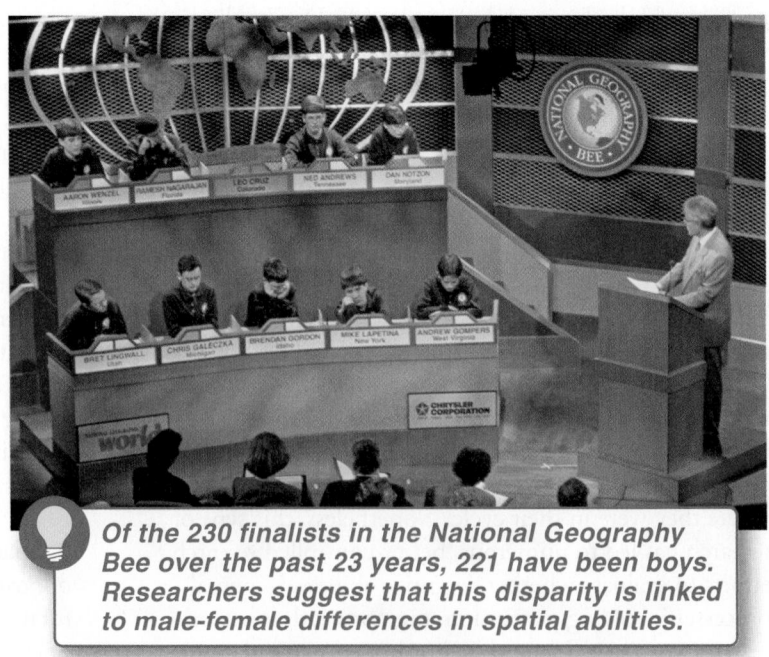

Of the 230 finalists in the National Geography Bee over the past 23 years, 221 have been boys. Researchers suggest that this disparity is linked to male-female differences in spatial abilities.

FIGURE 24-23 Showing an interest in geography.

abilities—based on the belief that spatial abilities translate into an ability to read and interpret maps. An author of the study, Lynn Liben, commented that "it's not true that every woman is worse than every man or every girl is worse than every boy. But at the group level, it is true." Conversely, girls remain more likely than males to make the honor roll in school.

Beyond tests of motor and verbal tasks and tests of spatial ability, another component of cognitive performance is memory. Numerous studies report a strong role for estrogen in memory, suggesting that estrogen increases the growth and connections of neurons. A recent study in rodents, for example, showed that treatment with a high dose of estrogen improved a maze-running task that tests memory.

The stress hormone cortisol has also been implicated in memory abilities. Most studies have reported a relationship that, when plotted as a graph, resembles an inverted "U": up to a point, increased cortisol improves memory, but excess cortisol and other stress hormones consistently reduce performance. (Removing the adrenal glands, which produce most of the body's cortisol, impairs performance on tests of memory, but abilities are restored when cortisol is supplemented to typical levels.) Optimum memory performance seems to require moderate levels of cortisol and other stress hormones.

TAKE-HOME MESSAGE 24·9

A great number of experimental studies demonstrate that cognitive abilities in humans are influenced by hormones, particularly the reproductive hormones estrogen and testosterone, but also the stress hormone cortisol.

24·10 Hormones can affect health and longevity.

Sometimes the links between cause and effect in biological systems appear straightforward. Take, for example, the results from one of the most appalling "experiments" ever conducted. In the early 1900s, many men committed to sanitariums were castrated. In a case-controlled study, the castrated men were compared with non-castrated, institutionalized men, born in the same year and with the same estimated IQ. It turned out that the median longevity of the 297 castrated men, at 69.3 years, was almost 14 years longer than that of the 735 men in the control group. Similarly, data from analyses of more than 1,000 cats (male and female) showed that sterilized cats live significantly longer than those not sterilized. Among males, for example, those not castrated lived a mean of 5.3 years, while castrated males had a mean life span of 8.1 years (**FIGURE 24-24**).

Laboratory mice, too, have significantly lengthened life spans when sterilized. And in similar experiments, female fruit flies exposed to high temperature or X rays experienced a dramatic reduction in ovary size, a severe drop in egg-laying rate, and an accompanying 73% increase in life span. Other researchers gave mice diets significantly reduced in calories and found that the amounts of reproductive hormones in the bloodstream were significantly reduced among calorie-restricted males and females compared with controls—animals given access to as much food as they wanted. Mice on the low-calorie diet lived more than 40%

longer than those with unlimited access to food. All of these results suggest that reducing the levels of circulating reproductive hormones increases longevity.

Hormones probably have their significant impact on longevity because the rate of cancer occurrence—in rodents as well as in humans—is closely related to the concentrations of circulating reproductive hormones, such as estrogen.

- Increased lifelong exposure to estrogen is associated with increased rates of cell division and, consequently, increased cancer risk.

- High concentrations of estrogen in the bloodstream are associated with an increased incidence of endometrial cancer.

- Women taking oral contraceptives and women giving birth to higher numbers of children—both of which reduce a woman's exposure to estrogen and other hormones produced by developing follicles—have decreased incidences of ovarian cancer. An analysis of 20 studies reported that five years of taking oral contraceptives reduced women's lifetime risk of cancer by approximately 50% (**FIGURE 24-25**).

There is similar evidence of increased cancer risk linked to circulating levels of progesterone and testosterone.

GRAPHIC CONTENT!
Thinking critically about visual displays of data.
Turn to p. 976 for a closer inspection of this figure.

STERILIZATION AND LONGEVITY

STERILIZATION AND LONGEVITY IN MALE CATS*

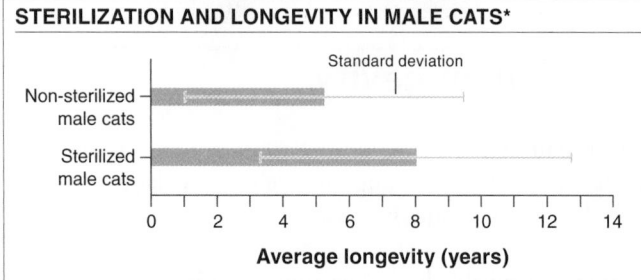

Standard deviation

Non-sterilized male cats

Sterilized male cats

Average longevity (years) (0, 2, 4, 6, 8, 10, 12, 14)

*Data included only for "protected" cats for which the cause of death was known and excluding deaths by trauma or poisoning, which are known to occur more commonly in non-castrated cats.

STERILIZATION AND LONGEVITY IN HUMAN MALES*

Interquartile range (a measure of variance for a median, ranging from the 25th percentile to the 75th percentile)

Non-sterilized male humans

Sterilized male humans

Median longevity (years) (0, 20, 40, 60, 80, 100)

*Data for human males are from patients living in a sanitarium in the United States, born between 1871 and 1932.

> 💡 *Research suggests that reducing the levels of circulating reproductive hormones increases longevity.*

FIGURE 24-24 Long-lived pets. Sterilization increases longevity in cats and humans.

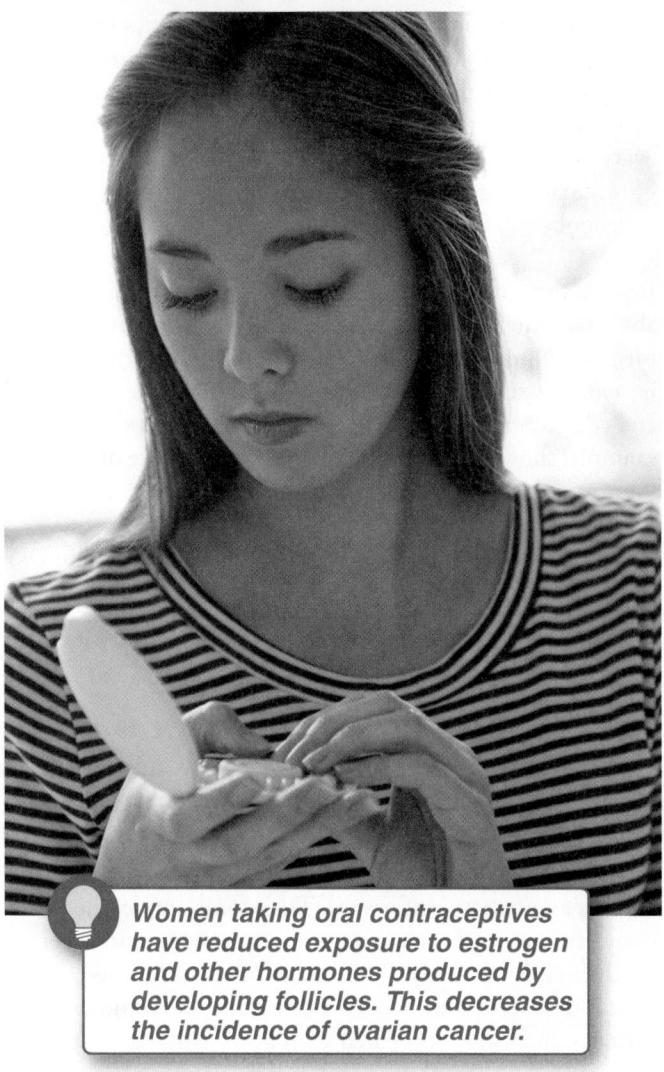

> 💡 *Women taking oral contraceptives have reduced exposure to estrogen and other hormones produced by developing follicles. This decreases the incidence of ovarian cancer.*

FIGURE 24-25 Use of birth control pills decreases the incidence of ovarian cancer.

These seemingly straightforward results, however, lead us to an example that illustrates the extreme complexity and interrelatedness of the body's physiological systems. It would seem, given the results above, that longevity should be decreased by hormone replacement therapy, which can take a variety of forms but generally involves supplementation of the hormone estrogen (or estrogen and progesterone), following menopause—which, typically beginning in the late forties to early fifties, is characterized by the cessation of monthly ovulation and a reduced production of estrogen and progesterone by the ovaries. In fact, though, almost all studies of hormone replacement have found that the treatment reduces the annual risk of death by about 25% and leads to increased longevity.

How can this increased longevity be reconciled with observations on the adverse effects of estrogen? It turns out that estrogen reduces circulating levels of cholesterol, which can reduce the risk of death from heart disease, the top killer of elderly women. Heart disease kills significantly more women than do breast cancer and reproductive-system cancers, so any treatment that reduces heart disease is likely to increase longevity, *even if it increases the risk of breast cancer and cancers of the reproductive system.*

Nonetheless, as a consequence of the complex nature of these results, there is still confusion and concern when it comes to hormone replacement therapy, and the debate continues. In 2009, a large analysis of 27 studies on the mortality risks of hormone replacement therapy concluded that for younger post-menopausal women (under 60 years of age), there is a significant reduction in mortality risk associated with hormone therapy, but that the benefit is reduced among older women. And so, while there are several strong links between hormones and health and longevity, the complex and myriad ways in which hormones can affect health make it difficult to make simple predictions about the influence of any hormone on health and longevity.

TAKE-HOME MESSAGE 24·10

Hormones affect health and longevity in complex ways. Sterilization of animals, for example, reduces levels of circulating reproductive hormones and increases longevity, usually due to reduced cancer mortality. But in other cases, such as hormone replacement therapy in women, the relationship appears to be reversed, with treatment reducing the annual risk of death by about 25%.

24·11 Environmental contaminants can disrupt normal hormone functioning.

Bald eagle adults and juvenile (Haliaeetus leucocephalus), *in Alaska.*

24·11 Chemicals in the environment can mimic or block hormones, with disastrous results.

Beginning in 1939 and continuing for more than three decades, the chemical DDT was used as a pesticide, with widespread agricultural use. It is extremely effective in killing a variety of insects, including mosquitoes, which made it popular in strategies against malaria—a disease transmitted by insects. Unfortunately, after DDT killed the intended insect pests, it remained in the environment. Animals that consumed insects exposed to DDT ingested the chemical, which was stored in their body tissues. And when those animals were consumed by others, the DDT was passed on. Because larger animals ate greater numbers of animals carrying DDT, they stored more and more of the toxic chemical.

In predatory birds such as bald eagles, peregrine falcons, and pelicans, DDT disrupted the development and functioning of the reproductive tract and impaired the birds' ability to produce normal eggshells—the shells would crack under the weight of the parent incubating the eggs (**FIGURE 24-26**). These problems led to serious population declines in many bird species and may have led to the extinction of some species.

Publication of *Silent Spring* by biologist Rachel Carson in 1962 called attention to the negative environmental effects of the widespread use of DDT. Carson's book represented the beginning of the environmental movement in the United States. It incited such a public outcry that DDT was eventually banned in the United States—a ban that is cited as instrumental in the rebound of bald eagle populations.

DDT is a synthetic chemical called an **endocrine disruptor.** When endocrine disruptors are taken up by organisms, they can mimic, block, or otherwise interfere with hormones, leading to harmful effects. These effects are a consequence of the close chemical similarity between endocrine disruptors and hormones, particularly estrogen. Often, endocrine disruptors can directly bind to the same receptors as estrogen.

Predatory birds consuming insects exposed to the pesticide DDT had reduced ability to produce properly functioning eggshells, leading to serious population declines.

FIGURE 24-26 Effects of DDT. The endocrine disruptor DDT causes thinning of eggshells in some birds.

THE ADVERSE EFFECTS OF ENDOCRINE DISRUPTORS

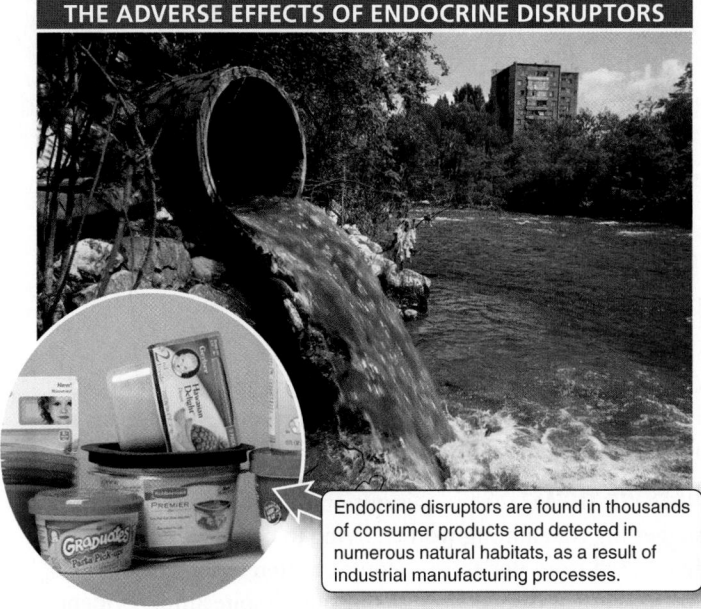

Endocrine disruptors are found in thousands of consumer products and detected in numerous natural habitats, as a result of industrial manufacturing processes.

A variety of animal groups appear to have been adversely affected by endocrine disruptors.

MAMMALS
In populations of Baltic ringed seals, endocrine disruptors have interfered with female reproductive functioning, leading to partial or complete sterility in 70% of the animals.

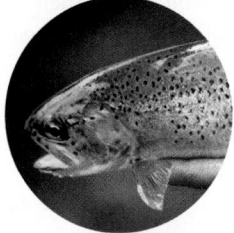

FISHES
In a variety of fish species, including carp, rainbow trout, and flounder, exposure to endocrine disruptors in sewage runoff has been shown to interfere with reproductive functioning.

INVERTEBRATES
In marine invertebrates, endocrine disruptors have led to the production of defective shells, as well as the masculinization of female genitals, reducing fertility.

FIGURE 24-27 Some consumer products contain chemicals that act as endocrine disruptors in wildlife.

There are several types of endocrine disruptors, in addition to DDT. These include **PCBs (polychlorinated biphenyls)**, which are effective as industrial coolants and lubricants; **phthalates,** commonly found in soft toys and cosmetics; and **bisphenol A (BPA),** found in some plastic water bottles and baby bottles (**FIGURE 24-27**).

Endocrine disruptors are found in thousands of other consumer products, too, and have been detected in numerous natural habitats, sometimes carried in runoff water from industrial manufacturing processes or as airborne pollutants. Exposure to endocrine disruptors has been implicated in a variety of adverse physiological effects, often related to the chemicals' feminizing effects, which has led to some endocrine disruptors being referred to as "gender-bending chemicals." Many animal groups seem to be adversely affected by endocrine disruptors.

1. Mammals. Populations of Baltic ringed seals have declined significantly over the past 100 years. This is due, in part, to the presence of large concentrations of pollutants, including PCBs and DDT, in their habitats, which has interfered with female reproductive functioning in many ways, leading to partial or complete sterility in 70% of the animals.

2. Fishes. In a variety of fish species, including carp, rainbow trout, and flounder, exposure to endocrine disruptors in sewage runoff is known to interfere with reproductive functioning. In some cases, the exposure causes males to produce egg proteins that are typically found in females.

3. Invertebrates. A group of chemicals called tributyltin compounds, or TBTs, are used to reduce the growth of organisms on the hulls of ships. TBTs act as endocrine disruptors in several marine species. Oysters, for example, when exposed to TBTs, produce defective shells, and in numerous other marine invertebrates, females' genitals become masculinized and the animals have reduced fertility. These impacts have led to a worldwide decline in populations of gastropods such as sea snails and limpets.

Large numbers of synthetic and natural chemicals have endocrine-disrupting functions in both natural and laboratory populations of animals. It remains controversial, however, whether these chemicals cause health problems in humans. Many studies are under way—so far, with conflicting or inconsistent results—and the U.S. government has taken many steps to restrict the use of the endocrine disruptors described here.

TAKE-HOME MESSAGE 24·11

Endocrine disruptors are chemicals used by humans that, when taken up by organisms, can mimic, block, or otherwise interfere with hormones and can lead to a variety of adverse physiological effects. Although endocrine disruptions affect many animal species, it remains controversial whether these chemicals cause health problems in humans.

HORMONES ARE CHEMICAL MESSENGERS · HORMONES ARE PRODUCED IN GLANDS · WIDE-RANGING EFFECTS OF HORMONES · CHEMICALS CAN DISRUPT HORMONE FUNCTION

973

StreetBIO
Knowledge You Can Use

ARE PHEROMONES REAL-LIFE "LOVE POTIONS"?

Q: WHAT ARE SEX PHEROMONES? Sex pheromones, such as those produced by female gypsy moths, are chemical messengers released into the environment to announce to males, over a wide area, that a female is ready to reproduce.

Q: DO HUMANS PRODUCE THEM? The jury is out on this question. In 1971, data were published suggesting that among women living in college dormitories, pheromones, probably released from underarms, could shorten or lengthen the reproductive cycle in other women (see Section 25-7). But, despite ample evidence of sex pheromones in other species, the evidence of their existence in humans is still hotly debated.

Q: WHAT ABOUT THE CLAIMS MADE IN OTHER STUDIES? A study published in 2002 claimed that human pheromones could increase the sexual attractiveness of women to men. In the double-blind, placebo-controlled study, one group of women had a purported human sex pheromone added to their perfume, while women in a control group had a placebo. The women then recorded, over the next three months, their "socio-sexual" behaviors—including kissing, dating, sexual activity, and male approaches—which were then compared with observations from the same women *prior* to receiving the pheromone or placebo. The results? More than three times as many pheromone users as placebo users (74% vs. 23%) experienced an increased frequency of socio-sexual behaviors. The researchers concluded that the pheromone acted as a sex attractant.

Q: CAN WE BE CERTAIN OF THE CLAIMS OF JUST ONE STUDY? The double-blind and placebo-controlled aspects of this study represent important attempts at making a rigorous test of the authors' hypothesis. But the study has been criticized on several grounds. The authors tested only a small number of women ($n = 36$), within a limited age range (27.8 ± 6.7 years), over only a three-month period. Perhaps more importantly, they did not disclose in their published report the chemical preparation added to the perfumes. Additionally, one of the study's authors synthesized the proprietary chemical and currently markets it for profit. And re-analyses of the results challenge their significance. Still, the results do suggest that there may be something in the air.

Big Ideas in ... Hormones

24·1–24·3 Hormones are chemical messengers regulating cell functioning.

- Hormones are chemical messengers, secreted by endocrine cells and endocrine glands into the circulatory system, that influence the actions of target cells elsewhere in the body—including by affecting gene transcription. They are part of an internal communication and regulation system.

- Most hormones are one of two types: (1) peptide and protein hormones, which cannot pass through cell membranes and bind to receptors embedded in the membranes; and (2) steroid hormones, which can diffuse through cell membranes and bind to receptors in the cytoplasm or nucleus.

- Emotions, physical characteristics, behaviors, and other traits can be influenced by hormones.

24·4–24·5 Hormones are produced in glands throughout the body.

- Endocrine glands throughout the body are responsible for detecting and responding to signals that reflect an organism's internal and external environments.

- The hypothalamus functions as a liaison between the nervous and endocrine systems, often directing the pituitary gland to release hormones with important regulatory effects on body tissues.

- The adrenal glands regulate organisms' responses to stress.

- The pineal gland regulates wake and sleep cycles.

- The thyroid gland influences the speed and efficiency of cellular metabolism.

- The pancreas maintains blood glucose levels.

- The gonads produce hormones responsible for numerous physical, behavioral, and emotional features, including much sexual behavior, development, and growth.

24·6–24·10 Hormones influence nearly every facet of an organism.

- Hormones affect a person's physique and physical performance, behavior, mood, and cognitive abilities, as well as health and longevity.

- Hormones produce these changes by influencing gene expression and protein synthesis in cells with appropriate receptors.

24·11 Environmental contaminants can disrupt normal hormone functioning.

- Endocrine disruptors are chemicals that, when taken up by organisms, can mimic, block, or otherwise interfere with their hormones. They can lead to a variety of adverse physiological outcomes, often related to the chemicals' feminizing effects.

- Although endocrine disruptions have been demonstrated in numerous animal species, it remains controversial whether these chemicals cause endocrine disruption and health problems in humans.

See the To-Go Guide (packaged with every new copy of this textbook) for an illustrated summary of the chapter.

Check Your Knowledge

1. What is the "take-home message" of these graphs? What additional data would be helpful? Why?

2. What are the scales used in the graphs? How would the graphs be perceived differently if the cat graph ranged from 0 to 100 years and the human graph ranged from 50 to 70 years? Would that be a misleading presentation? Why?

3. What is the percentage longevity increase resulting from sterilization in cats? What is it in humans?

4. In non-technical terms, what does "standard deviation" mean?

5. For populations with the same average value for a trait, what is the difference between having a large and a small standard deviation?

6. In the lower graph, longevity is measured as median longevity. What does this mean? How does it differ from average longevity?

7. What does the 25th percentile mean? What does 75th percentile mean?

8. Why do you think the data for the lower graph were collected from sanitarium patients?

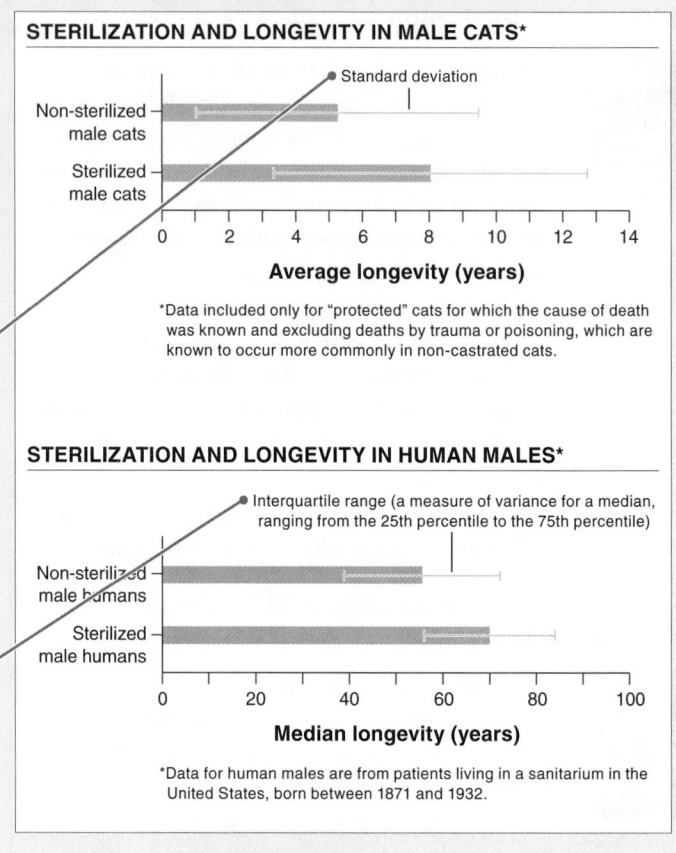

STERILIZATION AND LONGEVITY IN MALE CATS*

Standard deviation

Non-sterilized male cats

Sterilized male cats

Average longevity (years)

*Data included only for "protected" cats for which the cause of death was known and excluding deaths by trauma or poisoning, which are known to occur more commonly in non-castrated cats.

STERILIZATION AND LONGEVITY IN HUMAN MALES*

Interquartile range (a measure of variance for a median, ranging from the 25th percentile to the 75th percentile)

Non-sterilized male humans

Sterilized male humans

Median longevity (years)

*Data for human males are from patients living in a sanitarium in the United States, born between 1871 and 1932.

See Answers at the back of the book.

Key Terms in Hormones

Multiple-Choice Questions

1. The target cells of the hormone _____ are located in a woman's uterus and breasts. This hormone causes its target cells to contract, which causes the uterine contractions that push out the newborn during labor and releases milk from the breast cells to feed the infant.

   a) oxytocin
   b) progesterone
   c) estrogen
   d) ACTH
   e) prolactin

   100 HARD
   35
   0 EASY

2. Human sex hormones are classified as which type of biological molecule?

   a) enzyme
   b) lipid
   c) protein
   d) carbohydrate
   e) nucleic acid

   100 HARD
   51
   0 EASY

3. Why are steroid hormone complexes with their receptors able to directly bind to DNA to influence gene expression, whereas peptide hormones must influence gene expression indirectly?

   a) Peptide hormones are made from amino acids, which are also used to make proteins, and proteins cannot bind to DNA. Steroid hormones are not made from amino acids, and therefore they can directly interact with DNA.
   b) Steroid hormones are lipid-based, allowing them to pass through the lipid-composed cell membrane to enter the cell and directly bind to DNA. Peptide hormones are not lipid-based and therefore cannot pass through the cell membrane.
   c) Steroid hormones are smaller than peptide hormones and can fit through the holes in the cell membrane to enter the cell.
   d) Steroid hormones are cholesterol-based and therefore can block arteries, causing cardiovascular disease. Directly binding to DNA allows them to complete their function and to be removed from the circulatory system as soon as possible.
   e) Neither steroid nor peptide hormones directly bind to DNA; both influence gene expression indirectly.

   100 HARD
   30
   0 EASY

4. The _____ is a pea-sized gland located below the hypothalamus in the brain and is one of the controlling glands of the endocrine system.

   a) testis
   b) pancreas
   c) thyroid gland
   d) pituitary gland
   e) adrenal gland

   100 HARD
   5
   0 EASY

5. The hypothalamus secretes which two hormones into the posterior pituitary gland, from where they enter the bloodstream and act on their target cells?

   a) ADH and TSH
   b) prolactin and oxytocin
   c) oxytocin and ADH
   d) pheromone and ACTH
   e) FSH and LH

   100 HARD
   56
   0 EASY

6. **The following pairs link a human gland with the hormone(s) it secretes. Which pairing is incorrect?**
   a) adrenal cortex: cortisol
   b) pancreas: insulin
   c) testis: testosterone
   d) ovary: estrogen and progesterone
   e) thyroid: oxytocin

7. **The pituitary gland is actually a fusion of two glands. Which of the following statements about its origins is correct?**
   a) The posterior pituitary is an outgrowth of the cerebellum; the anterior pituitary develops from the pineal gland.
   b) The anterior pituitary is an outgrowth of the hypothalamus; the posterior pituitary is an outgrowth of the cerebellum.
   c) The posterior pituitary is an outgrowth of the hypothalamus; the anterior pituitary is an outgrowth of the cerebellum.
   d) The posterior pituitary is an outgrowth of the hypothalamus; the anterior pituitary develops from a fold of tissue at the roof of the embryonic mouth.
   e) The anterior pituitary is an outgrowth of the hypothalamus; the posterior pituitary develops from a fold of tissue at the roof of the embryonic mouth.

8. **The _____ gland releases melatonin, which is a hormone important in regulating circadian cycles in numerous mammalian species.**
   a) pineal
   b) adrenal
   c) pituitary
   d) thyroid
   e) pancreatic

9. **The target tissues or organs of insulin are:**
   a) the testes and ovaries.
   b) blood and the pancreas.
   c) muscles and the liver.
   d) blood and bones.
   e) muscles and the pancreas.

10. **Blood samples from an individual who has fasted for 24 hours would have:**
    a) high levels of insulin and low levels of glucagon.
    b) high levels of both insulin and glucagon.
    c) high levels of glucagon and standard levels of insulin.
    d) low levels of both insulin and glucagon.
    e) high levels of glucagon and low levels of insulin.

11. **Many female bodybuilders take steroids (testosterone) to increase muscle mass and achieve their desired body shape. The consequences can include all of the following except:**
    a) increased competitiveness and aggressiveness.
    b) increased hair growth.
    c) decreased object memory.
    d) increased concentration.
    e) decreased fertility.

12. **If a high dose of time-released testosterone is given to a male songbird, which of the following is not a likely effect?**
    a) He would obtain a larger territory than males with lower levels of circulating testosterone.
    b) He would get into many fights with larger males.
    c) He would have a longer life span than most other males.
    d) He would enjoy increased reproductive success.
    e) He would develop a greater muscle mass than other males of similar body weight.

Short-Answer Questions

1. Compare and contrast peptide and protein hormones with steroid hormones.

2. How do the hypothalamus, posterior pituitary, and anterior pituitary interact, and what role do they play in the endocrine system?

3. In what ways do estrogen and testosterone influence mood? How can sex hormones, including these two hormones, affect life expectancy?

4. What are the general effects of endocrine disruptors? Why can even small quantities in the environment be harmful to some organisms?

See Answers at the back of the book.
For additional study questions, go to www.prep-u.com.

From two parents to
one embryo to one baby

25

Reproduction and Development

981

Takhi mare (Equus caballus przewalskii) *interacting with offspring, in Hustain Nuruu National Park, Mongolia.*

25·1

Reproductive options (and ethical issues) are on the rise.

Thirty-year-old Diane Blood wanted to have a child with her husband, Stephen. And then the High Court in England ruled that she could not. The problem: her husband was dead.

Stephen Blood had died two years earlier, but when he was in a coma, his wife asked the doctors to freeze a sperm sample from him the day before he died. The Human Fertilisation and Embryology Authority, however, ruled that because he hadn't given written consent, his sperm could not be used.

This case illustrates a type of ethical and legal quandary that is becoming increasingly common (**FIGURE 25-1**). Technology is making pregnancy possible in many situations where it previously was not. But along with many happy outcomes, there are also numerous complex legal battles and, as yet, few consistent legal decisions on such matters. Here are some examples.

Are frozen embryos divided up like other marital assets at divorce?

- Do couples have the right to make contracts with a surrogate mother, a woman who carries and gives birth to their child? And, if so, can they pay her? In North Dakota,

the surrogate actually becomes the legal parent of the child. In Washington, DC, and in many states, a couple can pay the surrogate's expenses, but nothing more.

- Do egg donors have any rights (and responsibilities) with respect to the children conceived with their eggs? Do sperm donors? States have ruled differently on these issues.

- Do children conceived from sperm or egg donors have a right to know who the donor was?

Q • If a couple has embryos frozen for later implantation but then gets divorced, who retains custody of the embryos? In one Tennessee case, custody was given to the mother, against the wishes of the father. A Texas court, on the other hand, refused to give frozen embryos to the mother. With almost half a million frozen embryos in the United States, this is likely to become a common case in courts.

In this chapter, we describe how men produce sperm and women produce eggs, as well as the process by which fertilization occurs (or does not occur). We also explore the early stages of development, following fertilization,

FIGURE 25-1 In the headlines: ethical issues and reproductive technologies.

including the steps by which an embryo is triggered to develop as a male or a female. Lastly, we investigate the perils and promise of a variety of assisted reproductive technologies.

But first, a happy resolution to the case we opened with. Diane Blood was eventually allowed to take the sperm to another country to be inseminated (after re-mortgaging her house to pay for the expensive legal battles). The law in England still prevents storage of sperm from a man without his written consent, but an appeals court made an exception in her case, and Diane Blood was able to conceive a child (and, three and a half years later, another child) with her husband's sperm.

TAKE-HOME MESSAGE 25·1

Technology is making pregnancy possible in many situations where it previously was not, but it is simultaneously giving rise to complex legal battles and ethical dilemmas.

25·2 There are costs and benefits to having a partner: sexual versus asexual reproduction.

The term "reproduction," the process by which new organisms are produced from existing organisms, usually conjures images of a male and a female, producing offspring together. And for most animals, this is how it's done. But recall from Section 6-14 that there are two fundamentally different ways in which organisms can reproduce. While the vast majority of plants and animals reproduce sexually, prokaryotes and many plant and animal species reproduce asexually—and some can reproduce in both ways.

Sexual reproduction involves two individuals contributing genetic material to produce offspring (**FIGURE 25-2**). The genetic material is contained in gametes, the reproductive cells. The male gamete is called a **sperm** (or sperm cell) and the female gamete is called an egg or **ovum** (*pl.* **ova**). Recall from Section 6-11 that the cellular division process of meiosis produces gametes, cells that contain only half as many sets of chromosomes as other body cells (the somatic

FIGURE 25-2 In sexual reproduction, two parents contribute genetic material to the offspring. The fusion of female gamete (egg) and male gamete (sperm) forms a zygote that potentially develops into offspring.

SEXUAL REPRODUCTION

Sexual reproduction involves two individuals contributing genetic material to produce offspring. The genetic material is contained in gametes, the reproductive cells.

EGG
• Female gamete
• Haploid (one copy of each chromosome)

SPERM
• Male gamete
• Haploid (one copy of each chromosome)

FERTILIZATION

FERTILIZED EGG (ZYGOTE)
• Diploid (two copies of each chromosome)

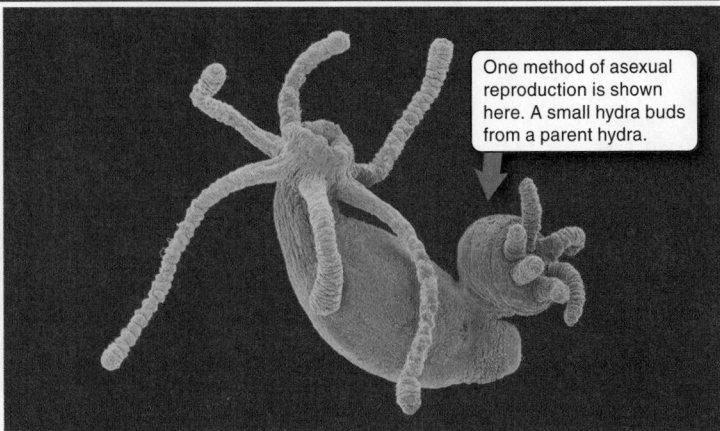

One method of asexual reproduction is shown here. A small hydra buds from a parent hydra.

SEXUAL REPRODUCTION

ADVANTAGES
- Offspring are genetically different from each other and from either parent—an evolutionary adaptation that can lead to increased fitness in changing environments.

DISADVANTAGES
- Finding a partner and mating can be difficult and time-consuming.
- Only half of an individual's alleles will be passed to its offspring.

ASEXUAL REPRODUCTION

ADVANTAGES
- Reproduction is fast and efficient.
- All of an individual's alleles are passed on to its offspring.

DISADVANTAGES
- With a changing environment, individuals producing genetically identical offspring are less likely to have offspring suited to the environment.

FIGURE 25-3 Genetic variation versus efficiency: advantages and disadvantages of sexual and asexual reproduction.

cells). When the male and female gametes fuse in **fertilization,** the full chromosome number is restored. Both the production of gametes and the combination of genetic material from two individuals tend to increase genetic diversity among offspring. We explore sexual reproduction in greater detail in the remainder of this chapter.

An important feature of sexual reproduction is that it leads to offspring that differ genetically from each other and from either parent (see Figure 6-24). This genetic diversity can be an evolutionary adaptation, increasing fitness in changing environments. If an environment is gradually changing, individuals producing diverse offspring increase the likelihood that one of their offspring will be suited, genetically, to the new environment. There are, however, disadvantages to sexual reproduction. The two main drawbacks are that (1) finding a partner and mating can be time-consuming and dangerous, and (2) an individual contributes only half of the alleles that its offspring carry (**FIGURE 25-3**).

In contrast to sexual reproduction, **asexual reproduction** involves the production of offspring by a single individual without a contribution of genetic material from another individual. There are several types of asexual reproduction in

Q Do female turkeys need males to reproduce?

animals, including parthenogenesis, budding, and fragmentation (**FIGURE 25-4**).

1. Parthenogenesis. In **parthenogenesis,** a female's egg develops into a new organism without having to be fertilized by a sperm cell. Some species, including the desert grassland whiptail lizard, are exclusively asexual, and all of the individuals in the species are female. Among these lizards, though, ovulation rates are increased by female-female courtship rituals and mating behavior. Other species can reproduce either asexually or sexually, depending on environmental conditions; parthenogenesis allows them to utilize resources as quickly as possible. For example, in the spring, when food is plentiful, aphids produce diploid maternal cells that develop into normal adults without fertilization. When food is limited, they produce haploid eggs that must be fertilized before development. Hammerhead sharks and, occasionally, turkeys also have the capability to reproduce by parthenogenesis (although turkeys resulting from asexual reproduction tend to be less healthy).

2. Budding. In budding, an offspring grows directly out of the body of the parent. Hydras, which are predatory cnidarians, reproduce by budding.

3. Fragmentation. In fragmentation, one individual breaks into multiple pieces, each of which develops into a fully

TYPES OF ASEXUAL REPRODUCTION

Asexual reproduction involves the production of offspring by a single individual without contribution of genetic material from another individual.

PARTHENOGENESIS
A female's egg develops into a new organism without ever having to be fertilized by a sperm cell.

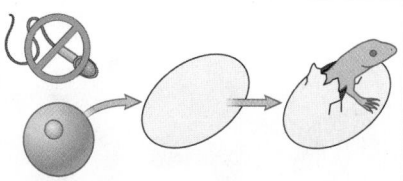

BUDDING
An offspring grows right out of the body of the parent.

FRAGMENTATION
A parent breaks into multiple pieces, and each develops into a fully functioning, independent individual.

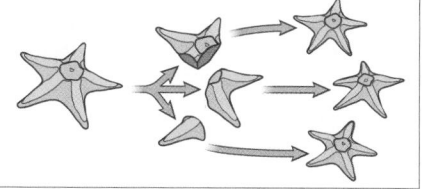

FIGURE 25-4 Asexual reproduction: parthenogenesis, budding, and fragmentation.

functioning, independent individual. Fragmentation is seen among many species of flatworms, as well as some sea stars. Among some sea stars, for example, if even a tiny part of one arm breaks off, it can develop into a complete individual.

Asexual reproduction can be fast and easy, because it involves only a single individual. And if an organism's environment is stable, it is beneficial for offspring to carry all of the genes that their parent carried. If an environment is changing, however, asexually reproducing organisms may be at a disadvantage.

TAKE-HOME MESSAGE 25·2

Organisms can reproduce sexually or asexually—or both. Sexual reproduction, which leads to offspring that are genetically different from each other and from both parents, occurs in the vast majority of plant and animal species. Asexual reproduction, which can be fast and efficient, leads to offspring genetically identical to the parent; it occurs in all prokaryotes and in many plant and animal species.

25·3
Fertilization can occur inside or outside a female's body.

Sexual reproduction, as we've seen, can have evolutionary advantages. But because it requires male and female gametes to come together at fertilization, it also presents a challenge: the male and female gametes must somehow get to each other. Two general strategies have evolved as a consequence: **external fertilization,** in which the sperm and eggs unite outside the male's and female's bodies, and **internal fertilization,** in which the sperm are deposited directly in the female's reproductive tract and unite with eggs inside her body (**FIGURE 25-5**).

The first vertebrates evolved in the oceans, where it was possible for females to release batches of eggs right into the water. Males could then release sperm into the water, and fertilization could take place. Many aquatic invertebrates—including sea urchins and clams—along with most fishes and amphibians use external fertilization to bring sperm and eggs together.

Male frogs clutch onto female frogs for months at a time without letting go. Why?

Although seawater is not harmful to sperm or eggs, one potential problem for organisms using external fertilization is that the tiny gametes of one sex can be very quickly washed away from those of the other sex. For this reason, the males and females of a species tend to produce very large numbers of gametes and release them, at the same time, very near each other. A variety of cues help synchronize their release of gametes, including water temperature, phase of the moon, day length, chemicals released by one or the other sex (pheromones), and courtship rituals.

Q Among the most extreme tactics employed for ensuring that sperm and eggs are released at the same time and place is something called amplexus, used by most species of frogs. In amplexus, the male embraces the female from behind, wrapping his front legs around her. He holds on until she releases her eggs, at which point he releases his sperm to fertilize them (externally). This doesn't sound all that

During amplexus, the male frog mounts and hangs onto the female until she lays her eggs, at which point he releases his sperm and fertilizes them.

EXTERNAL FERTILIZATION
The sperm and egg unite outside the male's and the female's body.

INTERNAL FERTILIZATION
Sperm are deposited directly in the female's reproductive tract and unite with eggs inside the female's body.

FIGURE 25-5 Methods of fertilization. Frogs deposit large quantities of sperm and eggs into the water, where some are fertilized. In mammals, such as the black rhinoceros, fertilization takes place within the reproductive tract of the female.

remarkable, except that males will sometimes hold on to a female for weeks or even months at a time!

As we learned in Chapter 11, vertebrates' colonization of land opened up a huge number of new niches but presented one huge problem. External fertilization just doesn't work well on land. First, gametes cannot be moved around (and thus toward each other) without water. Second, and even more important, gametes quickly dry out. For these reasons, there was strong selective pressure on land-colonizing vertebrates for a new method to evolve: internal fertilization.

Used by nearly all terrestrial animals, internal fertilization solves the problem of gamete desiccation (drying out) by having males deposit their sperm directly inside the females. This deposit is usually accomplished by the male placing his reproductive organ within the female's reproductive tract, in the act of **copulation.** Inside the female's body, there is sufficient moisture for the sperm to remain viable until one or more are able to fertilize her eggs.

Once an egg is fertilized by a sperm, the fertilized egg is called a **zygote.** Following the first division into two cells (and continuing until approximately 8 weeks of

development in humans), it is called an **embryo.** The offspring must, at some point in its development, leave the female's body. There are three different strategies for this (**FIGURE 25-6**).

1. Oviparity, a strategy in which the fertilized egg moves outside the body, where most embryonic development continues. The embryos are nourished by nutrients in the egg's yolk, and live offspring emerge from the egg. This developmental strategy is most familiar to us among birds (all bird species are oviparous), but it also occurs among most fishes, amphibians, reptiles, insects, and spiders.

2. Ovoviviparity, a less common strategy, in which most embryonic development takes place inside an egg, with the embryo nourished by the egg's yolk, but the egg itself remains in the female's body until it hatches (or is released just before hatching). This strategy is used by many aquatic organisms, including sharks and some other fishes, and by some species of amphibians, reptiles, and invertebrates.

3. Viviparity, a strategy in which the embryo develops inside the mother, nourished by nutrients in her blood, and live offspring are born. This strategy is perhaps

EMBRYONIC DEVELOPMENT

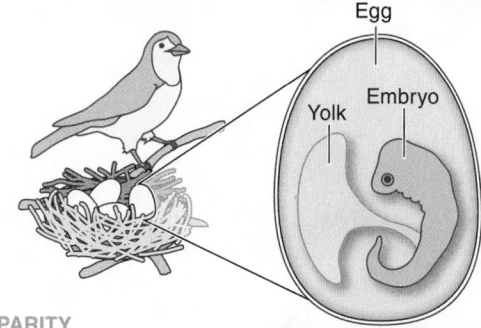

OVIPARITY

- Most embryonic development takes place within an egg outside the mother's body
- Embryo is nourished by nutrients in the egg's yolk
- Examples: all birds; also some fishes, amphibians, reptiles, insects, and spiders

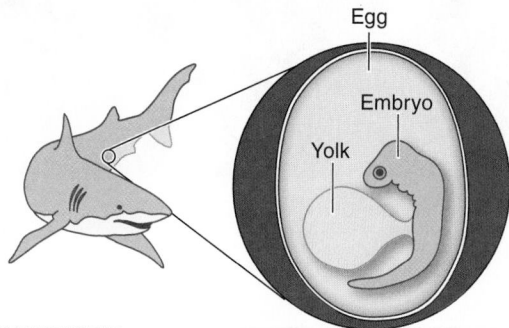

OVOVIVIPARITY

- Most embryonic development takes place within an egg that remains in the mother's body until it hatches (or is released just before hatching)
- Embryo is nourished by nutrients in the egg's yolk
- Examples: some sharks, fishes, amphibians, reptiles, and invertebrates

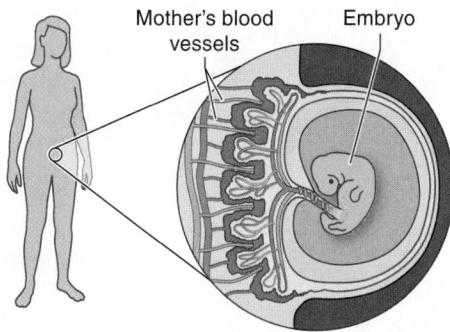

VIVIPARITY

- Most embryonic development takes place inside the mother, and live offspring are born
- Embryo is nourished by nutrients in the mother's blood
- Examples: nearly all mammals; also some fishes, amphibians, and reptiles

FIGURE 25-6 Three strategies for protecting and nourishing a developing embryo.

Although kangaroos are viviparous, offspring emerge from the mother's womb after about 33 days, blind, hairless, and just a few centimeters long. They finish development (for many months) in the mother's protective pouch.

FIGURE 25-7 The kangaroo is a viviparous animal.

most familiar because it is used by humans and nearly all other mammals (including marsupials; **FIGURE 25-7**), but it also occurs among some reptiles, amphibians, and fishes.

TAKE-HOME MESSAGE 25·3

Sexual reproduction requires fertilization, which occurs externally in most fishes and amphibians, and internally in most other vertebrates, including humans. Among those species having internal fertilization, development of the embryo can be nourished by yolk within an egg (that may or may not be retained within the female's body during development) or, remaining in the mother's body, by nutrients in her blood.

25·4–25·7 Male and female reproductive systems have important similarities and differences.

From Here to Eternity, *1953*.

25·4
Sperm are made in the testes.

Beginning at puberty and continuing for their entire lives, men produce sperm, often more than 100 million per day. The process of sperm production, called **spermatogenesis,** is similar among most mammals and requires 9–10 weeks in humans. In this section, we examine the male reproductive system and the production of sperm and semen, a fluid expelled at ejaculation that usually contains sperm. We begin with the male reproductive structures and the role that each plays in the process of sperm formation and fertilization (**FIGURE 25-8**).

Male reproductive structures Externally, a male has just two reproductive structures, the penis and the scrotum. The **penis** has three columns of tissue—one along each side and a third underneath—that can become engorged with blood, causing erection and making copulation possible. In most animal species, including dogs, walruses, and most primates other than humans, a bone (known as a baculum) is present in the penis and contributes to its stiffness. The **scrotum,** generally on the outside of the body, is a sac containing the two **testes** (*sing.* **testis;** also called testicles), the site of sperm production. Each testis is made up of highly coiled **seminiferous tubules,** lined with cells, called

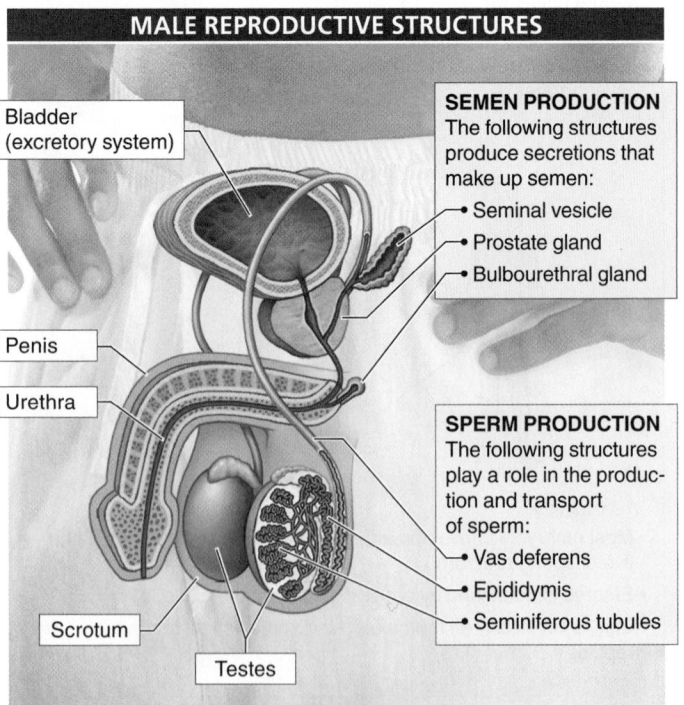

MALE REPRODUCTIVE STRUCTURES

Bladder (excretory system)

Penis

Urethra

Scrotum

Testes

SEMEN PRODUCTION
The following structures produce secretions that make up semen:
- Seminal vesicle
- Prostate gland
- Bulbourethral gland

SPERM PRODUCTION
The following structures play a role in the production and transport of sperm:
- Vas deferens
- Epididymis
- Seminiferous tubules

FIGURE 25-8 The structures of the male reproductive system.

spermatogonia, that are the site of sperm production. It is in cells between the seminiferous tubules that **testosterone,** the principal male sex hormone, and other androgens are produced. Testosterone stimulates sperm production.

Connected to the seminiferous tubules is the **epididymis,** a 15- to 20-foot-long coiled tube, in each testis, where sperm mature. The epididymis in each testis is linked to a **vas deferens,** a tube of smooth muscle tissue that passes from the testis into the body. The vas deferens from each testis connects to a single ejaculatory duct, which continues into the urethra, a duct passing through the penis and through which semen and urine are expelled.

Three other important male reproductive structures produce secretions that make up semen. These include the **prostate gland,** located just below the urinary bladder, which secretes into the urethra a milky, basic (as opposed to acidic) fluid

containing enzymes and sperm nutrients that makes up just under one-third of the volume of the ejaculate. A pair of **seminal vesicles** secrete into the semen nutrients for the sperm, as well as substances that increase sperm motility and make the female reproductive tract more hospitable to the sperm. And finally, a pair of **bulbourethral glands,** located just below the urethra near the base of the penis, contribute the remaining 1% or so of the ejaculate, as well as a mixture of mucus and sugar that lubricates the tip of the penis prior to copulation.

Gametogenesis in males
Recall from Sections 6-10 through 6-14 that gametes are produced by cells that undergo meiosis. Diploid cells, the spermatogonia, are present in the highly coiled seminiferous tubules of the testes (**FIGURE 25-9**). Each spermatogonium divides by mitosis to produce two cells. One of these cells is another spermatogonium, so the male never runs out of a store of

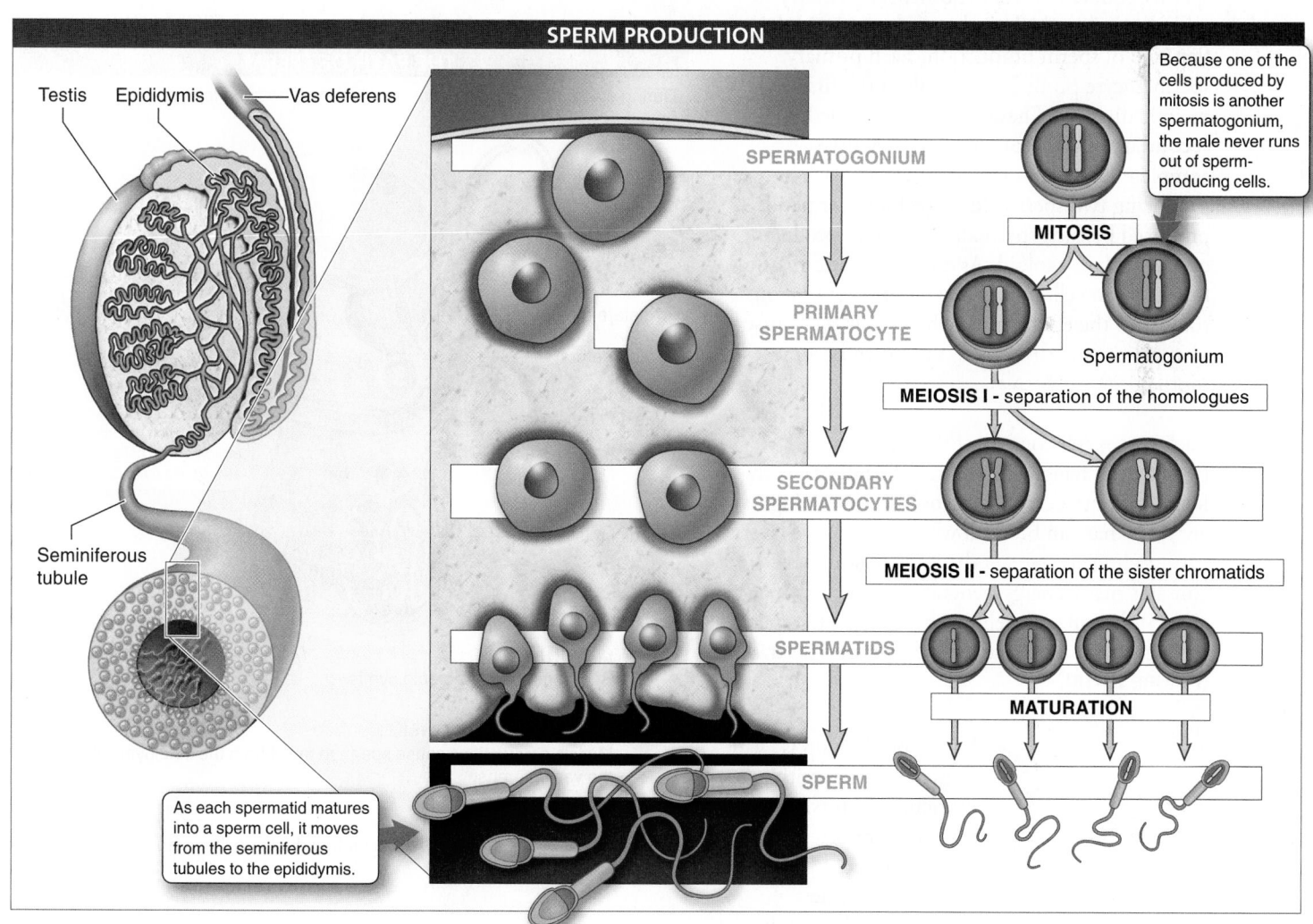

FIGURE 25-9 Gametogenesis in males. Sperm are continuously produced in the testis by meiosis.

HOW DO ANIMALS REPRODUCE?

MALE AND FEMALE REPRODUCTIVE SYSTEMS

SEX CAN LEAD TO FERTILIZATION

HUMAN DEVELOPMENT

REPRODUCTIVE TECHNOLOGY

989

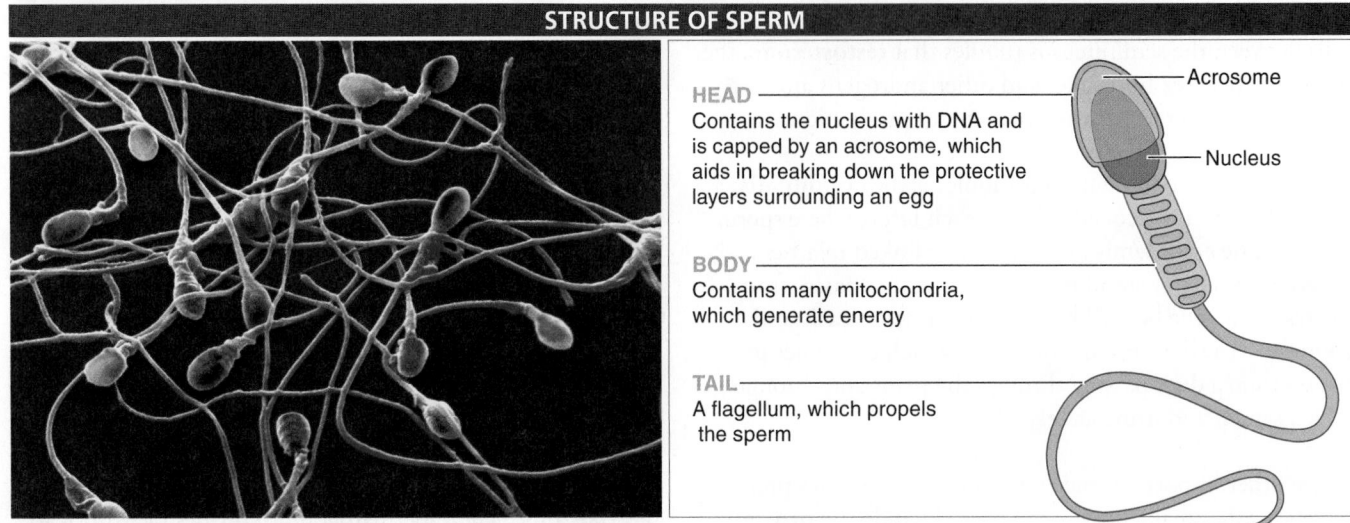

HEAD — Contains the nucleus with DNA and is capped by an acrosome, which aids in breaking down the protective layers surrounding an egg

Acrosome

Nucleus

BODY — Contains many mitochondria, which generate energy

TAIL — A flagellum, which propels the sperm

FIGURE 25-10 Sperm structure reflects its function.

sperm-producing cells; the other is a **primary spermatocyte,** which undergoes meiosis, in the first step of sperm production. Each primary spermatocyte produces two cells in the first meiotic division. These two cells are called **secondary spermatocytes,** and they then complete the second meiotic division, each producing two spermatids. The four spermatids produced by each spermatogonium, as products of meiosis, are haploid. As each spermatid matures into a sperm cell, it moves from the seminiferous tubules to the epididymis, where, over the course of approximately 18 hours, the sperm become motile.

Each sperm cell consists of three primary parts: (1) the head region, containing the nucleus with its DNA, plus a cap-like **acrosome** containing enzymes that can break down the protective layers surrounding an egg; (2) the body region, which contains many energy-generating mitochondria; and (3) the tail, a flagellum that propels the sperm through the fluid in the female reproductive tract (**FIGURE 25-10**).

Q Do hot tubs reduce a man's fertility?

Sperm production is tremendously sensitive to numerous factors. Two of the most important are hormones and temperature. The optimum temperature for sperm production is approximately two degrees lower than body

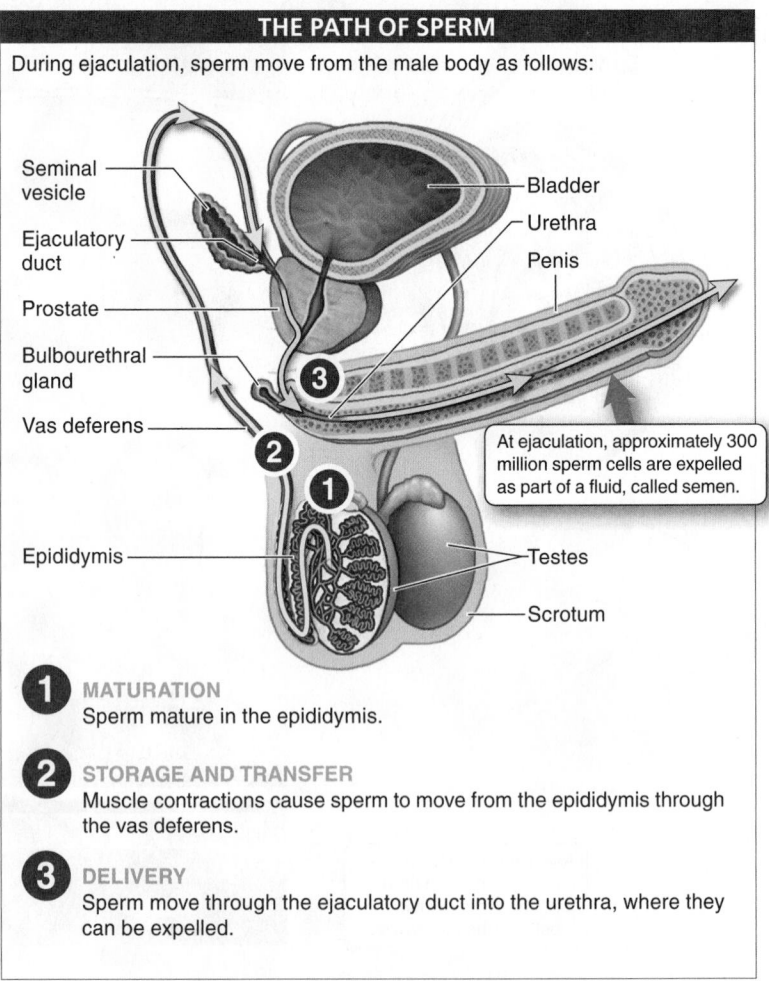

THE PATH OF SPERM

During ejaculation, sperm move from the male body as follows:

Seminal vesicle

Ejaculatory duct

Prostate

Bulbourethral gland

Vas deferens

Epididymis

Bladder

Urethra

Penis

At ejaculation, approximately 300 million sperm cells are expelled as part of a fluid, called semen.

Testes

Scrotum

1 MATURATION
Sperm mature in the epididymis.

2 STORAGE AND TRANSFER
Muscle contractions cause sperm to move from the epididymis through the vas deferens.

3 DELIVERY
Sperm move through the ejaculatory duct into the urethra, where they can be expelled.

FIGURE 25-11 The pathway taken by sperm during ejaculation.

temperature. This accounts for why, in most mammals, the testes hang outside the body, where their temperature can be controlled by moving them closer to or farther from the heat of the body. It also accounts for the fact that men exposed to hot tubs or hot baths for 30 minutes or more each week generally show signs of infertility, with lower sperm count and motility. Fortunately, the condition can almost always be reversed by reducing exposure to the hot tubs or baths.

The path that sperm take from the male to the female is as follows (**FIGURE 25-11**):

1. **Maturation:** sperm mature in the epididymis, within each testis.

2. **Storage and transfer:** during ejaculation, sperm move from the epididymis (in each testis) through the vas deferens as a result of contractions of the muscular tissue of the vas deferens.

3. **Delivery:** sperm moving from each vas deferens then pass through the ejaculatory duct and into the urethra. During copulation, sperm are ejected from the urethra into the female reproductive tract.

At ejaculation, the sperm are expelled as part of the semen. Although there are approximately 300 million sperm cells in the fluid of a single ejaculation, the sperm make up only about 1% to 5% of the total volume of ejaculated fluid. In the next section, we explore why so many sperm are present in an ejaculation.

> ### TAKE-HOME MESSAGE 25·4
>
> In adult men, sperm are continuously produced in the testes by meiosis. Semen—consisting of sperm cells and fluids that nurture and aid the sperm in fertilization—is ejaculated during copulation.

25·5
There is unseen conflict among sperm cells.

In *The Chimpanzees of Gombe: Patterns of Behavior,* Jane Goodall reported female copulatory rates of "an average of between five and six copulations per female per hour in the early morning, after which the rate dropped gradually to about two per hour in the midmorning, rose very slightly during the afternoon, and tapered off to one per hour in the evening." These observations were relevant to the realization reached by earlier researchers that if females (of any species, not just chimps) mate with more than one male, there may be competition among the males' sperm.

Q chimp's testicles e 15 times gger, relative to dy weight, than a rilla's! Why?

The idea of sperm competition, or "sperm wars" as this has been called, gives rise to several testable predictions. One simple prediction is this: when a female is likely to mate with more than one male, the males that produce more sperm are more likely to be successful at fertilizing the female's eggs. Some interesting observations support this prediction. For example, gorillas have golf-ball-sized testes, while chimpanzees' testes are closer in size to baseballs. Gorilla testicles account for only 0.02% of body weight, whereas chimp testes account for 0.30%, 15 times as much. Why the huge difference? Gorilla groups are relatively small, and all females within a group mate with just one male, the dominant silverback. In

contrast, as Jane Goodall noted, fertile chimpanzee females may have sex dozens of times a day with many different males. Consequently, the tiny testes of the gorilla are perfectly adequate, but for a chimp male to win these sperm competitions, he must produce significantly more sperm (**FIGURE 25-12**). Similarly, among fruit bats, males of species that live in large social groups have significantly larger testes than males of species that live in smaller groups.

Sperm competition has given rise to several other adaptations.

- Physical barriers to copulation, such as the mating plugs produced by the coagulation of semen in many species (including some squirrels, mice, scorpions, and spiders) that prevent other males' sperm from entering the female's reproductive tract.

- Toxic semen components, such as the protein in fruit fly semen that suppresses further mating by the female for several days (ensuring a male's paternity), as well as the fruit fly semen components that can incapacitate the sperm of other males (and even decrease the female's lifespan by about 10%).

Q Why *do* male fruit flies produce toxic semen?

- Genital morphology, such as the claspers and scrapers of dung flies, as well as the "shovel penis" of some dragonfly

> A female's mating with more than one male leads to sperm competition and the evolution of increased sperm production and testis size.

FIGURE 25-12 The evolutionary consequences of sperm competition among males. The inset shows the size of a male chimp's brain (top) relative to one of its testicles.

FIGURE 25-13 Sperm wars. Male and female damselflies *(Calopteryx virgo)* mating. The inset shows a micrograph of a damselfly penis, which is described as a "shovel penis" and can scrape away the sperm deposited by a rival.

species that make it possible for males to dislodge the sperm of other males that have already mated with a female (**FIGURE 25-13**).

This unseen conflict between males is an area of considerable investigation, as researchers try to understand the physical and behavioral consequences of such competition. And females are not passive players in these battles; research studies have documented how, in many cases, the female will eject the sperm from undesirable males.

TAKE-HOME MESSAGE 25·5

When females mate with more than one male, sperm competition occurs and can lead to a variety of adaptations, including increased sperm production and testis size, semen that can create a physical barrier to subsequent mating, toxic semen components, and penis morphology that aids in the displacement of rival males' sperm.

25·6 Eggs are made in the ovaries (and the process can take decades).

From a genetic perspective, making eggs barely differs from making sperm. In the female gonads—the **ovaries**—diploid cells undergo meiosis to produce haploid eggs, and in the

process, a great deal of variation is generated so that each haploid egg has a unique genetic makeup. When the haploid egg is fertilized by a sperm, the diploid condition is restored.

But the process of egg production differs from sperm production in several key ways. Eggs are produced in much smaller numbers; each egg is considerably larger than a sperm cell; and the production process can take decades rather than days, even though it begins at a much younger age. Let's explore the specifics, beginning with a description of the female reproductive system (**FIGURE 25-14**).

Female reproductive structures

Externally, a female's clitoris and labia develop from the same embryonic tissue that, in males, produces the penis and scrotum. There is also a vaginal opening. Internally, the **vagina** is a tube-like chamber into which sperm are released during copulation. The vagina connects with the **uterus,** also called the womb, where an embryo develops throughout pregnancy. The lower, narrowest portion of the uterus is called the **cervix.** The lining of the uterus, rich with blood vessels, is the **endometrium,** where the fertilized egg implants and is nourished.

Connecting to the top of the uterus on both sides are the **Fallopian tubes,** or **oviducts.** The Fallopian tubes extend outward and are funnel-shaped near the end where the ovaries lie. Each ovary is about the size of a large olive.

Gametogenesis in females

The process of gametogenesis in females, called **oogenesis** (pronounced oh-oh-GEN-eh-sis), starts in the ovaries while the female is still a fetus (**FIGURE 25-15**). Here, diploid cells called **oogonia** (*sing.* **oogonium**) multiply by mitosis. Each oogonium then begins meiosis, but stops at prophase I, at which point the cell is called a **primary oocyte** and is contained within a **follicle**—the small structure in which an egg will form. At birth, there are approximately one million follicles in a female's ovaries, each follicle containing a primary oocyte.

The primary oocytes remain in their hibernation-like state until puberty. At that point, periodic bursts of **follicle-stimulating hormone (FSH)** cause several primary oocytes to complete meiosis I. Unlike in the production of sperm, however, when the primary oocyte divides into two cells, although the pairs of homologous chromosomes split evenly, nearly all of the cytoplasm goes to one of the cells, now called a **secondary oocyte.** The other cell, known as a **polar body,** gets almost no cytoplasm and eventually disintegrates. At this point, meiosis again stops.

When females **ovulate,** generally a single follicle in one ovary ruptures, releasing the secondary oocyte—which still has not completed meiosis. The secondary oocyte, now called an egg, is swept by cilia into the Fallopian tube and carried down toward the uterus. If sperm have been deposited in the vagina during copulation, it is in the Fallopian tube that the sperm, swimming up from the vagina and through the uterus, are most likely to fertilize the egg. It is only *after* fertilization that a secondary oocyte is triggered to finally complete meiosis—once again with an

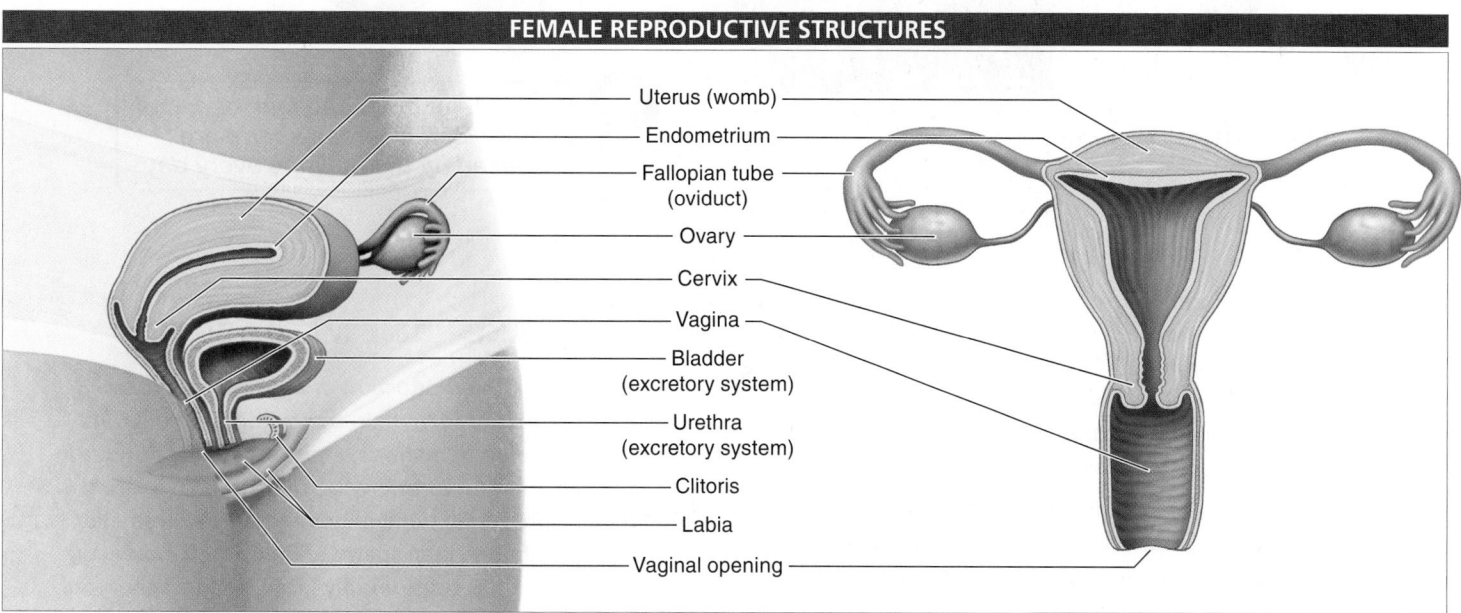

FEMALE REPRODUCTIVE STRUCTURES

Uterus (womb)
Endometrium
Fallopian tube (oviduct)
Ovary
Cervix
Vagina
Bladder (excretory system)
Urethra (excretory system)
Clitoris
Labia
Vaginal opening

FIGURE 25-14 The structures of the female reproductive system.

FIGURE 25-15 Gametogenesis in females.

Egg development can take decades to complete, whereas sperm are produced by the millions every day.

unequal division of cytoplasm. One of the resulting cells, the ovum, receives most of the cytoplasm, while the other receives almost none. This second polar body disintegrates just as the first polar body did. The haploid ovum now fuses with the haploid nucleus of the sperm, forming a diploid fertilized egg, called a zygote.

In the next section, we see how the development of follicles, preparation of the uterus for implantation, and ovulation are coordinated by hormone secretions.

TAKE-HOME MESSAGE 25·6

Genetically, the production of eggs barely differs from sperm production. In the ovaries, diploid cells begin to undergo meiosis, a process that continues in the Fallopian tubes following ovulation, producing genetically varied haploid gametes. A much smaller number of eggs than sperm are produced, however, and each egg is considerably larger than a sperm cell.

If you are female, here's something you may have noticed if you are living in a dormitory (or a prison): when women live in close proximity, their reproductive cycles become synchronized over time so that they menstruate and—perhaps less obviously—ovulate at approximately the same time. This issue was first addressed in 1971, when Martha McClintock published findings, inspired by her own experiences, based on data from 135 female students living in a dormitory at Wellesley College in Massachusetts. Similar observations have been reported for other animal species, and subsequent studies implicate airborne chemicals, called **pheromones** (probably released from women's underarms), that can shorten or lengthen the reproductive cycle in other women (**FIGURE 25-16**).

It's not clear why such synchrony of reproductive cycles would occur, however. And other researchers have been critical of the original data analyses and have argued that the different lengths of women's cycles make it impossible for them to become truly synchronized. Results from recent studies have been conflicting; several have found evidence for menstrual synchrony, while others have not. The jury is still out on this hotly contested issue.

Hormones regulate the timing and development of egg production, called the **ovarian cycle,** which occurs approximately every 28 days. Hormones also regulate the **menstrual cycle,** during which the uterus prepares for the possible implantation and nurturing of a fertilized egg, and sheds its lining when fertilization does not occur. We describe each of these cycles and how each influences the other (**FIGURE 25-17**).

In the normal monthly cycle, hormones direct the development of a follicle and the release of an egg (ovulation), while simultaneously preparing the uterus for implantation. Let's follow the changes in hormone levels and their effects during the 28-day cycle (see Figure 25-17).

1. **Menstruation.** Traditionally, the first day of menstrual bleeding, a woman's "period," or **menstruation,** is considered the first day of the menstrual cycle. Three to five days of bleeding occur as the lining of the uterus (the endometrium) is sloughed off.

2. **FSH produced.** As the uterine lining sheds, the levels of **estrogen,** the chief female sex hormone, drop. Reduced levels of estrogen cause the pituitary gland to release follicle-stimulating hormone (FSH).

MENSTRUAL SYNCHRONY IN DORMS

Increased menstrual synchrony occurs among women living together.

GRAPHIC CONTENT!
Thinking critically about visual displays of data.
Turn to p. 1016 for a closer inspection of this figure.

FIGURE 25-16 Synchronizing menstrual cycles.

THE REPRODUCTIVE CYCLE

OVARIAN CYCLE

Follicle

Corpus luteum (cells—still in ovary—that had surrounded the egg)

Ovulation

0   7   14   21   28
Day

MENSTRUAL CYCLE

0   7   14   21   28
Day

Menstruation

HORMONE LEVELS

Follicle-stimulating hormone (FSH)

Luteinizing hormone (LH)

Estrogen

Progesterone

0   7   14   21   28
Day

FIGURE 25-17 The stages of the female reproductive cycle and associated hormonal changes.

3. **Follicle develops.** FSH, just as its name indicates, causes a few follicles in the ovaries to grow and develop, although only one follicle reaches full maturity. Within this one follicle, the primary oocyte completes its first meiotic division and becomes a secondary oocyte.

4. **Estrogen produced.** As the follicles develop, they produce estrogen, gradually increasing the level of estrogen in the blood.

5. **LH released.** The high levels of estrogen trigger the release of a burst of luteinizing hormone (LH) and more FSH.

6. **Ovulation.** The burst of LH triggers ovulation, causing the secondary oocyte to erupt from the follicle and out of the ovary. This release occurs approximately halfway through the menstrual cycle, around day 14, and signals the end of the **follicular phase.**

7. **Progesterone produced.** As the second half, or **luteal phase,** of the reproductive cycle begins, the follicle cells that had surrounded the oocyte develop into a structure called the **corpus luteum** (Latin for "yellow body"). These cells begin secreting smaller amounts of estrogen, but increasing amounts of progesterone.

8. **Endometrium thickens.** Just as its name suggests, **progesterone** (*pro* = for; *gestare* = to bear) causes the body to prepare for gestation of an embryo, in case fertilization occurs. Progesterone's primary effect is to cause a thickening of the endometrium, or lining of the uterus. The endometrium becomes increasingly rich with blood vessels and deposits of glycogen that can nourish a developing embryo.

At this point, the process can go in one of two directions, depending on whether or not the egg is fertilized (**FIGURE 25-18**).

If the egg is not fertilized, the egg disintegrates and the corpus luteum degenerates, sloughs off, and is shed, along with the disintegrating egg, as menstruation begins. Abruptly removing this source of estrogen and progesterone causes the lining of the uterus to slough off, and menstruation begins. With continuing reduction in estrogen levels, the pituitary gland is spurred to release FSH, and the process begins again.

If the egg is fertilized, which usually occurs in the Fallopian tube, the zygote begins development and after several days begins to secrete **human chorionic gonadotropin (hCG).** This hormone prevents degradation of the corpus luteum, which continues to secrete progesterone, thereby maintaining the endometrium. In the next section, we investigate what happens next in development of the embryo.

Females have about one million follicles, or potential eggs, when they are born, but most women ovulate fewer than 500 times over the course of their life. This leaves a lot of potential eggs lying around. In the normal course of events, these follicles just disintegrate, but in recent decades, modern medicine has made it possible for a woman to donate her eggs to another woman. The process involves several steps.

Q What does the process of being an egg donor entail?

TWO POSSIBLE FATES OF AN EGG

The fate of an egg and the preparation of the endometrium can go in one of two directions, depending on whether or not the egg is fertilized.

IF THE EGG IS NOT FERTILIZED

The corpus luteum degenerates.

Progesterone levels decrease.

The endometrium sloughs off and is shed, along with the egg, as menstruation begins.

IF THE EGG IS FERTILIZED

The zygote secretes hCG, preserving the corpus luteum.

Progesterone levels remain high.

The endometrium thickens in preparation for implantation.

FIGURE 25-18 An egg's fate can go in one of two directions. The photo shows an egg moving down the oviduct.

First, if you choose to be a donor, each day for about a week you have an injection of a drug that suppresses your own reproductive cycle. The suppression is followed by a week of injections of a fertility drug that contains large amounts of two hormones, LH (luteinizing hormone) and FSH (follicle-stimulating hormone), which induces one to two dozen follicles to develop in your ovaries. A doctor examines your ovaries by ultrasound to estimate the size and number of developing follicles. Finally, you are injected with human chorionic gonadotropin, which stimulates ovulation, the night before the egg "retrieval." The following morning, before the eggs have been released from the follicles, guided with the aid of ultrasound, the doctor inserts a tiny needle through the vagina into each follicle within the ovaries and sucks out the eggs, one by one. This process takes about half an hour. The eggs are placed in a Petri dish, fertilized with sperm, and allowed to divide for 2–6 days before several are transferred to the recipient's uterus.

Normal reproductive cycling continues from puberty until **menopause**—the cessation of ovulation and menstruation—usually between ages 45 and 55. It is not clear whether there is any evolutionarily adaptive value to menopause. In most species other than humans, females remain fertile throughout their entire adult life. Menopause may be a consequence of the relatively recent (on an evolutionary time scale) increase in human longevity. Regardless of the evolutionary explanation, oocyte depletion seems to influence the onset of menopause.

TAKE-HOME MESSAGE 25·7

In the ovaries, a cell within a follicle is stimulated to develop into a fertile egg by coordinated secretions of the hormones estrogen, FSH, and LH. Preparation of the uterus for implantation of a fertilized egg is coordinated by progesterone.

25·8–25·10 Sex can lead to fertilization, but it can also spread sexually transmitted diseases.

Human sperm fertilizing an egg.

25·8

In fertilization, two cells become one.

It's not enough for sperm cells to be in the same general location as an egg—there are some specific events that must occur for fertilization. The process of fertilization in vertebrates involves three separate steps: activation, penetration, and fusion of the nuclei (**FIGURE 25-19**). And before a sperm can take that first step and then penetrate an egg, it must find it. Recently, researchers discovered that sperm have receptors, like chemical sensors, that cause the sperm cells to swim toward a chemical attractant released by the egg. This attractant, in essence, says, "I'm over here!"

After ovulation, the egg is still surrounded by some smaller cells, called granulosa cells. These cells stand between the sperm and the egg, but they're not the only barrier. Between the granulosa cells and the egg's membrane, there is a glycoprotein layer called the **zona pellucida** (pronounced puh-LOO-sih-duh). As sperm approach the egg, release of calcium by cells surrounding the egg seems to increase the swimming speed and tail movements of the sperm, in a process known as sperm activation. A second phase of sperm

activation occurs as a sperm cell pushes its way through the granulosa cells, and the acrosome (at the head of the sperm) dissolves and releases digestive enzymes that help the sperm penetrate the zona pellucida.

Once the sperm gets through the zona pellucida, the oocyte is activated, and the plasma membranes of the sperm and egg fuse. This activation and fusion has a couple of important consequences. First, it changes the egg's membrane in such a way that it is impossible for any other sperm to also fertilize the egg. After all, it would be a genetic disaster for the fertilized egg to have more than two sets of chromosomes. Second, fusion of the plasma membranes induces the egg to complete its second meiotic division. On doing so, one haploid egg, the ovum, is formed, along with one smaller polar body. The latter disintegrates or is ejected from the egg.

And, finally, the haploid nucleus of the egg fuses with the haploid nucleus of the sperm, creating a diploid cell—the zygote.

FIGURE 25-19 **Fertilization is the fusion of one sperm with an egg.**

Within the figure:

FERTILIZATION

SPERM

Granulosa cells

Zona pellucida

Enzymes   Acrosome

EGG

Plasma membrane

Sperm nucleus

Egg nucleus

Zygote nucleus

1 PENETRATION
A sperm pushes its way through the granulosa cells, and enzymes within its acrosome digest the zona pellucida.

2 ACTIVATION
The plasma membrane of the sperm and egg fuse, making it impossible for other sperm to fuse with the egg.

3 NUCLEI FUSION
The haploid nucleus of the egg fuses with the haploid nucleus of the sperm, forming a diploid zygote.

In many species, stripping away the zona pellucida makes it possible for the egg to be fertilized by sperm from a different species. This suggests that something in the zona pellucida, perhaps recognition sites, ensures that the egg can be fertilized only by sperm from the same species.

TAKE-HOME MESSAGE 25·8

At fertilization, a sperm penetrates the protective zone around the egg, the egg blocks additional sperm entry, and the sperm and egg membranes fuse. The egg then completes its second meiotic division, and the haploid nuclei of the egg and sperm fuse, forming a diploid zygote.

25·9 Numerous strategies can help prevent fertilization.

Pregnancy depends on the occurrence of a great many events, relating to the production of sperm and eggs, fertilization, and implantation of the zygote in the uterus. **Contraception,** or birth control, is the attempt to prevent pregnancy. Although a wide variety of contraception methods are used—with varying degrees of effectiveness—each method generally represents one of three general strategies: (1) preventing ovulation, (2) preventing fertilization, or (3) preventing implantation. **FIGURE 25-20** summarizes various methods of contraception, how they work, and their effectiveness rates.

Preventing Ovulation

Birth control pills. Available since 1960, "the pill" is among the most effective of all methods of contraception, with a failure rate of 1% to 8%; that is, among 100 women using

birth control pills over the course of one year, there would be 1–8 pregnancies. (If taken every day at exactly the same time, the pills are more than 99% effective; the problem is that not all women are consistent in taking them.) Among 100 women using no contraception, there would be about 85 pregnancies during one year.

Two chief varieties of birth control pills, or oral contraceptives, are available, one that contains synthetic versions of estrogen and progesterone, and one that contains only a synthetic progesterone. The estrogen-progesterone pill prevents ovulation by keeping estrogen levels just high enough that the release of FSH by the pituitary gland is never triggered. As long as FSH is never released, eggs never develop and ovulation does not occur. The progesterone component

Q How do birth control pills work?

	METHOD	HOW IT WORKS
PREVENTING OVULATION	• Birth control pills	A pill containing synthetic hormones prevents the release of FSH by the pituitary gland, thus preventing egg development and ovulation (effectiveness: 92–99%).
	• Hormone injections or implants	Synthetic hormones are inserted under the skin to prevent the release of FSH by the pituitary gland, thus preventing egg development and ovulation (effectiveness: 97–99%).
PREVENTING FERTILIZATION	• Condoms	A thin rubber or natural membrane sheath placed on the penis or inside the vagina prevents sperm from coming in contact with an egg (effectiveness: male condoms: 85–98%; female condoms: 79–95%).
	• Diaphragm/cervical cap	A dome-shaped piece of rubber placed in the vagina blocks the cervix and prevents sperm from coming in contact with an egg (effectiveness: 84–94%).
	• Sterilization	A medical procedure permanently alters the reproductive system to prevent the release of sperm or block the movement of eggs down the Fallopian tubes (effectiveness: >99%).
	• Abstinence	Individuals refrain from sexual intercourse (effectiveness: complete abstinence: 100%; abstinence during days when fertility is likely, based on analysis of female's menstrual cycle pattern: 75–99%).
PREVENTING IMPLANTATION	• Intrauterine device (IUD)	A small plastic or metal device inserted into the uterus by a doctor prevents a fertilized egg from implanting (effectiveness: >99%).
	• "Morning-after" pills	A pill containing a dose of estrogen 50 times higher than that found in birth control pills can stop ovum development or implantation (effectiveness: >75%).

FIGURE 25-20 Preventing pregnancy.

of the pill causes just enough development of the lining of the uterus that a plug of mucus forms at the connection between the vagina and uterus, blocking sperm from getting through.

Taking the pill at the same time every day is essential. If more than 24 hours go by between pills, the estrogen level in the body begins to drop; if it gets below a critical level, FSH release by the pituitary is triggered, which can lead to ovulation and the risk of pregnancy.

The long-term health consequences of using birth control pills include a slightly elevated risk of cardiovascular disease, particularly among women who smoke. However, because birth control users have a reduced risk of pregnancy—a condition that carries with it some significant health risks— and a reduced risk of ovarian and endometrial cancers, women's overall mortality risk is reduced while on the pill (see Section 24-10).

Although the birth control pill is one of the most commonly used contraceptives, recent research has revealed that its hormones may actually alter women's attraction to men. When not taking birth control pills, most women prefer the odor of men possessing certain genetic combinations that are most different from their own. When taking the pill, however, their preference switches to the odor of men with genetic combinations most similar to their own. Much additional research in this area is under way.

Hormone injections or implants. Injections or capsule implants, just under the skin, of synthetic estrogen and progesterone, or progesterone only, represent a slight variation on birth control pills. The prevention of pregnancy works in the same way, but with the added convenience of not having to take a pill every day. Some implants, in fact, need to be replaced only once every three years. These methods are slightly more effective than birth control pills, because much of the user error is eliminated.

Preventing Fertilization

Condoms. The condom—a thin rubber or natural membrane sheath placed on the penis or inside the vagina, covering the cervix—is one of several barrier methods of contraception, which keep sperm from coming in contact with an egg. Condoms have the added benefit of being one of the only methods of contraception that offer effective protection against sexually transmitted diseases, including HIV/AIDS. (See the next section for further discussion of this topic.)

FIGURE 25-21 X ray of intrauterine contraceptive device (IUD).

Temporary abstinence during the times when conception is most likely (often called the "rhythm method"), while theoretically effective, has a failure rate as high as 25%, probably due to variation in the time of ovulation and the longevity of sperm in the female reproductive system (72 hours or more).

Preventing Implantation

Intrauterine device (IUD). The intrauterine device, or IUD, is a small, T-shaped plastic or metal device inserted by a doctor into the uterus (**FIGURE 25-21**). The IUD (which can be left in for 3–4 years) does not prevent fertilization but instead prevents a fertilized egg from implanting in the uterus. IUDs have a failure rate of just under 1%. Some women experience side effects from IUDs (including cramps and other pain) and may need to have the device removed.

Diaphragm or cervical cap. A diaphragm or cervical cap—a dome-shaped piece of rubber placed in the vagina, blocking the cervix—also prevents pregnancy by blocking sperm from reaching an egg. The use of spermicidal creams with a diaphragm or cervical cap (and with a condom as well) can increase its effectiveness.

Sterilization. Sterilization is the permanent alteration of the reproductive system to prevent the release of sperm or the movement of eggs down the Fallopian tubes. In a tubal ligation, the woman's oviducts are cut and tied so that eggs cannot reach the uterus. In a vasectomy, the man's vas deferens on each side is cut and tied so that sperm cannot reach the urethra, thereby causing the semen to carry no sperm. There are no side effects in either case. Each of these procedures, however, should be considered permanent (although in rare cases, the procedure can be successfully reversed).

Abstinence. Abstinence—not having sexual intercourse—is the most effective method of preventing pregnancy. In practice, however, abstaining from intercourse can prove difficult, particularly in the context of a long-term relationship.

"Morning-after" pills. Although not recommended as a long-term strategy for contraception, the morning-after pill, a dose of estrogen 50 times greater than that in birth control pills, can stop ovum development or implantation. The morning-after pill has a failure rate of up to 25% and is recommended only for cases of rape and emergencies in which other methods of contraception have failed. In contrast to the large hormone content of morning-after drugs, another drug, known as RU486, is considered an anti-hormone drug. It blocks progesterone receptors in the uterus, thereby causing the lining of the uterus to be sloughed off. This can end a pregnancy any time during the first seven weeks. In addition to causing abdominal pain and cramping, RU486 can also have other adverse effects, including nausea, vomiting, and fever.

Q { **What is the "morning-after" pill?**

TAKE-HOME MESSAGE 25·9

Pregnancy can be prevented by numerous methods, each of which acts in one or more ways to prevent ovulation, fertilization, or implantation.

25·10 Sexually transmitted diseases reveal battles between microbes and humans.

To many microbes, the human genitals and reproductive tract represent a desirable place to find shelter, nourishment, and opportunities for reproducing and dispersing. Unfortunately, these microbes can cause problems for humans in the form of **sexually transmitted diseases (STDs).** STDs produce symptoms of varying severity, from

mild to extreme discomfort to sterility or even death. It is estimated that more than 300 million new cases of STDs occur each year worldwide.

Sexually transmitted diseases are caused by bacteria, viruses, fungi, protists, and even some arthropods. The organisms are passed from the mucous membranes (of the genitals, as well as of the anus and mouth) of one individual to those of another during sexual contact; sometimes they are transmitted by needles used for drug injections.

Some of the most common STDs, with their symptoms and treatments, are listed in **FIGURE 25-22**. Although most are curable with antibiotics, antifungal drugs, or anti-protozoan drugs, two characteristics of STDs make them nearly impossible to completely eradicate from a population: (1) their symptoms may be mild or completely absent at times, causing many people to unwittingly pass an infection to their partners, and (2) to prevent reinfection, both partners must be treated simultaneously. Furthermore, because most microbes have such high reproductive rates, populations of a

microbe can evolve quickly and become resistant to existing drugs, reducing the long-term effectiveness of treatments. Consequently, the treatment of STDs represents one of the most pressing public health issues in the world today.

TAKE-HOME MESSAGE 25·10

Sexually transmitted diseases (STDs) are caused by a variety of organisms, including bacteria, viruses, protists, fungi, and arthropods. Worldwide, more than 300 million people are infected each year. The symptoms of STDs range from nonexistent to mild to extreme discomfort, sterility, or even death.

SEXUALLY TRANSMITTED DISEASES

CAUSE	EXAMPLES	SYMPTOMS	TREATMENT
BACTERIUM	• Gonorrhea	Often none; sometimes painful urination, genital discharge, or irregular menstruation	Several antibiotics can successfully cure gonorrhea; however, drug-resistant strains are increasing.
	• Syphilis	Often no symptoms for years; eventual sores, skin rash, and if untreated, organ damage	Penicillin, an antibiotic, can cure syphilis in the early stages.
	• Chlamydia	Often none; sometimes painful urination, genital discharge	Chlamydia can be easily treated and cured with antibiotics.
VIRUS	• HIV/AIDS	Initial symptoms range from none to flu-like; late stages involve severe infections and death	Currently no cure. Antiretroviral treatment can slow progression. Drug-resistant strains occur.
	• Genital herpes	Often none; outbreaks include sores on genitals, flu-like symptoms	Currently no cure. Antiviral medications can shorten and prevent outbreaks.
	• Human papilloma virus (HPV)	Often none; some types can lead to genital warts, others can cause cervical cancer	A vaccine prevents HPV and is recommended for girls age 11–12. Warts and cancerous lesions can be removed.
	• Hepatitis	Initial symptoms range from none to fever, fatigue, and abdominal pain; can develop into a chronic disease that may cause liver cancer.	Antiviral drugs can help chronic disease; regular monitoring needed to identify liver damage or cancer.
PROTIST	• Trichomoniasis	Painful urination and/or vaginal discharge in women; often no symptoms in men	Trichomoniasis can usually be cured with prescription drugs.
FUNGUS	• Yeast infections	Genital itching or burning and/or vaginal discharge in women; genital itching in men	Yeast infections can usually be cured with antifungal suppositories or creams.
ARTHROPOD	• Crab lice	Visible lice eggs or lice crawling or attached to pubic hair, itching in the pubic and groin area	Crab lice infection can be treated with over-the-counter lotions.

FIGURE 25-22 The most common STDs.

25·11–25·15 Human development occurs in specific stages.

A developing human fetus, five months after fertilization.

25·11

Early embryonic development occurs during cleavage, gastrulation, and neurulation.

How do you build a complete human, with specialized cells, tissues, and organs, when at fertilization there is just a zygote, a single cell that doesn't resemble a human at all? The field of developmental biology seeks to understand and explain how a complex organism develops from a single cell. To be sure, the genes in that initial cell are important, and the environmental conditions in which the cell develops are also critical. These factors interact as the development of humans and most other vertebrates proceeds in a carefully coordinated sequence of three stages: cleavage, gastrulation, and neurulation.

Cleavage The first phase, **cleavage,** is the early cell division, by mitosis, of the zygote, beginning shortly after fertilization (**FIGURE 25-23**). It starts about 30 hours after fertilization, as the zygote divides into two cells. Then, after another 30 hours or so, it divides again, becoming four cells, and then again, through numerous divisions. Although the number of cells increases significantly during cleavage, there is little or no growth in overall size. Rather, the fertilized egg is partitioned into more and more cells that are smaller and smaller. These multiple cell divisions are fueled by nutrients that were in the egg. At the cleavage stage, it is difficult to distinguish between species as dissimilar as sea urchins and humans.

After about six days of continuous cell division, the cells form a hollow ball, called a **blastula**—the mammalian version is called a **blastocyst**—of approximately a thousand cells. The cells secrete fluid into the center of the ball, where there is an inner mass of cells that form the embryo. The outer cells also produce human chorionic gonadotropin (hCG), which keeps the corpus luteum from disintegrating.

The blastocyst grows rapidly and forms membranes that surround and protect it. These include the **amnion,** which surrounds the embryo, and the **chorion,** which, along with the endometrium, forms the **placenta,** the structure that connects the developing embryo to the wall of the uterus (see Figure 25-29). The placenta is packed with blood vessels that bring nourishment to the embryo and remove wastes generated by the embryo (**FIGURE 25-24**).

Gastrulation In the second phase of development, **gastrulation,** three distinct **germ layers** of tissue form. Picture a beach ball—a hollow sphere. Now imagine making a fist and slowly pushing inward on the beach ball. This resembles the process of gastrulation. The entire mass of cells is called a gastrula (**FIGURE 25-25**), and the indentation is called the blastopore. The blastopore is located almost

Shortly after fertilization, cleavage—the early cell division, by mitosis, of the zygote—begins.

Inner cell mass

Zygote

Blastula

0 hours   30 hours   60 hours   6 days

Time

Cleavage results in a blastula (the mammalian version is called a blastocyst), a hollow ball of cells that contains an inner cellular mass, which will form the embryo.

FIGURE 25-23 Cleavage: formation of the blastula (blastocyst). During cleavage, cells divide continuously, eventually forming a hollow ball filled with fluid.

opposite the point at which the sperm entered the egg and, in vertebrates, becomes the anus.

Three distinct layers of tissue form during gastrulation. The cells in these layers have not yet differentiated (that is, they all look similar to one another), but they have become determined, which means that the type of tissue they will become, their ultimate developmental fate, is irreversibly decided. Prior to determination, cells are referred to as

"totipotent" and have the capacity to develop into any type of tissue in the body.

Here's a summary of what happens during gastrulation.

1. First, the blastocyst begins to fold inward forming an indentation, the blastopore.

2. As the cells continue to push inward, they are called **endoderm,** and they form the lining of what will eventually become the digestive tract. Endoderm cells will also form the liver, the pancreas, and the lining of the respiratory tract. At this point, the entire mass of cells is called a **gastrula.**

3. The cells that remain on the outer surface of the gastrula are called **ectoderm** and will ultimately form the outer layer of skin, the hair, the lining of the nose and mouth, and the nervous system.

4. Some additional cells migrate inward, between the endoderm and ectoderm, forming a third type of tissue, called **mesoderm,** which gives rise to the muscles and skeleton.

FIGURE 25-24 Tiny, but with tremendous potential. A human embryo in the blastocyst stage on the tip of a pin. *Inset:* photomicrograph of a human embryo at the same stage.

The specific details of gastrulation differ slightly from one species to the next. The general outcome, however—the formation of endoderm, mesoderm, and ectoderm—is the same throughout the vertebrates.

Neurulation In the third week of embryonic development, the three types of tissue formed during gastrulation begin to develop into the various organs and tissues. At this time, within the mesoderm and running the length of the embryo, just above the digestive tract, the notochord forms. The **notochord** is a flexible rod that develops in all chordates and

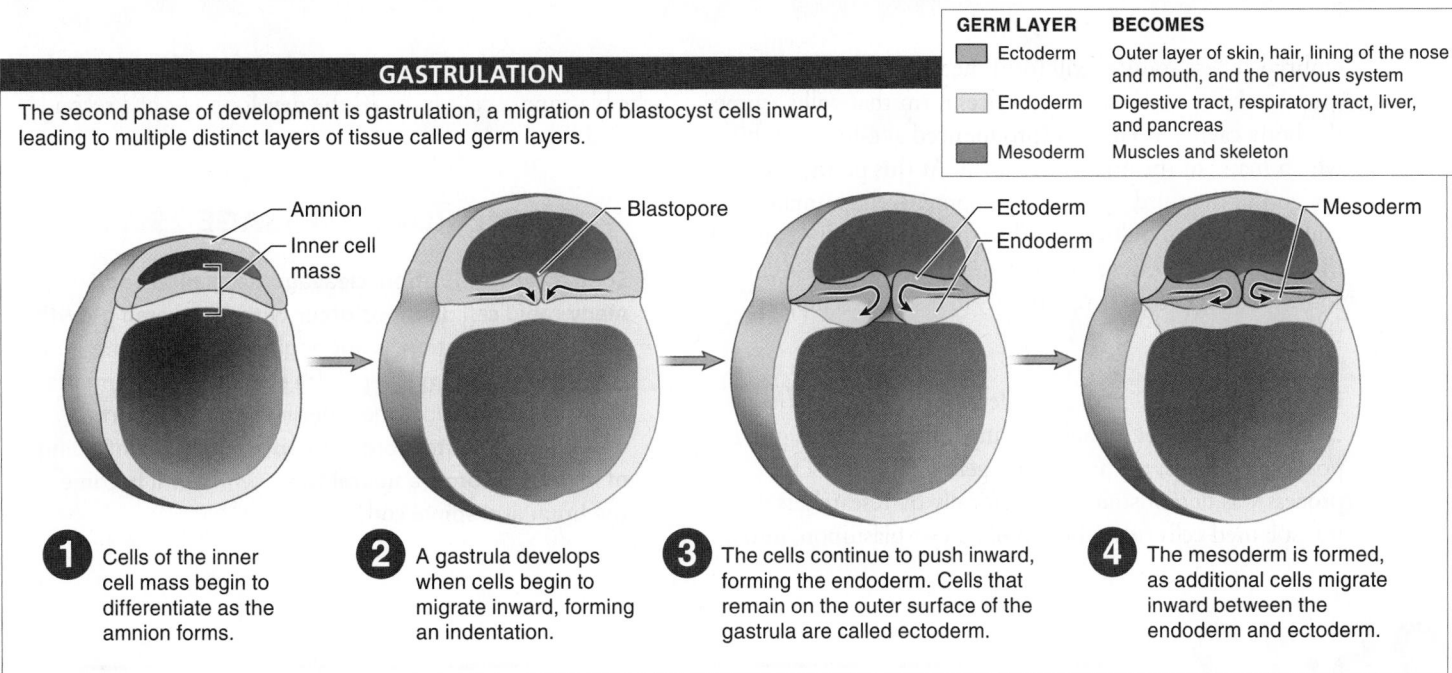

GERM LAYER | BECOMES

GERM LAYER	BECOMES
Ectoderm	Outer layer of skin, hair, lining of the nose and mouth, and the nervous system
Endoderm	Digestive tract, respiratory tract, liver, and pancreas
Mesoderm	Muscles and skeleton

GASTRULATION

The second phase of development is gastrulation, a migration of blastocyst cells inward, leading to multiple distinct layers of tissue called germ layers.

1 Cells of the inner cell mass begin to differentiate as the amnion forms.

2 A gastrula develops when cells begin to migrate inward, forming an indentation.

3 The cells continue to push inward, forming the endoderm. Cells that remain on the outer surface of the gastrula are called ectoderm.

4 The mesoderm is formed, as additional cells migrate inward between the endoderm and ectoderm.

FIGURE 25-25 Gastrulation: formation of three germ layers. During gastrulation, three distinct layers of tissue form that will eventually make up the structures of the body.

gives support to surrounding tissue. In vertebrates, the notochord's function is ultimately taken over by the backbone.

Just above the notochord, ectoderm folds in for the entire length of the embryo, first forming a groove and then becoming a long hollow tube, called the **neural tube.** The process is referred to as **neurulation,** and the resulting neural tube ultimately develops into the entire nervous system, including the brain and the spinal cord (**FIGURE 25-26**).

As the neural tube is developing, blocks of mesoderm tissue, called somites, begin to form down the length of the

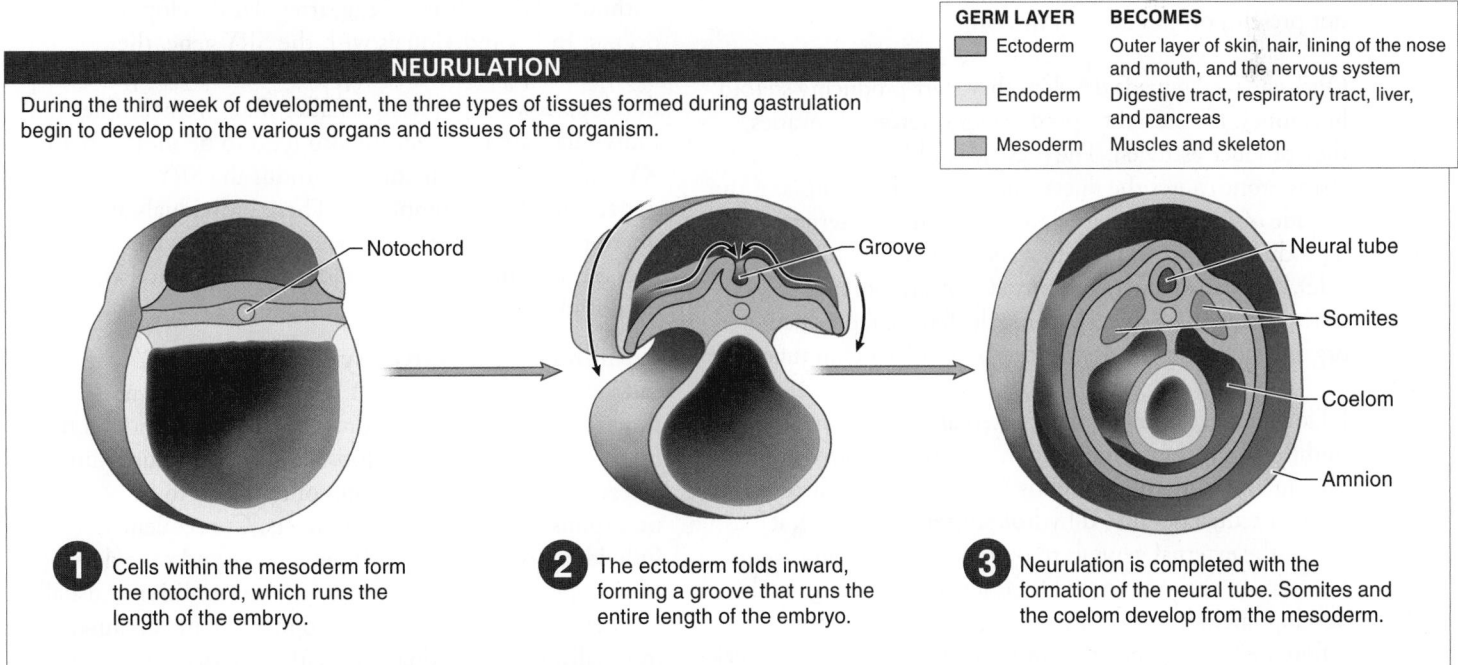

GERM LAYER	BECOMES
Ectoderm	Outer layer of skin, hair, lining of the nose and mouth, and the nervous system
Endoderm	Digestive tract, respiratory tract, liver, and pancreas
Mesoderm	Muscles and skeleton

NEURULATION

During the third week of development, the three types of tissues formed during gastrulation begin to develop into the various organs and tissues of the organism.

1 Cells within the mesoderm form the notochord, which runs the length of the embryo.

2 The ectoderm folds inward, forming a groove that runs the entire length of the embryo.

3 Neurulation is completed with the formation of the neural tube. Somites and the coelom develop from the mesoderm.

FIGURE 25-26 Neurulation: formation of organs and tissues from the germ layers. During neurulation, the germ layers begin to develop into the organs and tissues of the body.

embryo. These somites will form the vertebrae and the muscles. Next to the somites, spaces form that will become the body cavity, or **coelom** (pronounced SEE-lum), within which many of the organs will form. At this point, toward the end of the third week of development, the human embryo is only 2 millimeters (less than one-tenth of an inch) in length. Further development and specialization occur as some cells are programmed to die, in essence "sculpting" the body.

Other cells may be induced to develop into one particular cell type or another by neighboring cells that send signals, possibly proteins, to turn certain genes on or off. This process was demonstrated dramatically by researchers who transplanted cells from the top of a newt blastopore into a different developing embryo. In the recipient embryo, the blastopore cells induced the development of a second neural tube!

TAKE-HOME MESSAGE 25·11

Soon after fertilization, cleavage takes place, and many rapid cell divisions occur without overall growth. Then, in gastrulation, a gut begins to form, along with three distinct germ layers with specific developmental fates. In neurulation, mesoderm forms a supporting rod called the notochord, and above that, an infolding of ectoderm forms a neural tube, which will become the brain and spinal cord.

25·12 How does an embryo become male or female?

During the first few weeks after fertilization, surprisingly little distinguishes males from females. Then, about four weeks into embryo development in mammals, a gene carried on the Y chromosome, called SRY (for **s**ex-determining **r**egion on the **Y** chromosome), can initiate development as a male (**FIGURE 25-27**). The gene is expressed in the tissue that will form the gonads, and usually, when SRY is expressed, the gonads develop as testes. (There is a gene on the X chromosome that also influences sex determination and, in rare cases, can alter typical sex development.) If SRY is not present, ovaries develop instead.

Once the fetal gonads develop, they start producing steroid hormones. If testes, they produce testosterone. If ovaries, they produce estrogen. The presence of high levels of testosterone causes the ducts connecting the gonads and the outside of the body to develop into the male internal reproductive organs, including the vas deferens (on each side), ejaculatory duct, and prostate. In the absence of testosterone, these ducts become the female reproductive organs, including the uterus, cervix, and Fallopian tubes.

Following development of the internal reproductive organs, undifferentiated external genitals develop. If testosterone is present and is modified slightly (by an enzyme called 5-alpha-reductase) into dihydrotestosterone (DHT), it causes the external genitals to become the penis and scrotum. In the absence of DHT, female external genitals develop, including the clitoris, labia, and vagina. Sex differentiation is generally complete by about the 12th week of development in humans.

At several points, the development of an embryo as male or female can be disrupted. Disruptions of this type occur in several genetic disorders.

1. Recombination leading to XX individuals with the SRY gene or XY individuals lacking SRY. It is possible, during the production of sperm, for crossing over to occur between the X and Y chromosomes. If this crossover causes the SRY gene to be moved to the X chromosome, and if the sperm cell carrying the X with SRY or the Y without SRY fertilizes an egg, irregular development occurs. In XX individuals with the SRY gene, the individual appears to develop as a male. Although testes develop, however, they are smaller than average. These individuals are infertile and also tend to be shorter than XY males. In XY individuals without the SRY gene, the gonads develop incompletely. These individuals appear to develop as female. At puberty, however, they are taller than average, do not develop secondary sex characteristics, and do not menstruate.

2. Androgen insensitivity syndrome. Some XY individuals (approximately 1 in 20,000) carry a non-functioning copy of the androgen receptor. Although the SRY gene triggers the development of testes, this X-linked recessive trait causes the tissues of the body to be unresponsive to testosterone's effects. Consequently, individuals with androgen insensitivity syndrome develop what appears to be a female body. The condition is usually not detected until the girl fails to menstruate, because, internally, this individual has neither uterus nor ovaries but, rather, internal testes.

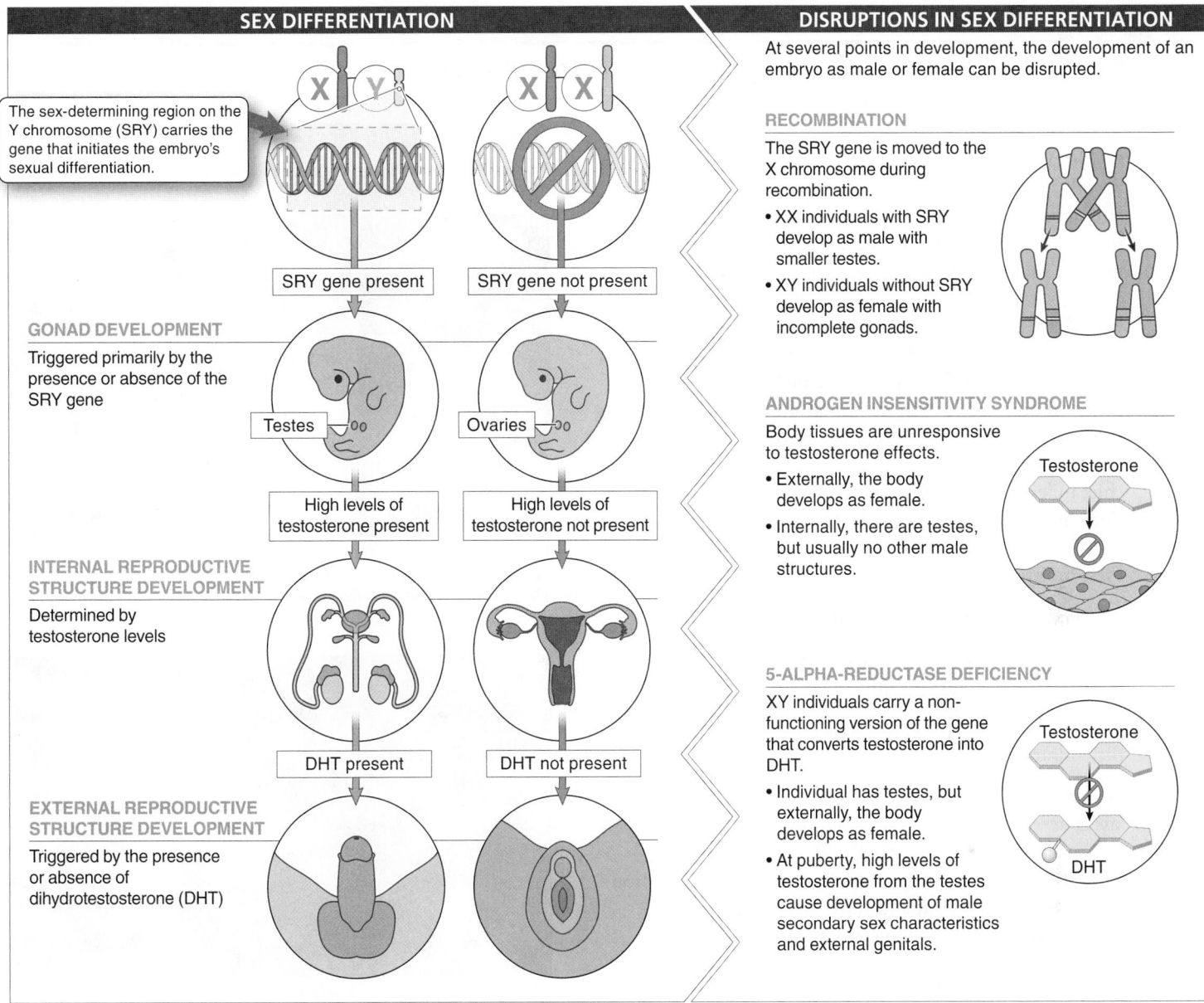

SEX DIFFERENTIATION

The sex-determining region on the Y chromosome (SRY) carries the gene that initiates the embryo's sexual differentiation.

SRY gene present

SRY gene not present

GONAD DEVELOPMENT

Triggered primarily by the presence or absence of the SRY gene

Testes

Ovaries

High levels of testosterone present

High levels of testosterone not present

INTERNAL REPRODUCTIVE STRUCTURE DEVELOPMENT

Determined by testosterone levels

DHT present

DHT not present

EXTERNAL REPRODUCTIVE STRUCTURE DEVELOPMENT

Triggered by the presence or absence of dihydrotestosterone (DHT)

DISRUPTIONS IN SEX DIFFERENTIATION

At several points in development, the development of an embryo as male or female can be disrupted.

RECOMBINATION

The SRY gene is moved to the X chromosome during recombination.

- XX individuals with SRY develop as male with smaller testes.
- XY individuals without SRY develop as female with incomplete gonads.

ANDROGEN INSENSITIVITY SYNDROME

Body tissues are unresponsive to testosterone effects.

- Externally, the body develops as female.
- Internally, there are testes, but usually no other male structures.

Testosterone

5-ALPHA-REDUCTASE DEFICIENCY

XY individuals carry a non-functioning version of the gene that converts testosterone into DHT.

- Individual has testes, but externally, the body develops as female.
- At puberty, high levels of testosterone from the testes cause development of male secondary sex characteristics and external genitals.

Testosterone

DHT

FIGURE 25-27 Typical and atypical sex development.

3. 5-Alpha-reductase deficiency. Some XY individuals carry a non-functioning version of the gene for the enzyme that converts testosterone into DHT. Without DHT to direct the development of external male genitals, these individuals possess testes, but the external genitals develop as they would in a female. Consequently, individuals with 5-alpha-reductase deficiency are generally identified as female at birth. At puberty, however, in response to increased testosterone production, they develop male secondary sex characteristics, including a deeper voice, facial hair, and increased muscle mass. The external genitals grow and often come to resemble a penis and scrotum more than a clitoris and labia.

TAKE-HOME MESSAGE 25·12

Mammalian embryos develop female internal and external reproductive organs unless a gene on the Y chromosome stimulates fetal gonads to develop as testes, leading to testosterone production, which then stimulates the development of male reproductive organs.

HOW DO ANIMALS REPRODUCE?

MALE AND FEMALE REPRODUCTIVE SYSTEMS

SEX CAN LEAD TO FERTILIZATION

HUMAN DEVELOPMENT

REPRODUCTIVE TECHNOLOGY

1007

There are three stages of pregnancy.

The development of a human embryo and fetus is usually divided into three equal periods of approximately three months each. (The **fetus** stage begins about 8 weeks after fertilization, when the organs and other major structures first form.) Each **trimester** is characterized by specific features and developmental milestones (**FIGURE 25-28**).

First trimester The first three months of development are characterized by relatively little growth, at the end of which the fetus is only about two or three inches long and weighs about an ounce. Much more important than growth during the first trimester is development and the differentiation of cells into specialized types of tissues. Here are some of the chief milestones (times indicate how much time has passed since fertilization).

First month

30 hours: The first cleavage occurs.

60 hours: The second cleavage occurs. In both cleavages, there is no overall growth, just cell division.

6–7 days: The embryo reaches the uterus for implantation in the endometrium.

2nd week: Gastrulation occurs, and three distinct tissue layers develop. The placenta also forms, as two membranes grow around the blastocyst—the amnion around the embryo and the chorion around the amnion. The chorion ultimately branches out and surrounds the lining of the uterus and, with the endometrium, forms the placenta (**FIGURE 25-29**), a mass of tissue in which nutrients, respiratory gases, and waste products are transferred between the circulatory systems of the mother and the developing embryo. (Although there is a yolk sac in placental mammals, its size is reduced and the placenta takes over the yolk sac's role of nourishing the embryo.) The embryo is connected to the chorion by the body stalk, which will become the **umbilical cord.**

Although the mother's blood and the embryo's blood do not mix, they come in very close contact at the placenta, and oxygen diffuses from mother to embryo as carbon dioxide diffuses from embryo to mother. The placenta also nourishes the embryo and secretes hormones, including hCG, which

FIGURE 25-28 Development of the human embryo and fetus. The nine months of human fetal development are divided into three-month trimesters.

HUMAN EMBRYO DEVELOPMENT

The nine months of human fetal development are divided into three-month trimesters.

FIRST TRIMESTER: MONTHS 1–3
- Cells begin to differentiate into specialized types of tissues.
- Major organs and structures begin to form, including the eyes, heart, liver, pancreas, and gallbladder, as well as the limbs.

SECOND TRIMESTER: MONTHS 4–6
- Significant muscle and bone growth occurs, with less new development relative to the first trimester.

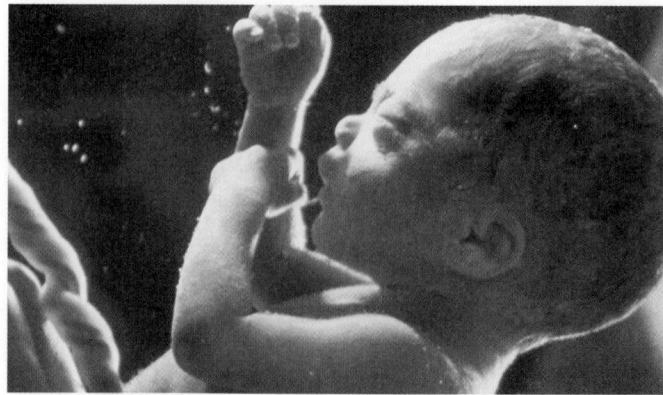

THIRD TRIMESTER: MONTHS 7–9
- Significant development of the nervous system takes place.

THE PLACENTA

The placenta is a mass of highly vascularized tissue in which nutrients, respiratory gases, and waste products are transferred between the mother and the developing embryo.

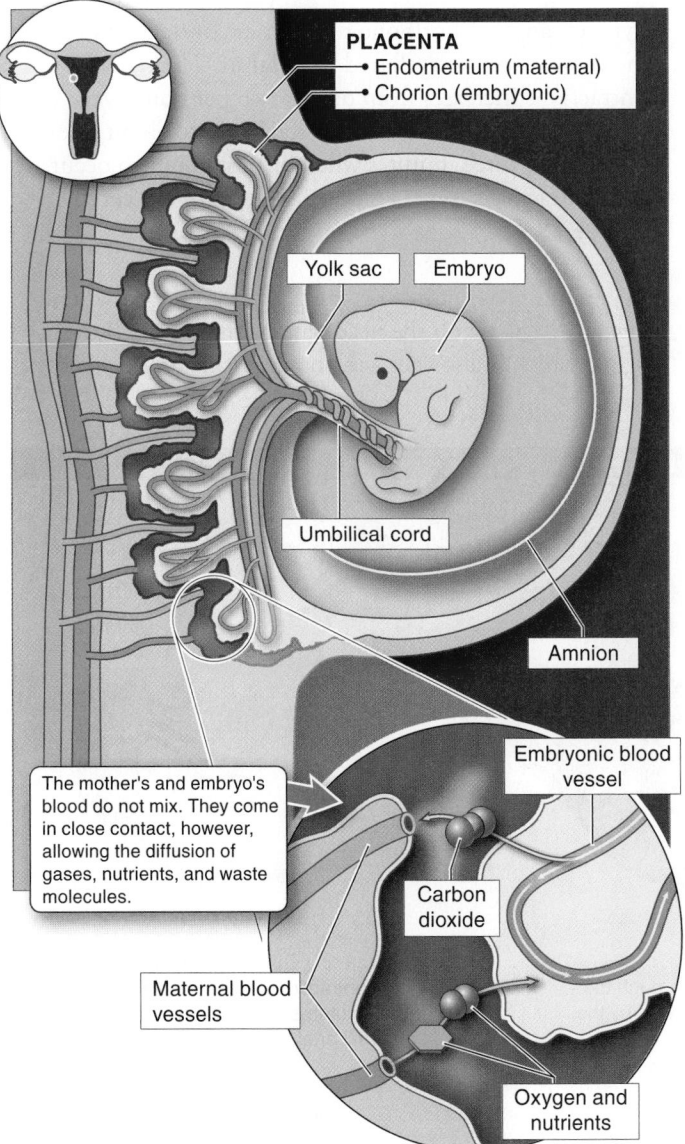

PLACENTA
- Endometrium (maternal)
- Chorion (embryonic)

Yolk sac   Embryo

Umbilical cord

Amnion

The mother's and embryo's blood do not mix. They come in close contact, however, allowing the diffusion of gases, nutrients, and waste molecules.

Embryonic blood vessel

Carbon dioxide

Maternal blood vessels

Oxygen and nutrients

FIGURE 25-29 Structure and function of the placenta.

maintains the corpus luteum, ensuring continued secretions of progesterone and, consequently, maintenance of the endometrium.

3rd week: Neurulation occurs.

4th week: Major structures and organs, including the eyes and heart, begin to form. At this point, it is also possible to see the arm and leg buds.

Second month

During this time, the limbs take shape. The major organs, including the liver, pancreas, and gallbladder, can also be seen. In spite of such dramatic development and differentiation, though, very little growth has occurred yet, and the weight of the embryo is about one gram, less than one-tenth of an ounce!

Third month

During the third month, the nervous system develops, as do some of the first reflexes, such as suckling. At this point, the corpus luteum finally degenerates. In the absence of the progesterone it has been producing, a new ovulatory cycle would typically (i.e., without pregnancy) occur, but because the placenta produces significant levels of estrogen and progesterone (which inhibit the production of FSH and LH), no ovulation occurs. Around the 10th week, the fetus's heartbeat usually becomes audible, and the development of mammary glands in the mother's breasts is also stimulated, in preparation for later milk production (**lactation**).

Second trimester Months 4, 5, and 6 of a pregnancy are a time of significant growth and less new development relative to the first trimester. During this time, as the bones get bigger and the muscles develop, the fetus moves around and the mother can often feel it kick. The heartbeat becomes much louder, and its "whooshing" can be heard easily with a stethoscope. Although the fetus cannot survive outside the womb at the end of the second trimester, its size has increased to about 600 grams (1.3 pounds) and 12 inches in length.

Third trimester The third trimester is all about growth, as the fetus ultimately becomes large enough to survive outside the mother (the minimum size for survival is generally about a pound and a half, or 680 g). Lung maturation also occurs during the third trimester and is associated with the production of increasing amounts of surfactant, compounds that reduce the surface tension and increase the lungs' ability to inflate and deflate without collapsing. The lungs of premature infants commonly have insufficient surfactant and are structurally immature. As a consequence, the infant may have difficulty with gas exchange and suffer from infant respiratory distress syndrome, which is the leading cause of death in premature infants. In addition to growth and lung maturation, during the third trimester there is significant development of the nervous system. The addition of new neurons occurs at the explosive rate of 15 million per hour, a rate that continues even after birth.

25·14 Pregnancy culminates in childbirth and the start of lactation.

Birth, also called parturition, is the culmination of pregnancy, and it occurs in three phases. The first is the initiation of contractions and the dilation, or opening, of the cervix. Toward the end of the third trimester, the fetus usually becomes positioned with its head down and its skull resting on the cervix. This positioning, along with the increasing size of the fetus, stretches the uterus. Although the exact process is not fully understood, fetal hormones cause the placenta to produce hormones, including estrogen and prostaglandin, that stimulate contractions. The stretching of the uterus causes the pituitary gland to release

oxytocin, another hormone that causes contractions. The contractions are referred to as **labor.** The rate of contractions increases from one or two per hour over many hours or even days before the birth, to about one every two to three minutes when birth is about to occur. The contractions cause a gradual dilation of the cervix (**FIGURE 25-30**).

The second phase of birth is the delivery of the baby. This generally occurs with the head passing first through the vagina, which is also called the birth canal. After delivery of

THE PHASES OF BIRTH

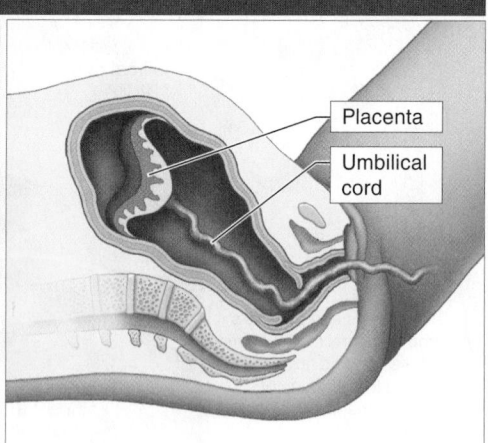

1 INITIATION OF CONTRACTIONS AND DILATION OF THE CERVIX
Hormones, including estrogen and prostaglandins, stimulate contractions in the uterus that cause a gradual opening of the cervix.

2 DELIVERY OF THE BABY
The baby's head passes through the vagina, or birth canal, followed by the rest of the body.

3 EXPULSION OF THE PLACENTA
Final contractions shear the placenta from the uterus wall and expel it through the birth canal.

FIGURE 25-30 Labor and birth.

Lactation, stimulated by prolactin and other hormones, nourishes the baby with protein, carbohydrates, and lipids, as well as with protective antibodies.

FIGURE 25-31 Complete nutrition. Breastfeeding provides an infant with all the nourishment it needs, along with antibody protection from some diseases.

the baby, its umbilical cord is clamped and cut, and clotting quickly stops any bleeding. There is a brief relaxation of the contractions before the third and final phase of the birth process. When the contractions resume, the placenta is sheared from the wall of the uterus and expelled.

During pregnancy, mammary gland development is stimulated by estrogen, progesterone, and other hormones.

After birth, the pituitary hormone prolactin stimulates milk production. Suckling by the infant, too, causes the release of prolactin and the hormone oxytocin, which further increases milk production. During the first few days, a yellowish fluid, called colostrum, is released. Colostrum is high in protein and contains numerous antibodies from the mother that protect the infant from some diseases (**FIGURE 25-31**). Gradually, the colostrum is replaced by milk, which is higher in fat and sugar, with less protein than colostrum. The median duration of breastfeeding varies a lot from one country, and one culture, to another. Published reports by the journal *Pediatrics* and by the World Health Organization, for example, note that the median duration of "any breastfeeding" is approximately 3 months in the United States and 33 to 34 months in Bangladesh and Nepal, respectively.

Q } How long does breastfeeding last?

During lactation, the suckling of the infant prevents the pituitary from releasing a sufficient surge of LH to cause ovulation. For this reason, during lactation, a woman's fertility is significantly reduced. As a successful method of birth control, this "lactational amenorrhea" depends on several conditions, including that the mother is exclusively breastfeeding (i.e., the baby is not getting nourishment in any other way), the baby is less than six months old, and no more than six hours pass between any two feedings.

Q } Can breast-feeding prevent pregnancy?

TAKE-HOME MESSAGE 25·14

Birth is the culmination of pregnancy and occurs in three phases. The first phase is initiation of contractions and dilation of the cervix. The second is delivery of the baby. The third is expulsion of the placenta. Lactation, stimulated by prolactin and other hormones, nourishes the infant with proteins, carbohydrates, and lipids and provides it with protective antibodies.

25·15 Reproductive technology has benefits and dangers.

The DNA from a single sperm is injected into the cytoplasm of an egg. At left is a pipette, which holds the egg in place. On the right, a needle is about to penetrate the egg and inject the genetic material.

25·15

Assisted reproductive technologies are promising and perilous.

Many methods exist that help otherwise infertile couples to have children. In this section we examine some of these techniques, beginning with the somewhat low-tech procedure that, more than a hundred years ago, started it all.

In 1884, a woman came to see Dr. William Pancoast because she had not been able to conceive a child. After examining the couple, Dr. Pancoast determined that the husband was infertile. In a discussion about the case with his medical students, someone suggested that semen be collected from "the best-looking" member of the class to inseminate the woman. Dr. Pancoast agreed and arranged to see the patient again, under the pretense of another examination, at which point he injected the semen into the woman's uterus. Only when it became clear that the woman was pregnant did the doctor inform the husband of what he had done. The husband, however, was happy and requested only that the doctor not tell his wife how she had become pregnant. Eventually, a healthy son was born, the first recorded child born as the result of artificial insemination with a donor's sperm. From these inauspicious beginnings, there have been tremendous advances in the technologies available to couples experiencing difficulty having children.

Infertility is defined as the inability to get pregnant after one year of trying. It affects approximately 7% of married couples in the United States in any given year. There are many causes of infertility—evenly divided between males and females—including low sperm counts and insufficient sperm motility, Fallopian tube damage or blockage, and ovulation problems. In 10% of cases, no cause can be found.

The reproductive technologies available are varied and include such interventions as surgery to repair blocked Fallopian tubes and hormone treatments to increase sperm counts or egg production. They also include a range of options called **assisted reproductive technology (ART),** the use of fertility treatments in which both sperm and egg are handled. These procedures typically involve removing eggs from a woman's ovaries, combining them with sperm to achieve fertilization in a Petri dish, and reinserting the fertilized eggs into the reproductive tract of that woman, or another woman. In many cases, the eggs, sperm, or fertilized eggs may be frozen for some period of time (**FIGURE 25-32**). The methods used in ART include the following:

1. IVF-ET. This stands for **in v**itro **f**ertilization–**e**mbryo **t**ransfer. It is the most common of all ART methods.

FIGURE 25-32 ART procedures.

Several secondary oocytes are collected and combined with sperm in a Petri dish. After several days, the fertilized eggs, at the eight-cell stage, are inserted into the woman's uterus.

2. ZIFT. Zygote **i**ntra-**F**allopian **t**ransfer differs from IVF-ET in only two respects. After fertilization in a Petri dish, the fertilized eggs are transferred not to the uterus but to one of the Fallopian tubes instead. Also, they are transferred earlier, at the one-cell stage. Perhaps because surgery is needed to place a fertilized egg within the Fallopian tube, ZIFT is used by only 1% of couples seeking ART. In some cases, transfer to the Fallopian tube is not made until the fertilized egg is in the two- to four-cell stage (this is referred to as tubal embryo transfer). Some studies have shown ZIFT to have a higher implantation rate than IVF-ET.

3. GIFT. The method known as **g**amete **i**ntra-**F**allopian **t**ransfer differs from ZIFT only in that the oocytes are mixed with sperm and immediately transferred to a Fallopian tube, so that fertilization occurs in the body, rather than in a Petri dish.

In some cases, if the male's sperm counts are particularly low or if his sperm have low motility, a procedure called ICSI, or **i**ntra**c**ytoplasmic **s**perm **i**njection, may be used in conjunction with IVF-ET or ZIFT. In this procedure, a single sperm is injected directly into an egg. While this method can be effective as a treatment for male infertility, there are concerns because sperm selection is bypassed. That

is, instead of one sperm "winning" the competition to fertilize the egg, a sperm is selected by the individual doing the procedure. This may be why there's an increased incidence of genetically carried birth defects with ICSI.

Outside the definition of ART is the increasingly effective process for selecting the sex of a baby, known as "sperm sorting." In this method, a fluorescent dye that binds to the DNA is applied to a sperm sample. Because the X chromosome is larger than the Y chromosome (by about 3%), the X-chromosome-bearing sperm bind more dye. The dyed sperm are then given a small electric charge, positive or negative, depending on which chromosome they carry, and as they are passed through a tube in single file, the sperm cells are deflected to a collecting tube on one side or the other, depending on their charge. The selected sperm carrying an X or Y sex chromosome can then be used in any of the ART methods described above. The purities of the X versus Y samples of sperm range from 70% to 90%.

TAKE-HOME MESSAGE 25·15

Assisted reproductive technology (ART) procedures typically involve removing eggs from a woman's ovaries, combining them with sperm to achieve fertilization, and reinserting the fertilized eggs into the woman's uterus or Fallopian tube. These technologies can enable previously infertile couples to have babies.

StreetBIO
Knowledge You Can Use

BUSINESS AND SCIENCE IN CONFLICT
Why is the number of multiple births—twins, triplets, and more—on the rise?

Q: MULTIPLE BIRTHS ARE IN THE NEWS A LOT. ARE THEY ON THE RISE? Yes! Between 1980 and 2008, the incidence of twins in the United States increased by 70%. The rate of triplets and higher increased even more.

Q: WHY ARE THERE SO MANY MORE MULTIPLE BIRTHS? Consider this: if you are running a fertility clinic, one of the most important pieces of information that will lead to the success or failure of your clinic is the percentage of treated couples who become pregnant. Unfortunately, in most ART procedures, this number is influenced by the number of embryos transferred into the woman: 5–10 transferred embryos are more likely to result in pregnancy than 1–4 transferred embryos. The problem is, though, that with 5–10 embryos transferred, the risk of "multiples"—twins, triplets, or more—also increases, as does the health risk to the mother and the babies. And so the decision regarding the number of embryos to transfer involves a trade-off between the perceived effectiveness of the clinic and the risk to the mother. This point was vividly illustrated in 2009 by the case of Nadya Suleman (called "Octomom" by the media), a California woman who gave birth to octuplets after eight embryos were implanted.

Q: ARE FERTILITY CLINICS BRINGING THE RATE BACK DOWN TO SAFER LEVELS? In the past 10 years, the proportion of in vitro fertilization cycles in which four or more embryos were transferred dropped from 62% to 21%. This has significantly reduced the incidence of triplets, but the rate of twins has remained high. And although, for women under 35, the American Society of Reproductive Medicine now recommends the transfer of just a single embryo during ART procedures, for women above 35, it still recommends three to five embryos be transferred.

Big Ideas in ... Reproduction and Development

25·1–25·3 How do animals reproduce?

- Animals can reproduce sexually or asexually.
- Sexual reproduction occurs in the vast majority of animal species and leads to offspring that are genetically different from one another and from either parent.
- Asexual reproduction can be fast and efficient, but leads to offspring genetically identical to the parent.

25·4–25·7 Male and female reproductive systems have important similarities and differences.

- In adult men, sperm are continuously produced in the testes by meiosis.
- Semen, consisting of sperm cells and accessory fluids that nurture the sperm and aid in fertilization, is ejaculated during copulation.
- In adult women, diploid cells in the ovaries undergo meiosis to produce genetically varied haploid eggs.
- Fewer eggs than sperm are produced, and eggs are much larger than sperm.

25·8–25·10 Sex can lead to fertilization, but it can also spread sexually transmitted diseases.

- At fertilization, a sperm penetrates the egg. The egg blocks additional sperm entry, and the sperm and egg membranes fuse. The haploid nuclei of the egg and sperm then fuse, forming a diploid zygote.
- Pregnancy can be prevented by preventing ovulation, fertilization, or implantation.
- Sexually transmitted diseases, which are caused by a variety of organisms, including bacteria, viruses, protists, fungi, and arthropods, infect more than 300 million people each year and can cause discomfort, sterility, or even death.

25·11–25·14 Human development occurs in specific stages.

- Fertilization is followed by cleavage of the zygote, with many rapid cell divisions but without growth.
- In gastrulation, a gut begins to form, along with three distinct germ layers with specific developmental fates.
- In neurulation, mesoderm forms the notochord, and ectoderm forms a neural tube, which will become the brain and spinal cord.
- Mammalian embryos develop female reproductive organs unless a gene on the Y chromosome stimulates the fetal gonads to develop as testes, leading to the further development of male reproductive organs.
- The development of human embryos is divided into three trimesters. The first is primarily a time of development and differentiation; the second and third are characterized mostly by significant growth.
- Birth is the culmination of pregnancy, and lactation, stimulated by prolactin and other hormones, nourishes the baby and provides protective antibodies.

25·15 Reproductive technology has benefits and dangers.

- Assisted reproductive technology can enable couples who previously would have been infertile to have babies.
- The procedures typically involve removing eggs from a woman's ovaries, combining them with sperm to achieve fertilization in a Petri dish, and reinserting the fertilized eggs into the woman.

See the To-Go Guide (packaged with every new copy of this textbook) for an illustrated summary of the chapter.

Check Your Knowledge

Thinking critically about visual displays of data.

1. In October, what was the average number of days between a woman's first day of menstruation and those of her 5–10 closest friends in the dorm? What was this number in April? By what percentage had it changed in six months?

2. If you assume that all women in the study had 28-day menstrual cycles, what is the highest value that would have been possible for the y-axis? Why?

3. Women on the pill were not excluded from this study. How might they influence the results? Why do you think they were included?

4. The data and the idea being tested were developed by a college undergraduate. Should that influence your interpretation of them? Why or why not?

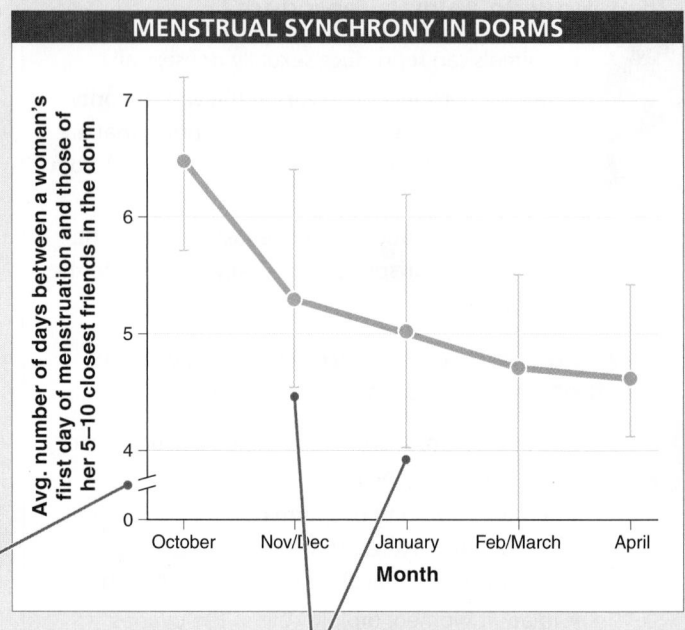

MENSTRUAL SYNCHRONY IN DORMS

5. What does the break in the y-axis (near the bottom) indicate? How would the graph appear different if this break were not made?

6. What do the vertical lines through each data point indicate? How would your evaluation of this graph change if the vertical lines through the data points were twice as long?

7. What is the "take-home message" of this graph? What additional data would be helpful? Why?

See Answers at the back of the book.

Key Terms in Reproduction and Development

Multiple-Choice Questions

1. Some animals are primarily asexual in their reproduction, but have the ability to switch to sexual reproduction under certain conditions. What might be the adaptive advantage to an animal that generally reproduces asexually to also be able to reproduce sexually?

   a) to increase the genetic diversity of its offspring during periods of stress

   b) to confuse its predators

   c) to give the animal some variety in its life

   d) to increase its own likelihood of survival

   e) Only a) and d) are correct.

   100 HARD **55** 0 EASY

2. Amplexus is a tactic that occurs in most species of frogs. The most likely reason that this tactic has evolved is:

   a) the gametes of terrestrial animals can quickly dry out in non-aquatic environments.

   b) it enables internal fertilization to occur without the necessity of viviparity.

   c) it ensures that the sperm and eggs are released at the same time and in the same place, increasing the likelihood of fertilization.

   d) it reduces the negative effect of salt water on gametes.

   e) All of the above are correct.

   100 HARD **41** 0 EASY

3. Meiosis occurs in the _____ in female humans and in the _____ in male humans.

   a) follicles; seminiferous tubules

   b) somatic cells; germ cells

   c) uterus; prostate gland

   d) follicles; prostate gland

   e) Fallopian tube; vas deferens

   100 HARD **72** 0 EASY

4. Which three sets of accessory glands add secretions to the semen in human males?

   a) the seminal vesicles, the prostate gland, and the bulbourethral glands

   b) the ejaculatory duct, the prostate gland, and the vas deferens

   c) the seminal vesicles, the prostate gland, and the urethra

   d) the seminal vesicles, the prostate gland, and the epididymis

   e) the ejaculatory duct, the prostate gland, and the bulbourethral glands

   100 HARD **38** 0 EASY

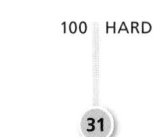
5. When individual females mate with multiple males within short periods of time:

   a) a male that produces more sperm than the other males has an increased probability of reproductive success.

   b) internal fertilization cannot occur.

   c) there is selection for a reduction in size of the male testes.

   d) the male gametes experience reduced desiccation.

   e) All of the above are correct.

   100 HARD **32** 0 EASY

6. The tissue that in males develops into the penis, in females develops into:

   a) the vagina.

   b) the labia.

   c) the clitoris.

   d) the oviduct.

   e) the ovary.

   100 HARD **31** 0 EASY

7. The completion of meiosis II in the oocyte of human females occurs:

a) before birth.

b) during menstruation.

c) after the oocyte is fertilized by a sperm.

d) a few hours before ovulation.

e) at ovulation.

8. The corpus luteum:

a) secretes chorionic gonadotropin.

b) is reabsorbed when fertilization occurs.

c) is the only source of the hormones that maintain pregnancy.

d) secretes progesterone but not estrogen.

e) is the initial source of progesterone during pregnancy.

9 In mammalian fertilization, the extracellular layer of the egg that functions, in part, as a sperm receptor is called the:

a) endoderm.

b) jelly coat.

c) acrosome.

d) egg plasma membrane.

e) zona pellucida.

10. The hormones present in birth control pills typically prevent pregnancy by:

a) preventing formation of the endometrial lining of the uterus.

b) preventing ovarian follicles from maturing.

c) preventing sperm from fertilizing the ovulated egg.

d) causing the endometrium to be shed once a fertilized egg has implanted.

e) preventing implantation of fertilized eggs in the endometrium.

11. Tying off the vas deferens leading from each testis will:

a) prevent formation of sperm.

b) decrease testosterone secretion.

c) reduce secretion from the seminal vesicles.

d) reduce secretions from the prostate gland.

e) None of the above.

12. When do cells begin to lose their totipotency?

a) anaphase of mitosis

b) gastrulation

c) late prophase I of meiosis

d) cleavage

e) neurulation

13. The phenotype of an individual who is genetically XY but is lacking the sex-determining region on the Y chromosome would be:

a) a person who does not have testes but does have male external sex organs.

b) completely male, because of low estrogen levels.

c) either male or female, depending on whether the person carries the gene for DHT, which directs development of the penis.

d) a person with ovaries and female secondary sex characteristics.

e) completely male, because the person will produce testosterone, which masculinizes the internal and external reproductive organs.

14. In humans, fetal growth is slowest during which trimester?

a) first

b) second

c) third

d) fourth

e) It occurs at the same rate in all trimesters.

15. In which of the following methods of assisted reproductive technology does fertilization occur within the woman's body?

a) intracytoplasmic sperm injection

b) in vitro fertilization–embryo transfer (IVF-ET)

c) zygote intra-Fallopian transfer (ZIFT)

d) gamete intra-Fallopian transfer (GIFT)

e) All of the above are correct.

Short-Answer Questions

1. In humans, how are male gametes formed? Where in the male reproductive system does this process occur?

2. What are germ layers? How many layers are there, what are they called, and what structures ultimately form from them?

3. Summarize the three stages of pregnancy and the major events that occur in each.

See Answers at the back of the book.
For additional study questions, go to www.prep-u.com.

How the body defends and maintains itself

26

Immunity and Health

26·1–26·4 Your body has different ways to protect you against disease-causing invaders.

Sneezing is one of the body's ways of expelling harmful substances that enter our body.

26·1

Three lines of defense prevent and fight pathogen attacks.

Most of us don't think about the germs that constantly attempt to invade our bodies, until we hear that an illness is "going around." For example, in the spring of 2009, Mexico alerted the world to an outbreak of the H1N1 virus that caused numerous deaths—particularly among people under 25 years old and pregnant women. This outbreak was caused by a new strain of the influenza virus that the world's current population had never before encountered. The media showed footage of Mexico City residents wearing face masks and reported that schools and businesses were closing for extended periods of time. Within weeks, the virus had spread to the United States and around the world. Fortunately, however, as the flu strain began infecting people worldwide, researchers noted that although this influenza strain was strong, it was not as virulent as first suggested (**FIGURE 26-1**).

When you first hear about an outbreak of a particularly dangerous flu, do you think about washing your hands more frequently, wearing a face mask, and staying away from people who are coughing? The H1N1 flu example demonstrates that when we are aware of **pathogens,** disease-causing microorganisms, molecules, and viruses (sometimes

referred to as "germs"), in our environment, we may take precautions to avoid them. But we fail to notice most of the germs in our everyday lives.

FIGURE 26-1 Outbreak. Indian girls wearing protective masks outside a museum in the Indian city of Bangalore in August 2009, just after a 26-year-old woman died of swine flu (H1N1 virus) in a nearby hospital.

Shopping cart surfaces have been shown to have significantly more illness-causing bacteria than even public restroom toilet seats and flush handles.

FIGURE 26-2 Everyday encounters with pathogens. Shopping cart handles harbor germs.

Think about the commonplace items that you and others touch. Did you know that shopping cart handles rank as one of the "germiest" items around? A 2006 study by the Centers for Disease Control and Prevention (CDC) found that for infants, riding in a shopping cart near meat

was one of the biggest risk factors for *Salmonella* infection (just below exposure to reptiles and eating partially cooked eggs)! Following up on this report, a 2010 study reported that 72% of the shopping carts the researchers sampled (across four states) tested positive for fecal bacteria, and the average contamination levels exceeded those measured on toilet seats and flush handles in public restrooms (**FIGURE 26-2**). Not surprisingly, many stores now offer disinfectant wipes, and some states have even proposed legislation to make providing these wipes mandatory.

The vast majority of the microscopic organisms found on everyday items will not cause disease, but some will. That we don't notice or pay attention to surfaces that may be covered with germs, we don't get sick frequently, and we don't think too much about how our immune system protects us is a testament to the efficacy of this body system.

The human **immune system** provides protection against an enormous variety of pathogens, including many bacteria, fungi, viruses, and parasitic protists and worms (**FIGURE 26-3**). To protect the body from pathogens, the immune system must be able to rapidly recognize what belongs in the body and what doesn't, as well as distinguish among specific disease-causing microbes or viruses. Once a pathogen enters the human body, the immune system works within minutes to begin destroying it. The three major divisions of the immune system undertake this challenging task of protecting us against the diverse threats (**FIGURE 26-4**).

PATHOGENS

Viruses   Bacteria   Fungi   Parasitic protists   Parasitic worms

FIGURE 26-3 Examples of the foreign, "non-self" microbes and viruses that can harm the body.

The immune system protects us from a diverse group of pathogens—disease-causing viruses and microorganisms, often referred to as "germs."

DIVISIONS OF THE IMMUNE SYSTEM

Skin wound

PHYSICAL BARRIERS
• Form a nearly impenetrable wall, keeping pathogens from entering body tissues
• Consist of skin, mucous membranes, and their associated anti-pathogen secretions

Pathogens

Skin

NON-SPECIFIC IMMUNITY
• Recognizes and destroys pathogens that breach external barriers
• Responds to all pathogens in the same way
• Responds to infection within minutes

Pathogens

Non-specific immune system cells

SPECIFIC IMMUNITY
• Destroys pathogens that are not killed by non-specific defenses
• Recognizes specific pathogens and forms a memory of each
• Responds to infection in hours to days

Pathogens

Specific immune system cells

After the specific immune system forms a "memory" of a pathogen, it fights off the same pathogen more quickly in the future, often resulting in lifelong protection from that pathogen.

FIGURE 26-4 Layered defenses of the immune system block entry and fight invaders.

1. Physical barriers provide the first defense against pathogens and can keep them out of the body. For example, skin acts as a nearly impenetrable barrier that keeps viruses, bacteria, and other pathogens from entering the body, and various chemicals secreted by skin surfaces and by cells within mucous membranes stop the growth of many pathogens.

2. Non-specific immunity is the part of the immune system that provides defense when pathogens make it past the physical barriers and into the body. The term "non-specific" indicates that the cells that are part of this system attack any and all pathogens that enter the body. This system is sometimes called the *innate system* (meaning "inborn"), because it is ready to function at birth. Cells of the non-specific division of the immune system rapidly recognize and attack any pathogen that breaches the body's external barriers. Non-specific immunity is found in virtually all multicellular organisms, including plants, nematode worms, fruit flies, and humans.

3. Specific immunity, also called *adaptive immunity,* is the division of the immune system that deals with pathogens that have been missed by the non-specific system or cannot be overcome by that system. The specific division recognizes very specific infectious agents—not just bacteria in general but, for example, the *Staphylococcus aureus* that causes common skin infections; not just viruses in general, but the specific varicella-zoster virus that causes chicken pox. Because the specific immunity part of your immune system must first recognize a specific threat and then manufacture specific weapons to combat it, there is a time lag of a few hours to a few days between your exposure to the pathogen and the specific immunity division's response to it. In contrast, non-specific immunity responds to a pathogen immediately or within minutes. Once activated, the cells of the specific division remember past infections and can then fight off the same infection more quickly in the future. As a result, an individual often has lifelong protection from a pathogen he or she has previously encountered.

The three divisions of the immune system work together to protect us against diseases and infections. Once an invader breaks through the physical barriers, it is usually recognized as a pathogen and attacked by the cells of the non-specific system, at the same time that chemical signals trigger the cells of the specific system to go to work.

TAKE-HOME MESSAGE 26·1

The immune system, which protects us from a diverse group of pathogens, has three basic parts: physical barriers, non-specific immunity, and specific immunity. Physical barriers and non-specific immunity are the first lines of defense, serving to distinguish a substance as a pathogen. Cells in the specific immunity line of defense recognize individual pathogens and remember them, so they can fight them more effectively in the future.

26·2 External barriers prevent pathogens from entering your body.

Just as a high-security building may have walls and barbed wire to keep out potential intruders, your body has ways to prevent pathogens from entering your body, tissues, and cells. The **integumentary system** is made up of skin, mucous membranes (such as those lining the respiratory system), sweat glands, oil glands, hair, and nails, all of which protect you from stress or injuries caused by external forces such as friction, pressure, sunlight, dehydration, and, of course, pathogens (**FIGURE 26-5**).

Q

How dangerous is it to sit directly on a toilet seat in a public restroom?

Have you ever sat down on a public toilet seat only to wonder if you were going to contract some horrible disease from it (**FIGURE 26-6**)? The good news is that most human pathogens cannot survive outside the body for very long, and a cold, smooth toilet seat is not an ideal place for them to survive.

Furthermore, pathogens need some way to get into your body, and the skin on your buttocks is generally a strong barrier to entry for any pathogens on the toilet seat. Many public bathrooms offer toilet seat covers that can act like a second skin, further reducing the already very low risk.

Skin is not just a passively protective wall, however. It's more like a wall with armed guards. In addition to forming a nearly impenetrable barrier, skin cells actively secrete chemicals that inhibit bacterial growth (**FIGURE 26-7**). Sweat secreted onto the skin's surface, for example, contains **lysozyme,** an enzyme that kills bacteria by damaging their cell walls. The protection provided by skin becomes really clear in burn victims: lacking skin in certain areas, they are susceptible to infection by numerous pathogenic bacteria and fungi. The external and internal surfaces of the body, such as eyes, ears, and the linings of the digestive and respiratory tracts, also protect us from environmental stresses and forces. These body areas, too, are shielded by the integumentary system (and, as we'll see, by the cells of the non-specific defense system).

Consider, for example, how the digestive tract is protected. Imagine that minutes after you push a germ-laden shopping cart, you put your finger in your mouth to bite your nail.

FIGURE 26-6 A safe place to sit. Public restrooms are generally safe to use (but be sure to thoroughly wash your hands!).

THE INTEGUMENTARY SYSTEM

Hair

Nails

Skin surface

Hair

Oil glands

Sweat glands

Fat cells

Nerve fiber

Blood vessel

The integumentary system protects you from pathogens and external stresses such as friction, pressure, sunlight, and dehydration.

FIGURE 26-5 Providing a nearly impenetrable barrier: the integumentary system.

Pathogens do not pass through intact skin. So, while there may be germs on a toilet seat, your skin acts as a barrier that prevents entry.

DEFENSE MECHANISMS OF THE INTEGUMENTARY SYSTEM

SKIN
This forms a nearly impenetrable barrier that keeps pathogens from entering the body.

LYSOZYME AND OTHER ENZYMES
Lysozyme in saliva and tears, and digestive enzymes in the small intestine, kill many bacteria.

ACIDIC SECRETIONS
Stomach acids, acidic vaginal secretions, and acidic urine, all protect the digestive, reproductive, and urinary tracts from bacterial pathogens.

CILIA
Hair-like extensions on the surface of the respiratory tract move mucus-entrapped pathogens up and out of the lungs.

TEARS
Fluid containing antiviral and antibacterial chemicals washes away microorganisms from around the eyes.

EAR WAX
This sticky substance can trap microorganisms in the ear canal.

FIGURE 26-7 Security barrier. The integumentary system provides multiple defenses to protect you from pathogens.

Are you guaranteed to get ill? No, because mucus (a major component of the saliva in your mouth) also contains the antibacterial chemical lysozyme. And even if lysozyme doesn't destroy potential invaders, the pathogens will quickly reach the stomach, a highly acidic environment flooded with digestive enzymes that can destroy a variety of pathogens.

In the respiratory tract, sticky mucus traps pathogens before they can reach the lungs. The epithelial cells that line the respiratory tract have hair-like extensions, called **cilia,** that continually move mucus-entrapped pathogens up and out of the lungs. As the mucus moves up into your throat, you continually swallow the germ-containing mucus and send it to your stomach, where the germs are destroyed. Mucus that's not swallowed continues up further into your throat until you feel the urge to "clear your throat" or cough.

The eyes produce tears that physically wash away microorganisms, and that also contain lysozyme and antiviral and antibacterial chemicals. Ear wax serves a protective function, too. Secretions produced by numerous glands inside the ear canal, combined with dead skin cells, make up this sticky substance that is effective at trapping microorganisms. The slight acidity and the lysozyme in ear wax also serve to inhibit the growth of some microorganisms that find their way into the ear canal.

Q What is the purpose of ear wax?

TAKE-HOME MESSAGE 26·2
Skin, part of the integumentary system, is a physical barrier that prevents pathogens from entering the body's cells. Cells that are not covered by skin but are exposed to the external environment are protected by defenses such as bacteria-destroying chemicals, acidic secretions, sticky mucus, and wax.

26·3 The non-specific division of the immune system recognizes and fights pathogens and signals for additional defenses.

Sometimes security measures fail. When intruders break through a defensive wall surrounding a secure building, the building's security guards need to (1) identify the security breach, (2) call for backup, and (3) attack and remove as many of the invaders as possible. Similarly, your body *recognizes* any

security breaches, such as a wound to the skin or some spoiled food you've eaten, and then *responds* instantly to prevent an infection (**FIGURE 26-8**). Chemical signals are put out to call for backup cells, and cellular and molecular weapons are used to destroy both the pathogens and any cells they've infected.

RESPONDING TO PATHOGENS IN THE BODY

1 IDENTIFY THE INTRUDER
Non-specific immune system cells recognize molecules found only on the surface of pathogens and bind to them, marking the pathogens as invaders.

2 CALL FOR BACKUP
Immune system cells secrete signaling proteins called cytokines that recruit more immune cells to the site of the infection or warn other cells to protect themselves.

3 ATTACK AND REMOVE
Specialized immune system cells destroy, break down, and ingest both the pathogens and any cells they've infected.

FIGURE 26-8 Sometimes the security measures fail. The body recognizes and responds to invading pathogens.

In this section, we examine the cells that perform these duties and the tools that they use to combat infection. **White blood cells** (introduced in Section 21-7) are specialized cells that play roles in both the specific and the non-specific divisions of the immune system. These cells are made in the bone marrow and released into the bloodstream, where they patrol the body's tissues and search for invaders.

An important first step in defending the body is recognition, in which white blood cells of the immune system distinguish the body's own cells ("self") from invaders ("non-self"). The surface receptors on the patrolling non-specific (innate) immune system cells recognize molecules, usually proteins, such as those found only on the surfaces of pathogens, and bind to them. Because your own cells do not contain these molecules, a cell that possesses any of them can be identified as an invader (non-self) by the cells of the non-specific part of the immune system.

This recognition is considered non-specific because immune cell receptors recognize and bind to classes of molecules shared by a wide array of organisms. For example, one receptor recognizes a protein contained in all bacterial flagella. Another receptor recognizes a molecule found in the cell walls of many types of fungi.

Once the immune system cells recognize these receptors and bind to them, the cells of the non-specific immune system begin to attack and destroy the invaders. There are four types of cells that mount the non-specific defense (**FIGURE 26-9**).

FIGURE 26-9 Hardworking cells. Several types of white blood cells defend the body in the non-specific division of the immune system.

THE WHITE BLOOD CELLS OF NON-SPECIFIC IMMUNITY

The non-specific immune system consists of several types of white blood cells that are made in the bone marrow and released into the bloodstream.

NEUTROPHILS
- Phagocytic cells that ingest small organisms, primarily bacteria
- Destroy both the pathogen and themselves in the process
- Nucleus is multi-lobed

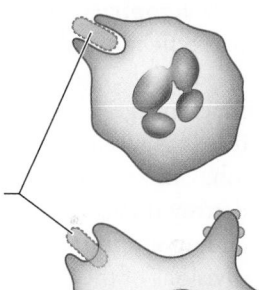

Pathogens

MACROPHAGES
- Phagocytic cells that ingest whole pathogens as well as large debris such as dead cells
- Present pieces of pathogens on their surface, advertising the infection to cells of the specific immune system

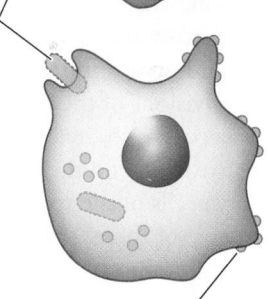

Presented pathogen fragments

DENDRITIC CELLS
- Phagocytic cells (named for their tentacle-like arms, called dendrites) that present ingested pathogens to cells of the specific immune system

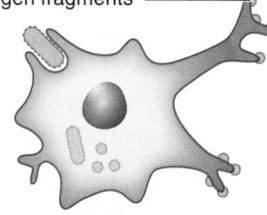

NATURAL KILLER (NK) CELLS
- Kill body cells infected by pathogens by poking holes in the cell membranes
- Also play a role in recognizing and killing cancer cells

Infected cell

1. **Neutrophils** circulate in the blood and exit blood vessels at sites of injury and infection in tissues. These cells are phagocytes, ingesting harmful particles or pathogens, primarily bacteria. Neutrophils normally make up between 50% and 70% of all white blood cells circulating in the bloodstream, and their numbers increase dramatically and rapidly during the first few days of some infections. Neutrophils destroy themselves as they ingest pathogens and live only 3–5 days, on average.

Q **What is pus?** After self-destruction, the dead neutrophils become a major part of **pus,** the thick yellowish fluid we often notice at the site of infection. (Other components of pus include damaged cell debris from the invaded tissue and both live and dead pathogens.) Often, our bodies can clear infections on their own or with some help from an **antiseptic,** a solution used on a body surface to kill or discourage growth of microorganisms, such as rubbing alcohol or hydrogen peroxide. But when there is excessive pus, combined with signs of a more serious infection, antibiotics might be needed to kill bacteria inside the body.

2. **Macrophages** are large ("macro") white blood cells that reside in and patrol the tissues (outside the blood vessels). They engulf and digest small pathogens whole. Macrophages also remove any pathogen and neutrophil debris that remains after the neutrophils have done their job. Unlike neutrophils, however, macrophages do not destroy themselves in the process. Instead, they serve as an important link between the non-specific and specific divisions of the immune system. Once they have ingested a pathogen, macrophages "present" digested pieces of the pathogen on their cell surface, "advertising" the infection to cells of the specific system. We'll learn more about the role of these "presenting cells" when we examine specific immunity (see Section 26-9).

Neutrophils and macrophages employ chemical warfare to destroy pathogens. For example, both types of cells can produce hydrogen peroxide and hypochlorous acid (also components of household bleach), two chemicals that are effective in killing bacteria and fungi.

3. **Dendritic cells** are phagocytes that link the non-specific and specific divisions of the immune system by "presenting" the cells of the specific system with foreign matter. These phagocytic cells migrate to the lymph nodes, which are populated by cells of the specific immunity system.

4. **Natural killer (NK) cells,** which are not phagocytes, are the first line of resistance to viruses. They kill virus-infected cells by poking holes in them, thereby killing the viruses inside the cells. The initial response of the NK cells may eliminate a viral infection, or at least slow it down until the specific system can respond to the virus in a more specific manner. NK cells also play a role in recognizing and killing cancer cells (**FIGURE 26-10**).

While the cells of the non-specific system are the initial responders to a pathogen, there are never enough of them at the initial site of infection to ingest and kill all the invading pathogens. Thus, after recognizing the security breach and starting the response, the patrolling cells of the non-specific system sound the alarm and call for backup.

The chief way that cells of the immune system—both the specific and non-specific divisions—talk to one another is by secreting signaling proteins called **cytokines** in response to pathogens in the body. Cytokines secreted by one immune cell can bind to receptors on other immune cells and signal them to respond in various ways. For example, cytokine binding can cause immune cells to move closer to the site where the cytokines are being produced (*cyto* = cell; *kine* = to move).

Interferons are an important type of cytokine produced by cells infected by a virus. An interferon alerts nearby healthy cells to turn on protective measures that help them resist viruses. These alerted cells take on an "antiviral state" in which they transcribe specific genes and translate them into proteins that can inhibit viral replication and can degrade viral RNA.

FIGURE 26-10 Attacking cancer. Natural killer cells are attaching to a cancer cell.

A collective group of circulating proteins, called complement proteins, recognize pathogens and help fight them in various ways, including by sticking to them and increasing the ability of phagocytes to consume them, and by directly destroying them (shown here).

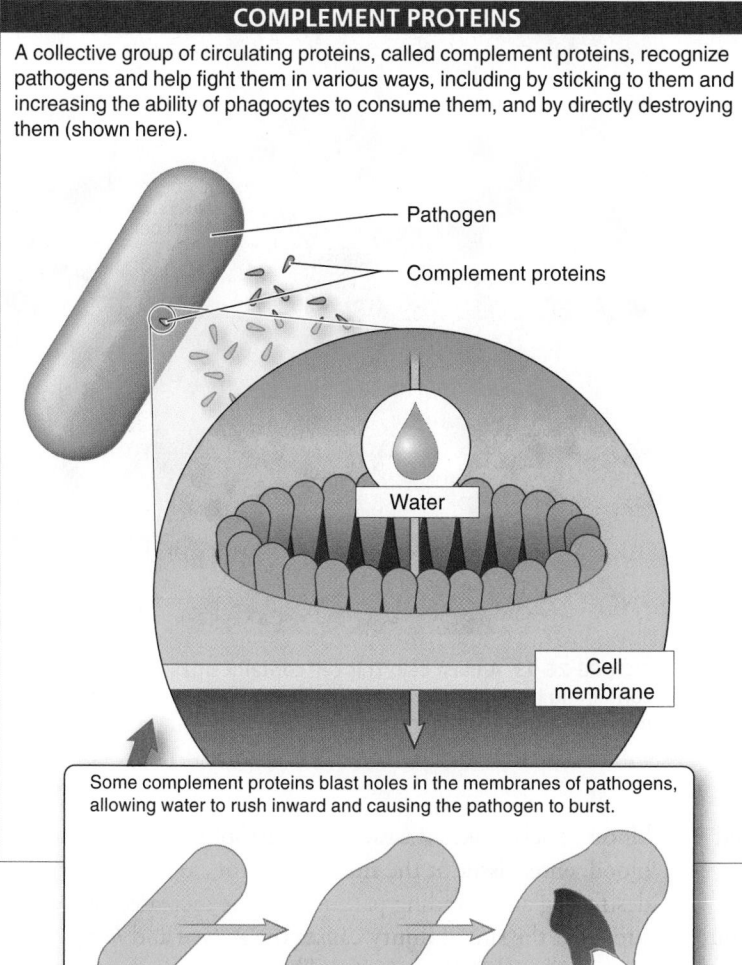

Some complement proteins blast holes in the membranes of pathogens, allowing water to rush inward and causing the pathogen to burst.

In addition to the cells we've learned about here, the non-specific system can also make use of some circulating defensive proteins, collectively called **complement proteins,** to quickly recognize and destroy invaders. These proteins

FIGURE 26-11 Defensive proteins "complement" the other cells of the non-specific system to combat pathogens.

"complement" (work with) the activities of cells in the non-specific and specific immunity systems and can link the two systems. Foreign molecules, such as the components of bacterial cell walls, activate the complement proteins (**FIGURE 26-11**). Once activated, the complement proteins fight pathogens in several ways. For example, a particular combination of complement proteins can blast holes in the cell membranes of pathogenic organisms, allowing water and ions to pass through, but not larger molecules such as proteins. As a result, water rushes inward and the pathogen swells and bursts. Other complement proteins help destroy pathogens by sticking to them and forming a coating that enhances the ability of phagocytes to bind and engulf them.

TAKE-HOME MESSAGE 26·3

Non-specific immunity provides defenses against pathogens by recognizing molecules on their cell surfaces and by recruiting other cells to the site of infection or warning them to protect themselves. White blood cells of the non-specific system include phagocytes (neutrophils, macrophages, and dendritic cells) that ingest and kill pathogens, cells (macrophages and dendritic cells) that display pathogens to cells of the specific immunity system, and cells (natural killer cells) that kill virus-infected cells and cancer cells. Complement proteins also non-specifically recognize invaders and help to destroy them.

26·4 The non-specific system responds to infection with the inflammatory response and with fever.

While we don't notice that our non-specific immunity system is constantly on patrol for invaders, we definitely do notice when it responds at the site of an infection. A little response is quickly amplified into a noticeable one. Think about what happens when you get a splinter. Initially, you might feel only the pain of the splinter going into your finger. Within minutes, though, you feel pain and warmth, and see that the area around the splinter is red and

swollen. The changes you are observing at the site of the splinter are the signs of an **inflammatory response.** The inflammatory response is a combination of events that leads to the recruitment of phagocytes and other immune cells to assist with pathogen destruction, followed by tissue healing. Whenever tissues are damaged by an invading pathogen, such as a virus infecting throat cells, or by a physical injury such as a burn, bug bite, or other

FIGURE 26-12 **An inflammatory response.** Following a wound—such as the cut shown here—the body responds with an inflammatory response that causes redness, heat, swelling, and pain. But the process clears away foreign invaders and allows for healing.

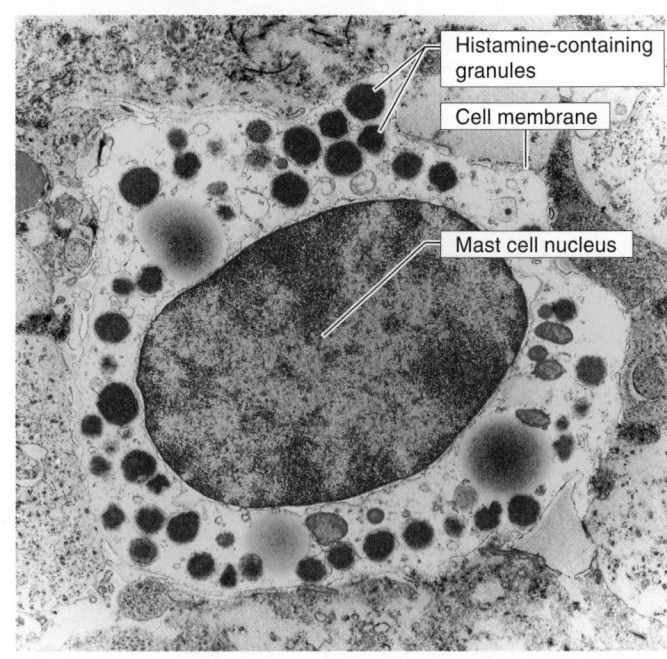

Histamine-containing granules

Cell membrane

Mast cell nucleus

FIGURE 26-13 **A mast cell.** This cell contains small round granules containing histamine. Release of histamine occurs at sites of infection as part of the immune response.

wound to the skin, the inflammatory response is triggered (**FIGURE 26-12**).

In the first century A.D., the Romans first described the four signs of inflammation: redness, heat, swelling, and pain—hence the term used today, "inflammation," which means, literally, "setting on fire." Whether it is a sore throat or wounded skin, these hallmarks of inflammation are always the same.

Let's imagine a scenario in which you cut your finger with a small knife while slicing a bagel. Three quick steps happen within a matter of minutes. First, invading pathogens from the knife and the skin surface are quickly engulfed by the macrophages that reside outside the blood vessels, in all tissues. Second, those macrophages release cytokines to recruit more phagocytes to the wound location. And, third, the cytokines also summon two other types of white blood cells, which initiate inflammation. **Basophils,** which circulate in the blood, and **mast cells,** found in the tissues (**FIGURE 26-13**), both release **histamine,** a molecule that produces inflammation by causing nearby non-injured blood vessels to (1) dilate (open up and become wider) and (2) become leaky.

When blood vessels dilate, the flow of blood increases and allows for a faster, greater supply of defensive molecules and cells that can fight infection. The increased leakiness of the

blood vessels makes it easier for neutrophils to exit the blood, enter tissue at the site of infection, and begin destroying any invading pathogens. The increased blood supply at the site of injury causes the *redness* and *heat* associated with inflammation. The leakiness is the reason for the *swelling,* because fluid leaking from the blood vessels accumulates in the tissue. And the increased pressure stimulates local *pain* receptors. Macrophages and neutrophils then begin an immediate response to destroy pathogens and also release cytokines that call more immune cells to the infection site (**FIGURE 26-14**).

Complement proteins also play a role in inflammation. Just as cytokines (secreted by macrophages) trigger the inflammatory response, activated complement proteins can also trigger initial inflammatory reactions. Activated complement proteins at the site of an infection cause mast cells to release histamine and further amplify the inflammatory response by attracting additional phagocytes. As mentioned in Section 26-3, complement proteins also directly affect pathogens by attacking their membranes and making it easier for phagocytes to engulf them.

So what about that cut on your finger? A scab—formed from dried, clotted blood and interstitial fluid—temporarily forms to cover the wound, much like a natural Band-Aid, and prevents more pathogens from entering. At the end of the inflammatory process, collagen fibers are secreted by

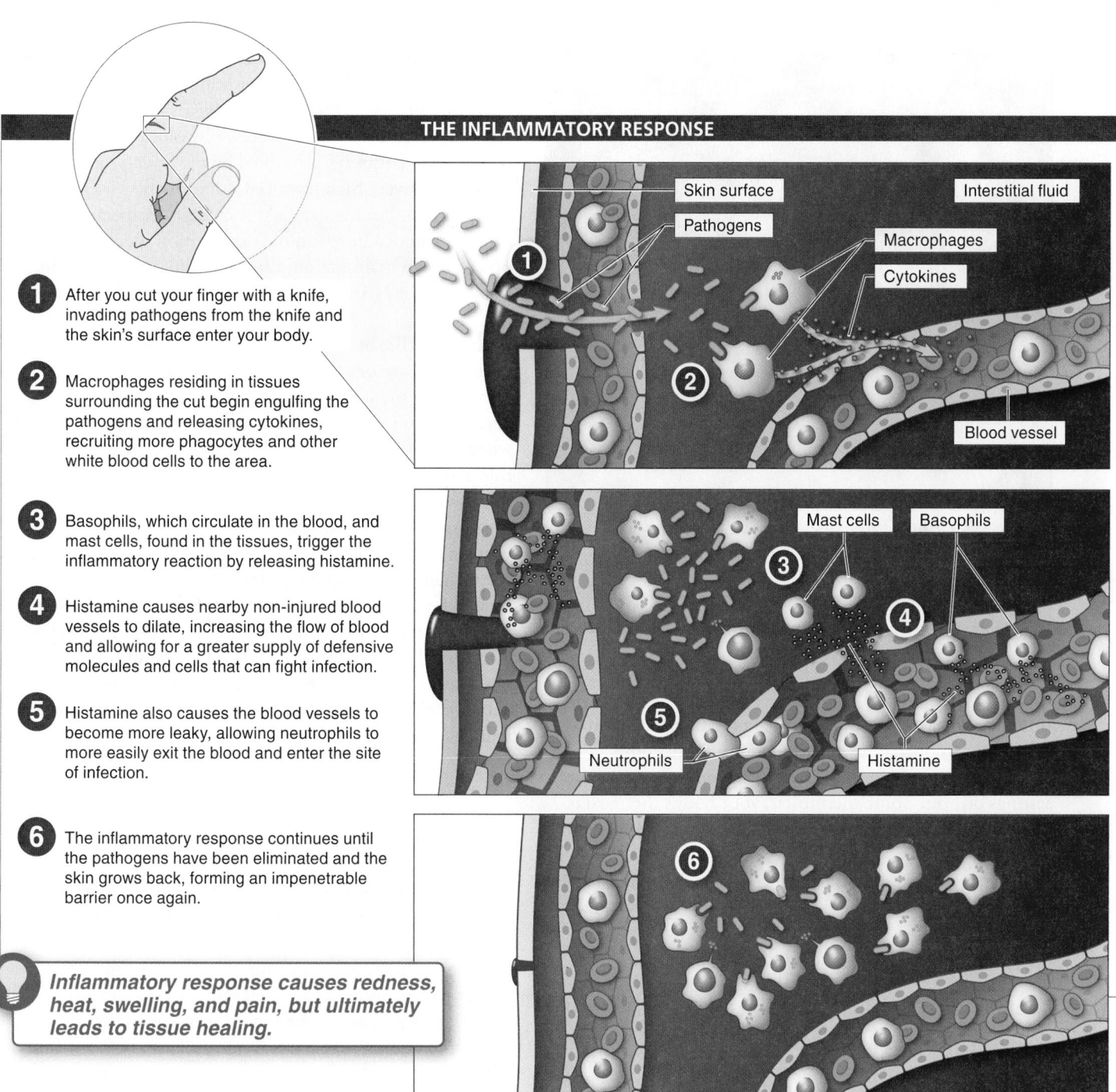

1 After you cut your finger with a knife, invading pathogens from the knife and the skin's surface enter your body.

2 Macrophages residing in tissues surrounding the cut begin engulfing the pathogens and releasing cytokines, recruiting more phagocytes and other white blood cells to the area.

3 Basophils, which circulate in the blood, and mast cells, found in the tissues, trigger the inflammatory reaction by releasing histamine.

4 Histamine causes nearby non-injured blood vessels to dilate, increasing the flow of blood and allowing for a greater supply of defensive molecules and cells that can fight infection.

5 Histamine also causes the blood vessels to become more leaky, allowing neutrophils to more easily exit the blood and enter the site of infection.

6 The inflammatory response continues until the pathogens have been eliminated and the skin grows back, forming an impenetrable barrier once again.

Inflammatory response causes redness, heat, swelling, and pain, but ultimately leads to tissue healing.

FIGURE 26-14 Reacting to injury. An inflammatory response causes redness, heat, swelling, and pain, but ultimately leads to tissue healing.

nearby cells to close the wound in a more stable fashion, and the scab falls off. Skin begins to grow back, once again forming an impenetrable barrier. And you are more cautious about cutting bagels!

Sometimes an infection is overcome quickly by the inflammatory response and is confined to the site of damage.

However, if pathogens are not quickly destroyed, macrophages will be constantly stimulated and will continue to release cytokines. Some cytokines can cause a **fever,** an elevated body temperature, if their concentration is high enough—a situation that both stimulates the immune response and reduces the rate at which many pathogenic bacteria can divide. The fever-causing cytokines travel

Chemicals released by immune system cells can trigger a fever, which can inhibit pathogen growth.

FIGURE 26-15 Turning up the thermostat. Fever slows the growth of pathogens.

through the bloodstream and affect a region of the brain, called the hypothalamus, that functions as the body's thermostat (see Section 23-17). Just as you can change the settings on your home thermostat, your body's thermostat can also be set higher, thus leading to a fever (**FIGURE 26-15**).

Q Why do chills and sweating sometimes occur together when you have a fever?

When your body's thermostat is set higher with a fever, you feel cold and your body responds with rapid periods of muscle contractions and relaxations (shivers and chills). Chills are the body's way of trying to warm up to the higher temperature setting of the thermostat. When your fever "breaks," the thermostat is

being reset to normal. You sweat because your body is now too hot, and sweating cools your body down. Anti-inflammatory medicines such as aspirin, acetaminophen, and ibuprofen help to lower a fever by blocking steps in the biochemical pathways promoted by the fever-producing cytokines. A very high fever (105° F or higher) is extremely dangerous and can be fatal. At such high temperatures, proteins can denature (unfold) and critical biochemical processes can malfunction, causing cellular stress and, in small children, seizures.

In the StreetBio at the end of Chapter 20, we described "Darwinian medicine," a new perspective on when to treat and when not to treat symptoms. From this perspective, many protective responses that have evolved in organisms are recognized as having value in fighting illness. And consequently, treating symptoms such as fever, which is actually part of the immune system response to infection, can hinder our efforts at fighting infection. This idea was supported, for example, by the observation that chicken pox lasted longer, on average, in patients taking aspirin than in patients taking a non-fever-reducing placebo.

Q Is it always wise to treat a fever with aspirin or other medication?

TAKE-HOME MESSAGE 26·4

Inflammation is a major way in which pathogens are eliminated by the non-specific immunity system. The four recognizable signs of the inflammatory response (redness, heat, swelling, and pain) are related to the changes in blood vessels that enhance the recruitment of phagocytes and complement proteins to the site of inflammation. Fever-promoting cytokines help the body fight infection by stimulating immune responses and inhibiting the growth of some pathogens.

A selection of cells from the bloodstream, including red blood cells (red) and white blood cells (yellow), as well as platelets (pink).

26·5 The specific division of the immune system forms a memory of specific pathogens.

Often, a pathogen can be eliminated completely by the non-specific system's inflammatory response. Sometimes, however, an infection is persistent or the pathogen molecularly "disguises" itself in some way and is not recognized as a pathogen by the non-specific system. Luckily, the specific division of the immune system is also there to protect us. Recall that non-specific defenses first *recognize* pathogens and then *respond*. The same is true for the specific division, but the recognition is more tailored to target particular pathogens, as opposed to all pathogens. The types of cells and molecular weapons used in the specific response differ greatly from those deployed by the non-specific division, especially in terms of response time. In a sense, there is a trade-off between the speed of the non-specific response and the slower, but much more precise, response of the specific immunity system. The specific immunity system also forms a memory, so the body's response to a specific pathogen occurs more quickly if it should invade the body again. Only by working together can the specific and non-specific systems

completely defend us from the constant barrage of pathogens that surround us.

The memory of the specific division of the immune system results in **immunity,** a state of long-term protection against a specific pathogen. There are two ways in which we can acquire immunity to a particular pathogen. The first is to become sick with the disease (**FIGURE 26-16**). For example, people who contract chicken pox when they are young cannot get chicken pox again; they are immune to it. Fortunately, there is a second way to gain immunity, without having to suffer through a disease and its unpleasant symptoms. A vaccine for chicken pox has been widely used since 1995 and, as a result, cases of chicken pox in the United States have fallen by about 75% from the approximately 4 million cases in 1995 (which resulted in more than 10,000 hospitalizations and 100 deaths).

A **vaccine** is a weakened or harmless form of a specific pathogen that is administered to an individual to induce

GETTING SICK
Exposure to a pathogen causes the body to form a memory of the pathogen, producing the cells necessary to rapidly respond to the pathogen if encountered again. Shown here: a toddler with chicken pox.

GETTING A VACCINATION
Exposure to a weakened or harmless form of a pathogen in a vaccine allows the body to form a memory of the pathogen without the risk of symptoms. The body then produces the cells necessary to rapidly respond to the pathogen if encountered again.

FIGURE 26-16 Two paths to immunity: contracting and fighting an illness, or receiving a vaccine.

immunity, without subjecting the individual to the disease. Vaccines trick the body into thinking it has the full-blown disease, and the body mounts a specific immunity response. An individual who receives the chicken pox vaccine and is later exposed to the virus will not get the disease, because the body already has a memory of this virus. It has manufactured a group of cells—called memory cells—that are already primed to recognize and rapidly respond to the virus. When the individual's immune system again encounters the virus, there will be no lag time in responding. Vaccine technology has been a major success in medicine.

Today we have vaccines against numerous viruses (including polio, measles, rubella, mumps, and rotavirus) and bacteria (including tetanus, cholera, and meningitis). These vaccines are less available in the developing world, and thus, worldwide, many people die each year from what are now preventable illnesses.

Let's investigate how the immune system recognizes and responds to pathogens. An **antigen** is any molecule or fragment of a molecule that induces a specific immune response. A single pathogen often contains many different antigens (for example, the different glycoproteins, lipoproteins, and polysaccharides of a single bacterium can all be antigens). The body responds to antigens by making **antibodies,** circulating proteins that recognize

specific antigens. (You can remember the difference between "antigen" and "antibody" by remembering that antigen is short for *anti*body *gen*erating.) Antibodies provide protection by enhancing the immune system's ability to recognize and destroy pathogens such as bacteria and viruses and the body cells they infect (**FIGURE 26-17**). But keep in mind that antibodies don't directly kill a pathogen. Instead, antibodies act as beacons that make pathogens conspicuous to patrolling phagocytes. Antibody levels peak within the first two weeks after encountering a pathogen or receiving a vaccine. We discuss the body's ability to recognize and destroy antigens in the next section.

Even though antibody production eventually diminishes, the specific immune system retains a memory of the disease. If the same antigen is encountered again, it will take the body only 1–2 days to begin producing large amounts of specific antibodies that aid in destruction of the pathogen; within just 7–9 days, there will be massive amounts of the antibodies. So, if a friend exposes you to chicken pox after you've already had the vaccine, your body won't need two weeks to respond: it will quickly kick into high gear and start producing antibodies immediately!

One of the most common infections fought off by the specific division of the immune system is influenza, an infectious disease caused by a virus. Each year there are

ANTIGENS AND ANTIBODIES

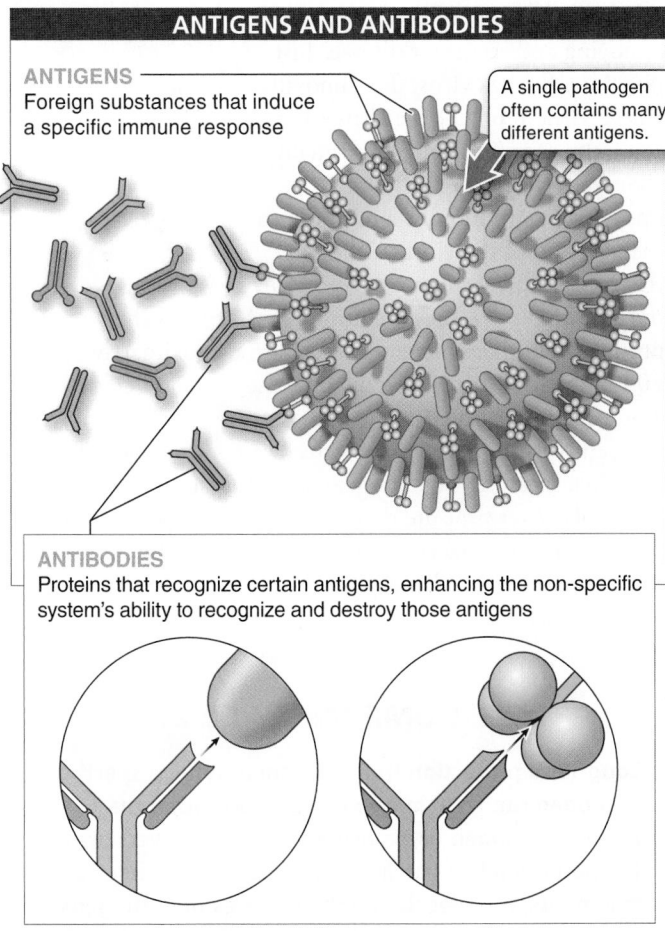

ANTIGENS
Foreign substances that induce a specific immune response

A single pathogen often contains many different antigens.

ANTIBODIES
Proteins that recognize certain antigens, enhancing the non-specific system's ability to recognize and destroy those antigens

FIGURE 26-17 Antibodies are proteins that recognize foreign molecules called antigens.

many different versions, or strains, of the influenza virus, which are constantly changing. With each new flu season, the body encounters a slightly different form of an influenza virus and, therefore, a different set of antigens.

As the virus adapts to changing conditions and evolves, the best protection is to get a flu shot each year (**FIGURE 26-18**). And in the case of the flu vaccine, because any vaccine must contain an antigen, the vaccine is commonly made from an influenza virus (of the most common current strain or a mixture of strains) that has been inactivated by heat or a live, weakened form of the virus that does not cause the flu. Although you can get the flu at any time of year, the flu season occurs in winter, so it makes sense to get vaccinated in autumn to give your body time to make antibodies that can protect you throughout the winter flu season. Every year a new flu vaccine is available in August or September.

Yet, even with these preventive measures, a person may still get the flu. Although it is commonly thought that the flu shot itself can give someone the flu, this is simply not true. So, why do individuals sometimes get the flu after having the vaccination? There are several possible reasons. First, scientists developing the vaccine must make predictions, well before the flu season, about how the influenza virus will change in the upcoming season. Sometimes the vaccine "matches" the current virus, and sometimes it may be less than perfect. Second, different strains of the flu virus circulate at the same time, and the vaccine may not protect

THE INFLUENZA VIRUS IS CONSTANTLY CHANGING

Inluenza virus   Antigens

Time

Strains of the influenza virus are constantly changing, so the body encounters a slightly different form with each new flu season, and therefore a different set of antigens.

FIGURE 26-18 Because the influenza virus changes so rapidly, flu vaccinations need to be given annually.

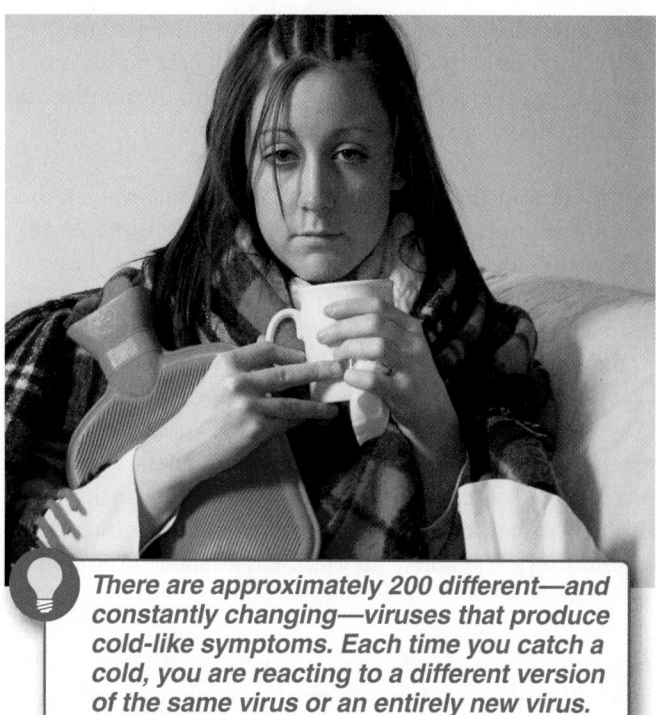

There are approximately 200 different—and constantly changing—viruses that produce cold-like symptoms. Each time you catch a cold, you are reacting to a different version of the same virus or an entirely new virus.

FIGURE 26-19 A constant challenge. Many different, rapidly changing viruses cause the common cold.

Q

Why don't people develop immunity to the common cold?

develop immunity to this most annoying and recurrent disease? Just like the influenza virus, the rhinovirus ("nose virus"), one of the viruses that cause the common cold, continually changes (**FIGURE 26-19**). Your immune system mounts a response to each version of the virus. Although rhinoviruses are a frequent cause of the common cold, they are not the only viruses that produce cold-like symptoms; there are approximately 200 different viruses that can cause the common cold. Thus, each time you catch a cold, you are reacting to a different version of the same virus or an entirely new virus. The sheer number of pathogens and their ability to adapt and evolve over time are two challenges that the immune system constantly faces. Nonetheless, the specific immune system stands up to this challenge, as detailed in the next few sections.

TAKE-HOME MESSAGE 26·5

Long-term protection from, or immunity to, a specific pathogen can form in two ways: exposure to the natural pathogen or exposure to an altered version of the pathogen in a vaccine. Antigens are molecules or fragments of molecules on the surfaces of pathogens that can be identified by disease-fighting proteins of the immune system, called antibodies. Antibodies are produced after exposure to a specific antigen. The specific immunity system is continually responding to numerous pathogens, many of which change over time.

---

an individual from all strains. Lastly, a person might already be infected with the flu at the time of vaccination.

If the specific immune response can protect a person from illness during a future encounter with a specific pathogen, why is it that every winter you develop the runny nose, cough, and sore throat of the common cold? Why don't you

26·6 ——— The structure of antibodies reflects their function.

We now examine the structure and function of antibodies to learn exactly how they work with the non-specific division of the immune system to protect us against pathogens. All antibodies are Y-shaped, and their diversity and specificity come from variations in the top of the "Y."

Each antibody consists of four polypeptide chains joined together: two long (also called heavy) chains and two short (or light) chains (**FIGURE 26-20**). The top of the "Y" is the region that varies from antibody to antibody. But there are only about five variants for the lower part, the base of the "Y," and so this is referred to as the constant region of an antibody. At the top of the "Y," the variable region, each

antibody has a unique three-dimensional shape that dictates which specific antigen it will "fit." An enormous diversity of antibodies is needed to recognize the correspondingly enormous group of antigens that the immune system may encounter. (And a given pathogen may have several different types of antigens on its surface.) Keep in mind that antibodies recognize *antigens,* not pathogens. And there are antigens that can get into the body that are not part of pathogens. An antigen is anything that an antibody recognizes as not being part of the body, as not being "self," including snake venom toxins, bacterial toxins that cause food poisoning, pollen, and various chemicals (such as those found in latex gloves).

ANTIBODY STRUCTURE

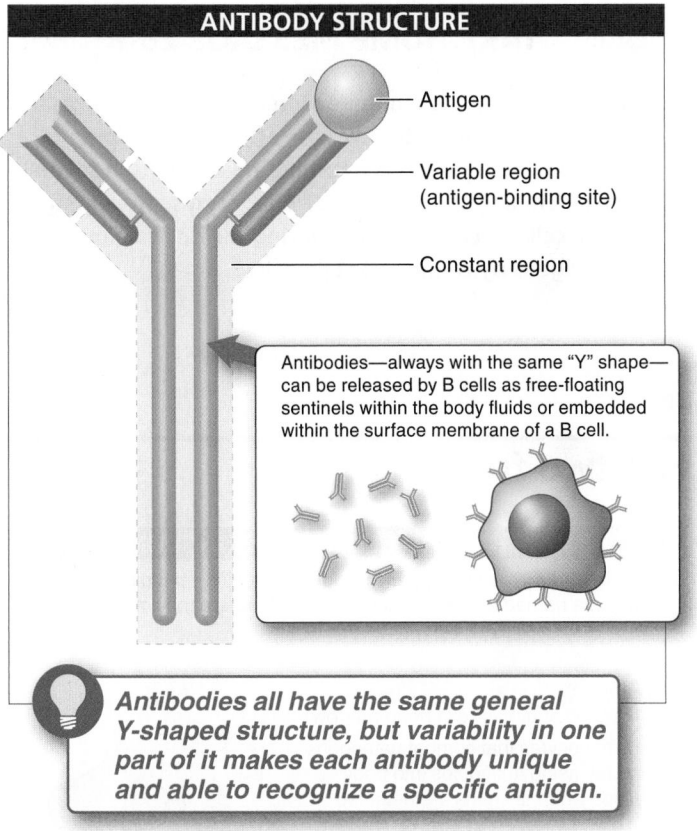

Antigen

Variable region (antigen-binding site)

Constant region

Antibodies—always with the same "Y" shape—can be released by B cells as free-floating sentinels within the body fluids or embedded within the surface membrane of a B cell.

Antibodies all have the same general Y-shaped structure, but variability in one part of it makes each antibody unique and able to recognize a specific antigen.

FIGURE 26-20 Variations on a molecular theme. The shape at the top of the "Y" varies from one antibody to another and fits with only one antigen.

Any foreign cells introduced into the body will elicit an immune response, even if the cells are part of a life-saving medical treatment. Consider organ transplants. Transplanted cells have surface molecules that are seen as antigens ("non-self") by the recipient's immune system. Although the transplanted cells are not pathogens, the recipient's immune system identifies them as invaders, and an immune response begins. Thus, medicines are needed to suppress the immune system's attack on and eventual destruction of a transplanted organ.

The immune system is also the reason that people in need of blood transfusions must have a proper match of blood type. As we saw in Section 7-10, if a transfusion is made between individuals with incompatible blood types, antibodies from the recipient will attach to antigens on the surface of the foreign (in this case, the donor's) red blood cells and mount an attack that can end in death.

Now let's consider the main ways in which the antibodies function (**FIGURE 26-21**). The immune system pumps out tons of antibodies following exposure to a pathogen, but

ANTIBODY FUNCTIONS

Antibodies function in several ways to help destroy pathogens and free-floating antigens.

PHAGOCYTE SIGNALING
Antibodies bind to antigens on the surface of pathogens, making it easier for phagocytes to find the pathogens and destroy them.

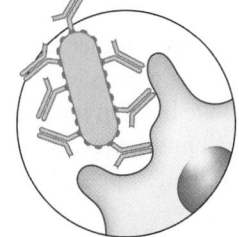

ANTIGEN CLUMPING
Antibodies make pathogens and free-floating antigens clump together, making it easier for phagocytes to find them and destroy them.

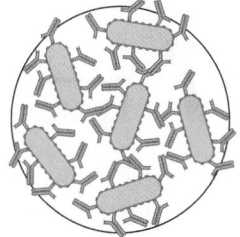

PREVENTION OF CELL ENTRY
Antibodies coating the surface of pathogens prevent the pathogens from entering body cells.

COMPLEMENT PROTEIN SIGNALING
Antibodies recruit complement proteins, which poke holes in pathogen membranes, causing the pathogen cells to burst.

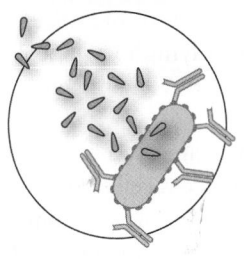

FIGURE 26-21 Antibodies fight pathogens in several ways.

remember that antibodies don't *directly* kill the pathogen. Instead, they use the cells of the non-specific immune system (such as macrophages and neutrophils) to kill the pathogen. When the antigens on the surface of a pathogen have an antibody attached to them, the pathogen is easily ingested by phagocytes of the non-specific immune system.

Besides "marking" for destruction the antigens on a pathogen, or marking free-floating antigens (such as snake venom toxin), antibodies act in two other important ways. (1) They cause pathogens or antigens to clump together, making it easier for phagocytes to find and ingest them. And (2) they coat the surfaces of pathogens and prevent them from binding to and entering body cells, and thus they block the infection from spreading.

Lastly, when antibodies are bound to the surface of a pathogen, they recruit another player of the non-specific system: complement proteins. Recall that some complement proteins can poke holes in membranes and cause the pathogenic cells to burst. Thus, by recruiting these complement proteins, antibodies indirectly destroy pathogens by causing them to burst.

TAKE-HOME MESSAGE 26·6

Each antibody has a unique structure that recognizes a specific antigen. Antibodies are effective in helping to destroy pathogens and free-floating antigens in several ways: enhancing ingestion by phagocytes, preventing more cell infection, and enhancing the destruction of pathogens by complement proteins.

26·7 Lymphocytes fight pathogens on two fronts.

Lymphocytes are the white blood cells responsible for the specific immunity response. These cells can be found circulating in the blood and lymphatic systems, and they reside in lymphatic organs such as the lymph nodes and spleen. (See Section 21-10 to review the lymphatic system.) In contrast to blood, which contains various types of white blood cells, 99% of the lymph is made up of lymphocytes. Lymphocytes have **antigen receptors,** proteins on their plasma membranes that stick out from the cell surface and can bind to specific antigens—each lymphocyte can bind to just one type of antigen. The presence of antigen receptors allows lymphocytes, collectively, to recognize and react to a wide array of antigens.

There are two major types of lymphocytes. Both develop from stem cells in the bone marrow, but one type leaves the bone marrow and continues to mature in the thymus, a lymphatic organ located in the upper chest. Lymphocytes are named for where they mature, so those that mature in the bone marrow are named B lymphocytes, or **B cells,** and those that mature in the thymus are called T lymphocytes, or **T cells** (FIGURE 26-22). The other cells that normally circulate in the lymphatic system are dendritic cells, which use the lymphatic system for the sole purpose of meeting up with lymphocytes.

Both B and T cells have antigen receptors on their surfaces. From lymphocyte to lymphocyte, these receptors differ in structure and are characterized by both diversity and specificity. There are endless variations of these receptors. It is estimated that our lymphocytes can recognize billions of different pathogens. But each individual lymphocyte doesn't have billions of different antigen receptors. Instead, each lymphocyte has just one type of receptor that recognizes just one antigen, and it has many copies of this receptor on its surface.

THE WHITE BLOOD CELLS OF SPECIFIC IMMUNITY

B cells and T cells are responsible for the specific immunity response. They are named for the location in the body where they mature (the bone marrow and thymus).

B CELLS
• Develop and mature in bone marrow
• Lymphocytes that combat pathogens by releasing antibodies into body fluids when antigens are detected

Bone marrow

Antigen receptors

T CELLS
• Develop in bone marrow and mature in the thymus
• Lymphocytes that combat pathogens by directly destroying the infected cells

Bone marrow   Thymus

FIGURE 26-22 B cells and T cells.

Immune system reactions are comparable to a military battle. In real-life combat, it is advantageous to attack by both land and air to win a battle. Like the armed forces, the specific immune system has major divisions, too. Lymphocytes fight pathogens on two fronts: humoral immunity and cell-mediated immunity (FIGURE 26-23).

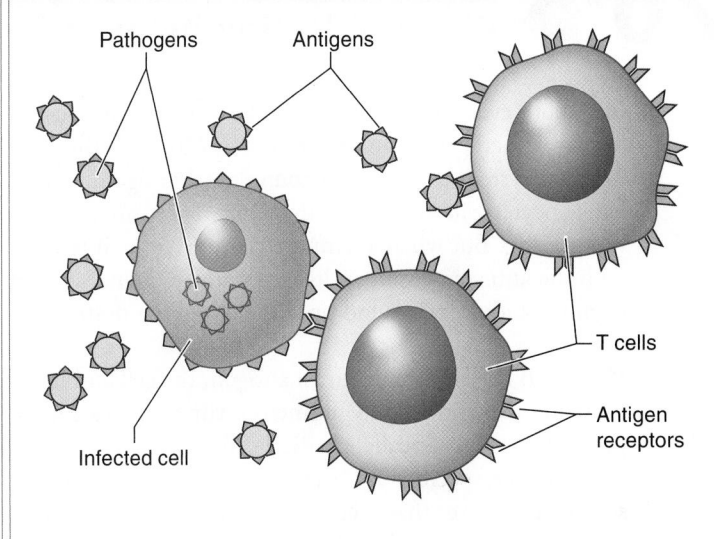

HUMORAL IMMUNITY
- Protection against pathogens and toxins found in body fluids, such as blood and lymph
- Carried out by B cells that secrete antibodies into body fluid, making it easier for phagocytes to engulf and destroy invading pathogens

CELL-MEDIATED IMMUNITY
- Protection against pathogens and toxins found within body cells
- Carried out by T cells that directly destroy invading pathogens as well as the infected cells

FIGURE 26-23 Fighting invaders in body fluids and within cells. B cells are responsible for humoral immunity (antibody-mediated immunity), and T cells are responsible for cell-mediated immunity.

1. In *humoral immunity*, also called antibody-mediated immunity, the individual is protected against pathogens and toxins found in body fluids, such as blood and lymph. The word *humoral* comes from "humors"—the term that Greeks and Romans used for body fluids. Blood was one of the four humors (the other three were phlegm, yellow bile, and black bile). When an antigen is detected by a B cell with the matching antigen receptors on its surface, the B cell secretes antibodies into the blood, lymph, and other body fluids. The circulating antibodies defend against specific pathogens and toxins and make it easier for phagocytes to engulf them.

2. In *cell-mediated immunity*, the individual is protected against pathogens located *inside* the body cells. All your body cells have molecules on their cell membranes that identify them as "self" to the cells of your immune system—as cells that belong. Body cells that have been infected by a pathogen (and many cancer cells) present some different proteins (antigens) on their membranes. When a T cell recognizes these antigens (because the T cell has the matching antigen receptors on its surface), it binds to them. This binding initiates an immune response that kills the infected cells and, usually, the pathogen within.

To defeat a specific pathogen, numerous identical lymphocytes (bearing the same antigen receptor) are needed. You may be starting to ask yourself, do we have trillions of immune cells? How does the body have room for all of these individual armies of lymphocytes ready to face any enemy it might—or might not ever—encounter? The answer is that the body doesn't store vast quantities of identical lymphocytes. Rather, for each of the billion or more different antigen-recognizing receptors, it has just a small number of lymphocytes with those receptors. It makes copies of these lymphocytes *only if* the antigen is encountered. In the next section, we see how the body does this.

TAKE-HOME MESSAGE 26·7

Lymphocytes are a type of white blood cell. Two types of lymphocytes are associated with the specific immunity system: B cells and T cells. B cells are responsible for the humoral (antibody-mediated) response, and T cells are responsible for the cell-mediated response. Because of the diversity and specificity of lymphocyte receptors, almost any pathogen can be recognized by the body's B and T cells.

26·8 Clonal selection helps in fighting infection now and later.

Just about every lymphocyte in an individual is unique, because of its specific antigen receptor. Although the immune system is *ready* to encounter any antigen, many lymphocytes will never meet the antigen they are capable of recognizing. But when a lymphocyte does come into contact with the antigen specific to its receptor, a sequence of events begins—and it doesn't end until the antigen is destroyed.

When a B or T cell binds to an antigen, the cell and its descendants rapidly divide numerous times to create a population of genetically identical cells (clones), all with the same antigen specificity. This process, known as **clonal selection,** ensures that there are enough B and T cells to recognize and respond to all of the specific pathogen that has invaded the body.

Recognizing a new pathogen is an important first step, but the specific immunity system has two additional challenges: to *respond* to and *remember* the invader. Clonal selection generates many lymphocytes that can recognize the same pathogen, and these lymphocytes then function in one of two ways. Some attack the antigen (these are called the effector cells), and some are involved in creating a memory of the invasion (the memory cells). We discuss the effector cells first.

The responders, or **effector cells,** recognize the antigen and immediately take some action that leads to its destruction. For example, **plasma cells,** derived from B cells, are the effector cells in the humoral response because they secrete antibodies. And T cells that directly kill infected cells are the effector cells in the cell-mediated response. During the immune system's first interaction with a pathogen, called the **primary response,** effector cells are not immediately available. The cells of the primary immune response must first be generated through clonal selection. On average, it takes two weeks to produce enough effector cells to combat and vanquish an infection (**FIGURE 26-24**).

Also produced during the primary response is the second type of lymphocyte, the **memory cells.** Like effector cells, memory cells are produced through clonal selection. The memory cells' job is to remember an antigen so that, if the body is infected with the same antigen in the future, it will be ready to attack the invader relatively quickly (in a matter of a couple of days rather than two weeks). Thus, memory cells hang around in the lymph and blood and wait for their specific antigen to show up again. There are both B and T memory cells, and they have the same antigen

THE PRIMARY RESPONSE TO INFECTION

1 RECOGNITION
When a lymphocyte comes into contact with the antigen specific to its receptor, the cell initiates a response that leads to the destruction of the antigen.

Antigens
Antigen receptor
Lymphocyte

2 CLONAL SELECTION
The lymphocyte divides numerous times, creating two populations of cells with the same antigen specificity.

3 EFFECTOR CELLS ATTACK
Effector cells immediately take action, leading to the destruction of the antigen.

Effector cells

4 MEMORY CELLS REMEMBER
Memory cells remember the antigen so that if the body is infected with the same antigen in the future, they will be ready to respond.

Memory cells

The primary response leads to destruction of an antigen and generation of memory cells to fight the antigen should it ever be encountered again.

FIGURE 26-24 Fighting now and later.

specificity as the effector cells produced in the primary response. While effector cells live less than a week, memory cells remain and circulate for a long time. The lifespan of memory cells is variable, but they may exist for years and possibly even for the individual's lifetime.

Memory cells produced during a primary immune response (such as to chicken pox) enable you to mount a faster, stronger secondary response following exposure to the virus later in life, preventing illness.

FIGURE 26-25 Another encounter with the same antigen.

With this understanding of how effector cells and memory cells act in the primary immune response, let's look at what happens when a five-year-old kindergartener comes to school not knowing that he has a chicken pox infection. Imagine that the kindergarten teacher had chicken pox as a small girl. At that time, her specific immunity system produced a population of chicken pox memory cells during her primary immune response. When the teacher interacts with the infected boy, these specific memory cells go through clonal selection and give rise to new B and T effector and memory cells armed to fight off the chicken pox virus. This **secondary response,** the creation of B and T effector cells, occurs rapidly (beginning after as little as 1–2 days) and produces a more intense response (peaking at 7–9 days) than the primary response that occurred in her childhood (**FIGURE 26-25**). Because the B cells of humoral immunity and the T cells of the cell-mediated response work immediately to destroy the virus, the teacher won't even miss a day of work, because this secondary immune response attacks the chicken pox virus so rapidly and effectively.

TAKE-HOME MESSAGE 26·8

When the body encounters a specific antigen, the lymphocytes recognizing this antigen divide to produce many identical cells through clonal selection. During a primary response, effector cells respond to and attack the antigen. Memory cells produced during the primary response are ready to go through clonal selection if a secondary response is necessary.

26·9 Cytotoxic T cells and helper T cells serve different functions.

The specific immune response, as we've seen, has two parts: the humoral response (B cells) and the cell-mediated response (T cells). Why the two-pronged approach? Aren't the antibodies secreted in the humoral response sufficient? In a word, *no.* Consider a viral infection. Free-floating antibodies, circulating in blood and lymph, can recognize and bind to a specific virus in these body fluids. And a virus that is coated with antibodies cannot effectively bind to and enter a host cell, which is a required event in viral infection. This antibody coating therefore is effective in slowing infection, but what about all the body cells that already have

viruses hiding inside them because they were infected before any antibodies could bind to the viruses? Antibodies cannot enter these (or any other) cells—it is the role of the T cell-mediated response to fight pathogens that are already inside cells. We focus here on this T cell-mediated response, and begin by examining the two major types of T cells, both of which are lymphocytes:

1. **Cytotoxic T cells,** which are the effectors of the cell-mediated response; they directly kill cells infected with pathogens.

2. **Helper T cells,** which do not directly kill infected cells but, instead, stimulate other immune cells. Helper T cells stimulate B cells to produce antibodies and cytotoxic T cells to kill infected cells.

We'll follow a viral infection through the cell-mediated response to demonstrate one example of how T cells function (**FIGURE 26-26**).

When a pathogen enters the body, the phagocytes and NK cells of the non-specific system respond. At the same time, dendritic cells and macrophages call on the specific system by "advertising" the presence of antigens to circulating lymphocytes. Dendritic cells and macrophages (as well as B cells) that "present" digested particles of pathogens on their cell surfaces as a means of advertising are called **antigen-presenting cells.** The role of presenting cells is essential to all T cell functioning, because T cells can recognize infected cells only by the "non-self" antigens presented on their plasma membranes.

Imagine a macrophage in your throat that has engulfed a respiratory virus and is presenting an antigen (from a digested virus particle) on its cell surface. If this presenting macrophage is to increase the likelihood of meeting up with a helper T cell that will recognize this specific antigen and stimulate a strong immune response to the virus, hanging out in the tissues of your throat is not very effective. It is more effective for the presenting cell to circulate through the lymph system, especially in the lymph nodes and spleen where lymphocytes circulate.

A macrophage circulating through a lymph node or the spleen may bump into helper T cells with specificity for the viral antigen being presented. The helper T cell receptor recognizes the antigen, and the T cell locks onto the antigen-presenting macrophage. Once this binding has taken place, the helper T cell has been activated. Activated helper T cells quickly ramp up an immune response by producing signaling molecules (cytokines) that activate the other type of T cell, the cytotoxic T cells. This is important because cytotoxic T cells are the only T cells that kill infected cells.

Both helper T cells and cytotoxic T cells then undergo clonal expansion, producing vast numbers of memory and effector cells with specificity for this

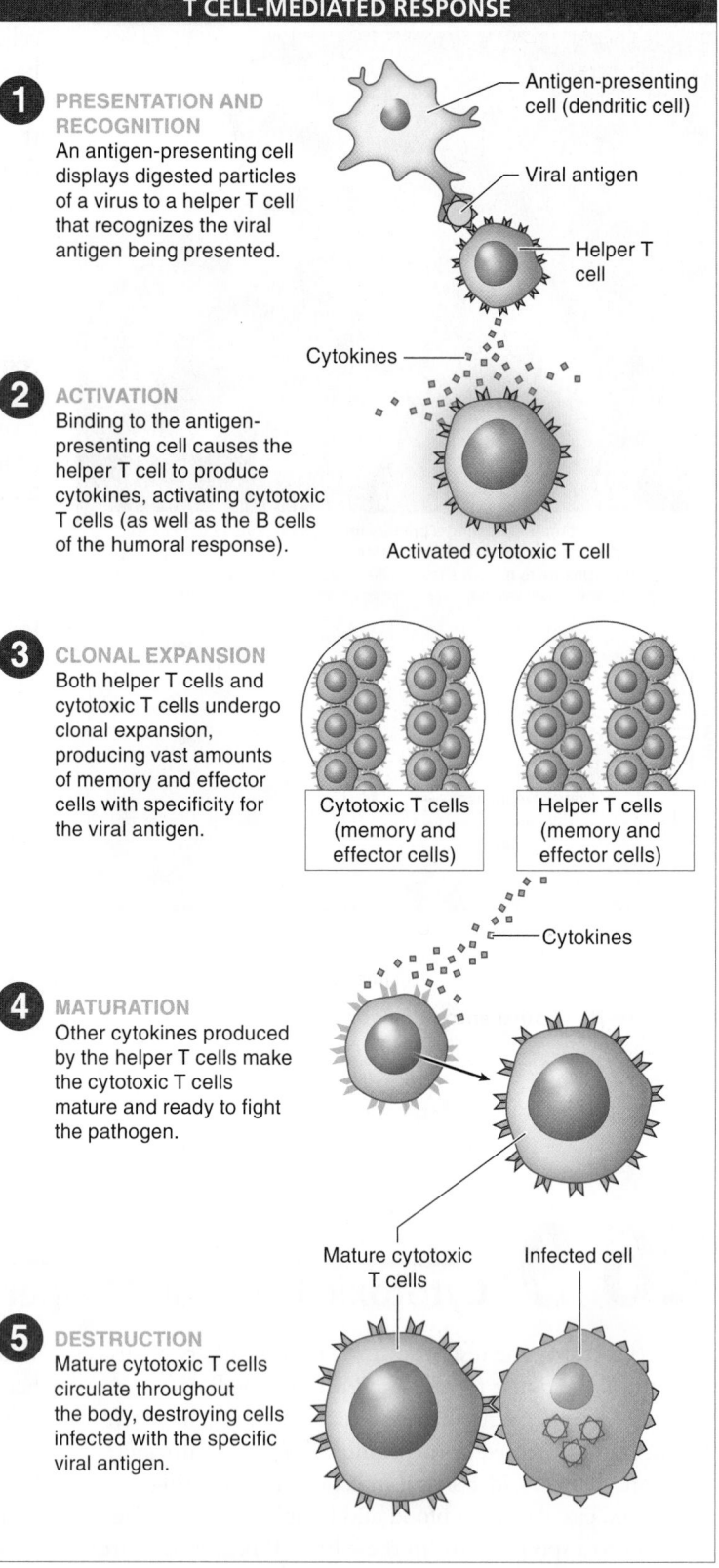

T CELL-MEDIATED RESPONSE

1 **PRESENTATION AND RECOGNITION**
An antigen-presenting cell displays digested particles of a virus to a helper T cell that recognizes the viral antigen being presented.

Antigen-presenting cell (dendritic cell)

Viral antigen

Helper T cell

Cytokines

2 **ACTIVATION**
Binding to the antigen-presenting cell causes the helper T cell to produce cytokines, activating cytotoxic T cells (as well as the B cells of the humoral response).

Activated cytotoxic T cell

3 **CLONAL EXPANSION**
Both helper T cells and cytotoxic T cells undergo clonal expansion, producing vast amounts of memory and effector cells with specificity for the viral antigen.

Cytotoxic T cells (memory and effector cells)

Helper T cells (memory and effector cells)

Cytokines

4 **MATURATION**
Other cytokines produced by the helper T cells make the cytotoxic T cells mature and ready to fight the pathogen.

Mature cytotoxic T cells

Infected cell

5 **DESTRUCTION**
Mature cytotoxic T cells circulate throughout the body, destroying cells infected with the specific viral antigen.

FIGURE 26-26 Helper T cells and cytotoxic T cells work together to recognize and respond to pathogens.

Leukocyte undergoing apoptosis

Extreme situations, extreme measures: cyototoxic effector cells can induce apoptosis, in which enzymes fragment and destroy an infected cell.

FIGURE 26-27 Programmed cell death. Shown are two leukocytes (white blood cells). The one on the right is undergoing apoptosis.

respiratory virus antigen. Other cytokines produced by the activated helper T cells provide the final signals that make the cytotoxic T cells "mature" and ready to fight the pathogen at the site of infection. You may notice this process occurring when you've been sick: the rapid division of lymphocytes in the lymph nodes causes the nodes to swell (usually called "swollen glands"). The helper T cells and cytotoxic T cells then leave the lymph nodes or spleen and circulate throughout the body. (Helper T cells also are required to stimulate B cells to produce antibodies; B cell development occurs only in response to these signals from helper T cells.)

Mature cytotoxic effector cells are like newly trained soldiers, ready to fight the enemy, but first they need to detect where the enemy is hiding. Consider that infected cell in the throat again. Is it revealing that it's under attack? Yes! The infected

cell displays some of the pathogen's molecules on its cell surface receptors, advertising the infection to the now numerous cytotoxic T cells that can recognize that specific respiratory virus.

How do the cytotoxic effector cells fight the internal pathogen? They do something drastic—they kill the throat cell that is infected. The weapons that they use are proteins: some punch holes in the cell's plasma membrane, and others promote the cell's self-destruction, or **apoptosis.** This programmed cell death does not explode the cell—sending virus particles everywhere. Just the opposite: it is a neatly organized, well-orchestrated process carried out by enzymes that break down macromolecules inside the cell (including the pathogen), fragment the cell into smaller pieces, and package the pieces in vesicles (**FIGURE 26-27**). The vesicles are then engulfed and digested by phagocytes. So, while some body cells are lost in the battle, ultimately it is for the good of the entire organism.

Because memory helper T cells and memory cytotoxic T cells are also made during the throat infection, this same virus cannot cause illness again. Remember, this is specific immunity, and memory cells will leap into action to make more effector cells if the virus is encountered again.

TAKE-HOME MESSAGE 26·9

Antibodies, produced by B cells, cannot destroy pathogens that are inside cells. The specialization of cytotoxic T cells is required to kill infected cells. Antigen-presenting cells, such as macrophages, display antigens to circulating helper T cells and cytotoxic T cells, to alert the specific immunity system that an infection is under way. In turn, helper T cells produce cytokines that instruct cytotoxic T cells to mature and respond to the infection.

A T lymphocyte (green) surrounded by HIV particles (red).

26·10–26·12 Malfunction of the immune system causes disease.

26·10 Autoimmune diseases occur when the body turns against its own tissues.

What happens when the immune system malfunctions? Genetic defects, environmental influences, and even viruses can trigger immune dysfunction. And in many cases, such as autoimmune diseases, a combination of causes is suspected, but not completely understood. **Autoimmunity** occurs when an individual's immune system responds inappropriately to the individual's own cells and tissues as if they were pathogens, mistaking "self" for "non-self." If immunity can be compared to warfare, then autoimmunity is equivalent to an army turning its weapons upon its own citizens. Lymphocyte receptors wrongly recognize an individual's own molecules or cellular structures as antigens, and the humoral and/or cell-mediated immune responses can be initiated by these antigens. Most autoimmune diseases result in significant tissue and organ damage, and some can even result in death.

Type 1 diabetes (or juvenile diabetes) is an example of an autoimmune disorder. It is diagnosed in more than 13,000 young people in the United States each year. Symptoms include high blood glucose levels, weight loss, unquenchable thirst, frequent urination, fatigue, and weakness. In this disease, cytotoxic T cells, complement proteins, and macrophages destroy the person's own pancreatic cells. Without a normal pancreas, a person cannot make insulin (**FIGURE 26-28**). Without insulin, cells in need of glucose are not able to take it up from the blood, even

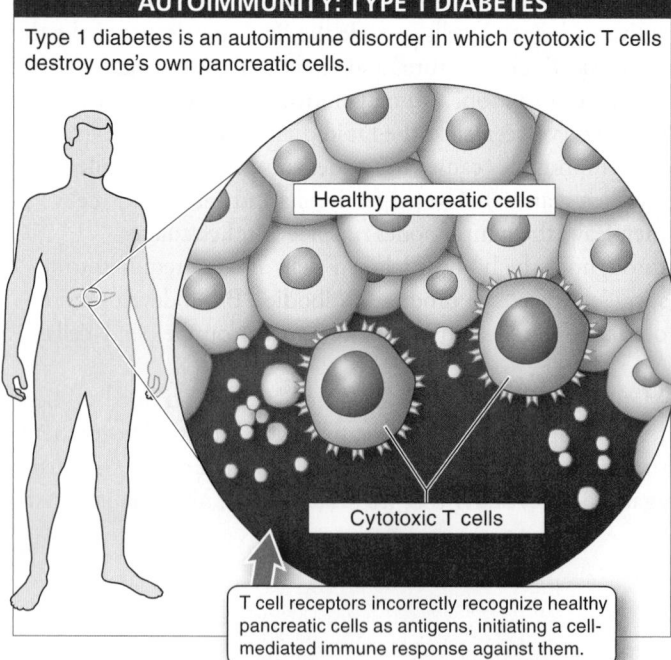

AUTOIMMUNITY: TYPE 1 DIABETES

Type 1 diabetes is an autoimmune disorder in which cytotoxic T cells destroy one's own pancreatic cells.

Healthy pancreatic cells

Cytotoxic T cells

T cell receptors incorrectly recognize healthy pancreatic cells as antigens, initiating a cell-mediated immune response against them.

FIGURE 26-28 Type 1 diabetes is an all-too-common autoimmune disorder.

though glucose is plentiful. In turn, the body breaks down muscle and fat tissues to provide cells with needed energy, and blood glucose levels remain high. The exact cause of this disorders, the damage is spread throughout the body. When the insulation that surrounds nerve fibers of the brain and spinal cord is under immune attack, the resulting disorder is called **multiple sclerosis (MS)** (see Section 23-5). Individuals with MS usually begin to exhibit symptoms between 20 and 40 years of age, and these symptoms include blurred vision, weakness in the arms and legs, trouble with balance, and tingling sensations (**FIGURE 26-29**). This disorder tends to affect women more than men, and it affects more than 300,000 people in the United States. There is no cure for MS, but anti-inflammatory drugs can reduce the severity of some symptoms. Many new drugs are being investigated, including some that block the inflammatory response.

Rheumatoid arthritis is another autoimmune disease that affects women more frequently than men, and it usually strikes between ages 40 and 60. (This form of arthritis is a far less common cause of joint inflammation than osteoarthritis, which is not an autoimmune disease.) The linings of joints are the targets of this immune attack—leading to pain and severe joint swelling that can result in deformities. Various pharmaceuticals are available to help reduce symptoms, and joint replacement surgeries also provide relief for individuals suffering from rheumatoid arthritis.

Multiple sclerosis results from an autoimmune attack on the insulation surrounding nerve fibers.

FIGURE 26-29 An autoimmune disorder: multiple sclerosis.

autoimmune reaction is not understood. Treatment for individuals with type 1 diabetes is insulin injections or implantation of an insulin pump, which directly monitors blood glucose levels and releases insulin as needed.

In some disorders, including type 1 diabetes, the immune system destroys a single cell type or a single organ. In other

TAKE-HOME MESSAGE 26·10

When lymphocytes bear receptors that inappropriately recognize structures of a person's own body as foreign invaders, autoimmunity develops. Autoimmune responses can do significant damage to specific organs or to tissues throughout the body, depending on where the antigens are located.

26·11 AIDS is an immune deficiency disease.

Autoimmune diseases demonstrate how immune recognition can fail and have devastating effects on the body. Here we examine a case in which recognition of a true pathogen occurs, but the *response* is deficient. Normally, the immune system destroys body cells that are infected with a virus. But what if the infected cells are immune cells that are critical for mounting a normal immune response? The **human immunodeficiency virus (HIV),** which causes **AIDS (acquired immune deficiency syndrome),** infects immune system cells, including helper T cells—cells that are crucial to survival. With AIDS, a deficiency of helper T cells leads to complete failure of the specific immunity response. As a result of this failure, individuals are prey to, and may die

from, infections that a healthy immune system would have no trouble defeating.

HIV infection occurs through contact with blood, semen, vaginal fluid, or breast milk from an infected person. Thus, using clean (not shared) intravenous needles and using condoms are effective precautionary measures against HIV infection. People who become infected with HIV often do not have immediate symptoms and often do not know they are infected. Because individuals are contagious once they are infected, this initial lack of symptoms contributes to the spread of the disease. Let's examine the details of how immunity diminishes as the immune system loses its battle against HIV.

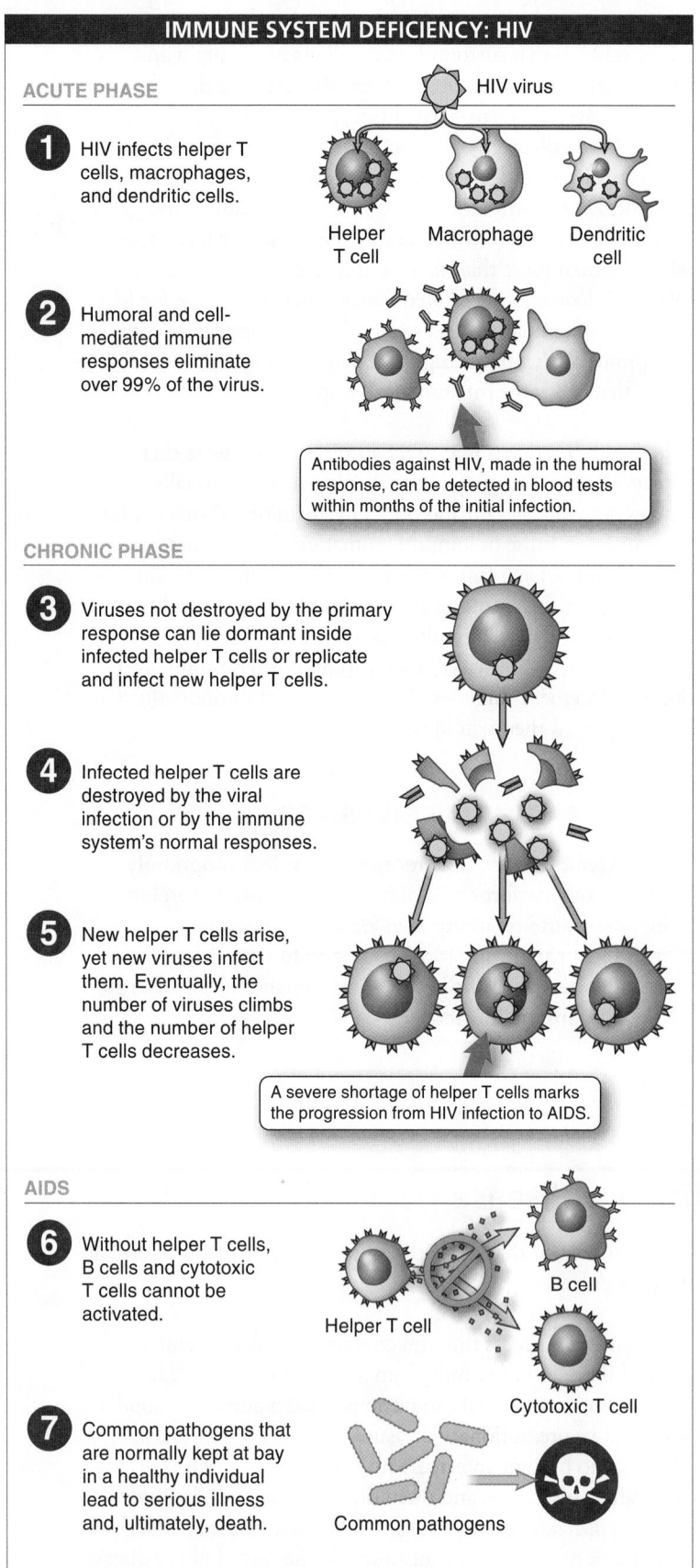

IMMUNE SYSTEM DEFICIENCY: HIV

ACUTE PHASE

HIV virus

1 HIV infects helper T cells, macrophages, and dendritic cells.

Helper T cell   Macrophage   Dendritic cell

2 Humoral and cell-mediated immune responses eliminate over 99% of the virus.

Antibodies against HIV, made in the humoral response, can be detected in blood tests within months of the initial infection.

CHRONIC PHASE

3 Viruses not destroyed by the primary response can lie dormant inside infected helper T cells or replicate and infect new helper T cells.

4 Infected helper T cells are destroyed by the viral infection or by the immune system's normal responses.

5 New helper T cells arise, yet new viruses infect them. Eventually, the number of viruses climbs and the number of helper T cells decreases.

A severe shortage of helper T cells marks the progression from HIV infection to AIDS.

AIDS

6 Without helper T cells, B cells and cytotoxic T cells cannot be activated.

Helper T cell   B cell   Cytotoxic T cell

7 Common pathogens that are normally kept at bay in a healthy individual lead to serious illness and, ultimately, death.

Common pathogens

FIGURE 26-30 The progression from HIV infection to AIDS.

Different viruses infect different kinds of body cells. HIV infects helper T cells and macrophages, among other cells. When an individual is first infected by HIV, a normal specific immunity response is mounted, and infected helper T cells are killed by both humoral and cell-mediated responses. More than 99% of the virus is destroyed in this primary response. Although many helper T cells are lost, new helper T cells arise. As you might expect, antibodies against HIV are made in a humoral response and can easily be detected in blood tests within months of the initial infection. Antibody detection marks the end of the first phase of HIV infection, the *acute phase* (**FIGURE 26-30**).

Unfortunately, the viruses that were not destroyed by the primary response can lie dormant inside infected helper T cells and macrophages. The infection then enters a period called the *chronic phase,* in which the person is infectious but doesn't have outward symptoms. This period is variable but rarely exceeds 12 years. Although the infection may seem inactive, a battle is going on within the immune system. Some of the HIV viruses lie dormant, but others replicate and infect new helper T cells. Helper T cells that are infected are killed by the viral infection or are destroyed by the immune system's normal responses. New helper T cells arise, and new viruses infect them. This cycle continues, but it is not a balanced situation. Sooner or later, the number of viruses climbs and the number of helper T cells decreases, and serious clinical symptoms appear. (This process is like an army valiantly fighting a battle but ultimately running out of soldiers.)

A severe shortage of helper T cells marks the progression from HIV infection to AIDS. Without helper T cells, B cells and cytotoxic T cells cannot be activated (recall from Section 26-9 that helper T cells stimulate the production of B cells and cytotoxic T cells). Common pathogens that are normally kept at bay in a healthy individual—such as a parasitic protist that causes diarrhea, a fungus that causes "thrush" on the tongue and throat, and viruses that can cause skin lesions and swelling—ultimately lead to debilitating illness and death.

As we saw in Section 13-19, HIV is a rapidly mutating, RNA-containing virus, with surface proteins that can change with each new round of replication (**FIGURE 26-31**). This ever-changing nature of HIV makes development of vaccines against it challenging. Consider a vaccine that is made using a surface glycoprotein of HIV as the antigen. The vaccine becomes obsolete immediately, because the viral antigen is changing too quickly. More than

Q Why is there no vaccine against AIDS yet?

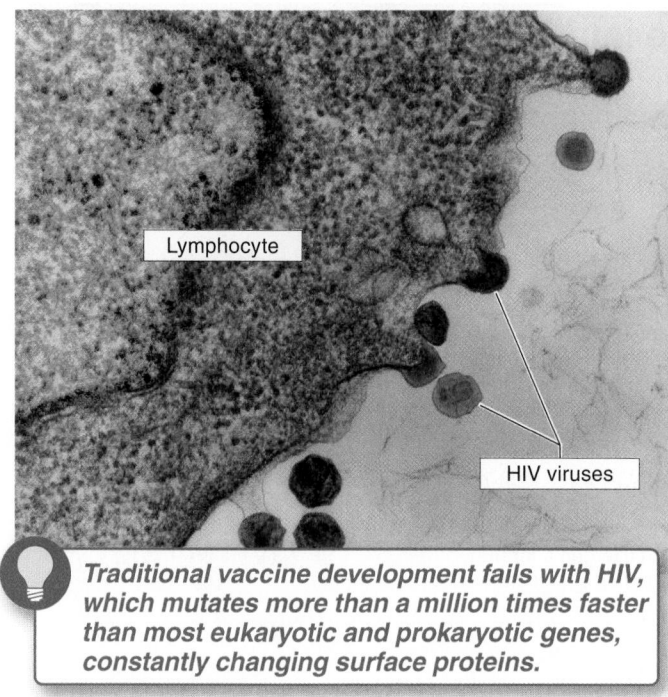

Lymphocyte

HIV viruses

Traditional vaccine development fails with HIV, which mutates more than a million times faster than most eukaryotic and prokaryotic genes, constantly changing surface proteins.

FIGURE 26-31 An ever-changing foe.

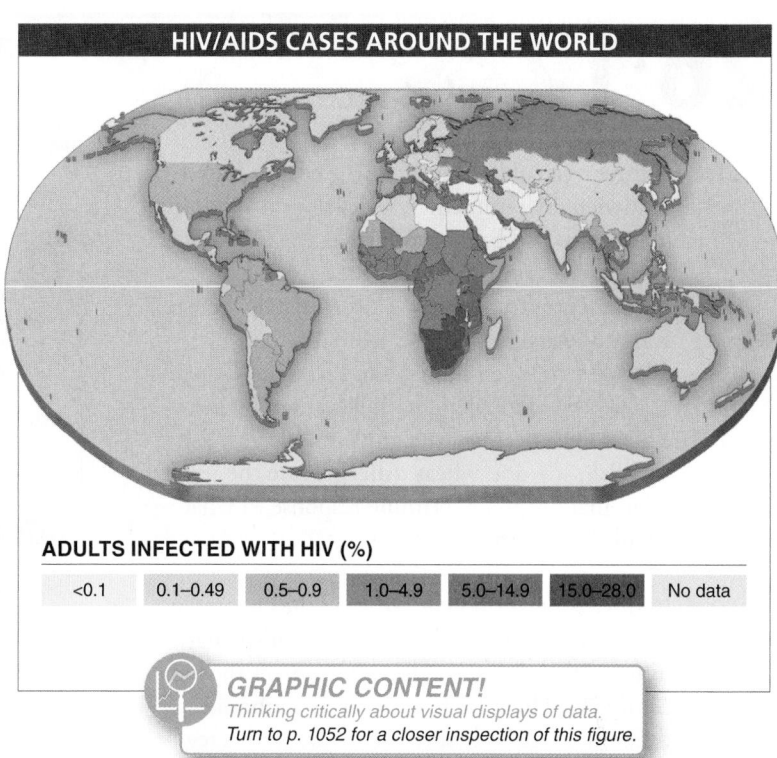

HIV/AIDS CASES AROUND THE WORLD

ADULTS INFECTED WITH HIV (%)

| <0.1 | 0.1–0.49 | 0.5–0.9 | 1.0–4.9 | 5.0–14.9 | 15.0–28.0 | No data |

GRAPHIC CONTENT!
Thinking critically about visual displays of data.
Turn to p. 1052 for a closer inspection of this figure.

FIGURE 26-32 HIV/AIDS is widespread in sub-Saharan Africa.

25 years after isolating the virus, the traditional method of making vaccines against viral antigens has failed because of the constantly mutating HIV. Interestingly, some people have a mutation in a T cell receptor that makes it more difficult for the virus to enter their helper T cells. Ongoing studies of individuals who are naturally resistant to HIV are helping scientists develop new potential vaccines and drug treatments.

Current therapies for HIV infection have been successful at increasing the length and quality of life for those infected. The regimen, called combination therapy, includes numerous drugs that affect HIV's ability to replicate or infect new cells. These drugs keep the number of viruses low and maintain a suitable number of helper T cells. HIV resistance to the drugs, however, is a fear shared by patients and clinicians. Nonetheless, the life span for individuals taking combination therapy is increasing and getting close to a normal length of life. Although there is not a cure yet, individuals who have access to treatment are able to live with HIV as a chronic condition. (Unfortunately, treatment is unavailable for millions of infected people in developing nations.) New therapies aim to find latent viruses that hide inside helper T cells, sometimes for decades, and eliminate them. In the future, HIV may be a disease that can be cured, but for now it continues to be a lifelong condition and a challenge to scientists.

Looking at a map depicting HIV/AIDS cases around the world, we can see just how widespread this virus is. Sub-Saharan Africa is the region most severely affected. In some countries in this region, such as Swaziland and Lesotho, close to 25% of the adult population is infected with HIV. In South Africa, more than 5 million people, or almost 20% of its adult population, are infected (**FIGURE 26-32**). In contrast, less than 1% of the U.S. population is infected with HIV. Not everyone who is HIV-infected has AIDS, however. For example, estimates indicate that of the more than one million people infected by HIV in the United States, in fewer than 40,000 cases has the infection progressed to AIDS.

TAKE-HOME MESSAGE 26·11

AIDS is an immune system disease caused by the human immunodeficiency virus (HIV), which infects helper T cells—immune cells that are crucial to survival. As helper T cells are killed by the infection or by the body's own immune cells in response to the infection, the deficiency of helper T cells leads to complete failure of the specific immunity response, resulting in illness and death from infections that a healthy immune system could defeat. There is currently no vaccine for HIV, because traditional vaccine methods do not work against this rapidly mutating virus, nor is there a cure for AIDS.

26·12 Allergies are an inappropriate immune response to a harmless substance.

A three-year-old girl bites into a peanut butter sandwich. She immediately develops hives around her mouth and begins vomiting. She is having an allergic reaction. This is only the second time she's eaten peanut butter. Unfortunately, her story is not unusual. The CDC estimates that approximately 3 million children in the United States have food allergies, 90% caused by just eight foods: peanuts, tree nuts, milk, eggs, fish, shellfish, soy, and wheat. **Allergies** are the result of an inappropriate immune response to what should be a harmless substance.

In discussing antibodies earlier in the chapter, we did not focus on the groups of antibodies that differ in their constant (heavy) region at the base of the "Y." There are five classes of antibodies, differing in their chemical structure in this region. When antibodies of one of these classes bind to mast cells (the white blood cells found in tissues), they cause the mast cells to release histamine and cytokines, both of which cause local blood vessels to become dilated and leaky (as we've seen, standard parts of the inflammatory response), and recruit other immune cells to the site.

This mast-cell-binding class of antibodies can cause much harm to the body if they are made in response to an **allergen,** an antigen that causes an allergic response. On first encounter, an allergen induces a normal humoral response: memory cells form and plasma cells secrete antibodies specific to the allergen. The antibodies bind to the surface of mast cells and can remain bound for months and maybe even years. The mast cells are now "sensitized" to the allergen. In a second exposure, the allergen binds to the antibodies that are still attached to the mast cells—which are now "activated." This time, allergen binding causes the mast cells to release histamine, which causes the blood vessels to dilate and become leaky, and inflammation ensues (**FIGURE 26-33**).

The effect of different allergens reflects which particular mast cells have been exposed to the allergen and thus activated. Most allergic reactions occur in the digestive or respiratory tracts, because this is where the body first encounters an allergen that is eaten or inhaled. Allergic reactions associated with food often lead to vomiting or

ALLERGIC REACTION

FIRST RESPONSE

Allergen

1 When the body first encounters an allergen, although the material (such as peanut proteins) is harmless, a humoral response occurs: memory cells form and plasma cells secrete antibodies specific to the allergen.

Plasma cell

Antibodies

2 Mast cells become "sensitized" to the allergen after the antibodies bind to their surface.

Mast cell

SECOND RESPONSE

Allergen

3 Allergens bind to the antibodies that are still attached to the mast cells, causing the mast cells to release histamine.

Mast cell

Histamine

4 Histamine causes the blood vessels to dilate and become leaky, and inflammation ensues.

Allergies result from overly sensitized mast cells releasing histamine and cytokines in response to allergens.

FIGURE 26-33 Allergens induce a humoral response in some individuals.

diarrhea, but can also lead to hives and other symptoms if the allergen enters the bloodstream. Respiratory allergens, such as pollen and dust, can cause a runny nose and teary eyes ("hay fever") in the upper respiratory tract, or can result in asthma, a chronic inflammatory disease of the lower respiratory tract that causes wheezing, coughing, and shortness of breath.

Taking an antihistamine can alleviate some allergies, as these medicines block the inflammatory effects of histamine.

FIGURE 26-34 Screening for allergies.

Allergies can be tested for by injecting microscopic amounts of allergens under the skin. If a bump or rash develops there, an allergy may be suspected.

the site of inflammation. Additionally, steroids can block the killing ability of these phagocytes, resulting in less damage to the inflamed tissue.

An individual with a severe allergic response may experience **anaphylactic shock,** a life-threatening allergic reaction that is systemic, meaning that it is not localized to the site of exposure. Anaphylactic shock can lead to severe respiratory distress, as the throat swells and asthma develops. Swelling in various tissues means there is less fluid in the blood system, and this can lead to dangerously low blood pressure. Individuals with severe allergies often carry with them a dose of adrenaline, also called epinephrine, a chemical found naturally in our bodies (see Section 24-5) and also manufactured by several drug companies. Epinephrine, which can be injected if needed, reverses the effects of histamine on blood vessels, but it must be injected quickly, because death can occur rapidly from anaphylactic shock.

A common method of testing for allergies is called *skin allergy testing,* in which microscopic amounts of one or more potential allergens are injected under the skin—usually on the back or the forearm. The development of a rash can indicate a hypersensitivity to that allergen, enabling the person to take steps to reduce exposure to the allergen (**FIGURE 26-34**).

TAKE-HOME MESSAGE 26·12

In individuals who are sensitive, an allergen induces a humoral response in which one class of antibodies binds to and activates mast cells. A second exposure to the allergen leads activated mast cells to release histamine and other chemicals, resulting in allergy-related symptoms. Swelling and inflammation can be localized or can be systemic and lead to anaphylactic shock.

Other medicines block mast cells from releasing histamine. Steroids are prescribed for more severe allergies. Steroids block the production of the chemicals released from immune cells, thus preventing the migration of more inflammatory cells, such as macrophages and neutrophils, to

FACTS OR FALLACIES? How best to avoid getting sick.

Q: CAN I CATCH A COLD FROM GOING OUT WITH WET HAIR IN THE WINTER? No. Your grandmother was wrong about this one! To catch a cold, you must be infected with a pathogen (such as a rhinovirus) that causes the common cold. Colds do tend to be more common in colder weather, because the viruses are more stable in colder air with low humidity. And droplets of water and virus (such as those that escape when we sneeze and cough) remain airborne slightly longer in dry air than in humid summer air. Also, because people are indoors more often during winter, the increased population in confined quarters increases the incidence and ease of transmission. So, while the virus is affected by the colder weather, your immune system is not. Dry your hair before you leave the house if you don't want icicles in it, but not as a strategy for combating the common cold.

Q: CAN I CATCH A COLD BECAUSE I AM NOT SLEEPING ENOUGH? This gets an emphatic *yes!* In randomized, controlled studies in which individuals were given nasal drops containing rhinovirus, individuals getting less sleep were significantly more likely to develop colds than those sleeping 7 hours or more. And simply resting in bed or having an interrupted night's sleep doesn't count. Seven hours or more of good-quality sleep seems to be important to the immune system, particularly for the production and functioning of cytokines. Interestingly, there is also evidence that individuals who sleep 7–8 hours a night have the lowest rates of heart disease. Although eating well and exercising are most often associated with good health, sleep, too, is important, and neglecting it can increase your vulnerability to illness.

Q: CAN DRINKING HERBAL TEAS, EATING CHICKEN SOUP, OR TAKING THE PRODUCT AIRBORNE HELP ME WARD OFF THE COMMON COLD? *Herbal teas and chicken soup?* Not exactly. There are some symptom-reducing benefits of hot fluids, including keeping nasal passages moist, preventing dehydration, and soothing a sore throat. And one study showed that chicken soup with vegetables seemed to have an anti-inflammatory effect. But while these effects can make an infection less unpleasant by reducing the symptoms, they don't decrease the likelihood of catching a cold or shorten its duration. *Airborne?* Remember the very first section of the first chapter of this book? There is not a shred of evidence that Airborne can ward off colds or boost your immune system.

Big Ideas in ...
Immunity and Health

26·1–26·4 Your body has different ways to protect you against disease-causing invaders.

- There are three collaborative divisions of the immune system: physical barriers, non-specific immunity, and specific immunity.

- Physical barriers, part of the integumentary system, prevent pathogens from entering the body's cells; cells exposed to the external environment are protected by defenses such as bacteria-destroying chemicals, acidic secretions, sticky mucus, and wax.

- Non-specific (innate) immunity defends against pathogens by recognizing combinations of receptors on their cell surfaces.

- White blood cells of the non-specific system include phagocytes—including neutrophils and macrophages that kill pathogens, and macrophages and dendritic cells that display pathogens to cells of the specific immunity system—and natural killer cells that kill cancer cells and virus-infected cells. Complement proteins non-specifically recognize invaders and help destroy them.

- Inflammation is a major way in which the innate system eliminates pathogens. The redness, heat, swelling, and pain of inflammation reflect changes in blood vessels that enhance recruitment of phagocytes and complement proteins to the site of inflammation.

26·5–26·9 Specific immunity develops after exposure to pathogens.

- Long-term protection, or immunity, from a specific pathogen can form by exposure to the natural pathogen or exposure to a vaccine with an altered version of the pathogen, both of which result in production of antibodies.

- The specific (adaptive) immunity system responds continually to numerous pathogens that can change over time, through the action of two types of lymphocytes. B cells are responsible for the humoral (antibody-mediated) response, and T cells for the cell-mediated response.

- Lymphocytes recognizing an antigen divide to produce many cells through clonal selection.

- During a primary response, effector cells respond to and facilitate removal of the antigen, and memory cells are produced that are ready to go through clonal selection if a secondary response is necessary.

- Plasma cells secrete antibodies into the blood and lymph. Each antibody has a unique structure that recognizes a specific antigen. Antibodies help destroy pathogens and free-floating antigens by enhancing ingestion by phagocytes, preventing more cell infection, and enhancing complement-driven cell lysis.

- Cytotoxic T cells undergo specialization to kill infected cells. Antigen-presenting cells display antigens to helper T cells and cytotoxic T cells, to alert the adaptive immune system to an infection. In turn, helper T cells produce cytokines that allow cytotoxic T cells to mature and respond to the infection.

26·10–26·12 Malfunction of the immune system causes disease.

- When lymphocytes bear antigen receptors that inappropriately recognize the body's own structures, autoimmunity develops and damages specific organs or tissues throughout the body.

- AIDS is an immune system disease caused by the human immunodeficiency virus (HIV), which infects helper T cells. The deficiency of helper T cells leads to complete failure of the specific immunity response and thus illness and death from infections that a healthy immune system could defeat.

- In individuals who are sensitive, allergens induce a humoral response in which one type of antibody binds to mast cells, activating them. With a second exposure to the allergen, activated mast cells release histamine and cytokines, resulting in allergy-related symptoms.

See the To-Go Guide (packaged with every new copy of this textbook) for an illustrated summary of the chapter.

Check Your Knowledge

Thinking critically about visual displays of data.

1. Based on this figure, what would you estimate is the number of adults in the United States who are infected with HIV? Show your work.

2. Can you identify which countries have the largest number of adults infected with HIV? Explain your answer.

3. From this figure, can you conclude that there are twice as many adults infected with HIV in the United States as there are in Canada? Explain your answer.

4. What can you conclude about the HIV infection rates in South America relative to the infection rates in South Africa?

5. Each of the first three colored bars covers ranges of less than 1 percentage point, while the darkest red bar covers almost 15 percentage points. Why? How might this difference mislead a reader? Why might this be a useful way to present the data?

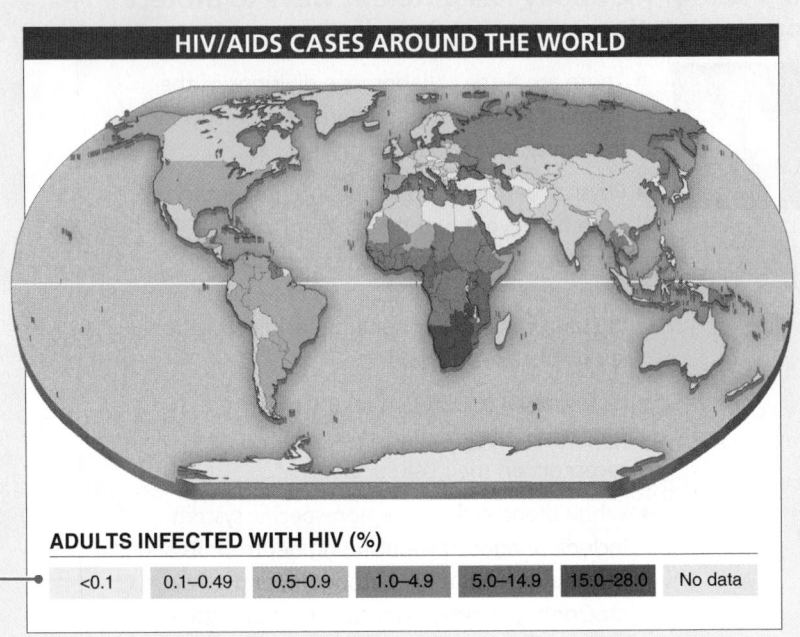

HIV/AIDS CASES AROUND THE WORLD

ADULTS INFECTED WITH HIV (%)

| <0.1 | 0.1–0.49 | 0.5–0.9 | 1.0–4.9 | 5.0–14.9 | 15.0–28.0 | No data |

See Answers at the back of the book.

Key Terms in Immunity and Health

AIDS (acquired immune deficiency syndrome), p. 1045
allergen, p. 1048
allergy, p. 1048
anaphylactic shock, p. 1049
antibody, p. 1034
antigen, p. 1034
antigen-presenting cell, p. 1042
antigen receptor, p. 1038
antiseptic, p. 1028

apoptosis, p. 1043
autoimmunity, p. 1044
B cell, p. 1038
basophil, p. 1030
cilia, p. 1026
clonal selection, p. 1040
complement protein, p. 1029
cytokine, p. 1028
cytotoxic T cell, p. 1041
dendritic cell, p. 1028
effector cell, p. 1040
fever, p. 1031

helper T cell, p. 1042
histamine, p. 1030
HIV (human immunodeficiency virus), p. 1045
immune system, p. 1023
immunity, p. 1033
inflammatory response, p. 1029
integumentary system, p. 1025
interferon, p. 1028

lymphocyte, p. 1038
lysozyme, p. 1025
macrophage, p. 1028
mast cell, p. 1030
memory cell, p. 1040
multiple sclerosis (MS), p. 1045
natural killer (NK) cell, p. 1028
neutrophil, p. 1028
non-specific immunity, p. 1024
pathogen, p. 1022

physical barriers (immune system), p. 1024
plasma cell, p. 1040
primary response, p. 1040
pus, p. 1028
secondary response, p. 1041
specific immunity, p. 1024
T cell, p. 1038
vaccine, p. 1033
white blood cell, p. 1027

Multiple-Choice Questions

1. **Which of the following statements about the integumentary system is incorrect?**

   a) It is one of the body's three lines of defense against infectious pathogens.

   b) It confers specific immunity on an individual, because it confers protection against individual pathogens.

   c) It includes sweat glands.

   d) It is responsible for the production of tears and ear wax.

   e) It helps protect the digestive system from pathogens.

   100 HARD
   61
   0 EASY

2. **Which of the following statements about how complement proteins kill bacteria is incorrect?**

   a) Bound complement proteins are able to recruit other complement proteins to come to the site of bacterial infection.

   b) Complement proteins aggregate to form larger protein complexes that create holes in the bacterial cell surface.

   c) Bacterial death results from membrane holes created by complexes between complement and surface proteins.

   d) Complement proteins surround and bind to the entire surface of a bacterium, marking it to be engulfed by phagocytes and cytotoxic T cells.

   e) Complement proteins are able to recognize and bind directly to the surface of bacteria's cell surface proteins.

   100 HARD
   65
   0 EASY

3. **Which of the following statements about the inflammatory response is incorrect?**

   a) The release of histamine by mast cells initiates inflammation.

   b) Cells lining blood vessels near inflamed tissue become "stickier" to neutrophils.

   c) Pain can occur with inflammation, as increased pressure in an inflamed area stimulates local neurons.

   d) The release of histamine causes blood vessels to constrict, reducing blood loss in an injured area.

   e) Four signs of inflammation are swelling, redness, heat, and pain.

   100 HARD
   53
   0 EASY

4. **Vaccines:**

   a) activate a primary response in the vaccinated individual.

   b) lead to the creation of memory B cells that provide a rapid secondary response against a specific infectious agent.

   c) are sometimes made of no more than the unique antigens from a pathogen's surface.

   d) All of the above are correct.

   e) Only b) and c) are correct.

   100 HARD
   62
   0 EASY

5. **The major difference between T cells and B cells is that:**

   a) T cells develop in the thymus, whereas B cells develop in the bone marrow.

   b) T cells do not interact with the innate immune system, but B cells do.

   c) T cells bind directly to foreign antigens, whereas B cells produce proteins (antibodies) that are secreted and bind to the foreign antigens.

   d) All of the above are major differences between T cells and B cells.

   e) Both a) and c) are major differences between T cells and B cells.

   100 HARD
   40
   0 EASY

6. Why don't people develop immunity to the common cold?

a) Actually, many people do develop immunity to the common cold and get sick only from bacterial infections.

b) There are at least 200 different viruses that can cause the common cold, and they change over time.

c) Only non-specific immunity helps individuals fight the common cold; specific immunity is not an effective defense against viruses.

d) The rhinovirus that causes the common cold has no surface antigens and so can move through the body without being detected.

e) The pathogen that causes the common cold attacks and kills memory cells, continually "erasing" the immune system's memory of it.

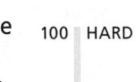

100 HARD

0 13 EASY

7. Antibodies:

a) are produced by helper B cells.

b) are produced by helper T cells.

c) are produced by the B cell bound by a specific antigen.

d) are produced by plasma cells.

e) are made in the bone marrow.

100 HARD

70

0 EASY

8. The polypeptides that make up the structure of an antibody consist of:

a) two heavy chains and two light chains, shaped like a "Y," with a lower constant region and an upper variable region.

b) two heavy chains and two light chains, shaped like a "Y," each with an upper constant region and a lower variable region.

c) one heavy chain and one light chain, shaped like a "Y," each with a lower constant region and an upper variable region.

d) one heavy chain and one light chain, shaped like a "Y," each with an upper constant region and a lower variable region.

e) Both b) and d) can be correct, depending on the type of antibody.

100 HARD

59

0 EASY

9. Which of the following is not a function of helper T cells?

a) They stimulate B cells to proliferate and produce antibodies.

b) They activate cytotoxic T cells.

c) They stimulate B cells to secrete cytokines.

d) They recognize antigens presented on macrophage surfaces.

e) All of the above are functions of helper T cells.

100 HARD

53

0 EASY

10. Autoimmunity is:

a) one of three lines of defense in the vertebrate immune system.

b) responsible for muscular dystrophy, which occurs when immune cells destroy the myelin sheath, reducing motor control and balance.

c) the culprit in rheumatoid arthritis, which occurs when immune attack on the linings of joints causes inflammation.

d) a consequence of a body's inability to produce antigens, leading it to attack its own cells as if they were pathogens.

e) All of the above statements about autoimmunity are correct.

100 HARD

71

0 EASY

11. As the human immunodeficiency virus (HIV) begins to kill the host's _____, the host's immune system begins to fail.

a) thymus cells

b) spleen cells

c) red blood cells

d) white blood cells

e) liver cells

100 HARD

23

0 EASY

12. Hay fever affects millions of individuals every year and is caused by an allergic reaction to pollen. Which of the following is not a step of the process in which a pollen grain causes an allergic reaction in an individual?

a) Mast cells burst when they encounter the pollen during the initial exposure, releasing histamine and other chemicals.

b) During the first exposure, B cells are activated by the pollen and differentiate into antibody-secreting plasma cells.

c) During the second exposure, the pollen grains are recognized by previously created antibodies on mast cells.

d) A type of antibody, specific to the pollen grain, is produced during the initial attack, and these antibodies adhere to mast cells, where they remain.

e) Histamine and other allergen chemicals cause itchy eyes and a runny nose.

100 HARD

68

0 EASY

Short-Answer Questions

1. Generally, the second time a person is exposed to a particular pathogen, his or her immune system is able to respond to the pathogen more quickly and effectively. Why?

2. Why is it necessary to get only a single vaccine against the pathogen causing chicken pox, while a flu shot is necessary every year?

See Answers at the back of the book.
For additional study questions, go to www.prep-u.com.

Periodic Table

THE PERIODIC TABLE OF ELEMENTS

GROUP

PERIOD

ELEMENT CATEGORIES

- Alkali metals
- Alkaline earth metals
- Transition metals
- Lanthanides
- Actinides
- Post-transition metals
- Metalloids
- Other nonmetals
- Halogens
- Nobel gases
- Unknown chemical properties

Atomic number
Element symbol
Element name
Atomic mass

Group	1	2	3	4	5	6	7	8	9	10	11	12	13	14	15	16	17	18
1	1 H Hydrogen 1.00794																	2 He Helium 4.00260
2	3 Li Lithium 6.941	4 Be Beryllium 9.01218											5 B Boron 10.811	6 C Carbon 12.0107	7 N Nitrogen 14.0067	8 O Oxygen 15.9994	9 F Fluorine 18.9984	10 Ne Neon 20.1797
3	11 Na Sodium 22.9898	12 Mg Magnesium 24.3050											13 Al Aluminum 26.9815	14 Si Silicon 28.0855	15 P Phosphorus 30.9738	16 S Sulfur 32.065	17 Cl Chlorine 35.453	18 Ar Argon 39.948
4	19 K Potassium 39.0983	20 Ca Calcium 40.078	21 Sc Scandium 44.9559	22 Ti Titanium 47.867	23 V Vanadium 50.9415	24 Cr Chromium 51.9961	25 Mn Manganese 54.9380	26 Fe Iron 55.845	27 Co Cobalt 58.9332	28 Ni Nickel 58.6934	29 Cu Copper 63.546	30 Zn Zinc 65.409	31 Ga Gallium 69.723	32 Ge Germanium 72.64	33 As Arsenic 74.9216	34 Se Selenium 78.96	35 Br Bromine 79.904	36 Kr Krypton 83.798
5	37 Rb Rubidium 85.4678	38 Sr Strontium 87.62	39 Y Yttrium 88.9059	40 Zr Zirconium 91.224	41 Nb Niobium 92.9064	42 Mo Molybdenum 95.94	43 Tc Technetium [98]	44 Ru Ruthenium 101.07	45 Rh Rhodium 102.906	46 Pd Palladium 106.42	47 Ag Silver 107.868	48 Cd Cadmium 112.411	49 In Indium 114.818	50 Sn Tin 118.710	51 Sb Antimony 121.760	52 Te Tellurium 127.60	53 I Iodine 126.904	54 Xe Xenon 131.293
6	55 Cs Cesium 132.905	56 Ba Barium 137.327	57-71	72 Hf Hafnium 178.49	73 Ta Tantalum 180.948	74 W Tungsten 183.84	75 Re Rhenium 186.207	76 Os Osmium 190.23	77 Ir Iridium 192.217	78 Pt Platinum 195.078	79 Au Gold 196.967	80 Hg Mercury 200.59	81 Tl Thallium 204.383	82 Pb Lead 207.2	83 Bi Bismuth 208.980	84 Po Polonium [209]	85 At Astatine [210]	86 Rn Radon [222]
7	87 Fr Francium [223]	88 Ra Radium [226]	89-103	104 Rf Rutherfordium [261]	105 Db Dubnium [262]	106 Sg Seaborgium [266]	107 Bh Bohrium [264]	108 Hs Hassium [277]	109 Mt Meitnerium [268]	110 Ds Darmstadtium [281]	111 Rg Roentgenium [272]	112 Cn Copernicium [285]	113 Uut Ununtrium [284]	114 Uuq Ununquadium [289]	115 Uup Ununpentium [288]	116 Uuh Ununhexium [292]	117 Uus Ununseptium ?	118 Uuo Ununoctium [294]

57 La Lanthanum 138.906	58 Ce Cerium 140.116	59 Pr Praseodymium 140.908	60 Nd Neodymium 144.24	61 Pm Promethium [145]	62 Sm Samarium 150.36	63 Eu Europium 151.964	64 Gd Gadolinium 157.25	65 Tb Terbium 158.925	66 Dy Dysprosium 162.5	67 Ho Holmium 164.930	68 Er Erbium 167.259	69 Tm Thulium 168.934	70 Yb Ytterbium 173.04	71 Lu Lutetium 174.967
89 Ac Actinium [227]	90 Th Thorium 232.038	91 Pa Protactinium 231.036	92 U Uranium 238.029	93 Np Neptunium [237]	94 Pu Plutonium [244]	95 Am Americium [243]	96 Cm Curium [247]	97 Bk Berkelium [247]	98 Cf Californium [251]	99 Es Einsteinium [252]	100 Fm Fermium [257]	101 Md Mendelevium [258]	102 No Nobelium [259]	103 Lr Lawrencium [262]

Answers

Chapter 1

1. b; 2. b; 3. d; 4. e; 5. c; 6. e; 7. a; 8. a; 9. b; 10. a; 11. d; 12. c; 13. a; 14. b; 15. e; 16. a; 17. d; 18. a

Short-Answer Questions

1. To provide proper controls, a group of participants must receive a placebo that superficially resembles the medication. The control group should be treated exactly the same as the experimental group, with one exception: the control group receives a placebo instead of the drug. This provides a basis of comparison between the experimental and control groups.

2. There are many possible answers. Four possibilities are: adding a control group; extending the test for a longer period of time; standardizing the subjects to make sure that other variables are not responsible for the weight loss; repeating the study.

Graphic Content Questions

1. The green portion represents the proportion of all papers published in the journal *Behavioral Ecology* that had a female first author. The blue portion represents the proportion of all papers published in *Behavioral Ecology* that had a male first author. Together, the green and blue portions represent all papers published in *Behavioral Ecology* (that is, 100%).

2. The pie chart on the left presents the proportion of all papers published in *Behavioral Ecology* that had a female first author (and, in blue, the proportion that had a male first author) during the years 1997–2001, when the journal had a "single-blind" review process in which reviewers knew the authors' identities (and, presumably, their sex). The pie chart on the right presents the same information, but for the years 2002–2005, when the journal had a "double-blind" review policy in which reviewers did *not* know the authors' identities or sex.

3. When the journal changed its review policy so that reviewers did not know the sex of the authors, the proportion of accepted papers that had female first authors increased from 23.7% to 31.6%. This suggests that when reviewers knew the sex of the authors, they were less likely to accept a paper with a female first author. This would seem to indicate that the reviewers for *Behavioral Ecology* at that time were biased against female authors.

4. It could be that, beginning in 2002, there was an increase in the proportion of papers submitted to *Behavioral Ecology* that had a female first author. This explanation seems unlikely, however, given the information in the text that a similar journal that did not change its review policy had no change in the proportion of published papers with a female first author. Another possible explanation is that the proportion of women in the field of behavioral ecology increased in the early 1990s, so that, during the second period measured, 2002–2005, there were more women at a more advanced stage in their careers, so the quality of the papers they submitted increased over time.

5. The increase in proportion of published papers with female first authors was 31.6% – 23.7%, or 7.9 percentage points. It could also be described as a 7.9%/23.7% = 33% increase (if you take one-third of 23.7% and add it to 23.7%, you get 31.6%).

6. The information given in the figure tells us what percentage of the papers *published* had a female first author. We cannot tell from this information whether 50% of the papers *submitted* had female first authors. If that were true, it would be reasonable to be concerned why the proportion published wasn't also 50%. But what if only 10% of the people working as behavioral ecologists are women? If that were the case, we might expect that only 10% of the papers published in the journal would have female first authors, and we might be concerned that with such a small proportion of female behavioral ecologists, more than one-quarter of the papers published in this journal had female first authors.

7. The graphs do not prove a general bias against female scientists. Because the data are drawn from just one journal in one field of science, we cannot be certain that they reflect a similar bias across all journals in biology, or in chemistry, physics, or other scientific fields. Nonetheless, the findings do suggest such a bias may exist. It would be valuable to collect additional data on this topic across all of the sciences.

Chapter 2

1. d; 2. e; 3. d; 4. b; 5. a; 6. c; 7. a; 8. d; 9. c; 10. b; 11. a; 12. a; 13. a; 14. a; 15. a; 16. a; 17. e; 18. e; 19. d; 20. b

Short-Answer Questions

1. a) The sodium atom has one electron in its outermost shell; the fluorine atom has seven electrons in its outermost shell. b) An ionic bond forms between these two atoms. Neither atom has a full outer electron shell, and both are unstable. The atoms interact to achieve a full outer shell of electrons: the single electron in the outermost shell of the sodium is transferred to the outermost shell of the fluorine. Each atom becomes an ion, and the oppositely charged ions attract each other.

2. First, cohesion is a result of polar water molecules easily bonding together by hydrogen bonds; this allows one water molecule to "connect" with the next as water makes its way up from the soil to the leaves of a tall tree. Second, water has a large capacity to hold heat and resists large fluctuations in temperature; this is because added energy, in the form of heat, does not increase the movement of water molecules, as occurs in most substances. Instead, hydrogen bonds between water molecules are briefly broken and then re-form with nearby water molecules. Third, ice is less dense than water, so it floats; this is because polar water molecules are held apart by hydrogen bonds when the temperature drops (see Figure 2-15). Fourth, water is an excellent solvent because water molecules are polar. Polar molecules with charged regions are attracted to the charged regions of other polar molecules. Many substances contain polar molecules, which easily dissolve in water.

3. Water is a polar molecule and is attracted to other polar molecules, or molecules with charged regions. Oil consists of nonpolar molecules. As a result, polar water molecules will not interact with oil, and water by itself will not be able to dissolve oily dirt.

4. Lettuce and celery contain carbohydrates, which provide a source of energy or fuel for the body. Strawberries also contain carbohydrates,

but more monosaccharides, versus the complex carbohydrates of lettuce and celery. Walnuts and chicken are sources of protein. The amino acid building blocks of protein are used to build many structures and molecules required by all cells. The salad dressing contains lipids, which provide the body with energy.

Graphic Content Questions

1. A blue dot in a column indicates that the food summarized in that column carries the optimal level of the amino acid(s) listed for that row. A white dot indicates that the food does not contain optimal levels of that amino acid(s). For example, lentils contain optimal levels of the amino acid cysteine, but white rice does not.

2. There is a large amount of information in this figure. One very important conclusion you can draw is that some food sources of protein contain all of the essential amino acids, but others, mostly from plants, do not contain all of the essential amino acids.

3. Although neither of these foods, alone, is a complete protein, consuming them together provides all of the essential amino acids at optimal levels.

4. You don't necessarily have to avoid such a food. It is not necessary to get all of the essential amino acids from each protein source. As long as you get all of the essential amino acids from *everything* you consume at a meal, you will not have any amino acid deficiencies.

5. Apples and white rice, consumed together, would contain all of the essential amino acids. Lentils and almonds would not, since neither of these foods contains methionine and cysteine.

6. The figure doesn't specify what the "optimal levels" of an essential amino acid are. The word "optimal" seems a bit subjective, and the figure doesn't specify who determined what constitutes an "optimal" level. This could be cause for some caution in interpreting the data. In fact, though, these levels were determined by the Institute of Medicine's Nutrition Advisory Board. The Institute of Medicine is the health arm of the U.S. National Academy of Sciences, a highly respected group of the country's most distinguished scientists.

7. The amount of a food you must consume to get a sufficient amount of all the essential amino acids is not given. We can assume that a standard serving is sufficient, but it would be helpful if specific amounts were given, such as "8 ounces" of 2% fat milk, or "6 ounces" of chicken breast.

Chapter 3

1. e; 2. b; 3. e; 4. a; 5. d; 6. d; 7. c; 8. a; 9. d; 10. d; 11. b; 12. d; 13. c; 14. e; 15. b; 16. b; 17. e; 18. e

Short-Answer Question

1. See Figure 3-41 on page 121.

Graphic Content Questions

1. The different cell types observed are the variables. For each cell type, the figure shows how many mitochondria it has.

2. It would be helpful to see data for more cell types, such as sperm cells, egg cells, or brain cells. Data on variation among cells of a particular type within an individual would also be helpful. In other words, do all liver cells have the same number of mitochondria, or does the number vary a lot? And does the number of mitochondria in a specific cell type of a person vary over time—such as when the person gets older, or in response to exercise?

3. Cells with high rates of metabolic activity seem to have more mitochondria.

4. First, perhaps "number of mitochondria per some measure of cell volume" would be better, which would be a measure of mitochondrial density. This would make it easier to compare energy-generating capacity for cells that differ greatly in size. Second, it is also possible that mitochondria can shrink or swell. If that's the case (and some researchers believe it is), maybe the energetic needs of a cell can be met by a few big mitochondria *or* by a large number of small mitochondria—in which case, the *number* of mitochondria wouldn't be the best measure. A measure of total mitochondrial *volume* might be better.

5. Some other cells with high metabolic activity might have relatively large numbers of mitochondria. Sperm cells, for example, might have larger numbers. Similarly, for one cell type, such as muscle cells, more active cells (such as leg muscles) might have more mitochondria than less used muscles (such as those controlling your baby toe).

Chapter 4

1. a; 2. e; 3. e; 4. c; 5. a; 6. c; 7. a; 8. b; 9. d; 10. c; 11. b; 12. e; 13. b; 14. b; 15. a; 16. a; 17. e; 18. d

Short-Answer Questions

1. The plant can split the water molecules in the "photo" reactions of photosynthesis, producing oxygen gas, which can be used for aerobic respiration by both the plant and the mouse. The carbon dioxide produced as a by-product of aerobic respiration by the plant and the mouse can be used by the plant in the "synthesis" reactions, which ultimately produce glucose for the plant.

2. a) Water molecules are split during the "photo" reactions and oxygen gas is released. Measuring the amount of O_2 provides an indication of the rate of the "photo" reactions. b) Plants incorporate CO_2 in the "synthesis" reactions. Using the energy from the "photo" reactions, plants modify the CO_2 to (eventually) form glucose. The "synthesis" reactions are driven by the energy from the "photo" reactions. c) With additional CO_2, the rate of the "synthesis" reactions will increase, which in turn will increase the amount of energy needed from the "photo" reactions.

3. Photosynthesis involves the production of glucose, and cellular respiration involves the breakdown of glucose. Growth in plants is dependent on the rate of photosynthesis. The faster this process occurs, the more glucose is made, the more plant material can be synthesized, and the more the plant grows. If a plant is growing, the rate of photosynthesis exceeds the rate of cellular respiration.

Graphic Content Questions

1. The *x*-axis is the horizontal axis, on which the photosynthetic pigments are listed. The *y*-axis is the vertical axis, which shows the height of each bar and is a measure of the amount of the pigment molecule (for each pigment on the *x*-axis) present in leaves.

2. The independent variable is the time at which the researcher measured the amounts of photosynthetic pigments in leaves. The researcher controlled this, by deciding when to make the measurements. The dependent variable is the measure of the amount of the pigment molecule (for each pigment on the *x*-axis) present in leaves. Based on the information in the graph, you cannot determine how the amounts of pigment molecules were measured. Presumably, this was done by some sort of biochemical assay, but you cannot be sure. The colors of the bars give an extra bit of information, showing the color of light reflected by each of the pigments.

3. The source of the data is not given. In this case, this probably does not reduce the value of the information in the graph by much. It can be important to know the source of a graph's data if the graph is being used to persuade the reader to believe something controversial, or is being used to advance some sort of political or social agenda. In the figure here, it's hard to imagine why the data would not be reliable or trustworthy. However, it would be useful to know whether the researcher had the technical training and skills to carry out the data collection appropriately.

4. The two graphs are measures of the amounts of pigment, for three different pigments, in spring versus fall. This allows us to evaluate differences in the photosynthetic pigments present in leaves at two different times of year, when the leaves appear green and when they have the red, orange, and yellow colors characteristic of fall foliage. We can see that the amount of yellow-reflecting carotenoids is the same in spring as in fall, but the green-reflecting chlorophylls *a* and *b* are present in much smaller amounts in fall than in spring.

5. The colors of leaves in the fall are a consequence of reduced amounts of chlorophylls *a* and *b* in the leaves, which reduces the green reflectance, but the amounts of yellow-reflecting pigments are unchanged.

6. First, in the fall, leaves have many colors, including yellow. It would be helpful to see measures of the amounts of other photosynthetic pigments in leaves in the fall and spring. Which ones are responsible for the other colors? Second, as with any graph, a standard deviation or standard error bar for each bar in the graph would be useful. This would indicate how much leaves vary in the amounts of each pigment they contain. Is it a lot? Or are the amounts relatively constant from leaf to leaf? From this figure, we don't know. Third, it might also be interesting to see the same pair of plots for several different species, including some trees whose leaves change color in the fall and other trees whose leaves do not change color.

7. These graphs show experimental results, namely, that the relative amounts of photosynthetic pigments differ at the two time periods measured. There are no control and experimental variables, however. Rather, there are just measures of the different pigments at different times.

Chapter 5

1. e; 2. e; 3. b; 4. c; 5. d; 6. d; 7. e; 8. b; 9. c; 10. b; 11. a; 12. e; 13. c; 14. a; 15. d

Short-Answer Questions

1. Thymine makes up 30% of the bases. Cytosine and thymine have only one complementary base, so the base and its complement occur in equal numbers. Because cytosine makes up 20%, its complementary base, guanine, is also 20%. The total of cytosine and guanine is 40%, so the remaining bases total 60%. Because thymine and adenine must occur in equal numbers, half of this total (30%) must be thymine and the other half (30%) adenine.

2. The mRNA is UAG CUG CCU AGG. mRNA allows instructions from DNA to be delivered to ribosomes in the cytoplasm, where it directs the assembly of the protein it encodes.

3. The sequence of codons of the mRNA is translated into a sequence of amino acids that forms a polypeptide chain. As each codon of the mRNA is read by a ribosome, a transfer RNA with an anticodon complementary to the mRNA codon adds a specific amino acid to the growing polypeptide chain.

4. This is an example of a point mutation. The adenine in the fourth codon from the left has been replaced with thymine. This change results in

coding for a different amino acid, changing the type of protein produced by the gene—because the amino acid sequence has changed.

5. First, recombinant DNA technology is used to make certain medicines, such as insulin, growth hormone, and erythropoietin, with much less expense; this enables more people to purchase and benefit from these medicines. Second, there have been many efforts to cure some diseases caused by genetic abnormalities by using gene therapy; although this technology has not met with success, the future still holds potential. Third, genetic testing can be conducted on parents to identify whether they are at risk of producing offspring with certain genetic diseases. Prenatal genetic screening can be conducted to determine whether a baby will be born with a genetic disease. Adults can also be tested to determine whether they carry genes that put them at risk of developing a disease. With genetic screening, preventive measures and treatments can be undertaken.

Graphic Content Questions

1. In the United States, 86% of the corn is genetically modified. The legend indicates that the blue portion of each pie chart represents the proportion of the crop that is genetically modified.

2. It is not possible to determine whether more genetically modified corn or more genetically modified cotton is produced in the United States. Although it might appear that more genetically modified cotton is produced (93% vs. 86%), that only tells you the *proportion* of each crop that is genetically modified. The figure doesn't give any information about the *total amount* produced for any of these crops. Recent data actually show that, in the United States, while corn is cultivated on 80 million acres, only about 12 million acres are used for cotton cultivation. So the absolute amount of genetically modified corn grown in the United States is much greater than the amount of genetically modified cotton.

3. The common theme across the three pie charts is that the vast majority of these crops, whether corn, cotton, or soybeans, are genetically modified. This may be a surprise to many people and may cause them to become interested in learning more about genetically modified crops, including whether they are nutritionally different or carry any health or environmental risks.

4. If absolute amounts were given, the figure would convey more information about the total size of the corn crop versus the cotton crop versus the soybean crop in the United States. While this might be interesting, it would deflect attention from the fact that the proportion of crops that are genetically modified is very high for all of these crops, independent of the total amount of each crop grown.

5. The information in the question suggests that the United States is relying much more heavily on genetically modified crops than is the rest of the world. This might prompt you to investigate not just why such large proportions of crops are genetically modified but why there is such a large disparity between practices in the United States and those in the rest of the world. Is it because genetically modified crops are more commonly developed in the United States? Or are there, perhaps, fewer regulations or limitations on the cultivation of genetically modified crops in the United States? Or do consumers' attitudes to genetically modified crops differ around the world?

6. There are several ways to present the data in the question. You could produce a series of pie charts, one for each year. Or you could produce a bar graph, with the *x*-axis indicating the year and the *y*-axis indicating the proportion of the corn crop that is genetically modified in each year,

showing one bar for each year. Or you could produce a line graph with the same axes as the bar graph, but with a point for each year's proportion and a line connecting them. In each of these representations, the dramatic rate of increase would be the most obvious trend.

Chapter 6

1. c; 2. b; 3. d; 4. d; 5. c; 6. a; 7. b; 8. e; 9. d; 10. b; 11. b; 12. c; 13. d; 14. e; 15. c; 16. a; 17. e; 18. d

Short-Answer Questions

1. Crossing over occurs as sister chromatids of homologous chromosomes come together and swap equivalent segments containing the same genes (but possibly different alleles) during the first prophase of meiosis. This results in an uneven distribution of genetic material from maternal and paternal chromosomes. Gametes could potentially receive more genes from one (either) biological parent than the other. Also, the random division of the homologues (with respect to whether they are maternal or paternal) at anaphase I can lead to gametes having greater than or less than exactly 50% maternal and 50% paternal genetic material. For every gamete having a higher percentage of its genetic material from the maternal side, there is a gamete having an equally higher percentage of paternal genetic material.

2. There cannot be any essential genetic information on the Y chromosome—because all females are able to live without a Y chromosome—but there is on the X chromosome. Receiving only the Y chromosome means that essential genetic information from the X chromosome is absent.

3. An organism is more likely to reproduce asexually in the absence of adverse environmental pressures. Should some environmental pressure develop, the organism may start reproducing sexually, producing genetically diverse offspring that are better able to survive environmental pressures. An experiment could be conducted with an organism that has the capacity to switch between sexual and asexual reproduction. This organism could be placed in an environment with ideal conditions and in another with adverse conditions. If the hypothesis is correct, the organism will reproduce asexually under ideal conditions and sexually under adverse conditions.

Graphic Content Questions

1. The probability that a 35-year-old woman giving birth will have a baby with Down syndrome is approximately 1 in 333 (i.e., 3/1,000).

2. A woman of age 45 giving birth is unlikely to have a baby with Down syndrome. In fact, according to the data in the graph, a woman of age 45 giving birth has a 98.1% probability of having a baby that does not have Down syndrome. This is because the incidence, according to the figure, is approximately 1.9% (19 in 1,000).

3. You cannot conclude from the figure that most babies with Down syndrome are born to mothers over 35. The figure shows only, for mothers of a given age, the proportion of babies born with Down syndrome. But because relatively few of the babies born in any year are born to mothers older than 35, the total number of babies with Down syndrome in this group of mothers is small. In fact, since so many more babies are born to women under 35, it turns out that 80% of babies with Down syndrome are born to mothers under 35.

4. Because the number of births to women older than 45 is much smaller than the number of births to younger women, it becomes increasingly difficult to make accurate estimates. For this reason, researchers restrict the data they present to situations for which they have sufficiently high confidence in the data accuracy.

5. Based on doctors' recommendations, women aged 35 and higher are likely to have amniocentesis, which will reveal whether a fetus has trisomy-21. Conversely, amniocentesis is not recommended for women under 35. As a consequence, women aged 35 and higher are more likely to learn that a baby will be born with Down syndrome and choose to terminate the pregnancy. This prenatal testing therefore reduces the incidence of babies born with Down syndrome among women 35 and over, but not among women under 35. Among women under 35, the rate of babies born with Down syndrome is much more likely to be almost the same as the incidence of fetuses having trisomy-21.

Chapter 7

1. a; 2. b; 3. e; 4. e; 5. a; 6. c; 7. e; 8. a; 9. c; 10. e; 11. e; 12. d; 13. d; 14. b; 15. d; 16. a

Short-Answer Questions

1. a) SMA must be a recessive genetic disorder, because the phenotype of both parents is normal—that is, they are not affected by SMA. For two unaffected parents to have children with the disease, both parents' genotypes must be heterozygous. This is an example of a disease-causing allele that doesn't always reveal itself in a population. b) Individuals who are heterozygous for a recessive genetic disorder (i.e., are carriers) will not necessarily have children with the disease. However, this example demonstrates heterozygous parents with children who inherit the disease-causing allele from both parents, resulting in SMA. The probability of having another biological child with SMA is the same as it was for each of the first two children. The probability of inheriting the recessive allele from the mother is 0.5, and the probability of inheriting the recessive allele from the father is 0.5. Therefore the overall probability is 0.25, 25%, or 1 in 4.

2. The phenotype, or color of the blooms, is affected by differences in the environment. Hydrangea flower color varies with the type of soil, because the pH of the soil affects the pigmentation of the blooms.

3. a) Genetic disorders that involve genes on the X chromosome affect men differently from women. If a female inherits an allele that produces a non-functional protein on one of her X chromosomes, she may not be affected *if* the second X chromosome has the normal allele. However, because males have only one X chromosome, they have only one chance to receive the normal allele.

b)

	X^H	X^H
X^h	X^hX^H	X^hX^H
Y	X^HY	X^HY

There is a 0% chance that a son will have hemophilia. A son inherits his X chromosome from his mother. Because the mother is carrying two functional alleles, either X would provide a functional allele.

Graphic Content Questions

1. A novelty-seeking score was measured for individuals with different genotypes. Measurement was based on the individuals' responses on a questionnaire. While this might be a fast and easy way to estimate one person's propensity for novelty-seeking relative to another person's propensity, it would have been better to observe individuals' actual behavior. If you are interested in behavior, it is always better to

see how someone behaves than to ask them how they think they would behave.

2. *CC* refers to a genotype for the promoter polymorphism –521 *C/T*, which alters the transcription rate of the dopamine receptor gene. This gene influences the activity of the brain's pleasure centers. There are two different alleles, *C* and *T*, and a person can have one of each or two copies of *C* or two copies of *T*. Having one or two copies of the *T* allele (that is, *CT* or *TT*) seems to lead to reduced transcription of the dopamine receptor gene, while having the *CC* genotype is associated with greater gene activity and, hence, greater novelty-seeking behavior.

3. The data reported for the initial study provide information on how much individuals with genotypes in the two groups (first group: *CC*, second group: *CT* or *TT*) varied in their score on the novelty-seeking questionnaire (since everyone would not be expected to score exactly the same). This information is useful because it helps us see that not only was the average novelty-seeking score higher among those with the *CC* genotype, but those with the lowest novelty-seeking scores in the *CC* genotype group had higher scores than those with the highest novelty-seeking scores in the *CT/TT* group. The smaller the variation observed in each group, the more likely it is that differences between the two groups reflect true differences in the measure between the groups.

4. A meta-study combines the results of several or many studies that address a related research hypothesis. This is commonly done because the results from a group of studies can allow more accurate data analysis, whereas a single study doesn't necessarily have enough power to reveal a true effect.

5. The 11 different studies did not include exactly the same subjects. In fact, they may have used groups of subjects that differed in significant ways, such as age, sex, profession, or ancestry. They may also have measured different numbers of subjects, or they may have used slightly different versions of novelty-seeking questionnaires.

6. The results of any one study showing that individuals with the *CC* genotype score higher on a novelty-seeking questionnaire than individuals with the *CT* or *TT* genotype might be interesting, but unconvincing. Questions might remain about the population from which the subjects were chosen, the number of subjects used, the laboratory methods used in determining genotypes, the conditions under which the questionnaire was administered, and a whole range of unconscious, inadvertent, or otherwise hidden biases that the researchers may have had. But it is powerful when the results of all 11 studies that tested this hypothesis are reported and most of the studies seem to show similar results. This means that you can be more certain about the conclusions drawn in any one of the studies. It's important that *all* of the studies conducted on this hypothesis were collected and analyzed, rather than the meta-study simply selecting studies that supported or rejected the hypothesis. We can have more confidence in concluding that an individual's genotype for this gene influences novelty-seeking behavior. (In fact, though, without information about how well a person's score on this questionnaire predicts actual behavior, it might be safer to simply conclude that an individual's genotype influences his or her score on a novelty-seeking questionnaire. This conclusion gives rise to numerous new hypotheses that could be tested.)

Chapter 8

1. e; 2. a; 3. b; 4. c; 5. d; 6. d; 7. e; 8. a; 9. e; 10. e; 11. b; 12. a; 13. c; 14. b; 15. d; 16. b; 17. b; 18. e; 19. d; 20. d; 21. c

Short-Answer Questions

1. Evolution is a change in allele frequencies in a population. Natural selection is one of four evolutionary agents, characterized by variation, heritability, and differential reproductive success for a trait.

2. Genetic drift is a random change in allele frequencies. In small populations, random deviations from the expected genotype frequencies among offspring are less likely to be counterbalanced by deviations in the opposite direction from the expected genotype frequencies.

3. First, environments can change quickly. Natural selection may be too slow to adapt the species to a constantly changing environment. Second, variation is needed as the raw material of selection. If there is no mutation to give rise to an allele that would help make an individual more fit, the species will never be perfectly adapted. (Why, for instance, are there no mammals with wheeled appendages?) Third, evolution produces "more fit" individuals in each generation. If the optimum solution required organisms to get worse before they could evolve to "perfection," selection would never lead to such a solution.

4. In the 1940s, when penicillin was first used to treat bacterial infections, it was uniformly effective in killing *Staphylococcus aureus*. Today, more than 90% of isolated *S. aureus* strains are resistant to penicillin. Because penicillin has become such a pervasive toxin in the environment of *Staphylococcus*, natural selection has led to an increase in the frequency of alleles that make the bacteria resistant. Today, nearly a third of "staph" infections are resistant to antibiotics. The meaning of such unintentional natural selection "experiments" is clear and consistent: evolution is occurring all around us.

Graphic Content Questions

1. The curvy line represents the average beak size of Galápagos finches, measured from 1976 to 1985.

2. The "average" beak size is calculated from measures of many birds. If more birds with large beaks die in a particular year, the average will be lower. If birds with larger beaks are healthier and reproduce at a higher rate than birds with small beaks during that year, the average will increase.

3. Each time there was a drought, the average beak size increased a bit. During the wet year, the average beak size decreased. It seems as though the environment is influencing which birds are most successful.

4. Based on this figure, it appears that when the climate gets drier, birds with larger beaks survive and reproduce better than birds with smaller beaks. Similarly, when the climate is wetter, birds with smaller beaks are more plentiful. So having information about annual rainfall would be useful in making predictions about average beak size in these finches

5. There is no "optimum" beak size. Rather, the beak size that leads to the greatest survival and reproduction varies from year to year and is dependent on the amount of rainfall.

6. Traits in a population can vary in fitness, depending on the environment. There is no such thing as a better trait or a worse trait. A trait is better or worse in a particular environment.

Chapter 9

1. b; 2. d; 3. e; 4. b; 5. d; 6. d; 7. c; 8. a; 9. d; 10. e; 11. c; 12. a; 13. a; 14. b; 15. e; 16. b

Short-Answer Question

1. Males provide more parental care, consistent with the two predictions about sex roles and parental investment. First, the sex that invests more

will be more discriminating. Second, members of the sex that invests less will compete among themselves for access to the higher-investing sex.

Graphic Content Questions

1. A female with one mate produces 60 offspring. This is the same number as for a male mating with one female. The two numbers are the same because they are measuring the same thing: one male mating with one female. Whatever the number of offspring produced, it is recorded in the left-most bar in each graph.

2. A female with two mates produces 50 offspring. It is not clear why females with two mates would produce fewer offspring than females with one mate. At least two explanations are possible. First, because these numbers are measured for different females—that is, a female's reproductive output can be measured when she has one mate or two mates, but not both—this may just be a consequence of natural variation among females. Maybe those in the two-mate group just happened to have fewer offspring, unrelated to the number of mates they had. Second, perhaps the presence of two males created stress, which somehow reduced either the female's or the males' fertility.

   For additional data, it would be useful to have error bars to determine why the number of offspring is lower for females with two mates. These would give us a sense of how much variation there is in reproductive output among females given access to two males (and among females given access to just one male). If there is much variation within those two groups, then the lower number seen here may just be an artifact of the individual females measured. In this case, if greater numbers of birds were used in the study, the average reproductive output would be the same for females given access to one mate or two mates.

3. Females with four mates would most likely still have about 60 offspring, while males with four mates would have about 150 offspring. These numbers assume the same trends shown in the graphs.

4. If a single male produces more sperm than the number of eggs a female produces, a female's having access to more sperm will not increase her number of offspring.

5. It appears that females are not limited by access to mates. Rather, they seem to be limited by their own production of eggs. Males' reproductive output, however, does seem to be constrained by the number of mates they have. If a male has more mates, he has greater reproductive output.

6. To make comparisons between the data in the two graphs, it is essential that they are measuring the same thing, using the same scales. Otherwise, it would be like comparing apples and oranges.

Chapter 10

1. a; 2. d; 3. e; 4. e; 5. a; 6. d; 7. d; 8. a; 9. e; 10. a; 11. d; 12. d; 13. e; 14. b; 15. c; 16. a; 17. c

Short-Answer Questions

1. The biological species concept focuses on reproductive populations, or groups of individuals that can mate with each other and are unable to breed with other reproductively isolated groups. The morphological species concept focuses on physical characteristics of the organisms to distinguish one species from another. Many living organisms don't fit neatly into a species as defined by the biological species concept. An example is many of the living organisms that divide asexually, such as bacteria. For these organisms, because they do not require a partner to mate, reproductive compatibility is not a useful diagnostic tool for discriminating among species.

2. Biologists would rely on physical features or characteristics to create evolutionary trees and establish relationships between groups of organisms. Today, with the advent of technology, DNA sequencing (examining the base-pair sequence of DNA) is used to construct evolutionary trees. In either case, the trees define which groups of organisms are most closely related, but not which groups are more advanced than others.

3. These adaptations could be considered an "evolutionary innovation" in which a specific trait or group of traits allows an organism to fill a new niche or an unoccupied niche. This is one trigger of adaptive radiation—the huge, rapid expansion of a species, often diversifying into many more species. The specific traits of tall, flat teeth and a square jaw allowed the horse to efficiently crop grasses and vegetation from the ground. With areas of grasslands plentiful, these mammals were able to expand and flourish in this niche.

Graphic Content Questions

1. The blue line hovers around a rate of 10% of families becoming extinct at any time during the period recorded on the graph.

2. There are several reasons why the graph may record data on the extinction of families rather than of species. First, because the events documented in the figure occurred millions or even hundreds of millions of years ago, it is difficult to estimate the total number of species present on earth at that time. (It is nearly impossible to do this even today, when we can, at least in theory, count all of the species.) Second, it is difficult to identify whether multiple fossils belong to the same or different species. But because all of the organisms within a family share basic similarities, it is possible to identify fossils as members of the same family with much more certainty. Third, due to the limited number of fossils found, researchers are much more likely to find at least one representative from each family that has existed across time than they are to find at least one representative of each species. This enables a more accurate identification of when all species within a family became extinct (because after that point, no fossils are found of any members of the family). Still, even if no fossils of a family are found after a certain point in time, we can't be sure whether extinction occurred *or* whether the environmental situation just changed so that members of that family were less likely to be fossilized.

3. The data points for background extinction rates never get much higher than 11% or 12% of all families becoming extinct at that point. In each of the mass extinctions shown on the graph, the rate is significantly higher—usually 20% or more, except for the most recent event, which is about 15%, but still significantly higher than the typical background rate.

4. Several factors influence whether a species or a family becomes extinct. These include competition with other species, the range over which the species can grow, and other aspects of the species' environment. For this reason, conditions leading to extinction won't necessarily occur at exactly the same rate. There will be variation over time, influenced by climate, population sizes of competitors and predators, and other factors, all leading to ups and down.

5. As described in Section 8-18, fossils are left only by certain types of organisms, and under a very limited range of environmental conditions. For this reason, the magnitude of mass extinctions noted on this graph may overestimate or underestimate the rate of extinctions of the many groups of organisms that did not leave fossils. This figure is an accurate measure of overall extinction rates only if our (unstated) assumption is true: that the extinction rates of the groups of organisms not leaving

fossils were proportional to the extinction rates of the groups that did leave fossils.

6. If the current rate begins to rise above typical background rates of extinction, we might be in the midst of another mass extinction. This is important in that it may be an indicator that human activities are causing a higher than usual rate of extinctions. If this is the case, it may signal a need to reduce the human impact on extinction rates so as to reduce the likelihood of large (and maybe catastrophic, for us) changes in the species composition of earth.

Chapter 11

1. d; 2. c; 3. e; 4. e; 5. d; 6. c; 7. b; 8. b; 9. a; 10. b; 11. d; 12. c; 13. a; 14. c; 15. b; 16. c; 17. e; 18. d

Short-Answer Questions

1. In all animals, the ability to obtain food, whatever method that may be, has evolved through natural selection. For the sloth, it would make no sense for it to have developed the ability to spring at great speeds, because its food source (vegetation) is stationary. The cheetah, by contrast, must use high speeds to catch its prey, which also can run fast. If the cheetah were to occupy the same niche as the sloth, its ability to run would not improve its ability to obtain vegetation, so it might lose this running ability over many generations.

2. Much of the energy derived from food is utilized for heat production, so endotherms require more food to maintain a constant internal temperature. Ectotherms depend on an external heat source to maintain their body temperature, so they do not need energy derived from food to generate heat.

3. The snake, like other ectotherms, depends on an outside source of heat, so placing an insulating sweater on the snake will prevent heat from reaching its body, keeping it from warming up. For the same reason, ectotherms do not have insulating feathers or fur.

4. The slug has a radula for scraping food from surfaces, has a broad foot on which it glides, and produces a protective slime. Slugs lack the body segmentation found in segmented worms.

Graphic Content Questions

1. We are of the species *Homo sapiens,* which has *Homo heidelbergensis* as an ancestor, which may have *Homo ergaster* as an ancestor, which may have *Homo habilis* as an ancestor, which may have *Australopithecus* (gracile) as an ancestor, which may have *Ardipithecus* as an ancestor. We seem less likely to be direct descendants of *Homo neanderthalensis* and *Australopithecus* (robust), which are dead-end branches that split off from our common ancestors and became extinct.

2. *Homo* appeared about 2.5 million years ago. It seems to have had a significantly larger skull (and so brain size) than its *Australopithecus* ancestors.

3. The solid lines represent transitions from one species to another that are better supported by fossils showing gradual changes. The dashed lines represent potential relationships that are not as well supported by transitional fossils. But the discovery of additional fossils may enable better clarification of the relationships.

4. About 1.6 million years ago, there were probably four different human species living at the same time: *Australopithecus* (robust), *Homo erectus, Homo ergaster,* and *Homo habilis.*

5. It's not long ago that our species became the only living representative of the genus *Homo.* From this figure, it appears to be approximately 10,000 years ago.

Chapter 12

1. a; 2. b; 3. b; 4. c; 5. a; 6. b; 7. e; 8. c; 9. c; 10. c; 11. d; 12. b; 13. d; 14. b; 15. d

Short-Answer Questions

1. Non-vascular plants lack tissue that can conduct water and dissolved nutrients, tissue that *is* found in vascular plants. Because diffusion can transport water only over very short distances, non-vascular plants are much smaller than vascular plants. Non-vascular plants must live in an environment that is wet for at least some parts of the year, and they become dormant when it is dry.

2. Mycorrhizal fungi are associated with the roots of plants, benefiting them by transporting phosphorus and nitrogen from the soil to the cells of the plant roots. In exchange, the fungus takes some sugar from the plant. This relationship enhances the overall health of the plant.

3. Plants expend considerable energy producing a fruit, which contains the seeds. Once a fruit is eaten, it is digested by the animal and the seeds are excreted unharmed, and thus relocated to an area distant from the parent plant. The plant pays the animal with a meal, and in return, the animal transports the seeds.

4. The most dramatic initial effect of the extinction of all animals would be the loss of pollinators and seed dispersers for most of the angiosperms on earth. This would lead to significant reduction in the flowering plants' rates of reproduction and population growth, if not outright extinction of animal-pollinated plants and plants with animal-dispersed seeds. Many such plants can grow vegetatively and many can self-fertilize, helping them to avoid immediate extinction, but these methods of growth and reproduction would lead to a rapid reduction in genetic diversity within populations, putting the plants at risk in changing environments. The reduction of herbivory would certainly help plants at first, reducing their mortality rates. But this benefit would be experienced by all plants, and so competition for limited resources (space, sun, soil, etc.) would probably increase.

Graphic Content Questions

1. At the most general level, you can conclude that having mycorrhizal fungi benefits a plant. To be more precise, you can conclude that plants with symbiotic mycorrhizal fungi have offspring that are more likely to survive than the offspring of plants without the fungi. This difference in offspring survival does not become apparent until sometime between 20 and 47 days after planting.

2. It appears that for the 10-day and 20-day bars, there is no variance at all. In other words, 100% of the offspring were alive in both groups.

3. Based on the number of individuals observed in each group, the difference in survival recorded is unlikely to have occurred if there were, in fact, no true difference in survival. In other words, there is less than a 5% chance that the researchers would have found such a difference between the two groups due to random chance.

4. For the parents with mycorrhizal fungi, about 60% of their offspring were surviving after 47 days. For parents without mycorrhizal fungi, only about 30% of their offspring were surviving after 47 days.

5. Because the difference in offspring survival appeared between 20 and 47 days after planting, it would be helpful to have data for some point within that interval, probably at the mid-point of 33 or 34 days after planting. This is the likely time when some significant differences in offspring quality appeared.

Chapter 13

1. a; 2. b; 3. c; 4. e; 5 d; 6. a; 7. a; 8. d; 9. b; 10. a; 11. c; 12. b; 13. e; 14. b; 15. e; 16. e; 17. e; 18. b

Short-Answer Question

	Prokaryotes		Eukaryotes	Viruses
	Bacteria	Archaea	Protists	
Unicellular, colonial, or multicellular?	Unicellular	Unicellular	Unicellular or colonial	Not cells
Plasma membrane?	Present	Present	Present	Absent
Peptidoglycan in cell wall?	Present	Absent	Absent	Absent
Flagella? What type?	Yes; spins like a propeller	Yes; spins like a propeller, but has a chemical composition different from that of bacteria	Yes; waves from side to side and has a chemical composition different from that of bacteria or archaea	No flagellum
Presence of nucleus?	Absent	Absent	Present	No nucleus
Intracellular organelles?	Absent	Absent	Present	No organelles
Type of genetic material (DNA, RNA, or both possible)?	DNA	DNA	DNA	DNA or RNA
Chromosome structure (linear or circular)?	Usually circular	Usually circular	Linear	Linear or circular

Graphic Content Questions

1. Although it may be surprising, the vast majority of cells in a human body are microbial cells—probably bacterial—rather than human cells. In fact, according to this figure, 90 percent of the 100 trillion cells in a human, or 90 trillion cells, are microbial.

2. A human has about 10 trillion human cells.

3. A human has about 90 trillion microbial cells.

4. One feature of bacteria that contributes to their ability to outnumber human cells even as a human still appears human is that bacterial cells are significantly smaller than eukaryotic cells.

5. It is not clear how the cell counts were obtained. The figure would be much more helpful if it included information on how the data were collected. For example, if the cell counts for multiple humans were determined, how much variation was there among individuals, both in the total number of cells *and* in the proportion of each type?

6. There are several other ways to convey these data. Here are two examples. First, because the data include two components (number of bacterial cells and number of human cells) that make up one entity (a human), you could present them as a pie chart, with 90% of the pie in one color, representing bacteria, and 10% of the pie in another color, representing human cells. A strength of this presentation is that it conveys nicely that most of the "pie" is bacterial rather than human. A weakness is that it conveys information on how each component represents some proportion of the whole, but no information on the absolute numbers of each cell type. Second, because there is a comparison of two entities, you could present side-by-side bar graphs, with a *y*-axis labeled "Number of cells (trillions)." The bar for "human cells" would extend to 10 trillion, and the bar for "bacterial cells" would extend to 90 trillion. One strength of this approach is that it makes it easier to compare the two numbers. A weakness is that it de-emphasizes that the two components together make up the whole of how many cells there are in a human body.

Chapter 14

1. a; 2. e; 3. a; 4. b; 5. e; 6. d; 7. b; 8. d; 9. c; 10. c; 11. e; 12. d; 13. a; 14. b; 15. c

Short-Answer Questions

1. Density-dependent factors are limitations on a population's growth resulting from competition among individuals for a finite amount of resources, such as food and space for living and breeding, and an increased risk of disease and predation. Density-independent factors are forces such as hurricanes and droughts that kill off many individuals in a population, regardless of the size of the population.

2. An organism with a type I survivorship curve is relatively large, has only a few offspring, invests a lot in each offspring, and lives a relatively long life. If the organism had a type III survivorship curve, it would have a high probability of dying early in life and would produce many offspring and provide very little parental care.

3. Species that lack natural enemies and live in an environment with low risk of mortality from other sources breed at a later age; late-onset genetic disorders are selected out and individuals are healthier in old age. Species that breed at an early age pass on adverse genetic traits that are expressed after their normal age of breeding; they do not live long after the normal age of breeding. If breeding is delayed, as in the fruit flies in the experiments described in the chapter, age-related disorders that interfere with breeding are selected out and the life span will be extended.

Graphic Content Questions

1. The graph shows how a population's size changes over time. Based on the graph's title, "Managing Natural Resources," it also is intended to reveal something about how knowledge of population growth can help resource managers be more effective. Specifically, it shows the size at which a population can most effectively be utilized for natural resources, which may involve cutting down some trees for wood or catching some lobsters for food, for example.

2. As a population gets closer to the carrying capacity of its environment, its growth slows and plateaus at that point.

3. A population can stay at the same size if the number of individuals arriving (through birth or immigration) is exactly the same as the number of individuals leaving (through death or emigration). This situation can persist indefinitely, even as organisms continue dying.

4. No data points appear on the graph. This suggests that perhaps the graph just presents a theoretical relationship. In this case, it appears to be the

relationship between population size and time, when a population is growing logistically, calculated as: $rN[(K − N)/K]$.

5. It would be helpful if some real data were presented for actual populations, showing how they grow over time. The data points could be overlaid on the graph, perhaps with points for different populations shown in different colors. This would give insight into how well the logistic growth equation predicts the actual growth of natural populations.

6. The graph described in the question will show a sort of inverted U, with the low points of growth rate at population sizes 0 and K, and with the maximum in the middle of the x-axis at $K/2$. The population grows fastest when it is at half its carrying capacity.

7. Implicit assumptions are, first, that carrying capacity does not change over time, and second, that a population's growth is restrained with perfect efficiency as it approaches its carrying capacity. In other words, growth slows exactly as required to avoid exceeding the carrying capacity—as opposed to the population growing so quickly that it overshoots its carrying capacity, after which it grows more slowly, possibly undershooting K, and ultimately oscillating around it.

Chapter 15

1. d; 2. e; 3. a; 4. a; 5. e; 6. d; 7. e; 8. a; 9. d; 10. a; 11. a; 12. a; 13. d; 14. e; 15. b; 16. b

Short-Answer Questions

1. Heated air rises and cools at the equator (0° latitude); as it cools, it cannot hold as much water and loses it as precipitation. Air moves north and south from the equator and begins to fall at about 30° latitude north and south, warming and absorbing moisture. This creates very dry conditions at these latitudes, and deserts are found there. Air continues to move toward the Poles and begins to rise again at 60° latitude, cooling and losing its moisture through precipitation, making these locations very wet. Air again falls near the Poles, making these areas very dry. Temperature and amount of rainfall are the primary determinants of the kind of biome found in any terrestrial location.

2. Energy flows through each trophic level. Photosynthetic organisms, the primary producers, trap energy from the sun in the chemical bonds of food. Primary consumers, the herbivores, eat photosynthetic organisms, and these animals are consumed by secondary consumers, the carnivores. Carnivores can be consumed by tertiary consumers, the top carnivores. A natural ecosystem can support only a few top carnivores, because only about 10% of the energy is available to each subsequent trophic level.

3. An organism's niche includes the space it requires to live in, the kinds and amount of food it eats, the time of day and time of year it reproduces, the amount of moisture and temperature it requires, as well as other criteria. Two organisms that occupy the same niche compete, with two different possible outcomes: one species may drive the other to extinction (competitive exclusion), or both species may change their behavior or undergo a morphological change so that they are restricted within their own niche, dividing the resources between them (resource partitioning).

Graphic Content Questions

1. The drawings are roughly proportional in size to the biomass of each level in the energy pyramid (i.e., primary producer, primary consumer, secondary consumer, tertiary consumer) for this particular type of ecosystem.

2. The size of the pie at each level in this diagram of energy flow reflects the biomass in an ecosystem of organisms fulfilling a particular role. The pies are different sizes because the biomass of primary producers is typically 10 times the biomass of primary consumers, and the biomass of each successive step up the pyramid is typically one-tenth of that at the previous level. This is due to inefficiencies of energy flow and conversion.

3. The pie slice, typically 10% of the size of the pie, represents the conversion efficiency of biomass at one level into biomass at the next level up the pyramid.

4. At the level of tertiary consumers, typically there is not sufficient biomass to support a viable population of quaternary consumers, given the 10% rule.

5. A secondary or tertiary consumer that also eats plants could have greater biomass than shown here because it could draw its energy not just from the animals it eats, but also from plants. The expected biomass of such a consumer would be 10% of the total biomass of the organisms it could consume. This would be much greater than for any of the consumers shown here.

6. There are likely to be many fewer predators than prey individuals (particularly herbivores), probably because the total biomass of predators is estimated to be one-tenth of the total biomass of prey organisms.

Chapter 16

1. e; 2. c; 3. d; 4. a; 5. e; 6. e; 7. d; 8. d; 9. b; 10. a; 11. e; 12. c; 13. b; 14. e

Short-Answer Questions

1. The greatest biodiversity, both aquatic and terrestrial, is in equatorial regions. Less biodiversity is found with increasing latitude. Habitat destruction and degradation are the greatest threats to biodiversity.

2. The biotic and abiotic nature of the habitat was altered, but species were not driven to extinction. If species had been made extinct, the ecosystem disturbances would not have been reversible.

3. Most of the deforestation of tropical rain forests is a result of clearing land to make way for agriculture; mining and pollution also contribute. The biodiversity of the planet is greatly affected by rain forest deforestation, because no other terrestrial ecosystem has the extent of biodiversity found in these forests.

Graphic Content Questions

1. There are two graphs. Each presents data on the number of species present at different latitudes, from the equator toward the Poles. The x-axis shows the number of species: in the top graph, the number of mammalian species, and in the bottom graph, the number of marine copepod species. The y-axis shows the latitude. In the top graph, data are presented for the numbers of species at 40° and 20° south, the equator, and 20°, 40°, and 60° north. In the bottom graph, data are presented for the equator and 20°, 40°, and 60° north.

2. The independent variable is latitude. The dependent variable is species number. Typically, the x-axis is used for the independent variable and the y-axis for the dependent variable. In these graphs, the variables are placed on the opposite axes. This is because the data are overlaid on a world map, which aids in identifying exactly where in the world 20°, 40°, and 60° latitudes fall. This makes it easy to see, for example, that 20° north latitude includes Central America, while 60° north latitude cuts across southern Alaska and northern Canada.

3. For mammalian species and for marine copepods, the largest numbers of species occur at 0°, which is the equator.

4. The value of having data both for mammalian species and for marine copepod species is that it enables us to see that the trend of decreasing species diversity toward the Poles holds true for a *terrestrial* species and for a *marine* species. This suggests that the phenomenon is robust and not just a quirk of one group of organisms. It would be helpful if data were presented for *all* species, but such data do not exist. (And, as we saw in Chapter 10, for prokaryotes and many other organisms it is difficult to even define what a species is.) Only a fraction of the world's species have been described. In this figure, it is more valuable to include animal groups for which most species have been described. Also important is that the figure uses groups of organisms for which any bias in the proportion of total species described at the equator versus the proportion described at higher latitudes is unlikely.

5. There are more mammalian species than marine copepod species at 20° north latitude. A person might answer this question incorrectly because the bar representing the number of copepod species is longer than the bar representing mammalian species—but this is because the scales for the axes differ. There are more than 300 mammalian species and about 70 copepod species at 20° north.

6. The bars here represent exact counts of species rather than some repeated measure of a variable (such as height), which would have a variance associated with it.

Chapter 17

1. b; 2. b; 3. d; 4. a; 5. d; 6. d; 7. a; 8. a; 9. b; 10. b; 11. a; 12. c; 13. e

Short-Answer Questions

1. Both groups are autotrophic, photosynthesizing plants that inhabit a wide range of environments, and play a vital role in human survival by providing foods, medicines, housing, and many other products. Monocots have one cotyledon, which distinguishes them from eudicots, which have two cotyledons. The venation, which is bundles of xylem and phloem, of leaves is another distinguishing characteristic, with monocots having parallel venation and eudicots having a branching pattern. Vascular bundles are arranged in a random pattern within stems of monocots, while they are arranged in a circular pattern in stems of eudicots. A vast majority of eudicots are capable of secondary growth, while only a small percentage of monocots are capable of secondary growth. Flowering parts of flowers occur in multiples of 3 for monocots and multiples of 4 and 5 for eudicots. Finally, monocots typically form fibrous root systems while eudicots form taproots from which rootlets grow.

2. Water is pulled from the roots up through xylem to the leaves. When a water molecule evaporates from a leaf it pulls on its neighboring water molecule, which is held together by hydrogen bonding. This in turn causes all the other water molecules within this xylem tube, which all have hydrogen bonds with their neighboring water molecules, forming an interconnected column of water, to be pulled up the xylem. The ability of water to form hydrogen bonds between water molecules allows it to have tension and cohesion and therefore the ability to be pulled up from leaves as water evaporates.

3. Since vascular bundles of monocots are randomly spread out within the stem, a shallow cut would sever only those vascular bundles near the surface. Vascular bundles of eudicots, on the other hand, usually form a ring structure, typically closer to the surface. Since their vascular tissue is close to the surface a shallow cut is likely to sever all

of their vascular tissue, preventing the movement of fluids and causing the plant to die.

Graphic Content Questions

1. As do all pie charts, this figure attempts to show the proportion of the whole that is contributed by each of several factors. In this case, the whole pie represents all of the material from which soil is composed. The parts it is divided into are minerals; organic materials; and water and air.

2. The source of the data presented is not given. This lack can be problematic because the reader must make several assumptions. In this figure, one important assumption is that all soil has approximately the same composition.

3. There is no information in the pie chart suggesting that different types of soil differ significantly in their composition. In other words, whether sandy soil at the beach or moist soil around a lake, from this figure the reader must conclude that both soils are consistently 50% minerals, 1% to 5% organic materials, and 45% to 50% water and air. To the extent that different soils *do* differ in their compositions, the data for several different soil types could be presented in a group of pie charts, all next to each other. That would allow for quick comparison and identification for the chief ways in which they differ. Alternatively, the data could be presented in a table. Each row could be a soil type, and for each there could be three columns: minerals, organic materials, and water and air.

4. Because there is no way to present an error bar reflecting variation in the size of a "piece" of the pie, it can be difficult to present information about the variability in a measure. For some phenomena, this can be important. In a pie chart, it is possible (but not commonly done) to show the borders between the pie pieces as fuzzy, with the size of the fuzzy region proportional to the variation in that measure. Alternatively, it is possible to draw the pie pieces precisely but in their labels to indicate the proportion that each represents, along with some measure of variation. In this pie chart, for example, the size of the water and air slice is given as 45% to 50%, although it is drawn as 45%. Similarly, the organic materials slice is drawn as 5%, but the text with the label for that slice indicates that it is 1% to 5%.

5. The benefit to presenting these data as a pie chart rather than a bar graph with three bars is that it is immediately clear that the greatest proportion of soil is made up from minerals, with water and air making up a proportion that is just slightly less, and organic materials not contributing much to soil. It is also immediately clear that the mineral component makes up half the soil. In general, if you wish to convey proportions of a whole made up of several component parts, a pie chart is effective. If the data were presented as a bar graph, the *y*-axis label would probably be "proportion of the whole," and each bar would represent a "soil component."

6. Making a pie chart three dimensional may make it more aesthetically pleasing, but it can also lead to deception. Because there are not actually three dimensions of data, the depth of the pie does not convey any actual data. A simple circle could convey exactly the same data as are shown.

Moreover, by rotating the pie so that a given slice (in this chart, "water and air" and, to a lesser extent, "organic materials") appears in the front, that slice is given more prominence because more of that slice's color or shading is visible than for the slice or slices in the back. This can cause a reader to misjudge the size of a slice, since the proportion of each color in the chart doesn't reflect the proportion of the whole made up from that component. In other words, it appears in this chart that the blue slice is larger than the purple slice because more blue is visible than purple. This method of data presentation can be used to mislead viewers into believing that one component is more or less significant than it actually is. The figure might then be used to persuade a reader to believe something that is not true.

Chapter 18

1. a; 2. b; 3. e; 4. a; 5. e; 6. a; 7. e; 8. e; 9. d; 10. a; 11. b; 12. c; 13. c; 14. b

Short-Answer Questions

1. A single strawberry plant, within a year or so, can completely fill a large area as the plant reproduces asexually and populates the patch with genetically identical, strawberry-producing clones.

2. Planting a potato produces a new plant asexually, so the new plant is genetically identical to the plant from which the potato came. If the parent plant is healthy and productive, this can help a farmer produce new crops that are equally productive. Seeds, on the other hand, are the product of sexual reproduction, so the new plant may not resemble the "mother plant" from which the seeds were collected; the properties of the new generation will depend also on the male parent, of unknown productivity. The farmer should choose potatoes for planting that come from the parent plant with the greatest productivity and vigor.

Graphic Content Questions

1. The fuzzy borders of each slice of the pie are meant to convey that the exact size of each slice is not certain. There are several other ways that uncertainty or variation can be conveyed in a graph. The pieces of the pie can have sharp borders, but within the slice (or its label) there can be a numerical indication of the size of the slice (i.e., 3–7%, 20-25%, etc.). Alternatively, instead of a pie chart, a bar graph can be used, with each slice shown as a separate bar having an error bar that reflects the uncertainty or variation around the estimate. A third way would be with a bar graph having just a single bar (representing 100% of flowering plant species), with the bar divided into regions representing each type of pollinator and the borders between regions being fuzzy, to represent uncertainty. And, perhaps, the labels associated with each region could indicate the size of that region, as a range (again, such as 3-7%, 20-25%, etc.).

2. The different colors in this pie chart represent a broad category of plant pollinators. All of the green slices, for example, represent insect pollinators, with each shade of green representing a different group of insects. Each of the blue slices represents a group of non-insect animal pollinators. This makes it possible to make quick comparisons about the relative proportions of non-insect animal pollinators versus insect pollinators, while also enabling a comparison of the relative proportions of pollinators from each group of insects (bees versus beetles, for example).

3. Actual percentages for each slice might make more precise comparisons of the size of each slice. In this figure, however, they may have been excluded because such precise data do not exist. The title above the pie chart suggests that this may be the reason.

4. From the pie chart, it appears that bees are the pollinators of the largest proportion of plant species. The slice representing bees indicates that about 45% of flowering plants are pollinated by bees. The second-largest slice is for birds, indicating that they pollinate the second-largest proportion of flowering plant species.

5. It would be useful to know which habitats (and how many of each) were surveyed to produce the data shown because it may be the case that in some habitats the majority of flowering plant species are pollinated by birds, while in other habitats the majority of flowering plant species are pollinated by bees or beetles. Or perhaps the proportions are the same across all habitats. More important, it is not possible to evaluate how much variation there is across different habitats (tropical versus arctic, for example) in the proportions of flowering plant species pollinated by each group of pollinators.

6. You can conclude many things from this pie chart. Most flowering plant species, for example, are pollinated by animals as opposed to wind or water. And you can conclude that, among animals, insects are the most common pollinators of flowering plants. Additional conclusions you could draw include that more flowering plant species are pollinated by birds than by bats; overall, more flowering plant species are pollinated by bees than by any other group of animals; among non-animal methods of pollination, wind pollination is much more common than water pollination.

7. An important detail to note in this figure is that the slices represent the proportion of flowering plant *species* rather than proportion of flowering plants. Because each species of flowering plant does not have the same number of individuals, an extremely common plant species with millions of individuals that is pollinated by flies counts as "one species, pollinated by flies" and a rare species with just a few hundred individuals that is pollinated by bats counts, similarly, as "one species, pollinated by bats." This means that if you were to survey just one habitat and count the number of plants pollinated by insects versus non-insect animals, it may be that you rarely see any of the non-insect animals pollinating plants if the plant species that they pollinate have much smaller population sizes than those pollinated by insects. If all flowering plant species had the same population sizes, on the other hand, approximately 75% of the plants being pollinated would be pollinated by insects and approximately 20% would be pollinated by non-insect animals.

8. Because the data here are described as "loose approximations," it is essential to understand that we cannot have complete confidence in their accuracy. Any interpretations should be made with caution and the understanding that they are subject to change. With the collection of additional observations and, perhaps, additional habitats, it may turn out that the size of any slice is actually a bit larger or smaller than shown here.

"Loose approximations" can still be valuable, however. From this pie chart, it is probably safe to assume that bees are in fact the pollinators of the largest proportion of flowering plants. Similarly, it's probably safe to conclude that more flowering plant species are pollinated by animals than by non-animal methods. And that among animals, insects represent a more important group of pollinators than do non-insect animals. Each of these conclusions can help us to understand the general patterns of pollination in nature. Moreover, the presentation of loose approximations can help to guide future studies aimed at gaining a deeper understanding of pollination.

Chapter 19

1. d; 2. a; 3. a; 4. c; 5. b; 6. b; 7. e; 8. a; 9. e; 10. d; 11. a

Short-Answer Questions

1. This phenomenon is called phototropism, growth in response to a light source. When light hits a plant from a particular direction, auxins produced in the plant move away from the light source and end up on the opposite, shaded side of the stem. There, the auxins stimulate a slightly

greater rate of growth than on the side with less auxin. As a consequence, the uneven growth causes the plant to bend toward the light.

2. The hormone ethylene is a gas that speeds the rate at which fruit ripens. Ethylene can help with shipping fruits internationally because if bananas, for example, are picked in Central America before they are ripe (when they are green), and just prior to their delivery, ethylene is injected into the cargo hold of the ship; this initiates the ripening of all the fruit simultaneously.

3. Spicy foods, such as mustard, frequently come from plants and get their flavor from secondary compounds that may make the plant toxic or unpalatable to an insect, representing an anti-herbivore adaptation. The fact that the chemicals are not, in some cases, toxic to humans may be a consequence of our larger body size relative to the intended herbivores'.

4. See Figure 19-9, page 744.

Graphic Content Questions

1. The dark purple region represents the months during which long-day plants typically flower: late March until late May. The height of the dark purple region represents the length of the night during that time period. Between late March and late May the length of night decreases, meaning that the days are getting longer.

2. The light purple region of the graph indicates the length of the night across all the months of the year. The yellow area represents the length of the day across all the months of the year. For this reason, when the amount of purple gets smaller, the amount of yellow at that point is greater; if the nights get shorter, the days must get longer.

3. Each graph includes a large amount of information. (1) The length of the day and of the night across the entire calendar year (and the pattern with which it changes). (2) The time of the year during which long-day plants flower (shown by the dark purple region in the top graph). (3) The time of the year during which short-day plants flower (shown by the dark purple region in the lower graph). (4) The rate and direction of change during the periods in which long-day plants flower and during which short-day plants flower.

4. It appears that two factors are responsible for long-day plants flowering: (1) that the length of the night is decreasing, and (2) that the length of the night falls within a particular range. Similarly, it appears that two factors are responsible for short-day plants flowering: (1) that the length of the night is increasing, and (2) that the length of the night falls within a particular range.

   These conclusions could be undermined if it turns out that some other environmental variable also has a similar pattern of change. If, for example, the amount of rain/precipitation varies in the same pattern throughout the year as the length of night, it may be the case that it is the amount of rainfall and the rate/direction of change in the amount of rainfall that triggers flowering in these types of plants. Or perhaps it is the temperature and the rate and direction of change in temperature during the year that is actually triggering flowering.

5. The reversed pattern of day/night length in the southern hemisphere relative to the northern hemisphere should alter the pattern of the light purple and the yellow bands in these graphs. In the southern hemisphere, the low point of the purple (corresponding to the shortest nights) would occur during late December, and the high point would occur during late June. This would lead to the timing of flowering in long-day and short-day plants to be six months later/earlier for each.

6. In order for landscape architects or gardeners to design gardens so that flowers are blooming at desired times during the year, they must understand the flowering patterns of various species and plant them accordingly. They may want to change their flower species throughout the year to showcase those that are best at different times, or they may want to plant both long-day and short-day species together in a garden.

Chapter 20

1. a; 2. d; 3. e; 4. b; 5. d; 6. a; 7. a; 8. c; 9. d; 10. a; 11. a

Short-Answer Questions

1. Cells of similar type are organized into tissues; tissues are organized into organs that perform specialized functions; and organs are organized into organ systems, arranged in an integrated manner to achieve common goals. There are four types of tissue. *Connective tissues* support and help form body structures. *Epithelial tissues* form internal and external body coverings, providing protection, synthesizing and releasing chemical products, and controlling movement of substances within the body. *Muscle tissues* have the ability to contract, generating body movements and moving materials within the body. *Nervous tissue* conducts electrical impulses, allowing communication within the organism.

2. *Connective tissue proper* includes (a) *loose connective tissue,* which has cells embedded in a semi-fluid matrix, with many collagen fibers that bind and hold organs in place, as well as storing fat and insulating, cushioning, and protecting the body; and (b) *dense connective tissue,* which has many more collagen fibers than loose connective tissue and thus has greater strength, forming tendons, which connect muscles to bones, and ligaments, which connect bones to each other. *Special connective tissue* includes (a) *bone,* composed of cells within a solid matrix interspersed with many collagen fibers, forming a rigid structure that supports and protects the body; (b) *cartilage,* composed of cells within a matrix (not as hard as bone) made up of collagen, elastin, and proteins connected to carbohydrate chains; and (c) *blood,* which has a fluid matrix called plasma, with suspended red blood cells, white blood cells, and platelets.

3. *Skeletal muscles* are made up of cells (fibers) that have alternating light and dark bands (striations) and contain many nuclei; the muscles are attached to bones, generating force for their movement, and are controlled voluntarily. *Smooth muscles,* which are not striated and have smaller cells, are found in the walls of hollow organs; contractions allow movement of liquids and solids within the organs, and are involuntary. *Cardiac muscle* is found in the walls of the heart and consists of striated, small, branched cells with a single nucleus; contractions generate pressure to move blood in the cardiovascular system, and are involuntary.

4. Homeostasis is the maintenance of a constant internal environment within a narrow range of conditions around a set point for variables such as temperature, pH, and concentrations of solute, water, CO_2, O_2, and glucose, among many others. Homeostasis allows for the normal functioning of an organism's cells. Body temperature is normally controlled by a negative feedback mechanism (thermoregulation). Hyperthermia occurs when the body temperature rises above its normal range. If high enough, this can interfere with the structure and activity of the enzymes involved in the body's metabolic activities, resulting in metabolic dysfunction, death of cells, organ failure, and, ultimately, death of the organism.

Graphic Content Questions

1. The line showing the cat body temperature (on the y-axis) as a function of ambient temperature (on the x-axis) shows a very slight increase. For this reason, you could say that cats' body temperature is influenced by the ambient temperature. However, the effect is very, very small. Over an increase of about 17°C, cats' body temperature rises by only one or two degrees. For this reason, it would be more accurate to say that cats' body temperature is almost completely unaffected by ambient temperature.

2. At 10°C, you would expect the lizard body temperature also to be 10°C. This is because at every other point on the graph showing the relationship between lizard body temperature and ambient temperature, the lizard body temperature is exactly the same as the ambient temperature.

3. Metabolic rate, as shown in the lower graph, is measured as the amount of oxygen consumption (in milliliters) per gram of body weight per hour. At any ambient temperature, cat metabolic rate is higher than lizard metabolic rate.

4. In order to make the comparison in metabolic rates meaningful, it is reported as a function of the animals' body weight. In other words, the difference in weight is factored out so that in both organisms, metabolism is measured as a *rate* rather than a total consumption of oxygen.

5. Between 27° and 36°C, lizard metabolic rate increases from about 0.15 ml O_2/g/hr to 0.35 ml O_2/g/hr. In other words, lizards' metabolic rate more than doubles. Across the same temperature range, the cat metabolic rate does not increase at all.

6. Lizard metabolic rate is considerably lower than cat metabolic rate at every temperature reported. Lizard metabolic rate, however, increases dramatically between 27° and 36°C while cat metabolic rate remains constant. In order to make this difference more apparent, for lizards you could use a y-axis with a different scale, perhaps multiplying the rate by 10. This would cause the steeper slope to be much more apparent, highlighting the greater influence of ambient temperature on metabolic rate in lizards as compared to cats. (Most textbooks do this.) A drawback to this method is that it may mislead readers into concluding that the metabolic rate itself is greater in lizards when it is not. It is only the rate of increase that is greater.

7. From this graph it appears that "thermoneutral zone" refers to a range of ambient temperatures across which an animal's metabolic rate remains unchanged. Cats have a clear thermoneutral zone, while it does not appear that lizards have such a thermoneutral zone. Any increase in ambient temperature is accompanied by an increase in metabolic rate.

8. From these graphs, we can conclude that at ambient temperatures between 27° and 36°C, it is more efficient to be a homeotherm. When the ambient temperature falls below 27°C or rises above 36°C, however, metabolic costs in homeotherms rise more dramatically than they do in ectotherms, suggesting that it is more efficient under such conditions to be an ectotherm.

Chapter 21

1. d; 2. c; 3. a; 4. b; 5. a; 6. e; 7. c; 8. e; 9. b; 10. e; 11. a; 12. b; 13. e; 14. c; 15. a; 16. d; 17. d; 18. a

Short-Answer Questions

1. Single-celled organisms, such as bacteria, are in direct contact with their environment, and direct diffusion of gases, nutrients, and wastes can take place at an adequate rate to maintain these organisms physiologically. In larger organisms made up of multiple cells, many of which are not in direct contact with the outside environment, direct diffusion is no longer feasible. With the development of a circulatory system, nutrients and gases can be brought in close proximity to cells, where diffusion can take place. An open circulatory system is characterized by having only one type of extracellular fluid; a closed circulatory system has two different extracellular fluids: interstitial fluid, bathing cells, and blood, which is contained only within the blood vessels.

2. In a single-circuit cardiovascular system, the heart has two chambers, one receiving blood that has traveled through the body, and the other moving blood to the gills and then through the blood vessels of the rest of the body. As blood moves through capillaries and other blood vessels, it slows down considerably, which slows down the delivery of substances to tissues and removal of waste products. A double-circuit system has one circuit that moves blood through the lungs and another that moves blood through the rest of the body. This system allows blood to be re-pressurized after it has traveled through the lungs, and this would be the better choice to supply tissues with high energy demands: blood can be delivered and removed at a faster rate.

3. *Red blood cells (erythrocytes):* Their primary function is to carry oxygen. They are suspended in plasma and contain iron-bearing hemoglobin, which binds, carries, and releases the oxygen. *White blood cells (leukocytes):* These are part of the body's immune system; their primary function is to seek out and destroy foreign organisms, including viruses and bacteria. *Platelets:* These cellular fragments circulate in blood and take part in plugging tears and holes in blood vessels and preventing leakage of blood. They do this by sticking together to form a clot.

4. Aquatic animals move water across their gills, which have capillaries that use a countercurrent mechanism. Blood moves through the capillaries in the opposite direction to the water flow, and this allows for a more efficient gas exchange: absorption of O_2 by and release of CO_2 from blood. In animals that breathe air, fresh air enters the lungs and moves into the alveoli. Gas exchange occurs there: O_2 in the air diffuses into capillaries in the walls of the alveoli, and CO_2 diffuses out of the blood and into the air, to be exhaled from the lungs.

Graphic Content Questions

1. The purpose of this graph is to illustrate the relationship between the partial pressure of oxygen and the degree to which hemoglobin is saturated with oxygen. As the partial pressure of oxygen increases, more oxygen binds to hemoglobin. And as the partial pressure of oxygen decreases, oxygen bound to hemoglobin is released.

2. Red shading indicates a high hemoglobin saturation of oxygen, whereas blue shading indicates low hemoglobin saturation with oxygen. The color at any point along the S-shaped curve reflects the degree to which hemoglobin is saturated with oxygen at that partial pressure of oxygen.

3. In this graph there are no individual data points included. However, the curve appears to represent the general relationship between the partial pressure of oxygen and the oxygen saturation in hemoglobin. This relationship could be determined only through the measurement

of the oxygen saturation in large amounts of hemoglobin across the range of oxygen partial pressure covered by the *x*-axis. We can assume, therefore, that the graph is based on data points that are not individually shown.

4. The curve's S-shape reveals that there is not a linear relationship between the partial pressure of oxygen and hemoglobin's saturation with oxygen. Rather, as the partial pressure decreases from 100 mm Hg, there is at first a very gradual decrease in the oxygen saturation in hemoglobin. But as the partial pressure is further reduced, to approximately 50 mm Hg, the rate at which oxygen saturation in hemoglobin drops is rapidly increasing. If the S-shaped curve were a straight line, organisms would release oxygen to tissue at a consistent rate as the partial pressure in the tissue decreased. With the S-shaped curve, hemoglobin stays relatively saturated with oxygen, even as the partial pressure is halved. But after that point, the rate at which oxygen is released from hemoglobin rapidly increases. Physical exertion, therefore, is accompanied by a rapid release of more oxygen than would occur if the curve were linear.

5. At a partial pressure of 60 mm Hg, the oxygen saturation of hemoglobin is approximately 90%. This would not make sense if we were considering just a single molecule of hemoglobin because the only possible states of saturation are 0%, 25%, 50%, 75%, or 100%, corresponding to 0, 1, 2, 3, or 4 oxygen molecules bound to the hemoglobin, which has just four binding sites. However, if numerous molecules of hemoglobin were analyzed for oxygen saturation, it is possible that some are at 75% saturation and others (most others) are at 100% saturation. When the *average* of these numbers is taken, it could be 90%.

6. When the curve is the steepest there is the greatest change in oxygen saturation for any change in the partial pressure of oxygen. From this graph, we can estimate this change to be approximately 25–45 mm Hg.

7. When people are at high elevation, the partial pressure of oxygen in the air they breathe is lower than it is at sea level. For this reason, their hemoglobin may not reach full saturation with each breath they take. As a consequence, they may not be able to deliver sufficient oxygen to their tissue, which may lead to shortness of breath and faster breathing. This oxygen deficiency can be exacerbated by the strenuous physical activity of climbing.

Chapter 22

1. a; 2. c; 3. d; 4. a; 5. a; 6. b; 7. b; 8. d; 9. a; 10. b; 11. b; 12. e; 13. d; 14. d; 15. e; 16. a

Short-Answer Questions

1. *Water:* important in the transport of nutrients and wastes; acts as a solvent for amino acids, sugars, minerals, and many vitamins; and takes part in some chemical reactions. *Proteins:* the source of amino acids, which are the building blocks of body proteins, such as hemoglobin, muscle cells, and enzymes. Proteins also can act as an energy source. *Carbohydrates:* energy-rich chemicals used by cells, through cellular respiration, as their primary energy source. Cellulose (fiber), which cannot be digested by humans, stimulates movement of food through the intestines. *Fats:* long-term energy-storage molecules, stored as fat tissue under the skin (which also provides body insulation) and elsewhere. *Vitamins and minerals:* required in very small quantities, but playing an important role in the proper functioning of enzymes and other processes.

2. *Ingestion:* intake of food through the mouth. The structures of the mouth cut food into small pieces and grind and mix it with saliva, so that it can be transported through the esophagus to the stomach by peristaltic action. *Digestion:* breakdown of food in the mouth, stomach, and small intestine into its most basic components, which can be readily absorbed and used by cells. Digestion is accomplished by a combination of physical breakdown of food into smaller pieces and chemical breakdown by enzymes. *Absorption:* uptake of usable nutrients through the wall of the small intestine and into the bloodstream, and then transport to cells of the body. *Elimination:* finally, in the large intestine, absorption of water, salts, and vitamins, storage of feces in the rectum, and elimination through defecation.

3. Animals that consume cellulose-containing foods such as grasses and leaves have, either in their stomach or in their cecum, bacteria that can break down cellulose into a usable form.

4. Type 1 diabetes, usually beginning in childhood, results from the inability of the pancreas to produce enough insulin; treatment is injection of insulin so that cells can absorb glucose. Type 2 diabetes, generally beginning later in life, occurs when cells become less responsive to insulin or the number of insulin receptors is reduced. Risk factors include obesity and chronic consumption of high amounts of sugar. Treatment includes weight loss and minimizing glucose fluctuations.

Graphic Content Questions

1. Each spice was tested to see whether it could kill or inhibit the growth of more than 30 species of common food-borne bacteria. The *x*-axis represents the proportion of those species killed or inhibited by the spice. The *x*-axis is calibrated in fractions of a whole, so the final value is 1.0. Thus, in this graph 1.0 means that all of the species of bacteria tested were killed or inhibited by the spice.

2. The spice that is the second most frequently used in recipes is black pepper (indicated in the text). The graph indicates the proportion of recipes that include garlic, onion, chili pepper, or black pepper. The other spices are used in a smaller proportion of recipes than the 24% of recipes that included chili peppers.

3. Garlic and onion are at the top of the chart because the spices are ordered on the basis of the proportion of bacteria species inhibited, rather than on the frequency of recipes in which they occur. Both garlic and onions inhibited 100% of the bacteria species tested.

4. You can conclude that oregano is used in less than 24% of recipes. This is because the graph indicates (in red type) the four most commonly used spices and indicates how frequently they are used. Because oregano is not among the four most commonly used spices, it must be used in a smaller proportion than the fourth most commonly used spice, which is chili pepper, in 24% of recipes.

5. You cannot conclude anything about the relative frequency of use of coriander versus ginger in recipes because this information is not given in the graph.

6. In a city close to the equator, you would expect fewer food poisoning cases to come from an Indian restaurant. This is because, according to the text, Indian recipes call for more spices, on average, than do recipes from countries farther from the equator. To the extent that greater spice use is associated with greater inhibition of bacterial growth, Indian food would be expected to support less bacterial growth. You

cannot be very certain of this prediction, however, because numerous factors influence the incidence of food poisoning—for example, general level of cleanliness in restaurants and the number of customers served at each restaurant.

7. It would be helpful to know the relationship between the amount of each spice used and the spice's effectiveness at killing bacteria. It would also be helpful to know how quickly each spice killed bacteria and the influence of heat and cooking on the effectiveness of each spice in killing bacteria. It would also be interesting to know whether any combinations of spices were more effective at killing bacteria than would be expected from the spices' antibacterial effectiveness on their own.

8. One alternative way of plotting the data would be a scatterplot, with proportion of bacteria inhibited on the x-axis and frequency of use on the y-axis. This graph would have the advantage of revealing the extent to which a spice's frequency of use was related to its antibacterial effectiveness. A disadvantage of a scatterplot would be the difficulty of including with each point the identity of the spice it represented. To put so many labels in the graph might obscure the information.

Another way of presenting these data would be to use bar graphs, showing two bars for each spice, with one indicating the proportion of bacteria inhibited and the other (perhaps in a different color) indicating the frequency of use in recipes. Again, this would make it easier to investigate the strength of the relationship between each spice's antibacterial effectiveness and its frequency of use. It would also make it easy to identify any spices for which the usage was significantly less than would be expected given the spices antibacterial effectiveness. That might help in identifying future research questions. A disadvantage of a bar graph would be the fact that most of the spices are used in less than 24% of all recipes. So the size of the bars reflecting spice usage might be too small, making it difficult to evaluate their relative usages. Instead, it might be helpful to *rank* the usage frequencies rather than using absolute numbers for the frequency of use.

Chapter 23

1. a; 2. e; 3. a; 4. a; 5. c; 6. e; 7. d; 8. d; 9. c; 10. d; 11. a; 12. a; 13. a; 14. d; 15. e; 16. e; 17. e; 18. d; 19. b; 20. e

Short-Answer Questions

1. Neurons are the impulse-conducting cells of the central and peripheral nervous systems. An impulse travels along the axon away from the cell body, eventually arriving at a synapse with another neuron, a muscle cell, or a gland cell. Glial cells are supporting cells found in the central and peripheral nervous systems. They help neurons function by protecting, insulating, and nourishing them, but do not play a direct role in impulse conduction. Without glial cells, neurons would not be able to function, survive, and grow. Glial cells are capable of dividing throughout life, while neurons, with a few exceptions, are not.

2. Each skeletal muscle fiber consists of numerous myofibrils, which are made up of many sarcomeres—the units of contraction. Each sarcomere contains thin and thick filaments, made of different types of protein. Thin filaments consist of two rows of small globular actin molecules, and thick filaments are made up of myosin; each myosin molecule looks much like a double-headed golf club. Myosin molecules are overlapping, with the globular heads projecting along the entire length of the fiber. The four-part change that allows contraction consists of: (1) *Detach:* A link between a myosin and an

actin filament parallel to it is broken as a molecule of ATP binds to the myosin. (2) *Reach:* As the ATP breaks down, energy released alters the shape of the myosin into a higher-energy shape. (3) *Reattach:* In its altered shape, the myosin reaches farther down the actin filament, where it reattaches. And (4) *Pull back:* The myosin then snaps back to its original shape, pulling the actin filament as it does so and shortening the fiber, in the "power stroke."

3. There are five primary types of sensory receptors. *Mechanoreceptors* measure mechanical stress and are associated with hearing and touch. *Thermoreceptors* measure temperature and are found in the skin; they are part of our perception of touch. *Photoreceptors* measure light and are found in the eyes, functioning in sight. *Pain receptors* detect pain, which can be caused by extremes of heat or tissue damage; they are part of the perception of touch. *Chemoreceptors* detect chemicals; they are found in the mouth and nose and function in taste and smell.

Graphic Content Questions

1. The take-home message of these graphs is that extensive and long-term usage of spatial memory for navigation seems to increase the size of the structure in the brain used in such mental processes.

2. In the middle measure, the bar for hippocampus body size in taxi drivers is larger than for non-taxi drivers, but the difference is not statistically significant. This might be because the variation among taxi drivers for this measure (as well as the variation for this measure among non-taxi drivers) might have been relatively large or because there was a true but small effect of being a taxi driver. In either case, using a larger sample size would likely lead to a determination that the difference between the groups was in fact significant.

3. Taxi drivers may have a larger posterior hippocampus because driving a cab (and the associated increase in usage of the posterior hippocampus for navigation and spatial memory usage) *causes* the posterior hippocampus to become larger. An alternative hypothesis is that (1) there is natural variation among individuals in the size of the posterior hippocampus, (2) that having a larger posterior hippocampus causes a person to be a better cab driver, and (3) those individuals with a smaller posterior hippocampus either fail at being a cab driver or give up, causing the remaining cab drivers to have larger than average posterior hippocampus size.

4. The lower graph reveals that the more time a person spends as a taxi driver, the larger the posterior hippocampus. This suggests that it is the first hypothesis above, rather than the second, that is true.

5. Each blue square represents the data on time as a taxi driver and relative posterior hippocampus size for one taxi driver in the study. The angle of the line represents a positive relationship between the variables plotted on the x-axis and the y-axis. The average amount of time spent as a taxi driver is just under 15 years.

6. If it is true that driving a cab *causes* the posterior hippocampus to become larger, measurements of individual drivers at two points in time should reveal that their posterior hippocampus has increased in size following additional years of driving.

7. The anterior hippocampus size is larger among non-taxi drivers than taxi drivers. A possible explanation of this is that driving a cab increases the size of the posterior hippocampus, but the fixed size of the skull makes it impossible for this increase to occur without a concurrent decrease in some other part of the hippocampus.

Chapter 24

1. b; 2. d; 3. c; 4. e; 5. b; 6. b; 7. d; 8. e; 9. b; 10. d; 11. b; 12. c

Short-Answer Questions

1. Both types of hormones circulate in extracellular fluids and influence changes in target cells (cells with a receptor for a particular hormone). Peptide and protein hormones cannot pass through the cell membrane of target cells; they attach to membrane receptors on the target cell, which causes a change within the cell. Steroid hormones, however, can pass through the cell membrane of target cells; they then attach to a receptor in the cytoplasm or nucleus.

2. The hypothalamus integrates sensory information, received by the brain, on the internal and external conditions of the organism. Once the hypothalamus has evaluated the information, it produces hormones that travel to the pituitary gland, which is attached by a thin stalk to the hypothalamus. These hormones cause the pituitary either to release or to stop the release of specific hormones. The pituitary gland is made up of two parts, the anterior and posterior pituitary; these produce hormones that influence other endocrine glands to produce other hormones.

3. Drops in estrogen level in females, such as during menopause and after giving birth, as well as the spike in estrogen that occurs at puberty, have been correlated with depression. In cases of low estrogen, supplements can be taken to help return estrogen levels to normal and reduce the occurrence of depression. Males who take supplemental testosterone may experience elevated self-esteem and overflowing of new ideas, and feel energetic, euphoric, confident, and charismatic; others find that they are more aggressive. Human and animal studies show that castrated males, who produce almost no testosterone, and females that have been sterilized and do not produce estrogen and other sex hormones, live longer than those producing normal levels of these hormones. However, among post-menopausal women taking hormone supplements, mortality decreases, illustrating the complexity of this issue.

4. Some manufactured chemicals, such as DDT and PCBs, can mimic, block, or interfere with the functioning of hormones. These endocrine disruptors can build up in organisms that feed on other, contaminated organisms, and collect in tissues (such as fat tissue, in the case of DDT). As a result, even in small quantities, the chemicals may harm some organisms.

Graphic Content Questions

1. The take-home message of these graphs is that sterilization seems to increase longevity in male mammals. In order to have greater confidence in this take-home message, it would be helpful to know whether there were similar changes in causes of mortality in cats and humans following sterilization. For example, if rates of death from cancer decreased similarly, that would support the take-home message while suggesting a possible mechanism for this effect.

2. The graphs use different scales because humans live much longer than do cats, whether they are sterilized or not. Because both graphs have an *x*-axis that begins at 0, however, it is possible to evaluate the *proportion* of increase in life span among sterilized males relative to non-sterilized males. If the human graph's *x*-axis went from 50 to 70 years, the magnitude of the increase would appear much more dramatic. That would be misleading because it would suggest that the *proportion* of the increase in longevity among sterilized males relative to non-sterilized males was much greater than it actually is.

3. Sterilized male cats lived about 8 years as opposed to 5 years for non-sterilized cats—a 60% increase in longevity. For humans, sterilized males lived about 70 years while non-sterilized males lived about 55 years—a 15/55, or 27%, increase in longevity.

4. Standard deviation is a measure of how much variation in the measure there is from one individual to another.

5. For populations with the same average value for a trait, in the population with the larger standard deviation individuals would be more likely to deviate from the average. In the population with the smaller standard deviation, individuals would be clustered much more closely around the average. For example, imagine two populations each having an average value of 5 for a trait. If one population has a standard deviation of 0, everyone would have the same value for the trait: 5. If a different population had a very high standard deviation, there could, for example, be many people with measures of 8 or 9, and these individuals would be balanced out by others with measures of 2 or 1, respectively, so that any two individuals would be more likely to differ for the measure (and to differ by a greater amount).

6. A median, like a mean (which is the same thing as an average), is a measure of the central tendency of a group of measures. The mean is the arithmetical average value, obtained by adding all the measures and dividing by the number of measures. The median is the number for which half of the measures are greater and half are less. The median is less influenced by extreme measures.

7. The 25th percentile is the number for which 25% of all the individuals fall below (and for which 75% of the individuals are above). The 75th percentile is the number for which 75% of all the individuals fall below (and for which 25% of the individuals are above).

8. The data from the lower graph were collected from sanitarium patients because at one time, many patients were castrated. The practice is now considered extremely unethical and is not performed. It is extremely rare for any individual to be castrated and it would not be ethical to coerce anyone to undergo castration. The data therefore were available only because the practice once occurred in sanitariums. This experiment certainly could not be conducted today.

Chapter 25

1. a; 2. c; 3. a; 4. a; 5. a; 6. c; 7. c; 8. e; 9. e; 10. b; 11. e; 12. b; 13. d; 14. a; 15. d

Short-Answer Questions

1. Human males produce sperm by the process of spermatogenesis, which occurs in the testes, located in the scrotum. Spermatogonia, cells in the seminiferous tubules, divide by mitosis, each cell producing a new spermatogonium and a primary spermatocyte. The primary spermatocyte undergoes a first meiotic division, producing two secondary spermatocytes, each of which divides by a second meiotic division to produce four haploid sperm. Sperm move to the epididymis, where they mature and become motile.

2. Germ layers are the three layers of tissue—endoderm, mesoderm, and ectoderm—that form in the embryo during gastrulation. *Endoderm* is the inner tissue layer that forms the digestive tract, liver, pancreas, and the lining of the respiratory tract. *Mesoderm* is the middle tissue layer that gives rise to muscle and the skeletal system. *Ectoderm* is the outer tissue that gives rise to the outer layer of skin, hair, the nervous system, and the lining of the nose and mouth.

3. *First trimester:* During the first three months of development, minimal growth of the embryo takes place, but vital cell differentiation and development occur. The fertilized egg (zygote) divides and eventually forms three cell layers, from which all the organs and their associated systems will develop, as well as all body structures. This is also the stage during which the zygote implants in the uterus and the placenta forms. *Second trimester:* Significant growth occurs during the fourth through six months. The bones of the skeletal system grow and muscles develop, making possible fetal movement. *Third trimester:* The fetus primarily grows during these last three months of pregnancy. Growth and development of the nervous system also take place. During this stage, the fetus becomes an individual that can survive outside the womb.

Graphic Content Questions

1. In October, the average number of days between a woman's "first day of menstruation" and those of her 5–10 closest friends in her dorm was 6.5 days. In April, this number was about 4.7. This is a decrease of approximately 28%.

2. If all women had a 28-day menstrual cycle, the highest value that would be possible on the *y*-axis is 14. This is because if a woman's first day of menstruation is more than 14 days *later* than her friend's (for example, 16 days later), it would then be considered to be some smaller number of days *earlier* than her friend's next "first day of menstruation." In other words, if her first day of menstruation occurs 16 days after her friend's first day, it would be reported as 12 days *earlier* than her friend's next "first day of menstruation."

3. The fact that women on the pill were not excluded from this study makes the results a bit more convincing. This is because it is likely that all women on the pill would have 28-day menstrual cycles that could not be altered. Consequently, the phenomenon of menstrual synchrony is not occurring among women on the pill, and so including them in the data makes it more difficult to detect the phenomenon among the other women. It's hard to be certain why women on the pill were included in this study. One possibility is the fact that, although their cycles could not change in length, they still were part of the environment of the other women and were potentially influencing the cycle length of those women—causing the cycles of women not on the pill to become more synchronized with cycles of those on the pill.

4. Just because these ideas and data were developed by an undergraduate should not influence our interpretation of them. One of the strengths of scientific thinking is that any study can be evaluated solely on its merits. On their own, the academic qualifications of the researcher do not make a study more or less accurate. That said, it might be true that the more experience researchers have, the more likely that they may anticipate difficulties in interpretation or appreciate complex issues relating to the development of experimental controls—thus enabling them to design a better-controlled experiment or to conduct a more powerful analysis of the results.

5. The break in the *y*-axis indicates that part of the scale (from 0 to 3) has been omitted. This was likely done because none of the data points or their associated error bars fell in that range, and so including this range on the graph would just reduce the proportion of the graph devoted to actual data. If this break were not made, however, the magnitude of the change conveyed by the data would appear smaller. This is because in the current form, the entire graph can cover the range of 4 to 7 days. If the graph covered 0 to 7 days, the portion in which the

data appear would be only about half as large. As a consequence, that magnitude of the change from October to April would appear less steep (although its actual value would remain unchanged).

6. The vertical lines through each data point represent the variation around the average. In other words, while the average number of days between a woman's "first day of menstruation" and that of her 5–10 closest friends in the dorm was 6.5 days, in some cases it was larger and in some cases it was smaller. The size of the error bars, which probably represent the standard deviation around the mean, gives an indication of how much variation there was among individuals in this measure. If the error bars were twice as long, it would indicate much more variation from one woman to another in the number of days between her first day of menstruation and those of her 5–10 closest friends. This would decrease our confidence that the increased synchrony observed represented a true physiological phenomenon as opposed to a coincidental change in means due to random chance.

7. The take-home message of this graph is that over the course of less than one academic year, women living together in dorms tend to become synchronized in their menstrual cycles, as evidenced by a reduced difference in the number of days between their first days of their menstrual cycles. It would be helpful to see data from women living together for longer periods than that shown. It also would be helpful to see data from these same women after they stop living together at the end of the academic year. We would expect, gradually, the average number of days to increase between a woman's "first day of menstruation" and those of her 5–10 closest friends in the dorm (but who are no longer living together), until it is no different from the number determined at the beginning of this study.

Chapter 26

1. b; 2. d; 3. d; 4. d; 5. e; 6. b; 7. d; 8. a; 9. e; 10. c; 11. d; 12. a

Short-Answer Questions

1. During the specific division of the immune system's primary response to an antigen on a pathogen, a type of lymphocyte called memory cells is produced through clonal selection. These lymphocytes "remember" an antigen. The second time a person is exposed to the pathogen, the memory cells, hanging around in the lymph and blood cells, are ready to attack it, mounting a much faster and more vigorous attack.

2. The specific division of the immune system recognizes very specific infectious agents, such as the virus that causes chicken pox. As a consequence of a vaccine for this illness, the immune system forms a "memory" of the virus that allows it to fight off the virus in the future before the virus can cause the chicken pox. The chicken pox virus antigens remain relatively constant over time. The influenza virus, on the other hand is not so constant. Each year there are many different versions, or strains, of the influenza virus, all of which are constantly changing. And so with each new flu season, the body encounters a slightly different form of influenza and, therefore, a different set of antigens. For this reason, previously formed memory cells are not helpful in fighting the new virus.

Graphic Content Questions

1. According to this figure, in the United States the percent of adults infected with HIV is 0.5% to 0.9%. In order to estimate the number of adults infected with HIV, we need to estimate the number of adults in the United States. Assuming that there are about 300 million people in

the United States (there were actually 313 million), we might estimate that three-quarters of people in the United States, or 225 million people, are adults. (The proportion of people in the United States who are under 18 years old is actually about 24% of the 313 million people, or 238 million.)

If there are 225 million adults in the United States, and 0.5% to 0.9% are infected with HIV, that works out to 1.125 million for the low estimate and 2.025 million for the high estimate. If we had to give one number, it would probably be best to take the average of these two numbers: 1.575 million.

2. It is difficult from this map and the associated data to determine which countries have the largest number of adults infected with HIV. Certain countries, those shown in dark red, clearly have a much higher percentage of adults infected with HIV than other countries. But the data shown here are meant to convey information about which countries have the highest *proportion* of their population infected with HIV. In order to know which country has the most infected adults, it is necessary to multiply the rate of infection in each country by the number of adults. But those data are not given. And so, at a glance, we cannot easily identify which countries have the largest number of adults infected with HIV.

3. Using the same logic as in the previous question/answer, from the information given it is not possible to determine whether there are twice as many adults infected with HIV in the United States as in Canada. The rate of infection in Canada is between 0.1% and 0.49% (or, to take the midpoint, approximately 0.3%). And in the United States the rate of infection is between 0.5% and 0.9% (or, to take the midpoint, approximately 0.75%). This suggests that the *rate* of infection

in the United States is about twice as high as in Canada. Given that the number of adults in the United States is much greater than in Canada, however, that would lead us to conclude that the total number of adults infected with HIV in the United States is more than double the number of infected adults in Canada.

4. From the map and associated data, it appears that the rate of adult HIV infection in South Africa is between 15% and 28%. (To take a midpoint, we could say 21.5%.) In South America, most of the countries have infection rates of 0.5% to 0.9%, although there appears to be at least one country with a rate of 1.0% to 4.9% and at least one with a rate of 0.1% to 0.49%. (To take a midpoint, we could say 0.75%.) From these data, we could conclude that the rate of HIV infection among adults is significantly higher in South Africa than in South America. Further, we could conclude that the rate of infection is almost 30 times higher in South Africa.

5. The different colors used to indicate successively increasing rates of infection of adults with HIV in the map do not represent consistent increases. Rather, each of the last three intervals is considerably broader than the previous, and each of those intervals is much larger than the first three intervals. While this might confuse or mislead a reader who does not carefully note the infection rates designated by each color, it serves an important purpose. In many cases, it is important to be able to convey a very large range of numbers. When doing so, it can be helpful to indicate when one data point is *double* the previous data point. And when the next data point is *double* that one. In this figure, the ranges used with each color make that possible. This makes it possible to show fine gradations at the low end, while also showing meaningful gradations at the high end, even when the high end is 100 times greater than the low end.

Glossary

A note about notation: The word or phrase being defined is in boldface type; it is followed by the number (in parentheses) of the chapter or chapters where it is discussed. In some cases, derivations are given. Abbreviations: Gk., Greek; Lat., Latin; *sing.,* singular; *pl.,* plural; *dim.,* diminutive (a smaller version of the object named); *pron.,* pronounced.

A

abiotic (15) Relating to the physical and chemical components in an environment. These include the chemical resources of the soil, water, and air (such as carbon, nitrogen, and phosphorus) and physical conditions (such as temperature, salinity, moisture, humidity, and energy sources).

abscisic acid (19) A plant hormone that has the general effect of inhibiting growth and reproductive activities.

absorption (22) The process by which biological macromolecules in food particles are taken up from the cells lining the digestive tract and then move into the bloodstream.

acid (2) Any fluid with a pH below 7.0, indicating the presence of more H^+ ions than OH^- ions. [Lat., *acidus,* sour]

acquired immune deficiency syndrome (AIDS) (13, 26) Infectious human disease caused by a retrovirus, HIV (human immunodeficiency virus), which compromises the immune system by attacking T cells, leaving an individual susceptible to infections, as well as cancers.

acrosome (25) Cap-like structure covering the head region of a sperm; it contains enzymes for penetrating the outer membrane of an egg, enabling fusion of the nuclei.

actin (23) A protein of muscle tissue; makes up the thin filaments.

action potential (23) An electrical signal that travels along an axon, from a neuron to another neuron, a muscle cell, or a gland cell.

activation energy (2) The minimum energy needed to initiate a chemical reaction (regardless of whether the reaction releases or consumes energy).

activator (2) A chemical within a cell that binds to an enzyme, altering the enzyme's shape or structure in a way that causes the enzyme to catalyze a reaction.

active site (2) The part of an enzyme to which reactants (or substrates) bind and undergo a chemical reaction.

active transport (3) Molecular movement that depends on the input of energy, which is necessary when the molecules to be moved are large or are being moved against their concentration gradient.

adaptation (8) The process by which, as a result of natural selection, a population's organisms become better matched to their environment; also, a specific feature, such as the quills of a porcupine, that makes an organism more fit.

adaptive radiation (10) The rapid diversification of a small number of species into a much larger number of species, able to live in a wide variety of habitats.

additive effects (7) Effects from alleles of multiple genes that all contribute to the ultimate phenotype for a given characteristic.

adenosine triphosphate (ATP) (4) A molecule that temporarily stores energy for cellular activity in all living organisms. ATP is composed of an adenine, a sugar molecule, and a chain of three negatively charged phosphate groups.

adrenal glands (24) Two glands of the endocrine system which sit just above the kidneys and help regulate an organism's response to stress, by secreting the hormones cortisol and adrenaline (also called *epinephrine*), among other hormones.

adrenocorticotropic hormone (ACTH) (24) A hormone produced by the anterior pituitary in mammals that stimulates the adrenal glands to produce cortisol and other stress-related hormones. Also known as corticotropin.

adult (11) (Pertaining to insect developmental stages) In complete metamorphosis, the third and final stage of insect development.

aging (14) An increased risk of mortality with increasing age; generally characterized by multiple physiological breakdowns.

alleles (5, 7) Alternative versions of a gene. [Gk., *allos,* another]

allergen (26) An antigen that causes an allergic response.

allergy (26) An inappropriate immune response to what should be a harmless substance.

allopatric speciation (10) Speciation that occurs as a result of a geographic barrier between groups of individuals that leads to reproductive isolation and then genetic divergence. [Gk., *allos,* another + *patris,* native land]

alternation of generations (18) In plants, the life cycle characterized by an extended period in which the plant has a multicellular haploid form and a period in which it has a multicellular diploid form.

altruistic behavior (9) A behavior that comes at a cost to the individual performing it and benefits another. [Lat., *alter,* the other]

amino acid (2) One of 20 molecules built of an amino group, a carboxyl group, and a unique side chain. Proteins are constructed of combinations of amino acids linked together.

amino group (2) A nitrogen atom bonded to three hydrogen atoms.

amnion (25) During animal development, the membrane enclosing the fluid-filled sac surrounding an embryo.

amniotes (11) Terrestrial vertebrates—reptiles, birds, and mammals—that produce eggs (called amniotic eggs) that are protected by a water-tight membrane and a shell.

amphibians (11) Members of the class Amphibia; ectotherms (that is, they are cold-blooded), with a moist skin, lacking scales, through which they can fully or partially absorb oxygen. They were the first terrestrial vertebrates. The young of most species are aquatic, and the adults are true land animals. [Gk., *bios,* life + *amphi,* on both sides]

amygdala (23) Part of the brain's limbic system; associates emotional feelings and sensory input with memories.

analogous traits (10) Characteristics (such as bat wings and insect wings) that are similar because they were produced by convergent evolution, not because they descended from a common structure in a shared ancestor. [Gk., *analogos,* proportionate]

anaphase (6) A phase in mitosis and meiosis in which chromosomes separate. In mitosis, it is the third phase, in which the sister chromatids are pulled apart by the spindle fibers, with a full set of chromosomes going to opposite sides of the cell. In meiosis, the homologues separate in anaphase I and the sister chromatids separate in anaphase II. [Gk., *ana,* up + *phasis,* appearance]

anaphylactic shock (26) A life-threatening allergic reaction that causes severe respiratory distress, as the throat swells and asthma develops. With swelling in various tissues, there is less fluid in the bloodstream, and this can lead to dangerously low blood pressure.

anecdotal observation (1) Observation of one or only a few instances of a phenomenon.

angiosperms (12) Vascular, seed-producing flowering and fruit-bearing plants, in which the seeds are enclosed in an ovule within the ovary. [Gk., *angeion*, vessel, jar + *sperma*, seed]

animals (11) Members of the kingdom Animalia; eukaryotic, multicellular, heterotrophic (that is, they cannot produce their own food) organisms. Many of these organisms have body parts specialized for different activities and can move during some stage of their lives. [Lat., *animal*, a living being]

annelid (11) Phylum of worms having segmented bodies; protostomes with defined tissues, which grow by adding segments rather than by molting. There are about 13,000 identified species of segmented worms, including earthworms and leeches.

anterior pituitary (24) A gland of the endocrine system that produces numerous hormones, including thyroid-stimulating hormone (TSH), luteinizing hormone (LH), follicle-stimulating hormone (FSH), prolactin, adrenocorticotropic hormone (ACTH), and growth hormone. Many of the hormones of the anterior pituitary gland direct endocrine glands elsewhere to release other hormones.

anther (12, 18) The part of the stamen, the male reproductive structure of a flower, that produces pollen. [Gk., *anthos*, blossom]

antibody (26) A protein produced by the specific immunity system in response to an antigen. Circulating antibodies recognize and bind to specific antigens.

antidiuretic hormone (ADH) (24) A peptide hormone produced in neurons within the hypothalamus and released by the posterior pituitary gland that influences water retention by the kidneys. With increased levels of ADH, more water is saved, reducing the amount of urine produced while increasing its concentration.

antigen (26) Any molecule that induces a specific immunity response.

antigen-presenting cells (26) Dendritic cells and macrophages that ingest bacteria and viruses, destroying them and "presenting" digested particles of the pathogens on their cell surface.

antigen receptor (26) Protein on the plasma membrane of a lymphocyte that sticks out from the cell surface and can bind one specific type of antigen.

antiseptic (26) Solution such as rubbing alcohol or hydrogen peroxide that discourages growth of microorganisms.

apical meristem (17) Growth region at the tip of a plant root or stem; division of cells in this meristem causes the root or stem to increase in length.

apoptosis (6, 26) Programmed cell death, which takes place particularly in parts of the body where the cells are likely to accumulate significant genetic damage over time and are therefore at high risk of becoming cancerous. [Gk., *apoptosis*, falling away]

archaea (*sing.* **archaeon**) (10) A group of prokaryotes that are evolutionarily distinct from bacteria and that thrive in some of the most extreme environments on earth; one of the three domains of life. [Gk., *archaios*, ancient]

arteriosclerosis (21) A disease process, following development of atherosclerosis, in which calcium deposits harden the arteries.

artery (21) A blood vessel that transports blood from the heart, at higher pressure than veins, to the capillaries of the body.

arthropods (11) Members of the invertebrate phylum Arthropoda; characterized by a segmented body, an exoskeleton, and jointed appendages. [Gk., *arthron*, joint + *pous*, foot]

asexual reproduction (6, 25) A type of reproduction common in prokaryotes and plants, and also occurring in many other multicellular organisms, in which the offspring inherit their DNA from a single parent.

assisted reproductive technology (ART) (25) The use of fertility treatments in which both sperm and egg are handled.

atherosclerosis (21) A disease process in which plaques develop in the arteries, reducing the flow of blood and increasing the risk of blood clots.

atom (2) A particle of matter than cannot be further subdivided without losing its essential properties. [Gk., *atomos*, indivisible]

atomic mass (2) The mass of an atom; the combined mass of the protons, neutrons, and electrons in an atom (the mass of the electrons is so small as to be almost negligible).

atomic number (2) The number of protons in the nucleus of an atom of a given element.

atrium (21) A chamber of the heart that collects blood returning from the lungs or the rest of the body.

autoimmunity (26) Inappropriate response of an individual's immune system to the individual's own cells and tissues as if they were pathogens.

autonomic nervous system (23) One of the two major divisions of the motor pathways of the peripheral nervous system (the somatic nervous system is the other); relays signals–not under conscious control–to glands and smooth muscle tissue (such as the muscle that moves food through the digestive tract) and cardiac muscle.

auxins (19) In plants, a small group of naturally occurring hormones (and a larger group of synthetic variants) that promote cell division, stem elongation, and formation of roots. Auxins also influence plant orientation, making sure the correct ends are up and down.

axon (20, 23) A projection from a neuron that transmits impulses away from the cell body.

B

B cell (26) A type of lymphocyte, maturing in the bone marrow, that is involved in humoral immunity; fights invaders in body fluids.

background extinctions (10) Extinctions that occur at lower rates than at times of mass extinctions; occur mostly as the result of aspects of the biology and competitive success of the species, rather than catastrophe.

basal metabolic rate (BMR) (22) The amount of energy expended by a living organism at rest in a neutral temperature environment.

base (chemistry) (2) Any fluid with a pH above 7.0, that is, with more OH^- ions than H^+ ions.

base (of DNA) (2, 5) One of the nitrogen-containing side-chain molecules attached to a sugar molecule in the sugar-phosphate backbone of DNA and RNA. The four bases in DNA are adenine (A), thymine (T), guanine (G), and cytosine (C); the four bases in RNA are adenine (A), uracil (U), guanine (G), and cytosine (C). The information in a molecule of DNA and RNA is determined by its sequence of bases.

base pair (5) Two nucleotides on complementary strands of DNA that form a pair, linked by hydrogen bonds. The pattern of pairing is adenine (A) with thymine (T) and cytosine (C) with guanine (G); the base-paired arrangement forms the "rungs" of the double-helix structure of DNA.

basophil (26) A type of white blood cell that initiates inflammation.

behavior (9) Any and all of the actions performed by an organism, often in response to its environment or to the actions of another organism.

bilateral symmetry (11) A body structure with left and right sides, which are mirror images. [Lat., *bi-*, two + *latus*, side]

bile (22) A juice that aids in the breakdown of fats; it is produced by the liver, sent to the gallbladder, and passed through a small duct into the small intestine, where it initiates the first step in fat digestion.

binary fission (6) A type of asexual reproduction in which the parent cell divides into two genetically identical daughter cells. Bacteria and other prokaryotes reproduce by binary fission. [Lat., *binarius,* consisting of two + *fissus,* divided]

biodiversity (10, 16) The variety and variability among all genes, species, and ecosystems. [Gk., *bios,* life + Lat., *diversus,* turned in different directions]

biodiversity hotspots (16) Regions of the world with significant reservoirs of biodiversity that are under threat of destruction.

biofuels (4) Fuels produced from plant and animal products.

biogeography (8) The study and interpretation of distribution patterns of living organisms around the world. [Gk. *bios,* life + *geo-,* earth + *graphein,* to write down]

biological literacy (1) The ability to use scientific inquiry to think creatively about problems with a biological component, to communicate these thoughts to others, and to integrate these ideas into one's decision making.

biological species concept (10) A definition of species described as populations of organisms that interbreed, or could possibly interbreed, with each other under natural conditions, and that cannot interbreed with organisms outside their own group.

biology (1) The study of living things. [Gk., *bios,* life + *logos,* discourse]

biomass (15) The total mass of all the living organisms in a given area. [Gk., *bios,* life]

biomes (15) The major ecological communities of earth. Terrestrial biomes, such as rain forest or desert, are defined and usually described by the predominant types of plant life in the area, which are mostly determined by the weather; aquatic biomes are usually defined by physical features such as salinity, water movement, and depth. [Gk., *bios,* life]

biotechnology (5) The modification of organisms, cells, and their molecules for practical benefits. [Gk., *bios,* life + *technologia,* systematic treatment]

biotic (15) Relating to living organisms; the biotic environment, or community, consists of all the living organisms in a given area. [Gk., *bios,* life]

bisphenol A (BPA) (24) A chemical found in some plastic water bottles and baby bottles; a known endocrine disruptor.

bivalve mollusk (11) Mollusks with two hinged shells; examples are clams, scallops, and oysters. [Lat., *bi-,* two]

blastocyst (25) The mammalian blastula.

blastula (25) An early stage of embryonic development produced by cleavage of a fertilized egg (zygote). A spherical layer of cells encloses a large fluid-filled space where the embryo forms. [Gk., *blastos,* sprout]

blind experimental design (1) An experimental design in which the subjects do not know what treatment (if any) they are receiving.

blood (20, 21) A connective tissue with a liquid extracellular matrix containing blood cells; contained in a closed circulatory system, and important in the transport of respiratory gases, vitamins and minerals, nutrients, hormones, components of the immune system, and metabolic wastes.

blood pressure (21) The force with which blood flows through the arteries.

body mass index (22) Body weight in kilograms divided by height in meters squared (kg/m^2); often used as an index of a healthy weight for an individual based on the person's height.

bond energy (2) The strength of a bond between two atoms, defined as the energy required to break the bond.

bone (20) A rigid connective tissue that protects and provides support.

bottleneck effect (8) A phenomenon by which genetic drift can occur; a sudden reduction in population size (often due to famine, disease, or rapid environmental disturbance) that can lead to changes in the allele frequencies of a population.

Bowman's capsule (20) A ball-like structure surrounding the blood-filtering unit of a nephron in the kidney. It is connected to a single, long, urine-collecting tube that excretes its filtered fluid into a collecting duct.

Broca's area (23) The discrete part of the brain, located, in most people, in the front part of the left frontal lobe, that is used for controlling the muscles responsible for the process of speaking.

bryophytes (12) Three groups of plants (the liverworts, hornworts, and mosses) that lack vascular tissue and move water and dissolved nutrients by diffusion. [Gk., *bruon,* tree-moss, liverwort + *phytas,* plant]

buffer (2) A chemical that can quickly absorb excess H^+ ions in a solution (preventing it from becoming too acidic) or quickly release H^+ ions (to counteract increases in OH^- concentration).

bulbourethral gland (25) A male reproductive gland, one on each side of the body, that contributes mucus and sugar to the ejaculate and lubricant to the tip of the penis prior to copulation.

C

C4 photosynthesis (4) A method (along with C3 and CAM photosynthesis) by which plants fix carbon dioxide, using the carbon to build sugar; serves as a more effective method than C3 for binding carbon dioxide under low carbon dioxide conditions, such as when plants in warmer climates close their stomata to reduce water loss.

calcitonin (24) A hormone released from the thyroid gland that causes bones to take up excess calcium from the bloodstream.

calorie (22) The energy required to raise the temperature of 1 gram of water by 1° C; the kilocalorie, which is 1,000 calories, is commonly used as a measure of the amount of energy in a particular food (and often is, inaccurately, referred to as a calorie).

Calvin cycle (4) In photosynthesis, a series of chemical reactions in the stroma of chloroplasts, in which sugar molecules are assembled. [From the name of one of its discoverers, Melvin Calvin, 1911–1997]

CAM (crassulacean acid metabolism) (4) Energetically expensive photosynthesis in which the stomata are open only at night to admit CO_2, which is bound to a holding molecule and released to enter the Calvin cycle to make sugar during the day. In this type of photosynthesis, found in many fleshy, juicy plants of hot, dry areas, water loss is reduced because the stomata are closed during the day.

cancer (6) Unrestrained cell growth and division. [Lat., *cancer,* crab]

capillaries (21) Tiny blood vessels that bring blood close enough to cells to allow the diffusion of molecules into and out of the blood.

capsid (13) The protein container surrounding the genetic material (DNA or RNA) of a virus. [Lat., *capsa,* box, case]

capsule (13) A layer surrounding the cell wall of many bacteria; it may restrict the movement of water out of the cell and thus allow bacteria to live in dry places, such as the surface of the skin. The capsule contributes to the virulent characteristics of some bacteria, making them resistant to phagocytosis by the host's immune system. [Lat., *capsula,* small box or case]

carbohydrate (2) One of the four types of biological macromolecule, containing mostly carbon, hydrogen, and oxygen. Carbohydrates are the primary fuel for cellular activity and form much of the cell structure in all life forms. [Lat., *carbo,* charcoal + *hydro-,* pertaining to water]

carboxyl group (2) A functional group characterized by a carbon atom double-bonded to one oxygen atom and single-bonded to another oxygen atom. Amino acids are made up of an amino group, a carboxyl group, and a side chain.

cardiac muscle (20) A type of muscle tissue, located only in the heart, that causes the heart to pump blood through the body. Cardiac muscle cells, which are fused together and connected by gap junctions, contain many more mitochondria than other types of muscle cells.

cardiovascular disease (21) Progressive deterioration of the arteries and other degradations of the circulatory system; the leading cause of death and disability in the United States.

carnivores (15, 22) Predatory animals (and some plants) that consume only animals. [Lat., *carnis,* of flesh + *vorare,* to devour]

carotenoids (4) Pigments that absorb blue-violet and blue-green wavelengths of light and reflect yellow, orange, and red wavelengths of light. [Lat., *carota,* carrot]

carpel (12, 18) The female reproductive structure of a flower, including the stigma, style, and ovary. [Gk., *karpos,* fruit]

carrier (7) An individual who carries one allele for a recessive trait and does not exhibit the trait; if two carriers mate, they may produce offspring who do exhibit the trait.

carrying capacity (*K*) (14) The ceiling on a population's growth imposed by the limitation of resources for a particular habitat over a period of time.

cartilage (20) A dense connective tissue with an extracellular matrix rich in collagen, elastin, and proteins bound to long carbohydrate chains, with a hardness between that of bone and of tendons; strong, but also flexible, cartilage is found in the ears and tip of the nose in humans, and it cushions the bones in joints throughout the body.

cartilaginous fishes (11) Fish species characterized by a skeleton made completely of cartilage, not bone. [Lat., *cartilago,* gristle]

cell (3) The smallest unit of life that can function independently; a three-dimensional structure, surrounded by a membrane and, in the case of prokaryotes and most plants, a cell wall, in which many of the essential chemical reactions of the life of an organism take place. [Lat., *cella,* room]

cell body (20, 23) The part of a cell, such as a neuron, that contains the nucleus and other organelles.

cell cycle (6) In a cell, the alternation of activities related to cell division and those related to growth and metabolism.

cell theory (3) A unifying and universally accepted theory in biology that holds that all living organisms are made up of one or more cells, and that all cells arise from other, preexisting cells.

cell wall (3) A rigid structure, outside the cell membrane, that protects and gives shape to the cell; found in many prokaryotes and plants.

cellular respiration (4) The process by which all living organisms extract energy stored in the chemical bonds of molecules and use it for fuel for their life processes.

cellulose (2) A complex carbohydrate, indigestible by humans, that serves as the structural material for a huge variety of plant structures. It is the single most prevalent organic compound on earth. [Lat., *cellula, dim.* of *cella,* room]

central nervous system (CNS) (20, 23) The part of an organism's nervous system that includes the brain and spinal cord and coordinates all nervous activity.

central vacuole (3) See **vacuole.**

centriole (6) A structure, located outside the nucleus in most animal cells, to which the spindle fibers are attached during cell division.

centromere (6) After replication, the region of contact between sister chromatids, which occurs near the center of the two strands. [Gk.,

centron, the stationary point of a pair of compasses, thus the center of a circle + *meris,* part]

cephalopods (11) Mollusks in which the head is prominent and the foot has been modified into tentacles; examples are octopuses and squids. Cephalopods have a reduced or absent shell and possess the most advanced nervous system of the invertebrates. [Gk., *kephale,* head + *pous,* foot]

cerebellum (23) The part of the vertebrate hindbrain that controls muscle coordination.

cerebral cortex (23) The part of the vertebrate brain involved in abstract thought, problem solving, language, and more; the brain structure most responsible for the traits that set humans apart from other animal species.

cervix (25) The low, narrow portion of the uterus leading to the vagina. [Lat., *cervix,* neck]

character displacement (15) An evolutionary divergence in one or more of the species that occupy a niche that leads to a partitioning of the niche between the species. Changes in characteristics, such as behavior or body plan, of two or more very similar species that have overlapping geographic locations result in a reduction of competition between the species.

chemical energy (4) A type of potential energy in which energy is stored in chemical bonds between atoms or molecules.

chemolithotrophs (13) Bacteria that can use inorganic molecules such as ammonia, hydrogen sulfide, hydrogen, and iron as sources of energy. [Gk., *lithos,* stone, rock + *trophē,* food]

chemoorganotrophs (13) Bacteria that consume organic molecules, such as carbohydrates, as an energy source. [Gk., *trophē,* food]

chemoreceptor (23) A type of sensory cell that detects chemical changes in the organism's internal or external environment.

chitin (2) (*pron.* KITE-in) A complex carbohydrate, indigestible by humans, that forms the rigid outer skeleton of most insects and crustaceans. [Gk., *chiton,* undershirt]

chlorophyll (4) A light-absorbing pigment molecule in chloroplasts. [Gk., *chloros,* pale green + *phyllon,* leaf]

chlorophyll *a* (4) The primary photosynthetic pigment. Chlorophyll *a* absorbs blue-violet and red light; because it cannot absorb green light and instead reflects those wavelengths, we perceive the reflected light as the color green.

chlorophyll *b* (4) A photosynthetic pigment similar in structure to chlorophyll *a.* Chlorophyll *b* absorbs blue and red-orange wavelengths and reflects yellow-green wavelengths.

chloroplast (3, 4) The organelle in plant cells in which photosynthesis occurs. [Gk., *chloros,* pale green + *plastos,* formed]

cholesterol (2, 3) One of the sterols, a group of lipids important in regulating growth and development; an important component of most cell membranes, helping the membrane maintain its flexibility. [Gk., *chole,* bile + *stereos,* solid + *-ol,* chemical suffix for an alcohol]

chorion (25) During animal development, the outer membrane surrounding an embryo, which, with the endometrium, forms the placenta.

chromatid (6) One of the two strands of a replicated chromosome. [Gk., *chroma,* color]

chromatin (3) A mass of long, thin fibers consisting of DNA and proteins in the nucleus of the cell. [Gk., *chroma,* color]

chromosomal aberration (5) A type of mutation characterized by a change in the overall organization of genes on a chromosome, such as the deletion of a section of DNA; the moving of a gene from one part of a chromosome to elsewhere on the same chromosome or to a different chromosome; or the duplication of a gene, with the new copy inserted elsewhere on the chromosome or on a different chromosome. [Lat., *aberrare,* to wander]

chromosome (5) A linear or circular strand of DNA on which are found specific sequences of base pairs. The human genome consists of two copies of each of 23 unique chromosomes, one from the mother and one from the father. [Gk., *chroma,* color + *soma,* body]

chyme (22) A liquid mass of partially digested food that passes from the stomach through the small intestine.

cilia (*sing.* **cilium**) (3, 26) Short projections from the cell surface, often occurring in large numbers on a single cell, that beat against the intercellular fluid to move the fluid past the cell. [Lat., *cilium,* eyelid]

class (10) In the hierarchical taxonomic system developed by Carolus Linnaeus (1707–1778), a classification of organisms consisting of related orders.

cleavage (25) In embryonic development, the early cell division of the zygote, which begins shortly after fertilization.

climax community (15) A stable and self-sustaining community that results from ecological succession.

clonal selection (26) Process in which a B cell or T cell binds to its antigen and divides numerous times to create a population of cells with the same antigen specificity. This process ensures that there are sufficient numbers of B and T cells to recognize and respond to a specific pathogen that has invaded the body.

clone (5) A genetically identical DNA fragment, cell, or organism produced by a single cell or organism. [Gk., *klon,* twig]

clone library (5) A collection of cloned DNA fragments; also known as a gene library.

cloning (5) The production of genetically identical cells, organisms, or DNA molecules.

closed circulatory system (21) A circulatory system in which blood is contained in vessels and is separate from the interstitial fluid that bathes cells.

code (5) In genetics, the base sequence of a gene.

codominance (7) The case in which the heterozygote displays characteristics of both alleles.

codons (5) Three-base sequences in mRNA that link with complementary tRNA molecules, which are attached to amino acids; a codon with yet another sequence ends the process of assembling a protein from amino acids.

coelom (25) (*pron.* SEE-lum) The body cavity; it forms from the mesoderm in embryonic development.

coevolution (15) The concurrent appearance and modification over time, through natural selection, of traits in interacting species that enable each species to become adapted to the other; an example is the 11-inch-long tongue of a moth that feeds from the 11-inch-long nectar tube of an orchid.

cohesion-tension mechanism (17) In vascular plants, the force driving fluid flow in the xylem; results from evaporation of water from leaves, which pulls water up from the roots.

collagen (20) A protein in the matrix of connective tissue, synthesized and secreted by connective tissue cells (fibroblasts).

collenchyma cell (17) A long, stringy cell with unevenly thickened cell walls that contributes to a plant's flexibility. Collenchyma cells are a type of ground tissue.

colon (22) See **large intestine.**

colonizers (15) Species introduced into an area that has been disturbed and is undergoing the process of either primary or secondary succession. The identity of a colonizing species varies, depending on the stage and type of succession.

color-blind (23) In humans, describes the inability to distinguish between colors that most individuals can see—most commonly, the inability to distinguish between the colors red and green; occurs mostly in males.

commensalism (15) A symbiotic relationship between species in which one benefits and the other neither benefits nor is harmed. [Lat., *com,* with + *mensa,* table]

communication (9) An action or signal on the part of one organism that alters the behavior of another organism.

community (in ecology) (15) The biotic environment; a geographic area defined as a loose assemblage of species with overlapping ranges.

competitive exclusion (15) The case in which two species battle for resources in the same niche until the more efficient of the two wins and the other is driven to extinction in that location.

competitive inhibitor (2) A chemical within a cell that binds to the active site of an enzyme, blocking substrate molecules from the site and thereby reducing the enzyme's ability to catalyze a reaction.

complement protein (26) A type of circulating, defensive protein that can create holes in the membranes of pathogens or destroy pathogens by sticking to them and forming a coating that enhances the ability of phagocytes to bind to and engulf them.

complementarity (6) The characteristic of double-stranded DNA that the base on one strand always has the same pairing partner, or complementary base, on the other strand.

complementary base (6) A base on a strand of double-stranded DNA that is a pairing partner to a base on the other strand: adenine (A) is the complementary base to thymine (T), and guanine (G) is the complementary base to cytosine (C).

complex carbohydrate (2) A carbohydrate that contains multiple simple carbohydrates linked together; examples are starch, which is the primary form of energy storage in plants, and glycogen, which is the primary form of short-term energy storage in animals.

composting (17) Deliberate mixing of decaying organic matter, from leaves, food scraps, and manure, used to provide nutrients to soil.

compound (2) A substance composed of atoms of different elements in specific ratios, held together by ionic bonds. [Lat., *componere,* to put together]

compound eye (23) A group of light-sensing cells found in many invertebrates, made up of dozens to thousands of separate light-sensing units, each with its own lens that focuses light onto about a dozen photoreceptors.

cone (23) In the retina, a highly light-sensitive cell type that enables color vision.

conformer (20) An organism that, for a given physiological variable, has no set point for the variable and allows it to fluctuate with external changes in the environment.

conjugation (13) The process by which a bacterium transfers a copy of some or all of its DNA to another bacterium, of the same or another species. [Lat., *coniugatio,* connection]

connective tissue (20) A type of animal tissue that consists of cells embedded in a large amount of extracellular material, called matrix, which together contribute to body structure and support; includes tendons, ligaments, fat, blood, bone, and cartilage.

connective tissue proper (20) A type of connective tissue, including fat tissue, tendons, and ligaments, that has a semi-fluid, flexible matrix and functions like packing material.

conservation biology (16) An interdisciplinary field, drawing on ecology, economics, psychology, sociology, and political science, that studies and devises ways of preserving and protecting biodiversity and other natural resources.

contact inhibition (3) The limiting factor of cell growth that occurs when normal cells come into contact; in cancer cells, contact inhibition does not take place and the cells continue to divide.

contraception (25) The attempt to prevent pregnancy by preventing ovulation, fertilization, or implantation. Also called *birth control.*

control group (1) In an experiment, the group of subjects not exposed to the treatment being studied but otherwise treated identically to the experimental group.

convergent evolution (8, 10) A process of natural selection in which features of organisms not closely related come to resemble each other as a consequence of similar selective forces. Many marsupial and placental species resemble each other as a result of convergent evolution. [Lat., *con-*, together with + *vergere*, turn + *evolvere*, to roll out]

coprophagy (22) A nutritional strategy, common in rabbits and rodents, in which animals consume some of their feces, thereby increasing their ability to extract energy from food by passing it through their digestive system twice.

copulation (25) The act of placing the male reproductive organ within the female's reproductive tract.

cork cell (17) A cell of the protective outer covering of some plants, containing a waxy substance impermeable to water and resistant to fire and decay.

coronary arteries (21) The blood vessels that deliver oxygen and nutrients to the heart.

corpus callosum (23) In the brain, the broad, thick band of neurons connecting the left hemisphere to the right hemisphere.

corpus luteum (25) A structure that develops from a follicle after ovulation; it secretes hormones to maintain pregnancy. [Lat., *corpus*, body + *luteum*, yellow]

cortex (17) In vascular plants, the ground tissue located between the epidermis and the xylem and phloem.

corticotropin (24) A hormone produced by the anterior pituitary in mammals that stimulates the adrenal glands to produce cortisol and other stress-related hormones. Also known as adrenocorticotropic hormone (ACTH).

cotyledon (17, 18) Part of the plant embryo within the seed; this structure usually becomes the first embryonic leaf or leaves of the plant. Also called *seed leaf.*

covalent bond (2) A strong bond formed when two atoms share electrons; the simplest example is the H_2 molecule, in which each of the two atoms in the molecule shares its lone electron with the other atom. [Lat., *con-*, together + *valere*, to be strong]

critical experiment (1) An experiment that makes it possible to determine decisively between alternative hypotheses.

cross (7) The breeding of organisms that differ in one or more traits.

crossing over (6) The exchange of some genetic material between a paternal homologous chromosome and a maternal homologous chromosome, leading to a chromosome carrying genetic material from each; also referred to as recombination.

cuticle (12, 17) A waxy layer produced by epidermal cells and found on leaves and shoots of terrestrial plants, protecting them from drying out. [Lat., *cuticula, dim.* of *cutis*, skin]

cytokine (26) A type of signaling protein secreted by cells of the immune system: the chief way in which cells of the specific and non-specific immunity systems communicate with one another.

cytokinesis (6) In the cell cycle, the stage following mitosis in which cytoplasm and organelles duplicate and are divided into approximately equal parts and the cell separates into two daughter cells. In meiosis, two diploid daughter cells are formed in cytokinesis following telophase I and four haploid daughter cells are formed in cytokinesis following telophase II. [Gk., *kytos*, container + *kinesis*, motion]

cytokinins (19) In plants, a group of hormones that stimulate cell division throughout the body and throughout the lifetime of the plant.

cytoplasm (3) The jelly-like fluid that fills the inside of the cell; in eukaryotes, the cytoplasm contains the organelles. [Gk., *kytos*, container + *plasma*, anything molded]

cytoskeleton (3) A network of protein structures in the cytoplasm of eukaryotes (and, to a lesser extent, prokaryotes) that serves as scaffolding, adding support and, in some cases, giving animal cells of different types their characteristic shapes. The cytoskeleton serves as tracks guiding the intercellular traffic flow and, because it is flexible and can generate force, gives cells some ability to control their movement.

cytotoxic T cell (26) A type of lymphocyte, acting in the cell-mediated response, that directly kills body cells infected with a pathogen.

D

daughter cells (6) Cells produced by the division of a parent cell.

decomposers (12, 15) Organisms, including bacteria, fungi, and detritivores, that break down and feed on once-living organisms.

decomposition (17) The process of breaking down organic material into the individual elements of which it is made.

demographic transition (14) A pattern of population growth characterized by the progression from high birth and death rates (slow growth) to high birth rates and low death rates (fast growth) to low birth and death rates (slow growth).

denaturation (2) The disruption of protein folding, in which secondary and tertiary structures are lost, caused by exposure to extreme conditions in the environment such as heat or extreme pH.

dendrite (20, 23) A branched projection from a neuron that receives signals from the external environment or from other neurons. [Gk., *dendron*, tree]

dendritic cell (26) A type of white blood cell that links the non-specific and specific divisions of the immune system by engulfing foreign matter and then presenting the digested remnants of the pathogen on its cell surface.

density-dependent factors (14) Limitations on a population's growth that are a consequence of population density.

density-independent factors (14) Limitations on a population's growth without regard to population size, such as floods, earthquakes, fires, and lightning.

deoxyribonucleic acid (DNA) (2, 5) A nucleic acid, DNA carries information about the production of particular proteins in the sequences of its nucleotide bases.

dependent variable (1) A measurable entity that is created by the process being observed and whose value cannot be controlled; generally represented on the *y*-axis in a graph and expected to change in response to a change in the independent variable.

dermal tissue (17) The outer covering that protects the surface of a plant.

desert (15) A type of terrestrial biome; a type of dry climate, with very little rainfall, in which water loss through evaporation exceeds water gain through precipitation; typically found at 30° north and south latitude.

desmosome (3) Irregularly spaced connections between adjacent animal cells that, in the manner of Velcro, hold cells together by attachments but are not water-tight. They provide mechanical strength and are found in muscle tissue and in much of the tissue that lines the cavities of animal bodies. [Gk., *desmos,* bond + *soma,* body]

detritivores (15) Organisms that break down and feed on once-living organic matter; this group includes scavengers such as vultures, worms, and a variety of arthropods. [Lat., *detritus,* worn out + *vorare,* to devour]

deuterostomes (11) Bilaterally symmetrical animals with defined tissues in which the gut develops from back to front; the anus forms first, and the second opening formed is the mouth of the adult animal. [Gk., *deuteros,* second + *stoma,* mouth]

diabetes (22) A condition in which an individual does not adequately regulate his or her blood sugar levels; usually results from insufficient insulin secretion from the pancreas in response to an increase in blood sugar, or inadequate response of the cells of the body to insulin in the bloodstream.

diaphragm (21) A large sheet of muscle that separates the chest cavity from the abdominal cavity, allowing for increased volume when contracted during inhalation. [Gk., *dia,* through + *phrasein,* to enclose]

diastolic pressure (21) The second blood pressure reading; a measure of the force that blood exerts on the artery walls while the heart is between beats.

differential reproductive success (8) The situation in which individuals have greater reproductive success than other individuals in a population; along with variation and heritability, differential reproductive success is one of the three conditions necessary for evolution by natural selection.

diffusion (3) Passive transport in which a particle (the solute) is dissolved in a gas or liquid (the solvent) and moves from an area of higher solute concentration to an area of lower solute concentration. [Lat., *diffundere,* to pour in different directions]

digestion (22) The physical and chemical breakdown of food into its fundamental macromolecular components for absorption or elimination.

diploid (6) Describes cells that have two copies of each chromosome (in many organisms, including humans, somatic cells are diploid). [Gk., *diplasiazein,* to double]

direct fitness (9) The total reproductive output of an individual.

directional selection (8) Selection that, for a given trait, increases fitness at one extreme of the phenotype and reduces fitness at the other, leading to an increase or decrease in the mean value of the trait.

disaccharides (2) Carbohydrates formed by the union of two simple sugars, such as sucrose (table sugar) and lactose (the sugar found in milk). [Gk., *di-,* two + *sakcharon,* sugar]

dispersers (15) Organisms able to move away from their original home.

disruptive selection (8) Selection that, for a given trait, increases fitness at both extremes of the phenotype distribution and reduces fitness at middle values.

DNA probe (5) A short sequence of radioactively tagged single-stranded DNA that contains part of the sequence of the gene of interest, used to locate that gene in a gene library. The probe binds to the complementary base pair on a gene in the library, which is identified by the radioactive tag on the probe.

domain (10) In modern classification, the highest level of the hierarchy; there are three domains, Bacteria, Archaea, and Eukarya.

dominant (7) Describes an allele that masks the phenotypic effect of the other, recessive, allele for a trait; the phenotype shows the effect of the dominant allele in both homozygous and heterozygous genotypes. [Lat., *dominari,* to rule]

dorsal hollow nerve cord (11) The central nervous system of vertebrates, consisting of the spinal cord and brain. [Lat., *dorsum,* back]

double-blind experimental design (1) An experimental design in which neither the subjects nor the experimenters know what treatment (if any) individual subjects are receiving.

double bond (2) The sharing of two electrons between two atoms; for example, the most common form of oxygen is the O_2 molecule, in which two electrons from each of the two atoms of oxygen are shared.

double fertilization (12, 18) In angiosperms, two sperm are released by a pollen grain: one fuses with an egg to form a zygote, and the other fuses with two nuclei, forming a triploid endosperm.

double helix (2) The spiraling ladder-like structure of DNA composed of two strands of nucleotides; the bases protruding from each strand like "half-rungs" meet in the center and bind to each other (via hydrogen bonds), holding the ladder together. [Gk., *heligmos,* wrapping]

E

ear canal (23) The channel from the outer ear to the middle ear that conducts sound waves.

eardrum (23) The thin membrane that divides the outer ear from the middle ear.

echolocation (23) The ability of some animals (including bats) to sense the location of objects by producing sounds and then detecting echoes bounced off the objects.

ecological footprint (14) A measure of the impact of an individual or population on the environment by calculation of the amount of resources—including land, food and water, and fuel—consumed.

ecology (14) The study of the interaction between organisms and their environments, at the level of individuals, populations, communities, and ecosystems. [Gk., *oikos,* home + *logos,* discourse]

ecosystem (15) A community of biological organisms and the non-living environmental components with which they interact.

ectoderm (25) The outermost embryonic cell layer during gastrulation; it eventually forms skin, hair, the nervous system, and the lining of the nose and mouth. [Gk., *ektos,* outside + *derma,* skin]

ectotherms (11, 20) Organisms that rely on the heat from an external source to raise their body temperature and seek the shade when the air is too warm. [Gk., *ektos,* outside + *thermē,* heat]

effector (20) A structure that can be triggered in response to a stimulus; aids in the maintenance of homeostasis by opposing or reducing changes in the internal environment in response to changes in the external environment.

effector cell (26) In the specific (adaptive) immunity system, a type of cell that recognizes an antigen and immediately takes some action that leads to its destruction. Plasma cells, which are antibody-secreting, modified B cells, are the effector cells of the cell-mediated response.

egg (25) See **ovum.**

El Niño (15) A sustained surface temperature change in the central Pacific Ocean that occurs every two to seven years; this event can start a chain reaction of unusual weather across the globe that can result in flooding, droughts, famine, and a variety of extreme climate disruptions. [Spanish, *the child;* a reference to the Christ child, because of the appearance of the phenomenon at Christmastime]

elastin (20) A protein in the matrix of connective tissue, synthesized and secreted by connective tissue cells (fibroblasts), that gives the tissue flexibility.

electromagnetic spectrum (4) The range of wavelengths that produce electromagnetic radiation, extending (in order of decreasing energy) from high-energy, short-wave, gamma rays and X rays, through ultraviolet light, visible light, and infrared light, to very long, low-energy, radio waves. [Lat., *specere*, to look at]

electron (2) A negatively charged particle that moves around the atomic nucleus.

electron transport chain (4) The path of high-energy electrons from one molecule within a membrane to another, coupled to the pumping of protons across the membrane, creating a concentration gradient that is used to make ATP; occurs in mitochondria and chloroplasts.

element (2) A pure substance that cannot be broken down chemically into any other substances; all atoms of an element have the same atomic number. [Lat., *elementum*, element, or first principle]

elimination (22) The last phase in the breakdown of food; the absorption of water, salts, and some vitamins in the large intestine, followed by defecation of remaining waste material.

embryo (25) The multicellular, developing, fertilized egg of a eukaryote. In humans, at about eight weeks following fertilization the embryo is called a fetus.

embryo sac (18) In flowering plants, the part of the female reproductive structure of a flower that contains an egg and is the site of fertilization.

empirical (1) Describes knowledge that is based on experience and observations that are rational, testable, and repeatable. [Gk., *empeiria*, experience]

endangered species (16) As defined by the Endangered Species Act, species in danger of extinction throughout all or a significant portion of their range.

Endangered Species Act (ESA) (16) A U.S. law that defines "endangered species" and is designed to protect those species from extinction.

endemic (16) Describes species peculiar to a particular region and not naturally found elsewhere. [Gk., *en*, in + *demos*, the people of a country]

endocrine cell (24) A hormone-secreting cell. Endocrine cells are part of the endocrine system.

endocrine disruptor (24) A chemical manufactured by humans that, when taken up by organisms, can mimic, block, or otherwise interfere with their hormones, leading to harmful effects.

endocrine gland (20, 24) A collection of epithelial cells that produces hormones and releases them into the bloodstream or other fluids of the body.

endocrine system (24) Organ system comprising glands and cells that secrete hormones, which are chemical messengers that act on target cells to regulate body functions and maintain homeostasis.

endocytosis (3) A cellular process in which large particles, solid or dissolved, outside the cell are surrounded by a fold of the plasma membrane, which pinches off, forming a vesicle, and the enclosed particle now moves into the cell. The three types of endocytosis are phagocytosis, pinocytosis, and receptor-mediated endocytosis. [Gk., *endon*, within + *kytos*, container]

endoderm (25) The innermost embryonic cell layer during gastrulation; it eventually forms the lining of the respiratory and digestive tracts, the liver, and the pancreas. [Gk., *endon*, within + *derma*, skin]

endomembrane system (3) A system of organelles (the rough endoplasmic reticulum, the smooth endoplasmic reticulum, and the Golgi apparatus) that surrounds the nucleus; it produces and modifies necessary molecules, breaks down toxic chemicals and cellular by-products, and is thus responsible for many of the fundamental functions of the cell. [Gk., *endon*, within + Lat., *membrana*, a thin skin]

endometrium (25) The lining of the uterus where a fertilized egg implants and is nourished.

endosperm (12, 18) Tissue of a mature seed that stores certain carbohydrates, proteins, and lipids that fuel the germination, growth, and development of the embryo and young seedling. [Gk., *endon*, within + *sperma*, seed]

endosymbiosis theory (3) Theory of the origin of eukaryotes that holds that, in the past, two different types of prokaryotes engaged in a close partnership and eventually one, capable of performing photosynthesis, was subsumed into the other, a larger prokaryote. The smaller prokaryote made some of its photosynthetic energy available to the host and, over time, the two became symbiotic and eventually became a single more complex organism in which the smaller prokaryote had evolved into the chloroplast of the new organism. A similar scenario can be developed for the evolution of mitochondria. [Gk., *endon*, within + *symbios*, living together]

endotherms (11, 20) Organisms that use the heat produced by their cellular respiration to raise and maintain their body temperature above air temperature. [Gk., *endon*, within + *thermē*, heat]

energy (4) The capacity to do work, which is the moving of matter against an opposing force. [Gk., *energeia*, activity]

energy pyramid (15) A diagram that illustrates the path of energy through the organisms of an ecosystem; each layer of the pyramid represents the biomass of a trophic level.

enzymatic protein (3) See **enzyme.**

enzyme (2, 3) A protein that initiates and accelerates a chemical reaction in a living organism; enzymatic proteins take part in chemical reactions on the inside and outside surfaces of the plasma membrane. [Gk., *en*, in + *zyme*, leaven]

epidermis (17) In plants, the layer of tightly packed, very thin cells that covers and protects roots, leaves, and stems.

epididymis (25) A tube in each testis where the sperm mature.

epithelial tissue (20) A thin tissue that covers and protects the surfaces of an animal's body. Also called *epithelium*.

epithelium (20) See **epithelial tissue.**

erythrocytes (21) See **red blood cells.**

esophagus (22) The passageway from the throat to the stomach through which food travels.

essential amino acid (22) An amino acid that is not made by the body and so must be consumed in food.

estrogen (24, 25) One of the primary female sex hormones; important in female development and the female reproductive cycle.

estuary (15) A tidal water passage, linked to the sea, in which salt water and fresh water mix; characterized by exceptionally high productivity. [Lat., *aestus*, tide]

ethanol (4) The end product of fermentation of yeast; the alcohol in beer, wine, and spirits. [contraction of the full chemical name, ethyl alcohol]

ethylene (19) In plants, a gas that functions as a hormone that speeds up fruit ripening.

eudicot (17) A large monophyletic subset of the dicots (plants in which two cotyledons form) and one of the two major groups of flowering plants (along with monocots).

ethylene (19) In plants, a gas that functions as a hormone that speeds up fruit ripening.

eudicot (17) A large monophyletic subset of the dicots (plants in which two cotyledons form) and one of the two major groups of flowering plants (along with monocots).

eukaryote (3) An organism composed of eukaryotic cells. [Gk., *eu,* good + *karyon,* nut, kernel]

eukaryotic cell (3) A cell with a membrane-surrounded nucleus containing DNA, membrane-surrounded organelles, and internal structures organized into compartments.

eutrophication (15) The process in which excess nutrients dissolved in a body of water lead to rapid growth of algae and bacteria, which consume much of the dissolved oxygen and, in time, can lead to large-scale die-offs. [Gk., *eu,* good + *trophē,* food]

evolution (8) A change in allele frequencies of a population. [Lat., *evolvere,* to roll out]

exocrine gland (20) A collection of epithelial cells that secretes products onto the surface of the epithelium.

exocytosis (3) A cellular process in which particles within the cell, solid or dissolved, are enclosed in a vesicle and transported to the plasma membrane, where the membrane of the vesicle merges with the plasma membrane and the material in the vesicle is expelled to the extracellular fluid for use throughout the body. [Gk., *ex,* out of + *kytos,* container]

exoskeleton (11) A rigid external covering such as is found in some invertebrates, including insects and crustaceans. [Gk., *ex,* out of]

exotic species (16) Species introduced by human activities to areas other than the species' native range.

experimental group (1) In an experiment, the group of subjects exposed to a particular treatment; also known as the treatment group.

exponential growth (14) Growth of a population at a rate that is proportional to its current size.

external fertilization (25) The process in which sperm and egg unite outside the bodies of the male and female.

extinction (10) The complete loss of all individuals in a species. [Lat., *extinguere,* to extinguish]

extracellular fluid (20) A body fluid that is outside the cells; as distinct from intracellular fluid. See also **blood; interstitial fluid.**

extremophiles (13) Bacteria and archaea that can live in extreme physical and chemical conditions. [Lat., *extremus,* outermost + Gk., *philios,* loving]

eye cup (23) A group of simple, light-sensing cells found in flatworms such as planaria.

F

facilitated diffusion (3) Diffusion of molecules through the phospholipid bilayer of the plasma membrane that takes place through a transport protein (a "carrier molecule") embedded in the membrane. Molecules that require the assistance of a carrier molecule are those that are too big to cross the membrane directly or are electrically charged and would be repelled by the middle layer of the membrane.

Fallopian tube (25) The tube that conveys eggs from an ovary to the uterus. Also called *oviduct.*

family (10) In the system developed by Carolus Linnaeus (1707–1778), a classification of organisms consisting of related genera.

fatty acid (2) A long hydrocarbon (a chain of carbon-hydrogen molecules); fatty acids form the tail region of triglyceride fat molecules.

female (9) In sexually reproducing organisms, a member of the sex that produces the larger gamete.

fermentation (4) The process by which glycolysis occurs in the absence of oxygen; the electron acceptor is pyruvate (in animals) or acetaldehyde (in yeast) rather than oxygen.

fertilization (6, 25) The fusion of two reproductive cells.

fetus (25) Developmental stage in humans, from the end of the embryonic period, approximately eight weeks after fertilization, until birth.

fever (26) An elevated body temperature in response to infection; enhances the immune response and slows the growth of pathogens.

fibrous roots (17) A root system in which numerous roots branch out directly from the plant stem; found primarily in monocots.

filament (12, 18) The supporting stalk of the anther of a stamen found in angiosperm flowers. [Lat., *filum,* thread]

filtrate (20) Fluid that accumulates in Bowman's capsule in the vertebrate kidney; it contains salts, sugars, amino acids, vitamins, and many other molecules, all at the same concentration as in the blood.

first law of thermodynamics (4) A physical law that states that energy cannot be created or destroyed; it can only change from one form to another.

fitness (8) A relative measure of the reproductive output of an individual with a given phenotype compared with the reproductive output of individuals with alternative phenotypes.

fixation (8) The point at which the frequency of an allele in a population is 100% and, therefore, there is no more variation in the population for this gene.

fixed action pattern (9) An innate sequence of behaviors, triggered under certain conditions, that requires no learning, does not vary, and once begun runs to completion; an example is egg-retrieval in geese.

flagellum (*pl.* **flagella**) (3) Long, thin, whip-like projection from the cell body of a prokaryote that aids in cell movement through the medium in which the organism lives; in animals, the only cell with a flagellum is the sperm cell. [Lat., *flagellum,* whip]

flatworms (11) Worms with flat bodies that are members of the phylum Platyhelminthes; characterized by well-defined head and tail regions, with some having clusters of light-sensitive cells for eyespots. Most are hermaphroditic and are protostomes that do not molt. Examples are tapeworms and flukes.

fleshy fruit (12) A fruit that consists of the ovary and some additional parts of the flower; when fleshy fruits, an attractive food, are eaten by animals, the seeds may be widely dispersed.

flower (12) The part of an angiosperm that contains the reproductive structures; consists of a supporting stem with modified leaves (the petals and sepals) and usually contains both male and female reproductive structures.

fluid mosaic (3) A term that describes the structure of the plasma membrane, which is made up of several different types of molecules, many of which are not fixed in place but float, held in proper orientation by hydrophilic and hydrophobic forces.

fMRI scan (23) Functional magnetic resonance imaging scan; a brain imaging technology. A giant magnet detects the relative amounts of oxygenated and deoxygenated blood in different parts of the brain, which vary with brain activity.

follicle (25) In an ovary, the small structure in which an egg forms.

follicle-stimulating hormone (FSH) (24, 25) A hormone that stimulates the production of eggs.

follicular phase (25) The first half of the reproductive cycle in women, culminating in ovulation.

food chain (15) The path of energy flow from primary producers to tertiary consumers.

food web (15) A more precisely described path of energy flow from primary producers to tertiary consumers than the food chain, reflecting the fact that many organisms are omnivores and occupy more than one position in the chain.

forebrain (23) The largest region of the vertebrate brain; includes two control and relay structures, the thalamus and hypothalamus, and the cerebrum.

fossil (8) The remains of an organism, usually its hard parts such as shell, bones, or teeth, which have been naturally preserved; also, traces of such an organism, such as footprints. [Lat., *fossilis,* that which is dug up]

fossil fuels (4) Fuels produced from the decayed remains of ancient plants and animals; include oil, natural gas, and coal.

founder effect (8) A phenomenon by which genetic drift can occur; the isolation of a small subgroup of a larger population which can lead to changes in the allele frequencies of a population because all the descendants of the smaller group will reflect the allele frequencies of the subgroup, which may be different from those of the larger source population.

fruit (18) The mature ovary of a flower that houses seeds for dispersal. See also **fleshy fruit.**

fundamental niche (15) The full range of environmental conditions under which an organism can live.

G

gamete (6) Cell (often haploid) that will combine at fertilization to produce offspring; also called a *reproductive cell.* [Gk., *gamete,* wife]

gametophyte (12) The structure in land plants and some algae that produces gametes (sperm and eggs); the haploid life stage of plants and some algae, which may be either male (producing sperm) or female (producing eggs). [Gk., *gamete,* wife + *phytas,* plant]

gap junction (3) A junction between adjacent animal cells in the form of a pore in each of the plasma membranes surrounded by a protein that links the two cells and acts like a channel between them, allowing materials to pass between the cells.

gastropods (11) Mollusks that are members of the class Gastropoda; most have a single shell, a muscular foot for locomotion, and a radula used for scraping food from surfaces; examples are snails and slugs. [Gk., *gaster,* belly + *pous,* foot]

gastrula (25) The mass of cells, made up of three layers, formed during the gastrulation phase of embryonic development.

gastrulation (25) The second phase of embryonic development in which cells form distinct layers.

gene (5) The basic unit of heredity; a sequence of DNA nucleotides on a chromosome that carries the information necessary for making a functional product, usually a protein or an RNA molecule. [Gk., *genos,* race, descent]

gene expression (5) The process by which information in a gene's sequence is used to synthesize a gene product (commonly a protein, but also RNA).

gene flow (8) A change in the allele frequencies of a population due to movement of some individuals of a species from one population to another, changing the allele frequencies of the population they join; also known as migration.

gene library (5) A collection of cloned DNA fragments; also known as a clone library.

gene regulation (5) The processes by which cells "turn on" or "turn off" genes, influencing the amount of gene products formed.

gene therapy (5) The process of inserting, altering, or deleting one or more of the genes in an individual's cells to correct defective versions of the gene(s).

genetic drift (8) A random change in allele frequencies over successive generations; a cause of evolution.

genetic engineering (5) The manipulation of an organism's genetic material by adding, deleting, or transplanting genes from one organism to another.

genome (5) The full set of DNA present in an individual organism; also can refer to the full set of DNA present in a species.

genotype (5, 7) The genes that an organism carries for a particular trait; also, collectively, an organism's genetic composition. [Gk., *genos,* race, descent + *typos,* impression, engraving]

genus (*pl.* **genera**) (10) In the system developed by Carolus Linnaeus (1707–1778), a classification of organisms consisting of closely related species. [Lat., *genus,* race, family, origin]

germ layers (25) The three distinct layers of cells formed during gastrulation.

germinate (18) In plant spores or seeds, to begin growing after a period of dormancy.

gibberellins (19) In plants, a large group of hormones that regulate a plant's growth processes, primarily by stimulating cell division and cell elongation.

gills (21) Organs in fishes and other aquatic animals in which gases are exchanged between water and blood capillaries.

gland (20) A collection of epithelial cells that produces secretions for use elsewhere in the body.

glial cells (20, 23) Cells of nervous tissue that support and provide nutrients to neurons. Also called *neuroglia.*

glomerulus (20) The blood-filtering unit of the nephron; a mass of capillaries, surrounded by Bowman's capsule and connected to a single, long, urine-collecting tube that excretes its filtered fluid into a collecting duct.

glucagon (24) A hormone produced by the pancreas and secreted in response to a low blood sugar level; has the reverse effect of insulin, causing the liver to convert stored glycogen into glucose, which is released into the bloodstream.

glycemic index (22) A measure of the extent to which foods cause a surge in blood sugar and subsequent release of insulin.

glycerol (2, 3) A small molecule that forms the head region of a triglyceride fat molecule. [Gk., *glykys,* sweet + *-ol,* chemical suffix for an alcohol]

glycogen (2) A complex carbohydrate consisting of stored glucose molecules linked to form a large web, which breaks down to release glucose when it is needed for energy. [Gk., *glykys,* sweet + Gk., *genos,* race, descent]

glycolysis (4) In all organisms, the first step in cellular respiration, in which one molecule of glucose is broken into two molecules of pyruvate. For some organisms, glycolysis is the only means of extracting energy from food; for others, including most plants and animals, it is followed by the Krebs cycle and the electron transport chain. [Gk., *glykys,* sweet + *lysis,* releasing]

Golgi apparatus (3) (*pron.* GOHL-jee) An organelle, part of the endomembrane system, structurally like a flattened stack of unconnected membranes, each known as a Golgi body. The Golgi apparatus processes molecules synthesized in the cell and packages those molecules that are destined for use elsewhere in the body. [From the name of the discoverer, Camillo Golgi, 1843–1926]

gonads (6) The ovaries and testes in sexually reproducing animals. [Gk., *gonē,* offspring]

Gram stain (13) A test used by microbiologists in identifying an unknown bacterium; the dye that is used stains the layer of peptidoglycan outside the cell wall purple, but those bacteria in which the layer of peptidoglycan is covered by a membrane are not colored by the dye. Bacteria that take a Gram stain are known as Gram-positive bacteria, those that do not are known as Gram-negative bacteria.

gravitropism (19) Growth in plants in response to the pull of gravity. [Lat., *gravidus*, heavy + Gk., *tropikos*, turn]

ground tissue (17) Those parts of a plant that are not dermal tissue or vascular tissue; makes up the bulk of the plant and is where most of the plant's metabolic activities take place.

group selection (9) The process, extremely uncommon in nature, that brings about an increase in the frequency of alleles for traits (e.g., behaviors) that are beneficial to the persistence of the species or population while simultaneously being detrimental to the fitness of the individual possessing the trait (or engaging in the behavior).

growth hormone (24) A peptide hormone secreted by cells in the anterior pituitary. It is a major participant in control of several processes, including growth and metabolism.

growth rate (*r*) (14) The birth rate minus the death rate; the change in the number of individuals in a population per unit of time.

guard cell (17) One of the pair of plant cells that surround and control the opening of stomata, through which carbon dioxide and water can pass.

gymnosperms (12) Vascular plants that do not produce their seeds in a protective structure; seeds are usually found on the surface of the scales of a cone-like structure. The gymnosperms include conifers, cycads, gnetophytes, and ginkgo. [Gk., *gymnos*, naked + *sperma*, seed]

H

habitat (15) The physical environment of organisms, consisting of the chemical resources of the soil, water, and air, and physical conditions such as temperature, salinity, humidity, and energy sources. [Lat., *habitare*, to dwell or inhabit]

hair (11) Dead cells filled with the protein keratin that collectively serve as insulation covering the body or a part of the body; present in all mammals.

haploid (6) Describes cells that have a single copy of each chromosome (in many species, including humans, gametes are haploid). [Gk., *haploeides*, single]

hazard factor (14) An external force on a population that increases the risk of death.

heart (21) A muscular pump that, with each contraction, propels blood at high pressure to lungs, gills, or other body organs and tissues.

heart murmur (21) A medical condition–usually non-life-threatening–resulting from the incomplete closure of the atrioventricular or semilunar valves of the heart, leading to some blood flowing back through the valves, making a swishing noise.

heat stroke (20) A potentially life-threatening medical condition caused by extreme hyperthermia, characterized by an inability of the organism to maintain homeostasis.

heliotropism (19) In plants, growth in response to a light source, in which leaves and flowers orient themselves in relationship to the sun's rays. [Gk., *helios*, sun + *tropikos*, turn]

helper T cell (26) A type of lymphocyte that stimulates B cells to produce antibodies and cytotoxic T cells to kill infected cells.

hematocrit (21) The proportion of blood that is made up from red blood cells; determined by spinning a blood sample in a centrifuge.

hemoglobin (21) An oxygen-carrying protein molecule in red blood cells. [Gk., *haima*, blood + Lat., *globus*, ball]

hemolymph (21) The single fluid of an open circulatory system that surrounds all cells and transports nutrients, gases, and waste products.

herbivores (15, 22) Animals that eat plants; also known as primary consumers. [Lat., *herba*, grass + *vorare*, to devour]

heredity (7) The greater resemblance of offspring to parents than to other individuals in the population, a consequence of the passing of characteristics from parents to offspring through their genes. [Lat., *heres*, heir]

heritability (8) The transmission of traits from parents to offspring via genetic information; also known as inheritance.

hermaphrodite (6) An organism that produces both male and female gametes. [From the names of the Greek god Hermes and goddess Aphrodite]

heterotherm (20) An animal that has a body temperature that fluctuates as the environmental temperature changes. [Gk., *heteros*, other + *thermē*, heat]

heterozygous (7) Describes the genotype of a trait for which the two alleles an individual carries differ from each other. [Gk., *heteros*, other + *zeugos*, pair]

hibernate (20) To go into a state of reduced metabolic activity for days or weeks, during which the animal's body temperature can drop considerably.

hindbrain (23) The region of the vertebrate brain that includes the medulla, pons, and cerebellum.

hippocampus (23) Part of the brain's limbic system; functions in long-term memory formation.

histamine (26) A molecule released by mast cells that assists in the inflammatory response by causing non-injured blood vessels to dilate and become leaky.

histones (6) Proteins around which the long, linear strands of DNA are wrapped; serve to keep the DNA untangled and to enable an orderly, tight, and efficient packing of the DNA within the cell.

homeostasis (20) The body's use of physical and chemical processes to maintain a consistent internal environment. [Gk., *homos*, same + *stasis*, standing]

homeotherm (20) An animal that maintains a relatively constant body temperature. [Gk., *homos*, same + *thermē*, heat]

homologous feature (10) A feature inherited from a common ancestor. [Gk., *homologia*, agreement]

homologous pair (homologues) (6) The maternal and paternal copies of a chromosome. [Gk., *homologia*, agreement]

homologous structures (8) Body structures in different organisms that, although they may have been modified over time to serve different functions in different species, are due to inheritance from a common evolutionary ancestor.

homozygous (7) Describes the genotype of a trait for which the two alleles are the same. [Gk., *homos*, same + *zeugos*, pair]

honest signal (9) A signal, which cannot be faked, that is given when both the individual making the signal and the individual responding to it have the same interests; it carries the most accurate information about an individual or situation.

horizontal gene transfer (10) The transfer of genetic material directly from one individual to another, not necessarily related, individual; common among bacteria.

hormone (19, 24) A chemical signal that responds to environmental variables, found in both plants and animals. In plants, hormones are produced in various locations and may have their effect in that location or may be transported to another part of the plant to regulate the plant's activities. In animals, hormones are usually secreted by endocrine glands and are transported by the bloodstream to target cells as part of an internal communication and regulation system. [Gk., *hormaō*, that which sets in motion or urges forward]

host (13, 15) An organism in or on which a parasite lives.

human chorionic gonadotropin (hCG) (25) A hormone secreted by the embryo that keeps the lining of the uterus thickened for implantation.

human immunodeficiency virus (HIV) (13, 26) The virus responsible for AIDS, a deadly disease that destroys the human immune system. HIV is a retrovirus, an RNA-containing virus that is thought to have been introduced to humans from chimpanzees.

humus (17) (*pron.* HYOO-muss) The decomposing remains of plants and animals found in the uppermost region of soil; absorbs and releases water easily and releases many nutrients.

hybridization (10) The interbreeding of closely related species. [Lat., *hybrida,* animal produced by two different species]

hybrids (10) Offspring of individuals of two different species. [Lat., *hybrida,* animal produced by two different species]

hydrogen bond (2) A type of weak chemical bond formed between the slightly positively charged hydrogen atoms of one molecule and the slightly negatively charged atoms of another (often oxygen or nitrogen atoms). Hydrogen bonds are important in building multi-atom molecules, such as complex proteins, and are responsible for many of the unique and important features of water.

hydrophilic (2, 3) Attracted to water, as, for example, polar molecules that readily form hydrogen bonds with water. [Lat., *hydro-,* pertaining to water; Gk., *philios,* loving]

hydrophobic (2, 3) Repelled by water, as, for example, nonpolar molecules that tend to minimize contact with water. [Lat., *hydro-,* pertaining to water, Gk., *phobos,* fearing]

hydroponically grown plant (17) A plant grown without soil, but in water enriched with essential plant nutrients.

hypertension (21) A medical condition characterized by consistently high blood pressure in the arteries; a potential health hazard due to the loss of arterial elasticity, and the associated increase in the risks of heart attacks and strokes.

hyperthermia (20) A condition in which high external environmental temperature and humidity overwhelm the body's ability to dissipate heat, and body temperature becomes abnormally high; can lead to death. [Gk., *hyper,* above + *thermē,* heat]

hypertonic (3) Of two solutions, that with a higher concentration of solutes. [Gk., *hyper,* above + *tonos,* tension]

hyphae (*sing.* **hypha**) (12) (*pron.* HIGH-fee) Long strings of cells that make up the mycelium of a multicellular fungus. [Gk., *hypha,* web]

hypotension (21) The condition of consistently low blood pressure; symptoms may include dizziness, particularly just after a person stands up; does not typically have long-term health risks.

hypothalamus (23, 24) A structure on the underside of the brain that functions as a liaison between the nervous and endocrine systems and serves as one of the chief regulatory centers of the brain. It regulates many fundamental drives, including hunger and thirst, sexual activity, and maintenance of body temperature. It also controls the hormone secretions of the pituitary gland, located next to it. [Gk., *hypo,* under + *thalamos,* inner room]

hypothermia (20) A condition in which body temperature becomes abnormally low; can lead to death. [Gk., *hypo,* under + *thermē,* heat]

hypothesis (*pl.* **hypotheses**) (1) A proposed explanation for an observed phenomenon. [Gk., *hypothesis,* a proposal]

hypotonic (3) Of two solutions, that with a lower concentration of solutes. [Gk., *hypo,* under + *tonos,* tension]

I

immune system (26) Body system consisting of disease-fighting white blood cells and external barriers such as skin, providing protection against an enormous variety of pathogens, such as bacteria, fungi, some viruses, parasitic protists, and worms.

immunity (26) State of long-term protection against a specific disease-causing microorganism or virus.

inclusive fitness (9) The sum of an individual's indirect and direct fitness.

incomplete dominance (7) The case in which the heterozygote has a phenotype intermediate between those of the two homozygotes; an example is pink snapdragons, with an appearance intermediate between homozygous for white flowers and homozygous for red flowers.

independent variable (1) A measurable entity that is available at the start of a process being observed and whose value can be changed as required; generally represented on the *x*-axis in a graph.

indirect fitness (9) The reproductive output that an individual brings about through apparently altruistic behaviors toward genetic relatives.

infertility (25) The inability of a couple to get pregnant after one year of trying.

inflammatory response (26) The recruitment of phagocytes and other immune cells to assist with pathogen destruction, followed by tissue healing. Signs of the inflammatory response include redness, heat, swelling, and pain.

ingestion (22) The intake of food via the mouth, teeth, tongue, and esophagus.

inheritance (8) The transmission of traits from parents to offspring via genetic information; also known as heritability.

inhibitor (2) A chemical within a cell that binds to an enzyme or substrate molecule and in doing so reduces the enzyme's ability to catalyze a reaction.

innate behaviors (9) Behaviors that do not require environmental input for their development. These behaviors are present in all individuals in a population and do not vary much from one individual to another or over an individual's life span; also known as instincts. [Lat., *innatus,* inborn]

instincts (9) Behaviors that do not require environmental input for their development. Instincts are present in all individuals in a population and do not vary much from one individual to another or over an individual's life span; also known as innate behaviors. [Lat., *instinctus,* impelled]

insulin (24) A hormone produced in the pancreas and released in response to an increased concentration of blood glucose. Insulin in the bloodstream causes the liver, muscle, and other tissues to take up glucose.

integumentary system (26) Body system consisting of skin, sweat glands, oil glands, hair, and nails that protects the body from mechanical stress caused by external forces such as friction or pressure, sunlight, dehydration, and pathogens. [Lat., *integere,* to cover]

interferon (26) An important cytokine produced by cells infected by a virus; alerts other cells to turn on protective measures that help them resist infection.

intermediate filaments (3) One of three types of protein fibers (the others are microtubules and microfilaments) that make up the eukaryotic cytoskeleton, providing it with structure and shape; a durable, rope-like system of numerous different overlapping proteins.

intermembrane space (3) In a mitochondrion, the region between the inner and outer membranes. [Lat., *inter,* between + *membrana,* a thin skin]

internal fertilization (25) The process in which sperm are deposited in the female's reproductive tract and unite with one or more eggs.

interneuron (23) A type of neuron that acts as a middleman, integrating the signals coming in from sensory neurons and relaying them to a motor neuron; located in the brain and spinal cord.

interphase (6) In the cell cycle, the phase during which the cell grows and functions; during this phase, replication of DNA occurs in preparation for cell division. [Lat., *inter,* between + Gk., *phasis,* appearance]

interstitial fluid (20) An extracellular fluid that surrounds and bathes cells; consists mainly of water and also contains nutrients, raw materials, and waste products.

intron (5) A non-coding region of DNA.

invagination (3) The folding in of a membrane or layer of tissue so that an outer surface becomes an inner surface. [Lat., *in*, in + *vagina*, sheath]

invertebrates (11) Animals that do not have a backbone; although commonly used in organizing the animals, invertebrates are not a monophyletic group.

ion (2) An atom that carries an electrical charge, positive or negative, because it has either lost or gained an electron or electrons from its normal, stable configuration. [Gk., *ion*, going]

ionic bond (2) A bond created by the transfer of one or more electrons from one atom to another; the resulting atoms, now called ions, are charged oppositely and so attract each other to form a compound.

iris (23) The colored portion of the vertebrate eye with an opening, called the pupil, that controls the amount of light reaching the eye's interior.

isotonic (3) Refers to solutions with equal concentrations of solutes. [Gk., *isos*, equal to + *tonos*, tension]

isotopes (2) Variants of atoms that differ in the number of neutrons they possess; isotopes do not vary in charge, because neutrons have no electrical charge, but the atom's mass changes with the loss or addition of a particle in the nucleus.

K

karyotype (6) A visual display of an individual's full set of chromosomes. [Gk., *karyon*, nut or kernel + *typos*, impression, engraving]

keystone species (15) A species that has an unusually large influence on the presence or absence of numerous other species in a community.

kilocalorie (kcal) (22) One thousand calories (cal).

kin selection (9) "Kindness" toward close relatives, which may evolve as apparently altruistic behavior toward them, but which in fact is beneficial to the fitness of the individual performing the behavior.

kinetic energy (4) The energy of moving objects, such as legs pushing the pedals of a bicycle or wings beating against the air. [Gk., *kinesis*, motion]

kingdom (10) In the system developed by Carolus Linnaeus (1707–1778), one of the three categories—animal, plant, and mineral—into which all organisms and substances on earth were placed. In modern classification, there are six kingdoms: bacteria, archaea, protists, plants, animals, and fungi.

Krebs cycle (4) The second step of cellular respiration, in which energy is extracted from sugar molecules as additional molecules of ATP and NADH are formed. [From the name of the discoverer, Hans Adolf Krebs, 1900–1981]

L

La Niña (15) The counterpart of the El Niño phenomenon, characterized by the reverse effects, including a decrease in surface temperature and air pressure at the surface of the western Pacific Ocean; the resulting climate effects are approximately opposite to El Niño effects.

labor (25) During childbirth, a series of contractions of the uterus.

lactation (25) Milk production in the mammary glands.

lamella (*pl.* **lamellae**) (21) Disk-like structure in gills, with elaborately branched capillaries.

landscape conservation (16) The conservation of habitats and ecological processes, as well as species.

language (9, 23) A type of communication in which arbitrary symbols represent concepts and grammar; a system of rules dictates how the symbols can be manipulated to communicate and express ideas.

large intestine (22) The last part of the vertebrate digestive system, larger in diameter but shorter in length than the small intestine. It serves to absorb water, salts, and some vitamins and, in its final compartment (the rectum), to store the indigestible parts of consumed food and symbiotic bacteria (the feces), which can then be defecated. Also called *colon*.

larva (11) In complete metamorphosis, the first stage of insect development; the larva is hatched from the egg and eats to grow large enough to enter the pupa stage. The larva (for example, a caterpillar) looks completely different from the adult (a butterfly or moth). [Lat., *larva*, ghost]

lateral meristem (17) Growth region of a plant consisting of a layer of cells called cambium; division in this meristem causes a stem or root to become thicker, as opposed to longer.

leaf (17) The chief site of photosynthesis in most plants; leaves and stems form the shoot system.

learning (9) The alteration and modification of behavior over time in response to experience.

left hemisphere (23) The region of the brain that, in most (but not all) humans, specializes in language, logic, and mathematical skills.

leukocytes (21) See **white blood cells.**

lichen (12) Symbiotic partnership between fungi and chlorophyll-containing algae or cyanobacteria, or both.

life (10) A physical state characterized by the ability to replicate and the presence of metabolic activity.

life cycle (18) The series of stages experienced by an individual of a species throughout its development, each stage following the preceding stage, through reproduction.

life history (14) The vital statistics of a species, including age at first reproduction, probabilities of survival and reproduction at each age, litter size and frequency, and longevity.

life table (14) A table presenting data on the mortality rates within defined age ranges for a population; used to determine an individual's probability of dying during any particular year.

ligament (20) A connective tissue that binds bone to bone.

light energy (4) A type of kinetic energy made up of energy packets called photons, which are organized into waves.

lignin (17) A chemical in the cell walls of sclerenchyma cells of woody plants; it is indigestible by nearly all organisms and gives sclerenchyma cells their strength.

limbic system (23) The brain region that includes parts of the cerebral cortex and two structures deeper in the center of the brain, the hippocampus and the amygdala; responsible for many physiological drives and instincts.

linked genes (7) Genes that are close to each other on a chromosome and so are more likely than others to be inherited together.

lipid (2) One of four types of macromolecules, lipids are insoluble in water and greasy to the touch; they are important in energy storage and insulation (fats), membrane formation (phospholipids), and regulating growth and development (sterols). [Gk., *lipos*, fat]

liver (22) An organ in vertebrates and some other animals that is important in the detoxification of toxic molecules, storage of glycogen, and synthesis of bile, hormones, and digestive enzymes.

lobe-finned fishes (11) Fish species characterized by two pairs of sturdy lobe-shaped fins on the underside of the body.

logistic growth (14) A pattern of population growth in which initially exponential growth levels off as the environment's carrying capacity is approached.

long-term depression (23) Long-lasting decrease in the sensitivity of a neuron, resulting from a period of intense stimulation.

long-term potentiation (23) Long-lasting increase in the sensitivity of a neuron, resulting from a period of intense stimulation.

lungs (21) Internal organs in most land vertebrates, with highly branched, moist respiratory surfaces where gases are exchanged between air and blood.

luteal phase (25) The second half of the reproductive cycle in women in which the follicle cell that had surrounded the ovum develops into the corpus luteum; culminates in pregnancy or the sloughing off of the uterine lining.

luteinizing hormone (LH) (24) An animal hormone produced in the anterior pituitary gland; a surge in luteinizing hormone triggers ovulation in females and testosterone production in males.

lymph (21) A clear fluid formed from interstitial fluid as it is filtered into the lymphatic vessels in vertebrates.

lymph nodes (21) In the lymphatic system, patches of connective tissue filled with pathogen-fighting white blood cells, through which lymph passes.

lymphocyte (26) A type of white blood cell that carries out the response of the specific division of the immune system.

lysosome (3) A round, membrane-enclosed, enzyme- and acid-filled vesicle in the cell that digests and recycles cellular waste products and consumed material. [Gk., *lysis,* releasing + *soma,* body]

lysozyme (26) An enzyme produced by skin cells and in tears that kills bacteria by damaging their cell walls.

M

macroevolution (10) Large-scale evolutionary change involving the origins of new groups of organisms; the accumulated effect of microevolution over a long period of time. [Gk., *macros,* large + Lat., *evolvere,* to roll out]

macromolecule (2) A large molecule, made up of smaller building blocks or subunits; four types of biological macromolecules are carbohydrates, lipids, proteins, and nucleic acids. [Gk., *macros,* large + Lat., *dim.* of *moles,* mass]

macrophage (26) A type of large ("macro") white blood cell that resides in tissues and ingests small organisms and large debris such as dead cells; serving as an important link between the non-specific and specific divisions of the immune system.

male (9) In sexually reproducing organisms, a member of the sex that produces the smaller gamete.

mammary glands (11) Glands in all female mammals that produce milk for the nursing of young. [Lat., *mamma,* breast]

marsupials (11) Mammals in which, in most species, after a short period of embryonic life in the uterus, the young complete their development in a pouch in the female. [Gk., *marsipos,* pouch]

mass (2) The amount of matter in a given sample of a substance.

mass extinctions (10) Extinctions in which a large number of species become extinct in a short period of time, usually because of extraordinary and sudden environmental change. [Lat., *extinguere,* to extinguish]

mast cell (26) A type of white blood cell found in tissues that triggers the inflammatory response by releasing histamine.

mate guarding (9) Behavior by an individual that reduces the opportunity for that individual's mate to interact with other potential mates.

mating system (9) The pattern of mating behavior in a species, ranging from polyandry to monogamy to polygyny; mating systems are influenced by the relative amounts of parental investment by males and by females.

matrix (connective tissue) (20) A mass of non-living, extracellular material in which connective tissue cells are embedded.

matrix (mitochondrial) (3, 4) The space within the inner membrane, where the carriers NADH and FADH$_2$ begin the electron transport chain by carrying high-energy electrons to molecules embedded in the inner membrane.

maximum sustainable yield (14) The point at which the maximum number of individuals are removed from a population without impairing its growth rate; it occurs at half the carrying capacity.

mechanoreceptor (23) A type of sensory cell that responds to mechanical pressure.

medulla (23) The part of the vertebrate hindbrain that connects to the spinal cord; controls functions such as respiration, heart rate, and digestion.

meiosis (6) In sexually reproducing organisms, a process of nuclear division in the gonads that, along with cytokinesis, produces reproductive cells that have half as much genetic material as the parent cell and that all differ from each other genetically. [Gk., *meioun,* to lessen]

memory cells (26) Long-lived B cells or T cells, produced in the primary immune response to a particular antigen, that enable rapid response to subsequent exposure to the same antigen.

Mendel's law of independent assortment (7) Allele pairs for different genes separate independently in meiosis, so the inheritance of one trait generally does not influence the inheritance of another trait (the exception, unknown to Mendel, occurs with linked genes). [From the name of its discoverer, Gregor Mendel, 1822–1884]

Mendel's law of segregation (7) During the formation of gametes, the two alleles for a gene separate, so that half the gametes carry one allele, and half the gametes carry the other. [From the name of its discoverer, Gregor Mendel, 1822–1884]

menopause (25) The permanent cessation of ovulation and menstruation, typically beginning in the late forties to early fifties in humans, and characterized by a reduced production of estrogen and progesterone by the ovaries.

menstrual cycle (25) The cycle in which the uterus prepares for the implantation and nurturing of a fertilized egg, and sheds its lining if fertilization does not occur.

menstruation (25) The shedding of the uterine lining.

meristem (17, 18) Growth region of a plant, made up of undifferentiated cells that divide to form both additional undifferentiated cells and other cells that differentiate to form specific plant tissues.

mesoderm (25) The middle embryonic cell layer during gastrulation; it eventually forms the muscles and skeleton. [Gk., *mesos,* middle + *derma,* skin]

messenger RNA (mRNA) (5) The ribonucleic acid that "reads" the sequence for a gene in DNA and then moves from the nucleus to the cytoplasm, where the next stage of protein synthesis will take place.

metamorphosis (11) The rebuilding of molecules from the larva stage to the adult, resulting in a change of form. *Complete metamorphosis* is the division of an organism's life history into three completely different stages; *incomplete metamorphosis* is the pattern of growth and development in which an organism does not pass through separate, dramatically different life stages. [Gk., *metamorphoun,* to transform]

metaphase (6) The second phase of mitosis, in which the sister chromatids line up at the center of the cell; in meiosis, the homologues line up at the center of the cell in metaphase I and the sister chromatids line up in metaphase II. [Gk., *meta,* in the midst of + *phasis,* appearance]

microbe (10, 13) A microscopic organism; not a monophyletic group, since it includes protists, archaea, and bacteria. [Gk., *micros,* small + *bios,* life]

microevolution (10) A slight change in allele frequencies in a population over one or a few generations. [Gk., *micros,* small + Lat., *evolvere,* to roll out]

microfilaments (3) One of three types of protein fibers (the others are intermediate filaments and microtubules) that make up the eukaryotic cytoskeleton, providing it with structure and shape, These are the thinnest elements in the cytoskeleton; long, solid, rod-like fibers that help generate forces, including those important in cell contraction and cell division.

microsphere (10) A membrane-enclosed, small, spherical unit containing a self-replicating molecule and carrying information, although no genetic material. Microspheres may have been an important stage in the development of life. [Gk., *micros,* small + *sphaira,* ball]

microtubules (3) One of three types of protein fibers (the others are intermediate filaments and microfilaments) that make up the eukaryotic cytoskeleton, providing it with structure and shape, These are the thickest elements in the cytoskeleton; they resemble rigid, hollow tubes, functioning as tracks to which molecules and organelles within the cell may attach and be moved along; also help pull chromosomes apart during cell division.

midbrain (23) Part of the brainstem; a sensory integration and relay center through which most of the sensory information and motor neuron connections entering and leaving the brain pass.

migration (8) A change in the allele frequencies of a population due to the movement of some individuals from one population to another; an agent of evolutionary change caused by the movement of individuals into or out of a population. [Lat., *migrare,* to move from place to place]

mimicry (15) The evolution of an organism to resemble another organism or object in its environment to help conceal itself from predators. [Gk., *mimesis,* imitation]

mineral (22) A chemical element other than those commonly found in organic molecules (carbon, hydrogen, oxygen, and nitrogen); some minerals are required in the diet, in small amounts.

mitochondrial matrix (4) See **matrix (mitochondrial).**

mitochondrion (*pl.* **mitochondria**) (3) The organelle in eukaryotic cells that converts the energy stored in food in the chemical bonds of carbohydrate, fat, and protein molecules into a form usable by the cell for all its functions and activities. [Gk., *mitos,* thread + *chondros,* cartilage]

mitosis (6) The division of a nucleus into two genetically identical nuclei that, along with cytokinesis, leads to the formation of two identical daughter cells. [Gk., *mitos,* thread + *phasis,* appearance]

mitotic phase (M phase) (6) The phase of the cell cycle during which first the genetic material and nucleus, and then the rest of the cellular contents, divide.

molecule (2) A group of atoms held together by covalent bonds. [Lat., *dim.* of *moles,* mass]

monocot (17) One of the two major groups of flowering plants; monocot seedlings have one cotyledon (seed leaf).

monogamy (9) A mating system in which most individuals mate and remain with just one other individual. [Gk., *monos,* single + *gamete,* wife]

monophyletic (10) A group containing a common ancestor and all of its descendants. [Gk., *monos,* single + *phylon,* race, tribe, class]

monosaccharides (2) The simplest carbohydrates and the building blocks of more complex carbohydrates; they cannot be broken down into other monosaccharides; examples are glucose, fructose, and galactose; also known as simple sugars. [Gk., *monos,* single + *sakcharon,* sugar]

monotremes (11) Present-day mammals that retain the ancestral condition of laying eggs. Monotremes are so called because they have a single duct, the cloaca, into which the reproductive system, the urinary system, and the digestive system (for defecation) open. [Gk., *monos,* single + *trema,* hole]

mood (24) A relatively long-lasting emotional state (shorter-lasting than a person's temperament, but longer-lasting and less specific than a single emotion).

morphological species concept (10) A concept that defines species on the basis of physical features such as body size and shape. [Gk., *morphē,* shape]

motor neuron (23) A type of neuron that stimulates action by conveying signals to muscles or glands and initiating a body's response to stimuli.

multiple allelism (7) The case in which a single gene has more than two possible alleles.

multiple sclerosis (MS) (26) An autoimmune disease in which the body attacks the myelin sheath surrounding nerve fibers of the brain and spinal cord, causing blurred vision, weakness in arms and legs, and trouble with balance.

muscle fiber (20) An individual muscle cell; typically contains multiple nuclei.

muscle tissue (20) A body tissue consisting of contractile cells (muscle fibers) that generate force and can facilitate movement.

mutation (5, 8) An alteration in the base-pair sequence of an individual's DNA; may arise spontaneously or following exposure to a mutagen. [Lat., *mutare,* to change]

mutualism (15) A symbiotic relationship in which both species benefit and neither is harmed. [Lat., *mutuus,* reciprocal]

mycelium (12) A mass of interconnecting hyphae that make up the structure of a multicellular fungus. [Gk., *mykes,* fungus]

mycorrhizae (12, 17) (*pron.* my-ko-RYE-zay) Root fungi, that is, symbiotic associations between roots and fungi in which fungal structures are closely associated with fine rootlets and root hairs. [Gk., *mykes,* fungus + *rhiza,* root]

myelin sheath (23) Fatty coating insulating the axon.

myofibril (23) A cylindrical organelle within muscle cells that can contract; contains repeating units, called sarcomeres, in which the contraction takes place.

myosin (23) A protein of muscle tissue; makes up the thick filaments.

N

NADPH (4) A molecule (nicotinamide adenine dinucleotide phosphate) that is a high-energy electron carrier involved in photosynthesis, which stores energy by accepting high-energy protons. It is formed when the electrons released from the splitting of water are passed to $NADP^+$.

natural killer (NK) cell (26) A type of white blood cell that kills body cells infected by a pathogen.

natural selection (8) A mechanism of evolution that occurs when there is heritable variation for a trait and individuals with one version of the trait have greater reproductive success than individuals with a different version of that trait.

nectar (18) A solution produced by a flower, rich in sugars and amino acids, that can serve as an attractant to animal pollinators.

negative feedback (20) A control mechanism in which sensors detect changes in the internal environment and trigger effectors to counteract the change; one of the chief strategies by which organisms maintain homeostasis.

nephron (20) The chief functional unit in the vertebrate kidney, consisting of a tubule and a mass of blood vessels that work together to accomplish the tasks of filtration, reabsorption, and excretion.

nerve (23) A group of neurons bundled together with connective tissue.

nervous system (23) Network of cells (neurons), present in all multicellular animals other than sponges, that collects information about the organism's internal and external environments, processes that information, and sends signals to muscles and glands in response to the information.

nervous tissue (20) A body tissue that specializes in storing and transmitting information.

neural tube (25) A long hollow tube formed during neurulation that ultimately develops into the nervous system.

neuroglia (20) See **glial cells.**

neuron (20, 23) The "excitable" cell within the nervous system that receives and transmits signals; made up of three distinctive elements: dendrites, a cell body, and an axon.

neurotransmitter (23) A chemical of the nervous system that transmits signals to adjacent cells.

neurulation (25) During embryonic development, the process of the folding in of the ectoderm for the entire length of the embryo, first forming a groove and then becoming the neural tube.

neutron (2) An electrically neutral particle in the atomic nucleus. [Lat., *neutro,* in neither direction]

neutrophil (26) A type of white blood cell that circulates in the blood and ingests small organisms, primarily bacteria. Neutrophils make up 50% to 70% of all white blood cells.

niche (15) The way an organism utilizes the resources of its environment, including the space it requires, the food it consumes, and timing of reproduction.

nitrogen fixation (17) Process by which the bonds between paired nitrogen atoms in molecules of nitrogen (N_2) are broken and the individual atoms are converted into a form, such as ammonia, that is usable by plants.

node (phylogeny) (10) The point on an evolutionary tree at which species diverge from a common ancestor. [Lat., *nodus,* knot]

node (plant structure) (17) A small lump of tissue on a stem from which a leaf, flower, cone, or additional stem (or branch) may grow.

nodule (17) In plant roots, a round lump containing plant cells and nitrogen-fixing bacteria.

noncompetitive inhibitor (2) A chemical within a cell that binds to part of an enzyme away from the active site, but alters the enzyme's shape so as to alter the active site, thereby reducing or blocking the enzyme's ability to bind with substrate.

nondisjunction (6) The unequal distribution of chromosomes during cell division; can lead to Down syndrome and other disorders caused by an individual's possession of too few or too many chromosomes.

non-essential amino acids (22) Amino acids that can be produced by the body and so are not needed in the diet.

nonpolar (3) Electrically uncharged.

non-specific immunity (26) Division of the immune system that, through various types of non-specific immune cells, rapidly recognizes as pathogens substances that breach external barriers and are not part of the body's own tissue, but does not distinguish between specific pathogens. Also called the *innate system* (meaning "inborn"), because it is functioning at birth and does not require any previous exposure to pathogens to act.

non-vascular plants (12) Plants that do not have vessels to transport water and dissolved nutrients, but instead rely on diffusion; bryophytes are non-vascular plants. [Lat., *vasculum, dim.* of *vas,* vessel]

notochord (11, 25) A rod of tissue from head to tail that stiffens the body when muscles contract during locomotion. Primitive chordates retain the notochord throughout life, but in advanced chordates it is present only in early embryos and is replaced by the vertebral column. [Gk., *notos,* back + Lat., *chorda,* cord]

nuclear membrane (3) A membrane that surrounds the nucleus of a cell, separating it from the cytoplasm, consisting of two bilayers and perforated by pores enclosed in embedded proteins that allow the passage of large molecules from nucleus to cytoplasm and from cytoplasm to nucleus; also called the *nuclear envelope.*

nucleic acid (2, 5) One of the four types of biological macromolecules; the nucleic acids DNA and RNA store genetic information in unique sequences of nucleotides.

nucleolus (3) An area near the center of the nucleus where subunits of the ribosomes are assembled. [Lat., *nucleolus, dim.* of *nucleus,* kernel, small nut]

nucleotide (2, 5) A molecule containing a phosphate group, a sugar molecule, and a nitrogen-containing molecule. Nucleotides are the individual units that together, in a unique sequence, constitute a nucleic acid.

nucleus (cell biology) (3) A membrane-enclosed structure in eukaryotic cells that contains the organism's genetic information as linear strands of DNA in the form of chromosomes. [Lat., *nucleus, dim.* of *nux,* nut]

nucleus (chemistry) (2) The central and most massive part of an atom, usually made up of two types of particles, protons and neutrons, which move about the nucleus. [Lat., *nucleus, dim.* of *nux,* nut]

null hypothesis (1) A hypothesis that proposes a lack of relationship between two factors. [Lat., *nullus,* none]

nuptial gift (9) A food item or other item presented to a potential mate as part of courtship. [Lat., *nuptialis,* of marriage]

nutrient (22) A substance used for energy, raw materials, and maintenance of the body's systems.

O

omnivores (15, 22) Animals that eat both plants and other animals and thus can occupy more than one position in the food chain. [Lat., *omnis,* all + *vorare,* to devour]

oogenesis (25) The process of egg production in females.

oogonium (*pl.* **oogonia**) (25) Diploid cell in the ovary that multiplies by mitosis. Each oogonium begins meiosis but pauses at prophase I, at which point the cell is called a primary oocyte.

open circulatory system (21) A circulatory system in which a single fluid, hemolymph, circulates to transport nutrients, gases, and waste products and also surrounds all cells.

operon (5) A group of several genes, along with the elements that control their expression as a unit, all within one section of DNA.

optic nerve (23) The nerve that transports visual information from the retina of the eye to the thalamus and other parts of the brain.

order (10) In the system developed by Carolus Linnaeus (1707–1778), a classification of organisms consisting of related families.

organ (20) A structure that serves specialized functions and contains several types of tissue.

organ system (20) A group of organs that work together to accomplish physiological functions.

organelles (3) Specialized structures in the cytoplasm of eukaryotic cells with specific functions, such as the rough and smooth endoplasmic reticulum, Golgi apparatus, and mitochondria. [Gk., *organon,* tool]

osmoconformer (20) An organism that regulates water loss and gain by maintaining the solute concentration of its body fluids at the solute concentration of its environment.

osmoregulation (20) The regulation of water content and of the concentrations of dissolved solutes that influence osmosis; an important component of homeostasis in animals.

osmoregulator (20) An organism that regulates water loss and gain by maintaining the solute concentration of its body fluids within a narrow range that differs from that of its environment.

osmosis (3) A type of passive transport in which water molecules move across a membrane, such as the plasma membrane of a cell; the direction of osmosis is determined by the relative concentrations of all solutes on either side of the membrane. [Gk., *osmos*, thrust]

ovarian cycle (25) The cycle in which a woman's hormones regulate the timing and development of egg production.

ovary (12, 18, 25) An enclosed chamber at the base of the carpel of a flower that contains the ovules; the female gonad. [Lat., *ovum*, egg]

oviduct (25) See **Fallopian tube.**

oviparity (25) A reproductive strategy in which the fertilized egg moves outside the body for embryonic development.

ovoviviparity (25) A reproductive strategy in which most embryonic development takes place in the female's body until the egg hatches (or is released just before hatching).

ovulate (25) To release a secondary oocyte from an ovarian follicle into a Fallopian tube, from where it moves to the uterus.

ovule (12, 18) The structure within the ovary of flowering plants that gives rise to female egg cells. [Lat., *ovum*, egg]

ovum (*pl.* **ova**) (25) A female gamete. Also called **egg.**

Oxygen Revolution (13) The accumulation in the atmosphere of oxygen released by cyanobacteria and other photosynthetic organisms.

oxytocin (24) A peptide hormone produced in neurons within the hypothalamus and released by the posterior pituitary that influences people's trust in others, increases the propensity to form social attachments, directs the ejection (or "let-down") of milk for nursing babies, and stimulates muscular contractions in the uterus during childbirth.

P

pair bond (9) A bond between an individual male and female in which they spend a high proportion of their time together, often over many years, sharing a nest or other refuge and contributing equally to the care of offspring.

pancreas (22, 24) An organ that secretes digestive juice into the small intestine and hormones into the blood.

paracrine regulator (24) A chemical that is secreted from a cell and acts locally. Paracrine regulators generally diffuse through intracellular fluid from the tissue in which they are produced to nearby tissue, binding to receptors of neighboring cells and influencing their activity.

parasite (13, 15) An organism that lives in or on another organism, the host, and damages it. [Gk., *para*, beside + *sitos*, grain, food]

parasitism (15) A symbiotic relationship in which one organism (the parasite) benefits while the other (the host) is harmed.

parasympathetic nervous system (23) One of two components to the autonomic nervous system (the sympathetic nervous system is the other); responsible for unconsciously controlling activities related to digesting food and eliminating waste, tending to slow the heart and breathing rates.

parathyroid glands (24) Endocrine glands embedded in the surface of the thyroid gland that produce parathyroid hormone, which plays a central role in regulating calcium levels in adults. [Gk. *para*, beside + *thyra*, door]

parenchyma cell (17) A type of cell that carries out most of a plant's metabolic activities. Parenchyma cells are a type of ground tissue.

parent cells (6) Cells that divide to form daughter cells, which are genetically identical to the parent cell.

parthenogenesis (25) The asexual reproductive process in which a female's egg develops into a new organism without fertilization by a sperm cell.

passive transport (3) Molecular movement that occurs spontaneously, without the input of energy; the two types of passive transport are diffusion and osmosis.

paternity uncertainty (9) Describes the fact that among species with internal fertilization in the female, a male cannot be 100% certain that any offspring a female produces are his. [Lat., *pater,* father]

pathogen (21, 26) A disease-causing substance or organism, such as infectious bacteria, viruses, and fungi. Pathogens are sometimes referred to as "germs."

pathogenic (13) Disease-causing.

PCBs (polychlorinated biphenyls) (24) Chemicals used in industrial coolants and lubricants; known endocrine disruptors.

pedigree (7) In genetics, a type of family tree that maps the occurrence of a trait in a family, often over many generations.

penis (25) External male reproductive structure.

pepsin (22) A protein-dismantling enzyme produced by cells in the stomach lining.

peptide bond (2) A bond in which the amino group of one amino acid is bonded to the carboxyl group of another; two amino acids so joined form a dipeptide, several amino acids so joined form a polypeptide. [Gk., *peptikos,* able to digest]

peptidoglycan (13) A glycoprotein that forms a thick layer on the outside of the cell wall of a bacterium; in some bacteria, the layer of peptidoglycan is covered by a membrane and so is not colored by a Gram stain.

periodic table (2) A tabular display in which all the known chemical elements are arranged in the order of their atomic number and on the basis of other aspects of their atomic structures.

peripheral nervous system (PNS) (20, 23) The part of an organism's nervous system that transmits information to and from the central nervous system; includes the sensory and motor neurons.

peristalsis (22) Waves of smooth muscle contractions that propel food along the digestive tract. [Gk., *peri,* around + *stellein,* to place]

permafrost (19) Soil that remains frozen for two or more years, so that plants' root growth is limited and any water that is present from precipitation or melting cannot drain well.

petal (18) One of the usually brightly colored leaf-like structures of a flower, located inside the ring of sepals; the color, shape, and size vary greatly among the flowering plants. The petals help to attract animal pollinators, with different colors generally appealing to different pollinator species.

pH (2) A logarithmic scale that measures the concentration of hydrogen ions (H^+) in a solution, with decreasing values indicating increasing acidity. Water, in which the concentration of hydrogen ions (H^+) equals the concentration of hydroxyl ions (OH^-), has pH = 7, the midpoint of the scale. [Abbreviation for "power of hydrogen"]

phagocyte (26) A type of white blood cell that can engulf, ingest, kill, and break down foreign pathogens and particles. [Gk., *phagein,* to eat + *kytos,* container]

phagocytosis (3, 13) One of the three types of endocytosis, in which relatively large solid particles are engulfed by the plasma membrane, a vesicle is formed, and the particle is moved into the cell.

pharyngeal slits (11) Slits in the pharyngeal region, between the back of the mouth and the top of the throat, for the passage of water for breathing and feeding. [Gk., *pharynx,* throat]

phenotype (5, 7) The manifested structure, function, and behaviors of an individual; the expression of the genotype of an organism. [Gk., *phainein,* to cause to appear + *typos* impression, engraving]

pheromones (9, 24, 25) Molecules released by an individual into the environment that trigger behavioral or physiological responses in other individuals. [Gk., *pherein,* to carry]

phloem (17) (*pron.* FLOW-uhm) In vascular plants, the tissue that conducts nutrients—sugar, in particular—throughout the plant.

phospholipid (2, 3) A lipid that is the major component of the plasma membrane; phospholipids are structurally similar to fats, but contain a phosphorus atom and have two, not three, fatty acid chains.

phospholipid bilayer (3) The structure of the plasma membrane; two layers of phospholipids, arranged tail to tail (the tails are hydrophobic and so avoid contact with water), with the hydrophilic head regions facing the watery extracellular fluid and intracellular fluid.

photoautotroph (13) Chlorophyll-containing bacteria, or other organisms, that use the energy from sunlight to convert carbon dioxide to glucose by photosynthesis. [Gk., *phos,* light + *autos,* self + *trophē,* food]

photon (4) The elementary particle that carries the energy of electromagnetic radiation of all wavelengths. [Gk., *phos,* light]

photoperiodism (19) A plant's response to the cycling of light and dark in a day; regulates flowering time and numerous other responses to seasonal changes.

photoreceptor cell (23) A type of cell that detects the presence of light.

photosynthesis (4) The process by which some organisms are able to capture energy from the sun and store it in the chemical bonds of sugars and other molecules that they produce. [Gk., *phos,* light + *syn,* together with + *tithenai,* to place or put]

photosystems (4) Two arrangements of light-absorbing pigments, including chlorophyll, within the chloroplast that capture energy from the sun and transform it first into the energy of excited electrons and ultimately into ATP and high-energy electron carriers such as NADPH. [Gk., *phos,* light + *systema,* a whole compounded of parts]

phototropism (19) A growth response in plants, toward or away from a light source. [Gk., *phos,* light + *tropikos,* turn]

phthalates (24) Chemicals commonly found in soft toys and cosmetics; known endocrine disruptors.

phylogenetic tree (5) A grouping of organisms in a hierarchical system that reflects the evolutionary history and relatedness of the organisms. [Gk., *phylon,* race, tribe, class + Lat., *genus,* race, family, origin]

phylogeny (10) The evolutionary history of organisms.

phylum (10) In the system developed by Carolus Linnaeus (1707–1778), a classification of organisms consisting of related classes. [Gk., *phylon,* race, tribe, class]

physical barriers (immune system) (26) The first defense against pathogens, to keep them out of the body; for example, skin acts as a nearly impenetrable barrier that keeps viruses and bacteria from entering the body, and various chemicals secreted by epithelial surfaces stop the growth of many pathogens. See also **integumentary system.**

physiology (2) The study of the functioning of living organisms and their parts, including the processes and systems necessary for growth, development, maintenance, and reproduction.

pigment (4) In photosynthesis, molecules that are able to absorb the energy of light of specific wavelengths, raising electrons to an excited state in the process. [Lat., *pigmentum,* paint]

pilus (*pl.* **pili**) (3) A thin, hair-like projection that helps a prokaryote attach to surfaces. [Lat., *pilus,* a single hair]

pineal gland (24) A gland (pea-sized in humans) located near the center of the brain in vertebrates; has neuron connections with the retina of the eye and controls secretion of the hormone melatonin, which affects circadian and seasonal cycles.

pinocytosis (3) One of the three types of endocytosis, in which dissolved particles and liquids are engulfed by the plasma membrane, a vesicle is formed, and the material is moved into the cell. The vesicles formed in pinocytosis are generally much smaller than those formed in phagocytosis. [Gk., *pinein,* to drink + *kytos,* container]

pith (17, 18) The ground tissue close to the center of a stem.

pituitary gland (24) An endocrine gland, consisting of anterior and posterior parts, attached to the hypothalamus by a thin stalk and regulated by secretions from the hypothalamus. See also **anterior pituitary; posterior pituitary.**

placebo (1) An inactive substance used in controlled experiments to test the effectiveness of another substance; the treatment group receives the substance being tested, the control group receives the placebo. [Lat., *placebo,* I shall please]

placebo effect (1) A frequently observed and poorly understood phenomenon in which there is a positive response to treatment with an inactive substance.

placenta (6, 25) The organ formed during pregnancy (and expelled at birth) that connects the developing embryo to the wall of the uterus and allows the transfer of gases, nutrients, and waste products between mother and fetus; the placenta is so called from its shape. [Lat., *placenta,* a flat cake]

placentals (11) Mammals in which the developing fetus takes its nourishment from the transfer of nutrients from the mother through the placenta, which also supplies respiratory gases and removes metabolic waste products. [Lat., *placenta,* a flat cake]

plants (12) Members of the kingdom Plantae; multicellular eukaryotes that have cell walls made up primarily of cellulose, contain true tissues, and produce their own food by photosynthesis. Plants are sessile, and most inhabit terrestrial environments.

plasma (21) The liquid part of blood that contains dissolved metabolites and wastes, salts and ions, proteins, vitamins, and other chemicals and transports them to the tissues where they are required.

plasma cell (26) A type of white blood cell (an effector B cell) that secretes antibodies as part of the specific immune system's response to a pathogen. Plasma cells can secrete hundreds to thousands of antibodies per second.

plasma membrane (3) A complex, thin, two-layered membrane that encloses the cytoplasm of the cell, holding the contents in place and regulating what enters and leaves the cell; also called the cell membrane. [Gk., *plasma,* anything molded]

plasmid (5, 13) A circular DNA molecule found outside the main chromosome in bacteria.

plasmodesma (*pl.* **plasmodesmata**) (3) In plants, microscopic tube-like channels connecting the cells and enabling communication and transport between them. [Gk., *plassein,* to mold + *desmos,* bond]

platelets (21) Cellular fragments, components of the blood, formed by the pinching off of fragments from large cells (megakaryocytes) in the bone marrow; they lack organelles but are filled with enzymes and chemicals important for blood clotting.

pleiotropy (7) A phenomenon in which an individual gene influences multiple traits. [Gk., *pleion,* more + *tropos,* turn]

point mutation (5) A mutation in which one base pair in DNA is replaced with another, or a base pair is either inserted or deleted.

polar (3) Having an electrical charge.

polar body (6, 25) One of the two cells formed when a primary oocyte divides; it gets almost no cytoplasm and eventually disintegrates.

pollen grain (12, 18) A structure that contains the male gametophyte of a seed plant. [Lat., *pollen,* fine dust]

pollen tube (18) A long, tube-like structure formed by the growth of a single cell of the pollen grain after germination; forms within the style of the female reproductive structure and carries the male gametes to the ovule.

pollination (12, 18) The transfer of pollen from the anther of one flower to the stigma of another flower. [Lat. pollen, *fine dust*]

polyandry (9) A polygamous mating system in which individual females mate with multiple males. [Gk., *polys,* many + *aner,* husband]

polygamy (9) A mating system in which, for one sex, some individuals attract multiple mates while other individuals of that sex attract none; among the opposite sex, all or nearly all of the individuals are able to attract a mate. [Gk., *polys,* many + *gamete,* wife]

polygenic (7) Describes a trait that is influenced by multiple different genes. [Gk., *polys,* many + *genos,* race, descent]

polygyny (9) A mating system in which, among the males, some individuals attract multiple mates while other males attract none; among the females, all or nearly all of the individuals are able to attract a mate. [Gk., *polys,* many + *gune,* woman]

polymerase chain reaction (PCR) (5) A laboratory technique in which a fragment of DNA can be duplicated repeatedly. [Gk., *polys,* many + *meris,* part]

polyploidy (10) The doubling of the number of sets of chromosomes in an individual. [Gk., *polys,* many + *ploion,* vessel]

polysaccharides (2) Complex carbohydrates formed by the union of many simple sugars. [Gk., *polys,* many + *sakcharon,* sugar]

pons (23) Part of the vertebrate hindbrain that acts with the medulla to control body functions related to respiration, heart rate, and digestion.

population (8) A group of organisms of the same species living in a particular geographic region.

population density (14) The number of individuals of a population in a given area.

population ecology (14) A subfield of ecology that studies the interactions between populations of organisms of a species and their environment.

positive correlation (1) A relationship between variables in which they increase (or decrease) together. [Lat., *com,* with + *relatio,* report]

positive feedback (20) A control mechanism in which a deviation from normal internal conditions causes an increase or acceleration of the change.

post-anal tail (11) A tail that extends beyond the end of the trunk, a point that is marked by the anus; a characteristic of chordates. [Lat., *post,* after]

posterior pituitary (24) A gland of the endocrine system; releases several important peptide hormones—including oxytocin and antidiuretic hormone—that are produced in neurons of the hypothalamus.

postsynaptic membrane (23) The cell membrane of a neuron on the receiving side of a synapse, across from the presynaptic membrane.

postzygotic barrier (10) A barrier to reproduction caused by the infertility of hybrid individuals or the inability of hybrid individuals to survive long after fertilization. [Lat., *post,* after]

potential energy (4) Stored energy; the capacity to do work that results from an object's location or position, as in the case of water held behind a dam. [Lat., *potentia,* power]

predation (15) An interaction between two species in which one species eats the other. [Lat., *praedari,* to plunder]

prepared learning (9) Behaviors that are learned easily by all, or nearly all, individuals of a species.

pressure-flow mechanism (17) In vascular plants, the force driving the movement of sugar in the phloem; osmotic pressure moves material from sugar-production sites (sources) to sites where sugar is needed or stored (sinks).

presynaptic membrane (23) The cell membrane of an axon at the synapse.

prezygotic barrier (10) A barrier to reproduction caused by the physical inability of individuals to mate with each other, or the inability of the male's reproductive cell to fertilize the female's reproductive cell. [Lat., *prae,* before]

primary active transport (3) Active transport using energy released directly from ATP.

primary consumers (15) Herbivores, which consume the output of primary producers.

primary electron acceptor (4) In photosynthesis, a molecule that accepts excited, high-energy electrons from chlorophyll *a,* beginning the series of electron handoffs known as an electron transport chain.

primary growth (18) Plant growth that originates in the apical meristems of shoots and roots, increasing the height of the shoot, increasing the length of roots and branches, and producing new tissues. See also **secondary growth.**

primary oocyte (25) In female gametogenesis, a cell produced by meiosis, which then completes meiosis; it can become an egg (ovum).

primary producers (15) The organisms responsible for primary productivity, such as grasses, trees, and agricultural crops, which convert light energy from the sun into chemical energy (that is, food) through photosynthesis.

primary productivity (15) The amount of organic matter produced by living organisms, primarily through photosynthesis.

primary response (26) The immune system's first interaction with a pathogen.

primary spermatocyte (25) In sperm production, one of the two cells resulting from division of the spermatogonium; it undergoes meiosis in the first step of sperm production.

primary structure (2) The sequence of amino acids in a polypeptide chain.

probiotic therapy (13) A method of treating infections by introducing benign bacteria in numbers large enough to overwhelm harmful bacteria in the body. [Lat., *pro,* for, on behalf of + Gk., *bios,* life]

progesterone (24, 25) A hormone, secreted by the corpus luteum of the ovary, that causes thickening of the endometrium to prepare for gestation. [Lat., *pro,* for + *gestare,* to bear]

prokaryote (3) An organism consisting of a prokaryotic cell (all prokaryotes are one-celled organisms). [Gk., *pro,* before + *karyon,* nut, kernel]

prokaryotic cell (3) A cell bound by a plasma membrane enclosing the cell contents (cytoplasm, DNA, and ribosomes); there is no nucleus or other organelles.

prolactin (24) Hormone secreted by the anterior pituitary which stimulates the production of milk in the mammary glands.

promoter site (5) Part of a DNA molecule that indicates where the sequence of base pairs that makes up a gene begins.

prophase (6) The first phase of mitosis, in which the nuclear membrane breaks down, sister chromatids condense, and the spindle forms. In meiosis, homologous pairs of sister chromatids come together and cross over in prophase I, and the chromosomes in daughter cells condense in prophase II. [Gk., *pro*, before + *phasis*, appearance]

prostate gland (25) A gland in males that secretes enzymes and nutrients into the semen.

protein (2) One of the four types of biological macromolecules; constructed of unique combinations of 20 amino acids that result in unique structures and chemical behavior. Proteins are the chief building blocks of tissues in most organisms. [Gk., *proteion*, of the first quality]

protein synthesis (5) The construction of a protein from its constituent amino acids, by the processes of transcription and translation.

prothallus (12) The free-living haploid life stage of a fern; produces haploid gametes. [Gk., *pro*, before + *thallia*, twig]

protists (10) In modern classification, one of the four eukaryotic kingdoms; includes all the single-celled eukaryotes.

proton (2) A positively charged particle in the atomic nucleus; it is identical to the nucleus of the hydrogen atom, which lacks a neutron and has atomic number 1. [Gk., *protos*, first]

protostomes (11) Bilaterally symmetrical animals with defined tissues in which the gut develops from front to back; the first opening formed is the mouth of the adult animal. [Gk., *protos*, first + *stoma*, mouth]

pseudoscience (1) Hypotheses and theories not supported by trustworthy and methodical scientific studies. [Gk., *pseudes*, false + Lat., *scientia*, knowledge]

pulmonary circuit (21) Flow of blood from the heart to the lungs and back to the heart; the returning blood is oxygenated.

punctuated equilibrium (10) A theory in biology about the tempo of evolution, suggesting that in many taxa long periods in which there is relatively little evolutionary change are punctuated by brief periods of rapid evolutionary change.

Punnett square (7) A diagram showing the possible outcomes of a cross between two individuals; the possible crosses are shown in the manner of a multiplication table. [From the name of its designer, Reginald C. Punnett, 1875–1967]

pupa (11) In complete metamorphosis, the second stage of insect development, in which the larva is enclosed in a case and its body structures are broken down into molecules that are reassembled into the adult form. [Lat., *pupa*, a little girl]

pus (26) The thick, yellowish fluid at the site of an infection, made up of neutrophils, damaged cell debris from the invaded tissue, and both live and dead pathogens.

pyruvate (4) The end product of glycolysis.

Q

quaternary structure (2) Two or more polypeptide chains bonded together in a single protein; an example is hemoglobin. [Lat., *quaterni*, four each]

R

radial symmetry (11) A body structure like that of a wheel, or pie, in which any cut through the center would divide the organism into identical halves. [Lat., *radius*, spoke of a wheel + Gk., *symmetria*, symmetry]

radioactive (2) The property of some elements or isotopes of having a nucleus that breaks down spontaneously, releasing tiny, high-speed particles that carry energy.

radiometric dating (8) A method of determining both the relative and the absolute ages of objects such as fossils by measuring both the radioactive isotopes they contain, which are known to decay at a constant rate, and their decay products.

rain shadow (15) An area in the lee of a mountain where there is no or reduced rainfall, because the air passing over the mountain falls, becoming warmer and thus increasing the amount of moisture it can hold.

randomized (1) Describes a manner of choosing subjects and assigning them to groups on the basis of chance, that is, randomly.

ray-finned fishes (11) Fish species characterized by rigid bones and a mouth at the apex of the body; they are so called because their fins are lined with hardened rays.

realized niche (15) The environmental conditions in which an organism is living at a given time.

receptor-mediated endocytosis (3) One of the three types of endocytosis, in which receptors on the surface of a cell bind to specific molecules; the plasma membrane then engulfs both molecule and receptor and draws them into the cell.

receptor protein (3) A protein in the plasma membrane that binds to specific chemicals in the cell's external environment to regulate processes within the cell; for example, cells in the heart have receptor proteins that bind to adrenaline.

recessive (7) Describes an allele whose phenotypic effect is masked by a dominant allele for a trait. [Lat., *recessus*, retreating]

reciprocal altruism (9) Costly behavior directed toward another individual that benefits the recipient, with the expectation that, at some later time, the recipient will behave in a similar manner, "returning the favor." [Lat., *reciprocare*, to move backward and forward + *alter*, the other]

recognition protein (3) A protein in the plasma membrane that provides a "fingerprint" on the outside-facing surface of the cell, making it recognizable to other cells. Recognition proteins make it possible for the immune system to distinguish the body's own cells from invaders that may produce infection, and also help cells bind to other cells or molecules.

recombinant DNA technology (5) Technology that depends on the combination of two or more sources of DNA into a product; an example is the production of human insulin from fast-dividing transgenic *E. coli* bacteria in which has been inserted the human DNA sequence that codes for insulin.

recombination (6) The exchange of some genetic material between a paternal homologous chromosome and a maternal homologous chromosome, leading to a chromosome carrying genetic material from each; also referred to as crossing over.

red blood cells (21) Hemoglobin-containing, oxygen-transporting blood cells, the most common type of blood cell. Also called *erythrocytes*.

reflex (23) An automatic response that occurs when signals travel directly from sensory neurons to the spinal cord, where they connect with motor neurons to stimulate a response to a sensation that does not need to be processed through the brain.

regulator (20) An organism that, for a given physiological variable, maintains homeostasis for that variable, keeping it within a narrow range, even in the face of changes in the external environment.

replication (6) The process in both eukaryotes and prokaryotes by which DNA duplicates itself in preparation for cell division.

reproductive cells (6) Haploid cells from two individuals that, as sperm and egg, will combine at fertilization to produce offspring; also called *gametes*.

reproductive investment (9, 14) Energy and material expended by an individual in the growth, feeding, and care of offspring.

reproductive isolation (10) The inability of individuals from two populations to produce fertile offspring together.

reproductive output (14) The number of offspring an individual or population produces.

resource partitioning (15) A division of resources that occurs when species overlap some portion of a niche in which one or more species differ in behavior or body plan in a way that divides the resources of the niche between the species.

resting potential (23) In a neuron, the state when the neuron is not transmitting a signal and during which, due to the action of sodium-potassium pumps, a greater positive charge is maintained outside the cell than inside the cell.

restriction enzymes (5) Enzymes that recognize and bind to different specific sequences of four to eight bases in DNA and cut the DNA at that point. Restriction enzymes are important in biotechnology because they permit the cutting of short lengths of DNA, which can be inserted into other chromosomes or otherwise utilized.

retina (23) Nervous tissue containing light-sensitive cells, on the inner surface of the vertebrate eye, which transmits impulses to the vision centers of the brain.

retrovirus (13) A virus containing RNA and also reverse transcriptase, a viral enzyme, which uses the viral RNA as a template to synthesize a single strand of DNA. [Lat., *retro*, backward + *virus*, slime]

ribonucleic acid (RNA) (2) A nucleic acid, RNA serves as a middleman in the process of converting genetic information in DNA into protein; messenger RNA (mRNA) takes instructions for production of a given protein from DNA to another part of the cell, whereas transfer RNA (tRNA) interprets the mRNA code and directs the construction of the protein from its constituent amino acids.

ribosomal subunits (5) The two structural parts of a ribosome, which function together to translate mRNA to build a chain of amino acids that will make up a protein.

ribosomes (3) Granular bodies in the cytoplasm, released from their initial positions on the rough endoplasmic reticulum, that copy the information in segments of DNA to provide instruction for the construction of proteins.

right hemisphere (23) The region of the brain dedicated, in most humans, to emotions, intuitive thinking, and artistic expression.

ring species (10) Populations that can interbreed with neighboring populations but not with populations separated by larger geographic distances. Because the non-interbreeding populations are connected by gene flow through geographically intermediate populations, there is no clear point at which one species stops and another begins, and for this reason, ring species are problematic for the biological species concept.

RNA world hypothesis (10) A hypothesis that proposes that the world may have been filled with RNA-based life before it became filled with life based on DNA, the life of today.

rod (23) In the retina, a type of cell that enables vision in dim light.

root (12, 17) The part of a vascular plant, usually below ground, that absorbs water and minerals from the soil and transports them through vascular tissue to the rest of the plant, and that anchors the plant in place. The overall structure of a plant's roots is called the root system.

root meristem (18) A cluster of active, dividing embryonic cells at the tips of roots that generates new tissue and increases root length.

rough endoplasmic reticulum (3) An organelle, part of the endomembrane system, structurally like a series of interconnected, flattened sacs connected to the nuclear envelope; called "rough" because its surface is studded with ribosomes. [Gk., *endon*, within + *plasma*, anything molded; Lat., *reticulum*, dim. of *rete*, net]

roundworms (11) A worm phylum with members characterized by a long, narrow, unsegmented body and growth by molting. Roundworms, also called nematodes, are protostomes with defined tissues; there are some 90,000 identified species.

rubisco (4) An enzyme (ribulose 1,5-bisphosphate carboxylase/oxygenase), important in photosynthesis, that fixes carbon atoms from CO_2 in the air, attaching them to an organic molecule in the stroma of the chloroplast. This fixation is the first step in the Calvin cycle, in which molecules of sugar are assembled. Rubisco is the most plentiful protein on earth.

ruminant (22) A mammal characterized by having a four-chambered stomach. Ruminants chew a cud consisting of regurgitated, partially digested food. Cows, sheep, goats, and bison are examples.

S

sap (17) In vascular plants, (1) the fluid in the xylem that consists of water and dissolved minerals and sometimes sugars; (2) the fluid in the phloem that consists of water and dissolved sugars and other nutrients.

sarcomere (23) The fundamental unit of muscle contraction, made up of actin and myosin.

saturated fat (2) A fat in which each carbon in the hydrocarbon chain forming the tail region of the fat molecule is bound to two hydrogen atoms; saturated fats are solid at room temperature.

savanna (15) A type of terrestrial biome; a tropical or subtropical grassland with scattered woody plants, characterized by hot climate and distinct wet and dry seasons (rainfall is less than in the tropical seasonal forest biome).

science (1) A body of knowledge based on observation, description, experimentation, and explanation of natural phenomena. [Lat., *scientia*, knowledge]

scientific literacy (1) A general, fact-based understanding of the basics of biology and other sciences, the scientific method, and the social, political, and legal implications of scientific information.

scientific method (1) A process of examination and discovery of natural phenomena that involves making observations, constructing hypotheses, testing predictions, experimenting, and drawing conclusions and revising them as necessary.

sclerenchyma cell (17) A type of cell that provides strength to plants, enabling them to grow tall; at maturity, the cell is not living. Sclerenchyma cells are a type of ground tissue.

scrotum (25) External sac that contains the testes.

second law of thermodynamics (4) A physical law that states that every conversion of energy is not perfectly efficient and invariably includes the transformation of some energy into heat.

secondary active transport (3) Active transport in which there is no direct involvement of ATP (adenosine triphosphate); the transport protein simultaneously moves one molecule against its concentration gradient while letting another flow down its concentration gradient.

secondary consumers (15) Animals that feed on herbivores; also known as carnivores.

secondary growth (18) In woody plants, plant growth that originates in lateral meristems, increasing the girth of stems and branches. It is the process by which dicots and some other angiosperms produce wood, acquiring increased water-conduction capacity and becoming thicker and sturdier. See also **primary growth.**

secondary oocyte (25) One of the two cells formed by division of a primary oocyte; it completes meiosis after fertilization.

secondary phloem (18) In woody plants, tissue produced by the vascular cambium, toward the outer circumference of the trunk or branch, during secondary growth; the cells conduct sugars throughout the plant body.

secondary response (26) The creation of B and T effector cells in the immune system's response to a second exposure to a pathogen. The secondary response occurs rapidly and produces a more intense response than the primary response.

secondary spermatocyte (25) One of the two cells produced by the first meiotic division of a primary spermatocyte, which then complete the second meiotic division; each produces two spermatids.

secondary structure (2) The corkscrew-like twists or folds formed by hydrogen bonds between amino acids in a polypeptide chain.

secondary xylem (18) In woody plants, tissue produced by the vascular cambium, toward the inside of the trunk or branch, during secondary growth; the cells conduct water and minerals, while also providing structural support. Also called *wood.*

seed (12, 18) An embryonic plant with its own supply of water and nutrients, encased within a protective coating.

segmented worms (11) A worm phylum with members characterized by grooves around the body that mark divisions between segments. Segmented worms, also called annelids, are protostomes with defined tissues and do not molt; examples are earthworms and leeches.

selective serotonin reuptake inhibitors (SSRIs) (23) Antidepressant medications (including Prozac and Zoloft) that block serotonin from being reabsorbed and recycled by the cells (neurons) that released it, prolonging its effect. The net result for the individual is generally an elevated mood, because of serotonin's prolonged stay in the synapse.

seminal vesicle (25) One of a pair of male reproductive glands that secrete sugar, enzymes, vitamin C, proteins, and immune suppressants into semen.

seminiferous tubules (25) Coiled tubes in the testes that are lined with the cells that divide to produce sperm.

sensory integration (23) The process of incorporating information from all of the senses to form a single perception.

sensory neuron (23) A type of neuron that collects information from an animal's environment; its dendrites are modified to respond directly to external stimulation—temperature, touch, taste, smell, light, or sound.

sepal (18) One of the leaf-like structures that grow in a ring around the outside of a flower, at the point where the flower is connected to the branch, stem, or stalk. Sepals protect the developing bud and usually are green, but sometimes are the same color as the petals.

sessile (11) Describes organisms that are fastened in place, such as adult mussels and barnacles. [Lat., *sedere,* to sit]

set point (20) A target value or range; in homeostasis, the normal range of values for a variable (such as temperature, pH, or solute concentration).

sex-linked trait (7) A trait controlled by a gene on a sex chromosome.

sexual dimorphism (9) The case in which the sexes of a species differ in size or appearance. [Gk., *di-*, two + *morphē,* shape]

sexual reproduction (6, 25) A type of reproduction in which offspring are produced by the fusion of gametes from two distinct sexes.

sexual selection (8) The process by which natural selection favors traits, such as ornaments or fighting behavior, that give an advantage to individuals of one sex in attracting mating partners.

sexually transmitted disease (STD) (13, 25) A disease passed from one person to another through sexual activity.

shoot (12, 17) The above-ground part of a plant, consisting of stems and leaves, and sometimes flowers and fruits. The stem contains vascular tissue and supports the leaves, the main photosynthetic organ of the plant. Also called *shoot system.*

shoot meristem (18) A cluster of active, dividing embryonic cells found at the tips of shoots that increases plant height and generates new tissues, including branches and buds.

short tandem repeat (STR) (5) Region in DNA in which a short sequence (commonly four or five nucleotides) repeats over and over, a dozen or more times. Variation among individuals in the number of times the sequence repeats makes it possible to use these regions as a DNA "fingerprint," unique to an individual and valuable as a forensic tool.

sieve tube (17) A tube structure formed from specialized cells in the phloem that conducts sugar throughout the plant.

sign stimulus (9) An external signal that triggers the innate behavior called a fixed action pattern.

simple diffusion (3) Diffusion of molecules directly through the phospholipid bilayer of the plasma membrane that takes place without the assistance of other molecules; oxygen and carbon dioxide, because they are small and carry no charge that would cause them to be repelled by the middle layer of the membrane, can pass through the membrane in this way.

simple sugars (2) Monosaccharide carbohydrates, generally containing three to seven carbon atoms, which store energy in their chemical bonds and which biological cells can break down; cannot be broken down into other simple sugars; examples are glucose, fructose, and galactose.

single-gene trait (7) A trait that is determined by instructions on only one gene; examples are a cleft chin, a widow's peak, and unattached earlobes.

single-lens eye (23) The image-forming eye found in jellyfish and some mollusks.

sister chromatids (6) The two identical strands of a replicated chromosome.

skeletal muscle (20) A type of muscle tissue, usually attached to bones, that is responsible for generating most of the movement in animals; accounts for about 40% of human body weight. Also called *voluntary muscle.*

small intestine (22) A long, thin tube of the digestive tract between the stomach and large intestine; the part of the digestive system where most digestion and absorption take place.

smooth endoplasmic reticulum (3) An organelle, part of the endomembrane system, structurally like a series of branched tubes; called "smooth" because its surface has no ribosomes. Smooth endoplasmic reticulum synthesizes lipids such as fatty acids, phospholipids, and steroids. [Gk., *endon,* within + *plasma,* anything molded; Lat., *reticulum, dim. of rete,* net]

smooth muscle (20) A type of muscle tissue found in the walls surrounding blood vessels, the stomach and intestines, bladder, and many other organs and inner "tubes" within the body. It generates slow, rhythmic contractions that can gradually move blood, food, or other substances through the organ; not under conscious control.

solute (3) A substance that is dissolved in a gas or liquid; in a solution of water and sugar, sugar is the solute. [Lat., *solvere,* to loosen]

solvent (3) The gas or liquid in which a substance is dissolved; in a solution of water and sugar, water is the solvent. [Lat., *solvere,* to loosen]

somatic cells (6) The (usually diploid) cells of the body of an organism (in contrast to the usually haploid reproductive cells). [Gk., *soma,* body]

somatic nervous system (23) One of the two major divisions of the motor pathways of the peripheral nervous system (the autonomic nervous system is the other); relays signals to your skeletal muscles and enables you to contract those muscles and move your limbs consciously.

special connective tissue (20) A type of connective tissue, including bone, cartilage, and blood, in which the matrix differs from that of connective tissue proper in that it is rigid or liquid.

speciation (10) The process by which one species splits into two distinct species; the first phase of speciation is reproductive isolation, the second is genetic divergence, in which two populations evolve over time as separate entities with physical and behavioral differences.

speciation event (10) A point in evolutionary history at which a given population splits into independent evolutionary lineages.

species (10) Natural populations of organisms that can interbreed and are reproductively isolated from other such groups; in the Linnaean system, the species is the narrowest classification for an organism. [Lat., *species,* kind, sort]

specific epithet (10) In the system developed by Carolus Linnaeus (1707–1778), a noun or adjective added to the genus name to distinguish a species; in the name *Homo sapiens, Homo* is the genus name and *sapiens* is the specific epithet. [Gk., *epithetos,* added]

specific immunity (26) Division of the immune system that recognizes and defends against very specific infectious agents—for example, not just all bacteria, but specific species, individually. Also called *adaptive immunity.*

sperm (18, 25) A male gamete.

spermatogenesis (25) The process of sperm production.

sphincter (22) A ring of muscle that opens or closes a passage between two chambers in the body, such as between the esophagus and the stomach.

spindle (6) A part of the cytoskeleton of a cell, formed in prophase (in mitosis) or in prophase I (in meiosis), from which extend the fibers that organize and separate the sister chromatids.

spindle fibers (6) Fibers that extend from one pole of a cell to the other, which pull the sister chromatids apart in the anaphase stage of mitosis or the anaphase II stage of meiosis.

sporangia (*sing.* **sporangium**) (12) In many ferns, the structures on the underside of the leaves in which the spores are produced. [Gk., *spora,* seed + *angeion,* vessel]

spore (12, 18) A reproductive structure of non-vascular and some vascular plants that have an alternation of generations; spores are typically haploid, unicellular, and develop into either a male (producing sperm) or female (producing eggs) gametophyte. The eggs and sperm produced by gametophytes unite to produce the diploid generation (sporophyte) of the plant. [Gk., *spora,* seed]

sporophyte (12) The multicellular diploid structure in non-vascular plants, some vascular plants, and some algae that produces asexual spores, the diploid life stage in organisms exhibiting alternation of generations.

stabilizing selection (8) Selection that, for a given trait, produces the greatest fitness at the intermediate point of the phenotypic range.

stamen (12, 18) The male reproductive structure of a flower, consisting of a head-like anther on a stalk-like filament. There are usually several stamens in a flower. [Lat., *stamen,* thread]

starch (2) A complex polysaccharide carbohydrate consisting of a large number of monosaccharides linked in line; in plants, starch is the primary form of energy storage.

statistics (1) A set of analytical and mathematical tools designed to further the understanding of numerical data.

stem (17) Plant structure that supports and positions the leaves and flowers. The stem and leaves (and flowers) make up the shoot system.

stem cells (5, 21) Undifferentiated cells that have the ability to develop into any type of cell in the body; this property makes stem cells useful in biotechnology.

sterol (2) A lipid important in regulating growth and development; the sterols include cholesterol and the steroid hormones testosterone and estrogen, and all are modifications of a basic structure of four interlinked rings of carbon atoms. [Gk., *stereos,* solid + *-ol,* chemical suffix for an alcohol]

stigma (18) The region of the carpel, the female reproductive structure of a flower, that has a flat, sticky surface that functions as a landing pad for pollen.

stomach (22) A J-shaped digestive organ with thick, elastic walls; the part of the digestive system where food is mixed and partially digested.

stomata (*sing.* **stoma**) (4, 17) Small pores, usually on the undersides of leaves, that are the primary sites for gas exchange in plants; carbon dioxide (for photosynthesis) enters and oxygen (a by-product of photosynthesis) exits through the stomata. [Gk., *stoma,* mouth]

stroma (3, 4) In the leaf of a green plant, the fluid in the inner compartment of a chloroplast, which contains DNA and protein-making machinery. [Gk., *stroma,* bed]

style (18) The long, thin part of the carpel, the female reproductive structure of a flower, that holds up the stigma for pollen capture and through which a pollen tube will grow down into the ovary.

substrate (2) The molecule on which an enzyme acts. The active site on the enzyme binds to the substrate, initiating a chemical reaction; for example, the active site on the enzyme lactase binds to the substrate lactose, breaking it down into the two simple sugars glucose and galactose. [Lat., *sub-,* under + *stratus,* spread]

succession (15) The change in the species composition of a community over time, following a disturbance.

superstition (1) The irrational belief that actions not related by logic to a course of events can influence an outcome.

surface protein (3) A protein that resides primarily on the inner or outer surface of the phospholipid bilayer that constitutes the plasma membrane of the cell.

survivorship curves (14) Graphs showing the proportion of individuals of particular ages now alive in a population; indicate an individual's likelihood of surviving through a given age interval.

sympathetic nervous system (23) One of two components to the autonomic nervous system (the parasympathetic nervous system is the other); responsible for unconsciously controlling activities related to coordinating the body's fight-or-flight response to stress, including increasing the heart and breathing rates and providing muscles with additional blood flow.

sympatric speciation (10) Speciation that results not from geographic isolation but from polyploidy or hybridization and allopolyploidy; this type of speciation is relatively uncommon in animals but is common among plants. [Gk., *syn,* together with + *patris,* native land]

synapse (23) The site where a neuron communicates with another neuron, muscle cell, or gland [Gk., *syn,* together with + *haptein,* to fasten]

synaptic cleft (23) The space at the synapse between the axon terminal and whatever is next to it (neuron, muscle cell, or gland cell).

systematics (10) The modern approach to classification, with the broader goal of reconstructing the evolutionary history, or phylogeny, of organisms. [Gk., *systema,* a whole compounded of parts]

systemic circuit (21) Flow of blood from the heart to the body (other than the lungs) and back to the heart; returning blood is low in oxygen and high in carbon dioxide.

systolic pressure (21) The first blood pressure reading; a measure of the pressure when the heart contracts, pumping blood into the arteries.

T

T cell (26) A type of lymphocyte, maturing in the thymus, that is involved in cell-mediated immunity; fights invaders in body cells.

taproot (17) A thick primary root that grows deep into the soil and has smaller roots branching out from it; found primarily in dicots.

target cell (24) A cell that responds to a chemical regulatory signal, such as a hormone, typically when the regulatory chemical interacts with a receptor on or in the target cell.

telomere (6) A non-coding, highly repetitive section of DNA at the tip of every eukaryotic chromosome that shortens with every cell division; if it becomes too short, additional cell division can cause the loss of functional, essential DNA and therefore almost certain cell death. [Gk., *telos,* end + *meris,* part]

telophase (6) The fourth and last phase of mitosis, in which the chromosomes begin to uncoil and the nuclear membrane is reassembled around them. In meiosis, the sister chromatids arrive at the cell poles and the nuclear membrane reassembles around them in telophase I; in telophase II, the sister chromatids have been pulled apart and the nuclear membrane reassembles around haploid numbers of chromosomes. [Gk., *telos,* end + *phasis,* appearance]

tendon (20) A connective tissue structure that joins muscle to bone.

tendril (19) A specialized thread-like leaf or stem or branch that wraps around whatever it touches. Tendrils support the stem of the plant.

terminal buttons (23) Knob-like ends of an axon. Also called *axon terminals.*

tertiary consumers (15) Animals that eat animals that eat herbivores; also known as top carnivores. [Lat., *tertius,* third]

tertiary structure (2) The unique and complex three-dimensional shape formed by multiple twists of the secondary structure of a protein as amino acids come together and form hydrogen bonds or covalent sulfur-sulfur bonds. [Lat., *tertius,* third]

test-cross (7) A mating in which a homozygous recessive individual is bred with individuals of unknown genotype, showing the dominant phenotype; this type of cross can reveal the unknown genotype by the observed characteristics, or phenotype, of the offspring.

testis (*pl.* **testes**) (25) The male gonad.

testosterone (24, 25) The principal male sex hormone; influences development of an embryo as male and the production of male secondary sex characteristics.

tetrapod (11) An organism with four limbs; all terrestrial vertebrates are tetrapods. [Gk., *tetra-,* four + *pous,* foot]

thalamus (23) One of the primary switchboards in the brain. It receives most of the visual, auditory, and touch input, and relays some signals to the cerebral cortex while blocking others.

theory (1) An explanatory hypothesis for a natural phenomenon that is exceptionally well supported by empirical data. [Gk., *theorein,* to consider]

thermodynamics (4) The study of the transformation of energy from one type to another, such as from potential energy to kinetic energy. [Gk., *thermē,* heat + *dynamis,* power]

thermoneutral zone (20) In endotherms, the temperature range (typically between 27° and 36° C) within which the organism is able to maintain a constant internal body temperature without any energy expenditures.

thermoregulation (20) The maintenance of body temperature within its normal range in homeostasis.

thigmotropism (19) Plant growth that occurs in response to touch or physical contact with an object. [Gk., *thigma,* touch + *tropikos,* turn]

thylakoids (3, 4) Interconnected membranous structures in the stroma of a chloroplast, where light energy is collected and the conversion of light energy to chemical energy in photosynthesis takes place. [Gk., *thylakis, dim.* of *thylakos,* bag]

thyroid gland (24) An endocrine gland, located in the neck in humans, that produces thyroxine, an iodine-containing hormone that influences growth and metabolism.

thyroid-stimulating hormone (24) An animal hormone, produced by the anterior pituitary gland, that causes the thyroid gland to produce thyroxine, which is important in regulating cellular respiration.

thyroxine (24) An animal hormone, produced and secreted by the thyroid gland, that influences metabolic speed and efficiency.

tight junction (3) A continuous, water-tight connection between adjacent animal cells. Tight junctions are particularly important in the small intestine, where digestion occurs, to ensure that nutrients do not leak between cells into the body cavity and so become lost as a source of energy.

tissue (20) A group of similar cells that act together to perform specific functions in the body.

tonicity (3) For a cell in solution, a measure of the concentration of solutes outside the cell relative to that inside the cell. [Gk., *tonos,* tension]

topography (15) The physical features of a region, including those created by humans. [Gk., *topos,* place + *graphein,* to write down]

total reproductive output (9) The lifetime number of offspring produced by an individual.

trachea (22) A structure in the respiratory system that conducts air to the lungs. Also called *windpipe.*

trait (5, 8) Any characteristic or feature of an organism, such as red petal color in a flower.

trans fat (2) An unsaturated fat that has been partially hydrogenated (meaning that hydrogen atoms have been added to make the fat more saturated and to improve a food's taste, texture, and shelf-life). The added hydrogen atoms are in a trans orientation, which differs from the cis ("near") orientation of hydrogen atoms in the unsaturated fat. [Lat., *trans,* on the other side of]

transcription (5) The process by which a gene's base sequence is copied to mRNA.

transduction (13) A method of lateral transfer of DNA from one bacterial cell to another by means of a virus containing pieces of bacterial DNA picked up from its previous host, which infects the recipient bacterium and passes along new genes to the recipient. [Lat., *trans,* on the other side of + *ducere,* to lead]

transfer RNA (tRNA) (5) The type of RNA molecules in the cytoplasm that link specific triplet base sequences on mRNA to specific amino acids.

transformation (13) A method of lateral transfer of DNA from one bacterial cell to another in which a bacterial cell scavenges DNA released from burst bacterial cells in the environment. [Lat., *trans,* on the other side of + *formare,* to shape]

transgenic organism (5) An organism that contains DNA from another species.

translation (5) The process by which mRNA, which encodes a gene's base sequence, directs the production of a protein.

transmembrane protein (3) A protein that can penetrate the phospholipid bilayer of a cell's plasma membrane.

transport protein (3) A transmembrane protein that provides a channel or passageway through which large or strongly charged molecules can pass. Transport proteins are of a number of shapes and sizes, making possible the transport of a wide variety of molecules.

treatment (1) Any condition applied to the subjects of a research study that is not applied to subjects in a control group.

triglyceride (2) A fat having three fatty acids linked to the glycerol molecule. [Gk., *tri-* three + *glykys,* sweet]

trimester (25) In human development, one of the three three-month periods of pregnancy.

trophic level (15) A step in the flow of energy through an ecosystem. [Gk., *trophē,* food]

tropical rain forest (15) A type of terrestrial biome, found between the Tropic of Cancer (23.5° north latitude) and Tropic of Capricorn (23.5º south latitude) and characterized by constant moisture and temperature that do not vary across the seasons; vegetation is dense.

tropical seasonal forest (15) A type of terrestrial biome; characterized by hot climate and distinct wet and dry seasons; trees shed their leaves in the dry season.

tropism (19) In plants, a growth response by which plants grow toward or away from environmental stimuli such as light, gravity, and physical impediments, by bending, curving, and twisting. [Gk., *tropikos,* turn] See also **gravitropism; heliotropism; phototropism; thigmotropism.**

true-breeding (7) Describes a population of organisms in which, for a given trait, the offspring of crosses of individuals within the population always show the same trait; for example, the offspring of pea plants that are true-breeding for round peas always have round peas.

turgor pressure (3) In plants, the pressure of the contents of the cell against the cell wall, which is maintained by osmosis as water rushes into the cell when it contains high concentrations of dissolved substances. Turgor pressure allows non-woody plants to stand upright, and its loss causes wilting. [Lat., *turgere,* to swell]

twitch (23) In a muscle contraction, the duration of the period between muscle contraction and relaxation.

U

umbilical cord (25) A mass of tissue that connects the embryo to the placenta and through which nutrients and wastes are exchanged.

unsaturated fat (2) A fat in which at least one carbon in the hydrocarbon chain forming the tail region of the fat molecule is bound to only one hydrogen atom; unsaturated fats are liquid at room temperature.

uterus (25) Reproductive organ in female mammals, the site where an embryo develops. Also called *womb.*

V

vaccine (26) Weakened or harmless form of a specific pathogen that is administered to an individual to induce immunity without subjecting the individual to the disease.

vacuole (central) (3) A membrane-enclosed, fluid-filled, multipurpose organelle prominent in most plant cells (but also present in some protists, fungi, and animals); functions vary but can include storing nutrients, retaining and degrading waste products, accumulating poisonous materials, containing pigments, and providing physical support. [Lat., *vacuus,* empty]

vagina (25) Tube-like chamber connecting the female external genitals to the uterus; the place where sperm are released during copulation.

variables (1) The characteristics of an experimental system subject to change; for example, time (the duration of treatment) or specific elements of the treatment, such as the substance or procedure administered or the temperature at which it takes place. [Lat., *variare,* to vary]

vas deferens (25) A tube of smooth muscle tissue that passes from each testis into the body.

vascular cambium (18) In woody plants, the layer of lateral meristem cells that produces secondary xylem and secondary phloem.

vascular plants (12) Plants that transport water and dissolved nutrients by means of vascular tissue, a system of tubes that extends from the roots through the stem and into the leaves. [Lat., *vasculum, dim.* of *vas,* vessel]

vascular tissue (17) The part of a plant that conducts food, water, and nutrients throughout the plant body.

vein (21) A blood vessel that transports blood, at lower pressure than in arteries, from capillaries in the body to the heart.

ventricle (21) A chamber of the heart from which blood is pumped to the lungs, gills, or the rest of the body.

vertebrates (11) Chordate animals that have a backbone (made of cartilage or hollow bones) and, at the front end of the organism, a head containing a skull, brain, and sensory organs.

vesicle (3, 23) A small, membrane-enclosed sac within a cell. In neurons, a chemical-filled sac in the axon terminal that fuses with the presynaptic cell membrane to release its contents into the synaptic cleft. [Lat., *vesicula,* dim. of *vesica,* bladder]

vestigial structure (8) A structure, once useful to organisms, but which has lost its function over evolutionary time; an example is molars in bats that now consume an exclusively liquid diet. [Lat., *vestigium,* footprint, trace]

viruses (10) Diverse and important biological entities that can replicate but can conduct metabolic activity only by taking over the metabolic processes of a host organism, and therefore fall outside the definition of life. [Lat., *virus,* slime]

vitamin (22) An organic compound that is an essential nutrient required by the body in small amounts.

viviparity (11, 25) The characteristic of bearing young alive, giving birth to babies (rather than laying eggs); the embryo develops inside the mother. [Lat., *vivus,* alive + *parere,* to bear]

W

waggle dance (9) Behavior of scout honeybees that indicates, by the angle of the body relative to the sun and by physical maneuvers of various duration, the direction to a distant source of food.

wax (2) A lipid similar in structure to fats but with only one long-chain fatty acid linked to the glycerol head of the molecule; because the fatty acid chain is highly nonpolar, waxes are strongly hydrophobic.

Wernicke's area (23) The area of the brain responsible for understanding speech; located, in most people, in the left temporal lobe.

white blood cells (21, 26) Blood cells that defend against pathogens; the primary components of the immune response system. Also called *leukocytes.*

X

X and Y chromosomes (6) The human sex chromosomes.

xylem (17) (*pron.* ZY-lum) In vascular plants, the tissue that conducts water and dissolved minerals throughout the plant.

Z

zona pellucida (25) The glycoprotein layer between the granulosa cells and the egg's membrane.

zygote (18, 25) Diploid cell resulting when the sperm and egg fuse during fertilization.

Photo Credits

Legend: *L*, left; *C*, center; *R*, right; *T*, top; *M*, middle; *B*, bottom

CHAPTER 1   pp. 0–1: Michael Nichols/National Geographic Stock. **p. 2:** Martin Barraud/Getty Images. **p. 3:** *Figure 1-1 (L to R)* AP Photo, Mike Fuentes/The New York Times/Redux Pictures, The Photo Works. **p. 4:** *Figure 1-2 (clockwise from L)* Reprinted through the courtesy of the Editors of TIME Magazine © 2008 Time Inc., Courtesy of The Economist, Newsweek/PRN/Newscom, AP Photo/Tony Gutierrez; headline used with permission of The Associated Press Copyright © 2011. All rights reserved. **p. 5:** *Figure 1-3* Walter Dawn/Photo Researchers. **p. 6:** *Figure 1-4 (TL)* Steven Puetzer/Getty Images, *(TR)* Ingolf Hatz/Corbis; *(ML)* Mark Scott/Getty Images, *(MR)* WireImage/Getty Images; *(B)* Louie Psihoyos/Corbis. **p. 7:** Frans Lanting Photography. **p. 8:** *Figure 1-6* AFP/Getty Images; *Figure 1-7* Digital Vision Photography/Veer. **p. 9:** *Figure 1-8* CDC/Photo Researchers, *(inset)* Nigel Cattlin/Alamy. **p. 10:** *Figure 1-9* LWA/Dann Tardif/Blend Images/Corbis. **p. 13:** *Figure 1-12* Peter Frank/Corbis. **p. 16:** Nigel Cattlin/Alamy. **p. 18:** *Figure 1-15* Topham/The Image Works. **p. 20:** *Figure 1-16 (L)* Courtesy of KCBD News Channel 11, *(R)* Courtesy of www.hivandhepatitis.com. **p. 22:** B. Boissonnet/age fotostock. **p. 24:** *Figure 1-20* Pacific Coast News. **p. 25:** *Figure 1-21 (L)* Image Source Black/Alamy, *(R)* Marni Rolfes. **p. 26:** *Figure 1-22* AP Photo/Paul Sakuma. **p. 27:** *Figure 1-23* Reprinted through the courtesy of the Editors of TIME Magazine © 2008 Time Inc. **p. 28:** *Figure 1-24* Waltraud Grubitzsch/epa/Corbis. **p. 29:** Patrick Landmann/Photo Researchers. **p. 30:** yellowdog/age fotostock.

CHAPTER 2   pp. 36–37: ©Tim Laman (www.TimLaman.com). **p. 38:** David Nicholls/Photo Researchers; *Figure 2-1 (L)* Stockfolio/Alamy, *(C)* Jeffrey Coolidge/Getty Images, *(R)* Alex Cao/Getty Images. **p. 44:** *Figure 2-10* Judith Collins/Alamy, *(inset)* Dennis Kunkel/Phototake. **p. 46:** imagewerks/Getty Images; *Figure 2-13 (L)* Kietmar Nill/Foto Natura/Minden Pictures, *(R)* R. B. Suter, Vassar College. **p. 52:** Keren Su/Getty Images. **p. 53:** *Figure 2-20* Dorling Kindersley/Getty Images. **p. 54:** *Figure 2-22 (T)* Frans Lemmens/Alamy, *(B)* Lew Robertson/Getty Images. **p. 55:** *Figure 2-25 (L)* Paul Geor/Stockxpert, *(R)* Alison Parks-Whitfield/Alamy. **p. 56:** *Figure 2-26 (T)* Lake County Museum/Corbis, *(B)* Masterfile; *Figure 2-27* Chassenet/age fotostock. **p. 57:** Jeff Foott/Discovery Channel Images/Getty Images. **p. 58:** *Figure 2-28* Bryan & Cherry Alexander Photography/Alamy. **p. 59:** *Figure 2-30* Gary Gladstone/Corbis; *Figure 2-31 (L)* Ellen Isaacs/Alamy, *(R)* Masterfile. **p. 60:** *Figure 2-32* Andrew O'Toole/Taxi/Getty Images. **p. 62:** *Figure 2-34* Hulton Archive/Getty Images. **p. 63:** Stephanie Pfriender Stylander. **p. 64:** *Figure 2-36 (T to B)* Steve Bloom Images/Alamy, Steve Gschmeissner/Photo Researchers, Dennis Kunkel/Phototake, Dennis Kunkel/Phototake/Alamy, Deco/Alamy. **p. 65:** *Figure 2-38* Michael Waring/Foodstock. **p. 67:** *Figure 2-41 (L)* Ryan McVay/Getty Images, *(R)* White Packert/Getty Images. **p. 71:** Driscoll, Youngquist, & Baldeschwieler/Caltech/Photo Researchers. **p. 74:** Gustavo Andrade/age fotostock.

CHAPTER 3   pp. 80–81: Marshall Sklar/Photo Researchers. **p. 82:** Alfred Pasieka/Photo Researchers; *Figure 3-1 (L)* Steve Taylor/Getty Images, *(C)* Frans Lanting/Corbis, *(R)* David Scharf/Peter Arnold Images. **p. 83:** *Figure 3-2 (T)* Clark Sumida, *(M)* Rosenfeld/age fotostock, *(B)* Clouds Hill Imaging Ltd./Corbis, *(inset)* Courtesy of Reproductive Solutions.

p. 85: *Figure 3-3* Dennis Kunkel/Getty Images. **p. 86:** *Figure 3-4 (L)* John Glover/age fotostock, *(C)* Juniors Bildarchiv/age fotostock, *(R)* Matt Meadows/Peter Arnold Images. **p. 87:** *Figure 3-5 (L)* Dr. Donald Fawcett/Visuals Unlimited, *(R)* Phototake/Alamy. **p. 89:** imagebroker/Alamy. **p. 90:** *Figure 3-8 (L)* Don W. Fawcett/Photo Researchers, *(R)* Caro/Alamy. **p. 93:** *Figure 13-12 (L)* Photo Researchers, *(R)* Jim Evans/Kennebec Journal & Morning Sentinel. **p. 94:** *Figure 3-13* Image Source/Veer. **p. 96:** *Figure 3-15* AP Photo/Jeffrey Boan. **p. 97:** Courtesy of Dr. G. M. Gaietta and T. J. Deerinck, CRBS/NCMIR, University of California, San Diego. **p. 101:** *Figure 3-20* Richard Keppel-Smith/Getty Images. **p. 102:** *Figure 3-21* Biophoto Associates/Photo Researchers. **p. 103:** *Figure 3-23 (L)* Chuck Brown/Photo Researchers, *(C)* Ed Reschke/Peter Arnold Images, *(R)* Carolina Biological Supply Company/Phototake. **p. 105:** Lorenz Britt/Alamy. **p. 106:** *Figure 3-25 (L)* Dennis Kunkel/Phototake, *(C)* Dennis Kunkel/Visuals Unlimited, *(R)* Courtesy of Dr. G. D. Griffin, Oak Ridge National Laboratory. **p. 107:** Dennis Kunkel/Visuals Unlimited, *Figure 3-26* Mary Ellen Mark. **p. 108:** *Figure 3-27* Phototake/Alamy. **p. 109:** *Figure 3-28* Lynne Chang/Visuals Unlimited. **p. 110:** *Figure 3-29 (L)* Dr. Yorgos Nikas/Phototake, *(R)* Juergen Berger/Photo Researchers. **p. 111:** *Figure 3-30* Dr. Donald Fawcett/Getty Images. **p. 113:** *Figure 3-32* Dr. Gopal Murti/Photo Researchers. **p. 114:** *Figure 3-33* Kevin Somerville/The Medical File/Peter Arnold Images. **p. 115:** *Figure 3-34* Dennis Kunkel/Visuals Unlimited; *Figure 3-35* Omikron/Photo Researchers. **p. 117:** *Figure 3-36* Dennis Kunkel/Visuals Unlimited. **p. 118:** *Figure 3-38* Perennou Nuridsany/Photo Researchers. **p. 119:** *Figure 3-39* Biophoto Associates/Photo Researchers. **p. 120:** *Figure 3-40* George Chapman/Visuals Unlimited. **p. 122:** Marco Garcia/Getty Images.

CHAPTER 4   pp. 128–129: Pete Saloutos/Corbis. **p. 130:** Inga Spence/Getty Images. **p. 131:** *Figure 4-1* Pat LaCroix/Getty Images. **p. 132:** *Figure 4-3 (TL)* David Madison/Getty Images, *(TC)* Konrad Wothe/Minden Pictures, *(TR)* Michel Gunther/Photolibrary, *(BL)* Bernhard Edmaier/Photo Researchers, *(BR)* David Stoecklein/Corbis. **p. 133:** *Figure 4-4* Michael Pohuski/Foodpix/Jupiterimages. **p. 134:** *Figure 4-5 (L)* Ed Gifford/Masterfile, *(R)* Walter Lockwood/Corbis; *Figure 4-6* David Allio/Icon SMI/Corbis. **p. 137:** Frans Lanting Photography. **p. 138:** *Figure 4-10 (L to R)* Wim van Egmond/Visuals Unlimited, Dennis Kunkel/Phototake, Dennis Kunkel/Visuals Unlimited, Norbert Wu/Minden Pictures. **p. 139:** *Figure 4-12 (T)* Value Stock Images/Fotosearch, *(B)* Dennis Kunkel/Visuals Unlimited. **p. 148:** *Figure 4-23* Wolfgang Dufner/age fotostock; *Figure 4-24 (L and R)* Dr. Jeremy Burgess/Science Photo Library. **p. 149:** *Figure 4-25 (L)* age fotostock/SuperStock, *(C)* Beth Perkins/Getty Images, *(R)* PBNJ Productions/Corbis. **p. 151:** ClassicStock/Alamy; *Figure 4-27 (L)* age fotostock/SuperStock, *(C)* Frans Lanting Photography, *(R)* Volker Steger/Photo Researchers. **p. 153:** *Figure 4-29 (L)* age fotostock/SuperStock, *(C)* Frans Lanting Photography, *(R)* A. Barry Dowsett/Photo Researchers. **p. 156:** *Figure 4-33* hybrid medical animation/Photo Researchers. **p. 159:** Martin Harvey/Getty Images; *Figure 4-36* Tobias Bernhard/Getty Images. **p. 160:** *Figure 4-38 (L)* Cephas Picture Library/Alamy, *(R)* Romilly Lockyer/Getty Images, *(inset)* SciMAT/Photo Researchers. **p. 161:** *Figure 4-39 (L)*

FoodCollection/age fotostock, (C) Tim Hill/Alamy, (R) D. Hurst/Alamy. **p. 162:** Plush Studios/Getty Images.

CHAPTER 5   pp. 168-169: Steven Puetzer/Getty Images. **p. 170:** Mario Tama/Getty Images; *Figure 5-1* Vasna Wilson/Virginian-Pilot. **p. 171:** *Figure 5-2 (L)* Reprinted with permission, September 2008, *Discover* magazine. Copyright © Discover Magazine. All rights reserved. *(R)* Reprinted through the courtesy of the Editors of TIME Magazine © 2008 Time Inc. *(B)* Reprinted by permission of The Wall Street Journal, © 2008 Dow Jones & Company, Inc. All rights reserved worldwide. **p. 172:** *Figure 5-3 (L)* A. Barrington Brown/Photo Researchers, *(R)* Science Source/Photo Researchers. **p. 174:** *Figure 5-5 (TL)* Courtesy of Jay Phelan, *(TC)* Sian Irvine/Getty Images, *(TR)* Eye of Science/Photo Researchers, *(BL)* Visuals Unlimited/Corbis, *(BR)* John White. **p. 177:** *Figure 5-8 (T to B)* Eye of Science/Photo Researchers, Courtesy of Jay Phelan, Sian Irvine/Getty Images, John White, Visuals Unlimited/Corbis. **p. 178:** *Figure 5-9 (T to B)* Courtesy of Jay Phelan, Eye of Science/Photo Researchers, Dennis Kunkel/Getty Images, Fancy/Veer/Corbis, Dennis Kunkel/Visuals Unlimited. **p. 180:** Denis Galante Photography, Inc. **p. 186:** *Figure 5-16* Zave Smith/Corbis. **p. 189:** © Uli Westphal 2008. **p. 190:** *Figure 5-20 (L)* Andrew Syred/Photo Researchers, *(R)* Ted Kinsman/Photo Researchers. **p. 192:** *Figure 5-22 (L)* Mika/zefa/Corbis, *(C)* Justin Pumfrey/Getty Images, *(R)* Ocean/Corbis. **p. 193:** *Figure 5-23 (L and R)* Marni Rolfes. **p. 194:** Peter Ginter/Science Faction/Corbis. **p. 198:** *Figure 5-30 (L)* John Doebley, *(R)* Ed Young/Corbis. **p. 199:** *Figure 5-31 (TL)* Martin Ruegner/Digital Vision/Getty Images, *(TR)* Scottish Crop Research Institute, Dundee, *(M and B)* Professor Peter Beyer/Humanitarian Board for Golden Rice/www.goldenrice.org. **p. 200:** *Figure 5-32 (L)* Wally Eberhart/Getty Images, *(C)* Lance Nelson/Corbis, *(R)* David Munns/Photo Researchers; *Figure 5-33* Nigel Cattlin/Visuals Unlimited. **p. 201:** *Figure 5-35* Frank Whitney/Getty Images. **p. 202:** *Figure 5-36* Dr. Garth Fletcher. **p. 203:** *Figures 5-37* and *5-38* Reuters/Corbis. **p. 205:** Karen Kasmauski/Corbis. **p. 206:** *Figure 5-39* AJPhoto/Photo Researchers, *Figure 5-40* MGM/Courtesy of Everett Collection. **p. 207:** *Figure 5-41* Robin Nelson/Photo Edit. **p. 208:** *Figure 5-42* Baylor Medical Center. **p. 210:** *Figure 5-44 (T)* AP Photo/John Chadwick, *(M)* AP Photo/Ben Margot, *(B)* AP Photo/Advanced Cell Technologies. **p. 211:** *Figure 5-45 (L)* Neville Chadwick/Science Photo Library, *(C)* Tom Grill/Corbis, *(R)* David Parker/Science Photo Library. **p. 215:** Anthony Marsland/Getty Images.

CHAPTER 6   pp. 220–221: Steve Schapiro/Corbis Outline. **p. 222:** Dennis Kunkel Microscopy/Visuals Unlimited. **p. 223:** *Figure 6-1* Dr. Peter Landsorp/Visuals Unlimited; *Figure 6-2* Barcroft/Fame Pictures. **p. 225:** *Figure 6-4* Dennis Kunkel Microscopy. **p. 229:** Indeed/Getty Images; *Figure 6-7 (L to R)* Dan Guravich/Photo Researchers, Biology Media/Photo Researchers, SPL/Photo Researchers, Alex Blackburn Clayton/Photolibrary. **p. 230:** *Figure 6-8* Micro Discovery/Corbis. **p. 231:** *Figure 6-9* David Scharf/Getty Images. **p. 232:** *Figure 6-11* Courtesy of T. Wittman. **p. 235:** *Figure 6-13* GJLP/CNRI/Science Photo Library. **p. 236:** *Figure 6-15* Kevin Laubacher/Taxi/Getty Images. **p. 237:** Dr. Yorgos Nikas/Photo Researchers. **p. 238:** *Figure 6-17* AP Photo. **p. 243:** *Figure 6-21* Dr. David Phillips/Visuals Unlimited. **p. 245:** *Figure 6-23* Margot Granitsas/Photo Researchers. **p. 246:** *Figure 6-25* James H. Robinson/Science Photo Library/Photo Researchers; *Figure 6-26* Dr. Kari Lounatmaa/Photo Researchers. **p. 247:** Cormac Hanley/Getty Images; *Figure 6-27* Biophoto Associates/Photo Researchers. **p. 249:** *Figure 6-29 (L)* Frans Lanting

Photography, *(C)* imagebroker/Alamy, *(R)* Michael Patrick O'Neill/Alamy. **p. 250:** Visuals Unlimited/Corbis. **p. 251:** *Figure 6-31* CNRI/Photo Researchers; *Figure 6-32* Saturn Stills/Science Photo Library/Photo Researchers. **p. 252:** *Figure 6-33 (L)* Mika/zefa/Corbis, *(R)* L. Willatt/East Anglian Regional Genetics Service/Photo Researchers. **p. 256:** Michael Elins.

CHAPTER 7   pp. 262–263: Exactostock/SuperStock. **p. 264:** Mitsuaki Iwago/Minden Pictures; *Figure 7-1* Felix Wirth/Corbis. **p. 266:** *Figure 7-4* Newspix/Rex USA. **p. 267:** *Figure 7-5 (row 1)* Les3photo8/Dreamstime .com, Custom Medical Stock Photo/Alamy, *(row 2)* Geoff du Feu/Alamy, Gabriela Medina/Getty Images, *(row 3)* Kevin Winter/Getty Images, Kevin Winter/Getty Images, *(row 4)* Dorling Kindersley/Getty Images, Beyond Fotomedia GmbH/Alamy. **p. 269:** *Figure 7-7* James King-Holmes/Photo Researchers. **p. 270:** *Figure 7-8 (L)* blickwinkel/Alamy, *(R)* Sally Reed/age fotostock. **p. 272:** *Figure 7-10* Reinhard Kunkel/Photolibrary. **p. 274:** Inspirestock/Corbis. **p. 276:** *Figure 7-14* Richard Ellis/Alamy. **p. 278:** *Figure 7-16* Courtesy of Michael Comte. **p. 279:** Photodisc. **p. 280:** *Figure 7-18* René Maltête/Gamma Rapho. **p. 283:** *Figure 7-22* Big Cheese Photo LLC/Alamy. **p. 285:** *Figure 7-23* Wellcome Images. **p. 287:** *Figure 7-25* Tommy Moorman. **p. 288:** *Figure 7-26 (T)* Juniors Bildarchiv/age fotostock, *(B)* Juniors Bildarchiv/Alamy. **p. 289:** Joel Meyerowitz/Gallerystock. **p. 291:** *Figure 7-28* Armando Gallo/Retna Ltd./Corbis. **p. 292:** Patrick J. Miller.

CHAPTER 8   pp. 298–299: Chris Johns/National Geographic Stock. **p. 300:** Frans Lanting Photography; *Figure 8-1* Graphic Science/Alamy. **p. 303:** Frans Lanting Photography. **p. 304:** *Figure 8-3 (L to R)* Leonard de Selva/Corbis, Sheila Terry/Photo Researchers, The Granger Collection, New York, The Granger Collection, New York, Mary Evans Picture Library/Alamy. **p. 305:** *Figure 8-5* Getty Images. **p. 308:** *Figure 8-7 (L)* The Granger Collection, New York, *(R)* Louie Fasciolo/Bernard J. Shapero Rare Books. **p. 309:** Manfred Danegger/Corbis; *Figure 8-9* Renee Lynn/Corbis. **p. 312:** *Figure 8-11 (L)* Juniors Bildarchiv/Alamy, *(R)* blickwinkel/Alamy. **p. 313:** *Figure 8-12* J. D. Talasek/Phototake. **p. 314:** *Figure 8-13* Lester V. Bergman/Corbis. **p. 315:** *Figure 8-14* Ross Warner/Alamy. **p. 317:** *Figure 8-16 (TL)* Annie Katz/Getty Images, *(TC)* Catherine Ledner/Getty Images, *(TR)* Deanne Fitzmaurice/Corbis, *(BL)* Jason Homa/Getty Images, *(BC)* Paul Costello/Getty Images, *(BR)* Jacob Langvad/Stone/Getty Images; *Figure 8-17* Max Nash/AFP/Getty Images. **p. 318:** *Figure 8-18* Benn Mitchell/Riser/Getty Images. **p. 322:** Terry Andrewartha/NPL/Minden Pictures. **p. 323:** *Figure 8-22 (L and R)* Lynn Johnson/National Geographic Stock. **p. 324:** *Figure 8-23* J. Sneesby/B. Wilkins/Getty Images. **p. 326:** *Figure 8-26* Patricia McDonough. **p. 327:** *Figure 8-27* Andrew Sacks/Getty Images. **p. 328:** *Figure 8-28* Walter B. McKenzie/Getty Images; *Figure 8-29* Tom & Pat Leeson. **p. 329:** *Figure 8-30* RubberBall/Alamy. **p. 330:** *Figure 8-31* Steve Allen/Getty Images. **p. 331:** Constantinos Petrinos/NPL/Minden Pictures. **p. 332:** *Figure 8-32 (L)* Jason Edwards/National Geographic/Getty Images, *(R)* Kjell Sandved/Visuals Unlimited. **p. 334:** *Figure 8-36 (T)* Joe McDonald/Visuals Unlimited, *(BL)* G. Armistead/Vireo, *(BC)* Aaron French, *(BR)* Jack Jeffrey. **p. 335:** *Figure 8-37 (TL)* Joe McDonald/Visuals Unlimited, *(TC)* Martin Pot, *(TR)* Dave Watts/Alamy, *(BL)* Kim Taylor/Minden Pictures, *(BC)* Morales/age fotostock, *(BR)* John W. Warden/age fotostock. **p. 336:** *Figure 8-38 (TL)* Jose I. Castro, *(TR)* Laboratory of Evolutionary Morphology, *(BL)* Courtesy of Bradley Smith, University of Michigan, *(BR)* S. K. Ackerley, Department of Integrative Biology, University of Guelph, Guelph, ON, Canada; *Figure*

8-39 (L to R) PBNJ Productions/PBNJ/age fotostock, Juniors Bildarchiv/age fotostock, Malcolm Schuyl/Alamy, Juniors Bildarchiv/age fotostock. **p. 337:** *Figure 8-40* Adrian Warren/Ardea; *Figure 8-41 (T)* Michael Durham/Minden Pictures/Getty Images, (B) Kevin Schafer/Getty Images. **p. 338:** *Figure 8-42 (L to R)* Getty Images, Arco Images/Alamy, PhotoSpin/Alamy, Danita Delimont/Alamy, Ulrike Klenke and Zeev Pancer, Center of Marine Biotechnology, Baltimore, MD.

CHAPTER 9 **pp. 346–347:** Harald Lange/zefa/Corbis. **p. 348:** DLILLC/Corbis; *Figure 9-1* AP Photo/Independence Daily Reporter/Rob Morgan. **p. 349:** *Figure 9-2* Radius Images/Alamy; *Figure 9-3* Isabel M. Smallegange. **p. 350:** *Figure 9-4 (L)* Juniors Bildarchiv/Alamy, (TR) Andrew Darrington/Alamy, (BR) ARCO/H. Reinhard/age fotostock. **p. 352:** *Figure 9-6 (T)* Sharon Dominick/Getty Images, (BL) Michael Fogden/Bruce Coleman Inc., (BR) Lew Robertson/Corbis. **p. 355:** tbkmedia.de/Alamy; *Figure 9-8* Dr. Theodore Evans. **p. 357:** *Figure 9-9* Pete Cairns/NPL/Minden Pictures. **p. 360:** *Figure 9-12* Courtesy of Gerald Carter. **p. 361:** *Figure 9-13* Ben Cranke/Getty Images. **p. 363:** *Figure 9-14* PA Wire URN:5620400 (Press Association via AP Images). **p. 365:** Tsuneo Hayashida/Nature Production/Minden Pictures; *Figure 9-16* David M. Phillips/Photo Researchers. **p. 367:** *Figure 9-18 (L)* Suzi Eszterhas/Minden Pictures, (C) Gregory Basco/Visuals Unlimited, (R) Frans Lanting/Corbis. **p. 368:** *Figure 9-19 (L)* Universal Pictures/Photofest, (R) Summit Entertainment/Photofest. **p. 369:** *Figure 9-20* Michael Fogden/Photolibrary. **p. 370:** *Figure 9-21 (TL)* Anthony Mercieca/Photo Researchers, (TR) Dr. John Alcock/Visuals Unlimited, (BL) Joe McDonald/Corbis, (BR) Miroslav Beneda/Alamy. **p. 372:** *Figure 9-22* Thomas Marent/Visuals Unlimited; *Figure 9-23* Heidi & Hans-Juergen Koch/Minden Pictures. **p. 373:** *Figure 9-24* Yva Momatiuk & John Eastcott/Minden Pictures. **p. 374:** *Figure 9-25* M. Botzek/age fotostock. **p. 376:** *Figure 9-27 (L)* Yva Momatiuk & John Eastcott/Minden Pictures, (R) Frans Lanting Photography. **p. 377:** Juniors Bildarchiv/Alamy. **p. 378:** *Figure 9-28 (L)* Thomas Marent/Minden Pictures, (C) David Ponton/Design Pics/Corbis, (R) Jupiterimages/Creatas/Alamy; *Figure 9-29 (L)* Scott Camazine/Alamy, (C) Ocean/Corbis, (R) Michael Newman/PhotoEdit. **p. 379:** *Figure 9-30* Werner Bollmann/age fotostock. **p. 380:** Titus Lacoste/Getty Images.

CHAPTER 10 **pp. 386–387:** Kellar Autumn, Lewis & Clark College. **p. 388:** Frans Lanting Photography. **p. 389:** *Figure 10-1* Peter Sawyer, NMNH, Smithsonian Institution; *Figure 10-2* Roger Ressmeyer/Corbis. **p. 390:** *Figure 10-3* Courtesy of Andrew Knoll. **p. 392:** Photodisc; *Figure 10-5 (L to R)* Peter Turnley/Corbis, Steve Sands/New York Newswire/Corbis, Plantography/Alamy, The Collection by Jan Smith Photography/Alamy, Frans Lanting Photography, Frans Lanting Photography. **p. 393:** *Figure 10-6* Galen Rowell/Corbis; *Figure 10-7* European Pressphoto Agency B.V.; *Figure 10-8 (L)* Juniors Bildarchiv/Alamy, (R) Masterfile. **p. 398:** *Figure 10-11 (L)* John Cancalosi/age fotostock, (R) Wildlife/Peter Arnold Images. **p. 399:** *Figure 10-12 (TL)* Minden Pictures/SuperStock, (TC) Tui De Roy/Minden Pictures, (TR) Hiroya Minakuchi/Minden Pictures, (BL) David Hosking/Alamy, (BC) Tui De Roy/Minden Pictures, (BR) Michael Woodruff. **p. 401:** Fred Habegger/Grant Heilman Photography. **p. 404:** *Figure 10-17 (L to R)* DLILLC/Corbis, Nigel Dennis/age fotostock, James Gritz/Getty Images, Altrendo/Getty Images. **p. 406:** *Figure 10-19* Michael Durham/Minden Pictures; *Figure 10-20 (L)* David Hosking/Alamy, (C) Galen Rathbun, California Academy of Sciences, www.afrotheria.net, (R) IFA-Bilderteam/Jupiterimages. **p. 407:** Michael & Patricia Fogden/Corbis;

Figure 10-21 David Edwards/Getty Images. **p. 412:** *Figure 10-26* Reuters/Corbis. **p. 413:** Frans Lanting Photography. **p. 416:** *Figure 10-29* Radius Images/Alamy. **p. 417:** *Figure 10-30* Steve Gschmeissner/Photo Researchers; *Figure 10-31* John Wang/Getty Images, (inset) Derek Lovley/Kazem Kashefi/Photo Researchers. **p. 419:** *Figure 10-32 (L to R)* Michael & Patricia Fogden/Corbis, from *Botanica* by Howard Schatz ©Schatz Ornstein 2005, Adam Jones/Photo Researchers, Frans Lanting/Corbis. **p. 420:** Lawrence Migdale/Photo Researchers.

CHAPTER 11 **pp. 426–427:** Frans Lanting Photography. **p. 428:** Frans Lanting Photography; *Figure 11-1 (L)* Bill Beatty/Visuals Unlimited, (C) Stephen Frink/zefa/Corbis, (R) Reinhard Dirscherl/Visuals Unlimited. **p. 431:** *Figure 11-3 (L)* Jef Meul/Minden Pictures, (R) Frans Lanting Photography. **p. 432:** Courtesy of Jay Phelan. **p. 433:** *Figure 11-4 (top row, L to R)* Barry Brown/Visuals Unlimited, Dirk Wiersma/Photo Researchers, Sinclair Stammers/Photo Researchers, Wayne G. Lawler/Photo Researchers, (bottom row, L to R) Matthew Oldfield/Scubazoo/Photo Researchers, Arthur Siegelman/Visuals Unlimited, Gerry Bishop/Visuals Unlimited, Brandon Cole/Visuals Unlimited. **p. 434:** Poul Beckmann. **p. 435:** *Figure 11-5 (L)* Juan Carlos Calvin/Photolibrary, (R) Robert Yin/Corbis; *Figure 11-6* Doug Perrine/NPL/Minden Pictures. **p. 436:** *Figure 11-7 (T)* Melissa Fiene Photography, (BL) Brandon Cole/Visuals Unlimited, (BR) Michael Pitts/NPL/Minden Pictures. **p. 437:** *Figure 11-9 (T)* ©Tim Laman (www.TimLaman.com), (B) Howard Hall/Photolibrary. **p. 439:** *Figure 11-10 (L)* Alamy, (R) Sinclair Stammers/Photo Researchers; *Figure 11-11 (T)* CNRI/Photo Researchers, (B) LSHTM/Photo Researchers. **p. 440:** *Figure 11-12 (T)* Ross & Diane Armstrong/Minden Pictures, (M) Konrad Wothe/Minden Pictures, (B) ARCO/H. Reinhard/age fotostock. **p. 442:** *Figure 11-13 (TL)* David B. Fleetham/SeaPics.com, (TR) Gerry Ellis/Minden Pictures, (BL) Jeff Rotman/Getty Images, (BR) Norbert Wu/Getty Images. **p. 443:** *Figure 11-14 (L)* David B. Fleetham/Photolibrary, (C) Reuters/Corbis, (R) Norbert Wu/Getty Images. **p. 444:** *Figure 11-15* Tomasz Machnik. **p. 445:** *Figure 11-16 (TL)* blickwinkel/Alamy, (TR) George Grall/Getty Images, (BL) Scott Leslie, (BR) Chris Newbert/Minden Pictures. **p. 446:** *Figure 11-17 (L to R)* Frans Lanting/Corbis, Alamy, Alamy, Nigel Cattlin/Visuals Unlimited, Satoshi Kuribayashi/Nature Production/Minden Pictures. **p. 447:** *Figure 11-18 (L to R)* Satoshi Kuribayashi/Nature Production/Minden Pictures, Gerold & Cynthia Merker/Visuals Unlimited, Mark Moffett/Minden Pictures, Gerald & Buff Corsi/Visuals Unlimited. **p. 449:** *Figure 11-19 (T)* Brandon Cole/Visuals Unlimited, (ML) Jeffrey L. Rotman/Corbis, (MR) Stephen Frink/Corbis, (B) Frans Lanting Photography. **p. 450:** Frans Lanting/Corbis. **p. 451:** *Figure 11-20 (TL)* Frans Lanting Photography, (TR) Ross Armstrong/Photolibrary, (BL) Art Wolfe/Getty Images, (BR) Images&Stories/Alamy. **p. 452:** *Figure 11-22 (L)* Georgette Douwma/Science Photo Library/Photo Researchers, (C) Natural Visions/Alamy, (R) Frans Lanting/Corbis. **p. 453:** *Figure 11-24 (L)* Reinhard H/Photolibrary, (inset) Darlyne A. Murawski/Getty Images, (R) Masa Ushioda/SeaPics.com. **p. 454:** *Figure 11-25 (L)* Paul Souders/Corbis, (C) Tim Fitzharris/Minden Pictures, (R) Rudie Kuiter/OceanwideImages.com. **p. 456:** Luciano Candisani/Minden Pictures; *Figure 11-27 (L)* Stephen Dalton/Minden Pictures, (C) Michael Redmer/Visuals Unlimited, (R) McDonald Wildlife Photography, Inc. **p. 458:** *Figure 11-29 (L)* John Cancalosi/Photolibrary, (R) © Tim Laman (www.TimLaman.com); *Figure 11-30* © Chuang Zhao and Lida Xing. **p. 460:** *Figure 11-32 (L)* Dave Watts/Alamy, (C) Martin Rugner/Photolibrary, (R) Joe McDonald/Visuals Unlimited. **p. 466:** Ariel Skelley/Blend Images/Corbis.

Howard Greenberg & Bryce Wolkowitz, New York. **p. 576:** Elke Hesser/Getty Images.

CHAPTER 15   pp. 582–583: Frans Lanting Photography. **p. 584:** Frans Lanting Photography; *Figure 15-1* © Tim Laman (www.TimLaman.com). **p. 585:** *Figure 15-2* Steve Allen/Getty Images. **p. 586:** *Figure 15-3 (TL)* Frans Lanting Photography, *(TC)* Gerry Ellis/Minden Pictures, *(TR)* Fritz Poelking/Photolibrary, *(ML)* John Warburton-Lee Photography/Alamy, *(MC)* Michael Melford/Getty Images, *(MR)* Frans Lanting Photography, *(BL)* Dan Lamont/Corbis, *(BC)* Peter Arnold/Alamy, *(BR)* Frans Lanting/Corbis. **p. 587:** *Figure 15-4 (TL)* James Randklev/Corbis, *(TR)* Frans Lanting/Corbis, *(BL)* Momatiuk–Eastcott/Corbis, *(BC)* Troy Plota/Getty Images, *(BR)* Mark Conlin/V&W/Image Quest Marine. **p. 588:** Steven Besserman. **p. 589:** *Figure 15-6* Mike Boyatt/AGStockUSA; *Figure 15-7* Frans Lanting Photography. **p. 590:** *Figure 15-8* Jacques Descloitres, MODIS Land Rapid Response Team, NASA/GSFC. **p. 591:** *Figure 15-9 (L)* Courtesy of NASA/Goddard Space Flight Center Scientific Visualization Studio, *(R)* Sandy Felsenthal/Corbis. **p. 594:** Scott Linstead/FN/Minden Pictures. **p. 595:** *Figure 15-13 (L)* AJPhoto/Photo Researchers, *(R)* Eye of Science/Photo Researchers. **p. 601:** *Figure 15-19* AP Photo/Gautam Singh. **p. 602:** Norbert Wu/Minden Pictures; *Figure 15-20* Mitsuhiko Imamori/Minden Pictures. **p. 603:** *Figure 15-21* Jim Brandenburg/Minden Pictures. **p. 606:** *Figure 15-24 (TL)* Anthony Bannister, Gallo Images/Corbis, *(TR)* Thomas Marent/Minden Pictures, *(BL)* Beata Slonecka/National Geographic My Shot/National Geographic Stock, *(BR)* Michael & Patricia Fogden/Minden Pictures. **p. 607:** *Figure 15-25 (T)* Fred Bavendam/Minden Pictures, *(B)* John Downer/naturepl.com. **p. 608:** *Figure 15-26* E. Widder/HBOI/Visuals Unlimited. **p. 609:** *Figure 15-27 (T)* Stephen Dalton/Photo Researchers, *(B)* Eye of Science/Photo Researchers. **p. 610:** *Figure 15-28* Biosphoto/Heuclin Daniel/Peter Arnold Images. **p. 611:** *Figure 15-29 (T)* Mitsuhiko Imamori/Minden Pictures, *(B)* Arco Images GmbH/Alamy. **p. 612:** Michael Melford/National Geographic Stock. **p. 614:** *Figure 15-31* Siede Preis/Getty Images. **p. 617:** NASA Image by Robert Simmon, based on Landsat data provided by the UMD Global Land Cover Facility.

CHAPTER 16   pp. 622–623: Emmanuel Coupé, Greece. **p. 624:** DeAgostini/Getty Images; *Figure 16-1* Inga Spence/Getty Images, *(inset)* Bristol-Myers Squibb. **p. 625:** *Figure 16-2* Daniel Beltrá for Greenpeace. **p. 626:** *Figure 16-3 (L to R)* Jupiterimages/Getty Images, Jeff Vanuga/Corbis, Jack Phelan, François Gohier/Photo Researchers. **p. 628:** *Figure 16-5* Dennis MacDonald/Photolibrary. **p. 630:** *Figure 16-8 (T)* blickwinkel/Alamy, *(BL)* Michael & Patricia Fogden/Corbis, *(BR)* Frans Lanting Photography. **p. 631:** *Figure 16-9* Courtesy of Edward O. Wilson. **p. 632:** *Figure 16-10* Danny Lehman/Corbis. **p. 634:** Gallo Images/Corbis; *Figure 16-12* Tom Uhlman/Alamy, *(inset)* Libraries of Saginaw, MI, Local History and Genealogical Collection. **p. 637:** *Figure 16-15* Gerry Ellis/Minden Pictures; *Figure 16-16* Frans Lanting Photography. **p. 638:** Frans Lanting Photography. **p. 639:** *Figure 16-17 (L and C)* USGS Photo by Harry Glicken, *(R)* Barry O'Neil; *Figure 16-18 (L)* E. J. Keller/National Zoo/Smithsonian Institution, *(C)* Mark Carwardine/NPL/Minden Pictures, *(R)* Denis Scott/Corbis. **p. 640:** *Figure 16-19* Jany Sauvanet/Photo Researchers, *(inset)* Gale S. Hanratty/Alamy. **p. 641:** *Figure 16-21 (L)* Michael & Patricia Fogden/Minden Pictures, *(C)* Michael P. Gadomski/Photo Researchers, *(R)* Peter Yates/Photo Researchers. **p. 642:** *Figure 16-22* Jack Picone/Alamy. **p. 643:** *Figure 16-23* Anil Risal Singh–UNEP/Peter Arnold Images. **p. 644:** *Figure 16-26* Will & Deni McIntyre/Corbis.

p. 646: *Figure 16-29 (T and B)* NASA/Goddard Space Flight Center Scientific Visualization Studio–Thanks to Rob Gerston (GSFC) for providing the data. **p. 648:** *Figure 16-31 (from L)* NASA Goddard Space Flight Center Scientific Visualization Studio, *(far R)* NASA; *Figure 16-32* AP Photo/Elise Amendola, *(inset)* New Line/Photofest. **p. 650:** *Figure 16-35* Frans Lanting/Corbis. **p. 651:** Jason Lee/X01757/Reuters/Corbis; *Figure 16-36 (T)* Mitsuaki Iwago/Minden Pictures, *(B)* Dennis Kunkel Microscopy. **p. 652:** *Figure 16 37 (L)* Frans Lanting Photography, *(R)* Florian Schultz/www.visionsofthewild.com. **p. 653:** *Figure 16-38* Tommy Moorman. **p. 656:** Corbis/SuperStock.

CHAPTER 17   pp. 662–663: Cindy Kassab/Corbis. **p. 664:** Tim Fitzharris/Minden Pictures. **p. 665:** *Figure 17-1 (L-R)* Lonely Planet Images/Getty Images, Stephen Belcher/Minden Pictures, De Agostini Picture Library/Getty Images, Koji Nakamura/amanaimages/Corbis. **p. 666:** *Figure 17-4* David T. Webb (Ph.D.), *(inset)* Carolina Biological Supply Co. Source/Visuals Unlimited. **p. 668:** *Figure 17-6 (L-R)* Eye of Science/Photo Researchers, *(inset)* Mark Bolton/Corbis, Dr. Gerald Van Dyke/Getty Images, Dennis Kunkel Microscopy/Visuals Unlimited, *(inset)* Doug Wilson/Corbis. **p. 669:** *Figure 17-7* Steve Gschmeissner/Photo Researchers. **p. 670:** *Figure 17-8 (L-R)* Image Source/Corbis, *(inset)* Dennis Kunkel Microscopy, Joe Petersburger/National Geographic Stock, *(inset)* Biophoto Associates/Photo Researchers, Wood Stock/Alamy, *(inset)* Cheryl Power/Photo Researchers. **p. 671:** Hand Colored Scanning Electron Micrograph. © Rob Kesseler. **p. 672:** *Figure 17-10* Yuji Sakai/Getty Images, Jim Richardson/Getty Images; *Figure 17-11* Susumu Nishinaga/Photo Researchers. **p. 673:** *Figure 17-12* Wayne Lawler/Ecopix. **p. 674:** *Figure 17-15 (L-R)* AgStock Images/Corbis, Dorling Kindersley/Getty Images, Gabor Geissler/Getty Images, Robert & Jean Pollock/Getty Images. **p. 676:** *Figure 17-17 (Top Row)* Anna Kern/Etsa/Corbis, Niall Benvie/Corbis, Tony Howell, *(Middle Row)* Michael Sedam/Photolibrary, John and Lisa Merrill/Corbis, Tony Howell, *(Bottom Row)* Frank Krahmer/Corbis, Micha Pawlitzki/Corbis, DLILLC/Corbis. **p. 677:** *Figure 17-18* Installation view of Claude Monet's Water Lilies (1914–26) Oil on canvas, three panels. The Museum of Modern Art. Mrs. Simon Guggenheim Fund. Photo © Jason Brownrigg. **p. 678:** *Figure 17-19 (L-R)* Grant Heilman Photography, Mark Bolton/Corbis, Jonathan Buckley/Getty Images, Martin Oeggerli/Visuals Unlimited. **p. 679:** Scott Sinklier/AgStock Images/Corbis. **p. 680:** *Figure 17-21* AP Photo/Minot Daily News, Marvin Baker. **p. 681:** *Figure 17-22* Jim Richardson/National Geographic Stock; *Figure 17-23* Darrell Gulin/Corbis. **p. 682:** *Figure 17-24* Mary Hobbs/Alamy, Jane Legate/Photolibrary; *Figure 17-25* Envision/Corbis. **p. 684:** *Figure 17-28* Clive Nichols/Getty Images, Coke Whitworth/Getty Images. **p. 685:** Tony Howell; *Figure 17-29* Dennis Drenner/Visuals Unlimited. **p. 686:** *Figure 17-31* Dr. Merton Brown/Visuals Unlimited. **p. 687:** *Figure 17-32* Adam Jones/Visuals Unlimited. **p. 689:** *Figure 17-35* Jerry & Marcy Monkman/Animals Animals/Earth Scenes, *(inset)* Radius Images/Corbis. **p. 691:** *Figure 17-37* George D. Lepp/Corbis. **p. 693:** Annie Corrigan/WFIU.

CHAPTER 18   pp. 698–699: Rob Kesseler. **p. 700:** Gerry Bishop/Visuals Unlimited; *Figure 18-1* Ingo Arndt/Minden Pictures. **p. 701:** *Figure 18-2* Andric/Gallery Stock, Copyright © Regents of the University of Minnesota. All rights reserved. **p. 702:** *Figure 18-3 (L-R)* Marc Vassallo © 2001 by The Taunton Press, Inc., Gregory G. Dimijian, M.D./Photo Researchers, Arco Images GmbH/Alamy. **p. 704:** *Figure 18-5* Jerry Harpur/Gap Photo/Visuals Unlimited; *Figure 18-6* Gunawan Kartapranata/Wikimedia Commons.

Index

Instructor's Resource Map

What Is Life? A Guide to Biology, Second Edition is s

extraordinary range of instructor resources. The Instr

makes it easy to locate and access the resources you

INSIDE THE BACK COVER you will find the full **Ins**

Map —an overview of all the resources accompanyin

FOLLOWING THIS PAGE you will find **Chapter R**

specific lecture, homework, assessment, and lab reso

each chapter.

Instructor's Resource Map

The Instructor's Resource Map for *What Is Life? A Guide to Biology,* Second Edition, is organized to help you:

- Prepare lectures
- Build assignments
- Engage students in hands-on active learning activities

- Assess your students' understanding of the concepts
- Direct students to helpful study tools
- Prepare lab activities
- Create a syllabus

The Instructor's Resource Map describes each resource in detail, and tells you where you can find the resource—online and/or offline. In addition to the full **Instructor's Resource Map** (inside back cover), there are also sixteen **Chapter Resource Maps**. Use the Instructor's Resource Map to see resources across the entire book, and the Chapter Resource Maps to see what is available for specific chapters.

KEY TO FINDING YOUR RESOURCES

The Instructor's Resource Map directs you to different Web sites, discs, and print supplements. The key below provides Web site links and instructions for accessing what you need.

ONLINE (You'll need your username and password to access these sites. Please contact your local sales representative if you do not know your password or need additional access information.)

- **BIOPORTAL**
  www.courses.bfwpub.com/phelan2e
  BioPortal helps you administer your course by combining our fully customizable eBook, student media, instructor resources, and homework management tools all in one place.

- **BOOK COMPANION SITE**
  www.whfreeman.com/phelan2e
  The Book Companion Site (BCS) is a free site that provides student study tools and instructor resources (password-protected) for every chapter of the book.

- **FACULTY LOUNGE**
  www.whfreeman.com/facultylounge/nonmajors
  At this publisher-provided site you can share ideas, videos, animations, and other resources with colleagues. Adopters can access instructor resources here as well.

- **STAND-ALONE RESOURCES**
  These resources are available in addition to the BioPortal, Book Companion Site, and Faculty Lounge:
  - eBook
    (ebooks.bfwpub.com/phelan2e)
  - Prep-U (www.prep-u.com)
  - Lab options (Virtual Labs, LabPartner, and Hayden McNeil Custom)

OFFLINE (Contact your local sales representative to request a copy of any of these resources, or sample a copy at www.whfreeman.com/phelaninstructorresources.)

- **INSTRUCTOR RESOURCE DVD (IRDVD)**
  The IRDVD contains all of the instructor resources found on the Book Companion Site, in a format that makes it easy to find and export files.

- **TEST BANK**
  The Test Bank is offered in print and on CD (Windows and Mac formats on one disc).

- **PRINTED**
  Some resources are available as printed supplements, including the *Instructor's Resource Manual* (IRM), the Overhead Transparency Set, and the following student resources:
  - Questions About Life Reader
  - Student Success Guide
  - Exploring Biology: Case Studies
  - Connecting Biology to Life

CHAPTER 1 INSTRUCTOR'S RESOURCE MAP

I WANT TO PREPARE A LECTURE

CLASSROOM CATALYSTS
ONLINE: BioPortal; Book Companion Site
OFFLINE: IRDVD; IRM

- **ACTIVITY ONE: THE SCIENTIFIC METHOD (30 MINUTES)** shows how a hypothesis is generated and the need for a "testable" hypothesis.

- **ACTIVITY TWO: EXPERIMENTAL DESIGN (15-30 MINUTES)** shows how an experiment is set up and the requirements of both control and experimental groups.

- **ACTIVITY THREE: THE SCIENTIFIC METHOD AND DRUG RESEARCH (10-20 MINUTES)** evaluates the relationship between the scientific method and drug marketing.

- **ACTIVITY FOUR: GOOD VS. BAD SCIENCE (10-15 MINUTES)** analyzes the validity of science that is presented to them from various media sources.

- **ACTIVITY FIVE: BIOETHICS AND INFORMED CONSENT (15-30 MINUTES)** discusses the need for the bioethical issues of informed consent in human experimental trials.

STUDENT WORKSHEETS
ONLINE: BioPortal; Book Companion Site. **OFFLINE:** IRDVD; IRM

- **FIGURE 1-11 "WHEN YOU NEED TO KNOW..."** considers a control group and an experimental group as two treatment groups as a printed worksheet.

- **FIGURE 1-20 HUMAN HEIGHT AND STATISTICS** considers random sampling and statistics as a printed worksheet.

I WANT TO ASSESS MY STUDENTS

CHECK YOUR KNOWLEDGE CHAPTER QUIZZES
ONLINE: Book Companion Site; BioPortal **OFFLINE:** IRDVD

- **SCIENTIFIC THINKING**
  Questions regarding the scientific method.

I WANT LAB RESOURCES

HANDS-ON BIOLOGY: LABORATORIES FOR DISTANCE LEARNING
ONLINE: Book Companion Site (Instructor's Edition Only)
OFFLINE: Printed Stand-Alone Resource

- **LAB 1: SCIENTIFIC METHOD** objectives include formulating a testable hypothesis, collecting and analyzing data, constructing graphs, and considering all of the scientific method through hands-on approach with simple household supplies.

CHAPTER 2 INSTRUCTOR'S RESOURCE MAP

I WANT TO PREPARE A LECTURE

Q ANIMATIONS
ONLINE: BioPortal; Book Companion Site; Faculty Lounge
OFFLINE: IRDVD

- ATOMS AND CHEMICAL BONDS: THE BIG PICTURE (01:33) provides an overview of atoms and chemical bonds.

- ATOMS AND CHEMICAL BONDS: THE STRUCTURE OF ATOMS (02:43) offers a guide to key elements and the basic structure of an atom.

- ATOMS AND CHEMICAL BONDS: CHEMICAL BONDING (05:51) defines molecules and compounds; summarizes covalent, ionic, and hydrogen bonds.

- ATOMS AND CHEMICAL BONDS: Q QUESTION (00:59) shows a Check Your Understanding question regarding chemical bonds and protein strands.

LECTURE LAUNCHER VIDEOS
ONLINE: BioPortal; Book Companion Site. OFFLINE: IRDVD

- FATS CAN ACCUMULATE OVER TIME (01:28) discusses saturated and unsaturated fats in the body, and includes Thought and Fact questions as clicker question assessment.

- FOODS PROVIDING ENERGY (04:20) discusses food and its value in terms of energy for the body, and includes Thought and Fact questions as clicker question assessment.

CLASSROOM CATALYSTS
ONLINE: BioPortal; Book Companion Site. OFFLINE: IRDVD; IRM

- ACTIVITY ONE: BUILDING THE ELEMENTS (15-30 MINUTES) demonstrates what particles make up the atoms of different elements.

- ACTIVITY TWO: CHEMICAL BONDS (30-60 MINUTES) demonstrates the different kinds of chemical bonds and the relevant strengths of these bonds.

- ACTIVITY THREE: THE POWER OF THE HYDROGEN BOND (15-30 MINUTES) explores the strength of the "weak" hydrogen bond.

- ACTIVITY FOUR: POTATOES—THE IRISH POTATO FAMINE (15-30 MINUTES) discusses the role of starch-based crops in providing energy for organisms (humans).

- ACTIVITY FIVE: PROTEIN ASSEMBLY (15-30 MINUTES) discusses the peptide bond and the orientation challenges of the secondary structure of proteins.

- ACTIVITY SIX: POLYMER STRUCTURE DIVERSITY (15-30 MINUTES) helps students explore the diversity of polymer structures that can be constructed from small sets of monomers.

- ACTIVITY SEVEN: WHY CAN'T WE DIGEST CELLULOSE? (15-30 MINUTES) discusses how the different orientations of chemical bonds between simple sugars in a complex carbohydrate affect how polysaccharides can be broken down by certain enzymes.

STUDENT WORKSHEETS
ONLINE: BioPortal; Book Companion Site. OFFLINE: IRDVD; IRM

- FIGURE 2-09 COVALENT BONDS: STRENGTH THROUGH SHARING considers each molecule and identifies its value as a graph (the advantage of drawing it that way) as a printed worksheet.

- FIGURE 2-13 "WALKING ON WATER!": WATER MOLECULES AND SURFACE TENSIONS OF WATER considers how water's polarity and its Mickey Mouse shape also account for its solvent properties, its high heat capacity, and its ability to float as solid ice as a printed worksheet.

I WANT TO CREATE HOMEWORK ASSIGNMENTS OR HANDS-ON ACTIVITIES

Q ANIMATIONS (See left column for listing)

CONNECTING BIOLOGY TO LIFE
ONLINE: BioPortal; Book Companion Site OFFLINE: IRDVD

- WHY DO WE CRAVE SALT? discusses the role sodium and chloride play in our diet, environment, and agriculture.

- LEAD IN OUR LIVES discusses signs and symptoms of lead poisoning; how and why lead was historically used; and lead exposure and its effects on the body and central nervous system specifically.

- MERCURY POISONING discusses mercury found in fish, mercury toxicity and illnesses, and mercury contamination in the environment.

- PLANTS SERVE UP USEFUL ENZYMES discusses the functions of papain, plants as a medicinal resource, enzymes' role in chemical reactions, and plant species in rain forests.

I WANT TO ASSESS MY STUDENTS

Q ANIMATIONS (See left column for listing)

CHECK YOUR KNOWLEDGE CHAPTER QUIZZES
ONLINE: Book Companion Site; BioPortal. OFFLINE: IRDVD

- ATOMS AND CHEMICAL BONDING
  Questions regarding the structure of atoms and chemical bonding.

I WANT STUDY TOOLS FOR MY STUDENTS

Q ANIMATIONS (See left column for listing)

I WANT LAB RESOURCES

HANDS-ON BIOLOGY: LABORATORIES FOR DISTANCE LEARNING
ONLINE: Book Companion Site (Instructor's Edition Only)
OFFLINE: Printed Stand-Alone Resource

- LAB 2: INTRODUCTION TO CHEMISTRY diagrams basic structure of atoms, distinguishes the different kinds of bonds, and defines several chemistry terms and formations using simple household and lab supplies.

CHAPTER 3 INSTRUCTOR'S RESOURCE MAP

I WANT TO PREPARE A LECTURE

Q ANIMATIONS
ONLINE: BioPortal; Book Companion Site; Faculty Lounge
OFFLINE: IRDVD

- **CELLS: THE BIG PICTURE (01:48)** provides an overview of cells.

- **CELLS: ORIGIN OF ORGANELLES (03:35)** offers a guide to organelles and the different kinds of cells.

- **CELLS: A ROAD MAP (12:03)** defines the nucleus, the cytoskeleton, plant chloroplasts, mitochondria, lysosomes, and other key terms.

- **CELLS: THE PLASMA MEMBRANE (05:41)** offers a guide to the plasma membrane, phospholipids, recognition proteins, enzymatic proteins, and cellular response.

- **CELLS: Q QUESTION (01:37)** shows a Check Your Understanding question regarding how proteins regulate cellular responses.

LECTURE LAUNCHER VIDEOS
ONLINE: BioPortal; Book Companion Site. OFFLINE: IRDVD

- **ANIMAL CELL STRUCTURE** discusses the structure of animal cells, and includes Thought and Fact clicker questions.

- **PLANT CELL STRUCTURE** discusses the structure of plant cells, and includes Thought and Fact clicker questions.

CLASSROOM CATALYSTS
ONLINE: BioPortal; Book Companion Site. OFFLINE: IRDVD; IRM

- **ACTIVITY ONE: FORM RELATES TO FUNCTION (10-15 MINUTES)** explores the relationship between a cell's form and its function.

- **ACTIVITY TWO: LIPID BILAYERS (15-20 MINUTES)** demonstrates how the amphipathic nature of phospholipid molecules can create a lipid bilayer that has semipermeable properties.

- **ACTIVITY THREE: MEMBRANE FLUIDITY AND OTHER PROPERTIES OF CELL MEMBRANES (15-30 MINUTES)** shows how different structures of the plasma membrane contribute to the properties of active and passive transport across a plasma membrane.

- **ACTIVITY FOUR: THE THREE AMOEBAS LOOK FOR AN ISOTONIC HOME (15-20 MINUTES)** explores the concepts of tonicity of water solutions and their effects on living organisms.

- **ACTIVITY FIVE: DESIGN YOUR OWN ORGANELLE ANALOGIES (10-30 MINUTES)** promotes student retention of the functions of the basic eukaryotic cell components by student analogy construction.

- **ACTIVITY SIX: A PROTEIN MOLECULE FOR EXPORT (15 MINUTES)** demonstrates how different organelles contribute to the synthesis and transport of proteins.

STUDENT WORKSHEETS
ONLINE: BioPortal; Book Companion Site. OFFLINE: IRDVD; IRM

- **FIGURE 3-07 HOW DID EUKARYOTIC CELLS BECOME SO STRUCTURALLY COMPLEX?** considers how the relative size of prokaryotic and eukaryotic cells supports or fails to support the theory of endosymbiosis as a printed worksheet.

- **FIGURE 3-16 DIFFUSION** considers the process of diffusion and the role molecules play as a printed worksheet.

- **FIGURE 3-36 THE ENDOMEMBRANE SYSTEM** considers how endocytosis and exocytosis processes contribute to the work of the endomembrane system.

- **FIGURE 3-39 REVIEW OF THE STRUCTURES AND FUNCTIONS OF CELLULAR ORGANISMS** considers cell types and their specific organelles as a printed worksheet.

I WANT TO CREATE HOMEWORK ASSIGNMENTS OR HANDS-ON ACTIVITIES

Q ANIMATIONS (See left column for listing)

CONNECTING BIOLOGY TO LIFE
ONLINE: BioPortal; Book Companion Site OFFLINE: IRDVD

- **OSMOSIS HAPPENS** discusses osmosis, absorption of water, and elimination of waste.

I WANT TO ASSESS MY STUDENTS

Q ANIMATIONS (See left column for listing)

CHECK YOUR KNOWLEDGE CHAPTER QUIZZES
ONLINE: Book Companion Site; BioPortal. OFFLINE: IRDVD

- **CELLS**
  Questions regarding cells.

I WANT STUDY TOOLS FOR MY STUDENTS

Q ANIMATIONS (See left column for listing)

I WANT LAB RESOURCES

HANDS-ON BIOLOGY: LABORATORIES FOR DISTANCE LEARNING
ONLINE: Book Companion Site (Instructor's Edition Only)
OFFLINE: Printed Stand-Alone Resource

- **LAB 4: CELLS AND CELL PROCESSES** objectives include prokaryotic and eukaryotic cells, cellular organelles, animal cells, protist cells, and plant cells through hands-on approach.

CHAPTER 4 INSTRUCTOR'S RESOURCE MAP

I WANT TO PREPARE A LECTURE

Q ANIMATIONS
ONLINE: BioPortal; Book Companion Site; Faculty Lounge
OFFLINE: IRDVD

- PHOTOSYNTHESIS: THE BIG PICTURE (01:29) provides an overview of photosynthesis.

- PHOTOSYNTHESIS: THE "PHOTO" REACTIONS (07:12) offers a detailed guide to photosynthesis, chlorophyll, and water's role in the process.

- PHOTOSYNTHESIS: Q QUESTION 1 (1:42) shows a Check Your Understanding question regarding why plants need water for photosynthesis to occur.

- PHOTOSYNTHESIS: THE "SYNTHESIS" REACTIONS (04:36) offers a guide to "photo" reactions and "synthesis" reactions, defines rubisco, and goes over the Calvin cycle.

- PHOTOSYNTHESIS: Q QUESTION 2 (00:35) shows a Check Your Understanding question regarding how feeding a cut flower sugar keeps it alive.

- CELLULAR RESPIRATION: THE BIG PICTURE (02:13) provides an overview of cellular respiration.

- CELLULAR RESPIRATION: GLYCOLYSIS (03:37) shows a detailed guide to glycolysis.

- CELLULAR RESPIRATION: THE KREBS CYCLE (05:03) shows a detailed guide to the Krebs cycle, the function of NADH, and mitochondria.

- CELLULAR RESPIRATION: Q QUESTION 1 (00:35) shows a Check Your Understanding question regarding mitochondria in muscle cells.

- CELLULAR RESPIRATION: THE ELECTRON TRANSPORT CHAIN (04:39) defines concentration gradient, goes over the electron transport chain, and the overall purpose of cellular respiration.

- CELLULAR RESPIRATION: Q QUESTION 2 (01:14) shows a Check Your Understanding question regarding cyanide as a deadly poison.

LECTURE LAUNCHER VIDEOS
ONLINE: BioPortal; Book Companion Site. OFFLINE: IRDVD

- AEROBIC AND ANAEROBIC PHOTOSYNTHESIS (04:00) discusses aerobic and anaerobic photosynthesis and includes Thought and Fact clicker questions.

- DISCOVERY OF PHOTOSYNTHESIS (02:19) discusses the discovery of photosynthesis, and includes Thought and Fact clicker questions.

- PHOTOSYNTHESIS (04:50) discusses photosynthesis, and includes Thought and Fact clicker questions.

CLASSROOM CATALYSTS
ONLINE: BioPortal; Book Companion Site. OFFLINE: IRDVD; IRM

- ACTIVITY ONE: KINETIC VERSUS POTENTIAL ENERGY (5-10 MINUTES) introduces different examples of kinetic and potential energy.

- ACTIVITY TWO: WHY IS ENERGY STORED IN SUGARS AND NOT ATP? (5 MINUTES) compares the differences in energy stored as sugars versus ATP.

- ACTIVITY THREE: WHY DO WE STORE MOST OF OUR ENERGY AS FATS INSTEAD OF SUGARS? (5-10 MINUTES) compares the differences in energy stored as lipids versus complex carbohydrates.

- ACTIVITY FOUR: SOLAR ENERGY VS. PHOTOSYNTHESIS (10-20 MINUTES) compares the function of a photovoltaic cell to the light-dependent reactions in photosynthesis.

- ACTIVITY FIVE: WHAT DO CHLOROPHYLL AND FIREWORKS HAVE IN COMMON? (15 MINUTES) compares the energy changes due to electron excitation in photosynthesis and fireworks.

- ACTIVITY SIX: FOLLOW THE ENERGY: THE MITOCHONDRION EDITION (10-15 MINUTES) makes the connection between the Laws of Thermodynamics and the energy transfer reactions in a mitochondrion.

- ACTIVITY SEVEN: DEMONSTRATING ELECTRON TRANSPORT AND THE CHEMIOSMOTIC HYPOTHESIS (15-30 MINUTES) helps students comprehend the transfer of energy and ions for the electron transport chain and chemiosmotic hypothesis.

- ACTIVITY EIGHT: NUMBER OF MITOCHONDRIA AND ENERGY DEMAND: A CLASSROOM DISCUSSION (15-30 MINUTES) compares the energy demands of various cells and how energy needs relate to number of mitochondria.

STUDENT WORKSHEETS
ONLINE: BioPortal; Book Companion Site. OFFLINE: IRDVD; IRM

- FIGURE 4-11 PHOTOSYNTHESIS: THE BIG PICTURE considers the simplest equation for photosynthesis.

- FIGURE 4-12 PHOTOSYNTHETIC FACTORIES examines the structure of a typical leaf, its features, and function.

- FIGURE 4-39 "MORE FLEXIBLE THAN AUTOS" covers cells and their supply of ATP.

I WANT TO CREATE HOMEWORK ASSIGNMENTS OR HANDS-ON ACTIVITIES

Q ANIMATIONS (See left column for listing)

CONNECTING BIOLOGY TO LIFE
ONLINE: BioPortal; Book Companion Site OFFLINE: IRDVD

- PICKLING AND FERMENTATION discusses bacteria, fermentation through pickling, preservation, and salt.

I WANT TO ASSESS MY STUDENTS

Q ANIMATIONS (See left column for listing)

CHECK YOUR KNOWLEDGE CHAPTER QUIZZES
ONLINE: Book Companion Site BioPortal. OFFLINE: IRDVD

- ENERGY AND CELLULAR RESPIRATION
  Questions regarding energy and cellular respiration.

I WANT STUDY TOOLS FOR MY STUDENTS

Q ANIMATIONS (See left column for listing)

I WANT LAB RESOURCES

HANDS-ON BIOLOGY: LABORATORIES FOR DISTANCE LEARNING
ONLINE: Book Companion Site (Instructor's Edition Only)
OFFLINE: Printed Stand-Alone Resource

- LAB 6: PHOTOSYNTHESIS AND CELLULAR RESPIRATION objectives include using chemical indicators to test for the presence of the end products of photosynthesis and cell respiration and comparing and contrasting those materials, predicting the effect of leaf coloration of starch, and how environmental factors affect photosynthesis and cellular respiration through hands-on activities and simple household and lab supplies.

CHAPTER 5 INSTRUCTOR'S RESOURCE MAP

I WANT TO PREPARE A LECTURE

Q ANIMATIONS

ONLINE: BioPortal; Book Companion Site; Faculty Lounge
OFFLINE: IRDVD

- **GENE EXPRESSION: THE BIG PICTURE (01:25)** provides an overview of gene expression.

- **GENE EXPRESSION: TRANSCRIPTION (03:44)** offer a detailed guide to transcription and RNA polymerase.

- **GENE EXPRESSION: TRANSLATION 1 (01:42)** offer a detailed guide to translation.

- **GENE EXPRESSION: Q QUESTION (04:36)** shows a Check Your Understanding question regarding "fast flush" responses to alcohol.

LECTURE LAUNCHER VIDEOS

ONLINE: BioPortal; Book Companion Site. OFFLINE: IRDVD

- **GENETICALLY MODIFIED CROPS (03:04)** discusses genetically modified crops and includes Thought and Fact clicker questions.

- **GMO CROP SCARE (01:08)** discusses the GMO crop scare, and includes Thought and Fact clicker questions.

- **HUMAN GENOME PROJECT (01:43)** discusses the Human Genome Project, and includes Thought and Fact clicker questions.

- **CLONING ANIMALS (01:46)** discusses animal cloning, and includes Thought and Fact clicker questions.

CLASSROOM CATALYSTS

ONLINE: BioPortal; Book Companion Site OFFLINE: IRDVD; IRM

- **ACTIVITY ONE: CENTRAL DOGMA OF MOLECULAR BIOLOGY (10-15 MINUTES)** reviews the central dogma of molecular biology.

- **ACTIVITY TWO: TRANSCRIPTION (10-15 MINUTES; FOR LARGE CLASS (15-30 MINUTES)** reviews the process of transcription.

- **ACTIVITY THREE: TRANSLATION (20-30 MINUTES)** reviews the process of translation.

- **ACTIVITY FOUR: SIMULATING TRANSLATION (20-40 MINUTES)** simulates the steps to assembling an amino acid.

- **ACTIVITY FIVE: STUDENT WORKSHEET ON DNA REPLICATION, TRANSCRIPTION, TRANSLATION, AND EXPRESSED TRAITS (10-15 MINUTES)** reviews process connecting the concepts of complementary base pairs in DNA and translation as well as connecting genotypes and phenotypes.

- **ACTIVITY SIX: POINT MUTATIONS (20-30 MINUTES)** reviews the different types of point mutations and how they cause shifts in the reading frame of the amino acid sequence.

- **ACTIVITY SEVEN: GENETICALLY MODIFIED FOODS (20-30 MINUTES)** discusses the merits and hazards of genetically modified foods.

- **ACTIVITY EIGHT: HUMAN GENOME AND GENETIC DISCRIMINATION (105-130 MINUTES)** discusses how the Human Genome Project information could be used to protect society or abused by limiting privacy and/or personal freedoms of individuals.

- **ACTIVITY NINE: POINT MUTATIONS (15-30 MINUTES)** examines the uses and abuses of genetic information by health insurance companies.

- **ACTIVITY TEN: COMPULSORY DNA FINGERPRINTING: CRIME PREVENTION OR A VIOLATION OF CIVIL LIBERTIES? (90-105 MINUTES)** discusses the merits and hazards of compulsory DNA fingerprinting for the entire population. Discusses the concepts of privacy of one's DNA versus the merits of criminal identification.

STUDENT WORKSHEETS

ONLINE: BioPortal; Book Companion Site OFFLINE: IRDVD; IRM

- **FIGURE 5-04 OVERVIEW OF THE STRUCTURE OF DNA** identifies molecule features and natural ways base pairs can pair up as a printed worksheet.

- **FIGURE 5-08 DOES THE SIZE OF AN ORGANISM'S GENOME RELATE TO ITS COMPLEXITY?** considers the relative numbers of base pairs (rungs on the DNA "ladder") among the fruit fly, newt, and human. Considers the process of diffusion and the role molecules play as a printed worksheet.

I WANT TO CREATE HOMEWORK ASSIGNMENTS OR HANDS-ON ACTIVITIES

Q ANIMATIONS (See left column for listing)

CONNECTING BIOLOGY TO LIFE

ONLINE: BioPortal, Book Companion Site. OFFLINE: IRDVD

- **BUSTING POACHERS WITH DNA BARCODING** Identifying endangered species through their genetic code.

I WANT TO ASSESS MY STUDENTS

Q ANIMATIONS (See left column for listing)

CHECK YOUR KNOWLEDGE CHAPTER QUIZZES

ONLINE: Book Companion Site BioPortal. OFFLINE: IRDVD

- **DNA, GENE EXPRESSION, AND BIOTECHNOLOGY** Multiple choice questions regarding DNA, gene expression, and biotechnology.

I WANT STUDY TOOLS FOR MY STUDENTS

Q ANIMATIONS (See left column for listing)

I WANT LAB RESOURCES

HANDS-ON BIOLOGY: LABORATORIES FOR DISTANCE LEARNING

ONLINE: Book Companion Site (Instructor's Edition Only)
OFFLINE: Printed Stand-Alone Resource

- **LAB 10: BIOLOGY IN FORENSIC INVESTIGATIONS** objectives include observing fingerprint patterns and details, analyzing the role of DNA in forensic investigations, and interpreting information in an STR profile through hands-on approach with simple household and lab kit supplies.

CHAPTER 6 INSTRUCTOR'S RESOURCE MAP

I WANT TO PREPARE A LECTURE

Q ANIMATIONS
ONLINE: BioPortal; Book Companion Site; Faculty Lounge
OFFLINE: IRDVD

- CELL DIVISION: THE BIG PICTURE (02:32) provides an overview of cell division.

- CELL DIVISION: DNA REPLICATION (04:38) offers a detailed guide to the cell cycle, DNA replication, and mutations in DNA sequences.

- CELL DIVISION: Q QUESTION 1 (02:22) shows a Check Your Understanding question regarding mutation and sickle cell disease.

- CELL DIVISION: MITOSIS AND CANCER (05:14) defines mitosis, telophase, and briefs on normal and cancer cells.

- CELL DIVISION: Q QUESTION 2 (02:36) shows a Check Your understanding question regarding cancer cells.

- CELL DIVISION: MEIOSIS AND SEXUAL REPRODUCTION (06:56) provides an overview of meiosis, sexual reproduction.

- CELL DIVISION: Q QUESTION 3 (02:20) shows a Check Your Understanding question regarding nondisjunction.

LECTURE LAUNCHER VIDEOS
ONLINE: BioPortal; Book Companion Site. OFFLINE: IRDVD

- MEIOSIS (01:56) discusses meiosis, and includes Thought and Fact clicker questions.

- MITOSIS (02:50) discusses mitosis, and includes Thought and Fact clicker questions.

CLASSROOM CATALYSTS
ONLINE: BioPortal; Book Companion Site. OFFLINE: IRDVD; IRM

- ACTIVITY ONE: CHROMOSOME CONDENSATION (10-15 MINUTES) reviews the need for chromosome condensation prior to mitosis.

- ACTIVITY TWO: CHROMOSOMES AND CELL DIVISION (15-20 MINUTES) reviews the need for chromosome condensation prior to mitosis.

- ACTIVITY THREE: CROSSING OVER IS EASY TO DO (15-20 MINUTES) reviews the process of crossing-over of homologous chromosomes that occurs during prophase one.

- ACTIVITY FOUR: CELL DIVISION—MITOSIS AND MEIOSIS—THE CARD GAME! (15-20 MINUTES) reviews the process of crossing-over of homologous chromosomes that occurs during prophase one.

- ACTIVITY FIVE: MEIOSIS AND MITOSIS (15-20 MINUTES) enhances student understanding of the cell division processes of mitosis and meiosis.

- ACTIVITY SIX: THE SPIDER PLANT—SEXUAL AND ASEXUAL REPRODUCTION (15-20 MINUTES) enhances student understanding of chromosomal distribution during the processes of mitosis and meiosis.

- ACTIVITY SEVEN: X-CHROMOSOME INACTIVATION (30-60 MINUTES) enhances student understanding of advantages and disadvantages to sexual versus asexual forms of reproduction.

- ACTIVITY EIGHT: TRISOMIES AND MONOSOMIES (30-60 MINUTES) enhances student understanding of inactivation of the X chromosome in humans and other animals.

STUDENT WORKSHEETS
ONLINE: BioPortal; Book Companion Site. OFFLINE: IRDVD; IRM

- FIGURE 6-09 MITOSIS: CELL DUPLICATION, STEP BY STEP

- FIGURE 6-10 "DIVIDING IN TWO"

- FIGURE 6-11 A SIMPLIFIED INTRODUCTION TO MITOSIS

- FIGURE 6-19 MEIOSIS reduces the genome by half in anticipation of combining it with another genome.

- FIGURE 6-20 MEIOSIS: GENERATING REPRODUCTIVE CELLS, STEP BY STEP identifies mitosis, eukaryotic cells, and prokaryotic cells as a printed worksheet.

- FIGURE 6-21 EGG AND SPERM examines all of the features of mitosis and meiosis in a compare and contrast as a printed worksheet.

- FIGURE 6-29 OTHER METHODS OF SEX DETERMINATION considers the differences between egg and sperm, and different meiosis outcomes as a printed worksheet.

- FIGURE 6-33 KARYOTYPE FOR DOWN'S SYNDROME goes over different ways to determine sex in all animals.

I WANT TO CREATE HOMEWORK ASSIGNMENTS OR HANDS-ON ACTIVITIES

Q ANIMATIONS (See left column for listing)

I WANT TO ASSESS MY STUDENTS

Q ANIMATIONS (See left column for listing)

CHECK YOUR KNOWLEDGE CHAPTER QUIZZES
ONLINE: Book Companion Site; BioPortal. OFFLINE: IRDVD

- CHROMOSOMES AND CELL DIVISION
  Questions regarding chromosomes and cell division.

I WANT STUDY TOOLS FOR MY STUDENTS

Q ANIMATIONS (See left column for listing)

I WANT LAB RESOURCES

Q ANIMATIONS (See left column for listing)

HANDS-ON BIOLOGY: LABORATORIES FOR DISTANCE LEARNING
ONLINE: Book Companion Site (Instructor's Edition Only)
OFFLINE: Printed Stand-Alone Resource

- LAB 7: MITOSIS AND MEIOSIS objectives include defining all cell division terminology and stages of mitosis and meiosis, and identifying genetic diversity in a population through a hands-on approach.

CHAPTER 7 INSTRUCTOR'S RESOURCE MAP

I WANT TO PREPARE A LECTURE

Q ANIMATIONS
ONLINE: BioPortal; Book Companion Site; Faculty Lounge
OFFLINE: IRDVD

- MENDELIAN INHERITANCE: MENDEL'S LAW OF SEGREGATION (03:06) introduces Mendel's Law of Segregation, additionally covering gene expression, dominant vs. recessive alleles, and meiosis.

- MENDELIAN INHERITANCE: PUNNETT SQUARES (06:03) discusses the method of Punnett square analysis and the test-cross.

- MENDELIAN INHERITANCE: Q QUESTION 1 (02:54) uses color-blindness to discuss sex-linked genes, and shows how to understand them by using a Punnett square.

- MENDELIAN INHERITANCE: MENDEL'S LAW OF INDEPENDENT ASSORTMENT (06:30) touches on important concepts including Mendel's Law of Independent Assortment, the 9:3:3:1 ratio, and crossing over.

- MENDELIAN INHERITANCE: Q QUESTION 2 (02:28) asks "why do most redheads have pale skin?" and uses concepts of independent assortment and linked genes to explain.

- MENDELIAN INHERITANCE: THE BIG PICTURE (02:48) reviews the broad picture of genetic inheritance, as well as the work Mendel performed to establish it.

LECTURE LAUNCHER VIDEOS
ONLINE: BioPortal; Book Companion Site. OFFLINE: IRDVD

- INHERITANCE OF TRAITS (01:50) discusses genetic inheritance, and includes Thought and Fact questions as clicker question assessment.

- MENDEL'S EXPERIMENTS ON INHERITANCE (02:19) discusses Mendel's experiments, and includes Thought and Fact questions as clicker question assessment.

CLASSROOM CATALYSTS
ONLINE: BioPortal; Book Companion Site. OFFLINE: IRDVD; IRM

- ACTIVITY ONE: GREGOR MENDEL (15-20 MINUTES) reviews the impact of Gregor Mendel's work on genetics.

- ACTIVITY TWO: MENDEL'S LAW OF INDEPENDENT ASSORTMENT (10-20 MINUTES) helps students understand the process of independent assortment.

- ACTIVITY THREE: MONOHYBRID AND DIHYBRID CROSSES (20-30 MINUTES) enhances understanding of genetic crosses using several practice monohybrid and dihybrid crosses.

- ACTIVITY FOUR: SIMULATING A TEST-CROSS OF LOLLYBOBS, A NEWLY DISCOVERED CREATURE (15-30 MINUTES) students utilize a test-cross on a fictitious animal.

- ACTIVITY FIVE: HUMAN GENETIC TRAITS (40-55 MINUTES) enhances understanding of human genetic traits and the probability of appearance based on the recessive or dominance of that trait.

- ACTIVITY SIX: HUMAN BALDNESS: SEX-LINKED GENETIC TRAIT? (30-60 MINUTES) enhances understanding of complex human genetic traits and the means by which traits appear.

STUDENT WORKSHEETS
ONLINE: BioPortal; Book Companion Site. OFFLINE: IRDVD; IRM

- FIGURE 7-03 UNLUCKY CATCH considers the chances that the nieces and nephews of a man with fish odor syndrome will inherit the condition, as a printed worksheet.

- FIGURE 7-06 THE "PRE-MADE HUMAN" presents the theories of the "ovists," who believed that within each ovum was a complete human being, and asks students for a logical critique of the theory, as a printed worksheet.

- FIGURE 7-13 THE CHANCE OF INHERITING TAY-SACHS DISEASE asks students to predict the outcome of pregnancies for two people who are both heterozygous for Tay-Sachs, as a printed worksheet.

- FIGURE 7-19 MULTIPLE ALLELISM considers possible blood types for the children of a couple who both have type AB blood.

I WANT TO CREATE HOMEWORK ASSIGNMENTS OR HANDS-ON ACTIVITIES

Q ANIMATIONS (See left column for listing)

EXPLORING BIOLOGY: CASE STUDIES
ONLINE: Book Companion Site; Faculty Lounge

- IT'S ALL IN THE FAMILY
This case study follows those who struggle with concerns about increased risk of genetic mutations in children of older parents. Their discussions with a genetic counselor show students how to use the laws of Mendelian inheritance to statistically evaluate the potential risks of heritable disease.

I WANT TO ASSESS MY STUDENTS

Q ANIMATIONS (See left column for listing)

CHECK YOUR KNOWLEDGE CHAPTER QUIZZES
ONLINE: Book Companion Site; BioPortal. OFFLINE: IRDVD

- MENDELIAN INHERITANCE
Questions regarding Mendelian inheritance.

I WANT STUDY TOOLS FOR MY STUDENTS

Q ANIMATIONS (See left column for listing)

I WANT LAB RESOURCES

HANDS-ON BIOLOGY: LABORATORIES FOR DISTANCE LEARNING
ONLINE: Book Companion Site (Instructor's Edition Only)
OFFLINE: Printed Stand-Alone Resource

- LAB 8: HUMAN GENETICS objectives include interpreting male and female karyotypes, explaining chromosomal abnormalities, understanding the Punnett square, and defining genetic terms through hands-on approach.

CHAPTER 8 INSTRUCTOR'S RESOURCE MAP

I WANT TO PREPARE A LECTURE

Q ANIMATIONS
ONLINE: BioPortal; Book Companion Site; Faculty Lounge
OFFLINE: IRDVD

- EVOLUTION IN ACTION: THE BIG PICTURE (03:57) covers comparative anatomy, differentiation of species, and the development of similar, but different, features.

- EVOLUTION IN ACTION: EVOLUTION (07:34) examines the process of evolution within a fruit fly population, touching on key points such as natural selection, fitness, and experimental design.

- EVOLUTION IN ACTION: Q QUESTION (01:48) shows a Check Your Understanding question regarding whether evolution occurs and looks for an answer by designing an experiment using bacteria.

LECTURE LAUNCHER VIDEOS
ONLINE: BioPortal; Book Companion Site. OFFLINE: IRDVD

- CHARLES DARWIN (01:55) discusses Darwin, and includes Thought and Fact questions as clicker question assessment.

- GALÁPAGOS ISLANDS AT RISK (01:32) discusses dangers faced by the Galápagos Islands, and includes Thought and Fact questions as clicker question assessment.

CLASSROOM CATALYSTS
ONLINE: BioPortal; Book Companion Site. OFFLINE: IRDVD; IRM

- ACTIVITY ONE: HAMMERS AND NATURAL SELECTION (15 MINUTES) shows how allele frequency changes in a population.

- ACTIVITY TWO: NATURAL SELECTION IN ACTION (OUT-OF-CLASS ACTIVITY) (60-90 MINUTES) explores natural selection in a small sample population of animals introduced to an island.

- ACTIVITY THREE: EVOLUTIONARY TRADE-OFFS (10–20 MINUTES) students will explore the trade-offs that can accompany evolutionary adaptations.

- ACTIVITY FOUR: ARTIFICIAL SELECTION (10–15 MINUTES) helps students to understand Darwin's idea of *descent with modification* by studying the artificial selection performed for centuries by plant and animal breeders.

- ACTIVITY FIVE: GENETIC DRIFT (30 MINUTES) illustrates genetic drift.

- ACTIVITY SIX: MUTATION (15-30 MINUTES) shows how genetic mutations permeate a population.

- ACTIVITY SEVEN: FITNESS (60-85 MINUTES) defines fitness.

- ACTIVITY EIGHT: PERFECT ORGANISMS (30-45 MINUTES) explores the consequences of genetic manipulation in human beings for the purpose of perfecting human beings.

- ACTIVITY NINE: VESTIGIAL STRUCTURES (30-60 MINUTES) explores the presence of vestigial organs in populations.

STUDENT WORKSHEETS
ONLINE: BioPortal; Book Companion Site. OFFLINE: IRDVD; IRM

- FIGURE 8-01 STARVATION RESISTANCE IN FRUIT FLIES presents a graphical approach to determining what percentage of a fly population will survive starvation, as a printed worksheet.

- FIGURE 8-02 EVOLUTION IN ACTION: INCREASING FRUIT FLY RESISTANCE TO STARVATION considers how a population's resistance to starvation can change over time, as a printed worksheet.

- FIGURE 8-14 GENETIC DRIFT: BOTTLENECK EFFECT considers allele frequency in a cheetah population after a hypothetical disaster, as a printed worksheet.

- FIGURE 8-41 AN EVOLUTIONARY CLOCK? considers differences in the beta globulin chains of various primates, as a printed worksheet.

I WANT TO CREATE HOMEWORK ASSIGNMENTS OR HANDS-ON ACTIVITIES

Q ANIMATIONS (See left column for listing)

EXPLORING BIOLOGY: CASE STUDIES
ONLINE: Book Companion Site; Faculty Lounge

- SCHOOL'S OUT FOR SUMMER
In this case study, students learn about the effects of toxic mushrooms, which interfere with RNA polymerase, in a story about friends making their own food on a camping trip. The friends' idyllic weekend turns into an epidemiological mystery, as they recount the events that led to severe illness, hospitalization, and, ultimately, a liver transplant.

I WANT TO ASSESS MY STUDENTS

CHECK YOUR KNOWLEDGE CHAPTER QUIZZES
ONLINE: Book Companion Site BioPortal. OFFLINE: IRDVD

- EVOLUTION AND NATURAL SELECTION
Questions regarding evolution and natural selection.

I WANT STUDY TOOLS FOR MY STUDENTS

Q ANIMATIONS (See left column for listing)

I WANT LAB RESOURCES

Q ANIMATIONS (See left column for listing)

HANDS-ON BIOLOGY: LABORATORIES FOR DISTANCE LEARNING
ONLINE: Book Companion Site (Instructor's Edition Only)
OFFLINE: Printed Stand-Alone Resource

- LAB 11: EVOLUTION objectives include analyzing the effect of pesticide applications on insect populations, understanding natural selection and the principles of evolution through a hands-on approach with simple household and lab kit supplies.

CHAPTER 9 INSTRUCTOR'S RESOURCE MAP

I WANT TO PREPARE A LECTURE

CLASSROOM CATALYSTS
ONLINE: BioPortal; Book Companion Site OFFLINE: IRDVD; IRM

- **ACTIVITY ONE: IMPRINTING AND LEARNING (45-75 MINUTES)** reviews the impact of imprinting and human influences on imprinting.

- **ACTIVITY TWO: ASSOCIATIVE LEARNING (15 MINUTES)** introduces students to the concept of associative learning, including Ivan Pavlov's classical conditioning experiments.

- **ACTIVITY THREE: THE ALTRUISM PARADOX (10-15 MINUTES)** helps students to explore how altruistic behavior benefits the population while potentially decreasing the environmental fitness of the altruistic individual.

- **ACTIVITY FOUR: MATE SELECTION AND THE COSTS OF REPRODUCTION (60-90 MINUTES)** reviews the concepts of mate selection and productive costs.

- **ACTIVITY FIVE: FIGHTING AND HIERARCHY (45-60 MINUTES)** reviews the impact of fighting on communication and hierarchy development.

- **ACTIVITY SIX: WHY DO YOUNG WOMEN CHOOSE OLDER MEN? (5-15 MINUTES)** reviews the development of mating behaviors and reproductive investment.

- **ACTIVITY SEVEN: WHY DO FIREFLIES FLASH? (15-30 MINUTES)** reviews the concepts of communication, including visual communication.

STUDENT WORKSHEETS
ONLINE: BioPortal; Book Companion Site. OFFLINE: IRDVD; IRM

- **FIGURE 9-07 PROGRAMMED TO RETRIEVE** considers the triggers, actions, and results of a particular behavior in geese, as a printed worksheet.

- **FIGURE 9-17 MAXIMIZING REPRODUCTIVE SUCCESS IN FRUIT FLIES** considers differing reproductive strategies of male and female fruit flies, as a printed worksheet.

- **FIGURE 9-24 KING OF THE BEACH** considers how genes are passed along in populations of fruit flies, as a printed worksheet.

I WANT TO CREATE HOMEWORK ASSIGNMENTS OR HANDS-ON ACTIVITIES

CONNECTING BIOLOGY TO LIFE
ONLINE: BioPortal; Book Companion Site; Faculty Lounge
OFFLINE: IRDVD

- **ELEPHANT COMMUNICATION**
Biologists discover that elephants use seismic waves to communicate over distances.

EXPLORING BIOLOGY: CASE STUDIES
ONLINE: Book Companion Site, Faculty Lounge

- **DOGS GONE WILD**
This case study tells the story of a young researcher who "bags and tags" fresh scat left by dogs and foxes in the local nature preserve. The results of his data collection, used to study diet and species interaction, produce unexpected results, demonstrating the unpredictability of research and opening avenues for future science.

I WANT TO ASSESS MY STUDENTS

CHECK YOUR KNOWLEDGE CHAPTER QUIZZES
ONLINE: Book Companion Site BioPortal. OFFLINE: IRDVD

- **EVOLUTION AND BEHAVIOR** questions assessing evolution and behavior.

I WANT LAB RESOURCES

HANDS-ON BIOLOGY: LABORATORIES FOR DISTANCE LEARNING
ONLINE: Book Companion Site (Instructor's Edition Only)
OFFLINE: Printed Stand-Alone Resource

- **LAB 11: EVOLUTION** objectives include analyzing the effect of pesticide applications on insect populations, understanding natural selection and the principles of evolution through a hands-on approach with simple household and lab kit supplies.

CHAPTER 10 INSTRUCTOR'S RESOURCE MAP

I WANT TO PREPARE A LECTURE

LECTURE LAUNCHER VIDEOS
ONLINE: BioPortal; Book Companion Site. OFFLINE: IRDVD

- **ANIMAL HYBRIDIZATION (01:09)** discusses animal hybridization, and includes Thought and Fact clicker questions.

- **ARE BUTTERFLIES FACING EXTINCTION? (01:41)** discusses the future of butterflies, and includes Thought and Fact clicker questions.

CLASSROOM CATALYSTS
ONLINE: BioPortal; Book Companion Site. OFFLINE: IRDVD; IRM

- **ACTIVITY ONE: PLAYING CARD CLASSIFICATION (15-30 MINUTES)** helps students comprehend the concepts and methods of classification.

- **ACTIVITY TWO: EXAMINING SPECIES AND SUBSPECIES (15-30 MINUTES)** helps students comprehend the concepts and definitions of species.

- **ACTIVITY THREE: HYBRIDIZATION AND SPECIES DEVELOPMENT (30-60 MINUTES)** helps students comprehend the concepts of hybridization and species development.

- **ACTIVITY FOUR: SPECIES DETERMINATION CONCEPTS (15-20 MINUTES)** helps students comprehend the methods of species determination.

- **ACTIVITY FIVE: ALLOPATRIC VS. SYMPATRIC SPECIATION (15-30 MINUTES)** helps students comprehend the concepts of and differences between allopatric and sympatric speciation.

- **ACTIVITY SIX: ONTOGENY RECAPITULATES PHYLOGENY (20-30 MINUTES)** asks students to compare and contrast ontogeny (developmental history) and phylogeny (genetic evolutionary history).

- **ACTIVITY SEVEN: THE DIVERSITY OF LIFE—ANIMAL DIVERSITY WEB (30-60 MINUTES)** helps students comprehend the concepts of biodiversity.

- **ACTIVITY EIGHT: CICHLIDS FISH DIVERSITY OF LAKE TANGANYIKA; AN EXAMPLE OF RADIATION (15-30 MINUTES)** Introduces students to cichlids as a model example of adaptive radiation.

STUDENT WORKSHEETS
ONLINE: BioPortal; Book Companion Site OFFLINE: IRDVD; IRM

- **FIGURE 10-13 SPECIATION WITHOUT GEOGRAPHIC ISOLATION** considers sympatric speciation and polyploidy in plants vs. animals, as a printed worksheet.

- **FIGURE 10-14 MAPPING COMMON ANCESTORS** considers levels of relation using phylogenetic trees, as a printed worksheet.

- **FIGURE 10-15 A GROWING TREE** considers the classification of fungi within the tree of life, as a printed worksheet.

- **FIGURE 10-28 FROM SELF-REPLICATING METABOLIZING CELLS TO COMPLEX ORGANISMS** considers the place of bacteria and archaea in the tree of life, as a printed worksheet.

I WANT TO CREATE HOMEWORK ASSIGNMENTS OR HANDS-ON ACTIVITIES

EXPLORING BIOLOGY: CASE STUDIES
ONLINE: Book Companion Site, Faculty Lounge

- **PLANT WARS**
  This case study is narrated by Josh, a protected species of cactus, who is uprooted from his native Arizona desert when "his people" move to a humid southern clime, bringing their plants with them. Josh and the other transplants grow sickly until a plant physician diagnoses the problem: while the photosynthetic ability of the CAM and C4 plants is unaffected by their new environment, they are absorbing too much water.

I WANT TO ASSESS MY STUDENTS

CONNECTING BIOLOGY TO LIFE
ONLINE: BioPortal; Book Companion Site OFFLINE: IRDVD

- **FROM COW MANURE TO ELECTRICITY** discusses the dairy industry, and the potential to harness its by-products for the production of electricity.

I WANT TO ASSESS MY STUDENTS

CHECK YOUR KNOWLEDGE CHAPTER QUIZZES
ONLINE: Book Companion Site BioPortal. OFFLINE: IRDVD

- **THE ORIGIN AND DIVERSIFICATION OF LIFE ON EARTH** Questions assessing the origin and diversification of life.

CHAPTER 11 INSTRUCTOR'S RESOURCE MAP

I WANT TO PREPARE A LECTURE

LECTURE LAUNCHER VIDEOS
ONLINE: BioPortal; Book Companion Site. OFFLINE: IRDVD

- HOW SMART IS AN OCTOPUS? (02:00) discusses animal intelligence in octopi, and includes Thought and Fact clicker questions.

CLASSROOM CATALYSTS
ONLINE: BioPortal; Book Companion Site. OFFLINE: IRDVD; IRM

- ACTIVITY ONE: HOW DO YOU KNOW WHAT KIND OF ORGANISM THAT IS? (15-30 MINUTES) helps students comprehend the diversity of what defines an animal species.

- ACTIVITY TWO: ANIMAL DIVERSITY AT THE ZOO (20-40 MINUTES) helps students comprehend the diversity of animals.

- ACTIVITY THREE: WHAT MAKES AN ANIMAL? CHALLENGE (30-60 MINUTES) helps students comprehend the diversity of organisms in the animal kingdom.

- ACTIVITY FOUR: VERTEBRATE LIMB DEVELOPMENT (60 MINUTES IN CLASS, OR ONE DAY IN A MUSEUM) explores the evolution of limb development in vertebrates.

- ACTIVITY FIVE: PLACENTAL VERSUS MARSUPIAL MAMMALS: A QUESTION OF FITNESS? (20-30 MINUTES) compares the fitness of marsupial mammals versus placental mammals.

- ACTIVITY SIX: HOMO SAPIENS: HYBRID OR UNIQUE SPECIES? (60-90 MINUTES) helps comprehend the hypotheses of evolution of Homo sapiens.

- ACTIVITY SEVEN: NEGATIVE EFFECTS OF EARTHWORMS ON ECOSYSTEMS (40-60 MINUTES) helps comprehend the adverse effects of earthworms on ecosystems.

STUDENT WORKSHEETS
ONLINE: BioPortal; Book Companion Site. OFFLINE: IRDVD; IRM

- FIGURE 11-11 AMNIOTIC VERTEBRATE PHYLOGENY considers family trees and levels of relation between animals, as a printed worksheet.

- FIGURE 11-17 PHYLOGENY OF PRIMATES considers family trees and levels of relation among primates, as a printed worksheet.

I WANT TO ASSESS MY STUDENTS

CHECK YOUR KNOWLEDGE CHAPTER QUIZZES
ONLINE: Book Companion Site BioPortal. OFFLINE: IRDVD

- ANIMAL DIVERSIFICATION
  Questions assessing animal diversification.

CHAPTER 12 INSTRUCTOR'S RESOURCE MAP

I WANT TO PREPARE A LECTURE

LECTURE LAUNCHER VIDEOS
ONLINE: BioPortal; Book Companion Site. OFFLINE: IRDVD

- BEES AS POLLINATORS (00:51) discusses the role of bees in pollination, and includes Thought and Fact questions as clicker question assessment.

CLASSROOM CATALYSTS
ONLINE: BioPortal; Book Companion Site. OFFLINE: IRDVD; IRM

- ACTIVITY ONE: VASCULAR TISSUE IN PLANTS (15-20 MINUTES) helps students comprehend the importance of vascular tissue in plant organisms.

- ACTIVITY TWO: SEED ANATOMY (15 MINUTES) helps students comprehend the structure of seeds.

- ACTIVITY THREE: SEED GERMINATION (15 MINUTES) analyzes the conditions for seed germination and growth.

- ACTIVITY FOUR: ARE FOREST FIRES A NATURAL PART OF A FOREST'S LIFE CYCLE? (40-60 MINUTES) compares the fitness of marsupial mammals versus placental mammals.

- ACTIVITY FIVE: PREDATORY FUNGI AND OTHER FORMS OF PREDATION (10-40 MINUTES) helps students comprehend the concept of fungal predation as well as other predatory organisms.

STUDENT WORKSHEETS
ONLINE: BioPortal; Book Companion Site. OFFLINE: IRDVD; IRM

- FIGURE 12-13 WHAT IS A SEED? considers photosynthesis and cellular respiration in seeds, as a printed worksheet.

- FIGURE 12-20 A FLOWER HOUSES A PLANT'S REPRODUCTIVE STRUCTURES considers the various parts of flowers and their functions, as a printed worksheet.

I WANT TO ASSESS MY STUDENTS

CHECK YOUR KNOWLEDGE CHAPTER QUIZZES
ONLINE: Book Companion Site; BioPortal. OFFLINE: IRDVD

- PLANT AND FUNGI DIVERSIFICATION
  Questions assessing plant and fungi diversification.

I WANT LAB RESOURCES

HANDS-ON BIOLOGY: LABORATORIES FOR DISTANCE LEARNING
ONLINE: Book Companion Site (Instructor's edition only)
OFFLINE: Printed Stand-Alone Resource

- LAB 13: GROWTH PATTERNS AND NUTRIENT TRANSPORT IN PLANTS objectives include analyzing a tree's ring growth, understanding water absorption by seeds and germination, and being able to explain the storage of energy reserves in plants with simple household supplies through hands-on approach.

CHAPTER 13 INSTRUCTOR'S RESOURCE MAP

I WANT TO PREPARE A LECTURE

CLASSROOM CATALYSTS
ONLINE: BioPortal; Book Companion Site. OFFLINE: IRDVD; IRM

- ACTIVITY ONE: BACTERIAL REPRODUCTION (15-20 MINUTES) helps students comprehend the reproduction rates of bacteria.

- ACTIVITY TWO: BENEFICIAL BACTERIA (65-80 MINUTES) helps students comprehend the beneficial role of bacteria flora in the body.

- ACTIVITY THREE: ANTIBIOTICS–MODES OF ACTION AND RESISTANCE (30-40 MINUTES) helps students comprehend the action of antibiotics on bacteria.

- ACTIVITY FOUR: ARCHAEA AND INTESTINAL GAS (15-20 MINUTES) helps students comprehend the action of Archaea in the human intestine.

- ACTIVITY FIVE: VIRUSES TO COMBAT BACTERIAL DISEASES (30-60 MINUTES) helps students comprehend the application of bacteria viruses (bacteriophages) to combat bacterial diseases.

- ACTIVITY SIX: CHOOSE A MICROBE! (15-30 MINUTES) helps students comprehend the diversity of microbiological organisms.

- ACTIVITY SEVEN: THE VIRUS YOU KNOW (10-20 MINUTES) students explore why the viral agents discussed in the media vary from year to year.

- ACTIVITY EIGHT: KNOW THIS PROTIST: AN ARTISTIC EXPLORATION (10-15 MINUTES) prompts students to explore the diverse organisms that make up the kingdom Protista.

STUDENT WORKSHEETS
ONLINE: BioPortal; Book Companion Site. OFFLINE: IRDVD; IRM

- FIGURE 13-23 MALARIA-INFECTED BLOOD CELLS AND SICKLED BLOOD CELLS considers relations between parasite and host, as a printed worksheet.

- FIGURE 13-25 MAKING MORE VIRUSES considers the evidence suggesting that viruses are not living organisms, as a printed worksheet.

I WANT TO CREATE HOMEWORK ASSIGNMENTS OR HANDS-ON ACTIVITIES

CONNECTING BIOLOGY TO LIFE
ONLINE: BioPortal; Book Companion Site OFFLINE: IRDVD

- THE OLDEST THING IN YOUR FRIDGE discusses the factors that contribute to a product's shelf life.
- WHY ARE ANTIBIOTICS FOR RESISTANT STRAINS SO HARD TO FIND? With resistant strains of bacteria on the rise, scientists are looking to new sources for antibiotics-even alligators!

I WANT TO ASSESS MY STUDENTS

CHECK YOUR KNOWLEDGE CHAPTER QUIZZES
ONLINE: Book Companion Site BioPortal. OFFLINE: IRDVD

- EVOLUTION AND DIVERSITY AMONG MICROBES
  Questions assessing evolution and diversity among microbes.

I WANT LAB RESOURCES

HANDS-ON BIOLOGY: LABORATORIES FOR DISTANCE LEARNING
ONLINE: Book Companion Site (Instructor's Edition Only)
OFFLINE: Printed Stand-Alone Resource

- LAB 11: EVOLUTION objectives include analyzing the effect of pesticide applications on insect populations, understanding natural selection and the principles of evolution through a hands-on approach with simple household and lab kit supplies.

CHAPTER 14 INSTRUCTOR'S RESOURCE MAP

I WANT TO PREPARE A LECTURE

LECTURE LAUNCHER VIDEOS
ONLINE: BioPortal; Book Companion Site. OFFLINE: IRDVD

- CROP YIELD INCREASE METHODS (01:48) discusses methods to increase crop yield, and includes Thought and Fact questions as clicker question assessment.

- LOCUST SWARMS (01:43) discusses the locust swarms, and includes Thought and Fact questions as clicker question assessment.

- WHAT IS SUSTAINABILITY? (01:15) discusses sustainability, and includes Thought and Fact questions as clicker question assessment.

CLASSROOM CATALYSTS
ONLINE: BioPortal; Book Companion Site. OFFLINE: IRDVD; IRM

- ACTIVITY ONE: DENSITY-DEPENDENT FACTORS (15-20 MINUTES) helps students comprehend the importance of density-dependent factors for population survival.

- ACTIVITY TWO: EXTENDING THE LIFE EXPECTANCY OF DOMESTICATED DOGS AND ITS CONSEQUENCES (15-30 MINUTES) helps students comprehend the impact of increasing life expectancy on population density.

- ACTIVITY THREE: WHY IS DEMENTIA, INCLUDING ALZHEIMER'S DISEASE, COMMON AMONG OLDER PEOPLE? (15-30 MINUTES) helps students comprehend the impact of increasing life expectancy on population density.

- ACTIVITY FOUR: HUMAN POPULATION GROWTH: WHAT HAPPENS TO GROWTH WHEN FAMILIES ARE LIMITED TO EITHER 2 OR 4 CHILDREN? (15-30 MINUTES) helps students comprehend the impact of family size on population growth over time.

STUDENT WORKSHEETS
ONLINE: BioPortal; Book Companion Site. OFFLINE: IRDVD; IRM

- FIGURE 14-21 CARRYING A TIME BOMB considers the possibility of genetic inheritance in heart disease, as a printed worksheet.

- FIGURE 14-27 WORLD POPULATION considers carrying capacity and logistic growth in the human population, as a printed worksheet.

I WANT TO CREATE HOMEWORK ASSIGNMENTS OR HANDS-ON ACTIVITIES

CONNECTING BIOLOGY TO LIFE
ONLINE: BioPortal; Book Companion Site OFFLINE: IRDVD

- TRACKING JAWS
  Researchers fear that the great white shark population is dwindling off the California coast, signaling that these fabled creatures may be facing extinction.

I WANT TO ASSESS MY STUDENTS

CHECK YOUR KNOWLEDGE CHAPTER QUIZZES
ONLINE: Book Companion Site; BioPortal. OFFLINE: IRDVD

- POPULATION ECOLOGY
  Questions assessing population ecology.

I WANT LAB RESOURCES

HANDS-ON BIOLOGY: LABORATORIES FOR DISTANCE LEARNING
ONLINE: Book Companion Site (Instructor's Edition Only)
OFFLINE: Printed Stand-Alone Resource

- LAB 12: DETERMINING YOUR ECOLOGICAL FOOTPRINT objectives include estimating household energy and water usage, analyzing usage patterns, and comparing local water usage to national averages with simple household supplies through a hands-on approach.

CHAPTER 15 INSTRUCTOR'S RESOURCE MAP

I WANT TO PREPARE A LECTURE

LECTURE LAUNCHER VIDEOS
ONLINE: BioPortal. **OFFLINE:** IRDVD

- **ENERGY FLOW IN A LOCUST (04:39)** discusses the flow of energy in a locust, and includes Thought and Fact clicker questions.

- **NITROGEN AND SOIL (03:15)** discusses the nitrogen in soil and includes Thought and Fact clicker questions.

- **THE NORTH AND SOUTH POLES (01:28)** discusses the polar regions, and includes Thought and Fact clicker questions.

- **THE VALUE OF FORESTS (04:12)** discusses the importance of forests, and includes Thought and Fact clicker questions.

CLASSROOM CATALYSTS
ONLINE: BioPortal; Book Companion Site. **OFFLINE:** IRDVD; IRM

- **ACTIVITY ONE: PREDICTING CLIMATES (15-30 MINUTES)** helps students comprehend the importance of climates on biomes.

- **ACTIVITY TWO: TROPHIC LEVELS AND THE PRESERVATION OF AN ECOSYSTEM (15-30 MINUTES)** helps students comprehend the interactions of trophic levels in a food chain.

- **ACTIVITY THREE: THE CARBON CYCLE: WHERE IS THE CARBON TODAY AND TOMORROW? (10-20 MINUTES)** helps students to understand the global cycling of carbon and its impact on global climate.

- **ACTIVITY FOUR: BUT I DON'T WANT TO BE EATEN (15-20 MINUTES)** learning how to demonstrate the correlation between the adaptations that a predator uses to hunt prey and the adaptations that the prey use to avoid being eaten. Students should also be able to explain how adaptations can drive natural selection in both predator and prey.

STUDENT WORKSHEETS
ONLINE: BioPortal; Book Companion Site. **OFFLINE:** IRDVD; IRM

- **FIGURE 15-14 INEFFICIENCES IN THE TRANSFER OF BIOMASS** considers inefficiency in the flow of matter and energy through an organism, as a printed worksheet.

- **FIGURE 15-23 ALLOWING ORGANISMS TO DIVIDE RESOURCES** considers conditions and selective forces on beak sizes in island bird populations, as a printed worksheet.

I WANT TO ASSESS MY STUDENTS

CHECK YOUR KNOWLEDGE CHAPTER QUIZZES
ONLINE: Book Companion Site; BioPortal **OFFLINE:** IRDVD

- **ECOSYSTEMS AND COMMUNITIES**
  Questions assessing ecosystems and communities.

CHAPTER 16 INSTRUCTOR'S RESOURCE MAP

I WANT TO PREPARE A LECTURE

LECTURE LAUNCHER VIDEOS
ONLINE: BioPortal; Book Companion Site. OFFLINE: IRDVD

- **ARCTIC MELTDOWN (01:25)** discusses the melting in the Arctic, and includes Thought and Fact questions as clicker question assessment.

- **BIG MELT: VIEWING THE EVIDENCE (02:00)** discusses ice melt, and includes Thought and Fact questions as clicker question assessment.

- **ENDANGERED WATER VOLE (01:00)** discusses the case of the endangered water vole, and includes Thought and Fact questions as clicker question assessment.

- **ENVIRONMENTALLY FRIENDLY QUARRY? (04:16)** discusses quarrying and the environment, and includes Thought and Fact questions as clicker question assessment.

- **EXOTIC PLANT SPECIES THREAT IN WALES (02:41)** discusses threatened plants in Wales, and includes Thought and Fact questions as clicker question assessment.

- **GREENHOUSE BIODIVERSITY PROJECT (03:48)** discusses the Greenhouse Biodiversity Project, and includes Thought and Fact questions as clicker question assessment.

- **OIL SPILL DEVASTATES HABITATS IN SPAIN (02:10)** discusses the effect of an oil spill in Spain, and includes Thought and Fact questions as clicker question assessment.

- **POLAR BEARS AFFECTED BY MELTING ICE (02:33)** discusses the effect of melting ice on polar bears, and includes Thought and Fact questions as clicker question assessment.

- **RED SEA CORAL REEF ENDANGERED (02:06)** discusses the threats to the Red Sea coral reef, and includes Thought and Fact questions as clicker question assessment.

- **RIVER IN DECLINE (05:22)** discusses river ecology, and includes Thought and Fact questions as clicker question assessment.

- **SEED BANK HELPS ENSURE BIODIVERSITY (01:45)** discusses the impact of seed banks, and includes Thought and Fact questions as clicker question assessment.

- **THREAT TO ANTARCTIC WILDLIFE (01:45)** discusses threats to Antarctic wildlife, and includes Thought and Fact questions as clicker question assessment.

- **VANISHING LAKE (02:30)** discusses a threatened lake biome, and includes Thought and Fact questions as clicker question assessment.

CLASSROOM CATALYSTS
ONLINE: BioPortal; Book Companion Site. OFFLINE: IRDVD; IRM

- **ACTIVITY ONE: EXAMINING AN ENDANGERED SPECIES (15-30 MINUTES)** helps students comprehend the factors that contribute to a species becoming endangered.

- **ACTIVITY TWO: DESIGNING A CONSERVATION PROGRAM FOR A HYPOTHETICAL SPECIES (30-60 MINUTES)** helps students comprehend the components that contribute to a conservation program for a species.

- **ACTIVITY THREE: MOUNT SAINT HELENS, AN EXAMPLE OF ENVIRONMENTAL DISTURBANCE AND RECOVERY (30-60 MINUTES)** helps students understand how an environment that has been extensively disturbed recovers.

- **ACTIVITY FOUR: NORTHERN SPOTTED OWLS VS LOGGERS (15-30 MINUTES)** helps students to better understand the issues associated with determining if a species should be conserved.

STUDENT WORKSHEETS
ONLINE: BioPortal; Book Companion Site. OFFLINE: IRDVD; IRM

- **FIGURE 16-10 THE LONELY ISLAND AND FIGURE 16-39 CAREFULLY PLANNED NATURE PRESERVES FOCUS ON FEATURES THAT MAXIMIZE BIODIVERSITY** consider the effect of corridors and buffer zones in island biogeography, as a printed worksheet.

- **FIGURE 16-11 OFFERING INSIGHT INTO POPULATION DYNAMICS: DYNAMIC EQUILIBRIUM** considers falling rate of immigration and rising rate of extinction on an island, as a printed worksheet.

I WANT TO CREATE HOMEWORK ASSIGNMENTS OR HANDS-ON ACTIVITIES

CONNECTING BIOLOGY TO LIFE
ONLINE: BioPortal; Book Companion Site. OFFLINE: IRDVD

- **USING ALGAE TO TREAT TOXINS** discusses various uses for algae such as cleaning up industrial waste and fueling water treatment plants.

I WANT TO ASSESS MY STUDENTS

CHECK YOUR KNOWLEDGE CHAPTER QUIZZES
ONLINE: Book Companion Site; BioPortal. OFFLINE: IRDVD

- **BIODIVERSITY AND CONSERVATION**
  Questions assessing biodiversity and conservation.

I WANT LAB RESOURCES

HANDS-ON BIOLOGY: LABORATORIES FOR DISTANCE LEARNING
ONLINE: Book Companion Site (Instructor's Edition Only)
OFFLINE: Printed Stand-Alone Resource

- **LAB 12: DETERMINING YOUR ECOLOGICAL FOOTPRINT** objectives include estimating household energy and water usage, analyzing usage patterns, and comparing local water usage to national averages with simple household supplies through a hands-on approach.

Look for the complete listing of chapter-by-chapter resources for chapters 1-26 on the website (www.whfreeman.com/phelan2e), BioPortal, (courses.bfwpub.com/phelan2e), and in the Phelan Essential Supplement Kit.
Contact your local sales rep if you need assistance accessing these sites.

Instructor's Resource Map

>

INSTRUCTOR'S RESOURCE MAP

I WANT TO PREPARE A LECTURE

RESOURCE	DESCRIPTION	CHAPTERS	ONLINE	OFFLINE
POWERPOINT IMAGES				
Optimized Art (JPEG/PPT)	All text figures, photos, and tables digitized for optimal readability in large lecture halls. Available in labeled and unlabeled versions.	All	BCS; BioPortal; Faculty Lounge	IRDVD
Stepped Art PowerPoints	Complex concepts and processes animated step by step.	All	BCS; BioPortal; Faculty Lounge	IRDVD
Lecture Outline PowerPoints	Key figures, photos, and bulleted text on the slide; lecture notes and captions in a Notes section.	All	BCS; BioPortal; Faculty Lounge	IRDVD
Active Learning Lecture Outline PowerPoints	Incorporates classroom catalyst activities and clicker questions into a lecture outline of the key figures and photos from the text.	All	BCS; BioPortal; Faculty Lounge	IRDVD
Clicker Question PowerPoints	Questions to use with clicker systems to engage students during lectures.	All	BCS; BioPortal; Faculty Lounge	IRDVD
Customized PowerPoints	Text figures with editable labels.	All	BCS; BioPortal; Faculty Lounge	IRDVD
Phelan's Favorites (JPEG/PPT)	Stunning photos not found in the book, selected by Jay Phelan.	All	BCS; BioPortal; Faculty Lounge	IRDVD
ANIMATIONS AND VIDEOS				
Q Animations (QuickTime; Flash)	Interactive animations modeled on the text art with built-in study questions. English and Spanish subtitles.	Select	BCS; BioPortal; Faculty Lounge	IRDVD
Lecture Launcher Videos	Video clips and questions to be used to introduce key biological concepts by highlighting some interesting or potentially controversial aspect of the topic.	Select	BCS; BioPortal	IRDVD
Phelan Lecture Videos	Text author Jay Phelan's ten minute video clips based on applied topics and case studies in non-majors biology. These engaging lectures include topics on caffeine, genetic variation, how much an animal needs to eat, and more.	Select	BCS; BioPortal	IRDVD
ADDITIONAL LECTURE TOOLS				
Launch Pad	Pre-built modules that offer a complete unit-by-unit breakdown of the textbook with carefully selected and arranged assignments, activities, and quizzes. Launch Pad modules can be used as is, or modified to suit your course.	All	BioPortal	
Chapter Outlines and Learning Objectives	The scope of each chapter at a glance.	All	BCS; BioPortal	IRDVD; IRM
Classroom Catalysts	Engaging activities (10-15 minutes each) incorporating Q Questions and working off common student misconceptions. Designed for classrooms of any size or budget.	All	BCS; BioPortal	IRDVD; IRM
Student Worksheets	Hand-out activities focused on concepts, based on textbook figures.	All	BCS; BioPortal	IRDVD; IRM
Overhead Transparency Set	Every figure from the text with labels enhanced for clear visibility in large lecture halls.	All		Print

I WANT TO CREATE HOMEWORK ASSIGNMENTS OR HANDS-ON ACTIVITIES

RESOURCE	DESCRIPTION	CHAPTERS	ONLINE	OFFLINE
Active Learning Lecture Outline PowerPoints	Incorporates classroom catalyst activities and clicker questions into a lecture outline of the key figures and photos from the text.	All	BCS; BioPortal; Faculty Lounge	IRDVD
Clicker Question PowerPoints	Questions to use with clicker systems to engage students during lectures.	All	BCS; BioPortal; Faculty Lounge	IRDVD
Q Animations (QuickTime; Flash)	Interactive animations modeled on the text art with built-in study questions. English and Spanish subtitles.	Select	BCS; BioPortal; Faculty Lounge	IRDVD
BioNews	A current newsfeed, updated weekly with articles relevant to various biology topics.	Select	BioPortal	
Exploring Biology: Case Studies	Designed for active learning, these topic-specific cases can be used for everything from brief lecture openers to large-scale multi-week projects.	Select	BCS; BioPortal; Faculty Lounge	
Connecting Biology to Life	Concept-based activities addressing real-life applications in an active learning style.	Select	BCS; BioPortal; Faculty Lounge	IRDVD
PRINT SUPPLEMENTS (Ask your local W. H. Freeman representative for a sample copy and packaging options..)				
Questions About Life Reader	Based on the Scientific American feature "Ask the Experts," the Reader is designed to pique students' interest in health, wellness, and the biological world around us.	All		Print
Student Success Guide	Provides students with all the tools they need to excel in biology, including learning objectives, engaging lecture outlines, key figures, assessment, and a visual glossary.	All		Print